America's Country & Western Tradition

CHARLES T. BROWN

Saginaw Valley State College

PRENTICE-HALL, Englewood Cliffs, New Jersey 07632

Library of Congress Cataloging-in-Publication Data

BROWN, CHARLES T.
Music U.S.A.

Discography: p. 206
Bibliography: p. 210
Includes index.
1. Country music—United States—History and criticism. 2. Country musicians—United States—Biography. I. Title. II. Title: Music USA.
ML3524.B76 1986 784.5'2'00973 85-12411
ISBN 0-13-608175-4
ISBN 0-13-608167-3 (pbk.)

Editorial/production supervision and
interior design: Patricia V. Amoroso
Cover design: Photo Plus Art
Manufacturing buyer: Ray Keating

Printed in the United States of America

10 9 8 7 6 5 4 3 2 1

ISBN 0-13-608175-4 01
ISBN 0-13-608167-3 (pbk.) 01

PRENTICE-HALL INTERNATIONAL (UK) LIMITED, *London*
PRENTICE-HALL OF AUSTRALIA PTY. LIMITED, *Sydney*
PRENTICE-HALL CANADA INC., *Toronto*
PRENTICE-HALL HISPANOAMERICANA, S.A., *Mexico City*
PRENTICE-HALL OF INDIA PRIVATE LIMITED, *New Delhi*
PRENTICE-HALL OF JAPAN, INC., *Tokyo*
PRENTICE-HALL OF SOUTHEAST ASIA PTE. LTD., *Singapore*
EDITORA PRENTICE-HALL DO BRASIL, LTDA., *Rio de Janeiro*
WHITEHALL BOOKS LIMITED, *Wellington, New Zealand*

Contents

ILLUSTRATIONS

Preface

I have appreciated country music for a long time, probably most of my life. However, until quite recently I did not realize how much I appreciated it. Like many things in our lives, country music is often treated like background information, satisfying us and entertaining us in ways we do not really understand. The purpose of this book is to make that understanding and appreciation a higher priority in the lives of those who read the book.

It will be my purpose to define country music in its various stages of evolution, to discuss the important practitioners in each period of development, and to analyze some of the important compositions they performed. Therefore, this book is fundamentally about country *music* and not about the country music lifestyle. There are many fine books in the bibliography that discuss the country music lifestyle and the kinds of concerns that country musicians have. Since we are dealing primarily with the music as opposed to its sociological influences, those who are interested in stories about the musicians' lives should probably consult these and other books. However, it is my contention that the main importance of country music is the music itself.

I tend to think in positive terms and therefore my treatment of country music is supportive. Country music should be understood not only as an expression of attitudes but also as a creative art form. While not all country music is high art, it all has an integrity as musical communication. Music is an alternate form of communication for some people. In some cases it can communicate values and ideas that would not be possible through other mediums. Country music should be appreciated for its uniqueness and quality rather than be treated as a lowly popular form. When country music is popular music and appeals to large masses of people, it is simply communication on a grander scale; it does not cease to be a unique form of communication.

The basic technique of structuring this book derives from the approach of many others. The content of this book is in fact derived from other fine books mentioned in the bibliography, together with listening to country music and thinking about it over many years. However, the information is recycled into a new form. The structure is chronological and is organized at times by topic, at times by artist. I believe that it has been the important musicians at particular points in time who have breathed life into country music.

It should be understood that this book does not claim to be a complete history of country music, but is rather a discussion of country music covering its full course in a selective manner. Even with the good representation in this book, there are important musicians who have been left out. The selections are a result of consensus among country writers and people with whom I have consulted in preparing the outline and the final writing. Therefore, if your favorite country musician is not mentioned, please read the book anyway. You can apply the information and the technique for listening to appreciation of your favorite musicians. Who knows—you may find people in this book who have not yet been a part of your life.

It should also be understood that this is a book about country music appreciation. As such, the book does some teaching even though it is not fundamentally designed as a textbook. I will try to explain techniques for appreciating music and, in particular, country music in all its various styles.

It is hoped that these words will be effective, for in this book I am attempting to illustrate the importance of country music, not only as an expression of the people who played or sang it, but also as a valid expression and art form of the American people. Country music's popularity cannot be doubted; what I am trying to show in this book is its artistry.

ACKNOWLEDGMENTS

I would like to acknowledge three country music scholars—Douglas Green, Bill Malone, and Greil Marcus. Greil Marcus is not known primarily for his country scholarship, but his book *Mystery Train* has been important to me. Douglas Green and Bill Malone have contributed greatly to my thinking about country music, although I have yet to have the pleasure of meeting them personally.

I would also like to thank Bill Ivey and Ronnie Pugh at the Country Music Hall of Fame. Both have been very helpful over time, especially Ronnie Pugh for correcting misstatements in this book during its first draft.

I would also like to thank the Foundation at Saginaw Valley State College for supporting one of my trips to Nashville. And I thank my dean, Bill Barnett, for his constant support. My students, especially those in my country course of Spring 1984, deserve special credit, for they each contributed to my thinking about country music.

I dedicate this book to Mr. George Becker of Saginaw Valley State College. George is a real country music fan, and it was George who worked on me for years to get me to take country music seriously. His exhortations were successful, and I thank him for his encouragement.

1 Introduction

ORIGINS OF COUNTRY MUSIC

To trace the history of country music and its early influences we really ought to go back to 1492, when our country was first discovered by Europeans. When Europeans first came to the land which would later be the United States, they brought their own culture, which included their own music. The early settlers set the tone for country music even though their musical preferences were very far from what that music evolved into towards the nineteenth century.

The original settlers in the northeastern part of the United States were Puritans, severe Protestants who had left Europe to seek religious freedom. Many were from northern European countries and were outcasts in their original countries. As such, they were tightly knit in their communities and expressed relatively homogeneous attitudes, especially in their musical activities. They had strong religious beliefs, and their musical tastes reflected conservative religious attitudes. Two of their guiding principles, a belief in original sin and an avoidance of sensual pleasure, translated musically into a preference for simplicity of melody, harmony, and rhythm.

The religious hymns that these settlers brought from Europe had simple one-line melodies. The message of the words was considered more important than the music itself. Quite often, the congregation could not read music, so the melodies were sung by the minister and the congregation repeated them afterward, a practice called *lining-out.* These hymns were regular in musical form, made up of four equal phrases consistent with the word organization. There were of course exceptions to this rule; irregular tunes were learned by the congregation as being the right presentation of particular hymns. This oral tradition influenced country music, which was at first primarily an oral art form.

Both the subject matter and the musical material of early Protestant hymns had an influence on all American popular music, and the strong Puritan roots of early American colony life are a continuing influence in the United States. The basic tendencies of this music as well as the religious attitudes were shared by German and French settlers in the United States whenever those settlers were of the conservative Protestant type.

It should be understood that Protestant settlers, whether they settled in Massachusetts or in Appalachia, all brought to the United States a relatively homogenous world view as influenced by their religious beliefs. This fundamentalism of spirit is a continuing influence in country music and should be understood as one of the earliest influences in American life.

It cannot be doubted that early settlers sang secular music as well, and these secular songs have been documented in various writings on early American life. Although the subject matter of these songs is quite different from that of Protestant hymns, the musical content is fairly similar. The song forms are made of equal-length phrases and they usually divide into two- and four-unit groups. Various European dance forms were important in the United States—the sarabande, the *basse danse,* the jig, and others.

There was some migration to the United States by other groups of settlers with different religious and philosophical attitudes, for instance, the French and Spanish Catholics who settled in the New Orleans area and the Irish Catholics in Boston. Wherever these groups settled they brought other influences with them and their music evolved differently.

In the South (which is the primary focus for early country music), most of the population growth took place near the ocean or major rivers; it was only in the middle of the eighteenth century that small encampments began to develop in the hills of the Appalachians and other such areas. Up until those rural developments, the South was largely like the North except for climate. Even in the early eighteenth century, the North was becoming industrialized. Although the South had textile and tobacco production quite early in its history, it was basically agricultural because of the climate. While people in northern settlements had to beat back the rigors of climate, people in southern towns could work outside all year long. Therefore, southern towns were easier to build and the South quite naturally took to agricultural production. Although the South certainly did not lack in sophistication or high culture, the lifestyle of its people tended to move towards farming and the land. It is my impression that many of the southern attitudes can be explained by this one fact.

In the eighteenth century settlements began to appear in more rural environments and it was from these environments that country music came, primarily because these people became isolated from urban settlements and retained many of the roots of early American attitudes. This is not to say that the rural southerner is a throwback, but simply to state that people who lived in small communities separate from large cities developed homogeneous cultural attitudes. Since they were not influenced by the rest of the world, the kind of attitudes and music they produced were a mirror of their culture.

BRIEF SURVEY OF SOUTHERN FOLK SONG

The folk music of the South in the sixteenth and seventeenth centuries was the same as in the North and was primarily religious in nature. The Puritan ethic, which dominated the South as well as the North, maintained a tight hold on nonreligious music from the perspective that the singing of anything other than psalms or hymns was considered bad for human nature.

The black slave population developed its own musical forms—field hollers, cries, and worksongs. Undoubtedly, such musical developments also occurred in white civilization in the South, especially since the southern economy was early tied to agriculture. English ballads were popular in the South; the greatest evidence of this is the writings about performances of the ballad opera in eighteenth-century southern towns. A particularly southern style of folk music started in a way that was similar to that which occurred in the North: from ballads and narrative songs that were particular to an ethnic group (such as Irish, British, German, French, or African), or to a certain location. Although there are notable examples of retention of original song types in the South, it was probably in the process of the melding of two or more ethnic types that a true southern style evolved.

By the nineteenth century the South had three distinct types of songs that would ultimately make up southern folk music: (1) ethnic folk songs (usually sung in the original foreign language), (2) Afro-American songs (most notably the early blues) and (3) a nostalgic white music in the nineteenth-century parlor style (such as the Stephen Foster tunes). These three types of folk songs ultimately came together to form a uniquely Southern style of folk music.

The Southern style that finally evolved towards the end of the nineteenth century was conservative, maintaining the older types of melodies (often modal or pentatonic, and frequently in the minor mode and sad in character). The music usually spoke of rural problems in a way that was quite different from northern folk music. Folk instruments were used for accompaniment, and that accompaniment was usually simple. The music was popularized throughout the South through minstrel shows, medicine shows, and vaudeville. It functioned to communicate local feelings, common problems, and a sense of regional pride about the South.

The most significant kinds of music which would ultimately influence country music were minstrel ("Rise When the Rooster Crows"); spiritual ("Go Down, Moses"); and mountain ("Kitty Wells"). These early types of southern folk songs were very important to the development of country music, and some of the old nineteenth-century repertoire continues to be played by country musicians (although not with the same instrumentation).

DEVELOPMENT OF THE BLUES

This particular explanation of the development of the blues will be rather short by comparison to what has been done in other sources, mainly because one could write a whole book on the blues alone. I will develop a short capsule of the blues development from the nineteenth century to the 1950s and then describe specifically how that influenced country music. The blues will be discussed throughout the text where that is appropriate. For more on the blues, consult the bibliography (in particular my book—*The Art of Rock and Roll*).[1]

The blues in its fully developed form (from the 1920s on) was a twelve-measure unit that had specific chord relationships in it. In order to understand the development, we must first explain what that means, and this will require a touch of technical discussion. However, this should not scare anyone off — or at least I hope that it does not. So stay with me.

Music is divided into units of time, and in order to understand what is happening in any country tune or other music, we must be able to perceive those units of time. Of course, music is communicated through time and any composition takes a certain amount of time to play. We will start with the blues because it will provide information that can be used in discussing country forms.

A *musical scale* is a set of notes leading from one to another. A *major scale* in the western world consists of eight notes, going either from a bottom note up or a top note down. The first and last note of any scale have the same letter name and are separated by a distance called an *octave*. The notes in a *major* scale could be obtained from singing the first eight notes of "Joy to the World."

[1]Brown, Charles, *The Art of Rock and Roll* (Englewood Cliffs, N.J.: Prentice-Hall, Inc., 1983).

Joy to the world the Lord is come.

C B A G F E D C
8 7 6 5 4 3 2 1

Notice that C and C are notes 1 and 8 and that this particular major scale is a descending one. There are actually very few songs that use a complete major scale in the opening eight notes.

You will notice that we are talking about the *melody* without considering how long each of the notes is held. If you have not yet understood what a melody is, here is an example: the pitches themselves, without the words, form a melody, in this case a descending major scale.

The letters represent the notes as they could be played on a guitar or a piano. The numbers represent the scale degrees, which could be used to describe the different pitches in the scale and the relationships among them.

The pitches of a scale have a relationship to each other in forming a melody or a *progression* of notes, such as the progression of notes which form the basis of the blues. A *progression* is a set of occurrences which happens more than once. It should not be confused with progressing from one place to another, although that is a meaning of the word as well. In music, *progression* usually refers to a set of chord changes which occurs over and over, serving as a basis for verses of a song or for improvisation. We will first set up the blues progression, explain a method by which to count it, and then refer to it as an example of a progression used in country music.

The basic blues progression normally consists of twelve measures, each of which has four pulsations. To produce a measure we simply clap our hands four times, keeping the distance between the claps the same. We can use the second hand on a clock if we wish, to keep the beats even. Next, we sing some note at the same time that we clap our hands—for instance, C, C, C, C or 1, 1, 1, 1. We have produced a measure with four notes and then can go on to create groups of two, four, eight, and twelve measures.

The blues progression follows a certain pattern of scale notes. Using both letters and numbers, we can represent the blues progression as follows:

CCCC/CCCC/CCCC/CCCC/FFFF/FFFF/CCCC/CCCC/GGGG/GGGG

/CCCC/CCCC

or

1111/1111/1111/1111/4444/4444/1111/1111/5555/5555

/1111/1111

Athough this is a scaled-down version of a complete explanation of the blues progression (for more see the bibliography), it should suffice as a model for understanding progressions and for counting beats. As we get to the actual analysis of music, we will give more suggestions on how to do this. It is important to understand one basic progression and how it works, and the blues progression is a good one to start with.

The term *blues* is used in a variety of ways to describe different phenomena. It can be used to describe a feeling of sadness or frustration. Certainly many of the early work songs illustrated such feelings as well as some of the note patterns, that is, blueslike melodies. However, this is not the same as the blues progression just defined.

The term can also be used to describe certain notes that exist in singing, not part of the major scale given above but rather halfway between scale degrees; these, when used, give color to a melody. Sometimes certain scale notes will give a melody the sound of African tribal music, and in a way that does not correspond to European scales at all (the blues progression given above is based on Western European scales). Actually, there are some notes on the piano that are not included in the major scale. The black notes on the piano are in between the scale degrees given above (which are all white keys). The note between A and B is a black key called B-flat (or B♭) because it is a half step below (or a flat of) B. A note halfway between B and B♭ is a *blue note*. The note halfway between E♭ and E is another common blue note. Putting the blue notes into a scale, we would get a blues scale that is used extensively in blues melodies:

C *E♭* F *F♯* G *B♭* C (E♭, F♯, and B♭ are altered.)

Although this concept is not necessary for an understanding of the material in this book, it is important to recognize that there are some melodic tendencies of blues songs that are incorporated into country music.

The *blues* can also refer to a feeling in a song, or it may be part of the title, even when the song does not follow a blues progression. This of course confuses the issue still further, but for our purposes we will talk of blues songs that follow the basic twelve-measure progression given previously.

The history of the blues is significant, especially as we slowly work our way toward country music. Early blues was rural blues, performed by rural musicians in rural settings, usually as a solo (with a guitar accompaniment played by the singer). It quite often followed patterns which were marginally like the blues progression presented as the basic model. Early blues forms had eight-measure lengths, ten-measure lengths, twelve, thirteen, fourteen, sixteen, twenty-four, and other odd lengths. Some were influenced by European dance forms and others were simply produced spontaneously. The only overriding consistency was that they began as simple songs and then were improvised (made up on the spot), both in lyrics and accompaniment, to fill out the remainder of the song. Improvisation is probably the most important trait of the blues.

Primitive blues was the primary form at the end of the nineteenth century. Classic blues (as defined by LeRoi Jones in *Urban Blues*), the form that followed primitive blues, was the acculturated form. It was still not urban blues in the commercial sense, but it did begin to solidify the style and move toward a standard blues form.

By the beginning of the twentieth century, there were significant blues singers and instrumentalists who were influential both in the blues and in most other forms available: Bill Broonzy, Leadbelly, Lightnin' Hopkins, Ma Rainey, Ethel Waters, Bessie Smith. Some later musicians in this same development are T-Bone Walker, Billie Holiday, Ella Fitzgerald, Muddy Waters, and B.B. King. Interestingly, some of these singers continued to employ eight-bar blues forms as well as the more standard twelve-measure blues. The point is that each of these musicians did things that influenced other blues singers and, parenthetically, country music. Even when they used progressions that did not follow the twelve-bar patterns, they used *one-to-five changes* and blues melodies.[2]

The basic chronology of the blues is as follows:

Primitive Blues	1800s
Classic Blues	1900–1930
Boogie Woogie	1926–
Urban Blues	1930–
Jump Blues	1940s
Rhythm and Blues	1940–

[2]*One-to-five changes* are chord progressions based on the first note of the musical scale and then on the fifth note—two chords make up this progression.

These various forms were influential in country music in the early period, during rockabilly and in various instrumental styles. Although the blues is thought to be primarily a development of black musicians, it is certain that white influences were present and that country music came from an interesting amalgam of traditional folk music, blues, and salon music of the nineteenth century. Therefore, in defining country music and its musical forms, we will need to consider continuing blues influences.

STRUCTURE OF MUSICAL FORMS

Assuming that the reader is now familiar with the information in the preceding section, especially the musical explanation of the blues progression, we can proceed to discuss some musical forms used in country music. At present, we will discuss these forms devoid of actual lyrics and musical accompaniment.

We have already discussed at length the standard twelve-measure blues form, each measure having four beats to it. We will also discuss other lengths of musical phrases, such as the eight-measure musical unit, which is the most common in country music. This musical phrase is usually made up of two equal four-measure phrases, measures having three or four beats in them, the two phrases fitting together into one complete eight-measure phrase. More often than not, the units start on the first degree of the scale for the first two measures, rise to the fifth degree of the scale for the next four measures, and then return to the first degree of the scale for the last two measures.

Before we go any further, let me clear up a possible area of confusion. The first degree of the scale, when it functions as an organization unit for a progression, does not make up the melody but rather serves as the basic note for the accompaniment. A better way to understand this is to listen to what the guitar plays when it is used as an accompaniment to singing. Typically in simple folk song, the guitar player strums chords and sings at the same time. The chords would be based on one of the scale degrees as previously described and would provide a pleasing background for the melody. For ease of comprehension we will not explain chord theory, as it really can get quite complicated. However, it should be understood that when we talk about a first-degree chord, we mean a chord played or implied by the background instruments that is based upon the first degree of the scale.

Country music also employs other forms of music, such as long ballad forms of up to thirty-two measures. A common ballad form has two eight-measure phrases, followed by an eight-measure contrasting section and a return to the original eight-measure phrase. The key to figuring out form will be given in the next section, but the easiest way to establish the skill is by listening to music that has lyrics, and especially some repetitious lyric. A section of lyrics that repeats, called a refrain, usually will help a person to understand the basic form. Counting beats is also a useful skill in analyzing forms.

Some country music, especially early country music and experimental country, uses odd lengths of phrases. This may cause some difficulty because the earliest country music discussed has uneven phrases. Since the analyzed pieces are contained in the appendices, you can skip that material if you wish. However, it would probably illuminate the development of country music for you if listening was connected with reading that material.

ANALYSIS TECHNIQUE USED IN TEXT

The analysis system I use and recommend in this book is one based on counting beats and figuring out repetition schemes. The conclusions that this system will yield are mostly descriptive, although some rather precise technical analysis of a simple nature can be achieved.

In analyzing music you will find that you have to listen to the piece more than once; the actual number of times will be determined by the complexity of the composition and by your developing skill. The first listening should reveal the types of instruments used as accompaniment and, if there is singing, the general meaning of the lyrics. I suggest that you concentrate first on songs with lyrics. You might determine if there is an instrumental introduction before the singing starts and instrumental interludes in between verses and at the end. Notate these on paper in a kind of time line.

Instrumental introduction
Singing
Instrumental interlude
Singing
Instrumental ending without singing

This is merely one model; your model should represent the piece you are analyzing.

Once you have done this analysis, try to determine if there are any repetition schemes in the lyrics. If there are, indicate where they are as follows:

Singing—Verse, Refrain, Verse, Refrain, *etc.*

The next step is to describe the instrumental background in relationship to the words. If there are any particularly distinctive instrumental activities, like a guitar or fiddle solo, be sure to note them. After this, try to count beats to the music and determine the phrase lengths.

Pay special attention to how the instrumentalists begin and end phrases because that will often give you information about the style of the particular period or musician. Pay attention to the chords as well, especially if you can hear the change from one scale degree to another. This will always increase your understanding and appreciation of any style of music, especially country music. You will quickly discover that if you use these techniques over the broad range of country music, you will be able to make valid judgments about stylistic changes over its sixty-plus years of history.

Lastly, I encourage you not to get discouraged in doing analysis. At first it may seem like the last thing in the world you would want to do. However, through careful analysis of country music over a period of time, you will reach a level of sophistication and ease. Therefore, I encourage all readers to read carefully the material in the Appendix, to purchase the recordings on which the analyses are based, and to think about the relationship between the sounds and the words in that section. You will not only know that country music is varied in style, commercially successful, and valid as a communication form, but you will also know why and how.

2 Instruments of Country Music

This chapter discusses the various instruments used in country music. This is intended as an introduction to the instruments; particular applications by specific musicians will be discussed in further chapters. However, it is probably a good idea to have a general description before we start the actual country music story. As you listen to country music you should try to pick out the sounds of each of the instruments, and perhaps this chapter will help you do that.

Guitar

The *guitar* is undoubtedly the most important instrument in country music and certainly has had the most applications. It is derived from the *lute* and is a very ancient instrument. In the fifteenth and sixteenth centuries, the lute went through various transformations; the Spanish version of the experimental lute was called a *vihuela*. This particular instrument was not oval in shape like the lute but was rather a flat-bodied instrument. Ultimately called the *guitarra* by folk musicians of Spain, this instrument was transported to the New World by the conquistadores.

The guitar, then, is a flat-bodied instrument with strings running the course of the body and up a reinforced neck. There is a sounding hole in the center of the body, which is hollow (except in a later development in the 1950s—see *electric bass*). The guitar can have from four to twelve strings, although the two most common types have six and twelve, respectively. The twelve-string guitar is usually tuned like the six-string, only there are two strings tuned to the same note.

The guitar is played by plucking the strings with the right hand (either strumming or picking) while the left hand stops the strings at various points (separated by frets) on the neckboard, effectively shortening the string by

Milly and Polly Good, the "Girls of the Golden West," with a guitar (*Photograph courtesy of the John Edwards Memorial Collection of the University of North Carolina at Chapel Hill*)

one-half pitch per fret and raising the pitch. Various sliding techniques are employed, and a number of special effects can be achieved by modifying the guitar, the tuning, or the normal playing technique.

The guitar is used for simple accompaniment, often just strumming chords. It is also used for countermelodies in back of a sung melody or as a part of an instrumental ensemble. It can also be a solo instrument, especially in the hands of a fine technician. It is found in every type of country music and has been one of the most important American folk and popular instruments of the last two centuries.

The *mandolin* and the *ukelele* are guitar variants which have been important in some styles of country music. The mandolin is a smaller guitar that produces a different sound and is higher in pitch. The ukelele has four strings and is a poor person's guitar. Originally a Hawaiian instrument, it found favor with a few country musicians, although not as many as ultimately embraced the other Hawaiian instrument in country music, the steel guitar.

Bill Monroe with a mandolin (*Photograph courtesy of the John Edwards Memorial Collection of the University of North Carolina at Chapel Hill*)

The *steel guitar* is one of the most important instruments in country music, often the character of the country sound is defined by the steel guitar. Also imported from Hawaii, the steel guitar was developed substantially in the United States, with pedals and electronic effects added. It has been used since the honky tonk period. It is played with a picking technique in combination with the use of a metal cylinder to stop the strings and produces a bending sound, similar in style to the bottleneck guitar playing of early blues musicians. The steel guitar is used both as a rhythm instrument and as a solo instrument.

Dobro

The *dobro* is a twentieth-century invention of John Dopyera, who in 1925 developed a guitar with a raised bridge and a resonator cone placed in the traditional sounding hole. This resonator cone caused the new instru-

Josh Graves and an example of a dobro (*Photograph courtesy of the John Edwards Memorial Collection of the University of North Carolina at Chapel Hill*)

ment to sound like a cross between a guitar and a steel guitar. In 1929 John and his two brothers formed a company specializing in dobros; the name came from *Do*pyera *Bro*thers. Variants of the dobro use four, six, and eight strings. The instrument has enjoyed a great deal of popularity in country music.

Banjo

The *banjo* is one of the most interesting instruments in American folk music because it is really a cross between a string instrument and a percussion instrument. Shaped like a guitar, it has a long neck and a round body. The body, which is really a circle of wood, has a membrane stretched over it like a drum, and quite often the head or membrane is struck like a drum during playing. As a folk instrument, the banjo was most important in the nineteenth century. More recently, its main use has been in bluegrass music, although most country fans would consider a banjo player to be imperative

Samantha Bumgarner plucking a banjo (*Photograph courtesy of the John Edwards Memorial Collection of the University of North Carolina at Chapel Hill*)

in country music. Actually, it is not used in all styles, but is one of those instruments clearly associated with country music. When the banjo is included in a bluegrass tune or other country ensemble its presence is obvious.

The banjo probably came to the New World in the eighteenth century or even earlier. It is debatable whether it is an instrument of African or European origin, but most accept the theory of African origin. The banjo was used by African slaves and was picked up by white musicians in the nineteenth century. The original banjo had four strings, but the American banjo has five strings. The five-string banjo was invented by Joe Sweeney, a Virginian, who lived from 1810 to 1860. In the twentieth century, the four-string banjo was reintroduced as a tenor banjo and used in jazz bands.

The American country banjo (the five-string variety) is played primarily with a picking style, although one can certainly play rhythmic chords on a banjo (used effectively as a part of a rhythm ensemble). The fifth string serves as a drone string, played by the thumb, to produce rhythmic and bass melody accompaniment to the faster style played by the other four strings. Bluegrass banjo picking is extremely virtuosic. Some of the important banjo experts were Uncle Dave Macon, Earl Scruggs, and Roy Clark.

Fiddle

Fiddle is the term applied to the violin when it is used as a folk instrument. Actually the term goes quite far back in time, when it was used for the ancestors of the violin. In country music, the fiddle (or violin) is a

Clayton McMichen and fiddle (*Photograph courtesy of the John Edwards Memorial Collection of the University of North Carolina at Chapel Hill*)

standard violin as would be used in a symphony orchestra. However, the playing technique is rather different.

The violin has four strings tuned a fourth apart and is played with a bow or, occasionally, plucked. The violin can bc played smoothly and slowly, or it can be played with amazing speed in what some musicians refer to as pyrotechnics. The fiddle is important to most country music styles, and until post-World War II it was the lead instrument. After 1945 the fiddle became a background instrument, playing countermelodies.

The importance of the fiddle should not be understated: for much of the nineteenth century and into the twentieth century, the solo fiddle provided all of the music necessary for a barn dance or country get-together. There were and still are fiddling contests held throughout the United States, and the virtuosity of a good fiddle player is amazing. Some of the noted practitioners have been Vern Dalhart, John Carson, and, again, Roy Clark.

Dulcimer

The *dulcimer* is a European instrument, although the American dulcimer is really quite different from its European ancestor. The *European dulcimer* is a flat box with many metal strings strung across the entire

Jean Ritchie with a dulcimer (*Photograph courtesy of the John Edwards Memorial Collection of the University of North Carolina at Chapel Hill*)

instrument. The strings are then struck with small wooden hammers. In this sense it is an early piano, although clearly the piano has a different striking action.

The *Appalachian* or *mountain dulcimer* is a smaller instrument with from three to six strings (most have three or four); it has a fret board so the strings can be stopped and raised by a half pitch per fret. It is a plucked instrument and in its shape and playing style it is akin to the steel guitar. It is primarily used in southern mountain music.

Autoharp

The *autoharp* is really an automatic harp. The typical American variety has forty to fifty metal strings that can be tuned individually. A series of chord bars runs across one side of the instrument; each, when pressed, produces one chord by blocking off certain strings. It is a rather rudimentary instrument, although the plucking styles of several musicians have brought its playing level up by quite a bit.

The autoharp, thought to be an American invention of the 1800s, was used extensively in rural southern music. Maybelle Carter of the Carter Family made the autoharp famous and some later musicians, such as Mike Seeger, popularized it in the 1950s and 1960s.

Maybelle Carter holding an autoharp (*Photograph courtesy of the John Edwards Memorial Collection of the University of North Carolina at Chapel Hill*)

Harmonica

The *harmonica* is a small wind instrument that produces sound by blowing wind through small metal reeds. Normally, blowing in will produce one note at any point on the instrument's surface, and drawing out will produce another note. There are some harmonicas that have various buttons which allow the player to produce complex chords, but the harmonica used in most country music is a simpler kind.

The harmonica was invented in the early 1800s. The name was originally given to an instrument invented by Benjamin Franklin, the *glass harmonica*. The glass harmonica has little relationship to the folk harmonica because it produces sound by friction on the edges of glass bowls. The harmonica as a folk instrument has been used primarily by blues and folk musicians, but it is occasionally used by musicians in a country context.

Accordion

The *accordion* is similar to the harmonica in its tone production. Air is blown through reeds by the bellows, which are worked by the player's left arm. There is a piano keyboard played by the right hand, and button chords (as on the autoharp) that are played by the left hand. The accordion is most important in Cajun music of the 1930s, where it was the distinctive trademark of that music. It has also been used occasionally in other contexts of country music.

Jug

The *jug band* has often been thought to be the province of jazz because it was developed in black areas of southern cities during the dixieland craze of the 1920s. The jug band is simply one that uses a variety of musical instruments, one of which is a *jug* that is blown into like a closed organ pipe. The jug produces one pitch—unless it has fluid in it and the player imbibes between solos.

Jug bands were quite popular in the 1920s and early 1930s, and again in the 1960s when there was a revival in folk music. Jug bands were popular in mountain areas in the South since the early part of the century and quite often appeared on the WSM Barn Dance, the Opry, and "Hee Haw."

Piano

The piano was invented in the early eighteenth century in Europe and was imported to the United States. Several significant piano builders came to the United States in the nineteenth century. By the mid–1800s, the piano was the second most popular instrument in America, the first being the banjo. The piano has been an important instrument in the development of classical music, salon music of the 19th century, and many jazz and blues forms.

As a country instrument, the piano was not used very much until the 1950s. It came into use in country music primarily through rockabilly, Jerry Lee Lewis being the first to popularize it in a semi-country vein. From Jerry Lee Lewis on, many country bands have used the piano, although its role in the music is always subordinant. With the advent of country rock of the 1970s, the piano has become a rather standard part of crossover and experimental country music.

Drums

A *drum set* was not used very much in country music prior to rockabilly. However, there has always been a percussive nature to country music, so much of it having strong rhythmic drive to it. The case for the use of drums is similar to the case made for the piano. As a traditional part of a rhythm section, a drum set has become necessary to country music, except in solos or string bands.

Electric Bass

The *electric bass* is perhaps a bit different from the other standard members of a contemporary rhythm section in that country music has used a bass instrument for quite a while. The traditional bass instrument was a stand-up *double bass violin;* it was used in country bands back to the bluegrass days. This instrument was used to support the high string band sound and also functioned as a rhythm instrument, instead of drums.

Musicians started to amplify the double bass in the 1940s. When the electric bass was developed in the 1950s it fit naturally into rockabilly and then into the later forms mentioned for the drums. The electric bass differs from other stringed instruments mentioned in this chapter in that it is a solid body instrument. Without amplification microphones situated near the sounding board and strings, the electric bass would make no sound. The invention of the solid-bodied guitar allowed technicians to put more tension on the strings and to produce many sound effects previously impossible.

Saxes, Trumpets, and Trombones

Saxes, trumpets, and *trombones* are among the musical instruments that have occasionally been used in country music. The best early example is the use of one lone trumpet as a novel effect in the Elton Britt hit of the 1940s, "There's a Star-Spangled Banner Waving Somewhere." Western music, especially where it was influenced by the Tex-Mex sound, often used pairs of trumpets to imitate the mariachi sound. Western swing used standard dance band instruments as well.

As country music moved into film, the background scores were set for full orchestras, and many of the standard orchestral instruments were used in a way that faithfully recreated a country sound. Experiments like the Nashville Brass suggest another interesting use of alternate instruments, and of course the honking saxophone of rockabilly is an imperative part of that style.

In conclusion, there are some instruments that are a standard part of country music; they were mentioned first in this chapter. Then there are other instruments that have been used occasionally. And lastly, there are a variety of instruments that have been used to enhance the appeal of country music, some of which have taken country music very far from its simple roots. The biggest change in country music in its over sixty-year history is that of fusion with other forms of music, and the best way to trace that is through changes in instrumentation.

3 Original Country Music

EARLY PRACTITIONERS

This chapter begins our discussion with some of the real pioneers of country music. All of these names are known to true country fans, although Uncle Dave Macon and Roy Acuff would be the best known. However, they were each important in their own way to the establishment of the style of music we now call country. They were not all commercial successes at their trade; but, like early pioneers of other fields, they provided the impetus for others who followed.

Much of the music of the following musicians was regionally popular. It was the early success of some of their recordings that caused country music to become commercial music. It took interest and foresight on the part of certain recording companies and their representatives to record this early music at all.

The country music of the 1920s was primarily mountain music and was termed *hillbilly music,* for a reason which will be examined in this chapter. That name did not stick to country music because ultimately it was thought to be insulting, although when the term was first coined the musicians themselves were the ones who used it.

Much of the mountain music was simple by comparison to other later country styles. It was only after country music had been influenced by music outside of the rural setting that it became more complex. In that very important sense, this early mountain or "hillbilly" music was perhaps both more honest and more representative of the people from which it sprang.

Alexander Robertson

Alexander Campbell Robertson was born in Amarillo, Texas in the 1880s and died in the mid–1970s; "Eck" Robertson was one of the first great fiddlers and was the first recorded country musician. Old-time fiddling was

Eck Robertson (*Photograph courtesy of the John Edwards Memorial Collection of the University of North Carolina at Chapel Hill*)

very popular in West Texas, where he grew up, and he travelled extensively to hear other fiddlers. By the late 1890s he was already making a living as a solo fiddler, and he continued in that career until the middle 1960s. He won his last national fiddling title in 1962.

In 1922 he met another fiddler in Virginia named Henry Gilliland. They decided to go to New York to the Victor Talking Machine Company, which recorded several songs for them in June 1922. Victor released some of those duets, the most successful of which is "Sally Goodin'." (See the analysis of the duet "Arkansas Traveler" in the Appendix.) Eck Robertson was also known because of his trick of appearing in full western costume, which very well may have started that trend.

He did not record again until 1929, and that recording session was unproductive because of the onset of the Depression. Ralph Peer, the person responsible for that later recording, was to be important for his many contributions to the country music industry. The interesting thing is that the 1922 recordings were not actually released until after the recordings of "Fiddlin'" John Carson were successful. Therefore, Robertson and Gilliland were the first recorded country musicians but not the first to have records released.

Eck Robertson was a major influence because he was a superb technician, even though his style might seem old-fashioned today. He had total mastery of the fiddle and could weave fascinating variations of basic tunes. The piece analyzed in the Appendix does not have much variation to it; it was chosen so first-time analyzers would not be lost by complexity. For a true mastery of variation technique, listen to "Sally Goodin'."

The fact that Robertson wore western garb was of course influential. He was a good showman and provided a desired service for the people for whom he played. Unfortunately, he made very little money for his recordings and died feeling bitter about that. He received some of the acclaim he deserved; unfortunately he was not adequately compensated for his contribution to country music.

William Henry Whitter

William Henry Whitter (1892–1941) was important in the early development of country music, although most critics do not evaluate him very kindly. He was born near Fries, Virginia. After completing the sixth grade he went to work in the cotton mills. Whitter took up music as a pastime and by the age of twenty had learned several instruments. However, he only recorded on the guitar and the harmonica.

In 1923 he traveled to New York to the General Phonograph Corporation to make some test recordings. After "Fiddlin' " John Carson had become successful, Whitter was recalled to New York. In that session he recorded nine songs, two of which were put on an Okeh record—"The Wreck on the Southern Old '97" and "Lonesome Road Blues." This recording went on sale in January of 1924 and was reasonably successful.

Whitter enjoyed considerable success during his career. He put together one of the first string bands, Whitter's Virginia Breakdowners (so named because they had constant breakdowns in their car). He also recorded with one of the first female country singers to record, Roba Stanley. He put out over a hundred recordings during his career. Although his musicianship suffers by comparison with others, he was competent for his time. He recorded in many genres: British ballads, instrumentals, minstrel music, and sentimental pieces. He even recorded some World War I tunes—for example, "The Kaiser and Uncle Sam."

John Carson

"Fiddlin' " John Carson was undoubtedly the most important musician in the establishment of the commercial value of country music. He was born in the Blue Ridge Mountains of Kentucky. He spent time as a racehorse jockey, a railroad worker and foreman, and a house painter. He did not make his first recording until he was fifty-five years of age; the country music "Johnny Carson" was a seasoned veteran by the time he started commercializing country music.

In the early 1900s he moved to Atlanta, where he quickly established himself as a premium-quality fiddle player. He had learned to play the fiddle from his family, and the violin he played was brought by his grandfather to America from Ireland. By the late 1910s he was the finest fiddle player in Atlanta; in fact, he won the Georgia State Fiddler's Championship seven times.

In March 1922, the first radio station in the South, WSB, came on the air; on September 9 Carson made his first appearance. This radio station was to have a major influence in promulgating and commercializing country music.

Henry Whitter (*Photograph courtesy of the John Edwards Memorial Collection of the University of North Carolina at Chapel Hill*)

In June 1923, Ralph Peer of Victor and Polk Brockman, Atlanta's Okeh distributor, met to record two tunes of Carson's, "The Little Old Log Cabin in the Lane" and "The Old Hen Cackled and the Rooster's Going to Crow." This was the first country music record released, and its sale convinced Ralph Peer that country music was marketable. This was a major step in the development of country music.

John Carson continued to record for the rest of his life, except for the period between 1930 and 1934 (during the Depression). He was a fine technician and an even better singer. His voice was clear, and he communicated the words in a way that could be easily understood. Although other musicians may have been better, his influence cannot be doubted. Both Robertson and Whitter recorded before Carson did, but the important point is that Carson sold the first records, and it was his example that allowed the other records to be released.

John Carson, who was quite a showman, was loved by his friends and by the politicians he supported. During the governorship of Herman Talmadge, Carson was given a job as the state capitol elevator operator, obviously in loving remembrance of his political support through his music and lyrics. As America's first country musician to sell records, he represented country music well—and, fascinatingly enough, he played a Stradivarius violin.

Fiddlin' John Carson in a photo originally from the Atlanta Historical Society, taken about 1920 (*Photograph courtesy of the John Edwards Memorial Collection of the University of North Carolina at Chapel Hill*)

Al Hopkins

Al Hopkins is put into this section because he was the leader of a band that actually first used the term *hillbilly* in relationship to country music. Al and his brother Joe went with a put-together group of musicians from Virginia and North Carolina to New York to do a string band recording for Okeh records. They recorded six numbers; when asked for the name of the band, they responded that they were just "hillbillies." The name stuck, although it was eventually changed to the "Original Hillbillies." Although this group was not to have lasting musical significance, it was important for giving the name to the original country music. In fact, the 1920s and early 1930s were later called the "Golden Age of Hillbilly Music."

Vernon Dalhart

Marion Try Slaughter (Dalhart's real name) was born in 1883 on a farm near Jefferson, Texas. The family moved to Jefferson in the 1890s. Interestingly enough, Vernon Dalhart (a recording name adopted from two Texas town names) was trained as a classical singer and in fact had his first professional experience in opera, not country music. He recorded first in 1915 for the Edison company, chosen personally by Thomas Edison. The first recording, released in 1917, was a black dialect tune. He also recorded operatic excerpts. In 1916, he recorded a patriotic tune for Columbia. He started recording with Victor in 1918. Obviously, in those days they did not have exclusive artist contracts.

Al Hopkins and the Original Hillbillies. Al Hopkins is second from the left, Joe Hopkins is third from the left (*Photograph courtesy of the John Edwards Memorial Collection of the University of North Carolina at Chapel Hill*)

The first country tune he made was for Victor in 1924, a cover (a rendition by a different artist) of "The Wreck of the Old '97"; this recording became the first million seller in country music. The flip side of that record, "The Prisoner's Song," is analyzed in the Appendix. From that time on, a great percentage of the Dalhart recordings were in the country vein. Some have suggested that the reason is that Dalhart knew where the money was.

With his lifetime record sales exceeding 75 million, Vernon Dalhart was a very successful musician by anyone's standards. His singing style was very smooth and clear by comparison with other singers of the day. Dalhart did a great deal to popularize country music; he was perhaps the first cross-over artist, capable of selling records even to urban audiences. His cover version of the 1924 recording was one indication of his clear head for business. He died of a heart attack in Bridgeport, Connecticut in 1948.

Dalhart was enormously successful up until the Depression and undoubtedly influenced a number of country singers of his time and later. However, after the Depression he was unable to pick up his career, and he spent much of the rest of his life trying to trump up another contract. At the time of his death he was a check-out clerk in a hotel. In retrospect, though, Vernon Dalhart was a great influence in country music because he smoothed out the country style, made it less nasal, and popularized it among audiences that might otherwise not have listened to a country or "hillbilly" tune (a designation that Dalhart insistently refused to accept).

Uncle Dave Macon

Each of the musicians discussed in this chapter has made his contribution to country music, but there can be little doubt that Uncle Dave Macon was among the most important. David Harrison Macon (1870–1952) was born in Smart Station, Tennessee; he moved to Nashville when he was thirteen. When his father died in 1886 the family moved near Murfreesboro;

Vernon Dalhart (*Photograph courtesy of the John Edwards Memorial Collection of the University of North Carolina at Chapel Hill*)

when Macon got married he purchased a farm nearby, where he resided until his death.

He ran a transportation company from 1900 to 1920; after giving up that business he set to the task of becoming a musician. He traveled the Loew show circuit, and by 1924 he made his first recording for Vocalion records. One of the recorded tunes, "Hill Billie Blues," was the first to include the words Hill Billie [*sic*]. He also did a cover version of John Carson's "The Little Old Log Cabin in the Lane." But it was his first tune, "Chewing Gum," which would establish his reputation as a solid performer and premier entertainer.

Dave Macon was one of the first real banjo virtuosos; Uncle Dave was also the first country comic. In fact, he was billed as banjoist and humorist. He did things with the banjo that no other person did. In 1927 he formed a string band, the Fruit Jar Drinkers. Unlike most string bands of the time, this band played with great rhythmic intensity and with obvious spirit. Their recordings are filled with spoken and shouted exclamations of joy. Where other musicians sang songs that were filled with depression, Uncle Dave Macon consistently made light of everything and seemed to take life pretty lightly.

Dave Macon appeared on radio station WSM in Nashville in 1926 be-

Uncle Dave Macon and his son Dorris (*Photograph courtesy of the John Edwards Memorial Collection of the University of North Carolina at Chapel Hill*)

fore it was called the WSM Barn Dance. When it was renamed the Grand Ole Opry he was the first vocal country star to join up. He was the main star for the first fifteen years of the Opry and stayed around long enough to be joined by a new breed of country singers. Uncle Dave was there when others came to the Opry and thus became the greatest influence in Nashville music.

The repertoire of Dave Macon on record is extensive, with well over 175 recordings, including both instrumental numbers and songs running the gamut of subjects. His banjo tunes are especially pleasing. His banjo style was clearly an influence on banjo players who followed him; he had a very impressive style of playing even in early recordings. The most important legacy of Uncle Dave Macon is his tunes, called Uncle Dave tunes, that country musicians continue to play. Uncle Dave Macon was one of the superstars of country music, an artistic and musical success. He showed human and humorous concern over being just an entertainer, and felt lucky to be what he was. His last appearance with the Grand Ole Opry was on March 1, 1952; he entered the hospital in Mulfreesboro the next day and died three weeks later.

Roy Acuff

Roy Acuff is certainly one of the most important people discussed in this book. His influence on country music was first felt through his most significant career and then as a publisher and industry executive. Roy Acuff is discussed in this chapter because he has always been a traditional country singer. He is somewhat conservative personally, but much more so in his music. Although he has been tremendously important in the industry and is in fact still performing today, he really must be considered an original practitioner. Much of his music is traditional, but, like many musicians of the 1930s and 1940s, he made a living playing in honky tonks. And even when his lyrics were not strong or progressive, his playing style was heavily influenced by, and influential in, the strengthening of country music during the honky tonk period.

From left to right: Clell Sumney (Cousin Jody), Jess Easterday, Tiny (Red Jones's wife), Roy Acuff, and Red Jones (*Photograph courtesy of the John Edwards Memorial Collection of the University of North Carolina at Chapel Hill*)

Roy Acuff was born in Maynardsville, Tennessee in 1903. He really never intended to become a musician, although his father was a champion fiddler. All through high school his goal was to be an athlete; he worked hard toward this goal, and had tremendous success. After high school he played semi-pro baseball. By his mid-twenties he was about to sign with a major league ball team, the New York Yankees. Unfortunately, he had very light skin and was easily sunburned. He developed three cases of very severe sunstroke. The last time he was very sick, and he realized that he simply could not endure being out in the sun, which was of course a job hazard of a professional baseball player.

In his late twenties he had to find a new career, so he started listening to his father's recordings and learning how to play the fiddle. Fortunately, he became reasonably competent and was able to sign on with a medicine show troupe in 1932. In 1934 he began regular broadcasts with two radio stations in Knoxville. He toured extensively in Tennessee throughout the 1930s and had some very popular recordings during that time. In February of 1938 he was invited to join the Grand Ole Opry, where he eventually became the major star, surpassing the first original star, Uncle Dave Macon.

Roy Acuff became the first living member of the Country Hall of Fame in 1962 although he did not even begin his professional career as a musician and entertainer until he was thirty. He began the highly influential Acuff-Rose Publishing Company, which has been instrumental in many musical careers and responsible for increasing by many times the financial earnings of country musicians. He himself is quite wealthy as well. He was nominated for governor of Tennessee in the 1940s (although as a Republican he had little chance in a Democratic state). He has entertained Presidents, and worked with Richard Nixon in 1974 on the Grand Ole Opry. One of his stage techniques, playing with a yo-yo, became the center of that skit. His career has created new practices in country music, popularizing the dobro and other electric instruments; he has been very important as an industry executive and spokesman for country music; and he has consistently remained true to country music and served as a tower of strength for that field. Roy Acuff well deserves to have a permanent collection of memorabilia in the Country Hall of Fame.

His band, the Smoky Mountain Boys, had many members over the years. A number of them have gone on to significant careers as members of other bands and as session men in Nashville. His band at one time or another included each of the following instruments: fiddle, guitar (rhythm and lead), mandolin, dobro, banjo, string bass, piano, jug, accordion, steel guitar, and even, occasionally, drums. The sound of the Smoky Mountain Boys is unusual because it generally features the dobro more than fiddle. Roy Acuff's band is really a string band that has evolved over the years, and at its basis is a really traditional country sound. The reason the fiddle is not emphasized is that Roy Acuff never became a great fiddle player, although late in life he improved tremendously. He used the fiddle more as a prop than anything else, often balancing the fiddle or the bow or both on his forehead, nose, or chin. It was part of the comic routine.

Of course, comedy and crowd interaction has always been an important part of country music. Roy Acuff had a marvelous ability to communicate to audiences and should be seen primarily as an entertainer. However, as a result of the way he used the fiddle (or did not use it), his group's sound was slightly different from that of other string bands, especially in the early period.

Although conservative, Roy Acuff did experiment over the years. He added electronic instruments when it seemed valid, although during several periods he went purely traditional. The instrumentation of the Smoky Mountain Boys went through interesting cycles, moving back and forth between traditional and progressive. Acuff also took part in the Nitty Gritty Dirt Band album which was so significant in the early 1970s.

From 1940 to 1949, Acuff was involved in eight movies, which obviously increased his popularity. In fact, many of the tunes his band sang in these movies became recording hits as a result. His first film, *Grand Ole Opry* was historic in many ways. The musicians dressed in traditional country garb in the movie and it was the practice at that time to make all country singers look like cowboys. This particular film popularized traditional country music, and especially Roy Acuff, who by this time was a star on the Grand Ole Opry.

His other films were *Hi Neighbor* (1942), *O' My Darling Clementine* (1943), *Cowboy Canteen* (1944—this film also featured Tex Ritter), *Sing Neighbor Sing* (1944), *Night Train to Memphis* (1946), *Smokey Mountain Melody* (1948), and *Home in San Antone* (1949). These films, although not artistic masterpieces, were highly successful, popularizing Acuff's band and making country music of a traditional style quite a bit more visible.

The intriguing thing about Roy Acuff is the way he kept up what he started in the 1930s. He could simply have stopped performing, since he is highly influential in his business dealings and really a very important man. However, his love of performing has been unabated, and his career has been uninterrupted except during brief bouts of illness. He went back to fiddling, and remained a show stopper as an entertainer. His singing voice, while never considered great, has a very unusual high quality to it, and with it he is able to communicate the emotions of the words, sometimes even crying while he delivers certain lines. He continues to perform on a regular basis in Opryland and is still very much a part of Nashville country music today.

4 The Marketing Era

THE BRISTOL RECORDING SESSION

This chapter discusses the Carter Family and Jimmie Rodgers, and the historic recording session that started the careers of these musicians. The man responsible for that particular occurrence in country music was Ralph Peer, then talent scout for Victor Talking Machine Company.

Ralph Peer (1892–1960) was the first important publisher in country music. In fact, he saw the potential of country music before it was called country music and before anyone else (including the musicians) thought there was a market for it. He could be considered a visionary—or if not that, at least very astute.

Peer was the son of a phonograph dealer, Abram Peer, and the exposure he gained to the music industry as a youth certainly had a major influence on him. He left Northwestern University after two years to work in the recording field. From 1911 to 1919 he worked for the Columbia Phonograph Company of Kansas City, where he was born. An assistant manager by 1919, he quit that company and went to work for General Phonograph Corporation in New York. He was the production director for that company and also held the same position for Okeh Records, a subsidiary, starting in 1920. It was with Okeh that he recorded many major blues artists in the "race" category (an early euphemism for music of black performers—typically blues). His influence as the director and talent scout for that record label was strongly felt in the earlier stages of country or hillbilly recordings.

In 1926, Okeh was absorbed by the American Recording Corporation (later Columbia Records), and Peer left to join Victor. His main job was to supervise on site recording sessions either in a sound truck or in a makeshift recording studio in a warehouse or hotel room. He sought out rural musicians in particular because he believed there was a real market for their

Ralph Peer, in a photo taken in the 1930s (*Photograph courtesy of the Country Music Foundation Library and Media Center, Nashville, Tennessee*)

recordings. In the process he discovered many important musicians, Jimmie Rodgers and the Original Carter Family being good examples.

In 1928 he formed the Southern Music Publishing Company and, in 1940, Peer International. These became the largest music publishing companies in the South and were responsible for the tremendous growth in country music. Peer in particular was a giant in music publishing and the commercialization of country music. He was elected to the Country Music Hall of Fame in 1984.

But the Bristol, Tennessee recording session of late July and early August 1927 was probably the most important single example of Ralph Peer's influence, for it was at this recording session that he recorded both Jimmie Rodgers and the Carter Family. It was historic because it was the first time that he moved on site for recordings; all previous recordings had been done in New York in a recording studio. He advertised this event through a local news story and advertisement for Victor talking machines (record players). The fact that it was done in the South and in a rural town is particularly important.

Much can be said for the local color of country music, and somehow it really is not the same when it is done in a recording studio outside of the cultural environment of the music. Although less true today (because most country music is produced in elaborate recording studios with studio musicians), at the time of the original country musicians this music did not lend itself to studio productions. In a very important sense, hillbilly music of 1927 could not be produced in a recording studio in New York; it would not have been authentic.

The historic recordings of 1927 were made in the cultural milieu of the musicians, in a recording studio on the top floor of an empty building. Later recordings of the artists would be made in Camden, New Jersey; but the fact that the first recordings were made in the South helped to establish a sense of southern style in the way they performed. When they finally did land in a professional recording studio, they were expected to perform in that style and continue a sense of true authenticity. Earlier recordings had often been watered-down versions of true southern music; these Bristol productions were not like that. In addition, a new process of recording and record production was used which vastly improved the final result. These recordings were not only more authentic but also better in sound quality.

The recording studio was probably set up some time between July 21 and 23; newspaper advertisements appeared on July 24, and the Carter family arrived on July 31 and recorded six tunes on August 1 and 2. Jimmie Rodgers arrived in town either on July 31 or August 1 and recorded on August 4.[3]

The Carter Family

The Original Carter Family musical group was made up of Alvin Pleasant Delaney Carter (1891–1960), Sara Carter (1899–1979), and Maybelle Addington Carter (1909–1978). They came to be called the Original Carter Family because Maybelle formed a group with her daughters in the 1940s which was also called the Carter Family. This group was important because of its early recordings, but also for its longevity in performance and influence in country music.

A. P. Carter and Sara were married in 1915; Sara was only fifteen years old. A. P. had been working on the railroad and, like Jimmie Rodgers, probably learned various chants and tunes from southern black railroaders. He had also learned ballads from his mother as a youth. When A. P. met Sara, she was playing an autoharp and singing "Engine One-Forty-Three." The couple got their musical start playing at church socials, school parties, and local events.

In 1926, A. P.'s brother Ezra Carter married Maybelle Addington, who was proficient on both the banjo and the guitar. By this time they lived in Maces Spring, Virginia, and began entertaining as the group that would ultimately become famous. In actuality, A. P. and Sara had been offered a recording possibility by Brunswick Records before joining up with Maybelle, but the deal fell through: Brunswick wanted them to record square dance tunes, and A. P. had religious convictions which would not allow him to do that. Like many southern musicians, the Carters performed certain kinds of music and not others for religious reasons.

In any event, the Carter family had only a local following at the time that A. P. saw the advertisement for the Bristol recording session. He did not meet with support from the other members. He and Sara had three children and Maybelle was two months away from delivering her first child. However, through a fortunate turn of good oratory, A. P. convinced them to make the twenty-five mile trip to Bristol.

In the two days-worth of recording they did six tunes, all of which were released: "Bury Me under the Weeping Willow," "Little Log Cabin by the Sea," "The Poor Orphan Child," "The Storms Are on the Ocean," "Single Girl, Married Girl," and "The Wandering Boy." Sara and Maybelle each played guitar. Sara sang the lead part, A. P. sang bass, and Maybelle sang the middle voice. Maybelle was the strongest on an instrument; her guitar playing would ultimately be influential on other musicians. A. P. had an enormous talent as a vocal arranger, that is, in the way he put the harmonies together for the voices. None of the Carters were strong composers— in fact, they probably lifted most of their tunes from other sources, a practice that

[3]See Brian Rush, *Victor Master Book* (London: Hatch End, 1969), Vol. 2, for timetable.

The Original Carter Family. From left to right: Maybelle, A. P., and Sara (*Photograph courtesy of the John Edwards Memorial Collection of the University of North Carolina at Chapel Hill*)

was common and accepted at the time. However, the Carter family was the first group to put the material together commercially.

Ralph Peer was so impressed with the Carter family that he asked them to come to the main studio in Camden, New Jersey to make more recordings, which they did in 1928. This session produced "Wildwood Flower," "Diamonds in the Rough," and the immortal "Foggy Mountain Top." Eight other compositions were also recorded at that session. In February of 1929 they recorded an additional twelve songs. Recording opportunities were infrequent during the Depression, but the Carter family's work picked up in 1934, and they continued to record as a group until October 14, 1941. It is interesting that they continued to record and tour as a group even though A. P. and Sara were divorced in 1939. In their career they recorded over 250 songs.

Maybelle Carter continued to be a force in country music after the breakup of the original group. Sara married one of A. P.'s cousins and retired completely from singing for nine years. In the early 1950s A. P. and Sara tried to return to singing but were rather unsuccessful. But it was really Maybelle who continued the Carter name. She and her three children, the Carter Sisters, went on to develop a very successful career, first out of

Mother Maybelle Carter (with autoharp) and her daughter Helen Carter (with guitar), members of the famous Carter family (*Photo taken in Saginaw, Michigan, on October 6, 1963. Courtesy of Tom Cederberg, Teddy Bear Record Exchange, Bay City, Michigan*)

Richmond, Virginia and later out of Nashville. They did radio shows in Richmond from 1943 to 1948 and then joined the Grand Ole Opry in 1950.

Maybelle Carter continued to record with great success, with the full support of the Nashville system (much more on this throughout the book). By the mid-1950s she had become a superstar on the autoharp, developing a system of playing in a standing position, picking with the right hand and working the chord bars with the left. She was known as the "Queen of the Autoharp."

In 1971, she made another historic recording, an album with the Nitty Gritty Dirt Band—*Will the Circle Be Unbroken.* Maybelle appeared in 1963 at the Newport Folk Festival, where Mike Seeger introduced her as the most influential performer to have appeared at the festival. In 1967 she and Sara appeared at the same festival, with Joe Carter substituting for his father, A. P., who had died in 1960. From the early 1960s on there has been a revival of interest in the Carter family, and as a result, practically all of their original recordings have been rereleased.

The Carter family has been influential, especially in bluegrass music where many of their songs have been recreated by bluegrass musicians. Many people have done Carter family songs, and the vocal arranging style of A. P. continues to influence. Maybelle's guitar and autoharp playing have affected other country musicians as well. Maybelle continued the legend by becoming an Opry star. Her daughter June, who married Johnny Cash, was herself an influential performer.

June Carter with banjo (*Photo taken in Saginaw, Michigan, on October 6, 1963. Courtesy of Tom Cederberg, Teddy Bear Record Exchange, Bay City, Michigan*)

The lasting legacy of the Carter family is the body of songs they popularized that continue to be done in modern versions. Their status as the most important group to record at the Bristol session (actually Ralph Peer was much more impressed with them than he was with Jimmie Rodgers) is enough to insure their position in country music history, but their influence did not stop there. They were inducted into the Country Music Hall of Fame in 1970 in recognition of their significant contribution to country music.

Albums of the Carter Family include *50 Years of Country Music, Happiest Days of All, Lonesome Pine Special, The Original and Great Carter Family, My Old Cottage Home, Smoky Mountain Ballads, Mid the Green Fields of Virginia,* and *More Golden Gems from the Original Carter Family.*

Jimmie Rodgers

Although the Carters were to have lasting influence in country music, they did not have the kind of instantaneous success that Jimmie Rodgers did. Jimmie Rodgers also served as an immediate model for others, and many country stars started out as Jimmie Rodgers imitators, the most obvious indication of influence in any musical style. And the most unique feature of Jimmie Rodgers' phenomenal success story is that his career only lasted six years, from 1927 to 1933, when he died.

James Charles Rodgers (1897–1933) was born in Meridian, Mississippi. Most of his spare time in boyhood years was spent at the Mobile and Ohio Railroad station, where his father was employed as a section foreman. As Jimmie's mother had died when he was only four years old, he had little else to do but to try to follow in his father's footsteps, even though his father was really not home enough for Jimmie to see what that meant. In any event, Jimmie was fascinated by trains, and his ambition was to be a railroad man.

In 1911, Jimmie dropped out of school and got a job at the railroad station as a water boy, carrying water to the laborers working on the tracks. Most of these laborers were blacks, and this interaction with black and poor workers was to have an influence on Jimmie. When he started singing, many of his songs were about poor conditions, and many were heavily influenced by black music, both in singing and in playing style. Through these workers, Jimmie learned the rudiments of playing the banjo and the guitar, as well as the style of black music which was popular with them.

Rodgers was married in 1916 and fathered a daughter; the marriage was annulled two years later. Meanwhile, he worked as a brakeman on the railroad, strumming his guitar and singing to his fellow workers; he was able to spend quite a bit of time singing because the brakeman's job was sporadic in nature. Although unable to read or write music, Rodgers was prompted by the death of a friend in 1918 to compose his first song, "The Soldier's Sweetheart." By 1919 he had developed a particular singing trait, a yodeling style which was half way between Swiss yodeling and country singing; this ultimately became his trademark and most important trick, "the blue yodel."

In 1920, Rodgers married Carrie Williamson, whose family was at first not too pleased with the idea. There were six sisters in her family, all of them trained in music. They were quite religious, and although poor by most standards, they perceived themselves as being a cut above Jimmie Rodgers. The marriage did work out, although Carrie certainly lived through some hardships as a result of her husband's work patterns and especially because of his tuberculosis. Rodgers spent quite a bit of time at the Williamson household, singing to the piano playing of Carrie's sister Elsie, who became his musical arranger and confidante.

Carrie and Jimmie's first child, Carrie Anita, was born in 1921; the second daughter, June Rebecca, was born in 1923. Tragedy struck the Rodgers family for the first time in 1923 when, two months after her birth, June died. Shortly after that, in 1924, Rodgers had a severe lung hemorrhage and was forced to leave the railroad. When the disease was diagnosed as tuberculosis, he knew he would have to pursue some different means by which to support his wife and child, although he still believed himself to be a railroad man and intended to return to railroading when he got better. Unfortunately, he never really got better, and his short returns to working on the railroad probably contributed to his early death.

From 1924 to 1927, Rodgers bounced from job to job and floated aimlessly. At the same time his health was rapidly failing. He continued to devote more time to music even though he was attached to the railroad. In early 1927, Rodgers formed a band called the Jimmie Rodgers Entertainers and played briefly on a radio station in Asheville, North Carolina. This band fell apart. In late July of 1927 (probably July 24) Carrie Rodgers spotted an ad in the Bristol, Tennessee *Herald Courier.* This ad (previously mentioned) announced that records would be made by the Victor Talking Machine Company for ten days at 621 State Street, Bristol, Tennessee.

Carrie immediately urged her husband to attend this recording session and he eventually took Carrie's advice. He went to Bristol with a group known as the Tenneva Ramblers. Friction in the group brought about separate tryouts, with the Ramblers performing by themselves and Jimmie Rodgers doing two tunes by himself. Although Carrie wanted him to sing "T for Texas," he chose to sing "Soldier's Sweetheart" and "Sleep Baby Sleep." The latter had been recorded two years earlier by Riley Pickett; some have asserted that Jimmie Rodgers thought he could do a better job.

Peer was not obviously convinced that Jimmie Rodgers had great sales potential, but he was convinced about the Carter Family. He simply told Jimmie Rodgers that he might get a hold of him later. Some sources indicate that Peer encouraged Jimmie Rodgers to move nearer to Camden, New Jersey, in case they wanted to record more. In any event, Peer did not contact Jimmie Rodgers. In the meantime, one of Carrie's sisters, Annie, contacted

Jimmie Rodgers, in a photo taken in the early 1930s (*Photograph courtesy of the John Edwards Memorial Collection of the University of North Carolina at Chapel Hill*)

the Rodgers' and suggested they come and stay with her in Washington, D. C. They left immediately.

Rodgers' first recording, released on October 7, was not highly successful. In November of 1927, he decided that if Ralph Peer was not going to call him, he would just try to set up another recording session himself. He called Peer and told him that he was in New York for a few days and that if Peer wanted to record him, this would be a good time. Peer was interested, and set up a date on November 30, 1927 at the Victor studio in Camden. At the first session he sang "Ben Dewberry's Final Run" and "Mother Was a Lady." At a second session, he did "T for Texas" and "Away Out on the Mountain." It was these recordings which really launched his career.

Ralph Peer knew by this time that he had a real winner on his hands and from that day guided Rodgers' career beyond expectations. These recordings alone prompted the largest payment Victor had ever made to a beginning solo singer.

In February of 1928 Rodgers recorded the following songs: "Dear Old

Sunny South by the Sea," "Treasures Untold," "The Sailor's Plea," "Brakeman's Blues," "Memphis Yodel," "Blue Yodel #2" ("T for Texas" was also called "Blue Yodel"), and "In the Jailhouse Now." In July of 1928 Jimmie Rodgers was in his first theater performance as an added attraction, singing "T for Texas," "Soldier's Sweetheart," and "Frankie and Johnnie." In September of 1929 Rodgers made his first film, *The Singing Brakeman.*

Rodgers continued to tour and do performances throughout the South even though he was constantly battling tuberculosis. Other singers, such as Gene Autry, began to imitate Rodgers' style. In June of 1931 the Original Carter family met with Rodgers and did recordings together in Louisville, Kentucky. Ernest Tubb began singing like Rodgers in 1932. By 1933 Rodgers knew that his health was rapidly failing. In order to provide for the future of his family, he made a last ditch effort to record as many songs as possible for later release. In fact, in those last recording sessions he would record one song and then lay down on a cot in the studio to rest up for another. He lost the battle with tuberculosis on May 26, 1933 at the age of thirty-five.

In a six-year span Jimmie Rodgers recorded 111 songs selling over 20 million copies. His death caused a wave of musical tributes, and in 1961 he was the first musician enshrined in the Country Hall of Fame. His mountain music with songs about trains poverty, and memories of his earlier years, has earned him the title "Father of Country Music." He had only a six-year career, at least half of which was during the Depression, yet he achieved enormous popularity.

Popular albums of Jimmie Rodgers include *Legendary Performer, Best of the Legendary Jimmie Rodgers, Country Music Hall of Fame, Jimmie Rodgers, Jimmie the Kid, My Rough and Rowdy Ways, My Time Ain't Long, Train Whistle Blues, This Is Jimmie Rodgers, Short but Brilliant Life of Jimmie Rodgers,* and *Never No Mo' Blues.*

THE FIRST COMMERCIAL PERIOD OF COUNTRY MUSIC

While the first period of commercial country music started with "Fiddlin' " John Carson, the real growth in commercialization was centered around the Carter Family and Jimmie Rodgers. At the end of the 1920s Jimmie Rodgers was created by Ralph Peer as a commercial entity. His emergence as a singing performer and film actor had a great deal to do with subsequent packaging of country singers, especially the singing cowboys, considered in the next chapter.

The career of Jimmie Rodgers survived through the Depression, even though not very much else survived during that period. If Jimmie Rodgers had lived longer, there can be little question that he would have been the first millionaire country musician. His records continued to sell well after his death and are still sold today.

This period of country music is marked not only with discovery but with the development of country music as a commercial enterprise. Although the commercial value of early careers was not as great as we see today, those early careers showed how country music could be packaged and sold to the public and an impressive sales market was created.

5 Western Music

SINGING COWBOYS

This particular subject warms my heart because I can remember growing up with the singing cowboys. They presented an image of life that captivated many young people from the mid–1930s into the 1960s. I'll bet that thousands of children in that era at one time or another said "I want to be a cowboy," and it was the singing cowboys of movie lore that made us feel that way.

The singing cowboy was more important than just the character that he represented in films; he was a symbol for the nation. He symbolized a hero who always made things better for the people he touched. It is doubtful whether the same kind of hero would be successful today because society has changed so much in the last fifteen years, but in the 1940s and 1950s the singing cowboy was an idyllic image for a nation that identified with heroes, especially heroes of the West.

The singing cowboy as a symbol of the Old West also served to remind us of the concept of western expansion that has always been so pivotal to the American identity. The Old West was the place where everyone could get rich, where lives were started anew and legends were made. The singing cowboy was a mystical figure for many people. He allowed us to escape to a world where everything was always better, and confirmed the rightness of the American feeling of superiority over the rest of the world.

The singing cowboy was recognized as a part of the American patriotism because he was always helping someone else, always optimistic, always saving the day. Anyone growing up during that era has to remember going to the movies for 25 cents, paying 10 cents for popcorn, and watching the new Flash Gordon serial and two cowboy movies. You could cheer the guy in the white hat, boo the evil characters in black hats. And you could always count on the story to end with the wrongs being righted, with the hero getting the girl, and both riding off into the sunset.

Gene Autry

Orvon "Gene" Autry was born in Tioga, Texas in 1907. He was raised primarily in Oklahoma but returned to Tioga for high school, from which he graduated in 1925. After graduation he took a job as a railroad telegraph operator in Sepulpa, Oklahoma, a job which ultimately became the springboard for his phenomenal career.

Gene Autry had learned a few songs while in Oklahoma and Texas, but music was simply not something he considered doing for a living. However, when he began working as a telegraph operator he discovered that he had a great deal of time without anything to do between telegrams. He bought a guitar and began singing songs and composing some of his own. The story goes that he was singing and playing the guitar one night when a fellow came in to send a telegram. After writing out the order and signing it, the guy said to Gene Autry that he ought to be on radio as a singer. The customer was Will Rogers, who was a big star.

Autry took his advice and soon after got a job on station KVOO as "Oklahoma's Singing Cowboy" (a name that stuck regardless of which state he was in at the time). He became popular in Oklahoma almost overnight, and soon was signed to make several cowboy records. In 1929 he was signed by the American Record Company, and he went to New York to cut six songs, one of which was "That Silver-Haired Daddy of Mine." In 1930 he left Oklahoma to begin working on WLS in Chicago; it was there that he became one of the most popular stars in the midwest. He remained in that position until 1934. His career expanded because of his radio jobs and his recordings. His first original recording, "That Silver-Haired Daddy of Mine," was used quite frequently in films and sold over 5 million copies.

In 1934 Autry moved to Hollywood to play a small singing role in a film, *In Old Santa Fe*. After this his film career took off, and he became one of the most important film stars of the 1930s and 1940s. He made over 100 films in his career and appeared in person all over the world. He was truly an international star, all based on singing cowboy songs.

He served in the army air corps from 1942 to 1945 as a pilot ferrying cargo and supplies to India and North Africa. His voluntary service, an act of patriotism, was important to his career but was also a very honest gesture. Gene Autry was believable as a hero because he had a hero quality about him personally. After his army service he returned to Hollywood and began making new movies. He returned to "Melody Ranch," a show he had started on radio in 1939 which later was on TV; this show was to run for seventeen years. Through this medium, he expanded his listening audience and further marketed country music. It was during this time that Sears began distributing the Gene Autry "Melody Ranch Roundup" guitar that influenced many young people into learning guitar.

Gene Autry recorded for Okeh, Vocalion, Victor, Gennet, ARC Group, and Conqueror until the late 1940s, when he signed with Columbia. Although primarily known for cowboy songs, he also had crossover hits, such as the Christmas tunes "Here Comes Santa Claus" in 1948 and "Rudolph the Red-Nosed Reindeer" in 1949, and the pop hit "Buttons and Bows" from 1948. During the 1950s he moved into other areas, although he kept performing and recording. By the 1960s he had become successful in many business ventures— he was the first musician to buy a baseball team, the California Angels, and owned radio stations, hotels, TV films, and other properties. By the time I met him in the late 1950s he was already a rich man, but since he is such a nice guy I figure he deserved it.

The film image of Gene Autry was supported by his horse Champion; the hero's horse was an integral part of the symbolism of the cowboy. Some of the films he starred in were *Boots and Saddles* (1937), *Under Western Stars* (1938), *Carolina Moon* (1940), *Back in the Saddle* (1941), *Sunset in Wyoming*

Gene Autry with his horse, Champion (*Photograph courtesy of the John Edwards Memorial Collection of the University of North Carolina at Chapel Hill*)

(1942), *Range War* (1946), *Sioux City Sue* (1947), *Guns and Saddles* (1949), and *Goldtown Ghost Riders* (1953).

The musical importance of Gene Autry is even more impressive than his life story. He started out in the late 1920s as a Jimmie Rodgers impersonator, but he gradually shifted to a style all his own. By the time he was established in Chicago he had a singing style which was very different from Rodgers'; his was smooth and full-voiced, whereas Rodgers always sang with a tight throat and a relatively thin sound. Also, as Autry developed as an individual, his lyric content began to change. He sang optimistic songs about the American West, speaking to people in a way they wanted to hear.

Probably the most important characteristic of his music and style was that it was optimistic; it made people feel good. I would venture to say that Gene Autry was the first really successful crossover musician, appealing to audiences which probably would not have listened to pure hillbilly music. He was also important because his career had many facets to it. He did everything that Jimmie Rodgers did, but in grander design and greater numbers. Gene Autry had everything—fan clubs, movies, million-selling records over

Jimmie Rodgers (left) and Will Rogers (right), in the early 1930s (*Photograph courtesy of the John Edwards Memorial Collection of the University of North Carolina at Chapel Hill)*

four decades, personal appearances, a town named after him (Gene Autry, Oklahoma), and more. He had a marketing strategy that served as a model for others who tried to imitate him, and he had plenty of imitators.

Many country singers after him tried to do things the way he did. He developed a new fad for singing in a clear voice without a noticeably western or southern twang. He also popularized the guitar through his movies. In many of the movies, which were pretty much formula films, he would be singing a song and something bad would happen. He would put the guitar down, go save the situation, and then come back and pick up the guitar as if nothing had happened. This was one of the grand appeals of Gene Autry's films. Some of the people that Gene Autry influenced directly were Roy Rogers, Johnny Bond, the Sons of the Pioneers, Eddie Dean, Rex Allen, and Tex Ritter. His career influenced many others, and I would conjecture that the force of country music would not have been the same without Gene Autry.

However, the chief importance of Gene Autry to country music is that he made it respectable. Other early country giants were self-effacing characters who seemed always down on their luck. Gene Autry, by contrast, was a real hero who had a tremendously strong ego. That is not to say that he was egotistical; he was just self-assured. When Gene Autry sang, it was from the heart. But unlike many down-home singers, Gene Autry did not sound sad when he sang, and he was obviously a winner. Many country musicians and writers about country music do not give Gene Autry the credit he deserves; in fact, Tex Ritter was elected to the Country Hall of Fame five years before Gene Autry was.

The lasting legacy of Gene Autry is that he was our hero at a time when we could have that kind of hero. He sold a lot of people on country music because he was so dynamic in person, on record, and on film. He popularized the guitar through the Sears connection, and provided a model for the marketing of a country musician. He captivated the hearts and minds of many children who wanted to be like the man in the white hat. In these days, when things seem to be so confusing, memories like those that Gene Autry gave us on Saturday afternoons can certainly help us make it through the hard times.

Roy Rogers

Leonard Franklin Slye was born in Cincinnati, Ohio in 1912. The son of a shoemaker, he lived in Cincinnati for seven years and then moved to a farm near Portsmouth, Ohio. His father worked in town, while his mother and three sisters worked on the farm. Although it did not seem important at the time, living on the farm gave Leonard (stage name Roy Rogers) a chance to learn to ride. As a youth, he was also captivated by the cowboy movies of Buck Jones and Tom Mix, which he saw at the local cinema on Saturday afternoons, little knowing that eventually he would become a star just like them.

Although he originally had visions of becoming a dentist, the family finances did not allow him to go to school. When the family moved back to Cincinnati, Roy went to work for his father in the shoe factory. The family drove to California during Roy's teenage years to visit one of his sisters who had recently gotten married. The trip was to be important because it placed in Roy's mind the notion that he should be in California.

He bought a guitar and learned to play it and sing. In fact, by 1928 he was already proficient enough to sing and double as a square dance caller for local dances. In 1930 he hitched a ride to California with a relative, fulfilling an earlier dream. At first he held a variety of jobs, such as picking peaches and driving a truck. But all the time he kept on singing and hoping for a break.

The first group that he joined was called the Rocky Mountaineers; the group lasted about two months. He then organized the International Cowboys, but this group was basically a failure as well. In the last part of 1933, he met two other performers, Tim Spencer and Bob Nolan, with whom he formed the Sons of the Pioneers; they did not fail but rather succeeded beyond their wildest dreams. Between 1934 and 1937, the Sons of the Pioneers became a very popular musical group. Their sound was very smooth and relaxed and appealed to many audiences other than just country audiences. But probably the most important feature of the group was their continuous output of major country tunes, compositions that would remain a part of the country repertoire; good examples are "Tumbling Tumbleweeds" and "Cool Water," both by Bob Nolan.

The music of the Sons of the Pioneers is very interesting (see the analysis later of "Tumbling Tumbleweeds") in that it sounds so smooth, yet is so irregular. They did music that was much closer to the fabric of country music than many country fans perceived, music like Jimmie Rodgers' in its closeness to folk roots. Even though the lyrics are different, the underlying style is similar. However, it was in their original vocal harmonies that they were at the height of their creativity. If A. P. Carter was a genius as an arranger for the Carter Family, Tim Spencer was the genius of the Sons of the Pioneers. In fact, the greatest contribution to American popular music of the Sons of the Pioneers was in vocal arrangement.

Building on a major career as a recording and performing star, Roy Rogers auditioned for a movie in 1937 called *Under Western Skies*. Through very good luck, he got the lead role. With Trigger, his white horse, and Dale Evans, his leading lady and wife in 1947, he went on to star in over 100 films. A sampling of his films include *Under Western Skies* (1938), *The Carson City Kid* (1940), *Dark Command* (1940), *Robin Hood of the Pecos* (1942), *The Man from Music Mountain* (1944), *Along the Navajo Trail* (1946), *Roll on Texas Moon* (1947), *Night Time in Nevada* (1949), *Trail of Robin Hood* (1951), *Son of Paleface* (1952), and *Pals of the Golden West* (1953). I even

Roy Rogers on his horse Trigger (*Photograph courtesy of the John Edwards Memorial Collection of the University of North Carolina at Chapel Hill*)

recall seeing an episode of "Fall Guy" in 1983 that featured Roy Rogers, a second generation Trigger, Dale Evans, and a whole hoard of western heroes.

Roy Rogers, like Gene Autry, went into business ventures after his film career slowed down. Investing wisely, he and Dale Evans moved to Apple Valley, California, fairly near the Roy Rogers Museum, where you can see a stuffed Trigger. Dale Evans was a constant source of inspiration to her husband, and her career rivaled his in popularity.

Roy Rogers was in many ways similar to Gene Autry, although his singing style was different. Gene Autry was primarily a solo artist, while Roy Rogers was primarily a group artist. Rogers did not have the same quality voice as Gene Autry, but it was expressive and successful. However, it was the unique close harmony sound of the Sons of the Pioneers that made Roy Rogers marketable as a film star. They were comparable to the Hi-Lo's of the 1930s and 1940s, a unique experiment using cowboy songs as their basic material. Of course, they had fine composers in the group, and their continuous production of solid hit material was responsible for their lasting popularity. The Sons of the Pioneers did not stop performing when Roy Rogers left the group. They backed up Roy in many of his movies, but they also grew themselves, up to six members in the 1940s. They also appeared on The Roy Rogers Show, a television series that lasted from 1952 to 1954.

Dale Evans (*Photograph courtesy of the John Edwards Memorial Collection of tne University of North Carolina at Chapel Hill*)

Although similar to Gene Autry in his image, Roy Rogers projected a slightly different character on the screen. Roy Rogers was scrappier. A small man, he at times looked like an imp when he got into a fight. His singing was different as well. Although quite smooth, he had more of a plaintive quality to him than did Autry. Roy Rogers' chief strength lay in the way he interacted with others. Often he was the star, but it was the way he worked with others, the relationship to his horse and to his girl, which made his movies impressive.

Tex Ritter

Maurice Woodward Ritter (1906–1974) was born in Panola County, Texas on a ranch that had been in his family since 1830. On the ranch they raised cotton, corn, peanuts, and cattle. As a result of this environment, "Tex" (as he would later be called) grew up around ranching, roping, and singing. In a sense, Tex Ritter was a more authentic cowboy than the others previously discussed.

In 1924 he enrolled at the University of Texas as a law major. He also showed a continuing interest in Texas folklore. While still a student, he worked out a singing and lecture program that he delivered to whoever was interested. His show, which was called "The Texas Cowboy and His Songs," was very popular, and he actually went on tour with it. He settled in Chicago, attending Northwestern University for a while. He then moved on to

Tex Ritter, in a photo from the 1960s (*Courtesy of Tom Cederberg, Teddy Bear Record Exchange, Bay City, Michigan*)

New York, where he landed a job on a radio station as a disc jockey. His strong Texas drawl, which at first was thought to be a liability by potential bosses, contributed to his overnight success. As both writer and performer for radio in the 1930s, he became one of the most important people in that medium. He had major input into the original "Lone Ranger" radio series and starred in "Death Valley Days," "Tex Ritter's Camp Fire," and "Cowboy Tom's Round Up."

In New York he was in a play called *Green Grow the Lilacs,* which was later turned into a musical called *Oklahoma.* He was one of the early stars on the New York version of the WHN Barn Dance. He had already become a very important star before he moved to Hollywood in 1936 to do his first film, *Song of the Gringo.* He was an active performer in westerns after that, making more than fifty films in the 1940s and 1950s. He also continued to tour extensively. His personal magnetism was responsible for his enormous success.

Some of his hits on record were "Jingle, Jangle, Jingle" (1942), "Jealous Heart" (1944), "There's a New Moon over My Shoulder" (1944), and "I Dreamed of a Hillbilly Heaven" (1961). Most of these tunes, especially the first and the last, were crossover hits. He appeared frequently on television throughout the 1950s and early 1960s, moving to Nashville in 1965, where he became a member of the Grand Ole Opry. He remained active as a touring musician, an officer of several recording industry organizations, a supporter of country music, and a member of the Country Hall of Fame, until his death of a heart attack in 1974. Tex Ritter was recognized by the Hall of Fame five years before the model for singing cowboys, Gene Autry, was recognized. This was probably because of his commitment to country music and his activities in the industry.

Tex Ritter was more identified with mainstream country music than were Gene Autry and Roy Rogers. He supported country music and moved to Nashville in the 1960s, while Gene Autry and Roy Rogers remained in California. His singing style and speaking voice do not hide his Texas background, whereas the other musicians sing without any noticeable accent. But probably the most important reason why he was appreciated is that he was personally captivating; he had charisma. And he used that charisma in a variety of ways—for entertainment purposes and for support of the country music industry. His involvement in Nashville towards the end of his life confirmed the earlier feeling that Tex Ritter was a singing cowboy who was at heart a country musician.

WESTERN SWING

Most authorities on country music, including the Country Music Association, agree that western swing is an important and influential type of country music. In this section we will discuss its constituent parts and try to illustrate why it was so important.

Western swing is western music first and country music second, at least in its growing stages. It is the first important fusion music of all the music discussed in this book. Although other styles had crossover popularity, western swing was a true mixture of western music (with its country and folk roots), string band music, and big band jazz music. Some jazz writers have included discussions of Bob Wills in their books. Most country writers include Bob Wills and give mention to Spade Cooley and Hank Thompson. But western swing does not fit conveniently into any category. The best proof of this is that Bob Wills was surprised when the Country Music Association voted him into the Country Hall of Fame in 1968; Wills did not believe that he was a country musician. Fortunately, he accepted the award.

Western swing developed out of fiddle music, and its practitioners were fiddlers. However, instrumentation went beyond the traditional string band, especially during the 1930s and 1940s. While southern fiddle players often engaged in lengthy variations on basic tunes, western fiddlers improvised or made up music based on the chord changes presented by a regular tune. Western fiddling was thus more akin to jazz, although the influence of southern music was clearly present in western swing fiddling. Almost by definition, much of western swing was more virtuosic than other styles of country music. One of the reasons for the continuing interest in western swing today is its technical quality.

Western swing was fundamentally music for dancing. While much of country music is designed for dancing, western swing is particularly appropriate for that function. Instrumental in character, it also served as an appropriate backdrop for vocalists, especially for featured soloists like Bing Crosby, who sang with the Bob Wills Band. In the 1930s and 1940s, western swing bands became big bands with the addition of saxophones, trumpets, and trombones. They were then in an excellent position to compete with other big bands of the day. Bob Wills and Spade Cooley and their bands both competed easily with the Dorsey Brothers, Glenn Miller, and Freddy Martin.

Like the singing cowboys, western swing musicians were featured in films and used as background musicians. In fact, Bob Wills made several film shorts that were used as intermission films between full-length features.

This was of course a marketing trick for western swing music. But since the lyrics of songs that were done by western swing bands were basically optimistic, these shorts produced a happy effect on the audiences. Similarly, the upbeat instrumental music produced good feelings in the crowds who came to listen and to dance.

In the 1930s and 1940s big band music was the thing; by the late 1940s many of the western swing bands had returned to a string band format. The jazzy feeling of western swing prevailed throughout its history, as well as its basic optimism. This was a music that fit all seasons.

Although there are many characteristics peculiar to western swing, the most obvious is that it has a different beat. It sounds more like jazz because it uses a standard jazz rhythm section, at least on recordings from 1935 to the mid–1940s. Unlike other forms of country music of the time, western swing used a piano, bass, guitars, and drums. The use of the drums was rather innovative; a drum set would become part of rockabilly and other country styles after the 1950s, but in the 1930s it was unheard of to use drums in a country recording. There were western swing tunes that did not use a full rhythm section, and the basis of the music was still the string sound. But when western swing bands had seventeen to twenty-four members and functioned as big bands, they used a full rhythm section.

Another major factor in the western swing sound was the incorporation of traditional big band instruments in full arrangements for the orchestra. During the big band era Bob Wills developed a seventeen-piece orchestra that used a traditional big band instrumentation, full rhythm section plus steel guitar. He played fiddle and often had one more fiddle player as well. This was a hybrid sound, appealing to big band audiences but also to western song fans. Spade Cooley had as many as twenty-four musicians in his band in the late 1940s, and consistently sold out performances, with as many as 6000 people in attendance. The music played by these large ensembles was completely written out, so there was a definite structure to the music (a fact that will make analysis of a few examples quite easy for us). There was still improvisation, but as in traditional big band music, it was controlled by the written arrangements, with a particular player allowed to improvise at a specified time in the tune.

But the most important quality of western swing was in the appeal of its hybrid nature. It had complete organization and show quality because of the large number of musicians and the style that evolved; it was quite predictable, and audiences could count on hearing specific arrangements done the same way each time. It had a folksy quality because of the nature of the western songs that made up the repertoire. And it had flashy fiddling, with vocalists galore. Western swing had so many elements that it succeeded in satisfying everyone. Although it could take on a formal quality, it was folk music in the sense that the common people could identify with it easily, whereas other forms of music might make some people feel out of place.

But the intriguing thing is that western swing had so much influence on other styles. Bill Haley, known primarily as a rock and roll musician, was first a country musician; he acknowledged the influence of western swing, as did jazz artists of the West Coast. Even classical composers made use of western swing pieces. And country musicians like Merle Haggard credit western swing with convincing them to take country music seriously. If the singing cowboys popularized and raised the respectability of country music, the western swing musicians made it technically credible.

Bob Wills

Occasionally it is appropriate to mention another book in a text; this is especially true in the case of Bob Wills. Charles R. Townsend wrote a book called *San Antonio Rose: The Life and Music of Bob Wills*[4]. This meticulous piece of scholarship represents some of the finest writing in country music,

[4]Urbana: University of Illinois Press, 1976.

and I would recommend it to anyone interested in further reading. Much of the information in this section is from that book.

James Robert Wills (1905–1975) was born near Kosse, Texas and grew up around a lot of musicians. His father was a champion old-style fiddler, and it was expected that his oldest son would follow in his footsteps. At first it did not happen, but after a move to West Texas Bob began playing the fiddle. He played in public for the first time when he was ten, although most of the time he accompanied his father, playing the mandolin. The kind of music they played was primarily ranching music, with a heavy dose of roundup songs, but there was also a clear influence of Tex-Mex music. In fact, his first two compositions, "San Antonio Rose" and "Spanish Two Step" of 1927, illustrate the influence of Mexican folk music.

Townsend considers black music to be the single most important influence on the beat of Wills' western swing. Wills worked in the cotton fields with the children of black farmhands, and this close association gave him an intimate knowledge of black music and, in particular, of rhythms associated with black music. Wills later credited those early experiences for his uncanny ability to maintain a sense of swing in his music; other musicians who worked with him recognized that special gift. The notion that western swing was a hybrid of western song, New Orleans dixieland, and the blues is undoubtedly true at least for Bob Wills.

Over the years he was to record many of the black songs that he first heard as a youth. His fiddle style also was largely derivative of this music. He slurred the notes in a blues style (like the singers he had heard) and used blue notes. He also used syncopation (irregular accents) and a pronounced beat in his playing. When he formed his own band, that rhythmic influence was to manifest itself in the instrumentation and style of playing.

In the summer of 1929 he formed the Wills Fiddle Band, himself on fiddle and Herman Arnspiger on guitar. In 1930, living in Fort Worth, he added three musicians, and they got work on several radio stations. In January 1931 his band started a program in which they advertised Light Crust Flour, and they changed their name to the Light Crust Doughboys. This first in country music history ultimately proved to be a springboard to success for Bob Wills. In 1932 the band made a recording for Victor: "Nancy Jane" and "Sunbonnet Sue."

In 1932 the owner of the company that made Light Crust Flour ordered the band to stop doing dances, causing a major confrontation. The singer, Milton Brown, quit the band to form his own band, Milton Brown and His Musical Brownies. Wills was fired from the band in August 1933 and formed his own band, Bob Wills and His Playboys, which eventually became the Texas Playboys. They moved to Tulsa, Oklahoma to radio station KVOO in 1934, where they advertised Play Boy Flour by General Mills. The radio program was shared by Bob Wills and his brother Johnnie Lee for twenty-four years.

The original Playboy band had six musicians. By 1935, when they did their first recording, there were thirteen musicians: a full rhythm section, a string band, trumpets, and sax/clarinet. This band would grow to the seventeen-musician band discussed earlier. It was from 1935 to the mid–1950s that Bob Wills was most prosperous. However, his Playboy band from 1935 to 1941 was the most exciting thing he ever did. They were billed as the most versatile big band because they could play standard string band music, big band music, and dixieland, and could improvise with the best of them. Their show was well organized and had high visibility. When they remade "San Antonio Rose" as a big band vocal in 1940, they were catapulted into national acclaim. A writer from *Metronome* came to Tulsa and described the band members as some of the best jazzmen one could find. In short, the Bob Wills Texas Playboys were hot.

The band disintegrated during World War II; Bob Wills served in the army for a short period. After the war, he put together a new band that was more of a string band, and continued to have success. He played steadily until 1969, when he had a massive stroke. In 1971 Merle Haggard recorded a

Bob Wills and the Texas Playboys; Wills is at far left with hand to ear (*Photograph courtesy of the John Edwards Memorial Collection of the University of North Carolina at Chapel Hill*)

tribute album with some old members of Wills' band, and there was a revival of interest in Wills' music. He recovered from the stroke, to be given countless awards and accolades from the public and from fellow musicians. In December 1973 he went to Dallas to record with the Texas Playboys, a recording session that included Merle Haggard. The night after the first day of recording he had a stroke in his sleep, and remained in a coma for seventeen months. He died on May 13, 1975.

Bob Wills will be remembered as an innovator and entertainer. He always recognized that his music was for dancing, and felt an obligation to the public for which he performed. Yet his music was complex and different from other music of the time. The reasons were the rather unique set of influences on Bob Wills and the strength and determination he used to get what he wanted.

Hank Thompson

Henry "Hank" Thompson was born in Waco, Texas in 1925. Obviously of the generation after Bob Wills, Hank Thompson was early influenced by western swing, then moving easily into more of a honky-tonk style in the late 1940s. His band, the Brazos Valley Boys, which has had enormous popularity in country music, has been specifically recognized as a western band. Their sound is an interesting hybrid of western swing, Tex-Mex music and, from the mid–1950s on, country rock and roll. The Brazos Valley Boys have traveled all over the world.

Hank Thompson started in radio while still in high school, returning to

Hank Thompson as he looked in the 1960s (*Courtesy of Tom Cederberg, Teddy Bear Record Exchange, Bay City, Michigan*)

it after serving in the navy during World War II. His first record was made in 1946, and from that time on his recordings have been successful. He is rich as a result of writing his own tunes and having other people sing them.

The relationship of Thompson's music to western swing is sometimes tenuous but nevertheless always there. Hank Thompson never had a large band, but western swing influence is present in his playing style. His sound, obviously Texan with Mexican influence, is characteristic of western swing. However, the most important western-swing characteristic of his music is the strong sense of beat. Eventually that strong beat would be characterized as honky-tonk, but Hank Thompson was influenced by other Texans prior to the time the term honky-tonk was used to describe musical characteristics.

Spade Cooley

Donnell C. Cooley (1910–1969) was born into a family of fiddle players in Grand, Oklahoma. Unlike the other musicians mentioned in this chapter, "Spade" Cooley (so named because of a poker game) was really not influenced that much by western cowboy life as a youth, but seems to have picked it up for professional reasons. He moved to Hollywood in the early 1930s and eventually became an extra in western films. His musical career was totally in southern California.

His first successful band did not begin until 1942. He put together the largest western swing band ever, which at times grew to twenty-four members. Cooley was a radio performer in the early 1940s, leased a ballroom in

Hank Thompson in the 1980s (*Courtesy of Churchill Records, Tulsa, Oklahoma*)

Santa Monica for dances in 1946, and started doing a TV show in 1948. He was a charismatic leader with great screen visibility, both on TV and film. The public was shocked to hear of his 1961 conviction for killing his wife, for which he was imprisoned from 1961 to 1969. Shortly after being paroled, he suffered a fatal heart attack while performing with a new band for a benefit.

Spade Cooley's band was the Mantovani strings of western swing. He used a full big band, a full string section and a rhythm section with extra country string instruments. His full violin section played in pop style, not country fiddling, with sustained chords and beautiful melodies. Quite a bit of the time, Spade Cooley's band played not like a western band at all, but rather like an extended dance band. On the whole, however, Spade Cooley's band played a mixture of jazz (western swing), country western, western, and dance band music. The only element he did not have that Bob Wills did was dixieland. And I do not recall Spade Cooley playing any blues or black-based music. Spade Cooley was very popular in southern California and eventually in other parts of the United States, but his music was perhaps more of an urban phenomenon than a rural one.

Spade Cooley was a western swing musician, especially in his fiddle playing. The composition analyzed in the Appendix, "Shame on You," was a big hit in 1945 and illustrated well the notion that crossover popularity could be had by country musicians, especially if they couched their tunes in western swing sounds. The logical conclusion to this is that western swing was more than just a playing technique; it was an attitude that incorporated

Spade Cooley, in a photo from the late 1940s (*Photograph courtesy of the Country Music Foundation Library and Media Center, Nashville, Tennessee*)

dancing and entertainment music in an upbeat and optimistic kind of sound. It was versatile, incorporating western songs with a strong rhythm section, sometimes in string band ensembles and sometimes in big bands. The Spade Cooley sound was the most sophisticated of the western swing music mentioned in this chapter, and his phenomenal success is illustrative of how good a model this sound was.

6 Instrumental Country

STRING BANDS TO BLUEGRASS

It is the point of view of this chapter that bluegrass developed from string band music. We will trace the growth of some early playing styles towards *bluegrass,* as it came to be known in 1945. Nothing just happens overnight, although in the case of bluegrass the style changed rather remarkably from string band music.

The typical bluegrass band consists of fiddle, mandolin, guitar, string bass, and the American-style five-string banjo. Occasionally bluegrass bands make use of one or more of the following: dobro, harmonica, accordion, or a second guitar. Some typical bluegrass bands do not use all the traditional instruments mentioned first, but they all use at least guitar and banjo. Therefore, the guitar and banjo are more or less prerequisites for a band to be called bluegrass. But of course it is the style of the music that makes it bluegrass, not just the presence or absence of certain instruments.

Typically one would think of bluegrass music as coming from the bluegrass region of Kentucky, and there are some fine bluegrass bands from that area. However, most of the important early bluegrass musicians came from the hill country of North Carolina, Tennessee, and Virginia.

Some of the early string bands had important influences on the development of bluegrass, and some of those musicians survived long enough to play bluegrass themselves. The Skillet Lickers (Gid Tanner and Riley Puckett) was a string band duo, performing on fiddle and guitar. Their style was simpler than bluegrass, but certainly the interaction of those two instruments began to establish the style in which fiddle and guitar would be used in a bluegrass ensemble. Fiddlin' John Carson performed with the Virginia Reelers and Henry Whitter with the Virginia Breakdowners. The style of the Breakdowners in particular would be influential in that much of bluegrass

Gid Tanner and the Skillet Lickers. From left to right are Gid Tanner, Clayton McMichen, Riley Puckett, and probably Fate Norris (*Photograph courtesy of the John Edwards Memorial Collection of the University of North Carolina at Chapel Hill*)

can be explained in terms of the instrumental *breakdown,* a rhythmically charged section in which the fiddle typically improvises around the basic melody in an intense style.

The Dixie Mountaineers with Ernest Stoneman and the North Carolina Ramblers with Charlie Poole also established styles that influenced bluegrass. Charlie Poole was especially important because he played banjo in the three-finger style that would become the staple of bluegrass through Earl Scruggs. Although the Original Hillbillies (previously discussed) used a piano, they also used fiddle, guitar, and banjo, and in a sense that group had the right instrumentation for bluegrass.

Many of these musicians (most of whom performed in the 1920s) played in a style that would ultimately influence the people who began the bluegrass movement. In the bluegrass playing style, we can certainly trace influences back to earlier times, particularly to string band musicians such as Charlie Poole. We can see that these significant influences came from Virginia, North Carolina, and Tennessee. We will also find that in selection of lyric topics many bluegrass tunes are really based on the traditional country tunes sung by string bands. Bands such as the Carter Family provided many of the lyrics for later bluegrass hits, even though the instrumental sound was radically different. Maybelle Carter's unique guitar-playing style provided another of the basic materials with which bluegrass musicians worked.

The characteristics of bluegrass music are high-pitched singing, closed-position harmony for ensemble singing (the notes sung are close together), intense vocal style, absence of any amplification, characteristic instrumentation (see above), and the extensive use of traditional songs (like those of the Carter family). The instrumental forces combine to create a polyphonic texture (having multiple melodies), and there is traditionally a good deal of improvisation, especially for the fiddle and the banjo.

The fiddle in bluegrass music is played in a style similar to fiddle playing from the string band era. Of course, much of bluegrass music is played at a faster tempo so it sounds like the fiddle is really going to town. The fiddle mainly plays variations of the basic melody or the chord patterns, quite often in an arpeggiated style. A C-chord would have three notes in it—

Fiddlin' John Carson and the Virginia Reelers, from the April 1927 Okeh catalogue supplement (*Photograph courtesy of the John Edwards Memorial Collection of the University of North Carolina at Chapel Hill*)

Charlie Poole (center) with the North Carolina Ramblers (*Photograph courtesy of the John Edwards Memorial Collection of the University of North Carolina at Chapel Hill*)

C E G. The fiddle player may run up and down those notes to create a continuous sound. The fiddle usually plays at a rate of two or four times the basic beat of the tune.

The guitar in bluegrass has primarily a rhythmic and harmonic role, seldom playing melodies or solos. In some senses, the guitar plays the role that the banjo used to play, with chords on all major beats. In some bluegrass bands the guitar is played in a picking style, although this is usually left to the mandolin and the banjo.

The mandolin, especially in the hands of a musician like Bill Monroe, is a virtuosic instrument in bluegrass, played primarily in a picking style creating countermelodies to what the fiddle does. Although it is not played at the same rate as either the fiddle or the banjo, it creates a very important part of the melodic texture. The mandolin, higher than the guitar, produces a very distinctive tone and makes the overall texture higher than that of a string band music.

The string bass provides harmonic foundation and basically plays a note within the chord on each beat. It serves as the tempo-keeping part of the ensemble, although occasionally we hear bass solos as breaks in the tune (for instance, in the tune by Bill Monroe analyzed in the Appendix).

Most fans would agree that the really important instrument in the bluegrass band is the banjo. The banjo was the instrument that made the sound of bluegrass into something quite different from string band music, although some banjo players had played the three-finger style before bluegrass. Some say that Earl Scruggs was the person responsible for creating the model bluegrass sound, for he did codify a style within the context of a bluegrass band.

Prior to bluegrass, the banjo usually played a role similar to that defined above for the guitar, playing on each beat and strumming a chord. The addition of the banjo in Bill Monroe's band in 1942 provided that type of playing. However, Earl Scruggs, who joined the band in 1946, played a picking style of banjo that provided an intensity to bluegrass it had not previously enjoyed. Classical bluegrass (post-1945) sounded different because of the added melodic line played by the banjo, elaborated in a style similar to the fiddle but in a plucked variation. The sound of the mandolin, fiddle, and banjo all playing elaborations of the basic melody or chord progression gave bluegrass an excitement never before heard in country music.

One school of bluegrass music called "hyper-bluegrass" accentuated this melodic interplay even further. The musicians played everything twice as fast and with such an intensity that it really tired out both performer and listener. This occurred when bluegrass became nationally popular, especially in the North with folk musicians and second-generation bluegrass musicians.

In short, the basic style of bluegrass has to do with the way the instruments interact (although most of the styles had been previously developed), strong singing styles featuring high vocal ranges and closed-position harmony, the selection of traditional country lyrics, and a disdain for amplification. Bluegrass was a conscious reaction to the tendency of country music to be influenced by other forms of the time and especially to big band pop music of the 1940s. It was a return to country and its roots, but with an exciting new vitality to the sound.

Bill Monroe

Bill Monroe was born near Rosine, Kentucky in 1911. His main musical influences were his mother and a black guitarist and railroad worker, Arnold Schultz. With his brothers Charlie and Birch, Bill became competent on a number of string instruments, but he specialized in the mandolin. He began performing in public in his twenties and formed a band with his brothers in 1925. Birch dropped out, and Bill and Charlie played together as the Monroe Brothers until 1938.

Bill wrote his first successful tune in 1934—"Kentucky Waltz" (recorded in 1945). The Monroe Brothers were well known in the 1930s, especially for the instrumental arrangements of their pieces, which Bill generally did. Their particular sound was snappy by comparison to other bands of that era, foreshadowing what Bill Monroe would do with his Bluegrass Boys. Charlie Monroe's guitar playing was important to their higher quality sound, although Charlie tends not to receive proper credit.

In 1938 Bill and Charlie split up, forming two separate bands—Charlie with his Kentucky Pardners, and Bill with his Bluegrass Boys. Charlie remained in performance until the mid–1950s, but it was Bill Monroe who would become famous. By 1939 Bill had been invited to join the Grand Ole Opry, where he remained for over forty years. The sound of his Bluegrass Boys, prior to the time they played real bluegrass music, was very full. Monroe's singing style has always been truly distinctive, a style that would ultimately be copied by many other musicians. He sang in a high tenor voice and used a crackling kind of yodel sound.

Bill Monroe and his group illustrated the continuing influence of black music, especially in the style of the fiddle player, but also in the selection of songs, many of which were blues tunes such as "Muleskinner Blues." There was always a great deal of syncopation in the Monroe band, especially in the guitar chording, which often came off the beat (highly unusual for country music). Bill Monroe had phenomenal success with the Bluegrass Boys from the very beginning, although his success would be even more remarkable after 1945.

The Bluegrass Boys did not use a banjo until 1942. When the first banjoist joined the group, he played in a strumming chord style, although with syncopation. In 1946, Earl Scruggs joined the band, and Scruggs played in the three-finger picking style. This addition to the band brought together all of the elements of classical bluegrass. With Scruggs, the sound was energized many times over, and bluegrass in the full-blown sense of the term was invented. The Bluegrass Boys were thus the most important band of the

Bill Monroe (*Courtesy of MCA Records*)

bluegrass movement; but if it had not been for Earl Scruggs, the bluegrass sound would not have been complete.

It is important to realize that Earl Scruggs codified a style that had been around for some time. But it is also important to give him credit for doing it better than anyone had ever done it before, and for influencing so many other players. The texture he created by combining banjo, mandolin, and fiddle was supercharged, and the relentless swing of bluegrass is certainly a result of this instrumental combination.

Most important bluegrass musicians of that era passed through the Bluegrass Boys—Lester Flatt, Earl Scruggs, and Don Reno, to name a few. Bill Monroe has had a lasting influence, mostly the direct influence he had on other musicians. He had the musical intelligence to imagine a particular sound and work towards it, as well as the foresight to trust other musicians in their experiments. The result was a new kind of southern music, one that would gain national attention like no other had before. Bill Monroe was elected to the Country Hall of Fame in 1970.

The major characteristics of the Bluegrass Boys were Bill Monroe's high-pitched singing, use of tight-chord ensemble singing, bass runs on the guitar and string bass, intense style in the mandolin part, three-finger picking style on the banjo, and a high level of energy in playing and singing style. In short, the elements of the Bluegrass Boys are an ideal model for bluegrass. Some other bands, like Flatt and Scruggs, may have been more popular. But not only did this band give the name to the movement; they were also the best example of the style.

Flatt and Scruggs

Lester Flatt was born in 1914 in Overton County, Tennessee, in the Appalachians. He grew up in a musical family of nine. Like many families in that region, they sang hymns after supper. Both of Lester's parents played the banjo, and his father, a sharecropper, also played the fiddle. Although Lester first started playing the banjo, he changed over to the guitar fairly early in life.

In 1931 he went to work in Sparta, where his family then resided. He met Gladys Stacey, who became his wife. He and his wife often listened to the radio to "hillbilly" hits; one of his favorite groups was the Monroe Brothers. By the mid–1930s Lester and Gladys Flatt had moved to Covington, Virginia, where they both worked at Burlington Mills. Several friends from Tennessee had also come to Covington to get work, and in 1938 they formed a band that started broadcasting on radio in 1939 as the Harmonizers. In the early 1940s Flatt sang with a group known as the Happy-Go-Lucky Boys. In 1943 he and his wife went to work with Charlie Monroe's Kentucky Pardners. In 1944 he quit the Pardners and retired from music. A few months after that he went back to music broadcasting on a radio station. He then received a telegram from Bill Monroe asking him to join the Bluegrass Boys on the Grand Ole Opry.

Earl Scruggs was born in 1924 at Flint Hill, North Carolina. Earl began performing with his brothers at the age of six, and by the age of fifteen he was performing professionally on radio with the Carolina Wildcats. His musical career was cut short by World War II and it was really not until after the war that he picked it up again.

He started performing again on radio in Knoxville, Tennessee in August of 1945 and was hired by Bill Monroe in 1946. Earl Scruggs was one of the great technicians of country music. However, his style of banjo playing was relatively unknown in the context of a string band (about to become a bluegrass band).

So Earl Scruggs and Lester Flatt were fellow members of the Bluegrass Boys for three years. During that time they were very important members of the group. Lester played fine guitar and was billed as one of the singers. Earl provided a new dimension to the Monroe band: he could solo as a banjo player. Ultimately they decided to form their own band and go out on the

Earl Scruggs (left) and Lester Flatt (right) in Saginaw, Michigan, on October 6, 1963 (*Courtesy of Tom Cederberg, Teddy Bear Record Exchange, Bay City, Michigan*)

road without Bill Monroe. Although they were an integral part of the creation of the bluegrass sound while with Bill Monroe, what they did after they left the band may have popularized bluegrass to a much greater extent than anything Monroe did. This is not to take credit away from Bill Monroe, for he was terribly important to country music. But the fact remains that to the general public bluegrass usually means Flatt and Scruggs.

The actual reason Earl and Lester quit the Monroe band was that they were tired and needed a rest. But it was not long before they got together and started doing radio work again. By the summer of 1938 they had formed a band for recording purposes, the Foggy Mountain Boys (a name derived from an old Carter family tune, "Foggy Mountain Top"). Between 1949 and 1955 they were an extremely popular act, and they continued to put out hit recordings.

In 1951 Earl Scruggs developed a special device for the banjo that allowed an instantaneous retuning of a string; the result was the "Scruggs Peg." In 1953 they started advertising Martha White Flour; from that association came "The Martha White Theme," which would eventually become the theme song of the Foggy Mountain Boys. In 1955 they became members of the Grand Ole Opry, with a band that had the same instrumentation as the Bluegrass Boys but also included Buck Graves ("Uncle Josh") on dobro. Their sound was slightly different; the mandolin player used a chordal rather than picking style, and the singing style of the Foggy Mountain Boys was lower and more mellow than the sound of Bill Monroe.

In the North there was a great deal of interest in bluegrass starting in 1954, with most of it centered around the banjo playing of Earl Scruggs. During the folksong revival of the late 1950s and 1960s, musicians like Pete Seeger and the Kingston Trio created a banjo revival. Earl Scruggs was their spiritual leader. This is especially fascinating because bluegrass had a strong southern identity. However, it was its simplicity of style combined with a mastery of technique that caused northerners to be in awe of Earl Scruggs.

In any event, the Foggy Mountain Boys and Earl Scruggs continued to be popular in the 1950s.

In the 1960s Flatt and Scruggs sold more country records than anyone else except Johnny Cash. They had one of their major hits in December of 1962—"The Ballad of Jed Clampett." This song was for the TV series "The Beverly Hillbillies." The association with that TV show was to have lasting consequences; the show can still be seen today in reruns. In 1968, the 1949 recording of "Foggy Mountain Breakdown" was used as the theme song and chase music for the movie *Bonnie and Clyde.* Although the band was highly successful, there were slow changes occurring in the late 1960s. They were using more Nashville studio musicians than members of the band for recording, and their recordings were beginning to sound less intense and more like the Nashville sound (see later chapters).

Lester Flatt was having health difficulties, especially after his heart attack in 1967. By 1969 the two musicians came to a peaceful parting of the ways. Lester formed a band called the Nashville Grass, which was a traditional bluegrass band. And in fact, many hard-core bluegrass fans like the Grass better than the post-1965 Foggy Mountain Boys. Earl Scruggs went into many ventures, most of them with his sons. One of the prime movers in establishing the Nitty Gritty Dirt Band, he was quick to move in the direction of rock and roll when the country rock movement got started. Earl Scruggs was too good to remain solely within the bluegrass tradition. He had been an innovator before, and in the early 1970s he found that it was time to take off in a new direction.

The Stanley Brothers

The Stanley Brothers was a popular bluegrass duo from the mid–1950s to 1966. Ralph Stanley was born in 1927 in Stratton, Virginia. His brother Carter was born in McClure in 1925 and died in Bristol, Virginia in 1966.

Flatt and Scruggs Band (*Courtesy of Tom Cederberg, Teddy Bear Record Exchange, Bay City, Michigan*)

The Stanley Brothers (*Photograph courtesy of the John Edwards Memorial Collection of the University of North Carolina at Chapel Hill*)

Carter played the guitar and Ralph played the banjo. Their mother was the primary musical inspiration, although the region of Virginia where they grew up was filled with good musicians—mainly traditional musicians.

The Stanley Brothers imitated the early style of Bill Monroe, and in many ways they were second generation Bill Monroes. However, their particular style of singing and playing was a combination of string band, traditional southern mountain, and bluegrass. Carter was a member of the Bluegrass Boys for a while before joining with his brother. When Carter died in 1966, Ralph formed a band called the Clinch Mountain Boys. The Stanley Brothers' style was more traditional than other bluegrass groups. There was always a sense of eeriness about the Stanley Brothers songs, and a mellow quality to the singing style.

The Virginia Boys

Jim McReynolds was born in Coeburn, Virginia in 1927; his brother Jesse was born there in 1929. They grew up in a musical family—in fact, their grandfather was a master old-time fiddler. They both learned all the string band instruments, with Jesse gravitating to the mandolin and Jim to the guitar. In the 1940s they played at local dances, and in 1947 they started working in radio broadcasting. They made professional recordings in the early 1950s for Kentucky and Capitol record companies.

In 1952 Jesse was drafted to serve in the Korean War. He and Jim got back together in 1954 with their band, The Virginia Boys, and they began to make real progress. However, this band would not really become successful until the flowering of interest in bluegrass in the late 1950s. The Virginia Boys were very good by 1954; as soon as the interest level in bluegrass grew to a sufficient point, they were right there to be recognized as one of the most talented bluegrass organizations.

They worked on the "Tennessee Barn Dance" in Knoxville, CBS Network's "Saturday Night Country Style," the Swannee River Jamboree of Florida, and the Lowndes County Jamboree in Valdosta, Georgia. In the early 1960s they started having a string of hit records, and were invited to the Newport Folk Festival in 1963. They joined the Grand Ole Opry in 1966; they had already settled in Nashville in 1965.

The Virginia Boys were versatile musicians: they performed bluegrass standards, rockabilly tunes (especially Chuck Berry's), trucking songs, gospel, and crossover pop. They were influenced by earlier bluegrass musicians; but, like Earl Scruggs, they were willing to change with the times.

THE TECHNICIANS

The period of the late 1940s and early 1950s was one of the most important in the development of country music. Many of the technological changes that began in this period would have a lasting influence on entertainment and popular music, and these influences would continue to change the way country music was played and marketed.

Economically, this period was one of the best periods in American history. Many had predicted a post-war depression coupled with inflation. In reality there was no depression; instead, there was tremendous growth in the economy and in the buying power of Americans. Industrialization and new technologies led to growth, and many Americans felt the power of having more money each year. More Americans bought homes for the first time than at any other period in American history. This economic strength caused a general feeling of optimism that was supported by our position in the world; we felt like winners.

There were tremendous technological advancements in this period, advancements that would have lasting importance. The postwar baby boom was certainly due in part to servicemen being home; but it was also due to a feeling of economic security. That security was enhanced by one of the strongest growth periods ever in technology.

The particular developments in electronics that would ultimately have major impact on country music were simply a part of the general growth in technologies. In particular, the development of advanced recording and transmitting equipment was influential, along with the development of television. Sound equipment was improved, especially amplification equipment and microphones. Electronic microphones were developed that accurately picked up the sound without the distortion present in prewar microphones. Much of the electronic development had to do with miniaturization and protection from heat distortion. Ultimately this led to the development of the transistor and solid-state electronics.

As the quality of sound equipment went up while its price went down, the average American was able to invest in home sound equipment. The result was a massive increase in the market for record sales. With the general state of the economy being so good, it was possible to market records for particular audiences, and this is certainly one of the reasons why rock and roll made it as a popular art form. And the market growth that came from better quality equipment produced the need for better and more diversified music.

Better equipment and more accurate recording and playback devices meant that audiences could hear more of a recording. Even if a bluegrass group continued to argue against amplification, that is exactly what happened when they recorded. The studio production of music forced musicians to play interesting lines because the listener could hear everything. The subtle process of technology changing the way that people communicate was certainly felt in country music, primarily because recording meant money, and if the audience who paid your paycheck could hear everything you did, then it behooved you, the musician, to play it right.

Studio recordings from the 1930s and early 1940s were pretty terrible because the equipment used was not adequate for the job. One simply could not pick up all the quality of the sound through inefficient microphones and amplifier reproduction machines. A properly adjusted audio system changes the way we perceive the sound coming out of a recording or live performance. The musicians who performed on records prior to the late 1940s were at a disadvantage, or, more properly, their recordings were different.

Although sound systems and the studio setting would become even more sophisticated in the 1970s, musicians in the late 1940s were already being influenced by what could be done electronically. As the technical level of the studio went up, so did the level of musicianship. The relationship between the technical studio musician within the confines of the studio itself and the resultant types of recorded music is an important one. And the economics of this particular period provided the environment in which both musicians and types of music improved and diversified.

One could see the development of both western swing and bluegrass as anticipating the day when technology would allow the fusion of musical styles. Both these types of music added legitimacy to country music, and both were more complicated than what had gone before them. In a sense, the developments of the late 1930s and the 1940s in these two areas showed that country music could envelop other markets and at the same time become much more complicated. Country music seems to have increased in crossover appeal in direct relationship to its complexity. The relationship of popularity to complexity does not always hold, but in the case of the late 1940s it seems to be true.

Specific technological applications will be discussed in later chapters, but suffice it to say that each individual adaptation or invention added a dimension to country music. The "Scruggs Peg" is an example of a mechanical device that changed the style of banjo playing. The invention of the dobro is a similar example. However, it was the development of the electronic pickup for guitars and other such technological advancements that would change the face of country music completely.

As a side remark, one should not read into this chapter that because of electronics country music became something totally different. While Earl Scruggs was strongly influenced by electronic music and in particular by country rock, his compatriot Lester Flatt remained true to the country sound. However, even Flatt was influenced by electronics because over the years his recordings with Scruggs and by himself were influenced by the steady advancement of studio technique and recording. There is a solid vein of traditional country music existing today that still has mass appeal, while some movements in country music are progressive and more influenced by changing technology. However, even the most traditional musicians use microphones.

Nashville continued to exert a tremendous influence on country music. The Grand Ole Opry and the complex surrounding it make Nashville the center of activity in country music. The Hall of Fame is there, and Nashville serves as a mecca for country musicians. Many of the major technological influences felt by country musicians from the 1940s until today were most strongly felt in Nashville, with both positive and negative results.

Nashville was the place where one did recordings and the best studio musicians were available there for those recordings. Nashville is not the only place where you can do a country recording, as some people in Austin, Texas might well argue. However, many country musicians have recorded in Nashville for years because the music industry there is geared toward country. As in other towns with strong music industries (New York, Los Angeles, or Los Vegas), this produces tremendous competition. And out of that competition normally comes some experts.

There are many fine musicians in Nashville and the two choices presented here are not the total representation, but they are good examples. In Nashville today one can hear countless superb technicians in any bar and wonder why they are not famous. Actually, in Nashville the chances are that such musicians are rather famous, since the competition is so keen. However, the purpose here is to illustrate the relationship between fine technicians and growing technology.

The two musicians I have selected are Chet Atkins and Roy Clark. Chet Atkins is discussed because of his technical mastery of the guitar as a country instrument and his contributions to guitar technique, to country music, and to the industry. It should be noted that Chet Atkins is one of the finest guitarists of the twentieth century and not just in country music. Roy Clark is chosen not only because he showed prodigious technique at an early age, but also because as an entertainer he has continued to be enjoyed by a great number of Americans who may not even realize how good he is.

Chet Atkins

Chet Atkins was born in Luttrell, Tennessee in 1924. His father was a piano and voice teacher. In his home Chet became acquainted with country music—particularly the music of Jimmie Rodgers—through the phonograph. He learned to play the guitar well by his teenage years. By the early 1940s he had a job on WNOX in Knoxville, where he worked as a solo act for three years. Chet's older brother, Jim, was also a fine guitarist who played with the Fred Waring Orchestra and the Les Paul Trio; undoubtedly, Jim was a major influence on Chet.

In 1944 Chet went to Nashville to audition for the Roy Acuff band but was not successful. In 1945 he went to work in Cincinnati at WLW, where he met his wife, who was performing as a vocalist on the radio station. After auditioning for Red Foley in 1946, he moved to Nashville, where he was a member of the Foley band on WSM's Grand Ole Opry. In 1947 he signed with RCA Victor to record; in his first session he recorded eight tunes, five of them vocals. These early recordings were not successful.

After these recordings Atkins returned to Knoxville and began working with Homer and Jethro (an important early duo), and also with the band that backed Maybelle Carter and her three daughters, then called the Carter Family. In 1949 he began doing session work in Nashville. Slowly he became the player representative for RCA because of his musical intelligence and playing ability. He became an assisting A & R man in 1952 and started building up a reputation for putting together background music and helping to solidify recording sessions. Chet Atkins combined an innate ability to communicate with other musicians with the ability to manage new and rising stars. He was responsible for the success of the first recording session of Elvis Presley with RCA, the session that produced "Heartbreak Hotel."

By 1960 he was A & R manager for Nashville, and he was promoted to vice-president of RCA Records in 1968. Part of the significance of Chet Atkins' career has been his influence on other musicians in the recording studio. He worked tirelessly to get himself into positions where he could have influence. Although not a vociferous man by nature, he talked when he had to and got his point across. He has been tremendously influential in pushing the interests of the music business, on behalf both of the musicians themselves and of the recording industry.

But of course, Chet Atkins' main importance was his phenomenal playing ability. He developed a style of guitar playing that has been described as touching the strings to play them rather than plucking them. Most guitarists play with a strumming or plucking technique. A few musicians developed

Chet Atkins (*Photo by Beverly Parker; used by courtesy of Columbia Records, Nashville*)

more complex ways of playing prior to the 1960s. Merle Travis is cited in the Atkins autobiography as being a tremendous influence on Atkins. Maybelle Carter had a picking style that was influential.

But Chet Atkins went quite a bit past his influencers in the development of his style of playing. He used the thumb of the right hand to play bass notes (much like what bluegrass musicians did) while leaving the rest of the right hand fingers free to play melodic embellishments. Chet Atkins always thoroughly studied anything that he wished to know, and his tremendous knowledge of the structure of music allowed him to develop melodic counterpoint just from his right hand. The touching technique he used (simply depressing the string to get the note) allowed him to move with a speed never before attained on the guitar. In some sense, he played the guitar like a banjo. The fact that he had learned to play the fiddle quite well as a child must also have had an effect on his guitar-playing ability.

But probably Chet Atkins' greatest single accomplishment was the development of a technique so good that he could produce more styles on the guitar than other musicians. He could play with great facility in classical, country, or jazz style.

He was the prototypical studio musician in that he could read music very well and produce at sight any kind of music needed at the moment. As a result of this tremendous versatility his recordings exhibited a great deal of musicality and complexity. As well, his particular style led to a manner of playing the guitar in a much softer way than did other musicians. The Chet Atkins' sound is really quite original, although a number of players have imitated it.

He was also one of the first country musicians to adopt the electric guitar, which certainly sets him apart from bluegrass and more traditional instrumentalists. He exhibited a fascination with electronics and technological advancement throughout his career and made personal studies of many associated subjects such as musical acoustics.

Roy Clark (*Courtesy of Churchill Records, Tulsa, Oklahoma*)

Chet Atkins has also been very much a commercial artist. He has recorded over 500 selections in his career and been responsible for the creation of thousands of recorded pieces. Since he is so concerned with communicating to the public and pushing the interests of the recording industry, he stands open to criticism from purists. However, there is no denying that he is a great technician.

Chet Atkins tried to play music that communicated easily to people, and he has had a major role in creating what is called the "Nashville sound." This certainly has caused him to think about his role in country music. But he has been concerned primarily with doing whatever he does to the highest level possible. He is a tireless worker and commands the respect of the people who work with him, yet he retains a simplicity of character and a sense of humor. Chet Atkins is truly a model musician in both his playing and influence through his position in the industry.

Roy Clark

This particular choice may surprise some people who were not surprised at all by Chet Atkins. But Roy Clark really has not received the kind of publicity that he should, so I am going to do something about that. I think it is important to discuss musicians who have had very successful careers as entertainers; and it is appropriate here to discuss Roy Clark because he is a tremendous technician on several different instruments.

Roy Clark was born in Meherrin, Virginia in 1933. His father, a tobacco farmer, taught Roy to play the guitar. By the age of ten Roy was better on the banjo, and in 1948 and 1949 he won the National Country Music Banjo Championship. In 1949 he appeared on the Grand Ole Opry, and seeing a videotape of that performance will convince anyone of the validity of including him in this chapter. Roy Clark must have been a child prodigy to have played so well at the age of fifteen or sixteen.

He moved to Washington, D.C. and appeared there with Jimmy Dean. In 1956 he appeared on the "Arthur Godfrey Show" and by this time had become well known not only in country music but also in general entertainment. He backed Wanda Jackson in 1960 and Hank Thompson in 1961. In 1962, he had a recording hit with "Lightning," and he was on the "Johnny Carson Show" for the first time in 1963. Late in 1963 he had a top-10 country western hit with "Tips of My Fingers." He toured with the "Andy Williams Show" in 1964 and 1965 and in 1969 became the co-host of the TV show "Hee Haw."

Roy Clark has won many major awards—Entertainer of the Year in 1972 and 1973, the Jim Reeves Memorial Award in 1976, Comedy Act of the Year in 1969, 1970, and 1971, Lead Guitar in 1977 (all from the Academy of Country Music). He also won the Country Music Association awards as Entertainer of the Year in 1973, Instrumental Group of the Year in 1975 and 1976, Instrumentalist of the Year in 1977, 1978, and 1980, and Comedian of the Year in 1970. Chet Atkins won the Instrumentalist Award in 1984.

The importance of Roy Clark as an entertainer should not be overlooked. He is more than just a musician or a singer; he is also a very funny comedian. Like Chet Atkins, Roy Clark wants to entertain people; even when he is playing or singing something that is simple, it is obvious that he wants people to understand and enjoy what he is doing.

Roy Clark is equally at home on banjo, fiddle, and guitar, and plays a few other instruments. He has a thorough mastery of each instrument and plays in a very complicated style on each. A trained musician can tell that Clark has made a careful study of playing techniques. Roy Clark is another fine example of a very technical musician who has worked long and hard to perfect his technique even though he already showed much natural talent during his childhood years.

The careers of Chet Atkins and Roy Clark are in many ways different. However, the similarities rest in their phenomenal technical ability, developed through years of very hard work. Both men have achieved enormous success based in part, it might appear, on the strength of their personalities. But while many factors in their careers led to their tremendous success and influence, the one essential was that they were and are great technicians.

7 Honky Tonk

THE PRACTITIONERS

The honky tonk period in country music is interesting because of its influence on the development of country music in the 1960s, but like most movements in country music it started long before its primary influence was felt. Honky tonk music is generally thought to be a phenomenon of the late 1940s, re-emerging in the 1960s, but in fact it really started much earlier, synchronous with the urbanization of both the South and the West.

Country writers are somewhat unclear on honky tonk music, and there is a tendency to identify it as something western or Texan in origin. There is also a tendency to identify it as a specific kind of music when in fact the term *honky tonk* has been applied to a rather diverse set of performers, as is evidenced by the selections for this chapter. The one thing that can be said with certainty is that it was connected with urbanization, although in many cases it was rural in its performance.

It would be more proper to consider *honky tonk* as a period in music that occurred roughly between 1933 and 1950, with a revival of interest in the 1960s. The term *honky tonk* comes from the kind of establishment in which this music was played—a bar. While mountain music occurred in county fair settings or family get-togethers and western swing took place in dance settings, honky tonk was clearly associated with wilder surroundings, where people were drinking and having a good time. Most of the musicians mentioned in this chapter made their successes in this environment.

Playing in a bar is different from playing in a family environment. Background sound is much louder, and the musician has to be aggressive in order to get the crowd's attention. If the crowd does not like you, they will either ignore you or become rude. Therefore, the style of music that evolved for this setting had to be stronger, with more of a show. The lyrics used for those tunes tended to be earthier, less nostalgic, and more up-to-date. Even when the bar in which this urban music was played was in a small town, the kinds of tunes that were done were for an audience that came to town to whoop it up, and not for a rural community with little identification to a town environment.

Honky tonk started in 1933 because that is when prohibition ended. Certainly there was music played for drinking audiences prior to 1933 because, rumor has it, there were some people who still drank during prohibition. However, as a general development it really did not get started until after drinking was again legal. By the late 1930s a distinct kind of music evolved, raw-edged in nature and speaking about different issues than "Turkey in the Straw." Instrumentation, too, started to change subtly with the addition of a string bass and electric instruments—first the steel guitar and then the electric guitar. Although real technological change would occur primarily in the 1940s and 1950s, the beginnings of change in the sound of country music happened with honky tonk musicians in the late 1930s.

Although drums were used rarely in early honky tonk, the instrumental forces that were used created a type of music that was much stronger and more rhythmic than earlier styles. Often honky tonk music was played in such a way that the lyrics could scarcely be heard, because it was really the sound of the music that was important for properly whooping it up. Many of the instruments (especially the guitar) were played in what was called a "sock rhythm": chords on each beat would be strummed or struck quite hard to produce a chopping regular beat that could be heard above the din produced by the crowd. This style would eventually influence rockabilly musicians (see the next chapter). The sound of honky tonk, with its insistent rhythmic pounding, was similar to what was happening on the black circuit with rhythm and blues; and the combination of honky tonk and rhythm and blues was to create rockabilly.

Rhythm and blues for black honky tonks and honky tonk country for white honky tonks both developed out of the same movement toward urbanization. The hopped-up rhythmic quality of both kinds of music came directly from the environment and because of the loudness of the bar setting. Lyrics of both honky tonk music and rhythm and blues were highly charged and pretty earthy by comparison to what had happened before them. It is also interesting that many of the honky tonk musicians were very influenced by Jimmie Rodgers, who was by his own account heavily influenced by black styles.

Honky tonk music then developed during the late 1930s with the style reaching maturity by the end of the second world war. It was very popular in the late 1940s, but began to decline during the 1950s, primarily because of rockabilly. However, it was to re-emerge as a vital force in country music in the 1960s. Although much of the music that was specifically called honky tonk either used the words "honky tonk" in the lyrics or had a driving beat to it, some of the music that was played in honky tonks was very traditional country music, seemingly not affected by urbanization. However, in playing style it was very different than the same material would have been in a non-honky tonk setting. Therefore, honky tonk performance is a combination of certain types of lyrics and playing style, with the playing style being its single most important quality.

Many performers such as Ernest Tubb and Hank Williams, Sr. were mainly known as honky tonkers. These two in particular made star status based on singing for honky tonks; ultimately they became stars in other milieus but their first successes were in honky tonks. Ballad singers of that era also had their first successes in bars, although they usually sang stronger music in those settings. Once their careers were started, they recorded ballads that received air play on radio stations. Other musicians were honky tonkers because of where and how they played.

These musicians are important because they established the basic style of traditional contemporary country music. Some of them are still around—George Jones, for instance. George, who will be considered in other chapters, started first as a honky tonk musician. With his unique vocal quality and his

Little Jimmie Dickens, in a photo from the early to mid-1940s *(Photograph courtesy of the Country Music Foundation Library and Media Center, Nashville, Tennessee)*

hard luck attitude, he was perfect as a honky tonk musician even as a young man. Later on he often still sounded like a honky tonk musician, but of course his career grew to include other kinds of music. Many musicians in this particular era continued to be popular past the era's prime, building on the careers they started as honky tonk musicians to become some of country music's most important stars.

The development of honky tonk country music also coincided with the economic good times discussed in the last chapter, when marketing considerations were important. But regardless of whether the times produced honky tonk or honky tonk took advantage of the times, it was a beneficial relationship. Honky tonk became big business, perhaps not as big as rockabilly, but definitely illustrating a growth industry in country music. And it is important to remember that the fundamental reason why country musicians played at honky tonks was that they wanted to make money. Honky tonk succeeded in doing that; country music had become a big business.

As we consider the careers of the following musicians, we should keep in mind the fundamental definition of honky tonk: music for an urbanized audience in a bar setting. We should also keep in mind the economic situation of the time and the different behavior and attitude of the audiences that went to hear honky tonk. We should consider instrumental changes and the difference in texture of honky tonk music. Lastly, we should think carefully about each of the musicians in this chapter because they were (and some still are) quite important to the making of country music.

Jim Dickens

"Little" Jimmy Dickens was born in West Virginia in 1920. He learned the guitar at an early age and became a performer with country and western bands in the mid–1940s. He is called "Little" because he stands just slightly under five feet tall. As a solo musician for radio he travelled through the Midwest from the mid–1940s on. In 1948 he joined the Grand Ole Opry.

Some of his hits over the years were "I'm Little but I'm Loud," "Out behind the Barn," "Lovin' Lies," "Salty Boogie," "Sea of Broken Dreams," and "May the Bird of Paradise Fly up Your Nose." This last tune, from 1965, was his all-time best-seller. His style is basically honky tonk because he sings stridently and not just traditional songs. He is known as a screaming country boy singer and therefore fits the classic model of a honky tonk musician, even though primarily a solo act.

Freddie Hart

Freddie Hart was born in Alabama in 1928. As a singer, guitarist, bandleader of the Heartbeats, and songwriter, he has had a successful career; his primary success was the in early 1970s, although he has continued to have hit records up into the 1980s. His style was late honky tonk, which he basically learned from touring with Buck Owens and Hank Williams.

He grew up in a poverty-ridden sharecropper family that was always on the move. He went to work early in life, and in fact served a stint in the Marines beginning at age fourteen. Like many honky tonk musicians, he had a hard early life that came through in many of his tunes and in his singing style. He became proficient as a musician, and was lucky in being involved with the Hank Williams-Lefty Frizzell touring group and also with Buck Owens. He became quite successful when he began making his own records.

Some of his recordings are "Born a Fool," "Togetherness," "If Fingerprints Showed Up on Skin," "My Hangup Is You," "Easy Lovin' " (top single of 1971 and 1972), "Sure Thing" and "Roses Are Red" from 1980, and "You Were There" from 1981. He won the Academy of Country Music's Entertainer of the Year award in 1971. As a major advocate of the Hank Williams style he has had an important career in country music.

George Jones

George Glenn Jones was born in Saratoga, Texas in 1931 in an area called the "Thicket" because it is so incredibly humid, filled with trees and inhabited by huge mosquitos. This particular area had really developed its own laws and customs; many of these were important early influences in George Jones' life, sometimes to his detriment. In 1942 the Joneses moved to Beaumont, where life was somewhat normalized for the family.

George had shown an early interest in music, singing in church, and he got his first guitar when he was eleven. He began singing in honky tonks or saloons at the age of sixteen and patterned himself after Hank Williams. In his late teens he joined the Marines, serving during the Korean War. After that he returned to Texas and worked as a housepainter, and as a singer at night. In 1954, he was signed by Starday Records out of Houston. In 1955 he had his first national hit, "Why Baby Why," which was a prototypical honky tonk song; it also illustrated the strong emotional character of that music. His first top-10 hit was "Treasure of Love" in 1958. Others to follow were "Who Shot Sam" in 1959, "White Lightning" in 1961, and "Where Does a Little Tear Come From" in 1964.

George Jones has had many hits over his performing career, which is still very active. He will be discussed in other chapters; however, his first major impact was with honky tonk in the Hank Williams style, although with his own unique way of performing. Much of George Jones' life has been peppered with sad times. He remains a pivotal character in country music, typifying the musician who sings about the troubles of the world and knowing full well what that means. A winner of many awards in 1980 and 1981 including Male Vocalist of the Year, George Jones remains a perennial favorite in country music. Although he has remained somewhat outside the Nashville circle, residing in Texas, he is regularly on the Nashville shows.

George Jones in the mid-1960s (*Courtesy of Tom Cederberg, Teddy Bear Record Exchange, Bay City, Michigan*)

Ray Price

Like George Jones, Ray Price was born in Texas, but in 1926. He grew up at approximately the same time as George Jones and had many of the same influences. Ray Price was a singer, guitarist, and songwriter, a combination one sees quite often in country music. When he was twelve, the family moved to Dallas, but he never forgot his roots in Cherokee Indian land; in fact he was called "The Cherokee Cowboy." After he graduated from high school in 1942, he served in the military until 1946.

He returned to attend college in Arlington, Texas and remained there until 1949. He started working as a radio entertainer in 1948 in Abilene and then in 1949 he began work on the "Big D Jamboree" broadcast from Dallas. He had several minor hit records in the early 1950s before becoming a regular on the Grand Ole Opry in 1952, when he also signed a recording contract with Columbia. In 1952 he had hits with "Talk to Your Heart" and "Don't Let the Stars Get in Your Eyes." Probably his most important hit was in 1954—"Release Me." After that he had one hit after another. Many of these tunes, such as "My Shoes Keep Walking Back to You" and "Heartaches by the Number," reveal his classic roots in honky tonk, although he had actually not performed in many bars.

Sometimes described as a crooner, Ray Price does indeed have a somewhat softer sound than most honky tonk singers, but the emotional quality of his music fits in ideally with the period under discussion. His enduring popularity is certainly supported by his songwriting, which has produced major hits, even when performed by other artists. His status as a regular on the Grand Ole Opry also did much to promote his career.

Ray Price in the mid-1960s (*Courtesy of Tom Cederberg, Teddy Bear Record Exchange, Bay City, Michigan*)

Hank Snow

Hank Snow, along with Wilf Carter ("Montana Slim"), proved that you did not have to be from the South, or even from the United States, to be a country singer. Snow, born in Nova Scotia, Canada, in 1914, showed that you could love country music (in his case western music through western movies) and make a career out of it wherever you happened to be. Although his rise to success was undoubtedly made more difficult because he was originally from Canada, his singing voice, with its distinctive Nova Scotian accent, ultimately proved to be his mark of success. In fact, during the 1950s and 1960s he was one of the top five hit-makers.

As a singer and guitarist he made his first record in 1936 after two years as a radio singer in Halifax as "Hank, the Yodeling Ranger." However, these early RCA Victor recordings were only released in Canada, and so did not bring him fame even though they did well there. In 1948 Ernest Tubb arranged for a WSM engagement for Hank Snow, who had previously moved to the United States to be on the WWVA Jamboree in Wheeling, West Virginia. However, until 1949 his recordings were still only released in Canada.

In 1949, through the assistance of some loyal fans, RCA Victor released his tune "Brand on My Heart," which was his first true success in the United States. In 1950, his "I'm Moving On" was even more successful. Many of Hank Snow's hit records after "I'm Moving On" were written by him, contributing to his influence and his earning potential. One tune of his from 1951, "Music Makin' Mama from Memphis," stands out as illustrating his honky tonk tendencies, although Hank Snow could also sing in a ballad style or as a singing cowboy.

Hank Snow (*Photograph courtesy of the John Edwards Memorial Collection of the University of North Carolina at Chapel Hill*)

Through the 1950s and 1960s there was seldom a year in which Hank Snow did not have a hit song, and this must be at least partially attributed to his remarkable sense of what songs would work for the times. Also, his distinctive singing style in which you could hear all of the words lent an air of credibility to his singing. He joined the Grand Ole Opry in 1950, primarily at the insistence of Ernest Tubb, who was his constant supporter. But the reason Hank Snow was so successful was that he was slightly different because of his accent and clear enunciation.

One need only listen to a little of "Music Makin' Mama from Memphis" to realize why Hank Snow should be discussed with the honky tonkers. In this tune he goes at the speed of light in a punctuated style that clearly fits in with the honky tonk tradition. Of course, Hank Snow did other kinds of tunes and continued well past the honky tonk stage; but it is in the honky tonk style that he clearly shines. Clearly, he was Texas-influenced, but it should always be remembered that he grew up very far from Texas.

Ernest Tubb

Ernest Tubb was born in 1914 about forty miles from Dallas. His childhood seemed to be happy although not extravagant. His mother was a primary musical influence, as she played piano and organ. Ernest sang as a youth and wrote stories that he claims led to his songwriting. He did not get a guitar until his late teens, but for most of his early life he had a passion for the music of Jimmie Rodgers. In fact, Jimmie Rodgers was probably the

Ernest Tubb signing autographs in Saginaw, Michigan, on October 27, 1963
(*Courtesy of Tom Cederberg, Teddy Bear Record Exchange, Bay City, Michigan*)

performer who caused Ernest Tubb to become a musician. The story as told by Carrie Rodgers, Jimmie's widow, is that Ernest Tubb came to visit her after Jimmie had died. Ernest Tubb showed that he knew every word of every Rodgers song, and Mrs. Rodgers was so impressed that she personally arranged for a recording session. During that recording session, Ernest Tubb used one of Jimmie's guitars.

Those first recording sessions were not highly successful, and although Tubb spent the next five years (1935 to 1940) performing in honky tonks, it still did not seem likely that he would have a successful career. His first recording sessions for Decca Records in 1940 led to a job advertising Gold Chain Flour, and he became the Gold Chain Troubadour. These early recordings, although not as successful as his "Walking the Floor over You" from 1941, led to a short movie career. His four movies were *Eight Buckaroos* (1941), *Ridin' West* (1942), *Jamboree* (1943), and *Hollywood Barn Dance* (1947). He also had a cameo role with Roy Acuff in *Coalminer's Daughter.*

Probably the most important occurrence in Ernest Tubb's career was a set of concerts he did in Birmingham, Alabama and Memphis, Tennessee. In Memphis, he was billed with Roy Acuff, who has remained a lifelong friend. Through an auspicious turn of events, Roy Acuff's fan club leader told a manager, Joe Frank, about Ernest Tubb; Frank ultimately arranged for Tubb to move to Nashville and to begin working on the Grand Ole Opry in December of 1942.

One of Ernest Tubb's significant impacts on country music was a subtle change he brought about at Decca Records, where he insisted that they refer to his music as country rather than as hillbilly. Some writers have contended

Kitty Wells in the 1950s (*Photograph courtesy of the John Edwards Memorial Collection of the University of North Carolina at Chapel Hill*)

that Tubb was solely responsible for that change. There can be little doubt that Ernest Tubb raised the stature of country music, if by no other means than by influencing the industry into taking seriously musicians like Hank Snow and later Johnny Cash, both of whom owe Ernest Tubb for their start.

In 1947 Tubb was the headline performer in the first country show at Carnegie Hall. He recorded with the Andrews Sisters in 1949 and with Loretta Lynn in the 1960s. He has continued to affect other country musicians through his singing, his energy, and his total dedication to country music. Unlike some, Ernest Tubb never cut back on performing schedules.

His singing style is pure honky tonk, and as soon as he got over his Jimmie Rodgers imitation, he developed a style that was distinctive in character. His vocal style is full-voiced, and after the early 1940s hits, he began to move towards stronger songs with a fuller background. He always played a picking style guitar, and by the late 1940s he was using a fuller instrumentation to back his songs (early recordings used only guitar). Hits like "Driving Nails in My Coffin" and "Two Glasses, Joe" illustrate the honky tonk quality of Tubb's music. Basically he has remained pretty true to this second style. With the possible exception of Hank Williams (whom Tubb influenced), he is the honky tonk musician who springs most quickly to people's minds. Although still respected as a performer, his record sales in the 1980s dropped off to the point where he lost his recording contract. He passed away in 1984.

Kitty Wells

Kitty Wells was born in Nashville in 1919, the first country musician mentioned so far who came from that venerable city. Kitty, whose real name is Muriel Deason, was a country fan early in life and had become an accomplished guitarist and singer by her teenage years. However, she did not develop as a country musician until she had traveled extensively with her husband, Johnny Wright (whom she had married in 1938). In 1947 she got a guest spot on the Grand Ole Opry. From 1948 until 1952 she was one of the stars of the "Louisiana Hayride" in Shreveport, Louisiana.

In 1952 she signed with Decca Records and turned out a hit that settled her in as the reigning queen of country music and a prototypical honky tonker—"It Wasn't God Who Made Honky Tonk Angels." This tune was clearly the number-one country hit of 1952. She turned out one hit after another until the mid–1960s, when she was eclipsed by Loretta Lynn. Kitty Wells never went pop country, but she was the model for many female singers who came after her. She was probably also one of the first women's libbers in country music. Her 1952 hit and other tunes after that blamed some of life's woes on men, a relatively new theme in country music during that time, providing a new dimension to country music. Her singing style spoke of pain and woe in a down-home voice that made you want to cry with her. Her emotional quality and hard-hitting style were absolutely representative of the times and of the prevailing honky tonk style, which by this time you can clearly understand did not abate during the 1950s.

Hank Williams

Hiram "Hank" Williams ("The Drifting Cowboy") was born in Alabama in 1923 and died in West Virginia in 1953. His father was a railroad engineer. His mother was a church organist and no doubt Hank learned some of his music from her. Williams credited a black street-singer named Tee-Tot (real name Rufe Payne) with teaching him harmonies and chords. However, his guitar technique was totally self-taught. He listened to all of the country singers on record at that time, but the lasting influences on his style were Ernest Tubb and Roy Acuff.

Until 1946 he performed in every possible kind of situation but mostly in honky tonks. Honky tonk music and a drinking environment were important to Hank's style, with the drinking part having unfortunate consequences. During this entire time he kept writing songs, and ultimately when he hit the big time he did so totally with his own songs. Most of these songs illustrate honky tonk subjects. These, coupled with his singing style, made Hank Williams the main example of a honky tonk musician. He also serves as a good transition figure to the next chapter on rockabilly.

In 1946, he met Fred Rose of Acuff-Rose Publishing in Nashville, who asked Hank Williams to audition for him. The recording part of that event was not impressive to Rose, but he was impressed with Williams' songwriting ability. Signing Hank Williams to his publishing company's staff proved to be one of the smartest moves Fred Rose ever made, certainly worth his Hall of Fame election in 1961. In 1948 Williams had an enormous hit with "Lovesick Blues," and the tragically short but phenomenal career of Hank Williams was off with a bang.

Hank Williams performed first on the "Louisiana Hayride" in Shreveport, because even with Fred Rose's influence he was not a big enough star to perform on the Grand Ole Opry. However, in 1949 he did perform at the Opry, singing "Lovesick Blues." During the remainder of 1949, he recorded "Mind Your Own Business," "You're Gonna Change," "My Bucket's Got a Hole in It," and "Wedding Bells." Other top hits include:

1950

"I Just Don't Like This Kind of Livin' "
"Long Gone Lonesome Blues"
"Moanin' the Blues"
"Why Don't You Love Me?"

Hank Williams (*Photograph courtesy of the John Edwards Memorial Collection of the University of North Carolina at Chapel Hill*)

1951

"Baby We're Really in Love"
"Crazy Heart"
"Dear John"
"Hey Good Lookin' "
"Howlin' at the Moon"
"I Can't Help It"
"Cold Cold Heart"

1952

"I'll Never Get Out of This World Alive"
"Jambalaya"
"Half as Much"
"Honky Tonk Blues"
"Setting the Woods on Fire"

Unfortunately, tragedy struck in 1952 when various problems caught up with him. He was suspended from the Grand Ole Opry, his first wife left him, and his life started falling apart. He was such a mess that his band ultimately refused to tour with him, so he went out as a solo act. He died in the back seat of his car during a trip through West Virginia on January 1, 1953.

His popularity did not stop with his death, and probably the greatest tribute to Hank Williams is that his records still sell today. He did over thirty albums and there are more cover albums of Williams' songs than the songs of any other deceased country musician. Charley Pride did a remake of "Honky Tonk Blues" in the early 1980s that was in the top 10 on an album called "There's a Little Bit of Hank in Me." In the years since his death, several of his albums have sold enough copies to go platinum.

His influence is rather broad because of his unique style. His voice had a very hard edge to it, but he combined with it a tremendous feel for good phrasing and musical sense. He was a consummate communicator even when he was having personal difficulties. Many have made a lot of his personal difficulties, suggesting that Hank Williams would not have made the audience feel so much if he had been personally happy. But regardless of whether or not that theory is correct, Hank Williams had a tremendous talent for holding audiences right in the palm of his hand. Even at the end, when his personal life was a shambles, he still had that ability.

The legacy of Hank Williams in country music is in his continued influence on people who do his songs. Summing up Hank Williams is probably done best by quoting the inscription on his plaque at the Country Hall of Fame. Since Hank Williams was elected at the same time as Jimmie Rodgers and Fred Rose in 1961, his election shows the priority he held for the country music industry. However, in the words on that plaque, "The simple, beautiful melodies and straightforward, plaintive stories in his lyrics of life as he knew it will never die."

8 Rockabilly

COUNTRY AND ROCK 'N' ROLL

The interrelationship between rock and roll and country music is an interesting one, if for no other reason than most country fans do not believe there is any relationship and rock fans feel the same way. However, there is a clear relationship between the two musical styles, and eventually the rock influence would become one of the most important factors in contemporary country music, even if one only considers the financial aspects of its evolution.

To trace the influence of rock on country music, we can go back to the roots of rock and roll. All rock writers give at least some credit to earlier music in the development of rock and roll. However, the history of rock and roll is clearly tied up in the development of American popular music, going back at least to the early nineteenth century, if not earlier. Tracing just the black or Afro-American influences on rock and roll, one can easily go back to work songs and field hollers of the early slaves in the colonies. These simple songs contain melodic patterns that show up in rock and roll and can be traced through the development of the blues from the late nineteenth century through rhythm and blues. Therefore, the same black elements that influenced Jimmie Rodgers and Bill Monroe can be seen as part of the evolution of rock and roll. And if that is not cause to believe in a relationship between the development of rock and roll and country, then there is certainly more evidence.

Rock and roll also had a clear relationship to the development of jazz, which was heavily influenced by the blues. Many of the early rock forms were based on things that jazz bands had done, and although the instrumentation was different, much blues-based jazz is very similar to early rock and roll. Although this is the same as quoting black influences, it is another good example of the earlier origin of rock and roll than the traditional date of 1951.

Jazz was also a clear influence on country music, particularly on western swing. The fact that certain country musicians had jazz experiences (such as Kenny Rogers very early in his career) and that others would attain major successes playing jazz (Chet Atkins is the best example) illustrates that jazz was more similar to country music than many country fans would think and much more than jazz fans would admit. The point is that country music is just one avenue in which American popular music developed. All of the forms share the same basic roots.

So, if rock and roll is a combination of black rhythm and blues, jazz, and country music, the only thing left is to prove the country influence. In order to do this effectively, we must take a slightly different perspective than most country writers and most rock writers as well. Most rock experts tend to treat early rock and roll as being relatively insignificant, although a few (such as Arnold Shaw in *Honkers and Shouters*) treat the early history of rhythm and blues in a very thorough manner. However, most tend to gloss over Bill Haley as being somehow a minor figure. There seems to be a nearsightedness about the influence of Bill Haley, with two points of view presented: (1) black rhythm and blues is really the important development, not rock and roll; and (2) rock and roll really began with Elvis Presley, so there is no reason to talk about what happened before 1956.

Neither point of view is completely accurate and neither gives adequate representation to the role of country music in the development of rock and roll. And unfortunately, most country writers have believed the rock experts, quoting the basic works in rock and roll as their sources. Many books suffer from this myopia, with the unfortunate result that people are led to believe that Elvis Presley is the only important rocker who had country roots. Of course, Elvis is important in the history of rock and roll, but he was not the first rockabilly musician by any means. He was the first southern rockabilly musician but not the first country rockabilly star; Bill Haley was.

This chapter discusses rockabilly, which is a rock and roll style. However, I will consistently try to weave into the fabric of this discussion the relationship to country music. So even if you are a dyed-in-the-wool country fan who hates rock and roll, read this anyway. Each of the musicians discussed in this chapter will be presented from a country perspective, even when their contribution to and success in rock and roll is acknowledged.

Early rock and roll is understood by everyone to mean *rockabilly,* a term coined to explain what rock and roll was. The term *rock and roll* was always thought to be an invention of Alan Freed for a show he ran in Cleveland, Ohio. Freed wanted to have a legitimate name for rhythm and blues, legitimate in the sense that it would not be recognized as being black music. Bill Haley also claimed credit for inventing the term. Both Freed and Haley were responsible for popularizing the term and its music, although it is highly debatable whether either one of them invented the term.

The phrase "rock and roll" has been used in black rhythm and blues lyrics back into the early 1940s, especially in the music of Louis Jordan. And the fact that many early rockers, Bill Haley included, were influenced by Jordan is undeniable. They all say so and their music reveals it. A listen to Jordan's "Choo Choo Ch' Boogie" illustrates full well the origin of Bill Haley's style. The jump blues, then, is the real origin of rock and roll, with the term deriving from lyrics from the 1940s.

Rockabilly, on the other hand, is a term probably originating in the early 1950s although the phenomenon it represents is also rather old. The term was invented to explain what Bill Haley did, a combination of rock and roll and hillbilly. The fact that *hillbilly* was still being used in the early 1950s is intriguing, as we know for a fact that Ernest Tubb had already waged his campaign in Nashville and won a change from *hillbilly* to *country.* To explain this, we must understand that rockabilly or early rock and roll happened first in the Midwest and not in the South. Of course, this confuses the issue still further in the reader's mind because we are supposed to be talking about country music. Well, the clear explanation is that country music was not just a southern phenomenon any longer.

The information on the musicians selected for discussion in this chapter will concern the events of the mid–1950s in greater detail, but for our purposes here we should outline some general data. Whether the Bill Haley model was followed or whether the kinds of instrumental changes came from the same types of developments in honky tonk of the time, country music in the South had evolved by the mid–1950s, with more extensive use of electric instruments and more effective studio techniques in recordings. Although much of the first southern rockabilly music was technically pretty bad, by 1956 it was being produced in high-class studios.

The particular studio that was most influential in Memphis was the Sun studio, where many of the musicians discussed in this chapter first recorded. Sam Phillips started Sun Records and was the initial impetus behind the careers of Elvis Presley, Johnny Cash, Jerry Lee Lewis, and a horde of others. The importance of this one individual's insight must be stressed. He saw a market for this kind of music, and worked with the managers of these musicians to make recordings that were technically solid, employing good session men to back them up.

The southern rockabilly sound was probably more country than Bill Haley's music; it was certainly stronger and more versatile. The second generation rockabillies turned out shouting tunes like Haley, but they also turned out straight country songs and, perhaps more importantly, ballads and novelty songs. While the original contribution of Bill Haley was important, it was the southern style that insured the ultimate success of rock and roll. The commercial career of Bill Haley—concerts, records, movies, fan clubs, and memorabilia—was a model of success which the southern musicians (in particular Elvis Presley) carried to the extreme. This southern rockabilly was at first in competition with country music, and while it caused a massive depression in country music record sales during the 1950s, its connection with the South and with country music would ultimately cause country music both to prosper and to change.

Rockabilly and *rock and roll* were interchangeable terms by now; early hits were called rockabilly and later ones, rock and roll. The rock and roll of Elvis Presley, Carl Perkins, Johnny Cash, and others was a great commercial success, and when these artists did straight country tunes the early success they had as rockers contributed to their crossover sales. Conway Twitty (discussed in a later chapter) is a good example of the formula of early success in rock and roll and later success as a straight country performer. The point is that rock and roll was a very important phenomenon in the 1950s, and a number of country musicians did rock tunes, even musicians who were not recognized as rockabillies at all.

Although other musicians are certainly important to both rock and roll and country and their contributions will be mentioned individually, the really important story is Elvis Presley. If Bill Haley can be said to have originated the rock model, it was Elvis Presley who made sure that the model would survive. A country musician first and at heart, Elvis was to change the course of rock history and at the same time insure his rightful place in popular music in America.

Reading the many articles and books about Elvis Presley leaves one in awe of his career, but one thing comes through those writings: When Elvis began to become a musician, he had no predetermined plan at all. In fact, when he graduated from high school he had no impression of his talent other than from singing for high school assemblies and impressing girls. His first recording was a demonstration record that he made as a birthday present for his mother. That recording (done by then engineer Sam Phillips) would ultimately become important, but he had no idea of that at the time. That record had two tunes on it, both country traditional songs.

When he made his first recording for sale, one side was a blues tune and the other a country tune, "Blue Moon of Kentucky," written by Bill Monroe. His first band, arranged for by Sam Phillips, was called the Starlight Wranglers and his second, the Blue Moon Boys. These bands were country bands—drums, bass, and Presley playing guitar. It was not until he had worked in honky tonks and at dances as a country musician that he did a rhythm and blues tune in what would become the Presley style.

All who write about Elvis give credit to his country roots. However, it is also necessary to give tremendous credit to black influences on Elvis Presley. He grew up in very poor surroundings and went to a predominantly black high school. He was influenced by black people and this certainly comes through in his early music. He was described by many people as a white man singing in a black style, interestingly reminiscent of what was said about Jimmie Rodgers in 1928. Elvis Presley can be quoted on his roots in a 1970 interview (on tape at the Country Music Hall of Fame Library): "I listened to a lot of country music, gospel, and rhythm and blues. I was influenced by all that and my style is a combination of these." Elvis indeed put together black music and country music, but he did it unconsciously. Bill Haley can be said to have experimented his way to rock and roll; Elvis did it because it came naturally to him. Unlike other musicians whose musical training was long and arduous, Elvis was a natural talent with little formal training or experience in music. In this sense, his rise to stardom is even more astounding. He really had not paid his dues, or at least not for very long.

He began singing in his own style in 1955, when it was obvious to his manager, Bob Neal, that Presley's band would not go anywhere as a purely country trio. Presley had experimented with some rhythm and blues tunes in rehearsal, and these were woven into the act. Those tunes, in combination with his unabashed physical activity while singing, made him first a regional, then a national, success. His first record—"Heartbreak Hotel"—in 1956 was an immediate gold record.

The significance of the Memphis crew is that they packaged rockabilly in a new kind of lyric. The lyric content of Bill Haley's music was stereotyped and homogeneous. Ultimately, the Memphis crew, with Elvis as the leader, branched out into other types of music, including novelty tunes and ballads, to produce a more marketable combination of records. The most obvious reaction to rock and roll in country music is the subject of the next three chapters—The Nashville Sound.

Rockabilly, then, is a very important subject in the appreciation of country music. It was pivotal to the economic growth of country music as an industry. It provided country music with a model for future growth and the impetus to create a more dynamic pure country sound. It lent validity to the use of electronic instruments (although country musicians had begun that long before a rock and roll came around). But most importantly, it showed country musicians and their industry that it was possible to create the ultimate in crossover art. While rock and roll went through some heavy times because of negative public reaction, it was ultimately accepted (partially as a result of Elvis going into the army and proving himself a "real" American in the eyes of some of his detractors). Usually one talks about rock and roll as the key story of the 1950s through the 1980s, but the interesting thing is that country music also grew as a result. It was the relationship developed between rock and roll and country music in rockabilly that created the demand for both forms.

The discussion of the following musicians is in alphabetical order, and the order in no way supposes a rank ordering or order of influence. Some of the examples are more pure country than rockabilly (Johnny Cash, for instance) and some are marginally country (Buddy Holly). However, they were all rockabilly musicians and at least partially influenced by country music.

Johnny Cash

Johnny Cash really is not a rockabilly musician; however, he must be represented in any book on country music and should be discussed with the other Memphis musicians because that is where he got his start. The kind of sound he used as background instrumental texture was very similar to what the Memphis rockabilly musicians used. Johnny Cash sang in such a way that he could have been a rockabilly musician; however, he developed a unique style that should probably be considered half way between rockabilly and traditional country.

Johnny Cash was born in Arkansas in 1932. His father was a sharecropper; the family lived in a shack, and John worked in the cotton fields with his family. This dirt-poor existence gave him a perspective on life similar to that of Elvis Presley. They were both poor white boys who would ultimately become successful beyond their wildest dreams. Like many who went from rags to riches, both Elvis Presley and Johnny Cash had difficulties coping with that success.

Cash served in the Air Force in the early 1950s and after that returned to Memphis, where he was a salesman. He had learned to play the guitar while in Germany and had intentions of becoming a radio announcer upon his return to Memphis. He managed to get an audition with Sam Phillips, the Sun records man who was so important in Memphis, and Sam immediately sensed that Cash had something unusual. He was a songwriter, which ultimately turned out to be very important to his financial success. Cash interestingly enough was somewhat displeased with his first tune, "I Walk the Line," because Phillips had insisted on speeding it up. In this sense, Johnny Cash was initially influenced by the developing concept of rockabilly, that is, the style that Phillips imagined and created. From that point on, Johnny Cash was an enormous success.

Cash's voice, a rich baritone, is very full for a country singer. It was the unique sound of his voice that made Cash, like Presley, so successful. His

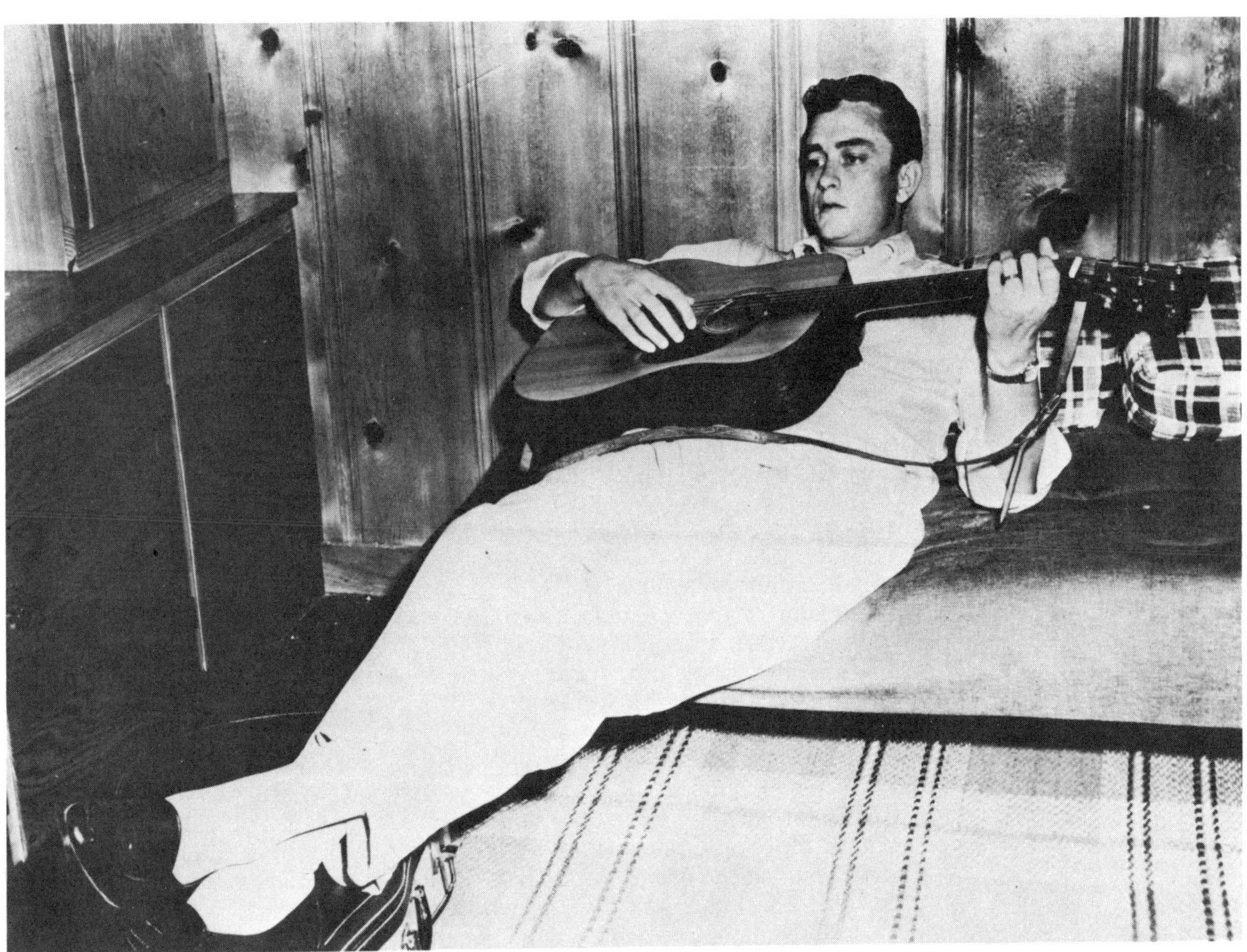

Johnny Cash as he looked in the 1950s (*Courtesy of John Singleton and the Sun International Corporation*)

Johnny Cash today (*Courtesy of John Singleton and the Sun International Corporation*)

overall sound is country, but heavily influenced by the powerful background of his band, which was always influenced by rockabilly (although sometimes referred to as honky tonk). He used a heavy amplification setup and driving rhythms, with his voice floating over a background with a rock beat.

Cash became more influential in folk music than anywhere else because his lyrics ran to the complex, especially after 1967. He has won numerous awards—Grammies from 1967 to 1970 and the Country Music Association Entertainer of the Year in 1969. He has had minor ups and downs in his career and in his life, but has been a major performer for almost thirty years. He has done hits with many other important musicians over his career, one of whom he married in 1967, June Carter of the Carter Family. Johnny Cash was elected to the Country Music Hall of Fame in 1980.

Bill Haley

Bill Haley was born in Detroit in 1927. In the mid–1940s he began playing country and western music; he was a relatively good guitar player. He toured with his band and also played on radio. At the end of the 1940s he began shaping his band, formerly the Saddle Pals and the four Aces of Western Swing, into the Comets, with a style based on pop, country and western, and rhythm and blues.

In the process of making the transition to a white version of rhythm and blues, which culminated in 1951, he listened carefully to its popularizers in the 1940s, in particular, Louis Jordan. Haley copied the beat pattern of the jump blues and some of the performing antics of Jordan. When Haley finally renamed his group the Comets, he had a clear view of what he wanted to do with his music and how he wanted it performed.

Haley's major contribution to the development of rock and roll was in what he did with lyrics. He took lyrics that were sexually obvious and toned them down so they would be acceptable to a white audience. He also worked

Johnny Cash and June Carter Cash (*Courtesy of Tom Cederberg, Teddy Bear Record Exchange, Bay City, Michigan*)

out elaborate stage routines, providing a dimension that white music had not previously had. Haley himself never really moved on stage that much, and in that sense he was more of a country musician. However, he had his musicians strike various poses and use their instruments as stage props (like Roy Acuff with his fiddle).

Haley was not original, although he felt that he had invented rock and roll. He simply put together available elements at the right time and had the good sense to get them before the public. But he was the catalyst necessary for rock and roll's success.

In 1951 he did quite well with a tune called "Rock the Joint." In 1952 he made "Crazy Man, Crazy," and in 1954 he did a cover version of Ivory Joe Hunter's "Shake, Rattle and Roll." Also in 1954 he made "Rock around the Clock." The 1955 release of the film *Blackboard Jungle* was aimed at a young audience. Its story of teenage decadence and alienation was backed up at the beginning by soundtrack music by Bill Haley, "Rock around the Clock." In 1956 he made a film called *Rock around the Clock,* which was an international success. After that he made another film called *Don't Knock the Rock* in which he was overshadowed by Little Richard. Although he continued to have some successful tunes, by 1957 he really had done all he could. After that he was clearly less significant than Elvis. He died in 1981, still remembered as the father of rock and roll.

The musical style of Bill Haley can be described pretty easily: a traditional 1950s rock and roll instrumental group that plays continuously (usually in a blues progression without variation). Haley sings in a slightly clipped style and plays an occasional guitar solo which is straight country.

Johnny Cash and the Statlers in the 1960s (*Photo taken in Saginaw, Michigan; used by courtesy of Tom Cederberg, Teddy Bear Record Exchange, Bay City, Michigan*)

The significance of his sound is that it provided a model for the rock and roll band. Given the country nature of the guitar solos and the types of lyrics, one can trace a continuous country element in rock and roll from the 1950s through today. It is especially present in blues-based rock and roll, punk, and the rockabilly revival (represented by the Stray Cats).

Buddy Holly

If Buddy Holly had only lived longer, he might certainly have been as important to the history of rockabilly as Presley was. Holly's career lasted only from 1956 to 1959. Born in Lubbock, Texas, he was at first a country musician, switching to rock and roll in the latter part of 1956. Between 1957 and his death in 1959, he recorded a great number of hits, both his own songs and the music of others. Some of his most important tunes were "Peggy Sue," "That'll Be the Day," "Early in the Morning," "Shake, Rattle and Roll," "Blue Suede Shoes," and "Rip It Up."

Holly, who could also be considered an early crooner, was similar to Elvis Presley in some ways, although Holly's country roots, and therefore his vocal inflections, were southwestern, or *Tex-Mex*. He was capable of using extreme contrast in his voice in order to create different moods, and although he did not have the range or perhaps the native talent of Presley, his performances took advantage of all of his technique. He looked like a person in pain while performing, and the main center of attention was his bobbing Adam's apple. His backup group, the Crickets, were pretty good, and at least one of them, Waylon Jennings, went on to great fame.

What was significant about Holly was his image as a performer and the way he elicited sympathy from the crowd. He seemed to be going through real pain while he was performing, which those present also felt and were affected by. Audience identification was high, not because Holly performed to entertain but because of the image he carried through his performances. At

Buddy Holly (on the right) and Waylon Jennings in 1958 *(Courtesy of William Griggs from the Buddy Holly Memorial Society collection)*

the time of his death he was second in popularity to Presley. For some people Buddy Holly was and still is a cult figure; some even feel he was the real central figure of rock and roll in the 1950s.

Jerry Lee Lewis

Jerry Lee Lewis was born in Louisiana in 1935. In many ways an Elvis imitator, he was originally a country western musician, and he returned to country western in the 1960s. He was probably the first important rock and roll piano player, which associated him with honky tonk country music because that was the only form that used a piano. He recorded for Sun Records and had his first success in 1956 with "End of the Road." His most popular song was "Great Balls of Fire" in 1957. He toured England in the late 1950s and failed miserably, primarily because of public scandal over his thirteen-year-old wife. He made a comeback in the 1960s as a country singer.

Lewis' style was straight shouting. He pounded the keyboard, used his fists and arms, and screamed at the audience. He sang a number of the same tunes that Presley did, but he usually recorded only the fast ones. Most of the songs were fast blues progressions (jump blues), which best fit his technique. Although successful as a rock and roll shouter, he did not show Presley's versatility, nor was he managed as well. His image was certainly right for a rock and roll star, but within a relatively limited spectrum. He has continued to be in the news, and has had eight wives at last count.

Jerry Lee Lewis (*Courtesy of John Singleton and the Sun International Corporation*)

Carl Perkins

Carl Perkins, a singer, guitarist, and songwriter, was born near Jackson, Tennessee, in 1932. He was poor as a child and his family were sharecroppers. In his teenage years he formed a band with his two brothers called the Perkins Brothers. He developed as a country singer in a traditional style and obtained a position in 1951 on the Big D Jamboree in Dallas, Texas. Better than average on the guitar, he quickly gained recognition as a country singer. As rock and roll increased in importance he quickly moved toward that kind of sound.

Moving back to Memphis, he started recording for Sun Records in 1955. He really hit it big in 1956 with his own composition, "Blue Suede Shoes." This particular song was a top-10 hit on country, pop, and rhythm and blues charts in 1956 and has been covered a number of times by other musicians. Carl continued to have some success in the 1950s and 1960s with hit records, but slowly moved into the position of songwriter and backup musician. He toured with Johnny Cash for years and is especially known for his fine guitar playing. His career suffered a setback when he was in a car accident on the way to perform on the Ed Sullivan Show; it was reported that he was going to do "Blue Suede Shoes."

Like Roy Orbison, Carl Perkins was a good example of a mainstream rockabilly musician who shows his country roots every time he plays or sings. The lyrics fit the rockabilly style and were very marketable at the time, but he eventually returned to country music. Carl Perkins took advantage of the popularity of rock and roll for a time and then returned to his first love.

Carl Perkins (*Courtesy of John Singleton and the Sun International Corporation*)

Elvis Presley

Elvis Presley was born in 1935 and died in 1977. Like many of the musicians in this chapter, he was born poor; however, Elvis Presley was to surpass everyone else in fame and earning power. Since the life of Elvis Presley is almost common knowledge, I will not repeat his biographical statistics except for a few.

His life until 1954 was basically like that of any kid from the South who was poor. He lived with his family in Tupelo, Mississippi. Although his family tried to provide him with everything they could, he just got by. He could sing and play the guitar, although no one including Elvis realized how talented he was. He went to high school in Memphis, where he was heavily influenced by black people because the high school was mostly black. However, at this point in his life he was just a very strange tall kid with long hair.

We have already discussed what happened to him from 1954 to 1956 (after which he was a star). He was a country singer and a southerner; that alone establishes him as playing a major part in the development of country music. But it was his overpowering success in the kind of music he did that makes him so important. He also did several albums of pure country music and gospel music; this is also quite important.

But the truly remarkable thing about Elvis was his voice and what he could do with it. He had a large range and tremendous control over volume and *vibrato* (wavering of the pitch). He could switch from a full voice to a thin voice instantaneously, and he used many emotional tricks to communicate. The beauty of his talent is that it was natural, not developed. If only

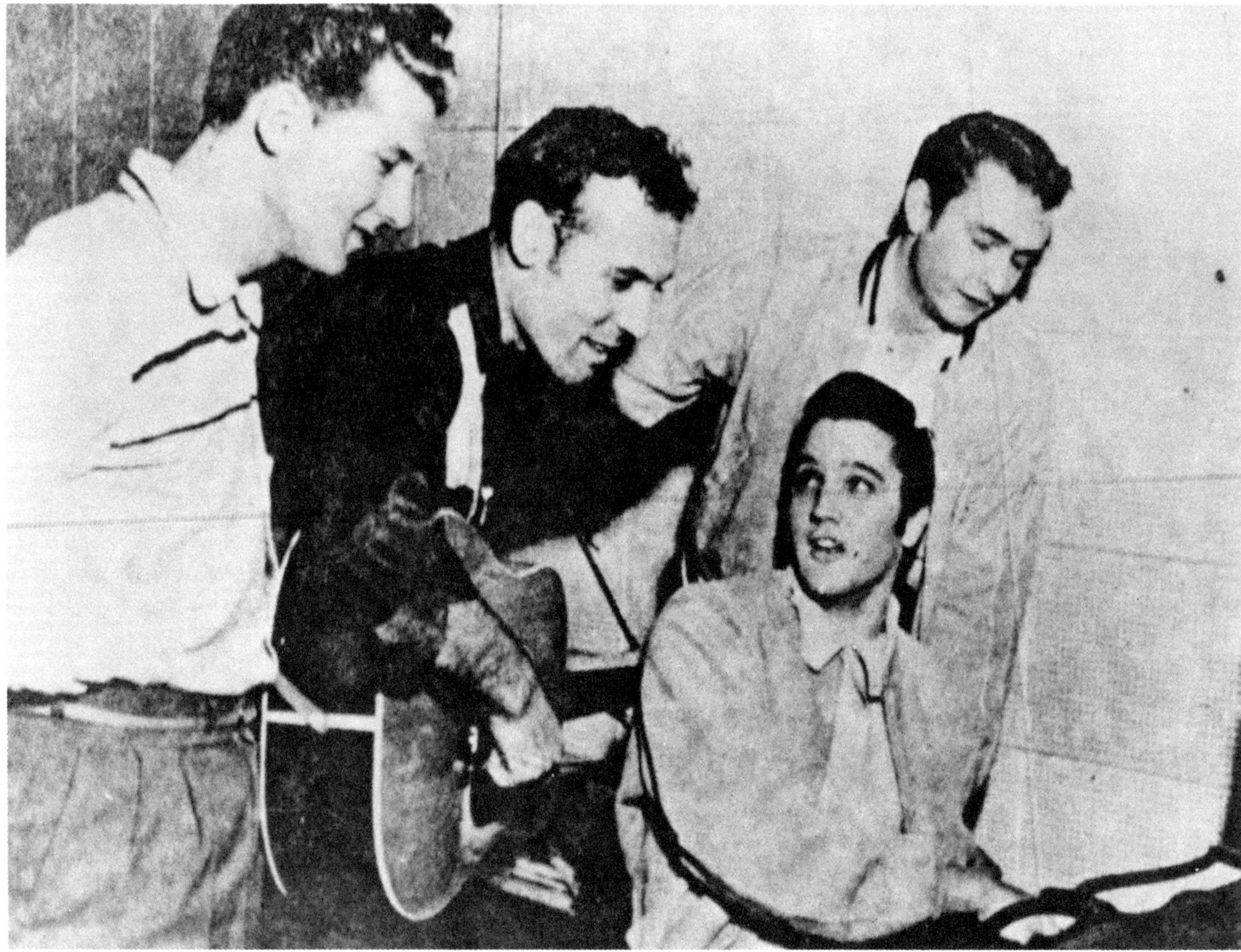

The Million Dollar Quartet; standing from left to right are Jerry Lee Lewis, Carl Perkins, and Johnny Cash, seated is Elvis Presley (*Courtesy of John Singleton and the Sun International Corporation*)

through the people who tried to imitate him, Elvis was a pivotal figure in American popular music. He was important because he served as a model for specific techniques.

Elvis was also important because he developed a stage routine that went way beyond anyone else's. When he took to the stage he commanded it, and the audience was immediately impressed by his tremendous charisma. He used his body and his voice as the whole act. He is important because he did so many things so well. His singing voice was a miracle, and he was undoubtedly one of the best natural singers of the twentieth century. And he was a country singer at heart.

Elvis always talked about himself as a simple country boy. That image really fits the way that country musicians tend to talk about themselves, and although some country musicians get to a level of popularity as Elvis did where they cannot really share themselves with the world, they always seem to want to be the simple country boy or girl. Elvis was for the most part a good symbol of Americana; he raised the level of rock and roll and undoubtedly helped country music through his enormous success. His manager, Colonel Tom Parker, was important before he met Elvis; Parker also managed Eddy Arnold and Hank Snow.

9 The Nashville Sound-Grand Ole Opry

TRADITIONAL COUNTRY

The next three chapters cover the Nashville sound under three different categories—traditional, the crooners, and country pop.

Before discussing the Nashville sound we probably ought to talk about the Grand Ole Opry. Of course, the Opry has been mentioned earlier in this book because many of the star performers gained national reputations through their work on the Opry. And the Opry has always represented the pinnacle of success for country musicians. However, it was during the late 1950s and early 1960s that the Opry would become the focal point of a development of a Nashville monopoly on country music, a monopoly that would ultimately produce a kind of music that was popular and standardized; it became recognizable as Nashville music. This style, so much associated with the Grand Ole Opry, became the norm for country music and assured the significance of Nashville as a financial and artistic center for the production of country music—so much so that people ultimately reacted against it.

The Opry was first known as the "WSM Barn Dance," founded by "Judge" George Hay in 1925. The show ran for an hour on Saturday evenings. It was first broadcast live from studio A of WSM and later shifted to studio B. In 1927 it was renamed the "Grand Ole Opry." The story is told that it was so named because it followed a "Music Appreciation Hour Show" that was purely classical. That show's announcer said that there is no place in the classics for realism. Judge Hay reacted by saying that his show would be called the Grand Ole Opry because, of course, country music has always been realistic.

The Grand Ole Opry has had many homes over the years; the first move after studio B was to Hillsboro Theatre to allow for an audience. The Opry later moved to the Dixie Tabernacle, then to the War Memorial Auditorium in 1939 and to the Ryman Auditorium in 1943. The Ryman was the location

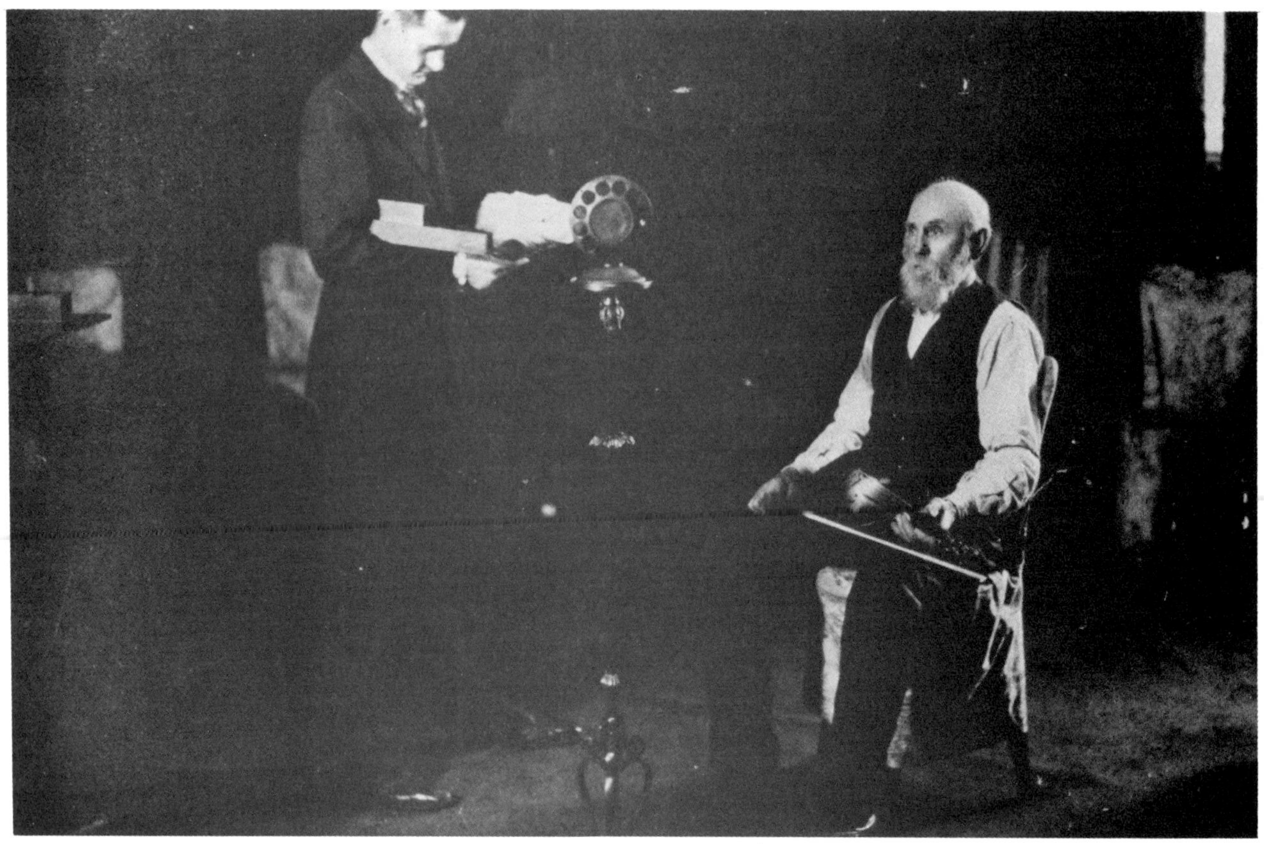

"Judge" George D. Hay and Uncle Jimmy Thompson in 1925 (*Photograph courtesy of the Country Music Foundation Library and Media Center, Nashville, Tennessee*)

where the Grand Ole Opry grew to become the central institution in country music and also where many stars were born. In 1974 a new location was built at Opryland, a combination performance center and amusement park. Although the new location is spectacular, many people still hold a warm place in their hearts for the Ryman, which is located in downtown Nashville.

The first real star of the Grand Ole Opry was Uncle Dave Macon, who first started playing on the WSM Barn Dance in 1926; he was a regular member of the Opry until his death in 1952. Although competent as a musician and singer, he was perhaps best known as an entertainer, and under Uncle Dave's watchful eye many Opry stars came to the program. It was quite important to have an established star in long-term residence and certainly part of Uncle Dave's legacy is his solid presence on the Opry during its formative years.

The Grand Ole Opry had local significance as a radio program; but until 1939 it was just another country show and there were a number of them in different towns. However, in 1939 the Grand Ole Opry began to make its move towards monopoly on this particular phenomenon when R. J. Reynolds Tobacco Company signed up the Opry for a half-hour radio program syndicated over the NBC Broadcasting Network. This commercial connection catapulted the Grand Ole Opry into millions of homes and also established the Opry as the frontrunner for popular radio country shows. The show was hosted first by Roy Acuff, a relative newcomer to the Opry, and later taken over by Ray Foley.

The formative years of the Opry corresponded to the growth of honky tonk music and were also aided by improving economic conditions. The 1940s saw the coming to the Opry of people like Minnie Pearl, Bill Monroe (1939),

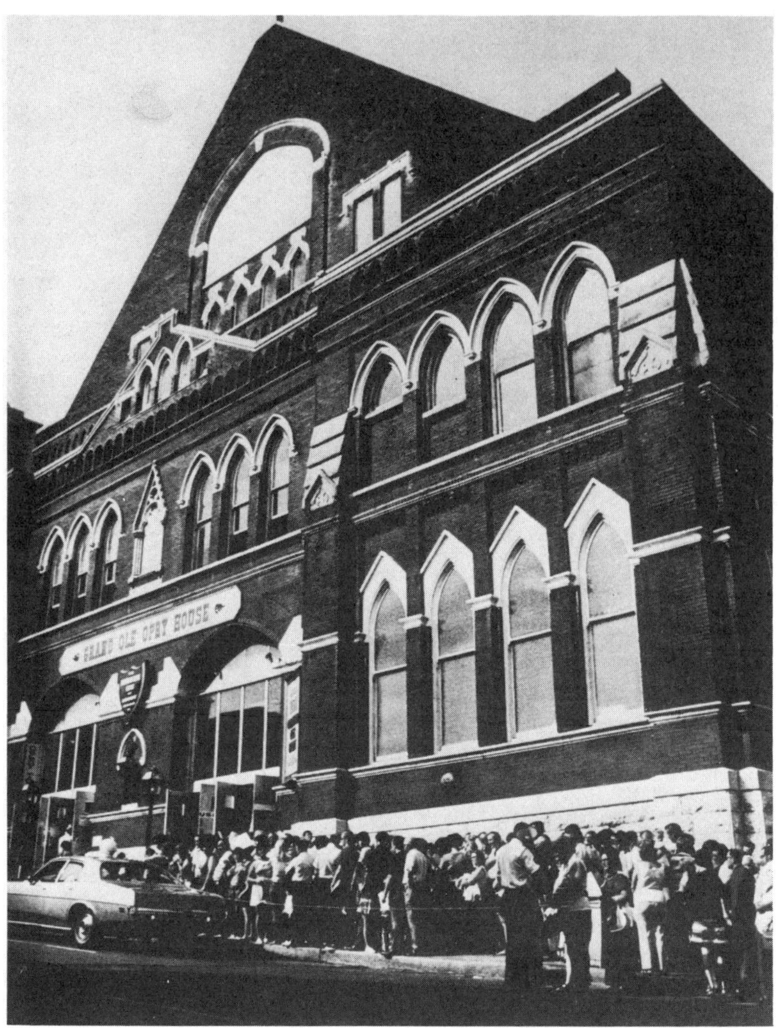

The Ryman Auditorium in the late 1960s (*Photograph courtesy of the Country Music Foundation Library and Media Center, Nashville, Tennessee*)

Ernest Tubb, Cowboy Copas, and Eddy Arnold. It was clearly attracting bright young stars and already becoming the center of country music activity. Of those just mentioned, Ernest Tubb was probably the most important continuing influence in the Opry if for no other reason than his longevity. It was also during this time that the benefits of being a regular Opry performer could be felt in the industry.

Regular performers used their Opry status as an advertising mechanism, and while that might not seem too important to us today, it was an important marketing tool for musicians in the 1940s. The exposure of being on a regular program—even if you did not get on the nationwide radio show very often—meant quite a bit. This early recognition of the Opry stars as being the country musicians with the industry's stamp of approval was one of the important reasons for the complete dominance of Nashville in country music. And that regular status was something that was to have lasting influence on the careers of musicians—you either had it or you suffered.

A most interesting phenomenon occurred in Nashville during the 1940s—a change in attitude toward country music. After all, Nashville had been a cultural center of the South and most old-time residents saw in Nashville "higher" cultural values than country music. However, as the strength and popularity of the Grand Ole Opry grew, Nashville people began

Opryland (*Photograph courtesy of the Country Music Foundation Library and Media Center, Nashville, Tennessee*)

to change their minds on this issue. What happened was a slow shift to a nationalistic or regionalistic feeling toward country music to the extent that country music is the most significant outward manifestation of Nashville today. And it was the Grand Ole Opry, or at least the economic side effects of its existence, which caused this change.

From the late 1940s on, many fine performers went to the Grand Ole Opry, and when television coverage was added for a brief period in the late 1950s it became even more popular. Spinoffs of the Grand Ole Opry are shows like "Hee Haw," which feature many musicians who first reached national prominence on the Opry. In short, the Opry is probably the number one institution in country music, with an existence that has spanned almost the complete history of country music. One need only go to Opryland to see the result of years of commercialization of country music; but of course it also served as an artistic focal point for the development of country music styles. Virtually every important new movement has been seen on the Opry except for a few rebellious styles, and even they are seen once they prove their commercial value.

If the Opry was the focal point for the development of country music, then Nashville was the center of the country music industry. Almost any other form of American popular music can be said to exist in many places in the United States. For instance, we can speak of jazz styles in New Orleans, Kansas City, Chicago, or Detroit, of New York bebop or West Coast cool jazz. And in each of those places, there are recording networks designed to support that particular development in popular music. The same can be said of rock and roll. However, in country music the main location has been Nashville, although that is really less true today. The main point is that Nashville

"Judge" George D. Hay (left) and Uncle Dave Macon (right) in Uncle Dave's home in the mid-1940s (*Photograph courtesy of the Country Music Foundation Library and Media Center, Nashville, Tennessee*)

is a thorough recording town devoted to country music. While other musicians may go there to record music from other fields with a country feel, the whole entertainment network of Nashville is geared towards country.

The importance of the Nashville recording industry is that it developed because of the presence of the musicians associated with the Opry. The growth of the recording industry came first because of out-of-town recording companies who set up recording studios in Nashville as outposts. Next came the development of publishing companies, the most important being Acuff-Rose, although certainly Southern was important as well. The people who started the publishing companies had great foresight because they saw that country music would be lucrative. Certainly the production and sales work that they did in signing writers and producing their work caused great growth of country music.

Recording studios and publishing companies increased the possibilities for musicians many times. Studio musicians developed under the watchful eyes of people like Chet Atkins. What developed was a very highly technical country musician who could play anything with a perfect performance. These developments, which led to the Nashville sound, began before the 1960s, probably by the mid–1940s. While country music was still not at the height of its marketability or its technical expertise by then, the development of higher standards in Nashville had already begun. The most distinguishing characteristic of the sound associated with Nashville is its sense of perfection.

Many people have made a big deal out of the Nashville sound developing because of rock and roll, but I believe that its constituent parts developed prior to the invention of rock and roll. In fact, Eddy Arnold did recordings in the late 1940s that have all of the attributes of the sound later called the reaction to rock and roll. It is also said in some country books that honky tonk developed as an important phenomenon in the late 1940s, died out during the 1950s, and then re-emerged as a new important sound in the 1960s. Sales sagged demonstrably in the 1950s, but honky tonk was still important to country music performance—Ernest Tubb, for instance. George Jones had his first major successes right in the middle of the rock era, and Ray Price was phenomenally successful during that period. Many musicians did turn to rock and roll during the 1950s, but a lot of country musicians had enormously popular careers during the heyday of rockabilly. It is my belief that the *Nashville sound* was a name given to country music of the 1960s, and that the term itself explains nothing. It is simply the logical extension of a phenomenon that had been developing since the 1940s and which was of pivotal importance. However, it was not invented in the 1960s; at most it was codified in the 1960s.

To define briefly what the *Nashville sound* is: (1) it is technically perfect music; (2) it tends to be rather smooth in sound even when the music has honky tonk lyrics; (3) it uses traditional country instrumentation with light amplification and light rhythmic activity—the instrumentation eventually expanding to include string sections, with choruses occasionally substituted for background groups; and (4) it uses regular phrase lengths of sung lyrics and is supported by instrumental activity, which reinforces the sense of regularity. These are all tendencies of the sound described and not absolute generalities. Traditional music in Nashville retains some semblance of the irregular phrases derived from old-time music, and occasionally something irregular will be added for emphasis. Dolly Parton has an extra half measure tossed in for her rendition of "Jolene." But for the most part, the Nashville sound is a commercialized product that is reduced to its simplest terms, designed for the average listener and intended to sell to as broad an audience as possible.

One must immediately be impressed with the relative conservative nature of this sound, designed to hit the broadest market possible. Part of the beauty and the danger of this kind of music is that it typically does not allow too much experimentation with the basic form. It is controlled music and its intention is clear: sell records. An interesting side story is that I tried to find out more about experimental country during my last trip to Nashville and I was told by someone that "we do not do experimental country in Nashville; we just pick and grin." Now I think that probably is not completely true, but it is at least partially so.

The Nashville sound then must be explained in terms of the various kinds of songs that are produced rather than as one particular type of music. It has general attributes, but it is in the way it manifests itself in specific styles that it can be more carefully defined.

Patsy Cline

Patsy Cline was born in 1932 in Winchester, Virginia and died in 1963 near Camden, Tennessee. Her important, although tragically brief, career was cut short by a plane crash that also killed Cowboy Copas and Hawkshaw Hawkins. She is a prototypical example of the early Nashville sound. She was very popular from 1957 until her death. Her kind of song was straight country, but the singing style was pop-oriented and the songs achieved crossover popularity.

Virginia Patterson Hensley (her real name) showed musical and entertaining talent early in life. She was first a tap dancer, started piano lessons at the age of eight, and was performing professionally by her teenage years. In the late 1940s she went to Nashville to try to break into the music scene

Patsy Cline in a photo taken in 1956 or 1957 (*Photograph courtesy of the Country Music Foundation Library and Media Center, Nashville, Tennessee*)

there, but she was unsuccessful. Returning home, she continued to work in country music and finally in 1957 she was on the Arthur Godfrey Talent Scouts program, a contest she won with her 1957 hit called "Walkin' after Midnight" (analyzed in the Appendix). From that point on she was a real contender in country music, becoming a recording artist in Nashville in the late 1950s, and appearing on the Grand Ole Opry for the first time in 1958.

She had seven hit songs in three years and seemed to be on her way to true stardom when she was tragically killed. She was elected posthumously to the Country Hall of Fame in 1973 and is considered one of country music's major female vocalists. Her voice was clear, although traditional, in sound. The music she performed had crossover popularity, regular phrasing, and very good quality backup work. Recording in Nashville, she produced good examples of the sophistication of Nashville music in the early 1960s.

Lefty Frizzell

William Orville "Lefty" Frizzell was born in Texas in 1928 and died in 1975. Deeply influenced by Jimmie Rodgers and the honky tonk musicians of Dallas and Waco, he emerged in the honky tonk field as a big hit in the early

Lefty Frizzell (*Courtesy of Columbia Records, Nashville*)

1950s. His first tune was "If You've Got the Money, I've Got the Time." He became an Opry regular in the early 1950s and had many hit tunes in 1951 and 1952.

Perhaps influenced by Hank Williams' death, he went into a slump until 1959, when he returned with tunes that were loosely labeled *saga* songs. He had a big hit in 1959 with "Long Black Veil" and again in 1964 with "Saginaw, Michigan." His career slumped again after that, and he was basically unrecognized at the time of his death in 1975. He was later recognized by the Country Hall of Fame by his election to it in 1982.

Frizzell's music is interesting because it had great popularity but few recognized its significance. He was basically a honky tonk singer. Most writers now recognize that a lot of people copied his vocal style, but unfortunately it was not until after his death that he was so recognized. Upon first hearing, tunes like "I Love You a Thousand Ways," "I Want to Be with You Always," and "I'm an Old, Old Man Trying to Live While I Can," one is tempted to write him off as simply another honky tonker singing about the traditional sad emotions of country music. But upon closer listening, one hears that his voice is really quite different from regular honky tonkers; it is much more mellow and has a clarity of communication not to be found in other musicians of that time.

As an early exponent of a developing sophistication in Nashville music, Lefty Frizzell illustrates the coming of age of Nashville music in 1959 with his "Long Black Veil." It is still a song of simple accompaniment, but there is a sophistication to the background and a rounded commercial quality to the singing.

Hawkshaw Hawkins

Harold "Hawkshaw" Hawkins was born in Huntington, West Virginia in 1921 and died in 1963 in the plane crash that also killed Patsy Cline and Cowboy Copas. He was a singer and guitar player and had achieved a regional following for his singing by the beginning of World War II. He served in the armed forces during the war, and after the Philippines were liberated he sang on a radio station there. In 1946 he returned to West Virginia and

Hawshaw Hawkins on the Opry in the 1950s (*Photograph courtesy of the John Edwards Memorial Collection of the University of North Carolina at Chapel Hill*)

began working at another radio station. Soon he signed a recording contract with King Records, for whom he produced many hits over the years, the last one, in 1963, being "Lonesome 7–7023." He became a regular on the Opry in 1955 and completely shifted his performing career to Nashville. Although he had begun his career before moving to Nashville, it was in the context of the Nashville complex that Hawkshaw Hawkins became a star.

Hawkshaw Hawkins lived long enough to become a mature performer and a very popular entertainer, even though he died in 1963. And while the Nashville complex was fully developed by that time, it is difficult to assess where Hawkins' career might have gone and what other types of music he might have done. In any event, he was very successful with what he did, which was a sophisticated honky tonk with a very smooth vocal style. Most of his tunes featured Nashville studio musicians in very slick arrangements. It sounds like traditional country, but the subtle influence of electric bass and drums is there, plus a Chet Atkins' style guitar background in most of his songs of the late 1950s and early 1960s. Another typical example of Nashville influence, when Hawkins moved to the Opry in 1955 he entered mainstream country music, and those influences are obvious in his music.

George Jones

George has been discussed previously in the honky tonk chapter and in a lot of ways he has been one of the few who have remained true to the honky tonk style. But so much of that style was assimilated into the Nashville sound that it is hard to distinguish between the two. Although George has consistently lived outside of Nashville (except during his marriage to Tammy Wynette), he does most of his recording there and has been heavily influenced by Nashville musicians. His singing style is very Texan, but the background sound and the perfection of his recordings are typically the sound of Nashville studios. Thus he is an example of the traditional Nashville sound of the late 1950s and 1960s as much as anyone is.

Some of his important hits in this style are the following: from 1959, "White Lightning," "Who Shot Sam," "Money to Burn"; from 1960, "The Window up Above"; from 1961, "Tender Years"; from 1962, "She Thinks I Still Care." He continued to have hits in this style throughout the 1960s and right up until today. In 1969 he married Tammy Wynette and their duet singing throughout the 1970s—even after they were divorced in 1975—continued the influence of the Nashville sound. George Jones is a good example of traditional Nashville music, even though he is really a Texan at heart.

Loretta Lynn

Country music has given many accolades to its stars over the years, and certainly Loretta Lynn has earned the many that it has bestowed on her. There is perhaps no female singer who has been more consistently important to country music since 1962. She has been influential in choice of material and has served as a model for women in country music. She is clearly a product of the Nashville sound of the 1960s and continues to illustrate her careful dedication to the development of her career within the context of Nashville as a center of country music.

Loretta Lynn was born in Butchers Hollow, Kentucky sometime in the mid–1930s (she has guardedly kept secret the exact date). She married her present husband, Oliver (Mooney) Lynn, when she was fourteen years old, and they had six children. Much of the credit for the development of her career should certainly go to her husband, a devoted family person who has quietly pushed and supported her for years. The daughter of a coal miner, she steadfastly holds on to her country roots and her roots in severe poverty. Although very wealthy and sophisticated now, she seems to be very sincere in her simplicity of attitude towards life. Loretta Lynn is a model for many reasons, but a big one is her humanity.

She first started singing professionally in Custer, Washington, where she had moved with her husband in the early 1950s. She won a talent contest in Tacoma, Washington that was hosted by Buck Owens. As a result of that show, she went to Los Angeles to record the tune "I'm a Honky Tonk Girl," and this record did well. Her manager at that time, Norman Burleigh, arranged for enough money for the Lynns to travel to Nashville to make a demo record. Doyle and Teddy Wilburn of Sure Fire Music, a new company in Nashville, decided to represent her.

Mooney, Loretta, and four of their children moved to Nashville from Washington because they believed in Loretta's music. A very risky decision because of the odds, this trip turned out to be successful. In 1962 she recorded "Success," which was a big hit, and she has had many hits ever since. "Coal Miner's Daughter" in 1970 is an autobiographical song. Although not one of her most successful tunes, it is an example of the impact of her recordings. She was named CMA Entertainer of the Year in 1972, Female Vocalist of the Year in 1967, 1972, and 1973, Music City News Female Artist of the Year from 1967 to 1978, Duet of the Year with Conway Twitty from 1971 to 1978 and again in 1980 and 1981, and the Academy of Country Music Artist of the Decade for the 1970s. She also won a Grammy in 1971. Interestingly, she never won a Most Promising award; she was already past "most promising" when she began.

Loretta Lynn is without doubt the most successful female country singer of all time. The reason is clear in her music. She combines a tradi-

Loretta Lynn (*Courtesy of MCA Records, Nashville*)

tional country sound in voice inflection and speech with a very sophisticated understanding of walking the line between a progressive and a traditional woman. She is not patronizing toward men, nor does she hide her head in shame. Although particular tunes like "The Pill" were controversial at the time, most of her songs are simple in character, while having a slightly deeper meaning than one might initially perceive. One of her songs, "Don't Come Home a-Drinkin' " from 1966, illustrates her way of threading the needle between being too strong and being a milquetoast. She speaks directly to the issue of drinking and what it can do to a relationship; she asserts her own position and yet manages to sound understanding at the same time. It is precisely within the context of the words that the true significance of Loretta Lynn can be found. They are contemporary lyrics, yet they retain the sense of country roots.

The backgrounds of Loretta's recordings are very slick, although one is not initially impressed with that fact. They are typical of the Nashville sound when it is really done to perfection: apparently simple but in actuality rather sophisticated. Since her recording has been done entirely in Nashville after the Nashville establishment was firmly in a position of monopoly, the recordings of Loretta Lynn represent precisely the topic of conversation of this chapter. It is a credit to her that she became so successful; but clearly the Nashville sound had something to do with enhancing the creative and

Tammy Wynette (*Photo by Harry Langdon; used by courtesy of Epic Records*)

financial potential of the move she and Mooney made because of their belief in her talent.

Tammy Wynette

Tammy Wynette Pugh was born near Tupelo, Mississippi in 1942. Due to her father's death when she was a baby she was raised by her grandparents on a farm. There she learned to play stringed instruments and learned to sing, southern style. She got married at the age of seventeen and had three children before that marriage dissolved. She moved to Birmingham, Alabama and began singing country music, playing both the guitar and the accordion. She appeared on the "Country Boy Eddie Show" on WBRC-TV and also on Porter Waggoner's syndicated TV series. She then began making trips to Nashville to try to get a contract as a solo musician, which ultimately led to success with Epic records. An important song of 1967, "Apartment Number Nine," was just the beginning of a long and illustrious career.

Porter Waggoner in the late 1960s *(Photograph courtesy of the Country Music Foundation Library and Media Center, Nashville, Tennessee)*

Tammy Wynette made her position in country music by singing songs that were traditional in attitude but contemporary in subject matter. Songs like "Stand By Your Man" in 1968 (the biggest selling single by a female country singer ever), "D-I-V-O-R-C-E," also in 1968, and "The Ways to Love a Man" reveal the traditional female role in country music and are markedly different in stance than those of Loretta Lynn. Tammy Wynette was early in her career noticeably proclaiming a traditional male-dominated view of her position as a woman, and this was responsible in great measure for her success. She was recognized as clearly expressing southern values.

She married George Jones in 1969. Although they were divorced in 1975 for some of the reasons that she had glorified in her early tunes, that marriage was also responsible for some of her success. They recorded together as a duet for much of the 1970s, even after the divorce. Their blend of traditional country with sophisticated Nashville backup musicians provided another model for the Nashville sound. Most of the music she has made on her own and with George Jones were story songs that were very popular. They fit the image of traditional country music although they were based on contemporary views.

10 Nashville Crossover

THE CROONERS

A very important part of the Nashville sound is the development of country crooners. However, the concept of crooning is not tied solely to country music nor is it just a style of the 1960s. It is a style of singing and not just a particular marketing technique. Crooning goes back at least to the middle of the nineteenth century in American music and will always be present to a certain extent in popular music.

Crooning can best be defined as beautiful singing, usually in a slower tempo and with a full rich voice. One often thinks of the Irish tenor when the word *crooner* is mentioned because the lovely vocal quality of an Irish tenor is a perfect example of crooning. Another example would be the *bel canto* or "beautiful singing" style of Italian opera, a style that helps define the word "romantic" as it describes nineteenth-century "serious" music. This romantic quality rubbed off on popular parlor music in both Europe and the United States. Similar kinds of music developed in Mexico and Latin America. In short, the emotional beautiful singing style of nineteenth-century music had influence on many kinds of music that ultimately influenced country music.

Probably the most important early crooner of twentieth-century popular music was Rudy Vallee. Vallee, who sang through a megaphone prior to the time of effective amplification, became known as the "Vagabond Lover" because of the song for which he became famous. He was quite a handsome man, with wavy hair; like many crooners, he had tremendous charisma and was a sex symbol. Through his emotional love songs he influenced numbers of people and probably established the crooning style as a part of American popular music in the twentieth century.

Important crooners of the Big Band era included Bing Crosby and Frank Sinatra. There were also vocal singing groups that had crooning qualities, such as the Mills Brothers. These crooners were of course associated with specific big bands, and their identification with these bands gave them true power in their communication; they were visible and well-known people as a result of the enormous popularity the bands had. That popularity also came from the nature of crooning; it allowed the musician to sing to an audience that felt as if the singer was singing to each person. In short, crooning was very personal music, and this is one of its greatest appeals.

There were some early examples of crooner-like voices in country music, Vernon Dalhart for instance. With his classically-trained voice, he had a much fuller sound than most traditional singers of that time. As well, he sang quite a number of songs that were not purely from the hillbilly tradition. Thus an important part of country crooning is the tendency for the lyrics to be sometimes less than pure country, imparting a crossover quality through both the vocal style and the choice of lyrics. Vernon Dalhart, a good example, was a rare exception in the earlier history of country music.

In trying to trace the time in country music when crooning had its major impact, most writers tend to think of it as being a phenomenon of the 1960s and as a reaction to rock and roll. But Eddy Arnold, a country crooner, had his first crooning hit in 1947. And in my estimation, country crooning had nothing to do with rock and roll; it was simply a logical development for much the same reason that crooning was developed in the rock and roll ballad.

In rock and roll, ballad singing developed partially as a result of Elvis doing ballads, but more so perhaps because rockabilly was a pretty homogeneous sound. It was based on a blues progression, usually sung to a fairly fast tempo, and featuring a specific set of instrumental characteristics in the playing style. Rockabilly was of course fascinating and very popular, but as American youths turned more toward dancing and less towards just listening, some kind of contrast tune was needed. Rock and roll ballads were developed to provide a change from the sameness of rockabilly. These slow songs were sung by people with rich voices and the lyrics were usually pop oriented. In fact, some of the most popular "rock and roll" ballads of the late 1950s were hardly rock and roll at all. But they served a purpose and therefore were included in the corpus of rock and roll music.

In this style of singing, musicians like Sam Cooke, Elvis Presley, Paul Anka, and Pat Boone were crooners. They had charisma and influenced people simply by their presence. They had rich voices with a full gamut of emotional singing techniques. The songs they sang were usually about simple emotions, but they fit the times for which they were written. In short, they did the same thing that Rudy Vallee and Frank Sinatra had done earlier.

It is my contention that crooning was a similar phenomenon in country music. That is, crooning or ballad singing developed because there was a function provided by that kind of music. I see crooning developing in country music as an outgrowth of honky tonk music, an urban form that began to speak to city, rather than rural, needs. Crooning, then, was music for people in an urban setting, and, as in rock and roll, it was designed for dancing. One can then understand the timing of Eddy Arnold and the country crooners of the 1950s, rather than saying they were just ahead of their time and that real crooning started as a reaction to rock and roll in the later 1950s or early 1960s.

Country crooning is of course different from rock and roll ballad singing and it is also different from straight pop singing. However, the differences are perhaps slighter than the differences between straight rock and roll and straight country. In short, the very quality of crooning imparts a similar character to songs in different styles. Country crooning differs from traditional country music in the vocal quality and subject matter. However, it can still be recognized as country music.

Many of the songs of Stephen Foster and other parlor song composers of the nineteenth century had crooner qualities to them. "No Place Like Home" has a dreamy quality to it best expressed by a beautiful singing voice. The crooner however also manifested another quality—charisma. Many crooners traveled with the vaudeville and minstrel shows of the nineteenth century; that particular tradition in the South supported some of our first country stars, although most of the country musicians who were part of minstrel or medicine shows sang in a high-pitched mountain style having little to do with crooning.

Crooning in country music started in the 1940s concurrently with the honky tonk movement. The emergence of the smooth singing style of Western musicians like Gene Autry certainly had something to do with the introduction of that kind of singing on the Grand Ole Opry. The connection of crooning with the Nashville sound then should be understood as being another part of the commercialized package that was developing in Nashville, centered first in the Grand Ole Opry, second in the publishing companies, and finally in the recording companies. The tremendous growth of recording studios in Nashville in the 1950s was very supportive of the great crooners spoken of in this chapter.

Country crooning is usually defined by the lyrics rather than by the singing style. The singing style is very much like pop music, a very smooth voice with clear pronunciation of the words. In fact, many of the songs of the important crooners were often felt to be sellouts from country music. Eddy Arnold, the first great crooner in country music, was condemned from 1950 on for selling out completely to crossover pop. This is rather unfair: Eddy Arnold was simply doing what came naturally, and the Country Music Association recognized that contribution. However, crooning does have a non-purist attitude to it because it attempts to present country lyrics in a less than pure country style. Country crooning expanded the market for country music and undoubtedly helped the cause of country music, so it fit right into the game plan of Nashville.

On that point, some newer writers have suggested rather maliciously that the Nashville sound was created by musicians like Chet Atkins who really could not make it in pure country. I doubt the validity of that last statement because it implies that Chet Atkins was less of a musician because of it. Atkins revolutionized guitar playing, as was shown in the discussion of him (see also Malone's *Stars of Country Music* and the chapter on Chet Atkins by Bill Ivey). The fact that he produced a new, softer sound of playing that ultimately influenced the Nashville sound does not make his contribution a negative one. The same writers have gone further to suggest that the Nashville sound was a canned effect, with all instrumental backings sounding the same. To an extent this is true because there was a great deal of similarity in the background sounds but that similarity is defined by the perfection of technique rather than by monotony. Crooning simply evolved because there was a market for it, and we should not blame Nashville for capitalizing on that market.

To conclude, country crooning features a singer with a beautiful voice who sings songs about relatively simple emotions. The background ensemble tends to be a standard rhythm section like that used in both honky tonk and standard Nashville sound country songs. By the mid–1960s there was some experimentation, with fiddles and steel guitars returning to the instrumental ensemble. Crooning songs are intended to have crossover popularity and many of them succeeded as pop tunes. However, they are still a part of country music, and their essential purpose is to provide programming contrast. At a dance crooning songs are used for slow dances and on radio or television, for diversity in programming. Thus, crooning songs are an important part of the development of the Nashville sound.

Eddy Arnold

Eddy Arnold was born in Henderson, Tennessee in 1918 to a farming family. His father died when Eddy was eleven but influenced him greatly: Eddy's father was a fiddle player and taught him about country music. Eddy Arnold's nickname, "The Tennessee Plowboy," came from the farm chores he did as a youth, and he has retained an active interest in farming throughout his life. Already an excellent guitar player, he played local engagements as a teenager, riding to and from the jobs on a mule.

In many ways, Eddy Arnold's early style was heavily influenced by singers from outside of the South; his favorites were Bing Crosby and Gene Autry, both clearly non-southern singers. The singing cowboy style of Autry was of course smoother than traditional country music and had crossover popularity. Bing Crosby was a classic crooner, first with big bands and then in films. While some writers have pointed to the heavy country influence in his early music, Eddy Arnold was always a pop singer with country influences from Tennessee.

Arnold's first job was with a fiddler, Speedy McNatt, on radio and in honky tonks in the mid–1930s. In 1940 he began working with Pee Wee King's Golden West Cowboys on the Grand Ole Opry, associating himself with the singing cowboy school of musicians. In 1942 he began working as a solo act on a radio station in Jackson, Tennessee and, in 1943, on WSM in Nashville, where he also received a recording contract with RCA. His first record, "Mommy Please Stay Home with Me," released in 1945, was a success. Probably the most important result of that record was that he acquired a manager, Colonel Tom Parker. Parker later managed Hank Snow and was responsible for the enormously successful career of Elvis Presley. However, Parker's first major success was with Eddy Arnold, who established the crooning style for country music, just as Elvis Presley ultimately established a crooning style for rock and roll.

In 1946 Eddy Arnold established himself as a major star. From that point on, he released a quantity of major hits each year through 1956. Very important as a singer and entertainer, he also made a significant contribution as a songwriter or co-writer; many of his hits were at least in part his own creation. If one were to examine the number of hits he had up until 1955 and then compare that with what he did after, one might conclude that his career went into decline after 1955. However, even during his so-called "declining" years, he had as many hits as did anyone else. In his career he has sold over 70 million records.

Eddy Arnold won the first Entertainer of the Year Award from the Country Music Association in 1967. He was elected to the Hall of Fame in 1966 at a time when there were only six members. He won the Academy of Country Music Pioneer Award in 1984. One of the first country entertainers

Eddy Arnold in the late 1940s or early 1950s (*Photograph courtesy of the John Edwards Memorial Collection of the University of North Carolina at Chapel Hill*)

to be featured on television shows as a pop singer, he appeared with Arthur Godfrey, Milton Berle, Perry Como, Bob Hope, and Dinah Shore. He had a syndicated TV show in the 1950s called "Eddy Arnold Time." He has also appeared in major nightclubs, including the Coconut Grove in Los Angeles. Eddy Arnold has consistently been quite visible over his more than forty years of performing.

The Arnold singing style is very easy to characterize. He has a rich voice in the baritone range. His phrasing is very smooth and in that sense like a pop singer. The background instrumentation in his early hits is more in a country style and light in texture. By the mid–1950s he was using a typical Nashville rhythm section, although with a rather subdued instrumental style. Some of his tunes use expanded instrumental backgrounds, especially the string of hits he had in the mid–1960s.

Jim Ed Brown in the 1970s (*Photograph courtesy of the Country Music Foundation Library and Media Center, Nashville, Tennessee*)

Some of his important songs are "Cattle Call," "I'm Throwing Rice at the Girl I Love," "Bouquet of Roses," "Anytime," "Texarkana Baby," "Will Santa Come to Shanty Town," "Kentucky Waltz," "Tennessee Stud," "Make the World Go Away," "What's He Doing in My World," and "Cowboy." Although traditionally thought of as a pop musician, about half of his recordings are country tunes with a pop singing style. Almost all of his songs are crooners, and he is best known in this style. I would go so far as to say that Eddy Arnold was one of the people responsible for the Nashville sound, at least the crooning part of it. He remains an important part of the country industry and he has retained close ties with Tennessee, his home state.

Jim Ed Brown

Jim Ed Brown performed with two sisters in a vocal trio that had its first success in 1955. Maxine, the oldest, was born in Louisiana in 1932; Jim Edward was born in Arkansas in 1934; and Bonnie was also born in Arkansas in 1937. Maxine and Jim Ed started as a duo in the early 1950s and Bonnie joined to make it a trio in 1955. The duo had already won a spot on the Louisiana Hayride in Shreveport, and after they became a trio they moved to the Ozark Jamboree in Springfield, Missouri. Their first hit recordings in 1955 were "Draggin' Main Street" and "I Was Looking Back to See." The latter record was done on Abbott Records, which had done the early recordings of Jim Reeves. Reeves suggested to Steve Sholes and Chet Atkins at RCA that they listen to the Browns, with the result that the Browns were signed by RCA.

Jim Edward spent two years in the army. After he returned, the trio continued to record and perform although it was not really well known. Their first major success was with "Jimmy Brown" in 1959, and from then until 1967 they were a very popular singing trio. In 1967, when the Browns had been Opry members for four years and had hit the top of their field, Jim Ed Brown started as a solo act.

While Jim Ed's style changed after 1967, the trio sang in a crooning style, as heard on their 1959 recording of "Jimmy Brown." The song is uptempo by comparison to other crooning tunes, but shifts back and forth between a slow speaking style and a quicker blending of voices. The emotional character and simplicity of communication put the song firmly in the crooning category, even though it had crossover popularity (as did many of the trio's tunes). Also, a careful listening to the background instrumentals on their tunes from 1959 to 1967 shows the influence of the Nashville sound. It is obvious that Chet Atkins had something to do with their recordings.

Tennessee Ernie Ford

Ernest Jennings Ford, born in Bristol, Tennessee in 1919, has been described as singer, songwriter, disc jockey, actor, and family man. One of the more successful entertainers of the 1940s and 1950s, he was very influential in popularizing country music to an audience that was much larger than the country audience. In the mid–1960s he effectively retired from show business, having made enough money to last the rest of his life.

His radio career started in 1937 and lasted into the late 1940s, interrupted by a four-year stint in the air corps as a bombardier and instructor. Ford spent most of 1938 studying voice at the Cincinnati Conservatory of Music, serious training that rounded out his singing style. His deep bass voice was to make a significant impression in the country field.

In 1949, Ford had two hit songs for Capitol Records, "Mule Train" and "Smokey Mountain Boogie"; he wrote the latter with Cliffie Stone, a bandleader on radio station KXLA in Pasadena, California, where Ford had moved with his new wife.

From 1949 until 1965 Tennessee Ernie Ford was a highly successful country musician—and much more as well. He had his own TV series from 1955 to 1961 and then again from 1962 to 1965, sponsored by the Ford Motor Company. The television and recording work supported and reinforced each other, and he was consistently successful during those periods. Ford had many top hits, including "I'll Never Be Free" with Kay Starr, "The Cry of the Wild Goose," "Shotgun Boogie" (a Ford original), "Ballad of Davy Crockett," and "Sixteen Tons" (a Merle Travis tune which broke existing record sales figures). During the 1960s he recorded a number of religious albums that were also extremely successful.

Tennessee Ernie Ford has definite crooning characteristics even when he is singing boogie tunes or upbeat tunes. Many of his songs had crossover popularity and some were just barely country tunes. For instance, "The Ballad of Davy Crockett" was used for the television series and, although about a western figure, was really done in a pop style. Even in that tune, however, Ford's rich and emotionally full voice had the quality of a crooner. Although Ford was born in Tennessee, his career as a singer and songwriter was totally in California. One might be tempted to say that he was an outlaw because he had little musical connection to Nashville, but that would be quite wrong.

His development was in a way very similar to that of country musicians in Nashville, but his main theater of performance was the Los Angeles national television and radio networks. He developed a sound similar to the Nashville sound, however, his deep bass voice with his classical training produced a vocal sound that was rather unique at the time. Johnny Cash would capitalize on a deep bass voice in somewhat the same fashion as Ford. Tennessee Ernie Ford was a crooner even when he was singing songs having little to do with crooning. He won a Grammy for a gospel song in 1964. His rich bass voice was very important in popularizing country music during the 1950s. If he had been in Nashville he might have been more mainstream country than he was.

Charley Pride

Charley Pride was born in Mississippi in 1938 to a cotton picking family. The most significant thing about "Country" Charley Pride is that he broke the color line for country musicians. As a black man, he sings in a totally country style, and although other black musicians had been involved in country music before, none have been so successful at just country music.

Pride began playing the guitar at the age of fourteen and immediately set to work learning how to play it based on recordings that he had heard. His first idol was Hank Williams, the reigning superstar at that time. However, it was not until much later that Pride turned to music seriously. As a well-built and athletic person, he always felt that baseball was where he belonged; inspired by Jackie Robinson's breakthrough, he decided to pursue professional baseball. He was on the Memphis Red Sox of the old Negro American League and then on a minor league team for a few years in Helena, Montana.

After performing during an intermission between innings at one of his ballgames, he got a job singing at a country bar in Helena, but he still concentrated on baseball. He had a tryout with the Los Angeles Angels in 1961 but was not successful. In 1963, Red Sovine heard him singing in Montana and later suggested that Chet Atkins audition him. Pride went to Nashville in 1964, auditioned for Chet Atkins, and the rest is history. Charley Pride has without doubt had a very successful career in country music, getting awards on a regular basis and doing for country music what Jackie Robinson did for baseball.

Pride's first record, "Snakes Crawl at Night," was released in 1966. "Just between You and Me" later that year was also a success. His first LP in 1966, *Country Charley Pride,* was his first gold record. In January of 1967 he made his first appearance on the Opry. His awards include CMA Entertainer of the Year (1971), CMA Male Vocalist of the Year (1971–1972), Music City News Male Artist of the Year (1969–1973) and Grammies (1971–1972).

His voice is rich and deep, and although he sings country and gospel hits, he is basically a crooner. He seems to fit a contemporary notion of the Nashville sound, especially since much of his career has existed after the formation of that concept. As he sings he clearly enunciates the words so that he is easy to understand. However, his music sounds like southern

Charley Pride (*Courtesy of RCA Records, Nashville*)

country music, perhaps because he is a southerner and grew up, as so many other Nashville stars, poor. It is very difficult to tell from recordings that he is black—his style is simply country. His gospel music (for which he has also won awards) shows more of the influence of black America. However, "Country" Charley Pride is a country crooner and that is what has made him so popular and successful.

Jim Reeves

Like the previously discussed star, Jim Reeves had intentions of becoming a baseball player. Born in 1924 in Panola County, Texas, he was a standout athlete by the time he was in junior high school. He learned to play the guitar as a young man and performed at local dances during his high school years. However, his dream was to be a professional baseball player. He went to the University of Texas at Austin, and after his sophomore year he was signed by the St. Louis Cardinals. He injured his leg during his first season with a farm team and had to resort to country music as a backup profession.

Reeves started as a radio announcer in Shreveport, Louisiana. He recorded for Abbott Records, where he made his earliest hit with "Mexican Joe." On Abbott Records in 1953 he had a hit with "Bimbo" and joined the Louisiana Hayride. A duet with Ginny Wright on Abbott Records, "I Love You," was a hit in 1954. At the end of 1954 he was signed by RCA in Nashville, and from that point on he was phenomenally successful.

He appeared first on the Opry in 1955 and became a regular from the late 1950s until his death in 1964. He also made USO tours and appeared on the shows of Ed Sullivan, Steve Allen, Dick Clark, and Jimmy Dean. He was also popular in Europe, especially Norway, and had multimillion album sales abroad. In his short career (1955–1964) he had phenomenal success, surpassed in record sales only by Eddy Arnold. His records continued to sell well after his death, and he had six number-one hits after his death (the last being in 1967). Like Jimmie Rodgers and Hank Williams, Jim Reeves left the greatest legacy of any country musician: posthumous popularity.

Jim Reeves had a very smooth and relaxed style of singing, extending the boundaries of country music toward middle-of-the road pop. However, his music was carefully controlled so that it always had country roots, and his band, the Blue Boys, had a real country sound. He was a crooner, as the titles of some of his songs bear out; he sang songs about simple emotions and did it with great clarity of singing style. With his velvet voice, he was an international success, communicating to people who did not even understand English. He was elected to the Country Music Hall of Fame in 1967, recognized as an artist of great taste and success. As a clear proponent of the Nashville crooning sound, Jim Reeves well deserved this award; unfortunately, he died too soon to win many others.

11 Nashville Pop

Frankly, the selection process of whom to include in this chapter is tough, and as I get closer to the end of the book the nagging suspicion that I have left someone out gets stronger. But, keeping in mind that we have to make selections, this chapter is offered as representative of the growing field of country pop as it was manifest from the late 1950s on. Some of the musicians mentioned are still around and doing music that might not always be defined as country pop, but they are included in this chapter because they did some tunes in that style.

The other problem with this particular discussion is how to define country pop. Most country numbers are in fact intended to be popular or the musician probably would not have done them in the first place. The Nashville sound was developed around a pop marketing concept. Therefore, everything in the previous two chapters is country pop, from the honky tonk tunes of George Jones to the pop ballads of Eddy Arnold. We will have to define the music for this chapter somewhat more narrowly in order to make sense of the classification.

Country pop (not to be confused with crossover pop) is music having some novel character to it, analogous to the novelty songs that developed in rock and roll. In the late 1950s rock and roll developed a number of novelty tunes, from "Itsy Bitsy Teeny Weenie Yellow Polka-Dot Bikini" to the "Monster Mash." These tunes were pop tunes and only parenthetically part of what people considered rock and roll. It was an important diversification of rock and roll programming. Many of these hits did not survive over time, but were done primarily for marketing reasons—quick to succeed and quick to be forgotten. However, many continue to have nostalgia value and are re-released occasionally on television offers.

The same can be said of country novelty tunes, starting with the Kingston Trio's "Tom Dooley" in 1958. The Kingston Trio was not a country group, but they did do a country novelty tune, and in that sense they are part of the country pop (defined as novelty) movement. In this chapter we will discuss straight country musicians and groups who did novelty tunes and also some non-country musicians who did country tunes in novelty style.

The importance of these tunes should not be minimized; novelty tunes come along at a time when a particular genre is really beginning to spread out in its commercial appeal. The emergence of novelty tunes in rock and roll from 1958 to 1962—the Golden Age of Novelty and Monster Songs—coincides with a commercialization of the rock and roll style. Some have referred to this era in rock and roll as a dead era in which nothing really happened. However, in hindsight it is my belief that this broadening of the form to include song types previously not considered part of the genre indicates the growing commercialization of the form and not its decay. Therefore, the emergence of novelty tunes in country music should be recognized as the same phenomenon, a broadening of the commercial appeal of country music.

It is interesting that the country pop movement was occurring pretty much in the same time frame as the rock novelty trend. The general economic situation, continued growth in the youth market, and specific technological changes in sound reproduction and recording were all contributing factors in making novelty tunes successful. The tunes were also very marketable for the radio programming at that time. But the most significant point is that country pop grew, especially as novelty tunes, because country music was in the process of gaining in sophistication. And even if the novelty tunes did not immediately convey the message of sophistication, that is the reason why they existed.

Novelty tunes have a "hook" of some kind with which the listener can immediately identify. The "yellow polka-dot bikini" is the hook of that tune, around which everything revolves. The "flying purple people eater" is a benevolent monster who really only comes down to earth to look at people, a friendly little character with whom people can have a good time. Most novelty tunes are basically fun tunes, not socially threatening, and simple to understand. But as in the case of the Nashville sound in general, one should not be fooled by the seeming lack of sophistication; these are tunes put together with imagination. The hook concept is ever-present in recording and publishing; any product must have some central focus that allows the perceiver to understand immediately what the whole thing is about. This is generally true for long works and always true for short works.

The novelty song is part of the Nashville sound, even when it happens to be done in Los Angeles or New York. The fact that some of the novelty tunes discussed in this chapter were done in places other than Nashville is an indication of how widespread the influence of Nashville was; it does not mean that Nashville was no longer in power. The sound of these novelty tunes is for the most part sophisticated and perfectly in accord with the Nashville sound. There are exceptions to this, like "Western Movies" by the Olympics. This black rhythm and blues group did a tune that is a country novelty hit, talking about the girlfriend who likes western movies. This novelty tune perhaps does not fit with the others because of its relative lack of sophistication. But even the fact that there were some rather unsophisticated hit country novelty tunes indicates the general marketability of the Nashville sound in novelty form.

Novelty songs are very word-oriented; the background instrumentals seldom have much impact on the song, although occasionally one will hear a particular instrumental technique supporting the words or some special phrase. There also tends to be a wide diversity of styles for accompaniment; many country novelty tunes use rhythmic accompaniments that are in fact not country at all. Similarly, "Yellow Polka-Dot Bikini" is a good example of that phenomenon in rock music because it uses a cha-cha beat, not normally considered to be rock and roll.

Many novelty songs are really *saga songs,* that is, songs with lyrics that tell a story about some person or set of events. "Tom Dooley," the classic hit from 1958 by the Kingston Trio, is like this, as is Jimmy Dean's "Big Bad John" and its sequel, "Big Bad Bruce." Saga songs were very popular at the end of the 1950s and in the early 1960s, so it should not be surprising that many novelty songs were saga songs. Saga songs are narratives in which the hook is the character discussed or the tragedy that occurs, as in "Tom Dooley."

But the most important characteristic of novelty tunes is their particularly catchy quality, usually coming from the main character and always from the lyrics. This catchy quality captures the attention of the disc jockey and his listeners. I believe that novelty songs were a quick way to get air play on radio, which at that time was considered the most important prerequisite for success. And in fact, many of the musicians discussed in this chapter—performers like Mel Tillis, Roger Miller, and Dolly Parton—made their first successes as comedians or novelty musicians, only to go on to round out their careers as first-rate country musicians.

Our discussion of novelty songs is based on particular musicians, and their contribution to novelty songs will be highlighted. We will also look at their contributions to country music in general and briefly outline their careers. It should be clearly understood that many of these musicians might have been successful without ever doing a novelty tune; they just happened to begin their careers or highlighted their careers with a novelty tune or two. In some cases, it catapulted them into stardom; in other cases, it simply helped pave the way on a road that probably would have led them to stardom anyway.

Jimmy Dean

Jimmy Dean was born in Texas in 1928. Like so many country musicians, Jimmy Dean grew up poor, doing farmwork—picking cotton and other manual labor. When he was ten his mother started teaching him the piano; he also learned to play the guitar, harmonica, and accordion. In the mid-1940s he was in the merchant marines and the air force, during which time he played and sang as a sideline. In 1948 he was discharged from the service and began working as a professional musician.

At first he was basically a honky tonk musician playing with fellow servicemen in a group called the Tennessee Haymakers. In 1952 he was sent with a new group called the Texas Wildcats to do a USO tour of the Caribbean. In 1953 he had his first hit single with "Bummin' Around." By 1955 he had gained a national reputation through a television show on which he was featured—"Town and Country Time." In 1957 he had a CBS network show, "The Jimmy Dean Show," which was popular but did not survive the season. He continued to record and perform through the 1950s and was a major star right through the 1960s.

Although Jimmy Dean's career has comprised much besides novelty tunes, he did have his biggest success in 1961 with a novelty tune, his own composition, "Big Bad John." This particular song (which is analyzed in the Appendix) is a perfect country novelty tune. It has the hero coming into town and saving everybody, and is sung in a real country style. However, it was an enormous crossover hit and was recognized as a pop tune. He followed that up with "Dear Ivan" and, in 1962, "The Cajun Queen" and "P.T.109"—based on the boat that President Kennedy captained during the war. These compositions were all enormously successful. The combination of songwriter and performer made Jimmy Dean an even greater star and, I might add, quite wealthy.

He had another television show from 1963 to 1966 on ABC and has appeared on many variety shows and country shows. Since 1966 he has had more hits, but they are not as frequent as those of the 1950s and 1960s. His last gold record was a single from 1976 called "I.O.U."

Jimmy Dean (center) with the Louvin Brothers (*Photograph courtesy of the John Edwards Memorial Collection of the University of North Carolina at Chapel Hill*)

Jimmy Dean was a significant country star who sang first in the honky tonk style and then as a traditional Nashville musician. However, he will be remembered in country music for his novelty tunes because of their great crossover popularity. He has a smooth voice that is emotive in style. His narration in "Big Bad John" immediately grabs your attention, and the song is a fine example of country novelty, seemingly simple yet very sophisticated in structure and emotional impact. In short, Jimmy Dean is both a fine country musician and an excellent example of a novelty song writer-performer.

Ferlin Husky

Ferin Husky was born in Missouri in 1927. He grew up on a farm, where he was exposed to guitar and fiddle music. When he finished school, he began work as a radio announcer, and although he played the guitar and sang, he really did not consider working as a musician. He worked for a number of different radio stations across the United States, eventually land-

Ferlin Husky in the mid-1960s in Saginaw, Michigan (*Courtesy of Tom Cederberg, Teddy Bear Record Exchange, Bay City, Michigan*)

ing in Bakersfield, California in 1949. It was at this time that he made up his first stage name, Terry Preston. When he finally began performing as a musician, he used that name.

As a part of his radio style, he developed a comic country character whose name was Simon Crum. With Capitol Records he made his first record as Simon Crum. These early recordings led to an opportunity to do straight country music, which he did under the name of Terry Preston. Also in 1953, he wrote a song called "Hank's Song" after his idol at that time, Hank Williams. He released this song under his own name, and its success led to the retirement of the Preston alias. If all this sounds confusing, it is. But Ferlin Husky combines a number of different and diverse talents. He is a first-rate songwriter, a fine straight country performer in traditional honky tonk style, hilarious comedian, and an actor. He was in a movie in 1958 called "Country Music Holiday" with Zsa Zsa Gabor and Faron Young; the movie, which is typical of the pictures of that time and similar to Presley movies, was successful. He toured the country throughout the 1950s and 1960s, appearing on TV shows in both the popular and the country fields.

Ferlin Husky is a fine straight country singer and could easily be discussed under other rubrics. However, he is being discussed here because of his alter-ego Simon Crum and especially for his big hit in 1958, "Country Music Is Here to Stay." This is a comedy tune and perfectly illustrates the novelty song of that era. It is a straight country tune and reminiscent of the comedians so much a part of the Opry and "Hee Haw."

Ferlin Husky continued to turn out major recordings throughout the 1960s and into the 1970s, both under his own name in straight country style and occasionally as Simon Crum. His significance as a country star is evi-

Faron Young in the mid 1960s (*Courtesy of Tom Cederberg, Teddy Bear Record Exchange, Bay City, Michigan*)

dent in the number of his gold records and of the songs he has written. His novelty songs may not have caused his career, since he was quite successful as himself. But he was first given a recording contract based on his comic presence, and one of his major hits at a time when his career was growing was a novelty tune.

Kingston Trio

The Kingston Trio was not a country group, but was one of the most important folk trios of the 1950s and early 1960s. The original members were Bob Sane from Hawaii, Dave Guard from San Francisco, and Nick Reynolds from Coronado, California. Shane and Guard went to school together in Hawaii, where they learned to play the ukelele and to sing Hawaiian folksongs. It was not until they both attended school in the San Francisco area that they met up with Reynolds and began singing at local events for extra cash. Their basic style was typical of folk music at that time, although the use of acoustic string instruments is similar to that in country music.

In the mid-1950s they began performing back in California, and by 1958 they had a long-term recording contract with Capitol Records. They appeared on a number of television shows and were probably the most popular folk group of the 1950s. But the biggest reason they were popular was their number-one hit of 1958, "Tom Dooley."

"Tom Dooley" was supposed to be a traditional ballad, based on a story of a Civil War soldier who returned to town to court two cousins. One was discovered dead, and Tom Dooley was eventually hanged for the murder. The story goes further: the other cousin eventually confessed, but not publicly, so Tom Dooley was "done wrong." When the song was done by the Kingston Trio almost a hundred years after the fact, public sentiment led to a petition campaign to save Tom Dooley from the Nevada gallows. One could conclude that the song was pretty believeable. The country writer Frank Proffitt was eventually declared the writer of the song in a historic legal battle over songwriter payments. The Kingston Trio had long made a practice of taking public domain material and resetting it. However, Proffitt had written the tune in a contemporary version and won the suit. (This particular lawsuit, while it has nothing to do with the novelty popularity of the song, set precedent for other lawsuits for songwriters.)

Although the Kingston Trio was not a country group by any stretch of the imagination, "Tom Dooley" was a country song even in its setting in the Old West. It was given a Grammy in 1958 as the top country western song of the year and has always been recognized as a country tune. The hook is the character of Tom Dooley and the unfairness of the fate that he met. In that sense, it is like many country songs in which characters meet with unfair fates. It is also one of the saga songs so popular both in traditional country music and in novelty hits.

But the most interesting thing about the song "Tom Dooley" is its lasting quality. People have forgotten many of the novelty hits of the late 1950s, but still know that song. It seems to transcend historical periods and continues to be performed in concert. It is a staple of the folk field and it is a country tune. While it did not serve as a pivot point for the entire career of the Kingston Trio, which continued as a group until 1967, it was one of their most significant hits.

Roger Miller

Roger Miller was born in Texas in 1936 but moved to Oklahoma as a small child because his father died. He was raised by his aunt and uncle. His early childhood was spent in meager surroundings. He claims that he always wanted to be a musician, admiring most Sheb Wooley, who was an in-law (and is discussed in this chapter as well). In Miller's teenage years, he wandered around Texas and Oklahoma working an assortment of jobs, most involving cattle herding or rodeos. Meanwhile he kept singing and playing the guitar, banjo, and piano.

He joined the army during the Korean War and managed to end up in Special Services in an entertainment unit. While he was not the star performer, he did have a chance to perfect his technique; and he kept writing songs and trying out new things. His group during the army experience was a hillbilly band in which Roger also played fiddle and drums. After the service he went to Texas for a short time, but eventually the drive of the music business caused him to go to Nashville. And frankly, he was at first very unsuccessful.

As a songwriter he is an interesting case because he does not read or write music. He plays or sings the song for someone else to write down. From the mid-1950s until the early 1960s he survived in Nashville, peddling songs, doing odd jobs, working whenever he could. He played a variety of instruments, including drums for Faron Young for two years. Many of his tunes were eventually recorded by great stars—Ernest Tubb, Jim Reeves, Ray Price. One of his earliest songs, "Invitation to the Blues," was recorded by Ray Price and later covered by Patti Page. Thus Roger Miller's initial success was as a songwriter, not as a performer.

RCA signed him as a performer in 1960 and a co-authored hit with Bill Anderson was released in 1961, "When Two Worlds Collide," a country pop tune. In 1962 he moved to Hollywood to pursue an acting career but changed his mind quickly when some of his compositions started scoring. He had a banner year in 1964 with "Dang Me" and "Chug-A-Lug." In 1965 he had four major hits, "King of the Road," "Engine Engine No. 9," "Kansas City Star," and "One Dyin' and One Buryin'."

Roger Miller in the mid-1960s in Saginaw, Michigan (*Courtesy of Tom Cederberg, Teddy Bear Record Exchange, Bay City, Michigan*)

Roger Miller was elected to the Songwriter's Hall of Fame in 1973. He won five Grammys in 1964 and six in 1965. In 1965 he was elected Country Music Man of the Year and Best Songwriter by the Academy of Country Music; he won their Best Single award in 1968 for "Little Green Apples." While his main awards came in the 1960s, he has had continuing influence in songwriting.

Roger Miller wrote mainly novelty tunes, although he was responsible for writing a number of mainstream country songs. Songs like "Dang Me," "Chug-A-Lug" and "Little Green Apples" are novelty tunes. They each have a hook—the words "dang me," a drinking style, and little green apples as a symbol of what God does not make. They are up-tempo tunes with catchy lyrics and a country style of singing. They are perfect examples of country novelty songs, and the number of awards he won for those tunes is rather impressive. His "King of the Road" is another novelty song telling the story of a guy who goes around the United States with no worries. A classic saga song, it had enormous popularity as a pop tune. Roger Miller's contribution to this particular segment of the country music story is most significant. He popularized the novelty country tune far more than did anyone else.

Dolly Parton

Dolly Parton was born in the foothills of the Smoky Mountains of Tennessee in 1946, the fourth of twelve children. Her father was a farmer and construction worker. Although the Partons were quite poor, Dolly has always had a very happy disposition. According to her, she was always musical and sang and played guitar from early youth. She also learned the banjo and started writing songs while still going to school. When she graduated from high school she moved to Nashville, intent on becoming a country star.

In Nashville she lived first with her Uncle Bill Owens, with whom she wrote songs. Their first success was with "Put It off until Tomorrow," which was recorded by Bill Phillips and became a hit in 1966. She signed with Monument Records as a singer and put out two albums with them. Two novelty singles in 1967 became hits—"Dumb Blonde" and "Something Fishy."

In 1967, she teamed up with Porter Wagoner, a partnership which lasted until 1974. As a member of one of the most successful duos of the 1970s, she racked up hit after hit, both of original material and of songs from other writers. Her acting career started off with the movie *9 to 5,* which used her own composition as the title song. Dolly Parton was a recording star from 1967 on, and her career became even more successful in the 1980s. Dolly Parton is one of the grandest stars of country music.

In the beginning of her career, her voice was thin, especially since she really is a high soprano. However, in her duet work with Porter Wagoner, she matured vocally. Her solo work since 1976 showcases a much more convincing voice. Her vocal inflections are true Tennessee, and her personally-motivated allegiance to Nashville is obvious. Her duet with Kenny Rogers on his BeeGees-inspired and -produced album is very convincing.

The following lists some of her awards: CMA Entertainer of the Year (1978), Female Vocalist of the Year (1975 and 1976), Vocal Duo of the Year (1970 and 1971); Music City News Most Promising Female Artist (1968) and Duet of the Year (1968 through 1970); Grammys (1978, 1981, and 1982); Academy of Country Music Entertainer of the Year (1977) and Female Vocalist of the Year (1980); and the Tex Ritter Award for her movie, *Best Little Whorehouse in Texas.*

Having briefly chronicled the enormous talent and success of Dolly Parton, I want to explain why I have categorized her as a novelty singer. Obviously, by the time she teamed up with Porter Wagoner she was not just a novelty singer, but her first successful single, "Dumb Blonde," was clearly a novelty tune. It had a hook which seemed at that time to be largely autobiographical, although it turns out not to coincide with her opinion of herself. Dolly Parton has always had more sense than most people give her credit for, because she realized that such a tune would work. She used an image of herself that would be understood and remembered by an audience, a classic definition of a novelty tune. Although she has done many songs during her career that have few novelty characteristics to them, certainly her "9 to 5" has novelty characteristics (see the analysis in the Appendix).

The Statler Brothers

The Statler Brothers could also be discussed as main proponents of the mainstream country style of the 1970s and 1980s. An important vocal quartet in the same vein as the Oakridge Boys and the Gatlin Brothers, the Statlers were essentially discovered by Johnny Cash, who used them as his warm-up band for seven years. However, they are mentioned in this chapter because of two clever novelty tunes they did in the 1960s—"Ruthless" and "You Can't Have Your Kate and Edith Too." The first of these is about a guy who loses his girl named Ruth and is now "Ruth-less." The second, a big hit in 1967, is about another guy who has two girls and sings that you can't have Kate and Edith too. Both are superb examples of novelty lyrics with a country setting. Both tunes came early in the Statler Brothers' career and, as do many novelty tunes, provided impetus for greater success. They won the CMA Vocal Group award in 1984.

The Statler Brothers (*Courtesy of PolyGram Records*)

Mel Tillis

Mel Tillis was born in Florida in 1932 and spent a very withdrawn childhood because of a case of malaria he contracted when he was three, which left him with a stuttering speech impediment. He had learned how to play the guitar as a youth and discovered that he could sing without the stutter. He was in the air force from 1951 to 1955 and then went to the University of Florida for one year. After that he worked as a truck driver and a strawberry picker. In 1956 he wrote a song entitled "I'm Tired," which was recorded by Webb Pierce. This number-one hit started Mel Tillis' career as a songwriter.

Although he recorded a folk classic, "It Takes a Worried Man," in the late 1950s, he was really only successful as a songwriter through the early 1960s. He recorded a number of tunes for Columbia in the early 1960s, most of which were by other songwriters. He shifted to Decca in the mid–1960s, recording one of his own tunes, "How Come Your Dog Don't Bite Nobody but Me." While this novelty tune was not a major success, it did sell well, and is responsible for Tillis' inclusion in this chapter.

From the mid–1960s on, Mel Tillis has been a consistently successful guitarist, singer, songwriter, actor, and music publisher. He has traveled the world for concerts and has been on many national television shows, including the Grand Ole Opry. His awards include CMA Entertainer of the Year in 1976 and Music City News Cover Award for Comedy Act of the Year in 1971, 1973, 1974, 1975, 1976, 1977, and 1978. If you get the idea that Mel Tillis is recognized as being funny, you are right.

Mel Tillis (*Courtesy of MCA Records, Nashville*)

Sheb Wooley

Sheb Wooley is one of the most interesting characters in country music, although he is not what one would call a household name. He was born in Erick, Oklahoma in 1921; he was related to an uncle of Roger Miller's and influenced Miller when he moved to Erick. Wooley grew up on a farm and, like Roger Miller, was influenced by fiddle and guitar music. While still in high school he performed with a band and had a radio show on a local station.

After graduating from high school he was a pipe welder in the oil business for a short time, but in the mid–1940s he packed up and moved to Nashville. He worked on radio and occasionally had guest spots on a midday show on WSM. However, he really was not succeeding in Nashville, so he moved to Fort Worth, Texas, where he landed a job on WBAP in 1946. The advertiser of his show was Calumet Baking Powder, and he created the advertising logo for that product, the Indian Chief. He toured with this show and did their advertising for three years.

After that, he went to Los Angeles where he continued to pursue a musical career; he also landed an MGM recording contract, which lasted into the 1970s. While in Los Angeles he began acting, ultimately appearing in over thirty films; including *Rocky Mountain, Little Big Horn, Man without a Star,* and *High Noon*. For five years he had a major part in the television series "Rawhide."

Webb Pierce in the mid-1960s (*Courtesy of Tom Cederberg, Teddy Bear Record Exchange, Bay City, Michigan*)

Wooley had a very successful career as an actor, but he did much more. During his film career, he kept writing songs. His 1953 hit for Hank Snow, "When Mexican Joe Met Jolie Blon," was a comedy parody on two other songs. He provided a number of hits for major artists during the 1950s. However, it was his composition and performance of "Purple People Eater" that really set him rolling. After that, he turned out one hit after another, and many of them were comic novelty tunes. In 1961 he did a top-selling country hit called "That's My Pa," which ingratiated him once again to the mainstream country establishment. It was recorded in Nashville.

While in Nashville, he recorded a number of comedy songs under the name Ben Colder, for which he is perhaps better known than as Sheb Wooley. He continued to record under the Colder name, with great hits like "Purple People Eater #2" in 1967, "Tie the Tiger Down" in 1968, and "The Lincoln's Parked at Margie's Again" in 1968. As Sheb Wooley he recorded a 1969 cover version of "Harper Valley P.T.A." He was featured on the Grand Ole Opry many times and was voted by the Country Music Association the Comedian of the Year in 1968. He joined the cast of "Hee Haw" in 1969, its debut year.

One never really knows where to place people like Sheb Wooley; he is so multi-talented that he is elusive. I can remember liking Ben Colder as a comedian and comic pop singer way before I realized that he had any relationship to Sheb Wooley or to country music. He was skilled and successful as an actor. And behind the scenes he also wrote many fine songs. But he is best remembered for the crossover popularity of his "Purple People Eater." An enormously popular song in 1958, it may well have started the novelty genre, at least as a big business. Although one might not realize it on first

Sheb Wooley performing as Ben Colder in the mid-to-late-1960s (*Photograph courtesy of the Country Music Foundation Library and Media Center, Nashville, Tennessee*)

listening, it really is a country tune with an unusual instrumental background. It does not sound like country music, nor is its lyric typically country. But the basic structure of the piece is like many country tunes. People were captivated by the clever tune and its benevolent monster. It proved its staying power when Wooley returned with "#2" nine years later.

Sheb Wooley/Ben Colder is a good person to end the chapter with because besides being a strong influence on Roger Miller, he may even have started the country novelty movement, or at least have provided the model for novelty tunes.

12 Alternatives to Nashville

AUSTIN, TEXAS

The next chapter describes the formation of two alternatives to Nashville: Austin, Texas and Bakersfield, California. These two locations should be considered centers of entertainment, performance, and perhaps specific attitudes, and not necessarily complete copies or variations of Nashville, because most of the recording of the musicians discussed still occurs in Nashville. The important point about these musicians is that they experimented with different versions of country songs, in some cases as a result of the perceived lack of freedom in Nashville, in others, simply because the individuals involved could not make it in Nashville.

It has been my position up until now that the Nashville sound was perfectly respectable and that the proponents of that type of music had everything to be proud of in creating that sound. My discussion of alternatives will not argue against that basic position, because the Nashville sound is undoubtedly the most important development in country music; it was that particular style of performing country music that popularized it and turned country music into an international phenomenon. All that being said, it is important to realize that the Nashville sound in itself defined the way that country music would be performed and recorded. Musicians who did not fit well into the Nashville sound either did not receive recording opportunities or were relegated to a different role in Nashville. This particular determinant is undoubtedly the main reason for the development of a concept called *outlawism*.

The term *outlaw* was developed from the 1972 song, "Ladies Love Outlaws," written by Lee Clayton and recorded by Waylon Jennings. It became the standard term for musicians who rebelled against the Nashville system. Interestingly enough, the term was publicized by Hazel Smith of Glaser

Studios as a public relations ploy. The concept of outlawism was partly a hype, although certainly some of the characteristics ascribed to outlaws were true. The term was first applied to Waylon Jennings and Tompall Glaser (of Glaser Studios), later to Willie Nelson, David Allan Coe, Kinky Friedman, and Kris Kristofferson. Much later, the term *outlaw* would be used to describe people like Hank Williams, Mel Tillis, Roger Miller, Johnny Cash, Glen Campbell, and even George Jones. In other words, once the term caught on, everyone was an outlaw.

That is the first and most important reason why the term is relatively meaningless; everyone became known as an outlaw. George Jones, for whose unique and continuing impact on country music I have the utmost respect, is not an outlaw by any stretch of the imagination. While retaining strong honky tonk roots, Jones has been very successful using a Nashville type of background as he sings songs from the 1940s to the 1980s. Hank Williams, Sr. (there is a successful son as well) sang in a style that was current at his time, and although he may have had some characteristics of an outlaw in his personal life, he did not rebel against the system, even when the system did not like his behavior. Glen Campbell was called an outlaw because of his recording of the 1967 hit, "Gentle on My Mind," which some considered a "dirty" song. Well, there is simply nothing in the singing style of the ever-clean Glen Campbell (once a member of the Beach Boys) that would suggest he was an outlaw. One might apply the term in a limited way, say, to the lifestyle and performance style of David Allen Coe, but when Glen Campbell and George Jones are included, it ceases to have much meaning.

The most annoying use of the label "outlaw" is with respect to the types of behavior in which "real" outlaws indulge. Hard drinking, drugs, and playing pinball have nothing to do with musical creativity; they are only diversions. Pinball probably does not hurt musical creativity; drinking in moderation does not either; but drugs certainly do. The suggestion that the real quality of outlawism has to do with excessive intake of foreign substances does real damage to the respectability of what some of these musicians created. The important point of this chapter is what Waylon and Willie did with songs; it is about songwriters and singers and not about outlaws.

Waylon Jennings was considered by most to be the central figure in this story, although he decried the use of the term outlaw. He simply wanted to do music that was satisfying to him, and that meant doing it differently than the way the recording companies wanted it done. While admitting his own difficulties with personal problems, he consistently refused to call himself an outlaw, even though it was a song that he sang that named the movement.

A complete history of the "outlaws," which would probably have to include many musicians, should actually be called a history of "experimental" country or "songs that could not be recorded." The first recording of "Ladies Love Outlaws" in 1972 and the historic platinum album *Wanted, the Outlaws* in 1976 could be considered to define the span of the Golden Age of Outlaws. This is when the term was marketed, fan clubs were formed, and personal images were honed. Although Waylon and Willie are discussed in this chapter, the most important person to the movement was Tompall Glaser, head of Glaser Studios (sometimes called Hillbilly Central); perhaps the most obvious "real" outlaw is David Allen Coe.

Actually there are three Glaser brothers, Tompall, Charles, and James, all born in the 1930s in Spalding, Nebraska. Their father taught them to play the guitar, and they formed a group that was to have major success in country music. In the mid–1950s they won a regional "Arthur Godfrey's Talent Scouts" contest and appeared on the national television show. In 1957 they met Marty Robbins and recorded their first song, and in 1958 they moved to Nashville. They signed with Decca Records in 1959 and served as a backup group to both Marty Robbins and Johnny Cash, appearing with Johnny Cash in an important Carnegie Hall show in New York. In 1962 they became regulars on the Grand Ole Opry, which as you recall was and still is an important step.

Tompall and the Glaser Brothers (*Photograph courtesy of the John Edwards Memorial Collection of the University of North Carolina at Chapel Hill*)

The Glaser Brothers were a very important vocal group throughout the 1960s, finally winning a Country Music Association award as Best Vocal Group of 1970. In the late 1960s they purchased or developed three publishing companies and built a recording studio, the Glaser Studios. By 1973 the pressures of road travel and Tompall's obsessive interest in studio production caused the group to break up. The group re-formed in 1979 and produced several hits soon thereafter.

But the importance of the Glaser Brothers to the experimental music discussed in this chapter is really in Tompall's contribution as a record producer. Many of the written explanations of what Tompall did are couched in terms of money, and he certainly succeeded in getting a bigger piece of the pie for himself and for his artists. But more importantly, he obtained control over a number of things that previously were controlled by others—in Tompall's terminology, the Nashville Establishment.

Tompall realized very early on that one of the problems faced by the kind of musician in which he had an interest was the matter of who controlled their record production and what kinds of songs they sang. He was also concerned about the amount of money that went to "middlemen"—the producers. Tompall was one of the writers in Nashville who hung out at Tootsie's. Writers like Tompall, Roger Miller, Mel Tillis, and Kris Kristofferson often wrote songs that they knew would never be recorded—because their lyrics were too sensitive or about the wrong subjects, suggested instru-

Marty Robbins and Jerry Reed in Saginaw, Michigan, in the mid-1960s (*Courtesy of Tom Cederberg, Teddy Bear Record Exchange, Bay City, Michigan*)

mental settings not like traditional Nashville sound backup groups, or were irregular in some way. For instance, many of Willie Nelson's later songs have unusual metric patterns. There was a kind of underground for songwriters, and most of these songs were destined not to be recorded. Tompall strove for a solution to this problem, and when he hooked up with Waylon Jennings his solution was found.

What he did was to incorporate himself as a recording company, with himself as the president. He negotiated directly with record companies for all producing rights, including control of the musicians. As he was a seasoned veteran of recording studios, starting in 1959 when he moved to Nashville, he knew that by controlling the musicians and the production itself he could create an environment in which some of those underground songs could be recorded. In essence, he set up his studio as the place where experimental records could be made. Unfortunately, he also capitalized on the use of the term *outlaw,* but I suppose we can forgive him that. In any event, what he did worked. Much of Waylon Jennings' music in the 1970s was recorded and produced by Glaser Studios, and the changed nature of Waylon's music as a recorded sound ultimately influenced other Nashville producers as well (although that took some time to happen).

Remembering carefully that the Nashville sound took some time to gain complete acceptance, we should see the formation of a progressive studio as simply another important development in country music. This "outlaw" movement was not designed to destroy country music, only to expand it. Experimentation allowed for increased rock influence (specifically the rockabilly-honky tonk sound of Waylon Jennings), increased use of other musical instruments such as the harmonica, and lyrics that were more expressive of contemporary views. Many people wrongly view this experimental music as giving approval to dirty words. Actually it simply allowed expanded subject matter, including a more frank appraisal of the world. In short, this progressive development on the part of Tompall Glaser helped ease country music into the contemporary world.

Therefore, outlaw music is not really destructive, nor is it inconsistent with the general development of country music, which has always flowed back and forth between traditional and progressive. Hank Williams was progressive, and so was Johnny Cash. Kris Kristofferson brought to country music the intelligence and breadth of a Rhodes Scholar, and although he may have seemed like an unusual country singer in the late 1960s and early 1970s, he broadened the scope of country music.

Instead of calling this movement progressive, outlaw, or destructive, let us simply call it alternative. What Waylon Jennings, Willie Nelson, David Allan Coe, Jessi Colter, and Tompall Glaser really did was to forge a logical extension of Nashville because so much of what they did was done right in Nashville. Their own discussions are filled with explanations of how they wanted to succeed, but on their own terms. The fact that Waylon and Willie went on to become the superstars of the 1980s is a good testament to the good fight or struggle that Tompall and friends went through during their rise to stardom. However, the most important point is that their music was and is valid and very artistic. As another part of the country music story, Waylon and Willie are both important because of the way they accomplished their success and the ultimate influence they have had on other country singers. Although they may have seemed to rebel against Nashville, they have creatively helped in the development of country music and Nashville.

Waylon Jennings

Wayon Jennings was born in Texas in 1937. He had a deep interest in music from an early age, learning to play guitar as a child and landing his first job as a disc jockey on a local radio station at the age of twelve. Interestingly enough, most of the records he played were pop, not country, records. In 1958 he moved to Lubbock, Texas to a larger radio station, where he met Buddy Holly. One of Waylon's early favorites was Elvis Presley, but it was with Buddy Holly that he was to do his first work as a musician; he was the electric bass player with the Crickets for the last part of 1958 until Holly's death in 1959.

Playing with Buddy Holly must have influenced Waylon Jennings; if you listen carefully to much of Jennings' music with the Waylors (his band) you will hear a strong rockabilly influence. Writers have called it honky tonk, but I hear it as rockabilly. Early Waylors recordings feature a strong electric bass and kicking drum beat, which clearly comes from the Buddy Holly backup band. In any event, his brief stint with Buddy Holly caused him to think of himself more as an entertainer and less as a disc jockey.

Jennings moved to Phoenix, Arizona in the early 1960s and formed his band, the Waylors. In 1964 Bobby Bare heard the band in Phoenix and recommended them to Chet Atkins. Chet Atkins, the chief proponent of the Nashville sound, signed Jennings and his group to a recording contract with RCA in 1965; the three singles produced showed their potential. The fact that Chet Atkins signed them to a recording contract suggests that the Nashville sound was not quite as all-pervasive as some have led us to believe. In 1966 Jennings moved in with another country singer on the rise in Nashville, Johnny Cash.

Waylon Jennings (*Courtesy of RCA Records, Nashville*)

Throughout the late 1960s and early 1970s Jennings toured extensively, was on many television shows, and continued to put out records. Always recognized as a star on the rise, known for his very powerful singing voice with its rough-edged quality, Waylon Jennings did not reach stardom immediately. He had number-one singles and did eight albums between 1966 and 1970. His song with the Kimberlys, "MacArthur Park," won him a Grammy Award for Best Country Performance by a Duo or Group.

Although Waylon Jennings had definite cult status in the late 1960s and early 1970s, he seemed to be doggedly refusing to become a star. Interestingly, he was often sought for performances for rather unusual circumstances for a country musician, for instance, with the Grateful Dead in San Francisco in 1973. His "Ladies Love Outlaws" in 1972 with Willie Nelson began to signal to people that Waylon Jennings would make it, but it would be on his own terms. It is hard to define precisely when stardom came for Waylon Jennings; it was probably in 1976 with the big album, *Wanted, the Outlaws,* although one could argue that it was a slow process that began much earlier. In any event, the Waylon Jennings' rise to stardom could have been predicted; his vocal quality places him in the ranks of few country stars. He has a unique big voice that allows him, like Johnny Cash, leeway to create many different moods through his singing.

In 1974 Waylon Jennings married Jessi Colter, who actually had a number-one hit before he did; her first single went to the top in 1975. His real recognition began in 1974, when he was nominated for Male Vocalist of the Year by the Country Music Association; he won the award in 1975. He won almost every award in 1976 with Willie Nelson for "Good Hearted Woman." By 1981 he was tied for most nominations for CMA awards with Chet Atkins and behind only five country musicians in the history of the awards.

The career of Waylon Jennings since the mid–1970s has been nothing but upward. He has had a number of hits with his own compositions and has performed hit records with Willie Nelson, Johnny Cash, and Jessi Colter. His 1980 "Theme from the Dukes of Hazzard" popularized Jennings' singing style to numerous people who might otherwise not have heard him. The cornerstone of his career has been his vocal quality and his ability to interpret the songs he sings. Although the early outlaw tune from 1972 may have helped his career, he was nominated for awards from 1974 until today because he was a fine singer, not because of his image. And the chances are pretty good that he would have won more of those awards if he had been willing to go to awards ceremonies to pick them up.

His singing style is fairly easy to define. He has a baritone vocal range with a full-bodied voice; he sometimes sounds like he has gravel in his throat, but that effect is systematically used to emphasize certain words. He sings everything from honky tonks to love songs, and occasionally sings fairly earthy lyrics. However, the honky tonk style predominates. He also sings a number of blues-based tunes, which further lends credence to the argument that he was influenced by his early rockabilly experience with Buddy Holly.

When one reads about Waylon Jennings, especially his interviews, or hears him talk on television, it might be easy to cross him off as a country bumpkin. However, that would be an error in judgment. Waylon Jennings has been continuously on the road as a working musician since 1958 and has worked hard, often under poor conditions. One can understand the complexity of Waylon Jennings by examining his lyrics; they usually are more complicated than they seem at first. Also, one should listen carefully to the vocal inflections he puts on certain words and phrases. He treats lyrics of a song verse as though they had a direction to them, putting a climax into his singing at the point at which the lyrics call for it from a structural point of view. Like many good musicians, Waylon Jennings has an instinctive ability to do the right things to make the lyric expressive. In fact, Willie Nelson once said that when Waylon sings one of Nelson's songs, Waylon makes it sound like it means something other than what he intended. That is the genius of Waylon Jennings; in his hands, any song becomes his own.

Willie Nelson

I might as well say it: Willie Nelson is my favorite country musician. I like his music a lot and I always have, but what I like most is that Willie Nelson is a real gentleman. Why anyone would call a person who is so self-effacing and soft spoken an outlaw will always elude me. In any event, Willie Nelson is a superstar, and I for one never doubted why.

Willie Nelson was born in 1933 in Forth Worth, Texas but was raised by his grandparents in Abbott, Texas. He grew up on a farm in a rural setting, working as a farm boy after school and playing guitar with everyone else. He sang songs that he heard on the Louisiana Hayride and the Grand Ole Opry. After high school he went into the air force, and then spent two years as a student at Baylor University. He then became a disc jockey, working in San Antonio, Texas, and in Oregon and California. In 1960 he moved to Nashville.

Willie had fooled around with writing music and performing it during his years as a disc jockey and was convinced that he could make it in country music. His first success did not come as a performer but as a songwriter. Although this is not an uncommon pattern in Nashville at the end of the 1950s and the early 1960s, it is somewhat unusual for Willie Nelson because he did not really have superstar success until the mid–1970s. Please notice that I said *superstar* status; Willie Nelson was successful as a performer starting in 1962, but it was not anything like what he experienced starting in the mid–1970s.

When he got to Nashville, he started hanging out at Tootsie's Orchid Lounge, a place that has been mentioned before as the location where young songwriters hung out in hopes of getting noticed or meeting people. Hank Cochran was impressed by Willie Nelson, who looked a lot different than we know him today; he had short hair and was relatively conservative. He introduced him to Ray Price and got Willie Nelson a writing contract with Pamper Music, which was partially owned by Price. Willie also became Ray Price's bass guitarist.

Beginning in 1961, he cranked out composition after composition that became hits for other artists—Patsy Cline with "Crazy" and "Funny How Time Slips Away," Faron Young with "Hello Walls," and others. He was signed as an artist by Liberty Records in 1962 and immediately had two top singles— "Touch Me" and "Willingly." He then began performing at major entertainment centers, including Las Vegas. In 1964 he became a regular member of the Grand Ole Opry and changed from Liberty to RCA. He put out thirteen albums for RCA from 1965 to 1972, as well as several more singles, including "The Party's Over" and "Blackjack Country" (1967) and "Little Things" (1968).

Although he had some success as a performer (frankly, more than most), his main source of income was royalties from the songs he wrote that others performed. A list of artists who have performed Willie Nelson tunes reads like a who's who in music (and not just country music): Frank Sinatra, Bing Crosby, Stevie Wonder, Lawrence Welk, and Aretha Franklin, to name a few. The point is that Willie Nelson enjoyed a successful career as a singer and a very successful career as a songwriter even during the time that most writers called him a failure.

In 1972 Willie Nelson made a career move: he moved to Austin, Texas. Perhaps Willie wanted to return to his home state, or perhaps he felt that Austin would be a place for progress. Whatever the reason, that move was to provide him with the appropriate setting for a quick rise to fame. He signed with Atlantic Records in 1972 and then with Columbia in 1974, where he eventually started his own label, Lone Star, and had complete artistic control over the production of his records. From 1975 on, Willie Nelson changed from a successful country musician to an innovator in country music.

The thing that had plagued Willie Nelson during his Nashville years was that people criticized his voice. He has a very soft singing voice and he does phrase the words in a distinctive and perhaps unusual way. One could also hypothesize that the timing of Willie Nelson's arrival in Nashville was wrong for him as an entertainer because the mid–1960s was the time of the crooners, singers who had robust and romantic voices. Their lyrics were also perfectly regular in their presentation, and even when Willie sang songs that would fit into a regular pattern he tended to sing them in an irregular way. In this sense Willie Nelson shared something with old-time singers, although clearly his presentation is quite contemporary. In any event, no record company really wanted to do his tunes with him performing because they thought his voice was wrong for a country star.

Therefore, during Willie's Nashville years (1960–1972) he was known primarily as a songwriter who also sang tunes, but only because he was such a successful songwriter. To my knowledge, no one including Willie has said that, but I think this explanation is the only valid conclusion one can make for the general perception on Willie's part that he was unsuccessful during those years, and for the rather uneven sales of his albums and singles during those years. There always has to be an explanation why a certain musician is not so popular during one era, only to emerge as a superstar ten years later.

The move to Austin has been explained by Willie as an attempt to change his life, and it certainly did. It is important to realize that Willie Nelson was not a failure in Nashville, even when other people said he was or he believed he was. By the time he moved to Austin, he was an extremely successful country musician and songwriter; Austin just helped him up the stakes of the game.

Austin, Texas is a fascinating town because it contains different life elements. It is a wealthy town in which many important families have major investments—the Lyndon Johnson family, for instance. Austin has a delightful mixture of old Texas and new, very "hip" Texas. As the state capital, it of course enjoys considerable prestige and power within the state; this undoubtedly causes Austin to be a cosmopolitan town. But that does not explain its extreme liberalness.

As the home of the prestigious University of Texas, Austin is a university town. And the districts of Austin surrounding this large institution contain the most diversified groups of people in Texas. Some have described the university section of Austin as the only place in the United States where people still live in the 1960s. That probably is not true, but there is a San Francisco-type atmosphere about the University of Texas.

Willie Nelson had a dream when he went back to Texas. He dreamed that there was a market for his performing style and that he would find it in Texas. When he moved to Austin he almost immediately went to the Tootsie's of Austin, The Armadillo World Headquarters. The Armadillo World Headquarters is a huge auditorium and in that sense is nothing like Tootsie's small bar, but the Armadillo World is the place in Austin for new music. When Willie went there in 1972 it was a rock auditorium, featuring primarily acts that will be discussed in later chapters.

Willie wanted to try out his brand of country music on the young and superhip audience of the Armadillo World. They loved him, and Willie knew that this was his audience. From that point on, country music and Austin, Texas had one common ingredient—Willie Nelson. This is not to suggest that there are not and were not other country musicians in Texas or even Austin because of course there were, but Willie created a new kind of country music that became associated with Austin. Like the Nashville sound, there was an Austin sound, and Willie was the one who started it. In all fairness, the Austin sound has become very experimental as of late (see Chapter 16).

Most of what Willie Nelson has done since 1972 is fairly common knowledge, so I will not repeat it all. By 1975, he had established as a regular occasion the Willie Nelson birthday parties and had formed his own record label. His major LP of 1975 was *Red-Headed Stranger,* followed in 1976 by his collaboration on the *Wanted, the Outlaws* album. From 1976 on he has never failed to have top singles, and his creative efforts have led him to compose even more complex lyrics than he was known for earlier in his career. He has done films—*Electric Horseman* with Robert Redford and Jane Fonda, and *Honeysuckle Rose* in 1979–1980; *Honeysuckle Rose* shows a side of Willie Nelson that everyone ought to see. He is a fine actor.

I heard Willie talk on a television interview in 1984, and he described the reason why he sings the way he does. He said that he sang a song the way he wanted to, the reason being that if it became a hit he would have to do it a lot. And he did not want to have to do anything that he did not like. This might seem like an odd explanation, but I think it has a strong ring of truth. Willie Nelson sings the way that he thinks.

Willie has also been described as a singer who just spits out the words until he runs out of breath. I do not believe that, even when he says it about himself. Even in his most complex statements, Willie Nelson sounds like he is singing simple country music. It probably would be fair to say that of the country musicians discussed in this chapter, Willie Nelson is the most conservative, regardless of his style of dress. He really goes to the roots of country style, but in his lyrics he goes quite a bit further than country musicians traditionally do. The subject matter is not so unusual, but the word and phrase choices are. Even more unusual is the way he delivers those phrases.

What I think Willie does is to deliver a phrase in one unit so that it speaks for an issue as one statement rather than as a set of words that are designed to be communicated through a melody. I think that traditional country music has a careful relationship between melody and word phrasing. Willie Nelson's music is much more word-oriented, and the melodic structure

Willie Nelson (*Courtesy of Columbia Records, Nashville*)

is second in importance to the words. When Willie Nelson sings, he is singing phrases rather than words. Willie Nelson is a folksinger or a narrator in the way he communicates to an audience.

Of course, Willie Nelson sings many different kinds of songs, and he has done a number of albums in tribute to others, such as his 1977 tribute to Lefty Frizzell, *To Lefty from Willie.* He also has worked with a number of other musicians: Waylon and Jessi of course, Ray Price, Danny Davis and the Nashville Brass (see Chapter 16), and Kris Kristofferson.

Although Willie has not been nominated for as many awards as Waylon Jennings, he actually has won more of them. So far, he has won two Grammys, CMA Album of the Year in 1976, CMA Entertainer of the Year in 1979, and Vocal Duo in 1984. It is fascinating to me that Willie Nelson has not won even more awards, but the thing one has to remember is that when Willie Nelson comes to Nashville (and he does) he wears a red headband and jeans. He has made his great success with a hip audience in Austin that expects Willie to be their symbol. He wore the company uniform of Nashville for twelve years, and now he wears the company uniform of Austin. Certainly a satisfied individual, Willie Nelson will undoubtedly win more awards over his professional career. His rise to superstardom was inevitable; however, it took a move to a different audience as an alternative to Nashville to provide the necessary catalyst.

BAKERSFIELD, CALIFORNIA

Although Bakersfield, California would not have the lasting influence on country music that Austin, Texas has enjoyed, this particular California town did have importance in country music in the 1960s and early 1970s. As an alternative to the Nashville sound, there was at one time a definite Bakersfield sound, basically an extension of the honky tonk sound at first but later developing into a mini-version of Nashville. Bakersfield had recording companies, publishing companies, and a full lineup of sidemen available for the bands that developed there. The two most important musicians to develop from Bakersfield were Merle Haggard and Buck Owens, but there were others as well.

Bakersfield, California is located on the northwest side of the Tehachapi Mountains and the southernmost part of the San Joaquin Valley. Described by some as an arid desert, Bakersfield is actually the southern entrance to a major agricultural center of California and is also a major crossroads for transportation and shipping. Although a first-time visitor to Bakersfield might see it as a godforsaken place where no one would live voluntarily, it actually has a fairly lengthy tradition in relation to California history. An old Spanish town, although it is in the high desert, it was an important location for early settlers to California.

However, like most southern Californian towns, it was not a large town until the twentieth century. The only town in California to have a rich tradition in the nineteenth century was San Francisco, although there were of course many towns that grew in California because of the gold rush. California was basically a rural state in the nineteenth century and Bakersfield was rich in Spanish hacienda history, like many other locations in southern California. The major expansion of Bakersfield occurred in the 1930s.

The dream of California was felt most strongly by Americans in the 1930s because of the Depression. Americans have always had a strong feeling towards going west, and certainly people did settle in the western part of the United States prior to the 1930s; but huge population resettlement occurred in the 1930s on a scale much larger than ever before. Of course, people from all over the United States moved to California in this particular westward expansion, but a large portion of this migration came from the middle and western parts of the South, especially Oklahoma and northern Texas. In particular, people from the dust bowl of Oklahoma moved to California because of the near-poverty of their existence in their original homes in Oklahoma.

Many of the people who settled in towns like Bakersfield came because of the railroad and other jobs available there. In particular, a large group of people from the dust bowl of Oklahoma settled in desert towns because unskilled labor jobs were available to them. Many of the people who migrated in the 1930s had tasted the bitter times of the Depression. For them, unskilled jobs were a gold mine after what they had been through in a state that had been hit by hard times.

The kind of society they created was in some senses similar to that of gold rush towns. People who arrived with nothing had to work hard to stay afloat. They brought whatever cultural values they had from their previous existence. The forces at work in these early settlements were the same forces that created honky tonk music in Texas. The only difference for the new population of Bakersfield was that honky tonk attitudes lasted longer. Men worked long hours at very difficult manual jobs; when they got paid they wanted to let off steam quickly. What resulted was a wild environment.

By the 1950s Bakersfield was a large town by California desert standards. Well over 70 percent of the town's business was associated with entertainment. Honky tonk bars, brothels, and gambling houses were rampant in Bakersfield in the 1950s, primarily as a result of the lifestyles and attitudes of the new and growing population. Bakersfield in the 1950s was a real western town and this certainly set the stage for it to become an alternative to Nashville.

It is important at this point to differentiate between Bakersfield and the American West at large. We have discussed western music previously, and we might have made a connection between singing cowboys and the

West. Bakersfield in the context of this chapter has very little to do with singing cowboys, because the kind of entertainment that developed in this town supported people who worked on oil rigs and in agriculture. The very definite kind of emotional singing that developed through the honky tonk Bakersfield style had little to do with the nostalgic and optimistic style of the singing cowboy. Gene Autry may have grown up in Oklahoma and moved to California, but he moved to Studio City, not Bakersfield.

So what we have in Bakersfield is an old Spanish town with a rich cultural heritage that, because of its particular location, its proximity to transportation systems, and the availability of work for migrants or immigrants, was environmentally suited to develop a rather particular style of entertainment. It was because of the population explosion and the particular population that moved there and what they did that Bakersfield developed into a western Nashville.

Because of the nature of the entertainment produced in Bakersfield and its audience, the music was fairly intense. The best analogy I can think of is when the Beatles went to perform in Hamburg, Germany before they became famous. They were singing for a rowdy and non-English speaking crowd. Therefore, they had to sing shouting tunes and develop a flamboyant stage technique. Honky tonk musicians from Ernest Tubb to Hank Williams did the same thing in Texas. The music had to be loud when people were shouting and generally raising hell.

The subject matter of songs sung for these kinds of crowds had to hit home and do it in a hard way. Some have said that honky tonk songs have to be about drinking, love, or something novel. This is interesting because this is the way that I broke up the Nashville sound—traditional, crooning, and novelty. Of course, honky tonk songs can be about other things as well, but for Bakersfield at least these general categories really fit pretty well.

Both a traditional and a progressive country sound were used in instrumentation. Fiddles were used extensively, both because of western swing influence and because of bluegrass. Electric guitars were used because the music needed to be loud; they were played in a style closer to rockabilly than to the Nashville sound.

Steel guitar was a standard part of the instrumental ensemble, and it was played in a very bluesy style—very much a part of the ensemble and not just as a filler instrument. There was no use of Nashville-type string sections nor of smooth backup vocal groups. Drums were present, as well as a strong electric bass. The Bakersfield sound was thus closely associated with rockabilly, although its lyrics were traditional honky tonk. The instrumentation was a hybrid of rockabilly and honky tonk. Saxophones were regularly used in this honky tonk style.

The most important musicians from Bakersfield other than Owens and Haggard were probably Tommy Collins, Dallas Frazier, Red Simpson, and Wynn Stewart. Although none of these are household names to country fans, they all had successful careers. Like any other musical milieu, Bakersfield would not have spawned the careers of two stars if there had not been other musicians around both before and during their careers. Leona Williams should probably be mentioned as well, although her achievement in recording happened in 1976, well after the prime of Bakersfield music.

In all fairness, we must admit that although Bakersfield was the proving ground for the above musicians, much of their recording was done in Los Angeles, which is not recognized as a center for country music. But Los Angeles does have some fine studio musicians, and they put out country music along with everything else. By the time Bakersfield had developed a reputation for a particular brand of country music, these musicians were making the hundred-mile trip to Los Angeles on a fairly regular basis to make recordings. Although Buck Owens built a very profitable publishing house centered in Bakersfield, an awful lot of the Bakersfield business somehow managed to happen in Los Angeles, one of the entertainment capitals of the world.

The distinctive quality of the Bakersfield sound was pretty well finished by the early 1970s but during its heyday in the 1960s the Bakersfield sound was still a stronghold of honky tonk. George Jones and other Texans continued to do honky tonk music, but Bakersfield did only honky tonk music and in a style that was true to the cultural characteristics of Bakersfield. The background sound was earthy and, although somewhat influenced by rockabilly, really retained more traditional country than rockabilly ever did. The West was important in the early 1960s for being the proving ground for musicians like Waylon Jennings in Phoenix, Arizona. But the groups in Bakersfield took their music past the proving ground; they institutionalized it into a distinctive philosophy and way of playing. And although it never really had the lasting impact that Austin did, for a time Bakersfield provided a real alternative to the Nashville sound. And the Nashville musicians knew it as well, because ultimately they opened up their doors for Merle Haggard.

Buck Owens

Alvis Edgar Owens, Jr., was born in Sherman, Texas in 1929, into a sharecropper family. Although not from Oklahoma like the immigrants to Bakersfield described earlier, the Owens family was from the Texas dust bowl. Not coming out of the Depression at all well, they decided to go West to California in the early 1930s; unfortunately, the family transportation only made it to Mesa, Arizona. Buck grew up in Mesa going to school until he was thirteen. He dropped out in that year to help haul produce and harvest crops.

During those years he learned to play the guitar, although he started on the mandolin. He got his first job as a musician at the age of sixteen on a Mesa radio station (KTYL) and joined a band called Mac's Skillet Lickers. One of the singers with that band was Bonnie Owens, whom he married when he was seventeen. Although his main goal was to be an entertainer, Buck Owens also worked at many other jobs. One of these was hauling produce between Arizona and the San Joaquin Valley in California. On one of those trips he talked with two uncles who lived in Bakersfield; they suggested that he move there if he wanted to work in music. When Buck Owens was twenty he moved his family to Bakersfield.

He started working in clubs in Bakersfield and was successful right away. He did session work in Los Angeles, including backup work for Tennessee Ernie Ford and others. He started singing at the Blackboard Club in Bakersfield and found that audiences liked him. The first band he was with decided to become a pop group, but Buck wanted to do country music. Therefore, he joined the band of Tommy Collins, taking Ferlin Husky's place (who had gone on to become a star). Unfortunately, while his career was escalating his marriage was disintegrating, and he was divorced from Bonnie.

In 1957 he got a recording contract from Capitol Records. His first singles did not do well. This was especially disappointing for him because many of the tunes he did for Capitol were originals. In 1958 he was so disgusted that he moved to Seattle, Washington for a disc jockey job. But then he had his first hit, "Under Your Spell." So it was back to Bakersfield and to commuting between there and Los Angeles. His career was off and running.

In 1960 he started having the kind of success that marked his career. He had two major hits that year and four the next. His only one-hit year was 1962, but that was also the year he formed his own band, the Buckaroos. From 1963 on, he had many hit singles and his compositions were being covered by other musicians. His 1965 hit, "I've Got a Tiger by the Tail" (analyzed in the Appendix), is probably the tune most associated with Buck Owens. He has run up an impressive list of hit singles and hit albums.

By the late 1960s he had started rather sizeable business holdings, including radio stations, a booking agency, cattle ranches, and his own song publishing house, Bluebook Music. He was on many television shows in the 1960s, including the "Ed Sullivan Show." And in 1969 he started as the co-

Buck Owens and the Buckaroos (*Photograph courtesy of the John Edwards Memorial Collection of the University of North Carolina at Chapel Hill*)

host of "Hee Haw," for which he is well known. He also had his own syndicated show, the "Buck Owens Ranch Show." Although some suggest that Buck Owens's career is in decline, the evidence suggests otherwise.

Some of his awards include Country Music Association Band of the Year in 1967 and 1968, Music City News Cover Awards Band of the Year in 1967, 1968, 1969, 1970 and 1974, Country Music TV Program of the Year for "Hee Haw" from 1969 through 1977 and 1983, and the Academy of Country Music Male Vocalist of the Year in 1965 and Band of the Year from 1965 through 1967. His biggest impact as illustrated by these awards has been for his band, the Buckaroos, and for "Hee Haw"; interestingly, these two aspects of his career are almost diametrically opposed. His band was very important in the late 1960s, known for its hard-hitting sound; the group influenced Nashville musicians of the 1970s.

"Hee Haw," on the other hand, was sometimes condemned by the country music establishment because of its often self-effacing attitude. But in some senses, the mere existence of "Hee Haw" gave country music wider visibility than anything prior to it, even the Grand Ole Opry and the singing cowboy movies. Buck Owens was always a showman and a businessman, and the commercial popularity of "Hee Haw" was another sign of his business acumen. Buck Owens was very successful in marketing his songs, most of which he wrote, but, like many other country musicians, he was also successful in building a business empire. In fact, Bakersfield became known as "Buckersfield," partially because of the financial ramifications of country music in the town but also because of the all-pervasive influence and impact of Buck Owens.

Merle Haggard

Buck Owens started to be less successful as a practicing musician by the mid–1970s, although he continued to be very wealthy from royalties and business enterprises. His compatriot in Bakersfield, Merle Haggard, has con-

Buck Owens (left) and George Jones in Saginaw, Michigan, in the 1960s
(*Courtesy of Tom Cederberg, Teddy Bear Record Exchange, Bay City, Michigan*)

tinued to be successful right up into the 1980s. The main reason for this is undoubtedly the sense of development that can easily be perceived in Haggard's career. While Buck Owens stayed with the fairly stock formula of his 1960s music, Merle Haggard has continued to develop. Perhaps a better technical musician than Buck Owens anyway, Merle Haggard has continued to improve, and his range of influence has certainly gone beyond Bakersfield.

Buck Owens was born in Texas and in some senses retained some Texas roots in the kind of music that he sang early in his career; some have said that he was one of the important continuations of the honky tonk tradition. Merle Haggard certainly sang some songs that might be placed in that tradition. But he was born in Bakersfield; his parents moved there during the Depression and lived in an abandoned railroad car. Merle was born in that railroad car in 1937.

Haggard's parents were originally from Oklahoma. His father was a fiddler, and although he died when Merle was nine, country music traditions must have been a part of his early childhood. Merle's existence as a child was fairly rough, and in fact he spent much of his early teenage life in juvenile detention centers. He finally ended up in San Quentin in 1957. After a parole in the early 1960s he came back to Bakersfield and began working as a musician.

He worked first as a sideman and then began recording for a local record company, Tally Records. In 1965 Tally Records was purchased by Capitol and Merle Haggard became one of their musicians. He had a few

Merle Haggard (*Photograph courtesy of the Country Music Foundation Library and Media Center, Nashville, Tennessee*)

successes with recordings in 1963 and 1964, but his first big hit was "Strangers" in 1965. This particular composition is very sentimental and describes the feelings of a man who is unlucky in love. Although Merle Haggard was born in California, the influence of an Oklahoma accent is readily apparent in his early music and in this hit in particular.

By this time Haggard had formed his own band, the Strangers, which used guitars, steel guitar, piano, and rhythm. The sound of his band was really quite folk-like and fit his singing style to a tee. By comparison with the Buckaroos, the sound of the Strangers was both softer and more intricate. There was a careful blending of the melodic lines, and the influence of Ralph Mooney on steel guitar was quite important. Mooney won an Academy of Country Music award for steel guitar in 1966. The same association voted the Strangers the best band of the year in 1969, 1970, 1971, 1972, 1974, 1975, and 1981. Interestingly, the Nashville awards of the Country Music Association only awarded the Strangers that distinction in 1971 and 1972. But regardless of that slight difference, the Buckaroos and the Strangers were two very hot bands and both influenced other musicians.

One of the more intriguing stories in country music history is the importance of Bonnie Owens to both Buck Owens and Merle Haggard. Divorced from Buck in the mid–1950s, she ultimately met and worked with Merle Haggard. They recorded a duet in 1964 called "Just between the Two of Us" on Tally Records. They were signed as a duet and as solo singers by Capitol in 1965 and they also got married. In 1965 they put out both separately and together several significant songs. In 1965, 1966, and 1967 they won awards from the Academy of Country Music. Although their marriage would also end in divorce, the team of Bonnie Owens and Merle Haggard was a major force in country music in the late 1960s, and they continued to perform together even after divorcing.

Merle's career took off in the late 1960s; he hit superstar status by 1970, especially with "Okie from Muskogee," a counter-counterculture song. In this tune he extols clean living and a rather traditional southern view. Although the symbol of an alternative Nashville musician, his major success really came from a song that could easily have been done in Nashville. However, he went on to do some tunes that were not mainstream at all.

His awards include Country Music Association—Entertainer of the Year in 1970, Single and Album of the Year in 1970 and Male Vocalist of the Year in 1970; Music City News Cover Awards—Male Artist of the Year in 1967 and 1968 and Songwriter of the Year in 1970; and Academy of Country Music—Entertainer of the Year in 1970, Male Vocalist of the Year in 1966, 1969, 1970, 1972, 1974, and 1981, Most Promising Male Vocalist in 1965, Song of the Year in 1969, and Single Record and Album of the Year in 1969. He was elected to the Songwriter's Hall of Fame in 1977.

Clearly, "Okie from Muskogee" was a pivotal song, and 1970 a pivotal time, for Merle Haggard; in fact, many of his awards are for that one song and the album. However, he had a clear record of achievement starting in 1965 and his band continued to win awards as late as 1981. His record sales have been consistently good over the years, and the development of his music from sappy emotionalism to experimental sophistication has been most satisfying to watch. He has also done some acting, including fine work in the miniseries for television, *Centennial,* from the book by James Michener.

His career in the 1970s concentrated primarily on touring with the Merle Haggard Show. However, by this time he was recording in Los Angeles and in Nashville. He worked with a variety of other musicians, and was on the tribute album to Bob Wills discussed in the chapter on western swing. He also worked with the Carter Family on an album entitled *Land of Many Churches.* He continued to have hit singles and major albums throughout the 1970s, with Capitol until 1977, MCA from 1977 to 1981, and Epic since 1981. In 1980, he did a duet with Clint Eastwood called "Bar Room Buddies," which appeared on Elektra Records. One can conclude that Merle Haggard has consistently sought to widen his career and at the same time stay on the road.

But by far the most important thing about Merle Haggard's twenty-odd years in the business is that he has grown over time. His first recordings were sentimental tunes based on previous tough experiences, like being in prison or being poor. In this sense, Merle Haggard was fairly conservative and certainly within the mainstream of country lyrics. His band, formed in 1965, was a strange combination of traditional string sounds and a more contemporary approach, folk-like in quality, yet lightly amplified to fit the honky tonk lyrics of his songs. It really was not until he began singing with Bonnie Owens that he got onto a commercial track that would separate him from the average musician. And at least at that time he was doing everything from outside of the mainstream of Nashville country music.

Even though he was recognized more often by the West Coast country music award groups, by 1969 he had hit it big with everyone with "Okie from Muskogee." From this point on, he had a history of success, most of his troubles seemed to be behind him, and he continued performing in concert tours, which enhanced his record sales. He took advantage of opportunities to record with major performers both old and new and therefore was constantly being influenced by the latest studio recording techniques and experimenting with unusual combinations. His playing continued to improve, and his singing style, although reasonably consistent, began to encompass more complex thoughts and a broader technique of expression. Even while continuing to sing songs that evoke feelings of sadness and frustration with the lot the world has given us, he quite often surprises us with songs that speak of other issues.

As a representative of the Nashville West, which is really no longer that significant, Merle Haggard is ideal. He was born there and continues to treat it as home. He developed a style of singing and playing that was very successful during the height of the influence of Bakersfield, and was one of the important reasons why Bakersfield was recognized at all. Outside of the rather limited definition of the Bakersfield style, Merle Haggard continued to develop over time and evolved in the instrumental style of his band (more and more like western swing) and in the lyric choices for his own compositions. His voice has remained largely the same—since it was originally such a tooled mechanism for singing the types of songs that he did, there was really no reason to change it.

Some have described Merle Haggard as a rugged individualist who refuses to compromise his ideals. While I think that is stretching the truth just a bit, there is no question that Merle is a solid character type. His acting in *Centennial* and his friendship with Clint Eastwood are indications of how he views himself. He really is a typical country singer in his background, his troubles, and his sense of reality. Had he lived and worked in Nashville he would simply have been one of the stars of that town. But Merle Haggard achieved his success in a relatively small town which, although it had a reputation for country music, was very far from the mainstream of Nashville. And Merle Haggard achieved his success during the 1960s, when Nashville had an even stronger hold on the development of country stars. Willie Nelson did not make the break to Austin until 1972, and "outlawism" did not come into vogue until Merle Haggard had already made it.

13 Country Rock

In the discussion of rockabilly we alluded to a difference between rockabilly and rock and roll; that distinction should be kept clearly in mind during the preliminary discussions of this chapter. Rockabilly was the first concrete combination of country music with rock and roll and was very significant in the development of both. In fact, rockabilly still exists today and is often defined by rock musicians as basic rock or the roots of rock. Rockabilly as a technique of punk or new wave musicians serves as the focal point for rock purity. The country rock discussed in this chapter, however, has little to do with trying to preserve the primary integrity of rock and roll; it is rather a conscious amalgamation of rock and country music.

Country rock is then analogous to rock music after the middle Beatles period (1965) in that it consciously uses elements of different kinds of music. Country rock is a combination of pop, folk, jazz, rock, and country music, and although most people think of country rock as being a specific type of music, it really encompasses a diverse group of musicians. This chapter discusses the cultural influencers of country rock, some of its specific technical advancements, and its main practitioners. This chapter is also quite condensed, as one could easily write a whole book on this subject.

Country rock has a few distinct style elements (although even these stylistic elements are occasionally missing from songs done by country rock groups—or groups that can be loosely defined as country rock). Country rock groups like Commander Cody and the Lost Planet Airmen usually do straight country music as well as country rock songs. The instrumentation of these groups is often versatile enough so that they can turn down the electronics, emphasize the violin or mandolin, and create mainstream country music in an effortless way. Therefore, the stylistic elements listed will define the way that country rock groups play when they are doing songs in a country rock style.

A country rock band normally uses rather heavy amplification of the guitar instruments, particularly the bass guitar. The bass guitar sound is stronger than in honky tonk or any other form of country music. The drum patterns show more rock influence, although usually the country drumming style is present. But it should be remembered that even the presence of a drum set is a rock influence—very traditional country music would not use drums at all. Country rock also uses a rock-influenced style of lead guitar playing, at least in the amplification of the sound. Solo work by the lead guitar player is normally more melodic and less arpeggiated than in the standard style for country music.

The most important quality of country rock is the lyric content, which is most uncharacteristic of straight country music. The folk influence in country rock can be heard in highly political, sometimes controversial and socially-aware lyrics, usually avoided by traditional country music. It is from country rock groups that we start hearing about drugs, social welfare, and ecology, and this shows a clear influence of the rock and folk world.

Like many of the "outlaws" described in the previous chapter, country rock musicians usually look different than traditional country musicians. Country rock musicians grow their hair long and have beards. The rough image they project is simply a part of being modern. Since image is certainly a part of the communication of music, this difference is as important as the longer hair and beards grown by the Beach Boys after the mid–1960s. In the image sense alone, country rock musicians defined themselves as being "hip" and contemporary; and although Southern influences remain present, country rock tends to be somewhat less regional in style than traditional country music.

It is important to understand the tremendous diversity of country rock and also that it is not totally relegated to groups that recognize themselves solely as country rock groups. There are many different kinds of music that could be labelled country rock, from Bob Dylan to the New Riders of the Purple Sage. A traditional country enthusiast might be tempted to say that a few of the musicians mentioned in this chapter do not fit their standard for inclusion in a book on country music. But they have been included because they sang country songs, did music that had country elements, or were influenced by country traditions. In some cases, a few of these musicians have been vastly influential, in country music and in popular music. In other cases, they have had little influence. But the main point of this chapter is to highlight some examples of musicians who were part of the general movement to amalgamate country music with other musical styles.

FOLK AND ROCK INFLUENCES IN THE LATE 1960s

There can be little doubt when viewing the cultural history of the United States in the late 1960s that folk music and rock were highly influential in communicating attitudes of the younger generation. There can be little doubt as well that both folk and rock influenced attitudes. Of course, this phenomenon started prior to the late 1960s and was a product of the turbulent times, but the real lasting influence was in the late 1960s. Country rock thus evolved from developments in music and society that were supercharged in attitudes.

One is always tempted to consider the South as a separate region in cultural discussions, and there is little doubt that some of the changes that occurred in the 1960s in San Francisco had little influence on small towns in the South. However, the attitudes of youth culture in the 1960s influenced people everywhere, although some places were affected later than others. Some of the significant shifts in attitudes during the 1960s were those regarding war, ecology, drugs, and dress standards.

Antiwar attitudes developed slowly during the 1960s. One could generally characterize the South as conservative (although Democratic) politically, and therefore pro-government or pro-war. However, this would be an overgeneralization because as in other parts of the United States, there are pockets of liberal attitudes in larger population areas such as Atlanta and Austin. The South was hugely affected by the Vietnam War. There was a general supportiveness given to the war effort early in the 1960s, and many southern boys volunteered for the service to support the position of the United States government. As a result, more people from the South were killed in Vietnam than from other parts of the United States.

Although many who have written on the pacifist movement in the 1960s have quoted moral and philosophical reasons for being opposed to war, the overriding reason many turned against the Vietnam War was the senselessness of the engagement. We had not declared war; we did not seem to be winning; and the combatants of North and South Vietnam did not seem to want us there. Also, it was an extremely sloppy war in the sense that enormous numbers of Americans were being killed without any real change in tactical positions. By the mid–1960s it was clear to many people that we would never win this war and that anyone who was sent there had a good chance of not returning. Even if that attitude was expressed more strongly by non-southerners, the fact that a larger percentage of southerners were being killed made that point obvious to southerners as well. To a younger and hipper southern generation of the late 1960s, antiwar feeling was strong, and that was expressed in the music of the time.

Ecology or concern for the environment was also a major shift in interest in this period, although it really started somewhat earlier. Many people became concerned with the process of erosion of our natural resources, and the South was, relatively speaking, important in that realization. The best examples of clear southern expression of this new attitude concerned strip mining and miners' safety. Also, the South has been responsible for major legislation protecting certain species of animals such as the alligator. A history of concern for the preservation of nature (if for no other reason than in support of agriculture) is old in the South; therefore, it was natural when a general sympathy towards ecology developed in the United States that the South would be a part of it. This particular attitude was also expressed strongly in folk music.

Drug use definitely increased in the 1960s and was and is a major theme in the music of folk. rock, and country rock. The author is not condoning or recommending the use of drugs. However, it is a fact that drug use was discussed by hippies, liberals, and other people of the 1960s, and as a result it became a constant theme in the music of those people. Ultimately, it became as common as beer drinking lyrics, even in country music.

Although it is the author's contention that the subject of drug use is very common in music past the mid–1960s, it is not always as blatant as the discussion of drinking or love. If you listen to country music a lot, you realize that love and drinking are the two big lyric issues. Drugs are discussed, but usually a bit more subtly. Drugs are more often the topic in country rock than in traditional country, and drugs are never mentioned by crossover musicians like Kenny Rogers or Barbara Mandrell. But in country rock, drugs exist, although their existence is usually somewhat more hidden than in the references made by the New Riders of the Purple Sage.

The kinds of drugs that were very popular in the 1960s were marijuana and hallucinogens such as LSD. Actual consumption of harder drugs did not rise during the 1960s and the cocaine revolution did not occur until the mid–1970s. Therefore, the kinds of drugs mentioned in 1960s and 1970s country rock were grass and LSD. At the time, the use of these drugs was a sign of rebellion against the establishment and thought to be good; it allowed one to leave reality and reach higher levels of understanding. Although this is most assuredly not true, it is what people thought.

This attitude probably started on the West Coast, in San Francisco. And certainly the development of psychedelic music, for which San Francisco was known, suggests that it was not originally a southern concept. But in fact, the style of psychedelic music probably comes from southern roots because it was so heavily country oriented (see the later discussion on Jerry Garcia of the Grateful Dead). However, the image of psychedelic music was that it was way-out rock; the truth is that it was a blending of folk, blues, rock, and country music with very hip lyrics. In short, psychedelic fits the earlier definition of country rock.

The evolution of psychedelic music into heavy metal and then its influence on country rock is a rather interesting one. In truth, the first psychedelic bands, emerging from San Francisco, were very heterogeneous in nature. Moby Grape and Big Brother and the Holding Company (with Janis Joplin) were blues-based, and although they did some loud music, they also performed rather subtle and soft music. The Grateful Dead was known as the model for psychedelic music, but in fact their music is based on blues and country. The Jefferson Airplane-Starship was probably the most psychedelic in performance and lyrics, but also did some music that was not at ear-shattering levels. Heavy metal bands that evolved from the early San Francisco groups would play at high volumes all the time; the actual psychedelic sound was much softer and certainly was heavily influenced by folk music.

Perhaps the most important musician in the psychedelic movement was Jimi Hendrix, who in fact had a strong influence on some southern bands, ZZ Top for instance. ZZ Top performed as the opening band with Hendrix in 1967, and the singing style and guitar playing of Hendrix certainly influenced the Texas-based band. In fact, Billy Gibbons, the leader of ZZ Top, did a totally psychedelic album with the band Moving Sidewalk in 1966. Some have also said that he invented the term *psychedelic rock,* although this is debatable. Jimi Hendrix had a unique style of playing and singing. His playing style was melodic and very blues-like, but it was also loud. In his singing style, totally unlike the rockabilly shouters, he almost seemed to push the words out of his throat.

From the Hendrix style came a wave of heavy metal bands. These were the continuation of the psychedelic sound. Precursors of the heavy metal style in England were the Who and the Yardbirds. British heavy metal bands included the Jeff Beck Group and Black Sabbath. Important American bands were Iron Butterfly, MC5, Grand Funk Railroad, and Alice Cooper. Later heavy metal bands were largely derivative of the original sound, in particular, Quiet Riot and Def Leppard.

This style of music is of course the ultimate in amplification, and appeals mainly to teenagers. As such, it has not received the best of reviews over time. Even Led Zeppelin, in its heavy metal stage, was universally condemned for its sound, regardless of its ultimate success. Although the strains of country influence are perhaps hard to hear in heavy metal, Led Zeppelin, for instance, has done very country-influenced tunes, and musicians like Eric Clapton have indulged in heavy metal sounds as well. Heavy metal was one clear development from San Francisco psychedelic music and, at least in lyric content, has influenced much of country rock. The high level of amplification of music has become a trademark of the hard country rock groups even when the lyric content is more country in orientation.

But the most important influence of heavy metal as a continuation of the San Francisco sound is the blues revival that has been apparent since Janis Joplin and Big Brother and the Holding Company. Blues has been a steady influence in country music in general, and especially so in the last fifteen years. The blues revival took place in both England and the United States and influenced rock, folk, and pop music in both countries. It was essentially an outgrowth of the folk music revival and the rapid politicisation of folk music. Folk music prior to the 1960s appealed to a fairly small audience (similar to that of pure traditional country music). The blues revival was partially a development of the amalgamation of rock and folk, and partially assisted by musicians like Bob Dylan performing with a rock band, but it was essentially a development of a musical form designed for a multiracial urban audience.

In Britain, the blues revival came out of an interest in jazz and folk music. Blues records were brought to England by American servicemen and sent for by mail order. The blues had cult following of small proportions, but in the 1960s the blues developed as a viable form of entertainment for London pubs. Musicians like Elton John got their start playing in blues bands. Groups like the Rolling Stones modeled themselves after the blues groups they heard on recordings, especially those playing rhythm and blues. There developed two camps of blues musicians in Britain, the purists and the commercial. The Rolling Stones, the Animals, and the Yardbirds were commercial groups; John Mayall and the Bluesbreakers were purists. John Mayall used a variety of musicians including Eric Clapton and Mick Fleetwood. Cream, Clapton's first group, was a direct descendant of the Mayall group. The Jeff Beck Group, blues and heavy metal put together, used the enormous talents of Jeff Beck and Rod Stewart. And it is interesting that many of these musicians have also been mentioned by southern rockers as early influences.

The American blues revival was similar to the British one in that there was a group of purists and a group of commercial blues musicians. The rediscovery of major musicians like John Lee Hooker, Blind Lemon Jefferson, and Lightnin' Slim was important for the redevelopment of black blues. B.B. King and Muddy Waters were important in this movement as well. The commercial side of black blues is best represented by groups like Earth, Wind and Fire, formed in 1968 in New York City by Al Kooper. Actually a jazz-rock band, it is a model for commercial black rhythm and blues and certainly came about because of the blues revival. The band is especially interesting because of its use of an expanded horn section.

The Paul Butterfield Blues Band from Chicago was quite important if for no other reason than they performed with Bob Dylan in 1965. The California band Canned Heat, with their song "Amphetamine Annie," illustrates the blues and psychedelic influences working together. Electric Flag, from Chicago, although relatively short-lived, was a very important blues and psychedelic band. The point of mentioning these bands is that their influence lasted. And the direct line of evolution was to southern rock.

Southern rock has the following main points of style: it comes directly from blues tradition, expresses southern "nationalism" and pride, uses the strong guitar solo tradition of Texas, and has a strong machismo and sexual context. Ideally suited to the blues, southern rock is either folk-like in quality or raucous, almost honky tonk, blues. In some senses, southern rock could be understood to be an extension of the honky tonk tradition. However, it goes further than does honky tonk music.

The influences of urban-based developments in folk and rock in the 1960s are apparent in southern rock, especially in groups like Marshall Tucker, Charlie Daniels, ZZ Top, and Alabama. The music is electrified, blues-based, and progressive in lyric content. Drug and sexual images are much more blatant than they are in more Nashville-oriented music, and this is a direct development from the blues revival that in turn developed directly from the psychedelic-to-heavy metal evolution. In short, southern rock did develop from rock of the 1960s. The southern or country part of it is the same part that gave rockabilly of the mid–1950s its Memphis flavor.

THE EMERGENCE OF THE SONGWRITER AS NARRATOR

The songwriter has always been important in country music, from the days of Jimmie Rodgers to today. But at no time in the history of contemporary popular music has songwriting as narration been more important. Of course, songwriters are always narrators of the human condition, and country music is one of the most conscious expressions of the human condition. But prior to the 1960s, country music was relatively limited in the scope of that narration. During the 1960s and into the 1970s, the subject matter of country music diversified; the leaders of that trend were the country rock lyricists.

One of the important characteristics of country rock in this context is the expression of southern pride. Much of country music prior to the development of the Nashville sound was fairly self deprecating, promoting the image of the southern hick. Nashville writers created a feeling of pride in lyrics. Interestingly, one of the examples of that type of lyric writer was Willie Nelson. But it was the country rock musicians who delivered not only a sense of pride but also a diversity of message.

A good example of the southern pride expressed in country rock was Lynyrd Skynyrd's "Sweet Home, Alabama," which was designed as a rebuttal to Neil Young's "Southern Man." Crosby, Stills, Nash and Young was a highly influential folk rock group of the late 1960s and early 1970s, but "Southern Man" was not particularly complimentary of the South. Lynyrd Skynyrd's "Sweet Home, Alabama" redressed that. For the most part, country music has become more sophisticated and has lost the image of being constantly depressing.

Diversity of image is quite important in 1970s country rock, and one hears a variety of messages—social, political, moral, and others. It is in this way that the songwriter has become a more diversified narrator of life in the South. Southern music of the 1970s begins to have national impact rather than being regionalistic. Although country music has always had adherents in other parts of the United States, prior to this time fans from the Midwest liked country music because it evoked southern feeling. With the changes that occurred in the 1970s, country music began to express feelings no longer firmly tied to the South and to speak to urban issues everywhere. And probably the best proof of that is the international popularity that country music has won in the last fifteen years.

The changing subject matter of country music in the 1970s has had a snowballing effect, and writers have had an increasing influence on the types of songs that are sung. Many people have followed with great interest the growth of crossover popular country tunes and the continuing growth of traditional country music. Although one could argue that marketing has been responsible for increasing the sales of and public access to country music, it must certainly be due also to songwriters who have opened up new subjects, increasing their impact to the point where they could affect trends themselves. At no time in earlier country music has the writer had so much influence on the thinking of the public.

MAIN PRACTITIONERS OF COUNTRY ROCK

In this section, we will consider some representative examples of country rock groups or musicians who have influenced or been influenced by country music. Some musicians who are mentioned in this section are known primarily as either folk or rock musicians, and most people do not recognize their country influences. They are mentioned to give credit to the country part of their performance.

Alabama

The name of this award-winning group comes from the fact that the original three members, Randy Owen, Jeff Cook, and Teddy Gentry, came from Alabama. As teenagers in 1969 they started jamming together in usual sloppy style. In 1970 they formed the group, so Alabama has actually been around for some time. Their first job was playing at a local tourist park, where they got the opportunity to back major performers who were brought in on the weekends.

Alabama (*Courtesy of RCA Records, Nashville*)

In 1973 the band moved to Myrtle Beach, South Carolina, where they worked local clubs for cheap wages. They made demo records and tried to get a recording contract. They were successful and got a contract from GRT Records in 1976, recording under the name Wild Country. Their first recording of "I Want to Be with You" did not sell a lot, but it got them a more permanent contract with MDJ Records out of Dallas, Texas. With MDJ they issued several singles that actually made the charts; in 1980 "My Home's in Alabama" made it into the top 20. But it actually was not until 1980 that Alabama made it to the big time with RCA Records.

In 1980 RCA released Alabama's single, "Tennessee River," their first album, *My Home's in Alabama,* and another single, "Why, Lady, Why." The last single made it to the top 10 on the country list in the fall. After 1981 the group had phenomenal success, with a number of gold and platinum records and numerous awards. In a day when it is rare for a country group to win awards, Alabama consistently hit the top of the charts and has collected a lot of trophies, for example Entertainer of the Year in 1984.

This fearsome foursome fits the image of a country rock group because they are very neat looking, yet have long hair and beards. They are definitely country, and the rock part of their sound is light rock. In some ways they are folksingers, and their vocal texture is really quite soft. They do nostalgic songs and show clearly that they are southerners. They are of course very popular in the South, but they also have a strong following in other parts of the United States.

Commander Cody and the Lost Planet Airmen

Commander Cody (George Frayne) and the Lost Planet Airmen is one of those groups that you will not find in a country encyclopedia because they are not from the South. The original members of the group were from Ann Arbor (Michigan), Boise (Idaho), Decatur (Alabama), New York, and St. Louis. When the band formed in 1968, all of them were living in Ann Arbor, where Frayne was an art student at the University of Michigan.

The campus area of the University of Michigan is very active, and Ann Arbor is a very liberal town. The town has even had an active hippie movement since the late 1960s. It was the perfect location to put together something different. But even in Ann Arbor, country rock was unusual in the late 1960s.

The group was fairly interesting in its instrumentation, using players on piano, guitars, steel guitar, and one player who doubled on fiddle, sax, and trombone. Even at its craziest, the band was made up of technically superior players. They played a combination of western swing rockabilly and country music. Although not highly successful, they did put out nine albums and charted three singles on the top 100 over their nine-year career. Only one album, *Lost in the Ozone,* is still available, but it belongs in every diversified country fan's library.

At times Commander Cody plays straight country music, but the band is known primarily for its novelty tunes. They do mention drugs in some of their tunes, for instance, "Stoned in the Ozone Again" or in their classic "Seeds and Stems." Novelty tunes like "Beat Me Daddy Eight to the Bar" and Tex Ritter's "Smoke, Smoke, Smoke" were good examples in 1972 and 1973. It is hard to tell whether they were talking about the same kind of tobacco that Ritter was, but regardless, they did the tune in a remarkable parody.

Commander Cody and the Lost Planet Airmen may have seemed like just a bunch of crazies. But the group, whose career essentially ended in the late 1970s, was composed of very good musicians, and they did a variety of types of music right in the appropriate style. A good example of country rock in its more unusual form, they illustrate well that even midwesterners can do country music.

Charlie Daniels Band

The Charlie Daniels Band is a more obvious example of a country rock band because it is from the South, sings about southern themes, and has a country feel to the playing and singing style. Charlie Daniels was born in 1937 in North Carolina and now resides in Tennessee. A fiddler and guitarist, he formed his first band, the Jaguars, in 1958. He toured with that band throughout the South, essentially as a honky tonker. He also did some writing during that period and in fact collaborated on a tune done by Elvis Presley—"It Hurts Me." In 1967 he dissolved the Jaguars and moved to Nashville, where he wrote songs for Tammy Wynette, among others, and played on recording sessions for Bob Dylan, Pete Seeger, and numerous country stars.

In 1971 he started the Charlie Daniels Band, which was basically an imitation of the instrumentation of the Allman Brothers Band—two drummers and two guitarists. This instrumentation (which expanded over time) gives the Charlie Daniels Band a fairly heavy sound, bluesy and strong, yet still country in orientation. Daniels recorded on a variety of labels up until 1975, when he was signed by Epic. Some of his early big hits were "Uneasy Rider" and "The South's Gonna Do It." The last tune was a song of Southern pride and clearly identifies Daniels with the South.

He politicized country rock when he toured for Jimmy Carter and, later, performed at the White House. Daniels, who has kept up a demanding touring schedule, won his first major award, a Grammy, in 1979. During the 1980 Iran crisis he had a major hit with "In America." This is a country rock group with a message, and Charlie Daniels, the main songwriter, functions as a narrator of the human condition in their political songs. The Charlie Daniels Band is highly respected and plays in a number of different styles, everything from country rock to traditional to Tex-Mex music.

Eagles

The Eagles were formed in 1971 and dissolved in 1981. The original four members, Don Henley, Glenn Frey, Bernie Leadon, and Randy Meisner, made up the backup band for Linda Ronstadt on her *Silk Purse* album. These musicians had strong backgrounds as session players and as performing musicians, coming from such bands as the Flying Burrito Brothers, Poco, Bob Seger, and Shiloh.

The Eagles were Los Angeles-based, and although one does not think of Los Angeles as a mecca for country music, there was a thriving country rock tradition there in the 1970s. What the Eagles did was to take the country rock tradition of the Byrds and the Flying Burrito Brothers more toward the hard rock side, although they always retained some country flavor with a Tex-Mex accent.

The Eagles had tremendous success during their eleven-year career, although the awards groups did not seem to notice it. They cultivated a following of people who were half way between country and rock, and became a model for California-based country music. Hard-edged vocals pushed this particular group closer to rock than country, but the roots of country were always there.

Flying Burrito Brothers

The Flying Burrito Brothers is one of the most interesting country rock groups. The personnel changes this band has gone through in their sixteen-plus years of existence reads like a phone book. But to make a very long story short, the Burrito Brothers use basically the following instrumentation: keyboards (electric and acoustic), guitar, bass, steel guitar, and drums. At times they have also used banjo, dobro, harmonica, and fiddle.

The Flying Burrito Brothers were only really important from 1968, when they were formed in Los Angeles, to 1970, when Gram Parsons quit the group to have a solo career (Parsons died tragically in 1973). The Parsons-led Flying Burrito Brothers was a swinging bluegrass band with perpetual rhythm and haunting lyrics that were very un-countrylike. The original group was folk-rock with a bluegrass instrumentation.

After 1970 and their real successes, the Flying Burrito Brothers went through numerous changes in personnel. In the 1980s they existed as a vocal duet working out of Nashville, but the original intensity of the Flying Burrito Brothers as an example of the strong country rock movement of southern California ended in the early 1970s. However, when they were hot, they were really hot.

Grateful Dead

The Grateful Dead was formed in San Francisco in 1965 and is the only psychedelic band to survive into the mid–1980s. They have never had a hit record or a top-10 single, but for true Dead Heads (Grateful Dead fans) that does not matter.

The real story of the Grateful Dead is the story of Jerry Garcia. He was born in San Francisco in 1942, started playing the guitar at the age of fifteen, and later learned to play the banjo. He began playing in bluegrass bands in 1962, and in 1964 was a member of Mother McCree's Uptown Jug

Champions (now if that does not show country roots, I give up). In 1965 the band changed their name to the Warlocks, and they were essentially the house band for LSD parties, chronicled in Wolfe's *Electric Kool-Aid Acid Test.* Then they changed their name to the Grateful Dead, were signed by MGM, and became a psychedelic band. In 1967 they changed to Warner Brothers, where their music was produced in a better way. They did start their own record label in 1973, although that really did not do any better than Warner Brothers had.

The Dead are not important for their commercial success but rather for the quality of their music. If you listen to even a smattering of Dead albums you will hear country guitar picking and country tunes (granted, you will also hear some tunes that are not country at all).

Jerry Garcia continued to work with other artists, especially the New Riders of the Purple Sage. He did session work with the Jefferson Airplane and Crosby, Stills, Nash and Young. He continues to play bluegrass banjo and peddle steel guitar (which he played when recording with the New Riders). The Dead's personnel has varied greatly over the years, but Jerry Garcia as the center of the group has kept the sound fairly consistent; and the country roots of Jerry Garcia are obvious in the sound of the Grateful Dead.

Lynyrd Skynyrd

Lynyrd Skynyrd (watch that spelling) was formed in 1966 in Jacksonville, Florida, rose to prominence in 1973, and ended abruptly in 1977 when the lead singer and a guitar player were killed in a plane crash. This band was made up of long-haired hard rockers, with a sound somewhat patterned after the Allman Brothers. They are usually left out of country rock discussions because they are very loud and heavy metal mostly.

The name of the band was a takeoff on the name of one of their schoolteachers, a gym teacher who punished students with long hair. From 1966 until 1972 they played the club and bar circuit; in 1972 Al Kooper of MCA signed them to a recording contract after hearing them in a bar. From 1973 to 1980 the band, with its heavy metal brand of southern rock, had a large following in the South as well as some national exposure. Its major contribution to the cause of southern music was undoubtedly the song from 1974, "Sweet Home Alabama."

Marshall Tucker Band

The Marshall Tucker Band is made up of six musicians, the original six being from Spartanburg, South Carolina. In 1971, the Caldwell Brothers (Toy and Tommy) joined with the other four original members in what would become one of the hottest country rock bands of the 1970s. Tommy died in 1980 and was replaced by a long-time friend of the Caldwells.

Actually the Marshall Tucker Band is one of the most diverse groups in this chapter because they play everything—traditional country, blues, rockabilly, and jazz-rock. Playing a variety of musical instruments, they are capable of shifting from one style to another with great ease. They use alto sax and flute, steel guitar and full rhythm section, but they also use combinations that give the string band flavor. The band's sound has often been described as middle-of-the-road or crossover, which perhaps explains their national and overseas following.

The Marshall Tucker Band signed first with Capricorn Records in 1972 and changed to Warner Brothers in 1978. They got their first gold record in 1975 and their first platinum in 1977. Many of the band members were fine writers, and the Caldwells in particular had many of their songs done by other artists—Waylon Jennings, Kitty Wells, and Hank Williams, Jr., to mention a few. From 1977 on the band consistently put out top-selling al-

The Marshall Tucker Band (*Courtesy of Warner Brothers Records, Nashville*)

bums and singles, and that creative impetus did not cease, even with the hard blow of Tommy's death.

The Marshall Tucker Band toured with the Allman Brothers Band in 1973 and many have said that they are simply Allman imitators. They have a strong bluesy sound, but the diversity of song styles makes them quite different from the Allmans.

New Riders of the Purple Sage

The New Riders of the Purple Sage were an invention of Jerry Garcia. He wanted an opportunity to play the pedal steel guitar, which he had taken up in the late 1960s. He joined with John Dawson, a guitarist and singer who had been in an earlier band, Mother McCree's Uptown Jug Champions. Soon the duo was joined by other Dead members and by David Nelson, who had been with Big Brother and the Holding Company.

The New Riders of the Purple Sage were a country alternative to the Dead. Their sound is folksy, with lots of country in it, although the subject matter is often fairly unconventional. Their most popular subject seems to be marijuana, in particular Panama Red. One of their songs from the first album talks about going to Mexico to collect golden "keys." A fairly short-lived band (most of the Grateful Dead members, including Garcia, dropped out of the band quickly because of time commitments), it was an interesting experiment in country rock—a band formed to allow its members to play a different kind of music.

After 1974 the initial popularity of the New Riders dwindled greatly and they ultimately lost their record contract. However, during the time they existed they were a great band, as entertaining to watch as to listen to. The sound of the New Riders was clearly country, but the subject matter of their songs was so completely out of the tradition that they were in a sense a novelty band. The novelty was very popular in liberal and college towns, and they enjoyed moderate record sales and good concert success. At one point, they served as the warmup band for the Grateful Dead.

The Nitty Gritty Dirt Band

The Dirt Band, as it has been called since 1976, was formed in Long Beach, California in 1966. The group members are mostly from Long Beach, with one from Detroit, one from Boston, and one from West Germany. It is one of the oddest congregations of musicians you could imagine, capable of playing jug band, string band, traditional country, western swing, and country rock. They are even more versatile than the Marshall Tucker Band, which is saying something.

The original name of the band was the Illegitimate Jug Band, but by 1967 they were known as the Nitty Gritty Dirt Band. At the beginning of their career they were decidedly confused about whether they were country musicians or rock musicians, even after their first eight albums one would have been hard pressed to make that decision for them. However, with their 1973 historic recording of *Will the Circle Be Unbroken,* which featured a number of traditional country musicians like Earl Scruggs, Maybelle Carter, Merle Travis, and Roy Acuff, they began to move more clearly into country. In 1977 they made another type of history by being the first country band to tour through Russia.

A public performance of this band was a delight to behold because they were constantly trading instruments and creating new musical textures. During the mid–1970s a young comedian named Steve Martin worked as the warmup act for the Dirt Band. Even after Martin attained star status himself, he occasionally returned to appear with the Dirt Band, playing banjo. The band's importance is that they have preserved the original integrity of a country string and jug band, while at the same time moving easily into the country rock sound.

The Dirt Band continued to sell albums into the 1980s and had some successful hits in 1980 and 1981. However, it is really mostly a historical group now. Although they have had some very lucrative recordings, probably their most important was the 1973 album with those other country stars. It received very positive reviews and helped to bridge the gap between traditional country music and the new wave of country music. Of course, many of the old-time stars were reluctant to get involved, but the ultimate result was a very pleasing experience for everyone.

14 Mainstream Country of the 1970s and 1980s

COUNTRY FUSION

This section of the book covers country music from the 1970s and 1980s that has not previously been covered. Although rock and other alternatives to Nashville continue to have influence in the 1970s and 1980s, they will basically be left out of this discussion, although occasionally an artist will be discussed who might have been considered earlier but was not. The attempt of this discussion is to point out the dignity of country music in the most contemporary period.

Other writers have used various words to describe current country music—words such as *countrypolitan* or *contemporary country.* I have chosen not to refer to it as *contemporary country* because that phrase only says that it has happened recently or is still happening today. Since much of country music is conservative at heart, we still have performers who sing or play in a relatively old style, yet their music is chronologically contemporary. The term *countrypolitan* is popular as well, but I have also rejected its use. Typically, writers use the word with a certain disdain, implying that country music has sold out to the big cities and that it has become one homogeneous mishmash. Country music has been modernized and also more heavily marketed in recent years, but that is not to its discredit. It has simply become familiar to and popular with a broader group of people.

My position is that country music of the 1970s and the 1980s should be referred to as *country fusion,* because of the influences and presence of other forms of music. One such fusion is country rock; other influences come from folk, classical, jazz, and pop music.

We will discuss country fusion in three separate chapters describing mainstream country, crossover pop, and experimental. *Mainstream country* refers to music that is clearly indentifiable as country music, usually performed by well-established country stars, but often with some type of expanded instrumental background (differing from Nashville sound backgrounds of the mid–1960s) or a subtle change in lyrics. *Crossover pop* shows country influences but has definite pop appeal. Often the singers will not even be widely recognized as country singers, although several of them regularly win awards at country music conventions. *Experimental music* is so called because of some quality in the music that is unusual or expands the horizons of country music. There is a certain catchall quality to the last chapter, because novelty music is also discussed, as well as one wonderful comedienne.

This last section of the book is probably the most important, but it may appear to be a bit short, the reason being that all of these musicians are still performing today, and their history is yet to be completely understood.

MAINSTREAM COUNTRY

The artists discussed in this chapter are all recognized as great country singers who, with the possible exception of Kris Kristofferson, have been thoroughly dedicated to the cause of country music. These stars were established prior to the 1970s but have remained quite active. Their roots are clearly in traditional, honky tonk, and Nashville music, but their creations of the 1970s and 1980s have been modernized.

I would like to make a subtle distinction between Nashville sound and mainstream country of the fusion period. While the Nashville sound contributed greatly to the survival and popularity of country music, it was really fairly limited. The kind of music we are looking at in this chapter derived from Nashville sound, but went quite a bit beyond. It would be fair to see it as an extension of Nashville (and in fact much of this music is created in Nashville), but it really does have influences from outside of Nashville.

One of the most interesting issues of this later period is the tremendous growth in popularity of country music in the late 1960s and early 1970s. There are of course many reasons for it, but certainly the slow shift from the Nashville sound to a more inclusive mainstream country approach was part of it. Some have explained this rise of country music as being a conscious reaction against folk and rock, which were after all pretty complicated and difficult to understand. Folk and rock of the late 1960s were also heavily political and quite liberal. Some have seen country music as being the conservative music of that era, much as the election of Richard Nixon in 1968 came at the end of a very progressive age.

Conservative backlash comes in waves throughout cultural history. Such cycles are evident in radio programming. For a while programming goes toward the most commercial; it then returns after a time to the more pure forms, whether adult-oriented rock, middle of the road, or country western. Country music enjoyed a major growth in popularity in the late 1960s and early 1970s because of the attitudes of the times.

Also important was the rapid rise of media in that period. Marketing certainly had something to do with the rise of country music. "Hee Haw" probably had a tremendous influence as well—after all, it started in 1969, just about the time there was an increase in interest in country music. A very optimistic and entertaining show, it featured the talents of Buck Owens, Roy Clark, and many others. This national attention must have had a snowballing effect on country music.

But perhaps the biggest reason country music enjoyed unprecedented popularity in the 1970s and the 1980s is that its diversity gave it credibility. I can remember the time that one would not admit to liking country music because it was thought to be low class; that is no longer the general feeling. I believe it was the modernization of country music in the 1970s, with the addition of extra instruments and advanced studio techniques, that ultimately led to a type of music that could have the kind of universality now enjoyed by country music. There is little question that by the 1980s country music had become increasingly more popular, and that its modernization in this country fusion period was a major factor.

The modernization can be seen in several ways, but usually not in the singing voice. In fact, one of the chief characteristics of musicians discussed in this chapter is that, with a few exceptions, they still sing in a very clear country style. The country roots can thus be clearly heard in the singing of Loretta Lynn, Tom T. Hall, and George Jones, regardless of the instrumental backup group.

In the backup group we usually hear more than a standard string band. The Nashville sound had already given us drum sets, electric basses, and a stronger sound, but country fusion gave us string sections, horn players, and special electronic effects. Full-sounding choirs replaced the relatively simple backup harmonies of earlier music. The modernization was countryfied by using steel guitar, fiddle and, occasionally, mandolin. And increasingly in the 1970s, these instruments played solo breaks. The country sound was present even when a large orchestra was used; yet the changing style of country music included more emphasis on improvisation.

Marketing, media support, and cultural attitudes produced a situation in which country music grew in leaps and bounds. And in the process, it kept pace with that growth by changing in sound. This is what led musicians to change the way they recorded and, at times, what they recorded. However, each of the musicians discussed was absolutely true to country music in its basic style; that is why they are called *mainstream*.

Merle Haggard

Merle Haggard, who was discussed in the Bakersfield chapter, continued to perform with his band the Strangers into the 1980s. His singing voice has mellowed out a bit, although that is probably due to age and to an increasing sense of security after his tough early life.

Merle Haggard continues to sing about the same topics, but there is an increased complexity to the lyrics, as in "The Way I Am." Apart from the growing complexity of his words and a slight mellowing of his voice, he is still a mainstream singer with a slight honky tonk flair. However, the recordings of the late 1970s illustrate a definite modernization of performance style.

One good example of this modernization is in the 1978 song, "I'm Always on a Mountain When I Fall." The first verse begins with a singer and a simple background band, but the refrain reveals modern studio techniques, especially in the use of background singers. The advanced studio techniques and the slickness of the recording show the song to be mainstream country or fusion music of the 1970s. Many of Haggard's tunes illustrate this.

The Strangers always used a fair amount of improvisation, but there is a heightened use of improvisation in Haggard's recordings of the 1970s and 1980s. He also made a number of duet recordings that used expanded backgrounds and electronic effects.

Tom T. Hall

Some people may wonder why Tom T. Hall has not been discussed earlier, since he has been so important to country music. However, he illustrates so well the phenomenon discussed in this chapter that I decided to save him to use as a pivotal figure for this discussion.

Tom T. Hall is a singer, songwriter, and also an author. He was born in Kentucky in 1936, the son of a minister. Although he was around music because of the church, music did not beckon him at first. In fact, he attended Roanoke College in Virginia, where he read books and studied journalism. His favorite authors were Americans such as Mark Twain and Ernest Hemingway. These would ultimately be important influences for his songwriting career, where he was known as the "Storyteller."

Tom T. Hall (*Courtesy of PolyGram Records, Nashville*)

In the mid–1950s he joined the army, serving for eight years, then he returned to Roanoke to become a disc jockey. He started writing songs in his spare time, and sent some to Jimmy Key in Nashville, who urged him to move there. He did, and in 1964 was given a contract agreement. In 1967 he started his solo career and his second single, "A Week in a Country Jail," went to number one on the country charts. His 1968 hit "Harper Valley PTA" was sung by Jeannie C. Riley and won a CMA award. A member of the Songwriter's Hall of Fame, Tom T. Hall has written songs recorded by Perry Como, George Jones, Loretta Lynn, Johnny Cash, Bobby Bare, George Burns, Patti Page, and many others.

Hall has also recorded successfully since 1967, with memorable songs like "Country Is," "Sneaky Snake," "I Love," "I Like Beer," and "The Ballad of Forty Dollars." He has also written four books, including an autobiographical work called *The Storyteller's Nashville* and two novels.

He is a member of the Grand Ole Opry and hosts his own syndicated television show, "Pop Goes the Country." He has been on numerous other television shows and appeared at the Smithsonian Institution American Country Music Series in Washington, D.C. He has served in humanitarian causes such as the American Lung Association, the Heart Association, and the Veterinary Medical Association of Tennessee. He runs his own publishing company called Hallnote Music in connection with Toy Box Recording Studio. He is a man of many concerns, and this is illustrated by his music.

Starting with "Harper Valley PTA" he shows himself to be a narrator, and many of his songs tell stories and comment on the human condition. In another of his songs, "Country Is," Tom talks about country music in its

George Jones (*Photo by Slick Lawson; used by courtesy of Epic Records, Nashville*)

conflicting or varying images, which fits so perfectly with the discussion of this chapter. He also does upbeat novelty tunes like "I Like Beer." Diversification is the main reason why he is a fusion writer and singer, but even the background sounds illustrate the modernization of his music.

Tom T. Hall has the voice of a traditional country singer. However, his music makes a contemporary point, and does so with contemporary studio techniques. Even when a song has a simple background, there is always something sophisticated about it; and more often than not if you listen carefully you will hear something that makes the background a modern one. But his true claim to modernity is in the lyric and in the intelligence that wrote the lyric.

George Jones

George Jones has been around for a long time; some readers might feel like he is the focal point of the book because he has been mentioned so many times. Forever true to the honky tonk tradition, George Jones has continued to modernize his music. If you listen to some of his old recordings and then listen to "He Stopped Loving Her Today" or "Still Doin' Time," that modernization is obvious.

His singing voice has not changed, and he is still very traditional in his presentation. The lyrics have become a little more complicated, although their message is fairly conservative. But his band backgrounds and recording techniques have been modernized. George Jones, live, sounds very conservative by comparison. He now uses an expanded band of six musicians, and the sound is quite a bit heavier than even some of his honky tonk hits of a long time ago. In short, George Jones has retained the roots of the honky tonkers while using today's technology. His awards sweeps of 1980 and 1981 indicate a recognition that he has kept up with the times.

Kris Kristofferson

Kris Kristofferson is undoubtedly one of the most talented and intelligent people ever to be involved in country music, although he always manages to hide some of his worldliness. He was born in Brownsville, Texas in 1937, the son of a two-star general. During his early life he was filled with a passion for literature. He attended Pomona College in California, where he majored in literature and played football and soccer. After graduation he received a prestigious Rhodes Scholarship and studied at Oxford.

After Oxford, he served in the army as a pilot for five years. In 1965 he decided to move to Nashville to work as a songwriter and nearly starved for four years trying to do it. But he persevered, and finally attracted the attention of both Roger Miller and Johnny Cash. Roger Miller recorded his "Me and Bobby McGee," and Janis Joplin covered it. Johnny Cash did his tune "Sunday Morning Coming Down." By 1970 Kris Kristofferson had become a very hot songwriter in Nashville. Johnny Cash had Kristofferson on his show several times in 1969 and 1970, and although his performing career was not as hot as his songwriting, he was a success in both.

He won numerous awards for songwriting and singing between 1970 and 1975. He also has had a very successful film career and has won many awards for his films, especially Foreign Press Association Best Actor for *A Star Is Born*. He has remained active, although not at the same level as in the 1970s.

Kristofferson has a most unusual voice. In some sense he is the country equivalent of Bob Dylan, with whom he did the movie *Pat Garrett and Billy the Kid* in 1973. His literary background is obvious in the way he strings complex thoughts together. He sings in a style similar to Dylan or perhaps Willie Nelson. His voice is not at all traditional country, although the basic style of his music is. He uses every type of background instrumental group imaginable, which clearly places him in the fusion category. Actually, Kris-

Kris Kristofferson (left) in the late 1960s (*Photograph courtesy of the Country Music Foundation Library and Media Center, Nashville, Tennessee*)

Conway Twitty (*Courtesy of Warner Brothers Records, Nashville*)

tofferson is hard to pin down, in part because his personal background seems so unlike a country musician's. But he is actually a mainstream country singer of the 1970s, even though some have called him an outlaw.

Roger Miller

Roger Miller was an enormously successful songwriter and singer in the 1960s. Unfortunately, his success seemed to diminish in the 1970s and 1980s. His lyrics show a very eccentric quality. He was doing fusion music with his novelty songs and with his straight country-pop tunes back in the early 1960s.

Miller has always recorded songs with expanded orchestras, and for that he has been recognized as a pop singer (for which he was awarded often in the mid–1960s). He is a perfect example of a country fusion singer, and is probably half way between mainstream country and crossover pop. He is clever, witty, and wise in his narration of the human condition—remember "King of the Road."

Conway Twitty

Harold Lloyd Jenkins was born in Arkansas in 1933, the son of a Mississippi riverboat captain. He learned to play the guitar by the time he was five, and started playing in a country band while still in high school. He considered going into the ministry, working in country music, or being a professional baseball player (he had a contract with the Philadelphia Phillies). But in 1950 the Korean War interrupted, so he went to Japan where he performed with a country band.

When he returned from the service he took the name Conway Twitty and decided to be a rock and roll star. Conway Twitty was one of the important pop stars of the 1950s. It was not until the mid–1960s, when rockabilly had been killed off by the Beatles, that he returned to country music. By 1968 he had become a regular on the Opry and had appeared on the "Johnny Cash Show" and "Hee Haw." Also in 1968, his own songs and his performances of other songs landed him on both the pop and the country charts.

In the early 1970s he continued to have crossover success, but by the mid–1970s he had actually gone more country than pop. An interesting phenomenon in this age of purists going pop is that Conway Twitty went the other way. In duet with Loretta Lynn, Conway Twitty won CMA awards every year from 1971 to 1981 except in 1979, when Kenny Rogers and Dottie West won.

Dottie West

Dottie West (Branch) was born in Tennessee in 1932. She was exposed early to country music in a farm family. Dottie had the good fortune to get a scholarship to college, having received formal training in music prior to college. She graduated from college with a major in music. She and her first husband, Bill West, formed a duet team that performed for five years before Dottie got a contract from Starday Records and they moved to Nashville.

When she first moved to Nashville she hung out with the songwriters, and she credits Willie Nelson, Hank Cochran, and Roger Miller with helping her to discover her talent as a songwriter. Although known primarily for her duet work with Jim Reeves, Don Gibson, Jimmy Dean, and Kenny Rogers, Dottie West has had a very productive career as a songwriter and solo singer. She earned her first BMI Writing award in 1961 for "Is This Me?," which was recorded by Jim Reeves. This led to an RCA recording contract conferred by Chet Atkins in 1962. Both husband and wife got songwriting contracts from Tree Publishing Company soon after that. In 1964, her composition "Here Comes My Baby" established her as a major talent.

Dottie West sang, wrote, and dueted her way to major accomplishments, although her only Grammy came in 1964. In 1970, she wrote a commercial for the Coca Cola Company, and they gave her a lifetime contract. Her song "Country Sunshine" won her a Clio Award for best commercial of 1973, a first for a country writer. Despite the breakup of two marriages, Dottie West has been a creative dynamo over two decades and does not seem to be giving up. Her daughter Shelly is a star in her own right.

In conclusion, the purpose of this chapter has been to illustrate that country music can remain true to its origin yet evolve with the times. We have seen examples of musicians evolving in very different ways, but they all share the same basic style characteristics. The next chapter discusses crossover pop musicians, who have gone a little further from the country tradition.

15 Crossover Pop

The subject of crossover pop is central to this section on country fusion. It is a subject to which many country purists take exception, condemning the music for its commercialism. At some point in my artistic thinking, I decided that being commercial was not so terrible after all, and that it was easy to accept such musicians as Kenny Rogers, the Statlers, the Oakridge Boys, and the Mandrell Sisters.

The purpose of music is to communicate ideas and feelings. The songwriter narrates life's existence through his or her particular communication medium. There are tangible reasons for doing this in a way that reaches the widest possible audience. First, if one believes that the message being communicated is important, clearly one should make sure that as many people as possible hear it. A second reason for seeking a large audience is more personal. Most musicians create music because they like to have an audience. Music is a means by which they can get attention. In fact, many are introverts and do not speak well; their main communication medium is music. A third reason for expanding the audience is to make money. Musicians seek to get paid for the enormous amount of time it takes to gain skills. Most working musicians do not make a bundle; they make enough to get by like everyone else. Even most of the superstars in this book lived modestly for years before making it big; can anyone really blame them for collecting while they can?

Much can be said about the tyranny of too much money. But a strong possibility exists when earnings are high that the artist will have greater artistic control and freedom. A musician will play whatever the bar owner or customers want if it means one more night of work. An unknown recording artist does whatever the system asks. It is only after some success that artists like the Beatles or the Jackson Five have been able to demand and receive some control over their own products. In this sense, success can beget both more success and greater creativity.

Commercialization, then, does not necessarily lower the artistic quality of the music. True, quite often very commercial or crossover music will have a tendency to be somewhat more regular than noncommercial music, but that does not in itself ruin its artistic integrity. As long as a piece of music is put together by an intelligent and innovative composer and lyricist, there is a reasonable chance that it will have artistic merit.

Commercialization has given country music an air of respectability, which of course it always deserved. The difference is that now no one can take it away. Country musicians now make as much money as rock stars do, and this gives them the clout to be treated the same way as rock stars are.

It is not new to country music to incorporate other influences, such as rhythm and blues, rock, or folk music. However, the crossover artists of the 1970s did it in a more complete way than country musicians had done previously, using stage presentation, personal appearance, orchestration, and the total marketing package. Crossover artists have often been seen as total entertainers rather than as simple country singers or pure blues singers. The whole experience becomes the show—as Marshall McLuhan said, "The medium is the message." So the crossover artist communicates through a variety of means by providing many different stylistic elements in one package, so that different audiences can take whatever elements work for them.

Crossover artists must achieve a successful mixture between stylistic elements that are contradictory. For instance, a pop singer normally tries for a fairly smooth voice, as opposed to the strained nasal quality of older traditional country music. Often the southern accent is lost when a singer is trying to communicate to a broader spectrum of people, that is, people not from the South. Instrumental forces are usually expanded, so the simplicity of the traditional string band is not necessarily a quality of crossover art (although the bluegrass sound of Flatt and Scruggs has been enormously popular with non-country audiences). Instrumental ensembles are generally bigger, including string sections and even big bands at times. This is probably part of the modernization of country music rather than just a crossover quality; at any rate, it communicates to a larger audience.

Crossover entertainment usually uses more slick stage routines, light shows, even film, during performances. Popular music history is filled with musicians who did something different in their stage routine and as a result were recognized.

So crossover pop does by definition make some concessions. But the question is, does it stop being country music? It stops being country music when it has no country quality at all. Just like a jazz musician who goes pop, the country musician could conceivably stop being country. But the crossover artists discussed in this chapter have never stopped being country in orientation. Many of their lyrics are about country themes. Most of the time, the instrumental group has some instruments played in a country style (Mandrell with fiddle, Rogers with steel guitar). And all of them express a country attitude in performance, even when Kenny Rogers ends with a laser light show and Barbara Mandrell reveals her southern Californian accent.

I am reminded of an old adage that I think fits the situation, that "You can take the boy out of the country but you cannot take the country out of the boy."

The following musicians then represent the phenomenon of crossover country or pop musicians. They are obviously not the only ones who could be discussed here, but they are the ones who immediately spring to mind. There are fewer musicians discussed in this chapter than are usually included, but it was my feeling that a few performers discussed at some length cover the crossover field pretty well; clearly there are many other musicians who could appear in this context.

One is initially reminded of two Mexican Americans who were big crossover artists in the early and mid–1970s—Johnny Rodriguez and Freddy Fender. Johnny Rodriguez was a Texan born in 1952 who developed a style of

Johnny Rodriguez (*Photo by Mark Tucker; used by courtesy of Epic Records, Nashville*)

singing Texas country music both in Spanish and in English. That particular phenomenon had actually occurred earlier with the singing cowboys, in particular Roy Rogers, but Johnny Rodriguez was doing something fairly unusual for his time.

Tom T. Hall discovered Rodriguez through a mutual friend and promised to call him when he needed another player. When he did, Rodriguez moved to Nashville, where he became a star. Starting in 1972, he had one hit after another, and many were crossover successes. He also did some television acting.

Baldemar G. Huerta (Freddy Fender) was born in Texas in 1937 and has had what certainly must be seen as a fascinating career. Born into a migrant worker family right on the southern Texas border, Fender grew up with Tex-Mex music. He played the guitar and sang wherever he went, which was all over. In 1953, he dropped out of school and joined the marines; after serving for three years he returned to Texas and became a Spanish-singing recording and performing star. In the late 1950s he turned to rockabilly, and in 1959 and 1960 he had three hit records—"Holy One," "Wasted Days and Wasted Nights," and "Crazy, Crazy Baby." In that period he was somewhat like Conway Twitty, although he had moved to rockabilly from Tex-Mex music.

Unfortunately, he was arrested for marijuana possession in 1960 and spent three years in prison, and his career was gone by the time he got out. He spent much of the 1960s playing club dates in New Orleans. In 1969 he returned home and spent some time going to school, working during the day as a mechanic and playing at night. In 1974, he contacted a producer in

Larry Gatlin and the Gatlin Brothers (*Photo by Alan Messer; used by courtesy of Columbia Records, Nashville*)

Houston, who arranged for him to cut a single—a country song called "Before the Next Teardrop Falls." The song was a local hit; DOT Records bought national rights to it, and by 1975 it was a gold record. Subsequent productions of Freddy Fender, singles and albums of 1975, had great success on both country and pop charts. One particular recording— "Secret Love"—was very successful; it was an old Doris Day hit, which illustrates the type of material that worked at that time.

Fender was nominated for numerous awards during 1975 as a result of his tremendous crossover popularity. He has since been involved in film acting and has continued to have success in singing, although not matching his 1975 success. Freddy Fender had impact because of his crossover success, a delightful mixture between Mexican influence, country music, and straight pop music.

It would be an error not to mention the Gatlin Brothers and the Oakridge Boys. Both these groups have a strong gospel tradition; in fact, the Oakridge Boys were gospel singers for the first part of their career. Both have been very successful lately in winning country awards. But they both also have enormous crossover popularity, because of the universality of their songs and the sophisticated blend of the musical texture.

But the real story of crossover pop music can be told by examining the successes of Barbara Mandrell and Kenny Rogers. They each had a significant impact on country music and they both deserve all the attention that they are getting. Both of these musicians also illustrate the characteristics of crossover artists; everything is honed down to perfection so that the crossover phenomenon becomes total performance.

The Oak Ridge Boys (*Courtesy of MCA Records, Nashville*)

Barbara Mandrell

Barbara Mandrell was born in Houston, Texas in 1948 as the first daughter of parents who were both professionally involved in music. She showed strong interest in music very early in life, and her first instrument was the accordion. When she was six the family moved to Oceanside, California, where her father bought a music store. Barbara became very proficient on the steel guitar, and later picked up banjo, guitar, bass guitar, and saxophone.

She became a regular player on the California-based TV show "Town Hall Party" at the age of eleven. At twelve she appeared on a national television program "Five Star Jubilee," broadcast from Missouri. Irby Mandrell, her father, formed the Mandrell Family Band, working club dates in southern California. In 1967 she married the drummer of that original band, Ken Dudney. It was her intention at that point to give up music, but her new husband was in the air force and was shipped overseas.

She went to live with her family, which by this time included two more sisters with whom she would ultimately create the Mandrell Sisters. In 1968 the family moved to Nashville so that Irby could become involved in contracting. They went to a Grand Ole Opry performance that changed her life.

Barbara Mandrell was pretty versatile in her formative years. In 1968 she was all of twenty years old, and had played country, western swing, rock and roll, and pop music. Although she had all the technical skills necessary for success in any of these fields, she by no means felt more strongly about one than another. She had many musical skills, had practiced long hours, and could read music very well.

Barbara Mandrell (*Photo by Harry Langdon; used by courtesy of MCA Records, Nashville*)

She started working with the Curly Chalker Trio in Nashville, and soon came to the attention of producers. At that time she played steel guitar and did some singing. She got her first recording contract with Mosrite Records in 1969. Her first tunes were mostly rhythm and blues. One favorite recording was a song by Otis Redding, who was very popular in southern California. Among her hits over the years, the rhythm and blues tunes have sold well to black audiences, which is fairly untypical for country music.

Mandrell began to do more country tunes than anything else, and by 1972 was asked to join the Opry. She recorded for Columbia for five years. During that time she was consistently on the charts and also had crossover success, pop and rhythm and blues. In 1975 she moved to Dot, a subsidiary of ABC, which was bought out by MCA in 1979. By October of 1978 the Country Music Association started to recognize her; she was nominated for awards and by 1979 she started winning: Female Vocalist and Entertainer of the Year, among others.

With her younger sisters, Louise and Irlene, she began her own television series, which survived two seasons. That show's format illustrated crossover popularity in that it had the occasional humor of "Hee Haw" and the cleverness in format of a variety show with high-powered acts. But at the center of it was this feisty woman who played and sang her heart out.

Barbara Mandrell sings with an almost accentless voice—her childhood years in California had an influence. Yet the country quality of the playing, even backed with big orchestra, is unmistakable. Her saxophone playing has pop sound, but the three sisters create a country context in what they do on stage. And the songs, even when they are rockabilly or light pop tunes, always have a country basis.

The Mandrell Sisters, and Barbara in particular, live up to the dress code of crossover pop: they look like stars. Barbara's performances on television, at awards ceremonies, and on records illustrate the crossover potential of her music, and she has been a consistently successful superstar in rhythm and blues, pop, and country since 1978. Behind her success is a diversified career, hard practice, and continuous focus on career growth.

Kenny Rogers

Like Barbara Mandrell, Kenny Rogers was born in Houston, Texas. He was born in 1937, and so is a little older than Mandrell. He was the fourth of eight children, and the Rogers family by Kenny's own account was really poor. Although his early childhood is not marked by the same kind of precocious development enjoyed by Barbara Mandrell, Kenny Rogers did spend much of his time playing guitar and singing. In fact, he formed his first band to play rockabilly while still in high school. And they recorded their music, including one album.

He went to college at the University of Houston, but dropped out to play string bass and sing in a jazz group, the Bobby Doyle Trio, which put out a recording for Columbia in 1962. He left them to work for the Kirby Stone Four, then in 1966 he moved to Los Angeles to work with the New Christy Minstrels. He put out several solo singles during that time, but they were not highly successful.

In 1967 he and another Minstrel, Mike Settle, decided to form what would eventually be a five-member singing group, the First Edition, later called Kenny Rogers and the First Edition. This group was a good response to the kind of music being done at that time, and Kenny Rogers became quite popular as a result. He did a number of tunes that have remained Kenny Rogers tunes over time, including "Reuben James" and "Ruby." The First Edition was on the "Johnny Cash Show" and had its own syndicated series called "Rollin' on the River."

However, the First Edition began to wane in popularity and finally ended in bankruptcy. Kenny Rogers went out on his own in 1975 and did very poorly for a few years. He played small clubs and did television commercials. He credits his meeting with Marianne Gordon on "Hee Haw" as the most important thing at that point in his life, but I think also that his time had come.

He had signed a contract with United Artists/Liberty in 1975 but later switched to RCA. A few singles came out in 1975 but did not sell. In 1977 his recording of "Lucille" went to the top of both country and pop charts. His own composition, "Sweet Music Man," followed, and was a success. In fact, he collects good royalties from that song because it has been re-recorded a number of times. In early 1978 he recorded a duet with Dottie West, "Every Time Two Fools Collide," which was massively successful and also won them the Country Music Association Top Vocal Duo of the Year award of 1978, interrupting Conway Twitty and Loretta Lynn's eight-year winning streak.

Little needs to be said about Rogers' career since 1978 because his success is common knowledge. He has been in a number of films, including *The Gambler*. His live performances are almost intimate in style, although they are played in front of thousands of people. The 1984 performance had light shows in it, home movies of his child, and Rogers throwing souvenir frisbees to the rafters. His charisma captivated the audience.

His band is fairly large by country standards and includes a woodwind player. The sound is unmistakably crossover country, with a strong pop emphasis, but also with the ever-present steel guitar. He does a delightful combination of old and new songs, with at least half of them being pure country with an expanded background. His duet performances with other stars, particularly female stars, are dynamite.

But what is most intriguing is Kenny Rogers' voice. He has said in interviews that his most distinctive vocal quality is a gravelly voice; this can certainly be heard even on First Edition recordings. But I believe that it is the way he uses the gravel sound, transferring back and forth between a smooth voice and that vocal harshness at the right times (emphasizing certain feelings and words).

Rogers always seems to be self-deprecating. He is a good musician who has worked long and hard to perfect his craft. He just seems not to want to admit it. He communicates a love for his crowd and a genuine appreciation that they are willing to accept him. He has said publicly that he knows this love affair will not go on forever. He has tasted defeat before, and he seems to intend to appreciate the success he now has. Obviously one of the most important forces in country music today, he has had the opportunity to influence numbers of other musicians. As one of the most important, if not the most important, country musician in the late 1970s and 1980s, Kenny Rogers deserves all the success he has achieved.

16 Experimental Country and the Future

Experimentalism is not highly rewarded in country music, perhaps because country music is by definition fairly conservative. It is sometimes said that experimental country music can be found only outside of the traditional country center, Nashville. It is particularly difficult for innovators to break into the business in the recording centers. However, much of the experimentation is eventually recorded in Nashville, even if the artists have to wait until they are successful before they can do so. And even then, the experimentalism of country music is probably more subtle than it is in other kinds of music.

Experimentalism means doing something different from the normal, that is, from the current style. In that sense, a reversion to an older style could be experimental, as in the return to straight country by Conway Twitty. Some experimentation involves fusion. Other times, a particular technique or novelty device is used. Probably the most interesting form of experimentation in country music of the 1970s was country rock. The impact of country rock was felt in other types of experimentation, such as the blues revival in Texas and California. Rock and roll has had a significant impact on country music and has enjoyed a revival in rockabilly in the 1980s.

Experimentation is the creative act of producing change. Virtually every important musician mentioned in this book has had an impact by making some kind of change. Therefore this short discussion of musicians who have experimented with country music in the 1970s and 1980s is dedicated to those earlier innovators from Jimmie Rodgers on.

Danny Davis and the Nashville Brass

The Nashville Brass should certainly be the first experimental group to spring to anyone's mind, because the idea of playing country music using

Danny Davis and the Nashville Brass (*Courtesy of Danny Davis and the Nashville Brass*)

mostly brass instruments was truly unique. And it was not accepted easily by the Nashville establishment, although it would ultimately have great influence on Nashville. This particular band won numerous awards from around 1960 up through the 1970s, and has continued to sell records into the 1980s.

Danny Davis (George Nowlan) has a somewhat unusual background for a Nashville-based musician. Born in Massachusetts in 1925, he was a classical trumpet player; his mother was a singing teacher. At the age of fourteen he was a member of the Massachusetts All-State Orchestra. At fifteen he became a student at the New England Conservatory of Music; during that year he was offered a job by Gene Krupa, which he took. He subsequently was on the road with the big bands of Bob Crosby, Freddy Martin, and others.

After years of playing on the road, he went into artists-and-production work in New York City for RCA. He subsequently moved to Nashville as executive A & R producer with RCA Nashville. He and Chet Atkins had become friends during their playing days, and Chet believed that he could be valuable in Nashville. He worked with many country stars during the late 1960s and has continued in that capacity.

But he had an idea to add more than just one horn to a studio recording; he wanted to do the whole thing with brass and a rhythm section (it had been common practice to use one wind instrument on a recording, although

Ricky Skaggs (*Photo by Leonard Kamsler; used by courtesy of Epic Records, Nashville*)

usually it was a reed instrument or French horn). His first album in late 1968, called *The Nashville Brass Featuring Danny Davis Plays Nashville Sounds,* created a furor and was very popular. It also had important crossover popularity.

An extremely intelligent and well-trained musician, Danny Davis was an experimentalist of the first order. The fact that he was able to convince Chet Atkins to go along with this idea argues against the position some take, that Chet Atkins was autocratic. The idea of using a brass group was really unusual for Nashville. It was also highly successful and added a new dimension to country music. And although this particular experimentation happened prior to the 1970s, it had the sophisticated ring of 1970s country fusion to it.

Ricky Skaggs

Ricky Skaggs was really hot in late 1983 and 1984. His major recording work started in 1981. Unabashedly a bluegrass musician in the times of rock fusion, he represents the conservative side of country music. Yet by melding bluegrass and honky tonk, as he does in "Don't Let Your Sweet Love Die" from his *Highways and Heartaches* album, he puts himself clearly into the fusion category. His 1984 popularity probably represented the conservative backlash that occurs cyclically in country music. His music is refreshing and quite experimental, given the time frame.

Emmy Lou Harris

Emmy Lou Harris, a superstar of country music, was born in Alabama in 1947. She grew up in the South, yet was drawn by folk music; her first musical endeavor after quitting college was to go to New York to become a folksinger. She was signed by Jubilee Records in 1969, but her first album was not really successful. She returned to her parents' home in Washington, D.C. and lived there until 1971.

In 1971 she was asked to join the Flying Burrito Brothers, who had heard her sing in a club. Unfortunately, the Burrito Brothers had one of their breakups, so that did not work out. However, ex-Burrito Brother Gram Parsons asked her to record with him, which she did. His death in 1973 was devastating to Harris, who had really begun to develop.

However, in mid–1974 she signed with Warner Brothers and began making albums and singles that charted both in country and pop. Her innovative music has been very influential, and her duets with Don Williams clearly show why. Emmy Lou Harris sings country music in a varied style, sometimes bluesy and sometimes folksy. She is a perfect model of an experimenter—in this case, one who has been very successful.

Minnie Pearl

Minnie Pearl was an experimentalist. Born in Centerville, Tennessee in 1912, she was a regular member of the Grand Ole Opry starting in 1940, and was elected to the Country Music Hall of Fame in 1975 as a comedienne. In her experimentation, which she started in the 1930s, she made up a character and explained the human condition through it. She was optimistic at a time when so many people were sad.

One Minnie Pearl line has got to be included: When asked how one tells the difference between a hillbilly musician and a country musician, she responds, pointing to her mink coat, "When you can afford one of these, you are a country musician!"

Moe Bandy and Joe Stampley

Actually, Bandy and Stampley are listed here for one tune they did in the summer of 1984, "Where's the Dress?" But they have been around for a while, doing primarily novelty tunes.

This particular tune is a takeoff on Boy George, the male rock singer who dresses in female clothes. In "Where's the Dress?" they talk about how much money they could make if they wore dresses, and then decide to do it. It is a great tune because it makes fun of and comments on rock at the same time. It shows what country attitudes are and why they are different from rock attitudes. And it comments on the amount of money that rock musicians make but also on what they have to go through in order to do it. One is left with the question of whether or not a country musician would do the same. The song even says at one point that "Roy would not like that," referring to Roy Acuff.

Bandy and Stampley deserve to be called experimentalists for this one tune. We have had "Big Bad John" and all the trucking songs, but this novelty song goes way beyond the others. It is not only clever but also much deeper than first hearing would suggest.

Earl Scruggs

Earl Scruggs is of course one of the most venerated names in country music. Scruggs went through a decided career change when he separated from Lester Flatt. The reason for the split was that Scruggs wanted to experiment with more electric material.

Ultimately this led him to form a new band called the Earl Scruggs Revue. This would become an all-Scruggs family affair in 1978, much as

Moe Bandy and Joe Stampley (*Photo by Larry Dixon; used by courtesy of Columbia Records, Nashville*)

Dave Brubeck's band included his sons. The Scruggs revue is a high-energy bluegrass-country band; although it is not as way out as some people think, it represents a clear departure from standard bluegrass. It uses a full rhythm section and has a modern sound. Sadly, Scruggs is probably not as well respected as a result of this experiment, but I suspect he is much happier. His past successes, however, made possible this experimentation.

The Stray Cats

I wanted to include at least one rockabilly group because in a sense rockabilly really is different from southern or country rock. Rockabilly is something that stayed alive in England in its original form. And while we have had certain nostalgia groups in the United States who have stayed true to the 1950s style, the true rockabilly revival in the United States came from England.

England has been responsible for punk and new wave rock (which most country fans could probably ignore without much effort). One element of both punk and new wave is a revival of original 1950s rock and roll. A few groups from England who were recognized as new wave bands were really in a sense very much like the Memphis rockabilly musicians, only with British accents. One classic example is the Stray Cats.

The Stray Cats were actually from New York. A trio, they formed into a simple rockabilly group in 1979, but were unsuccessful. So they moved to London with their manager. They were very successful in England because of

Sawyer Brown (*Courtesy of James Scholten of Sawyer Brown*)

their almost cartoon caricature of 1950s rock and roll. They became a very popular club act and were recorded by Arista U.K. Their first single, "Runaway Boy," was successful in 1980 and their next two songs, "Stray Cat Strut" and "Rock This Joint," were even more so. So in order for this American group to make it big with an experiment in going back in time, they had to go to London.

There are many other blue-rockabilly bands that could be discussed in this same context: Rank and File, the LeRoi Brothers, and others.

Rank and File

Rank and File is a six-member group that was founded in late 1982. One of their compositions is discussed in the Appendix as an example of new wave rock/country. In some ways they were a country rock band because they played both rock tunes and country tunes. But it was their new wave sound when they did country rock that made them experimental. They had two albums out by 1984 and enjoyed some success with both country and rock progressive audiences.

Sawyer-Brown

This last group represents an entirely different kind of experiment. They did not come from Nashville; of the five musicians, three are from Michigan, one from Maine, and one from Florida. They won the TV "Star Search" contest, for which they were rewarded with a recording contract in Nashville. Their music that came out in late 1984 is definitely country music, but if you listen carefully you can hear subtle funk overtones (Michigan influence) and an occasional lick from the group Chicago. The way they got their recording contract is itself highly experimental: they won it on a television show. I think this new means by which to make it in Nashville is interesting and encouraging to the many musicians who have been told that one can only succeed in Nashville by being family or by knowing somebody (which may very well often be true).

Country music is big in many parts of the United States, but differs from one place to another. And Sawyer-Brown plays with an emphasis and set of stylistic characteristics very different from a typical Nashville band. The singer of the group is from Florida, but the band's sound is basically not southern.

Sawyer-Brown was on the Ralph Emery "Nashville Now" show several times in 1984; their enthusiastic reception suggests that their experiment worked. Actually, there is one more reason why I have mentioned Sawyer-Brown. The bass player was one of my students at one time. It is always nice to have your students make good.

CONCLUSION

We have arrived at the end of an arduous but enjoyable task. We have tried to tell the story of country music and to place its movements and influences into perspective. Where it has been logically necessary to disagree with standard conceptions of country music, we have not shirked our responsibility to do so.

However, in order to fully appreciate what has been written here and in order to make sense of the musical analysis, it is necessary to listen to country music on recordings, at concerts, and on television. I recommend the Nashville Network; I also recommend going to Nashville whenever possible. And I recommend country music as a source of inspiration; it has so many facets that it is capable of producing whatever is needed by the human spirit.

Appendix: For Musicians Only

This section contains discussions of representative compositions for chapters Three through Sixteen; two examples have been chosen for most chapters. This material has been placed here rather than in each chapter so the reading flow will not be broken. However, it is quite important that this material be used, perhaps in conjunction with reading the chapter. Further, although this appendix has been entitled *For Musicians Only,* please do not stop reading. Even if you have no previous musical training, the chances are very good that you can use the information and that it will enhance your understanding of country music. It may take a little more work for those without previous musical training, but the effort would be well worth it.

For ease in collecting the records necessary for this section, many of the examples have been chosen from either the *60 Years of Country Music* cassette or the six-album series called *History of Country Music*. However, there are some examples that are not on those two sources for some of the following reasons: (1) the artist is not represented because of permission problems; (2) it was desirable to include some examples from after the mid–1970s; or (3) the example chosen comes from a cassette or record that would be an extremely valuable addition to a basic country library. Some of the recordings are also available in the Smithsonian collection (see the discography) and the inclusion in that collection has been noted next to the title. However, please be advised that in many cases the version discussed and illustrated in the descriptive chart may differ from the Smithsonian version.

The specific form of the analysis of these pieces is designed to communicate to the broadest possible audience and is therefore rudimentary in nature. In a few instances, I have included actual chord changes based on the system used to explain the blues in Chapter One; this occurs later in each section and only where the chord changes are relatively simple to hear and to provide some assistance in understanding the composition. Many of the people reading this part of the book, especially those using it as a textbook, will want to flesh out the analyses further.

More information could be conveyed if one could quote the lyrics completely on top of a time line that gives the other information contained in the descriptions. However, quoting lyrics is simply cost-prohibitive. The individual copyright holders of these tunes charge a tremendous amount of money to quote lyrics or melody lines. I would heartily recommend that you write in above the descriptions in this appendix specific words that fit at certain points in the charts. I cannot for copyright reasons.

Many of the irregularities that exist in these tunes can be explained easily in terms of the needs of the lyric for extra beats—for example, a certain line of text may need more than four beats, say five beats. In many cases, for instance, in the Tom T. Hall song and in most of Jimmie Rodgers's compositions, that is exactly what happens. I have indicated where these irregularities occur. If I could write in the lyrics, I could illustrate the reason for the irregularity; but since I cannot, you will have to supply that information to make the descriptions more complete. It is a better learning experience if the learner actually does some of the work.

Lastly, some of you will be able to do much more in terms of analysis than I have done here. Of course, you are fortunate because you will be able to get even more out of country music than the majority of country music appreciators. In any event, this section is intended to provide some structural models for the way that country music functions and communicates, which is one of the primary aims of this book.

CHAPTER THREE

The first two compositions we will discuss are "Arkansas Traveler" by Eck Robertson and "The Prisoner's Song" (Smithsonian Side 1, No. 5) by Vernon Dalhart. These selections can both be found on *60 Years of Country Music* (RCA CPK2–4351).

"Arkansas Traveler" by Eck Robertson and Henry Gilliland

This is a fiddle duet played by Eck Robertson and Henry Gilliland, recorded in 1922. The playing style is fairly unimaginative but it is highly representative of that period. I might have chosen "Sally Goddin'" because it is more interesting musically, but I wanted to select a composition that would be fairly easy to hear for the first analysis.

The most important characteristic of this music that will help you understand my chart is the speed at which it moves or how to count beats. This piece moves along at a little over 210 beats per minute. The best way to figure out what that means is to watch a second hand on a clock and try even claps of your hands or tapping a hard surface so that you get seven claps in two seconds and then start the cycle over again on the third second. That is about the speed of this composition and the chart fits that rate of beats. The numbers below each section refer to the number of beats in each section. However, if in counting the whole piece you get half the number of beats, that is fine. You are just counting at half the speed that I did.

The rest of the chart refers to parts of the melody; in this case there are two parts to the melody (A and B). Each part is repeated (AABB) and this pattern happens five times with the first part stated just once for the ending. If you can listen to the piece, make sure that you listen to it enough times so that the chart makes sense to you. Then you will be able to handle all the remaining analyses without any problems. However, if you do not understand this one even after listening several times, the next piece might help.

If that one makes sense to you, then come back to this one and it probably will as well.

The piece is a typical old-style fiddle duet. It is similar to fiddle tunes that were brought to the colonies and transferred into fife music for the Revolutionary War. There is not much variation, but the melody is basically repeated with slight changes in the way the two fiddlers interact. It is a good example of old-time mountain instrumental style and that is why we considered it first.

210 beats/minute

Part A 16	Part A 16	Part B 16	Part B 16
Part A 16	Part A 16	Part B 16	Part B 16
Part A 16	Part A 16	Part B 16	Part B 16
Part A 16	Part A 16	Part B 16	Part B 16
Part A 16	Part A 16	Part B 16	Part B 16
Part A 16			

"The Prisoner's Song" by Vernon Dalhart

This lovely song is backed by guitar and violin and is in a much slower tempo than the previous tune. The speed is about 84 beats per minute or a little less than three beats per two seconds. The following chart describes this composition in the same format just used, with a few descriptive additions.

This particular style of playing is more classical in orientation, in that the fiddle (perhaps a viola rather than a violin, actually, given its low range) plays an obbligato line against the guitar chords. This particular fits much better with Dalhart's style, for after all he was also an operatic singer. It is a rather good example of using an instrumental style to fit the sound of the voice, or an early example of crossover style in country music.

84 beats/minute

Instrumental introduction—Fiddle and guitar
16 + 16 beats

Verse 1—Singing with guitar accompaniment
16 + 16

Verse 2—Singing with guitar accompaniment
16 + 16

Fiddle solo-Guitar accompaniment
16 + 16

Verse 3—Singing with guitar accompaniment
16 + 16

Verse 4—Singing with guitar accompaniment plus fiddle countermelody
16 + 16

Verse 5—Singing with guitar accompaniment plus fiddle countermelody

At the end there is an ascending plucked figure on the guitar that fits in beats 15 and 16 of the last section. The guitar accompaniment is otherwise consistent throughout and the vocal or fiddle melody is the same in all seven sections of the piece.

CHAPTER FOUR

"Blue Yodel No. 2" by Jimmie Rodgers

The first song analyzed is by Jimmie Rodgers, "Blue Yodel No. 2" ("T for Texas") (on *60 Years of Country Music*). This is a simple tune accompanied by guitar. It has six verses, with a simple yodeling figure that serves as a refrain. As a narrative tune it communicates a whole story and is delightful in its seeming simplicity. It is based on the following blues progression: 1 4 1 5 1. However, the simplicity stops here. This is a pretty hard tune to analyze and you may have some difficulty coming up with the same answer that I got. If you get a slightly different number of two-beat measures for each unit, do not be concerned; you might be right. The irregularity of this composition is a perfect example of the rhythmic accompaniment fitting the words and it would be fruitful to place the words on top of the specific number of measures suggested in the chart. It is a good example of orally transmitted music because it does not attempt to produce sameness but rather functionally uses the number of guitar chords necessary to communicate the entire lyric line. Although this was very popular it does represent an older style of composition; interestingly, this style is still done today because it represents the roots of country music (plus it is influenced by primitive blues).

In the following chart, I am assuming that the song goes about 84 beats per minute and that the measures are $^2/_4$ measures, that is, with two beats per measure. There is a short guitar introduction, followed by six verse and refrain patterns. No verse length is the same as any other although they work out to between 14½ to 16½ measures. The refrains are also flexible, with two of them having some extended guitar filler material. The black influence on Jimmie Rodgers is exemplified by the flexible rural style represented in the piece. Although other Jimmie Rodgers tunes would be easier to analyze, this is his most popular and probably best represents his actual style. The irregularity of the performance should not be considered as weak; it is characteristic of the style at that time.

84 beats/minute   2 beats/measure

Guitar introduction
3 measures

Verse 1	Yodel refrain
15	4½
Verse 2	Yodel refrain
16½	3½
Verse 3	Yodel refrain
16¼	4¾
Verse 4	Yodel refrain
14	6 guitar fill
Verse 5	Yodel refrain
16½	8 guitar fill
Verse 6	Yodel refrain
14½	4

N.B. If you try to count this you might listen carefully to the changes in the blues progression (if you can hear them); chords or basic notes change at different points in various verses to accommodate the words.

"Wildwood Flower" (Smithsonian Side 2, No. 7) by the Carter Family

This piece is simple by comparison to the Jimmie Rodgers tune and may well have exhibited the style that so captivated Ralph Peer. This recording was made in 1928 and features guitar accompaniment of a fairly complicated nature for that time. The lead singing is done by Sara Carter in a sweet song that is fairly regular (although it does have one irregularity). The sections of music are the same throughout, starting with guitar alone and then a verse. The speed is about 120 beats per minute, with two beats per measure in the chart.

Each section of music is nineteen measures long, divided as follows: 5 + 5 + 4 + 5. The music for each of the sections with five-measures is the same and the music for the four-measure section is different, yielding an AABA structure, which is fairly common. The five-measure phrase could be explained as an elongation, but it probably would be best to say simply that this was the style of this piece. Although more regular in section repetitions, this piece exhibits its rural and folk-like character in the use of the five-measure phrase.

120 beats/minute   2 beats/measure

Guitar
5 5 4 5 = 19 measures
Verse 1
19
Guitar
19
Verse 2
19
Guitar
19
Verse 3
19
Guitar
19
Verse 4
19
Guitar
19

CHAPTER FIVE

Two selections I will analyze here are by the Sons of the Pioneers and Gene Autry and they are the same song, "Tumbling Tumbleweeds" (Smithsonian Side 5, No. 2). They can be found on the following cassette tapes: *Way Out West: The Sons of the Pioneers* available from the Country Music Foundation, 4 Music Square East, Nashville, TN, 37203; and *Gene Autry* Columbia Historic Edition, FCT 37465.

I decided to do two versions of the same song because I wanted to show the comparison between the two, which are so different. These differences clearly illustrate the stylistic traits of the Sons of the Pioneers as basically a folk group and Gene Autry as a pop artist. The Sons of the Pioneers version is irregular and somewhat similar to the Jimmie Rodgers tune we analyzed. The Gene Autry version is absolutely regular and is analogous to the Carter Family composition of the same chapter.

Frankly, you might want to skip trying to reconcile my chart of the first version with your own hearing of it, although I would advocate getting the cassette and listening to it. The composition is so incredibly irregular that it almost defies analysis. Without analyzing it, one would never guess it was so irregular because the style sounds so smooth. Undoubtedly, this is a fine example of musicians working so closely with each other that they could sing something this disjointed and make it sound so smooth. Everything in the recording is so well done that it sounds like it is perfectly straightforward when in fact the underlying structure is terribly complicated.

On the other hand, the Gene Autry version is a typical example of crossover music because it is so regular it is almost predictable. Even after listening to it only once, you can almost tell what will happen next. And that is the mark of good commercial music (or music that will appeal to a large audience). Only occasionally does music that is not perfectly regular have mass appeal. Fortunately, the Sons of the Pioneers sold lots of records anyway because the complexity was disguised.

"Tumbling Tumbleweeds" by the Sons of the Pioneers

This piece goes about 92 beats per minute in measures of four beats each. Guitar and fiddle are used for accompaniment and the guitar plays throughout. The numbers below each section refer to measures with actual number of beats in parentheses. Again, my suggestion is not to try to reconcile the number of measures and beats that I have. You will undoubtedly come up with different answers but you would find that it is fairly irregular. What we find in this piece is an extension of five beats at the end of each phrase and then beginning the next phrase right after that. The precise reason for the irregularity is the length of the line "Drifting along with the tumbling tumbleweeds." The Sons of the Pioneers take five beats to sing that line, causing the irregularity discussed previously.

92 beats/minute   4 beats/measure

Guitar and fiddle intro (starts with one guitar chord)
  4 measures (16 beats)
Group vocal refrain
  3¼ (13)
Solo vocal
  12 (48)
Group vocal
  27¾ (111)
Fiddle solo
  4 (16)
Group vocal refrain
  2 (8)
Indeterminate ending

"Tumbling Tumbleweeds" by Gene Autry

This tune is the easiest to count yet, and if you have not understood the analysis so far, this piece should make it obvious. The piece goes about 96 beats per minute with clear measures of four beats each. In fact, the piece starts with four guitar chords, one beat each, which set up the tempo. So if you are listening to the piece, just listen to those four guitar chords and you will have the beat speed.

Everything is sung, either by the vocal group or as a solo by Gene Autry. There are three different melodies that can be heard very easily. One serves as a refrain attached to each different verse. But the main thing is to count beats and try to follow the chart. Although the first version of this song by the Sons of the Pioneers actually has the same lyric structure as the Gene Autry version, the even-measured units in the second version illustrate the verse, verse, refrain, verse or AABA form in a clearer fashion.

96 beats/minute   4 beats/measure

Short guitar intro—four beats for four chords.
  1 measure
Verse 1 Group vocal accompanied by mandolin and guitar
  8 + 8
Solo bridge with violin
  4 (melody 2)
Verse 2 Group vocal
  8 + 8
Vocal solo
  8 (melody 3) + 4 (melody 2)
Vocal group (repetition of verse 1)
  8 + 8
Solo vocal
  4 (melody 2, same words as before)
Vocal group (part of verse 2)
  8

"Right or Wrong" by Bob Wills and the Texas Playboys

This next piece for consideration can be found on a cassette titled *Bob Wills,* Columbia Historic Edition, FCT 37468. This is a re-issue of a 1936 recording that appeared on several original 78s. The instrumentation in this piece is as follows: two fiddles, guitar, steel guitar, banjo, bass, piano, drums, two saxophones, and trumpet. The lead vocalist in this piece is Tommy Duncan. This is a good early representative of the Bob Wills style in that the western string band influence is there, but also present is the beginning of a big band style. There is little improvisation, but the sense of early swing style is present throughout.

The piece is fairly regular and the speed is about 92 beats per minute in measures of two beats each. You might hear the piece as going twice as fast, in which case double the number of measures given in the chart. The melody is broken into four eight-measure phrases, with the first and third phrases being basically the same; the second and fourth phrases are different. Therefore, the basic structure of the melody is ABAC. There is one slight iregularity in the piece because before each sung verse there is a one-beat extension for the pickup to the words. The instrumental section starts right on the first beat. In the first sung verse there are vocal answers by an unnamed person. In the second sung verse the lead singer is on his own; one hears a change in the melody to higher notes for emphasis, and a little yodelling. Be sure to notice the fiddle playing of Bob Wills and the examples of blues-like slurring of notes.

92 beats/minute   2 beats/measure

Instrumental chorus—fiddle playing the lead melody
  32 measures (1 extra beat at end of phrase)
Verse 1—lead vocalist with responding words
  32
Instrumental chorus—trumpet lead with sax harmonies
  32 (1 extra beat at end of phrase)
Verse 2—Lead vocalist with yodelling and change of melody
  32
Standard big band ending

"Shame on You" by Spade Cooley

Cooley's big hit of 1945 can be found on *Spade Cooley,* a Columbia History Edition cassette, FCT 37467. This piece uses a fairly extended western swing orchestra that mainly features a large string section, full rhythm section, and a standard string band. No information on personnel or instrumentation was available on this recording; I do not hear any horns but I think I hear an accordion. Take a listen and see what you think.

The piece moves along at about 100 beats per minute in measures of two beats each, just a little faster than the Bob Wills piece. It definitely is in big band style and sounds like pop hits from that era. However, it does have some fairly standard western song characteristics as well, in particular the predominance of solo fiddle and the violin section. In fact, the Spade Cooley trademark was the extensive use of violin sections.

This composition has eight equal sections, with a four-measure introduction. The eight sections have sixteen measures each and the piece is perfectly regular; this very well may have been one of the reasons why it was such a smash hit. The four-measure intro is a fiddle rendition of the melody (or part of it) that is joined by the violin section toward the end of the third measure. Sections 1, 2, 4, 6, and 8 are sung with basically the same pattern each time—twelve measures of solo voice and then four measures of ensemble response. Each verse is slightly different, but the ensemble response is always the same. Section 3 is a steel guitar solo, first pretty close to the melody and then clearly improvised toward the end. Section 5 is a repetition of the melody by violins in harmony. Section 7 is full ensemble with the steel guitar playing the lead, then breaking into another solo section for the steel guitar.

The final ensemble voice response changes the vocal harmonies to provide a conclusive ending, and then someone says "Oh lady, shame on you." This piece is a very satisfying example of full-orchestrated western swing of the mid–1940s, partly because of its popularity but also because it contains so many elements discussed in this appendix. It is also a good example because the sections are very clear and it is easy to analyze.

100 beats/minute   2 beats/measure

Introduction—fiddles
  4

1. Verse 1	Solo singer	Ensemble singing
	12	4
2. Verse 2	Solo singer	Ensemble singing
	12	4
3. Steel Guitar solo		
	16	
4. Verse 3	Solo singer	Ensemble singing

12 4

5. Violins play melody in harmony

16

6. Verse 4 Solo singer Ensemble singing

12 4

7. Ensemble plays melody; steel guitar lead, then Solo

16

8. Verse 5 Solo singer Ensemble singing

16 4 (with altered ending)

Spoken ending: "Oh lady, shame on you"

CHAPTER SIX

"Y'All Come" by the Bluegrass Boys

The first piece we will consider here can be found on MCAC-17, an MCA cassette called *Bill Monroe's Greatest Hits.* This particular piece is in classic Bill Monroe bluegrass style. The piece moves along about 138 beats per minute in measures of two beats each. There are nine units of sixteen measures each and the piece is perfectly regular. There are solos for the banjo and the fiddle and a refrain that no one will miss. There are three different verses of text, sung to the same musical accompaniment each time. There is relatively little change in the musical texture in this piece. Notice especially the high singing character of Bill Monroe and the closed-position harmony of the ensemble voices that respond to the refrain solo.

138 beats/min 2 beats/measure

Banjo solo with group accompaniment

16

Verse 1—solo voice

16

Refrain—solo voice with ensemble vocal response

16

Fiddle solo with group accompaniment

16

Verse 2—solo voice

16

Refrain—same as before

16

Banjo solo with group accompaniment

16

Verse 3—solo voice

16

Refrain—same as before

16

"Foggy Mountain Special" by the Foggy Mountain Boys

This piece can be found on a cassette entitled *Flatt and Scruggs,* Columbia Historic Edition FCT 37469. It moves at 120 beats per minute or two beats per second. The music is in nine sections of twelve measures each and, interestingly, follows a straight blues progression. Therefore, it should be fairly easy to track. However, the problem is that there are no words in this tune, so the technique I suggest is to listen for the solo instruments. The design makes it obvious who was in control in the Flatt and Scruggs band, as five out of nine choruses are for banjo.

This piece illustrates well the technique of Earl Scruggs, and you might want to listen to the piece with just that in mind. However, do not fail to listen to the bass solo in which the performer plays by himself, with occasional punctuated chords to keep the rhythm going; this technique is called *stop-time* and can be found in black rhythm and blues of the 1940s and rock and roll of the 1950s. Ray Charles used this technique extensively. All in all, this piece is a good example of bluegrass because it shows each of its elements rather satisfactorily. You can also hear an example of improvisation by each of the traditional bluegrass instruments.

120 beats/minute	2 beats/measure	
1. Banjo	12	
2. Banjo	12	
3. Fiddle	12	
4. Banjo	12	octave leap and chromatic
5. Bass	12	stop time
6. Banjo	12	
7. Guitar	12	
8. Mandolin	12	
9. Banjo	12	listen for bending notes at the end

"Yakety Axe" by Chet Atkins

The title of the next piece discussed is a takeoff on Boots Randolph's "Yakety Sax." It is totally instrumental, with most of the work being guitar solo, a basic melody at the beginning and end with improvisation in the middle. The piece moves along at about 132 beats per minute in measures of two beats each. There is a short instrumental introduction of four measures followed by seven sections of sixteen measures each. A two-measure tag ending provides the conclusion. As a pop instrumental, this particular tune had crossover success and illustrates Chet Atkins's complicated yet soft country sound.

One should listen especially for the types of improvisations Chet does on this tune, and also to the harmonica solo. The instrumental group backing this is a standard rhythm section. This piece is nicely structured and is satisfying from the listener's point of view. You can hear the melody even when it is changed in section 3, and the improvisation is clearly marked off with a nice return to the original melody for the last two sections. This piece can be found on the cassette *60 Years of Country Music.*

132 beats/minute	2 beats/measure	
1. Instrumental introduction	4	
2. Guitar plays melody	16	
3. Guitar repeats melody	16	
4. Guitar with new melody	16	
5. Guitar Improvisation	16	notice use of bass notes
6. Harmonica solo	16	
7. Original Guitar melody	16	
8. Original Guitar melody	16	
9. Short tag ending (notes are 8 5565 78)	2 measures	

"Yesterday When I Was Young" by Roy Clark

The next piece, done by Roy Clark in 1969, is very commercial. In fact, "Yesterday When I Was Young" was successful in both the country and pop fields, for good reason. It is country only in some ways. It uses guitar rather extensively but it also uses a full string section. The piece can be found on Volume 6 of the *History of Country Music* series.

The piece is a ballad and moves at about 112 beats per minute in four-beat measures. It starts with spoken lyrics after a short guitar sequence. There are eight sections of eight measures each; only section 5 is light guitar improvisation. Everything else is sung. The main interest in this piece from a structural perspective is the way in which the verses are each backed with different instrumental forces. The piece moves nicely to a textural climax in the middle sections, where a light rock beat takes over, with the beginning and the ending being subdued and accompanied by acoustic guitar. The guitar solo is very tasty and, although it does not sound difficult, is very well played by Roy Clark. There is a very fine figure on the guitar to end the piece.

112 beats/minute 4 beats/measure

Guitar introduction

Spoken dialogue over guitar background

Section 1—sung with guitar accompaniment

8

Section 2—sung with addition of strings

8

Section 3—sung with background voices and full orchestra; rock beat is added

8

Section 4—sung with same vocal ensemble and backup but slightly more intense

8

Section 5—tasty guitar solo with string accompaniment

8

Section 6—sung with same background as section 3

8

Section 7—sung with similar background to section 6

8

Section 8—sung with acoustic guitar and thin texture, slowing down toward the end and dissolving into a simple guitar figure for the ending

8

CHAPTER SEVEN

"I'm Moving On" (Smithsonian Side 9, No. 6) by Hank Snow

The first piece can be found on the cassette entitled *60 Years of Country Music*. A typical example of honky tonk music, this piece features Hank Snow singing, with a fiddle break and a guitar break. It is fairly easy to follow if you do not try to count the beats. The sung verses and the two solo breaks are thirteen measures long each and have irregular phrasing within the section unit. The piece moves along (joke) at about 108 beats per minute in two-beat measures.

108 beats/minute 2 beats/measure

1. Instrumental introduction	8
2. Verse 1—sung	13
3. Verse 2—sung	13
4. Fiddle break	13
5. Verse 3—sung	13
6. Verse 4—sung	13
7. Guitar break	13
8. Verse 5—sung	13
9. Verse 6—sung	13
10. Verse 7—sung	13
11. Instrumental interlude	4
12. Verse 8—sung	13
13. Instrumental ending and fade-out	13 8

"Your Cheating Heart" by Hank Williams

This song can be found in the *History of Country Music* series. It is a fairly short song, full of poignant feelings and definitely honky tonk. It is absolutely regular in structure, moved along at about 144 beats per minute in four-beat measures. It is a standard ballad form with a main melody of eight measures and a repeat, then a different bridge melody of eight measures and a repeat of the first melody of eight measures. There are two complete renditions of the ballad form, with an interlude of guitar on the bridge and then fiddle on the first melody.

144 beats/minute 4 beats/measure

1. Instrumental interlude 4				
2. Verse 1—sung	first melody 8	first melody 8	bridge 8	first melody 8
3. Guitar lead	bridge melody 8			
4. Fiddle lead	first melody 8			
5. Verse 2—sung	same structure as verse 1 8	8	8	8

CHAPTER EIGHT

The two tunes selected for this chapter are Elvis Presley's "Heartbreak Hotel" and Conway Twitty's "I Can't Stop Loving You." They both can be found on the *60 Years of Country Music* cassette. One is a good example of a rockabilly shouter and the other, a rockabilly ballad. As such they perfectly illustrate the style of the Memphis connection.

"Heartbreak Hotel" by Elvis Presley

This piece is backed by piano, bass, drums, and guitar and moves along at about 104 beats per minute in measures of four beats each. It is unusual in not having an instrumental introduction. There are six sections of eight measures each and the progression is a standard country progression with some blues overtones to it: 1 1 1 1 4 4 5 1.

There are of course some specific vocal qualities in this piece that illustrate well points made in the chapter. The song features a large vocal range, the first half of the song is in a high wailing sound and the second half is low and more subdued. Presley uses vibrato very effectively in this tune and uses a voice quiver on the word "baby." He also switches from thin voice to full voice. And he uses an emotional trick in gasping right after the word "baby."

104 beats/minute   4 beats/measure

Verse 1 sung in stop time (singing, then two chords)
8
Verse 2
8
Verse 3
8
Verse 4
8
Guitar solo, then piano
4   4
Verse 5
8

"I Can't Stop Loving You" by Conway Twitty

The next piece features a four-beat measure, but each of the beats is divided into three parts, giving a twelve-beat feeling, which you can hear in the piano part. Just listen for something that is very repetitious. The piece moves at about the same speed as the previous one, although it is clearly a ballad rather than a shouter. It uses background vocal singing and the same instrumentation as the previous piece. The instrumentation is especially indicative of the southern rockabilly style and the ballad is a good example of that style. Melody 1 is supported by the chord progression 1 1 4 4 1 5 1-5 1; Melody 2 is supported by the chord progression 4 4 1 1 5 5 1 1.

104 beats/minute   4 beats/measure

Instrumental introduction
4
Singing with background vocals—Melody 1
8
Singing with background vocals—Melody 1
8
Singing with background vocals—Melody 2
8
Singing with background vocals—Melody 2
8
Singing with background vocals—Melody 1
8
Singing with background vocals—Melody 1
8

CHAPTER NINE

The two pieces we will discuss in this section are Patsy Cline's 1957 hit "Walking after Midnight" and Hawkshaw Hawkins's "Lonesome 7–7203" from 1963. These are chosen as early examples of the Nashville sound. They both illustrate the new sophistication of the sound emanating from Nashville. The two recordings can be found in the *History of Country Music* Series, Volume 6.

"Walking after Midnight" by Patsy Cline

This first song is a sophisticated honky tonk tune. It was clearly influenced by the pop movement in country music and in fact did have crossover popularity. However, the lyric and playing style are pure traditional country. Set in a fairly slow tempo (about 106 beats per minute in four-beat measures), it is a typical example of a sophisticated structure and excellent backup work that so typified the Nashville sound. Accompanied by drums, bass, steel guitar, and fiddle, Patsy sings about walking around searching for love. After an instrumental beginning, Patsy sings the main lyric in a 32-measure form. There is one eight-measure melody that is repeated, then an eight-measure bridge or different melody, followed by one more version of the first melody. This sung section is followed by a four-measure instrumental section and then Patsy concludes with the eight-measure bridge and one more eight-measure repetition of the first melody. The song is perfectly regular and counting it is quite easy.

The singing style is very clear and precise. It is a relatively simple song conveying feelings that were quite current at the time and also typical of country songs. Nashville presence is obvious in this tune; although the recording quality is old-fashioned to us now, it was quite good for its time. This is a commercial recording and fits the model previously described for Nashville sound.

106 beats/minute	4 beats/measure			
Instrumental introduction			Fiddle dominant	
4				
Vocal section	Melody 1	Melody 1	Bridge	Melody 1
	8	8	8	8
Fiddle extemporizes throughout the song				
Instrumental Interlude				
4	Steel guitar + fiddle			
Vocal section	Bridge	Melody 1		
	8	8		

Stock Nashville ending—one chord allowed to ring and decay to silence.

"Lonesome 7–7203" by Hawkshaw Hawkins

This next song was recorded in 1963 shortly before Hawkins's death. The background instrumental group is a typical rhythm section but also includes a piano, which has an extensive role in this piece; over all, the vocals are dominant. The speed is about 126 beats per minute in four-beat measures. The lyric is about a phone number and the suggestion that if his girl is ever lonesome she can call this number. It is a platonic song in that it talks about boy-girl relationships but in a rather nonphysical sense. It is clearly a traditional country song and not honky tonk influenced in lyric so much as in the background playing style, which is very reminiscent of barrelhouse piano style.

Hawkins uses a very clear voice, slight vocal slides, and a light vibrato. Although his vocal inflections are clearly southern, this piece features very clear diction, another mark of the Nashville influence. It is pretty typical Nashville sound of the early 1960s in instrumentation, quality of vocal presentation, and subject matter. Perfectly regular in phrase lengths, it communicates through a structure that is very easy to follow.

126 beats/minute 4 beats/measure

Instrumental introduction
 4
Verse 1—voice
 16
Verse 2—voice
 16
Instrumental interlude—mainly piano
 4 (the music is taken from the last four measures of the previous phrase)
Verse 3—voice
 16
Verse 4—voice
 16 + 4 (last 4 measures of phrase are repeated)

CHAPTER TEN

The two pieces selected for analysis of crooning tunes are "He'll Have to Go" (Smithsonian Side 11, No. 6) by Jim Reeves from 1959 and "Make the World Go Away" by Eddy Arnold from 1965. I picked these tunes because they are both contained on the *60 Years of Country Music* tape, and usually the tunes that people from the Country Hall of Fame pick for inclusion on an anthology are the most important tunes from that era. But also I picked them because one is a tune from the late 1950s with a relatively simple instrumental background, and the other is from the mid–1960s and uses a bigger orchestra. The vocal quality of the singing voices is unmistakably crooning.

"He'll Have to Go" by Jim Reeves

This first piece has a simple rhythm section of piano, bass, drums, and vibraphone. A vibraphone, which is a jazz rather than a country instrument, is similar to a xylophone. Its set of metallic keys are hit with round mallets; underneath the keys are metal resonating tubes, with vibrating disks in each tube. When amplified it can produce a percussive organ effect. The vibraphone is very effective in this piece in its support of the emotional content.

The piece moves along at about 90 beats per minute in measures of three beats each (quite often, country crooning songs, and in fact many old time country tunes, are in three-beat measures). The piece starts with a four-measure introduction, then singing by the soloist and a background group. There are two verses of sixteen measures each, an eight-measure bridge with different music, and the concluding sixteen-measure verse with a slowing down effect at the end. The piece is perfectly regular and is very easy to hear the first time. Note especially the places where the background vocals are used (primarily at the ends of phrases) and the way the vibraphone is used to fill out phrases as well.

90 beats/minute 3 beats/measure

Instrumental introduction

4

Verse 1—voice

16

Verse 2—voice

16

Bridge—voice

8

Verse 3—voice (slowing down)

16

"Make the World Go Away" by Eddy Arnold

"Make the World Go Away" is a classic mid–1960s crooning tune with a prototypical Nashville sound: big orchestra and smooth quality. Although Eddy Arnold had been around since the 1940s and helped develop that sound, he is at his best in this recording. The composition defines the style for mainstream Nashville sound in the middle of its most influential period. The orchestral sound is most impressive and certainly illustrates the tremendous crossover popularity of Nashville sound recordings and especially the crooning tunes.

The composition moves along in four-beat measures at a speed of about 86 beats per minute. The piece uses a standard rhythm section for Nashville sound recordings, with piano being dominant. Also, a full string section is employed. The main filling instrument are the piano and, occasionally, the strings. Especially in crooning tunes it is essential to have a filling instrument because there tends to be some notes at the ends of phrases that are long in duration. This is where you will hear the most piano playing.

The composition itself is rather nicely structured into eight-measure units. The only difficulty is that the singing starts immediately without an instrumental introduction; counting this tune requires counting three beats at the beginning and then starting the eight-measure units. In essence, the whole piece is displaced by three-beat units but it really should be counted that way. At the end the last measures of the refrain are simply repeated. In my estimation, the only weakness in the piece is its ending, which sounds anticlimactic and somewhat like an afterthought.

86 beats/minute   4 beats/measure

Refrain

3 beats + 8 measures

Verse 1

8

Refrain

8

Verse 2

8

Refrain

8 + 4 (last four measures repeated)

CHAPTER ELEVEN

"Big Bad John" by Jimmy Dean

This 1961 hit was written on the way to a recording session. An experimental tune, it is also a saga song because it tells the story of a mining accident and a hero, but it is spoken in parts. In charting the piece we quickly see it is rather complicated because of the narration. However, since we have had so much practice by now, we should be able to follow it. This piece can be found on the *History of Country Music* series on Volume 3.

There is a rather obvious refrain repeated many times during the piece; in fact, the refrain is sung first. Generally the refrain should be counted as a one-beat beginning and then four full measures. The piece moves at about 92 beats per minute in four-beat measures and the piece has a modulation or change of key at the end of the fourth rendition of the refrain. After that the orchestra gets bigger and there is a fiddle obbligato in back of the speaking. This is obviously a studio recording because we have a number of different instrumental textures including a full big-band ending at the conclusion.

92 beats/minute   4 beats/measure

Refrain—sung by vocal group with speaking/singing at the end by Dean
  1 beat + 4 measures (or 1/4 + 4)
Verse 1—spoken
  5 + 4 3/4
Refrain
  1/4 + 4
Verse 2
  5 + 4 3/4
Refrain
  1/4 + 4
Verse 3
  5 + 4 3/4
Refrain—modulation in last measure
  1/4 + 3 + 1 (change of key and bigger orchestra)
Verse 4 (fiddle background)
  5 + 4 3/4
Refrain
  1/4 + 4
Verse 5 (lighter texture)
  5 + 4 3/4
Refrain
  1/4 + 4 + 1
Spoken section and big band ending

"9 to 5" by Dolly Parton

This song might seem a little out of place with older novelty tunes, but it really is a good example of the genre, and one which few readers will have trouble identifying. Other than its novelty factor—the hook "9 to 5"—the lyrics speak to common feelings of frustration. It is a delightful country tune, successfully designed for crossover popularity. The song won many awards. This recording is available at your local record store and has not yet been made a part of a recorded anthology.

Musically the composition is not very complicated, unlike the previous composition, "Big Bad John," which was complicated because of the speaking part and in that sense was more like traditional country music than most novelty tunes. "9 to 5" has a big band introduction, which is consistent with contemporary crossover Nashville music. After a four-measure introduction there are two basic melodies, a verse and a refrain, "9 to 5." The refrain is repeated six times during the piece, with alternating words in between the words "9 to 5."

The piece moves along at about 116 beats per minute (or about disco tempo) in measures of four beats each. The background group is a full studio dance band type of orchestra with heavy drums and bass; the whole composition has a funk or disco feel to it. The composition uses a number of electronic effects, including overdubbing of voices.

After the four-measure instrumental introduction, the first verse (eight measures) is sung without background voices and with light instrumentation. When the refrain starts, extra voices are added and the instrumentation gets heavier (along with the beat). The refrain is done twice and is eight measures long for the basic unit. After the refrain there is a two-measure instrumental interlude. A second verse is sung by Parton alone, with a light steel guitar figure in back of it. Then the refrain is repeated four times; during the last time it fades out slowly into nothingness and in fact you cannot hear the last measure of the fourth version.

116 beats/minute   4 beats/measure

Introduction Big band
 4
Verse 1—Solo
 8
Refrain—overdubbed voices
 8
Refrain
 8
Instrumental interlude
 2
Verse 2—solo with steel guitar background
 8
Refrain
 8
Refrain
 8
Refrain
 8
Refrain—fading out
 6 or 7 (depends on how sensitive your record player is)

CHAPTER TWELVE

"Good Hearted Woman" by Waylon Jennings

The first piece for this section is located on the *60 Years of Country Music* cassette; it is an excellent example of the style of Waylon Jennings and his band, the Waylors. It features a rock rhythm section with steel guitar in a song based on eight-measure units. The chord progression for this eight-measure unit is 1 1 4 4 5 5 1 1. The song moves along at 115 beats per minute in four-beat measures.

The singing style of Waylon Jennings is illustrated well on this recording: he sings the song in such a way that most of the words are done early in the musical phrase with instrumental filler toward the end of each phrase. From an instrumental and textural point of view, the song builds to the first refrain, where there is a stronger double-time feel. Then verse 2 gets gradually softer towards the end, when a bass note is held and the song actually stops. Next there is a modulation from the original key of D major and the refrain begins in E major. This particular kind of modulation is rather unusual in that most country modulations go up a half step, while this one is a whole step. From that point on the refrain is done four times, the last time fading out to silence.

Of great interest is the timing of entrance of the drums in the second half of the first verse. Then the background singers enter in the first refrain with steel guitar countermelodies. The singers first sing the words with Waylon and then hum to provide a choral texture behind the singing of the refrain. The bass part is strong throughout the piece but is further emphasized as other instruments are added.

115 beats/minute	4 beats/measure			
Introduction	2			instrumental (D major)
Verse 1	8	+	8	solo singing with drums added in second 8
Refrain	8	+	8	background singing, steel guitar fills and doubletime feel
Verse 2	8	+	8	solo singing ending with held bass note
modulation to E major				
Refrain	8 + 8 + 8 + 8			fadeout at end of phrase

"So You Think You're a Cowboy" by Willie Nelson

This song can be found on the album *Outlaw Country* (Realistic Cat. No. 51-7004 by Radio Shack). I selected this particular recording because it is an excellent example of Willie Nelson, both vocally and instrumentally, and also because I think this is a good basic country album to own. It also has a George Jones tune on it that I discussed under Chapter Fourteen. You can get this recording on other albums but I think you ought to get this album.

The piece uses rhythm guitar, bass, drums, electric piano, and harmonica. It is in three-beat measures, at a speed of about 138 beats per minute. There are two chord progressions, one for the verse and one for the refrain, as follows: verse —1 1 4 1 5 5 1 1 and refrain—4 4 1 1 5 5 1 1. From the following chart you can tell that the piece does build up instrumentally until the harmonica solo takes over. That solo is interesting in style, sort of a cross between a country and a blues solo.

The lyrics discuss a dream and perhaps the futility of that dream. Typical of Willie Nelson tunes, it is somewhat more complicated than one might think at first. Willie sings in a soft style that has some variation to it. The song is a continuous narrative in the way that he sings the words at beginnings of phrases and then leaves blank spots, similar to Waylon's style.

138 beats/minute	3 beats/measure	
(No introduction)		
Refrain	8 + 8	acoustic guitar and light bass
Verse 1	8 + 8	drums added
Refrain	8 + 8	electric piano added
No singing	8 + 8	harmonica solo
Verse 2	8 + 8	
Refrain	8 + 8	adds harmonica for fills
Refrain	4	last four measures of refrain to held note

"My Heart Skips a Beat" by Buck Owens

This 1964 Buck Owens hit is a delightful example of the kinds of hits Buck Owens turned out, making Bakersfield the important town that it was to country music in the 1960s. This song illustrates the character of the Bakersfield sound. It is not smooth in style like Nashville music was, although it does use a background chorus. What we near is a pop rhythm section with a much stronger drum role than would exist in Nashville music of the same era. The drummer actually provides the instrumental hook of this piece with the fills before the word "skips," which occurs at the beginning of each eight-measure phrase or before the verse. The guitar solo as well is in a much different style than was being used in Nashville. Of great interest is the opening phrase, which is an intro of 2 1/2 measures or ten beats (seven are instrumental and three, a vocal lead-in to the word "skips"). Other than this, the song divides evenly into eight-measure phrases.

The song moves at about 94 beats per measure in four-beat measures. The background chorus is used only for the refrain, so it will be easy to identify the refrain; in fact, you cannot help but hear it because of the growth in textural sound at that point.

94 beats/minute	4 beats/measure	
Introduction	2 1/2 (10 beats)	7 beats instrumental/3 vocal
Refrain	8	background chorus
Verse 1	8	solo singing
Refrain	8	background chorus
Guitar	8	solo
Verse 2	8	solo singing
Refrain	8	background chorus

Stock ending with guitar leading the melody to a held note

"I Think I'll Just Stay Here and Drink" by Merle Haggard

"I Think I'll Just Stay Here and Drink" can be found on Merle Haggard's *Greatest Hits* album (MCA 5386). This 1980 composition is a fine example of contemporary Merle Haggard; another good example is his 1984 top single "Let's Chase Each Other Round the Room." This piece is a standard country drinking song, a genre for which Merle is justifiably famous. However, the most interesting quality of this particular tune is the way the instrumental forces are used because it is in this area that Merle Haggard made a special contribution.

The piece moves at about 96 beats per minute in four-beat measures and is honky tonk country rock. The singing style is pure honky tonk country, but the playing style is halfway between country and rock. It uses drums, bass, guitar, piano (barrelhouse style), saxophone, and steel guitar. The actual formal structure of the composition is not that complicated; the chord progression of the eight-measure phrase used twelve times is as follows: 4 4 1 1 5 5 1 1. The most interesting character of that progression is that in the sixth measure only the first beat is played by the rhythm section. This gives a stop-time characteristic to the lyric, and clearly this is the instrumental hook of the piece.

Instrumentally, the piece builds nicely to the steel guitar solo following the third verse. It gets funkier as it goes along, and moves more and more toward a rock style. The entire second half of the piece is taken over by solos, first a guitar solo in a rockabilly style with a fuzz pedal, then a tenor sax solo in funk style, and finally a very jazzy steel guitar solo that extends for twenty-four measures to a fadeout ending. The steel guitar solo is especially interesting toward the end, where the improvised line extends to melodic passages that are less like country than like mainstream jazz.

96 beats/minute   4 beats/measure

Intro	1 beat	chord on the guitar (1 beat)
Verse 1	8	solo singing with barrelhouse piano
Verse 2	8	more piano fills
Verse 3	8	alto sax fills, stronger drums
Steel guitar	8	solo
Piano	8	solo in barrelhouse style with funk bass
Verse 4	8	solo singing with strong bass
Guitar	8	rock solo
Guitar	8	rock solo
Tenor sax	8	sax player changes to tenor rock and roll
Steel Guitar	8 + 8 + 8	extended solo with barrelhouse piano—interesting melodic figures towards fadeout ending

CHAPTER THIRTEEN

It was difficult to select only two compositions for this chapter because, as I am sure the reader can tell, I am quite interested in rock influences. However, I decided to discuss one tune by Alabama, first, because the group has been so popular and successful in the 1980s and second, because they are represented on the *60 Years of Country Music* cassette (interestingly, no other contemporary country rock bands are represented on the series materials). I also chose "Lost in the Ozone" by Commander Cody and the Lost Planet Airmen because I feel it is a delightful example of an early country rock experiment. That composition is available on the album of the same title (see discography).

Both these selections illustrate the mixing of rock and country music, through either singing style or instrumentation. In all fairness, a number of tunes from 1970 on have this mixture, including a song by Rank and File discussed under Chapter Sixteen. Alabama and Commander Cody are clearly labeled as country rock bands, by publicity and by the kinds of songs they do. However, they both also do straight country songs, as do many of the groups discussed in this chapter.

"Old Flame" by Alabama

The song of Alabama I chose is "Old Flame." Although its musical presentation clearly has rock ballad styling, the lyric itself is rather typical of country music. About the flame in the eyes of a woman, the song talks of no disguise for the inner feelings. This is a contemporary way of expressing a common country music theme, platonic feelings for a woman.

The composition breaks up nicely into verses and refrains, with two different chord progressions (the verse is based on 1 to 1 and the refrain on 4 to 1). The actual chord progression is reasonably complicated by the vocal harmonies but the tendencies are typical, the verse being based on 1 and the refrain starting on 4 working its way back to one. Like much country music, the song is broken down into eight-measure units with the verse taking sixteen measures and the refrain taking sixteen as well. Vocal harmony, the trademark of Alabama, is used throughout the song after the introductory solo singing of verse 1. There is a six-measure acoustic piano introduction and a four-measure guitar interlude after the first refrain.

The song moves at about 118 beats per minute in four-beat measures and formally is an AABA form (the verse repeats A music and verse progression twice, then the refrain begins with the B and the refrain progression and then finishes with another eight-measure phrase of A music and the verse progression). The song ends with a fadeout on a repetition of part of the B structure.

118 beats/minute	4 beats/measure	
Introduction	6	piano
Verse 1	8 + 8	solo singing
Refrain (A)	8	refrain progression—vocal harmony
Refrain (B)	8	verse progression—vocal harmony
Guitar	4	solo interlude
Verse 2	8 + 8	vocal harmony
Refrain (A)	8	
Refrain (B)	8	
Refrain (A)	8	
Refrain (B)	to a fadeout	

"Lost in the Ozone" by Commander Cody and the Lost Planet Airmen

"Lost in the Ozone" was like a theme song for the band. It is structured exactly like a country song in eight-measure phrases. Like many other country tunes, it breaks down into two sets of chord progressions: verse 1 5 5 1 1 4 1-5 1 and refrain 1 1 1 5 1 4 1-5 1. The singing style is group singing for the refrain, which is obvious on first listening. The refrain lyric is typical of country music in that it is basically a drinking song with the bizarre touch of using the ozone as a metaphor. Solo fills are used in country style and in rock style, which suggests the mixture of rock and country. There is a decided double-time feel or bluegrass texture of the instrumental style. The song moves at about 126 beats per minute in four-beat measures.

126 beats/minute	4 beats/measure	
Intro	2	steel guitar
Verse 1	8	solo singing with steel guitar fills
Refrain	8	group singing with guitar fills
Steel guitar	8	refrain progression—country style
Verse 2	8	solo singing
Refrain	8	piano solo in background
Guitar	8	rockabilly solo
Refrain	8	steel guitar fills
Refrain	8	fiddle fills and funk walking bass

CHAPTER FOURTEEN

The two selections from Chapter Fourteen are "Bartender's Blues" of 1978 by George Jones and "Everything from Jesus to Jack Daniels" of 1983 by Tom T. Hall. The George Jones tune is on the *Outlaw Country* album mentioned in the material for Chapter Twelve and the Tom T. Hall recording is available on the album of the same name (see discography). These tunes are especially appropriate for this section because they are both traditional tunes done with the sophistication of 1970s and 1980s instrumental character and recording techniques. Also, they both illustrate the styles of these two musicians.

"Bartender's Blues" by George Jones

"Bartender's Blues" is actually sung in duet with the composer, James Taylor, who is also an important country singer and songwriter. However, the duet is only during the refrain, so the song is basically George Jones singing by himself. It is an interesting tune because it is so like the honky tonk style of Jones and it is a drinking song as well. The singing style is a bit smoother than his 1950s and 1960s hits, but the clear narrative strikes one immediately. It is slightly autobiographical and the lyrics, about a woman, are typically country and very easy to understand.

This slow ballad is in three-beat measures and moves at about 94 beats per measure. It is broken down into eight-measure units, with the same chord progression throughout. Probably the most interesting thing musically is the change up a half step after the guitar solo. The tune has an ending, going from 4 to 1 and then slowing down to a held note. The song starts with three bass notes, then Jones takes over with Verse 1.

94 beats/minute	3 beats/measure	
Intro	1	3 beats (A major)
Verse 1	8 + 8	solo singing
Refrain	8 + 8	two measure units of duet/solo with steel guitar fills and stronger bass figure
Verse 2	8 + 8	guitar fills
Refrain	8 + 8	
Guitar	8	at the end a modulation up a half step (to B♭ major)
Verse 3	8 + 8	piano fills
Refrain	8 + 8	slowing down for *amen* ending and then a held note

"Everything from Jesus to Jack Daniels" by Tom T. Hall

"Everything from Jesus to Jack Daniels" is a complicated song because its lyrics can be understood on many different levels. What I perceive is a statement of confusion about the conflicting attitudes that are expressed by people in the world. The solution seems to be Jack Daniels, but that is really not what Tom T. Hall is saying; he is saying that there may be no solutions to the myriad of forces impinging on us. Therefore, the lyric is very contemporary, certainly for country music. The musical presentation is very traditional in structure. Hall allows the lyrics to rule the music, so this piece is not terribly regular. Like earlier tunes of Jimmie Rodgers or Roy Rogers ("Tumblin' Tumbleweeds"), this song has uneven phrases to allow for the words; in fact, even the refrain has two extra beats.

The piece uses a standard rhythm section, plus fiddle and steel guitar. The fiddle style is especially bluegrass in orientation, although there is one section in the refrain that is old-time obbligato playing (like the Vernon Dalhart tune discussed in Chapter Three). The steel guitar playing is fairly contemporary. The song moves along at about 116 beats per minute in four-beat measures. It starts with a fiddle bluegrass opening and has a blues-type breakdown instrumental ending. The verse typically starts on a 1-chord and the refrain on a 4-chord.

116 beats/minute	4 beats/measure	
Introduction	4 1/2 (18 beats)	fiddle bluegrass sound
Verse 1	9	solo singing breaks into two 4 1/2 beat phrases

Verse 2	9	steel guitar background/ fiddle at ends
Refrain	8½	chorus with responses/ fiddle obbligato
Fiddle break	3½	old style
Verse 3	9	
Verse 4	9	steel guitar background
Refrain	8½	
Verse 5	9	
Refrain	8 + 1	7 ½ singing and 1 ½ fiddle to breakdown blues ending with fiddle and bass to held chord

CHAPTER FIFTEEN

For this chapter, I selected "Kiss the Hurt Away" by Barbara Mandrell, available on *The Best of Barbara Mandrell* (Col. 34876) and Kenny Rogers's "The Gambler," available on his *Greatest Hits* (Liberty LOO-1072). Both these selections are good examples of crossover songs because they communicate messages that are broader than very traditional country music, and they use background choruses and extra-musical effects. The tunes are both from the late 1970s and were both successful.

"Kiss the Hurt Away" by Barbara Mandrell

"Kiss the Hurt Away" is especially delightful because it sounds so simple yet is musically so complicated. Moving at about 72 beats per minute in four-beat measure, this song can also be felt in a twelve-beat measure with each of the beats in the four-beat measure broken up into three pulses. In this sense, it is a typical rock and roll ballad with country influences. Basically divided into eight-measure units, it slides from unit to unit with a great deal of flexibility, as will be shown by the chart. The chord progression is quite difficult although there is clearly a verse progression and a refrain progression. Probably the most interesting musical quality of the verse structure is the way the eight-measure unit is divided:

measure #	1	2	3	4	5	6	7	8
texture	chorus		solo		inst/solo		steel guitar	

This structure is consistent throughout the piece.

There is also a modulation for a repeat of the A section of the piece from G major to A♭ major just before the ending. However, the lyric structure is basically one long song form rather than separate verses, so the piece should be understood in eight-measure units of AABA, then a modulation and another A.

72 beats/minute	4 beats/measure	
A section	8	divided as above illustration
A section	8	new words, same structure
B section	1 + 2+ 5	1 of instrumental, 2 sung for transition to five measures of B section, strong feel with piano
A section	8	same structure

modulation on last two beats of previous section

A section	8	slight change sung through measure six and 2 measures guitar fill for choral ending

"The Gambler" by Kenny Rogers

"The Gambler" is one of those delightful tunes in country music that communicates to everyone. The lyric is very simple and it talks about things we all understand: basically, about the way that one does something right in life. Therefore, the lyric is narrative, but in the mode of much crossover art, its presentation is absolutely straightforward.

The piece moves along at about 98 beats per minute in four-measure phrases and has a decided two-beat feel. It uses a full country band, plus chorus, temple blocks, and other added instruments and electronic effects. It has a strong bass pattern and builds in textural depth up to the modulation after the refrain and before verse 4. It is structured in eight-measure phrases, with the same progression used nine times. There is a two-measure instrumental introduction, two extra beats at the end of verse 2, and a six-beat instrumental modulation. Therefore, it has an irregularity even if it does not sound like it.

98 beats/minute		4 beats/measure
Intro	2	acoustic guitar
Verse 1	8	
Verse 2	8 + ½	rhythm, bass, temple blocks
Verse 3	8	bass in double time, adds drums
Refrain	8	chorus in background
modulation		6 beats instrumental
Verse 4	8	steel guitar more important
Verse 5	8	steel guitar more important
Refrain	8 +	chorus
Refrain	8	rhythm stops, only drums, vocal breakdown between Rogers and chorus responding to him
Refrain	8	held note at end

CHAPTER SIXTEEN

The two compositions I have selected for this section are very dissimilar. First is the Nashville Brass arrangement of "Tennessee Waltz," available on the 1976 album *Down Yonder* (Camden ACL-7034). The second is "Amanda Ruth" by Rank and File (Slash cassette WS 23833-4). These are both experimental tunes, the first because of the brass arrangement and the second because of the new wave country sound. However, it should be understood that they are here mainly for the purpose of analysis; you may disagree on their experimental qualities.

"The Tennessee Waltz" by the Nashville Brass

"The Tennessee Waltz" is an old country song; the lyric was written by Pee Wee King in 1946 and was popularized in 1948. It moves at 92 beats per minute and, since it is a waltz, has three beats per measure. There is nothing experimental about the music's standard thirty-two-measure ballad form (AABA). The song is presented in such a way that the most can be made of different instrumental textures. The basic style of trumpet playing is like the Tijuana Brass, using a solo muted trumpet. The trumpets and trombones use a very extensive vibrato, especially the solo trumpet.

92 beats/minute 3 beats/measure

Intro	8	piano with background trombone chords
A	8	trumpet muted melody with piano background
A	8	4 brass section + 4 trumpet solo
B	8	4 trombone section and background chorus + 4 trumpet solo
A	8	2 trombone section + 2 open trumpet section + 4 trumpet solo
B	8	guitar solo (Chet Atkins style)
A	8	4 brass section + 4 trumpet solo
	2	measure piano and bass ending with trombones in chord

"Amanda Ruth" by Rank and File

The last tune is by a relatively new band who put out their first album, *Sundown,* in 1983. In truth, their second album, *Long Gone Dead,* which came out in 1984, is actually more country than the first, but even in the first album and "Amanda Ruth" they illustrate strong country influences within a new wave way of playing. They could of course be categorized as a country rock band, but I prefer to think of them as experimental.

In their first album they use bass, drums, and two guitars with singers. In their second album they add fiddle and steel guitar. Certain selections on their first album are slightly more country than "Amanda Ruth," but what I wish to illustrate is the new wave style rather than just country sounds. However, the vocal singing is clearly country in style, as is the short guitar solo toward the end. Also, the eight-measure phrases in the song suggest country influence.

The piece moves quickly, at 152 beats per minute in four-beat measures. It has three clear units to it: a set of instrumental changes without singing, a verse, and a refrain. Other than one extra measure right before the guitar solo, the piece is perfectly regular. Vocal harmony is typically used only during the refrain. The singing style of the verses is more rock than country.

152 beats/minute 4 beats/measure

Intro	4	
Inst. Ch	4	
Refrain	4	vocal harmony
Refrain	4	
Verse 1	4 + 4	solo singing
Refrain	4 + 4	
Verse 2	4 + 4	
Refrain	4 + 4	
Inst. Ch	4 + 1	extension
Guitar	12	solo
Inst. Ch	4	
Refrain	4 + 4	
Verse 3	4 + 4	
Refrain	4 + 4 + 4 + 4	
Inst. Ch	4 + 4	held chord at end

Discography

This discography represents a basic collection of country music. It also includes all the records from which longer discussions of particular pieces in the text were drawn. One should not consider this a complete discography of country music; that would require a multi-volume set of books. You will find some of these recordings available under different record labels because country artists tend to change companies rather often, and major record companies go in and out of the country field with great regularity.

Many of these records are available at discount prices if you look around used record stores. I would encourage you to invest in the Smithsonian set of records; you have to order it from the Smithsonian Institute (Order #3025, Smithsonian Customer Services, P. O. Box 10229, Des Moines, Iowa 50336—(800)-247-5072); it costs 54.95 for either records or tapes with a 56-page booklet by Bill Malone. Also, many fine tapes are available from the Country Music Hall of Fame in Nashville.

Roy Acuff, *Greatest Hits*—Col. PC-1034E.

Rex Allen, *Golden Songs of the Old West*—Voc. 73885E.

The Allman Brothers, *The Allman Brothers Band*—2-Pol. CPN-0196.

Eddy Arnold, *Eddy Arnold: Legendary Performances*—RCA CPL 2-4885.

Chet Atkins, *Chet Atkins: Legendary Performances*— CPL1-2503.

Gene Autry, *Gene Autry*—Columbia Historic Edition, FCT 37465.

Bobby Bare, *Bare*—Col. KC-35314.

Blue Sky Boys, *Sunny Side of Life*—Roun. 1006.

Big Bill Broonzy, *Sings Country Blues*—Folk. 31005E.

Milton Brown, *Pioneer Western Swing Band*—MCA 1509.

The Byrds, *Sweetheart of the Rodeo*—Col. PC-9670.

Glen Campbell, *Rhinestone Cowboy*-Cap SN-16030.

Carolina Tar Heels —Folk. Leg. 124.

Fiddlin' John Carson, *The Old Hen Cackled*—Roun. 1003.

The Carter Family, *Mid the Green Fields of Virginia*—RCA ANL 1-1107.

Johnny Cash, *Country Gold*—Power 246E.

———*Superbilly*—Sun 1002.

Roy Clark, *Best of Roy Clark*—Dot 25986.

Patsy Cline, *Portrait*—MCA 224.

Commander Cody and the Lost Planet Airmen, *Lost in the Ozone*—Para. 6017.

Spade Cooley—Columbia Historic Edition, FCT 37467.

Cowboy Copas, *16 Greatest Hits*—Star. 3012E.

Country Gentlemen—Vol. 1, 2, and 3, Folk. 2409-10-11, 884, 885, 886.

Cryin' in the Morning: An Anthology of Post-War Blues— Muse 5212.

Vernon Dalhart, *First Singing Cowboy*—Mark 56 793.

Charlie Daniels, *Charlie Daniels*—Cap. SN-16039.

Danny Davis and the Nashville Brass, *Best*—RCA AYL1-4069.

Delmore Brothers, *Best of the Delmore Brothers*—Star 962E.

Dirt Band, *Will the Circle Be Unbroken*—UAS 9801.

Bob Dylan, *Nashville Skyline*—Col. JC-9825.

Freddy Fender, *Your Cheatin' Heart*—Pick. 6195.

Lester Flatt and Earl Scruggs, *Flatt and Scruggs*—Columbia Historic Edition, FCT 37469.

Flying Burrito Brothers, *Close Up Honky Tonks*—A & M 4258.

Tennessee Ernie Ford, *Country Hits Feelin' Blue*—Cap. SM-2097.

Kinky Friedman, *Sold American*—Van. 79333.

Lefty Frizzell, *Greatest Hits*—Col. CS-9288.

Larry Gatlin, *Greatest Hits, Vol. 1*—Col. JC-36488.

———, *Larry Gatlin & The Gatlin Brothers Band*—Col. PCT-38340.

Crystal Gayle, *Crystal*—UA LN-10004.

Merle Haggard, *Best of Merle Haggard*—Cap. SN-16054.

———, *Greatest Hits*—MCA 5386.

———, *Okie from Muskogee*—Cap. ST-384.

———, *Tribute to the Best Damn Fiddle Player*—Cap. ST-638.

Bill Halley, *Rock and Roll Revival*—Pick. 3280.

Tom T. Hall, *Greatest Hits*—Mer. 61369.

———, *Everything from Jesus to Jack Daniels*—Mercury 422.

Freddie Hart, *The Best of Freddie Hart*—2-MCA 4088.

Hawkshaw Hawkins, *16 Greatest Hits*—Star. 3013E.

Lightnin' Hawkins, *Texas Blues Man*—Arhoo. 1034.

History of Country Music—RRC-1011-1016. Vols. I–VI from Radiant Record Corp., Box 1438, Radio City Station, New York, NY 10019.

Buddy Holly, *The Complete Buddy Holly*—6-MCA 80000.

Waylon Jennings, *Ladies Love Outlaws*—RCA AFL1-4751.

George Jones, *16 Greatest Hits*—Star. 3021E.

———, *All Time Greatest Hits, Vol. 1*—Epic PE-34692.

George Jones and Tammy Wynette, *Golden Ring*—Epic PE-34291.

Grandpa Jones, *Old Time Country Music*—2-CMH 9010.

Jerry Lee Lewis, *Memories*—Mer. 5004.

Loretta Lynn, *Greatest Hits Vol. 1-2*—MCA 2341/2353.

Loretta Lynn and Conway Twitty, *Loretta and Conway*—CSP RRC 1010 (Radiant Record Corp., Box 1438, Radio City Station, New York, NY 10019).

Louisiana Cajun Music, Vol. 1-5—Old Timey 108/9/10/11/14.

Lynyrd Skynyrd, *Bullets*—MCA 37070.

Dave Macon, *Uncle Dave Macon, 1926-39: Wait Till the Clouds Roll By* — Hist. 8006.

Barbara Mandrell, *Best of Barbara Mandrell* — Col. PC-34876.

——, *Live* — MCA 5243.

Marshall Tucker Band, *Marshall Tucker Band* — War. 3606.

Roger Miller, *Golden Hits* — Smash 67073.

Ronnie Milsap, *Live*—RCA AHL1-2043.

Bill Monroe, *Bill Monroe's Greatest Hits*—MCAC-17.

Monroe Brothers, *Feast Here Tonight*—2-Blueb. AXM2-5510.

Bill Monroe, *Sixteen All Time Greatest Hits—Bill Monroe*—Columbia CS-1065.

Bill Monroe, Lester Flatt, and Earl Scruggs, *Original Bluegrass Band*—Roun. SS06.

Nashville Brass, *Down Yonder*—Camden ACL-7034.

Willie Nelson, *Best*—Lib. LN-10118.

——, *Yesterday's Wine*—RCA AYL1-3800.

Willie Nelson and Roger Miller, *Old Friends*—Col. PC-38013.

Willie Nelson and Webb Pierce, *In the Jailhouse Now*—Col. PC-38095.

New Riders of the Purple Sage, *Best*—Col. PC-34367.

Roy Orbison, *Original Sound*—Sun 113E.

Outlaw Country—Realistic 51-7004 (Radio Shack).

Buck Owens, *Best of Buck Owens Vol. 1*—Cap. SM-11827.

——, *My Heart Skips a Beat*—Capitol SF-534.

Dolly Parton, *Best of Dolly Parton—RCA LSP-4449*.

——, *Jolene*—RCA AYL1-3898.

——, *Nine to Five and Odd Jobs*—RCA AYL1-3852.

Carl Perkins, *Original Golden Hits*—Sun 111E.

Webb Pierce, *Best of Webb Pierce*—2-MCA 4087.

Charlie Poole, *Boy Left Home*—Hist. 8005.

Elvis Presley *Elvis Country*—RCA AYL1-3956.

——, *Elvis Sun Sessions*—AYM1-3893.

——, *Worldwide 50 Gold Award Hits, Vol.* 1—4-RCA LPM-6401.

Ray Price, *Greatest Hits*—Col. CS-8866.

Charley Pride, *Best of Charley Pride, Vols. 1 & 2*—RCA AYL1-4223/4682.

Boots Randolph, *Yakety Sax*—Monu. 6600.

Rank and File, *Sundown*—Slash 4-23833.

——, *Long Gone Dead*—Slash 1-25087.

Jim Reeves, *Jim Reeves—Legendary Performances*—CPL1-1891.

Charlie Rich, *Greatest Hits of Charlie Rich*—Epic PE-34240.

Tex Ritter, *Tex Ritter: An American Legend*—Capitol SKC 11241.

Marty Robbins, *Greatest Hits, Vol. 4*—Col. KC-35629.

Jimmie Rodgers, *This Is Jimmie Rodgers*—RCA VPS 6091.

Johnny Rodriguez, *Greatest Hits of Johnny Rodriguez*—Mer. 1078.

Kenny Rogers, *Greatest Hits*—Lib. L00-1072.

The Earl Scruggs Revue, *Live From Austin City Limits*—Col. PC-34464.

60 Years of Country Music—RCA CPK2-4351.

Ricky Skaggs, *Family and Friends*—Roun. 0151.

Smithsonian Collection of Classic Country Music—Smithsonian Institution.

Hank Snow, *Best of Hank Snow*—RCA ANL1-3470E.

Sons of the Pioneers, *Way Out West: The Sons of the Pioneers* —Country Music Foundation, 4 Music Square

Bibliography

ARTIS, BOB. *Bluegrass: From the Lonesome Wail of a Mountain Love Song to the Hammering Drive of the Scruggs-Style Banjo—The Story of an American Musical Tradition.* New York: Hawthorn Books, Inc., 1975.

ATKINS, CHET, and BILL NEELY. *Country Gentlemen.* Chicago: Henry Regnery Co., 1974.

AUTRY, GENE, and MICKEY HERSKOWITZ. *Back in the Saddle Again.* New York: Doubleday & Co., 1978.

BLAUSTEIN, RICHARD. "WOPI: The Pioneer Voice of the Appalachians." *The Journal of Country Music* 6:3 (Fall 1975): 122–29.

BOND, JOHNNY. *The Recordings of Jimmie Rodgers: An Annotated Discography.* JEMF Special Series No. 11, 1978.

——— *The Tex Ritter Story.* New York: Chappell Music Co., 1976.

BRONNER, SIMON. "Old Time Tunes on Edison Records." *The Journal of Country Music* 8:1 (May 1979): 95–100.

BROWN, CHARLES T. *The Art of Rock and Roll.* Englewood Cliffs, N.J.: Prentice-Hall, Inc., 1983.

CARR, PATRICK, ed. *The Illustrated History of Country Music.* Garden City, N.Y.: A Country Music Magazine Press Book, Doubleday & Co., Inc., 1979.

COHEN, NORMAN. "The Skillet Lickers: A Study of a Hillbilly String Band and Its Repertoire." *Journal of American Folklore* 78:309 (July-September 1965): 229–44.

COMBER, CHRIS. "Tex Ritter." *Folk Style* 17. Surrey, London: Society for the Preservation and Promotion of Traditional Country Music, 1969.

DELMORE, ALTON. *Truth Is Stranger Than Publicity: Alton Delmore's Autobiography.* Nashville: Country Music Foundation Press, 1977.

DUNKLEBERGER, A. C. *King of Country Music: The Life Story of Roy Acuff.* Nashville: Williams Printing Co., 1977.

East, Nashville, TN 37203.

——, *Sons of the Pioneers: Empty Saddles*—MCA 1563.

Stanley Brothers, *Banjo in the Hills,* King 872.

Stars of the Grand Ole Opry—2-RCA LSP-6015/2-RCA CPL2-0466.

Statler Brothers, *The World of the Statler Brothers*—2-Col CG-31557.

———, *The Statler Brothers Sing the Big Hits*—Col. PCT-09519.

Gid Tanner, *Gid Tanner and the Skillet Lickers*—Vetco 107.

This Is the Nashville Sound—2-RCA VPS-6037.

Hank Thompson, *The Best of Hank Thompson and His Brazos Valley Boys*—Cap. SM-1

Mel Tillis, *Greatest Hits*—MGM 4970(6).

———, *Detroit City*—Pick. 6153.

Tompall and the Glaser Brothers, *Lovin' Her Was Easier*—Elek. 542.

Merle Travis, *Best of Merle Travis*—Cap. SM 2662.

Ernest Tubb, *Ernest Tubb: Honky Tonk Classics*—Rounder SS-14.

Conway Twitty, *Greatest Hits, Vol.* 2—MCA 2235.

Conway Twitty and Loretta Lynn, *Lead Me On*—MCA 9.

Kitty Wells, *Greatest Hits of Kitty Wells*—MCA 121.

Dottie West, *Once You Were Mine*—RCA AYL1-4302.

Hank Williams, *Hank Williams 24 Greatest Hits*—MGM 4755-2.

Bob Wills, *Bob Wills*—Columbia Historic Edition, FCT 37468.

——, *The Bob Wills Anthology*—Columbia-32416.

Tammy Wynette, *Greatest Hits*—Epic PC-26486.

Faron Young, *Hello Walls*—Picca.3547.

EVANS, DAVID. "Black Musicians Remember Jimmie Rodgers." *Old Time Music* 7 (Winter 1972–73): 12–15.

FORD, ERNEST J. *This Is My Story—This Is My Song*. Englewood Cliffs, N.J.: Prentice-Hall, Inc., 1963.

GREEN, DOUGLAS. "The Blue Sky Boys on Radio, 1939-1940: A Newly Discovered Log of Their Daily Program, Kept by Ruth Walker." *The Journal of Country Music* 4:4 (Winter 1973): 108–58.

——— "Bob Wills and His Texas Playboys on Radio, 1942." *The Journal of Country Music* 5:4 (Winter 1974): 108–58.

——— *Country Roots: The Origins of Country Music*. New York: Hawthorn Books, Inc., 1976.

HAGAN, CHET. *The Great Country Music Book*. New York: Simon & Schuster, Inc., 1983.

HALL, TOM T. *The Storyteller's Nashville*. New York: Doubleday & Co., Inc., 1979.

HAMM, CHARLES. *Music in the New World*. New York: W. W. Norton & Co., Inc., 1983.

HATCHER, DANNY. "Bob Wills: Discography of the Columbia Years." *The Journal of Country Music* 3:3–4 (Fall and Winter 1972): 114–30.

HEMPHILL, PAUL. *The Nashville Sound: Bright Lights and Country Music*. New York: Simon & Schuster, Inc., 1970.

HURST, JACK. *Nashville's Grand Ole Opry*. New York: Harry N. Abrams, Inc., 1975.

LYNN, LORETTA, and GEORGE VECSEY. *Loretta Lynn: Coal Miner's Daughter*. Chicago: Henry Regnery Co., 1976.

MALONE, BILL C. *Country Music, U.S.A. A Fifty-Year History*. Austin: The University of Texas Press, 1968.

——. *Southern Music: American Music*. Lexington: The University Press of Kentucky, 1979.

MALONE, BILL C., and JUDITH MCCULLOH, eds. *Stars of Country Music: Uncle Dave Macon to Johnny Rodriguez*. Urbana: University of Illinois Press, 1975.

MARCUS, GREIL. *Mystery Train: Images of America in Rock 'n' Roll Music*. New York: E.P. Dutton & Co., Inc., 1975.

NORTHLAND, JOHN. *The Best of Country Music*. Garden City, N.Y.: Doubleday & Co., Inc., 1984.

O'DONNELL, RED. *Chet Atkins*. Nashville: Athens Music Co., 1967.

PARELES, JOHN, and PATRICIA ROMANOWSKI, eds. *The Rolling Stone Encyclopedia of Rock and Roll*. New York: Simon & Schuster, Inc., 1983.

PARIS, MIKE, and CHRIS COMBER. *Jimmie the Kid: The Life of Jimmie Rodgers*. London: Eddison Press Ltd., 1977.

PATTERSON, TIMOTHY. "Hillbilly Music among the Flatlanders:. Early Midwestern Radio and Barn Dances." *The Journal of Country Music* 6:1 (Spring 1975): 12–18.

PEARL, MINNIE, and JOAN DEW. *Minnie Pearl: An Autobiography*. New York: Simon & Schuster, Inc., 1980.

PORTERFIELD, NOLAN. *Jimmie Rodgers: The Life and Times of America's Blue Yodeler*. Urbana: University of Illinois Press, 1979.

RINZLER, RALPH, and NORMAN COHEN. *Uncle Dave Macon: A Bio-Discography*, No. 3. Los Angeles: John Edwards Memorial Foundation, UCLA, 1970.

RODGERS, MRS. JIMMIE. *My Husband, Jimmie Rodgers*. Nashville: The Country Music Foundation Press, 1975.

RORRER, CLIFFORD K. *Charlie Poole and the North Carolina Ramblers*. Reidsville, N.C.: Reidsville Printing Co., Inc., 1968.

ROSENBERG, NEIL V. *Bill Monroe and His Blue Grass Boys: An Illustrated Discography*. Nashville: The Country Music Foundation Press, 1974.

ROTHEL, DAVID. *The Singing Cowboys*. Cranbury, N.J.: A.S. Barnes & Co., 1978.

RUST, BRIAN. *The Victor Master Book: Volume 2 (1925-1936)*. Published by the author. Hatch End, Eng.: 1969.

SCHLAPPI, ELIZABETH. *Roy Acuff: The Smokey Mountain Boy*. Gretna, La.: Pelican Publishing Co., Inc., 1978.

SMITH, JOHN L. "I Ain't No Ordinary Dude: A Bio-Discography of Waylon Jennings." *The Journal of Country Music* 6:2 (Summer 1975): 45–95.

——. *Johnny Cash Discography and Recording History 1955–1968*, No. 2. Los Angeles: John Edwards Memorial Foundation, UCLA, 1969.

STOWERS, CARLTON. *Happy Trails: The Story of Roy Rogers and Dale Evans.* Waco, Tex.: Word, Inc., 1979.

STRICKLIN, AL, and JON McCONAL. *My Years with Bob Wills.* San Antonio: The Naylor Co., 1976.

TOWNSEND, CHARLES R. *San Antonio Rose: The Life and Music of Bob Wills.* Urbana: University of Illinois Press, 1976.

WELLS, PAUL E. *Presenting the Blue Sky Boys.* Los Angeles: John Edwards Memorial Foundation, UCLA, 1977.

WHITE, JOHN I. *Git Along, Little Dogies: Songs and Songmakers of the American West.* Urbana: University of Illinois Press, 1975.

WILLIAMS, HANK, JR., and MICHAEL BONE. *Living Proof: An Autobiography.* New York: G. P. Putnam's Sons, 1979.

WILLIAMS, ROGER M. *Sing a Sad Song: The Life of Hank Williams.* New York: Doubleday & Co., lnc., 1970.

WOLFE, CHARLES. "Early Nashville Media and Its Response to Old-Time Music." *The Journal of Country Music* 4:1 (Spring 1973): 2–60.

——. "The Delmore Brothers: A Pre-War Discography." *The Journal of Country Music* 6:1 (Spring 1975): 2–11.

——. *The Grand Ole Opry: The Early Years, 1925-35.* London: Old Time Music, 1975.

——. *Tennessee Strings: The Story of Country Music in Tennessee.* Knoxville: The University of Tennessee Press, 1977.

——. "Up North with the Blue Ridge Ramblers: Jennie Bowman's 1931 Tour Diary." *The Journal of Country Music* 6:3 (Fall 1975): 136-45.

Wynette, Tammy. *Stand by Your Man.* New York: Simon & Schuster, Inc., 1979.

Index

PERMUTATIONS

The number of permutations of n elements taken r at a time, where $r \leq n$, is

$$_nP_r = \frac{n!}{(n-r)!}.$$

COMBINATIONS

The number of combinations of n elements taken r at a time, where $r \leq n$, is

$$\binom{n}{r} = {}_nC_r = \frac{n!}{(n-r)!r!}.$$

BINOMIAL PROBABILITY

If p is the probability of success in a single trial of a binomial experiment, the probability of x successes and $n - x$ failures in n independent repeated trials of the experiment is

$$\binom{n}{x} p^x (1-p)^{n-x}.$$

MEAN

The mean of the n numbers, $x_1, x_2, x_3, \ldots, x_n$, is

$$\bar{x} = \frac{x_1 + x_2 + \cdots + x_n}{n} = \frac{\Sigma(x)}{n}.$$

SAMPLE STANDARD DEVIATION

The standard deviation of a sample of n numbers, $x_1, x_2, x_3, \ldots, x_n$, with mean $\bar{x}$, is

$$s = \sqrt{\frac{\Sigma(x - \bar{x})^2}{n-1}}.$$

BINOMIAL DISTRIBUTION

Suppose an experiment is a series of n independent repeated trials, where the probability of a success in a single trial is always p. Let x be the number of successes in the n trials. Then the probability that exactly x successes will occur in n trials is given by

$$\binom{n}{x} p^x (1-p)^{n-x}.$$

The mean μ and variance σ^2 of a binomial distribution are, respectively,

$$\mu = np \quad \text{and} \quad \sigma^2 = np(1-p).$$

The standard deviation is

$$\sigma = \sqrt{np(1-p)}.$$

Mathematics with Applications

In the Management, Natural, and Social Sciences

Graphing Technology Version

Thomas W. Hungerford
Cleveland State University

Margaret L. Lial
American River College

An imprint of Addison Wesley Longman, Inc.

Reading, Massachusetts • Menlo Park, California • New York • Harlow, England
Don Mills, Ontario • Sydney • Mexico City • Madrid • Amsterdam

Publisher: Greg Tobin
Editorial Project Manager: Christine O'Brien
Developmental Editor: Sandi Goldstein
Managing Editor: Karen Guardino
Production Supervisor: Rebecca Malone
Production Services: Elm Street Publishing Services, Inc.
Marketing Manager: Carter Fenton
Marketing Coordinator: Michael Boezi
Prepress Services Buyer: Caroline Fell
Manufacturing Manager: Ralph Mattivello
Manufacturing Buyer: Evelyn Beaton
Text Design: Jeanne Wolfgeher
Senior Designer: Barbara T. Atkinson
Cover Designer: Jeannet Leendertse
Cover Photography: Art Wolfe © Tony Stone Images

Library of Congress Cataloging-in-Publication Data

Hungerford, Thomas W.
Mathematics with applications: in the management, natural, and social sciences: graphing technology version/Thomas W. Hungerford, Margaret L. Lial.
p. cm.
Includes index.
ISBN 0-321-01621-1
1. Mathematics. 2. Mathematics—Graphic methods. I. Lial, Margaret L. II. Title.
QA37.2.H85 1999
510—dc21 98-21684
CIP

1 2 3 4 5 6 7 8 9 10—DOW—01009998

Contents

Preface

Mathematics with Applications: Graphing Technology Version provides the mathematical topics needed by students in the fields of business, social science, and natural science. It integrates graphing technology into the course without losing sight of the fact that the underlying mathematics is the crucial issue. The book enables students to become active participants in developing their understanding of mathematics, but it avoids the danger of making technology an end in itself. We have done our best to present sound mathematics in an informal manner that stresses meaningful motivation, careful explanations, and numerous examples, with an ongoing focus on real-world problem solving.

The book is written at a level appropriate for the intended audience. Topics are presented by proceeding from what is already known to new material, from concrete examples to general rules and formulas. Almost every section includes pertinent applications. The only prerequisite for using this book is a course in algebra. Chapters 1 and 2 provide a thorough review of algebra and an introduction to graphing technology.

GRAPHING TECHNOLOGY

Graphing technology is an integral part of this text. This technology makes it possible for students to explore mathematical ideas from graphical, numerical, and algebraic perspectives. It also allows students and instructors to spend less time on "mechanics" and more on the underlying concepts. Students can focus on essentials without getting bogged down in calculations that obscure the key ideas.

Although graphing technology doesn't change the underlying mathematics, it does affect the pedagogical approach to many topics and the order in which topics are covered. For example, graphs are now introduced before equations and inequalities so that graphical means can be used in solving them.

By interpreting the solutions of the equation $f(x) = 0$ as the x-intercepts of the graph of $y = f(x)$, the power of graphing technology can be brought into play to approximate solutions with a high degree of accuracy. The crucial connection between graphical and algebraic information is emphatically brought home to students. Even the basic algebraic techniques for solving inequalities are more easily explained and better understood when considered from a graphical point of view. More importantly, problems and applications are no longer artificially restricted to situations that involve relatively simple equations.

CONTENT HIGHLIGHTS

In addition to the changes necessary to incorporate graphing technology into the text, several topics are treated differently than they were in the sixth edition of *Mathematics with Applications.*

- The introductory algebraic material that formerly constituted a very long first chapter has been rearranged and dispersed over two chapters. Rather than introducing all the basic algebra at the beginning, these topics are introduced as they are needed in the development of the course.
- The discussion of polynomial and rational functions (Chapter 4) includes a section on optimization and other applications of polynomial functions. This section uses the graphing calculator rather than calculus to approximate local extrema.
- The treatment of standard deviation in Chapter 11 has been rewritten so that the distinction between the population and the sample standard deviations is more fully explained. In addition, the treatment of various statistical graphs has been expanded in Chapters 10 and 11.
- Chapter 13, Applications of the Derivative, has been significantly reordered to produce a better organized, more cohesive discussion of the first and second derivatives and their use in optimization applications.

PEDAGOGICAL FEATURES

Several features designed to assist students in the learning process are used in this book.

Technology Tips Many students fail to make full use of their graphing calculators, often because they don't realize what these calculators can do. Some students also have difficulty in implementing certain procedures on their calculators. Consequently, we have placed *Technology Tips* at appropriate places in the discussion. Some of these Tips inform students of various features of their calculators. Others provide specific directions for accessing certain features on particular models of TI, Casio, HP, and Sharp calculators (e.g., "look in the NUM submenu of the MATH menu on TI-83"). The Technology Tips can be easily omitted by those who don't need them, but they should provide significant assistance to others.

Program Appendix This appendix contains programs of two types: programs to update older calculators (e.g., a table program for TI-85 and a root-finder for TI-81 and older Casio models) and programs to do specific tasks discussed in the text (e.g., programs to create amortization tables, to carry out the simplex method, and to approximate a definite integral by using the areas of rectangles). Depending on which parts of the text an instructor covers, some of these programs are likely to prove extremely useful.

Artwork In addition to the usual color figures prepared by professional artists, there are many black-and-white representations of graphing calculator screens that duplicate exactly what students see on their own calculators. These screens help students to interpret the images produced by their calculators and make clear the difference between an "ideal" graph and the sometimes less than ideal ones produced by calculators or computers.

Other Features We have retained popular features from the conventional version of this book, *Mathematics with Applications* (whose seventh edition is being published concurrently and in which graphing technology is optional):

- Extensive examples
- Exercises keyed to the text
- Conceptual and writing exercises
- Realistic and timely applications, many based on real data
- End-of-chapter case studies
- Margin problems
- Highlighted rules, definitions, and summaries
- Connection exercises that involve material from earlier sections (marked with a 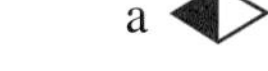)

COURSE FLEXIBILITY

This book can be used for a variety of courses, including the following:

Finite Mathematics and Calculus (one year or less). Use the entire book; cover topics from Chapters 1–5 as needed before proceeding to further topics.

Finite Mathematics (one semester or two quarters). Use as much of Chapters 1–5 as needed, then go into Chapters 6–11 as time permits and local needs require.

Calculus (one semester or quarter). Cover the precalculus topics in Chapters 1–5 as necessary, and then use Chapters 12–15.

College Algebra with Applications (one semester or quarter). Use Chapters 1–9, with the topics in Chapters 8 and 9 being optional.

Chapter interdependence is as follows:

	Chapter	*Prerequisite*
1	Algebra and Graphs	None
2	Equations and Inequalities	Chapter 1
3	Functions and Graphs	Chapters 1 and 2
4	Polynomial and Rational Functions	Chapter 3
5	Exponential and Logarithmic Functions	Chapter 3
6	Mathematics of Finance	Chapter 5
7	Systems of Linear Equations and Matrices	Chapters 1 and 2
8	Linear Programming	Chapters 3 and 7
9	Sets and Probability	None
10	Further Topics in Probability	Chapter 9
11	Introduction to Statistics	Chapter 9
12	Differential Calculus	Chapters 1–5
13	Applications of the Derivative	Chapter 12
14	Integral Calculus	Chapters 12 and 13
15	Multivariate Calculus	Chapters 12–14

Contact your Addison Wesley Longman sales representative to order a customized version of this text.

SUPPLEMENTS

FOR THE INSTRUCTOR

Instructor's Resource Guide and Solutions Manual (ISBN 0-321-03958-0) The Manual contains detailed solutions to all text problems and test items with their answers.

Answer Book (ISBN 0-321-04315-4) The Answer Book contains the answers to all the problems in the text.

TestGen-EQ with QuizMaster (ISBN for Windows: 0-321-03563-1; ISBN for Macintosh: 0-321-03564-X) TestGen-EQ is a computerized test generator with algorithmically defined problems organized specifically for this textbook. Its user-friendly graphical interface enables instructors to select, view, edit, and add test items, then print tests in a variety of fonts and forms. Seven question types are available, and search and sort features let the instructor quickly locate questions and arrange them in a preferred order. A built-in question editor gives the user the power to create graphs, import graphics, insert mathematical symbols and templates, and insert variable numbers or text. An "Export to HTML" feature lets instructors create practice tests that can be posted to a Web site. Tests created with TestGen-EQ can be used with QuizMaster-EQ, which enables students to take exams on a computer network. QuizMaster-EQ automatically grades the exams, stores results on disk, and allows the instructor to view or print a variety of reports for individual students, classes, or courses. This program, available in Windows and Macintosh formats, is free to adopters of the text.

Printed Test Bank (ISBN 0-321-04316-2) The Test Bank provides prepared tests for each chapter.

FOR THE STUDENT

Student's Solutions Manual (ISBN 0-321-03957-2) The Student's Solutions Manual contains detailed, carefully worked-out solutions to all odd-numbered section and chapter review exercises, and all case study exercises. Also included are the *Explorations in Finite Mathematics* and *Visual Calculus* software programs, by David Schneider of the University of Maryland. These are Windows/DOS programs that contain several routines directly tied to this text. Many routines allow for application and discovery.

Graphing Calculator Manual (ISBN 0-321-03959-9) The Graphing Calculator Manual provides step-by-step instructions for using graphing calculators to work through examples from the main text.

Web Site A Web site to accompany this text contains additional application problems (and their answers) and TI-83 graphing calculator programs that can be downloaded to a computer and transferred to a TI-83 calculator using TI-Graph Link. http://hepg.awl.com Keyword: CalcZone or FiniteZone

ACKNOWLEDGMENTS

We thank the following instructors who reviewed the manuscript and made many helpful suggestions for improvement.

James F. Brown, *Midland College*
James E. Carpenter, *Iona College*
Faith Y. Chao, *Golden Gate University*
Frank Fitzgerald, *Boston University*
Leland J. Fry, *Kirkwood Community College*
Joseph A. Guthrie, *University of Texas–El Paso*
Jeremy Haefner, *University of Colorado at Colorado Springs*
Beata Hebda, *Gainesville College*
Phil Huneke, *Ohio State University*
Alec Ingraham, *New Hampshire College*
Norman Lindquist, *Western Washington University*
Jim Loats, *Metropolitan State College of Denver*
Sarah L. Mabrouk, *Boston University*
Kevin McDougal, *University of Wisconsin–Oshkosh*
C.G. Mendez, *Metropolitan State College of Denver*
Kandasamy Muthuvel, *University of Wisconsin–Oshkosh*
Michael I. Ratliff, *Northern Arizona University*
Cheryl Slayden, *Pellissippi State Technical Community College*
Giovanni Viglino, *Ramapo College of New Jersey*
Bhushan Wadhwa, *Cleveland State University*

We also wish to thank our accuracy checkers who did an excellent job of checking all of the exercise answers: James E. Carpenter, *Iona College,* Beata Hebda, *Gainesville College,* Alec Ingraham, *New Hampshire College,* Kevin McDougal, *University of Wisconsin–Oshkosh,* Kandasamy Muthuvel, *University of Wisconsin–Oshkosh,* and Michael I. Ratliff, *Northern Arizona University.*

Special thanks go to Laurel Technical Services and Paula Young, who did an outstanding job preparing the print supplements; to Terry McGinnis, whose careful proofreading has helped eliminate errors from the text; to Paul Van Erden, who created an accurate and complete index for us; and to Becky Troutman, who carefully compiled the Index of Applications.

We want to thank both the former employees of HarperCollins who initiated this project, George Duda, Anne Kelly, and Kevin Connors, and the current staff of Addison Wesley Longman who carried it to completion, particularly Greg Tobin, Christine O'Brien, and Becky Malone. Finally we express our deep appreciation to freelance editor Sandi Goldstein, who kept us on schedule and on target, and to Cathy Wacaser of Elm Street Publishing Services, who did her usual fine production work.

Thomas W. Hungerford
Margaret L. Lial

To the Student

In order to use this book effectively, you must have a graphing calculator or a computer with appropriate graphing software. In the text, the term "calculator" means "graphing calculator." It is understood that, with obvious modification, all discussions of calculators apply equally well to computer graphing software. The book is not written for a specific calculator, so the calculator screens pictured in the text may not look exactly like yours.

Several features of the text are designed to assist you in understanding the concepts and learning the mathematical procedures involved. First of all, there are *Technology Tips* throughout the book. These Tips describe the proper menus or keys to be used on specific calculators in order to carry out a particular procedure. When these Tips are not sufficient, consult the instruction manual for your calculator.

To help you learn new concepts and reinforce your understanding, there are numerous *side problems* in the margin. They are referred to in the text by numbers in colored squares, such as **2**. When you see that symbol, you should work the indicated problem in the margin before going on.

The key to succeeding in this course is to remember that

mathematics is not a spectator sport.

You can't expect to learn mathematics without *doing* mathematics any more than you could learn to swim without getting wet. You have to take an active role, making use of all the resources at your disposal: your instructor, your fellow students, your calculator (and its instruction manual), and this book.

There is no way that your instructor can possibly cover every aspect of a topic during class time. You simply won't develop the level of understanding you need to succeed unless you read the text carefully. In particular, you should read the text *before* starting the exercises. However, you can't read a math book the way you read a novel. You should have pencil, paper, and calculator handy to do the side problems, work out the statements you don't understand, and make notes on things to ask your fellow students and/or your instructor.

Finally, remember the words of the great Hillel: "The bashful do not learn." There is no such thing as a "dumb question" (assuming, of course, that you have read the book and your class notes and attempted the homework). Your instructor will welcome questions that arise from a serious effort on your part. So get your money's worth: Ask questions.

CHAPTER 1

Algebra and Graphs

This book deals with the application of mathematics to business, social science, and biology. Because algebra is vital to understanding these applications, we begin with a review of the fundamental ideas of algebra. Later in the chapter we shall see how technology—particularly the graphing calculator—enables us to deal with many problems graphically as well as algebraically.

Technology cannot be used with maximum efficiency unless you have a sound foundation in basic algebra. If you have not used your algebraic skills for some time, it is important for you to study the review material in the first half of this chapter carefully; your success in covering the material that follows will depend on your algebraic skills.

1.1 THE REAL NUMBERS

Only real numbers will be used in this book.* The names of the most common types of real numbers are as follows.

THE REAL NUMBERS

Natural (counting) numbers	1, 2, 3, 4, . . .
Whole numbers	0, 1, 2, 3, 4, . . .
Integers	. . . , −3, −2, −1, 0, 1, 2, 3, . . .
Rational numbers	All numbers of the form p/q, where p and q are integers, with $q \neq 0$
Irrational numbers	Real numbers that are not rational

The relationships among these types of numbers are shown in Figure 1.1 on the next page. Notice, for example, that the integers are also rational numbers and real numbers, but the integers are not irrational numbers.

*Not all numbers are real numbers. An example of a number that is not a real number is $\sqrt{-1}$.

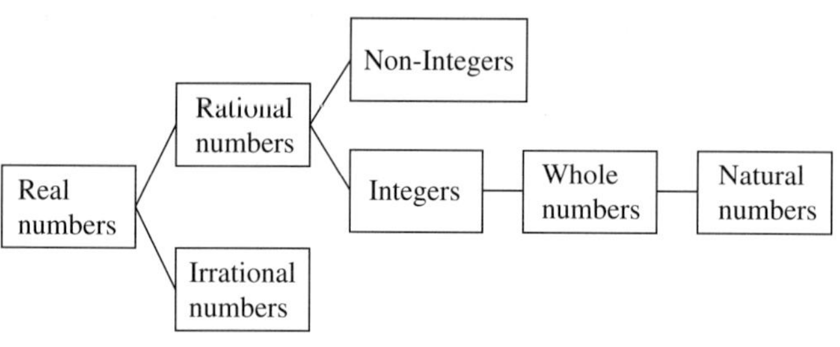

FIGURE 1.1

One example of an irrational number is π, the ratio of the circumference of a circle to its diameter. The number π can be approximated by writing $\pi \approx 3.14159$ ($\approx$ means "is approximately equal to"), but there is no rational number that is exactly equal to π.

1 Name all the types of numbers that apply to the following.

(a) -2

(b) $-5/8$

(c) $\pi/5$

Answers:

(a) Integer, rational, real

(b) Rational, real

(c) Irrational, real

EXAMPLE 1 What kind of number is each of the following?

(a) 6

The number 6 is a natural number, whole number, integer, rational number, and real number.

(b) 3/4

This number is rational and real.

(c) 3π

Because π is not a rational number, 3π is irrational and real. ■ 1*

All real numbers can be written in decimal form. A rational number, when written in decimal form, is either a terminating decimal, such as .5 or .128, or a repeating decimal in which some block of digits eventually repeats forever, such as 1.3333. . . or 4.7234234234. . . .† Irrational numbers are decimals that neither terminate nor repeat.

The only real numbers that can be entered exactly into a calculator are those rational numbers that are terminating decimals of no more than 10 or 12 digits (depending on the calculator). Similarly, the answers produced by a calculator are often 10–12 digit decimal *approximations*—accurate enough for most applications. As a general rule, *you should not round off any numbers during a long calculator computation,* so that your final answer will be as accurate as possible. For convenience, however, we usually round off the final answer to three or four decimal places.

The important basic properties of the real numbers are as follows.

PROPERTIES OF THE REAL NUMBERS

For all real numbers, a, b, and c, the following properties hold true.

Commutative properties	$a + b = b + a$	$ab = ba$

continued

*The use of margin problems is explained in the "To the Student" section preceding this chapter.

†Some calculators have a FRAC key that automatically converts some repeating decimals to fraction form. FRAC programs for other calculators are in the Program Appendix.

Associative properties	$(a + b) + c = a + (b + c)$ $\quad (ab)c = a(bc)$
Identity properties	There exists a unique real number 0, called the **additive identity,** such that $$a + 0 = a \quad \text{and} \quad 0 + a = a.$$ There exists a unique real number 1, called the **multiplicative identity,** such that $$a \cdot 1 = a \quad \text{and} \quad 1 \cdot a = a.$$
Inverse properties	For each real number a, there exists a unique real number $-a$, called the **additive inverse** of a, such that $$a + (-a) = 0 \quad \text{and} \quad (-a) + a = 0.$$ If $a \neq 0$, there exists a unique real number $1/a$, called the **multiplicative inverse** of a, such that $$a \cdot \frac{1}{a} = 1 \quad \text{and} \quad \frac{1}{a} \cdot a = 1.$$
Distributive property	$a(b + c) = ab + ac$

2 Name the property illustrated in each of the following examples.

(a) $(2 + 3) + 9 = (3 + 2) + 9$

(b) $(2 + 3) + 9 = 2 + (3 + 9)$

(c) $(2 + 3) + 9 = 9 + (2 + 3)$

(d) $(4 \cdot 6)p = (6 \cdot 4)p$

(e) $4(6p) = (4 \cdot 6)p$

Answers:

(a) Commutative property

(b) Associative property

(c) Commutative property

(d) Commutative property

(e) Associative property

EXAMPLE 2 The following statements are examples of the commutative properties. Notice that the order of the numbers changes from one side of the equals sign to the other. Thus, the order in which two numbers are added or multiplied is unimportant.

(a) $(6 + x) + 9 = (x + 6) + 9$

(b) $(6 + x) + 9 = 9 + (6 + x)$

(c) $5 \cdot (9 \cdot 8) = (9 \cdot 8) \cdot 5$

(d) $5 \cdot (9 \cdot 8) = 5 \cdot (8 \cdot 9)$ ■

EXAMPLE 3 The following statements are examples of the associative properties. Here the order of the numbers does not change, but the placement of the parentheses does change. This means that when three numbers are to be added, the sum of any two can be found first, then that result is added to the remaining number.

(a) $4 + (9 + 8) = (4 + 9) + 8$

(b) $3(9x) = (3 \cdot 9)x$ ■ 2

EXAMPLE 4 By the identity properties,

(a) $-8 + 0 = -8$, **(b)** $(-9)1 = -9$. ■

TECHNOLOGY TIP To enter a negative number, such as −8, on most calculators, use the negation key, which is usually labeled (−). If you use the subtraction key and enter [−] [8], the display will read "Ans − 8" which tells the calculator to subtract 8 from the previous answer. ✔

EXAMPLE 5 By the inverse properties, the statements in parts (a) through (d) are true.

(a) $9 + (-9) = 0$

(b) $-15 + 15 = 0$

(c) $-8 \cdot \left(\frac{1}{-8}\right) = 1$

(d) $\frac{1}{\sqrt{5}} \cdot \sqrt{5} = 1$ ■

NOTE There is no real number x such that $0 \cdot x = 1$, so 0 has no inverse for multiplication. ◆ 3

3 Name the property illustrated in each of the following examples.

(a) $2 + 0 = 2$

(b) $-\frac{1}{4} \cdot (-4) = 1$

(c) $-\frac{1}{4} + \frac{1}{4} = 0$

(d) $1 \cdot \frac{2}{3} = \frac{2}{3}$

Answers:

(a) Identity property

(b) Inverse property

(c) Inverse property

(d) Identity property

One of the most important properties of the real numbers, and the only one that involves both addition and multiplication, is the distributive property. The next example shows how this property is applied.

EXAMPLE 6 By the distributive property,

(a) $9(6 + 4) = 9 \cdot 6 + 9 \cdot 4$

(b) $3(x + y) = 3x + 3y$

(c) $-8(m + 2) = (-8)(m) + (-8)(2) = -8m - 16$

(d) $(5 + x)y = 5y + xy$. ■

NOTE As shown in Example 6(d), by the commutative property, the distributive property can also be written as $(a + b)c = ac + bc$. ◆ 4

4 Use the distributive property to complete each of the following.

(a) $4(-2 + 5)$

(b) $2(a + b)$

(c) $-3(p + 1)$

(d) $(8 - k)m$

(e) $5x + 3x$

Answers:

(a) $4(-2) + 4(5) = 12$

(b) $2a + 2b$

(c) $-3p - 3$

(d) $8m - km$

(e) $(5 + 3)x = 8x$

ORDER OF OPERATIONS We avoid possible ambiguity when working problems with real numbers by using the following *order of operations,* which has been agreed on as the most useful. This order of operations is used by computers and graphing calculators.

ORDER OF OPERATIONS

If parentheses or square brackets are present:

1. Work separately above and below any fraction bar.
2. Use the rules below within each set of parentheses or square brackets. Start with the innermost set and work outward.

If no parentheses are present:

1. Find all powers and roots, working from left to right.
2. Do any multiplications or divisions in the order in which they occur, working from left to right.
3. Do any additions or subtractions in the order in which they occur, working from left to right.

EXAMPLE 7 Use the order of operations to evaluate each expression if $x = -2$, $y = 5$, and $z = -3$.

(a) $-4x^2 - 7y + 4z$

5 Evaluate the following if $m = -5$ and $n = 8$.

(a) $-2mn - 2m^2$

(b) $\frac{4(n-5)^2 - m}{m+n}$

Answers:

(a) 30

(b) $\frac{41}{3}$

Use parentheses when replacing letters with numbers.

$$-4x^2 - 7y + 4z = -4(\mathbf{-2})^2 - 7(\mathbf{5}) + 4(\mathbf{-3})$$
$$= -4(\mathbf{4}) - 7(5) + 4(-3) = \mathbf{-16} - \mathbf{35} - \mathbf{12} = -63$$

(b) $$\frac{2(x-5)^2 + 4y}{z+4} = \frac{2(\mathbf{-2} - 5)^2 + 4(\mathbf{5})}{\mathbf{-3} + 4}$$
$$= \frac{2(\mathbf{-7})^2 + 20}{1} = 2(\mathbf{49}) + 20 = 118$$ ■ 5

6 Simplify the following.

(a) $4^2 \div 8 + 3^2 \div 3$

(b) $[-7 + (-9)](-4) - 8(3)$

(c) $\frac{-11 - (-12) - 4 \cdot 5}{4(-2) - (-6)(-5)}$

(d) $\frac{36 \div 4 \cdot 3 \div 9 + 1}{9 \div (-6) \cdot 8 - 4}$

Answers:

(a) 5

(b) 40

(c) $\frac{19}{38} = \frac{1}{2} = .5$

(d) $-\frac{1}{4} = -.25$

EXAMPLE 8 Use a calculator to evaluate

$$\frac{-9(-3) + (-5)}{3(-4) - 5(2)}.$$

Use extra parentheses around the numerator and denominator and enter the expression into your calculator in the following form, being careful to distinguish the negation key from the subtraction key.

$$(-9(-3) + (-5))/(3(-4) - 5(2))$$

Negation key (arrows point to the minus signs in -9, (-3), (-5), (-4)); Subtraction key (arrow points to the minus before $5(2)$)

Then press ENTER (or EXE) to obtain the answer, -1. ■ 6

SQUARE ROOTS There are two numbers whose square is 16, namely, 4 and -4. The positive one, 4, is called the *square root* of 16. Similarly, the square root of a nonnegative number d is defined to be the *nonnegative* number whose square is d; it is denoted $\sqrt{d}$. For instance,

$$\sqrt{36} = 6 \text{ because } 6^2 = 36 \quad \text{and} \quad \sqrt{1.44} = 1.2 \text{ because } (1.2)^2 = 1.44.$$

No negative number has a square root in the real numbers. For instance, there is no real number whose square is -4, so -4 has no square root.

Every nonnegative real number has a square root. Unless an integer is a perfect square (such as $64 = 8^2$), its square root is an irrational number. A calculator can be used to obtain a rational approximation of these square roots.

7 Estimate each of the following.

(a) $\sqrt{73}$

(b) $\sqrt{22} + 3$

(c) Confirm your estimates in parts (a) and (b) with a calculator.

Answers:

(a) Between 8 and 9

(b) Between 7 and 8

(c) 8.5440; 7.6904

EXAMPLE 9 Estimate each of the following quantities. Verify your estimates with a calculator.

(a) $\sqrt{40}$

Since $6^2 = 36$ and $7^2 = 49$, $\sqrt{40}$ must be a number between 6 and 7. A typical calculator shows that $\sqrt{40} \approx 6.32455532$.

(b) $5\sqrt{7}$

$\sqrt{7}$ is between 2 and 3 because $2^2 = 4$ and $3^2 = 9$, so $5\sqrt{7}$ must be a number between $5 \cdot 2 = 10$ and $5 \cdot 3 = 15$. A calculator shows that $5\sqrt{7} \approx 13.22875656$. ■ 7

CAUTION If c and d are positive real numbers, then $\sqrt{c+d}$ is *not* equal to $\sqrt{c} + \sqrt{d}$. For example, $\sqrt{9+16} = \sqrt{25} = 5$, but $\sqrt{9} + \sqrt{16} = 3 + 4 = 7$. ◆

8 Draw a number line and graph the numbers $-4, -1, 0, 1, 2.5,$ and $13/4$ on it.

Answer:

THE NUMBER LINE The real numbers can be illustrated geometrically with a diagram called a **number line.** Each real number corresponds to exactly one point on the line and vice-versa. A number line with several sample numbers located (or **graphed**) on it is shown in Figure 1.2. 8

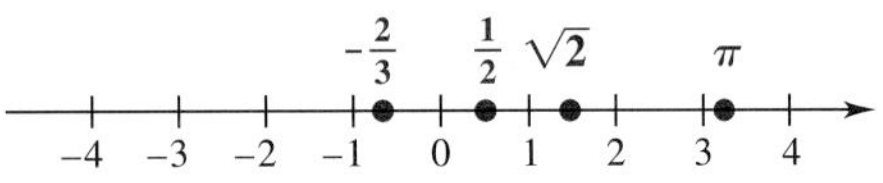

FIGURE 1.2

Comparing two real numbers requires symbols that indicate their order on the number line. The following symbols are used to indicate that one number is greater than or less than another number.

$<$ means *is less than*	$\leq$ means *is less than or equal to*
$>$ means *is greater than*	$\geq$ means *is greater than or equal to*

The following definitions show how the number line is used to decide which of two given numbers is the greater.

> For real numbers a and b,
> if a is to the left of b on a number line, then $a < b$;
> if a is to the right of b on a number line, then $a > b$.

9 Write *true* or *false* for the following.

(a) $-9 \leq -2$

(b) $8 > -3$

(c) $-14 \leq -20$

Answers:

(a) True

(b) True

(c) False

EXAMPLE 10 Write *true* or *false* for each of the following.

(a) $8 < 12$

This statement says that 8 is less than 12, which is true.

(b) $-6 > -3$

The graph in Figure 1.3 shows that -6 is to the *left* of -3. Thus, $-6 < -3$, and the given statement is false.

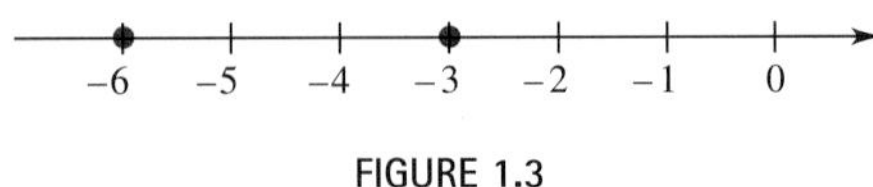

FIGURE 1.3

(c) $-2 \leq -2$

Because $-2 = -2$, this statement is true. ■ 9

TECHNOLOGY TIP If your calculator has inequality symbols (usually located on the TEST menu), you can key in statements such as "$5 < 12$" or "$-2 \geq 3$." When you press ENTER, the calculator will display 1 if the statement is true and 0 if it is false. ✔

10 Graph all integers x such that

(a) $-3 < x < 5$

(b) $1 \le x \le 5$.

Answers:

(a) −3 −2 −1 0 1 2 3 4 5

(b) 0 1 2 3 4 5 6

11 Graph all real numbers x such that

(a) $-5 < x < 1$

(b) $4 < x < 7$.

Answers:

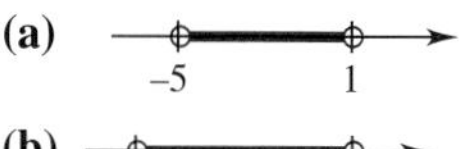

A number line can be used to draw the graph of a set of numbers, as shown in the next few examples.

EXAMPLE 11 Graph all integers x such that $1 < x < 5$.

The only integers between 1 and 5 are 2, 3, and 4. These integers are graphed on the number line in Figure 1.4. ■ **10**

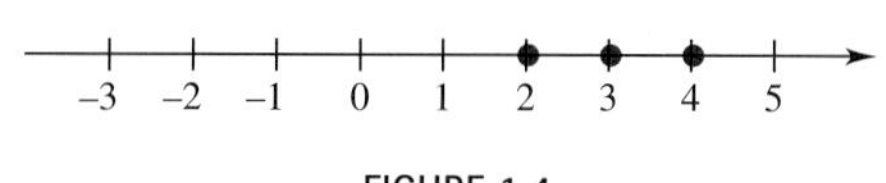

FIGURE 1.4

EXAMPLE 12 Graph all real numbers x such that $1 < x < 5$.

The graph includes all the real numbers between 1 and 5 and not just the integers. Graph these numbers by drawing a heavy line from 1 to 5 on the number line, as in Figure 1.5. Open circles at 1 and 5 show that neither of these points belongs to the graph. ■ **11**

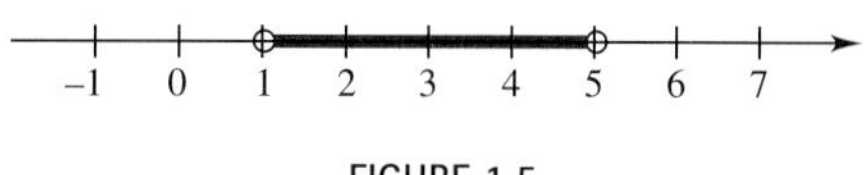

FIGURE 1.5

A set that consists of all the real numbers between two points, such as $1 < x < 5$ in Example 12, is called an **interval.** A special notation called **interval notation** is used to indicate an interval on the number line. For example, the interval including all numbers x, where $-2 < x < 3$, is written as $(-2, 3)$. The parentheses indicate that the numbers -2 and 3 are *not* included. If -2 and 3 are to be included in the interval, square brackets are used, as in $[-2, 3]$. The chart below shows several typical intervals, where $a < b$.

Inequality	*Interval Notation*	*Explanation*
$a \le x \le b$	$[a, b]$	Both a and b are included.
$a \le x < b$	$[a, b)$	a is included, b is not.
$a < x \le b$	$(a, b]$	b is included, a is not.
$a < x < b$	(a, b)	Neither a nor b is included.

Interval notation is also used to describe sets such as the set of all numbers x, with $x \ge -2$. This interval is written $[-2, \infty)$.

EXAMPLE 13 Graph the interval $[-2, \infty)$.

Start at -2 and draw a heavy line to the right, as in Figure 1.6 on the next page. Use a solid circle at -2 to show that -2 itself is part of the graph. The symbol, ∞, read "infinity," *does not* represent a number. This notation simply indicates that *all*

[12] Graph all real numbers x such that

(a) $[4, \infty)$;

(b) $[-2, 1]$.

Answers:

(a)

(b)

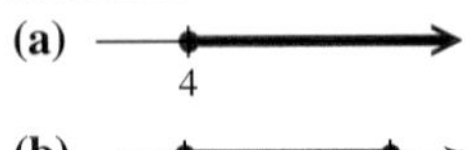

numbers greater than -2 are in the interval. Similarly, the notation $(-\infty, 2)$ indicates the set of all numbers x with $x < 2$. ■ [12]

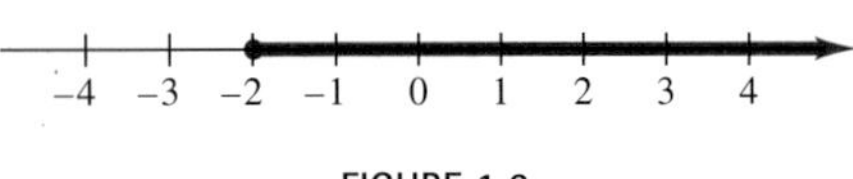

FIGURE 1.6

ABSOLUTE VALUE Distance is always a nonnegative number. For example, the distance from 0 to -2 on a number line is 2, the same as the distance from 0 to 2. The **absolute value** of a number a gives the distance on the number line from a to 0. Thus, the absolute value of both 2 and -2 is 2. We write the absolute value of the real number a as $|a|$. For example, the distance on the number line from 9 to 0 is 9, as is the distance from -9 to 0. (See Figure 1.7.) By definition, $|9| = 9$ and $|-9| = 9$.

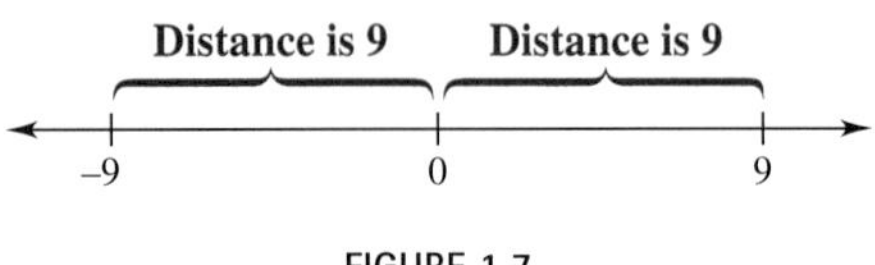

FIGURE 1.7

The facts that $|9| = 9$ and that $|-9| = 9 = -(-9)$ suggest the following algebraic definition of absolute value.

> **ABSOLUTE VALUE**
>
> For any real number a,
>
> $$|a| = a \quad \text{if } a \geq 0$$
> $$|a| = -a \quad \text{if } a < 0.$$

[13] Find the following.

(a) $|-6|$

(b) $-|7|$

(c) $-|-2|$

(d) $|-3 - 4|$

(e) $|2 - 7|$

Answers:

(a) 6

(b) -7

(c) -2

(d) 7

(e) 5

Note the second part of the definition: for a negative number, say -5, the negative of -5 is the positive number $-(-5) = 5$. Similarly, if a is any negative number, then $-a$ is a *positive* number. Thus, *for every real number a, $|a|$ is nonnegative.*

EXAMPLE 14 To evaluate $|8 - 9|$, you should first simplify the expression within the absolute value bars:

$$|8 - 9| = |-1| = 1.$$

Similarly, $-|-5 - 8| = -|-13| = -13$. ■ [13]

EXAMPLE 15 Use a calculator to compute $|9 - 3k|$, when $k = 5.789$.

The absolute value key on a calculator is labeled ABS (on the keyboard or in the math menu or one of its submenus) and should be used with parentheses whenever more than one number is involved. So substitute 5.789 for k and key in ABS(9 − 3 · 5.789). The calculator then displays the answer, 8.367. ■

1.1 EXERCISES

Label each of the following as true *or* false.

1. Every integer is a rational number.
2. Every integer is a whole number.
3. Every whole number is an integer.
4. No whole numbers are rational.

Identify the properties that are illustrated in each of the following. Some may require more than one property. Assume all variables represent real numbers. (See Examples 2–6.)

5. $-7 + 0 = -7$
6. $3 + (-3) = (-3) + 3$
7. $0 + (-7) = -7 + 0$
8. $8 + (12 + 6) = (8 + 12) + 6$
9. $[5(-8)](-3) = 5[(-8)(-3)]$
10. $8(m + 4) = 8m + 8 \cdot 4$
11. $x(y + 2) = xy + 2x$
12. $8(4 + 2) = (2 + 4)8$
13. How is the additive inverse property related to the additive identity property? the multiplicative inverse property to the multiplicative identity property?
14. Explain the distinction between the commutative and associative properties.

Evaluate each of the following if $p = -2$, $q = 4$, and $r = -5$. (See Example 7.)

15. $-3(p + 5q)$
16. $2(q - r)$
17. $\dfrac{q + r}{q + p}$
18. $\dfrac{3q}{3p - 2r}$
19. $\dfrac{\frac{q}{r} - \frac{r}{5}}{\frac{p}{2} + \frac{q}{2}}$
20. $\dfrac{\frac{3r}{10} - \frac{5p}{2}}{q + \frac{2r}{5}}$

Evaluate each expression, using the order of operations given in the text. (See Example 8.)

21. $8 - 4^2 - (-12)$
22. $8 - (-4)^2 - (-12)$
23. $-(3 - 5) - [2 - (3^2 - 13)]$
24. $\dfrac{2(3 - 7) + 4(8)}{4(-3) + (-3)(-2)}$
25. $\dfrac{2(-3) + 3/(-2) - 2/(-\sqrt{16})}{\sqrt{64} - 1}$
26. $\dfrac{6^2 - 3\sqrt{25}}{\sqrt{6^2 + 13}}$

State whether each of the following numbers is rational *or* irrational. *If the number is irrational, approximate it to four decimal places.*

27. 3π
28. $2/\pi$
29. $\sqrt{3}$
30. $\sqrt{4^2 - 3^2}$
31. $-\sqrt{4 + 5^2 - 13}$
32. $\dfrac{\sqrt{4} - 6}{3^2 + 7}$

Express each of the following statements in symbols, using $<$, $>$, $\leq$, or $\geq$.

33. 5 is less than 7.
34. -4 is greater than -9.
35. y is less than or equal to 8.3.
36. z is greater than or equal to -3.
37. t is positive.
38. c is at most 14.

Graph each of the following on a number line. (See Examples 11 and 12.)

39. All integers x such that $-4 < x < 4$
40. All integers x such that $-4 \leq x < 2$
41. All natural numbers x such that $-2 < x < 5$
42. All natural numbers x such that $x \leq 2$
43. All real numbers x such that $-2 < x \leq 3$
44. All real numbers x such that $x \geq -3$

Graph the following intervals. (See Example 13.)

45. $(3, \infty)$
46. $(-\infty, 5)$
47. $(-\infty, -2]$
48. $[-4, \infty)$
49. $(-8, -1)$
50. $[-1, 10]$
51. $[-2, 2)$
52. $(3, 7]$

Physical Science *The wind-chill factor is a measure of the cooling effect that the wind has on a person's skin. It calculates the equivalent cooling temperature if there were no wind. The table gives the wind-chill factor for various wind speeds and temperatures.**

°F\Wind	5 mph	10 mph	15 mph	20 mph	25 mph	30 mph	35 mph	40 mph
40°	37	28	22	18	16	13	11	10
30°	27	16	9	4	0	−2	−4	−6
20°	16	4	−5	−10	−15	−18	−20	−21
10°	6	−9	−18	−25	−29	−33	−35	−37
0°	−5	−21	−36	−39	−44	−48	−49	−53
−10°	−15	−33	−45	−53	−59	−63	−67	−69
−20°	−26	−46	−58	−67	−74	−79	−82	−85
−30°	−36	−58	−72	−82	−88	−94	−98	−100
−40°	−47	−70	−85	−96	−104	−109	−113	−116
−50°	−57	−83	−99	−110	−118	−125	−129	−132

Suppose that we wish to determine the difference between two of these entries, and we are interested only in the magnitude, or absolute value, of this difference. Then we subtract the two entries and find the absolute value. For example, the difference in wind-chill factors for wind at 20 miles per hour with a 20° temperature and wind at 30 miles per hour with a 40° temperature is $|-10° - 13°| = 23°$, *or equivalently,* $|13° - (-10°)| = 23°$.

Find the absolute value of the difference of the two indicated wind-chill factors.

53. Wind at 15 miles per hour with a 30° temperature and wind at 10 miles per hour with a −10° temperature

54. Wind at 20 miles per hour with a −20° temperature and wind at 5 miles per hour with a 30° temperature

55. Wind at 30 miles per hour with a −30° temperature and wind at 15 miles per hour with a −20° temperature

56. Wind at 40 miles per hour with a 40° temperature and wind at 25 miles per hour with a −30° temperature

Evaluate each of the following. (See Examples 14 and 15.)

57. $|8| - |-4|$ **58.** $|-9| - |-12|$

59. $-|-4| - |-1 - 14|$ **60.** $-|6| - |-12 - 4|$

*Source: Miller, A. and J. Thompson, *Elements of Meteorology,* 2e, Charles E. Merrill Publishing Co., 1975.

In each of the following problems, fill in the blank with either =, <, or >, so that the resulting statement is true.

61. $|5|$ ____ $|-5|$ **62.** $-|-4|$ ____ $|4|$

63. $|10 - 3|$ ____ $|3 - 10|$

64. $|6 - (-4)|$ ____ $|-4 - 6|$

65. $|-2 + 8|$ ____ $|2 - 8|$

66. $|3 + 1|$ ____ $|-3 - 1|$

67. $|3| \cdot |-5|$ ____ $|3(-5)|$

68. $|3| \cdot |2|$ ____ $|3(2)|$

69. $|3 - 2|$ ____ $|3| - |2|$

70. $|5 - 1|$ ____ $|5| - |1|$

Write the expression without using absolute values.

71. $|a - 7|$ if $a < 7$

72. $|b - c|$ if $b \geq c$

73. In general, if a and b are any real numbers having the same sign (both negative or both positive), is it always true that $|a + b| = |a| + |b|$? Explain your answer.

74. If a and b are any two real numbers, is it always true that $|a - b| = |b - a|$? Explain your answer.

75. If a and b are any real numbers, is it always true that $|a + b| = |a| + |b|$? Explain your answer.

76. For which real numbers b does $|2 - b| = |2 + b|$? Explain your answer.

Social Science *Use inequality symbols to rewrite each of the following statements, which are based on an article in* The Sacramento Bee *newspaper.* Using x as the variable, describe what x represents in each exercise and then write an inequality. Example: At least 4000 foreign students attend the University of Southern California (USC). Let x represent the number of foreign students attending USC. Then* $x \geq 4000$.

77. Foreign students contribute more than $1 billion annually to the California economy.

78. More than 60% of the international students come from Asian countries.

79. Less than 7.5% of foreign students in the United States now come from Middle Eastern countries.

80. No more than 10% of the foreign students in the United States come from Japan.

*"State colleges drawing foreigners despite cuts" by Lisa Lapin from *The Sacramento Bee,* December 2, 1992. Copyright, The Sacramento Bee, 1994. Reprinted by permission.

81. California has more than 13% of all foreign students in the United States.

82. Foreign students must prove they have at least \$22,000 in cash to spend here each year.

Social Science *Sociologists measure the status of an individual within a society by evaluating for that individual the number x, which gives the percentage of the population with less income than the given person, and the number y, the percentage of the population with less education. The average status is defined as* $(x + y)/2$, *while the individual's status incongruity is defined by* $|(x - y)/2|$. *People with high status incongruities would include unemployed Ph.D.'s (low x, high y) and millionaires who didn't make it past the second grade (high x, low y).*

83. What is the highest possible average status for an individual? The lowest?

84. What is the highest possible status incongruity for an individual? The lowest?

85. Jolene Rizzo makes more money than 56% of the population and has more education than 78%. Find her average status and status incongruity.

86. A popular movie star makes more money than 97% of the population and is better educated than 12%. Find the average status and status incongruity for this individual.

1.2 FIRST-DEGREE EQUATIONS

One of the main uses of algebra is to solve equations. An **equation** is a statement that two mathematical expressions are equal; for example,

$$3x^2 - 2x + 4 = 7x - 2, \quad 4y^3 + 8 = 12, \quad 2z + 6 = -9.$$

The letter in each equation is called the **variable.**

In this section we concentrate on **first-degree equations,** which are equations that can be written in the form $ax + b = c$, where a, b, and c are constants (real numbers) and $a \neq 0$. Examples of first-degree equations are

$$5x - 3 = 13, \quad 8y = 4, \quad -3p + 5 = -8.$$

Examples of equations that are *not* first-degree include $x^3 = 15$, $2x^2 = 5x + 6$ and $\sqrt{x + 2} = 4$ (because of the radical).

A **solution** of an equation is a number that can be substituted for the variable in the equation to produce a true statement. For example, substituting the number 9 for x in the equation $2x + 1 = 19$ gives

$$2x + 1 = 19$$

$$2(9) + 1 = 19 \qquad \text{Let } x = 9.$$

$$18 + 1 = 19. \qquad \text{True}$$

This true statement indicates that 9 is a solution of $2x + 1 = 19$. [1]

[1] Is -4 a solution of the following equations?

(a) $3x + 5 = -7$

(b) $2x - 3 = 5$

(c) Is there more than one solution of the equation in part (a)?

Answers:

(a) Yes

(b) No

(c) No

The following properties are used to solve equations.

PROPERTIES OF EQUALITY

1. The same number may be added to or subtracted from both sides of an equation:

$$\text{If } a = b, \text{ then } a + c = b + c \quad \text{and} \quad a - c = b - c.$$

2. Both sides of an equation may be multiplied or divided by the same nonzero number:

$$\text{If } a = b \text{ and } c \neq 0, \text{ then } ac = bc \quad \text{and} \quad \frac{a}{c} = \frac{b}{c}.$$

EXAMPLE 1 Solve the equation $5x - 3 = 12$.

Using the first property of equality, add 3 to both sides. This isolates the term containing the variable on one side of the equals sign.

$$5x - 3 = 12$$
$$5x - 3 + \mathbf{3} = 12 + \mathbf{3} \qquad \text{Add 3 to both sides.}$$
$$5x = 15$$

Now arrange for the coefficient of x to be 1 by using the second property of equality.

$$5x = 15$$
$$\frac{5x}{5} = \frac{15}{5} \qquad \text{Divide both sides by 5.}$$
$$x = 3$$

The solution of the original equation, $5x - 3 = 12$, is 3. Check the solution by substituting 3 for x in the original equation. ■ [2]

[2] Solve the following.

(a) $3p - 5 = 19$

(b) $4y + 3 = -5$

(c) $-2k + 6 = 2$

Answers:

(a) 8

(b) -2

(c) 2

EXAMPLE 2 Solve $2k + 3(k - 4) = 2(k - 3)$.

First simplify the equation by using the distributive property on the left-side term $3(k - 4)$ and the right-side term $2(k - 3)$:

$$2k + 3(k - 4) = 2(k - 3)$$
$$2k + 3k - 12 = 2k - 6.$$

On the left, $2k + 3k = (2 + 3)k = 5k$, again by the distributive property, which gives

$$5k - 12 = 2k - 6.$$

One way to proceed is to add $-2k$ to both sides.

$$5k - 12 + \mathbf{(-2k)} = 2k - 6 + \mathbf{(-2k)} \qquad \text{Add } -2k \text{ to both sides.}$$
$$3k - 12 = -6$$
$$3k - 12 + \mathbf{12} = -6 + \mathbf{12} \qquad \text{Add 12 to both sides.}$$
$$3k = 6$$
$$\frac{\mathbf{1}}{\mathbf{3}}(3k) = \frac{\mathbf{1}}{\mathbf{3}}(6) \qquad \text{Multiply both sides by } \frac{1}{3}.$$
$$k = 2$$

The solution is 2. Check this result by substituting 2 for k in the original equation. ■ [3]

[3] Solve the following.

(a) $3(m - 6) + 2(m + 4) = 4m - 2$

(b) $-2(y + 3) + 4y = 3(y + 1) - 6$

Answers:

(a) 8

(b) -3

EXAMPLE 3 Use a calculator to solve $42.19x + 121.34 = 16.83x + 19.15$.

To avoid round-off errors in the intermediate steps, do all the algebra first, without using the calculator.

$$42.19x = 16.83x + 19.15 - 121.34 \qquad \text{Subtract 121.34 from both sides.}$$
$$42.19x - 16.83x = 19.15 - 121.34 \qquad \text{Subtract } 16.83x \text{ from both sides.}$$

$$(42.19 - 16.83)x = 19.15 - 121.34 \qquad \text{Distributive property}$$

$$x = \frac{19.15 - 121.34}{42.19 - 16.83} \qquad \text{Divide both sides by } (42.19 - 16.83).$$

Now use the calculator and determine that $x \approx -4.0296$. Because this answer is approximate, it may not check exactly when substituted in the original equation. ■

The next three examples show how to simplify the solution of first-degree equations involving fractions. We solve these equations by multiplying both sides of the equation by a **common denominator,** a number that can be divided (with remainder 0) by each denominator in the equation. This step will eliminate the fractions.

CAUTION Because this is an application of the multiplication property of *equality,* it can be done *only in an equation.* ◆

EXAMPLE 4 Solve $\frac{r}{10} - \frac{2}{15} = \frac{3r}{20} - \frac{1}{5}$.

Here the denominators are 10, 15, 20, and 5. Each of these numbers can be divided into 60; therefore, 60 is a common denominator. Multiply both sides of the equation by 60.

$$60\left(\frac{r}{10} - \frac{2}{15}\right) = 60\left(\frac{3r}{20} - \frac{1}{5}\right)$$

Use the distributive property to eliminate the denominators.

$$60\left(\frac{r}{10}\right) - 60\left(\frac{2}{15}\right) = 60\left(\frac{3r}{20}\right) - 60\left(\frac{1}{5}\right)$$

$$6r - 8 = 9r - 12$$

Add $-6r$ and 12 to both sides.

$$6r - 8 + (-6r) + 12 = 9r - 12 + (-6r) + 12$$

$$4 = 3r$$

Multiply both sides by 1/3 to get the solution.

$$r = \frac{4}{3}$$

Check this solution in the original equation. ■ 4

4 Solve the following.

(a) $\frac{x}{2} - \frac{x}{4} = 6$

(b) $\frac{2x}{3} + \frac{1}{2} = \frac{x}{4} - \frac{9}{2}$

Answers:

(a) 24

(b) -12

EXAMPLE 5 Solve $\frac{4}{3(k+2)} - \frac{k}{3(k+2)} = \frac{5}{3}$.

Multiply both sides of the equation by the common denominator $3(k + 2)$. Here $k \neq -2$, since $k = -2$ would give a 0 denominator, making the fraction undefined.

$$3(k+2) \cdot \frac{4}{3(k+2)} - 3(k+2) \cdot \frac{k}{3(k+2)} = 3(k+2) \cdot \frac{5}{3}$$

Simplify each side and solve for k.

$$4 - k = 5(k + 2)$$

$$4 - k = 5k + 10 \quad \text{Distributive property}$$

$$4 - k + k = 5k + 10 + k \quad \text{Add } k \text{ to both sides.}$$

$$4 = 6k + 10$$

$$4 + (-10) = 6k + 10 + (-10) \quad \text{Add } -10 \text{ to both sides.}$$

$$-6 = 6k$$

$$-1 = k \quad \text{Multiply by } \frac{1}{6}.$$

The solution is -1. Substitute -1 for k as a check.

$$\frac{4}{3(-1+2)} - \frac{-1}{3(-1+2)} \stackrel{?}{=} \frac{5}{3}$$

$$\frac{4}{3} - \frac{-1}{3} \stackrel{?}{=} \frac{5}{3}$$

$$\frac{5}{3} = \frac{5}{3}$$

The check shows that -1 is the solution. ■ 5

5 Solve the equation.

$$\frac{5p + 1}{3(p + 1)} = \frac{3p - 3}{3(p + 1)} + \frac{9p - 3}{3(p + 1)}$$

Answer:
1

CAUTION Because the equation in Example 5 has a restriction on k, it is *essential* to check the solution. ◆

EXAMPLE 6 Solve $\frac{x}{x - 2} = \frac{2}{x - 2} + 2$.

Multiply both sides of the equation by $x - 2$, assuming that $x - 2 \neq 0$. This gives

$$x = 2 + 2(x - 2)$$

$$x = 2 + 2x - 4$$

$$x = 2.$$

Recall the assumption that $x - 2 \neq 0$. Because $x = 2$, we have $x - 2 = 0$, and the multiplication property of equality does not apply. To see this, substitute 2 for x in the original equation—this substitution produces a 0 denominator. Since division by zero is not defined, there is no solution for the given equation. ■ 6

6 Solve each equation.

(a) $\frac{3p}{p + 1} = 1 - \frac{3}{p + 1}$

(b) $\frac{8y}{y - 4} = \frac{32}{y - 4} - 3$

Answer:
Neither equation has a solution.

Sometimes an equation with several variables must be solved for one of the variables. This process is called **solving for a specified variable.**

EXAMPLE 7 Solve for x: $3(ax - 5a) + 4b = 4x - 2$.

Use the distributive property to get

$$3ax - 15a + 4b = 4x - 2.$$

7 Solve for x.

(a) $2x - 7y = 3xk$

(b) $8(4 - x) + 6p = -5k - 11yx$

Answers:

(a) $x = \dfrac{7y}{2 - 3k}$

(b) $x = \dfrac{5k + 32 + 6p}{8 - 11y}$

Treat x as the variable, the other letters as constants. Get all terms with x on one side of the equals sign, and all terms without x on the other side.

$$3ax - 4x = 15a - 4b - 2 \qquad \text{Isolate terms with } x \text{ on the left.}$$
$$(3a - 4)x = 15a - 4b - 2 \qquad \text{Distributive property}$$
$$x = \frac{15a - 4b - 2}{3a - 4} \qquad \text{Multiply by } \frac{1}{3a - 4}.$$

The final equation is solved for x, as required. ■ 7

Recall from Section 1.1 that the absolute value of the number a, written $|a|$, gives the distance on a number line from a to 0. For example, $|4| = 4$, and $|-7| = 7$.

EXAMPLE 8 Solve the equation $|x| = 3$.

There are two numbers whose absolute value is 3, namely 3 and -3. The solutions of the given equation are 3 and -3. ■

8 Solve each equation.

(a) $|y| = 9$

(b) $|r + 3| = 1$

(c) $|2k - 3| = 7$

Answers:

(a) 9, -9

(b) $-2, -4$

(c) 5, -2

EXAMPLE 9 Solve $|p - 4| = 2$.

The only numbers with absolute value 2 are 2 and -2. So this equation will be satisfied if the expression inside the absolute value bars, $p - 4$, equals either 2 or -2:

$$p - 4 = 2 \quad \text{or} \quad p - 4 = -2.$$

Solving these two equations produces

$$p = 6 \quad \text{or} \quad p = 2,$$

so that 6 and 2 are solutions for the original equation. As before, check by substituting in the original equation. ■ 8

EXAMPLE 10 Solve $|4m - 3| = |m + 6|$.

The quantities in absolute value bars must either be equal or be negatives of one another to satisfy the equation. That is,

$$\begin{aligned} 4m - 3 &= m + 6 &\quad \text{or} \quad 4m - 3 &= -(m + 6) \\ 3m &= 9 & 4m - 3 &= -m - 6 \\ m &= 3 & 5m &= -3 \\ & & m &= -\frac{3}{5}. \end{aligned}$$

Check that the solutions for the original equation are 3 and $-3/5$. ■ 9

9 Solve each equation.

(a) $|r + 6| = |2r + 1|$

(b) $|5k - 7| = |10k - 2|$

Answers:

(a) 5, $-7/3$

(b) -1, 3/5

APPLIED PROBLEMS One of the main reasons for learning mathematics is to be able to use it to solve practical problems. There are no hard and fast rules for dealing with real-world applications, except perhaps to use common sense. However, you will find it much easier to deal with such problems if you don't try to do everything at once. After reading the problem carefully, attack it in stages, as suggested in the following guidelines.

SOLVING APPLIED PROBLEMS

1. Decide on the unknown. Name it with some variable that you *write down.* Many students try to skip this step. They are eager to get on with the writing of the equation. But this is an important step. If you don't know what the variable represents, how can you write a meaningful equation or interpret a result?
2. Draw a sketch or make a chart, if appropriate, showing the information given in the problem.
3. Decide on a variable expression to represent any other unknowns in the problem. For example, if x represents the width of a rectangle, and you know that the length is one more than twice the width, then *write down* that the length is $1 + 2x$.
4. Using the results of Steps 1–3, write an equation that expresses a condition that must be satisfied.
5. Solve the equation.
6. Check the solution in the words of the *original problem,* not just in the equation you have written.

The following examples illustrate this approach.

EXAMPLE 11 If the length of a side of a square is increased by 3 centimeters, the new perimeter is 40 centimeters more than twice the length of the side of the original square. Find the length of a side of the original square.

Step 1 What should the variable represent? To find the length of a side of the original square, let

$$x = \text{length of a side of the original square.}$$

Step 2 Draw a sketch, as in Figure 1.8.

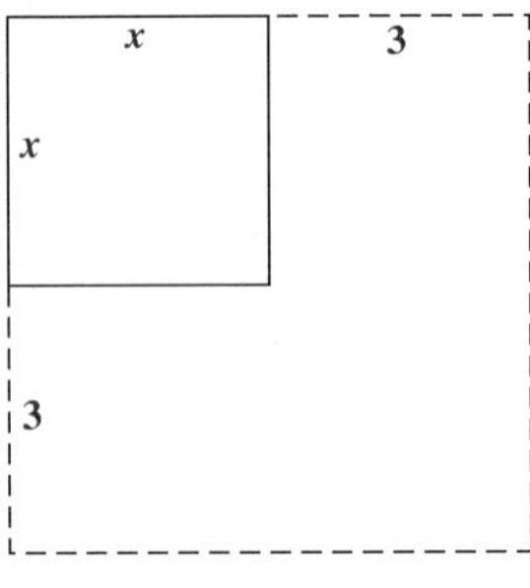

FIGURE 1.8

Step 3 The length of a side of the new square is 3 centimeters more than the length of a side of the old square, so

$$x + 3 = \text{length of a side of the new square.}$$

Now write a variable expression for the new perimeter. Since the perimeter of a square is four times the length of a side,

$$4(x + 3) = \text{the perimeter of the new square.}$$

Step 4 Write an equation by looking again at the information in the problem. The new perimeter is 40 more than twice the length of a side of the original square, so the equation is

$$\begin{array}{ccccc} \left(\begin{array}{c}\text{the new}\\ \text{perimeter}\end{array}\right) & \text{is} & 40 & \left(\begin{array}{c}\text{more}\\ \text{than}\end{array}\right) & \left(\begin{array}{c}\text{twice the side of}\\ \text{the original square}\end{array}\right) \\ 4(x+3) & = & 40 & + & 2x. \end{array}$$

Step 5 Solve the equation.

$$4(x + 3) = 40 + 2x$$
$$4x + 12 = 40 + 2x$$
$$2x = 28$$
$$x = 14$$

Step 6 Check the solution using the wording of the original problem. The length of a side of the new square would be $14 + 3 = 17$ centimeters; its perimeter would be $4(17) = 68$ centimeters. Twice the length of the side of the original square is $2(14) = 28$ centimeters. Because $40 + 28 = 68$ centimeters, the solution checks with the words of the original problem. ■ 10

10 **(a)** A triangle has a perimeter of 45 centimeters. Two of the sides of the triangle are equal in length, with the third side 9 centimeters longer than either of the two equal sides. Find the lengths of the sides of the triangle.

(b) A rectangle has a perimeter which is five times its width. The length is 4 more than the width. Find the length and width of the rectangle.

Answers:

(a) 12 centimeters, 12 centimeters, 21 centimeters

(b) Length is 12, width is 8

EXAMPLE 12 Chuck travels 80 kilometers in the same time that Mary travels 180 kilometers. Mary travels 50 kilometers per hour faster than Chuck. Find the speed of each person.

Use the steps given earlier.

Step 1 Use x to represent Chuck's speed and $x + 50$ to represent Mary's speed, which is 50 kilometers per hour faster than Chuck's.

Steps 2 and 3 Constant rate problems of this kind require the distance formula

$$d = rt,$$

where d is the distance traveled in t hours at a constant rate of speed r. The distance traveled by each person is given, along with the fact that the time traveled by each person is the same. Solve the formula $d = rt$ for t.

$$d = rt$$
$$\mathbf{\frac{1}{r}} \cdot d = \mathbf{\frac{1}{r}} \cdot rt$$
$$\frac{d}{r} = t$$

For Chuck, $d = 80$ and $r = x$, giving $t = 80/x$. For Mary, $d = 180$, $r = x + 50$, and $t = 180/(x + 50)$. Use these facts to complete a chart, which organizes the information given in the problem.

	d	r	t
Chuck	80	x	$\frac{80}{x}$
Mary	180	$x + 50$	$\frac{180}{x + 50}$

Step 4 Because both people traveled for the *same time,* the equation is

$$\frac{80}{x} = \frac{180}{x + 50}.$$

Step 5 Multiply both sides of the equation by $x(x + 50)$.

$$x(x + 50)\frac{80}{x} = x(x + 50)\frac{180}{x + 50}$$

$$80(x + 50) = 180x$$

$$80x + 4000 = 180x$$

$$4000 = 100x$$

$$40 = x$$

Step 6 Since x represents Chuck's speed, Chuck went 40 kilometers per hour. Mary's speed is $x + 50$, or $40 + 50 = 90$ kilometers per hour. Check these results in the words of the original problem. ■ 11

11 **(a)** Tom and Dick are in a run for charity. Tom runs at 7 mph and Dick runs at 5 mph. If they start at the same time, how long will it be until they are 1/2 mile apart?

(b) In part (a), suppose the run has a staggered start. If Dick starts first, and Tom starts 10 minutes later, how long will it be until they are neck and neck?

Answers:
(a) 15 minutes (1/4 hour)
(b) Tom runs 25 minutes.

EXAMPLE 13 A financial manager has \$14,000 to invest for her company. She plans to invest part of the money in tax-free bonds at 6% interest and the remainder in taxable bonds at 9%. She wants to earn \$1005 per year in interest from the investments. Find the amount she should invest at each rate.

Let x represent the amount to be invested at 6%, so that $14{,}000 - x$ is the amount to be invested at 9%. Interest is given by the product of principal, rate, and time in years ($i = prt$). Summarize this information in a chart.

Investment	*Amount Invested*	*Interest Rate*	*Interest Earned in 1 Year*
Tax-free Bonds	x	$6\% = .06$	$.06x$
Taxable Bonds	$14{,}000 - x$	$9\% = .09$	$.09(14{,}000 - x)$
Totals	14,000		1005

Because the total interest is to be \$1005,

$$.06x + .09(14{,}000 - x) = 1005.$$

Solve this equation.

$$.06x + 1260 - .09x = 1005$$

$$-.03x = -255$$

$$x = 8500$$

The manager should invest \$8500 at 6%, and \$14,000 − \$8500 = \$5500 at 9%. ■ 12

12 An investor owns two pieces of property. One, worth twice as much as the other, returns 6% in annual interest, while the other returns 4%. Find the value of each piece of property if the total annual interest earned is \$8000.

Answer:
6% return: \$100,000; 4% return: \$50,000

1.2 EXERCISES

Solve each equation. (See Examples 1–6.)

1. $3x + 5 = 20$
2. $4 - 5y = 9$
3. $.6k - .3 = .5k + .4$
4. $2.5 + 5.04m = 8.5 - .06m$
5. $\frac{2}{5}r + \frac{1}{4} - 3r = \frac{6}{5}$
6. $\frac{2}{3} - \frac{1}{4}p = \frac{3}{2} + \frac{1}{3}p$
7. $2a - 1 = 3(a + 1) + 7a + 5$
8. $3(k - 2) - 6 = 4k - (3k - 1)$
9. $2[x - (3 + 2x) + 9] = 2x + 4$
10. $-2[4(k + 2) - 3(k + 1)] = 14 + 2k$
11. $\frac{3x}{5} - \frac{4}{5}(x + 1) = 2 - \frac{3}{10}(3x - 4)$
12. $\frac{4}{3}(x - 2) - \frac{1}{2} = 2\left(\frac{3}{4}x - 1\right)$
13. $\frac{5y}{6} - 8 = 5 - \frac{2y}{3}$
14. $\frac{x}{2} - 3 = \frac{3x}{5} + 1$
15. $\frac{m}{2} - \frac{1}{m} = \frac{6m + 5}{12}$
16. $-\frac{3k}{2} + \frac{9k - 5}{6} = \frac{11k + 8}{k}$
17. $\frac{4}{x - 3} - \frac{8}{2x + 5} + \frac{3}{x - 3} = 0$
18. $\frac{5}{2p + 3} - \frac{3}{p - 2} = \frac{4}{2p + 3}$
19. $\frac{3}{2m + 4} = \frac{1}{m + 2} - 2$
20. $\frac{8}{3k - 9} - \frac{5}{k - 3} = 4$

Use a calculator to solve each of the following equations. Round your answer to the nearest hundredth. (See Example 3.)

21. $9.06x + 3.59(8x - 5) = 12.07x + .5612$
22. $-5.74(3.1 - 2.7p) = 1.09p + 5.2588$
23. $\frac{2.63r - 8.99}{1.25} - \frac{3.90r - 1.77}{2.45} = r$
24. $\frac{8.19m + 2.55}{4.34} - \frac{8.17m - 9.94}{1.04} = 4m$

Solve each equation for x. (See Example 7. In Exercises 29 and 30, recall that $a^2 = a \cdot a$.)

25. $4(a - x) = b - a + 2x$
26. $(3a + b) - bx = a(x - 2)$
27. $5(b - x) = 2b + ax$
28. $bx - 2b = 2a - ax$
29. $x = a^2x + ax - 3a + 3$
30. $a^2x - 2a^2 = 3x$

Solve each equation for the specified variable. Assume all denominators are nonzero. (See Example 7.)

31. $PV = k$ for V
32. $i = prt$ for p
33. $V = V_0 + gt$ for g
34. $S = S_0 + gt^2 + k$ for g
35. $A = \frac{1}{2}(B + b)h$ for B
36. $C = \frac{5}{9}(F - 32)$ for F
37. $\frac{1}{R} = \frac{1}{r_1} + \frac{1}{r_2}$ for R
38. $m = \frac{Ft}{v_1 - v_2}$ for v_2

Solve each equation. (See Examples 8–10.)

39. $|2h + 1| = 5$
40. $|4m - 3| = 12$
41. $|6 - 2p| = 10$
42. $|-5x + 7| = 15$
43. $\left|\frac{5}{r - 3}\right| = 10$
44. $\left|\frac{3}{2h - 1}\right| = 4$
45. $\left|\frac{6y + 1}{y - 1}\right| = 3$
46. $\left|\frac{3a - 4}{2a + 3}\right| = 1$
47. $|3y - 2| = |4y + 5|$
48. $|1 - 3z| = |z + 2|$
49. **Natural Science** The excess lifetime cancer risk R is a measure of the likelihood that an individual will develop cancer from a particular pollutant. For example, if $R = .01$, then a person has a 1% increased chance of developing cancer during a lifetime. The value of R for formaldehyde can be calculated using the linear equation $R = kd$, where k is a constant and d is the daily dose in parts per million. The constant k for formaldehyde can be calculated using the formula $k = .132\left(\frac{B}{W}\right)$, where B is the total number of cubic meters of air a person breathes in one day and W is a person's weight in kilograms.*

---

*Hines, A., Ghosh, T., Layalka, S., and Warder, R., *Indoor Air Quality & Control*, Prentice Hall, 1993. (TD 883.1.I476 1993)

(a) Find k for a person that breathes in 20 cubic meters of air per day and weighs 75 kg.
(b) Mobile homes in Minnesota were found to have a mean daily dose d of .42 parts per million. Calculate R.*
(c) For every 5000 people, how many cases of cancer could be expected each year from these levels of formaldehyde? Assume an average life expectancy of 72 years.

50. Refer to Exercise 29. Suppose someone tells you that there is no reason to solve for x, because the left side of the equation is already equal to x. Is this correct? Explain.

Management *The approximate annual interest rate of a loan paid off with monthly payments is given by*

$$A = \frac{24f}{b(p + 1)},$$

where f is the finance charge on the loan, p is the total number of payments, and b is the original balance of the loan. Use the formula to find the requested value in the following. Round A to the nearest percent and round other variables to the nearest whole numbers. (This formula is not accurate enough for the requirements of federal law.)

51. $f = \$800, b = \$4000, p = 36$; find A

52. $A = 5\%, b = \$1500, p = 24$; find f

53. $A = 6\%, f = \$370, p = 36$; find b

54. $A = 10\%, f = \$490, p = 48$; find b

Management *When a loan is paid off early, a portion of the finance charge must be returned to the borrower. By one method of calculating finance charge (called the* rule of 78*), the amount of unearned interest (finance charge to be returned) is given by*

$$u = f \cdot \frac{n(n + 1)}{q(q + 1)},$$

where u represents unearned interest, f is the original finance charge, n is the number of payments remaining when the loan is paid off, and q is the original number of payments. Find the amount of the unearned interest in each of the following.

55. Original finance charge = \$800, loan scheduled to run 36 months, paid off with 18 payments remaining

56. Original finance charge = \$1400, loan scheduled to run 48 months, paid off with 12 payments remaining

Solve each applied problem. (See Examples 11–13.)

57. A closed recycling bin is in the shape of a rectangular box. Find the height of the bin if its length is 18 feet, its width is 8 feet, and its surface area is 496 square feet.

(a) Choose a variable and write down what it represents.
(b) Write an equation relating the height, length, and width of a box to its surface area.
(c) Solve the equation and check the solution in the wording of the original problem.

58. The length of a rectangular label is 3 centimeters less than twice the width. The perimeter is 54 centimeters. Find the width. Follow the steps outlined in Exercise 57.

59. A puzzle piece in the shape of a triangle has a perimeter of 30 centimeters. Two sides of the triangle are each twice as long as the shortest side. Find the length of the shortest side.

60. A triangle has a perimeter of 27 centimeters. One side is twice as long as the shortest side. The third side is seven centimeters longer than the shortest side. Find the length of the shortest side.

61. A plane flies nonstop from New York to London, which are about 3500 miles apart. After one hour and six minutes in the air, the plane passes over Halifax, Nova Scotia, which is 600 miles from New York. Estimate the flying time from New York to London.

62. On vacation, Le Hong averaged 50 mph traveling from Denver to Minneapolis. Returning by a different route that covered the same number of miles, he averaged 55 mph. What is the distance between the two cities, if his total traveling time was 32 hours?

63. Russ and Janet are running in the Apple Hill Fun Run. Russ runs at 7 mph, Janet at 5 mph. If they start at the same time, how long will it be before they are 2/3 mile apart?

64. If the run in Exercise 63 has a staggered start and Janet starts first, with Russ starting 15 minutes later, how long will it be before he catches up with her?

65. Joe Gonzalvez received \$52,000 profit from the sale of some land. He invested part at 5% interest, and the rest at 4% interest. He earned a total of \$2290 interest per year. How much did he invest at 5%?

66. Weijen Luan invests \$20,000 received from an insurance settlement in two ways: some at 6%, and some at 4%. Altogether, she makes \$1040 per year interest. How much is invested at 4%?

67. Maria Martinelli bought two plots of land for a total of \$120,000. On the first plot, she made a profit of 15%. On the second, she lost 10%. Her total profit was \$5500. How much did she pay for each piece of land?

68. Suppose \$20,000 is invested at 5%. How much additional money must be invested at 4% to produce a yield of 4.8% on the entire amount invested?

69. Cathy Wacaser earns take-home pay of \$592 a week. If her deductions for taxes, retirement, union dues, and medical plan amount to 26% of her wages, what is her weekly pay before deductions?

---

*Ritchie, I and R. Lehnen, "An Analysis of Formaldehyde Concentration in Mobile and Conventional Homes." *J. Env. Health* 47: 300–305.

70. Barbara Dalton gives 10% of her net income to the church. This amounts to \$80 a month. In addition, her paycheck deductions are 24% of her gross monthly income. What is her gross monthly income?

Natural Science *Exercises 71 and 72 depend on the idea of the octane rating of gasoline, a measure of its antiknock qualities. Actual gasoline blends are compared to standard fuels. In one measure of octane, a standard fuel is made with only two ingredients: heptane and isooctane. For this fuel, the octane rating is the percent of isooctane; i.e., a gasoline with an octane rating of 98 has the same antiknock properties as a standard fuel that is 98% isooctane.*

71. How many liters of 94 octane gasoline should be mixed with 200 liters of 99 octane gasoline to get a mixture that is 97 octane?

72. A service station has 92 octane and 98 octane gasoline. How many liters of each gasoline should be mixed to provide 12 liters of 96 octane gasoline for a chemistry experiment?

1.3 POLYNOMIALS

We begin with exponents, whose properties are essential for understanding polynomials. You are familiar with the usual notation for squares and cubes:

$$5^2 = 5 \cdot 5 \quad \text{and} \quad 6^3 = 6 \cdot 6 \cdot 6.$$

We now extend this convenient notation to other cases.

> If n is a natural number and a is any real number, then
>
> $$\boldsymbol{a^n} \quad \text{denotes the product} \quad \boldsymbol{a \cdot a \cdot a \cdots a} \ (n \text{ factors}).$$
>
> The number a is the **base** and n is the **exponent.**

EXAMPLE 1 4^6, which is read "four to the sixth" is the number

$$4 \cdot 4 \cdot 4 \cdot 4 \cdot 4 \cdot 4 = 4096.$$

Similarly, $(-5)^3 = (-5)(-5)(-5) = -125$ and

$$\left(\frac{3}{2}\right)^4 = \frac{3}{2} \cdot \frac{3}{2} \cdot \frac{3}{2} \cdot \frac{3}{2} = \frac{81}{16}. \quad \blacksquare$$

EXAMPLE 2 Use a calculator to approximate the following.

(a) $(1.2)^8$

Key in 1.2, then use the x^y key (labeled $\wedge$ on some calculators), and finally key in the exponent 8. The calculator displays the (exact) answer 4.29981696.

(b) $\left(\frac{12}{7}\right)^{23}$

Don't compute 12/7 separately. Use parentheses and key in (12/7), followed by the x^y key and the exponent 23 to obtain the approximate answer 242,054.822. ■ [1]

[1] Evaluate the following.

(a) 6^3

(b) 5^{12}

(c) 1^9

(d) $\left(\frac{7}{5}\right)^8$

Answers:

(a) 216

(b) 244,140,625

(c) 1

(d) 14.75789056

CAUTION A common error in using exponents occurs with expressions such as $4 \cdot 3^2$. The exponent 2 applies only to the base 3, so that

$$4 \cdot \mathbf{3^2} = 4 \cdot \mathbf{3} \cdot \mathbf{3} = 36.$$

On the other hand,

$$(\mathbf{4 \cdot 3})^2 = (\mathbf{4 \cdot 3})(\mathbf{4 \cdot 3}) = 12 \cdot 12 = 144,$$

2 Evaluate the following.

(a) $3 \cdot 6^2$

(b) $5 \cdot 4^3$

(c) -3^6

(d) $(-3)^6$

(e) $-2 \cdot (-3)^5$

Answers:

(a) 108

(b) 320

(c) -729

(d) 729

(e) 486

and so

$$4 \cdot 3^2 \neq (4 \cdot 3)^2.$$

Be careful to distinguish between expressions like -2^4 and $(-2)^4$.

$$-2^4 = -(2^4) = -(2 \cdot 2 \cdot 2 \cdot 2) = -16$$
$$(-2)^4 = (-2)(-2)(-2)(-2) = 16$$

and so

$$-2^4 \neq (-2)^4. \blacklozenge$$ 2

By the definition of an exponent,

$$3^4 \cdot 3^2 = (3 \cdot 3 \cdot 3 \cdot 3)(3 \cdot 3) = 3^6.$$

This suggests the following property for the product of two powers of a number.

> If m and n are natural numbers and a is a real number, then
>
> $$a^m \cdot a^n = a^{m+n}.$$

3 Simplify the following.

(a) $5^3 \cdot 5^6$

(b) $(-3)^4 \cdot (-3)^{10}$

(c) $(5p)^2 \cdot (5p)^8$

Answers:

(a) 5^9

(b) $(-3)^{14}$

(c) $(5p)^{10}$

EXAMPLE 3 Simplify the following.

(a) $7^4 \cdot 7^6 = 7^{4+6} = 7^{10}$

(b) $(-2)^3 \cdot (-2)^5 = (-2)^{3+5} = (-2)^8$

(c) $(3k)^2 \cdot (3k)^3 = (3k)^5$

(d) $(m+n)^2 \cdot (m+n)^5 = (m+n)^7$ ■ 3

POLYNOMIALS A polynomial is an algebraic expression like

$$5x^4 + 2x^3 + 6x, \quad 8m^3 + 9m^2 - 6m + 3, \quad 10p, \quad \text{or} \quad -9.$$

More formally, a **polynomial** in one variable is an expression of the form

$$a_n x^n + a_{n-1}x^{n-1} + \cdots + a_1 x + a_0, \qquad (1)$$

where n is a whole number, x is a **variable,** and $a_0, a_1, a_2, \ldots, a_n$ are real numbers (called the **coefficients** of the polynomial). For example, the polynomial

$$8x^3 + 9x^2 - 6x + 3$$

is of the form

$$a_n x^n + a_{n-1}x^{n-1} + \cdots + a_1 x + a_0,$$

with $n = 3$, $a_n = a_3 = 8$, $a_{n-1} = a_2 = 9$, $a_1 = -6$, and $a_0 = 3$. Each of the expressions $8x^3$, $9x^2$, $-6x$, and 3 is called a **term** of the polynomial $8x^3 + 9x^2 - 6x + 3$. The coefficient a_0 of a polynomial (for instance, 3 in the polynomial $8x^3 + 9x^2 - 6x + 3$) is called the **constant term.** Letters other than x may be used for the variable of a polynomial.

Only expressions that can be put in the form (1) are polynomials. Consequently, the following expressions are *not* polynomials:

$$8x^3 + \frac{6}{x}, \quad \frac{9 + x}{2 - x}, \quad \text{and} \quad \frac{-p^2 + 5p + 3}{2p - 1}.$$

The **degree of a nonzero term** with only one variable is the exponent on the variable. For example, the term $9p^4$ has degree 4. The **degree of a polynomial** is the highest degree of any of its nonzero terms. Thus, the degree of $-p^2 + 5p + 3$ is 2. The **zero polynomial** consists of the constant term 0 and no other terms. No degree is assigned to the zero polynomial because it has no nonzero terms. A polynomial with two terms, such as $5x + 2$ or $x^3 + 7$, is called a **binomial** and a polynomial with three terms, such as $3x^2 - 4x + 7$, is called a **trinomial.**

ADDITION AND SUBTRACTION Two terms having the same variable with the same exponent are called **like terms;** other terms are called **unlike terms.** Polynomials can be added or subtracted by using the distributive property to combine like terms. Only like terms can be combined. For example,

$$12\mathbf{y^4} + 6\mathbf{y^4} = (12 + 6)\mathbf{y^4} = 18y^4$$

and

$$-2\mathbf{m^2} + 8\mathbf{m^2} = (-2 + 8)\mathbf{m^2} = 6m^2.$$

The polynomial $8y^4 + 2y^5$ has unlike terms, so it cannot be further simplified. Polynomials are subtracted using the fact that $a - b = a + (-b)$. The next example shows how to add and subtract polynomials by combining terms.

EXAMPLE 4 Add or subtract as indicated.

(a) $(8x^3 - 4x^2 + 6x) + (3x^3 + 5x^2 - 9x + 8)$
Combine like terms.

$$\begin{aligned}&(8x^3 - 4x^2 + 6x) + (3x^3 + 5x^2 - 9x + 8)\\ &\quad = (8x^3 + 3x^3) + (-4x^2 + 5x^2) + (6x - 9x) + 8 && \text{Commutative property and associative property}\\ &\quad = 11x^3 + x^2 - 3x + 8 && \text{Distributive property}\end{aligned}$$

(b) $(-4x^4 + 6x^3 - 9x^2 - 12) + (-3x^3 + 8x^2 - 11x + 7)$
$= -4x^4 + 3x^3 - x^2 - 11x - 5$

(c) $(2x^2 - 11x + 8) - (7x^2 - 6x + 2)$
Use the definition of subtraction: $a - b = a + (-b)$. Here a and b are polynomials, and $-b$ is

$$-(7x^2 - 6x + 2) = -7x^2 + 6x - 2.$$

Now perform the subtraction.

$$\begin{aligned}&(2x^2 - 11x + 8) - (7x^2 - 6x + 2)\\ &\quad = (2x^2 - 11x + 8) + (-7x^2 + 6x - 2)\\ &\quad = -5x^2 - 5x + 6\end{aligned}$$

■ 4

4 Add or subtract.

(a) $(-2x^2 + 7x + 9) + (3x^2 + 2x - 7)$

(b) $(4x + 6) - (13x - 9)$

(c) $(9x^3 - 8x^2 + 2x) - (9x^3 - 2x^2 - 10)$

Answers:

(a) $x^2 + 9x + 2$

(b) $-9x + 15$

(c) $-6x^2 + 2x + 10$

MULTIPLICATION The distributive property is also used to multiply polynomials. For example, the product of $8x$ and $6x - 4$ is found as follows.

$$\begin{aligned} \mathbf{8x}(6x - 4) &= \mathbf{8x}(6x) - \mathbf{8x}(4) && \text{Distributive property} \\ &= 48x^2 - 32x && x \cdot x = x^2 \end{aligned}$$

5 Find the following products.

(a) $-6r(2r - 5)$

(b) $(8m + 3)(m^4 - 2m^2 + 6m)$

Answers:

(a) $-12r^2 + 30r$

(b) $8m^5 + 3m^4 - 16m^3 + 42m^2 + 18m$

EXAMPLE 5 Find each product.

(a) $2p^3(3p^2 - 2p + 5) = \mathbf{2p^3}(3p^2) + \mathbf{2p^3}(-2p) + \mathbf{2p^3}(5)$
$= 6p^5 - 4p^4 + 10p^3$

(b) $(3k - 2)(k^2 + 5k - 4) = 3k(k^2 + 5k - 4) - 2(k^2 + 5k - 4)$
$= 3k^3 + 15k^2 - 12k - 2k^2 - 10k + 8$
$= 3k^3 + 13k^2 - 22k + 8$ ■ 5

EXAMPLE 6 The product $(2x - 5)(3x + 4)$ can be found by using the distributive property twice.

$$\begin{aligned} (2x - 5)(3x + 4) &= 2x(3x + 4) - 5(3x + 4) \\ &= 2x \cdot 3x + 2x \cdot 4 + (-5) \cdot 3x + (-5) \cdot 4 \\ &= 6x^2 + \underbrace{8x - 15x} - 20 \\ &= 6x^2 - \quad 7x \quad - 20 \end{aligned}$$ ■

Observe the pattern in the second line of Example 6 and its relationship to the terms being multiplied.

$$(\mathbf{2x} - 5)(\mathbf{3x} + 4) = 2x \cdot 3x + 2x \cdot 4 + (-5) \cdot 3x + (-5) \cdot 4$$

- $(\mathbf{2x} - 5)(\mathbf{3x} + 4)$ → First terms ($2x \cdot 3x$)
- $(\mathbf{2x} - 5)(3x + \mathbf{4})$ → Outside terms ($2x \cdot 4$)
- $(2x - \mathbf{5})(\mathbf{3x} + 4)$ → Inside terms ($(-5) \cdot 3x$)
- $(2x - \mathbf{5})(3x + \mathbf{4})$ → Last terms ($(-5) \cdot 4$)

This pattern is easy to remember by using the acronym **FOIL** (**F**irst, **O**utside, **I**nside, **L**ast). The FOIL method makes it easy to find products such as this one mentally, without the necessity of writing out the intermediate steps.

6 Use FOIL to find these products.

(a) $(5k - 1)(2k + 3)$

(b) $(7z - 3)(2z + 5)$

Answers:

(a) $10k^2 + 13k - 3$

(b) $14z^2 + 29z - 15$

EXAMPLE 7

$$(3x + 2)(x + 5) = \underset{\text{First}}{3x^2} + \underset{\text{Outside}}{15x} + \underset{\text{Inside}}{2x} + \underset{\text{Last}}{10} = 3x^2 + 17x + 10$$ ■ 6

The profit from the sales of an item is the difference between the revenue R received from the sales and the cost C to sell the item. Thus, profit P is found from the equation $P = R - C$.

7 Write an expression for profit if revenue is $7x^2 - 3x + 8$ and cost is $3x^2 + 5x - 2$.

Answer:
$4x^2 - 8x + 10$

EXAMPLE 8 Suppose the cost to sell x compact discs is $2x^2 - 2x + 10$ and the revenue from the sale of x discs is $5x^2 + 12x - 1$. Write an expression for the profit.

Because profit equals revenue less cost, or $P = R - C$, the profit is

$$\begin{aligned} P &= (5x^2 + 12x - 1) - (2x^2 - 2x + 10) \\ &= 3x^2 + 14x - 11. \end{aligned}$$ ■ 7

1.3 EXERCISES

Use a calculator to evaluate the following, approximating when necessary.

1. 17^9 **2.** $(-6.54)^{11}$ **3.** $(-18/7)^6$ **4.** $(7/9)^8$

5. Explain how the value of -3^2 differs from $(-3)^2$. Do -3^3 and $(-3)^3$ differ in the same way? Why or why not?

6. Describe the steps used to multiply 4^3 and 4^5. Is the product of 4^3 and 3^4 found in the same way? Explain.

Simplify each of the following. Leave answers with exponents. (See Example 3.)

7. $2^4 \cdot 2^3$ **8.** $3^8 \cdot 3^3$

9. $(-5)^2 \cdot (-5)^5$ **10.** $(-4)^4 \cdot (-4)^6$

11. $(-3)^5 \cdot 3^4$ **12.** $8^2 \cdot (-8)^3$

13. $(2z)^5 \cdot (2z)^6$ **14.** $(6y)^3 \cdot (6y)^5$

Add or subtract as indicated. (See Example 4.)

15. $(3x^3 + 2x^2 - 5x) + (-4x^3 - x^2 + 8x)$

16. $(-2p^3 - 5p + 7) + (-4p^2 + 8p + 2)$

17. $(-4y^2 - 3y + 8) - (2y^2 - 6y - 2)$

18. $(7b^2 + 2b - 5) - (3b^2 + 2b - 6)$

19. $(2x^3 - 2x^2 + 4x - 3) - (2x^3 + 8x^2 - 1)$

20. $(3y^3 + 9y^2 - 11y + 8) - (-4y^2 + 10y - 6)$

Find each of the following products and sums. (See Examples 5–7.)

21. $-9m(2m^2 + 3m - 1)$

22. $2a(4a^2 - 6a + 3)$

23. $(3z + 5)(4z^2 - 2z + 1)$

24. $(2k + 3)(4k^3 - 3k^2 + k)$

25. $(6k - 1)(2k - 3)$

26. $(8r + 3)(r - 1)$

27. $(3y + 5)(2y - 1)$

28. $(5r - 3s)(5r + 4s)$

29. $(9k + q)(2k - q)$

30. $(.012x - .17)(.3x + .54)$

31. $(6.2m - 3.4)(.7m + 1.3)$

32. $2p - 3[4p - (3p + 1)]$

33. $5k - [k + (-3 + 5k)]$

34. $(3x - 1)(x + 2) - (2x + 5)^2$

35. $(4x + 3)(2x - 1) - (x + 3)^2$

Management *The accompanying bar graph depicts the number of North American users, in millions, of on-line services, as reported by Forrester Research, Inc. Using these figures, it can be determined that the polynomial*

$$.035x^4 - .266x^3 + 1.005x^2 + .509x + 2.986$$

gives a good approximation of the number of users in the year x, where x = 0 corresponds to 1992, x = 1 corresponds to 1993, and so on. For the given year (a) *use the bar graph to determine the number of users and then* (b) *use the polynomial to determine the number of users.*

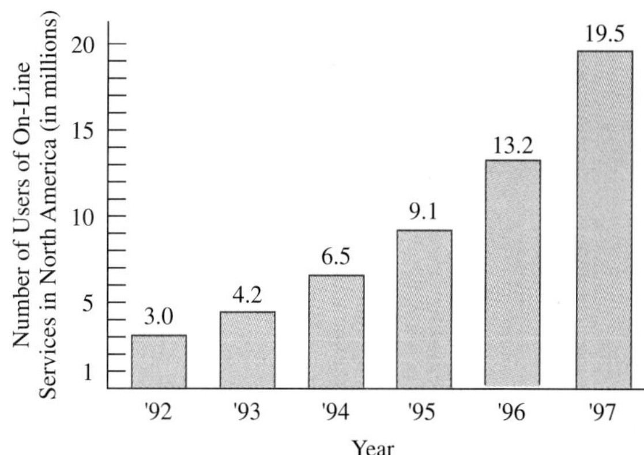

36. 1992 **37.** 1993

38. 1994 **39.** 1997

40. Physical Science One of the most amazing formulas in all of ancient mathematics is the formula discovered by the Egyptians to find the volume of the frustum of a square pyramid shown in the figure on the next page. Its volume is given by $(1/3)h(a^2 + ab + b^2)$, where b is the length of the base, a is the length of the top, and h is the height.*

*Freebury, H. A., *A History of Mathematics.* MacMillan Company, New York, 1968.

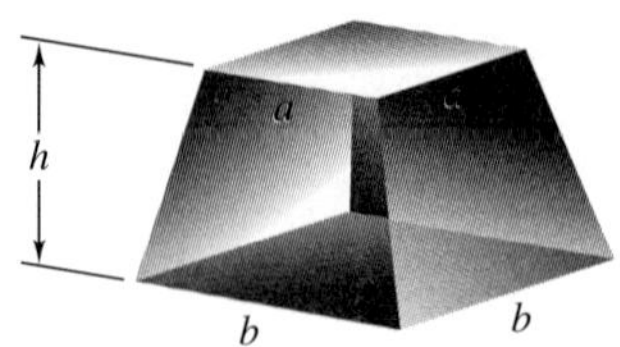

(a) When the Great Pyramid in Egypt was partially completed to a height h of 200 feet, b was 756 feet, and a was 314 feet. Calculate its volume at this stage of construction.

(b) Try to visualize the figure if $a = b$. What is the resulting shape? Find its volume.

(c) Let $a = b$ in the Egyptian formula and simplify. Are the results the same?

41. **Physical Science** Refer to the formula and the discussion in Exercise 40.

(a) Use the expression $(1/3)h(a^2 + ab + b^2)$ to determine a formula for the volume of a pyramid with a square base b and height h by letting $a = 0$.

(b) The Great Pyramid in Egypt had a square base of 756 feet and a height of 481 feet. Find the volume of the Great Pyramid. Compare it with the 273-foot-tall Superdome in New Orleans, which has an approximate volume of 100 million cubic feet.*

(c) The Superdome covers an area of 13 acres. How many acres does the Great Pyramid cover? (*Hint:* 1 acre = 43,560 ft^2.)

42. Suppose one polynomial has degree 3 and another also has degree 3. Find all possible values for the degree of their
(a) sum
(b) difference
(c) product.

43. If one polynomial has degree 3 and another has degree 4, find all possible values for the degree of their
(a) sum
(b) difference
(c) product.

44. Generalize the results of Exercise 43: Suppose one polynomial has degree m and another has degree n, where m and n are natural numbers with $n < m$. Find all possible values for the degree of their
(a) sum
(b) difference
(c) product.

45. Find $(a + b)(a - b)$. Then state in words a formula for the result of the product $(3x + 2y)(3x - 2y)$.

46. Find $(a - b)^2$. Then state in words a formula for finding $(2x - 5)^2$.

Management *Write an expression for profit given the following expressions for revenue and cost. (See Example 8.)*

47. Revenue: $5x^3 - 3x + 1$; cost: $4x^2 + 5x$

48. Revenue: $3x^3 + 2x^2$; cost: $x^3 - x^2 + x + 10$

49. Revenue: $2x^2 - 4x + 50$; cost: $x^2 + 3x + 10$

50. Revenue: $10x^2 + 8x + 12$; cost: $2x^2 - 3x + 20$

The Guinness Book of Records 1995.

1.4 FACTORING

The number 18 can be written as a product in several ways: $9 \cdot 2$, $(-3)(-6)$, $1 \cdot 18$, etc. The numbers in each product (9, 2, −3, etc.) are called **factors** and the process of writing 18 as a product of factors is called **factoring.** Thus, factoring is the reverse of multiplication.

Factoring of polynomials is also important. It provides a means to simplify many situations and to solve certain types of equations. As is the usual custom, factoring of polynomials in this book will be restricted to finding factors with *integer* coefficients (otherwise there are an infinite number of possible factors).

GREATEST COMMON FACTOR The algebraic expression $15m + 45$ is made up of two terms, $15m$ and 45. Each of these terms can be divided by 15. In fact, $15m = 15 \cdot m$ and $45 = 15 \cdot 3$. By the distributive property,

$$15m + 45 = \mathbf{15} \cdot m + \mathbf{15} \cdot 3 = \mathbf{15}(m + 3).$$

Both 15 and $m + 3$ are factors of $15m + 45$. Since 15 divides into all terms of $15m + 45$ and is the largest number that will do so, it is called the **greatest common factor** for the polynomial $15m + 45$. The process of writing $15m + 45$ as $15(m + 3)$ is called **factoring out** the greatest common factor.

EXAMPLE 1 Factor out the greatest common factor.

(a) $12p - 18q$

Both $12p$ and $18q$ are divisible by 6, and

$$12p - 18q = \mathbf{6} \cdot 2p - \mathbf{6} \cdot 3q = \mathbf{6}(2p - 3q).$$

(b) $8x^3 - 9x^2 + 15x$

Each of these terms is divisible by x.

$$8x^3 - 9x^2 + 15x = (8x^2) \cdot \boldsymbol{x} - (9x) \cdot \boldsymbol{x} + 15 \cdot \boldsymbol{x}$$
$$= \boldsymbol{x}(8x^2 - 9x + 15)$$

(c) $5(4x - 3)^3 + 2(4x - 3)^2$

The quantity $(4x - 3)^2$ is a common factor. Factoring it out gives

$$5(4x - 3)^3 + 2(4x - 3)^2 = (4x - 3)^2[5(4x - 3) + 2]$$
$$= (4x - 3)^2(20x - 15 + 2)$$
$$= (4x - 3)^2(20x - 13).$$ ■ [1]

[1] Factor out the greatest common factor.

(a) $12r + 9k$

(b) $75m^2 + 100n^2$

(c) $6m^4 - 9m^3 + 12m^2$

(d) $3(2k + 1)^3 + 4(2k + 1)^4$

Answers:

(a) $3(4r + 3k)$

(b) $25(3m^2 + 4n^2)$

(c) $3m^2(2m^2 - 3m + 4)$

(d) $(2k + 1)^3(7 + 8k)$

FACTORING TRINOMIALS Factoring is the opposite of multiplication. Because the product of two binomials is usually a trinomial, we can expect factorable trinomials (that have terms with no common factor) to have two binomial factors. Thus, factoring trinomials requires using FOIL backwards.

EXAMPLE 2 Factor each trinomial.

(a) $4y^2 - 11y + 6$

To factor this trinomial, we must find integers a, b, c, and d such that

$$4y^2 - 11y + 6 = (ay + b)(cy + d)$$
$$= acy^2 + ady + bcy + bd$$
$$= acy^2 + (ad + bc)y + bd.$$

Since the coefficients of y^2 must be the same on both sides, we see that $ac = 4$. Similarly, the constant terms show that $bd = 6$. The positive factors of 4 are 4 and 1 or 2 and 2. Since the middle term is negative, we consider only negative factors of 6. The possibilities are -2 and -3 or -1 and -6. Now we try various arrangements of these factors until we find one that gives the correct coefficient of y.

$$(2y - 1)(2y - 6) = 4y^2 - \mathbf{14y} + 6 \quad \text{Incorrect}$$
$$(2y - 2)(2y - 3) = 4y^2 - \mathbf{10y} + 6 \quad \text{Incorrect}$$
$$(y - 2)(4y - 3) = 4y^2 - \mathbf{11y} + 6 \quad \text{Correct}$$

The last trial gives the correct factorization.

(b) $6p^2 - 7pq - 5q^2$

Again, we try various possibilities. The positive factors of 6 could be 2 and 3 or 1 and 6. As factors of -5 we have only -1 and 5 or -5 and 1. Try different combinations of these factors until the correct one is found.

$$(2p - 5q)(3p + q) = 6p^2 - \mathbf{13pq} - 5q^2 \quad \text{Incorrect}$$
$$(3p - 5q)(2p + q) = 6p^2 - \mathbf{7pq} - 5q^2 \quad \text{Correct}$$

Finally, $6p^2 - 7pq - 5q^2$ factors as $(3p - 5q)(2p + q)$. ■ [2]

[2] Factor the following.

(a) $r^2 - 5r - 14$

(b) $3m^2 + 5m - 2$

(c) $6p^2 + 13pq - 5q^2$

Answers:

(a) $(r - 7)(r + 2)$

(b) $(3m - 1)(m + 2)$

(c) $(2p + 5q)(3p - q)$

NOTE In Example 2, we chose positive factors of the positive first term. Of course, we could have used two negative factors, but the work is easier if positive factors are used. ◆

The method shown above can be used to factor a **perfect square trinomial,** one that is the square of a binomial. The binomial can be predicted by observing the following patterns that always apply to a perfect square trinomial.

$$\left.\begin{aligned} x^2 + 2xy + y^2 &= (x + y)^2 \\ x^2 - 2xy + y^2 &= (x - y)^2 \end{aligned}\right\} \quad \text{Perfect square trinomials}$$

EXAMPLE 3 Factor each trinomial.

(a) $16p^2 - 40pq + 25q^2$

Because $16p^2 = (4p)^2$ and $25q^2 = (5q)^2$, use the second pattern shown above with $4p$ replacing x and $5q$ replacing y to get

$$\begin{aligned} 16p^2 - 40pq + 25q^2 &= (\mathbf{4p})^2 - 2(\mathbf{4p})(\mathbf{5q}) + (\mathbf{5q})^2 \\ &= (4p - 5q)^2. \end{aligned}$$

Make sure that the middle term of the trinomial being factored, $-40pq$ here, is twice the product of the two terms in the binomial $4p - 5q$.

$$-40pq = 2(\mathbf{4p})(\mathbf{-5q})$$

(b) $169x^2 + 104xy^2 + 16y^4 = (13x + 4y^2)^2$, since $2(13x)(4y^2) = 104xy^2$. ■ 3

3 Factor each trinomial.

(a) $4m^2 + 4m + 1$

(b) $25z^2 - 80zt + 64t^2$

Answers:

(a) $(2m + 1)^2$

(b) $(5z - 8t)^2$

FACTORING BINOMIALS Three special factoring patterns are listed below. Each can be verified by multiplying on the right side of the equation. These formulas should be memorized.

$x^2 - y^2 = (x + y)(x - y)$	Difference of two squares
$x^3 - y^3 = (x - y)(x^2 + xy + y^2)$	Difference of two cubes
$x^3 + y^3 = (x + y)(x^2 - xy + y^2)$	Sum of two cubes

EXAMPLE 4 Factor each of the following.

(a) $4m^2 - 9$

Notice that $4m^2 - 9$ is the difference of two squares, since $4m^2 = (2m)^2$ and $9 = 3^2$. Use the pattern for the difference of two squares, letting $2m$ replace x and 3 replace y. Then the pattern $x^2 - y^2 = (x + y)(x - y)$ becomes

$$\begin{aligned} 4m^2 - 9 &= (\mathbf{2m})^2 - \mathbf{3}^2 \\ &= (2m + 3)(2m - 3). \end{aligned}$$

(b) $128p^2 - 98q^2$

First factor out the common factor of 2.

$$\begin{aligned}128p^2 - 98q^2 &= 2(64p^2 - 49q^2)\\ &= 2[(\mathbf{8p})^2 - (\mathbf{7q})^2]\\ &= 2(8p + 7q)(8p - 7q)\end{aligned}$$

(c) $x^2 + 36$

The *sum* of two squares usually cannot be factored. To see this, check some possibilities.

$$(x + 6)(x + 6) = (x + 6)^2 = x^2 + 12x + 36$$
$$(x + 4)(x + 9) = x^2 + 13x + 36$$

Any product of two binomials will always have a middle term unless it is the *difference* of two squares.

(d) $4z^2 + 12z + 9 - w^2$

Notice that the first three terms can be factored as a perfect square.

$$\mathbf{4z^2 + 12z + 9} - w^2 = \mathbf{(2z + 3)^2} - w^2$$

Written in this form, the expression is the difference of squares, which can be factored as

$$\begin{aligned}(2z + 3)^2 - w^2 &= [(2z + 3) + w][(2z + 3) - w]\\ &= (2z + 3 + w)(2z + 3 - w).\end{aligned}$$

(e) $256k^4 - 625m^4$

Use the difference of two squares pattern twice, as follows:

$$\begin{aligned}256k^4 - 625m^4 &= (\mathbf{16k^2})^2 - (\mathbf{25m^2})^2\\ &= (16k^2 + 25m^2)(16k^2 - 25m^2)\\ &= (16k^2 + 25m^2)(4k + 5m)(4k - 5m).\end{aligned}$$ ■ 4

4 Factor the following.

(a) $9p^2 - 49$

(b) $y^2 + 100$

(c) $9r^2 + 12r + 4 - t^2$

(d) $81x^4 - 16y^4$

Answers:

(a) $(3p + 7)(3p - 7)$

(b) Cannot be factored

(c) $(3r + 2 + t)(3r + 2 - t)$

(d) $(9x^2 + 4y^2)(3x + 2y) \cdot (3x - 2y)$

EXAMPLE 5 Factor each of the following.

(a) $k^3 - 8$

Use the pattern for the difference of two cubes, since $k^3 = (k)^3$ and $8 = (2)^3$, to get

$$k^3 - 8 = \mathbf{k^3 - 2^3} = (k - 2)(k^2 + 2k + 4).$$

(b) $m^3 + 125 = m^3 + 5^3 = (m + 5)(m^2 - 5m + 25)$

(c) $8k^3 - 27z^3 = (2k)^3 - (3z)^3 = (2k - 3z)(4k^2 + 6kz + 9z^2)$ ■ 5

5 Factor the following.

(a) $a^3 + 1000$

(b) $z^3 - 64$

(c) $100m^3 - 27z^3$

Answers:

(a) $(a + 10)(a^2 - 10a + 100)$

(b) $(z - 4)(z^2 + 4z + 16)$

(c) $(10m - 3z) \cdot (100m^2 + 30mz + 9z^2)$

EXAMPLE 6 Factor each of the following.

(a) $12x^2 - 26x - 10$

Look first for a common factor. Here there is a common factor of 2: $12x^2 - 26x - 10 = \mathbf{2}(6x^2 - 13x - 5)$. Now try to factor $6x^2 - 13x - 5$. Possible factors of 6 are 3 and 2 or 6 and 1. The only factors of -5 are -5 and 1 or 5 and -1. Try various combinations. You should find the trinomial factors as $(3x + 1)(2x - 5)$. Thus,

$$12x^2 - 26x - 10 = 2(3x + 1)(2x - 5).$$

(b) $16a^2 - 100 - 48ac + 36c^2$
Factor out the common factor of 4 first.

$$16a^2 - 100 - 48ac + 36c^2 = 4[4a^2 - 25 - 12ac + 9c^2]$$
$$= 4[(4a^2 - 12ac + 9c^2) - 25]$$ Rearrange terms and group.
$$= 4[(2a - 3c)^2 - 25]$$ Factor the trinomial.
$$= 4(2a - 3c + 5)(2a - 3c - 5)$$ Factor the difference of squares. ■

6 Factor.
(a) $6x^2 - 27x - 15$
(b) $18 - 8xy - 2y^2 - 8x^2$

Answers:
(a) $3(2x + 1)(x - 5)$
(b) $2(3 - 2x - y)(3 + 2x + y)$

CAUTION Remember always to look first for a common factor. ◆ 6

1.4 EXERCISES

Factor out the greatest common factor in each of the following. (See Example 1.)

1. $12x^2 - 24x$
2. $5y - 25xy$
3. $r^3 - 5r^2 + r$
4. $t^3 + 3t^2 + 8t$
5. $2m - 5n + p$
6. $4k + 6h - 5c$
7. $6z^3 - 12z^2 + 18z$
8. $5x^3 + 35x^2 + 10x$
9. $25p^4 - 20p^3q + 100p^2q^2$
10. $60m^4 - 120m^3n + 50m^2n^2$
11. $3(2y - 1)^2 + 5(2y - 1)^3$
12. $(3x + 7)^5 - 2(3x + 7)^3$
13. $3(x + 5)^4 + (x + 5)^6$
14. $3(x + 6)^2 + 2(x + 6)^4$

Factor each of the following completely. Factor out the greatest common factor as necessary. (See Examples 2–4 and 6.)

15. $2a^2 + 3a - 5$
16. $6a^2 - 48a - 120$
17. $x^2 - 64$
18. $x^2 + 17xy + 72y^2$
19. $9p^2 - 24p + 16$
20. $3r^2 - r - 2$
21. $r^2 - 3rt - 10t^2$
22. $2a^2 + ab - 6b^2$
23. $m^2 - 6mn + 9n^2$
24. $8k^2 - 16k - 10$
25. $4p^2 - 9$
26. $8r^2 + r + 6$
27. $3x^2 - 24xz + 48z^2$
28. $9m^2 - 25$
29. $a^2 + 4ab + 5b^2$
30. $6y^2 - 11y - 7$
31. $-x^2 + 7x + 12$
32. $4y^2 + y - 3$
33. $3a^2 - 13a - 30$
34. $3k^2 + 2k - 8$
35. $21m^2 + 13mn + 2n^2$
36. $81y^2 - 100$
37. $20y^2 + 39yx - 11x^2$
38. $12s^2 + 11st - 5t^2$
39. $64z^2 + 25$
40. $p^2q^2 - 10 - 2q^2 + 5p^2$
41. $y^2 - 4yz - 21z^2$
42. $49a^2 + 9$
43. $3n^2 - 4m^2 + m^2n^2 - 12$
44. $y^2 + 20yx + 100x^2$
45. $121x^2 - 64$
46. $4z^2 + 56zy + 196y^2$
47. $24a^4 + 10a^3b - 4a^2b^2$
48. $10x^2 + 34x + 12$
49. $18x^5 + 15x^4z - 75x^3z^2$
50. $16m^2 + 40m + 25$
51. $5m^3(m^3 - 1)^2 - 3m^5(m^3 - 1)^3$
52. $9(x - 4)^5 - (x - 4)^3$
53. When asked to factor $6x^4 - 3x^2 - 3$ completely, a student gave the following result:
$$6x^4 - 3x^2 - 3 = (2x^2 + 1)(3x^2 - 3).$$
Is this answer correct? Explain why.
54. When can the sum of two squares be factored? Give examples.

Factor each of the following. (See Example 5.)

55. $a^3 - 216$
56. $b^3 + 125$
57. $8r^3 - 27s^3$
58. $1000p^3 + 27q^3$
59. $64m^3 + 125$
60. $216y^3 - 343$
61. $1000y^3 - z^3$
62. $125p^3 + 8q^3$
63. Explain why $(x + 2)^3$ is not the correct factorization of $x^3 + 8$ and give the correct factorization.
64. Describe how factoring and multiplication are related. Give examples.

1.5 GRAPHS

Just as the number line associates the points on a line with real numbers, a similar construction in two dimensions associates points in the plane with *ordered pairs* of real numbers. A **Cartesian coordinate system,** as shown in Figure 1.9, consists of a horizontal number line (usually called the **x-axis**) and a vertical number line (usually called the **y-axis**). The point where the number lines meet is called the **origin.** Each point in a Cartesian coordinate system is labeled with an **ordered pair** of real numbers, such as $(-2, 4)$ or $(3, 2)$. Several points and their corresponding ordered pairs are shown in Figure 1.9.

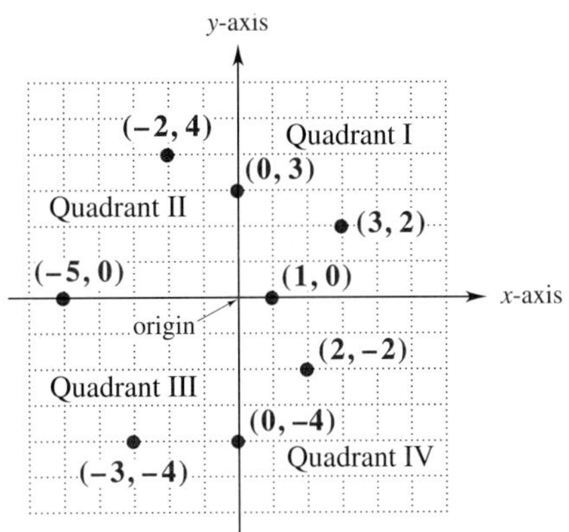

FIGURE 1.9

1 Locate $(-1, 6)$, $(-3, -5)$, $(4, -3)$, $(0, 2)$, and $(-5, 0)$ on a coordinate system.

Answer:

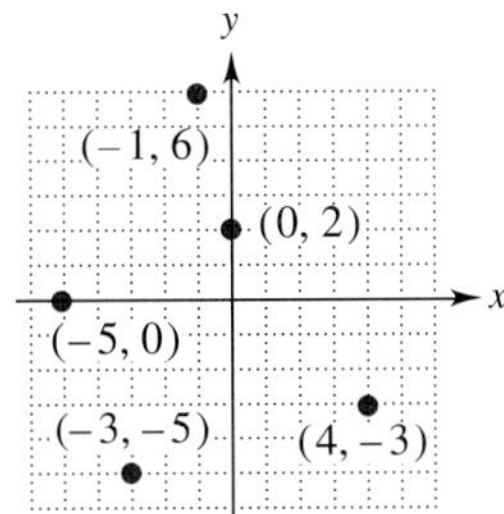

For the point $(-2, 4)$, for example, -2 is the **x-coordinate** and 4 is the **y-coordinate.** You can think of these coordinates as directions telling you how to move to this point from the origin: you go 2 horizontal units to the left (x-coordinate) and 4 vertical units upward (y-coordinate). From now on, instead of referring to "the point labeled by the ordered pair $(-2, 4)$," we will say "the point $(-2, 4)$." 1

The x-axis and the y-axis divide the plane into four parts, or **quadrants,** which are numbered as shown in Figure 1.9. The points on the coordinate axes belong to no quadrant.

EQUATIONS AND GRAPHS A **solution of an equation** in two variables, such as

$$y = -2x + 3 \quad \text{or} \quad y = x^2 + 7x - 2,$$

is an ordered pair of numbers such that the substitution of the first number for x and the second number for y produces a true statement.

2 Which of the following are solutions of $y = x^2 + 7x - 2$?

(a) $(1, 6)$

(b) $(-2, -20)$

(c) $(-1, -8)$

Answer:
Parts (a) and (c)

EXAMPLE 1 Which of the following are solutions of $y = -2x + 3$?

(a) $(2, -1)$
This is a solution of $y = -2x + 3$ because "$-1 = -2 \cdot 2 + 3$" is a true statement.

(b) $(4, 7)$
Since $-2 \cdot 4 + 3 = -5$ and not 7, the ordered pair $(4, 7)$ is not a solution of $y = -2x + 3$. ■ 2

Equations in two variables, such as $y = -2x + 3$, typically have an infinite number of solutions. To find one, choose a number for x and then compute the value of y that produces a solution. For instance, if $x = 5$, then $y = -2 \cdot 5 + 3 = -7$, so that

3 Graph $x = 5y$.

Answer:

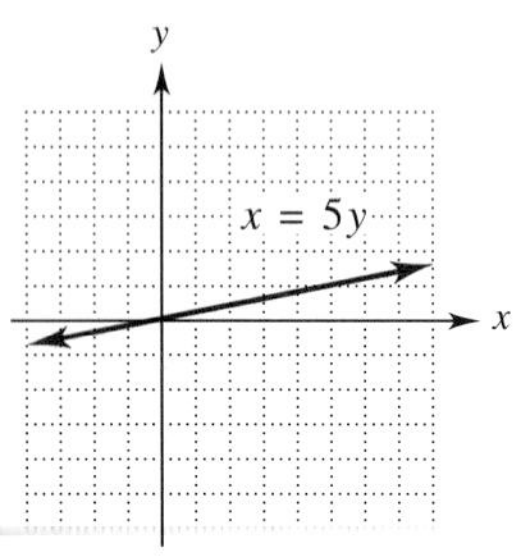

$(5, -7)$ is a solution of $y = -2x + 3$. Similarly, if $x = 0$, then $y = -2 \cdot 0 + 3 = 3$, so that $(0, 3)$ is also a solution.

The **graph** of an equation in two variables is the set of points in the plane whose coordinates (ordered pairs) are solutions of the equation. Thus, the graph of an equation is a picture of its solutions. Since a typical equation has infinitely many solutions, its graph has infinitely many points.

EXAMPLE 2 Sketch the graph of $y = -2x + 5$ by hand.

Since we cannot plot infinitely many points, we construct a table of y-values for a reasonable number of x-values, plot the corresponding points, and make an "educated guess" about the rest. The table of values and points in Figure 1.10 suggest that the graph is a straight line, as shown in Figure 1.11. ■ 3

x	$-2x + 5$
−1	7
0	5
2	1
4	−3
5	−5

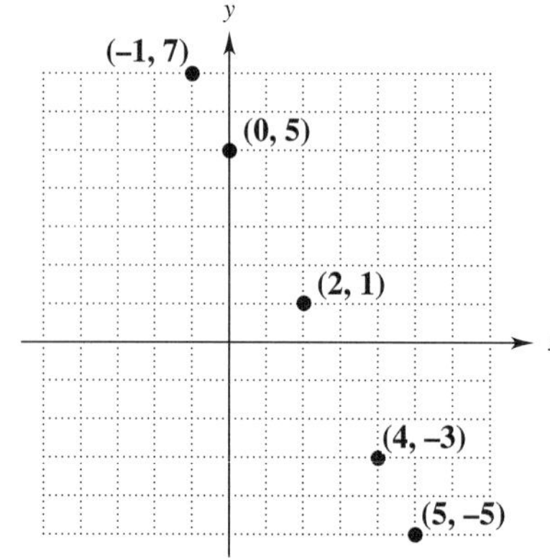

FIGURE 1.10

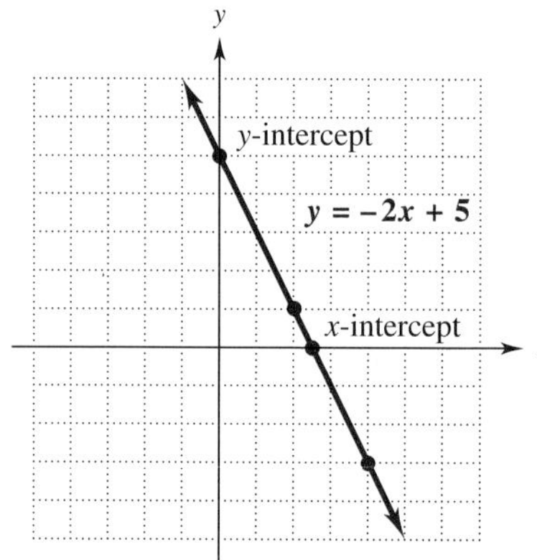

FIGURE 1.11

4 What are the x-intercepts and y-intercepts of this graph?

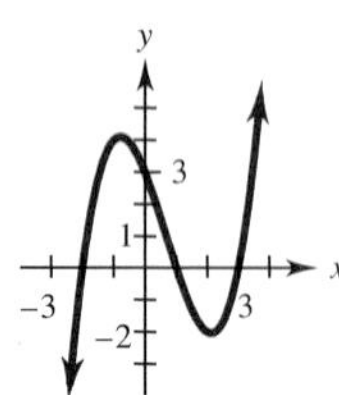

Answer:
x-intercepts -2, 1, and 3;
y-intercept 3

An ***x*-intercept** of a graph is the x-coordinate of a point where the graph meets the x-axis (the y-coordinate of this point is 0 since it's on the axis). Similarly, a ***y*-intercept** of a graph is the y-coordinate of a point where the graph meets the y-axis (the x-coordinate of this point is 0). For example, the graph in Figure 1.11 has x-intercept 5/2 and y-intercept 5. 4

TECHNOLOGY AND GRAPHS A graphing calculator or computer graphing program follows essentially the same procedure used when graphing by hand: the calculator selects a large number of x-values (95 or more) equally spaced along the x-axis and plots the corresponding points, simultaneously connecting them with line segments. By plotting far more points than could conveniently be plotted by hand, the calculator generally produces very accurate graphs. As we shall see below, however, technology can sometimes produce misleading graphs and mathematical knowledge is needed to interpret some of these screen images. The basics of calculator graphing are presented in the following examples.

EXAMPLE 3 Use a graphing calculator to sketch the graph of the equation $2x^3 - 2y - 10x + 2 = 0$.*

First, set the ***viewing window***—the portion of the coordinate plane that will appear on the screen. A certain amount of trial and error may be involved here,

*With obvious modifications all discussions of graphing calculators in this book apply equally well to computer graphing programs.

because you may not know in advance what part of the plane the graph is in. We shall talk more about this problem below (see Examples 4(a) and 7), but as a general rule, start with a window that has the origin at its center. In this example, we have already experimented with various windows and are presenting only the final result to illustrate how a viewing window is entered in the calculator. Press the WINDOW key (labeled RANGE or PLOT-SETUP on some calculators) and enter the appropriate numbers as in Figure 1.12 (which shows a TI-83; other calculators are similar). This tells the calculator to display the portion of the plane in Figure 1.13, that is, the points (x, y) with $-9 \leq x \leq 9$ and $-6 \leq y \leq 6$.*

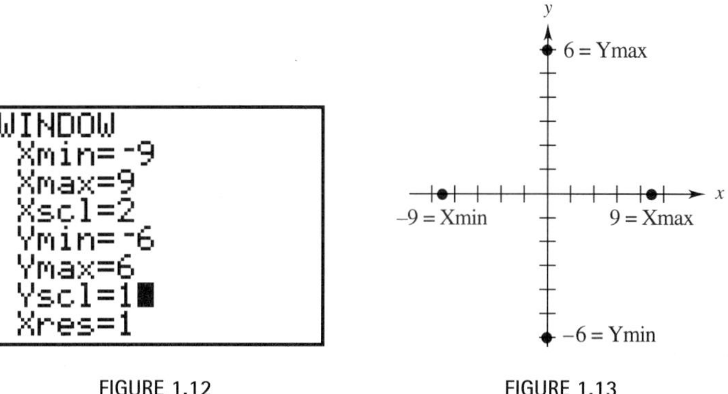

FIGURE 1.12

FIGURE 1.13

In Figure 1.12 we have set Xscl $= 2$ and Yscl $= 1$, which means the **tick marks** on the x-axis are two units apart and the tick marks on the y-axis are one unit apart (Figure 1.13).

Second, enter the equation to be graphed in the equation memory. To do this, you must first solve the equation for y (because a calculator only accepts equations of the form $y =$ expression in x):

$$2y = 2x^3 - 10x + 2$$
$$y = x^3 - 5x + 1.$$

Now press the Y= key (labeled SYMB or EQTN on some calculators) and enter the equation, using the "variable key" for x. (This key is labeled X,T,θ or X,θ,T or x-VAR or X|T, depending on the calculator.) Figure 1.14 shows how it looks on a TI-83; other calculators are similar. Now press GRAPH (or PLOT or DRW on some calculators) and obtain Figure 1.15.

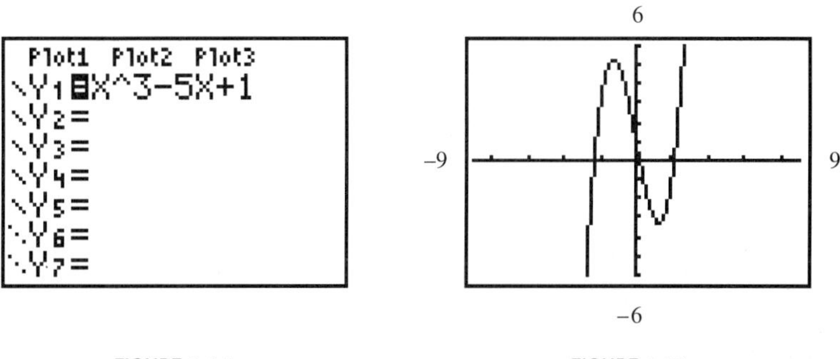

FIGURE 1.14

FIGURE 1.15

*Some calculators do not have an Xres setting; on those that do, it should normally be 1.

5 Graph $y = 18x - 3x^3$ in the following viewing windows.

(a) $-10 \leq x \leq 10$ and $-10 \leq y \leq 10$, with Xscl = 1, Yscl = 1

(b) $-5 \leq x \leq 5$ and $-20 \leq y \leq 20$, with Xscl = 1, Yscl = 5

Answers:

(a)

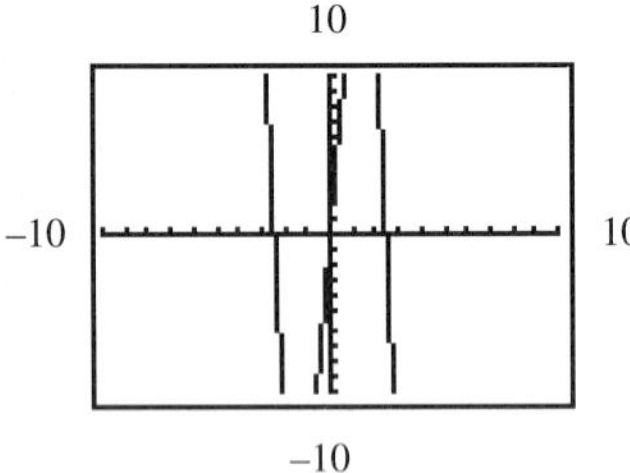

(b)

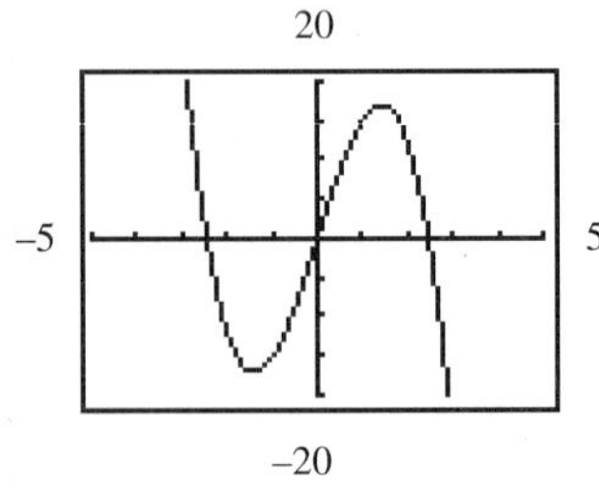

Finally, if necessary, change the viewing window to obtain a more readable graph. It is difficult to see the y-intercept in Figure 1.15, so press WINDOW and change the viewing window (Figure 1.16); then press GRAPH to obtain Figure 1.17, in which the y-intercept at $y = 1$ is clearly shown. (It isn't necessary to re-enter the equation.) ■ 5

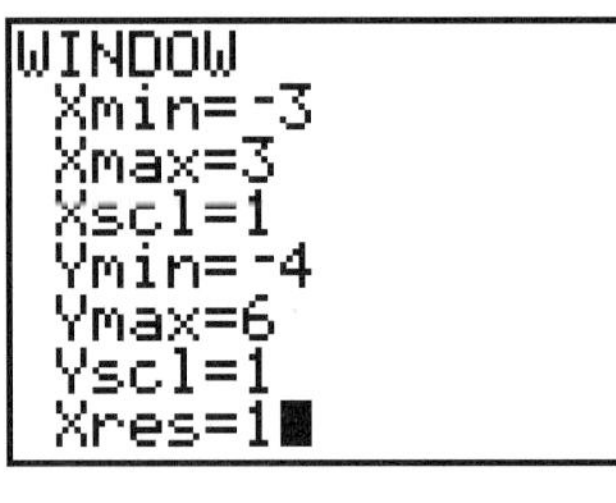

FIGURE 1.16

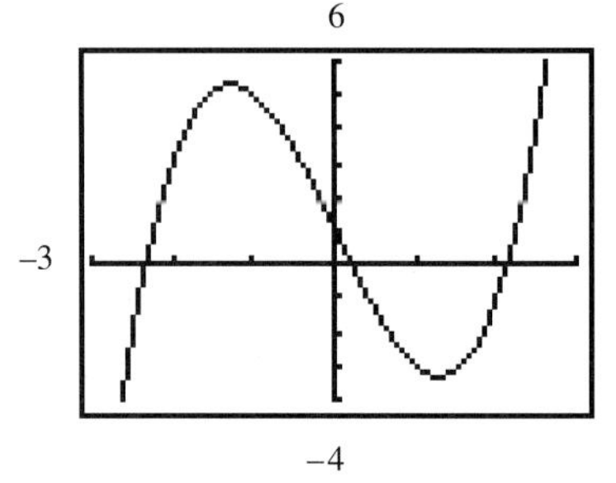

FIGURE 1.17

Because of the limited resolution of a calculator screen, the graphs in Figures 1.15 and 1.17 consist of adjacent line segments, rather than the unbroken smooth curves that they are. Nevertheless, calculator generated graphs can be used to answer a number of questions that previously required more time-consuming algebraic techniques.

EXAMPLE 4 The monthly profit at Connors Coffee Company is given by the equation $y = -.00027x^2 + 8.4x - 750$, where x is the number of cases of coffee sold and y is the profit. The plant can produce no more than 25,000 cases of coffee per month.

(a) Estimate graphically the number of cases that should be produced each month in order to make the largest possible profit.

The number of cases, x, is nonnegative and no more than 25,000 can be produced. The profit, y, may be positive or negative (the company could lose money). So we try the window with $0 \leq x \leq 25{,}000$ and $-10{,}000 \leq y \leq 75{,}000$ and graph the equation (Figure 1.18). For each point on the graph in Figure 1.18,

the x-coordinate is the number of cases produced;

the y-coordinate is the profit on that number of cases.

The maximum profit occurs at the point with the largest y-coordinate, that is, at the highest point on the graph. This point can be estimated as follows. Press the TRACE key and use the *left* and *right* arrow keys to move the flashing cursor along the graph.* As you do this, the coordinates of the point the cursor is on are displayed at the bot-

*On some calculators (such as Sharp 9300) pressing the left or right arrow key starts the trace feature; on others (such as HP-38), the trace feature is automatically on after graphing.

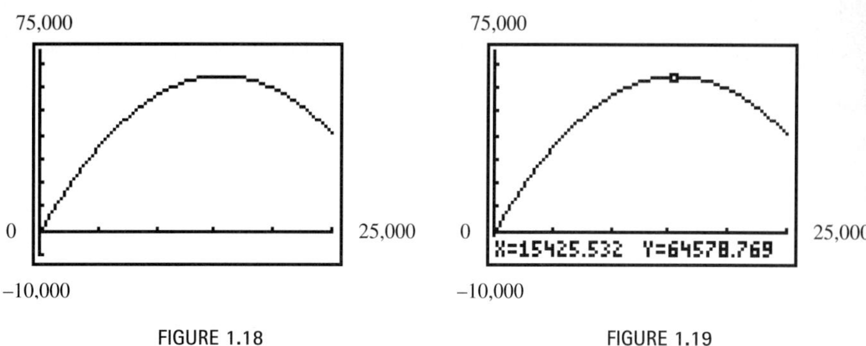

FIGURE 1.18

FIGURE 1.19

tom of the screen. Move the cursor until its y-coordinate is as large as possible. Since the trace cursor only lands on the points the calculator actually plotted in making this graph, this is not necessarily the highest point on the graph, but only the highest point that the calculator plotted. Nevertheless, it is a reasonable *estimate* of the actual highest point. With this particular calculator that occurs when $x = 15{,}425.532$ and $y = 64{,}578.769$ (Figure 1.19; other calculators may plot different points and give slightly different results). So approximately 15,426 cases will result in an estimated maximum profit of about $64,579.

6 The amount y of sheet metal (in square inches) needed to make a one-quart cylindrical can is given by the equation $y = 116/x + 2\pi x^2$, where x is the radius of the can (in inches) and $0 < x \le 5$. Estimate graphically the radius that uses the least amount of sheet metal.

Answer:
About 2.1 inches

(b) Graphically determine, as precisely as possible, the number of cases that should be produced in order to have maximum profit.

Graph the equation as in part (a) and use the "maximum finder" on your calculator (see the Tip below). It approximates the highest point on the graph with the greatest precision that the calculator is capable of. A typical finder shows that the highest point is $x = 15{,}555.558$ and $y = 64{,}583.333$ (Figure 1.20). Since they only sell whole cases, they should produce 15,556 cases for a maximum profit of approximately $64,583. ■ 6

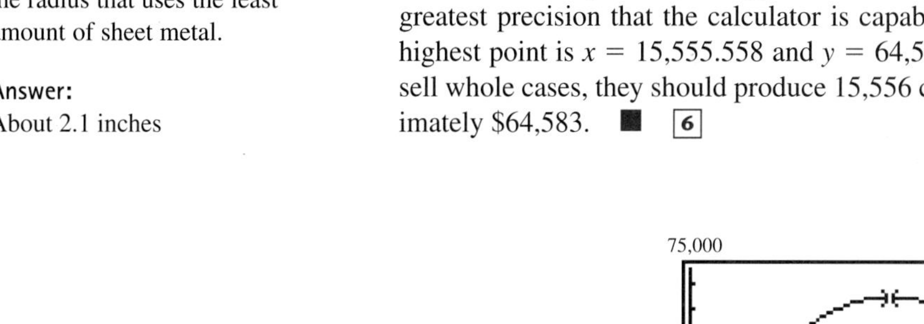

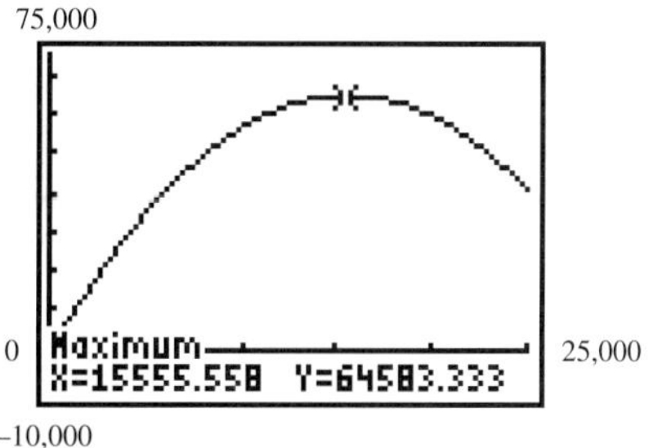

FIGURE 1.20

TECHNOLOGY TIP Depending on the calculator, the maximum finder is on the CALC or MATH or FCN or G-SOLVE or JUMP menu and is labeled "maximum" or "extremum"; check your instruction manual. A maximum finder program for TI-81 is in the Program Appendix. ✔

CAUTION On some calculators (such as HP-38 and all TI's) you can move the cursor around the screen using the arrow keys, without using TRACE. In this case, the cursor may appear to be on the graph when it is only *near* a point on the graph, so the displayed coordinates may not be the coordinates of a point on the graph as they are when TRACE is used. ◆

SPECIAL VIEWING WINDOWS The viewing window with $-10 \le x \le 10$ and $-10 \le y \le 10$ is called the **standard viewing window** (Figure 1.21). On some calculators it can be chosen with a single keystroke (in the ZOOM menu).

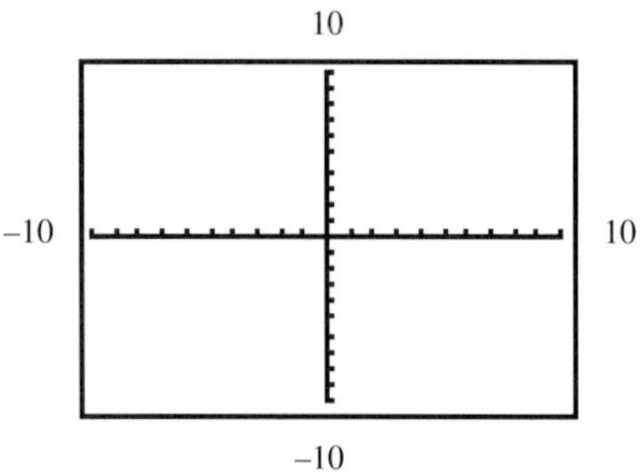

FIGURE 1.21

A **square viewing window** is one in which one-unit segments have the same length on both axes. A typical calculator screen is wider than it is high, so setting the same range of values for both x and y (as in the standard window) does *not* produce a square window because a one-unit segment on the y-axis is shorter than a one-unit segment on the x-axis, as you can see in Figure 1.21.

EXAMPLE 5 **(a)** Using the standard viewing window, graph both of these equations on the same screen:

$$y = 2x - 6 \quad \text{and} \quad y = -.5x + 4.$$

Enter the range settings for the standard window, enter the equations into the function memory (as y_1 and y_2, as in Figure 1.22), and press GRAPH (or PLOT or DRW). The calculator will graph them both (Figure 1.23). As we shall see in Section 1.6, the graphs should be straight lines, but they appear somewhat jagged on a calculator screen.

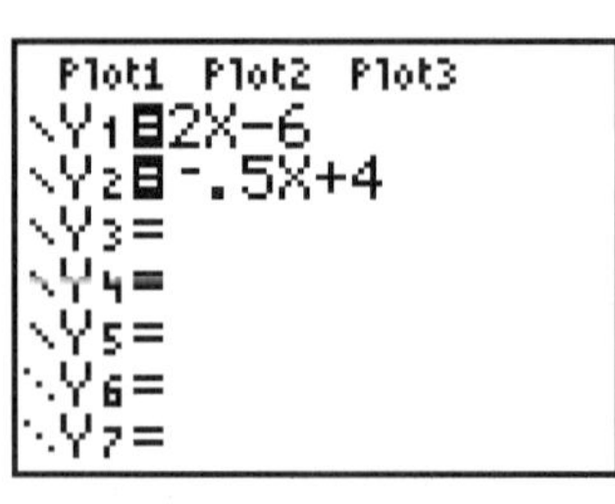

FIGURE 1.22

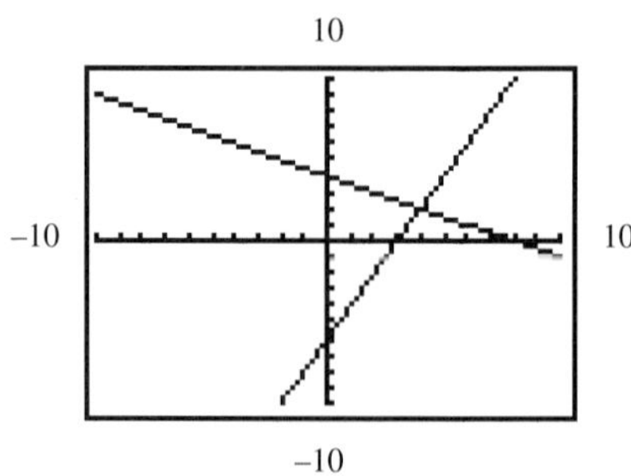

FIGURE 1.23

(b) Now graph both equations in a square viewing window.

Most calculator screens (including the ones shown in this book) are about two-thirds as high as they are wide, so a square window can be obtained by displaying a y-axis that is about 2/3 the length of the x-axis.* We set the range values at $-15 \leq x \leq 15$ and $-10 \leq y \leq 10$ and obtain Figure 1.24, which suggests that the two lines are actually perpendicular (which is indeed the case, as we shall see in Section 1.6).

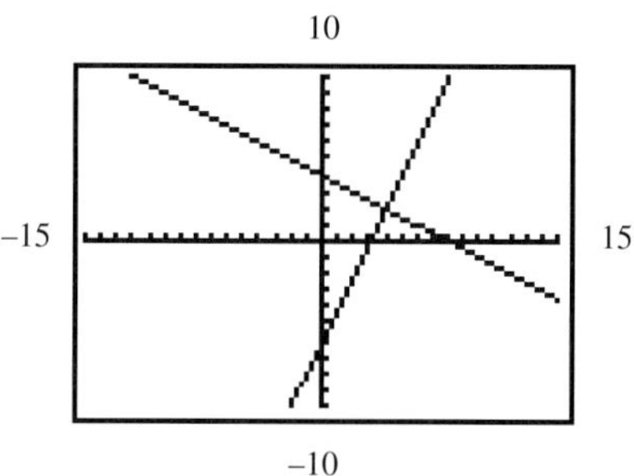

FIGURE 1.24

(c) Graph $y = 2x - 6$ in the square window of part (b).

Leave the range settings as they were in part (b). Both equations that were graphed there are already in the equation memory and both are "on" (which is indicated either by a shaded equals sign, as in Figure 1.25, or by a small check mark on some other calculators). In order to graph only y_1, but not y_2, you must "turn off" y_2. Do this by putting the cursor over the equals sign in y_2 and pressing ENTER to obtain Figure 1.26 (on calculators where a check mark is used, move the cursor to y_2 and press SELECT or CHECK to remove it). Now when you press GRAPH, only y_1 will be graphed. (Do it!) ■

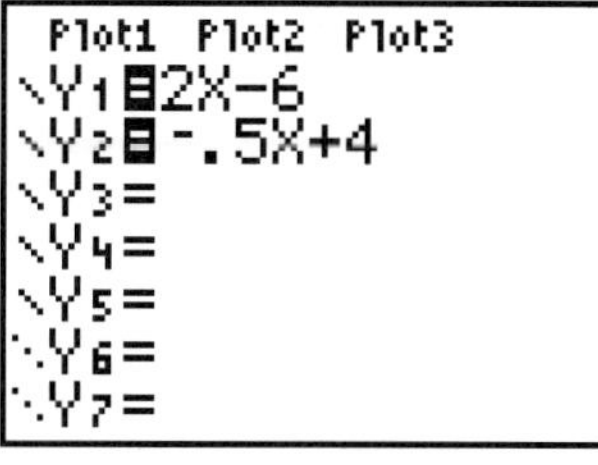

FIGURE 1.25

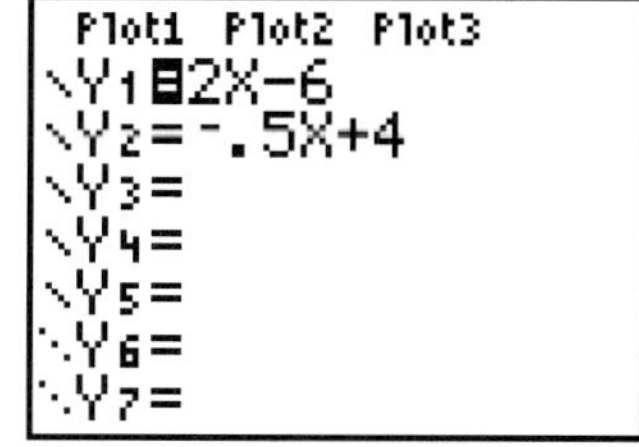

FIGURE 1.26

TECHNOLOGY TIP On many calculators you can change the current viewing window to a square window with a single key (usually labeled SQUARE in the ZOOM menu). ✔

---

*To obtain a square window on wide-screen calculators (such as TI-85/86, TI-92, and HP-38), the y-axis should be approximately 1/2 to 3/5 as long as the x-axis.

You should use square viewing windows when you want perpendicular lines to look perpendicular (as in Example 5), circles to look round, etc., but use any convenient window for the rest of your graphs.

EXAMPLE 6 Determine graphically whether the following factorizations could possibly be correct.

(a) $3x^3 - 4x^2 + 13x + 6 = (x - 3)(x - 1)(3x + 2)$

Enter the left side into the function memory as $y_1 = 3x^3 - 4x^2 + 13x + 6$ and the right side as $y_2 = (x - 3)(x - 1)(3x + 2)$. If the left side of the factorization is equal to the right side, then the graphs of y_1 and y_2 should be identical. Test this by graphing y_1 and y_2 on the same screen. Figure 1.27 shows that the graphs are not the same. Therefore the given factorization must be incorrect.

(b) $2x^3 - 9x^2 + 7x + 6 = (x - 2)(x - 3)(2x + 1)$

Graph the left and right sides on the same screen, as in part (a). The two graphs appear to be identical, that is, only one graph appears on the screen (Figure 1.28). This strongly suggests that the factorization is correct. You can confirm that it is correct algebraically by multiplying out the right side. ■ 7

7 Determine graphically whether the following factorizations could possibly be correct.

(a) $x^3 + 4x^2 - 16x - 64 = (x + 4)(x + 4)(x - 4)$

(b) $x^3 + 2x^2 + x - 6 = (x + 1)(x - 2)(x + 3)$

Answers:

(a) Possibly correct

(b) Incorrect

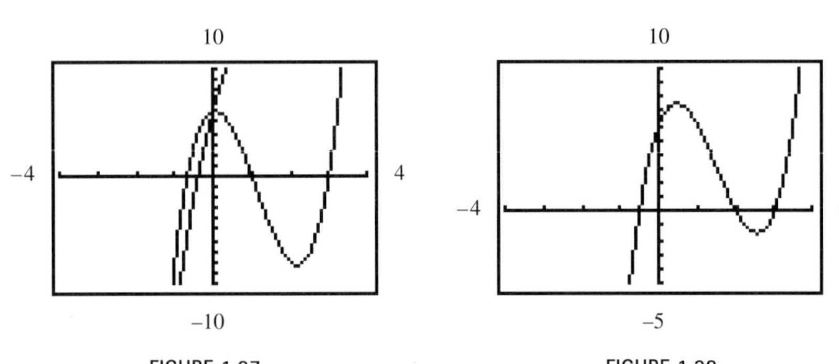

FIGURE 1.27

FIGURE 1.28

CAUTION The fact that two graphs *appear* identical on a calculator screen does not guarantee that they actually *are* identical. When two graphs appear the same, all you can conclude is that they *might* be identical. ◆

COMPLETE GRAPHS Graphing equations on a calculator is analogous to photographing a building with a camera with a zoom lens. Depending on the zoom lens setting (which determines the viewing window of the camera), the resulting photograph may only show a small portion that gives no idea what the rest of the building looks like, or it may show all the important features and give a good idea what the entire building looks like. We shall say that a viewing window on a calculator gives a **complete graph** if it shows all the important features of a graph (such as x- and y-intercepts, peaks, and valleys) and suggests the general shape of any portions of the graph that aren't shown. Many different viewing windows may show a complete graph. It's usually best to use one that is small enough to show as much detail as possible.

Eventually we shall develop some algebraic facts that will assist in obtaining complete graphs of many types of equations. For now, however, you should try various viewing windows to assemble evidence that suggests that a particular graph is probably complete.

8 Graph the equation in Example 7 in the following windows.

(a) $-30 \le x \le 30$; $-500 \le y \le 1500$

(b) $-60 \le x \le 60$; $-6000 \le y \le 6000$

(c) Does the general shape of the graph (one peak, one valley, one x-intercept, rising sharply to the left, and falling sharply to the right) remain the same? What does this suggest?

Answers:

(a)

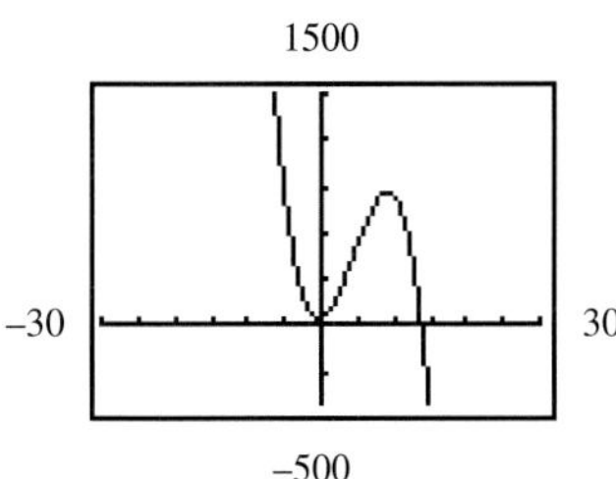

(b)

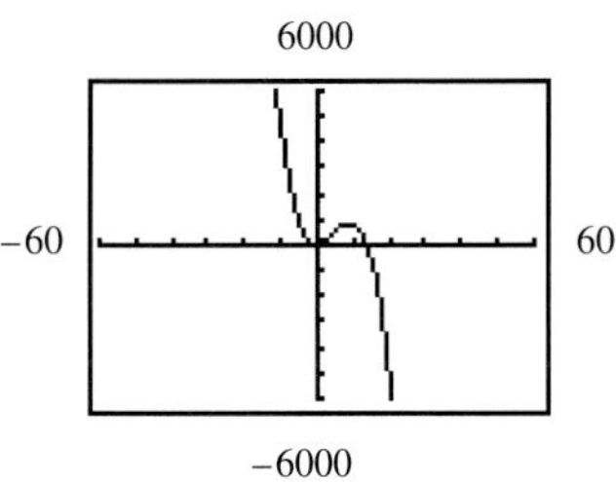

(c) Yes; it suggests that these graphs and the one in Figure 1.30 are probably complete.

EXAMPLE 7 Find a graph of $y = -2x^3 + 26x^2 + 18x + 50$ that appears to be complete.

If you graph the equation in the standard viewing window, you obtain a blank screen (try it!). Don't panic; this just means that no part of the graph is in this particular window. When this happens, you can find at least one point on the graph by finding the y-intercept (set $x = 0$ and compute y). In this case, if $x = 0$, then $y = 50$ so that (0, 50) is on the graph. Figure 1.29, which shows a viewing window that includes this point, *might be* a complete graph. Just to be sure, however, we try a larger window (Figure 1.30). Problem 8 in the margin provides evidence that the graph in Figure 1.30 probably is complete. ■ **8**

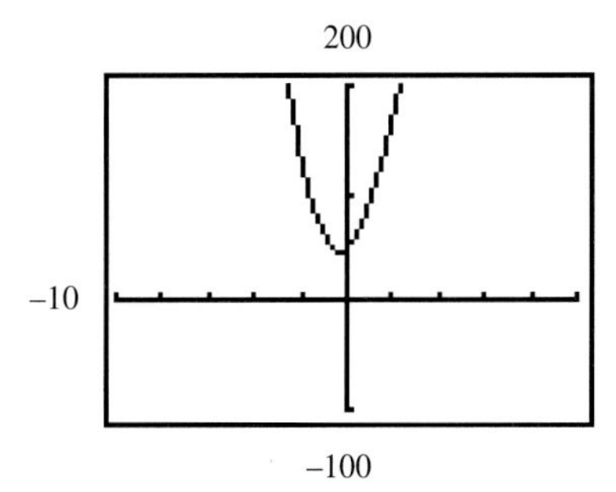

FIGURE 1.29

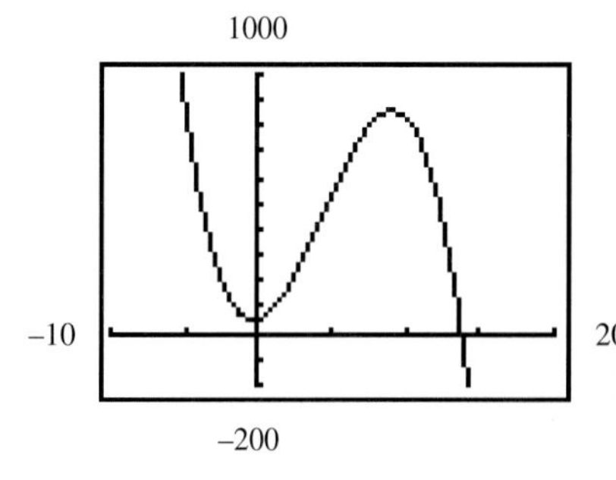

FIGURE 1.30

TECHNOLOGY TIP When you get a blank screen, press TRACE. On most calculators the coordinates of the location of the trace cursor will be displayed even though that point is not in the viewing window. Moving the trace cursor and watching its coordinates will enable you to find a viewing window that does display the graph. ✔

As a general rule, you should follow the directions below when graphing equations.

GRAPHING CONVENTIONS

1. Unless directed otherwise, use a calculator or computer for graphing.
2. Complete graphs are required unless a viewing window is specified or the context of a problem indicates that a partial graph is acceptable.
3. If the directions say "obtain the graph," "find the graph," or "graph the equation," you need not actually draw the graph on paper. For review purposes, however, it may be helpful to record the viewing window used.
4. The directions "sketch the graph" mean "draw the graph on paper, indicating the scale on each axis." This may involve simply copying the display on the calculator screen, or it may require more work if the calculator display is misleading.

1.5 EXERCISES

Exercises 1–4 are designed to help you become familiar with the graphing calculator and its capabilities.

1. Turn off all the functions in the function memory and select a viewing window with $-500 \le x \le 500$ and Xscl = 1. Press GRAPH (or PLOT) and the coordinate plane will be displayed.
   (a) Can you distinguish the tick marks on the x-axis?
   (b) By experimenting with different values for Xscl, find the smallest one that produces clearly distinguishable tick marks that appear to be equally spaced along the x-axis.
   (c) Select a viewing window with $-500 \le y \le 500$ and Yscl = 1. Do parts (a) and (b) for the y-axis. Do you get the same answer in part (b)? Why?
2. Calculator screens consist of tiny rectangles that are darkened to produce graphs. A typical screen will measure 95–239 pixels wide and 63–102 pixels high. Determine the size of the screen on your calculator. (If you can't find the answer in your instruction manual, try moving the cursor across the screen and counting.)
3. Graph the equations $y = .3x^2 - 5$ and $y = x + 3$ in the standard viewing window and turn on the trace feature.
   (a) If you use the left and right arrow keys, which graph does the cursor move along?
   (b) If you use the up or down arrow keys, what happens?
4. Learn how to use the maximum/minimum finders on your calculator. Then use the minimum finder to find the x-coordinate of the lowest point on the graph of $y = x^3 - 2x + 5$ in the viewing window with $0 \le x \le 5$ and $-3 \le y \le 8$. The correct answer is $x = \sqrt{2/3} \approx .816496580928$. How good is your approximation?

List the Xscl and Yscl settings and find the approximate coordinates of P and Q in each of these calculator representations of the coordinate plane.

5.

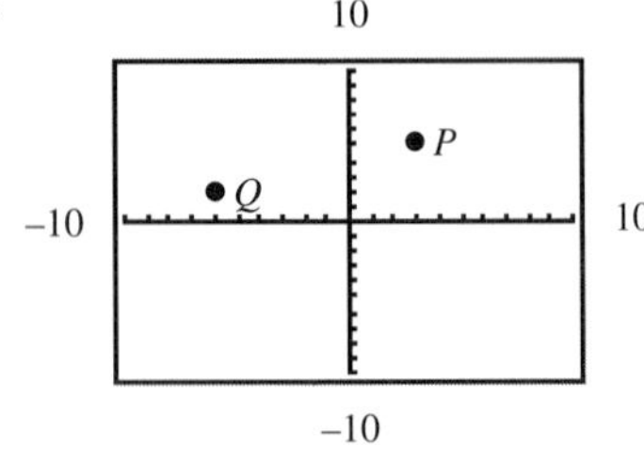

6.

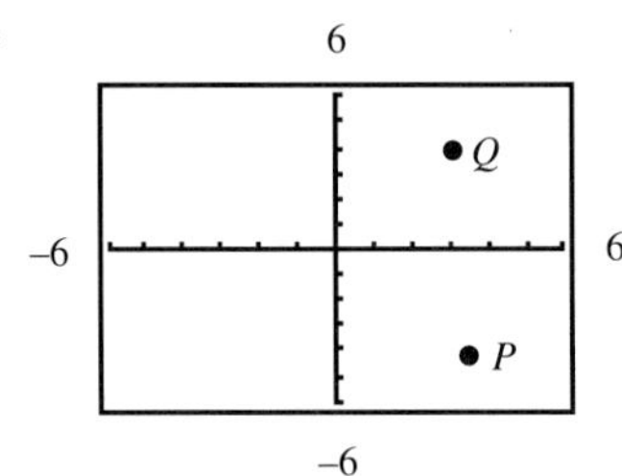

7.

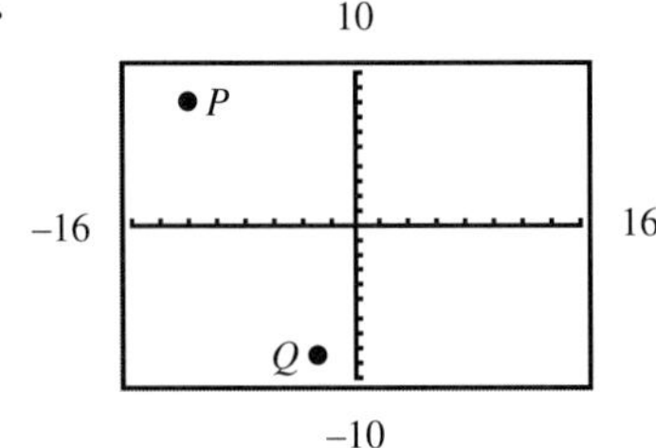

8.

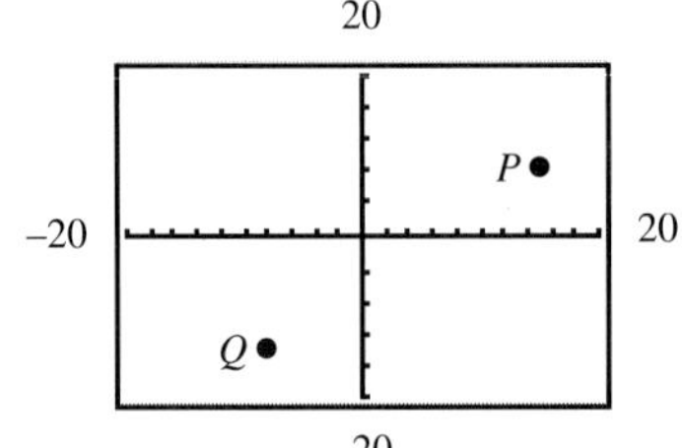

Determine whether the given ordered pair is a solution of the given equation. (See Example 1.)

9. $(1, -2)$; $3x - y - 5 = 0$
10. $(2, -1)$; $x^2 + y^2 - 6x + 8y = -15$
11. $(3, 4)$; $(x - 2)^2 + (y + 5)^2 = 4$
12. $(1, -1)$; $\dfrac{x^2}{2} + \dfrac{y^2}{3} = 1$
13. What is the equation whose graph is the x-axis?
14. What is the equation whose graph is the y-axis?

Sketch the graph of each of these equations by hand. (See Example 2.)

15. $4y + 3x = 12$
16. $2x + 7y = 14$
17. $8x + 3y = 12$
18. $9y - 4x = 12$
19. $x = 2y + 3$
20. $x - 3y = 0$

List the x-intercepts and y-intercepts of each graph.

21.

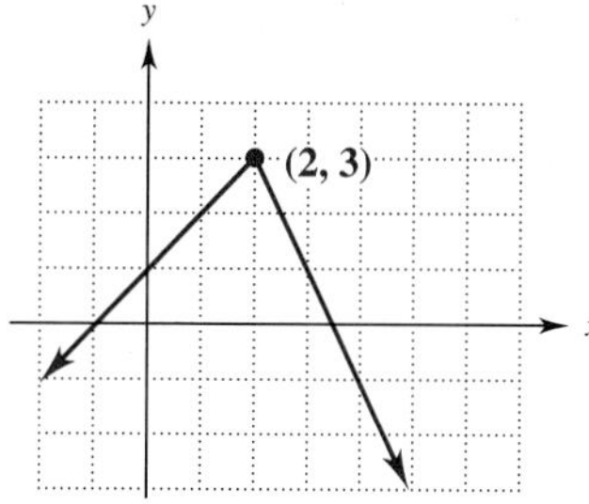

22.

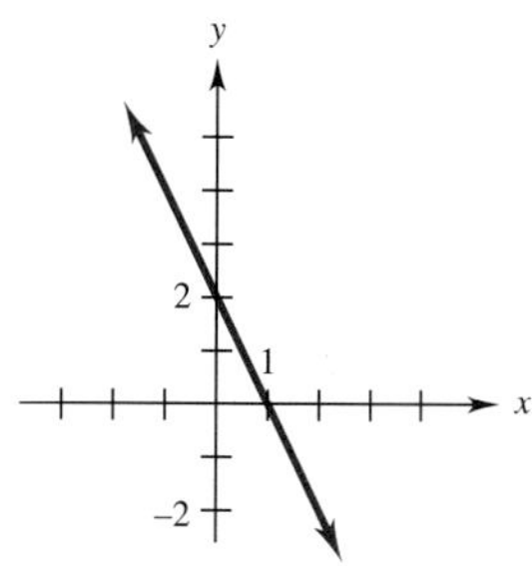

23.

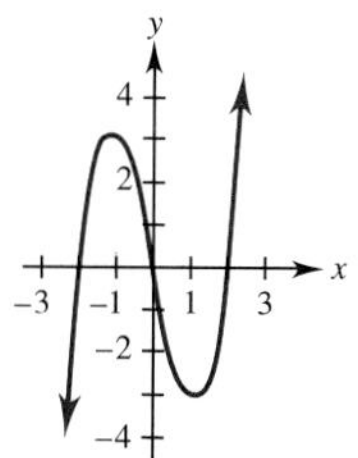

24.

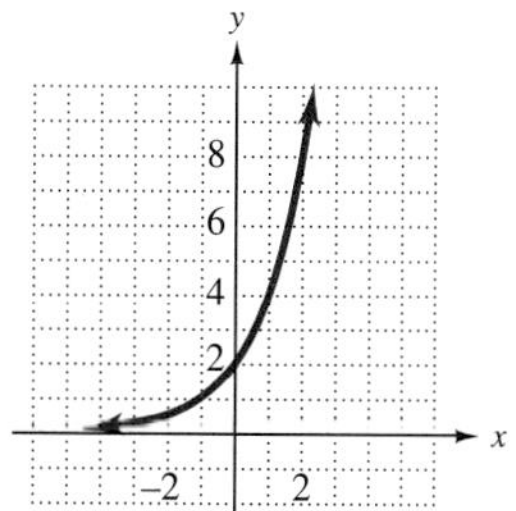

Find the graph of the equation. (See Examples 3–5.)

25. $y = x^2 + x + 1$

26. $y = 2 - x - x^2$

27. $y = (x - 3)^3$

28. $y = x^3 + 2x^2 + 2$

29. $y = x^3 - 3x^2 + x - 1$

30. $y = x^4 - 5x^2 - 2$

31. Graph $y = x^4 - 2x^3 + 2x$ in a window with $-3 \le x \le 3$. Is the "flat" part of the graph near $x = 1$ really a horizontal line segment? (*Hint:* Use trace to move along the "flat" part and watch the y-coordinates. Do they remain the same (as they should on a horizontal segment)?)

32. **(a)** Graph $y = x^4 - 2x^3 + 2x$ in the standard viewing window. Use trace to approximate the coordinates of the lowest point on the graph.

(b) Use a minimum finder to obtain an accurate approximation of the lowest point. How does this compare with your answer in part (a)?

In each of the following situations, find an appropriate viewing window—one that includes all points relevant to the problem, but does not include large regions that are irrelevant to the problem, and one that has easily readable tick marks on the axes. Explain why you chose this window. (See Example 4(a).)

33. A cardiac test measures the concentration y of a dye x seconds after a known amount is injected into a vein near the heart. In a normal heart $y = -.006x^4 + .14x^3 - .053x^2 + 179x$.

34. Beginning in 1905 the deer population in a region of Arizona rapidly increased because of a lack of natural predators. Eventually food resources were depleted to such a degree that the deer population completely died out. In the equation $y = -.125x^5 + 3.125x^4 + 4000$, y is the number of deer in year x, where $x = 0$ corresponds to 1905.

35. A winery can produce x barrels of red wine and y barrels of white wine, where

$$y = \frac{200{,}000 - 50x}{2000 + x}.$$

36. The concentration of a certain medication in the bloodstream at time x hours is approximated by the equation

$$y = \frac{375x}{.1x^3 + 50},$$

where y is measured in milligrams per liter. After two days the medication has no effect.

Determine graphically whether the given factorization could possibly be correct. If it could, determine algebraically whether or not it actually is correct. (See Example 6.)

37. $16x^4 - 32x^3 + 24x^2 - 8x + 1 = (2x - 1)^4$

38. $-27x^3 + 54x^2 - 18x + 8 = (2 - 3x)^3$

39. $2x^4 - 9x^3 + 9x^2 - 16x - 12 = (x - 2)^2(x + 1)(2x - 3)$

40. $x^5 - 2x^4 - x + 2 = (x + 1)(x - 1)(x - 2)(x^2 + 1)$

41. $x^6 - 6x^5 + 15x^4 - 20x^3 + 15x^2 - 6x + 1 = (1 - x)^6$

42. $x^5 - 8x^4 + 16x^3 - 5x^2 + 4x - 20 = (x - 2)^2(x - 5)(x^2 + x + 1)$

Determine graphically whether the given statement is possibly true or definitely false. (See Example 6.)

43. $(x + 2)^3 = x^3 + 8$

44. $\left(\frac{1}{\sqrt{x}} + \frac{1}{\sqrt{5}}\right)^2 = \frac{1}{x} + \frac{1}{5}$

45. $\frac{1}{x^2 + 2} = \frac{1}{x^2} + \frac{1}{2}$

46. $\sqrt{x + 9} = \sqrt{x} + 3$

Decide which of the following viewing windows (a)–(e) gives the best complete graph of the given equation. (See Example 7.)

(a) $-10 \le x \le 10; -10 \le y \le 10$
(b) $-5 \le x \le 25; 0 \le y \le 20$
(c) $-10 \le x \le 10; -100 \le y \le 100$
(d) $-20 \le x \le 15; -60 \le y \le 400$
(e) *None of (a), (b), (c), or (d) gives a complete graph.*

47. $y = 18x - 3x^2$

48. $y = 4x^2 + 80x + 350$

49. $y = \frac{1}{3}x^3 - 25x + 100$

50. $y = x^4 + x - 5$

51. $y = x^2 + 50x + 625$

52. $y = .01(x - 15)^4$

Obtain a complete graph of the equation by trying various viewing windows, as in Example 7. List a viewing window that shows this complete graph. (Many correct answers are possible; consider your answer correct if it shows all the features in the window given in the answer section.)

53. $y = 7x^3 + 35x + 10$

54. $y = x^3 - 5x^2 + 5x - 6$

55. $y = -.1x^4 + x^3 + x^2 + x + 50$

56. $y = .002x^5 + .06x^4 - .001x^3 + .04x^2 - .2x + 15$

Physical Science *According to an article in the December 1994 issue of* Scientific American, *the coast-down time for a typical 1993 car as it drops 10 miles per hour from an initial speed depends on variations from the standard condition (automobile in neutral; average drag and tire pressure). The accompanying graph illustrates some of these conditions with coast-down time in seconds graphed as a function of initial speed in miles per hour.*

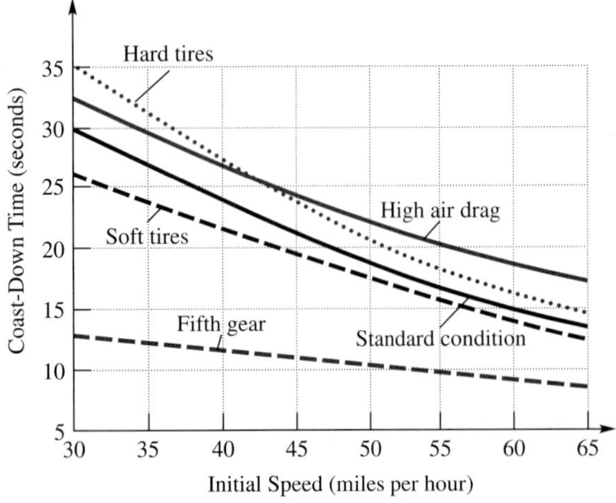

Use the graph to answer the following questions.

57. What is the approximate coast-down time in fifth gear if the initial speed is 40 miles per hour?

58. For what speed is the coast-down time the same for the conditions of high air drag and hard tires?

Management *Work the following problems. (See Example 4.)*

59. Since 1990 Congress has authorized more than \$700 million for research and development of "smart highways."* The approximate spending each year is given by the equation

$$y = -19.321x^2 + 3608.7x - 168{,}310,$$

where x is the number of years since 1900 and y is the amount spent (in millions).

(a) How much was spent in 1991 (that is, $x = 91$)? In 1995?

(b) In what year was the maximum amount spent?

60. An office supply manufacturer has found that the profit y (in dollars) from selling x boxes of staples is given by the equation $y = -.0002x^2 + 1.4x - 300$. How many boxes of staples must be sold in order to make as large a profit as possible? What is the maximum profit?

61. A manufacturer has found that the average cost y per computer when x computers per day are produced is given by the equation $y = .13x^2 - 70x + 10{,}000$. How many computers should be produced to make the average cost as low as possible? What is the minimum average cost?

62. The surface area of a rectangular box with a square base, no top, and a volume of 30,000 cubic cm is given by the equation $y = x^2 + 120{,}000/x$, where x is the length of a side of the base (in cm) and y is the surface area (in square cm). How long should a side of the base be in order for the surface area to be as small as possible? What is the minimum surface area?

63. A hardware store sells ladders throughout the year. In addition to the wholesale cost of the ladders there are shipping and storage charges each time ladders are ordered. The yearly total shipping and storage cost y, when ladders are ordered x times per year, is given by the equation $y = 20x + 3000/x$. How many times per year should ladders be ordered in order to keep shipping and storage costs at a minimum? (Your answer must be a whole number.)

64. A novelty company has determined that its daily profit y from making x hundred bookmarks is given by the equation $y = -x^3 + 8x^2 + 122x - 40$.

(a) Because of other projects, a maximum of 600 bookmarks per day can be manufactured. Assuming the company can sell all the bookmarks it makes, how many should it make each day to maximize profit?

(b) Due to a change in orders, as many as 1600 bookmarks can now be made each day. How many should be made to maximize profit?

*I.V.H.S. America.

1.6 SLOPE AND THE EQUATIONS OF A LINE

Straight lines, which are the simplest graphs, play an important role in a wide variety of applications. They are considered here from both a geometric and an algebraic point of view.

The key geometric feature of a nonvertical straight line is how steeply it rises or falls as you move from left to right. The "steepness" of a line can be represented numerically by a number called the *slope* of the line.

To see how slope is defined, start with Figure 1.31, which shows a line passing through the two different points $(x_1, y_1) = (-3, 5)$ and $(x_2, y_2) = (2, -4)$. The difference in the two x-values,

$$x_2 - x_1 = 2 - (-3) = 5$$

in this example, is called the **change in *x*.** The Greek letter Δ (delta) is used to denote change. The symbol Δx (read "delta x") represents the change in x. In the same way, Δy represents the **change in *y*.** In this example,

$$\Delta y = y_2 - y_1 = -4 - 5 = -9.$$

The **slope** of the line through the two points (x_1, y_1) and (x_2, y_2), where $x_1 \neq x_2$, is defined as the quotient of the change in y and the change in x, or

$$\textbf{slope} = \frac{\textbf{change in } y}{\textbf{change in } x} = \frac{\Delta y}{\Delta x} = \frac{y_2 - y_1}{x_2 - x_1}.$$

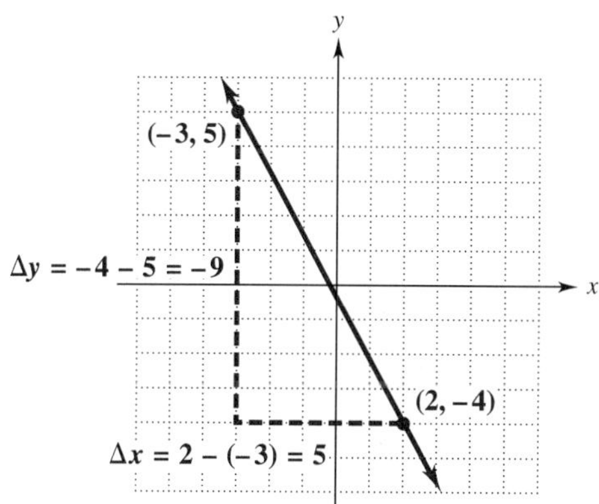

FIGURE 1.31

The slope of the line in Figure 1.31 is

$$\text{slope} = \frac{\Delta y}{\Delta x} = \frac{-4 - 5}{2 - (-3)} = -\frac{9}{5}.$$

Using similar triangles from geometry, it can be shown that the slope is independent of the choice of points on the line. That is, the same value of the slope will be obtained for *any* choice of two different points on the line.

EXAMPLE 1 Find the slope of the line through the points $(-7, 6)$ and $(4, 5)$.

Let $(x_1, y_1) = (-7, 6)$. Then $(x_2, y_2) = (4, 5)$. Use the definition of slope.

$$\text{slope} = \frac{\Delta y}{\Delta x} = \frac{5 - 6}{4 - (-7)} = -\frac{1}{11}$$

The slope can also be found by letting $(x_1, y_1) = (4, 5)$ and $(x_2, y_2) = (-7, 6)$. In that case,

$$\text{slope} = \frac{6 - 5}{-7 - 4} = -\frac{1}{11},$$

the same answer. ■ [1]

[1] Find the slope of the line through

(a) $(6, 11), (-4, -3)$;

(b) $(-3, 5), (-2, 8)$.

Answers:

(a) 7/5

(b) 3

CAUTION When finding the slope of a line, be careful to subtract the x-values and the y-values in the same order. For example, with the points $(4, 3)$ and $(2, 9)$, if you use $9 - 3$ for the numerator, you must use $2 - 4$ (*not* $4 - 2$) for the denominator. ◆

EXAMPLE 2 Find the slope of the horizontal line in Figure 1.32.

Every point on the line has the same y-coordinate, -5. Choose any two of them to compute the slope, say $(x_1, y_1) = (-3, -5)$ and $(x_2, y_2) = (2, -5)$:

$$\text{slope} = \frac{-5 - (-5)}{2 - (-3)} = \frac{0}{5} = 0. \quad ■$$

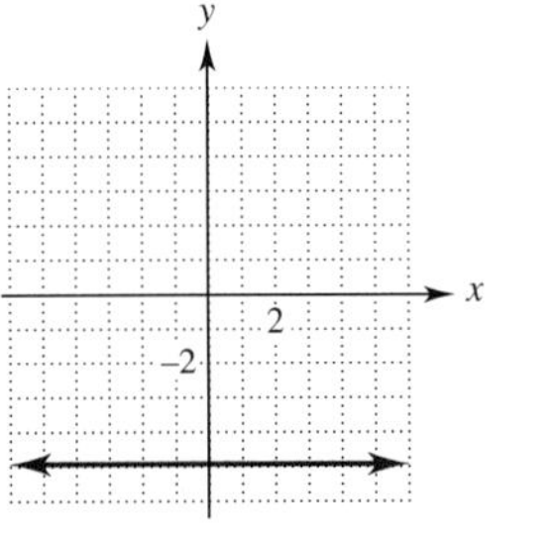

FIGURE 1.32

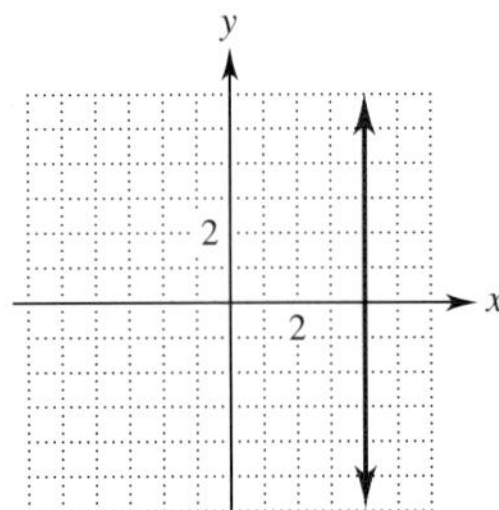

FIGURE 1.33

EXAMPLE 3 What is the slope of the vertical line in Figure 1.33?

Every point on the line has the same x-coordinate, 4. If you attempt to compute the slope with two of these points, say $(x_1, y_1) = (4, -2)$ and $(x_2, y_2) = (4, 1)$, you obtain

$$\text{slope} = \frac{1 - (-2)}{4 - 4} = \frac{3}{0}.$$

Division by 0 is not defined, so the slope of this line is undefined. ■

The arguments used in Examples 2 and 3 work in the general case and lead to the following conclusion.

> The slope of every horizontal line is 0.
>
> The slope of every vertical line is undefined.

SLOPE-INTERCEPT FORM Slope can be used to develop an algebraic description of nonvertical straight lines. Assume that a line with slope m has y-intercept b, so that it goes through the point $(0, b)$ (see Figure 1.34). Let (x, y) be any point on the line other than $(0, b)$.

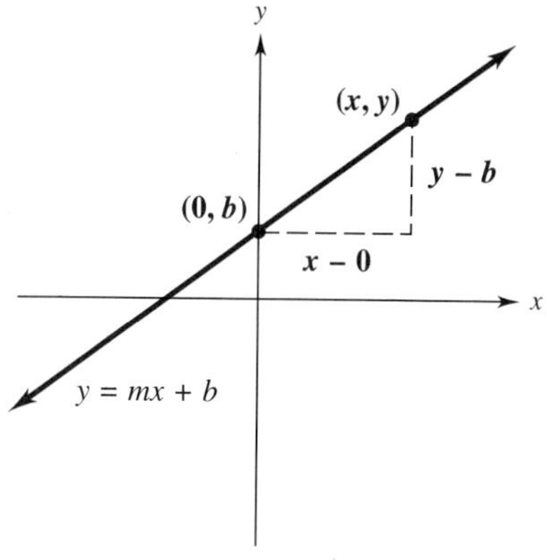

FIGURE 1.34

Using the definition of slope with the points $(0, b)$ and (x, y) gives

$$m = \frac{y - b}{x - 0}$$

$$m = \frac{y - b}{x}$$

$$mx = y - b \qquad \text{Multiply by } x.$$

$$y = mx + b. \qquad \text{Add } b\text{. Reverse the equation.}$$

In other words, the coordinates of any point on the line satisfy the equation $y = mx + b$.

> **SLOPE-INTERCEPT FORM**
>
> If a line has slope m and y-intercept b, then it is the graph of the equation
>
> $$y = mx + b.$$
>
> This equation is called the **slope-intercept form** of the equation of the line.

EXAMPLE 4 Find an equation for the line with y-intercept 7/2 and slope $-5/2$.

Use the slope-intercept form with $b = 7/2$ and $m = -5/2$.

$$y = mx + b$$

$$y = -\frac{5}{2}x + \frac{7}{2} \quad ■$$

2 Find an equation for the line with

(a) y-intercept -3 and slope $2/3$;

(b) y-intercept $1/4$ and slope $-3/2$.

Answers:

(a) $y = \frac{2}{3}x - 3$

(b) $y = -\frac{3}{2}x + \frac{1}{4}$

3 Find the slope and y-intercept for

(a) $x + 4y = 6$;

(b) $3x - 2y = 1$.

Answers:

(a) Slope $-1/4$; y-intercept $3/2$

(b) Slope $3/2$; y-intercept $-1/2$

4 **(a)** List the slopes of the following lines:

$$y_1 = -.3x, \quad y_2 = -x, \quad y_3 = -2x, \quad y_4 = -5x.$$

(b) Using the standard viewing window, graph all four lines on the same screen.

(c) How are the slopes of the lines related to their steepness?

Answers:

(a) Slope $y_1 = -.3$; slope $y_2 = -1$; slope $y_3 = -2$; slope $y_4 = -5$.

(b)

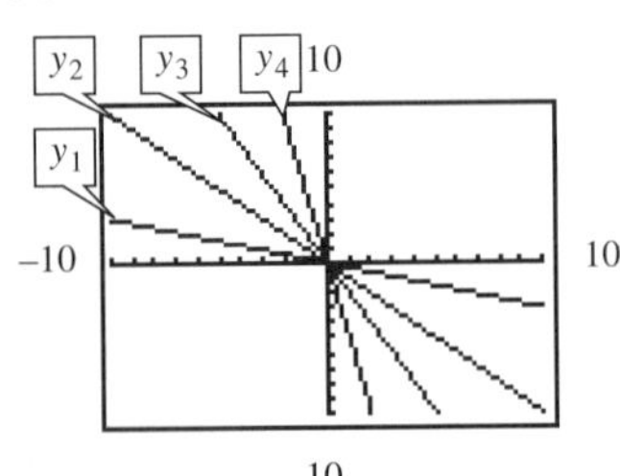

(c) The larger the slope in absolute value, the more steeply the line falls from left to right.

EXAMPLE 5 Find the equation of the horizontal line with y-intercept 3.

The slope of the line is 0 (why?) and its y-intercept is 3, so its equation is

$$y = mx + b$$
$$y = 0x + 3$$
$$y = 3$$ ■ 2

The argument in Example 5 also works in the general case.

> If k is a constant, then the graph of the equation $y = k$ is the horizontal line with y-intercept k.

EXAMPLE 6 Find the slope and y-intercept for each of the following lines.

(a) $5x - 3y = 1$

Solve for y.

$$5x - 3y = 1$$
$$-3y = -5x + 1$$
$$y = \frac{5}{3}x - \frac{1}{3}$$

This equation is in the form $y = mx + b$, with $m = 5/3$ and $b = -1/3$. So the slope is $5/3$ and the y-intercept is $-1/3$.

(b) $-9x + 6y = 2$

Solve for y.

$$-9x + 6y = 2$$
$$6y = 9x + 2$$
$$y = \frac{3}{2}x + \frac{1}{3}$$

The slope is $3/2$ (coefficient of x) and the y-intercept is $1/3$. ■ 3

The slope-intercept form can be used with a graphing calculator to show how the slope measures the steepness of a line. Using the standard viewing window, graph the following four equations on the same screen. Each graph is a straight line with y-intercept 0 and slope as indicated.

$y_1 = .5x$,	$y_2 = x$,	$y_3 = 3x$,	$y_4 = 7x$
Slope .5	Slope 1	Slope 3	Slope 7

Figure 1.35 shows that the bigger the slope, the more steeply the line rises from left to right. 4

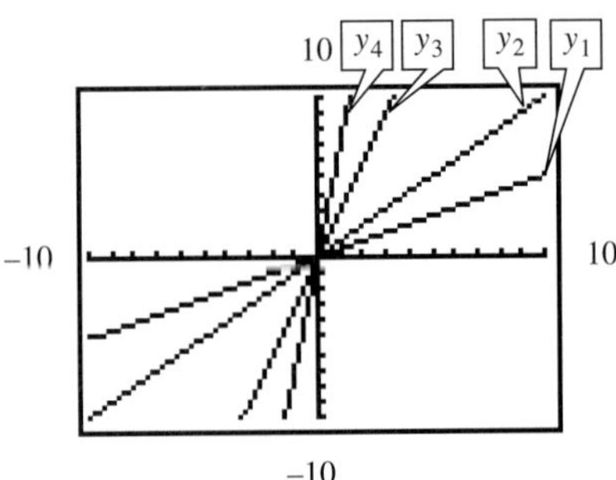

FIGURE 1.35

The preceding discussion and Problem 4 in the margin may be summarized as follows.

Direction of Line (moving from left to right)	*Slope*
Upward	**Positive** (larger for steeper lines)
Horizontal	**0**
Downward	**Negative** (larger in absolute value for steeper lines)
Vertical	**Undefined**

When the equation of a line is written in slope-intercept form, it is easily graphed on a calculator. Graphing lines by hand is just as easy.

EXAMPLE 7 Sketch the graph of $x + 2y = 5$ and label the intercepts.

Find the x-intercept by setting $y = 0$ and solving for x.

$$x + 2 \cdot 0 = 5$$
$$x = 5$$

The x-intercept is 5 and (5, 0) is on the graph. The y-intercept is found similarly, by setting $x = 0$ and solving for y.

$$0 + 2y = 5$$
$$y = 5/2$$

The y-intercept is 5/2 and (0, 5/2) is on the graph. The points (5, 0) and (0, 5/2) can be used to sketch the graph (Figure 1.36).

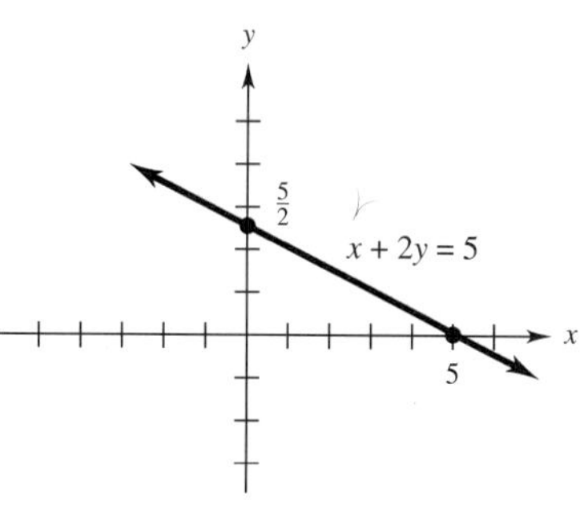

FIGURE 1.36

To avoid error, plot a third point (if it's not on the line, recheck your work) or use your calculator to confirm the accuracy of Figure 1.36. ■ 5

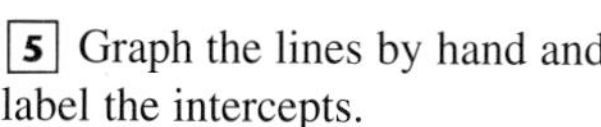
5 Graph the lines by hand and label the intercepts.

(a) $3x + 4y = 12$

(b) $5x - 2y = 8$

Answers:

(a)

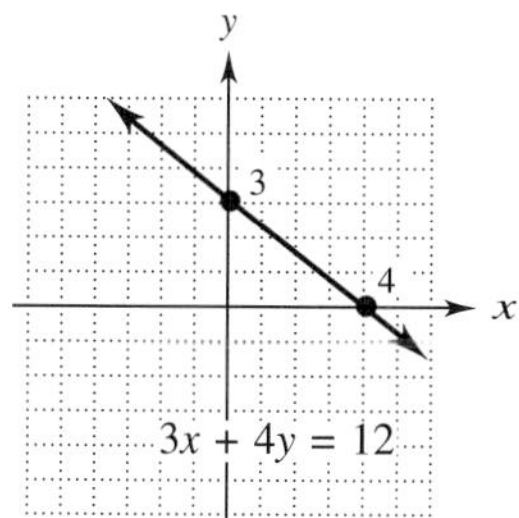

(b)

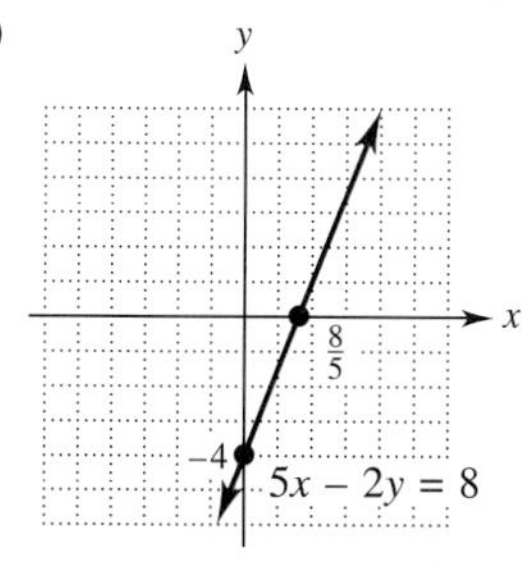

PARALLEL AND PERPENDICULAR LINES We shall assume the following facts without proof. The first one is a consequence of the fact that slope measures steepness and parallel lines have the same steepness.

> Two nonvertical lines are parallel whenever they have the same slope.
>
> Two nonvertical lines are perpendicular whenever the product of their slopes is -1.

EXAMPLE 8 Determine whether each of the following pairs of lines are *parallel, perpendicular,* or *neither.*

(a) $2x + 3y = 5$ and $4x + 5 = -6y$

Put each equation in slope-intercept form by solving for y.

$$3y = -2x + 5 \qquad -6y = 4x + 5$$

$$y = -\frac{2}{3}x + \frac{5}{3} \qquad y = -\frac{2}{3}x - \frac{5}{6}$$

In each case the slope (coefficient of x) is $-2/3$, so the lines are parallel.

(b) $3x = y + 7$ and $x + 3y = 4$

The slope of $3x = y + 7$ is 3 (why?). Verify that the slope of $x + 3y = 4$ is $-1/3$. Since $3(-1/3) = -1$, these lines are perpendicular. 6

(c) $x + y = 4$ and $x - 2y = 3$

Verify that the slope of the first line is -1 and the slope of the second is $1/2$. The slopes are not equal and their product is not -1, so the lines are neither parallel nor perpendicular. ■ 7

6 Graph the lines in Example 8(b) in a square viewing window with $-6 \le x \le 6$, so that they look perpendicular.

Answer:

For standard width screens:

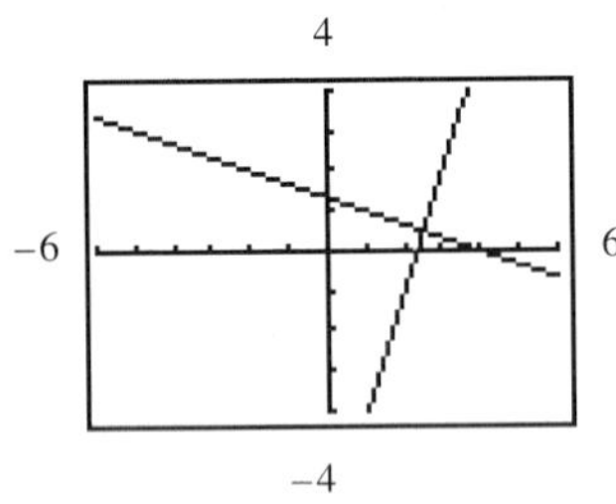

For wide screens, try $-3.5 \le y \le 3.5$ or $-3 \le y \le 3$.

7 Tell if the lines in each of the following pairs are *parallel, perpendicular,* or *neither.*

(a) $x - 2y = 6$ and $2x + y = 5$

(b) $3x + 4y = 8$ and $x + 3y = 2$

(c) $2x - y = 7$ and $2y = 4x - 5$

Answers:

(a) Perpendicular

(b) Neither

(c) Parallel

POINT-SLOPE FORM The slope-intercept form of the equation of a line involves the slope and the y-intercept. Sometimes, however, the slope of a line is known, together with one point on the line (perhaps *not* the y-intercept). The *point-slope form* of the equation of a line is used to find an equation in this case. Let (x_1, y_1) be any fixed point on the line and let (x, y) represent any other point on the line. If m is the slope of the line, then, by the definition of slope,

$$\frac{y - y_1}{x - x_1} = m.$$

Multiplying both sides by $x - x_1$ shows that

$$y - y_1 = m(x - x_1).$$

> POINT-SLOPE FORM
>
> If a line has slope m and passes through the point (x_1, y_1), then
>
> $$\mathbf{y - y_1 = m(x - x_1)}$$
>
> is the **point-slope form** of the equation of the line.

EXAMPLE 9 Find an equation of the line with the given slope and going through the given point.

(a) $(-4, 1)$, $m = -3$

Use the point-slope form because a point on the line, together with the slope of the line, is known. Substitute the values $x_1 = -4$, $y_1 = 1$, and $m = -3$ into the point-slope form.

$$y - y_1 = m(x - x_1)$$

$$y - 1 = -3[x - (-4)] \qquad \text{Point-slope form}$$

Using algebra we obtain the slope-intercept form of this equation.

$$y - 1 = -3(x + 4)$$

$$y - 1 = -3x - 12 \qquad \text{Distributive property}$$

$$y = -3x - 11 \qquad \text{Slope-intercept form}$$

(b) $(3, -7)$, $m = 5/4$

$$y - y_1 = m(x - x_1)$$

$$y - (-7) = \frac{5}{4}(x - 3) \qquad \text{Let } y_1 = -7, m = \frac{5}{4}, x_1 = 3.$$

$$y + 7 = \frac{5}{4}(x - 3) \qquad \text{Point-slope form}$$

$$y + 7 = \frac{5}{4}x - \frac{15}{4}$$

$$y = \frac{5}{4}x - \frac{43}{4} \qquad \text{Slope-intercept form}$$

■ 8

8 Find both the point-slope and the slope-intercept forms of the equation of the line having the given slope and passing through the given point.

(a) $m = -3/5$, $(5, -2)$

(b) $m = 1/3$, $(6, 8)$

Answers:

(a) $y + 2 = -\frac{3}{5}(x - 5)$; $y = -\frac{3}{5}x + 1$.

(b) $y - 8 = \frac{1}{3}(x - 6)$; $y = \frac{1}{3}x + 6$.

The point-slope form can also be used to find an equation of a line when two different points on the line are given.

EXAMPLE 10 Find an equation of the line through $(5, 4)$ and $(-10, -2)$.

Begin by using the definition of slope to find the slope of the line that passes through the two points.

$$\text{slope} = m = \frac{-2 - 4}{-10 - 5} = \frac{-6}{-15} = \frac{2}{5}$$

Use $m = 2/5$ and either of the given points in the point-slope form. If $(x_1, y_1) = (5, 4)$, then

$$y - y_1 = m(x - x_1)$$

$$y - 4 = \frac{2}{5}(x - 5) \qquad \text{Let } y_1 = 4, m = \frac{2}{5}, x_1 = 5.$$

$$5(y - 4) = 2(x - 5) \qquad \text{Multiply both sides by 5.}$$

$$5y - 20 = 2x - 10 \qquad \text{Distributive property}$$

$$5y = 2x + 10.$$

Check that the result is the same when $(x_1, y_1) = (-10, -2)$. ■ 9

9 Find an equation of the line through

(a) $(2, 3)$ and $(-4, 6)$;

(b) $(-8, 2)$ and $(3, -6)$.

Answers:

(a) $2y = -x + 8$

(b) $11y = -8x - 42$

EXAMPLE 11 In an experiment testing a person's reaction time y (in seconds) after undergoing x hours of stressful activity, the linear equation $y = .1957x + .1243$ was found to be a good approximation of the relationship between stress and reaction time during the first 5 hours. Assuming that reaction times continue to follow this pattern, what would be the approximate reaction time after eight and a half hours?

The question can be answered algebraically by substituting $x = 8.5$ into the equation of the line and solving for y. It can be answered graphically by graphing $y = .1957x + .1243$ (Figure 1.37) and using the trace feature (Figure 1.38). The viewing window was chosen so that each time the arrow key is pushed, the x-coordinate of the trace cursor changes by exactly .1.* Moving the cursor along the graph to the point with x-coordinate 8.5, we see that the corresponding reaction time is approximately 1.79 seconds. ■

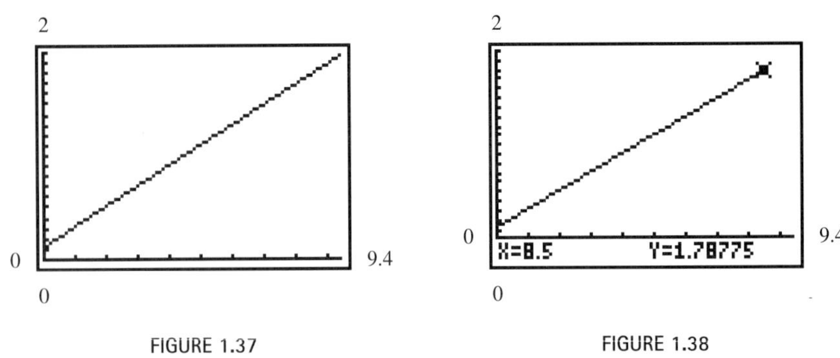

FIGURE 1.37

FIGURE 1.38

VERTICAL LINES The equation forms developed above do not apply to vertical lines because slope is not defined for such lines. However, vertical lines can easily be described as graphs of equations.

EXAMPLE 12 Find the equation whose graph is the vertical line in Figure 1.39.

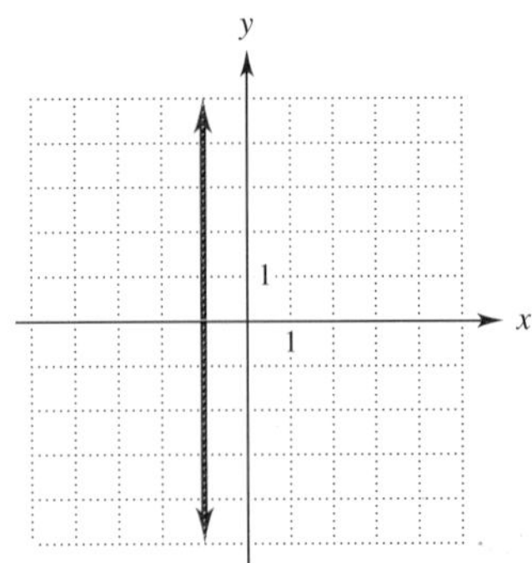

FIGURE 1.39

*To get the same effect on some standard screen calculators it may be necessary to change the Xmax setting from 9.4 to 9.5. For wide screen calculators, try Xmax = 12.6 or 13 or 23.8. For the reason *why* these windows have this property, see Exercise 1.

Every point on the line has x-coordinate -1 and hence has the form $(-1, y)$. Thus every point is a solution of the equation $x + 0y = -1$, which is usually written simply as $x = -1$. Note that -1 is the x-intercept of the line. ■

The argument in Example 12 also works in the general case.

> If k is a constant, then the graph of the equation $x = k$ is the vertical line with x-intercept k.

A **linear equation** is an equation in two variables that can be put in the form $ax + by = c$ for some constants a, b, c, with at least one of a, b nonzero. These equations are so named because their graph is always a straight line. For instance, when $b \neq 0$, then $ax + by = c$ can be written

$$by = -ax + c$$

$$y = -\frac{a}{b}x + \frac{c}{b},$$

which is the equation of a line with slope $-a/b$ and y-intercept c/b. Similarly, when $b = 0$, then $a \neq 0$ and $ax + by = c$ becomes $x = c/a$, whose graph is a vertical line. Conversely, the equation of every line is a linear equation. For example, the line with slope -3 and y-intercept 5 has the equation $y = -3x + 5$ (why?), which can be written $3x + 1y = 5$. Here is a summary of the basic facts about linear equations and their graphs.

Equation	*Description*
$ax + by = c$	If $a \neq 0$ and $b \neq 0$, the line has x-intercept c/a and y-intercept c/b.
$x = k$	**Vertical line,** x-intercept k, no y-intercept, undefined slope
$y = k$	**Horizontal line,** y-intercept k, no x-intercept, slope 0
$y = mx + b$	**Slope-intercept form,** slope m, y-intercept b
$y - y_1 = m(x - x_1)$	**Point-slope form,** slope m, the line passes through (x_1, y_1)

1.6 EXERCISES

Exercises 1–2 are designed to help you become familiar with the graphing calculator and its capabilities.

1. If your calculator screen is 95 pixels wide (for example, a TI-82 or Casio 9800 or Sharp 9300) and you set the viewing window so that $0 \leq x \leq 94$, then the pixels on the x-axis represent the 95 numbers 0, 1, 2, . . . , 94. Since the trace cursor moves one horizontal pixel at a time, its x-coordinate will change by one unit each time you press the left or right arrow key. Similarly, on other size screens, setting the x-range to go from 0 to one less than the pixel-width of the screen will cause the x-coordinate of the trace cursor to change by one unit at a time.
   (a) If your screen is 95 pixels wide, find Xmax so that $0 \leq x \leq$ Xmax and the x-coordinate of the trace cursor changes by two units each time you press an arrow key.

(exercise continues)

(b) If your screen is 95 pixels wide, find, Xmin and Xmax so that 0 is in the middle of the x-axis and the x-coordinate of the trace cursor changes by one unit each time you press an arrow key.
(c) If your screen is 95 pixels wide, find Xmin and Xmax so that 0 is in the middle of the x-axis and the x-coordinate of the trace cursor changes by *one-tenth* of a unit each time you press an arrow key.
(d) Do parts (a)–(c) for a calculator with a 131-pixel wide screen (such as an HP-38).
(e) Do parts (a)–(c) for a calculator with a 127-pixel wide screen (such as a TI-85).

2. From our work in this section, we know that the lines $y = .2x + 4$ and $y = -5x - 6$ are perpendicular (the product of their slopes is -1).
(a) Graph both lines in the standard viewing window. Do they look perpendicular?
(b) Find a viewing window with $-10 \le x \le 10$ in which the lines do look perpendicular (think square).
(c) Find a viewing window with $-10 \le y \le 10$ in which the lines do look perpendicular.

Find the slope of the line, if it is defined. (See Examples 1–3.)

3. Through $(-4, 7)$ and $(3, 0)$

4. Through $(-5, -2)$ and $(-4, 11)$

5. Through the origin and $(-4, 6)$

6. Through the origin and $(8, -2)$

7. Through $(-1, 4)$ and $(-1, 8)$

8. Through $(-3, 5)$ and $(2, 5)$

Find an equation of the line with the given y-intercept and slope m. (See Examples 4 and 5.)

9. $5, m = 3$

10. $-3, m = -7$

11. $1.5, m = -2.3$

12. $-4.5, m = 1.5$

13. $4, m = -3/4$

14. $-3, m = 2/3$

Find the slope and the y-intercept of the line whose equation is given. (See Example 6.)

15. $2x - y = 7$

16. $x + 2y = 7$

17. $6x = 2y + 4$

18. $4x + 3y = 12$

19. $6x - 9y = 14$

20. $4x + 2y = 0$

21. $2x - 3y = 0$

22. $y = 5$

23. On one graph, sketch six straight lines that meet at a single point and satisfy this condition: one line has slope 0, two lines have positive slope, two lines have negative slope, and one line has undefined slope.

24. For which of the line segments in the following figure is the slope
(a) largest? (b) smallest?
(c) largest in absolute value? (d) closest to 0?

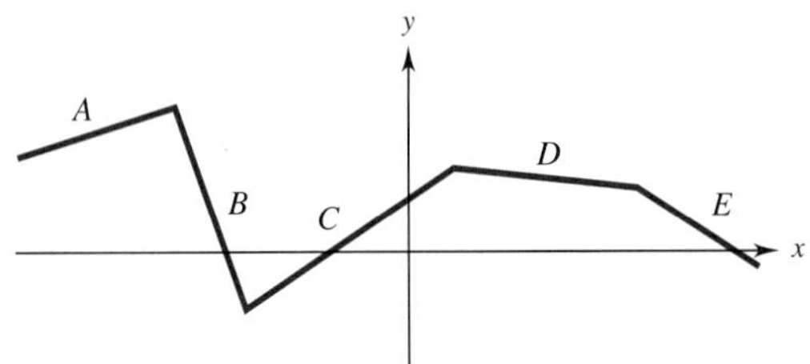

25. (a) Graph $y = 2x + 4$ in the standard viewing window.
(b) Graph $y = 6x - 3$ in the window with $-10 \le x \le 10$ and $-60 \le y \le 60$.
(c) Which of the lines in parts (a) and (b) *appears* to rise more steeply? Which has the largest slope?
(d) Explain why your answer in part (c) does not contradict the properties of slope in the box on page 47.

26. Match each equation with the line that most closely resembles its graph. (*Hint:* Consider the signs of m and b in the slope-intercept form.)

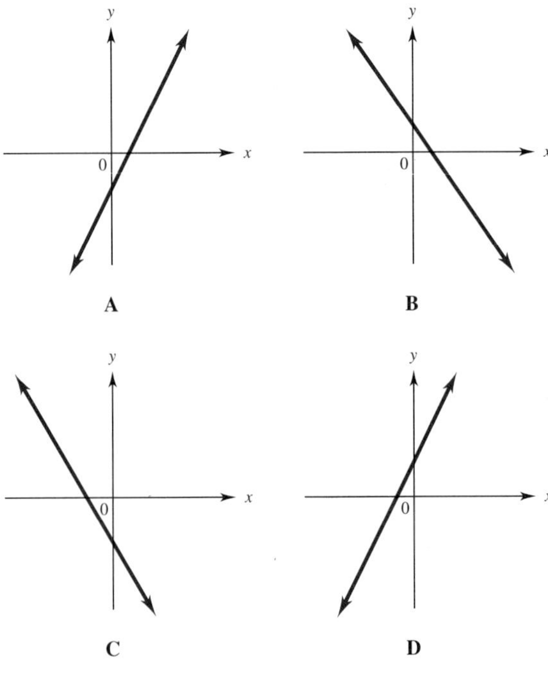

(a) $y = 3x + 2$ (b) $y = -3x + 2$
(c) $y = 3x - 2$ (d) $y = -3x - 2$

Sketch the graph of the equation and label the intercepts. (See Example 7.)

27. $2x - y = -2$

28. $2y + x = 4$

29. $2x + 3y = 4$

30. $-5x + 4y = 3$

31. $4x - 5y = 2$

32. $3x + 2y = 8$

Determine whether each pair of lines is parallel, perpendicular, or neither. (See Example 8.)

33. $4x - 3y = 6$ and $3x + 4y = 8$

34. $2x - 5y = 7$ and $15y - 5 = 6x$

35. $3x + 2y = 8$ and $6y = 5 - 9x$

36. $x - 3y = 4$ and $y = 1 - 3x$

37. $4x = 2y + 3$ and $2y = 2x + 3$

38. $2x - y = 6$ and $x - 2y = 4$

39. **(a)** Find the slope of each side of the triangle with vertices $(9, 6)$, $(-1, 2)$, and $(1, -3)$.
(b) Is this triangle a right triangle? (*Hint:* Are two sides perpendicular?)

40. **(a)** Find the slope of each side of the quadrilateral with vertices $(-5, -2)$, $(-3, 1)$, $(3, 0)$, and $(1, -3)$.
(b) Is this quadrilateral a parallelogram?

41. **Physical Science** The graph shows the winning times (in minutes) at the Olympic Games for the 5000-meter run, together with a linear approximation of the data.*

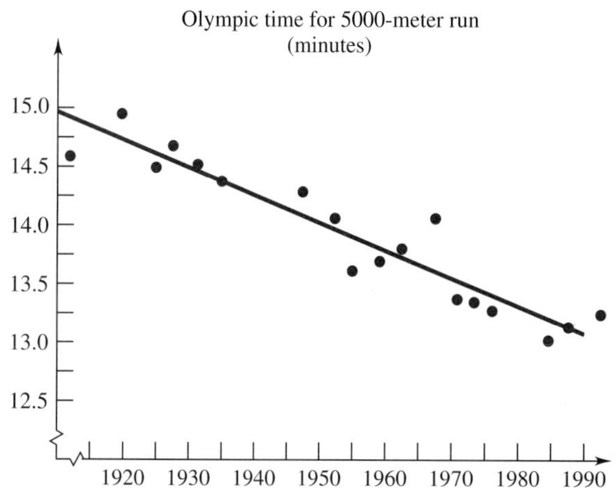

(a) The equation for the linear approximation is $y = -.0221x + 57.14$. What does the slope of this line represent? Why is the slope negative?
(b) Can you think of any reason why there are no data points for the years 1940 and 1944?

42. **Management** The graph in the next column shows the number of U.S. radio stations on the air along with a linear approximation of the data.†

*United States Olympic Committee.

†National Association of Broadcasters.

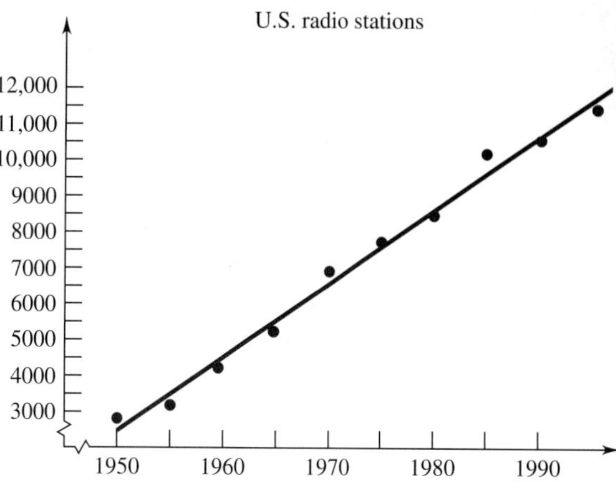

(a) Discuss the accuracy of the linear approximation.
(b) Use the two data points (1950, 2773) and (1994, 11600) to find the approximate slope of the line shown. Interpret this number.

Find an equation of the line that passes through the given point and has the given slope. (See Examples 9 and 12.)

43. $(-1, 2)$, $m = -2/3$

44. $(-4, -3)$, $m = 5/4$

45. $(-2, -2)$, $m = 2$

46. $(-2, 3)$, $m = -1/2$

47. $(8, 2)$, $m = 0$

48. $(2, -4)$, $m = 0$

49. $(6, -5)$, undefined slope

50. $(-8, 9)$, undefined slope

Find an equation of the line that passes through the given points. (See Example 10.)

51. $(-1, 1)$ and $(2, 5)$

52. $(2, 5)$ and $(0, 6)$

53. $(1, 2)$ and $(3, 7)$

54. $(-1, -2)$ and $(2, -1)$

Find an equation of the line satisfying the given conditions.

55. Through the origin with slope 7

56. Through the origin and horizontal

57. Through $(5, 8)$ and vertical

58. Through $(7, 11)$ and parallel to $y = 6$

59. Through $(3, 4)$ and parallel to $4x - 2y = 5$

60. Through $(6, 8)$ and perpendicular to $y = 2x - 3$

61. x-intercept 5; y-intercept -5

62. Through $(-5, 2)$ and parallel to the line through $(1, 2)$ and $(4, 3)$

63. Through $(-1, 3)$ and perpendicular to the line through $(0, 1)$ and $(2, 3)$

64. y-intercept 3 and perpendicular to $2x - y + 6 = 0$

65. **Management** Ral Corp. has an incentive compensation plan under which a branch manager receives 10% of the branch's income after deduction of the bonus but before deduction of income tax.* Branch income for 1988 before the bonus and income tax was \$165,000. The tax rate was 30%. The 1988 bonus amounted to
(a) \$12,600 **(b)** \$15,000
(c) \$16,500 **(d)** \$18,000

Management *The lost value of equipment over a period of time is called* **depreciation.** *The simplest method for calculating depreciation is* **straight-line depreciation.** *The annual straight-line depreciation on an item that cost x dollars with a useful life of n years is* $D = (1/n)x$. *Find the depreciation for items with the following characteristics.*

66. Cost: \$12,482; life 10 yr

67. Cost: \$39,700; life 12 yr

68. Cost: \$145,000; life 28 yr

69. **Management** In a recent issue of *Business Week,* the president of InstaTune, a chain of franchised automobile tune-up shops, says that people who buy a franchise and open a shop pay a weekly fee (in dollars) of

$$y = .07x + 135$$

to company headquarters. Here y is the fee and x is the total amount of money taken in during the week by the tune-up center. Find the weekly fee if x is
(a) \$0; **(b)** \$1000; **(c)** \$2000;
(d) \$3000. **(e)** Graph y.

70. **Management** In a recent issue of *The Wall Street Journal,* we are told that the relationship between the amount of money that an average family spends on food eaten at home, x, and the amount of money it spends on eating out, y, is approximated by the model $y = .36x$. Find y if x is
(a) \$40; **(b)** \$80;
(c) \$120. **(d)** Graph y.

*Uniform CPA Examination, May, 1989, American Institute of Certified Public Accountants.

Use graphical approximation to answer the following. (See Example 11.)

71. **Physical Science** Kitchen gas ranges are a source of indoor pollutants such as carbon monoxide and nitrogen dioxide. One of the most effective ways of removing contaminants from the air while cooking is to use a *vented* range hood. If a range hood removes F liters of air per second, the percentage P of contaminants that are also removed from the surrounding air is given by $P = 1.06F + 7.18$, where $10 \leq F \leq 75$.* For instance, if $F = 10$, then $10.6 + 7.18 = 17.78$ percent of the contaminants are removed. To the nearest liter, what rate F is needed to remove at least 58 percent of the contaminants from the air?

72. **Management** An insurance company determines that the amount of damage y a building sustains in a fire is related to the distance x from the building to the nearest fire station and is given by the equation $y = 9.879x + 5.117$, where x is in miles and y is in thousands of dollars. To the nearest tenth of a mile, how far from the fire station is a building that sustains more than \$60,000 worth of damage?

73. **Social Science** The capital outlay for education by state and local governments during the period from 1985 to 1992 can be approximated by the equation $y = 2480x + 12{,}726$, where $x = 0$ corresponds to 1985 and y is in millions of dollars.† Based on this model, in what year did this amount first exceed 22,600 million dollars?

74. **Social Science** The number of farms with milk cows in the United States has steadily declined since 1985. The equation $y = -13.5x + 261.5$ gives a good approximation of the number of such farms in each year from 1985 to 1992, with $x = 0$ representing 1985 and with y in thousands.‡ If these trends continued, in what year would the number of such farms first fall below 150 thousand?

*R. L. Rezvan, "Effectiveness of Local Ventilation in Removing Simulated Pollutants from Point Sources" in *Proceedings of the Third International Conference on Indoor Air Quality and Climate,* 1984.

†U.S. Bureau of the Census, *Historical Statistics on Governmental Finances and Employment,* and *Government Finance,* Series GF, annual.

‡U.S. Dept. of Agriculture, National Agricultural Statistics Service, *Dairy Products,* annual; and *Milk: Production, Disposition, and Income,* annual.

1.7 APPLICATIONS OF LINEAR EQUATIONS

When mathematics is used to solve real-world problems, there are no hard and fast rules that can be used in every case. You must use the given information, your common sense, and the mathematics available to you to build an appropriate mathematical model (such as an equation or inequality) that describes the situation. The examples in this section, which are restricted to models given by linear equations, illustrate this process in several situations.

In most cases, linear (or any other reasonably simple) equations provide only *approximations* to the real-world situations. Nevertheless, these approximations are often remarkably useful. Furthermore, the concepts and procedures presented here are applicable to more complicated situations, as we shall see later.

TEMPERATURE Recall that water freezes at a temperature of 32° Fahrenheit and at 0° Celsius, while it boils at 212° Fahrenheit and 100° Celsius.

EXAMPLE 1 The relation between the Celsius and Fahrenheit temperature scales is known to be linear.

(a) Find the equation that relates the Celsius temperature y to the corresponding Fahrenheit temperature x and display its graph.

The fact that 32° Fahrenheit corresponds to 0° Celsius means that the point (32, 0) is on the graph. Similarly, (212, 100) is also on the graph. The graph is a straight line whose slope can be found from these two points.

$$\text{slope} = m = \frac{100 - 0}{212 - 32} = \frac{100}{180} = \frac{5}{9}$$

Use $m = 5/9$ and either of the given points in the point-slope form to find the equation. Using $(x_1, y_1) = (32, 0)$, we have

$$y - y_1 = m(x - x_1)$$

$$y - 0 = \frac{5}{9}(x - 32)$$

$$y = \frac{5}{9}(x - 32).$$

The graph is in Figure 1.40.

(b) Find the Celsius temperatures corresponding to 50° and 75° Fahrenheit.

This can be done algebraically by substituting $x = 50$ or $x = 75$ in the equation $y = \frac{5}{9}(x - 32)$ and solving for y. It can be done graphically by using the trace feature. The viewing window in Figure 1.40 was chosen so that each time the arrow key is pushed, the x-coordinate of the trace cursor changes by exactly 1.* Moving the cursor along the graph we see that 50° Fahrenheit corresponds to 10° Celsius, and 75° Fahrenheit corresponds to approximately 23.89° Celsius (Figure 1.41). ■ 1

1 Determine either algebraically or graphically the Celsius temperature corresponding to 23° Fahrenheit.

Answer:
−5°

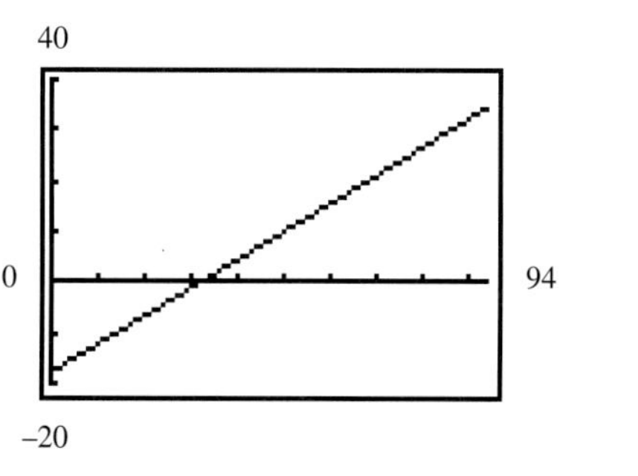

FIGURE 1.40

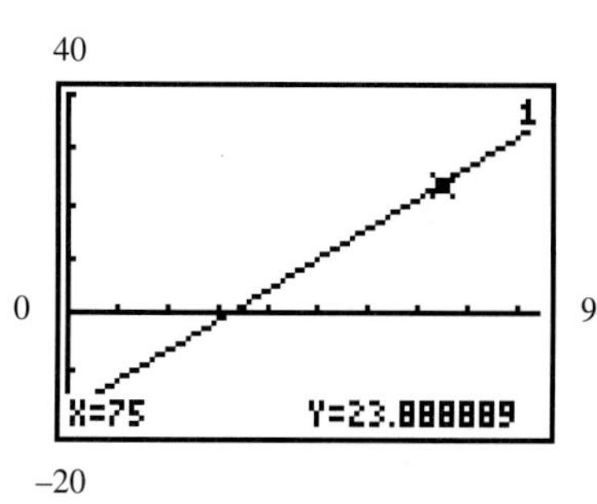

FIGURE 1.41

*A different X-max setting may be needed to accomplish this on other calculators; try 95, 126, 130, or 238. For the reason why these windows have this property, see Exercise 1 in Section 1.6.

BREAK-EVEN ANALYSIS In a manufacturing and sales situation the basic relationship is

$$\textbf{Profit} = \textbf{Revenue} - \textbf{Cost.}$$

Typically, revenue and cost can be described in terms of equations. Here, as in many applications, we use as variables letters that suggest what they represent, rather than the letters x or y: r for revenue, c for cost, and p for profit.

EXAMPLE 2 The cost c (in dollars) of making x leaf-blowers is given by the equation $c = 45x + 6000$. Each leaf-blower can be sold for $60.

(a) Find an equation that expresses the revenue r from selling x leaf-blowers.

The revenue r from selling x leaf-blowers is the product of the price per item, $60, and the number of units sold, x. So $r = 60x$.

(b) What is the revenue from selling 500 leaf-blowers?

Using the revenue equation of part (a) with $x = 500$, we have

$$r = 60 \cdot 500 = \$30{,}000.$$

(c) Find an equation that expresses the profit p from selling x leaf-blowers.

The profit is the difference between revenue and cost, that is,

$$p = r - c = 60x - (45x + 6000) = 15x - 6000.$$

(d) What is the profit from selling 500 leaf-blowers?

Using the profit equation of part (c) with $x = 500$, we have

$$p = 15 \cdot 500 - 6000 = 7500 - 6000 = \$1500. \blacksquare$$

A company can make a profit only if the revenue received from its customers exceeds the cost of producing its goods and services. The number of units at which revenue equals cost (that is, profit is 0) is the **break-even point.**

EXAMPLE 3 A firm producing poultry feed finds that the total cost c of producing x units is given by

$$c = 20x + 100.$$

Management plans to charge $24 per unit for the feed. How many units must be sold for the firm to break even?

The revenue equation is $r = 24x$ (price per unit times number of units). The firm will break even (0 profit) as long as revenue equals cost, that is, when

$$\begin{aligned} r &= c. \\ 24x &= 20x + 100 \\ 4x &= 100 \\ x &= 25 \end{aligned}$$

The firm breaks even by selling 25 units. The graphs of the revenue and cost equations are shown in Figure 1.42. The break-even point (where $x = 25$) is shown on the graph. If the company produces more than 25 units ($x > 25$), it makes a profit. If it produces less than 25 units, it loses money (that is, profit is negative). ■ 2

2 For a certain magazine, the cost equation is $c = .70x + 1200$, where x is the number of magazines sold. The magazine sells for $1 per copy. Find the break-even point.

Answer:
4000 magazines

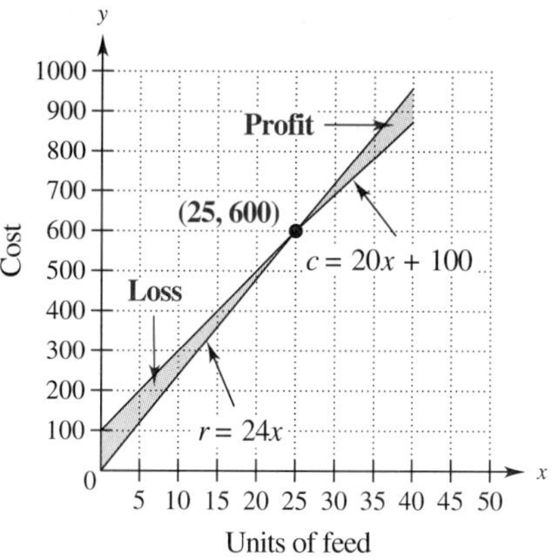

FIGURE 1.42

The break-even point can be found algebraically, as in Example 3, or graphically, as in the next example.

EXAMPLE 4 The cost (in millions of dollars) to produce x units of a new frozen food product is given by $c = .7x + 18.4$. The revenue from selling x units is given by $r = 1.5x$. Find the break-even point graphically.

Graph the revenue and cost functions in an appropriate viewing window (Figure 1.43). The break-even point occurs where the two graphs intersect. This cannot be easily read from the graph, but can be found by using the "intersection finder" on your calculator (see the Tip below). The intersection finder shows that the break-even point occurs when $x = 23$ (Figure 1.44).

3 A Seattle company finds that the cost (in thousands of dollars) of producing x thousand pounds of coffee is given by $c = 3.461x + 7.98$. The revenue (in thousands of dollars) from selling x thousand pounds is given by $r = 5.974x$. What is the break-even point?

Answer:
About 3175 pounds

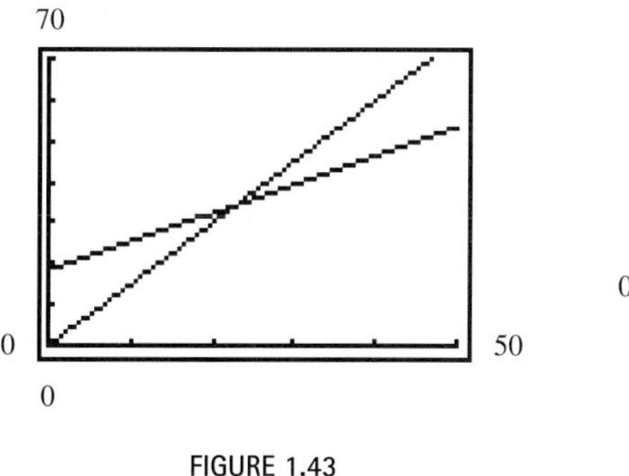

FIGURE 1.43

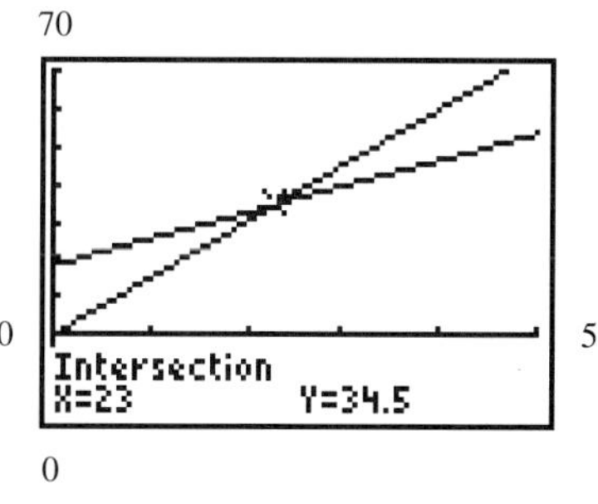

FIGURE 1.44

Therefore selling more than 23 units will produce a profit. ■ 3

TECHNOLOGY TIP Depending on the calculator, the intersection finder is on the CALC or MATH or FCN or G-SOLVE or JUMP menu; check your instruction manual to see how to use it. An intersection finder program for TI-81 is in the Program Appendix. ✔

SUPPLY AND DEMAND The supply of and demand for an item are usually related to its price. Producers will supply large numbers of the item at a high price, but consumer demand will be low. As the price of the item decreases, consumer demand increases, but producers are less willing to supply large numbers of the item. The curves that show the quantity that will be supplied at a given price and the quantity that will be demanded at a given price are called **supply and demand curves.** Straight lines often appear as supply and demand curves, as in the next example. In supply and demand problems, we use p for price and q for quantity. We will discuss the economic concepts of supply and demand in more detail in later chapters.

EXAMPLE 5 Bill Cornett, an economist, has studied the supply and demand for aluminum siding and has determined that price per unit,* p, and the quantity demanded, q, are related by the linear equation

$$p = 60 - \frac{3}{4}q.$$

(a) Find the demand at a price of $40 per unit.
Let $p = 40$.

$$p = 60 - \frac{3}{4}q$$

$$\mathbf{40} = 60 - \frac{3}{4}q \qquad \text{Let } p = 40.$$

$$-20 = -\frac{3}{4}q \qquad \text{Add } -60 \text{ on both sides.}$$

$$\frac{80}{3} = q \qquad \text{Multiply both sides by } -\frac{4}{3}.$$

At a price of $40 per unit, 80/3 (or $26\frac{2}{3}$) units will be demanded.

(b) Find the price if the demand is 32 units.
Let $q = 32$.

$$p = 60 - \frac{3}{4}q$$

$$p = 60 - \frac{3}{4}(\mathbf{32}) \qquad \text{Let } q = 32.$$

$$p = 60 - 24$$

$$p = 36$$

With a demand of 32 units, the price is $36.

(c) Graph $p = 60 - \frac{3}{4}q$.

It is customary to use the horizontal axis for quantity q and the vertical axis for price p. In part (a) we saw that 80/3 units would be demanded at a price of $40 per unit; this gives the ordered pair (80/3, 40). Part (b) shows that with a demand of 32 units, the price is $36, which gives the ordered pair (32, 36). Use the points (80/3, 40)

*An appropriate unit here might be, for example, one thousand square feet of siding.

4 Suppose price and demand are related by $p = 100 - 4q$.

(a) Find the price if the demand is 10 units.

(b) Find the demand if the price is \$80.

(c) Write the corresponding ordered pairs.

Answers:

(a) \$60

(b) 5 units

(c) (10, 60); (5, 80)

and (32, 36) to get the demand graph shown in Figure 1.45. Only the portion of the graph in Quadrant I is shown, because supply and demand are meaningful only for positive values of p and q. 4

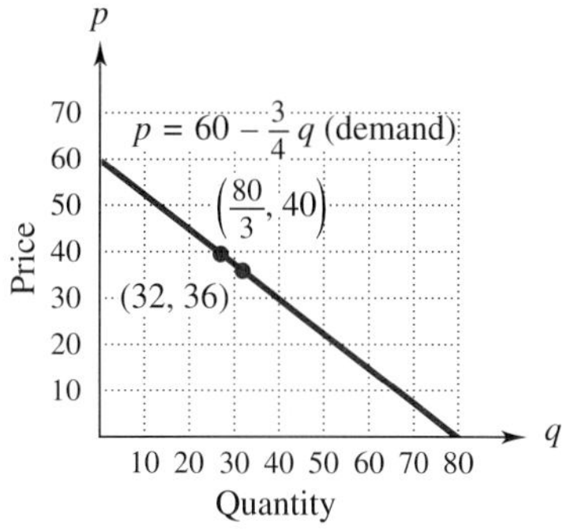

FIGURE 1.45

(d) From Figure 1.45, at a price of \$30, what quantity is demanded?

Price is located on the vertical axis. Look for 30 on the p-axis and read across to where the horizontal line $p = 30$ crosses the demand graph. As the graph shows, this occurs where the demand is 40.

(e) At what price will 60 units be demanded?

Quantity is located on the horizontal axis. Find 60 on the q-axis and read up to where the vertical line $q = 60$ crosses the demand graph. This occurs where the price is \$15 per unit.

(f) What quantity is demanded at a price of \$60 per unit?

The point (0, 60) on the demand graph shows that the demand is 0 at a price of \$60 (that is, there is no demand at such a high price). ■

EXAMPLE 6 Suppose the economist of Example 5 concludes that the supply q of siding is related to its price p by the equation

$$p = .85q.$$

(a) Find the supply if the price is \$51 per unit.

$$51 = .85q \qquad \text{Let } p = 51.$$
$$60 = q$$

If the price is \$51 per unit, then 60 units will be supplied to the marketplace. Thus the ordered pair (60, 51) is on the graph of the supply equation.

(b) Find the price per unit if the supply is 20 units.

$$p = .85(20) = 17 \qquad \text{Let } q = 20.$$

If the supply is 20 units, then the price is \$17 per unit.

(c) Graph the supply equation $p = .85q$ on a calculator.

As with demand, each point on the graph has quantity q as its first coordinate and the corresponding price p as its second coordinate. On a calculator (where x denotes first coordinates and y denotes second coordinates), the equation $p = .85q$ must be entered as $y = .85x$. Its graph is shown in Figure 1.46.

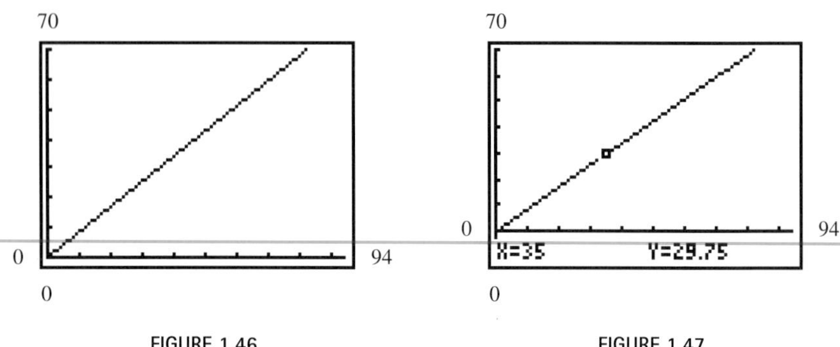

FIGURE 1.46

FIGURE 1.47

(d) Use the graph in Figure 1.46 to find the price at which 35 units will be supplied.

Use the trace feature. The viewing window in Figure 1.46 was chosen so that the trace cursor on our calculator would move one unit at a time horizontally (for other calculators, see the footnote on page 55). Moving the trace cursor to the point with first coordinate 35, we see that the second coordinate is 29.75 (Figure 1.47). Therefore 35 units will be supplied when the price is $29.75. ■

EXAMPLE 7 The supply and demand curves of Examples 5 and 6 are shown in Figure 1.48. Graphically determine whether there is a surplus or a shortage of supply at a price of $38 per unit.

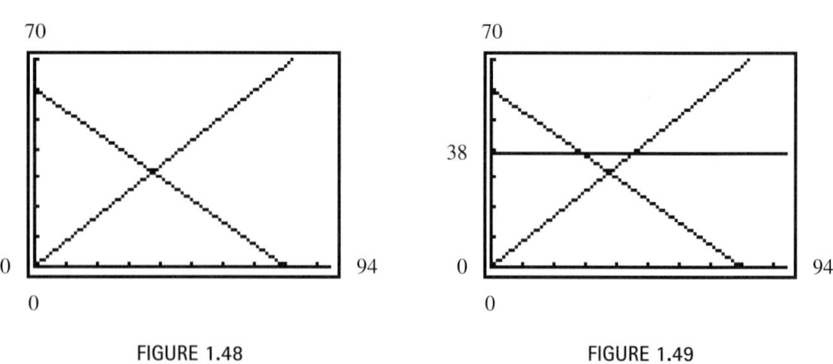

FIGURE 1.48

FIGURE 1.49

The idea is to find 38 on the vertical axis and read across to the point where the horizontal line $p = 38$ crosses the supply graph. This is difficult to do visually, so graph the line $y = 38$ on the same screen as the supply and demand curves (Figure 1.49). You can then easily see that the point on the supply curve corresponding to a price of $38 (the intersection of the supply curve with the horizontal line $y = 38$) lies above the demand curve. At this point supply is greater than demand and there is a surplus of supply. ■

Supply and demand are equal at the point where the supply curve intersects the demand curve. This is the *equilibrium point.* Its second coordinate is the **equilibrium price,** the price at which the same quantity will be supplied as is demanded. Its first coordinate is the quantity that will be demanded and supplied at the equilibrium price; this number is called either the **equilibrium demand** or the **equilibrium supply.**

EXAMPLE 8 In the situation described in Examples 5–7, what is the equilibrium demand? What is the equilibrium price?

The equilibrium point is where the two curves in Figure 1.48 intersect. Its coordinates may be found either algebraically or graphically.

Algebraic Method To find the quantity q at which the price given by the supply equation $p = 60 - .75q$ (Example 5) is the same as that given by the demand equation $p = .85q$ (Example 6), set these two expressions for p equal and solve the resulting equation.

$$\begin{aligned} 60 - .75q &= .85q \\ 60 &= 1.6q \\ 37.5 &= q \end{aligned}$$

Therefore, the equilibrium demand is 37.5 units, the number of units for which supply will equal demand. Substituting $q = 37.5$ in either the supply or demand equation shows that

$$p = 60 - .75(37.5) = 31.875 \quad \text{or} \quad p = .85(37.5) = 31.875.$$

So the equilibrium price is $31.88 (rounded). (To avoid error, it's a good idea to substitute in both equations, as we did here, to be sure the same value of p results; if it doesn't, a mistake has been made.)

Graphical Method Use the intersection finder on a calculator to find the equilibrium point where the supply and demand curves intersect (Figure 1.50). It is (37.5, 31.875), which provides the same answer found algebraically: equilibrium demand is 37.5 units and the equilibrium price is $31.88 per unit (rounded). ■ 5

5 The demand for a certain commodity is related to the price by $p = 80 - (2/3)q$. The supply is related to the price by $p = (4/3)q$. Find

(a) the equilibrium demand;

(b) the equilibrium price.

Answers:

(a) 40

(b) $160/3 \approx \$53.33$

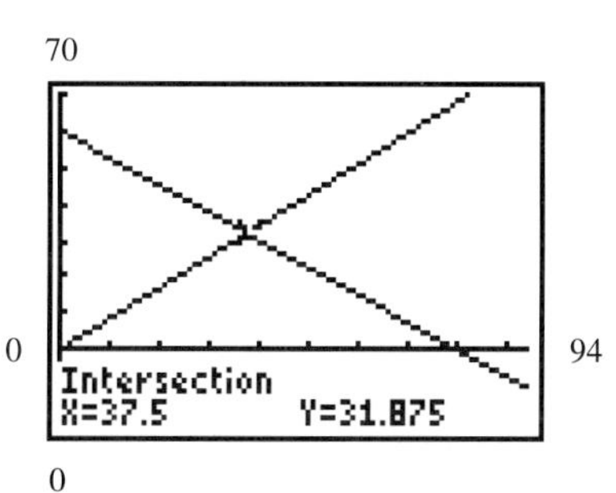

FIGURE 1.50

1.7 EXERCISES

Physical Science *Use the equation derived in Example 1 for conversion between Fahrenheit and Celsius temperatures.*

1. Convert each temperature.
   (a) 58°F to Celsius **(b)** 50°C to Fahrenheit
   (c) −10°C to Fahrenheit **(d)** −20°F to Celsius
2. According to the *1995 Guinness Book of Records,* Venus is the hottest planet, with a surface temperature of 864° Fahrenheit. What is this temperature in Celsius?
3. Find the temperature at which Celsius and Fahrenheit temperatures are numerically equal.
4. You may have heard that the average temperature of the human body is 98.6°. Recent experiments show that the actual figure is closer to 98.2°.* The figure of 98.6 comes from experiments done by Carl Wunderlich in 1868. But Wunderlich measured the temperatures in degrees Celsius and rounded the average to the nearest degree, giving 37°C as the average temperature.
   (a) What is the Fahrenheit equivalent of 37°C?
   (b) Given that Wunderlich rounded to the nearest degree Celsius, his experiments tell us that the actual average human temperature is somewhere between 36.5°C and 37.5C°. Find what this range corresponds to in degrees Fahrenheit.

In each of the following problems, assume that the data can be closely approximated by a straight line. Find the equation of the line and then answer the question. (See Example 1.)

5. **Management** Assume that the sales of a certain appliance dealer are approximated by a linear function. Suppose that sales were $850,000 in 1987 and $1,262,500 in 1992. Let $x = 0$ represent 1987.
   (a) Find an equation giving the dealer's yearly sales.
   (b) Estimate the sales in 1999.
   (c) The dealer estimates that a new store will be necessary once sales exceed $2,170,000. When is this expected to occur?
6. **Management** Assume that the sales of a certain automobile parts company are approximated by a linear function. Suppose that sales were $200,000 in 1985 and $1,000,000 in 1992. Let $x = 0$ represent 1985 and $x = 7$ represent 1992.
   (a) Find the equation giving the company's yearly sales.
   (b) Estimate the sales in 1996.
   (c) The company wants to negotiate a new contract with the automobile company once sales reach $2,000,000. When is this expected to occur?
7. **Social Science** The graph, in which $x = 0$ corresponds to 1980, shows an idealized linear relationship for the average monthly family payment to families with dependent children in 1994 dollars. Based on this information, what was the average payment in 1987? (*Hint:* Use the graph to find two points, from which the equation can be found.)

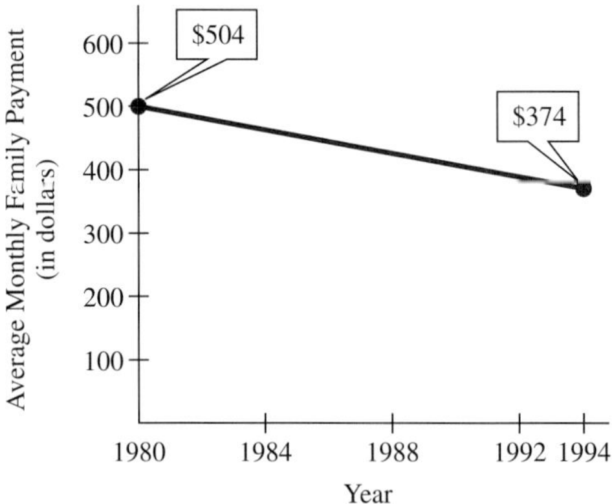

Source: Office of Financial Management, Administration for Children and Families.

8. **Management** Consumer prices in the United States at the beginning of each year, measured as a percent of the 1967 average, have produced a graph that is approximately linear. In 1984 the consumer price index was 300% and in 1987 it was 333%. Let y represent the consumer price index in year x, where $x = 0$ corresponds to 1980. In what year will the consumer price index reach 350%?
9. **Physical Science** Suppose a baseball is thrown at 85 miles per hour. The ball will travel 320 feet when hit by a bat swung at 50 miles per hour and will travel 440 feet when hit by a bat swung at 80 miles per hour. Let y be the number of feet traveled by the ball when hit by a bat swung at x miles per hour. (*Note:* This is valid for $50 \le x \le 90$, where the bat is 35 inches long, weighs 32 ounces, and strikes a waist-high pitch so the place of the swing lies at 10° from the diagonal.*) How much farther will a ball travel for each mile per hour increase in the speed of the bat?
10. **Natural Science** The amount of tropical rain forests in Central America decreased from 130,000 square miles to about 80,000 square miles from 1969 to 1985. Let y be the amount (in ten thousands of square miles) x years after 1965. How large were the rain forests in the year 1997?
11. **Physical Science** Ski resorts require large amounts of water in order to make snow. Snowmass Ski Area in Colorado plans to pump at least 1120 gallons of water per minute for at least 12 hours a day from Snowmass Creek

**Science News,* Nov. 7, 1992, p. 399.

*Adair, Robert K, *The Physics of Baseball:* Harper & Row 1990.

between mid-October and late December.* Environmentalists are concerned about the effects on the ecosystem. Find the minimum amount of water pumped in 30 days. (*Hint:* Let y be the total number of gallons pumped x days after pumping begins. Note that (0, 0) is on the graph of the equation.)

12. Physical Science Suppose that instead of making snow in Exercise 11, the water being pumped from Snowmass Creek was used to fill swimming pools. If the average backyard pool holds 20,000 gallons of water, how many pools could be filled each day? In how many days could at least 1000 pools be filled? (*Hint:* Let y be the number of pools filled after x days.)

13. Physical Science In 1994 Leroy Burrell (USA) set a world record in the 100-meter dash with a time of 9.85 seconds.† If this pace could be maintained for an entire 26-mile, 385-yard marathon, how would this time compare to the fastest time for a marathon, 2 hours, 6 minutes, 50 seconds? (*Hint:* Let x be the distance in meters and y the time in seconds. Use the point (0, 0) and the point obtained from the data in the problem to obtain the equation of a line. To answer the question, remember that 1 meter = 3.281 ft.)

14. Natural Science In 1990, the Intergovernmental Panel on Climate Change predicted that the average temperature on the earth would rise .3°C per decade in the absence of international controls on greenhouse emissions.‡ The average global temperature was 15°C in 1970. Let y be the average global temperature t years after 1970. Scientists have estimated that the sea level will rise by 65 centimeters, if the average global temperature rises to 19°C. From your equation, when will this occur?

15. Physical Science Ventilation is an effective method of removing air pollutants. According to the American Society of Heating, Refrigerating and Air-Conditioning Engineers, Inc., a nonsmoking classroom should have a ventilation rate of 15 cubic feet per minute for each person in the classroom. How much ventilation (in cubic feet per hour) is needed for a classroom with 30 people in it?

16. Physical Science A common unit of ventilation is an air exchange per hour (ach). 1 ach is equivalent to replacing all of the air in the room every hour. If a classroom with a volume of 15,000 cubic feet has 40 people in it, how many air exchanges per hour are necessary to keep the room properly ventilated? (*Hint:* Let x be the number of people and y the number of ach. Use the information developed in Exercise 15.)

17. Management The U.S. is China's largest export market. Imports from China have grown from about 8 billion dollars in 1988 to 39 billion dollars in 1995.* This growth has been approximately linear. Use the given data pairs to write a linear equation that describes this growth in imports over the years. Let $x = 88$ represent 1988 and $x = 95$ represent 1995.

18. Management U.S. exports to China have grown (although at a slower rate than imports) since 1988. In 1988, about 8 billion dollars of goods were exported to China. By 1995, this amount had grown to 15.9 billion dollars. Write a linear equation describing the number of exports each year, with $x = 88$ representing 1988 and $x = 95$ representing 1995.

Use algebra to find the intersection points of the graphs of the given equations. (See Examples 3 and 8.)

19. $2x - y = 7$ and $y = 8 - 3x$

20. $6x - y = 2$ and $y = 4x + 7$

21. $y = 3x - 7$ and $y = 7x + 4$

22. $y = 3x + 5$ and $y = 12 - 2x$

Graphically find the intersection points of the graphs of the given equations. (See Examples 4 and 8.)

23. $y = x^2 + x - 3$ and $y = x^3$

24. $y = .2x^2 + .5x - 3$ and $y = -x^5 + 2x + 1$

25. $y = .2x^2 + .5x - 3$ and $9x - 2y = 6$

26. $y = \sqrt{x^2 + 1}$ and $y = x^3 - 15x^2 + .8x - 6$

Management *Work the following problems. (See Examples 2–4.)*

27. For x thousand policies, an insurance company claims that their monthly revenue in dollars is given by $R = 125x$ and their monthly cost in dollars is given by $C = 100x + 5000$.
(a) Find the break-even point.
(b) Graph the revenue and cost equations on the same axes.
(c) From the graph, estimate the revenue and cost when $x = 100$ (100 thousand policies).

28. The owners of a parking lot have determined that their weekly revenue and cost in dollars are given by $R = 80x$ and $C = 50x + 2400$, where x is the number of long-term parkers.
(a) Find the break-even point.
(b) Graph R and C on the same axes.
(c) From the graph, estimate the revenue and cost when there are 60 long-term parkers.

29. The revenue (in millions of dollars) from the sale of x units at a home supply outlet is given by $r = .21x$. The profit (in millions of dollars) from the sale of x units is given by $p = .084x - 1.5$.

* York Snow Incorporated.

†International Amateur Athletic Association.

‡ *Science News,* June 23, 1990, p. 391.

*Problems 17 and 18 from *Economist,* U.S.-China Business Council, *China Business Review,* U.S. Commerce Department.

(a) Find the cost equation.
(b) What is the cost of producing 7 units?
(c) What is the break-even point?

30. The profit (in millions of dollars) from the sale of x million units of Blue Glue is given by $p = .7x - 25.5$. The cost is given by $c = .9x + 25.5$.
(a) Find the revenue equation.
(b) What is the revenue from selling 10 million units?
(c) What is the break-even point?

Management *Suppose you are the manager of a firm. The accounting department has provided cost estimates and the sales department sales estimates on a new product. You must analyze the data they give you, determine what it will take to break even, and decide whether or not to go ahead with production of the new product. (See Examples 3 and 4.)*

31. Cost estimate is given by $c = 80x + 7000$ and revenue estimate by $r = 95x$; no more than 400 units can be sold.

32. Cost is $c = 140x + 3000$ and revenue is $r = 125x$.

33. Cost is $c = 125x + 42{,}000$ and revenue is $r = 165.5x$; no more than 2000 units can be sold.

34. Cost is $c = 1750x + 95{,}000$ and revenue is $r = 1975x$; no more than 600 units can be sold.

35. **Management** The graph shows the productivity of U.S. and Japanese workers in appropriate units over a 35-year period. Estimate the break-even point (the point at which workers in the two countries produced the same amounts).*

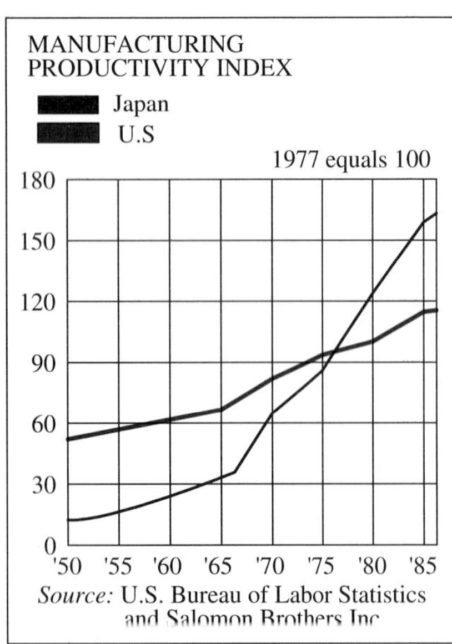

36. **Management** The graph gives U.S. imports and exports in billions of dollars over a five-year period. Estimate the break-even point.

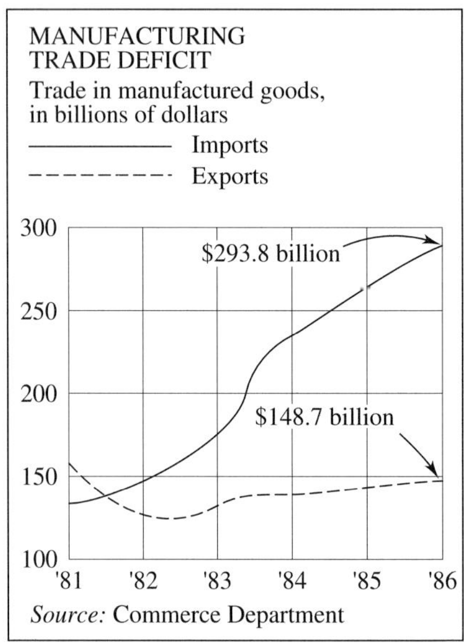

37. **Management** Canadian and Japanese investment in the United States in billions of dollars in 1980 and 1990 are shown in the chart.*

	1980	*1990*
Canada	12.1	27.7
Japan	4.7	108.1

(a) Assuming the change in investment in each case is linear, write an equation giving the investment in year x for each country. Let x be the number of years since 1980.
(b) Graph the equations from part (a) on the same coordinate axes.
(c) Find the intersection point where the graphs in part (b) cross and interpret your answer.

38. **Social Science** The median family income (in thousands of dollars) for the white population in the United States is given by $y = (4/3)x + 8$, where x is the number of years since 1973. The median family income (in thousands of dollars) for the black population in the United States is given by $y = (2/3)x + 6$.

*The figures for Exercises 35 and 36 appeared in *The Sacramento Bee*, December 21, 1987. Reprinted by permission of The Associated Press.

*Data reprinted with permission from *The World Almanac and Book of Facts*, 1992. Copyright © 1991. All rights reserved. The World Almanac is an imprint of Funk & Wagnalls Corporation.

(a) Graph both equations on the same coordinate axes.
(b) Do the graphs intersect? If so, in what year was median family income the same for white and black populations?
(c) What can you infer from the two graphs in part (a)?

Management *Use the supply and demand curves graphed below to answer Exercises 39–42. (See Examples 5–8.)*

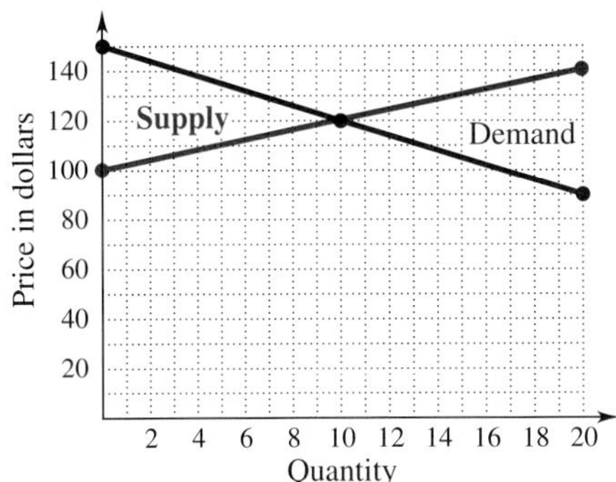

39. At what price are 20 items supplied?

40. At what price are 20 items demanded?

41. Find the equilibrium supply and the equilibrium demand.

42. Find the equilibrium price.

Management *Work the following exercises. (See Examples 5–8.)*

43. Suppose that the demand and price for a certain brand of shampoo are related by

$$p = 16 - \frac{5}{4}q,$$

where p is price, in dollars, and q is demand. Find the price for a demand of
(a) 0 units; **(b)** 4 units; **(c)** 8 units.
Find the demand for the shampoo at a price of
(d) \$6; **(e)** \$11; **(f)** \$16.
(g) Graph $p = 16 - (5/4)q$.
Suppose the price and supply of the shampoo are related by

$$p = \frac{3}{4}q,$$

where q represents the supply and p the price. Find the supply when the price is
(h) \$0; **(i)** \$10; **(j)** \$20.
(k) Graph $p = (3/4)q$ on the same axes used for part (g).
(l) Find the equilibrium supply.
(m) Find the equilibrium price.

44. Let the supply and demand for radial tires in dollars be given by

$$\text{supply: } p = \frac{3}{2}q \quad \text{and} \quad \text{demand: } p = 81 - \frac{3}{4}q.$$

(a) Graph these on the same axes.
(b) Find the equilibrium demand.
(c) Find the equilibrium price.

45. Let the supply and demand for bananas in cents per pound be given by

$$\text{supply: } p = \frac{2}{5}q \quad \text{and} \quad \text{demand: } p = 100 - \frac{2}{5}q.$$

(a) Graph these on the same axes.
(b) Find the equilibrium demand.
(c) Find the equilibrium price.
(d) On what interval does demand exceed supply?

46. Let the supply and demand for sugar be given by

$$\text{supply: } p = 1.4q - .6$$

and

$$\text{demand: } p = -2q + 3.2,$$

where p is in dollars.
(a) Graph these on the same axes.
(b) Find the equilibrium demand.
(c) Find the equilibrium price.
(d) On what interval does supply exceed demand?

Work the following problems.

47. Management The sales of a certain furniture company in thousands of dollars are shown in the chart below.

x (year)	*y* (sales)
0	48
1	59
2	66
3	75
4	80
5	90

(a) Graph this data, plotting years on the x-axis and sales on the y-axis. (Note that the data points can be closely approximated by a straight line.)
(b) Draw a line through the points (2, 66) and (5, 90). The other four points should be close to this line. (These two points were selected as "best" representing the line that could be drawn through the data points.)

(exercise continues)

(c) Use the two points from part (b) to find an equation for the line that approximates the data.

(d) Complete the following chart.

Year	*Sales (actual)*	*Sales (predicted from equation of (c))*	*Difference, Actual Minus Predicted*
0			
1			
2			
3			
4			
5			

(e) Use the result from part (c) to predict sales in year 7.

(f) Do the same for year 9.

48. Social Science Some scientists believe there is a limit to how long humans can live.* One supporting argument is that during the last century, life expectancy from age 65 has increased more slowly than life expectancy from birth, so eventually these two will be equal, at which point, according to these scientists, life expectancy should increase no further. In 1900, life expectancy at birth was 46 years, and life expectancy at age 65 was 76. In 1975, these figures had risen to 75 and 80, respectively. In both cases, the increase in life expectancy has been linear. Using these assumptions and the data given, find the maximum life expectancy for humans.

*See *Science,* November 15, 1991, pp. 936–38.

CHAPTER 1 SUMMARY

Key Terms and Symbols

1.1 $\approx$ is approximately equal to
π pi
$|a|$ absolute value of a
real number
natural (counting) number
whole number
integer
rational number
irrational number
properties of real numbers
additive inverse
multiplicative inverse
order of operations
number line
interval
interval notation
absolute value

1.2 variable
first-degree equation
solution
properties of equality
solving for a specified variable

1.3 a^n a to the power n
exponent or power
base
polynomial
term
coefficient
constant term
degree of a nonzero term
degree of a polynomial
zero polynomial
binomial
trinomial
variable
like terms
FOIL

1.4 factoring
factor
greatest common factor
perfect square trinomial
difference of two squares
sum and difference of two cubes

1.5 Cartesian coordinate system
x-axis
y-axis
origin
ordered pair
x-coordinate
y-coordinate
quadrant
solution of an equation
graph
x-intercept
y-intercept
viewing window
tick marks
trace feature
minimum/maximum finder
standard viewing window
square viewing window
complete graph

1.6 Δx change in x
Δy change in y
slope
slope-intercept form

parallel and perpendicular lines
point-slope form
vertical lines
linear equation

1.7 revenue
profit
break-even point
supply and demand curves
equilibrium price
equilibrium supply/demand

Key Concepts

Absolute Value

Assume a and b are real numbers with $b > 0$.

The solutions of $|a| = b$ or $|a| = |b|$ are $a = b$ or $a = -b$.

The solutions of $|a| < b$ are $-b < a < b$.

The solutions of $|a| > b$ are $a < -b$ or $a > b$.

Factoring

$x^2 + 2xy + y^2 = (x + y)^2$ $\quad$ $x^3 - y^3 = (x - y)(x^2 + xy + y^2)$

$x^2 - 2xy + y^2 = (x - y)^2$ $\quad$ $x^3 + y^3 = (x + y)(x^2 - xy + y^2)$

$x^2 - y^2 = (x + y)(x - y)$

The **slope** of the line through the points (x_1, y_1) and (x_2, y_2), where $x_1 \neq x_2$ is $m = \dfrac{y_2 - y_1}{x_2 - x_1}$.

Nonvertical **parallel lines** have the same slope and **perpendicular lines,** if neither is vertical, have slopes with a product of -1.

The line with equation $\boldsymbol{ax + by = c}$ has x-intercept c/a and y-intercept c/b.
The line with equation $\boldsymbol{x = k}$ is vertical with x-intercept k, no y-intercept, and undefined slope.
The line with equation $\boldsymbol{y = k}$ is horizontal, with y-intercept k, no x-intercept, and slope 0.
The line with equation $\boldsymbol{y = mx + b}$ has slope m and y-intercept b.
The line with equation $\boldsymbol{y - y_1 = m(x - x_1)}$ has slope m and goes through (x_1, y_1).

If one equation gives the price per unit when q units can be supplied, and a second equation gives the price per unit when q units are demanded, then the **equilibrium price, supply,** and **demand** occur at the point where the graphs of the supply and demand equations intersect.

Chapter 1 Review Exercises

Name the numbers from the list $-12, -6, -9/10, -\sqrt{7}, -\sqrt{4}, 0, 1/8, \pi/4, 6, \sqrt{11}$ that are

1. whole numbers; **2.** integers;

3. rational numbers; **4.** irrational numbers.

Identify the properties of real numbers that are illustrated in each of the following.

5. $7[(-3)4] = 7[4(-3)]$

6. $9(4 + 5) = (4 + 5)9$

7. $6(x + y - 3) = 6x + 6y + 6(-3)$

8. $11 + (8 + 3) = (11 + 8) + 3$

Express each statement in symbols.

9. x is at least 6. **10.** x is negative.

Write the following numbers in numerical order from smallest to largest.

11. $-7, -3, 8, \pi, -2, 0$

12. $\frac{5}{6}, \frac{1}{2}, -\frac{2}{3}, -\frac{5}{4}, -\frac{3}{8}$

13. $|6 - 4|, -|-2|, |8 + 1|, -|3 - (-2)|$

14. $\sqrt{7}, -\sqrt{8}, -|\sqrt{16}|, |-\sqrt{12}|$

Write without absolute value bars.

15. $-|-6| + |3|$ **16.** $|-5| + |-9|$

17. $7 - |-8|$ **18.** $|-2| - |-7 + 3|$

Graph each of the following on a number line.

19. $x \geq -3$

20. $-4 < x \leq 6$

21. $x < -2$

22. $x \leq 1$

Use the order of operations to simplify.

23. $(-6 + 2 \cdot 5)(-2)$

24. $-4(-7 - 9 \div 3)$

25. $\dfrac{-8 + (-6)(-3) \div 9}{6 - (-2)}$

26. $\dfrac{20 \div 4 \cdot 2 \div 5 - 1}{-9 - (-3) - 12 \div 3}$

Solve each equation.

27. $2x - 5(x - 4) = 3x + 2$

28. $5y + 6 = -2(1 - 3y) + 4$

29. $\dfrac{2z}{5} - \dfrac{4z - 3}{10} = \dfrac{-z + 1}{10}$

30. $\dfrac{p}{p + 2} - \dfrac{3}{4} = \dfrac{2}{p + 2}$

31. $\dfrac{2m}{m - 3} = \dfrac{6}{m - 3} + 4$

32. $\dfrac{15}{k + 5} = 4 - \dfrac{3k}{k + 5}$

Solve for x.

33. $5ax - 1 = x$

34. $6x - 3y = 4bx$

35. $\dfrac{2x}{3 - c} = ax + 1$

36. $b^2x - 2x = 4b^2$

Solve each equation.

37. $|m - 3| = 9$

38. $|6 - x| = 12$

39. $\left|\dfrac{2 - y}{5}\right| = 8$

40. $\left|\dfrac{3m + 5}{7}\right| = 15$

41. $|4k + 1| = |6k - 3|$

Management *Solve each of the following problems.*

42. A computer printer is on sale for 15% off. The sale price is \$425. What was the original price?

43. To make a special mix for Valentine's Day, the owner of a candy store wants to combine chocolate hearts which sell for \$5 per pound with candy kisses which sell for \$3.50 per pound. How many pounds of each kind should be used to get 30 pounds of a mix that can be sold for \$4.50 per pound?

44. A real estate firm invests the \$100,000 proceeds from a sale in two ways. The first portion is invested in a shopping center that provides an annual return of 8%. The rest is invested in a small apartment building with an annual return of 5%. The firm wants an annual income of \$6800 from these investments. How much should be put into each investment?

Perform each of the indicated operations.

45. $(3x^4 - x^2 + 5x) - (-x^4 + 3x^2 - 8x)$

46. $(-8y^3 + 8y^2 - 3y) - (2y^3 - 4y^2 - 10)$

47. $-2(q^4 - 3q^3 + 4q^2) + 4(q^4 + 2q^3 + q^2)$

48. $5(3y^4 - 4y^5 + y^6) - 3(2y^4 + y^5 - 3y^6)$

49. $(5z + 2)(3z - 2)$

50. $(8p - 4)(5p + 3)$

51. $(4k - 3h)(4k + 3h)$

52. $(2r - 5y)(2r + 5y)$

53. $(6x + 3y)^2$

54. $(2a - 5b)^2$

Which of the ordered pairs $(-2, 3)$, $(0, -5)$, $(2, -3)$, $(3, -2)$, $(4, 3)$, $(7, 2)$ are solutions of the given equation?

55. $y = x^2 - 2x - 5$

56. $x - y = 5$

57. Find an appropriate viewing window for the graph of the equation in the following situation. A person who weighs 180 lbs at sea level will weigh y pounds at a height of x miles above sea level, where

$$y = \frac{2,808,450,000}{(x + 3950)^2}.$$

The highest point on Earth is 5.5 miles above sea level and a person's weight there is within one pound of his or her weight at sea level.

58. What kind of viewing window should be used to obtain an accurate graph of perpendicular lines?

59. Management The profit y from selling x carloads of fertilizer is given by the equation $y = -.1x^3 + 39x^2 + 420x - 97,600$. To the nearest whole number, how many carloads should be sold in order to guarantee a maximum profit?

60. Management The storage and delivery costs y for a certain manufacturer are given by $y = .1x^3 - 25x^2 - 10x + 750,000$, where x is the number of truckloads produced. To the nearest whole number, how many truckloads should be produced if storage and delivery costs are to be as small as possible?

Find a viewing window that appears to display a complete graph of the equation.

61. $y = .0003x^3 + .015x^2 - .25x + 5$

62. $y = .2x^3 - 42x^2 + 98x - 6000$

Factor as completely as possible.

63. $2kh^2 - 4kh + 5k$

64. $2m^2n^2 + 6mn^2 + 16n^2$

65. $3a^4 + 13a^3 + 4a^2$

66. $24x^3 + 4x^2 - 4x$

67. $10y^2 - 11y + 3$

68. $8q^2 + 3m + 4qm + 6q$

69. $144p^2 - 169q^2$

70. $81z^2 - 25x^2$

71. $8y^3 - 1$

72. $125a^3 + 216$

Determine graphically whether the statement is definitely false *or possibly true.*

73. $6x^5 - 23x^4 + 24x^3 + x^2 - 12x + 4 = (3x + 2)(2x - 1)(x - 2)(x - 1)^2$

74. $-6x^5 + 5x^4 + 14x^3 - 8x^2 - 8x + 3 = (2x - 3)(3x - 1)(x - 1)(x + 1)^2$

Graph each of the following linear equations by hand.

75. $5x - 3y = 15$

76. $2x + 7y - 21 = 0$

77. $y + 3 = 0$

78. $y - 2x = 0$

79. In your own words, define the slope of a line.

Find the slope of the line.

80. Through $(-1, 4)$ and $(2, 3)$

81. Through $(5, -3)$ and $(-1, 2)$

82. Through $(7, -2)$ and the origin

83. Through $(8, 5)$ and $(0, 3)$

84. $2x + 3y = 30$

85. $4x - y = 7$

86. $x + 5 = 0$

87. $y = 3$

88. Parallel to $3x + 8y = 0$

89. Perpendicular to $x = 3y$

90. Graph the line through $(0, 5)$ with $m = -2/3$.

91. Graph the line through $(-4, 1)$ with $m = 3$.

92. What information is needed to determine the equation of a line?

Find an equation for each of the following lines.

93. Through $(5, -1)$, slope $2/3$

94. Through $(8, 0)$, slope $-1/4$

95. Through $(5, -2)$ and $(1, 3)$

96. Through $(2, -3)$ and $(-3, 4)$

97. Undefined slope, through $(-1, 4)$

98. Slope 0, through $(-2, 5)$

99. x-intercept -3, y-intercept 5

100. x-intercept $-2/3$, y-intercept $1/2$

101. Social Science The percent of children living with a never-married parent was 4.2 in 1960 and 30.6 in 1990.

(a) Assuming that this growth was linear, write an equation that relates the percentage y and the year x. Let 1960 correspond to $x = 0$, 1961 to $x = 1$, and so on.

(b) Graph the equation for the years from 1960 to 2000.

(c) Is the slope of the line positive or negative? Why?

102. Social Science In 1960 the percent of children living with two parents was 87.7 and in 1990 it was 72.5.

(a) Assuming the decrease was linear, write an equation that relates the percent y with the year x, with 1960 corresponding to $x = 0$.

(b) Graph the equation for the years from 1960 to 2000.

(c) Is the slope of the line positive or negative? Why?

103. Management The cost c of producing x units of a product is given by the equation $c = 20x + 100$. The product sells for $40 per unit.

(a) What is the revenue equation?

(b) Graph the cost and revenue equations on the same screen.

(c) Find the break-even point.

(d) If the company sells exactly the number of units needed to break even, what will its revenue be?

(e) Find the equation that gives the profit p gained from selling x units.

104. Management A product can be sold for $25 per unit. The cost c of producing x units in the Zanesville plant is given by $c = 24x + 5000$.

(a) What is the revenue equation?

(b) How many units must be sold for the company to break even?

105. Management For producing x tons of crushed rock, a quarry has average monthly costs given by the equation $c = 56.75x + 192.44$. The rock can be sold for $102.50 per ton. How many tons must be sold each month for the quarry to break even?

106. Natural Science Lead is a neurotoxin found in drinking water, old paint, and the air. It is particularly hazardous to people because it is not easily eliminated from the body. As directed by the Safe Drinking Water Act of 1974, the EPA proposed a maximum lead level in public drinking water of .05 milligram per liter. This standard assumes that an individual consumes two liters of water per day.*

(a) If EPA guidelines are followed, write an equation that expresses the maximum amount y of lead that could be ingested in x years. Assume that there are 365.25 days in a year.

(b) If the average life expectancy is 75 years, what is the EPA maximum lead intake from water over an average lifetime?

107. Natural Science Ground level ozone is toxic to both plants and animals and causes respiratory problems and eye irritation in humans. Automobiles are a major source of this type of ozone, which often occurs when smog levels are significant. Ozone from outside air can enter buildings through ventilation systems. Guideline levels for indoor ozone recommend less than 50 parts per billion (ppb). In a scientific study, a purafil air filter was found to remove 43% of the ozone.†

(a) Write an equation that expresses the amount y of ozone remaining from an initial concentration of x ppb when this filter is used.

(b) If the initial concentration is 140 ppb, does this type of filter reduce the ozone to acceptable levels?

(c) What is the maximum initial concentration of ozone that this filter will reduce to an acceptable level?

---

*Nemerow, N. and Dasgupta, A., *Industrial and Hazardous Waste Treatment,* New York: Van Nostrand Reinhold, 1991.

†Parmar and Grosjean, *Removal of Air Pollutants from Museum Display Cases,* Marina del Rey, CA: Getty Conservation Institute, 1989.

108. Management The supply and demand for a certain commodity are related by

$$\text{supply: } p = 6q + 3 \quad \text{demand: } p = 19 - 2q,$$

where p represents the price at a supply or demand of q units. Find the supply and the demand when the price is as follows.

(a) \$10 **(b)** \$15 **(c)** \$18

(d) Find the equilibrium price.

(e) Find the equilibrium quantity (supply/demand).

109. Management For a particular product, 72 units will be supplied at a price of \$34, while 16 units will be supplied at a price of \$6.

(a) Write a linear supply equation for this product.

(b) The demand for this product is given by the equation $p = 12 - .5q$. Find the equilibrium price and quantity.

CASE 1

Consumers Often Defy Common Sense*

Imagine two refrigerators in the appliance section of a department store. One sells for \$700 and uses \$85 worth of electricity a year. The other is \$100 more expensive but costs only \$25 a year to run. Given that either refrigerator should last at least 10 years without repair, consumers would overwhelmingly buy the second model, right?

Well, not exactly. Many studies by economists have shown that in a wide range of decisions about money—from paying taxes to buying major appliances—consumers consistently make decisions that defy common sense.

In some cases—as in the refrigerator example—this means that people are generally unwilling to pay a little more money up front to save a lot of money in the long run. At times, psychological studies have shown, consumers appear to assign entirely whimsical values to money, values that change depending on time and circumstances.

In recent years, these apparently irrational patterns of human behavior have become a subject of intense interest among economists and psychologists, both for what they say about the way the human mind works and because of their implications for public policy.

How, for example, can the United States move toward a more efficient use of electricity if so many consumers refuse to buy energy-efficient appliances even when such a move is in their own best interest?

At the heart of research into the economic behavior of consumers is a concept known as the discount rate. It is a measure of how consumers compare the value of a dollar received today with one received tomorrow.

Consider, for example, if you won \$1000 in a lottery. How much more money would officials have to give you before you would agree to postpone cashing the check for a year?

Some people might insist on at least another \$100, or 10 percent, since that is roughly how much it would take to make up for the combined effects of a year's worth of inflation and lost interest.

But the studies show that someone who wants immediate gratification might not be willing to postpone receiving the \$1000 for 20 percent or 30 percent or even 40 percent more money.

In the language of economists, this type of person has a high discount rate: He or she discounts the value of \$1000 so much over a year that it would take hundreds of extra dollars to make waiting as attractive as getting the money immediately.

Of the two alternatives, waiting a year for more money is clearly more rational than taking the check now. Why would people turn down \$1400 dollars next year in favor of \$1000 today? Even if they needed the \$1000 immediately, they would be better off borrowing it from a bank, even at 20 percent or even 30 percent interest. Then, a year later, they could pay off the loan—including the interest—with the \$1400 and pocket the difference.

The fact is, however, that economists find numerous examples of such high discount rates implicit in consumer behavior.

While consumers were very much aware of savings to be made at the point of purchase, they so heavily discounted the value of monthly electrical costs that they would pay over the lifetime of their dryer or freezer that they were oblivious of the potential for greater savings.

*"Consumers often defy common sense" by Malcolm Gladwell from *The Washington Post*. Copyright © 1990, The Washington Post. Reprinted with permission.

Gas water heaters, for example, were found to carry an implicit discount rate of 100 percent. This means that in deciding which model was cheapest over the long run, consumers acted as if they valued a \$100 gas bill for the first year as if it were really \$50. Then, in the second year, they would value the next \$100 gas bill as if it were really worth \$25, and so on through the life of the appliance.

Few consumers actually make this formal calculation, of course. But there are clearly bizarre behavioral patterns in evidence.

Some experiments, for example, have shown that the way in which consumers make decisions about money depends a great deal on how much is at stake. Few people are willing to give up \$10 now for \$15 next year. But they are if the choice is between \$100 now and \$150 next year, a fact that would explain why consumers appear to care less about many small electricity bills—even if they add up to a lot—than one big initial outlay.

EXERCISES

1. Suppose a refrigerator that sells for \$700 costs \$85 a year for electricity. Write an expression for the cost to buy and run the refrigerator for x years.
2. Suppose another refrigerator costs \$1000 and \$25 a year for electricity. Write an expression for the total cost for this refrigerator over x years.
3. Over 10 years which refrigerator costs the most? By how much?
4. In how many years will the total costs for the two refrigerators be equal?

CHAPTER 2 Equations and Inequalities

Many applied problems reduce to solving equations and inequalities. Although algebraic solution methods play an essential role, many complicated equations that arise in real-world applications cannot be readily solved algebraically. However, their solutions can be approximated to a high degree of accuracy by graphical or numerical techniques, all of which depend on technology for effective implementation. This chapter presents a variety of algebraic, graphical, and numerical methods for solving equations and inequalities.

2.1 GRAPHICAL AND NUMERICAL SOLUTIONS OF EQUATIONS

One graphical method for solving equations is the **intersection method,** which is illustrated in the next example.

EXAMPLE 1 Solve $|x^2 - 3x| = 5$

Let $y_1 = |x^2 - 3x|$ and let $y_2 = 5$ and graph both equations on the same screen (Figure 2.1). For each number x, the point (x, y_1) is on the graph of y_1 and the point (x, y_2) is on the graph of y_2. A point with first coordinate x that is on *both* graphs must satisfy $(x, y_1) = (x, y_2)$. Thus, the first coordinate of such an intersection point is a value of x for which $y_1 = y_2$, that is, for which $|x^2 - 3x| = 5$. In other words, *the solutions of the equation are the first coordinates of the points where the graphs of y_1 and y_2 intersect.* Using the intersection finder on a calculator, we find that one of these solutions is $x \approx 4.1925824$ (Figure 2.2). ■ [1]

[1] Use the intersection method to approximate the second solution of the equation in Example 1.

Answer:
$x \approx -1.192582$

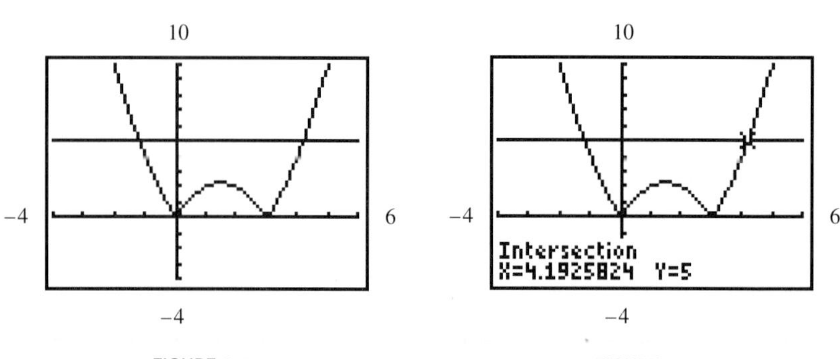

FIGURE 2.1

FIGURE 2.2

EXAMPLE 2 Use the intersection method to solve $x^2 - x - 3 = \sqrt{2x + 7}$.

Graph $y_1 = x^2 - x - 3$ and $y_2 = \sqrt{2x + 7}$ on the same screen. Then use an intersection finder to show that the approximate solutions (the x-coordinates of the intersection points) are $x = -1.7616$ and $x = 3.1249$ (Figure 2.3). ■

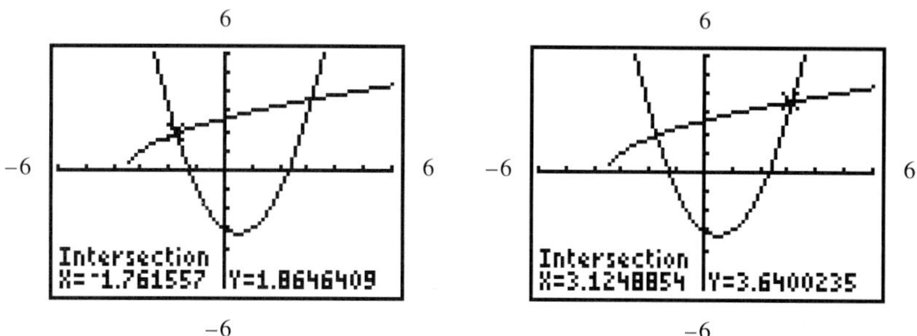

FIGURE 2.3

THE INTERCEPT METHOD An extremely useful graphical solution technique is a special case of the intersection method.

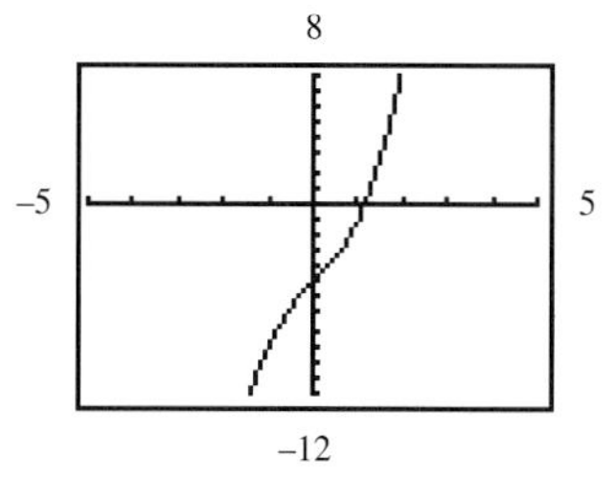

FIGURE 2.4

EXAMPLE 3 Solve $x^3 + 3x - 5 = 0$.

If we were to solve this equation by the intersection method, we would find the x-coordinate of the point where the graph of $y = x^3 + 3x - 5$ intersects the graph of $y = 0$ (Figure 2.4). But the graph of $y = 0$ is the x-axis. So the solution of the equation is the x-coordinate of the point where the graph of $y = x^3 + 3x - 5$ meets the x-axis, that is, the x-intercept of the graph. This x-intercept can be approximated in several different ways, each of which is illustrated here.

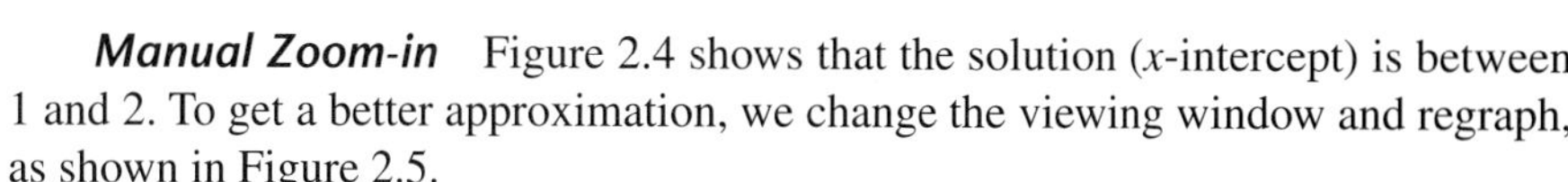

Manual Zoom-in Figure 2.4 shows that the solution (x-intercept) is between 1 and 2. To get a better approximation, we change the viewing window and regraph, as shown in Figure 2.5.

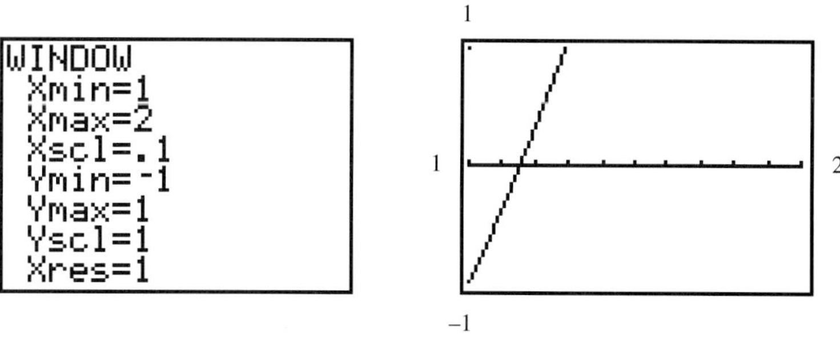

FIGURE 2.5

Note that the Xscl has been changed in Figure 2.5 so that the tick marks on the axis are .1 unit apart. So we see that the solution is between 1.1 and 1.2, approximately 1.16. Greater accuracy can be achieved by changing the viewing window (and Xscl) again (Figure 2.6 on the next page). The Yscl setting need not be changed because there is no need to read the tick marks on the y-axis.

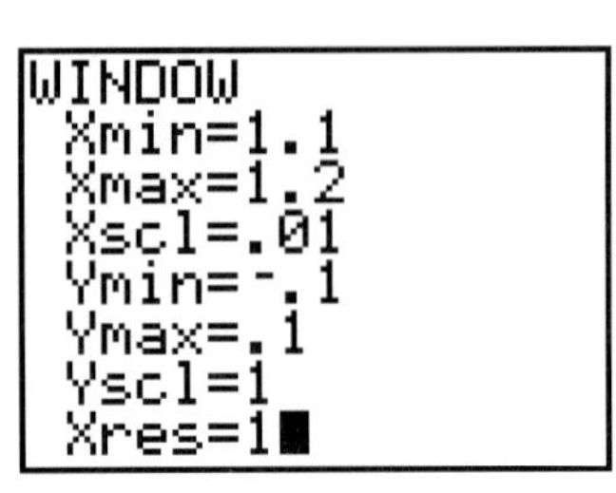

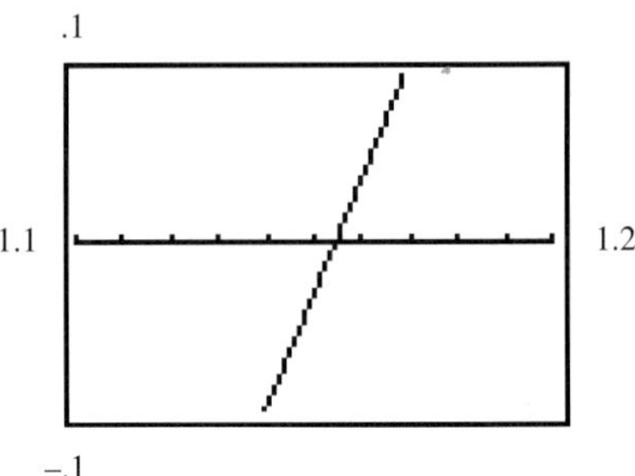

FIGURE 2.6

The tick marks in Figure 2.6 are .01 unit apart and the x-intercept (solution) is between 1.15 and 1.16. So any number between 1.15 and 1.16 will approximate the solution with an error of at most .01 (the distance between adjacent tick marks). Figure 2.6 suggests that 1.155 would be a reasonable approximation. One can continue in this manner to obtain more accurate approximations of the solution.

2 Use automatic or manual zoom-in to solve $x^3 + x^2 - 7 = 0$.

Answer:
$x \approx 1.6311$

Automatic Zoom-in Many steps in the manual zoom-in procedure can be done much more quickly by using either the "zoom-in" or "box zoom" feature on your calculator. Look on the ZOOM menu of your calculator and check your instruction manual for details. If the tick marks on the axis "disappear" after a few steps, you will have to change the Xscl setting manually in order to estimate the accuracy of your approximation. 2

Graphical Root Finder The easiest way to find the solution (x-intercept) on most calculators is to use a "graphical root finder." This feature can approximate an x-intercept to a very high degree of accuracy with just a few keystrokes. Look on the CALC or MATH or FCN or G-SOLVE or JUMP menu of your calculator for "root" or "zero" or "x-intercept." The syntax varies depending on the calculator, so check your instruction manual.* A typical root finder produced Figure 2.7, which shows that the solution (x-intercept) is approximately $x = 1.1542$. ■

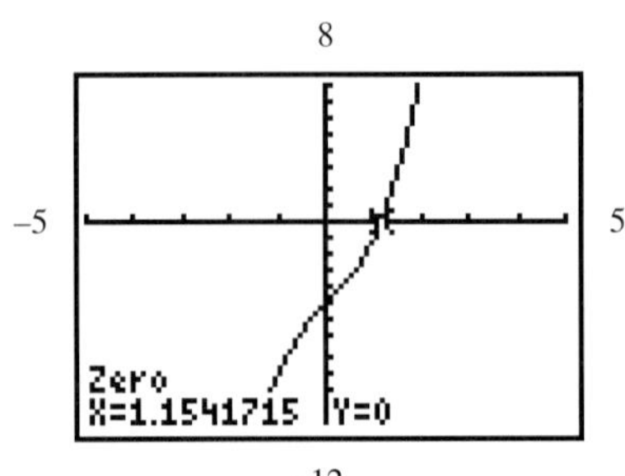

FIGURE 2.7

*A root finder program for TI-81 is in the Program Appendix.

The procedure used in Example 3 works equally well in the general case.

> **SOLUTIONS AND INTERCEPTS**
>
> The real number solutions of a one-variable equation of the form
>
> $$\text{Expression in } x = 0$$
>
> are the x-intercepts of the graph of the two-variable equation
>
> $$y = \text{Expression in } x.$$
>
> These solutions (x-intercepts) may be approximated by manual zoom-in, automatic zoom-in, or by the use of a graphical root finder.

EXAMPLE 4 Use the intercept method to solve $x^4 + x^2 = x^3 + x + 5$.
First rewrite the equation so that one side is 0.

$$x^4 - x^3 + x^2 - x - 5 = 0$$

Then graph $y = x^4 - x^3 + x^2 - x - 5$ in the standard viewing window. Figure 2.8 shows that there are x-intercepts (solutions) near -1 and between 1 and 2. Assuming that Figure 2.8 includes all the x-intercepts of the graph, the original equation has exactly two real solutions.* Using zoom-in or a graphical root finder, we see that one solution is $x \approx -1.0913$ (Figure 2.9). ■ 3

3 Use a graphical root finder to approximate the second solution of the equation in Example 4.

Answer:
$x \approx 1.72699$

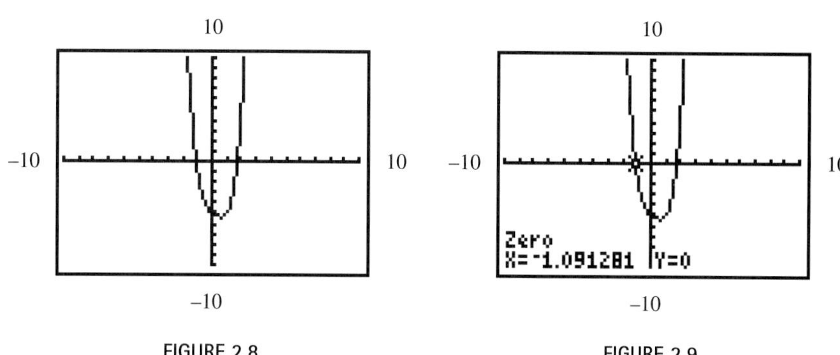

FIGURE 2.8

FIGURE 2.9

CAUTION Graphical root finders may fail to find some solutions of an equation (which they usually indicate by displaying an error message). See Exercise 2. ◆

*Unless stated otherwise in the examples and exercises in this section, you may assume that the standard viewing window includes all the x-intercepts of a graph.

Graphical solution methods can be very helpful in dealing with applied problems.

EXAMPLE 5 A manufacturing firm needs to design an open-topped box with a square base and a volume of 32 cubic inches. What should the dimensions of the box be if it is to be made from 57.45 square inches of cardboard and each side of the base is less than 5 inches long?

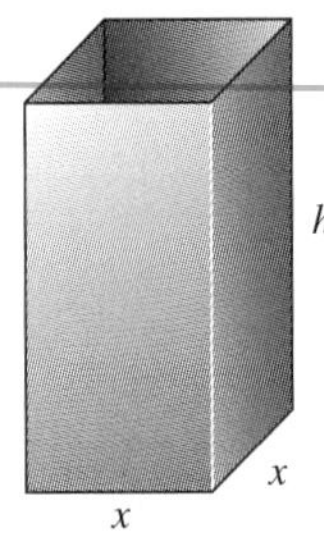

FIGURE 2.10

Let x be the length of one side of the base and h the height of the box, as in Figure 2.10. Then

$$\text{length} \times \text{width} \times \text{height} = \text{volume of box}$$
$$x \cdot x \cdot h = 32$$
$$x^2h = 32. \qquad (1)$$

The surface area of the open box (the amount of cardboard to be used) consists of the base (which measures x by x inches) and four sides, each of which measures x by h inches. Since this must total 57.45 square inches, we have:

$$x^2 + 4xh = 57.45. \qquad (2)$$

From equation (1) we know that $h = 32/x^2$. Substitute this in equation (2).

$$x^2 + 4xh = 57.45$$
$$x^2 + 4x\left(\frac{32}{x^2}\right) = 57.45$$
$$x^2 + \frac{128}{x} = 57.45$$

This last equation can be solved either by the intersection or the intercept method. To use the intercept method, write the equation as $x^2 + 128/x - 57.45 = 0$ and graph the left side. A complete graph is not necessary because x is positive (it is a length) and $x < 5$ by hypothesis. So any window with $0 \le x \le 5$ that includes the y-axis will do. The graph in Figure 2.11 shows that the equation has a solution (x-intercept) between 2 and 3. Zoom-in or a graphical root finder shows that this solution is

4 If the base of the box in Example 5 must have sides of length greater than 5, what are the dimensions of the box?

Answer:
Approximately 6.014 by 6.014 by .88 inches, not a very practical size

$x = 2.5$. (This is an exact solution that you can verify by substituting it in the equation.) Now use equation (1) to find h.

$$h = \frac{32}{x^2} = \frac{32}{(2.5)^2} = \frac{32}{6.25} = 5.12$$

Therefore the dimensions of the box should be 2.5 by 2.5 by 5.12 inches. ■ 4

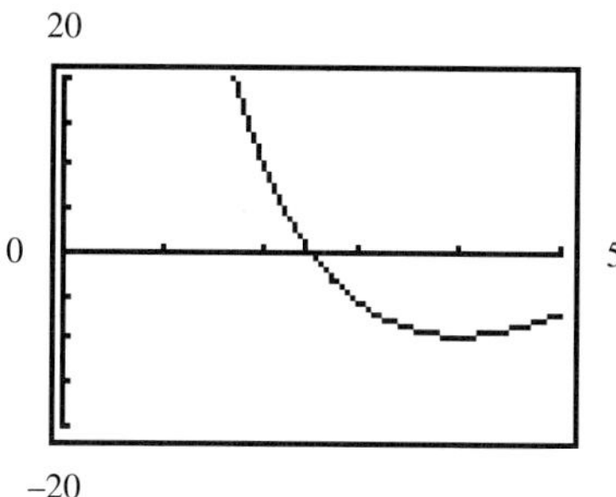

FIGURE 2.11

NUMERICAL METHODS Other techniques for approximating solutions of equations are used on calculators that have built-in "equation solvers" (no graphing required). If your calculator has an equation solver, learn how to use it. Most equation solvers find one solution at a time, but some calculators (such as TI-85 and HP-38) have a second solver that will find all the solutions of a polynomial equation in one step; these are usually labeled POLY or POLYROOT. Check your instruction manual.

2.1 EXERCISES

Exercises 1 and 2 are designed to help you become familiar with the graphing calculator and its capabilities.

1. (a) Verify graphically that the equation $x^5 - 2x^4 - x^3 + 3x + 1 = 0$ has a solution between -1 and 0.
   (b) Find this solution graphically.
   (c) Now use the equation solver on your calculator (if it has one) to find this same solution. How well does your answer agree with the one you obtained in part (b)?
2. Some graphical root finders have difficulty finding x-intercepts when the graph touches, but does not cross, the x-axis. Can your calculator's graphical root finder solve the following equations?
   (a) $\sqrt{x-2} = 0$ (If you are asked to specify a starting point or make an initial guess, use a number other than 2.)
   (b) $x^2 = 0$

Use the intersection method to find a solution of the equation that lies in the given interval. (See Examples 1 and 2.)

3. $x^5 + x^2 = 7$; $(1, 2)$
4. $12x^3 - 28x^2 - 7x = 10$; $(2, 3)$
5. $x^3 + 9 = 3x^2 + 6x$; $(1, 2)$
6. $x^3 + 10x = -4x^2 - 15$; $(-3, -2)$

Use the intersection method to find all solutions of the equation. (See Examples 1 and 2.)

7. $|x^2 + 4x - 1| = 4$
8. $|x^2 + 2x - 9| = 6$
9. $|x^2 - 5x + 1| = 3$
10. $|2x^2 + 5x - 7| = 4$

Use manual or automatic zoom-in to find a solution of the equation that lies in the given interval; your solution should have a maximum error of .01 (that is, the x-intercept should lie between two tick marks that are .01 unit apart). Consider your answer correct if it is within .01 of the answer in the back of the book. (See Example 3.)

11. $x^4 + x - 3 = 0; (0, \infty)$

12. $x^3 - 3x^2 + 1 = 0; (1, \infty)$

13. $x^5 - 3x^4 - x + 5 = 0; (-\infty, 1)$

14. $x^3 - 3x + 1 = 0; (-\infty, -1)$

Determine graphically the number of real solutions of the given equation (by counting either intersection points or x-intercepts). You need not solve the equation, but you may need a viewing window other than the standard one to find all the solutions. (See Examples 1–4.)

15. $x^5 + 5 = 3x^4 + x$

16. $x^3 + 5 = 3x^2 + 24x$

17. $x^7 - 10x^5 + 15x + 10 = 0$

18. $x^5 + 36x + 25 = 13x^3$

19. $x^4 + 500x^2 - 8000x = 16x^3 - 32{,}000$

20. $6x^5 + 80x^3 + 45x^2 + 30 = 45x^4 + 86x$

Find all real solutions of the equation. (See Examples 1–4.)

21. $x^3 - 3x^2 + 5 = 0$

22. $x^3 + x - 1 = 0$

23. $2x^3 - 4x^2 + x - 3 = 0$

24. $6x^3 - 5x^2 + 3x - 2 = 0$

25. $x^5 - 6x + 6 = 0$

26. $x^3 - 3x^2 + x - 1 = 0$

27. $10x^5 - 3x^2 + x - 6 = 0$

28. $\frac{1}{4}x^4 - x - 4 = 0$

29. $2x - \frac{1}{2}x^2 - \frac{1}{12}x^4 = 0$

30. $\frac{1}{4}x^4 + \frac{1}{3}x^2 + 3x - 1 = 0$

31. $x^6 + x^2 - 2x - 1 = 0$

32. $x^4 + x - 3 = 0$

Find an exact solution of the equation in the given interval. (For example, if the graphical approximation of a solution begins .3333, check to see if 1/3 is the exact solution. Similarly, since $\sqrt{2} \approx 1.414$, if your approximation begins 1.414, check to see if $\sqrt{2}$ is a solution.)

33. $3x^3 - 2x^2 + 3x - 2 = 0; (0, 1)$

34. $12x^4 - x^3 - 12x^2 + 25x - 2 = 0; (0, 1)$

35. $4x^4 - 13x^2 + 3 = 0; (1, 2)$

36. $x^3 + x^2 - 2x - 2 = 0; (1, 2)$

37. Physical Science The surface area S of the right circular cone in the figure is given by $S = \pi r\sqrt{r^2 + h^2}$. What radius should be used to produce a cone of height 5 inches and surface area 100 square inches?

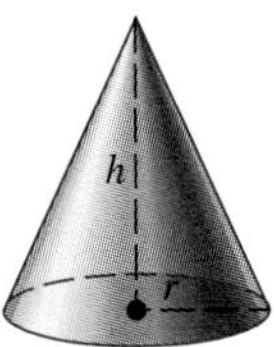

38. Physical Science The surface area of the right square pyramid in the figure is given by $S = b\sqrt{b^2 + 4h^2}$. If the pyramid has height 10 ft and surface area 100 sq ft, what is the length of a side b of its base?

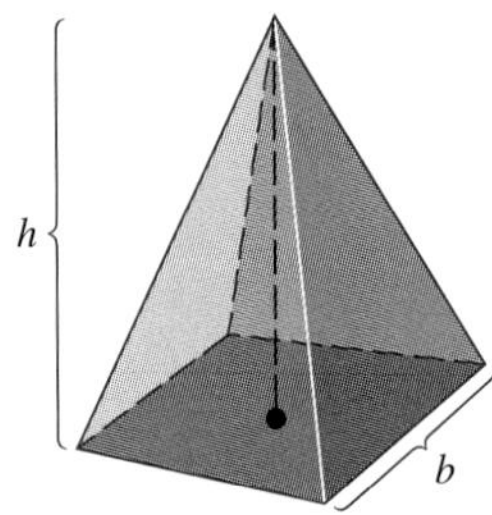

39. Management A manufacturer's revenue (in dollars) from selling x units is given by $r = 2x - .0002x^2$. The cost (in dollars) of producing x units is given by $c = .6x + 300$. The plant can produce a maximum of 5000 units per week.

(a) Find the profit equation.

(b) How many units should be made each week in order to make a profit of $1100?

40. Management A manufacturer has found that the average cost per computer when x computers per day are produced is given by the equation $c = .13x^2 - 70x + 10{,}000$. How many should be produced each day if the average cost is to be $1516 per computer?

41. Natural Science During the years from 1930 to 1990 the rate of breast cancer has been nearly constant at 30 cases per 100,000 females, whereas the rate of lung cancer in females has increased. The number y of lung cancer cases per 100,000 females in the year x (where $x = 0$ corresponds to 1930) is approximated by the equation $y = .00028x^3 - .011x^2 + .23x + .93$.*

(a) What equation approximates the rate of breast cancer?

(b) Graph the breast cancer and lung cancer rate equations on the same screen for the years 1930 to 1995 (that is, for $0 \le x \le 65$).

(c) In what year is the breast cancer rate equal to the lung cancer rate?

---

*Valanis, B., *Epidemiology in Nursing and Health Care.* Norwalk, CT: Appleton & Lange, 1992.

42. Management On Saturday afternoons, cars line up to get into the parking lot of an amusement park. Under certain circumstances, the average waiting time y (in minutes) for each vehicle arriving at the gate is given by the equation

$$y = \frac{2x - 25}{2x^2 - 50x},$$

where x is the average number of vehicles admitted per minute by the gate attendants.*

(a) Assuming that at least 25 cars are admitted per minute, what admittance rate is necessary to keep the average waiting time y at 30 seconds?

(b) If one gate attendant can serve an average of 5.3 vehicles per minute, how many attendants will be needed to keep the average waiting time at 30 seconds?

43. Natural Science Carbon monoxide combines with the hemoglobin of the blood to form carboxyhemoglobin (COHb), which reduces transport of oxygen to tissue. A 4% to 6% COHb level in the blood (typical for smokers) can cause symptoms such as blood flow alterations, visual impairment, and poorer vigilance ability. When $50 \le x \le 100$, the equation $T = .00787x^2 - 1.528x + 75.89$ approximates the exposure time T (in hours) necessary to reach this 4% to 6% level, where x is the amount of carbon monoxide present in the air in parts per million (ppm).†

(a) A kerosene heater or a room full of smokers is capable of producing 50 ppm of carbon monoxide. How long would it take for a nonsmoking person to start feeling the above symptoms?

(b) What carbon monoxide concentration will cause a person to reach a 4% to 6% COHb level in three hours?

44. Natural Science The exposure time T (in hours) required for a person to reach a COHb level capable of causing a coma (see Exercise 43) can be approximated by the equation $T = .0002x^2 - .316x + 127.9$, where x is the carbon monoxide concentration (in ppm) and $500 \le x \le 800$.†

(a) What is the exposure time when $x = 600$ ppm?

(b) What concentration of carbon monoxide will produce a coma in four hours?

Physical Science *Work the following problems. (See Example 5.)*

45. A firm wants to make an open-top box with a square base, whose sides do not exceed 30 cm, and a volume of 30,000 cubic centimeters. If the surface area of the box is 6000 square centimeters, what are its dimensions (to the nearest tenth of a centimeter)?

46. An open-top box with a square base is to be constructed from 120 square inches of aluminum. If each side of the base is no more than 5 inches long and if the volume of the box is 100 cubic inches, what are its dimensions (to the nearest tenth of an inch)?

47. The dimensions of a rectangular box are consecutive integers. If the box has a volume of 17,550 cubic inches, what are its dimensions?

*Based on Mannering, F. and W. Kilareski, *Principles of Highway Engineering and Traffic Control,* John Wiley and Sons, Inc., 1990.

†*Indoor Air Quality Environmental Information Handbook: Combustion Sources,* Report No. DOE/EV/10450-1, U.S. Department of Energy, 1985.

2.2 QUADRATIC EQUATIONS

An equation that can be put in the form

$$ax^2 + bx + c = 0,$$

where a, b, and c are real numbers with $a \neq 0$, is called a **quadratic equation.** For example, each of

$$2x^2 + 3x + 4 = 0, \quad x^2 = 6x - 9, \quad 3x^2 + x = 6, \quad \text{and} \quad x^2 = 5$$

is a quadratic equation. A solution of an equation that is a real number is said to be a **real solution** of the equation.

EXAMPLE 1 Determine graphically the *number* of real solutions of the quadratic equation.

(a) $3x^2 + x = 6$

Rewrite the equation as $3x^2 + x - 6 = 0$ and graph $y = 3x^2 + x - 6$. The graph (Figure 2.12 on the next page) has two x-intercepts. Therefore the equation has two real solutions (why?).

1 How many real solutions does each equation have?

(a) $x^2 + 3 = -8x$

(b) $2x^2 + x + 3 = 0$

Answers:

(a) 2

(b) 0

(b) $x^2 - 6x + 10 = 0$

The graph of $y = x^2 - 6x + 10$ (Figure 2.13) has no x-intercepts, and hence the equation has no real solutions.

(c) $9x^2 + 30x + 25 = 0$

The graph of $y = 9x^2 + 30x + 25$ in Figure 2.14 appears to have just one x-intercept, which would mean that the equation has a single real solution. This is indeed the case, as we shall verify algebraically in Example 6. ■ 1

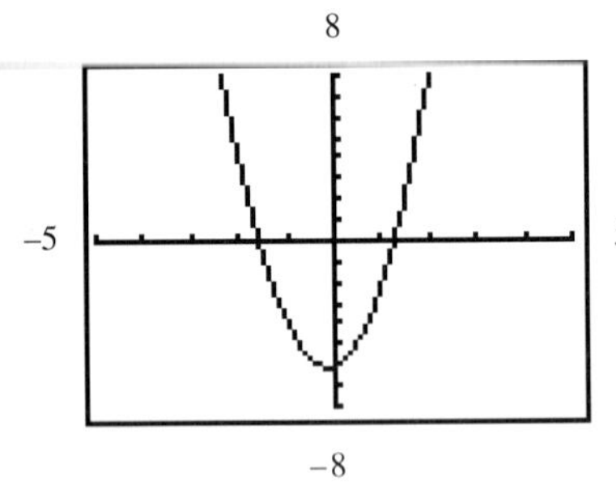

FIGURE 2.12

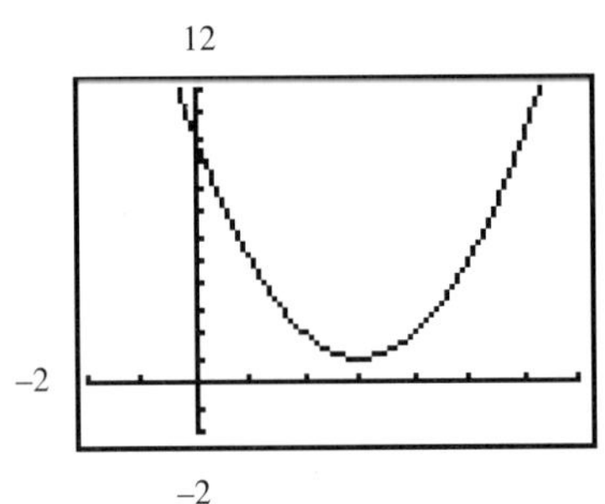

FIGURE 2.13

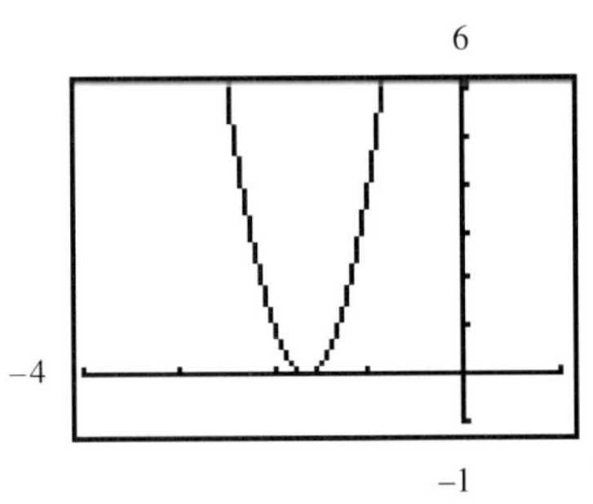

FIGURE 2.14

Example 1 illustrates this fact:

Every quadratic equation has either two or one or no real solutions.

Although the solutions of a quadratic equation can be approximated graphically, it is often faster to use algebraic methods, which give exact solutions. One algebraic method is based on factoring and the following property of real numbers.

ZERO-FACTOR PROPERTY

If a and b are real numbers, with $ab = 0$, then $a = 0$ or $b = 0$ or both.

EXAMPLE 2 Solve $6r^2 + 7r = 3$.

Rewrite the equation as

$$6r^2 + 7r - 3 = 0.$$

Now factor $6r^2 + 7r - 3$ to get

$$(3r - 1)(2r + 3) = 0.$$

By the zero-factor property, the product $(3r - 1)(2r + 3)$ can equal 0 only if

$$3r - 1 = 0 \quad \text{or} \quad 2r + 3 = 0.$$

Solving each of these equations separately gives the solutions of the original equation.

$$3r = 1 \quad \text{or} \quad 2r = -3$$

$$r = \frac{1}{3} \qquad\qquad r = -\frac{3}{2}$$

2 Solve each equation by factoring.

(a) $y^2 + 3y = 10$

(b) $2r^2 + 9r = 5$

(c) $4k^2 = 9k$

Answers:

(a) 2, −5

(b) 1/2, −5

(c) 9/4, 0

Verify that both 1/3 and −3/2 are solutions by substituting them in the original equation. ■ 2

An equation such as $x^2 = 5$ has two solutions, $\sqrt{5}$ and $-\sqrt{5}$. The same idea is true in general.

SQUARE-ROOT PROPERTY

If $b > 0$, then the solutions of $\boldsymbol{x^2 = b}$ are $\boldsymbol{\sqrt{b}}$ and $\boldsymbol{-\sqrt{b}}$.

The two solutions are sometimes abbreviated $\pm\sqrt{b}$.

3 Solve each equation by using the square root property.

(a) $p^2 = 21$

(b) $(m + 7)^2 = 15$

(c) $(2k - 3)^2 = 5$

Answers:

(a) $\pm\sqrt{21}$

(b) $-7 \pm \sqrt{15}$

(c) $(3 \pm \sqrt{5})/2$

EXAMPLE 3 Solve each equation.

(a) $m^2 = 17$

By the square-root property, the solutions are $\sqrt{17}$ and $-\sqrt{17}$, abbreviated $\pm\sqrt{17}$.

(b) $(y - 4)^2 = 11$

Use a generalization of the square-root property, working as follows:

$$(y - 4)^2 = 11$$

$$y - 4 = \sqrt{11} \quad \text{or} \quad y - 4 = -\sqrt{11}$$

$$y = 4 + \sqrt{11} \qquad\qquad y = 4 - \sqrt{11}.$$

Abbreviate the solutions as $4 \pm \sqrt{11}$. ■ 3

As suggested by Example 3(b), any quadratic equation can be solved using the square-root property if the equation can be written in the form $(x + n)^2 = k$. For instance, to write $4x^2 - 24x + 19 = 0$ in this form, we need to write the left side as a perfect square, $(x + n)^2$. To get a perfect square trinomial, first add −19 to both sides of the equation, then multiply both sides by 1/4, so that x^2 has a coefficient of 1.

$$4x^2 - 24x + 19 = 0$$

$$4x^2 - 24x = -19$$

$$x^2 - 6x = -\frac{19}{4}$$

Adding 9 to both sides will make the left side a perfect square, so the equation can be written in the desired form.

$$x^2 - 6x + 9 = -\frac{19}{4} + 9$$

$$(x - 3)^2 = \frac{17}{4}$$

Use the square-root property to complete the solution.

$$x - 3 = \pm\sqrt{\frac{17}{4}} = \pm\frac{\sqrt{17}}{2}$$

$$x = 3 \pm \frac{\sqrt{17}}{2} = \frac{6 \pm \sqrt{17}}{2}$$

The two solutions are $\frac{6+\sqrt{17}}{2}$ and $\frac{6-\sqrt{17}}{2}$.

Notice that the number 9 added to both sides of $x^2 - 6x = -19/4$ is found by taking half the coefficient of x, $(1/2)(-6) = -3$, and squaring it: $(-3)^2 = 9$. This always works because

$$\left(x+\frac{b}{2}\right)^2 = x^2 + 2\left(\frac{b}{2}\right)x + \left(\frac{b}{2}\right)^2 = x^2 + bx + \left(\frac{b}{2}\right)^2.$$

The process of changing $4x^2 - 24x + 19 = 0$ to $(x-3)^2 = 17/4$ is called **completing the square.***

The method of completing the square can be used on the general quadratic equation

$$ax^2 + bx + c = 0 \quad (a \neq 0)$$

to convert it to one whose solution can be found by the square-root property. This will give a general formula for solving any quadratic equation. Going through the necessary algebra produces the following important result.

QUADRATIC FORMULA

The solutions of the quadratic equation $ax^2 + bx + c = 0$, where $a \neq 0$, are given by

$$x = \frac{-b \pm \sqrt{b^2 - 4ac}}{2a}.$$

CAUTION When using the quadratic formula, remember the equation must be in the form $ax^2 + bx + c = 0$. Also, notice that the fraction bar in the quadratic formula extends under *both* terms in the numerator. Be sure to add $-b$ to $\pm\sqrt{b^2 - 4ac}$ *before* dividing by $2a$. ◆

EXAMPLE 4 Solve $x^2 + 1 = 4x$.

First add $-4x$ to both sides, to get 0 alone on the right side.

$$x^2 - 4x + 1 = 0$$

Now identify the letters a, b, and c. Here $a = 1$, $b = -4$, and $c = 1$. Substitute these numbers into the quadratic formula.

$$x = \frac{-(-4) \pm \sqrt{(-4)^2 - 4(1)(1)}}{2(1)}$$

$$= \frac{4 \pm \sqrt{16-4}}{2}$$

$$= \frac{4 \pm \sqrt{12}}{2}$$

$$= \frac{4 \pm 2\sqrt{3}}{2} \qquad \sqrt{12} = \sqrt{4\cdot 3} = \sqrt{4}\cdot\sqrt{3} = 2\sqrt{3}$$

*Completing the square is discussed further in Section 3.4.

$$= \frac{2(2 \pm \sqrt{3})}{2} \qquad \text{Factor } 4 \pm 2\sqrt{3}.$$

$$x = 2 \pm \sqrt{3}$$

The $\pm$ sign represents the two solutions of the equation. First use $+$ and then use $-$ to find each of the solutions: $2 + \sqrt{3}$ and $2 - \sqrt{3}$. ■ 4

4 Use the quadratic formula to solve each equation.

(a) $x^2 - 2x = 2$

(b) $u^2 - 6u + 4 = 0$

Answers:

(a) $x = 1 + \sqrt{3}$ or $1 - \sqrt{3}$

(b) $u = 3 + \sqrt{5}$ or $3 - \sqrt{5}$

Example 4 shows that the quadratic formula produces exact solutions of quadratic equations that do not readily factor. In many real-world situations, however, accurate decimal approximations of solutions are needed. A calculator is ideal for this. In Example 4, for instance, we can use a calculator to determine that approximate solutions (accurate to seven decimal places) are

$$x = 2 + \sqrt{3} \approx 3.7320508 \quad \text{and} \quad x = 2 - \sqrt{3} \approx .2679492.$$

Experiment with your calculator to find the most efficient keystroke sequence for using the quadratic formula.

EXAMPLE 5 Use the quadratic formula and a calculator to solve

$$3.2x^2 + 15.93x - 7.1 = 0.$$

Compute $\sqrt{b^2 - 4ac} = \sqrt{15.93^2 - 4(3.2)(-7.1)} \approx 18.56461419$ and store the result in memory D. Then the solutions of the equation are given by

$$\frac{-15.93 + D}{2(3.2)} \approx .411658467 \quad \text{and} \quad \frac{-15.93 - D}{2(3.2)} \approx -5.38978347.$$

Remember that these answers are *approximations,* so they may not check exactly when substituted in the original equation. ■ 5

5 Find approximate solutions for $5.1x^2 - 3.3x - 240.624 = 0$.

Answer:

$x = 7.2$ or $x \approx -6.5529$

An even easier way to approximate the solutions of quadratic equations is to program your calculator to do it (or use a built-in quadratic equation solver if your calculator has one). Then you need only enter the coefficients *a, b,* and *c* to obtain the approximate solutions. See the Program Appendix for details.

EXAMPLE 6 Solve $9x^2 + 30x + 25 = 0$.

Graphical analysis in Example 1(c) suggests that this equation has just one real solution. The quadratic formula provides an algebraic proof of this. Applying the formula with $a = 9$, $b = 30$, and $c = 25$, we have

$$x = \frac{-(\mathbf{30}) \pm \sqrt{(\mathbf{30})^2 - 4(\mathbf{9})(\mathbf{25})}}{2(\mathbf{9})}$$

$$= \frac{-30 \pm \sqrt{900 - 900}}{18} = \frac{-30 \pm 0}{18} = \frac{-30}{18} = -\frac{5}{3}.$$

Therefore, the given equation has only one real solution. The fact that the solution is a rational number indicates that this equation could have been solved by factoring. ■

EXAMPLE 7 Solve $x^2 - 6x + 10 = 0$.

In Example 1(b) we determined graphically that this equation has no real solutions. The quadratic formula provides an algebraic confirmation of this fact. Apply the formula with $a = 1$, $b = -6$, and $c = 10$.

$$x = \frac{-(-6) \pm \sqrt{(-6)^2 - 4(1)(10)}}{2(1)} = \frac{6 \pm \sqrt{36 - 40}}{2} = \frac{6 \pm \sqrt{-4}}{2}$$

Since no negative number has a square root in the real number system, $\sqrt{-4}$ is not a real number. Hence the equation has no real solutions. ■ 6

6 Solve each equation.

(a) $9k^2 - 6k + 1 = 0$

(b) $4m^2 + 28m + 49 = 0$

(c) $2x^2 - 5x + 5 = 0$

Answers:

(a) 1/3

(b) $-7/2$

(c) No real number solutions

Examples 4–7 show that $b^2 - 4ac$, the quantity under the radical in the quadratic formula, determines the number of real solutions of the equation as follows.

If $b^2 - 4ac > 0$ (as in Examples 4 and 5), there are two real solutions.

If $b^2 - 4ac = 0$ (as in Example 6), there is one real solution.

If $b^2 - 4ac < 0$ (as in Example 7), there are no real solutions.

This provides algebraic confirmation of the fact that a quadratic equation has two, one, or no real solutions. The number $b^2 - 4ac$ is called the **discriminant** of the equation $ax^2 + bx + c = 0$. 7

7 Use the discriminant to determine the number of real solutions of each equation.

(a) $x^2 + 8x + 3 = 0$

(b) $2x^2 + x + 3 = 0$

(c) $x^2 - 194x + 9409 = 0$

Answers:

(a) 2

(b) 0

(c) 1

EXAMPLE 8 A landscape architect wants to make an exposed gravel border of uniform width around a small shed behind a company plant. The shed is 10 feet by 6 feet. He has enough gravel to cover 36 square feet. How wide should the border be?

Follow the steps given in Section 1.2 for solving applied problems. A sketch of the shed with border is given in Figure 2.15. Let x represent the width of the border. Then the width of the large rectangle is $6 + 2x$ and its length is $10 + 2x$.

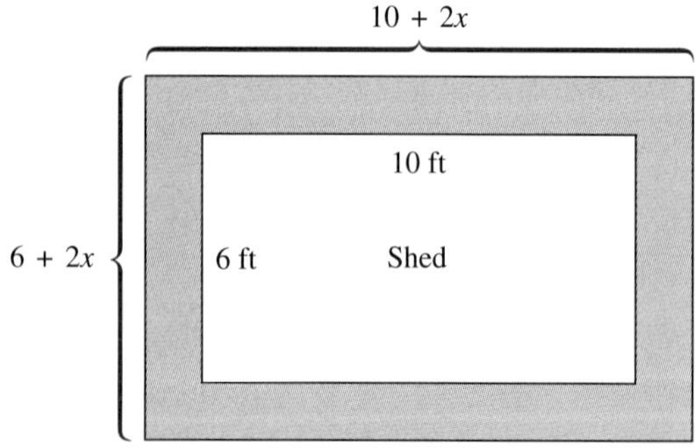

FIGURE 2.15

We must write an equation relating the given areas and dimensions. The area of the large rectangle is $(6 + 2x)(10 + 2x)$. The area occupied by the shed is $6 \cdot 10 = 60$.

The area of the border is found by subtracting the area of the shed from the area of the large rectangle. This difference should be 36 square feet, giving the equation

$$(6 + 2x)(10 + 2x) - 60 = 36.$$

Solve this equation with the following sequence of steps.

$$60 + 32x + 4x^2 - 60 = 36$$
$$4x^2 + 32x - 36 = 0$$
$$x^2 + 8x - 9 = 0$$
$$(x + 9)(x - 1) = 0$$

The solutions are -9 and 1. The number -9 cannot be the width of the border, so the solution is to make the border 1 foot wide. ■ 8

8 The length of a picture is 2 inches more than the width. It is mounted on a mat that extends 2 inches beyond the picture on all sides. What are the dimensions of the picture if the area of the mat is 99 square inches?

Answer:
5 inches by 7 inches

Some equations that are not quadratic can be solved as quadratic equations by making a suitable substitution. Such equations are called **quadratic in form.**

EXAMPLE 9 Solve $4m^4 - 9m^2 + 2 = 0$.

Use the substitutions

$$x = m^2 \quad \text{and} \quad x^2 = m^4$$

to rewrite the equation as

$$4\mathbf{x}^2 - 9\mathbf{x} + 2 = 0.$$

This quadratic equation can be solved by factoring.

$$4x^2 - 9x + 2 = 0$$
$$(x - 2)(4x - 1) = 0$$
$$x - 2 = 0 \quad \text{or} \quad 4x - 1 = 0$$
$$\mathbf{x} = 2 \quad \text{or} \quad 4x = 1$$
$$\mathbf{x} = \frac{1}{4}$$

Because $x = m^2$,

$$\mathbf{m}^2 = 2 \quad \text{or} \quad \mathbf{m}^2 = \frac{1}{4}$$

$$m = \pm\sqrt{2} \quad \text{or} \quad m = \pm\frac{1}{2}.$$

There are four solutions: $-\sqrt{2}$, $\sqrt{2}$, $-1/2$, and $1/2$. ■ 9

9 Solve each equation.

(a) $9x^4 - 23x^2 + 10 = 0$

(b) $4x^4 = 7x^2 - 3$

Answers:

(a) $-\sqrt{5/3}, \sqrt{5/3}, -\sqrt{2}, \sqrt{2}$

(b) $-\sqrt{3/2}, \sqrt{3/2}, -1, 1$

EXAMPLE 10 Solve $4 + \frac{1}{z - 2} = \frac{3}{2(z - 2)^2}$.

First, substitute u for $z - 2$ to get

$$4 + \frac{1}{\mathbf{z - 2}} = \frac{3}{2(\mathbf{z - 2})^2}$$

$$4 + \frac{1}{\mathbf{u}} = \frac{3}{2\mathbf{u}^2}.$$

Now multiply both sides of the equation by the common denominator $2u^2$; then solve the resulting quadratic equation.

$$2u^2\left(4 + \frac{1}{u}\right) = 2u^2\left(\frac{3}{2u^2}\right)$$

$$8u^2 + 2u = 3$$

$$8u^2 + 2u - 3 = 0$$

$$(4u + 3)(2u - 1) = 0$$

$$4u + 3 = 0 \quad \text{or} \quad 2u - 1 = 0$$

$$u = -\frac{3}{4} \quad \text{or} \quad u = \frac{1}{2}$$

$$z - 2 = -\frac{3}{4} \quad \text{or} \quad z - 2 = \frac{1}{2} \qquad \text{Replace } u \text{ with } z - 2.$$

$$z = -\frac{3}{4} + 2 \qquad z = \frac{1}{2} + 2$$

$$z = \frac{5}{4} \quad \text{or} \quad z = \frac{5}{2}.$$

The solutions are 5/4 and 5/2. Check both solutions in the original equation. ■ 10

10 Solve each equation.

(a) $\frac{13}{3(p + 1)} + \frac{5}{3(p + 1)^2} = 2$

(b) $1 + \frac{1}{a} = \frac{5}{a^2}$

Answers:

(a) $-4/3$, $3/2$

(b) $(-1 + \sqrt{21})/2$, $(-1 - \sqrt{21})/2$

The next example shows how to solve an equation for a specified variable when the equation is quadratic in that variable.

EXAMPLE 11 Solve $v = mx^2 + x$ for x. (Assume $m \neq 0$.)

The equation is quadratic in x because of the x^2 term. Use the quadratic formula, first writing the equation in standard form.

$$v = mx^2 + x$$

$$0 = mx^2 + x - v$$

Let $a = m$, $b = 1$, and $c = -v$. Then the quadratic formula gives

$$x = \frac{-1 \pm \sqrt{1^2 - 4(m)(-v)}}{2m}$$

$$x = \frac{-1 \pm \sqrt{1 + 4mv}}{2m}. \quad ■ \quad 11$$

11 Solve each of the following equations for the indicated variable. Assume no variable equals 0.

(a) $k = mp^2 - bp$ for p

(b) $r = \frac{APk^2}{3}$ for k

Answers:

(a) $p = \frac{b \pm \sqrt{b^2 + 4mk}}{2m}$

(b) $k = \pm\sqrt{\frac{3r}{AP}} = \frac{\pm\sqrt{3rAP}}{AP}$

2.2 EXERCISES

Determine graphically the number of solutions of the equation. You need not solve the equation. (See Example 1.)

1. $9z^2 - 12z - 1 = 0$
2. $3x^2 + 2 = x$
3. $2x^2 = x - 1$
4. $x^2 - 5x = 28$
5. $x^2 - 2.2x + 1.2 = 0$
6. $x^2 + 2.4x + 1.46 = 0$

Use factoring to solve each equation. (See Example 2.)

7. $y^2 + 15y + 56 = 0$
8. $k^2 - 4k - 5 = 0$
9. $2x^2 = 5x - 3$
10. $2 = 12z^2 + 5z$
11. $6r^2 + r = 1$
12. $3y^2 = 16y - 5$
13. $2m^2 + 20 = 13m$
14. $10a^2 + 17a + 3 = 0$
15. $m(m - 7) = -10$
16. $z(2z + 7) = 4$
17. $9x^2 - 16 = 0$
18. $25y^2 - 64 = 0$
19. $16x^2 - 16x = 0$
20. $12y^2 - 48y = 0$

Solve each equation by the square-root property. (See Example 3.)

21. $(r - 2)^2 = 7$
22. $(b + 5)^2 = 8$
23. $(4x - 1)^2 = 20$
24. $(3t + 5)^2 = 11$

Use the quadratic formula to solve each equation. If the solutions involve square roots, give both the exact and approximate solutions. (See Examples 4–7.)

25. $2x^2 + 5x + 1 = 0$

26. $3x^2 - x - 7 = 0$

27. $4k^2 + 2k = 1$

28. $r^2 = 3r + 5$

29. $5y^2 + 6y = 2$

30. $2z^2 + 3 = 8z$

31. $6x^2 + 6x + 5 = 0$

32. $3a^2 - 2a + 2 = 0$

33. $2r^2 - 7r + 5 = 0$

34. $8x^2 = 8x - 3$

35. $6k^2 - 11k + 4 = 0$

36. $8m^2 - 10m + 3 = 0$

37. $2x^2 - 7x + 30 = 0$

38. $3k^2 + k = 6$

Use the discriminant to determine the number of real solutions of each equation. You need not solve the equations.

39. $25t^2 + 49 = 70t$

40. $9z^2 - 12z = 1$

41. $13x^2 + 24x - 6 = 0$

42. $22x^2 + 19x + 5 = 0$

Use a calculator and the quadratic formula to find approximate solutions of the equation. (See Example 5.)

43. $4.42x^2 - 10.14x + 3.79 = 0$

44. $3x^2 - 82.74x + 570.4923 = 0$

45. $7.63x^2 + 2.79x = 5.32$

46. $8.06x^2 + 25.8726x = 25.047256$

Give all real number solutions of the following equations. (See Examples 9 and 10. Hint: In Exercise 51, let $u = p - 3$.)

47. $z^4 - 2z^2 = 15$

48. $6p^4 = p^2 + 2$

49. $2q^4 + 3q^2 - 9 = 0$

50. $4a^4 = 2 - 7a^2$

51. $6(p - 3)^2 + 5(p - 3) - 6 = 0$

52. $12(q + 4)^2 - 13(q + 4) - 4 = 0$

53. $1 + \frac{7}{2a} = \frac{15}{2a^2}$

54. $5 - \frac{4}{k} - \frac{1}{k^2} = 0$

55. $-\frac{2}{3z^2} + \frac{1}{3} + \frac{8}{3z} = 0$

56. $2 + \frac{5}{x} + \frac{1}{x^2} = 0$

Students often confuse expressions with equations. In part **(a)**, *add or subtract the expressions as indicated. In part* **(b)**, *solve the equation. Compare the results.*

57. **(a)** $\frac{6}{r} - \frac{5}{r - 2} - 1$ **(b)** $\frac{6}{r} = \frac{5}{r - 2} - 1$

58. **(a)** $\frac{8}{z - 1} - \frac{5}{z} + \frac{2z}{z - 1}$ **(b)** $\frac{8}{z - 1} = \frac{5}{z} + \frac{2z}{z - 1}$

Solve the following problems. (See Example 8.)

59. An ecology center wants to set up an experimental garden. It has 300 meters of fencing to enclose a rectangular area of 5000 square meters. Find the length and width of the rectangle.

(a) Let x = the length and write an expression for the width.

(b) Write an equation relating the length, width, and area, using the result of part (a).

(c) Solve the problem.

60. A shopping center has a rectangular area of 40,000 square yards enclosed on three sides for a parking lot. The length is 200 yards more than twice the width. Find the length and width of the lot. Let x equal the width and follow steps similar to those in Exercise 59.

61. A landscape architect has included a rectangular flower bed measuring 9 ft by 5 ft in her plans for a new building. She wants to use two colors of flowers in the bed, one in the center and the other for a border of the same width on all four sides. If she can get just enough plants to cover 24 sq ft for the border, how wide can the border be?

62. Joan wants to buy a rug for a room that is 12 feet by 15 feet. She wants to leave a uniform strip of floor around the rug. She can afford 108 square feet of carpeting. What dimensions should the rug have?

63. In 1991 Rick Mears won the (500 mi) Indianapolis 500 race. His speed (rate) was 100 mph (to the nearest mph) faster than that of the 1911 winner, Ray Harroun. Mears completed the race in 3.74 hours less time than Harroun. Find Mears's rate to the nearest whole number.

64. Chris and Josh have received walkie-talkies for Christmas. If they leave from the same point at the same time, Chris walking north at 2.5 mph and Josh walking east at 3 mph, how long will they be able to talk to each other if the range of the walkie-talkies is 4 mi? Round your answer to the nearest minute.

65. **Management** The manager of a bicycle shop knows that the cost of selling x bicycles is $C = 20x + 60$ and the revenue from selling x bicycles is $R = x^2 - 8x$. Find the break-even value of x.

66. **Management** A company that produces breakfast cereal has found that its operating cost in dollars is $C = 40x + 150$ and its revenue in dollars is $R = 65x - x^2$. For what value(s) of x will the company break even?

67. **Physical Science** If a ball is thrown upward with an initial velocity of 64 feet per second, then its height after t seconds is $h = 64t - 16t^2$. In how many seconds will the ball reach

(a) 64 ft?

(b) 28 ft?

(c) Why are two answers possible?

68. **Physical Science** A particle moves horizontally with its distance from a starting point in centimeters at t seconds given by $d = 11t^2 - 10t$.

(a) How long will it take before the particle returns to the starting point?

(b) When will the particle be 100 centimeters from the starting point?

Solve each of the following equations for the indicated variable. Assume all denominators are nonzero, and that all variables represent positive real numbers. (See Example 11.)

69. $S = \frac{1}{2}gt^2$ for t

70. $a = \pi r^2$ for r

71. $L = \frac{d^4k}{h^2}$ for h

72. $F = \frac{kMv^2}{r}$ for v

73. $P = \frac{E^2R}{(r + R)^2}$ for R

74. $S = 2\pi rh + 2\pi r^2$ for r

2.3 LINEAR INEQUALITIES

An **inequality** is a statement that one mathematical expression is greater than (or less than) another. Inequalities are very important in applications. For example, a company wants revenue to be *greater than* costs and must use *no more than* the total amount of capital or labor available.

Inequalities may be solved using algebraic or geometric methods. In this section we shall concentrate on algebraic methods of solving **linear inequalities,** such as

$$4 - 3x \le 7 + 2x \quad \text{and} \quad -2 < 5 + 3m < 20,$$

and absolute value inequalities, such as $|x - 2| < 5$. The following properties are the basic algebraic tools for working with inequalities.

PROPERTIES OF INEQUALITY

For real numbers a, b, and c,

(a) if $a < b$, then $a + c < b + c$

(b) if $a < b$, and if $c > 0$, then $ac < bc$

(c) if $a < b$, and if $c < 0$, then $ac > bc$.

Throughout this section, definitions are given only for $<$; but they are equally valid for $>$, $\le$, or $\ge$.

CAUTION Pay careful attention to part (c): If both sides of an inequality are multiplied by a negative number, the direction of the inequality symbol must be *reversed.* For example, starting with the true statement $-3 < 5$ and multiplying both sides by the positive number 2 gives

$$-3 \cdot 2 < 5 \cdot 2,$$

or

$$-6 < 10,$$

still a true statement. On the other hand, starting with $-3 < 5$ and multiplying both sides by the negative number -2 gives a true result only if the direction of the inequality symbol is reversed:

$$-3(-2) > 5(-2)$$
$$6 > -10. \blacklozenge \quad \boxed{1}$$

$\boxed{1}$ **(a)** First multiply both sides of $-6 < -1$ by 4, and then multiply both sides of $-6 < -1$ by -7.

(b) First multiply both sides of $9 \ge -4$ by 2, and then multiply both sides of $9 \ge -4$ by -5.

(c) First add 4 to both sides of $-3 < -1$, and then add -6 to both sides of $-3 < -1$.

Answers:

(a) $-24 < -4$; $42 > 7$

(b) $18 \ge -8$; $-45 \le 20$

(c) $1 < 3$; $-9 < -7$

EXAMPLE 1 Solve $3x + 5 > 11$. Graph the solution.

First, add -5 to both sides.

$$3x + 5 + (-5) > 11 + (-5)$$
$$3x > 6$$

Now multiply both sides by 1/3.

$$\frac{1}{3}(3x) > \frac{1}{3}(6)$$
$$x > 2$$

(Why was the direction of the inequality symbol not changed?) As a check, note that 0, which is not part of the solution, makes the inequality false, while 3, which is part of the solution, makes it true.

$$3(0) + 5 > 11 \qquad\qquad 3(3) + 5 > 11$$
$$5 > 11 \quad \text{False} \qquad\qquad 14 > 11 \quad \text{True}$$

In interval notation (introduced in Section 1.1), the solution is the interval $(2, \infty)$, which is graphed on the number line in Figure 2.16. An open circle at 2 shows that 2 is not included. ■ [2]

FIGURE 2.16

[2] Solve these inequalities. Graph each solution.

(a) $5z - 11 < 14$

(b) $-3k \leq -12$

(c) $-8y \geq 32$

Answers:

(a) $z < 5$

(b) $k \geq 4$

(c) $y \leq -4$

EXAMPLE 2 Solve $4 - 3x \leq 7 + 2x$.

Add -4 to both sides to obtain

$$-3x \leq 3 + 2x.$$

Add $-2x$ to both sides. (Remember that *adding* to both sides never changes the direction of the inequality symbol.)

$$-3x + (-2x) \leq 3 + 2x + (-2x)$$
$$-5x \leq 3$$

Multiply both sides by $-1/5$. Since $-1/5$ is negative, change the direction of the inequality symbol.

$$-\frac{1}{5}(-5x) \geq -\frac{1}{5}(3)$$
$$x \geq -\frac{3}{5}$$

Figure 2.17 shows a graph of the solution $[-3/5, \infty)$. The solid circle in Figure 2.17 shows that $-3/5$ is included in the solution. ■ [3]

FIGURE 2.17

[3] Solve these inequalities. Graph each solution.

(a) $8 - 6t \geq 2t + 24$

(b) $-4r + 3(r + 1) < 2r$

Answers:

(a) $t \leq -2$

(b) $r > 1$

4 Solve each of the following. Graph each solution.

(a) $9 < k + 5 < 13$

(b) $-6 \le 2z + 4 \le 12$

Answers:

(a) $4 < k < 8$

(b) $-5 \le z \le 4$

EXAMPLE 3 Solve $-2 < 5 + 3m < 20$. Graph the solution.

The inequality $-2 < 5 + 3m < 20$ says that $5 + 3m$ is *between* -2 and 20. We can solve this inequality with an extension of the properties given above. Work as follows, first adding -5 to each part.

$$-2 + (\mathbf{-5}) < 5 + 3m + (\mathbf{-5}) < 20 + (\mathbf{-5})$$
$$-7 < 3m < 15$$

Now multiply each part by 1/3.

$$-\frac{7}{3} < m < 5$$

A graph of the solution, $(-7/3, 5)$, is given in Figure 2.18. ■ 4

FIGURE 2.18

EXAMPLE 4 The formula for converting from Celsius to Fahrenheit temperature is

$$F = \frac{9}{5}C + 32.$$

What Celsius temperature range corresponds to the range from 32°F to 77°F?

The Fahrenheit temperature range is $32 < F < 77$. Since $F = (9/5)C + 32$,

$$32 < \mathbf{\frac{9}{5}C + 32} < 77.$$

Solve the inequality for C.

$$32 < \frac{9}{5}C + 32 < 77$$
$$0 < \frac{9}{5}C < 45$$
$$0 < C < \frac{5}{9} \cdot 45$$
$$0 < C < 25$$

5 In Example 4, what Celsius temperatures correspond to 5°F to 95°F?

Answer:

−15°C to 35°C

The corresponding Celsius temperature range is 0°C to 25°C. ■ 5

A product will break even, or produce a profit, only if the revenue R from selling the product at least equals the cost C of producing it, that is if $R \ge C$.

EXAMPLE 5 A company analyst has determined that the cost to produce and sell x units of a certain product is $C = 20x + 1000$. The revenue for that product is $R = 70x$. Find the values of x for which the company will break even or make a profit on the product.

Solve the inequality $R \geq C$.

$$
\begin{aligned}
R &\geq C \\
70x &\geq 20x + 1000 \qquad \text{Let } R = 70x,\ C = 20x + 1000. \\
50x &\geq 1000 \\
x &\geq 20
\end{aligned}
$$

The company must produce and sell 20 items to break even and more than 20 to make a profit. ■

The next examples show how to solve inequalities with absolute value.

EXAMPLE 6 Solve each inequality.

(a) $|x| < 5$

Because absolute value gives the distance from a number to 0, the inequality $|x| < 5$ is true for all real numbers whose distance from 0 is less than 5. This includes all numbers from -5 to 5, or numbers in the interval $(-5, 5)$. A graph of the solution is shown in Figure 2.19.

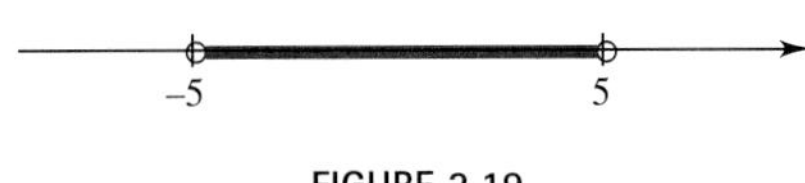

FIGURE 2.19

(b) $|x| > 5$

In a similar way, the solution of $|x| > 5$ is given by all those numbers whose distance from 0 is *greater* than 5. This includes the numbers satisfying $x < -5$ or $x > 5$. A graph of the solution, all numbers in

$$(-\infty, -5) \quad \text{or} \quad (5, \infty),$$

is shown in Figure 2.20. ■ 6

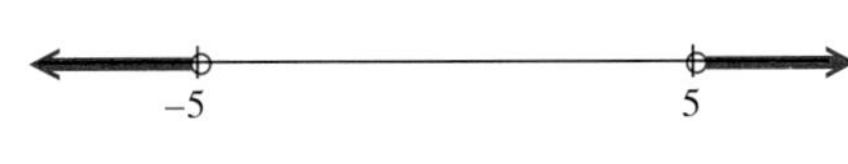

FIGURE 2.20

6 Solve each inequality. Graph each solution.

(a) $|x| \leq 1$

(b) $|y| \geq 3$

Answers:

(a) $[-1, 1]$

(b) All numbers in $(-\infty, -3]$ or $[3, \infty)$

The examples above suggest the following generalizations.

> Assume a and b are real numbers with b positive.
>
> **1.** Solve $|a| = |b|$ by solving $a = b$ or $a = -b$.
>
> **2.** Solve $|a| < b$ by solving $-b < a < b$.
>
> **3.** Solve $|a| > b$ by solving $a < -b$ or $a > b$.

7 Solve each inequality. Graph each solution.

(a) $|p + 3| < 4$

(b) $|2k - 1| \leq 7$

Answers:

(a) $(-7, 1)$

(b) $[-3, 4]$

8 Solve each inequality. Graph each solution.

(a) $|y - 2| > 5$

(b) $|3k - 1| \geq 2$

(c) $|2 + 5r| - 4 \geq 1$

Answers:

(a) All numbers in $(-\infty, -3)$ or $(7, \infty)$

(b) All numbers in $\left(-\infty, -\frac{1}{3}\right]$ or $[1, \infty)$

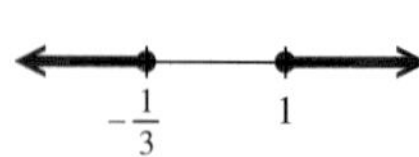

(c) All numbers in $\left(-\infty, -\frac{7}{5}\right]$ or $\left[\frac{3}{5}, \infty\right)$

9 Solve each inequality.

(a) $|5m - 2| > -1$

(b) $|2 + 3a| < -3$

(c) $|6 + r| > 0$

Answers:

(a) All real numbers

(b) No solution

(c) All real numbers except -6

EXAMPLE 7 Solve $|x - 2| < 5$.

Replace a with $x - 2$ and b with 5 in property (2) above. Now solve $|x - 2| < 5$ by solving the inequality

$$-5 < x - 2 < 5.$$

Add 2 to each part, getting the solution

$$-3 < x < 7,$$

which is graphed in Figure 2.21. ■ **7**

FIGURE 2.21

EXAMPLE 8 Solve $|2 - 7m| - 1 > 4$.

First add 1 on both sides.

$$|2 - 7m| > 5$$

Now use property (3) from above to solve $|2 - 7m| > 5$ by solving the inequality

$$2 - 7m < -5 \quad \text{or} \quad 2 - 7m > 5.$$

Solve each part separately.

$$-7m < -7 \quad \text{or} \quad -7m > 3$$

$$m > 1 \quad \text{or} \quad m < -\frac{3}{7}$$

The solution, all numbers in $\left(-\infty, -\frac{3}{7}\right)$ or $(1, \infty)$, is graphed in Figure 2.22. ■ **8**

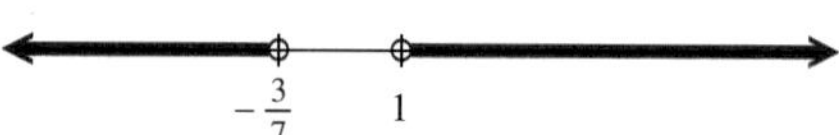

FIGURE 2.22

EXAMPLE 9 Solve $|2 - 5x| \geq -4$.

The absolute value of a number is always nonnegative. Therefore, $|2 - 5x| \geq -4$ is always true, so that the solution is the set of all real numbers. Note that the inequality $|2 - 5x| < -4$ has no solution, because the absolute value of a quantity can never be less than a negative number. ■ **9**

Absolute value inequalities can be used to indicate how far a number may be from a given number. The next example illustrates this use of absolute value.

EXAMPLE 10 Write each statement using absolute value.

(a) k is at least 4 units from 1.

If k is at least 4 units from 1, then the distance from k to 1 is greater than or equal to 4. See Figure 2.23(a). Since k may be on either side of 1 on the number line, k may be less than -3 or greater than 5. Write this statement using absolute value as follows:

$$|k - 1| \geq 4.$$

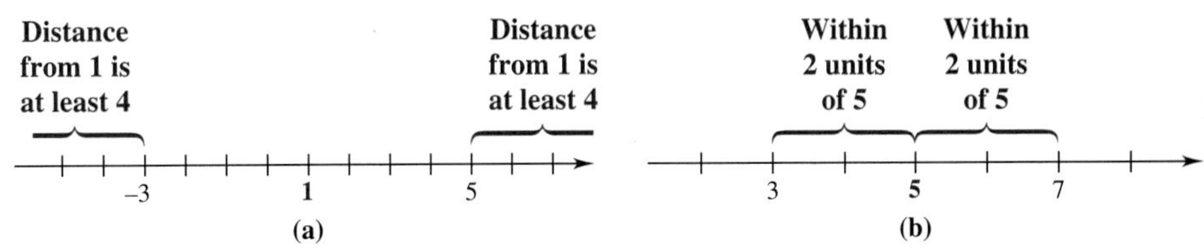

FIGURE 2.23

10 Write each statement using absolute value.

(a) m is at least 3 units from 5.

(b) t is within .01 of 4.

Answers:

(a) $|m - 5| \geq 3$

(b) $|t - 4| \leq .01$

(b) p is within 2 units of 5.

This statement means that the difference between p and 5 must be less than or equal to 2. See Figure 2.23(b). Using absolute value notation, the statement is written as

$$|p - 5| \leq 2. \quad ■ \quad \boxed{10}$$

2.3 EXERCISES

1. Explain how to determine whether an open circle or a solid circle is used when graphing the solution of a linear inequality.

2. The three-part inequality $p < x < q$ means "p is less than x and x is less than q." Which one of the following inequalities is not satisfied by any real number x? Explain why.

(a) $-3 < x < 5$ **(b)** $0 < x < 4$

(c) $-7 < x < -10$ **(d)** $-3 < x < -2$

Solve each inequality. Graph each solution in Exercises 3–32. (See Examples 1–3.)

3. $-8k \leq 32$ **4.** $-6a \leq 36$

5. $-2b > 0$ **6.** $6 - 6z < 0$

7. $3x + 4 \leq 12$ **8.** $2y - 5 < 9$

9. $-4 - p \geq 3$ **10.** $5 - 3r \leq -4$

11. $7m - 5 < 2m + 10$ **12.** $6x - 2 > 4x - 8$

13. $m - (4 + 2m) + 3 < 2m + 2$

14. $2p - (3 - p) \leq -7p - 2$

15. $-2(3y - 8) \geq 5(4y - 2)$

16. $5r - (r + 2) \geq 3(r - 1) + 5$

17. $3p - 1 < 6p + 2(p - 1)$

18. $x + 5(x + 1) > 4(2 - x) + x$

19. $-7 < y - 2 < 4$

20. $-3 < m + 6 < 2$

21. $8 \leq 3r + 1 \leq 13$ **22.** $-6 < 2p - 3 \leq 5$

23. $-4 \leq \frac{2k - 1}{3} \leq 2$ **24.** $-1 \leq \frac{5y + 2}{3} \leq 4$

25. $\frac{3}{5}(2p + 3) \geq \frac{1}{10}(5p + 1)$

26. $\frac{8}{3}(z - 4) \leq \frac{2}{9}(3z + 2)$

27. $42.75x > 7.460$ **28.** $15.79y < 6.054$

29. $8.04z - 9.72 < 1.72z - .25$

30. $3.25 + 5.08k > .76k + 6.28$

31. $-(1.42m + 7.63) + 3(3.7m - 1.12) \leq 4.81m - 8.55$

32. $3(8.14a - 6.32) - (4.31a - 4.84) > .34a + 9.49$

33. Natural Science Federal guidelines require drinking water to have fewer than .050 milligram per liter of lead. A test using 21 samples of water in a midwestern city found that the average amount of lead in the samples was .040 milligram per liter. All samples had lead content within 5% of the average. Did all the samples meet the federal requirement?

(a) Select a variable and write down what it represents.

(b) Write a three-part inequality to express the sample results.

(c) Answer the question.

34. Management The federal income tax for an income of \$24,651 to \$59,750 is 28% times (net income − 24,650) + \$3697.50.

(a) Choose two variables and state what they represent (see parts (b) and (c)).
(b) Write this income bracket as an inequality.
(c) Write the tax range in dollars for this income bracket as an inequality.

35. **Natural Science** Exposure to radon gas is a known lung cancer risk. According to the Environmental Protection Agency (EPA), the individual lifetime excess cancer risk R for radon exposure is between .0015 and .006, where $R = .01$ represents a 1% increase in risk of developing cancer.*
(a) Write the preceding information as an inequality.
(b) Determine the range of individual annual risk by dividing R by an average life expectancy of 75 years.

Solve each inequality. Graph each solution. (See Examples 6–8.)

36. $|p| > 7$
37. $|m| < 1$
38. $|r| \leq 4$
39. $|a| < -2$
40. $|b| > -5$
41. $|2x + 5| < 3$
42. $\left|x - \frac{1}{2}\right| < 2$
43. $|3z + 1| \geq 7$
44. $|8b + 5| \geq 7$
45. $\left|5x + \frac{1}{2}\right| - 2 < 5$
46. $\left|x + \frac{2}{3}\right| + 1 < 4$

47. **Physical Science** The temperatures on the surface of Mars in degrees Celsius approximately satisfy the inequality $|C + 84| \leq 56$. What range of temperatures corresponds to this inequality?

48. **Natural Science** Dr. Tydings has found that, over the years, 95% of the babies he has delivered have weighed y pounds, where $|y - 8.0| \leq 1.5$. What range of weights corresponds to this inequality?

49. **Physical Science** The industrial process that is used to convert methanol to gasoline is carried out at a temperature range of 680°F to 780°F. Using F as the variable, write an absolute value inequality that corresponds to this range.

50. **Physical Science** When a model kite was flown across the wind in tests to determine its limits of power extraction, it attained speeds of 98 to 148 feet per second in winds of 16 to 26 feet per second. Using x as the variable in each case, write absolute value inequalities that correspond to these ranges.

51. **Natural Science** Human beings emit carbon dioxide when they breathe. In one study, the emission rates of carbon dioxide by college students were measured both during lectures and exams. The average individual rate R_L (in grams per hour) during a lecture class satisfied the inequality $|R_L - 26.75| \leq 1.42$, whereas during an exam the rate R_E satisfied the inequality $|R_E - 38.75| \leq 2.17$.*
(a) Find the range of values for R_L and R_E.
(b) The class had 225 students. If T_L and T_E represent the total amounts of carbon dioxide (in grams) emitted during a one-hour lecture and one-hour exam respectively, write inequalities that describe the ranges for T_L and T_E.

52. **Social Science** When administering a standard intelligence test, we expect about 1/3 of the scores to be more than 12 units above 100 or more than 12 units below 100. Describe this situation by writing an absolute value inequality.

Management *Work the following problems. (See Example 4.)*

53. In 1993 Pacific Bell charged 15 cents for the first minute plus 14 cents for each additional minute (or part of a minute) for a dial-direct call from Sacramento to North Highland, California.† How many minutes could a person talk for no more than $2.00?

54. A student has a total of 970 points before the final exam in her algebra class. She must have 81% of the 1300 points possible in order to get a B. What is the lowest score she can earn on the 100-point final to get a B in the class?

55. Bill Bradkin went to a conference in Montreal, Canada for a week. He decided to rent a car and checked with two rental firms. Avery wanted $56 per day, with no mileage fee. Hart wanted $216 per week and $.28 per mile (or part of a mile). How many miles must Bradkin drive before the Avery car is the better deal?

56. After considering the situation in Exercise 55, Bradkin contacted Lowcost Rental Cars and was offered a car for $198 per week plus $.30 a mile (or part of a mile). With this offer, can he travel more miles for the same price as Avery charges? How many more or fewer miles?

Management *In Exercises 57–62, find all values of x where the following products will at least break even. (See Example 5.)*

57. The cost to produce x units of wire is $C = 50x + 5000$, while the revenue is $R = 60x$.

58. The cost to produce x units of squash is $C = 100x + 6000$, while the revenue is $R = 500x$.

59. $C = 85x + 900$; $R = 105x$

60. $C = 70x + 500$; $R = 60x$

61. $C = 1000x + 5000$; $R = 900x$

62. $C = 2500x + 10{,}000$; $R = 102{,}500x$

**Indoor-Air-Assessment: A Review of Indoor Air Quality Risk Characterization Studies,* Report No. EPA/600/8-90/044, Environmental Protection Agency, 1991.

*Wang, T.C., *ASHRAE Transactions* 81 (Part 1), 32 (1975).

†Pacific Bell White Pages, January 1996–January 1997.

Write each of the following statements using absolute value. (See Example 10.)

63. x is within 4 units of 2.

64. m is no more than 8 units from 9.

65. z is no less than 2 units from 12.

66. p is at least 5 units from 9.

67. If x is within .0004 unit of 2, then y is within .00001 unit of 7.

68. y is within .001 unit of 10 whenever x is within .02 unit of 5.

2.4 POLYNOMIAL AND RATIONAL INEQUALITIES

Polynomial and rational inequalities, such as

$$x^2 - x \leq 12, \quad x^3 - 5x^2 + x + 6 > 0, \quad \text{and} \quad \frac{2x - 1}{3x + 4} < 5,$$

may be solved by algebraic or graphical methods, both of which are discussed here.

GRAPHICAL METHODS The basic graphical technique, which can be used with any inequality, is illustrated in the following example.

EXAMPLE 1 Solve $x^3 - 5x^2 + x + 6 > 0$.

Begin by graphing $y = x^3 - 5x^2 + x + 6$ (Figure 2.24) and finding the x-intercepts of the graph. Zoom-in or a root finder shows that they are approximately $-.9254$, 1.4481, and 4.4774.

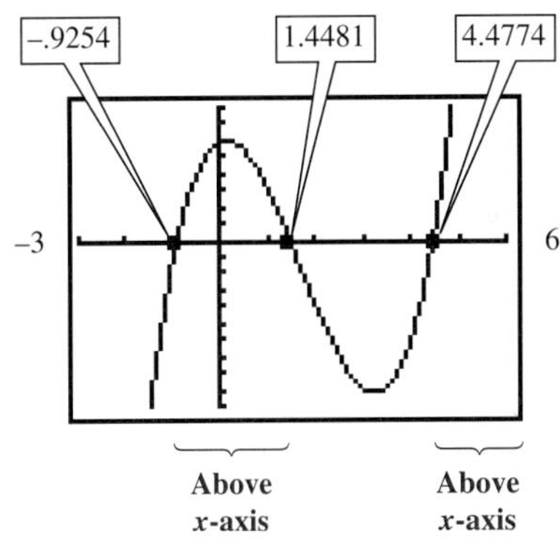

FIGURE 2.24

A typical point on the graph has coordinates $(x, x^3 - 5x^2 + x + 6)$. The number x is a solution of the inequality precisely when the second coordinate of this point is *positive,* that is, when this point lies *above* the x-axis. So to solve the inequality, we need only find the first coordinates of points on the graph that are above the x-axis. This information can be read from the graph in Figure 2.24 and its x-intercepts: The graph is above the x-axis when $-.9254 < x < 1.4481$ and also when $x > 4.4774$. Therefore the approximate solutions of the inequality are all numbers in the intervals

$$(-.9254, 1.4481) \quad \text{or} \quad (4.4774, \infty). \blacksquare$$

EXAMPLE 2 Solve $x^3 - 5x^2 + x + 6 < 0$.

Except for the direction of the inequality sign, this is the inequality of Example 1. A typical point on the graph of $y = x^3 - 5x^2 + x + 6$ in Figure 2.24 has

1 Use graphical methods to find approximate solutions of these inequalities.

(a) $x^2 - 6x + 2 > 0$

(b) $x^2 - 6x + 2 < 0$

Answers:

(a) All numbers in $(-\infty, .3542)$ or $(5.6458, \infty)$

(b) All numbers in $(.3542, 5.6458)$

coordinates $(x, x^3 - 5x^2 + x + 6)$. The number x is a solution of this inequality precisely when the second coordinate of this point is *negative,* that is, when this point lies *below* the x-axis. From Figure 2.24, we see that the solutions of the inequality are all numbers in the intervals

$$(-\infty, -.9254) \quad \text{or} \quad (1.4481, 4.4774). \quad ■ \quad \boxed{1}$$

Exact solutions of inequalities can sometimes be obtained by combining algebra with graphical techniques.

EXAMPLE 3 Solve the following inequalities.

(a) $x^3 \geq 4x$

Begin by rewriting the inequality as $x^3 - 4x \geq 0$ and graphing $y = x^3 - 4x$ (Figure 2.25). Since the inequality is ≥ 0, that is, positive or 0, the solutions are the first coordinates of points that lie *on* the x-axis or *above* the x-axis. In this case, however, there is no need to approximate the x-intercepts of the graph because they can easily be found by solving the equation.

$$x^3 - 4x = 0$$
$$x(x^2 - 4) = 0$$
$$x(x + 2)(x - 2) = 0$$
$$x = 0 \quad \text{or} \quad x + 2 = 0 \quad \text{or} \quad x - 2 = 0$$
$$x = 0 \qquad x = -2 \qquad x = 2$$

The graph is on or above the x-axis when $-2 \leq x \leq 0$ or when $x \geq 2$. So the solutions of the inequality are the numbers in the intervals $[-2, 0]$ or $[2, \infty)$.

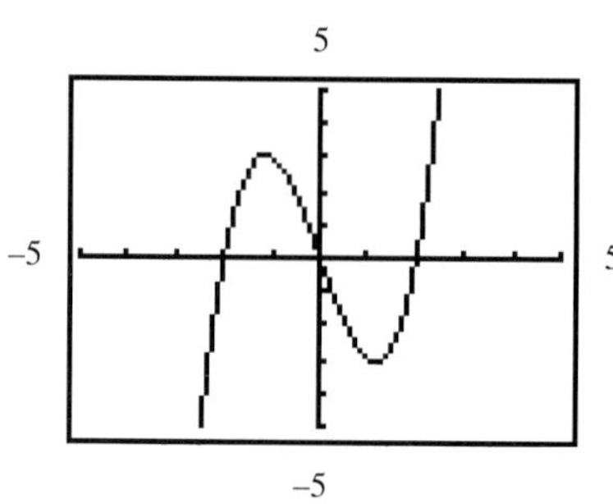

FIGURE 2.25

2 Use algebraic and graphical methods to find exact solutions of $x^3 - 2x^2 - 3x \geq 0$.

Answer:

All numbers in $[-1, 0]$ or $[3, \infty)$

(b) $x^3 \leq 4x$

This is equivalent to solving $x^3 - 4x \leq 0$, that is, finding the intervals where the graph of $y = x^3 - 4x$ is *on* or *below* the x-axis. The x-intercepts were found in part (a) and Figure 2.25 shows that the solutions of this inequality are the numbers in the intervals $(-\infty, -2]$ or $[0, 2]$. ■ $\boxed{2}$

EXAMPLE 4 Solve $(x + 4)(x^2 - 2x - 3) < 0$.

Find the x-intercepts of the graph $y = (x + 4)(x^2 - 2x - 3)$ by solving the equation

$$(x + 4)(x^2 - 2x - 3) = 0$$
$$(x + 4)(x + 1)(x - 3) = 0$$
$$x = -4 \quad \text{or} \quad x = -1 \quad \text{or} \quad x = 3.$$

The graph of y in Figure 2.26 is below the x-axis when $x < -4$ or $-1 < x < 3$. Therefore, the solutions of the inequality are the numbers in the intervals $(-\infty, -4)$ or $(-1, 3)$. ■

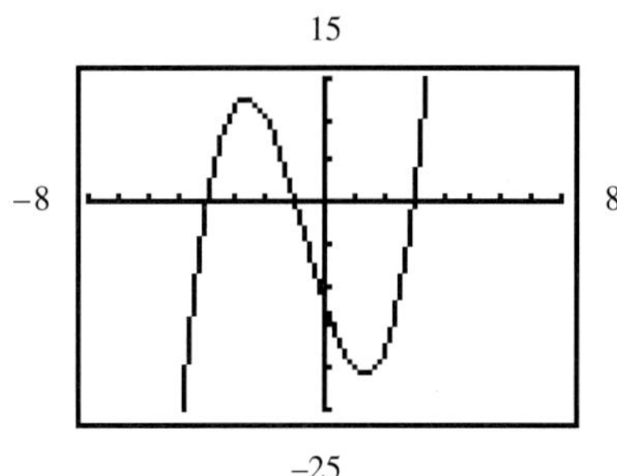

FIGURE 2.26

The graphical techniques in Examples 1–4 can be used to solve any inequality, with exact solutions whenever the x-intercepts can be determined precisely and approximate solutions otherwise.

ALGEBRAIC METHODS Polynomial inequalities that can be factored can be solved algebraically, as illustrated in the next example. Although this method is algebraic and requires no graphing, there are graphical reasons *why* it works, which are noted in parentheses in the example.

EXAMPLE 5 Solve the quadratic inequality $x^2 - x < 12$.

First rewrite the inequality so that one side is 0.

$$x^2 - x < 12$$

$$x^2 - x - 12 < 0 \qquad \text{Add } -12 \text{ to both sides.}$$

Now solve the *equation* $x^2 - x - 12 = 0$.

$$x^2 - x - 12 = 0$$

$$(x + 3)(x - 4) = 0$$

$$x = -3 \quad \text{or} \quad x = 4$$

These numbers (which are the x-intercepts of the graph of $y = x^2 - x - 12$) separate the x-axis into three intervals, as shown in Figure 2.27.

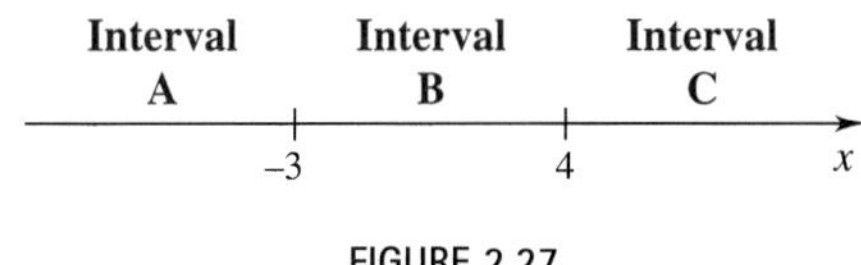

FIGURE 2.27

(As in the previous examples, over any one of these three intervals, the graph will be entirely above or entirely below the x-axis because it can cross the axis only at the intercepts -3 or 4.) In other words, on any one of these intervals, the quantity

3 Use the algebraic method of Example 5 to solve each inequality.

(a) $x^2 - x - 12 > 0$

(b) $2x^2 + 3x - 2 < 0$

Answers:

(a) All numbers in $(-\infty, -3)$ or $(4, \infty)$

(b) All numbers in $(-2, 1/2)$

$x^2 - x - 12$ will be always positive or always negative. We can determine its sign in each interval by choosing a number in each interval and evaluating it there.

Let $x = -5$ from interval A: $(-5)^2 - (-5) - 12 = 18 > 0$.

Let $x = 0$ from interval B: $(0)^2 - (0) - 12 = -12 < 0$.

Let $x = 5$ from interval C: $(5)^2 - (5) - 12 = 8 > 0$.

Therefore, $x^2 - x - 12$ is positive (graph above the x-axis) for *all* numbers in intervals A or C and negative (graph below the x-axis) for *all* numbers in interval B. Hence, the solutions of $x^2 - x - 12 < 0$ are all numbers in interval B, that is, in $(-3, 4)$. ■ 3

RATIONAL INEQUALITIES Inequalities involving quotients of polynomials are called **rational inequalities.** These inequalities can be solved in much the same way as polynomial inequalities.

EXAMPLE 6 Solve the rational inequality $\dfrac{5}{x+4} \geq 1$.

There are three ways to solve this inequality.

Graphical Rewrite the inequality as $\dfrac{5}{x+4} - 1 \geq 0$ and graph $y = \dfrac{5}{x+4} - 1$ (Figure 2.28). The solutions of the inequality are the x-coordinates of the points on the graph that lie on or above the x-axis. The graph is not defined at $x = -4$ (because the denominator is 0 there) and appears to be above the x-axis to the right of -4 until it crosses the axis near the origin. Use zoom-in or a root finder to determine that the x-intercept of the graph is at $x = 1$. Hence the graph is on or above the x-axis when $-4 < x \leq 1$. So the solutions of the inequality are all numbers in the interval $(-4, 1]$. Note that we do not use a square bracket to the left of -4, because $5/(x + 4)$ is not defined when $x = -4$.

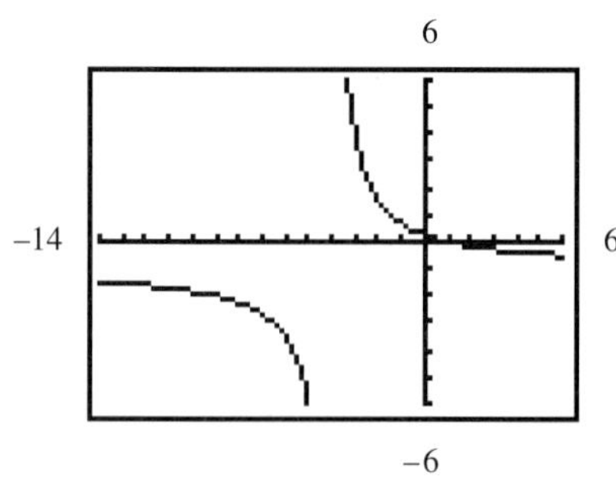

FIGURE 2.28

Algebraic Begin by putting all nonzero terms on the left side of the inequality and writing them as a single fraction.

$$\frac{5}{x+4} - 1 \geq 0$$

$$\frac{5}{x+4} - \frac{x+4}{x+4} \geq 0 \qquad \text{Get a common denominator.}$$

$$\frac{5-(x+4)}{x+4} \geq 0 \qquad \text{Subtract fractions.}$$

$$\frac{5-x-4}{x+4} \geq 0 \qquad \text{Distributive property}$$

$$\frac{1-x}{x+4} \geq 0$$

The quotient on the left can change sign only when the denominator is 0 or the numerator is 0, that is, when $x = -4$ or $x = 1$.* These numbers separate the x-axis into three intervals, as shown in Figure 2.29.

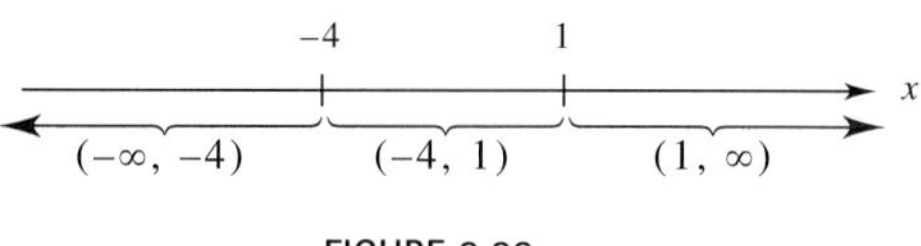

FIGURE 2.29

On each of these three intervals, $\dfrac{1-x}{x+4}$ is either always positive or always negative. Determine its sign in each interval by choosing a number in each interval and evaluating it there.

$$\text{Let } x = -5 \text{ in } (-\infty, -4): \quad \frac{1-(-5)}{-5+4} = \frac{6}{-1} = -6 < 0.$$

$$\text{Let } x = 0 \text{ in } (-4, 1): \quad \frac{1-0}{0+4} = \frac{1}{4} > 0.$$

$$\text{Let } x = 2 \text{ in } (1, \infty): \quad \frac{1-2}{2+4} = \frac{-1}{6} < 0.$$

These tests show that every number in $(-4, 1)$ satisfies the inequality. Since $x = 1$ is also a solution (why?), all solutions of the inequality are the numbers in $(-4, 1]$.

Graphical/Algebraic Proceed as in the algebraic method to write the left side of the inequality as a single fraction and the right side as 0.

$$\frac{1-x}{x+4} \geq 0$$

The graph of the left side will be the same as the graph in Figure 2.28 (if you have doubts, graph it yourself). However, when the inequality is written in this form, you can easily see that the left side is 0 when $x = 1$ (that is, that 1 is the x-intercept of the graph), so there is no need to find the intercept graphically. Once again, then, the solutions (numbers where the graph is above the x-axis) are all numbers in the interval $(-4, 1]$. ■

*Figure 2.28 illustrates this: The graph changes from above to below the x-axis or vice versa at the undefined point where $x = -4$ and at the x-intercept $x = 1$.

4 Solve each inequality.

(a) $\dfrac{3}{x-2} \geq 4$

(b) $\dfrac{p}{1-p} < 3$

(c) Why is 2 excluded from the solution in part (a)?

Answers:

(a) $(2, 11/4]$

(b) All numbers in $(-\infty, 3/4)$ or $(1, \infty)$

(c) When $x = 2$, the fraction is undefined.

CAUTION As suggested by Example 6, be very careful with the endpoints of the intervals in the solutions of rational inequalities. A number at which the inequality is undefined cannot be a solution. ◆ 4

TECHNOLOGY TIP The graph of $y = \dfrac{5}{x+4} - 1$ in Figure 2.28 is accurate, but in some viewing windows, this graph may contain an erroneous vertical line, as in Figure 2.30. In Figure 2.28 the calculator computed the value of y when $x = -4$, discovered that it was not defined, and plotted no point there. In Figure 2.30, however, it did not evaluate y at -4; it evaluated y just to the left of -4 and just to the right of -4, and erroneously connected the two points, thus producing the vertical line segment. On most calculators such erroneous lines can usually be avoided by choosing a viewing window that has the undefined number at the middle of the x-axis because y is always evaluated at the middle number. That's what was done in Figure 2.28, where -4 is midway between -14 and 6. ✔

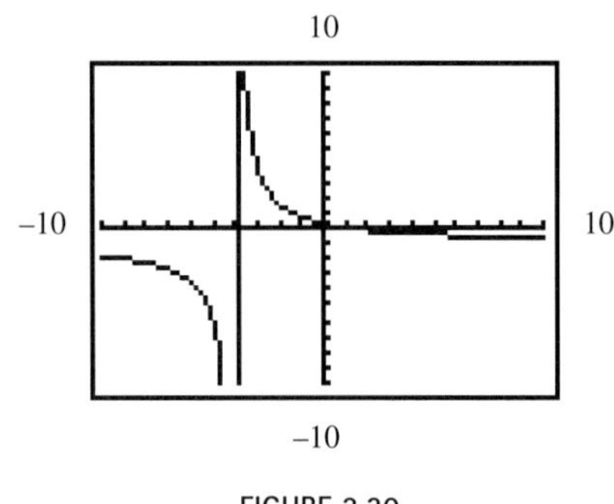

FIGURE 2.30

EXAMPLE 7 Solve $\dfrac{2x+1}{3x+4} < 5$.

Rewrite the inequality so that there is a single fraction on one side and 0 on the other.

$$\frac{2x-1}{3x+4} < 5$$

$$\frac{2x-1}{3x+4} - 5 < 0 \qquad \text{Get 0 on one side.}$$

$$\frac{2x-1-5(3x+4)}{3x+4} < 0 \qquad \text{Subtract.}$$

$$\frac{-13x-21}{3x+4} < 0 \qquad \text{Combine terms.}$$

Now determine the x-intercepts and undefined points of the graph of $y = \dfrac{-13x-21}{3x+4}$ by setting the numerator and denominator equal to 0 and solving the two equations.

***x*-intercept**	**Undefined Point**
$-13x - 21 = 0$	$3x + 4 = 0$
$x = -\dfrac{21}{13}$	$x = -\dfrac{4}{3}$

The graph of $y = \dfrac{-13x - 21}{3x + 4}$ in Figure 2.31 contains an erroneous vertical line, but we can still read the necessary information: The graph is below the x-axis to the left of the x-intercept $-21/13$ and to the right of the undefined point at $-4/3$. Therefore the solutions of the inequality are all numbers in the intervals $(-\infty, -21/13)$ or $(-4/3, \infty)$. ■

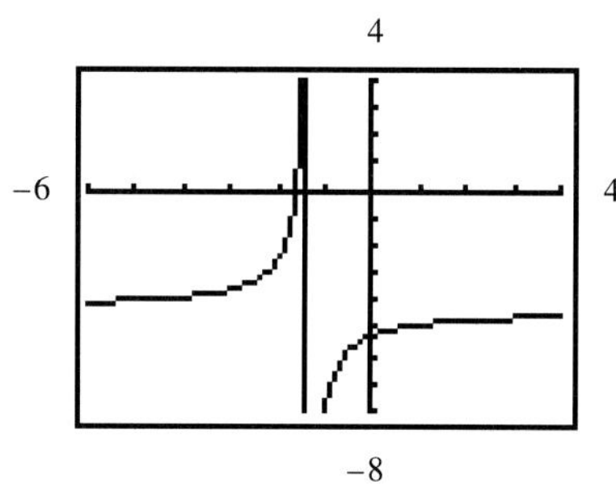

FIGURE 2.31

5 Solve each rational inequality.

(a) $\dfrac{3y - 2}{2y + 5} < 1$

(b) $\dfrac{3c - 4}{2 - c} \geq -5$

Answers:

(a) $(-5/2, 7)$

(b) All numbers in $(-\infty, 2)$ or $[3, \infty)$

CAUTION In problems like Examples 6 and 7, we cannot treat the inequality as if it were an equation and multiply both sides by the denominator to simplify it because we do not know whether the variable denominator is positive or negative. ◆ 5

EXAMPLE 8 A computer store has determined that the cost C of ordering and storing x printers is given by the equation

$$C = 2x + \frac{300{,}000}{x}.$$

If the delivery truck can bring at most 450 printers per order, how many printers should be ordered at a time to keep the cost below \$1600?

To find the values of x that make C less than 1600, we must solve the inequality.

$$2x + \frac{300{,}000}{x} < 1600$$

$$2x + \frac{300{,}000}{x} - 1600 < 0$$

The only solutions that make sense in this context are those between 0 and 450, so we choose the viewing window in Figure 2.32 on the next page and graph the left side of the last inequality. The solutions (corresponding to the points below the x-axis) are the numbers between the x-intercept and 450. Zoom-in or a root finder or good old fashioned algebra shows that the x-intercept is 300. Therefore, to keep costs under \$1600, x printers should be ordered each time, with $300 < x \leq 450$. ■

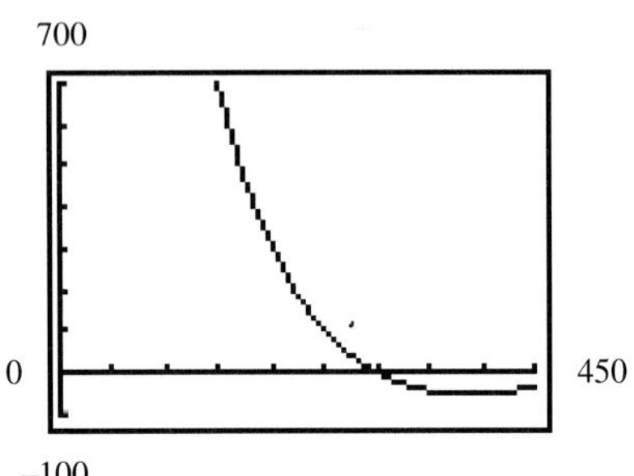

FIGURE 2.32

2.4 EXERCISES

Solve each inequality graphically, but use algebra to find exact solutions when possible. (See Examples 1–4.)

1. $6m^2 + m > 1$ **2.** $10r^2 + r \leq 2$

3. $2y^2 + 5y \leq 3$ **4.** $3a^2 + a > 10$

5. $x^2 \leq 25$ **6.** $y^2 \geq 4$

7. $3x^2 + 4x > 5$ **8.** $3x + 7 < 2x^2$

9. $.5x^2 - 1.2x < .1$ **10.** $3.1x^2 - 7.4x + 3.2 > 0$

11. $x^3 - 9x \geq 0$ **12.** $p^3 - 25p \leq 0$

13. $6k^3 - 5k^2 < 4k$ **14.** $2m^3 + 7m^2 > 4m$

15. $x^3 - 2x^2 - 5x + 7 \geq 2x + 1$

16. $x^4 - 6x^3 + 2x^2 > 5x - 2$

17. $2x^4 + 3x^3 < 2x^2 + 4x - 2$

18. $x^5 + 5x^4 > 4x^3 - 3x^2 - 2$

19. $3.02x^3 - 6.47x^2 + 2.4x > 6$

20. $x^4 + 10x^3 + 21x^2 + 8 > 40x + 88$

Solve each inequality algebraically. (See Example 5.)

21. $4m^2 + 7m - 2 \leq 0$ **22.** $6p^2 - 11p + 3 \geq 0$

23. $4x^2 + 3x - 1 > 0$ **24.** $3x^2 - 5x > 2$

25. $(x + 6)(x + 1)(x - 4) \geq 0$ **26.** $(2x + 5)(x^2 - 1) \leq 0$

27. A student solved the inequality $p^2 < 16$ by taking the square root of both sides to get $p < 4$. She wrote the solution as $(-\infty, 4)$. Is her solution correct?

In each of the following inequalities, the intervals on the number line are $(-\infty, 2)$, $(2, 5)$, and $(5, \infty)$. Without actually solving the inequality, state whether the numbers 2 and 5 will be included in or excluded from the solution of the inequality.

28. $(x - 5)(x - 2) \leq 0$ **29.** $\frac{x - 2}{x - 5} > 0$ **30.** $\frac{x - 5}{x - 2} \geq 0$

Solve each rational inequality. (See Examples 6 and 7.)

31. $\frac{a - 2}{a - 5} < -1$ **32.** $\frac{1}{3k - 5} < \frac{1}{3}$

33. $\frac{1}{p - 2} < \frac{1}{3}$ **34.** $\frac{2y + 3}{y - 5} \leq 1$

35. $\frac{a + 2}{3 + 2a} \leq 5$ **36.** $\frac{7}{k + 2} \geq \frac{1}{k + 2}$

37. $\frac{2x - 1}{x - 5} > 2x - 1$ **38.** $\frac{x + 3}{x - 5} < x + 3$

39. $\frac{x^2 - 4}{x} > 0$ **40.** $\frac{x^2 - x - 6}{x} < 0$

41. $\frac{x^2 + x - 2}{x^2 - 2x - 3} < 0$ **42.** $\frac{2x^2 + x - 1}{x^2 - 4x + 4} \leq 0$

Management *Solve each problem. (See Example 8.)*

43. An analyst has found that his company's profits, in hundreds of thousands of dollars, are given by $P = 3x^2 - 35x + 50$, where x is the amount, in hundreds of dollars, spent on advertising. For what values of x does the company make a profit?

44. The commodities market is very unstable; money can be made or lost quickly on investments in soybeans, wheat, and so on. Suppose that an investor kept track of her total profit, P, at time t, in months, after she began investing, and found that $P = 4t^2 - 29t + 30$. Find the time intervals where she has been ahead.

45. The manager of a large apartment complex has found that the profit is given by $P = -x^2 + 250x - 15{,}000$, where x is the number of apartments rented. For what values of x does the complex produce a profit?

Management *In recent years, many states have increased their maximum speed limit on rural highways to 75 miles per hour or more, which affects the costs of large trucking companies. The cost of shipping can be simply expressed as the cost G of gas plus the cost of paying the driver an hourly wage W. If D represents the distance of the trip and M_x represents the gas mileage at a speed of x miles per hour, then the cost C is given by the equation $C = G(D/M_x) + (D/x)W$. To compare the cost of driving at 55 mph to the cost of driving 75 mph, use the following inequality in Exercises 46–48.*

$$G\left(\frac{D}{M_{75}}\right) + \left(\frac{D}{75}\right)W < G\left(\frac{D}{M_{55}}\right) + \left(\frac{D}{55}\right)W$$

46. Suppose gas is \$1.30 per gallon and the gas mileage for a 400-mile trip at 55 mph is 25, while gas mileage for the same trip at 75 mph is 16. At what hourly wage would it be more cost effective for the driver's speed to be 75 mph?

47. If gas costs \$1.25 per gallon and gas mileage for a 200-mile trip at 55 mph is 27, while gas mileage for the same trip at 75 mph is 18, at what hourly wage would it be more cost effective for the driver's speed to be 75 mph?

48. If the driver is paid \$9 per hour in Exercise 47 and all other variables remain the same except the price of gasoline, determine the prices at which it is more cost effective for the driver to travel at 75 mph.

49. Physical Science The length of a rectangle is 6 inches longer than its width. If its area is at least 667 square inches, what are its possible widths?

50. Physical Science A farmer wants to use 200 feet of fencing to enclose a rectangular region with an area of less than 1000 square feet. What are the possible lengths for the shortest side of the rectangle?

CHAPTER 2 SUMMARY

Key Terms and Symbols

2.1 intersection method
intercept method
zoom-in
root finder

2.2 quadratic equation
real solution
number of solutions
zero-factor property
square-root property
completing the square
quadratic formula
discriminant

2.3 $<$ is less than
$\leq$ is less than or equal to
$>$ is greater than
$\geq$ is greater than or equal to
linear inequality
properties of inequality
absolute value inequality

2.4 polynomial inequality
graphical solution methods
algebraic solution methods
rational inequality

Key Concepts

Solving Quadratic Equations

Let a, b, and c be real numbers.

Factoring: If $ab = 0$, then $a = 0$ or $b = 0$ or both.

Square-Root Property: If $b > 0$, then the solutions of $x^2 = b$ are $\sqrt{b}$ and $-\sqrt{b}$.

Quadratic Formula: The solutions of $ax^2 + bx + c$ $(a \neq 0)$ are

$$x = \frac{-b \pm \sqrt{b^2 - 4ac}}{2a}.$$

Discriminant: There are two real solutions if $b^2 - 4ac > 0$, one real solution if $b^2 - 4ac = 0$, and no real solutions if $b^2 - 4ac < 0$.

Chapter 2 Review Exercises

Use the graphical intersection method to solve the equation. Find exact solutions when possible.

1. $|x^2 - 4x + 1| = 6$

2. $|x^2 + 6x - 2| = 14$

3. $x^3 - x + 3 = 2x - 3$

4. $x^3 - 2x^2 + 3 = -x + 6$

Use graphical methods to find an approximate solution of the equation that lies in the given interval.

5. $x^3 + 2x^2 - 11x = 6; [1, \infty)$

6. $x^3 + 2x^2 - 11x = 6; (-\infty, -1]$

7. $x^4 + x^3 - 10x^2 - 8x + 16 = 0; [2, \infty)$

8. $2x^4 + x^3 - 2x^2 + 6x + 2 = 0; (-\infty, -1)$

9. $x^3 + 2x^2 - 3x + 4 = 0; (-10, \infty)$

10. $3x^4 + x^3 - 6x^2 - 2x = 0; [1, \infty)$

11. $x^3 + 2x^2 - 3x - 5 = 0; [0, \infty)$

12. $1 + 2x - 3x^2 + 4x^3 - x^4 = 0; (0, 5)$

13. Management The average cost c (in dollars) of manufacturing x cases of pens is given by the equation

$$c = \frac{600x + 600}{x^2 + 1}.$$

How many cases should be produced to have an average cost of \$25?

14. Management The top and bottom margins of a rectangular political poster are 5 inches and each side margin is 3 inches. The printed material on the poster takes up a rectangular area of 600 square inches. If the entire poster has an area of 1040 square inches and is more than 19 inches wide, what are the dimensions of the printed material? Of the entire poster?

Determine the number of real solutions of the quadratic equation.

15. $x^2 - 6x = 4$

16. $-3x^2 + 5x + 2 = 0$

17. $4x^2 - 12x + 9 = 0$

18. $5x^2 + 2x + 1 = 0$

Find all real solutions of the equation.

19. $(b + 7)^2 = 5$

20. $(2p + 1)^2 = 7$

21. $2p^2 + 3p = 2$

22. $2y^2 = 15 + y$

23. $x^2 - 2x = 2$

24. $r^2 + 4r = 1$

25. $2m^2 - 12m = 11$

26. $9k^2 + 6k = 2$

27. $2a^2 + a - 15 = 0$

28. $12x^2 = 8x - 1$

29. $2q^2 - 11q = 21$

30. $3x^2 + 2x = 16$

31. $6k^4 + k^2 = 1$

32. $21p^4 = 2 + p^2$

33. $2x^4 = 7x^2 + 15$

34. $3m^4 + 20m^2 = 7$

35. $3 = \dfrac{13}{z} + \dfrac{10}{z^2}.$

36. $1 + \dfrac{13}{p} + \dfrac{40}{p^2} = 0$

37. $\dfrac{15}{x - 1} + \dfrac{18}{(x - 1)^2} = -2$

38. $\dfrac{5}{(2t + 1)^2} = 2 - \dfrac{9}{2t + 1}$

Solve each equation for the specified variable.

39. $p = \dfrac{E^2R}{(r + R)^2}$ for r

40. $p = \dfrac{E^2R}{(r + R)^2}$ for E

41. $K = s(s - a)$ for s

42. $kz^2 - hz - t = 0$ for z

43. Management A landscaper wants to put a cement walk of uniform width around a rectangular garden that measures 24 by 40 feet. She has enough cement to cover 660 square feet. To the nearest tenth of a foot, how wide should the walk be in order to use up all the cement?

44. Management A corner lot measures 25 by 40 yards. The city plans to take a strip of uniform width along the two sides bordering the streets in order to widen these roads. To the nearest tenth of a yard, how wide should the strip be if the remainder of the lot is to have an area of 844 square yards?

45. Management A recreation director wants to fence off a rectangular playground beside an apartment building. The building forms one boundary, so she needs to fence only the other three sides. The area of the playground is to be 11,250 square meters. She has enough material to build 325 meters of fence. Find the length and width of the playground.

46. Two cars leave an intersection at the same time. One travels north and the other heads west traveling 10 mph faster. After 1 hour they are 50 miles apart. What are their speeds?

Solve each inequality.

47. $-6x + 3 < 2x$

48. $12z \geq 5z - 7$

49. $2(3 - 2m) \geq 8m + 3$

50. $6p - 5 > -(2p + 3)$

51. $-3 \leq 4x - 1 \leq 7$

52. $0 \leq 3 - 2a \leq 15$

Solve each inequality.

53. $|b| \leq 8$

54. $|a| > 7$

55. $|2x - 7| \geq 3$

56. $|4m + 9| \leq 16$

57. $|5k + 2| - 3 \leq 4$

58. $|3z - 5| + 2 \geq 10$

59. Natural Science Dr. Ryan has found that, over the years, 95% of the babies he has delivered have weighed y pounds, where $|y - 7.5| \leq 2$. What range of weights corresponds to this inequality?

60. Natural Science The number of milligrams of a certain substance per liter in drinking water samples all tested within .05 of 40 milligrams per liter. Write this information as an inequality, using absolute value.

61. Management One automobile rental firm charges \$75 for a weekend rental (Friday afternoon through Monday morning) with unlimited mileage. A second firm charges \$50 plus 5 cents per mile. For what range of miles driven is the second firm cheaper?

62. **Management** A nearby business college charges an annual tuition of \$6400. Jack plans to save \$150 from each monthly paycheck, which he receives at the end of each month. What is the least number of months it will take him to save enough for one year's tuition?

Solve each inequality, finding exact solutions when possible and approximate ones otherwise.

63. $r^2 + r - 6 < 0$

64. $y^2 + 4y - 5 \geq 0$

65. $2z^2 + 7z \geq 15$

66. $3k^2 \leq k + 14$

67. $(x - 3)(x^2 + 7x + 10) \leq 0$

68. $(x + 4)(x^2 - 1) \geq 0$

69. $x^3 + 4x^2 - 6x > 0$

70. $2x^3 - 5x^2 - 4x < 0$

71. $x^4 - 2x^3 + 2x < 3$

72. $x^4 + x^3 - x^2 > 2$

73. $\dfrac{m + 2}{m} \leq 0$

74. $\dfrac{q - 4}{q + 3} > 0$

75. $\dfrac{5}{p + 1} > 2$

76. $\dfrac{6}{a - 2} \leq -3$

77. $\dfrac{2}{r + 5} \leq \dfrac{3}{r - 2}$

78. $\dfrac{1}{z - 1} > \dfrac{2}{z + 1}$

CASE 2

Depreciation

Straight-Line (Linear) Depreciation Because machines and equipment wear out or become obsolete over time, business firms must take into account the value that equipment has lost during each year of its useful life. This lost value, called **depreciation,** may be calculated in several ways.

Historically, to find the annual straight-line depreciation, the net cost was first found by deducting any estimated residual or **salvage value.** The depreciation was then divided by the number of years of useful life. For example, a \$10,000 item, with a salvage value of \$2000 and a useful life of 4 years would have an annual depreciation of

$$\frac{\$10{,}000 - \$2000}{4} = \$2000.$$

The \$8000 difference in the numerator is called the **depreciable basis.** However, from a practical viewpoint, it is often difficult to determine the salvage value when the item is new. Also, for many items, such as computers, there is no residual dollar value at the end of the useful life due to obsolescence.

The tendency now is to focus away from salvage value. In actual practice, it is customary to determine the annual straight-line depreciation by simply dividing the cost by the number of years of useful life.* In the example above, then, the annual straight-line depreciation would be

$$\frac{\$10{,}000}{4} = \$2500.$$

*Joel E. Halle, CPA.

In general, the annual straight-line depreciation is given by

$$D = \frac{1}{n}x.$$

Suppose a copier costs \$4500 and has a useful life of 3 years. Because the useful life is 3 years, 1/3 of the cost of the copier is depreciated each year.

$$D = \frac{1}{3}(\$4500) = \$1500.$$

Straight-line depreciation is the easiest method of depreciation to use, but it often does not accurately reflect the rate at which assets actually lose value. Some assets, such as new cars, lose more value annually at the beginning of their useful life than at the end. For this reason, two other methods of depreciation, the *sum-of-the-years'-digits* method and the *double declining balance* method (a nonlinear method) are permitted by the Internal Revenue Service.

Sum-of-the-Years'-Digits Depreciation With sum-of-the-years'-digits depreciation, a successively smaller fraction is applied each year to the cost of the asset. The denominator of the fraction, which remains constant, is the "sum of the years' digits" that gives the method its name. For example, if the asset has a 5-year life, the denominator is $5 + 4 + 3 + 2 + 1 = 15$. The numerator of the fraction, which changes each year, is the number of years of life that remain. For the first year the numerator is 5, for the second year it is 4, and so on. For example, for an asset with a cost of \$15,000 and a 5-year life, the depreciation in each year is shown in the following table.

Year	*Fraction*	*Depreciation*	*Accumulated Depreciation*
1	5/15	\$5000	\$ 5000
2	4/15	\$4000	\$ 9000
3	3/15	\$3000	\$12,000
4	2/15	\$2000	\$14,000
5	1/15	\$1000	\$15,000

Now, let us develop a model (or formula) for the depreciation D in year j of an asset with a cost of x dollars and a life of n years. The constant denominator will be the sum

$$n + (n - 1) + (n - 2) + \cdots + 2 + 1.$$

We can simplify this expression for the sum as follows.

$$\begin{aligned} S &= 1 + 2 + 3 + \cdots + (n-1) + n \\ S &= n + (n-1) + \cdots + 3 + 2 + 1 \\ \hline 2S &= (n+1) + (n+1) + \cdots + (n+1) \end{aligned}$$

There are n terms, so adding term by term gives n sums of $n + 1$.

$$2S = n(n+1)$$

$$S = \frac{n(n+1)}{2}$$

Since the numerator is the number of years of life that remain, in the first year (when $j = 1$), the numerator is n; when $j = 2$, the numerator is $n - 1$; when $j = 3$, the numerator is $n - 2$; and so on. In each case, the value of j plus the numerator equals $n + 1$, so the numerator can be written as $n + 1 - j$. Thus, the fraction for the year j is

$$\frac{n+1-j}{\frac{n(n+1)}{2}} = \frac{2(n+1-j)}{n(n+1)},$$

and the depreciation in year j (denoted D_j) is

$$D_j = \frac{2(n+1-j)}{n(n+1)}x.$$

Double Declining Balance Depreciation Another common method is double declining balance depreciation. In the first year, the depreciation is found by multiplying the cost x by $2/n$, double the amount of value lost each year. Thus, the depreciation in year 1 is

$$\frac{2}{n}x.$$

The depreciation in later years of an asset's life can be found by multiplying the depreciation from the previous year by $1 - 2/n$. For example, an asset costing \$5000 with a life of 5 years would lead to a depreciation of 5000(2/5), or \$2000, during the first year of its life. To find the depreciation in year 2, multiply the depreciation in year 1 by $1 - 2/5$, as follows.

$$\begin{aligned} \text{depreciation in year 2} &= (\text{depreciation in year 1}) \times \left(1 - \frac{2}{n}\right) \\ &= 2000\left(1 - \frac{2}{5}\right) \qquad \text{Let } n = 5. \\ &= 2000\left(\frac{3}{5}\right) = 1200, \end{aligned}$$

or \$1200. To find the depreciation in year 3, multiply this result by $1 - 2/5$, or $3/5$, to get \$720.

The depreciation by the double declining balance method in each of the first four years of the life of an asset is shown in the following table.

Year	1	2	3	4
Amount of depreciation	$\frac{2}{n} \cdot x$	$\frac{2}{n} \cdot x \cdot \left(1 - \frac{2}{n}\right)$	$\frac{2}{n} \cdot x \cdot \left(1 - \frac{2}{n}\right)^2$	$\frac{2}{n} \cdot x \cdot \left(1 - \frac{2}{n}\right)^3$

As the table suggests, each entry is found by multiplying the preceding entry by $1 - 2/n$. Based on this, the depreciation in year j, written D_j, is the amount

$$D_j = \frac{2}{n} \cdot x \cdot \left(1 - \frac{2}{n}\right)^{j-1}.$$

This result is a general formula for the entries in the table above. It is a mathematical model for double declining balance depreciation. If double declining balance depreciation were to be used for each year of the life of an asset, then the total depreciation would be less than the net cost of the asset. For this reason, it is permissible to switch to straight-line depreciation toward the end of the useful life of the asset.

In the example above, the total amount depreciated after 3 years is $2000 + 1200 + 720 = 3920$, leaving an undepreciated balance of $5000 - 3920 = 1080$. If we switch to straight-line depreciation after 3 years, we would depreciate $1080/2 = 540$, or \$540, in each of the last two years.

EXERCISES

1. A machine tool costs \$55,000 and has a useful life of 5 years. For each of the methods discussed, find the depreciation in each year. The total depreciation at the end of the 5 years should be \$55,000 for each method. For the double declining balance method, switch to straight-line depreciation in the last 2 years.
2. A new airplane costs \$600,000 and has a useful life of 10 years. Find the depreciation in years 1 and 4 by each of the three methods discussed.
3. Which method gives the largest deductions in the early years?

CHAPTER 3 Functions and Graphs

Functions are an extremely useful way of describing many real-world situations in which the value of one quantity varies with, depends on, or determines the value of another. In this chapter you will be introduced to functions, learn how to use functional notation, develop skill in constructing and interpreting the graphs of functions, and, finally, learn to apply this knowledge in a variety of situations.

3.1 FUNCTIONS

To understand the origin of the concept of function, we consider some "real life" situations in which one numerical quantity depends on, corresponds to, or determines another.

EXAMPLE 1 The amount of income tax you pay depends on the amount of your income. The way in which the income determines the tax is given by the tax law. ■

EXAMPLE 2 The weather bureau records the temperature over a 24-hour period in the form of a graph (see Figure 3.1). The graph shows the temperature that corresponds to each given time. ■

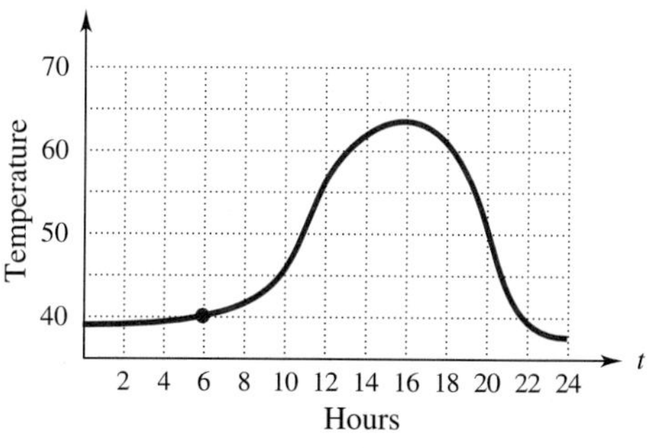

FIGURE 3.1

EXAMPLE 3 Suppose a rock is dropped straight down from a high point. From physics we know that the distance traveled by the rock in t seconds is $16t^2$ feet. So the distance depends on the time. ■

The first common feature shared by these examples is that each involves two sets of numbers, which we can think of as a set of inputs and a set of outputs.

	Set of Inputs	*Set of Outputs*
Example 1	All incomes	All tax amounts
Example 2	Hours since midnight	Temperatures during the day
Example 3	Seconds elapsed after dropping the rock	Distances rock travels

The second common feature is that in each example there is a definite *rule* by which each input determines an output. In Example 1 the rule is given by the tax law, which specifies how each income (input) determines a tax amount (output). Similarly, the rule is given by the time/temperature graph in Example 2 and by the formula (distance $= 16t^2$) in Example 3.

Each of these examples could be represented by an idealized calculator that has a single operation key and can receive or display any real number. When a number is entered (*input*), and the "rule key" is pressed, an answer is displayed (*output*). (See Figure 3.2.) The formal definition of function has these same common features (input/rule/output), with a slight change of terminology.

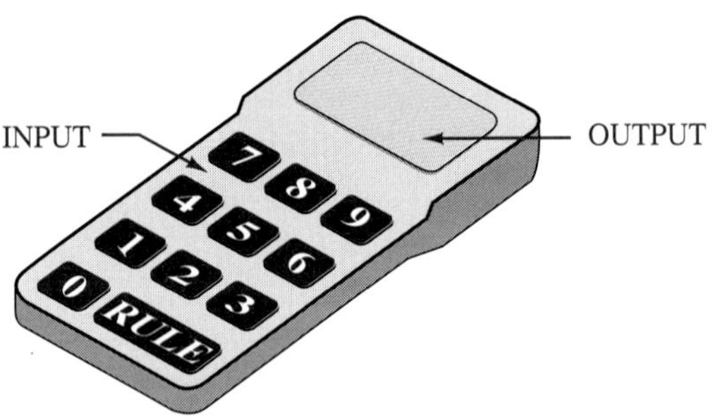

FIGURE 3.2

> A **function** consists of a set of input numbers called the **domain,** a set of output numbers called the **range,** and a rule by which each input (number in the domain) determines exactly one output (number in the range).

The domain in Example 1 consists of all possible income amounts; the rule is given by the tax law, and the range consists of all possible tax amounts. In Example 2 the domain is the set of hours in the day (that is, all real numbers from 0 to 24); the rule is given by the time/temperature graph, which shows the temperature at each time. The graph also shows that the range (the temperatures that actually occur during the day) includes all the numbers from 38 to 63.

In Example 2, for each time of day (number in the domain) there is one and only one temperature (number in the range). Notice, however, that it is possible to have the same temperature (number in the range) corresponding to two different times (numbers in the domain).

By the rule of a function, each number in the domain determines *one and only one* number in the range. But several different numbers in the domain may determine the same number in the range.

In other words, exactly one output is produced for each input, but different inputs may produce the same output.

EXAMPLE 4 Which of the following rules describe functions?

(a) Use the optical reader at the checkout counter of the supermarket to convert codes to prices.

For each code, the reader produces exactly one price, so this is a function.

(b) Enter a number in a calculator and press the x^2 key.

This is a function because the calculator produces just one number x^2 for each number x that is entered.

(c) Assign to each number x the number y given by this table.

x	1	1	2	2	3	3
y	3	−3	5	−5	8	−8

Since at least one x-value corresponds to more than one y-value, this table does not define a function.

(d) Assign to each number x the number y given by this equation: $y = 3x - 5$.

Because the equation determines a unique value of y for each value of x, it defines a function. ■ 1

1 Do the following define functions?

(a) The correspondence defined by the rule $y = x^2 + 5$

(b) The $1/x$ key on a calculator

(c) The correspondence between a computer, x, and several users of the computer, y

Answers:

(a) Yes

(b) Yes

(c) No

The preceding examples show that there are many ways to define a function. Almost all of the functions used in this book will be defined by equations, as in part (d) of Example 4, and *x will be assumed to represent the input variable.*

The domain and range may or may not be the same set. For instance, in the function given by the x^2 key on a calculator, the domain consists of all numbers (positive, negative, or 0) that can be entered in the calculator, but the range consists only of *nonnegative* numbers (since $x^2 \geq 0$ for every x). In the function given by the equation $y = 3x - 5$, both the domain and range are the set of all real numbers because of the following *agreement on domains.*

Unless otherwise stated, assume that the domain of any function defined by an equation is the largest set of real numbers that are meaningful replacements for the input variable.

For example, suppose

$$y = \frac{-4x}{2x - 3}.$$

Any real number can be used for x except $x = 3/2$, which makes the denominator equal 0. By the agreement on domains, the domain of this function is the set of all real numbers except 3/2.

2 Do the following define y as a function of x?

(a) $y = -6x + 1$

(b) $y = x^2$

(c) $x = y^2 - 1$

(d) $y < x + 2$

Answers:

(a) Yes

(b) Yes

(c) No

(d) No

EXAMPLE 5 Decide whether each of the following equations defines y as a function of x. Give the domain of any functions.

(a) $y = -4x + 11$

For a given value of x, calculating $-4x + 11$ produces exactly one value of y. (For example, if $x = -7$, then $y = -4(-7) + 11 = 39$.) Because one value of the input variable leads to exactly one value of the output variable, $y = -4x + 11$ defines a function. Since x may take on any real-number values, the domain is the set of all real numbers, written $(-\infty, \infty)$.

(b) $y^2 = x$

Suppose $x = 36$. Then $y^2 = x$ becomes $y^2 = 36$, from which $y = 6$ or $y = -6$. Since one value of x can lead to two values of y, $y^2 = x$ does not define y as a function of x. ■ **2**

3 Give the domain.

(a) $y = 3x + 1$

(b) $y = x^2$

(c) $y = \sqrt{-x}$

Answers:

(a) $(-\infty, \infty)$

(b) $(-\infty, \infty)$

(c) $(-\infty, 0]$

EXAMPLE 6 Find the domain of each of the following functions.

(a) $y = x^4$

Any number may be raised to the fourth power so the domain is $(-\infty, \infty)$.

(b) $y = \sqrt{6 - x}$

For y to be a real number, $6 - x$ must be nonnegative. This happens only when $6 - x \geq 0$, or $6 \geq x$, making the domain the interval $(-\infty, 6]$.

(c) $y = \dfrac{1}{x + 3}$

Because the denominator cannot be 0, $x \neq -3$ and the domain consists of all numbers in the intervals

$$(-\infty, -3) \quad \text{or} \quad (-3, \infty).$$ ■ **3**

CAUTION Notice the difference between the rule $y = \sqrt{6 - x}$ in Example 6(b) and the rule $y^2 = 6 - x$. For a particular x-value, say 2, the radical expression in the first rule represents a single positive number. The second rule, however, when $x = 2$, produces *two* numbers, $y = 2$ or $y = -2$. ◆

FUNCTIONAL NOTATION In actual practice, functions are seldom presented in the style of domain, rule, range, as they have been here. Functions are usually denoted by a letter (f is frequently used). If x is an input (number in the domain), then $f(x)$ denotes the output number that the function f produces from the input x. The symbol $f(x)$ is read "f of x." The rule is usually given by a formula, such as $f(x) = \sqrt{x^2 + 1}$. This formula can be thought of as a set of directions.

Name of function Input number

$$\underbrace{f(x)}_{\text{Output number}} = \underbrace{\sqrt{x^2 + 1}}$$

Output number Directions that tell you what to do with input x in order to produce the corresponding output $f(x)$; namely, "square it, add 1, and take the square root of the result."

For example, to find $f(3)$, (the output number produced by the input 3), simply replace x by 3 in the formula:

$$f(\mathbf{3}) = \sqrt{\mathbf{3}^2 + 1} = \sqrt{10}.$$

Similarly, replacing x by -5 and 0 shows that

$$f(-5) = \sqrt{(-5)^2 + 1} = \sqrt{26} \quad \text{and} \quad f(0) = \sqrt{0^2 + 1} = 1.$$

These directions can be applied to any quantities, such as $a + b$ or c^4 (where a, b, c are real numbers). Thus, to compute $f(a + b)$, the output corresponding to input $a + b$, we square the input [obtaining $(a + b)^2$], add 1 [obtaining $(a + b)^2 + 1$] and take the square root of the result:

$$f(\mathbf{a + b}) = \sqrt{(\mathbf{a + b})^2 + 1} = \sqrt{a^2 + 2ab + b^2 + 1}.$$

Similarly, the output $f(c^4)$ corresponding to the input c^4 is computed by squaring the input $[(c^4)^2]$, adding 1 $[(c^4)^2 + 1]$, and taking the square root of the result:

$$f(c^4) = \sqrt{(c^4)^2 + 1} = \sqrt{c^8 + 1}.$$

EXAMPLE 7 Let $g(x) = -x^2 + 4x - 5$. Find each of the following.

(a) $g(-2)$

Replace x with -2.

$$\begin{aligned} g(\mathbf{-2}) &= -(\mathbf{-2})^2 + 4(\mathbf{-2}) - 5 \\ &= -4 - 8 - 5 \\ &= -17 \end{aligned}$$

(b) $g(x + h)$

Replace x by the quantity $x + h$ in the rule of g.

$$\begin{aligned} g(\mathbf{x + h}) &= -(\mathbf{x + h})^2 + 4(\mathbf{x + h}) - 5 \\ &= -(x^2 + 2xh + h^2) + (4x + 4h) - 5 \\ &= -x^2 - 2xh - h^2 + 4x + 4h - 5 \end{aligned}$$

(c) $g(x + h) - g(x)$

Use the result from part (b) and the rule for $g(x)$.

$$\begin{aligned} g(x + h) - g(x) &= (-x^2 - 2xh - h^2 + 4x + 4h - 5) - (-x^2 + 4x - 5) \\ &= -2xh - h^2 + 4h \end{aligned}$$

4 Let $f(x) = 5x^2 - 2x + 1$. Find the following.

(a) $f(1)$

(b) $f(3)$

(c) $f(1 + 3)$

(d) $f(1) + f(3)$

(e) $f(m)$

(f) $f(x + h) - f(x)$

Answers:

(a) 4

(b) 40

(c) 73

(d) 44

(e) $5m^2 - 2m + 1$

(f) $10xh + 5h^2 - 2h$

(d) $\dfrac{g(x + h) - g(x)}{h}$

The numerator was found in part (c). Divide it by h as follows.

$$\frac{g(x + h) - g(x)}{h} = \frac{-2xh - h^2 + 4h}{h}$$
$$= \frac{h(-2x - h + 4)}{h}$$
$$= -2x - h + 4 \quad \blacksquare$$

The quotient found in Example 7(d)

$$\frac{g(x + h) - g(x)}{h}$$

is important in calculus, and we will see it again in Chapter 12. 4

CAUTION Functional notation is *not* the same as ordinary algebraic notation. You cannot simplify an expression such as $f(x + h)$ by writing $f(x) + f(h)$. To see why, consider the answers to Problems 4(c) and (d) at the side, which show that

$$f(1 + 3) \neq f(1) + f(3). \blacklozenge$$

EVALUATING FUNCTIONS WITH A CALCULATOR To illustrate the possibilities, several ways of evaluating the function $f(x) = 1.2x^2 + 5.6x - 6$ are described in the following paragraphs.

Direct Computation On all calculators, you can find $f(4)$ by keying in $1.2(4)^2 + 5.6(4) - 6$ ENTER. To find $f(5)$, you need not key in everything again. Use the instant replay feature: press 2nd ENTER or "left arrow" or "up arrow" COPY, depending on the calculator. Your screen will display the previous calculation (without the answer). Just change each 4 to a 5 (using the left/right arrow or delete or insert key as needed) and press ENTER.

X-memory The following method works on the majority of calculators. Enter the function f in the function memory as $y_1 = 1.2x^2 + 5.6x - 6$ and return to the home screen (on some calculators, you use f_1 in place of y_1). To evaluate $f(4)$, store the number 4 in memory X, then key in y_1 ENTER. (On some calculators you type in $y1$, but on others you must get this symbol from the Y-VARS menu.)

Functional Notation Many calculators allow you to use functional notation. Enter the function f in the function memory as $y_1 = 1.2x^2 + 5.6x - 6$ and return to the home screen. Now key in $y_1(4)$. When you press ENTER, the value of the function at 4 is displayed, and similarly for other values (Figure 3.3).

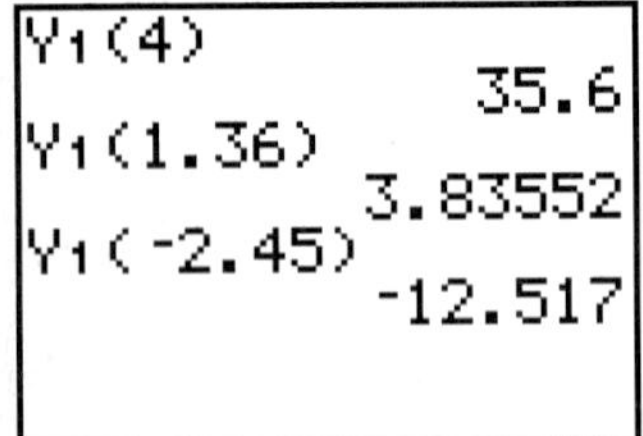

FIGURE 3.3

CAUTION The preceding method does not work on some calculators. These calculators interpret $y_1(4)$ to mean $y_1 \cdot 4$. They evaluate y_1 at whatever number happens to be stored in the X-memory and multiply the result by 4. You can check your calculator by computing $f(4)$, $f(1.36)$, and $f(-2.45)$ and comparing the results with Figure 3.3. Some calculators on which this method fails do have an [EVAL] key that can be used instead to evaluate functions. ◆

Table Most calculators have a built-in table feature, which displays a table of values for the function, as in Figure 3.4. (Table programs for some other calculators are in the Program Appendix.) Usually you can "scroll" through the table by using the up/down arrow keys. You can also change the increment (the amount by which the x-values change in successive entries). In Figure 3.4, for example, the increment is 1 and in Figure 3.5 it is .2. The syntax using tables varies from calculator to calculator, so check your instruction manual. Note that table entries in Figures 3.4 and 3.5 are sometimes rounded off, but that the full value of the shaded number is displayed at the bottom; the shaded rectangle can be moved with the arrow keys.

X	Y1
-2	-12.4
-1	[illegible]
0	-6
1	.8
2	10
3	21.6
4	35.6

Y1=-10.4

FIGURE 3.4

X	Y1
-2.6	-12.45
-2.4	-12.53
-2.2	-12.51
-2	-12.4
-1.8	-12.19
-1.6	[illegible]
-1.4	-11.49

Y1=-11.888

FIGURE 3.5

[5] A developer estimates that the total cost of building x large apartment complexes in a year is approximated by

$$A(x) = x^2 + 80x + 60,$$

where $A(x)$ represents the cost in hundred thousands of dollars. Find the cost of building

(a) 4 complexes;

(b) 10 complexes.

Answers:

(a) \$39,600,000

(b) \$96,000,000

EXAMPLE 8 Suppose the projected sales (in thousands of dollars) of a small company over the next ten years are approximated by the function

$$S(x) = .08x^4 - .04x^3 + x^2 + 9x + 54.$$

(a) What are the projected sales this year?

The current year corresponds to $x = 0$ and the sales this year are given by $S(0)$. Substituting 0 for x in the rule of S, we see that $S(0) = 54$. So the projected sales are \$54,000.

(b) What will sales be in three years?

The sales three years from now are given by $S(3)$, which can be computed by hand or with a calculator:

$$\begin{aligned} S(x) &= .08x^4 - .04x^3 + x^2 + 9x + 54 \\ S(3) &= .08(3)^4 - .04(3)^3 + 3^2 + 9(3) + 54 \qquad \text{Let } x = 3. \\ &= 95.4, \end{aligned}$$

which means that sales are projected to be \$95,400.

(c) What are the sales projections for years four through ten?

Using the table feature on a calculator, we obtain Figure 3.6, which shows that sales are projected to rise from \$123,920 in year four to \$1,004,000 in year ten. ■ [5]

X	Y1
4	123.92
5	169
6	239.04
7	344.36
8	497.2
9	711.72
10	1004

X=4

FIGURE 3.6

3.1 EXERCISES

Which of the following rules define y as a function of x? (See Examples 1–5.)

1.

x	3	2	1	0	−1	−2	−3
y	9	4	1	0	1	4	9

2.

x	9	4	1	0	1	4	9
y	3	2	1	0	−1	−2	−3

3. $y = x^3$ **4.** $y = \sqrt{x - 1}$

5. $x = |y + 2|$ **6.** $x = y^2 + 3$

7. $y = \dfrac{-1}{x - 1}$ **8.** $y = \dfrac{4}{2x + 3}$

State the domain of each function. (See Examples 5 and 6.)

9. $f(x) = 4x - 1$

10. $f(x) = 2x + 7$

11. $f(x) = x^4 - 1$

12. $f(x) = (2x + 5)^2$

13. $f(x) = \sqrt{-x + 3}$

14. $f(x) = \sqrt{4 - x}$

15. $f(x) = \dfrac{1}{x - 1}$

16. $f(x) = \dfrac{1}{x - 3}$

17. $f(x) = |5 - 4x|$

18. $f(x) = |-x - 6|$

For each of the following functions, find (a) $f(4)$, (b) $f(-3)$, (c) $f(2.7)$, *and* (d) $f(-4.9)$.

19. $f(x) = 6$

20. $f(x) = 0$

21. $f(x) = 2x^2 + 4x$

22. $f(x) = x^2 - 2x$

23. $f(x) = \sqrt{x + 3}$

24. $f(x) = \sqrt{5 - x}$

25. $f(x) = x^3 - 6.2x^2 + 4.5x - 1$

26. $f(x) = x^4 + 5.5x^2 - .3x$

27. $f(x) = |x^2 - 6x - 4|$

28. $f(x) = |x^3 - x^2 + x - 1|$

29. $f(x) = \dfrac{\sqrt{x - 1}}{x^2 - 1}$

30. $f(x) = \sqrt{-x} + \dfrac{2}{x + 1}$

If your calculator has table making ability, display a table showing the (approximate) values of the given function at 3.5, 3.9, 4.3, 4.7, 5.1, and 5.5. (See Example 8.)

31. $g(x) = 3x^4 - x^3 + 2x$ **32.** $f(x) = \sqrt{x^2 - 2.4x + 8}$

For each of the following functions, find (a) $f(p)$, (b) $f(-r)$, *and* (c) $f(m + 3)$. *(See Example 7.)*

33. $f(x) = 5 - x$

34. $f(x) = 3x + 7$

35. $f(x) = \sqrt{4 - x}$

36. $f(x) = \sqrt{-2x}$

37. $f(x) = x^3 + 1$

38. $f(x) = 2 - x^3$

39. $f(x) = \dfrac{3}{x - 1}$

40. $f(x) = \dfrac{-1}{2 + x}$

For each of the following find

$$\frac{f(x + h) - f(x)}{h}.$$

(See Example 7.)

41. $f(x) = 2x - 4$ **42.** $f(x) = 2 - 3x$

43. $f(x) = x^2 + 1$ **44.** $f(x) = x^2 - x$

Work the following problems. (See Example 8.)

45. Natural Science The table contains incidence ratios by age for death from coronary heart disease (CHD) and lung cancer (LC) when comparing smokers (21–39 cigarettes per day) to nonsmokers.*

Age	*CHD*	*LC*
55–64	1.9	10
65–74	1.7	9

The incidence ratio of 10 means that smokers are 10 times more likely than nonsmokers to die of lung cancer between the ages of 55 and 64. If the incidence ratio is x, then the percentage P (expressed as a decimal) of deaths caused by smoking is given by the function $P(x) = \dfrac{x - 1}{x}$.

(a) What is the percentage of lung cancer deaths that can be attributed to smoking between the ages of 65 and 74?

(b) What is the percentage of coronary heart disease deaths that can be attributed to smoking between the ages of 55 and 64?

*Walker, A., *Observations and Inference: An Introduction to the Methods of Epidemiology*, Newton Lower Falls, MA: Epidemiology Resources, Inc., 1991.

46. Management The number of fliers on commuter airlines (10- to 30-seat planes) was 1.4 million in 1975 and 3.1 million in 1994. It is estimated that there will be 9.3 million fliers in the year 2006.* Here are three possible functions that model this data (where $x = 0$ corresponds to 1975 and $f(x)$ is in millions):

$$f(x) = .24x + 1.4,$$
$$g(x) = .0138x^2 - .172x + 1.4,$$
$$h(x) = .0125x^2 - .193x + 1.4.$$

Make a table or otherwise evaluate each function at the three values of x corresponding to 1975, 1994, and 2006. Use this information to decide which of the three functions best approximates the given data.

47. Social Science The table lists the number of Americans (in thousands) that are or are expected to be over 100 years old in selected years.†

Year	*Number*
1994	50
1996	56
1998	65
2000	75
2002	94
2004	110

Here are three possible functions that model this data (where $x = 0$ corresponds to 1994):

$$f(x) = 6.057x + 44.714,$$
$$g(x) = -.06x^3 + .506x^2 + 1.659x + 50.238,$$
$$h(x) = .4018x^2 + 2.039x + 50.017.$$

(a) Determine which of the three functions best approximates the given data by making a table or otherwise evaluating each function at the six values of x corresponding to the years shown in the table.

(b) Use your answer in part (a) to predict the number of Americans that will be over 100 years old in the year 2008.

*Federal Aviation Administration (in *USA Today,* March 27, 1995).

†U.S. Census Bureau.

48. Management The table shows the total annual amount (in millions of dollars) of government guaranteed student loans from 1986 to 1994.*

Year	*Amount*
1986	8.6
1987	9.8
1988	11.8
1989	12.5
1990	12.3
1991	13.5
1992	14.7
1993	16.5
1994	18.2

Which of the following functions best approximates this data?

$$f(x) = 1.088(x - 1986) + 8.6,$$
$$g(x) = .4(x - 1986)^2 + 8.6,$$
$$h(x) = 1.455\sqrt{x - 1986} + 8.6.$$

49. Physical Science The distance from Chicago to Seattle is approximately 2000 miles. A plane flying directly to Seattle passes over Chicago at noon. If the plane travels at 475 mph, find the rule of the function $f(t)$ that gives the distance of the plane from Seattle at time t hours (with $t = 0$ corresponding to noon).

50. Management A pretzel factory has daily fixed costs of \$1800. In addition, it costs 50 cents to produce each bag of pretzels. A bag of pretzels sells for \$1.20.

(a) Find the rule of the cost function $c(x)$ that gives the total daily cost of producing x bags of pretzels.

(b) Find the rule of the revenue function $r(x)$ that gives the daily revenue from selling x bags of pretzels.

(c) Find the rule of the profit function $p(x)$ that gives the daily profit from x bags of pretzels.

**USA Today.*

3.2 GRAPHS OF FUNCTIONS

The **graph** of a function $f(x)$ is defined to be the graph of the *equation* $y = f(x)$. For example, the graph of $f(x) = x^3 + x + 5$ is the graph of the equation $y = x^3 + x + 5$. Thus, the graph consists of all points in the coordinate plane whose coordinates are of the form $(x, x^3 + x + 5)$, that is, all points $(x, f(x))$. The same thing is true in the general case: Each point on the graph of a function f is an ordered pair whose first coordinate is an input number from the domain of f and whose second coordinate is the corresponding output number.

Many functions can be quickly and accurately graphed on a calculator. However, there is more to graphing functions than simply plotting points and connecting them, which is essentially all that a calculator does. To deal effectively with functions, you must use algebra and other mathematical information in order to select appropriate viewing windows and correctly interpret misleading screen images.

EXAMPLE 1 Graph $g(x) = \sqrt{4x - 8} + 10$.

If you graph this function in the standard viewing window, you get a blank screen (try it). Algebra can help to find a useful window. The rule of the function is defined only when the quantity under the radical is nonnegative, that is, when

$$\begin{aligned} 4x - 8 &\geq 0 \\ 4x &\geq 8 \\ x &\geq 2. \end{aligned}$$

Since all square roots are nonnegative, the value of $g(x)$ is always greater than or equal to 10. Therefore a window that shows a tall enough portion of the first quadrant will be suitable, as in Figure 3.7. ■

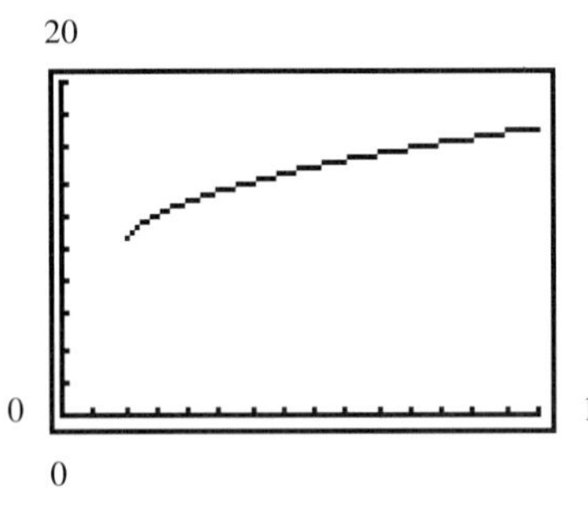

FIGURE 3.7

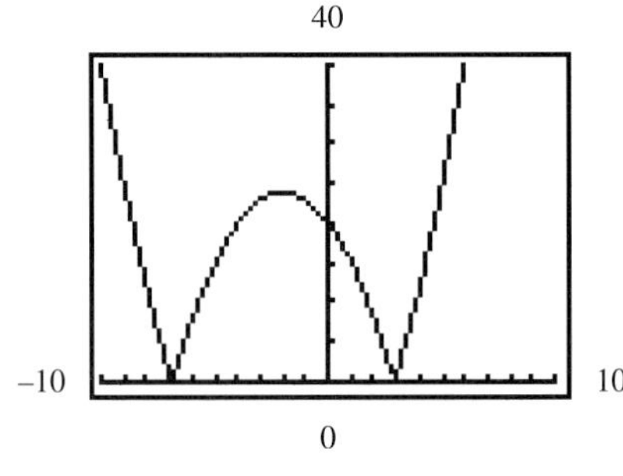

FIGURE 3.8

1 Find a viewing window that appears to show a complete graph of $g(x) = \sqrt{-x - 10}$.

Answer:
Any window that shows the part of the second quadrant to the left of $x = -10$, such as $-30 \leq x \leq 0$ and $0 \leq y \leq 10$.

EXAMPLE 2 Graph $g(x) = |x^2 + 4x - 20|$.

Since $g(x)$ is defined for every real number x, we should use a window that includes both positive and negative values of x. A good place to start might be $-10 \leq x \leq 10$. The absolute value of *any* quantity is nonnegative, so the graph lies entirely on or above the x-axis. Hence we should choose a window with $y \geq 0$. When $x = 0$, then $g(0) = 20$, so the graph crosses the y-axis at 20 and our window should show this. Based on these facts, we try the window in Figure 3.8, which does produce an accurate graph. ■ 1

PIECEWISE LINEAR FUNCTIONS We now consider functions whose graphs consist of straight line segments. Such functions are called **piecewise linear functions** and are typically defined with different equations for different parts of the domain.

EXAMPLE 3 Graph the following function by hand and by using a calculator.

$$f(x) = \begin{cases} x + 1 & \text{if } x \leq 2 \\ -2x + 7 & \text{if } x > 2 \end{cases}$$

When $x \le 2$, the graph consists of the part of the line $y = x + 1$ that lies to the left of $x = 2$. When $x > 2$, the graph consists of the part of the line $y = -2x + 7$ that lies to the right of $x = 2$. These line segments can be graphed by plotting the points determined by the following tables.

$x \le 2$

x	-2	0	2
$y = x + 1$	-1	1	3

$x > 2$

x	2	3	4
$y = -2x + 7$	3	1	-1

Note that even though 2 is not in the interval $x > 2$, we found the ordered pair for that endpoint because the graph will extend right up to that point. Because this endpoint (2, 3) agrees with the endpoint for the interval $x \le 2$, the two parts of the graph are joined at that point as shown in Figure 3.9.

In order to obtain this graph on a calculator, as in Figure 3.10, you must use special syntax. On TI and HP-38 calculators, graph this equation:

$$y = (x + 1)(x \le 2) + (-2x + 7)(x > 2),$$

using the symbols $\le$ and $>$ from the TEST (or CHAR) menu. Other calculators use a different syntax. Check your instruction manual. ■

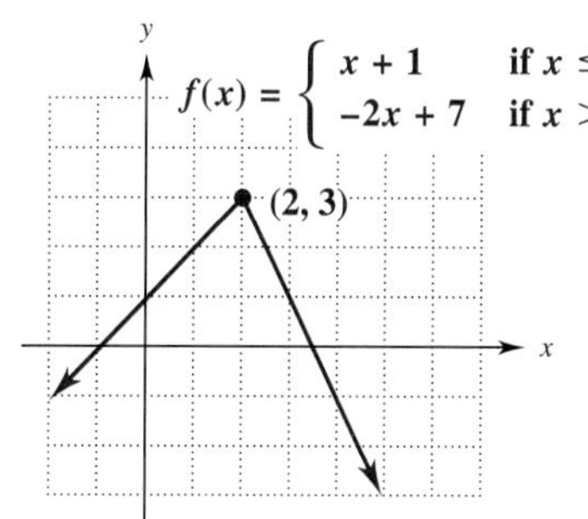

FIGURE 3.9

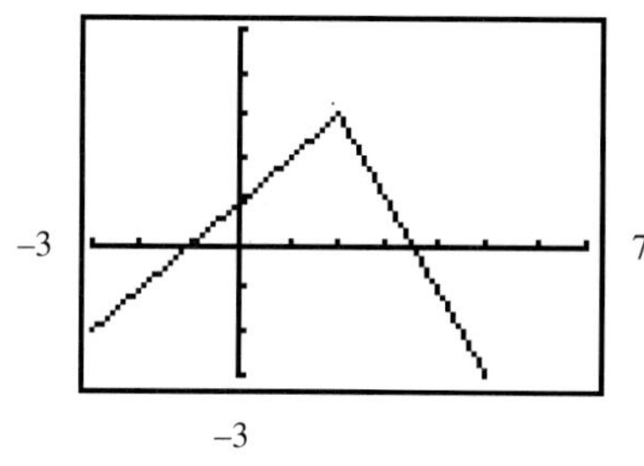

FIGURE 3.10

2 Graph each function.

(a) $f(x) = 2 - |x|$

(b) $f(x) = |5x - 7|$

Answers:

(a)

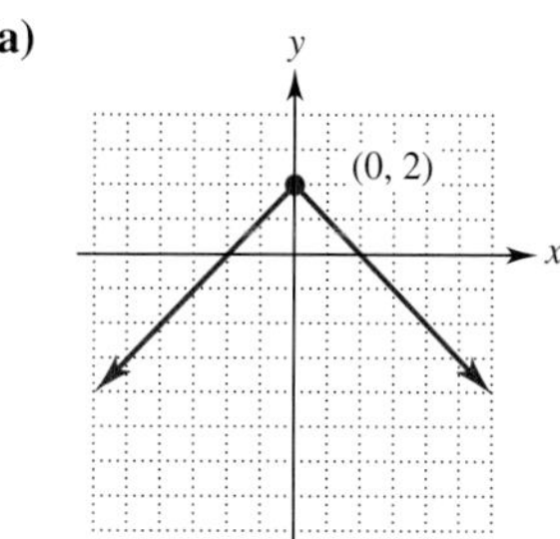

(b)

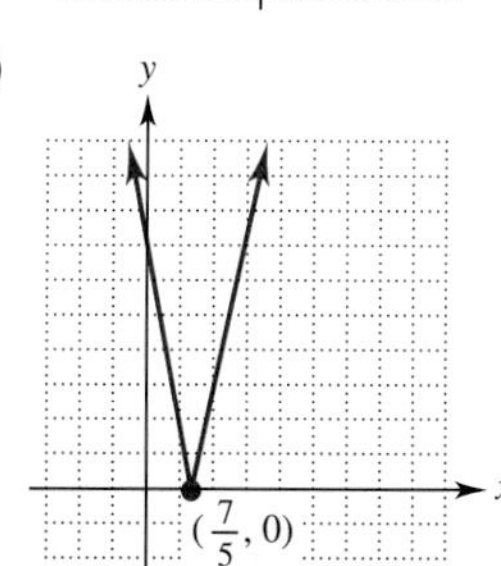

CAUTION In Example 3, notice that we did not graph the entire lines but only those portions with domain as given. Graphs of these functions should *not* be two intersecting lines. ◆

EXAMPLE 4 Graph the **absolute value function,** whose rule is $f(x) = |x|$.

The function f is a piecewise linear function because from the definition of $|x|$,

$$f(x) = \begin{cases} x & \text{if } x \ge 0 \\ -x & \text{if } x < 0. \end{cases}$$

When graphing by hand, use the technique in Example 3. On a calculator, absolute value is denoted by ABS (if it's not on the keyboard, look in the MATH menu or its NUM submenu). You can obtain the graph in Figure 3.11 on the next page by graphing the equation $y = \text{abs}(x)$. ■ **2**

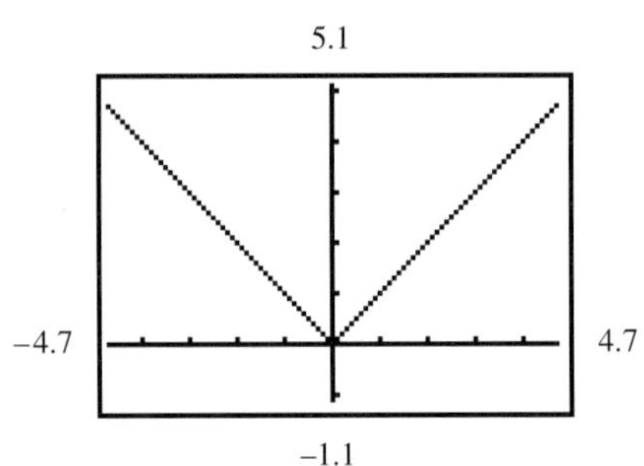

FIGURE 3.11

EXAMPLE 5 Graph the function

$$f(x) = \begin{cases} x - 2 & \text{if } x \le 3 \\ -x + 8 & \text{if } x > 3. \end{cases}$$

The ordered pairs $(-2, -4)$, $(0, -2)$, and $(3, 1)$ satisfy $y = x - 2$ and the pairs $(4, 4)$ and $(6, 2)$ satisfy $y = -x + 8$. Use them to graph the two straight line segments that make up the graph of the function. The point $(3, 5)$, where the right half of the graph begins, is an endpoint, but is *not* part of the graph, as indicated by the open circle in Figure 3.12. If you use the standard syntax to enter this function on a calculator (as in Example 3), the resulting graph usually contains an erroneous vertical line segment, as in Figure 3.13. This is because the calculator mistakenly connects all the points it plots instead of leaving a gap at $x = 3$. With most calculators, you can avoid this problem by graphing two separate equations on the same screen. On TI or HP calculators, graph:

$$y_1 = (x - 2)/(x \le 3) \quad \text{and} \quad y_2 = (-x + 8)/(x > 3).$$

The syntax varies for other calculators, but the same idea should work. However, no calculator indicates which endpoints are included and which are excluded. ■ 3

3 Graph $f(x)$, where

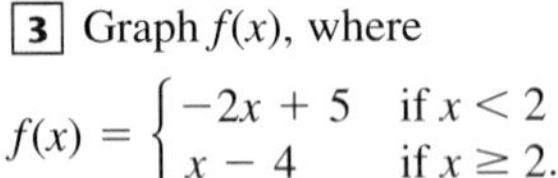

$$f(x) = \begin{cases} -2x + 5 & \text{if } x < 2 \\ x - 4 & \text{if } x \ge 2. \end{cases}$$

Answer:

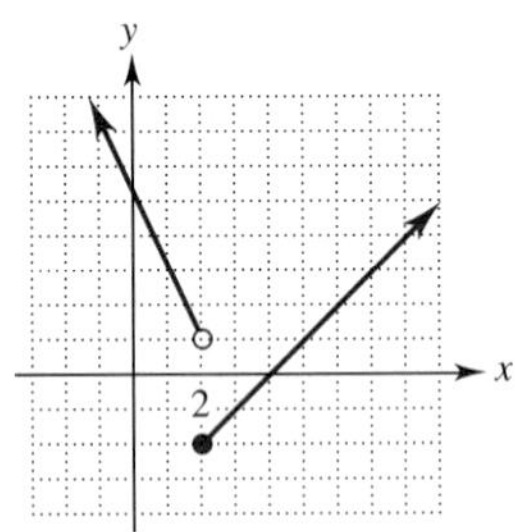

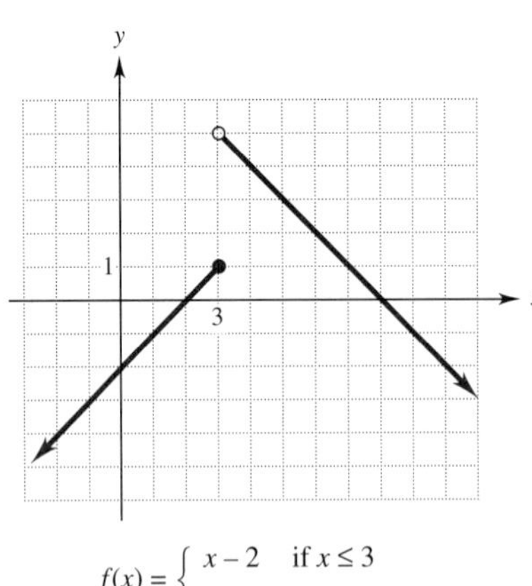

FIGURE 3.12

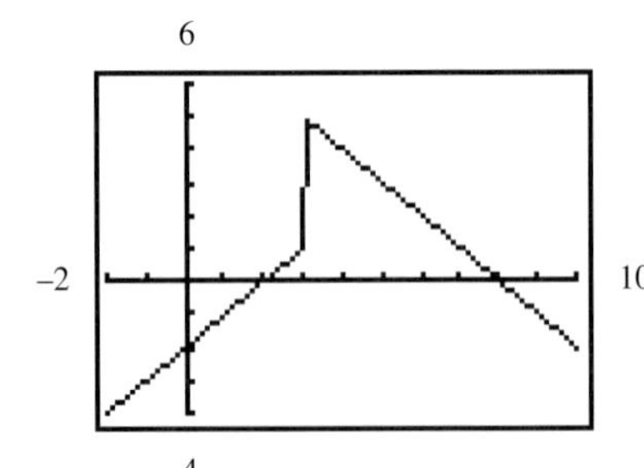

FIGURE 3.13

Graphs used in business and economics are often graphs of piecewise linear functions. It is just as important to know how to *read* such graphs as it is to construct them.

EXAMPLE 6 The graph in Figure 3.14 shows the per capita personal income in the greater Sacramento area from 1980 to 1992. What does it say about the rate of income growth?

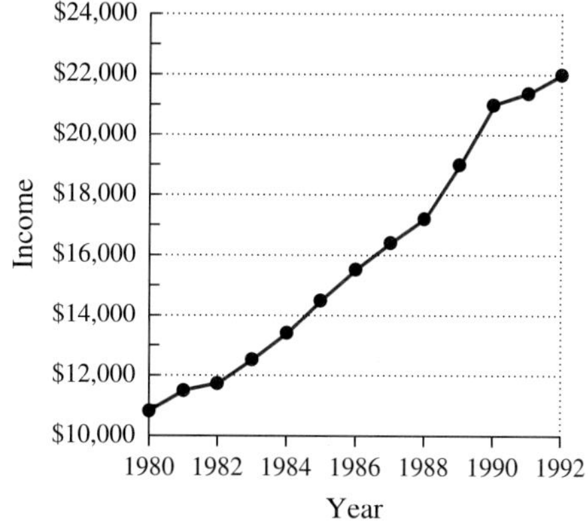

Graph showing per capita personal income in the greater Sacramento area, *Economic Profile Greater Sacramento Area* from Sacramento Area Commerce and Trade Organization, Summer, 1992. Reprinted by permission.

FIGURE 3.14

After increasing slightly from 1980 to 1982, income rose at about the same steady rate from 1982 to 1988, which is indicated by the fact that a straight line connecting these two points would be virtually identical to the graph for this period. Income increased quite sharply from 1988 to 1990, then tended to level off, increasing much more slowly from 1990 to 1992. ■

EXAMPLE 7 China's economy boomed during the late 80s and early 90s. Figure 3.15 shows the graphs of two piecewise linear functions representing China's exports and imports (in billions of dollars) during this period.* The rules of these functions are

$E(x)$ = total exports in year x (in billions of dollars)

$I(x)$ = total imports in year x (in billions of dollars).

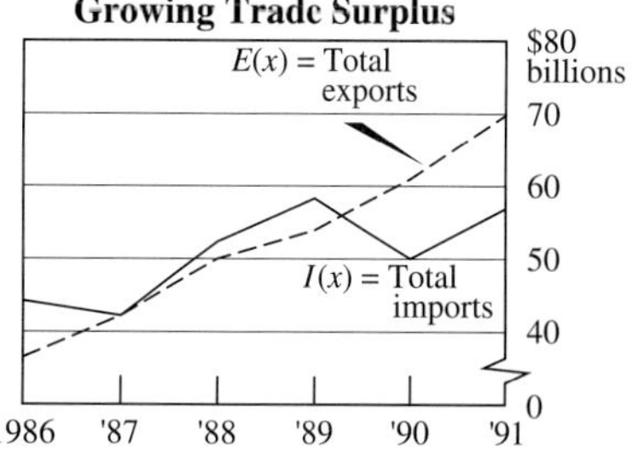

FIGURE 3.15

*The graph is from "China's Booming Economy" in *U.S. News and World Report,* October 19, 1992. Copyright © 1992 by U.S. News and World Report. Reprinted by permission.

(a) Find the function values $E(1988)$ and $E(1991)$ and interpret them.

$E(1988) = 50$ and $E(1991) \approx 70$, because the points (1988, 50) and (1991, 70) are on the graph of E. This means that exports totaled 50 billion dollars in 1988 and 70 billion in 1991.

(b) Find the function values $I(1986)$ and $I(1991)$ and interpret them.

$I(1986) \approx 44$ and $I(1991) \approx 57$, because the (approximate) points (1986, 44) and (1991, 57) are on the graph of I. This means that total imports were 44 billion dollars in 1986 and 57 billion in 1991.

(c) What was the difference between exports and imports in 1991? What does this mean?

In functional notation, we must find $E(1991) - I(1991)$. Using parts (a) and (b), we have $E(1991) - I(1991) = 70 - 57 = 13$. Therefore, China had a positive net balance of trade of 13 billion dollars. ■

4 Use a calculator to graph $f(x) = [x]$ (that is, $f(x) = \text{int}(x)$ or $\text{floor}(x)$ or $\text{intg}(x)$) in the window with $-5 \le x \le 5$ and $-5 \le y \le 5$. How does the calculator graph differ from the graph in Figure 3.16?

Answer:
The calculator graph probably contains many erroneous vertical line segments, so that the graph looks like a staircase. You can avoid the vertical segments by using "dot" graphing mode instead of the usual "connected" mode. Try it.

STEP FUNCTIONS The **greatest integer function,** usually written $f(x) = [x]$, is defined by saying that $[x]$ denotes the largest integer that is less than or equal to x, for example, $[8] = 8$, $[7.45] = 7$, $[\pi] = 3$, $[-1] = -1$, $[-2.6] = -3$, and so on. On most calculators the greatest integer function is denoted INT or FLOOR (look on the MATH menu or its NUM submenu). However, a few calculators use INT for a different function and INTG for the greatest integer function. Experiment or check your instruction manual.

EXAMPLE 8 Graph $f(x) = [x]$.

If $-1 \le x < 0$, then $[x] = -1$. If $0 \le x < 1$, then $[x] = 0$. If $1 \le x < 2$, then $[x] = 1$, and so on. Thus, the graph, as shown in Figure 3.16, consists of a series of horizontal line segments. In each one, the left endpoint is included and the right endpoint is excluded. The shape of the graph is the reason that this function is called a **step function.** A calculator is likely to produce a more evocative, but less accurate, graph of a step function. ■ 4

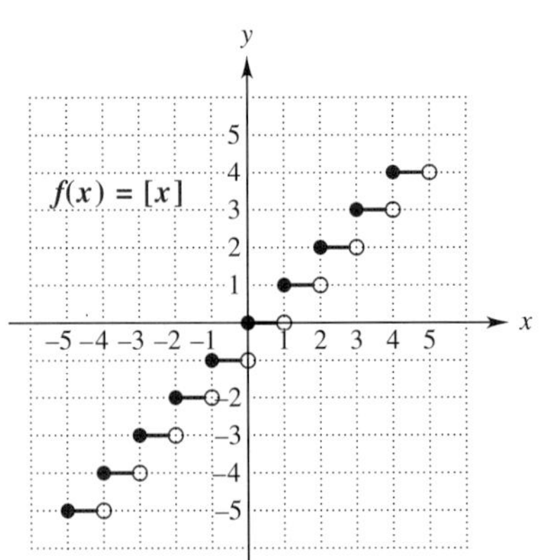

FIGURE 3.16

EXAMPLE 9 An overnight delivery service charges \$25 for a package weighing up to 2 pounds. For each additional pound or fraction of a pound there is an additional charge of \$3. Let $D(x)$ represent the cost to send a package weighing x pounds. Graph $D(x)$ for x in the interval $(0, 6]$.

5 Assume that the post office charges 30¢ per ounce, or fraction of an ounce, to mail a letter. Graph the ordered pairs (ounces, cost).

Answer:

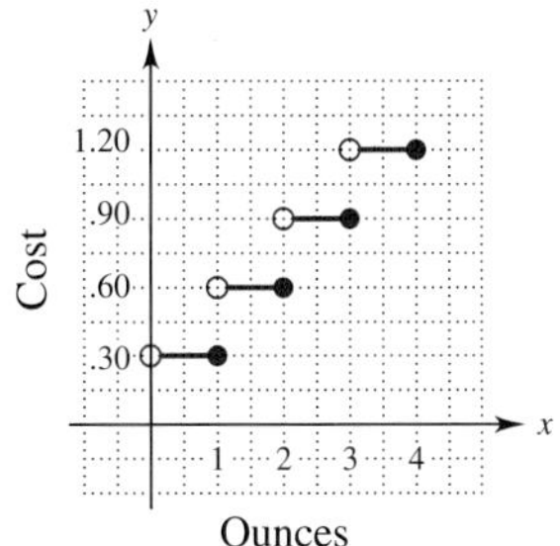

For x in the interval (0, 2], $y = 25$. For x in (2, 3], $y = 25 + 3 = 28$. For x in (3, 4], $y = 28 + 3 = 31$, and so on. The graph, which is that of a step function, is shown in Figure 3.17. ■ 5

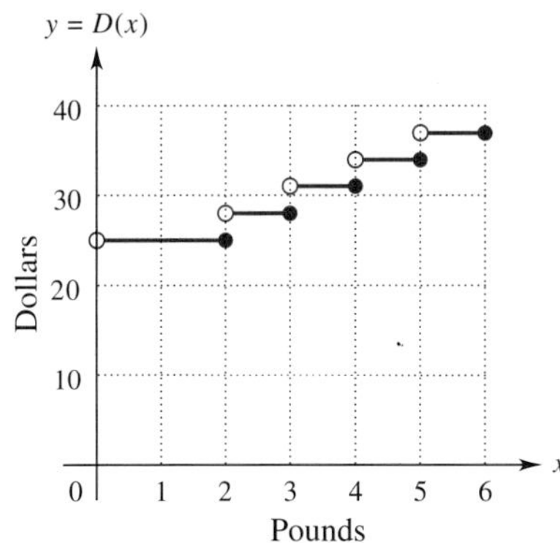

FIGURE 3.17

OTHER FUNCTIONS The following fact, which distinguishes function graphs from other graphs, is sometimes useful for interpreting calculator generated graphs.

VERTICAL LINE TEST

No vertical line intersects the graph of a function more than once.

In other words, if a vertical line intersects a graph at more than one point, the graph is not the graph of a function. To see why this is true, consider the graph in Figure 3.18. The vertical line $x = 3$ intersects the graph at two points. If this were the graph of a function f, this would mean that $f(3) = 2$ (because (3, 2) is on the graph) *and* that $f(3) = -1$ (because (3, -1) is on the graph). This is impossible because a *function* can have only one value when $x = 3$ (each input determines exactly one output). Therefore, this cannot be the graph of a function. A similar argument works in the general case.

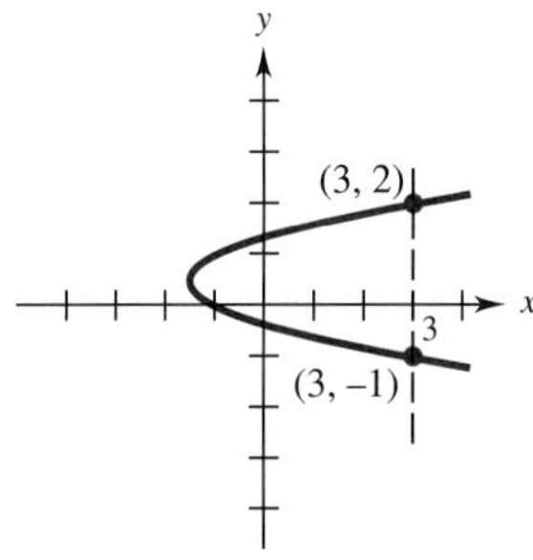

FIGURE 3.18

6 Find a viewing window that indicates the actual shape of the graph of the function $f(x) = 15x^{11} - 2$ of Example 10 near the point $(-1, -17)$.

Answer:
There are many correct answers, including $-1.4 \le x \le -.6$ and $-30 \le y \le 0$.

EXAMPLE 10 In the standard viewing window, the graph of the function $f(x) = 15x^{11} - 2$ (Figure 3.19) contains several vertical line segments, apparently contradicting the vertical line test. Explain this.

To see what's really going on near $x = 1$, for example, look at the table in Figure 3.20. It shows that as x gets larger, so does $f(x)$, meaning that the graph moves to the right as it moves upward, as shown in Figure 3.21 which includes all the points obtained from the table. This detail is lost in the standard viewing window (Figure 3.19), however, because all the x-values in Figure 3.20 occupy only a single pixel width, so the calculator plots the corresponding points in a vertical line. A similar explanation accounts for the other apparent vertical line segments. ■ 6

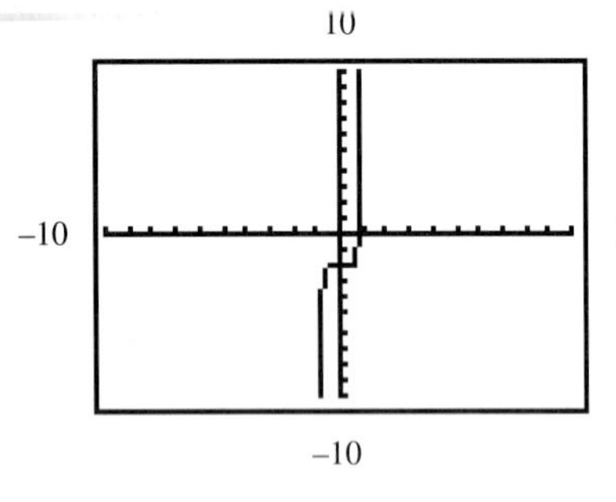

FIGURE 3.19

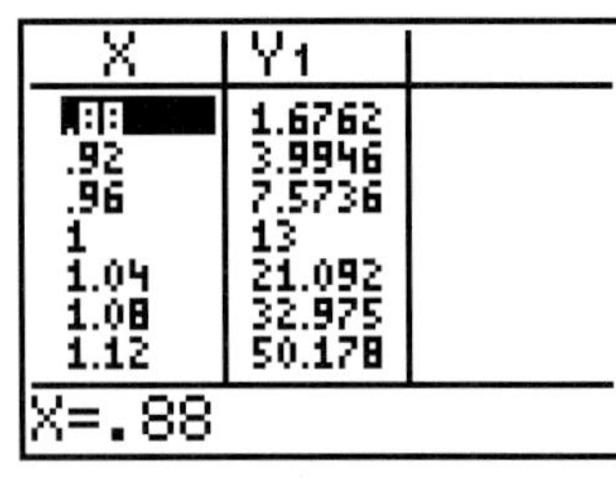

X	Y1
.88	1.6762
.92	3.9946
.96	7.5736
1	13
1.04	21.092
1.08	32.975
1.12	50.178

X=.88

FIGURE 3.20

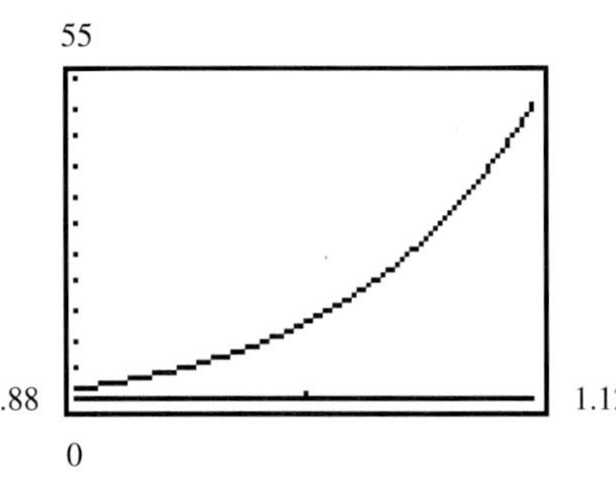

FIGURE 3.21

We have seen that the graph of a function may contain horizontal line segments (Examples 8 and 9). Nevertheless, horizontal line segments in calculator generated graphs often mask hidden behavior, rather than accurately displaying the graph.

7 Graph the function in Figure 3.22 on your own calculator, using the window shown in the figure. Use the trace feature to move along the "horizontal" segment to the right of the y-axis. Do the y-coordinates remain the same?

Answer:
No, they increase, then decrease, then increase as you move from left to right.

EXAMPLE 11 The graph of $f(x) = x^3 - 1.8x^2 + x + 2$ in Figure 3.22 contains a horizontal segment just to the right of the y-axis. To test whether this segment is actually horizontal, do margin problem 7 now. 7

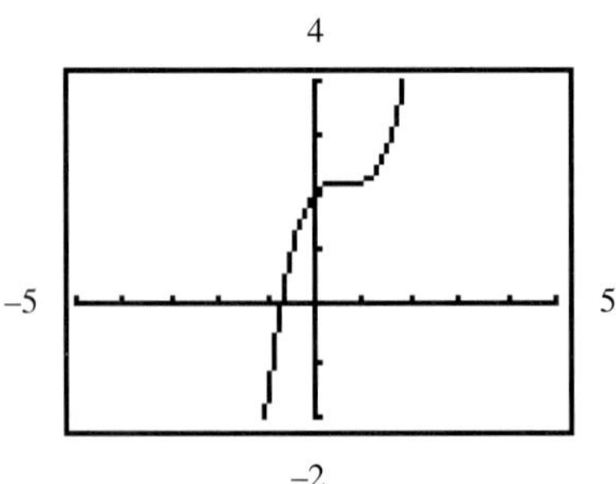

FIGURE 3.22

The answer to margin problem 7 indicates that this segment is not horizontal after all (if it were, the y-coordinates would be the same throughout the segment). To see what's really going on, graph this portion of the graph in a new viewing window (Figure 3.23). Then you can see that the graph of f actually has a tiny hill and valley just to the right of the y-axis. ■

2.2

.2 1

2.1

FIGURE 3.23

3.2 EXERCISES

Find an appropriate viewing window for displaying the graph of the function. It should include the coordinate axes, but not those quadrants of the plane in which there are no points of the graph. Consider your answer correct if your window shows the shape and graph features that appear in the window listed in the answer section. (See Examples 1 and 2.)

1. $f(x) = \sqrt{-x}$ **2.** $g(x) = -\sqrt{x^2 + 100}$

3. $h(x) = 20 - |x^2 - 6x + 8|$ **4.** $f(x) = \sqrt{|x^3 - 3|}$

5. $g(x) = -5(x^4 + x^2 + 8)$ **6.** $h(x) = x^6 + 2x^4 + x^2 + 50$

Graph each of the following functions. (See Examples 3–5.)

7. $f(x) = \begin{cases} x + 2 & \text{if } x \le 1 \\ 3 & \text{if } x > 1 \end{cases}$ **8.** $g(x) = \begin{cases} 2x - 1 & \text{if } x < 0 \\ -1 & \text{if } x \ge 0 \end{cases}$

9. $y = \begin{cases} 3 - x & \text{if } x \le 0 \\ 2x + 3 & \text{if } x > 0 \end{cases}$ **10.** $y = \begin{cases} x + 5 & \text{if } x \le 1 \\ 2 - 3x & \text{if } x > 1 \end{cases}$

11. $f(x) = \begin{cases} |x| & \text{if } x \le 2 \\ -x & \text{if } x > 2 \end{cases}$ **12.** $g(x) = \begin{cases} -|x| & \text{if } x \le 1 \\ 2x & \text{if } x > 1 \end{cases}$

13. $f(x) = |x - 4|$ **14.** $g(x) = |4 - x|$

15. $f(x) = |3 - 4x|$ **16.** $g(x) = -|x|$

17. $y = -|x - 1|$ **18.** $f(x) = |x| - 2$

19. $y = |x| + 3$

20. $|x| + |y| = 1$. (*Hint:* This is not the graph of a function, but is made up of four straight line segments. Find them by using the definition of absolute value in these four cases: $x \ge 0$ and $y \ge 0$; $x \ge 0$ and $y < 0$; $x < 0$ and $y \ge 0$; $x < 0$ and $y < 0$.)

Graph each of the following functions. (See Examples 8 and 9.)

21. $f(x) = [x - 3]$ **22.** $g(x) = [x + 2]$

23. $g(x) = [-x]$ **24.** $f(x) = -[x]$

25. $f(x) = [x] + [-x]$ (The graph contains horizontal segments, but is *not* a horizontal line.)

26. Assume that postage rates are 32¢ for the first ounce, plus 23¢ for each additional ounce and that each letter carries one 32¢ stamp and as many 23¢ stamps as necessary. Graph the *postage stamp function* whose rule is

$p(x)$ = the number of stamps on a letter weighing x ounces.

Which of these are graphs of functions?

27.

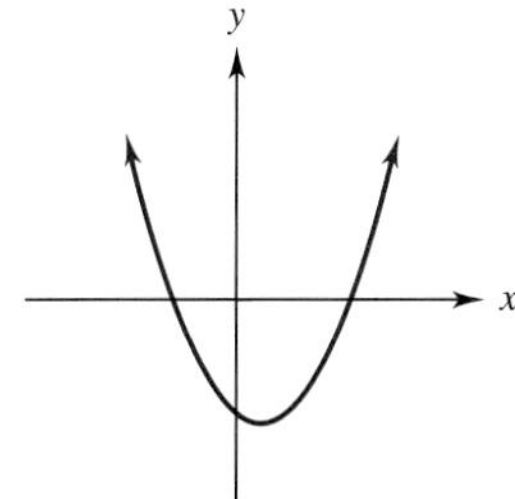

28.

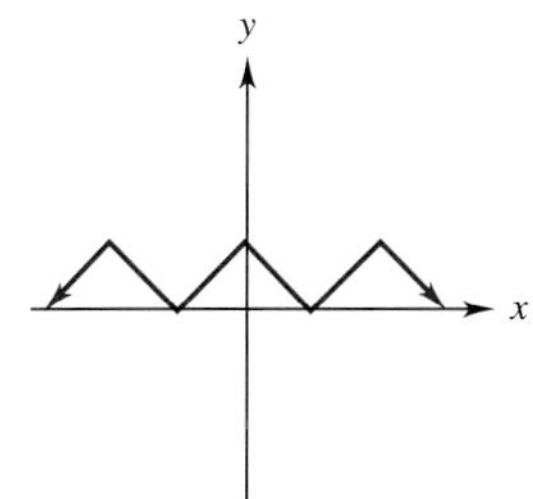

29.

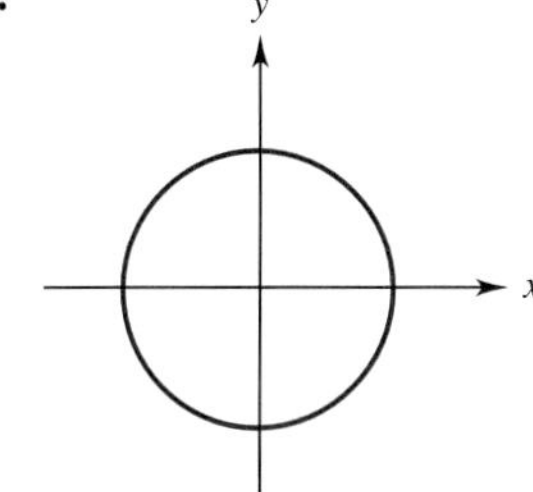

30.

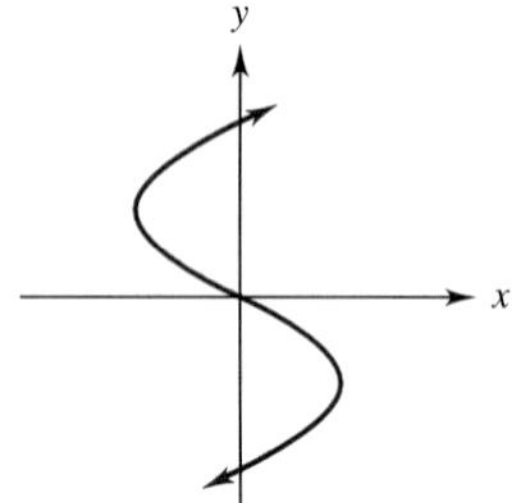

31.

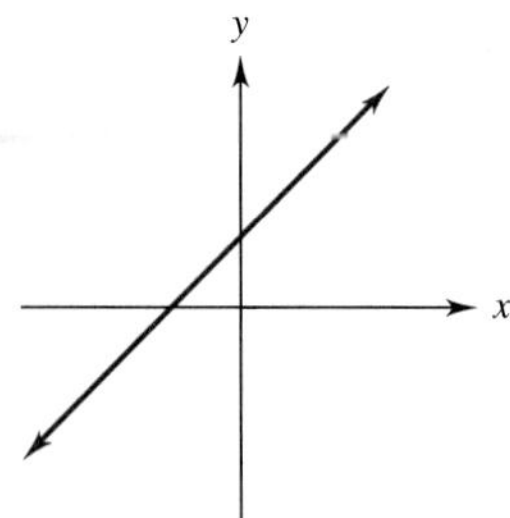

32.

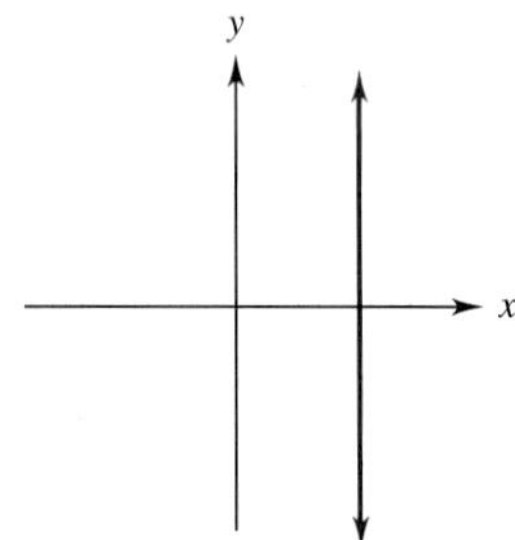

In the standard viewing window, the graph of each of the following functions contains a horizontal segment. Use TRACE to determine whether the segment is actually horizontal. If it is not, describe this region of the graph and find a viewing window that illustrates your description. (See Example 11.)

33. $f(x) = .02x^3 - .02x^2 - .03x - .5$

34. $g(x) = .01x^4 - .02x^2 - .01$

35. $g(x) = x^6 - 1$

36. $f(x) = x^5 - 2$

Work the following problems. (See Examples 3–5.)

37. Social Science United States health care costs as a percent of the gross national product from 1960 to 1992 are given by

$$y = \begin{cases} .22x + 5.5 & \text{for 1960 to 1985} \\ .29x + 3.75 & \text{for 1985 to 1990.} \end{cases}$$

Let $x = 0$ represent 1960 and graph this function. What does the graph suggest about health care costs?

38. Social Science Personal taxes in the United States from 1960 to 1990 are approximated by

$$f(x) = \begin{cases} 7.9x + 50.4 & \text{from 1960 to 1975} \\ 35.4x - 361.6 & \text{from 1975 to 1990.} \end{cases}$$

Let $x = 0$ represent 1960 and graph the function. What happened to personal taxes in 1975?

39. Natural Science The snow depth in Michigan's Isle Royale National Park varies throughout the winter. In a typical winter, the snow depth in inches is approximated by the following function.

$$f(x) = \begin{cases} 6.5x & \text{if } 0 \le x \le 4 \\ -5.5x + 48 & \text{if } 4 < x \le 6 \\ -30x + 195 & \text{if } 6 < x \le 6.5 \end{cases}$$

Here, x represents the time in months with $x = 0$ representing the beginning of October, $x = 1$ representing the beginning of November, and so on.

(a) Graph $f(x)$.

(b) In what month is the snow deepest? What is the deepest snow depth?

(c) In what months does the snow begin and end?

40. Natural Science A factory begins emitting particulate matter into the atmosphere at 8 A.M. each workday, with the emissions continuing until 4 P.M. The level of pollutants, $P(t)$, measured by a monitoring station 1/2 mile away, is approximated as follows, where t represents the number of hours since 8 A.M.

$$P(t) = \begin{cases} 75t + 100 & \text{if } 0 \le t \le 4 \\ 400 & \text{if } 4 < t < 8 \\ -100t + 1200 & \text{if } 8 \le t \le 10 \\ -\dfrac{50}{7}t + \dfrac{1900}{7} & \text{if } 10 < t < 24 \end{cases}$$

Find the level of pollution at

(a) 9 A.M. **(b)** 11 A.M. **(c)** 5 P.M.

(d) 7 P.M. **(e)** Midnight.

(f) Graph $y = P(t)$.

(g) From the graph in part (f), at what time(s) is the pollution level highest? lowest?

41. Natural Science The table shows the percentage of babies delivered by Caesarean section in 1970, 1980, and 1990.*

Year	*Percentage*
1970	5%
1980	17%
1990	23%

(a) Let $x = 0$ correspond to 1970 and $x = 20$ to 1990. Find the rule of a piecewise linear function f that models this

*Teutsch, S. and R. Churchill, *Principles and Practice of Public Health Surveillance*, New York: Oxford University Press, 1994.

data, that is, a piecewise linear function with $f(0) = .05$, $f(10) = .17$, and $f(20) = .23$.

(b) Graph the function f when $0 \le x \le 20$.

(c) Use the function f to estimate the percentage of Caesarean deliveries in 1975 and 1982.

42. Management The graph (from the Office of Management and Budget) shows the total federal debt from 1982 to 1994 (in billions of dollars). Note that the straight line segment joining the endpoints of this piecewise linear graph is a very good approximation of the graph.

(a) Let $x = 0$ correspond to 1982 and $x = 12$ to 1994. Find the rule of the function g whose graph is the straight line that approximates the federal debt graph when $0 \le x \le 12$.

(b) Use the function g to find the approximate federal debt in 1990. How does this compare with the actual debt that year of 3190 billion dollars?

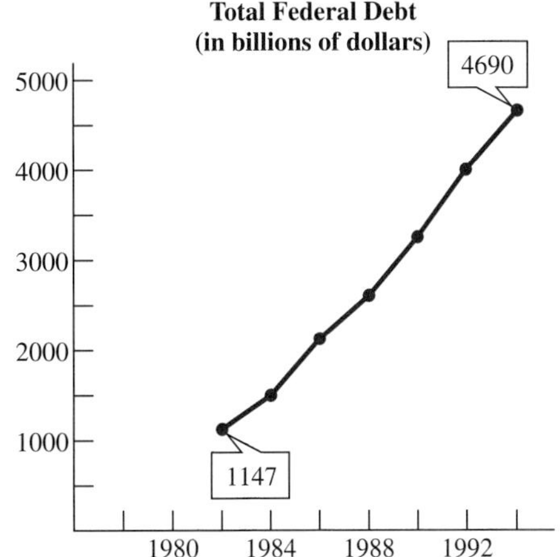

Work the following problems. (See Examples 6 and 7.)

43. Management The graph* at the top of the next column shows two functions of time. The first, which we will designate $I(t)$, shows the energy intensity of the United States, which is defined as the thousands of BTUs of energy consumed per dollar of Gross National Product (GNP) in year t (in 1982 dollars). The second, which we will designate $S(t)$, represents the national savings per year (also in 1982 dollars) due to a decreased use of energy.

(a) Find $I(1976)$. **(b)** Find $S(1984)$.

(c) Find $I(t)$ and $S(t)$ at the time when the two graphs intersect. In what year does this occur?

(d) What significance, if any, is there to the point at which the two graphs intersect?

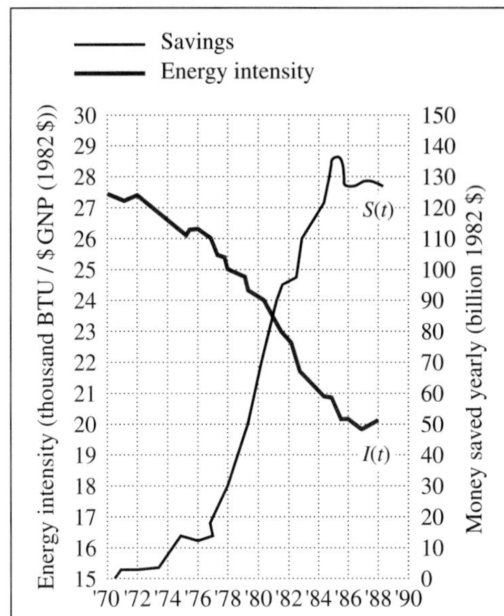

44. Management A chain-saw rental firm charges $7 per day or fraction of a day to rent a saw, plus a fixed fee of $4 for resharpening the blade. Let $S(x)$ represent the cost of renting a saw for x days. Find each of the following.

(a) $S\left(\frac{1}{2}\right)$ **(b)** $S(1)$ **(c)** $S\left(1\frac{1}{4}\right)$ **(d)** $S\left(3\frac{1}{2}\right)$

(e) What does it cost to rent a saw for $4\frac{9}{10}$ days?

(f) A portion of the graph of $y = S(x)$ is shown here. Explain how the graph could be continued.

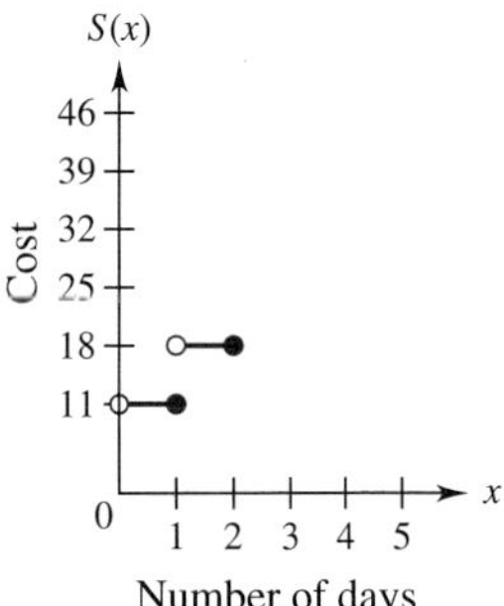

(g) What is the domain variable?

(h) What is the range variable?

(i) Write a sentence or two explaining what part (c) and its answer represent.

(j) We have left $x = 0$ out of the graph. Discuss why it should or shouldn't be included. If it were included, how would you define $S(0)$?

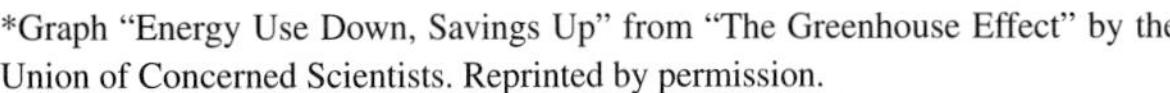

*Graph "Energy Use Down, Savings Up" from "The Greenhouse Effect" by the Union of Concerned Scientists. Reprinted by permission.

45. **Natural Science** The table gives estimates of the percent of ozone change from 1985 for several years in the future, if chlorofluorocarbon production is reduced 80% globally.

Year	*Percent*
1985	0
2005	1.5
2025	3
2065	4
2085	5

(a) Plot these ordered pairs on a grid.
(b) The points from part (a) should lie approximately on a straight line. Use the points (2005, 1.5) and (2085, 5) to write an equation of the line.
(c) Letting $f(x)$ represent the percent of ozone change and x represent the year, write your equation from part (b) as a rule that defines a function.
(d) Find $f(2065)$. Does it agree fairly closely with the number in the table that corresponds to 2065? Do you think the expression from part (c) describes this function adequately?

46. **Management** The graph below, based on data given in *Business Week* magazine, shows the number of aircraft with airfones since 1984.*
(a) Is this graph that of a function?
(b) What does the domain represent?
(c) Estimate the range.

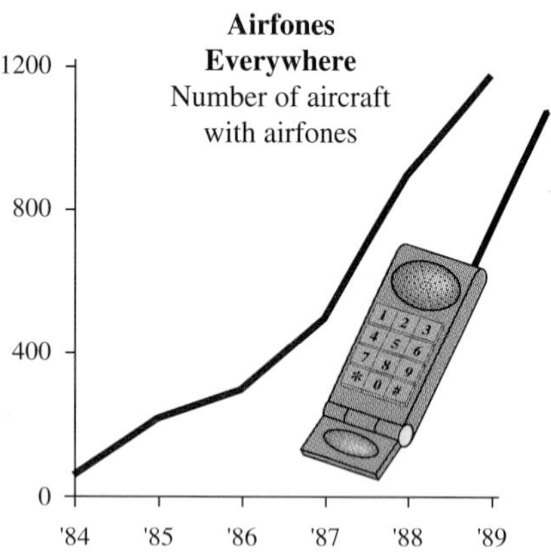

*"Airfones Everywhere" reprinted from February 15, 1990 issue of *Business Week* by special permission, copyright © 1990 by McGraw-Hill, Inc.

47. **Natural Science** A laboratory culture contains about one million bacteria at midnight. The culture grows very rapidly until noon, when a bactericide is introduced and the bacteria population plunges. By 4 P.M. the bacteria have adapted to the bactericide, and the culture slowly increases in population until 9 P.M. when the culture is accidently destroyed by the clean-up crew. Let $g(t)$ denote the bacteria population at time t (with $t = 0$ corresponding to midnight) and draw a plausible graph of the function g. (Many correct answers are possible.)

48. **Management** A plane flies from Austin, Texas, to Cleveland, Ohio, a distance of 1200 miles. Let f be the function whose rule is:

$$f(t) = \text{distance (in miles) from Austin at time } t \text{ hours,}$$

with $t = 0$ corresponding to the 4 P.M. takeoff. In each of the following, draw a plausible graph of f under the given circumstances. (There are many correct answers for each part.)
(a) The flight is nonstop and takes between 3.5 and 4 hours.
(b) Bad weather forces the plane to land in Dallas (about 200 miles from Austin) at 5 P.M., remain overnight and leave at 8 A.M. the next morning, flying nonstop to Cleveland.
(c) The plane flies nonstop, but due to heavy traffic it must fly in a holding pattern for an hour over Cincinnati (about 200 miles from Cleveland), then go on to Cleveland.

Management *Work the following problems. (See Examples 8 and 9.)*

49. The charge to rent a Haul-It-Yourself Trailer is \$25 plus \$2 per hour or portion of an hour. Find the cost to rent a trailer for
(a) 2 hours; (b) 1.5 hours; (c) 4 hours;
(d) 3.7 hours.
(e) Graph the ordered pairs (hours, cost).

50. A delivery company charges \$3 plus 50¢ per mile or part of a mile. Find the cost for a trip of
(a) 3 miles; (b) 3.4 miles; (c) 3.9 miles;
(d) 5 miles.
(e) Graph the ordered pairs (miles, cost).
(f) Is this a function?

51. A college typing service charges \$3 plus \$7 per hour or fraction of an hour. Graph the ordered pairs (hours, cost).

52. A parking garage charges \$1 plus 50¢ per hour or fraction of an hour. Graph the ordered pairs (hours, cost).

Work these exercises.

53. **Management** Since 1990 Congress has authorized more than \$700 million for research and development of "smart" highways, with the goal of enabling cars to drive them-

selves.* The spending per year is approximated by the function $f(x) = -19.321x^2 + 3608.7x - 168{,}310$, where $x = 90$ corresponds to 1990 and $f(x)$ is in millions of dollars.

(a) In what year was the maximum amount spent?

(b) What is the maximum amount spent?

(c) Sketch a graph of the function from 1991 through 1996.

54. Physical Science According to data from the National Traffic Safety Institute,† the stopping distance $g(x)$ of a car traveling x mph is given by $g(x) = .056057x^2 + 1.06657x$.

(a) Find the stopping distance for a car traveling 25 mph.

(b) How fast can you drive if you need to be certain of stopping within 150 ft?

55. Social Science According to data from the National Highway Traffic Safety Administration, the accident rate as a function of the age x of the driver (in years) can be approximated by the function

$$f(x) = 60 - 2.28x + .0232x^2 \quad (16 \le x \le 85).$$

Find the age at which the accident rate is a minimum.

*Exercises 53 and 55 are from Ralph DeMarr, University of New Mexico.

†*National Traffic Safety Institute Student Workbook,* 1993, p. 7.

3.3 APPLICATIONS OF LINEAR FUNCTIONS

In Chapter 1, we saw that the graph of an equation of the form $y = ax + b$ is a straight line. This equation also defines y as a function of x, which leads to the following terminology.

> A **linear function** is a function whose rule can be written in the form
>
> $$f(x) = ax + b$$
>
> for some constants a and b.

In this section we show how linear functions can be applied to a variety of real-world situations.

LINEAR MODELS In real-world situations it is sometimes possible to use discrete data to construct a linear function that approximates the data. Such a function provides a **linear model** of the situation which can be used (within limits) to predict future behavior.

EXAMPLE 1 The average annual cost of tuition and fees at public four-year colleges has been rising steadily, as illustrated in the following table from the College Board.

TECHNOLOGY TIP You can plot single points on a calculator screen by using PT-ON (in the Catalogue or Draw menu of TI calculators) or PLOT (on the Casio 9800 and Sharp 9300 keyboards). ✔

Year	1981	1983	1985	1987	1989	1991	1993
Cost	\$909	\$1148	\$1318	\$1537	\$1781	\$2137	\$2527

(a) Display this information graphically.

Let $x = 0$ represent the year 1980, $x = 1$ represent 1981, and so on. Using the Tip in the margin, plot the points given by the table: (1, 909), (3, 1148), (5, 1318), etc. (See Figure 3.24 on the next page.)

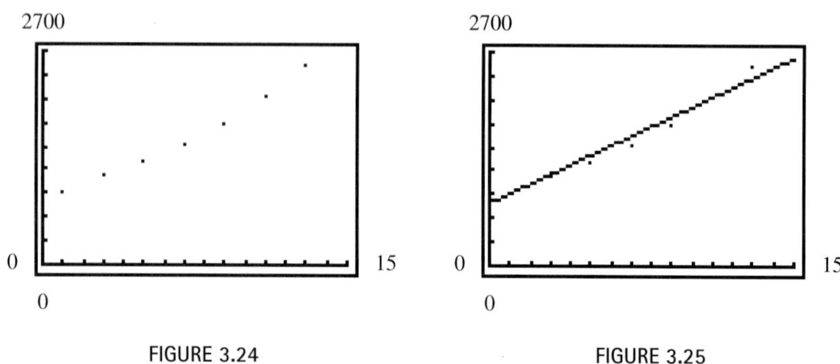

FIGURE 3.24

FIGURE 3.25

(b) The points in Figure 3.24 do not lie on a straight line, but they come close. Find a linear model for this data.

There are a variety of sophisticated methods of finding a straight line that "best fits" data that is almost linear. We shall use a simpler approach. Choose two of the points in Figure 3.24, say (1, 909) and (11, 2137), and draw the straight line they determine. All the data points lie reasonably close to this line (Figure 3.25). The line through (1, 909) and (11, 2137) has slope

$$\frac{y_2 - y_1}{x_2 - x_1} = \frac{2137 - 909}{11 - 1} = \frac{1228}{10} = 122.8.$$

Its equation can be found by using the point-slope form (see Section 1.6).

$$\begin{aligned} y - y_1 &= m(x - x_1) \\ y - 909 &= 122.8(x - 1) \\ y &= 122.8x + 786.2 \end{aligned}$$

Therefore, the function $f(x) = 122.8x + 786.2$ provides a linear model of the situation.

(c) Use the linear model in part (b) to estimate the average annual cost of tuition and fees in 1984 and 2001.

According to the model, the average cost in 1984 (that is, $x = 4$) was

$$f(4) = 122.8(4) + 786.2 = 1277.4$$

or \$1277.40, which is a bit higher than the actual cost of \$1228 that year. Since 2001 corresponds to $x = 21$, the average cost in 2001 is given by

$$f(21) = 122.8(21) + 786.2 = \$3365. \quad \blacksquare$$

CAUTION A linear model need not be accurate for all values of x. The model in Example 1, for instance, suggests that the average cost in 1970 (corresponding to $x = -10$) is the negative number $f(-10) = -441.8$, which is obviously nonsense. Similarly, this model may not accurately predict costs far in the future. ◆

COMPARING RATES OF CHANGE One way to compare the change in some quantity in two or more situations is to compare the rates at which the quantity changes in the two cases. If the increase or decrease in a quantity can be approximated (or modeled) by a linear function, we can use the work in Section 1.6 to find the rate of change of the quantity with respect to time.

EXAMPLE 2 The chart below shows sales in two different years for two stores of a major chain of discount stores:

Store	*Sales in 1992*	*Sales in 1995*
A	\$100,000	\$160,000
B	50,000	140,000

A study of company records suggests that the sales of both stores have increased linearly (that is, the sales can be closely approximated by a linear function). Find a linear equation describing the sales for Store A.

To find a linear equation describing the sales, let $x = 0$ represent 1992 so that 1995 corresponds to $x = 3$. Then, by the chart above, the line representing the sales for Store A passes through the points (0, 100000) and (3, 160000). The slope of the line through these points is

$$\frac{160{,}000 - 100{,}000}{3 - 0} = 20{,}000.$$

1 Find a linear equation describing the sales for Store B from Example 2.

Answer:
$y = 30{,}000x + 50{,}000$

Using the point-slope form of the equation of a line gives

$$y - 100{,}000 = 20{,}000(x - 0)$$
$$y = 20{,}000x + 100{,}000$$

as an equation describing the sales of Store A. ■ 1

AVERAGE RATE OF CHANGE Notice that the sales for Store A in Example 2 increased from \$100,000 to \$160,000 over the period from 1992 to 1995 representing a total increase of \$60,000 in 3 years.

$$\text{Average rate of change in sales} = \frac{\$60{,}000}{3} = \$20{,}000 \text{ per year}$$

This is the same as the slope found in Example 2. Verify that the average annual rate of change in sales for Store B over the 3-year period also agrees with the slope of the equation found in Problem 1 at the side. Management needs to watch the rate of change in sales closely in order to be aware of any unfavorable trends. If the rate of change is decreasing, then sales growth is slowing down, and this trend may require some response.

Example 2 illustrates a useful fact about linear functions. If $f(x) = mx + b$ is a *linear* function, then the **average rate of change** in y with respect to x (the change in y divided by the corresponding change in x) is the slope of the line $y = mx + b$. In particular, the average rate of change of a linear function is constant. (See Exercises 12 and 13 in this section for examples of functions where the average rate of change is not constant.)

2 A certain new anticholesterol drug is related to the blood cholesterol level by the linear model

$$y = 280 - 3x,$$

where x is the dosage of the drug (in grams) and y is the blood cholesterol level.

(a) Find the blood cholesterol level if 12 grams of the drug are administered.

(b) In general, an increase of 1 gram in the dose causes what change in the blood cholesterol level?

Answers:

(a) 244

(b) A decrease of 3 units

EXAMPLE 3 Average family health care costs in dollars y over the 10-year period of the 90s are expected to increase each year as given by

$$y = 510x + 4300,$$

where x is the number of years since 1990. By this estimate, how much did health care cost the average family in 1996? What is the average rate of increase?

Let $x = 1996 - 1990 = 6$. The health care costs were

$$y = 510(6) + 4300 = 7360 \quad \text{or} \quad \$7360.$$

The average rate of increase in cost is given by the slope of the line. The slope is 510, so this model indicates that each year costs will increase $510. ■ 2

COST ANALYSIS The cost of manufacturing an item commonly consists of two parts. The first is a **fixed cost** for designing the product, setting up a factory, training workers, and so on. Within broad limits, the fixed cost is constant for a particular product and does not change as more items are made. The second part is a *cost per item* for labor, materials, packing, shipping, and so on. The total value of this second cost *does* depend on the number of items made.

EXAMPLE 4 Suppose that the cost of producing clock-radios can be approximated by the linear model

$$C(x) = 12x + 100,$$

where $C(x)$ is the cost in dollars to produce x radios. The cost to produce 0 radios is

$$C(0) = 12(0) + 100 = 100,$$

or $100. This amount, $100, is the fixed cost.

Once the company has invested the fixed cost into the clock-radio project, what is the additional cost per radio? To find out, first find the cost of a total of 5 radios:

$$C(5) = 12(5) + 100 = 160,$$

or $160. The cost of 6 radios is

$$C(6) = 12(6) + 100 = 172,$$

or $172. The sixth radio costs $172 − $160 = $12 to produce. In the same way, the 81st radio costs $C(81) - C(80) = \$1072 - \$1060 = \$12$ to produce. In fact, the $(n + 1)$st radio costs

$$C(n + 1) - C(n) = [12(n + 1) + 100] - [12n + 100] = 12,$$

or $12 to produce. Because each additional radio costs $12 to produce, $12 is the variable cost per radio. The number 12 is also the slope of the cost function, $C(x) = 12x + 100$. ■

Example 4 can easily be generalized. Suppose the total cost to make x items is given by the linear cost function $C(x) = mx + b$. Then the fixed cost (the cost which occurs even if no items are produced) is found by letting $x = 0$.

$$C(0) = m \cdot 0 + b = b$$

Thus, the fixed cost is the y-intercept of the cost function.

3 The cost in dollars to produce x kilograms of chocolate candy is given by $C(x)$, where in dollars

$$C(x) = 3.5x + 800.$$

Find each of the following.

(a) The fixed cost

(b) The total cost for 12 kilograms

(c) The marginal cost per kilogram

(d) The marginal cost of the 40th kilogram

Answers:

(a) \$800

(b) \$842

(c) \$3.50

(d) \$3.50

In economics, **marginal cost** is the rate of change of cost. Marginal cost is important to management in making decisions in areas such as cost control, pricing, and production planning. If the cost function is $C(x) = mx + b$, then its graph is a straight line with slope m. Since the slope represents the average rate of change, the marginal cost is the number m. 3

In Example 4, the marginal cost (slope) 12 was also the cost of producing one more radio. We now show that the same thing is true for any linear cost function $C(x) = mx + b$. If n items have been produced, the cost of the $(n + 1)$st item is the difference between the cost of producing $n + 1$ items and the cost of producing n items, namely, $C(n + 1) - C(n)$. Because $C(x) = mx + b$,

$$\begin{aligned}\text{Cost of one more item} &= C(n + 1) - C(n)\\ &= [m(n + 1) + b] - [mn + b]\\ &= mn + m + b - mn - b = m\\ &= \text{marginal cost.}\end{aligned}$$

This discussion is summarized as follows.

> In a **linear cost function** $C(x) = mx + b$, m represents the marginal cost and b the fixed cost. The marginal cost is the cost of producing one more item.
>
> Conversely, if the fixed cost is b and the marginal cost is always the same constant m, then the cost function for producing x items is $C(x) = mx + b$.

EXAMPLE 5 The marginal cost to produce an anticlot drug is \$10 per unit, while the cost to produce 100 units is \$1500. Find the cost function $C(x)$, given that it is linear.

Since the cost function is linear, it can be written in the form $C(x) = mx + b$. The marginal cost is \$10 per unit, which gives the value for m, leading to $C(x) = 10x + b$. To find b, use the fact that the cost of producing 100 units of the drug is \$1500, or $C(100) = 1500$. Substituting $x = 100$ and $C(x) = 1500$ into $C(x) = 10x + b$ gives

$$\begin{aligned}C(x) &= 10x + b\\ 1500 &= 10(100) + b\\ 1500 &= 1000 + b\\ 500 &= b.\end{aligned}$$

The cost function is $C(x) = 10x + 500$, where the fixed cost is \$500. ■ 4

4 The total cost of producing 10 business calculators is \$100. The marginal cost per calculator is \$4. Find the cost function, $C(x)$, if it is linear.

Answer:

$C(x) = 4x + 60$

If $C(x)$ is the total cost to manufacture x items, then the **average cost** per item is given by

$$\overline{C}(x) = \frac{C(x)}{x}.$$

In Example 4, the average cost per clock-radio is

$$\overline{C}(x) = \frac{C(x)}{x} = \frac{12x + 100}{x} = 12 + \frac{100}{x}.$$

Note what happens to the term $100/x$ as x gets larger.

$$\overline{C}(100) = 12 + \frac{100}{100} = 12 + 1 = \$13$$

$$\overline{C}(500) = 12 + \frac{100}{500} = 12 + \frac{1}{5} = \$12.20$$

$$\overline{C}(1000) = 12 + \frac{100}{1000} = 12 + \frac{1}{10} = \$12.10$$

As more and more items are produced, $100/x$ gets smaller and the average cost per item decreases. However, the average cost is never less than \$12.

EXAMPLE 6 Find the average cost per unit to produce 50 units and 500 units of the anticlot drug in Example 5.

The cost function from Example 5 is $10x + 500$, so the average cost per unit is

$$\overline{C}(x) = \frac{C(x)}{x} = \frac{10x + 500}{x} = 10 + \frac{500}{x}.$$

If 50 units of the drug are produced, the average cost is

$$\overline{C}(50) = 10 + \frac{500}{50} = 20,$$

or \$20 per unit. Producing 500 units of the drug will lead to an average cost of

$$\overline{C}(500) = 10 + \frac{500}{500} = 11,$$

or \$11 per unit. ■ 5

5 In Problem 4, at the side, find the average cost per calculator to produce 100 calculators.

Answer:
\$4.60

3.3 EXERCISES

1. **Social Science** The number of children in the U.S. from 5 to 13 years old decreased from 31.2 million in 1980 to 30.3 million in 1986.
   (a) Write a linear function describing this population y in terms of year x for the given period.
   (b) What was the average rate of change in this population over the period from 1980 to 1986?

2. **Social Science** According to the U.S. Census Bureau, the poverty level income for a family of four was \$5500 in 1975, \$8414 in 1980, and \$13,359 in 1990.
   (a) Let $x = 0$ correspond to 1975 and use the points (0, 5500) and (15, 13359) to find a linear model for this data.
   (b) Compare the poverty level given by the model for 1985 with the actual level of \$10,989. How accurate is the model?
   (c) How accurate is the level given by the model for 1970, when the actual poverty level was \$3968?
   (d) According to this model, what will the poverty level income be in 2000?

3. **Physical Science** The table lists the distances (in megaparsecs) and velocities (in km/sec) of four galaxies moving rapidly away from Earth.*

Galaxy	*Distance*	*Velocity*
Virgo	15	1,600
Ursa Minor	200	15,000
Corona Borealis	290	24,000
Bootes	520	40,000

*Acker, A. and C. Jaschek, *Astronomical Methods and Calculations*, John Wiley & Sons, 1986. Karttunen, H. (editor), *Fundamental Astronomy*, Springer Verlag, 1994.

(a) Plot the data using distance for the x-values and velocity for the y-values. What type of relationship seems to hold for this data?

(b) Use the points (0, 0) and (520, 40000) to find a linear function that models this data.

(c) Graph the linear model from part (b) and the original data on the same coordinate axes.

(d) The galaxy Hydra has a velocity of 60,000 km/sec. About how far away is it?

(e) The constant m in the rule of the function is called the Hubble constant. The Hubble constant can be used to estimate the age of the universe A (in years), with the formula

$$A = \frac{9.5 \times 10^{11}}{m}.$$

Approximate A using your value of m.

4. **Social Science** The table lists the average annual cost (in dollars) of tuition and fees at private four-year colleges for selected years.*

Year	*Tuition and Fees*
1981	4,113
1983	5,093
1985	6,121
1987	7,116
1989	8,446
1991	10,017
1993	11,025

Let $x = 1$ correspond to 1981 and let $f(x)$ be the tuition and fees in year x.

(a) Determine a linear function $f(x) = mx + b$ that models the data, using the points (1, 4113) and (13, 11025).

(b) Graph f and the data on the same coordinate axes.

(c) What does the slope of the graph of f indicate?

(d) Use this function to approximate the tuition and fees in the year 1990. Compare it with the true value of $9340.

5. **Natural Science** In one study of HIV patients who were infected by intravenous drug use, it was found that after four years 17% of the patients had AIDS and after seven years 33% had AIDS.†

(a) Use the points (4, .17) and (7, .33) to find a linear function that models the relationship between the time interval and the percentage of patients with AIDS.

(b) Predict the number of years until half of these patients have AIDS.

*The College Board

†Alcabes, P., A. Munoz, D. Vlahov, and G. Friedland, "Incubation Period of Human Immunodeficiency Virus," *Epidemiologic Review,* Vol. 15, No. 2, The Johns Hopkins University School of Hygiene and Public Health, 1993.

6. **Management** The table lists the total federal debt (in billions of dollars) from 1985 to 1989.*

Year	*Federal Debt*
1985	1828
1986	2130
1987	2354
1988	2615
1989	2881

(a) Plot the data by letting $x = 0$ correspond to 1985. Discuss any trends of the federal debt over this time period.

(b) Find a linear function $f(x) = mx + b$ that approximates the data, using the points (0, 1828) and (4, 2881). What does the slope of the graph of f represent? Graph f and the data on the same coordinate axes.

(c) Use f to predict the federal debt in the years 1984 and 1990. Compare your results to the true values of 1577 and 3191 billion dollars.

(d) Now use f to predict the federal debt in the years 1980 and 1994. Compare your results to the true values of 914 and 4690 billion dollars.

7. **Natural Science** To achieve the maximum benefit for the heart when exercising, your heart rate (in beats per minute) should be in the Target Heart Rate Zone. The lower limit of this zone is found by taking 70% of the difference between 220 and your age. The upper limit is found by using 85%.†

(a) Find formulas for the upper and lower limits ($u(x)$ and $l(x)$) as a function of age x.

(b) What is the Target Heart Rate Zone for a 20-year-old?

(c) What is the Target Heart Rate Zone for a 40-year-old?

(d) Two women in an aerobics class stop to take their pulse, and are surprised to find that they have the same pulse. One woman is 36 years older than the other and is working at the upper limit of her Target Heart Rate Zone. The younger woman is working at the lower limit of her Target Heart Rate Zone. What are the ages of the two women, and what is their pulse?

(e) Run for 10 minutes, take your pulse, and see if it is in your Target Heart Rate Zone. (After all, this is listed as an exercise!)

8. **Management** In deciding whether to set up a new manufacturing plant, company analysts have established that a reasonable function for the total cost to produce x items is

$$C(x) = 500{,}000 + 4.75x.$$

(a) Find the total cost to produce 100,000 items.

(b) Find the rate of change of the cost of the items to be produced in this plant.

*U.S. Office of Management and Budget.

†*The New York Times,* August 17, 1994, p. B9.

9. Management Suppose the sales of a particular brand of electric guitar satisfy the relationship

$$S(x) = 300x + 2000,$$

where $S(x)$ represents the number of guitars sold in year x, with $x = 0$ corresponding to 1987.
Find the sales in each of the following years.

(a) 1987 **(b)** 1990 **(c)** 1991

(d) The manufacturer needed sales to reach 4000 guitars by 1996 to pay off a loan. Did sales reach that goal?

(e) Find the annual rate of change of sales.

10. Management In the early 1990s, the Office of Management and Budget made the estimates for future Medicare costs (in billions of dollars) shown in the table.

Year	*Costs*
1995	157
1996	178
1997	194
1998	211
1999	229
2000	247

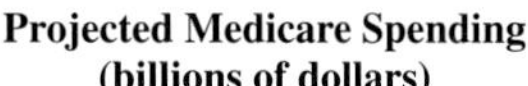

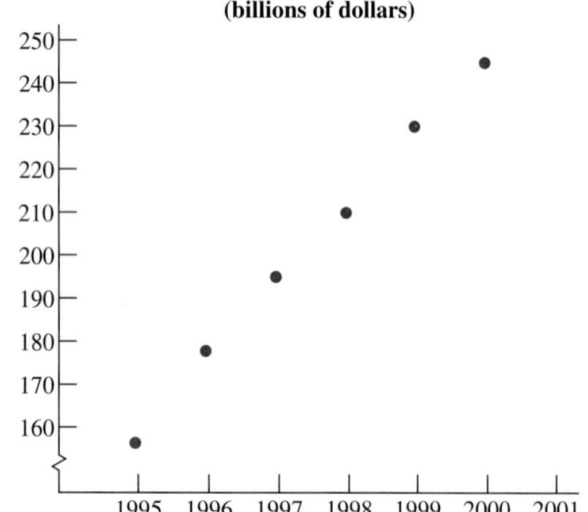

(a) The graph shows that the data are approximately linear. Use the data from 1995 and 2000 to find a linear function $f(x)$ that approximates the cost in year x.

(b) According to this function f, at what rate are costs increasing? How is this number related to the graph of the function?

11. Management Used car "superstores" that compete in the used car market with new car dealers are a recent phenomenon.*

(a) The figure shows the total number of new car dealers selling used cars in thousands. Describe what the graph tells us about the number of dealers selling used cars over this time period. From the data in the figure, what was the average rate of change in dealers from 1990 to 1995?

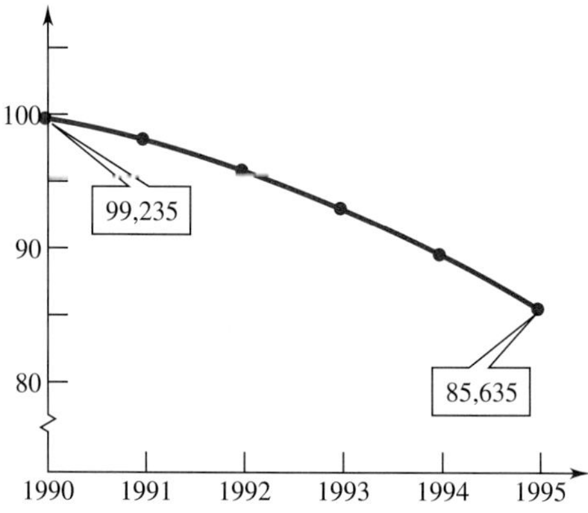

(b) The sales graph showing the number of used vehicles (in millions) sold by used car "superstores" is approximately linear, as shown in the figure. What does the slope of this line indicate about the sales of these superstores?

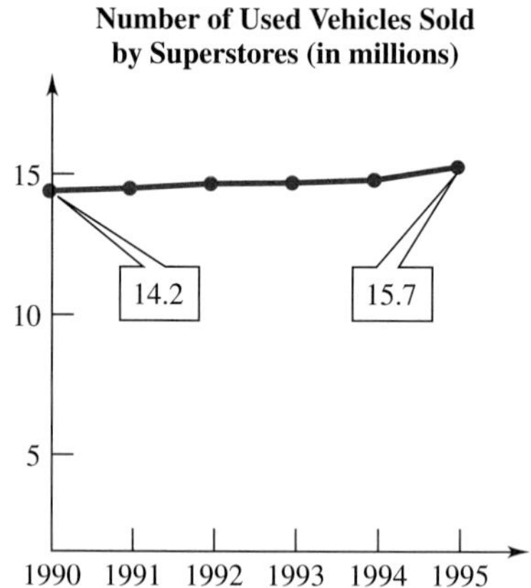

(c) Compare the graphs in parts (a) and (b). Describe a possible connection between the number of new car dealers selling used cars and the number of used cars sold in superstores.

12. Management The graph on the next page shows the total sales, in thousands of dollars from the distribution of x thousand catalogs. Find the average rate of change of sales with respect to the number of catalogs distributed for the following changes in x.

(a) 10 to 20 **(b)** 10 to 40

(c) 20 to 30 **(d)** 30 to 40

*"A Revolution in Car Buying," *Chicago Tribune,* February 18, 1996.

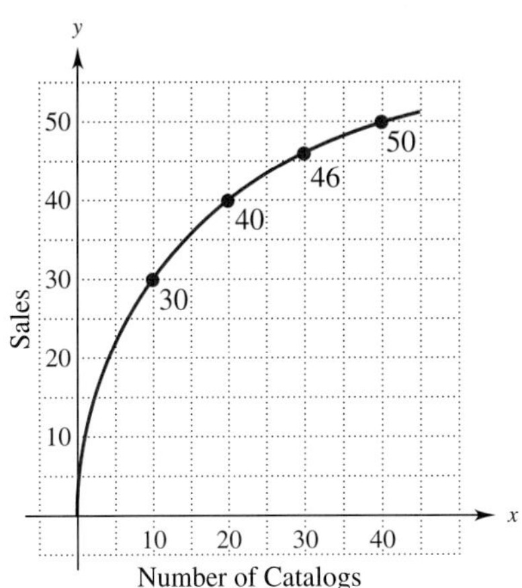

13. **Management** The graph below shows annual sales (in appropriate units) of a typical product. Sales increase slowly at first to some peak, hold steady for a while, and then decline as the product goes out of style. Find the average annual rate of change in sales for the following changes in years.
(a) 1 to 3 **(b)** 2 to 4 **(c)** 3 to 6
(d) 5 to 7 **(e)** 7 to 9 **(f)** 8 to 11
(g) 9 to 10 **(h)** 10 to 12

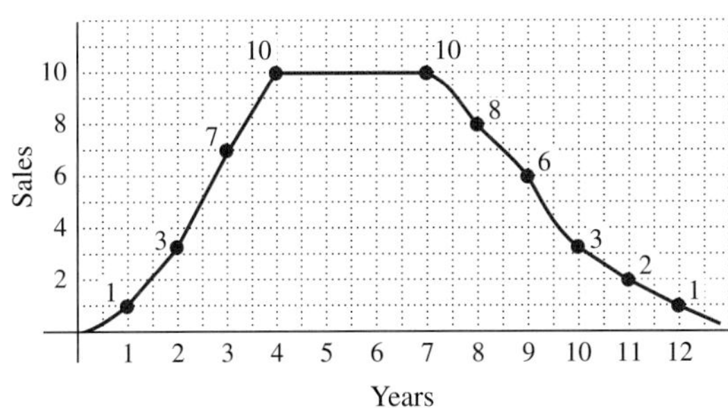

14. What is the meant by the marginal cost of a product? the fixed cost?

Management *Write a cost function for each of the following. Identify all variables used. (See Example 5.)*

15. A chain-saw rental firm charges \$12 plus \$1 per hour.
16. A trailer-hauling service charges \$45 plus \$2 per mile.
17. A parking garage charges 35¢ plus 30¢ per half hour.
18. For a 1-day rental, a car rental firm charges \$14 plus 6¢ per mile.

Management *Assume that each of the following can be expressed as a linear cost function. Find the appropriate cost function in each case. (See Example 5.)*

19. Fixed cost, \$100; 50 items cost \$1600 to produce.
20. Fixed cost, \$1000; 40 items cost \$2000 to produce.
21. Marginal cost, \$120; 100 items cost \$15,800 to produce.
22. Marginal cost, \$90; 150 items cost \$16,000 to produce.
23. **Management** The total cost (in dollars) to produce x algebra books is $C(x) = 5.25x + 40{,}000$.
(a) What is the marginal cost per book?
(b) What is the total cost to produce 5000 books?
24. **Management** In Exercise 8, we were given the following function for the total cost in dollars to produce x items.

$$C(x) = 500{,}000 + 4.75x$$

(a) Find the marginal cost per item of the items to be produced in this plant.
(b) Find the average cost per item.

Management *Assume that each of the following can be expressed as a linear cost function. Find* (a) *the cost function;* (b) *the revenue function.*

	Fixed Cost	*Marginal Cost per Item*	*Item Sells for*
25.	\$500	\$10	\$35
26.	\$180	\$11	\$20
27.	\$250	\$18	\$28
28.	\$1500	\$30	\$80

29. **Management** In the profit-volume chart below, EF and GH represent the profit-volume graphs of a single-product company for 1989 and 1990, respectively.*

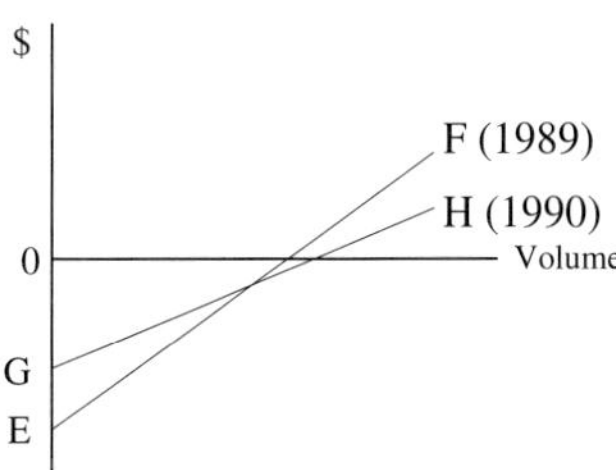

If 1989 and 1990 unit sales prices are identical, how did total fixed costs and unit variable costs of 1990 change compared to 1989?

	1990 Total Fixed Costs	*1990 Unit Variable Costs*
(a)	Decreased	Increased
(b)	Decreased	Decreased
(c)	Increased	Increased
(d)	Increased	Decreased

*Uniform CPA Examination, May, 1991, American Institute of Certified Public Accountants.

3.4 QUADRATIC FUNCTIONS

A **quadratic function** is a function whose rule is given by a quadratic polynomial, such as

$$f(x) = x^2, \qquad g(x) = 3x^2 + 30x + 67, \qquad \text{and} \qquad h(x) = -x^2 - 4x.$$

Thus, a quadratic function is one whose rule can be written in the form

$$f(x) = ax^2 + bx + c$$

for some constants a, b, c, with $a \neq 0$.

EXAMPLE 1 Using the standard viewing window, graph each of these quadratic functions.

(a) $f(x) = x^2$ **(b)** $k(x) = -.4x^2 + 1.6x + 5$

The graphs are shown in Figure 3.26. ■ 1

1 Graph these quadratic functions in the standard viewing window.

(a) $f(x) = x^2 - 2x + 3$

(b) $h(x) = -x^2 - 4x$

Answers:

(a)

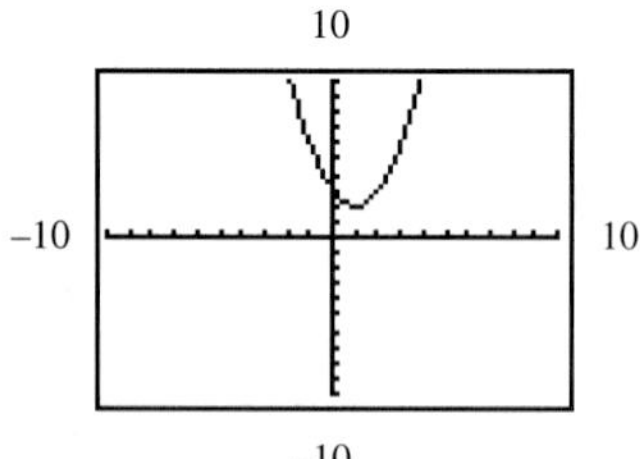

(b)

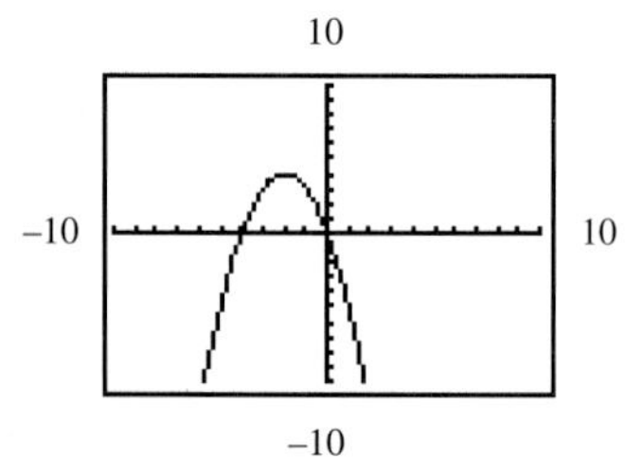

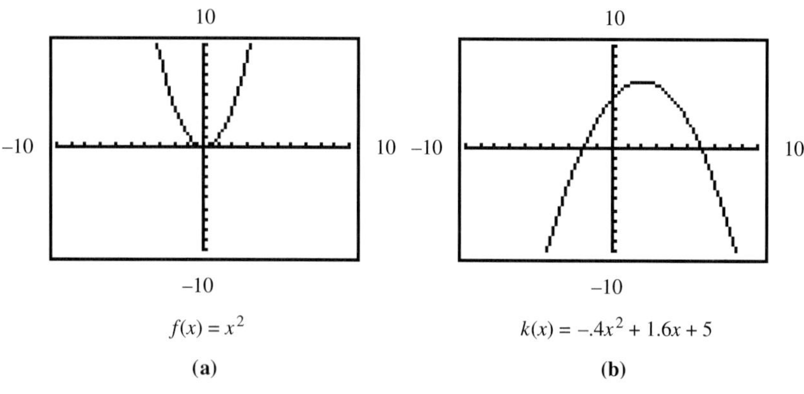

FIGURE 3.26

The curves in Figure 3.26 and in problem 1 in the margin are called **parabolas.** It can be shown that the graph of every quadratic function is a parabola. All parabolas have the same basic "cup" shape, though the cup may be broad or narrow. The parabola opens upward when the coefficient of x^2 is positive and downward when this coefficient is negative.

Parabolas have many useful properties. Cross sections of radar dishes and spotlights form parabolas. Discs often visible on the sidelines of televised football games are microphones having reflectors with parabolic cross sections. These microphones are used by the television networks to pick up the shouted signals of the quarterbacks.

When a parabola opens upward (as in Figure 3.26(a)), its lowest point is called the **vertex.** When a parabola opens downward (as in Figure 3.26(b)), its highest point is called the **vertex.** The vertical line through the vertex of a parabola is called the **axis of the parabola.** For example, (0, 0) is the vertex of the parabola in Figure 3.26(a) and its axis is the y-axis. If you were to fold this graph along its axis, the two halves of the parabola would match exactly. This means that a parabola is *symmetric* about its axis.

The vertex of a parabola can be roughly approximated by using the trace feature or accurately approximated by using the minimum or maximum finder on a calculator. However, there are algebraic techniques for finding the vertex precisely.

EXAMPLE 2 The function $g(x) = 2(x - 3)^2 + 1$ is a quadratic because its rule can be written in the required form:

$$g(x) = 2(x - 3)^2 + 1 = 2(x^2 - 6x + 9) + 1 = 2x^2 - 12x + 19.$$

Its graph (Figure 3.27) is an upward-opening parabola. Note that

$$g(3) = 2(3 - 3)^2 + 1 = 1,$$

so that (3, 1) is on the graph. Figure 3.27 suggests that (3, 1) is the vertex of the parabola. This can be proved algebraically as follows. When $x \neq 3$, the quantity $2(x - 3)^2$ is positive and hence

$$g(x) = 2(x - 3)^2 + 1 = (\text{a positive number}) + 1,$$

so that $g(x) > 1$. Therefore, every point $(x, g(x))$ on the graph with $x \neq 3$ has second coordinate $g(x)$ larger than 1 and hence lies *above* the point (3, 1). In other words, (3, 1) is the lowest point on the graph, the vertex of the parabola. Consequently, the vertical line $x = 3$ is the axis of the parabola. ■

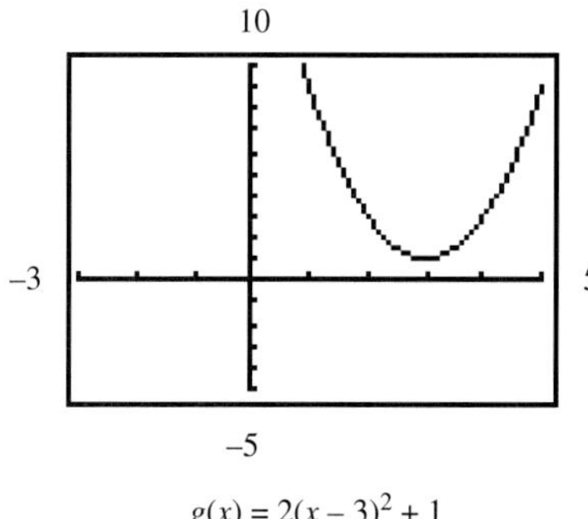

$g(x) = 2(x - 3)^2 + 1$

FIGURE 3.27

Example 2 illustrates some of the following facts, whose proofs are omitted.

> If f is a quadratic function defined by $y = a(x - h)^2 + k$, then the graph of the function f is a parabola having its vertex at (h, k) and axis of symmetry $x = h$.
>
> If $a > 0$, the parabola opens upward; if $a < 0$, it opens downward.
>
> If $0 < |a| < 1$, the parabola is "broader" than $y = x^2$, while if $|a| > 1$, the parabola is "narrower" than $y = x^2$.

EXAMPLE 3 Determine algebraically whether the parabola opens upward or downward and find its vertex.

(a) $f(x) = -3(x - 4)^2 - 7$

The rule of the function is in the form $f(x) = a(x - h)^2 + k$ (with $a = -3$, $h = 4$, and $k = -7$). The parabola opens downward ($a < 0$) and its vertex is $(h, k) = (4, -7)$. You can use your calculator and its maximum finder to confirm these results graphically.

2 Determine the vertex of the parabola algebraically and graph it.

(a) $f(x) = (x + 4)^2 - 3$

(b) $f(x) = -2(x - 3)^2 + 1$

Answers:

(a)

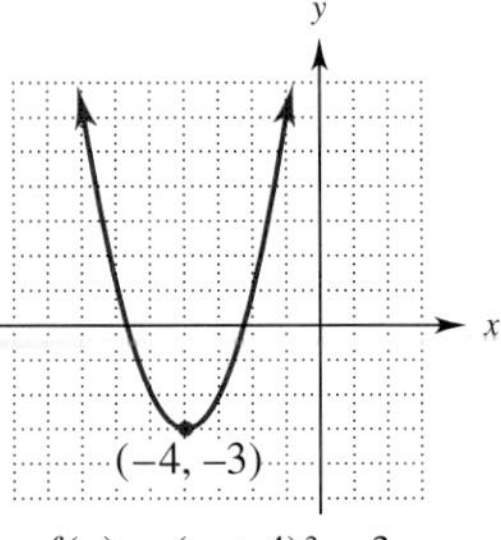

$f(x) = (x + 4)^2 - 3$

(b)

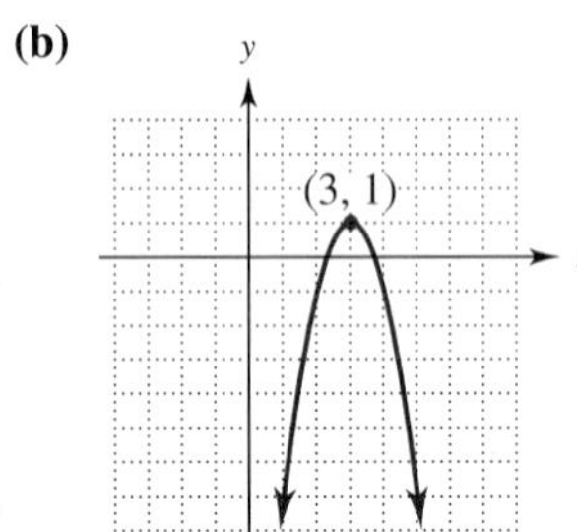

$f(x) = -2(x - 3)^2 + 1$

(b) $g(x) = 2(x + 3)^2 + 5$

Be careful here; the vertex is *not* (3, 5), as you should verify by graphing. To put the rule of $g(x)$ in the form $a(x - h)^2 + k$, we must rewrite it so that there is a minus sign inside the parentheses:

$$g(x) = 2(x + 3)^2 + 5 = 2(x - (-3))^2 + 5.$$

This is the required form with $a = 2$, $h = -3$, and $k = 5$. The parabola opens upward and its vertex is $(-3, 5)$. ■ 2

EXAMPLE 4 Find the rule of a quadratic function whose graph has vertex (3, 4) and passes through the point (6, 22).

The graph of $f(x) = a(x - h)^2 + k$ has vertex (h, k). We want $h = 3$ and $k = 4$, so that $f(x) = a(x - 3)^2 + 4$. Since (6, 22) is on the graph, we must have $f(6) = 22$. Therefore

$$\begin{aligned} f(x) &= a(x - 3)^2 + 4 \\ f(6) &= a(6 - 3)^2 + 4 \\ 22 &= a(3)^2 + 4 \\ 9a &= 18 \\ a &= 2. \end{aligned}$$

Thus, the graph of $f(x) = 2(x - 3)^2 + 4$ is a parabola with vertex (3, 4) that passes through (6, 22). ■

The vertex of each parabola in Examples 2 and 3 was easily determined because the rule of the function had the form

$$f(x) = a(x - h)^2 + k.$$

The rule of *any* quadratic function can be put in this form by using the technique of completing the square, which was discussed in Section 2.2.

EXAMPLE 5 By completing the square, determine the vertex of the graph of $f(x) = x^2 - 2x + 3$. Then graph the parabola.

Rewrite the equation in the form $f(x) = a(x - h)^2 + k$ by first writing $f(x) = x^2 - 2x + 3$ as

$$f(x) = (x^2 - 2x \qquad) + 3.$$

Now complete the square for the expression in parentheses. Take half the coefficient of x, namely $(\frac{1}{2})(-2) = -1$, and square the result: $(-1)^2 = 1$. In order to complete the square we must add 1 inside the parentheses, but in order not to change the rule of the function we must also subtract 1:

$$f(x) = (x^2 - 2x + \mathbf{1} - \mathbf{1}) + 3.$$

By the associative property,

$$f(x) = (x^2 - 2x + \mathbf{1}) + (\mathbf{-1} + 3).$$

Factor $x^2 - 2x + 1$ as $(x - 1)^2$, to get

$$f(x) = (x - 1)^2 + 2.$$

With the rule in this form, we can see that the graph is an upward-opening parabola with vertex (1, 2), as shown in Figure 3.28. ■ 3

3 Rewrite the rule of the function by completing the square, and use this form to find the vertex of the graph.

(a) $f(x) = x^2 - 6x + 11$

(b) $g(x) = x^2 + 8x + 18$

Answers:

(a) $f(x) = (x - 3)^2 + 2$; (3, 2)

(b) $g(x) = (x + 4)^2 + 2$; (−4, 2)

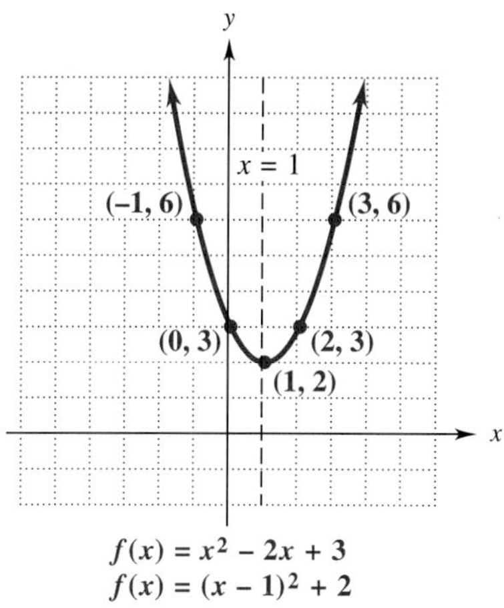

FIGURE 3.28

EXAMPLE 6 Find the vertex of the graph of $f(x) = -2x^2 + 12x - 19$ and graph the parabola.

Get $f(x)$ in the form $f(x) = a(x - h)^2 + k$ by first factoring -2 from $-2x^2 + 12x$.

$$f(x) = -2x^2 + 12x - 19 = -2(x^2 - 6x) - 19$$

Working inside the parentheses, take half of -6 (which is the coefficient of x): $(\frac{1}{2})(-6) = -3$. Square this result: $(-3)^2 = 9$. Add and subtract 9 inside the parentheses.

$$y = -2(x^2 - 6x + 9 - 9) - 19$$

$$y = \mathbf{-2}(x^2 - 6x + 9) + (\mathbf{-2})(-9) - 19 \qquad \text{Distributive property}$$

Simplify and factor to get

$$y = -2(x - 3)^2 - 1.$$

Since $a = -2$ is negative, the parabola opens downward. The vertex is at $(3, -1)$, and the parabola is narrower than $y = x^2$. Use these results and plot additional ordered pairs as needed to get the graph of Figure 3.29. ■ [4]

[4] Complete the square, find the vertex, and graph the following.

(a) $f(x) = 3x^2 - 12x + 14$

(b) $f(x) = -x^2 + 6x - 12$

Answers:

(a) $f(x) = 3(x - 2)^2 + 2$

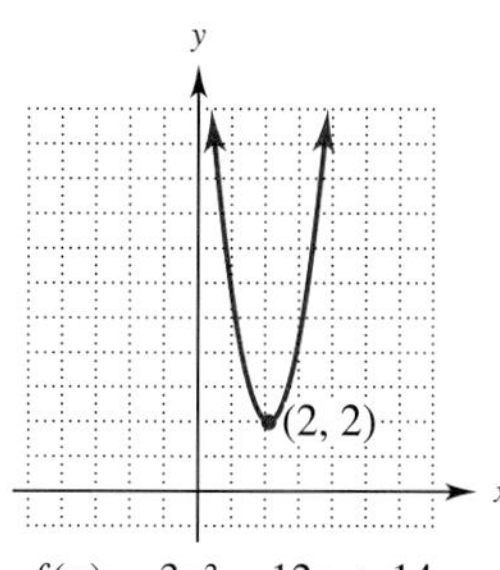

(b) $f(x) = -(x - 3)^2 - 3$

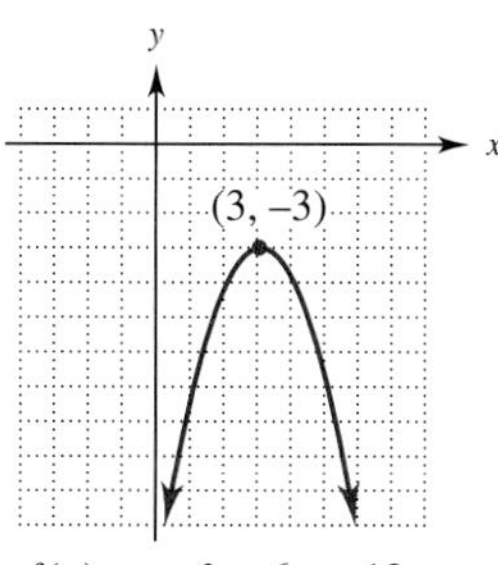

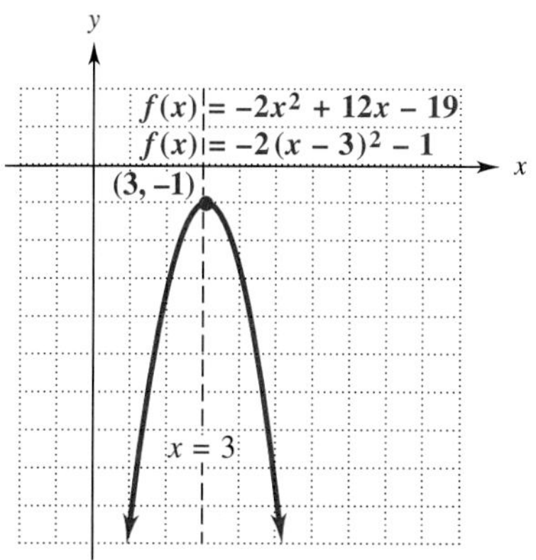

FIGURE 3.29

The technique of completing the square can be used to rewrite the general equation $f(x) = ax^2 + bx + c$ in the form $f(x) = a(x - h)^2 + k$, as is shown in Exercise 40. When this is done we obtain a formula for the coordinates of the vertex.

> The graph of $f(x) = ax^2 + bx + c$ is a parabola with vertex (h, k), where
>
> $$h = \frac{-b}{2a} \quad \text{and} \quad k = f(h).$$

EXAMPLE 7 Find the vertex, the axis, and the x- and y-intercepts of the graph of $f(x) = x^2 - x - 6$.

Since $a = 1$ and $b = -1$, the x-value of the vertex is

$$\frac{-b}{2a} = \frac{-(\mathbf{-1})}{2 \cdot \mathbf{1}} = \frac{1}{2}.$$

The y-value of the vertex is

$$f\left(\frac{1}{2}\right) = \left(\frac{1}{2}\right)^2 - \frac{1}{2} - 6 = -\frac{25}{4}.$$

The vertex is $(1/2, -25/4)$ and the axis of the parabola is $x = 1/2$, as shown in Figure 3.30. The intercepts are found by setting each variable equal to 0.

Set $f(x) = y = 0$;

$$\mathbf{0} = x^2 - x - 6$$
$$0 = (x + 2)(x - 3)$$
$$x + 2 = 0 \quad \text{or} \quad x - 3 = 0$$
$$x = -2 \qquad\qquad x = 3$$

Set $x = 0$:

$$f(x) = y = \mathbf{0}^2 - \mathbf{0} - 6 = -6$$

The y-intercept is -6.

The x-intercepts are -2 and 3. ■ 5

5 Find the vertex of the graph.

(a) $f(x) = 2x^2 - 7x + 12$

(b) $k(x) = -.4x^2 + 1.6x + 5$

Answers:

(a) $(7/4, 47/8)$

(b) $(2, 6.6)$

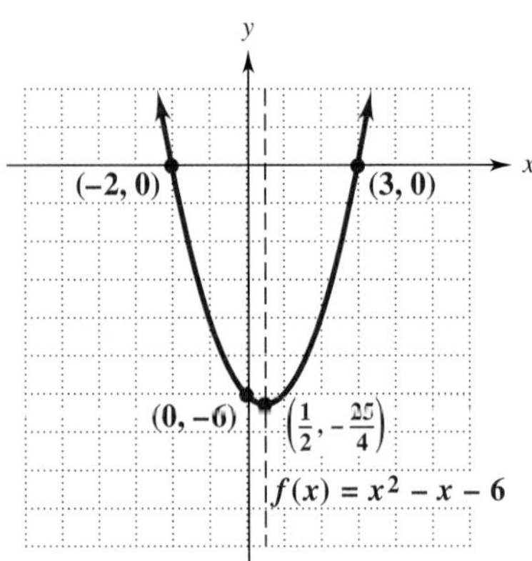

FIGURE 3.30

3.4 EXERCISES

Without graphing, determine the vertex of each of the following parabolas and state whether it opens upward or downward. (See Examples 2, 3, 5–7.)

1. $f(x) = 3(x - 5)^2 + 2$
2. $g(x) = -6(x - 2)^2 - 5$
3. $f(x) = -(x - 1)^2 + 2$
4. $g(x) = x^2 + 1$
5. $f(x) = x^2 + 12x + 1$
6. $g(x) = x^2 - 10x + 3$
7. $f(x) = 2x^2 + 4x + 1$
8. $g(x) = -3x^2 + 6x + 5$

Without graphing, determine the x- and y-intercepts of each of the following parabolas. (See Example 7.)

9. $f(x) = 3(x - 2)^2 - 3$
10. $f(x) = x^2 - 4x - 1$
11. $g(x) = 2x^2 + 8x + 6$
12. $g(x) = x^2 - 10x + 20$

Find the rule of a quadratic function whose graph has the given vertex and passes through the given point. (See Example 4.)

13. Vertex $(3, -5)$; point $(5, -9)$
14. Vertex $(2, 4)$; point $(0, -8)$
15. Vertex $(1, 2)$; point $(5, 6)$
16. Vertex $(-3, 2)$; point $(2, 1)$
17. Vertex $(-1, -2)$; point $(1, 2)$
18. Vertex $(2, -4)$; point $(5, 2)$

Graph each of the following parabolas. Find the vertex and axis of symmetry of each. (See Examples 1–7.)

19. $f(x) = (x + 2)^2$
20. $f(x) = -(x + 5)^2$
21. $f(x) = (x - 1)^2 - 3$
22. $f(x) = (x - 2)^2 + 1$
23. $f(x) = x^2 - 4x + 6$
24. $f(x) = x^2 + 6x + 3$
25. $f(x) = 2x^2 - 4x + 5$
26. $f(x) = -3x^2 + 24x - 46$
27. $f(x) = -x^2 + 6x - 6$
28. $f(x) = -x^2 + 2x + 5$

Determine the vertex of the parabola and find a viewing window that includes the origin and the vertex and shows the shape of the parabola.

29. $f(x) = 5x^2 - 72x + 271.2$
30. $f(x) = 3x^2 - 30x + 27$
31. $f(x) = .3x^2 - 57x + 12$
32. $f(x) = .005x^2 - .002x + .16$

In Exercises 33–38, graph the functions in parts (a)–(d) on the same set of axes; then answer part (e).

33. **(a)** $k(x) = x^2$ **(b)** $f(x) = 2x^2$
(c) $g(x) = 3x^2$ **(d)** $h(x) = 3.5x^2$
(e) Explain how the coefficient a in the function given by $f(x) = ax^2$ affects the shape of the graph, in comparison with the graph of $k(x) = x^2$, when $a > 1$.

34. **(a)** $k(x) = x^2$ **(b)** $f(x) = .8x^2$
(c) $g(x) = .5x^2$ **(d)** $h(x) = .3x^2$
(e) Explain how the coefficient a in the function given by $f(x) = ax^2$ affects the shape of the graph, in comparison with the graph of $k(x) = x^2$, when $0 < a < 1$.

35. **(a)** $k(x) = -x^2$ **(b)** $f(x) = -2x^2$
(c) $g(x) = -3x^2$ **(d)** $h(x) = -3.5x^2$
(e) Compare these graphs to the ones in Exercise 33 and explain how changing the sign of the coefficient a in the function given by $f(x) = ax^2$ affects the graph.

36. **(a)** $k(x) = x^2$ **(b)** $f(x) = x^2 + 2$
(c) $g(x) = x^2 + 3$ **(d)** $h(x) = x^2 + 5$
(e) Explain how the graph of $f(x) = x^2 + c$ (where c is a positive constant) can be obtained from the graph of $k(x) = x^2$.

37. **(a)** $k(x) = x^2$ **(b)** $f(x) = x^2 - 1$
(c) $g(x) = x^2 - 2$ **(d)** $h(x) = x^2 - 4$
(e) Explain how the graph of $f(x) = x^2 - c$ (where c is a positive constant) can be obtained from the graph of $k(x) = x^2$.

38. **(a)** $k(x) = x^2$ **(b)** $f(x) = (x + 2)^2$
(c) $g(x) = (x - 2)^2$ **(d)** $h(x) = (x - 4)^2$
(e) Explain how the graph of $f(x) = (x + c)^2$ and $f(x) = (x - c)^2$ (where c is a positive constant) can be obtained from the graph of $k(x) = x^2$.

39. Find the rule of a quadratic function whose graph is a parabola with vertex $(0, 0)$ that includes the point $(2, 12)$.

40. Verify that the right side of the equation $ax^2 + bx + c = a\left(x - \left(\frac{-b}{2a}\right)\right)^2 + \left(c - \frac{b^2}{4a}\right)$ equals the left side. Since the right side is in the form $a(x - h)^2 + k$, we conclude that the vertex of the parabola $f(x) = ax^2 + bx + c$ has x-coordinate $h = -b/2a$.

3.5 APPLICATIONS OF QUADRATIC FUNCTIONS

The fact that the vertex of a parabola $y = ax^2 + bx + c$ is the highest or lowest point on the graph can be used in applications to find a maximum or a minimum value. When $a > 0$, the graph opens upward, so the function has a minimum. When $a < 0$, the graph opens downward, producing a maximum.

EXAMPLE 1 Leslie Lahr owns and operates Aunt Emma's Blueberry Pies. She has hired a consultant to analyze her business operations. The consultant tells her that her profits, $P(x)$, from the sale of x units of pies, are given by

$$P(x) = 120x - x^2.$$

How many units of pies should be sold in order to maximize profit? What is the maximum profit?

The profit function can be rewritten as $P(x) = -x^2 + 120x$. Its graph is a downward-opening parabola (Figure 3.31). Its vertex, which may be found algebraically (as in Section 3.4) or graphically with a calculator's maximum finder, is (60, 3600). For each point on the graph,

the x-coordinate is the number of units of pies;

the y-coordinate is the profit on that number of units.

Only the portion of the graph of Quadrant I (where both coordinates are positive) is relevant here because she cannot sell a negative number of pies and she is not interested in a negative profit. *Maximum* profit occurs at the point with the largest y-coordinate, namely, the vertex, as shown in Figure 3.31. The maximum profit of \$3600 is obtained when 60 units of pies are sold. ■ 1

1 When a company sells x units of a product, its profit is $P(x) = -2x^2 + 40x + 280$. Find

(a) the number of units that should be sold so that maximum profit is received;

(b) the maximum profit.

Answers:

(a) 10 units

(b) \$480

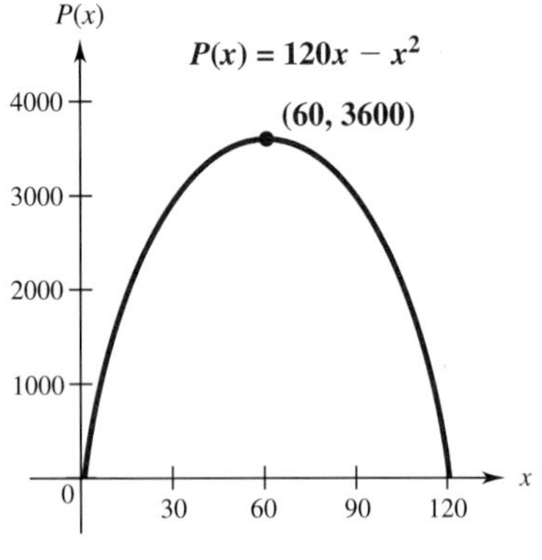

FIGURE 3.31

Supply and demand curves were introduced in Section 1.7. Here is a quadratic example.

EXAMPLE 2 Suppose that the price and demand for an item are related by

$$p = 150 - 6q^2, \qquad \text{Demand function}$$

where p is the price (in dollars) and q is the number of items demanded (in hundreds). The price and supply are related by

$$p = 10q^2 + 2q, \qquad \text{Supply function}$$

where q is the number of items supplied (in hundreds). Find the equilibrium demand (and supply) and the equilibrium price.

The graphs of both of these equations are parabolas (Figure 3.32). Only those portions of the graphs that lie in the first quadrant are included, because neither supply, demand, nor price can be negative.

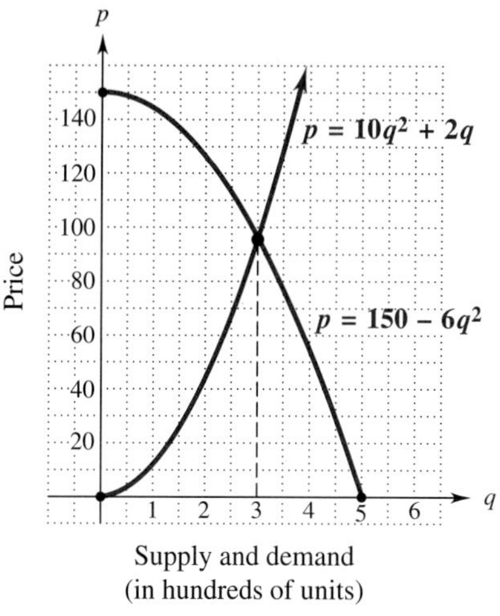

FIGURE 3.32

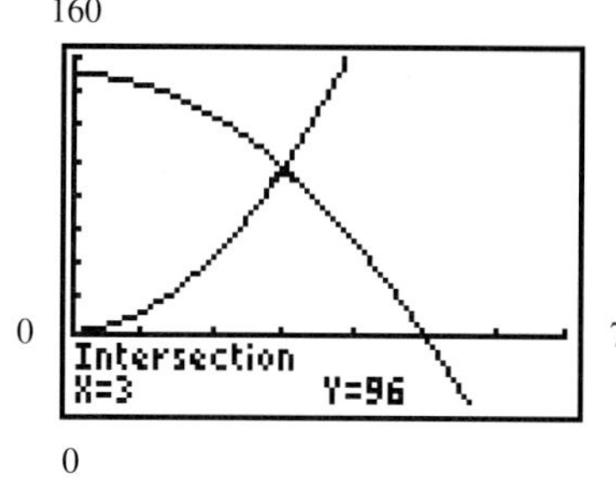

FIGURE 3.33

The point where the demand and supply curves intersect is the equilibrium point. Its first coordinate is the equilibrium demand (and supply) and its second coordinate is the equilibrium price. These coordinates may be found graphically or algebraically.

Graphical Method Graph the two functions on your calculator and use its intersection finder to determine that the equilibrium point is (3, 96), as in Figure 3.33. Since q represents quantity in hundreds, the equilibrium demand (and supply) is 300 items. The equilibrium price is \$96.

Algebraic Method At the equilibrium point, the second coordinate of the demand curve must be the same as the second coordinate of the supply curve so that

$$150 - 6q^2 = 10q^2 + 2q.$$

Write this quadratic equation in standard form as follows.

$$0 = 16q^2 + 2q - 150 \qquad \text{Add } -150 \text{ and } 6q^2 \text{ to both sides.}$$

$$0 = 8q^2 + q - 75 \qquad \text{Multiply both sides by } \frac{1}{2}.$$

This equation can be solved by the quadratic formula given in Section 2.2. Here $a = 8$, $b = 1$, and $c = -75$.

$$q = \frac{-1 \pm \sqrt{1^2 - 4(8)(-75)}}{2(8)}$$

$$= \frac{-1 \pm \sqrt{1 + 2400}}{16} \qquad -4(8)(-75) = 2400$$

$$= \frac{-1 \pm 49}{16} \qquad \sqrt{1 + 2400} = \sqrt{2401} = 49$$

$$q = \frac{-1 + 49}{16} = \frac{48}{16} = 3 \quad \text{or} \quad q = \frac{-1 - 49}{16} = -\frac{50}{16} = -\frac{25}{8}$$

2 The price and demand for an item are related by $p = 32 - x^2$, while price and supply are related by $p = x^2$. Find

(a) the equilibrium supply;

(b) the equilibrium price.

Answers:

(a) 4

(b) 16

It is not possible to make $-25/8$ units, so discard that answer and use only $q = 3$. Once again, the equilibrium demand (and supply) is 300. Find the equilibrium price by substituting 3 for q in either the supply or the demand function (and check your answer by using the other one). Using the supply function gives

$$p = 10q^2 + 2q$$

$$p = 10 \cdot \mathbf{3}^2 + 2 \cdot \mathbf{3} \qquad \text{Let } q = 3.$$

$$= 10 \cdot 9 + 6$$

$$p = 96. \quad \blacksquare \quad \boxed{2}$$

EXAMPLE 3 The rental manager of a small apartment complex with 16 units has found from experience that each \$40 increase in the monthly rent results in an empty apartment. All 16 apartments will be rented at a monthly rent of \$500. How many \$40 increases will produce maximum monthly income for the complex?

Let x represent the number of \$40 increases. Then the number of apartments rented will be $16 - x$. Also, the monthly rent per apartment will be $500 + 40x$. (There are x \$40 increases for a total increase of $40x$.) The monthly income, $I(x)$, is given by the number of apartments rented times the rent per apartment, so

$$I(x) = (16 - x)(500 + 40x)$$

$$= 8000 + 640x - 500x - 40x^2$$

$$= 8000 + 140x - 40x^2.$$

Since x represents the number of \$40 increases and each \$40 increase causes one empty apartment, x must be a whole number. Since there are only 16 apartments, $0 \le x \le 16$. Because there is a small number of possibilities, the value of x that produces maximum income may be found in two ways.

Table Method Use the table making feature of your calculator to find all the values of $I(x)$ for $x = 0, 1, 2, \ldots, 16$, as in Figure 3.34.

X	Y1
0	8000
1	8100
2	8120
3	8060
4	7920
5	7700
6	7400

X=0

X	Y1
7	7020
8	6560
9	6020
10	5400
11	4700
12	3920
13	3060

X=7

X	Y1
14	2120
15	1100
16	0
17	-1180
18	-2440
19	-3780
20	-5200

X=14

FIGURE 3.34

The tables show that a maximum income of \$8120 occurs when $x = 2$. So the manager should charge a rent of $500 + 2(40) = \$580$ and leave 2 apartments vacant.

Algebraic Method The graph of $I(x) = 8000 + 140x - 40x^2$ is a downward-opening parabola (why?) and the value of x that produces maximum income occurs at the vertex. The methods of Section 3.4 show that the vertex is (1.75, 8122.50).

Since x must be a whole number, evaluate $I(x)$ at $x = 1$ and $x = 2$ to see which one gives the best result.

$$\text{If } x = 1, \text{ then } I(1) = 8000 + 140(1) - 40(1)^2 = 8100.$$
$$\text{If } x = 2, \text{ then } I(2) = 8000 + 140(2) - 40(2)^2 = 8120.$$

Once again, two rent increases of \$40 each produce a maximum income of \$8120. ■

QUADRATIC MODELS Real-world data can sometimes be used to construct a quadratic function that approximates the data. Such **quadratic models** can then be used (subject to limitations) to predict future behavior.

EXAMPLE 4 The table below lists the cumulative number of AIDS cases diagnosed in the United States during 1982–1993.* It shows, for example, that 22,620 cases were diagnosed in 1982–1985.

Year	*AIDS Cases*	*Year*	*AIDS Cases*
1982	1,563	1988	105,489
1983	4,647	1989	147,170
1984	10,845	1990	193,245
1985	22,620	1991	248,023
1986	41,662	1992	315,329
1987	70,222	1993	361,509

(a) Display this information graphically.

Let $x = 0$ represent the year 1980, $x = 1$ represent 1981, and so on. Then plot the points given by the table: (2, 1563), (3, 4647), etc. (Figure 3.35).

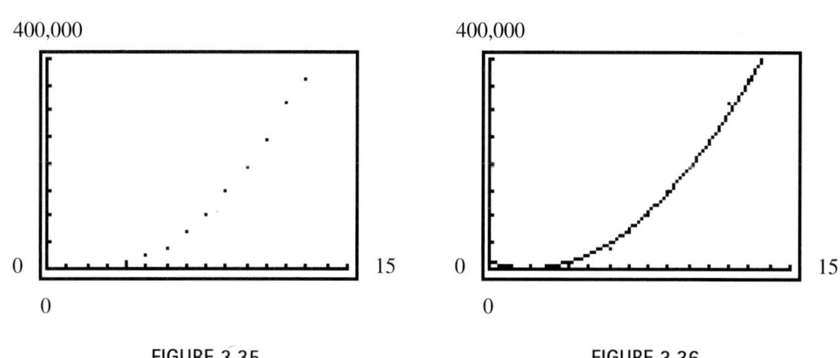

FIGURE 3.35

FIGURE 3.36

*U.S. Dept. of Health and Human Services, Centers for Disease Control and Prevention, *HIV/AIDS Surveillance*, March 1994.

(b) The shape of the data points in Figure 3.35 resembles the right half of an upward-opening parabola. Find a quadratic model $f(x) = a(x - h)^2 + k$ for this data.

Based on Figure 3.35, we let (2, 1563) be the vertex of the parabola, so that $f(x) = a(x - 2)^2 + 1563$. Use another point, say (13, 361509), to find a (another choice here would lead to a different quadratic model).

$$f(x) = a(x - 2)^2 + 1563$$
$$361{,}509 = a(13 - 2)^2 + 1563$$
$$121a = 359{,}946$$
$$a \approx 2974.76$$

Therefore $f(x) = 2974.76(x - 2)^2 + 1563$ is a quadratic model for the data. The graph of $f(x)$ in Figure 3.36 appears to be a reasonable approximation of the data.

(c) Use the quadratic model in part (b) to estimate the total number of AIDS cases diagnosed by 2000.

The year 2000 corresponds to $x = 20$, so the number is approximately

$$f(20) = 2974.76(20 - 2)^2 + 1563 \approx 965{,}385. \quad ■ \quad \boxed{3}$$

$\boxed{3}$ Find another quadratic model in Example 4(b) by using (2, 1563) as vertex and (11, 248023) as the other point.

Answer:
$f(x) = 3042.72(x - 2)^2 + 1563$

3.5 EXERCISES

Work these problems. (See Example 1.)

1. **Management** Shannise Cole makes and sells candy. She has found that the cost per box for making x boxes of candy is given by

$$C(x) = x^2 - 10x + 32.$$

   (a) How much does it cost per box to make 2 boxes? 4 boxes? 10 boxes?
   (b) Graph the cost function $C(x)$ and mark the points corresponding to 2, 4, and 10 boxes.
   (c) What point on the graph corresponds to the number of boxes that will make the cost per box as small as possible?
   (d) How many boxes should she make in order to keep the cost per box at a minimum? What is the minimum cost per box?

2. **Management** Greg Tobin sells bottled water. He has found that the average amount of time he spends with each customer is related to his weekly sales volume by the function

$$f(x) = x(60 - x),$$

   where x is the number of minutes per customer and $f(x)$ is the number of cases sold per week.
   (a) How many cases does he sell if he spends 10 minutes with each customer? 20 minutes? 45 minutes?
   (b) Choose an appropriate scale for the axes and sketch the graph of $f(x)$. Mark the points on the graph corresponding to 10, 20, and 45 minutes.
   (c) Explain what the vertex of the graph represents.
   (d) How long should Greg spend with each customer in order to sell as many cases per week as possible? In this case, how many cases will he sell?

3. **Management** French fries produce a tremendous profit (150% to 300%) for many fast food restaurants. Management, therefore, desires to maximize the number of bags sold. Suppose that a mathematical model connecting p, the profit per day from french fries (in tens of dollars), and x, the price per bag (in dimes), is $p = -2x^2 + 24x + 8$.
   (a) Find the price per bag that leads to maximum profit.
   (b) What is the maximum profit?

4. **Natural Science** A researcher in physiology has decided that a good mathematical model for the number of impulses fired after a nerve has been stimulated is given by $y = -x^2 + 20x - 60$, where y is the number of responses per millisecond and x is the number of milliseconds since the nerve was stimulated.
   (a) When will the maximum firing rate be reached?
   (b) What is the maximum firing rate?

5. **Physical Science** If an object is thrown upward with an initial velocity of 32 feet per second, then its height, in feet, above the ground after t seconds is given by

$$h = 32t - 16t^2.$$

   Find the maximum height attained by the object. Find the number of seconds it takes for the object to hit the ground.

6. **Management** Colleen Davis owns a factory that manufactures souvenir key chains. Her weekly profit (in hundreds of dollars) is given by $P(x) = -2x^2 + 60x - 120$, where x is the number of cases of key chains sold.
   (a) What is the largest number of cases she can sell and still make a profit?
   (b) Explain how it is possible for her to lose money if she sells more cases than your answer in part (a).
   (c) How many cases should she make and sell in order to maximize her profits?

7. **Management** The manager of a bicycle shop has found that, at a price (in dollars) of $p(x) = 150 - \frac{x}{4}$ per bicycle, x bicycles will be sold.
   (a) Find an expression for the total revenue from the sale of x bicycles. (*Hint:* revenue = demand × price.)
   (b) Find the number of bicycle sales that leads to maximum revenue.
   (c) Find the maximum revenue.

8. **Management** If the price (in dollars) of a videotape is $p(x) = 40 - \frac{x}{10}$, then x tapes will be sold.
   (a) Find an expression for the total revenue from the sale of x tapes.
   (b) Find the number of tapes that will produce maximum revenue.
   (c) Find the maximum revenue.

9. **Management** The demand for a certain type of cosmetic is given by

$$p = 500 - x,$$

where p is the price when x units are demanded.
   (a) Find the revenue, $R(x)$, that would be obtained at a demand of x.
   (b) Graph the revenue function, $R(x)$.
   (c) From the graph of the revenue function, estimate the price that will produce the maximum revenue.
   (d) What is the maximum revenue?

Work the following problem. (See Example 2.)

10. **Management** Suppose the price p of widgets is related to the quantity q that is demanded by

$$p = 640 - 5q^2,$$

where q is measured in hundreds of widgets. Find the price when the number of widgets demanded is
(a) 0; (b) 5; (c) 10.
Suppose the supply function for widgets is given by $p = 5q^2$, where q is the number of widgets (in hundreds) that are supplied at price p.
   (d) Graph the demand function $p = 640 - 5q^2$ and the supply function $p = 5q^2$ on the same axes.
   (e) Find the equilibrium supply.
   (f) Find the equilibrium price.

Management *Suppose the supply and demand for a certain textbook are given by:*

$$\text{supply: } p = \frac{1}{5}q^2; \quad \text{demand: } p = -\frac{1}{5}q^2 + 40,$$

where p is price and q is quantity.

11. How many books are demanded at a price of
(a) 10? (b) 20? (c) 30? (d) 40?
How many books are supplied at a price of
(e) 5? (f) 10? (g) 20? (h) 30?
(i) Graph the supply and demand functions on the same axes.

12. Find the equilibrium demand and the equilibrium price in Exercise 11.

Management *Work each problem. (See Example 3.)*

13. A charter flight charges a fare of \$200 per person, plus \$4 per person for each unsold seat on the plane. If the plane holds 100 passengers and if x represents the number of unsold seats, find the following.
   (a) An expression for the total revenue received for the flight. (*Hint:* Multiply the number of people flying, $100 - x$, by the price per ticket.)
   (b) The graph for the expression of part (a).
   (c) The number of unsold seats that will produce the maximum revenue.
   (d) The maximum revenue.

14. The revenue of a charter bus company depends on the number of unsold seats. If 100 seats are sold, the price is \$50. Each unsold seat increases the price per seat by \$1. Let x represent the number of unsold seats.
   (a) Write an expression for the number of seats that are sold.
   (b) Write an expression for the price per seat.
   (c) Write an expression for the revenue.
   (d) Find the number of unsold seats that will produce the maximum revenue.
   (e) Find the maximum revenue.

15. Farmer Linton wants to find the best time to take her hogs to market. The current price is 88 cents per pound and her hogs weigh an average of 90 pounds. The hogs gain 5 pounds per week and the market price for hogs is falling each week by 2 cents per pound. How many weeks should Ms. Linton wait before taking her hogs to market in order to receive as much money as possible? At this time, how much money (per hog) will she get?

Work these problems. (See Example 4.)

16. Management Federal government revenues (in billions of dollars) for selected years are shown in the table.*

Year	*Revenue*
1960	92.5
1965	116.8
1970	192.8
1975	279.1
1980	517.1
1985	734.1

(a) Let $x = 0$ correspond to 1960. Use (0, 92.5) as the vertex and the data from 1985 to find a quadratic function $f(x) = a(x - h)^2 + k$ that models this data.

(b) Use the quadratic model to estimate government revenue in the years 1981, 1988, and 1991. How well do the estimates compare to the actual revenues of 599.3, 909, and 1119.1? Does this model seem reasonable?

(c) Estimate government revenue in 1999.

17. Natural Science The table lists the total cumulative number of deaths in the United States to date known to have been caused by AIDS.†

Year	*Deaths*
1982	620
1983	2,122
1984	5,600
1985	12,529
1986	24,550
1987	40,820
1988	61,723
1989	89,172
1990	119,821
1991	154,567
1992	191,508
1993	220,592

(a) Let $x = 0$ correspond to 1980 and plot the data points.

(b) Use (2, 620) as the vertex and (13, 220592) as the other point to find a quadratic model $g(x) = a(x - h)^2 + k$ for this data.

(c) Plot the data and the graph of $g(x)$ on the same coordinate plane. How well does g model the data?

(d) Use g to estimate the numbers of deaths by the year 2000.

18. Management The gross national product (GNP) of the United States in billions of 1982 dollars was 2416.2 in 1970, 3187.1 in 1980, and 4155.8 in 1990.*

(a) Use the points corresponding to 1970 (vertex) and 1990 to construct a quadratic model for this data, with $x = 0$ corresponding to 1970.

(b) Estimate the GNP in 1980, 1985, 1995, and 2000. How good is the 1980 estimate?

19. A field bounded on one side by a river is to be fenced on three sides to form a rectangular enclosure. There are 320 ft of fencing available. What should the dimensions be to have an enclosure with the maximum possible area?

20. A rectangular garden bounded on one side by a river is to be fenced on the other three sides. Fencing material for the side parallel to the river costs \$30 per foot and material for the other two sides costs \$10 per foot. What are the dimensions of the garden of largest possible area, if \$1200 is to be spent for fencing material?

21. A trough is to be made by bending a long, flat piece of metal 10 inches wide into a rectangular shape. What depth should the trough be to have maximum possible cross-sectional area?

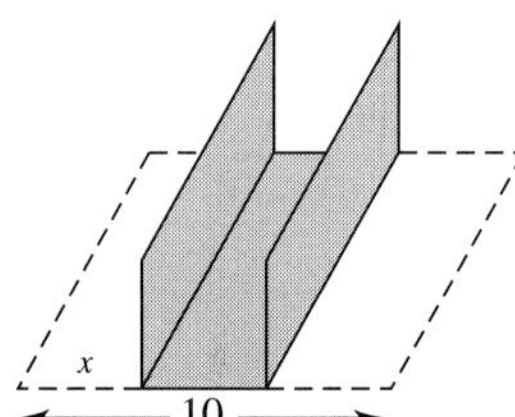

22. A culvert is shaped like a parabola, 18 centimeters across the top and 12 centimeters deep. How wide is the culvert 8 centimeters from the top?

Management *Recall that profit equals revenue minus cost. In Exercises 23 and 24 find the following.*

(a) *The break-even point (to the nearest tenth)*

(b) *The x-value that makes revenue a maximum*

(c) *The x-value that makes profit a maximum*

(d) *The maximum profit*

(e) *For what x-values will a loss occur?*

(f) *For what x-values will a profit occur?*

23. $R(x) = 60x - 2x^2$; $C(x) = 20x + 80$

24. $R(x) = 75x - 3x^2$; $C(x) = 21x + 65$

*Economic Reports of the President, 1960–1991.

†U.S. Dept. of Health and Human Services, Centers for Disease Control and Prevention, *HIV/AIDS Surveillance,* March 1994.

*Economic Reports of the President, 1970–1991.

CHAPTER 3 SUMMARY

Key Terms and Symbols

3.1 function
domain
range
functional notation
function evaluation

3.2 graph
piecewise linear function
absolute value function
step function
greatest integer function
vertical line test
hidden behavior

3.3 linear function
linear model
average rate of change
fixed cost
marginal cost
linear cost function
average cost

3.4 quadratic function
parabola
vertex
axis

3.5 quadratic model

Key Concepts

A **function** consists of a set of input numbers called the **domain,** a set of output numbers called the **range,** and a rule by which each number in the domain determines exactly one number in the range.

If a vertical line intersects a graph in more than one point, the graph is not that of a function.

A **linear cost function** has equation $C(x) = mx + b$ where m is the **marginal cost** (the cost of producing one more item) and b is the **fixed cost.**

The **quadratic function** defined by $y = a(x - h)^2 + k$ has a graph that is a **parabola** with vertex (h, k) and axis of symmetry $x = h$. The parabola opens upward if $a > 0$, downward if $a < 0$. If the equation is in the form $f(x) = ax^2 + bx + c$, the vertex is $\left(-\frac{b}{2a}, f\left(-\frac{b}{2a}\right)\right)$.

Chapter 3 Review Exercises

Which of the following rules defines a function?

1.

x	3	2	1	0	1	2
y	8	5	2	0	−2	−5

2.

x	2	1	0	−1	−2
y	5	3	1	−1	−3

3. $y = \sqrt{x}$ **4.** $x = |y|$

5. $x = y^2 + 1$ **6.** $y = 5x - 2$

For each function, find (a) $f(6)$, (b) $f(-2)$, (c) $f(p)$, (d) $f(r + 1)$.

7. $f(x) = 4x - 1$ **8.** $f(x) = 3 - 4x$

9. $f(x) = -x^2 + 2x - 4$ **10.** $f(x) = 8 - x - x^2$

11. Let $f(x) = 5x - 3$ and $g(x) = -x^2 + 4x$. Find each of the following.
(a) $f(-2)$ **(b)** $g(3)$ **(c)** $g(-k)$
(d) $g(3m)$ **(e)** $g(k - 5)$ **(f)** $f(3 - p)$

12. Let $f(x) = 1.4x^3 - 3.88x^2 + 5x + 6.32$. Construct a table that shows the (approximate) values of the function when $x = 2.1, 4.45, 6.8, 9.15, 11.5$, and 13.85.

Graph each function.

13. $f(x) = |x| - 3$ **14.** $f(x) = -|x| - 2$

15. $f(x) = -|x + 1| + 3$ **16.** $f(x) = 2|x - 3| - 4$

17. $f(x) = [x - 3]$ **18.** $f(x) = \left[\frac{1}{2}x - 2\right]$

19. $f(x) = \begin{cases} -4x + 2 & \text{if } x \le 1 \\ 3x - 5 & \text{if } x > 1 \end{cases}$

20. $f(x) = \begin{cases} 3x + 1 & \text{if } x < 2 \\ -x + 4 & \text{if } x \ge 2 \end{cases}$

21. $f(x) = \begin{cases} |x| & \text{if } x < 3 \\ 6 - x & \text{if } x \ge 3 \end{cases}$

If the graph of the function in the standard viewing window contains any horizontal line segments, determine what the graph actually looks like along these segments and find a window that shows this behavior.

22. $f(x) = x^7 + x^5 - .3x^3 + 3$

23. $g(x) = x^3 - .1x^2 - .003x + 1$

24. $f(x) = x^3 - .1x^2 + .005x - 2$

Management *In Exercises 25–28 find the following.*
(a) *the linear cost function*
(b) *the marginal cost*
(c) *the average cost per unit to produce 100 units*

25. Eight units cost \$300; fixed cost is \$60.

26. Fixed cost is \$2000; 36 units cost \$8480.

27. Twelve units cost \$445; 50 units cost \$1585.

28. Thirty units cost \$1500; 120 units cost \$5640.

29. Management The graph shows the percent of car owners who own foreign cars since 1975. Estimate the average rate of change in the percent over the following intervals.
(a) 1975 to 1983 **(b)** 1983 to 1987
(c) 1975 to 1991 **(d)** 1987 to 1991

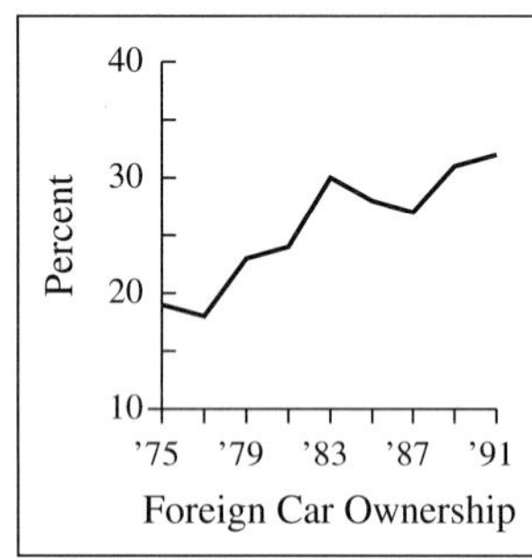

Foreign Car Ownership

30. Management Let f be a function that gives the cost to rent a floor polisher for x hours. The cost is a flat \$3 for renting the polisher plus \$4 per day or fraction of a day for using the polisher.
(a) Graph f.
(b) Give the domain and range of f.
(c) David Fleming wants to rent a polisher, but he can spend no more than \$15. At most how many days can he use it?

31. Management A trailer hauling service charges \$45, plus \$2 per mile or part of a mile.
(a) Is \$90 enough for a 20-mile haul?
(b) Graph the ordered pairs (miles, cost).
(c) Give the domain and range.

32. Social Sciences The birth rate per thousand in developing countries, for 1775–1977, can be approximated by

$$f(x) = \begin{cases} 42 & \text{from 1775 to 1925} \\ 67.5 - .17x & \text{from 1925 to 1977.} \end{cases}$$

Graph the function. Let $x = 0$ correspond to 1775. What does the graph suggest about the birth rate in developing countries?

Without graphing, determine whether each of the following parabolas opens upward or downward and find its vertex.

33. $f(x) = 3(x - 2)^2 + 6$ **34.** $f(x) = 2(x + 3)^2 - 5$

35. $g(x) = -4(x + 1)^2 + 8$ **36.** $g(x) = -5(x - 4)^2 - 6$

Graph each of the following and label its vertex.

37. $f(x) = x^2 - 4$ **38.** $f(x) = 6 - x^2$

39. $f(x) = x^2 + 2x - 3$ **40.** $f(x) = -x^2 + 6x - 3$

41. $f(x) = -x^2 - 4x + 1$ **42.** $f(x) = 4x^2 - 8x + 3$

43. $f(x) = 2x^2 + 4x - 3$ **44.** $f(x) = -3x^2 - 12x - 8$

Determine whether each of the following functions has a minimum or a maximum value and find that value.

45. $f(x) = x^2 + 6x - 2$ **46.** $f(x) = x^2 + 4x + 5$

47. $g(x) = -4x^2 + 8x + 3$ **48.** $g(x) = -3x^2 - 6x + 3$

Solve each problem.

49. Management The commodity market is very unstable; money can be made or lost quickly when investing in soybeans, wheat, pork bellies, and the like. Suppose that an investor kept track of her total profit, P, at time t, measured in months, after she began investing and found that $P = -4t^2 + 32t - 20$. At what point was her profit largest? (*Hint:* $t > 0$ in this case.)

50. Physical Science The height h (in feet) of a rocket at time t seconds is given by $h = -16t^2 + 800t$.
(a) How long does it take the rocket to reach 3200 feet?
(b) What is the maximum height of the rocket?

51. Management The Hopkins Company's profit in thousands of dollars is given by $P = -4x^2 + 88x - 259$, where x is the number of hundreds of cases produced. How many cases should be produced if the company is to make a profit?

52. Management The manager of a large apartment complex has found that the profit is given by $P = -x^2 + 250x - 15{,}000$, where x is the number of units rented. For what value of x does the complex produce the largest profit?

53. Find the dimensions of the rectangular region of maximum area that can be enclosed with 200 meters of fencing.

54. A rectangular enclosure is to be built with three sides made out of redwood fencing at a cost of \$15 per running foot and the fourth side made out of cement blocks at a cost of \$30 per running foot. \$900 is available for the project. What are the dimensions of the enclosure with maximum possible area?

CASE 3

Marginal Cost—Booz, Allen and Hamilton*

Booz, Allen and Hamilton is a large management consulting firm. One of the services it provides to client companies is profitability studies, which show ways in which the client can increase profit levels. The client company requesting the analysis presented in this case is a large producer of a staple food. The company buys from farmers, and then processes the food in its mills, resulting in a finished product. The company sells both at retail and under its own brands, and in bulk to other companies who use the product in the manufacture of convenience foods.

The client company has been reasonably profitable in recent years, but the management retained Booz, Allen and Hamilton to see whether its consultants could suggest ways of increasing company profits. The management of the company had long operated with the philosophy of trying to process and sell as much of its product as possible, since they felt this would lower the average processing cost per unit sold. However, the consultants found that the client's fixed mill costs were quite low, and that, in fact, processing extra units made the cost per unit start to increase. (There are several reasons for this: the company must run three shifts, machines break down more often, and so on.)

In this case, we shall discuss the marginal cost of two of the company's products. The marginal cost (cost of producing an extra unit) of production for product A was found by the consultants to be approximated by the linear function

$$y = .133x + 10.09,$$

where x is the number of units produced (in millions) and y is the marginal cost.

For example, at a level of production of 3.1 million units, an additional unit of product A would cost about

$$\begin{aligned} y &= .133(3.1) + 10.09 \\ &\approx \$10.50. \end{aligned}$$

At a level of production of 5.7 million units, an extra unit costs \$10.85. Figure 1 shows a graph of the marginal cost function from $x = 3.1$ to $x = 5.7$, the domain to which the function above was found to apply.

The selling price for product A is \$10.73 per unit, so that, as shown on the graph of Figure 1, the company was losing money on many units of the product that it sold. Since the selling price could not be raised if the company was to remain competitive, the consultants recommended that production of product A be cut.

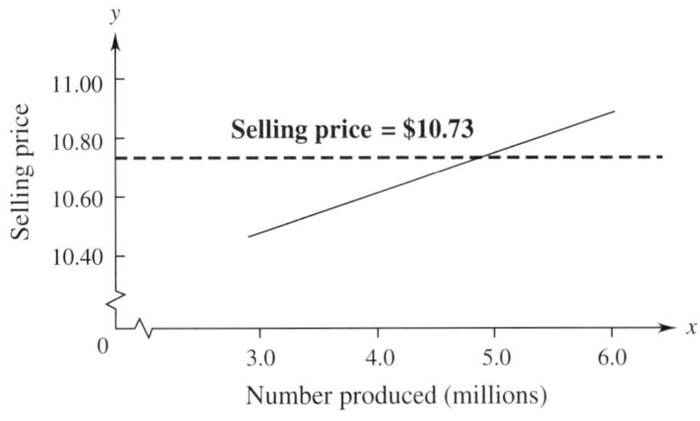

FIGURE 1

For product B, the Booz, Allen and Hamilton consultants found a marginal cost function given by

$$y = .0667x + 10.29,$$

with x and y as defined above. Verify that at a production level of 3.1 million units, the marginal cost is \$10.50, while at a production level of 5.7 million units, the marginal cost is \$10.67. Since the selling price of this product is \$9.65, the consultants again recommended a cutback in production.

The consultants ran similar cost analyses of other products made by the company, and then issued their recommendations: the company should reduce total production by 2.1 million units. The analysts predicted that this would raise profits for the products under discussion from \$8.3 million annually to \$9.6 million, which is very close to what actually happened when the client took this advice.

EXERCISES

1. At what level of production, x, was the marginal cost of a unit of product A equal to the selling price?
2. Graph the marginal cost function for product B from $x = 3.1$ million units to $x = 5.7$ million units.
3. Find the number of units for which marginal cost equals the selling price for product B.
4. For product C, the marginal cost of production is
$$y = .133x + 9.46.$$
   (a) Find the marginal cost at a level of production of 3.1 million units; of 5.7 million units.
   (b) Graph the marginal cost function.
   (c) For a selling price of \$9.57, find the level of production for which the cost equals the selling price.

*Case study, "Marginal Cost—Booz, Allen and Hamilton" supplied by John R. Dowdle of Booz, Allen & Hamilton, Inc. Reprinted by permission.

Polynomial and Rational Functions

Polynomial functions (that is, functions defined by polynomial expressions) arise naturally in many real world applications. They are also useful for approximating many complicated functions in applied mathematics. In Chapter 3 we considered linear and quadratic polynomial functions. In this chapter we examine polynomial functions of higher degree, as well as rational functions (whose rules are given by quotients of polynomials).

1 Graph these functions in the viewing window used in Example 1.

(a) $f(x) = -x^5$

(b) $g(x) = 2x^6$

Answers:

(a)

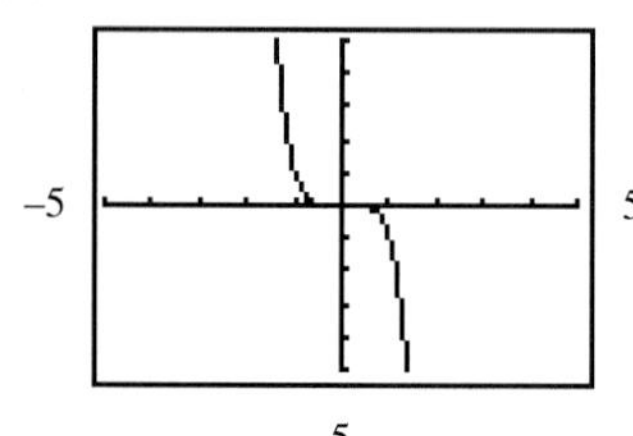

(b)

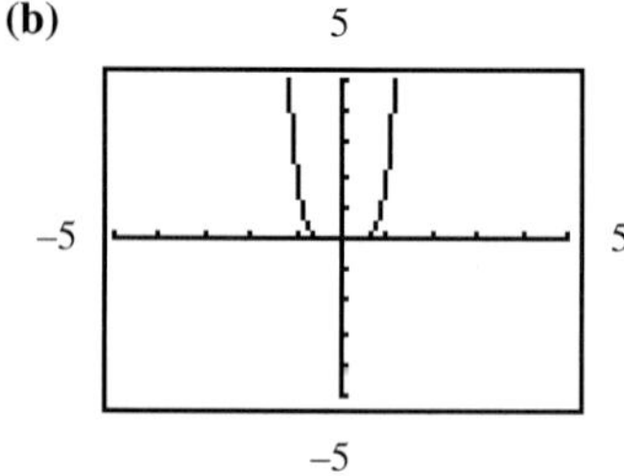

4.1 POLYNOMIAL FUNCTIONS

A **polynomial function of degree *n*** is a function whose rule is given by a polynomial of degree n.* For example, linear functions, such as

$$f(x) = 3x - 2 \quad \text{and} \quad g(x) = 7x + 5,$$

are polynomial functions of degree 1 and quadratic functions, such as

$$f(x) = 3x^2 + 4x - 6 \quad \text{and} \quad g(x) = -2x^2 + 9,$$

are polynomial functions of degree 2. Similarly, the function given by

$$f(x) = 2x^4 + 5x^3 - 6x^2 + x - 3$$

is a polynomial function of degree 4.

The simplest polynomial functions are those whose rules are of the form $f(x) = ax^n$ (where a is constant).

EXAMPLE 1 Graph each of these functions in the viewing window with $-5 \le x \le 5$ and $-5 \le y \le 5$.

(a) $f(x) = 1.5x^3$ **(b)** $g(x) = -.7x^4$

The graphs are shown in Figure 4.1. ■ 1

*The degree of a polynomial was defined on page 23.

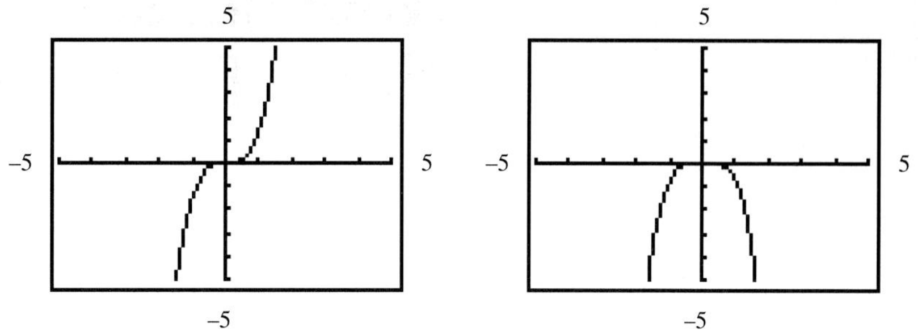

$f(x) = 1.5x^3$

(a)

$g(x) = -.7x^4$

(b)

FIGURE 4.1

The graph of $f(x) = ax^n$ has the same general shape as one of the graphs in Figure 4.1 or Problem 1 in the margin.

GRAPH OF $f(x) = ax^n$

If the exponent n is even, then the graph of $f(x) = ax^n$ is cup-shaped with the bottom of the cup at the origin and the y-axis through the middle; it opens upward when $a > 0$ and downward when $a < 0$.

If the exponent n is odd, then the graph of $f(x) = ax^n$ moves upward from left to right when $a > 0$ and downward when $a < 0$, with a single bend at the origin.

The domain of every polynomial function is the set of all real numbers. The range of a polynomial function of odd degree (1, 3, 5, 7, and so on) is also the set of all real numbers. Graphs typical of polynomial functions of odd degree are shown in Figure 4.2.

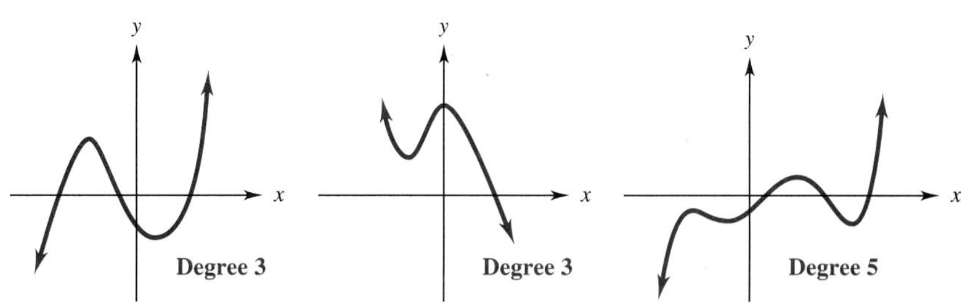

FIGURE 4.2

A polynomial function of even degree has a range that takes the form $y \leq k$ or $y \geq k$, for some real number k. Figure 4.3 on the next page shows two graphs of typical polynomial functions of even degree.

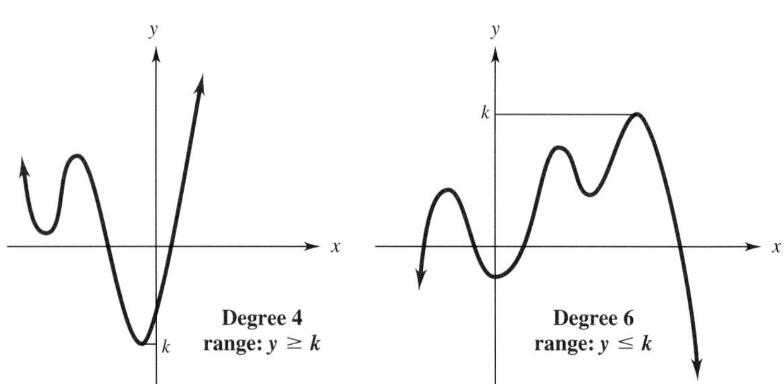

FIGURE 4.3

As illustrated in the preceding figures, the graph of a typical polynomial function moves sharply away from the x-axis at the far left and far right and may have several "peaks" and "valleys." For instance, the right-hand graph in Figure 4.3 has 3 peaks and 2 valleys. Note that this is the graph of a polynomial of degree 6 and that there are a total of 5 peaks and valleys. The location of peaks and valleys on a graph can be approximated with a high degree of accuracy by a maximum or minimum finder on a calculator. Calculus is needed to determine their exact locations.

Since the domain of a polynomial function is the set of all real numbers, every polynomial graph extends forever to the left and to the right, although this isn't always apparent in some viewing windows. However, there is an easy way of determining the general shape of the graph at the far left and right (that is, when $|x|$ is very large).

2 Find a viewing window larger than the standard window in which the graphs of $g(x) = x^4$ and $f(x) = x^4 - 2x^2 - 3$ extend to the left and right edges of the window. Do the graphs appear to coincide in this window?

Answer:
There are many correct answers, including the window with $-12 \leq x \leq 12$ and $-5000 \leq y \leq 25{,}000$, in which the graphs appear to coincide.

EXAMPLE 2 If you graph $f(x) = 2x^3$ and $g(x) = 2x^3 + x^2 - 6x - 2$ in the standard viewing window (Figure 4.4), the graphs are distinct, but only visible for $-2 \leq x \leq 2$. The larger viewing window in Figure 4.5, which includes both graphs, shows that they do extend to the left and right. On this scale, the peak and valley in the graph of $g(x)$ that were visible in Figure 4.4 can no longer be seen and the graphs now appear to coincide. This does *not* mean that the graphs are identical (they aren't, as you can confirm with the trace feature), but it does mean that when $|x|$ is very large, the graph of $g(x) = 2x^3 + x^2 - 6x - 2$ has the *same shape* as the graph of its "highest degree term," $f(x) = 2x^3$. ■ 2

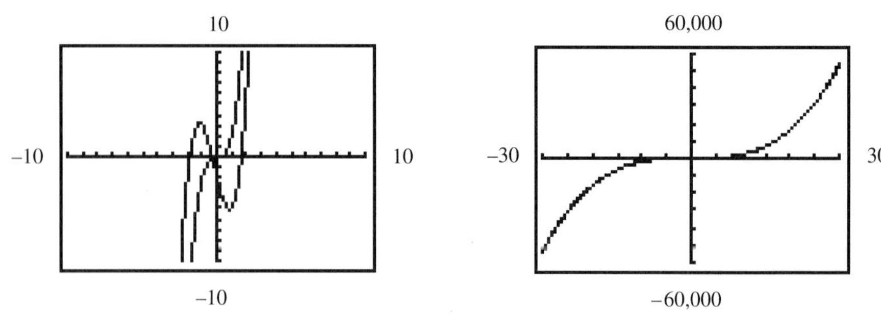

FIGURE 4.4

FIGURE 4.5

The preceding discussion illustrates the following facts, which require calculus for their proof.

POLYNOMIAL GRAPHS

The graph of a polynomial function $f(x)$ is a smooth, unbroken curve that extends forever to the left and right.

When $|x|$ is large, the graph of $f(x)$ resembles the graph of its highest degree term and moves sharply away from the x-axis.

If $f(x)$ has degree n, then

the number of x-intercepts of its graph is $\leq n$ and
the total number of peaks and valleys on its graph is $\leq n - 1$.

The facts in the preceding box can often be used to determine that a particular viewing window shows a complete graph of a polynomial function (that is, shows all the important features of the graph).

EXAMPLE 3 Find a complete graph of $g(x) = 1.5x^3 + 5x^2 - x - 6$.

The graph of $g(x)$ in Figure 4.6 shows all the possible peaks and valleys because $g(x)$ has degree 3 and therefore the total number of peaks and valleys must be ≤ 2 (by the last fact in the preceding box, with $n = 3$). Similarly, the graph in Figure 4.6 has the maximum possible number of x-intercepts for a polynomial of degree 3. Finally, the far left and right ends of the graph resemble the graph of the highest degree term $f(x) = 1.5x^3$, whose graph is in Figure 4.1(a). Therefore, Figure 4.6 (or any viewing window showing all these features) provides a complete graph. ■

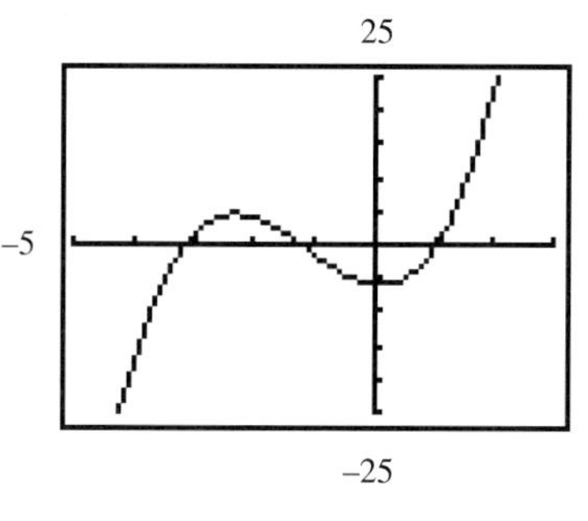

FIGURE 4.6

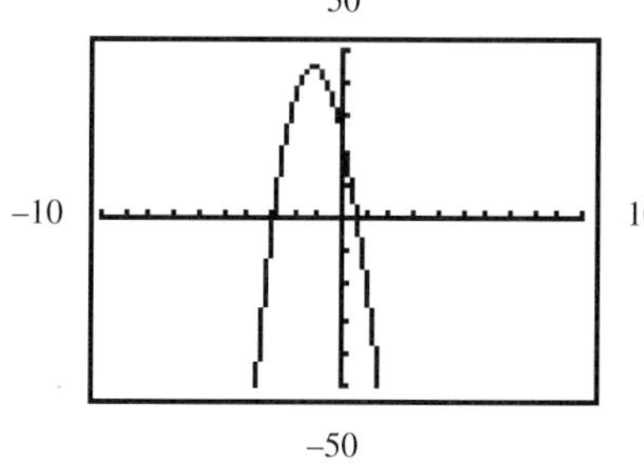

FIGURE 4.7

EXAMPLE 4 Is the graph of $g(x) = x^3 - 11x^2 - 32x + 24$ in Figure 4.7 complete? If not, find a complete graph.

The far ends of the graph of $g(x)$ should resemble the graph of its highest degree term, $f(x) = x^3$, which you can easily find on your calculator. In particular, the graph should move upward at the far right, which it does not do in this viewing window. So this is not a complete graph.

A viewing window that shows a complete graph must extend beyond $x = 10$ since the graph must eventually start rising on the right side. You can use trial and error to find one, or use the trace or table feature of your calculator to get some idea about the values of the function. The window in Figure 4.8 shows all the peaks and valleys (total of 2) and x-intercepts (3) that are possible in the graph of a polynomial

[3] Find a viewing window that shows a complete graph of the function.

(a) $f(x) = x^4 + x^3 - 13x^2 - x + 12$

(b) $g(x) = .2x^5 + x^4 - 4x^3 + x^2 - 4x - 60$

Answers:

(a) Any window showing all the features visible in the window with $-5 \leq x \leq 5$ and $-50 \leq y \leq 50$.

(b) Any window showing all the features visible in the window with $-9 \leq x \leq 5$ and $-300 \leq y \leq 700$.

of degree 3. At the far ends, the graph of $g(x)$ resembles the graph of $f(x) = x^3$. So the graph in Figure 4.8 is complete. ■ [3]

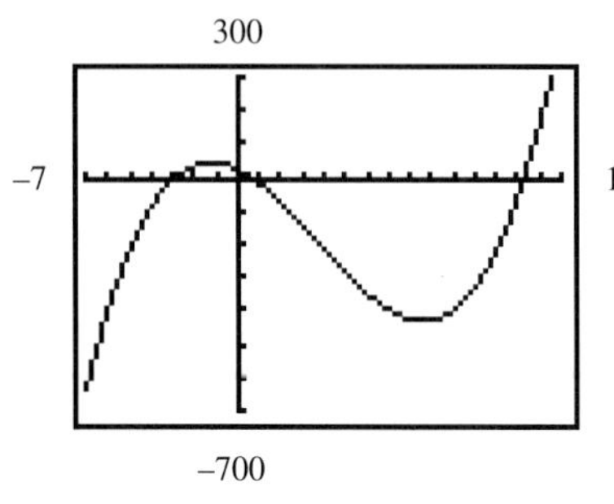

FIGURE 4.8

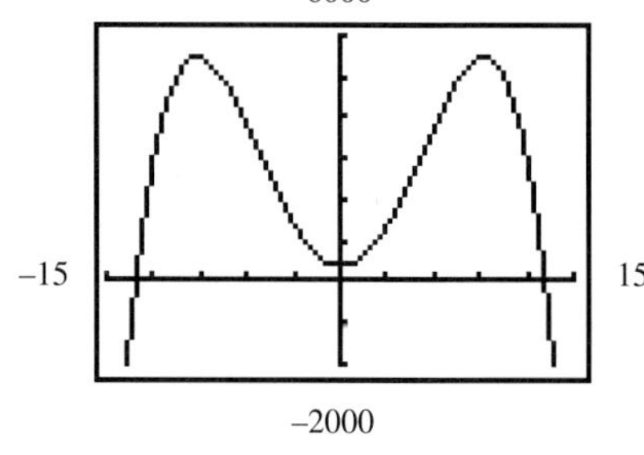

FIGURE 4.9

EXAMPLE 5 Find a complete graph of $f(x) = -.7x^4 + 119x^2 + 400$.

By experimenting with various windows, we obtain Figure 4.9. At the far ends the graph has the same shape as the graph of $g(x) = -.7x^4$ (see Figure 4.1(b)). The graph has a total of 3 peaks and valleys, the maximum possible for a polynomial of degree 4, but has only two x-intercepts. There cannot be any other x-intercepts because if there were, the graph would have to turn toward the x-axis again, thus producing another peak or valley, which is impossible. Therefore, this graph is complete. ■

When a polynomial can be factored, the general shape of its graph can be determined by using algebra and plotting a few points. Although determining the exact location of the peaks and valleys requires calculus, this approach is a reasonable way to graph polynomial functions by hand.

EXAMPLE 6 Sketch the graph of $f(x) = 3x^4 + x^3 - 2x^2$.

The polynomial can be factored as follows:

$$3x^4 + x^3 - 2x^2 = x^2(3x^2 + x - 2) = x^2(3x - 2)(x + 1).$$

By letting $f(x) = 0$ we find that the x-intercepts are at $x = 0$, $x = 2/3$, and $x = -1$. Between any two adjacent intercepts, the graph must be entirely above or entirely below the x-axis. We can determine whether the graph is above or below the x-axis in each interval by evaluating the function at a "test number" in that interval, as summarized in the following chart.

Region	*Test Number*	*Value of f(x)*	*Sign of f(x)*	*Graph*
$x < -1$	-2	32	positive	above x-axis
$-1 < x < 0$	$-\frac{1}{2}$	$-\frac{7}{16}$	negative	below x-axis
$0 < x < \frac{2}{3}$	$\frac{1}{2}$	$-\frac{3}{16}$	negative	below x-axis
$\frac{2}{3} < x$	1	2	positive	above x-axis

[4] Graph by hand:
$f(x) = x^3 - 4x$.

Answer:

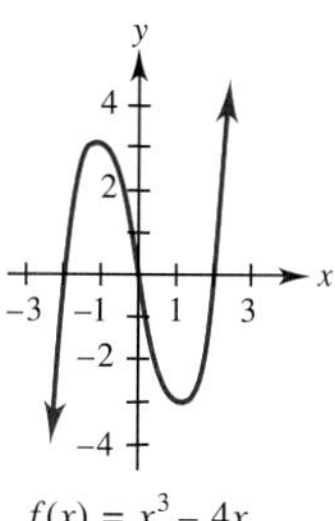

By plotting the x-intercepts and the points determined by the test numbers and using the fact that there can be a total of at most 3 peaks and valleys (why?), we obtain the graph in Figure 4.10. ■ [4]

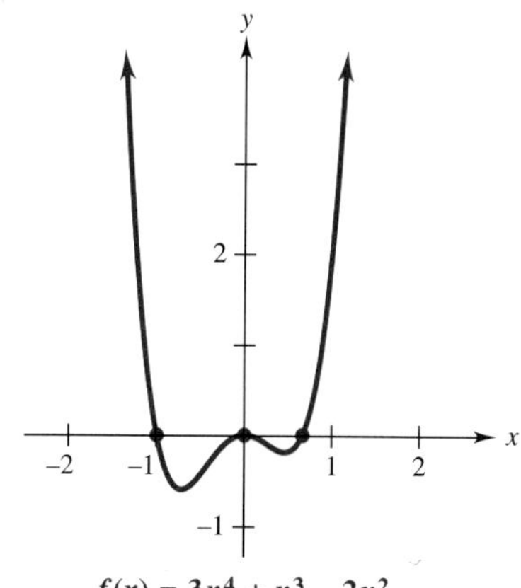

$f(x) = 3x^4 + x^3 - 2x^2$

FIGURE 4.10

4.1 EXERCISES

Find a viewing window larger than the standard window in which the graph of the given function appears to coincide with the graph of its highest degree term, thus demonstrating that the two graphs have the same shape when $|x|$ is large. (See Example 2.)

1. $f(x) = -2x^3 + 5x - 3$ **2.** $g(x) = .03x^4 + 2x^2 - 3x$

In Exercises 3–10, state whether the graph could possibly be the graph of (a) some polynomial function; (b) a polynomial function of degree 3; (c) a polynomial function of degree 4; (d) a polynomial function of degree 5. (See the box preceding Example 3.)

3.

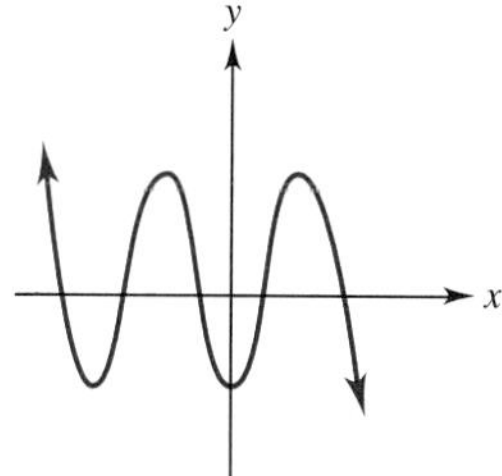

4.

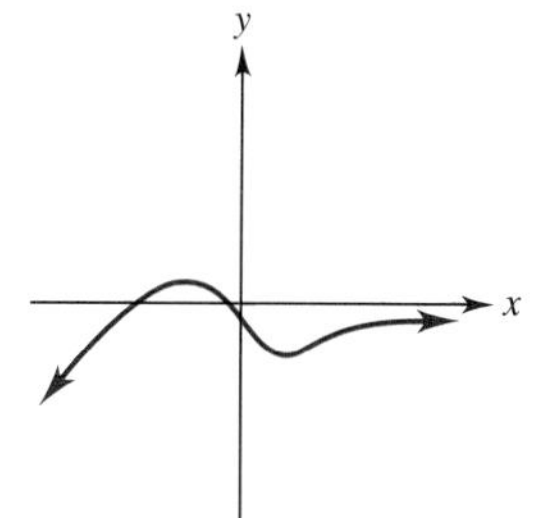

5.

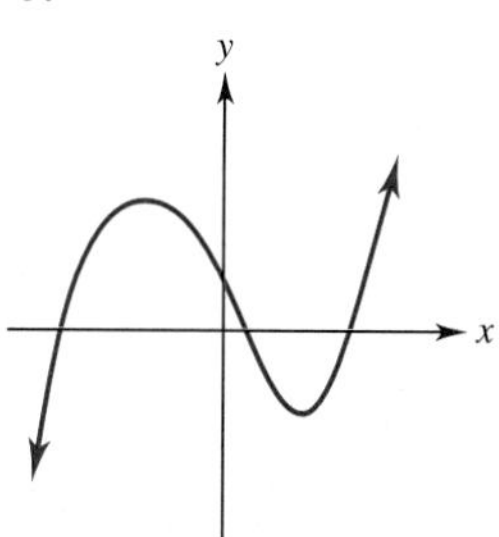

6.

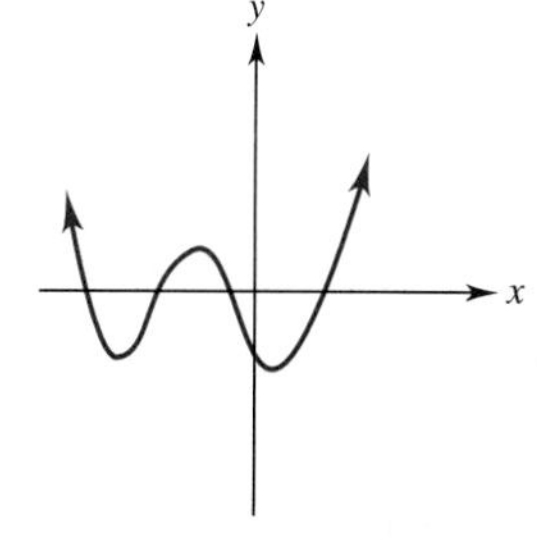

7.

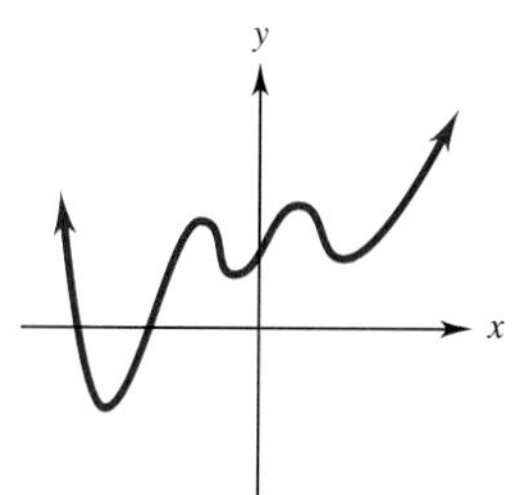

8.

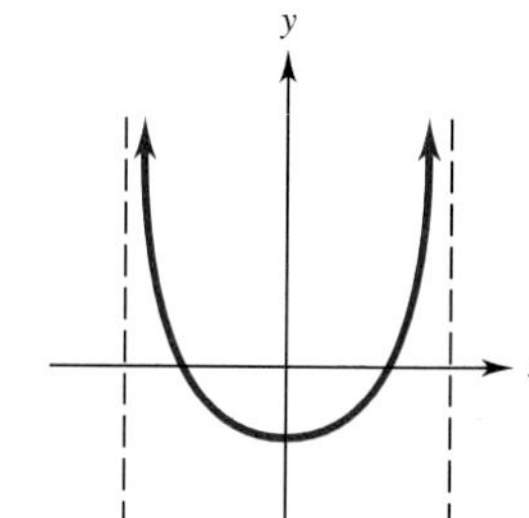

9.

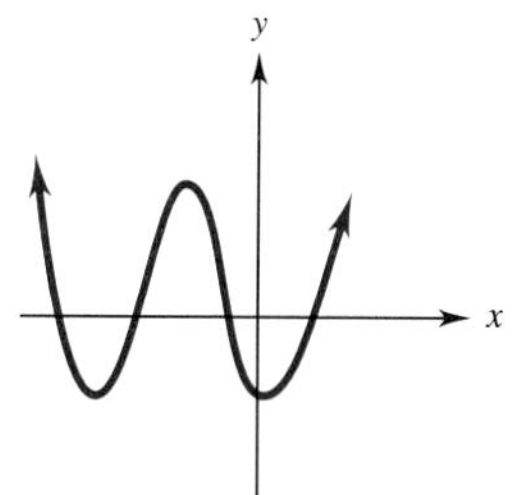

10.

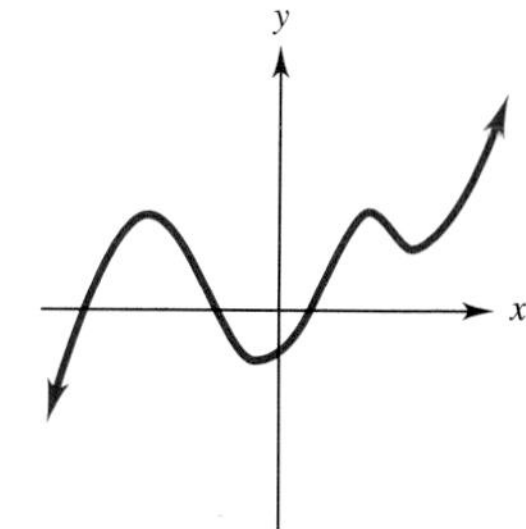

Find a viewing window that shows a complete graph of the function. Consider your answer correct if it shows all the features that appear in the window given in the answers. (See the box preceding Example 3.)

11. $g(x) = x^3 - 3x^2 - 4x - 5$

12. $f(x) = x^4 - 10x^3 + 35x^2 - 50x + 24$

13. $f(x) = 2x^5 - 3.5x^4 - 10x^3 + 5x^2 + 12x + 6$

14. $g(x) = x^5 + 8x^4 + 20x^3 + 9x^2 - 27x - 7$

Find a complete graph of each of these polynomial functions. (See Examples 3–5.)

15. $f(x) = x^3 + x^2 - 6x$

16. $f(x) = x^3 - 2x^2 - 8x$

17. $f(x) = x^3 + 3x^2 - 4x$

18. $f(x) = x^4 - 5x^2$

19. $f(x) = x^4 - 2x^2$

20. $f(x) = x^4 - 7x^2 + 12$

21. $f(x) = x^3 + 8x^2 + 5x - 14$

22. $g(x) = -x^4 - 3x^3 + 24x^2 + 80x + 15$

23. $f(x) = x^4 + 10x^3 + 21x^2 - 40x - 80$

24. $g(x) = 4x^5 - x^3 + x^2 - x + 2$

Graph each of these functions by hand. (See Example 6.)

25. $f(x) = 2x(x - 3)(x + 2)$

26. $f(x) = -x(2x + 1)(x - 3)$

27. $f(x) = (x + 2)(x - 3)(x + 4)$

28. $f(x) = (x - 3)(x - 1)(x + 1)$

29. $f(x) = x^2(x - 2)(x + 3)$

30. $f(x) = x^2(x + 1)(x - 1)$

31. A partial graph of a cubic polynomial function $f(x)$ is shown on the calculator screen below. The coefficient of x^3 in the rule of $f(x)$ is negative. Sketch a graph that has the same shape as the entire graph of $f(x)$.

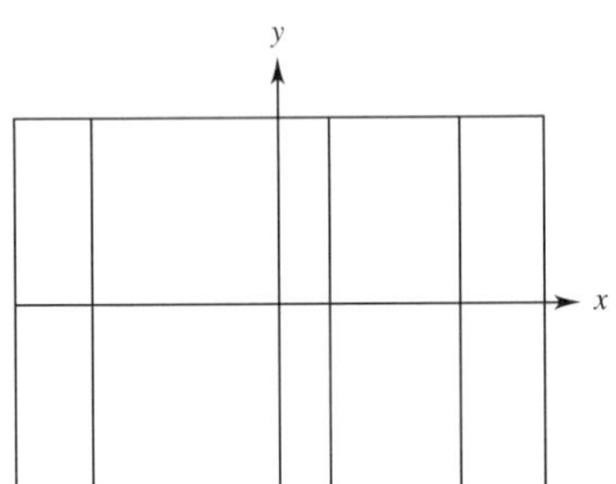

32. A partial graph of a fourth degree polynomial $g(x)$ is shown on the calculator screen below. Sketch a graph that has the same shape as the entire graph of $g(x)$.

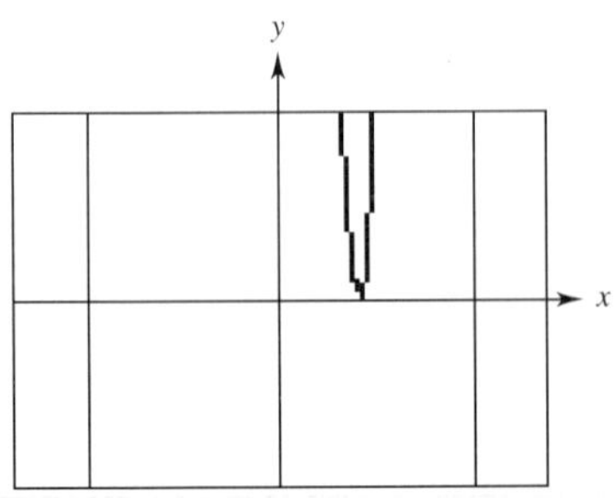

Work these problems.

33. Natural Science A technique for measuring cardiac output depends on the concentration of a dye after a known amount is injected into a vein near the heart. In a normal heart, the concentration of the dye at time x (in seconds) is given by the function defined by

$$g(x) = -.006x^4 + .140x^3 - .053x^2 + 1.79x.$$

(a) Find the following: $g(0)$; $g(1)$; $g(2)$; $g(3)$.
(b) Graph $g(x)$ for $x \geq 0$.

34. Natural Science The pressure of the oil in a reservoir tends to drop with time. By taking sample pressure readings for a particular oil reservoir, petroleum engineers have found that the change in pressure is given by

$$P(t) = t^3 - 18t^2 + 81t,$$

where t is time in years from the date of the first reading.
(a) Find the following: $P(0)$; $P(3)$; $P(7)$; $P(10)$.
(b) Graph $P(t)$.
(c) For what time period is the change in pressure (drop) increasing? decreasing?

35. Natural Science During the early part of the 20th century, the deer population of the Kaibab Plateau in Arizona experienced a rapid increase because hunters had reduced the number of natural predators. The increase in population depleted the food resources and eventually caused the population to decline. For the period from 1905 to 1930, the deer population was approximated by

$$D(x) = -.125x^5 + 3.125x^4 + 4000,$$

where x is time in years from 1905.
(a) Find the following: $D(0)$; $D(5)$; $D(10)$; $D(15)$; $D(20)$; $D(25)$.
(b) Graph $D(x)$.
(c) From the graph, over what period of time (from 1905 to 1930) was the population increasing? relatively stable? decreasing?

36. Management According to data for the years 1983–1994 in *Insider Flyer Magazine,* the number of frequent flier miles (in billions) earned by customers of various airlines, but not yet redeemed in year x, could be approximated by the polynomial function

$$f(x) = .015x^4 - .68x^3 + 11.33x^2 - 20.15x \quad (3 \leq x \leq 14),$$

where $x = 0$ corresponds to 1980.
(a) How many unredeemed miles were there in 1985? In 1990?
(b) Assume this model remains valid through 2003 ($x = 23$). How many unredeemed frequent flier miles are there in 1998? In 2000?
(c) If all the unredeemed miles in 2002 are redeemed for jumbo jet flights from New York to Los Angeles (each requiring 30,000 frequent flier miles) and each plane holds 400 people, how many planes would be needed?

37. Natural Science From 1930 to 1990 the rate of breast cancer was nearly constant at 30 cases per 100,000 women, whereas the rate of lung cancer in women over the same period increased. The number of lung cancer cases per 100,000 women in the year t (where $t = 0$ corresponds to 1930) can be approximated by the function

$$f(t) = .00028t^3 - .011t^2 + .23t + .93.^*$$

(a) State the rule of the function g that gives the rate of breast cancer per 100,000 women in year t.

(b) Graph the functions f and g on the same screen for the years 1930–1990.

(c) In what year did the rate of lung cancer first exceed the rate for breast cancer?

38. Physical Science The following table contains the average distance D from the sun for the first eight planets and their period P of revolution around the sun in years.† The distances are given in astronomical units (A.U.); 1 A.U. is the average distance from Earth to the sun. For example, since Jupiter's distance is 5.2 A.U., its distance from the sun is 5.2 times farther than Earth's.

Planet	*Distance D*	*Period P*
Mercury	.39	.24
Venus	.72	.62
Earth	1	1
Mars	1.52	1.89
Jupiter	5.20	11.9
Saturn	9.54	29.5
Uranus	19.2	84.0
Neptune	30.1	164.8

(a) Find a constant k (rounded to two decimal places) such that the function given by $P = kD$ fits the data for Neptune.

(b) Do part (a) for $P = kD^{1.5}$ and for $P = kD^2$.

(c) Graph the data in the table and the three functions found in parts (a) and (b) on the same screen. Which of these functions best fits the data?

(d) Use the best fitting function from part (c) to predict the period of the planet Pluto, which has a distance from the sun of 39.5 A.U. How does your answer compare to the true value of 248.5 years?

(e) If your calculator has a power regression feature, use it to find a function of the form $P = kD^n$ that approximates the data. How does this answer compare with the answer to part (c)?

*Valanis, B., *Epidemiology in Nursing and Health Care*, Appleton & Lange, 1992.

†Ronan, C., *The Natural History of the Universe*, MacMillan, 1991.

4.2 APPLICATIONS OF POLYNOMIAL FUNCTIONS

Higher degree polynomial functions often provide better models for such applications as supply and demand problems or break-even analysis than do the linear and quadratic models studied in previous chapters.

EXAMPLE 1 When $q \leq 500$, the price and demand for a particular type of graphing calculator are related by

$$p = .0000014q^3 - .0014q^2 - .05q + 202, \qquad \text{Demand function}$$

where p is the price (in dollars) and q is the number of calculators demanded (in thousands). Also, when $q \leq 500$, the price and supply are related by

$$p = .00000069q^3 - .000069q^2 + .24q, \qquad \text{Supply function}$$

where q is the number of calculators supplied (in thousands). Find the equilibrium demand (and supply) and the equilibrium price.

As before, this problem may be solved graphically or algebraically.

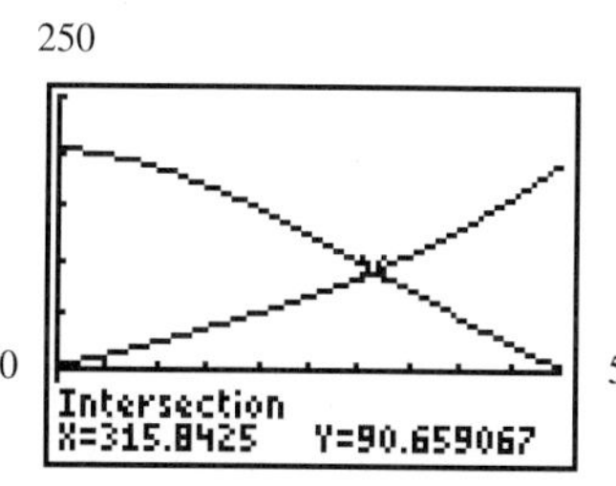

FIGURE 4.11

Graphical Method Graph the supply and demand functions in the first quadrant (since neither supply nor demand can be negative). Then use an intersection finder to determine the equilibrium point, that is, the point where the graphs intersect. Figure 4.11 shows that the equilibrium point is approximately (315.843, 90.659). Therefore, the equilibrium demand (supply) is approximately 315,843 (remember q is measured in thousands) and the equilibrium price is about \$90.66.

1 Find the equilibrium quantity and price when the demand function is

$$p = -.000011q^3 + .0014q^2 - .15q + 80$$

and the supply function is

$$p = -.000009q^3 + .003q^2 + .34q + .5.$$

Answer:
The equilibrium quantity is approximately 113.87 and the equilibrium price is approximately \$64.83.

Algebraic Method Set the two expressions for p in the supply and demand functions equal to each other (which they will be at the equilibrium point):

$$.00000069q^3 - .000069q^2 + .24q = .0000014q^3 - .0014q^2 - .05q + 202$$

which is equivalent to

$$-.00000071q^3 + .001331q^2 + .29q - 202 = 0.$$

Now solve this equation by using a solver or graphical solution methods. There are two positive solutions

$$q \approx 315.8425 \quad \text{and} \quad q \approx 2007.5135.$$

The second solution is not relevant in this situation since the supply and demand equations are valid only when $q \leq 500$. So $q \approx 315.843$ once again gives the equilibrium quantity of 315,843. Evaluating either the supply or demand functions at $q = 315.843$ gives the equilibrium price of \$90.66. ■ 1

Many real-life situations require that the largest or smallest quantity satisfying certain conditions be found. For instance, automobile companies want to design engines with maximum fuel efficiency. Similarly, a cereal manufacturer might want to find a box that uses the least amount of cardboard (and hence is cheapest). Polynomial functions often provide useful models of such situations and graphing technology produces accurate approximate solutions. The exact solution of such problems usually requires calculus.

EXAMPLE 2 When items are manufactured, the average cost per item is quite high at first, but as production increases, economies of scale bring down the average cost per item. When production reaches too high a level, however, the average cost per item begins to rise. Magtex Company, which can produce up to 55,000 electric pencil sharpeners per month, has found that its average cost per sharpener for producing x thousand sharpeners is given by the function $A(x) = -.000018x^4 + .0014x^3 + .02x^2 - 2.3x + 40$. If the average cost is to be as small as possible, how many sharpeners should be produced each month?

Graph the cost function $A(x)$ in a viewing window with $0 \leq x \leq 55$ (because x is measured in thousands and Magtex can't make more than 55,000). For each point on the graph in Figure 4.12,

the x-coordinate is the number of thousands of sharpeners produced;

the y-coordinate is the average cost per sharpener.

Use the minimum finder on your calculator to find the point with the smallest y-coordinate, which is approximately (23.288, 9.672), as shown in Figure 4.13. Consequently, Magtex should produce 23,288 sharpeners per month at an average cost of approximately \$9.67 each. ■

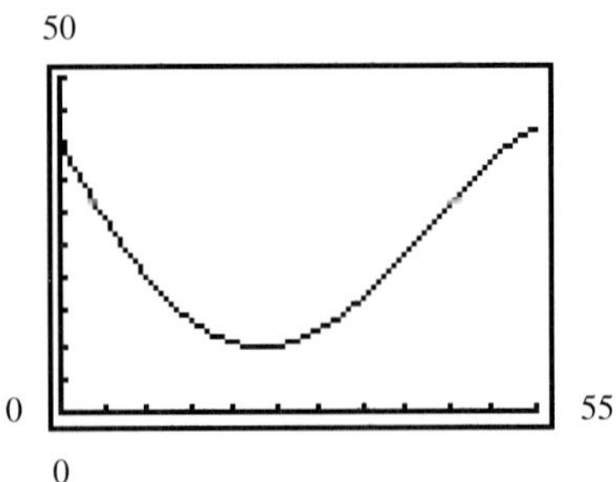

FIGURE 4.12

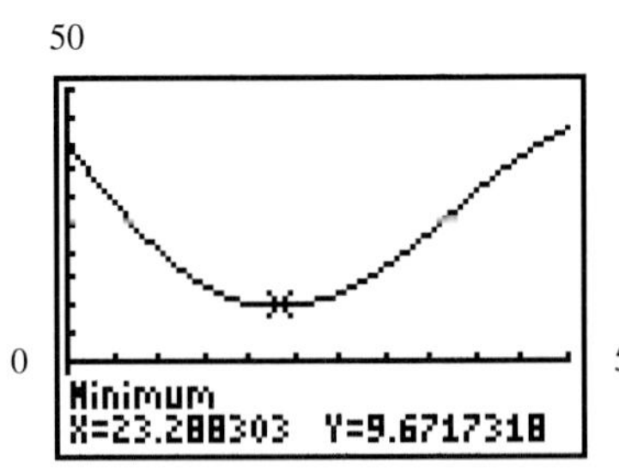

FIGURE 4.13

In the preceding examples, the rules of the appropriate functions were given. More often, however, you must use the known information to find a function that models the situation.

EXAMPLE 3 Tags-R-Us sells name tags for \$29 per thousand. The company has found that the cost (in dollars) of manufacturing x thousand name tags is given by the function $C(x) = .001x^3 + .06x^2 - 1.5x + 1000$.

(a) Find the rules of the revenue function and the profit function.

Since name tags sell for \$29 per thousand, the revenue from selling x thousand of them is given by $R(x) = 29x$. Profit is the difference between revenue and cost, so the profit function is given by

$$P(x) = R(x) - C(x) = 29x - (.001x^3 + .06x^2 - 1.5x + 1000)$$
$$P(x) = -.001x^3 - .06x^2 + 30.5x - 1000.$$

(b) What is the smallest number of name tags that can be made without losing money? The largest number?

The company makes money whenever $P(x)$ is positive, that is, whenever the graph of $P(x)$ is above the x-axis. Figure 4.14 shows that this occurs between the two x-intercepts. A root-finder shows that the x-intercepts of the graph are at approximately 37.196 (Figure 4.14) and 122.418. Therefore, they must make between 37,196 and 122,418 tags in order to make a profit.

(c) What number of tags should be made to guarantee a maximum profit? What will that profit be?

For each point on the graph of the profit function $P(x)$ in Figure 4.14,

the x-coordinate is the number of thousands of tags;

the y-coordinate is the profit on that number of tags.

Use the maximum finder on a calculator to find the point with the largest y-coordinate. Figure 4.15 shows that it is approximately (82.794, 546.39). So the company should make 82,794 tags for a maximum profit of \$546.39. ■ 2

2 An item sells for \$4 per hundred and the cost of making x hundred is given by

$$C(x) = -.00004x^3 + .05x^2 - .6x + 5.$$

(a) Find the revenue and profit functions.

(b) How many items should be made to have maximum profit?

Answers:

(a) $R(x) = 4x$ and

$$P(x) = .00004x^3 - .05x^2 + 4.6x - 5.$$

(b) About 4887

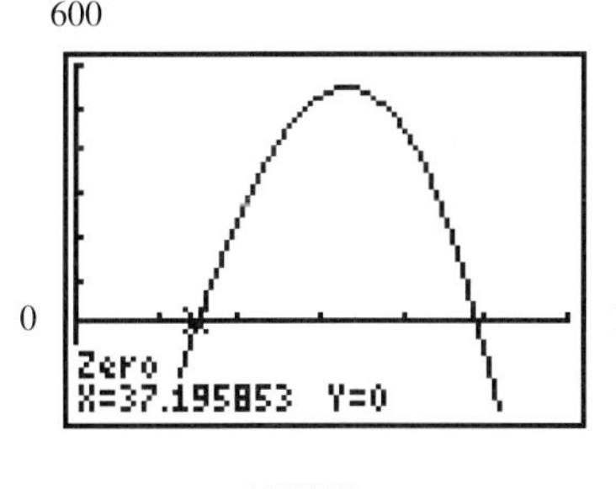

FIGURE 4.14

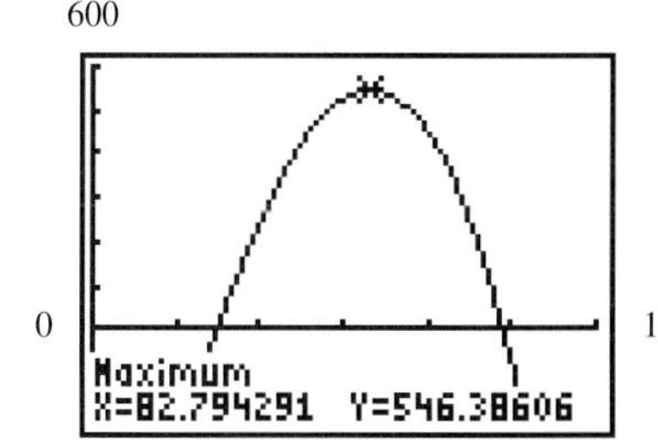

FIGURE 4.15

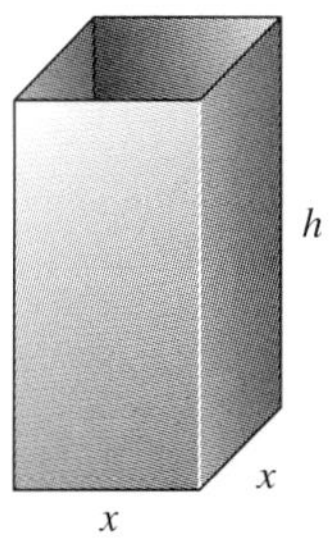

FIGURE 4.16

EXAMPLE 4 A rectangular box with a square base and no top (Figure 4.16) is to be manufactured from 729 square centimeters of sheet plastic. If the box is to have as large a volume as possible, find its dimensions.

The volume V of the box is given by

$$V = \text{length} \times \text{width} \times \text{height} = x \cdot x \cdot h = x^2h.$$

We must find the values of x and h that make V as large as possible. To do this, we must first write V as a function of just one variable. We do this by using the fact that the amount of material is given by the surface area of the box. The bottom of the box has area x^2 and each side has area xh, so the total surface area is

$$729 = x^2 + 4xh$$

so that

$$4xh = 729 - x^2$$
$$h = \frac{729 - x^2}{4x}.$$

Substituting this result in the volume formula, we have

$$V = x^2h = x^2\left(\frac{729 - x^2}{4x}\right) = \frac{x}{4}(729 - x^2)$$
$$= \frac{729}{4}x - \frac{x^3}{4} = 182.25x - .25x^3.$$

Now graph the function $V(x) = 182.25x - .25x^3$ and use the maximum finder to find the highest point on the graph (corresponding to maximum volume). Figure 4.17 shows that this is approximately (15.59, 1894). So the maximum volume of 1894 cubic centimeters occurs when $x \approx 15.59$ cm. In this case

$$h = \frac{729 - x^2}{4x} = \frac{729 - 15.59^2}{4(15.59)} \approx 7.79 \text{ cm.}$$

So the box should measure 15.59 by 15.59 by 7.79 centimeters. ■

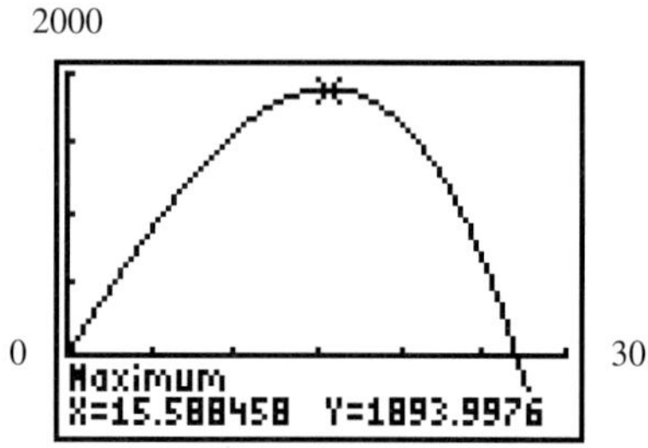

FIGURE 4.17

4.2 EXERCISES

Management *Find the equilibrium demand and the equilibrium price. (See Example 1.)*

1. Demand: $p = .0000028q^3 - .0022q^2 - .015q + 70$ $(q \leq 200)$
   Supply: $p = .0026q^2 + .005q$

2. Demand: $p = -.004q^2 - .03q + 90$ $(q \leq 145)$
   Supply: $p = .000037q^3 - .004q^2 + .4q$

3. Demand: $p = .00000034q^3 - .00055q^2 - .085q + 200$ $(q \leq 660)$
   Supply: $p = -.00000028q^3 + .0004q^2 + .07q$

4. Demand: $p = .00000028q^3 + .002q^2 - 5q + 2700$ $(q \leq 930)$
   Supply: $p = .000019q^3 - .019q^2 + 9.2q$

Work these problems. (See Example 2.)

5. **Management** An electronics company, which can produce up to 10,000 personal disc players per month, has found that its average cost per player for producing x hundred players is given by the function $C(x) = .000000000001x^4 - .000089x^2 + 2010$. If the average cost is to be as small as possible, how many players should be produced each month? In this case, what is the average cost?

6. **Management** The firm in Exercise 5 also makes inexpensive tape decks, as many as 13,000 a month. Its average cost per tape deck when x hundred are produced is given by $C(x) = .000000000216x^3 - .000002196x^2 + .000042x + 83$. How many should be made in order to minimize the average cost per item? What is this minimum average cost?

7. **Natural Science** The polynomial function $A(x) = -.015x^3 + 1.058x$ gives the approximate alcohol concentration (in tenths of a percent) in an average person's bloodstream x hours after drinking about eight ounces of 100 proof whiskey. The function provides a reasonably accurate model when $0 \le x \le 8$.
   (a) Sketch the graph of $A(x)$ for $0 \le x \le 8$.
   (b) Display a table that gives the value of $A(x)$ when $x = 1, 3, 5, 7$.
   (c) Find the time of maximum alcohol concentration.
   (d) In some states a person is considered legally drunk if the blood alcohol concentration exceeds .15%. In this situation, during what time period is this average person legally drunk?

8. **Physical Science** For speeds up to 75 mph, the amount $P(x)$ of a certain pollutant (in parts per thousand) emitted by an automobile traveling at x miles per hour is approximated by the function $P(x) = -.000074x^3 + .011x^2 - .4x + 9$. At what speed between 0 and 75 mph is the amount of the pollutant emitted a minimum and at what speed is it a maximum?

Work these problems. (See Example 3.)

9. **Management** An auto parts manufacturer makes radiators that sell for \$350 each. The cost of producing x radiators is approximated by the function $C(x) = 600{,}000 - 25x + .01x^2$.
   (a) Find the revenue and profit functions.
   (b) What is the break-even point, that is, what is the minimum number of radiators that must be sold in order to make a profit?
   (c) What is the maximum number of radiators that can be sold without losing money?
   (d) What number of radiators will produce the largest possible profit?

10. **Management** Martex Company has found that the cost (in thousands of dollars) of producing x thousand address stickers is given by $C(x) = .00024x^3 - .046x^2 + 3x + 82$. The stickers can be sold for \$3.20 per thousand.
   (a) Find the revenue and profit functions.
   (b) How many stickers must be made and sold to break even?
   (c) What is the maximum number of stickers that can be sold without losing money?
   (d) What number of stickers will produce the largest possible profit?

11. **Management** The Premier Pen Company has found that its revenue and profit (in thousands of dollars) from selling x thousand pens are approximated by these functions:

   Revenue: $R(x) = -.000004x^3 - .007x^2 + 2x$;
   Profit: $P(x) = -.000029x^3 + .001x^2 + x - 30$.

   (a) Find and graph the cost function.
   (b) How much does it cost to produce 50,000 pens? 150,000? 200,000?
   (c) What is the profit on 50,000 pens? On 150,000? On 200,000?
   (d) How many pens should be sold to have maximum profit?

12. **Management** Sorewell Inc. makes adhesive bandages. Their cost and profit (in thousands of dollars) from making x thousand bandages are given by

   Cost: $C(x) = .00024x^3 - .026x^2 + 1.4x + 60$;
   Profit: $P(x) = -.00004x^3 - .034x^2 + 3.6x - 60$.

   (a) Find the revenue function.
   (b) What is the revenue from selling 40,000 bandages? From 60,000? From 80,000?
   (c) What is the profit on 40,000 bandages? On 60,000? On 80,000?
   (d) How many bandages should be sold to have maximum profit? What is the maximum profit?

Work these problems. (See Example 4.)

13. **Physical Science** An open-top box with a square base is to be constructed from 120 square centimeters of material. The side of its base must be less than 7 cm. What dimensions will produce a box with
   (a) a volume of 100 cubic centimeters?
   (b) the largest possible volume?

14. **Physical Science** A 20-inch square piece of metal is to be used to make an open-top box by cutting equal-sized squares from each corner and folding up the sides. The length, width, and height of the box are each to be less than 12 inches. What size squares should be cut out to produce a box with
   (a) a volume of 550 cubic inches?
   (b) the largest possible volume?

15. **Management** An open-top box with a square base is to be constructed. The material for the bottom costs \$.025 (that is, 2.5 cents) per square centimeter and the material for the sides costs \$.005 per square centimeter. What are the dimensions of the largest box that can be built for \$7? What is its volume?

16. **Physical Science** A 24 cm by 45 cm piece of metal is to be used to make an open-top box by cutting equal-sized squares from each corner and folding up the sides. What size squares should be cut out to produce a box with maximum volume?

17. **Natural Science** As much as one-half of the world's population carry the *H. pylori* bacteria that can cause gastritis, ulcers, and cancer. According to data in the February 1996 issue of *Scientific American,* the percentage of the population of developing countries infected with *H. pylori* at age x years is approximated by the function $g(x) = -.0000186x^4 + .0036x^3 - .25x^2 + 7.4x \quad (0 \le x \le 80)$.
   (a) What percentage are infected at age 10? At age 40? At age 70?
   (b) At what age is the largest number of people infected? What percentage of people is infected at that age?

18. **Management** A local club is arranging a charter flight to Hawaii. The cost of the trip is \$425 each for 75 passengers, with a refund of \$5 per passenger for each passenger in excess of 75.
   (a) How many passengers are needed to maximize the revenue received by the airline?
   (b) What is the maximum revenue?

19. **Management** When there are 22 apple trees per acre, the average yield is 500 apples per tree. For each additional tree planted per acre, the yield per tree decreases by 15 apples. How many additional trees per acre should be planted to maximize the yield?

4.3 RATIONAL EXPRESSIONS

In order to prepare for the functions to be considered in the next section, we now consider **rational expressions,** such as

$$\frac{8}{x-1}, \quad \frac{3x^2+4x}{5x-6}, \quad \text{and} \quad \frac{2+\frac{1}{y}}{y}.$$

Because rational expressions involve quotients, it is important to keep in mind values of the variables that make denominators 0. For example, 1 cannot be used as a replacement for x in the first rational expression above, and 6/5 cannot be used in the second one, since these values make the respective denominators equal 0. 1

1 What values of the variable make each denominator equal 0?

(a) $\frac{5}{x-3}$

(b) $\frac{2x-3}{4x-1}$

(c) $\frac{x+2}{x}$

(d) Why do we need to determine these values?

Answers:

(a) 3

(b) 1/4

(c) 0

(d) Because division by 0 is undefined.

OPERATIONS WITH RATIONAL EXPRESSIONS The rules for operations with rational expressions are the usual rules for fractions.

OPERATIONS WITH RATIONAL EXPRESSIONS

For all mathematical expressions P, $Q \neq 0$, R, and $S \neq 0$,

(a) $\frac{P}{Q} = \frac{PS}{QS}$ Fundamental property

(b) $\frac{P}{Q} \cdot \frac{R}{S} = \frac{PR}{QS}$ Multiplication

(c) $\frac{P}{Q} + \frac{R}{Q} = \frac{P+R}{Q}$ Addition

(d) $\frac{P}{Q} - \frac{R}{Q} = \frac{P-R}{Q}$ Subtraction

(e) $\frac{P}{Q} \div \frac{R}{S} = \frac{P}{Q} \cdot \frac{S}{R}, \quad R \neq 0.$ Division

The following examples illustrate these operations.

EXAMPLE 1 Write each of the following rational expressions in lowest terms (so that the numerator and denominator have no common factor with integer coefficients except 1 or -1).

(a) $\dfrac{12m}{-18}$

Both $12m$ and -18 are divisible by 6. By operation (a) above,

$$\frac{12m}{-18} = \frac{2m \cdot \mathbf{6}}{-3 \cdot \mathbf{6}} = \frac{2m}{-3} = -\frac{2m}{3}.$$

(b) $\dfrac{8x+16}{4} = \dfrac{8(x+2)}{4} = \dfrac{\mathbf{4} \cdot 2(x+2)}{\mathbf{4}} = \dfrac{2(x+2)}{1} = 2(x+2)$

The numerator, $8x + 16$, was factored so that the common factor could be identified. The answer could also be written as $2x + 4$, if desired.

(c) $\dfrac{k^2+7k+12}{k^2+2k-3} = \dfrac{(k+4)(\boldsymbol{k+3})}{(k-1)(\boldsymbol{k+3})} = \dfrac{k+4}{k-1}$ ■ [2]

The values of k in Example 1(c) are restricted to $k \neq 1$ and $k \neq -3$. From now on, such restrictions will be assumed when working with rational expressions.

[2] Write each of the following in lowest terms.

(a) $\dfrac{12k+36}{18}$

(b) $\dfrac{15m+30m^2}{5m}$

(c) $\dfrac{2p^2+3p+1}{p^2+3p+2}$

Answers:

(a) $\dfrac{2(k+3)}{3}$ or $\dfrac{2k+6}{3}$

(b) $3(1+2m)$ or $3+6m$

(c) $\dfrac{2p+1}{p+2}$

EXAMPLE 2

(a) Multiply $\dfrac{2}{3} \cdot \dfrac{y}{5}$.

Multiply the numerators and then the denominators.

$$\frac{2}{3} \cdot \frac{y}{5} = \frac{2 \cdot y}{3 \cdot 5} = \frac{2y}{15}$$

The result, $2y/15$, is in lowest terms.

(b) $\dfrac{3y+9}{6} \cdot \dfrac{18}{5y+15}$

Factor where possible.

$$\frac{3y+9}{6} \cdot \frac{18}{5y+15} = \frac{3(y+3)}{6} \cdot \frac{18}{5(y+3)}$$

$$= \frac{3 \cdot 18(y+3)}{6 \cdot 5(y+3)} \qquad \text{Multiply numerators and denominators.}$$

$$= \frac{3 \cdot \mathbf{6} \cdot 3(\boldsymbol{y+3})}{\mathbf{6} \cdot 5(\boldsymbol{y+3})} \qquad 18 = 6 \cdot 3$$

$$= \frac{3 \cdot 3}{5} \qquad \text{Write in lowest terms.}$$

$$= \frac{9}{5}$$

3 Multiply.

(a) $\dfrac{3r^2}{5} \cdot \dfrac{20}{9r}$

(b) $\dfrac{y-4}{y^2-2y-8} \cdot \dfrac{y^2-4}{3y}$

Answers:

(a) $\dfrac{4r}{3}$

(b) $\dfrac{y-2}{3y}$

(c) $\dfrac{m^2+5m+6}{m+3} \cdot \dfrac{m^2+m-6}{m^2+3m+2}$

$$= \frac{(m+2)(m+3)}{m+3} \cdot \frac{(m-2)(m+3)}{(m+2)(m+1)} \qquad \text{Factor.}$$

$$= \frac{\mathbf{(m+2)(m+3)}(m-2)(m+3)}{\mathbf{(m+3)(m+2)}(m+1)} \qquad \text{Multiply.}$$

$$= \frac{(m-2)(m+3)}{m+1} \qquad \text{Lowest terms}$$

$$= \frac{m^2+m-6}{m+1}$$ ■ **3**

EXAMPLE 3

(a) Divide $\dfrac{8x}{5} \div \dfrac{11x^2}{20}$.

Invert the second expression and multiply.

$$\frac{8x}{5} \div \frac{11x^2}{20} = \frac{8x}{5} \cdot \frac{20}{11x^2} \qquad \text{Invert and multiply.}$$

$$= \frac{8x \cdot 20}{5 \cdot 11x^2} \qquad \text{Multiply.}$$

$$= \frac{32}{11x} \qquad \text{Lowest terms}$$

4 Divide.

(a) $\dfrac{5m}{16} \div \dfrac{m^2}{10}$

(b) $\dfrac{2y-8}{6} \div \dfrac{5y-20}{3}$

(c) $\dfrac{m^2-2m-3}{m(m+1)} \div \dfrac{m+4}{5m}$

Answers:

(a) $\dfrac{25}{8m}$

(b) $\dfrac{1}{5}$

(c) $\dfrac{5(m-3)}{m+4}$

(b) $\dfrac{9p-36}{12} \div \dfrac{5(p-4)}{18}$

$$= \frac{9p-36}{12} \cdot \frac{18}{5(p-4)} \qquad \text{Invert and multiply.}$$

$$= \frac{9(p-4)}{12} \cdot \frac{18}{5(p-4)} \qquad \text{Factor.}$$

$$= \frac{27}{10} \qquad \text{Multiply and write in lowest terms.}$$ ■ **4**

EXAMPLE 4 Add or subtract as indicated.

(a) $\dfrac{4}{5k} - \dfrac{11}{5k}$

When two rational expressions have the same denominators, subtract by subtracting the numerators and keeping the common denominator.

$$\frac{4}{5k} - \frac{11}{5k} = \frac{4-11}{5k} = -\frac{7}{5k}$$

(b) $\dfrac{7}{p} + \dfrac{9}{2p} + \dfrac{1}{3p}$

These three denominators are different; addition requires the same denominators. Find a common denominator, one which can be divided by p, $2p$, and $3p$. A common denominator here is $6p$. Rewrite each rational expression, using operation (a), with a denominator of $6p$. Then, using operation (c), add the numerators and keep the common denominator.

$$\frac{7}{p} + \frac{9}{2p} + \frac{1}{3p} = \frac{\mathbf{6} \cdot 7}{\mathbf{6} \cdot p} + \frac{\mathbf{3} \cdot 9}{\mathbf{3} \cdot 2p} + \frac{\mathbf{2} \cdot 1}{\mathbf{2} \cdot 3p} \qquad \text{Operation (a)}$$

$$= \frac{42}{6p} + \frac{27}{6p} + \frac{2}{6p}$$

$$= \frac{42 + 27 + 2}{6p} \qquad \text{Operation (c)}$$

$$= \frac{71}{6p}$$

(c) $\dfrac{k^2}{k^2 - 1} - \dfrac{2k^2 - k - 3}{k^2 + 3k + 2}$

Factor the denominators to find a common denominator.

$$\frac{k^2}{k^2 - 1} - \frac{2k^2 - k - 3}{k^2 + 3k + 2} = \frac{k^2}{(k + 1)(k - 1)} - \frac{2k^2 - k - 3}{(k + 1)(k + 2)}$$

The common denominator is $(k + 1)(k - 1)(k + 2)$. Write each fraction with the common denominator.

$$\frac{k^2}{(k + 1)(k - 1)} - \frac{2k^2 - k - 3}{(k + 1)(k + 2)}$$

$$= \frac{k^2(\mathbf{k + 2})}{(k + 1)(k - 1)(\mathbf{k + 2})} - \frac{(2k^2 - k - 3)(\mathbf{k - 1})}{(k + 1)(\mathbf{k - 1})(k + 2)}$$

$$= \frac{k^3 + 2k^2 - (2k^2 - k - 3)(k - 1)}{(k + 1)(k - 1)(k + 2)} \qquad \text{Subtract fractions.}$$

$$= \frac{k^3 + 2k^2 - (2k^3 - 3k^2 - 2k + 3)}{(k + 1)(k - 1)(k + 2)} \qquad \text{Multiply } (2k^2 - k - 3)(k - 1).$$

$$= \frac{k^3 + 2k^2 - 2k^3 + 3k^2 + 2k - 3}{(k + 1)(k - 1)(k + 2)} \qquad \text{Polynomial subtraction}$$

$$= \frac{-k^3 + 5k^2 + 2k - 3}{(k + 1)(k - 1)(k + 2)} \qquad \text{Combine terms.}$$ ■ 5

5 Add or subtract.

(a) $\dfrac{3}{4r} + \dfrac{8}{3r}$

(b) $\dfrac{1}{m - 2} - \dfrac{3}{2(m - 2)}$

(c) $\dfrac{p + 1}{p^2 - p} - \dfrac{p^2 - 1}{p^2 + p - 2}$

Answers:

(a) $\dfrac{41}{12r}$

(b) $\dfrac{-1}{2(m - 2)}$

(c) $\dfrac{-p^3 + p^2 + 4p + 2}{p(p - 1)(p + 2)}$

COMPLEX FRACTIONS Any quotient of two rational expressions is called a **complex fraction.** Complex fractions can be simplified by the methods shown in the following examples.

EXAMPLE 5 Simplify each complex fraction.

(a) $\dfrac{6 - \dfrac{5}{k}}{1 + \dfrac{5}{k}}$

Multiply both numerator and denominator by the common denominator k.

$$\frac{6-\frac{5}{k}}{1+\frac{5}{k}} = \frac{k\left(6-\frac{5}{k}\right)}{k\left(1+\frac{5}{k}\right)} \quad \text{Multiply by } \frac{k}{k}.$$

$$= \frac{6k - k\left(\frac{5}{k}\right)}{k + k\left(\frac{5}{k}\right)} \quad \text{Distributive property}$$

$$= \frac{6k-5}{k+5} \quad \text{Simplify.}$$

(b) $\dfrac{\frac{a}{a+1}+\frac{1}{a}}{\frac{1}{a}+\frac{1}{a+1}}$

Multiply both numerator and denominator by the common denominator of all the fractions, in this case $a(a + 1)$. Doing so gives

$$\frac{\frac{a}{a+1}+\frac{1}{a}}{\frac{1}{a}+\frac{1}{a+1}} = \frac{\left(\frac{a}{a+1}+\frac{1}{a}\right)a(a+1)}{\left(\frac{1}{a}+\frac{1}{a+1}\right)a(a+1)} = \frac{a^2+(a+1)}{(a+1)+a} = \frac{a^2+a+1}{2a+1}.$$

As an alternative method of solution, first perform the indicated additions in the numerator and denominator, and then divide.

$$\frac{\frac{a}{a+1}+\frac{1}{a}}{\frac{1}{a}+\frac{1}{a+1}} = \frac{\frac{a^2+1(a+1)}{a(a+1)}}{\frac{1(a+1)+1(a)}{a(a+1)}} = \frac{\frac{a^2+a+1}{a(a+1)}}{\frac{2a+1}{a(a+1)}}$$

$$= \frac{a^2+a+1}{a(a+1)} \cdot \frac{a(a+1)}{2a+1} = \frac{a^2+a+1}{2a+1}$$ ■ 6

6 Simplify each complex fraction.

(a) $\dfrac{t-\frac{1}{t}}{2t+\frac{3}{t}}$

(b) $\dfrac{\frac{m}{m+2}+\frac{1}{m}}{\frac{1}{m}-\frac{1}{m+2}}$

Answers:

(a) $\dfrac{t^2-1}{2t^2+3}$

(b) $\dfrac{m^2+m+2}{2}$

4.3 EXERCISES

Write each of the following in lowest terms. Factor as necessary. (See Example 1.)

1. $\dfrac{8x^2}{40x}$
2. $\dfrac{27m}{81m^3}$
3. $\dfrac{20p^2}{35p^3}$
4. $\dfrac{18y^4}{27y^2}$
5. $\dfrac{5m+15}{4m+12}$
6. $\dfrac{10z+5}{20z+10}$
7. $\dfrac{4(w-3)}{(w-3)(w+3)}$
8. $\dfrac{-6(x+2)}{(x-4)(x+2)}$
9. $\dfrac{3y^2-12y}{9y^3}$
10. $\dfrac{15k^2+45k}{9k^2}$
11. $\dfrac{8x^2+16x}{4x^2}$
12. $\dfrac{36y^2+72y}{9y}$
13. $\dfrac{m^2-4m+4}{m^2+m-6}$
14. $\dfrac{r^2-r-6}{r^2+r-12}$
15. $\dfrac{x^2+3x-4}{x^2-1}$
16. $\dfrac{z^2-5z+6}{z^2-4}$

Multiply or divide as indicated in each of the following. Write all answers in lowest terms. (See Examples 2 and 3.)

17. $\dfrac{4p^3}{49} \cdot \dfrac{7}{2p^2}$
18. $\dfrac{24n^4}{6n^2} \cdot \dfrac{18n^2}{9n}$
19. $\dfrac{21a^5}{14a^3} \div \dfrac{8a}{12a^2}$
20. $\dfrac{2x^3}{6x^2} \div \dfrac{10x^2}{15x}$

21. $\frac{2a+b}{2c} \cdot \frac{15}{4(2a+b)}$

22. $\frac{4(x+2)}{w} \cdot \frac{3w}{8(x+2)}$

23. $\frac{15p-3}{6} \div \frac{10p-2}{3}$

24. $\frac{6m-18}{18} \cdot \frac{20}{4m-12}$

25. $\frac{2k+8}{6} \div \frac{3k+12}{2}$

26. $\frac{5m+25}{10} \cdot \frac{12}{6m+30}$

27. $\frac{9y-18}{6y+12} \cdot \frac{3y+6}{15y-30}$

28. $\frac{12r+24}{36r-36} \div \frac{6r+12}{8r-8}$

29. $\frac{4a+12}{2a-10} \div \frac{a^2-9}{a^2-a-20}$

30. $\frac{6r-18}{9r^2+6r-24} \cdot \frac{12r-16}{4r-12}$

31. $\frac{k^2-k-6}{k^2+k-12} \cdot \frac{k^2+3k-4}{k^2+2k-3}$

32. $\frac{n^2-n-6}{n^2-2n-8} \div \frac{n^2-9}{n^2+7n+12}$

33. In your own words, explain how to find the least common denominator for two fractions.

34. Describe the steps required to add three rational expressions. You may use an example to illustrate.

Add or subtract as indicated in each of the following. Write all answers in lowest terms. (See Example 4.)

35. $\frac{3}{5z} - \frac{2}{3z}$

36. $\frac{7}{4z} - \frac{5}{3z}$

37. $\frac{r+2}{3} - \frac{r-2}{3}$

38. $\frac{3y-1}{8} - \frac{3y+1}{8}$

39. $\frac{4}{x} + \frac{1}{3}$

40. $\frac{6}{r} - \frac{3}{4}$

41. $\frac{2}{y} - \frac{1}{4}$

42. $\frac{6}{11} + \frac{3}{a}$

43. $\frac{1}{6m} + \frac{2}{5m} + \frac{4}{m}$

44. $\frac{8}{3p} + \frac{5}{4p} + \frac{9}{2p}$

45. $\frac{1}{m-1} + \frac{2}{m}$

46. $\frac{8}{y+2} - \frac{3}{y}$

47. $\frac{8}{3(a-1)} + \frac{2}{a-1}$

48. $\frac{5}{2(k+3)} + \frac{2}{k+3}$

49. $\frac{2}{5(k-2)} + \frac{3}{4(k-2)}$

50. $\frac{11}{3(p+4)} - \frac{5}{6(p+4)}$

51. $\frac{2}{x^2-2x-3} + \frac{5}{x^2-x-6}$

52. $\frac{3}{m^2-3m-10} + \frac{5}{m^2-m-20}$

53. $\frac{2y}{y^2+7y+12} - \frac{y}{y^2+5y+6}$

54. $\frac{-r}{r^2-10r+16} - \frac{3r}{r^2+2r-8}$

55. $\frac{3k}{2k^2+3k-2} - \frac{2k}{2k^2-7k+3}$

56. $\frac{4m}{3m^2+7m-6} - \frac{m}{3m^2-14m+8}$

In each of the following exercises, simplify the complex fraction. (See Example 5.)

57. $\dfrac{1+\frac{1}{x}}{1-\frac{1}{x}}$

58. $\dfrac{2-\frac{2}{y}}{2+\frac{2}{y}}$

59. $\dfrac{\frac{1}{x+h}-\frac{1}{x}}{h}$

60. $\dfrac{\frac{1}{(x+h)^2}-\frac{1}{x^2}}{h}$

61. $\dfrac{1+\frac{1}{1-b}}{1-\frac{1}{1+b}}$

62. $\dfrac{m-\frac{1}{m^2-4}}{\frac{1}{m+2}}$

4.4 RATIONAL FUNCTIONS

A **rational function** is a function whose rule is the quotient of two polynomials, such as

$$f(x) = \frac{2}{1+x}, \quad g(x) = \frac{3x+2}{2x+4}, \quad h(x) = \frac{x^2-2x-4}{x^3-2x^2+x}.$$

Thus a rational function is one whose rule can be written in the form

$$f(x) = \frac{P(x)}{Q(x)},$$

where $P(x)$ and $Q(x)$ are polynomials, with $Q(x) \neq 0$. The function is undefined for any values of x that make $Q(x) = 0$, so there are breaks in the graph at these numbers.

Calculators sometimes do a poor job of graphing rational functions. If you know how rational functions behave, however, and you analyze each function before graphing it, you will be able to interpret screen images correctly. So the emphasis here will be on algebraic analysis of rational functions.

LINEAR RATIONAL FUNCTIONS We begin with rational functions in which both numerator and denominator are first-degree or constant polynomials. Such functions are sometimes called **linear rational functions.**

EXAMPLE 1 Graph the rational function defined by $f(x) = \dfrac{2}{1 + x}$.

This function is undefined for $x = -1$, since -1 leads to a 0 denominator. For this reason, the graph of this function will not intersect the vertical line $x = -1$. Since x can take on any value except -1, the values of x can approach -1 as closely as desired from either side of -1, as shown in the following table of values.

x approaches -1 ↓

x	-1.5	-1.2	-1.1	-1.01	$-.99$	$-.9$	$-.8$	$-.5$
$1 + x$	$-.5$	$-.2$	$-.1$	$-.01$	$.01$	$.1$	$.2$	$.5$
$\dfrac{2}{1 + x}$	-4	-10	-20	-200	200	20	10	4

↑ $|f(x)|$ gets larger and larger

The table above suggests that as x gets closer and closer to -1 from either side, the denominator $1 + x$ gets closer and closer to 0, and $|2/(1 + x)|$ gets larger and larger. The part of the graph in Figure 4.18 near $x = -1$ shows this behavior. The vertical line $x = -1$ that is approached by the curve is called a *vertical asymptote.* For convenience, the vertical asymptote is indicated by a dashed line in Figure 4.18, but this line is *not* part of the graph of the function.

As $|x|$ gets larger and larger so does the absolute value of the denominator $1 + x$. Hence $y = 2/(1 + x)$ gets closer and closer to 0, as shown in the table below.

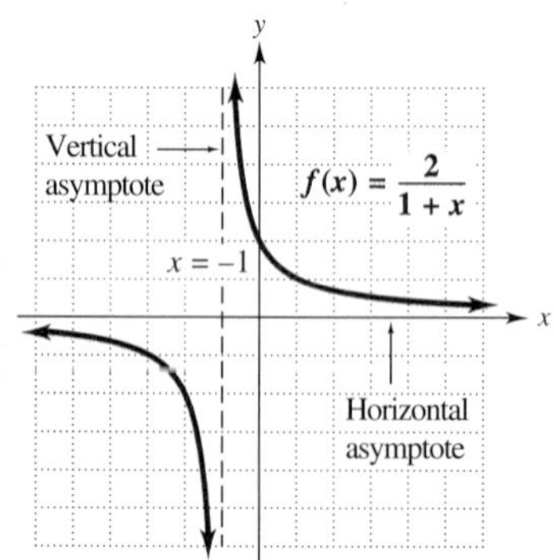

FIGURE 4.18

x	-101	-11	-2	0	9	99
$1 + x$	-100	-10	-1	1	10	100
$\dfrac{2}{1 + x}$	$-.02$	$-.2$	-2	2	$.2$	$.02$

The horizontal line $y = 0$ is called a *horizontal asymptote* for this graph. Using the asymptotes and plotting the intercept and other points gives the graph of Figure 4.18. ■

Depending on the viewing window, a calculator may not accurately represent the graph of a rational function, particularly near a vertical asymptote. For example, one calculator produced the graphs of $f(x) = \dfrac{2}{1 + x}$, in Figure 4.19, two of which do not look like Figure 4.18 as they should.

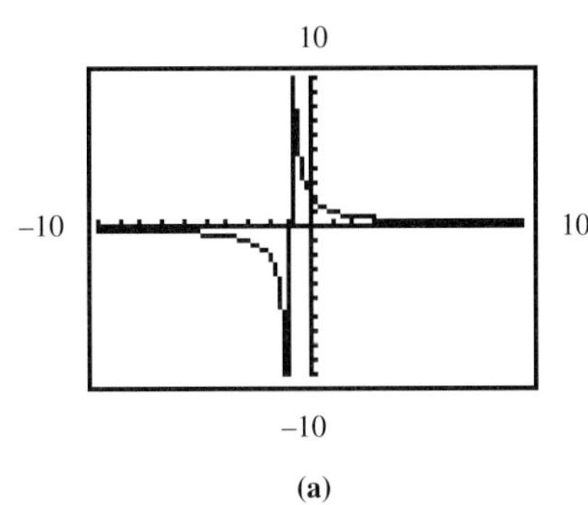

(a)

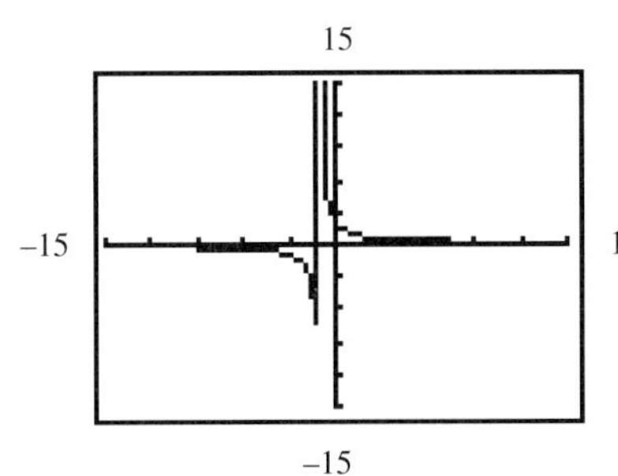

(b)

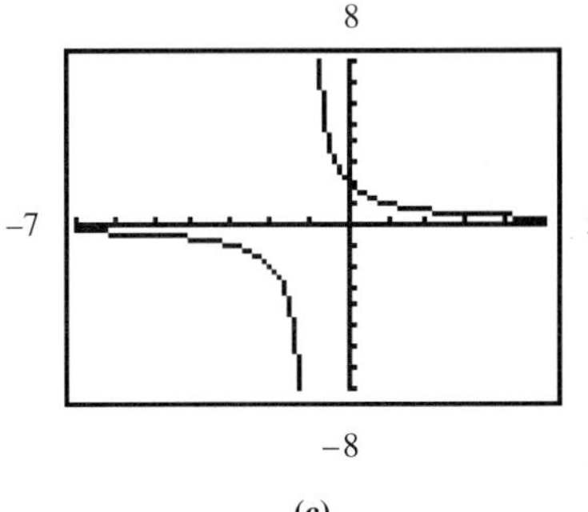

(c)

FIGURE 4.19

The vertical line segments in graphs (a) and (b) of Figure 4.19 are *not* representations of the vertical asymptote. They are a result of the calculator evaluating $f(x)$ just to the left of $x = -1$ and just to the right of $x = -1$, but not at $x = -1$, and then erroneously connecting these points with a near vertical segment that looks like an asymptote. In the accurate graph in Figure 4.19(c), the calculator attempted to plot a point with $x = -1$ and, when it found that $f(-1)$ was not defined, skipped a pixel and did not join the points on either side of the skipped one. The window in Figure 4.19(c) was found by using the Technology Tip on page 100. 1

1 Find a viewing window that displays the graph of the function with no erroneous vertical lines.

(a) $f(x) = \dfrac{3}{5 - x}$

(b) $g(x) = \dfrac{-4}{x + 4}$

Answers:
Windows with the vertical asymptote at the center of the x-axis will work on most calculators:

(a) $-1 \leq x \leq 11$ and $-10 \leq y \leq 10$;

(b) $-10 \leq x \leq 2$ and $-10 \leq y \leq 10$.

On TI-92, be sure Xres = 1 (in the WINDOW menu) and on HP-38, use a window in which the x-axis is 13 units long, such as $-1.5 \leq x \leq 11.5$ in part (a) or $-10.5 \leq x \leq 2.5$ in part (b).

Example 1 suggests the following conclusion.

If a number c makes the denominator 0 but the numerator nonzero in the expression defining a rational function, then the line $x = c$ is a **vertical asymptote** for the graph of the function.

Also, wherever the values of y approach but do not equal some number k as $|x|$ gets larger and larger, the line $y = k$ is a **horizontal asymptote** for the graph.

EXAMPLE 2 Graph $f(x) = \dfrac{3x + 2}{2x + 4}$.

Find the vertical asymptote by setting the denominator equal to 0, then solving for x.

$$2x + 4 = 0$$
$$x = -2$$

In order to see what the graph looks like when $|x|$ is very large, we rewrite the rule of the function. When $x \neq 0$, dividing both numerator and denominator by x does not change the value of the function:

$$f(x) = \frac{3x + 2}{2x + 4} = \frac{\dfrac{3x + 2}{x}}{\dfrac{2x + 4}{x}}$$

$$= \frac{\dfrac{3x}{x} + \dfrac{2}{x}}{\dfrac{2x}{x} + \dfrac{4}{x}} = \frac{3 + \dfrac{2}{3}}{2 + \dfrac{4}{x}}.$$

Now when $|x|$ is very large, the fractions $2/x$ and $4/x$ are very close to 0 (for instance, when $x = 200$, $4/x = 4/200 = .02$). Therefore the numerator of $f(x)$ is very close to $3 + 0 = 3$ and the denominator is very close to $2 + 0 = 2$. Hence $f(x)$ is very close to $3/2$ when $|x|$ is large, so the line $y = 3/2$ is the horizontal asymptote of the graph, as shown in Figure 4.20. ■

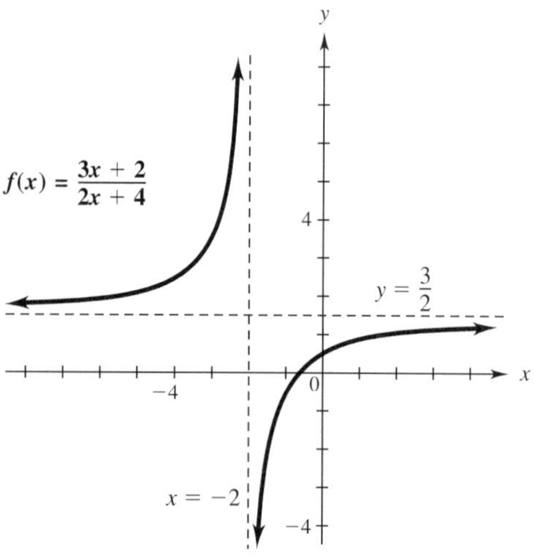

FIGURE 4.20

In Examples 1 and 2, each graph has a single vertical asymptote, determined by the root of the denominator, and a horizontal asymptote determined by the coefficients of x. In Example 2, for instance, $f(x) = \dfrac{3x + 2}{2x + 4}$ has horizontal asymptote

$y = \frac{3}{2}$, and in Example 1, $f(x) = \frac{2}{1+x} = \frac{0x+2}{1x+1}$ has horizontal asymptote $y = \frac{0}{1} = 0$ (the x-axis). Similar arguments work for any linear rational function.

> The graph of $f(x) = \frac{ax+b}{cx+d}$ (where $c \neq 0$ and $ad \neq bc$) has a vertical asymptote at the root of the denominator and horizontal asymptote $y = \frac{a}{c}$.

OTHER RATIONAL FUNCTIONS When the numerator or denominator of a rational function has degree greater than 1, its graph can be more complicated than those in Examples 1 and 2. These graphs may have several vertical asymptotes, as well as peaks and valleys.

EXAMPLE 3 Graph $f(x) = \frac{2x^2}{x^2+x-2}$.

Find the vertical asymptotes by setting the denominator equal to 0 and solving for x.

$$\begin{aligned} x^2 + x - 2 &= 0 \\ (x+2)(x-1) &= 0 \\ x + 2 = 0 \quad &\text{or} \quad x - 1 = 0 \\ x = -2 \quad & \qquad\quad x = 1 \end{aligned}$$

Since neither of these numbers make the numerator 0, the lines $x = -2$ and $x = 1$ are vertical asymptotes of the graph. The horizontal asymptote can be determined by dividing both the numerator and denominator of $f(x)$ by x^2 (the highest power of x that appears in either one).

$$f(x) = \frac{2x^2}{x^2+x-2} = \frac{\frac{2x^2}{x^2}}{\frac{x^2+x-2}{x^2}} = \frac{\frac{2x^2}{x^2}}{\frac{x^2}{x^2} + \frac{x}{x^2} - \frac{2}{x^2}} = \frac{2}{1 + \frac{1}{x} - \frac{2}{x^2}}.$$

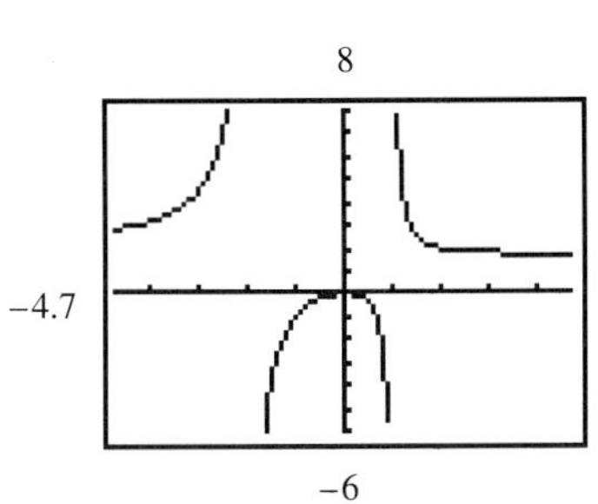

FIGURE 4.21

When $|x|$ is very large, the fractions $1/x$ and $2/x^2$ are very close to 0 so that the denominator is very close to 1 and $f(x)$ is very close to 2. So the line $y = 2$ is the horizontal asymptote of the graph. Using this information and selecting a viewing window that will accurately portray the graph near the vertical asymptotes (see the Technology Tip on the next page), we obtain Figure 4.21. ■

Technology Tip The viewing window in Figure 4.21 is an example of a *decimal window*, that is, one in which the horizontal distance between adjacent pixels is .1, so that the calculator evaluates the function at $-2.2, -2.1, -2, -1.9, -1.8$, etc., and thus catches the undefined points at $x = -2$ and $x = 1$. On many calculators such windows can be produced with a single keystroke. Look for "decimal" in the ZOOM menu of TI or the VIEWS menu of HP calculators. Look for "initial" in the Casio RANGE menu or "default" in the Sharp RANGE MENU (two keys).

On wide-screen calculators (such as TI-85/92 and HP-38), the x-range of the decimal window may differ from that in Figure 4.21 (which was produced by a TI-83). On all calculators, the y-range of the decimal window may have to be enlarged to see the graph, as was done in Figure 4.21.

Doubling the Xmin and Xmax settings for a decimal window produces a window in which the distance between adjacent pixels is .2, so that the calculator evaluates at $-1.2, -1, -.8$, etc. ✔

2 List the vertical and horizontal asymptotes of the function and find a viewing window that accurately displays its graph near the asymptotes.

(a) $f(x) = \dfrac{3x + 5}{x + 5}$

(b) $g(x) = \dfrac{2 - x^2}{x^2 - 4}$

Answers:

(a) Vertical $x = -5$; horizontal $y = 3$; a window with the vertical asymptote at the center of the x-axis, such as $-20 \le x \le 10$ and $-20 \le y \le 20$, works for most calculators. Other windows also work.

(b) Vertical $x = -2$ and $x = 2$; horizontal $y = -1$; the decimal window (with the y-range lengthened to $-6 \le y \le 4$) works for most calculators. Other windows also work.

The arguments used to find the horizontal asymptotes in Examples 1–3 work in the general case and lead to this conclusion.

If the numerator of the rational function $f(x)$ has *smaller* degree than the denominator, then the x-axis (the line $y = 0$) is the horizontal asymptote of the graph. If the numerator and denominator have the *same* degree, say $f(x) = \dfrac{ax^n + \cdots}{cx^n + \cdots}$, then the line $y = \dfrac{a}{c}$ is the horizontal asymptote.*

The preceding facts make it easier to select appropriate viewing windows and to interpret calculator-generated graphs of rational functions. 2

APPLICATIONS Rational functions have a variety of applications, some of which are explored here.

EXAMPLE 4 In many situations involving environmental pollution, much of the pollutant can be removed from the air or water at a fairly reasonable cost, but the last, small part of the pollutant can be very expensive to remove.

Cost as a function of the percentage of pollutant removed from the environment can be calculated for various percentages of removal, with a curve fitted through the resulting data points. This curve then leads to a function that approximates the situation. Rational functions often are a good choice for these **cost-benefit functions.**

For example, suppose a cost-benefit function is given by

$$f(x) = \frac{18x}{106 - x},$$

where $f(x)$ or y is the cost (in thousands of dollars) of removing x percent of a certain pollutant. The domain of x is the set of all numbers from 0 to 100, inclusive; any

*When the numerator has larger degree than the denominator, the graph has no horizontal asymptote, but may have non-horizontal lines or other curves as asymptotes; see Exercises 33 and 34 for examples.

3 Using the function of Example 4, find the cost to remove the following percents of pollutants.

(a) 70%

(b) 85%

(c) 98%

Answers:

(a) \$35,000

(b) About \$73,000

(c) About \$221,000

amount of pollutant from 0% to 100% can be removed. To remove 100% of the pollutant here would cost

$$y = \frac{18(100)}{106 - 100} = 300,$$

or \$300,000. Check that 95% of the pollutant can be removed for \$155,000, 90% for \$101,000, and 80% for \$55,000, as shown in Figure 4.22. ■ 3

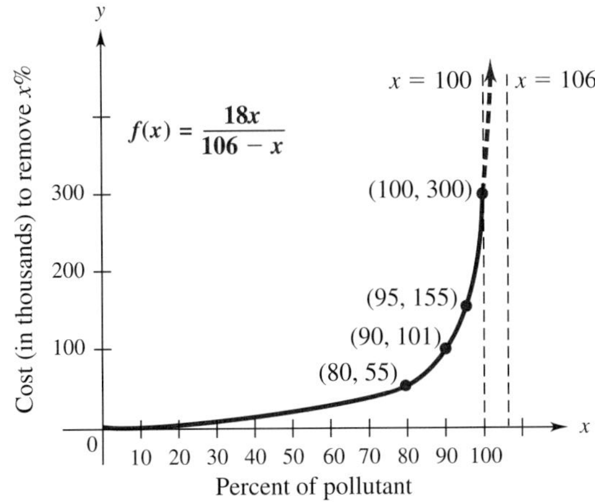

FIGURE 4.22

In management, **product-exchange functions** give the relationship between quantities of two items that can be produced by the same machine or factory. For example, an oil refinery can produce gasoline, heating oil, or a combination of the two; a winery can produce red wine, white wine, or a combination of the two. The next example discusses a product-exchange function.

EXAMPLE 5 The product-exchange function for the Golden Grape Winery for red wine x and white wine y, in tons, is

$$y = \frac{100{,}000 - 50x}{1000 + x}.$$

Graph the function and find the maximum quantity of each kind of wine that can be produced.

Only nonnegative values of x and y make sense in this situation, so we shall graph the function in the first quadrant. Note that the y-intercept of the graph (found by setting $x = 0$) is 100, and the x-intercept (found by setting $y = 0$ and solving for x) is 2000. Since we are interested only in the Quadrant I portion of the graph, we can find a few more points in Quadrant I and complete the graph as shown in Figure 4.23 on the next page.

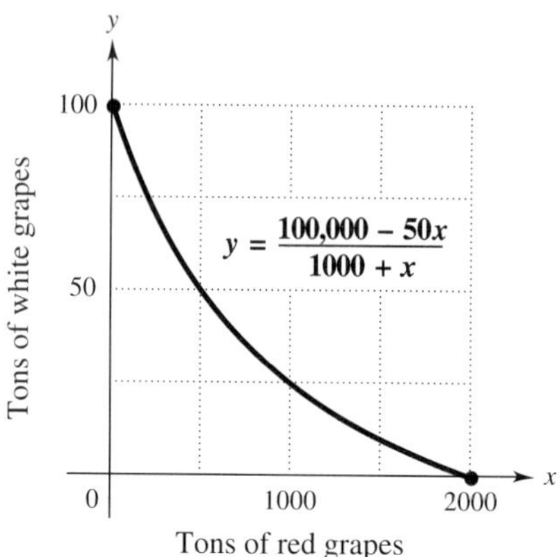

FIGURE 4.23

4 Rework Example 5 with the product-exchange function

$$y = \frac{60{,}000 - 10x}{60 + x}$$

to find the maximum amount of each wine that can be produced.

Answer:
6000 tons of red, 1000 tons of white

The maximum value of y occurs when $x = 0$, so the maximum amount of white wine that can be produced is 100 tons, given by the y-intercept. The x-intercept gives the maximum amount of red wine that can be produced, 2000 tons. ■ 4

EXAMPLE 6 A retailer buys 2500 light bulbs from a distributor each year. In addition to the cost of each bulb, there is an order fee for each order, so she wants to order as few times as possible. On the other hand, storage costs are higher when there are fewer orders (and hence more bulbs per order to store). Past experience shows that the total annual cost (for the bulbs, ordering fees, and storage costs) is given by the rational function

$$C(x) = \frac{.98x^2 + 1200x + 22{,}000}{x},$$

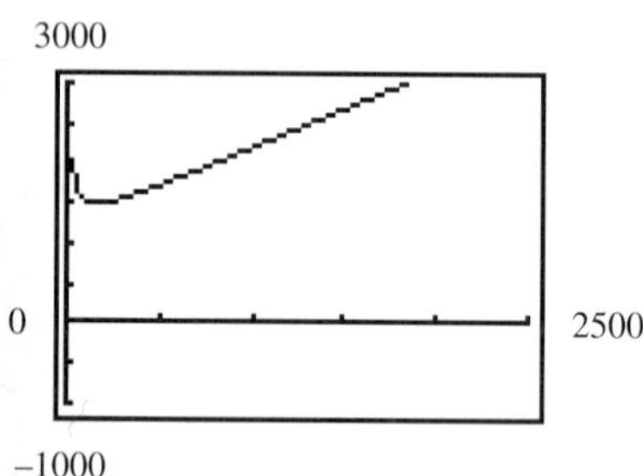
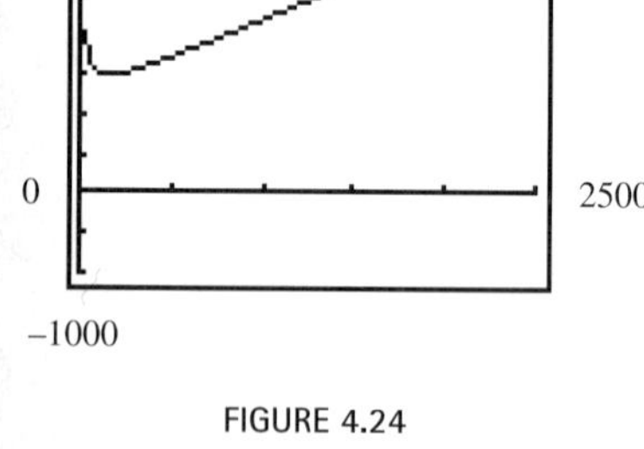

FIGURE 4.24

where x is the number of bulbs ordered each time. How many bulbs should be ordered each time in order to have the smallest possible cost?

Graph the cost function $C(x)$ in a window with $0 \le x \le 2500$ (because she can't order a negative number and needs only 2500 for the year). For each point on the graph in Figure 4.24,

the x-coordinate is the number of bulbs ordered each time;

the y-coordinate is the annual cost when x bulbs are ordered each time.

Use the minimum finder on your calculator to find the point with smallest y-coordinate, which is approximately (149.83, 1493.67), as shown in Figure 4.25. Since the retailer can't order part of a light bulb, she should order 150 bulbs each time for an approximate annual cost of \$1494. ■

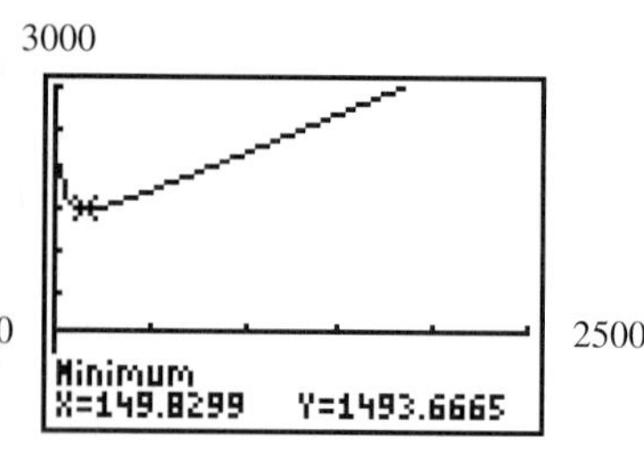

FIGURE 4.25

4.4 EXERCISES

Graph each function. Give the equations of the vertical and horizontal asymptotes (see Examples 1–3).

1. $f(x) = \frac{1}{x + 5}$

2. $g(x) = \frac{-7}{x - 6}$

3. $f(x) = \frac{-3}{2x + 5}$

4. $h(x) = \frac{-4}{2 - x}$

5. $f(x) = \frac{2 - x}{x - 3}$

6. $g(x) = \frac{3x - 2}{x + 3}$

7. $f(x) = \frac{2x - 1}{4x + 2}$

8. $f(x) = \frac{3x - 6}{6x - 1}$

9. $h(x) = \frac{x + 1}{x^2 + 3x - 4}$

10. $g(x) = \frac{x^2 + 2}{x^2 - 4x + 3}$

11. $f(x) = \dfrac{x^2 + 1}{x^2 - 1}$ **12.** $g(x) = \dfrac{1}{x^3 + 3x}$

13. $f(x) = \dfrac{x^2 + x}{x^2 - 2x + 4}$ **14.** $f(x) = \dfrac{1 - 4x^2}{x^2}$

Find a viewing window, or windows, that shows a complete graph of the function (if possible, with no erroneous vertical line segments). Be alert for hidden behavior (such as tiny peaks or valleys).

15. $h(x) = \dfrac{2x + 3}{x^2 + 3x}$ **16.** $f(x) = \dfrac{x + 3}{x^2 + 2x - 15}$

17. $f(x) = \dfrac{x - 3}{x^2 + x - 2}$ **18.** $g(x) = \dfrac{x + 2}{x^2 - 1}$

19. $f(x) = \dfrac{x - 4}{2x^3 - 5x^2 - 4x + 12}$

20. $g(x) = \dfrac{x^3 + 4x^2 - 5x}{x^4 - 13x^2 + 36}$

21. Natural Science Suppose a cost-benefit model (see Example 4) is given by

$$f(x) = \frac{4.3x}{100 - x},$$

where $f(x)$ is the cost in thousands of dollars of removing x percent of a given pollutant. Find the cost of removing each of the following percents of pollutants.

(a) 50% **(b)** 70% **(c)** 80% **(d)** 90%
(e) 95% **(f)** 98% **(g)** 99%
(h) Is it possible, according to this model to remove *all* the pollutant?
(i) Graph the function.

22. Natural Science Suppose a cost-benefit model is given by

$$f(x) = \frac{4.5x}{101 - x},$$

where $f(x)$ is the cost in thousands of dollars of removing x percent of a certain pollutant. Find the cost of removing the following percents of pollutants.

(a) 0% **(b)** 50% **(c)** 80% **(d)** 90%
(e) 95% **(f)** 99% **(g)** 100%
(h) Graph the function.

23. Management SuperStar Cablevision Company recently began service to the city of Megapolis. Based on past experience, it estimates that the number $N(x)$ of subscribers (in thousands) at the end of x months is

$$N(x) = \frac{250x}{x + 6}.$$

Find the number of subscribers at the end of

(a) 6 months **(b)** 18 months **(c)** two years.
(d) Graph $N(x)$.
(e) What part of the graph is relevant to this situation?
(f) What is the horizontal asymptote of the graph? What does this suggest that the maximum possible number of subscribers will be?

24. Social Science The average waiting time in a line (or queue) before getting served is given by

$$W = \frac{S(S - A)}{A},$$

where A is the average rate that people arrive at the line and S is the average service time. At a certain fast food restaurant, the average service time is 3 minutes. Find W for each of the following average arrival times.

(a) 1 minute **(b)** 2 minutes **(c)** 2.5 minutes
(d) What is the vertical asymptote?
(e) Graph the equation on the interval (0, 3].
(f) What happens to W when $A > 3$? What does this mean?

25. Management At Ewing's Clothing Store, daily sales of shirts (in dollars) after x days of newspaper ads are given by

$$S = \frac{600x + 3800}{x + 1}.$$

(a) Graph the first quadrant portion of the sales function.
(b) Assuming that the ads keep running, will sales tend to level off? What is the minimum amount of sales to be expected? What feature of the graph gives this information?
(c) If newspaper ads cost $1000 per day, at what point should they be discontinued? Why?

Management *Sketch the Quadrant I portion of the graph of each of the functions defined below, and then estimate the maximum quantities of each product that can be produced. (See Example 5.)*

26. The product-exchange function for gasoline, x, and heating oil, y, in hundreds of gallons per day, is

$$y = \frac{125{,}000 - 25x}{125 + 2x}.$$

27. A drug factory found the product-exchange function for a red tranquilizer, x, and a blue tranquilizer, y, is

$$y = \frac{900{,}000{,}000 - 30{,}000x}{x + 90{,}000}.$$

28. Physical Science The failure of several O-rings in field joints was the cause of the fatal crash of the *Challenger* space shuttle in 1986. NASA data from 24 successful launches prior to *Challenger* suggested that O-ring failure was related to launch temperature by a function similar to

$$N(t) = \frac{600 - 7t}{4t - 100} \quad (50 \le t \le 85),$$

where t is the temperature (in °F) at launch and N is the approximate number of O-rings that fail. Assume that this function accurately models the number of O-ring failures that would occur at lower launch temperatures (an assumption NASA did not make).

(a) Does $N(t)$ have a vertical asymptote? At what value of t does it occur?
(b) Without graphing, what would you conjecture that the graph would look like just to the right of the vertical

asymptote? What does this suggest about the number of O-ring failures that might be expected near that temperature? (The temperature at the *Challenger* launching was 31°.)

(c) Confirm your conjecture by graphing $N(t)$ between the vertical asymptote and $t = 85$.

29. Management When no more than 110 units are produced, the cost of producing x units is given by $C(x) = .2x^3 - 25x^2 + 1531x + 25{,}000$. How many units should be produced in order to have the lowest possible average cost? (Average cost was defined on page 131.)

30. Management A company has fixed costs of \$40,000 and marginal cost of \$2.60 per unit.

(a) Find the linear cost function.

(b) Find the average cost function. (Average cost was defined on page 131.)

(c) Graph the average cost function in a window with $0 \le x \le 100{,}000$ and $0 \le y \le 20$.

(d) Find the horizontal asymptote of the average cost function. Explain what the asymptote means in this situation (how low can the average cost possibly be?).

31. Physical Science An open-top box with a square base and a volume of 1000 cubic inches is to be constructed. What are the dimensions of the box that uses the least possible amount of material? (*Hint:* Use the volume and surface area formulas to get two equations, as in Example 4 of Section 4.2, then solve the volume equation for h and substitute this in the surface area equation; then find the value of x that makes surface area a minimum.)

32. Physical Science It costs 2.5 cents per square inch to make the bottom of the box in Exercise 31. The sides cost 1.5 cents per square inch. What are the dimensions of the cheapest possible box?

33. (a) Graph $f(x) = \dfrac{x^3 + 3x^2 + x + 1}{x^2 + 2x + 1}$.

(b) Does the graph appear to have a horizontal asymptote? Does the graph appear to have some nonhorizontal straight line as an asymptote?

(c) Graph $f(x)$ and the line $y = x + 1$ on the same screen. Does this line appear to be an asymptote of the graph of $f(x)$?

34. (a) Graph $g(x) = \dfrac{x^3 - 2}{x - 1}$ in the window with $-4 \le x \le 6$ and $-6 \le y \le 12$.

(b) Graph $g(x)$ and the parabola $y = x^2 + x + 1$ on the same screen. How do the two graphs compare when $|x| \ge 2$?

CHAPTER 4 SUMMARY

Key Terms and Symbols

4.1 polynomial function
graph of $f(x) = ax^n$
properties of polynomial graphs

4.2 optimization problems

4.3 rational expression
operations with rational expressions
complex fraction

4.4 rational function
linear rational function
vertical asymptote
horizontal asymptote
cost-benefit function
product exchange function

Key Concepts

If a number c makes the denominator of a **rational function** 0, but the numerator nonzero, then the line $x = c$ is a **vertical asymptote** for the graph.

Whenever $y = f(x)$ and the values of y approach, but never equal, some number k as $|x|$ gets larger and larger, the line $y = k$ is a **horizontal asymptote** for the graph of f.

Chapter 4 Review Exercises

Find a complete graph of each polynomial function and list the x-intercepts.

1. $g(x) = x^3 - x$

2. $g(x) = x^4 - x^2$

3. $f(x) = 2x^3 - 3x^2 - 2x$

4. $f(x) = x^3 - 3x^2 - 4x$

5. $f(x) = x^4 - 5x^2 - 6$

6. $f(x) = x^4 - 7x^2 - 8$

Find a viewing window (or windows) that shows a complete graph of the function. Be alert for hidden behavior.

7. $g(x) = .5x^3 - 4x^2 + x + 1$

8. $g(x) = .3x^5 - 4x^4 + x^3 - 4x^2 + 5x + 1$

9. $f(x) = 4x^3 - 85x^2 + 600x - 1000$

10. $f(x) = 32x^3 - 99x^2 + 101x - 28$

11. Management The demand equation for automobile oil filters is

$$p = -.000012q^3 - .00498q^2 + .1264q + 1508,$$

where p is in dollars and q is in thousands of items. The supply equation is

$$p = -.000001q^3 + .00097q^2 + 2q.$$

Find the equilibrium quantity and the equilibrium price.

12. Management The average cost (in dollars) per item of manufacturing x thousand cans of spray paint is given by

$$A(x) = -.000006x^4 + .0017x^3 + .03x^2 - 24x + 1110.$$

How many cans should be manufactured if the average cost is to be as low as possible? What is the average cost in that case?

13. Management Plastic racks for holding compact discs sell for \$23 each. The cost of manufacturing x racks is given by $C(x) = -.000006x^3 + .07x^2 + 2x + 1200$. At most 600 racks can be produced.
(a) Find the revenue and profit functions.
(b) What is the break-even point?
(c) What is the maximum number of racks that can be made without losing money?
(d) How many racks should be made in order to have as large a profit as possible? What is that profit?

14. Physical Science A box with a top and a square base is to be made from 500 square inches of material. In order for the box to have as large a volume as possible, what should its dimensions be?

Perform each operation.

15. $\frac{4x}{5} \cdot \frac{35x}{12}$ **16.** $\frac{5k^2}{24} - \frac{75k}{36}$

17. $\frac{c^2 - 3c + 2}{2c(c - 1)} \div \frac{c - 2}{8c}$

18. $\frac{p^3 - 2p^2 - 8p}{3p(p^2 - 16)} \div \frac{p^2 + 4p + 4}{9p^2}$

19. $\frac{2y - 10}{5y} \cdot \frac{20y - 25}{12}$

20. $\frac{m^2 - 2m}{15m^3} \cdot \frac{5}{m^2 - 4}$

21. $\frac{2m^2 - 4m + 2}{m^2 - 1} \div \frac{6m + 18}{m^2 + 2m - 3}$

22. $\frac{x^2 + 6x + 5}{4(x^2 + 1)} \cdot \frac{2x(x + 1)}{x^2 - 25}$

23. $\frac{6}{15z} + \frac{2}{3z} - \frac{9}{10z}$ **24.** $\frac{5}{y - 2} - \frac{4}{y}$

25. $\frac{2}{5q} + \frac{10}{7q}$ **26.** $\dfrac{\frac{1}{x} - \frac{2}{y}}{3 - \frac{1}{xy}}$

List the vertical and horizontal asymptotes of each function and sketch its graph.

27. $f(x) = \frac{1}{x - 3}$ **28.** $f(x) = \frac{-2}{x + 4}$

29. $f(x) = \frac{-3}{2x - 4}$ **30.** $f(x) = \frac{5}{3x + 7}$

31. $g(x) = \frac{5x - 2}{4x^2 - 4x - 3}$ **32.** $g(x) = \frac{x^2}{x^2 - 1}$

33. $f(x) = \frac{3x^2 + 1}{2x^2 - x - 1}$ **34.** $f(x) = \frac{3 - x^2}{x^2 + 2x - 3}$

Find a viewing window (or windows) that shows a complete graph of the function. Be alert for hidden behavior.

35. $f(x) = \frac{x^4 + 4}{x^4 - 99x^2 - 100}$

36. $g(x) = \frac{x^2 - x - 6}{x^3 - 3x^2 + 3x - 1}$

37. Management The average cost per unit of producing x cartons of cocoa is given by

$$C(x) = \frac{650}{2x + 40}.$$

Find the average cost per carton to make the following number of cartons.
(a) 10 cartons **(b)** 50 cartons **(c)** 70 cartons
(d) 100 cartons **(e)** Graph $C(x)$.

38. Management The cost and revenue functions (in dollars) for a frozen yogurt shop are given by

$$C(x) = \frac{400x + 400}{x + 4} \quad \text{and} \quad R(x) = 100x,$$

where x is measured in hundreds of units.
(a) Graph $C(x)$ and $R(x)$ on the same axes.
(b) What is the break-even point for this shop?
(c) If the profit function is given by $P(x)$, does $P(1)$ represent a profit or a loss?
(d) Does $P(4)$ represent a profit or a loss?

39. Management The supply and demand functions for the yogurt shop in Exercise 38 are as follows:

$$\text{supply: } p = \frac{q^2}{4} + 25; \quad \text{demand: } p = \frac{500}{q},$$

where p is the price in dollars for q hundred units of yogurt.

(exercise continues)

(a) Graph both functions on the same axes, and from the graph, estimate the equilibrium point.
(b) Give the q-intervals where supply exceeds demand.
(c) Give the q-intervals where demand exceeds supply.

40. **Natural Science** The survival rate s of seedlings in the vicinity of a parent tree is given by

$$s = \frac{.5x}{1 + .4x^2},$$

where x is the distance from the seedlings to the parent tree (in meters) and $0 < x \leq 10$.
(a) For what distances is the survival rate at least .21?
(b) What distance produces the maximum survival rate? What is that rate?

CASE 4

Error-Correcting Codes*

Both the *Voyager* satellite and musical CDs send data over "noisy" channels, so that error-correcting techniques are needed to get the original information. To see how these techniques work, consider a simple 2-word message coded as the numbers 2.6 and 5.7. This information will be interpreted as the ordered pairs (1, 2.6) and (2, 5.7), where the first numbers indicate the position of the word in the message.

These two pairs determine a straight line, whose equation can be found to be $y = 3.1x - .5$. This equation can be used to find more pairs: (3, 8.8), (4, 11.9), (5, 15.0), and (6, 18.1), for example. Now the message is sent encoded as (2.6, 5.7, 8.8, 11.9, 15.0, 18.1). This establishes a strong pattern that makes it possible to recover any data that has been incorrectly received. For instance, if the data was received as (5.7, 2.6, 8.8, 11.9, 15.0, 18.1), after plotting the points, the four collinear points could be used to determine the equation of the line containing them. Then, by substituting the x-coordinates of the points that don't fit, the correct y-values can be determined.

*Linda Kurz, "Error-Correcting Codes," given in "Snapshots of Applications in Mathematics" edited by Dennis Callas and David J. Hildreth in the *AMATYC Review*, Fall 1995.

Messages with more words require higher-order polynomials, but the same procedure can be used. A graphing calculator with a polynomial regression feature can be used to find a polynomial through the points. (For the correct syntax, look for "regression" in the index of your instruction manual.)

EXERCISES

1. Use the method discussed here to determine the correct 2-word message if (2.9, 14.1, 8.5, 11.3, 5.7, 16.9) is received.
2. A 3-word message requires a quadratic equation. Suppose the message to be sent is (1.2, 2.5, 3.7). Use quadratic regression on a calculator to find a quadratic equation that satisfies the corresponding ordered pairs, (1, 1.2), (2, 2.5), (3, 3.7). Find the points (4, y), (5, y), (6, y), and (7, y). What message would be sent?
3. If your calculator can do cubic regression, create a strong pattern with eight points for sending the following message: (2.3, 1.1, 1.7, 2.4).

CHAPTER 5

Exponential and Logarithmic Functions

Exponential and logarithmic functions play a key role in management, economics, the social and physical sciences, and engineering. They are used to study the growth of money and organizations; learning curves; the growth of human, animal, and bacterial populations; the spread of disease; and radioactive decay.

5.1 EXPONENTS AND RADICALS

To prepare for our study of the exponential and logarithmic functions, we begin by reviewing the definitions and properties of real number exponents. Earlier we showed that $a^m \cdot a^n = a^{m+n}$ for positive integer values of m and n. Now we develop further definitions and properties of exponents, beginning with a rule for quotients.

INTEGER EXPONENTS By definition

$$\frac{6^5}{6^2} = \frac{\mathbf{6 \cdot 6 \cdot 6 \cdot 6 \cdot 6}}{\mathbf{6 \cdot 6}} = 6 \cdot 6 \cdot 6 = 6^3.$$

Because there are 5 factors of 6 in the numerator and 2 factors of 6 in the denominator, the quotient has $5 - 2 = 3$ factors of 6. In general, if $m > n$, then

$$\frac{a^m}{a^n} = a^{m-n}.$$

Using this rule, $$\frac{3^5}{3^5} = 3^{5-5} = 3^0.$$

On the other hand, $3^5/3^5 = 1$. Therefore, it is reasonable to define $3^0 = 1$.

ZERO EXPONENT

If a is any nonzero real number, then

$$\mathbf{a^0 = 1.}$$

The symbol 0^0 is not defined.

EXAMPLE 1 Evaluate the following.

(a) $6^0 = 1$

(b) $(-9)^0 = 1$

(c) $-(4^0) = -(1) = -1$ ■ 1

1 Evaluate the following.

(a) 17^0

(b) 30^0

(c) $(-10)^0$

(d) $-(12^0)$

Answers:

(a) 1

(b) 1

(c) 1

(d) −1

If m is less than n in the quotient rule given above, the result has a negative exponent. For example,

$$\frac{3^2}{3^4} = 3^{2-4} = 3^{-2}.$$

However,

$$\frac{3^2}{3^4} = \frac{3 \cdot 3}{3 \cdot 3 \cdot 3 \cdot 3} = \frac{1}{3^2},$$

which suggests that 3^{-2} should be defined to be $1/3^2$. Thus, we have the following definition of a negative exponent.

NEGATIVE EXPONENT

If n is a natural number, and if $a \neq 0$, then

$$a^{-n} = \frac{1}{a^n}.$$

EXAMPLE 2 Evaluate the following.

(a) $5^{-4} = \frac{1}{5^4} = \frac{1}{625}$

(b) $7^{-1} = \frac{1}{7^1} = \frac{1}{7}$

(c) $-4^{-2} = -\frac{1}{4^2} = -\frac{1}{16}$

(d) $(-4)^{-2} = \frac{1}{(-4)^2} = \frac{1}{16}$

(e) $\left(\frac{3}{4}\right)^{-1} = \frac{1}{\left(\frac{3}{4}\right)^1} = \frac{1}{\frac{3}{4}} = \frac{4}{3}$

(f) $\left(\frac{2}{3}\right)^{-3} = \frac{1}{\left(\frac{2}{3}\right)^3} = \frac{1}{\left(\frac{2^3}{3^3}\right)} = 1 \cdot \frac{3^3}{2^3} = \frac{3^3}{2^3} = \frac{27}{8}$ ■

2 Evaluate the following.

(a) 6^{-2}

(b) -6^{-3}

(c) -3^{-4}

(d) $\left(\frac{5}{8}\right)^{-1}$

(e) $\left(\frac{1}{2}\right)^{-4}$

(f) $\left(\frac{7}{3}\right)^{-2}$

Answers:

(a) 1/36

(b) −1/216

(c) −1/81

(d) 8/5

(e) 16

(f) 9/49

Parts (e) and (f) of Example 2 involve work with fractions that can lead to error. For a useful shortcut with such fractions, use the properties of division of rational numbers and the definition of a negative exponent to get

$$\left(\frac{a}{b}\right)^{-n} = \frac{1}{\left(\frac{a}{b}\right)^n} = \frac{1}{\left(\frac{a^n}{b^n}\right)} = 1 \cdot \frac{b^n}{a^n} = \frac{b^n}{a^n} = \left(\frac{b}{a}\right)^n.$$ 2

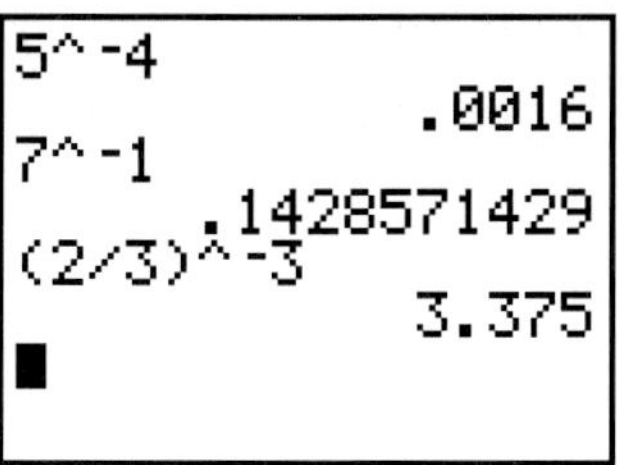

FIGURE 5.1

A calculator can be very helpful for evaluating expressions with exponents, provided that you are aware of how it operates. When entering negative exponents on a calculator, you must use the negative key (−) and not the subtraction key −. When the base is negative, you must use parentheses around it, as in $(-4)^{-2}$. To see what may happen if you don't, look at the difference between parts (c) and (d) of Example 2. In other parts of Example 2 we saw that

$$5^{-4} = 1/625, \quad 7^{-1} = 1/7, \quad \text{and} \quad (2/3)^{-3} = 27/8.$$

On a typical calculator screen, however, these results look like Figure 5.1.

TECHNOLOGY TIP On many calculators, repeating decimals, such as those in Figure 5.1, can be changed into equivalent fractions. Depending on the calculator, use the FRAC key (in the MATH menu) or change the number display format (in the MODES menu) to "fraction" or "exact." Check your instruction manual. A FRAC program for calculators that do not have this feature built-in is given in the Program Appendix. ✔

ROOTS AND RATIONAL EXPONENTS The definition of a^n will now be extended to include rational values of n, such as 1/2 and 5/4. In order to do this, we need some terminology.

There are two numbers whose square is 16, 4 and −4. The positive one, 4, is called the **square root** (or second root) of 16.* Similarly, there are two numbers whose fourth power is 16, 2 and −2. We call 2 the **fourth root** of 16. This suggests the following generalization.

If n is even, the ***n*th root of *a*** is the positive real number whose nth power is a.

All nonnegative numbers have nth roots for every natural number n, but *no negative number has a real, even nth root.* For example there is no real number whose square is −16, so −16 has no square root.

We say that the **cube root** (or third root) of 8 is 2 because $2^3 = 8$. Similarly, since $(-2)^3 = -8$, we say −2 is the cube root of −8. Again, we can generalize.

If n is odd, the ***n*th root of *a*** is the real number whose nth power is a.

Every real number has an nth root for every *odd* natural number n.

*Sometimes the positive square root is called the *principal* square root.

We can now define rational exponents. If they are to have the same properties as integer exponents, we want $a^{1/2}$ to be a number such that

$$(a^{1/2})^2 = a^{1/2} \cdot a^{1/2} = a^{1/2+1/2} = a^1 = a.$$

Thus, $a^{1/2}$ should be a number whose square is a and it is reasonable to *define* $a^{1/2}$ to be the square root of a (if it exists). Similarly, $a^{1/3}$ is defined to be the cube root of a, and $a^{1/n}$ is defined to be the nth root of a (if it exists).

3 Evaluate the following.

(a) $16^{1/2}$

(b) $16^{1/4}$

(c) $-256^{1/2}$

(d) $(-256)^{1/2}$

(e) $-8^{1/3}$

(f) $243^{1/5}$

Answers:

(a) 4

(b) 2

(c) -16

(d) Not a real number

(e) -2

(f) 3

EXAMPLE 3 Evaluate the following roots.

(a) $36^{1/2} = 6$ because $6^2 = 36$

(b) $-100^{1/2} = -10$

(c) $-(225^{1/2}) = -15$

(d) $625^{1/4} = 5$ because $5^4 = 625$

(e) $(-1296)^{1/4}$ is not a real number, but $-1296^{1/4} = -6$ because $6^4 = 1296$

(f) $27^{1/3} = 3$

(g) $-32^{1/5} = -2$ ■ 3

A calculator can be used to evaluate expressions with fractional exponents. Whenever it's easy to do so, enter the fractional exponents in their equivalent decimal form. For instance, to find $625^{1/4}$, enter $625^{.25}$ on the calculator. When the decimal equivalent of a fraction is an infinitely repeating decimal, however, it is best to enter the fractional exponent directly, using parentheses, as in Figure 5.2. If you omit the parentheses or use a shortened decimal approximation (such as .333 for 1/3), you will not get the correct answers because the calculator will not interpret these exponents as you intended, as shown in Figure 5.3.

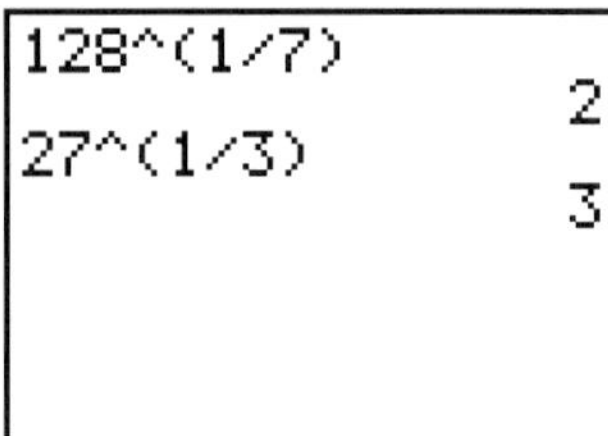

FIGURE 5.2

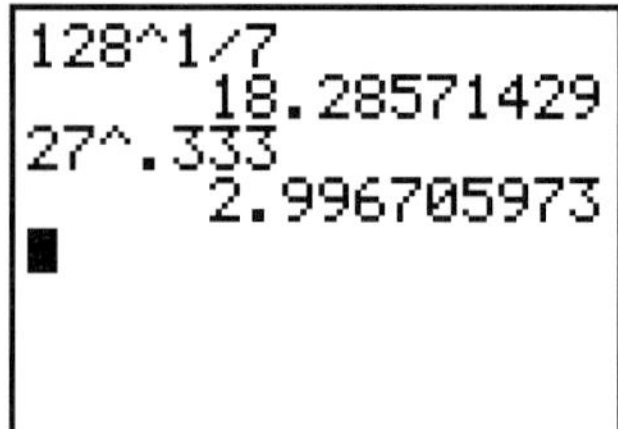

FIGURE 5.3

For more general rational exponents, the symbol $a^{m/n}$ should be defined so that the properties for exponents still hold. For example, by the product property, we want

$$(a^{1/3})^2 = a^{1/3} \cdot a^{1/3} = a^{2/3}.$$

This suggests the following definition.

For all integers m and all positive integers n, and for all real numbers a for which $a^{1/n}$ is a real number,

$$a^{m/n} = (a^{1/n})^m.$$

4 Evaluate the following.

(a) $16^{3/4}$

(b) $25^{5/2}$

(c) $32^{7/5}$

(d) $100^{3/2}$

Answers:

(a) 8

(b) 3125

(c) 128

(d) 1000

EXAMPLE 4 Evaluate the following.

(a) $27^{2/3} = (27^{1/3})^2 = 3^2 = 9$

(b) $32^{2/5} = (32^{1/5})^2 = 2^2 = 4$

(c) $64^{4/3} = (64^{1/3})^4 = 4^4 = 256$

(d) $25^{3/2} = (25^{1/2})^3 = 5^3 = 125$ ■ 4

The definitions and properties discussed above are summarized below, together with three power rules that follow from the definition of an exponent.

PROPERTIES OF EXPONENTS

For any rational numbers m and n, and any real numbers a and b for which the following exist.

(a) $a^m \cdot a^n = a^{m+n}$ Product property

(b) $\dfrac{a^m}{a^n} = a^{m-n}$ Quotient property

(c) $(a^m)^n = a^{mn}$

(d) $(ab)^m = a^m \cdot b^m$

(e) $\left(\dfrac{a}{b}\right)^m = \dfrac{a^m}{b^m}$

(c)–(e): Power properties

(f) $a^0 = 1$

(g) $a^{-n} = \dfrac{1}{a^n}$

(h) $\left(\dfrac{b}{a}\right)^{-m} = \left(\dfrac{a}{b}\right)^m$.

5 Simplify the following.

(a) $9^6 \cdot 9^{-4}$

(b) $\dfrac{8^7}{8^{-3}}$

(c) $(13^4)^{-3}$

(d) $6^{2/5} \cdot 6^{3/5}$

(e) $\dfrac{8^{2/3} \cdot 8^{-4/3}}{8^2}$

Answers:

(a) 9^2

(b) 8^{10}

(c) $\dfrac{1}{13^{12}}$

(d) 6

(e) $\dfrac{1}{8^{8/3}}$ or $\dfrac{1}{2^8}$

EXAMPLE 5 Use the properties of exponents to simplify each of the following. Write answers with positive exponents.

(a) $7^{-4} \cdot 7^6 = 7^2$ Product property

(b) $\dfrac{9^{14}}{9^{-6}} = 9^{14-(-6)} = 9^{20}$ Quotient property

(c) $(2^{-3})^{-4} = 2^{(-3)(-4)} = 2^{12}$ Power property

(d) $\dfrac{27^{1/3} \cdot 27^{5/3}}{27^3} = \dfrac{27^{1/3+5/3}}{27^3}$ Product property

$= \dfrac{27^2}{27^3} = 27^{2-3}$ Quotient property

$= 27^{-1} = \dfrac{1}{27}$ Property (g) ■ 5

You can use a calculator to check computations, such as those in Example 5, by computing the left and right sides separately and confirming that the answers are the same in each case. Figure 5.4 shows this for part (a) of Example 5.

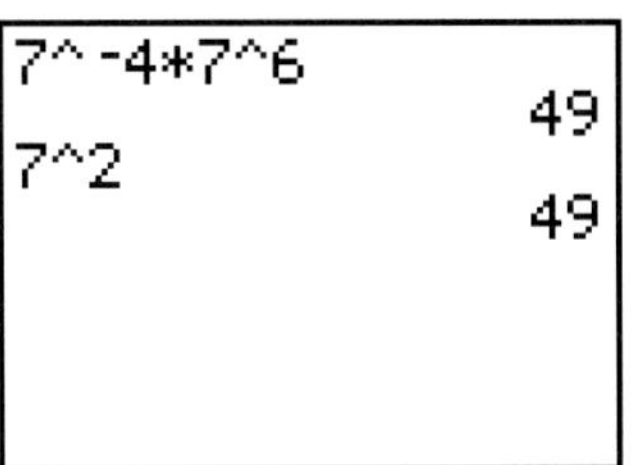

FIGURE 5.4

6 Simplify the following. Give answers with only positive exponents. Assume all variables represent positive real numbers.

(a) $\frac{(t^{-1})^2}{t^{-5}}$

(b) $\frac{(3z)^{-1}z^4}{z^2}$

(c) $3x^{1/4} \cdot 5x^{5/4}$

(d) $\left(\frac{2k^{1/3}}{p^{5/4}}\right)^2 \cdot \left(\frac{4k^{-2}}{p^5}\right)^{3/2}$

(e) $a^{5/8}(2a^{3/8} + a^{-1/8})$

Answers:

(a) t^3

(b) $z/3$

(c) $15x^{3/2}$

(d) $32/(p^{10}k^{7/3})$

(e) $2a + a^{1/2}$

TECHNOLOGY TIP There is another way to check the accuracy of computations on some calculators. When an equation or inequality is keyed into TI or HP calculators and ENTER is pressed, the calculator displays 1 if the statement is true and 0 if it is false. The symbols =, <, etc., are in the TEST or CHARS menu. ✔

EXAMPLE 6 Simplify each expression. Give answers with only positive exponents. Assume all variables represent positive real numbers.

(a) $\frac{(m^3)^{-2}}{m^4} = \frac{m^{-6}}{m^4} = m^{-6-4} = m^{-10} = \frac{1}{m^{10}}$

(b) $6y^{2/3} \cdot 2y^{-1/2} = 12y^{2/3-1/2} = 12y^{1/6}$

(c) $\left(\frac{3m^{5/6}}{y^{3/4}}\right)^2 = \frac{3^2m^{5/3}}{y^{3/2}} = \frac{9m^{5/3}}{y^{3/2}}$

(d) $m^{2/3}(m^{7/3} + 2m^{1/3}) = (m^{2/3+7/3} + 2m^{2/3+1/3}) = m^3 + 2m$ ■ 6

RADICALS The nth root of a was denoted above as $a^{1/n}$. An alternative notation for nth roots uses **radicals.**

> If n is an even natural number and $a \ge 0$, or n is an odd natural number,
> $$a^{1/n} = \sqrt[n]{a}.$$

In the radical expression, $\sqrt[n]{a}$, a is called the **radicand,** and n is called the **index.** The familiar symbol $\sqrt{a}$ is used instead of $\sqrt[2]{a}$. Although some calculators have an $\sqrt[n]{a}$ key in their MATH menus or on their keyboards, it is usually much easier to calculate nth roots by using fractional exponents.

7 Simplify.

(a) $\sqrt[3]{27}$

(b) $\sqrt[4]{625}$

(c) $\sqrt[6]{64}$

(d) $\sqrt[3]{\frac{64}{125}}$

Answers:

(a) 3

(b) 5

(c) 2

(d) 4/5

EXAMPLE 7 Simplify the following.

(a) $\sqrt[4]{16} = 16^{1/4} = 2$

(b) $\sqrt[5]{-32} = -2$

(c) $\sqrt[3]{1000} = 10$

(d) $\sqrt[6]{\frac{64}{729}} = \frac{2}{3}$ ■ 7

The symbol $a^{m/n}$ also can be written in an alternative notation using radicals.

For all rational numbers m/n and all real numbers a for which $\sqrt[n]{a}$ exists,

$$a^{m/n} = (\sqrt[n]{a})^m \quad \text{or} \quad a^{m/n} = \sqrt[n]{a^m}.$$

Notice that $\sqrt[n]{x^n}$ cannot be written simply as x when n is even. For example, if $x = -5$,

$$\sqrt{x^2} = \sqrt{(-5)^2} = \sqrt{25} = 5 \neq x.$$

However, $|-5| = 5$, so that $\sqrt{x^2} = |x|$ when x is -5. This is true in general.

For any real number a and any natural number n,

$$\sqrt[n]{a^n} = |a| \text{ if } n \text{ is even}$$

and

$$\sqrt[n]{a^n} = a \text{ if } n \text{ is odd.}$$

To avoid this difficulty that $\sqrt[n]{a^n}$ is not necessarily equal to a, we shall assume that all variables in radicands represent only nonnegative numbers, as they usually do in applications.

The properties of exponents can be written with radicals as shown below.

For all real numbers a and b and positive integers n for which all indicated roots exist,

(a) $\sqrt[n]{a} \cdot \sqrt[n]{b} = \sqrt[n]{ab}$ **(b)** $\dfrac{\sqrt[n]{a}}{\sqrt[n]{b}} = \sqrt[n]{\dfrac{a}{b}}$ $(b \neq 0)$.

EXAMPLE 8 Simplify the following.

(a) $\sqrt{6} \cdot \sqrt{54} = \sqrt{6 \cdot 54} = \sqrt{324} = 18$

Alternatively, simplify $\sqrt{54}$ first.

$$\begin{aligned} \sqrt{6} \cdot \sqrt{54} &= \sqrt{6} \cdot \sqrt{9 \cdot 6} \\ &= \sqrt{6} \cdot 3\sqrt{6} = 3 \cdot 6 = 18 \end{aligned}$$

(b) $\sqrt{\dfrac{7}{64}} = \dfrac{\sqrt{7}}{\sqrt{64}} = \dfrac{\sqrt{7}}{8}$

8 Simplify.

(a) $\sqrt{3} \cdot \sqrt{27}$

(b) $\sqrt{\frac{3}{49}}$

(c) $\sqrt{25 - 4}$

(d) $\sqrt{25} - \sqrt{4}$

Answers:

(a) 9

(b) $\frac{\sqrt{3}}{7}$

(c) $\sqrt{21}$

(d) 3

(c) $\sqrt{9 + 16} = \sqrt{25} = 5$

When using a calculator to evaluate radical expressions, be sure to use parentheses. To compute $\sqrt{9 + 16}$ on a calculator, for example, you must enter it as $\sqrt{\ }(9 + 16)$ in order to get the correct answer 5. If you enter $\sqrt{\ }9 + 16$, most calculators will interpret it as $\sqrt{9} + 16$ and display $3 + 16 = 19$ as the answer, as shown in Figure 5.5. ■ 8

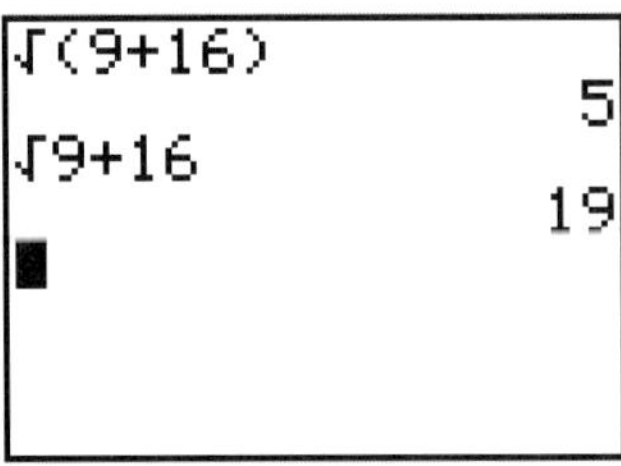

FIGURE 5.5

5.1 EXERCISES

Evaluate each expression. Write all answers without exponents. (See Examples 1–2.)

1. 5^0 **2.** 8^0 **3.** 6^{-1} **4.** 10^{-3}

5. 2^{-5} **6.** 5^{-2} **7.** -4^{-3} **8.** -7^{-4}

9. $(7.94)^{-3}$ **10.** $(12.5)^{-2}$ **11.** $\left(\frac{1}{3}\right)^{-2}$ **12.** $\left(\frac{1}{6}\right)^{-3}$

13. $\left(\frac{2}{5}\right)^{-4}$ **14.** $\left(\frac{4}{3}\right)^{-2}$

15. Explain why $-2^{-4} = -1/16$, but $(-2)^{-4} = 1/16$.

16. Explain the reason a negative exponent is defined as a reciprocal: $a^{-n} = 1/a^n$.

Evaluate each expression. Write all answers without exponents. Write decimal answers to the nearest tenth. (See Examples 3–4.)

17. $49^{1/2}$ **18.** $8^{1/3}$

19. $(7.51)^{1/4}$ **20.** $(68.93)^{1/5}$

21. $27^{2/3}$ **22.** $243^{3/2}$

23. $(947)^{2/5}$ **24.** $(58.1)^{3/4}$

25. $-64^{2/3}$ **26.** $-64^{3/2}$

27. $(9/25)^{1/2}$ **28.** $(2401/16)^{1/4}$

29. $(16/9)^{-3/2}$ **30.** $(8/27)^{-4/3}$

31. Explain why the following input will lead to an error message on a graphing calculator that works only with real numbers.

(-9)^(1/2)

Simplify each expression. Write all answers using only positive exponents. (See Example 5.)

32. $\frac{4^{-2}}{4^3}$ **33.** $\frac{9^{-4}}{9^{-3}}$

34. $4^{-3} \cdot 4^6$ **35.** $5^{-9} \cdot 5^{10}$

36. $8^{2/3} \cdot 8^{-1/3}$ **37.** $12^{-3/4} \cdot 12^{1/4}$

38. $\frac{8^9 \cdot 8^{-7}}{8^{-3}}$ **39.** $\frac{5^{-4} \cdot 5^6}{5^{-1}}$

40. $\frac{9^{-5/3}}{9^{2/3} \cdot 9^{-1/5}}$ **41.** $\frac{3^{5/3} \cdot 3^{-3/4}}{3^{-1/4}}$

Simplify each expression. Assume all variables represent positive real numbers. Write answers with only positive exponents. (See Example 6.)

42. $\frac{z^5 \cdot z^2}{z^4}$ **43.** $\frac{k^6 \cdot k^9}{k^{12}}$

44. $\frac{2^{-1}(p^{-1})^3}{2p^{-4}}$ **45.** $\frac{(5x^3)^{-2}}{x^4}$

46. $(q^{-5}r^2)^{-1}$ **47.** $(2y^2z^{-2})^{-3}$

48. $(2p^{-1})^3 \cdot (5p^2)^{-2}$ **49.** $(5^{-1}m^2)^{-3} \cdot (3m^{-2})^4$

50. $(2p)^{1/2} \cdot (2p^3)^{1/3}$ **51.** $(5k^2)^{3/2} \cdot (5k^{1/3})^{3/4}$

52. $p^{2/3}(2p^{1/3} + 5p)$ **53.** $2z^{1/2}(3z^{-1/2} + z^{1/2})$

Match the rational exponent expression in Column I with the equivalent radical expression in Column II. Assume that x is not zero.

I	II
54. $(-3x)^{1/3}$	**(a)** $\frac{3}{\sqrt[3]{x}}$
55. $-3x^{1/3}$	**(b)** $-3\sqrt[3]{x}$
56. $(-3x)^{-1/3}$	**(c)** $\frac{1}{\sqrt[3]{3x}}$
57. $-3x^{-1/3}$	**(d)** $\frac{-3}{\sqrt[3]{x}}$
58. $(3x)^{1/3}$	**(e)** $3\sqrt[3]{x}$
59. $3x^{-1/3}$	**(f)** $\sqrt[3]{-3x}$
60. $(3x)^{-1/3}$	**(g)** $\sqrt[3]{3x}$
61. $3x^{1/3}$	**(h)** $\frac{1}{\sqrt[3]{-3x}}$

62. Some graphing calculators will not compute a value for expressions like $(-8)^{2/3}$, having a negative base and a rational exponent with an odd denominator and an even numerator. Check to see whether your model is one of these. If it is, use the fact that $(-8)^{2/3} = [(-8)^{1/3}]^2$ to calculate it. What rule for exponents applies here?

63. Graph $y = x^{2/3}$ in the standard window of your calculator. If you get no graph for negative values of x, refer to Exercise 62 to explain why. How could you get the graph for the entire domain $(-\infty, \infty)$?

Simplify each of the following. (See Examples 7 and 8.)

64. $\sqrt[3]{64}$ **65.** $\sqrt[4]{625}$

66. $\sqrt[5]{-243}$ **67.** $\sqrt[7]{-128}$

68. $\sqrt{44} \cdot \sqrt{11}$ **69.** $\sqrt[3]{81} \cdot \sqrt[3]{9}$

70. $\sqrt{49 - 16}$ **71.** $\sqrt{81 - 4}$

72. $\sqrt{49} - \sqrt{16}$ **73.** $\sqrt{81} - \sqrt{4}$

74. What is wrong with the statement $\sqrt[3]{4} \cdot \sqrt[3]{4} = 4$?

75. Does the calculator screen shown indicate that the number π is exactly equal to $\sqrt[4]{2143/22}$? Explain.

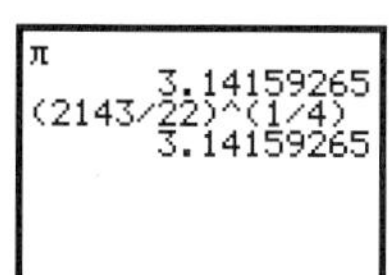

76. Consider the number $16^{-3/4}$.

(a) Simplify this expression without the use of a calculator. Give the answer in both decimal and $\frac{a}{b}$ forms.

(b) Write two different radical expressions that are equivalent to it, and use your calculator to evaluate them to show that the result is the same as the decimal form you found in part (a).

(c) If your calculator has the capability to convert decimal numbers to fractions, use it to verify your results in part (a).

77. If a number is raised to a negative rational power, should we consider the negative sign to be in the numerator or in the denominator of the exponent to simplify the expression without the use of a calculator? Explain.

78. If we wish to compute a radical expression whose root index is a power of 2, we may simply use the $\boxed{\sqrt{\ }}$ key repeatedly to do so. For example,

$$\sqrt[4]{16} = \sqrt{\sqrt{16}} = 2 \quad \text{and} \quad \sqrt[8]{6561} = \sqrt{\sqrt{\sqrt{6561}}} = 3.$$

Explain why this is so, and calculate $\sqrt[16]{65{,}536}$ using this method. Then support your result by calculating $65{,}536^{1/16}$.

79. Consider the expression $5^{.47}$.

(a) Use the exponentiation capability of your calculator to find an approximation. Give as many digits as your calculator displays.

(b) Use the fact that $.47 = \frac{47}{100}$ to write the expression as a radical, and then use the root-finding capability of your calculator to find an approximation that agrees with the one found in part (a).

The following exercises are applications of exponentiation and radicals.

80. Management The theory of economic lot size shows that, under certain conditions, the number of units to order to minimize total cost is

$$x = \sqrt{\frac{kM}{f}}.$$

Here k is the cost to store one unit for one year, f is the (constant) setup cost to manufacture the product, and M is the total number of units produced annually. (See Section 13.3.) Find x for the following values of f, k, and M.

(a) $k = \$1$, $f = \$500$, $M = 100{,}000$

(b) $k = \$3$, $f = \$7$, $M = 16{,}700$

(c) $k = \$1$, $f = \$5$, $M = 16{,}800$

81. Social Science The threshold weight T for a person is the weight above which the risk of death increases greatly. One researcher found that the threshold weight in pounds for men aged 40–49 is related to height in inches by the equation $h = 12.3T^{1/3}$. What height corresponds to a threshold of 216 pounds for a man in this age group?

82. Social Science The length L of an animal is related to its surface area S by the equation

$$L = \left(\frac{S}{a}\right)^{1/2},$$

where a is a constant that depends on the type of animal. Find the length of an animal with a surface area of 1000 square centimeters if $a = 2/5$.

Natural Science *The wind-chill factor is a measure of the cooling effect that the wind has on a person's skin. It calculates the equivalent cooling temperature if there were no wind. The table gives the wind-chill factor for various wind speeds and temperatures.**

°F/Wind	5 mph	10 mph	15 mph	20 mph	25 mph	30 mph
40°	37	28	22	18	16	13
30°	27	16	9	4	0	−2
20°	16	4	−5	−10	−15	−18
10°	6	−9	−18	−25	−29	−33
0°	−5	−21	−36	−39	−44	−48
−10°	−15	−33	−45	−53	−59	−63
−20°	−26	−46	−58	−67	−74	−79
−30°	−36	−58	−72	−82	−88	−94
−40°	−47	−70	−85	−96	−104	−109
−50°	−57	−83	−99	−110	−118	−125

*Miller, A. and J. Thompson, *Elements of Meteorology*, 2e, Charles E. Merrill Publishing Co., 1975.

83. One model of the wind-chill factor is

$$C = T - \left(\frac{v}{4} + 7\sqrt{v}\right)\left(1 - \frac{T}{90}\right),$$

where T represents the temperature and v represents the wind velocity. Evaluate C for **(a)** $T = -10$ and $v = 30$, and **(b)** $T = -40$ and $v = 5$.

84. Refer to Exercise 83. Another model of the wind-chill factor is

$$C = 91.4 - (91.4 - T)(.478 + .301\sqrt{v} - .02v).$$

Repeat parts (a) and (b) of Exercise 83 using this model.

85. Use the chart to find the wind-chill factor for the information in parts (a) and (b) of Exercise 83. Which expression in Exercises 83 and 84 models the wind-chill factor better?

86. Management Using a technique from statistics called *exponential regression,* it can be shown that the equation $y = 386(1.18)^x$ provides a fairly good model for product sales generated by infomercials, where y is in millions of dollars and $x = 0$ corresponds to the year 1988, $x = 1$ corresponds to 1989, and so on through the year 1993.* Use a calculator to estimate, to the nearest million dollars, the amount generated during the following years.
(a) 1988 **(b)** 1990 **(c)** 1992

*National Infomercial Marketing Association.

5.2 EXPONENTIAL FUNCTIONS

In polynomial functions, the variable is raised to various constant exponents; for instance, $f(x) = x^2 + 3x - 5$. In exponential functions, such as

$$f(x) = 10^x \quad \text{or} \quad g(x) = 2^{-x^2} \quad \text{or} \quad h(x) = 3^{.6x},$$

the variable is in the exponent and the base is a positive constant. Exponential functions can be used to model situations such as national expenditures for health care as we shall see in Exercise 63. We begin our discussion with the simplest type of exponential function.

If a is a positive constant other than 1, then the function defined by

$$f(x) = a^x$$

is called an **exponential function with base *a*.**

The function $f(x) = 1^x$ is the constant function $f(x) = 1^x = 1$. Exponential functions with negative bases are not of interest because when a is negative, a^x may not be defined for some values of x; for instance, $(-4)^{1/2} = \sqrt{-4}$ is not a real number.

EXAMPLE 1 Graph each exponential function and discuss its characteristics.

(a) $f(x) = 2^x$

The graph is shown in Figure 5.6. From the graph we can see that $f(x)$ (or y) gets larger as x increases. We should expect this, because 2^x increases as the exponent increases. However, there is no vertical asymptote. The graph approaches the negative x-axis, but will never touch it because *every power* of 2 is positive. Thus, the x-axis is a horizontal asymptote. Since x may take any real number value, the domain is the set of all real numbers. Because 2^x is always positive, the range is the set of positive real numbers.

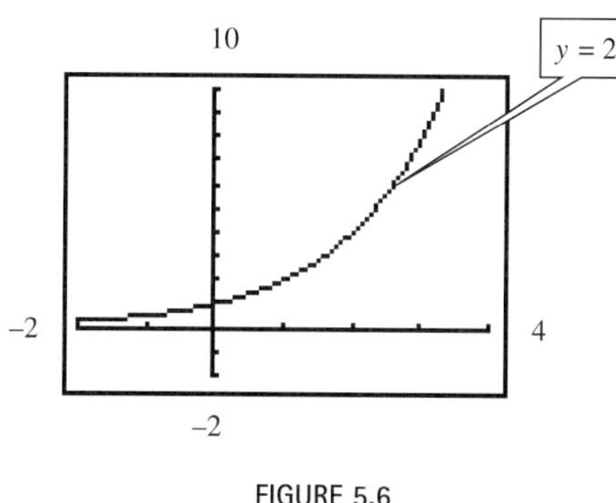

FIGURE 5.6

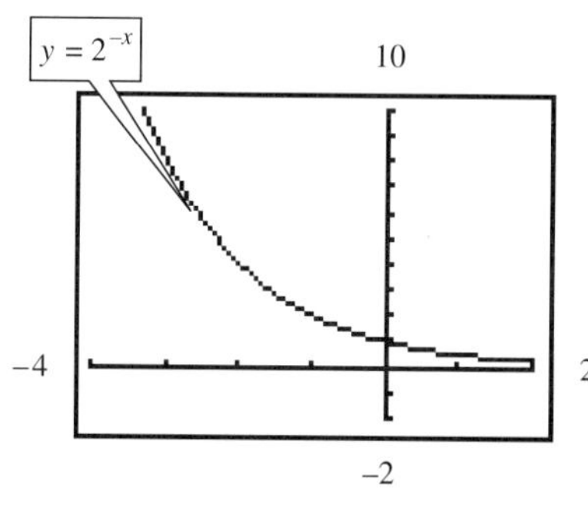

FIGURE 5.7

1 Graph $f(x) = \left(\frac{1}{5}\right)^x$.

Answer:

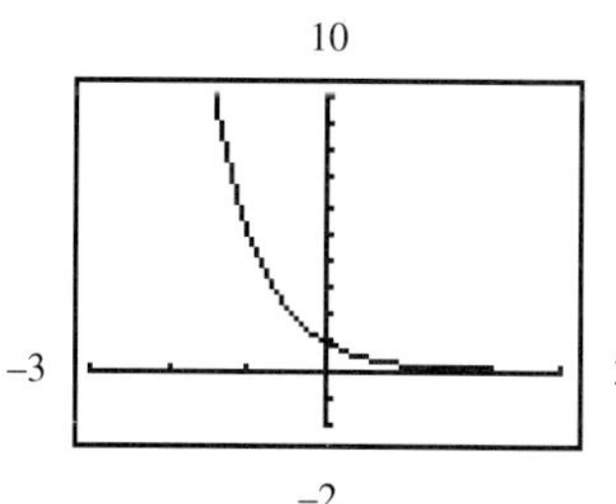

(b) $g(x) = 2^{-x}$

The graph in Figure 5.7 approaches the positive x-axis, so the x-axis is again a horizontal asymptote. This graph indicates that $g(x)$ decreases as x increases. Notice that

$$2^{-x} = \frac{1}{2^x} = \left(\frac{1}{2}\right)^x,$$

by properties of exponents. The graph of $g(x) = (1/2)^x$ is the mirror image of the graph of $f(x) = 2^x$, with the y-axis as the mirror. The domain and range are the same as for $f(x)$. ■ 1

The graph of $f(x) = 2^x$ in Figure 5.6 illustrates **exponential growth,** which is far more explosive than polynomial growth. For example, if the graph in Figure 5.6 were extended on the same scale to include the point $(50, 2^{50})$, the graph would be more than 1.5 billion *miles* high! Similarly, the graph of $g(x) = 2^{-x} = (1/2)^x$ illustrates **exponential decay.**

When $a > 1$, the graph of the exponential function $g(x) = a^x$ has the same basic characteristics as the graph of $f(x) = 2^x$. The larger the base a is, the more steeply the graph rises, as illustrated in Figure 5.8(a).

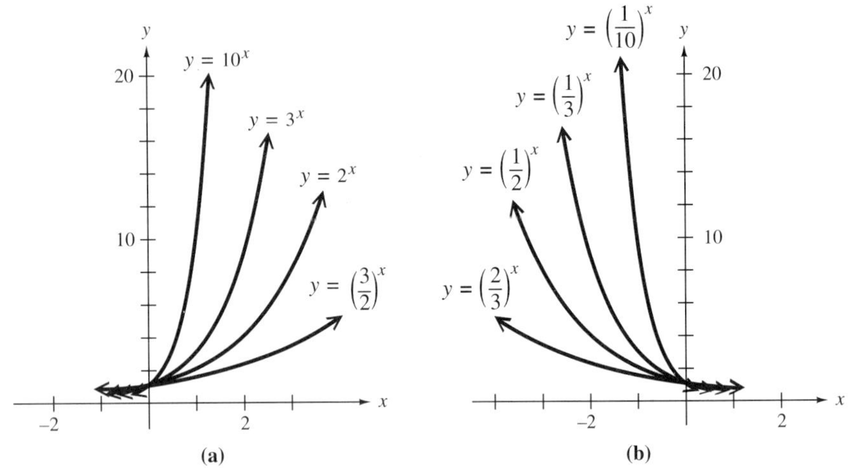

FIGURE 5.8

When $0 < a < 1$, the graph of $h(x) = a^x$ has the same basic shape as the graph of $g(x) = (1/2)^x$ in Figure 5.7. Graphs of some typical exponential functions with $0 < a < 1$ are shown in Figure 5.8(b).

The graphs of exponential functions such as $f(x) = 3^{1-x}$ or $g(x) = 2^{.6x}$ have the same general shape as the exponential graphs above. The only differences are that the graph may rise or fall at a different rate or the entire graph may be shifted vertically or horizontally.

EXAMPLE 2 Graph $f(x)$ and $g(x)$ as defined below and explain how the two graphs are related.

(a) $f(x) = 3^{1-x}$ and $g(x) = 3^{-x}$

The graphs are shown in Figure 5.9. The graph of $f(x) = 3^{1-x}$ in Figure 5.9(a) has the same shape as the graph of $g(x) = 3^{-x}$ in Figure 5.9(b), but is shifted 1 unit to the right, making the y-intercept (0, 3) rather than (0, 1).

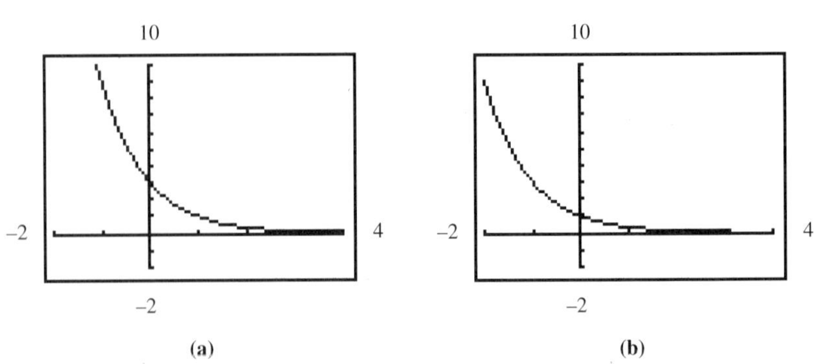

FIGURE 5.9

2 Graph $f(x) = 2^{x+1}$.

Answer:

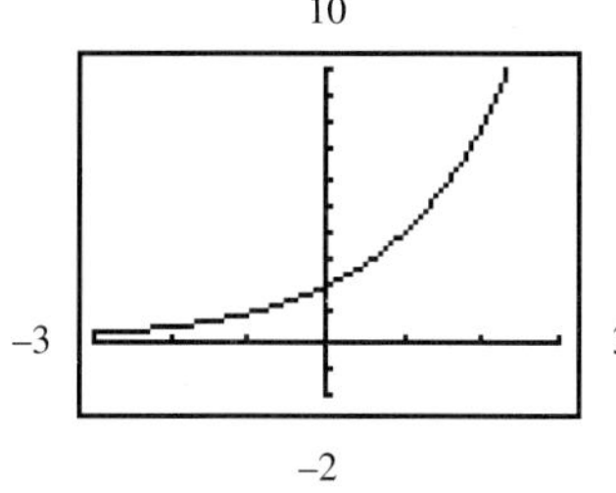

(b) $f(x) = 2^{.6x}$ and $g(x) = 2^x$

Comparing the graph of $f(x) = 2^{.6x}$, shown in Figure 5.10(a), to that of $g(x) = 2^x$ in Figure 5.10(b), we see that the graphs are both increasing, but the graph of $f(x)$ rises at a slower rate. This happens because of the .6 in the exponent. If the coefficient of x were greater than 1, the graph would rise at a faster rate than the graph of $f(x) = 2^x$. ■ 2

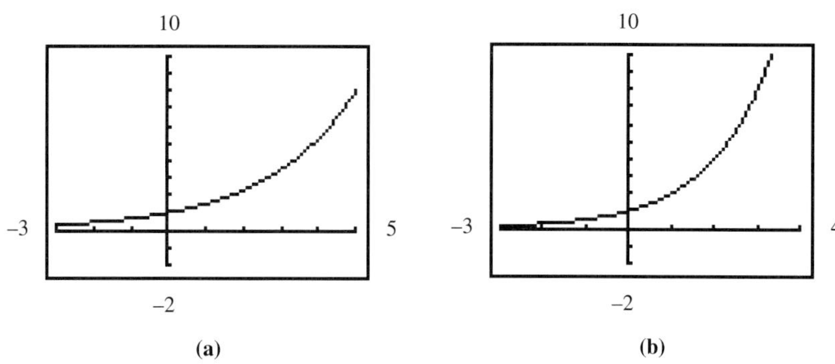

FIGURE 5.10

3 Graph $f(x) = .5^{-x^2}$.

Answer:

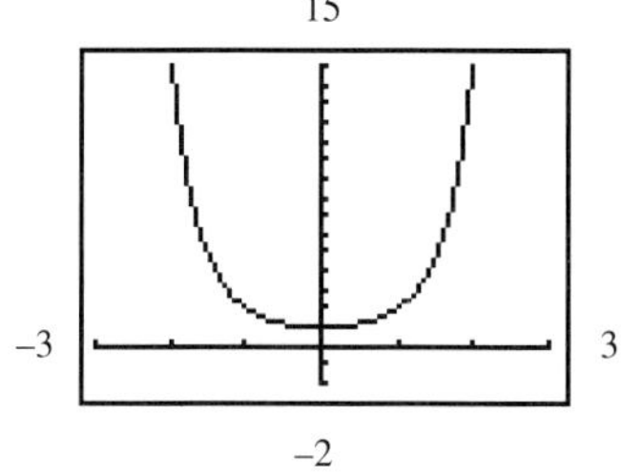

When the exponent involves a nonlinear expression in x, an exponential function graph may have a much different shape than the preceding ones.

EXAMPLE 3 Graph $f(x) = 2^{-x^2}$.

As Figure 5.11 suggests, the graph is symmetrical about the y-axis—that is, if the figure were folded on the y-axis, the two halves would match. Like the graphs above, this graph also has the x-axis as a horizontal asymptote. The domain is still all real numbers, but here the range is $0 < y \leq 1$.* ■ 3

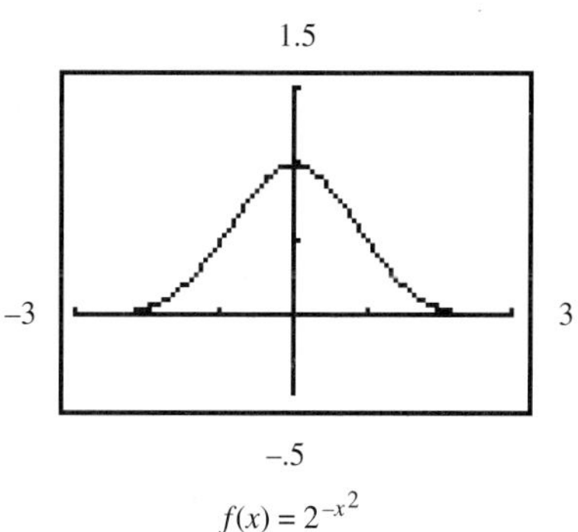

$f(x) = 2^{-x^2}$

FIGURE 5.11

The graphs of typical exponential functions $y = a^x$ in Figures 5.9 and 5.10 suggest that every value of x leads to exactly one value of a^x and each value of a^x corresponds to exactly one value of x. Because of this, an equation with a variable in the exponent, called an **exponential equation,** can often be solved using the following property.

*As Figure 5.11 suggests, the graph has a "bell shape" and is related to the bell-shaped curve studied in probability.

If $a > 0$, $a \neq 1$, and $a^x = a^y$, then $x = y$.

4 Solve each equation.

(a) $6^x = 6^4$

(b) $3^{2x} = 3^9$

(c) $5^{-4x} = 5^3$

Answers:

(a) 4

(b) 9/2

(c) $-3/4$

CAUTION Both bases must be the same. The value $a = 1$ is excluded because $1^2 = 1^3$, for example, even though $2 \neq 3$.

As an example, we can solve $2^{3x} = 2^7$ using this property as follows:

$$2^{3x} = 2^7$$
$$3x = 7$$
$$x = \frac{7}{3}. \quad \blacklozenge \quad \boxed{4}$$

5 Solve each equation.

(a) $8^{2x} = 4$

(b) $5^{3x} = 25^4$

(c) $36^{-2x} = 6$

Answers:

(a) 1/3

(b) 8/3

(c) $-1/4$

EXAMPLE 4 Solve $9^x = 27$.

First rewrite both sides of the equation so the bases are the same. Since $9 = 3^2$ and $27 = 3^3$,

$$(3^2)^x = 3^3$$
$$3^{2x} = 3^3$$
$$2x = 3$$
$$x = \frac{3}{2}. \quad \blacksquare \quad \boxed{5}$$

Exponential functions have many practical applications. For example, in situations that involve growth or decay of a quantity, the amount of the quantity present at a given time t often is determined by an exponential function of t.

Year	*Carbon Dioxide*
1990	353
2000	375
2075	590
2175	1090
2275	2000

EXAMPLE 5 The International Panel on Climate Change (IPCC) in 1990 published its finding that if current trends of burning fossil fuel and deforestation continue, then future amounts of atmospheric carbon dioxide in parts per million (ppm) will increase as shown in the table at the side.*

(a) Plot the data. Do the carbon dioxide levels appear to grow exponentially?

We show a calculator-generated graph for the data in Figure 5.12(a). The data do appear to have the shape of the graph of an increasing exponential function.

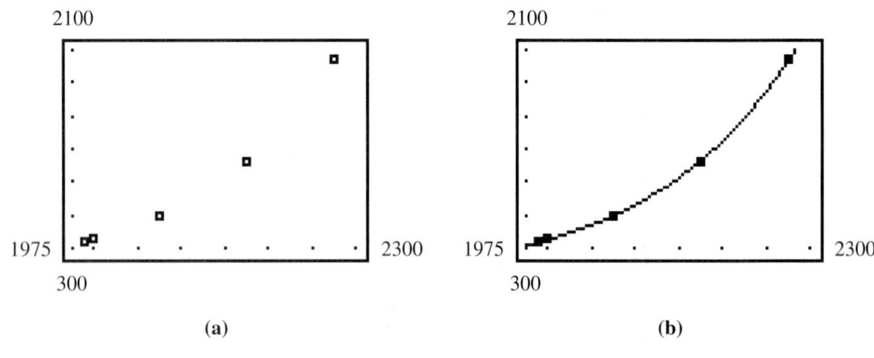

FIGURE 5.12

*International Panel on Climate Change (IPCC) 1990.

6 The number of organisms present at time t is given by $f(t) = 75(2.5)^{.5t}$.

(a) Is this a growth function or a decay function?

(b) How many organisms are present at time 0?

(c) For what value of t will the number of organisms reach 400? (Use a graph to decide.)

Answers:

(a) A growth function

(b) 75

(c) At about $t = 3.65$

(b) The function defined by $y = 353e^{.0060857(t-1990)}$ is a good model for the data. A graph of this function in Figure 5.12(b) shows that it is very close to the data points. From the graph, estimate when future levels of carbon dioxide will double and triple over the preindustrial level of 280 ppm.

In Figure 5.13, we graph $y = 560$ $(2 \cdot 280)$ and $y = 840$ $(3 \cdot 280)$ on the same coordinate axes as the function in Figure 5.12(b), and use the calculator to find the intersection points. The graph of the function intersects the horizontal lines at approximately 2065.8 and 2132.5. This means that carbon dioxide levels will double and triple the preindustrial level of 280 during 2065 and 2132, respectively. ■ 6

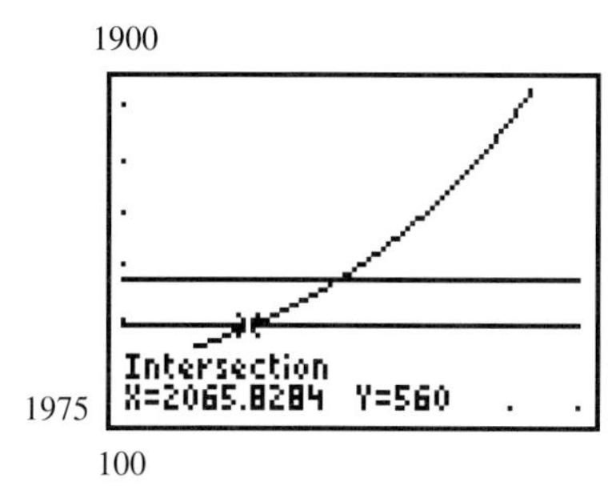

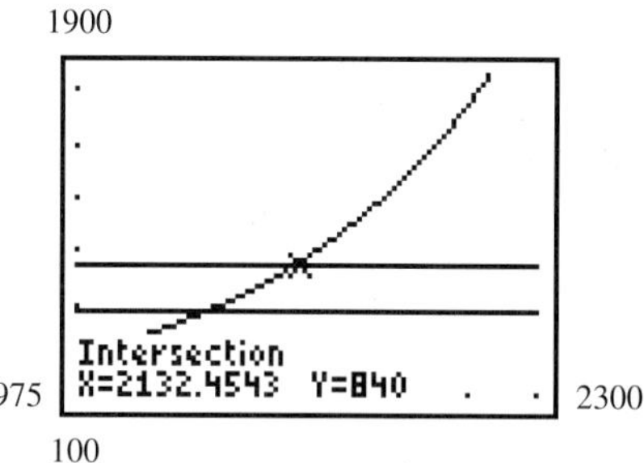

FIGURE 5.13

TECHNOLOGY TIP One way to plot points is discussed in the Technology Tip on page 127. The statistical graphing function of a calculator can also be used to plot points. Check your instruction manual. ✓

Further examples of exponential growth or decay are given in the next section.

5.2 EXERCISES

Use a calculator whenever necessary to do these exercises.

Classify each function as linear, quadratic, or exponential.

1. $f(x) = 2x^2 + x - 3$ **2.** $g(x) = 5^{x-3}$

3. $h(x) = 3 \cdot 6^{2x^2+4}$ **4.** $f(x) = 3x + 1$

Without graphing, **(a)** *describe the shape of the graph of each function, and* **(b)** *complete these ordered pairs for each function: (0,) and (1,).*

5. $f(x) = .8^x$ **6.** $g(x) = 6^{-x}$

7. $f(x) = 5^{.4x}$ **8.** $g(x) = -(2^x)$

Graph each function. (See Examples 1–3.)

9. $f(x) = 3^x$ **10.** $g(x) = 3^{.5x}$

11. $f(x) = 2^{x/2}$ **12.** $g(x) = 4^{-x}$

13. $g(x) = 2^{-x^2+2}$ **14.** $f(x) = 2^{x^2-2}$

15. $h(x) = x \cdot 2^x$ **16.** $f(x) = x^2 \cdot 2^x$

The figure shows the graphs of $y = a^x$ for $a = 1.8, 2.3, 3.2, .4, .75,$ and .31. They are identified by letter, but not necessarily in the same order as the values of a just given. Use your knowledge of how the exponential function behaves for various powers of a to match each lettered graph with the correct value of a.

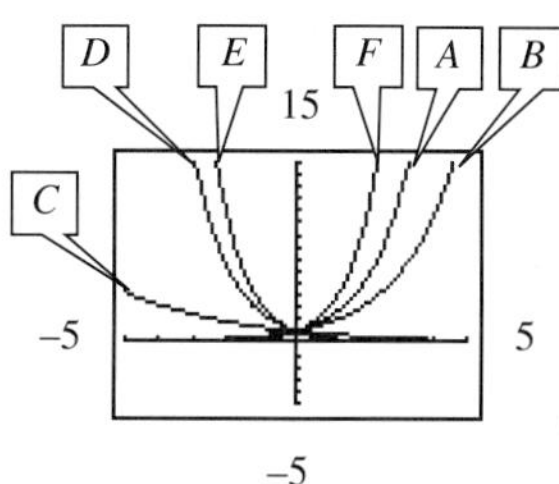

17. A **18.** B **19.** C

20. D **21.** E **22.** F

In Exercises 23 and 24, the graph of an exponential function with base a is given. Follow the directions in parts (a)–(f) in each exercise.

23.

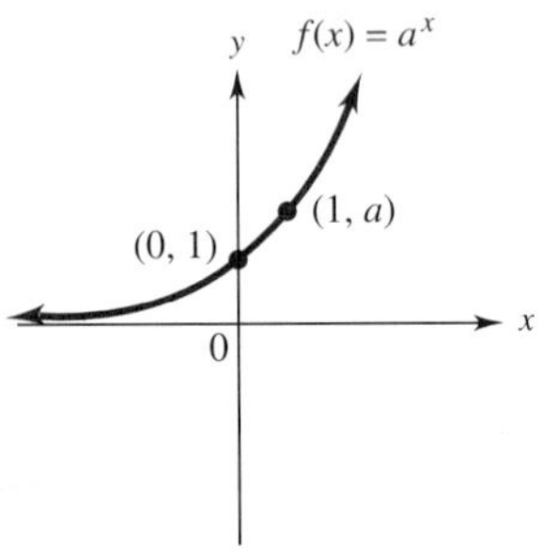

(a) Is $a > 1$ or is $0 < a < 1$?
(b) Give the domain and range of f.
(c) Sketch the graph of $g(x) = -a^x$.
(d) Give the domain and range of g.
(e) Sketch the graph of $h(x) = a^{-x}$.
(f) Give the domain and range of h.

24.

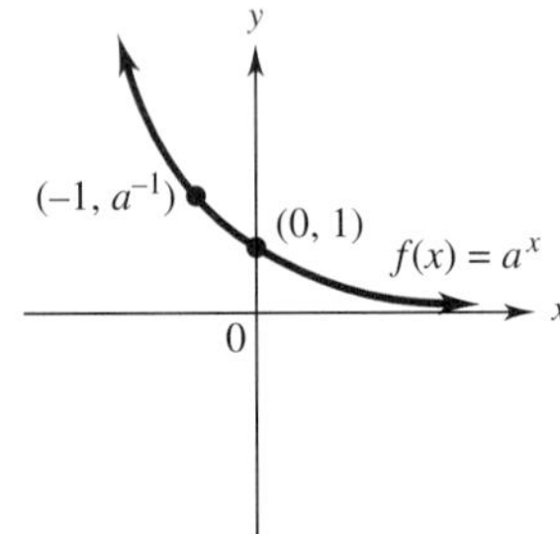

(a) Is $a > 1$ or is $0 < a < 1$?
(b) Give the domain and range of f.
(c) Sketch the graph of $g(x) = a^x + 2$.
(d) Give the domain and range of g.
(e) Sketch the graph of $h(x) = a^{x+2}$.
(f) Give the domain and range of h.

25. Graph each function on the same axes.
(a) $f(x) = 2^x$ **(b)** $g(x) = 2^{x+3}$
(c) $h(x) = 2^{x-4}$
(d) If c is a positive constant, explain how the graphs of $y = 2^{x+c}$ and $y = 2^{x-c}$ are related to the graph of $f(x) = 2^x$.

26. Graph each function on the same axes.
(a) $f(x) = 3^x$ **(b)** $g(x) = 3^x + 2$
(c) $h(x) = 3^x - 4$
(d) If c is a positive constant, explain how the graphs of $y = 3^x + c$ and $y = 3^x - c$ are related to the graph of $f(x) = 3^x$.

27. To graph $f(x) = 2^{.5x}$, a student entered [2] [^] [.] [5] [x] in her calculator. She got the graph shown in the figure. Is this correct? Explain why or why not. If not correct, what was her error?

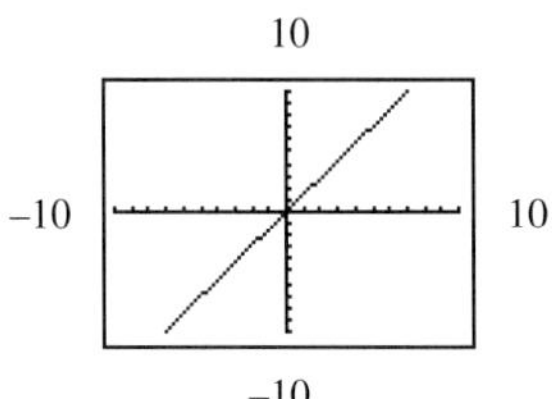

28. If $f(x) = a^x$ and $f(3) = 27$, find the following values of $f(x)$.
(a) $f(1)$ **(b)** $f(-1)$ **(c)** $f(2)$ **(d)** $f(0)$

Give an equation of the form $f(x) = a^x$ to define the exponential function whose graph contains the given point.

29. $(3, 8)$ **30.** $(-3, 64)$

Solve each equation. (See Example 4.)

31. $5^x = 25$ **32.** $3^x = \frac{1}{9}$

33. $4^x = 64$ **34.** $a^x = a^2 \quad (a > 0)$

35. $16^x = 64$ **36.** $\left(\frac{3}{4}\right)^x = \frac{16}{9}$

37. $5^{-2x} = \frac{1}{25}$ **38.** $3^{x-1} = 9$

39. $16^{-x+1} = 8$ **40.** $25^{-2x} = 3125$

41. $81^{-2x} = 3^{x-1}$ **42.** $7^{-x} = 49^{x+3}$

43. $2^{|x|} = 16$ **44.** $5^{-|x|} = \frac{1}{25}$

45. $2^{x^2-4x} = \frac{1}{16}$ **46.** $5^{x^2+x} = 1$

Use a graphical method to solve each equation. Give the solution to the nearest hundredth.

47. $7^x = 12$

48. $3^x = 5$

49. $2^{x-1} = 9$

50. $10^x = 2^{x+1}$

51. Use the graph of $f(x) = 2^x$ to explain why the solution of $2^x = 12$ must be a number between 3.5 and 3.6.

52. Explain why the equation $4^{x^2+1} = 2$ has no solutions.

53. Graph both $f(x) = 2^x$ and $g(x) = 2^x + 2^{-x}$ in the window with $-4 \le x \le 4$ and $-1 \le y \le 10$. Explain why the graphs appear to coincide when $x > 2$.

Work each applied problem.

54. Management If money loses value at the rate of 3% per year, the value of \$1 in x years is given by $y = (1 - .03)^x = (.97)^x$. If money loses value, then it takes more dollars to buy the same item.

(a) Use the TABLE feature of your calculator with a minimum x-value of 0 and an increment of 1 to get a table of values of X and Y.

(b) Suppose a house costs \$85,000 today. Use the table to estimate the cost of a similar house in 10 years. (*Hint:* Solve the equation $bx = 85{,}000$, where b is the value of 1 dollar in ten years.)

(c) Estimate the cost of a \$40 textbook in 8 years.

55. Social Science If the world population continues to grow at the present rate, the population in billions in year x is given by the function

$$P(x) = 4.2(2^{.0285(x-1980)}), \quad x \geq 1980.$$

(a) There were fewer than a billion people on earth when Thomas Jefferson died in 1826. What was the population of the world in 1980?

(b) If this model is accurate, what will the world population be in the year 2000? in 2040?

(c) Use a graph of the population function to estimate how many years it will take for the world population in 2000 to triple. Is it likely that you will be alive then?

56. Natural Science The amount of plutonium remaining from one kilogram after x years is given by the function $W(x) = 2^{-x/24360}$. How much will be left after

(a) 1000 years? **(b)** 10,000 years?

(c) 15,000 years?

(d) Estimate how long it will take for the one kilogram to decay to half its original weight. This may help to explain why nuclear waste disposal is a serious problem.

Management *The scrap value of a machine is the value of the machine at the end of its useful life. By one method of calculating scrap value, where it is assumed a constant percentage of value is lost annually, the scrap value S is given by*

$$S = C(1 - r)^n,$$

where C is the original cost, n is the useful life of the machine in years, and r is the constant annual percentage of value lost. Find the scrap value for each of the following machines.

57. Original cost, \$54,000; life, 8 years; annual rate of value loss, 12%

58. Original cost, \$178,000; life, 11 years; annual rate of value loss, 14%

59. Management Midwest Creations finds that its total sales $T(x)$, in thousands, from the distribution of x catalogs, where x is measured in thousands, is approximated by

$$T(x) = \frac{2500}{1 + 24 \cdot 2^{-x/4}}.$$

(a) Graph $T(x)$. Use Xmin = 0, Xmax = 50, Ymin = 0, and Ymax = 3000.

(b) Use the graph to find the total sales if 0 catalogs are distributed.

(c) Find the total sales if 20,000 catalogs are distributed.

(d) From the graph, what happens to the total sales as the number of catalogs approaches 50,000 ($x = 50$)?

60. Natural Science The population of fish in a certain lake at time t months is given by the function

$$p(t) = \frac{20{,}000}{1 + 24(2^{-.36t})}.$$

(a) Graph the population function from $t = 0$ to $t = 48$ (a four-year period).

(b) What was the population at the beginning?

(c) Use the graph to estimate the one-year period in which the population grew most rapidly.

(d) When do you think the population will reach 25,000? What factors in nature might explain your answer?

61. Natural Science The number of fruit flies present after t days of a laboratory experiment is $p(t) = 100 \cdot 3^{t/10}$. How many flies will be present after

(a) 15 days? **(b)** 25 days?

(c) When will the fly population reach 3500?

62. Physical Science The atmospheric pressure (in millibars) at a given altitude (in meters) is listed in the table.

Altitude	*Pressure*
0	1,013
1,000	899
2,000	795
3,000	701
4,000	617
5,000	541
6,000	472
7,000	411
8,000	357
9,000	308
10,000	265

(a) Use your calculator to plot the data for atmospheric pressure P at altitude x.

(b) Would a linear or exponential function fit the data better?

(c) Graph the function defined by $P(x) = 1013(2.78)^{-.0001341x}$ on the same axes as the data in part (a). Does this graph "fit" the data points?

(d) Use P to predict the pressure at 1500 m and 11,000 m and compare the results to the actual values of 846 millibars and 227 millibars, respectively.

63. **Natural Science** The national expenditures for health care (in millions of dollars) in the United States from 1970 to 1993 are shown in the table.*

Year	1970	1975	1980	1985	1990	1993
Expenditure	74.3	132.9	251.1	434.5	696.6	884.2

Use the exponential regression feature of your calculator to find an exponential function in the form $y = a \cdot b^x$ for real numbers a and b, with $x = 0$ in 1970, that models this data.

*_The Universal Almanac, 1996,_ John W. Wright, General Editor, Andrews and McMeel, Kansas City, p. 212.

5.3 APPLICATIONS OF EXPONENTIAL FUNCTIONS

1 Evaluate the following powers of e.

(a) $e^{.06}$

(b) $e^{-.06}$

(c) $e^{2.30}$

(d) $e^{-2.30}$

Answers:

(a) 1.06184

(b) .94176

(c) 9.97418

(d) .10026

A certain irrational number, denoted e, arises naturally in a variety of mathematical situations (much the same way that the number π appears when you consider the area of a circle).* To nine decimal places,

$$e = 2.718281828.$$

Perhaps the single most useful exponential function is the function defined by $f(x) = e^x$.

To evaluate powers of e with a graphing calculator, we use the e^x key. For example, your calculator should show that $e^{-14} \approx 1.150273799$ (to 8 places). 1

NOTE To display the decimal expansion of e on your calculator screen, calculate e^1. ◆

In Figure 5.14 the functions defined by

$$g(x) = 2^x, \quad f(x) = e^x, \quad \text{and} \quad h(x) = 3^x$$

are graphed for comparison.

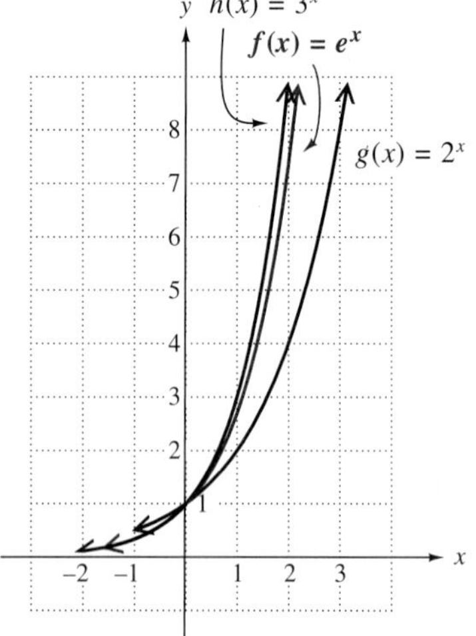

FIGURE 5.14

In many situations in biology, economics, and the social sciences, a quantity changes at a rate proportional to the quantity present. In such cases, the amount present at time t is a function of t called the *exponential growth function.*

*See pages 233 and 234 for an example.

> **EXPONENTIAL GROWTH FUNCTION**
>
> Under normal conditions, growth is described by the function
>
> $$f(t) = y_0e^{kt},$$
>
> where $f(t)$ is the amount or quantity present at time t, y_0 is the amount present at time $t = 0$, and k is a constant that depends on the rate of growth.

It is understood in this context that "growth" can involve either growing larger or growing smaller. Here is an example of growing larger.

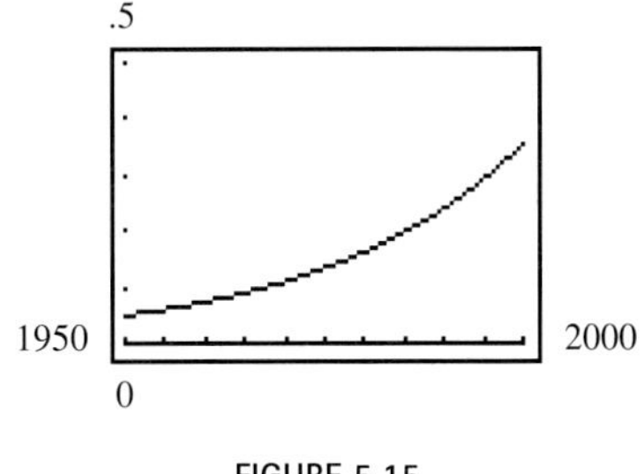

FIGURE 5.15

EXAMPLE 1 Chlorofluorocarbons (CFCs) are greenhouse gases that were produced by humans after 1930. CFCs are found in refrigeration units, foaming agents, and aerosols. They have great potential for destroying the ozone layer. As a result, governments have agreed to phase out their production by the year 2000. CFC-11 is a CFC which has increased faster than any other greenhouse gas. The exponential function $f(x) = .05e^{.03922(x-1950)}$ models the concentration of atmospheric CFC-11 in parts per billion (ppb) from 1950 to 2000, where x is the year. This is an example of an exponential growth function with $k = .03922$ and $y_0 = .05$. The graph of $f(x)$ is shown in Figure 5.15.

(a) What was the concentration of atmospheric CFC-11 in 1950?

Evaluating $f(1950)$ gives

$$f(1950) = .05e^{.03922(1950-1950)} = .05e^0 = .05.$$

This confirms that .05 is y_0.

(b) What will the concentration be in 2000?

$$f(2000) = .05e^{.03922(2000-1950)} \approx .355 \text{ ppb}$$

(c) In what year did the concentration reach .25?

Use the TABLE feature of your calculator (see Figure 5.16(a)) or find the intersection point of the graph of $f(x)$ with the line $y = .25$ (Figure 5.16(b)). Both show that the concentration reached .25 during 1991.* ■ 2

2 In Example 1,

(a) what was the atmospheric concentration of CFC-11 in 1990?

(b) In what year was there .20 ppb of CFC-11 in the atmosphere?

Answers:

(a) About .24 ppb

(b) 1985

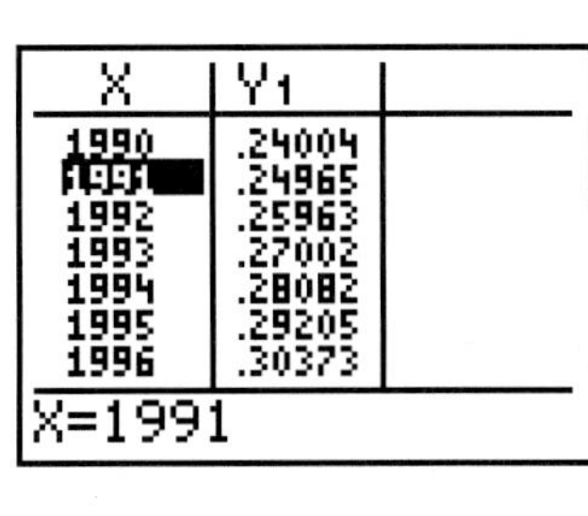

X	Y1
1990	.24004
1991	.24965
1992	.25963
1993	.27002
1994	.28082
1995	.29205
1996	.30373

X=1991

(a)

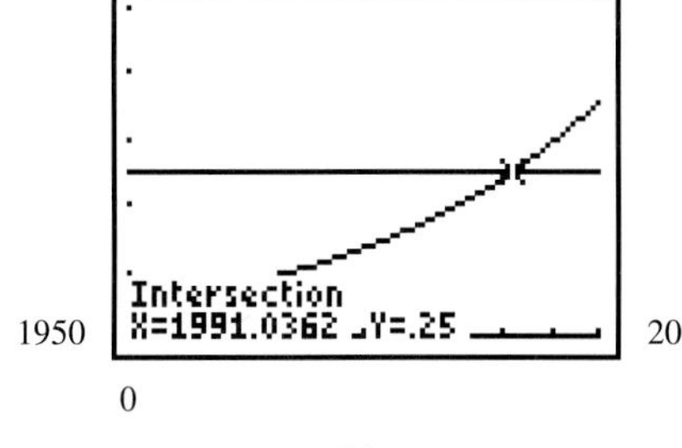

(b)

FIGURE 5.16

*Nilsson, A., *Greenhouse Earth,* John Wiley & Sons, New York, 1992.

3 Suppose the number of bacteria in a culture at time t is

$$y = 500e^{.4t},$$

where t is measured in hours.

(a) How many bacteria are present initially?

(b) How many bacteria are present in 10 hours?

Answers:

(a) 500

(b) About 27,300

When the constant k in the exponential growth function is negative, the quantity will *decrease* over time, that is, grow smaller.

EXAMPLE 2 Radioactive lead-210 decays to polonium-210. The amount y of radioactive lead-210 at time t is given by $y = y_0e^{-.032t}$, where t is time in years. How much of an initial 500 grams of lead-210 will remain after 5 years?

Since the initial amount is 500 grams, $y_0 = 500$. Substitute 500 for y_0 and 5 for t in the definition of the function.

$$y = 500e^{-.032(5)} \approx 426$$

About 426 grams will remain. ■ 3

The exponential growth function deals with quantities that eventually either grow very large or decrease practically to 0. Other exponential functions are needed to deal with different patterns of growth.

EXAMPLE 3 Sales of a new product often grow rapidly at first and then begin to level off, as illustrated in Figure 5.17. The figure shows both the graph of the horizontal line $y = 1000$ and the graph of the function $S(x) = 1000 - 800e^{-x}$, which gives the sales of a new model calculator in year x.

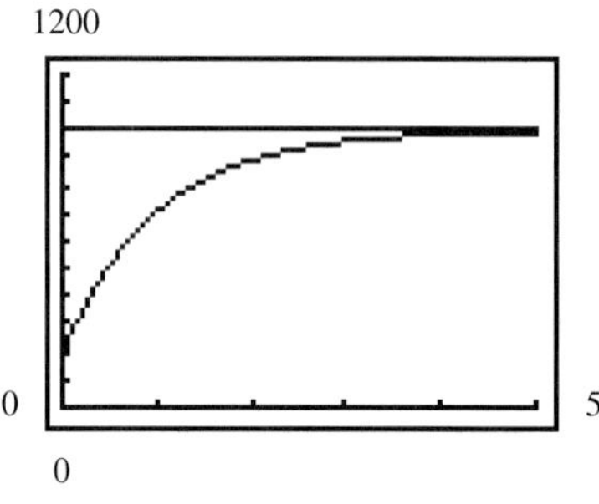

FIGURE 5.17

4 Suppose the value of the assets of a certain company at time t are given by

$$f(t) = 100{,}000 - 75{,}000e^{-.2t}.$$

(a) What is the limiting value of the assets?

(b) What is the initial value of the assets?

(c) Use the graph of f to find the year when the asset value is \$72,000.

Answers:

(a) \$100,000

(b) \$25,000

(c) The 5th year

The graph of $S(x)$ suggests that sales are approaching 1000 units and will not increase beyond that number. Note that

$$S(0) = 1000 - 800e^{-0} = 1000 - 800 = 200$$

gives the initial sales. As the number of years increases, e^{-x} decreases and $S(x)$ gets closer and closer to the limiting value of 1000 units. ■ 4

The sales graph in Figure 5.17 is typical of the graphs of *limited growth functions.* Another example of a limited growth function is a **learning curve.** Certain types of skills involving the repetitive performance of the same task characteristically improve rapidly, but then the learning tapers off and approaches some upper limit. (See Exercises 16–17.) The next example shows a **forgetting curve.**

EXAMPLE 4 Psychologists have measured people's ability to remember facts that they have memorized. In one such experiment, it was found that the number of facts $N(t)$ remembered after t days was given by

$$N(t) = 10\left(\frac{1 + e^{-8}}{1 + e^{.8t-8}}\right).$$

At the beginning of the experiment, $t = 0$ and

$$N(0) = 10\left(\frac{1 + e^{-8}}{1 + e^{.8(0)-8}}\right) = 10\left(\frac{1 + e^{-8}}{1 + e^{-8}}\right) = 10.$$

So 10 facts were known at the beginning. In the expression for $N(t)$, as t gets larger, the denominator increases and the fraction decreases, so fewer facts are remembered as time goes on. The graph of $N(t)$ in Figure 5.18 illustrates the situation. ■ 5

5 In Example 4,

(a) find the number of facts remembered after 10 days.

(b) When will just 2 facts be remembered?

Answers:

(a) 5

(b) After 11.7 days

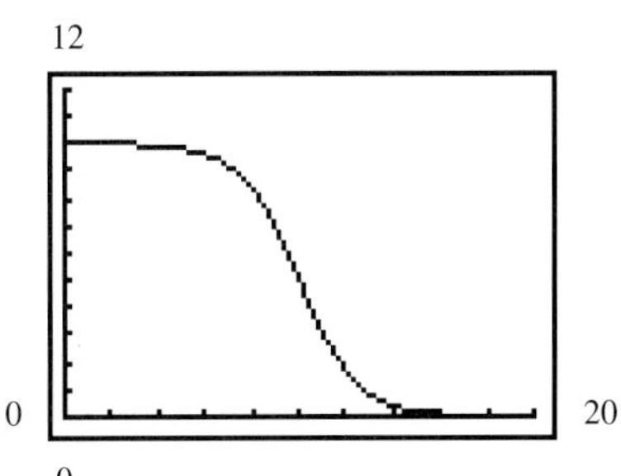

FIGURE 5.18

5.3 EXERCISES

Work each problem. (See Examples 1 and 2.)

1. **Social Science** The population of U.S. residents of Hispanic origin is given in thousands by
$$P(x) = 14{,}700e^{.0421x},$$
where x is years since 1980. Find the population in
(a) 1980. **(b)** 1990.
(c) Predict the population in 2000.

2. **Natural Science** A sealed box contains radium. The number of grams present at time t is given by
$$Q(t) = 100e^{-.00043t},$$
where t is measured in years. Find the amount of radium in the box at the following times.
(a) $t = 0$ **(b)** $t = 800$ **(c)** $t = 1600$
(d) $t = 5000$

3. **Natural Science** The amount of a chemical in grams that will dissolve in a solution is given by
$$C(t) = 10e^{.02t},$$
where t is the temperature of the solution. Find each of the following.
(a) $C(0°)$ **(b)** $C(10°)$ **(c)** $C(30°)$
(d) $C(100°)$

4. **Management** In Chapter 6, it is shown that P dollars compounded continuously (every instant) at an annual rate of interest i would amount to
$$A = Pe^{ni}$$
at the end of n years. How much would \$20,000 amount to at 8% compounded continuously for the following number of years?
(a) 1 year **(b)** 5 years **(c)** 10 years
(d) Use a graph to estimate how long it will take for the initial \$20,000 to triple.

5. **Management** The estimated number of units that will be sold by the Goldstein Widget Works t months from now is given by
$$N(t) = 100{,}000e^{-.09t}.$$
(a) What are current sales ($t = 0$)?
(b) What will sales be in 2 months? In 6 months?
(c) Will sales ever regain their present level? (What does the graph of $N(t)$ look like?)

Natural Science *When physicians prescribe medication they must consider how the drug's effectiveness decreases over time. If, each hour, a drug is only 90% as effective as the previous hour, at some point the patient will not be receiving enough medication and must receive another dose. This situation can be modeled by an exponential function with $y = y_0a^n$, where y_0 is the original dose, a is the percent of effectiveness after one hour (as a decimal), and n is the number of hours since the drug was administered less one. Use this information for Exercises 6 and 7.*

6. If 250 mg of a drug are administered, and the drug is only 75% as effective each subsequent hour, how much effective medicine will remain in the person's system after 6 hours?

7. A new drug has been introduced which is 80% as effective each hour as the previous hour. A minimum of 20 mg must remain in the patient's bloodstream during the course of treatment. If 100 mg are administered, how many hours may elapse before another dose is necessary?

8. **Management** The number of books, in millions, sold per year in the United States between 1985 and 1990, can be approximated by the function $A(t) = 1757e^{.0264t}$, where $t = 0$ corresponds to the year 1985. Based on this model, how many books were sold in 1996?*

9. **Management** Personal consumption expenditures for recreation in billions of dollars in the United States during the years 1984 through 1990 can be approximated by the function $A(t) = 185.4e^{.0587t}$, where $t = 0$ corresponds to the year 1984. Based on this model, how much were personal consumption expenditures in 1996?†

10. **Social Science** Vehicle theft in the United States has been rising exponentially since 1972. The number of stolen vehicles, in millions, is given by
$$f(x) = .88(1.03)^x,$$
where $x = 0$ represents the year 1972. Find the number of vehicles stolen in the following years.
(a) 1980 **(b)** 1990
(c) In what year were 2 million vehicles stolen?

Natural Science *The pressure of the atmosphere, p(h), in pounds per square inch, is given by*
$$p(h) = p_0e^{-kh},$$
where h is the height above sea level and p_0 and k are constants. The pressure at sea level is 15 pounds per square inch and the pressure is 9 pounds per square inch at a height of 12,000 feet.

11. Find the pressure at an altitude of 6000 feet.

12. At what height would a spaceship encounter a pressure of .025 pound per square inch?

13. **Management** India has become an important exporter of software to the United States. The chart shows India's software exports (in millions of U.S. dollars) in the years since 1985. The figure for 1997 is an estimate. Letting y represent the value of software exported (in millions of dollars) and x represent the number of years since 1900, we find the function with
$$f(x) = 6.2(10)^{-12}(1.4)^x$$
approximates the data reasonably well. According to this function, when will software exports double their 1997 value?*

Year (x)	1985	1987	1989	1991	1993	1995	1997
\$ (y)	6	39	67	128	225	483	1000

14. **Social Science** The probability P percent of having an automobile accident is related to the alcohol level of the driver's blood t by the function $P(t) = e^{21.459t}$.
(a) Graph $P(t)$ in a viewing window with $0 \le t \le .2$ and $0 \le P(t) \le 100$.
(b) At what blood alcohol level is the probability of an accident at least 50 percent? What is the legal blood alcohol level in your state?

Work each problem. (See Examples 3 and 4.)

15. **Natural Science** The number (in hundreds) of fish in a small commercial pond is given by
$$F(t) = 27 - 15e^{-.8t},$$
where t is in years. Find each of the following.
(a) $F(0)$ **(b)** $F(1)$ **(c)** $F(5)$
(d) The limiting value of $F(x)$

16. **Social Science** The number of words per minute that an average typist can type is given by
$$W(t) = 60 - 30e^{-.5t},$$
where t is time in months after the beginning of a typing class. Find the number of words typed per minute
(a) at the beginning of the class.
(b) after 2 months.
(c) What is the maximum number of words per minute according to this model?
(d) When will 45 words per minute be achieved?

17. **Management** Assembly line operations tend to have a high turnover of employees, forcing the companies involved to spend much time and effort in training new workers. It has been found that a worker new to the operation of a certain task on the assembly line will produce items according to
$$P(x) = 25 - 25e^{-.3x},$$

*Book Industry Study Group.

†U.S. Bureau of Economic Analysis.

*NIIT, NASSCOM and *Scientific American*, September, 1994, page 95.

where $P(x)$ is the number of items produced by the worker on day x. How many items will be produced by the worker on

(a) day 1?

(b) day 8?

(c) According to the model, what is the maximum number of items these workers can produce?

(d) When will a worker produce 20 items per day?

18. Management Sales of a new model can opener are approximated by

$$S(x) = 5000 - 4000e^{-x},$$

where x represents the number of years that the can opener has been on the market, and $S(x)$ represents sales in thousands. Find each of the following.

(a) $S(0)$

(b) $S(1)$

(c) $S(2)$

(d) $S(5)$

(e) $S(10)$

(f) Find the horizontal asymptote for the graph.

(g) Graph $y = S(x)$.

19. Natural Science The beaver population in a certain lake in year t is approximately

$$p(t) = \frac{2000}{1 + e^{-.5544t}}.$$

(a) What is the population now ($t = 0$)?

(b) What will the population be in five years?

20. Social Science A sociologist has shown that the fraction $y(t)$ of people in a group who have heard a rumor after t days is approximated by

$$y(t) = \frac{y_0e^{kt}}{1 - y_0(1 - e^{kt})},$$

where y_0 is the fraction of people who have heard the rumor at time $t = 0$, and k is a constant. A graph of $y(t)$ for a particular value of k is shown in the figure.

(a) If $k = .1$ and $y_0 = .05$, find $y(10)$.

(b) If $k = .2$ and $y_0 = .10$, find $y(5)$.

(c) Describe the fraction of people who have heard the rumor as the number of days increases.

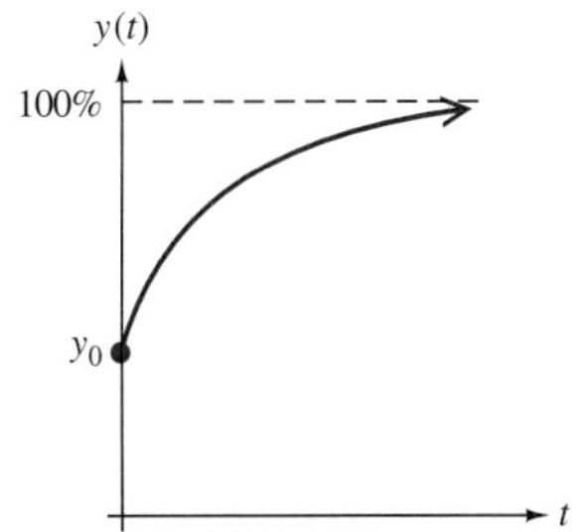

21. Social Science Data from the National Highway Traffic Safety Administration for the period 1982–1992* indicates that the approximate percentage of people who use seat belts when driving is given by

$$f(t) = \frac{880}{11 + 69e^{-.3(t-1982)}}.$$

What percentage used seat belts in

(a) 1982?

(b) 1989?

(c) 1992?

Assuming this function is accurate after 1992, what percentage of people used or will use seat belts in

(d) 1997?

(e) 2000?

(f) 2005?

(g) If this function remains accurate in the future, will there ever be a time when 95% of people use seat belts?

22. Social Science The graph shows that the percent y of American children growing up without a father has increased rapidly since 1950. If x represents the number of years since 1900, the function defined by

$$y = \frac{25}{1 + 1364.3e^{-x/9.316}}$$

models the data fairly well.†

(a) From the graph, in what year were 20% of these children living without a father? Using the function, when did this happen?

(b) According to the function, will the percent ever increase to 30? Explain why or why not.

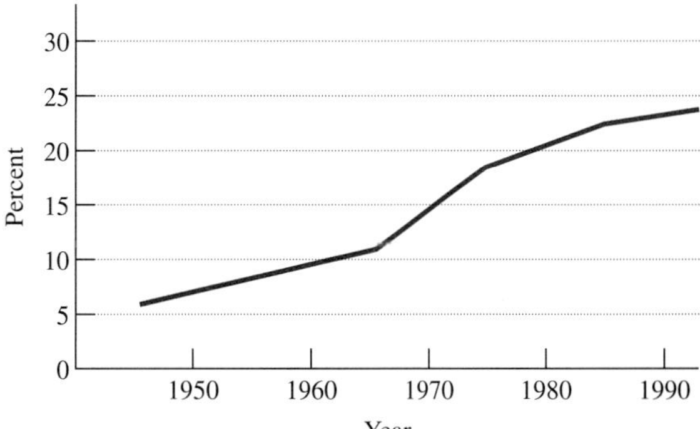

USA Today, December 30, 1992.

†National Longitudinal Survey of Youth, U.S. Department of Commerce, Bureau of the Census.

Management *The national debt has grown from 65 million dollars at the beginning of the Civil War to more than 4 trillion dollars by 1992. The graph of the debt, in which the horizontal axis represents time and the vertical axis dollars, has the approximate shape of an exponential growth function.* Over the past thirty years, the amount of debt (in billions of dollars) has been roughly approximated by the function*

$$D(t) = e^{.1293(t+36)} + 150,$$

where t is measured in years with $t = 0$ representing 1964.

23. Use this function to estimate the debt in each of the following years. Compare your results with the graph.
(a) 1972 **(b)** 1982 **(c)** 1992

24. (a) The Congressional Budget Office has projected that the national debt will be less than 6 trillion dollars at the turn of the century. How does this figure compare with the one predicted by the function D? What might explain the difference?
(b) Experiment with your calculator and various exponential functions to see if you can find a model for the national debt for the decade 1992–2002. Your model should indicate a debt of approximately 4077 billion in 1992 and approximately 6000 billion in 2002.

25. Social Science A class in elementary Tibetan is given a final exam worth 100 points. Then as part of an experiment they are tested weekly thereafter to see how much they remember. The average score on the test taken after t weeks is given by

$$T(x) = 77\left(\frac{1 + e^{-1}}{1 + e^{.08x-1}}\right).$$

(a) What was the average score on the original exam?
(b) What was the average score on the exam after 3 weeks? after 8 weeks?
(c) Do the students remember much Tibetan after a year?

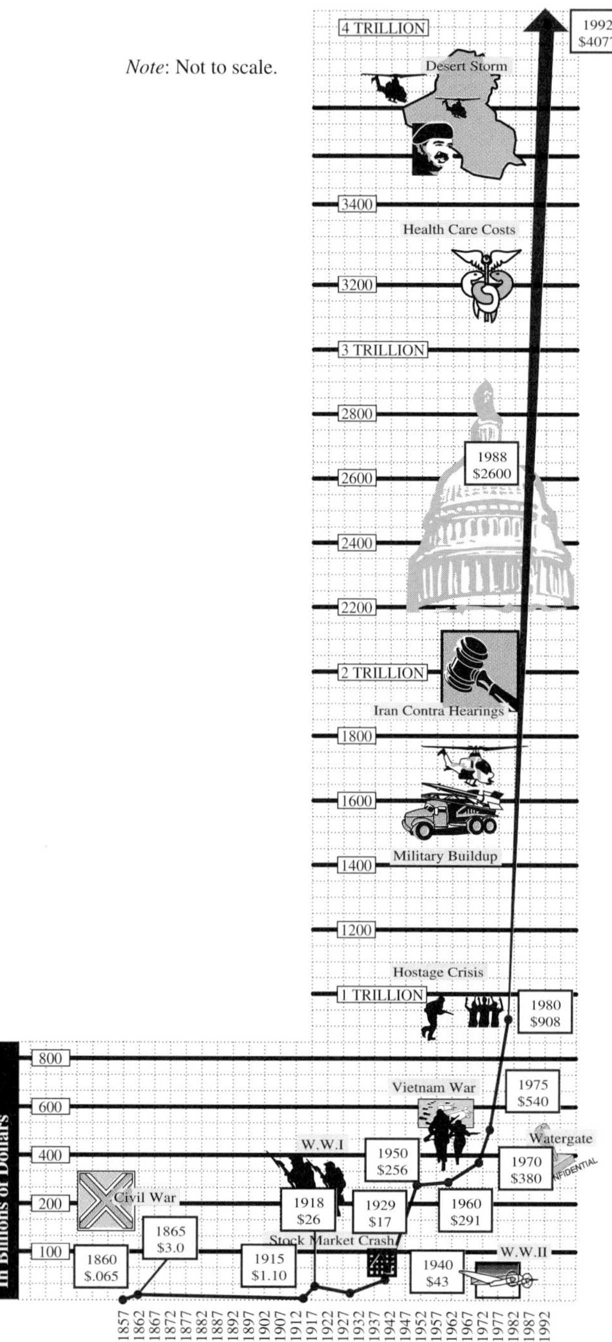

---

*Graph from "Debt Dwarfs Deficit" by Sam Hodges as appeared in *The Mobile Register.* Reprinted by permission of Newhouse News Service.

5.4 LOGARITHMIC FUNCTIONS

Until the development of computers and calculators, logarithms were the only effective tool for large-scale numerical computations. They are no longer needed for this, but logarithmic functions still play a crucial role in many applications.

COMMON LOGARITHMS Logarithms are simply a *new language for old ideas*—essentially a special case of exponents.

DEFINITION OF COMMON (BASE 10) LOGARITHMS

$$y = \log x \quad \text{means} \quad 10^y = x.$$

"Log x," which is read "the logarithm of x," is the answer to the question

To what exponent must 10 be raised to produce x?

1 Find each common logarithm.

(a) log 100

(b) log 1000

(c) log .1

Answers:

(a) 2

(b) 3

(c) −1

EXAMPLE 1 To find log 10,000 ask yourself, "To what exponent must 10 be raised to produce 10,000?" Since $10^4 = 10{,}000$, we see that $\log 10{,}000 = 4$. Similarly,

$$\log 1 = 0 \quad \text{because} \quad 10^0 = 1;$$

$$\log .01 = -2 \quad \text{because} \quad 10^{-2} = \frac{1}{10^2} = \frac{1}{100} = .01;$$

$$\log \sqrt{10} = 1/2 \quad \text{because} \quad 10^{1/2} = \sqrt{10}.$$ ■ 1

EXAMPLE 2 Log (−25) is the exponent to which 10 must be raised to produce −25. But every power of 10 is positive! So there is no exponent that will produce −25. *Logarithms of negative numbers and 0 are not defined.* ■

2 Find each common logarithm.

(a) log 27

(b) log 1089

(c) log .00426

Answers:

(a) 1.4314

(b) 3.0370

(c) −2.3706

EXAMPLE 3 **(a)** We know that log 359 must be a number between 2 and 3 because $10^2 = 100$ and $10^3 = 1000$. By pressing the log key, followed by 359, we find that log 359 (to four decimal places) is 2.5551. You can verify this by computing $10^{2.5551}$; the answer (rounded) is 359. See Figure 5.19.

(b) When 10 is raised to a negative exponent, the result is a number less than 1. Consequently, the logarithms of numbers between 0 and 1 are negative. For instance, Figure 5.19 shows that $\log .026 \approx -1.5850$. ■ 2

```
log(359)
         2.555094449
10^(2.5551)
           359.004589
log(.026)
        -1.585026652
```

FIGURE 5.19

NATURAL LOGARITHMS Although common logarithms still have some uses (one of which is discussed in Section 5.5), the most widely used logarithms today are defined in terms of the number e (whose decimal expansion begins 2.71828 . . .) rather than 10. They have a special name and notation.

DEFINITION OF NATURAL (BASE e) LOGARITHMS

$$y = \ln x \quad \text{means} \quad e^y = x.$$

Thus the number $\ln x$ (which may be read "el-en x") is the exponent to which e must be raised to produce the number x. For instance, $\ln 1 = 0$ because $e^0 = 1$. Although logarithms to base e may not seem as "natural" as common logarithms, there are several reasons for using them, some of which are discussed in Section 5.5.

3 Find the following.

(a) ln 6.1

(b) ln 20

(c) ln .8

(d) ln .1

Answers:

(a) 1.8083

(b) 2.9957

(c) $-.2231$

(d) -2.3026

EXAMPLE 4 **(a)** To find ln 85 use the ln key on your calculator followed by 85. The result is approximately 4.4427. Thus, 4.4427 is the exponent (to 4 decimal places) to which e must be raised to produce 85. You can verify this by computing $e^{4.4427}$; the answer (rounded) is 85.

(b) A calculator shows that $\ln .38 = -.9676$ (rounded), which means that $e^{-.9676} \approx .38$.

These results are shown in Figure 5.20. ■ 3

```
ln(85)
           4.442651256
e^(4.4427)
           85.0041433
ln(.38)
          -.9675840263
```

FIGURE 5.20

EXAMPLE 5 You don't need a calculator to find $\ln e^8$. Just ask yourself, "To what exponent must e be raised to produce e^8?" The answer, obviously, is 8. Thus, $\ln e^8 = 8$. ■

Example 5 is an illustration of the following fact.

$\ln e^k = k$ for every real number k.

OTHER LOGARITHMS The procedure used to define common and natural logarithms can be carried out with any positive number $a \neq 1$ as the base (in place of 10 or e).

DEFINITION OF LOGARITHMS TO THE BASE a

$$y = \log_a x \quad \text{means} \quad a^y = x.$$

Read $y = \log_a x$ as "y is the logarithm of x to the base a." For example, the exponential statement $2^4 = 16$ can be translated into the equivalent logarithmic statement $4 = \log_2 16$. Thus, $\log_a x$ is an *exponent;* it is the answer to the question

To what power must a be raised to produce x?

This key definition should be memorized. It is important to remember the location of the base and exponent in each part of the definition.

4 Write the logarithmic form of
(a) $5^3 = 125$;
(b) $3^{-4} = 1/81$;
(c) $8^{2/3} = 4$.

Answers:
(a) $\log_5 125 = 3$
(b) $\log_3(1/81) = -4$
(c) $\log_8 4 = 2/3$

Logarithmic form: $y = \log_a x$ (Exponent: y; Base: a)

Exponential form: $a^y = x$ (Exponent: y; Base: a)

Common and natural logarithms are the special cases when $a = 10$ and when $a = e$ respectively. Both $\log u$ and $\log_{10} u$ mean the same thing. Similarly, $\ln u$ and $\log_e u$ mean the same thing.

5 Write the exponential form of
(a) $\log_{16} 4 = 1/2$;
(b) $\log_3(1/9) = -2$;
(c) $\log_{16} 8 = 3/4$.

Answers:
(a) $16^{1/2} = 4$
(b) $3^{-2} = 1/9$
(c) $16^{3/4} = 8$

EXAMPLE 6 This example shows several statements written in both exponential and logarithmic forms.

Exponential Form	*Logarithmic Form*
(a) $3^2 = 9$	$\log_3 9 = 2$
(b) $(1/5)^{-2} = 25$	$\log_{1/5} 25 = -2$
(c) $10^5 = 100{,}000$	$\log_{10} 100{,}000$ (or $\log 100{,}000$) $= 5$
(d) $4^{-3} = 1/64$	$\log_4(1/64) = -3$
(e) $2^{-4} = 1/16$	$\log_2(1/16) = -4$
(f) $e^0 = 1$	$\log_e 1$ (or $\ln 1$) $= 0$

■ 4 5

PROPERTIES OF LOGARITHMS The usefulness of logarithmic functions depends in large part on the following *properties of logarithms.* These properties will be needed to solve exponential and logarithmic equations analytically in this section and the next.

PROPERTIES OF LOGARITHMS

Let x and y be any positive real numbers and r be any real number. Let a be a positive real number, $a \neq 1$. Then

(a) $\log_a xy = \log_a x + \log_a y$; **(b)** $\log_a \dfrac{x}{y} = \log_a x - \log_a y$;

(c) $\log_a x^r = r \log_a x$; **(d)** $\log_a a = 1$;

(e) $\log_a 1 = 0$; **(f)** $\log_a a^r = r$;

(g) $a^{\log_a x} = x$.

NOTE Because these properties are so useful, they should be memorized. ◆

To prove property (a), let

$$m = \log_a x \quad \text{and} \quad n = \log_a y.$$

Then, by the definition of logarithm,

$$a^m = x \quad \text{and} \quad a^n = y.$$

Multiply to get

$$a^m \cdot a^n = x \cdot y,$$

or, by a property of exponents,

$$a^{m+n} = xy.$$

Use the definition of logarithm to rewrite this last statement as

$$\log_a xy = m + n.$$

Replace m with $\log_a x$ and n with $\log_a y$ to get

$$\log_a xy = \log_a x + \log_a y.$$

Properties (b) and (c) can be proven in a similar way. Since $a^1 = a$ and $a^0 = 1$, properties (d) and (e) come from the definition of logarithm.

6 Simplify, using the properties of logarithms.

(a) $\log_a 5x + \log_a 3x^4$

(b) $\log_a 3p - \log_a 5q$

(c) $4 \log_a k - 3 \log_a m$

Answers:

(a) $\log_a 15x^5$

(b) $\log_a(3p/5q)$

(c) $\log_a(k^4/m^3)$

EXAMPLE 7 If all the following variable expressions represent positive numbers, then for $a > 0$, $a \neq 1$,

(a) $\log_a x + \log_a(x - 1) = \log_a x(x - 1)$;

(b) $\log_a \dfrac{x^2 + 4}{x + 6} = \log_a(x^2 + 4) - \log_a(x + 6)$;

(c) $\log_a 9x^5 = \log_a 9 + \log_a x^5 = \log_a 9 + 5 \log_a x$. ■ 6

CAUTION There is no logarithm property that allows you to simplify the logarithm of a sum, such as $\log_a (x^2 + 4)$. In particular, $\log_a(x^2 + 4)$ is *not* equal to $\log_a x^2 + \log_a 4$. Property (a) of logarithms in the box above shows that $\log_a x^2 + \log_a 4 = \log_a 4x^2$. ◆

Calculators give values only for base 10 or base e logarithms. Sometimes an application requires logarithms to other bases. The following theorem allows us to evaluate a logarithm to any base.

CHANGE OF BASE THEOREM

For positive numbers a and x (with $a \neq 1$),

$$\log_a x = \frac{\ln x}{\ln a}.$$

EXAMPLE 8 To find $\log_7 3$ with a calculator, use the theorem with $a = 7$ and $x = 3$:

$$\log_7 3 = \frac{\ln 3}{\ln 7} \approx \frac{1.0986}{1.9459} \approx .5646.$$

You can check this by verifying that $7^{.5646} \approx 3$. ■

LOGARITHMIC EQUATIONS Equations involving logarithms are often solved by using the fact that a logarithmic equation can be rewritten (with the definition of logarithm) as an exponential equation. In other cases, the properties of logarithms may be useful in simplifying an equation involving logarithms.

EXAMPLE 9 Solve each of the following equations.

(a) $\log_x 8/27 = 3$

First, use the definition of logarithm and write the expression in exponential form.

$$x^3 = \frac{8}{27} \qquad \text{Definition of logarithm}$$

$$x^3 = \left(\frac{2}{3}\right)^3 \qquad \text{Write } \frac{8}{27} \text{ as a cube.}$$

$$x = \frac{2}{3} \qquad \text{Set the bases equal.}$$

The solution is 2/3.

(b) $\log_4 x = 5/2$

In exponential form, the given statement becomes

$$4^{5/2} = x \qquad \text{Definition of logarithm}$$

$$(4^{1/2})^5 = x \qquad \text{Definition of rational exponent}$$

$$2^5 = x$$

$$32 = x.$$

The solution is 32. ■ 7

7 Solve each equation.

(a) $\log_x 6 = 1$

(b) $\log_5 25 = m$

(c) $\log_{27} x = 2/3$

Answers:

(a) 6

(b) 2

(c) 9

In the next example, properties of logarithms are needed to solve equations.

EXAMPLE 10 Solve each equation.

(a) $\log_2 x - \log_2 (x - 1) = 1$

By a property of logarithms, the left-hand side can be simplified as

$$\log_2 x - \log_2(x - 1) = \log_2 \frac{x}{x - 1}.$$

The original equation then becomes

$$\log_2 \frac{x}{x - 1} = 1.$$

Use the definition of logarithm to write this last result in exponential form.

$$\frac{x}{x - 1} = 2^1 = 2$$

Solve this equation.

$$\frac{x}{x-1} \cdot (x-1) = 2(x-1)$$
$$x = 2(x-1)$$
$$x = 2x - 2$$
$$-x = -2$$
$$x = 2$$

The domain of logarithmic functions includes only positive real numbers, so it is *necessary* to check this proposed solution in the original equation.

$$\log_2 x - \log_2(x-1) \stackrel{?}{=} 1$$
$$\log_2 2 - \log_2(2-1) \stackrel{?}{=} 1 \qquad \text{Let } x = 2.$$
$$1 - 0 = 1 \qquad \text{Definition of logarithm}$$

The solution, 2, checks.

(b) $\log x + \log 8.5463 = .7258$
To solve the equation graphically,

$$\text{let } Y_1 = \log x + \log 8.5463,$$
$$Y_2 = .7258,$$

and graph both functions in the same window. Use your intersection point locater to see that the graphs cross at $x = .62233162$, as shown in Figure 5.21. Thus, the solution of the equation is about .6223. ■ 8

8 Solve each equation.

(a) $\log_5 x + 2 \log_5 x = 3$

(b) Use a calculator to solve

$$\log(a+2) - \log\frac{a-7}{5} = 1.$$

Answers:

(a) 5

(b) 16

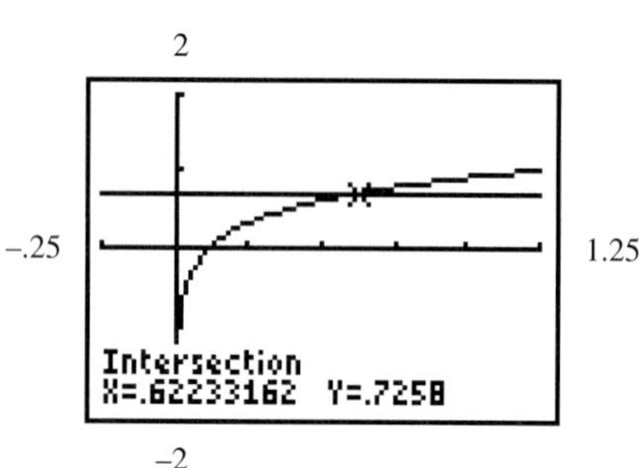

FIGURE 5.21

LOGARITHMIC FUNCTIONS For a given *positive* value of x, the definition of logarithm leads to exactly one value of y, so that $y = \log_a x$ defines a logarithmic function of base a. (The base a must be positive, with $a \neq 1$.)

> If $a > 0$ and $a \neq 1$, the **logarithmic function** with base a is defined as
>
> $$f(x) = \log_a x.$$

The most important logarithmic function is the natural logarithmic function.

9 Using a square window, graph $f(x) = \log_{10} x$ and $g(x) = 10^x$ on the same axes. Include the graph of $y = x$.

Answer:

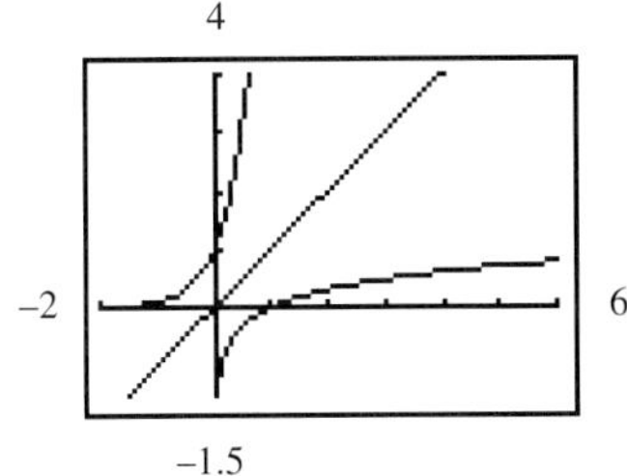

EXAMPLE 11 Graph $f(x) = \ln x$ and $g(x) = e^x$ on the same axes.

The graphs are shown in Figure 5.22. The straight line is the graph of $y = x$. Notice that the graph of $f(x) = \ln x$ is the mirror image of the graph of $g(x) = e^x$, with the line $y = x$ as the mirror. ■ 9

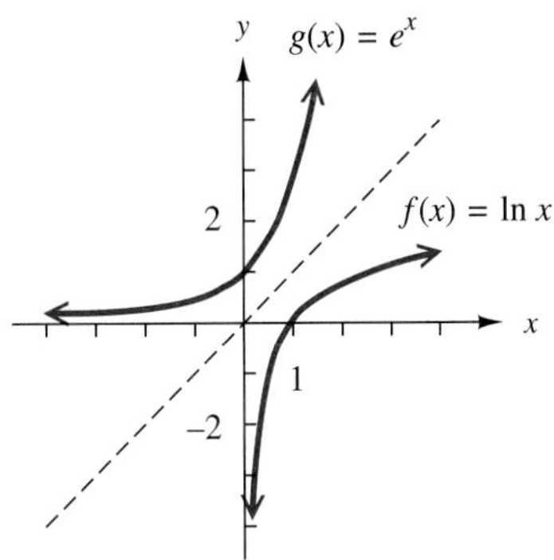

FIGURE 5.22

CAUTION In the answer to Problem 9 at the side, it would be easy to misinterpret the calculator-generated graph in the answer by thinking that there are endpoints on the two curves. ◆

When the base $a > 1$, the graph of $f(x) = \log_a x$ has the same basic shape as the graph of the natural logarithmic function in Figure 5.22, as summarized below.

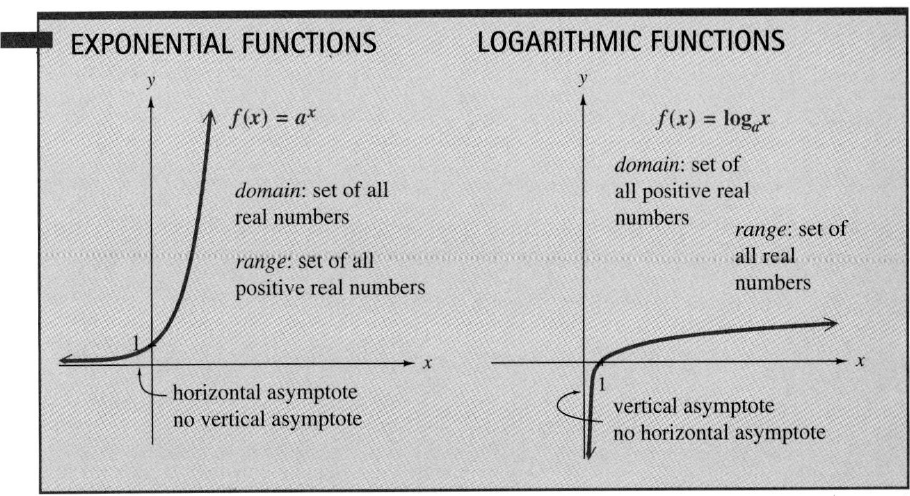

Finally, the graph of $f(x) = \log_a x$ is the mirror image of the graph of $g(x) = a^x$, with the line $y = x$ being the mirror. Functions whose graphs are related in this way are said to be **inverses** of each other. A more complete discussion of inverse functions is given in most standard college algebra books.

5.4 EXERCISES

Complete each statement in Exercises 1–4.

1. $y = \log_a x$ means $x =$ ________.
2. The statement $\log_5 125 = 3$ tells us that ________ is the power of ________ that equals ________.
3. What is wrong with the expression $y = \log_b$?
4. Logarithms of negative numbers are not defined because ________.

Translate each logarithmic statement into an equivalent exponential statement. (See Examples 1, 5, 6.)

5. $\log 100{,}000 = 5$
6. $\log .001 = -3$
7. $\log_3 81 = 4$
8. $\log_2(1/4) = -2$

Translate each exponential statement into an equivalent logarithmic statement. (See Examples 5 and 6.)

9. $10^{1.8751} = 75$
10. $e^{3.2189} = 25$
11. $3^{-2} = 1/9$
12. $16^{1/2} = 4$

Without using a calculator, evaluate each of the following. (See Examples 1, 5, 6.)

13. $\log 100$
14. $\log .0001$
15. $\log_5 25$
16. $\log_9 81$
17. $\log_4 64$
18. $\log_6 216$
19. $\log_2 \frac{1}{4}$
20. $\log_3 \frac{1}{27}$
21. $\ln \sqrt{e}$
22. $\ln(1/e)$
23. $\ln e^{3.78}$
24. $\log 10^{56.9}$

Use a calculator to evaluate each logarithm to three decimal places. (See Examples 3 and 4.)

25. $\log 47$
26. $\log .004$
27. $\ln .351$
28. $\ln 2160$
29. Why does $\log_a 1$ always equal 0 for any valid base a?

Write each expression as the logarithm of a single number or expression with a coefficient of 1. Assume all variables represent positive numbers. (See Example 7.)

30. $\log 15 - \log 3$
31. $\log 4 + \log 8 - \log 2$
32. $3 \ln 2 + 2 \ln 3$
33. $2 \ln 5 - \frac{1}{2} \ln 25$
34. $3 \log x - 2 \log y$
35. $2 \log u + 3 \log w - 6 \log v$
36. $\ln(3x + 2) + \ln(x + 4)$
37. $2 \ln(x + 1) - \ln(x + 2)$
38. Graph $y_1 = \log x$ and $y_2 = \log(x/4)$ in the window with $-2 \le x \le 10$ and $-3 \le y \le 3$. How are these graphs related? How does the quotient rule support your answer?

Write each expression as a sum and/or a difference of logarithms with all variables to the first degree.

39. $\log 5x^2y^3$
40. $\ln \sqrt{6m^4n^2}$
41. $\ln \frac{3x}{5y}$
42. $\log \frac{\sqrt{xz}}{z^3}$

Express each of the following in terms of u and v, where $u = \ln x$ and $v = \ln y$. For example, $\ln x^3 = 3(\ln x) = 3u$.

43. $\ln(x^2y^5)$
44. $\ln(\sqrt{x} \cdot y^2)$
45. $\ln(x^3/y^2)$
46. $\ln(\sqrt{x}/y)$

Evaluate each expression. (See Example 8.)

47. $\log_6 543$
48. $\log_{20} 97$
49. $\log_{35} 6874$
50. $\log_5 50 - \log_{50} 5$

Find numerical values for b and c for which the given statement is FALSE.

51. $\log(b + c) = \log b + \log c$
52. $\frac{\ln b}{\ln c} = \ln\left(\frac{b}{c}\right)$

Solve each of the following equations. (See Examples 9 and 10.)

53. $\log_x 25 = -2$
54. $\log_x \frac{1}{16} = -2$
55. $\log_9 27 = m$
56. $\log_8 4 = z$
57. $\log_y 8 = \frac{3}{4}$
58. $\log_r 7 = \frac{1}{2}$
59. $\log_3(5x + 1) = 2$
60. $\log_5(9x - 4) = 1$
61. $\log x - \log(x + 3) = -1$
62. $\log m - \log(m - 4) = -2$
63. $\log_3(y + 2) = \log_3(y - 7) + \log_3 4$
64. $\log_8(z - 6) = 2 - \log_8(z + 15)$
65. $\ln(x + 9) - \ln x = 1$
66. $\ln(2x + 1) - 1 = \ln(x - 2)$
67. $\log x + \log(x - 3) = 1$
68. $\log(x - 1) + \log(x + 2) = 1$
69. Suppose you overhear the following statement: "I must reject any negative answer when I solve an equation involving logarithms." Is this correct? Write an explanation of why it is or is not correct.
70. What values of x could not possibly be solutions of the following equation?

$$\log_a(4x - 7) + \log_a(x^2 + 4) = 0$$

Graph each of the following. (See Example 11.)

71. $y = \ln(x + 2)$
72. $y = \ln x + 2$
73. $y = \log(x - 3)$
74. $y = \log x - 3$
75. Solve $e^{\ln x} - \ln(x + 2.954) = \ln 10.304$ by graphing. (See Example 10(b).)
76. The graph of $y = \log x$ is shown with the coordinates of a point displayed at the bottom of the screen. Write the

logarithmic and exponential equations associated with the display.

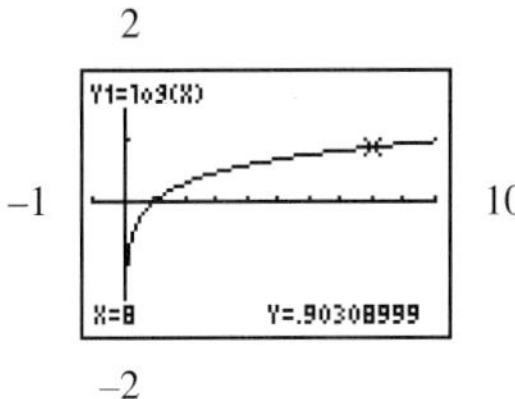

77. The graph of $y = \ln x$ is shown with the coordinates of a point displayed at the bottom of the screen. Write the logarithmic and exponential equations associated with the display.

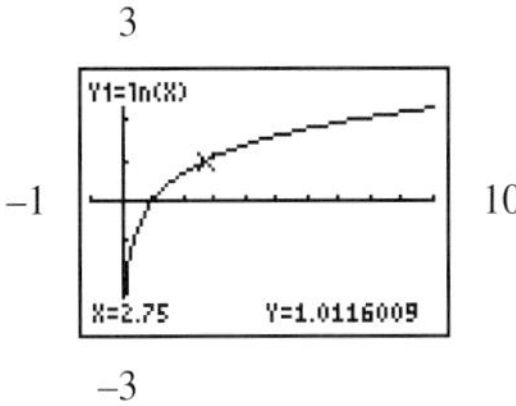

78. Match each equation with its graph. In each case the window has $-2 \leq x \leq 6$ and $-1.5 \leq y \leq 4$.

(a) $y = \log x$ **(b)** $y = 10^x$ **(c)** $y = \ln x$ **(d)** $y = e^x$

A.
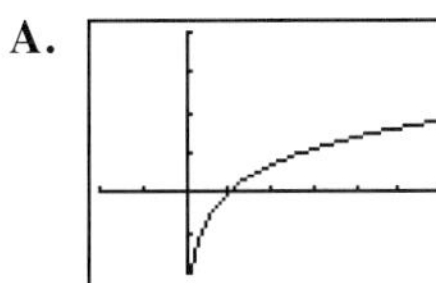

B.
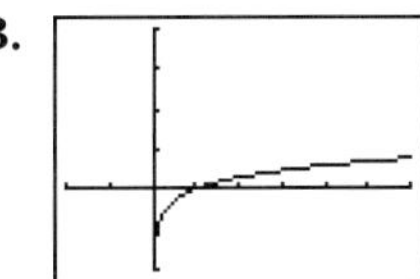

C.
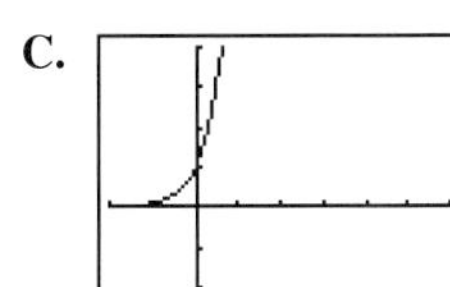

D.
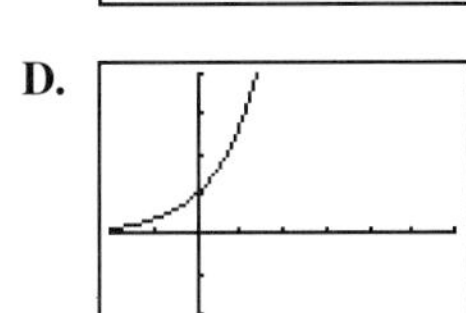

79. The calculator-generated table in the figure is for $y_1 = \log(4 - x)$. Why do the values in the y_1 column show ERROR for $x \geq 4$?

X	Y1
0	.60206
1	.47712
2	.30103
3	0
4	ERROR
5	ERROR
6	ERROR

X=4

80. How might one misinterpret the domain of a logarithmic function of the form $f(x) = \log_a x$ by simply observing the calculator-generated graph of the function?

Work the following exercises.

81. Natural Science Two people with the flu visited the campus of Big State U. The number of days T that it took for the flu virus to infect n people is given by

$$T = -1.43 \ln\left(\frac{10{,}000 - n}{4998n}\right).$$

How many days will it take for the virus to infect

(a) 500 people? **(b)** 5000 people?

82. Natural Science

(a) Graph the "flu function" in Exercise 81 in a viewing window with $0 \leq n \leq 11{,}000$.

(b) How many people are infected on the 16th day?

(c) Explain why this model is not realistic when large numbers of people are involved.

83. Management The graph shows the percent increase in commercial rents in California from 1992 to 1999 (1997–1999 figures are estimates). In the two-year period 1990–1992 commercial rents had decreased by about 6%. They started to increase in 1992 as the state finally began an economic recovery.

(a) Describe the growth in rents during the period shown in the graph.

(b) The graph can be approximated by $f(x) = -650 + 143 \ln x$, where x is the number of years since 1900 and y is the corresponding percent change in rents. Find $f(92)$ and $f(99)$. Compare your results with the corresponding y-values from the graph.

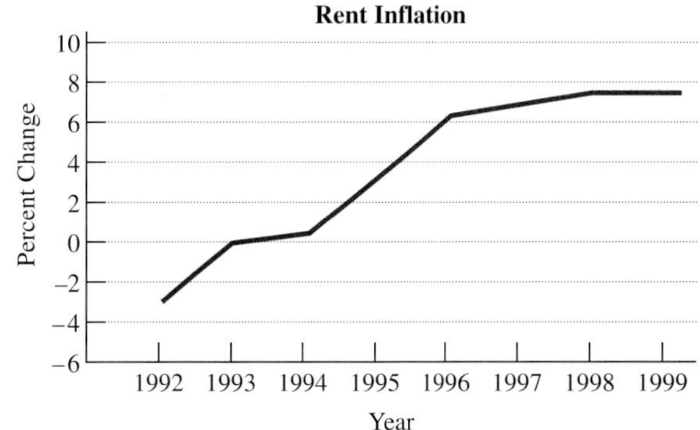

Source: CB Commercial/Torto Wheaton Research.

84. Management The following table lists the interest rates for various U.S. Treasury Securities on February 1, 1996.*

Time	*Yield*
3-month	4.99%
6-month	4.92%
1-year	4.84%
2-year	4.90%
3-year	4.99%
5-year	5.18%
10-year	5.59%
30-year	6.07%

(a) Use your calculator to plot the data.

(b) Discuss which type of function will model this data best: linear, exponential, or logarithmic.

*Merrill Lynch.

5.5 APPLICATIONS OF LOGARITHMIC FUNCTIONS

We begin this section by introducing and illustrating a powerful method of solving exponential and logarithmic equations. We then show some applications that require this method of solution. The method depends on the following fact.

> Let x and y be positive numbers. Let a be a positive number, $a \neq 1$.
>
> If $x = y$, then $\log_a x = \log_a y$.
>
> If $\log_a x = \log_a y$, then $x = y$.

1 Solve each equation. Round solutions to the nearest thousandth.

(a) $2^x = 7$

(b) $5^m = 50$

(c) $3^y = 17$

Answers:

(a) 2.807

(b) 2.431

(c) 2.579

EXAMPLE 1 Solve $3^x = 5$.

Since 3 and 5 cannot easily be written with the same base, the methods of Section 5.2 cannot be used to solve this equation. Instead, use the result given above and take natural logarithms of both sides.

$$3^x = 5$$

$$\ln 3^x = \ln 5$$

$$x \ln 3 = \ln 5 \qquad \text{Property (c) of logarithms}$$

$$x = \frac{\ln 5}{\ln 3} \approx 1.465$$

To check, evaluate $3^{1.465}$; the answer should be approximately 5, which verifies that the solution of the given equation is 1.465 to the nearest thousandth. ■ **1**

CAUTION There are no logarithm properties that enable you to simplify $\frac{\ln 5}{\ln 3}$; this number is *not* equal to $\ln\left(\frac{5}{3}\right)$ or $\ln 5 - \ln 3$. ◆

2 Solve each equation. Round solutions to the nearest thousandth.

(a) $6^m = 3^{2m-1}$

(b) $5^{6a-3} = 2^{4a+1}$

Answers:

(a) 2.710

(b) .802

EXAMPLE 2 Solve $3^{2x-1} = 4^{x+2}$.

Taking natural logarithms on both sides gives

$$\ln 3^{2x-1} = \ln 4^{x+2}.$$

Now use property (c) of logarithms and the fact that ln 3 and ln 4 are constants to rewrite the equation.

$$(2x - 1)(\ln 3) = (x + 2)(\ln 4) \qquad \text{Property (c)}$$

$$2x(\ln 3) - 1(\ln 3) = x(\ln 4) + 2(\ln 4) \qquad \text{Distributive property}$$

$$2x(\ln 3) - x(\ln 4) = 2(\ln 4) + 1(\ln 3) \qquad \text{Collect terms with } x \text{ on one side.}$$

Factor out x on the left side to get

$$[2(\ln 3) - \ln 4]x = 2(\ln 4) + \ln 3.$$

Divide both sides by the coefficient of x:

$$x = \frac{2(\ln 4) + \ln 3}{2(\ln 3) - \ln 4}.$$

Using a calculator to evaluate this last expression, we find that

$$x = \frac{2 \ln 4 + \ln 3}{2 \ln 3 - \ln 4} \approx 4.774. \quad ■ \quad \boxed{2}$$

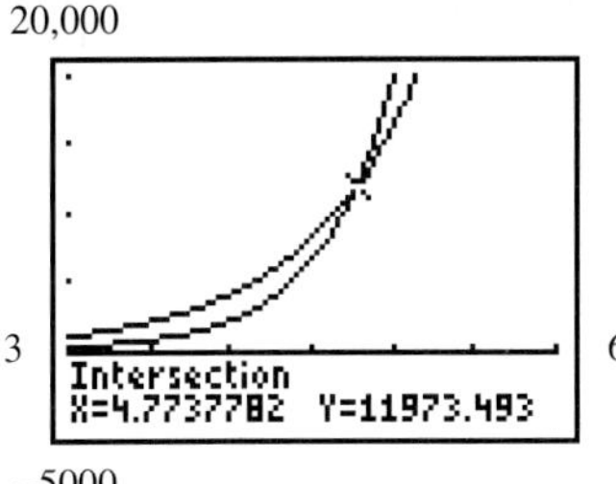

FIGURE 5.23

Earlier, we saw that a graphing calculator can be used to solve an equation. One way to solve Example 2 using a calculator is to graph $y_1 = 3^{2x-1}$ and $y_2 = 4^{x+2}$, then locate the x-value of the intersection point. (Be careful to put parentheses around the quantities in the exponents.) The graphs and the intersection point are shown in Figure 5.23. It will be necessary to experiment a bit to find a suitable window. Since exponential expressions get large very quickly, we should expect y to assume large values, as is the case here. The solution, $x = 4.774$, agrees with the answer we found analytically in Example 2.

In the remaining examples in this section, we show only the algebraic solutions, because here we want to emphasize the use of the properties of logarithms to solve equations. Of course, these equations also can be solved graphically.

Recall that $\ln e = 1$ (because 1 is the exponent to which e must be raised to produce e). This fact simplifies the solution of equations involving powers of e.

EXAMPLE 3 Solve $3e^{x^2} = 600$.

First divide each side by 3 to get

$$e^{x^2} = 200.$$

Now take natural logarithms on both sides; then use properties of logarithms.

$$\begin{aligned} e^{x^2} &= 200 \\ \ln e^{x^2} &= \ln 200 \\ x^2 \ln e &= \ln 200 && \text{Property (c)} \\ x^2 &= \ln 200 && \ln e = 1 \\ x &= \pm\sqrt{\ln 200} \\ x &\approx \pm 2.302 \end{aligned}$$

The solutions are ± 2.302, rounding to the nearest thousandth. (The symbol $\pm$ is used as a shortcut for writing the two solutions, 2.302 and -2.302.) ■ 3

3 Solve each equation. Round solutions to the nearest thousandth.

(a) $e^{.1x} = 11$

(b) $e^{3+x} = .893$

(c) $e^{2x^2-3} = 9$

Answers:

(a) 23.979

(b) -3.113

(c) ± 1.612

The fact given at the beginning of this section, along with the properties of logarithms from Section 5.4, is useful in solving logarithmic equations, as shown in the next examples.

EXAMPLE 4 Solve $\log(x + 4) - \log(x + 2) = \log x$.

Using property (b) of logarithms, rewrite the equation as

$$\log \frac{x + 4}{x + 2} = \log x.$$

Then

$$\begin{aligned} \frac{x + 4}{x + 2} &= x \\ x + 4 &= x(x + 2) \\ x + 4 &= x^2 + 2x \\ x^2 + x - 4 &= 0. \end{aligned}$$

By the quadratic formula,

$$x = \frac{-1 \pm \sqrt{1 + 16}}{2},$$

4 Solve each equation.

(a) $\log_2(p + 9) - \log_2 p = \log_2(p + 1)$

(b) $\log_3(m + 1) - \log_3(m - 1) = \log_3 m$

Answers:

(a) 3

(b) $1 + \sqrt{2} \approx 2.414$

so that

$$x = \frac{-1 + \sqrt{17}}{2} \quad \text{or} \quad x = \frac{-1 - \sqrt{17}}{2}.$$

Log x cannot be evaluated for $x = (-1 - \sqrt{17})/2$, because this number is negative and not in the domain of log x. By substitution, verify that $(-1 + \sqrt{17})/2$ is a solution. ■ 4

A radioactive substance decays according to a function of the form $y = y_0e^{-kt}$, where y_0 is the amount present initially (at time $t = 0$) and k is a positive number. The **half-life** of a radioactive substance is the time it takes for exactly half of the substance to decay. We find the half-life by finding the value of t such that $y = (1/2)y_0$. Similarly, we can find the time for any proportion of A_0 to remain.

EXAMPLE 5 Carbon 14, also known as radiocarbon, is a radioactive form of carbon that is found in all living plants and animals. After a plant or animal dies, the radiocarbon disintegrates with a half-life of approximately 5600 years. Scientists can determine the age of the remains by comparing the amount of radiocarbon with the amounts present in living plants and animals. This technique is called *carbon dating.* The amount of radiocarbon present after t years is given by

$$y = y_0e^{-(\ln 2)(1/5600)t},$$

where y_0 is the amount present in living plants and animals.

A round table hanging in Winchester Castle (England) was alleged to belong to King Arthur, who lived in the 5th century. A recent chemical analysis showed that the table had 91% of the amount of radiocarbon present in living wood. How old is the table?

The amount of radiocarbon present in the round table after y years is $.91y_0$. Therefore, in the equation

$$y = y_0e^{-(\ln 2)(1/5600)t},$$

replace y with $.91y_0$ and solve for t.

$$.91y_0 = y_0e^{-(\ln 2)(1/5600)t}$$

$$.91 = e^{-(\ln 2)(1/5600)t} \qquad \text{Divide both sides by } y_0.$$

$$\ln .91 = \ln e^{-(\ln 2)(1/5600)t} \qquad \text{Take logarithms on both sides.}$$

$$\ln .91 = \frac{(-\ln 2)t}{5600} \qquad \text{Property (c) of logarithms and } \ln e = 1$$

$$t = \frac{(5600)\ln .91}{-\ln 2} \approx 761.94$$

The table is about 762 years old and therefore could not have belonged to King Arthur.

We could also solve this problem by graphing after y_0 has been eliminated. The quantities .91 and $e^{-(\ln 2)(1/5600)t}$ will be equal if their difference is 0. So let $Y_1 = e^{-(\ln 2)(1/5600)t} - .91$. Graph Y_1 and find the value of x where the graph crosses the x-axis. Figure 5.24 shows that $Y_1 = 0$ when $x = 761.94$. ■ 5

5 What is the age of a specimen in which $y = (1/3)y_0$?

Answer:

About 8880 years

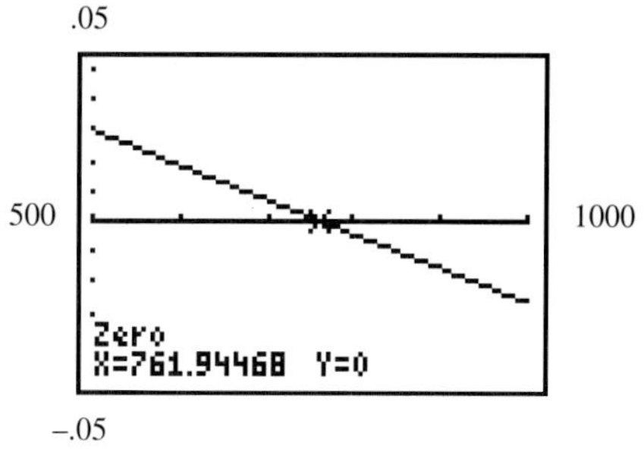

.05

500

1000

Zero
X=761.94468 Y=0

−.05

FIGURE 5.24

Our next example uses common logarithms (base 10).

EXAMPLE 6 The intensity $R(i)$ of an earthquake, measured on the Richter scale, is given by

$$R(i) = \log\left(\frac{i}{i_0}\right),$$

where i is the intensity of the ground motion of the earthquake and i_0 is the intensity of the ground motion of the so-called *zero earthquake* (the smallest detectable earthquake, against which others are measured). The 1989 San Francisco earthquake measured 7.1 on the Richter scale.

(a) How did the ground motion of this earthquake compare with that of the zero earthquake?

In this case $R(i) = 7.1$, that is, $\log(i/i_0) = 7.1$. Thus 7.1 is the exponent to which 10 must be raised to produce i/i_0. In other words,

$$10^{7.1} = \frac{i}{i_0}, \quad \text{or equivalently,} \quad i = 10^{7.1}i_0.$$

So this earthquake had $10^{7.1}$ (approximately 12.6 million) times more ground motion than the zero earthquake.

(b) What is the Richter scale intensity of an earthquake with 10 times as much ground motion as the 1989 San Francisco earthquake?

Using the result from (a), the ground motion of such a quake would be

$$i = 10(10^{7.1}i_0) = 10^1 \cdot 10^{7.1}i_0 = 10^{8.1}i_0$$

so that its Richter scale intensity would be

$$R(i) = \log\left(\frac{i}{i_0}\right) = \log\left(\frac{10^{8.1}i_0}{i_0}\right) = \log 10^{8.1} = 8.1.$$

Therefore, a ten-fold increase in ground motion increases the Richter scale intensity by just 1. ■ 6

6 Find the Richter scale intensity of an earthquake whose ground motion is 100 times greater than the ground motion of the 1989 San Francisco earthquake discussed in Example 6.

Answer:
9.1

In the final example we solve a base e logarithmic equation.

EXAMPLE 7 One action that government could take to reduce carbon emissions into the atmosphere is to place a tax on fossil fuel. This tax would be based on the amount of carbon dioxide that is emitted into the air when the fuel is burned. The *cost-benefit* equation $\ln(1 - P) = -.0034 - .0053T$ describes the approximate

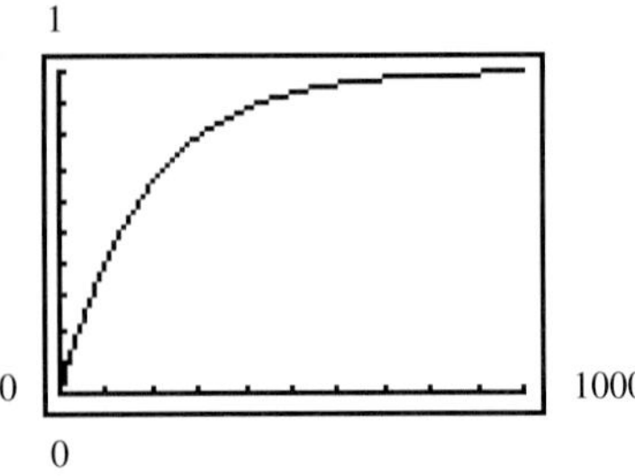

FIGURE 5.25

relationship between a tax of T dollars per ton of carbon dioxide and the corresponding percent reduction P (in decimals) of emission of carbon dioxide.*

(a) Write P as a function of T.
We begin by writing the cost-benefit equation in exponential form.

$$\ln(1 - P) = -.0034 - .0053T$$
$$1 - P = e^{-.0034-.0053T}$$
$$P = P(T) = 1 - e^{-.0034-.0053T}$$

(b) Graph $P(T)$ for $0 \le T \le 1000$.
The graph is shown in Figure 5.25.

(c) Discuss the benefit of continuing to raise taxes on carbon dioxide emissions.
From the graph we see that initially there is a rapid reduction of carbon dioxide emissions. However, after a while there is little benefit in raising taxes further. ■

The most important applications of exponential and logarithmic functions for the fields of management and economics are considered in Chapter 6 (Mathematics of Finance).

*Nordhause, W., "To Slow or Not to Slow: The Economics of the Greenhouse Effect." Yale University, New Haven, Connecticut.

5.5 EXERCISES

Solve each exponential equation. Round to the nearest thousandth. (See Examples 1–3.)

1. $3^x = 5$
2. $5^x = 4$
3. $2^x = 3^{x-1}$
4. $4^{x+2} = 2^{x-1}$
5. $3^{1-2x} = 5^{x+5}$
6. $4^{3x-1} = 3^{x-2}$
7. $e^{2x} = 5$
8. $e^{-3x} = 2$
9. $2e^{5a+2} = 8$
10. $10e^{3z-7} = 5$
11. $2^{x^2-1} = 12$
12. $3^{2-x^2} = 4$
13. $2(e^x + 1) = 10$
14. $5(e^{2x} - 2) = 15$

Solve each equation for c.

15. $10^{4c-3} = d$
16. $3 \cdot 10^{2c+1} = 4d$
17. $e^{2c-1} = b$
18. $3e^{5c-7} = b$

Solve each logarithmic equation. (See Example 4.)

19. $\ln(3x - 1) - \ln(2 + x) = \ln 2$
20. $\ln(8k - 7) - \ln(3 + 4k) = \ln(9/11)$
21. $\ln x + 1 = \ln(x - 4)$
22. $\ln(4x - 2) = \ln 4 - \ln(x - 2)$
23. $2\ln(x - 3) = \ln(x + 5) + \ln 4$
24. $\ln(k + 5) + \ln(k + 2) = \ln 14k$
25. $\log_5(r + 2) + \log_5(r - 2) = 1$
26. $\log_4(z + 3) + \log_4(z - 3) = 1$
27. $\log_3(a - 3) = 1 + \log_3(a + 1)$
28. $\log w + \log(3w - 13) = 1$
29. $\log_2 \sqrt{2y^2} - 1 = 1/2$
30. $\log_2(\log_2 x) = 1$
31. $\log z = \sqrt{\log z}$
32. $\log x^2 = (\log x)^2$

Solve each equation for c.

33. $\log(3 + b) = \log(4c - 1)$
34. $\ln(b + 7) = \ln(6c + 8)$
35. $2 - b = \log(6c + 5)$
36. $8b + 6 = \ln(2c) + \ln c$
37. Explain why the equation $3^x = -4$ has no solutions.
38. Explain why the equation $\log(-x) = -4$ does have a solution and find that solution.

Work these exercises. (See Example 5.)

39. Natural Science The amount of cobalt-60 (in grams) in a storage facility at time t is given by

$$C(t) = 25e^{-.14t},$$

where time is measured in years.
(a) How much cobalt-60 was present initially?
(b) What is the half life of cobalt-60?

40. Natural Science An American Indian mummy was found recently. It had 73.6% of the amount of radiocarbon present in living beings. Approximately how long ago did this person die?

41. Natural Science How old is a piece of ivory that has lost 36% of its radiocarbon?

42. **Natural Science** A large cloud of radioactive debris from a nuclear explosion has floated over the Pacific Northwest, contaminating much of the hay supply. Consequently, farmers in the area are concerned that the cows who eat this hay will give contaminated milk. (The tolerance level for radioactive iodine in milk is 0.) The percent of the initial amount of radioactive iodine still present in the hay after t days is approximated by $P(t)$, which is given by the function

$$P(t) = 100e^{-.1t}.$$

(a) Find the percent remaining after 4 days.
(b) Find the percent remaining after 10 days.
(c) Some scientists feel that the hay is safe after the percent of radioactive iodine has declined to 10% of the original amount. Solve the equation $10 = 100e^{-.1t}$ to find the number of days before the hay may be used.
(d) Other scientists believe that the hay is not safe until the level of radioactive iodine has declined to only 1% of the original level. Find the number of days that this would take.

Work these exercises. (See Example 6.)

43. **Natural Science** Find the Richter scale intensity of earthquakes whose ground motion is
(a) $1000i_0$ (b) $100{,}000i_0$ (c) $10{,}000{,}000i_0$.
(d) Fill the blank in this statement: Increasing the ground motion by a factor of 10^k increases the Richter intensity by______ units.

44. **Natural Science** The great San Francisco earthquake of 1906 measured 8.3 on the Richter scale. How much greater was the ground motion in 1906 than in the 1989 earthquake, which measured 7.1 on the Richter scale?

45. **Natural Science** The loudness of sound is measured in units called decibels. The decibel rating of a sound is given by

$$D(i) = 10 \cdot \log\left(\frac{i}{i_0}\right),$$

where i is the intensity of the sound and i_0 is the minimum intensity detectable by the human ear (the so-called *threshold sound*). Find the decibel rating of each of the following sounds whose intensities are given. Round answers to the nearest whole number.
(a) Whisper, $115i_0$
(b) Busy street, $9{,}500{,}000i_0$
(c) Rock music, $895{,}000{,}000{,}000i_0$
(d) Jetliner at takeoff, $109{,}000{,}000{,}000{,}000i_0$

46. (a) How much more intense is a sound that measures 100 decibels than the threshold sound?
(b) How much more intense is a sound that measures 50 decibels than the threshold sound?
(c) How much more intense is a sound measuring 100 decibels than one measuring 50 decibels?

47. **Natural Science** (Refer to Example 7.)
(a) Determine P when $T = \$60$.
(b) What value of T will give a 50% reduction in carbon dioxide emissions?

48. **Natural Science** In the central Sierra Nevada of California, the percent of moisture that falls as snow rather than rain is approximated reasonably well by

$$p = 86.3 \ln h - 680,$$

where p is the percent of moisture as snow at an altitude of h feet (with $3000 \le h < 8500$).
(a) Graph p.
(b) At what altitude is 50 percent of the moisture snow?

49. **Social Science** The number of years, $N(r)$, since two independently evolving languages split off from a common ancestral language is approximated by

$$N(r) = -5000 \ln r,$$

where r is the proportion of the words from the ancestral language that is common to both languages now. Find each of the following.
(a) $N(.9)$ (b) $N(.5)$ (c) $N(.3)$
(d) How many years have elapsed since the split if 70% of the words of the ancestral language are common to both languages today?
(e) If two languages split off from a common ancestral language about 1000 years ago, find r.

50. **Social Science** The number of visitors (in millions) to U.S. National Parks from 1950 through 1993 can be approximated by the logarithmic function with $f(x) = -266 + 72 \ln x$.* Here, x represents the number of years since 1900; thus, 1950 corresponds to 50, 1960 corresponds to 60, and so on.
(a) Use this function to estimate the number of visitors in the year 2000. What assumption must we make to estimate the number of visitors beyond 1993?
(b) According to the function, in what year will the number of visitors reach 70 million?

51. **Natural Science** The growth of outpatient surgery as a percent of total surgeries at hospitals is approximated by $f(x) = -1317 + 304 \ln x$, where x represents the number of years since 1900.†
(a) What does this function predict for the percent of outpatient surgeries in 1998?
(b) When did outpatient surgeries reach 50%?

52. **Natural Science** In an earlier exercise set, we discussed how a drug's effectiveness decreases over time. If each hour a drug is only 90% as effective as the previous hour, at some point the patient will not be receiving enough medication and must receive another dose. This situation can be modeled by an exponential function with $y = y_0(.90)^t$. In this equation, y_0 is the amount of the initial dose and y is the percent of medication still available t hours after the drug was administered. Note that t is the number of hours since the drug was administered less one. Suppose 200 mg of the drug is administered. How long will it take for this initial dose to reach the dangerously low level of 50 mg?

*Statistical Abstract of the United States 1994, p. 249.

†American Hospital Association, Chicago.

53. **Physical Science** The table gives some of the planets' average distances D from the sun and their period P of revolution around the sun in years. The distances have been normalized so that Earth is one unit from the sun. Thus, Jupiter's distance of 5.2 means that Jupiter's distance from the sun is 5.2 times farther than Earth's.*

Planet	*D*	*P*
Earth	1	1
Jupiter	5.2	11.9
Saturn	9.54	29.5
Uranus	19.2	84.0

(a) Plot the points (D, P) for these planets. Would a straight line or an exponential curve fit these points best?

(b) Plot the points $(\ln D, \ln P)$ for these planets. Do these points appear to lie on a line?

(c) Determine a linear equation that approximates the data points with $x = \ln D$ and $y = \ln P$. Use the data points $(0, 0)$ and $(2.95, 4.43)$. Graph your line and the data on the same coordinate axes.

(d) Use the linear equation to predict the period of the planet Pluto if its distance is 39.5. Compare your answer to the true value of 248.5 years.

*Ronan, C. *The Natural History of the Universe*, MacMillan Publishing Co., New York, 1991.

Natural Science *Many environmental situations place effective limits on the growth of the number of an organism in an area. Many such limited growth situations are described by the logistic function, defined by*

$$G(t) = \frac{MG_0}{G_0 + (M - G_0)e^{-kMt}}$$

where G_0 is the initial number present, M is the maximum possible size of the population, and k is a positive constant. Assume $G_0 = 100$, $M = 2500$, $k = .0004$, and t is time in decades (10-yr periods).

54. Graph the S-shaped limited growth function using $0 \le t \le 8$, $0 \le y \le 2500$.

55. Estimate the value of $G(2)$ from the graph. Then evaluate $G(2)$ to find the population after 20 years.

56. Find the x-coordinate of the intersection of the curve with the horizontal line $y = 1000$ to estimate the number of decades required for the population to reach 1000. Then solve $G(t) = 1000$ algebraically to obtain the exact value of t.

CHAPTER 5 SUMMARY

Key Terms and Symbols

5.1 a^{-n} negative exponent
$a^{1/n}$ nth root of a
$\sqrt[n]{a}$ nth root of a
radical
radicand
index

5.2 exponential function
exponential growth and decay
exponential equation

5.3 the number $e \approx 2.71828\ldots$
exponential growth function
learning curve
forgetting curve

5.4 $\log x$ common logarithm (base 10 logarithm) of x
$\ln x$ natural logarithm (base e logarithm) of x
$\log_a x$ base a logarithm of x
logarithmic equation
logarithmic function
inverses

5.5 half-life
Richter scale

Key Concepts

Rules for Exponents

Let a, b, r, and s be any real numbers for which the following exist.

$$a^{-r} = \frac{1}{a^r} \qquad a^0 = 1 \qquad \left(\frac{a}{b}\right)^r = \frac{a^r}{b^r}$$

$$a^r \cdot a^s = a^{r+s} \qquad (a^r)^s = a^{rs} \qquad a^{1/r} = \sqrt[r]{a}$$

$$\frac{a^r}{a^s} = a^{r-s} \qquad (ab)^r = a^r b^r \qquad \left(\frac{a}{b}\right)^{-r} = \left(\frac{b}{a}\right)^r$$

Rules for Radicals

Let a and b be real numbers, n be a positive integer, and m be any integer for which the following exist.

$a^{m/n} = \sqrt[n]{a^m} = (\sqrt[n]{a})^m$ $\quad \sqrt[n]{a^n} = |a|$ if n is even $\quad \sqrt[n]{a^n} = a$ if n is odd

$\sqrt[n]{a} \cdot \sqrt[n]{b} = \sqrt[n]{ab}$ $\quad \dfrac{\sqrt[n]{a}}{\sqrt[n]{b}} = \sqrt[n]{\dfrac{a}{b}} \quad (b \neq 0)$

An important application of exponents is the **exponential growth function,** defined as $f(t) = y_0e^{kt}$, where y_0 is the amount of a quantity present at time $t = 0$, $e \approx 2.71828$, and k is a constant.

The **logarithm** of x to the base a is defined as follows. For $a > 0$ and $a \neq 1$, $y = \log_a x$ means $a^y = x$. Thus, $\log_a x$ is an *exponent,* the power to which a must be raised to produce x.

Properties of Logarithms

Let x, y, and a be positive real numbers, $a \neq 1$, and let r be any real number.

$\log_a xy = \log_a x + \log_a y \qquad \log_a \dfrac{x}{y} = \log_a x - \log_a y$

$\log_a x^r = r \log_a x \qquad \log_a 1 = 0$

$\log_a a = 1 \qquad a^{\log_a x} = x$

$\log_a a^r = r$

Solving Exponential and Logarithmic Equations

Let $a > 0$, $a \neq 1$.

If $a^x = a^y$, then $x = y$ and if $x = y$, then $a^x = a^y$.

If $x = y$, then $\log_a x = \log_a y$, $\quad x > 0, y > 0$.

If $\log_a x = \log_a y$, then $x = y$, $\quad x > 0, y > 0$.

Chapter 5 Review Exercises

Simplify each expression. Assume all variables represent positive real numbers.

1. $\dfrac{5^{1/3} \cdot 5^{1/2}}{5^{-3/2}}$ **2.** $\dfrac{2^{3/4} \cdot 2^{-1/2}}{2^{1/4}}$

3. $(4p)^{2/3} \cdot (2p^3)^{3/2}$ **4.** $\sqrt[4]{64a^5b^3}$

5. $\sqrt{\dfrac{5n^2}{6m}}$ **6.** $\sqrt{\dfrac{3x^3}{2z}}$

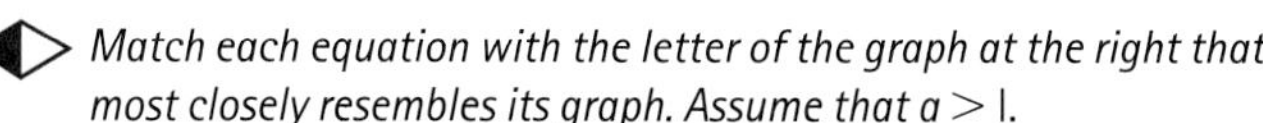
Match each equation with the letter of the graph at the right that most closely resembles its graph. Assume that $a > 1$.

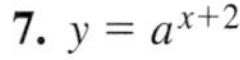
7. $y = a^{x+2}$ **8.** $y = a^x + 2$

9. $y = -a^x + 2$ **10.** $y = a^{-x} + 2$

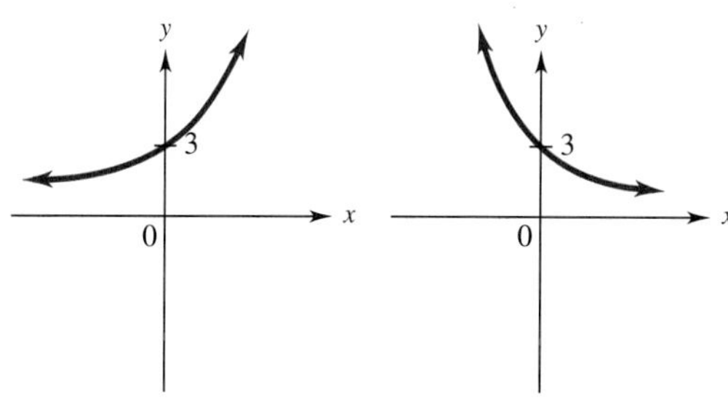

Solve each equation.

11. $2^{3x} = \dfrac{1}{8}$ **12.** $9^{2y-1} = 27^y$

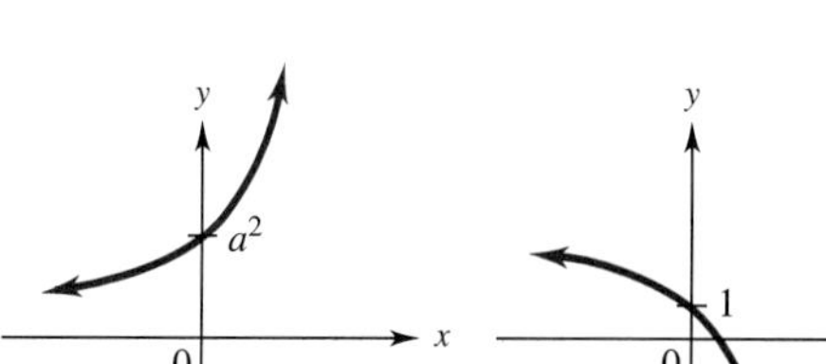
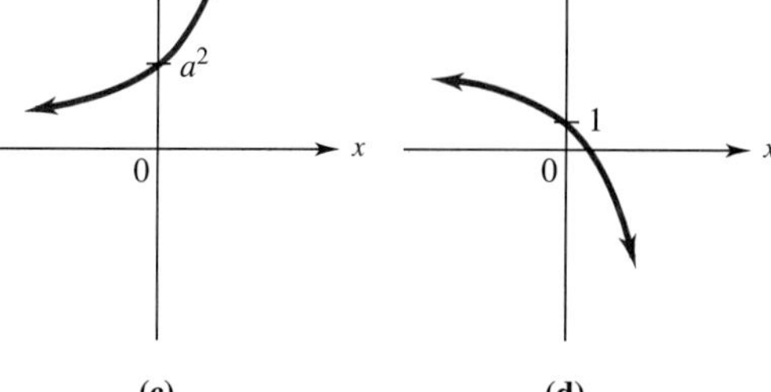

Graph each function.

13. $f(x) = 4^x$ **14.** $g(x) = 4^{-x}$

15. $f(x) = \ln x + 5$ **16.** $g(x) = \log x - 3$

Work these problems.

17. Management A person learning certain skills involving repetition tends to learn quickly at first. Then learning tapers off and approaches some upper limit. Suppose the number of symbols per minute a textbook typesetter can produce is given by $p(t) = 250 - 120(2.8)^{-.5t}$, where t is the number of months the typesetter has been in training. Find each of the following:
(a) $p(2)$ **(b)** $p(4)$ **(c)** $p(10)$.
(d) Graph $y = p(t)$ in the window with $0 \le x \le 10$ and $0 \le y \le 300$ and support the answer of part (a).

18. Natural Science The growth of atmospheric carbon dioxide is modeled by the exponential function $y = 353e^{.00609t}$, where t is the number of years since 1990.* Use this model to estimate the year when the levels of carbon dioxide in the air will be 2.5 times the preindustrial level of 280 ppm, assuming no changes are made.

Translate each exponential statement into an equivalent logarithmic one.

19. $10^{1.6721} = 47$ **20.** $5^4 = 625$

21. $e^{3.6636} = 39$ **22.** $5^{1/2} = \sqrt{5}$

Translate each logarithmic statement into an equivalent exponential one.

23. $\log 1000 = 3$ **24.** $\log 16.6 = 1.2201$

25. $\ln 95.4 = 4.5581$ **26.** $\log_2 64 = 6$

Evaluate each expression without using a calculator.

27. $\ln e^3$ **28.** $\log \sqrt{10}$ **29.** $10^{\log 7.4}$

30. $\ln e^{4k}$ **31.** $\log_8 16$ **32.** $\log_{25} 5$

Write each expression as a single logarithm. Assume all variables represent positive quantities.

33. $\log 4k + \log 5k^3$ **34.** $4 \log x - 2 \log x^3$

35. $2 \log b - 3 \log c$ **36.** $4 \ln x - 2(\ln x^3 + 4 \ln x)$

Solve each equation. Round to the nearest thousandth.

37. $8^p = 19$ **38.** $3^z = 11$

39. $5 \cdot 2^{-m} = 35$ **40.** $2 \cdot 15^{-k} = 18$

41. $e^{-5-2x} = 5$ **42.** $e^{3x-1} = 12$

43. $6^{2-m} = 2^{3m+1}$ **44.** $5^{3r-1} = 6^{2r+5}$

45. $(1 + .003)^k = 1.089$ **46.** $(1 + .094)^z = 2.387$

47. $\log(m + 2) = 1$ **48.** $\log x^2 = 2$

49. $\log_2(3k - 2) = 4$ **50.** $\log_5\left(\frac{5z}{z - 2}\right) = 2$

51. $\log x + \log(x + 3) = 1$ **52.** $\log_2 r + \log_2(r - 2) = 3$

53. $\ln(m + 3) - \ln m = \ln 2$

54. $2 \ln(y + 1) = \ln(y^2 - 1) + \ln 5$

Work these problems.

55. Management Suppose the gross national product (GNP) of a small country (in millions of dollars) is approximated by $G(t) = 15 + 2 \log t$ where t is time in years, for $1 \le t \le 6$. Find the GNP at the following times.
(a) 1 year **(b)** 2 years **(c)** 5 years

56. Natural Science A population is increasing according to the growth law $y = 2e^{.02t}$, where y is in millions and t is in years. Match each of the questions (a), (b), (c), and (d) with one of the solutions (A), (B), (C), or (D).

(a) How long will it take for the population to triple?	**(A)** Evaluate $2e^{.02(1/3)}$.
(b) When will the population reach 3 million?	**(B)** Solve $2e^{.02t} = 3 \cdot 2$ for t.
(c) How large will the population be in 3 years?	**(C)** Evaluate $2e^{.02(3)}$.
(d) How large will the population be in 4 months?	**(D)** Solve $2e^{.02t} = 3$ for t.

57. Natural Science The amount of polonium (in grams) present after t days is given by

$$A(t) = 10e^{-.00495t}.$$

(a) How much polonium was present initially?
(b) What is the half-life of polonium?
(c) How long will it take for the polonium to decay to 3 grams?

58. Natural Science One earthquake measures 4.6 on the Richter scale. A second earthquake has ground motion 1000 times greater than the first. What does the second one measure on the Richter scale?

Natural Science *Newton's Law of Cooling says that the rate at which a body cools is proportional to the difference in temperature between the body and an environment into which it is introduced. Using calculus, the temperature $F(t)$ of the body at time t after being introduced into an environment having constant temperature T_0 is*

$$F(t) = T_0 + Ce^{-kt},$$

where C and k are constants. Use this result in Exercises 59–61.

59. A piece of metal is heated to 300°C and then placed in a cooling liquid at 50°C. After 4 minutes the metal has cooled to 175°C. Find its temperature after 12 minutes.

60. Boiling water, at 100°C, is placed in a freezer at 0°C. The temperature of the water is 50°C after 24 minutes. Find the temperature of the water after 96 minutes.

61. Christine O'Brien refuses to drink coffee cooler than 95°F. She makes coffee with a temperature of 170°F in a room with a temperature of 70°F. The coffee cools to 120°F in 10 minutes. What is the longest time she can let the coffee sit before she drinks it?

*International Panel on Climate Change (IPCC) 1990.

CASE 5

Characteristics of the Monkeyface Prickleback*

The monkeyface prickleback (*Cebidichthys violaceus*), known to anglers as the monkeyface "eel," is found in rocky intertidal and subtidal habitats ranging from San Quintin Bay, Baja California, to Brookings, Oregon. Pricklebacks are prime targets of the few sports anglers who "poke pole" in the rocky intertidal zone at low tide. Little is known about the life history of this species. The results of a study of the length, weight, and age of this species is discussed in this case.

Data on standard length (*SL*) and total length (*TL*) were collected. Early in the study only *TL* was measured, so a conversion to *SL* was necessary. The equation relating the two lengths, calculated from 177 observations for which both lengths had been measured, is

$$SL = TL(.931) + 1.416.$$

Ages (determined by standard aging techniques) were used to estimate parameters of the von Bertanfany growth model

$$L_t = L_x(1 - e^{-kt}) \qquad (1)$$

where

L_t = length at age t,
L_x = asymptotic age of the species,
k = growth completion rate, and
t_0 = theoretical age at zero length.

The constants a and b in the model

$$W = aL^b \qquad (2)$$

where

W = weight in g,
L = standard length in cm,

were determined using 139 fish ranging from 27 cm and 145 g to 60 cm and 195 g.

Growth curves giving length as a function of age are shown in Figure 1. For the data marked opercle, the lengths were computed from the ages using Equation (1).

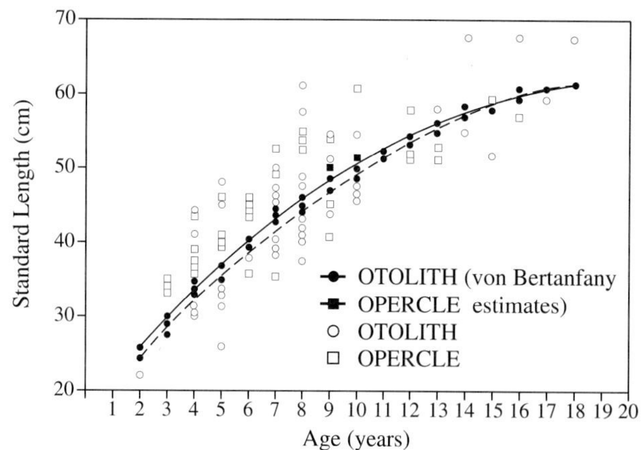

FIGURE 1

Estimated length from Equation (1) at a given age was larger for males than females after age eight. See the table. Weight/length relationships found with Equation (2) are shown in Figure 2 on the next page, along with data from other studies.

Structure/ Sex	*Age (yr)*	*Length (cm)*	L_x	k	t_0	n
Otolith						
Est.	2–18	23–67	72	.10	−1.89	91
S.D.			8	.03	1.08	
Opercle						
Est.	2–18	23–67	71	.10	−2.63	91
S.D.			8	.04	1.31	
Opercle-Females						
Est.	0–18	15–62	62	.14	−1.95	115
S.D.			2	.02	.28	
Opercle-Males						
Est.	0–18	13–67	70	.12	−1.91	74
S.D.			5	.02	.29	

**Characteristics of the Monkeyface Prickleback,* by William H. Marshall and Tina Wyllie Echeverria as appeared in *California Fish & Game,* Vol. 78, Spring 1992, Number 2.

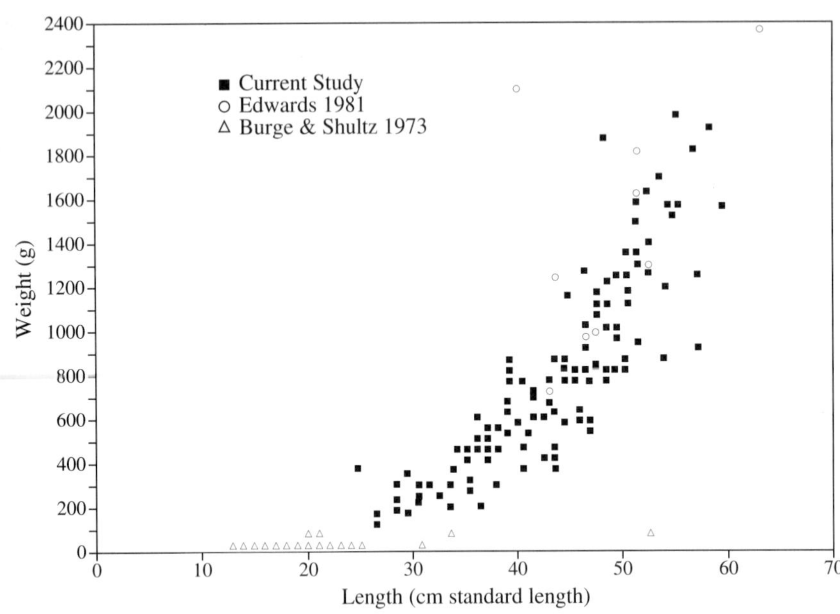

FIGURE 2

EXERCISES

1. Use Equation (1) to estimate the lengths of ages 4, 11, and 17. Let $L_x = 71.5$ and $k = .1$. Compare your answers with the results in Figure 1. What do you find?
2. Use Equation (2) with $a = .01289$ and $b = 2.9$ to estimate the weights for lengths of 25 cm, 40 cm, and 60 cm. Compare with the results in Figure 2. Are your answers reasonable compared to the curve?

CHAPTER 6

Mathematics of Finance

Whether you are in a position to invest money or to borrow money, it is important for both business managers and consumers to understand *interest.* The formulas for interest are developed in this chapter.

6.1 SIMPLE INTEREST AND DISCOUNT

Interest is the fee paid for the use of someone else's money. For example, you might pay interest to a bank for money you borrow or the bank might pay you interest on the money in your savings account. The amount of money that is borrowed or deposited is called the **principal.** The fee paid as interest depends on the interest **rate** and the length of **time** for which you have the use of the money. Unless stated otherwise, the time, t, is measured in years and the interest rate, r, is in percent per year, expressed as a decimal; for instance, 8% = .08 or 9.5% = .095.

There are two common ways of computing interest, the first of which we study in this section. **Simple interest** is interest paid only on the amount deposited and not on past interest.

> The **simple interest,** I, on an amount of P dollars at a rate of interest r per year for t years is
>
> $$I = Prt.$$

(Interest is rounded to the nearest cent, as is customary in financial problems.)

1 Find the simple interest for the following.

(a) $1000 at 8% for 2 years

(b) $5500 at 10.5% for $1\frac{1}{2}$ years

Answers:

(a) $160

(b) $866.25

EXAMPLE 1 To buy furniture for a new apartment, Sylvia Chang borrowed $5000 at 11% simple interest for 11 months. How much interest will she pay?

From the formula, $I = Prt$, with $P = 5000$, $r = .11$, and $t = 11/12$ (in years). The total interest she will pay is

$$I = 5000(.11)(11/12) = 504.17,$$

or $504.17. ■ 1

A deposit of P dollars today at a rate of interest r for t years produces interest of $I = Prt$. The interest, added to the original principal P, gives

$$P + Prt = P(1 + rt).$$

This amount is called the **future value** of P dollars at an interest rate r for time t in years. When loans are involved, the future value is often called the **maturity value** of the loan. This idea is summarized as follows.

> The **future value** or **maturity value,** A, of P dollars for t years all at a rate of interest r per year is
>
> $$\mathbf{A = P(1 + rt).}$$

EXAMPLE 2 Find the maturity value for each of the following loans at simple interest.

(a) A loan of \$2500 to be repaid in 9 months with interest at 12.1%
The loan is for 9 months, or $9/12 = .75$ of a year. The maturity value is

$$\begin{aligned} A &= P(1 + rt) \\ A &= 2500[1 + .121(.75)] \\ &\approx 2500(1.09075) = 2726.875, \end{aligned}$$

or \$2726.88. Because the maturity value is the sum of principal and interest, the interest paid on this loan is

$$\$2726.88 - \$2500 = \$226.88.$$

(b) A loan of \$11,280 for 85 days at 11% interest
It is common to assume 360 days in a year when working with simple interest. We shall usually make such an assumption in this book. The maturity value in this example is

$$A = 11{,}280\left[1 + .11\left(\frac{85}{360}\right)\right] \approx 11{,}280[1.0259722] \approx 11{,}572.97,$$

or \$11,572.97. ■ 2

2 Find the maturity value of each loan.

(a) \$10,000 at 10% for 6 months

(b) \$8970 at 11% for 9 months

(c) \$95,106 at 9.8% for 76 days

Answers:

(a) \$10,500

(b) \$9710.03

(c) \$97,073.64

TECHNOLOGY TIP The table feature of a graphing calculator makes it easy to compare the effect on the future value of a loan of a small difference in the interest rate. The screen in Figure 6.1 shows the portion of a year in the X column, and the future value of the loan in Example 2(a) with interest rates of 12.1% in the Y_1 column and 11.6% in the Y_2 column. From the table we see that when X = .75 the future value is \$9.40 less at 11.6% than at 12.1%. ✔

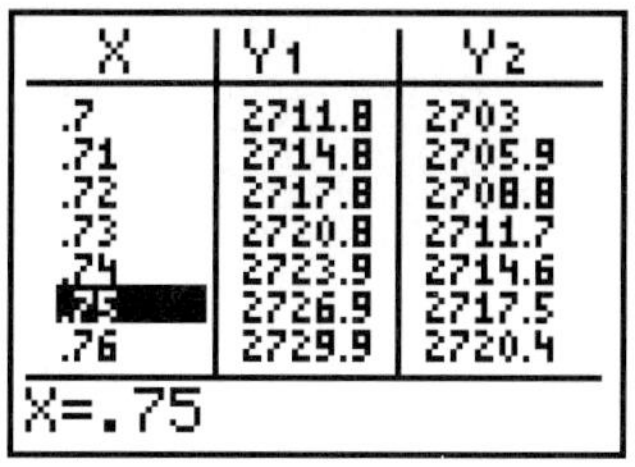

X	Y_1	Y_2
.7	2711.8	2703
.71	2714.8	2705.9
.72	2717.8	2708.8
.73	2720.8	2711.7
.74	2723.9	2714.6
.75	2726.9	2717.5
.76	2729.9	2720.4

X=.75

FIGURE 6.1

PRESENT VALUE A sum of money that can be deposited today to yield some larger amount in the future is called the **present value** of that future amount. Present value refers to the principal to be invested or loaned, so we use the same variable P as we did for principal. In interest problems, P always represents the amount at the beginning of the time period, and A always represents the amount at the end of the time period. To find a formula for P, we begin with the future value formula

$$A = P(1 + rt).$$

Dividing each side by $1 + rt$ gives the following formula for present value.

$$P = \frac{A}{1 + rt}$$

> The **present value** P of a future amount of A dollars at a simple interest rate r for t years is
>
> $$\mathbf{P = \frac{A}{1 + rt}}.$$

3 Find the present value of the following future amounts. Assume 12% interest.

(a) \$7500 in 1 year

(b) \$89,000 in 5 months

(c) \$164,200 in 125 days

Answers:

(a) \$6696.43

(b) \$84,761.90

(c) \$157,632.00

EXAMPLE 3 Find the present value of \$32,000 in 4 months at 9% interest.

$$P = \frac{32{,}000}{1 + (.09)\left(\frac{4}{12}\right)} = \frac{32{,}000}{1.03} = 31{,}067.96$$

A deposit of \$31,067.96 today, at 9% interest, would produce \$32,000 in 4 months. These two sums, \$31,067.96 today and \$32,000.00 in 4 months, are equivalent (at 9%) because the first amount becomes the second amount in 4 months. ■ 3

4 Jerrell Davis is owed \$19,500 by Christine O'Brien. The money will be paid in 11 months, with no interest. If the current interest rate is 10%, how much should Davis be willing to accept today in settlement of the debt?

Answer:
\$17,862.60

EXAMPLE 4 Because of a court settlement, Charlie Dawkins owes \$5000 to Joshua Parker. The money must be paid in 10 months, with no interest. Suppose Dawkins wishes to pay the money today. What amount should Parker be willing to accept? Assume an interest rate of 5%.

The amount that Parker should be willing to accept is given by the present value:

$$P = \frac{5000}{1 + (.05)\left(\frac{10}{12}\right)} = 4800.00.$$

Parker should be willing to accept \$4800.00 today in settlement of the obligation. ■ 4

EXAMPLE 5 Suppose you borrow \$40,000 today and are required to pay \$41,400 in 4 months to pay off the loan and interest. What is the simple interest rate?

We can use the future value formula, with $P = 40{,}000$, $A = 41{,}400$, and $t = 4/12 = 1/3$, and solve for r.

$$A = P(1 + rt)$$

$$41{,}400 = 40{,}000\left(1 + r \cdot \frac{1}{3}\right)$$

$$41{,}400 = 40{,}000 + \frac{40{,}000r}{3}$$

$$1400 = \frac{40{,}000r}{3}$$

$$40{,}000r = 3 \cdot 1400 = 4200$$

$$r = \frac{4200}{40{,}000} = .105$$

Therefore, the interest rate is 10.5%. ■

SIMPLE DISCOUNT NOTES The loans discussed up to this point are called **simple interest notes,** where interest on the face value of the loan is added to the loan and paid at maturity. Another common type of note, called a **simple discount note,** has the interest deducted in advance from the amount of a loan before giving the *balance* to the borrower. The *full* value of the note must be paid at maturity. The money that is deducted is called the **bank discount** or just the **discount,** and the money actually received by the borrower is called the **proceeds.**

For example, consider a loan of \$3000 at 6% interest for 9 months. We can compare the two types of loan arrangements as follows.

	Simple Interest Note	*Bank Discount Note*
Interest on the note	3000(.06)(9/12) = \$135	3000(.06)(9/12) = \$135
Borrower receives	**\$3000**	\$2865
Borrower pays back	\$3135	**\$3000**

EXAMPLE 6 Theresa DePalo needs a loan from her bank and agrees to pay \$8500 to her banker in 9 months. The banker subtracts a discount of 12% and gives the balance to DePalo. Find the amount of the discount and the proceeds.

As shown above, the discount is found in the same way that simple interest is found, except that it is based on the amount to be repaid.

$$\textbf{Discount} = 8500(.12)\left(\frac{9}{12}\right) = \mathbf{765.00}$$

The proceeds are found by subtracting the discount from the original amount.

$$\textbf{Proceeds} = \$8500 - \$765.00 = \mathbf{\$7735.00}$$ ■ 5

5 Kelly Bell signs an agreement at her bank to pay the bank \$25,000 in 5 months. The bank charges a 13% discount rate. Find the amount of the discount and the amount Bell actually receives.

Answer:
\$1354.17; \$23,645.83

In Example 6, the borrower was charged a discount of 12%. However, 12% is *not* the interest rate paid, since 12% applies to the \$8500, while the borrower actually received only \$7735. In the next example, we find the rate of interest actually paid by the borrower.

EXAMPLE 7 Find the actual rate of interest paid by DePalo in Example 6.

Use the formula for simple interest, $I = Prt$, with r the unknown. Since the borrower received only \$7735 and must repay \$8500, $I = 8500 - 7735 = 765$. Here, $P = 7735$ and $t = 9/12 = .75$. Substitute these values into $I = Prt$.

$$I = Prt$$
$$765 = 7735(r)(.75)$$
$$\frac{765}{7735(.75)} = r$$
$$.132 \approx r$$

The actual interest rate paid by the borrower is about 13.2%. ■ 6

6 Refer to Problem 5 and find the actual rate of interest paid by Bell.

Answer:
13.7% (to the nearest tenth)

Let D represent the amount of discount on a loan. Then $D = Art$, where A is the maturity value of the loan (the amount borrowed plus interest), and r is the stated rate of interest. The amount actually received, the proceeds, can be written as $P = A - D$, or $P = A - Art = A(1 - rt)$.

The formulas for discount are summarized below.

DISCOUNT

If D is the discount on a loan having a maturity value A at a rate of interest r for t years, and if P represents the proceeds, then

$$P = A - D \quad \text{or} \quad P = A(1 - rt).$$

EXAMPLE 8 John Young owes \$4250 to Meg Holden. The loan is payable in 1 year at 10% interest. Holden needs cash to buy a new car, so 3 months before the loan is payable she goes to the bank to have the loan discounted. That is, she sells the loan (note) to the bank. The bank charges an 11% discount fee. Find the amount of cash she will receive from the bank.

First find the maturity value of the loan, the amount (with interest) Young must pay Holden. By the formula for maturity value,

$$A = P(1 + rt)$$
$$= 4250[1 + (.10)(1)]$$
$$= 4250(1.10) = 4675$$

or \$4675.00.

The bank applies its discount rate to this total:

$$\text{Amount of discount} = 4675(.11)(3/12) \approx 128.56.$$

(Remember that the loan was discounted 3 months before it was due.) Holden actually receives

$$\$4675 - \$128.56 = \$4546.44$$

in cash from the bank. Three months later, the bank will get \$4675.00 from Young. ■ 7

7 A firm accepts a \$21,000 note due in 7 months with interest of 10.5%. Suppose the firm discounts the note at a bank 75 days before it is due. Find the amount the firm would receive if the bank charges a 12.4% discount rate. (Use 360 days in a year.)

Answer:
\$21,710.52

6.1 EXERCISES

1. What factors determine the amount of interest earned on a fixed principal?

Find the simple interest in Exercises 2–5. (See Example 1.)

2. \$25,000 at 7% for 9 mo
3. \$3850 at 9% for 8 mo
4. \$1974 at 6.3% for 7 mo
5. \$3724 at 8.4% for 11 mo

Find the simple interest. Assume a 360-day year and a 30-day month.

6. \$5147.18 at 10.1% for 58 days
7. \$2930.42 at 11.9% for 123 days
8. \$7980 at 10%; loan made on May 7 and due September 19
9. \$5408 at 12%; loan made on August 16 and due December 30

Find the simple interest. Assume 365 days in a year, and use the exact number of days in a month. (Assume 28 days in February.)

10. \$7800 at 11%; made on July 7 and due October 25
11. \$11,000 at 10%; made on February 19 and due May 31
12. \$2579 at 9.6%; made on October 4 and due March 15
13. \$37,098 at 11.2%; made on September 12 and due July 30
14. In your own words, describe the *maturity value* of a loan.
15. What is meant by the *present value* of money?

Find the present value of each of the future amounts in Exercises 16–19. Assume 360 days in a year. (See Example 3.)

16. \$15,000 for 8 mo; money earns 6%
17. \$48,000 for 9 mo; money earns 5%
18. \$15,402 for 125 days; money earns 6.3%
19. \$29,764 for 310 days; money earns 7.2%

Find the proceeds for the amounts in Exercises 20–23. Assume 360 days in a year. (See Example 6.)

20. \$7150; discount rate 12%; length of loan 11 mo
21. \$9450; discount rate 10%; length of loan 7 mo
22. \$35,800; discount rate 9.1%; length of loan 183 days
23. \$50,900; discount rate 8.2%; length of loan 238 days
24. Why is the discount rate charged on a simple discount note different from the actual interest rate paid on the proceeds?

Find the interest rate to the nearest tenth on the proceeds for the following simple discount notes. (See Example 7.)

25. \$6200; discount rate 10%; length of loan 8 mo
26. \$5000; discount rate 8.1%; length of loan 6 mo
27. \$58,000; discount rate 10.8%; length of loan 9 mo
28. \$43,000; discount rate 9%; length of loan 4 mo

Management *Work the following applied problems.*

29. Linda Davis borrowed \$25,900 from her father to start a flower shop. She repaid him after 11 mo, with interest of 8.4%. Find the total amount she repaid.
30. An accountant for a corporation forgot to pay the firm's income tax of \$725,896.15 on time. The government charged a penalty of 12.7% interest for the 34 days the money was late. Find the total amount (tax and penalty) that was paid. (Use a 365-day year.)
31. A \$100,000 certificate of deposit held for 60 days is worth \$101,133.33. To the nearest tenth of a percent, what interest rate was earned?
32. Tuition of \$1769 will be due when the spring term begins in 4 mo. What amount should a student deposit today, at 6.25%, to have enough to pay the tuition?
33. A firm of accountants has ordered 7 new computers at a cost of \$5104 each. The machines will not be delivered for 7 mo. What amount could the firm deposit in an account paying 6.42% to have enough to pay for the machines?
34. Sun Kang needs \$5196 to pay for remodeling work on his house. He plans to repay the loan in 10 mo. His bank loans money at a discount rate of 13%. Find the amount of his loan.

35. Joan McKee decides to go back to college. To get to school, she buys a small car for $6100. She decides to borrow the money from a bank that charges an 11.8% discount rate. If she will repay the loan in 7 months, find the amount of the loan.

36. John Matthews signs a $4200 note at the bank. The bank charges a 12.2% discount rate. Find the net proceeds if the note is for 10 mo. Find the actual interest rate (to the nearest hundredth) charged by the bank.

37. A stock that sold for $22 at the beginning of the year was selling for $24 at the end of the year. If the stock paid a dividend of $.50 per share, what is the simple interest rate on an investment in this stock? (*Hint:* Consider the interest to be the increase in value plus the dividend.)

38. A bond with a face value of $10,000 in 10 yr can be purchased now for $5988.02. What is the simple interest rate?

39. A building contractor gives a $13,500 note to a plumber. (The plumber loans $13,500 to the contractor.) The note is due in 9 mo, with interest of 9%. Three months after the note is signed, the plumber discounts it at the bank. The bank charges a 10.1% discount rate. How much will the plumber receive? Will it be enough to pay a bill for $13,582?

40. Maria Lopez owes $7000 to the Eastside Music Shop. She has agreed to pay the amount in 7 mo at an interest rate of 10%. Two months before the loan is due, the store needs $7350 to pay a wholesaler's bill. The bank will discount the note at a rate of 10.5%. How much will the store receive? Is it enough to pay the bill?

41. Fay, Inc., received a $30,000, six-month, 12% interest-bearing note from a customer.* The note was discounted the same day by Carr National Bank at 15%. The amount of cash received by Fay from the bank was

(a) $30,000 **(b)** $29,550
(c) $29,415 **(d)** $27,750.

*Uniform CPA Examination, May, 1989, American Institute of Certified Public Accountants.

6.2 COMPOUND INTEREST

Simple interest is normally used for loans or investments of a year or less. For longer periods *compound interest* is used. With **compound interest,** interest is charged (or paid) on interest as well as on principal. For example, if $1000 is deposited at 5% compounded annually, then the interest for the first year is $1000(.05) = $50, just as with simple interest, so that the account balance is $1050 at the end of the year. During the second year, interest is paid on the entire $1050 (not just on the original $1000 as with simple interest), so the amount in the account at the end of the second year is $1050 + $1050(.05) = $1102.50. This is more than simple interest would produce. 1

1 Use the formula

$$A = P(1 + rt)$$

to find the amount in the account after 2 years at 5% simple interest.

Answer:
$1100

To find a formula for compound interest, suppose that P dollars are deposited at interest rate r per year. The amount A on deposit after 1 year is found by the simple interest formula.

$$A = P[1 + r(1)] = P(1 + r)$$

If the deposit earns compound interest, the interest for the second year is paid on the total amount on deposit at the end of the first year, $P(1 + r)$. Using the formula $A = P(1 + rt)$ again, with $P = P(1 + r)$ and $t = 1$ gives the total amount on deposit at the end of the second year.

$$A = [P(1 + r)](1 + r \cdot 1) = P(1 + r)^2$$

In the same way, the total amount on deposit at the end of the third year is

$$P(1 + r)^3.$$

Continuing in this way, the total amount on deposit after t years is

$$A = P(1 + r)^t,$$

called the **compound amount.**

NOTE Compare this formula for compound interest with the formula for simple interest from the previous section.

Compound interest $A = P(1 + r)^t$

Simple interest $A = P(1 + rt)$

The important distinction between the two formulas is that in the compound interest formula, the number of years t is an *exponent,* so that money grows much more rapidly when interest is compounded. ◆

Figure 6.2 shows calculator-generated graphs of these two formulas with $P = 1000$ and $r = 10\%$ from 0 to 20 years. The future value after 15 years is shown for each graph. After 15 years at compound interest, \$1000 grows to \$4177.25, whereas with simple interest, it amounts to \$2500.00, a difference of \$1677.25.

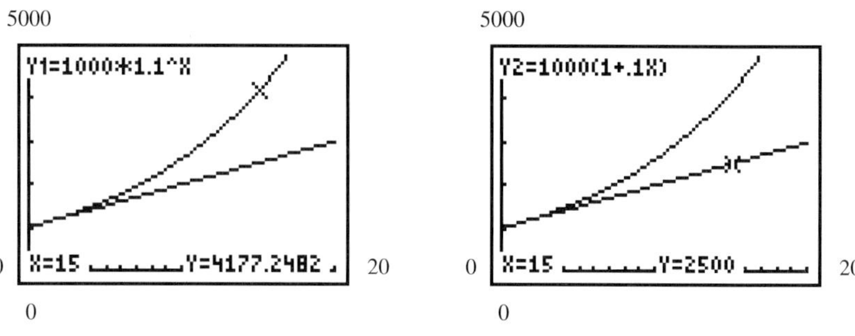

FIGURE 6.2

Interest can be compounded more than once a year. Common **compounding periods** include *semiannually* (two periods per year), *quarterly* (four periods per year), *monthly* (twelve periods), and *daily* (usually 365 periods per year). To find the *interest rate per period, i,* we *divide* the annual interest rate r by the number of compounding periods, m, per year. The total number of compounding periods, n, is found by *multiplying* the number of years t by the number of compounding periods per year, m. Then the general formula can be derived in much the same way as the formula given above.

COMPOUND INTEREST FORMULA

If P dollars are deposited for n compounding periods at a rate of interest i per period, the compound amount (or future value) A is

$$\boldsymbol{A = P(1 + i)^n}.$$

In particular, if the annual interest rate r is compounded m times per year and the number of years is t, then $i = r/m$ and $n = mt$.

EXAMPLE 1 Suppose \$1000 is deposited for 6 years in an account paying 8.31% per year compounded annually.

(a) Find the compound amount.

In the formula above, $P = 1000$, $i = .0831$, and $n = 6$. The compound amount is

$$A = P(1 + i)^n$$
$$A = 1000(1.0831)^6$$
$$A = \$1614.40.$$

2 Suppose $17,000 is deposited at 4% compounded semiannually for 11 years.

(a) Find the compound amount.

(b) Find the amount of interest earned.

Answers:

(a) $26,281.65

(b) $9281.65

3 Find the compound amount.

(a) $10,000 at 8% compounded quarterly for 7 years

(b) $36,000 at 6% compounded monthly for 2 years

Answers:

(a) $17,410.24

(b) $40,577.75

(b) Find the amount of interest earned.
Subtract the initial deposit from the compound amount.

$$\text{Amount of interest} = \$1614.40 - \$1000 = \$614.40$$ ■ 2

EXAMPLE 2 Find the amount of interest earned by a deposit of $2450 for 6.5 years at 5.25% compounded quarterly.

Interest compounded quarterly is compounded 4 times a year. In 6.5 years, there are 6.5(4) = 26 periods. Thus, $n = 26$. Interest of 5.25% per year is 5.25/4 per quarter, so $i = .0525/4$. Now use the formula for compound amount.

$$A = P(1 + i)^n$$
$$A = 2450(1 + .0525/4)^{26} = 3438.78$$

Rounded to the nearest cent, the compound amount is $3438.78, so the interest is $3438.78 − $2450 = $998.78. ■ 3

CAUTION As shown in Example 2, compound interest problems involve two rates—the nominal or stated annual rate r and the rate per compounding period i. Be sure you understand the distinction between them. When interest is compounded annually, these rates are the same. In all other cases, $i \neq r$. ◆

The more often interest is compounded within a given time period, the more interest will be earned. Surprisingly, however, there is a limit on the amount of interest, no matter how often it is compounded. To see this, suppose that $1 is invested at 100% interest per year, compounded n times per year. Then the interest rate (in decimal form) is 1.00 and the interest rate per period is $1/n$. According to the formula (with $P = 1$), the compound amount at the end of 1 year will be $A = \left(1 + \frac{1}{n}\right)^n$. A computer gives the following results for various values of n.

Interest Is Compounded	n	$\left(1 + \frac{1}{n}\right)^n$
Annually	1	$\left(1 + \frac{1}{1}\right)^1 = 2$
Semiannually	2	$\left(1 + \frac{1}{2}\right)^2 = 2.25$
Quarterly	4	$\left(1 + \frac{1}{4}\right)^4 \approx 2.4414$
Monthly	12	$\left(1 + \frac{1}{12}\right)^{12} \approx 2.6130$
Daily	365	$\left(1 + \frac{1}{365}\right)^{365} \approx 2.71457$
Hourly	8760	$\left(1 + \frac{1}{8760}\right)^{8760} \approx 2.718127$
Every minute	525,600	$\left(1 + \frac{1}{525{,}600}\right)^{525{,}600} \approx 2.7182792$
Every second	31,536,000	$\left(1 + \frac{1}{31{,}536{,}000}\right)^{31{,}536{,}000} \approx 2.7182818$

Because interest is rounded to the nearest penny, the compound amount never exceeds \$2.72, no matter how big n is.

NOTE Try computing the values in the table with your calculator. You may notice your answers do not agree exactly. This is because of round-off error. ◆

The table above suggests that as n takes larger and larger values, then the corresponding values of $\left(1 + \frac{1}{n}\right)^n$ get closer and closer to a specific real number, whose decimal expansion begins 2.71828. . . . This is indeed the case, as is shown in calculus, and the number 2.71828 . . . is denoted e.

The preceding example is typical of what happens when interest is compounded n times per year, with larger and larger values of n. It can be shown that no matter what interest rate or principal is used, there is always an upper limit on the compound amount, which is called the compound amount from **continuous compounding.**

CONTINUOUS COMPOUNDING

The compound amount A for a deposit of P dollars at interest rate r per year compounded continuously for t years is given by

$$A = Pe^{rt}.*$$

Many calculators have an e^x key for computing powers of e. See Chapter 5 for more details on using a calculator to evaluate e^x.

4 Find the compound amount, assuming continuous compounding.

(a) \$12,000 at 10% for 5 years

(b) \$22,867 at 7.2% for 9 years

Answers:

(a) \$19,784.66

(b) \$43,715.15

EXAMPLE 3 Suppose \$5000 is invested at an annual rate of 4% compounded continuously for 5 years. Find the compound amount.

In the formula for continuous compounding, let $P = 5000$, $r = .04$ and $t = 5$. Then a calculator with an e^x key shows that

$$A = 5000e^{(.04)5} = 5000e^{.2} = \$6107.01.$$

You can readily verify that daily compounding would have produced a compound amount about 6¢ less. ■ 4

EFFECTIVE RATE If \$1 is deposited at 4% compounded quarterly, a calculator can be used to find that at the end of one year, the compound amount is \$1.0406, an increase of 4.06% over the original \$1. The actual increase of 4.06% in the money is somewhat higher than the stated increase of 4%. To differentiate between these two numbers, 4% is called the **nominal** or **stated rate** of interest, while 4.06% is called the **effective rate.** To avoid confusion between stated rates and effective rates, we shall continue to use r for the stated rate and we will use r_e for the effective rate.

EXAMPLE 4 Find the effective rate corresponding to a stated rate of 6% compounded semiannually.

*Other applications of the exponential function $f(x) = e^x$ are discussed in Chapter 5.

5 Find the effective rate corresponding to a nominal rate of

(a) 12% compounded monthly;

(b) 8% compounded quarterly.

Answers:

(a) 12.68%

(b) 8.24%

A calculator shows that \$100 at 6% compounded semiannually will grow to

$$A = 100\left(1 + \frac{.06}{2}\right)^2 = 100(1.03)^2 = \$106.09.$$

Thus, the actual amount of compound interest is \$106.09 − \$100 = \$6.09. Now if you earn \$6.09 interest on \$100 in 1 year with annual compounding, your rate is 6.09/100 = .0609 = 6.09%. Thus, the effective rate is $r_e = 6.09\%$. ■ 5

In the preceding example we found the effective rate by dividing compound interest for 1 year by the original principal. The same thing can be done with any principal P and rate r compounded m times per year.

$$\text{Effective rate} = \frac{\text{compound interest}}{\text{principal}}$$

$$r_e = \frac{\text{compound amount} - \text{principal}}{\text{principal}}$$

$$= \frac{P\left(1 + \frac{r}{m}\right)^m - P}{P} = \frac{P\left[\left(1 + \frac{r}{m}\right)^m - 1\right]}{P}$$

$$r_e = \left(1 + \frac{r}{m}\right)^m - 1$$

The **effective rate** corresponding to a stated rate of interest r per year compounded m times per year is

$$r_e = \left(1 + \frac{r}{m}\right)^m - 1.\text{*}$$

Using the effective rate formula, a graphing calculator generated the table in Figure 6.3, in which the interest rate r is 10%, Y_1 denotes the effective rate, and X the number of compoundings.

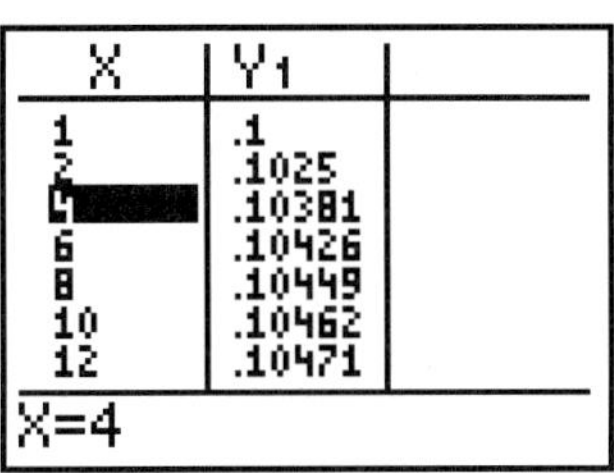

X	Y1
1	.1
2	.1025
4	.10381
6	.10426
8	.10449
10	.10462
12	.10471

X=4

FIGURE 6.3

*When applied to consumer finance, the effective rate is called the annual percentage rate, APR, or annual percentage yield, APY.

6 Find the effective rate corresponding to a nominal rate of

(a) 15% compounded monthly;

(b) 10% compounded quarterly.

Answers:

(a) 16.08%

(b) 10.38%

EXAMPLE 5 A bank pays interest of 4.9% compounded monthly. Find the effective rate.

Use the formula given above with $r = .049$ and $m = 12$. The effective rate is

$$r_e = \left(1 + \frac{.049}{12}\right)^{12} - 1$$

$$= 1.050115575 - 1 \approx .0501,$$

or 5.01%. ■ 6

EXAMPLE 6 Bank A is now lending money at 13.2% interest compounded annually. The rate at Bank B is 12.6% compounded monthly and the rate at Bank C is 12.7% compounded quarterly. If you need to borrow money, at which bank will you pay the least interest?

Compare the effective rates.

$$\text{Bank A:} \quad \left(1 + \frac{.132}{1}\right)^{1} - 1 = .132 = 13.2\%$$

$$\text{Bank B:} \quad \left(1 + \frac{.126}{12}\right)^{12} - 1 \approx .13354 = 13.354\%$$

$$\text{Bank C:} \quad \left(1 + \frac{.127}{4}\right)^{4} - 1 \approx .13318 = 13.318\%$$

The lowest effective interest rate is at Bank A, which has the highest nominal rate. ■

PRESENT VALUE WITH COMPOUND INTEREST The formula for compound interest, $A = P(1 + i)^n$, has four variables, A, P, i, and n. Given the values of any three of these variables, the value of the fourth can be found. In particular, if A (the future amount), i, and n are known, then P can be found. Here P is the amount that should be deposited today to produce A dollars in n periods.

EXAMPLE 7 Joan Ailanjian must pay a lump sum of \$6000 in 5 years. What amount deposited today at 6.2% compounded annually will amount to \$6000 in 5 years?

Here $A = 6000$, $i = .062$, $n = 5$, and P is unknown. Substituting these values into the formula for the compound amount gives

$$6000 = P(1.062)^5$$

$$P = \frac{6000}{(1.062)^5} = 4441.49,$$

or \$4441.49. If Ailanjian leaves \$4441.49 for 5 years in an account paying 6.2% compounded annually, she will have \$6000 when she needs it. To check your work, use the compound interest formula with $P = \$4441.49$, $i = .062$, and $n = 5$. You should get $A = \$6000.00$. ■ 7

7 Find P in Example 7 if the interest rate is

(a) 6%;

(b) 10%.

Answers:

(a) \$4483.55

(b) \$3725.53

As Example 7 shows, \$6000 in 5 years is the same as \$4441.49 today (if money can be deposited at 6.2% annual interest). An amount that can be deposited today to yield a given amount in the future is called the *present value* of the future amount.

Generalizing from Example 7, by solving $A = P(1 + i)^n$ for P, we get the following formula for present value.

> The **present value** of A dollars compounded at an interest rate i per period for n periods is
>
> $$\mathbf{P = \frac{A}{(1+i)^n} \quad \text{or} \quad P = A(1+i)^{-n}.}$$

Compare this with the present value of an amount at simple interest r for t years, given in the previous section:

$$P = \frac{A}{1 + rt}.$$

NOTE This is just the compound interest formula solved for P. It is not necessary to remember a new formula for present value. You can use the compound interest formula, if you understand what each of the variables represents. ◆

EXAMPLE 8 Find the present value of \$16,000 in 9 years if money can be deposited at 6% compounded semiannually.

In 9 years there are $2 \cdot 9 = 18$ semiannual periods. A rate of 6% per year is 3% in each semiannual period. Apply the formula with $A = 16{,}000$, $i = .03$, and $n = 18$.

$$P = \frac{A}{(1+i)^n} = \frac{16{,}000}{(1+.03)^{18}} \approx \frac{16{,}000}{1.702433} \approx 9398.31$$

A deposit of \$9398.31 today, at 6% compounded semiannually, will produce a total of \$16,000 in 9 years. ■ 8

8 Find the present value in Example 8 if money is deposited at 10% compounded semiannually.

Answer:
\$6648.33

The formula for compound amount also can be solved for n.

EXAMPLE 9 Suppose the general level of inflation in the economy averages 8% per year. Find the number of years it would take for the overall level of prices to double.

To find the number of years it will take for \$1 worth of goods or services to cost \$2, we must solve for n in the equation

$$2 = 1(1 + .08)^n,$$

where $A = 2$, $P = 1$, and $i = .08$. This equation simplifies to

$$2 = (1.08)^n.$$

To solve for n, we will use base 10 logarithms as in Chapter 5.

$$\log 2 = \log (1.08)^n \qquad \text{Take the logarithm of each side.}$$

$$\log 2 = n \log 1.08 \qquad \text{Property (c) of logarithms}$$

$$n = \frac{\log 2}{\log 1.08} \qquad \text{Divide both sides by log 1.08.}$$

$$n \approx 9.01$$

To check, use a calculator to get $1.08^{9.01} = 2.00$ to the nearest hundredth. ■ 9

9 Using a calculator, find the number of years it will take for \$500 to increase to \$750 in an account paying 6% interest compounded semiannually.

Answer:
About 7 years

When interest is compounded continuously, the present value can be found by solving the continuous compounding formula $A = Pe^{rt}$ for P.

EXAMPLE 10 How much must be deposited today in an account paying 7.5% interest compounded continuously in order to have $10,000 in 4 years?

Here the future value is $A = 10{,}000$, the interest rate is $r = .075$, and the number of years is $t = 4$. The present value P is found as follows.

$$A = Pe^{rt}$$

$$10{,}000 = Pe^{(.075)4}$$

$$10{,}000 = Pe^{.3}$$

$$P = \frac{10{,}000}{e^{.3}} \approx \$7408.18 \quad \blacksquare$$

At this point, it seems helpful to summarize the notation and the most important formulas for simple and compound interest. We use the following variables.

P = principal or present value

A = future or maturity value

r = annual (stated or nominal) interest rate

t = number of years

m = number of compounding periods per year

i = interest rate per period ($i = r/m$)

r_e = effective rate

n = total number of compounding periods ($n = tm$)

Simple Interest	*Compound Interest*	*Continuous Compounding*
$A = P(1 + rt)$	$A = P(1 + i)^n$	$A = Pe^{rt}$
$P = \dfrac{A}{1 + rt}$	$P = \dfrac{A}{(1 + i)^n} = A(1 + i)^{-n}$	$P = \dfrac{A}{e^{rt}}$
	$r_e = \left(1 + \dfrac{r}{m}\right)^m - 1$	

6.2 EXERCISES

1. Explain the difference between simple interest and compound interest.
2. In the compound interest formula, how do r and i differ? How do t and n differ?

Find the compound amount for each of the following deposits. (See Examples 1–2.)

3. $1000 at 6% compounded annually for 8 yr
4. $1000 at 7% compounded annually for 10 yr
5. $470 at 10% compounded semiannually for 12 yr
6. $15,000 at 6% compounded semiannually for 11 yr
7. $6500 at 12% compounded quarterly for 6 yr
8. $9100 at 8% compounded quarterly for 4 yr

Find the amount of interest earned by each of the following deposits. (See Examples 1–2.)

9. $26,000 at 7% compounded annually for 5 years
10. $32,000 at 5% compounded annually for 10 years
11. $8000 at 4% compounded semiannually for 6.4 years
12. $2500 at 4.5% compounded semiannually for 8 years
13. $5124.98 at 6.3% compounded quarterly for 5.2 years
14. $27,630.35 at 7.1% compounded quarterly for 3.7 years

Find the compound amount if \$25,000 is invested at 6% compounded continuously for the following number of years. (See Example 3.)

15. 1 **16.** 5

17. 10 **18.** 15

19. In Figure 6.2, one graph is a straight line and the other is curved. Explain why this is so, and which represents each type of interest (simple or compound).

20. How do the nominal or stated interest rate and the effective interest rate differ?

Find the effective rate corresponding to the following nominal rates. (See Examples 4–6.)

21. 4% compounded semiannually

22. 8% compounded quarterly

23. 8% compounded semiannually

24. 10% compounded semiannually

25. 12% compounded semiannually

26. 12% compounded quarterly

Find the present value of the following future amounts. (See Examples 7 and 8.)

27. \$12,000 at 5% compounded annually for 6 years

28. \$8500 at 6% compounded annually for 9 years

29. \$4253.91 at 6.8% compounded semiannually for 4 years

30. \$27,692.53 at 4.6% compounded semiannually for 5 years

31. \$17,230 at 4% compounded quarterly for 10 years

32. \$5240 at 8% compounded quarterly for 8 years

33. If money can be invested at 8% compounded quarterly, which is larger: \$1000 now or \$1210 in 5 years? Use present value to decide.

34. If money can be invested at 6% compounded annually, which is larger: \$10,000 now or \$15,000 in 10 years? Use present value to decide.

Find the present value of \$17,200 for the following number of years, if money can be deposited at 11.4% compounded continuously.

35. 2 **36.** 4

37. 7 **38.** 10

Under certain conditions, Swiss banks pay negative interest—they charge you. (You didn't think all that secrecy was free?) Suppose a bank "pays" −2.4% interest compounded annually. Use a calculator and find the compound amount for a deposit of \$150,000 after the following.

39. 2 years **40.** 4 years

41. 8 years **42.** 12 years

Management *Work the following applied problems.*

43. A New York bank offered the following special on C.D. (certificate of deposit) rates. The rates are annual percentage yield, or effective rates, which are higher than the corresponding nominal rates. Assume quarterly compounding. Solve for r to approximate the corresponding nominal rates to the nearest hundredth.

Term	6 mo	1 yr	18 mo	2 yr	3 yr
APY (%)	5.00	5.30	5.45	5.68	5.75

44. The pie graph shows the percent of baby boomers ages 46 to 49 who said they had investments with a total value as shown in each category.* Note that 30% say they have saved less than \$10,000 and 28% don't know or gave no answer. Assume the money is invested at an average rate of 8% compounded quarterly for 20 years, when this age group will be ready for retirement. Find the range of amounts each group (except the "don't know or no answer" group) in the graph will have saved for retirement if no more is added.

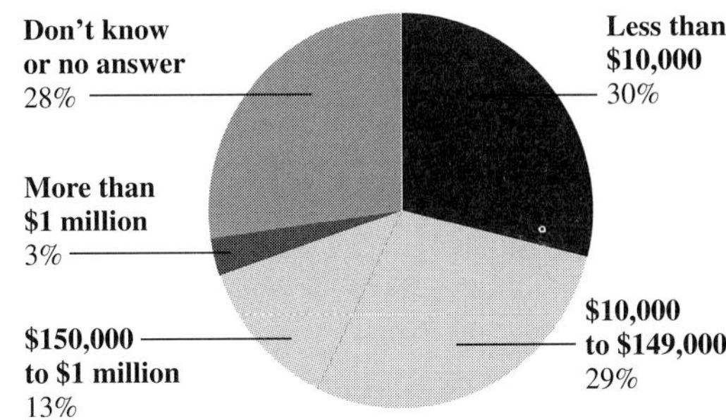

Note: Figures add to more than 100% because of rounding.

Sources: Census Bureau (age distribution); Merrill Lynch Baby Boom Retirement Index (investments); William M. Mercer Inc. (life expectancy).

45. When Lindsay Branson was born, her grandfather made an initial deposit of \$3000 in an account for her college education. Assuming an interest rate of 6% compounded quarterly, how much will the account be worth in 18 yr?

46. Frank Capek has \$10,000 in an Individual Retirement Account (IRA). Because of new tax laws, he decides to make no further deposits. The account earns 6% interest compounded semiannually. Find the amount on deposit in 15 yr.

47. A small business borrows \$50,000 for expansion at 12% compounded monthly. The loan is due in 4 yr. How much interest will the business pay?

48. A developer needs \$80,000 to buy land. He is able to borrow the money at 10% per year compounded quarterly. How much will the interest amount to if he pays off the loan in 5 yr?

49. A company has agreed to pay \$2.9 million in 5 yr to settle a lawsuit. How much must they invest now in an account paying 8% compounded monthly to have that amount when it is due?

*From *The New York Times*, December 31, 1995, Section 3, p. 5.

50. Bill Poole wants to have \$20,000 available in 5 yr for a down payment on a house. He has inherited \$15,000. How much of the inheritance should he invest now to accumulate the \$20,000, if he can get an interest rate of 8% compounded quarterly?

51. Two partners agree to invest equal amounts in their business. One will contribute \$10,000 immediately. The other plans to contribute an equivalent amount in 3 yr, when she expects to acquire a large sum of money. How much should she contribute at that time to match her partner's investment now, assuming an interest rate of 6% compounded semiannually?

52. As the prize in a contest, you are offered \$1000 now or \$1210 in 5 yr. If money can be invested at 6% compounded annually, which is larger?

53. The consumption of electricity has increased historically at 6% per year. If it continues to increase at this rate indefinitely, find the number of years before the electric utilities will need to double their generating capacity.

54. Suppose a conservation campaign coupled with higher rates cause the demand for electricity to increase at only 2% per year, as it has recently. Find the number of years before the utilities will need to double generating capacity.

Use the approach in Example 9 to find the time it would take for the general level of prices in the economy to double at the average annual inflation rates in Exercises 55 and 56.

55. 4%

56. 5%

57. In 1995, O. G. McClain of Houston, Texas, mailed a \$100 check to a descendant of Texas independence hero Sam Houston to repay a \$100 debt of McClain's great-great-grandfather, who died in 1835, to Sam Houston.* A bank estimated the interest on the loan to be \$420 million for the 160 years it was due. Find the interest rate the bank was using, assuming interest is compounded annually.

58. In the New Testament, Jesus commends a widow who contributed 2 mites to the temple treasury (Mark 12:42–44). A mite was worth roughly 1/8 of a cent. Suppose the temple had invested those 2 mites at 4% interest compounded quarterly. How much would the money be worth 2000 years later?

59. On January 1, 1980, Jack deposited \$1000 into Bank X to earn interest at the rate of j per annum compounded semiannually. On January 1, 1985, he transferred his account to Bank Y to earn interest at the rate of k per annum compounded quarterly. On January 1, 1988, the balance at Bank Y was \$1990.76. If Jack could have earned interest at the rate of k per annum compounded quarterly from January 1, 1980, through January 1, 1988, his balance would have been \$2203.76. Which of the following represents the ratio k/j?*

(a) 1.25 **(b)** 1.30 **(c)** 1.35 **(d)** 1.40
(e) 1.45

60. On January 1, 1987, Tone Company exchanged equipment for a \$200,000 noninterest bearing note due on January 1, 1990. The prevailing rate of interest for a note of this type at January 1, 1987, was 10%. The present value of \$1 at 10% for three periods is 0.75. What amount of interest revenue should be included in Tone's 1988 income statement?†

(a) \$7500 **(b)** \$15,000 **(c)** \$16,500
(d) \$20,000

**The New York Times,* March 30, 1995.

*Problem from "Course 140 Examination, Mathematics of Compound Interest" of the Education and Examination Committee of The Society of Actuaries. Reprinted by permission of The Society of Actuaries.

†Uniform CPA Examination, May, 1989, American Institute of Certified Public Accountants.

6.3 ANNUITIES

So far in this chapter, only lump sum deposits and payments have been discussed. But many financial situations involve a sequence of equal payments at regular intervals, such as weekly deposits in a savings account or monthly payments on a mortgage or car loan. In order to develop formulas to deal with periodic payments like these, we must first discuss sequences.

GEOMETRIC SEQUENCES If a and r are fixed nonzero numbers, then the infinite list of numbers, $a, ar, ar^2, ar^3, ar^4, \ldots$ is called a **geometric sequence.** For instance, if $a = 5$ and $r = 2$, we have the sequence

$$5, 5 \cdot 2, 5 \cdot 2^2, 5 \cdot 2^3, 5 \cdot 2^4, \ldots,$$

or

$$5, 10, 20, 40, 80, \ldots.$$

In the sequence $a, ar, ar^2, ar^3, ar^4, \ldots,$ the number a is the first term of the sequence, ar the second term, ar^2 the third term, ar^3 the fourth term, and so on. Thus, for any $n \geq 1$,

$$ar^{n-1} \textbf{ is the } n\textbf{th term of the sequence.}$$

Each term in the sequence is r times the preceding term. The number r is called the **common ratio** of the sequence.

EXAMPLE 1 Find the seventh term of the geometric sequence with $a = 6$ and $r = 4$. Using ar^{n-1}, with $n = 7$, the **seventh** term is

$$ar^6 = 6(4)^6 = 6(4096) = 24{,}576. \quad \blacksquare$$

TECHNOLOGY TIP Some graphing calculators have the ability to produce a list of the terms of a sequence, given the expression for the nth term. With other calculators you can use the TABLE feature by entering the expression for the nth term as a function. The first four terms of the sequence discussed in Example 1 are shown in Figure 6.4. ✔

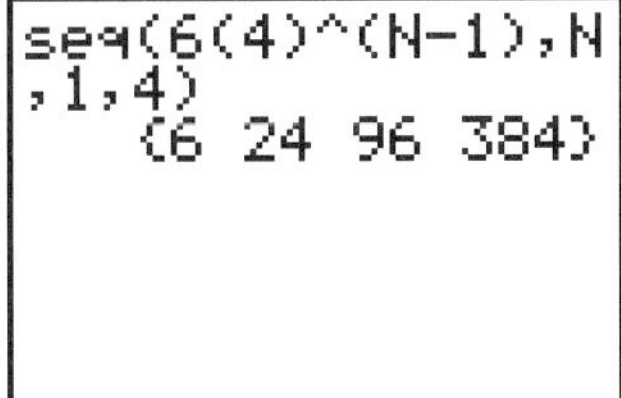

FIGURE 6.4

EXAMPLE 2 \$100 is deposited in an account that pays interest of 10% compounded annually. How much is in the account at the beginning of each of the first five years?

According to the compound interest formula (with $P = 100$ and $i = .01$), the value of the account at the beginning of each of the first five years is given by the first five terms of the geometric sequence with $a = 100$ and $r = 1.1$. The first five terms are

$$100, \quad 100(1.1), \quad 100(1.1)^2, \quad 100(1.1)^3, \quad 100(1.1)^4,$$

so the value of the account at the beginning of each of the five years is

$$\$100, \quad \$110, \quad \$121, \quad \$133.10, \quad \$146.41. \quad \blacksquare \quad \boxed{1}$$

$\boxed{1}$ Write the first four terms of the geometric sequence with $a = 5$ and $r = -2$. Then find the seventh term.

Answer:
5, −10, 20, −40; 320

Next we find the sum S_n of the first n terms of a geometric sequence. That is, we find S_n, where

$$S_n = a + ar + ar^2 + ar^3 + \cdots + ar^{n-1}. \tag{1}$$

If $r = 1$, this is easy because

$$S_n = \underbrace{a + a + a + \cdots + a}_{n \text{ terms}} = na.$$

If $r \neq 1$, multiply both sides of equation (1) by r, obtaining

$$rS_n = ar + ar^2 + ar^3 + ar^4 + \cdots + ar^n. \qquad (2)$$

Now subtract corresponding sides of equation (1) from equation (2):

$$\begin{aligned} rS_n &= \quad ar + ar^2 + ar^3 + \cdots + ar^{n-1} + ar^n \\ -S_n &= -(a + ar + ar^2 + ar^3 + \cdots + ar^{n-1}) \\ \hline rS_n - S_n &= ar^n - a \\ S_n(r-1) &= a(r^n - 1) \\ S_n &= \frac{a(r^n - 1)}{r - 1}. \end{aligned}$$

Hence, we have this useful formula.

> If a geometric sequence has first term a and common ratio r, then the **sum of the first n terms** is given by
>
> $$S_n = \frac{a(r^n - 1)}{r - 1}, \quad r \neq 1.$$

EXAMPLE 3 Find the sum of the first six terms of the geometric sequence 3, 12, 48, ...

Here $a = 3$ and $r = 4$. Find S_6 by the result above.

$$S_6 = \frac{3(4^6 - 1)}{4 - 1} \qquad \text{Let } n = 6, a = 3, r = 4.$$

$$= \frac{3(4096 - 1)}{3}$$

$$= 4095$$ ■ [2]

[2] (a) Find S_4 and S_7 for the geometric sequence 5, 15, 45, 135, ...

(b) Find S_5 for the geometric sequence having $a = -3$ and $r = -5$.

Answers:

(a) $S_4 = 200$, $S_7 = 5465$

(b) $S_5 = -1563$

TECHNOLOGY TIP Graphing calculators with sequence capability can also find the sum of the first n terms of a sequence, given the expression for the nth term. ✔

ORDINARY ANNUITIES A sequence of equal payments made at equal periods of time is called an **annuity.** If the payments are made at the end of the time period, and if the frequency of payments is the same as the frequency of compounding, the annuity is called an **ordinary annuity.** The time between payments is the **payment period,** and the time from the beginning of the first payment period to the end of the last period is called the **term of the annuity.** The **future value of the annuity,** the final sum on deposit, is defined as the sum of the compound amounts of all the payments, compounded to the end of the term.

Two common uses of annuities are to accumulate funds for some goal or to withdraw funds from an account. For example, an annuity may be used to save money for a large purchase, such as an automobile, an expensive trip, or a down payment on a home. An annuity also may be used to provide monthly payments for retirement. We explore these options in this and the next section.

For example, suppose \$1500 is deposited at the end of the year for the next 6 years in an account paying 8% per year compounded annually. Figure 6.5 shows this annuity schematically.

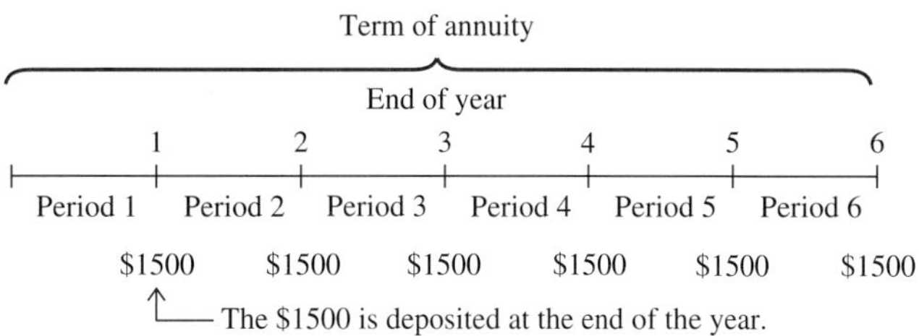

FIGURE 6.5

3 Complete these steps for an annuity of \$2000 at the end of each year for 3 years. Assume interest of 8% compounded annually.

(a) The first deposit of \$2000 produces a total of ______.

(b) The second deposit becomes ______.

(c) No interest is earned on the third deposit, so the total in the account is ______.

Answers:

(a) \$2332.80

(b) \$2160.00

(c) \$6492.80

To find the future value of this annuity, look separately at each of the \$1500 payments. The first of these payments will produce a compound amount of

$$1500(1 + .08)^5 = 1500(1.08)^5.$$

Use 5 as the exponent instead of 6 since the money is deposited at the *end* of the first year and earns interest for only 5 years. The second payment of \$1500 will produce a compound amount of $1500(1.08)^4$. As shown in Figure 6.6, the future value of the annuity is

$$1500(1.08)^5 + 1500(1.08)^4 + 1500(1.08)^3 + 1500(1.08)^2 + 1500(1.08)^1 + 1500.$$

(The last payment earns no interest at all.) Reading this in reverse order, we see that it is just the sum of the first six terms of a geometric sequence with $a = 1500$, $r = 1.08$, and $n = 6$. Therefore, the sum is

$$\frac{a(r^n - 1)}{r - 1} = \frac{1500[(1.08)^6 - 1]}{1.08 - 1} = \$11{,}003.89. \quad \boxed{3}$$

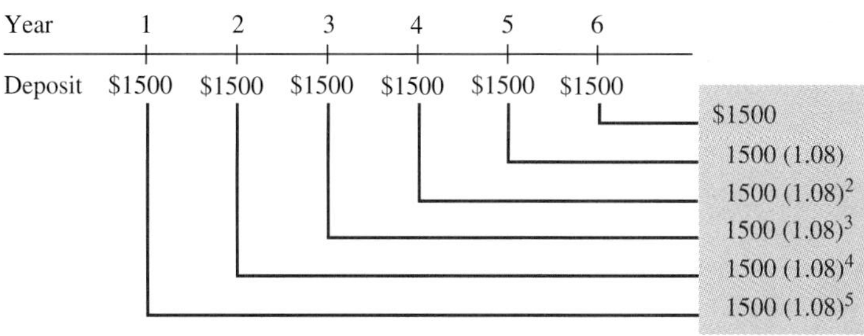

FIGURE 6.6

To generalize this result, suppose that payments of R dollars each are deposited into an account at the *end of each period* for *n periods,* at a rate of interest *i per period.* The first payment of R dollars will produce a compound amount of $R(1 + i)^{n-1}$ dollars, the second payment will produce $R(1 + i)^{n-2}$ dollars, and so on; the final payment earns no interest and contributes just R dollars to the total. If S represents the future value of the annuity, then (as shown in Figure 6.7),

$$S = R(1 + i)^{n-1} + R(1 + i)^{n-2} + R(1 + i)^{n-3} + \cdots + R(1 + i) + R$$

or, written in reverse order,

$$S = R + R(1 + i)^1 + R(1 + i)^2 + \cdots + R(1 + i)^{n-1}.$$

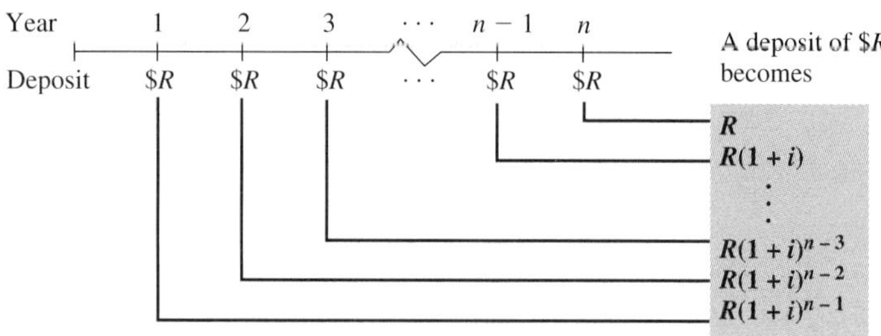

FIGURE 6.7

This result is the sum of the first n terms of the geometric sequence having first term R and common ratio $1 + i$. Using the formula for the sum of the first n terms of a geometric sequence,

$$S = \frac{R[(1 + i)^n - 1]}{(1 + i) - 1} = \frac{R[(1 + i)^n - 1]}{i} = R\left[\frac{(1 + i)^n - 1}{i}\right].$$

The quantity in brackets is commonly written $s_{\overline{n}|i}$ (read "s-angle-n at i"), so that

$$S = R \cdot s_{\overline{n}|i}.$$

We can summarize the preceding work as follows.*

FUTURE VALUE OF AN ORDINARY ANNUITY

$$\mathbf{S = R\left[\frac{(1 + i)^n - 1}{i}\right]} \quad \text{or} \quad \mathbf{S = R \cdot s_{\overline{n}|i}}$$

where

S is future value,
R is the payment at the end of each period,
i is the interest rate per period,
n is the number of periods.

*We use S for the future value here, instead of A as in the compound interest formula, to help avoid confusing the two formulas.

TECHNOLOGY TIP A calculator will be very helpful in computations with annuities. The TI-83 graphing calculator has a special finance menu that is designed to give any desired result after the basic information is entered. If your calculator does not have this feature, it probably can be programmed to evaluate the formulas introduced in this section and the next. These programs are in the Program Appendix. ✔

4 Johnson Building Materials deposits \$2500 at the end of each year into an account paying 8% per year compounded annually. Find the total amount on deposit after

(a) 6 years;

(b) 10 years.

Answers:

(a) \$18,339.82

(b) \$36,216.41

EXAMPLE 4 Athan Lee Lewis is an athlete who feels that his playing career will last 7 years. To prepare for his future, he deposits \$22,000 at the end of each year for 7 years in an account paying 6% compounded annually. How much will he have on deposit after 7 years?

His payments form an ordinary annuity with $R = 22{,}000$, $n = 7$, and $i = .06$. The future value of this annuity (by the formula above) is

$$S = 22{,}000\left[\frac{(1.06)^7 - 1}{.06}\right] = \$184{,}664.43. \quad \blacksquare \quad \boxed{4}$$

EXAMPLE 5 Experts say that the baby boom generation (born between 1946 and 1960) cannot count on a company pension or Social Security to provide a comfortable retirement, as their parents did. It is recommended that they start to save early and regularly. Michael Karelius, a baby boomer, has decided to deposit \$200 at the end of each month in an account that pays interest of 7.2% compounded monthly for retirement in 20 years.

(a) How much will be in the account at that time?

This savings plan is an annuity with $R = 200$, $i = .072/12$, and $n = 12(20)$. The future value is

$$S = 200\left[\frac{1 + (.072/12)^{12(20)} - 1}{.072/12}\right] = 106{,}752.47,$$

or \$106,752.47.

(b) Michael believes he needs to accumulate \$130,000 in the 20-year period to have enough for retirement. What interest rate would provide that amount?

Once again we have an annuity with $R = 200$ and $n = 12(20)$. Now the future value $S = 130{,}000$ is given and we must find the interest rate. If x is the annual interest rate, then the interest rate per month is $i = x/12$ and we have

$$R\left[\frac{(1+i)^n - 1}{i}\right] = S$$

$$200\left[\frac{(1 + x/12)^{12(20)} - 1}{x/12}\right] = 130{,}000. \qquad (1)$$

5 Helen's Dry Goods deposits \$5800 at the end of each quarter for 4 years.

(a) Find the final amount on deposit if the money earns 6.4% compounded quarterly.

(b) Helen wants to accumulate \$110,000 in the four-year period. What interest rate (to the nearest tenth) will be required?

Answers:

(a) \$104,812.44

(b) 8.9%

This last equation is difficult to solve algebraically. We can get a rough approximation by using a calculator to compute the left side of the equation for various values of x, to see which one comes closest to producing \$130,000. For example, $x = .08$ produces 117,804 and $x = .09$ produces 133,577, so the solution is between .08 and .09. Further experimentation of this type leads to the approximate solution $x = .0879$, that is, 8.79%. A more exact approximation can be obtained with a graphing calculator (see the following Technology Tip). ■ 5

TECHNOLOGY TIP To solve equation (1) in Example 5 with a graphing calculator, graph the equations

$$y = 200\left[\frac{[(1 + x/12)^{12(20)} - 1]}{x/12}\right] \quad \text{and} \quad y = 130{,}000$$

on the same screen and find the intersection of their graphs, as in Figure 6.8. The same result can be obtained on the TI-83 without graphing, by using the TVM solver in the FINANCE menu. ✔

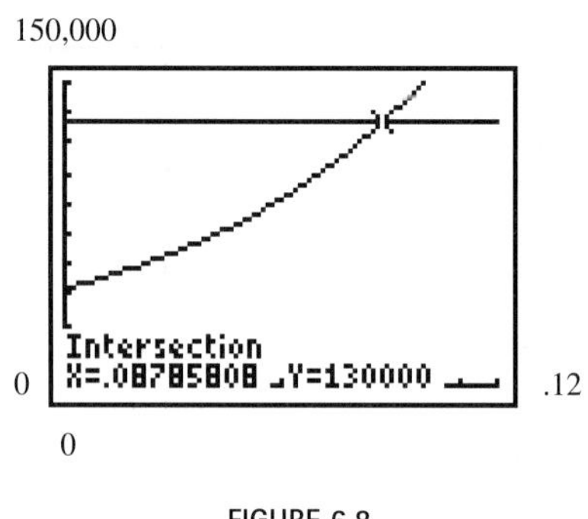

FIGURE 6.8

ANNUITIES DUE The formula developed above is for *ordinary annuities*—those with payments at the *end* of each time period. These results can be modified slightly to apply to **annuities due**—annuities where payments are made at the *beginning* of each time period.

To find the future value of an annuity due, treat each payment as if it were made at the end of the *preceding* period, that is, find $s_{\overline{n}|i}$ for *one additional period.* No payment is made at the end of the last period, so to compensate for this, subtract the amount of one payment. Thus, the **future value of an annuity due** of n payments of R dollars each at the beginning of consecutive interest periods with interest compounded at the rate of i per period is

$$S = R\left[\frac{(1 + i)^{n+1} - 1}{i}\right] - R \quad \text{or} \quad S = R \cdot s_{\overline{n+1}|i} - R.$$

EXAMPLE 6 Payments of \$500 are made at the beginning of each quarter for 7 years in an account paying 12% compounded quarterly.

(a) Find the future value of this annuity due.

In 7 years there are 28 quarterly periods. Add one period to get $n = 29$, and use the formula with $i = 12\%/4 = 3\%$.

$$S = 500\left[\frac{(1.03)^{29} - 1}{.03}\right] - 500$$

$$S \approx 500(45.21885) - 500 = \$22{,}109.43$$

The account will contain a total of \$22,109.43 after 7 years.

6 (a) Ms. Black deposits $800 at the beginning of each 6-month period for 5 years. Find the final amount if the account pays 6% compounded semiannually.

(b) Find the final amount if this account were an ordinary annuity.

Answers:

(a) $9446.24

(b) $9171.10

(b) Compare the result from part (a) with the future value of an ordinary annuity. In this case the future value is given by

$$S = 500\left[\frac{1.03^{28} - 1}{.03}\right] = \$21{,}465.46.$$

The future amount is a little less because the payments are each made one month later than the payments for an annuity due. ■ 6

SINKING FUNDS A fund set up to receive periodic payments is called a **sinking fund.** The periodic payments, together with the interest earned by the payments, are designed to produce a given sum at some time in the future. For example, a sinking fund might be set up to receive money that will be needed to pay off the principal on a loan at some future time. If the payments are all the same amount and are made at the end of a regular time period, they form an ordinary annuity.

EXAMPLE 7 The Chinns are close to retirement. They agree to sell an antique urn to the local museum for $17,000. Their tax adviser suggests that they defer receipt of this money until they retire, 5 years in the future. (At that time, they might well be in a lower tax bracket.) Find the amount of each payment the museum must make into a sinking fund so that it will have the necessary $17,000 in 5 years. Assume that the museum can earn 6% compounded annually on its money. Also, assume that the payments are made annually.

These payments are the periodic payments into an ordinary annuity. The annuity will amount to $17,000 in 5 years at 6% compounded annually. Using the formula and a calculator,

$$17{,}000 = R\left[\frac{(1.06)^5 - 1}{.06}\right]$$

$$17{,}000 \approx R(5.637093)$$

$$R \approx \frac{17{,}000}{5.637093} = 3015.74$$

or $3015.74. If the museum management deposits $3015.74 at the end of each year for 5 years in an account paying 6% compounded annually, it will have the total amount needed. This result is shown in the following sinking fund table. In these tables the last payment may differ slightly from the others because of rounding in the preceding lines.

Payment Number	*Amount of Deposit*	*Interest Earned*	*Total in Account*
1	$3015.74	$0	$3,015.74
2	3015.74	180.94	6,212.42
3	3015.74	372.75	9,600.91
4	3015.74	576.05	13,192.70
5	3015.74	791.56	17,000.00

7 Francisco Arce needs $8000 in 6 years so that he can go on an archeological dig. He wants to deposit equal payments at the end of each quarter so that he will have enough to go on the dig. Find the amount of each payment if the bank pays

(a) 12% compounded quarterly;

(b) 8% compounded quarterly.

Answers:

(a) $232.38

(b) $262.97

To construct the table, notice that the first payment does not earn interest until the second payment is made. Line 2 of the table shows the second payment, 6% interest of $180.94 on the first payment, and the sum of these amounts added to the total in line 1. Line 3 shows the third payment, 6% interest of $372.75 on the total from line 2, and the new total found by adding these amounts to the total in line 2. This procedure is continued to complete the table. ■ 7

6.3 EXERCISES

Find the fourth term of each of the following geometric sequences. (See Example 1.)

1. $a = 5, r = 3$ **2.** $a = 20, r = 2$

3. $a = 48, r = .5$ **4.** $a = 80, r = .1$

5. $a = 2000, r = 1.05$ **6.** $a = 10{,}000, r = 1.01$

Find the sum of the first four terms for each of the following geometric sequences. (See Example 3.)

7. $a = 1, r = 2$ **8.** $a = 3, r = 3$

9. $a = 5, r = .2$ **10.** $a = 6, r = .5$

11. $a = 128, r = 1.1$ **12.** $a = 100, r = 1.05$

Find each of the following values.

13. $s_{\overline{12}|.05}$ **14.** $s_{\overline{20}|.06}$ **15.** $s_{\overline{16}|.04}$

16. $s_{\overline{40}|.02}$ **17.** $s_{\overline{20}|.01}$ **18.** $s_{\overline{18}|.015}$

19. Explain the difference between an ordinary annuity and an annuity due.

Find the future value of the following ordinary annuities. Payments are made and interest is compounded as given. (See Examples 4 and 5.)

20. $R =$ \$1500, 4% interest compounded annually for 8 years

21. $R =$ \$680, 5% interest compounded annually for 6 years

22. $R =$ \$12,000, 6.2% interest compounded annually for 10 years

23. $R =$ \$20,000, 5.5% interest compounded annually for 12 years

24. $R =$ \$865, 6% interest compounded semiannually for 8 years

25. $R =$ \$7300, 9% interest compounded semiannually for 6 years

26. $R =$ \$1200, 8% interest compounded quarterly for 10 years

27. $R =$ \$20,000, 6% interest compounded quarterly for 12 years

Find the future value of each annuity due. (See Example 6.)

28. Payments of \$500 for 10 years at 5% compounded annually

29. Payments of \$1050 for 6 years at 3.5% compounded annually

30. Payments of \$16,000 for 8 years at 4.7% compounded annually

31. Payments of \$25,000 for 12 years at 6% compounded annually

32. Payments of \$1000 for 9 years at 8% compounded semiannually

33. Payments of \$750 for 15 years at 6% compounded semiannually

34. Payments of \$100 for 7 years at 12% compounded quarterly

35. Payments of \$1500 for 11 years at 12% compounded quarterly

Find the periodic payment that will amount to the given sums under the given conditions, if payments are made at the end of each period. (See Example 7.)

36. $S =$ \$14,500, interest is 5% compounded semiannually for 8 years

37. $S =$ \$43,000, interest is 6% compounded semiannually for 5 years

38. $S =$ \$62,000, interest is 8% compounded quarterly for 6 years

39. $S =$ \$12,800, interest is 6% compounded monthly for 4 years

40. What is meant by a sinking fund? Give an example of a sinking fund.

Find the amount of each payment to be made into a sinking fund to accumulate the following amounts. Payments are made at the end of each period. (See Example 7.)

41. \$11,000, money earns 6% compounded semiannually, for 6 years

42. \$75,000, money earns 6% compounded semiannually, for $4\frac{1}{2}$ years

43. \$50,000, money earns 10% compounded quarterly, for $2\frac{1}{2}$ years

44. \$25,000, money earns 12% compounded quarterly, for $3\frac{1}{2}$ years

45. \$6000, money earns 8% compounded monthly, for 3 years

46. \$9000, money earns 12% compounded monthly, for $2\frac{1}{2}$ years

Management *Work the following applied problems.*

47. A typical pack-a-day smoker spends about \$55 per month on cigarettes. Suppose the smoker invests that amount at the end of each month in a savings account at 4.8% compounded monthly. What would the account be worth after 40 years?

48. Pat Quinlan deposits \$6000 at the end of each year for 4 years in an account paying 5% interest compounded annually.

(a) Find the final amount she will have on deposit.

(b) Pat's brother-in-law works in a bank that pays 4.8% compounded annually. If she deposits her money in this bank instead of the one above, how much will she have in her account?

(c) How much would Quinlan lose over 5 years by using her brother-in-law's bank?

49. A father opened a savings account for his daughter on the day she was born, depositing $1000. Each year on her birthday he deposits another $1000, making the last deposit on her twenty-first birthday. If the account pays 9.5% interest compounded annually, how much is in the account at the end of the day on the daughter's twenty-first birthday?

50. A 45-year-old man puts $1000 in a retirement account at the end of each quarter until he reaches the age of 60 and makes no further deposits. If the account pays 11% interest compounded quarterly, how much will be in the account when the man retires at age 65?

51. At the end of each quarter a 50-year-old woman puts $1200 in a retirement account that pays 7% interest compounded quarterly. When she reaches age 60, she withdraws the entire amount and places it in a mutual fund that pays 9% interest compounded monthly. From then on she deposits $300 in the mutual fund at the end of each month. How much is in the account when she reaches age 65?

52. Jasspreet Kaur deposits $2435 at the beginning of each semiannual period for 8 years in an account paying 6% compounded semiannually. She then leaves that money alone, with no further deposits, for an additional 5 years. Find the final amount on deposit after the entire 13-year period.

53. Chuck Hickman deposits $10,000 at the beginning of each year for 12 years in an account paying 5% compounded annually. He then puts the total amount on deposit in another account paying 6% compounded semiannually for another 9 years. Find the final amount on deposit after the entire 21-year period.

54. David Horwitz needs $10,000 in 8 years.

(a) What amount should he deposit at the end of each quarter at 8% compounded quarterly so that he will have his $10,000?

(b) Find Horwitz's quarterly deposit if the money is deposited at 6% compounded quarterly.

55. Harv's Meats knows that it must buy a new deboner machine in 4 years. The machine costs $12,000. In order to accumulate enough money to pay for the machine, Harv decides to deposit a sum of money at the end of each 6 months in an account paying 6% compounded semiannually. How much should each payment be?

56. Karin Sandberg wants to buy an $18,000 car in 6 years. How much money must she deposit at the end of each quarter in an account paying 12% compounded quarterly so that she will have enough to pay for her car?

In Exercises 57 and 58, use a graphing calculator to find the value of i that produces the given value of S. (See Example 5(b).)

57. To save for retirement, Karla Harby put $300 each month into an ordinary annuity for 20 years. Interest was compounded monthly. At the end of the 20 years, the annuity was worth $147,126. What annual interest rate did she receive?

58. Jennifer Wall made payments of $250 per month at the end of each month to purchase a piece of property. At the end of 30 years, she completely owned the property, which she sold for $330,000. What annual interest rate would she need to earn on an ordinary annuity for a comparable rate of return?

59. In a 1992 Virginia lottery, the jackpot was $27 million. An Australian investment firm tried to buy all possible combinations of numbers, which would have cost $7 million. In fact, the firm ran out of time and was unable to buy all combinations, but ended up with the only winning ticket anyway. The firm received the jackpot in 20 equal annual payments of $1.35 million.* Assume these payments meet the conditions of an ordinary annuity.

(a) Suppose the firm can invest money at 8% interest compounded annually. How many years would it take until the investors would be further ahead than if they had simply invested the $7 million at the same rate? (*Hint:* Experiment with different values of n, the number of years, or use a graphing calculator to plot the value of both investments as a function of the number of years.)

(b) How many years would it take in part (a) at an interest rate of 12%?

60. Diane Gray sells some land in Nevada. She will be paid a lump sum of $60,000 in 7 yr. Until then, the buyer pays 8% simple interest quarterly.

(a) Find the amount of each quarterly interest payment.

(b) The buyer sets up a sinking fund so that enough money will be present to pay off the $60,000. The buyer wants to make semiannual payments into the sinking fund; the account pays 6% compounded semiannually. Find the amount of each payment into the fund.

(c) Prepare a table showing the amount in the sinking fund after each deposit.

61. Joe Seniw bought a rare stamp for his collection. He agreed to pay a lump sum of $4000 after 5 yr. Until then, he pays 6% simple interest semiannually.

(a) Find the amount of each semiannual interest payment.

(b) Seniw sets up a sinking fund so that enough money will be present to pay off the $4000. He wants to make annual payments into the fund. The account pays 8% compounded annually. Find the amount of each payment.

(c) Prepare a table showing the amount in the sinking fund after each deposit.

**The Washington Post,* March 10, 1992, p. A1.

6.4 PRESENT VALUE OF AN ANNUITY; AMORTIZATION

Suppose that at the end of each year, for the next 10 years, \$500 is deposited in a savings account paying 7% interest compounded annually. This is an example of an ordinary annuity. The **present value** of this annuity is the amount that would have to be deposited in one lump sum today (at the same compound interest rate) in order to produce exactly the same balance at the end of 10 years. We can find a formula for the present value of an annuity as follows.

Suppose deposits of R dollars are made at the end of each period for n periods at interest rate i per period. Then the amount in the account after n periods is the future value of this annuity:

$$S = R\left[\frac{(1+i)^n - 1}{i}\right].$$

On the other hand, if P dollars are deposited today at the same compound interest rate i, then at the end of n periods, the amount in the account is $P(1+i)^n$. This amount must be the same as the amount S in the formula above, that is,

$$P(1+i)^n = R\left[\frac{(1+i)^n - 1}{i}\right].$$

To solve this equation for P, multiply both sides by $(1+i)^{-n}$.

$$P = R\,\mathbf{(1+i)^{-n}}\left[\frac{(1+i)^n - 1}{i}\right]$$

Use the distributive property; also recall that $(1+i)^{-n}(1+i)^n = (1+i)^0 = 1$.

$$P = R\left[\frac{\mathbf{(1+i)^{-n}}(1+i)^n - \mathbf{(1+i)^{-n}}}{i}\right]$$

$$P = R\left[\frac{1-(1+i)^{-n}}{i}\right]$$

The amount P is called the **present value of the annuity.** The quantity in brackets is abbreviated as $a_{\overline{n}|i}$, (read "a-angle-n at i"), so

$$a_{\overline{n}|i} = \frac{1-(1+i)^{-n}}{i}.$$

Compare this quantity with $s_{\overline{n}|i}$ in the previous section.

Here is a summary of what we have done.

PRESENT VALUE OF AN ANNUITY

The present value P of an annuity of n payments of R dollars each at the end of consecutive interest periods with interest compounded at a rate of interest i per period is

$$\mathbf{P = R\left[\frac{1-(1+i)^{-n}}{i}\right] \quad \text{or} \quad P = R \cdot a_{\overline{n}|i}.}$$

CAUTION Don't confuse the formula for the present value of an annuity with the one for the future value of an annuity. Notice the difference: the numerator of the fraction in the present value formula is $1 - (1 + i)^{-n}$, but in the future value formula, it is $(1 + i)^n - 1$. ◆

1 What lump sum deposited today would be equivalent to equal payments of

(a) \$650 at the end of each year for 9 years at 4% compounded annually?

(b) \$1000 at the end of each quarter for 4 years at 4% compounded quarterly?

Answers:

(a) \$4832.97

(b) \$14,717.87

EXAMPLE 1 Paul Eldersveld and Maria Gonzalez are both graduates of the Forestvire Institute of Technology. They both agree to contribute to the endowment fund of FIT. Eldersveld says that he will give \$500 at the end of each year for 9 years. Gonzalez prefers to give a lump sum today. What lump sum can she give that will equal the present value of Eldersveld's annual gifts, if the endowment fund earns 7.5% compounded annually?

Here $R = 500$, $n = 9$, and $i = .075$ and we have

$$P = 500\left[\frac{1 - (1.075)^{-9}}{.075}\right]$$

$$= 3189.44.$$

Therefore, Gonzalez must donate a lump sum of \$3189.44 today. ■ **1**

TECHNOLOGY TIP It would be useful to store a program for finding present value in your calculator (if one is not built-in); refer to the Program Appendix. ✔

2 Kelly Erin buys a small business for \$174,000. She agrees to pay off the cost in payments at the end of each semiannual period for 7 years, with interest of 10% compounded semiannually on the unpaid balance. Find the amount of each payment.

Answer:

\$17,578.17

EXAMPLE 2 A car costs \$12,000. After a down payment of \$2000, the balance will be paid off in 36 equal monthly payments with interest of 12% per year on the unpaid balance. Find the amount of each payment.

A single lump sum payment of \$10,000 today would pay off the loan. So, \$10,000 is the present value of an annuity of 36 monthly payments with interest of $12\%/12 = 1\%$ per month. Thus, $P = 10{,}000$, $n = 36$, $i = .01$, and we must find the monthly payment R in the formula

$$P = R\left[\frac{1 - (1 + i)^{-n}}{i}\right]$$

$$10{,}000 = R\left[\frac{1 - (1.01)^{-36}}{.01}\right]$$

$$R \approx 332.1430981.$$

A monthly payment of \$332.14 will be needed. ■ **2**

AMORTIZATION A loan is **amortized** if both the principal and interest are paid by a sequence of equal periodic payments. In Example 2 above, a loan of \$10,000 at 12% interest compounded monthly could be amortized by paying \$332.14 per month for 36 months.

The periodic payment needed to amortize a loan may be found, as in Example 2, by solving the present value equation for R.

AMORTIZATION PAYMENTS

A loan of P dollars at interest rate i per period may be amortized in n equal periodic payments of R dollars made at the end of each period, where

$$R = \frac{P}{a_{\overline{n}|i}} = \frac{P}{\left[\frac{1-(1+i)^{-n}}{i}\right]} = \frac{Pi}{1-(1+i)^{-n}}.$$

EXAMPLE 3 The Beckenstein family buys a house for \$94,000 with a downpayment of \$16,000. They take out a 30-year mortgage for \$78,000 at an annual interest rate of 9.6%.

(a) Find the amount of the monthly payment needed to amortize this loan.

Here $P = 78{,}000$ and the monthly interest rate is $9.6\%/12 = .096/12 = .008$.* The number of monthly payments is $12 \cdot 30 = 360$. Therefore,

$$R = \frac{78{,}000}{a_{\overline{360}|.008}} = \frac{78{,}000}{\left[\frac{1-(1.008)^{-360}}{.008}\right]} \approx \frac{78{,}000}{117.90229} = 661.56.$$

Monthly payments of \$661.56 are required to amortize the loan.

(b) Find the total amount of interest paid when the loan is amortized over 30 years.

The Beckenstein family makes 360 payments of \$661.56 each, for a total of \$238,161.60. Since the amount of the loan was \$78,000, the total interest paid is

$$\$238{,}161.60 - \$78{,}000 = \$160{,}161.60.$$

This large amount of interest is typical of what happens with a long mortgage. A 15-year mortgage would have higher payments but would involve significantly less interest. [3]

[3] If the mortgage in Example 3 runs for 15 years, find

(a) the monthly payment;

(b) the total amount of interest paid.

Answers:

(a) \$819.21

(b) \$69,457.80

(c) Find the part of the first payment that is interest and the part that is applied to reducing the debt.

As we saw in part (a), the monthly interest rate is .008. During the first month, the entire \$78,000 is owed. Interest on this amount for 1 month is found by the formula for simple interest.

$$I = Prt = 78{,}000(.008)(1) = 624$$

At the end of the month, a payment of \$661.56 is made; since \$624 of this is interest, a total of

$$\$661.56 - \$624 = \$37.56$$

is applied to the reduction of the original debt. ■

AMORTIZATION SCHEDULES In Example 3, 360 payments are made to amortize a \$78,000 loan. The loan balance after the first payment is reduced by only \$37.56, which is much less than $(1/360)(78{,}000) \approx \$216.67$. Therefore, even though equal *payments* are made to amortize a loan, the loan *balance* does not decrease in equal steps. This fact is very important if a loan is paid off early.

*Mortgage rates are quoted in terms of annual interest, but it is always understood that the monthly rate is 1/12 of the annual rate and that interest is compounded monthly.

EXAMPLE 4 Jill Stuart borrows \$1000 for 1 year at 12% annual interest compounded monthly.

(a) What is her monthly loan payment?
The monthly interest rate is 12%/12 = 1% = .01, so that her payment is

$$R = \frac{1000}{a_{\overline{12}|.01}} = \frac{1000}{\left[\frac{1-(1.01)^{-12}}{.01}\right]} \approx \frac{1000}{11.25508} = \$88.85.$$

(b) After making three payments, she decides to pay off the remaining balance all at once. How much must she pay?

Since nine payments remain to be paid, they can be thought of as an annuity consisting of nine payments of \$88.25 at 1% interest per period. The present value of this annuity is

$$88.85\left[\frac{1-(1.01)^{-9}}{.01}\right] = 761.09.$$

So Jill's remaining balance, computed by this method, is \$761.09.

An alternative method of figuring the balance is to consider the payments already made as an annuity of three payments. At the beginning, the present value of this annuity was

$$88.85\left[\frac{1-(1.01)^{-3}}{.01}\right] = 261.31.$$

That is, if she had borrowed only \$261.31, the loan would be repaid after these 3 payments. Considered this way, she has paid nothing toward the rest of her loan, so she still owes the difference \$1000 − \$261.31 = \$738.69. Furthermore, she owes the interest on this amount for 3 months, for a total of

$$(738.69)(1.01)^3 = \$761.07.$$

This balance due differs from the one obtained by the first method by 2¢ because the monthly payment and the other calculations were rounded to the nearest penny. ■ 4

4 Find the following for a car loan of \$10,000 for 48 months at 9% interest compounded monthly.

(a) the monthly payment

(b) How much is still due after 12 payments have been made?

Answers:

(a) \$248.85

(b) \$7825.54 or \$7825.56

Although most people wouldn't quibble about a 2¢ difference in the balance due in Example 4, the difference in other cases (larger amounts or longer terms) might be more than that. A bank or business must keep its books accurately to the nearest penny, so it must determine the balance due in cases like this unambiguously and exactly. This is done by means of an **amortization schedule,** which lists how much of each payment is interest, how much goes to reduce the balance, and how much is owed after *each* payment.

EXAMPLE 5 Determine the exact amount Jill Stuart in Example 4 owes after three monthly payments.

An amortization table for the loan is shown on the next page. It is obtained as follows. The annual interest rate is 12% compounded monthly, so the interest rate per month is 12%/12 = 1% = .01. When the first payment is made, 1 month's interest, namely .01(1000) = \$10, is owed. Subtracting this from the \$88.85 payment leaves \$78.85 to be applied to repayment. Hence, the principal at the end of the first payment period is 1000 − 78.85 = \$921.15, as shown in the "payment 1" line of the table.

When payment 2 is made, 1 month's interest on \$921.15 is owed, namely .01(921.15) = \$9.21. Subtracting this from the \$88.85 payment leaves \$79.64 to reduce the principal. Hence, the principal at the end of payment 2 is 921.15 − 79.64 = \$841.51. The interest portion of payment 3 is based on this amount and the remaining lines of the table are found in a similar fashion.

Payment Number	*Amount of Payment*	*Interest for Period*	*Portion to Principal*	*Principal at End of Period*
0	—	—	—	\$1000.00
1	\$88.85	\$10.00	\$78.85	921.15
2	88.85	9.21	79.64	841.51
3	88.85	8.42	80.43	761.08
4	88.85	7.61	81.24	679.84
5	88.85	6.80	82.05	597.79
6	88.85	5.98	82.87	514.92
7	88.85	5.15	83.70	431.22
8	88.85	4.31	84.54	346.68
9	88.85	3.47	85.38	261.30
10	88.85	2.61	86.24	175.06
11	88.85	1.75	87.10	87.96
12	88.84	.88	87.96	0

The schedule shows that after three payments, she still owes \$761.08, an amount that differs slightly from that obtained by either method in Example 4. ■

The amortization schedule in Example 5 is typical. In particular, note that all payments are the same except the last one. It is often necessary to adjust the amount of the final payment to account for rounding off earlier and to ensure that the final balance is exactly 0.

An amortization schedule also shows how the periodic payments are applied to interest and principal. The amount going to interest decreases with each payment, while the amount going to reduce the principal owed increases with each payment.

TECHNOLOGY TIP Programs to produce amortization schedules are in the Program Appendix. ✔

6.4 EXERCISES

1. Which of the following is represented by $a_{\overline{n}|i}$?

(a) $\frac{(1+i)^{-n}-1}{i}$ (b) $\frac{(1+i)^{n}-1}{i}$

(c) $\frac{1-(1+i)^{-n}}{i}$ (d) $\frac{1-(1+i)^{n}}{i}$

2. Which of the choices in Exercise 1 represents $s_{\overline{n}|i}$?

Find each of the following.

3. $a_{\overline{15}|.06}$ 4. $a_{\overline{10}|.03}$ 5. $a_{\overline{18}|.04}$

6. $a_{\overline{30}|.01}$ 7. $a_{\overline{16}|.01}$ 8. $a_{\overline{32}|.02}$

9. Explain the difference between the present value of an annuity and the future value of an annuity. For a given annuity, which is larger? Why?

Find the present value of each ordinary annuity. (See Example 1.)

10. Payments of \$5200 are made annually for 6 years at 5% compounded annually.

11. Payments of \$1250 are made annually for 8 years at 4% compounded annually.

12. Payments of \$675 are made semiannually for 10 years at 6% compounded semiannually.

13. Payments of \$750 are made semiannually for 8 years at 6% compounded semiannually.

14. Payments of \$16,908 are made quarterly for 3 years at 4.4% compounded quarterly.

15. Payments of \$12,125 are made quarterly for 5 years at 5.6% compounded quarterly.

Find the lump sum deposited today that will yield the same total amount as payments of \$10,000 at the end of each year for 15 yr, at each of the given interest rates. (See Example 1.)

16. 4% compounded annually

17. 5% compounded annually

18. 6% compounded annually

19. What does it mean to amortize a loan?

Find the payment necessary to amortize each of the following loans. (See Example 2.)

20. \$800, 10 annual payments at 5%

21. \$12,000, 8 quarterly payments at 6%

22. \$25,000, 8 quarterly payments at 6%

23. \$35,000, 12 quarterly payments at 4%

24. \$5000, 36 monthly payments at 12%

25. \$472, 48 monthly payments at 12%

Find the monthly house payment necessary to amortize the following loans. Interest is calculated on the unpaid balance. (See Examples 3 and 4.)

26. \$49,560 at 10.75% for 25 years

27. \$70,892 at 11.11% for 30 years

28. \$53,762 at 12.45% for 30 years

29. \$96,511 at 10.57% for 25 years

Use the amortization table in Example 5 to answer the questions in Exercises 30–33.

30. How much of the fifth payment is interest?

31. How much of the tenth payment is used to reduce the debt?

32. How much interest is paid in the first 5 months of the loan?

33. How much interest is paid in the last 5 months of the loan?

34. What sum deposited today at 5% compounded annually for 8 yr will provide the same amount as \$1000 deposited at the end of each year for 8 yr at 6% compounded annually?

35. What lump sum deposited today at 8% compounded quarterly for 10 yr will yield the same final amount as deposits of \$4000 at the end of each six-month period for 10 yr at 6% compounded semiannually?

Management *Work the following applied problems.*

36. Stereo Shack sells a stereo system for \$600 down and monthly payments of \$30 for the next 3 yr. If the interest rate is 1.25% per month on the unpaid balance, find
(a) the cost of the stereo system;
(b) the total amount of interest paid.

37. Hong Le buys a car costing \$6000. He agrees to make payments at the end of each monthly period for 4 years. He pays 12% interest, compounded monthly.
(a) What is the amount of each payment?
(b) Find the total amount of interest Le will pay.

38. A speculator agrees to pay \$15,000 for a parcel of land; this amount, with interest, will be paid over 4 yr, with semiannual payments, at an interest rate of 10% compounded semiannually. Find the amount of each payment.

39. In the Million-Dollar Lottery, a winner is paid a million dollars at the rate of \$50,000 per year for 20 yr. Assume that these payments form an ordinary annuity, and that the lottery managers can invest money at 6% compounded annually. Find the lump sum that the management must put away to pay off the million-dollar winner.

40. The Adams family bought a house for \$81,000. They paid \$20,000 down and took out a 30-year mortgage for the balance at 11%. Use one of the methods in Example 4 to estimate the mortgage balance after 100 payments.

41. After making 180 payments on their mortgage, the Adams family of Exercise 40 sells their house for \$136,000. They must pay closing costs of \$3700 plus 2.5% of the sale price of the house. Approximately how much money will they receive at the close of the sale after their current mortgage is paid off and closing costs are deducted?

In Exercises 42–45, prepare an amortization schedule showing the first 4 payments for each loan. (See Example 5.)

42. An insurance firm pays \$4000 for a new printer for its computer. It amortizes the loan for the printer in 4 annual payments at 8% compounded annually.

43. Large semitrailer trucks cost \$72,000 each. Ace Trucking buys such a truck and agrees to pay for it by a loan that will be amortized with 9 semiannual payments at 6% compounded semiannually.

44. One retailer charges \$1048 for a computer monitor. A firm of tax accountants buys 8 of these monitors. They make a down payment of \$1200 and agree to amortize the balance with monthly payments at 12% compounded monthly for 4 yr.

45. Joan Varozza plans to borrow \$20,000 to stock her small boutique. She will repay the loan with semiannual payments for 5 yr at 7% compounded semiannually.

Student borrowers now have more options to choose from when selecting repayment plans. The standard plan repays the loan in 10 years with equal monthly payments. The extended plan allows from 12 to 30 years to repay the loan. A student borrows $35,000 at 7.43% compounded monthly.*

46. Find the monthly payment and total interest paid under the standard plan.

47. Find the monthly payment and total interest paid under the extended plan with 20 years to pay off the loan.

48. When Teresa Flores opened her law office, she bought $14,000 worth of law books and $7200 worth of office furniture. She paid $1200 down and agreed to amortize the balance with semiannual payments for 5 yr, at 12% compounded semiannually.

(a) Find the amount of each payment.

(b) When her loan had been reduced below $5000, Flores received a large tax refund and decided to pay off the loan. How many payments were left at this time?

49. Kareem Adams buys a house for $285,000. He pays $60,000 down and takes out a mortgage at 9.5% on the balance. Find his monthly payment and the total amount of interest he will pay if the length of the mortgage is

(a) 15 yr; **(b)** 20 yr; **(c)** 25 yr.

(d) When will half the 20-year loan be paid off?

50. Sandi Goldstein has inherited $25,000 from her grandfather's estate. She deposits the money in an account offering 6% interest compounded annually. She wants to make equal annual withdrawals from the account so that the money (principal and interest) lasts exactly 8 years.

(a) Find the amount of each withdrawal.

(b) Find the amount of each withdrawal if the money must last 12 years.

**The New York Times*, April 2, 1995, "Money and College," Saul Hansell, p. 28.

51. The Beyes plan to purchase a home for $212,000. They will pay 20% down and finance the remainder for 30 years at 8.9% interest, compounded monthly.*

(a) How large are their monthly payments?

(b) What will be their loan balance right after they have made their 96th payment?

(c) How much interest will they pay during the 7th year of the loan?

(d) If they were to increase their monthly payments by $150, how long would it take to pay off the loan?

52. Jeni Ramirez plans to retire in 20 years. She will make 240 equal monthly contributions to her retirement account. One month after her last contribution, she will begin the first of 120 monthly withdrawals from the account. She expects to withdraw $3500 per month. How large must her monthly contributions be in order to accomplish her goal if her account is assumed to earn interest of 10.5%, compounded monthly throughout the life of this problem?

53. Ron Okimura also plans to retire in 20 years. Ron will make 120 equal monthly contributions to his account. Ten years after his last contribution (120 months) he will begin the first of 120 monthly withdrawals from his account. Ron also expects to withdraw $3500 per month. His account also earns interest of 10.5%, compounded monthly throughout the life of this problem. How large must Ron's monthly contributions be in order to accomplish his goals?

54. Madeline and Nick Swenson took out a 30-year mortgage for $160,000 at 9.8% interest, compounded monthly. After they had made 12 years of payments (144 payments) they decided to refinance the remaining loan balance for 25 years at 7.2% interest, compounded monthly. What will be the balance on their loan 5 years after they refinance?

*Exercises 51–54 were supplied by Norman Lindquist at Western Washington University.

6.5 APPLYING FINANCIAL FORMULAS

We have presented a lot of new formulas in this chapter. By answering the following questions, you can decide which formula to use for a particular problem.

1. Is simple or compound interest involved?
   Simple interest is normally used for investments or loans of a year or less; compound interest is normally used in all other cases.
2. If simple interest is being used, what is being sought: interest amount, future value, present value, or discount?
3. If compound interest is being used, does it involve a lump sum (single payment) or an annuity (sequence of payments)?
   (a) For a lump sum,
      (i) Is ordinary compound interest or continuous interest involved?
      (ii) What is being sought: present value, future value, number of periods, or effective rate?

(b) For an annuity,

(i) Is it an ordinary annuity (payment at the end of each period) or an annuity due (payment at the beginning of each period)?

(ii) What is being sought: present value, future value, or payment amount?

Once you have answered these questions, choose the appropriate formula from the Chapter Summary, as in the following examples.

EXAMPLE 1 Karen La Bonte must pay \$27,000 in settlement of an obligation in 3 years. What amount can she deposit today, at 4% compounded monthly, to have enough?

In this problem, the future value of \$27,000 is known, and the present value must be found. Because the time is more than one year, we should use the formula for the present value of compound interest. ■

EXAMPLE 2 A bond sells for \$800 and pays interest of 7.5%. How much interest is earned in 6 months?

The time period is for less than a year, so use the simple interest formula. The cost of the bond is the principal P, so $P = 800$, $i = .075$, and $t = 6/12 = 1/2$ year. ■

EXAMPLE 3 A new car is priced at \$11,000. The buyer must pay \$3000 down and pay the balance in 48 equal monthly payments at 12% compounded monthly. Find the payment.

The payments form an ordinary annuity with a present value of $11{,}000 - 3000 = 8000$. Use the formula for the present value of an annuity with $P = 8000$, $i = .01$, and $n = 48$ to find R, the amount of the payment. ■

EXAMPLE 4 Hassi is paid on the first of each month and \$80 is automatically deducted from his pay and deposited in a savings account. If the account pays 4.5% interest compounded monthly, how much will be in the account after 3 years and 9 months?

The time period is for more than a year, so we use compound interest. There will be $3(12) + 9 = 45$ monthly deposits of \$80, so this is an annuity due (the payments are at the first of each month). We want the future value of the annuity. Use the formula for an annuity due with $R = 80$, $i = .045$, and $n = 45$. ■

After you have analyzed the situation and chosen the correct formula, as in the preceding examples, work the problem. As a final step, consider whether the answer you get makes sense. For instance, present value should always be less than future value. Similarly, the future value of an annuity (which includes interest) should be larger than the sum of the payments.

6.5 EXERCISES

For the exercises in this section, round money amounts to the nearest cent, time to the nearest day, and rates to the nearest tenth of a percent.

Find the present value of \$82,000 for the following number of years, if the money can be deposited at 12% compounded quarterly.

1. 5 years

2. 7 years

Find the amount of the payment necessary to amortize the following amounts.

3. \$4250, 13 quarterly payments at 4%

4. \$58,000, 23 quarterly payments at 6%

Find the compound amount for each of the following.

5. \$4792.35 at 4% compounded semiannually for $5\frac{1}{2}$ years

6. \$2500 at 6% compounded quarterly for $3\frac{3}{4}$ years

Find the simple interest for each of the following. Assume 360 days in a year.

7. \$42,500 at 5.75% for 10 months

8. \$32,662 at 6.882% for 225 days

Find the amount of interest earned by each of the following deposits.

9. \$22,500 at 6% compounded quarterly for $5\frac{1}{4}$ years

10. \$53,142 at 8% compounded monthly for 32 months

Find the compound amount and the amount of interest earned by a deposit of \$32,750 at 5% compounded continuously for the following number of years.

11. $7\frac{1}{2}$ years

12. 9.2 years

Find the present value of the following future amounts. Assume 360 days in a year and use simple interest.

13. \$17,320 for 9 months, money earns 3.5%

14. \$122,300 for 138 days, money earns 4.75%

Find the proceeds for the following. Assume 360 days in a year and use simple interest.

15. \$23,561 for 112 days, discount rate 4.33%

16. \$267,100 for 271 days, discount rate 5.72%

Find the future value of each of the following annuities.

17. \$2500 is deposited at the end of each semiannual period for $5\frac{1}{2}$ years, money earns 7% compounded semiannually

18. \$800 is deposited at the end of each month for $1\frac{1}{4}$ years, money earns 8% compounded monthly

19. \$250 is deposited at the end of each quarter for $7\frac{1}{4}$ years, money earns 4% compounded quarterly

20. \$100 is deposited at the beginning of each year for 5 years, money earns 8% compounded yearly

Find the amount of each payment to be made to a sinking fund to accumulate the indicated amounts.

21. \$10,000, money earns 5% compounded annually, 7 annual payments at the end of each year

22. \$42,000, money earns 4% compounded quarterly, 13 quarterly payments at the end of each quarter

23. \$100,000, money earns 6% compounded semiannually, 9 semiannual payments at the end of each semiannual period

24. \$53,000, money earns 6% compounded monthly, 35 monthly payments at the end of each month

Find the present value of each ordinary annuity.

25. Payments of \$1200 are made annually for 7 years at 5% compounded annually

26. Payments of \$500 are made semiannually at 4% compounded semiannually for $3\frac{1}{2}$ years

27. Payments of \$1500 are made quarterly for $5\frac{1}{4}$ years at 6% compounded quarterly

28. Payments of \$905.43 are made monthly for $2\frac{11}{12}$ years at 8% compounded monthly

Prepare an amortization schedule for each of the following loans. Interest is calculated on the unpaid balance.

29. \$8500 loan repaid in semiannual payments for $3\frac{1}{2}$ years at 8%

30. \$40,000 loan repaid in quarterly payments for $1\frac{3}{4}$ years at 9%

Management *Solve the following applied problems.*

31. A 10-month loan of \$42,000 at simple interest produces \$1785 interest. Find the interest rate.

32. Willa Burke deposits \$803.47 at the end of each quarter for $3\frac{3}{4}$ years in an account paying 4% compounded quarterly. Find the final amount in the account and the amount of interest earned.

33. Makarim Wibison owes \$7850 to a relative. He has agreed to pay the money in 5 months at simple interest of 7%. One month before the loan is due, the relative discounts the loan at the bank. The bank charges a 9.2% discount rate. How much money does the relative receive?

34. A small resort must add a swimming pool to compete with a new resort built nearby. The pool will cost \$28,000. The resort borrows the money and agrees to repay it with equal payments at the end of each quarter for $6\frac{1}{2}$ years at an interest rate of 6% compounded quarterly. Find the amount of each payment.

35. According to the terms of a divorce settlement, one spouse must pay the other a lump sum of \$2800 in 17 months. What lump sum can be invested today, at 6% compounded monthly, so that enough will be available for the payment?

36. An accountant loans \$28,000 at simple interest to her business. The loan is at 9% and earns \$3255 interest. Find the time of the loan in months.

37. A firm of attorneys deposits \$5000 of profit sharing money at the end of each semiannual period for $7\frac{1}{2}$ years. Find the final amount in the account if the deposit earns 5% compounded semiannually. Find the amount of interest earned.

38. Find the principal that must be invested at 5.25% simple interest to earn \$937.50 interest in 8 months.

39. In 3 years Ms. Thompson must pay a pledge of \$7500 to her college's building fund. What lump sum can she deposit today, at 4% compounded semiannually, so that she will have enough to pay the pledge?

40. The owner of Eastside Hallmark borrows \$48,000 to expand the business. The money will be repaid in equal payments at the end of each year for 7 years. Interest is 8%. Find the amount of each payment.

41. To buy a new computer, Mark Nguyen borrows \$3250 from a friend at 9% interest compounded annually for 4 years. Find the compound amount he must pay back at the end of the 4 years.

42. A small business invests some spare cash for 3 months at 5.2% simple interest and earns \$244 in interest. Find the amount of the investment.

43. When the Lee family bought their home, they borrowed \$115,700 at 10.5% compounded monthly for 25 years. If they make all 300 payments, repaying the loan on schedule, how much interest will they pay? Assume the last payment is the same as the previous ones.

44. Suppose \$84,720 is deposited for 7 months and earns \$2372.16 in interest. Find the rate of interest.

CHAPTER 6 SUMMARY

Key Terms and Symbols

6.1 interest
principal
rate
time
simple interest
future value (maturity value)
present value
discount (bank discount)
proceeds

6.2 compound interest
compound amount
compounding period
continuous compounding
nominal rate (stated rate)
effective rate

6.3 geometric sequence
common ratio
annuity
ordinary annuity
payment period
term of an annuity
future value of an annuity
annuity due
sinking fund

6.4 present value of an annuity
amortize a loan
amortization schedule

Key Concepts

Simple Interest

The **simple interest** I on an amount of P dollars for t years at interest rate r per year is $\boldsymbol{I = Prt}$.

The **future value** A of P dollars at simple interest rate r for t years is $\boldsymbol{A = P(1 + rt)}$.

The **present value** P of a future amount of A dollars at simple interest rate r for t years is

$$P = \frac{A}{1 + rt}.$$

If D is the **discount** on a loan having maturity value A at simple interest rate r for t years, then $\boldsymbol{D = Art}$. If D is the discount and P the **proceeds** of a loan having maturity value A at simple interest rate r for t years, then $\boldsymbol{P = A - D}$ or $\boldsymbol{P = A(1 - rt)}$.

Compound Interest

If P dollars is deposited for n time periods at compound interest rate i per period, the **compound amount (future value)** A is $A = P(1+i)^n$.

The **present value** P of A dollars at compound interest rate i per period for n periods is

$$P = \frac{A}{(1+i)^n} = A(1+i)^{-n}.$$

The **effective rate** corresponding to a stated interest rate r per year, compounded m times per year, is

$$r_e = \left(1 + \frac{r}{m}\right)^m - 1.$$

Continuous Compound Interest

If P dollars is deposited for t years at interest rate r per year, compounded continuously, the **compound amount (future value)** A is $A = Pe^{rt}$.

The **present value** P of A dollars at interest rate r per year compounded continuously for t years is

$$P = \frac{A}{e^{rt}}.$$

Annuities

The **future value S of an ordinary annuity** of n payments of R dollars each at the end of consecutive interest periods with interest compounded at rate i per period is

$$S = R\left[\frac{(1+i)^n - 1}{i}\right] \quad \text{or} \quad S = R \cdot s_{\overline{n}|i}.$$

The **present value P of an ordinary annuity** of n payments of R dollars each at the end of consecutive interest periods with interest compounded at rate i per period is

$$P = R\left[\frac{1 - (1+i)^{-n}}{i}\right] \quad \text{or} \quad P = R \cdot a_{\overline{n}|i}.$$

To find the payment, solve the formula for R.

The **future value S of an annuity due** of n payments of R dollars each at the beginning of consecutive interest periods with interest compounded at rate i per period is

$$S = R\left[\frac{(1+i)^{n+1} - 1}{i}\right] - R \quad \text{or} \quad S = R \cdot s_{\overline{n+1}|i} - R.$$

Chapter 6 Review Exercises

Find the simple interest for the following loans.

1. \$4902 at 9.5% for 11 months
2. \$42,368 at 15.22% for 5 months
3. \$3478 at 7.4% for 88 days (assume a 360-day year)
4. \$2390 at 18.7% from May 3 to July 28 (assume 365 days in a year)
5. What is meant by the present value of an amount A?

Find the present value of the following future amounts. Assume 360 days in a year; use simple interest.

6. \$459.57 in 7 months, money earns 8.5%
7. \$80,612 in 128 days, money earns 6.77%
8. Explain what happens when a borrower is charged a discount. What are the proceeds?

Find the proceeds in Exercises 9 and 10. Assume 360 days in a year.

9. \$802.34; discount rate 8.6%; length of loan 11 mo

10. \$12,000; discount rate 7.09%; length of loan 145 days

11. For a given amount of money at a given interest rate for a given time period greater than 1 year, does simple interest or compound interest produce more interest? Explain.

Find the compound amount and the amount of interest earned in each of the following.

12. \$2800 at 6% compounded annually for 10 yr

13. \$57,809.34 at 4% compounded quarterly for 5 yr

14. \$12,903.45 at 6.37% compounded quarterly for 29 quarters

15. \$4677.23 at 4.57% compounded monthly for 32 mo

Find the present value of the following amounts.

16. \$42,000 in 7 yr, 12% compounded monthly

17. \$17,650 in 4 yr, 8% compounded quarterly

18. \$1347.89 in 3.5 yr, 6.77% compounded semiannually

19. \$2388.90 in 44 mo, 5.93% compounded monthly

20. Write the first five terms of the geometric sequence with $a = 2$ and $r = 3$.

21. Write the first four terms of the geometric sequence with $a = 4$ and $r = 1/2$.

22. Find the sixth term of the geometric sequence with $a = -3$ and $r = 2$.

23. Find the fifth term of the geometric sequence with $a = -2$ and $r = -2$.

24. Find the sum of the first four terms of the geometric sequence with $a = -3$ and $r = 3$.

25. Find the sum of the first five terms of the geometric sequence with $a = 8000$ and $r = -1/2$.

26. Find $s_{\overline{30}|.01}$.

27. What is meant by the future value of an annuity?

Find the future value of each annuity.

28. \$1288 deposited at the end of each year for 14 yr; money earns 8% compounded annually

29. \$4000 deposited at the end of each quarter for 7 yr; money earns 6% compounded quarterly

30. \$233 deposited at the end of each month for 4 yr; money earns 12% compounded monthly

31. \$672 deposited at the beginning of each quarter for 7 yr; money earns 8% compounded quarterly

32. \$11,900 deposited at the beginning of each month for 13 mo; money earns 12% compounded monthly

33. What is the purpose of a sinking fund?

Find the amount of each payment that must be made into a sinking fund to accumulate the following amounts. Assume payments are made at the end of each period.

34. \$6500; money earns 5% compounded annually; 6 annual payments

35. \$57,000; money earns 6% compounded semiannually for $8\frac{1}{2}$ yr

36. \$233,188; money earns 5.7% compounded quarterly for $7\frac{3}{4}$ yr

37. \$56,788; money earns 6.12% compounded monthly for $4\frac{1}{2}$ yr

Find the present value of each ordinary annuity.

38. Payments of \$850 annually for 4 yr at 5% compounded annually

39. Payments of \$1500 quarterly for 7 yr at 8% compounded quarterly

40. Payments of \$4210 semiannually for 8 yr at 8.6% compounded semiannually

41. Payments of \$877.34 monthly for 17 mo at 6.4% compounded monthly

42. Give two examples of the types of loans that are commonly amortized.

Find the amount of the payment necessary to amortize each of the following loans.

43. \$32,000 at 9.4% compounded quarterly, 10 quarterly payments

44. \$5607 at 7.6% compounded monthly, 32 monthly payments

Find the monthly house payments for the following mortgages.

45. \$56,890 at 10.74% for 25 yr

46. \$77,110 at 8.45% for 30 yr

A portion of an amortization table is given below for a \$127,000 loan at 8.5% interest compounded monthly for 25 yr.

Payment Number	*Amount of Payment*	*Interest for Period*	*Portion to Principal*	*Principal at End of Period*
0	—	—	—	\$127,000.00
1	\$1022.64	\$899.58	\$123.06	126,876.94
2	1022.64	898.71	123.93	126,753.02
3	1022.64	897.83	124.80	126,628.21
4	1022.64	896.95	125.69	126,502.53
5	1022.64	896.06	126.58	126,375.95
6	1022.64	895.16	127.48	126,248.47

Use the table to answer the following questions.

47. How much of the fifth payment is interest?

48. How much of the sixth payment is used to reduce the debt?

49. How much interest is paid in the first 3 months of the loan?

50. How much has the debt been reduced at the end of the first 6 months?

Management *Work the following applied problems.*

51. Larry DiCenso needs $9812 to buy new equipment for his business. The bank charges a discount rate of 12%. Find the amount of DiCenso's loan if he borrows the money for 7 mo.

52. A florist borrows $1400 at simple interest to pay taxes. The loan is at 11.5% and costs $120.75 in interest. Find the time of the loan in months.

53. A developer deposits $84,720 for 7 mo and earns $4055.46 in interest. Find the interest rate.

54. Tom Wilson owes $5800 to his mother. He has agreed to pay back the money in 10 mo, at an interest rate of 10%. Three months before the loan is due, Tom's mother discounts the loan at the bank to get cash for $6000 worth of new furniture. The bank charges a 13.45% discount rate. How much money does Tom's mother receive? Is it enough to buy the furniture?

55. In 3 yr Ms. Flores must pay a pledge of $7500 to her favorite charity. What lump sum can she deposit today, at 10% compounded semiannually, so that she will have enough to pay the pledge?

56. Each year a firm must set aside enough funds to provide employee retirement benefits of $52,000 in 20 years. If the firm can invest money at 7.5% compounded monthly, what amount must be invested at the end of each month for this purpose?

57. Chalon Bridges deposits semiannual payments of $3200, received in payment of a debt, in an ordinary annuity at 6.8% compounded semiannually. Find the final amount in the account and the interest earned at the end of 3.5 years.

58. To finance the $15,000 cost of their kitchen remodeling, the Chews will make equal payments at the end of each month for 36 months. They will pay interest at the rate of 7.2% compounded monthly. Find the amount of each payment.

59. To expand her business, the owner of a small restaurant borrows $40,000. She will repay the money in equal payments at the end of each semiannual period for 8 years at 9% interest compounded semiannually. What payments must she make?

60. Pension experts recommend that you start drawing at least 40% of your full pension as early as possible.* Suppose you have built up a pension with $12,000 annual payments by working 10 years for a company, when you leave to accept a better job. The company gives you the option of collecting half the full pension when you reach age 55 or the full pension at age 65. Assume an interest rate of 8% compounded annually. By age 75, how much will each plan produce? Which plan would produce the larger amount?

Smart Money, October, 1994, "Pocket That Pension," p. 33.

61. The Taggart family bought a house for $91,000. They paid $20,000 down and took out a 30-yr mortgage for the balance at 9%.

(a) Find their monthly payment.

(b) How much of the first payment is interest?

After 180 payments, the family sells their house for $136,000. They must pay closing costs of $3700 plus 2.5% of the sale price.

(c) Estimate the current mortgage balance at the time of the sale using one of the methods from Example 4 in Section 6.4.

(d) Find the total closing costs.

(e) Find the amount of money they receive from the sale after paying off the mortgage.

62. The proceeds of a $10,000 death benefit are left on deposit with an insurance company for 7 yr at an annual effective interest rate of 5%.* The balance at the end of 7 yr is paid to the beneficiary in 120 equal monthly payments of X, with the first payment made immediately. During the payout period, interest is credited at an annual effective interest rate of 3%. Calculate X.

(a) 117 **(b)** 118 **(c)** 129 **(d)** 135 **(e)** 158

63. Gene deposits $500 per quarter to his nest egg account. The account earns interest of 9%, compounded quarterly. Right after Gene makes his 16th deposit, he loses his job and cannot make any deposits for the next 5 years (20 quarters). Eventually Gene gets another job and again begins making deposits to his account. Since he missed so many deposits while he was out of work, Gene now deposits $750 per quarter. His first $750 deposit comes exactly 20 quarters after his last $500 deposit. What will be Gene's account balance right after he has made his 32nd $750 deposit?†

64. Cathy wants to retire on $55,000 per year for her life expectancy of 20 years. She estimates that she will be able to earn interest of 9%, compounded annually, throughout her lifetime. To reach her retirement goal, Cathy will make annual contributions to her account for the next 25 years. One year after making her last contribution, she will take her first retirement check. How large must her yearly contributions be?

*Problem from "Course 140 Examination, Mathematics of Compound Interest" of the Education and Examination Committee of The Society of Actuaries. Reprinted by permission of The Society of Actuaries.

†Exercises 63 and 64 supplied by Norman Lindquist, Western Washington University.

CASE 6

Time, Money, and Polynomials*

A *time line* is often helpful for evaluating complex investments. For example, suppose you buy a $1000 CD at time t_0. After one year $2500 is added to the CD at t_1. By time t_2, after another year, your money has grown to $3851 with interest. What rate of interest, called *yield to maturity* (*YTM*), did your money earn? A time line for this situation is shown in Figure 1.

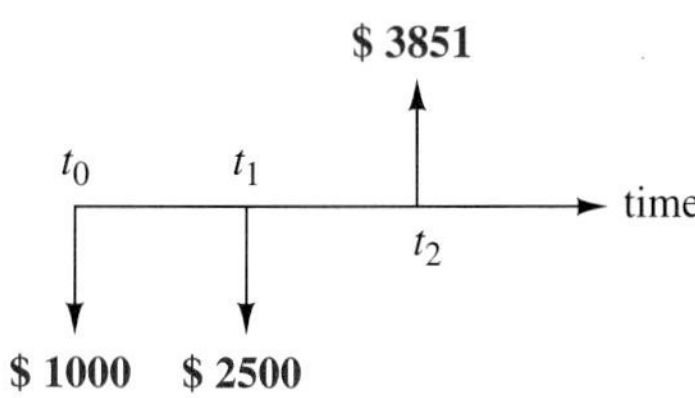

FIGURE 1

Assuming interest is compounded annually at a rate i, and using the compound interest formula gives the following description of the YTM.

$$1000(1 + i)^2 + 2500(1 + i) = 3851$$

To determine the yield to maturity, we must solve this equation for i. Since the quantity $1 + i$ is repeated, let $x = 1 + i$ and first solve the second-degree (quadratic) polynomial equation for x.

$$1000x^2 + 2500x - 3851 = 0$$

We can use the quadratic formula with $a = 1000$, $b = 2500$, and $c = -3851$.

$$x = \frac{-2500 \pm \sqrt{2500^2 - 4(1000)(-3851)}}{2(1000)}$$

We get $x = 1.0767$ and $x = -3.5767$. Since $x = 1 + i$, the two values for i are $.0767 = 7.67\%$ and $-4.5767 = -457.67\%$. We reject the negative value because the final accumulation is greater than the sum of the deposits. In some applications, however, negative rates may be meaningful. By checking in the first equation, we see that the yield to maturity for the CD is 7.67%.

Now let us consider a more complex but realistic problem. Suppose Curt Reynolds has contributed for four years to a retirement fund. He contributed $6000 at the beginning of the first year. At the beginning of the next three years, he contributed $5840, $4000, and $5200, respectively. At the end of the fourth year, he had $29,912.38 in his fund. The interest rate earned by the fund varied between 21% and −3%, so Reynolds would like to know the YTM $= i$ for his hard-earned retirement dollars. From a time line (see Figure 2), we set up the following equation in $1 + i$ for Reynolds' savings program.

$$6000(1 + i)^4 + 5840(1 + i)^3 + 4000(1 + i)^2 + 5200(1 + i) = 29{,}912.38$$

Let $x = 1 + i$. We need to solve the fourth-degree polynomial equation

$$f(x) = 6000x^4 + 5840x^3 + 4000x^2 + 5200x - 29{,}912.38 = 0.$$

There is no simple way to solve a fourth-degree polynomial equation, so we will use a guess and check method.

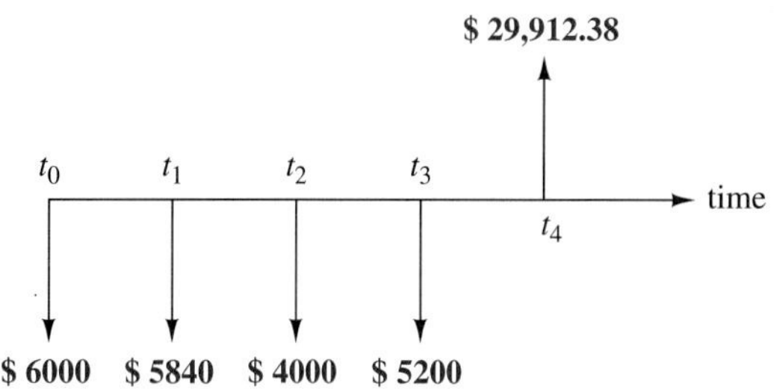

FIGURE 2

We expect that $0 < i < 1$, so that $1 < x < 2$. Let us calculate $f(1)$ and $f(2)$. If there is a change of sign, we will know that there is a solution to $f(x) = 0$ between 1 and 2. We find that

$$f(1) = -8872.38 \text{ and } f(2) = 139{,}207.62.$$

There is a change in sign as expected. Now we find $f(1.1)$, $f(1.2)$, $f(1.3)$, and so on, and look for another change in sign. (A computer or calculator program would help here to try values of x between 1 and 2.) Right away we find

$$f(1.1) = -2794.74 \quad \text{and} \quad f(1.2) = 4620.74.$$

This process can be repeated for values of x between 1.1 and 1.2, to get $f(1.11) = -2116.59$, $f(1.12) = -1424.88$, $f(1.13) = -719.42$, and $f(1.14) = 0$. We were lucky; the solution for $f(x) = 0$ is exactly 1.14, so $i = \text{YTM} = .14 = 14\%$.

*From *Time, Money, and Polynomials*, COMAP.

EXERCISES

1. Lucinda Turley received \$50 on her 16th birthday, and \$70 on her 17th birthday, both of which she immediately invested in the bank with interest compounded annually. On her 18th birthday, she had \$127.40 in her account. Draw a time line, set up a polynomial equation, and calculate the YTM.

2. At the beginning of the year, Jay Beckenstein invested \$10,000 at 5% for the first year. At the beginning of the second year, he added \$12,000 to the account. The total account earned 4.5% for the second year.

(a) Draw a time line for this investment.

(b) How much was in the fund at the end of the second year?

(c) Set up and solve a polynomial equation and determine the YTM. What do you notice about the YTM?

3. On January 2 each year for three years, Earl Karn deposited bonuses of \$1025, \$2200, and \$1850, respectively, in an account. He received no bonus the following year, so he made no deposit. At the end of the fourth year, there was \$5864.17 in the account.

(a) Draw a time line for these investments.

(b) Write a polynomial equation in x ($x = 1 + i$) and use the guess and check method to find the YTM for these investments.

4. Pat Kelley invested yearly in a fund for his children's college education. At the beginning of the first year, he invested \$1000; at the beginning of the second year, \$2000; at the third through the sixth, \$2500 each year; and at the beginning of the seventh, he invested \$5000. At the beginning of the eighth year, there was \$21,259 in the fund.

(a) Draw a time line for this investment program.

(b) Write a seventh-degree polynomial equation in $1 + i$ that gives the YTM for this investment program.

(c) Use a graphing calculator to show that the YTM is less than 5.07% and greater than 5.05%.

(d) Use a graphing calculator to calculate the solution for $1 + i$ and find the YTM.

5. People often lose money on investments. Jim Carlson invested \$50 at the beginning of each of two years in a mutual fund, and at the end of two years his investment was worth \$90.

(a) Draw a time line and set up a polynomial equation in $1 + i$. Solve for i.

(b) Examine each negative solution (rate of return on the investment) to see if it has a reasonable interpretation in the context of the problem. To do this, use the compound interest formula on each value of i to trace each \$50 payment to maturity.

CHAPTER 7

Systems of Linear Equations and Matrices

Many applications of mathematics require finding the solution of a *system* of first-degree equations. This chapter presents methods for solving such systems, including matrix methods. Matrix algebra and other applications of matrices are also discussed.

7.1 SYSTEMS OF LINEAR EQUATIONS

This section deals with **linear** (or **first-degree**) **equations** such as

$$2x + 3y = 14 \quad \text{linear equation in two variables,}$$
$$4x - 2y + 5z = 8 \quad \text{linear equation in three variables,}$$

and so on. A **solution** of such an equation is an ordered set of numbers that when substituted for the variables in the order they appear produces a true statement. For instance, (1, 4) is a solution of the equation $2x + 3y = 14$ because substituting $x = 1$ and $y = 4$ produces the true statement $2(1) + 3(4) = 14$. Similarly, $(0, -4, 0)$ is a solution of $4x - 2y + 5z = 8$ because $4(0) - 2(-4) + 5(0) = 8$.

Many applications involve **systems of linear equations,** such as these two:

Two equations in two variables	Three equations in four variables
$5x - 3y = 7$	$2x + y + z = 3$
$2x + 4y = 8$	$x + y + z + w = 5$
	$-4x + z + w = 0$

A **solution of a system** is a solution that satisfies *all* the equations in the system. For instance, in the right-hand system of equations above, (1, 0, 1, 3) is a solution of all three equations (check it) and hence is a solution of the system. On the other hand, (1, 1, 0, 3) is a solution of the first two equations but not the third. Hence (1, 1, 0, 3) is not a solution of the system. [1]

[1] Which of $(-8, 3, 0)$, $(8, -2, -2)$, $(-6, 5, -2)$ are solutions of the system

$$x + 2y + 3z = -2$$
$$2x + 6y + z = 2$$
$$3x + 3y + 10z = -2?$$

Answer:
Only $(8, -2, -2)$

SYSTEMS OF TWO EQUATIONS IN TWO VARIABLES The graph of a linear equation in two variables is a straight line. Earlier we saw that the coordinates of each point on the graph represent a solution of the equation. Thus, the solution of a system of two such equations is represented by the point or points where the two lines intersect. There are exactly three geometric possibilities for two lines: they intersect at a single point, or they coincide, or they are distinct and parallel. As illustrated in Figure 7.1, each of these geometric possibilities corresponds to an algebraic outcome for which special terminology is used.

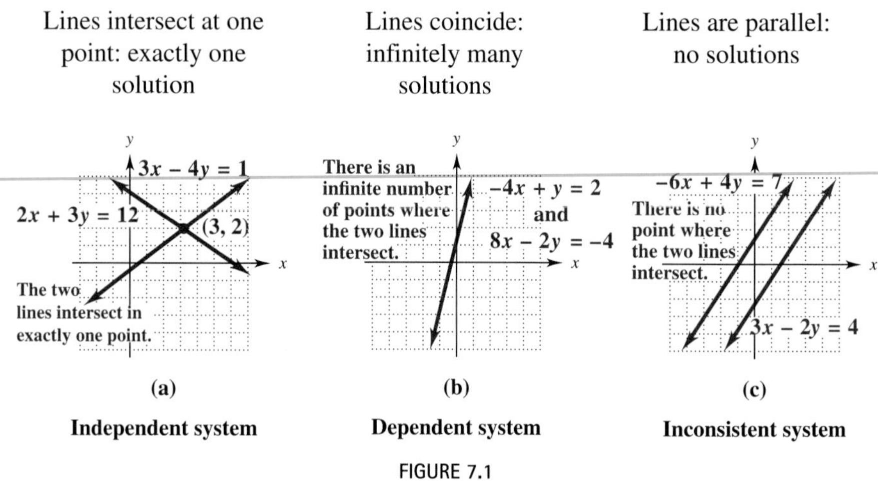

FIGURE 7.1

In theory, every system of two equations in two variables can be solved by graphing the lines and finding their intersection points (if any). In practice, however, algebraic techniques are usually needed to determine the solutions precisely. Such systems can be solved by the **elimination method,** as illustrated in the following examples.

EXAMPLE 1 Solve the system

$$3x - 4y = 1 \qquad (1)$$
$$2x + 3y = 12. \qquad (2)$$

To eliminate one variable by addition of the two equations, the coefficients of either x or y in the two equations must be additive inverses. For example, let us choose to eliminate x. We multiply both sides of equation (1) by 2 and both sides of equation (2) by -3 to get

$$6x - 8y = 2$$
$$-6x - 9y = -36.$$

Adding these equations gives a new equation with just one variable, y. This equation can be solved for y.

$$\begin{array}{r} 6x - 8y = 2 \\ \underline{-6x - 9y = -36} \\ -17y = -34 \end{array} \qquad \text{Variable } x \text{ is eliminated.}$$

$$y = 2$$

2 Solve the system of equations

$$3x + 2y = -1$$
$$5x - 3y = 11.$$

Draw the graph of each equation on the same axes.

Answer:
(1, −2)

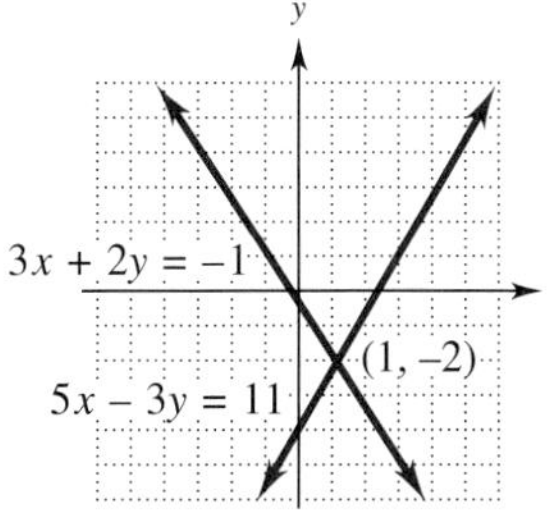

To find the corresponding value of x, substitute 2 for y in either of equations (1) or (2). We choose equation (1).

$$3x - 4(2) = 1$$
$$3x - 8 = 1$$
$$x = 3$$

Therefore, the solution of the system is (3, 2). The graphs of both equations of the system are shown in Figure 7.1(a). They intersect at the point (3, 2), the solution of the system. ■ 2

TECHNOLOGY TIP To find approximate solutions of a system of two equations in two variables with a graphing calculator, solve each equation for y and graph both of them on the same screen. In Example 1, for instance, we would graph

$$y_1 = \frac{3x - 1}{4} \quad \text{and} \quad y_2 = \frac{12 - 2x}{3}.$$

The point where the graphs intersect (the solution of the system) can then be found by using the calculator's intersection finder, as shown in Figure 7.2. ✔

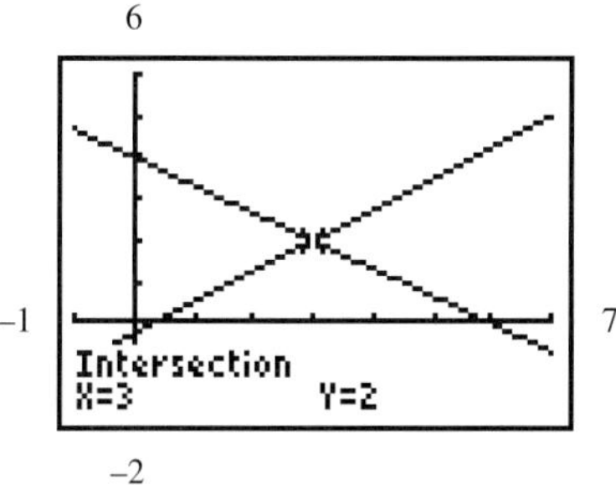

FIGURE 7.2

EXAMPLE 2 Solve the system

$$-4x + y = 2$$
$$8x - 2y = -4.$$

Eliminate x by multiplying both sides of the first equation by 2 and adding the results to the second equation.

$$-8x + 2y = 4$$
$$8x - 2y = -4$$
$$0 = 0 \quad \text{Both variables eliminated.}$$

3 Solve the following system.

$$3x - 4y = 13$$
$$12x - 16y = 52$$

Answer:
All ordered pairs that satisfy the equation $3x - 4y = 13$ (or $12x - 16y = 52$)

Although both variables have been eliminated, the resulting statement "0 = 0" is true, which is the algebraic indication that the two equations have the same graph, as shown in Figure 7.1(b). Therefore the system is dependent and has an infinite number of solutions: every ordered pair that is a solution of the equation $-4x + y = 2$ is a solution of the system. ■ 3

4 Solve the system

$$x - y = 4$$
$$2x - 2y = 3.$$

Draw the graph of each equation on the same axes.

Answer:
No solution

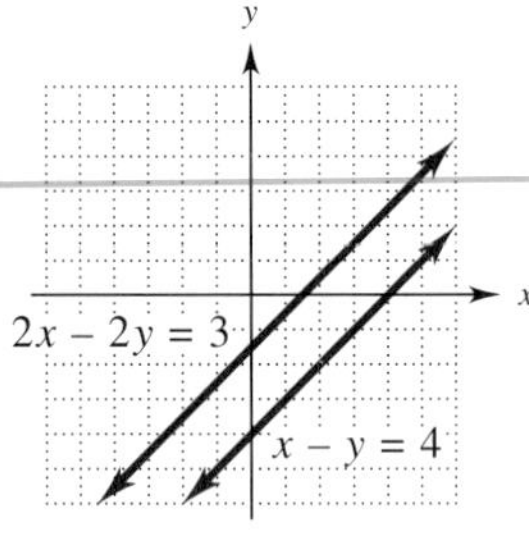

EXAMPLE 3 Solve the system

$$3x - 2y = 4$$
$$-6x + 4y = 7.$$

The graphs of these equations are parallel lines (each has slope 3/2), as shown in Figure 7.1(c). Therefore the system has no solution. However, you do not need the graphs to discover this fact. If you try to solve the system algebraically by multiplying both sides of the first equation by 2 and adding the results to the second equation, you obtain

$$\begin{aligned} 6x - 4y &= 8 \\ -6x + 4y &= 7 \\ \hline 0 &= 15. \end{aligned}$$

The false statement "$0 = 15$" is the algebraic signal that the system is inconsistent and has no solution. ■ 4

LARGER SYSTEMS OF LINEAR EQUATIONS Two systems of equations are said to be **equivalent** if they have the same solutions. The basic procedure for solving a large system of equations is to use properties of algebra to transform the system into a simpler, equivalent system and then solve this simpler system.

5 Verify that $x = 2, y = 1$ is the solution of the system

$$x - 3y = -1$$
$$3x + 2y = 8.$$

(a) Replace the second equation by the sum of itself and -3 times the first equation.

(b) What is the solution of the system in part (a)?

Answers:

(a) The system becomes

$$x - 3y = -1$$
$$11y = 11.$$

(b) $x = 2, y = 1$

Performing any one of the following **elementary operations** on a system of linear equations produces an equivalent system.

1. Interchange any two equations.
2. Multiply both sides of an equation by a nonzero constant.
3. Replace an equation by the sum of itself and a constant multiple of another equation in the system.

Performing either of the first two elementary operations produces an equivalent system because rearranging the order of the equations or multiplying both sides of an equation by a constant does not affect the solutions of the individual equations, and hence does not affect the solutions of the system. No formal proof will be given here that performing the third elementary operation produces an equivalent system, but Side Problem 5 illustrates this fact. 5

Example 4 shows how to use elementary operations on a system to eliminate certain variables and produce an equivalent system that is easily solved. The italicized statements provide an outline of the procedure.

EXAMPLE 4 Use the elimination method to solve the system

$$2x + y - z = 2$$
$$x + 3y + 2z = 1$$
$$x + y + z = 2.$$

First, *use elementary operations to produce an equivalent system in which 1 is the coefficient of x in the first equation.* One way to do this is to interchange the first two equations (another would be to multiply both sides of the first equation by 1/2).

$$\begin{aligned} x + 3y + 2z &= 1 \qquad \text{Interchange } R_1, R_2. \\ 2x + y - z &= 2 \\ x + y + z &= 2 \end{aligned}$$

Here and below we use R_1 to denote the first equation in a system, R_2 the second equation, and so on.

Next, *use elementary operations to produce an equivalent system in which the x-term has been eliminated from the second and third equations.* To eliminate the x term from the second equation above, replace the second equation by the sum of itself and -2 times the first equation.

$$\begin{array}{r|r} -2R_1 & -2x - 6y - 4z = -2 \\ R_2 & 2x + y - z = 2 \\ \hline -2R_1 + R_2 & -5y - 5z = 0 \end{array}$$

$$\begin{aligned} x + 3y + 2z &= 1 \\ -5y - 5z &= 0 \qquad -2R_1 + R_2 \leftarrow \\ x + y + z &= 2 \end{aligned}$$

To eliminate the x-term from the third equation of this last system, replace the third equation by the sum of itself and -1 times the first equation.

$$\begin{array}{r|r} -1R_1 & -x - 3y - 2z = -1 \\ R_3 & x + y + z = 2 \\ \hline -1R_1 + R_3 & -2y - z = 1 \end{array}$$

$$\begin{aligned} x + 3y + 2z &= 1 \\ -5y - 5z &= 0 \\ -2y - z &= 1 \qquad -1R_1 + R_3 \leftarrow \end{aligned}$$

Now that x has been eliminated from all but the first equation, we ignore the first equation and work on the remaining ones. *Use elementary operations to produce an equivalent system in which 1 is the coefficient of y in the second equation.* This can be done by multiplying the second equation in the system above by $-1/5$.

$$\begin{aligned} x + 3y + 2z &= 1 \\ y + z &= 0 \qquad -\frac{1}{5}R_2 \\ -2y - z &= 1 \end{aligned}$$

Then *use elementary operations to obtain an equivalent system in which y has been eliminated from the third equation:* replace the third equation by the sum of itself and 2 times the second equation:

$$\begin{aligned} x + 3y + 2z &= 1 \\ y + z &= 0 \\ z &= 1. \qquad 2R_2 + R_3 \end{aligned}$$

This last system is said to be in **triangular form,** a form in which the solution of the third equation is obvious: $z = 1$. Now work backward in the system. Substitute 1 for

z in the second equation and solve for y, obtaining $y = -1$. Finally, substitute 1 for z and -1 for y in the first equation and solve for x, obtaining $x = 2$. This process is known as **back substitution.** When it is finished we have the solution of the original system, namely, $(2, -1, 1)$. It is always wise to check the solution by substituting the values for x, y, and z in all equations of the original system. ■

The procedure used in Example 4 to eliminate variables and produce a system in which back substitution works can be carried out with any system, as summarized below. In this summary, the first variable that appears in an equation with nonzero coefficient is called the **leading variable** of that equation and its nonzero coefficient is called the **leading coefficient.**

THE ELIMINATION METHOD FOR SOLVING LARGE SYSTEMS OF LINEAR EQUATIONS

Use elementary operations to transform the given system into an equivalent one in which the leading coefficient in each equation is 1 and the leading variable in each equation does not appear in any later equations. This can be done systematically as follows:

1. Make the leading coefficient of the first equation 1.
2. Eliminate the leading variable of the first equation from each later equation by replacing the later equation by the sum of itself and a suitable multiple of the first equation.
3. Repeat Steps 1 and 2 for the second equation: make its leading coefficient 1 and eliminate its leading variable from each later equation by replacing the later equation by the sum of itself and a suitable multiple of the second equation.
4. Repeat Steps 1 and 2 for the third equation, fourth equation, and so on, until it is not possible to go further.

Then solve the resulting system by back substitution.

6 Use the elimination method to solve each system.

(a) $$\begin{aligned} 2x + y &= -1 \\ x + 3y &= 2 \end{aligned}$$

(b) $$\begin{aligned} 2x - y + 3z &= 2 \\ x + 2y - z &= 6 \\ -x - y + z &= -5 \end{aligned}$$

Answers:

(a) $(-1, 1)$

(b) $(3, 1, -1)$

At various stages in the elimination process, you may have a choice of elementary operations that can be used. As long as the final result is a system in which back substitution can be used, the choice does not matter. To avoid unnecessary errors, choose elementary operations that minimize the amount of computation and, as far as possible, avoid complicated fractions. 6

MATRIX METHODS You may have noticed that the variables in a system of equations remain unchanged during the solution process. We really need to keep track of just the coefficients and the constants. For instance, consider the system in Example 4:

$$\begin{aligned} 2x + y - z &= 2 \\ x + 3y + 2z &= 1 \\ x + y + z &= 2. \end{aligned}$$

7 (a) Write the augmented matrix of this system.

$$\begin{aligned} 4x - 2y + 3z &= 4 \\ 3x + 5y + z &= -7 \\ 5x - y + 4z &= 6 \end{aligned}$$

(b) Write the system of equations associated with this augmented matrix.

$$\left[\begin{array}{cc|c} 2 & -2 & -2 \\ 1 & 1 & 4 \\ 3 & 5 & 8 \end{array}\right]$$

Answers:

(a) $\left[\begin{array}{ccc|c} 4 & -2 & 3 & 4 \\ 3 & 5 & 1 & -7 \\ 5 & -1 & 4 & 6 \end{array}\right]$

(b) $\begin{aligned} 2x - 2y &= -2 \\ x + y &= 4 \\ 3x + 5y &= 8 \end{aligned}$

8 Perform the following row operations on the matrix

$$\begin{bmatrix} -1 & 5 \\ 3 & -2 \end{bmatrix}.$$

(a) Interchange R_1 and R_2.

(b) $2R_1$

(c) Replace R_2 by $-3R_1 + R_2$.

(d) Replace R_1 by $2R_2 + R_1$.

Answers:

(a) $\begin{bmatrix} 3 & -2 \\ -1 & 5 \end{bmatrix}$

(b) $\begin{bmatrix} -2 & 10 \\ 3 & -2 \end{bmatrix}$

(c) $\begin{bmatrix} -1 & 5 \\ 6 & -17 \end{bmatrix}$

(d) $\begin{bmatrix} 5 & 1 \\ 3 & -2 \end{bmatrix}$

This system can be written in an abbreviated form as

$$\begin{bmatrix} 2 & 1 & -1 & 2 \\ 1 & 3 & 2 & 1 \\ 1 & 1 & 1 & 2 \end{bmatrix}.$$

Such a rectangular array of numbers, consisting of horizontal **rows** and vertical **columns,** is called a **matrix** (plural **matrices**). Each number in the array is an **element** or **entry.** To separate the constants in the last column of the matrix from the coefficients of the variables, we may use a vertical line, producing the following **augmented matrix.**

$$\left[\begin{array}{ccc|c} 2 & 1 & -1 & 2 \\ 1 & 3 & 2 & 1 \\ 1 & 1 & 1 & 2 \end{array}\right]$$ 7

The rows of the augmented matrix can be transformed in the same way as the equations of the system, since the matrix is just a shortened form of the system. The following **row operations** on the augmented matrix correspond to the elementary operations used on systems of equations.

> Performing any one of the following **row operations** on the augmented matrix of a system of linear equations produces the augmented matrix of an equivalent system.
>
> 1. Interchange any two rows.
> 2. Multiply each element of a row by a nonzero constant.
> 3. Replace a row by the sum of itself and a constant multiple of another row of the matrix.

Row operations on a matrix are indicated by the same notation we used for elementary operations on a system of equations. For example, $2R_3 + R_1$ indicates the sum of 2 times row 3 and row 1. 8

EXAMPLE 5 Use matrices to solve the system

$$\begin{aligned} x - 2y &= 6 - 4z \\ x + 13z &= 6 - y \\ -2x + 6y - z &= -10. \end{aligned}$$

First, put the system in the required form, with the constants on the right side of the equals sign and the terms with variables in the same order in each equation on the left side of the equals sign. Then write the augmented matrix of the system.

$$\begin{aligned} x - 2y + 4z &= 6 \\ x + y + 13z &= 6 \\ -2x + 6y - z &= -10 \end{aligned} \qquad \left[\begin{array}{ccc|c} 1 & -2 & 4 & 6 \\ 1 & 1 & 13 & 6 \\ -2 & 6 & -1 & -10 \end{array}\right]$$

The matrix method is the same as the elimination method, except that row operations are used on the augmented matrix instead of elementary operations on the corresponding system of equations, as shown in this side-by-side comparison.

Equation Method	*Matrix Method*
Replace the second equation by the sum of itself and −1 times the first equation.	Replace the second row by the sum of itself and −1 times the first row.

$$\begin{aligned} x - 2y + 4z &= 6 \\ 3y + 9z &= 0 \\ -2x + 6y - z &= -10 \end{aligned} \quad \xleftarrow{\;} -1R_1 + R_2 \rightarrow \quad \left[\begin{array}{ccc|c} 1 & -2 & 4 & 6 \\ 0 & 3 & 9 & 0 \\ -2 & 6 & -1 & -10 \end{array}\right]$$

Replace the third equation by the sum of itself and 2 times the first equation.	Replace the third row by the sum of itself and 2 times the first row.

$$\begin{aligned} x - 2y + 4z &= 6 \\ 3y + 9z &= 0 \\ 2y + 7z &= 2 \end{aligned} \quad \leftarrow 2R_1 + R_3 \rightarrow \quad \left[\begin{array}{ccc|c} 1 & -2 & 4 & 6 \\ 0 & 3 & 9 & 0 \\ 0 & 2 & 7 & 2 \end{array}\right]$$

Multiply both sides of the second equation by 1/3.	Multiply each element of row 2 by 1/3.

$$\begin{aligned} x - 2y + 4z &= 6 \\ y + 3z &= 0 \\ 2y + 7z &= 2 \end{aligned} \quad \leftarrow \frac{1}{3}R_2 \rightarrow \quad \left[\begin{array}{ccc|c} 1 & -2 & 4 & 6 \\ 0 & 1 & 3 & 0 \\ 0 & 2 & 7 & 2 \end{array}\right]$$

Replace the third equation by the sum of itself and −2 times the second equation.	Replace the third row by the sum of itself and −2 times the second row.

$$\begin{aligned} x - 2y + 4z &= 6 \\ y + 3z &= 0 \\ z &= 2 \end{aligned} \quad \leftarrow -2R_2 + R_3 \rightarrow \quad \left[\begin{array}{ccc|c} 1 & -2 & 4 & 6 \\ 0 & 1 & 3 & 0 \\ 0 & 0 & 1 & 2 \end{array}\right]$$

The system is now in triangular form. Using back substitution shows that the solution of the system is $(-14, -6, 2)$. ■ 9

9 Complete the matrix solution of the system with this augmented matrix.

$$\left[\begin{array}{ccc|c} 1 & 1 & 1 & 2 \\ 1 & -2 & 1 & -1 \\ 0 & 3 & 1 & 5 \end{array}\right]$$

Answer:
$(-1, 1, 2)$

TECHNOLOGY TIP Virtually all graphing calculators have matrix capabilities. You should consult your instruction manual to learn how to enter a matrix and perform row operations. With most calculators you will need to enter the matrix dimensions (the number of rows and columns). For example, a matrix with three rows and four columns has dimensions 3×4.

A matrix can be put in triangular form in a single step on TI-83/85/86/92 calculators by using REF (in the MATH or OPS submenu of the MATRIX menu). "REF" stands for "Row Echelon Form," which is the triangular form in which 1 is the first nonzero entry in each row. ✔

DEPENDENT AND INCONSISTENT SYSTEMS The possible number of solutions of a system with more than two variables or equations is the same as for smaller systems. Such a system has exactly one solution (independent system); or infinitely many solutions (dependent system); or no solutions (inconsistent system). Both the equation method and the matrix method always produce the unique solution of an independent system. The matrix method also provides a useful way of describing the infinitely many solutions of a dependent system, as we now see.

EXAMPLE 6 Solve the system

$$\begin{aligned} 2x - 3y + 4z &= 6 \\ x - 2y + z &= 9. \end{aligned}$$

Use the steps of the matrix method as far as possible. The augmented matrix is

$$\left[\begin{array}{ccc|c} 2 & -3 & 4 & 6 \\ 1 & -2 & 1 & 9 \end{array}\right].$$

$$\left[\begin{array}{ccc|c} 1 & -2 & 1 & 9 \\ 2 & -3 & 4 & 6 \end{array}\right] \quad \text{Interchange } R_1 \text{ and } R_2.$$

$$\left[\begin{array}{ccc|c} 1 & -2 & 1 & 9 \\ 0 & 1 & 2 & -12 \end{array}\right] \quad -2R_1 + R_2 \qquad \begin{aligned} x - 2y + z &= 9 \\ y + 2z &= -12 \end{aligned}$$

The last augmented matrix above represents the system shown to its right. Since there are only two rows in the matrix, it is not possible to continue the process. The fact that the corresponding system has one variable (namely z) that is not the leading variable of an equation indicates a dependent system. Its solutions can be found as follows. Solve the second equation for y.

$$y = -2z - 12$$

Now substitute the result for y in the first equation, and solve for x.

$$\begin{aligned} x - 2\mathbf{y} + z &= 9 \\ x - 2(\mathbf{-2z - 12}) + z &= 9 \\ x + 4z + 24 + z &= 9 \\ x + 5z &= -15 \\ x &= -5z - 15 \end{aligned}$$

Each choice of a value for z leads to values for x and y. For example,

if $z = 1$, then $x = -20$ and $y = -14$;
if $z = -6$, then $x = 15$ and $y = 0$;
if $z = 0$, then $x = -15$ and $y = -12$.

There are infinitely many solutions for the original system, since z can take on infinitely many values. The solutions are all ordered triples in the form

$$(-5z - 15, -2z - 12, z),$$

where z is any real number. ■ 10

10 Use the following values of z to find additional solutions for the system of Example 6.

(a) $z = 7$

(b) $z = -14$

(c) $z = 5$

Answers:

(a) $(-50, -26, 7)$

(b) $(55, 16, -14)$

(c) $(-40, -22, 5)$

Since both x and y in Example 6 were expressed in terms of z, the variable z is called a **parameter.** If we solved the system in a different way, x or y could be the parameter. The system in Example 6 had one more variable than equations. If there are two more variables than equations, there usually will be two parameters, and so on.

Whenever there are more variables than equations, as in Example 6, then the system cannot have a unique solution. It must be either dependent (infinitely many solutions) or inconsistent (no solutions).

When a system is inconsistent, the matrix method will indicate this fact, too, as in the next example.

EXAMPLE 7 Solve the system

$$\begin{aligned} 4x + 12y + 8z &= -4 \\ 2x + 8y + 5z &= 0 \\ 3x + 9y + 6z &= 2 \\ 3x + 2y - z &= 6. \end{aligned}$$

Write the augmented matrix and go through the steps of the matrix method.

$$\left[\begin{array}{ccc|c} 4 & 12 & 8 & -4 \\ 2 & 8 & 5 & 0 \\ 3 & 9 & 6 & 2 \\ 3 & 2 & -1 & 6 \end{array}\right]$$

$$\left[\begin{array}{ccc|c} 1 & 3 & 2 & -1 \\ 2 & 8 & 5 & 0 \\ 3 & 9 & 6 & 2 \\ 3 & 2 & -1 & 6 \end{array}\right] \quad (1/4)R_1$$

$$\left[\begin{array}{ccc|c} 1 & 3 & 2 & -1 \\ 0 & 2 & 1 & 2 \\ 3 & 9 & 6 & 2 \\ 3 & 2 & -1 & 6 \end{array}\right] \quad -2R_1 + R_2$$

$$\left[\begin{array}{ccc|c} 1 & 3 & 2 & -1 \\ 0 & 2 & 1 & 2 \\ 0 & 0 & 0 & 5 \\ 3 & 2 & -1 & 6 \end{array}\right] \quad -3R_1 + R_3$$

Stop! The third row has all zeros to the left of the vertical bar, so the corresponding equation is $0x + 0y + 0z = 5$. This equation has no solution because its left side is 0 and its right side is 5, resulting in the false statement "$0 = 5$." Therefore the entire system cannot have any solutions and is inconsistent. ■ 11

11 Complete the matrix solution of the system.

$$\left[\begin{array}{ccc|c} -1 & 3 & -2 & -1 \\ 1 & -2 & 3 & 1 \\ 2 & -4 & 6 & 5 \end{array}\right]$$

Answer:
No solution

CAUTION It is possible for the elimination method to result in an equation that is 0 on *both* sides, such as $0x + 0y + 0z = 0$. Unlike the situation in Example 7, such an equation has infinitely many solutions, so a system that contains it may also have solutions.

As a general rule, there is no way to determine in advance whether a system is independent, dependent, or inconsistent. So you should carry out the elimination process as far as necessary. If you obtain an equation of the form $0 = c$ for some nonzero c (as in Example 7), then the system is inconsistent and has no solutions. Otherwise, the system will either be independent with a unique solution (Example 4) or dependent with infinitely many solutions (Example 6). ◆

APPLICATIONS The mathematical techniques in this text will be useful to you only if you are able to apply them to practical problems. To do this, always begin by reading the problem carefully. Next, identify what must be found. Let each unknown quantity be represented by a variable. (It is a good idea to *write down* exactly what each variable represents.) Now reread the problem, looking for all necessary data. Write that down, too. Finally, look for one or more sentences that lead to equations or inequalities.

12 **(a)** Write the augmented matrix for the system of equations in Example 8.

(b) List a sequence of row operations that will transform the matrix in part (a) into triangular form, and give the triangular form.

Answers:

(a) $\left[\begin{array}{ccc|c} 10 & 20 & 60 & 440 \\ 10 & 8 & 28 & 248 \end{array}\right]$

(b) Many sequences are possible, including this one:

replace R_1 by $\frac{1}{10}R_1$;

replace R_2 by $\frac{1}{2}R_2$;

replace R_2 by $-5R_1 + R_2$;

replace R_2 by $-\frac{1}{6}R_2$.

$\left[\begin{array}{ccc|c} 1 & 2 & 6 & 44 \\ 0 & 1 & \frac{8}{3} & 16 \end{array}\right]$

EXAMPLE 8 Kelly Karpet Kleaners sells rug cleaning machines. The EZ model weighs 10 pounds and comes in a 10 cubic ft box. The compact model weighs 20 pounds and comes in an 8 cubic ft box. The commercial model weighs 60 pounds and comes in a 28 cubic ft box. Each of their delivery vans has 248 cubic feet of space and can hold a maximum of 440 pounds. In order for a van to be fully loaded, how many of each model should it carry?

Let x be the number of EZ, y the number of compact, and z the number of commercial models carried by a van. Then we can summarize the information in this chart.

Model	*Number*	*Weight*	*Volume*
EZ	x	10	10
Compact	y	20	8
Commercial	z	60	28
Total for a load		440	248

Since a fully loaded van can carry 440 pounds and 248 cubic feet, we must solve this system of equations.

$$10x + 20y + 60z = 440 \qquad \text{Weight equation}$$
$$10x + 8y + 28z = 248 \qquad \text{Volume equation}$$ 12

As shown in Problem 12 at the side, this system is equivalent to the following one.

$$x + 2y + 6z = 44$$
$$y + \frac{8}{3}z = 16$$

Solving this dependent system by back substitution, we have

$$y = 16 - \frac{8}{3}z$$

$$x = 44 - 2y - 6z = 44 - 2\left(16 - \frac{8}{3}z\right) - 6z = 12 - \frac{2}{3}z,$$

so that all solutions of the system are given by $\left(12 - \frac{2}{3}z, 16 - \frac{8}{3}z, z\right)$. The only solutions that apply in this situation, however, are those given by $z = 0, 3,$ or 6 because all other values of z lead to fractions or negative numbers (you can't deliver a negative number of boxes, or part of a box). Hence, there are three ways to have a fully loaded van.

Solution	*Van Load*
(12, 16, 0)	12 EZ, 16 compact, 0 commercial
(10, 8, 3)	10 EZ, 8 compact, 3 commercial
(8, 0, 6)	8 EZ, 0 compact, 6 commercial ■

7.1 EXERCISES

Determine whether the given ordered set of numbers is a solution of the system of equations.

1. $(-1, 3)$

$$\begin{aligned} 2x + y &= 1 \\ -3x + 2y &= 9 \end{aligned}$$

2. $(2, 1.5, -.5)$

$$\begin{aligned} 3x + 4y - 2z &= -.5 \\ .5x + 8z &= -3 \\ x - 3y + 5z &= -5 \end{aligned}$$

Solve each of the following systems of two equations in two variables. (See Examples 1–3.)

3. $\begin{aligned} x - 2y &= 5 \\ 2x + y &= 3 \end{aligned}$

4. $\begin{aligned} 3x - y &= 1 \\ -x + 2y &= 4 \end{aligned}$

5. $\begin{aligned} 2x - 2y &= 12 \\ -2x + 3y &= 10 \end{aligned}$

6. $\begin{aligned} 3x + 2y &= -4 \\ 4x - 2y &= -10 \end{aligned}$

7. $\begin{aligned} x + 3y &= -1 \\ 2x - y &= 5 \end{aligned}$

8. $\begin{aligned} 4x - 3y &= -1 \\ x + 2y &= 19 \end{aligned}$

9. $\begin{aligned} 2x + 3y &= 15 \\ 8x + 12y &= 40 \end{aligned}$

10. $\begin{aligned} 2x + 5y &= 8 \\ 6x + 15y &= 18 \end{aligned}$

11. $\begin{aligned} 2x - 8y &= 2 \\ 3x - 12y &= 3 \end{aligned}$

12. $\begin{aligned} 3x - 2y &= 4 \\ 6x - 4y &= 8 \end{aligned}$

13. $\begin{aligned} 3x + 2y &= 5 \\ 6x + 4y &= 8 \end{aligned}$

14. $\begin{aligned} 9x - 5y &= 1 \\ -18x + 10y &= 1 \end{aligned}$

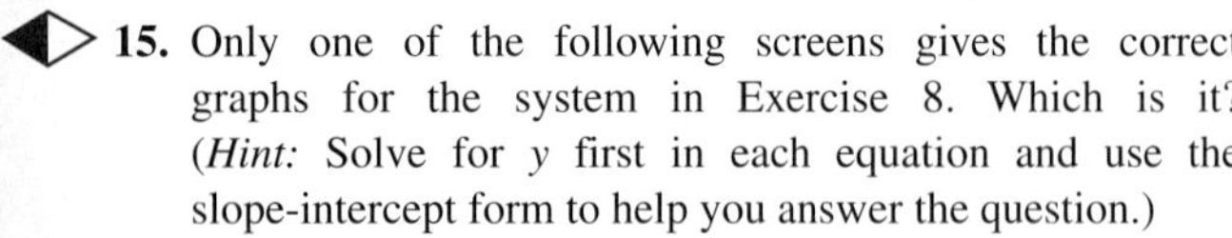

15. Only one of the following screens gives the correct graphs for the system in Exercise 8. Which is it? (*Hint:* Solve for y first in each equation and use the slope-intercept form to help you answer the question.)

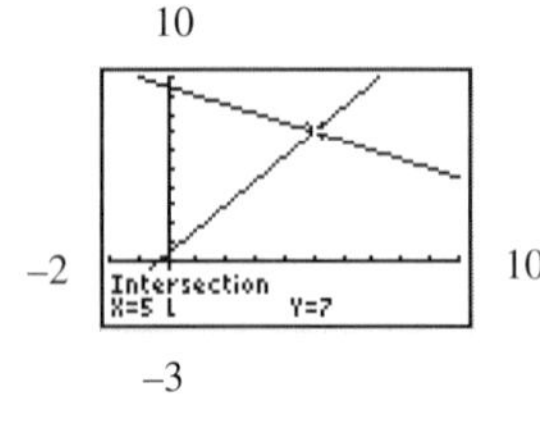

(a)

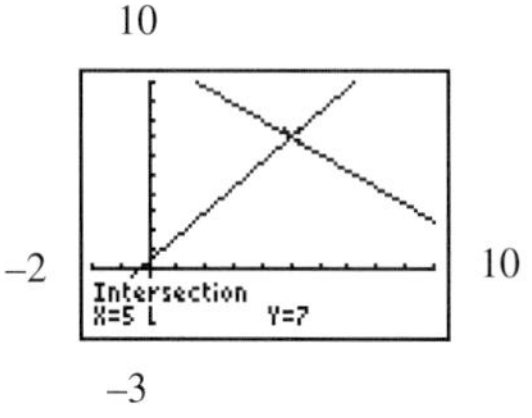

(b)

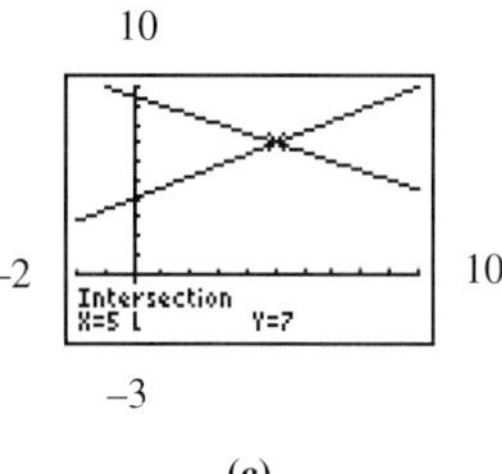

(c)

In Exercises 16–19, multiply both sides of each equation by a common denominator to eliminate the fractions. Then solve the system.

16. $\begin{aligned} \frac{x}{2} + \frac{y}{3} &= 8 \\ \frac{2x}{3} + \frac{3y}{2} &= 17 \end{aligned}$

17. $\begin{aligned} \frac{x}{5} + 3y &= 31 \\ 2x - \frac{y}{5} &= 8 \end{aligned}$

18. $\begin{aligned} \frac{x}{2} + y &= \frac{3}{2} \\ \frac{x}{3} + y &= \frac{1}{3} \end{aligned}$

19. $\begin{aligned} x + \frac{y}{3} &= -6 \\ \frac{x}{5} + \frac{y}{4} &= -\frac{7}{4} \end{aligned}$

In Exercises 20–25, perform row operations on the augmented matrix as far as necessary to determine whether the system is independent, dependent, or inconsistent. (See Examples 6 and 7.)

20. $\begin{aligned} x + 2y &= 0 \\ y - z &= 2 \\ x + y + z &= -2 \end{aligned}$

21. $\begin{aligned} x + 2y + z &= 0 \\ y + 2z &= 0 \\ x + y - z &= 0 \end{aligned}$

22. $\begin{aligned} x + 2y + 4z &= 6 \\ y + z &= 1 \\ x + 3y + 5z &= 10 \end{aligned}$

23. $\begin{aligned} x + y + 2z + 3w &= 1 \\ 2x + y + 3z + 4w &= 1 \\ 3x + y + 4z + 5w &= 2 \end{aligned}$

24. $\begin{aligned} a - 3b - 2c &= -3 \\ 3a + 2b - c &= 12 \\ -a - b + 4c &= 3 \end{aligned}$

25. $\begin{aligned} 2x + 2y + 2z &= 6 \\ 3x - 3y - 4z &= -1 \\ x + y + 3z &= 11 \end{aligned}$

Write the augmented matrix of the system and use the matrix method to solve the system. If the system is dependent, express the solutions in terms of the parameter z. (See Examples 4–7.)

26. $\begin{aligned} x + y + z &= 2 \\ 2x + y - z &= 5 \\ x - y + z &= -2 \end{aligned}$

27. $\begin{aligned} 2x + y + z &= 9 \\ -x - y + z &= 1 \\ 3x - y + z &= 9 \end{aligned}$

28. $\begin{aligned} x + 3y + 4z &= 14 \\ 2x - 3y + 2z &= 10 \\ 3x - y + z &= 9 \end{aligned}$

29. $\begin{aligned} 4x - y + 3z &= -2 \\ 3x + 5y - z &= 15 \\ -2x + y + 4z &= 14 \end{aligned}$

30. $\begin{aligned} x + 2y + 3z &= 8 \\ 3x - y + 2z &= 5 \\ -2x - 4y - 6z &= 5 \end{aligned}$

31. $\begin{aligned} 3x - 2y - 8z &= 1 \\ 9x - 6y - 24z &= -2 \\ x - y + z &= 1 \end{aligned}$

32. $\begin{aligned} 2x - 4y + z &= -4 \\ x + 2y - z &= 0 \\ -x + y + z &= 6 \end{aligned}$

33. $\begin{aligned} 4x - 3y + z &= 9 \\ 3x + 2y - 2z &= 4 \\ x - y + 3z &= 5 \end{aligned}$

34. $\begin{aligned} 5x + 3y + 4z &= 19 \\ 3x - y + z &= -4 \end{aligned}$

35. $\begin{aligned} 3x + y - z &= 0 \\ 2x - y + 3z &= -7 \end{aligned}$

36. $\begin{aligned} 11x + 10y + 9z &= 5 \\ x + 2y + 3z &= 1 \\ 3x + 2y + z &= 1 \end{aligned}$

37. $\begin{aligned} x + y &= 3 \\ 5x - y &= 3 \\ 9x - 4y &= 1 \end{aligned}$

38. Find constants a, b, c such that the points $(2, 3)$, $(-1, 0)$, and $(-2, 2)$ lie on the graph of the equation $y = ax^2 + bx + c$. (*Hint:* Since $(2, 3)$ is on the graph, we must have $3 = a(2^2) + b(2) + c$, that is, $4a + 2b + c = 3$. Similarly, the other two points lead to two more equations. Solve the resulting system for a, b, c.)

39. **(a)** Find the equation of the straight line through $(1, 2)$ and $(3, 4)$.
(b) Find the equation of the line through $(-1, 1)$ with slope 3.
(c) Find a point that lies on both the lines in (a) and (b).

40. Graph the equations in the following system. Then explain why the graphs show that the system is inconsistent.

$$\begin{aligned} 2x + 3y &= 8 \\ x - y &= 4 \\ 5x + y &= 7 \end{aligned}$$

41. Explain why a system with more variables than equations cannot have a unique solution (that is, be an independent system). (*Hint:* When you apply the elimination method to such a system, what must necessarily happen?)

Work the following problems by writing and solving a system of equations. (See Example 8.)

42. Physical Science Linear systems occur in the design of roof trusses for new homes and buildings. The simplest type of roof truss is a triangle. The truss shown in the figure is used to frame roofs of small buildings. If a 100-pound force is applied at the peak of the truss, then the forces or weights W_1 and W_2 exerted parallel to each rafter of the truss are determined by the following linear system of equations.

$$\frac{\sqrt{3}}{2}(W_1 + W_2) = 100$$

$$W_1 - W_2 = 0$$

Solve the system to find W_1 and W_2.*

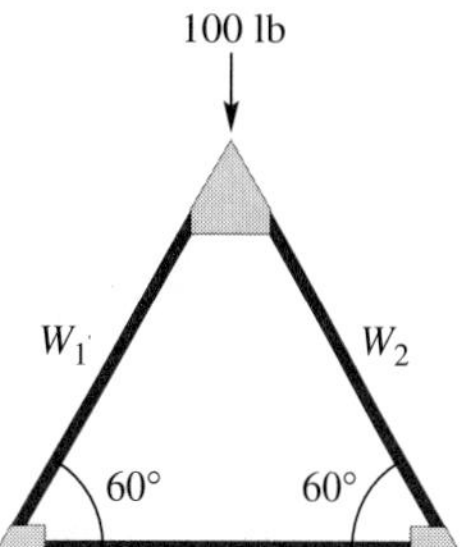

43. Physical Science (Refer to Exercise 42.) Use the following system of equations to determine the forces or weights W_1 and W_2 exerted on each rafter for the truss shown in the figure.

$$\begin{aligned} W_1 + \sqrt{2}W_2 &= 300 \\ \sqrt{3}W_1 - \sqrt{2}W_2 &= 0 \end{aligned}$$

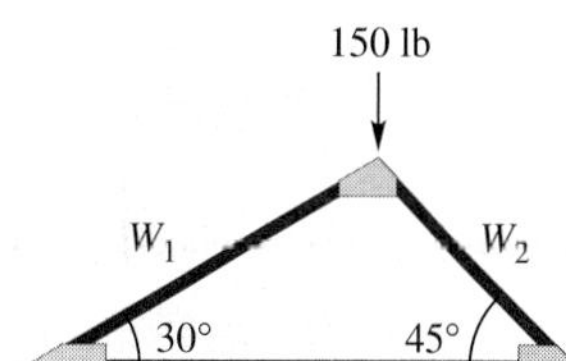

44. Management Shirley Cicero has \$16,000 invested in Boeing and GE stock. The Boeing stock currently sells for \$30 a share and the GE stock for \$70 a share. If GE stock triples in value and Boeing stock goes up 50%, her stock will be worth \$34,500. How many shares of each stock does she own?

45. Management A flight leaves New York at 8 P.M. and arrives in Paris at 9 A.M. (Paris time). This 13-hour difference includes the flight time plus the change in time zones. The return flight leaves Paris at 1 P.M. and arrives in New

*Hibbeler R., *Structural Analysis*, Prentice-Hall, Englewood Cliffs, 1995.

York at 3 P.M. (New York time). This 2-hour difference includes the flight time *minus* the time zones, plus an extra hour due to the fact that flying westward is against the wind. Find the actual flight time eastward and the difference in time zones.

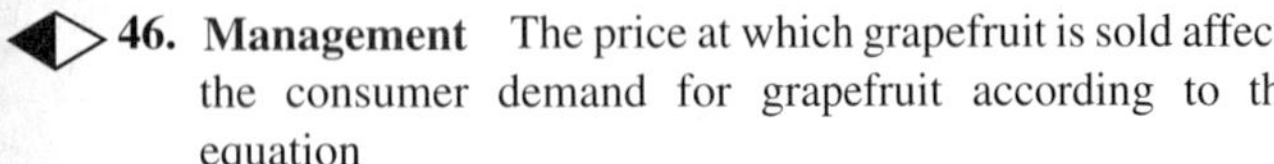

46. Management The price at which grapefruit is sold affects the consumer demand for grapefruit according to the equation

$$2p = -.2q + 5,$$

where p is the price per pound (in dollars) at which consumers will demand q thousand pounds of grapefruit. The amount q of grapefruit that producers will supply at price p is governed by the equation $5p = .3q + 5.3$. Find the equilibrium quantity and the equilibrium price. (That is, find the quantity and price at which supply equals demand, or the values of p and q that satisfy both equations.)

47. Management If 20 pounds of rice and 10 pounds of potatoes cost \$16.20 and 30 pounds of rice and 12 pounds of potatoes cost \$23.04, how much will 10 pounds of rice and 50 pounds of potatoes cost?

48. Management An apparel shop sells skirts for \$45 and blouses for \$35. Its entire stock is worth \$51,750. But sales are slow and only half the skirts and two-thirds of the blouses are sold, for a total of \$30,600. How many skirts and blouses are left in the store?

49. Management A company produces two models of bicycles, model 201 and model 301. Model 201 requires 2 hours of assembly time and model 301 requires 3 hours of assembly time. The parts for model 201 cost \$25 per bike and the parts for model 301 cost \$30 per bike. If the company has a total of 34 hours of assembly time and \$365 available per day for these two models, how many of each can be made in a day?

50. Social Science The relationship between a professional basketball player's height H (in inches) and weight W (in pounds) was modeled using two different samples of players. The resulting equations that modeled each sample were $W = 7.46H - 374$ and $W = 7.93H - 405$.

(a) Use both equations to predict the weight of a 6′11″ professional basketball player.

(b) According to each model, what change in weight is associated with a 1-inch increase in height?

(c) Determine the weight and height where the two models agree.

51. Management Juanita invests \$10,000, received from her grandmother, in three ways. With one part, she buys mutual funds which offer a return of 8% per year. The second part, which amounts to twice the first, is used to buy government bonds at 9% per year. She puts the rest in the bank at 5% annual interest. The first year her investments bring a return of \$830. How much did she invest in each way?

52. Management To get the necessary funds for a planned expansion, a small company took out three loans totaling \$25,000. The company was able to borrow some of the money at 16%. They borrowed \$2000 more than one half the amount of the 16% loan at 20%, and the rest at 18%. The total annual interest was \$4440. How much did they borrow at each rate?

53. Natural Science Three brands of fertilizer are available that provide nitrogen, phosphoric acid, and soluble potash to the soil. One bag of each brand provides the following units of each nutrient.

	NUTRIENT		
Brand	*Nitrogen*	*Phosphoric Acid*	*Potash*
A	1	3	2
B	2	1	0
C	3	2	1

For ideal growth, the soil in a certain country needs 18 units of nitrogen, 23 units of phosphoric acid, and 13 units of potash per acre. How many bags of each brand of fertilizer should be used per acre for ideal growth?

54. Management A company produces three color television sets: models X, Y, and Z. Each model X set requires 2 hours of electronics work and 2 hours of assembly time. Each model Y requires 1 hour of electronics work and 3 hours of assembly time. Each model Z requires 3 hours of electronics work and 2 hours of assembly time. There are 100 hours available for electronics and assembly each per week. How many of each model should be produced each week if all available time must be used?

55. Management A restaurant owner orders a replacement set of knives, forks, and spoons. The box arrives containing 40 utensils and weighing 141.3 ounces (ignoring the weight of the box). A knife, fork, and spoon weigh 3.9 ounces, 3.6 ounces, and 3.0 ounces, respectively.

(a) How many solutions are there for the number of knives, forks, and spoons in the box? What are the possible number of spoons?

(b) Which solution has the smallest number of spoons?

56. Management Turley Tailor Inc. makes long-sleeve, short-sleeve, and sleeveless blouses. A sleeveless blouse requires .5 hour of cutting and .6 hour of sewing. A short-sleeve blouse requires 1 hour of cutting and .9 hour of sewing. A long-sleeve blouse requires 1.5 hours of cutting and 1.2 hours of sewing. There are 380 hours of labor available in the cutting department each day and 330 hours in the sewing department. If the plant is to run at full capacity, how many of each type of blouse should be made each day?

7.2 THE GAUSS-JORDAN METHOD

In Example 5 of the previous section, we used matrix methods to rewrite the system

$$\begin{aligned} x - 2y &= 6 - 4z \\ x + 13z &= 6 - y \\ -2x + 6y - z &= -10 \end{aligned}$$

as an augmented matrix. We carried out the steps of the matrix method until the final matrix was

$$\left[\begin{array}{rrr|r} 1 & -2 & 4 & 6 \\ 0 & 1 & 3 & 0 \\ 0 & 0 & 1 & 2 \end{array}\right].$$

We then used back substitution to solve it. In the **Gauss-Jordan method,** we continue the process with additional elimination of variables replacing back substitution as follows.

$$\left[\begin{array}{rrr|r} 1 & -2 & 4 & 6 \\ 0 & 1 & 0 & -6 \\ 0 & 0 & 1 & 2 \end{array}\right] \quad -3R_3 + R_2$$

$$\left[\begin{array}{rrr|r} 1 & -2 & 0 & -2 \\ 0 & 1 & 0 & -6 \\ 0 & 0 & 1 & 2 \end{array}\right] \quad -4R_3 + R_1$$

$$\left[\begin{array}{rrr|r} 1 & 0 & 0 & -14 \\ 0 & 1 & 0 & -6 \\ 0 & 0 & 1 & 2 \end{array}\right] \quad 2R_2 + R_1$$

The solution of the system is now obvious; it is $(-14, -6, 2)$. Note that this solution is the last column of the final augmented matrix.

In the Gauss-Jordan method row operations can be performed in any order, provided they eventually lead to the augmented matrix of a system in which the leading variable of each equation is not the leading variable in any other equation of the system. When there is a unique solution, as in the example above, this final system will be of the form $x =$ constant, $y =$ constant, $z =$ constant, and so on. [1]

[1] Use the Gauss-Jordan method to solve the system

$$\begin{aligned} x + 2y &= 11 \\ -4x + y &= -8, \end{aligned}$$

as follows. Give the shorthand notation and the new matrix in (b)–(d).

(a) Set up the augmented matrix.

(b) Get 0 in row two, column one.

(c) Get 1 in row two, column two.

(d) Finally, get 0 in row one, column two.

(e) The solution for the system is ______.

Answers:

(a) $\left[\begin{array}{rr|r} 1 & 2 & 11 \\ -4 & 1 & -8 \end{array}\right]$

(b) $4R_1 + R_2$; $\left[\begin{array}{rr|r} 1 & 2 & 11 \\ 0 & 9 & 36 \end{array}\right]$

(c) $\frac{1}{9}R_2$; $\left[\begin{array}{rr|r} 1 & 2 & 11 \\ 0 & 1 & 4 \end{array}\right]$

(d) $-2R_2 + R_1$; $\left[\begin{array}{rr|r} 1 & 0 & 3 \\ 0 & 1 & 4 \end{array}\right]$

(e) (3, 4)

It is best to transform the matrix systematically. Either follow the procedure in the example (which first puts the system in a form where back substitution could be used and then eliminates additional variable terms) or work column by column from left to right, as in the next example.

EXAMPLE 1 Use the Gauss-Jordan method to solve the system

$$\begin{aligned} x \qquad + 5z &= -6 + y \\ 3x + 3y \qquad &= 10 + z \\ x + 3y + 2z &= 5. \end{aligned}$$

The system must first be rewritten in proper form as follows.

$$\begin{aligned} x - y + 5z &= -6 \\ 3x + 3y - z &= 10 \\ x + 3y + 2z &= 5 \end{aligned}$$

Begin the solution by writing the augmented matrix of the linear system.

$$\left[\begin{array}{rrr|r} 1 & -1 & 5 & -6 \\ 3 & 3 & -1 & 10 \\ 1 & 3 & 2 & 5 \end{array}\right]$$

The first element in column one is already 1. Get 0 for the second element in column one by multiplying each element in the first row by -3 and adding the results to the corresponding elements in row two.

$$\left[\begin{array}{rrr|r} 1 & -1 & 5 & -6 \\ 0 & 6 & -16 & 28 \\ 1 & 3 & 2 & 5 \end{array}\right] \quad -3R_1 + R_2$$

Now, change the first element in row three to 0 by multiplying each element of the first row by -1 and adding the results to the corresponding elements of the third row.

$$\left[\begin{array}{rrr|r} 1 & -1 & 5 & -6 \\ 0 & 6 & -16 & 28 \\ 0 & 4 & -3 & 11 \end{array}\right] \quad -1R_1 + R_3$$

This transforms the first column. Transform the second column in a similar manner, as directed in Side Problem 2. 2

2 Continue the solution of the system in Example 1 as follows. Give the shorthand notation and the matrix for each step.

(a) Get 1 in row two, column two.

(b) Get 0 in row one, column two.

(c) Now get 0 in row three, column two.

Answers:

(a) $\frac{1}{6}R_2$;

$$\left[\begin{array}{rrr|r} 1 & -1 & 5 & -6 \\ 0 & 1 & -\frac{8}{3} & \frac{14}{3} \\ 0 & 4 & -3 & 11 \end{array}\right]$$

(b) $R_2 + R_1$;

$$\left[\begin{array}{rrr|r} 1 & 0 & \frac{7}{3} & -\frac{4}{3} \\ 0 & 1 & -\frac{8}{3} & \frac{14}{3} \\ 0 & 4 & -3 & 11 \end{array}\right]$$

(c) $-4R_2 + R_3$;

$$\left[\begin{array}{rrr|r} 1 & 0 & \frac{7}{3} & -\frac{4}{3} \\ 0 & 1 & -\frac{8}{3} & \frac{14}{3} \\ 0 & 0 & \frac{23}{3} & -\frac{23}{3} \end{array}\right]$$

(Solution continued in the text.)

Complete the solution by transforming the third column of the matrix in part (c) of Side Problem 2.

$$\left[\begin{array}{rrr|r} 1 & 0 & \frac{7}{3} & -\frac{4}{3} \\ 0 & 1 & -\frac{8}{3} & \frac{14}{3} \\ 0 & 0 & 1 & -1 \end{array}\right] \quad \frac{3}{23}R_3$$

$$\left[\begin{array}{rrr|r} 1 & 0 & 0 & 1 \\ 0 & 1 & -\frac{8}{3} & \frac{14}{3} \\ 0 & 0 & 1 & -1 \end{array}\right] \quad -\frac{7}{3}R_3 + R_1$$

$$\left[\begin{array}{rrr|r} 1 & 0 & 0 & 1 \\ 0 & 1 & 0 & 2 \\ 0 & 0 & 1 & -1 \end{array}\right] \quad \frac{8}{3}R_3 + R_2$$

The linear system associated with this last augmented matrix is

$$\begin{aligned} x &= 1 \\ y &= 2 \\ z &= -1, \end{aligned}$$

and the solution is $(1, 2, -1)$. ■

3 Use the Gauss-Jordan method to solve

$$x + y - z = 6$$
$$2x - y + z = 3$$
$$-x + y + z = -4.$$

Answer:
$(3, 1, -2)$

NOTE Notice that the first two row operations are used to get the ones and the third row operation is used to get the zeros. ◆ 3

EXAMPLE 2 Use the Gauss-Jordan method to solve the system

$$2x + 4y = 4$$
$$3x + 6y = 8$$
$$2x + y = 7.$$

Write the augmented matrix and perform row operations to obtain a first column whose entries (from top to bottom) are 1, 0, 0.

$$\left[\begin{array}{cc|c} 2 & 4 & 4 \\ 3 & 6 & 8 \\ 2 & 1 & 7 \end{array}\right]$$

$$\left[\begin{array}{cc|c} 1 & 2 & 2 \\ 3 & 6 & 8 \\ 2 & 1 & 7 \end{array}\right] \quad \frac{1}{2}R_1$$

$$\left[\begin{array}{cc|c} 1 & 2 & 2 \\ 0 & 0 & 2 \\ 2 & 1 & 7 \end{array}\right] \quad -3R_1 + R_2$$

Stop! The second row of this augmented matrix denotes the equation $0x + 0y = 2$. Since the left side of this equation is always 0 and the right side is 2, it has no solutions. Hence, the original system has no solutions. ■ 4

4 Solve each system.

(a) $x - y = 4$
$-2x + 2y = 1$

(b) $3x - 4y = 0$
$2x + y = 0$

Answers:
(a) No solution
(b) $(0, 0)$

Whenever the Gauss-Jordan method produces a row whose elements are all 0 except the last one, such as $[0 \quad 0 \mid 2]$ in Example 2, the system is inconsistent and has no solutions. On the other hand, if a row with *every* element 0 is produced, the system may have solutions. In that case, continue carrying out the Gauss-Jordan method. 5

5 Use the Gauss-Jordan method to solve the system.

$$x + 3y = 4$$
$$4x + 8y = 4$$
$$6x + 12y = 6$$

Answer:
$(-5, 3)$

EXAMPLE 3 Use the Gauss-Jordan method to solve the system

$$x + 2y - z = 0$$
$$3x - y + z = 6.$$

Start with the augmented matrix and use row operations to obtain a first column whose entries (from top to bottom) are 1, 0.

$$\left[\begin{array}{ccc|c} 1 & 2 & -1 & 0 \\ 3 & -1 & 1 & 6 \end{array}\right]$$

$$\left[\begin{array}{ccc|c} 1 & 2 & -1 & 0 \\ 0 & -7 & 4 & 6 \end{array}\right] \quad -3R_1 + R_2$$

Now use row operations to obtain a second column whose entries (from top to bottom) are 0, 1.

$$\left[\begin{array}{ccc|c} 1 & 2 & -1 & 0 \\ 0 & 1 & -\frac{4}{7} & -\frac{6}{7} \end{array}\right] \quad -\frac{1}{7}R_2$$

$$\left[\begin{array}{ccc|c} 1 & 0 & \frac{1}{7} & \frac{12}{7} \\ 0 & 1 & -\frac{4}{7} & -\frac{6}{7} \end{array}\right] \quad -2R_2 + R_1$$

This last matrix is the augmented matrix of the system

$$x + \frac{1}{7}z = \frac{12}{7}$$

$$y - \frac{4}{7}z = -\frac{6}{7}.$$

Solving the first equation for x and the second for y gives the solution

z arbitrary

$$y = -\frac{6}{7} + \frac{4}{7}z$$

$$x = \frac{12}{7} - \frac{1}{7}z,$$

or $(12/7 - z/7, -6/7 + 4z/7, z)$. ■ 6

6 Use the Gauss-Jordan method to solve the following.

(a) $3x + 9y = -6$
$-x - 3y = 2$

(b) $2x + 9y = 12$
$4x + 18y = 5$

Answers:

(a) y arbitrary,
$x = -3y - 2$
or $(-3y - 2, y)$

(b) No solution

The techniques used in Examples 1–3 can be summarized as follows.

THE GAUSS-JORDAN METHOD FOR SOLVING A SYSTEM OF LINEAR EQUATIONS

1. Arrange the equations with the variable terms in the same order on the left of the equals sign and the constants on the right.
2. Write the augmented matrix of the system.
3. Use row operations to transform the augmented matrix into this form:
   (a) The rows consisting entirely of zeros are grouped together at the bottom of the matrix.
   (b) In each row that does not consist entirely of zeros, the leftmost nonzero element is 1 (called a *leading* 1).
   (c) Each column that contains a leading 1 has zeros in all other entries.
   (d) The leading 1 in any row is to the left of any leading 1's in the rows below it.
4. Stop the process in Step 3 if you obtain a row whose elements are all zero except the last one. In that case, the system is inconsistent and has no solutions. Otherwise, finish Step 3 and read the solutions of the system from the final matrix.

When doing Step 3, try to choose row operations so that as few fractions as possible are carried through the computation. This makes calculation easier when working by hand and avoids introducing round-off errors when using a calculator or computer.

TECHNOLOGY TIP The Gauss-Jordan method can be carried out in a single step on some calculators by using RREF (in the MATH or OPS submenu of the MATRIX menu of TI-83/85/86/92 and the MATRIX submenu of the MATH menu of HP-38). ✔

EXAMPLE 4 An animal feed is to be made from corn, soybeans, and cottonseed. Determine how many units of each ingredient are needed to make a feed that supplies 1800 units of fiber, 2800 units of fat, and 2200 units of protein, given that one unit of each ingredient provides the numbers of units shown in the table below. The table states, for example, that a unit of corn provides 10 units of fiber, 30 units of fat, and 20 units of protein.

	Corn	*Soybeans*	*Cottonseed*	*Totals*
Units of Fiber	10	20	30	1800
Units of Fat	30	20	40	2800
Units of Protein	20	40	25	2200

7 List a sequence of row operations that will transform the augmented matrix of system (1) in Example 4 into the augmented matrix of system (2).

Answer:

Many sequences are possible, including this one:

replace R_1 by $\frac{1}{10}R_1$;

replace R_2 by $\frac{1}{10}R_2$;

replace R_3 by $\frac{1}{5}R_3$;

replace R_2 by $-3R_1 + R_2$;
replace R_3 by $-4R_1 + R_3$;

replace R_2 by $-\frac{1}{4}R_2$;

replace R_3 by $-\frac{1}{7}R_3$.

Let x represent the required number of units of corn, y the number of units of soybeans, and z the number of units of cottonseed. Since the total amount of fiber is to be 1800,

$$10x + 20y + 30z = 1800.$$

The feed must supply 2800 units of fat, so

$$30x + 20y + 40z = 2800.$$

Finally, since 2200 units of protein are required,

$$20x + 40y + 25z = 2200.$$

Thus we must solve this system of equations.

$$\begin{aligned} 10x + 20y + 30z &= 1800 \\ 30x + 20y + 40z &= 2800 \\ 20x + 40y + 25z &= 2200 \end{aligned} \qquad (1)$$

The elimination method or a matrix method leads to the following equivalent system, as shown in Problem 7 at the side. 7

$$\begin{aligned} x + 2y + 3z &= 180 \\ y + \frac{5}{4}z &= 65 \\ z &= 40 \end{aligned} \qquad (2)$$

Back substitution now shows that $z = 40$,

$$y = 65 - \frac{5}{4}(40) = 15 \quad \text{and} \quad x = 180 - 2(15) - 3(40) = 30.$$

Thus, the feed should contain 30 units of corn, 15 units of soybeans, and 40 units of cottonseed. ■

EXAMPLE 5 The U-Drive Rent-a-Truck Company plans to spend 3 million dollars on 200 new vehicles. Each van will cost $10,000, each small truck, $15,000, and each large truck, $25,000. Past experience shows that they need twice as many vans as small trucks. How many of each kind of vehicle can they buy?

Let x be the number of vans, y the number of small trucks, and z the number of large trucks. Then $x + y + z = 200$. The cost of x vans at \$10,000 each is $10{,}000x$, the cost of y small trucks is $15{,}000y$, and the cost of z large trucks is $25{,}000z$, so that $10{,}000x + 15{,}000y + 25{,}000z = 3{,}000{,}000$. Dividing this equation on each side by 5000 makes it $2x + 3y + 5z = 600$. Finally, the number of vans is twice the number of small trucks: $x = 2y$, or equivalently, $x - 2y = 0$.

To solve the system

$$\begin{aligned} x + y + z &= 200 \\ 2x + 3y + 5z &= 600 \\ x - 2y \quad &= 0, \end{aligned}$$

we form the augmented matrix and use the indicated row operations.

$$\left[\begin{array}{ccc|c} 1 & 1 & 1 & 200 \\ 2 & 3 & 5 & 600 \\ 1 & -2 & 0 & 0 \end{array}\right]$$

$$\left[\begin{array}{ccc|c} 1 & 1 & 1 & 200 \\ 0 & 1 & 3 & 200 \\ 0 & -3 & -1 & -200 \end{array}\right] \quad \begin{array}{l} \\ -2R_1 + R_2 \\ -R_1 + R_3 \end{array}$$

$$\left[\begin{array}{ccc|c} 1 & 0 & -2 & 0 \\ 0 & 1 & 3 & 200 \\ 0 & 0 & 8 & 400 \end{array}\right] \quad \begin{array}{l} -R_2 + R_1 \\ \\ 3R_2 + R_3 \end{array}$$

$$\left[\begin{array}{ccc|c} 1 & 0 & -2 & 0 \\ 0 & 1 & 3 & 200 \\ 0 & 0 & 1 & 50 \end{array}\right] \quad \begin{array}{l} \\ \\ \frac{1}{8}R_3 \end{array}$$

$$\left[\begin{array}{ccc|c} 1 & 0 & 0 & 100 \\ 0 & 1 & 0 & 50 \\ 0 & 0 & 1 & 50 \end{array}\right] \quad \begin{array}{l} 2R_3 + R_1 \\ -3R_3 + R_2 \\ \end{array}$$

The final matrix corresponds to the system

$$\begin{aligned} x &= 100 \\ y &= 50 \\ z &= 50. \end{aligned}$$

Therefore, U-Drive should buy 100 vans, 50 small trucks, and 50 large trucks. ■ 8

8 In Example 5, suppose the U-Drive Company can spend only 2 million dollars on 150 new vehicles, and that they need three times as many vans as small trucks. Write a system of equations to express these conditions.

Answer:

$$\begin{aligned} x + y + z &= 150 \\ 2x + 3y + 5z &= 400 \\ x - 3y \quad &= 0 \end{aligned}$$

7.2 EXERCISES

Write the augmented matrix of each of the following systems. Do not solve the systems.

1. $$\begin{aligned} 2x + y + z &= 3 \\ 3x - 4y + 2z &= -5 \\ x + y + z &= 2 \end{aligned}$$

2. $$\begin{aligned} 3x + 4y - 2z - 3w &= 0 \\ x - 3y + 7z + 4w &= 9 \\ 2x \quad + 5z - 6w &= 0 \end{aligned}$$

Write the system of equations associated with the following augmented matrices. Do not solve the systems.

3. $$\left[\begin{array}{ccc|c} 2 & 3 & 8 & 20 \\ 1 & 4 & 6 & 12 \\ 0 & 3 & 5 & 10 \end{array}\right]$$

4. $$\left[\begin{array}{ccc|c} 3 & 2 & 6 & 18 \\ 2 & -2 & 5 & 7 \\ 1 & 0 & 5 & 20 \end{array}\right]$$

Use the indicated row operation to transform each matrix.

5. Interchange R_2 and R_3.

$$\left[\begin{array}{ccc|c} 1 & 2 & 3 & -1 \\ 6 & 5 & 4 & 6 \\ 2 & 0 & 7 & -4 \end{array}\right]$$

6. Replace R_3 by $-3R_1 + R_3$.

$$\left[\begin{array}{cccc|c} 1 & 5 & 2 & 0 & -1 \\ 8 & 5 & 4 & 6 & 6 \\ 3 & 0 & 7 & 1 & -4 \end{array}\right]$$

7. Replace R_2 by $2R_1 + R_2$.

$$\left[\begin{array}{cccc|c} -4 & -3 & 1 & -1 & 2 \\ 8 & 2 & 5 & 0 & 6 \\ 0 & -2 & 9 & 4 & 5 \end{array}\right]$$

8. Replace R_3 by $\frac{1}{4}R_3$.

$$\left[\begin{array}{ccc|c} 2 & 5 & 1 & -1 \\ -4 & 0 & 4 & 6 \\ 6 & 0 & 8 & -4 \end{array}\right]$$

Use the Gauss-Jordan method to solve each of the following systems of equations. (See Examples 1–3.)

9. $$\begin{aligned} x + 2y + z &= 5 \\ 2x + y - 3z &= -2 \\ 3x + y + 4z &= -5 \end{aligned}$$

10. $$\begin{aligned} 3x - 2y + z &= 6 \\ 3x + y - z &= -4 \\ -x + 2y - 2z &= -8 \end{aligned}$$

11. $$\begin{aligned} x + 3y - 6z &= 7 \\ 2x - y + 2z &= 0 \\ x + y + 2z &= -1 \end{aligned}$$

12. $$\begin{aligned} x &= 1 - y \\ 2x &= z \\ 2z &= -2 - y \end{aligned}$$

13. $$\begin{aligned} 3x + 5y - z &= 0 \\ 4x - y + 2z &= 1 \\ -6x - 10y + 2z &= 0 \end{aligned}$$

14. $$\begin{aligned} x + y &= -1 \\ y + z &= 4 \\ x + z &= 1 \end{aligned}$$

15. $$\begin{aligned} x + y - z &= 6 \\ 2x - y + z &= -9 \\ x - 2y + 3z &= 1 \end{aligned}$$

16. $$\begin{aligned} y &= x - 1 \\ y &= 6 + z \\ z &= -1 - x \end{aligned}$$

17. $$\begin{aligned} x - 2y + z &= 5 \\ 2x + y - z &= 2 \\ -2x + 4y - 2z &= 2 \end{aligned}$$

18. $$\begin{aligned} 2x + 3y + z &= 9 \\ 4x + y - 3z &= -7 \\ 6x + 2y - 4z &= -8 \end{aligned}$$

19. $$\begin{aligned} -8x - 9y &= 11 \\ 24x + 34y &= 2 \\ 16x + 11y &= -57 \end{aligned}$$

20. $$\begin{aligned} 2x + y &= 7 \\ x - y &= 3 \\ x + 3y &= 4 \end{aligned}$$

21. $$\begin{aligned} x + y - z &= -20 \\ 2x - y + z &= 11 \end{aligned}$$

22. $$\begin{aligned} 4x + 3y + z &= 1 \\ -2x - y + 2z &= 0 \end{aligned}$$

23. $$\begin{aligned} 2x + y + 3z - 2w &= -6 \\ 4x + 3y + z - w &= -2 \\ x + y + z + w &= -5 \\ -2x - 2y + 2z + 2w &= -10 \end{aligned}$$

24. $$\begin{aligned} x + y + z + w &= -1 \\ -x + 4y + z - w &= 0 \\ x - 2y + z - 2w &= 11 \\ -x - 2y + z + 2w &= -3 \end{aligned}$$

25. $$\begin{aligned} x + 2y - z \qquad &= 3 \\ 3x + y \qquad + w &= 4 \\ 2x - y + z + w &= 2 \end{aligned}$$

26. $$\begin{aligned} x - 2y - z - 3w &= -3 \\ -x + y + z \qquad &= 2 \\ 4y + 3z - 6w &= -2 \end{aligned}$$

Set up a system of equations and use the Gauss-Jordan method to solve it. (See Examples 4 and 5.)

27. **Management** McFrugal Snack Shops plan to hire two public relations firms to survey 500 customers by phone, 750 by mail, and 250 by in-person interviews. The Garcia firm has personnel to do 10 phone surveys, 30 mail surveys, and 5 interviews per hour. The Wong firm can handle 20 phone surveys, 10 mail surveys, and 10 interviews per hour. For how many hours should each firm be hired to produce the exact number of surveys needed?

28. **Management** A knitting shop ordered yarn from three suppliers, I, II, and III. One month the shop ordered a total of 100 units of yarn from these suppliers. The delivery costs were \$80, \$50, and \$65 per unit for the orders from suppliers I, II, and III, respectively, with total delivery costs of \$5990. The shop ordered the same amount from suppliers I and III. How many units were ordered from each supplier?

29. **Management** An electronics company produces three models of stereo speakers, models A, B, and C, and can deliver them by truck, van, or station wagon. A truck holds 2 boxes of model A, 1 of model B, and 3 of model C. A van holds 1 box of model A, 3 boxes of model B, and 2 boxes of model C. A station wagon holds 1 box of model A, 3 boxes of model B, and 1 box of model C. If 15 boxes of model A, 20 boxes of model B, and 22 boxes of model C are to be delivered, how many vehicles of each type should be used so that all operate at full capacity?

30. **Management** Pretzels cost \$3 per pound, dried fruit \$4 per pound, and nuts \$8 per pound. How many pounds of each should be used to produce 140 pounds of trail mix costing \$6 per pound in which there are twice as many pretzels (by weight) as dried fruit?

31. **Management** A manufacturer purchases a part for use at both of its two plants—one in Canoga Park, California, the other in Wooster, Ohio. The part is available in limited quantities from two suppliers. Each supplier has 75 units available. The Canoga Park plant needs 40 units and the Wooster plant requires 75 units. The first supplier charges \$70 per unit delivered to Canoga Park and \$90 per unit delivered to Wooster. Corresponding costs from the second supplier are \$80 and \$120. The manufacturer wants to order a total of 75 units from the first, less expensive, supplier, with the remaining 40 units to come from the second supplier. If the company spends \$10,750 to purchase the required number of units for the two plants, find the number of units that should be purchased from each supplier for each plant as follows.
   (a) Assign variables to the four unknowns.
   (b) Write a system of five equations with the four variables. (Not all equations will involve all four variables.)
   (c) Solve the system of equations.

32. **Management** An auto manufacturer sends cars from two plants, I and II, to dealerships A and B located in a midwestern city. Plant I has a total of 28 cars to send, and plant II has 8. Dealer A needs 20 cars, and dealer B needs 16. Transportation costs based on the distance of each dealership from each plant are \$220 from I to A, \$300 from I to B, \$400 from II to A, and \$180 from II to B. The

manufacturer wants to limit transportation costs to $10,640. How many cars should be sent from each plant to each of the two dealerships?

33. Management The electronics company in Exercise 29 no longer makes model C. Each kind of delivery vehicle can now carry one more box of model B than previously and the same number of boxes of model A. If 16 boxes of model A and 22 boxes of model B are to be delivered, how many vehicles of each type should be used so that all operate at full capacity?

34. Natural Science An animal breeder can buy four types of tiger food. Each case of Brand A contains 25 units of fiber, 30 units of protein, and 30 units of fat. Each case of Brand B contains 50 units of fiber, 30 units of protein, and 20 units of fat. Each case of Brand C contains 75 units of fiber, 30 units of protein, and 20 units of fat. Each case of Brand D contains 100 units of fiber, 60 units of protein, and 30 units of fat. How many cases of each brand should the breeder mix together to obtain a food that provides 1200 units of fiber, 600 units of protein, and 400 units of fat?

35. Management An investment firm recommends that a client invest in AAA, A, and B rated bonds. The average yield on AAA bonds is 6%, on A bonds 7%, and on B bonds 10%. The client wants to invest twice as much in AAA bonds as in B bonds. How much should be invested in each type of bond under the following conditions?

(a) The total investment is $25,000, and the investor wants an annual return of $1810 on the three investments.

(b) The values in part (a) are changed to $30,000 and $2150, respectively.

(c) The values in part (a) are changed to $40,000 and $2900, respectively.

36. Management An electronics company produces transistors, resistors, and computer chips. Each transistor requires 3 units of copper, 1 unit of zinc, and 2 units of glass. Each resistor requires 3, 2, and 1 units of the three materials, and each computer chip requires 2, 1, and 2 units of these materials, respectively. How many of each product can be made with the following amounts of materials?

(a) 810 units of copper, 410 units of zinc, and 490 units of glass

(b) 765 units of copper, 385 units of zinc, and 470 units of glass

(c) 1010 units of copper, 500 units of zinc, and 610 units of glass

37. Management At a pottery factory, fuel consumption for heating the kilns varies with the size of the order being fired. In the past, the company recorded these figures.

x = *Number of Platters*	y = *Fuel Cost per Platter*
6	$2.80
8	2.48
10	2.24

(a) Find an equation of the form $y = ax^2 + bx + c$ whose graph contains the three points corresponding to the data in the table.

(b) How many platters should be fired at one time in order to minimize the fuel cost per platter? What is the minimum fuel cost per platter?

38. Management A convenience store sells 23 sodas one summer afternoon in 12, 16, and 20 ounce cups (small, medium, and large). The total volume of soda sold was 376 ounces.

(a) Suppose that the prices for a small, medium, and large soda are $1, $1.25, and $1.40, respectively, and that the total sales were $28.45. How many of each size did the store sell?

(b) Suppose the prices for a small, medium, and large soda are changed to $1, $2, and $3, respectively, but all other information is the same. How many of each size did the store sell?

(c) Suppose the prices are the same as in part (b), but the total revenue is $48. Now how many of each size did the store sell?

39. Management According to data from a 1984 Texas agricultural report, the amount of nitrogen (in lbs/acre), phosphate (in lbs/acre), and labor (in hrs/acre) needed to grow honeydews, yellow onions, and lettuce is given by the following table.*

	Honeydews	*Yellow Onions*	*Lettuce*
Nitrogen	120	150	180
Phosphate	180	80	80
Labor	4.97	4.45	4.65

(a) If the farmer has 220 acres, 29,100 lbs of nitrogen, 32,600 lbs of phosphate, and 480 hours of labor, is it possible to use all resources completely? If so, how many acres should he allot for each crop?

(b) Suppose everything is the same as in part (a), except that 1061 hours of labor are available. Is it possible to use all resources completely? If so, how many acres should he allot for each crop?

40. Management The business analyst for Melcher Manufacturing wants to find an equation that can be used to project sales of a relatively new product. For the years 1995, 1996, and 1997, sales were $15,000, $32,000, and $123,000, respectively.

(a) Graph the sales for the years 1995, 1996, and 1997, letting the year 1995 equal 0 on the x-axis. Let the values on the vertical axis be in thousands. (For example, the point (1996, 32,000) will be graphed as (1, 32).)

*Paredes, Miguel, Fatehi, Mohammad, and Hinthorn, Richard, "The Transformation of an Inconsistent Linear System into a Consistent System," *The AMATYC Review*, Vol 13, No. 2, Spring 1992.

(b) Find the equation of the straight line $ax + by = c$ through the points for 1995 and 1997.

(c) Find the equation of the parabola $y = ax^2 + bx + c$ through the three given points.

(d) Find the projected sales for 2000 first by using the equation from part (b) and then by using the equation from part (c). If you were to estimate sales of the product in 2000, which result would you choose? Why?

41. **Natural Science** Determining the amount of carbon dioxide in the atmosphere is important because carbon dioxide is known to be a greenhouse gas. Carbon dioxide concentrations (in parts per million) have been measured at Mauna Loa, Hawaii, over the past 30 years. The concentrations have increased quadratically.* The table lists readings for three years.

Year	CO_2
1958	315
1973	325
1988	352

(a) If the relationship between the carbon dioxide concentration C and the year t is expressed as $C = at^2 + bt + c$, where $t = 0$ corresponds to 1958, use a linear system of equations to determine the constants a, b, and c.

(b) Predict the year when the amount of carbon dioxide in the atmosphere will double from its 1958 level.

*Nilsson, A., *Greenhouse Earth*, John Wiley & Sons, New York, 1992.

42. **Physical Science** For certain aircraft there exists a quadratic relationship between an airplane's maximum speed S (in knots) and its ceiling C, its highest altitude possible (in thousands of feet).* The table lists three airplanes that conform to this relationship.

Airplane	*Maximum Speed*	*Ceiling*
Hawkeye	320	33
Corsair	600	40
Tomcat	1283	50

(a) If the relationship between C and S is written as $C = aS^2 + bS + c$, use a linear system of equations to determine the constants a, b, and c.

(b) A new aircraft of this type has a ceiling of 45,000 feet. Predict its top speed.

*Sanders, D., *Statistics: A First Course*, Fifth Edition, McGraw Hill, Inc., 1995.

7.3 BASIC MATRIX OPERATIONS

Until now we have used matrices only as a convenient shorthand to solve systems of equations. However, matrices are also important in the fields of management, natural science, engineering, and social science as a way to organize data, as Example 1 demonstrates.

EXAMPLE 1 The EZ Life Company manufactures sofas and armchairs in three models, A, B, and C. The company has regional warehouses in New York, Chicago, and San Francisco. In its August shipment, the company sends 10 model A sofas, 12 model B sofas, 5 model C sofas, 15 model A chairs, 20 model B chairs, and 8 model C chairs to each warehouse.

This data might be organized by first listing it as follows.

Sofas	10 model A	12 model B	5 model C
Chairs	15 model A	20 model B	8 model C

Alternatively, we might tabulate the data in a chart.

		MODEL		
		A	B	C
FURNITURE	**Sofa**	10	12	5
	Chair	15	20	8

1 Rewrite this information in a matrix with three rows and two columns.

Answer:
$$\begin{bmatrix} 10 & 15 \\ 12 & 20 \\ 5 & 8 \end{bmatrix}$$

With the understanding that the numbers in each row refer to the furniture type (sofa, chair) and the numbers in each column refer to the model (A, B, C), the same information can be given by a matrix, as follows.

$$M = \begin{bmatrix} 10 & 12 & 5 \\ 15 & 20 & 8 \end{bmatrix} \quad ■ \quad \boxed{1}$$

A matrix with m rows and n columns has dimensions or size $m \times n$. The number of rows is always given first.

2 Give the size of each of the following matrices.

(a) $\begin{bmatrix} 2 & 1 & -5 & 6 \\ 3 & 0 & 7 & -4 \end{bmatrix}$

(b) $\begin{bmatrix} 1 & 2 & 3 \\ 4 & 5 & 6 \\ 9 & 8 & 7 \end{bmatrix}$

Answers:
(a) 2×4
(b) 3×3

EXAMPLE 2 **(a)** The matrix $\begin{bmatrix} 6 & 5 \\ 3 & 4 \\ 5 & -1 \end{bmatrix}$ is a 3×2 matrix.

(b) $\begin{bmatrix} 5 & 8 & 9 \\ 0 & 5 & -3 \\ -4 & 0 & 5 \end{bmatrix}$ is a 3×3 matrix.

(c) $[1 \quad 6 \quad 5 \quad -2 \quad 5]$ is a 1×5 matrix.

(d) A graphing calculator displays a 4×1 matrix like this. ■ 2

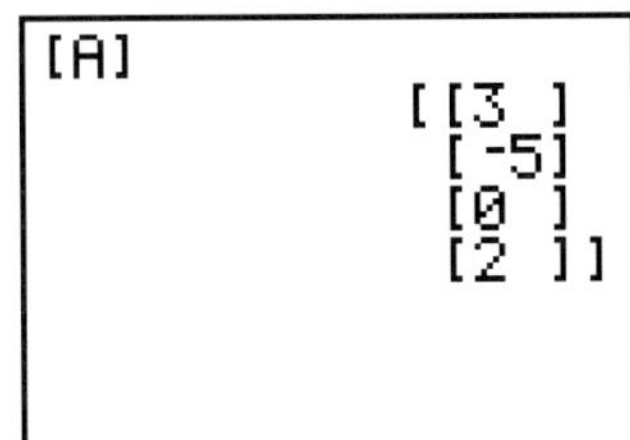

3 Use the numbers 2, 5, −8, 4 to write
(a) a row matrix;
(b) a column matrix;
(c) a square matrix.

Answers:
(a) $[2 \quad 5 \quad -8 \quad 4]$
(b) $\begin{bmatrix} 2 \\ 5 \\ -8 \\ 4 \end{bmatrix}$
(c) $\begin{bmatrix} 2 & 5 \\ -8 & 4 \end{bmatrix}$ or $\begin{bmatrix} 2 & -8 \\ 5 & 4 \end{bmatrix}$

(Other answers are possible.)

A matrix with only one row, as in Example 2(c), is called a **row matrix** or **row vector.** A matrix with only one column, as in Example 2(d), is called a **column matrix** or **column vector.** A matrix with the same number of rows as columns is called a **square matrix.** The matrix in Example 2(b) above is a square matrix, as are

$$A = \begin{bmatrix} -5 & 6 \\ 8 & 3 \end{bmatrix} \quad \text{and} \quad B = \begin{bmatrix} 0 & 0 & 0 & 0 \\ -2 & 4 & 1 & 3 \\ 0 & 0 & 0 & 0 \\ -5 & -4 & 1 & 8 \end{bmatrix}. \quad \boxed{3}$$

When a matrix is denoted by a single letter, such as the matrix A above, then the element in row i and column j is denoted a_{ij}. For example, $a_{21} = 8$ (the element in row 2, column 1). Similarly, in matrix B above, $b_{42} = -4$ (the element in row 4, column 2).

ADDITION The matrix given in Example 1,

$$M = \begin{bmatrix} 10 & 12 & 5 \\ 15 & 20 & 8 \end{bmatrix},$$

shows the August shipment from the EZ Life plant to each of its warehouses. If matrix N below gives the September shipment to the New York warehouse, what is the total shipment for each item of furniture to the New York warehouse for these two months?

$$N = \begin{bmatrix} 45 & 35 & 20 \\ 65 & 40 & 35 \end{bmatrix}$$

If 10 model A sofas were shipped in August and 45 in September, then altogether 55 model A sofas were shipped in the 2 months. Adding the other corresponding entries gives a new matrix, Q, that represents the total shipment to the New York warehouse for the 2 months.

$$Q = \begin{bmatrix} 55 & 47 & 25 \\ 80 & 60 & 43 \end{bmatrix}$$

It is convenient to refer to Q as the "sum" of M and N.

The way these two matrices were added illustrates the following definition of addition of matrices.

> The **sum** of two $m \times n$ matrices X and Y is the $m \times n$ matrix $X + Y$ in which each element is the sum of the corresponding elements of X and Y.

4 Find each sum when possible.

(a) $\begin{bmatrix} 2 & 5 & 7 \\ 3 & -1 & 4 \end{bmatrix} + \begin{bmatrix} -1 & 2 & 0 \\ 10 & -4 & 5 \end{bmatrix}$

(b) $\begin{bmatrix} 1 \\ 2 \\ 3 \end{bmatrix} + \begin{bmatrix} 2 & -1 \\ 4 & 5 \\ 6 & 0 \end{bmatrix}$

(c) $[5 \quad 4 \quad -1] + [-5 \quad 2 \quad 3]$

Answers:

(a) $\begin{bmatrix} 1 & 7 & 7 \\ 13 & -5 & 9 \end{bmatrix}$

(b) Not possible

(c) $[0 \quad 6 \quad 2]$

It is important to remember that only matrices that are the same size can be added.

TECHNOLOGY TIP Sums (and differences) of matrices that have the same dimensions can be found with a graphing calculator that has matrix capability. See your instruction manual for details. ✔

EXAMPLE 3 Find each sum if possible.

(a) $$\begin{bmatrix} 5 & -6 \\ 8 & 9 \end{bmatrix} + \begin{bmatrix} -4 & 6 \\ 8 & -3 \end{bmatrix} = \begin{bmatrix} 5 + (-4) & -6 + 6 \\ 8 + 8 & 9 + (-3) \end{bmatrix} = \begin{bmatrix} 1 & 0 \\ 16 & 6 \end{bmatrix}$$

(b) The matrices

$$A = \begin{bmatrix} 5 & 8 \\ 6 & 2 \end{bmatrix} \quad \text{and} \quad B = \begin{bmatrix} 3 & 9 & 1 \\ 4 & 2 & 5 \end{bmatrix}$$

are different sizes, so it is not possible to find the sum $A + B$. ■ 4

EXAMPLE 4 The September shipments of the three models of sofas and chairs from the EZ Life Company to the New York, San Francisco, and Chicago warehouses are given in matrices N, S, and C below.

$$N = \begin{bmatrix} 45 & 35 & 20 \\ 65 & 40 & 35 \end{bmatrix}, \quad S = \begin{bmatrix} 30 & 32 & 28 \\ 43 & 47 & 30 \end{bmatrix}, \quad C = \begin{bmatrix} 22 & 25 & 38 \\ 31 & 34 & 35 \end{bmatrix}$$

What was the total amount shipped to the three warehouses in September?

5 From the result of Example 4, find the total number of the following shipped to the three warehouses.

(a) Model A chairs

(b) Model B sofas

(c) Model C chairs

Answers:

(a) 139

(b) 92

(c) 100

The total of the September shipments is represented by the sum of the three matrices N, S, and C.

$$N + S + C = \begin{bmatrix} 45 & 35 & 20 \\ 65 & 40 & 35 \end{bmatrix} + \begin{bmatrix} 30 & 32 & 28 \\ 43 & 47 & 30 \end{bmatrix} + \begin{bmatrix} 22 & 25 & 38 \\ 31 & 34 & 35 \end{bmatrix}$$

$$= \begin{bmatrix} 97 & 92 & 86 \\ 139 & 121 & 100 \end{bmatrix}$$

For example, from this sum the total number of model C sofas shipped to the three warehouses in September was 86. ■ 5

As mentioned in Section 1.1, the additive inverse of the real number a is $-a$; a similar definition is given for the additive inverse of a matrix.

The **additive inverse** (or *negative*) of a matrix X is the matrix $-X$ in which each element is the additive inverse of the corresponding element of X.

If

$$A = \begin{bmatrix} 1 & 2 & 3 \\ 0 & -1 & 5 \end{bmatrix} \quad \text{and} \quad B = \begin{bmatrix} -2 & 3 & 0 \\ 1 & -7 & 2 \end{bmatrix},$$

then by the definition of the additive inverse of a matrix,

$$-A = \begin{bmatrix} -1 & -2 & -3 \\ 0 & 1 & -5 \end{bmatrix} \quad \text{and} \quad -B = \begin{bmatrix} 2 & -3 & 0 \\ -1 & 7 & -2 \end{bmatrix}.$$

TECHNOLOGY TIP A graphing calculator with matrix capability gives the additive inverse of a matrix by preceding the matrix with a negative sign. See Figure 7.3. ✔

```
[A]
        [[2 3  ]
         [1 1.5]]
-[A]
       [[-2 -3  ]
        [-1 -1.5]]
```

FIGURE 7.3

By the definition of matrix addition, for each matrix X, the sum $X + (-X)$ is a **zero matrix,** O, whose elements are all zeros. There is an $m \times n$ zero matrix for each pair of values of m and n.

$$\begin{bmatrix} 0 & 0 \\ 0 & 0 \end{bmatrix} \qquad \begin{bmatrix} 0 & 0 & 0 & 0 \\ 0 & 0 & 0 & 0 \end{bmatrix}$$

2×2 zero matrix $\qquad$ 2×4 zero matrix

Zero matrices have the following *identity property.*

If O is the $m \times n$ zero matrix, and A is any $m \times n$ matrix, then

$$A + O = O + A = A.$$

Compare this with the identity property for real numbers: for any real number a, $a + 0 = 0 + a = a$.

SUBTRACTION The **subtraction** of matrices can be defined in a manner comparable to subtraction for real numbers.

For two $m \times n$ matrices X and Y, the **difference** of X and Y is the $m \times n$ matrix $X - Y$ in which each element is the difference of the corresponding elements of X and Y, or, equivalently,

$$X - Y = X + (-Y).$$

According to this definition, matrix subtraction can be performed by subtracting corresponding elements. For example, using A and B as defined above,

$$A - B = \begin{bmatrix} 1 & 2 & 3 \\ 0 & -1 & 5 \end{bmatrix} - \begin{bmatrix} -2 & 3 & 0 \\ 1 & -7 & 2 \end{bmatrix}$$

$$= \begin{bmatrix} 1-(-2) & 2-3 & 3-0 \\ 0-1 & -1-(-7) & 5-2 \end{bmatrix}$$

$$= \begin{bmatrix} 3 & -1 & 3 \\ -1 & 6 & 3 \end{bmatrix}.$$

6 Find each of the following differences when possible.

(a) $\begin{bmatrix} 2 & 5 \\ -1 & 0 \end{bmatrix} - \begin{bmatrix} 6 & 4 \\ 3 & -2 \end{bmatrix}$

(b) $\begin{bmatrix} 1 & 5 & 6 \\ 2 & 4 & 8 \end{bmatrix} - \begin{bmatrix} 2 & 1 \\ 10 & 3 \end{bmatrix}$

(c) $[5 \quad -4 \quad 1] - [6 \quad 0 \quad -3]$

Answers:

(a) $\begin{bmatrix} -4 & 1 \\ -4 & 2 \end{bmatrix}$

(b) Not possible

(c) $[-1 \quad -4 \quad 4]$

EXAMPLE 5 **(a)** $[8 \quad 6 \quad -4] - [3 \quad 5 \quad -8] = [5 \quad 1 \quad 4]$

(b) The matrices

$$\begin{bmatrix} -2 & 5 \\ 0 & 1 \end{bmatrix} \quad \text{and} \quad \begin{bmatrix} 3 \\ 5 \end{bmatrix}$$

are different sizes and cannot be subtracted. ■ 6

EXAMPLE 6 During September the Chicago warehouse of the EZ Life Company shipped out the following numbers of each model.

$$K = \begin{bmatrix} 5 & 10 & 8 \\ 11 & 14 & 15 \end{bmatrix}$$

What was the Chicago warehouse inventory on October 1, taking into account only the number of items received and sent out during the month?

The number of each kind of item received during September is given by matrix C from Example 4; the number of each model sent out during September is given by matrix K above. The October 1 inventory will be represented by the matrix $C - K$ as shown below.

$$\begin{bmatrix} 22 & 25 & 38 \\ 31 & 34 & 35 \end{bmatrix} - \begin{bmatrix} 5 & 10 & 8 \\ 11 & 14 & 15 \end{bmatrix} = \begin{bmatrix} 17 & 15 & 30 \\ 20 & 20 & 20 \end{bmatrix} \blacksquare$$

EXAMPLE 7 A drug company is testing 200 patients to see if Painoff (a new headache medicine) is effective. Half the patients receive Painoff and half receive a placebo. The data on the first 50 patients is summarized in this matrix.

	Pain Relief Obtained Yes	No
Patient took Painoff	22	3
Patient took placebo	8	17

For example, row 2 shows that of the people who took the placebo, 8 got relief, but 17 did not. The test was repeated on three more groups of 50 patients each, with the results summarized by these matrices.

$$\begin{bmatrix} 21 & 4 \\ 6 & 19 \end{bmatrix} \quad \begin{bmatrix} 19 & 6 \\ 10 & 15 \end{bmatrix} \quad \begin{bmatrix} 23 & 2 \\ 3 & 22 \end{bmatrix}$$

The total results of the test can be obtained by adding these four matrices.

$$\begin{bmatrix} 22 & 3 \\ 8 & 17 \end{bmatrix} + \begin{bmatrix} 21 & 4 \\ 6 & 19 \end{bmatrix} + \begin{bmatrix} 19 & 6 \\ 10 & 15 \end{bmatrix} + \begin{bmatrix} 23 & 2 \\ 3 & 22 \end{bmatrix} = \begin{bmatrix} 85 & 15 \\ 27 & 73 \end{bmatrix}$$

Because 85 of 100 patients got relief with Painoff and only 27 of 100 with the placebo, it appears that Painoff is effective. ■ 7

7 Later it was discovered that the data in the last group of 50 patients in Example 7 was invalid. Use a matrix to represent the total test results after those data were eliminated.

Answer:

$$\begin{bmatrix} 62 & 13 \\ 24 & 51 \end{bmatrix}$$

Suppose one of the EZ Life Company warehouses receives the following order, written in matrix form, where the entries have the same meaning as given earlier.

$$\begin{bmatrix} 5 & 4 & 1 \\ 3 & 2 & 3 \end{bmatrix}$$

Later, the store that sent the order asks the warehouse to send six more of the same order. The six new orders can be written as one matrix by multiplying each element in the matrix by 6, giving the product

$$6\begin{bmatrix} 5 & 4 & 1 \\ 3 & 2 & 3 \end{bmatrix} = \begin{bmatrix} 30 & 24 & 6 \\ 18 & 12 & 18 \end{bmatrix}.$$

8 Find each product.

(a) $-3\begin{bmatrix} 4 & -2 \\ 1 & 5 \end{bmatrix}$

(b) $4\begin{bmatrix} 2 & 4 & 7 \\ 8 & 2 & 1 \\ 5 & 7 & 3 \end{bmatrix}$

Answers:

(a) $\begin{bmatrix} -12 & 6 \\ -3 & -15 \end{bmatrix}$

(b) $\begin{bmatrix} 8 & 16 & 28 \\ 32 & 8 & 4 \\ 20 & 28 & 12 \end{bmatrix}$

In work with matrices, a real number, like the 6 in the multiplication above, is called a **scalar.**

The **product** of a scalar k and a matrix X is the matrix kX, each of whose elements is k times the corresponding element of X.

For example,

$$(-3)\begin{bmatrix} 2 & -5 \\ 1 & 7 \end{bmatrix} = \begin{bmatrix} -6 & 15 \\ -3 & -21 \end{bmatrix}.$$ **8**

7.3 EXERCISES

Find the size of each of the following. Identify any square, column, or row matrices. (See Example 2.) Give the additive inverse of each matrix.

1. $\begin{bmatrix} 7 & -8 & 4 \\ 0 & 13 & 9 \end{bmatrix}$

2. $\begin{bmatrix} -7 & 23 \\ 5 & -6 \end{bmatrix}$

3. $\begin{bmatrix} -3 & 0 & 11 \\ 1 & \frac{1}{4} & -7 \\ 5 & -3 & 9 \end{bmatrix}$

4. $\begin{bmatrix} 6 & -4 & \frac{2}{3} & 12 & 2 \end{bmatrix}$

5. $\begin{bmatrix} 7 \\ 11 \end{bmatrix}$

6. $[-5]$

7. If A is a 5×3 matrix and $A + B = A$, what do you know about B?

8. If C is a 3×3 matrix and D is a 3×4 matrix, then $C + D$ is ______.

Perform the indicated operations where possible. (See Examples 3–6.)

9. $\begin{bmatrix} 1 & 2 & 5 & -1 \\ 3 & 0 & 2 & -4 \end{bmatrix} + \begin{bmatrix} 8 & 10 & -5 & 3 \\ -2 & -1 & 0 & 0 \end{bmatrix}$

10. $\begin{bmatrix} 1 & 5 \\ 2 & -3 \\ 3 & 7 \end{bmatrix} + \begin{bmatrix} 2 & 3 \\ 8 & 5 \\ -1 & 9 \end{bmatrix}$

11. $\begin{bmatrix} 1 & 5 & 7 \\ 2 & 2 & 3 \end{bmatrix} + \begin{bmatrix} 4 & 8 & -7 \\ 1 & -1 & 5 \end{bmatrix}$

12. $\begin{bmatrix} 2 & 4 \\ -8 & 1 \end{bmatrix} + \begin{bmatrix} 9 & -3 \\ 8 & 5 \end{bmatrix}$

13. $\begin{bmatrix} 4 & -2 & 5 \\ 3 & 7 & 0 \end{bmatrix} - \begin{bmatrix} 1 & 5 & -2 \\ -1 & 3 & 8 \end{bmatrix}$

14. $\begin{bmatrix} 9 & 1 \\ 0 & -3 \\ 4 & 10 \end{bmatrix} - \begin{bmatrix} 1 & 9 & -4 \\ -1 & 1 & 0 \end{bmatrix}$

Let $A = \begin{bmatrix} -2 & 4 \\ 0 & 3 \end{bmatrix}$ *and* $B = \begin{bmatrix} -6 & 2 \\ 4 & 0 \end{bmatrix}$. *Find each of the following.*

15. $2A$ **16.** $-3B$ **17.** $-4B$

18. $5A$ **19.** $-4A + 5B$ **20.** $3A - 10B$

Let $A = \begin{bmatrix} 1 & -2 \\ 4 & 3 \end{bmatrix}$ *and* $B = \begin{bmatrix} 2 & -1 \\ 0 & 5 \end{bmatrix}$. *Find a matrix X satisfying the given equation.*

21. $2X = 2A + 3B$ **22.** $3X = A - 3B$

Using matrices

$$O = \begin{bmatrix} 0 & 0 \\ 0 & 0 \end{bmatrix},\ P = \begin{bmatrix} m & n \\ p & q \end{bmatrix},\ T = \begin{bmatrix} r & s \\ t & u \end{bmatrix}, \text{ and}$$

$$X = \begin{bmatrix} x & y \\ z & w \end{bmatrix},$$

verify that the statements in Exercises 23–28 are true.

23. $X + T$ is a 2×2 matrix.

24. $X + T = T + X$ (Commutative property of addition of matrices)

25. $X + (T + P) = (X + T) + P$ (Associative property of addition of matrices)

26. $X + (-X) = O$ (Inverse property of addition of matrices)

27. $P + O = P$ (Identity property of addition of matrices)

28. Which of the above properties are valid for matrices that are not square?

29. Management An investment group planning a shopping center decided to include a market, a barber shop, a variety store, a drug store, and a bakery. They estimated the initial cost and the guaranteed rent (both in dollars per square foot) for each type of store, respectively, as follows. Initial cost: 18, 10, 8, 10, and 10; guaranteed rent: 2.7, 1.5, 1.0, 2.0, and 1.7. Write this information first as a 5×2 matrix and then as a 2×5 matrix. (See Example 1.)

30. Natural Science A dietician prepares a diet specifying the amounts a patient should eat of four basic food groups: group I, meats; group II, fruits and vegetables; group III, breads and starches; group IV, milk products. Amounts are given in "exchanges" which represent 1 ounce (meat), 1/2 cup (fruits and vegetables), 1 slice (bread), 8 ounces (milk), or other suitable measurements.

(a) The number of "exchanges" for breakfast for each of the four food groups, respectively, are 2, 1, 2, and 1; for lunch, 3, 2, 2, and 1; and for dinner, 4, 3, 2, and 1. Write a 3×4 matrix using this information.

(b) The amounts of fat, carbohydrates, and protein in each food group respectively are as follows.

Fat: 5, 0, 0, 10
Carbohydrates: 0, 10, 15, 12
Protein: 7, 1, 2, 8

Use this information to write a 4×3 matrix.

(c) There are 8 calories per unit of fat, 4 calories per unit of carbohydrates, and 5 calories per unit of protein; summarize this data in a 3×1 matrix.

31. Natural Science At the beginning of a laboratory experiment, five baby rats measured 5.6, 6.4, 6.9, 7.6, and 6.1 centimeters in length, and weighed 144, 138, 149, 152, and 146 grams, respectively.

(a) Write a 2×5 matrix using this information.

(b) At the end of 2 weeks, their lengths were 10.2, 11.4, 11.4, 12.7, and 10.8 centimeters, and they weighed 196, 196, 225, 250, and 230 grams. Write a 2×5 matrix with this information.

(c) Use matrix subtraction and the matrices found in (a) and (b) to write a matrix that gives the amount of change in length and weight for each rat. (See Examples 5, 6, and 7.)

(d) The following week the rats grew 1.8, 1.5, 2.3, 1.8, and 2.0 centimeters, respectively, and gained 25, 22, 29, 33, and 20 grams, respectively. Set up a matrix with these increases and use matrix addition to find their lengths and weights at the end of this week.

32. Management There are three convenience stores in Gambier. This week, Store I sold 88 loaves of bread, 48 quarts of milk, 16 jars of peanut butter, and 112 pounds of cold cuts. Store II sold 105 loaves of bread, 72 quarts of milk, 21 jars of peanut butter, and 147 pounds of cold cuts. Store III sold 60 loaves of bread, 40 quarts of milk, no peanut butter, and 50 pounds of cold cuts.

(a) Use a 3×4 matrix to express the sales information for the three stores.

(b) During the following week, sales on these products at Store I increased by 25%; sales at Store II increased by 1/3; and sales at Store III increased by 10%. Write the sales matrix for that week.

(c) Write a matrix that represents total sales over the two-week period.

33. Management A toy company has plants in Boston, Chicago, and Seattle that manufacture toy rockets and robots. The matrix below gives the production costs (in dollars) for each item at the Boston plant:

$$\begin{array}{c} \\ \text{Material} \\ \text{Labor} \end{array} \begin{array}{c} \text{Rockets} \quad \text{Robots} \\ \begin{bmatrix} 4.27 & 6.94 \\ 3.45 & 3.65 \end{bmatrix} \end{array}$$

(a) In Chicago, a rocket costs \$4.05 for materials and \$3.27 for labor; a robot costs \$7.01 for material and \$3.51 for labor. In Seattle, material costs are \$4.40 for rockets and \$6.90 for robots; labor costs are \$3.54 for rockets and \$3.76 for robots. Write the production cost matrices for Chicago and Seattle.

(b) Assume each plant makes the same number of each item. Write a matrix that expresses the average production costs for all three plants.

(c) Suppose labor costs increase by \$.11 per item in Chicago and material costs there increase by \$.37 for a rocket and \$.42 for a robot. What is the new production cost matrix for Chicago?

(d) After the Chicago cost increases, the Boston plant is closed and production divided evenly among the other two plants. What is the matrix that now expresses the average production costs for the entire country?

34. Social Sciences The following table gives the educational attainment of the U.S. population 25 years and older.*

	MALE		FEMALE	
	Four Years of High School or More	*Four Years of College or More*	*Four Years of High School or More*	*Four Years of College or More*
1940	22.7%	5.5%	26.3%	3.8%
1950	32.6	7.3	36.0	5.2
1959	42.2	10.3	45.2	6.0
1970	55.0	14.1	55.4	8.2
1980	69.1	20.8	68.1	13.5
1987	76.0	23.6	75.3	16.5
1991	78.5	24.3	78.3	18.8

(a) Write a matrix for the educational attainment of males.

(b) Write a matrix for the educational attainment of females.

(c) Use the matrices from parts (a) and (b) to write a matrix showing how much more (or less) education males have attained than females.

*"Educational Attainment by Percentage of Population 25+ Years, 1940–91" from "The Universal Almanac, 1993," John W. Wright, General Editor, Kansas City, New York: Andrews and McMeel.

7.4 MATRIX PRODUCTS AND INVERSES

In the previous section we showed how to multiply a matrix by a scalar. Finding the product of two matrices is more involved, but is important in solving practical problems. To understand the reasoning behind the definition of matrix multiplication, look again at the EZ Life Company. Suppose sofas and chairs of the same model are often sold as sets with matrix W showing the number of each model set in each warehouse.

$$\begin{array}{l} \\ \text{New York} \\ \text{Chicago} \\ \text{San Francisco} \end{array} \begin{array}{c} \begin{array}{ccc} \text{A} & \text{B} & \text{C} \end{array} \\ \begin{bmatrix} 10 & 7 & 3 \\ 5 & 9 & 6 \\ 4 & 8 & 2 \end{bmatrix} \end{array} = W$$

If the selling price of a model A set is \$800, of a model B set \$1000, and of a model C set \$1200, find the total value of the sets in the New York warehouse as follows.

Type	*Number of Sets*		*Price of Set*		*Total*
A	10	×	\$ 800	=	\$ 8,000
B	7	×	1000	=	7,000
C	3	×	1200	=	3,600
			Total for New York		\$18,600

1 In this example of the EZ Life Company, find the total value of the New York sets if model A sets sell for \$1200, model B for \$1600, and model C for \$1300.

Answer:
\$27,100

The total value of the three kinds of sets in New York is \$18,600. 1

The work done in the table above is summarized as follows:

$$10(\$800) + 7(\$1000) + 3(\$1200) = \$18{,}600.$$

In the same way, the Chicago sets have a total value of

$$5(\$800) + 9(\$1000) + 6(\$1200) = \$20{,}200,$$

and in San Francisco, the total value of the sets is

$$4(\$800) + 8(\$1000) + 2(\$1200) = \$13{,}600.$$

The selling prices can be written as a column matrix, P, and the total value in each location as a column matrix, V.

$$\begin{bmatrix} 800 \\ 1000 \\ 1200 \end{bmatrix} = P \quad \text{and} \quad \begin{bmatrix} 18{,}600 \\ 20{,}200 \\ 13{,}600 \end{bmatrix} = V$$

Consider how the first row of the matrix W and the single column P lead to the first entry of V.

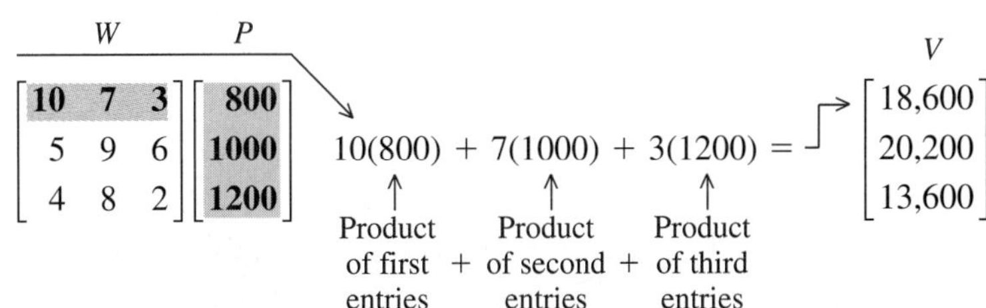

Similarly, adding the products of corresponding entries in the second row of W and the column P produces the second entry in V. The third entry in V is obtained in the same way by using the third row of W and column P. This suggests that it is reasonable to *define* the product WP to be V.

$$WP = \begin{bmatrix} 10 & 7 & 3 \\ 5 & 9 & 6 \\ 4 & 8 & 2 \end{bmatrix} \begin{bmatrix} 800 \\ 1000 \\ 1200 \end{bmatrix} = \begin{bmatrix} 18{,}600 \\ 20{,}200 \\ 13{,}600 \end{bmatrix} = V$$

Note the sizes of the matrices here: the product of a 3×3 matrix and a 3×1 matrix is a 3×1 matrix.

MULTIPLYING MATRICES We first define the **product of a row of a matrix and a column of a matrix** (with the same number of entries in each) to be the *number* obtained by multiplying the corresponding entries (first by first, second by second, and so on) and adding the results. For instance,

$$[3 \quad -2 \quad 1] \cdot \begin{bmatrix} 4 \\ 5 \\ 0 \end{bmatrix} = 3 \cdot 4 + (-2) \cdot 5 + 1 \cdot 0 = 12 - 10 + 0 = 2.$$

Now **matrix multiplication** is defined as follows.

> Let A be an $m \times n$ matrix and let B be an $n \times k$ matrix. The **product matrix** AB is the $m \times k$ matrix whose entry in the ith row and jth column is
>
> the product of the ith row of A and the jth column of B.

CAUTION Be careful when multiplying matrices. Remember that the number of *columns* of A must equal the number of *rows* of B in order to get the product matrix AB. The final product will have as many rows as A and as many columns as B. ◆

EXAMPLE 1 Suppose matrix A is 2×2 and matrix B is 2×4. Can the product AB be calculated? What is the size of the product?

The following diagram helps decide the answers to these questions.

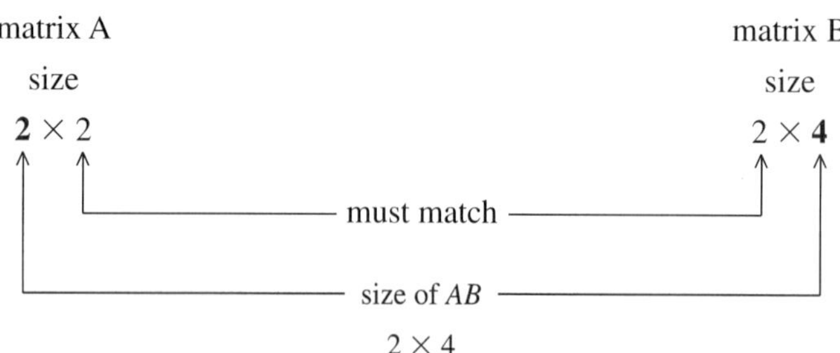

The product AB can be calculated because A has two columns and B has two rows. The product will be a 2×4 matrix. ■ 2

2 Matrix A is 4×6 and matrix B is 2×4.

(a) Can AB be found? If so, give its size.

(b) Can BA be found? If so, give its size.

Answers:

(a) No

(b) Yes; 2×6

EXAMPLE 2 Find the product CD given

$$C = \begin{bmatrix} -3 & 4 & 2 \\ 5 & 0 & 4 \end{bmatrix} \quad \text{and} \quad D = \begin{bmatrix} -6 & 4 \\ 2 & 3 \\ 3 & -2 \end{bmatrix}.$$

Here matrix C is 2×3 and matrix D is 3×2, so matrix CD can be found and will be 2×2.

Step 1

$$\begin{bmatrix} \mathbf{-3} & \mathbf{4} & \mathbf{2} \\ 5 & 0 & 4 \end{bmatrix} \begin{bmatrix} \mathbf{-6} & 4 \\ \mathbf{2} & 3 \\ \mathbf{3} & -2 \end{bmatrix} \quad (-3) \cdot (-6) + 4 \cdot 2 + 2 \cdot 3 = 32$$

Step 2

$$\begin{bmatrix} \mathbf{-3} & \mathbf{4} & \mathbf{2} \\ 5 & 0 & 4 \end{bmatrix} \begin{bmatrix} -6 & \mathbf{4} \\ 2 & \mathbf{3} \\ 3 & \mathbf{-2} \end{bmatrix} \quad (-3) \cdot 4 + 4 \cdot 3 + 2 \cdot (-2) = -4$$

Step 3

$$\begin{bmatrix} -3 & 4 & 2 \\ \mathbf{5} & \mathbf{0} & \mathbf{4} \end{bmatrix} \begin{bmatrix} \mathbf{-6} & 4 \\ \mathbf{2} & 3 \\ \mathbf{3} & -2 \end{bmatrix} \quad 5 \cdot (-6) + 0 \cdot 2 + 4 \cdot 3 = -18$$

Step 4

$$\begin{bmatrix} -3 & 4 & 2 \\ \mathbf{5} & \mathbf{0} & \mathbf{4} \end{bmatrix} \begin{bmatrix} -6 & \mathbf{4} \\ 2 & \mathbf{3} \\ 3 & \mathbf{-2} \end{bmatrix} \quad 5 \cdot 4 + 0 \cdot 3 + 4 \cdot (-2) = 12$$

Step 5 The product is

$$CD = \begin{bmatrix} -3 & 4 & 2 \\ 5 & 0 & 4 \end{bmatrix} \begin{bmatrix} -6 & 4 \\ 2 & 3 \\ 3 & -2 \end{bmatrix} = \begin{bmatrix} 32 & -4 \\ -18 & 12 \end{bmatrix}.$$ ■ 3

EXAMPLE 3 Find BA given

$$A = \begin{bmatrix} 1 & -3 \\ 7 & 2 \end{bmatrix} \quad \text{and} \quad B = \begin{bmatrix} 1 & 0 & -1 \\ 3 & 1 & 4 \end{bmatrix}.$$

Since B is a 2×3 matrix and A is a 2×2 matrix, the product BA cannot be found. ■ 4

TECHNOLOGY TIP Graphing calculators can find matrix products. However, if you use a graphing calculator to try to find the product in Example 3, the calculator will display an error message. ✔

Matrix multiplication has some similarities with the multiplication of numbers.

3 Find the product CD given

$$C = \begin{bmatrix} 1 & 3 & 5 \\ 2 & -4 & -1 \end{bmatrix}$$

and

$$D = \begin{bmatrix} 2 & -1 \\ 4 & 3 \\ 1 & -2 \end{bmatrix}.$$

Answer:

$$CD = \begin{bmatrix} 19 & -2 \\ -13 & -12 \end{bmatrix}$$

4 Give the size of each of the following products that can be found.

(a) $\begin{bmatrix} 2 & 4 \\ 6 & 8 \end{bmatrix} \begin{bmatrix} 1 & 2 & 3 \\ 0 & -1 & 2 \end{bmatrix}$

(b) $\begin{bmatrix} 1 & 2 \\ 5 & 10 \\ 12 & 7 \end{bmatrix} \begin{bmatrix} 2 & 4 \\ 3 & 6 \\ 9 & 1 \end{bmatrix}$

(c) $\begin{bmatrix} 5 \\ 2 \\ 4 \end{bmatrix} [1 \quad 0 \quad 6]$

Answers:

(a) 2×3

(b) Not possible

(c) 3×3

For any matrices A, B, C, such that all the indicated sums and products exist, matrix multiplication is associative and distributive.

$$A(BC) = (AB)C \quad A(B + C) = AB + AC \quad (B + C)A = BA + CA$$

However, there are important differences between matrix multiplication and multiplication of numbers. (See Exercises 19–22 at the end of this section.) In particular, matrix multiplication is *not* commutative.

If A and B are matrices such that the products AB and BA exist,

AB may not equal BA.

The next example illustrates matrix multiplication used in an application.

EXAMPLE 4 A contractor builds three kinds of houses, models A, B, and C, with a choice of two styles, Spanish or contemporary. Matrix P shows the number of each kind of house planned for a new 100-home subdivision.

$$\begin{array}{l} \\ \text{Model A} \\ \text{Model B} \\ \text{Model C} \end{array} \begin{array}{c} \begin{array}{cc} \text{Spanish} & \text{Contemporary} \end{array} \\ \begin{bmatrix} 0 & 30 \\ 10 & 20 \\ 20 & 20 \end{bmatrix} \end{array} = P$$

The amounts for each of the exterior materials used depend primarily on the style of the house. These amounts are shown in matrix Q. (Concrete is in cubic yards, lumber in units of 1000 board feet, brick in 1000s, and shingles in units of 100 square feet.)

$$\begin{array}{l} \\ \text{Spanish} \\ \text{Contemporary} \end{array} \begin{array}{c} \begin{array}{cccc} \text{Concrete} & \text{Lumber} & \text{Brick} & \text{Shingles} \end{array} \\ \begin{bmatrix} 10 & 2 & 0 & 2 \\ 50 & 1 & 20 & 2 \end{bmatrix} \end{array} = Q$$

Matrix R gives the cost for each kind of material.

$$\begin{array}{l} \\ \text{Concrete} \\ \text{Lumber} \\ \text{Brick} \\ \text{Shingles} \end{array} \begin{array}{c} \text{Cost per Unit} \\ \begin{bmatrix} 20 \\ 180 \\ 60 \\ 25 \end{bmatrix} \end{array} = R$$

(a) What is the total cost for each model house?

First find PQ. The product PQ shows the amount of each material needed for each model house.

$$PQ = \begin{bmatrix} 0 & 30 \\ 10 & 20 \\ 20 & 20 \end{bmatrix} \begin{bmatrix} 10 & 2 & 0 & 2 \\ 50 & 1 & 20 & 2 \end{bmatrix}$$

$$PQ = \begin{bmatrix} 1500 & 30 & 600 & 60 \\ 1100 & 40 & 400 & 60 \\ 1200 & 60 & 400 & 80 \end{bmatrix} \begin{matrix} \text{Model A} \\ \text{Model B} \\ \text{Model C} \end{matrix}$$

(columns: Concrete, Lumber, Brick, Shingles)

Now multiply PQ and R, the cost matrix, to get the total cost for each model house.

$$\begin{bmatrix} 1500 & 30 & 600 & 60 \\ 1100 & 40 & 400 & 60 \\ 1200 & 60 & 400 & 80 \end{bmatrix} \begin{bmatrix} 20 \\ 180 \\ 60 \\ 25 \end{bmatrix} = \overset{\text{Cost}}{\begin{bmatrix} 72{,}900 \\ 54{,}700 \\ 60{,}800 \end{bmatrix}} \begin{matrix} \text{Model A} \\ \text{Model B} \\ \text{Model C} \end{matrix}$$

(b) How much of each of the four kinds of material must be ordered?

The totals of the columns of matrix PQ will give a matrix whose elements represent the total amounts of each material needed for the subdivision. Call this matrix T, and write it as a row matrix.

$$T = [3800 \quad 130 \quad 1400 \quad 200]$$

(c) What is the total cost for material?

Find the total cost of all the materials by taking the product of matrix T, the matrix showing the total amounts of each material, and matrix R, the cost matrix. (To multiply these and get a 1×1 matrix, representing total cost, we must multiply a 1×4 matrix by a 4×1 matrix. This is why T was written as a row matrix in (b) above.)

$$TR = [3800 \quad 130 \quad 1400 \quad 200] \begin{bmatrix} 20 \\ 180 \\ 60 \\ 25 \end{bmatrix} = [188{,}400]$$

(d) Suppose the contractor builds the same number of homes in five subdivisions. Calculate the total amount of each material for each model for all five subdivisions.

Multiply PQ by the scalar 5, as follows.

$$5\begin{bmatrix} 1500 & 30 & 600 & 60 \\ 1100 & 40 & 400 & 60 \\ 1200 & 60 & 400 & 80 \end{bmatrix} = \begin{bmatrix} 7500 & 150 & 3000 & 300 \\ 5500 & 200 & 2000 & 300 \\ 6000 & 300 & 2000 & 400 \end{bmatrix}$$ ■

We can introduce a notation to help keep track of the quantities a matrix represents. For example, we can say that matrix P, from Example 4, represents models/styles, matrix Q represents styles/materials, and matrix R represents materials/cost. In each case, the meaning of the rows is written first and the columns second. When we found the product PQ in Example 4, the rows of the matrix represented models and the columns represented materials. Therefore, we can say the matrix product PQ represents models/materials. The common quantity, styles, in both P and Q was eliminated in the product PQ. Do you see that the product $(PQ)R$ represents models/cost?

In practical problems this notation helps decide in what order to multiply two matrices so that the results are meaningful. In Example 4(c) we could have found either product RT or product TR. However, since T represents subdivisions/materials and R represents materials/cost, the product TR gives subdivisions/cost. 5

5 Let matrix A be

$$\textit{Brand}\ \begin{matrix} X \\ Y \end{matrix} \overset{\substack{\textit{Vitamin} \\ C\ \ E\ \ K}}{\begin{bmatrix} 2 & 7 & 5 \\ 4 & 6 & 9 \end{bmatrix}}$$

and matrix B be

$$\textit{Vitamin}\ \begin{matrix} C \\ E \\ K \end{matrix} \overset{\substack{\textit{Cost} \\ X\ \ Y}}{\begin{bmatrix} 12 & 14 \\ 18 & 15 \\ 9 & 10 \end{bmatrix}}.$$

(a) What quantities do matrices A and B represent?

(b) What quantities does the product AB represent?

(c) What quantities does the product BA represent?

Answers:

(a) A = brand/vitamin, B = vitamin/cost

(b) AB = brand/cost

(c) Not meaningful, although the product BA can be found

6 Let $A = \begin{bmatrix} 3 & -2 \\ 4 & -1 \end{bmatrix}$

and $I = \begin{bmatrix} 1 & 0 \\ 0 & 1 \end{bmatrix}$.

Find IA and AI.

Answer:

$IA = \begin{bmatrix} 3 & -2 \\ 4 & -1 \end{bmatrix} = A$ and

$AI = \begin{bmatrix} 3 & -2 \\ 4 & -1 \end{bmatrix} = A$

IDENTITY AND INVERSE MATRICES Recall from Section 1.1 that the real number 1 is the identity element for multiplication of real numbers: for any real number a, $a \cdot 1 = 1 \cdot a = a$. In this section, an **identity matrix I** is defined that has properties similar to those of the number 1.

If I is to be the identity matrix, the products AI and IA must both equal A. The 2×2 identity matrix that satisfies these conditions is

$$I = \begin{bmatrix} \mathbf{1} & \mathbf{0} \\ \mathbf{0} & \mathbf{1} \end{bmatrix}. \quad \boxed{6}$$

To check that I is really the 2×2 identity matrix, let

$$A = \begin{bmatrix} a & b \\ c & d \end{bmatrix}.$$

Then AI and IA should both equal A.

$$AI = \begin{bmatrix} a & b \\ c & d \end{bmatrix}\begin{bmatrix} 1 & 0 \\ 0 & 1 \end{bmatrix} = \begin{bmatrix} a(1) + b(0) & a(0) + b(1) \\ c(1) + d(0) & c(0) + d(1) \end{bmatrix} = \begin{bmatrix} a & b \\ c & d \end{bmatrix} = A$$

$$IA = \begin{bmatrix} 1 & 0 \\ 0 & 1 \end{bmatrix}\begin{bmatrix} a & b \\ c & d \end{bmatrix} = \begin{bmatrix} 1(a) + 0(c) & 1(b) + 0(d) \\ 0(a) + 1(c) & 0(b) + 1(d) \end{bmatrix} = \begin{bmatrix} a & b \\ c & d \end{bmatrix} = A$$

This verifies that I has been defined correctly. (It can also be shown that I is the only 2×2 identity matrix.)

The identity matrices for 3×3 matrices and 4×4 matrices, respectively, are

$$I = \begin{bmatrix} 1 & 0 & 0 \\ 0 & 1 & 0 \\ 0 & 0 & 1 \end{bmatrix} \quad \text{and} \quad I = \begin{bmatrix} 1 & 0 & 0 & 0 \\ 0 & 1 & 0 & 0 \\ 0 & 0 & 1 & 0 \\ 0 & 0 & 0 & 1 \end{bmatrix}.$$

By generalizing, an identity matrix can be found for any n by n matrix: this identity matrix will have 1's on the main diagonal from upper left to lower right, with all other entries equal to 0.

TECHNOLOGY TIP On Casio 9850, HP-38, and most TI calculators you can display an $n \times n$ identity matrix by using IDENTITY n or IDENT n or IDENMAT(n). Look in the MATH or OPS submenu of the TI MATRIX menu, or the OPTN MAT menu of Casio 9850, or the MATRIX submenu of the HP-38 MATH menu. ✔

Recall that for every nonzero real number a, the equation $ax = 1$ has a solution, namely, $x = 1/a = a^{-1}$. Similarly, for a square matrix A it is natural to consider the matrix equation $AX = I$. This equation does not always have a solution, but when it does, we use special terminology. If there is a matrix A^{-1} satisfying

$$AA^{-1} = I,$$

(that is A^{-1} is a solution of $AX = I$), then A^{-1} is called the **inverse matrix** of A. In this case it can be proved that $A^{-1}A = I$ and that A^{-1} is unique (that is, a square matrix has no more than one inverse). When a matrix has an inverse, it can be found by using the row operations given in Section 7.2, as we shall see below.

CAUTION Only square matrices have inverses, but not every square matrix has one. A matrix that does not have an inverse is called a **singular matrix.** Note that the symbol A^{-1} (read A-inverse) does *not* mean $1/A$ or I/A; the symbol A^{-1} is just the notation for the inverse of matrix A. There is no such thing as matrix division. ◆

7 Given

$$A = \begin{bmatrix} 1 & 2 \\ 4 & 6 \end{bmatrix}$$

and

$$B = \begin{bmatrix} -3 & 1 \\ 2 & -\frac{1}{2} \end{bmatrix},$$

decide if they are inverses.

Answer:
Yes because $AB = BA = I$.

EXAMPLE 5 Given matrices A and B below, decide if they are inverses.

$$A = \begin{bmatrix} 2 & 3 \\ 1 & 8 \end{bmatrix} \qquad B = \begin{bmatrix} -1 & 3 \\ 1 & -2 \end{bmatrix}$$

The matrices are inverses if AB and BA both equal I.

$$AB = \begin{bmatrix} 2 & 3 \\ 1 & 8 \end{bmatrix}\begin{bmatrix} -1 & 3 \\ 1 & -2 \end{bmatrix} = \begin{bmatrix} 1 & 0 \\ 7 & -13 \end{bmatrix} \neq I$$

Since $AB \neq I$, the two matrices are not inverses of each other. ■ 7

To see how to find the multiplicative inverse of a matrix, let us look for the inverse of

$$A = \begin{bmatrix} 2 & 4 \\ 1 & -1 \end{bmatrix}.$$

Let the unknown inverse matrix be

$$A^{-1} = \begin{bmatrix} x & y \\ z & w \end{bmatrix}.$$

By the definition of matrix inverse, $AA^{-1} = I$, or

$$AA^{-1} = \begin{bmatrix} 2 & 4 \\ 1 & -1 \end{bmatrix}\begin{bmatrix} x & y \\ z & w \end{bmatrix} = \begin{bmatrix} 1 & 0 \\ 0 & 1 \end{bmatrix}.$$

Use matrix multiplication to get

$$\begin{bmatrix} 2x + 4z & 2y + 4w \\ x - z & y - w \end{bmatrix} = \begin{bmatrix} 1 & 0 \\ 0 & 1 \end{bmatrix}.$$

Setting corresponding elements equal gives the system of equations

$$2x + 4z = 1 \qquad (1)$$
$$2y + 4w = 0 \qquad (2)$$
$$x - z = 0 \qquad (3)$$
$$y - w = 1. \qquad (4)$$

Since equations (1) and (3) involve only x and z, while equations (2) and (4) involve only y and w, these four equations lead to two systems of equations,

$$\begin{aligned} 2x + 4z &= 1 \\ x - z &= 0 \end{aligned} \quad \text{and} \quad \begin{aligned} 2y + 4w &= 0 \\ y - w &= 1. \end{aligned}$$

Writing the two systems as augmented matrices gives

$$\left[\begin{array}{cc|c} 2 & 4 & 1 \\ 1 & -1 & 0 \end{array}\right] \quad \text{and} \quad \left[\begin{array}{cc|c} 2 & 4 & 0 \\ 1 & -1 & 1 \end{array}\right].$$

Each of these systems can be solved by the Gauss-Jordan method. However, since the elements to the left of the vertical bar are identical, the two systems can be combined into one matrix

$$\left[\begin{array}{cc|cc} 2 & 4 & 1 & 0 \\ 1 & -1 & 0 & 1 \end{array}\right] \tag{5}$$

and solved simultaneously as follows.

$$\left[\begin{array}{cc|cc} 1 & -1 & 0 & 1 \\ 2 & 4 & 1 & 0 \end{array}\right] \quad \text{Interchange } R_1, R_2$$

$$\left[\begin{array}{cc|cc} 1 & -1 & 0 & 1 \\ 0 & 6 & 1 & -2 \end{array}\right] \quad -2R_1 + R_2$$

$$\left[\begin{array}{cc|cc} 1 & -1 & 0 & 1 \\ 0 & 1 & \frac{1}{6} & -\frac{1}{3} \end{array}\right] \quad \frac{1}{6}R_2$$

$$\left[\begin{array}{cc|cc} 1 & 0 & \frac{1}{6} & \frac{2}{3} \\ 0 & 1 & \frac{1}{6} & -\frac{1}{3} \end{array}\right] \quad R_2 + R_1 \tag{6}$$

The left half of the augmented matrix (6) is the identity matrix, so the Gauss-Jordan process is finished and the solutions can be read from the right half of the augmented matrix. The numbers in the first column to the right of the vertical bar give the values of x and z. The second column to the right of the bar gives the values of y and w. That is,

$$\left[\begin{array}{cc|cc} 1 & 0 & x & y \\ 0 & 1 & z & w \end{array}\right] = \left[\begin{array}{cc|cc} 1 & 0 & \frac{1}{6} & \frac{2}{3} \\ 0 & 1 & \frac{1}{6} & -\frac{1}{3} \end{array}\right]$$

so that

$$A^{-1} = \begin{bmatrix} x & y \\ z & w \end{bmatrix} = \begin{bmatrix} \frac{1}{6} & \frac{2}{3} \\ \frac{1}{6} & -\frac{1}{3} \end{bmatrix}.$$

Thus the original augmented matrix (5) has A as its left half and the identity matrix as its right half, while the final augmented matrix (6), at the end of the Gauss-Jordan process, has the identity matrix as its left half and the inverse matrix A^{-1} as its right half.

$$[A \mid I] \rightarrow [I \mid A^{-1}]$$

Check by multiplying A and A^{-1}. The result should be I.

$$AA^{-1} = \begin{bmatrix} 2 & 4 \\ 1 & -1 \end{bmatrix}\begin{bmatrix} \frac{1}{6} & \frac{2}{3} \\ \frac{1}{6} & -\frac{1}{3} \end{bmatrix} = \begin{bmatrix} \frac{1}{3} + \frac{2}{3} & \frac{4}{3} - \frac{4}{3} \\ \frac{1}{6} - \frac{1}{6} & \frac{2}{3} + \frac{1}{3} \end{bmatrix} = \begin{bmatrix} 1 & 0 \\ 0 & 1 \end{bmatrix} = I$$ 8

8 (a) Find A^{-1} if

$$A = \begin{bmatrix} 2 & 2 \\ 4 & 1 \end{bmatrix}.$$

(b) Check your answer by finding AA^{-1}.

Answers:

(a) $\begin{bmatrix} -\frac{1}{6} & \frac{1}{3} \\ \frac{2}{3} & -\frac{1}{3} \end{bmatrix}$

(b) $\begin{bmatrix} 1 & 0 \\ 0 & 1 \end{bmatrix}$

This procedure for finding the inverse of a matrix can be generalized as follows.

To obtain an **inverse matrix** A^{-1} for any $n \times n$ matrix A for which A^{-1} exists, follow these steps.

1. Form the augmented matrix $[A \mid I]$ where I is the $n \times n$ identity matrix.
2. Perform row operations on $[A \mid I]$ to get a matrix of the form $[I \mid B]$.
3. Matrix B is A^{-1}.

EXAMPLE 6 Find A^{-1} if $A = \begin{bmatrix} 1 & 0 & 1 \\ 2 & -2 & -1 \\ 3 & 0 & 0 \end{bmatrix}$.

First write the augmented matrix $[A \mid I]$.

$$[A \mid I] = \left[\begin{array}{ccc|ccc} 1 & 0 & 1 & 1 & 0 & 0 \\ 2 & -2 & -1 & 0 & 1 & 0 \\ 3 & 0 & 0 & 0 & 0 & 1 \end{array}\right]$$

The augmented matrix already has 1 in the upper left-hand corner as needed, so begin by selecting the row operation which will result in a 0 for the first element in row two. Multiply row one by -2 and add the result to row two. This gives

$$\left[\begin{array}{ccc|ccc} 1 & 0 & 1 & 1 & 0 & 0 \\ 0 & -2 & -3 & -2 & 1 & 0 \\ 3 & 0 & 0 & 0 & 0 & 1 \end{array}\right]. \quad -2R_1 + R_2$$

Get 0 for the first element in row three by multiplying row one by -3 and adding to row three as directed in Side Problem 9. 9

9 **(a)** Complete this step.

(b) Write this row transformation as ______.

Answers:

(a)

$$\left[\begin{array}{ccc|ccc} 1 & 0 & 1 & 1 & 0 & 0 \\ 0 & -2 & -3 & -2 & 1 & 0 \\ 0 & 0 & -3 & -3 & 0 & 1 \end{array}\right]$$

(b) $-3R_1 + R_3$

Get 1 for the second element in row two by multiplying row two of the matrix found in Problem 9 at the side by $-1/2$, obtaining the new matrix

$$\left[\begin{array}{ccc|ccc} 1 & 0 & 1 & 1 & 0 & 0 \\ 0 & 1 & \frac{3}{2} & 1 & -\frac{1}{2} & 0 \\ 0 & 0 & -3 & -3 & 0 & 1 \end{array}\right]. \quad -\frac{1}{2}R_2$$

Get 1 for the third element in row three by multiplying row three by $-1/3$, with the result

$$\left[\begin{array}{ccc|ccc} 1 & 0 & 1 & 1 & 0 & 0 \\ 0 & 1 & \frac{3}{2} & 1 & -\frac{1}{2} & 0 \\ 0 & 0 & 1 & 1 & 0 & -\frac{1}{3} \end{array}\right]. \quad -\frac{1}{3}R_3$$

Now do Side Problem 10 to get 0s for the third elements in rows one and two. 10

10 **(a)** Complete these steps.

(b) Write these row transformations as ______.

Answers:

(a)

$$\left[\begin{array}{ccc|ccc} 1 & 0 & 0 & 0 & 0 & \frac{1}{3} \\ 0 & 1 & 0 & -\frac{1}{2} & -\frac{1}{2} & \frac{1}{2} \\ 0 & 0 & 1 & 1 & 0 & -\frac{1}{3} \end{array}\right]$$

(b) $-1R_3 + R_1$; $-\frac{3}{2}R_3 + R_2$

The answer for Problem 10(a) at the side gives the desired inverse:

$$A^{-1} = \begin{bmatrix} 0 & 0 & \frac{1}{3} \\ -\frac{1}{2} & -\frac{1}{2} & \frac{1}{2} \\ 1 & 0 & -\frac{1}{3} \end{bmatrix}.$$

Verify that AA^{-1} is I. ■

TECHNOLOGY TIPS **1.** With 3×3 or larger matrices, a graphing calculator is a much easier way to find an inverse. For a matrix A, A^{-1} is found by defining A and using the x^{-1} key. The calculator-generated inverse matrix for Example 6 is shown in Figure 7.4. The inverse is given with decimal approximations for 1/3 and 1/2. The three dots at the end of each row indicate that more of the matrix can be seen by moving the cursor to the right.

```
[A]-1
[[0    0    .3333...
 [-.5  -.5  .5   ...
 [1    0    -.333...
```

FIGURE 7.4

2. On TI calculators, you can use FRAC (in the MATH menu) to display the matrix A^{-1} shown in Figure 7.4 in the more conventional fractional form shown in Figure 7.5. On HP calculators you can do the same thing by changing the "number format" (in the MODES menu) to "fraction."

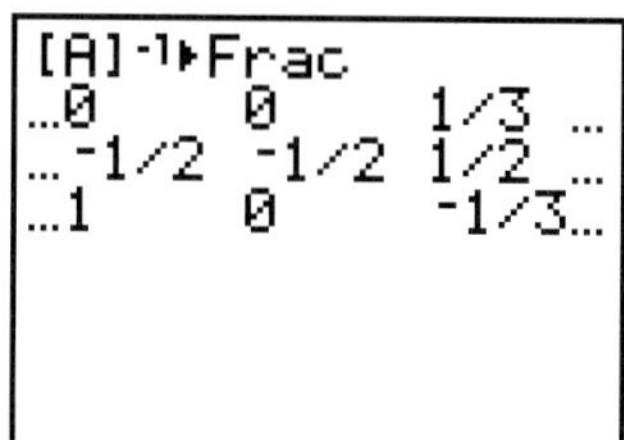

FIGURE 7.5

3. If you attempt to find the inverse of a singular matrix (one without an inverse) with a calculator, it will produce an error message. Sometimes, however, because of round-off error, the calculator will display a matrix that it erroneously says is A^{-1}. To verify, you should multiply A by A^{-1} to see if the product is the identity matrix. If it is not, then A does not have an inverse. ✔

7.4 EXERCISES

In Exercises 1–6, the sizes of two matrices A and B are given. Find the sizes of the product AB and the product BA whenever these products exist. (See Example 1.)

1. A is 2×2 and B is 2×2.
2. A is 3×3 and B is 3×3.
3. A is 3×5 and B is 5×2.
4. A is 4×3 and B is 3×6.
5. A is 4×2 and B is 3×4.
6. A is 7×3 and B is 2×7.
7. To find the product matrix AB, the number of ______ of A must be the same as the number of ______ of B.
8. The product matrix AB has the same number of ______ as A and the same number of ______ as B.

Find each of the following matrix products. (See Examples 2–4.)

9. $\begin{bmatrix} 1 & 2 \\ 3 & 4 \end{bmatrix}\begin{bmatrix} -1 \\ 7 \end{bmatrix}$

10. $\begin{bmatrix} -1 & 5 \\ 7 & 0 \end{bmatrix}\begin{bmatrix} 6 \\ 2 \end{bmatrix}$

11. $\begin{bmatrix} 2 & 2 & -1 \\ 3 & 0 & 1 \end{bmatrix}\begin{bmatrix} 0 & 2 \\ -1 & 4 \\ 0 & 2 \end{bmatrix}$

12. $\begin{bmatrix} -9 & 2 & 1 \\ 3 & 0 & 0 \end{bmatrix}\begin{bmatrix} 2 \\ -1 \\ 4 \end{bmatrix}$

13. $\begin{bmatrix} -4 & 1 \\ 2 & -3 \end{bmatrix}\begin{bmatrix} 1 & 0 \\ 0 & 1 \end{bmatrix}$

14. $\begin{bmatrix} 1 & 0 \\ 0 & 1 \end{bmatrix}\begin{bmatrix} 3 & -2 \\ 1 & -5 \end{bmatrix}$

15. $\begin{bmatrix} 1 & 0 & 0 \\ 0 & 1 & 0 \\ 0 & 0 & 1 \end{bmatrix}\begin{bmatrix} 3 & -5 & 7 \\ -2 & 1 & 6 \\ 0 & -3 & 4 \end{bmatrix}$

16. $\begin{bmatrix} -8 & 9 \\ 3 & -4 \\ -1 & 6 \end{bmatrix}\begin{bmatrix} 1 & 0 & 0 \\ 0 & 1 & 0 \end{bmatrix}$

17. $\begin{bmatrix} 1 & 2 & 3 \\ 4 & 5 & 6 \\ 7 & 8 & 9 \end{bmatrix}\begin{bmatrix} -1 & 5 \\ 7 & 0 \\ 1 & 2 \end{bmatrix}$

18. $\begin{bmatrix} -2 & 0 & 3 \\ 5 & -3 & -1 \end{bmatrix}\begin{bmatrix} 2 & 0 & -1 & 3 \\ 0 & 1 & 0 & -1 \\ 4 & 2 & 5 & -4 \end{bmatrix}$

In Exercises 19–21, use the matrices

$$A = \begin{bmatrix} -3 & -9 \\ 2 & 6 \end{bmatrix} \quad \text{and} \quad B = \begin{bmatrix} 4 & 6 \\ 2 & 3 \end{bmatrix}.$$

19. Show that $AB \neq BA$. Hence, matrix multiplication is not commutative.

20. Show that $(A + B)^2 \neq A^2 + 2AB + B^2$.

21. Show that $(A + B)(A - B) \neq A^2 - B^2$.

22. Show that $D^2 = D$, where

$$D = \begin{bmatrix} 1 & 0 & 0 \\ \frac{1}{2} & 0 & \frac{1}{2} \\ 0 & 0 & 1 \end{bmatrix}.$$

Given matrices

$$P = \begin{bmatrix} m & n \\ p & q \end{bmatrix}, \quad X = \begin{bmatrix} x & y \\ z & w \end{bmatrix}, \quad T = \begin{bmatrix} r & s \\ t & u \end{bmatrix},$$

verify that the statements in Exercises 23–26 are true.

23. $(PX)T = P(XT)$ (Associative property)

24. $P(X + T) = PX + PT$ (Distributive property)

25. $k(X + T) = kX + kT$ for any real number k

26. $(k + h)P = kP + hP$ for any real numbers k and h

Determine whether the given matrices are inverses of each other by computing their product. (See Example 5.)

27. $\begin{bmatrix} 5 & 2 \\ 3 & -1 \end{bmatrix}$ and $\begin{bmatrix} -1 & 2 \\ 3 & -4 \end{bmatrix}$

28. $\begin{bmatrix} 0 & 1 \\ 1 & 0 \end{bmatrix}$ and $\begin{bmatrix} 3 & 5 \\ 7 & 9 \end{bmatrix}$

29. $\begin{bmatrix} 3 & -1 \\ -4 & 2 \end{bmatrix}$ and $\begin{bmatrix} 1 & \frac{1}{2} \\ 2 & \frac{3}{2} \end{bmatrix}$

30. $\begin{bmatrix} 1 & 1 \\ .1 & .2 \end{bmatrix}$ and $\begin{bmatrix} 2 & -10 \\ -1 & 10 \end{bmatrix}$

31. $\begin{bmatrix} 1 & 1 & 1 \\ 2 & 3 & 0 \\ 1 & 2 & 1 \end{bmatrix}$ and $\begin{bmatrix} 1.5 & .5 & -1.5 \\ -1 & 0 & 1 \\ .5 & -2 & 2 \end{bmatrix}$

32. $\begin{bmatrix} 2 & 5 & 4 \\ 1 & 4 & 3 \\ 1 & 3 & 2 \end{bmatrix}$ and $\begin{bmatrix} 1 & 2 & 1 \\ -5 & 8 & 2 \\ 7 & -11 & -3 \end{bmatrix}$

Find the inverse, if it exists, for each of the following matrices. (See Example 6.)

33. $\begin{bmatrix} 2 & 3 \\ 1 & 2 \end{bmatrix}$

34. $\begin{bmatrix} -1 & 2 \\ 1 & -1 \end{bmatrix}$

35. $\begin{bmatrix} 2 & 4 \\ 3 & 6 \end{bmatrix}$

36. $\begin{bmatrix} -3 & -5 \\ 6 & 10 \end{bmatrix}$

37. $\begin{bmatrix} 2 & 6 \\ 1 & 4 \end{bmatrix}$

38. $\begin{bmatrix} 1 & 2 \\ 3 & 4 \end{bmatrix}$

39. $\begin{bmatrix} 1 & -1 & 1 \\ 0 & 2 & -1 \\ 2 & 3 & 0 \end{bmatrix}$

40. $\begin{bmatrix} 1 & 2 & 3 \\ 1 & 1 & 2 \\ 0 & 1 & 2 \end{bmatrix}$

41. $\begin{bmatrix} 1 & 4 & 3 \\ 1 & -3 & -2 \\ 2 & 5 & 4 \end{bmatrix}$

42. $\begin{bmatrix} 1 & 2 & 0 \\ 3 & -1 & 2 \\ -2 & 3 & -2 \end{bmatrix}$

43. $\begin{bmatrix} 1 & -3 & 4 \\ 2 & -5 & 7 \\ 0 & -1 & 1 \end{bmatrix}$

44. $\begin{bmatrix} 5 & 0 & 2 \\ 2 & 2 & 1 \\ -3 & 1 & -1 \end{bmatrix}$

Use a graphing calculator to find the inverse of each matrix.

45. $\begin{bmatrix} 2 & 4 & 6 \\ -1 & -4 & -3 \\ 0 & 1 & -1 \end{bmatrix}$

46. $\begin{bmatrix} 2 & 2 & -4 \\ 2 & 6 & 0 \\ -3 & -3 & 5 \end{bmatrix}$

47. $\begin{bmatrix} 1 & -2 & 3 & 0 \\ 0 & 1 & -1 & 1 \\ -2 & 2 & -2 & 4 \\ 0 & 2 & -3 & 1 \end{bmatrix}$

48. $\begin{bmatrix} 1 & 1 & 0 & 2 \\ 2 & -1 & 1 & -1 \\ 3 & 3 & 2 & -2 \\ 1 & 2 & 1 & 0 \end{bmatrix}$

49. **Management** Burger Barn's three locations sell hamburgers, fries, and soft drinks. Barn I sells 900 burgers, 600 orders of fries, and 750 soft drinks each day. Barn II sells 1500 burgers a day and Barn III sells 1150. Soft drink sales number 900 a day at Barn II and 825 a day at Barn III. Barn II sells 950 and Barn III sells 800 orders of fries per day.
   (a) Write a 3×3 matrix S that displays daily sales figures for all locations.
   (b) Burgers cost \$1.50 each, fries \$.90 an order, and soft drinks \$.60 each. Write a 1×3 matrix P that displays the prices.
   (c) What matrix product displays the daily revenue at each of the three locations?
   (d) What is the total daily revenue from all locations?

50. **Management** The four departments of Stagg Enterprises need to order the following amounts of the same products.

	Paper	*Tape*	*Printer Ribbon*	*Memo Pads*	*Pens*
Department 1	10	4	3	5	6
Department 2	7	2	2	3	8
Department 3	4	5	1	0	10
Department 4	0	3	4	5	5

The unit price (in dollars) of each product is given below for two suppliers.

	Supplier A	*Supplier B*
Paper	2	3
Tape	1	1
Printer Ribbon	4	3
Memo Pads	3	3
Pens	1	2

(a) Use matrix multiplication to get a matrix showing the comparative costs for each department for the products from the two suppliers.

(b) Find the total cost to buy products from each supplier. From which supplier should the company make the purchase?

51. Management The Perulli Candy Company makes three types of chocolate candy: Cheery Cherry, Mucho Mocha, and Almond Delight. The company produces its products in San Diego, Mexico City, and Managua using two main ingredients: chocolate and sugar.

(a) Each kilogram of Cheery Cherry requires .5 kg of sugar and .2 kg of chocolate; each kilogram of Mucho Mocha requires .4 kg of sugar and .3 kg of chocolate; and each kilogram of Almond Delight requires .3 kg of sugar and .3 kg of chocolate. Put this information into a 2×3 matrix, labeling the rows and columns.

(b) The cost of 1 kg of sugar is \$3 in San Diego, \$2 in Mexico City, and \$1 in Managua. The cost of 1 kg of chocolate is \$3 in San Diego, \$3 in Mexico City, and \$4 in Managua. Put this information into a matrix in such a way that when you multiply it with your matrix from part (a), you get a matrix representing the ingredient cost of producing each type of candy in each city.

(c) Multiply the matrices in parts (a) and (b), labeling the product matrix.

(d) From part (c) what is the combined sugar-and-chocolate cost to produce 1 kg of Mucho Mocha in Managua?

(e) Perulli Candy needs to quickly produce a special shipment of 100 kg of Cheery Cherry, 200 kg of Mucho Mocha, and 500 kg of Almond Delight, and it decides to select one factory to fill the entire order. Use matrix multiplication to determine in which city the total sugar-and-chocolate cost to produce the order is the smallest.

52. Natural Science Label the matrices $\begin{bmatrix} 2 & 1 & 2 & 1 \\ 3 & 2 & 2 & 1 \\ 4 & 3 & 2 & 1 \end{bmatrix}$, $\begin{bmatrix} 5 & 0 & 7 \\ 0 & 10 & 1 \\ 0 & 15 & 2 \\ 10 & 12 & 8 \end{bmatrix}$, and $\begin{bmatrix} 8 \\ 4 \\ 5 \end{bmatrix}$ found in parts (a), (b), and (c) of Section 7.3 Exercise 30, respectively, X, Y, and Z.

(a) Find the product matrix XY. What do the entries of this matrix represent?

(b) Find the product matrix YZ. What do the entries represent?

(c) Find the products $(XY)Z$ and $X(YZ)$ and verify that they are equal. What do the entries represent?

53. Social Sciences The average birth and death rates per million for several regions and the world population (in millions) by region are given below.*

	Births	*Deaths*
Asia	.027	.009
Latin America	.030	.007
North America	.015	.009
Europe	.013	.011
Soviet Union	.019	.011

	Asia	*Latin America*	*North America*	*Europe*	*USSR*
1960	1596	218	199	425	214
1970	1996	286	226	460	243
1980	2440	365	252	484	266
1990	2906	455	277	499	291

(a) Write the information in each table as a matrix.

(b) Use the matrices from part (a) to find the total number (in millions) of births and deaths in each year.

(c) Using the results of part (b), compare the number of births in 1960 and in 1990. Also compare the birth rates from part (a). Which gives better information?

(d) Using the results of part (b), compare the number of deaths in 1980 and in 1990. Discuss how this comparison differs from comparing death rates from part (a).

54. Explain why the system of equations

$$\begin{aligned} x - 3y &= 4 \\ 2x + y &= 1 \end{aligned}$$

is equivalent to the matrix equation $AX = B$, where $A = \begin{bmatrix} 1 & -3 \\ 2 & 1 \end{bmatrix}$, $X = \begin{bmatrix} x \\ y \end{bmatrix}$, and $B = \begin{bmatrix} 4 \\ 1 \end{bmatrix}$. (*Hint:* What is the product AX?)

Solve the matrix equation $AX = B$. (See Exercise 54.)

55. $A = \begin{bmatrix} 1 & 2 \\ 5 & -4 \end{bmatrix}$, $X = \begin{bmatrix} x \\ y \end{bmatrix}$, $B = \begin{bmatrix} 3 \\ -6 \end{bmatrix}$.

56. $A = \begin{bmatrix} 1 & 2 & 3 \\ 2 & 6 & 1 \\ 3 & 3 & 10 \end{bmatrix}$, $X = \begin{bmatrix} x \\ y \\ z \end{bmatrix}$, $B = \begin{bmatrix} -2 \\ 2 \\ -2 \end{bmatrix}$.

*"Vital Events and Rates by Region and Development Category, 1987" and "World Population by Region and Development Category, 1950–2025" from U.S. Bureau of the Census, *World Population Profile: 1987*.

7.5 APPLICATIONS OF MATRICES

1 Write the matrix of coefficients, the matrix of variables, and the matrix of constants for the system

$$2x + 6y = -14$$
$$-x - 2y = 3.$$

Answers:

$$A = \begin{bmatrix} 2 & 6 \\ -1 & -2 \end{bmatrix},$$

$$X = \begin{bmatrix} x \\ y \end{bmatrix},$$

$$B = \begin{bmatrix} -14 \\ 3 \end{bmatrix}.$$

This section gives a variety of applications of matrices.

SOLVING SYSTEMS WITH MATRICES Consider this system of linear equations.

$$2x - 3y = 4$$
$$x + 5y = 2$$

Let $A = \begin{bmatrix} 2 & -3 \\ 1 & 5 \end{bmatrix}, \quad X = \begin{bmatrix} x \\ y \end{bmatrix}, \quad B = \begin{bmatrix} 4 \\ 2 \end{bmatrix}.$

Since $AX = \begin{bmatrix} 2 & -3 \\ 1 & 5 \end{bmatrix}\begin{bmatrix} x \\ y \end{bmatrix} = \begin{bmatrix} 2x - 3y \\ x + 5y \end{bmatrix}$ and $B = \begin{bmatrix} 4 \\ 2 \end{bmatrix},$

the original system is equivalent to the single matrix equation $AX = B$. Similarly, any system of linear equations can be written as a matrix equation $AX = B$. The matrix A is called the **coefficient matrix.** 1

A matrix equation $AX = B$ can be solved if A^{-1} exists. Assuming A^{-1} exists and using the facts that $A^{-1}A = I$ and $IX = X$ along with the associative property of multiplication of matrices gives

$$AX = B$$
$$A^{-1}(AX) = A^{-1}B \qquad \text{Multiply both sides by } A^{-1}.$$
$$(A^{-1}A)X = A^{-1}B \qquad \text{Associative property}$$
$$IX = A^{-1}B \qquad \text{Inverse property}$$
$$X = A^{-1}B. \qquad \text{Identity property}$$

When multiplying by matrices on both sides of a matrix equation, be careful to multiply in the same order on both sides of the equation, since multiplication of matrices is not commutative (unlike multiplication of real numbers). This discussion is summarized below.

> A system of equations $AX = B$, where A is the matrix of coefficients, X is the matrix of variables, and B is the matrix of constants, is solved by first finding A^{-1}. Then, if A^{-1} exists, $X = A^{-1}B$.

This method is very efficient when a graphing calculator with matrix capability is available. The elimination method (the matrix version) or the Gauss-Jordan method is the best choice when solving a system by hand.

EXAMPLE 1 Use the inverse of the coefficient matrix to solve the system

$$-x - 2y + 2z = 9$$
$$2x + y - z = -3$$
$$3x - 2y + z = -6.$$

We use the fact that $X = A^{-1}B$, with

$$A = \begin{bmatrix} -1 & -2 & 2 \\ 2 & 1 & -1 \\ 3 & -2 & 1 \end{bmatrix} \quad \text{and} \quad B = \begin{bmatrix} 9 \\ -3 \\ -6 \end{bmatrix}.$$

Using either the method explained in Section 7.4 or a graphing calculator,

$$A^{-1} = \begin{bmatrix} \frac{1}{3} & \frac{2}{3} & 0 \\ \frac{5}{3} & \frac{7}{3} & -1 \\ \frac{7}{3} & \frac{8}{3} & -1 \end{bmatrix}$$

and

$$X = A^{-1}B = \begin{bmatrix} \frac{1}{3} & \frac{2}{3} & 0 \\ \frac{5}{3} & \frac{7}{3} & -1 \\ \frac{7}{3} & \frac{8}{3} & -1 \end{bmatrix} \begin{bmatrix} 9 \\ -3 \\ -6 \end{bmatrix} = \begin{bmatrix} 1 \\ 14 \\ 19 \end{bmatrix}.$$

Thus, the solution is (1, 14, 19). ■ 2

2 Use the inverse matrix to solve the system in Example 1, if the constants for the three equations are 12, 0, and 8, respectively.

Answer:
(4, 12, 20)

EXAMPLE 2 Use the inverse of the coefficient matrix to solve the system

$$\begin{aligned} x + 1.5y &= 8 \\ 2x + \quad 3y &= 10. \end{aligned}$$

The coefficient matrix is $A = \begin{bmatrix} 1 & 1.5 \\ 2 & 3 \end{bmatrix}$. A calculator will indicate that A^{-1} does not exist. If we try to carry out the row operations, we see why.

$$\left[\begin{array}{cc|cc} 1 & 1.5 & 1 & 0 \\ 2 & 3 & 0 & 1 \end{array}\right]$$

$$\left[\begin{array}{cc|cc} 1 & 1.5 & 1 & 0 \\ 0 & 0 & -2 & 1 \end{array}\right]$$

The next step cannot be performed because of the zero in the second row second column. Verify that the original system has no solution. ■ 3

3 Solve the system in Example 2 if the constants are, respectively, 3 and 6.

Answer:
$(3 - 1.5y, y)$ for all real numbers y

INPUT-OUTPUT ANALYSIS An interesting application of matrix theory to economics was developed by Nobel Prize winner Wassily Leontief. His application of matrices to the interdependencies in an economy is called **input-output** analysis. In practice, input-output analysis is very complicated with many variables. We shall discuss only simple examples with a few variables.

Input-output models are concerned with the production and flow of goods (and perhaps services). In an economy with n basic commodities (or sectors), the production of each commodity uses some (perhaps all) of the commodities in the economy as inputs. The amounts of each commodity used in the production of 1 unit of each commodity can be written as an $n \times n$ matrix A, called the **technological** or **input-output matrix** of the economy.

EXAMPLE 3 Suppose a simplified economy involves just three commodity categories: agriculture, manufacturing, and transportation, all in appropriate units.

Production of 1 unit of agriculture requires 1/2 unit of manufacturing and 1/4 unit of transportation. Production of 1 unit of manufacturing requires 1/4 unit of agriculture and 1/4 unit of transportation; while production of 1 unit of transportation requires 1/3 unit of agriculture and 1/4 unit of manufacturing. Write the input-output matrix of this economy.

The matrix is shown below.

		Output		
		Agriculture	**Manufacturing**	**Transportation**
Input	**Agriculture**	0	$\frac{1}{4}$	$\frac{1}{3}$
	Manufacturing	$\frac{1}{2}$	0	$\frac{1}{4}$
	Transportation	$\frac{1}{4}$	$\frac{1}{4}$	0

$$\begin{bmatrix} 0 & \frac{1}{4} & \frac{1}{3} \\ \frac{1}{2} & 0 & \frac{1}{4} \\ \frac{1}{4} & \frac{1}{4} & 0 \end{bmatrix} = A$$

The first column of the input-output matrix represents the amount of each of the three commodities consumed in the production of 1 unit of agriculture. The second column gives the corresponding amounts required to produce 1 unit of manufacturing, and the last column gives the amounts needed to produce 1 unit of transportation. (Although it is unrealistic, perhaps, that production of 1 unit of a commodity requires none of that commodity, the simpler matrix involved is useful for our purposes.) ■ [4]

[4] Write a 2 × 2 technological matrix in which 1 unit of electricity requires 1/2 unit of water and 1/3 unit of electricity, while 1 unit of water requires no water but 1/4 unit of electricity.

Answer:

	Elec.	Water
Elec.	$\frac{1}{3}$	$\frac{1}{4}$
Water	$\frac{1}{2}$	0

Another matrix used with the input-output matrix is a matrix giving the amount of each commodity produced, called the **production matrix,** or the **vector of gross output.** In an economy producing n commodities, the production matrix can be represented by a column matrix x with entries $x_1, x_2, x_3, \ldots, x_n$.

EXAMPLE 4 In Example 3, suppose the production matrix is

$$X = \begin{bmatrix} 60 \\ 52 \\ 48 \end{bmatrix}.$$

Then 60 units of agriculture, 52 units of manufacturing, and 48 units of transportation are produced. As 1/4 unit of agriculture is used for each unit of manufacturing produced, $1/4 \times 52 = 13$ units of agriculture must be used up in the "production" of manufacturing. Similarly, $1/3 \times 48 = 16$ units of agriculture will be used up in the "production" of transportation. Thus $13 + 16 = 29$ units of agriculture are used for production in the economy. Look again at the matrices A and X. Since X gives the number of units of each commodity produced and A gives the amount (in units) of each commodity used to produce 1 unit of the various commodities, the matrix product AX gives the amount of each commodity used up in production.

$$AX = \begin{bmatrix} 0 & \frac{1}{4} & \frac{1}{3} \\ \frac{1}{2} & 0 & \frac{1}{4} \\ \frac{1}{4} & \frac{1}{4} & 0 \end{bmatrix} \begin{bmatrix} 60 \\ 52 \\ 48 \end{bmatrix} = \begin{bmatrix} 29 \\ 42 \\ 28 \end{bmatrix}$$

This product shows that 29 units of agriculture, 42 units of manufacturing, and 28 units of transportation are used to produce 60 units of agriculture, 52 units of manufacturing, and 48 units of transportation. ■

5 **(a)** Write a 2×1 matrix X to represent gross production of 9000 units of electricity and 12,000 units of water.

(b) Find AX using A from the last side problem.

(c) Find D using $D = X - AX$.

Answers:

(a) $\begin{bmatrix} 9000 \\ 12{,}000 \end{bmatrix}$

(b) $\begin{bmatrix} 6000 \\ 4500 \end{bmatrix}$

(c) $\begin{bmatrix} 3000 \\ 7500 \end{bmatrix}$

We have seen that the matrix product AX represents the amount of each commodity used in the production process. The remainder (if any) must be enough to satisfy the demand for the various commodities from outside the production system. In an n-commodity economy, this demand can be represented by a **demand matrix** D with entries $d_1, d_2, \ldots, d_n$. The difference between the production matrix, X, and the amount, AX, used in the production process must equal the demand, D, or

$$D = X - AX.$$

In Example 4,

$$D = \begin{bmatrix} 60 \\ 52 \\ 48 \end{bmatrix} - \begin{bmatrix} 29 \\ 42 \\ 28 \end{bmatrix} = \begin{bmatrix} 31 \\ 10 \\ 20 \end{bmatrix}.$$

This result shows that production of 60 units of agriculture, 52 units of manufacturing, and 48 units of transportation would satisfy a demand of 31, 10, and 20 units of each, respectively. 5

In practice, A and D usually are known and X must be found. That is, we need to decide what amounts of production are necessary to satisfy the required demands. Matrix algebra can be used to solve the equation $D = X - AX$ for X.

$$\begin{aligned} D &= X - AX & \\ D &= IX - AX & \text{Identity property} \\ D &= (I - A)X & \text{Distributive property} \end{aligned}$$

If the matrix $I - A$ has an inverse, then

$$\boldsymbol{X = (I - A)^{-1}D.}$$

EXAMPLE 5 Suppose, in the 3-commodity economy of Examples 3 and 4, there is a demand for 516 units of agriculture, 258 units of manufacturing, and 129 units of transportation. What should production of each commodity be?

The demand matrix is

$$D = \begin{bmatrix} 516 \\ 258 \\ 129 \end{bmatrix}.$$

Find the production matrix by first calculating $I - A$.

$$I - A = \begin{bmatrix} 1 & 0 & 0 \\ 0 & 1 & 0 \\ 0 & 0 & 1 \end{bmatrix} - \begin{bmatrix} 0 & \frac{1}{4} & \frac{1}{3} \\ \frac{1}{2} & 0 & \frac{1}{4} \\ \frac{1}{4} & \frac{1}{4} & 0 \end{bmatrix} = \begin{bmatrix} 1 & -\frac{1}{4} & -\frac{1}{3} \\ -\frac{1}{2} & 1 & -\frac{1}{4} \\ -\frac{1}{4} & -\frac{1}{4} & 1 \end{bmatrix}.$$

Using a calculator with matrix capability or row operations, find the inverse of $I - A$.

$$(I - A)^{-1} = \begin{bmatrix} 1.3953 & .4961 & .5891 \\ .8372 & 1.3643 & .6202 \\ .5581 & .4651 & 1.3023 \end{bmatrix}$$

(The entries are rounded to four decimal places.)* Since $X = (I - A)^{-1}D$,

$$X = \begin{bmatrix} 1.3953 & .4961 & .5891 \\ .8372 & 1.3643 & .6202 \\ .5581 & .4651 & 1.3023 \end{bmatrix} \begin{bmatrix} 516 \\ 258 \\ 129 \end{bmatrix} = \begin{bmatrix} 924 \\ 864 \\ 576 \end{bmatrix},$$

(rounded to the nearest whole numbers).

From the last result, we see that production of 924 units of agriculture, 864 units of manufacturing, and 576 units of transportation is required to satisfy demands of 516, 258, and 129 units, respectively. ■

TECHNOLOGY TIP If you are using a graphing calculator to determine X, you can calculate $(I - A)^{-1}D$ in one step without finding the intermediate matrices $I - A$ and $(I - A)^{-1}$. ✔

6 A simple economy depends on just two products, beer and pretzels.

(a) Suppose 1/2 unit of beer and 1/2 unit of pretzels are needed to make 1 unit of beer, and 3/4 unit of beer is needed to make 1 unit of pretzels. Write the technological matrix A for the economy.

(b) Find $I - A$.

(c) Find $(I - A)^{-1}$.

(d) Find the gross production X that will be needed to get a net production of

$$D = \begin{bmatrix} 100 \\ 1000 \end{bmatrix}.$$

Answers:

(a) $\begin{bmatrix} \frac{1}{2} & \frac{3}{4} \\ \frac{1}{2} & 0 \end{bmatrix}$

(b) $\begin{bmatrix} \frac{1}{2} & -\frac{3}{4} \\ -\frac{1}{2} & 1 \end{bmatrix}$

(c) $\begin{bmatrix} 8 & 6 \\ 4 & 4 \end{bmatrix}$

(d) $\begin{bmatrix} 6800 \\ 4400 \end{bmatrix}$

EXAMPLE 6 An economy depends on two basic products, wheat and oil. To produce 1 metric ton of wheat requires .25 metric tons of wheat and .33 metric tons of oil. Production of 1 metric ton of oil consumes .08 metric tons of wheat and .11 metric tons of oil. Find the production that will satisfy a demand of 500 metric tons of wheat and 1000 metric tons of oil.

The input-output matrix, A, and the matrix $I - A$, are

$$A = \begin{bmatrix} .25 & .08 \\ .33 & .11 \end{bmatrix} \quad \text{and} \quad I - A = \begin{bmatrix} .75 & -.08 \\ -.33 & .89 \end{bmatrix}.$$

Next, calculate $(I - A)^{-1}$.

$$(I - A)^{-1} = \begin{bmatrix} 1.3882 & .1248 \\ .5147 & 1.1699 \end{bmatrix} \quad \text{(rounded)}$$

To find the production matrix X, use the equation $X = (I - A)^{-1}D$, with

$$D = \begin{bmatrix} 500 \\ 1000 \end{bmatrix}.$$

The production matrix is

$$X = \begin{bmatrix} 1.3882 & .1248 \\ .5147 & 1.1699 \end{bmatrix} \begin{bmatrix} 500 \\ 1000 \end{bmatrix} = \begin{bmatrix} 819 \\ 1427 \end{bmatrix}.$$

The production numbers were rounded to the nearest whole number. Production of 819 metric tons of wheat and 1427 metric tons of oil is required to satisfy the indicated demand. ■ 6

CODE THEORY Governments need sophisticated methods of coding and decoding messages. One example of such an advanced code uses matrix theory. Such a code takes the letters in the words and divides them into groups. (Each space between words is treated as a letter; punctuation is disregarded.) Then, numbers are assigned to the letters of the alphabet. For our purposes, let the letter a correspond to 1, b to 2, and so on. Let the number 27 correspond to a space between words.

*Although we show the matrix $(I - A)^{-1}$ with entries rounded to four decimal places, we did not round off in calculating $(I - A)^{-1}D$. If the rounded figures are used, the numbers in the product may vary slightly in the last digit.

For example, the message

mathematics is for the birds

can be divided into groups of three letters each.

mat hem ati cs– is– for –th e–b ird s––

(We used – to represent a space between words.) We now write a column matrix for each group of three symbols using the corresponding numbers, as determined above, instead of letters. For example, the letters *mat* can be encoded as

$$\begin{bmatrix} 13 \\ 1 \\ 20 \end{bmatrix}.$$

7 Write the message "*when*" using 2×1 matrices.

Answer:

$$\begin{bmatrix} 23 \\ 8 \end{bmatrix}, \begin{bmatrix} 5 \\ 14 \end{bmatrix}$$

The coded message then consists of the 3×1 column matrices:

$$\begin{bmatrix} 13 \\ 1 \\ 20 \end{bmatrix}, \begin{bmatrix} 8 \\ 5 \\ 13 \end{bmatrix}, \begin{bmatrix} 1 \\ 20 \\ 9 \end{bmatrix}, \begin{bmatrix} 3 \\ 19 \\ 27 \end{bmatrix}, \begin{bmatrix} 9 \\ 19 \\ 27 \end{bmatrix}, \begin{bmatrix} 6 \\ 15 \\ 18 \end{bmatrix}, \begin{bmatrix} 27 \\ 20 \\ 8 \end{bmatrix}, \begin{bmatrix} 5 \\ 27 \\ 2 \end{bmatrix}, \begin{bmatrix} 9 \\ 18 \\ 4 \end{bmatrix}, \begin{bmatrix} 19 \\ 27 \\ 27 \end{bmatrix}.$$ 7

We can further complicate the code by choosing a matrix that has an inverse (in this case a 3×3 matrix, call it M) and finding the products of this matrix and each of the above column matrices. The size of each group, the assignment of numbers to letters, and the choice of matrix M must all be predetermined.

Suppose we choose

$$M = \begin{bmatrix} 1 & 3 & 3 \\ 1 & 4 & 3 \\ 1 & 3 & 4 \end{bmatrix}.$$

8 Use the matrix given below to find the 2×1 matrices to be transmitted for the message you encoded in Problem 7 at the side.

$$\begin{bmatrix} 2 & 1 \\ 5 & 0 \end{bmatrix}$$

Answer:

$$\begin{bmatrix} 54 \\ 115 \end{bmatrix}, \begin{bmatrix} 24 \\ 25 \end{bmatrix}$$

If we find the products of M and the column matrices above, we have a new set of column matrices,

$$\begin{bmatrix} 1 & 3 & 3 \\ 1 & 4 & 3 \\ 1 & 3 & 4 \end{bmatrix}\begin{bmatrix} 13 \\ 1 \\ 20 \end{bmatrix} = \begin{bmatrix} 76 \\ 77 \\ 96 \end{bmatrix}, \text{ and so on.}$$

The entries of these matrices can then be transmitted to an agent as the message 76, 77, 96, and so on. 8

When the agent receives the message, it is divided into groups of three numbers with each group formed into a column matrix. After multiplying each column matrix by the matrix M^{-1}, the message can be read. For example,

$$M^{-1} \cdot \begin{bmatrix} 76 \\ 77 \\ 96 \end{bmatrix} = \begin{bmatrix} 13 \\ 1 \\ 20 \end{bmatrix}.$$

Although this type of code is relatively simple, it is actually difficult to break. Many complications are possible. For example, a long message might be placed in groups of 20, thus requiring a 20×20 matrix for coding and decoding. Finding the inverse of such a matrix would require an impractical amount of time if calculated by hand. For this reason some of the largest computers are used by government agencies involved in coding.

ROUTING The diagram in Figure 7.6 shows the roads connecting four cities. Another way of representing this information is shown in matrix A, where the entries represent the number of roads connecting two cities without passing through another city.* For example, from the diagram we see that there are two roads connecting city 1 to city 4 without passing through either city 2 or 3. This information is entered in row one, column four and again in row four, column one of matrix A.

$$A = \begin{bmatrix} 0 & 1 & 2 & 2 \\ 1 & 0 & 1 & 0 \\ 2 & 1 & 0 & 1 \\ 2 & 0 & 1 & 0 \end{bmatrix}$$

Note that there are zero roads connecting each city to itself. Also, there is one road connecting cities 3 and 2.

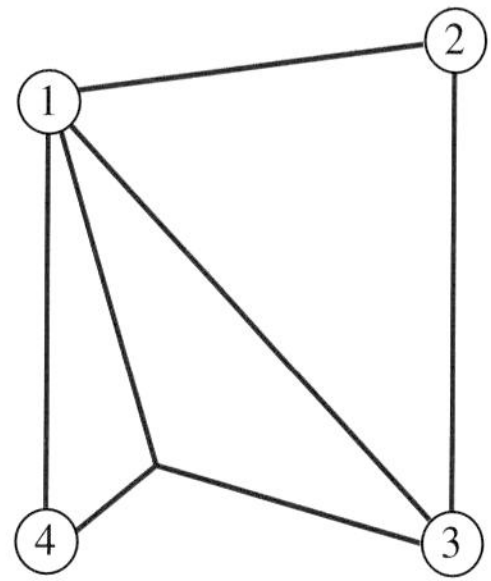

FIGURE 7.6

How many ways are there to go from city 1 to city 2, for example, by going through exactly one other city? Because we must go through one other city, we must go through either city 3 or city 4. On the diagram in Figure 7.6, we see that we can go from city 1 to city 2 through city 3 in two ways. We can go from city 1 to city 3 in two ways and then from city 3 to city 2 in one way, so there are $2 \cdot 1 = 2$ ways to get from city 1 to city 2 through city 3. It is not possible to go from city 1 to city 2 through city 4, because there is no direct route between cities 4 and 2.

The matrix A^2 gives the number of ways to travel between any two cities by passing through exactly one other city. Multiply matrix A by itself, to get A^2. Let the first row, second column entry of A^2 be b_{12}. (We use a_{ij} to denote the entry in the ith row and jth column of matrix A.) The entry b_{12} is found as follows.

$$\begin{aligned} b_{12} &= a_{11}a_{12} + a_{12}a_{22} + a_{13}a_{32} + a_{14}a_{42} \\ &= 0 \cdot 1 + 1 \cdot 0 + 2 \cdot 1 + 2 \cdot 0 \\ &= 2 \end{aligned}$$

The first product $0 \cdot 1$ in the calculations above represents the number of ways to go from city 1 to city 1, (that is, 0), and then from city 1 to city 2, (that is, 1). The 0 result indicates that such a trip does not involve a third city. The only nonzero product $(2 \cdot 1)$

*From *Matrices with Applications,* section 3.2, example 5, by Hugh G. Campbell, Copyright © 1968, pp. 50–51. Adapted by permission of Prentice-Hall, Englewood Cliffs, New Jersey.

represents the two routes from city 1 to city 3 and the one route from city 3 to city 2 which result in the $2 \cdot 1$ or 2 routes from city 1 to city 2 by going through city 3.

Similarly, A^3 gives the number of ways to travel between any two cities by passing through exactly two cities. Also, $A + A^2$ represents the total number of ways to travel between two cities with at most one intermediate city.

The diagram can be given many other interpretations. For example, the lines could represent lines of mutual influence between people or nations, or they could represent communication lines such as telephone lines.

7.5 EXERCISES

Solve the matrix equation AX = B for X. (See Example 1.)

1. $A = \begin{bmatrix} 1 & -1 \\ 5 & -6 \end{bmatrix}, B = \begin{bmatrix} 2 \\ 4 \end{bmatrix}$

2. $A = \begin{bmatrix} 3 & -2 \\ -1 & 1 \end{bmatrix}, B = \begin{bmatrix} -3 \\ 5 \end{bmatrix}$

3. $A = \begin{bmatrix} 3 & 1 \\ 4 & 2 \end{bmatrix}, B = \begin{bmatrix} 3 & 4 \\ 5 & 6 \end{bmatrix}$

4. $A = \begin{bmatrix} 7 & -3 \\ -2 & 1 \end{bmatrix}, B = \begin{bmatrix} 0 & 8 \\ 4 & 1 \end{bmatrix}$

5. $A = \begin{bmatrix} 1 & -2 & -3 \\ -1 & 4 & 6 \\ 1 & -1 & -2 \end{bmatrix}, B = \begin{bmatrix} 2 \\ 7 \\ 4 \end{bmatrix}$

6. $A = \begin{bmatrix} 3 & -1 & 0 \\ 0 & 1 & 2 \\ 6 & 0 & 5 \end{bmatrix}, B = \begin{bmatrix} -6 \\ 12 \\ 15 \end{bmatrix}$

Use the inverse of the coefficient matrix to solve each system of equations. (The inverses for Exercises 9–14 were found in Exercises 41 and 44–48 of Section 7.4.) (See Example 1.)

7. $\begin{aligned} x + 2y + 3z &= 5 \\ 2x + 3y + 2z &= 2 \\ -x - 2y - 4z &= -1 \end{aligned}$

8. $\begin{aligned} x + y - 3z &= 4 \\ 2x + 4y - 4z &= 8 \\ -x + y + 4z &= -3 \end{aligned}$

9. $\begin{aligned} x + 4y + 3z &= -12 \\ x - 3y - 2z &= 0 \\ 2x + 5y + 4z &= 7 \end{aligned}$

10. $\begin{aligned} 5x + 2z &= 3 \\ 2x + 2y + z &= 4 \\ -3x + y - z &= 5 \end{aligned}$

11. $\begin{aligned} 2x + 4y + 6z &= 4 \\ -x - 4y - 3z &= 8 \\ y - z &= -4 \end{aligned}$

12. $\begin{aligned} 2x + 2y - 4z &= 12 \\ 2x + 6y &= 16 \\ -3x - 3y + 5z &= -20 \end{aligned}$

13. $\begin{aligned} x - 2y + 3z &= 4 \\ y - z + w &= -8 \\ -2x + 2y - 2z + 4w &= 12 \\ 2y - 3z + w &= -4 \end{aligned}$

14. $\begin{aligned} x + y + 2w &= 3 \\ 2x - y + z - w &= 3 \\ 3x + 3y + 2z - 2w &= 5 \\ x + 2y + z &= 3 \end{aligned}$

Use matrix algebra to solve the following matrix equations for X. Then use the given matrices to find X and check your work.

15. $N = X - MX, N = \begin{bmatrix} 8 \\ -12 \end{bmatrix}, M = \begin{bmatrix} 0 & 1 \\ -2 & 1 \end{bmatrix}$

16. $A = BX + X, A = \begin{bmatrix} 4 & 6 \\ -2 & 2 \end{bmatrix}, B = \begin{bmatrix} -2 & -2 \\ 3 & 3 \end{bmatrix}$

Find the production matrix given the following input-output and demand matrices. (See Examples 3–6.)

17. $A = \begin{bmatrix} \frac{1}{2} & \frac{2}{5} \\ \frac{1}{4} & \frac{1}{5} \end{bmatrix}, D = \begin{bmatrix} 2 \\ 4 \end{bmatrix}$

18. $A = \begin{bmatrix} \frac{1}{5} & \frac{1}{25} \\ \frac{3}{5} & \frac{1}{20} \end{bmatrix}, D = \begin{bmatrix} 3 \\ 10 \end{bmatrix}$

19. $A = \begin{bmatrix} .1 & .03 \\ .07 & .6 \end{bmatrix}, D = \begin{bmatrix} 5 \\ 10 \end{bmatrix}$

20. $A = \begin{bmatrix} .01 & .03 \\ .05 & .05 \end{bmatrix}, D = \begin{bmatrix} 100 \\ 200 \end{bmatrix}$

21. $A = \begin{bmatrix} .4 & 0 & .3 \\ 0 & .8 & .1 \\ 0 & .2 & .4 \end{bmatrix}, D = \begin{bmatrix} 1 \\ 3 \\ 2 \end{bmatrix}$

22. $A = \begin{bmatrix} .1 & .5 & 0 \\ 0 & .3 & .4 \\ .1 & .2 & .1 \end{bmatrix}, D = \begin{bmatrix} 10 \\ 4 \\ 2 \end{bmatrix}$

Write a system of equations and use the inverse of the coefficient matrix to solve the system.

23. **Management** Felsted Furniture makes dining room furniture. A buffet requires 30 hours for construction and 10 hours for finishing. A chair requires 10 hours for construction and 10 hours for finishing. A table requires 10 hours for construction and 30 hours for finishing. The construction department has 350 hours of labor and the finishing department 150 hours of labor available each week. How many pieces of each type of furniture should be produced each week if the factory is to run at full capacity?

24. **Natural Science** **(a)** A hospital dietician is planning a special diet for a certain patient. The total amount per meal of food groups A, B, and C must equal 400 grams. The diet should include one-third as much of group A as of group B, and the sum of the amounts of group A and group C should equal twice the amount of group B. How many grams of each food group should be included?
    (b) Suppose we drop the requirement that the diet include one-third as much of group A as of group B. Describe the set of all possible solutions.
    (c) Suppose that, in addition to the conditions given in part (a), foods A and B cost 2 cents per gram and food C costs 3 cents per gram, and that a meal must cost $8. Is a solution possible?

25. **Natural Science** Three species of bacteria are fed three foods, I, II, and III. A bacterium of the first species consumes 1.3 units each of foods I and II and 2.3 units of food III each day. A bacterium of the second species consumes 1.1 units of food I, 2.4 units of food II, and 3.7 units of food III each day. A bacterium of the third species consumes 8.1 units of I, 2.9 units of II, and 5.1 units of III each day. If 16,000 units of I, 28,000 units of II, and 44,000 units of III are supplied each day, how many of each species can be maintained in this environment?

26. **Management** A company produces three combinations of mixed vegetables which sell in 1 kilogram packages. Italian style combines .3 kilogram of zucchini, .3 of broccoli, and .4 of carrots. French style combines .6 kilogram of broccoli and .4 of carrots. Oriental style combines .2 kilogram of zucchini, .5 of broccoli, and .3 of carrots. The company has a stock of 16,200 kilograms of zucchini, 41,400 kilograms of broccoli, and 29,400 kilograms of carrots. How many packages of each style should they prepare to use up their supplies?

Exercises 27 and 28 refer to Example 6.

27. **Management** If the demand is changed to 690 metric tons of wheat and 920 metric tons of oil, how many units of each commodity should be produced?

28. **Management** Change the technological matrix so that production of 1 metric ton of wheat requires 1/5 metric ton of oil (and no wheat), and the production of 1 metric ton of oil requires 1/3 metric ton of wheat (and no oil). To satisfy the same demand matrix, how many units of each commodity should be produced?

29. **Management** A simplified economy has only two industries, the electric company and the gas company. Each dollar's worth of the electric company's output requires $.40 of its own output and $.50 of the gas company's output. Each dollar's worth of the gas company's output requires $.25 of its own output and $.60 of the electric company's output. What should the production of electricity and gas be (in dollars) if there is a $12 million demand for gas and a $15 million demand for electricity?

30. **Management** A two-segment economy consists of manufacturing and agriculture. To produce one unit of manufacturing output requires .40 unit of its own output and .20 unit of agricultural output. To produce one unit of agricultural output requires .30 unit of its own output and .40 unit of manufacturing output. If there is a demand of 240 units of manufacturing and 90 units of agriculture, what should be the output of each segment?

31. **Management** A primitive economy depends on two basic goods, yams and pork. Production of 1 bushel of yams requires 1/4 bushel of yams and 1/2 of a pig. To produce 1 pig requires 1/6 bushel of yams. Find the amount of each commodity that should be produced to get
    (a) 1 bushel of yams and 1 pig;
    (b) 100 bushels of yams and 70 pigs.

32. **Management** A simplified economy is based on agriculture, manufacturing, and transportation. Each unit of agricultural output requires .4 unit of its own output, .3 unit of manufacturing, and .2 unit of transportation output. One unit of manufacturing output requires .4 unit of its own output, .2 unit of agricultural, and .3 unit of transportation output. One unit of transportation output requires .4 unit of its own output, .1 unit of agricultural, and .2 unit of manufacturing output. There is demand for 35 units of agricultural, 90 units of manufacturing, and 20 units of transportation output. How many units should each segment of the economy produce?

33. **Management** How many units of each segment should the economy in Exercise 32 produce, if the demand is for 55 units of agricultural, 20 units of manufacturing, and 10 units of transportation output?

34. **Social Science** Use the method discussed in the text to encode the message

Anne is home.

Break the message into groups of two letters and use the matrix

$$M = \begin{bmatrix} 1 & 3 \\ 2 & 7 \end{bmatrix}.$$

35. **Social Science** Use the matrix of Exercise 34 to encode the message

Head for the hills!

36. **Social Science** Decode the following message, which was encoded by using the matrix M of Exercise 34.

$$\begin{bmatrix} 90 \\ 207 \end{bmatrix}, \begin{bmatrix} 39 \\ 87 \end{bmatrix}, \begin{bmatrix} 26 \\ 57 \end{bmatrix}, \begin{bmatrix} 66 \\ 145 \end{bmatrix}, \begin{bmatrix} 61 \\ 142 \end{bmatrix}, \begin{bmatrix} 89 \\ 205 \end{bmatrix}.$$

37. **Social Science** Use matrix A in the discussion on routing in the text to find A^2. Then answer the following questions. How many ways are there to travel from
    - **(a)** City 1 to city 3 by passing through exactly one city?
    - **(b)** City 2 to city 4 by passing through exactly one city?
    - **(c)** City 1 to city 3 by passing through at most one city?
    - **(d)** City 2 to city 4 by passing through at most one city?

38. **Social Science** Find A^3. (See Exercise 37.) Then answer the following questions.
    - **(a)** How many ways are there to travel between cities 1 and 4 by passing through exactly two cities?
    - **(b)** How many ways are there to travel between cities 1 and 4 by passing through at most two cities?

39. **Management** A small telephone system connects three cities. There are four lines between cities 3 and 2, three lines connecting city 3 with city 1, and two lines between cities 1 and 2.
    - **(a)** Write a matrix B to represent this information.
    - **(b)** Find B^2.
    - **(c)** How many lines which connect cities 1 and 2 go through exactly one other city (city 3)?
    - **(d)** How many lines which connect cities 1 and 2 go through at most one other city?

40. **Management** The figure shows four southern cities served by Supersouth Airlines.

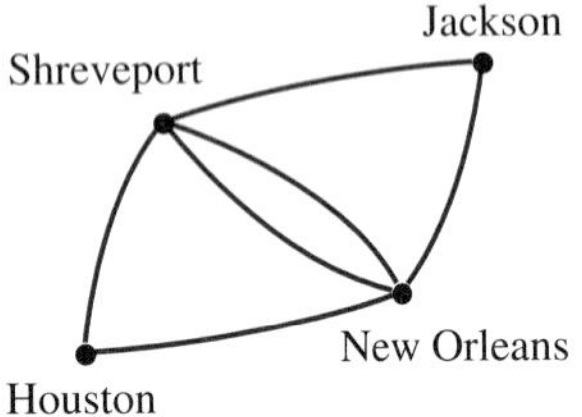

- **(a)** Write a matrix to represent the number of nonstop routes between cities.
- **(b)** Find the number of one-stop flights between Houston and Jackson.
- **(c)** Find the number of flights between Houston and Shreveport which require at most one stop.
- **(d)** Find the number of one-stop flights between New Orleans and Houston.

41. **Natural Science** The figure shows a food web. The arrows indicate the food sources of each population. For example, cats feed on rats and on mice.

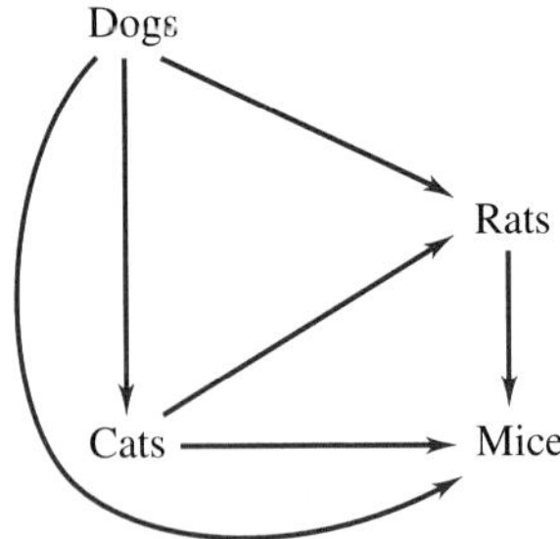

- **(a)** Write a matrix C in which each row and corresponding column represents a population in the food chain. Enter a 1 when the population in a given row feeds on the population in the given column.
- **(b)** Calculate and interpret C^2.

CHAPTER 7 SUMMARY

Key Terms and Symbols

7.1 linear equation
system of linear equations
solution of a system
independent system
dependent system
inconsistent system
elimination method
equivalent systems
elementary operations
triangular form
row
column
matrix (matrices)
element (entry)
augmented matrix
row operations
parameter

7.2 Gauss-Jordan method

7.3 row matrix (row vector)
column matrix (column vector)
square matrix
additive inverse of a matrix
zero matrix
scalar
product of a scalar and a matrix

7.4 product matrix
identity matrix
inverse matrix
singular matrix

7.5 coefficient matrix
input-output model
technological matrix (input-output matrix)
production matrix (vector of gross output)
demand matrix
code theory
routing theory

Key Concepts

Solving Systems of Equations

The following **elementary operations** are used to transform a system of equations into a simpler equivalent system.

1. Interchange any two equations.
2. Multiply both sides of an equation by a nonzero constant.
3. Replace an equation by the sum of itself and a constant multiple of another equation in the system.

The **elimination method** is a systematic way of using elementary operations to transform a system into an equivalent system that can be solved by **back substitution.** See Section 7.1 for details.

The matrix version of the elimination method uses the following **matrix row operations** that correspond to using elementary row operations with back substitution on a system of equations.

1. Interchange any two rows.
2. Multiply each element of a row by a nonzero constant.
3. Replace a row by the sum of itself and a constant multiple of another row in the matrix.

The **Gauss-Jordan method** is an extension of the elimination method for solving a system of linear equations. It uses row operations on the augmented matrix of the system. See Section 7.2 for details.

Operations on Matrices

The **sum** of two $m \times n$ matrices X and Y is the $m \times n$ matrix $X + Y$ in which each element is the sum of the corresponding elements of X and Y. The **difference** of two $m \times n$ matrices X and Y is the $m \times n$ matrix $X - Y$ in which each element is the difference of the corresponding elements of X and Y.

The **product** of a scalar k and a matrix X is the matrix kX, with each element k times the corresponding element of X.

The **product matrix** AB of an $m \times n$ matrix A and an $n \times k$ matrix B is the $m \times k$ matrix whose entry in the ith row and jth column is the product of the ith row of A and the jth column of B.

The **inverse matrix** A^{-1} for any $n \times n$ matrix A for which A^{-1} exists is found as follows. Form the augmented matrix $[A \mid I]$; perform row operations on $[A \mid I]$ to get the matrix $[I \mid A^{-1}]$.

Chapter 7 Review Exercises

Use the elimination or matrix method to solve each of the following systems. Identify any dependent or inconsistent systems.

1. $-5x - 3y = 4$
   $2x + y = -3$

2. $3x - y = 6$
   $2x + 3y = 7$

3. $3x - 5y = 10$
   $4x - 3y = 6$

4. $\frac{1}{4}x - \frac{1}{3}y = -\frac{1}{4}$
   $\frac{1}{10}x + \frac{2}{5}y = \frac{2}{5}$

5. $x - 2y = 1$
   $4x + 4y = 2$
   $10x + 8y = 4$

6. $x + y - 4z = 0$
   $2x + y - 3z = 2$

7. $3x + y - z = 13$
   $x + 2z = 9$
   $-3x - y + 2z = 9$

8. $4x - y - 2z = 4$
   $x - y - \frac{1}{2}z = 1$
   $2x - y - z = 8$

9. **Management** An office supply manufacturer makes two kinds of paper clips, standard and extra large. To make 1000 standard paper clips requires 1/4 hr on a cutting machine and 1/2 hr on a machine that shapes the clips. One thousand extra large paper clips require 1/3 hr on each machine. The manager of paper clip production has 4 hr per day available on the cutting machine and 6 hr per day on the shaping machine. How many of each kind of clip can he make?

10. **Management** Gretchen Schmidt plans to buy shares of two stocks. One costs $32 per share and pays dividends of $1.20 per share. The other costs $23 per share and pays dividends of $1.40 per share. She has $10,100 to spend and wants to earn dividends of $540. How many shares of each stock should she buy?

11. **Management** Joyce Pluth has money in two investment funds. Last year the first fund paid a dividend of 8% and the second a dividend of 2% and Joyce received a total of $780. This year the first fund paid a 10% dividend and the second only 1% and Joyce received $810. How much does she have invested in each fund?

12. You are given $144 in one, five, and ten dollar bills. There are 35 bills. There are two more ten dollar bills than five dollar bills. How many bills of each type are there?

13. **Social Science** A social service agency provides counseling, meals, and shelter to clients referred by sources I, II, and III. Clients from source I require an average of $100 for food, $250 for shelter, and no counseling. Source II clients require an average of $100 for counseling, $200 for food, and nothing for shelter. Source III clients require an average of $100 for counseling, $150 for food, and $200 for shelter. The agency has funding of $25,000 for counseling, $50,000 for food, and $32,500 for shelter. How many clients from each source can be served?

14. **Management** The Waputi Indians make woven blankets, rugs, and skirts. Each blanket requires 24 hr for spinning the yarn, 4 hr for dying the yarn, and 15 hr for weaving. Rugs require 30, 5, and 18 hr and skirts 12, 3, and 9 hr, respectively. If there are 306, 59, and 201 hr available for spinning, dying, and weaving, respectively, how many of each item can be made? (*Hint:* Simplify the equations you write, if possible, before solving the system.)

Use the Gauss-Jordan method to solve the following systems.

15. $x - z = -3$
    $y + z = 6$
    $2x - 3z = -9$

16. $2x - y + 4z = -1$
    $-3x + 5y - z = 5$
    $2x + 3y + 2z = 3$

17. $5x - 8y + z = 1$
    $3x - 2y + 4z = 3$
    $10x - 16y + 2z = 3$

18. $x - 2y + 3z = 4$
    $2x + y - 4z = 3$
    $-3x + 4y - z = -2$

19. $3x + 2y - 6z = 9$
    $x + y + 2z = 4$
    $2x + 2y + 5z = 0$

20. **Management** Each week at a furniture factory, there are 2000 work hours available in the construction department, 1400 work hours in the painting department, and 1300 work hours in the packing department. Producing a chair requires 2 hours of construction, 1 hour of painting, and 2 hours for packing. Producing a table requires 4 hours of construction, 3 hours of painting, and 3 hours for packing. Producing a chest requires 8 hours of construction, 6 hours of painting, and 4 hours for packing. If all available time is used in every department, how many of each item are produced each week?

For each of the following, find the dimensions of the matrix and identify any square, row, or column matrices.

21. $\begin{bmatrix} 2 & 3 \\ 5 & 9 \end{bmatrix}$

22. $\begin{bmatrix} 2 & -1 \\ 4 & 6 \\ 5 & 7 \end{bmatrix}$

23. $[12 \quad 4 \quad -8 \quad -1]$

24. $\begin{bmatrix} -7 & 5 & 6 \\ 3 & 2 & -1 \\ -1 & 12 & 8 \end{bmatrix}$

25. $\begin{bmatrix} 6 & 8 & 10 \\ 5 & 3 & -2 \end{bmatrix}$

26. $\begin{bmatrix} -9 \\ 15 \\ 4 \end{bmatrix}$

27. **Natural Science** The activities of a grazing animal can be classified roughly into three categories: grazing, moving, and resting. Suppose horses spend 8 hours grazing, 8 moving, and 8 resting; cattle spend 10 grazing, 5 moving, and 9 resting; sheep spend 7 grazing, 10 moving, and 7 resting; and goats spend 8 grazing, 9 moving, and 7 resting. Write this information as a 4×3 matrix.

28. **Management** The New York Stock Exchange reports in the daily newspapers give the dividend, price-to-earnings ratio, sales (in hundreds of shares), last price, and change in price for each company. Write the following stock reports as a 4×5 matrix. American Telephone & Telegraph: 5, 7, 2532, $52\frac{3}{8}$, $-\frac{1}{4}$. General Electric: 3, 9, 1464, 56, $+\frac{1}{8}$. Gulf Oil: 2.50, 5, 4974, 41, $-1\frac{1}{2}$. Sears: 1.36, 10, 1754, 18, $+\frac{1}{2}$.

Given the matrices

$$A = \begin{bmatrix} 4 & 10 \\ -2 & -3 \\ 6 & 9 \end{bmatrix}, \quad B = \begin{bmatrix} 2 & 3 & -2 \\ 2 & 4 & 0 \\ 0 & 1 & 2 \end{bmatrix}, \quad C = \begin{bmatrix} 5 & 0 \\ -1 & 3 \\ 4 & 7 \end{bmatrix},$$

$$D = \begin{bmatrix} 6 \\ 1 \\ 0 \end{bmatrix}, \quad E = [1 \quad 3 \quad -4], \quad F = \begin{bmatrix} -1 & 4 \\ 3 & 7 \end{bmatrix},$$

$$G = \begin{bmatrix} 2 & 5 \\ 1 & 6 \end{bmatrix},$$

find each of the following (if possible).

29. $-B$
30. $-D$
31. $3A - 2C$
32. $F + 3G$
33. $2B - 5C$
34. $G - 2F$

35. **Management** Refer to Exercise 28. Write a 4×2 matrix using the sales and price changes for the four companies. The next day's sales and price changes for the same four companies were 2310, 1258, 5061, 1812 and $-1/4$, $-1/4$, $+1/2$, $+1/2$, respectively. Write a 4×2 matrix using these new sales and price change figures. Use matrix addition to find the total sales and price changes for the two days.

36. **Management** An oil refinery in Tulsa sent 110,000 gallons of oil to a Chicago distributor, 73,000 to a Dallas distributor, and 95,000 to an Atlanta distributor. Another refinery in New Orleans sent the following amounts to the same three distributors: 85,000, 108,000, 69,000. The next month the two refineries sent the same distributors new shipments of oil as follows: from Tulsa, 58,000 to Chicago, 33,000 to Dallas, and 80,000 to Atlanta; from New Orleans, 40,000, 52,000, and 30,000, respectively.
   (a) Write the monthly shipments from the two distributors to the three refineries as 3×2 matrices.
   (b) Use matrix addition to find the total amounts sent to the refineries from each distributor.

Use the matrices given above Exercise 29 to find each of the following (if possible).

37. AG
38. EB
39. GF
40. CA
41. AGF
42. B^2D

43. **Management** An office supply manufacturer makes two kinds of paper clips, standard and extra large. To make a unit of standard paper clips requires 1/4 hour on a cutting machine and 1/2 hour on a machine that shapes the clips. A unit of extra large paper clips requires 1/3 hour on each machine.
   (a) Write this information as a 2×2 matrix (size/machine).
   (b) If 48 units of standard and 66 units of extra large clips are to be produced, use matrix multiplication to find out how many hours each machine will operate. (*Hint:* Write the units as a 1×2 matrix.)

44. **Management** Theresa DePalo buys shares of three stocks. Their cost per share and dividend earnings per share are \$32, \$23, and \$54, and \$1.20, \$1.49, and \$2.10, respectively. She buys 50 shares of the first stock, 20 shares of the second, and 15 shares of the third.
   (a) Write the cost per share and earnings per share of the stocks as a 3×2 matrix.
   (b) Write the number of shares of each stock as a 1×3 matrix.
   (c) Use matrix multiplication to find the total cost and total dividend earnings of these stocks.

45. If $A = \begin{bmatrix} 3 & 0 \\ 2 & 1 \end{bmatrix}$, find a matrix B such that both AB and BA are defined and $AB \neq BA$.

46. Is it possible to do Exercise 45 if $A = \begin{bmatrix} 4 & 0 \\ 0 & 4 \end{bmatrix}$? Explain why.

Find the inverse of each of the following matrices that has an inverse.

47. $\begin{bmatrix} -4 & 2 \\ 0 & 3 \end{bmatrix}$

48. $\begin{bmatrix} 2 & 1 \\ 5 & 3 \end{bmatrix}$

49. $\begin{bmatrix} 6 & 4 \\ 3 & 2 \end{bmatrix}$

50. $\begin{bmatrix} 2 & 0 \\ -1 & 5 \end{bmatrix}$

51. $\begin{bmatrix} 2 & 0 & 4 \\ 1 & -1 & 0 \\ 0 & 1 & -2 \end{bmatrix}$

52. $\begin{bmatrix} 2 & -1 & 0 \\ 1 & 0 & 1 \\ 1 & -2 & 0 \end{bmatrix}$

53. $\begin{bmatrix} 2 & 3 & 5 \\ -2 & -3 & -5 \\ 1 & 4 & 2 \end{bmatrix}$

54. $\begin{bmatrix} 1 & 3 & 6 \\ 4 & 0 & 9 \\ 5 & 15 & 30 \end{bmatrix}$

55. $\begin{bmatrix} 1 & 3 & -2 & -1 \\ 0 & 1 & 1 & 2 \\ -1 & -1 & 1 & -1 \\ 1 & -1 & -3 & -2 \end{bmatrix}$

56. $\begin{bmatrix} 3 & 2 & 0 & -1 \\ 2 & 0 & 1 & 2 \\ 1 & 2 & -1 & 0 \\ 2 & -1 & 1 & 1 \end{bmatrix}$

Refer again to the matrices given above Exercise 29 to find each of the following (if possible).

57. F^{-1}
58. G^{-1}
59. $(G - F)^{-1}$
60. $(F + G)^{-1}$
61. B^{-1}

62. Explain why the matrix $\begin{bmatrix} a & 0 \\ c & 0 \end{bmatrix}$, where a and c are nonzero constants, cannot possibly have an inverse.

Solve each of the following matrix equations $AX = B$ for X.

63. $A = \begin{bmatrix} 2 & 4 \\ -1 & -3 \end{bmatrix}, B = \begin{bmatrix} 8 \\ 3 \end{bmatrix}$

64. $A = \begin{bmatrix} 1 & 3 \\ -2 & 4 \end{bmatrix}, B = \begin{bmatrix} 15 \\ 10 \end{bmatrix}$

65. $A = \begin{bmatrix} 1 & 0 & 2 \\ -1 & 1 & 0 \\ 3 & 0 & 4 \end{bmatrix}, B = \begin{bmatrix} 8 \\ 4 \\ -6 \end{bmatrix}$

66. $A = \begin{bmatrix} 2 & 4 & 0 \\ 1 & -2 & 0 \\ 0 & 0 & 3 \end{bmatrix}, B = \begin{bmatrix} 72 \\ -24 \\ 48 \end{bmatrix}$

Use the method of matrix inverses to solve each of the following systems.

67. $\begin{aligned} x + y &= 4 \\ 2x + 3y &= 10 \end{aligned}$

68. $\begin{aligned} 5x - 3y &= -2 \\ 2x + 7y &= -9 \end{aligned}$

69. $\begin{aligned} 2x + y &= 5 \\ 3x - 2y &= 4 \end{aligned}$

70. $\begin{aligned} x - 2y &= 7 \\ 3x + y &= 7 \end{aligned}$

71. $\begin{aligned} x + y + z &= 1 \\ 2x - y \quad &= -2 \\ 3y + z &= 2 \end{aligned}$

72. $\begin{aligned} x &= -3 \\ y + z &= 6 \\ 2x - 3z &= -9 \end{aligned}$

73. $\begin{aligned} 3x - 2y + 4z &= 4 \\ 4x + y - 5z &= 2 \\ -6x + 4y - 8z &= -2 \end{aligned}$

74. $\begin{aligned} x + 2y \quad &= -1 \\ 3y - z &= -5 \\ x + 2y - z &= -3 \end{aligned}$

Solve each of the following problems by any method.

75. Management A wine maker has two large casks of wine. One is 8% alcohol and the other is 18% alcohol. How many liters of each wine should be mixed to produce 30 liters of wine that is 12% alcohol?

76. Management A gold merchant has some 12 carat gold (12/24 pure gold), and some 22 carat gold (22/24 pure). How many grams of each could be mixed to get 25 grams of 15 carat gold?

77. Natural Science A chemist has some 40% acid solution and some 60% solution. How many liters of each should be used to get 40 liters of a 45% solution?

78. Management How many pounds of tea worth \$4.60 a pound should be mixed with tea worth \$6.50 a pound to get 10 pounds of a mixture worth \$5.74 a pound?

79. Management A machine in a pottery factory takes 3 minutes to form a bowl and 2 minutes to form a plate. The material for a bowl costs \$.25 and the material for a plate costs \$.20. If the machine runs for 8 hours and exactly \$44 is spent for material, how many bowls and plates can be produced?

80. A boat travels at a constant speed a distance of 57 km downstream in 3 hours, then turns around and travels 55 km upstream in 5 hours. What is the speed of the boat and of the current?

81. Management Ms. Tham invests \$50,000 three ways—at 8%, $8\frac{1}{2}$%, and 11%. In total, she receives \$4436.25 per year in interest. The interest from the 11% investment is \$80 more than the interest on the 8% investment. Find the amount she has invested at each rate.

82. Tickets to a band concert cost \$2 for children, \$3 for teenagers, and \$5 for adults. 570 people attended the concert and total ticket receipts were \$1950. Three fourths as many teenagers as children attended. How many children, teenagers, and adults were at the concert?

Find the production matrix given the following input-output and demand matrices.

83. $A = \begin{bmatrix} .01 & .05 \\ .04 & .03 \end{bmatrix}, D = \begin{bmatrix} 200 \\ 300 \end{bmatrix}$

84. $A = \begin{bmatrix} .2 & .1 & .3 \\ .1 & 0 & .2 \\ 0 & 0 & .4 \end{bmatrix}, D = \begin{bmatrix} 500 \\ 200 \\ 100 \end{bmatrix}$

85. Given the input-output matrix $A = \begin{bmatrix} 0 & \frac{1}{4} \\ \frac{1}{2} & 0 \end{bmatrix}$ and the demand matrix $D = \begin{bmatrix} 2100 \\ 1400 \end{bmatrix}$, find each of the following.

(a) $I - A$ **(b)** $(I - A)^{-1}$

(c) the production matrix X

86. Management An economy depends on two commodities, goats and cheese. It takes 2/3 of a unit of goats to produce 1 unit of cheese and 1/2 unit of cheese to produce 1 unit of goats.

(a) Write the input-output matrix for this economy.

(b) Find the production required to satisfy a demand of 400 units of cheese and 800 units of goats.

87. Management In a simple economic model, a country has two industries: agriculture and manufacturing. To produce \$1 of agricultural output requires \$.10 of agricultural output and \$.40 of manufacturing output. To produce \$1 of manufacturing output requires \$.70 of agricultural output and \$.20 of manufacturing output. If agricultural demand is \$60,000 and manufacturing demand is \$20,000, what must each industry produce? (Round answers to the nearest whole number.)

88. Management The matrix below represents the number of direct flights between four cities.

$$\begin{array}{c} \\ A \\ B \\ C \\ D \end{array} \begin{array}{c} \begin{array}{cccc} A & B & C & D \end{array} \\ \begin{bmatrix} 0 & 1 & 0 & 1 \\ 1 & 0 & 0 & 1 \\ 0 & 0 & 0 & 1 \\ 1 & 1 & 1 & 0 \end{bmatrix} \end{array}$$

(a) Find the number of one-stop flights between cities A and C.

(b) Find the total number of flights between cities B and C that are either direct or one-stop.

(c) Find the matrix that gives the number of two-stop flights between these cities.

89. Social Science **(a)** Use the matrix $M = \begin{bmatrix} 2 & 6 \\ 1 & 4 \end{bmatrix}$ to encode the message "leave now."

(b) What matrix should be used to decode this message?

CASE 7

Leontief's Model of the American Economy

In the April 1965 issue of *Scientific American,* Wassily Leontief explained his input-output system using the 1958 American economy as an example.* He divided the economy into 81 sectors, grouped into six families of related sectors. In order to keep the discussion reasonably simple, we will treat each family of sectors as a single sector and so, in effect, work with a six-sector model. The sectors are listed in Table 1.

Table 1

Sector	*Examples*
Final Nonmetal (FN)	Furniture, processed food
Final Metal (FM)	Household appliances, motor vehicles
Basic Metal (BM)	Machine-shop products, mining
Basic Nonmetal (BN)	Agriculture, printing
Energy (E)	Petroleum, coal
Services (S)	Amusements, real estate

The workings of the American economy in 1958 are described in the input-output table (Table 2) based on Leontief's figures. We will demonstrate the meaning of Table 2 by considering the first left-hand column of numbers. The numbers in this column mean that 1 unit of final nonmetal production requires the consumption of .170 unit of (other) final nonmetal production, .003 unit of final metal output, .025 unit of basic metal products, and so on down the column. Since the unit of measurement that Leontief used for this table is millions of dollars, we conclude that the production of $1 million worth of final nonmetal production consumes $.170 million, or $170,000, worth of other final nonmetal products, $3000 of final metal products, $25,000 of basic metal products, and so on. Similarly, the entry in the column headed FM and opposite S of .074 means that $74,000 worth of input from the service industries goes into the production of $1 million worth of final metal products, and

*Adapted from *Applied Finite Mathematics* by Robert F. Brown and Brenda W. Brown. Copyright © 1977 by Robert F. Brown and Brenda W. Brown. Reprinted by permission.

Table 2

	FN	*FM*	*BM*	*BN*	*E*	*S*
FN	.170	.004	0	.029	0	.008
FM	.003	.295	.018	.002	.004	.016
BM	.025	.173	.460	.007	.011	.007
BN	.348	.037	.021	.403	.011	.048
E	.007	.001	.039	.025	.358	.025
S	.120	.074	.104	.123	.173	.234

the number .358 in the column headed E and opposite E means that $358,000 worth of energy must be consumed to produce $1 million worth of energy.

By the underlying assumption of Leontief's model, the production of n units (n = any number) of final nonmetal production consumes $.170n$ units of final nonmetal output, $.003n$ units of final metal output, $.025n$ units of basic metal production, and so on. Thus, production of $50 million worth of products from the final nonmetal section of the 1958 American economy required $(.170)(50) = 8.5$ units ($8.5 million) worth of final nonmetal input, $(.003)(50) = .15$ units of final metal input, $(.025)(50) = 1.25$ units of basic metal production, and so on.

EXAMPLE 1 According to the simplified input-output table for the 1958 American economy, how many dollars worth of final metal products, basic nonmetal products, and services are required to produce $120 million worth of basic metal products?

Each unit ($1 million worth) of basic metal products requires .018 units of final metal products because the number in the BM column of the table opposite FM is .018. Thus, $120 million, or 120 units, requires $(.018)(120) = 2.16$ units, or $2.16 million worth of final metal products. Similarly, 120 units of basic metal production uses $(.021)(120) = 2.52$ units of basic nonmetal production and $(.104)(120) = 12.48$ units of services, or $2.52 million and $12.48 million worth of basic nonmetal output and services, respectively. ■

The Leontief model also involves a *bill of demands,* that is, a list of requirements for units of output beyond that required for its inner workings as described in the input-output table. These demands represent exports, surpluses, government and individual consumption, and the like. The bill of demands (in millions) for the simplified version of the 1958 American economy we have been using is shown below.

FN	$99,640
FM	$75,548
BM	$14,444
BN	$33,501
E	$23,527
S	$263,985

We can now use the methods developed in Section 7.5 to answer this question: How many units of output from each sector are needed in order to run the economy and fill the bill of demands? The units of output from each sector required to run the economy and fill the bill of demands is unknown, so we denote them by variables. In our example, there are six quantities which are, at the moment, unknown. The number of units of final nonmetal production required to solve the problem will be our first unknown, because this sector is represented by the first row of the input-output matrix. The unknown quantity of final nonmetal units will be represented by the symbol x_1. Following the same pattern, we represent the unknown quantities in the following manner.

x_1 = units of final nonmetal production required
x_2 = units of final metal production required
x_3 = units of basic metal production required
x_4 = units of basic nonmetal production required
x_5 = units of energy required
x_6 = units of services required

These six numbers are the quantities we are attempting to calculate, and the variables will make up the entries in our production matrix.

To find these numbers, first let A be the 6×6 matrix corresponding to the input-output table.

$$A = \begin{bmatrix} .170 & .004 & 0 & .029 & 0 & .008 \\ .003 & .295 & .018 & .002 & .004 & .016 \\ .025 & .173 & .460 & .007 & .011 & .007 \\ .348 & .037 & .021 & .403 & .011 & .048 \\ .007 & .001 & .039 & .025 & .358 & .025 \\ .120 & .074 & .104 & .123 & .173 & .234 \end{bmatrix}$$

A is the input-output matrix. The bill of demands leads to a 6×1 demand matrix D, and X is the matrix of unknowns.

$$D = \begin{bmatrix} 99{,}640 \\ 75{,}548 \\ 14{,}444 \\ 33{,}501 \\ 23{,}527 \\ 263{,}985 \end{bmatrix} \quad \text{and} \quad X = \begin{bmatrix} x_1 \\ x_2 \\ x_3 \\ x_4 \\ x_5 \\ x_6 \end{bmatrix}$$

To use the formula $D = (I - A)X$, or $X = (I - A)^{-1}D$, we need to find $I - A$.

$$I - A = \begin{bmatrix} 1 & 0 & 0 & 0 & 0 & 0 \\ 0 & 1 & 0 & 0 & 0 & 0 \\ 0 & 0 & 1 & 0 & 0 & 0 \\ 0 & 0 & 0 & 1 & 0 & 0 \\ 0 & 0 & 0 & 0 & 1 & 0 \\ 0 & 0 & 0 & 0 & 0 & 1 \end{bmatrix} - \begin{bmatrix} .170 & .004 & 0 & .029 & 0 & .008 \\ .003 & .295 & .018 & .002 & .004 & .016 \\ .025 & .173 & .460 & .007 & .011 & .007 \\ .348 & .037 & .021 & .403 & .011 & .048 \\ .007 & .001 & .039 & .025 & .358 & .025 \\ .120 & .074 & .104 & .123 & .173 & .234 \end{bmatrix}$$

$$= \begin{bmatrix} .830 & -.004 & 0 & -.029 & 0 & -.008 \\ -.003 & .705 & -.018 & -.002 & -.004 & -.016 \\ -.025 & -.173 & .540 & -.007 & -.011 & -.007 \\ -.348 & -.037 & -.021 & .597 & -.011 & -.048 \\ -.007 & -.001 & -.039 & -.025 & .642 & -.025 \\ -.120 & -.074 & -.104 & -.123 & -.173 & .766 \end{bmatrix}$$

By the method given in Section 7.5, we find the inverse (actually an approximation).

$$(I - A)^{-1} = \begin{bmatrix} 1.234 & .014 & .007 & .064 & .006 & .017 \\ .017 & 1.436 & .056 & .014 & .019 & .032 \\ .078 & .467 & 1.878 & .036 & .044 & .031 \\ .752 & .133 & .101 & 1.741 & .065 & .123 \\ .061 & .045 & .130 & .083 & 1.578 & .059 \\ .340 & .236 & .307 & .315 & .376 & 1.349 \end{bmatrix}$$

Therefore,

$$X = (I - A)^{-1}D = \begin{bmatrix} 1.234 & .014 & .007 & .064 & .006 & .017 \\ .017 & 1.436 & .056 & .014 & .019 & .032 \\ .078 & .467 & 1.878 & .036 & .044 & .031 \\ .752 & .133 & .101 & 1.741 & .065 & .123 \\ .061 & .045 & .130 & .083 & 1.578 & .059 \\ .340 & .236 & .307 & .315 & .376 & 1.349 \end{bmatrix} \begin{bmatrix} 99{,}640 \\ 75{,}548 \\ 14{,}444 \\ 33{,}501 \\ 23{,}527 \\ 263{,}985 \end{bmatrix}$$

$$= \begin{bmatrix} 131{,}033 \\ 120{,}459 \\ 80{,}681 \\ 178{,}732 \\ 66{,}929 \\ 431{,}562 \end{bmatrix}.$$

From this result,

$$x_1 = 131{,}033$$
$$x_2 = 120{,}459$$
$$x_3 = 80{,}681$$
$$x_4 = 178{,}732$$
$$x_5 = 66{,}929$$
$$x_6 = 431{,}562.$$

In other words, it would require 131,033 units ($131,033 million worth) of final nonmetal production, 120,459 units of final metal output, 80,681 units of basic metal products, and so on to run the 1958 American economy and completely fill the stated bill of demands.

EXERCISES

Use a graphing calculator to work the following problems.

1. A much simplified version of Leontief's 42-sector analysis of the 1947 American economy divides the economy into just 3 sectors: agriculture, manufacturing, and the household (i.e., the sector of the economy that produces labor). It is summarized in the following input-output table.

	Agriculture	*Manufacturing*	*Household*
Agriculture	.245	.102	.051
Manufacturing	.099	.291	.279
Household	.433	.372	.011

The bill of demands (in billions of dollars) is shown below.

Agriculture	2.88
Manufacturing	31.45
Household	30.91

(a) Write the input-output matrix A, the demand matrix D, and the matrix X.

(b) Compute $I - A$.

(c) Check that $(I - A)^{-1} = \begin{bmatrix} 1.453 & .291 & .157 \\ .532 & 1.762 & .525 \\ .836 & .790 & 1.277 \end{bmatrix}$ is an approximation of the inverse of $I - A$ by calculating $(I - A)^{-1}(I - A)$.

(d) Use the matrix of part (c) to compute X.

(e) Explain the meaning of the numbers in X in dollars.

2. An analysis of the 1958 Israeli economy* is here simplified by grouping the economy into three sectors: agriculture, manufacturing, and energy. The input-output table is given below.

	Agriculture	*Manufacturing*	*Energy*
Agriculture	.293	0	0
Manufacturing	.014	.207	.017
Energy	.044	.010	.216

Exports (in thousands of Israeli pounds) were as follows.

Agriculture	138,213
Manufacturing	17,597
Energy	1,786

(a) Write the input-output matrix A and the demand (export) matrix D.

(b) Compute $I - A$.

(c) Check that $(I - A)^{-1} = \begin{bmatrix} 1.414 & 0 & 0 \\ .027 & 1.261 & .027 \\ .080 & .016 & 1.276 \end{bmatrix}$ is an approximation of the inverse of $I - A$ by calculating $(I - A)^{-1}(I - A)$.

(d) Use the matrix of part (c) to determine the number of Israeli pounds worth of agricultural products, manufactured goods, and energy required to run this model of the Israeli economy and export the stated value of products.

*Leontief, Wassily, *Input-Output Economics* (New York: Oxford University Press, 1966), pp. 54–57.

CHAPTER 8

Linear Programming

Many realistic problems involve inequalities. For example, a factory may have no more than 200 workers on a shift and must manufacture at least 3000 units at a cost of no more than $35 each. How many workers should it have per shift in order to produce the required units at minimal cost? *Linear programming* is a method for finding the optimal (best possible) solution for such problems, if there is one.

In this chapter we shall study two methods of solving linear programming problems: the graphical method and the simplex method. The graphical method requires a knowledge of **linear inequalities,** those involving only first-degree polynomials in x and y. So we begin with a study of such inequalities.

8.1 GRAPHING LINEAR INEQUALITIES IN TWO VARIABLES

Examples of linear inequalities in two variables include

$$x + 2y < 4, \quad 3x + 2y > 6, \quad \text{and} \quad 2x - 5y \geq 10.$$

A solution of a linear inequality is an ordered pair that satisfies the inequality. For example (4, 4) is a solution of

$$3x - 2y \leq 6.$$

(Check by substituting 4 for x and 4 for y.) A linear inequality has an infinite number of solutions, one for every choice of a value for x. The best way to show these solutions is with a graph that consists of all the points in the plane whose coordinates satisfy the inequality.

EXAMPLE 1 Graph the linear inequality $3x - 2y \leq 6$.

Because of the "=" portion of $\leq$, the points of the line $3x - 2y = 6$ satisfy the linear inequality $3x - 2y \leq 6$ and are part of its graph. As in Chapter 2, we find the intercepts by first letting $x = 0$ and then letting $y = 0$; we use these points to get the graph of $3x - 2y = 6$ shown in Figure 8.1.

FIGURE 8.1

1 Graph.

(a) $2x + 5y \leq 10$

(b) $x - y \geq 4$

Answers:

(a)

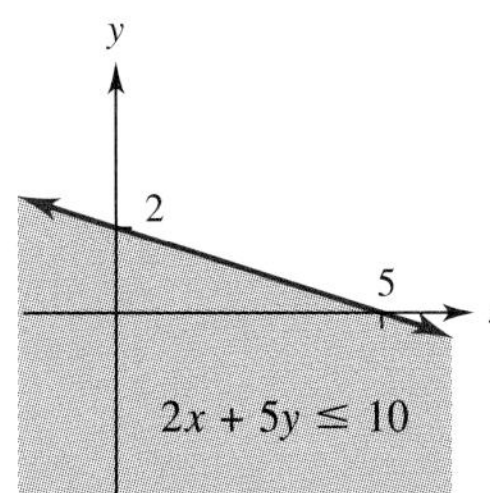

(b)

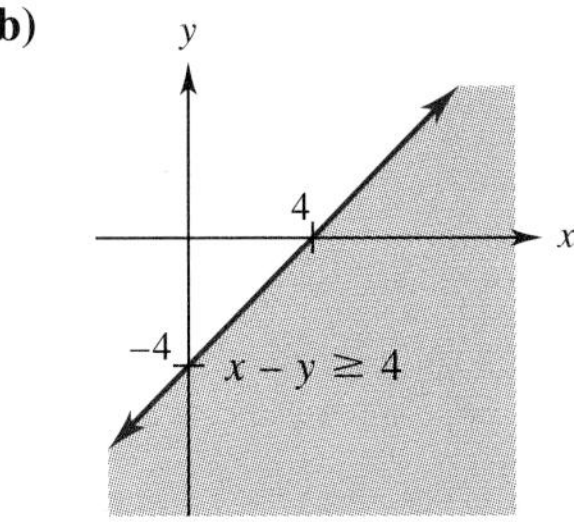

The points on the line satisfy "$3x - 2y$ *equals* 6." The points satisfying "$3x - 2y$ *is less than* 6" can be found by first solving $3x - 2y \leq 6$ for y.

$$3x - 2y \leq 6$$

$$-2y \leq -3x + 6$$

$$y \geq \frac{3}{2}x - 3 \qquad \text{Multiply by } -1/2; \text{ reverse the inequality.}$$

As shown in Figure 8.2, the points *above* the line $3x - 2y = 6$ satisfy

$$y > \frac{3}{2}x - 3,$$

while those below the line satisfy

$$y < \frac{3}{2}x - 3.$$

The line itself is the **boundary.** In summary, the inequality $3x - 2y \leq 6$ is satisfied by all points *on or above* the line $3x - 2y = 6$. Indicate the points above the line by shading, as in Figure 8.3. The line and shaded region of Figure 8.3 make up the graph of the linear inequality $3x - 2y \leq 6$. ■ **1**

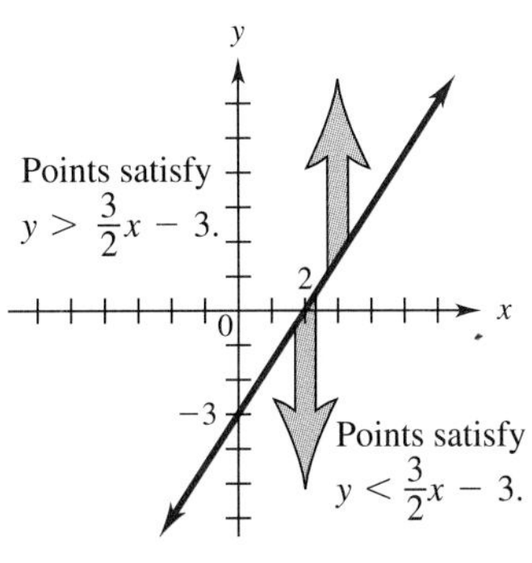

FIGURE 8.2

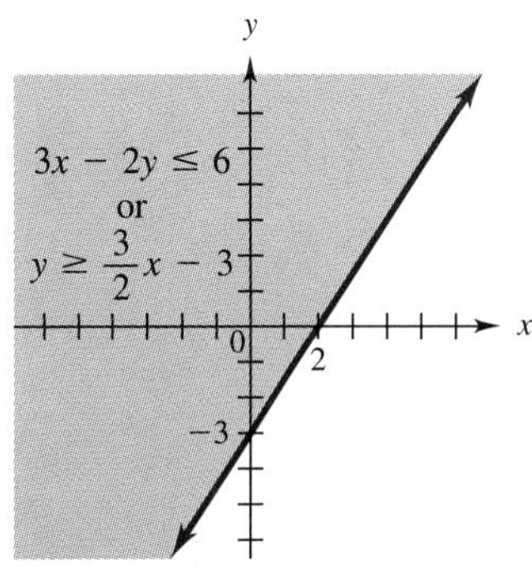

FIGURE 8.3

2 Graph.

(a) $2x + 3y > 12$

(b) $3x - 2y < 6$

Answers:

(a)

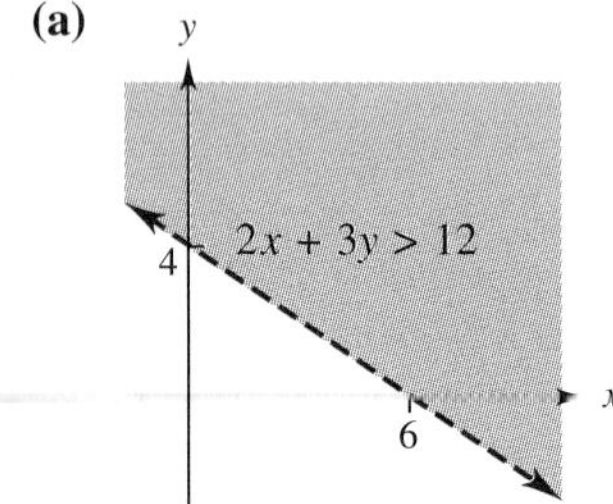

(b)

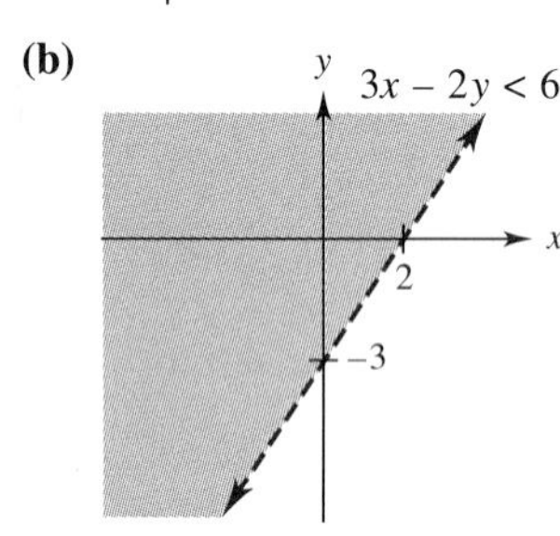

EXAMPLE 2 Graph $x + 4y < 4$.

The boundary here is the line $x + 4y = 4$. Since the points on this line do not satisfy $x + 4y < 4$, when drawing the graph by hand we use a dashed line, as in Figure 8.4. Solving the inequality for y gives $y < -(1/4)x + 1$. The $<$ symbol tells us we should shade the region below the line, as in Figure 8.4. ■ 2

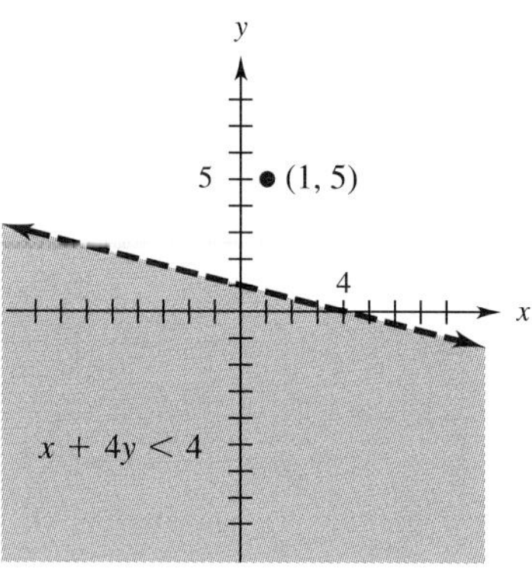

FIGURE 8.4

In Example 2, another way to decide which region to shade is to use a test point. For example, test the coordinates of the point (1, 5) in the inequality.

$$\mathbf{1} + 4(\mathbf{5}) = 21 \not< 4$$

Since the coordinates do not satisfy the inequality, shade the region on the other side of the boundary line, as shown in Figure 8.4.

As these examples suggest, the graph of a linear inequality is a region in the plane, perhaps including the line that is the boundary of the region. Each of the shaded regions is an example of a **half-plane,** a region on one side of a line. For example, in Figure 8.5 line r divides the plane into half-planes P and Q. The points of line r belong to neither P nor Q. Line r is the boundary of each half-plane.

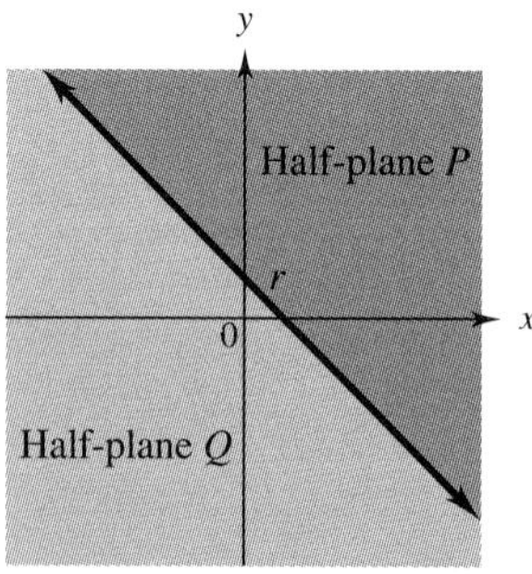

FIGURE 8.5

EXAMPLE 3 Graph each of the following.

(a) $x \leq -1$

Recall that the graph of $x = -1$ is the vertical line through $(-1, 0)$. The points where $x < -1$ lie in the half-plane to the left of the boundary line, as shown in Figure 8.6(a).

3 Graph each of the following.

(a) $x \geq 3$

(b) $y - 3 \leq 0$

Answers:

(a)

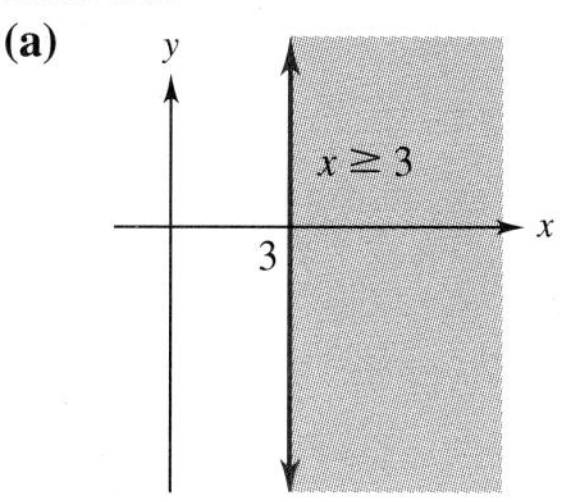

(b)

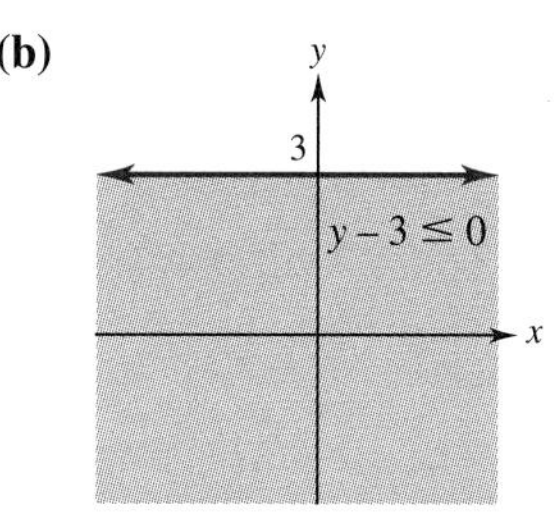

4 Use your calculator to graph $2x < y$.

Answer:

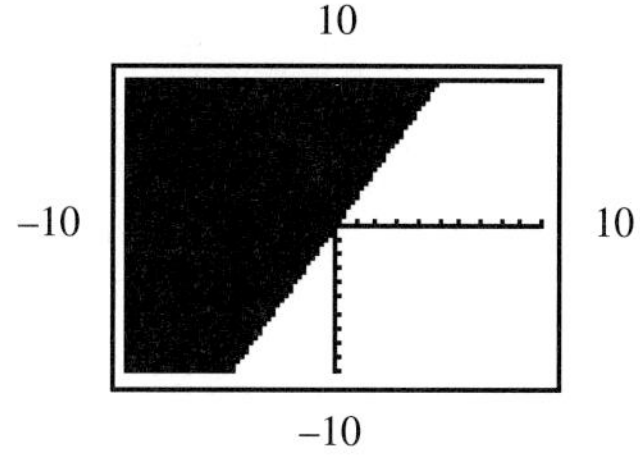

(b) $y \geq 2$

The graph of $y = 2$ is the horizontal line through (0, 2). The points where $y \geq 2$ lie in the half-plane above this boundary line or on the line, as shown in Figure 8.6(b). ■ 3

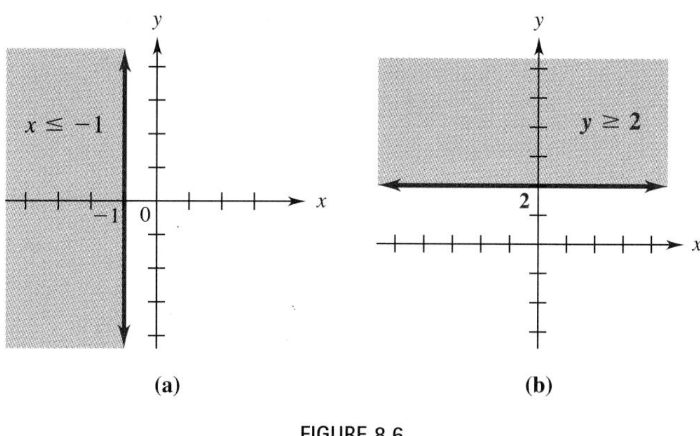

FIGURE 8.6

A graphing calculator can be used to shade regions in the plane as shown in the next example.

EXAMPLE 4* Use a graphing calculator to graph $x \geq 3y$.

Begin by solving the inequality for y to get $y \leq (1/3)x$. Use your calculator to graph the corresponding line $y = (1/3)x$. Because of the $\leq$ sign, we want to shade below the line. Use your calculator and the Technology Tip on the next page to shade this area, as in Figure 8.7. Note that you cannot tell from the graph if the boundary line is solid or dashed (it should be solid here). In fact, because of the way the calculator graphs, the boundary looks like a staircase (with very tiny stairs) rather than a straight line. ■ 4

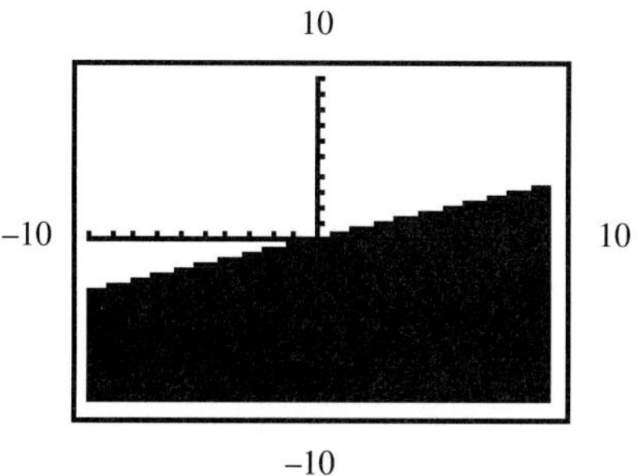

FIGURE 8.7

*If you don't have a graphing calculator, skip this example.

Technology Tip Most calculators can shade the region under or over a graph in the plane. On TI calculators, use SHADE in the DRAW menu. On Sharp 9300, use FILL BELOW or FILL ABOVE in the EQTN menu. On HP-38, use AREA in the FCN menu that appears after graphing. On some Casio calculators, use inequality graphing mode. Check your instruction manual for the correct syntax and procedure. On TI calculators and HP-38, you must shade the area *between* two graphs. So to shade the area below the graph of $y = f(x)$, as in Example 4, have the calculator shade the area between the graph of y and the horizontal line at the bottom of the screen. In Figure 8.7, for example, the calculator shaded the area between $y = (1/3)x$ and the horizontal line $y = -10$. ✔

The steps used to graph a linear inequality are summarized below.

GRAPHING A LINEAR INEQUALITY

1. Graph the boundary line. Decide whether the line is part of the solution. (If graphing by hand, make the line solid if the inequality involves $\leq$ or $\geq$; make it dashed if the inequality involves $<$ or $>$.)
2. Solve the inequality for y: Shade the region above the line if $y > mx + b$; shade the region below the line if $y < mx + b$.

SYSTEMS OF INEQUALITIES Realistic problems often involve many inequalities. For example, a manufacturing problem might produce inequalities resulting from production requirements, as well as inequalities about cost requirements. A set of at least two inequalities is called a **system of inequalities.** The graph of a system of inequalities is made up of all those points that satisfy all the inequalities of the system at the same time. The next example shows how to graph a system of linear inequalities.

5 Graph the system
$x + y \leq 6$, $2x + y \geq 4$.

Answer:

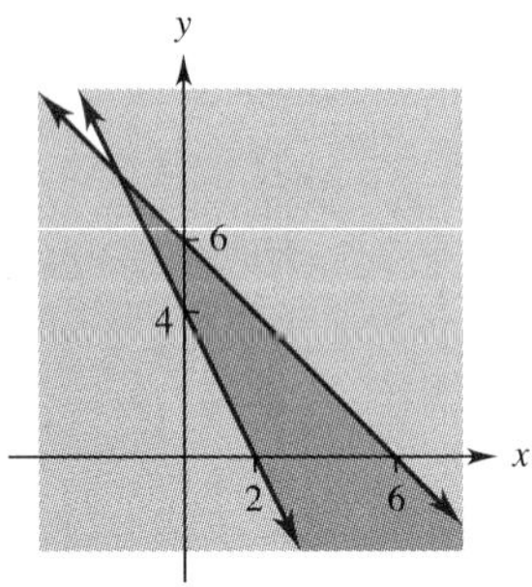

EXAMPLE 5 Graph the system

$$y < -3x + 12$$
$$x < 2y.$$

First, graph the solution of $y < -3x + 12$. The boundary, the line with equation $y = -3x + 12$, is dashed. The points below the boundary satisfy $y < -3x + 12$. Now graph the solution of $x < 2y$ on the same axes. Again, the boundary line $x - 2y$ is dashed. Use a test point to see that the region above the boundary satisfies $x < 2y$. The heavily shaded region in Figure 8.8 shows all the points that satisfy both inequalities of the system. ■ 5

Solution:
$y < -3x + 12$
$x < 2y$

FIGURE 8.8

The heavily shaded region of Figure 8.8 is sometimes called the **region of feasible solutions,** or just the **feasible region,** since it is made up of all the points that satisfy (are feasible for) each inequality of the system.

6 Graph the feasible region of the system

$$x + 4y \le 8$$
$$x - y \ge 3$$
$$x \ge 0,\ y \ge 0.$$

Answer:

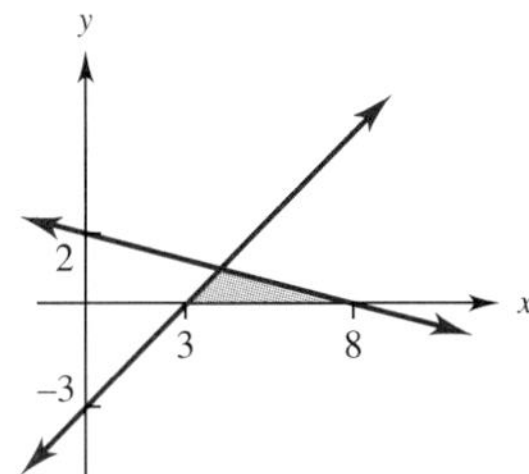

EXAMPLE 6 Graph the feasible region for the system

$$2x - 5y \le 10$$
$$x + 2y \le 8$$
$$x \ge 0,\ y \ge 0.$$

On the same axes, graph each inequality by graphing the boundary and choosing the appropriate half-plane. Graph the solid boundary line $2x - 5y = 10$ by first locating the intercepts that give the points (5, 0) and (0, −2). Use a test point to see that $2x - 5y < 10$ is satisfied by the points above the boundary. In the same way, the solid boundary line $x + 2y = 8$ goes through (8, 0) and (0, 4). A test point will show that the graph of $x + 2y < 8$ includes all points below the boundary. The inequalities $x \ge 0$ and $y \ge 0$ restrict the feasible region to the first quadrant. Find the feasible region by locating the intersection (overlap) of *all* the half-planes. This feasible region is shaded in Figure 8.9(a). ■ 6

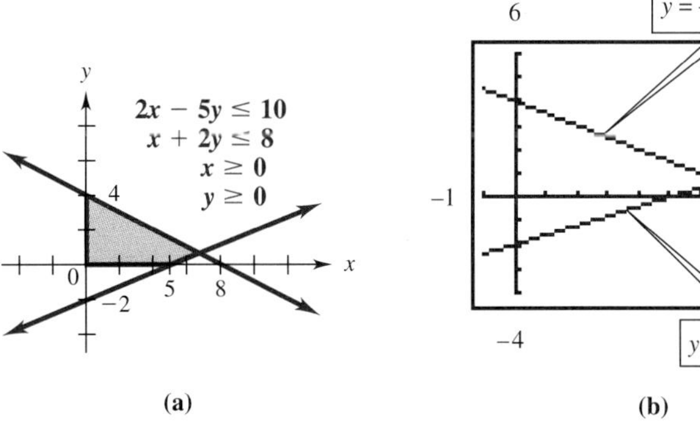

FIGURE 8.9

TECHNOLOGY TIP To use a graphing calculator to solve the system in Example 6, solve the first two inequalities for y to get

$$y \ge .4x - 2 \quad \text{and} \quad y \le -.5x + 4.$$

Graph the boundary lines $y = .4x - 2$ and $y = -.5x + 4$ in the same window. See Figure 8.9(b). Because $x \geq 0$ and $y \geq 0$, the feasible region consists of all points that are in the first quadrant, above $y = .4x - 2$ and below $y = -.5x + 4$, as shown in Figure 8.9(a). ✔

APPLICATIONS As we shall see in the rest of this chapter, many realistic problems lead to systems of linear inequalities. The next example is typical of such problems.

EXAMPLE 7 Midtown Manufacturing Company makes plastic plates and cups, both of which require time on two machines. A unit of plates requires 1 hour on machine A and 2 on machine B, while a unit of cups requires 3 hours on machine A and 1 on machine B. Each machine is operated for at most 15 hours per day. Write a system of inequalities expressing these conditions and graph the feasible region.

Let x represent the number of units of plates to be made, and y represent the number of units of cups. Then make a chart that summarizes the given information.

	Number Made	TIME ON MACHINE	
		A	B
Plates	x	1	2
Cups	y	3	1
Maximum time available		15	15

On machine A, x units of plates require a total of $1 \cdot x = x$ hours while y units of cups require $3 \cdot y = 3y$ hours. Since machine A is available no more than 15 hours a day,

$$x + 3y \leq 15. \qquad \text{Machine A}$$

The requirement that machine B be used no more than 15 hours a day gives

$$2x + y \leq 15. \qquad \text{Machine B}$$

It is not possible to produce a negative number of cups or plates, so that

$$x \geq 0 \quad \text{and} \quad y \geq 0.$$

The feasible region for this system of inequalities is shown in Figure 8.10. ■

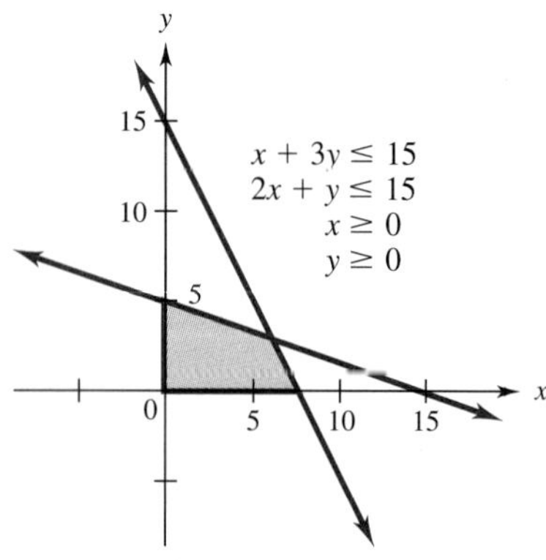

FIGURE 8.10

8.1 EXERCISES

Graph each of the following linear inequalities. (See Examples 1–4.)

1. $y < 5 - 2x$
2. $y > x + 3$
3. $3x - 2y \geq 18$
4. $2x + 5y \leq 10$
5. $2x - y \leq 4$
6. $4x - 3y \geq 24$
7. $y \leq -4$
8. $x \geq -2$
9. $x + 4y \leq 2$
10. $3x + 2y \geq 6$
11. $4x + 3y > -3$
12. $5x + 3y > 15$
13. $2x - 4y < 3$
14. $4x - 3y < 12$
15. $x \leq 5y$
16. $2x \geq y$
17. $-3x < y$
18. $-x > 6y$
19. $y < x$
20. $y > -2x$
21. In your own words, explain how to determine whether the boundary of an inequality is solid or dashed.
22. When graphing $y \leq 3x - 6$, would you shade above or below the line $y = 3x - 6$? Explain your answer.

Graph the feasible region for the following systems of inequalities. (See Examples 5 and 6.)

23. $x - y \geq 1$
    $x \leq 3$
24. $2x + y \leq 5$
    $x + 2y \leq 5$
25. $4x + y \geq 9$
    $2x + 3y \leq 7$
26. $2x + y > 8$
    $4x - y < 3$
27. $x + y > 5$
    $x - 2y < 2$
28. $3x - 4y < 6$
    $2x + 5y > 15$
29. $2x - y < 1$
    $3x + y < 6$
30. $x + 3y \leq 6$
    $2x + 4y \geq 7$
31. $-x - y < 5$
    $2x - y < 4$
32. $6x - 4y > 8$
    $3x + 2y > 4$
33. $3x + y \geq 6$
    $x + 2y \geq 7$
    $x \geq 0$
    $y \geq 0$
34. $2x + 3y \geq 12$
    $x + y \geq 4$
    $x \geq 0$
    $y \geq 0$
35. $-2 < x < 3$
    $-1 \leq y \leq 5$
    $2x + y < 6$
36. $-2 < x < 2$
    $y > 1$
    $x - y > 0$
37. $2y - x \geq -5$
    $y \leq 3 + x$
    $x \geq 0$
    $y \geq 0$
38. $2x + 3y \leq 12$
    $2x + 3y > -6$
    $3x + y < 4$
    $x \geq 0$
    $y \geq 0$
39. $3x + 4y > 12$
    $2x - 3y < 6$
    $0 \leq y \leq 2$
    $x \geq 0$
40. $0 \leq x \leq 9$
    $x - 2y \geq 4$
    $3x + 5y \leq 30$
    $y \geq 0$

In Exercises 41 and 42, find a system of inequalities whose feasible region is the interior of the given polygon.

41. Rectangle with vertices (2, 3), (2, −1), (7, 3), (7, −1)
42. Triangle with vertices (2, 4), (−4, 0), (2, −1)
43. **Management** Cindi Herring and Kent Merrill produce handmade shawls and afghans. They spin the yarn, dye it, and then weave it. A shawl requires 1 hour of spinning, 1 hour of dyeing, and 1 hour of weaving. An afghan needs 2 hours of spinning, 1 of dyeing, and 4 of weaving. Together, they spend at most 8 hours spinning, 6 hours dyeing, and 14 hours weaving.
    (a) Complete the following chart.

	Number	*Hours Spinning*	*Hours Dyeing*	*Hours Weaving*
Shawls	x			
Afghans	y			
Maximum number of hours available		8	6	14

    (b) Use the chart to write a system of inequalities that describe the situation.
    (c) Graph the feasible region of this system of inequalities.
44. **Management** An electric shaver manufacturer makes two models, the regular and the flex. Because of demand, the number of regular shavers made is never more than half the number of flex shavers. The factory's production cannot exceed 1200 shavers per week.
    (a) Write a system of inequalities that describe the possibilities for making x regular and y flex shavers per week.
    (b) Graph the feasible region of this system of inequalities.

In each of the following, write a system of inequalities that describes all the conditions and graph the feasible region of the system. (See Example 7.)

45. **Management** Southwestern Oil supplies two distributors located in the Northwest. One distributor needs at least 3000 barrels of oil, and the other needs at least 5000 barrels. Southwestern can send out at most 10,000 barrels. Let x = the number of barrels of oil sent to distributor 1 and y = the number sent to distributor 2.
46. **Management** The California Almond Growers have 2400 boxes of almonds to be shipped from their plant in Sacramento to Des Moines and San Antonio. The Des Moines market needs at least 1000 boxes, while the San Antonio market must have at least 800 boxes. Let x = the

number of boxes to be shipped to Des Moines and y = the number of boxes to be shipped to San Antonio.

47. **Management** A cement manufacturer produces at least 3.2 million barrels of cement annually. He is told by the Environmental Protection Agency that his operation emits 2.5 pounds of dust for each barrel produced. The EPA has ruled that annual emissions must be reduced to 1.8 million pounds. To do this, the manufacturer plans to replace the present dust collectors with two types of electronic precipitators. One type would reduce emissions to .5 pound per barrel and would cost 16¢ per barrel. The other would reduce the dust to .3 pound per barrel and would cost 20¢ per barrel. The manufacturer does not want to spend more than .8 million dollars on the precipitators. He needs to know how many barrels he should produce with each type. Let x = the number of barrels in millions produced with the first type and y = the number of barrels in millions produced with the second type.

48. **Natural Science** A dietician is planning a snack package of fruit and nuts. Each ounce of fruit will supply 1 unit of protein, 2 units of carbohydrates, and 1 unit of fat. Each ounce of nuts will supply 1 unit of protein, 1 unit of carbohydrates, and 1 unit of fat. Every package must provide at least 7 units of protein, at least 10 units of carbohydrates, and no more than 9 units of fat. Let x be the ounces of fruit and y the ounces of nuts to be used in each package.

8.2 LINEAR PROGRAMMING: THE GRAPHICAL METHOD

Many problems in business, science, and economics involve finding the optimal value of a function (for instance, the maximum value of the profit function or the minimum value of the cost function) subject to various **constraints** (such as transportation costs, environmental protection laws, availability of parts, interest rates, etc.). **Linear programming** deals with such situations in which the function to be optimized, called the **objective function,** is linear and the constraints are given by linear inequalities. Linear programming problems that involve only two variables can be solved by the graphical method, explained in Example 1.

EXAMPLE 1 Find the maximum and minimum values of the objective function $z = 2x + 5y$, subject to the following constraints.

$$\begin{aligned} 3x + 2y &\leq 6 \\ -2x + 4y &\leq 8 \\ x + y &\geq 1 \\ x \geq 0, y &\geq 0 \end{aligned}$$

First, graph the feasible region of the system of inequalities (Figure 8.11). The points in this region or on its boundaries are the only ones that satisfy all the constraints. However, each such point may produce a different value of the objective function. For instance, the points (.5, 1) and (1, 0) in the feasible region lead to the values

$$z = 2(.5) + 5(1) = 6 \quad \text{and} \quad z = 2(1) + 5(0) = 2.$$

We must find the points that produce the maximum and minimum values of z.

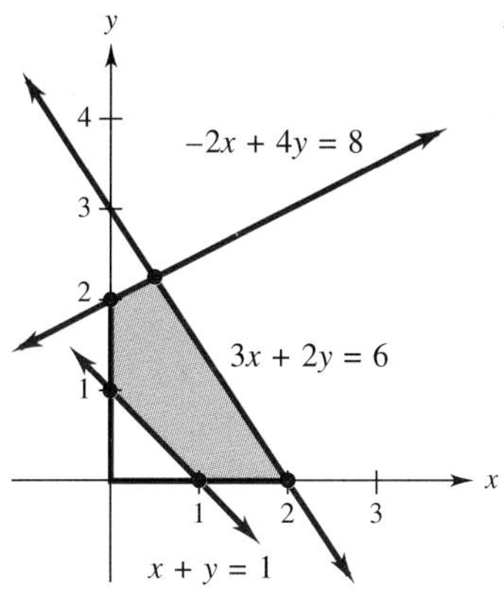

FIGURE 8.11

To find the maximum value, consider various possible values for z. For instance, when $z = 0$, then the objective function is $0 = 2x + 5y$, whose graph is a straight line. Similarly, when z is 5, 10, and 15, the objective function becomes (in turn)

$$5 = 2x + 5y, \qquad 10 = 2x + 5y, \qquad 15 = 2x + 5y.$$

These four lines are graphed in Figure 8.12. (All the lines are parallel because they have the same slope.) The figure shows that z cannot take on the value 15 because the graph for $z = 15$ is entirely outside the feasible region. The maximum possible value of z will be obtained from a line parallel to the others and between the lines representing the objective function when $z = 10$ and $z = 15$. The value of z will be as large as possible and all constraints will be satisfied if this line just touches the feasible region. This occurs at point A.

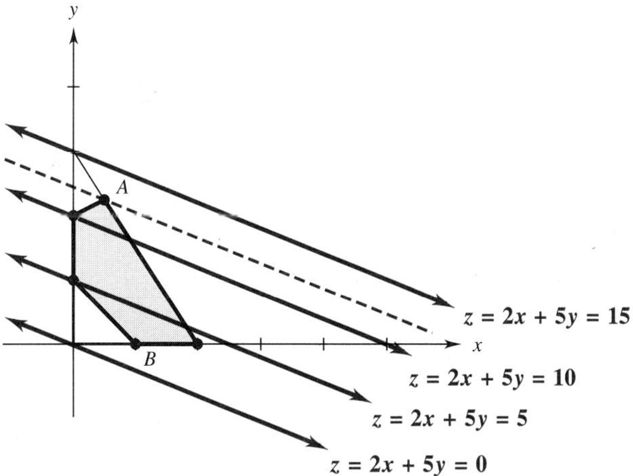

FIGURE 8.12

The point A is the intersection of the graphs of $3x + 2y = 6$ and $-2x + 4y = 8$. Its coordinates can be found either algebraically or graphically (using a graphing calculator).

1 Suppose the objective function in Example 1 is changed to $z = 5x + 2y$.

(a) Sketch the graphs of the objective function when $z = 0$, $z = 5$, and $z = 10$ on the region of feasible solutions given in Figure 8.11.

(b) From the graph, decide what values of x and y will maximize the objective function.

Answers:

(a)

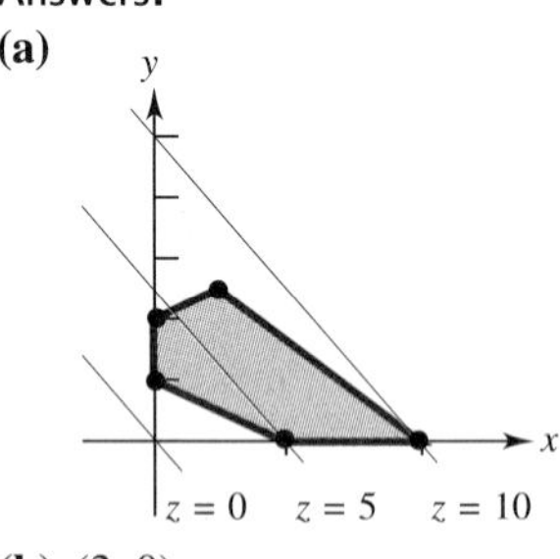

(b) (2, 0)

Algebraic Method

Solve the system

$$3x + 2y = 6$$
$$-2x + 4y = 8,$$

as in Section 7.1, to get $x = 1/2$ and $y = 9/4$. Hence A has coordinates $(1/2, 9/4) = (.5, 2.25)$.

Graphical Method

Solve the two equations for y.

$$y = -1.5x + 3$$
$$y = .5x + 2$$

Graph both equations on the same screen and use the intersection finder to find that the coordinates of the intersection point A are $(.5, 2.25)$.

The value of z at the point A is

$$z = 2x + 5y = 2(.5) + 5(2.25) = 12.25.$$

Thus, the maximum possible value of z is 12.25. Similarly, the minimum value of z occurs at point B, which has coordinates (1, 0). The minimum value of z is $2(1) + 5(0) = 2$. ■ 1

Points such as A and B in Example 1 are called corner points. A **corner point** is a point in the feasible region where the boundary lines of two constraints cross. The feasible region in Figure 8.11 is **bounded,** because the region is enclosed by boundary lines on all sides. Linear programming problems with bounded regions always have solutions. However, if Example 1 did not include the constraint $3x + 2y \leq 6$, the feasible region would be **unbounded,** and there would be no way to *maximize* the value of the objective function.

Some general conclusions can be drawn from the method of solution used in Example 1. Figure 8.13 shows various feasible regions and the lines that result from various values of z. (Figure 8.13 shows the situation in which the lines are in order from left to right as z increases.) In part (a) of the figure, the objective function takes on its minimum value at corner point Q and its maximum value at P. The minimum is again at Q in part (b), but the maximum occurs at P_1 or P_2, or any point on the line segment connecting them. Finally, in part (c), the minimum value occurs at Q, but the objective function has no maximum value because the feasible region is unbounded.

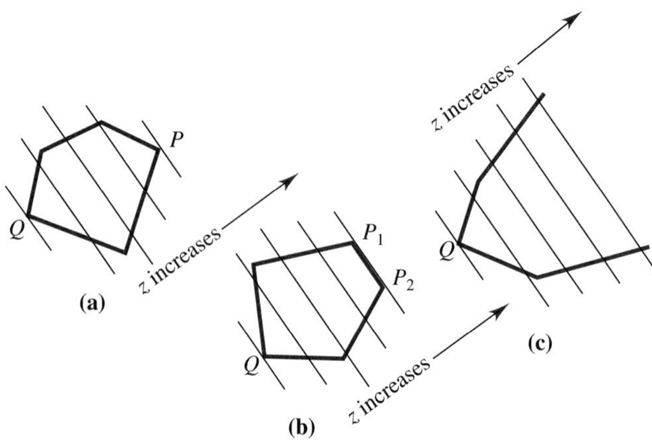

FIGURE 8.13

The preceding discussion suggests the truth of the **corner point theorem.**

CORNER POINT THEOREM

If the feasible region is bounded, then the objective function has both a maximum and a minimum value and each occurs at one or more corner points.

If the feasible region is unbounded, the objective function may not have a maximum or minimum. But if a maximum or minimum value exists, it will occur at one or more corner points.

This theorem simplifies the job of finding an optimum value: First, graph the feasible region and find all corner points. Then test each point in the objective function. Finally, identify the corner point producing the optimum solution.

With the theorem, the problem in Example 1 could have been solved by identifying the five corner points of Figure 8.11: (0, 1), (0, 2), (.5, 2.25), (2, 0), and (1, 0). Then, substituting each of these points into the objective function $z = 2x + 5y$ would identify the corner points that produce the maximum and the minimum values of z.

Corner Point	*Value of* $z = 2x + 5y$
(0, 1)	$2(0) + 5(1) = 5$
(0, 2)	$2(0) + 5(2) = 10$
(.5, 2.25)	$\mathbf{2(.5) + 5(2.25) = 12.25}$ **(maximum)**
(2, 0)	$2(2) + 5(0) = 4$
(1, 0)	$\mathbf{2(1) + 5(0) = 2}$ **(minimum)**

From these results, the corner point (.5, 2.25) yields the maximum value of 12.25 and the corner point (1, 0) gives the minimum value of 2. These are the same values found earlier. 2

2 **(a)** Identify the corner points in the graph.

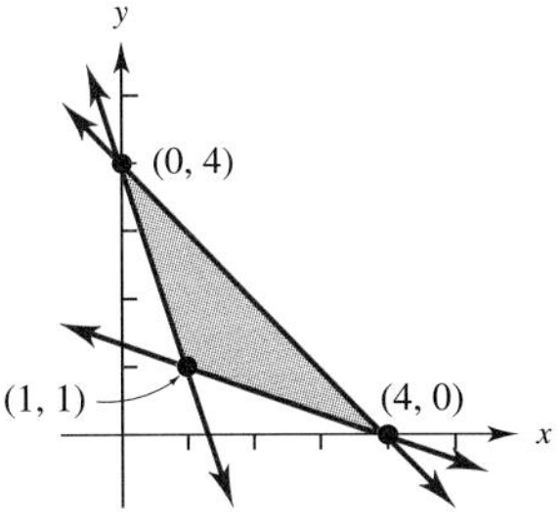

(b) Which corner point would minimize $z = 2x + 3y$?

Answers:

(a) (0, 4), (1, 1), (4, 0)

(b) (1, 1)

A summary of the steps in solving a linear programming problem by the graphical method is given here.

SOLVING A LINEAR PROGRAMMING PROBLEM GRAPHICALLY

1. Write the objective function and all necessary constraints.
2. Graph the feasible region.
3. Determine the coordinates of each of the corner points.
4. Find the value of the objective function at each corner point.
5. If the feasible region is bounded, the solution is given by the corner point producing the optimum value of the objective function.
6. If the feasible region is an unbounded region in the first quadrant and both coefficients of the objective function are positive,* then the minimum value of the objective function occurs at a corner point and there is no maximum value.

*This is the only case of an unbounded region that occurs in the applications considered here.

EXAMPLE 2 Sketch the feasible region for the following set of constraints:

$$3y - 2x \geq 0$$
$$y + 8x \leq 52$$
$$y - 2x \leq 2$$
$$x \geq 3.$$

Then find the maximum and minimum values of the objective function $z = 5x + 2y$.

The graph in Figure 8.14(a) shows that the feasible region is bounded. The corner points are found by solving systems of two equations either algebraically using the methods of Chapter 7 or graphically using the intersection finder on a graphing calculator. Figure 8.14(b) shows the calculator graphs of the first three inequalities. With the graphical method, corner points on the line $x = 3$ are found by observation.

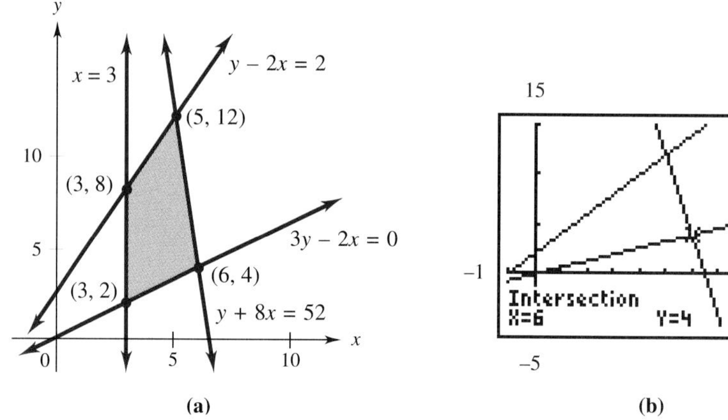

FIGURE 8.14

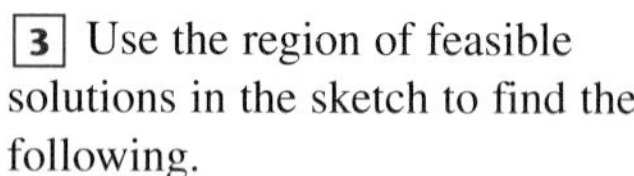
3 Use the region of feasible solutions in the sketch to find the following.

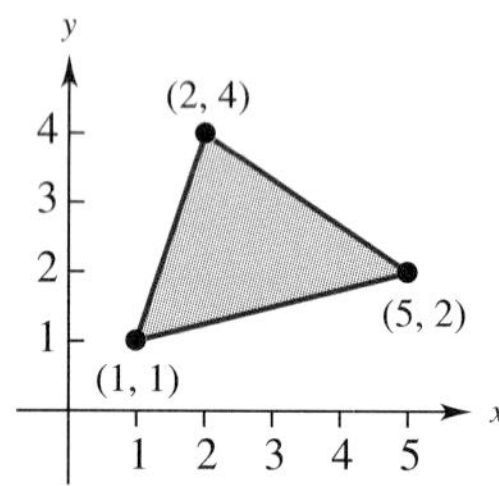

(a) The values of x and y that maximize $z = 2x - y$.

(b) The maximum value of $z = 2x - y$.

(c) The values of x and y that minimize $z = 4x + 3y$.

(d) The minimum value of $z = 4x + 3y$.

Answers:

(a) (5, 2)

(b) 8

(c) (1, 1)

(d) 7

Use the corner points from the graph to find the maximum and minimum values of the objective function.

Corner Point	*Value of $z = 5x + 2y$*
(3, 2)	**$5(3) + 2(2) = 19$ (minimum)**
(6, 4)	$5(6) + 2(4) = 38$
(5, 12)	**$5(5) + 2(12) = 49$ (maximum)**
(3, 8)	$5(3) + 2(8) = 31$

The minimum value of $z = 5x + 2y$ is 19 at the corner point (3, 2). The maximum value is 49 at (5, 12). ■ 3

EXAMPLE 3 Solve the following linear programming problem.

Minimize $z = x + 2y$

subject to:
$$x + y \leq 10$$
$$3x + 2y \geq 6$$
$$x \geq 0,\ y \geq 0.$$

The feasible region is shown in Figure 8.15. From the figure, the corner points are (0, 3), (0, 10), (10, 0), and (2, 0). These corner points give the following values of z.

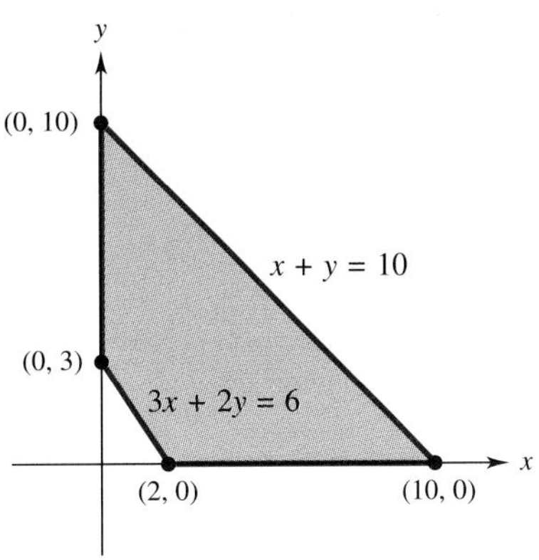

FIGURE 8.15

Corner Point	*Value of $z = x + 2y$*
(0, 3)	$0 + 2(3) = 6$
(0, 10)	$0 + 2(10) = 20$
(10, 0)	$10 + 2(0) = 10$
(2, 0)	$\mathbf{2 + 2(0) = 2}$ **(minimum)**

The minimum value of z is 2; it occurs at (2, 0). ■ [4]

[4] The sketch shows a feasible region. Let $z = x + 3y$. Use the sketch to find the values of x and y that

(a) minimize z;

(b) maximize z.

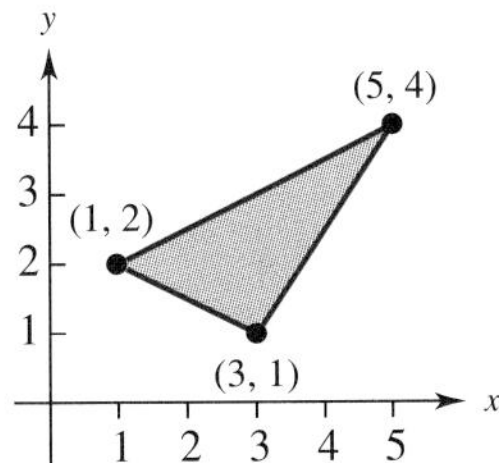

Answers:

(a) (3, 1)

(b) (5, 4)

EXAMPLE 4 Solve the following linear programming problem.

$$\begin{aligned} \text{Minimize} \quad & z = 2x + 4y \\ \text{subject to:} \quad & x + 2y \geq 10 \\ & 3x + y \geq 10 \\ & x \geq 0, y \geq 0. \end{aligned}$$

Figure 8.16 shows the hand-drawn graph with corner points (0, 10), (2, 4), and (10, 0), as well as the calculator graph with the corner point (2, 4). Find the value of z for each point.

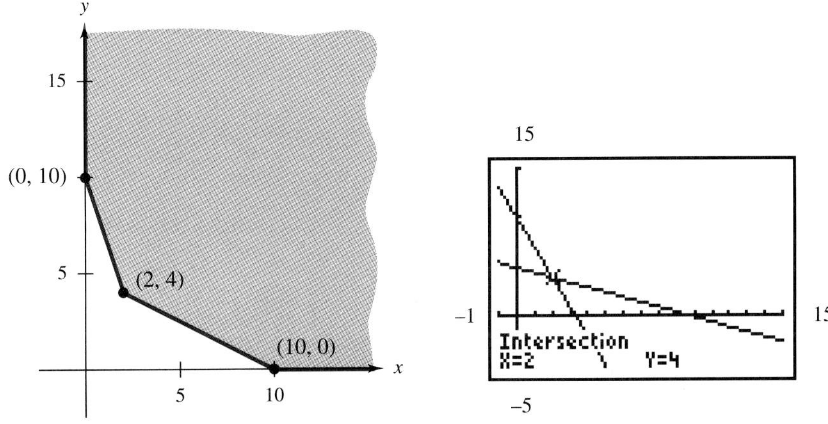

FIGURE 8.16

5 The sketch below shows a region of feasible solutions. From the sketch decide what ordered pair would minimize $z = 2x + 4y$.

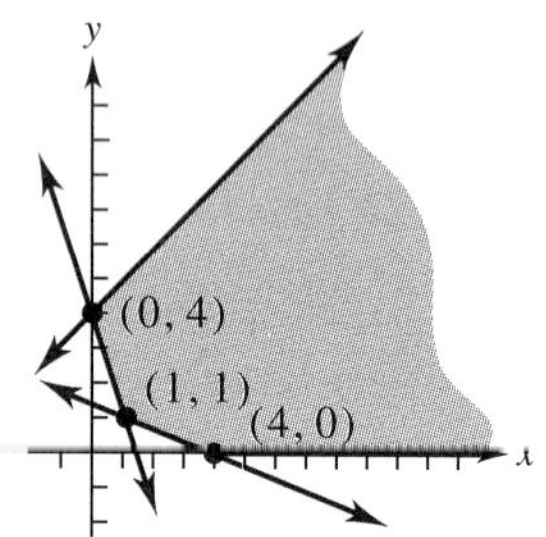

Answer:
(1, 1)

Corner Point	*Value of $z = 2x + 4y$*
(0, 10)	2(0) + 4(10) = 40
(2, 4)	**2(2) + 4(4) = 20 (minimum)**
(10, 0)	**2(10) + 4(0) = 20 (minimum)**

In this case, both (2, 4) and (10, 0), as well as all the points on the boundary line between them, give the same optimum value of z. There is an infinite number of equally "good" values of x and y which give the same minimum value of the objective function $z = 2x + 4y$. The minimum value is 20. ■ 5

8.2 EXERCISES

Exercises 1–6 show regions of feasible solutions. Use these regions to find maximum and minimum values of each given objective function. (See Examples 1–2.)

1. $z = 3x + 5y$

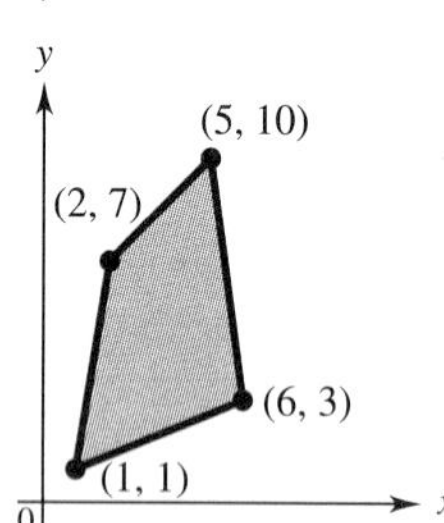

2. $z = 6x + y$

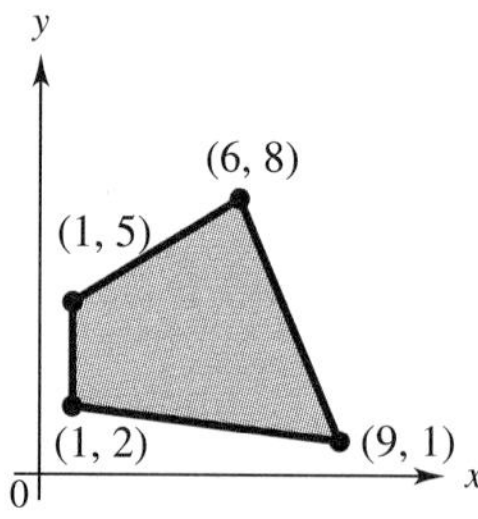

3. $z = .40x + .75y$

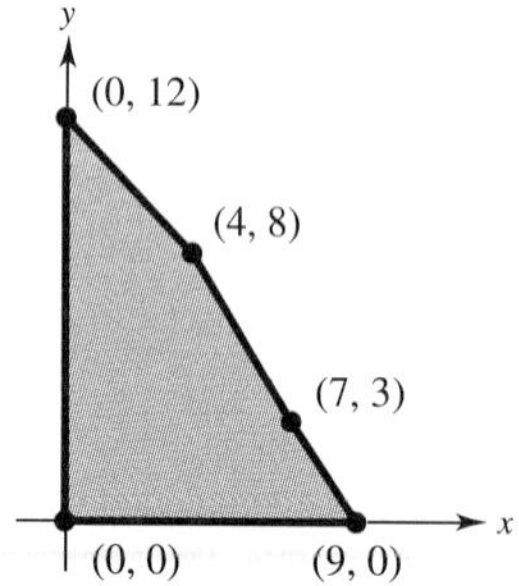

4. $z = .35x + 1.25y$

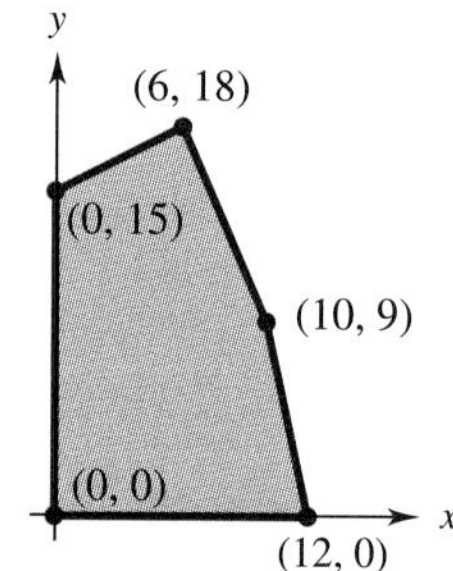

5. **(a)** $z = 4x + 2y$
(b) $z = 2x + yy$
(c) $z = 2x + 4y$
(d) $z = x + 4y$

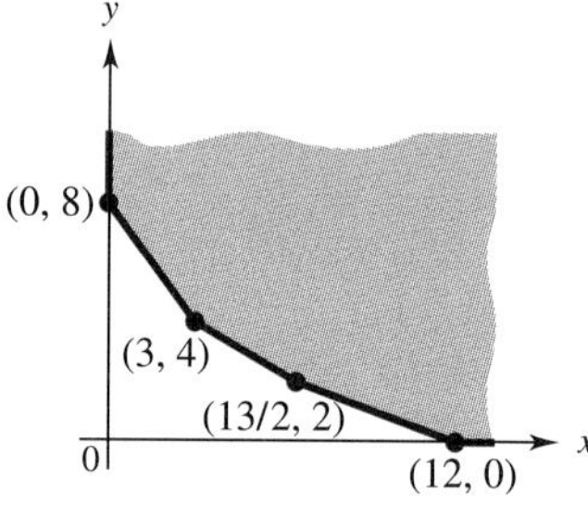

6. **(a)** $z = 4x + y$
(b) $z = 5x + 6y$
(c) $z = x + 2y$
(d) $z = x + 6y$

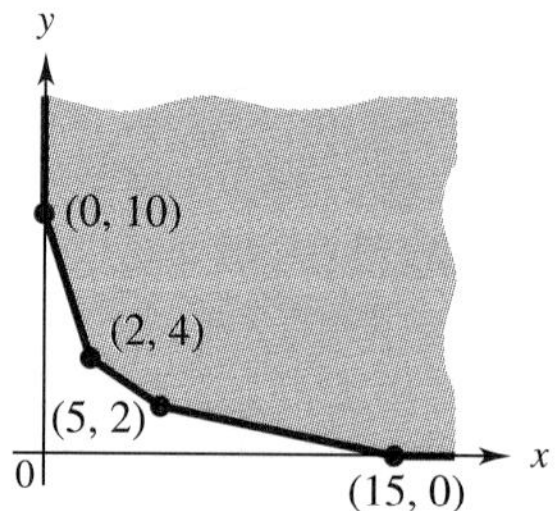

Use graphical methods to solve Exercises 7–12. (See Examples 2–4.)

7. Maximize $z = 5x + 2y$
subject to:
$$2x + 3y \le 6$$
$$4x + y \le 6$$
$$x \ge 0, y \ge 0.$$

8. Minimize $z = x + 3y$
subject to:
$$2x + y \le 10$$
$$5x + 2y \ge 20$$
$$-x + 2y \ge 0$$
$$x \ge 0, y \ge 0.$$

9. Minimize $z = 2x + y$
subject to:
$$3x - y \ge 12$$
$$x + y \le 15$$
$$x \ge 2, y \ge 3.$$

10. Maximize $z = x + 3y$
subject to:
$$2x + 3y \le 100$$
$$5x + 4y \le 200$$
$$x \ge 10, y \ge 20.$$

11. Maximize $z = 4x + 2y$
subject to:
$$x - y \le 10$$
$$5x + 3y \le 75$$
$$x \ge 0, y \ge 0.$$

12. Maximize $z = 4x + 5y$
subject to:
$$10x - 5y \le 100$$
$$20x + 10y \ge 150$$
$$x \ge 0, y \ge 0.$$

Find the minimum and maximum values of $z = 3x + 4y$ (if possible) for each of the following sets of constraints. (See Examples 2–4.)

13.
$$3x + 2y \ge 6$$
$$x + 2y \ge 4$$
$$x \ge 0, y \ge 0$$

14.
$$2x + y \le 20$$
$$10x + y \ge 36$$
$$2x + 5y \ge 36$$

15.
$$x + y \le 6$$
$$-x + y \le 2$$
$$2x - y \le 8$$

16.
$$-x + 2y \le 6$$
$$3x + y \ge 3$$
$$x \ge 0, y \ge 0$$

17. Find values of $x \ge 0$ and $y \ge 0$ that maximize $z = 10x + 12y$ subject to each of the following sets of constraints.

(a) $x + y \le 20$
$x + 3y \le 24$

(b) $3x + y \le 15$
$x + 2y \le 18$

(c) $x + 2y \ge 10$
$2x + y \ge 12$
$x - y \le 8$

18. Find values of $x \ge 0$ and $y \ge 0$ that minimize $z = 3x + 2y$ subject to each of the following sets of constraints.

(a) $10x + 7y \le 42$
$4x + 10y \ge 35$

(b) $6x + 5y \ge 25$
$2x + 6y \ge 15$

(c) $2x + 5y \ge 22$
$4x + 3y \le 28$
$2x + 2y \le 17$

19. Explain why it is impossible to maximize the function $z = 3x + 4y$ subject to the constraints:
$$x + y \ge 8$$
$$2x + y \le 10$$
$$x + 2y \le 8$$
$$x \ge 0, \ y \ge 0$$

20. You are given the following linear programming problem:*

Maximize $z = c_1x_1 + c_2x_2$
subject to:
$$2x_1 + x_2 \le 11$$
$$-x_1 + 2x_2 \le 2$$
$$x_1 \ge 0, x_2 \ge 0.$$

If $c_2 > 0$, determine the range of c_1/c_2 for which $(x_1, x_2) = (4, 3)$ is an optimal solution.

(a) $[-2, 1/2]$

(b) $[-1/2, 2]$

(c) $[-11, -1]$

(d) $[1, 11]$

(e) $[-11, 11]$

---

*Problem from "Course 130 Examination Operations Research" of the *Education and Examination Committee of The Society of Actuaries.* Reprinted by permission of The Society of Actuaries.

8.3 APPLICATIONS OF LINEAR PROGRAMMING

In this section we show several applications of linear programming with two variables.

EXAMPLE 1 A 4-H Club member raises only geese and pigs. She wants to raise no more than 16 animals including no more than 10 geese. She spends \$15 to raise a goose and \$45 to raise a pig, and has \$540 available for this project. Find the maximum profit she can make if each goose produces a profit of \$7 and each pig a profit of \$20.

The total profit is determined by the number of geese and pigs. So let x be the number of geese to be produced, and let y be the number of pigs. Then summarize the information of the problem in a table.

	Number	*Cost to Raise*	*Profit Each*
Geese	x	\$ 15	\$ 7
Pigs	y	45	20
Maximum available	16	\$540	

Use this table to write the necessary constraints. Since the total number of animals cannot exceed 16, the first constraint is

$$x + y \leq 16.$$

"No more than 10 geese" leads to

$$x \leq 10.$$

The cost to raise x geese at \$15 per goose is $15x$ dollars, while the cost for y pigs at \$45 each is $45y$ dollars. Only \$540 is available, so

$$15x + 45y \leq 540.$$

Dividing both sides by 15 gives the equivalent inequality

$$x + 3y \leq 36.$$

The number of geese and pigs cannot be negative, so

$$x \geq 0, \quad y \geq 0.$$

The 4-H Club member wants to know the number of geese and the number of pigs that should be raised for maximum profit. Each goose produces a profit of \$7 and each pig, \$20. If z represents total profit, then

$$z = 7x + 20y$$

is the objective function, which is to be maximized.

We must solve the following linear programming problem.

$$\begin{aligned} \text{Maximize} \quad & z = 7x + 20y && \text{Objective function} \\ \text{subject to:} \quad & \left.\begin{aligned} x + y &\le 16 \\ x &\le 10 \\ x + 3y &\le 36 \\ x \ge 0,\ y &\ge 0. \end{aligned}\right\} && \text{Constraints} \end{aligned}$$

Using the methods of the previous section, graph the feasible region for the system of inequalities given by the constraints as in Figure 8.17.

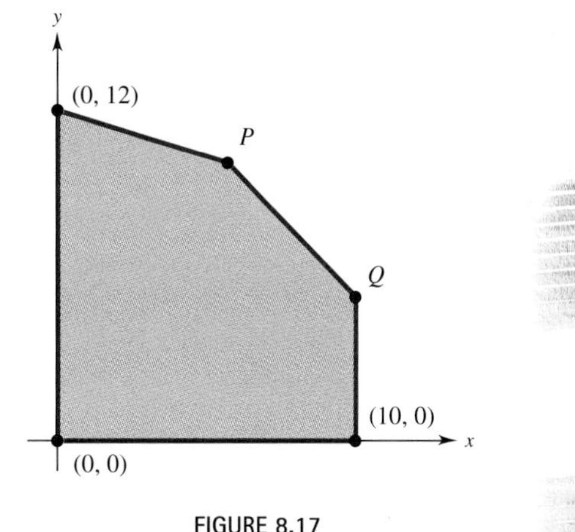

FIGURE 8.17

1 Find the corner points P and Q in Figure 8.17.

Answer:
$P = (6, 10)$
$Q = (10, 6)$

The corner points (0, 12), (0, 0), and (10, 0) can be read directly from the graph. Find the coordinates of the other corner points by solving a system of equations or with a graphing calculator. 1

Test each corner point in the objective function to find the maximum profit.

Corner Point	$z = 7x + 20y$
(0, 12)	7(0) + 20(12) = 240
(6, 10)	**7(6) + 20(10) = 242 (maximum)**
(10, 6)	7(10) + 20(6) = 190
(10, 0)	7(10) + 20(0) = 70
(0, 0)	7(0) + 20(0) = 0

The maximum value for z of 242 occurs at (6, 10). Thus 6 geese and 10 pigs will produce a maximum profit of $242. ■

EXAMPLE 2 An office manager needs to purchase new filing cabinets. He knows that Ace cabinets cost $40 each, require 6 square feet of floor space, and hold 8 cubic feet of files. On the other hand, each Excello cabinet costs $80, requires 8 square feet of floor space, and holds 12 cubic feet. His budget permits him to spend no more than

\$560 on files, while the office has room for no more than 72 square feet of cabinets. The manager desires the greatest storage capacity within the limitations imposed by funds and space. How many of each type of cabinet should he buy?

Let x represent the number of Ace cabinets to be bought and let y represent the number of Excello cabinets. The information given in the problem can be summarized as follows.

	Number	*Cost of Each*	*Space Required*	*Storage Capacity*
Ace	x	\$ 40	6 sq ft	8 cu ft
Excello	y	\$ 80	8 sq ft	12 cu ft
Maximum available		\$560	72 sq ft	

The constraints imposed by cost and space are

$$40x + 80y \leq 560 \quad \text{Cost}$$
$$6x + 8y \leq 72. \quad \text{Floor space}$$

The number of cabinets cannot be negative, so $x \geq 0$ and $y \geq 0$. The objective function to be maximized gives the amount of storage capacity provided by some combination of Ace and Excello cabinets. From the information in the chart, the objective function is

$$\text{Storage space} = z = 8x + 12y.$$

2 Find the corner point labeled Q on the region of feasible solutions given below.

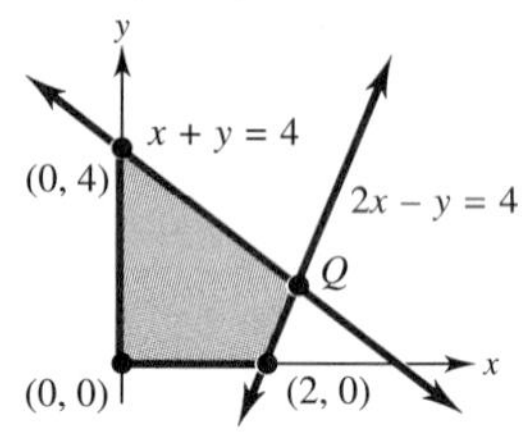

Answer:
(8/3, 4/3)

In summary, the given problem has produced the following linear programming problem.

$$\begin{aligned} \text{Maximize} \quad & z = 8x + 12y \\ \text{subject to:} \quad & 40x + 80y \leq 560 \\ & 6x + 8y \leq 72 \\ & x \geq 0, y \geq 0. \end{aligned}$$

A graph of the feasible region is shown in Figure 8.18. Three of the corner points can be identified from the graph as (0, 0), (0, 7), and (12, 0). The fourth corner point, labeled Q in the figure, can be found algebraically or with a graphing calculator to be (8, 3). 2

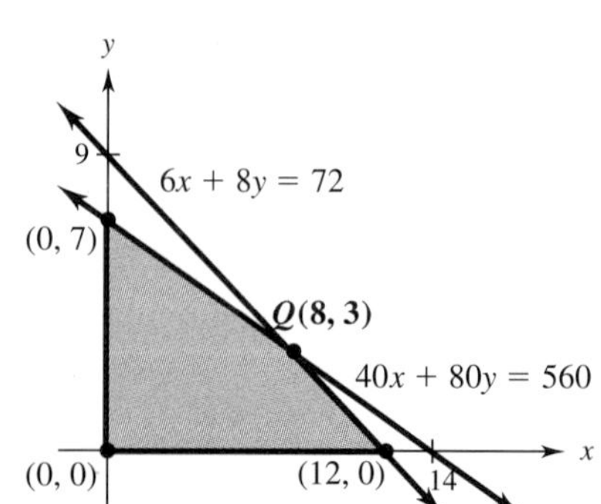

FIGURE 8.18

Use the corner point theorem to find the maximum value of z.

3 A popular cereal combines oats and corn. At least 27 tons of the cereal is to be made. For the best flavor, the amount of corn should be no more than twice the amount of oats. Corn costs \$200 per ton and oats cost \$300 per ton. How much of each grain should be used to minimize the cost?

(a) Make a chart to organize the information given in the problem.

(b) Write an equation for the objective function.

(c) Write four inequalities for the constraints.

Answers:

(a)

	Number of Tons	*Cost/Ton*
Oats	x	\$300
Corn	y	200
	27	

(b) $z = 300x + 200y$

(c) $x + y \geq 27$
$y \leq 2x$
$x \geq 0$
$y \geq 0$

Corner Point	*Value of* $z = 8x + 12y$
(0, 0)	0
(0, 7)	84
(12, 0)	96
(8, 3)	**100 (maximum)**

The objective function, which represents storage space, is maximized when $x = 8$ and $y = 3$. The manager should buy 8 Ace cabinets and 3 Excello cabinets. ■ 3

EXAMPLE 3 Certain laboratory animals must have at least 30 grams of protein and at least 20 grams of fat per feeding period. These nutrients come from food A, which costs 18¢ per unit and supplies 2 grams of protein and 4 of fat, and food B, with 6 grams of protein and 2 of fat, costing 12¢ per unit. Food B is bought under a long-term contract requiring that at least 2 units of B be used per serving. How much of each food must be bought to produce minimum cost per serving?

Let x represent the amount of food A needed, and y the amount of food B. Use the given information to produce the following table.

Food	*Number of Units*	*Grams of Protein*	*Grams of Fat*	*Cost*
A	x	2	4	18¢
B	y	6	2	12¢
Minimum required		30	20	

The linear programming problem can be stated as follows.

$$\begin{aligned} \text{Minimize} \quad & z = .18x + .12y \\ \text{subject to:} \quad & 2x + 6y \geq 30 \\ & 4x + 2y \geq 20 \\ & y \geq 2 \\ & x \geq 0,\ y \geq 0. \end{aligned}$$

(The constraint $y \geq 0$ is redundant because of the constraint $y \geq 2$.) A graph of the feasible region with the corner points identified is shown in Figure 8.19.

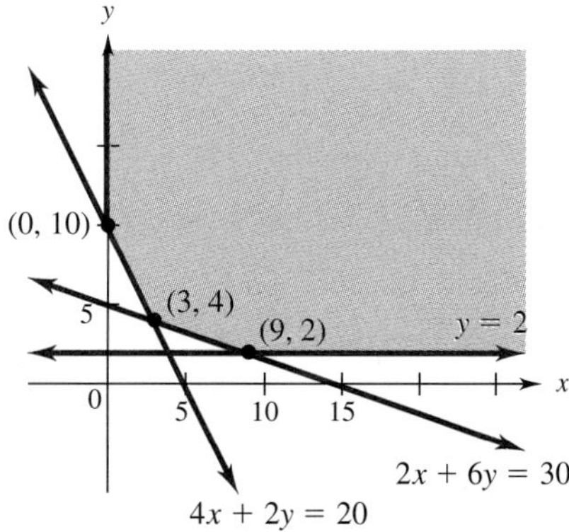

FIGURE 8.19

4 Use the information in Side Problem 3 to do the following.

(a) Graph the feasible region and find the corner points.

(b) Determine the minimum value of the objective function and the point where it occurs.

(c) Is there a maximum cost?

Answers:

(a)

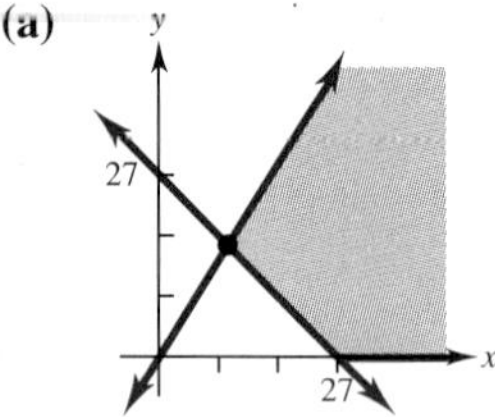

Corner points: (27, 0), (9, 18)

(b) \$6300 at (9, 18)

(c) No

Use the corner point theorem to find the minimum value of z as shown in the chart below.

Corner Points	$z = .18x + .12y$
(0, 10)	.18(0) + .12(10) = 1.20
(3, 4)	**.18(3) + .12(4) = 1.02 (minimum)**
(9, 2)	.18(9) + .12(2) = 1.86

The minimum value of 1.02 occurs at (3, 4). Thus, 3 units of A and 4 units of B will produce a minimum cost of \$1.02 per serving. ■ 4

The feasible region in Figure 8.19 is an unbounded feasible region—the region extends indefinitely to the upper right. With this region it would not be possible to *maximize* the objective function, because the total cost of the food could always be increased by encouraging the animals to eat more.

8.3 EXERCISES

Write the constraints in Exercises 1–5 as linear inequalities and identify all variables used. In some instances, not all of the information is needed to write the constraints. (See Examples 1–3.)

1. A canoe requires 6 hours of fabrication and a rowboat 4 hours. The fabrication department has at most 90 hours of labor available each week.
2. Doug Gilbert needs at least 2400 mg of Vitamin C per day. Each Supervite pill provides 250 mg and each Vitahealth pill provides 350 mg.
3. A candidate can afford to spend no more than \$8500 on radio and TV advertising. Each radio spot costs \$150 and each TV ad costs \$750.
4. A hospital dietician has two meal choices, one for patients on solid food that costs \$2.25, and one for patients on liquids that costs \$3.75. There are a maximum of 400 patients in the hospital.
5. Cashews costing \$8 per pound are to be mixed with peanuts costing \$3 per pound to obtain at least 30 pounds of mixed nuts.
6. An agricultural advisor looks at the results of Example 1 and claims that it cannot possibly be correct. He says that since the 4-H Club member could raise 16 animals, but is only raising 12, she could earn more profit by raising all 16 animals. How would you respond?

Solve the following linear programming problems. (See Examples 1–3.)

7. **Management** Audio City Corporation has warehouses in Meadville and Cambridge. It has 80 stereo systems stored in Meadville and 70 in Cambridge. Superstore orders 35 systems and ValueHouse orders 60. It costs \$8 to ship a system from Meadville to Superstore and \$12 to ship one to ValueHouse. It costs \$10 to ship a system from Cambridge to Superstore and \$13 to ship one to ValueHouse. How should the orders be filled to keep shipping costs as low as possible? What is the minimum shipping cost? (*Hint:* If x systems are shipped from Meadville to Superstore, then $35 - x$ systems are shipped from Cambridge to Superstore.)
8. **Management** A manufacturer of refrigerators must ship at least 100 refrigerators to its two West Coast warehouses. Each warehouse holds a maximum of 100 refrigerators. Warehouse A holds 25 refrigerators already, and warehouse B has 20 on hand. It costs \$12 to ship a refrigerator to warehouse A and \$10 to ship one to warehouse B. Union rules require that at least 300 workers be hired. Shipping a refrigerator to Warehouse A requires 4 workers, while shipping a refrigerator to Warehouse B requires 2 workers. How many refrigerators should be shipped to each warehouse to minimize costs? What is the minimum cost?

9. **Management** A company is considering two insurance plans with the types of coverage and premiums shown in the table below.

	Policy A	*Policy B*
Fire/Theft	\$10,000	\$15,000
Liability	\$180,000	\$120,000
Premium	\$50	\$40

(For example, this means that \$50 buys one unit of plan A, consisting of \$10,000 fire and theft insurance and \$180,000 of liability insurance.)

(a) The company wants at least \$300,000 fire/theft insurance and at least \$3,000,000 liability insurance from these plans. How many units should be purchased from each plan to minimize the cost of the premiums? What is the minimum premium?

(b) Suppose the premium for policy A is reduced to \$25. Now how many units should be purchased from each plan to minimize the cost of the premiums? What is the minimum premium?

10. **Management** Hotnews Magazine publishes a U.S. and a Canadian edition each week. There are 30,000 subscribers in the United States and 20,000 in Canada. Other copies are sold at newsstands. Postage and shipping costs average \$80 per thousand copies for the U.S. and \$60 per thousand copies for Canada. Surveys show that no more than 120,000 copies of each issue can be sold (including subscriptions) and that the number of copies of the Canadian edition should not exceed twice the number of copies of the U.S. edition. The publisher can spend at most \$8400 a month on postage and shipping. If the profit is \$200 for each thousand copies of the U.S. edition and \$150 for each thousand copies of the Canadian edition, how many copies of each version should be printed to earn as large a profit as possible? What is that profit?

11. **Management** The manufacturing process requires that oil refineries must manufacture at least 2 gallons of gasoline for every gallon of fuel oil. To meet the winter demand for fuel oil, at least 3 million gallons a day must be produced. The demand for gasoline is no more than 6.4 million gallons per day. It takes .25 hour to ship each million gallons of gasoline and 1 hour to ship each million gallons of fuel oil out of the warehouse. No more than 4.65 hours are available for shipping. If the refinery sells gasoline for \$1.25 per gallon and fuel oil for \$1 per gallon, how much of each should be produced to maximize revenue? Find the maximum revenue.

12. **Natural Science** Kim Walrath has a nutritional deficiency and is told to take at least 2400 mg of iron, 2100 mg of Vitamin B-1, and 1500 mg of Vitamin B-2. One Maxivite pill contains 40 mg of iron, 10 mg of B-1, and 5 mg of B-2, and costs 6¢. One Healthovite pill provides 10 mg of iron, 15 mg of B-1, and 15 mg of B-2, and costs 8¢. What combination of Maxivite and Healthovite pills will meet the requirement at lowest cost? What is the minimum cost?

13. **Management** A machine shop manufactures two types of bolts. The bolts require time on each of three groups of machines, but the time required on each group differs, as shown in the table below.

		MACHINE GROUP		
		I	*II*	*III*
BOLTS	Type 1	.1 min	.1 min	.1 min
	Type 2	.1 min	.4 min	.02 min

Production schedules are made up one day at a time. In a day there are 240, 720, and 160 min available, respectively, on these machines. Type 1 bolts sell for 10¢ and type 2 bolts for 12¢. How many of each type of bolt should be manufactured per day to maximize revenue? What is the maximum revenue?

14. **Management** The Miers Company produces small engines for several manufacturers. The company receives orders from two assembly plants for their Topflight engine. Plant I needs at least 50 engines, and plant II needs at least 27 engines. The company can send at most 85 engines to these two assembly plants. It costs \$20 per engine to ship to plant I and \$35 per engine to ship to plant II. Plant I gives Miers \$15 in rebates towards its products for each engine they buy, while plant II gives similar \$10 rebates. Miers estimates that they need at least \$1110 in rebates to cover products they plan to buy from the two plants. How many engines should be shipped to each plant to minimize shipping costs? What is the minimum cost?

15. **Management** A small country can grow only two crops for export, coffee and cocoa. The country has 500,000 hectares of land available for the crops. Long-term contracts require that at least 100,000 hectares be devoted to coffee and at least 200,000 hectares to cocoa. Cocoa must be processed locally, and production bottlenecks limit cocoa to 270,000 hectares. Coffee requires two workers per hectare, with cocoa requiring five. No more than 1,750,000 people are available for working with these crops. Coffee produces a profit of \$220 per hectare and cocoa a profit of \$310 per hectare. How many hectares should the country devote to each crop in order to maximize profit? Find the maximum profit.

16. **Management** 60 pounds of chocolates and 100 pounds of mints are available to make up 5-pound boxes of candy. A regular box has 4 pounds of chocolates and 1 pound of mints and sells for \$10. A deluxe box has 2 pounds of chocolates and 3 pounds of mints and sells for \$16. How

many boxes of each kind should be made to maximize revenue?

17. Management A greeting card manufacturer has 370 boxes of a particular card in warehouse I and 290 boxes of the same card in warehouse II. A greeting card shop in San Jose orders 350 boxes of the card, and another shop in Memphis orders 300 boxes. The shipping costs per box to these shops from the two warehouses are shown in the following table.

		DESTINATION	
		San Jose	*Memphis*
WAREHOUSE	I	\$.25	\$.22
	II	\$.23	\$.21

How many boxes should be shipped to each city from each warehouse to minimize shipping costs? What is the minimum cost? (*Hint:* Use x, $350 - x$, y, and $300 - y$ as the variables.)

18. Management A pension fund manager decides to invest at most \$40 million in U.S. Treasury Bonds paying 8% annual interest and in mutual funds paying 12% annual interest. He plans to invest at least \$20 million in bonds and at least \$15 million in mutual funds. Bonds have an initial fee of \$300 per million dollars, while the fee for mutual funds is \$100 per million. The fund manager is allowed to spend no more than \$8400 on fees. How much should be invested in each to maximize annual interest? What is the maximum annual interest?

19. Natural Science A certain predator requires at least 10 units of protein and 8 units of fat per day. One prey of Species I provides 5 units of protein and 2 units of fat; one prey of Species II provides 3 units of protein and 4 units of fat. Capturing and digesting each Species II prey requires 3 units of energy, and capturing and digesting each Species I prey requires 2 units of energy. How many of each prey would meet the predator's daily food requirements with the least expenditure of energy? Are the answers reasonable? How could they be interpreted?

20. Management In a small town in South Carolina, zoning rules require that the window space (in square feet) in a house be at least one-sixth of the space used up by solid walls. The cost to build windows is \$10 per square foot, while the cost to build solid walls is \$20 per square foot. The total amount available for building walls and windows is no more than \$12,000. The estimated monthly cost to heat the house is \$.32 for each square foot of windows and \$.20 for each square foot of solid walls. Find the maximum total area (windows plus walls) if no more than \$160 per month is available to pay for heat.

21. Social Science Students at Upscale U are required to take at least 3 humanities and 4 science courses. The maximum allowable number of science courses is 12. Each humanities course carries 4 credits and each science course 5 credits. The total number of credits in science and humanities cannot exceed 80. Quality points for each course are assigned in the usual way: the number of credit hours times 4 for an A grade; times 3 for a B grade; times 2 for a C grade. Susan Katz expects to get B's in all her science courses. She expects to get C's in half her humanities courses, B's in one-fourth of them, and A's in the rest. Under these assumptions, how many courses of each kind should she take in order to earn the maximum possible number of quality points?

22. Social Science In Exercise 21, find Susan's grade point average (the total number of quality points divided by the total number of credit hours) at each corner point of the feasible region. Does the distribution of courses that produces the highest number of quality points also yield the highest grade point average? Is this a contradiction?

*The importance of linear programming is shown by the inclusion of linear programming problems on most qualification examinations for Certified Public Accountants. Exercises 23–25 are reprinted from one such examination.**

The Random Company manufactures two products, Zeta and Beta. Each product must pass through two processing operations. All materials are introduced at the start of Process No. 1. There are no work-in-process inventories. Random may produce either one product exclusively or various combinations of both products subject to the following constraints.

	Process No. 1	*Process No. 2*	*Contribution Margin Per Unit*
Hours required to produce 1 unit of:			
Zeta	1 hour	1 hour	\$4.00
Beta	2 hours	3 hours	5.25
Total capacity in hours per day	1000 hours	1275 hours	

A shortage of technical labor has limited Beta production to 400 units per day. There are no constraints on the production of Zeta other than the hour constraints in the above schedule. Assume that all the relationships between capacity and production are linear.

*Material from *Uniform CPA Examinations and Unofficial Answers,* copyright © 1973, 1974, 1975 by the American Institute of Certified Public Accountants, Inc., is reprinted with permission.

23. Given the objective to maximize total contribution margin, what is the production constraint for Process No. 1?
(a) Zeta + Beta ≤ 1000
(b) Zeta + 2 Beta ≤ 1000
(c) Zeta + Beta ≥ 1000
(d) Zeta + 2 Beta ≥ 1000

24. Given the objective to maximize total contribution margin, what is the labor constraint for production of Beta?
(a) Beta ≤ 400 (b) Beta ≥ 400
(c) Beta ≤ 425 (d) Beta ≥ 425

25. What is the objective function of the data presented?
(a) Zeta + 2 Beta = \$9.25
(b) \$4.00 Zeta + 3(\$5.25) Beta = total contribution margin
(c) \$4.00 Zeta + \$5.25 Beta = total contribution margin
(d) 2(\$4.00) Zeta + 3(\$5.25) Beta = total contribution margin

8.4 THE SIMPLEX METHOD: MAXIMIZATION

For linear programming problems with more than two variables or with two variables and many constraints, the graphical method is usually too inefficient, so the **simplex method** is used. The simplex method, which is introduced here, was developed for the U.S. Air Force by George B. Danzig in 1947. It was used successfully during the Berlin airlift in 1948–49 to maximize the amount of cargo delivered under very severe constraints and is widely used today in a variety of industries.

Because the simplex method is used for problems with many variables, it usually is not convenient to use letters such as x, y, z, or w as variable names. Instead, the symbols x_1 (read "x-sub-one"), x_2, x_3, and so on, are used. In the simplex method, all constraints must be expressed in the linear form

$$a_1x_1 + a_2x_2 + a_3x_3 + \cdots \le b,$$

where $x_1, x_2, x_3, \ldots$ are variables, $a_1, a_2, a_3, \ldots$ are coefficients, and b is a constant.

We first discuss the simplex method for linear programming problems in *standard maximum form.*

STANDARD MAXIMUM FORM

A linear programming problem is in **standard maximum form** if

1. the objective function is to be maximized;
2. all variables are nonnegative ($x_i \ge 0$, $i = 1, 2, 3, \ldots$);
3. all constraints involve $\le$;
4. the constants on the right side in the constraints are all nonnegative ($b \ge 0$).

Problems that do not meet all of these conditions are considered in Sections 8.6 and 8.7.

The "mechanics" of the simplex method are demonstrated in Examples 1–5. Although the procedures to be followed will be made clear, as will the fact that they result in an optimal solution, the reasons why these procedures are used may not be immediately apparent. Examples 6 and 7 will supply these reasons and explain the connection between the simplex method and the graphical method used in Section 8.3.

SETTING UP THE PROBLEM The first step is to convert each constraint, a linear inequality, into a linear equation. This is done by adding a nonnegative variable, called a **slack variable,** to each constraint. For example, convert the inequality $x_1 + x_2 \leq 10$ into an equation by adding the slack variable x_3, to get

$$x_1 + x_2 + x_3 = 10, \quad \text{where } x_3 \geq 0.$$

The inequality $x_1 + x_2 \leq 10$ says that the sum $x_1 + x_2$ is less than or perhaps equal to 10. The variable x_3 "takes up any slack" and represents the amount by which $x_1 + x_2$ fails to equal 10. For example, if $x_1 + x_2$ equals 8, then x_3 is 2. If $x_1 + x_2 = 10$, the value of x_3 is 0.

CAUTION A different slack variable must be used for each constraint. ◆

EXAMPLE 1 Restate the following linear programming problem by introducing slack variables.

$$\begin{aligned} \text{Maximize} \quad & z = 2x_1 + 3x_2 + x_3 \\ \text{subject to:} \quad & x_1 + x_2 + 4x_3 \leq 100 \\ & x_1 + 2x_2 + x_3 \leq 150 \\ & 3x_1 + 2x_2 + x_3 \leq 320 \\ \text{with} \quad & x_1 \geq 0, x_2 \geq 0, x_3 \geq 0. \end{aligned}$$

Rewrite the three constraints as equations by introducing nonnegative slack variables x_4, x_5, and x_6, one for each constraint. Then the problem can be restated as

$$\begin{aligned} \text{Maximize} \quad & z = 2x_1 + 3x_2 + x_3 \\ \text{subject to:} \quad & x_1 + x_2 + 4x_3 + x_4 = 100 \\ & x_1 + 2x_2 + x_3 + x_5 = 150 \\ & 3x_1 + 2x_2 + x_3 + x_6 = 320 \\ \text{with} \quad & x_1 \geq 0, x_2 \geq 0, x_3 \geq 0, x_4 \geq 0, x_5 \geq 0, x_6 \geq 0. \end{aligned}$$ ■ 1

1 Rewrite the following set of constraints as equations by adding nonnegative slack variables.

$$\begin{aligned} x_1 + x_2 + x_3 &\leq 12 \\ 2x_1 + 4x_2 &\leq 15 \\ x_2 + 3x_3 &\leq 10 \end{aligned}$$

Answer:

$$\begin{aligned} x_1 + x_2 + x_3 + x_4 &= 12 \\ 2x_1 + 4x_2 + x_5 &= 15 \\ x_2 + 3x_3 + x_6 &= 10 \end{aligned}$$

Adding slack variables to the constraints converts a linear programming problem into a system of linear equations. These equations should have all variables on the left of the equals sign and all constants on the right. All the equations of Example 1 satisfy this condition except for the objective function, $z = 2x_1 + 3x_2 + x_3$, which may be written with all variables on the left as

$$-2x_1 - 3x_2 - x_3 + z = 0.$$

Now the equations of Example 1 (with the constraints listed first) can be written as the following augmented matrix.

$$\begin{array}{ccccccc|c} x_1 & x_2 & x_3 & x_4 & x_5 & x_6 & z & \\ 1 & 1 & 4 & 1 & 0 & 0 & 0 & 100 \\ 1 & 2 & 1 & 0 & 1 & 0 & 0 & 150 \\ 3 & 2 & 1 & 0 & 0 & 1 & 0 & 320 \\ \hline -2 & -3 & -1 & 0 & 0 & 0 & 1 & 0 \end{array}$$

Indicators

2 Set up the initial simplex tableau for the following linear programming problem:

Maximize $z = 2x_1 + 3x_2$

subject to:

$$x_1 + 2x_2 \le 85$$
$$2x_1 + x_2 \le 92$$
$$x_1 + 4x_2 \le 104$$

with $x_1 \ge 0, x_2 \ge 0$.

Answer:

x_1	x_2	x_3	x_4	x_5	z	
1	2	1	0	0	0	85
2	1	0	1	0	0	92
1	4	0	0	1	0	104
−2	−3	0	0	0	1	0

This matrix is the initial **simplex tableau.** Except for the last entries, the 1 and 0 on the right end, the numbers in the bottom row of a simplex tableau are called **indicators.** 2

This simplex tableau represents a system of 4 linear equations in 7 variables. Since there are more variables than equations, the system is dependent and has infinitely many solutions. Our goal is to find a solution in which all the variables are nonnegative and z is as large as possible. This will be done by using row operations to replace the given system by an equivalent one in which certain variables are eliminated from some of the equations. The process will be repeated until the optimum solution can be read from the matrix, as explained below.

SELECTING THE PIVOT Recall how row operations are used to eliminate variables in the Gauss-Jordan method. A particular nonzero entry in the matrix is chosen and changed to a 1; then all other entries in that column are changed to zeros. A similar process is used in the simplex method. The chosen entry is called the **pivot.** The procedure for selecting the appropriate pivot in the simplex method is explained in the next example. The reason why this procedure is used is discussed in Example 7.

TECHNOLOGY TIP A graphing calculator provides an efficient method for doing the row operations in the discussion below, so you may want to enter the initial simplex tableau of Example 1 on your calculator and perform the various operations on it as you read the following examples. Because of its size this simplex tableau will not fit on a calculator screen. Instead, you will see something like Figure 8.20(a), which shows only the left half of the tableau. Use the left and right arrow keys to scroll through the entire matrix and obtain its other half, as in Figure 8.20(b). Note that the calculator does not put a vertical line before the last column, as we do when working by hand. ✔

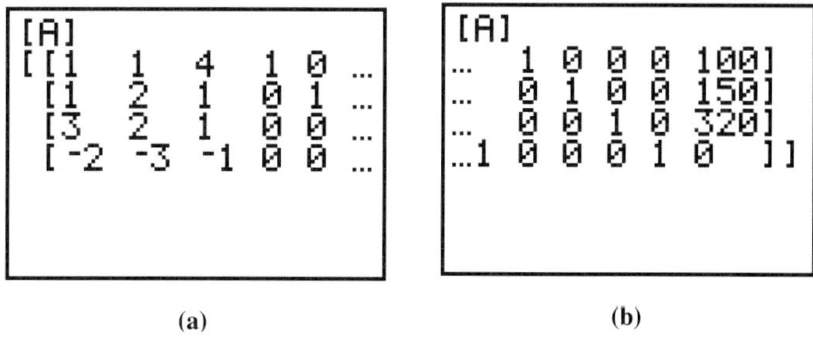

(a) (b)

FIGURE 8.20

EXAMPLE 2 Determine the pivot in the simplex tableau for the problem in Example 1.

Look at the indicators (the last row of the tableau) and choose the most negative one.

x_1	x_2	x_3	x_4	x_5	x_6	z	
1	1	4	1	0	0	0	100
1	2	1	0	1	0	0	150
3	2	1	0	0	1	0	320
−2	**−3**	−1	0	0	0	1	0

↑ Most negative indicator

The most negative indicator identifies the variable that is to be eliminated from all but one of the equations (rows), in this case x_2. The column containing the most negative indicator is called the **pivot column.** Now for each *positive* entry in the pivot column, divide the number in the far right column of the same row by the positive number in the pivot column.

x_1	x_2	x_3	x_4	x_5	x_6	z		Quotients
1	**1**	4	1	0	0	0	**100**	100/1 = 100
1	**2**	1	0	1	0	0	**150**	150/2 = 75← Smallest
3	**2**	1	0	0	1	0	**320**	320/2 = 160
−2	−3	−1	0	0	0	1	0	

The row with the smallest quotient (in this case, the second row) is called the **pivot row.** The entry in the pivot row and pivot column is the pivot.

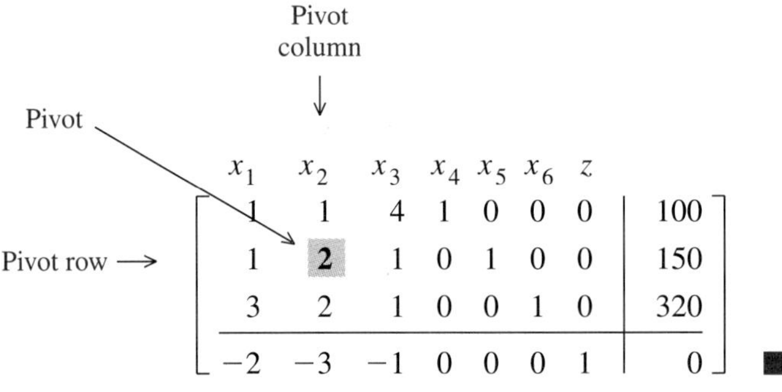

x_1	x_2	x_3	x_4	x_5	x_6	z	
1	1	4	1	0	0	0	100
1	**2**	1	0	1	0	0	150
3	2	1	0	0	1	0	320
−2	−3	−1	0	0	0	1	0

■

3 Find the pivot for the following tableau.

x_1	x_2	x_3	x_4	x_5	z	
0	1	1	0	0	0	50
−2	3	0	1	0	0	78
2	4	0	0	1	0	65
−5	−3	0	0	0	1	0

Answer:
2 (in first column)

CAUTION In some simplex tableaus the pivot column may contain zeros or negative entries. Only the positive entries in the pivot column should be used to form the quotients and determine the pivot row. If there are no positive entries in the pivot column (so that a pivot row cannot be chosen), then no maximum solution exists. ◆ 3

PIVOTING Once the pivot has been selected, row operations are used to replace the initial simplex tableau by another simplex tableau in which the pivot column variable is eliminated from all but one of the equations. Since this new tableau is obtained by row operations, it represents an equivalent system of equations (that is, a system with the same solutions as the original system). This process, which is called **pivoting,** is explained in the next example.

EXAMPLE 3 Use the indicated pivot, 2, to perform the pivoting on the simplex tableau of Example 2:

x_1	x_2	x_3	x_4	x_5	x_6	z	
1	1	4	1	0	0	0	100
1	**2**	1	0	1	0	0	150
3	2	1	0	0	1	0	320
−2	−3	−1	0	0	0	1	0

.

Start by multiplying each entry of row two by 1/2 in order to change the pivot to 1.

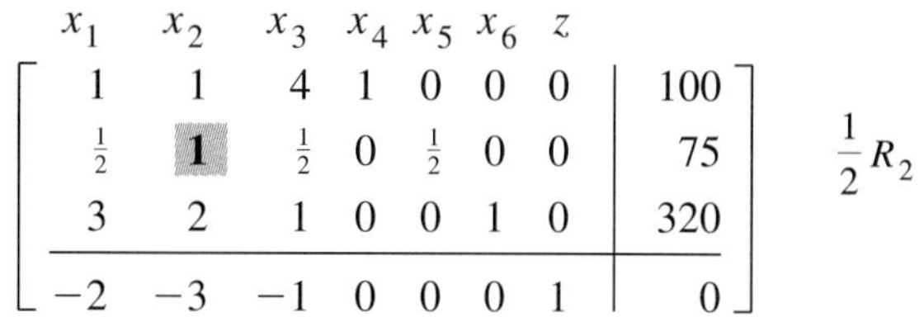

$$\begin{array}{ccccccc|c} x_1 & x_2 & x_3 & x_4 & x_5 & x_6 & z & \\ 1 & 1 & 4 & 1 & 0 & 0 & 0 & 100 \\ \frac{1}{2} & \boxed{1} & \frac{1}{2} & 0 & \frac{1}{2} & 0 & 0 & 75 \\ 3 & 2 & 1 & 0 & 0 & 1 & 0 & 320 \\ \hline -2 & -3 & -1 & 0 & 0 & 0 & 1 & 0 \end{array} \quad \frac{1}{2}R_2$$

Now use row operations to make the entry in row one, column two a 0.

$$\begin{array}{ccccccc|c} x_1 & x_2 & x_3 & x_4 & x_5 & x_6 & z & \\ \frac{1}{2} & 0 & \frac{7}{2} & 1 & -\frac{1}{2} & 0 & 0 & 25 \\ \frac{1}{2} & 1 & \frac{1}{2} & 0 & \frac{1}{2} & 0 & 0 & 75 \\ 3 & 2 & 1 & 0 & 0 & 1 & 0 & 320 \\ \hline -2 & -3 & -1 & 0 & 0 & 0 & 1 & 0 \end{array} \quad -R_2 + R_1$$

Change the 2 in row three, column two to a 0 by a similar process.

$$\begin{array}{ccccccc|c} x_1 & x_2 & x_3 & x_4 & x_5 & x_6 & z & \\ \frac{1}{2} & 0 & \frac{7}{2} & 1 & -\frac{1}{2} & 0 & 0 & 25 \\ \frac{1}{2} & 1 & \frac{1}{2} & 0 & \frac{1}{2} & 0 & 0 & 75 \\ 2 & 0 & 0 & 0 & -1 & 1 & 0 & 170 \\ \hline -2 & -3 & -1 & 0 & 0 & 0 & 1 & 0 \end{array} \quad -2R_2 + R_3$$

Finally, add 3 times row 2 to the last row in order to change the indicator -3 to 0.

$$\begin{array}{ccccccc|c} x_1 & x_2 & x_3 & x_4 & x_5 & x_6 & z & \\ \frac{1}{2} & 0 & \frac{7}{2} & 1 & -\frac{1}{2} & 0 & 0 & 25 \\ \frac{1}{2} & 1 & \frac{1}{2} & 0 & \frac{1}{2} & 0 & 0 & 75 \\ 2 & 0 & 0 & 0 & -1 & 1 & 0 & 170 \\ \hline -\frac{1}{2} & 0 & \frac{1}{2} & 0 & \frac{3}{2} & 0 & 1 & 225 \end{array} \quad 3R_2 + R_4$$

The pivoting is now complete because the pivot column variable x_2 has been eliminated from all equations except the one represented by the pivot row. The initial simplex tableau has been replaced by a new simplex tableau, which represents an equivalent system of equations. ■

CAUTION During pivoting, do not interchange rows of the matrix. Make the pivot entry 1 by multiplying the pivot row by an appropriate constant, as in Example 3. ◆ 4

4 For the simplex tableau below,

(a) find the pivot.

(b) Perform the pivoting and write the new tableau.

$$\begin{array}{cccccc|c} x_1 & x_2 & x_3 & x_4 & x_5 & z & \\ 1 & 2 & 6 & 1 & 0 & 0 & 16 \\ 1 & 3 & 0 & 0 & 1 & 0 & 25 \\ \hline -1 & -4 & -3 & 0 & 0 & 1 & 0 \end{array}$$

Answers:

(a) 2

(b)

$$\begin{array}{cccccc|c} x_1 & x_2 & x_3 & x_4 & x_5 & z & \\ \frac{1}{2} & 1 & 3 & \frac{1}{2} & 0 & 0 & 8 \\ -\frac{1}{2} & 0 & -9 & -\frac{3}{2} & 1 & 0 & 1 \\ \hline 1 & 0 & 9 & 2 & 0 & 1 & 32 \end{array}$$

When at least one of the indicators in the last row of a simplex tableau is negative (as is the case with the tableau obtained in Example 3), the simplex method requires that a new pivot be selected and the pivoting be performed again. This procedure is repeated until a simplex tableau with no negative indicators in the last row is obtained or a tableau is reached in which no pivot row can be chosen.

EXAMPLE 4 In the simplex tableau obtained in Example 3, select a new pivot and perform the pivoting.

First, locate the pivot column by finding the most negative indicator in the last row. Then locate the pivot row by computing the necessary quotients and finding the smallest one, as shown here.

$$\text{Pivot row} \longrightarrow \begin{array}{c} \begin{array}{ccccccc} x_1 & x_2 & x_3 & x_4 & x_5 & x_6 & z \end{array} \\ \left[\begin{array}{ccccccc|c} \frac{1}{2} & 0 & \frac{7}{2} & 1 & -\frac{1}{2} & 0 & 0 & 25 \\ \frac{1}{2} & 1 & \frac{1}{2} & 0 & \frac{1}{2} & 0 & 0 & 75 \\ 2 & 0 & 0 & 0 & -1 & 1 & 0 & 170 \\ \hline -\frac{1}{2} & 0 & \frac{1}{2} & 0 & \frac{3}{2} & 0 & 1 & 225 \end{array}\right] \end{array} \quad \begin{array}{l} \text{Quotients} \\ \dfrac{25}{1/2} = 50 \quad \text{Smallest} \\ \dfrac{75}{1/2} = 150 \\ 170/2 = 85 \\ \\ \end{array}$$

↑ Pivot column

So the pivot is the number 1/2 in row one, column one. Begin the pivoting by multiplying every entry in row one by 2. Then continue as indicated below, to obtain the following simplex tableau.

$$\begin{array}{c} \begin{array}{ccccccc} x_1 & x_2 & x_3 & x_4 & x_5 & x_6 & z \end{array} \\ \left[\begin{array}{ccccccc|c} 1 & 0 & 7 & 2 & -1 & 0 & 0 & 50 \\ 0 & 1 & -3 & -1 & 1 & 0 & 0 & 50 \\ 0 & 0 & -14 & -4 & 1 & 1 & 0 & 70 \\ \hline 0 & 0 & 4 & 1 & 1 & 0 & 1 & 250 \end{array}\right] \end{array} \quad \begin{array}{l} 2R_1 \\ -\frac{1}{2}R_1 + R_2 \\ -2R_1 + R_3 \\ \frac{1}{2}R_1 + R_4 \end{array}$$

Since there are no negative indicators in the last row, no further pivoting is necessary and we call this the **final simplex tableau.** ■

READING THE SOLUTION The next example shows how to read an optimal solution of the original linear programming problem from the final simplex tableau.

EXAMPLE 5 Solve the linear programming problem introduced in Example 1.

Look at the final simplex tableau for this problem, which was obtained in Example 4.

$$\begin{array}{c} \begin{array}{ccccccc} x_1 & x_2 & x_3 & x_4 & x_5 & x_6 & z \end{array} \\ \left[\begin{array}{ccccccc|c} 1 & 0 & 7 & 2 & -1 & 0 & 0 & 50 \\ 0 & 1 & -3 & -1 & 1 & 0 & 0 & 50 \\ 0 & 0 & -14 & -4 & 1 & 1 & 0 & 70 \\ \hline 0 & 0 & 4 & 1 & 1 & 0 & 1 & 250 \end{array}\right] \end{array}$$

The last row of this matrix represents the equation

$$4x_3 + x_4 + x_5 + z = 250, \quad \text{or equivalently,} \quad z = 250 - 4x_3 - x_4 - x_5.$$

If x_3, x_4, and x_5 are all 0, then the value of z is 250. If any one of x_3, x_4, or x_5 is positive, then z will have a smaller value than 250 (why?). Consequently, since we want a solution for this system in which all the variables are nonnegative and z is as large as possible, we must have

$$x_3 = 0, \quad x_4 = 0, \quad x_5 = 0.$$

When these values are substituted in the first equation (represented by the first row of the final simplex tableau), the result is

$$x_1 + 7 \cdot 0 + 2 \cdot 0 - 1 \cdot 0 = 50, \quad \text{that is,} \quad x_1 = 50.$$

Similarly, substituting 0 for x_3, x_4, and x_5 in the last three equations represented by the final simplex tableau shows that

$$x_2 = 50, \quad x_6 = 70, \quad z = 250.$$

Therefore, the maximum value of $z = 2x_1 + 3x_2 + x_3$ occurs when

$$x_1 = 50, \quad x_2 = 50, \quad x_3 = 0,$$

in which case $z = 2 \cdot 50 + 3 \cdot 50 + 0 = 250$. (The values of the slack variables are irrelevant in stating the solution of the original problem.) ■

In any simplex tableau, some columns look like columns of an identity matrix (one entry is 1, the rest are 0). The variables corresponding to these columns are called **basic variables** and the variables corresponding to the other columns **nonbasic variables.** In the tableau of Example 5, for instance, the basic variables are x_1, x_2, x_6, and z (shown in color below), and the nonbasic variables are x_3, x_4, and x_5.

$$\begin{array}{c} \begin{matrix} x_1 & x_2 & x_3 & x_4 & x_5 & x_6 & z & \end{matrix} \\ \left[\begin{array}{ccccccc|c} 1 & 0 & 7 & 2 & -1 & 0 & 0 & 50 \\ 0 & 1 & -3 & -1 & 1 & 0 & 0 & 50 \\ 0 & 0 & -14 & -4 & 1 & 1 & 0 & 70 \\ \hline 0 & 0 & 4 & 1 & 1 & 0 & 1 & 250 \end{array}\right] \end{array}$$

5 A linear programming problem with slack variables x_4 and x_5 has the final simplex tableau shown below. What is the optimal solution?

$$\begin{array}{c} \begin{matrix} x_1 & x_2 & x_3 & x_4 & x_5 & z & \end{matrix} \\ \left[\begin{array}{cccccc|c} 0 & 3 & 1 & 5 & 2 & 0 & 9 \\ 1 & -2 & 0 & 4 & 1 & 0 & 6 \\ \hline 0 & 5 & 0 & 1 & 0 & 1 & 21 \end{array}\right] \end{array}$$

Answer:
$z = 21$ when $x_1 = 6$, $x_2 = 0$, $x_3 = 9$.

The optimal solution in Example 5 was obtained from the final simplex tableau by setting the nonbasic variables equal to 0 and solving for the basic variables. Furthermore, the values of the basic variables are easy to read off the matrix: find the 1 in the column representing a basic variable; the last entry in that row is the value of that basic variable in the optimal solution. In particular, *the entry in the lower right-hand corner of the final simplex tableau is the maximum value of z.* **5**

CAUTION If there are two identical columns in a tableau, each of which is a column in an identity matrix, only one of the variables corresponding to these columns can be a basic variable. The other is treated as a nonbasic variable. You may choose either one to be the basic variable, unless one of them is z, in which case z must be the basic variable. ◆

The steps involved in solving a standard maximum linear programming problem by the simplex method have been illustrated in Examples 1–5 and are summarized here.

SIMPLEX METHOD

1. Determine the objective function.
2. Write all necessary constraints.
3. Convert each constraint into an equation by adding slack variables.
4. Set up the initial simplex tableau.
5. Locate the most negative indicator. If there are two such indicators, choose one. This indicator determines the pivot column.
6. Use the positive entries in the pivot column to form the quotients necessary for determining the pivot. If there are no positive entries in the pivot column,

continued

no maximum solution exists. If two quotients are equally the smallest, let either determine the pivot.*

7. Multiply every entry in the pivot row by the reciprocal of the pivot to change the pivot to 1. Then use row operations to change all other entries in the pivot column to 0 by adding suitable multiples of the pivot row to the other rows. (These steps can be done with a graphing calculator.)
8. If the indicators are all positive or 0, this is the final tableau. If not, go back to Step 5 above and repeat the process until a tableau with no negative indicators is obtained.†
9. Determine the basic and nonbasic variables and read the solution from the final tableau. The maximum value of the objective function is the number in the lower right-hand corner of the final tableau.

6 A linear programming problem has the initial tableau given below. Use the simplex method to solve the problem.

x_1	x_2	x_3	x_4	z	
1	1	1	0	0	40
2	1	0	1	0	24
−300	−200	0	0	1	0

Answer:
$x_1 = 0, x_2 = 24, x_3 = 16,$
$x_4 = 0, z = 4800$

The solution found by the simplex method may not be unique, especially when choices are possible in steps 5, 6, or 9. There may be other solutions that produce the same maximum value of the objective function. (See Exercises 37 and 38.) 6

GEOMETRIC INTERPRETATION OF THE SIMPLEX METHOD Although it may not be immediately apparent, the simplex method is based on the same geometrical considerations as the graphical method. This can be seen by looking at a problem that can be readily solved by both methods.

EXAMPLE 6 In Example 2 of Section 8.3 the following problem was solved graphically (using x, y instead of x_1, x_2):

$$\begin{aligned} \text{Maximize} \quad & z = 8x_1 + 12x_2 \\ \text{subject to:} \quad & 40x_1 + 80x_2 \le 560 \\ & 6x_1 + 8x_2 \le 72 \\ & x_1 \ge 0, x_2 \ge 0. \end{aligned}$$

Graphing the feasible region (Figure 8.21) and evaluating z at each corner point shows that the maximum value of z occurs at (8, 3).

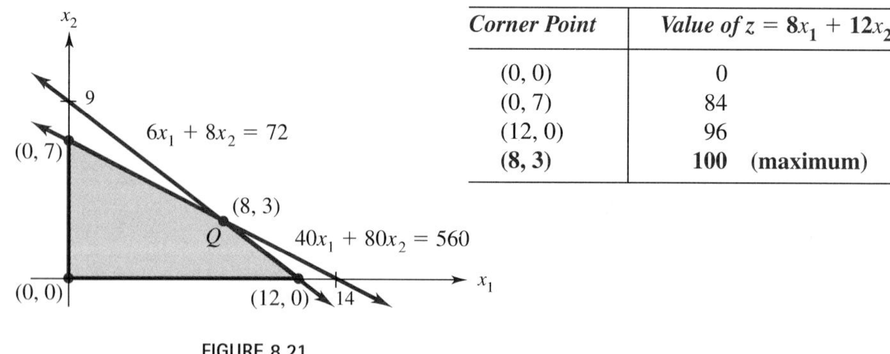

FIGURE 8.21

Corner Point	*Value of* $z = 8x_1 + 12x_2$
(0, 0)	0
(0, 7)	84
(12, 0)	96
(8, 3)	**100 (maximum)**

*It may be that the first choice of a pivot does not produce a solution. In that case try the other choice.

†Some special circumstances are noted at the end of Section 8.7.

To solve the same problem by the simplex method, add a slack variable to each constraint.

$$\begin{aligned} 40x_1 + 80x_2 + x_3 \quad\quad &= 560 \\ 6x_1 + \ 8x_2 \quad\quad + x_4 &= 72 \end{aligned}$$

Then write the initial simplex tableau.

$$\begin{array}{c} \begin{matrix} x_1 & x_2 & x_3 & x_4 & z & \end{matrix} \\ \left[\begin{array}{rrrrr|r} 40 & 80 & 1 & 0 & 0 & 560 \\ 6 & 8 & 0 & 1 & 0 & 72 \\ \hline -8 & -12 & 0 & 0 & 1 & 0 \end{array}\right] \end{array}$$

In this tableau the basic variables are x_3, x_4, and z (why?). By setting the nonbasic variables (namely, x_1 and x_2) equal to 0 and solving for the basic variables, we obtain the following solution (which will be called a **basic feasible solution**):

$$x_1 = 0, \quad x_2 = 0, \quad x_3 = 560, \quad x_4 = 72, \quad z = 0.$$

Since $x_1 = 0$ and $x_2 = 0$, this solution corresponds to the corner point at the origin in the graphical solution (Figure 8.21). The value $z = 0$ at the origin is obviously not maximal and pivoting in the simplex method is designed to improve it.

The most negative indicator in the initial tableau is -12 and the necessary quotients are

$$\frac{560}{80} = 7 \quad \text{and} \quad \frac{72}{8} = 9.$$

The smaller quotient is 7, giving 80 as the pivot. Performing the pivoting leads to this tableau.

$$\begin{array}{c} \begin{matrix} x_1 & x_2 & x_3 & x_4 & z & \end{matrix} \\ \left[\begin{array}{rrrrr|r} \frac{1}{2} & 1 & \frac{1}{80} & 0 & 0 & 7 \\ 2 & 0 & -\frac{1}{10} & 1 & 0 & 16 \\ \hline -2 & 0 & \frac{3}{20} & 0 & 1 & 84 \end{array}\right] \end{array} \quad \begin{array}{l} \frac{1}{80}R_1 \\ -8R_1 + R_2 \\ 12R_1 + R_3 \end{array}$$

The basic variables here are x_2, x_4, and z and the basic feasible solution (found by setting the nonbasic variables equal to 0 and solving for the basic variables) is

$$x_1 = 0, \quad x_2 = 7, \quad x_3 = 0, \quad x_4 = 16, \quad z = 84,$$

which corresponds to the corner point (0, 7) in Figure 8.21. Note that the new value of the pivot variable x_2 is precisely the smallest quotient, 7, that was used to select the pivot row. Although this value of z is better, further improvement is possible.

Now the most negative indicator is -2 and the quotients are

$$\frac{7}{1/2} = 14 \quad \text{and} \quad \frac{16}{2} = 8.$$

Since 8 is smaller, the pivot is the number 2 in row two, column one. Pivoting produces the final tableau.

$$\begin{array}{c} \begin{matrix} x_1 & x_2 & x_3 & x_4 & z & & \end{matrix} \\ \left[\begin{array}{ccccc|c} 0 & 1 & \frac{3}{80} & -\frac{1}{4} & 0 & 3 \\ 1 & 0 & -\frac{1}{20} & \frac{1}{2} & 0 & 8 \\ \hline 0 & 0 & \frac{1}{20} & 1 & 1 & 100 \end{array}\right] \begin{array}{l} -\frac{1}{2}R_2 + R_1 \\ \frac{1}{2}R_2 \\ 2R_2 + R_3 \end{array} \end{array}$$

Here the basic feasible solution is

$$x_1 = 8, \quad x_2 = 3, \quad x_3 = 0, \quad x_4 = 0, \quad z = 100,$$

which corresponds to the corner point (8, 3) in Figure 8.21. Once again, the new value of the pivot variable x_1 is the smallest quotient, 8, that was used to select the pivot. From the graphical method we know that this solution provides the maximum value of the objective function. This fact can also be seen algebraically by using an algebraic argument similar to the one used in Example 5. Thus there is no need to move to another corner point and the simplex method ends. ■

As illustrated in Example 6, the basic feasible solution obtained from a simplex tableau corresponds to a corner point of the feasible region. Pivoting, which replaces one tableau with another, is a systematic way of moving from one corner point to another, each time improving the value of the objective function. The simplex method ends when a corner point that produces the maximum value of the objective function is reached (or when it becomes clear that the problem has no maximum solution).

When there are three or more variables in a linear programming problem, it may be difficult or impossible to draw a picture, but it can be proved that the optimal value of the objective function occurs at a basic feasible solution (corresponding to a corner point in the two variable case). The simplex method provides a means of moving from one basic feasible solution to another until one that produces the optimal value of the objective function is reached.

EXPLANATION OF PIVOTING The rules for selecting the pivot in the simplex method can be understood by examining how the first pivot was chosen in Example 6.

EXAMPLE 7 The initial simplex tableau of Example 6 provides a basic feasible solution with $x_1 = 0, x_2 = 0$.

$$\begin{array}{c} \begin{matrix} x_1 & x_2 & x_3 & x_4 & z & \end{matrix} \\ \left[\begin{array}{ccccc|c} 40 & 80 & 1 & 0 & 0 & 560 \\ 6 & 8 & 0 & 1 & 0 & 72 \\ \hline -8 & -12 & 0 & 0 & 1 & 0 \end{array}\right] \end{array}$$

This solution certainly does not give a maximum value for the objective function $z = 8x_1 + 12x_2$. Since x_2 has the largest coefficient, z will be increased most if x_2 is increased. In other words, the most negative indicator in the tableau (which corresponds to the largest coefficient in the objective function) identifies the variable that will provide the greatest change in the value of z.

To determine how much x_2 can be increased without leaving the feasible region, look at the first two equations

$$\begin{aligned} 40x_1 + 80x_2 + x_3 \quad\quad &= 560 \\ 6x_1 + \ \ 8x_2 \quad\quad + x_4 &= 72 \end{aligned}$$

and solve for the basic variables x_3 and x_4.

$$\begin{aligned} x_3 &= 560 - 40x_1 - 80x_2 \\ x_4 &= 72 - 6x_1 - 8x_2 \end{aligned}$$

Now x_2 is to be increased while x_1 is to keep the value 0. Hence

$$\begin{aligned} x_3 &= 560 - 80x_2 \\ x_4 &= 72 - 8x_2. \end{aligned}$$

Since $x_3 \geq 0$ and $x_4 \geq 0$, we must have:

$$\begin{aligned} 0 \leq 560 - 80x_2 \quad &\text{and} \quad 0 \leq 72 - 8x_2 \\ 80x_2 \leq 560 \quad & \quad 8x_2 \leq 72 \\ x_2 \leq \frac{560}{80} = 7 \quad & \quad x_2 \leq \frac{72}{8} = 9. \end{aligned}$$

The right sides of these last inequalities are the quotients used to select the pivot row. Since x_2 must satisfy both inequalities, x_2 can be at most 7. In other words, the smallest quotient formed from positive entries in the pivot column identifies the value of x_2 that produces the largest change in z while remaining in the feasible region. By pivoting with the pivot determined in this way, we obtain the second tableau and a basic feasible solution in which $x_2 = 7$, as was shown in Example 6. ■

An analysis similar to that in Example 7 applies to each occurrence of pivoting in the simplex method. The idea is to improve the value of the objective function by adjusting one variable at a time. The most negative indicator identifies the variable that will account for the largest increase in z. The smallest quotient determines the largest value of that variable that will produce a feasible solution. Pivoting leads to a solution in which the selected variable has this largest value.

The simplex method is easily implemented on a computer and some graphing calculators. A computer is essential for the simplex method in any situation where there are a large number of variables and constraints (and hence an enormous number of corner points to check).

TECHNOLOGY TIP Simplex method programs for several calculators are in the Program Appendix. ✔

8.4 EXERCISES

In Exercises 1–4, **(a)** *determine the number of slack variables needed;* **(b)** *name them;* **(c)** *use the slack variables to convert each constraint into a linear equation. (See Example 1.)*

1. Maximize $z = 32x_1 + 9x_2$
subject to: $4x_1 + 2x_2 \leq 20$
$5x_1 + x_2 \leq 50$
$2x_1 + 3x_2 \leq 25$
$x_1 \geq 0, x_2 \geq 0.$

2. Maximize $z = 3.7x_1 + 4.3x_2$
subject to: $2.4x_1 + 1.5x_2 \leq 10$
$1.7x_1 + 1.9x_2 \leq 15$
$x_1 \geq 0, x_2 \geq 0.$

3. Maximize $z = 8x_1 + 3x_2 + x_3$
subject to: $3x_1 - x_2 + 4x_3 \le 95$
$7x_1 + 6x_2 + 8x_3 \le 118$
$4x_1 + 5x_2 + 10x_3 \le 220$
$x_1 \ge 0, x_2 \ge 0, x_3 \ge 0.$

4. Maximize $z = 12x_1 + 15x_2 + 10x_3$
subject to: $2x_1 + 2x_2 + x_3 \le 8$
$x_1 + 4x_2 + 3x_3 \le 12$
$x_1 \ge 0, x_2 \ge 0, x_3 \ge 0.$

Introduce slack variables as necessary and then write the initial simplex tableau for each of these linear programming problems.

5. Maximize $z = 5x_1 + x_2$
subject to: $2x_1 + 3x_2 \le 6$
$4x_1 + x_2 \le 6$
$5x_1 + 2x_2 \le 15$
$x_1 \ge 0, x_2 \ge 0.$

6. Maximize $z = 5x_1 + 3x_2 + 4x_3$
subject to: $4x_1 + 3x_2 + 2x_3 \le 60$
$3x_1 + 4x_2 + x_3 \le 24$
$x_1 \ge 0, x_2 \ge 0, x_3 \ge 0.$

7. Maximize $z = x_1 + 5x_2 + 10x_3$
subject to: $x_1 + 2x_2 + 3x_3 \le 10$
$2x_1 + x_2 + x_3 \le 8$
$3x_1 + 2x_3 \le 6$
$x_1 \ge 0, x_2 \ge 0, x_3 \ge 0.$

8. Maximize $z = 5x_1 - x_2 + 3x_3$
subject to: $3x_1 + 2x_2 + x_3 \le 36$
$x_1 + 4x_2 + x_3 \le 24$
$x_1 - x_2 - x_3 \le 32$
$x_1 \ge 0, x_2 \ge 0, x_3 \ge 0.$

Find the pivot in each of the following simplex tableaus. (See Example 2.)

9.

x_1	x_2	x_3	x_4	x_5	z	
2	2	0	3	1	0	15
3	4	1	6	0	0	20
−2	−1	0	1	0	1	10

10.

x_1	x_2	x_3	x_4	x_5	z	
0	2	1	1	3	0	5
1	−5	0	1	2	0	8
0	−2	0	−1	1	1	10

11.

x_1	x_2	x_3	x_4	x_5	x_6	z	
6	2	1	3	0	0	0	8
0	2	0	1	0	1	0	7
2	1	0	3	1	0	0	6
−3	−2	0	2	0	0	1	12

12.

x_1	x_2	x_3	x_4	x_5	x_6	z	
0	2	0	1	2	2	0	3
0	3	1	0	1	2	0	2
1	4	0	0	3	5	0	5
0	−4	0	0	4	−3	1	20

In Exercises 13–16, use the indicated entry as the pivot and perform the pivoting. (See Examples 3 and 4.)

13.

x_1	x_2	x_3	x_4	x_5	z	
1	2	4	1	0	0	56
2	**2**	1	0	1	0	40
−1	−3	−2	0	0	1	0

14.

x_1	x_2	x_3	x_4	x_5	x_6	z	
2	2	**1**	1	0	0	0	12
1	2	3	0	1	0	0	45
3	1	1	0	0	1	0	20
−2	−1	−3	0	0	0	1	0

15.

x_1	x_2	x_3	x_4	x_5	x_6	z	
1	1	1	1	0	0	0	60
3	1	**2**	0	1	0	0	100
1	2	3	0	0	1	0	200
−1	−1	−2	0	0	0	1	0

16.

x_1	x_2	x_3	x_4	x_5	x_6	z	
4	2	3	1	0	0	0	22
2	2	**5**	0	1	0	0	28
1	3	2	0	0	1	0	45
−3	−2	−4	0	0	0	1	0

For each simplex tableau in Exercises 17–20, **(a)** *list the basic and the nonbasic variables;* **(b)** *find the basic feasible solution determined by setting the nonbasic variables equal to 0;* **(c)** *decide whether this is a maximum solution. (See Examples 5 and 6.)*

17.

x_1	x_2	x_3	x_4	x_5	z	
3	2	0	−3	1	0	29
4	0	1	−2	0	0	16
−5	0	0	−1	0	1	11

18.

x_1	x_2	x_3	x_4	x_5	x_6	z	
−3	0	$\frac{1}{2}$	1	−2	0	0	22
2	0	−3	0	1	1	0	10
4	1	4	0	$\frac{3}{4}$	0	0	17
−1	0	0	0	1	0	1	120

19.

$$\begin{array}{ccccccc|c} x_1 & x_2 & x_3 & x_4 & x_5 & x_6 & z & \\ 1 & 0 & 2 & \frac{1}{2} & 0 & \frac{1}{3} & 0 & 6 \\ 0 & 1 & -1 & 5 & 0 & -1 & 0 & 13 \\ 0 & 0 & 1 & \frac{3}{2} & 1 & -\frac{1}{3} & 0 & 21 \\ \hline 0 & 0 & 2 & \frac{1}{2} & 0 & 3 & 1 & 18 \end{array}$$

20.

$$\begin{array}{cccccccc|c} x_1 & x_2 & x_3 & x_4 & x_5 & x_6 & x_7 & z & \\ -1 & 0 & 0 & 1 & 0 & 3 & -2 & 0 & 47 \\ 2 & 0 & 1 & 0 & 0 & 2 & -\frac{1}{2} & 0 & 37 \\ 3 & 0 & 0 & 0 & 1 & -1 & 6 & 0 & 43 \\ \hline 4 & 1 & 0 & 0 & 0 & 6 & 0 & 1 & 86 \end{array}$$

Use the simplex method to solve Exercises 21–36.

21. Maximize $z = x_1 + 3x_2$
subject to: $x_1 + x_2 \le 10$
$5x_1 + 2x_2 \le 20$
$x_1 + 2x_2 \le 36$
$x_1 \ge 0, x_2 \ge 0.$

22. Maximize $z = 5x_1 + x_2$
subject to: $2x_1 + 3x_2 \le 8$
$4x_1 + 8x_2 \le 12$
$5x_1 + 2x_2 \le 30$
$x_1 \ge 0, x_2 \ge 0.$

23. Maximize $z = 2x_1 + x_2$
subject to: $x_1 + 3x_2 \le 12$
$2x_1 + x_2 \le 10$
$x_1 + x_2 \le 4$
$x_1 \ge 0, x_2 \ge 0.$

24. Maximize $z = 4x_1 + 2x_2$
subject to: $-x_1 - x_2 \le 12$
$3x_1 - x_2 \le 15$
$x_1 \ge 0, x_2 \ge 0.$

25. Maximize $z = 5x_1 + 4x_2 + x_3$
subject to: $-2x_1 + x_2 + 2x_3 \le 3$
$x_1 - x_2 + x_3 \le 1$
$x_1 \ge 0, x_2 \ge 0, x_3 \ge 0.$

26. Maximize $z = 3x_1 + 2x_2 + x_3$
subject to: $2x_1 + 2x_2 + x_3 \le 10$
$x_1 + 2x_2 + 3x_3 \le 15$
$x_1 \ge 0, x_2 \ge 0, x_3 \ge 0.$

27. Maximize $z = 2x_1 + x_2 + x_3$
subject to: $x_1 - 3x_2 + x_3 \le 3$
$x_1 - 2x_2 + 2x_3 \le 12$
$x_1 \ge 0, x_2 \ge 0, x_3 \ge 0.$

28. Maximize $z = 4x_1 + 5x_2 + x_3$
subject to: $x_1 + 2x_2 + 4x_3 \le 10$
$2x_1 + 2x_2 + x_3 \le 10$
$x_1 \ge 0, x_2 \ge 0, x_3 \ge 0.$

29. Maximize $z = 2x_1 + 2x_2 - 4x_3$
subject to: $3x_1 + 3x_2 - 6x_3 \le 51$
$5x_1 + 5x_2 + 10x_3 \le 99$
$x_1 \ge 0, x_2 \ge 0, x_3 \ge 0.$

30. Maximize $z = 4x_1 + x_2 + 3x_3$
subject to: $x_1 + 3x_3 \le 6$
$6x_1 + 3x_2 + 12x_3 \le 40$
$x_1 \ge 0, x_2 \ge 0, x_3 \ge 0.$

31. Maximize $z = 300x_1 + 200x_2 + 100x_3$
subject to: $x_1 + x_2 + x_3 \le 100$
$2x_1 + 3x_2 + 4x_3 \le 320$
$2x_1 + x_2 + x_3 \le 160$
$x_1 \ge 0, x_2 \ge 0, x_3 \ge 0.$

32. Maximize $z = x_1 + 5x_2 - 10x_3$
subject to: $8x_1 + 4x_2 + 12x_3 \le 18$
$x_1 + 6x_2 + 2x_3 \le 45$
$5x_1 + 7x_2 + 3x_3 \le 60$
$x_1 \ge 0, x_2 \ge 0, x_3 \ge 0.$

33. Maximize $z = 4x_1 - 3x_2 + 2x_3$
subject to: $2x_1 - x_2 + 8x_3 \le 40$
$4x_1 - 5x_2 + 6x_3 \le 60$
$2x_1 - 2x_2 + 6x_3 \le 24$
$x_1 \ge 0, x_2 \ge 0, x_3 \ge 0.$

34. Maximize $z = 3x_1 + 2x_2 - 4x_3$
subject to: $x_1 - x_2 + x_3 \le 10$
$2x_1 - x_2 + 2x_3 \le 30$
$-3x_1 + x_2 + 3x_3 \le 40$
$x_1 \ge 0, x_2 \ge 0, x_3 \ge 0.$

35. Maximize $z = x_1 + 2x_2 + x_3 + 5x_4$
subject to: $x_1 + 2x_2 + x_3 + x_4 \le 50$
$3x_1 + x_2 + 2x_3 + x_4 \le 100$
$x_1 \ge 0, x_2 \ge 0, x_3 \ge 0, x_4 \ge 0.$

36. Maximize $z = x_1 + x_2 + 4x_3 + 5x_4$
subject to: $x_1 + 2x_2 + 3x_3 + x_4 \le 115$
$2x_1 + x_2 + 8x_3 + 5x_4 \le 200$
$x_1 + x_3 \le 50$
$x_1 \ge 0, x_2 \ge 0, x_3 \ge 0, x_4 \ge 0.$

37. The initial simplex tableau of a linear programming problem is given below.

$$\begin{array}{cccccc|c} x_1 & x_2 & x_3 & x_4 & x_5 & z & \\ 1 & 1 & 1 & 1 & 0 & 0 & 12 \\ 2 & 1 & 2 & 0 & 1 & 0 & 30 \\ \hline -2 & -2 & -1 & 0 & 0 & 1 & 0 \end{array}$$

(a) Use the simplex method to solve the problem, with column one as the first pivot column.

(b) Now use the simplex method to solve the problem, with column two as the first pivot column.

(c) Does this problem have a unique maximum solution? Why?

38. The final simplex tableau of a linear programming problem is given here.

$$\begin{array}{ccccc|c} x_1 & x_2 & x_3 & x_4 & z & \\ \hline 1 & 1 & 2 & 0 & 0 & 24 \\ 2 & 0 & 2 & 1 & 0 & 8 \\ \hline 4 & 0 & 0 & 0 & 1 & 40 \end{array}$$

(a) What is the solution given by this tableau?

(b) Even though all the indicators are nonnegative, perform one more round of pivoting on this tableau, using column three as the pivot column and choosing the pivot row by forming quotients in the usual way.

(c) Show that there is more than one solution to the linear programming problem by comparing your answer in part (a) to the basic feasible solution given by the tableau found in part (b). Does it give the same value of z as the solution in part (a)?

8.5 MAXIMIZATION APPLICATIONS

Applications of linear programming that use the simplex method are considered in this section. First, however, we make a slight change in notation. You have probably noticed that the column representing z in a simplex tableau never changes during pivoting. Furthermore, the value of z in the basic feasible solution associated with the tableau is the number in the lower right-hand corner. Consequently, the z column is unnecessary and will be omitted from all simplex tableaus hereafter.

EXAMPLE 1 A farmer has 100 acres of available land he wishes to plant with a mixture of potatoes, corn, and cabbage. It costs him \$400 to produce an acre of potatoes, \$160 to produce an acre of corn, and \$280 to produce an acre of cabbage. He has a maximum of \$20,000 to spend. He makes a profit of \$120 per acre of potatoes, \$40 per acre of corn, and \$60 per acre of cabbage. How many acres of each crop should he plant to maximize his profit?

Begin by summarizing the given information as follows.

Crop	*Number of Acres*	*Cost per Acre*	*Profit per Acre*
Potatoes	x_1	\$400	\$120
Corn	x_2	160	40
Cabbage	x_3	280	60
Maximum available	100	\$20,000	

If the number of acres allotted to each of the three crops is represented by x_1, x_2, and x_3, respectively, then the constraints can be expressed as

$$\begin{aligned} x_1 + x_2 + x_3 &\le 100 && \text{Number of acres} \\ 400x_1 + 160x_2 + 280x_3 &\le 20{,}000 && \text{Production costs} \end{aligned}$$

where x_1, x_2, and x_3 are all nonnegative. The first of these constraints says that $x_1 + x_2 + x_3$ is less than or perhaps equal to 100. Use x_4 as the slack variable, giving the equation

$$x_1 + x_2 + x_3 + x_4 = 100.$$

Here x_4 represents the amount of the farmer's 100 acres that will not be used. (x_4 may be 0 or any value up to 100.)

In the same way, the constraint $400x_1 + 160x_2 + 280x_3 \leq 20{,}000$ can be converted into an equation by adding a slack variable, x_5:

$$400x_1 + 160x_2 + 280x_3 + x_5 = 20{,}000.$$

The slack variable x_5 represents any unused portion of the farmer's \$20,000 capital. (Again, x_5 may have any value from 0 to 20,000.)

The farmer's profit on potatoes is the product of the profit per acre (\$120) and the number x_1 of acres, that is, $120x_1$. His profit on corn and cabbage is computed similarly. Hence his total profit is given by

$$z = \text{profit on potatoes} + \text{profit on corn} + \text{profit on cabbage}$$
$$z = 120x_1 + 40x_2 + 60x_3.$$

The linear programming problem can now be stated as follows:

$$\begin{aligned} \text{Maximize} \quad & z = 120x_1 + 40x_2 + 60x_3 \\ \text{subject to:} \quad & x_1 + x_2 + x_3 + x_4 = 100 \\ & 400x_1 + 160x_2 + 280x_3 + x_5 = 20{,}000 \\ \text{with} \quad & x_1 \geq 0, x_2 \geq 0, x_3 \geq 0, x_4 \geq 0, x_5 \geq 0. \end{aligned}$$

The initial simplex tableau (without the z column) is

$$\begin{array}{c} \begin{matrix} x_1 & x_2 & x_3 & x_4 & x_5 \end{matrix} \\ \left[\begin{array}{ccccc|c} 1 & 1 & 1 & 1 & 0 & 100 \\ 400 & 160 & 280 & 0 & 1 & 20{,}000 \\ \hline -120 & -40 & -60 & 0 & 0 & 0 \end{array}\right]. \end{array}$$

The most negative indicator is -120; column one is the pivot column. The quotients needed to determine the pivot row are $100/1 = 100$ and $20{,}000/400 = 50$. So the pivot is 400 in row two, column one. Multiplying row two by 1/400 and completing the pivoting leads to the final simplex tableau.

$$\begin{array}{c} \begin{matrix} x_1 & x_2 & x_3 & x_4 & x_5 \end{matrix} \\ \left[\begin{array}{ccccc|c} 0 & .6 & .3 & 1 & -.0025 & 50 \\ 1 & .4 & .7 & 0 & .0025 & 50 \\ \hline 0 & 8 & 24 & 0 & .3 & \mathbf{6000} \end{array}\right] \end{array} \quad \begin{array}{l} -1R_2 + R_1 \\ \frac{1}{400}R_2 \\ 120R_2 + R_3 \end{array}$$

Setting the nonbasic variables x_2, x_3, and x_5 equal to 0, solving for the basic variables x_1 and x_4, and remembering that the value of z is in the lower right-hand corner leads to this maximum solution:

$$x_1 = 50, \quad x_2 = 0, \quad x_3 = 0, \quad x_4 = 50, \quad x_5 = 0, \quad z = 6000.$$

Therefore, the farmer will make a maximum profit of \$6000 by planting 50 acres of potatoes, and no corn or cabbage. Thus 50 acres are left unplanted (represented by x_4, the slack variable for potatoes). The farmer has spent his \$20,000 most effectively in this way and has no more money to plant the remaining 50 acres. If he had more cash, he would plant more crops. ■

EXAMPLE 2 Set up the initial simplex tableau for the following problem.

Ana Pott, who is a candidate for the state legislature, has \$96,000 to buy TV advertising time. Ads cost \$400 per minute on a local cable channel, \$4000 per minute on a regional independent channel, and \$12,000 per minute on a national network channel. Because of existing contracts the TV stations can provide at most 30 minutes of advertising time, with a maximum of 6 minutes on the national network channel. At any given time during the evening, approximately 100,000 people watch the cable channel, 200,000 the independent channel, and 600,000 the network channel. To get maximum exposure, how much time should Ana buy from each station?

Let x_1 be the number of minutes of ads on the cable channel, x_2 the number of minutes on the independent channel, and x_3 the number of minutes on the network channel. Exposure is measured in viewer-minutes. For instance, 100,000 people watching x_1 minutes of ads on the cable channel produces $100{,}000x_1$ viewer-minutes. The amount of exposure is given by the total number of viewer-minutes for all three channels, namely,

$$100{,}000x_1 + 200{,}000x_2 + 600{,}000x_3.$$

Since 30 minutes are available,

$$x_1 + x_2 + x_3 \leq 30.$$

The fact that only 6 minutes can be used on the network channel means that

$$x_3 \leq 6.$$

Expenditures are limited to \$96,000, so

$$\begin{aligned} \text{Cable cost} + \text{independent cost} + \text{network cost} &\leq 96{,}000 \\ 400x_1 \quad + \quad 4000x_2 \quad + \quad 12{,}000x_3 &\leq 96{,}000. \end{aligned}$$

Therefore, Ana must solve the following linear programming problem:

$$\begin{aligned} \text{Maximize} \quad z = 100{,}000x_1 + 200{,}000x_2 + 600{,}000x_3 & \\ \text{subject to:} \quad x_1 + x_2 + x_3 &\leq 30 \\ x_3 &\leq 6 \\ 400x_1 + 4000x_2 + 12{,}000x_3 &\leq 96{,}000 \\ \text{with} \quad x_1 \geq 0, x_2 \geq 0, x_3 \geq 0. & \end{aligned}$$

Introducing slack variables x_4, x_5, and x_6 (one for each constraint), rewriting the constraints as equations, and expressing the objective function as

$$-100{,}000x_1 - 200{,}000x_2 - 600{,}000x_3 + z = 0,$$

leads to the initial simplex tableau:

$$\begin{array}{c} \begin{matrix} x_1 & \quad x_2 & \quad x_3 & x_4 & x_5 & x_6 & \end{matrix} \\ \left[\begin{array}{cccccc|c} 1 & 1 & 1 & 1 & 0 & 0 & 30 \\ 0 & 0 & 1 & 0 & 1 & 0 & 6 \\ 400 & 4000 & 12{,}000 & 0 & 0 & 1 & 96{,}000 \\ \hline -100{,}000 & -200{,}000 & -600{,}000 & 0 & 0 & 0 & 0 \end{array}\right]. \end{array}$$

1 What is the optimal solution in Example 2?

Answer:
Buying 20 minutes of time on the cable channel, 4 minutes on the independent channel, and 6 minutes on the network channel produces the maximum of 6,400,000 viewer-minutes.

Working by hand or using a computer or graphing calculator simplex method program leads to the final simplex tableau:

$$\begin{array}{cccccc} x_1 & x_2 & x_3 & x_4 & x_5 & x_6 \end{array}$$
$$\left[\begin{array}{cccccc|c} 1 & 0 & 0 & \frac{10}{9} & \frac{20}{9} & \frac{-25}{90,000} & 20 \\ 0 & 0 & 1 & 0 & 1 & 0 & 6 \\ 0 & 1 & 0 & -\frac{1}{9} & -\frac{29}{9} & \frac{25}{90,000} & 4 \\ \hline 0 & 0 & 0 & \frac{800,000}{9} & \frac{1,600,000}{9} & \frac{250}{9} & 6,400,000 \end{array}\right].$$ ■ 1

Technology Tip When using a graphing calculator, you can minimize scrolling and make the final simplex tableau in Example 2 easier to read by using the FRAC key (on most TI calculators) or by setting the number format mode to "fraction" (on HP-38). Doing so will convert most (but not necessarily all) the entries in the tableau into fractional form. ✔

8.5 EXERCISES

Set up the initial simplex tableau for each of the following problems.

1. **Management** A cat breeder has the following amounts of cat food: 90 units of tuna, 80 units of liver, and 50 units of chicken. To raise a Siamese cat, the breeder must use 2 units of tuna, 1 of liver, and 1 of chicken per day, while raising a Persian cat requires 1, 2, and 1 units, respectively, per day. If a Siamese cat sells for \$12 while a Persian cat sells for \$10, how many of each should be raised in order to obtain maximum gross income? What is the maximum gross income?

2. **Management** Banal, Inc., produces art for motel rooms. Its painters can turn out mountain scenes, seascapes, and pictures of clowns. Each painting is worked on by three different artists, T, D, and H. Artist T works only 25 hours per week, while D and H work 45 and 40 hours per week, respectively. Artist T spends 1 hour on a mountain scene, 2 hours on a seascape, and 1 hour on a clown. Corresponding times for D and H are 3, 2, and 2 hours, and 2, 1, and 4 hours respectively. Banal makes \$20 on a mountain scene, \$18 on a seascape, and \$22 on a clown. The head painting packer can't stand clowns, so that no more than 4 clown paintings may be done in a week. Find the number of each type of painting that should be made weekly in order to maximize profit. Find the maximum possible profit.

3. **Management** A manufacturer makes two products, toy trucks and toy fire engines. Both are processed in four different departments, each of which has a limited capacity. The sheet metal department can handle at least $1\frac{1}{2}$ times as many trucks as fire engines. The truck assembly department can handle at most 6700 trucks per week, while the fire engine assembly department assembles at most 5500 fire engines weekly. The painting department, which finishes both toys, has a maximum capacity of 12,000 per week. If the profit is \$8.50 for a toy truck and \$12.10 for a toy fire engine, how many of each item should the company produce to maximize profit?

4. **Natural Science** A lake is stocked each spring with three species of fish, A, B, and C. The average weights of the fish are 1.62, 2.12, and 3.01 kilograms for species A, B, and C, respectively. Three foods, I, II, and III, are available in the lake. Each fish of species A requires 1.32 units of food I, 2.9 units of food II, and 1.75 units of food III on the average each day. Species B fish each require 2.1 units of food I, .95 units of food II, and .6 units of food III daily. Species C fish require .86, 1.52, and 2.01 units of I, II, and III per day, respectively. If 490 units of food I, 897 units of food II, and 653 units of food III are available daily, how should the lake be stocked to maximize the weight of the fish supported by the lake?

Use the simplex method to solve the following problems.

5. **Management** A manufacturer of bicycles builds one-, three-, and ten-speed models. The bicycles need both aluminum and steel. The company has available 91,800 units of steel and 42,000 units of aluminum. The one-, three-, and ten-speed models need, respectively, 20, 30, and 40 units of steel and 12, 21, and 16 units of aluminum. How many of each type of bicycle should be made in order to maximize profit if the company makes \$8 per one-speed bike, \$12 per three-speed, and \$24 per ten-speed? What is the maximum possible profit?

6. **Social Science** Jayanta is working to raise money for the homeless by sending information letters and making

follow-up calls to local labor organizations and church groups. She discovered that each church group requires 2 hours of letter writing and 1 hour of follow-up, while for each labor union she needs 2 hours of letter writing and 3 hours of follow-up. Jayanta can raise $100 from each church group and $200 from each union local, and she has a maximum of 16 hours of letter-writing time and a maximum of 12 hours of follow-up time available per month. Determine the most profitable mixture of groups she should contact and the most money she can raise in a month.

7. **Management** A baker has 60 units of flour, 132 units of sugar, and 102 units of raisins. A loaf of raisin bread requires 1 unit of flour, 1 unit of sugar, and 2 units of raisins, while a raisin cake needs 2, 4, and 1 units respectively. If raisin bread sells for $3 a loaf and a raisin cake for $4, how many of each should be baked so that the gross income is maximized? What is the maximum gross income?

8. **Management** Mellow Sounds Inc. produces three types of compact discs: easy listening, jazz, and rock. Each easy listening disc requires 6 hours of recording, 12 hours of mixing, and 2 hours of editing. Each jazz disc requires 8 hours of recording, 8 hours of mixing, and 4 hours of editing. Each rock disc requires 3 hours of recording, 6 hours of mixing, and 1 hour of editing. Each week 288 hours of recording studio time are available, 312 hours of mixing board time are available, and editors are available for at most 124 hours. Mellow Sounds receives $6 for each easy listening and rock disc and $8 for each jazz disc. How many of each type of disc should the company produce each week to maximize their income? What is the maximum income?

9. **Management** The Cut-Right Company sells sets of kitchen knives. The Basic Set consists of 2 utility knives and 1 chef's knife. The Regular Set consists of 2 utility knives, 1 chef's knife, and 1 slicer. The Deluxe Set consists of 3 utility knives, 1 chef's knife, and 1 slicer. Their profit is $30 on a Basic Set, $40 on a Regular Set, and $60 on a Deluxe Set. The factory has on hand 800 utility knives, 400 chef's knives, and 200 slicers. Assuming that all sets will be sold, how many of each type should be made up in order to maximize profit? What is the maximum profit?

10. **Management** Super Souvenir Company makes paper weights, plaques, and ornaments. Each paperweight requires 8 units of plastic, 3 units of metal, and 2 units of paint. Each plaque requires 4 units of plastic, and 1 unit each of metal and paint. Each ornament requires 2 units each of plastic and metal, and 1 unit of paint. They make a profit of $3 on each paperweight and each ornament, and $4 on each plaque. If 36 units of plastic, 24 units of metal, and 30 units of paint are available today, how many of each kind of souvenir should be made in order to maximize profit?

11. **Management** The Fancy Fashions Store has $8000 available each month for advertising. Newspaper ads cost $400 each and no more than 20 can be run per month. Radio ads cost $200 each and no more than 30 can run per month. TV ads cost $1200 each, with a maximum of 6 available each month. Approximately 2000 women will see each newspaper ad, 1200 will hear each radio commercial, and 10,000 will see each TV ad. How much of each type of advertising should be used if the store wants to maximize its ad exposure?

12. **Management** Caroline's Quality Candy Confectionery is famous for fudge, chocolate cremes, and pralines. Its candy-making equipment is set up to make 100-pound batches at a time. Currently there is a chocolate shortage and the company can get only 120 pounds of chocolate in the next shipment. On a week's run, the confectionery's cooking and processing equipment is available for a total of 42 machine hours. During the same period the employees have a total of 56 work hours available for packaging. A batch of fudge requires 20 pounds of chocolate while a batch of cremes uses 25 pounds of chocolate. The cooking and processing take 120 minutes for fudge, 150 minutes for chocolate cremes, and 200 minutes for pralines. The packaging times measured in minutes per 1-pound box are 1, 2, 3, respectively, for fudge, cremes, and pralines. Determine how many batches of each type of candy the confectionery should make, assuming that the profit per pound box is 50¢ on fudge, 40¢ on chocolate cremes, and 45¢ on pralines. Also, find the maximum profit for the week.

Management *The next two problems come from past CPA examinations.* Select the appropriate answer for each question.*

13. The Ball Company manufactures three types of lamps, labeled A, B, and C. Each lamp is processed in two departments, I and II. Total available man-hours per day for departments I and II are 400 and 600, respectively. No additional labor is available. Time requirements and profit per unit for each lamp type are as follows.

	A	B	C
Man-hours in I	2	3	1
Man-hours in II	4	2	3
Profit per unit	$5	$4	$3

The company has assigned you as the accounting member of its profit planning committee to determine the numbers of types of A, B, and C lamps that it should produce in order to maximize its total profit from the sale of lamps. The following questions relate to a linear programming model that your group has developed.

*Material from *Uniform CPA Examination Questions and Unofficial Answers*, copyright © 1973, 1974, 1975 by the American Institute of Certified Public Accountants, Inc., is reprinted with permission.

(a) The coefficients of the objective function would be
(1) 4, 2, 3;
(2) 2, 3, 1;
(3) 5, 4, 3;
(4) 400,600.
(b) The constraints in the model would be
(1) 2, 3, 1;
(2) 5, 4, 3;
(3) 4, 2, 3;
(4) 400,600.
(c) The constraint imposed by the available man-hours in department I could be expressed as
(1) $4X_1 + 2X_2 + 3X_3 \leq 400$;
(2) $4X_1 + 2X_2 + 3X_3 \geq 400$;
(3) $2X_1 + 3X_2 + 1X_3 \leq 400$;
(4) $2X_1 + 3X_2 + 1X_3 \geq 400$.

14. The Golden Hawk Manufacturing Company wants to maximize the profits on products A, B, and C. The contribution margin for each product follows.

Product	*Contribution Margin*
A	\$2
B	5
C	4

The production requirements and departmental capacities, by departments, are as follows.

	PRODUCTION REQUIREMENTS BY PRODUCT (HOURS)			DEPARTMENTAL CAPACITY (TOTAL HOURS)
Department	A	B	C	
Assembling	2	3	2	30,000
Painting	1	2	2	38,000
Finishing	2	3	1	28,000

(a) What is the profit-maximization formula for the Golden Hawk Company?
(1) \$2A + \$5B + \$4C = X (where X = profit)
(2) 5A + 8B + 5C ≤ 96,000
(3) \$2A + \$5B + \$4C ≤ X
(4) \$2A + \$5B + \$4C = 96,000
(b) What is the constraint for the Painting Department of the Golden Hawk Company?
(1) 1A + 2B + 2C ≥ 38,000
(2) \$2A + \$5B + \$4C ≥ 38,000
(3) 1A + 2B + 2C ≤ 38,000
(4) 2A + 3B + 2C ≤ 30,000

15. Solve the problem in Exercise 1.

Use a graphing calculator or a computer program for the simplex method to solve the following linear programming problems.

16. Exercise 2. Your final answer should consist of whole numbers (Banal can't sell half a painting).

17. Exercise 3

18. Exercise 4

8.6 THE SIMPLEX METHOD: DUALITY AND MINIMIZATION

In this section the simplex method is extended to linear programming problems satisfying the following conditions.

1. The objective function is to be *minimized*.
2. All the coefficients of the objective function are nonnegative.
3. All constraints involve ≥ .
4. All variables are nonnegative.

The method of solving minimization problems presented here is based on an interesting connection between maximizing and minimizing problems: any solution of a maximizing problem produces the solution of an associated minimizing problem, or vice-versa. Each of the associated problems is called the **dual** of the other. Thus, duals enable us to solve minimization problems of the type described above by the simplex method introduced in Section 8.4. (An alternative approach for solving minimization problems is given in the next section.)

When dealing with minimization problems, we use y_1, y_2, y_3, etc. as variables and denote the objective function by w. An example will explain the idea of a dual.

EXAMPLE 1 Minimize $w = 8y_1 + 16y_2$

subject to:

$$y_1 + 5y_2 \geq 9$$
$$2y_1 + 2y_2 \geq 10$$
$$y_1 \geq 0, y_2 \geq 0.$$

Before considering slack variables, write the augmented matrix of the system of inequalities, and include the coefficients of the objective function (not their negatives) as the last row in the matrix.

$$\left[\begin{array}{cc|c} 1 & 5 & 9 \\ 2 & 2 & 10 \\ \hline 8 & 16 & 0 \end{array}\right]$$

(Constants: last column; Objective function: last row)

Look now at the following new matrix, obtained from the one above by interchanging rows and columns.

$$\left[\begin{array}{cc|c} 1 & 2 & 8 \\ 5 & 2 & 16 \\ \hline 9 & 10 & 0 \end{array}\right]$$

(Constants: last column; Objective function: last row)

1 Use the corner points in Figure 8.22(a) to find the minimum value of $w = 8y_1 + 16y_2$ and where it occurs.

Answer:
48 when $y_1 = 4, y_2 = 1$

2 Use Figure 8.22(b) to find the maximum value of $z = 9x_1 + 10x_2$ and where it occurs.

Answer:
48 when $x_1 = 2, x_2 = 3$

The *rows* of the first matrix (for the minimizing problem) are the *columns* of the second matrix.

The entries in this second matrix could be used to write the following maximizing problem in standard form (again ignoring the fact that the numbers in the last row are not negative).

Maximize $z = 9x_1 + 10x_2$

subject to:

$$x_1 + 2x_2 \leq 8$$
$$5x_1 + 2x_2 \leq 16$$
$$x_1 \geq 0, x_2 \geq 0.$$

Figure 8.22(a) shows the region of feasible solutions for the minimization problem given above, while Figure 8.22(b) shows the region of feasible solutions for the maximization problem produced by exchanging rows and columns. ■ 1 2

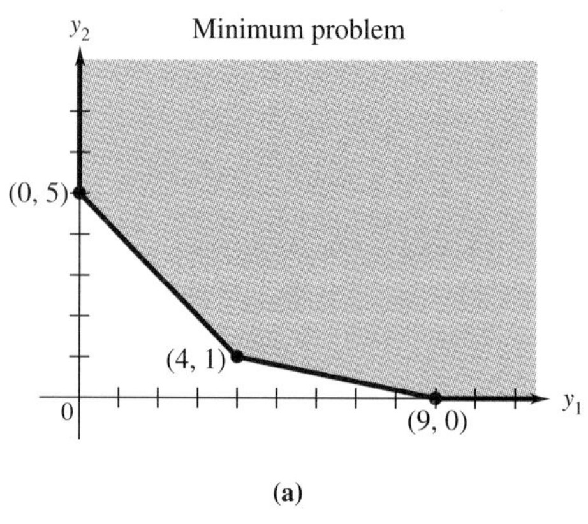

(a)

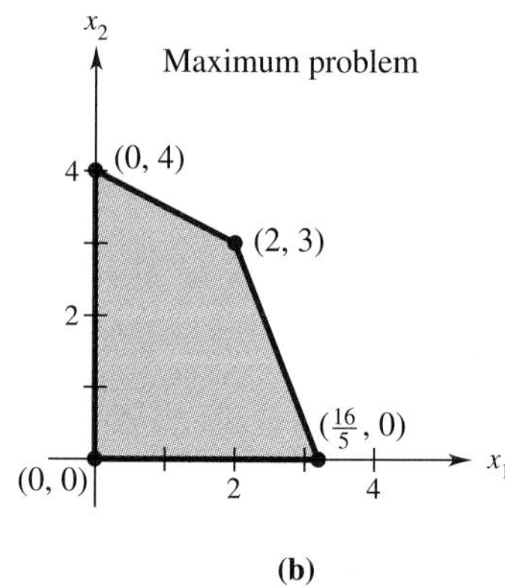

(b)

FIGURE 8.22

The two feasible regions in Figure 8.22 are different and the corner points are different, but the values of the objective functions found in Problems 1 and 2 at the side are equal—both are 48. An even closer connection between the two problems is shown by using the simplex method to solve the maximization problem given above.

Maximization problem

$$\begin{array}{c} \begin{matrix} x_1 & x_2 & x_3 & x_4 & \end{matrix} \\ \left[\begin{array}{cccc|c} 1 & \boxed{2} & 1 & 0 & 8 \\ 5 & 2 & 0 & 1 & 16 \\ \hline -9 & -10 & 0 & 0 & 0 \end{array}\right] \end{array}$$

$$\begin{array}{c} \begin{matrix} x_1 & x_2 & x_3 & x_4 & \end{matrix} \\ \left[\begin{array}{cccc|c} \frac{1}{2} & 1 & \frac{1}{2} & 0 & 4 \\ \boxed{4} & 0 & -1 & 1 & 8 \\ \hline -4 & 0 & 5 & 0 & 40 \end{array}\right] \end{array} \quad \begin{array}{l} \frac{1}{2}R_1 \\ -2R_1 + R_2 \\ 10R_1 + R_3 \end{array}$$

$$\begin{array}{c} \begin{matrix} x_1 & x_2 & x_3 & x_4 & \end{matrix} \\ \left[\begin{array}{cccc|c} 0 & 1 & \frac{5}{8} & -\frac{1}{8} & \mathbf{3} \\ 1 & 0 & -\frac{1}{4} & \frac{1}{4} & \mathbf{2} \\ \hline 0 & 0 & \mathbf{4} & \mathbf{1} & 48 \end{array}\right] \end{array} \quad \begin{array}{l} -\frac{1}{2}R_2 + R_1 \\ \frac{1}{4}R_2 \\ 4R_2 + R_3 \end{array}$$

The maximum is 48 when $x_1 = 2, x_2 = 3$.

Notice that the solution to the *minimization problem* (namely, $y_1 = 4, y_2 = 1$) is found in the bottom row and slack variable columns of the final simplex tableau for the maximization problem. This result suggests that a minimization problem can be solved by forming the dual maximization problem, solving it by the simplex method, and then reading the solution for the minimization problem from the bottom row of the final simplex tableau.

Before using this method to solve a minimization problem, let us find the duals of some typical linear programming problems. The process of exchanging the rows and columns of a matrix, which is used to find the dual, is called **transposing** the matrix, and each of the two matrices is the **transpose** of the other.

3 Give the transpose of each matrix.

(a) $\begin{bmatrix} 2 & 4 \\ 6 & 3 \\ 1 & 5 \end{bmatrix}$

(b) $\begin{bmatrix} 4 & 7 & 10 \\ 3 & 2 & 6 \\ 5 & 8 & 12 \end{bmatrix}$

Answers:

(a) $\begin{bmatrix} 2 & 6 & 1 \\ 4 & 3 & 5 \end{bmatrix}$

(b) $\begin{bmatrix} 4 & 3 & 5 \\ 7 & 2 & 8 \\ 10 & 6 & 12 \end{bmatrix}$

EXAMPLE 2 Find the transpose of each matrix.

(a) $A = \begin{bmatrix} 2 & -1 & 5 \\ 6 & 8 & 0 \\ -3 & 7 & -1 \end{bmatrix}$

Write the rows of matrix A as the columns of the transpose.

$$\text{Transpose of } A = \begin{bmatrix} 2 & 6 & -3 \\ -1 & 8 & 7 \\ 5 & 0 & -1 \end{bmatrix}$$

(b) The transpose of $\begin{bmatrix} 1 & 2 & 4 & 0 \\ 2 & 1 & 7 & 6 \end{bmatrix}$ is $\begin{bmatrix} 1 & 2 \\ 2 & 1 \\ 4 & 7 \\ 0 & 6 \end{bmatrix}$. ■ 3

TECHNOLOGY TIP Most graphing calculators can find the transpose of a matrix. Look for this feature in the MATRIX MATH menu (TI) or the OPTN MAT menu (Casio 9850) or the MATH MATRIX menu (HP-38). The transpose of matrix *A* from Example 2(a) is shown in Figure 8.23. ✔

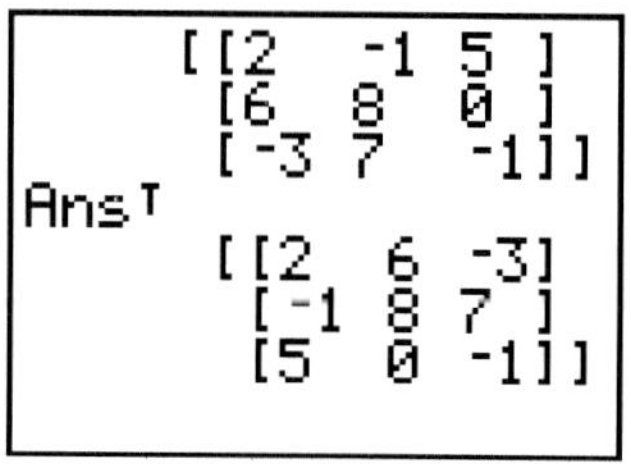

```
          [[2   -1 5 ]
           [6   8  0 ]
           [-3  7  -1]]
AnsT
          [[2  6 -3]
           [-1 8 7 ]
           [5  0 -1]]
```

FIGURE 8.23

EXAMPLE 3 Write the duals of the following minimization linear programming problems.

(a) Minimize $w = 10y_1 + 8y_2$

subject to:

$$\begin{aligned} y_1 + 2y_2 &\geq 2 \\ y_1 + y_2 &\geq 5 \\ y_1 \geq 0, y_2 &\geq 0. \end{aligned}$$

Begin by writing the augmented matrix for the given problem.

$$\left[\begin{array}{cc|c} 1 & 2 & 2 \\ 1 & 1 & 5 \\ \hline 10 & 8 & 0 \end{array}\right]$$

Form the transpose of this matrix to get

$$\left[\begin{array}{cc|c} 1 & 1 & 10 \\ 2 & 1 & 8 \\ \hline 2 & 5 & 0 \end{array}\right].$$

The dual problem is stated from this second matrix as follows (using x instead of y).

Maximize $z = 2x_1 + 5x_2$

subject to:

$$\begin{aligned} x_1 + x_2 &\leq 10 \\ 2x_1 + x_2 &\leq 8 \\ x_1 \geq 0, x_2 &\geq 0. \end{aligned}$$

(b) Minimize $w = 7y_1 + 5y_2 + 8y_3$

subject to:

$$\begin{aligned} 3y_1 + 2y_2 + y_3 &\geq 10 \\ y_1 + y_2 + y_3 &\geq 8 \\ 4y_1 + 5y_2 \quad &\geq 25 \\ y_1 \geq 0, y_2 > 0, y_3 &\geq 0. \end{aligned}$$

4 Write the dual of the following linear programming problem.
Minimize $w = 2y_1 + 5y_2 + 6y_3$
subject to:

$$\begin{aligned} 2y_1 + 3y_2 + y_3 &\geq 15 \\ y_1 + y_2 + 2y_3 &\geq 12 \\ 5y_1 + 3y_2 &\geq 10 \\ y_1 \geq 0, y_2 \geq 0, y_3 &\geq 0. \end{aligned}$$

Answer:
Maximize $z = 15x_1 + 12x_2 + 10x_3$
subject to:

$$\begin{aligned} 2x_1 + x_2 + 5x_3 &\leq 2 \\ 3x_1 + x_2 + 3x_3 &\leq 5 \\ x_1 + 2x_2 &\leq 6 \\ x_1 \geq 0, x_2 \geq 0, x_3 &\geq 0. \end{aligned}$$

The dual problem is stated as follows.

$$\begin{aligned} \text{Maximize} \quad z &= 10x_1 + 8x_2 + 25x_3 \\ \text{subject to:} \quad 3x_1 + x_2 + 4x_3 &\leq 7 \\ 2x_1 + x_2 + 5x_3 &\leq 5 \\ x_1 + x_2 &\leq 8 \\ x_1 \geq 0, x_2 \geq 0, x_3 &\geq 0. \end{aligned}$$ ■ 4

In Example 3, all the constraints of the minimization problems were $\geq$ inequalities, while all those in the dual maximization problems were $\leq$ inequalities. This is generally the case; inequalities are reversed when the dual problem is stated.

The following table shows the close connection between a problem and its dual.

Given Problem	*Dual Problem*
m variables	n variables
n constraints	m constraints
Coefficients from objective function	Constants
Constants	Coefficients from objective function

The next theorem, whose proof requires advanced methods, guarantees that a minimization problem can be solved by forming a dual maximization problem.

THEOREM OF DUALITY

The objective function w of a minimizing linear programming problem takes on a minimum value if and only if the objective function z of the corresponding dual maximizing problem takes on a maximum value. The maximum value of z equals the minimum value of w.

This method is illustrated in the following example.

EXAMPLE 4 Minimize $w = 3y_1 + 2y_2$

$$\begin{aligned} \text{subject to:} \quad y_1 + 3y_2 &\geq 6 \\ 2y_1 + y_2 &\geq 3 \\ y_1 \geq 0, y_2 &\geq 0. \end{aligned}$$

Use the given information to write the matrix.

$$\left[\begin{array}{cc|c} 1 & 3 & 6 \\ 2 & 1 & 3 \\ \hline 3 & 2 & 0 \end{array}\right]$$

Transpose to get the following matrix for the dual problem.

$$\left[\begin{array}{cc|c} 1 & 2 & 3 \\ 3 & 1 & 2 \\ \hline 6 & 3 & 0 \end{array}\right]$$

Write the dual problem from this matrix, as follows.

$$\begin{aligned} \text{Maximize} \quad & z = 6x_1 + 3x_2 \\ \text{subject to:} \quad & x_1 + 2x_2 \le 3 \\ & 3x_1 + x_2 \le 2 \\ & x_1 \ge 0, x_2 \ge 0. \end{aligned}$$

Solve this standard maximization problem using the simplex method. Start by introducing slack variables to give the system

$$\begin{aligned} x_1 + 2x_2 + x_3 \quad\quad\quad &= 3 \\ 3x_1 + x_2 \quad\quad + x_4 \quad &= 2 \\ -6x_1 - 3x_2 - 0x_3 - 0x_4 + z &= 0 \end{aligned}$$

with $x_1 \ge 0, x_2 \ge 0, x_3 \ge 0, x_4 \ge 0.$

The initial tableau for this system is given below with the pivot as indicated.

$$\begin{array}{c} \begin{matrix} x_1 & x_2 & x_3 & x_4 & & \end{matrix} \\ \left[\begin{array}{cccc|c} 1 & 2 & 1 & 0 & 3 \\ \boxed{3} & 1 & 0 & 1 & 2 \\ \hline -6 & -3 & 0 & 0 & 0 \end{array}\right] \end{array} \quad \begin{array}{l} \text{Quotients} \\ 3/1 = 3 \\ 2/3 \\ \\ \end{array}$$

The simplex method gives the following final tableau.

$$\begin{array}{c} \begin{matrix} x_1 & x_2 & x_3 & x_4 & & \end{matrix} \\ \left[\begin{array}{cccc|c} 0 & 1 & \frac{3}{5} & -\frac{1}{5} & \frac{7}{5} \\ 1 & 0 & -\frac{1}{5} & \frac{2}{5} & \frac{1}{5} \\ \hline 0 & 0 & \frac{3}{5} & \frac{9}{5} & \frac{27}{5} \end{array}\right] \end{array}$$

The last row of this final tableau shows that the solution of the given minimization problem is as follows:

The minimum value of $w = 3y_1 + 2y_2$, subject to the given constraints, is 27/5 and occurs when $y_1 = 3/5$ and $y_2 = 9/5$.

The minimum value of w, 27/5, is the same as the maximum value of z. ■ 5

5 Minimize $w = 10y_1 + 8y_2$ subject to:

$$\begin{aligned} y_1 + 2y_2 &\ge 2 \\ y_1 + y_2 &\ge 5 \\ y_1 \ge 0, y_2 &\ge 0. \end{aligned}$$

Answer:

$y_1 = 0, y_2 = 5$, for a minimum of 40

A minimizing problem that meets the conditions listed at the beginning of the section can be solved by the method of duals, as illustrated in Examples 1 and 4 and summarized here.

SOLVING MINIMUM PROBLEMS WITH DUALS

1. Find the dual standard maximum problem.*
2. Solve the maximum problem using the simplex method.
3. The minimum value of the objective function w is the maximum value of the objective function z.
4. The optimum solution is given by the entries in the bottom row of the columns corresponding to the slack variables.

*The coefficients of the objective function in the minimization problem are the constants on the right side of the constraints in the dual maximization problem. So when all these coefficients are nonnegative (condition 2), the dual problem is in standard maximum form.

FURTHER USES OF THE DUAL The dual is useful not only in solving minimization problems, but also in seeing how small changes in one variable will affect the value of the objective function. For example, suppose an animal breeder needs at least 6 units per day of nutrient A and at least 3 units of nutrient B and that the breeder can choose between two different feeds, feed 1 and feed 2. Find the minimum cost for the breeder if each bag of feed 1 costs \$3 and provides 1 unit of nutrient A and 2 units of B, while each bag of feed 2 costs \$2 and provides 3 units of nutrient A and 1 of B.

If y_1 represents the number of bags of feed 1 and y_2 represents the number of bags of feed 2, the given information leads to

$$\begin{aligned} \text{Minimize} \quad & w = 3y_1 + 2y_2 \\ \text{subject to:} \quad & y_1 + 3y_2 \ge 6 \\ & 2y_1 + y_2 \ge 3 \\ & y_1 \ge 0,\ y_2 \ge 0. \end{aligned}$$

This minimization linear programming problem is the one we solved in Example 4 of this section. In that example, we formed the dual and reached the following final tableau.

$$\begin{array}{c} \begin{matrix} x_1 & x_2 & x_3 & x_4 \end{matrix} \\ \left[\begin{array}{cccc|c} 0 & 1 & \frac{3}{5} & -\frac{1}{5} & \frac{7}{5} \\ 1 & 0 & -\frac{1}{5} & \frac{2}{5} & \frac{1}{5} \\ \hline 0 & 0 & \frac{3}{5} & \frac{9}{5} & \frac{27}{5} \end{array}\right] \end{array}$$

This final tableau shows that the breeder will obtain minimum feed costs by using 3/5 bag of feed 1 and 9/5 bags of feed 2 per day, for a daily cost of 27/5 = 5.40 dollars.

Now look at the data from the feed problem shown in the table below.

	UNITS OF NUTRIENT (PER BAG)		*Cost per Bag*
	A	B	
Feed 1	1	2	\$3
Feed 2	3	1	\$2
Minimum nutrient needed	6	3	

If x_1 and x_2 are the cost per unit of nutrients A and B, the constraints of the dual problem can be stated as follows.

$$\begin{aligned} \text{Cost of feed 1:} \quad & x_1 + 2x_2 \le 3 \\ \text{Cost of feed 2:} \quad & 3x_1 + x_2 \le 2 \end{aligned}$$

The solution of the dual problem, which maximizes nutrients, also can be read from the final tableau:

$$x_1 = \frac{1}{5} = .20 \quad \text{and} \quad x_2 = \frac{7}{5} = 1.40,$$

6 The final tableau of the dual of the problem about filing cabinets in Example 2, Section 8.3 and Example 6, Section 8.4 is given below.

$$\begin{array}{cccc|c} x_1 & x_2 & x_3 & x_4 & \\ 0 & 1 & \frac{1}{2} & -\frac{1}{4} & 1 \\ 1 & 0 & -\frac{1}{20} & -\frac{1}{80} & \frac{1}{20} \\ \hline 0 & 0 & 8 & 3 & 100 \end{array}$$

(a) What are the imputed amounts of storage for each unit of cost and floor space?

(b) What are the shadow values of the cost and the floor space?

Answers:

(a) Cost: 28 sq ft
floor space: 72 sq ft

(b) $\frac{1}{20}$, 1

which means that a unit of nutrient A costs 1/5 of a dollar = \$.20, while a unit of nutrient B costs 7/5 dollars = \$1.40. The minimum daily cost, \$5.40, is found by the following procedure.

(\$.20 per unit of A) × (6 units of A) =	\$1.20
+ (\$1.40 per unit of B) × (3 units of B) =	\$4.20
Minimum daily cost =	\$5.40

The numbers .20 and 1.40 are called the **shadow costs** of the nutrients. These two numbers from the dual, \$.20 and \$1.40, also allow the breeder to estimate feed costs for "small" changes in nutrient requirements. For example, an increase of 1 unit in the requirement for each nutrient would produce total cost as follows.

\$5.40	6 units of A, 3 of B
.20	1 extra unit of A
1.40	1 extra unit of B
\$7.00	Total cost per day 6

8.6 EXERCISES

Find the transpose of each matrix. (See Example 2.)

1. $\begin{bmatrix} 3 & -4 & 5 \\ 1 & 10 & 7 \\ 0 & 3 & 6 \end{bmatrix}$

2. $\begin{bmatrix} 3 & -5 & 9 & 4 \\ 1 & 6 & -7 & 0 \\ 4 & 18 & 11 & 9 \end{bmatrix}$

3. $\begin{bmatrix} 3 & 0 & 14 & -5 & 3 \\ 4 & 17 & 8 & -6 & 1 \end{bmatrix}$

4. $\begin{bmatrix} 15 & -6 & -2 \\ 13 & -1 & 11 \\ 10 & 12 & -3 \\ 24 & 1 & 0 \end{bmatrix}$

State the dual problem for each of the following, but do not solve it. (See Example 3.)

5. Minimize $w = 3y_1 + 5y_2$
subject to:
$3y_1 + y_2 \geq 4$
$-y_1 + 2y_2 \geq 6$
$y_1 \geq 0, y_2 \geq 0.$

6. Minimize $w = 4y_1 + 7y_2$
subject to:
$y_1 + y_2 \geq 17$
$3y_1 + 6y_2 \geq 21$
$2y_1 + 4y_2 \geq 19$
$y_1 \geq 0, y_2 \geq 0.$

7. Minimize $w = 2y_1 + 8y_2$
subject to:
$y_1 + 7y_2 \geq 18$
$4y_1 + y_2 \geq 15$
$5y_1 + 3y_2 \geq 20$
$y_1 > 0, y_2 > 0.$

8. Minimize $w = 5y_1 + y_2 + 3y_3$
subject to:
$7y_1 + 6y_2 + 8y_3 \geq 18$
$4y_1 + 5y_2 + 10y_3 \geq 20$
$y_1 \geq 0, y_2 \geq 0, y_3 \geq 0.$

9. Minimize $w = y_1 + 2y_2 + 6y_3$
subject to:
$3y_1 + 4y_2 + 6y_3 \geq -8$
$y_1 + 5y_2 + 2y_3 \geq 12$
$y_1 \geq 0, y_2 \geq 0, y_3 \geq 0.$

10. Minimize $w = 4y_1 + 3y_2 + y_3$
subject to:
$y_1 + 2y_2 + 3y_3 \geq 115$
$2y_1 + y_2 + 8y_3 \geq 200$
$y_1 - y_3 \geq 50$
$y_1 \geq 0, y_2 \geq 0, y_3 \geq 0.$

11. Minimize $w = 8y_1 + 9y_2 + 3y_3$
subject to:
$y_1 + y_2 + y_3 \geq 5$
$y_1 + y_2 \geq 4$
$2y_1 + y_2 + 3y_3 \geq 15$
$y_1 \geq 0, y_2 \geq 0, y_3 \geq 0.$

12. Minimize $w = y_1 + 2y_2 + y_3 + 5y_4$
subject to:
$y_1 + y_2 + y_3 + y_4 \geq 50$
$3y_1 + y_2 + 2y_3 + y_4 \geq 100$
$y_1 \geq 0, y_2 \geq 0, y_3 \geq 0, y_4 \geq 0.$

Use duality to solve the following problems. (See Example 4.)

13. Minimize $w = 2y_1 + y_2 + 3y_3$
subject to:
$$\begin{aligned} y_1 + y_2 + y_3 &\geq 100 \\ 2y_1 + y_2 \quad\;\; &\geq 50 \\ y_1 \geq 0, y_2 \geq 0, y_3 &\geq 0. \end{aligned}$$

14. Minimize $w = 2y_1 + 4y_2$
subject to:
$$\begin{aligned} 4y_1 + 2y_2 &\geq 10 \\ 4y_1 + y_2 &\geq 8 \\ 2y_1 + y_2 &\geq 12 \\ y_1 \geq 0, y_2 &\geq 0. \end{aligned}$$

15. Minimize $w = 3y_1 + y_2 + 4y_3$
subject to:
$$\begin{aligned} 2y_1 + y_2 + y_3 &\geq 6 \\ y_1 + 2y_2 + y_3 &\geq 8 \\ 2y_1 + y_2 + 2y_3 &\geq 12 \\ y_1 \geq 0, y_2 \geq 0, y_3 &\geq 0. \end{aligned}$$

16. Minimize $w = y_1 + y_2 + 3y_3$
subject to:
$$\begin{aligned} 2y_1 + 6y_2 + y_3 &\geq 8 \\ y_1 + 2y_2 + 4y_3 &\geq 12 \\ y_1 \geq 0, y_2 \geq 0, y_3 &\geq 0. \end{aligned}$$

17. Minimize $w = 6y_1 + 4y_2 + 2y_3$
subject to:
$$\begin{aligned} 2y_1 + 2y_2 + y_3 &\geq 2 \\ y_1 + 3y_2 + 2y_3 &\geq 3 \\ y_1 + y_2 + 2y_3 &\geq 4 \\ y_1 \geq 0, y_2 \geq 0, y_3 &\geq 0. \end{aligned}$$

18. Minimize $w = 12y_1 + 10y_2 + 7y_3$
subject to:
$$\begin{aligned} 2y_1 + y_2 + y_3 &\geq 7 \\ y_1 + 2y_2 + y_3 &\geq 4 \\ y_1 \geq 0, y_2 \geq 0, y_3 &\geq 0. \end{aligned}$$

19. Minimize $w = 20y_1 + 12y_2 + 40y_3$
subject to:
$$\begin{aligned} y_1 + y_2 + 5y_3 &\geq 20 \\ 2y_1 + y_2 + y_3 &\geq 30 \\ y_1 \geq 0, y_2 \geq 0, y_3 &\geq 0. \end{aligned}$$

20. Minimize $w = 4y_1 + 5y_2$
subject to:
$$\begin{aligned} 10y_1 + 5y_2 &\geq 100 \\ 20y_1 + 10y_2 &\geq 150 \\ y_1 \geq 0, y_2 &\geq 0. \end{aligned}$$

21. Minimize $w = 4y_1 + 2y_2 + y_3$
subject to:
$$\begin{aligned} y_1 + y_2 + y_3 &\geq 4 \\ 3y_1 + y_2 + 3y_3 &\geq 6 \\ y_1 + y_2 + 3y_3 &\geq 5 \\ y_1 \geq 0, y_2 \geq 0, y_3 &\geq 0. \end{aligned}$$

22. Minimize $w = 3y_1 + 2y_2$
subject to:
$$\begin{aligned} 2y_1 + 3y_2 &\geq 60 \\ y_1 + 4y_2 &\geq 40 \\ y_1 \geq 0, y_2 &\geq 0. \end{aligned}$$

23. Natural Science Glenn Russell, who is dieting, requires two food supplements, I and II. He can get these supplements from two different products, A and B, as shown in the following table.

		SUPPLEMENT (GRAMS PER SERVING)	
		I	II
PRODUCT	A	4	2
	B	2	5

Glenn's physician has recommended that he include at least 20 grams of supplement I and 18 grams of supplement II in his diet. If product A costs 24¢ per serving and product B costs 40¢ per serving, how can he satisfy these requirements most economically?

24. Management An animal food must provide at least 54 units of vitamins and 60 calories per serving. One gram of soybean meal provides at least 2.5 units of vitamins and 5 calories. One gram of meat byproducts provides at least 4.5 units of vitamins and 3 calories. One gram of grain provides at least 5 units of vitamins and 10 calories. If a gram of soybean meal costs 8¢, a gram of meat byproducts 9¢, and a gram of grain 10¢, what mixture of these three ingredients will provide the required vitamins and calories at minimum cost?

25. Management A furniture company makes tables and chairs. Union contracts require that the total number of tables and chairs produced must be at least 60 per week. Sales experience has shown that at least 1 table must be made for every 3 chairs that are made. If it costs \$152 to make a table and \$40 to make a chair, how many of each should be produced each week to minimize the cost? What is the minimum cost?

26. Management Brand X canners produce canned corn, beans, and carrots. Labor contracts require them to produce at least 1000 cases per month. Based on past sales, they should produce at least twice as many cases of corn as of beans. At least 340 cases of carrots must be produced to fulfill commitments to a major distributor. It costs \$10 to produce a case of beans, \$15 to produce a case of corn, and \$25 to produce a case of carrots. How many cases of each vegetable should be produced to minimize costs?

27. Management Refer to the end of this section, to the text on minimizing the daily cost of feeds.

(a) Find a combination of feeds that will cost \$7.00 and give 7 units of A and 4 units of B.

(b) Use the dual variables to predict the daily cost of feed if the requirements change to 5 units of A and 4 units of B. Find a combination of feeds to meet these requirements at the predicted price.

28. Management A small toy manufacturing firm has 200 squares of felt, 600 ounces of stuffing, and 90 feet of trim available to make two types of toys, a small bear and a monkey. The bear requires 1 square of felt and 4 ounces of stuffing. The monkey requires 2 squares of felt, 3 ounces of stuffing, and 1 foot of trim. The firm makes $1 profit on each bear and $1.50 profit on each monkey. The linear program to maximize profit is

$$\begin{aligned} \text{Maximize} \quad & x_1 + 1.5x_2 = z \\ \text{subject to:} \quad & x_1 + 2x_2 \leq 200 \\ & 4x_1 + 3x_2 \leq 600 \\ & x_2 \leq 90 \\ & x_1 \geq 0, x_2 \geq 0. \end{aligned}$$

The final simplex tableau is

$$\left[\begin{array}{ccccc|c} 0 & 1 & .8 & -.2 & 0 & 40 \\ 1 & 0 & -.6 & .4 & 0 & 120 \\ 0 & 0 & -.8 & .2 & 1 & 50 \\ \hline 0 & 0 & .6 & .1 & 0 & 180 \end{array}\right].$$

(a) What is the corresponding dual problem?
(b) What is the optimal solution to the dual problem?
(c) Use the shadow values to estimate the profit the firm will make if their supply of felt increases to 210 squares.
(d) How much profit will the firm make if their supply of stuffing is cut to 590 ounces and their supply of trim is cut to 80 feet?

29. Refer to Example 1 in Section 8.5.
(a) Give the dual problem.
(b) Use the shadow values to estimate the farmer's profit if land is cut to 90 acres but capital increases to $21,000.
(c) Suppose the farmer has 110 acres but only $19,000. Find the optimum profit and the planting strategy that will produce this profit.

Use duality and a graphing calculator or a computer program for doing the simplex method to solve this problem.

30. Management Natural Brand plant food is made from three chemicals. In a batch of the plant food there must be at least 81 kilograms of the first chemical and the ratio of the second chemical to the third chemical must be at least 4 to 3. If the three chemicals cost $1.09, $.87, and $.65 per kilogram, respectively, how much of each should be used to minimize the cost of producing at least 750 kilograms of the plant food?

8.7 THE SIMPLEX METHOD: NONSTANDARD PROBLEMS

So far we have used the simplex method to solve linear programming problems in standard maximum or minimum form only. Now this work is extended to include linear programming problems with mixed $\leq$ and $\geq$ constraints.

The first step is to write each constraint so that the constant on the right side is nonnegative. For instance, the inequality

$$4x_1 + 5x_2 - 12x_3 \leq -30$$

can be replaced by the equivalent one obtained by multiplying both sides by -1 and reversing the direction of the inequality sign:

$$-4x_1 - 5x_2 + 12x_3 \geq 30.$$

The next step is to write each constraint as an equation. Recall that constraints involving $\leq$ are converted to equations by adding a nonnegative slack variable. Similarly, constraints involving $\geq$ are converted to equations by *subtracting* a nonnegative **surplus variable.** For example, the inequality $2x_1 - x_2 + 5x_3 \geq 12$ means that

$$2x_1 - x_2 + 5x_3 - x_4 = 12$$

for some nonnegative x_4. The surplus variable x_4 represents the amount by which $2x_1 - x_2 + 5x_3$ exceeds 12.

1 **(a)** Restate this problem in terms of equations:

$$\begin{aligned} \text{Maximize} \quad & z = 3x_1 - 2x_2 \\ \text{subject to:} \quad & 2x_1 + 3x_2 \le 8 \\ & 6x_1 - 2x_2 \ge 3 \\ & x_1 + 4x_2 \ge 1 \\ & x_1 \ge 0, x_2 \ge 0. \end{aligned}$$

(b) Write the initial simplex tableau.

Answers:

(a) Maximize $z = 3x_1 - 2x_2$ subject to:

$$\begin{aligned} 2x_1 + 3x_2 + x_3 \qquad\qquad &= 8 \\ 6x_1 - 2x_2 \qquad - x_4 \qquad &= 3 \\ x_1 + 4x_2 \qquad\qquad - x_5 &= 1 \end{aligned}$$

$x_1 \ge 0, x_2 \ge 0, x_3 \ge 0, x_4 \ge 0, x_5 \ge 0.$

(b)

x_1	x_2	x_3	x_4	x_5	
2	3	1	0	0	8
6	−2	0	−1	0	3
1	4	0	0	−1	1
−3	2	0	0	0	0

2 State the basic solution given by each tableau. Is it feasible?

(a)

x_1	x_2	x_3	x_4	x_5	
3	−5	1	0	0	12
4	7	0	1	0	6
1	3	0	0	−1	5
−7	4	0	0	0	0

(b)

x_1	x_2	x_3	x_4	x_5	
9	8	−1	1	0	12
−5	3	0	0	1	7
4	2	3	0	0	0

Answers:

(a) $x_1 = 0, x_2 = 0, x_3 = 12, x_4 = 6, x_5 = -5$; no.

(b) $x_1 = 0, x_2 = 0, x_3 = 0, x_4 = 12, x_5 = 7$; yes.

EXAMPLE 1 Restate the following problem in terms of equations and write its initial simplex tableau.

$$\begin{aligned} \text{Maximize} \quad & z = 4x_1 + 10x_2 + 6x_3 \\ \text{subject to:} \quad & x_1 + 4x_2 + 4x_3 \ge 8 \\ & x_1 + 3x_2 + 2x_3 \le 6 \\ & 3x_1 + 4x_2 + 8x_3 \le 22 \\ & x_1 \ge 0, x_2 \ge 0, x_3 \ge 0. \end{aligned}$$

In order to write the constraints as equations, subtract a surplus variable from the $\ge$ constraint and add a slack variable to each $\le$ constraint. So the problem becomes

$$\begin{aligned} \text{Maximize} \quad & z = 4x_1 + 10x_2 + 6x_3 \\ \text{subject to:} \quad & x_1 + 4x_2 + 4x_3 - x_4 \qquad\qquad = 8 \\ & x_1 + 3x_2 + 2x_3 \qquad + x_5 \qquad = 6 \\ & 3x_1 + 4x_2 + 8x_3 \qquad\qquad + x_6 = 22 \\ & x_1 \ge 0, x_2 \ge 0, x_3 \ge 0, x_4 \ge 0, x_5 \ge 0, x_6 \ge 0. \end{aligned}$$

Write the objective function as $z - 4x_1 - 10x_2 - 6x_3 = 0$ and use the coefficients of the four equations to write the initial simplex tableau (omitting the z column):

x_1	x_2	x_3	x_4	x_5	x_6	
1	4	4	−1	0	0	8
1	3	2	0	1	0	6
3	4	8	0	0	1	22
−4	−10	−6	0	0	0	0

. ■ 1

The tableau in Example 1 resembles those that have appeared previously, and similar terminology is used. The variables whose columns have one entry ± 1 and the rest 0 will be called **basic variables;** the other variables are nonbasic. A solution obtained by setting the nonbasic variables equal to 0 and solving for the basic variables (by looking at the constants in the right-hand column) will be called a **basic solution.** A basic solution that is feasible is called a **basic feasible solution.** In the tableau of Example 1, for instance, the basic variables are x_4, x_5, and x_6, and the basic solution is:

$$x_1 = 0, \quad x_2 = 0, \quad x_3 = 0, \quad x_4 = -8, \quad x_5 = 6, \quad x_6 = 22.$$

However, because one variable is negative, this solution is not feasible. 2

Stage I of the two-stage method for nonstandard maximization problems consists of finding a basic *feasible* solution that can be used as the starting point for the simplex method. (This stage is unnecessary in a standard maximization problem because the solution given by the initial tableau is always feasible.) There are many systematic ways of finding a feasible solution, all of which depend on the fact that row operations (such as pivoting) produce a tableau that represents a system with the same solutions as the original one. One such technique is explained in the next example. Since the immediate goal is to find a feasible solution, not necessarily an optimal one, the procedures for choosing pivots differ from those in the ordinary simplex method.

EXAMPLE 2 Find a basic feasible solution for the problem in Example 1, whose initial tableau is

$$\begin{array}{cccccc|c} x_1 & x_2 & x_3 & x_4 & x_5 & x_6 & \\ 1 & 4 & 4 & -1 & 0 & 0 & 8 \\ 1 & 3 & 2 & 0 & 1 & 0 & 6 \\ 3 & 4 & 8 & 0 & 0 & 1 & 22 \\ \hline -4 & -10 & -6 & 0 & 0 & 0 & 0 \end{array}.$$

In the basic solution given by this tableau, x_4 has a negative value. The only nonzero entry in its column is the -1 in row one. Choose any *positive* entry in row one except the entry on the far right. The column that the chosen entry is in will be the pivot column. We choose the first positive entry in row one, the 1 in column one. The pivot row is determined in the usual way by considering quotients (constant at the right end of the row divided by the positive entry in the pivot column) in each row except the objective row:

$$8/1 = 8, \quad 6/1 = 6, \quad 22/3 = 7\frac{1}{3}.$$

The smallest quotient is 6, so the pivot is the 1 in row two, column one. Pivoting in the usual way leads to this tableau

$$\begin{array}{cccccc|cl} x_1 & x_2 & x_3 & x_4 & x_5 & x_6 & & \\ 0 & 1 & 2 & -1 & -1 & 0 & 2 & -R_2 + R_1 \\ 1 & 3 & 2 & 0 & 1 & 0 & 6 & \\ 0 & -5 & 2 & 0 & -3 & 1 & 4 & -3R_2 + R_3 \\ \hline 0 & 2 & 2 & 0 & 4 & 0 & 24 & 4R_2 + R_4 \end{array}$$

and the basic solution

$$x_1 = 6, \quad x_2 = 0, \quad x_3 = 0, \quad x_4 = -2, \quad x_5 = 0, \quad x_6 = 4.$$

Since the basic variable x_4 is negative, this solution is not feasible. So we repeat the pivoting process described above. The x_4 column has a -1 in row one, so we choose a positive entry in that row, namely, the 1 in row one, column two. This choice makes column two the pivot column. The pivot row is determined by the quotients $2/1 = 2$ and $6/3 = 2$ (negative entries in the pivot column and the entry in the objective row are not used). Since there is a tie, we can choose either row one or row two. We choose row one and use the 1 in row one, column 2 as the pivot. Pivoting produces this tableau

$$\begin{array}{cccccc|cl} x_1 & x_2 & x_3 & x_4 & x_5 & x_6 & & \\ 0 & 1 & 2 & -1 & -1 & 0 & 2 & \\ 1 & 0 & -4 & 3 & 4 & 0 & 0 & -3R_1 + R_2 \\ 0 & 0 & 12 & -5 & -8 & 1 & 14 & 5R_1 + R_3 \\ \hline 0 & 0 & -2 & 2 & 6 & 0 & 20 & -2R_1 + R_4 \end{array}$$

and the basic *feasible* solution

$$x_1 = 0, \quad x_2 = 2, \quad x_3 = 0, \quad x_4 = 0, \quad x_5 = 0, \quad x_6 = 14. \quad \blacksquare$$

Once a basic feasible solution has been found, Stage I is ended. The procedures used in Stage I are summarized below.*

3 The initial tableau of a maximization problem is given below. Use column one as the pivot column for carrying out Stage I and state the basic feasible solution that results.

x_1	x_2	x_3	x_4	
1	3	1	0	70
2	4	0	−1	50
−8	−10	0	0	0

Answer:

x_1	x_2	x_3	x_4	
0	1	1	$\frac{1}{2}$	45
1	2	0	$-\frac{1}{2}$	25
0	6	0	−4	200

$x_1 = 25, x_2 = 0, x_3 = 45, x_4 = 0.$

FINDING A BASIC FEASIBLE SOLUTION

1. If any basic variable has a negative value, locate the −1 in that variable's column and note the row it is in.
2. In the row determined in Step 1, choose a positive entry (other than the one at the far right) and note the column it is in. This is the pivot column.
3. Use the positive entries in the pivot column (except in the objective row) to form quotients and select the pivot.
4. Pivot as usual, which results in the pivot column's having one entry 1 and the rest 0s.
5. Repeat Steps 1–4 until every basic variable is nonnegative, so that the basic solution given by the tableau is feasible. If it ever becomes impossible to continue, then the problem has no feasible solution.

One way to make the required choices systematically is to choose the first possibility in each case (going from the top for rows or from the left for columns). However, any choice meeting the required conditions may be used. For maximum efficiency, it is usually best to choose the pivot column in Step 2 so that the pivot is in the same row chosen in Step 1, if this is possible. 3

In **Stage II,** the simplex method is applied as usual to the tableau that produced the basic feasible solution in Stage I. Just as in Section 8.4, each round of pivoting replaces the basic feasible solution of one tableau with the basic feasible solution of a new tableau in such a way that the value of the objective function is increased, until an optimal value is obtained (or it becomes clear that no optimal solution exists).

EXAMPLE 3 Solve the linear programming problem in Example 1.

A basic feasible solution for this problem was found in Example 2 by using the tableau shown below. However, this solution is not maximal because there is a negative indicator in the objective row. So we use the simplex method: the most negative indicator determines the pivot column and the usual quotients determine that the number 2 in row one, column three is the pivot.

x_1	x_2	x_3	x_4	x_5	x_6		Quotients
0	1	**2**	−1	−1	0	2	2/2 ← Smallest
1	0	−4	3	4	0	0	
0	0	12	−5	−8	1	14	14/12
0	0	−2	2	6	0	20	
		↑ Most negative indicator					

*Except in rare cases that do not occur in this book, this method eventually produces a basic feasible solution or shows that one does not exist. The *two-phase method* using artificial variables, which is discussed in more advanced texts, works in all cases and often is more efficient.

Pivoting leads to the final tableau.

$$\begin{array}{cccccc|c} x_1 & x_2 & x_3 & x_4 & x_5 & x_6 & \\ 0 & \frac{1}{2} & 1 & -\frac{1}{2} & -\frac{1}{2} & 0 & 1 \\ 1 & 0 & -4 & 3 & 4 & 0 & 0 \\ 0 & 0 & 12 & -5 & -8 & 1 & 14 \\ \hline 0 & 0 & -2 & 2 & 6 & 0 & 20 \end{array} \quad \frac{1}{2}R_1$$

$$\begin{array}{cccccc|c} x_1 & x_2 & x_3 & x_4 & x_5 & x_6 & \\ 0 & \frac{1}{2} & 1 & -\frac{1}{2} & -\frac{1}{2} & 0 & 1 \\ 1 & 2 & 0 & 1 & 2 & 0 & 4 \\ 0 & -6 & 0 & 1 & -2 & 1 & 2 \\ \hline 0 & 1 & 0 & 1 & 5 & 0 & 22 \end{array} \quad \begin{array}{l} \\ \\ 4R_1 + R_2 \\ -12R_1 + R_3 \\ 2R_1 + R_4 \end{array}$$

4 Complete Stage II and find an optimal solution for Side Problem 3 above. What is the optimal value of the objective function z?

Answer:
The optimal value $z = 560$ occurs when $x_1 = 70, x_2 = 0, x_3 = 0, x_4 = 90$.

Therefore, the maximum value of z occurs when $x_1 = 4, x_2 = 0$, and $x_3 = 1$, in which case $z = 22$. ■ 4

The two-stage method for maximization problems illustrated in Examples 1–3 also provides a means of solving minimization problems. To see why, consider this simple fact: when a number t gets smaller, then $-t$ gets larger, and vice-versa. For instance, if t goes from 6 to 1 to 0 to -8, then $-t$ goes from -6 to -1 to 0 to 8. Thus, if w is the objective function of a linear programming problem, the feasible solution that produces the minimum value of w also produces the maximum value of $-w$, and vice-versa. Therefore, to solve a minimization problem with objective function w, we need only solve the maximization problem with the same constraints and objective function $z = -w$.

EXAMPLE 4 Minimize $w = 2y_1 + y_2 - y_3$

subject to:

$$\begin{aligned} -y_1 - y_2 + y_3 &\le -4 \\ y_1 + 3y_2 + 3y_3 &\ge 6 \\ y_1 \ge 0, y_2 \ge 0, y_3 &\ge 0. \end{aligned}$$

Make the constant in the first constraint positive by multiplying both sides by -1. Then solve this maximization problem:

Maximize $z = -w = -2y_1 - y_2 + y_3$

subject to:

$$\begin{aligned} y_1 + y_2 - y_3 &\ge 4 \\ y_1 + 3y_2 + 3y_3 &\ge 6 \\ y_1 \ge 0, y_2 \ge 0, y_3 &\ge 0. \end{aligned}$$

Convert the constraints to equations by subtracting surplus variables, and set up the first tableau.

$$\begin{array}{ccccc|c} y_1 & y_2 & y_3 & y_4 & y_5 & \\ 1 & 1 & -1 & -1 & 0 & 4 \\ 1 & 3 & 3 & 0 & -1 & 6 \\ \hline 2 & 1 & -1 & 0 & 0 & 0 \end{array}$$

The basic solution given by this tableau, $y_1 = 0, y_2 = 0, y_3 = 0, y_4 = -4, y_5 = -6$ is not feasible, so the procedures of Stage I must be used to find a basic feasible solution. In the column of the negative basic variable y_4, there is a -1 in row one; we choose the first positive entry in that row, so that column one will be the pivot column. The quotients $4/1 = 4$ and $6/1 = 6$ show that the pivot is the 1 in row one, column one. Pivoting produces this tableau:

$$\begin{array}{c} \begin{matrix} y_1 & y_2 & y_3 & y_4 & y_5 & \end{matrix} \\ \left[\begin{array}{rrrrr|r} 1 & 1 & -1 & -1 & 0 & 4 \\ 0 & 2 & 4 & 1 & -1 & 2 \\ \hline 0 & -1 & 1 & 2 & 0 & -8 \end{array}\right]. \end{array} \quad \begin{array}{l} \\ -R_1 + R_2 \\ -2R_1 + R_3 \end{array}$$

The basic solution $y_1 = 4, y_2 = 0, y_3 = 0, y_4 = 0, y_5 = -2$ is not feasible because y_5 is negative, so we repeat the process. We choose the first positive entry in row two (the row containing the -1 in the y_5 column), which is in column two, so that column two is the pivot column. The relevant quotients are $4/1 = 4$ and $2/2 = 1$, so the pivot is the 2 in row two, column two. Pivoting produces a new tableau.

$$\begin{array}{c} \begin{matrix} y_1 & y_2 & y_3 & y_4 & y_5 & \end{matrix} \\ \left[\begin{array}{rrrrr|r} 1 & 1 & -1 & -1 & 0 & 4 \\ 0 & 1 & 2 & \frac{1}{2} & -\frac{1}{2} & 1 \\ \hline 0 & -1 & 1 & 2 & 0 & -8 \end{array}\right] \end{array} \quad \begin{array}{l} \\ \frac{1}{2}R_2 \\ \\ \end{array}$$

$$\begin{array}{c} \begin{matrix} y_1 & y_2 & y_3 & y_4 & y_5 & \end{matrix} \\ \left[\begin{array}{rrrrr|r} 1 & 0 & -3 & -\frac{3}{2} & \frac{1}{2} & 3 \\ 0 & 1 & 2 & \frac{1}{2} & -\frac{1}{2} & 1 \\ \hline 0 & 0 & 3 & \frac{5}{2} & -\frac{1}{2} & -7 \end{array}\right] \end{array} \quad \begin{array}{l} -R_2 + R_1 \\ \\ R_2 + R_3 \end{array}$$

The basic solution $y_1 = 3, y_2 = 1, y_3 = 0, y_4 = 0, y_5 = 0$, is feasible, so Stage I is complete. However, this solution is not optimal because the objective row contains the negative indicator $-1/2$ in column five. According to the simplex method, column five is the next pivot column. The only positive ratio $3/\frac{1}{2} = 6$ is in row one, so the pivot is 1/2 in row one, column five. Pivoting produces the final tableau.

$$\begin{array}{c} \begin{matrix} y_1 & y_2 & y_3 & y_4 & y_5 & \end{matrix} \\ \left[\begin{array}{rrrrr|r} 2 & 0 & -6 & -3 & 1 & 6 \\ 0 & 1 & 2 & \frac{1}{2} & -\frac{1}{2} & 1 \\ \hline 0 & 0 & 3 & \frac{5}{2} & -\frac{1}{2} & -7 \end{array}\right] \end{array} \quad \begin{array}{l} 2R_1 \\ \\ \\ \end{array}$$

$$\begin{array}{c} \begin{matrix} y_1 & y_2 & y_3 & y_4 & y_5 & \end{matrix} \\ \left[\begin{array}{rrrrr|r} 2 & 0 & -6 & -3 & 1 & 6 \\ 1 & 1 & -1 & -1 & 0 & 4 \\ \hline 1 & 0 & 0 & 1 & 0 & -4 \end{array}\right] \end{array} \quad \begin{array}{l} \\ \frac{1}{2}R_1 + R_2 \\ \frac{1}{2}R_1 + R_3 \end{array}$$

Since there are no negative indicators, the solution given by this tableau ($y_1 = 0$, $y_2 = 4, y_3 = 0, y_4 = 0, y_5 = 6$) is optimal. The maximum value of $z = -w$ is -4.

5 Minimize $w = 2y_1 + 3y_2$
subject to:

$$y_1 + y_2 \geq 10$$
$$2y_1 + y_2 \geq 16$$
$$y_1 \geq 0, y_2 \geq 0.$$

Answer:
$y_1 = 10, y_2 = 0; w = 20$

Therefore, the minimum value of the original objective function w is $-(-4) = 4$, which occurs when $y_1 = 0, y_2 = 4, y_3 = 0$. ■ 5

Here is a summary of the two-stage method that was illustrated in Examples 1–4.

SOLVING NONSTANDARD PROBLEMS

1. If necessary, write each constraint with a positive constant and convert the problem to a maximum problem by letting $z = -w$.
2. Add slack variables and subtract surplus variables as needed to convert the constraints into equations.
3. Write the initial simplex tableau.
4. Find a basic feasible solution for the problem, if one exists (Stage I).
5. When a basic feasible solution is found, use the simplex method to solve the problem (Stage II).

NOTE It may happen that the tableau that gives the basic feasible solution in Stage I has no negative indicators in its last row. In this case, the solution found is already optimal and Stage II is not necessary. ◆

EXAMPLE 5 A college textbook publisher has received orders from two colleges, C_1 and C_2. C_1 needs at least 500 books, and C_2 needs at least 1000. The publisher can supply the books from either of two warehouses. Warehouse W_1 has 900 books available and warehouse W_2 has 700. The costs to ship a book from each warehouse to each college are given below.

		TO	
		C_1	C_2
FROM	W_1	$1.20	$1.80
	W_2	$2.10	$1.50

How many books should be sent from each warehouse to each college to minimize the shipping costs?

To begin, let

y_1 = the number of books shipped from W_1 to C_1;
y_2 = the number of books shipped from W_2 to C_1;
y_3 = the number of books shipped from W_1 to C_2;
y_4 = the number of books shipped from W_2 to C_2.

C_1 needs at least 500 books, so

$$y_1 + y_2 \geq 500.$$

Similarly,

$$y_3 + y_4 \geq 1000.$$

Since W_1 has 900 books available and W_2 has 700 available,

$$y_1 + y_3 \le 900 \quad \text{and} \quad y_2 + y_4 \le 700.$$

The company wants to minimize shipping costs, so the objective function is

$$w = 1.20y_1 + 2.10y_2 + 1.80y_3 + 1.50y_4.$$

Now write the problem as a system of linear equations, adding slack or surplus variables as needed, and let $z = -w$.

$$\begin{aligned}
y_1 + y_2 \qquad\qquad\qquad - y_5 \qquad\qquad &= 500\\
y_3 + y_4 \qquad - y_6 \qquad &= 1000\\
y_1 \qquad + y_3 \qquad\qquad\qquad + y_7 \qquad &= 900\\
y_2 \qquad + y_4 \qquad\qquad\qquad + y_8 &= 700\\
1.20y_1 + 2.10y_2 + 1.80y_3 + 1.50y_4 \qquad\qquad\qquad + z &= 0
\end{aligned}$$

Set up the initial simplex tableau.

y_1	y_2	y_3	y_4	y_5	y_6	y_7	y_8	
1	1	0	0	−1	0	0	0	500
0	0	1	1	0	−1	0	0	1000
1	0	1	0	0	0	1	0	900
0	1	0	1	0	0	0	1	700
1.20	2.10	1.80	1.50	0	0	0	0	0

The indicated solution is

$$y_5 = -500, \quad y_6 = -1000, \quad y_7 = 900, \quad y_8 = 700,$$

which is not feasible since y_5 and y_6 are negative.

There is a −1 in row one of the y_5 column. We choose the first positive entry in row one, which makes column one the pivot column. The quotients 500/1 = 500 and 900/1 = 900 show that the pivot is the 1 in row one, column one. Pivoting produces this tableau.

y_1	y_2	y_3	y_4	y_5	y_6	y_7	y_8	
1	1	0	0	−1	0	0	0	500
0	0	1	1	0	−1	0	0	1000
0	−1	1	0	1	0	1	0	400
0	1	0	1	0	0	0	1	700
0	.9	1.8	1.5	1.2	0	0	0	−600

The basic variable y_6 is negative and there is a −1 in row two of its column. We choose the first positive entry in that row, which makes column three the pivot column. The quotients 1000/1 = 1000 and 400/1 = 400 show that the pivot is the 1 in row three, column three. Pivoting leads to the next tableau.

$$\begin{array}{cccccccc|c} y_1 & y_2 & y_3 & y_4 & y_5 & y_6 & y_7 & y_8 & \\ 1 & 1 & 0 & 0 & -1 & 0 & 0 & 0 & 500 \\ 0 & 1 & 0 & 1 & -1 & -1 & -1 & 0 & 600 \\ 0 & -1 & 1 & 0 & 1 & 0 & 1 & 0 & 400 \\ 0 & 1 & 0 & 1 & 0 & 0 & 0 & 1 & 700 \\ \hline 0 & 2.7 & 0 & 1.5 & -.6 & 0 & -1.8 & 0 & -1320 \end{array}$$

The basic variable y_6 is still negative, so we must choose a positive entry in row two (the row containing the -1 in the y_6 column). If we choose the first positive entry, as we usually have done, then the quotients for determining the pivot will be 500/1 and 700/1 so that the pivot will be in row one. However, it is usually more efficient to have the pivot in the same row as the -1 of the basic variable (in this case row two). So we choose the 1 in row two, column four. Then the quotients for determining the pivot are 600/1 and 700/1 and the pivot is the 1 in row two, column four. Pivoting produces this tableau

$$\begin{array}{cccccccc|c} y_1 & y_2 & y_3 & y_4 & y_5 & y_6 & y_7 & y_8 & \\ 1 & 1 & 0 & 0 & -1 & 0 & 0 & 0 & 500 \\ 0 & 1 & 0 & 1 & -1 & -1 & -1 & 0 & 600 \\ 0 & -1 & 1 & 0 & 1 & 0 & 1 & 0 & 400 \\ 0 & 0 & 0 & 0 & 1 & 1 & 1 & 1 & 100 \\ \hline 0 & 1.2 & 0 & 0 & .9 & 1.5 & -.3 & 0 & -2220 \end{array}$$

and the basic feasible solution $y_1 = 500, y_2 = 0, y_3 = 400, y_4 = 600, y_5 = 0, y_6 = 0, y_7 = 0, y_8 = 100$. Hence Stage I is ended. This solution is not optimal because there is a negative indicator in the objective row, so we proceed to Stage II and the usual simplex method. Column seven has the only negative indicator, $-.3$, and row four the smallest quotient, $100/1 = 100$. Pivoting on the 1 in row four, column seven produces the final simplex tableau.

$$\begin{array}{cccccccc|c} y_1 & y_2 & y_3 & y_4 & y_5 & y_6 & y_7 & y_8 & \\ 1 & 1 & 0 & 0 & -1 & 0 & 0 & 0 & 500 \\ 0 & 1 & 0 & 1 & 0 & 0 & 0 & 1 & 700 \\ 0 & -1 & 1 & 0 & 0 & -1 & 0 & -1 & 300 \\ 0 & 0 & 0 & 0 & 1 & 1 & 1 & 1 & 100 \\ \hline 0 & 1.2 & 0 & 0 & 1.2 & 1.8 & 0 & .3 & -2190 \end{array}$$

Since there are no negative indicators, the solution given by this tableau ($y_1 = 500$, $y_3 = 300$, $y_4 = 700$) is optimal. The publisher should ship 500 books from W_1 to C_1, 300 books from W_1 to C_2, and 700 books from W_2 to C_2 for a minimum shipping cost of \$2190 (remember that the optimal value for the original minimization problem is the negative of the optimal value for the associated maximization problem). ■

Although they will not occur in this book, various complications can arise in using the simplex method. Some of the possible difficulties, which are treated in more advanced texts, include the following:

1. Some of the constraints may be *equations* instead of inequalities. In this case, *artificial variables* must be used.
2. Occasionally, a transformation will cycle—that is, produce a "new" solution which was an earlier solution in the process. These situations are known as *degeneracies* and special methods are available for handling them.
3. It may not be possible to convert a nonfeasible basic solution to a feasible basic solution. In that case, no solution can satisfy all the constraints. Graphically, this means there is no region of feasible solutions.

A linear programming model on preparing a fertilizer mix to certain specifications is presented at the end of this chapter. The model illustrates the usefulness of linear programming. In most real applications, the number of variables is so large that these problems could not be solved without the use of a method, like the simplex method, that can be adapted to a computer.

8.7 EXERCISES

In Exercises 1–4, (a) restate the problem in terms of equations by introducing slack and surplus variables; (b) write the initial simplex tableau. (See Example 1.)

1. Maximize $z = 5x_1 + 2x_2 - x_3$
subject to:
$$2x_1 + 3x_2 + 5x_3 \geq 8$$
$$4x_1 - x_2 + 3x_3 \leq 7$$
$$x_1 \geq 0, x_2 \geq 0, x_3 \geq 0.$$

2. Maximize $z = x_1 + 4x_2 + 6x_3$
subject to:
$$5x_1 + 8x_2 - 5x_3 \leq 10$$
$$6x_1 + 2x_2 + 3x_3 \geq 7$$
$$x_1 \geq 0, x_2 \geq 0, x_3 \geq 0.$$

3. Maximize $z = 2x_1 - 3x_2 + 4x_3$
subject to:
$$x_1 + x_2 + x_3 \leq 100$$
$$x_1 + x_2 + x_3 \geq 75$$
$$x_1 + x_2 \geq 27$$
$$x_1 \geq 0, x_2 \geq 0, x_3 \geq 0.$$

4. Maximize $z = -x_1 + 5x_2 + x_3$
subject to:
$$2x_1 + x_3 \leq 40$$
$$x_1 + x_2 \geq 18$$
$$x_1 + x_3 \geq 20$$
$$x_1 \geq 0, x_2 \geq 0, x_3 \geq 0.$$

Convert Exercises 5–8 into maximization problems with positive constants on the right side of each constraint and write the initial simplex tableau. (See Example 4.)

5. Minimize $w = 2y_1 + 5y_2 - 3y_3$
subject to:
$$y_1 + 2y_2 + 3y_3 \geq 115$$
$$2y_1 + y_2 + y_3 \leq 200$$
$$y_1 + y_3 \geq 50$$
$$y_1 \geq 0, y_2 \geq 0, y_3 \geq 0.$$

6. Minimize $w = 7y_1 + 6y_2 + y_3$
subject to:
$$y_1 + y_2 + y_3 \geq 5$$
$$-y_1 + y_2 \leq -4$$
$$2y_1 + y_2 + 3y_3 \geq 15$$
$$y_1 \geq 0, y_2 \geq 0, y_3 \geq 0.$$

7. Minimize $w = y_1 - 4y_2 + 2y_3$
subject to:
$$-7y_1 + 6y_2 - 8y_3 \leq -18$$
$$4y_1 + 5y_2 + 10y_3 \geq 20$$
$$y_1 \geq 0, y_2 \geq 0, y_3 \geq 0.$$

8. Minimize $w = y_1 + 2y_2 + y_3 + 5y_4$
subject to:
$$-y_1 + y_2 + y_3 + y_4 \leq -50$$
$$3y_1 + y_2 + 2y_3 + y_4 \geq 100$$
$$y_1 \geq 0, y_2 \geq 0, y_3 \geq 0, y_4 \geq 0.$$

Use the two-stage method to solve Exercises 9–18. (See Examples 1–4.)

9. Maximize $z = 12x_1 + 10x_2$
subject to:
$$x_1 + 2x_2 \geq 24$$
$$x_1 + x_2 \leq 40$$
$$x_1 \geq 0, x_2 \geq 0.$$

10. Find $x_1 \geq 0$, $x_2 \geq 0$, and $x_3 \geq 0$ such that
$$x_1 + x_2 + x_3 \leq 150$$
$$x_1 + x_2 + x_3 \geq 100$$
and $z = 2x_1 + 5x_2 + 3x_3$ is maximized.

11. Find $x_1 \geq 0$, $x_2 \geq 0$, and $x_3 \geq 0$ such that
$$x_1 + x_2 + 2x_3 \leq 38$$
$$2x_1 + x_2 + x_3 \geq 24$$
and $z = 3x_1 + 2x_2 + 2x_3$ is maximized.

12. Maximize $z = 6x_1 + 8x_2$
subject to: $3x_1 + 12x_2 \geq 48$
$2x_1 + 4x_2 \leq 60$
$x_1 \geq 0, x_2 \geq 0.$

13. Find $x_1 \geq 0$ and $x_2 \geq 0$ such that

$$x_1 + 2x_2 \leq 18$$
$$x_1 + 3x_2 \geq 12$$
$$2x_1 + 2x_2 \leq 30$$

and $z = 5x_1 + 10x_2$ is maximized.

14. Find $x_1 \geq 0$ and $x_2 \geq 0$ such that

$$x_1 + x_2 \leq 100$$
$$x_1 + x_2 \geq 50$$
$$2x_1 + x_2 \leq 110$$

and $z = 2x_1 + 3x_2$ is maximized.

15. Find $y_1 \geq 0, y_2 \geq 0$ such that

$$10y_1 + 5y_2 \geq 100$$
$$20y_1 + 10y_2 \geq 160$$

and $w = 4y_1 + 5y_2$ is minimized.

16. Minimize $w = 3y_1 + 2y_2$
subject to: $2y_1 + 3y_2 \geq 60$
$y_1 + 4y_2 \geq 40$
$y_1 \geq 0, y_2 \geq 0.$

17. Minimize $w = 3y_1 + 4y_2$
subject to: $y_1 + 2y_2 \geq 10$
$y_1 + y_2 \geq 8$
$2y_1 + y_2 \leq 22$
$y_1 \geq 0, y_2 \geq 0.$

18. Minimize $w = 4y_1 + 2y_2$
subject to: $y_1 + y_2 \geq 20$
$y_1 + 2y_2 \geq 25$
$-5y_1 + y_2 \leq 4$
$y_1 \geq 0, y_2 \geq 0.$

In Exercises 19–22, set up the initial simplex tableau, but do not solve the problem. (See Example 5.)

19. **Management** The manufacturer of a popular personal computer has orders from two dealers. Dealer D_1 wants at least 32 computers, and dealer D_2 wants at least 20 computers. The manufacturer can fill the orders from either of two warehouses, W_1 or W_2. W_1 has 25 of the computers on hand, and W_2 has 30. The costs (in dollars) to ship one computer to each dealer from each warehouse are given below.

		TO	
		D_1	D_2
FROM	W_1	\$14	\$22
	W_2	\$12	\$10

How should the orders be filled to minimize shipping costs?

20. **Natural Science** Mark, who is ill, takes vitamin pills. Each day he must have at least 16 units of vitamin A, 5 units of vitamin B_1, and 20 units of vitamin C. He can choose between pill #1 which costs 10¢ and contains 8 units of A, 1 of B_1, and 2 of C, and pill #2 which costs 20¢ and contains 2 units of A, 1 of B_1, and 7 of C. How many of each pill should he buy in order to minimize his cost?

21. **Management** A company is developing a new additive for gasoline. The additive is a mixture of three liquid ingredients, I, II, and III. For proper performance, the total amount of additive must be at least 10 ounces per gallon of gasoline. However, for safety reasons, the amount of additive should not exceed 15 ounces per gallon of gasoline. At least 1/4 ounce of ingredient I must be used for every ounce of ingredient II and at least 1 ounce of ingredient III must be used for every ounce of ingredient I. If the costs of I, II, and III are \$.30, \$.09, and \$.27 per ounce, respectively, find the mixture of the three ingredients that produces the minimum cost of the additive. How much of the additive should be used per gallon of gasoline?

22. **Management** A popular soft drink called Sugarlo, which is advertised as having a sugar content of no more than 10%, is blended from five ingredients, each of which has some sugar content. Water may also be added to dilute the mixture. The sugar content of the ingredients and their costs per gallon are given below.

	INGREDIENT					
	1	2	3	4	5	*Water*
Sugar content (%)	.28	.19	.43	.57	.22	0
Cost (\$/gal.)	.48	.32	.53	.28	.43	.04

At least .01 of the content of Sugarlo must come from ingredients 3 or 4, .01 must come from ingredients 2 or 5, and .01 from ingredients 1 or 4. How much of each ingredient should be used in preparing at least 15,000 gallons of Sugarlo to minimize the cost?

Use the two-stage method to solve Exercises 23–30. (See Example 5.)

23. **Management** Southwestern Oil supplies two distributors in the Northwest from two outlets. Distributor D_1 needs at least 3000 barrels of oil, and distributor D_2 needs at least 5000 barrels. The two outlets can each furnish up to 5000 barrels of oil. The costs per barrel to send the oil are given below.

		TO	
		D_1	D_2
FROM	S_1	\$30	\$20
	S_2	\$25	\$22

How should the oil be supplied to minimize shipping costs?

24. Management Change Exercise 23 so that there is also a shipping tax per barrel as given in the table below. Southwestern Oil is determined to spend no more than $40,000 on shipping tax.

	D_1	D_2
S_1	$2	$6
S_2	$5	$4

How should the oil be supplied to minimize shipping costs?

25. Management A bank has set aside a maximum of $25 million for commercial and home loans. Every million dollars in commercial loans requires 2 lengthy application forms, while every million dollars in home loans requires 3 lengthy application forms. The bank cannot process more than 72 application forms at this time. The bank's policy is to loan at least four times as much for home loans as for commercial loans. Because of prior commitments, at least $10 million will be used for these two types of loans. The bank earns 12% on home loans and 10% on commercial loans. What amount of money should be allotted for each type of loan to maximize the interest income?

26. Management Virginia Keleske has decided to invest a $100,000 inheritance in government securities that earn 7% per year, municipal bonds that earn 6% per year, and mutual funds that earn an average of 10% per year. She will spend at least $40,000 on government securities, and she wants at least half the inheritance to go to bonds and mutual funds. Government securities have an initial fee of 2%, municipal bonds have an initial fee of 1%, and mutual funds have an initial fee of 3%. Virginia has $2400 available to pay initial fees. How much should be invested in each way to maximize the interest yet meet the constraints? What is the maximum interest she can earn?

27. Management Brand X Canners produce canned whole tomatoes and tomato sauce. This season, they have available 3,000,000 kilograms of tomatoes for these two products. To meet the demands of regular customers, they must produce at least 80,000 kilograms of sauce and 800,000 kilograms of whole tomatoes. The cost per kilogram is $4 to produce canned whole tomatoes and $3.25 to produce tomato sauce. Labor agreements require that at least 110,000 person hours be used. Each can of sauce requires 3 minutes for one worker, and each can of whole tomatoes requires 6 minutes for one worker. How many kilograms of tomatoes should Brand X use for each product to minimize cost? (For simplicity, assume production of y_1 kg of canned whole tomatoes and y_2 kilograms of tomato sauce requires $y_1 + y_2$ kg of tomatoes.)

28. Management A brewery produces regular beer and a lower-carbohydrate "light" beer. Steady customers of the brewery buy 12 units of regular beer and 10 units of light beer. While setting up the brewery to produce the beers, the management decides to produce extra beer, beyond that needed to satisfy the steady customers. The cost per unit of regular beer is $36,000 and the cost per unit of light beer is $48,000. The number of units of light beer should not exceed twice the number of units of regular beer. At least 20 additional units of beer can be sold. How much of each type beer should be made so as to minimize total production costs?

29. Management The chemistry department at a local college decides to stock at least 800 small test tubes and 500 large test tubes. It wants to buy at least 1500 test tubes to take advantage of a special price. Since the small tubes are broken twice as often as the larger, the department will order at least twice as many small tubes as large. If the small test tubes cost 15¢ each and the large ones, made of a cheaper glass, cost 12¢ each, how many of each size should they order to minimize cost?

30. Management Topgrade Turf lawn seed mixture contains three types of seeds: bluegrass, rye, and bermuda. The costs per pound of the three types of seed are 12¢, 15¢ and 5¢. In each mixture there must be at least 20% bluegrass seed, and the amount of bermuda must be no more than 2/3 the amount of rye. To fill current orders, the company must make at least 5000 pounds of the mixture. How much of each kind of seed should be used to minimize cost?

CHAPTER 8 SUMMARY

Key Terms and Symbols

8.1 linear inequality
boundary
half-plane
system of inequalities
region of feasible solutions (feasible region)

8.2 linear programming
objective function
constraints
corner point
bounded feasible region
unbounded feasible region
corner point theorem

8.4 standard maximum form
slack variable
simplex tableau

indicator
pivot and pivoting
final simplex tableau
basic variables
nonbasic variables
basic feasible solution
8.6 dual
transpose of a matrix

theorem of duality
shadow costs
8.7 surplus variable
basic variables
basic solution
basic feasible solution
Stage I
Stage II

Key Concepts

Graphing a Linear Inequality

Graph the boundary line as a solid line if the inequality includes "or equal," a dashed line otherwise. Shade the half-plane that includes a test point that makes the inequality true. The graph of a system of inequalities, called the **region of feasible solutions,** includes all points that satisfy all the inequalities of the system at the same time.

Solving Linear Programming Problems

Graphically: Determine the objective function and all necessary constraints. Graph the region of feasible solutions. The maximum or minimum value will occur at one or more of the corner points of this region.

Simplex Method: Determine the objective function and all necessary constraints. Convert each constraint into an equation by adding slack variables. Set up the initial simplex tableau. Locate the most negative indicator. Form the quotients to determine the pivot. Use row operations to change the pivot to 1 and all other numbers in that column to 0. If the indicators are all positive or 0, this is the final tableau. If not, choose a new pivot and repeat the process until no indicators are negative. Read the solution from the final tableau. The optimum value of the objective function is the number in the lower right corner of the final tableau. For problems with **mixed constraints,** add surplus variables as well as slack variables. In Stage I, use row operations to transform the matrix until the solution is feasible. In Stage II, use the simplex method as described above. For **minimum** problems, let the objective function be w and set $-w = z$. Then proceed as with mixed constraints.

Solving Minimum Problems with Duals

Find the dual maximum problem. Solve the dual using the simplex method. The minimum value of the objective function w is the maximum value of the dual objective function z. The optimal solution is found in the entries in the bottom row of the columns corresponding to the slack variables.

Chapter 8 Review Exercises

Graph each of the following linear inequalities.

1. $y \le 3x + 2$

2. $2x - y \ge 6$

3. $3x + 4y \ge 12$

4. $y \le 4$

Graph the solution of each of the following systems of inequalities.

5. $x + y \le 6$
$2x - y \ge 3$

6. $4x + y \ge 8$
$2x - 3y \le 6$

7. $2 \le x \le 5$
$1 \le y \le 7$
$x - y \le 3$

8. $x + 2y \le 4$
$2x - 3y \le 6$
$x \ge 0$
$y \ge 0$

Set up a system of inequalities for each of the following problems; then graph the region of feasible solutions.

9. Management A bakery makes both cakes and cookies. Each batch of cakes requires 2 hours in the oven and 3 hours in the decorating room. Each batch of cookies needs $1\frac{1}{2}$ hours in the oven and 2/3 of an hour in the decorating room. The oven is available no more than 15 hours a day, while the decorating room can be used no more than 13 hours a day.

10. Management A company makes two kinds of pizza, special and basic. The special has toppings of cheese, tomatoes, and vegetables. Basic has just cheese and tomatoes.

The company sells at least 6 units a day of the special pizza and 4 units a day of the basic. The cost of the vegetables (including tomatoes) is \$2 per unit for special and \$1 per unit for basic. No more than \$32 per day can be spent on vegetables (including tomatoes). The cheese used for the special is \$5 per unit, and the cheese for the basic is \$4 per unit. The company can spend no more than \$100 per day on cheese.

Use the given regions to find the maximum and minimum values of the objective function $z = 2x + 4y$.

11.

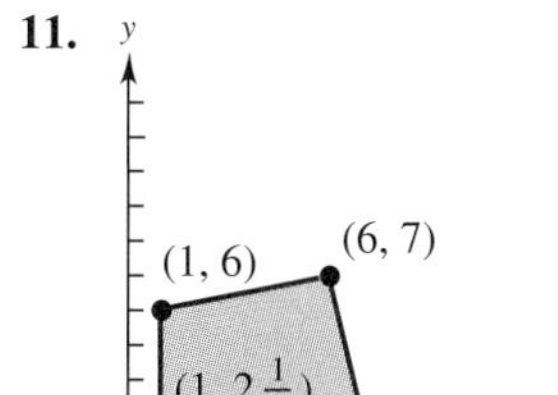

12.

y
(0, 8)
(8, 8)
(5, 2)
(2, 0)
x

Use the graphical method to solve Exercises 13–16.

13. Maximize $z = 3x + 2y$
subject to:
$$2x + 7y \le 14$$
$$2x + 3y \le 10$$
$$x \ge 0,\ y \ge 0.$$

14. Find $x \ge 0$ and $y \ge 0$ such that
$$8x + 9y \ge 72$$
$$6x + 8y \ge 72$$
and $w = 4x + 12y$ is minimized.

15. Find $x \ge 0$ and $y \ge 0$ such that
$$x + y \le 50$$
$$2x + y \ge 20$$
$$x + 2y \ge 30$$
and $w = 8x + 3y$ is minimized.

16. Maximize $z = 2x - 5y$
subject to:
$$3x + 2y \le 12$$
$$5x + y \ge 5$$
$$x \ge 0,\ y \ge 0.$$

17. Management How many batches of cakes and cookies should the bakery of Exercise 9 make in order to maximize profits if cookies produce a profit of \$20 per batch and cakes produce a profit of \$30 per batch?

18. Management How many units of each kind of pizza should the company of Exercise 10 make in order to maximize profits if special sells for \$20 per unit and basic for \$15 per unit?

For Exercises 19–22, **(a)** *select appropriate variables,* **(b)** *write the objective function,* **(c)** *write the constraints as inequalities.*

19. Management Roberta Hernandez sells three items, A, B, and C, in her gift shop. Each unit of A costs her \$2 to buy, \$1 to sell, and \$2 to deliver. For each unit of B, the costs are \$3, \$2, and \$2, respectively, and for each unit of C the costs are \$6, \$2, and \$4, respectively. The profit on A is \$4, on B it is \$3, and on C, \$3. How many of each should she order to maximize her profit if she can spend \$1200 to buy, \$800 on selling costs, and \$500 on delivery costs?

20. Management An investor is considering three types of investment: a high-risk venture into oil leases with a potential return of 15%, a medium-risk investment in bonds with a 9% return, and a relatively safe stock investment with a 5% return. He has \$50,000 to invest. Because of the risk, he will limit his investment in oil leases and bonds to 30% and his investment in oil leases and stock to 50%. How much should he invest in each to maximize his return, assuming investment returns are as expected?

21. Management The Aged Wood Winery makes two white wines, Fruity and Crystal, from two kinds of grapes and sugar. The wines require the following amounts of each ingredient per gallon and produce a profit per gallon as shown below.

	Grape A (bushels)	*Grape B (bushels)*	*Sugar (pounds)*	*Profit (dollars)*
Fruity	2	2	2	12
Crystal	1	3	1	15

The winery has available 110 bushels of grape A, 125 bushels of grape B, and 90 pounds of sugar. How much of each wine should be made to maximize profit?

22. Management A company makes three sizes of plastic bags: 5 gallon, 10 gallon and 20 gallon. The production time in hours for cutting, sealing, and packaging a unit of each size is shown below.

Size	*Cutting*	*Sealing*	*Packaging*
5 gallon	1	1	2
10 gallon	1.1	1.2	3
20 gallon	1.5	1.3	4

There are at most 8 hours available each day for each of the three operations. If the profit per unit is \$1 for 5-gallon bags, \$.90 for 10-gallon bags, and \$.95 for 20-gallon bags, how many of each size should be made per day to maximize the profit?

23. When is it necessary to use the simplex method rather than the graphical method?

24. What types of problems can be solved using slack, surplus, and artificial variables?

25. What kind of problem can be solved using the method of duals?

26. In solving a linear programming problem, you are given the following initial tableau.

$$\left[\begin{array}{cccccc|c} 4 & 2 & 3 & 1 & 0 & 0 & 9 \\ 5 & 4 & 1 & 0 & 1 & 0 & 10 \\ \hline -6 & -7 & -5 & 0 & 0 & 1 & 0 \end{array}\right]$$

(a) What is the problem being solved?
(b) If the 1 in row 1, column 4 were a -1 rather than a 1, how would it change your answer to part (a)?
(c) After several steps of the simplex algorithm, the following tableau results.

$$\left[\begin{array}{cccccc|c} 3 & 0 & 5 & 2 & -1 & 0 & 8 \\ 11 & 10 & 0 & -1 & 3 & 0 & 21 \\ \hline 47 & 0 & 0 & 13 & 11 & 10 & 227 \end{array}\right]$$

What is the solution? (List only the values of the original variables and the objective function. Do not include slack or surplus variables.)
(d) What is the dual of the problem you found in part (a)?
(e) What is the solution of the dual you found in part (d)? (Do not perform any steps of the simplex algorithm; just examine the tableau given in part (c).)

For each of the following problems, (a) *add slack variables and* (b) *set up the initial simplex tableau.*

27. Maximize $z = 2x_1 + 7x_2$
subject to:
$$\begin{aligned} 3x_1 + 5x_2 &\le 47 \\ x_1 + x_2 &\le 25 \\ 5x_1 + 2x_2 &\le 35 \\ 2x_1 + x_2 &\le 30 \\ x_1 \ge 0, x_2 &\ge 0. \end{aligned}$$

28. Maximize $z = 15x_1 + 10x_2$
subject to:
$$\begin{aligned} 2x_1 + 5x_2 &\le 50 \\ x_1 + 3x_2 &\le 25 \\ 4x_1 + x_2 &\le 18 \\ x_1 + x_2 &\le 12 \\ x_1 \ge 0, x_2 &\ge 0. \end{aligned}$$

29. Maximize $z = 4x_1 + 6x_2 + 3x_3$
subject to:
$$\begin{aligned} x_1 + x_2 + x_3 &\le 100 \\ 2x_1 + 3x_2 &\le 500 \\ x_1 + 2x_3 &\le 350 \\ x_1 \ge 0, x_2 \ge 0, x_3 &\ge 0. \end{aligned}$$

30. Maximize $z = x_1 + 4x_2 + 2x_3$
subject to:
$$\begin{aligned} x_1 + x_2 + x_3 &\le 90 \\ 2x_1 + 5x_2 + x_3 &\le 120 \\ x_1 + 3x_2 &\le 80 \\ x_1 \ge 0, x_2 \ge 0, x_3 &\ge 0. \end{aligned}$$

For each of the following, use the simplex method to solve the maximization linear programming problems with initial tableaus as given.

31.
$$\begin{array}{c} \begin{array}{ccccc} x_1 & x_2 & x_3 & x_4 & x_5 \end{array} \\ \left[\begin{array}{ccccc|c} 1 & 2 & 3 & 1 & 0 & 28 \\ 2 & 4 & 8 & 0 & 1 & 32 \\ \hline -5 & -2 & -3 & 0 & 0 & 0 \end{array}\right] \end{array}$$

32.
$$\begin{array}{c} \begin{array}{cccc} x_1 & x_2 & x_3 & x_4 \end{array} \\ \left[\begin{array}{cccc|c} 2 & 1 & 1 & 0 & 10 \\ 9 & 3 & 0 & 1 & 15 \\ \hline -2 & -3 & 0 & 0 & 0 \end{array}\right] \end{array}$$

33.
$$\begin{array}{c} \begin{array}{cccccc} x_1 & x_2 & x_3 & x_4 & x_5 & x_6 \end{array} \\ \left[\begin{array}{cccccc|c} 1 & 2 & 2 & 1 & 0 & 0 & 50 \\ 4 & 24 & 0 & 0 & 1 & 0 & 20 \\ 1 & 0 & 2 & 0 & 0 & 1 & 15 \\ \hline -5 & -3 & -2 & 0 & 0 & 0 & 0 \end{array}\right] \end{array}$$

34.
$$\begin{array}{c} \begin{array}{ccccc} x_1 & x_2 & x_3 & x_4 & x_5 \end{array} \\ \left[\begin{array}{ccccc|c} 1 & -2 & 1 & 0 & 0 & 38 \\ 1 & -1 & 0 & 1 & 0 & 12 \\ 2 & 1 & 0 & 0 & 1 & 30 \\ \hline -1 & -2 & 0 & 0 & 0 & 0 \end{array}\right] \end{array}$$

Convert the following problems into maximization problems without using duals.

35. Minimize $w = 18y_1 + 10y_2$
subject to:
$$\begin{aligned} y_1 + y_2 &\ge 17 \\ 5y_1 + 8y_2 &\ge 42 \\ y_1 \ge 0, y_2 &\ge 0. \end{aligned}$$

36. Minimize $w = 12y_1 + 20y_2 - 8y_3$
subject to:
$$\begin{aligned} y_1 + y_2 + 2y_3 &\ge 48 \\ y_1 + y_2 &\ge 12 \\ y_3 &\ge 10 \\ 3y_1 + y_3 &\ge 30 \\ y_1 \ge 0, y_2 \ge 0, y_3 &\ge 0. \end{aligned}$$

37. Minimize $w = 6y_1 - 3y_2 + 4y_3$
subject to:
$$\begin{aligned} 2y_1 + y_2 + y_3 &\geq 112 \\ y_1 + y_2 + y_3 &\geq 80 \\ y_1 + y_2 \quad &\geq 45 \\ y_1 \geq 0, y_2 \geq 0,& \; y_3 \geq 0. \end{aligned}$$

Use the simplex method to solve the following mixed constraint problems.

38. Maximize $z = 2x_1 + 4x_2$
subject to:
$$\begin{aligned} 3x_1 + 2x_2 &\leq 12 \\ 5x_1 + x_2 &\geq 5 \\ x_1 \geq 0, x_2 &\geq 0. \end{aligned}$$

39. Minimize $w = 4y_1 - 8y_2$
subject to:
$$\begin{aligned} y_1 + y_2 &\leq 50 \\ 2y_1 - 4y_2 &\geq 20 \\ y_1 - y_2 &\leq 22 \\ y_1 \geq 0, y_2 &\geq 0. \end{aligned}$$

The following tableaus are the final tableaus of minimizing problems solved by letting $w = -z$. Give the solution and the minimum value of the objective function for each problem.

40.
$$\left[\begin{array}{cccccc|c} 0 & 1 & 0 & 2 & 5 & 0 & 17 \\ 0 & 0 & 1 & 3 & 1 & 1 & 25 \\ 1 & 0 & 0 & 4 & 2 & \frac{1}{2} & 8 \\ \hline 0 & 0 & 0 & 2 & 5 & 0 & -427 \end{array}\right]$$

41.
$$\left[\begin{array}{ccccccc|c} 0 & 0 & 2 & 1 & 0 & 6 & 6 & 92 \\ 1 & 0 & 3 & 0 & 0 & 0 & 2 & 47 \\ 0 & 1 & 0 & 0 & 0 & 1 & 0 & 68 \\ 0 & 0 & 4 & 0 & 1 & 0 & 3 & 35 \\ \hline 0 & 0 & 5 & 0 & 0 & 2 & 9 & -1957 \end{array}\right]$$

The tableaus in Exercises 42–44 are the final tableaus of minimizing problems solved by the method of duals. State the solution and the minimum value of the objective function for each problem.

42.
$$\left[\begin{array}{cccccc|c} 1 & 0 & 0 & 3 & 1 & 2 & 12 \\ 0 & 0 & 1 & 4 & 5 & 3 & 5 \\ 0 & 1 & 0 & -2 & 7 & -6 & 8 \\ \hline 0 & 0 & 0 & 5 & 7 & 3 & 172 \end{array}\right]$$

43.
$$\left[\begin{array}{cccccc|c} 0 & 0 & 1 & 6 & 3 & 1 & 2 \\ 1 & 0 & 0 & 4 & -2 & 2 & 8 \\ 0 & 1 & 0 & 10 & 7 & 0 & 12 \\ \hline 0 & 0 & 0 & 9 & 5 & 8 & 62 \end{array}\right]$$

44.
$$\left[\begin{array}{cccc|c} 1 & 0 & 7 & -1 & 100 \\ 0 & 1 & 1 & 3 & 27 \\ \hline 0 & 0 & 7 & 2 & 640 \end{array}\right]$$

45. Solve Exercise 19.

46. Solve Exercise 20.

47. Solve Exercise 21.

48. Solve Exercise 22.

Management *Solve the following minimization problems.*

49. A contractor builds boathouses in two basic models, the atlantic and pacific. Each atlantic model requires 1000 feet of framing lumber, 3000 cubic feet of concrete, and \$2000 for advertising. Each pacific model requires 2000 feet of framing lumber, 3000 cubic feet of concrete, and \$3000 for advertising. Contracts call for using at least 8000 feet of framing lumber, 18,000 cubic feet of concrete, and \$15,000 worth of advertising. If the total spent on each atlantic model is \$3000 and the total spent on each pacific model is \$4000, how many of each model should be built to minimize costs?

50. A steel company produces two types of alloys. A run of type I requires 3000 pounds of molybdenum and 2000 tons of iron ore pellets as well as \$2000 in advertising. A run of type II requires 3000 pounds of molybdenum and 1000 tons of iron ore pellets as well as \$3000 in advertising. Total costs are \$15,000 on a run of type I and \$6000 on a run of type II. Because of various contracts, the company must use at least 18,000 pounds of molybdenum and 7000 tons of iron ore pellets and spend at least \$14,000 on advertising. How much of each type should be produced to minimize costs?

CASE 8

A Minimum Cost Balanced Organic Fertilizer Mix*

Organic fertilizers build on three key elements that are essential to plant growth and health. Nitrogen (N) promotes plant growth and resistance to insects. Phosphorus (P) is essential for proper root growth. Potassium (K) aids in plant growth and resistance to disease. The percent of these three elements in a fertilizer is always listed in the order N-P-K. Thus, a 3-2-2 fertilizer is 3% nitrogen, 2% phosphorus, and 2% potassium.

Many garden centers and seed catalogs sell pre-mixed organic fertilizers. However, to get a mixture with a specific N-P-K combination at a minimum cost, a gardener must solve an optimization problem. A fertilizer with a b-b-b mix for some number b, is called a balanced fertilizer. To get a balanced organic fertilizer with a b-b-b mix, a gardener must use a combination of the following choices.

Blood Meal (11-0-0) @ \$6.00 per five-pound bag
Bone Meal (6-12-0) @ \$5.00 per five-pound bag
Greensand (0-1-7) @ \$3.00 per five-pound bag
Sul-Po-Mag (0-0-22) @ \$2.80 per five-pound bag
Sustane (5-2-4) @ \$4.25 per five-pound bag

Linear programming can be used to model this problem. Let x_1 represent the number of pounds of blood meal to be used, x_2 represent the number of pounds of bone meal to be used, and so on. The gardener should minimize the objective function (using costs per pound)

$$z = 1.20x_1 + 1.00x_2 + .60x_3 + .56x_4 + .85x_5,$$

subject to the constraints

$$\begin{aligned} .11x_1 + .06x_2 \qquad\qquad\qquad\quad + .05x_5 &= 1 \\ .12x_2 + .01x_3 \qquad\quad + .02x_5 &= 1 \\ .07x_3 + .22x_4 + .04x_5 &= 1, \end{aligned}$$

where the element proportions are expressed as percents in decimal form. By setting all three sums equal to the same number, we ensure that the percents will be equal to provide a balanced fertilizer, as required. We use 1 on the right hand side to indicate 1 unit of mixed fertilizer. This makes the calculations easier. The nonnegativity constraints are

$$x_1 \geq 0, \quad x_2 \geq 0, \quad x_3 \geq 0, \quad x_4 \geq 0, \quad x_5 \geq 0.$$

Using a graphing calculator or a computer with linear programming software, we get the following solution.

$$x_1 = 4.5454, \quad x_2 = 8.3333, \quad x_3 = 0, \quad x_4 = 4.5454, \quad x_5 = 0$$

This mixture would cost \$16.33 (rounded), and since the mixture weighs 17.4242 pounds, the minimum cost per pound is \$.94 (rounded). Verify that a minimum cost organic fertilizer can be obtained by mixing 6 parts blood meal with 11 parts bone meal and 6 parts sul-po-mag.

EXERCISES

1. Show that the minimum cost mixture has proportions 6-11-6.
2. To determine the number b, the percent of each nutrient present in the fertilizer, we must divide the sum on the right of each constraint by the weight of the total mixture. (The results should be equal.) Do this and express the results in the form N-P-K. Is the result a balanced fertilizer?

*Turner, Steven J., "Using Linear Programming to Obtain a Minimum Cost Balanced Organic Fertilizer Mix," *The AMATYC Review*, Vol. 14, No. 2, Spring 1993, pp. 21–25.

CHAPTER 9 Sets and Probability

Federal officials cannot predict exactly how traffic deaths are affected by the trends toward fewer drunken drivers and increased use of seat belts. Economists cannot tell exactly how stricter federal regulations on bank loans affect the U.S. economy. The number of traffic deaths and the growth of the economy are subject to many factors that cannot be predicted precisely.

Probability theory enables us to deal with uncertainty. The basic concepts of probability are discussed in this chapter and applications of probability are discussed in the next chapter. Sets and set operations are the basic tools for the study of probability, so we begin with them.

9.1 SETS

Think of a **set** as a collection of objects. For example, a set of coins might contain one of each type of coin now put out by the United States government. Another set might include all the students in a class. The set containing the numbers 3, 4, and 5 is written

$$\{3, 4, 5\},$$

where **set braces,** { }, are used to enclose the numbers belonging to the set. The numbers, 3, 4, and 5 are called the **elements** or **members** of this set. To show that 4 is an element of the set {3, 4, 5}, we use the symbol $\in$ and write

$$4 \in \{3, 4, 5\},$$

read "4 is an element of the set containing 3, 4, and 5."

Also, $5 \in \{3, 4, 5\}$. Place a slash through the symbol $\in$ to show that 8 is *not* an element of this set.

$$8 \notin \{3, 4, 5\}$$

This is read "8 is not an element of the set {3, 4, 5}."

1 Write *true* or *false*.

(a) $9 \in \{8, 4, -3, -9, 6\}$

(b) $4 \notin \{3, 9, 7\}$

(c) If $M = \{0, 1, 2, 3, 4\}$, then $0 \in M$.

Answers:

(a) False

(b) True

(c) True

Sets are often named with capital letters, so that if

$$B = \{5, 6, 7\},$$

then, for example, $6 \in B$ and $10 \notin B$. 1

Sometimes a set has no elements. Some examples are the set of woman presidents of the United States in the period 1788–2000, the set of counting numbers less than 1, and the set of men more than 10 feet tall. A set with no elements is called the **empty set.** The symbol $\emptyset$ is used to represent the empty set.

CAUTION Be careful to distinguish between the symbols 0, $\emptyset$ and $\{0\}$. The symbol 0 represents a *number;* $\emptyset$ represents a *set* with no elements; and $\{0\}$ represents a *set* with one element, the number 0. Do not confuse the empty set symbol $\emptyset$ with the zero Ø on a computer screen or printout. ◆

Two sets are **equal** if they contain exactly the same elements. The sets $\{5, 6, 7\}$, $\{7, 6, 5\}$, and $\{6, 5, 7\}$ all contain exactly the same elements and are equal. In symbols,

$$\{5, 6, 7\} = \{7, 6, 5\} = \{6, 5, 7\}.$$

This means that the ordering of the elements in a set is unimportant. Sets that do not contain exactly the same elements are *not equal.* For example, the sets $\{5, 6, 7\}$ and $\{5, 6, 7, 8\}$ do not contain exactly the same elements and are not equal. We show this by writing

$$\{5, 6, 7\} \neq \{5, 6, 7, 8\}.$$

Sometimes we describe a set by a common property of its elements rather than by a list of elements. This common property can be expressed with **set-builder notation;** for example,

$$\{x \mid x \text{ has property } P\}$$

(read "the set of all elements x such that x has property P") represents the set of all elements x having some property P.

2 List the elements in the following sets.

(a) $\{x \mid x$ is a counting number more than 5 and less than 8$\}$

(b) $\{x \mid x$ is an integer, $-3 < x \leq 1\}$

Answers:

(a) $\{6, 7\}$

(b) $\{-2, -1, 0, 1\}$

EXAMPLE 1 List the elements belonging to each of the following sets.

(a) $\{x \mid x$ is a natural number less than 5$\}$
The natural numbers less than 5 make up the set $\{1, 2, 3, 4\}$.

(b) $\{x \mid x$ is a state that borders Florida$\}$ = {Alabama, Georgia} ■ 2

The **universal set** in a particular discussion is a set that contains all of the objects being discussed. In grade-school arithmetic, for example, the set of whole numbers might be the universal set, whereas in a college calculus class the universal set might be the set of all real numbers. When it is necessary to consider the universal set being used, it will be clearly specified or easily understood from the context of the problem.

Sometimes every element of one set also belongs to another set. For example, if

$$A = \{\mathbf{3, 4, 5, 6}\}$$

and

$$B = \{2, \mathbf{3, 4, 5, 6}, 7, 8\},$$

then every element of A is also an element of B. This is an example of the following definition.

> A set A is a **subset** of a set B (written $A \subseteq B$) provided that every element of A is also an element of B.

3 Write *true* or *false*.

(a) $\{3, 4, 5\} \subseteq \{2, 3, 4, 6\}$

(b) $\{x \mid x \text{ is an automobile}\} \subseteq \{x \mid x \text{ is a motor vehicle}\}$

(c) $\{3, 6, 9, 10\} \subseteq \{3, 9, 11, 13\}$

Answers:

(a) False

(b) True

(c) False

EXAMPLE 2 Decide whether or not $M \subseteq N$.

(a) M is the set of all small businesses with less than 20 employees. N is the set of all businesses.

Each business with less than 20 employees is also a business, so $M \subseteq N$.

(b) M is the set of all fourth-grade students in a school at the end of the school year, and N is the set of all nine-year-old students in the school at the end of the school year.

By the end of the school year, some fourth-grade students are ten years old, so there are elements in M that are not in N. Thus, M is not a subset of N, written $M \not\subseteq N$. ■ 3

Every set A is a subset of itself because the statement "every element of A is also an element of A" is always true. It is also true that the empty set is a subset of every set.*

> For any set A,
>
> $$\emptyset \subseteq A \quad \text{and} \quad A \subseteq A.$$

EXAMPLE 3 List all possible subsets for each of the following sets.

(a) $\{7, 8\}$

There are 4 subsets of $\{7, 8\}$:

$$\emptyset, \quad \{7\}, \quad \{8\}, \quad \{7, 8\}.$$

(b) $\{a, b, c\}$

There are 8 subsets of $\{a, b, c\}$:

$$\emptyset, \quad \{a\}, \quad \{b\}, \quad \{c\}, \quad \{a, b\}, \quad \{a, c\}, \quad \{b, c\}, \quad \{a, b, c\}. \quad ■$$

4 List all subsets of $\{w, x, y, z\}$.

Answer:

$\emptyset$, $\{w\}$, $\{x\}$, $\{y\}$, $\{z\}$, $\{w, x\}$, $\{w, y\}$, $\{w, z\}$, $\{x, y\}$, $\{x, z\}$, $\{y, z\}$, $\{w, x, y\}$, $\{w, x, z\}$, $\{w, y, z\}$, $\{x, y, z\}$, $\{w, x, y, z\}$

In Example 3, the subsets of $\{7, 8\}$ and the subsets of $\{a, b, c\}$ were found by trial and error. An alternative method uses a **tree diagram,** a systematic way of listing all the subsets of a given set. Figures 9.1(a) and (b) on the next page show tree diagrams for finding the subsets of $\{7, 8\}$ and $\{a, b, c\}$. 4

*This fact is not intuitively obvious to most people. If you wish, you can think of it as a convention that we agree to adopt in order to simplify the statements of several results later.

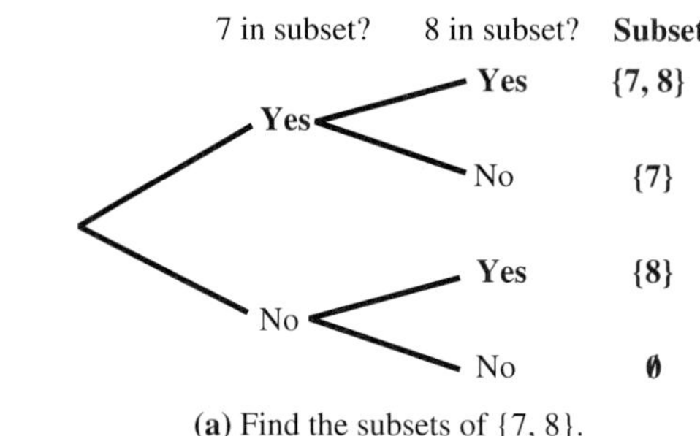

(a) Find the subsets of {7, 8}.

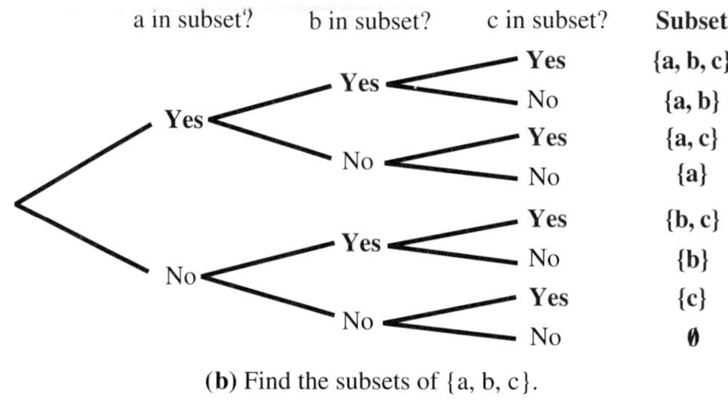

(b) Find the subsets of {a, b, c}.

FIGURE 9.1

5 Find the number of subsets for each of the following sets.

(a) $\{x \mid x \text{ is a season of the year}\}$

(b) $\{-6, -5, -4, -3, -2, -1, 0\}$

(c) $\{6\}$

Answers:

(a) 16

(b) 128

(c) 2

6 Refer to sets A, B, C, and U in the diagram.

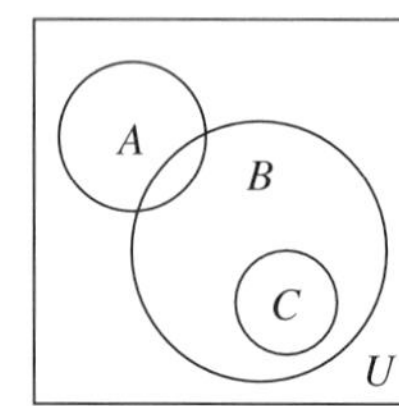

(a) Is $A \subseteq B$?

(b) Is $C \subseteq B$?

(c) Is $C \subseteq U$?

(d) Is $\emptyset \subseteq A$?

Answers:

(a) No

(b) Yes

(c) Yes

(d) Yes

By using the fact that there are two possibilities for each element (either it is in the subset or it is not) we have found that a set with 2 elements has 4 ($= 2^2$) subsets and a set with 3 elements has 8 ($= 2^3$) subsets. Similar arguments work for any finite set and lead to this conclusion.

> A set of n distinct elements has 2^n subsets.

EXAMPLE 4 Find the number of subsets for each of the following sets.

(a) $\{3, 4, 5, 6, 7\}$

Since this set has 5 elements, it has 2^5 or 32 subsets.

(b) $\{x \mid x \text{ is a day of the week}\}$

This set has 7 elements and therefore has $2^7 = 128$ subsets.

(c) $\emptyset$

Since the empty set has 0 elements, it has $2^0 = 1$ subset, $\emptyset$ itself. ■ 5

Figure 9.2 shows a set A, which is a subset of a set B, because A is entirely in B. (The areas of the regions are not meant to be proportional to the size of the corresponding sets.) The rectangle represents the universal set, U. Such diagrams, called **Venn diagrams,** are used to illustrate relationships among sets. 6

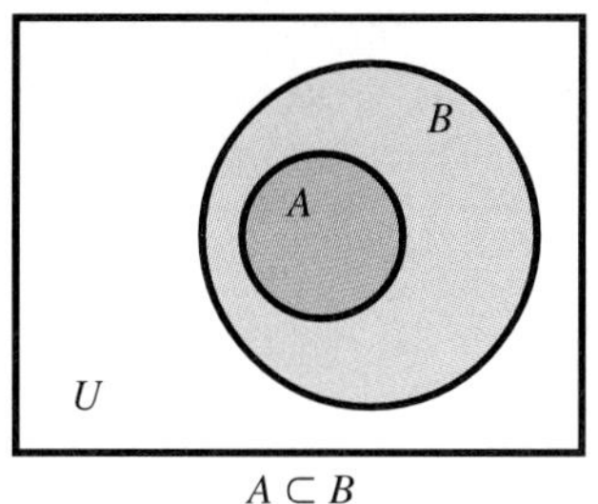

$A \subseteq B$

FIGURE 9.2

We can operate on sets to get other sets, just as operations on numbers (such as finding the negative, addition, and multiplication) produce other numbers. For example, given a set A and a universal set U, the set of all elements of U which do *not* belong to A is called the **complement** of set A. For example, if set A is the set of all the female students in your class and U is the set of all students in the class, then the complement of A would be the set of all male students in the class. The complement of set A is written A' (read "A-prime"). The Venn diagram of Figure 9.3 shows a set B. Its complement, B', is shown in color.

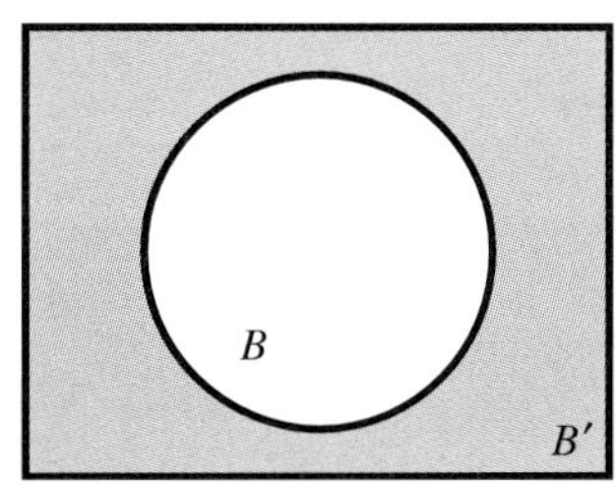

FIGURE 9.3

7 Let $U = \{a, b, c, d, e, f, g\}$, with $K = \{c, d, f, g\}$ and $R = \{a, c, d, e, g\}$. Find

(a) K';

(b) R'.

Answers:

(a) $\{a, b, e\}$

(b) $\{b, f\}$

EXAMPLE 5 Let $U = \{1, 2, 3, 4, 5, 6, 7\}$, $A = \{1, 3, 5, 7\}$, and $B = \{3, 4, 6\}$. Find the following sets.

(a) A'

Set A' contains the elements of U that are not in A.

$$A' = \{2, 4, 6\}$$

(b) $B' = \{1, 2, 5, 7\}$

(c) $\emptyset' = U$ and $U' = \emptyset$ ■ 7

Given two sets A and B, the set of all elements belonging to *both* set A and set B is called the **intersection** of the two sets, written $A \cap B$. For example, the elements that belong to both $A = \{1, 2, 4, 5, 7\}$ and $B = \{2, 4, 5, 7, 9, 11\}$ are 2, 4, 5, and 7, so that

$$A \cap B = \{1, 2, 4, 5, 7\} \cap (2, 4, 5, 7, 9, 11\} = \{2, 4, 5, 7\}.$$

The Venn diagram of Figure 9.4 shows two sets A and B with their intersection, $A \cap B$, shown in color.

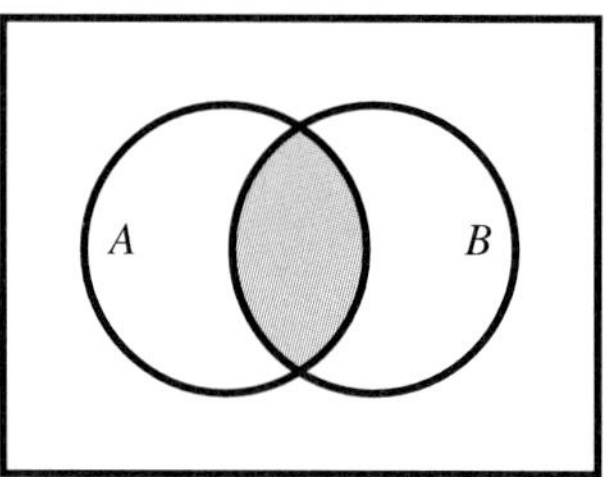

$A \cap B$

FIGURE 9.4

EXAMPLE 6 **(a)** $\{9, 15, 25, 36\} \cap \{15, 20, 25, 30, 35\} = \{15, 25\}$

The elements 15 and 25 are the only ones belonging to both sets.

(b) $\{x \mid x \text{ is a teen-ager}\} \cap \{x \mid x \text{ is a senior citizen}\}$ is an empty set. ■ 8

8 Find the following.

(a) $\{1, 2, 3, 4\} \cap \{3, 5, 7, 9\}$

(b) Suppose set K is the set of all blue-eyed blondes in a class and J is the set of all blue-eyed brunettes in the class. If the class has only blondes or brunettes, describe $K \cap J$ in words.

(c) Let $P = \{x \mid x \text{ is a brown-eyed redhead}\}$. Describe $K \cap P$.

Answers:

(a) $\{3\}$

(b) All members of the class with blue eyes

(c) $\emptyset$

Two sets that have no elements in common are called **disjoint sets.** For example, there are no elements common to both $\{50, 51, 54\}$ and $\{52, 53, 55, 56\}$, so that these two sets are disjoint, and

$$\{50, 51, 54\} \cap \{52, 53, 55, 56\} = \emptyset.$$

The result of this example can be generalized:

> For any sets A and B,
>
> if A and B are disjoint sets then $A \cap B = \emptyset$.

Figure 9.5 is a Venn diagram of disjoint sets.

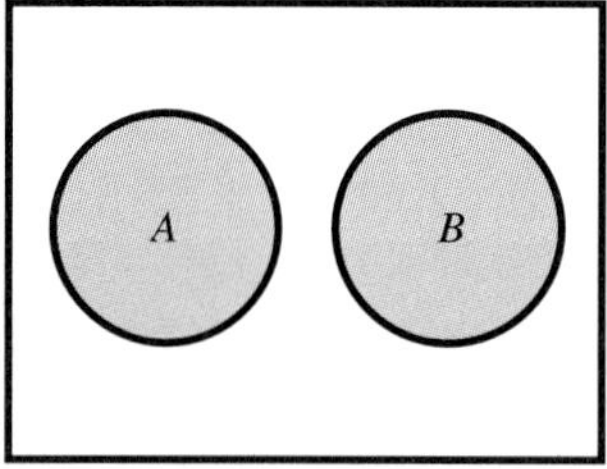

A and B are disjoint sets.

FIGURE 9.5

The set of all elements belonging to set A, to set B, or to both sets is called the **union** of the two sets, written $A \cup B$. For example,

$$\{1, 3, 5\} \cup \{3, 5, 7, 9\} = \{1, 3, 5, 7, 9\}.$$

The Venn diagram of Figure 9.6 shows two sets A and B, with their union $A \cup B$ shown in color.

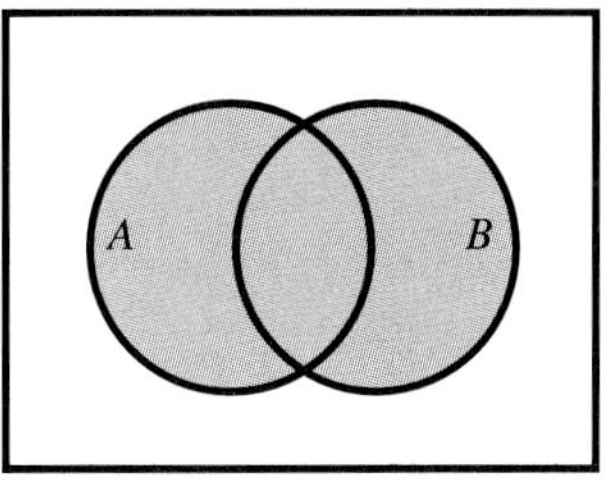

$A \cup B$

FIGURE 9.6

9 Find the following.

(a) $\{a, b, c\} \cup \{a, c, e\}$

(b) Describe $K \cup J$ in words for the sets given in Side Problem 8(b).

Answers:

(a) $\{a, b, c, e\}$

(b) All members of the class

EXAMPLE 7 **(a)** Find the union of $\{1, 2, 5, 9, 14\}$ and $\{1, 3, 4, 8\}$.

Begin by listing the elements of the first set, $\{1, 2, 5, 9, 14\}$. Then include any elements from the second set *that are not already listed.* Doing this gives

$$\{1, 2, 5, 9, 14\} \cup \{1, 3, 4, 8\} = \{1, 2, 3, 4, 5, 8, 9, 14\}.$$

(b) {terriers, spaniels, chows, dalmatians} $\cup$ {spaniels, collies, bulldogs} = {terriers, spaniels, chows, dalmatians, collies, bulldogs} ■ 9

Finding the complement of a set, the intersection of two sets, or the union of two sets are examples of *set operations.*

The set operations are summarized below.

OPERATIONS ON SETS

Let A and B be any sets with U the universal set. Then

the **complement** of A, written A', is

$$A' = \{x \mid x \notin A \text{ and } x \in U\};$$

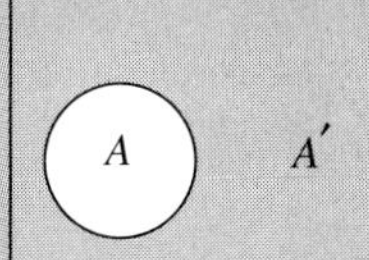

the **intersection** of A and B is

$$A \cap B = \{x \mid x \in A \text{ and } x \in B\};$$

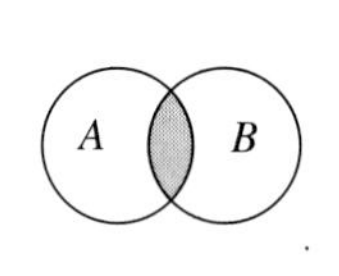

the **union** of A and B is

$$A \cup B = \{x \mid x \in A \text{ or } x \in B \text{ or both}\}.$$

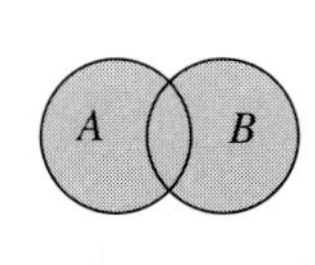

CAUTION As shown in the definitions given above, an element is in the *intersection* of sets A and B if it is in *both A and B*. On the other hand, an element is in the *union* of sets A and B if it is in *A or B or both*. ◆

EXAMPLE 8 The table gives the annual high and low prices, the last price, and the weekly change for six stocks, as listed on the New York Stock Exchange at the end of a recent week.*

Stock	*High*	*Low*	*Last*	*Change*
ATT	68 7/8	49 1/4	51 7/8	−1 1/2
GnMill	60 1/2	50 3/8	53 1/2	−1 1/4
Hershey	81 1/4	56 1/2	78 3/8	+5 1/2
IBM	128 7/8	83 1/8	103 7/8	+10 1/8
Mobil	120 1/8	93 1/2	109 5/8	−5 1/2
PepsiCo	35 7/8	22 1/8	31 7/8	−5/8

Let set A include all stocks with a high price greater than $100; B all stocks with a last price between $75 and $100; C all stocks with a positive price change. Find the following.

(a) A'

Set A' contains all the listed stocks outside set A, those with a high price less than or equal to $100, so

$$A' = \{\text{ATT, GnMill, Hershey, PepsiCo}\}.$$

(b) $A \cap C$

The intersection of A and C will contain those stocks with a high price greater than $100 and a positive price change.

$$A \cap C = \{\text{IBM}\}$$

(c) $A \cup B$

The union of A and B contains all stocks with a high price greater than $100 or a last price between $75 and $100.

$$A \cup C = \{\text{Hershey, IBM, Mobil}\}$$ ■ 10

10 If $U = \{-3, -2, -1, 0, 1, 2, 3\}$, $A = \{-1, -2, -3\}$, and $B = \{-2, 0, 2\}$, find

(a) $A \cup B$;

(b) B';

(c) $A \cap B$.

Answers:

(a) $\{-3, -2, -1, 0, 2\}$

(b) $\{-3, -1, 1, 3\}$

(c) $\{-2\}$

The Sacramento Bee, July 27, 1996, pp. F4 and F7.

9.1 EXERCISES

Write true *or* false *for each statement.*

1. $3 \in \{2, 5, 7, 9, 10\}$

2. $6 \in \{-2, 6, 9, 5\}$

3. $9 \notin \{2, 1, 5, 8\}$

4. $3 \notin \{7, 6, 5, 4\}$

5. $\{2, 5, 8, 9\} = \{2, 5, 9, 8\}$

6. $\{3, 7, 12, 14\} = \{3, 7, 12, 14, 0\}$

7. {all whole numbers greater than 7 and less than 10} = $\{8, 9\}$

8. {all counting numbers not greater than 3} = $\{0, 1, 2\}$

9. $\{x \mid x \text{ is an odd integer}, 6 \le x \le 18\} = \{7, 9, 11, 15, 17\}$

10. $\{x \mid x \text{ is a vowel}\} = \{a, e, i, o, u\}$

11. The elements of a set may be sets themselves, as in $\{1, \{1, 3\}, \{2\}, 4\}$. Explain why the set $\{\emptyset\}$ is not the same set as $\{0\}$.

12. What is set-builder notation? Give an example.

Let $A = \{-3, 0, 3\}$, $B = \{-2, -1, 0, 1, 2\}$, $C = \{-3, -1\}$, $D = \{0\}$, $E = \{-2\}$, and $U = \{-3, -2, -1, 0, 1, 2, 3\}$. Insert $\subseteq$ or $\not\subseteq$ to make the following statements true. (See Example 2.)

13. A ______ U **14.** E ______ A

15. A ______ E **16.** B ______ C

17. $\emptyset$ ______ A **18.** $\{0, 2\}$ ______ D

19. D ______ B **20.** A ______ C

Find the number of subsets for each set. (See Example 4.)

21. $\{A, B, C\}$

22. {red, yellow, blue, black, white}

23. $\{x \mid x$ is an integer between 0 and 7$\}$

24. $\{x \mid x$ is a whole number less than 4$\}$

25. Describe the intersection and union of sets. How do they differ?

Insert $\cap$ or $\cup$ to make each statement true. (See Examples 6 and 7.)

26. $\{5, 7, 9, 19\}$ ______ $\{7, 9, 11, 15\} = \{7, 9\}$

27. $\{8, 11, 15\}$ ______ $\{8, 11, 19, 20\} = \{8, 11\}$

28. $\{2, 1, 7\}$ ______ $\{1, 5, 9\} = \{1\}$

29. $\{6, 12, 14, 16\}$ ______ $\{6, 14, 19\} = \{6, 14\}$

30. $\{3, 5, 9, 10\}$ ______ $\emptyset = \emptyset$

31. $\{3, 5, 9, 10\}$ ______ $\emptyset = \{3, 5, 9, 10\}$

32. $\{1, 2, 4\}$ ______ $\{1, 2, 4\} = \{1, 2, 4\}$

33. $\{1, 2, 4\}$ ______ $\{1, 2\} = \{1, 2, 4\}$

34. Is it possible for two nonempty sets to have the same intersection and union? If so, give an example.

Let $U = \{2, 3, 4, 5, 7, 9\}$; $X = \{2, 3, 4, 5\}$; $Y = \{3, 5, 7, 9\}$; and $Z = \{2, 4, 5, 7, 9\}$.

List the members of each of the following sets, using set braces. (See Example 5–7.)

35. $X \cap Y$ **36.** $X \cup Y$

37. X' **38.** Y'

39. $X' \cap Y'$ **40.** $X' \cap Z$

41. $X \cup (Y \cap Z)$ **42.** $Y \cap (X \cup Z)$

Let $U = \{$all students in this school$\}$; $M = \{$all students taking this course$\}$; $N = \{$all students taking accounting$\}$; $P = \{$all students taking zoology$\}$.

Describe each of the following sets in words.

43. M' **44.** $M \cup N$

45. $N \cap P$ **46.** $N' \cap P'$

47. Refer to the sets listed in the directions for Exercises 13–20. Which pairs of sets are disjoint?

48. Refer to the sets listed in the directions for Exercises 35–42. Which pairs are disjoint?

Refer to Example 8 in the text. Describe each of the sets in Exercises 49–52 in words; then list the elements of each set.

49. B' **50.** $A \cap B$

51. $(A \cup B)'$ **52.** $(A \cap C)'$

Management *A department store classifies credit applicants by sex, marital status, and employment status. Let the universal set be the set of all applicants, M be the set of male applicants, S be the set of all single applicants, and E be the set of employed applicants. Describe the following sets in words.*

53. $M \cap E$ **54.** $M' \cap S$ **55.** $M' \cup S'$

Management *Computing power of personal computers has increased dramatically as a result of the ability to place an increasing number of transistors on a single processor chip. The table lists the number of transistors on some popular computer chips made by Intel.**

Year	*Chip*	*Transistors*
1971	4004	2,300
1986	386DX	275,000
1989	486DX	1,200,000
1993	Pentium	3,300,000
1995	P6	5,500,000

List the elements of each set.

56. The set of chips produced in the 1980s.

57. The years listed when there were more than 1 million transistors on a chip.

58. The chips with names consisting of both letters and numerals.

Social Science *The top five pay-cable services in 1994 are listed below.† Use this information for Exercises 59–64.*

Network	*Subscribers (in thousands)*	*Content*
Home Box Office (HBO)	19,200	Movies, variety sports, documentaries
The Disney Channel	12,600	Movies, cartoons
Showtime/The Movie Channel	11,900	Movies, variety, comedy, specials
Spice	11,000	Adult movies
Cinemax	7,800	Movies, comedy, specials

*Intel.

†"Top Five Pay-Cable Services, 1994" from *The Universal Almanac 1996,* edited by John W. Wright (Kansas City and New York: Andrews and McMeel, 1996).

List the elements of the following sets.

59. F, the set of networks with more than 12,000 thousand subscribers

60. G, the set of networks that show cartoons

61. H, the set of networks that show adult movies

62. $F \cap G$ **63.** $H \cup G$ **64.** F'

Natural Science *The table below shows some symptoms of an overactive thyroid and an underactive thyroid.*

Underactive Thyroid	*Overactive Thyroid*
Sleepiness, s	Insomnia, i
Dry hands, d	Moist hands, m
Intolerance of cold, c	Intolerance of heat, h
Goiter, g	Goiter, g

Let U be the smallest possible set that includes all the symptoms listed, N be the set of symptoms for an underactive thyroid, and O be the set of symptoms for an overactive thyroid. Use the italic letters to list the elements of each set.

65. O'

66. N'

67. $N \cap O$

68. $N \cup O$

69. $N \cap O'$

9.2 APPLICATIONS OF VENN DIAGRAMS

Venn diagrams were used in the last section to illustrate set union and intersection. The rectangular region in a Venn diagram represents the universal set, U. Including only a single set, A, inside the universal set, as in Figure 9.7, divides U into two nonoverlapping regions. Region 1 represents A', those elements outside set A, while region 2 represents those elements belonging to set A. (The numbering of these regions is arbitrary.)

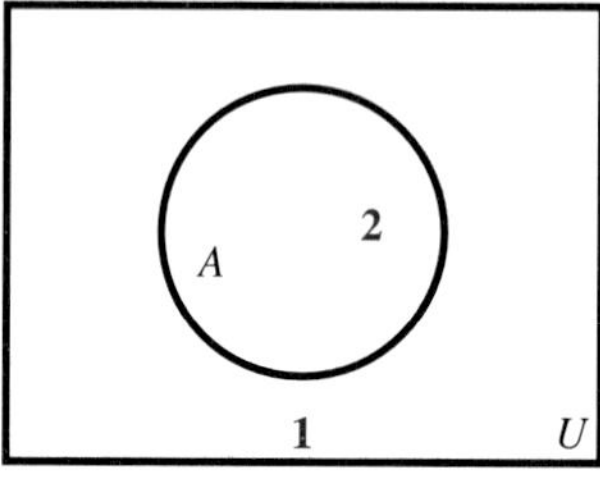

One set leads to 2 regions (numbering is arbitrary).

FIGURE 9.7

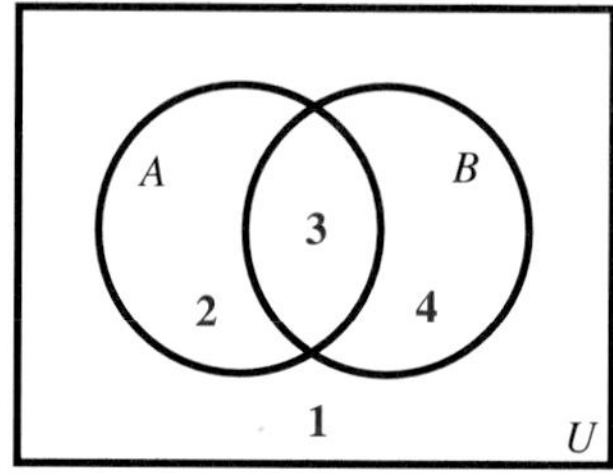

Two sets lead to 4 regions (numbering is arbitrary).

FIGURE 9.8

The Venn diagram of Figure 9.8 shows two sets inside U. These two sets divide the universal set into four nonoverlapping regions. As labeled in Figure 9.8, region 1 includes those elements outside both set A and set B. Region 2 includes those elements belonging to A and not to B. Region 3 includes those elements belonging to both A and B. Which elements belong to region 4? (Again, the numbering is arbitrary.)

1 Draw Venn diagrams for the following.

(a) $A \cup B'$

(b) $A' \cap B'$

Answers:

(a)

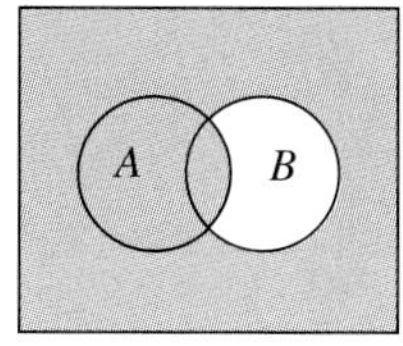

$A \cup B'$

(b)

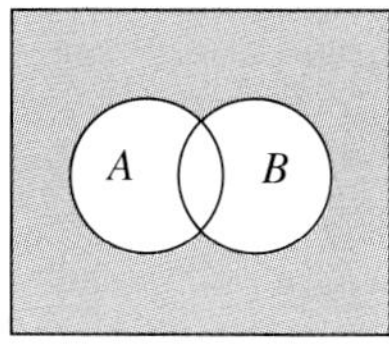

$A' \cap B'$

EXAMPLE 1 Draw Venn diagrams similar to Figure 9.8 and shade the regions representing the following sets.

(a) $A' \cap B$

Set A' contains all the elements outside set A. As labeled in Figure 9.8, A' is represented by regions 1 and 4. Set B is represented by the elements in regions 3 and 4. The intersection of sets A' and B, the set $A' \cap B$, is given by the region common to regions 1 and 4 and regions 3 and 4. The result, region 4, is shaded in Figure 9.9.

(b) $A' \cup B'$

Again, set A' is represented by regions 1 and 4, and set B' by regions 1 and 2. To find $A' \cup B'$, identify the region that represents the set of all elements in A', B', or both. The result, which is shaded in Figure 9.10, includes regions 1, 2, and 4. ■ 1

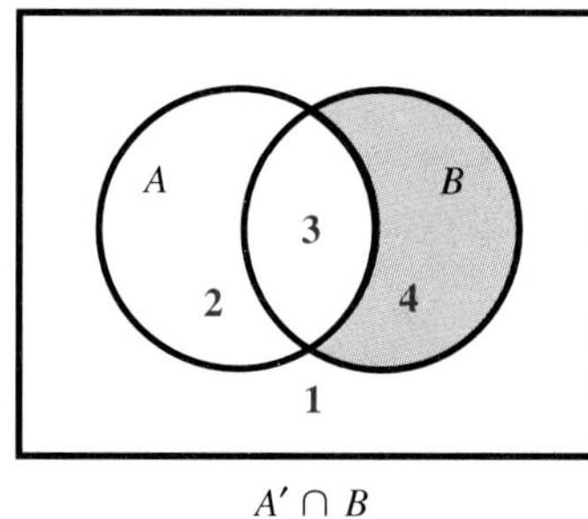

$A' \cap B$

FIGURE 9.9

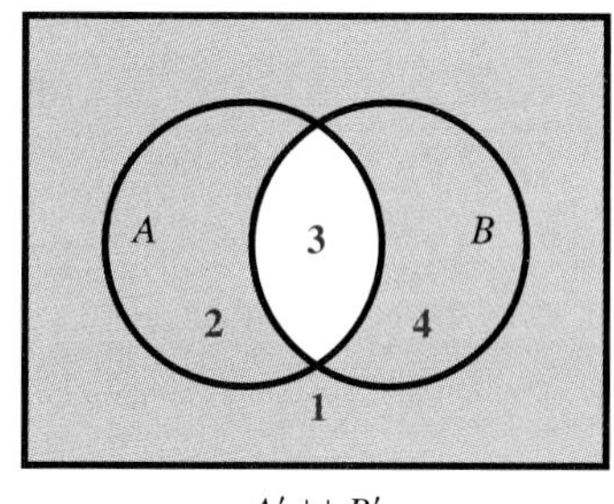

$A' \cup B'$

FIGURE 9.10

Venn diagrams also can be drawn with three sets inside U. These three sets divide the universal set into eight nonoverlapping regions which can be numbered (arbitrarily) as in Figure 9.11.

2 Draw a Venn diagram for the following.

(a) $B' \cap A$

(b) $(A \cup B)' \cap C$

Answers:

(a)

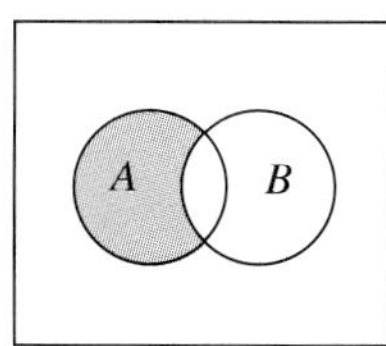

$B' \cap A$

(b)

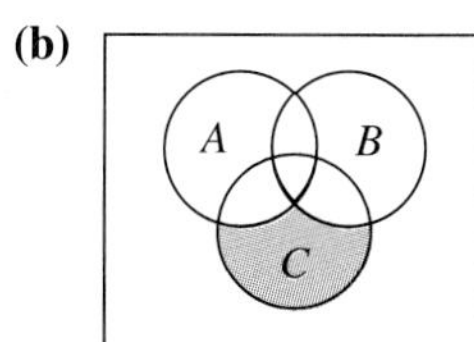

$(A \cup B)' \cap C$

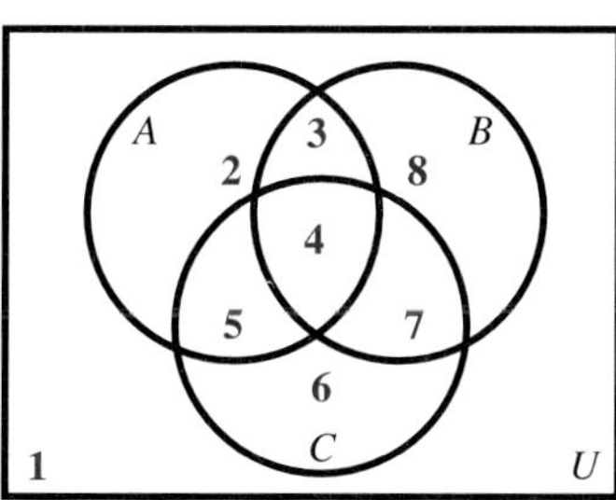

Three sets lead to 8 regions.

FIGURE 9.11

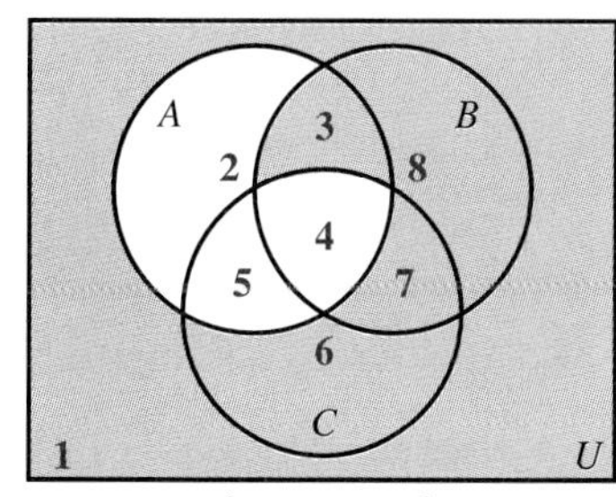

$A' \cup (B \cap C')$

FIGURE 9.12

EXAMPLE 2 Shade $A' \cup (B \cap C')$ on a Venn diagram.

First find $B \cap C'$. See Figure 9.12. Set B is represented by regions 3, 4, 7, and 8, and C' by regions 1, 2, 3, and 8. The overlap of these regions, regions 3 and 8, represents the set $B \cap C'$. Set A' is represented by regions 1, 6, 7, and 8. The union of regions 3 and 8 and regions 1, 6, 7, and 8 includes regions 1, 3, 6, 7, and 8, which are shaded in Figure 9.12. ■ 2

Venn diagrams can be used to solve problems that result from surveying groups of people. As an example, suppose a researcher collecting data on 100 households finds that

21 have a home computer;

56 have a videocassette recorder (VCR); and

12 have both.

The researcher wants to answer the following questions.

(a) How many do not have a VCR?
(b) How many have neither a computer nor a VCR?
(c) How many have a computer but not a VCR?

A Venn diagram like the one in Figure 9.13 will help sort out the information. In Figure 9.13(a), we put the number 12 in the region common to both a VCR and a computer, because 12 households have both. Of the 21 with a home computer, $21 - 12 = 9$ have no VCR, so in Figure 9.13(b) we put 9 in the region for a computer but no VCR. Similarly, $56 - 12 = 44$ households have a VCR but not a computer, so we put 44 in that region. Finally, the diagram shows that $100 - 44 - 12 - 9 = 35$ households have neither a VCR nor a computer. Now we can answer the questions:

(a) $35 + 9 = 44$ do not have a VCR;
(b) 35 have neither;
(c) 9 have a computer but not a VCR. 3

3 **(a)** Place numbers in the regions on a Venn diagram if the data on the 100 households showed

29 home computers;

63 VCRs;

20 with both.

(b) How many have a VCR but not a computer?

Answers:

(a)

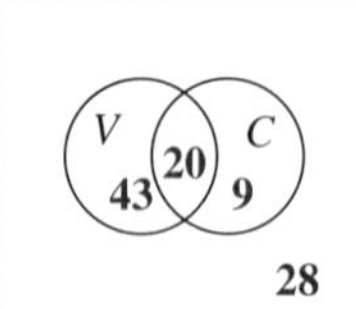

(b) 43

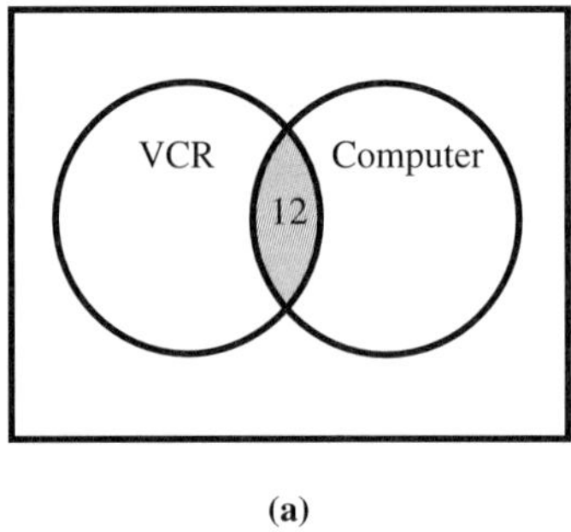

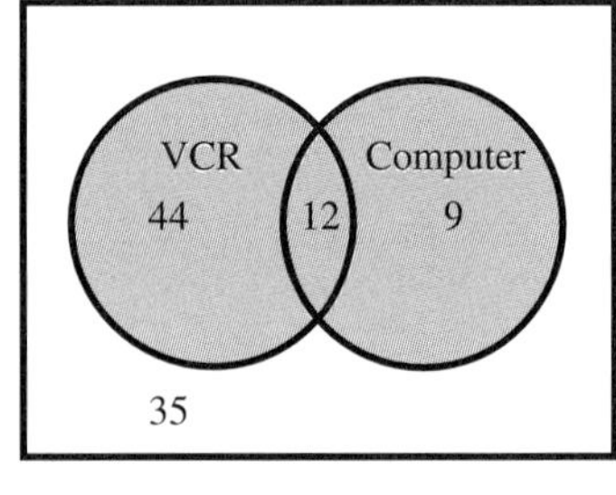

(a) **(b)**

FIGURE 9.13

EXAMPLE 3 A group of 60 freshman business students at a large university was surveyed, with the following results.

19 of the students read *Business Week;*

18 read *The Wall Street Journal;*

50 read *Fortune;*

13 read *Business Week* and *The Journal;*

11 read *The Journal* and *Fortune;*

13 read *Business Week* and *Fortune;*

9 read all three.

Use these data to answer the following questions.

(a) How many students read none of the publications?
(b) How many read only *Fortune?*
(c) How many read *Business Week* and *The Journal,* but not *Fortune?*

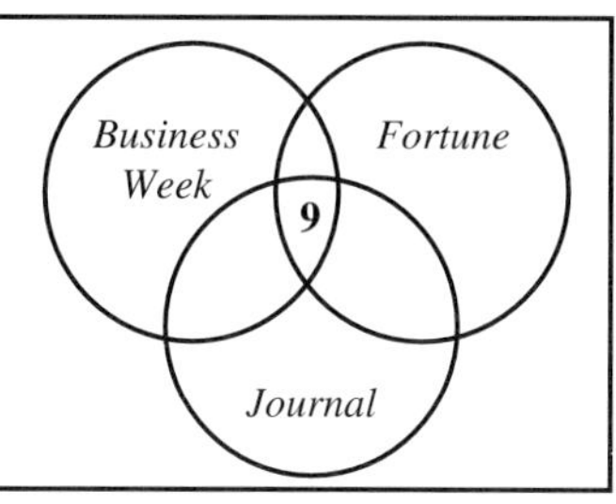

FIGURE 9.14(a)

Once again, use a Venn diagram to represent the data. Since 9 students read all three publications, begin by placing 9 in the area in Figure 9.14(a) that belongs to all three regions.

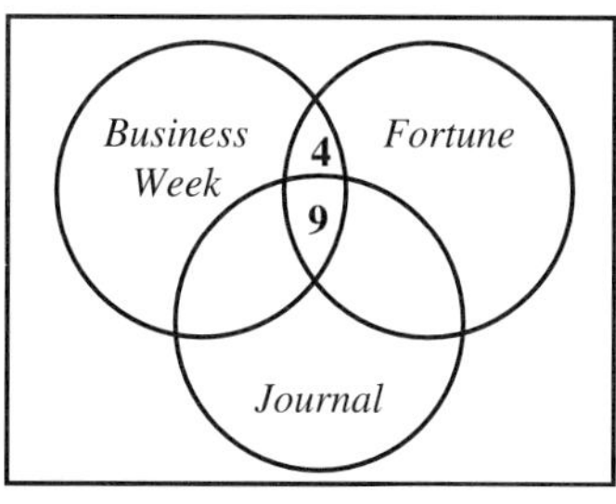

FIGURE 9.14(b)

Of the 13 students who read *Business Week* and *Fortune,* 9 also read *The Journal.* Therefore only $13 - 9 = 4$ students read just *Business Week* and *Fortune.* So place a 4 in the region common only to *Business Week* and *Fortune* readers, as in Figure 9.14(b).

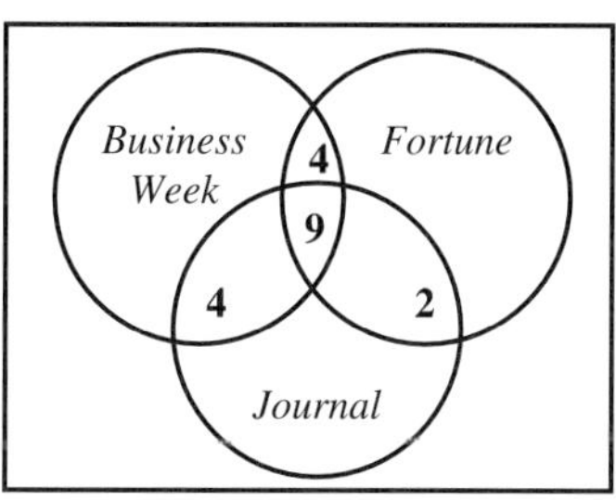

FIGURE 9.14(c)

In the same way, place a 4 in the region of Figure 9.14(c) common only to *Business Week* and *The Journal,* and 2 in the region common only to *Fortune* and *The Journal.*

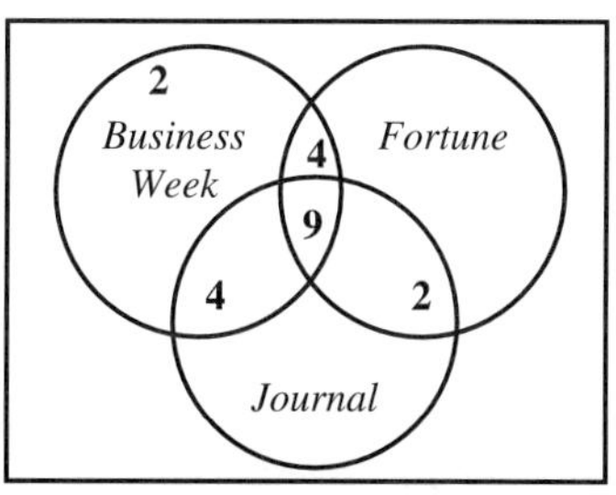

FIGURE 9.14(d)

The data show that 19 students read *Business Week.* However, $4 + 9 + 4 = 17$ readers have already been placed in the *Business Week* region. The balance of this region in Figure 9.14(d) will contain only $19 - 17 = 2$ students. These 2 students read *Business Week* only—not *Fortune* and not *The Journal.*

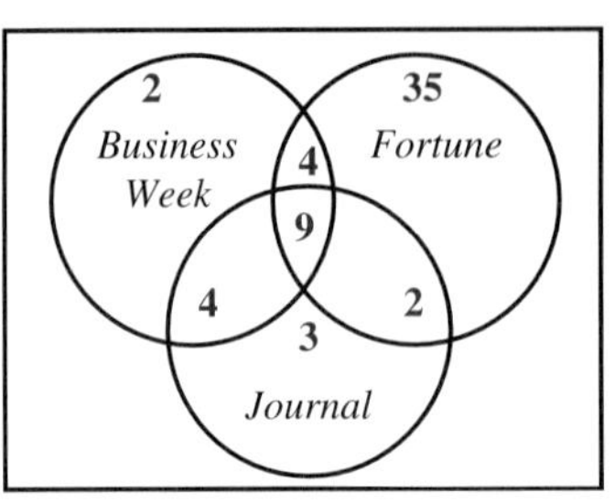

FIGURE 9.14(e)

In the same way, 3 students read only *The Journal* and 35 read only *Fortune,* as shown in Figure 9.14(e).

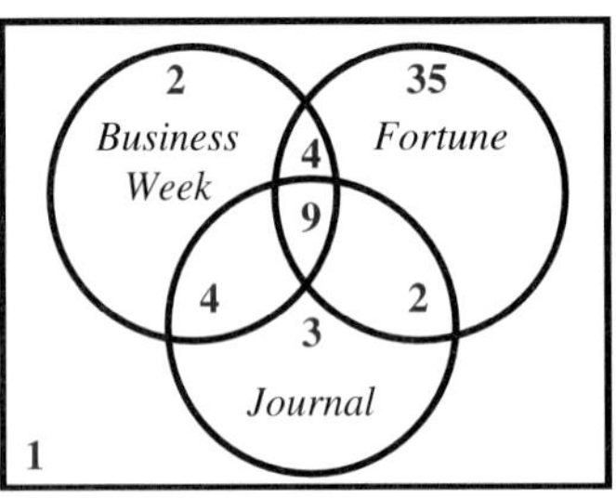

FIGURE 9.14(f)

A total of $2 + 4 + 3 + 4 + 9 + 2 + 35 = 59$ students are placed in the various regions of Figure 9.14(f). Since 60 students were surveyed, $60 - 59 = 1$ student reads none of the three publications and 1 is placed outside the other regions in Figure 9.14(f).

4 In the example about the three publications, how many students read exactly

(a) 1 of the publications;

(b) 2 of the publications?

Answers:

(a) 40

(b) 10

Figure 9.14(f) can now be used to answer the questions asked above.

(a) Only 1 student reads none of the publications.
(b) There are 35 students who read only *Fortune.*
(c) The overlap of the regions representing *Business Week* and *The Journal* shows that 4 students read *Business Week* and *The Journal* but not *Fortune.* ■ 4

EXAMPLE 4 Jeff Friedman is a section chief for an electric utility company. The employees in his section cut down tall trees, climb poles, and splice wire. Friedman reported the following information to the management of the utility.

> Of the 100 employees in my section,
>
> 45 can cut tall trees;
>
> 50 can climb poles;
>
> 57 can splice wire;
>
> 28 can cut trees and climb poles;
>
> 20 can climb poles and splice wire;
>
> 25 can cut trees and splice wire;
>
> 11 can do all three;
>
> 9 can't do any of the three (management trainees).

The data supplied by Friedman lead to the numbers shown in Figure 9.15. Add the numbers from all the regions to get the total number of Friedman's employees.

$$9 + 3 + 14 + 23 + 11 + 9 + 17 + 13 = 99$$

Friedman claimed to have 100 employees, but his data indicate only 99. The management decided that Friedman didn't qualify as a section chief, and reassigned him as a nightshift meter reader in Guam. (Moral: He should have taken this course.) ■ 5

5 In Example 4, suppose 46 employees can cut tall trees. Then how many

(a) can only cut tall trees?

(b) can cut trees or climb poles?

(c) can cut trees or climb poles or splice wire?

Answers:

(a) 4

(b) 68

(c) 91

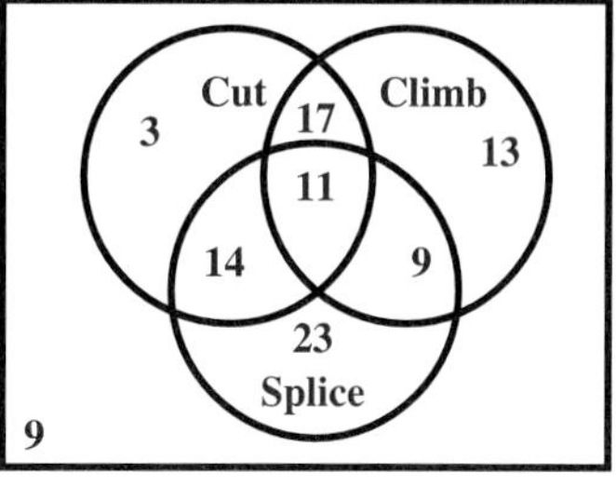

FIGURE 9.15

CAUTION Note that in all the examples above, we started in the innermost region with the intersection of the categories. This is usually the best way to begin solving problems of this type. ◆

We use the symbol $n(A)$ to denote the *number* of elements in A. For instance, if $A = \{w, x, y, z\}$, then $n(A) = 4$. The following useful fact is proved below.

UNION RULE FOR COUNTING

$$n(A \cup B) = n(A) + n(B) - n(A \cap B)$$

For example, if $A = \{r, s, t, u, v\}$ and $B = \{r, t, w\}$, then $A \cap B = \{r, t\}$, so that $n(A) = 5$, $n(B) = 3$, and $n(A \cap B) = 2$. By the formula in the box, $n(A \cup B) = 5 + 3 - 2 = 6$, which is certainly true since $A \cup B = \{r, s, t, u, v, w\}$.

Here is a proof of the statement in the box: let x be the number of elements in A that are not in B, y the number of elements in $A \cap B$, and z be the number of elements in B that are not in A, as indicated in Figure 9.16. That diagram shows that $n(A \cup B) = x + y + z$. It also shows that $n(A) = x + y$ and $n(B) = y + z$, so that

$$\begin{aligned} n(A) + n(B) - n(A \cap B) &= (x + y) + (z + y) - y \\ &= x + y + z \\ &= n(A \cup B). \end{aligned}$$

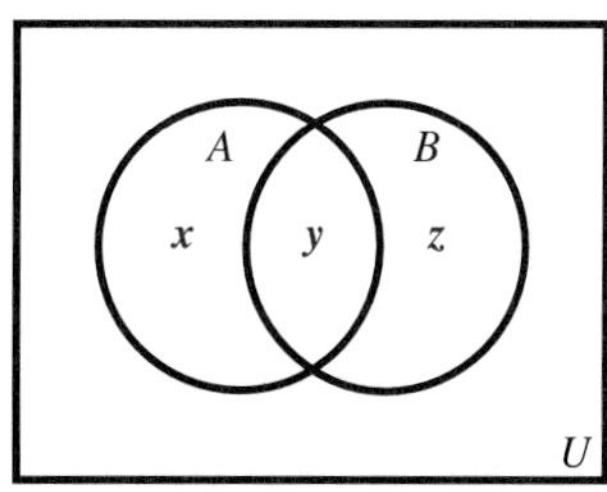

FIGURE 9.16

EXAMPLE 5 A group of 10 students meets to plan a school function. All are majors in accounting or economics or both. Five of the students are economics majors and 7 are majors in accounting. How many major in both subjects?

Use the union rule, with $n(A) = 5$, $n(B) = 7$, and $n(A \cup B) = 10$. We must find $n(A \cap B)$.

$$n(A \cup B) = n(A) + n(B) - n(A \cap B)$$
$$10 = 5 + 7 - n(A \cap B),$$

so

$$n(A \cap B) = 5 + 7 - 10 = 2. \blacksquare \quad \boxed{6}$$

6 If $n(A) = 10$, $n(B) = 7$, and $n(A \cap B) = 3$, find $n(A \cup B)$.

Answer:
14

EXAMPLE 6 Suppose a random sample of 200 voters was selected in the 1994 elections for the U.S. House of Representatives. The approximate numbers from the East, Midwest, South, or West who voted Democrat or Republican is given by the following table.*

	East (E)	*Midwest (M)*	*South (S)*	*West (W)*	*Total*
Democrat (*D*)	24	22	27	26	99
Republican (*R*)	22	28	33	18	101
Total	46	50	60	44	200

Using the letters given in the table, find the number of people in each of the following sets.

(a) $D \cap S$

The set $D \cap S$ consists of all those who voted Democrat *and* were from the South. From the table, we see that there were 27 such people.

(b) $D \cup S$

The set $D \cup S$ consists of all those who voted Democrat *or* were from the South. We include all 99 who voted Democrat, plus the 33 who were from the South and did not vote Democrat, for a total of 132. Alternatively, we could use the formula $n(D \cup S) = n(D) + n(S) - n(D \cap S) = 99 + 60 - 27 = 132$.

(c) $(E \cup W) \cap R'$

Begin with the set $E \cup W$, which is everyone from the East or the West. This consists of the four categories with 24, 22, 26, and 18 people. Of this set, take those who did *not* vote Republican, for a total of $24 + 26 = 50$ people. This is the number of people from the East or the West who did not vote Republican. ■ **7**

7 Find the number of people in each set.

(a) $R \cup M$

(b) $(R \cap W) \cup E'$

Answers:

(a) 123

(b) 154

The New York Times, Nov. 13, 1994, p. 24.

9.2 EXERCISES

Sketch a Venn diagram like the one at the right and use shading to show each of the following sets. (See Example 1.)

1. $B \cap A'$

2. $A \cup B'$

3. $A' \cup B$

4. $A' \cap B'$

5. $B' \cup (A' \cap B')$

6. $(A \cap B) \cup B'$

7. U'

8. $\emptyset'$

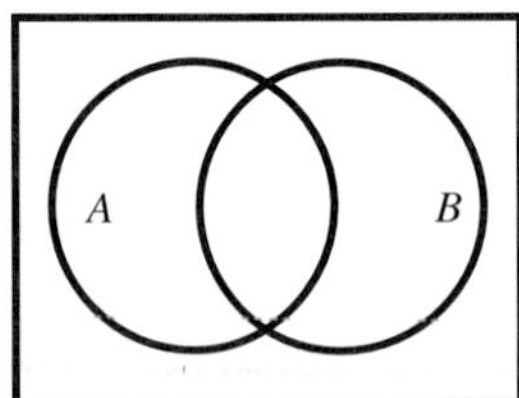

Sketch a Venn diagram like the one shown, and use shading to show each of the following sets. (See Example 2.)

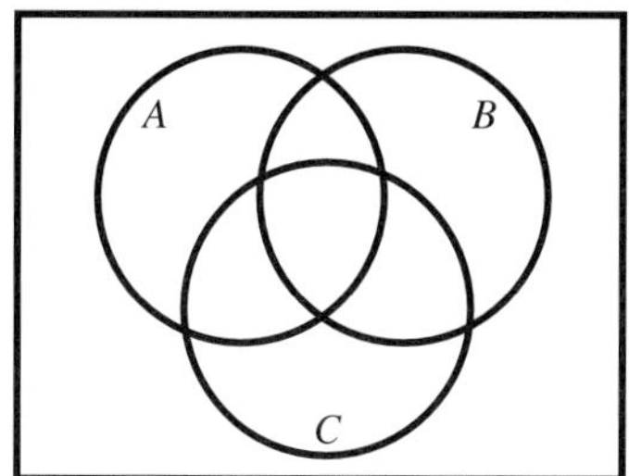

9. $(A \cap B) \cap C$ **10.** $(A \cap C') \cup B$ **11.** $A \cap (B \cup C')$

12. $A' \cap (B \cap C)$ **13.** $(A' \cap B') \cap C$ **14.** $(A \cap B') \cup C$

15. $(A \cap B') \cap C$ **16.** $A' \cap (B' \cup C)$

Use Venn diagrams to answer the following questions. (See Examples 3 and 4.)

17. Social Science A survey of people attending a Lunar New Year celebration in Chinatown yielded the following results:

120 were women;
150 spoke Cantonese;
170 lit firecrackers;
108 of the men spoke Cantonese;
100 of the men did not light firecrackers;
18 of the non-Cantonese-speaking women lit firecrackers;
78 non-Cantonese-speaking men did not light firecrackers;
30 of the women who spoke Cantonese lit firecrackers.

(a) How many attended?
(b) How many of those who attended did not speak Cantonese?
(c) How many women did not light firecrackers?
(d) How many of those who lit firecrackers were Cantonese-speaking men?

18. Management Jeff Friedman, of Example 4 in the text, was again reassigned, this time to the home economics department of the electric utility. He interviewed 140 people in a suburban shopping center to find out some of their cooking habits. He obtained the following results. Should he be reassigned yet one more time?

58 use microwave ovens;
63 use electric ranges;
58 use gas ranges;
19 use microwave ovens and electric ranges;
17 use microwave ovens and gas ranges;
4 use both gas and electric ranges;
1 uses all three;
2 cook only with solar energy.

19. Social Science A recent nationwide survey revealed the following data concerning unemployment in the United States. Out of the total population of people who are working or seeking work,

9% are unemployed;
11% are black;
30% are youths;
1% are unemployed black youths;
5% are unemployed youths;
7% are employed black adults;
23% are nonblack employed youths.

What percent are
(a) not black?
(b) employed adults?
(c) unemployed adults?
(d) unemployed black adults?
(e) unemployed nonblack youths?

20. Country-western songs emphasize three basic themes: love, prison, and trucks. A survey of the local country-western radio station produced the following data.

12 songs were about a truck driver who was in love while in prison;
13 about a prisoner in love;
28 about a person in love;
18 about a truck driver in love;
3 about a truck driver in prison who was not in love;
2 about a prisoner who was not in love and did not drive a truck;
8 about a person out of jail who was not in love, and did not drive a truck;
16 about truck drivers who were not in prison.

(a) How many songs were surveyed?
Find the number of songs about
(b) truck drivers;
(c) prisoners;
(d) truck drivers in prison;
(e) people not in prison;
(f) people not in love.

21. Natural Science After a genetics experiment, the number of pea plants having certain characteristics was tallied, with the results as follows.

22 were tall;
25 had green peas;
39 had smooth peas;
9 were tall and had green peas;
17 were tall and had smooth peas;
20 had green peas and smooth peas;
6 had all three characteristics;
4 had none of the characteristics.

(a) Find the total number of plants counted.
(b) How many plants were tall and had peas that were neither smooth nor green?
(c) How many plants were not tall but had peas that were smooth and green?

22. Natural Science Human blood can contain either no antigens, the A antigen, the B antigen, or both the A and B antigens. A third antigen, called the Rh antigen, is important in human reproduction, and again may or may not be present in an individual. Blood is called type A-positive if the individual has the A and Rh antigens, but not the B antigen. A person having only the A and B antigens is said to have type AB-negative blood. A person having only the Rh antigen has type O-positive blood. Other blood types are defined in a similar manner. Identify the blood type of the individuals in regions (a)–(g) of the Venn diagram.

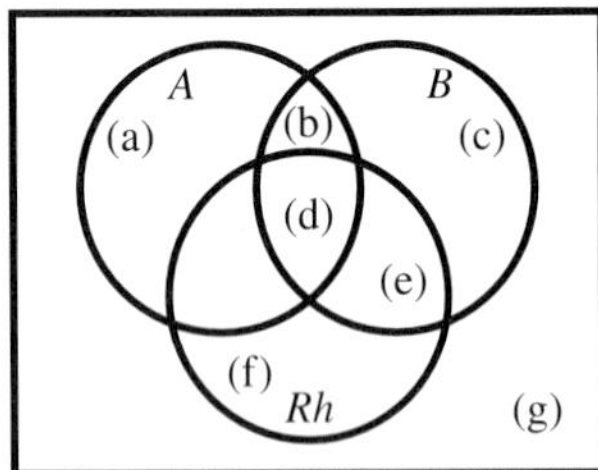

23. Natural Science Use the diagram from Exercise 22. In a certain hospital, the following data were recorded.

25 patients had the A antigen;
17 had the A and B antigens;
27 had the B antigen;
22 had the B and Rh antigens;
30 had the Rh antigen;
12 had none of the antigens;
16 had the A and Rh antigens;
15 had all three antigens.

How many patients
(a) were represented?
(b) had exactly one antigen?
(c) had exactly two antigens?
(d) had O-positive blood?
(e) had AB-positive blood?
(f) had B-negative blood?
(g) had O-negative blood?
(h) had A-positive blood?

24. Social Science At a pow-wow in Arizona, Native Americans from all over the Southwest came to participate in the ceremonies. A coordinator of the pow-wow took a survey and found that

15 families brought food, costumes, and crafts;
25 families brought food and crafts;
42 families brought food;
20 families brought costumes and food;
6 families brought costumes and crafts, but not food;
4 families brought crafts, but neither food nor costumes;
10 families brought none of the three items;
18 families brought costumes but not crafts.

(a) How many families were surveyed?
(b) How many families brought costumes?
(c) How many families brought crafts, but not costumes?
(d) How many families did not bring crafts?
(e) How many families brought food or costumes?

25. Social Science The U.S. population by age and race in 1995 (in millions) is given in the table.*

	Non-Hispanic White (A)	*Hispanic (B)*	*African-American (C)*	*Asian-American (D)*	*Total*
Under 45 (E)	124.5	21.6	23.9	7.0	177.0
45–64 (F)	40.8	3.7	5.0	1.6	51.1
65 and over (G)	28.6	1.5	2.7	.6	33.4
Total	193.9	26.8	31.6	9.2	261.5

Using the letters given in the table, find the number of people in each set.
(a) $A \cap E$ **(b)** $F \cup B$ **(c)** $F \cup (C \cap G)$
(d) $E' \cap (B \cup G)$ **(e)** $G' \cup D$ **(f)** $F' \cap (A' \cap C')$

26. Social Science The projected U.S. population by age and race in 2025 (in millions) is given in the table.*

	Non-Hispanic White (A)	*Hispanic (B)*	*African-American (C)*	*Asian-American (D)*	*Total*
Under 45 (E)	110.5	33.9	30.0	15.9	190.3
45–64 (F)	52.2	11.0	9.2	5.2	77.6
65 and over (G)	47.2	6.0	5.5	2.9	61.6
Total	209.9	50.9	44.7	24.0	329.5

Using the letters given in the table, find the number of people in each set.
(a) $D \cap E$ **(b)** $F \cup B$ **(c)** $G \cap (C \cup B)$
(d) $E' \cup (A \cup D)$ **(e)** $(F' \cup G') \cap B$

27. Restate the union rule in words.

Use Venn diagrams to answer the following questions. (See Example 5.)

28. If $n(A) = 5$, $n(B) = 8$, and $n(A \cap B) = 4$, what is $n(A \cup B)$?

**Projections of Hispanic and Non-Hispanic Populations by Age and Sex: 1995 to 2025,* U.S. Bureau of the Census.

29. If $n(A) = 12$, $n(B) = 27$, and $n(A \cup B) = 30$, what is $n(A \cap B)$?

30. Suppose $n(B) = 7$, $n(A \cap B) = 3$, and $n(A \cup B) = 20$. What is $n(A)$?

31. Suppose $n(A \cap B) = 5$, $n(A \cup B) = 35$, and $n(A) = 13$. What is $n(B)$?

Draw a Venn diagram and use the given information to fill in the number of elements for each region.

32. $n(U) = 38$, $n(A) = 16$, $n(A \cap B) = 12$, $n(B') = 20$

33. $n(A) = 26$, $n(B) = 10$, $n(A \cup B) = 30$, $n(A') = 17$

34. $n(A \cup B) = 17$, $n(A \cap B) = 3$, $n(A) = 8$, $n(A' \cup B') = 21$

35. $n(A') = 28$, $n(B) = 25$, $n(A' \cup B') = 45$, $n(A \cap B) = 12$

36. $n(A) = 28$, $n(B) = 34$, $n(C) = 25$, $n(A \cap B) = 14$, $n(B \cap C) = 15$, $n(A \cap C) = 11$, $n(A \cap B \cap C) = 9$, $n(U) = 59$

37. $n(A) = 54$, $n(A \cap B) = 22$, $n(A \cup B) = 85$, $n(A \cap B \cap C) = 4$, $n(A \cap C) = 15$, $n(B \cap C) = 16$, $n(C) = 44$, $n(B') = 63$

38. $n(A \cap B) = 6$, $n(A \cap B \cap C) = 4$, $n(A \cap C) = 7$, $n(B \cap C) = 4$, $n(A \cap C') = 11$, $n(B \cap C') = 8$, $n(C) = 15$, $n(A' \cap B' \cap C') = 5$

39. $n(A) = 13$, $n(A \cap B \cap C) = 4$, $n(A \cap C) = 6$, $n(A \cap B') = 6$, $n(B \cap C) = 6$, $n(B \cap C') = 11$, $n(B \cup C) = 22$, $n(A' \cap B' \cap C') = 5$

*In Exercises 40–43, show that the statements are true by drawing Venn diagrams and shading the regions representing the sets on each side of the equals signs.**

40. $(A \cup B)' = A' \cap B'$

41. $(A \cap B)' = A' \cup B'$

42. $A \cap (B \cup C) = (A \cap B) \cup (A \cap C)$

43. $A \cup (B \cap C) = (A \cup B) \cap (A \cup C)$

*The statements in Exercises 40 and 41 are known as De Morgan's laws. They are named for the English mathematician Augustus De Morgan (1806–71).

9.3 PROBABILITY

If you go to a supermarket and buy five pounds of peaches at \$1.26 per pound, you can easily find the *exact* price of your purchase: \$6.30. On the other hand, the produce manager of the market is faced with the problem of ordering peaches. The manager may have a good estimate of the number of pounds of peaches that will be sold during the day, but there is no way to know *exactly*. The number of pounds that customers will purchase during a day cannot be predicted exactly.

Many problems that come up in applications of mathematics involve phenomena for which exact prediction is impossible. The best that we can do is to determine the *probability* of the possible outcomes. In this section and the next we introduce some of the terminology and basic premises of probability theory.

In probability, an **experiment** is an activity or occurrence with an observable result. Each repetition of an experiment is called a **trial.** The possible results of each trial are called **outcomes.** An example of a probability experiment is the tossing of a coin. Each trial of the experiment (each toss) has two possible outcomes: heads, h, and tails, t. If the outcomes h and t are equally likely to occur, then the coin is not "loaded" to favor one side over the other. Such a coin is called **fair.** For a coin that is fair, this "equally likely" assumption is made for each trial.

Because *two* equally likely outcomes are possible, h and t, theoretically a coin tossed many, many times should come up heads approximately 1/2 of the time. Also, the more times the coin is tossed, the closer the occurrence of heads should be to 1/2. Therefore, it is reasonable to define the probability of a head coming up to be 1/2. Similarly, we define the probability of tails coming up to be 1/2.

For now we shall concentrate on experiments, like coin tossing, in which each outcome is equally likely and use the probabilities suggested by this fact.

If there are n equally likely outcomes of an experiment, then the probability of any one outcome is $1/n$.

EXAMPLE 1 Suppose a spinner like the one shown in Figure 9.17 is spun.

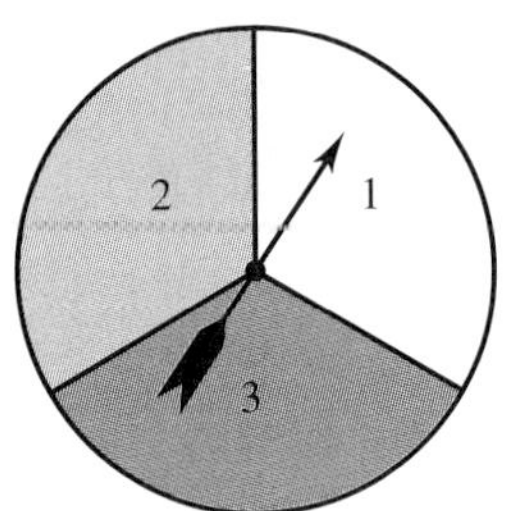

FIGURE 9.17

1 Find the probability that the spinner of Figure 9.17

(a) points to 3;

(b) does not point to 1.

Answers:

(a) 1/3

(b) 2/3

(a) Find the probability that the spinner will point to 1.

It is natural to assume that if this spinner were spun many, many times, it would point to 1 about 1/3 of the time, so that the required probability is 1/3.

(b) Find the probability that the spinner will point to 2.

Since 2 is one of three possible outcomes, the probability is 1/3. ■ 1

2 A jar holds a red marble, a blue marble, and a green marble. If one marble is drawn at random, what is the probability it is

(a) green?

(b) red?

Answers:

(a) 1/3

(b) 1/3

An ordinary die is a cube whose six faces show the following numbers of dots: 1, 2, 3, 4, 5, and 6. If the die is not "loaded" to favor certain faces over others (a fair die), then any one of the six faces is equally likely to come up when the die is rolled.

EXAMPLE 2 **(a)** If a single fair die is rolled, find the probability of rolling the number 4.

One out of six faces is a 4, so the required probability is 1/6.

(b) Using the same die, find the probability of rolling a 6.

One out of the six faces shows a 6, so the probability is 1/6. ■ 2

SAMPLE SPACES The set of all possible outcomes for an experiment is called the **sample space** for the experiment. A sample space for the experiment of tossing a coin has two outcomes: heads, h, and tails, t. If S represents this sample space, then

$$S = \{h, t\}.$$

EXAMPLE 3 Give a sample space for each experiment.

(a) A spinner like the one in Figure 9.17 is spun.

The three outcomes are 1, 2, or 3, so one sample space is

$$\{1, 2, 3\}.$$

(b) For the purposes of a public opinion poll, people are classified as young, middle-aged, or older, and as male or female.

A sample space for this poll could be written as a set of ordered pairs of these types.

$$\{(\text{young, male}), (\text{young, female}), (\text{middle-aged, male}),$$
$$(\text{middle-aged, female}), (\text{older, male}), (\text{older, female})\}$$

(c) An experiment consists of studying the number of boys and girls in families with exactly 3 children. Let b represent *boy* and g represent *girl.*

A 3-child family can have 3 boys, written bbb, 3 girls, ggg, or various combinations, such as bgg. A sample space with four outcomes (not equally likely) is

$$S_1 = \{3 \text{ boys, } 2 \text{ boys and } 1 \text{ girl, } 1 \text{ boy and } 2 \text{ girls, } 3 \text{ girls}\}.$$

Another sample space that considers the ordering of the births of the 3 children with, for example, bgg different from gbg or ggb, is

$$S_2 = \{bbb, bbg, bgb, gbb, bgg, gbg, ggb, ggg\}.$$

The second sample space, S_2, has equally likely outcomes; S_1 does not, since there is more than one way to get a family with 2 boys and 1 girl or a family of 2 girls and 1 boy, but only one way to get 3 boys or 3 girls. ■

3 **(a)** Write an equally likely sample space for the experiment of rolling a single fair die.

(b) Write an equally likely sample space for the experiment of tossing 2 fair coins.

(c) Write a sample space for the experiment of tossing 2 fair coins, if we are interested only in the number of heads. Are the outcomes in this sample space equally likely?

Answers:

(a) $\{1, 2, 3, 4, 5, 6\}$

(b) {hh, ht, th, tt}

(c) $\{0, 1, 2\}$; no

CAUTION An experiment may have more than one sample space, as shown in Example 3(c). The most useful sample spaces have equally likely outcomes, but it is not always possible to choose such a sample space. ◆ 3

EVENTS An **event** is a subset of outcomes from a sample space. If the sample space for tossing a coin is $S = \{h, t\}$, then one event is the subset $\{h\}$, which represents the outcome "heads." For the experiment of rolling a single fair die, with $S = \{1, 2, 3, 4, 5, 6\}$, some possible events are listed below.

The die shows an even number: $E_1 = \{2, 4, 6\}$.

The die shows a 1: $E_2 = \{1\}$.

The die shows a number less than 5: $E_3 = \{1, 2, 3, 4\}$.

The die shows a multiple of 3: $E_4 = \{3, 6\}$.

EXAMPLE 4

For the sample space S_2 in Example 3(c), write the following events.

(a) Event H: the family has exactly 2 girls.
Families can have exactly 2 girls with either bgg, gbg, or ggb, so that event H is

$$H = \{bgg, gbg, ggb\}.$$

(b) Event K: the 3 children are the same sex.
Two outcomes satisfy this condition, all boys or all girls.

$$K = \{bbb, ggg\}$$

(c) Event J: the family has 3 girls.
Only ggg satisfies this condition, so

$$J = \{ggg\}.$$ ■ 4

4 Suppose a die is tossed. Write the following events.

(a) The number showing is less than 3.

(b) The number showing is 5.

(c) The number showing is 8.

Answers:

(a) $\{1, 2\}$

(b) $\{5\}$

(c) $\emptyset$

In Example 4(c), event J had only one possible outcome, ggg. Such an event, with only one possible outcome, is a **simple event.** If an event E equals the sample space S, then E is a **certain event.** If event $E = \emptyset$, then E is an **impossible event.**

5 Which of the events listed in Side Problem 4 is

(a) simple?

(b) certain?

(c) impossible?

Answers:

(a) Part (b)

(b) None

(c) Part (c)

EXAMPLE 5 Suppose a die is rolled. As shown in Side Problem 3(a), the sample space is $\{1, 2, 3, 4, 5, 6\}$.

(a) The event "the die shows a 4," $\{4\}$, has only one possible outcome. It is a simple event.

(b) The event "the number showing is less than 10" equals the sample space $S = \{1, 2, 3, 4, 5, 6\}$. This event is a certain event; if a die is rolled the number showing (either 1, 2, 3, 4, 5, or 6) must be less than 10.

(c) The event "the die shows a 7" is the empty set, $\emptyset$; this is an impossible event. ■ 5

PROBABILITY For sample spaces with *equally likely* outcomes, the *probability of an event* is defined as follows.

BASIC PROBABILITY PRINCIPLE

Suppose event E is a subset of a sample space S. Then the **probability that event E occurs,** written $P(E)$, is

$$P(E) = \frac{n(E)}{n(S)}.$$

This definition means that the probability of an event is a number that indicates the relative likelihood of the event.

EXAMPLE 6 Suppose a single fair die is rolled. Use the sample space $S = \{1, 2, 3, 4, 5, 6\}$ and give the probability of each of the following events.

(a) E: the die shows an even number.
Here, $E = \{2, 4, 6\}$, a set with three elements. Because S contains six elements,

$$P(E) = \frac{3}{6} = \frac{1}{2}.$$

(b) F: the die shows a number greater than 4.
Since F contains two elements, 5 and 6,

$$P(F) = \frac{2}{6} = \frac{1}{3}.$$

(c) G: the die shows a number less than 10.
Event G is a certain event, with

$$G = \{1, 2, 3, 4, 5, 6\}, \quad \text{so} \quad P(G) = \frac{6}{6} = 1.$$

(d) H: the die shows an 8.
This event is impossible, so

$$P(H) = \frac{0}{6} = 0.$$ ■ 6

6 A fair die is rolled. Find the probability of rolling

(a) an odd number;

(b) 2, 4, 5, or 6;

(c) a number greater than 5;

(d) the number 7.

Answers:

(a) 1/2

(b) 2/3

(c) 1/6

(d) 0

EXAMPLE 7 If a single card is drawn at random from an ordinary well-shuffled, 52-card deck (shown in Figure 9.18), find the probability of each of the following events.

(a) Drawing an ace

There are 4 aces in the deck. The event "drawing an ace" is

$$\{\text{heart ace, diamond ace, club ace, spade ace}\}.$$

Therefore,

$$P(\text{ace}) = \frac{4}{52} = \frac{1}{13}.$$

(b) Drawing a face card (K, Q, J of any suit)

Since there are 12 face cards,

$$P(\text{face card}) = \frac{12}{52} = \frac{3}{13}.$$

(c) Drawing a spade

The deck contains 13 spades, so

$$P(\text{spade}) = \frac{13}{52} = \frac{1}{4}.$$

(d) Drawing a spade or a heart

Besides the 13 spades, the deck contains 13 hearts, so

$$P(\text{spade or heart}) = \frac{26}{52} = \frac{1}{2}.$$ ■ 7

7 A single playing card is drawn at random from an ordinary 52-card deck. Find the probability of drawing

(a) a queen;

(b) a diamond;

(c) a red card.

Answers:

(a) 1/13

(b) 1/4

(c) 1/2

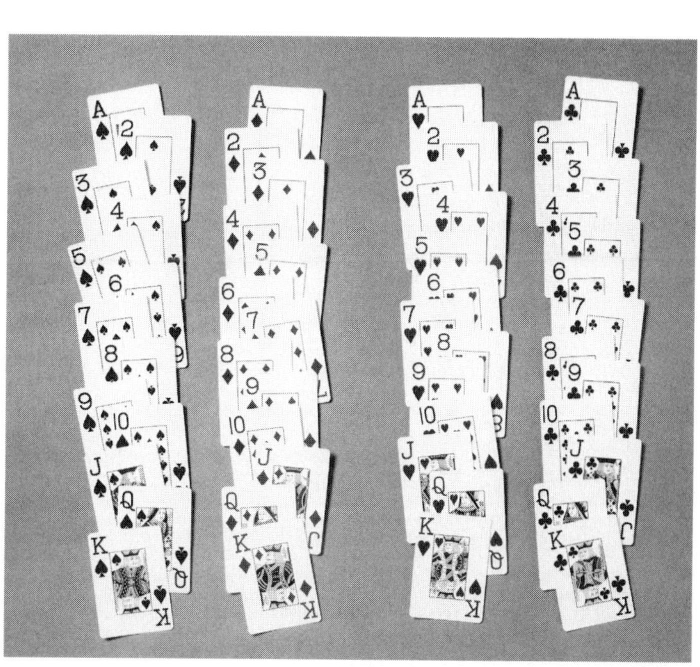

FIGURE 9.18

The probability of each event in the preceding examples was a number between 0 and 1, inclusive. The same thing is true in the general case. If an event E consists of m of the possible n outcomes, then $0 \le m \le n$ and hence, $0 \le m/n \le 1$. Since $P(E) = m/n$, $P(E)$ is between 0 and 1, inclusive.

For any event E, $\mathbf{0 \le P(E) \le 1}$.

For any sample space S, $\mathbf{P(S) = 1}$ **and** $\mathbf{P(\emptyset) = 0}$.

EXAMPLE 8 The table gives the number of bachelor's and graduate degrees granted in the U.S. in millions.*

Year	*Degrees*
1989–90	1.49
1990–91	1.54
1991–92	1.60
1992–93	1.62
1993–94	1.65
1994–95	1.67

8 Find the probability that a randomly selected person with a degree from the years shown in Example 8 received the degree in 1990–91.

Answer:
.161

Find the probability that a randomly selected person with a degree granted during these years received the degree in the 1993–94 year.

We must first find the total number of degrees granted during 1989–95. Verify that the amounts in the table add up to 9.57. Then,

$$P(1993\text{–}94) = \frac{1.65}{9.57} = .172. \quad \blacksquare \quad \boxed{8}$$

*_The Universal Almanac, 1996,_ John W. Wright, General Editor, Andrews and McMeel, Kansas City, p. 244.

9.3 EXERCISES

1. What is meant by a "fair" coin or die?
2. What is meant by the sample space for an experiment?

Write sample spaces for the experiments in Exercises 3–8. (See Example 3.)

3. A day in June is chosen for a picnic.
4. At a sleep center, a person is asked the number of hours (to the nearest hour) he slept yesterday.
5. The manager of a small company must decide whether to buy office space or lease it.
6. A student must decide which one of three courses that interest her to take.
7. A CPA chooses a month as the end of the fiscal year for a new corporation.
8. A coin is tossed and a die is rolled.
9. Define an event.
10. What is a simple event?

For the experiments in Exercises 11–16, write out an equally likely sample space, and then write the indicated events in set notation. (See Examples 3–5.)

11. A marble is drawn at random from a bowl containing 3 yellow, 4 white, and 8 blue marbles.
    (a) A yellow marble is drawn.
    (b) A blue marble is drawn.
    (c) A white marble is drawn.
    (d) A black marble is drawn.

12. Slips of paper marked with the numbers 1, 2, 3, 4, and 5 are placed in a box. After being mixed, two slips are drawn.
    (a) Both slips are marked with even numbers.
    (b) One slip is marked with an odd number and the other is marked with an even number.
    (c) Both slips are marked with the same number.
13. An unprepared student takes a three-question true/false quiz in which he guesses the answers to all three questions.
    (a) The student gets three answers wrong.
    (b) The student gets exactly two answers correct.
    (c) The student gets only the first answer correct.
14. A die is tossed twice, with the tosses recorded as ordered pairs.
    (a) The first die shows a 3.
    (b) The sum of the numbers showing is 8.
    (c) The sum of the numbers showing is 13.
15. One urn contains four balls, labeled 1, 2, 3, and 4. A second urn contains five balls, labeled 1, 2, 3, 4, and 5. An experiment consists of taking one ball from the first urn, and then taking a ball from the second urn.
    (a) The number on the first ball is even.
    (b) The number on the second ball is even.
    (c) The sum of the numbers on the two balls is 5.
    (d) The sum of the numbers on the two balls is 1.
16. From 5 employees, Strutz, Martin, Hampton, Williams, and Ewing, 2 are selected to attend a conference.
    (a) Hampton is selected.
    (b) Strutz and Martin are not both selected.
    (c) Both Williams and Ewing are selected.

A single fair die is rolled. Find the probabilities of the following events. (See Example 6.)

17. Getting a 5
18. Getting a number less than 4
19. Getting a number greater than 4
20. Getting a 2 or a 5

A card is drawn from a well-shuffled deck of 52 cards. Find the probability of drawing each of the following. (See Example 7.)

21. A 9
22. A black card
23. A black 9
24. A heart
25. The 9 of hearts
26. A 2 or a queen
27. A black 7 or a red 8
28. A red face card

A jar contains 5 red, 4 black, 7 purple, and 9 green marbles. If a marble is drawn at random, what is the probability that the marble is

29. red?
30. black?
31. green?
32. purple?
33. not black?
34. not purple?
35. red or black?
36. black or purple?

Solve each problem. (See Example 8.)

37. **Management** The table gives U.S. advertising volume in millions of dollars by medium in 1994.*

Medium	*Expenditures*
Newspapers	34.4
Magazines	7.9
Television	34.2
Radio	10.5
Direct Mail	29.6
Yellow Pages	9.8
Other	23.6
	Total 150.0

Find the probability that a company randomly decides to spend its advertising dollars on
    (a) direct mail,
    (b) television,
    (c) newspapers.

38. **Social Science** The population of the United States by race in 1995, and the projected population by race for the year 2025 are given below.†

U.S. Population by Race (in thousands)

Race	*1995*	*2025*
White	193,900	209,900
Hispanic	26,800	50,900
African-Amer.	31,600	44,700
Asian-Amer.	9,200	24,000
Other	1,900	2,800

Find the probability of a randomly selected person being each of the following.
    (a) Hispanic in 1995
    (b) Hispanic in 2025
    (c) African-American in 1995
    (d) African-American in 2025

**The Universal Almanac, 1996,* John W. Wright, General Editor, Andrews and McMeel, Kansas City, p. 270.

†Projections of Hispanic and Non-Hispanic Populations, by Age and Sex: 1995 to 2025, from U.S. Bureau of the Census, *Current Population Reports.*

9.4 BASIC CONCEPTS OF PROBABILITY

We discuss the probability of more complex events in this section. Since events are sets, we can use set operations to find unions, intersections, and complements of events.

EXAMPLE 1 Suppose a die is tossed. Let E be the event "the die shows a number greater than 3," and let F be the event "the die shows an even number." Then

$$E = \{4, 5, 6\} \quad \text{and} \quad F = \{2, 4, 6\}.$$

Find each of the following events (sets).

(a) The die shows an even number greater than 3.
We are looking for an even number *and* a number that is greater than 3. The event $E \cap F$ includes the outcomes common to *both* E and F. Here,

$$E \cap F = \{4, 6\}.$$

(b) The die shows an even number or a number greater than 3.
We want numbers that are even, or greater than 3, *or* both even and greater than 3, which is the event $E \cup F$.

$$E \cup F = \{2, 4, 5, 6\}$$

(c) The die shows a number less than or equal to 3.
This set is the complement of E,

$$E' = \{1, 2, 3\}.$$

The Venn diagrams of Figure 9.19 show the events $E \cap F$, $E \cup F$, and E'. ■ 1

1 Give the following events for the experiment of Example 1 if $E = \{1, 3\}$ and $F = \{2, 3, 4, 5\}$.

(a) $E \cap F$

(b) $E \cup F$

(c) E'

Answers:

(a) $\{3\}$

(b) $\{1, 2, 3, 4, 5\}$

(c) $\{2, 4, 5, 6\}$

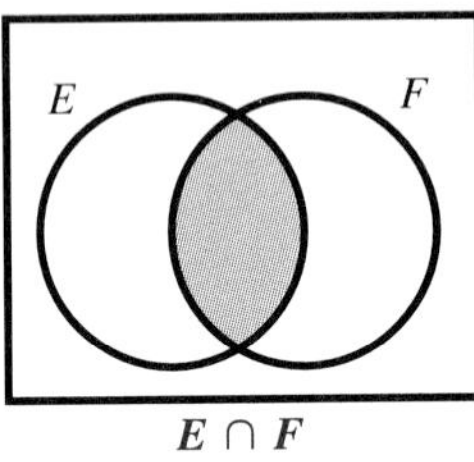

$E \cap F$

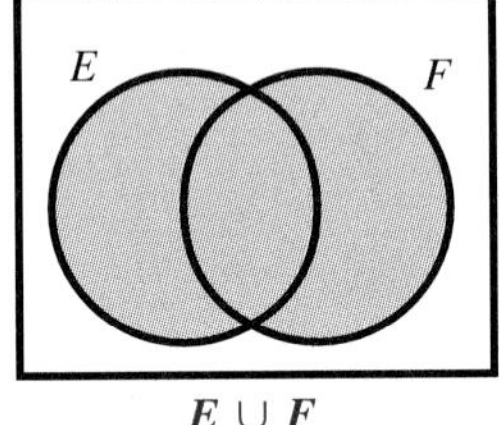

$E \cup F$

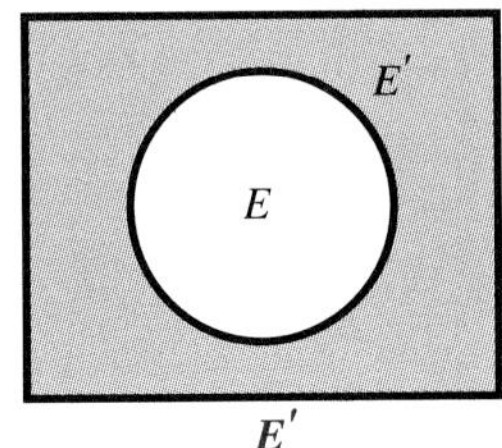

E'

FIGURE 9.19

Two events that cannot both occur at the same time, such as getting both a head and a tail on the same toss of a coin, are called **mutually exclusive events.**

Events A and B are mutually exclusive events if $A \cap B = \emptyset$.

For any event E, the events E and E' are mutually exclusive. See Figure 9.19. By definition, mutually exclusive events are disjoint sets.

2 In Example 2, let $F = \{2, 4, 6\}$, $K = \{1, 3, 5\}$, and G remain the same. Are the following events mutually exclusive?

(a) F and K

(b) F and G

Answers:

(a) Yes

(b) No

EXAMPLE 2 Let $S = \{1, 2, 3, 4, 5, 6\}$, the sample space for tossing a die. Let $E = \{4, 5, 6\}$, and let $G = \{1, 2\}$. Then E and G are mutually exclusive events because they have no outcomes in common; $E \cap G = \emptyset$. See Figure 9.20. ■ 2

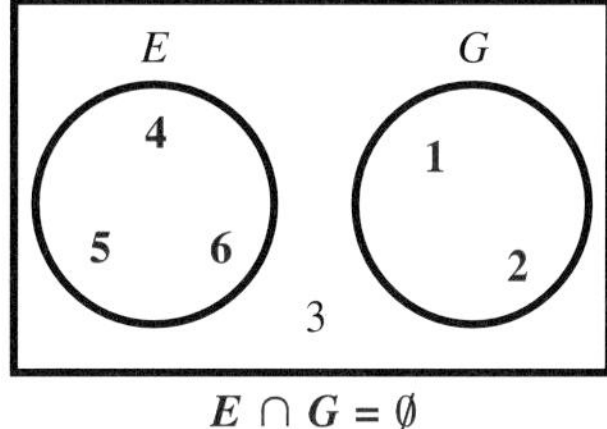

$E \cap G = \emptyset$

FIGURE 9.20

A summary of the set operations for events is given below.

> Let E and F be events for a sample space S.
>
> $E \cap F$ occurs when both E and F occur.
>
> $E \cup F$ occurs when either E or F or both occur.
>
> E' occurs when E does not.
>
> E and F are mutually exclusive if $E \cap F = \emptyset$.

To determine the probability of the union of the two events E and F in a sample space S, we use the union rule for counting from Section 9.2:

$$n(E \cup F) = n(E) + n(F) - n(E \cap F).$$

Dividing both sides by $n(S)$ shows that

$$\frac{n(E \cup F)}{n(S)} = \frac{n(E)}{n(S)} + \frac{n(F)}{n(S)} - \frac{n(E \cap F)}{n(S)}$$

$$P(E \cup F) = P(E) + P(F) - P(E \cap F).$$

This discussion is summarized below.

> **UNION RULE FOR PROBABILITY**
>
> For any events E and F from a sample space S,
>
> $$\mathbf{P(E \cup F) = P(E) + P(F) - P(E \cap F).}$$

EXAMPLE 3 If a single card is drawn from an ordinary deck of cards, find the probability that it will be red or a face card.

Let R represent the event "red card" and F the event "face card." There are 26 red cards in the deck, so $P(R) = 26/52$. There are 12 face cards in the deck, so

3 A single card is drawn from an ordinary deck. Find the probability that it is black or a 9.

Answer:
7/13

$P(F) = 12/52$. Since there are 6 red face cards in the deck, $P(R \cap F) = 6/52$. By the union rule, the probability that the card will be red or a face card is

$$P(R \cup F) = P(R) + P(F) - P(R \cap F)$$
$$= \frac{26}{52} + \frac{12}{52} - \frac{6}{52} = \frac{32}{52} = \frac{8}{13}. \quad \blacksquare \quad \boxed{3}$$

CAUTION Recall from Section 9.1, the word "or" always indicates a *union.* ◆

EXAMPLE 4 Suppose two fair dice (plural of *die*) are rolled. Find each of the following probabilities.

(a) The first die shows a 2 or the sum of the results is 6 or 7.

The sample space for the throw of two dice is shown in Figure 9.21, where 1-1 represents the event "the first die shows a 1 and the second die shows a 1," 1-2 represents "the first die shows a 1 and the second die shows a 2," and so on. Let A represent the event "the first die shows a 2" and B represent the event "the sum of the results is 6 or 7." These events are indicated in Figure 9.21. From the diagram, event A has 6 elements, B has 11 elements, and the sample space has 36 elements. Thus,

$$P(A) = \frac{6}{36}, \quad P(B) = \frac{11}{36}, \quad \text{and} \quad P(A \cap B) = \frac{2}{36}.$$

By the union rule,

$$P(A \cup B) = P(A) + P(B) - P(A \cap B),$$
$$P(A \cup B) = \frac{6}{36} + \frac{11}{36} - \frac{2}{36} = \frac{15}{36} = \frac{5}{12}.$$

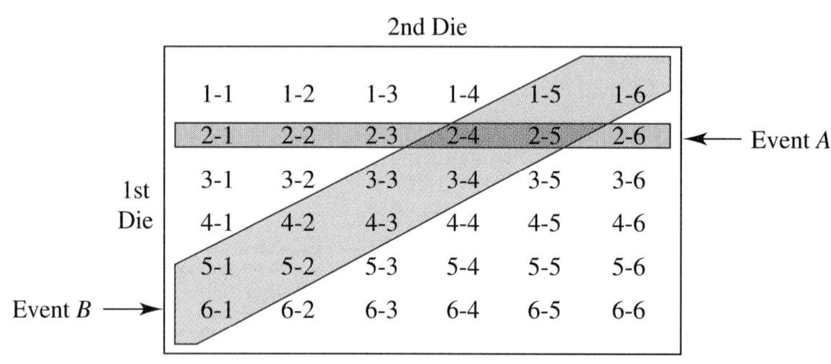

FIGURE 9.21

4 In the experiment of Example 4, find the following probabilities.

(a) The sum is 5 or the second die shows a 3.

(b) Both dice show the same number or the sum is at least 11.

Answers:
(a) 1/4
(b) 2/9

(b) The sum is 11 or the second die is 5.

$P(\text{sum is 11}) = 2/36$, $P(\text{second die is 5}) = 6/36$, and $P(\text{sum is 11 and second die is 5}) = 1/36$, so

$$P(\text{sum is 11 or second die is 5}) = \frac{2}{36} + \frac{6}{36} - \frac{1}{36} = \frac{7}{36}. \quad \blacksquare \quad \boxed{4}$$

When events E and F are mutually exclusive, then $E \cap F = \emptyset$ by definition; hence, $P(E \cap F) = 0$. The converse of this fact can be used to determine that two events are mutually exclusive.

For any events E and F, if $P(E \cap F) = 0$, then E and F are mutually exclusive.

Applying the union rule to mutually exclusive events yields a special case.

> For mutually exclusive events E and F,
>
> $$P(E \cup F) = P(E) + P(F).$$

EXAMPLE 5 Assume that the probability of a couple having a boy is the same as the probability of their having a girl. If the couple has 3 children, find the probability that at least 2 of them are girls.

The event of having at least 2 girls is the union of the mutually exclusive events E = "the family has exactly 2 girls" and F = "the family has exactly 3 girls." Using the equally likely sample space

$$\{ggg, ggb, gbg, bgg, gbb, bgb, bbg, bbb\},$$

we see that $P(2 \text{ girls}) = 3/8$ and $P(3 \text{ girls}) = 1/8$. Therefore,

$$P(\text{at least 2 girls}) = P(2 \text{ girls}) + P(3 \text{ girls}) = \frac{3}{8} + \frac{1}{8} = \frac{1}{2}.$$ ■ 5

5 In Example 5, find the probability of no more than 2 girls.

Answer:
7/8

By definition of E', for any event E from a sample space S,

$$E \cup E' = S \quad \text{and} \quad E \cap E' = \emptyset.$$

Because $E \cap E' = \emptyset$, events E and E' are mutually exclusive, so that

$$P(E \cup E') = P(E) + P(E').$$

However, $E \cup E' = S$, the sample space, and $P(S) = 1$. Thus

$$P(E \cup E') = P(E) + P(E') = 1.$$

Rearranging these terms gives the following useful rule.

> **COMPLEMENT RULE**
>
> For any event E,
>
> $$P(E') = 1 - P(E) \quad \text{and} \quad P(E) = 1 - P(E').$$

6 **(a)** Let $P(K) = 2/3$. Find $P(K')$.

(b) If $P(X') = 3/4$, find $P(X)$.

Answers:
(a) 1/3
(b) 1/4

EXAMPLE 6 If a fair die is rolled, what is the probability that any number but 5 will come up?

If E is the event that 5 comes up, then E' is the event that any number but 5 comes up. $P(E) = 1/6$, so we have $P(E') = 1 - 1/6 = 5/6$. ■ 6

EXAMPLE 7 If two fair dice are rolled, find the probability that the sum of the numbers showing is greater than 3.

To calculate this probability directly, we must find the probabilities that the sum is 4, 5, 6, 7, 8, 9, 10, 11, or 12 and then add them. It is much simpler to first find the probability of the complement, the event that the sum is less than or equal to 3.

$$P(\text{sum} \le 3) = P(\text{sum is } 2) + P(\text{sum is } 3)$$
$$= \frac{1}{36} + \frac{2}{36} = \frac{3}{36} = \frac{1}{12}$$

Now use the fact the $P(E) = 1 - P(E')$ to get

$$P(\text{sum} > 3) = 1 - P(\text{sum} \le 3) = 1 - \frac{1}{12} = \frac{11}{12}.$$ ■ 7

7 In Example 7, find the probability that the sum of the numbers rolled is at least 5.

Answer:
5/6

Venn diagrams are useful in finding probabilities, as shown in the next example.

EXAMPLE 8 Susan is a college student who receives heavy sweaters from her aunt at the first sign of cold weather. She estimates that the probability that a sweater is the wrong size is .47, the probability that it is a loud color is .59, and the probability that it is both the wrong size and a loud color is .31.

(a) Find the probability that the sweater is the correct size and not a loud color.

Let W be the event "wrong size" and L be the event "loud color." Draw a Venn diagram and determine the probabilities of the mutually exclusive events I–IV in Figure 9.22 as follows. We are given $P(\text{II}) = P(W \cap L) = .31$. Because regions I and II are mutually exclusive, $P(W) = P(\text{I}) + P(\text{II})$, so that $P(\text{I}) = P(W) - P(\text{II}) = .47 - .31 = .16$. Similarly, $P(\text{III}) = P(L) - P(\text{II}) = .59 - .31 = .28$. Finally, since IV is the complement of $W \cup L$, we have

$$P(\text{IV}) = 1 - P(W \cup L) = 1 - (.16 + .31 + .28) = .25.$$

The event "correct size *and* not a loud color" is region IV, the area outside of both W and L. Therefore, its probability is .25.

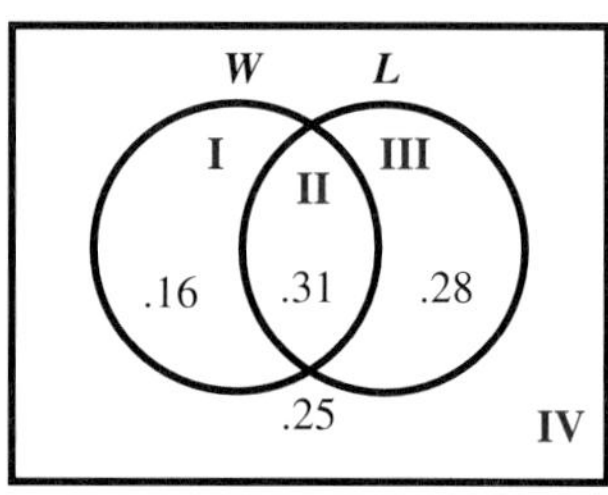

FIGURE 9.22

8 Find the probability that the sweater in Example 8 is

(a) not a loud color;

(b) the correct size *and* a loud color.

Answers:
(a) .41
(b) .28

(b) Find the probability that the sweater is the correct size *or* not a loud color.

The event "correct size *or* not a loud color" is the region outside of region II (in II every sweater is both the wrong size and a loud color), that is, the complement of II. Hence, its probability is $1 - .31 = .69$. ■ 8

In many realistic problems, it is not possible to establish exact probabilities for events. Useful approximations, however, often can be found by using past experience as a guide to the future, as in the next example.

EXAMPLE 9 The manager of a store has decided to make a study of the amounts of money spent by people coming into the store. To begin, he chooses a day that seems fairly typical and gathers the following data. (Purchases have been rounded to the nearest dollar, with sales tax ignored.)

Amount Spent	*Number of Customers*
\$0	158
\$1–10	94
\$11–20	203
\$21–50	126
\$51–100	47
\$101–200	38
\$201 and over	53

First, the manager might add the numbers of customers to find that 719 people came into the store that day. Of these 719 people, $126/719 \approx .175$ made a purchase of at least \$21 but no more than \$50. Also, $53/719 \approx .074$ of the customers spent \$201 or more. For this day, the probability that a customer entering the store will spend from \$21 to \$50 is .175, and the probability that the customer will spend \$201 or more is .074. Probabilities for the other purchase amounts can be assigned in the same way, giving the results below.

Amount Spent	*Probability*
\$0	.220
\$1–10	.131
\$11–20	.282
\$21–50	.175
\$51–100	.065
\$101–200	.053
\$201 and over	.074
	Total 1.000

The categories in the table are mutually exclusive simple events. Thus, by the union rule,

$$P(\text{spending} < \$21) = .220 + .131 + .282 = .633.$$

From the table, .282 of the customers spend from \$11 to \$20, inclusive. Since this price range attracts more than a quarter of the customers, perhaps the store's advertising should emphasize items in, or near, this price range.

The manager should use this table of probabilities to help in predicting the results on other days only if the manager is reasonably sure that the day when the measurements were made is fairly typical of the other days the store is open. For example, on the last few days before Christmas the probabilities might be quite different. ■ 9

9 A traffic engineer gathered the following data on the number of accidents at four busy intersections.

Intersection	*Number of Accidents*
1	25
2	32
3	28
4	35

If an accident occurs at one of these four intersections, what is the probability that it occurs at intersections 1 or 3?

Answer:

.44

In this section and the previous one, we have used more than one way to assign probabilities of events. There are three types of probability: *theoretical* (or *classical*); *empirical;* and *subjective.* We use theoretical probability when we assign probabilities for experiments with a coin or with dice, as in Examples 1–7. Probabilities determined by the data from experiments, using the frequency definition, $P(E) = n(E)/n(S)$, are empirical probabilities. See Example 9. Subjective probabilities are assigned when no experimental results or long-run frequencies are available. Since these probabilities are based on individual experience, different people may assign different probabilities to the same event. Example 8 gives an example of subjective probability. In the next chapter the use of subjective probability is discussed in more detail. No matter how probabilities are assigned, they must satisfy the following properties.

PROPERTIES OF PROBABILITY

Let S be a sample space consisting of n distinct outcomes $s_1, s_2, \ldots, s_n$. An acceptable probability assignment consists of assigning to each outcome s_i a number p_i (the probability of s_i) according to these rules.

1. The probability of each outcome is a number between 0 and 1.

$$0 \le p_1 \le 1, \quad 0 \le p_2 \le 1, \ldots, \quad 0 \le p_n \le 1$$

2. The sum of the probabilities of all possible outcomes is 1.

$$p_1 + p_2 + p_3 + \cdots + p_n = 1.$$

ODDS Sometimes probability statements are given in terms of **odds,** a comparison of $P(E)$ with $P(E')$. For example, suppose $P(E) = \frac{4}{5}$. Then $P(E') = 1 - \frac{4}{5} = \frac{1}{5}$. These probabilities predict that E will occur 4 out of 5 times and E' will occur 1 out of 5 times. Then we say the **odds in favor** of E are 4 to 1 or 4:1. This ratio may be found from the fraction $P(E)/P(E') = \frac{4}{5}/\frac{1}{5} = 4/1$.

ODDS

The **odds in favor** of an event E are defined as the ratio of $P(E)$ to $P(E')$, or

$$\frac{P(E)}{P(E')}, \quad P(E') \neq 0.$$

EXAMPLE 10 Suppose the weather forecaster says that the probability of rain tomorrow is 1/3. Find the odds in favor of rain tomorrow.

Let E be the event "rain tomorrow." Then E' is the event "no rain tomorrow." Since $P(E) = 1/3$, $P(E') = 2/3$. By the definition of odds, the odds in favor of rain are

$$\frac{1/3}{2/3} = \frac{1}{2}, \quad \text{written 1 to 2 or 1:2.}$$

[10] Suppose $P(E) = 9/10$. Find the odds

(a) in favor of E;

(b) against E.

Answers:

(a) 9 to 1

(b) 1 to 9

On the other hand, the odds that it will *not* rain, or the odds *against* rain, are

$$\frac{2/3}{1/3} = \frac{2}{1}, \quad \text{written 2 to 1.} \blacksquare \quad [10]$$

If the odds in favor of an event are, say, 3 to 5, then the probability of the event is 3/8, while the probability of the complement of the event is 5/8. (Odds of 3 to 5 indicate 3 outcomes in favor of the event out of a total of 8 outcomes.) This example suggests the following generalization.

> If the odds favoring event E are m to n, then
>
> $$P(E) = \frac{m}{m+n} \quad \text{and} \quad P(E') = \frac{n}{m+n}.$$

EXAMPLE 11 The odds that a particular bid will be the low bid are 4 to 5.

(a) Find the probability that the bid will be the low bid.

Odds of 4 to 5 show 4 favorable chances out of $4 + 5 = 9$ chances altogether.

$$P(\text{bid will be low bid}) = \frac{4}{4+5} = \frac{4}{9}$$

[11] If the odds in favor of event E are 1 to 5, find

(a) $P(E)$;

(b) $P(E')$.

Answers:

(a) 1/6

(b) 5/6

(b) Find the odds against that bid being the low bid.

There is a 5/9 chance that the bid will not be the low bid, so the odds against a low bid are

$$\frac{P(\text{bid will not be low})}{P(\text{bid will be low})} = \frac{5/9}{4/9} = \frac{5}{4},$$

or 5:4. $\blacksquare$ [11]

9.4 EXERCISES

Decide whether the events in Exercises 1–6 are mutually exclusive. (See Example 2.)

1. Being 15 and being a teenager
2. Wearing jogging shoes and wearing sandals
3. Being male and being a dancer
4. Owning a bicycle and owning a car
5. Being a U.S. Senator and being a U.S. Congressman concurrently
6. Being female and owning a truck
7. If the probability of an event is .857, what is the probability that the event will not occur?
8. Given $P(A) = .5$, $P(B) = .35$, $P(A \cup B) = .85$. Can this be correct? Explain under what conditions it is correct and under what conditions it is not correct.

Find the probabilities in Exercises 9–16. (See Examples 3–7.)

9. If a marble is drawn from a bag containing 2 yellow, 5 red, and 3 blue marbles, what are the probabilities of the following?
   (a) The marble is red.
   (b) The marble is either yellow or blue.
   (c) The marble is yellow or red.
   (d) The marble is green.
10. The law firm of Alam, Bartolini, Chinn, Dickinson, and Ellsberg has two senior partners, Alam and Bartolini. Two of the attorneys are to be selected to attend a conference. Assuming that all are equally likely to be selected, find the following probabilities.

(exercise continues)

(a) Chinn is selected.
(b) Ellsberg is not selected.
(c) Alam and Dickinson are selected.
(d) At least one senior partner is selected.

11. Ms. Bezzone invites 10 relatives to a party: her mother, two uncles, three brothers, and four cousins. If the chances of any one guest arriving first are equally likely, find the following probabilities.
(a) The first guest is an uncle or a cousin.
(b) The first guest is a brother or a cousin.
(c) The first guest is an uncle or her mother.

12. A card is drawn from a well-shuffled deck of 52 cards. Find the probability that the card is the following.
(a) a queen
(b) red
(c) a black 3
(d) a club or red

13. In Exercise 12, find the probability of the following.
(a) a face card (K, Q, J of any suit)
(b) red or a 3
(c) less than a four (consider aces as 1s)

14. Two dice are rolled. Find the probability of the following.
(a) The sum of the points is at least 10.
(b) The sum of the points is either 7 or at least 10.
(c) The sum of the points is 3 or the dice both show the same number.

15. Management The management of a firm wants to survey its workers, who are classified as follows for the purpose of an interview: 30% have worked for the company more than 5 years; 28% are female; 65% contribute to a voluntary retirement plan; 1/2 of the female workers contribute to the retirement plan. Find the following probabilities.
(a) A male worker is selected.
(b) A worker with less than 5 years in the company is selected.
(c) A worker who contributes to the retirement plan or a female worker is selected.

16. The numbers 1, 2, 3, 4, and 5 are written on five slips of paper, and two slips are drawn at random without replacement. Find the probability of each of the following.
(a) Both numbers are even.
(b) One of the numbers is even or greater than 3.
(c) The sum of the two numbers is 5 or the second number is 2.

Use Venn diagrams to work Exercises 17–22. (See Example 8.)

17. Social Science In a refugee camp in southern Mexico, it was found that 90% of the refugees came to escape political oppression, 80% came to escape abject poverty, and 70% came to escape both. What is the probability that a refugee in the camp was not poor nor seeking political asylum?

18. Social Science A study on body types gave the following results: 45% were short, 25% were short and overweight, and 24% were tall and not overweight. Find the probability that a person is
(a) overweight;
(b) short, but not overweight;
(c) tall and overweight.

19. Social Science A teacher found that 85% of the students in her math class had passed a course in algebra, 60% had passed a course in geometry, and 55% had passed both courses. Find the probability that a student selected randomly from the math class has passed at least one of the two courses.

20. Social Science The following data were gathered for 130 adult U.S. workers: 55 were women, 3 women earned more than $40,000, 62 men earned less than $40,000. Find the probability that an individual is
(a) a woman earning less than $40,000;
(b) a man earning more than $40,000;
(c) a man or is earning more than $40,000;
(d) a woman or is earning less than $40,000.

21. Management Suppose that 8% of a certain batch of calculators have a defective case, and that 11% have defective batteries. Also, 3% have both a defective case and defective batteries. A calculator is selected from the batch at random. Find the probability that the calculator has a good case and good batteries.

22. Social Science Fifty students in a Texas school were interviewed with the following results: 45 spoke Spanish, 10 spoke Vietnamese, and 8 spoke both languages. Find the probability that a randomly selected student from this group
(a) speaks both languages;
(b) speaks neither language;
(c) speaks only one of the two languages.

Work Exercises 23–29 on odds. (See Examples 10–11.)

23. A single die is rolled. Find the odds in favor of getting the following results.
(a) 3
(b) 5 or 6
(c) a number greater than 3
(d) a number less than 2

24. A marble is drawn from a box containing 3 yellow, 4 white, and 8 blue marbles. Find the odds in favor of drawing the following.
(a) A yellow marble
(b) A blue marble
(c) A white marble

25. The probability that a company will make a profit this year is .74. Find the odds against the company making a profit.

26. If the odds that a given candidate will win an election are 3 to 2, what is the probability that the candidate will lose?

27. **Social Science** A nationwide survey showed that the odds that an individual uses a seat belt when in a car's front seat are 17:8.* What is the probability that such an individual does not use a seat belt?

28. **Social Science** The survey mentioned in Exercise 27 also showed that the odds that a driver does not drink or does not drive after drinking are 4:1.* What is the probability that a driver was drinking?

29. On page 134 of Roger Staubach's autobiography, *First Down, Lifetime to Go,* Staubach makes the following statement regarding his experience in Vietnam: "Odds against a direct hit are very low but when your life is in danger, you don't worry too much about the odds." Is this wording consistent with our definition of odds for and against? How could it have been said so as to be technically correct?

An experiment is conducted for which the sample space is $S = \{s_1, s_2, s_3, s_4, s_5\}$. Which of the probability assignments in Exercises 30–35 is possible for this experiment? If an assignment is not possible, tell why.

30.

Outcomes	s_1	s_2	s_3	s_4	s_5
Probabilities	.02	.27	.35	.22	.14

31.

Outcomes	s_1	s_2	s_3	s_4	s_5
Probabilities	.50	.30	.10	.08	.02

32.

Outcomes	s_1	s_2	s_3	s_4	s_5
Probabilities	1/8	1/6	1/5	1/3	1/2

33.

Outcomes	s_1	s_2	s_3	s_4	s_5
Probabilities	1/10	1/8	1/5	1/5	1/4

34.

Outcomes	s_1	s_2	s_3	s_4	s_5
Probabilities	.23	.17	.32	.38	−.10

35.

Outcomes	s_1	s_2	s_3	s_4	s_5
Probabilities	.3	.4	−.4	.4	.3

Work the following problems. (See Example 9.)

36. **Social Science** A consumer survey randomly selects 2000 people and asks them about their income and their TV-watching habits. The results are shown in this table.

	HOURS OF TV WATCHED PER WEEK				
Annual Income	*0–8*	*9–15*	*16–22*	*23–30*	*More than 30*
Less than $12,000	11	15	8	14	120
$12,000–$24,999	10	19	28	96	232
$25,000–$39,999	18	32	88	327	189
$40,000–$59,999	31	85	160	165	100
$60,000 or more	73	60	52	55	12

As a reward for participation, each person questioned is given a small prize. Then the names of all participants are placed in a box and one name is randomly drawn to receive the grand prize of a free vacation trip. What is the probability that the winner of the grand prize
(a) watches TV at least 16 hours per week?
(b) has an income of at least $25,000?
(c) has an income of at least $40,000 and watches TV at least 16 hours per week?
(d) has an income of $0–$24,999 and watches TV more than 30 hours per week?

37. **Management** GT Global Theme Funds has world-wide assets distributed as follows.*

Geographic Location	*Percent*
Africa & Middle East	4.2
Latin America	6.0
Asia-Pacific	18.7
Europe	23.1
U.S. & Canada	48.0

If an asset is chosen randomly, what is the probability that it is from the following regions?
(a) Asia-Pacific
(b) North or South America
(c) Not from Europe

38. **Management** GT Global Health Care Fund has invested in the following sectors.*

Sector	*Percent*
Biotechnology	30.7
Pharmaceuticals	25.4
Medical Technology & Supplies	22.3
Health Care Services	8.2
Short-term & Other	13.4

Find the probability that an investment selected at random from this fund is as follows.
(a) In biotechnology or health care services
(b) In pharmaceuticals or medical technology & supplies
(c) Not in biotechnology

39. **Natural Science** The results of a study relating blood cholesterol level to coronary disease are given in the following table.

(exercise continues)

*Exercises 27 and 28 based on an article in *The Sacramento Bee,* June 4, 1992.

*Exercises 37 and 38 from GT Global Theme Funds Annual Report, October 31, 1996.

Cholesterol Level	Probability of Coronary Disease
Under 200	.10
200–219	.15
220–239	.20
240–259	.26
Over 259	.29

Find the probability of coronary disease if the cholesterol level is
(a) less than 240;
(b) 220 or more;
(c) from 200 to 239;
(d) from 220 to 259.

Natural Science *Color blindness is an inherited characteristic which is sex-linked, so that it is more common in males than in females. If M represents male and C represents red-green color blindness, using the relative frequencies of the incidence of males and red-green color blindness as probabilities,* $P(C) = .049$, $P(M \cap C) = .042$, $P(M \cup C) = .534$. *Find the following. (Hint: Use a Venn diagram with two circles labeled M and C.)*

40. $P(C')$

41. $P(M)$

42. $P(M')$

43. $P(M' \cap C')$

44. $P(C \cap M')$

45. $P(C \cup M')$

Natural Science *Gregor Mendel, an Austrian monk, was the first to use probability in the study of genetics. In an effort to understand the mechanisms of character transmittal from one generation to the next in plants, he counted the number of occurrences of various characteristics. Mendel found that the flower color in certain pea plants obeyed this scheme:*

Pure red crossed with pure white produces red.

The red offspring received from its parents genes for both red (R) and white (W), but in this case red is dominant and white recessive, so the offspring exhibits the color red. However, the offspring still carries both genes, and when two such offspring are crossed, several things can happen in the third generation, as shown in the table below, which is called a Punnet square.

		2ND PARENT	
		R	*W*
1ST PARENT	*R*	*RR*	*RW*
	W	*WR*	*WW*

This table shows the possible combinations of genes. Use the fact that red is dominant over white to find

46. $P(\text{red})$;

47. $P(\text{white})$.

Natural Science *Mendel found no dominance in snapdragons, with one red gene and one white gene producing pink-flowering offspring. These second-generation pinks, however, still carry one red and one white gene, and when they are crossed, the next generation still yields the Punnet square above. Find*

48. $P(\text{red})$;

49. $P(\text{pink})$;

50. $P(\text{white})$.

(Mendel verified these probability ratios experimentally with large numbers of observations, and did the same for many character units other than flower color. The importance of his work, published in 1866, was not recognized until 1900.)

Natural Science *In most animals and plants, it is very unusual for the number of main parts of the organism (arms, legs, toes, flower petals, etc.) to vary from generation to generation. Some species, however, have meristic variability, in which the number of certain body parts varies from generation from generation. One researcher* studied the front feet of certain guinea pigs and produced the probabilities shown below.*

$$P(\text{only four toes, all perfect}) = .77$$
$$P(\text{one imperfect toe and four good ones}) = .13$$
$$P(\text{exactly five good toes}) = .10$$

Find the probability of having the following.

51. No more than four good toes

52. Five toes, whether perfect or not

One way to solve a probability problem is to repeat the experiment (or a simulation of the experiment) many times, keeping track of the results. Then the probability can be approximated using the basic definition of the probability of an event E: $P(E) = m/n$, *where m favorable outcomes occur in n trials of an experiment. This is called the* **Monte Carlo method** *of approximating probabilities.*

Use a calculator with a random number generator or appropriate computer software and the Monte Carlo method to simulate the experiments in Exercises 53–58.

Approximate the probabilities in Exercises 53 and 54 if five coins are tossed. Then calculate the theoretical probabilities using the methods of the text and compare the results.

53. $P(4 \text{ heads})$

54. $P(2 \text{ heads}, 1 \text{ tail}, 2 \text{ heads})$ (in the order given)

*From "An Analysis of Variability in Guinea Pigs" by J. R. Wright, from *Genetics*, Vol. 19, 1934, pp. 506–36. Reprinted by permission.

Approximate the following probabilities if 4 cards are drawn from a 52-card deck.

55. P(any 2 cards and then 2 kings)

56. P(exactly 2 kings)

Approximate the probabilities in Exercises 57 and 58.

57. A jeweler received 8 identical watches each in a box marked with the series number of the watch. An assistant, who does not know that the boxes are marked, is told to polish the watches and then put them back in the boxes. She puts them in the boxes at random. What is the probability that she gets at least one watch in the right box?

58. A check room attendant has 10 hats but has lost the numbers identifying them. If he gives them back randomly, what is the probability that at least 2 of the hats are given back correctly?

9.5 CONDITIONAL PROBABILITY; INDEPENDENT EVENTS

The training manager for a large brokerage firm has noticed that some of the firm's brokers use the firm's research advice, while other brokers tend to go with their own beliefs about which stocks will go up. To see whether the research department performs better than the beliefs of the brokers, the manager conducted a survey of 100 brokers, with results as shown in the following table.

1 Use the data in the table to find

(a) $P(B)$,

(b) $P(A')$,

(c) $P(B')$.

Answers:

(a) .45

(b) .4

(c) .55

	Picked a Stock that Went Up	*Didn't Pick a Stock that Went Up*	*Totals*
Used Research	30	15	45
Didn't Use Research	30	25	55
Totals	60	40	100

Letting A be the event "picked a stock that went up" and letting B be the event "used research," $P(A)$, $P(A')$, $P(B)$, and $P(B')$ can be found. For example, the chart shows that a total of 60 brokers picked stocks that went up, so $P(A) = 60/100 = .6$. 1

Suppose we want to find the probability that a broker using research will pick a stock that goes up. From the table above, of the 45 brokers who use research, there are 30 who picked stocks that went up, so

$$P(\text{broker who uses research picks stocks that go up}) = \frac{30}{45} \approx .667.$$

This is a different number than the probability that a broker picks a stock that goes up, .6, because *we have additional information* (the broker uses research) *that has reduced the sample space.* In other words, we found the probability that a broker picks a stock that goes up, A, given the additional information that the broker uses research, B. This is called the *conditional probability* of event A, given that event B has occurred, written $P(A \mid B)$. ($P(A \mid B)$ may also be read as "the probability of A given B.")

In the example above,

$$P(A \mid B) = \frac{30}{45}.$$

If we divide the numerator and denominator by 100 (the size of the sample space), this can be written as

$$P(A \mid B) = \frac{\frac{30}{100}}{\frac{45}{100}} = \frac{P(A \cap B)}{P(B)},$$

where $P(A \cap B)$ represents, as usual, the probability that both A and B will occur.

To generalize this result, assume that E and F are two events for a particular experiment. Assume that the sample space S for this experiment has n possible equally likely outcomes. Suppose event F has m elements, and $E \cap F$ has k elements ($k \leq m$). Using the fundamental principle of probability,

$$P(F) = \frac{m}{n} \quad \text{and} \quad P(E \cap F) = \frac{k}{n}.$$

We now want $P(E \mid F)$, the probability that E occurs given that F has occurred. Since we assume F has occurred, reduce the sample space to F: look only at the m elements inside F. (See Figure 9.23.) Of these m elements, there are k elements where E also occurs, because $E \cap F$ has k elements. This makes

$$P(E \mid F) = \frac{k}{m}.$$

Divide numerator and denominator by n to get

$$P(E \mid F) = \frac{k/n}{m/n} = \frac{P(E \cap F)}{P(F)}.$$

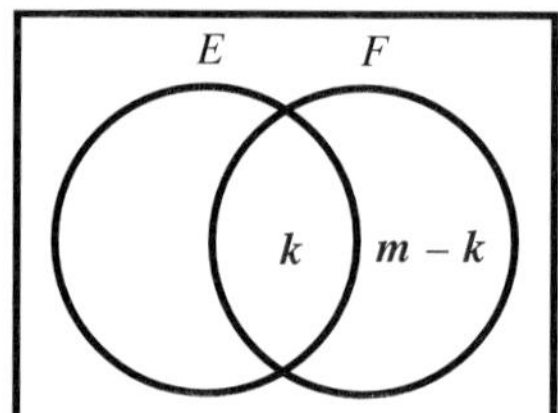

Event F has a total of m elements.

FIGURE 9.23

The last result gives the definition of conditional probability.

The **conditional probability** of an event E given event F, written $P(E \mid F)$, is

$$\mathbf{P(E \mid F) = \frac{P(E \cap F)}{P(F)}, \quad P(F) \neq 0.}$$

This definition tells us that, for equally likely outcomes, conditional probability is found by *reducing the sample space to event F,* and then finding the number of outcomes in F that are also in event E. Thus,

$$P(E \mid F) = \frac{n(E \cap F)}{n(F)}.$$

2 The table shows the results of a survey of a buffalo herd.

	Males	*Females*	*Totals*
Adults	500	1300	1800
Calves	520	500	1020
Totals	1020	1800	2820

Let M represent "male" and A represent "adult." Find each of the following.

(a) $P(M \mid A)$

(b) $P(M' \mid A)$

(c) $P(A \mid M')$

(d) $P(A' \mid M)$

(e) State the probability in part (d) in words.

Answers:

(a) 5/18

(b) 13/18

(c) 13/18

(d) 26/51

(e) The probability that a buffalo is a calf given that it is a male

EXAMPLE 1 Use the chart in the stockbroker's problem at the beginning of this section to find the following probabilities, where A is the event "picked a stock that went up" and B is the event "used research."

(a) $P(B \mid A)$

This represents the probability that the broker used research, given that the broker picked a stock that went up. Reduce the sample space to A. Then find $n(A \cap B)$ and $n(A)$.

$$P(B \mid A) = \frac{P(B \cap A)}{P(A)} = \frac{n(A \cap B)}{n(A)} = \frac{30}{60} = \frac{1}{2}$$

If a broker picked a stock that went up, then the probability is 1/2 that the broker used research.

(b) $P(A' \mid B)$

In words, this is the probability that a broker picks a stock that does not go up, even though he used research.

$$P(A' \mid B) = \frac{n(A' \cap B)}{n(B)} = \frac{15}{45} = \frac{1}{3}$$

(c) $P(B' \mid A')$

Here, we want the probability that a broker who picked a stock that did not go up did not use research.

$$P(B' \mid A') = \frac{n(B' \cap A')}{n(A')} = \frac{25}{40} = \frac{5}{8}$$ ■ 2

Venn diagrams can be used to illustrate problems in conditional probability. A Venn diagram for Example 1, in which the probabilities are used to indicate the number in the set defined by each region, is shown in Figure 9.24. In the diagram, $P(B \mid A)$ is found by *reducing the sample space to just set A.* Then $P(B \mid A)$ is the ratio of the number in that part of set B which is also in A to the number in set A, or $.3/.6 = .5$.

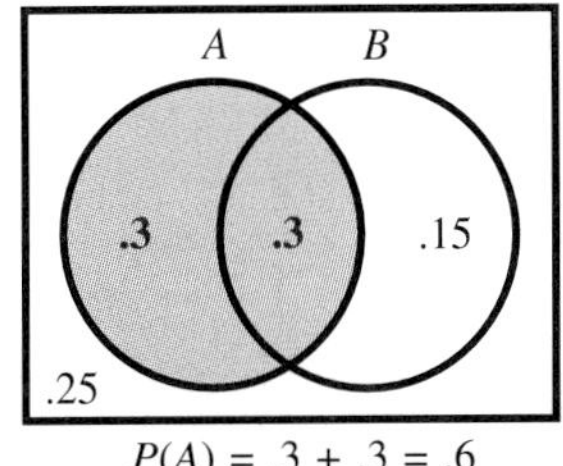

FIGURE 9.24

EXAMPLE 2 Given $P(E) = .4$, $P(F) = .5$, and $P(E \cup F) = .7$, find $P(E \mid F)$.

Find $P(E \cap F)$ first. Then use a Venn diagram to find $P(E \mid F)$. By the union rule,

$$\begin{aligned} P(E \cup F) &= P(E) + P(F) - P(E \cap F) \\ .7 &= .4 + .5 - P(E \cap F) \\ P(E \cap F) &= .2. \end{aligned}$$

3 Find $P(F \mid E)$ if $P(E) = .3$, $P(F) = .4$, and $P(E \cup F) = .6$.

Answer:
1/3

Now use the probabilities to indicate the number in each region of the Venn diagram in Figure 9.25. $P(E \mid F)$ is the ratio of the probability of that part of E which is in F to the probability of F or

$$P(E \mid F) = \frac{P(E \cap F)}{P(F)} = \frac{.2}{.5} = \frac{2}{5} = .4. \quad \blacksquare \quad \boxed{3}$$

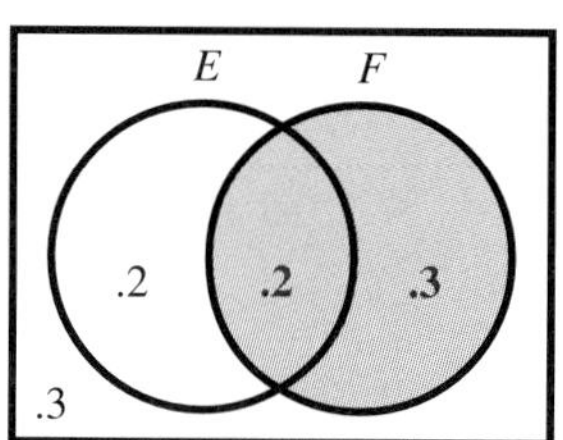

FIGURE 9.25

EXAMPLE 3 Two fair coins were tossed, and it is known that at least one was a head. Find the probability that both were heads.

The sample space has four equally likely outcomes, $S = \{hh, ht, th, tt\}$. Define two events:

$$E_1 = \text{at least 1 head} = \{hh, ht, th\}$$

and

$$E_2 = \text{2 heads} = \{hh\}.$$

Because there are four equally likely outcomes, $P(E_1) = 3/4$. Also, $P(E_1 \cap E_2) = 1/4$. We want the probability that both were heads, given that at least one was a head: that is, we want to find $P(E_2 \mid E_1)$. Because of the condition that at least one coin was a head, the reduced sample space is

$$\{hh, ht, th\}.$$

Since only one outcome in this reduced sample space is 2 heads,

4 In Example 3, find the probability that exactly one coin showed a head, given that at least one was a head.

Answer:
2/3

$$P(E_2 \mid E_1) = \frac{1}{3}.$$

Alternatively, use the definition given above.

$$P(E_2 \mid E_1) = \frac{P(E_2 \cap E_1)}{P(E_1)} = \frac{1/4}{3/4} = \frac{1}{3} \quad \blacksquare \quad \boxed{4}$$

PRODUCT RULE If $P(E) \neq 0$ and $P(F) \neq 0$, then the definition of conditional probability shows that

$$P(E \mid F) = \frac{P(E \cap F)}{P(F)} \quad \text{and} \quad P(F \mid E) = \frac{P(F \cap E)}{P(E)}.$$

Using the fact that $P(E \cap F) = P(F \cap E)$, and solving each of these equations for $P(E \cap F)$, we obtain the following rule.

PRODUCT RULE OF PROBABILITY

If E and F are events, then $P(E \cap F)$ may be found by either of these formulas.

$$\boldsymbol{P(E \cap F) = P(F) \cdot P(E \mid F)} \quad \text{or} \quad \boldsymbol{P(E \cap F) = P(E) \cdot P(F \mid E).}$$

The **product rule** gives a method for finding the probability that events E and F both occur, as illustrated by the next few examples.

EXAMPLE 4 In a class with 2/5 women and 3/5 men, 25% of the women are business majors. Find the probability that a student chosen at random from the class is a female business major.

Let B and W represent the events "business major" and "women," respectively. We want to find $P(B \cap W)$. By the product rule,

$$P(B \cap W) = P(W) \cdot P(B \mid W).$$

From the given information, $P(W) = 2/5 = .4$ and the probability that a woman is a business major is $P(B \mid W) = .25$. Then

$$P(B \cap W) = .4(.25) = .10. \quad ■ \quad \boxed{5}$$

5 In a litter of puppies, 3 were female and 4 were male. Half the males were black. Find the probability that a puppy chosen at random from the litter would be a black male.

Answer:
2/7

In Section 9.1 we used a tree diagram to find the number of subsets of a given set. By including the probabilities for each branch of a tree diagram, we convert it to a **probability tree.** The next examples show how conditional probability is used with probability trees.

EXAMPLE 5 A company needs to hire a new director of advertising. It has decided to try to hire either person A or person B, who are assistant advertising directors for its major competitor. To decide between A and B, the company does research on the campaigns managed by A or B (none are managed by both), and finds that A is in charge of twice as many advertising campaigns as B. Also, A's campaigns have satisfactory results three out of four times, while B's campaigns have satisfactory results only two out of five times. Suppose one of the competitor's advertising campaigns (managed by A or B) is selected randomly.

We can represent this situation schematically as follows. Let A denote the event "Person A does the job" and B the event "Person B does the job." Let S be the event "satisfactory results" and U the event "unsatisfactory results." Then the given information can be summarized in the probability tree in Figure 9.26 on the next page. Since A does twice as many jobs as B, $P(A) = 2/3$ and $P(B) = 1/3$, as noted on the first-stage branches of the tree. When A does a job, the probability of satisfactory results is 3/4 and of unsatisfactory results 1/4, as noted on the second-stage branches. Similarly, the probabilities when B does the job are noted on the remaining second-stage branches. The composite branches labeled 1–4 represent the four mutually exclusive possibilities for the running and outcome of the campaign.

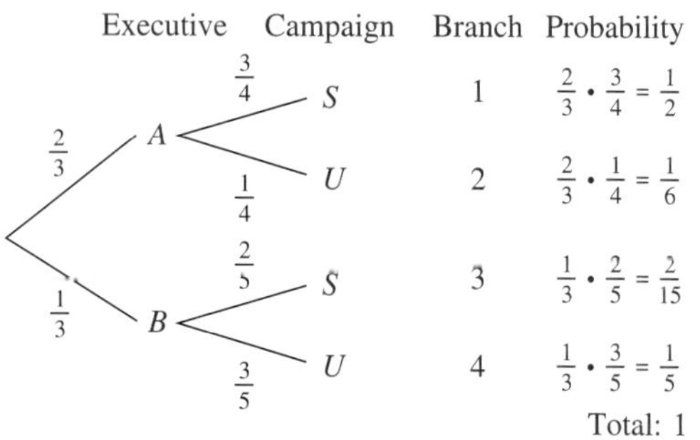

FIGURE 9.26

(a) Find the probability that A is in charge of a campaign that produces satisfactory results.

We are asked to find $P(A \cap S)$. We know that when A does the job, the probability of success is 3/4, that is, $P(S \mid A) = 3/4$. Hence, by the product rule,

$$P(A \cap S) = P(A) \cdot P(S \mid A) = \frac{2}{3} \cdot \frac{3}{4} = \frac{1}{2}.$$

The event $A \cap S$ is represented by branch 1 of the tree, and as we have just seen, its probability is the product of the probabilities that make up that branch.

(b) Find the probability that B runs a campaign that produces satisfactory results.

We must find $P(B \cap S)$. The event is represented by branch 3 of the tree and, as before, its probability is the product of the probabilities of the pieces of that branch:

$$P(B \cap S) = P(B) \cdot P(S \mid B) = \frac{1}{3} \cdot \frac{2}{5} = \frac{2}{15}.$$

(c) What is the probability that the campaign is satisfactory?

The event S is the union of the mutually exclusive events $A \cap S$ and $B \cap S$, which are represented by branches 1 and 3 of the tree diagram. By the union rule,

$$P(S) = P(A \cap S) + P(B \cap S) = \frac{1}{2} + \frac{2}{15} = \frac{19}{30}.$$

Thus, the probability of an event that appears on several branches is the sum of the probabilities of each of these branches.

(d) What is the probability that the campaign is unsatisfactory?

$P(U)$ can be read from branches 2 and 4 of the tree.

$$P(U) = \frac{1}{6} + \frac{1}{5} = \frac{11}{30}$$

Alternatively, because U is the complement of S,

$$P(U) = 1 - P(S) = 1 - \frac{19}{30} = \frac{11}{30}.$$

(e) Find the probability that either A runs the campaign or the results are satisfactory (or possibly both).

Event A combines branches 1 and 2, while event S combines branches 1 and 3, so use branches 1, 2, and 3.

$$P(A \cup S) = \frac{1}{2} + \frac{1}{6} + \frac{2}{15} = \frac{4}{5} \quad \blacksquare \quad \boxed{6}$$

$\boxed{6}$ Find each of the following probabilities for Example 5.

(a) $P(U \mid A)$

(b) $P(U \mid B)$

Answers:

(a) 1/4

(b) 3/5

EXAMPLE 6 From a box containing 1 red, 3 white, and 2 green marbles, two marbles are drawn one at a time without replacing the first before the second is drawn. Find the probability that one white and one green marble are drawn.

A probability tree showing the various possible outcomes is given in Figure 9.27. In this diagram, W represents the event "drawing a white marble" and G represents "drawing a green marble." On the first draw, $P(W \text{ on the 1st}) = 3/6 = 1/2$ because three of the six marbles in the box are white. On the second draw, $P(G \text{ on the 2nd} \mid W \text{ on the 1st}) = 2/5$. One white marble has been removed, leaving 5, of which 2 are green.

We want to find the probability of drawing exactly one white marble and exactly one green marble. Two events satisfy this condition: drawing a white marble first and then a green one (branch 2 of the tree), or drawing a green marble first and then a white one (branch 4). For branch 2,

$$P(W \text{ on 1st}) \cdot P(G \text{ on 2nd} \mid W \text{ on 1st}) = \frac{1}{2} \cdot \frac{2}{5} = \frac{1}{5}. \quad \boxed{7}$$

$\boxed{7}$ Find the probability of drawing a green marble and then a white marble.

Answer:

1/5

For branch 4, where the green marble is drawn first,

$$P(G \text{ first}) \cdot P(W \text{ second} \mid G \text{ first}) = \frac{1}{3} \cdot \frac{3}{5} = \frac{1}{5}.$$

Since these two events are mutually exclusive, the final probability is the sum of the two probabilities.

$$P(\text{one } W, \text{one } G) = P(W \text{ on 1st}) \cdot P(G \text{ on 2nd} \mid W \text{ on 1st}) + P(G \text{ on 1st}) \cdot P(W \text{ on 2nd} \mid G \text{ on 1st}) = \frac{2}{5} \quad \blacksquare \quad \boxed{8}$$

$\boxed{8}$ In Example 6, find the probability of drawing 1 white and 1 red marble.

Answer:

1/5

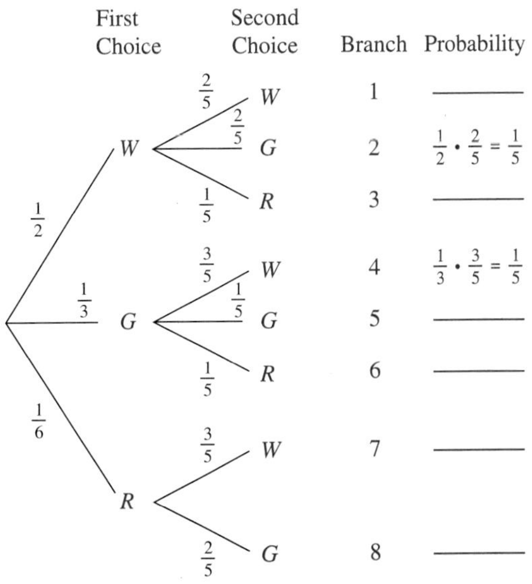

FIGURE 9.27

The product rule is often used when dealing with *stochastic processes,* which are mathematical models that evolve over time in a probabilistic manner. For example, drawing different colored marbles from a box (without replacing them) is such a process, in which the probabilities change with each successive draw. (Particular stochastic processes are studied further in Section 10.4.)

EXAMPLE 7 Two cards are drawn without replacement from an ordinary deck (52 cards). Find the probability that the first card is a heart and the second card is red.

Start with the probability tree of Figure 9.28. (You may wish to refer to the deck of cards shown in Figure 9.18.) On the first draw, since there are 13 hearts in the 52 cards, the probability of drawing a heart first is 13/52 = 1/4. On the second draw, since a (red) heart has been drawn already, there are 25 red cards in the remaining 51 cards. Thus the probability of drawing a red card on the second draw, given that the first is a heart, is 25/51. By the product rule of probability,

$$
\begin{aligned}
&P(\text{heart on 1st and red on 2nd}) \\
&\quad = P(\text{heart on 1st}) \cdot P(\text{red on 2nd} \mid \text{heart on 1st}) \\
&\quad = \frac{1}{4} \cdot \frac{25}{51} = \frac{25}{204} \approx .1225. \quad \blacksquare \quad \boxed{9}
\end{aligned}
$$

9 Find the probability of drawing a heart on the first draw and a black card on the second, if two cards are drawn without replacement.

Answer:
13/102 or .1275

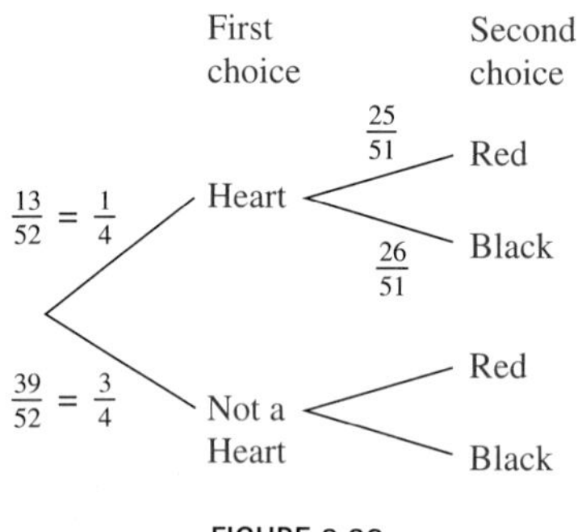

FIGURE 9.28

EXAMPLE 8 Three cards are drawn, without replacement, from an ordinary deck. Find the probability that exactly 2 of the cards are red.

Here we need a probability tree with three stages, as shown in Figure 9.29. The three branches indicated with arrows produce exactly 2 red cards from the draws. Multiply the probabilities along each of these branches and then add.

$$
\begin{aligned}
P(\text{exactly 2 red cards}) &= \frac{26}{52} \cdot \frac{25}{51} \cdot \frac{26}{50} + \frac{26}{52} \cdot \frac{26}{51} \cdot \frac{25}{50} + \frac{26}{52} \cdot \frac{26}{51} \cdot \frac{25}{50} \\
&= \frac{50{,}700}{132{,}600} = \frac{13}{34} \approx .382 \quad \blacksquare \quad \boxed{10}
\end{aligned}
$$

10 Use the tree in Example 8 to find the probability that exactly one of the cards is red.

Answer:
13/34 ≈ .382

INDEPENDENT EVENTS Suppose a fair coin is tossed and shows heads. The probability of heads on the next toss is still 1/2; the fact that heads was the result on a given toss has no effect on the outcome of the next toss. Coin tosses are **independent events,** since the outcome of one toss does not help decide the outcome of the next toss. Rolls of a fair die are independent events; the fact that a 2 came up on one

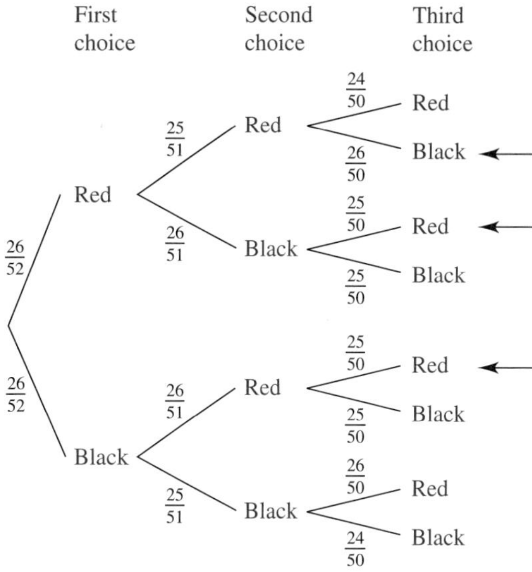

FIGURE 9.29

roll does not increase our knowledge of the outcome of the next roll. On the other hand, the events "today is cloudy" and "today is rainy" are **dependent events;** if it is cloudy, then there is an increased chance of rain. Similarly, in the example at the beginning of this section, the events A (broker picked a stock that went up) and B (broker used research) are dependent events, because information about the use of research affects the probability of picking a stock that goes up. That is, $P(A \mid B)$ is different from $P(A)$.

If events E and F are independent, then the knowledge that E has occurred gives no additional (probability) information about the occurrence or nonoccurrence of event F. That is, $P(F)$ is exactly the same as $P(F \mid E)$, or

$$P(F \mid E) = P(F).$$

In fact, this is the formal definition of independent events.

> E and F are **independent events** if
>
> $$\mathbf{P(F \mid E) = P(F)} \quad \text{or} \quad \mathbf{P(E \mid F) = P(E).}$$

When E and F are independent events, then $P(F \mid E) = P(F)$ and the product rule becomes

$$P(E \cap F) = P(E) \cdot P(F \mid E) = P(E) \cdot P(F).$$

Conversely, if this equation holds, then it follows that $P(F) = P(F \mid E)$. Consequently, we have this useful fact.

> PRODUCT RULE FOR INDEPENDENT EVENTS
>
> E and F are independent events if and only if
>
> $$\mathbf{P(E \cap F) = P(E) \cdot P(F).}$$

EXAMPLE 9 A calculator requires a key-stroke assembly and a logic circuit. Assume that 99% of the key-stroke assemblies are satisfactory and 97% of the logic circuits are satisfactory. Find the probability that a finished calculator will be satisfactory.

If the failure of a key-stroke assembly and the failure of a logic circuit are independent events, then

$$P(\text{satisfactory calculator})$$
$$= P(\text{satisfactory key-stroke assembly}) \cdot P(\text{satisfactory logic circuit})$$
$$= (.99)(.97) \approx .96.$$ ■ 11

11 Find the probability of getting 4 successive heads on 4 tosses of a fair coin.

Answer:
1/16

CAUTION It is common for students to confuse the ideas of *mutually exclusive* events and *independent* events. Events E and F are mutually exclusive if $E \cap F = \emptyset$. For example, if a family has exactly one child, the only possible outcomes are $B = \{\text{boy}\}$ and $G = \{\text{girl}\}$. These two events are mutually exclusive. However, the events are *not* independent, since $P(G \mid B) = 0$ (if a family with only one child has a boy, the probability it has a girl is then 0). Since $P(G \mid B) \neq P(G)$, the events are not independent. Of all the families with exactly *two* children, the events $G_1 = \{\text{first child is a girl}\}$ and $G_2 = \{\text{second child is a girl}\}$ are independent, because $P(G_2 \mid G_1)$ equals $P(G_2)$. However, G_1 and G_2 are not mutually exclusive, since $G_1 \cap G_2 = \{\text{both children are girls}\} \neq \emptyset$. ◆

To show that two events E and F are independent, we can show that $P(F \mid E) = P(F)$ or that $P(E \mid F) = P(E)$ or that $P(E \cap F) = P(E) \cdot P(F)$. Another way is to observe that knowledge of one outcome does not influence the probability of the other outcome, as we did for coin tosses.

EXAMPLE 10 On a typical January day in Manhattan the probability of snow is .10, the probability of a traffic jam is .80, and the probability of snow or a traffic jam (or both) is .82. Are the event "it snows" and the event "a traffic jam occurs" independent?

Let S represent the event "it snows" and T represent the event "a traffic jam occurs." We must determine whether

$$P(T \mid S) = P(T) \quad \text{or} \quad P(S \mid T) = P(S).$$

We know $P(S) = .10$, $P(T) = .8$, and $P(S \cup T) = .82$. We can use the union rule (or a Venn diagram) to find $P(S \cap T) = .08$, $P(T \mid S) = .8$, and $P(S \mid T) = .1$. Since

$$P(T \mid S) = P(T) = .8 \quad \text{and} \quad P(S \mid T) = P(S) = .1,$$

the events "it snows" and "a traffic jam occurs" are independent. ■ 12

12 In the U.S. population, the probability of being Hispanic is .11, the probability of living in California is .12, and the probability of being a Hispanic living in California is .04. Are the events being Hispanic and living in California independent?

Answer:
No

Although we showed $P(T \mid S) = P(T)$ and $P(S \mid T) = P(S)$ in Example 10, only one of these results is needed to establish independence.

It is important not to confuse $P(A \mid B)$ with $P(B \mid A)$. For example, in a criminal trial, a prosecutor may point out to the jury that the probability of the defendant's DNA profile matching that of a sample taken at the scene of the crime, given that the defendant is innocent, is very small. What the jury must decide, however, is the probability that the defendant is innocent, given that the defendant's DNA profile matches the sample. Confusing the two is an error sometimes called "the prosecutor's fallacy," and the 1990 conviction of a rape suspect in England was overturned by a panel of judges, who ordered a retrial, because the fallacy made the original trial unfair.*

In the next section, we will see how to compute $P(A \mid B)$ when we know $P(B \mid A)$.

*"Who's the DNA fingerprinting pointing at?", David Pringle, *New Scientist*, Jan. 29, 1994, pp. 51–52.

9.5 EXERCISES

If a single fair die is rolled, find the probability of rolling the following. (See Examples 1–3.)

1. 3, given that the number rolled was odd

2. 5, given that the number rolled was even

3. An odd number, given that the number rolled was 3

If two fair dice are rolled (recall the 36-outcome sample space), find the probability of rolling the following.

4. A sum of 8, given the sum was greater than 7

5. A sum of 6, given the roll was a "double" (two identical numbers)

6. A double, given that the sum was 9

If two cards are drawn without replacement from an ordinary deck (see Example 7), find the following probabilities.

7. The second is a heart, given that the first is a heart.

8. The second is black, given that the first is a spade.

9. The second is a face card, given that the first is a jack.

10. The second is an ace, given that the first is not an ace.

11. A jack and a 10 are drawn.

12. An ace and a 4 are drawn.

13. Two black cards are drawn.

14. Two hearts are drawn.

15. In your own words, explain how to find the conditional probability $P(E \mid F)$.

16. Your friend asks you to explain how the product rule for independent events differs from the product rule for dependent events. How would you respond?

17. Another friend asks you to explain how to tell whether two events are dependent or independent. How would you reply? (Use your own words.)

18. A student reasons that the probability in Example 3 of both coins being heads is just the probability that the other coin is a head, that is, 1/2. Explain why this reasoning is wrong.

Use a probability tree or Venn diagram in Exercises 19–30. (See Examples 2 and 5–8.)

Social Science *Marriages between cousins are very common in some countries, where about 50% of marriages are consanguineous (between first cousins or people even more closely related). A recent study in Pakistan has shown that 16% of children from unrelated marriages died by age 10, while 21% of children from consanguineous marriages died by age 10. Find the following probabilities.*

19. a child survives

20. a child from a consanguineous marriage survives

Management *Among users of automated teller machines (ATMs), 92% use ATMs to withdraw cash, and 32% use them to check their account balance.* Suppose that 96% use ATMs to either withdraw cash or check their account balance (or both). Find the probability that*

21. An ATM user withdraws funds if that person uses the ATM to check an account balance.

22. An ATM user checks an account balance given that the ATM is used to withdraw funds.

Natural Science *The following table based on data from the World Health Organization, gives the number of people (in thousands) infected with the AIDS virus by geographical location and method of transmission.†*

	United States	*Rest of World*	*Totals*
Homosexual transmission	1410	1090	2,500
Heterosexual transmission	90	7410	7,500
Totals	1500	8500	10,000

23. **(a)** Find the probability that a resident of the United States with AIDS received it via homosexual transmission.

(b) Find the probability that a person with AIDS who is not a resident of the United States received it via homosexual transmission.

**Chicago Tribune*, Sec. 4, p. 1, Dec. 18, 1995.

†Jane M. Watson, "Conditional Probability: Its Place in the Mathematics Curriculum," *The Mathematics Teacher*, Jan. 1995, Vol. 88, No. 1, pp. 12–17.

24. (a) Find the probability a person with AIDS is a resident of the United States.
(b) Find the probability a person who received AIDS via homosexual transmission is a resident of the United States.
(c) Are the events that a person with AIDS is a United States resident and that the person received AIDS via homosexual transmission independent? Explain your answer.

Social Science *A survey has shown that 52% of the women in a certain community work outside the home. Of these women, 64% are married, while 86% of the women who do not work outside the home are married. Find the probability that a woman in that community is*

25. married;

26. a single woman working outside the home.

Social Science *A study showed that, in 1991, 31.6% of men and 35.0% of women were obese.* Given that 48.7% of Americans are men and 51.3% are women, find the probability that a randomly selected adult fits the following description.*

27. An obese man

28. Obese

Management *A shop that produces custom kitchen cabinets has two employees, Sitlington and Capek. 95% of Capek's work is satisfactory and 10% of Sitlington's work is unsatisfactory. 60% of the shop's cabinets are made by Capek (the rest by Sitlington). Find the following probabilities.*

29. An unsatisfactory cabinet was made by Capek.

30. A finished cabinet is unsatisfactory.

Management *The table below shows employment figures for managerial/professional occupations in 1991 for U.S. civilians with four or more years of college.†*

	White	*Black*	*Totals*
Women	6,813	617	7,430
Men	9,453	435	9,888
Totals	16,266	1052	17,318

Letting A represent white, B represent black, C represent women, and D represent men, express each of the following probabilities in words and find its value. (See Example 1.)

31. $P(A \mid D)$

32. $P(C \mid A)$

33. $P(B \mid C)$

34. $P(D \cap A)$

**The New York Times,* July 17, 1994, p. 18.

†U.S. Bureau of the Census, Statistical Abstract of the United States: 1992 (112th edition), Washington, D.C., 1992.

Natural Science *The following table shows frequencies for red-green color blindness, where M represents male and C represents color-blind.*

	M	*M′*	*Totals*
C	.042	.007	.049
C′	.485	.466	.951
Totals	.527	.473	1.000

Use this table to find the following probabilities.

35. $P(M)$

36. $P(C)$

37. $P(M \cap C)$

38. $P(M \cup C)$

39. $P(M \mid C)$

40. $P(M' \mid C)$

41. Are the events C and M described above dependent? (Recall that two events E and F are dependent if $P(E \mid F) \neq P(E)$. See Example 10.)

42. Natural Science A scientist wishes to determine if there is any dependence between color blindness (C) and deafness (D). Given the probabilities listed in the table below, what should his findings be? (See Example 10.)

	D	*D′*	*Totals*
C	.0004	.0796	.0800
C′	.0046	.9154	.9200
Totals	.0050	.9950	1.0000

Social Science *The Motor Vehicle Department has found that the probability of a person passing the test for a driver's license on the first try is .75. The probability that an individual who fails on the first test will pass on the second try is .80, and the probability that an individual who fails the first and second tests will pass the third time is .70. Find the probability that an individual*

43. fails both the first and second tests;

44. will fail three times in a row;

45. will require at least two tries to pass the test.

Natural Science *Four different medications, C, D, E, and F, may be used to control high blood pressure. A physician usually prescribes C first because it is least likely to cause side effects. If blood pressure remains high, the patient is switched to D. If this fails to work, the patient is switched to E, and if necessary to F. The probability that C will work is .7. If C fails, the probability that D will work is .8. If D fails, the probability that E will work is .62. If E fails, the probability that F will work is .45. Find the probability that*

46. A patient's blood pressure will not be reduced by any of the medications.

47. A patient will have to take at least two medications and will have his or her blood pressure reduced.

48. If medications C and D fail, what is the probability that a patient's blood pressure will be reduced by medication E or F?

Management *The number of vehicles (in thousands) on the road from the major worldwide producers in selected years is shown in the following table.*

	U.S.	*Europe*	*Japan*	*Canada*
1975	4495	6,737	3,471	712
1980	6008	11,584	8,282	1031
1985	9322	12,767	9,817	1546
1990	9291	17,683	12,812	1801

Find the following probabilities for a vehicle selected at random.

49. It was made in the U.S.

50. It was made in 1990.

51. It was made in Japan in 1985.

52. It was made in 1980, given that it was made in Europe.

The probability that the first record by a singing group will be a hit is .32. If their first record is a hit, so are all their subsequent records. If their first record is not a hit, the probability of their second record and all subsequent ones being hits is .16. If the first two records are not hits, the probability that the third is a hit is .08. The probability of a hit continues to decrease by half with each successive nonhit record. Find the probability that

53. the group will have at least one hit in their first four records.

54. the group will have exactly one hit in their first three records.

55. the group will have a hit in their first six records if the first three are not hits.

Work the following problems on independent events. (See Examples 9 and 10.)

56. Management Corporations such as banks, where a computer is essential to day-to-day operations, often have a second, backup computer in case of failure by the main computer. Suppose that there is a .003 chance that the main computer will fail in a given time period and a .005 chance that the backup computer will fail while the main computer is being repaired. Assume these failures represent independent events, and find the fraction of the time that the corporation can assume it will have computer service. How realistic is our assumption of independence?

57. Management According to a booklet put out by Eastwest Airlines, 98% of all scheduled Eastwest flights actually take place. (The other flights are canceled due to weather, equipment problems, and so on.) Assume that the event that a given flight takes place is independent of the event that another flight takes place.

(a) Elisabeta Guervara plans to visit her company's branch offices; her journey requires 3 separate flights on Eastwest Airlines. What is the probability that all of these flights will take place?

(b) Based on the reasons we gave for a flight to be canceled, how realistic is the assumption of independence that we made?

58. Social Science In one area, 4% of the population drives luxury cars. However, 17% of the CPAs drive luxury cars. Are the events "person drives a luxury car" and "person is a CPA" independent?

59. Social Science The probability that a key component of a space rocket will fail is .03.

(a) How many such components must be used as backups to ensure that the probability of at least one of the components' working is .999999?

(b) Is it reasonable to assume independence here?

60. Natural Science A medical experiment showed that the probability that a new medicine is effective is .75, the probability that a patient will have a certain side effect is .4, and the probability that both events occur is .3. Decide whether these events are dependent or independent.

61. Social Science A teacher has found that the probability that a student studies for a test is .6, the probability that a student gets a good grade on a test is .7, and the probability that both occur is .52. Are these events independent?

9.6 BAYES' FORMULA

Suppose the probability that a person gets lung cancer, given that the person smokes a pack or more of cigarettes daily, is known. For a research project, it might be necessary to know the probability that a person smokes a pack or more of cigarettes daily, given that the person has lung cancer. More generally, if $P(E \mid F)$ is known for two events E and F, can $P(F \mid E)$ be found? The answer is yes, we can find $P(F \mid E)$ using the formula to be developed in this section. To develop this formula, we can use a probability tree to find $P(F \mid E)$. Since $P(E \mid F)$ is known, the first outcome is either F or F'. Then for each of these outcomes, either E or E' occurs, as shown in Figure 9.30.

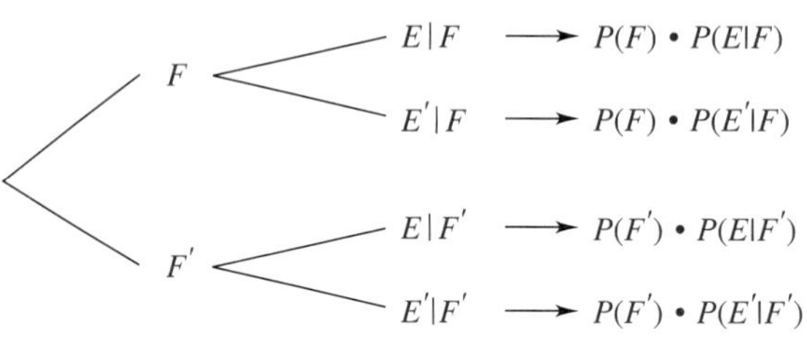

FIGURE 9.30

The four cases have the probabilities shown on the right. Notice that $P(E)$ is the sum of the first and third cases. By the definition of conditional probability and the product rule

$$P(F \mid E) = \frac{P(F \cap E)}{P(E)} = \frac{P(F) \cdot P(E \mid F)}{P(F) \cdot P(E \mid F) + P(F') \cdot P(E \mid F')}.$$

We have proved a special case of Bayes' formula, which is generalized later in this section.

[1] Use the special case of Bayes' formula to find $P(F \mid E)$ if $P(F) = .2$, $P(E \mid F) = .1$, and $P(E \mid F') = .3$. (*Hint:* $P(F') = 1 - P(F)$.)

Answer:
$1/13 \approx .077$

BAYES' FORMULA (SPECIAL CASE)

$$\mathbf{P(F \mid E) = \frac{P(F) \cdot P(E \mid F)}{P(F) \cdot P(E \mid F) + P(F') \cdot P(E \mid F')}}. \quad \boxed{1}$$

EXAMPLE 1 For a fixed length of time, the probability of worker error on a certain production line is .1, the probability that an accident will occur when there is a worker error is .3, and the probability that an accident will occur when there is no worker error is .2. Find the probability of a worker error if there is an accident.

Let E represent the event of an accident, and let F represent the event of worker error. From the information above,

$$P(F) = .1, \quad P(E \mid F) = .3, \quad \text{and} \quad P(E \mid F') = .2.$$

These probabilities are shown on the probability tree in Figure 9.31.

			Branch	Probability
$P(F) = .1$ → F	$P(E \mid F) = .3$	E	1	$P(F) \cdot P(E \mid F)$
	$P(E' \mid F) = .7$	E'	2	$P(F) \cdot P(E' \mid F)$
$P(F') = .9$ → F'	$P(E \mid F') = .2$	E	3	$P(F') \cdot P(E \mid F')$
	$P(E' \mid F') = .8$	E'	4	$P(F') \cdot P(E' \mid F')$

FIGURE 9.31

Find $P(F \mid E)$ using the tree or Bayes' formula.

$$P(F \mid E) = \frac{P(F) \cdot P(E \mid F)}{P(F) \cdot P(E \mid F) + P(F') \cdot P(E \mid F')}$$

$$= \frac{(.1)(.3)}{(.1)(.3) + (.9)(.2)} \approx .143 \quad \blacksquare \quad \boxed{2}$$

$\boxed{2}$ In Example 1, find $P(F' \mid E)$.

Answer:
$6/7 \approx .857$

Bayes' formula can be generalized to more than two possibilities with the probability tree of Figure 9.32. This diagram shows the paths that can produce an event E. We assume that events $F_1, F_2, \ldots, F_n$ are pairwise mutually exclusive events (that is, events which, taken two at a time, are disjoint), whose union is the sample space, and E is an event that has occurred. See Figure 9.33.

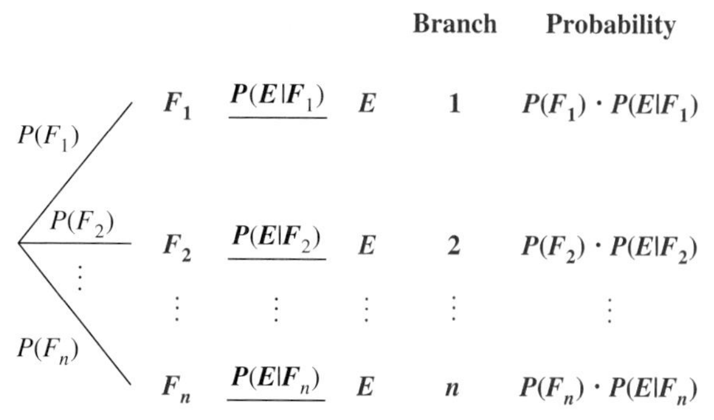

				Branch	Probability
$P(F_1)$	F_1	$P(E \mid F_1)$	E	1	$P(F_1) \cdot P(E \mid F_1)$
$P(F_2)$	F_2	$P(E \mid F_2)$	E	2	$P(F_2) \cdot P(E \mid F_2)$
$\vdots$	$\vdots$	$\vdots$	$\vdots$	$\vdots$	$\vdots$
$P(F_n)$	F_n	$P(E \mid F_n)$	E	n	$P(F_n) \cdot P(E \mid F_n)$

FIGURE 9.32

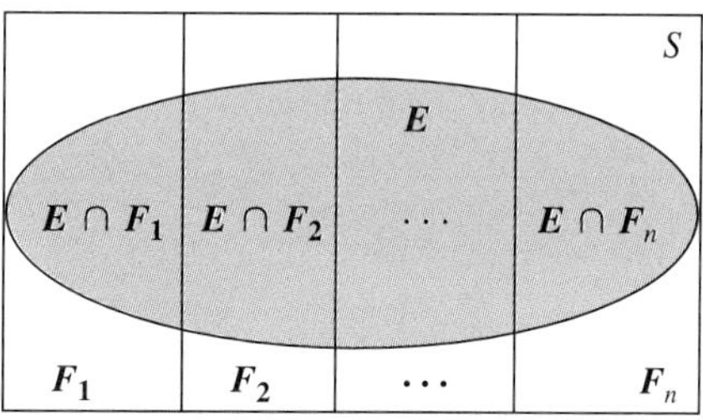

FIGURE 9.33

The probability $P(F_i \mid E)$, where $1 \le i \le n$, can be found by dividing the probability for the branch containing $P(E \mid F_i)$ by the sum of the probabilities of all the branches producing event E.

BAYES' FORMULA

$$P(F_i \mid E) = \frac{P(F_i) \cdot P(E \mid F_i)}{P(F_1) \cdot P(E \mid F_1) + \cdots + P(F_n) \cdot P(E \mid F_n)}.$$

This result is known as **Bayes' formula,** after the Reverend Thomas Bayes (1702–61), whose paper on probability was published about two hundred years ago.

The statement of Bayes' formula can be daunting. Actually, it is easier to remember the formula by thinking of the probability tree that produced it. Go through the following steps.

USING BAYES' FORMULA

Step 1 Start a probability tree with branches representing events F_1, $F_2, \ldots, F_n$. Label each branch with its corresponding probability.

Step 2 From the end of each of these branches, draw a branch for event E. Label this branch with the probability of getting to it, or $P(E \mid F_i)$.

Step 3 There are now n different paths that result in event E. Next to each path, put its probability—the product of the probabilities that the first branch occurs, $P(F_i)$, and that the second branch occurs, $P(E \mid F_i)$: that is, $P(F_i) \cdot P(E \mid F_i)$.

Step 4 $P(F_i \mid E)$ is found by dividing the probability of the branch for F_i by the sum of the probabilities of all the branches producing event E.

EXAMPLE 2 Based on past experience, a company knows that an experienced machine operator (one or more years of experience) will produce a defective item 1% of the time. Operators with some experience (up to one year) have a 2.5% defect rate, while new operators have a 6% defect rate. At any one time, the company has 60% experienced employees, 30% with some experience, and 10% new employees. Find the probability that a particular defective item was produced by a new operator.

Let E represent the event "item is defective," with F_1 representing "item was made by an experienced operator," F_2 "item was made by an operator with some experience," and F_3 "item was made by a new operator." Then

$$\begin{aligned} P(F_1) &= .60 \qquad & P(E \mid F_1) &= .01 \\ P(F_2) &= .30 \qquad & P(E \mid F_2) &= .025 \\ P(F_3) &= .10 \qquad & P(E \mid F_3) &= .06. \end{aligned}$$

We need to find $P(F_3 \mid E)$, the probability that an item was produced by a new operator, given that it is defective. First, draw a probability tree using the given information, as in Figure 9.34 on the next page. The steps leading to event E are shown.

Find $P(F_3 \mid E)$ using the bottom branch of the tree in Figure 9.34: divide the probability for this branch by the sum of the probabilities of all the branches leading to E.

$$P(F_3 \mid E) = \frac{.10(.06)}{.60(.01) + .30(.025) + .10(.06)} = \frac{.006}{.0195} \approx .3077 \quad \blacksquare \quad \boxed{3}$$

After working Problem 3 at the side, check that $P(F_1 \mid E) + P(F_2 \mid E) + P(F_3 \mid E) = 1$. (That is, the defective item was made by *someone.*)

$\boxed{3}$ In Example 2, find

(a) $P(F_1 \mid E)$;

(b) $P(F_2 \mid E)$.

Answers:

(a) $4/13 \approx .3077$

(b) $5/13 \approx .3846$

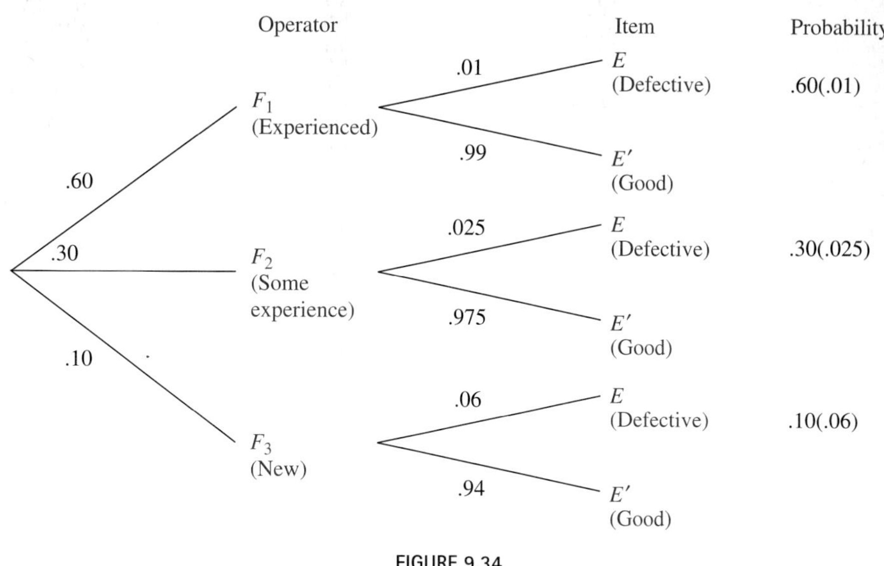

FIGURE 9.34

EXAMPLE 3 A manufacturer buys items from six different suppliers. The fraction of the total number of items obtained from each supplier, along with the probability that an item purchased from that supplier is defective, is shown in the following table.

Supplier	*Fraction of Total Supplied*	*Probability of Defective*
1	.05	.04
2	.12	.02
3	.16	.07
4	.23	.01
5	.35	.03
6	.09	.05

Find the probability that a defective item came from supplier 5.

Let F_1 be the event that an item came from supplier 1, with F_2, F_3, F_4, F_5, and F_6 defined in a similar manner. Let E be the event that an item is defective. We want to find $P(F_5 \mid E)$. Use the probabilities in the table above to prepare a probability tree. By Bayes' formula,

$$P(F_5 \mid E)$$

$$= \frac{(.35)(.03)}{(.05)(.04) + (.12)(.02) + (.16)(.07) + (.23)(.01) + (.35)(.03) + (.09)(.05)}$$

$$= \frac{.0105}{.0329} \approx .319.$$

There is about a 32% chance that a defective item came from supplier 5. ■ 4

4 In Example 3, find the probability that the defective item came from

(a) supplier 3;

(b) supplier 6.

Answers:

(a) .340

(b) .137

9.6 EXERCISES

For two events, M and N, $P(M) = .4$, $P(N \mid M) = .3$, and $P(N \mid M') = .4$. Find each of the following. (See Example 1.)

1. $P(M \mid N)$
2. $P(M' \mid N)$

For mutually exclusive events R_1, R_2, R_3, $P(R_1) = .05$, $P(R_2) = .6$, and $P(R_3) = .35$. In addition, $P(Q \mid R_1) = .40$, $P(Q \mid R_2) = .30$, and $P(Q \mid R_3) = .60$. Find each of the following. (See Examples 2 and 3.)

3. $P(R_1 \mid Q)$
4. $P(R_2 \mid Q)$
5. $P(R_3 \mid Q)$
6. $P(R_1' \mid Q)$

Suppose three jars have the following contents: 2 black balls and 1 white ball in the first; 1 black ball and 2 white balls in the second; 1 black ball and 1 white ball in the third. If the probability of selecting one of the three jars is 1/2, 1/3, and 1/6, respectively, find the probability that if a white ball is drawn, it came from the

7. second jar;
8. third jar.

Social Science *In 1990, 1% of the United States population was Native American. The probability that a Native American lives in the West or South is .76. The probability is .56 that a person who is not Native American lives in the West or South. Find the following probabilities.*

9. A person living in the West or South is Native American.
10. A person who does not live in the West or South is not Native American.

Social Science *A federal study showed that in 1990, 49% of all those involved in a fatal car crash wore seat belts. Of those in a fatal crash who wore seat belts, 44% were injured and 27% were killed. For those not wearing seat belts, the comparable figures were 41% and 50%, respectively.**

11. Find the probability that a randomly selected person who was killed in a car crash was wearing a seat belt.
12. Find the probability that a randomly selected person who was unharmed in a fatal crash was not wearing a seat belt.

Management *The probability that a customer of a local department store will be a "slow pay" is .02. The probability that a "slow pay" will make a large down payment when buying a refrigerator is .14. The probability that a person who is not a "slow pay" will make a large down payment when buying a refrigerator is .50. Suppose a customer makes a large down payment on a refrigerator. Find the probability that the customer is*

13. a "slow pay";
14. not a "slow pay."

*National Highway Traffic Safety Administration, Office of Driver and Pedestrian Research: "Occupant Protection Trends in 19 Cities" (November 1989) and "Use of Automatic Safety Belt Systems in 19 Cities" (February 1991).

Management *Companies A, B, and C produce 15%, 40%, and 45%, respectively, of the major appliances sold in a certain area. In that area, 1% of the Company A appliances, $1\frac{1}{2}$% of the Company B appliances, and 2% of the Company C appliances need service within the first year. Suppose an appliance that needs service within the first year is chosen at random; find the probability that it was manufactured by Company*

15. A;
16. B.

Management *On a given weekend in the fall, a tire company can buy television advertising time for a college football game, a baseball game, or a professional football game. If the company sponsors the college game, there is a 70% chance of a high rating, a 50% chance if they sponsor a baseball game, and a 60% chance if they sponsor a professional football game. The probability of the company sponsoring these various games is .5, .2, and .3, respectively. Suppose the company does get a high rating; find the probability that it sponsored*

17. a college game;
18. a professional football game.

19. **Social Science** A 1995 survey showed that of Baby Boomers (Americans born between 1946 and 1960), 78% own a home and 56% have a family income of more than $40,000.* The probability that a Baby Boomer's family own their own home if their income is over $40,000 is .51, while the probability that they own their home if the family income is less than or equal to $40,000 is .27. Find the probability that a Baby Boomer has family income over $40,000, if it is known that the family owns its home.
20. **Social Science** During the murder trial of O.J. Simpson, Alan Dershowitz, an advisor to the defense team, stated on television that only about .1% of men who batter their wives actually murder them. Statistician I. J. Good observed that even if, given that a husband is a batterer, the probability he is guilty of murdering his wife is .001, what we really want to know is the probability that the husband is guilty, given that the wife was murdered.† Good estimates the probability of a battered wife being murdered, given that her husband is not guilty, as .001. The probability that she is murdered if her husband is guilty is 1, of course. Using these numbers and Dershowitz' .001 probability of the husband being guilty, find the probability that the husband is guilty, given that the wife was murdered.
21. **Management** A manufacturing firm finds that 70% of its new hires turn out to be good workers and 30% poor

**The New York Times*, Sec. 3, p. 1, Dec. 31, 1995.

†I. J. Good, "When Batterer Turns Murderer," *Nature*, Vol. 375, No. 15, June 15, 1995, p. 541.

workers. All current workers are given a reasoning test. Of the good workers, 80% pass it; 40% of the poor workers pass it. Assume that these figures will hold true in the future. If the company makes the test part of its hiring procedure and only hires people who meet the previous requirements and pass the test, what percent of the new hires will turn out to be good workers?

22. **Management** A bank finds that the relationship between mortgage defaults and the size of the down payment is given by this table.

Down Payment (%)	*5%*	*10%*	*20%*	*25%*
Number of mortgages with this down payment	1260	700	560	280
Probability of default	.05	.03	.02	.01

If a default occurs, what is the probability that it is on a mortgage with a 5% down payment? (See Examples 2 and 3.)

23. **Management** The following information pertains to three shipping terminals operated by Krag Corp.:*

Terminal	*Percentage of Cargo Handled*	*Percentage of Error*
Land	50	2
Air	40	4
Sea	10	14

Krag's internal auditor randomly selects one set of shipping documents, ascertaining that the set selected contains an error. Which of the following gives the probability that the error occurred in the Land Terminal?

(a) .02 **(b)** .10 **(c)** .25 **(d)** .50

Natural Science *In a test for toxemia, a disease that affects pregnant women, the woman lies on her left side and then rolls over on her back. The test is considered positive if there is a 20 mm rise in her blood pressure within one minute. The results have produced the following probabilities, where T represents having toxemia at some time during the pregnancy, and N represents a negative test.*

$$P(T' \mid N) = .90 \quad \text{and} \quad P(T \mid N') = .75$$

Assume that $P(N') = .11$, *and find each of the following.*

24. $P(N \mid T)$

25. $P(N' \mid T)$

26. **Natural Science** The probability that a person with certain symptoms has hepatitis is .8. The blood test used to confirm this diagnosis gives positive results for 90% of those who have the disease and 5% of those without the disease. What is the probability that an individual with the symptoms who reacts positively to the test has hepatitis?

27. **Natural Science** Suppose the probability that an individual has AIDS is .01, the probability of a person testing positive if he or she has AIDS is .95, and the probability of a person testing positive if he or she does not have AIDS is .05.
    (a) Find the probability that a person who tests positive has AIDS.
    (b) It has been argued that everyone should be tested for AIDS. Based on the results of part (a), how useful would the results of such testing be?

Social Science *The following table gives the proportions of adult men and women in the U.S. population, and the proportions of adult men and women who have never married, in 1987.**

	MEN	
Age	*Proportion of Men*	*Proportion Never Married*
18–24	.151	.875
25–29	.126	.433
30–34	.126	.250
35–39	.110	.140
40 or over	.487	.054
	WOMEN	
Age	*Proportion of Women*	*Proportion Never Married*
18–24	.142	.752
25–29	.117	.295
30–34	.116	.161
35–39	.103	.090
40 or over	.522	.033

28. Find the probability that a randomly selected man who has never married is between 30 and 34 years old (inclusive).

29. Find the probability that a randomly selected woman who has been married is between 18 and 24 (inclusive).

*Uniform CPA Examination, November 1989.

*From *The Sacramento Bee*, September 10, 1987.

30. Find the probability that a randomly selected woman who has never been married is between 35 and 39 (inclusive).

31. **Natural Science** A recent study by the Harvard School of Public Health reported that 86% of male students who live in a fraternity house are binge drinkers. The figure for fraternity members who are not residents of a fraternity house is 71%, while the figure for men who do not belong to a fraternity is 45%.* Suppose that 10% of U.S. students live in a fraternity house, 15% belong to a fraternity, but do not live in a fraternity house, and 75% do not belong to a fraternity.
(a) What is the probability that a randomly selected male student is a binge drinker?
(b) If a randomly selected male student is a binge drinker, what is the probability that he lives in a fraternity house?

*New York Times, December 6, 1995, p. B16.

CHAPTER 9 SUMMARY

Key Terms and Symbols

$\{\ \}$ set braces
$\in$ is an element of
$\notin$ is not an element of
$\emptyset$ empty set
$\subseteq$ is a subset of
$\not\subseteq$ is not a subset of
A' complement of set A
$\cap$ set intersection
$\cup$ set union

9.1 set
element (member) of a set
empty set
equal sets
set-builder notation
universal set
subset
tree diagram
Venn diagram
complement
intersection
disjoint sets
union

9.2 Union Rule for Counting

9.3 $P(E)$ probability of event E
experiment
trial
outcome
fair coin
sample space
event
simple event
certain event
impossible event
basic probability principle
probability of an event

9.4 mutually exclusive events
Union Rule for Probability
Complement Rule
odds in favor

9.5 $P(F \mid E)$ probability of F, given that E has occurred
conditional probability
Product Rule of Probability
probability tree
independent events
dependent events
Product Rule for Independent Events

9.6 Bayes' formula

Key Concepts

Sets

Set A is a **subset** of set B if every element of A is also an element of B.

A set of n elements has 2^n subsets.

Let A and B be any sets with universal set U.
The **complement** of A is $A' = \{x \mid x \notin A \text{ and } x \in U\}$.
The **intersection** of A and B is $A \cap B = \{x \mid x \in A \text{ and } x \in B\}$.
The **union** of A and B is $A \cup B = \{x \mid x \in A \text{ or } x \in B \text{ or both}\}$.

$n(A \cup B) = n(A) + n(B) - n(A \cap B)$

Probability

If $n(S) = n$ and $n(E) = m$, where S is the sample space, then $P(E) = \frac{m}{n}$.

The probability of any outcome is a number between 0 and 1, inclusive.

The sum of the probabilities of all possible distinct outcomes in a sample space is 1.

Let E and F be events from a sample space S.

$$P(E') = 1 - P(E) \text{ and } P(E) = 1 - P(E')$$

$$P(E \cup F) = P(E) + P(F) - P(E \cap F)$$

$$P(E \mid F) = \frac{P(E \cap F)}{P(F)}, \quad P(F) \neq 0$$

$$P(E \cap F) = P(F) \cdot P(E \mid F) \quad \text{or} \quad P(E \cap F) = P(E) \cdot P(F \mid E)$$

Odds: The odds in favor of event E are given by the ratio of $P(E)$ to $P(E')$.

Events E and F are **mutually exclusive** if $E \cap F = \emptyset$. In that case, $P(E \cup F) = P(E) + P(F)$.

Events E and F are **independent events** if $P(F \mid E) = P(F)$ or $P(E \mid F) = P(E)$. In that case, $P(E \cap F) = P(E) \cdot P(F)$.

Bayes' Formula: $P(F_i \mid E) = \dfrac{P(F_i) \cdot P(E \mid F_i)}{P(F_1) \cdot P(E \mid F_1) + \cdots + P(F_n) \cdot P(E \mid F_n)}$

Chapter 9 Review Exercises

Write true *or* false *for each of the following.*

1. $9 \in \{8, 4, -3, -9, 6\}$
2. $4 \in \{3, 9, 7\}$
3. $2 \notin \{0, 1, 2, 3, 4\}$
4. $0 \notin \{0, 1, 2, 3, 4\}$
5. $\{3, 4, 5\} \subseteq \{2, 3, 4, 5, 6\}$
6. $\{1, 2, 5, 8\} \subseteq \{1, 2, 5, 10, 11\}$
7. $\emptyset \subseteq \{1\}$
8. $0 \subseteq \emptyset$

List the elements in the following sets.

9. $\{x \mid x \text{ is a national holiday}\}$
10. $\{x \mid x \text{ is an integer}, -3 \leq x < 1\}$
11. {all counting numbers less than 5}
12. $\{x \mid x \text{ is a leap year between 1989 and 1999}\}$

Let $U = \{$Vitamins $A, B_1, B_2, B_3, B_6, B_{12}, C, D, E\}$, $M = \{A, C, D, E\}$, and $N = \{A, B_1, B_2, C, E\}$. Find the following.

13. M'
14. N'
15. $M \cap N$
16. $M \cup N$
17. $M \cup N'$
18. $M' \cap N$

Let $U = \{$all students in a class$\}$, $A = \{$all male students$\}$, $B = \{$all A students$\}$, $C = \{$all students with red hair$\}$, and $D = \{$all students younger than 21$\}$. Describe the following sets in words.

19. $A \cap C$

20. $B \cap D$

21. $A \cup D$

22. $A' \cap D$

23. $B' \cap C'$

Draw a Venn diagram and shade the given set.

24. $B \cup A'$

25. $A' \cap B$

26. $A' \cap (B' \cap C)$

27. $(A \cup B)' \cap C$

Social Science *A survey of a group of military personnel revealed the following information.*

20 officers
27 minorities
19 women
5 women officers
8 minority women
10 minority officers
3 women minority officers
6 Caucasian male enlisted personnel

28. How many were interviewed?

29. How many were enlisted minority women?

30. How many were male minority officers?

Write sample spaces for the following.

31. A die is rolled and the number of points showing is noted.

32. A card is drawn from a deck containing only 4 aces.

33. A color is selected from the set {red, blue, green}, and then a number is chosen from the set {10, 20, 30}.

A jar contains 5 discs labeled 2, 4, 6, 8, 10, and another jar contains 2 blue and 3 yellow balls. One disc is drawn and then a ball is drawn. Give the following.

34. The sample space

35. Event F, the ball is blue.

36. Event E, the disc shows a number greater than 5.

37. Are the outcomes in this sample space equally likely?

Management *A company sells typewriters and copiers. Let E be the event "a customer buys a typewriter," and let F be the event "a customer buys a copier." In Exercises 38 and 39, write each of the following using ∩, ∪, or ′, as necessary.*

38. A customer buys neither.

39. A customer buys at least one.

40. A student gives the answer to a probability problem as 6/5. Explain why this answer must be incorrect.

41. Describe what is meant by disjoint sets and give an example.

42. Describe what is meant by mutually exclusive events and give an example.

43. How are disjoint sets and mutually exclusive events related?

A single card is drawn from an ordinary deck. Find the probability of drawing each of the following.

44. A black king

45. A face card

46. A red card or a face card

47. A black card, given it is a 2

48. A jack, given it is a face card

49. A face card, given it is a jack

Find the odds in favor of drawing the following.

50. A spade

51. A red queen

52. A black face card or a 7

Management *A sample shipment of five electric motors is chosen at random. The probability of exactly 0, 1, 2, 3, 4, or 5 motors being defective is given in the following table.*

Number defective	0	1	2	3	4	5
Probability	.31	.25	.18	.12	.08	.06

Find the probability that

53. no more than 3 are defective.

54. at least 3 are defective.

Natural Science *The square shows the four possible (equally likely) combinations when both parents are carriers of the sickle cell anemia trait. Each carrier parent has normal cells (N) and trait cells (T).*

		2ND PARENT	
		N_2	T_2
1ST PARENT	N_1		N_1T_2
	T_1		

55. Complete the table.

56. If the disease occurs only when two trait cells combine, find the probability that a child born to these parents will have sickle cell anemia.

57. The child will carry the trait but not have the disease if a normal cell combines with a trait cell. Find this probability.

58. Find the probability that the child is neither a carrier nor has the disease.

Find the probabilities for the following sums when two fair dice are rolled.

59. 8

60. At least 10

61. No more than 5

62. Odd and greater than 8

63. 12, given the sum is greater than 10

64. 7, given that at least one die shows a 4

Suppose $P(E) = .51$, $P(F) = .37$, and $P(E \cap F) = .22$. Find each of the following probabilities.

65. $P(E \cup F)$

66. $P(E \cap F')$

67. $P(E' \cup F)$

68. $P(E' \cap F')$

69. For the events E and F, $P(E) = .2$, $P(E \mid F) = .3$, and $P(F \mid E') = .2$. Find each of the following.

(a) $P(E \mid F)$ **(b)** $P(E \mid F')$

70. Define independent events and give an example.

71. Are independent events always mutually exclusive? Are they ever mutually exclusive? Give examples.

Management *Of the appliance repair shops listed in the phone book, 80% are competent and 20% are not. A competent shop can repair an appliance correctly 95% of the time; an incompetent shop can repair an appliance correctly 60% of the time. Suppose an appliance was repaired correctly. Find the probability that it was repaired by*

72. a competent shop;

73. an incompetent shop.

Suppose an appliance was repaired incorrectly. Find the probability that it was repaired by

74. a competent shop;

75. an incompetent shop.

76. Four red and one orange slips of paper are placed in a box. Two red and three orange slips are placed in a second box. A box is chosen at random, and a slip of paper is selected from it. The probability of choosing the first box is 3/8. If the selected slip of paper is orange, what is the probability that it came from the first box?

77. Find the probability that the slip of paper in Exercise 76 came from the second box, given that it is red.

78. **Management** A manufacturer buys items from four different suppliers. The fraction of the total number of items that is obtained from each supplier, along with the probability that an item purchased from that supplier is defective, is shown in the following table.

Supplier	*Fraction of Total Supplied*	*Probability of Defective*
1	.17	.04
2	.39	.02
3	.35	.07
4	.09	.03

(a) Find the probability that a defective item came from supplier 4.

(b) Find the probability that a defective item came from supplier 2.

79. **Management** The table below shows the results of a survey of buyers of a certain model of car.

Car Type	*Satisfied*	*Not Satisfied*	*Totals*
New	300	100	
Used	450		600
Totals		250	

(a) Complete the table.

(b) How many buyers were surveyed?

(c) How many bought a new car and were satisfied?

(d) How many were not satisfied?

(e) How many bought used cars?

(f) How many of those who were not satisfied had bought a used car?

(g) Rewrite the event stated in part (f) using the expression "given that."

(h) Find the probability of the outcome in parts (f) and (g).

(i) Find the probability that a used-car buyer is not satisfied.

(j) You should have different answers in parts (h) and (i). Explain why.

CASE 9

Medical Diagnosis

When a patient is examined, information, typically incomplete, is obtained about his or her state of health. Probability theory provides a mathematical model appropriate for this situation, as well as a procedure for quantitatively interpreting such partial information to arrive at a reasonable diagnosis.*

To do this, list the states of health that can be distinguished in such a way that the patient can be in one and only one state at the time of the examination. Each state of health H is associated with a number $P(H)$ between 0 and 1 such that the sum of all these numbers is 1. This number $P(H)$ represents the probability, before examination, that a patient is in the state of health H, and $P(H)$ may be chosen subjectively from medical experience, using any information available prior to the examination. The probability may be most conveniently established from clinical records; that is, a mean probability is established for patients in general, although the number would vary from patient to patient. Of course, the more information that is brought to bear in establishing $P(H)$, the better the diagnosis.

For example, limiting the discussion to the condition of a patient's heart, suppose there are exactly 3 states of health, with probabilities as follows.

	State of Health H	*P(H)*
H_1	patient has a normal heart	.8
H_2	patient has minor heart irregularities	.15
H_3	patient has a severe heart condition	.05

Having selected $P(H)$, the information from the examination is processed. First, the results of the examination must be classified. The examination itself consists of observing the state of a number of characteristics of the patient. Let us assume that the examination for a heart condition consists of a stethoscope examination and a cardiogram. The outcome of such an examination, C, might be one of the following:

C_1 = stethoscope shows normal heart and cardiogram shows normal heart;

C_2 = stethoscope shows normal heart and cardiogram shows minor irregularities;

and so on.

It remains to assess for each state of health H the conditional probability $P(C \mid H)$ of each examination outcome C using only the knowledge that a patient is in a given state of health. (This may be based on the medical knowledge and clinical experience of the doctor.) The conditional probabilities $P(C \mid H)$ will not vary from patient to patient, so that they may be built into a diagnostic system, although they should be reviewed periodically.

Suppose the result of the examination is C_1. Let us assume the following probabilities.

$$P(C_1 \mid H_1) = .9$$
$$P(C_1 \mid H_2) = .4$$
$$P(C_1 \mid H_3) = .1$$

Now, for a given patient, the appropriate probability associated with each state of health H, after examination, is $P(H \mid C)$ where C is the outcome of the examination. This can be calculated by using Bayes' formula. For example, to find $P(H_1 \mid C_1)$—that is, the probability that the patient has a normal heart given that the examination showed a normal stethoscope examination and a normal cardiogram—we use Bayes' formula as follows.

$$P(H_1 \mid C_1)$$
$$= \frac{P(C_1 \mid H_1)P(H_1)}{P(C_1 \mid H_1)P(H_1) + P(C_1 \mid H_2)P(H_2) + P(C_1 \mid H_3)P(H_3)}$$
$$= \frac{(.9)(.8)}{(.9)(.8) + (.4)(.15) + (.1)(.05)} \approx .92$$

Hence, the probability is about .92 that the patient has a normal heart on the basis of the examination results. This means that in 8 out of 100 patients, some abnormality will be present and not be detected by the stethoscope or the cardiogram.

EXERCISES

1. Find $P(H_2 \mid C_1)$.
2. Assuming the following probabilities, find $P(H_1 \mid C_2)$:
   $P(C_2 \mid H_1) = .2, \quad P(C_2 \mid H_2) = .8, \quad P(C_2 \mid H_3) = .3.$
3. Assuming the probabilities of Exercise 2, find $P(H_3 \mid C_2)$.

*From "Probabilistic Medical Diagnosis," Roger Wright, *Some Mathematical Models in Biology*, Robert M. Thrall, ed., (The University of Michigan, 1967), by permission of Robert M. Thrall.

CHAPTER 10 Further Topics in Probability

A survey by *Money* magazine found that supermarket scanners are overcharging customers at 30% of stores. If you shop at 3 supermarkets that use scanners, what is the probability that you will be overcharged? Techniques for finding this probability and solving other special kinds of probability problems are introduced in this chapter.

10.1 PERMUTATIONS AND COMBINATIONS

Up to this point we have simply listed the outcomes in a sample space S and an event E in order to find $P(E)$. However, when S has many outcomes, listing them becomes very tedious. In this section we discuss counting methods that do not require listing.

Let us begin with a simple example. If there are 3 roads from town A to town B and 2 roads from town B to town C, in how many ways can someone travel from A to C by way of B? For each of the 3 roads from A there are 2 different routes leading from B to C, making $3 \cdot 2 = 6$ different trips, as shown in Figure 10.1.

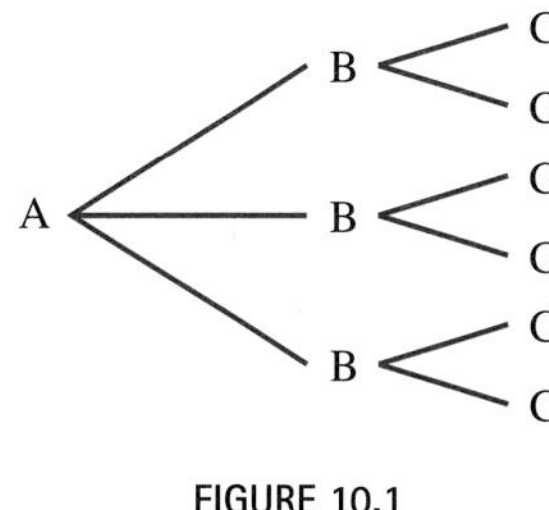

FIGURE 10.1

This example illustrates a general principle of counting called the *multiplication principle.*

MULTIPLICATION PRINCIPLE

Suppose n choices must be made, with

$$m_1 \text{ ways to make choice } 1,$$

and for each of these,

$$m_2 \text{ ways to make choice } 2,$$

and so on, with

$$m_n \text{ ways to make choice } n.$$

Then there are

$$m_1 \cdot m_2 \cdot \cdots \cdot m_n$$

different ways to make the entire sequence of choices.

EXAMPLE 1 A combination lock can be set to open to any 3-letter sequence. How many such sequences are possible?

Since there are 26 letters in the alphabet, there are 26 choices for each of the 3 letters, and, by the multiplication principle, $26 \cdot 26 \cdot 26 = 17{,}576$ different sequences. ■

EXAMPLE 2 Morse code uses a sequence of dots and dashes to represent letters and words. How many sequences are possible with at most 3 symbols?

"At most 3" means "1 or 2 or 3." Each symbol may be either a dot or a dash. Thus, the following number of sequences are possible in each case.

Number of Symbols	*Number of Sequences*
1	2
2	$2 \cdot 2 = 4$
3	$2 \cdot 2 \cdot 2 = 8$

Altogether, $2 + 4 + 8 = 14$ different sequences of at most 3 symbols are possible. Because there are 26 letters in the alphabet, some letters must be represented by 4 symbols in Morse code. ■

1 **(a)** In how many ways can 6 business tycoons line up their golf carts at the country club?

(b) How many ways can 4 pupils be seated in a row with 4 seats?

Answers:

(a) $6 \cdot 5 \cdot 4 \cdot 3 \cdot 2 \cdot 1 = 720$

(b) $4 \cdot 3 \cdot 2 \cdot 1 = 24$

EXAMPLE 3 A teacher has 5 different books to be arranged side by side. How many different arrangements are possible?

Five choices will be made, 1 for each space that will hold a book. Any of the 5 possible books could be chosen for the first space. There are 4 possible choices for the second space, since 1 book has already been placed in the first space, 3 possible choices for the third space, and so on. By the multiplication principle, the number of different possible arrangements (sequence of choices) is $5 \cdot 4 \cdot 3 \cdot 2 \cdot 1 = 120$. ■ 1

The use of the multiplication principle often leads to products such as $5 \cdot 4 \cdot 3 \cdot 2 \cdot 1$, the product of all the natural numbers from 5 down to 1. If n is a natural number, the symbol $n!$ (read "*n factorial*") denotes the product of all the natural numbers from n down to 1. If $n = 1$, this formula is understood to give $1! = 1$.

n-FACTORIAL

For any natural number n,

$$n! = n(n-1)(n-2) \cdot\cdot\cdot (3)(2)(1).$$

Also, $0!$ is defined to be the number 1.

2 Evaluate:

(a) $4!$

(b) $6!$

(c) $1!$

(d) $6!/4!$

Answers:

(a) 24

(b) 720

(c) 1

(d) 30

With this symbol, the product $5 \cdot 4 \cdot 3 \cdot 2 \cdot 1$ can be written as $5!$. Also, $3! = 3 \cdot 2 \cdot 1 = 6$. The definition of $n!$ could be used to show that $n! = n \cdot (n-1)!$ for all natural numbers $n \geq 2$. It is helpful if this result also holds for $n = 1$. This can only happen if $0!$ equals 1, as defined above. 2

Many scientific calculators and all graphing calculators can find the exact value of $n!$ for small values of n (typically, $n \leq 13$) and the approximate value of $n!$ for larger values of n (typically, $14 \leq n \leq 69$). Some graphing calculators can approximate $n!$ for much larger values of n.

TECHNOLOGY TIP The factorial key on a graphing calculator is usually located in the PROB submenu of the MATH menu. ✔

3 In how many ways can 3 of 7 items be arranged?

Answer:

$7 \cdot 6 \cdot 5 = 210$

EXAMPLE 4 Suppose the teacher in Example 3 wishes to place only 3 of the 5 books on his desk. How many arrangements of 3 books are possible?

The teacher again has 5 ways to fill the first space, 4 ways to fill the second space, and 3 ways to fill the third. Because he wants to use only 3 books, there are only 3 spaces to be filled giving $5 \cdot 4 \cdot 3 = 60$ arrangements. ■ 3

PERMUTATIONS The answer 60 in Example 4 is called the number of *permutations* of 5 things taken 3 at a time. A **permutation** of r elements (where $r \geq 1$) from a set of n elements is any arrangement, *without repetition,* of the r elements. The number of permutations of n things taken r at a time (with $r \leq n$) is written ${}_nP_r$.* Based on the work in Example 4,

$${}_5P_3 = 5 \cdot 4 \cdot 3 = 60.$$

Factorial notation can be used to express this product as follows.

$$5 \cdot 4 \cdot 3 = 5 \cdot 4 \cdot 3 \cdot \frac{2 \cdot 1}{2 \cdot 1} = \frac{5 \cdot 4 \cdot 3 \cdot 2 \cdot 1}{2 \cdot 1} = \frac{5!}{2!} = \frac{5!}{(5-3)!}$$

This example illustrates the general rule of permutations, which is stated below.

*Another notation that is sometimes used is $P(n, r)$.

> **PERMUTATIONS**
>
> If ${}_nP_r$ (where $r \le n$) is the number of permutations of n elements taken r at a time, then
>
> $$ {}_nP_r = \frac{n!}{(n-r)!}. $$

4 Find the number of permutations of

(a) 5 things taken 2 at a time;

(b) 9 things taken 3 at a time.

Find each of the following.

(c) ${}_3P_1$

(d) ${}_7P_3$

(e) ${}_{12}P_2$

Answers:

(a) 20

(b) 504

(c) 3

(d) 210

(e) 132

TECHNOLOGY TIP The permutation function on a graphing calculator is also in the PROB submenu of the MATH menu. As with $n!$, for large values of n and r, the calculator display for ${}_nP_r$ may be an approximation. ✔

To find ${}_nP_r$, we can use either the rule above or direct application of the multiplication principle, as the following example shows.

EXAMPLE 5 Early in 1996, eight candidates sought the Republican nomination for president. In how many ways could voters rank their first, second, and third choices?

This is the same as finding the number of permutations of 8 elements taken 3 at a time. Since there are 3 choices to be made, the multiplication principle gives ${}_8P_3 = 8 \cdot 7 \cdot 6 = 336$. Alternatively, by the formula for ${}_nP_r$,

$$ {}_8P_3 = \frac{8!}{(8-3)!} = \frac{8!}{5!} = \frac{8 \cdot 7 \cdot 6 \cdot 5 \cdot 4 \cdot 3 \cdot 2 \cdot 1}{5 \cdot 4 \cdot 3 \cdot 2 \cdot 1} = 8 \cdot 7 \cdot 6 = 336. \quad \blacksquare $$ 4

EXAMPLE 6 Find each of the following.

(a) The number of permutations of the letters A, B, and C

By the formula for ${}_nP_r$ with both n and r equal to 3,

$$ {}_3P_3 = \frac{3!}{(3-3)!} = \frac{3!}{0!} = \frac{3!}{1} = 3! = 6. $$

The 6 permutations (or arrangements) are

ABC, ACB, BAC, BCA, CAB, CBA.

5 Find the number of permutations of the letters C, O, D, and E

(a) using all the letters;

(b) using 2 of the 4 letters;

(c) using 3 of the 4 letters. (Can you find this without calculating?)

Answers:

(a) 24

(b) 12

(c) 24 (yes)

(b) The number of permutations possible using just 2 of the letters A, B, and C

Find ${}_3P_2$:

$$ {}_3P_2 = \frac{3!}{(3-2)!} = \frac{3!}{1!} = 3! = 6. $$

This result is exactly the same answer as in part (a). This is because, in the case of ${}_3P_3$, after the first 2 choices are made, the third is already determined, as shown in the table below.

First two letters	AB	AC	BA	BC	CA	CB
Third letter	C	B	C	A	B	A

$\blacksquare$ 5

EXAMPLE 7 A televised talk show will include 4 women and 3 men as panelists.

(a) In how many ways can the panelists be seated in a row of 7 chairs?
Find ${}_7P_7$, the total number of ways to seat 7 panelists in 7 chairs.

$${}_7P_7 = \frac{7!}{(7-7)!} = \frac{7!}{0!} = \frac{7!}{1} = 7 \cdot 6 \cdot 5 \cdot 4 \cdot 3 \cdot 2 \cdot 1 = 5040$$

There are 5040 ways to seat the 7 panelists.

(b) In how many ways can the panelists be seated if the men and women are to be alternated?

In order to alternate men and women, a woman must be seated in the first chair (since there are 4 women and only 3 men), any of the men next, and so on. Thus, there are 4 ways to fill the first seat, 3 ways to fill the second seat, 3 ways to fill the third seat (with any of the 3 remaining women), and so on. Use the multiplication principle. There are

$$4 \cdot 3 \cdot 3 \cdot 2 \cdot 2 \cdot 1 \cdot 1 = 144$$

ways to seat the panelists. ■ 6

6 A collection of 3 paintings by one artist and 2 by another is to be displayed. In how many ways can the paintings be shown

(a) in a row?

(b) if the works of the artists are to be alternated?

Answers:

(a) 120

(b) 12

COMBINATIONS In Example 4, we found that there are 60 ways that a teacher can arrange 3 of 5 different books on a desk. That is, there are 60 permutations of 5 things taken 3 at a time. Suppose now that the teacher does not wish to arrange the books on his desk, but rather wishes to choose, at random, any 3 of the 5 books to give to a book sale to raise money for his school. In how many ways can he do this?

At first glance, we might say 60 again, but this is incorrect. The number 60 counts all possible *arrangements* of 3 books chosen from 5. However, the following arrangements would all lead to the same set of 3 books being given to the book sale.

mystery-biography-textbook	biography-textbook-mystery
mystery-textbook-biography	textbook-biography-mystery
biography-mystery-textbook	textbook-mystery-biography

The list shows 6 different *arrangements* of 3 books, but only one subset of 3 books selected from the 5 books for the book sale. A subset of items selected *without regard to order* is called a **combination.** The number of combinations of 5 things taken 3 at a time is written $\binom{5}{3}$ or ${}_5C_3$. Since they are subsets, combinations are *not ordered.*

To evaluate $\binom{5}{3}$, start with the $5 \cdot 4 \cdot 3$ *permutations* of 5 things taken 3 at a time. Combinations are unordered, therefore, find the number of combinations by dividing the number of permutations by the number of ways each group of 3 can be ordered—that is, by 3!.

$$\binom{5}{3} = \frac{5 \cdot 4 \cdot 3}{3!} = \frac{5 \cdot 4 \cdot 3}{3 \cdot 2 \cdot 1} = 10$$

There are 10 ways that the teacher can choose 3 books at random for the book sale.

Generalizing this discussion gives the formula for the number of combinations of n elements taken r at a time, written $\binom{n}{r}$ or ${}_nC_r$.

7 Evaluate $\frac{{}_nP_r}{r!}$ for the following values.

(a) $n = 6, r = 2$

(b) $n = 8, r = 4$

(c) $n = 7, r = 0$

Answers:

(a) 15

(b) 70

(c) 1

$$\binom{n}{r} = {}_nC_r = \frac{{}_nP_r}{r!}$$
$$= \frac{n!}{(n-r)!} \cdot \frac{1}{r!} \qquad \text{Definition of } {}_nP_r$$
$$= \frac{n!}{(n-r)!r!}$$

This last form is the most useful for setting up the calculation. 7

COMBINATIONS

The number of combinations of n elements taken r at a time, where $r \leq n$, is

$$\binom{n}{r} = {}_nC_r = \frac{n!}{(n-r)!r!}.$$

TECHNOLOGY TIP The combination function on a graphing calculator is in the PROB submenu of the MATH menu. ✔

Replacing r by $n - r$ in the combinations formula gives

$$\binom{n}{n-r} = \frac{n!}{(n - [n-r])!\,(n-r)!}$$
$$= \frac{n!}{r!\,(n-r)!} = \frac{n!}{(n-r)!\,r!}.$$

8 Use $\frac{n!}{(n-r)!r!}$ to evaluate $\binom{n}{r}$.

(a) $\binom{6}{2}$

(b) $\binom{8}{4}$

(c) $\binom{7}{0}$

Compare your answers with the answers for Side Problem 7.

Answers:

(a) 15

(b) 70

(c) 1

Therefore,

$$\binom{n}{r} = \binom{n}{n-r}, \quad \text{or equivalently,} \quad {}_nC_r = {}_nC_{n-r}.$$

For example, by this result,

$$\binom{5}{3} = \binom{5}{2} \quad \text{and} \quad \binom{10}{4} = \binom{10}{6}.$$

EXAMPLE 8 How many committees of 3 people can be formed from a group of 8 people?

A committee is an unordered group, so find $\binom{8}{3}$. By the formula for combinations,

$$\binom{8}{3} = \frac{8!}{5!\,3!} = \frac{8 \cdot 7 \cdot 6 \cdot 5 \cdot 4 \cdot 3 \cdot 2 \cdot 1}{5 \cdot 4 \cdot 3 \cdot 2 \cdot 1 \cdot 3 \cdot 2 \cdot 1} = \frac{8 \cdot 7 \cdot 6}{3 \cdot 2 \cdot 1} = 56. \blacksquare$$ 8

EXAMPLE 9 Three managers are to be selected from a group of 30 to work on a special project.

(a) In how many different ways can the managers be selected?

Here we wish to know the number of 3-element combinations that can be formed from a set of 30 elements. (We want combinations and not permutations, since order within the group of 3 does not matter.)

$$\binom{30}{3} = 4060$$

There are 4060 ways to select the project group.

(b) In how many ways can the group of 3 be selected if a certain manager must work on the project?

Since 1 manager has already been selected for the project, the problem is reduced to selecting 2 more from the remaining 29 managers.

$$\binom{29}{2} = 406$$

In this case, the project group can be selected in 406 ways.

(c) In how many ways can a nonempty group of at most 3 managers be selected from these 30 managers?

The group is to be nonempty; therefore, "at most 3" means "1 or 2 or 3." Find the number of ways for each case.

Case	*Number of Ways*
1	$\binom{30}{1} = \frac{30!}{29!\,1!} = \frac{30 \cdot 29!}{29!\,(1)!} = 30$
2	$\binom{30}{2} = \frac{30!}{28!\,2!} = \frac{30 \cdot 29 \cdot 28!}{28! \cdot 2 \cdot 1} = 435$
3	$\binom{30}{3} = \frac{30!}{27!\,3!} = \frac{30 \cdot 29 \cdot 28 \cdot 27!}{27! \cdot 3 \cdot 2 \cdot 1} = 4060$

The total number of ways to select at most 3 managers will be the sum

$$30 + 435 + 4060 = 4525.$$ ■ 9

9 Five orchids from a collection of 20 are to be selected for a flower show.

(a) In how many ways can this be done?

(b) In how many different ways can the group of 5 be selected if 2 particular orchids must be included?

(c) In how many ways can at least 1 and at most 5 orchids be selected? (*Hint:* Use a calculator or refer to Table 1 in Appendix B.)

Answers:

(a) $\binom{20}{5} = 15{,}504$

(b) $\binom{18}{3} = 816$

(c) 21,699

The formulas for permutations and combinations given in this section will be very useful in solving probability problems in later sections. Any difficulty in using these formulas usually comes from being unable to differentiate between them. Both permutations and combinations give the number of ways to choose r objects from a set of n objects. The differences between permutations and combinations are outlined below.

PERMUTATIONS	COMBINATIONS
Different orderings or arrangements of the r objects are different permutations.	Each choice or subset of r objects gives 1 combination. Order within the r objects does not matter.
$_nP_r = \frac{n!}{(n-r)!}$	$\binom{n}{r} = {_nC_r} = \frac{n!}{(n-r)!\,r!}$
Clue words: Arrangement, Schedule, Order	Clue words: Group, Committee, Sample

In the next examples, concentrate on recognizing which of the formulas should be applied.

EXAMPLE 10 For each of the following problems, tell whether permutations or combinations should be used to solve the problem.

(a) How many 4-digit code numbers are possible if no digits are repeated?

Since changing the order of the 4 digits results in a different code, we use permutations.

(b) A sample of 3 light bulbs is randomly selected from a batch of 15 bulbs. How many different samples are possible?

The order in which the 3 light bulbs are selected is not important. The sample is unchanged if the bulbs are rearranged, so combinations should be used.

(c) In a basketball tournament with 8 teams, how many games must be played so that each team plays every other team exactly once?

Selection of 2 teams for a game is an *unordered* subset of 2 from the set of 8 teams. Use combinations again.

(d) In how many ways can 4 patients be assigned to 6 hospital rooms so that each patient has a private room?

The room assignments are an *ordered* selection of 4 rooms from the 6 rooms. Exchanging the rooms of any 2 patients within a selection of 4 rooms gives a different assignment, so permutations should be used. ■ 10

10 Solve the problems in Example 10.

Answers:

(a) 5040

(b) 455

(c) 28

(d) 360

EXAMPLE 11 A manager must select 4 employees for promotion. 12 employees are eligible.

(a) In how many ways can the 4 be chosen?

Because there is no reason to differentiate among the 4 who are selected, we use combinations.

$$\binom{12}{4} = \frac{12!}{4!\,8!} = 495$$

(b) In how many ways can 4 employees be chosen (from 12) to be placed in 4 different jobs?

In this case, once a group of 4 is selected, they can be assigned in many different ways (or arrangements) to the 4 jobs. Therefore, this problem requires permutations.

$${}_{12}P_4 = \frac{12!}{8!} = 11{,}880 \quad ■ \quad 11$$

11 A salesman has the names of 6 prospects.

(a) In how many ways can he arrange his schedule if he calls on all 6?

(b) In how many ways can he do it if he decides to call on only 4 of the 6?

Answers:

(a) 720

(b) 360

The following problems involve a standard deck of 52 playing cards, shown in Figure 9.18 on page 413.

EXAMPLE 12 In how many ways can a full house of aces and eights (3 aces and 2 eights) be dealt in 5-card poker?

The arrangement of the 3 aces or the 2 eights does not matter, so use combinations and the multiplication principle. There are $\binom{4}{3}$ ways to get 3 aces from the 4

12 In how many ways can 4 aces and any other card be dealt?

Answer:
48

aces in the deck, and $\binom{4}{2}$ ways to get 2 eights. By the multiplication principle, the number of ways to get 3 aces *and* 2 eights is

$$\binom{4}{3} \cdot \binom{4}{2} = 4 \cdot 6 = 24. \quad \blacksquare \quad \boxed{12}$$

EXAMPLE 13 Five cards are dealt from a standard 52-card deck.

(a) How many such hands have all face cards?

The face cards are the king, queen, and jack of each suit. There are 4 suits, so there are 12 face cards. The arrangement of the 5 cards is not important, so use combinations to get

$$\binom{12}{5} = \frac{12!}{5!\,7!} = 792.$$

(b) How many 5-card hands have all cards of the same suit?

The arrangement of the 5 cards is not important, so use combinations. The total number of ways that 5 cards of a particular suit of 13 cards can be dealt is $\binom{13}{5}$.

Since there are 4 different suits, by the multiplication principle, there are

13 In how many ways can 5 red cards be dealt?

Answer:
65,780

$$4 \cdot \binom{13}{5} = 4 \cdot 1287 = 5148$$

ways to deal 5 cards of the same suit. ■ 13

As Examples 12 and 13 show, often both combinations and the multiplication principle must be used in the same problem.

EXAMPLE 14 To illustrate the differences between permutations and combinations in another way, suppose 2 cans of soup are to be selected from 4 cans on a shelf: noodle (N), bean (B), mushroom (M), and tomato (T). As shown in Figure 10.2(a), there are 12 ways to select 2 cans from the 4 cans if the order matters (if noodle first and bean second is considered different from bean, then noodle, for example). On the other hand, if order is unimportant, then there are 6 ways to choose 2 cans of soup from the 4, as illustrated in Figure 10.2(b). ■

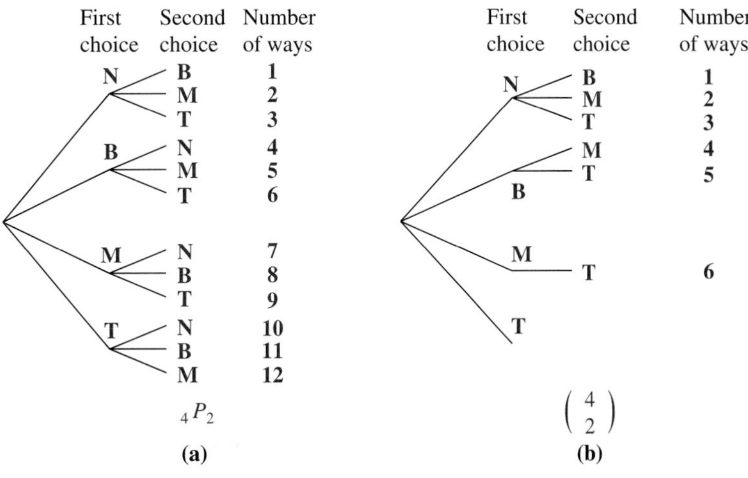

FIGURE 10.2

CAUTION It should be stressed that not all counting problems lend themselves to either permutations or combinations. Whenever a tree diagram or the multiplication principle can be used directly, as in the example at the beginning of this section, then use it. ◆

10.1 EXERCISES

Evaluate the following factorials, permutations, and combinations.

1. ${}_4P_2$
2. $3!$
3. $\binom{8}{3}$
4. $7!$
5. ${}_8P_1$
6. $\binom{8}{1}$
7. $4!$
8. ${}_4P_4$
9. ${}_{12}C_5$
10. $\binom{10}{8}$
11. ${}_{13}P_2$
12. ${}_{12}P_3$

Use a calculator to find values for Exercises 13–20.

13. ${}_{25}P_5$
14. ${}_{38}P_4$
15. ${}_{14}P_5$
16. ${}_{17}P_8$
17. $\binom{21}{10}$
18. $\binom{34}{25}$
19. ${}_{25}C_{16}$
20. $\binom{30}{15}$

Use the multiplication principle to solve the following problems. (See Examples 1–4.)

21. **Social Science** A social security number has 9 digits. How many social security numbers are there? The United States population in 1989 was about 248 million. Was it possible for every U.S. resident to have a unique social security number? (Assume no restrictions.)

22. **Social Science** The United States Postal Service uses 5-digit zip codes in most areas. How many zip codes are possible if there are no restrictions on the digits used? How many would be possible if the first number could not be 0?

23. **Social Science** The Postal Service is encouraging the use of 9-digit zip codes in some areas, adding 4 digits after the usual 5-digit code. How many such zip codes are possible with no restrictions?

24. **Management** How many different types of homes are available if a builder offers a choice of 5 basic plans, 3 roof styles, and 2 exterior finishes?

25. **Management** An auto manufacturer produces 7 models, each available in 6 different colors, with 4 different upholstery fabrics, and 5 interior colors. How many varieties of the auto are available?

26. **Management** How many different 4-letter radio station call letters can be made
    (a) if the first letter must be K or W and no letter may be repeated?
    (b) if repeats are allowed (but the first letter is K or W)?
    (c) How many of the 4-letter call letters (starting with K or W) with no repeats end in R?

27. **Social Science** For many years, the state of California used 3 letters followed by 3 digits on its automobile license plates.
    (a) How many different license plates are possible with this arrangement?
    (b) When the state ran out of new numbers, the order was reversed to 3 digits followed by 3 letters. How many new license plate numbers were then possible?
    (c) Several years ago, the numbers described in part (b) were also used up. The state then issued plates with 1 letter followed by 3 digits and then 3 letters. How many new license plate numbers will this provide?

Social Science *The United States is rapidly running out of telephone numbers. In large cities, telephone companies have introduced new area codes as numbers are used up.*

28. **(a)** Until recently, all area codes had a 0 or a 1 as the middle digit and the first digit could not be 0 or 1. How many area codes were possible with this arrangement? How many telephone numbers does the current 7-digit sequence permit per area code? (The 3-digit sequence that follows the area code cannot start with 0 or 1. Assume there are no other restrictions.)
    (b) The actual number of area codes under the previous system was 152. Explain the discrepancy between this number and your answer to part (a).

29. The shortage of area codes under the previous system was avoided by removing the restriction on the second digit. How many area codes are available under this new system?

30. A problem with the plan in Exercise 29 was that the second digit in the area code had been used to tell phone company equipment that a long-distance call was being made. To avoid changing all equipment, an alternative plan proposed a 4-digit area code and restricted the first and second digits as before. How many area codes would this plan have provided?

31. Still another alternative solution is to increase the local dialing sequence to 8 digits instead of 7. How many additional numbers would this plan create? (Assume the same restrictions.)

32. Define permutation in your own words.

Use permutations to solve each of the following problems. (See Examples 5–7.)

33. A baseball team has 20 players. How many 9-player batting orders are possible?

34. In a game of musical chairs, 12 children will sit in 11 chairs arranged in a row (one will be left out). In how many ways can the 11 children find seats?

35. Management From a carton of 12 cans of a soft drink, 2 are selected for 2 people. In how many ways can this be done?

36. Social Science In an election with 3 candidates for one office and 5 candidates for another office, how many different ballot orders may be used?

37. Management From a pool of 7 secretaries, 3 are selected to be assigned to 3 managers. In how many ways can they be selected?

38. A chapter of union Local 715 has 35 members. In how many different ways can the chapter select a president, a vice-president, a treasurer, and a secretary?

39. The television schedule for a certain evening shows 8 choices from 8 to 9 P.M., 5 choices from 9 to 10 P.M., and 6 choices from 10 to 11 P.M. In how many different ways could a person schedule that evening of television viewing from 8 to 11 P.M.? (Assume each program that is selected is watched for an entire hour.)

40. In a club with 15 members, how many ways can a slate of 3 officers consisting of president, vice-president, and secretary/treasurer be chosen?

Use combinations to solve each of the following problems. (See Examples 8–9 and 12–13.)

41. Management Five items are to be randomly selected from the first 50 items on an assembly line to determine the defect rate. How many different samples of 5 items can be chosen?

42. Social Science A group of 3 students is to be selected from a group of 12 students to take part in a class in cell biology.
(a) In how many ways can this be done?
(b) In how many ways can the group which will *not* take part be chosen?

43. Natural Science From a group of 16 smokers and 20 nonsmokers, a researcher wants to randomly select 8 smokers and 8 nonsmokers for a study. In how many ways can the study group be selected?

44. Five cards are drawn from an ordinary deck. In how many ways is it possible to draw
(a) all queens;
(b) all face cards (face cards are the Jack, Queen, and King);
(c) no face card;
(d) exactly 2 face cards;
(e) 1 heart, 2 diamonds, and 2 clubs.

Exercises 45–64 are mixed problems that may require permutations, combinations, or the multiplication principle. (See Examples 10, 11, and 14.)

45. Use a tree diagram to find the number of ways 2 letters can be chosen from the set {L, M, N} if order is important and
(a) if repetition is allowed;
(b) if no repeats are allowed.
(c) Find the number of combinations of 3 elements taken 2 at a time. Does this answer differ from parts (a) or (b)?

46. Repeat Exercise 45 using the set {L, M, N, P}.

47. Explain the difference between a permutation and a combination.

48. Padlocks with digit dials are often referred to as "combination locks." According to the mathematical definition of combination, is this an accurate description? Explain.

49. Social Science A legislative committee consists of 5 Democrats and 4 Republicans. A delegation of 3 is to be selected to visit a small Pacific Island republic.
(a) How many different delegations are possible?
(b) How many delegations would have all Democrats?
(c) How many delegations would have 2 Democrats and 1 Republican?
(d) How many delegations would include at least 1 Republican?

50. Natural Science In an experiment on plant hardiness, a researcher gathers 6 wheat plants, 3 barley plants, and 2 rye plants. She wishes to select 4 plants at random.
(a) In how many ways can this be done?
(b) In how many ways can this be done if 2 wheat plants must be included?

51. Baskin-Robbins advertises that it has 31 flavors of ice cream.
(a) How many different double-scoop cones can be made?
(b) How many different triple-scoop cones can be made?

52. A concert to raise money for an economics prize is to consist of 5 works: 2 overtures, 2 sonatas, and a piano concerto.
(a) In how many ways can the program be arranged?
(b) In how many ways can the program be arranged if an overture must come first?

53. A state lottery game requires that you pick 6 different numbers from 1 to 99. If you pick all 6 winning numbers, you win \$1 million.
(a) How many ways are there to choose 6 numbers if order is not important?
(b) How many ways are there to choose 6 numbers if order matters?

54. In Exercise 53, if you pick 5 of the 6 numbers correctly, you win $250,000. In how many ways can you pick exactly 5 of the 6 winning numbers without regard to order?

55. The game of Sets* consists of a special deck of cards. Each card has on it either one, two, or three shapes. The shapes on each card are all the same color, either green, purple, or red. The shapes on each card are the same style, either solid, shaded, or outline. There are three possible shapes: squiggle, diamond, and oval, and only one type of shape appears on a card. The deck consists of all possible combinations of shape, color, style, and number. How many cards are in a deck?

56. A bag contains 5 black, 1 red, and 3 yellow jelly beans; you take 3 at random. How many samples are possible in which the jelly beans are
(a) all black; **(b)** all red;
(c) all yellow; **(d)** 2 black, 1 red;
(e) 2 black, 1 yellow; **(f)** 2 yellow, 1 black;
(g) 2 red, 1 yellow.

57. In Example 6, there are six 3-letter permutations of the letters A, B, and C. How many 3-letter subsets (unordered groups of letters) are there?

58. In Example 6, how many unordered 2-letter subsets of the letters A, B, and C are there?

59. Natural Science Eleven drugs have been found to be effective in the treatment of a disease. It is believed that the sequence in which the drugs are administered is important in the effectiveness of the treatment. In how many orders can 5 of the 11 drugs be administered?

60. Natural Science A biologist is attempting to classify 52,000 species of insects by assigning 3 initials to each species. Is it possible to classify all the species in this way? If not, how many initials should be used?

61. One play in a state lottery consists of choosing 6 numbers from 1 to 44. If your 6 numbers are drawn (in any order), you win the jackpot.
(a) How many possible ways are there to draw the 6 numbers?
(b) If you get 2 plays for a dollar, how much would it cost to guarantee that 1 of your choices would be drawn?
(c) Assuming that you work alone and can fill out a betting ticket (for 2 plays) every second and the lotto drawing will take place 3 days from now, can you place enough bets to guarantee that 1 of your choices will be drawn?

62. Powerball is a lottery game played in 15 states across the United States. For $1 a ticket, a player selects five numbers from 1 to 45 and one Powerball number from 1 to 45. A match of all six numbers wins the jackpot. How many different selections are possible?

*Copyright © Marsha J. Falco.

63. In the game of Bingo, each card has five columns. Column 1 has spaces for 5 numbers, chosen from 1 to 15. Column 2 similarly has 5 numbers, chosen from 16 to 30. Column 3 has a free space in the middle, plus 4 numbers chosen from 31 to 45. The 5 numbers in columns 4 and 5 are chosen from 46 to 60 and from 61 to 75, respectively. The numbers in each card can be in any order. How many different Bingo cards are there?

64. A television commercial for Little Caesars pizza announced that with the purchase of two pizzas, one could receive free any combination of up to five toppings on each pizza. The commercial shows a young child waiting in line at Little Caesars who calculates that there are 1,048,576 possibilities for the toppings on the two pizzas.* Verify the child's calculation. Use the fact that Little Caesars has 11 toppings to choose from. Assume that the order of the two pizzas matters; that is, if the first pizza has combination 1 and the second pizza has combination 2, that is different from combination 2 on the first pizza and combination 1 on the second.

If the n objects in a permutations problem are not all distinguishable, that is, there are n_1 of type 1, n_2 of type 2, and so on for r different types, then the number of **distinguishable permutations** *is*

$$\frac{n!}{n_1!\, n_2! \ldots n_r!}.$$

Example *In how many ways can you arrange the letters in the word* Mississippi?

This word contains 1 m, 4 i's, 4 s's, and 2 p's. To use the formula, let $n = 11$, $n_1 = 1$, $n_2 = 4$, $n_3 = 4$, *and* $n_4 = 2$ *to get*

$$\frac{11!}{1!\,4!\,4!\,2!} = 34{,}650$$

arrangements. The letters in a word with 11 different letters can be arranged in $11! = 39{,}916{,}800$ *ways.*

65. Find the number of distinguishable permutations of the letters in each of the following words.
(a) initial **(b)** little **(c)** decreed

66. A printer has 5 A's, 4 B's, 2 C's, and 2 D's. How many different "words" are possible which use all these letters? (A "word" does not have to have any meaning here.)

67. Mike has 4 blue, 3 green, and 2 red books to arrange on a shelf. In how many distinguishable ways can this be done
(a) if they can be arranged in any order?
(b) if books of the same color are identical and must be grouped together?
(c) if books of the same color are identical but need not be grouped together?

*Joseph F. Heiser, "Pascal and Gauss meet Little Caesars," *The Mathematics Teacher*, Vol. 87, Sept. 1994, p. 389. In a letter to *The Mathematics Teacher*, Heiser argued that the two combinations should be counted as the same, so the child has actually overcounted. In that case there would be 524,800 possibilities.

68. A child has a set of different shaped plastic objects. There are 3 pyramids, 4 cubes, and 7 spheres. In how many ways can she arrange them in a row
(a) if they are all different colors?
(b) if the same shapes must be grouped?
(c) In how many distinguishable ways can they be arranged in a row if objects of the same shape are also the same color, but need not be grouped?

10.2 APPLICATIONS OF COUNTING

Many of the probability problems involving *dependent* events that were solved with probability trees in Chapter 9 can also be solved by using combinations. Combinations are especially helpful when the numbers involved would require a tree with a large number of branches.

The use of combinations to solve probability problems depends on the basic probability principle introduced in Section 9.3 and repeated here.

If event E is a subset of sample space S, then the probability that event E occurs, written $P(E)$, is

$$P(E) = \frac{n(E)}{n(S)}$$

It is also helpful to keep in mind that in probability statements

"and" corresponds to multiplication,

"or" corresponds to addition.

To compare the method of using combinations with the method of probability trees used in Section 9.5, the first example repeats Example 6 from that section.

EXAMPLE 1 From a box containing 3 white, 2 green, and 1 red marble, 2 marbles are drawn one at a time without replacement. Find the probability that 1 white and 1 green marble are drawn.

In Example 6 of Section 9.5, it was necessary to consider the order in which the marbles were drawn. With combinations, it is not necessary. Simply count the number of ways in which 1 white and 1 green marble can be drawn from the given selection. The white marble can be drawn from the 3 white marbles in $\binom{3}{1}$ ways, and the green marble can be drawn from the 2 green marbles in $\binom{2}{1}$ ways. By the multiplication principle, both results can occur in

$$\binom{3}{1} \cdot \binom{2}{1} \text{ ways,}$$

giving the numerator of the probability fraction, $P(E) = m/n$. For the denominator, 2 marbles are to be drawn from a total of 6 marbles. This can occur in $\binom{6}{2}$ ways. The required probability is

$$P(\mathbf{1}\text{ white and }\mathbf{1}\text{ green}) = \frac{\binom{3}{1}\binom{2}{1}}{\binom{6}{2}} = \frac{\frac{3!}{2!\,1!} \cdot \frac{2!}{1!\,1!}}{\frac{6!}{4!\,2!}} = \frac{6}{15} = \frac{2}{5}.$$

This agrees with the answer found earlier. ■

EXAMPLE 2 From a group of 22 nurses, 4 are to be selected to present a list of grievances to management.

(a) In how many ways can this be done?

Four nurses from a group of 22 can be selected in $\binom{22}{4}$ ways. (Use combinations, since the group of 4 is an unordered set.)

$$\binom{22}{4} = \frac{22!}{4!\,18!} = \frac{22(21)(20)(19)}{4(3)(2)(1)} = 7315$$

There are 7315 ways to choose 4 people from 22.

(b) One of the nurses is Michael Branson. Find the probability that Branson will be among the 4 selected.

The probability that Branson will be selected is given by m/n, where m is the number of ways the chosen group includes him, and n is the total number of ways the group of 4 can be chosen. If Branson must be one of the 4 selected, the problem reduces to finding the number of ways that the 3 additional nurses can be chosen. The 3 are chosen from 21 nurses; this can be done in

$$\binom{21}{3} = \frac{21!}{3!\,18!} = 1330$$

ways, so $m = 1330$. Since n is the number of ways 4 nurses can be selected from 22,

$$n = \binom{22}{4} = 7315.$$

The probability that Branson will be one of the 4 chosen is

$$P(\text{Branson is chosen}) = \frac{1330}{7315} \approx .182.$$

(c) Find the probability that Branson will not be selected.

The probability that he will not be chosen is $1 - .182 = .818$. ■ 1

1 A jar contains 1 white and 4 red jelly beans.

(a) What is the probability that out of 2 jelly beans selected at random from the jar, 1 will be white?

(b) What is the probability of choosing 3 red jelly beans?

Answers:

(a) 2/5

(b) 2/5

EXAMPLE 3 When shipping diesel engines abroad, it is common to pack 12 engines in 1 container which is then loaded on a railcar and sent to a port. Suppose that a company has received complaints from its customers that many of the engines arrive in nonworking condition. To help solve this problem, the company decides to make a spot check of containers after loading—the company will test 3 engines from a container at random; if any of the 3 is nonworking, the container will not be shipped until each engine in it is checked. Suppose a given container has 2 nonworking engines. Find the probability that the container will not be shipped.

The container will not be shipped if the sample of 3 engines contains 1 or 2 defective engines. Thus, letting $P(1\text{ defective})$ represent the probability of exactly 1 defective engine in the sample,

$$P(\text{not shipping}) = P(1\text{ defective}) + P(2\text{ defectives}).$$

There are $\binom{12}{3}$ ways to choose the 3 engines for testing:

$$\binom{12}{3} = \frac{12!}{3!\,9!} = \frac{12(11)(10)}{3(2)(1)} = 220.$$

There are $\binom{2}{1}$ ways of choosing 1 defective engine from the 2 in the container, and for each of these ways, there are $\binom{10}{2}$ ways of choosing 2 good engines from among the 10 in the container. By the multiplication principle, there are

2 Calculate $\binom{2}{1}\binom{10}{2}$.

Answer:
90

$$\binom{2}{1}\binom{10}{2}$$

ways of choosing a sample of 3 engines containing 1 defective. 2

Using the result from Problem 2 at the side,

$$P(1\text{ defective}) = \frac{90}{220}.$$

There are $\binom{2}{2}$ ways of choosing 2 defective engines from the 2 defective engines in the container, and $\binom{10}{1}$ ways of choosing 1 good engine from among the 10 good engines, giving

3 Calculate $\binom{2}{2}\binom{10}{1}$.

Answer:
10

$$\binom{2}{2}\binom{10}{1}$$

ways of choosing a sample of 3 engines containing 2 defectives. 3

Then, using the result from Problem 3 at the side,

$$P(2\text{ defectives}) = \frac{10}{220}$$

and

$$\begin{aligned} P(\text{not shipping}) &= P(1\text{ defective}) + P(2\text{ defectives}) \\ &= \frac{90}{220} + \frac{10}{220} = \frac{100}{220} = \frac{5}{11} \approx .455. \end{aligned}$$

The probability is $1 - .455 = .545$ that the container *will* be shipped, even though it has 2 defective engines. The management must decide if this probability is acceptable; if not, it may be necessary to test more than 3 engines from a container. ■

Instead of finding the sum $P(1\text{ defective}) + P(2\text{ defectives})$, the result in Example 3 could be found by calculating $1 - P(\text{no defectives})$.

$$\begin{aligned} P(\text{not shipping}) &= 1 - P(\text{no defectives in sample}) \\ &= 1 - \frac{\binom{2}{0}\binom{10}{3}}{\binom{12}{3}} = 1 - \frac{1(120)}{220} \\ &= 1 - \frac{120}{220} = \frac{100}{220} \approx .455 \end{aligned}$$ 4

4 In Example 3, if a sample of 2 engines is tested, what is the probability that the container will not be shipped?

Answer:
.318

EXAMPLE 4 In a common form of the card game *poker,* a hand of 5 cards is dealt to each player from a deck of 52 cards. There are a total of

$$\binom{52}{5} = \frac{52!}{5!47!} = 2{,}598{,}960$$

such hands possible. Find each of the following probabilities.

(a) A hand containing only hearts, called a *heart flush*

There are 13 hearts in a deck; there are

$$\binom{13}{5} = \frac{13!}{5!8!} = \frac{13(12)(11)(10)(9)}{5(4)(3)(2)(1)} = 1287$$

different hands containing only hearts. The probability of a heart flush is

$$P(\text{heart flush}) = \frac{1287}{2{,}598{,}960} = \frac{33}{66{,}640} \approx .000495.$$

(b) A flush of any suit (5 cards, all from 1 suit)

There are 4 suits to a deck, so

$$P(\text{flush}) = 4 \cdot P(\text{heart flush}) = 4(.000495) \approx .00198.$$

(c) A full house of aces and eights (3 aces and 2 eights)

There are $\binom{4}{3}$ ways to choose 3 aces from among the 4 in the deck, and $\binom{4}{2}$ ways to choose 2 eights.

$$P(3 \text{ aces, } 2 \text{ eights}) = \frac{\binom{4}{3} \cdot \binom{4}{2}}{2{,}598{,}960} = \frac{1}{108{,}290} \approx .00000923$$

(d) Any full house (3 cards of one value, 2 of another)

There are 13 values in a deck, so there are 13 choices for the first value mentioned, leaving 12 choices for the second value (order *is* important here, since a full house of aces and eights, for example, is not the same as a full house of eights and aces). Because, from part (c), the probability of any particular full house is .00000923,

$$P(\text{full house}) = 13 \cdot 12(.00000923) \approx .00144.$$ ■ 5

5 Find the probability of being dealt a poker hand (5 cards) with 4 kings.

Answer:
.00001847

EXAMPLE 5 A music teacher has 3 violin pupils, Fred, Carl, and Helen. For a recital, the teacher selects a first violinist and a second violinist. The third pupil will play with the others, but not solo. If the teacher selects randomly, what is the probability that Helen is first violinist, Carl is second violinist, and Fred does not solo?

Use *permutations* to find the number of arrangements in the sample space.

$${}_3P_3 = 3! = 6$$

The 6 arrangements are equally likely, since the teacher will select randomly. Thus, the required probability is 1/6. ■ 6

6 An office manager must select 4 employees, A, B, C, and D, to work on a project. Each employee will be responsible for a specific task and 1 will be the coordinator.

(a) If the manager assigns the tasks randomly, what is the probability that B is the coordinator?

(b) What is the probability of one specific assignment of tasks?

Answers:
(a) 1/4
(b) 1/24

EXAMPLE 6 Suppose a group of 5 people is in a room. Find the probability that at least 2 of the people have the same birthday.

"Same birthday" refers to the month and the day, not necessarily the same year. Also, ignore leap years, and assume that each day in the year is equally likely as a birthday. First find the probability that *no 2 people* among 5 people have the same birthday. There are 365 different birthdays possible for the first of the 5 people, 364 for the second (so that the people have different birthdays), 363 for the third, and so on. The number of ways the 5 people can have different birthdays is thus the number of permutations of 365 things (days) taken 5 at a time or

$$_{365}P_5 = 365 \cdot 364 \cdot 363 \cdot 362 \cdot 361.$$

The number of ways that the 5 people can have the same or different birthdays is

$$365 \cdot 365 \cdot 365 \cdot 365 \cdot 365 = (365)^5.$$

Finally, the *probability* that none of the 5 people have the same birthday is

$$\frac{_{365}P_5}{(365)^5} = \frac{365 \cdot 364 \cdot 363 \cdot 362 \cdot 361}{365 \cdot 365 \cdot 365 \cdot 365 \cdot 365} \approx .973.$$

The probability that at least 2 of the 5 people *do* have the same birthday is $1 - .973 = .027$. ■

7 Evaluate $1 - \frac{_{365}P_n}{(365)^n}$ for

(a) $n = 3$;

(b) $n = 6$.

Answers:

(a) .008

(b) .040

Example 6 can be extended for more than 5 people. In general, the probability that no 2 people among n people have the same birthday is

$$\frac{_{365}P_n}{(365)^n}.$$

The probability that at least 2 of the n people *do* have the same birthday is

$$1 - \frac{_{365}P_n}{(365)^n}.$$ 7

The following table shows this probability for various values of n.

Number of People, n	*Probability that 2 Have the Same Birthday*
5	.027
10	.117
15	.253
20	.411
22	.476
23	.507
25	.569
30	.706
35	.814
40	.891
50	.970
365	1

8 Set up (do not calculate) the probability that at least 2 of the 7 astronauts in the Mercury project have the same birthday.

Answer:

$1 - {_{365}P_7}/365^7$

The probability that 2 people among 23 have the same birthday is .507, a little more than half. Many people are surprised at this result—somehow it seems that a larger number of people should be required. 8

10.2 EXERCISES

Management *Refer to Example 3. The management feels that the probability of .545 that a container will be shipped even though it contains 2 defectives is too high. They decide to increase the sample size chosen. Find the probability that a container will be shipped even though it contains 2 defectives if the sample size is increased to*

1. 4. **2.** 5.

Management *A shipment of 9 computers contains 2 with defects. Find the probability that a sample of the following size, drawn from the 9, will not contain a defective. (See Example 3.)*

3. 1 **4.** 2 **5.** 3 **6.** 4

A grab-bag contains 10 \$1 prizes, 6 \$5 prizes, and 2 \$20 prizes. Three prizes are randomly drawn. Find the following probabilities. (See Examples 1 and 2.)

7. All \$1 prizes
8. All \$5 prizes
9. Exactly two \$20 prizes
10. One prize of each kind
11. At least one \$20 prize
12. No \$1 prize

Two cards are drawn at random from an ordinary deck of 52 cards. (See Example 4.)

13. How many 2-card hands are possible?

Find the probability that the two-card hand in Exercise 13 contains the following.

14. 2 queens
15. No aces
16. 2 face cards
17. Different suits
18. At least 1 black card
19. No more than 1 heart

20. Discuss the relative merits of using probability trees versus combinations to solve probability problems. When would each approach be most appropriate?

21. Several examples in this section used the rule $P(E') = 1 - P(E)$. Explain the advantage (especially in Example 6) of using this rule.

A bridge hand consists of 13 cards from a deck of 52. Set up the probabilities that a bridge hand includes each of the following.

22. 6 face cards

23. 2 aces and 3 kings

24. 7 cards of one suit and 6 of another

25. In Exercise 53 in the previous section, we found the number of ways to pick 6 different numbers from 1 to 99 in a state lottery.
(a) Assuming order is unimportant, what is the probability of picking all 6 numbers correctly to win the big prize?
(b) What is the probability, if order matters?

26. In Exercise 25, what is the probability of picking exactly 5 of the 6 numbers correctly?

27. In December 1993, Percy Ray Pridgen, a District of Columbia resident, and Charles Gill of Richmond, Virginia shared a \$90 million Powerball jackpot. The winning numbers were 1, 3, 13, 15, and 29. The Powerball number was 12. The answer to Exercise 62 in Section 10.1 gives the number of ways to win a Powerball jackpot as about 55 million. What is the probability of two individuals independently selecting the winning numbers?

28. Management A cellular phone manufacturer randomly selects 5 of every 50 phones from the assembly line and tests them. If at least 4 of the 5 pass inspection, the batch of 50 is considered acceptable. Find the probability that a batch is considered acceptable if it contains the following.
(a) 2 defective phones
(b) No defective phones
(c) 3 defective phones

29. Social Science Of the 16 members of President Clinton's first cabinet, 4 were women. Suppose the president randomly selected 4 advisors from the cabinet for a meeting. Find the probability that the group of 4 would be composed as follows.
(a) 2 women and 2 men
(b) All men
(c) At least 1 woman

30. Management A car dealer has 8 red, 11 gray, and 9 blue cars in stock. Ten cars are randomly chosen to be displayed in front of the dealership. Find the probability that
(a) 4 are red and the others are blue.
(b) 3 are red, 3 are blue, and 4 are gray.
(c) exactly 5 are gray and none are blue.
(d) all 10 are gray.

31. Social Science The teacher of a multicultural first-grade class on the first day of school found that in her class of 25 students, 10 spoke only English, 6 spoke only Spanish, 4 spoke only Russian, 3 spoke only Vietnamese, and 2 spoke only Hmong. The children were assigned randomly to groups of 5. Find the probability that a group included the following.
(a) 2 English-speaking and 3 Russian-speaking children
(b) All English-speaking children
(c) No English-speaking children
(d) At least two children who spoke Vietnamese or Hmong

For Exercises 32–34 refer to Example 6 in this section.

32. Set up the probability that at least 2 of the 41 men who have served as president of the United States have had the same birthday.*

33. Set up the probability that at least 2 of the 100 U.S. Senators have the same birthday.

*In fact, James Polk and Warren Harding were both born on November 2.

34. What is the probability that 2 of the 435 members of the House of Representatives have the same birthday?

35. An elevator has 4 passengers and stops at 7 floors. It is equally likely that a person will get off at any one of the 7 floors. Find the probability that no 2 passengers leave at the same floor.

36. Show that the probability that in a group of n people *exactly one pair* have the same birthday is

$$\binom{n}{2} \cdot \frac{{}_{365}P_{n-1}}{(365)^n}.$$

37. On National Public Radio, the "Weekend Edition" program on Sunday, September 7, 1991, posed the following probability problem: Given a certain number of balls, of which some are blue, pick 5 at random. The probability that all 5 are blue is 1/2. Determine the original number of balls and decide how many were blue.

38. The Big Eight Conference during the 1988 college football season ended the season in a "perfect progression," as shown in the table below.*

Won	*Lost*	*Team*
7	0	Nebraska (NU)
6	1	Oklahoma (OU)
5	2	Oklahoma State (OSU)
4	3	Colorado (CU)
3	4	Iowa State (ISU)
2	5	Missouri (MU)
1	6	Kansas (KU)
0	7	Kansas State (KSU)

Someone wondered what the probability of such an outcome might be.

(a) Assuming no ties and that each team had an equally likely probability of winning each game, find the probability of the perfect progression shown above.

(b) Find a general expression for the probability of a perfect progression in an n-team league with the same assumptions.

39. Use a computer or a graphing calculator and the Monte Carlo method with $n = 50$ to estimate the probabilities of the following hands at poker. (See the directions for Exercises 53–58 on page 426.) Assume aces are either high or low. Since each hand has 5 cards, you will need $50 \cdot 5 = 250$ random numbers to "look at" 50 hands. Compare these experimental results with the theoretical results.

(a) A pair of aces

(b) Any two cards of the same value

(c) Three of a kind

40. Use a computer or a graphing calculator and the Monte Carlo method with $n = 20$ to estimate the probabilities of the following 13-card bridge hands. Since each hand has 13 cards, you will need $20 \cdot 13 = 260$ random numbers to "look at" 20 hands.

(a) No aces

(b) 2 kings and 2 aces

(c) No cards of any one suit—that is, only 3 suits represented

*From Richard Madsen. "On the Probability of a Perfect Progression," *The American Statistician,* August 1991, vol. 45, no. 3, p. 214.

10.3 BINOMIAL PROBABILITY

Many probability problems are concerned with experiments in which an event is repeated many times. Some examples include finding the probability of getting 7 heads in 8 tosses of a coin, of hitting a target 6 times out of 6, and of finding 1 defective item in a sample of 15 items. Probability problems of this kind are called **Bernoulli trials** problems, or **Bernoulli processes,** named after the Swiss mathematician Jakob Bernoulli (1654–1705). In each case, some outcome is designated a success, and any other outcome is considered a failure. Thus, if the probability of a success in a single trial is p, the probability of failure will be $1 - p$. A Bernoulli trials problem, or **binomial experiment,** must satisfy the following conditions.

BINOMIAL EXPERIMENT

1. The same experiment is repeated several times.
2. There are only two possible outcomes, success or failure.
3. The repeated trials are independent so that the probability of each outcome remains the same for each trial.

Consider a typical problem of this type: find the probability of getting 5 ones on 5 rolls of a die. Here, the experiment, rolling a die, is repeated 5 times. If getting a one is designated as a success, then getting any other outcome is a failure. The 5 trials are independent; the probability of success (getting a one) is 1/6 on each trial, while the probability of a failure (any other result) is 5/6. Thus, the required probability is

$$P(5 \text{ ones in 5 rolls}) = P(1) \cdot P(1) \cdot P(1) \cdot P(1) \cdot P(1) = \left(\frac{1}{6}\right)^5$$
$$\approx .00013.$$

Now suppose the problem is changed to that of finding the probability of getting a one exactly 4 times in 5 rolls of the die. Again, a success on any roll of the die is defined as getting a one, and the trials are independent, with the same probability of success each time. The desired outcome for this experiment can occur in more than one way, as shown below, where s represents a success (getting a one), and f represents a failure (getting any other result), and each row represents a different outcome.

$$\begin{matrix} s & s & s & s & f \\ s & s & s & f & s \\ s & s & f & s & s \\ s & f & s & s & s \\ f & s & s & s & s \end{matrix}$$

Using combinations, the total number of ways in which 4 successes (and 1 failure) can occur is $\binom{5}{4} = 5$. The probability of each of these 5 outcomes is

$$\left(\frac{1}{6}\right)^4\left(\frac{5}{6}\right).$$

Since the 5 outcomes represent mutually exclusive alternative events, add the 5 probabilities, or multiply by $\binom{5}{4} = 5$.

$$P(4 \text{ ones in 5 rolls}) = \binom{5}{4}\left(\frac{1}{6}\right)^4\left(\frac{5}{6}\right)^{5-4} = 5\left(\frac{1}{6}\right)^4\left(\frac{5}{6}\right)^1 = \frac{5^2}{6^5} \approx .0032$$

The probability of rolling a one exactly 3 times in 5 rolls of a die can be computed in the same way. The probability of any one way of achieving 3 successes and 2 failures will be

$$\left(\frac{1}{6}\right)^3\left(\frac{5}{6}\right)^2.$$

1 Find the probability of rolling a one

(a) exactly twice in 5 rolls of a die;

(b) exactly once in 5 rolls of a die.

(c) Do the probabilities found in the text, plus the two probabilities found here cover all possible outcomes for this experiment? If not, what other outcomes are possible?

Answers:

(a) .161

(b) .402

(c) No; 0 ones

Again the desired outcome can occur in more than one way. The number of ways in which 3 successes (and 2 failures) can occur, using combinations, is $\binom{5}{3} = 10$.

$$P(\mathbf{3} \text{ ones in } 5 \text{ rolls}) = \binom{5}{\mathbf{3}}\left(\frac{1}{6}\right)^{3}\left(\frac{5}{6}\right)^{5-\mathbf{3}} = 10\left(\frac{1}{6}\right)^{3}\left(\frac{5}{6}\right)^{2} = \frac{250}{6^5} \approx .032$$ 1

A similar argument works in the general case.

BINOMIAL PROBABILITY

If p is the probability of success in a single trial of a binomial experiment, the probability of x successes and $n - x$ failures in n independent repeated trials of the experiment is

$$\binom{n}{x}p^x(1-p)^{n-x}.$$

This formula plays an important role in the study of *binomial distributions,* which are discussed in Section 11.4.

TECHNOLOGY TIP On the TI-83 calculator, use "binompdf(n,p,x)" in the DISTR menu to compute the probability of exactly x successes in n trials (where p is the probability of success in a single trial). Use "binomcdf(n,p,x)" to compute the probability of at most x successes in n trials. ✔

EXAMPLE 1 The advertising agency that handles the Diet Supercola account believes that 40% of all consumers prefer this product over its competitors. Suppose a random sample of 6 people is chosen. Assume that all responses are independent of each other. Find the probability of the following.

(a) Exactly 4 of the 6 people prefer Diet Supercola.

We can think of the 6 responses as 6 independent trials. A success occurs if a person prefers Diet Supercola. Then this is a binomial experiment with $p = P(\text{success}) = P(\text{prefer Diet Supercola}) = .4$. The sample is made up of 6 people, so $n = 6$. To find the probability that exactly 4 people prefer this drink, we let $x = 4$ and use the result in the box.

$$\begin{aligned} P(\text{exactly } \mathbf{4}) &= \binom{6}{\mathbf{4}}(.4)^{\mathbf{4}}(1-.4)^{6-\mathbf{4}} \\ &= 15(.4)^4(.6)^2 \\ &= 15(.0256)(.36) \qquad \text{Use a calculator.} \\ &= .13824 \end{aligned}$$

(b) None of the 6 people prefers Diet Supercola.

Let $x = 0$.

$$\begin{aligned} P(\text{exactly } \mathbf{0}) &= \binom{6}{\mathbf{0}}(.4)^{\mathbf{0}}(1-.4)^{6} \\ &= 1(1)(.6)^6 \\ &\approx .0467 \end{aligned}$$ ■ 2

2 Eighty percent of all students at a certain school ski. If a sample of 5 students at this school is selected, and if their responses are independent, find the probability that exactly

(a) 1 of the 5 students skis;

(b) 4 of the 5 students ski.

Answers:

(a) $\binom{5}{1}(.8)^1(.2)^4 = .0064$

(b) $\binom{5}{4}(.8)^4(.2)^1 = .4096$

3 Find the probability of getting 2 fours in 8 tosses of a die.

Answer:

$\binom{8}{2}\left(\frac{1}{6}\right)^2\left(\frac{5}{6}\right)^6 \approx .2605$

EXAMPLE 2 Find the probability of getting exactly 7 heads in 8 tosses of a fair coin.

The probability of success, getting a head in a single toss, is 1/2, so the probability of failure, getting a tail, is 1/2.

$$P(7 \text{ heads in } 8 \text{ tosses}) = \binom{8}{7}\left(\frac{1}{2}\right)^7\left(\frac{1}{2}\right)^1 = 8\left(\frac{1}{2}\right)^8 = .03125 \quad \blacksquare$$ 3

EXAMPLE 3 Assuming that selection of items for a sample can be treated as independent trials, and that the probability that any 1 item is defective is .01, find the following.

(a) The probability of 1 defective item in a random sample of 15 items from a production line

Here, a "success" is a defective item. Selecting each item for the sample is assumed to be an independent trial, so the binomial probability formula applies. The probability of success (a defective item) is .01, while the probability of failure (an acceptable item) is .99. This makes

$$\begin{aligned} P(1 \text{ defective in } 15 \text{ items}) &= \binom{15}{1}(.01)^1(.99)^{14} \\ &= 15(.01)(.99)^{14} \\ &\approx .130. \end{aligned}$$

(b) The probability of at most 1 defective item in a random sample of 15 items from a production line

"At most 1" means 0 defective items or 1 defective item. Since 0 defective items is equivalent to 15 acceptable items,

$$P(0 \text{ defective}) = (.99)^{15} \approx .860.$$

Use the union rule, noting that 0 defective and 1 defective are mutually exclusive events, to get

$$\begin{aligned} P(\text{at most 1 defective}) &= P(0 \text{ defective}) + P(1 \text{ defective}) \\ &\approx .860 + .130 \\ &= .990. \quad \blacksquare \end{aligned}$$ 4

4 Five percent of the clay pots fired in a certain way are defective. Find the probability of getting exactly 2 defective pots in a sample of 12.

Answer:

$\binom{12}{2}(.05)^2(.95)^{10} \approx .0988$

In the next example we return to the problem posed at the beginning of this chapter.

EXAMPLE 4 A survey by *Money* magazine found that supermarket scanners are overcharging customers at 30% of stores.* Assume all such scanners consistently overcharge. If you shop at 3 supermarkets that use the scanners, what is the probability that you will be overcharged in at least one store?

We can treat this as a binomial experiment, letting $n = 3$ and $p = .3$. At least 1 of 3 means 1 or 2 or 3. It will be simpler here to find the probability of being

*"Don't Get Cheated by Supermarket Scanners," pp. 132–138, by Vanessa O'Connell reprinted from the April 1993 issue of *Money* by special permission (reprinted in the *Chicago Tribune* as "Beware, When Scanners Err, You Pay Price"). Copyright © 1993, Time Inc.

5 In Example 4, find the probability that

(a) you are overcharged in more than 1 store.

(b) you are overcharged in less than 1 store.

Answers:

(a) .216

(b) .343

overcharged in none of the 3 stores, that is, $P(0 \text{ overcharges})$, and then find the probability of at least $1 = 1 - P(0 \text{ overcharges})$.

$$\begin{aligned} P(0 \text{ overcharges}) &= \binom{3}{0}(.3)^0(.7)^3 \\ &= 1(1)(.343) \\ &= .343 \\ P(\text{at least } 1) &= 1 - P(0 \text{ overcharges}) \\ &= 1 - .343 \\ &= .657 \end{aligned}$$

■ 5

10.3 EXERCISES

Social Science *In 1995 12.7% of the U.S. population was 65 or older, an increase from 4.1% in 1900.* Find the probabilities that the following number of persons selected at random from 20 U.S. residents in 1995 were 65 or older. (See Examples 1–3.)*

1. Exactly 5 **2.** Exactly 1

3. None **4.** All

5. At least 1 **6.** At most 3

A die is rolled 12 times. Find the probability of rolling

7. Exactly 12 ones; **8.** Exactly 6 ones;

9. Exactly 1 one; **10.** Exactly 2 ones;

11. No more than 3 ones; **12.** No more than 1 one.

A coin is tossed 5 times. Find the probability of getting

13. All heads; **14.** Exactly 3 heads;

15. No more than 3 heads; **16.** At least 3 heads.

17. How do you identify a probability problem that involves a binomial experiment?

18. Why do combinations occur in the binomial probability formula?

Management *The survey discussed in Example 4 also found the following:*

> *Customers overpay for 1 out of every 10 items, on average. Scanner errors account for more than half of supermarket profits. In 7% of the stores customers were undercharged.*

Suppose a customer purchases 15 items. Find the following probabilities.

19. A customer overpays on 3 items.

20. A customer is not overcharged for any item.

21. A customer overpays on no more than one item.

Suppose a customer shops in 15 stores that use scanners. Find the following probabilities.

22. A customer underpays in 3 stores.

23. A customer underpays in no stores.

24. A customer underpays in at least one store.

Management *The insurance industry has found that the probability is .9 that a life insurance applicant will qualify at the regular rates. Find the probabilities that of the next 10 applicants for life insurance, the following numbers will qualify at the regular rates.*

25. Exactly 10 **26.** Exactly 9

27. At least 9 **28.** Less than 8

Natural Science *The probability that a birth will result in twins is .012. Assuming independence (perhaps not a valid assumption), what are the probabilities that out of 100 births in a hospital, there will be the following numbers of sets of twins?*

29. Exactly 2 sets of twins **30.** At most 2 sets of twins

Natural Science *Six mice from the same litter, all suffering from a vitamin A deficiency, are fed a certain dose of carrots. If the probability of recovery under such treatment is .70, find the probabilities of the following results.*

31. None of the mice recover.

32. Exactly 3 of the 6 mice recover.

33. All of the mice recover.

34. No more than 3 mice recover.

35. Natural Science In an experiment on the effects of a radiation dose on cells, a beam of radioactive particles is aimed at a group of 10 cells. Find the probability that 8 of the cells will be hit by the beam if the probability that any single cell will be hit is .6. (Assume independence.)

36. Natural Science The probability of a mutation of a given gene under a dose of 1 roentgen of radiation is approximately 2.5×10^{-7}. What is the probability that in 10,000 genes, at least 1 mutation occurs?

37. Social Science The probability that an American falls asleep with the TV on at least three nights a week is 1/4.*

(exercise continues)

*U.S. Bureau of the Census, *Population Reports.*

**Harper's Magazine,* March 1996, p. 13.

Suppose a researcher selects 5 Americans at random and is interested in the probability that one or more is a "TV sleeper." Find the following probabilities.

(a) All 5 are TV sleepers.

(b) Three of the 5 are TV sleepers.

38. **Natural Science** Children in a certain school are monitored for a year and it is found that 30% of those who do not brush their teeth regularly don't have a cavity during the year. A child who brushes regularly has a 70% chance of having no cavities during the year.

(a) If 10 children brush regularly, what is the probability that at least 9 will have no cavities during the year?

(b) 150 children who brush regularly are divided into 15 groups of 10 each. What is the probability that in at least one group of 10, at least 9 will have no cavities during the year?

39. **Social Science** A recent study found that 33% of women would prefer to work part time rather than full time if money were not a concern.* Find the probability that if 10 women are selected at random, at least 3 of them would prefer to work part time.

40. **Social Science** A study several years ago by the College Board and the Western Interstate Commission for Higher Education predicted that by 1995, one-third of U.S. public elementary and secondary school students would belong to ethnic minorities. Assuming independence, find the probability that of 5 students selected at random in 1995 from schools throughout the nation, no more than 3 belonged to ethnic minorities.

41. **Social Science** According to the state of California, 33% of all state community college students belong to ethnic minorities. Find the probabilities of the following results in a random sample of 10 California community college students.

(a) Exactly 2 belong to an ethnic minority.

(b) Three or fewer belong to an ethnic minority.

(c) Exactly 5 do not belong to an ethnic minority.

(d) Six or more do not belong to an ethnic minority.

Use a calculator or computer to calculate each of the following probabilities.

42. **Natural Science** A flu vaccine has a probability of 80% of preventing a person who is inoculated from getting flu. A county health office inoculates 134 people. What is the probability that

(a) exactly 10 of them get the flu?

(b) no more than 10 get the flu?

(c) none of them get the flu?

43. **Natural Science** The probability that a male will be color-blind is .042. What is the probability that in a group of 53 men

(a) exactly 5 are color-blind?

(b) no more than 5 are color-blind?

(c) at least 1 is color-blind?

44. **Management** The probability that a certain machine turns out a defective item is .05. What is the probability that in a run of 75 items

(a) exactly 5 defectives are produced?

(b) no defectives are produced?

(c) at least 1 defective is produced?

45. **Management** A company is taking a survey to find out if people like their product. Their last survey indicated that 70% of the population likes their product. Based on that, of a sample of 58 people, what is the probability that

(a) all 58 like the product?

(b) from 28 to 30 (inclusive) like the product?

*Cathleen Ferraro, "Feelings of the Working Women," *The Sacramento Bee,* May 11, 1995, p. A1, A22.

10.4 MARKOV CHAINS

In Section 9.5, we touched on **stochastic processes,** mathematical models that evolve over time in a probabilistic manner. In this section we study a special kind of stochastic process called a **Markov chain,** where the outcome of an experiment depends only on the outcome of the previous experiment. In other words, the next **state** of the system depends only on the present state, not on preceding states. Such experiments are common enough in applications to make their study worthwhile. Markov chains are named after the Russian mathematician A. A. Markov, 1856–1922, who started the theory of stochastic processes. To see how Markov chains work, we look at an example.

EXAMPLE 1 A small town has only two dry cleaners, Johnson and NorthClean. Johnson's manager hopes to increase the firm's market share by an extensive advertising campaign. After the campaign, a market research firm finds that there is a probability of .8 that a Johnson customer will bring his next batch of dirty items to Johnson, and a .35 chance that a NorthClean customer will switch to Johnson for his next batch. Assume that the probability that a customer comes to a given cleaners depends only on where the last load of clothes was taken. If there is an .8 chance that a Johnson customer will return to Johnson, then there must be a 1 − .8 = .2 chance that the customer will switch to NorthClean. In the same way, there is a 1 − .35 = .65 chance that a NorthClean customer will return to NorthClean. If an individual bringing a load to Johnson is said to be in state 1 and an individual bringing a load to NorthClean is said to be in state 2, then these probabilities of change from one cleaner to the other are as shown in the following table.

		SECOND LOAD	
	State	*1*	*2*
FIRST LOAD	1	.8	.2
	2	.35	.65

■

[1] Given the transition matrix

$$\begin{array}{cc} & \textit{State} \\ & \begin{array}{cc} 1 & 2 \end{array} \\ \textit{State}\ \begin{array}{c} 1 \\ 2 \end{array} & \begin{bmatrix} .3 & .7 \\ .1 & .9 \end{bmatrix}. \end{array}$$

(a) What is the probability of changing from state 1 to state 2?

(b) What does the number .1 represent?

(c) Draw a transition diagram for this information.

Answers:

(a) .7

(b) The probability of changing from state 2 to state 1

(c)

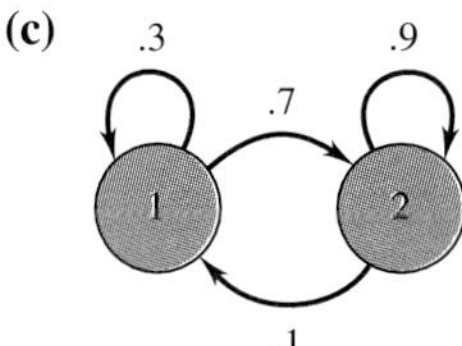

The information from the table can be written in other forms. Figure 10.3 is a **transition diagram** that shows the two states and the probabilities of going from one state to another.

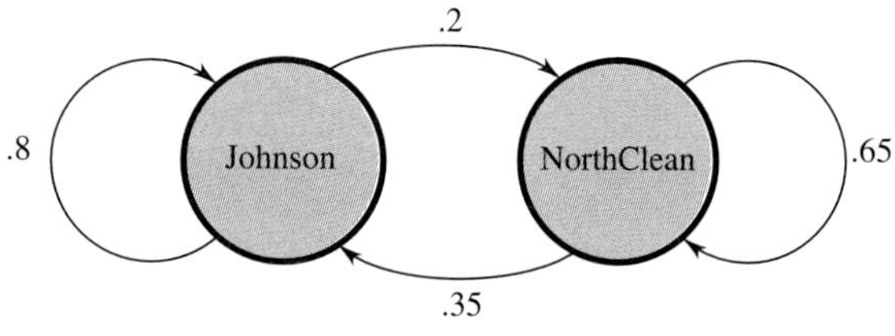

FIGURE 10.3

In a **transition matrix,** the states are indicated at the side and top, as follows.

$$\begin{array}{ccc} & & \begin{array}{cc} \textit{Second Load} \\ \text{Johnson} & \text{NorthClean} \end{array} \\ \textit{First Load} & \begin{array}{c} \text{Johnson} \\ \text{NorthClean} \end{array} & \begin{bmatrix} .8 & .2 \\ .35 & .65 \end{bmatrix} \end{array}$$ [1]

A **transition matrix** has the following features.

1. It is square, since all possible states must be used both as rows and as columns.
2. All entries are between 0 and 1, inclusive, because all entries represent probabilities.
3. The sum of the entries in any row must be 1, because the numbers in the row give the probability of changing from the state at the left to one of the states indicated across the top.

EXAMPLE 2 Suppose that when the new promotional campaign began, Johnson had 40% of the market and NorthClean had 60%. Use the probability tree in Figure 10.4 to find how these proportions would change after another week of advertising.

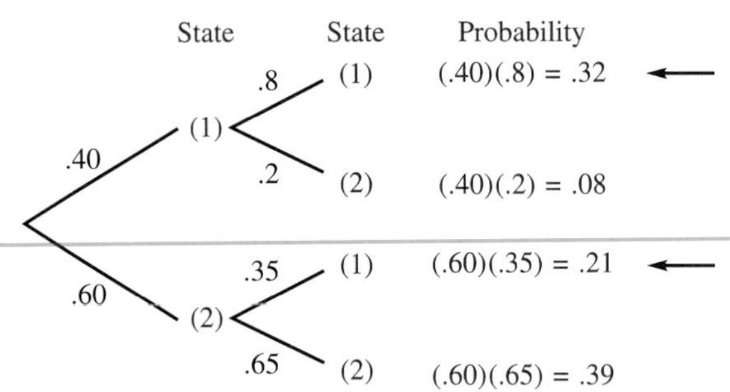

State 1: taking cleaning to Johnson
State 2: taking cleaning to NorthClean

FIGURE 10.4

Add the numbers indicated with arrows to find the proportion of people taking their cleaning to Johnson after 1 week.

$$.32 + .21 = .53$$

Similarly, the proportion taking their cleaning to NorthClean is

$$.08 + .39 = .47.$$

The initial distribution of 40% and 60% becomes, after 1 week, 53% and 47%. ■

These distributions can be written as the *probability vectors*

$$[.40 \quad .60] \quad \text{and} \quad [.53 \quad .47].$$

A **probability vector** is a matrix of only one row, having nonnegative entries with the sum of the entries equal to 1.

The results from the probability tree above are exactly the same as the result of multiplying the initial probability vector by the transition matrix. (Multiplication of matrices was discussed in Section 7.3.)

$$[.4 \quad .6]\begin{bmatrix} .8 & .2 \\ .35 & .65 \end{bmatrix} = [.53 \quad .47]$$

Find the market share after 2 weeks by multiplying the vector [.53 .47] and the transition matrix. 2

The product from Problem 2 at the side (with the numbers rounded to the nearest hundredth) shows that after 2 weeks of advertising, Johnson's share of the market has increased to 59%. To get the share after 3 weeks, multiply the probability vector [.59 .41] and the transition matrix. Continuing this process gives each cleaner's share of the market after any number of weeks. 3

2 Find the product

$$[.53 \quad .47]\begin{bmatrix} .8 & .2 \\ .35 & .65 \end{bmatrix}.$$

Answer:
[.59 .41] (rounded)

3 Find each cleaner's market share after 3 weeks.

Answer:
[.62 .38] (rounded)

The following table gives the market share (rounded) for each cleaner at the end of week n for several values of n.

Week	*Johnson*	*NorthClean*
Start	.4	.6
1	.53	.47
2	.59	.41
3	.62	.38
4	.63	.37
5	.63	.37
12	.64	.36

The results seem to approach the probability vector $[.64 \quad .36]$. This vector is called the **equilibrium vector** or **fixed vector** for the given transition matrix. The equilibrium vector gives a long-range prediction—the shares of the market will stabilize (under the same conditions) at 64% for Johnson and 36% for NorthClean.

Starting with some other initial probability vector and going through the steps above would give the same equilibrium vector. In fact, the long-range trend is the same no matter what the initial vector is. The long-range trend depends only on the transition matrix, not on the initial distribution.

One of the many applications of Markov chains is in finding these long-range predictions. It is not possible to make long-range predictions with all transition matrices, but there is a large set of transition matrices for which long-range predictions *are* possible. Such predictions are always possible with *regular transition matrices.* A transition matrix is **regular** if some power of the matrix contains all positive entries. A Markov chain is a **regular Markov chain** if its transition matrix is regular. A regular Markov chain always has an equilibrium vector.

EXAMPLE 3 Decide whether the following transition matrices are regular.

(a) $A = \begin{bmatrix} .75 & .25 & 0 \\ 0 & .5 & .5 \\ .6 & .4 & 0 \end{bmatrix}$

Square the matrix A by multiplying it by itself.

$$A^2 = \begin{bmatrix} .5625 & .3125 & .125 \\ .3 & .45 & .25 \\ .45 & .35 & .2 \end{bmatrix}$$

All entries in A^2 are positive, so that matrix A is regular.

(b) $B = \begin{bmatrix} .5 & 0 & .5 \\ 0 & 1 & 0 \\ 0 & 0 & 1 \end{bmatrix}$

Find various powers of B.

$$B^2 = \begin{bmatrix} .25 & 0 & .75 \\ 0 & 1 & 0 \\ 0 & 0 & 1 \end{bmatrix} \quad B^3 = \begin{bmatrix} .125 & 0 & .875 \\ 0 & 1 & 0 \\ 0 & 0 & 1 \end{bmatrix} \quad B^4 = \begin{bmatrix} .0625 & 0 & .9375 \\ 0 & 1 & 0 \\ 0 & 0 & 1 \end{bmatrix}$$

Notice that all of the powers of B shown here have zeros in the same locations. Thus, further powers of B will still give the same zero entries, so that no power of matrix B contains all positive entries. For this reason, B is not regular. ■ 4

4 Decide if the following transition matrices are regular.

(a) $\begin{bmatrix} 0 & 1 \\ 1 & 0 \end{bmatrix}$

(b) $\begin{bmatrix} .3 & .7 \\ 1 & 0 \end{bmatrix}$

Answers:

(a) No

(b) Yes

The equilibrium vector can be found without doing all the work shown above. Let $V = [v_1 \quad v_2]$ represent the desired vector. Let P represent the transition matrix. By definition, V is the fixed probability vector if $VP = V$. In our example,

$$[v_1 \quad v_2]\begin{bmatrix} .8 & .2 \\ .35 & .65 \end{bmatrix} = [v_1 \quad v_2].$$

Multiply on the left to get

$$[.8v_1 + .35v_2 \quad .2v_1 + .65v_2] = [v_1 \quad v_2].$$

Set corresponding entries from the two matrices equal to get

$$.8v_1 + .35v_2 = v_1 \qquad .2v_1 + .65v_2 = v_2.$$

Simplify each of these equations.

$$-.2v_1 + .35v_2 = 0 \qquad .2v_1 - .35v_2 = 0$$

These last two equations are really the same. (The equations in the system obtained from $VP = V$ are always dependent.) To find the values of v_1 and v_2, recall that $V = [v_1 \quad v_2]$ is a probability vector, so that

$$v_1 + v_2 = 1.$$

Find v_1 and v_2 by solving the system

$$\begin{aligned} -.2v_1 + .35v_2 &= 0 \\ v_1 + \quad v_2 &= 1. \end{aligned}$$

5 Solve the equation for v_2. Round to the nearest thousandth.

Answer:

.364

From the second equation, $v_1 = 1 - v_2$. Substitute for v_1 in the first equation:

$$-.2(1 - v_2) + .35v_2 = 0. \quad \boxed{5}$$

Since $v_2 = .364$ (from Problem 5 at the side) and $v_1 = 1 - v_2$, then $v_1 = 1 - .364 = .636$ and the equilibrium vector is $[.636 \quad .364]$.

EXAMPLE 4 Find the equilibrium vector for the transition matrix

$$P = \begin{bmatrix} \frac{1}{3} & \frac{2}{3} \\ \frac{3}{4} & \frac{1}{4} \end{bmatrix}.$$

Look for a vector $[v_1 \quad v_2]$ such that

$$[v_1 \quad v_2]\begin{bmatrix} \frac{1}{3} & \frac{2}{3} \\ \frac{3}{4} & \frac{1}{4} \end{bmatrix} = [v_1 \quad v_2].$$

Multiply on the left, obtaining the two equations

$$\frac{1}{3}v_1 + \frac{3}{4}v_2 = v_1 \qquad \frac{2}{3}v_1 + \frac{1}{4}v_2 = v_2.$$

Simplify each of these equations.

$$-\frac{2}{3}v_1 + \frac{3}{4}v_2 = 0 \qquad \frac{2}{3}v_1 - \frac{3}{4}v_2 = 0$$

We know that $v_1 + v_2 = 1$, so $v_1 = 1 - v_2$. Substitute this into either of the two given equations. Using the first equation gives

$$-\frac{2}{3}(1 - v_2) + \frac{3}{4}v_2 = 0$$

$$-\frac{2}{3} + \frac{2}{3}v_2 + \frac{3}{4}v_2 = 0$$

$$-\frac{2}{3} + \frac{17}{12}v_2 = 0$$

$$\frac{17}{12}v_2 = \frac{2}{3}$$

$$v_2 = \frac{8}{17},$$

and $v_1 = 1 - 8/17 = 9/17$. The equilibrium vector is $[9/17 \quad 8/17]$. ■ 6

6 Find the equilibrium vector for the transition matrix

$$P = \begin{bmatrix} .3 & .7 \\ .5 & .5 \end{bmatrix}.$$

Answer:
$[5/12 \quad 7/12]$

EXAMPLE 5 The probability that a complex assembly line works correctly depends on whether or not the line worked correctly the last time it was used. The various probabilities are as given in the following transition matrix.

	Works Properly Now	Does Not
Worked Properly Before	.9	.1
Did Not	.7	.3

Find the long-range probability that the assembly line will work properly.

Begin by finding the equilibrium vector $[v_1 \quad v_2]$, where

$$[v_1 \quad v_2]\begin{bmatrix} .9 & .1 \\ .7 & .3 \end{bmatrix} = [v_1 \quad v_2].$$

Multiplying on the left and setting corresponding entries equal gives the equations

$$.9v_1 + .7v_2 = v_1 \quad \text{and} \quad .1v_1 + .3v_2 = v_2$$

or

$$-.1v_1 + .7v_2 = 0 \quad \text{and} \quad .1v_1 - .7v_2 = 0.$$

Substitute $v_1 = 1 - v_2$ in the first of these equations to get

$$-.1(1 - v_2) + .7v_2 = 0$$

$$-.1 + .1v_2 + .7v_2 = 0$$

$$-.1 + .8v_2 = 0$$

$$.8v_2 = .1$$

$$v_2 = \frac{1}{8},$$

and $v_1 = 1 - 1/8 = 7/8$. The equilibrium vector is $[7/8 \quad 1/8]$. In the long run, the company can expect the assembly line to run properly 7/8 of the time. ■ 7

7 In Example 5, suppose the company modifies the line so that the transition matrix becomes

$$\begin{bmatrix} .95 & .05 \\ .8 & .2 \end{bmatrix}.$$

Find the long-range probability that the assembly line will work properly.

Answer:
16/17

The examples suggest the following generalization. If a regular Markov chain has transition matrix P and initial probability vector v, the products

$$\begin{aligned} &vP \\ &vPP = vP^2 \\ &vP^2P = vP^3 \\ &\vdots \\ &vP^n \end{aligned}$$

lead to the equilibrium vector V. The results of this section can be summarized as follows.

> Suppose a regular Markov chain has a transition matrix P.
>
> **1.** For any initial probability vector v, the products vP^n approach a unique vector V as n gets larger and larger. Vector V is called the equilibrium or fixed vector.
>
> **2.** Vector V has the property that $VP = V$.
>
> **3.** Vector V is found by solving a system of equations obtained from the matrix equation $VP = V$ and from the fact that the sum of the entries of V is 1.

10.4 EXERCISES

Decide which of the following could be a probability vector.

1. $\begin{bmatrix} \frac{1}{2} & \frac{2}{3} \end{bmatrix}$

2. $\begin{bmatrix} \frac{3}{4} & \frac{1}{2} \end{bmatrix}$

3. $[0 \quad 1]$

4. $[.4 \quad .2 \quad 0]$

5. $[.3 \quad -.1 \quad .6]$

6. $\begin{bmatrix} \frac{1}{4} & \frac{1}{8} & \frac{5}{8} \end{bmatrix}$

Decide which of the following could be a transition matrix. Sketch a transition diagram for any transition matrices.

7. $\begin{bmatrix} .7 & .1 \\ .5 & .5 \end{bmatrix}$

8. $\begin{bmatrix} \frac{1}{4} & \frac{3}{4} \\ 0 & 1 \end{bmatrix}$

9. $\begin{bmatrix} \frac{2}{3} & \frac{1}{3} \\ \frac{1}{5} & \frac{4}{5} \end{bmatrix}$

10. $\begin{bmatrix} 0 & 1 & 0 \\ \frac{1}{3} & \frac{1}{3} & \frac{1}{3} \\ 1 & 0 & 0 \end{bmatrix}$

11. $\begin{bmatrix} \frac{1}{2} & \frac{1}{4} & 1 \\ \frac{2}{3} & 0 & \frac{1}{3} \\ \frac{1}{3} & 1 & 0 \end{bmatrix}$

12. $\begin{bmatrix} .2 & .3 & .5 \\ 0 & 0 & 1 \\ .1 & .9 & 0 \end{bmatrix}$

In Exercises 13–15, write any transition diagrams as transition matrices.

13.

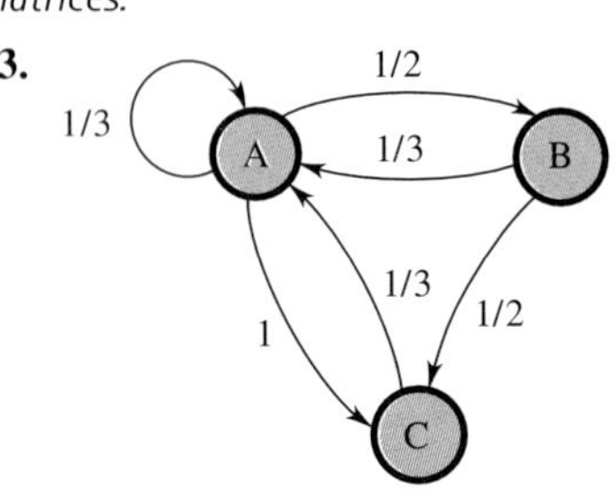

14.

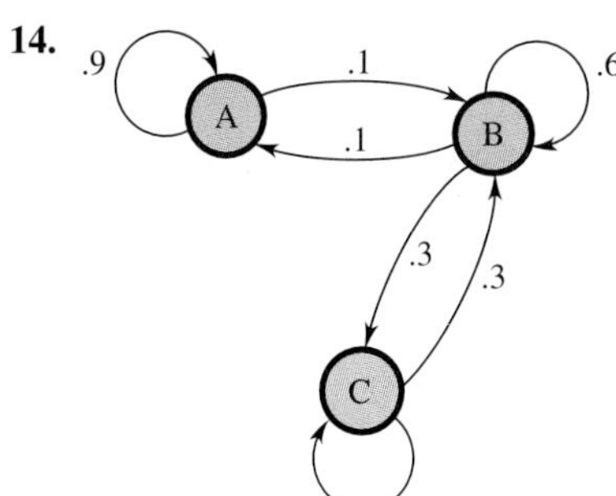

15.

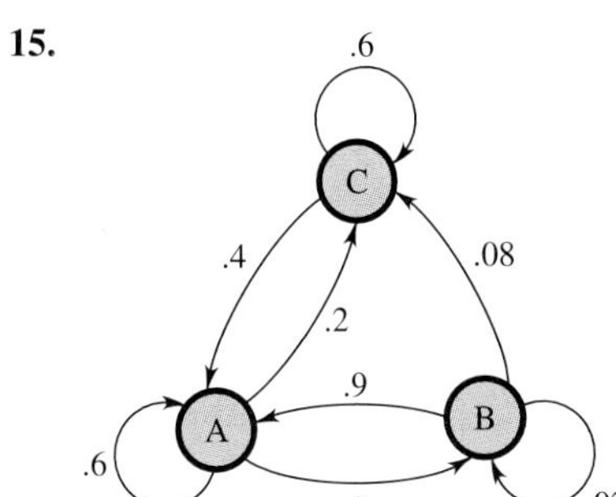

Decide whether the following transition matrices are regular. (See Example 3.)

16. $\begin{bmatrix} 1 & 0 \\ .6 & .4 \end{bmatrix}$

17. $\begin{bmatrix} .2 & .8 \\ .9 & .1 \end{bmatrix}$

18. $\begin{bmatrix} .3 & .5 & .2 \\ 1 & 0 & 0 \\ .5 & .1 & .4 \end{bmatrix}$

19. $\begin{bmatrix} 0 & 1 & 0 \\ .4 & .2 & .4 \\ 1 & 0 & 0 \end{bmatrix}$

20. $\begin{bmatrix} .25 & .40 & .30 & .05 \\ .18 & .23 & .59 & 0 \\ 0 & .15 & .36 & .49 \\ .28 & .32 & .24 & .16 \end{bmatrix}$

21. $\begin{bmatrix} .12 & .68 & 0 & .20 \\ 0 & .33 & .40 & .27 \\ 0 & 0 & 1 & 0 \\ .52 & 0 & .43 & .05 \end{bmatrix}$

Find the equilibrium vector for each of the following transition matrices. (See Examples 4 and 5.)

22. $\begin{bmatrix} .3 & .7 \\ .4 & .6 \end{bmatrix}$

23. $\begin{bmatrix} .8 & .2 \\ .1 & .9 \end{bmatrix}$

24. $\begin{bmatrix} \frac{1}{4} & \frac{3}{4} \\ \frac{1}{2} & \frac{1}{2} \end{bmatrix}$

25. $\begin{bmatrix} \frac{2}{3} & \frac{1}{3} \\ \frac{1}{8} & \frac{7}{8} \end{bmatrix}$

26. $\begin{bmatrix} .25 & .35 & .4 \\ .1 & .3 & .6 \\ .55 & .4 & .05 \end{bmatrix}$

27. $\begin{bmatrix} .16 & .28 & .56 \\ .43 & .12 & .45 \\ .86 & .05 & .09 \end{bmatrix}$

28. $\begin{bmatrix} .1 & .1 & .8 \\ .4 & .4 & .2 \\ .1 & .2 & .7 \end{bmatrix}$

29. $\begin{bmatrix} .5 & .2 & .3 \\ .1 & .4 & .5 \\ .2 & .2 & .6 \end{bmatrix}$

For each of the following transition matrices, use a graphing calculator or computer to find the first five powers of the matrix. Then find the probability that state 2 changes to state 4 after 5 repetitions of the experiment.

30. $\begin{bmatrix} .1 & .2 & .2 & .3 & .2 \\ .2 & .1 & .1 & .2 & .4 \\ .2 & .1 & .4 & .2 & .1 \\ .3 & .1 & .1 & .2 & .3 \\ .1 & .3 & .1 & .1 & .4 \end{bmatrix}$

31. $\begin{bmatrix} .3 & .2 & .3 & .1 & .1 \\ .4 & .2 & .1 & .2 & .1 \\ .1 & .3 & .2 & .2 & .2 \\ .2 & .1 & .3 & .2 & .2 \\ .1 & .1 & .4 & .2 & .2 \end{bmatrix}$

32. **Social Science** The following chart shows the percent of the poor, middle class, and affluent that change into another class. The first graph shows the figures for 1967–1979, and the second for 1980–1991.* For each time period, assume the number of people who move directly from poor to affluent or from affluent to poor is essentially 0.
  (a) Find the long-range percent of poor, middle class, and affluent people if the 1967–1979 trends were to continue.
  (b) Find the long-range percent of poor, middle class, and affluent people if the 1980–1991 trends were to continue.

The poor are more likely to stay poor and the affluent are more likely to stay affluent.

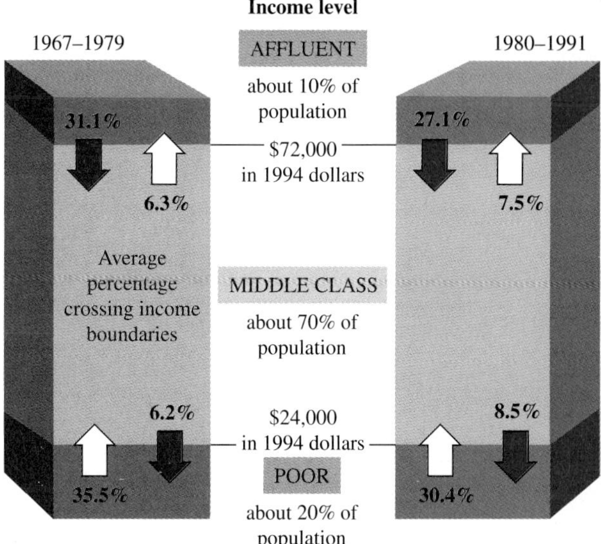

All figures are for household after-tax income, including wages, salaries, and some Government assistance programs like food stamps.

Sources: Greg Duncan, Northwestern University; Timothy Smeeding, Syracuse University

**The New York Times,* June 4, 1995, p. E4.

33. **Management** In 1992, many homeowners refinanced their mortgages to take advantage of lower interest rates. Most of the mortgages could be classified into three groups: 30-year fixed-rate, 15-year fixed-rate, and adjustable rate. (For this exercise, the small number of loans that are not of those three types will be classified with the adjustable rate loans.) Sometimes when a homeowner refinanced, the new loan was the same type as the old loan, and sometimes it was different. The breakdown of the percent in each category is shown in the following table.*

	NEW LOAN		
OLD LOAN	*30-year Fixed*	*15-year Fixed*	*Adjustable*
30-year fixed	.444	.479	.077
15-year fixed	.150	.802	.048
Adjustable	.463	.367	.170

If these conversion rates were to persist, find the long-range trend for the percent of loans of each type.

34. **Management** The probability that a complex assembly line works correctly depends on whether the line worked correctly the last time it was used. There is a .95 chance that the line will work correctly if it worked correctly the time before, and a .7 chance that it will work correctly if it did *not* work correctly the time before. Set up a transition matrix with this information and find the long-run probability that the line will work correctly. (See Example 5.)

35. **Management** Suppose improvements are made in the assembly line of Exercise 34, so that the transition matrix becomes

$$\begin{array}{l} \\ \text{Works} \\ \text{Doesn't Work} \end{array} \begin{array}{c} \begin{array}{cc} \text{Works} & \text{Doesn't Work} \end{array} \\ \begin{bmatrix} .95 & .05 \\ .85 & .15 \end{bmatrix} \end{array}.$$

Find the new long-run probability that the line will work properly.

36. **Natural Science** In Exercises 46 and 47 of Section 9.4 we discussed the effect on flower color of cross-pollinating pea plants. As shown there, since the gene for red is dominant and the gene for white is recessive, 75% of these pea plants have red flowers and 25% have white flowers, because plants with 1 red and 1 white gene appear red. If a red-flowered plant is crossed with a red-flowered plant known to have 1 red and 1 white gene, then 75% of the offspring will be red and 25% will be white. Crossing a red-flowered plant that has 1 red and 1 white gene with a white-flowered plant produces 50% red-flowered offspring and 50% white-flowered offspring.

(a) Write a transition matrix using this information.
(b) Write a probability vector for the initial distribution of colors.
(c) Find the distribution of colors after 4 generations.
(d) Find the long-range distribution of colors.

37. **Natural Science** Snapdragons with 1 red gene and 1 white gene produce pink-flowered offspring. If a red snapdragon is crossed with a pink snapdragon, the probabilities that the offspring will be red, pink, or white are 1/2, 1/2, and 0, respectively. If 2 pink snapdragons are crossed, the probabilities of red, pink, or white offspring are 1/4, 1/2, and 1/4, respectively. For a cross between a white and a pink snapdragon, the corresponding probabilities are 0, 1/2, and 1/2. Set up a transition matrix and find the long-range prediction for the fraction of red, pink, and white snapdragons.

38. Many phenomena can be viewed as examples of a random walk. Consider the following simple example. A security guard can stand in front of any one of three doors 20 ft apart in front of a building, and every minute he decides whether to move to another door chosen at random. If he is at the middle door, he is equally likely to stay where he is, move to the door to the left, or move to the door to the right. If he is at the door on either end, he is equally likely to stay where he is or move to the middle door.

(a) Verify that the transition matrix is given by

$$\begin{array}{c} \\ 1 \\ 2 \\ 3 \end{array} \begin{array}{c} \begin{array}{ccc} 1 & 2 & 3 \end{array} \\ \begin{bmatrix} \frac{1}{2} & \frac{1}{2} & 0 \\ \frac{1}{3} & \frac{1}{3} & \frac{1}{3} \\ 0 & \frac{1}{2} & \frac{1}{2} \end{bmatrix} \end{array}.$$

(b) Find the long-range trend for the fraction of time the guard spends in front of each door.

39. **Social Science** The probability that a homeowner will become a renter in five years is .03. The probability that a renter will become a homeowner in five years is .1. Suppose the proportions in the population are 64% homeowners (O), 35.5% renters (R), and .5% homeless (H), with the following transition matrix. Assume that these figures continue to apply.

$$\begin{array}{c} \\ O \\ R \\ H \end{array} \begin{array}{c} \begin{array}{ccc} O & R & H \end{array} \\ \begin{bmatrix} .97 & .03 & 0 \\ .1 & .899 & .001 \\ 0 & .4 & .6 \end{bmatrix} \end{array}$$

Find the long-range probabilities for the three categories.

40. **Management** An insurance company classifies its drivers into three groups: G_0 (no accidents), G_1 (one accident), and G_2 (more than one accident). The probability that a driver in G_0 will stay in G_0 after 1 year is .85, that he will become a G_1 is .10, and that he will become a G_2 is .05. A driver in G_1 cannot move to G_0 (this insurance company has a long memory). There is an .80 probability that a G_1 driver

**The New York Times,* Nov. 18, 1992, p. D2.

will stay in G_1 and a .20 probability that he will become a G_2. A driver in G_2 must stay in G_2.

(a) Write a transition matrix using this information.

Suppose that the company accepts 50,000 new policyholders, all of whom are in group G_0. Find the number in each group

(b) after 1 year; **(c)** after 2 years;
(d) after 3 years; **(e)** after 4 years.
(f) Find the equilibrium vector here. Interpret your result.

41. Management The difficulty with the mathematical model of Exercise 40 is that no "grace period" is provided; there should be a certain probability of moving from G_1 or G_2 back to G_0 (say, after 4 years with no accidents). A new system with this feature might produce the following transition matrix.

$$\begin{bmatrix} .85 & .10 & .05 \\ .15 & .75 & .10 \\ .10 & .30 & .60 \end{bmatrix}$$

Suppose that when this new policy is adopted, the company has 50,000 policyholders in group G_0. Find the number of these in each group

(a) after 1 year; **(b)** after 2 years;
(c) after 3 years.
(d) Find the equilibrium vector here. Interpret your result.

42. Management Research done by the Gulf Oil Corporation* produced the following transition matrix for the probability that a person with one form of home heating would switch to another.

		Will Switch to		
		Oil	Gas	Electric
Now Has	Oil	.825	.175	0
	Gas	.060	.919	.021
	Electric	.049	0	.951

The current share of the market held by these three types of heat is given by [.26 .60 .14]. Find the share of the market held by each type of heat after

(a) 1 year; **(b)** 2 years; **(c)** 3 years.
(d) What is the long-range prediction?

43. The results of cricket matches between England and Australia have been found to be modeled by a Markov chain.† The probability that England wins, loses, or draws is based on the result of the previous game, with the following transition matrix.

	Wins	Loses	Draws
Wins	.443	.364	.193
Loses	.277	.436	.287
Draws	.266	.304	.430

(a) Compute the transition matrix for the game after the next one, based on the result of the last game.
(b) Use your answer from part (a) to find the probability that, if England won the last game, England will win the game after the next one.
(c) Use your answer from part (a) to find the probability that, if Australia won the last game, England will win the game after the next one.

44. Social Science At one liberal arts college, students are classified as humanities majors, science majors, or undecided. There is a 20% chance that a humanities major will change to a science major from one year to the next, and a 45% chance that a humanities major will change to undecided. A science major will change to humanities with probability .15, and to undecided with probability .35. An undecided will switch to humanities or science with probabilities of .5 and .3, respectively. Find the long-range prediction for the fraction of students in each of these three majors.

45. Management In the queuing chain, we assume that people are queuing up to be served by, say, a bank teller. For simplicity, let us assume that once two people are in line, no one else can enter the line. Let us further assume that one person is served every minute, as long as someone is in line. Assume further that in any minute, there is a probability of $\frac{1}{2}$ that no one enters the line, a probability of $\frac{1}{3}$ that exactly one person enters the line, and a probability of $\frac{1}{6}$ that exactly two people enter the line, assuming there is room. If there is not enough room for two people, then the probability that one person enters the line is $\frac{1}{2}$. Let the state be given by the number of people in line.

(a) Verify that the transition matrix is

$$\begin{array}{c} \\ 0 \\ 1 \\ 2 \end{array}\begin{array}{c} \begin{array}{ccc} 0 & 1 & 2 \end{array} \\ \begin{bmatrix} \frac{1}{2} & \frac{1}{3} & \frac{1}{6} \\ \frac{1}{2} & \frac{1}{3} & \frac{1}{6} \\ 0 & \frac{1}{2} & \frac{1}{2} \end{bmatrix} \end{array}.$$

(b) Find the transition matrix for a two-minute period.
(c) Use your result from part (b) to find the probability that a queue with no one in line has two people in line two minutes later.

Use a calculator or computer for Exercises 46 and 47.

46. Management A company with a new training program classified each employee in one of four states: s_1, never in the program; s_2, currently in the program; s_3, discharged;

(exercise continues)

*From "Forecasting Market Shares of Alternative Home-Heating Units by Markov Process Using Transition Probabilities Estimates from Aggregate Time Series Data" by Ali Ezzati, from *Management Science,* Vol. 21, No. 4, December 1974. Copyright © 1974 The Institute of Management Sciences. Reprinted by permission.

†From Derek Colwell, Brian Jones, and Jack Gillett, "A Markov Chain in Cricket," *The Mathematical Gazette,* June 1991.

s_4, completed the program. The transition matrix for this company is given below.

$$\begin{array}{c} \\ s_1 \\ s_2 \\ s_3 \\ s_4 \end{array} \begin{array}{c} \begin{array}{cccc} s_1 & s_2 & s_3 & s_4 \end{array} \\ \begin{bmatrix} .4 & .2 & .05 & .35 \\ 0 & .45 & .05 & .5 \\ 0 & 0 & 1 & 0 \\ 0 & 0 & 0 & 1 \end{bmatrix} \end{array}$$

(a) What percent of employees who had never been in the program (state s_1) completed the program (state s_4) after the program had been offered five times?

(b) If the initial percent of employees in each state was [.5 .5 0 0], find the corresponding percents after the program had been offered four times.

47. Management Find the long-range prediction for the percent of employees in each state for the company training program from Exercise 46.

10.5 PROBABILITY DISTRIBUTIONS; EXPECTED VALUE

In this section we shall see that the *expected value* of a probability distribution is a kind of average. Probability distributions were introduced briefly in Chapter 9. A probability distribution depends on the idea of a *random variable,* so we begin with that.

Suppose a bank is interested in improving its services to the public. The manager decides to begin by finding the amount of time tellers spend on each transaction, rounded to the nearest minute. To each transaction, then, will be assigned one of the numbers 0, 1, 2, 3, 4, ... That is, if t represents an outcome of the experiment of timing a transaction, then t may take on any of the values from the list 0, 1, 2, 3, 4, ... The value that t takes on for a particular transaction is random, so t is called a random variable.

A **random variable** is a function that assigns a real number to each outcome of an experiment.

PROBABILITY DISTRIBUTIONS Suppose that the bank manager in our example records the times for 75 different transactions, with results as shown in Table 1. As the table shows, the shortest transaction time was 1 minute, with 3 transactions of 1-minute duration. The longest time was 10 minutes. Only 1 transaction took that long.

In Table 1, the first column gives the 10 values assumed by the random variable t, and the second column shows the number of occurrences corresponding to each of these values, the *frequency* of that value. Table 1 is an example of a **frequency distribution,** a table listing the frequencies for each value a random variable may assume.

TABLE 1

Time	*Frequency*
1	3
2	5
3	9
4	12
5	15
6	11
7	10
8	6
9	3
10	1
	Total: 75

Now suppose that several weeks after starting new procedures to speed up transactions, the manager takes another survey. This time she observes 57 transactions, and she records their times as shown in the frequency distribution in Table 2.

TABLE 2

Time	*Frequency*
1	4
2	5
3	8
4	10
5	12
6	17
7	0
8	1
9	0
10	0
	Total: 57

Do the results in Table 2 indicate an improvement? It is hard to compare the two tables, since one is based on 75 transactions and the other on 57. To make them comparable, we can add a column to each table that gives the *relative frequency* of each transaction time. These results are shown in Tables 3 and 4. Where necessary, decimals are rounded to the nearest hundredth. To find a **relative frequency,** divide each frequency by the total of the frequencies. Here the individual frequencies are divided by 75 or 57. Many of these frequencies have been rounded.

TABLE 3

Time	*Frequency*	*Relative Frequency*
1	3	$3/75 = .04$
2	5	$5/75 \approx .07$
3	9	$9/75 = .12$
4	12	$12/75 = .16$
5	15	$15/75 = .20$
6	11	$11/75 \approx .15$
7	10	$10/75 \approx .13$
8	6	$6/75 = .08$
9	3	$3/75 = .04$
10	1	$1/75 \approx .01$

TABLE 4

Time	*Frequency*	*Relative Frequency*
1	4	$4/57 \approx .07$
2	5	$5/57 \approx .09$
3	8	$8/57 \approx .14$
4	10	$10/57 \approx .18$
5	12	$12/57 \approx .21$
6	17	$17/57 \approx .30$
7	0	$0/57 = 0$
8	1	$1/57 \approx .02$
9	0	$0/57 = 0$
10	0	$0/57 = 0$

1 Complete the probability distribution below. (f represents frequency and p represents probability.)

x	f	p
1	3	
2	7	
3	9	
4	3	
5	2	

Answer:

x	f	p
1	3	.13
2	7	.29
3	9	.38
4	3	.13
5	2	.08
	Total: 24	

The results shown in the two tables are easier to compare using the relative frequencies. We will return to this problem later in this section.

The relative frequencies in Tables 3 and 4 can be considered probabilities. Such a table that lists all the possible values of a random variable, together with the corresponding probabilities, is called a **probability distribution.** The sum of the probabilities in a probability distribution must always be 1. (The sum in an actual distribution may vary slightly from 1 because of rounding.) 1

EXAMPLE 1 Many plants have seed pods with variable numbers of seeds. One variety of green beans has no more than 6 seeds per pod. Suppose that examination of 30 such bean pods gives the results shown in Table 5. Here the random variable x tells the number of seeds per pod. Give a probability distribution for these results.

The probabilities are found by computing the relative frequencies. A total of 30 bean pods were examined, so each frequency should be divided by 30 to get the probability distribution shown as Table 6. Some of the results have been rounded to the nearest hundredth.

TABLE 5

x	*Frequency*
0	3
1	4
2	6
3	8
4	5
5	3
6	1
	Total: 30

TABLE 6

x	*Frequency*	*Probability*
0	3	$3/30 = .10$
1	4	$4/30 \approx .13$
2	6	$6/30 = .20$
3	8	$8/30 \approx .27$
4	5	$5/30 \approx .17$
5	3	$3/30 = .10$
6	1	$1/30 \approx .03$
	Total: 30	

2 In Example 1, what is

(a) $P(x = 0)$?

(b) $P(x = 1)$?

Answers:

(a) .10

(b) .13

As shown in Table 6, the probability that the random variable x takes on the value 2 is 6/30, or .20. This is often written as

$$P(x = 2) = .20.$$

Also, $P(x = 5) = .10$, and $P(x = 6) \approx .03$. ■ 2

Instead of writing the probability distribution in Example 1 as a table, we could write the same information as a set of ordered pairs:

$$\{(0, .10), (1, .13), (2, .20), (3, .27), (4, .17), (5, .10), (6, .03)\}.$$

There is just one probability for each value of the random variable. Thus, a probability distribution defines a function, called a **probability distribution function** or simply a **probability function.** We shall use the terms "probability distribution" and "probability function" interchangeably.

The information in a probability distribution is often displayed graphically as a special kind of bar graph called a **histogram.** The bars of a histogram all have the same width, usually 1. The heights of the bars are determined by the frequencies. A histogram for the data in Table 3 is given in Figure 10.5. A histogram shows important characteristics of a distribution that may not be readily apparent in tabular form, such as the relative sizes of the probabilities and any symmetry in the distribution.

The area of the bar above $t = 1$ in Figure 10.5 is the product of 1 and .04, or $.04 \times 1 = .04$. Since each bar has a width of 1, its area is equal to the probability that corresponds to that value of t. The probability that a particular value will occur is thus given by the area of the appropriate bar of the graph. For example, the probability that a transaction will take less than 4 minutes is the sum of the areas for $t = 1$, $t = 2$, and $t = 3$. This area, shown in color in Figure 10.6, corresponds to 23% of the total area, since

$$\begin{aligned} P(t < 4) &= P(t = 1) + P(t = 2) + P(t = 3) \\ &= .04 + .07 + .12 = .23. \end{aligned}$$

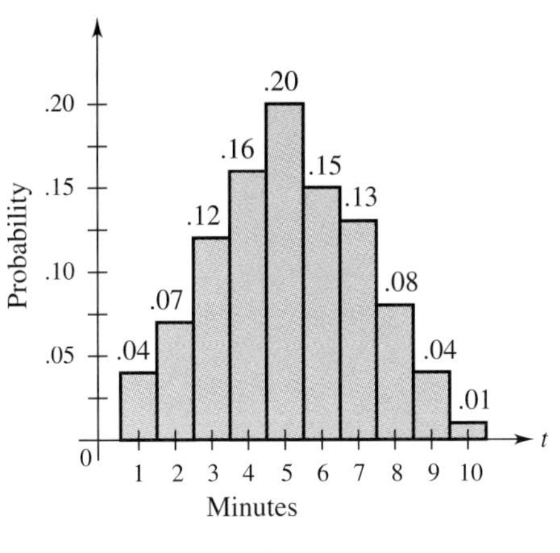

FIGURE 10.5

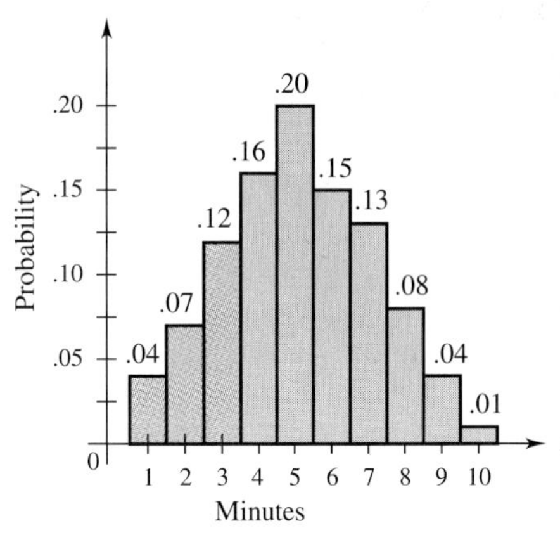

FIGURE 10.6

3 **(a)** Prepare a histogram for the probability distribution in Problem 1 at the side.

(b) Find $P(x \leq 2)$.

Answers:

(a)

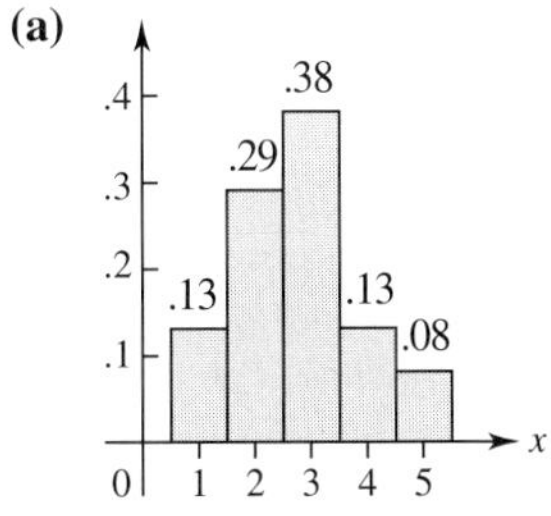

(b) .42

EXAMPLE 2 Construct a histogram for the probability distribution in Example 1. Find the area that gives the probability that the number of seeds will be more than 4.

A histogram for this distribution is shown in Figure 10.7. The portion of the histogram in color represents

$$\begin{aligned} P(x > 4) &= P(x = 5) + P(x = 6) \\ &= .10 + .03 \\ &= .13, \end{aligned}$$

or 13% of the total area. ■ 3

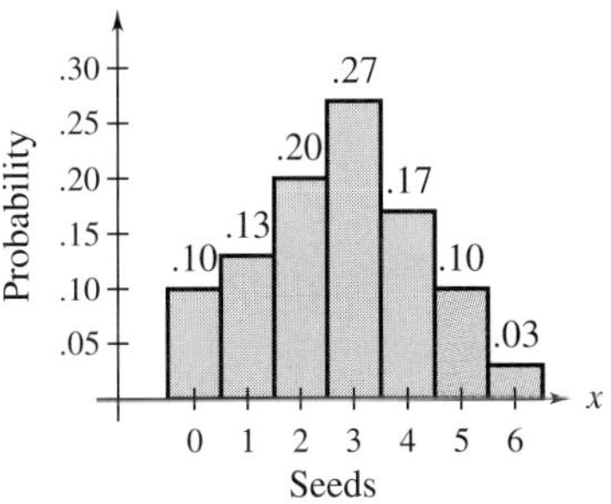

FIGURE 10.7

TECHNOLOGY TIP Virtually all graphing calculators can produce histograms. The procedures differ on various calculators, but usually require you to enter the outcomes in one list and the corresponding frequencies in a second list. Depending on the viewing window chosen, the histogram bars may not always be centered over the corresponding x-value. For specific details, check your instruction manual under "statistics graphs," or "statistical plotting." ✔

EXAMPLE 3 **(a)** Give the probability distribution for the number of heads showing when 2 coins are tossed.

Let x represent the outcome "number of heads." Then x can take on the values 0, 1, or 2. Now find the probability of each outcome. The results are shown in Table 7.

TABLE 7

x	$P(x)$
0	1/4
1	1/2
2	1/4

(b) Find the probability that at least one coin comes up heads.

$$P(x \geq 1) = P(x = 1) + P(x = 2)$$
$$= \frac{1}{2} + \frac{1}{4} = \frac{3}{4}$$

(c) Draw a histogram for the distribution in Table 7.

Two graphing calculator versions of the histogram are shown in Figure 10.8, both having bars of width 1. (See the Technology Tip below.) ■ 4

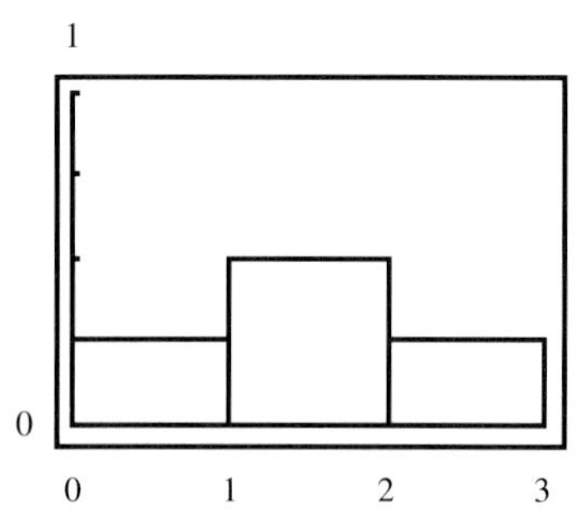

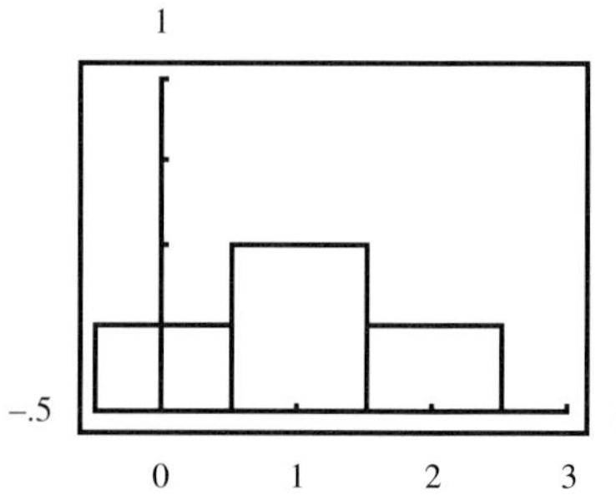

FIGURE 10.8

TECHNOLOGY TIP To obtain the histograms in Figure 10.8 on most graphing calculators, enter the outcomes 0, 1, and 2 on the first list and enter the probabilities .25, .5, and .25 on a second list. Use the second list as "frequencies" when graphing and use a window with $0 \leq y \leq 1$. On TI-81/82/85, however, frequencies must be integers. So make the entries of the second list 1, 2, and 1 (corresponding to 1/4, 2/4, and 1/4) and use a window with $0 \leq y \leq 4$. ✔

4 **(a)** Give the probability distribution for the number of heads showing when 3 coins are tossed.

(b) Find the probability that no more than 1 coin shows heads.

Answers:

(a)

x	$P(x)$
0	1/8
1	3/8
2	3/8
3	1/8

(b) 1/2

In working with experimental data, it is often useful to have a typical or "average" number that represents the entire set of data. For example, we compare our heights and weights to those of the typical or "average" person on weight charts. Students are familiar with the "class average" and their own "average" in a given course.

In a recent year, a citizen of the United States could expect to complete about 13 years of school, to be a member of a household earning $35,400 per year, and to live in a household of 2.6 people. What do we mean here by "expect"? Many people have completed less than 13 years of school; many others have completed more. Many households have less income than $35,400 per year; many others have more. The idea of a household of 2.6 people is a little hard to swallow. The numbers all refer to *averages.* When the term "expect" is used in this way, it refers to *mathematical expectation,* which is a kind of average.

EXPECTED VALUE What about an average value for a random variable? As an example, let us find the average number of offspring for a certain species of pheasant, given the probability distribution in Table 8.

TABLE 8

Number of Offspring	*Frequency*	*Probability*
0	8	.08
1	14	.14
2	29	.29
3	32	.32
4	17	.17
	Total: 100	

We might be tempted to find the typical number of offspring by averaging the numbers 0, 1, 2, 3, and 4, which represent the numbers of offspring possible. This won't work, however, since the various numbers of offspring do not occur with equal probability; for example, a brood with 3 offspring is much more common than one with 0 or 1 offspring. The differing probabilities of occurrence can be taken into account with a **weighted average,** found by multiplying each of the possible numbers of offspring by its corresponding probability, as follows.

$$\begin{aligned}\textbf{Typical number of offspring} &= 0(.08) + 1(.14) + 2(.29) + 3(.32) + 4(.17)\\ &= 0 + .14 + .58 + .96 + .68\\ &= \mathbf{2.36}\end{aligned}$$

Based on the data given above, a typical brood of pheasants includes 2.36 offspring.

It is certainly not possible for a pair of pheasants to produce 2.36 offspring. If the numbers of offspring produced by many different pairs of pheasants are found, however, the average of these numbers will be about 2.36.

We can use the results of this example to define the mean, or *expected value,* of a probability distribution as follows. (We will have more to say about the mean in Chapter 11.)

EXPECTED VALUE

Suppose the random variable x can take on the n values $x_1, x_2, x_3, \ldots, x_n$. Also, suppose the probabilities that these values occur are respectively $p_1, p_2, p_3, \ldots, p_n$. Then the **expected value** of the random variable is

$$\boldsymbol{E(x) = x_1p_1 + x_2p_2 + x_3p_3 + \cdots + x_np_n.}$$

As in the example above, the expected value of a random variable may be a number that can never occur in any one trial of the experiment.

Physically, the expected value of a probability distribution represents a balance point. Figure 10.9 shows a histogram for the distribution of the pheasant offspring. If the histogram is thought of as a series of weights with magnitudes represented by the heights of the bars, then the system would balance if supported at the point corresponding to the expected value.

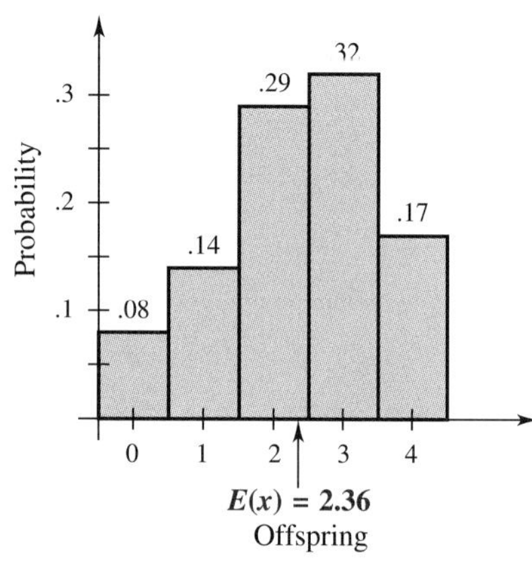

FIGURE 10.9

EXAMPLE 4 Find the expected transaction time for each of the survey results from the bank example at the beginning of this section. What can we conclude from the results?

Refer to Tables 3 and 4. From Table 3, using the relative frequencies as probabilities, the expected transaction time is

$$1(.04) + 2(.07) + 3(.12) + 4(.16) + 5(.20) + 6(.15) + 7(.13) + 8(.08) + 9(.04) + 10(.01) = 5.09. \quad \boxed{5}$$

5 Using Table 4, find the expected transaction time for the second survey.

Answer:
4.4

From Problem 5 at the side, the expected transaction time for the second survey is 4.4. The expected values give us a useful way to compare the results of the two surveys. The second survey had a smaller expected transaction time, so the new procedures may have sped up transactions. ■

EXAMPLE 5 Suppose a local church decides to raise money by raffling a microwave oven worth \$400. A total of 2000 tickets are sold at \$1 each. Find the expected value of winning for a person who buys 1 ticket in the raffle.

Here the random variable represents the possible amounts of net winnings, where net winnings = amount won − cost of ticket. The net winnings of the person winning the oven are \$400 (amount won) − \$1 (cost of ticket) = \$399. The net winnings for each losing ticket are \$0 − \$1 = −\$1.

The probability of winning is 1 in 2000, or 1/2000, while the probability of losing is 1999/2000. See Table 9.

TABLE 9

Outcome (net winnings)	*Probability*
\$399	$\frac{1}{2000}$
−\$1	$\frac{1999}{2000}$

The expected winnings for a person buying 1 ticket are

$$399\left(\frac{1}{2000}\right) + (-1)\left(\frac{1999}{2000}\right) = \frac{399}{2000} - \frac{1999}{2000}$$
$$= -\frac{1600}{2000}$$
$$= -.80.$$

On the average, a person buying 1 ticket in the raffle will lose \$.80, or 80¢.

It is not possible to lose 80¢ in this raffle—either you lose \$1, or you win a \$400 prize. If you bought tickets in many such raffles over a long period of time, however, you would lose 80¢ per ticket, on the average. ■ 6

6 Suppose you buy 1 of 1000 tickets at 10¢ each in a lottery where the prize is \$50. What are your expected net winnings? What does this answer mean?

Answer:
−5¢. On the average you lose 5¢ per ticket purchased.

EXAMPLE 6 Each day Donna and Mary toss a coin to see who buys the coffee (60¢ a cup). One tosses and the other calls the outcome. If the person who calls the outcome is correct, the other buys the coffee; otherwise the caller pays. Find Donna's expected winnings.

Assume that an honest coin is used, that Mary tosses the coin, and that Donna calls the outcome. The possible results and corresponding probabilities are shown below.

	Possible Results			
Result of toss	Heads	Heads	Tails	Tails
Call	Heads	Tails	Heads	Tails
Caller Wins?	Yes	No	No	Yes
Probability	1/4	1/4	1/4	1/4

Donna wins a 60¢ cup of coffee whenever the results and calls match, and she loses a 60¢ cup when there is no match. Her expected winnings are

$$(.60)\left(\frac{1}{4}\right) + (-.60)\left(\frac{1}{4}\right) + (-.60)\left(\frac{1}{4}\right) + (.60)\left(\frac{1}{4}\right) = 0.$$

On the average, over the long run, Donna neither wins nor loses. ■ 7

7 Find Mary's expected winnings.

Answer:
0

A game with an expected value of 0 (such as the one in Example 6) is called a **fair game.** Casinos do not offer fair games. If they did, they would win (on the average) \$0, and have a hard time paying the help! Casino games have expected winnings for the house that vary from 1.5¢ per dollar to 60¢ per dollar. Exercises 37–42 at the end of the section ask you to find the expected winnings for certain games of chance.

The idea of expected value can be very useful in decision making, as shown by the next example.

EXAMPLE 7 At age 50, Earl Karn receives a letter from the Mutual of Mauritania Insurance Company. According to the letter, he must tell the company immediately which of the following two options he will choose: take \$20,000 at age 60 (if he is alive, \$0 otherwise) or \$30,000 at age 70 (again, if he is alive, \$0 otherwise). Based *only* on the idea of expected value, which should he choose?*

Life insurance companies have constructed elaborate tables showing the probability of a person living a given number of years in the future. From a recent such table, the probability of living from age 50 to age 60 is .88, while the probability of living from age 50 to 70 is .64. The expected values of the two options are given below.

$$\text{First Option:} \quad (20{,}000)(.88) + (0)(.12) = 17{,}600$$

$$\text{Second Option:} \quad (30{,}000)(.64) + (0)(.36) = 19{,}200$$

Based strictly on expected values, Karn should choose the second option. ■ 8

8 A person can take one of two jobs. With job A, there is a 50% chance of making \$60,000 per year after 5 years and a 50% chance of making \$30,000. With job B, there is a 30% chance of making \$90,000 per year after 5 years and a 70% chance of making \$20,000. Based strictly on expected value, which job should be taken?

Answer:
Job A has an expected salary of \$45,000; job B, \$41,000. Take job A.

*Other considerations might affect the decision, such as the rate at which Karn might invest the \$20,000 at age 60 for 10 years.

10.5 EXERCISES

In Exercises 1–4 (a) give the probability distribution, and (b) sketch its histogram. (See Examples 1–3.)

1. The number of accidents at a certain intersection in a metropolitan area were counted each day for 7 days with the following results.

Number of Accidents	*Frequency*
0	2
1	3
2	1
3	0
4	1

2. A teacher polled a finite mathematics class each semester for 10 semesters to see how many students were business majors. The results are given in the table.

Number of Business Majors	*Frequency*
13	1
14	0
15	3
16	3
17	2
18	1

3. At a training program for police officers, each member of a class of 25 took 6 shots at a target. The numbers of bullseyes shot are shown in the table.

Number of Bullseyes	*Frequency*
0	0
1	1
2	0
3	4
4	10
5	8
6	2
	Total: 25

4. Five people are given a pain reliever. After a certain time period, the number who experience relief is noted. The experiment is repeated 20 times with the results shown in the table.

Number Who Experience Relief	*Frequency*
0	3
1	5
2	6
3	3
4	2
5	1
	Total: 20

For each of the experiments below, let x represent a random variable, and use your knowledge of probability to prepare a probability distribution.

5. The numbers 1 to 5 are written on cards, placed in a basket, mixed up, and then 2 cards are drawn. The number of even numbers are counted.

6. A bowl contains 5 yellow, 8 orange, and 3 white jelly beans. Two jelly beans are drawn at random and the number of white jelly beans is counted.

7. Two dice are rolled, and the total number of points is recorded.

8. Three cards are drawn from a deck. The number of aces is counted.

9. Two balls are drawn from a bag in which there are 4 white balls and 2 black balls. The number of black balls is counted.

10. Five cards are drawn from a deck. The number of black threes is counted.

Draw a histogram for each of the following, and shade the region that gives the indicated probability. (See Example 2.)

11. Exercise 7; $P(x \geq 11)$

12. Exercise 8; P(at least one ace)

13. Exercise 9; P(at least one black ball)

14. Exercise 10; $P(x = 1 \text{ or } x = 2)$

15. Exercise 5; $P(1 \leq x \leq 2)$

16. Exercise 10; $P(0 \leq x \leq 1)$

Find the expected value for each random variable. (See Example 4.)

17.

x	5	6	7	8
$P(x)$	.3	.1	.4	.2

18.

y	10	11	12	13	14
$P(y)$	.1	.05	.15	.4	.3

19.

z	22	23	24	25	26
$P(z)$	.15	.23	.34	.20	.08

20.

x	0	1	2	3	4
$P(x)$	.31	.35	.20	.11	.03

In Exercises 21–22, **(a)** *give a probability distribution,* **(b)** *sketch its histogram, and* **(c)** *find the expected value.*

21. Management According to officials of Mars, the makers of M & M Plain Chocolate Candies, 20% of the candies in each bag are red.* 4 candies are selected from a bag and the number of red candies is recorded.

22. Social Science In 1992, the Big 10 collegiate sports conference moved to have women compose at least 40% of its athletes within five years.† Suppose they exactly achieved the 40% figure, and that 5 athletes are picked at random from Big 10 universities. The number of women is recorded.

23. Refer to Example 6. Suppose one day Mary brings a two-headed coin and uses it to toss for the coffee. Since Mary tosses, Donna calls.
(a) Is this still a fair game?
(b) What is Donna's expected gain if she calls heads?
(c) What is it if she calls tails?

Find the expected values for the random variables x having the probability functions graphed below.

24.

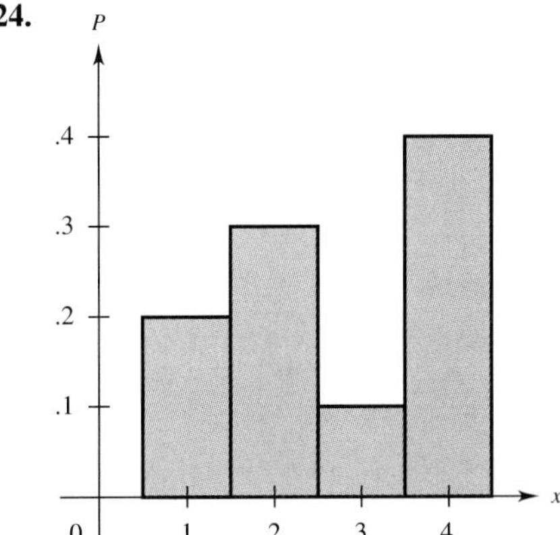

25.

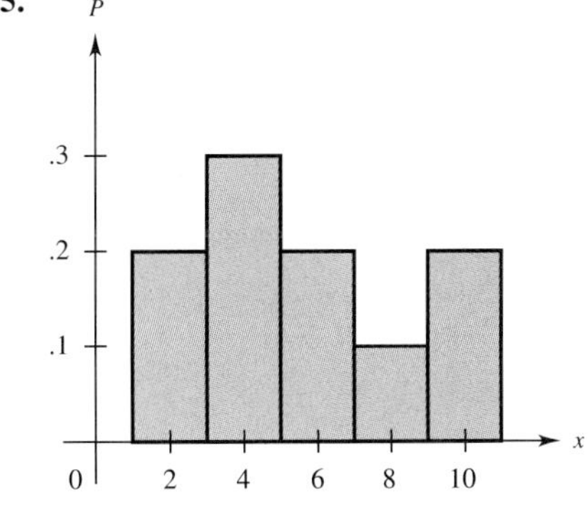

NCTM News Bulletin, Feb. 1995, p. 5.

†*Chicago Tribune*, April 28, 1993, p. 19.

26.

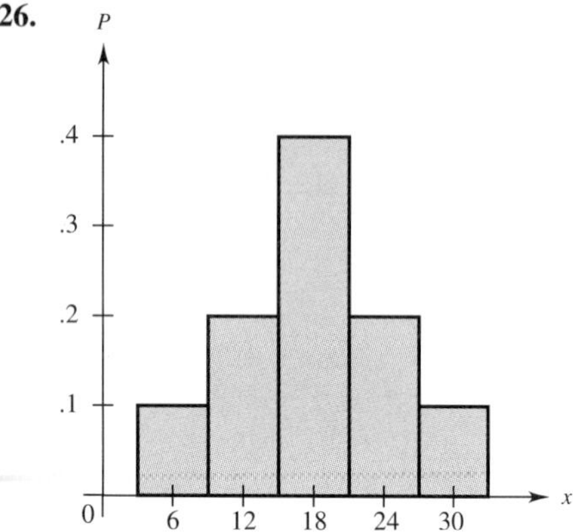

27.

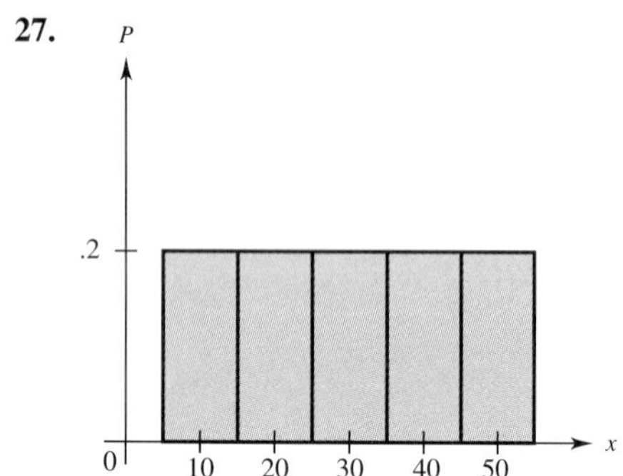

28. A raffle offers a first prize of \$100, and two second prizes of \$40 each. One ticket costs \$1, and 500 tickets are sold. Find the expected winnings for a person who buys 1 ticket. (See Example 5.)

29. A raffle offers a first prize of \$1000, two second prizes of \$300 each, and twenty prizes of \$10 each. If 10,000 tickets are sold at 50¢ each, find the expected winnings for a person buying 1 ticket.

Many of the following exercises use the idea of combinations discussed in Section 10.1.

30. If 3 marbles are drawn from a bag containing 3 yellow and 4 white marbles, what is the expected number of yellow marbles in the sample?

31. **Management** The shipping manager at a company receives a package of one dozen computer monitors, of which, unknown to him, three are broken. He checks four of the monitors at random to see how many are broken in his sample of four. What is the expected number of broken monitors in the sample?

32. **Social Science** According to the National Center for Education Statistics, 79% of the U.S. holders of Bachelor's degrees in Education in 1992–1993 were women.* What is the expected number of women in a random sample of five people holding U.S. Bachelor's degrees in Education?

33. If 2 cards are drawn at one time from a deck of 52 cards, what is the expected number of diamonds?

34. Suppose someone offers to pay you \$5 if you draw 2 diamonds in the game of Exercise 33. He says that you should pay 50¢ for the chance to play. Is this a fair game?

The following chart shows the number of times in a recent 52-week period that each possible number was chosen in any of the four digit positions in the Pick-4 game of the Illinois lottery.

No.	*1st*	*2nd*	*3rd*	*4th*	*Any*
0	38	29	32	34	133
1	32	35	39	40	146
2	35	37	39	39	150
3	46	43	35	42	166
4	33	50	38	40	161
5	31	35	28	37	131
6	46	35	36	32	149
7	41	37	42	33	153
8	26	28	43	35	132
9	35	34	31	31	131

Find each of the following expected values.

35. the expected number in first position

36. the expected number in any position

Find the expected winnings for the following games of chance.

37. A state lottery requires you to choose 1 heart, 1 club, 1 diamond, and 1 spade in that order from the 13 cards in each suit. If all four choices are correct, you win \$5000. It costs \$1 to play.

38. If exactly 3 of the 4 selections in Exercise 37 are correct, the player wins \$200. (It still costs \$1 to play.)

39. In one form of roulette, you bet \$1 on "even." If 1 of the 18 even numbers comes up, you get your dollar back, plus another one. If 1 of the 20 noneven (18 odd, 0, and 00) numbers comes up, you lose.

40. In another form of roulette, there are only 19 noneven numbers (no 00).

41. Numbers is an illegal game in which you bet \$1 on any 3-digit number from 000 to 999. If your number comes up, you get \$500.

42. In Keno, the house has a pot containing 80 balls, each marked with a different number from 1 to 80. You buy a ticket for \$1 and mark 1 of the 80 numbers on it. The house then selects 20 numbers at random. If your number is among the 20, you get \$3.20 (for a net winning of \$2.20).

43. Your friend missed class the day probability distributions were discussed. How would you explain to him what a probability distribution is?

44. How is the relative frequency of a random variable found?

**The New York Times*, Jan. 7, 1996, Education Life, p. 24.

45. The expected value of a random variable is
(a) the most frequent value of the random variable;
(b) the average of all possible values of the random variable;
(c) the sum of the products formed by multiplying each value of the random variable by its probability;
(d) the product of the sum of all values of the random variable and the sum of the probabilities.

46. Management An insurance company has written 100 policies of $10,000, 500 of $5000, and 1000 policies of $1000 on people of age 20. If experience shows that the probability of dying during the 20th year of life is .001, how much can the company expect to pay out during the year the policies were written?

47. Jack must choose at age 40 to inherit $25,000 at age 50 (if he is still alive) or $30,000 at age 55 (if he is still alive). If the probabilities for a person of age 40 to live to be 50 and 55 are .90 and .85, respectively, which choice gives him the larger expected inheritance? (See Example 7.)

48. Management A magazine distributor offers a first prize of $100,000, two second prizes of $40,000 each, and two third prizes of $10,000 each. A total of 2,000,000 entries are received in the contest. Find the expected winnings if you submit 1 entry to the contest. If it would cost you 35¢ in time, paper, and stamps to enter, would it be worth it?

49. Management Levi Strauss and Company* uses expected value to help its salespeople rate their accounts. For each account, a salesperson estimates potential additional volume and the probability of getting it. The product of these gives the expected value of the potential, which is added to the existing volume. The totals are then classified as *A*, *B*, or *C* as follows: below $40,000, class *C*; between $40,000 and $55,000 inclusive, class *B*; above $55,000, class *A*. Complete the chart below for one of its salespeople.

Account Number	*Existing Volume*	*Potential Additional Volume*	*Probability of Additional Volume*	*Expected Value of Potential*	*Existing Volume + Expected Value of Potential*	*Class*
1	$15,000	$10,000	.25	$2,500	$17,500	*C*
2	40,000	0	—	—	40,000	*B*
3	20,000	10,000	.20			
4	50,000	10,000	.10			
5	5,000	50,000	.50			
6	0	100,000	.60			
7	30,000	20,000	.80			

50. Natural Science One of the few methods that can be used in an attempt to cut the severity of a hurricane is to *seed* the storm. In this process, silver iodide crystals are dropped into the storm. Unfortunately, silver iodide crystals sometimes cause the storm to *increase* its speed. Wind speeds may also increase or decrease even with no seeding. The probabilities and amounts of property damage shown in the probability tree are from an article by R. A. Howard, J. E. Matheson, and D. W. North, "The Decision to Seed Hurricanes."*
(a) Find the expected amount of damage under each option, "seed" and "do not seed."
(b) To minimize total expected damage, what option should be chosen?

		Change in wind speed	Property damage (millions of dollars)
Seed	0.038	+32%	335.8
	0.143	+16%	191.1
	0.392	0	100.0
	0.255	−16%	46.7
	0.172	−34%	16.3
Do not seed	0.054	+32%	335.8
	0.206	+16%	191.1
	0.480	0	100.0
	0.206	−16%	46.7
	0.054	−34%	16.3

*This example was supplied by James McDonald, Levi Strauss and Company, San Francisco.

*Figure, "The Decision to Seed Hurricanes," by R. A. Howard from *Science*, Vol. 176, pp. 1191–1202, Copyright 1972 by the American Association for the Advancement of Science and the author.

51. **Social Science** Mr. Statistics (a feature in *Fortune* magazine) investigated the claim of the United States Postal Service that 83% of first class mail in New York City arrives by the next day.* (The figure is 87% nationwide.) He mailed a letter to himself on ten consecutive days; only four were delivered by the next day.

(a) Find the probability distribution for the number of letters delivered by the next day if the overall probability of next-day delivery is 83%.
(b) Using your answer to part (a), find the probability that four or fewer out of 10 letters would be delivered by the next day.
(c) Based on your answer to part (b), do you think it is likely that the 83% figure is accurate? Explain.
(d) Find the number of letters out of 10 that you would expect to be delivered by the next day if the 83% figure is accurate.

*Daniel Seligman, "Ask Mr. Statistics," *Fortune,* July 24, 1995, pp. 170–171.

10.6 DECISION MAKING

John F. Kennedy once remarked he had assumed that as president it would be difficult to choose between distinct, opposite alternatives when a decision needed to be made. Actually, however, he found that such decisions were easy to make; the hard decisions came when he was faced with choices that were not as clear-cut. Most decisions fall in this last category—decisions which must be made under conditions of uncertainty. In the previous section we saw how to use expected values to help make a decision. These ideas are extended in this section, where we consider decision making in the face of uncertainty. Let us begin with an example.

EXAMPLE 1 Freezing temperatures are endangering the orange crop in central California. A farmer can protect his crop by burning smudge pots—the heat from the pots keeps the oranges from freezing. However, burning the pots is expensive; the cost is \$4000. The farmer knows that if he burns smudge pots he will be able to sell his crop for a net profit (after smudge pot costs are deducted) of \$10,000, provided that the freeze does develop and wipes out other orange crops in California. If he does nothing he will either lose \$2000 already invested in the crop if it does freeze, or make a profit of \$9600 if it does not freeze. (If it does not freeze, there will be a large supply of oranges, and thus his profit will be lower than if there was a small supply.) What should the farmer do?

He should begin by carefully defining the problem. First, he must decide on the **states of nature,** the possible alternatives over which he has no control. Here there are two: freezing temperatures, or no freezing temperatures. Next, the farmer should list the things he can control—his actions or **strategies.** He has two possible strategies; to use smudge pots or not. The consequences of each action under each state of nature, called **payoffs,** are summarized in a **payoff matrix,** as shown below. The payoffs in this case are the profits for each possible combination of events.

1 Explain how each of the following payoffs in the matrix were obtained.
(a) −\$2000
(b) \$10,000

Answers:
(a) If it freezes and smudge pots are not used, the farmer's profit is −\$2000 for labor costs.
(b) If it freezes and smudge pots are used, the farmer makes a profit of \$10,000.

		States of Nature	
		Freeze	No Freeze
Strategies of Farmer	Use Smudge Pots	\$10,000	\$5600
	Do Not Use Pots	−\$2000	\$9600

To get the \$5600 entry in the payoff matrix, use the profit if there is no freeze, \$9600, and subtract the \$4000 cost of using the pots. 1

Once the farmer makes the payoff matrix, what then? The farmer might be an optimist (some might call him a gambler); in this case he might assume that the best will happen and go for the biggest number of the matrix ($10,000). For this profit, he must adopt the strategy "use smudge pots."

On the other hand, if the farmer is a pessimist, he would want to minimize the worst thing that could happen. If he uses smudge pots, the worst thing that could happen to him would be profit of $5600, which will result if there is no freeze. If he does not use smudge pots, he might face a loss of $2000. To minimize the worst, he once again should adopt the strategy "use smudge pots."

Suppose the farmer decides that he is neither an optimist nor a pessimist, but would like further information before choosing a strategy. For example, he might call the weather forecaster and ask for the probability of a freeze. Suppose the forecaster says that this probability is only .1. What should the farmer do? He should recall the discussion of expected value from the previous section and work out the expected profit for each of his two possible strategies. If the probability of a freeze is .1, then the probability that there is no freeze is .9. This information leads to the following expected values.

2 What should the farmer do if the probability of a freeze is .6? What is his expected profit?

Answer:
Use smudge pots; $8240

If smudge pots are used: $10{,}000(.1) + 5600(.9) = 6040$

If no smudge pots are used: $-2000(.1) + 9600(.9) = 8440$

Here the maximum expected profit, $8440, is obtained if smudge pots are not used. ■ 2

As the example shows, the farmer's beliefs about the probabilities of a freeze affect his choice of strategies.

EXAMPLE 2 A small manufacturer of Christmas cards must decide in February about the type of cards she should emphasize in her fall line. She has three possible strategies: emphasize modern cards, emphasize old-fashioned cards, or a mixture of the two. Her success is dependent on the state of the economy in December. If the economy is strong, she will do well with her modern cards, while in a weak economy people long for the old days and buy old-fashioned cards. In an in-between economy, her mixture of lines would do the best. She first prepares a payoff matrix for all three possibilities. The numbers in the matrix represent her profits in thousands of dollars.

		States of Nature		
		Weak Economy	In-between	Strong Economy
	Modern	40	85	120
Strategies	Old-fashioned	106	46	83
	Mixture	72	90	68

(a) What would an optimist do?

If the manufacturer is an optimist, she should aim for the biggest number on the matrix, 120 (representing $120,000 in profit). Her strategy in this case would be to produce modern cards.

(b) How would a pessimist react?

A pessimistic manufacturer wants to find the best of the worst of all bad things that can happen. If she produces modern cards, the worst that can happen is a profit of $40,000. For old-fashioned cards, the worst is a profit of $46,000. From a mixture, the worst is a profit of $68,000. Her strategy here is to use a mixture.

3 Suppose the manufacturer reads another article which gives the following predictions: 35% chance of a weak economy, 25% chance of an in-between economy, and a 40% chance of a strong economy. What is the best strategy now? What is the expected profit?

Answer:
Modern; $83,250

(c) Suppose the manufacturer reads in a business magazine that leading experts believe there is a 50% chance of a weak economy at Christmas, a 20% chance of an in-between economy, and a 30% chance of a strong economy. How might she use this information?

The manufacturer can now find her expected profit for each possible strategy.

Modern:	$40(.50) + 85(.20) + 120(.30) = 73$
Old-fashioned:	$106(.50) + 46(.20) + 83(.30) = 87.1$
Mixture:	$72(.50) + 90(.20) + 68(.30) = 74.4$

Here the best strategy is old-fashioned cards; the expected profit is 87.1, or $87,100. ■ 3

10.6 EXERCISES

1. **Management** A developer has $100,000 to invest in land. He has a choice of two parcels (at the same price), one on the highway and one on the coast. With both parcels, his ultimate profit depends on whether he faces light opposition from environmental groups or heavy opposition. He estimates that the payoff matrix is as follows (the numbers represent his profit).

	Opposition Light	Heavy
Highway	$70,000	$30,000
Coast	$150,000	−$40,000

What should the developer do if he is
(a) an optimist? **(b)** a pessimist?
(c) Suppose the probability of heavy opposition is .8. What is his best strategy? What is the expected profit?
(d) What is the best strategy if the probability of heavy opposition is only .4?

2. Hillsdale College has sold out all tickets for a jazz concert to be held in the stadium. If it rains, the show will have to be moved to the gym, which has a much smaller seating capacity. The dean must decide in advance whether to set up the seats and the stage in the gym or in the stadium, or both, just in case. The payoff matrix below shows the net profit in each case.

Strategies		*States of Nature* Rain	No Rain
	Set up in Stadium	−$1550	$1500
	Set up in Gym	$1000	$1000
	Set up Both	$750	$1400

What strategy should the dean choose if she is
(a) an optimist? **(b)** a pessimist?

(c) If the weather forecaster predicts rain with a probability of .6, what strategy should she choose to maximize expected profit? What is the maximum expected profit?

3. **Management** An analyst must decide what fraction of the items produced by a certain machine are defective. He has already decided that there are three possibilities for the fraction of defective items: .01, .10, and .20. He may recommend two courses of action: repair the machine or make no repairs. The payoff matrix below represents the *costs* to the company in each case, in hundreds of dollars.

Strategies		*States of Nature* .01	.10	.20
	Repair	130	130	130
	No Repair	25	200	500

What strategy should the analyst recommend if he is
(a) an optimist? **(b)** a pessimist?
(c) Suppose the analyst is able to estimate probabilities for the three states of nature as follows.

Fraction of Defectives	*Probability*
.01	.70
.10	.20
.20	.10

Which strategy should he recommend? Find the expected cost to the company if this strategy is chosen.

4. **Management** The research department of the Allied Manufacturing Company has developed a new process which it believes will result in an improved product. Management must decide whether or not to go ahead and

market the new product. The new product may be better than the old or it may not be better. If the new product is better and the company decides to market it, sales should increase by $50,000. If it is not better and they replace the old product with the new product on the market, they will lose $25,000 to competitors. If they decide not to market the new product they will lose $40,000 if it is better, and research costs of $10,000 if it is not.

(a) Prepare a payoff matrix.

(b) If management believes the probability that the new product is better to be .4, find the expected profits under each strategy and determine the best action.

5. **Management** A businessman is planning to ship a used machine to his plant in Nigeria. He would like to use it there for the next 4 years. He must decide whether or not to overhaul the machine before sending it. The cost of overhaul is $2600. If the machine fails when in operation in Nigeria, it will cost him $6000 in lost production and repairs. He estimates the probability that it will fail at .3 if he does not overhaul it, and .1 if he does overhaul it. Neglect the possibility that the machine might fail more than once in the 4 years.

   (a) Prepare a payoff matrix.

   (b) What should the businessman do to minimize his expected costs?

6. **Management** A contractor prepares to bid on a job. If all goes well, his bid should be $30,000, which will cover his costs plus his usual profit margin of $4500. However, if a threatened labor strike actually occurs, his bid should be $40,000 to give him the same profit. If there is a strike and he bids $30,000, he will lose $5500. If his bid is too high, he may lose they job entirely, while if it is too low, he may lose money.

   (a) Prepare a payoff matrix.

   (b) If the contractor believes that the probability of a strike is .6, how much should he bid?

7. **Natural Science** A community is considering an anti-smoking campaign.* The city council will choose one of three possible strategies: a campaign for everyone over age 10 in the community, a campaign for youths only, or no campaign at all. The two states of nature are a true cause-effect relationship between smoking and cancer and no cause-effect relationship. The costs to the community (including loss of life and productivity) in each case are as shown at the top of the next column.

	States of Nature	
Strategies	Cause-Effect Relationship	No Cause-Effect Relationship
Campaign for All	$100,000	$800,000
Campaign for Youth	$2,820,000	$20,000
No Campaign	$3,100,100	$0

What action should the city council choose if it is

(a) optimistic? **(b)** pessimistic?

(c) If the Director of Public Health estimates that the probability of a true cause-effect relationship is .8, which strategy should the city council choose?

8. **Management** An investor has $20,000 to invest in stocks. She has two possible strategies: buy conservative blue-chip stocks or buy highly speculative stocks. There are two states of nature: the market goes up or the market goes down. The following payoff matrix shows the net amounts she will have under the various circumstances.

	Market Up	Market Down
Buy Blue-Chip	$25,000	$18,000
Buy Speculative	$30,000	$11,000

What should the investor do if she is

(a) an optimist? **(b)** a pessimist?

(c) Suppose there is a .7 probability of the market going up. What is the best strategy? What is the expected profit?

(d) What is the best strategy if the probability of a market rise is .2?

Sometimes the numbers (or payoffs) in a payoff matrix do not represent money (profits or costs, for example), but utility. A **utility** *is a number that measures the satisfaction (or lack of it) that results from a certain action. The numbers must be assigned by each individual, depending on how he or she feels about a situation. For example, one person might assign a utility of +20 for a week's vacation in San Francisco, with −6 being assigned if the vacation were moved to Sacramento. Work the following problems in the same way as those above.*

9. **Social Science** A politician must plan her reelection strategy. She can emphasize jobs or she can emphasize the environment. The voters can be concerned about jobs or about the environment. A payoff matrix showing the utility of each possible outcome is shown below.

		Voters	
		Jobs	Environment
Candidate	Jobs	+25	−10
	Environment	−15	+30

The political analysts feel that there is a .35 chance that the voters will emphasize jobs. What strategy should the candidate adopt? What is its expected utility?

*This problem is based on an article by B. G. Greenberg in the September 1969 issue of the *Journal of the American Statistical Association*.

10. In an accounting class, the instructor permits the students to bring a calculator or a reference book (but not both) to an examination. The examination itself can emphasize either problems or definitions. In trying to decide which aid to take to an examination, a student first decides on the utilities shown in the following payoff matrix.

		Exam Emphasizes	
		Numbers	Definitions
Student Chooses	Calculator	+50	0
	Book	+10	+40

(a) What strategy should the student choose if the probability that the examination will emphasize numbers is .6? What is the expected utility in this case?

(b) Suppose the probability that the examination emphasizes numbers is .4. What strategy should be chosen by the student?

CHAPTER 10 SUMMARY

Key Terms and Symbols

10.1 $n!$ n factorial
multiplication principle
permutations
combinations

10.3 Bernoulli trials (processes)
binomial experiment

10.4 stochastic processes
Markov chain
state
transition diagram
transition matrix
probability vector
equilibrium vector (fixed vector)
regular transition matrix
regular Markov chain

10.5 random variable
frequency distribution
relative frequency
probability distribution
probability function (probability distribution function)
histogram
weighted average
expected value
fair game

10.6 states of nature
strategies
payoffs
payoff matrix

Key Concepts

Multiplication Principle: If there are m_1 ways to make a first choice, m_2 ways to make a second choice, and so on, where none of the choices depend on any of the others, then there are $m_1 m_2 \cdots m_n$ different ways to make the entire sequence of choices.

The number of **permutations** of n elements taken r at a time is ${}_nP_r = \dfrac{n!}{(n-r)!}$.

The number of **combinations** of n elements taken r at a time is

$${}_nC_r = \binom{n}{r} = \frac{n!}{(n-r)!r!}.$$

Binomial experiments have the following characteristics: The same experiment is repeated several times. There are only *two* outcomes, labeled success and failure. The trials are independent so that the probability of success is the same for each trial. If the probability of success in a single trial is p, then the probability of x successes in n trials is

$$\binom{n}{x}p^x(1-p)^{n-x}.$$

Markov Chains: A **transition matrix** must be square, with all entries between 0 and 1 inclusive, and the sum of the entries in any row must be 1. A Markov chain is *regular* if some power of its transition matrix P contains all positive entries. The long-range probabilities for a regular Markov chain are given by the **equilibrium** or **fixed vector** V, where for any initial probability vector v, the products vP^n approach V as n gets larger and larger, and $VP = V$. To find V, solve the system of equations formed by $VP = V$ and the fact that the sum of the entries of V is 1.

Expected Value of a Probability Distribution: For a random variable x with values $x_1, x_2, \ldots, x_n$ and probabilities $p_1, p_2, \ldots, p_n$, respectively, the expected value is

$$E(x) = x_1p_1 + x_2p_2 + \cdots + x_np_n.$$

Decision Making: A **payoff matrix** which includes all available strategies and states of nature is used in decision making to define the problem and the possible solutions. The expected value of each strategy can help to determine the best course of action.

Chapter 10 Review Exercises

1. In how many ways can 5 shuttle vans line up at the airport?
2. How many variations in first-, second-, and third-place finishes are possible in a 100-yard dash with 7 runners?
3. In how many ways can a sample of 3 pears be taken from a basket containing a dozen pears?
4. If 2 of the pears in Exercise 3 are spoiled, in how many ways can the sample of 3 include the following?
   (a) 1 spoiled pear **(b)** No spoiled pears
   (c) At most 1 spoiled pear
5. In how many ways can 3 pictures, selected from a group of 6 pictures, be arranged in a row on a wall?
6. In how many ways can the 6 pictures in Exercise 5 be arranged in a row, if a certain one must be first?
7. In how many ways can the 6 pictures in Exercise 5 be arranged if 3 are landscapes and 3 are puppies, and if
   (a) like types must be kept together?
   (b) landscapes and puppies are alternated?
8. A representative is to be selected from each of 3 departments in a large company. There are 7 people in the first department, 5 in the second department, and 8 in the third department.
   (a) How many different groups of 3 representatives are possible?
   (b) How many groups are possible, if any number (at least 1) up to 3 representatives can form a group?
9. Explain under what circumstances a permutation should be used in a probability problem, and under what circumstances a combination should be used.
10. Discuss under what circumstances the binomial probability formula should be used in a probability problem.

Suppose a family plans to have 4 children, and the probability that a particular child is a boy is 1/2. Find the probability that the family will have the following.

11. Exactly 2 boys
12. All girls
13. At least 2 boys
14. No more than 3 girls

Suppose 2 cards are drawn without replacement from an ordinary deck of 52 cards. Find the probabilities of the following results.

15. Both cards are black.
16. Both cards are hearts.
17. Exactly 1 is a face card.
18. At most 1 is an ace.

A collection of golf balls contains 4 yellow, 2 blue, and 6 white balls. A golfer selects 3 balls at random. Find the probability that the selection includes the following.

19. All white balls
20. All yellow balls
21. At least 1 blue ball
22. 1 ball of each color

Decide whether each of the following is a regular transition matrix.

23. $\begin{bmatrix} 0 & 1 \\ .8 & .2 \end{bmatrix}$
24. $\begin{bmatrix} -.1 & .4 \\ .3 & .7 \end{bmatrix}$
25. $\begin{bmatrix} .3 & 0 & .7 \\ .5 & .1 & .4 \\ 1 & 0 & 0 \end{bmatrix}$
26. $\begin{bmatrix} .2 & .3 & .5 \\ .4 & .4 & .2 \\ .5 & .1 & .4 \end{bmatrix}$

Management *A bottle capping machine has an error rate of .01. A random sample of 20 bottles is selected. Find the following probabilities.*

27. Exactly 4 bottles are improperly capped.
28. No more than 3 bottles are improperly capped.
29. At least 1 bottle is improperly capped.

30. Management A credit card company classifies its customers in three groups: nonusers in a given month, light users, and heavy users. The transition matrix for these states is

	Nonuser	Light	Heavy
Nonuser	.8	.15	.05
Light	.25	.55	.2
Heavy	.04	.21	.75

Suppose the initial distribution for the three states is [.4 .4 .2]. Find the distribution after

(a) 1 month; **(b)** 2 months.

(c) What is the long-range prediction for the distribution of users?

31. Management Savmor Investments starts a heavy advertising campaign. At the start of the campaign, Savmor sells 35% of all mutual funds sold in the area, while 65% are sold by the Highrate Company. The campaign produces the following transition matrix.

		After Campaign	
		Savmor	Highrate
Before Campaign	Savmor	.8	.2
	Highrate	.4	.6

(a) Find the market share for each company after the campaign.

(b) Find the share of the market for each company after three such campaigns.

(c) Predict the long-range market share for Savmor.

In Exercises 32–36, (a) give a probability distribution, and (b) sketch its histogram.

32.

x	6	7	8	9	10
Frequency	3	7	9	3	2

33.

x	1	2	3	4	5	6
Frequency	1	0	2	5	8	4

34. A coin is tossed 3 times and the number of heads is recorded.

35. A pair of dice are rolled and the sum of the results for each roll is recorded.

36. Natural Science Patients in groups of 5 are given a new cancer treatment. The experiment is repeated 10 times with the following results.

Number with Significant Improvement	*Frequency*
0	1
1	1
2	2
3	3
4	3
5	0
	Total: 10

In Exercises 37 and 38, give the probability that corresponds to the shaded region of each histogram.

37.

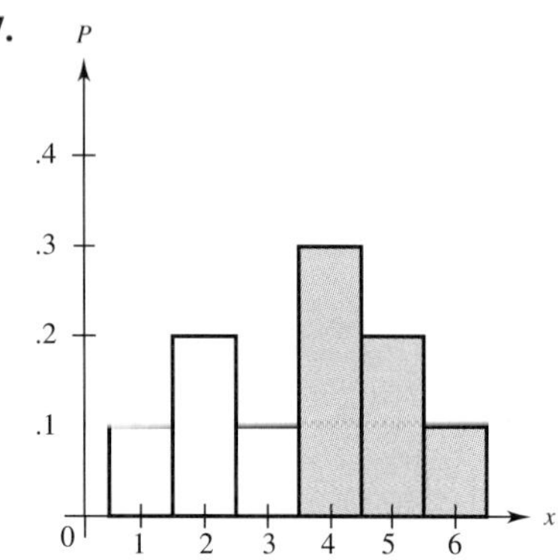

38.

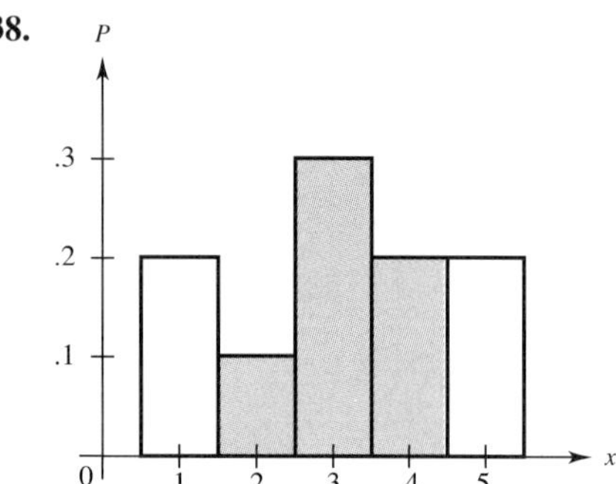

Solve the following problems.

39. Suppose someone offers to pay you $100 if you draw 3 cards from a standard deck of 52 cards and all the cards are clubs. What should you pay for the chance to win if it is a fair game?

40. You pay $6 to play in a game where you will roll a die, with payoffs as follows: $8 for a 6, $7 for a 5, and $4 for any other results. What are your expected winnings? Is the game fair?

41. A lottery has a first prize of $5000, two second prizes of $1000 each, and two $100 third prizes. A total of 10,000 tickets is sold, at $1 each. Find the expected winnings of a person buying 1 ticket.

42. Find the expected number of girls in a family of 5 children.

43. Three cards are drawn from a standard deck of 52 cards.

(a) What is the expected number of aces?

(b) What is the expected number of clubs?

44. Management In labor-management relations, both labor and management can adopt either a friendly or a hostile attitude. The results are shown in the following payoff matrix. The numbers give the wage gains made by an average worker.

		Management	
		Friendly	Hostile
Labor	Friendly	\$600	\$800
	Hostile	\$400	\$950

(a) Suppose the chief negotiator for labor is an optimist. What strategy should he choose?
(b) What strategy should he choose if he is a pessimist?
(c) The chief negotiator for labor feels that there is a 70% chance that the company will be hostile. What strategy should he adopt? What is the expected payoff?
(d) Just before negotiations begin, a new management is installed in the company. There is only a 40% chance that the new management will be hostile. What strategy should be adopted by labor?

45. **Social Science** A candidate for city council can come out in favor of a new factory, be opposed to it, or waffle on the issue. The change in votes for the candidate depends on what her opponent does, with payoffs as shown.

		Opponent		
		Favors	Waffles	Opposes
Candidate	Favors	0	−1000	−4000
	Waffles	1000	0	−500
	Opposes	5000	2000	0

(a) What should the candidate do if she is an optimist?
(b) What should she do if she is a pessimist?
(c) Suppose the candidate's campaign manager feels there is a 40% chance that the opponent will favor the plant, and a 35% chance that he will waffle. What strategy should the candidate adopt? What is the expected change in the number of votes?
(d) The opponent conducts a new poll which shows strong opposition to the new factory. This changes the probability he will favor the factory to 0 and the probability he will waffle to .7. What strategy should our candidate adopt? What is the expected change in the number of votes now?

*Exercises 46 and 47 are taken from actuarial examinations given by the Society of Actuaries.**

46. **Management** A company is considering the introduction of a new product that is believed to have probability .5 of being successful and probability .5 of being unsuccessful. Successful products pass quality control 80% of the time. Unsuccessful products pass quality control 25% of the time. If the product is successful, the net profit to the company will be \$40 million; if unsuccessful, the net loss will be \$15 million. Determine the expected net profit if the product passes quality control.
(a) \$23 million (b) \$24 million
(c) \$25 million (d) \$26 million
(e) \$27 million

47. **Management** A merchant buys boxes of fruit from a grower and sells them. Each box of fruit is either Good or Bad. A Good box contains 80% excellent fruit and will earn \$200 profit on the retail market. A Bad box contains 30% excellent fruit and will produce a loss of \$1000. The a priori probability of receiving a Good box of fruit is .9. Before the merchant decides to put the box on the market, he can sample one piece of fruit to test whether it is excellent. Based on that sample, he has the option of rejecting the box without paying for it. Determine the expected value of the right to sample. (*Hint:* If the merchant samples the fruit, what are the probabilities of accepting a Good box, accepting a Bad box, and not accepting the box? What are these probabilities if he does not sample the fruit?)
(a) 0 (b) \$16 (c) \$34
(d) \$72 (e) \$80

48. **Management** The March 1982 issue of *Mathematics Teacher* included "Overbooking Airline Flights," an article by Joe Dan Austin. In this article, Austin developed a model for the expected income for an airline flight. With appropriate assumptions, the probability that exactly x of n people with reservations show up at the airport to buy a ticket is given by the binomial probability formula. Assume the following: 6 reservations have been accepted for 3 seats, $p = .6$ is the probability that a person with a reservation will show up, a ticket costs \$100, and the airline must pay \$100 to anyone with a reservation who does not get a ticket. Complete the following table.

Number Who Show Up (x)	0	1	2	3	4	5	6
Airline's Income							
P(x)							

(a) Use the table to find $E(I)$, the expected airline income from the 3 seats.
(b) Find $E(I)$ for $n = 3$, $n = 4$, and $n = 5$. Compare these answers with $E(I)$ for $n = 6$. For these values of n, how many reservations should the airline book for the 3 seats in order to maximize the expected revenue?

*Problem from "Course 130 Examination, Operations Research," of the *Education and Examination Committee of the Society of Actuaries*. Reprinted by permission of the Society of Actuaries.

CASE 10

Optimal Inventory for a Service Truck

For many different items it is difficult or impossible to take the item to a central repair facility when service is required. Washing machines, large television sets, office copiers, and computers are only a few examples of such items. Service for items of this type is commonly performed by sending a repair person to the item, with the person driving to the location in a truck containing various parts that might be required in repairing the item. Ideally, the truck should contain all the parts that might be required. However, most parts would be needed only infrequently, so that inventory costs for the parts would be high.

An optimum policy for deciding on which parts to stock on a truck would require that the probability of not being able to repair an item without a trip back to the warehouse for needed parts be as low as possible, consistent with minimum inventory costs. An analysis similar to the one below was developed at the Xerox Corporation.*

To set up a mathematical model for deciding on the optimum truck-stocking policy, let us assume that a broken machine might require one of 5 different parts (we could assume any number of different parts—we use 5 to simplify the notation). Suppose also that the probability that a particular machine requires part 1 is p_1; that it requires part 2 is p_2; and so on. Assume also that failures of different part types are independent, and that at most one part of each type is used on a given job.

Suppose that, on the average, a repair person makes N service calls per time period. If the repair person is unable to make a repair because at least one of the parts is unavailable, there is a penalty cost, L, corresponding to wasted time for the repair person, an extra trip to the parts depot, customer unhappiness, and so on. For each of the parts carried on the truck, an average inventory cost is incurred. Let H_i be the average inventory cost for part i, where $1 \le i \le 5$.

Let M_1 represent a policy of carrying only part 1 on the repair truck, M_{24} represent a policy of carrying only parts 2 and 4, with M_{12345} and M_0 representing policies of carrying all parts and no parts, respectively.

For policy M_{35}, carrying parts 3 and 5 only, the expected cost per time period per repair person, written $C(M_{35})$, is

$$C(M_{35}) = (H_3 + H_5) + NL[1 - (1 - p_1)(1 - p_2)(1 - p_4)].$$

(The expression in brackets represents the probability of needing at least one of the parts not carried, 1, 2, or 4 here.) As further examples,

$$C(M_{125}) = (H_1 + H_2 + H_5) + NL[1 - (1 - p_3)(1 - p_4)],$$

while

$$\begin{aligned} C(M_{12345}) &= (H_1 + H_2 + H_3 + H_4 + H_5) + NL[1 - 1] \\ &= H_1 + H_2 + H_3 + H_4 + H_5, \end{aligned}$$

and

$$C(M_0) = NL[1 - (1 - p_1)(1 - p_2)(1 - p_3)(1 - p_4)(1 - p_5)].$$

To find the best policy, evaluate $C(M_0)$, $C(M_1)$, . . . , $C(M_{12345})$, and choose the smallest result. (A general solution method is in the *Management Science* paper.)

EXAMPLE Suppose that for a particular item, only 3 possible parts might need to be replaced. By studying past records of failures of the item, and finding necessary inventory costs, suppose that the following values have been found.

p_1	p_2	p_3
.09	.24	.17

H_1	H_2	H_3
\$15	\$40	\$9

Suppose $N = 3$ and L is \$54. Then, as an example,

$$\begin{aligned} C(M_1) &= H_1 + NL[1 - (1 - p_2)(1 - p_3)] \\ &= 15 + 3(54)[1 - (1 - .24)(1 - .17)] \\ &= 15 + 3(54)[1 - (.76)(.83)] \\ &\approx 15 + 59.81 \\ &= 74.81. \end{aligned}$$

*Reprinted by permission of Stephen Smith, John Chambers, and Eli Shlifer. "Optimal Inventories Based on Job Completion Rate for Repairs Requiring Multiple Items." *Management Science*, Vol. 26, No. 8, August 1980, copyright © 1980 by The Institute of Management Sciences.

Thus, if policy M_1 is followed (carrying only part 1 on the truck), the expected cost per repair person per time period is \$74.81. Also,

$$\begin{aligned} C(M_{23}) &= H_2 + H_3 + NL[1 - (1 - p_1)] \\ &= 40 + 9 + 3(54)(.09) \\ &= 63.58, \end{aligned}$$

so that M_{23} is a better policy than M_1. By finding the expected values for all other possible policies (see the exercises), the optimum policy may be chosen. ■

EXERCISES

1. Refer to the example and find each of the following.
(a) $C(M_0)$ **(b)** $C(M_2)$ **(c)** $C(M_3)$
(d) $C(M_{12})$ **(e)** $C(M_{13})$ **(f)** $C(M_{123})$

2. Which policy leads to the lowest expected cost?

3. In the example, $p_1 + p_2 + p_3 = .09 + .24 + .17 = .50$. Why is it not necessary that the probabilities add up to 1?

4. Suppose an item to be repaired might need one of n different parts. How many different policies would then need to be evaluated?

CHAPTER 11 Introduction to Statistics

Statistics is a branch of mathematics that deals with the collection and summarization of data. Methods of statistical analysis make it possible to draw conclusions about a population based on data from a sample of the population. Statistical models have become increasingly useful in manufacturing, government, agriculture, medicine, and the social sciences, and in all types of research. An Indianapolis race-car team is using statistics to improve performance by gathering data on each run around the track. They sample data 300 times a second, and use computers to process the data. In this chapter we give a brief introduction to some of the key topics from statistical theory.

In the previous chapter, we saw that a frequency distribution can be transformed into a probability distribution by using the relative frequency of each value of the random variable as its probability. Sometimes it is convenient to work directly with a frequency distribution.

11.1 FREQUENCY DISTRIBUTIONS; MEASURES OF CENTRAL TENDENCY

Often, a researcher wishes to learn something about a characteristic of a population, but because the population is very large or mobile, it is not possible to examine all of its elements. Instead, a limited sample drawn from the population is studied to determine the characteristics of the population. For example, a book by Frances Cerra Whittelsey, *Why Women Pay More,* published by Ralph Nader's Center for Responsive Law, documents how women are charged more than men for the same service. In the studies cited in this book, the population is U.S. women. The studies involved data collected from a sample of U.S. women.

For these inferences to be correct, the sample chosen must be a **random sample.** Random samples are representative of the population because they are chosen so that every element of the population is equally likely to be selected. For example, a hand dealt from a well-shuffled deck of cards is a random sample.

After a sample has been chosen and all data of interest are collected, the data must be organized so that conclusions may be more easily drawn. One method of organization is to group the data into intervals; equal intervals are usually chosen.

EXAMPLE 1 A survey asked 30 business executives how many college units in management each had. The results are shown below. Group the data into intervals and find the frequency of each interval.

3	25	22	16	0	9	14	8	34	21
15	12	9	3	8	15	20	12	28	19
17	16	23	19	12	14	29	13	24	18

The highest number in the list is 34 and the lowest is 0; one convenient way to group the data is in intervals of size 5, starting with 0–4 and ending with 30–34. This gives an interval for each number in the list and results in seven equal intervals of a convenient size. Too many intervals of smaller size would not simplify the data enough, while too few intervals of larger size would conceal information that the data might provide. A rule of thumb is to use from six to fifteen intervals.

First tally the number of college units falling into each interval. Then total the tallies in each interval, as in the table below. This table is an example of a **grouped frequency distribution.**

College Units	*Tally*	*Frequency*
0–4	III	3
5–9	IIII	4
10–14	~~IIII~~ I	6
15–19	~~IIII~~ III	8
20–24	~~IIII~~	5
25–29	III	3
30–34	I	1
		Total: 30

■ 1

1 An accounting firm selected 24 complex tax returns prepared by a certain tax preparer. The number of errors per return were as follows.

8	12	0	6	10	8	0	14
8	12	14	16	4	14	7	11
9	12	7	15	11	21	22	19

Prepare a grouped frequency distribution for this data. Use intervals 0–4, 5–9, and so on.

Answer:

Interval	*Frequency*
0–4	3
5–9	7
10–14	9
15–19	3
20–24	2
	Total: 24

The frequency distribution in Example 1 shows information about the data that might not have been noticed before. For example, the interval with the largest number of units is 15–19, and 19 executives (more than half) had between 9 and 25 units. Also, the frequency in each interval increases rather evenly (up to 8) and then decreases at about the same pace. However, some information has been lost; for example, we no longer know how many executives had 12 units.

The information in a grouped frequency distribution can be displayed in a histogram similar to the histograms for probability distributions in the previous chapter. The intervals determine the widths of the bars; if equal intervals are used, all the bars have the same width. The heights of the bars are determined by the frequencies.

A **frequency polygon** is another form of graph that illustrates a grouped frequency distribution. The polygon is formed by joining consecutive midpoints of the tops of the histogram bars with straight line segments. Sometimes the midpoints of the first and last bars are joined to endpoints on the horizontal axis where the next midpoint would appear. (See Figure 11.1 on the next page.)

2 Make a histogram and a frequency polygon for the distribution found in Side Problem 1 above.

Answer:

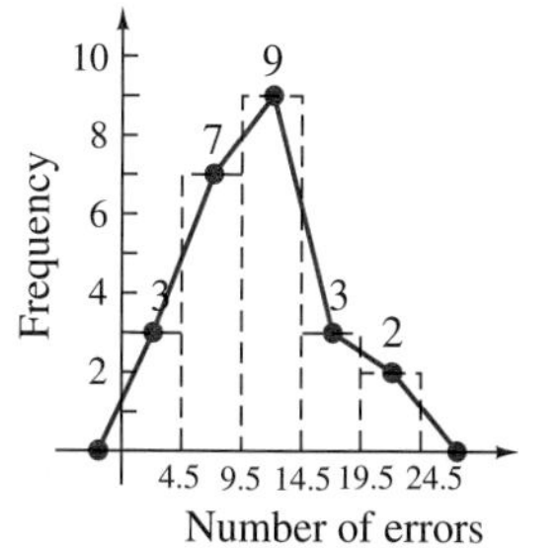

EXAMPLE 2 A grouped frequency distribution of college units was found in Example 1. Draw a histogram and a frequency polygon for this distribution.

First, draw a histogram, shown in black in Figure 11.1. To get a frequency polygon, connect consecutive midpoints of the tops of the bars. The frequency polygon is shown in color. ■ 2

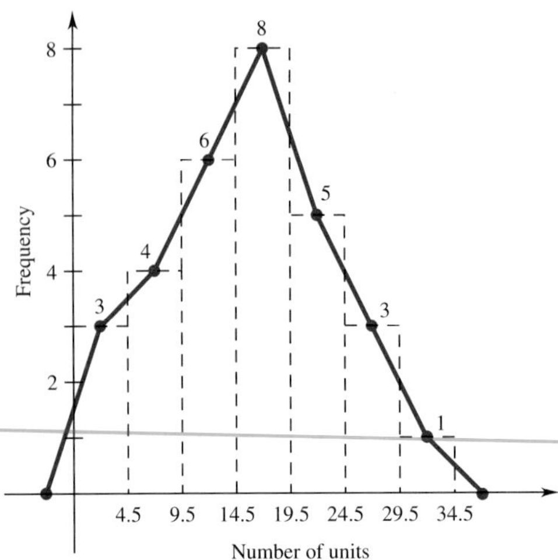

FIGURE 11.1

TECHNOLOGY TIP As noted in Section 10.5, most graphing calculators can display histograms. Many will also display frequency polygons (which are usually labeled LINE or xyLINE in calculator menus). When dealing with grouped frequency distributions, however, certain adjustments must be made on a calculator.

1. *A calculator list of outcomes must consist of single numbers, not intervals.* The table in Example 1, for example, cannot be entered as shown. To convert the first column of the table for calculator use, choose one number in each interval, say 2 in the interval 0–4, 7 in the interval 5–9, 12 in the interval 10–14, etc. Then use 2, 7, 12, . . . as the list of outcomes to be entered into the calculator. The frequency list (the last column of the table) remains the same.
2. *The histogram bar width affects the shape of the graph.* If you use a bar width of 4 in Example 1, the calculator may produce a histogram with gaps in it. To avoid this use the interval $0 \leq x < 5$ in place of $0 \leq x \leq 4$, and similarly for the other intervals and make 5 the bar width.

Following this procedure, we obtain the calculator-generated histogram and frequency polygon in Figure 11.2 for the data from Example 1. Note that the width of each histogram bar is 5. Some calculators cannot display both the histogram and the frequency polygon on the same screen as is done here. ✔

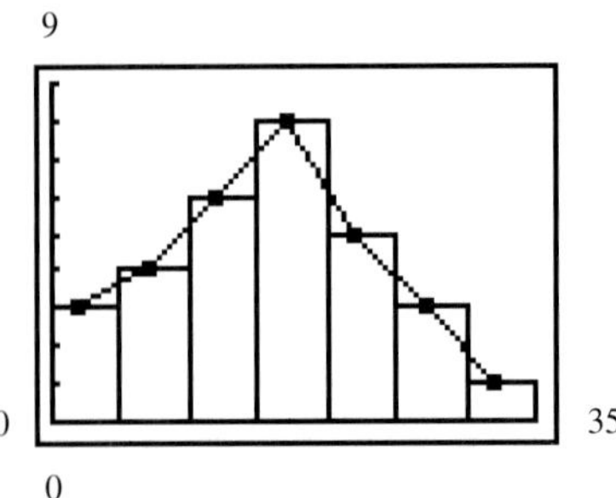

FIGURE 11.2

NOTE The remainder of this section deals with topics that are generally referred to as "measures of central tendency." Computing these various measures is greatly simplified by the statistical capabilities of most scientific and graphing calculators. Calculators vary considerably in how data is entered, so read your instruction manual to learn how to enter lists of data and the corresponding frequencies. On scientific calculators with statistical capabilities, there are keys for finding most of the measures of central tendency discussed below. On graphing calculators, most or all of these measures can be obtained with a single keystroke (look for *one-variable statistics,* which is often labeled 1-VAR, in the STAT menu or its CALC submenu). ◆

MEAN The average value of a probability distribution is the expected value of the distribution. Three measures of central tendency, or "averages," are used with frequency distributions: the mean, the median, and the mode. The most important of these is the mean, which is similar to the expected value of a probability distribution. The **mean** (the arithmetic average) of a set of numbers is the sum of the numbers, divided by the total number of numbers. We write the sum of n numbers $x_1, x_2, x_3, \ldots, x_n$ in a compact way using **summation notation,** also called **sigma notation.** With the Greek letter Σ (sigma), the sum

$$x_1 + x_2 + x_3 + \cdots + x_n$$

is written

$$x_1 + x_2 + x_3 + \cdots + x_n = \sum_{i=1}^{n} x_i.$$

In statistics, $\Sigma_{i=1}^{n} x_i$ is often abbreviated as just Σx. The symbol $\bar{x}$ (read "x-bar") is used to represent the mean of a sample.

MEAN

The mean of the n numbers $x_1, x_2, x_3, \ldots, x_n$ is

$$\bar{x} = \frac{x_1 + x_2 + \cdots + x_n}{n} = \frac{\Sigma x}{n}.$$

EXAMPLE 3 The number of bankruptcy petitions (in thousands) filed in the United States in the fiscal years 1988–1993 are given in the table on the next page.* Find the mean number of bankruptcy petitions filed annually during this period.

*Administrative Offices of the U.S. Courts, *Annual Report of the Director.*

Year	Petitions Filed
1988	594
1989	643
1990	725
1991	880
1992	973
1993	919

3 Find the mean of the following list of sales at a boutique.

\$25.12	\$42.58
\$76.19	\$32
\$81.11	\$26.41
\$19.76	\$59.32
\$71.18	\$21.03

Answer:
\$45.47

Let $x_1 = 594$, $x_2 = 643$, and so on. Here, $n = 6$, since there are 6 numbers in the list.

$$\bar{x} = \frac{594 + 643 + 725 + 880 + 973 + 919}{6} = 789$$

The mean number of bankruptcy petitions filed during the given years is 789,000. ■ 3

TECHNOLOGY TIP The mean of the six numbers in Example 3 is easily found by using the $\bar{x}$ key on a scientific calculator or the one-variable statistics key on a graphing calculator. A graphing calculator will also display additional information, which will be discussed in the next section. ✔

The mean of data that have been arranged in a frequency distribution is found in a similar way. For example, suppose the following data are collected.

Value	Frequency
84	2
87	4
88	7
93	4
99	3
	Total: 20

The value 84 appears twice, 87 four times, and so on. To find the mean, first add 84 two times, 87 four times, and so on; or get the same result faster by multiplying 84 by 2, 87 by 4, and so on, and then by adding the results. Dividing the sum by 20, the total of the frequencies, gives the mean.

$$\bar{x} = \frac{(84 \cdot 2) + (87 \cdot 4) + (88 \cdot 7) + (93 \cdot 4) + (99 \cdot 3)}{20}$$

$$= \frac{168 + 348 + 616 + 372 + 297}{20}$$

$$= \frac{1801}{20}$$

$$\bar{x} = 90.05$$

Verify that your calculator gives the same result.

EXAMPLE 4 Find the mean for the data shown in the following frequency distribution.

Value	*Frequency*	*Value × Frequency*
30	6	30 · 6 = 180
32	9	32 · 9 = 288
33	7	33 · 7 = 231
37	12	37 · 12 = 444
42	6	42 · 6 = 252
	Total: 40	**Total: 1395**

4 Find $\bar{x}$ for the following frequency distribution.

Value	*Frequency*
7	2
9	3
11	6
13	4
15	1
17	4

Answer:
$\bar{x} = 12.1$

A new column, "Value × Frequency," has been added to the frequency distribution. Adding the products from this column gives a total of 1395. The total from the frequency column is 40. The mean is

$$\bar{x} = \frac{1395}{40} = 34.875. \quad \blacksquare \quad \boxed{4}$$

NOTE The mean in Example 4 is found in the same way as was the expected value of a probability distribution in the previous chapter. In fact, the words *mean* and *expected value* are often used interchangeably. ◆

The mean of grouped data is found in a similar way. For grouped data, intervals are used rather than single values. To calculate the mean, it is assumed that all these values are located at the midpoint of the interval. The letter x is used to represent the midpoints and f represents the frequencies, as shown in the next example.

EXAMPLE 5 Find the mean for the following grouped frequency distribution.

Interval	*Midpoint, x*	*Frequency, f*	*Product, xf*
40–49	44.5	2	89
50–59	54.5	4	218
60–69	64.5	7	451.5
70–79	74.5	9	670.5
80–89	84.5	5	422.5
90–99	94.5	3	283.5
		Total: 30	Total: 2135

A column for the midpoint of each interval has been added. The numbers in this column are found by adding the endpoints of each interval and dividing by 2. For the interval 40–49, the midpoint is $(40 + 49)/2 = 44.5$. The numbers in the product column on the right are found by multiplying frequencies and corresponding midpoints. Finally, we divide the total of the product column by the total of the frequency column to get

$$\bar{x} = \frac{2135}{30} = 71.2 \text{ (to the nearest tenth).} \quad \blacksquare$$

The formula for the **mean of a grouped frequency distribution** is given below.

5 Find the mean of the following grouped frequency distribution.

Interval	*Frequency*
0–4	6
5–9	4
10–14	7
15–19	3

Answer:
8.75

MEAN OF A GROUPED DISTRIBUTION

The mean of a distribution where x represents the midpoints, f the frequencies, and $n = \Sigma f$, is

$$\bar{x} = \frac{\Sigma(xf)}{n}.$$

CAUTION Note that in the formula above, n is the sum of the frequencies in the entire data set, not the number of intervals. ◆ 5

MEDIAN Asked by a reporter to give the average height of the players on his team the Little League coach lined up his 15 players by increasing height. He picked out the player in the middle and pronounced this player to be of average height. This kind of average, called the **median,** is defined as the middle entry in a set of data arranged in either increasing or decreasing order. If there is an even number of entries, the median is defined to be the mean of the two center entries. The following table shows how to find the median for two sets of data: {8, 7, 4, 3, 1} and {2, 3, 4, 7, 9, 12}.

Odd Number of Entries	*Even Number of Entries*
8	2
7	3
Median = 4	4 } Median = $\frac{4+7}{2} = 5.5$
3	7 }
1	9
	12

NOTE As shown in the table above, when there are an even number of entries, the median is not always equal to one of the data entries. ◆

The procedure for finding the median of a grouped frequency distribution is more complicated. We omit it here because it is more common to find the mean when working with grouped frequency distributions.

EXAMPLE 6 Find the median for the following lists of numbers.

(a) 11, 12, 17, 20, 23, 28, 29

The median is the middle number, in this case 20. (Note that the numbers are already arranged in numerical order.) In this list, three numbers are smaller than 20 and three are larger.

(b) 15, 13, 7, 11, 19, 30, 39, 5, 10

First arrange the numbers in numerical order, from smallest to largest.

5, 7, 10, 11, 13, 15, 19, 30, 39

The middle number can now be determined; the median is 13.

[6] Find the median for each of the following lists of numbers.

(a) 12, 15, 17, 19, 35, 42, 58

(b) 28, 68, 7, 15, 47, 59, 13, 74, 32, 25

Answers:

(a) 19

(b) 30

(c) 47, 59, 32, 81, 74, 153

Write the numbers in numerical order.

32, 47, 59, 74, 81, 153

There are six numbers here; the median is the mean of the two middle numbers, or

$$\text{Median} = \frac{59 + 74}{2} = \frac{133}{2} = 66.5. \quad ■$$

CAUTION Remember, the data must be arranged in numerical order before locating the median. ◆ [6]

TECHNOLOGY TIP Many graphing calculators (including TI-82/83/86, HP-38, Casio 9800/9850) display the median when doing one-variable statistics. You may have to scroll down to a second screen to find it. ✔

In some situations, the median gives a truer representative or typical element of the data than the mean. For example, suppose in an office there are 10 salespersons, 4 secretaries, the sales manager, and Ms. Daly, who owns the business. Their annual salaries are as follows: secretaries, $15,000 each; salespersons, $25,000 each; manager, $35,000; and owner, $200,000. The mean salary is

$$\bar{x} = \frac{(15{,}000)4 + (25{,}000)10 + 35{,}000 + 200{,}000}{16} = \$34{,}062.50.$$

However, since 14 people earn less than $34,062.50 and only 2 earn more, this does not seem very representative. The median salary is found by ranking the salaries by size: $15,000, $15,000, $15,000, $15,000, $25,000, $25,000, . . . , $200,000. There are 16 salaries (an even number) in the list, so the mean of the 8th and 9th entries will give the value of the median. The 8th and 9th entries are both $25,000, so the median is $25,000. In this example, the median is more representative of the distribution than the mean.

MODE Sue's scores on ten class quizzes include one 7, two 8's, six 9's and one 10. She claims that her average grade on quizzes is 9, because most of her scores are 9's. This kind of "average," found by selecting the most frequent entry, is called the **mode.**

[7] Find the mode for each of the following lists of numbers.

(a) 29, 35, 29, 18, 29, 56, 48

(b) 13, 17, 19, 20, 20, 13, 25, 27, 13, 20

(c) 512, 546, 318, 729, 854, 253

Answers:

(a) 29

(b) 13 and 20

(c) No mode

EXAMPLE 7 Find the mode for each list of numbers.

(a) 57, 38, **55**, **55**, 80, 87, 98

The number 55 occurs more often than any other, so it is the mode. It is not necessary to place the numbers in numerical order when looking for the mode.

(b) 182, **185**, 183, **185**, **187**, **187**, 189

Both 185 and 187 occur twice. This list has *two* modes.

(c) 10,708, 11,519, 10,972, 17,546, 13,905, 12,182

No number occurs more than once. This list has no mode. ■ [7]

The mode has the advantages of being easily found and not being influenced by data that are very large or very small compared to the rest of the data. It is often used in samples where the data to be "averaged" are not numerical. The major disadvantage of the mode is that there may be more than one, in case of ties, or there may be no mode at all when all entries occur with the same frequency.

The mean is the most commonly used measure of central tendency. Its advantages are that it is easy to compute, it takes all the data into consideration, and it is reliable—that is, repeated samples are likely to give very similar means. A disadvantage of the mean is that it is influenced by extreme values, as illustrated in the salary example above.

The median can be easy to compute and is influenced very little by extremes. Like the mode, the median can be found in situations where the data are not numerical. A disadvantage of the median is the need to rank the data in order; this can be tedious when the number of items is large.

11.1 EXERCISES

For Exercises 1–4, (a) group the data as indicated; (b) prepare a frequency distribution with columns for intervals and frequencies; (c) construct a histogram; (d) construct a frequency polygon. (See Examples 1 and 2.)

1. Use six intervals, starting with 0–24.

74	133	4	127	20	30
103	27	139	118	138	121
149	132	64	141	130	76
42	50	95	56	65	104
4	140	12	88	119	64

2. Use seven intervals, starting with 30–39.

79	71	78	87	69	50	63	51	60	46
65	65	56	88	94	56	74	63	87	62
84	76	82	67	59	66	57	81	93	93
54	88	55	69	78	63	63	48	89	81
98	42	91	66	60	70	64	70	61	75
82	65	68	39	77	81	67	62	73	49
51	76	94	54	83	71	94	45	73	95
72	66	71	77	48	51	54	57	69	87

3. Use 70–74 as the first interval.

79	84	88	96	102	104	110	108	106	106	
104	99	97	92	94	90	82	74	72	83	
84	92	100	99	101	107	111	102	97	94	92

4. Use 140–149 as the first interval.

174	190	172	182	179	186	171	152	174	185
180	170	160	173	163	177	165	157	149	167
169	182	178	158	182	169	181	173	183	176
170	162	159	147	150	192	179	165	148	188

5. How does a frequency polygon differ from a histogram?

6. Discuss the advantages and disadvantages of the mean as a measure of central tendency.

Find the mean for each list of numbers. Round to the nearest tenth.

7. 8, 10, 16, 21, 25

8. 44, 41, 25, 36, 67, 51

9. 21,900, 22,850, 24,930, 29,710, 28,340, 40,000

10. 38,500, 39,720, 42,183, 21,982, 43,250

11. 9.4, 11.3, 10.5, 7.4, 9.1, 8.4, 9.7, 5.2, 1.1, 4.7

12. 30.1, 42.8, 91.6, 51.2, 88.3, 21.9, 43.7, 51.2

Find the mean for each of the following. Round to the nearest tenth. (See Example 4.)

13.

Value	*Frequency*
3	4
5	2
9	1
12	3

14.

Value	*Frequency*
9	3
12	5
15	1
18	1

15.

Value	*Frequency*
12	4
13	2
15	5
19	3
22	1
23	5

16.

Value	*Frequency*
25	1
26	2
29	5
30	4
32	3
33	5

Find the median for each of the following lists of numbers. (See Example 6.)

17. 12, 18, 32, 51, 58, 92, 106

18. 596, 604, 612, 683, 719

19. 100, 114, 125, 135, 150, 172

20. 1072, 1068, 1093, 1042, 1056, 1005, 1009

21. 28.4, 9.1, 3.4, 27.6, 59.8, 32.1, 47.6, 29.8

22. .6, .4, .9, 1.2, .3, 4.1, 2.2, .4, .7, .1

Find the mode or modes for each of the following lists of numbers. (See Example 7.)

23. 4, 9, 8, 6, 9, 2, 1, 3

24. 21, 32, 46, 32, 49, 32, 49

25. 74, 68, 68, 68, 75, 75, 74, 74, 70

26. 158, 162, 165, 162, 165, 157, 163

27. 6.8, 6.3, 6.3, 6.9, 6.7, 6.4, 6.1, 6.0

28. 12.75, 18.32, 19.41, 12.75, 18.30, 19.45, 18.33

29. When is the median the most appropriate measure of central tendency?

30. Under what circumstances would the mode be an appropriate measure of central tendency?

For grouped data, the modal class *is the interval containing the most data values. Give the mean and modal class for each of the following collections of grouped data. (See Example 5.)*

31. The distribution in Exercise 3.

32. The distribution in Exercise 4.

For each set of ungrouped data, **(a)** *Find the mean, median, and mode.* **(b)** *Discuss which of the three measures best represents the data and why.*

33. The weight gains of 10 experimental rats fed on a special diet were −1, 0, −3, 7, 1, 1, 5, 4, 1, 4.

34. A sample of 7 measurements of the thickness of a copper wire were .010, .010, .009, .008, .007, .009, .008.

35. The times in minutes that 12 patients spent in a doctor's office were 20, 15, 18, 22, 10, 12, 16, 17, 19, 21, 23, 13.

36. The scores on a 10-point botany quiz were 6, 6, 8, 10, 9, 7, 6, 5, 6, 8, 3.

37. Management A firm took a random sample of the number of days absent in a year for 40 employees, with results as shown below.

Days Absent	*Frequency*
0–2	23
3–5	11
6–8	5
9–11	0
12–14	1

Sketch a histogram and a frequency polygon for the data.

38. Natural Science The size of the home ranges (in square kilometers) of several pandas were surveyed over a year's time, with the following results.

Home Range	*Frequency*
.1–.5	11
.6–1.0	12
1.1–1.5	7
1.6–2.0	6
2.1–2.5	2
2.6–3.0	1
3.1–3.5	1

Sketch a histogram and frequency polygon for the data.

39. Social Science The histogram below shows the percent of the U.S. population in each age group in 1980.* What percent of the population was in each of the following age groups?
(a) 10–19 **(b)** 60–69
(c) What age group had the largest percent of the population?

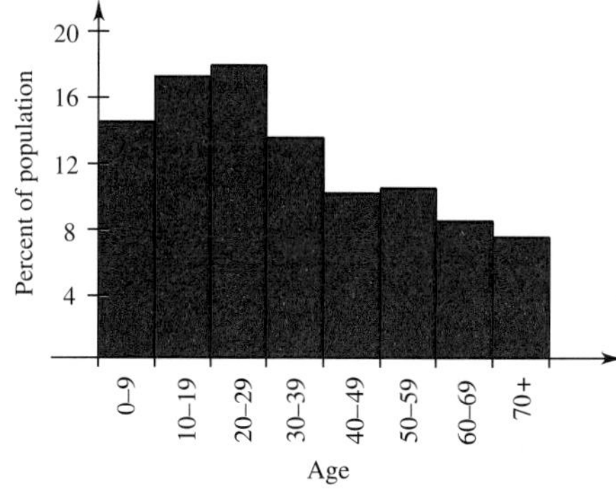

40. Social Science The histogram below shows the estimated percent of the U.S. population in each age group in the year 2000.* What percent of the population is estimated to be in each of the following age groups then?
(a) 20–29 **(b)** 70+
(c) What age group will have the largest percent of the population?
(d) Compare the histogram in Exercise 39 with the histogram below. What seems to be true of the U.S. population?

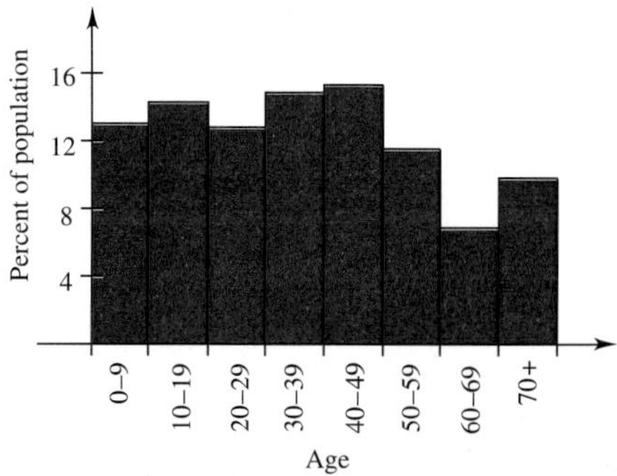

*Data from Census Bureau statistics.

Management *U.S. wheat prices and production figures for a recent decade are given below.*

Year	Price ($ per bushel)	Production (millions of bushels)
1982	2.70	2200
1983	2.30	2000
1984	2.95	1750
1985	3.80	2200
1986	3.90	2400
1987	3.60	2800
1988	3.55	2800
1989	3.50	2450
1990	3.35	2600
1991	3.20	2750

Find the mean for each of the following.

41. Price per bushel of wheat

42. Wheat production

43. Social Science The table shows the median age at first marriage in the U.S. over the last 50 years.*

Year	Male	Female
1990	26.1	23.9
1980	24.7	22.0
1970	23.2	20.8
1960	22.8	20.3
1950	22.8	20.3
1940	24.3	21.5

(a) Find the mean of the median ages for males.
(b) Find the mean of the median ages for females.

*U.S. National Center for Health Statistics of the United States, *Vital Statistics of the United States,* annual, *Monthly Vital Statistics Report.*

44. Social Science The number of nations participating in the winter Olympic games, from 1968 to 1992, is given below.*

Year	Nations Participating
1968	37
1972	35
1976	37
1980	37
1984	49
1988	57
1992	64

Find the following measures for the data.
(a) Mean **(b)** Median **(c)** Mode
(d) Which of these measures best represents the data? Explain your reasoning.

45. Social Science Washington Post writer John Schwartz pointed out that if Microsoft Corp. cofounder Bill Gates, who was reportedly worth $10 billion in 1995, lived in a town with 10,000 totally penniless people, the average personal wealth in the town would make it seem as if everyone were a millionaire.†
(a) Verify Schwartz' statement.
(b) What would be the median personal wealth in this town?
(c) What would be the mode for the personal wealth in this town?
(d) In this example, which average is most representative: the mean, the median, or the mode?

46. According to an article in the *Chance* electronic newsletter, the mean salary for National and American League baseball players in 1994 was $1,183,416, while the median salary was $500,000.‡ What might explain the large discrepancy between the mean and the median?

**The Universal Almanac,* John C. Wright, General Editor, Andrews and McMeel, Kansas City, p. 682.

†John Schwartz, "Mean Statistics: When is Average Best?" *The Washington Post,* Jan. 11, 1995, p. H7.

‡*Chance,* Aug. 13, 1994.

11.2 MEASURES OF VARIATION

The mean gives a measure of central tendency of a list of numbers, but tells nothing about the *spread* of the numbers in the list. For example, look at the following three samples.

I	3	5	6	3	3
II	4	4	4	4	4
III	10	1	0	0	9

Each of these three samples has a mean of 4, and yet they are quite different; the amount of dispersion or variation within the samples is different. Therefore, in addition to a measure of central tendency, another kind of measure is needed that describes how much the numbers vary.

The largest number in sample I is 6, while the smallest is 3, a difference of 3. In sample II this difference is 0; in sample III it is 10. The difference between the largest and smallest number in a sample is called the **range,** one example of a measure of variation. The range of sample I is 3, of sample II is 0, and of sample III is 10. The range has the advantage of being very easy to compute and gives a rough estimate of the variation among the data in the sample. However, it depends only on the two extremes and tells nothing about how the other data are distributed between the extremes.

EXAMPLE 1 Find the range for each list of numbers.

(a) 12, 27, 6, 19, 38, 9, 42, 15

The highest number here is 42; the lowest is 6. The range is the difference of these numbers, or

$$42 - 6 = 36.$$

(b) 74, 112, 59, 88, 200, 73, 92, 175

$$\text{Range} = 200 - 59 = 141$$ ■ 1

1 Find the range for the numbers 159, 283, 490, 390, 375, 297.

Answer:
331

TECHNOLOGY TIP Many graphing calculators list the largest and smallest numbers in a list when displaying one-variable statistics, usually on the second screen of the display. ✔

The most useful measure of variation is the *standard deviation.* Before defining it, however, we must find the **deviations from the mean,** the differences found by subtracting the mean from each number in a distribution.

EXAMPLE 2 Find the deviations from the mean for the numbers

32, 41, 47, 53, 57.

Adding these numbers and dividing by 5 gives a mean of 46. To find the deviations from the mean, subtract 46 from each number in the list. For example, the first deviation from the mean is $32 - 46 = -14$; the last is $57 - 46 = 11$.

Number	*Deviation from Mean*
32	−14
41	−5
47	1
53	7
57	11

To check your work, find the sum of these deviations. It should always equal 0. (The answer is always 0 because the positive and negative numbers cancel each other.) ■ 2

2 Find the deviations from the mean for each set of numbers.

(a) 19, 25, 36, 41, 52, 61

(b) 6, 9, 5, 11, 3, 2

Answers:

(a) Mean is 39; deviations are −20, −14, −3, 2, 13, 22.

(b) Mean is 6; deviations from the mean are 0, 3, −1, 5, −3, −4.

To find a measure of variation, we might be tempted to use the mean of the deviations. However, as mentioned above, this number is always 0, no matter how widely the data are dispersed. To avoid the problem of the positive and negative deviations averaging 0, statisticians square each deviation (producing a list of nonnegative numbers) and then find the mean.

Number	*Deviation from Mean*	*Square of Deviation*
32	−14	196
41	−5	25
47	1	1
53	7	49
57	11	121

In this case the mean of the squared deviations is

$$\frac{196 + 25 + 1 + 49 + 121}{5} = \frac{392}{5} = 78.4.$$

This number is called the **population variance,** because the sum was divided by $n = 5$, the number of items in the original list.

In most applications, however, it isn't practical to use the entire population, so a sample is used instead to estimate the variance and other measures. Since a random sample may not include extreme entries from the list, statisticians prefer to divide the sum of the squared deviations in a sample by $n - 1$, rather than n, to create what is called an *unbiased estimator.* The informal idea behind this is that using $n - 1$ increases the value of the variance, as would be the case if extreme entries were used. Using $n - 1$ in the distribution above gives

$$\frac{196 + 25 + 1 + 49 + 121}{5 - 1} = \frac{392}{4} = 98.$$

This number 98 is called the **sample variance** of the distribution and is denoted s^2 because it is found by averaging a list of squares. In this case, the population and sample variances differ by quite a bit. But when n is relatively large, as is the case in real-life applications, the difference between them is rather small.

SAMPLE VARIANCE

The variance of a sample of n numbers $x_1, x_2, x_3, \ldots, x_n$, with mean $\bar{x}$, is

$$s^2 = \frac{\Sigma(x - \bar{x})^2}{n - 1}.$$

When computing the sample variance by hand, it is often convenient to use the following shortcut formula, which can be derived algebraically from the definition in the box above.

$$s^2 = \frac{\Sigma x^2 - n\bar{x}^2}{n - 1}$$

To find the sample variance, we square the deviations from the mean, so the variance is in squared units. To return to the same units as the data, we use the *square root* of the variance, called the **sample standard deviation,** denoted s.

SAMPLE STANDARD DEVIATION

The standard deviation of a sample of n numbers $x_1, x_2, x_3, \ldots, x_n$, with mean $\bar{x}$, is

$$s = \sqrt{\frac{\Sigma(x - \bar{x})^2}{n - 1}}.$$

Similarly, the **population standard deviation** is the square root of the population variance (just replace $n - 1$ by n in the denominator in the box above).

TECHNOLOGY TIP When a graphing calculator computes one-variable statistics for a list of data, it usually displays the following information (not necessarily in this order and sometimes on two screens), and possibly other information as well.

Information	*Notation*
Number of data entries	n or $N\Sigma$
Mean	$\bar{x}$ or mean Σ
Sum of all data entries	Σx or TOT Σ
Sum of the squares of all data entries	Σx^2
Sample standard deviation	Sx or sx or $x\sigma_{n-1}$ or SSDEV
Population standard deviation	σx or $x\sigma_n$ or PSDEV
Largest / smallest data entries	maxX / minX or MAXΣ/MINΣ
Median	Med or MEDIAN

✔

NOTE Hereafter we shall deal exclusively with the sample variance and the sample standard deviation. So whenever standard deviation is mentioned, it means "sample standard deviation." ◆

As its name indicates, the standard deviation is the most commonly used measure of variation. The standard deviation is a measure of the variation from the mean. The size of the standard deviation indicates how spread out the data are from the mean.

EXAMPLE 3 Find the standard deviation of the numbers

$$7, \quad 9, \quad 18, \quad 22, \quad 27, \quad 29, \quad 32, \quad 40$$

by hand, using the shortcut variance formula at the bottom of page 518.

Arrange the work in columns, as shown in the table.

Number	*Square of the Number*
7	49
9	81
18	324
22	484
27	729
29	841
32	1024
40	1600
184	5132

Now find the mean.

$$\bar{x} = \frac{\Sigma x}{8} = \frac{184}{8} = 23$$

The total of the second column gives $\Sigma x^2 = 5132$. The variance is

$$s^2 = \frac{\Sigma x^2 - n\bar{x}^2}{n - 1}$$

$$= \frac{5132 - 8(23)^2}{8 - 1}$$

$$= 128.6 \quad \text{(rounded)},$$

and the standard deviation is

$$s \approx \sqrt{128.6} \approx 11.3.$$

Use your calculator to verify this result. ■ 3

3 Find the standard deviation of each set of numbers. The deviations from the mean were found in Problem 2 at the side.

(a) 19, 25, 36, 41, 52, 61

(b) 6, 9, 5, 11, 3, 2

Answers:

(a) 15.9

(b) 3.5

One way to interpret the standard deviation uses the fact that, for many populations, most of the data are within three standard deviations of the mean. (See Section 11.3.) This implies that, in Example 3, most of the population from which this sample is taken is between

$$\bar{x} - 3s = 23 - 3(11.3) = -10.9$$

and

$$\bar{x} + 3s = 23 + 3(11.3) = 56.9.$$

This has important implications for quality control. If the sample in Example 3 represents measurements of a product that the manufacturer wants to be between 5 and 45, the standard deviation is too large, even though all the numbers are within these bounds.

For data in a grouped frequency distribution, a slightly different formula for the standard deviation is used.

STANDARD DEVIATION FOR A GROUPED DISTRIBUTION

The standard deviation for a distribution with mean $\bar{x}$, where x is an interval midpoint with frequency f, and $n = \Sigma f$, is

$$s = \sqrt{\frac{\Sigma fx^2 - n\bar{x}^2}{n - 1}}.$$

The formula indicates that the product fx^2 is to be found for each interval. Then these products are summed, n times the square of the mean is subtracted, and the difference is divided by one less than the total frequency; that is, by $n - 1$. The square root of this result is s, the standard deviation. The standard deviation found by this formula may (probably will) differ somewhat from the standard deviation found from the original data.

CAUTION In calculating the standard deviation for either a grouped or ungrouped distribution, using a rounded value for the mean or variance may produce an inaccurate value. ◆

EXAMPLE 4 Find s for the grouped data of Example 5, Section 11.1. Begin by including columns for x^2 and fx^2 in the table.

Interval	f	x	x^2	fx^2
40–49	2	44.5	1980.25	3,960.50
50–59	4	54.5	2970.25	11,881.00
60–69	7	64.5	4160.25	29,121.75
70–79	9	74.5	5550.25	49,952.25
80–89	5	84.5	7140.25	35,701.25
90–99	3	94.5	8930.25	26,790.75
	Total: 30			Total: 157,407.50

Recall from Section 11.1 that $\bar{x} = 71.2$. Use the formula above with $n = 30$ to find s.

$$s = \sqrt{\frac{\Sigma fx^2 - n\bar{x}^2}{n - 1}}$$

$$= \sqrt{\frac{157{,}407.50 - 30(71.2)^2}{30 - 1}}$$

$$\approx 13.5$$ ■ 4

4 Find the standard deviation for the grouped data that follows. (*Hint:* $\bar{x} = 28.5$)

Value	*Frequency*
20–24	3
25–29	2
30–34	4
35–39	1

Answer:
5.3

NOTE A calculator is almost a necessity for finding a standard deviation. With a non-graphing calculator, a good procedure to follow is to first calculate $\bar{x}$. Then for each x, square that number, then multiply the result by the appropriate frequency. If your calculator has a key that accumulates a sum, use it to accumulate the total in the last column of the table. With a graphing calculator, simply enter the midpoints and the frequencies, then ask for the 1-variable statistics. ◆

11.2 EXERCISES

1. How are the variance and the standard deviation related?
2. Why can't we use the sum of the deviations from the mean as a measure of dispersion of a distribution?

Find the range and standard deviation for each of the following sets of numbers. (See Examples 1 and 3.)

3. 6, 8, 9, 10, 12
4. 12, 15, 19, 23, 26
5. 7, 6, 12, 14, 18, 15
6. 4, 3, 8, 9, 7, 10, 1
7. 42, 38, 29, 74, 82, 71, 35
8. 122, 132, 141, 158, 162, 169, 180
9. 241, 248, 251, 257, 252, 287
10. 51, 58, 62, 64, 67, 71, 74, 78, 82, 93

Find the standard deviation for the grouped data in Exercises 11 and 12. (See Example 4.)

11. (From Exercise 1, Section 11.1)

College Units	*Frequency*
0–24	4
25–49	3
50–74	6
75–99	3
100–124	5
125–149	9

12. (From Exercise 2, Section 11.1)

Scores	*Frequency*
30–39	1
40–49	6
50–59	13
60–69	22
70–79	17
80–89	13
90–99	8

13. **Natural Science** Twenty-five laboratory rats, used in an experiment to test the food value of a new product, made the following weight gains in grams.

5.25	5.03	4.90	4.97	5.03
5.12	5.08	5.15	5.20	4.95
4.90	5.00	5.13	5.18	5.18
5.22	5.04	5.09	5.10	5.11
5.23	5.22	5.19	4.99	4.93

Find the mean gain and the standard deviation of the gains.

14. **Management** An assembly-line machine turns out washers with the following thicknesses (in millimeters).

1.20	1.01	1.25	2.20	2.58	2.19	1.29	1.15
2.05	1.46	1.90	2.03	2.13	1.86	1.65	2.27
1.64	2.19	2.25	2.08	1.96	1.83	1.17	2.24

Find the mean and standard deviation of these thicknesses.

An application of standard deviation is given by **Chebyshev's theorem.** *(P. L. Chebyshev was a Russian mathematician who lived from 1821 to 1894.) This theorem applies to any distribution of numerical data. It states:*

> *For any distribution of numerical data, at least $1 - 1/k^2$ of the numbers lie within k standard deviations of the mean.*

Example *For any distribution, at least*

$$1 - \frac{1}{3^2} = 1 - \frac{1}{9} = \frac{8}{9}$$

of the numbers lie within 3 standard deviations of the mean. Find the fraction of all the numbers of a data set lying within the following numbers of standard deviations from the mean.

15. 2
16. 4
17. 5

In a certain distribution of numbers, the mean is 50 with a standard deviation of 6. Use Chebyshev's theorem to tell what percent of the numbers are

18. between 32 and 68;
19. between 26 and 74;
20. less than 38 or more than 62;
21. less than 32 or more than 68;
22. less than 26 or more than 74.
23. **Management** The Britelite Company conducted tests on the life of its light bulbs and those of a competitor (Brand X) with the following results for samples of 10 bulbs of each brand.

	Hours of Use (in 100s)									
Britelite	20	22	22	25	26	27	27	28	30	35
Brand X	15	18	19	23	25	25	28	30	34	38

Compute the mean and standard deviation for each sample. Compare the means and standard deviations of the two brands and then answer the questions below.
(a) Which bulbs have a more uniform life in hours?
(b) Which bulbs have the highest average life in hours?

24. **Management** The weekly wages of the six employees of Harold's Hardware Store are \$300, \$320, \$380, \$420, \$500, and \$2000.

(a) Find the mean and standard deviation of this distribution.

(b) How many of the employees earn within one standard deviation of the mean? How many earn within two standard deviations of the mean?

25. **Social Science** The number of unemployed workers in the United States in 1988–1993 (in millions) is given below.*

Year	*Number Unemployed*
1988	6.70
1989	6.53
1990	6.87
1991	8.43
1992	9.38
1993	8.73

(a) Find the mean number unemployed (in millions) in this period. Which year has unemployment closest to the mean?

(b) Find the standard deviation for the data.

(c) In how many of these years is unemployment within 1 standard deviation of the mean?

26. **Social Science** In an article comparing national mathematics examinations in the U.S. and some European countries, a researcher found the results shown in the histogram for the number of minutes allowed for each open-ended question.†

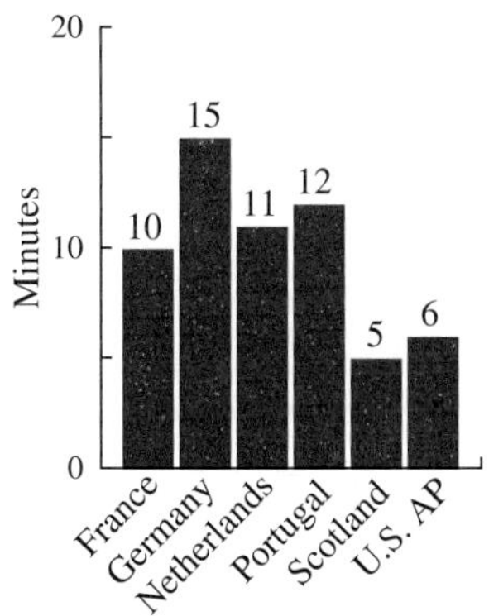

(a) Find the mean and standard deviation. (*Hint:* Do not use the rounded value of the mean to find the standard deviation.)

(b) How many standard deviations from the mean is the largest number of minutes?

(c) How many standard deviations from the mean is the U.S. AP examination?

27. **Social Science** For all questions, the researcher in Exercise 26 found the following results for Scotland and the United States, the countries with the least rigorous examinations.

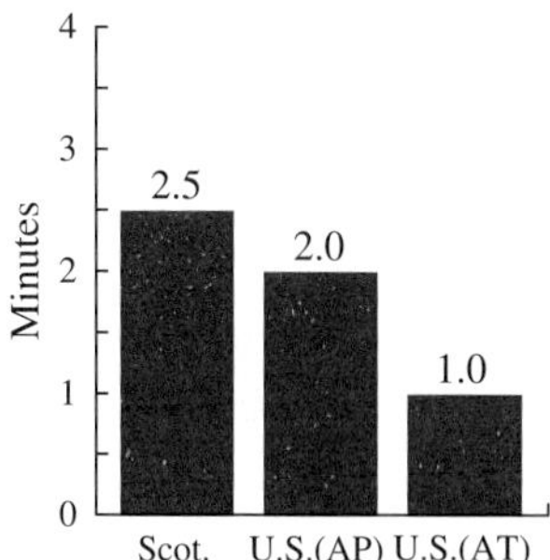

(a) Find the mean and standard deviation.

(b) How many standard deviations from the mean is the AT (achievement test)?

(c) How many standard deviations from the mean is the Scottish test?

28. **Social Science** Recently Germany has endured rioting and disruption because of the increasing numbers of immigrants. The nine top countries of origin of German immigrants are shown in the histogram.

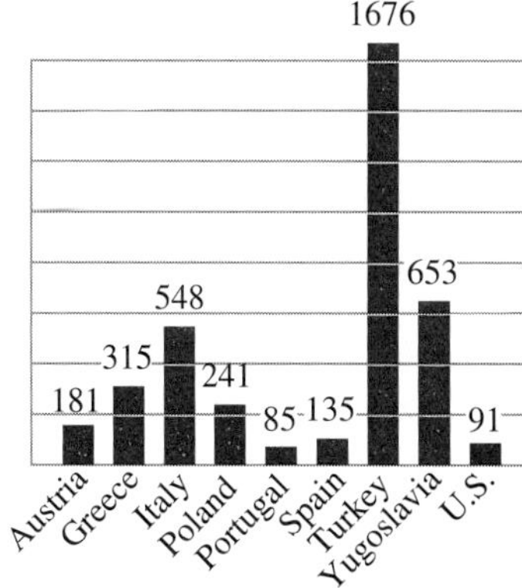

(a) Find the mean and standard deviation of this data.

(b) How many standard deviations from the mean is the largest number of immigrants? the smallest? Which country of origin is closest to the mean?

*U.S. Bureau of Labor Statistics, Bulletin 2307; and *Employment and Earnings*, monthly.

†Information from article comparing national mathematics examinations in the U.S. and some European countries as appeared in FOCUS, June 1993. Reprinted by permission of the Mathematical Association of America.

29. Social Science The numbers of immigrants to the United States (in thousands) from selected parts of the world in 1990 are shown in the table.*

Region	*Immigrants*
Europe	145.4
Asia	357.0
Canada	15.2
Mexico	213.8
Other America	210.3

(a) Find the mean number of immigrants from these regions. Which region produces the number of immigrants closest to the mean?

(b) Find the standard deviation. Are any of the data more than 2 standard deviations from the mean? If so, which ones? Are any of the data more than 1 standard deviation from the mean? If so, which ones?

30. Management The Quaker Oaks Company conducted a survey to determine if a proposed premium, to be included in their cereal, was appealing enough to generate new sales.† Four cities were used as test markets, where the cereal was distributed with the premium, and four cities as control markets, where the cereal was distributed without the premium. The eight cities were chosen on the basis of their similarity in terms of population, per capita income, and total cereal purchase volume. The results were as follows.

		Percent Change in Average Market Shares per Month
Test Cities	1	+18
	2	+15
	3	+7
	4	+10
Control Cities	1	+1
	2	−8
	3	−5
	4	0

(a) Find the mean of the change in market share for the four test cities.

(b) Find the mean of the change in market share for the four control cities.

(c) Find the standard deviation of the change in market share for the test cities.

(d) Find the standard deviation of the change in market share for the control cities.

(e) Find the difference between the mean of part (a) and the mean of part (b). This represents the estimate of the percent change in sales due to the premium.

(f) The two standard deviations from part (c) and part (d) were used to calculate an "error" of ± 7.95 for the estimate in part (e). With this amount of error what is the smallest and largest estimate of the increase in sales? (*Hint:* Use the answer to part (e).)

On the basis of the results of Exercise 30, the company decided to mass produce the premium and distribute it nationally.

31. Management The following table gives 10 samples, of three measurements, made during a production run.

SAMPLE NUMBER									
1	*2*	*3*	*4*	*5*	*6*	*7*	*8*	*9*	*10*
2	3	−2	−3	−1	3	0	−1	2	0
−2	−1	0	1	2	2	1	2	3	0
1	4	1	2	4	2	2	3	2	2

(a) Find the mean $\bar{x}$ for each sample of three measurements.

(b) Find the standard deviation s for each sample of three measurements.

(c) Find the mean $\bar{X}$ of the sample means.

(d) Find the mean $\bar{s}$ of the sample standard deviations.

(e) The upper and lower control limits of the sample means here are $\bar{X} \pm 1.954\bar{s}$. Find these limits. If any of the measurements are outside these limits, the process is out of control. Decide if this production process is out of control.

32. Discuss what the standard deviation tells us about a distribution.

Social Science *The reading scores of a second-grade class given individualized instruction are shown below. The table also shows the reading scores of a second-grade class given traditional instruction in the same school.*

Scores	*Individualized Instruction*	*Traditional Instruction*
50–59	2	5
60–69	4	8
70–79	7	8
80–89	9	7
90–99	8	6

33. Find the mean and standard deviation for the individualized instruction scores.

*Source: U.S. Immigration and Naturalization Service, *Statistics Yearbook,* annual; and releases.

†This example was supplied by Jeffrey S. Berman, Senior Analyst, Marketing Information, Quaker Oats Company.

34. Find the mean and standard deviation for the traditional instruction scores.

35. Discuss a possible interpretation of the differences in the means and the standard deviations in Exercises 33 and 34.

36. Social Science In 1998, nineteen state governors earned $100,000 or more (not counting expense allowances) as listed in the following table. (Salaries are given in thousands of dollars and are rounded to the nearest $1000.)*

(a) Find the mean salary of these governors. Which state has the governor with the salary closest to the mean?

(b) Find the standard deviation for the data.

(c) What percent of the governors have salaries within 1 standard deviation of the mean?

(d) What percent of the governors have salaries within 2 standard deviations of the mean?

State	*Salary*
California	131
Delaware	107
Florida	111
Georgia	103
Illinois	123
Maryland	120
Massachusetts	100
Michigan	127
Minnesota	115
Missouri	107
New York	130
North Carolina	107
Ohio	116
Pennsylvania	125
South Carolina	106
Texas	115
Virginia	110
Washington	121
Wisconsin	102

**World Almanac and Book of Facts*, 1998.

11.3 NORMAL DISTRIBUTIONS

The general idea of a probability distribution was first discussed in Section 10.5. In this section, we consider an important specific type of probability distribution.

Figure 11.3(a) shows a histogram and frequency polygon for the bank transaction example in Section 10.5. The heights of the bars are the probabilities. The transaction times in the example were given to the nearest minute. Theoretically, at least, they could have been timed to the nearest tenth of a minute, or hundredth of a minute, or even more precisely. In each case, a histogram and frequency polygon could be drawn. If the times are measured with smaller and smaller units, there are more bars in the histogram, and the frequency polygon begins to look more and more like the curve in Figure 11.3(b) instead of a polygon. Actually it is possible for the transaction times to take on any real number value greater than 0. A distribution in which the outcomes can take any real number value within some interval is a **continuous distribution.** The graph of a continuous distribution is a curve.

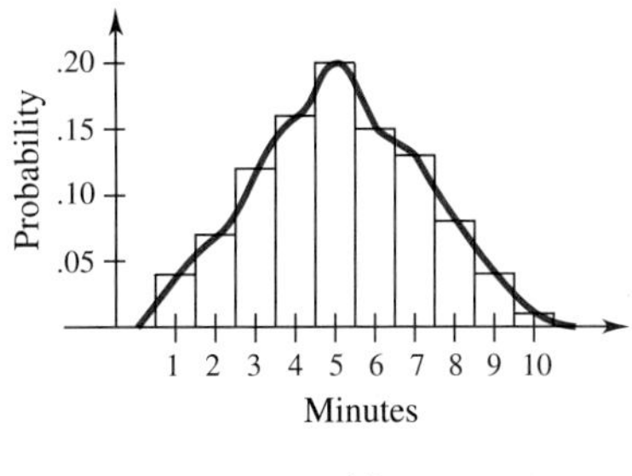

(a)

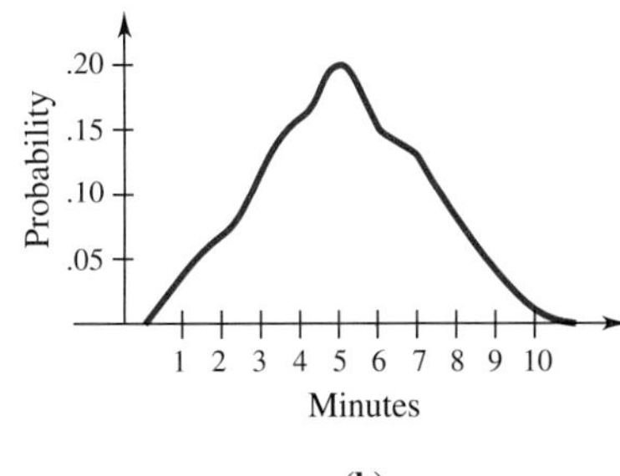

(b)

FIGURE 11.3

The distribution of heights (in inches) of college women is another example of a continuous distribution, since these heights include infinitely many possible measurements, such as 53, 58.5, 66.3, 72.666, . . . , and so on. Figure 11.4 shows the continuous distribution of heights of college women. Here the most frequent heights occur near the center of the interval shown.

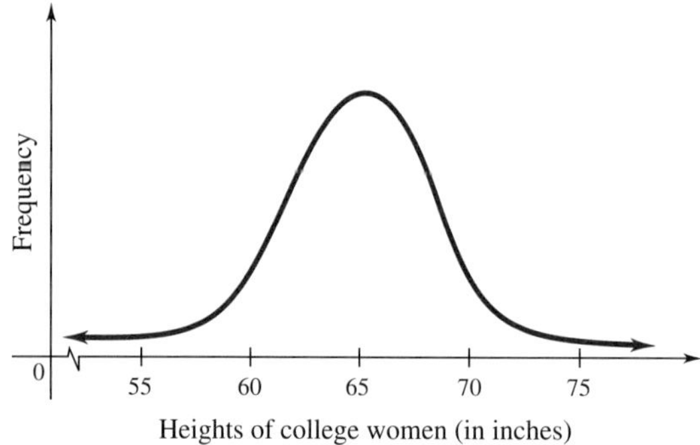

FIGURE 11.4

Another continuous curve, which approximates the distribution of yearly incomes in the United States, is given in Figure 11.5. The graph shows that the most frequent incomes are grouped near the low end of the interval. This kind of distribution, where the peak is not at the center, is called **skewed.**

FIGURE 11.5

Many natural and social phenomena produce continuous probability distributions whose graphs are approximated very well by bell-shaped curves, such as those shown in Figure 11.6. Such distributions are called **normal distributions** and their graphs are called **normal curves.** Examples of distributions that are approximately normal are the heights of college women and the errors made in filling 1-pound cereal boxes. We use the Greek letters μ (mu) to denote the mean and σ (sigma) to denote the standard deviation of a normal distribution.

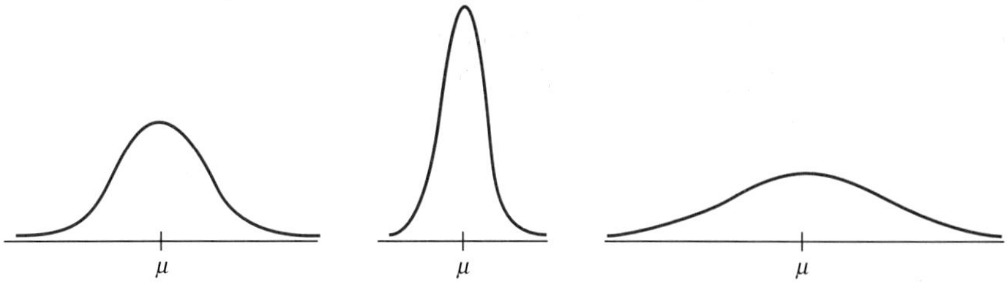

Three normal distributions

FIGURE 11.6

There are many normal distributions. Some of the corresponding normal curves are tall and thin and others short and wide, as shown in Figure 11.6. But every normal curve has the following properties.

1. Its peak occurs directly above the mean μ.
2. The curve is symmetric about the vertical line through the mean (that is, if you fold the page along this line, the left half of the graph will fit exactly on the right half).
3. The curve never touches the x-axis—it extends indefinitely in both directions.
4. The area under the curve (and above the horizontal axis) is 1. (As is shown in calculus, this is a consequence of the fact that the sum of the probabilities in any distribution is 1.)

It can be shown that a normal distribution is completely determined by its mean μ and standard deviation σ.* A small standard deviation leads to a tall, narrow curve like the one in the center of Figure 11.6, because most of the data are close to the mean. A large standard deviation means the data are very spread out, producing a flat wide curve like the one on the right in Figure 11.6.

Since the area under a normal curve is 1, parts of this area can be used to determine certain probabilities. For instance, Figure 11.7(a) on the next page is the probability distribution of the annual rainfall in a certain region. The probability that the annual rainfall will be between 25 and 35 inches is the area under the curve from 25 to 35. The general case, shown in Figure 11.7(b), can be stated as follows.

> The area of the shaded region under the normal curve from a to b is the probability that an observed data value will be between a and b.

*As is shown in more advanced courses, its graph is the graph of the function

$$f(x) = \frac{1}{\sigma\sqrt{2\pi}} e^{-(x-\mu)^2/(2\sigma^2)},$$

where $e \approx 2.71828$ is the real number discussed in Section 5.3.

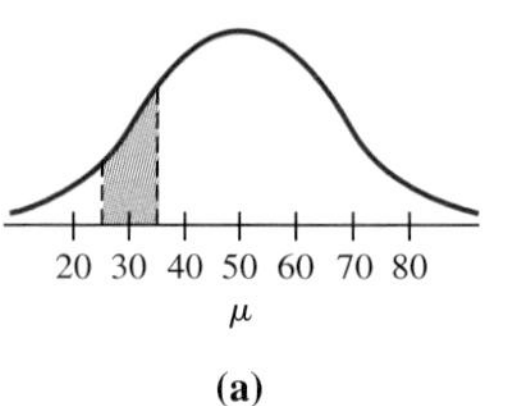

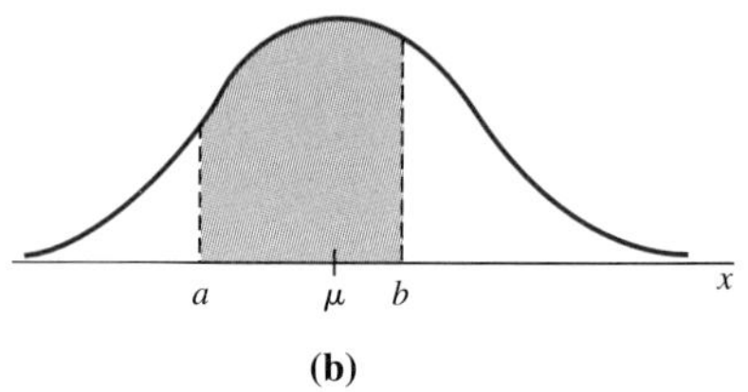

FIGURE 11.7

To use normal curves effectively we must be able to calculate areas under portions of these curves. These calculations have already been done for the normal curve with mean $\mu = 0$ and standard deviation $\sigma = 1$ (which is called the **standard normal curve**) and are available in Table 2 at the back of the book. The following examples demonstrate how to use Table 2 to find such areas. Later we shall see how the standard normal curve may be used to find areas under any normal curve.

The horizontal axis of the standard normal curve is usually labeled z. Since the standard deviation of the standard normal curve is 1, the numbers along the horizontal axis (the z-values) measure the number of standard deviations above or below the mean $z = 0$.

TECHNOLOGY TIP Some graphing calculators (such as the TI-83 and Casio 9800/9850) have the ability to graph a normal distribution given its mean and standard deviation and to find areas under the curve between two x-values. For an area under the curve, some calculators will give the corresponding z-value. For details, see your instruction book. (Look for "distribution" or "probability distribution.") A calculator-generated graph of the standard normal curve is shown in Figure 11.8. ✔

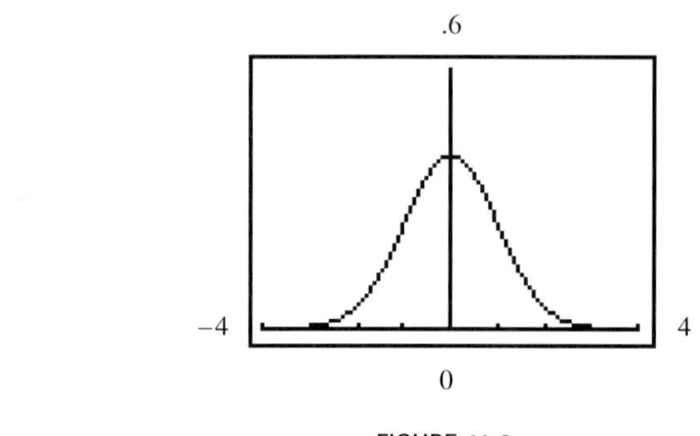

FIGURE 11.8

EXAMPLE 1 Find the following areas under the standard normal curve.

(a) The area between $z = 0$ and $z = 1$, the shaded region in Figure 11.9

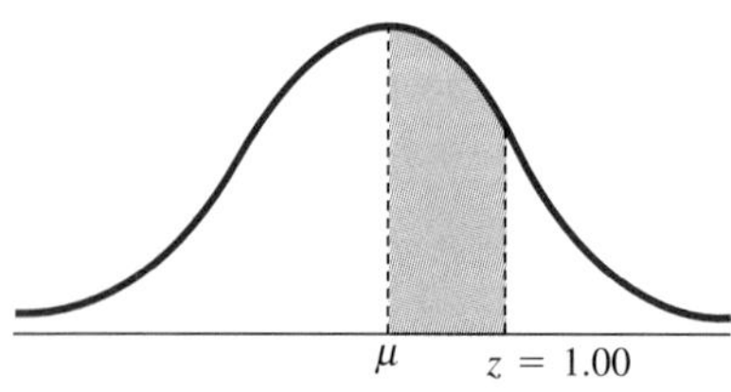

FIGURE 11.9

1 Find the percent of area between the mean and

(a) $z = 1.51$;

(b) $z = -2.04$.

(c) Find the percent of area in the shaded region.

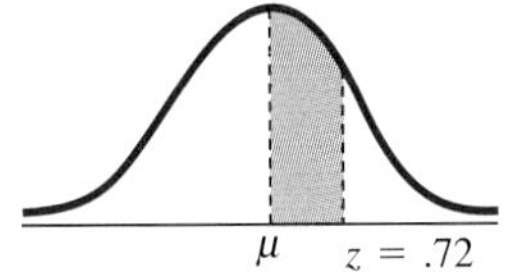

Answers:

(a) 43.45%

(b) 47.93%

(c) 26.42%

2 If your calculator can graph probability distributions and find area, use it to find the areas required in Example 1.

Answers:

(a) 34.13%

(b) 49.25%

Find the entry 1 in the z-column of Table 2. The entry next to it in the A-column is .3413, which means that the area between $z = 0$ and $z = 1$ is .3413. Since the total area under the curve is 1, the shaded area in Figure 11.9 is 34.13% of the total area under the normal curve.

(b) The area between $z = -2.43$ and $z = 0$

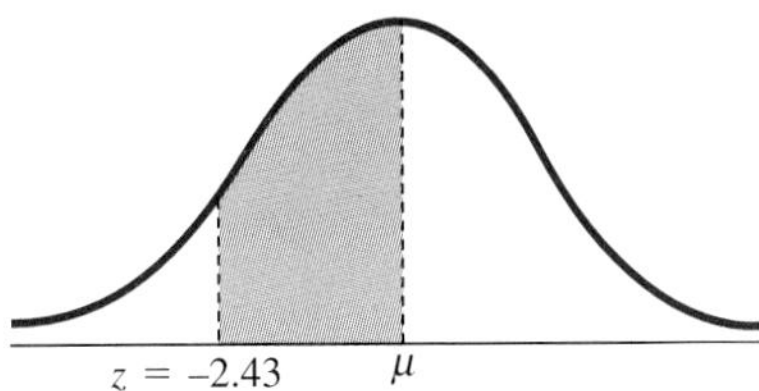

FIGURE 11.10

Table 2 lists only positive values of z. But the normal curve is symmetric around the mean $z = 0$, so the area between $z = 0$ and $z = -2.43$ is the same as the area between $z = 0$ and $z = 2.43$. Find 2.43 in the z-column of Table 2. The entry next to it in the A-column shows that the area is .4925. Hence, the shaded area in Figure 11.10 is 49.25% of the total area under the curve. ■ 1 2

EXAMPLE 2 Use a calculator or Table 2 to find the percent of the total area for the following areas under the standard normal curve.

(a) The area between 1.41 standard deviations *below* the mean and 2.25 standard deviations *above* the mean (that is, between $z = -1.41$ and $z = 2.25$)

First, draw a sketch showing the desired area, as in Figure 11.11. From Table 2, the area between the mean and 1.41 standard deviations below the mean is .4207. Also, the area from the mean to 2.25 standard deviations above the mean is .4878. As the figure shows, the total desired area can be found by *adding* these numbers.

$$\begin{array}{r} .4207 \\ +\ .4878 \\ \hline .9085 \end{array}$$

The shaded area in Figure 11.11 represents 90.85% of the total area under the normal curve.

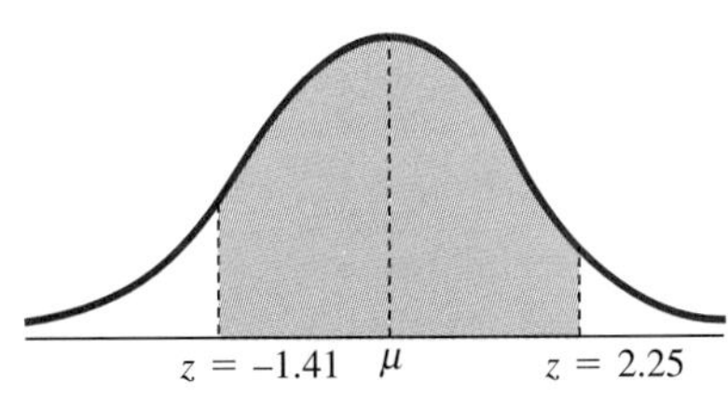

FIGURE 11.11

3 Find the following standard normal curve areas as percents of the total area.

(a) Between .31 standard deviations below the mean and 1.01 standard deviations above the mean

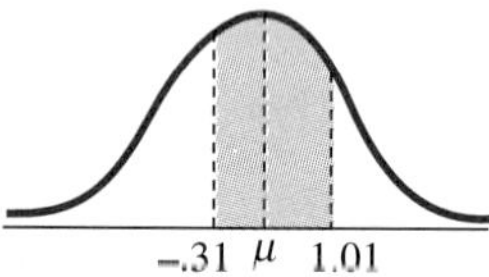

(b) Between .38 and 1.98 standard deviations below the mean

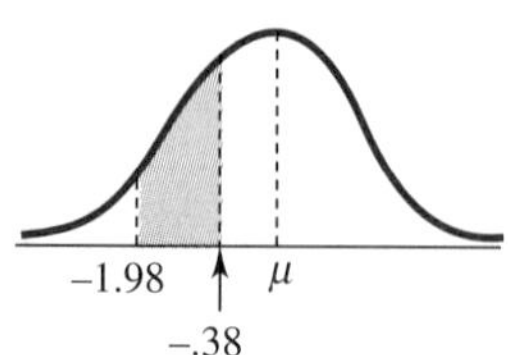

(c) To the right of 1.49 standard deviations above the mean

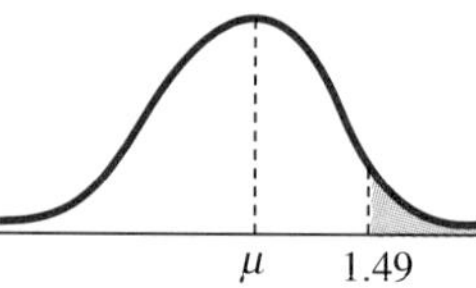

(d) What percent of the area is within 1 standard deviation of the mean? within 2 standard deviations of the mean? within 3 standard deviations of the mean? What can you conclude from the last answer?

Answers:

(a) 46.55%

(b) 32.82%

(c) 6.81%

(d) 68.3%, 95.47%, 99.7% Almost all the data lies within 3 standard deviations of the mean.

4 Find each z-score using the information in Example 3.

(a) $x = 36$

(b) $x = 55$

Answers:

(a) -3.5

(b) 1.25

(b) The area between .58 standard deviation above the mean and 1.94 standard deviations above the mean

Figure 11.12 shows the desired area. The area between the mean and .58 standard deviation above the mean is .2190. The area between the mean and 1.94 standard deviations above the mean is .4738. As the figure shows, the desired area is found by *subtracting* the two areas.

$$\begin{array}{r} .4738 \\ -\ .2190 \\ \hline .2548 \end{array}$$

The shaded area of Figure 11.12 represents 25.48% of the total area under the normal curve.

(c) The area to the right of 2.09 standard deviations above the mean

The total area under a normal curve is 1. Thus, the total area to the right of the mean is 1/2, or .5000. From Table 2, the area from the mean to 2.09 standard deviations above the mean is .4817. The area to the right of 2.09 standard deviations is found by subtracting .4817 from .5000.

$$\begin{array}{r} .5000 \\ -\ .4817 \\ \hline .0183 \end{array}$$

A total of 1.83% of the total area is to the right of 2.09 standard deviations above the mean. Figure 11.13 (which is not to scale) shows the desired area. ■ 3

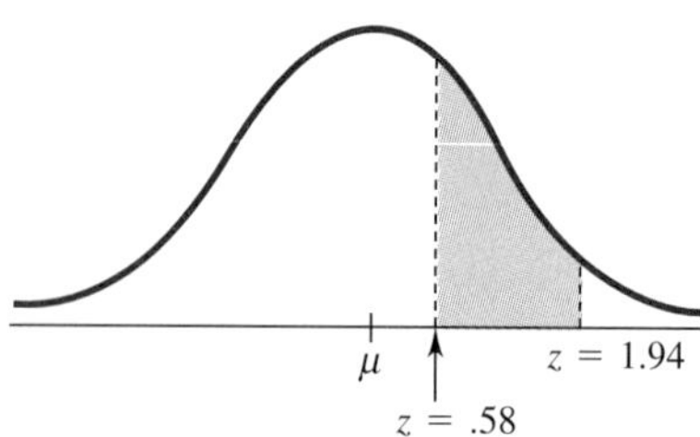

FIGURE 11.12

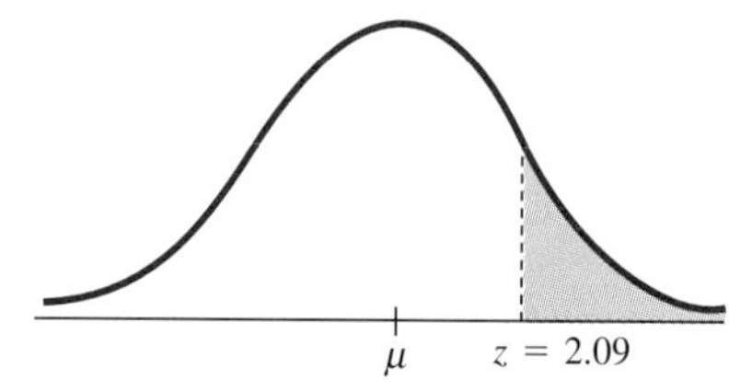

FIGURE 11.13

The key to finding areas under *any* normal curve is to express each number x on the horizontal axis in terms of standard deviations above or below the mean. The **z-score** for x is the number of standard deviations that x lies from the mean (positive if x is above the mean, negative if x is below the mean).

EXAMPLE 3 If a normal distribution has mean 50 and standard deviation 4, find the following z-scores.

(a) The z-score for $x = 46$

Since 46 is 4 units below 50 and the standard deviation is 4, 46 is 1 standard deviation below the mean. So, its z-score is -1.

(b) The z-score for $x = 60$

The z-score is 2.5 because 60 is 10 units above the mean (since $60 - 50 = 10$) and 10 units is 2.5 standard deviations (since $10/4 = 2.5$). ■ 4

In Example 3(b) we found the z-score by taking the difference between 60 and the mean and dividing this difference by the standard deviation. The same procedure works in the general case.

If a normal distribution has mean μ and standard deviation σ, then the z-score for the number x is

$$z = \frac{x - \mu}{\sigma}.$$

The importance of z-scores is the following fact, whose proof is omitted.

AREA UNDER A NORMAL CURVE

The area under a normal curve between $x = a$ and $x = b$ is the same as the area under the standard normal curve between the z-score for a and the z-score for b.

Therefore, by converting to z-scores and using a graphing calculator or Table 2 for the standard normal curve, we can find areas under any normal curve. Since these areas are probabilities (as explained earlier), we can now handle a variety of applications.

Graphing calculators, computer programs, and CAS programs (such as DERIVE) can be used to find areas under the normal curve and hence, probabilities. The equation of the standard normal curve, with $\mu = 0$ and $\sigma = 1$, is $f(x) = (1/\sqrt{2\pi})e^{-x^2/2}$. A good approximation of the area under this curve (and above $y = 0$) can be found by using the x-interval $[-4, 4]$. See Chapter 14 for more information on finding such areas.

EXAMPLE 4 Dixie Office Supplies finds that its sales force drives an average of 1200 miles per month per person, with a standard deviation of 150 miles. Assume that the number of miles driven by a salesperson is closely approximated by a normal distribution.

(a) Find the probability that a salesperson drives between 1200 and 1600 miles per month.

Here $\mu = 1200$ and $\sigma = 150$, and we must find the area under the normal distribution curve between $x = 1200$ and $x = 1600$. We begin by finding the z-score for $x = 1200$.

$$z = \frac{x - \mu}{\sigma} = \frac{1200 - 1200}{150} = \frac{0}{150} = 0$$

The z-score for $x = 1600$ is

$$z = \frac{x - \mu}{\sigma} = \frac{1600 - 1200}{150} = \frac{400}{150} = 2.67.*$$

*All z-scores here are rounded to two decimal places.

So the area under the curve from $x = 1200$ to $x = 1600$ is the same as the area under the standard normal curve from $z = 0$ to $z = 2.67$, as indicated in Figure 11.14. A graphing calculator or Table 2 shows that this area is .4962. Therefore, the probability that a salesperson drives between 1200 and 1600 miles per month is .4962.

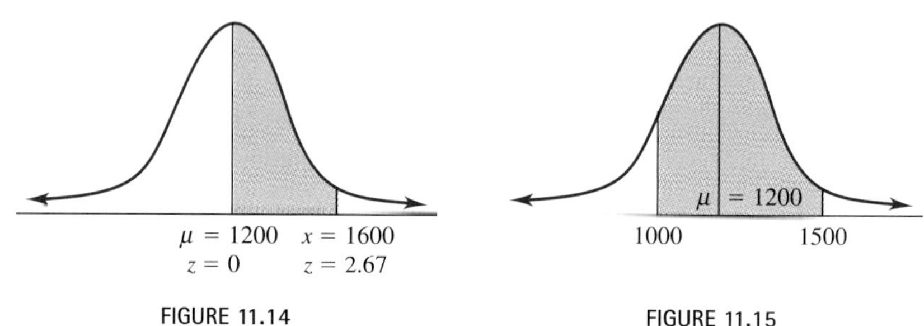

FIGURE 11.14

FIGURE 11.15

5 The heights of female sophomore college students at one school have $\mu = 172$ centimeters, with $\sigma = 10$ centimeters. Find the probability that the height of such a student is

(a) between 172 cm and 185 cm;

(b) between 160 cm and 180 cm;

(c) less than 165 cm.

Answers:

(a) .4032

(b) .6730

(c) .2420

(b) Find the probability that a salesperson drives between 1000 and 1500 miles per month.

As shown in Figure 11.15, z-scores for both $x = 1000$ and $x = 1500$ are needed.

For $x = 1000$,

$$z = \frac{1000 - 1200}{150} = \frac{-200}{150} = -1.33.$$

For $x = 1500$,

$$z = \frac{1500 - 1200}{150} = \frac{300}{150} = 2.00.$$

From the table $z = 1.33$ leads to an area of .4082, while $z = 2.00$ corresponds to .4773. A total of $.4082 + .4773 = .8855$, or 88.55%, of all drivers travel between 1000 and 1500 miles per month. From this, the probability that a driver travels between 1000 and 1500 miles per month is .8855. ■ 5

EXAMPLE 5 A tire store finds that the tread life of its tires is normally distributed, with a mean of 26,640 miles and a standard deviation of 4000 miles. The store sold 9000 tires this month. How many of them can be expected to last more than 35,000 miles?

Here $\mu = 26{,}640$ and $\sigma = 4000$. The probability that a tire will last more than 35,000 miles is the area under the normal curve to the right of $x = 35{,}000$. The z-score for $x = 35{,}000$ is

$$z = \frac{x - \mu}{\sigma} = \frac{35{,}000 - 26{,}640}{4000} = \frac{8360}{4000} = 2.09.$$

Example 2(c) and Figure 11.13 show that the area to the right of $z = 2.09$ is .0183, which is 1.83% of the total area under the curve. Therefore, 1.83% of the tires can be expected to last more than 35,000 miles. Thus,

$$1.83\% \text{ of } 9000 = .0183 \cdot 9000 = 164.7,$$

or approximately 165 tires can be expected to last more than 35,000 miles. ■

As mentioned above, z-scores are standard deviations, so $z = 1$ corresponds to 1 standard deviation above the mean, and so on. As found in Side Problem 3(d) of this section, 68.3% of the area under a normal curve lies within 1 standard deviation of the mean. Also, 95.47% lies within 2 standard deviations of the mean, and 99.7% lies within 3 standard deviations of the mean. These results, summarized in Figure 11.16, can be used to get a quick estimate of results when working with normal curves.

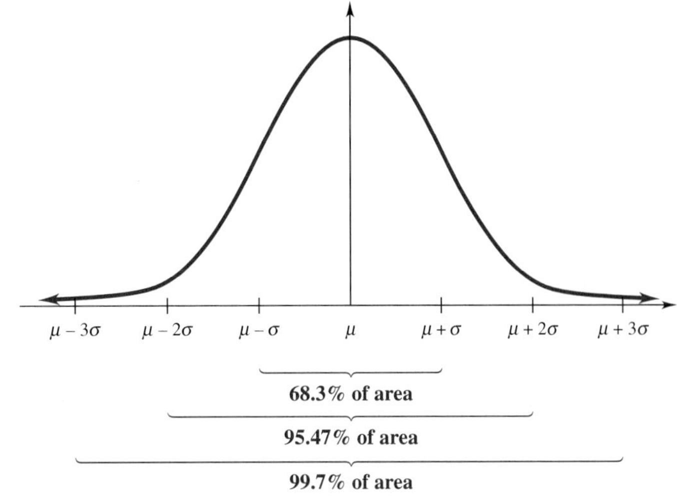

FIGURE 11.16

11.3 EXERCISES

1. In your own words, discuss the characteristics of a normal curve, mentioning the area under the curve, the location of the peak, and the end-behavior.

2. Explain how z-scores are found for normal distributions where

$$\mu \neq 0 \quad \text{or} \quad \sigma \neq 1.$$

3. Explain how the standard normal curve is used to find probabilities for other normal distributions.

Find the percent of the area under a normal curve between the mean and the following number of standard deviations from the mean. (See Example 2.)

4. 1.75
5. .23
6. −.43
7. −2.1
8. 3.1

Find the percent of the total area under the standard normal curve between the following z-scores. (See Examples 1 and 2.)

9. $z = 1.41$ and $z = 2.83$
10. $z = .64$ and $z = 2.11$
11. $z = -2.48$ and $z = -.05$
12. $z = -1.74$ and $z = -1.02$
13. $z = -3.11$ and $z = 1.44$
14. $z = -2.94$ and $z = -.43$

Find a z-score satisfying each of the following conditions. (Hint: Use Table 2 backwards or a graphing calculator.)

15. 5% of the total area is to the right of z.
16. 1% of the total area is to the left of z.
17. 15% of the total area is to the left of z.
18. 25% of the total area is to the right of z.

Use a graphing calculator or a computer to find the following probabilities by finding the comparable area under a standard normal curve.

19. $P(1.372 \leq z \leq 2.548)$
20. $P(-2.751 \leq z \leq 1.693)$
21. $P(z > -2.476)$
22. $P(z < 1.692)$

Use a graphing calculator or a computer to find the following probabilities for a distribution with a mean of 35.693 and a standard deviation of 7.104.

23. $P(12.275 < x < 28.432)$

24. $P(x > 38.913)$

25. $P(x < 17.462)$

26. $P(17.462 \le x \le 53.106)$

Assume the following distributions are all normal, and use the areas under the normal curve given in Table 2 or a graphing calculator to answer the questions. (See Example 4.)

27. Management According to the label, a regular can of Campbell's soup holds an average of 305 grams with a standard deviation of 4.2 grams. What is the probability that a can will be sold that holds more than 306 grams?

28. Management A jar of Adams Old Fashioned Peanut Butter contains 453 grams with a standard deviation of 10.1 grams. Find the probability that one of these jars contains less than 450 grams.

29. Management A General Electric soft white 3-way bulb has an average life of 1200 hours with a standard deviation of 50 hours. Find the probability that the life of one of these bulbs will be between 1150 and 1300 hours.

30. Management A 100-watt light bulb has an average brightness of 1640 lumens with a standard deviation of 62 lumens. What is the probability that a 100-watt bulb will have a brightness between 1600 and 1700 lumens?

31. Social Science The scores on a standardized test in a suburban high school have a mean of 80 with a standard deviation of 12. What is the probability that a student will have a score less than 60?

32. Social Science The average time to complete the test in Exercise 31 is 40 minutes with a standard deviation of 5.2 minutes. Find the probability that a student will require more than 50 minutes to finish the test.

33. A 120-minute video tape has a standard deviation of .7 minute. Find the probability that a 118-minute movie will not be entirely copied.

34. Natural Science The distribution of low temperatures for a city has an average of 44° with a standard deviation of 6.7°. What is the probability that the low temperature will be above 55°?

Social Science *New studies by Federal Highway Administration traffic engineers suggest that speed limits on many thoroughfares are set arbitrarily and often are artificially low. According to traffic engineers, the ideal limit should be the "85th percentile speed." This means the speed at or below which 85 percent of the traffic moves. Assuming speeds are normally distributed, find the 85th percentile speed for roads with the following conditions.*

35. The mean speed is 50 mph with a standard deviation of 10 mph.

36. The mean speed is 30 mph with a standard deviation of 5 mph.

Social Science *One professor uses the following system for assigning letter grades in a course.*

Grade	*Total Points*
A	Greater than $\mu + \frac{3}{2}\sigma$
B	$\mu + \frac{1}{2}\sigma$ to $\mu + \frac{3}{2}\sigma$
C	$\mu - \frac{1}{2}\sigma$ to $\mu + \frac{1}{2}\sigma$
D	$\mu - \frac{3}{2}\sigma$ to $\mu - \frac{1}{2}\sigma$
F	Below $\mu - \frac{3}{2}\sigma$

What percent of the students receive the following grades?

37. A

38. B

39. C

40. Do you think the system in Exercises 37–39 would be more likely to be fair in a large freshmen class in psychology or in a graduate seminar of five students? Why?

Natural Science *In nutrition, the recommended daily allowance of vitamins is a number set by the government as a guide to an individual's daily vitamin intake. Actually, vitamin needs vary drastically from person to person, but the needs are very closely approximated by a normal curve. To calculate the recommended daily allowance, the government first finds the average need for vitamins among people in the population and then the standard deviation. The recommended daily allowance is defined as the mean plus 2.5 times the standard deviation.*

Find the recommended daily allowance for the following vitamins.

41. Mean = 500 units, standard deviation = 50 units

42. Mean = 1800 units, standard deviation = 140 units

43. Mean = 159 units, standard deviation = 12 units

44. Mean = 1200 units, standard deviation = 92 units

Social Science *The mean performance score of a large group of fifth-grade students on a math achievement test is 88. The scores are known to be normally distributed. What percent of the students had scores as follows?*

45. More than 1 standard deviation above the mean

46. More than 2 standard deviations above the mean

Social Science *A teacher gives a test to a large group of students. The results are closely approximated by a normal curve. The mean is 74, with a standard deviation of 6. The teacher wishes to give A's to the top 8% of the students and F's to the bottom 8%. A grade of B is given to the next 15%, with D's given similarly. All other students get C's. Find the bottom cutoff (rounded to the* *nearest whole number) for the following grades. (Hint: Use Table 2 backwards.)*

47. A

48. B

49. C

50. D

Social Science *Studies have shown that women are charged an average of \$500 more than men for cars.* Assume a normal distribution of overcharges with a mean of \$500 and a standard deviation of \$60. Find the probability of a woman's paying the following additional amounts for a car.*

51. Less than \$500

52. At least \$600

53. Between \$400 and \$600

Social Science *Women earn an average of \$.74 for every \$1 earned by a man, a difference of \$.26. Assume differences in pay are normally distributed with a mean of \$.26 and a standard deviation of \$.08. Find the probability that a woman earns the following amounts less than a man in the same job.*

54. Between \$.20 and \$.30

55. More than \$.19

56. At most \$.26

Management *At a ranch in the Sacramento valley, the tomato crop yields an average of 25 tons per acre with a standard deviation of 2.2 tons per acre. Find the probability of each of the following yields in tons per acre.*

57. At least 24

58. At most 25.7

59. Between 24.5 and 25.5

Management *According to the manufacturer, a certain automobile averages 28.2 miles per gallon of gasoline with a standard deviation of 2.1 miles per gallon. Find the probability of each of the following miles per gallon.*

60. Between 27 and 29

61. At least 28

62. At most 29

*"From repair shops to cleaners, women pay more," by Bob Dart as appeared in *The Chicago Tribune,* May 27, 1993. Reprinted by permission of the author.

11.4 BINOMIAL DISTRIBUTIONS

Many practical experiments have only two possible outcomes, *success* or *failure.* Such experiments are called *binomial experiments* or *Bernoulli trials* and were first studied in Section 10.3. Examples of binomial experiments include flipping a coin (with heads being a success, for instance, and tails a failure) or testing TVs coming off the assembly line to see whether or not they are defective.

A **binomial distribution** is a probability distribution that satisfies the following conditions.

1. The experiment is a series of repeated independent trials.
2. There are only two possible outcomes for each trial, success or failure.
3. The probability of success is constant from trial to trial.

For example, suppose a fair die is tossed 5 times, with 1 or 2 considered a success and 3, 4, 5, or 6 a failure. Each trial is independent of the others and the probability of success in each trial is $p = \frac{2}{6} = \frac{1}{3}$. In 5 tosses there can be any number of successes from 0 through 5. But these 6 possible results are not equally likely, as shown in the chart at the side, which was obtained by using the following formula from Section 10.3.

x	$P(x)$
0	$\binom{5}{0}\left(\frac{1}{3}\right)^0\left(\frac{2}{3}\right)^5 = \frac{32}{243}$
1	$\binom{5}{1}\left(\frac{1}{3}\right)^1\left(\frac{2}{3}\right)^4 = \frac{80}{243}$
2	$\binom{5}{2}\left(\frac{1}{3}\right)^2\left(\frac{2}{3}\right)^3 = \frac{80}{243}$
3	$\binom{5}{3}\left(\frac{1}{3}\right)^3\left(\frac{2}{3}\right)^2 = \frac{40}{243}$
4	$\binom{5}{4}\left(\frac{1}{3}\right)^4\left(\frac{2}{3}\right)^1 = \frac{10}{243}$
5	$\binom{5}{5}\left(\frac{1}{3}\right)^5\left(\frac{2}{3}\right)^0 = \frac{1}{243}$

$$P(x) = \binom{n}{x}p^x(1-p)^{n-x},$$

where n is the number of trials (here, $n = 5$), x is the number of successes, p is the probability of success in a single trial (here, $p = \frac{1}{3}$), and $P(x)$ is the probability that exactly x of the n trials result in success.

TECHNOLOGY TIP The TI-83 computes binomial probabilities. See the Technology Tip on page 471. ✔

The expected value of this experiment (that is, the expected number of successes in 5 trials) is the sum

$$0 \cdot P(0) + 1 \cdot P(1) + 2 \cdot P(2) + 3 \cdot P(3) + 4 \cdot P(4) + 5 \cdot P(5)$$
$$= 0\left(\frac{32}{243}\right) + 1\left(\frac{80}{243}\right) + 2\left(\frac{80}{243}\right) + 3\left(\frac{40}{243}\right) + 4\left(\frac{10}{243}\right) + 5\left(\frac{1}{243}\right)$$
$$= \frac{405}{243} = 1\frac{2}{3} \quad \text{or} \quad \frac{5}{3}.$$

This result agrees with our intuition because there is, on average, 1 success in 3 trials; so we would expect 2 successes in 6 trials, and a bit less than 2 in 5 trials. From another point of view, since the probability of success is 1/3 in each trial and 5 trials were performed, the expected number of successes should be $5 \cdot (1/3) = 5/3$. More generally, we can show the following.

The expected number of successes in n binomial trials is np, where p is the probability of success in a single trial.

The expected value of any probability distribution is actually its mean. To show this, suppose an experiment has possible numerical outcomes $x_1, x_2, \ldots, x_k$, which occur with frequencies $f_1, f_2, \ldots, f_k$, respectively. If n is the total number of items, then (as shown in Section 11.1) the mean of this grouped distribution is

$$\mu = \frac{x_1 f_1 + x_2 f_2 + \cdots + x_k f_k}{n} = \frac{x_1 f_1}{n} + \frac{x_2 f_2}{n} + \cdots + \frac{x_k f_k}{n}$$
$$= x_1\left(\frac{f_1}{n}\right) + x_2\left(\frac{f_2}{n}\right) + \cdots + x_k\left(\frac{f_k}{n}\right).$$

But in each case, the fraction f_i/n (frequency over total number) is the probability p_i of outcome x_i. Hence,

$$\mu = x_1 p_1 + x_2 p_2 + \cdots + x_k p_k,$$

which is the expected value.

We saw above that the expected value (mean) of a binomial distribution is np. It can be shown that the variance and standard deviation of a binomial distribution are also given by convenient formulas.

$$\boldsymbol{\sigma^2 = np(1 - p) \quad \text{and} \quad \sigma = \sqrt{np(1 - p)}}$$

1 Find μ and σ for a binomial distribution having $n = 120$ and $p = 1/6$.

Answer:
$\mu = 20$; $\sigma = 4.08$

Substituting the appropriate values for n and p from the example into this new formula gives

$$\sigma^2 = 5\left(\frac{1}{3}\right)\left(\frac{2}{3}\right) = \frac{10}{9},$$

and $\sigma = \sqrt{10/9} \approx 1.05$. 1

A summary of these results follows.

BINOMIAL DISTRIBUTION

Suppose an experiment is a series of n independent repeated trials, where the probability of a success in a single trial is always p. Let x be the number of successes in the n trials. Then the probability that exactly x successes will occur in n trials is given by

$$\binom{n}{x} p^x (1-p)^{n-x}.$$

The mean μ and variance σ^2 of a binomial distribution are, respectively,

$$\mu = np \quad \text{and} \quad \sigma^2 = np(1-p).$$

The standard deviation is

$$\sigma = \sqrt{np(1-p)}.$$

EXAMPLE 1 The probability that a plate picked at random from the assembly line in a china factory will be defective is .01. A sample of 3 is to be selected. Write the distribution for the number of defective plates in the sample, and give its mean and standard deviation.

Since 3 plates will be selected, the possible number of defective plates ranges from 0 to 3. Here, n (the number of trials) is 3; p (the probability of selecting a defective on a single trial) is .01. The distribution and the probability of each outcome are shown below.

x	$P(x)$
0	$\binom{3}{0}(.01)^0(.99)^3 \approx .970$
1	$\binom{3}{1}(.01)(.99)^2 \approx .029$
2	$\binom{3}{2}(.01)^2(.99) \approx .0003$
3	$\binom{3}{3}(.01)^3(.99)^0 \approx .000001$

The mean of the distribution is

$$\mu = np = 3(.01) = .03.$$

The standard deviation is

$$\sigma = \sqrt{np(1-p)} = \sqrt{3(.01)(.99)} = \sqrt{.0297} \approx .17.$$ ■ 2

2 The probability that a can of soda from a certain plant is defective is .005. A sample of 4 cans is selected at random. Write a distribution for the number of defective cans in the sample, and give its mean and standard deviation.

Answer:

x	$P(x)$
0	.98
1	.0197
2	.00015
3	.0000005
4	6.25×10^{-10}

$\mu = .02$, $\sigma = .14$

Binomial distributions are very useful, but the probability calculations become difficult if n is large. If you do not have a calculator or computer that does binomial distributions, the standard normal distribution of the previous section (which shall be referred to as the normal distribution from now on) can be used to get a good approximation of binomial distributions.

As an example, to show how the normal distribution is used, consider the distribution for the expected number of heads if 1 coin is tossed 15 times. This is a binomial distribution with $p = 1/2$ and $n = 15$. The distribution is shown with Figure 11.17. The mean of the distribution is

$$\mu = np = 15\left(\frac{1}{2}\right) = 7.5.$$

The standard deviation is

$$\sigma = \sqrt{np(1-p)} = \sqrt{15\left(\frac{1}{2}\right)\left(1-\frac{1}{2}\right)}$$
$$= \sqrt{15\left(\frac{1}{2}\right)\left(\frac{1}{2}\right)} = \sqrt{3.75} \approx 1.94.$$

In Figure 11.17 the normal curve with $\mu = 7.5$ and $\sigma = 1.94$ has been superimposed over the histogram of the binomial distribution.

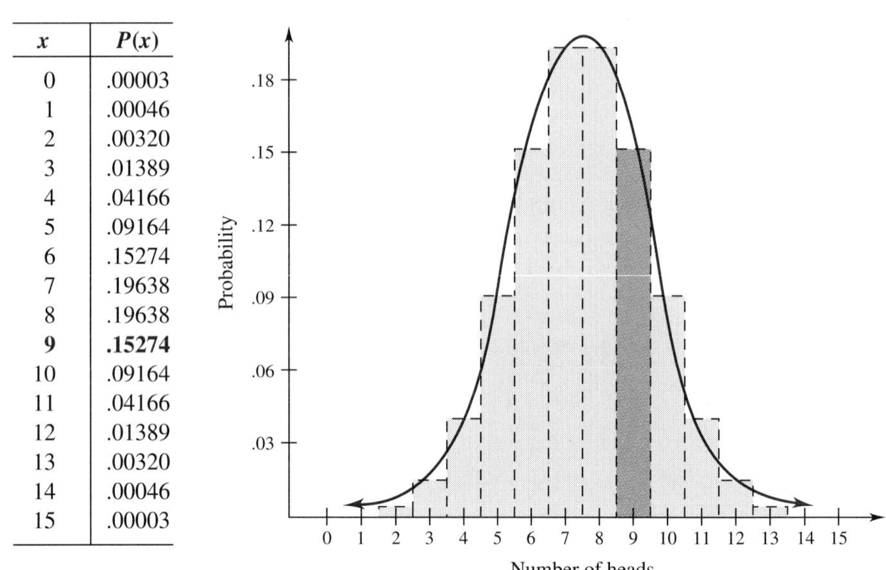

x	$P(x)$
0	.00003
1	.00046
2	.00320
3	.01389
4	.04166
5	.09164
6	.15274
7	.19638
8	.19638
9	**.15274**
10	.09164
11	.04166
12	.01389
13	.00320
14	.00046
15	.00003

FIGURE 11.17

As shown in the distribution, the probability of getting exactly 9 heads in the 15 tosses is approximately .153. This answer is about the same fraction that would be found by dividing the area of the bar in color in Figure 11.17 by the total area of all 16 bars in the graph. (Some of the bars at the extreme left and right ends of the graph are too short to show up.)

As the graph suggests, the area in color is approximately equal to the area under the normal curve from $x = 8.5$ to $x = 9.5$. The normal curve is higher than the top of the bar in the left half but lower in the right half.

To find the area under the normal curve from $x = 8.5$ to $x = 9.5$, first find z-scores, as in the previous section. Use the mean and the standard deviation for the distribution, which we have already calculated, to get z-scores for $x = 8.5$ and $x = 9.5$.

$$\text{For } x = 8.5, \quad z = \frac{8.5 - 7.5}{1.94} = \frac{1.00}{1.94}, \quad z \approx .52.$$

$$\text{For } x = 9.5, \quad z = \frac{9.5 - 7.5}{1.94} = \frac{2.00}{1.94}, \quad z \approx 1.03.$$

From Table 2, $z = .52$ gives an area of .1985, while $z = 1.03$ gives .3485. Find the required result by subtracting these two numbers.

$$.3485 - .1985 = .1500$$

This answer, .1500, is close to the answer, .153, found above. [3]

[3] Use the normal distribution to find the probability of getting exactly the following number of heads in 15 tosses of a coin.

(a) 7

(b) 10

Answers:

(a) .1985

(b) .0909

TECHNOLOGY TIP If your graphing calculator does not give binomial distribution values, but does compute areas under the normal curve, it can be used to approximate binomial distribution values in the same way. Choose the option that gives the area under the normal curve between two z-values: enter .52 and 1.03. The result is .1500267505, which agrees with the answer found using the table. ✔

EXAMPLE 2 About 6% of the bolts of cloth produced by a certain machine have defects.

(a) Find the approximate probability that in a sample of 100 bolts, 3 or fewer have defects.

This problem satisfies the conditions of the definition of a binomial distribution, so the normal curve approximation can be used. First find the mean and the standard deviation using $n = 100$ and $p = 6\% = .06$.

$$\mu = 100(.06) \qquad \mu = 6$$

$$\sigma = \sqrt{100(.06)(1 - .06)} = \sqrt{100(.06)(.94)} = \sqrt{5.64}, \quad \sigma \approx 2.37$$

As the graph of Figure 11.18 on the next page shows, the area to the left of $x = 3.5$ (since we want 3 or fewer bolts with defects) must be found. For $x = 3.5$,

$$z = \frac{3.5 - 6}{2.37} = \frac{-2.5}{2.37} \approx -1.05.$$

From Table 2, $z = -1.05$ corresponds to an area of .3531. Find the area to the left of z by subtracting .3531 from .5000 to get .1469. The approximate probability of 3 or fewer bolts with defects in a sample of 100 bolts is .1469, or 14.69%. (If you use a graphing calculator to approximate the area, use -4 as the lower bound. This works because the area under the normal curve between -4 and 4 is essentially equal to 1.)

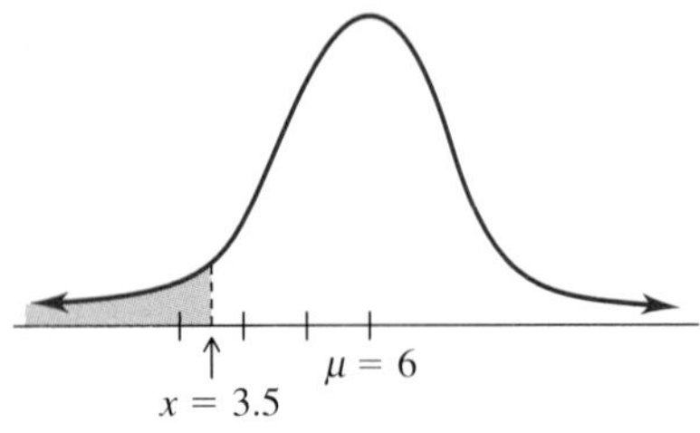

FIGURE 11.18

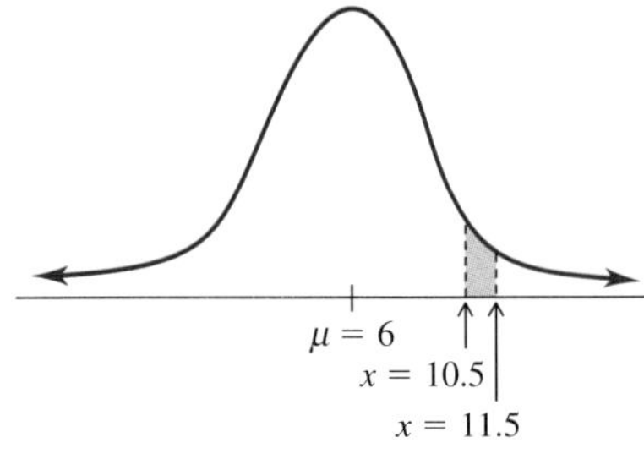

FIGURE 11.19

(b) Find the probability of exactly 11 bolts with defects in a sample of 100 bolts. As Figure 11.19 shows, the area between $x = 10.5$ and $x = 11.5$ must be found.

$$\text{If } x = 10.5, \text{ then } z = \frac{10.5 - 6}{2.37} = 1.90.$$

$$\text{If } x = 11.5, \text{ then } z = \frac{11.5 - 6}{2.37} = 2.32.$$

Look in Table 2; $z = 1.90$ gives an area of .4713, while $z = 2.32$ yields, .4898. The final answer is the difference of these numbers, or

$$.4898 - .4713 = .0185.$$

The probability of having exactly 11 bolts with defects is .0185. ■ 4

4 About 9% of the transistors produced by a certain factory are defective. Find the approximate probability that in a sample of 200, the following numbers of transistors will be defective. (*Hint:* $\sigma = 4.05$)

(a) Exactly 11

(b) 16 or fewer

(c) More than 14

Answers:

(a) .0226

(b) .3557

(c) .8051

CAUTION The normal curve approximation to a binomial distribution is quite accurate *provided that* n is large and p is not close to 0 or 1. As a rule of thumb, the normal curve approximation can be used as long as both np and $n(1 - p)$ are at least 5. ◆

11.4 EXERCISES

1. What three conditions must be satisfied for a distribution to be binomial?

2. What must be known to find the mean and standard deviation of a binomial distribution?

In Exercises 3–6, binomial experiments are described. For each one **(a)** *write the distribution;* **(b)** *find the mean;* **(c)** *find the standard deviation. (See Example 1.)*

3. **Management** According to a recent survey, fifty percent of cereals are bought with a coupon. Six cereal purchases are selected randomly and checked for use of a coupon. Write the distribution for the number purchased with a coupon.*

4. **Management** Private labels (not nationally advertised) account for 7% of cold cereal sales. The label on each of six randomly selected purchases is noted. Write the distribution of the number with a private label.*

5. **Social Science** In the United States 14% of people ages five and older speak a language other than English at home. Five people are interviewed. Write the distribution of the number speaking a language other than English at home.

6. **Management** To maintain quality control on the production line, the Bright Lite Company randomly selects three light bulbs each day for testing. Experience has shown a defective rate of .02. Write the distribution for the number of defectives in the daily samples.

Natural Science *Work the following exercises involving binomial experiments.*

7. The probability that an infant will die in the first year of life is about .025. In a group of 500 babies, what are the mean and standard deviation of the number of babies who can be expected to die in their first year of life?

*"Promotion costs soften cereal profit," by George Lazarus from *The Chicago Tribune*,

8. The probability that a particular kind of mouse will have a brown coat is 1/4. In a litter of 8, assuming independence, how many could be expected to have a brown coat? With what standard deviation?

9. The probability that a newborn infant will be a girl is .49. If 50 infants are born on Susan B. Anthony's birthday, how many can be expected to be girls? With what standard deviation?

10. What is the rule of thumb for using the normal distribution to approximate a binomial distribution?

11. **Social Science** According to the National Center for Education Statistics, 79% of the U.S. holders of Bachelor's degrees in Education in 1992–1993 were women.* Suppose five holders of Bachelor's degrees in Education are picked at random.
   (a) Find the expected value of the number of women selected.
   (b) Find the probability that four of the five are women.
   (c) Find the probability that at least two of the five are women.

For the remaining exercises, use the normal curve approximation to a binomial distribution. (See Example 2.)

Suppose 16 coins are tossed. Find the probability of getting exactly

12. 8 heads;
13. 7 heads;
14. 10 tails.

Suppose 1000 coins are tossed. Find the probability of getting each of the following.

15. Exactly 500 heads
16. Exactly 510 heads
17. 480 heads or more
18. Fewer than 470 tails
19. Fewer than 518 heads
20. More than 550 tails

A die is tossed 120 times. Find the probability of getting each of the following. (Hint: $\sigma = 4.08$)

21. Exactly 20 fives
22. Exactly 24 sixes
23. Exactly 17 threes
24. Exactly 22 twos
25. More than 18 threes
26. Fewer than 22 sixes

Management *Two percent of the quartz heaters produced in a certain plant are defective. Suppose the plant produced 10,000 such heaters last month. Find the probability that among these heaters, the following numbers were defective.*

27. Fewer than 170
28. More than 222

29. **Natural Science** For certain bird species, with appropriate assumptions, the number of nests escaping predation has a binomial distribution.† Suppose the probability of success (that is, a nest escaping predation) is .3. Find the probability that at least half of 26 nests escape predation.

30. **Natural Science** Under certain appropriate assumptions, the probability of a competing young animal eating x units of food is binomially distributed, with n equal to the maximum number of food units the animal can acquire, and p equal to the probability per time unit that an animal eats a unit of food.* Suppose $n = 120$ and $p = .6$.
   (a) Find the probability that an animal consumes 80 units of food.
   (b) Suppose the animal must consume at least 70 units of food to survive. What is the probability that this happens?

31. **Social Science** In a random sample of 100 drivers on Interstate 10 in Texas, 29% of the drivers exceeded the 70-mph speed limit. Find the probability of finding between 30 and 35 speeders in a random sample of 100.

32. **Social Science** A recent study of minimum wage earners found that 25.6% of them are teenagers.† Suppose a random sample of 60 minimum wage earners is selected. What is the probability that more than one-third of them are teenagers?

Use a graphing calculator or computer and the normal curve to approximate the following binomial probabilities. Compare these answers with those obtained by other methods in Exercises 42–45 of Section 10.3.

33. **Natural Science** A flu vaccine has a probability of 80% of preventing a person who is inoculated from getting the flu. A county health office inoculates 134 people. Find the probabilities of the following.
   (a) Exactly 10 of the people inoculated get the flu.
   (b) No more than 10 of the people inoculated get the flu.
   (c) None of the people inoculated get the flu.

34. **Natural Science** The probability that a male will be color-blind is .042. Find the probabilities that in a group of 53 men, the following will be true.
   (a) Exactly 5 are color-blind.
   (b) No more than 5 are color-blind.
   (c) At least 1 is color-blind.

35. **Management** The probability that a certain machine turns out a defective item is .05. Find the probabilities that in a run of 75 items, the following results are obtained.
   (a) Exactly 5 defectives
   (b) No defectives
   (c) At least 1 defective

36. **Management** A company is taking a survey to find out whether people like its product. Their last survey indicated that 70% of the population likes the product. Based on that, of a sample of 58 people, find the probabilities of the following.
   (a) All 58 like the product.
   (b) From 28 to 30 (inclusive) like the product.

**The New York Times,* Jan. 7, 1996, Education Life, p. 24.

†From H. M. Wilbur, *American Naturalist,* vol. 111.

*From G. deJong, *American Naturalist,* vol. 110.

†*The Chicago Tribune,* Dec. 28, 1995, pp. 1, 14.

CHAPTER 11 SUMMARY

Key Terms and Symbols

11.1 Σ summation (sigma) notation
$\bar{x}$ sample mean
random sample
grouped frequency distribution
frequency polygon
mean (arithmetic average)
median
mode

11.2 s^2 sample variance
s sample standard deviation
range
deviations from the mean
population variance
population standard deviation

11.3 μ mean of a normal distribution
σ standard deviation of a normal distribution
continuous distribution
skewed distribution
normal distributions
normal curves
standard normal curve
z-score

11.4 binomial distribution

Key Concepts

To organize the data from a sample, we use a **grouped frequency distribution,** a set of intervals with their corresponding frequencies. The same information can be displayed with a histogram, a bar graph with a bar for each interval. Each bar has width 1 and height equal to the probability of the corresponding interval. Another way to display this information is with a **frequency polygon,** which is formed by connecting the midpoints of consecutive bars of the histogram with straight line segments.

The **mean** $\bar{x}$ of a frequency distribution is the expected value.

For n numbers $x_1, x_2, \ldots, x_n$

$$\bar{x} = \frac{\Sigma x}{n}.$$

For a grouped distribution

$$\bar{x} = \frac{\Sigma(xf)}{n}.$$

The **median** is the middle entry in a set of data arranged in either increasing or decreasing order.

The **mode** is the most frequent entry in a set of numbers.

The **range** of a distribution is the difference between the largest and smallest numbers in the distribution.

The **sample standard deviation** s is the square root of the **variance.**

For n numbers

$$s = \sqrt{\frac{\Sigma x^2 - n\bar{x}^2}{n-1}}.$$

For a grouped distribution

$$s = \sqrt{\frac{\Sigma fx^2 - n\bar{x}^2}{n-1}}.$$

A **normal distribution** is a continuous distribution with the following properties: The highest frequency is at the mean; the graph is symmetric about a vertical line through the mean; the total area under the curve, above the x-axis, is 1. If a normal distribution has mean μ and standard deviation σ, then the z-score for the number x is $z = \frac{x - \mu}{\sigma}$.

Area Under a Normal Curve The area under a normal curve between $x = a$ and $x = b$ gives the probability that an observed data value will be between a and b.

The **binomial distribution** is a distribution with the following properties: For n independent repeated trials, where the probability of success in a single trial is p, the probability of x successes is $\binom{n}{x}p^x(1-p)^{n-x}$. The mean is $\mu = np$ and the standard deviation is

$$\sigma = \sqrt{np(1-p)}.$$

Chapter 11 Review Exercises

1. Discuss some reasons for organizing data into a grouped frequency distribution.

2. What is the rule of thumb for an appropriate interval in a grouped frequency distribution?

In Exercises 3 and 4, **(a)** *write a frequency distribution;* **(b)** *draw a histogram;* **(c)** *draw a frequency polygon.*

3. The following numbers give the sales in dollars for the lunch hour at a local hamburger store for the last twenty Fridays. (Use intervals 450–474, 475–499, and so on.)

480	451	501	478	512	473	509	515	458	566
516	535	492	558	488	547	461	475	492	471

4. The number of units carried in one semester by the students in a business mathematics class was as follows. (Use intervals of 9–10, 11–12, 13–14, 15–16.)

10	9	16	12	13	15	13	16	15	11	13
12	12	15	12	14	10	12	14	15	15	13

Find the mean for each of the following.

5. 41, 60, 67, 68, 72, 74, 78, 83, 90, 97

6. 105, 108, 110, 115, 106, 110, 104, 113, 117

7.

Interval	*Frequency*
10–19	6
20–29	12
30–39	14
40–49	10
50–59	8

8.

Interval	*Frequency*
40–44	2
45–49	5
50–54	7
55–59	10
60–64	4
65–69	1

9. What do the mean, median, and mode of a distribution have in common? How do they differ? Describe each in a sentence or two.

Find the median and the mode (or modes) for each of the following.

10. 32, 35, 36, 44, 46, 46, 59

11. 38, 36, 42, 44, 38, 36, 48, 35

The modal class is the interval containing the most data values. Find the modal class for the distributions of

12. Exercise 7 above;

13. Exercise 8 above.

14. What is meant by the range of a distribution?

15. How are the variance and the standard deviation of a distribution related? What is measured by the standard deviation?

Find the range and standard deviation for each of the following distributions.

16. 14, 17, 18, 19, 32

17. 26, 43, 51, 29, 37, 56, 29, 82, 74, 93

Find the standard deviation for the following.

18. Exercise 7 above

19. Exercise 8 above

20. Describe the characteristics of a normal distribution.

21. What is meant by a skewed distribution?

22. Find the percent of the area under a normal curve within 2.5 standard deviations of the mean.

Find the following areas under the standard normal curve.

23. Between $z = 0$ and $z = 1.27$

24. To the left of $z = .41$

25. Between $z = -1.88$ and $z = 2.10$

26. Find a z-score such that 8% of the area under the curve is to the right of z.

27. Why is the normal distribution not a good approximation of a binomial distribution that has a value of p close to 0 or 1?

Management *The table gives the probability distribution of U.S. buyers of recorded music in 1995 by age.**

Age	*Probability*
10–14	.08
15–19	.171
20–24	.153
25–29	.121
30–34	.123
35–39	.108
40–44	.075
45 & up	.169

28. **(a)** Draw a histogram for this distribution.

(b) From the shape of the histogram, is this a normal distribution?

*Recording Industry Association of America.

29. As shown in the distribution above, 16.9% of buyers of recorded music are age 45 or over. Assume a binomial distribution with $n = 6$ and $p = .169$.
(a) Find the probability that 4 of 6 randomly selected recorded music buyers are age 45 or over.
(b) Find the mean and standard deviation of the binomial distribution. Interpret your results.

30. Management The annual returns of two stocks for three years are given below.

	1997	*1998*	*1999*
Stock I	11%	−1%	14%
Stock II	9%	5%	10%

(a) Find the mean and standard deviation for each stock over the three-year period.
(b) If you are looking for security with an 8% return, which of these two stocks would you choose?

31. Natural Science The weight gains of two groups of 10 rats fed on two different experimental diets were as follows.

	Weight Gains									
Diet A	1	0	3	7	1	1	5	4	1	4
Diet B	2	1	1	2	3	2	1	0	1	0

Compute the mean and standard deviation for each group and compare them to answer the questions below.
(a) Which diet produced the greatest mean gain?
(b) Which diet produced the most consistent gain?

32. Social Science Between 1980 and 1990 HMO enrollment in the United States increased as shown below.

Location	*Gains*
South	7%
Midwest	10%
Northeast	13%
West	12%

(a) Compute the mean and standard deviation of the gains.
(b) How many standard deviations from the mean is the greatest gain? the smallest gain?

Social Science *On standard IQ tests, the mean is 100, with a standard deviation of 15. The results are very close to fitting a normal curve. Suppose an IQ test is given to a very large group of people. Find the percent of people whose IQ score is*

33. more than 130;

34. less than 85;

35. between 85 and 115.

36. Management A machine that fills quart orange juice cartons is set to fill them with 32.1 oz. If the actual contents of the cartons vary normally, with a standard deviation of .1 oz, what percent of the cartons contains less than a quart (32 oz)?

Management *About 60% of the blended coffee produced by a certain company contains cheap coffee. Assume a binomial distribution and use the normal distribution to find the probability that, in a sample of 500 bags of coffee, the following is true.*

37. 310 or fewer contain cheap coffee.

38. Exactly 300 contain cheap coffee.

Natural Science *An area infested with fruit flies is to be sprayed with a chemical which is known to be 98% effective for each application. A sample of 100 flies is checked. Assume a binomial distribution and use the normal distribution to approximate the following probabilities.*

39. 95% of the flies are killed in one application.

40. At least 95% of the flies are killed in one application.

41. At least 90% of the flies are killed in one application.

42. All the flies are killed in one application. Compare your answer with the probability found using the binomial distribution.

In Exercises 43–47, assume a binomial distribution and use the normal distribution approximation.

Natural Science *Twenty percent of third-world women would like to avoid pregnancy but are not using birth control. For 50 such women, use the normal curve approximation to find the probability of each of the following.*

43. Exactly 10 are not using birth control.

44. At least 20 are using birth control.

45. Social Science About 19% of the U.S. population older than 100 are African-Americans. Find the probability that in a group of 10 Americans older than 100, 4 are African-American.

46. Social Science A poll of 2000 teenagers found that 1 in 8 reported carrying a weapon for protection.* In a typical high school with 1200 students, what is the probability that more than 120 students, but fewer than 180, carry a weapon?

**The New York Times*, Jan. 12, 1996, p. A6.

47. **Social Science** Only 1 out of 12 American parents requires that children do their homework before watching TV.* In a typical neighborhood, what is the probability that out of 51 parents, 5 or fewer require their children to do homework before watching TV?

48. Much of our work in Chapters 10 and 11 is interrelated. Note the similarities in the following parallel treatments of a frequency distribution and a probability distribution.

Frequency Distribution

Complete the table below for the following data. (Recall that x is the midpoint of the interval.)

14, 7, 1, 11, 2, 3, 11, 6, 10, 13, 11, 11, 16, 12, 9, 11, 9, 10, 7, 12, 9, 6, 4, 5, 9, 16, 12, 12, 11, 10, 14, 9, 13, 10, 15, 11, 11, 1, 12, 12, 6, 7, 8, 2, 9, 12, 10, 15, 9, 3

Interval	*Tally*	x	f	$x \cdot f$
1–3				
4–6				
7–9				
10–12				
13–15				
16–18				

Probability Distribution

A binomial distribution has $n = 10$ and $p = .5$. Complete the table below.

x	$P(x)$	$x \cdot P(x)$
0	.001	
1	.010	
2	.044	
3	.117	
4		
5		
6		
7		
8		
9		
10		

(a) Find the mean (or expected value) for each distribution.
(b) Find the standard deviation for each distribution.
(c) For both distributions, use Chebyshev's theorem to find the interval that contains 75% of the distribution. (See Section 11.2 exercises.)
(d) Use the normal approximation of the binomial probability distribution to find the interval that contains 95.44% of that distribution.
(e) Why can't we use the normal distribution to answer probability questions about the frequency distribution?

*"Harper's Index," *Harper's*, Sept. 1996, p. 15.

CASE 11

Statistical Process Control

Statistical process control is a method of determining when a manufacturing process is out of control, producing defective items. The procedure involves taking samples of a measurement on a product over a production run and calculating the mean and standard deviation of each sample. These results are used to determine when the manufacturing process is out of control. For example, three sample measurements from a manufacturing process on each of four days are given in the table below. The mean $\bar{x}$ and standard deviation s are calculated for each sample.

DAY	1			2			3			4		
Sample Number	*1*	*2*	*3*	*1*	*2*	*3*	*1*	*2*	*3*	*1*	*2*	*3*
	−3	0	4	5	−2	4	3	−1	0	4	−2	1
Measurements	0	5	3	4	0	3	−2	0	0	3	0	3
	2	2	2	3	1	4	0	1	−2	3	−1	0
$\bar{x}$	−1/3	7/3	3	4	−1/3	11/3	1/3	0	−2/3	10/3	−1	4/3
s	2.5	2.5	1	1	1.5	.6	2.5	1	1.2	.6	1	1.5

Next, the mean of the 12 sample means, $\overline{X}$, and the mean of the 12 sample standard deviations, $\bar{s}$, are found (using the formula for $\bar{x}$). Here, these measures are

$$\overline{X} = 1.3 \quad \text{and} \quad \bar{s} = 1.41.$$

The control limits for the sample means are given by

$$\overline{X} \pm k_1\bar{s},$$

where k_1 is a constant found from a manual. For samples of size 3, $k_1 = 1.954$, so the control limits for the sample means are

$$1.3 \pm (1.954)(1.41).$$

The upper control limit is 4.06, and the lower control limit is -1.46.

Similarly, the control limits for the sample standard deviations are given by $k_2 \cdot \bar{s}$ and $k_3 \cdot \bar{s}$, where k_2 and k_3 also are values given in the same manual. Here, $k_2 = 2.568$ and $k_3 = 0$, with the upper and lower control limits for the sample standard deviations equal to 2.568(1.41) and 0(1.41), or 3.62 and 0. As long as the sample means are between -1.46 and 4.06 and the sample standard deviations are between 0 and 3.62, the process is in control.

EXERCISES

1. The following table gives 10 samples, of three measurements, made during a production run.

SAMPLE NUMBER									
1	*2*	*3*	*4*	*5*	*6*	*7*	*8*	*9*	*10*
2	3	−2	−3	−1	3	0	−1	2	0
−2	−1	0	1	2	2	1	2	3	0
1	4	1	2	4	2	2	3	2	2

(a) Find the mean $\bar{x}$ for each sample of three measurements.

(b) Find the standard deviation s for each sample of three measurements.

(c) Find the mean $\overline{X}$ of the sample means.

(d) Find the mean $\bar{s}$ of the sample standard deviations.

(e) Using $k_1 = 1.954$, find the upper and lower control limits for the sample means.

(f) Using $k_2 = 2.568$ and $k_3 = 0$, find the upper and lower control limits for the sample standard deviations.

2. Given the following measurements from later samples on the process in Exercise 1, decide whether the process is out of control. (*Hint:* Use the results of Exercise 1(e) and (f).)

SAMPLE NUMBER					
1	*2*	*3*	*4*	*5*	*6*
3	−4	2	5	4	0
−5	2	0	1	−1	1
2	1	1	−4	−2	−6

CHAPTER 12

Differential Calculus

The algebraic problems considered in earlier chapters dealt with *static* situations.

What is the revenue when x items are sold?

How much interest is earned in 2 years?

What is the equilibrium price?

Calculus, on the other hand, deals with *dynamic* situations.

At what rate is the economy growing?

How fast is a rocket going at any instant after liftoff?

How quickly can production be increased without adversely affecting profits?

The techniques of calculus will allow us to answer many questions like these that deal with rates of change.

The key idea underlying the development of calculus is the concept of limit. So we begin by studying limits.

12.1 LIMITS

We have often dealt with a problem like this: Find the value of the function $f(x)$ when $x = a$. The underlying idea of "limit," however, is to examine what the function does *near* $x = a$, rather than what it does *at* $x = a$.

EXAMPLE 1 The function

$$f(x) = \frac{.4x^3 - x^2 + .8}{x - 2}$$

is not defined when $x = 2$ (why?). What happens to the values of $f(x)$ when x is *very close* to 2?

1 Graph $f(x)$ in the viewing window of Figure 12.1(b). Then use the trace feature to move the cursor along the graph, and watch what happens to the y-coordinate (the value of $f(x)$) when the x-coordinate gets close to 2.

Answer:
Your results should be consistent with the following table.

x	$f(x)$
1.99	.78604
1.999	.79860
1.9999	.79986
2	—
2.0001	.80014
2.001	.80140
2.01	.81404

First, graph $f(x)$ in the two viewing windows shown in Figure 12.1. Because $x = 2$ is at the center of the x-axis in both windows, the graphs correctly show a tiny gap when $x = 2$ (the gap may not be visible on some calculators, particularly if the "XRes" setting is not 1). 1

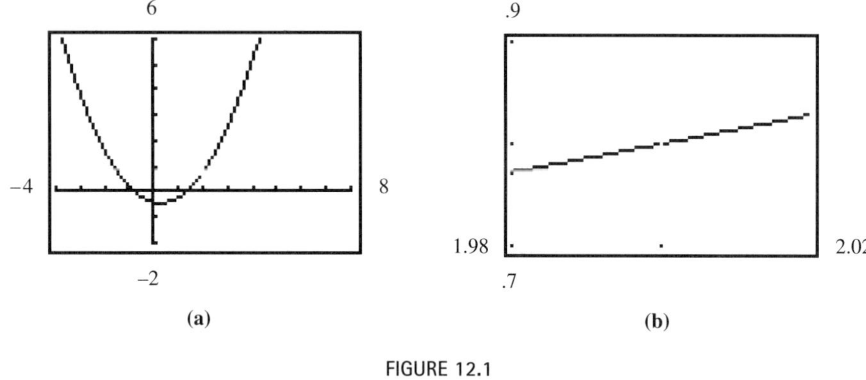

FIGURE 12.1

The results of the Margin Problem suggest that

> as x gets very close to 2, from either direction, the corresponding value of $f(x)$ gets very close to .8.

In fact, by experimenting further (by using the graph, a table, or function evaluation), you can convince yourself that the values of $f(x)$ can be made *as close as you want* to .8 by taking values of x close enough to 2. This situation is usually described by saying "the *limit* of $f(x)$ as x approaches 2 is the number .8," which is written symbolically as

$$\lim_{x\to 2} f(x) = .8, \quad \text{or equivalently,} \quad \lim_{x\to 2} \frac{.4x^3 - x^2 + .8}{x - 2} = .8. \quad ■$$

The following informal definition of "limit" is similar to the situation in Example 1, but now f is any function, and a and L are fixed real numbers (in Example 1, $a = 2$ and $L = .8$). The phrase "arbitrarily close" means "as close as you want."

LIMIT OF A FUNCTION

Let f be a function and let a and L be real numbers. Suppose that

> as x takes values very close (but not equal) to a (on both sides of a), the corresponding values of $f(x)$ are very close (and possibly equal) to L;

and that

> the values of $f(x)$ can be made arbitrarily close to L for all values of x that are close enough to a.

Then the number L is the **limit** of the function $f(x)$ as x approaches a, which is written

$$\lim_{x\to a} f(x) = L.$$

2 Graph $f(x) = x^2 + x + 1$ in the window with $2.8 \leq x \leq 3.2$ and $11 \leq y \leq 15$. Use trace to move along the graph. As the x-coordinate gets closer and closer to 3, what number does the y-coordinate (the value of $f(x)$) get close to?

Answer:
It appears to get very close to 13, which suggests that $\lim_{x \to 3} f(x) = 13$.

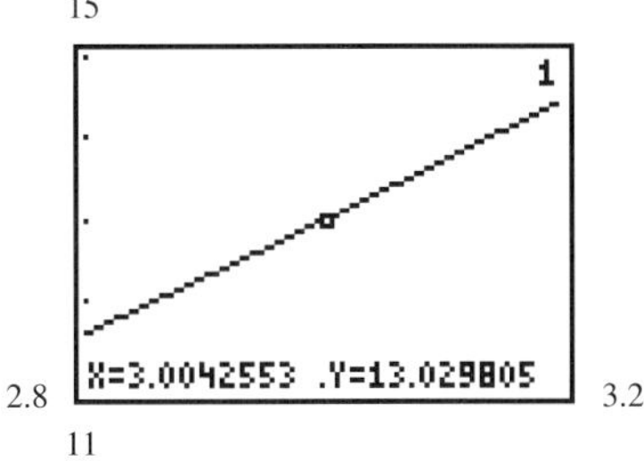

This definition is *informal* because the expressions "very close" and "arbitrarily close" have not been precisely defined. In particular, the tables and graphs used in Example 1 and the examples below provide strong intuitive confirmation, but not a rigorous proof, that the limits are as claimed.

EXAMPLE 2

If $f(x) = x^2 + x + 1$, what is $\lim_{x \to 3} f(x)$?

There are two ways to estimate the limit.

Graphical Method Graph $f(x)$ in a very narrow window and use the trace feature to find the values of $f(x)$ when x is very close to 3. 2

Numerical Method Make a table showing the values of the function at numbers very close to 3.

x approaches 3 from the left → 3 ← x approaches 3 from the right

x	2.9	2.99	2.9999	3	3.0001	3.01	3.1
$f(x)$	12.31	12.9301	12.9993 . . .		13.0007 . . .	13.0701	13.71

The table suggests that as x approaches 3 from either direction, $f(x)$ gets closer and closer to 13 and, hence, that

$$\lim_{x \to 3} f(x) = 13, \quad \text{or equivalently,} \quad \lim_{x \to 3} (x^2 + x + 1) = 13.$$

Note that the function $f(x)$ is defined when $x = 3$ and $f(3) = 3^2 + 3 + 1 = 13$. So in this case, the limit of $f(x)$ as x approaches 3 is $f(3)$, the value of the function at 3. ■

EXAMPLE 3

Find $\lim_{x \to 3} f(x)$, where f is the function whose rule is

$$f(x) = \begin{cases} 0 & \text{if } x \text{ is an integer} \\ 1 & \text{if } x \text{ is not an integer} \end{cases}$$

and whose graph is shown in Figure 12.2.

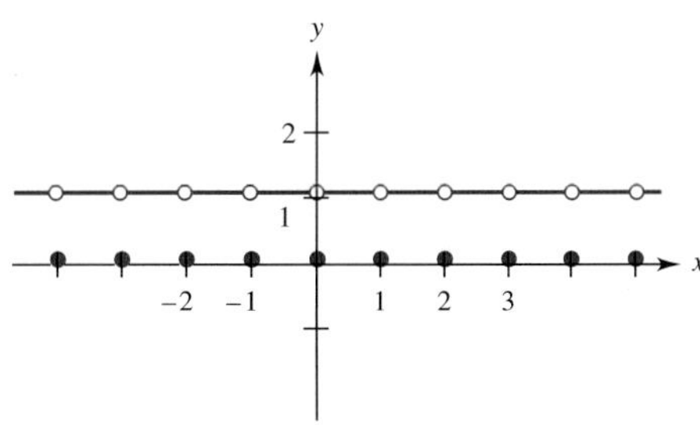

FIGURE 12.2

The definition of the limit as x approaches 3 involves only values of x that are close to, but not equal to 3—corresponding to the part of the graph on either side of 3, but not at 3 itself. Now $f(x) = 1$ for all these numbers (because the numbers very near 3, such as 2.99995 or 3.00002, are not integers). Thus for all x very close to 3, the corresponding value of $f(x)$ is 1, so $\lim_{x \to 3} f(x) = 1$. However, since 3 is an integer, $f(3) = 0$. Therefore, $\lim_{x \to 3} f(x) \neq f(3)$. ■

Examples 1–3 illustrate the following facts about limits.

LIMITS AND FUNCTION VALUES

If the limit of a function $f(x)$ as x approaches a exists, this limit need *not* be equal to the number $f(a)$. In fact, $f(a)$ may not even be defined.

FINDING LIMITS ALGEBRAICALLY As we have seen, graphs and tables are very useful for estimating limits. However, it often is more efficient and accurate to find limits algebraically by using the following properties of limits.

PROPERTIES OF LIMITS

Let a, k, A, and B be real numbers, and let f and g be functions such that

$$\lim_{x\to a} f(x) = A \quad \text{and} \quad \lim_{x\to a} g(x) = B.$$

1. $\lim_{x\to a} k = k$ (for any constant k)
   (The limit of a constant is the constant.)
2. $\lim_{x\to a} x = a$ (for any real number a)
3. $\lim_{x\to a} [f(x) \pm g(x)] = A \pm B = \lim_{x\to a} f(x) \pm \lim_{x\to a} g(x)$
   (The limit of a sum or difference is the sum or difference of the limits.)
4. $\lim_{x\to a} [f(x) \cdot g(x)] = A \cdot B = \lim_{x\to a} f(x) \cdot \lim_{x\to a} g(x)$
   (The limit of a product is the product of the limits.)
5. $\lim_{x\to a} \dfrac{f(x)}{g(x)} = \dfrac{A}{B} = \dfrac{\lim_{x\to a} f(x)}{\lim_{x\to a} g(x)}$ $(B \neq 0)$
   (The limit of a quotient is the quotient of the limits, provided the limit of the denominator is nonzero.)
6. For any real number r for which A^r exists,
   $$\lim_{x\to a} [f(x)]^r = A^r = [\lim_{x\to a} f(x)]^r.$$

Although we won't prove these properties (a rigorous definition of limit is needed for that), you should find most of them very plausible. For instance, if the values of $f(x)$ get very close to A and the values of $g(x)$ get very close to B when x approaches a, it is reasonable to expect that the corresponding values of $f(x) + g(x)$ will get very close to $A + B$ (Property 3) and that the corresponding values of $f(x)g(x)$ will get very close to AB (Property 4).

EXAMPLE 4 Find $\lim_{x\to 2}(3x^2+5x-1)$.

$$\lim_{x\to 2}(3x^2+5x-1)$$

$$= \lim_{x\to 2} 3x^2 + \lim_{x\to 2} 5x + \lim_{x\to 2}(-1) \qquad \text{Property 3}$$

$$= \lim_{x\to 2} 3 \cdot \lim_{x\to 2} x^2 + \lim_{x\to 2} 5 \cdot \lim_{x\to 2} x + \lim_{x\to 2}(-1) \qquad \text{Property 4}$$

$$= \lim_{x\to 2} 3 \cdot [\lim_{x\to 2} x]^2 + \lim_{x\to 2} 5 \cdot \lim_{x\to 2} x + \lim_{x\to 2}(-1) \qquad \text{Property 6}$$

$$= 3 \cdot 2^2 + 5 \cdot 2 + (-1) = 21 \qquad \text{Properties 1 and 2} \blacksquare$$

Example 4 shows that $\lim_{x\to 2} f(x) = 21$, where $f(x) = 3x^2 + 5x - 1$. Note that $f(2) = 3 \cdot 2^2 + 5 \cdot 2 - 1 = 21$. In other words, the limit as x approaches 2 is the value of the function at 2, that is

$$\lim_{x\to 2} f(x) = f(2).$$

The same analysis used in Example 4 works with any polynomial function and leads to the following conclusion.

3 If $f(x) = 2x^4 - 4x^3 + 3x$, find

(a) $\lim_{x\to 2} f(x)$;

(b) $\lim_{x\to -1} f(x)$.

Answers:

(a) 6

(b) 3

POLYNOMIAL LIMITS

If $f(x)$ is a polynomial function and a is a real number, then

$$\lim_{x\to a} f(x) = f(a).$$

This property will be used frequently. 3

EXAMPLE 5 Find each limit.

(a) $\lim_{x\to 2}[(x^2+1)+(x^3-x+3)]$

$$\lim_{x\to 2}[(x^2+1)+(x^3-x+3)]$$

$$= \lim_{x\to 2}(x^2+1) + \lim_{x\to 2}(x^3-x+3) \qquad \text{Property 3}$$

$$= (2^2+1)+(2^3-2+3) = 5+9-14 \qquad \text{Polynomial limit}$$

(b) $\lim_{x\to -1}(x^3+4x)(2x^2-3x)$

$$\lim_{x\to -1}(x^3+4x)(2x^2-3x)$$

$$= \lim_{x\to -1}(x^3+4x) \cdot \lim_{x\to -1}(2x^2-3x) \qquad \text{Property 4}$$

$$= [(-1)^3+4(-1)] \cdot [2(-1)^2-3(-1)] \qquad \text{Polynomial limit}$$

$$= (-1-4)(2+3) = -25$$

(c) $\lim_{x\to -1} 5(3x^2+2)$

$$\lim_{x\to -1} 5(3x^2+2) = \lim_{x\to -1} 5 \cdot \lim_{x\to -1}(3x^2+2) \qquad \text{Property 4}$$

$$= 5[3(-1)^2+2] \qquad \text{Property 1 and polynomial limit}$$

$$= 25$$

(d) $\lim_{x \to 4} \frac{x}{x+2}$

$$\lim_{x \to 4} \frac{x}{x+2} = \frac{\lim_{x \to 4} x}{\lim_{x \to 4} (x+2)} \quad \text{Property 5}$$

$$= \frac{4}{4+2} = \frac{2}{3} \quad \text{Polynomial limit}$$

(e) $\lim_{x \to 9} \sqrt{4x - 11}$

Begin by writing the square root in exponential form.

$$\lim_{x \to 9} \sqrt{4x - 11} = \lim_{x \to 9} [4x - 11]^{1/2}$$

$$= [\lim_{x \to 9} (4x - 11)]^{1/2} \quad \text{Property 6}$$

$$= [4 \cdot 9 - 11]^{1/2} \quad \text{Polynomial limit}$$

$$= [25]^{1/2} = \sqrt{25} = 5. \quad ■ \quad \boxed{4}$$

$\boxed{4}$ Use the limit properties to find the following.

(a) $\lim_{x \to 4} (3x - 9)$

(b) $\lim_{x \to -1} (2x^2 - 4x + 1)$

(c) $\lim_{x \to 2} \frac{x-1}{3x+2}$

(d) $\lim_{x \to 2} \sqrt{3x + 3}$

Answers:

(a) 3

(b) 7

(c) 1/8

(d) 3

The definition of the limit as x approaches a involves only the values of the function when x is *near a,* but not the value of the function *at a.* So two functions that agree for all values of x, except possibly at $x = a$, will necessarily have the same limit when x approaches a. Thus we have this fact:

> **LIMIT THEOREM**
>
> If f and g are functions that have limits as x approaches a, and $f(x) = g(x)$ for all $x \neq a$, then
>
> $$\lim_{x \to a} f(x) = \lim_{x \to a} g(x).$$

EXAMPLE 6 Find $\lim_{x \to 2} \frac{x^2 + x - 6}{x - 2}$.

Property 5 cannot be used here, because

$$\lim_{x \to 2} (x - 2) = 0.$$

You can, however, simplify the function by rewriting the fraction as

$$\frac{x^2 + x - 6}{x - 2} = \frac{(x+3)(x-2)}{x-2}.$$

When $x \neq 2$, the quantity $x - 2$ is nonzero and may be cancelled, so that

$$\frac{x^2 + x - 6}{x - 2} = x + 3 \quad \text{for all} \quad x \neq 2.$$

Now the Limit Theorem can be used.

$$\lim_{x \to 2} \frac{x^2 + x - 6}{x - 2} = \lim_{x \to 2} (x + 3) = 2 + 3 = 5 \quad ■ \quad \boxed{5}$$

$\boxed{5}$ Find $\lim_{x \to 1} \frac{2x^2 + x - 3}{x - 1}$.

Answer:

5

EXAMPLE 7 Find $\lim\limits_{x \to 4} \dfrac{\sqrt{x} - 2}{x - 4}$.

As $x \to 4$, the numerator approaches 0 and the denominator also approaches 0, giving the meaningless expression 0/0. To change the form of the expression, algebra can be used to rationalize the numerator by multiplying both the numerator and the denominator by $\sqrt{x} + 2$. This gives

$$\frac{\sqrt{x}-2}{x-4} = \frac{\sqrt{x}-2}{x-4} \cdot \frac{\sqrt{x}+2}{\sqrt{x}+2} = \frac{\sqrt{x}\cdot\sqrt{x} + 2\sqrt{x} - 2\sqrt{x} - 4}{(x-4)(\sqrt{x}+2)}$$

$$= \frac{x-4}{(x-4)(\sqrt{x}+2)} = \frac{1}{\sqrt{x}+2} \quad \text{for all } x \neq 4.$$

Now use the Limit Theorem and the properties of limits.

$$\lim_{x \to 4} \frac{\sqrt{x}-2}{x-4} = \lim_{x \to 4} \frac{1}{\sqrt{x}+2} = \frac{1}{\sqrt{4}+2} = \frac{1}{2+2} = \frac{1}{4} \quad ■ \quad \boxed{6}$$

$\boxed{6}$ Find the following.

(a) $\lim\limits_{x \to 1} \dfrac{\sqrt{x} - 1}{x - 1}$

(b) $\lim\limits_{x \to 9} \dfrac{\sqrt{x} - 3}{x - 9}$

Answers:

(a) 1/2

(b) 1/6

EXISTENCE OF LIMITS It is possible that $\lim\limits_{x \to a} f(x)$ may not exist, that is, there may be no number L satisfying the definition of $\lim\limits_{x \to a} f(x) = L$. This can happen in several ways, two of which are illustrated in the following examples.

EXAMPLE 8 Let $g(x) = \dfrac{x^2 + 4}{x - 2}$ and find $\lim\limits_{x \to 2} g(x)$.

Property 5 cannot be used since $\lim\limits_{x \to 2} (x - 2) = 0$. Furthermore, there is no way to simplify $g(x)$ algebraically (because $x^2 + 4$ doesn't factor). Hence, the Limit Theorem cannot be used. So try to estimate the limit by numerical or graphical means. Make a table of values, such as the one below, or graph the function. Remember that negative numbers far from 0 (such as -1000 or -5000) are very small numbers (even though their absolute values may be large).

	x approaches 2 from the left →				2	← *x* approaches 2 from the right		
x	1.8	1.9	1.99	1.999	2	2.001	2.01	2.05
$g(x)$	−36.2	−76.1	−796	−7996		8004	804	164
	g(*x*) gets smaller and smaller					*g*(*x*) gets larger and larger		

The table above and the graph of $g(x)$ in Figure 12.3 show that as x approaches 2 from the left, $g(x)$ gets smaller and smaller, but as x approaches 2 from the right, $g(x)$ gets larger and larger.

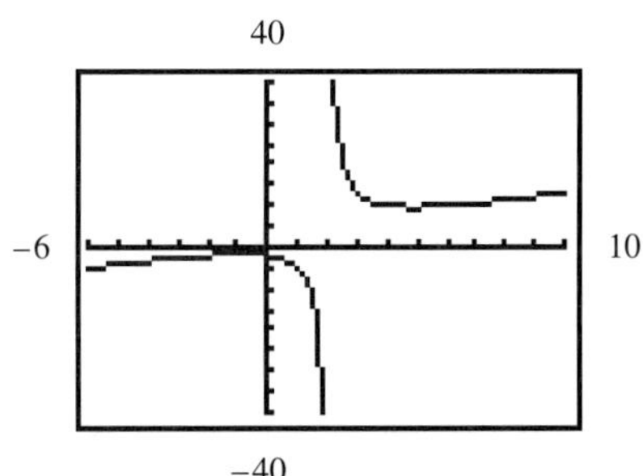

FIGURE 12.3

7 Let $f(x) = \frac{x^2 + 9}{x - 3}$. Find the following.

(a) $\lim_{x \to 3} f(x)$

(b) $\lim_{x \to 0} f(x)$

Answers:

(a) Does not exist

(b) -3

Since $g(x)$ does not get closer and closer to a single real number as x approaches 2 from either side,

$$\lim_{x \to 2} \frac{x^2 + 4}{x - 2} \text{ does not exist.}$$ ■ 7

EXAMPLE 9 What is $\lim_{x \to 0} \frac{|x|}{x}$?

The function $f(x) = |x|/x$ is not defined when $x = 0$. When $x > 0$, then the definition of absolute value shows that $f(x) = |x|/x = x/x = 1$. When $x < 0$, then $|x| = -x$ and $f(x) = -x/x = -1$. The graph of f is shown in Figure 12.4. As x approaches 0 from the right, x is always positive and the corresponding value of $f(x)$ is 1. But as x approaches 0 from the left, x is always negative and the corresponding value of $f(x)$ is -1. Thus, as x approaches 0 from *both* sides, the corresponding values of $f(x)$ do not get closer and closer to a *single* real number. Therefore, the limit does not exist.* ■

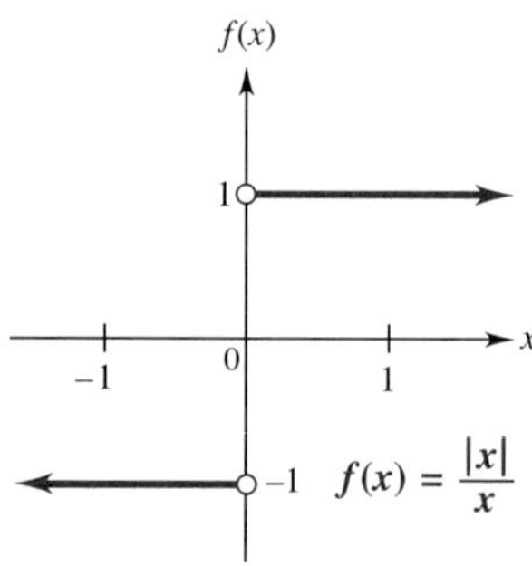

FIGURE 12.4

Examples 8 and 9 illustrate the following facts.

EXISTENCE OF LIMITS

The limit of a function f as x approaches a may fail to exist if

1. $f(x)$ becomes infinitely large in absolute value as x approaches a from either side (Example 8); or
2. $f(x)$ gets closer and closer to a number L as x approaches a from the left, but $f(x)$ gets closer and closer to a different number M as x approaches a from the right (Example 9).

*In a situation like this, one sometimes says that -1 is the *limit of $f(x)$ from the left* and that 1 is the *limit of $f(x)$ from the right*. The concept of limit as we have defined it is sometimes called a *two-sided limit*.

The function f whose graph is shown in Figure 12.5 illustrates various facts about limits that were discussed in this section.

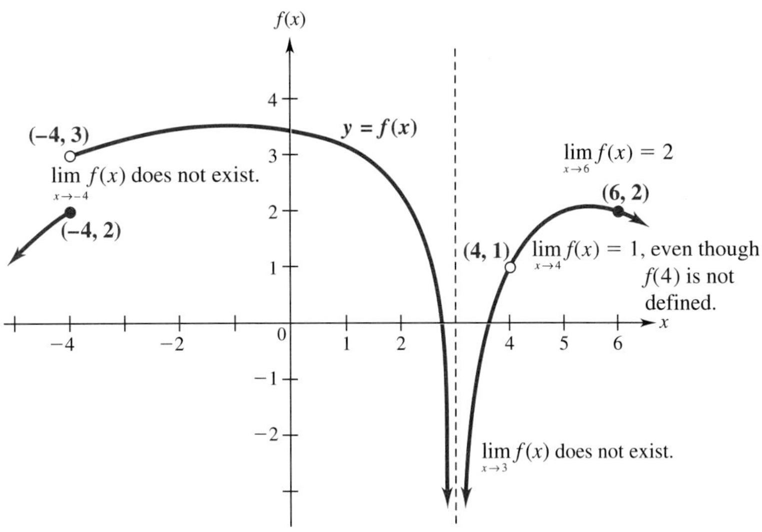

FIGURE 12.5

12.1 EXERCISES

In each of the following, use the graph to determine the value of the indicated limits. (See Examples 2, 3, 8, and 9 and Figure 12.5.)

1. (a) $\lim_{x\to 3} f(x)$ **(b)** $\lim_{x\to -1.5} f(x)$

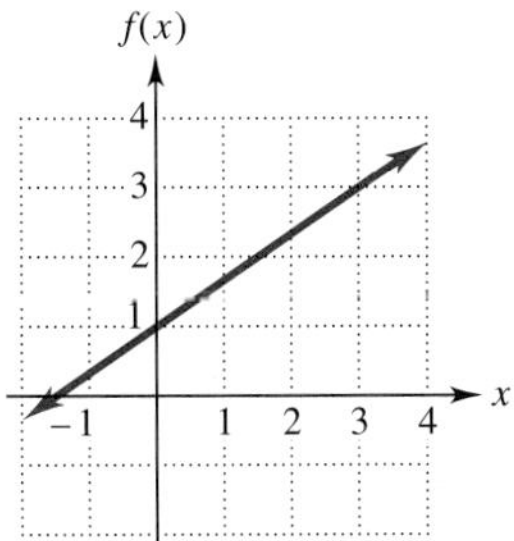

2. (a) $\lim_{x\to 2} F(x)$ **(b)** $\lim_{x\to -1} F(x)$

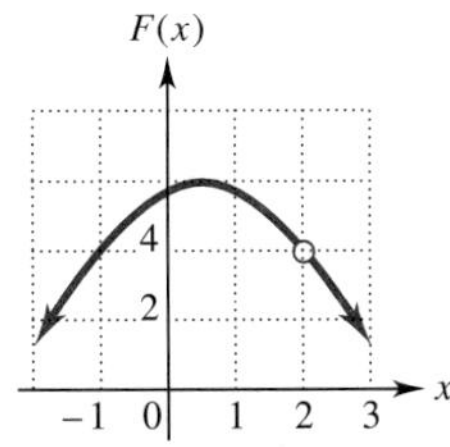

3. (a) $\lim_{x\to -2} f(x)$ **(b)** $\lim_{x\to 1} f(x)$

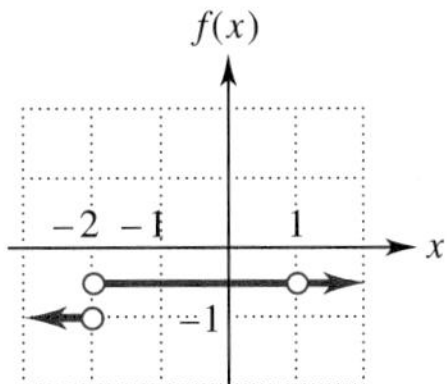

4. (a) $\lim_{x\to -1} g(x)$ **(b)** $\lim_{x\to 3} g(x)$

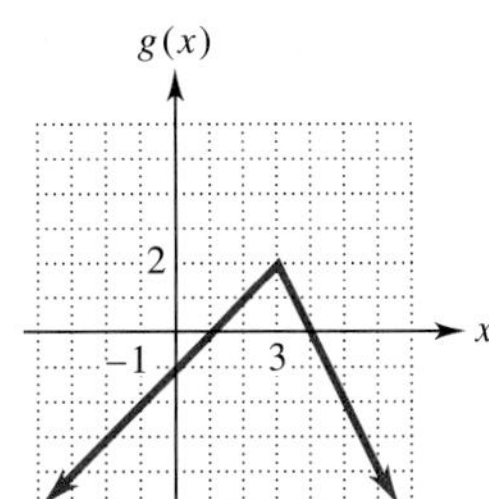

5. **(a)** $\lim_{x\to 0} f(x)$ **(b)** $\lim_{x\to -1} f(x)$

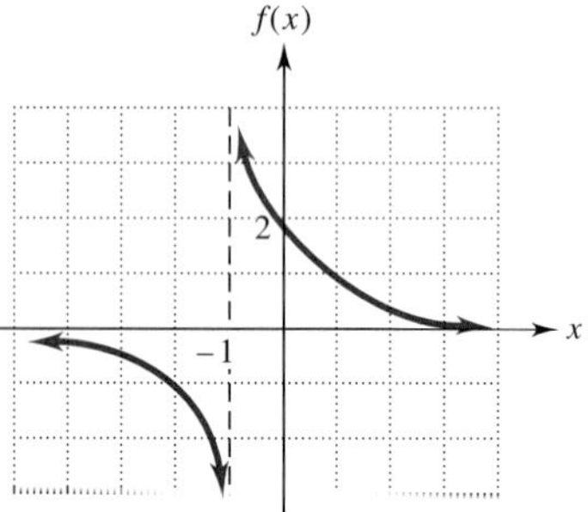

6. **(a)** $\lim_{x\to 1} h(x)$ **(b)** $\lim_{x\to 2} h(x)$

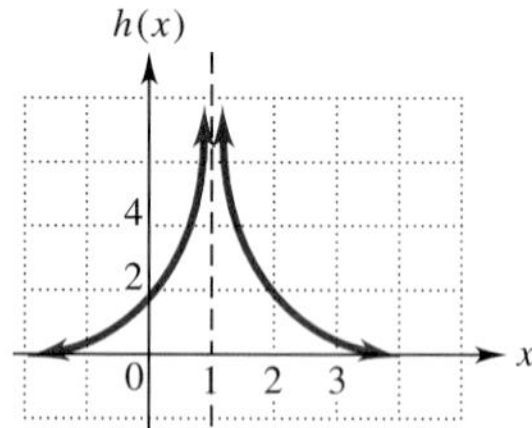

7. **(a)** $\lim_{x\to 1} g(x)$ **(b)** $\lim_{x\to -1} g(x)$

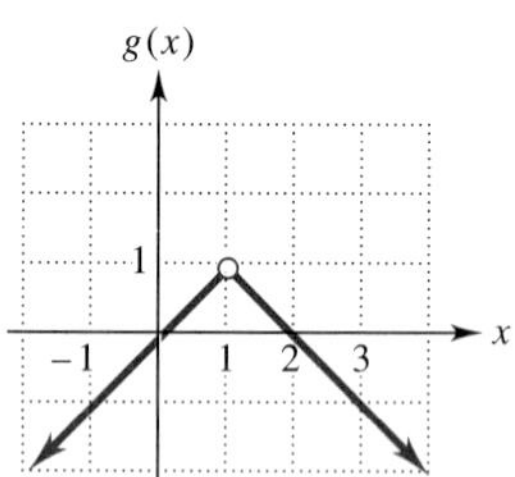

8. **(a)** $\lim_{x\to 3} f(x)$ **(b)** $\lim_{x\to 0} f(x)$

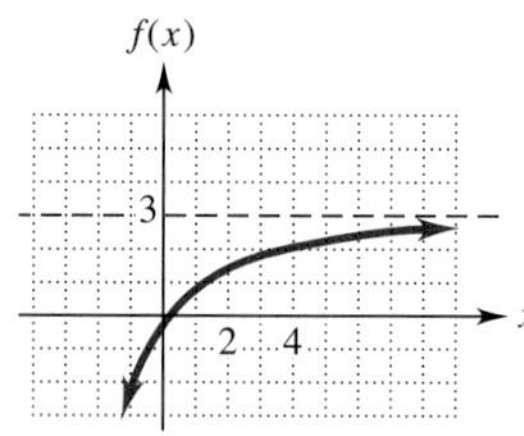

9. Explain why $\lim_{x\to 2} F(x)$ in Exercise 2(a) exists, but $\lim_{x\to -2} f(x)$ in Exercise 3(a) does not.

10. In Exercise 7(a), why does $\lim_{x\to 1} g(x)$ exist even though $g(1)$ is not defined?

Use a calculator and either the graphical method or the numerical method to estimate the limit. (See Examples 1, 2, 8, and 9.)

11. $\lim_{x\to 1} \dfrac{\ln x}{x-1}$

12. $\lim_{x\to 3} \dfrac{\ln x - \ln 3}{x-3}$

13. $\lim_{x\to 0} \dfrac{e^{2x}-1}{x}$

14. $\lim_{x\to 0} (x/\ln|x|)$

15. $\lim_{x\to 0} (x \ln|x|)$

16. $\lim_{x\to 0} \dfrac{x}{e^x - 1}$

17. $\lim_{x\to 3} \dfrac{x^3 - 3x^2 - x + 3}{x-3}$

18. $\lim_{x\to 4} \dfrac{.1x^4 - .8x^3 + 1.6x^2 + 2x - 8}{x-4}$

19. $\lim_{x\to -2} \dfrac{x^4 + 2x^3 - x^2 + 3x + 1}{x+2}$

20. $\lim_{x\to 0} \dfrac{e^{2x} + e^x - 2}{e^x - 1}$

Suppose $\lim_{x\to 4} f(x) = 16$ and $\lim_{x\to 4} g(x) = 8$. Use the limit properties to find the following limits.

21. $\lim_{x\to 4} [f(x) - g(x)]$

22. $\lim_{x\to 4} [g(x) \cdot f(x)]$

23. $\lim_{x\to 4} \dfrac{f(x)}{g(x)}$

24. $\lim_{x\to 4} [3 \cdot f(x)]$

25. $\lim_{x\to 4} \sqrt{f(x)}$

26. $\lim_{x\to 4} [g(x)]^3$

27. $\lim_{x\to 4} \dfrac{f(x) + g(x)}{2g(x)}$

28. $\lim_{x\to 4} \dfrac{5g(x) + 2}{1 - f(x)}$

29. **(a)** Graph the function f whose rule is

$$f(x) = \begin{cases} 3 - x & \text{if } x < -2 \\ x + 2 & \text{if } -2 \le x < 2. \\ 1 & \text{if } x \ge 2 \end{cases}$$

Use the graph in part (a) to find these limits.

(b) $\lim_{x\to -2} f(x)$ **(c)** $\lim_{x\to 1} f(x)$ **(d)** $\lim_{x\to 2} f(x)$

30. **(a)** Graph the function g whose rule is

$$g(x) = \begin{cases} x^2 & \text{if } x < -1 \\ x + 2 & \text{if } -1 \le x < 1. \\ 3 - x & \text{if } x \ge 1 \end{cases}$$

Use the graph in part (a) to find these limits.

(b) $\lim_{x\to -1} g(x)$ **(c)** $\lim_{x\to 0} g(x)$ **(d)** $\lim_{x\to 1} g(x)$

Use algebra and the properties of limits as needed to find the following limits. If the limit does not exist, say so. (See Examples 4–9.)

31. $\lim_{x\to 2} (2x^3 + 5x^2 + 2x + 1)$

32. $\lim_{x\to -1} (4x^3 - x^2 + 3x - 1)$

33. $\lim_{x\to 3} \dfrac{5x-6}{2x+1}$

34. $\lim_{x\to -2} \dfrac{2x+1}{3x-4}$

35. $\lim_{x\to 3} \dfrac{x^2 - 9}{x-3}$

36. $\lim_{x\to -2} \dfrac{x^2 - 4}{x+2}$

37. $\lim_{x\to -2} \dfrac{x^2 - x - 6}{x+2}$

38. $\lim_{x\to 5} \dfrac{x^2 - 3x - 10}{x-5}$

39. $\lim_{x\to 2} \frac{x^2 - 5x + 6}{x^2 - 6x + 8}$

40. $\lim_{x\to -2} \frac{x^2 + 3x + 2}{x^2 - x - 6}$

41. $\lim_{x\to 4} \frac{(x + 4)^2(x - 5)}{(x - 4)(x + 4)^2}$

42. $\lim_{x\to -3} \frac{(x + 3)(x - 3)(x + 4)}{(x + 8)(x + 3)(x - 4)}$

43. $\lim_{x\to 3} \sqrt{x^2 - 4}$

44. $\lim_{x\to 3} \sqrt{x^2 - 5}$

45. $\lim_{x\to 4} \frac{-6}{(x - 4)^2}$

46. $\lim_{x\to -2} \frac{3x}{(x + 2)^3}$

47. $\lim_{x\to 0} \frac{[1/(x + 3)] - 1/3}{x}$

48. $\lim_{x\to 0} \frac{[-1/(x + 2)] + 1/2}{x}$

49. $\lim_{x\to 25} \frac{\sqrt{x} - 5}{x - 25}$

50. $\lim_{x\to 36} \frac{\sqrt{x} - 6}{x - 36}$

51. $\lim_{x\to 5} \frac{\sqrt{x} - \sqrt{5}}{x - 5}$

52. $\lim_{x\to 8} \frac{\sqrt{x} - \sqrt{8}}{x - 8}$

53. **Management** The cost of manufacturing a particular videotape is

$$c(x) = 20{,}000 + 5x,$$

where x is the number of tapes produced. The average cost per tape, denoted by $\overline{c}(x)$, is found by dividing $c(x)$ by x. Find the following.
(a) $\overline{c}(1000)$ **(b)** $\overline{c}(100{,}000)$
(c) $\lim_{x\to 10{,}000} \overline{c}(x)$

54. **Management** A company training program has determined that a new employee can do an average of $P(s)$ pieces of work per day after s days of on-the-job training, where

$$P(s) = \frac{90s}{s + 6}.$$

Find the following.
(a) $P(1)$ **(b)** $P(11)$ **(c)** $\lim_{x\to 11} P(s)$

55. **Management** When the price of an essential commodity (such as gasoline) rises rapidly, consumption drops slowly at first. If the price continues to rise, however, a "tipping" point may be reached, at which consumption takes a sudden, substantial drop. Suppose the accompanying graph shows the consumption of gasoline, $G(t)$, in millions of gallons, in a certain area. We assume that the price is rising rapidly. Here t is time in months after the price began rising. Use the graph to find the following.
(a) $\lim_{t\to 12} G(t)$ **(b)** $\lim_{t\to 16} G(t)$ **(c)** $G(16)$
(d) The tipping point (in months)

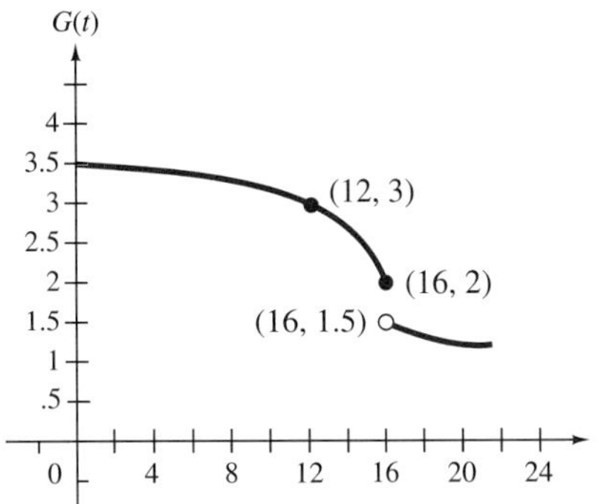

56. **Management** The graph below shows the profit from the daily production of x thousand kilograms of an industrial chemical. Use the graph to find the following limits.
(a) $\lim_{x\to 6} P(x)$ **(b)** $\lim_{x\to 10} P(x)$ **(c)** $\lim_{x\to 15} P(x)$
(d) Use the graph to estimate the number of units of the chemical that must be produced before the second shift is beneficial.

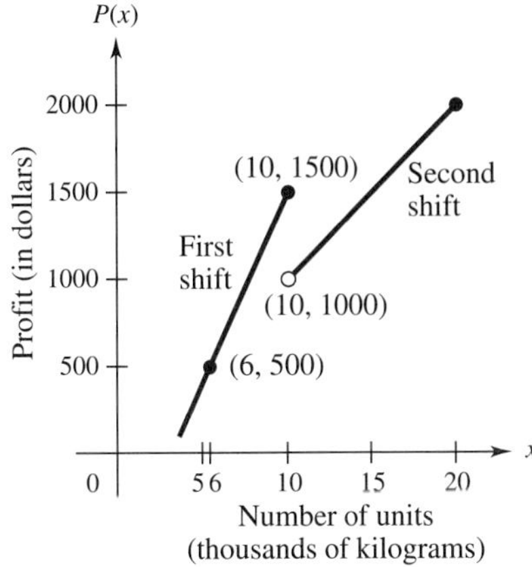

57. **Natural Science** The concentration of a drug in a patient's bloodstream h hours after it was injected is given by

$$A(h) = \frac{.2h}{h^2 + 2}.$$

Find the following.
(a) $A(.5)$ **(b)** $A(1)$ **(c)** $\lim_{h\to 1} A(h)$

58. **Management** Weekly sales (in dollars) at Sam's Shoppe x weeks after the end of an advertising campaign are given by

$$S(x) = 5000 + \frac{3600}{x + 2}.$$

Find the following.
(a) $S(2)$ **(b)** $\lim_{x\to 5} S(x)$ **(c)** $\lim_{x\to 16} S(x)$

12.2 RATES OF CHANGE

One of the main applications of calculus is determining how one variable changes in relation to another. A person in business wants to know how profit changes with respect to advertising, while a person in medicine wants to know how a patient's reaction to a drug changes with respect to the dose.

We begin the discussion with a familiar situation. A driver makes the 168-mile trip from Cleveland to Columbus, Ohio, in 3 hours. The following table shows how far the driver has traveled from Cleveland at various times.

Time (in hours)	0	.5	1	1.5	2	2.5	3
Distance (in miles)	0	22	52	86	118	148	168

If f is the function whose rule is

$$f(x) = \text{distance from Cleveland at time } x,$$

then the table shows, for example, that $f(2) = 118$ and $f(3) = 168$. So the distance traveled from time $x = 2$ to $x = 3$ is $168 - 118$, that is, $f(3) - f(2)$. In a similar fashion, we obtain the other entries in the following chart.

Time Interval	*Distance Traveled*
$x = 2$ to $x = 3$	$f(3) - f(2) = 168 - 118 = 50$
$x = 1$ to $x = 3$	$f(3) - f(1) = 168 - 52 = 116$
$x = 0$ to $x = 2.5$	$f(2.5) - f(0) = 148 - 0 = 148$
$x = .5$ to $x = 1$	$f(1) - f(.5) = 52 - 22 = 30$
$x = a$ to $x = b$	$f(b) - f(a)$

The last line of the chart shows how to find the distance traveled in any time interval $(0 \le a < b \le 3)$.

Since distance = average speed × time,

$$\text{Average speed} = \frac{\text{distance traveled}}{\text{time interval}}.$$

In the chart above, you can compute the length of each time interval by taking the difference between the two times. Thus, for example, from $x = 1$ to $x = 3$ is a time interval of length $3 - 1 = 2$ hours and, hence, the average speed over this interval is $116/2 = 58$ mph. Similarly, we have the following information.

Time Interval	*Average Speed* = $\dfrac{\textit{Distance Traveled}}{\textit{Time Interval}}$
$x = 2$ to $x = 3$	$\dfrac{f(3) - f(2)}{3 - 2} = \dfrac{168 - 118}{3 - 2} = \dfrac{50}{1} = 50$ mph
$x = 1$ to $x = 3$	$\dfrac{f(3) - f(1)}{3 - 1} = \dfrac{168 - 52}{3 - 1} = \dfrac{116}{2} = 58$ mph
$x = 0$ to $x = 2.5$	$\dfrac{f(2.5) - f(0)}{2.5 - 0} = \dfrac{148 - 0}{2.5 - 0} = \dfrac{148}{2.5} = 59.2$ mph
$x = .5$ to $x = 1$	$\dfrac{f(1) - f(.5)}{1 - .5} = \dfrac{52 - 22}{1 - .5} = \dfrac{30}{.5} = 60$ mph
$x = a$ to $x = b$	$\dfrac{f(b) - f(a)}{b - a}$ mph

1 Find the average speed

(a) from $t = 1.5$ to $t = 2$;

(b) from $t = s$ to $t = r$.

Answers:

(a) 64 mph

(b) $\frac{f(r) - f(s)}{r - s}$

The last line of the chart shows how to compute the average speed over any time interval ($0 \le a < b \le 3$). 1

Now speed (miles per hour) is simply the *rate of change* of distance with respect to time and what was done for the distance function f in the preceding discussion can be done with any function.

Quantity	*Meaning for the Distance Function*	*Meaning for an Arbitrary Function f*
$b - a$	Time interval = change in time from $x = a$ to $x = b$	Change in x from $x = a$ to $x = b$
$f(b) - f(a)$	Distance traveled = corresponding change in distance as time changes from a to b	Corresponding change in $f(x)$ as x changes from a to b
$\frac{f(b) - f(a)}{b - a}$	Average speed = average rate of change of distance with respect to time as time changes from a to b	**Average rate of change** of $f(x)$ with respect to x as x changes from a to b (where $a < b$)

EXAMPLE 1 If $f(x) = x^2 + 4x + 5$, find the average rate of change of $f(x)$ with respect to x as x changes from -2 to 3.

This is the situation described in the last line of the chart above, with $a = -2$ and $b = 3$. The average rate of change is

$$\frac{f(3) - f(-2)}{3 - (-2)} = \frac{26 - 1}{5} = \frac{25}{5} = 5. \blacksquare$$ 2

2 Find the average rate of change of $f(x)$ in Example 1 when x changes from

(a) 0 to 4;

(b) 2 to 7.

Answers:

(a) 8

(b) 13

EXAMPLE 2 The graph in Figure 12.6 on the next page shows the average price of steel $P(t)$, measured in dollars per ton, as a function of time t, measured in years.* The average rate of change of price with respect to time on an interval is the average rate of change of the function $P(t)$.

Chicago Tribune, December 12, 1995, Sec. 5, p. 1.

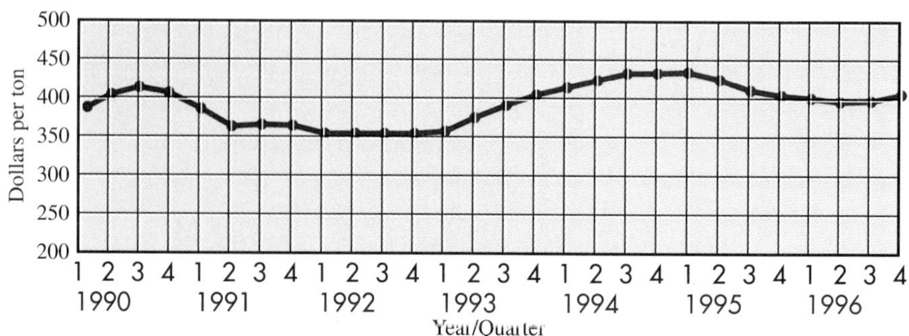

Sources: American Iron and Steel Institute; *Purchasing* magazine

FIGURE 12.6

(a) Approximate the average rate of change of price with respect to time from the first quarter of 1992 to the third quarter of 1995.

We denote the first quarter of 1992 by 92.00, the second quarter by 92.25, the third quarter by 92.50, and the fourth quarter by 92.75. Prices must be estimated from the graph. Verify that the price in the first quarter of 1992 is approximately \$355 and the price in the third quarter of 1995 is approximately \$410. Therefore, the average rate of change over this interval is

$$\frac{P(95.50) - P(92.00)}{95.50 - 92.00} = \frac{410 - 355}{95.50 - 92.00} = \frac{55}{3.5} \approx \$15.71.$$

On the average during this period, the price of a ton of steel increased at the rate of \$15.71 per year.

(b) Approximate the average rate of change of price with respect to time from the first quarter of 1990 to the first quarter of 1992.

The graph shows that the approximate price of a ton of steel was \$390 in the first quarter of 1990, so that the average rate of change is

$$\frac{P(92.00) - P(90.00)}{92.00 - 90.00} = \frac{355 - 390}{92.00 - 90.00} = \frac{-35}{2} = -\$17.50.$$

The negative number means that the price of a ton of steel *decreased* at the rate of \$17.50 per year during this period.

(c) Approximate the average rate of change of price with respect to time from the fourth quarter of 1990 to the fourth quarter of 1993.

Using the graph to approximate the values of the function P, we find that the average rate of change is

$$\frac{P(93.75) - P(90.75)}{93.75 - 90.75} = \frac{405 - 405}{93.75 - 90.75} = \frac{0}{3} = 0.$$

On the average, the price of a ton of steel did not change during this period. ■ 3

3 Use Figure 12.6 to find the average rate of change of price with respect to time

(a) from the first quarter of 1990 to the third quarter of 1995;

(b) from the fourth quarter of 1990 to the first quarter of 1992;

(c) from the fourth quarter of 1993 to the fourth quarter of 1994.

Answers:

(a) Increasing about \$3.64 per year

(b) Decreasing about \$40 per year

(c) Increasing about \$35 per year

INSTANTANEOUS RATE OF CHANGE Suppose a car is stopped at a traffic light. When the light turns green, the car begins to move along a straight road. Assume that the distance traveled by the car is given by the function

$$s(t) = 2t^2 \quad (0 \le t \le 30),$$

where time t is measured in seconds and the distance $s(t)$ at time t is measured in feet. We know how to find the *average* speed of the car over any time interval, so we now turn to a different problem: determining the *exact* speed of the car at a particular instant, say $t = 10$.*

The intuitive idea is that the exact speed at $t = 10$ is very close to the average speed over a very short time interval near $t = 10$. If we take shorter and shorter time intervals near $t = 10$, the average speeds over these intervals should get closer and closer to the exact speed at $t = 10$. In other words,

> the exact speed at $t = 10$ is the limit of the average speeds over shorter and shorter time intervals near $t = 10$.

The following chart illustrates this idea.

Interval	*Average Speed*
$t = 10$ to $t = 10.1$	$\dfrac{s(10.1) - s(10)}{10.1 - 10} = \dfrac{204.02 - 200}{.1} = 40.2$
$t = 10$ to $t = 10.01$	$\dfrac{s(10.01) - s(10)}{10.01 - 10} = \dfrac{200.4002 - 200}{.01} = 40.02$
$t = 10$ to $t = 10.001$	$\dfrac{s(10.001) - s(10)}{10.001 - 10} = \dfrac{200.040002 - 200}{.001} = 40.002$

The chart suggests that the exact speed at $t = 10$ is 40 ft/sec. We can confirm this intuition by computing the average speed from $t = 10$ to $t = 10 + h$, where h is any very small nonzero number. (The chart does this for $h = .1$, $h = .01$, and $h = .001$.) The average speed from $t = 10$ to $t = 10 + h$ is

$$\begin{aligned}
\frac{s(10 + h) - s(10)}{(10 + h) - 10} &= \frac{s(10 + h) - s(10)}{h} \\
&= \frac{2(10 + h)^2 - 2 \cdot 10^2}{h} \\
&= \frac{2(100 + 20h + h^2) - 200}{h} \\
&= \frac{200 + 40h + 2h^2 - 200}{h} \\
&= \frac{40h + 2h^2}{h} = \frac{h(40 + 2h)}{h} \qquad (h \ne 0) \\
&= 40 + 2h.
\end{aligned}$$

*As distance is measured in feet and time in seconds here, speed is measured in feet per second. It may help to know that 15 mph is equivalent to 22 ft/sec and 60 mph to 88 ft/sec.

Saying that the time interval from 10 to $10 + h$ gets shorter and shorter is equivalent to saying h gets closer and closer to 0. Hence, the exact speed at $t = 10$ is the limit as h approaches 0 of the average speeds over the intervals from $t = 10$ to $t = 10 + h$; that is,

$$\lim_{h \to 0} \frac{s(10 + h) - s(10)}{h} = \lim_{h \to 0} (40 + 2h)$$
$$= 40 \text{ ft/sec.}$$

The preceding example can easily be generalized. Suppose an object is moving in a straight line with its position (distance from some fixed point) at time t given by the function $s(t)$. The speed of the object is called its **velocity** and its exact speed at time t is called the **instantaneous velocity at time t** (or just velocity at time t).

Let t_0 be a constant. By replacing 10 by t_0 in the discussion above, we see that the average velocity of the object from time $t = t_0$ to time $t = t_0 + h$ is the quotient

$$\frac{s(t_0 + h) - s(t_0)}{(t_0 + h) - t_0} = \frac{s(t_0 + h) - s(t_0)}{h}.$$

The instantaneous velocity at time t_0 is the limit of this quotient as h approaches 0.

VELOCITY

If an object moves along a straight line, with position $s(t)$ at time t, then the **velocity** of the object at $t = t_0$ is

$$\lim_{h \to 0} \frac{s(t_0 + h) - s(t_0)}{h},$$

provided this limit exists.

EXAMPLE 3 The distance in feet of an object from a starting point is given by $s(t) = 2t^2 - 5t + 40$, where t is time in seconds.

(a) Find the average velocity of the object from 2 seconds to 4 seconds.
The average velocity is

$$\frac{s(4) - s(2)}{4 - 2} = \frac{52 - 38}{2} = \frac{14}{2} = 7$$

feet per second.

(b) Find the instantaneous velocity at 4 seconds.
For $t = 4$, the instantaneous velocity is

$$\lim_{h \to 0} \frac{s(4 + h) - s(4)}{h}$$

feet per second. We have

$$\begin{aligned} s(4 + h) &= 2(4 + h)^2 - 5(4 + h) + 40 \\ &= 2(16 + 8h + h^2) - 20 - 5h + 40 \\ &= 32 + 16h + 2h^2 - 20 - 5h + 40 \\ &= 2h^2 + 11h + 52 \end{aligned}$$

and

$$s(4) = 2(4)^2 - 5(4) + 40 = 52.$$

Thus,

$$s(4 + h) - s(4) = (2h^2 + 11h + 52) - 52 = 2h^2 + 11h$$

and the instantaneous velocity at $t = 4$ is

$$\lim_{h \to 0} \frac{2h^2 + 11h}{h} = \lim_{h \to 0} \frac{h(2h + 11)}{h}$$

$$= \lim_{h \to 0} (2h + 11) = 11 \text{ ft/sec.} \quad \blacksquare \quad \boxed{4}$$

$\boxed{4}$ In Example 3, if $s(t) = s^2 + 3$, find

(a) the average velocity from 1 second to 5 seconds;

(b) the instantaneous velocity at 5 seconds.

Answers:

(a) 6 ft per second

(b) 10 ft per second

EXAMPLE 4 The velocity of blood cells is of interest to physicians; a slower velocity than normal might indicate a constriction, for example. Suppose the position of a red blood cell in a capillary is given by

$$s(t) = 1.2t + 5,$$

where $s(t)$ gives the position of a cell in millimeters from some reference point and t is time in seconds. Find the velocity of this cell at time $t = t_0$.

Evaluate the limit given above. To find $s(t_0 + h)$, substitute $t_0 + h$ for the variable t in $s(t) = 1.2t + 5$.

$$s(t_0 + h) = 1.2(t_0 + h) + 5$$

Now use the definition of velocity.

$$v(t) = \lim_{h \to 0} \frac{s(t_0 + h) - s(t_0)}{h}$$

$$= \lim_{h \to 0} \frac{1.2(t_0 + h) + 5 - (1.2t_0 + 5)}{h}$$

$$= \lim_{h \to 0} \frac{1.2t_0 + 1.2h + 5 - 1.2t_0 - 5}{h} = \lim_{h \to 0} \frac{1.2h}{h} = 1.2$$

The velocity of the blood cell at $t = t_0$ is 1.2 millimeters per second, regardless of the value of t_0. In other words, the blood velocity is a constant 1.2 millimeters per second at any time. $\blacksquare$ $\boxed{5}$

$\boxed{5}$ Repeat Example 4 with $s(t) = .3t - 2$.

Answer:

The velocity is .3 millimeter per second.

The ideas underlying the concept of the velocity of a moving object can be extended to any function $f(x)$. In place of average velocity at time t, we have the average rate of change of $f(x)$ with respect to x as x changes from one value to another. Taking limits leads to this definition.

> The **instantaneous rate of change** for a function f when $x = x_0$ is
>
> $$\lim_{h \to 0} \frac{f(x_0 + h) - f(x_0)}{h},$$
>
> provided this limit exists.

EXAMPLE 5 A company determines that the cost in hundreds of dollars of manufacturing x units of a certain item is

$$C(x) = -.2x^2 + 8x + 40 \quad (0 \le x \le 20).$$

(a) Find the average rate of change of cost per item for manufacturing between 5 and 10 items.

Use the formula for average rate of change. The cost to manufacture 5 items is

$$C(5) = -.2(5^2) + 8(5) + 40 = 75,$$

or \$7500. The cost to manufacture 10 items is

$$C(10) = -.2(10^2) + 8(10) + 40 = 100,$$

or \$10,000. The average rate of change of cost is

$$\frac{C(10) - C(5)}{10 - 5} = \frac{100 - 75}{5} = 5.$$

Thus, on the average, cost is increasing at the rate of \$500 per item when production is increased from 5 to 10 units.

(b) Find the instantaneous rate of change with respect to the number of items produced when 5 items are produced.

The instantaneous rate of change when $x = 5$ is given by

$$\lim_{h\to 0} \frac{C(5 + h) - C(5)}{h}$$

$$= \lim_{h\to 0} \frac{[-.2(5 + h)^2 + 8(5 + h) + 40] - [-.2(5^2) + 8(5) + 40]}{h}$$

$$= \lim_{h\to 0} \frac{[-5 - 2h - .2h^2 + 40 + 8h + 40] - [75]}{h}$$

$$= \lim_{h\to 0} \frac{6h - .2h^2}{h} \qquad \text{Combine terms.}$$

$$= \lim_{h\to 0} (6 - .2h) \qquad \text{Divide by } h.$$

$$= 6. \qquad \text{Calculate the limit.}$$

When 5 items are manufactured, the cost is increasing at the rate of \$600 per item. ■

The rate of change of the cost function is called the **marginal cost.*** Similarly, **marginal revenue** and **marginal profit** are the rates of change of the revenue and profit functions, respectively. Part (b) of Example 5 shows that the marginal cost when 5 items are manufactured is \$600.

EXAMPLE 6 The function whose rule is $S(x) = 2.5(1.0185)^x$, gives the (approximate) population of the world (in billions) in year x, where $x = 0$ corresponds to 1950. The graph of $S(x)$ in Figure 12.7 shows that the population is steadily increasing. At what *rate* is the population increasing in the year 2000?

---

*Marginal cost for linear cost functions was discussed in Section 3.3.

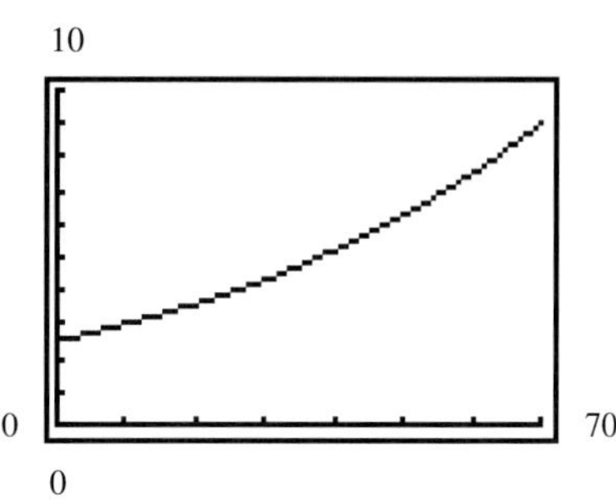

FIGURE 12.7

The year 2000 corresponds to $x = 50$ and the instantaneous rate of change of $S(x)$ when $x = 50$ is

$$\lim_{h\to 0} \frac{S(50 + h) - S(50)}{h} = \lim_{h\to 0} \frac{2.5(1.0185)^{50+h} - 2.5(1.0185)^{50}}{h}.$$

Although there is no algebraic way to compute this limit, it can be approximated either graphically (using trace) or numerically. The graph and the table in Figure 12.8 suggest that the limit is about .1146.* Since $S(x)$ is measured in billions, this means that world population is increasing at a rate of .1146 billion per year, that is, 114,600,000 people per year. ■

X	Y1
-.003	.11459
-.002	.1146
-.001	[illegible]
0	ERROR
.001	.1146
.002	.1146
.003	.1146

Y1=.1145968875

FIGURE 12.8

*Since the function variable on a calculator is denoted X, we enter the function as

$$y_1 = \frac{2.5(1.0185)^{50+X} - 2.5(1.0185)^{50}}{X}$$

and consider the limit as X approaches 0.

12.2 EXERCISES

Find the average rate of change for the following functions over the given closed intervals. (See Example 1.)

1. $f(x) = x^2 + 2x$ between $x = 0$ and $x = 5$

2. $f(x) = -4x^2 - 6$ between $x = 2$ and $x = 5$

3. $f(x) = 2x^3 - 4x^2 + 6x$ between $x = -1$ and $x = 2$

4. $f(x) = -3x^3 + 2x^2 - 4x + 1$ between $x = 0$ and $x = 1$

5. $f(x) = \sqrt{x}$ between $x = 1$ and $x = 4$

6. $f(x) = \sqrt{3x - 2}$ between $x = 1$ and $x = 3$

7. $f(x) = \dfrac{1}{x - 1}$ between $x = -2$ and $x = 0$

8. **Management** Data in an article in *The New York Times* suggests that the number of personal computers with

CD-ROM drives (in millions) is approximately given by the function $f(x) = .4525e^{1.556\sqrt{x}}$, where x is the number of years since 1990.* Find the average rate of change of this function for the first half of 1994 (that is, from $x = 4$ to $x = 4.5$).

Solve Exercises 9–16 by reading the necessary information from the graphs. (See Example 2.)

9. Use the graph of the function f to find each of the following.
(a) $f(1)$ **(b)** $f(3)$ **(c)** $f(5) - f(1)$
(d) The average rate of change of $f(x)$ as x changes from 1 to 5
(e) The average rate of change of $f(x)$ as x changes from 3 to 5

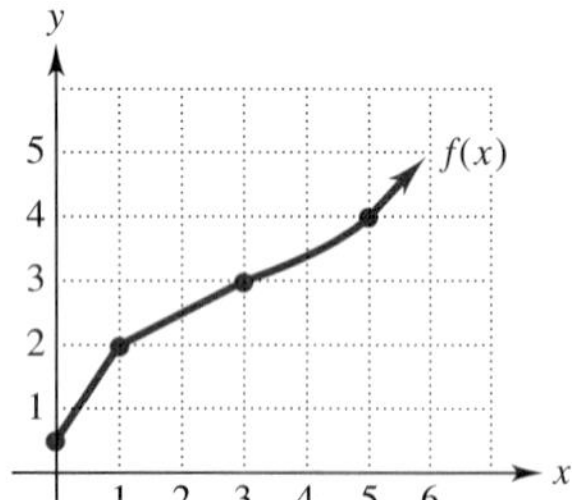

10. Management The graph shows the total sales in thousands of dollars from the distribution of x thousand catalogs. Find and interpret the average rate of change of sales with respect to the number of catalogs distributed for the following changes in x.
(a) 10 to 20 **(b)** 20 to 30 **(c)** 30 to 40
(d) What is happening to the average rate of change of sales as the number of catalogs distributed increases?
(e) Explain why part (d) might happen.

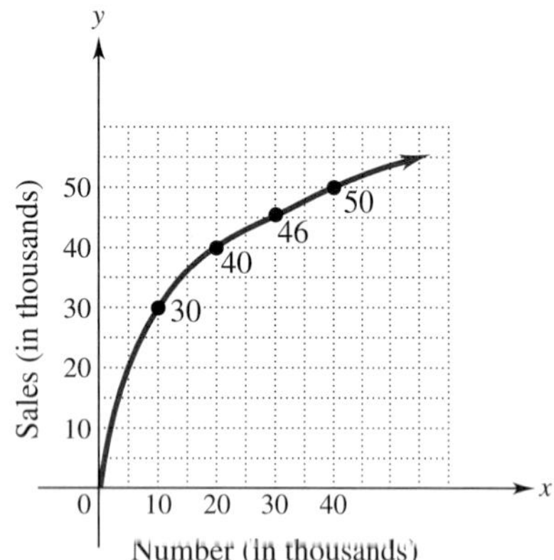

11. Management The graph shows annual sales (in appropriate units) of a computer game. Find the average annual rate of change in sales for the following changes in years.
(a) 1 to 4 **(b)** 4 to 7 **(c)** 7 to 12
(d) What do your answers for parts (a)–(c) tell you about the sales of this product?
(e) Give an example of another product that might have such a sales curve.

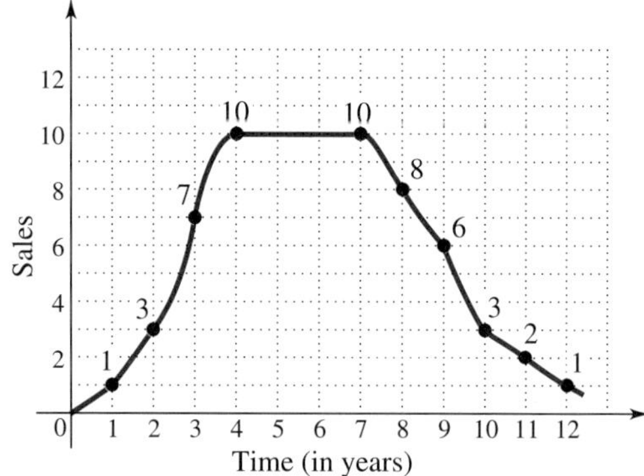

12. Management IBM Europe steadily lost its share of the market from 1985 to 1990, as shown in the figure.* Estimate the average drop in market share (in percent) over the following intervals.
(a) 1985 to 1986 **(b)** 1986 to 1988
(c) 1988 to 1989 **(d)** 1989 to 1990
(e) From your answers to parts (a)–(d), did the decline in market share seem to be increasing or tapering off?
(f) In which one-year period was the decline the greatest?

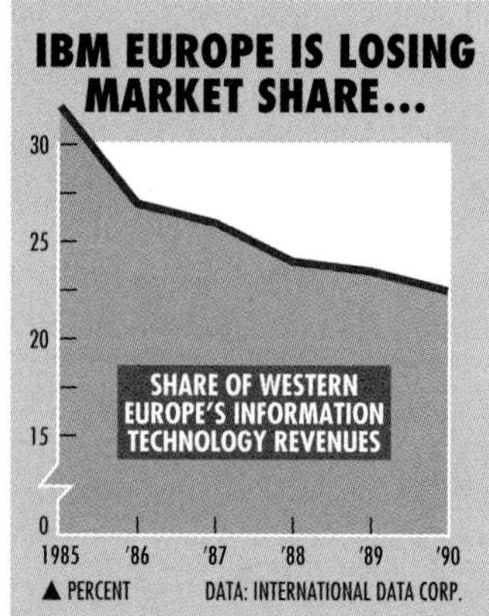

13. Management The graph shows the number of McDonald's restaurants in the United States as a function of time.† Find and interpret the average rate of change in the

The New York Times, December 28, 1993, p. D1.

*"IBM Europe Is Losing Market Share . . . and Feeling a Profit Pinch" reprinted from May 6, 1991 issue of *Business Week* by special permission, copyright © 1991 by McGraw-Hill, Inc.

†*Chicago Tribune*, Jan. 20, 1996, Sec. 5, p. 1.

number of restaurants with respect to time over the following intervals.

(a) 1955 to 1965
(b) 1965 to 1975
(c) 1975 to 1985
(d) 1985 to 1995
(e) 1955 to 1995
(f) What is happening to the average rate of change in the number of restaurants as time increases?
(g) How can the answer to part (e) be derived from the answers to parts (a)–(d)?

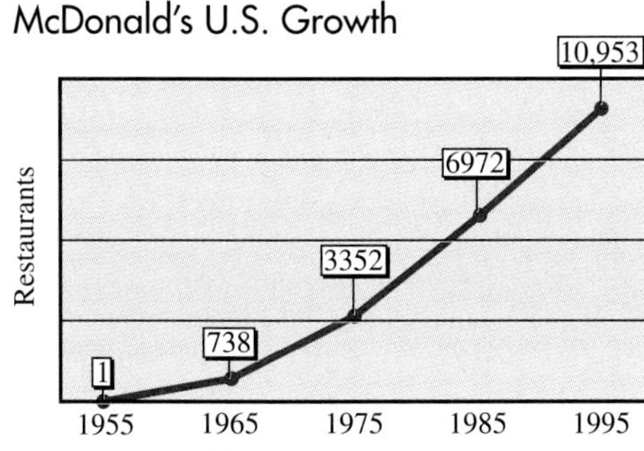

14. **Management** The graph* shows the amount spent by the Federal government and state Medicaid on prescription drugs during an eleven-year period. Spending went from 1.6 billion dollars in 1981 to 4.4 billion in 1990 to 6.7 billion in 1992. What was the average rate of change in spending (in billions of dollars per year) from

(a) 1981 to 1984?
(b) 1984 to 1987?
(c) 1987 to 1990?
(d) 1990 to 1992?
(e) How does the rate of change in the first three years of the period shown on the graph compare with the rate during the last two years?

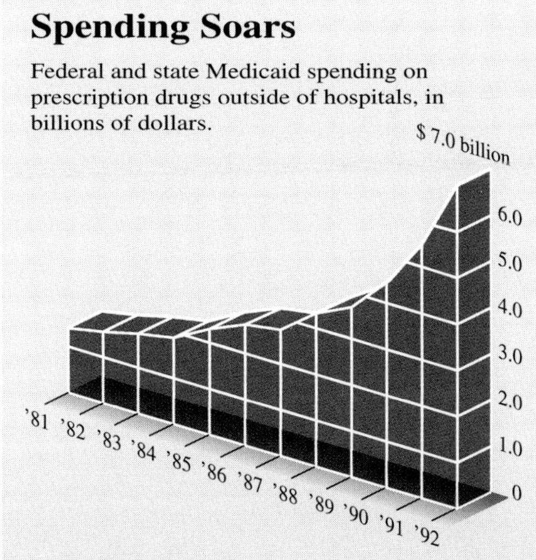

15. **Social Science** The graph* shows the amounts paid to the U.S. Treasury in fines by polluters during the 80s.

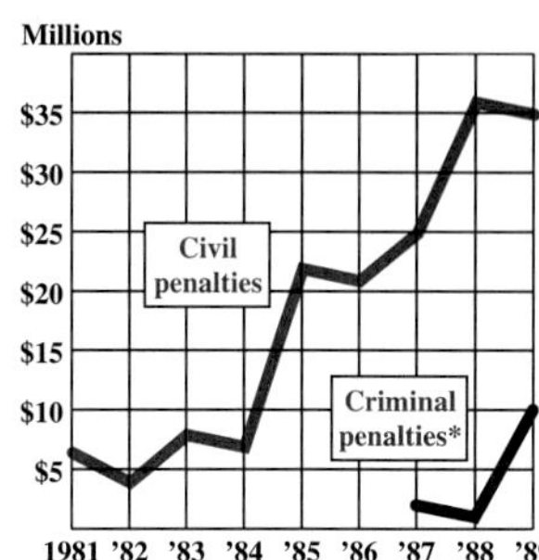

*Accurate data not available before 1987.
Source: EPA; art by Mark Holmes, NGS staff.

(a) Find the average rate of change for civil penalties from 1987 to 1988, and from 1988 to 1989.
(b) Find the average rate of change of criminal penalties from 1987 to 1988, and from 1988 to 1989.
(c) Compare your results for parts (a) and (b). What do they tell you? What might account for the differences?
(d) Find the average rate of change for civil penalties from 1981 to 1989. What was the general trend over this eight-year period? What might explain this trend?

16. Use the graph of the function g to answer these questions.

(a) Between which pair of consecutive points (P, Q, R, S, T) is the average rate of change of $g(x)$ the smallest?
(b) Between which pair of consecutive points is the average rate of change of $g(x)$ the largest?
(c) Between which pair of consecutive points is the average rate of change of $g(x)$ closest to 0?

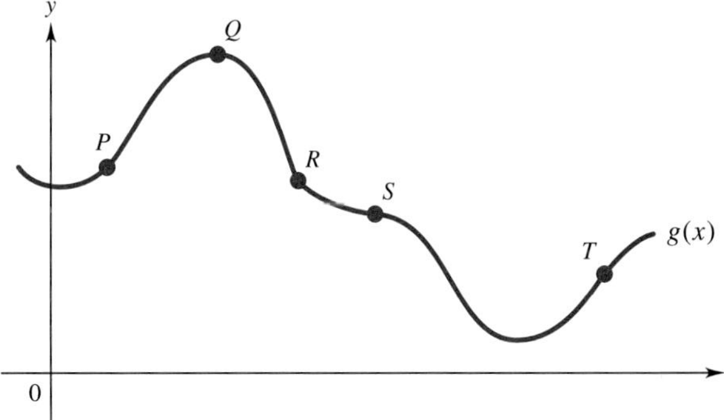

17. Explain the difference between the average rate of change of $y = f(x)$ as x changes from a to b, and the instantaneous rate of change of y at $x = a$.

18. If the instantaneous rate of change of $f(x)$ with respect to x is positive when $x = 1$, is f increasing or decreasing there?

*"Spending Soars" from *The New York Times*, July 7, 1993. Copyright © 1993 by the New York Times Company. Reprinted by permission.

*Graph entitled "Higher EPA Fines Make Pollution Costly" by Mark Holmes from *National Geographic*, February 1991. Copyright © 1991 by National Geographic Society. Reprinted by permission.

Exercises 19–21 deal with a car moving along a straight road, as discussed on pages 561–562. At time t seconds the distance of the car (in feet) from the starting point is $s(t) = 2t^2$. Find the instantaneous velocity (speed) of the car at

19. $t = 5$; **20.** $t = 20$.

21. What was the average speed of the car during the first 30 seconds?

An object moves along a straight line; its distance (in feet) from a fixed point at time t seconds is $s(t) = t^2 + 5t + 2$. Find the instantaneous velocity of the object at the following times. (See Example 3.)

22. $t = 6$ **23.** $t = 1$ **24.** $t = 10$

In each of the following exercises, find: (a) $f(x_0 + h)$; (b) $\frac{f(x_0 + h) - f(x_0)}{h}$; (c) *the instantaneous rate of change of f when $x_0 = 5$. (See Examples 3–5.)*

25. $f(x) = x^2 + 1$ **26.** $f(x) = x^2 + x$

27. $f(x) = x^2 - x - 1$ **28.** $f(x) = x^2 + 2x + 2$

29. $f(x) = x^3$ **30.** $f(x) = x^3 - x$

Solve Exercises 31 and 32 by algebraic methods. (See Examples 3–5.)

31. Management The revenue (in thousands of dollars) from producing x units of an item is

$$R(x) = 10x - .002x^2.$$

(a) Find the average rate of change of revenue when production is increased from 1000 to 1001 units.
(b) Find the marginal revenue when 1000 units are produced.
(c) Find the additional revenue if production is increased from 1000 to 1001 units.
(d) Compare your answers for parts (a) and (c). What do you find?

32. Management Suppose customers in a hardware store are willing to buy $N(p)$ boxes of nails at p dollars per box, as given by

$$N(p) = 80 - 5p^2, \quad 1 \le p \le 4.$$

(a) Find the average rate of change of demand for a change in price from \$2 to \$3.
(b) Find the instantaneous rate of change of demand when the price is \$2.
(c) Find the instantaneous rate of change of demand when the price is \$3.
(d) As the price is increased from \$2 to \$3, how is demand changing? Is the change to be expected?

In Exercises 33–36, use graphical or numerical methods to estimate the instantaneous rates of change. (See Example 6.)

33. Physical Science The distance (in ft) of a particle from a fixed point is given by

$$s(t) = .01t^4 - .3t^3 + 3t^2 + 2t + 2,$$

where the time t is measured in seconds. Find the average velocity over each of the following intervals.
(a) 8 to 12 sec **(b)** 9 to 11 sec **(c)** 9.5 to 10.5 sec
(d) 9.9 to 10.1 sec
(e) What is the instantaneous velocity when $t = 10$?

34. Physical Science A car is moving along a straight test track. The distance $s(t)$, in feet, traveled by the car at time t seconds is given by $s(t) = .01t^3 - .3t^2 + 4t$. Find the average velocity (speed) of the car over the following intervals.
(a) $t = 0$ to $t = 6$ **(b)** $t = 2$ to $t = 12$
(c) $t = 6$ to $t = 18$
What is the instantaneous velocity of the car when
(d) $t = 10$? **(e)** $t = 20$?

35. Management Based on figures from the first half of the decade, a small firm projects that its yearly profits (in dollars) between 1992 and 2002 are approximated by the function

$$P(x) = 25x^3 - 309x^2 + 1391x + 5000,$$

where $0 \le x \le 10$ and $x = 0$ corresponds to 1992.
(a) Find the average rate of change of profit from 1992 to 1996.
(b) What is the marginal profit in 1996?
(c) What is the marginal profit in 2000?

36. Social Science In an experiment, teenagers memorize a list of 15 words and then listen to rock music for certain periods of time. After t minutes of listening to rock music, the typical subject can remember approximately

$$R(t) = 15 - 4 \ln x$$

of the words, where $0 \le t \le 25$. Find the instantaneous rate at which the typical student remembers the words at the following times.
(a) $t = 5$ **(b)** $t = 15$

12.3 TANGENT LINES AND DERIVATIVES

We now develop a geometric interpretation of the rates of change considered in the previous section. In geometry, a tangent line to a circle at a point P is defined to be the line through P that is perpendicular to the radius OP, as in Figure 12.9 (which shows only the top half of the circle). If you think of this circle as a road on which you are driving at night, then the tangent line indicates the direction of the light beam from your headlights as you pass through the point P. This suggests a way of extending the idea of a tangent line to any curve: the tangent line to the curve at a point P indicates the "direction" of the curve as it passes through P. Using this intuitive idea of direction, we see, for example, that the lines through P_1 and P_3 in Figure 12.10 appear to be tangent lines, whereas the lines through P_2 and P_4 do not.

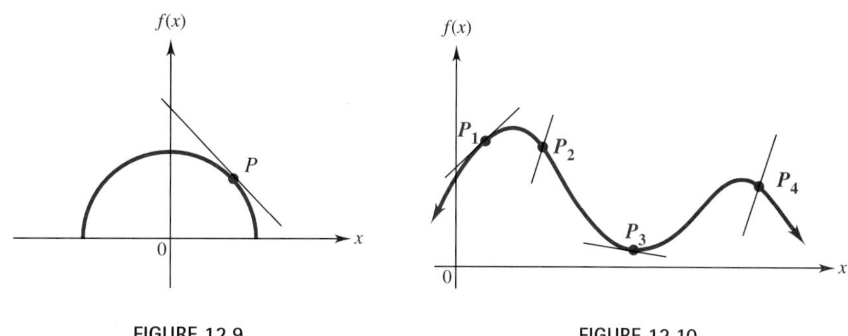

FIGURE 12.9 FIGURE 12.10

The tangent line through P_1 in Figure 12.10 appears to coincide with the graph near that point, and similarly at P_3. This suggests another informal way to think about tangent lines. Consider the graph of the function $f(x) = x^3 - 4x^2 + x + 3$ in Figure 12.11(a). Since $f(2) = -3$, the point $(2, -3)$ is on the graph. By using a calculator's zoom-in feature at $(2, -3)$, we obtain Figure 12.11(b), which looks very much like a straight line.

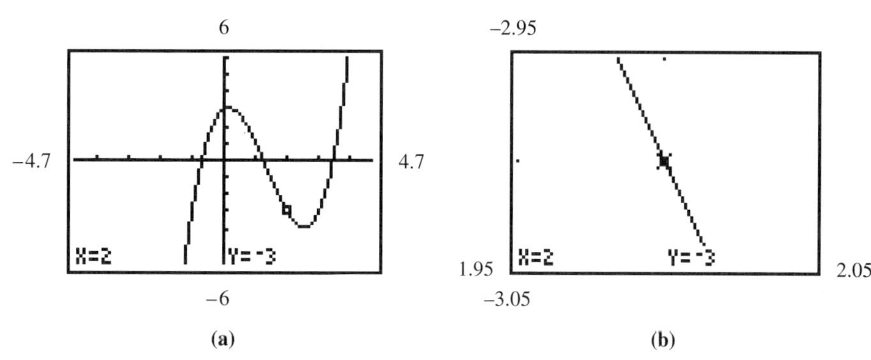

FIGURE 12.11

1 Find a viewing window in which the graph of

$$f(x) = -x^3 + 4x^2 - x - 5$$

near the point (2, 1) appears to be a straight line.

Answer:
Many possible correct answers, including $1.95 \le x \le 2.05$ and $.95 \le y \le 1.05$.

Although the tiny portion of the graph in Figure 12.11(b) is not actually a straight line, it suggests that near the point $(2, -3)$, the graph of f can be *approximated* by a line. You can think of the tangent line as the line through $(2, -3)$ that best approximates the graph near that point. 1

We now find the tangent line to the graph of a function f at the point R. As shown in Figure 12.12 on the next page, choose a second point S on the graph and draw the line through R and S. This line is called a **secant line.** You can think of this secant line as a rough approximation of the tangent line.

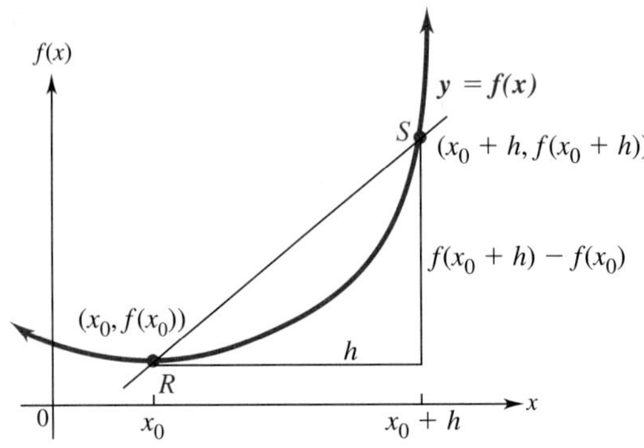

FIGURE 12.12

Now suppose that the point S slides down the curve closer to R. Figure 12.13 shows successive positions S_1, S_2, S_3, S_4 of the point S. The closer S gets to R, the better the secant line RS approximates our intuitive idea of the tangent line at R.

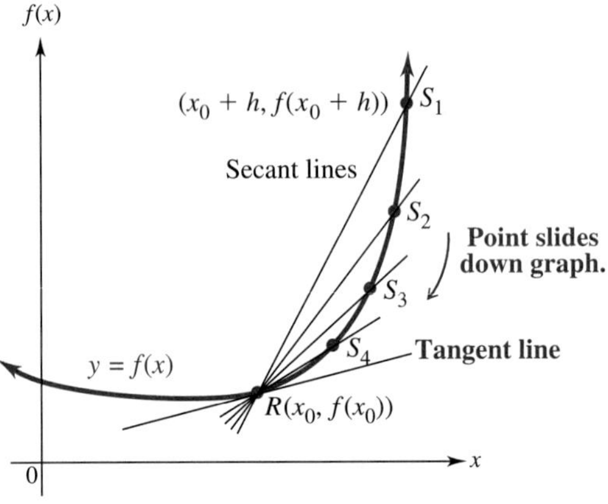

FIGURE 12.13

In particular, the closer S gets to R, the closer the slope of the secant line gets to the slope of the tangent line. Informally we say that

The slope of tangent line at R = The limit of the slope of secant line RS as S gets closer and closer to R.

In order to make this more precise, suppose the first coordinate of R is x_0. Then the first coordinate of S can be written as $x_0 + h$ for some number h (in Figure 12.12, h is the distance on the x-axis between the two first coordinates). Thus R has coordinates $(x_0, f(x_0))$ and S has coordinates $(x_0 + h, f(x_0 + h))$, as shown in Figure 12.12. Consequently, the slope of the secant line RS is

$$\frac{f(x_0 + h) - f(x_0)}{(x_0 + h) - x_0} = \frac{f(x_0 + h) - f(x_0)}{h}.$$

Now as S moves closer to R, their first coordinates move closer to each other, that is, h gets smaller and smaller. Hence

$$\begin{aligned}\text{Slope of tangent line at } R &= \text{The limit of slope of secant line } RS \\ &\quad \text{as } S \text{ gets closer and closer to } R; \\ &= \text{The limit of } \frac{f(x_0 + h) - f(x_0)}{h} \\ &\quad \text{as } h \text{ gets closer and closer to } 0; \\ &= \lim_{h \to 0} \frac{f(x_0 + h) - f(x_0)}{h}.\end{aligned}$$

This intuitive development suggests the following formal definition.

TANGENT LINE

The **tangent line** to the graph of $y = f(x)$ at the point $(x_0, f(x_0))$ is the line through this point having slope

$$\lim_{h \to 0} \frac{f(x_0 + h) - f(x_0)}{h}$$

provided this limit exists. If this limit does not exist, then there is no tangent at the point.

The slope of the tangent line at a point is also called the **slope of the curve** at that point. Since the slope of a line indicates its direction (see the box on page 47), the slope of the tangent line at a point indicates the direction of the curve at that point.

EXAMPLE 1 Find the slope of the tangent line to the graph of $y = x^2 + 2$ when $x = -1$. Find the equation of the tangent line.

Use the definition above, with $f(x) = x^2 + 2$ and $x_0 = -1$. The slope of the tangent line is

$$\begin{aligned}\text{Slope of tangent} &= \lim_{h \to 0} \frac{f(x_0 + h) - f(x_0)}{h} \\ &= \lim_{h \to 0} \frac{[(-1 + h)^2 + 2] - [(-1)^2 + 2]}{h} \\ &= \lim_{h \to 0} \frac{[1 - 2h + h^2 + 2] - [1 + 2]}{h} \\ &= \lim_{h \to 0} \frac{-2h + h^2}{h} = \lim_{h \to 0} (-2 + h) = -2.\end{aligned}$$

The slope of the tangent line at $(-1, f(-1)) = (-1, 3)$ is -2. The equation of the tangent line can be found with the point-slope form of the equation of a line from Chapter 1.

$$\begin{aligned} y - y_1 &= m(x - x_1) \\ y - 3 &= -2[x - (-1)] \\ y - 3 &= -2(x + 1) \\ y - 3 &= -2x - 2 \\ y &= -2x + 1 \end{aligned}$$

Figure 12.14 shows a graph of $f(x) = x^2 + 2$, along with a graph of the tangent line at $x = -1$. ■

2 Let $f(x) = x^2 + 2$.

(a) Find the equation of the tangent line to the graph at the point where $x = 1$.

(b) Confirm your answer by graphing $f(x)$ and the tangent line on the same screen.

Answers:

(a) $y = 2x + 1$

(b)

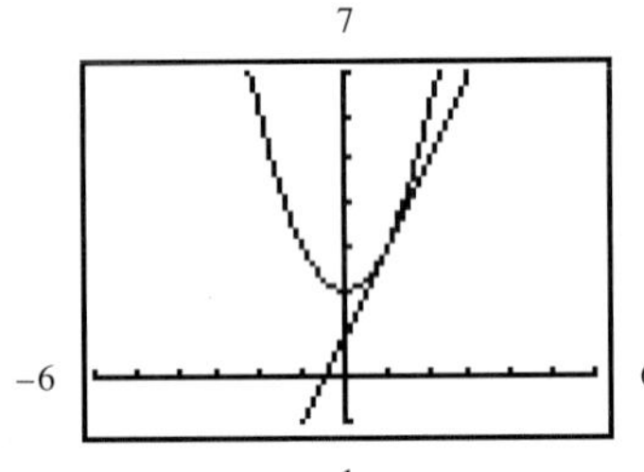

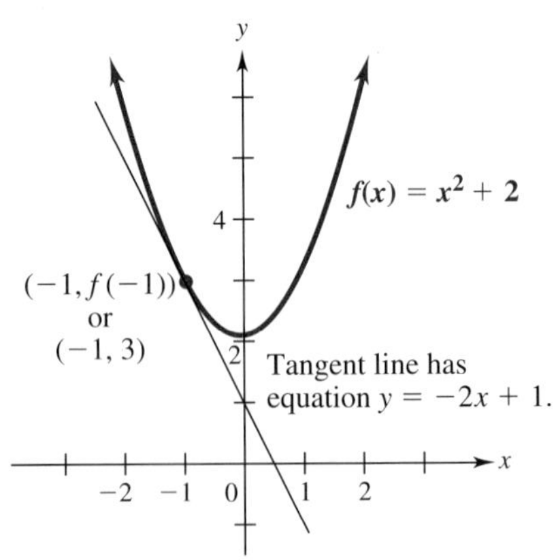

FIGURE 12.14

When finding the equation of a tangent line algebraically, it's a good idea to confirm your answer graphically, as we did in Figure 12.14, by graphing both the function and the tangent line on the same screen to see if the tangent line appears to be correct. 2

EXAMPLE 2 Find the equation of the tangent line to the graph of $f(x) = 5x + 2$ at the point where $x = c$.

Recall the intuitive idea that the tangent line at a point is the straight line that best approximates the graph of f at that point. In this case, however, the graph of f is itself a straight line (why?). So, from an intuitive viewpoint, the tangent line at any point should be the graph of f itself. We now show that this is indeed the case. According to the definition with $x_0 = c$, the slope of the tangent line is

$$\begin{aligned} \lim_{h \to 0} \frac{f(c + h) - f(c)}{h} &= \lim_{h \to 0} \frac{[5(c + h) + 2] - [5c + 2]}{h} \\ &= \lim_{h \to 0} \frac{[5c + 5h + 2] - 5c - 2}{h} \\ &= \lim_{h \to 0} \frac{5h}{h} = \lim_{h \to 0} 5 = 5. \end{aligned}$$

Hence the equation of the tangent line at the point $(c, f(c))$ is

$$\begin{aligned} y - y_1 &= m(x - x_1) \\ y - f(c) &= 5(x - c) \\ y &= 5x - 5c + f(c) \\ y &= 5x - 5c + 5c + 2 \\ y &= 5x + 2 \end{aligned}$$

Thus the tangent line is precisely the graph of $f(x) = 5x + 2$. ■

Secant lines and tangent lines (or more precisely, their slopes) are the geometric analogues of the average and instantaneous rates of change studied in the previous section, as summarized in the following chart.

Quantity	*Algebraic Interpretation*	*Geometric Interpretation*
$\dfrac{f(x_0 + h) - f(x_0)}{h}$	Average rate of change of f from $x = x_0$ to $x = x_0 + h$	Slope of the secant line through $(x_0, f(x_0))$ and $(x_0 + h, f(x_0 + h))$
$\lim\limits_{h \to 0} \dfrac{f(x_0 + h) - f(x_0)}{h}$	Instantaneous rate of change of f at $x = x_0$	Slope of the tangent line to the graph of f at $(x_0, f(x_0))$

THE DERIVATIVE If $y = f(x)$ is a function and x_0 is a number in its domain, then we shall use the symbol $f'(x_0)$ to denote the special limit

$$\lim_{h \to 0} \frac{f(x_0 + h) - f(x_0)}{h},$$

provided that it exists. In other words, to each number x_0, we can assign the number $f'(x_0)$ obtained by calculating this limit. This process defines an important new function.

> The **derivative** of the function f is the function denoted f' whose value at the number x is defined to be the number
>
> $$f'(x) = \lim_{h \to 0} \frac{f(x + h) - f(x)}{h},$$
>
> provided this limit exists.

The derivative function f' has as its domain all the points at which the specified limit exists, and the value of the derivative function at the number x is the number $f'(x)$. Using x instead of x_0 here is similar to the way that $g(x) = 2x$ denotes the function that assigns to each number x_0 the number $2x_0$.

If $y = f(x)$ is a function, then its derivative is denoted either by f' or by y'. If x is a number in the domain of $y = f(x)$ such that $y' = f'(x)$ is defined, then the function f is said to be **differentiable** at x. The process that produces the function f' from the function f is called **differentiation.**

The derivative function may be interpreted in many ways, two of which were discussed above.

1. The derivative function f' gives the *instantaneous rate of change* of $y = f(x)$ with respect to x. This instantaneous rate of change can be interpreted as marginal cost, revenue, or profit (if the original function represents cost, revenue, or profit) or as velocity (if the original function represents displacement along a line). From now on we will use "rate of change" to mean "instantaneous rate of change."

2. The derivative function f' gives the *slope* of the graph of f at any point. If the derivative is evaluated at $x = x_0$, then $f'(x_0)$ is the slope of the tangent line to the curve at the point $(x_0, f(x_0))$.

EXAMPLE 3 Use the graph of the function $f(x)$ in Figure 12.15 to answer the questions below.

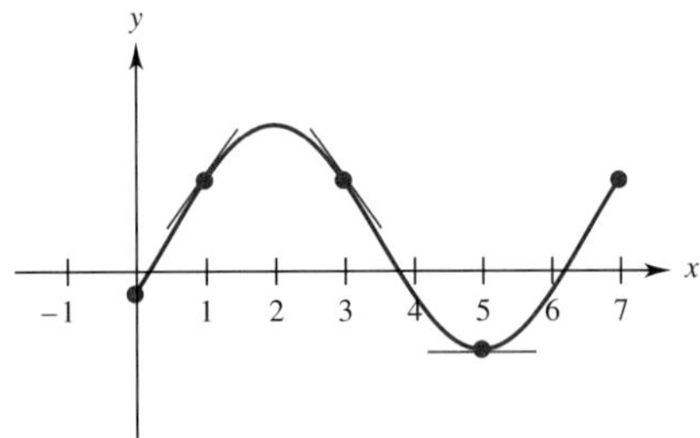

FIGURE 12.15

3 The graph of a function g is shown below. Determine whether the following numbers are *positive, negative*, or *zero*.

(a) $g'(0)$

(b) $g'(-1)$

(c) $g'(3)$

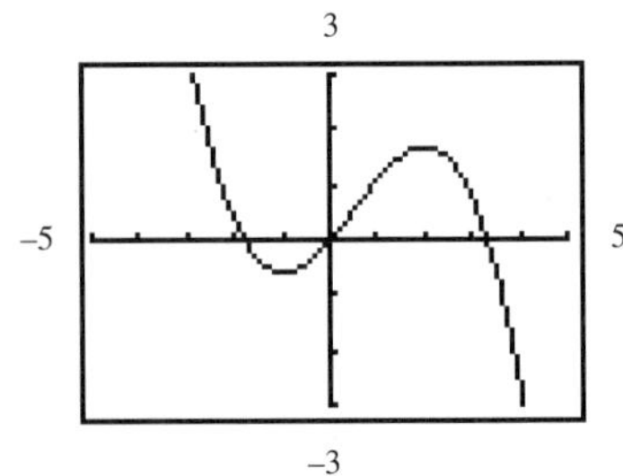

Answers:

(a) Positive

(b) 0

(c) Negative

(a) Is $f'(3)$ positive or negative?

We know that $f'(3)$ is the slope of the tangent line to the graph at the point where $x = 3$. Figure 12.15 shows that this tangent line slants downward from left to right, meaning that its slope is negative. Hence, $f'(3) < 0$.

(b) Which is larger, $f'(1)$ or $f'(5)$?

Figure 12.15 shows that the tangent line to the graph at the point where $x = 1$ slants upward from left to right, meaning that its slope, $f'(1)$, is a positive number. The tangent line at the point where $x = 5$ is horizontal, so it has slope 0, that is, $f'(5) = 0$. Therefore, $f'(1) > f'(5)$.

(c) For what values of x is $f'(x)$ positive?

Find the points on the graph, where the tangent line has positive slope (slants upward from left to right). At each such point, $f'(x) > 0$. Figure 12.15 shows that this occurs when $0 < x < 2$ and when $5 < x < 7$. ■ 3

The rule of a derivative function can be found by using the definition of derivative and the following four-step procedure.

FINDING $f'(x)$ FROM THE DEFINITION OF THE DERIVATIVE

Step 1 Find $f(x + h)$.

Step 2 Find $f(x + h) - f(x)$.

Step 3 Divide by h to get $\dfrac{f(x + h) - f(x)}{h}$.

Step 4 Let $h \to 0$; $f'(x) = \lim\limits_{h \to 0} \dfrac{f(x + h) - f(x)}{h}$ if this limit exists.

EXAMPLE 4 Let $f(x) = x^3 - 4x$.

(a) Find the derivative $f'(x)$.
By definition

$$f'(x) = \lim_{h \to 0} \frac{f(x + h) - f(x)}{h}.$$

Step 1 Find $f(x + h)$.
Replace x with $x + h$ in the rule of $f(x)$.

$$\begin{aligned} f(x) &= x^3 - 4x \\ f(x + h) &= (x + h)^3 - 4(x + h) \\ &= (x^3 + 3x^2h + 3xh^2 + h^3) - 4(x + h) \\ &= x^3 + 3x^2h + 3xh^2 + h^3 - 4x - 4h. \end{aligned}$$

Step 2 Find $f(x + h) - f(x)$.
Since $f(x) = x^3 - 4x$,

$$\begin{aligned} f(x + h) - f(x &= (x^3 + 3x^2h + 3xh^2 + h^3 - 4x - 4h) - (x^3 - 4x) \\ &= x^3 + 3x^2h + 3xh^2 + h^3 - 4x - 4h - x^3 + 4x \\ &= 3x^2h + 3xh^2 + h^3 - 4h. \end{aligned}$$

Step 3 Form and simplify the quotient $\dfrac{f(x + h) - f(x)}{h}$.

$$\begin{aligned} \frac{f(x + h) - f(x)}{h} &= \frac{3x^2h + 3xh^2 + h^3 - 4h}{h} \\ &= \frac{h(3x^2 + 3xh + h^2 - 4)}{h} \\ &= 3x^2 + 3xh + h^2 - 4. \end{aligned}$$

Step 4 Find the limit of the result in Step 3 as h approaches 0.

$$\begin{aligned} f'(x) = \lim_{h \to 0} \frac{f(x + h) - f(x)}{h} &= \lim_{h \to 0} (3x^2 + 3xh + h^2 - 4) \\ &= 3x^2 - 4. \end{aligned}$$

Therefore, the derivative of $f(x) = x^3 - 4x$ is $f'(x) = 3x^2 - 4$.

4 Let $f(x) = -2x^2 + 7$. Find the following.

(a) $f(x + h)$

(b) $f(x + h) - f(x)$

(c) $\dfrac{f(x + h) - f(x)}{h}$

(d) $f'(x)$

(e) $f'(4)$

(f) $f'(0)$

Answers:

(a) $-2x^2 - 4xh - 2h^2 + 7$

(b) $-4xh - 2h^2$

(c) $-4x - 2h$

(d) $-4x$

(e) -16

(f) 0

(b) Calculate and interpret $f'(1)$.

The procedure in part (a) works for *every* x and $f'(x) = 3x^2 - 4$. Hence, when $x = 1$,

$$f'(1) = 3 \cdot 1^2 - 4 = -1.$$

The number -1 is the slope of the tangent line to the graph of $f(x) = x^3 - 4x$ at the point where $x = 1$, that is, at $(1, f(1)) = (1, -3)$.

(c) Find the equation of the tangent line to the graph of $f(x) = x^3 - 4x$ at the point where $x = 1$.

By part (b), the point on the graph where $x = 1$ is $(1, -3)$ and the slope of the tangent line is $f'(1) = -1$. Therefore, the equation is

$$y - (-3) = (-1)(x - 1) \quad \text{Point-slope form}$$
$$y = -x - 2. \quad \text{Slope-intercept form}$$

Both $f(x)$ and the tangent line are shown in Figure 12.16. ■ 4

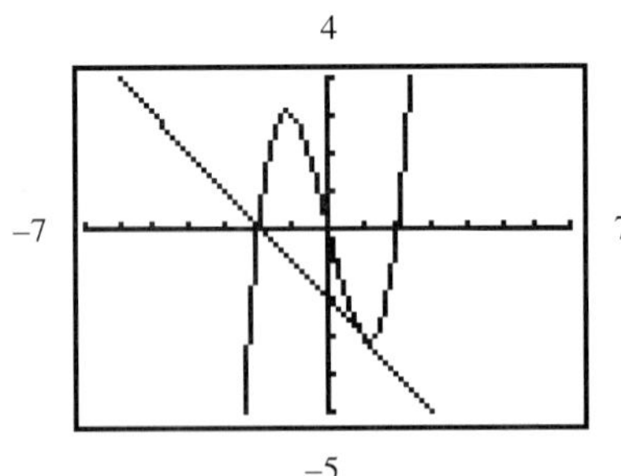

FIGURE 12.16

CAUTION

1. In Example 4(a) note that $f(x + h) \neq f(x) + h$ because by Step 1,

$$f(x + h) = x^3 + 3x^2h + 3xh^2 + h^3 - 4x - 4h,$$

but

$$f(x) + h = (x^3 - 4x) + h = x^3 - 4x + h.$$

2. In Example 4(b), do not confuse $f(1)$ and $f'(1)$. $f(1)$ is the value of the original function $f(x) = x^3 - 4x$ at $x = 1$, namely, -3, whereas $f'(1)$ is the value of the derivative function $f'(x) = 3x^2 - 4$ at $x = 1$, namely, -1. ◆

EXAMPLE 5 Let $f(x) = 1/x$. Find $f'(x)$.

Step 1 $f(x + h) = \dfrac{1}{x + h}$

Step 2 $f(x + h) - f(x) = \dfrac{1}{x + h} - \dfrac{1}{x}$

$$= \frac{x - (x + h)}{x(x + h)} \quad \text{Find a common denominator.}$$

5 Let $f(x) = -5/x$. Find the following.

(a) $f(x+h)$

(b) $f(x+h) - f(x)$

(c) $\dfrac{f(x+h) - f(x)}{h}$

(d) $f'(x)$

(e) $f'(-1)$

Answers:

(a) $\dfrac{-5}{x+h}$

(b) $\dfrac{5h}{x(x+h)}$

(c) $\dfrac{5}{x(x+h)}$

(d) $\dfrac{5}{x^2}$

(e) 5

$$= \frac{x - x - h}{x(x+h)} \qquad \text{Simplify the numerator.}$$

$$= \frac{-h}{x(x+h)}$$

Step 3 $$\frac{f(x+h) - f(x)}{h} = \frac{\dfrac{-h}{x(x+h)}}{h}$$

$$= \frac{-h}{x(x+h)} \cdot \frac{1}{h} \qquad \text{Invert and multiply.}$$

$$= \frac{-1}{x(x+h)}$$

Step 4 $$f'(x) = \lim_{h \to 0} \frac{f(x+h) - f(x)}{h} = \lim_{h \to 0} \frac{-1}{x(x+h)}$$

$$= \frac{-1}{x(x+0)} = \frac{-1}{x(x)} = \frac{-1}{x^2} \quad \blacksquare \quad \boxed{5}$$

EXAMPLE 6 Let $g(x) = \sqrt{x}$. Find $g'(x)$.

Step 1 $g(x+h) = \sqrt{x+h}$

Step 2 $g(x+h) - g(x) = \sqrt{x+h} - \sqrt{x}$

Step 3 $$\frac{g(x+h) - g(x)}{h} = \frac{\sqrt{x+h} - \sqrt{x}}{h}$$

At this point, in order to be able to divide by h, multiply both numerator and denominator by $\sqrt{x+h} + \sqrt{x}$; that is, rationalize the *numerator.*

$$\frac{g(x+h) - g(x)}{h} = \frac{\sqrt{x+h} - \sqrt{x}}{h} \cdot \frac{\sqrt{x+h} + \sqrt{x}}{\sqrt{x+h} + \sqrt{x}}$$

$$= \frac{(\sqrt{x+h})^2 - (\sqrt{x})^2}{h(\sqrt{x+h} + \sqrt{x})}$$

$$= \frac{x + h - x}{h(\sqrt{x+h} + \sqrt{x})} = \frac{1}{\sqrt{x+h} + \sqrt{x}}$$

Step 4 $$g'(x) = \lim_{h \to 0} \frac{1}{\sqrt{x+h} + \sqrt{x}} = \frac{1}{\sqrt{x} + \sqrt{x}} = \frac{1}{2\sqrt{x}} \quad \blacksquare$$

EXAMPLE 7 A sales representative for a textbook publishing company frequently makes a 4-hour drive from her home in a large city to a university in another city. If $s(t)$ represents her distance (in miles) from home t hours into the trip, then $s(t)$ is given by

$$s(t) = -5t^3 + 30t^2.$$

(a) How far from home will she be after 1 hour? After $1\frac{1}{2}$ hours?
Her distance from home after 1 hour is

$$s(1) = -5(1)^3 + 30(1)^2 = 25,$$

or 25 miles. After $1\frac{1}{2}$ (or 3/2) hours, it is

$$s\left(\frac{3}{2}\right) = -5\left(\frac{3}{2}\right)^3 + 30\left(\frac{3}{2}\right)^2 = \frac{405}{8} = 50.625,$$

or 50.625 miles.

(b) How far apart are the two cities?
Since the trip takes 4 hours and the distance is given by $s(t)$, the university city is $s(4) = 160$ miles from her home.

6 Go through the four steps to find $s'(t)$, the velocity of the car at any time t.

Answer:
$s'(t) = -15t^2 + 60t$

(c) How fast is she driving 1 hour into the trip? $1\frac{1}{2}$ hours into the trip?
Velocity (or speed) is the instantaneous rate of change in position with respect to time. We need to find the value of the derivative $s'(t)$ at $t = 1$ and $t = 1\frac{1}{2}$. **6**

From Problem 6 at the side, $s'(t) = -15t^2 + 60t$. At $t = 1$, the velocity is

$$s'(1) = -15(1)^2 + 60(1) = 45,$$

or 45 miles per hour. At $t = 1\frac{1}{2}$, the velocity is

$$s'\left(\frac{3}{2}\right) = -15\left(\frac{3}{2}\right)^2 + 60\left(\frac{3}{2}\right) = 56.25,$$

about 56 miles per hour.

(d) Does she ever exceed the speed limit of 65 miles per hour on the trip?
To find the maximum velocity, notice that the graph of the velocity function $s'(t) = -15t^2 + 60t$ is a parabola opening downward (Figure 12.17). The maximum velocity will occur at the vertex. Use graphical or algebraic methods to verify that the vertex of the parabola is (2, 60). Thus, her maximum velocity during the trip is 60 miles per hour, so she never exceeds the speed limit. ■

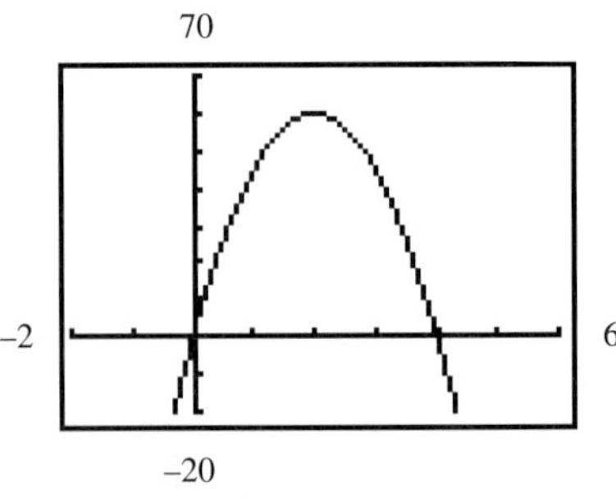

FIGURE 12.17

EXISTENCE OF THE DERIVATIVE The definition of the derivative includes the phrase "provided this limit exists." If the limit used to define $f'(x)$ does not exist, then of course the derivative does not exist at that x. For example, a derivative cannot exist at a point where the function itself is not defined. If there is no function value for a particular value of x, there can be no tangent line for that value. This was the case in Example 5—there was no tangent line (and no derivative) when $x = 0$.

Derivatives also do not exist at "corners" or "sharp points" on a graph. For example, the function graphed in Figure 12.18 is the *absolute value function*, defined by

$$f(x) = \begin{cases} x & \text{if } x \geq 0 \\ -x & \text{if } x < 0 \end{cases}$$

and written $f(x) = |x|$.

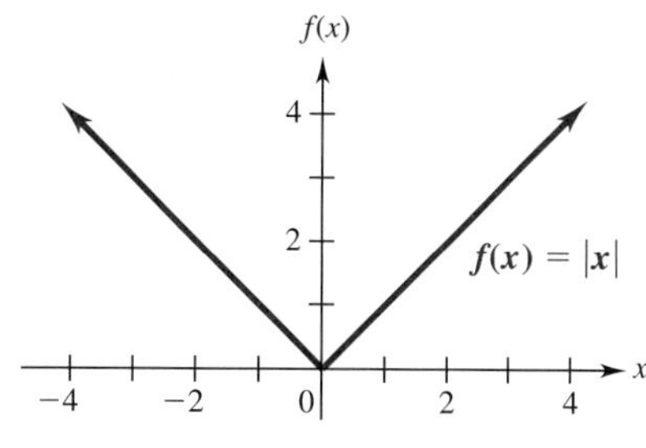

FIGURE 12.18

By the definition of derivative, the derivative at any value of x is given by

$$\lim_{h \to 0} \frac{f(x + h) - f(x)}{h},$$

provided this limit exists. To find the derivative at 0 for $f(x) = |x|$, replace x with 0 and $f(x)$ with $|0|$ to get

$$\lim_{h \to 0} \frac{|0 + h| - |0|}{h} = \lim_{h \to 0} \frac{|h|}{h}.$$

In Example 9 of Section 12.1 (with x in place of h) we showed that

$$\lim_{h \to 0} \frac{|h|}{h} \text{ does not exist.}$$

Therefore, there is no derivative at 0. However, the derivative of $f(x) = |x|$ *does* exist for all values of x other than 0.

Since a vertical line has an undefined slope, the derivative cannot exist at any point where the tangent line is vertical, as at x_5 in Figure 12.19. Figure 12.19 summarizes the various ways that a derivative can fail to exist.

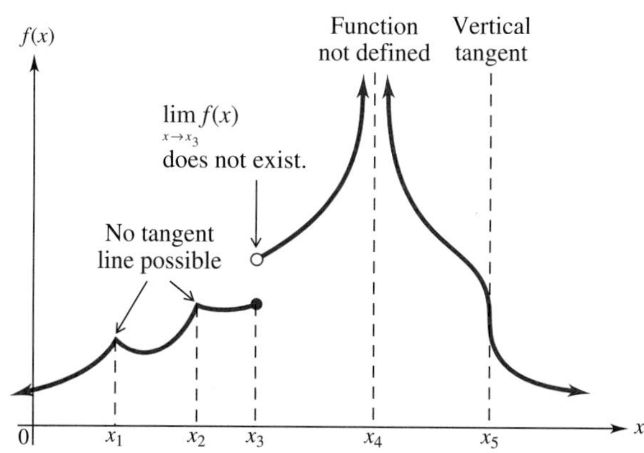

FIGURE 12.19

NUMERICAL METHODS If your calculator can do symbolic manipulations, learn how to use it to find derivatives. If your calculator does not do symbolic manipulations, you can find the *approximate* value of the derivative function at any number where it is defined by using the **numerical derivative** feature. It is labeled NDeriv or d/dx or nDer and is usually in the math menu or one of its submenus.* Exercise 38 explains how a calculator computes the numerical derivative and why it is a good approximation of the derivative.

7 If $f(x) = x^{3/4} - 7x^2 + 3^x$, find the (approximate) value of

(a) $f'(1)$;

(b) $f'(4.5)$;

(c) $f'(8)$.

Answers:

(a) -9.9542

(b) 91.646

(c) 7096.4412

EXAMPLE 8 If $f(x) = x^3 + x^{3/2} + 6 \ln x$, find the approximate value of $f'(4)$.

Check your instruction manual for the correct syntax, but on many calculators entering either

$$\text{NDeriv}(x^3 + x^{3/2} + 6 \ln x, x, 4) \quad \text{or} \quad \text{d/dx}(x^3 + x^{3/2} + 6 \ln x, 4)$$

produces the (approximate) value of $f'(4)$. Depending on the calculator, you are likely to get one of these answers:

$$52.4999982 \quad \text{or} \quad 52.5 \quad \text{or} \quad 52.50000102.$$

It can be shown that the exact value is $f'(4) = 52.5$. ■ 7

TECHNOLOGY TIP On many calculators, if you have the function $f(x)$ stored in the function memory as y_1, say, you can use y_1 with the NDeriv key, instead of typing in the rule of $f(x)$. ✔

EXAMPLE 9 The cost (in thousands of dollars) to manufacture x thousand graphing calculators is given by

$$C(x) = .002x^4 + .1x^3 + .3x^2 - .1x + 50 \quad (0 \le x \le 13).$$

Find the marginal cost (rate of change of cost) when 5000 and when 9000 calculators are made.

The marginal cost function is the derivative of the cost function and 5000 calculators corresponds to $x = 5$, so the marginal cost is $C'(5)$. In later sections you will learn how to find it exactly, but for now use the numerical derivative to approximate $C'(5)$. A typical calculator shows that $C'(5) \approx 11.4$, meaning that costs are changing at the rate of \$11,400 per thousand calculators. When 9000 calculators are made, the marginal cost is

$$C'(9) \approx 35.432; \text{ that is, \$35,432 per thousand calculators.} \quad ■$$

CAUTION Because of the approximation methods used, the NDeriv key may display an answer at numbers where the derivative is not defined. For instance, we saw above that the derivative of $f(x) = |x|$ is not defined when $x = 0$. But the NDeriv key on most calculators produces 1 or 0 or -1 as $f'(0)$. ◆

*An NDeriv program for calculators that do not have this feature is in the Program Appendix.

12.3 EXERCISES

Find the slope of the tangent line to each of the following curves when x has the given value. (See Example 1.) (Hint for Exercise 5: In Step 3, multiply numerator and denominator by $\sqrt{16+h}+\sqrt{16}$.)

1. $f(x) = -4x^2 + 11x; x = -3$

2. $f(x) = 6x^2 - 4x; x = -2$

3. $f(x) = -\frac{2}{x}; x = 4$

4. $f(x) = \frac{6}{x}; x = -1$

5. $f(x) = \sqrt{x+1}; x = 15$

6. $f(x) = -3\sqrt{x}; x = 1$

Find the equation of the tangent line to each of these curves at the given point. Confirm your answer graphically by graphing both f(x) and the tangent line on the same screen. (See Examples 1, 2, and 4.)

7. $f(x) = x^2 + 2x; x = 2$

8. $f(x) = 6 - x^2; x = -2$

9. $f(x) = \frac{5}{x}; x = 2$

10. $f(x) = -\frac{3}{x+1}; x = 1$

11. $f(x) = 4\sqrt{x}; x = 9$

12. $f(x) = \sqrt{x}; x = 25$

Find all points where the functions whose graphs are shown do not have derivatives.

13.

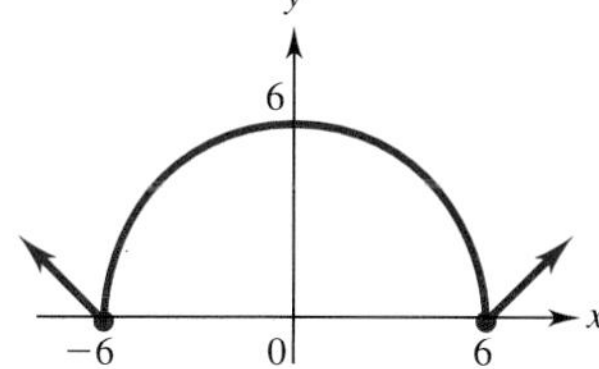

14.

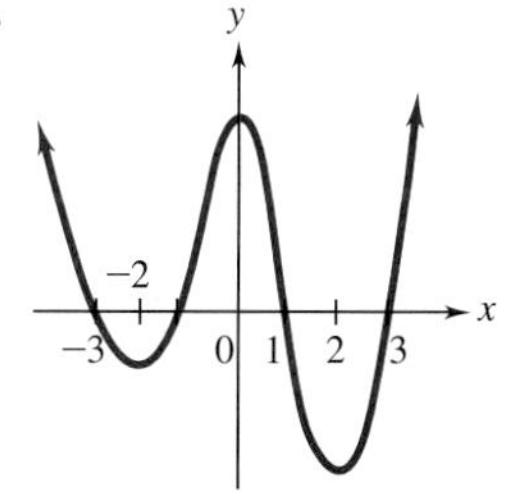

15.

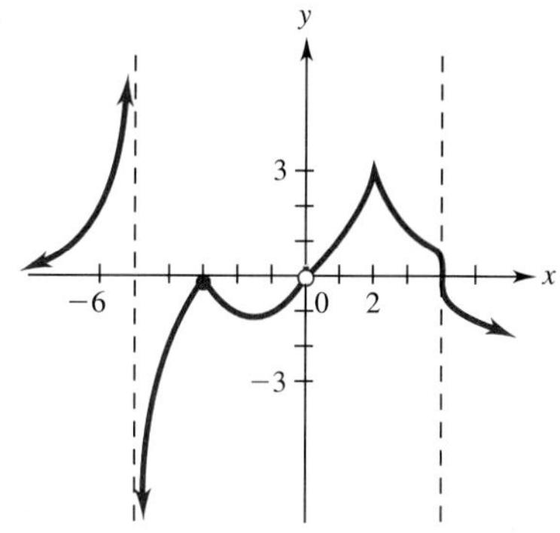

16. (a) Sketch the graph of $g(x) = \sqrt[3]{x}$ for $-1 \le x \le 1$.

(b) Explain why the derivative of $g(x)$ is not defined at $x = 0$. (*Hint:* What is the slope of the tangent line at $x = 0$?)

Use the fact that $f'(c)$ is the slope of the tangent line to the graph of f(x) at x = c to work these exercises. (See Example 3.)

17. In the graph of the function f, at which of the labeled x-values is

(a) $f(x)$ the largest?

(b) $f(x)$ the smallest?

(c) $f'(x)$ the smallest?

(d) $f'(x)$ the closest to 0?

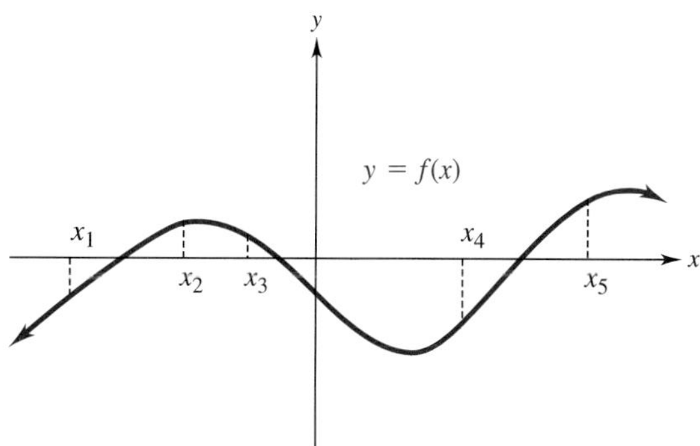

18. Draw the graph of a function f which has the following properties. (Many correct answers are possible.)

(a) $f'(x) > 0$ for $x < -2$

(b) $f'(x) = 0$ at $x = -2$

(c) $f'(x) < 0$ for $-2 < x < 3$

(d) $f'(x) = 0$ at $x = -3$

(e) $f'(x) > 0$ for $x > 3$

19. Sketch the graph of the *derivative* of the function g whose graph is shown. (*Hint*: Consider the slope of the tangent line at each point along the graph of g. Are there any points where there is no tangent line?)

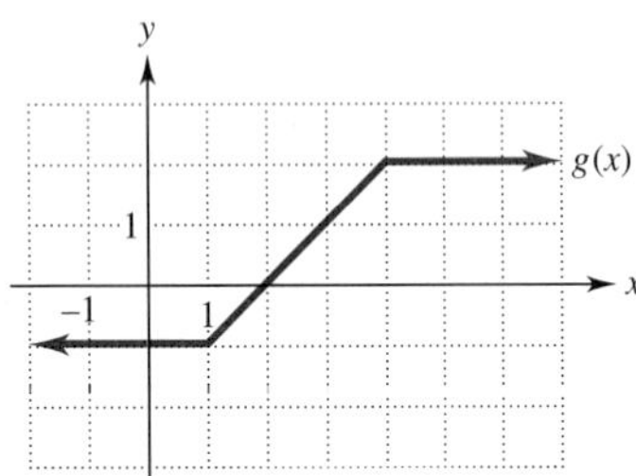

20. Sketch the graph of a function g with the property that $g'(x) > 0$ for $x < 0$ and $g'(x) < 0$ for $x > 0$. Many correct answers are possible.

In Exercises 21–22, tell which graph, (a) or (b), represents velocity and which represents distance from a starting point. (Hint: *Consider where the derivative is zero, positive, or negative.*)

21. (a)

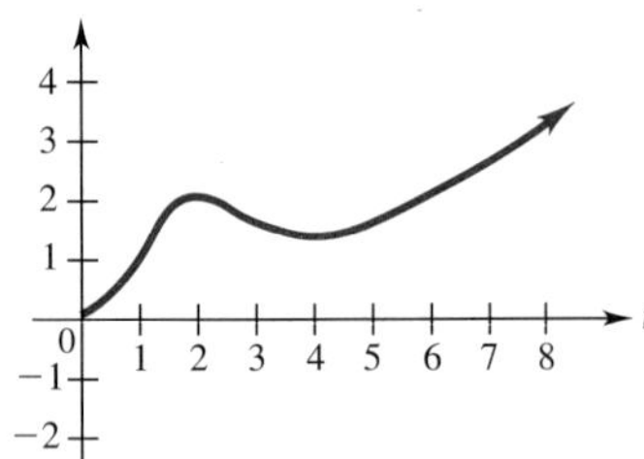

(b)

22. (a)

(b)

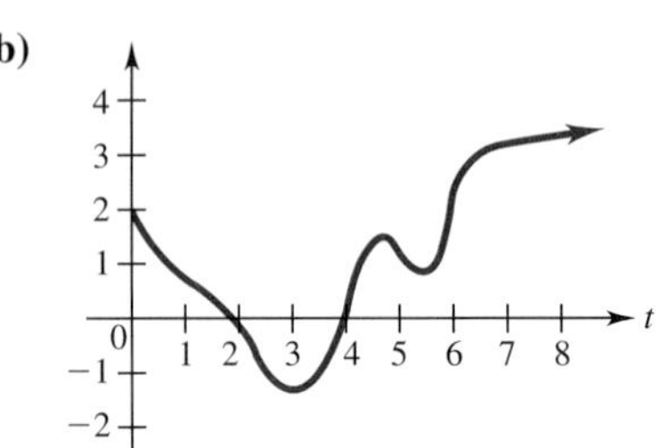

Find $f'(x)$ for each function. (Many of these derivatives were found in Exercises 1–6.) Then find $f'(2)$, $f'(0)$, and $f'(-3)$. (See Examples 4–6.)

23. $f(x) = -4x^2 + 11x$

24. $f(x) = 6x^2 - 4x$

25. $f(x) = 8x + 6$

26. $f(x) = x^3 + 3x$

27. $f(x) = -\dfrac{2}{x}$

28. $f(x) = \dfrac{6}{x}$

29. $f(x) = \dfrac{4}{x-1}$

30. $f(x) = \sqrt{x}$

*Graph the (numerical) derivative of each function by graphing $y =$ NDeriv(f(x),x).**

31. $f(x) = x^2 - 3x + 5$

32. $f(x) = .5x^3 + 3x^2 - x + 4$

33. $f(x) = \ln x$

34. $f(x) = e^x + 2$

35. (a) Graph the derivative of $f(x) = .5x^5 - 2x^3 + x^2 - 3x + 2$ for $-3 \le x \le 3$.

(b) Graph $g(x) = 2.5x^4 - 6x^2 + 2x - 3$ on the same screen.

(c) How do the graphs of $f'(x)$ and $g(x)$ compare? What does this suggest that the derivative of $f(x)$ is?

36. Repeat Exercise 35 for $f(x) = (x^2 + x + 1)^{1/3}$ (with $-6 \le x \le 6$) and $g(x) = \dfrac{2x+1}{3(x^2+x+1)^{2/3}}$.

37. By comparing graphs, as in Exercises 35 and 36, decide which of the following functions could *possibly* be the derivative of $y = \dfrac{4x^2 + x}{x^2 + 1}$?

(a) $f(x) = \dfrac{2x+1}{2x}$

(b) $g(x) = \dfrac{x^2 + x}{2x}$

(c) $h(x) = \dfrac{2x+1}{x^2+1}$

(d) $k(x) = \dfrac{-x^2 + 8x + 1}{(x^2+1)^2}$

38. If f is a function such that $f'(x)$ is defined, then it can be proved that

$$f'(x) = \lim_{h \to 0} \frac{f(x+h) - f(x-h)}{2h}.$$

*On some calculators you must use NDeriv(f(x),x,x) or d/dx(f(x),x); check your instruction manual.

Consequently, when h is very small, say $h = .001$, then

$$f'(x) \approx \frac{f(x+h) - f(x-h)}{2h} = \frac{f(x+.001) - f(x-.001)}{.002}.$$

(a) In Example 6 we saw that the derivative of $f(x) = \sqrt{x}$ is the function $f'(x) = 1/(2\sqrt{x})$. Make a table in which the first column lists $x = 1, 6, 11, 16, 21$; the second column lists the corresponding values of $f'(x)$ and the third column the corresponding values of

$$\frac{f(x+.001) - f(x-.001)}{.002}.$$

(b) How do the second and third columns of the table compare? (If you used the table feature on your calculator, the entries in the table are rounded off, so move the cursor over each entry to see it fully displayed at the bottom of the screen.) Your answer to this question may explain why most calculators use the method in the third column to compute numerical derivatives.

Use algebra, not a calculator, to work these exercises. (See Examples 4–7.)

39. Management The revenue generated from the sale of x picnic tables is given by

$$R(x) = 20x - \frac{x^2}{500}.$$

(a) Find the marginal revenue when $x = 1000$ units.
(b) Determine the actual revenue from the sale of the 1001st item.
(c) Compare the answers to parts (a) and (b). How are they related?

40. Management The cost of producing x tacos is $C(x) = 1000 + .24x^2, 0 \le x \le 30{,}000$.
(a) Find the marginal cost, $C'(x)$.
(b) Find and interpret $C'(100)$.
(c) Find the exact cost to produce the 101st taco.
(d) Compare the answers to parts (b) and (c). How are they related?

Use algebraic or numerical methods to work these exercises. (See Examples 7–9.)

41. Management Suppose the demand for a certain item is given by $D(p) = -2p^2 + 4p + 6$, where p represents the price of the item in dollars.
(a) Find the rate of change of demand with respect to price.
(b) Find and interpret the rate of change of demand when the price is \$10.

42. Management The profit (in dollars) from the expenditure of x thousand dollars on advertising is given by $P(x) = 1000 + 32x - 2x^2$. Find the marginal profit at the following expenditures. In each case, decide whether the firm should increase the expenditure.
(a) \$8000 **(b)** \$6000 **(c)** \$12,000
(d) \$20,000

43. Natural Science A biologist has estimated that if a bactericide is introduced into a culture of bacteria, the number of bacteria, $B(t)$, present at time t (in hours) is given by $B(t) = 1000 + 50t - 5t^2$ million. Find the rate of change of the number of bacteria with respect to time after each of the following numbers of hours:
(a) 3 **(b)** 5 **(c)** 6.
(d) When does the population of bacteria start to decline?

Use numerical derivatives to work these exercises. (See Examples 8 and 9.)

44. Natural Science In a research study, the population of shellfish in an area at time t (months) was approximated by the function $f(t) = 10{,}000(1 - e^{-.2t}) + 2000$.
(a) Estimate the value of the derivative function when $t = 2$, $t = 10$, $t = 30$, and $t = 60$.
(b) What does your answer to part (a) say about the rate at which the shellfish population is increasing?

45. Natural Science An inversion layer is formed when air at a higher altitude is warmer than air at sea level. For altitudes up to 10,000 ft, the function

$$T(h) = .014h^4 - .42h^3 + 3.72h^2 - 10h + 18$$

gives the temperature T (in degrees Celsius) at altitude h thousand ft during a recent inversion layer over Southern California. Estimate and interpret the value of the derivative at the following altitudes: 1000, 4000, and 8000 ft.

46. Management Over the past twenty years, the yearly profit (in thousands of dollars) from making a certain tool can be approximated by the function $P(t) = -.0013t^3 - .38t^2 + 10t - 25$.
(a) Find the marginal profit in years 3, 7, 12, 16, and 20.
(b) Describe the rate at which profit has been changing over this period. If the trends continue as they have during the past five years, what is likely to happen to profits?

47. Management A small firm has begun a major cost cutting initiative. Their cost of operation in thousands of dollars (excluding salaries) in month t is given by $C(t) = 25e^{-.2t} + 45$. At what rate are costs decreasing at the beginning of the program, and at the end of the first, second, and third years? What do these numbers mean?

Work these exercises. (See Example 3.)

48. Management The figure on the next page gives the percent of outstanding credit card loans that were at least 30 days past due from June 1989 to March 1991.* Assume the function changes smoothly.

(exercise continues)

*"Credit Card Defaults Pose Worry for Banks" as appeared in *The Sacramento Bee*, June 1991. Reprinted by permission of The Associated Press.

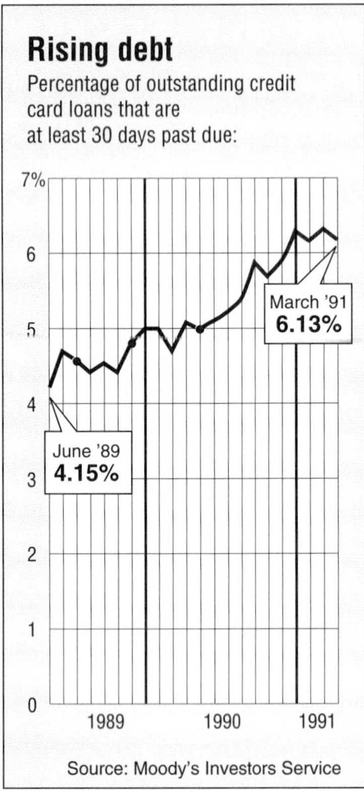

(a) Estimate and interpret the rate of change in the debt level at the indicated points on the curve.

(b) During which months in 1990 did the rate of change indicate a decreasing debt level?

(c) The overall direction of the curve is upward. What does this say about the average rate of change of outstanding loans over the time period shown in the figure?

49. Physical Science The graph shows the temperature in an oven during a self-cleaning cycle.* (The open circles on the graph are not points of discontinuity, but merely the times when the thermal door lock turns on and off.) The oven temperature is 100° when the cycle begins and 600° after half an hour. Let $T(x)$ be the temperature (in degrees Fahrenheit) after x hours.

(a) Find the approximate values of x at which the derivative T' does not exist.

(b) Find and interpret $T'(.5)$.

(c) Find and interpret $T'(2)$.

(d) Find and interpret $T'(3.5)$.

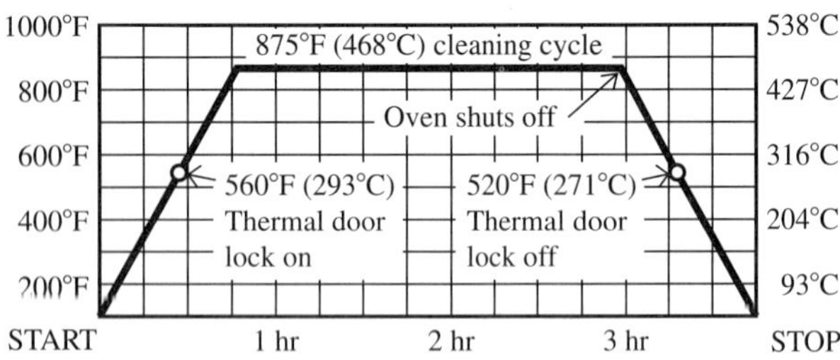

50. Natural Science The graph shows the relationship between the speed of the arctic tern in flight and the required power expended by its flight muscles.* Several significant flight speeds are indicated on the curve.

(a) The speed V_{mp} minimizes energy costs per unit of time. What is the slope of the line tangent to the curve at the point corresponding to V_{mp}? What is the physical significance of the slope at that point?

(b) The speed V_{mr} minimizes the energy costs per unit of distance covered. Estimate the slope of the curve at the point corresponding to V_{mr}. Give the significance of the slope at that point.

(c) The speed V_{opt} minimizes the total duration of the migratory journey. Estimate the slope of the curve at the point corresponding to V_{opt}. Relate the significance of this slope to the slopes found in parts (a) and (b).

(d) By looking at the shape of the curve, describe how the power level decreases and increases for various speeds.

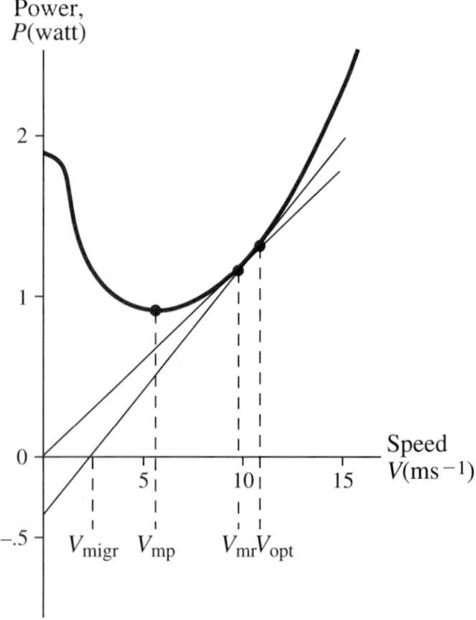

*Whirlpool Use and Care Guide, Self-Cleaning Electric Range.

*"Bird Flight and Optimal Migration" by Thomas Alerstam from *Trends in Ecology and Evolution,* July 1991, Volume 6, Number 7. Reprinted by permission of Elsevier Trends Journals and Thomas Alerstam.

12.4 TECHNIQUES FOR FINDING DERIVATIVES

In the previous section, the derivative of a function was defined as a special limit. The mathematical process of finding this limit, called *differentiation*, resulted in a new function that was interpreted in several different ways. Using the definition to calculate the derivative of a function is a very involved process even for simple functions. In this section we develop rules that make the calculation of derivatives much easier. Keep in mind that even though the process of finding a derivative will be greatly simplified with these rules, *the interpretation of the derivative will not change*.

In addition to y' and $f'(x)$, there are several other commonly used notations for the derivative.

1 Use the results of some of Exercises 26–30 in the previous section to find each of the following.

(a) $\frac{d}{dx}(x^3 + 3x)$

(b) $\frac{d}{dx}\left(-\frac{2}{x}\right)$

(c) $D_x\left(\frac{4}{x-1}\right)$

(d) $D_x(\sqrt{x})$

Answers:

(a) $3x^2 + 3$

(b) $\frac{2}{x^2}$

(c) $\frac{-4}{(x-1)^2}$

(d) $\frac{1}{2\sqrt{x}}$

NOTATIONS FOR THE DERIVATIVE

The derivative of the function $y = f(x)$ may be denoted in any of the following ways.

$$f'(x),\quad y',\quad \frac{dy}{dx},\quad \frac{d}{dx}[f(x)],\quad D_x y,\quad D_x[f(x)]$$

The *dy/dx* notation for the derivative is sometimes referred to as *Leibniz notation*, named after one of the co-inventors of calculus, Gottfried Wilhelm Leibniz (1646–1716). (The other was Sir Isaac Newton (1642–1727).)

For example, the derivative of $y = x^3 - 4x$, which we found in Example 4 of the last section to be $y' = 3x^2 - 4$, can also be written

$$\frac{dy}{dx} = 3x^2 - 4$$

$$\frac{d}{dx}(x^3 - 4x) = 3x^2 - 4$$

$$D_x(x^3 - 4x) = 3x^2 - 4.$$ 1

A variable other than x may be used as the independent variable. For example, if $y = f(t)$ gives population growth as a function of time, then the derivative of y with respect to t could be written

$$f'(t),\quad \frac{dy}{dt},\quad \frac{d}{dt}[f(t)],\quad \text{or}\quad D_t[f(t)].$$

In this section the definition of the derivative,

$$f'(x) = \lim_{h\to 0}\frac{f(x+h) - f(x)}{h},$$

is used to develop some rules for finding derivatives more easily than by the four-step process of the previous section. The first rule tells how to find the derivative of a constant function such as $f(x) = 5$. Since $f(x + h)$ is also 5, by definition $f'(x)$ is

$$f'(x) = \lim_{h\to 0}\frac{f(x+h) - f(x)}{h}$$

$$= \lim_{h\to 0}\frac{5-5}{h} = \lim_{h\to 0}\frac{0}{h} = \lim_{h\to 0} 0 = 0.$$

The same argument works for $f(x) = k$, where k is a constant real number, establishing the following rule.

CONSTANT RULE

If $f(x) = k$, where k is any real number, then

$$f'(x) = 0.$$

(The derivative of a constant function is 0.)

Figure 12.20 illustrates the constant rule; it shows a graph of the horizontal line $y = k$. At any point P on this line, the tangent line at P is the line itself. Since a horizontal line has a slope of 0, the slope of the tangent line is 0. This agrees with the result above: the derivative of a constant is 0.

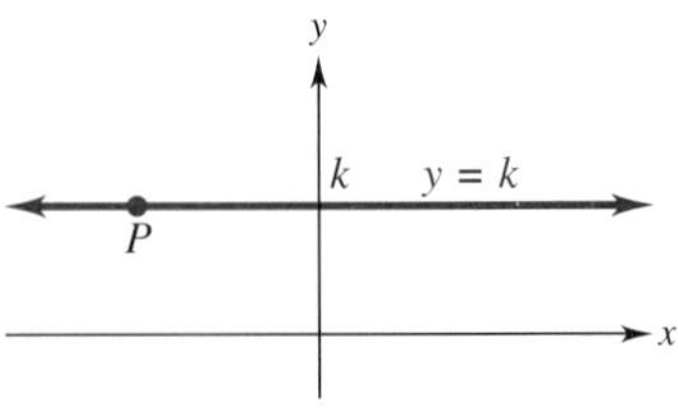

FIGURE 12.20

2 Find the derivatives of the following.

(a) $y = -4$

(b) $f(x) = \pi^3$

(c) $y = 0$

Answers:

(a) 0

(b) 0

(c) 0

EXAMPLE 1 **(a)** If $f(x) = 9$, then $f'(x) = 0$.

(b) If $y = \pi$, then $y' = 0$.

(c) If $y = 2^3$, then $dy/dx = 0$. ■ 2

Functions of the form $y = x^n$, where n is a fixed real number, are very common in applications. We now find the derivative functions when $n = 2$ and $n = 3$.

$$\begin{aligned} f(x) &= x^2 \\ f'(x) &= \lim_{h\to 0} \frac{f(x+h) - f(x)}{h} \\ &= \lim_{h\to 0} \frac{(x+h)^2 - x^2}{h} \\ &= \lim_{h\to 0} \frac{(x^2 + 2xh + h^2) - x^2}{h} \\ &= \lim_{h\to 0} \frac{2xh + h^2}{h} \\ &= \lim_{h\to 0} (2x + h) = 2x \end{aligned}$$

$$\begin{aligned} f(x) &= x^3 \\ f'(x) &= \lim_{h\to 0} \frac{f(x+h) - f(x)}{h} \\ &= \lim_{h\to 0} \frac{(x+h)^3 - x^3}{h} \\ &= \lim_{h\to 0} \frac{(x^3 + 3x^2h + 3xh^2 + h^3) - x^3}{h} \\ &= \lim_{h\to 0} \frac{3x^2h + 3xh^2 + h^3}{h} \\ &= \lim_{h\to 0} (3x^2 + 3xh + h^2) = 3x^2 \end{aligned}$$

Similar calculations show that

$$\frac{d}{dx}(x^4) = 4x^3 \quad \text{and} \quad \frac{d}{dx}(x^5) = 5x^4.$$

The pattern here (the derivative is the product of the exponent on the original function and a power of x that is one less) suggests that the derivative of $y = x^n$ is $y' = nx^{n-1}$, which is indeed the case (Exercise 67). Moreover, the pattern holds even when n is not an integer, as can be seen from translating Examples 5 and 6 of the last section into exponential notation. They show that

$$\text{if } f(x) = \frac{1}{x} = x^{-1}, \text{ then } f'(x) = -\frac{1}{x^2} = (-1)x^{-2} = (-1)x^{-1-1}$$

and

$$\text{if } g(x) = \sqrt{x} = x^{1/2}, \text{ then } g'(x) = \frac{1}{2\sqrt{x}} = \frac{1}{2}\cdot\frac{1}{\sqrt{x}} = \frac{1}{2}\cdot x^{-1/2} = \frac{1}{2}\cdot x^{(1/2)-1}.$$

These results suggest the following rule.

POWER RULE

If $f(x) = x^n$ for any nonzero real number n, then

$$f'(x) = nx^{n-1}.$$

(The derivative of $f(x) = x^n$ is found by multiplying by the exponent n and decreasing the exponent on x by 1.)

EXAMPLE 2 **(a)** If $y = x^6$, find y'.

Multiply x^{6-1} by 6.

$$y' = 6 \cdot x^{6-1} = 6x^5$$

(b) If $y = x = x^1$, find y'.

$$y' = 1 \cdot x^{1-1} = 1 \cdot x^0 = 1 \cdot 1 = 1.$$

(Recall that $x^0 = 1$ if $x \neq 0$.)

(c) If $y = t^{-3}$, find dy/dt.

$$\frac{dy}{dt} = -3 \cdot t^{-3-1} = -3 \cdot t^{-4} = -\frac{3}{t^4}.$$

(d) Find $D_t(t^{4/3})$.

$$D_t(t^{4/3}) = \frac{4}{3}t^{(4/3)-1} = \frac{4}{3}t^{1/3}.$$

(e) If $y = \sqrt[3]{x}$, find dy/dx.

First, write the rule of the function in exponent form, $y = x^{1/3}$. Then

$$\frac{dy}{dx} = \frac{1}{3}\cdot x^{(1/3)-1} = \frac{1}{3}x^{-2/3} = \frac{1}{3x^{2/3}} = \frac{1}{3\sqrt[3]{x^2}}.$$ ■ 3

3 Find the following.

(a) $y = x^4$; find y'

(b) $y = x^{17}$; find y'

(c) $y = x^{-2}$; find dy/dx

(d) $y = t^{-5}$; find dy/dt

(e) $D_t(t^{3/2})$

Answers:

(a) $y' = 4x^3$

(b) $y' = 17x^{16}$

(c) $dy/dx = -2/x^3$

(d) $dy/dt = -5/t^6$

(e) $D_t(t^{3/2}) = (3/2)t^{1/2}$

The next rule shows how to find the derivative of the product of a constant and a function.

CONSTANT TIMES A FUNCTION

Let k be a real number. If $g'(x)$ exists, then the derivative of $f(x) = k \cdot g(x)$ is

$$f'(x) = k \cdot g'(x).$$

(The derivative of a constant times a function is the constant times the derivative of the function.)

EXAMPLE 3 **(a)** If $y = 8x^4$, find y'.

Since the derivative of $g(x) = x^4$ is $g'(x) = 4x^3$ and $y = 8x^4 = 8g(x)$,

$$y' = 8g'(x) = 8(4x^3) = 32x^3.$$

(b) If $y = -\frac{3}{4}t^{12}$, find dy/dt.

$$\frac{dy}{dt} = -\frac{3}{4}\left[\frac{dy}{dt}(t^{12})\right] = -\frac{3}{4}(12t^{11}) = -9t^{11}$$

(c) Find $D_x(15x)$.

$$D_x(15x) = 15 \cdot D_x(x) = 15(1) = 15$$

(d) If $y = 6/x^2$, find y'.

Replace $\frac{6}{x^2}$ by $6 \cdot \frac{1}{x^2}$, or $6x^{-2}$. Then

$$y' = 6(-2x^{-3}) = -12x^{-3} = -\frac{12}{x^3}.$$

(e) Find $D_x(10x^{3/2})$ and confirm your answer numerically and graphically.

$$D_x(10x^{3/2}) = 10\left(\frac{3}{2}x^{1/2}\right) = 15x^{1/2}.$$

To confirm this result numerically make a table of values for $y_1 = 15x^{1/2}$ and y_2 = the numerical derivative of $10x^{3/2}$; check your instruction manual for the correct syntax for y_2, which is probably one of the following:

NDeriv($10x^{3/2}$,x) or NDeriv($10x^{3/2}$,x,x) or d/dx($10x^{3/2}$) or d/dx($10x^{3/2}$,x).

Figure 12.21(a) indicates that the corresponding values are identical to three decimal places. To confirm this result graphically, graph y_1 and y_2 on the same screen and verify that the graphs appear to be the same. (See Figure 12.21(b)). ■ 4

4 Find the derivatives of the following.

(a) $y = 12x^3$

(b) $f(t) = 30t^7$

(c) $y = -35t$

(d) $y = 5\sqrt{x}$

(e) $y = -10/t$

Answers:

(a) $36x^2$

(b) $210t^6$

(c) -35

(d) $(5/2)x^{-1/2}$ or $5/(2\sqrt{x})$

(e) $10t^{-2}$ or $10/t^2$

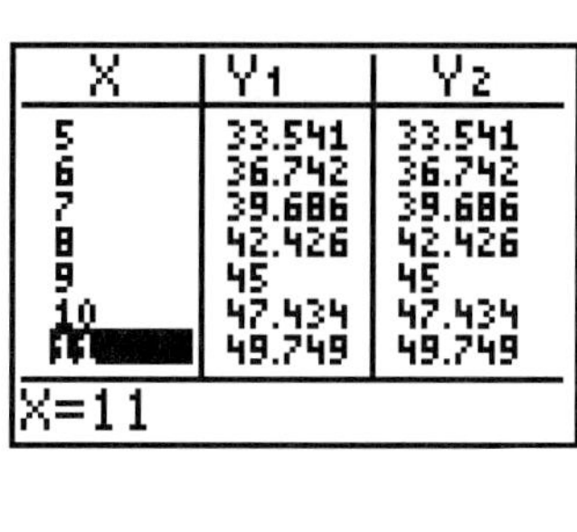

X	Y1	Y2
5	33.541	33.541
6	36.742	36.742
7	39.686	39.686
8	42.426	42.426
9	45	45
10	47.434	47.434
11	49.749	49.749

X=11

(a)

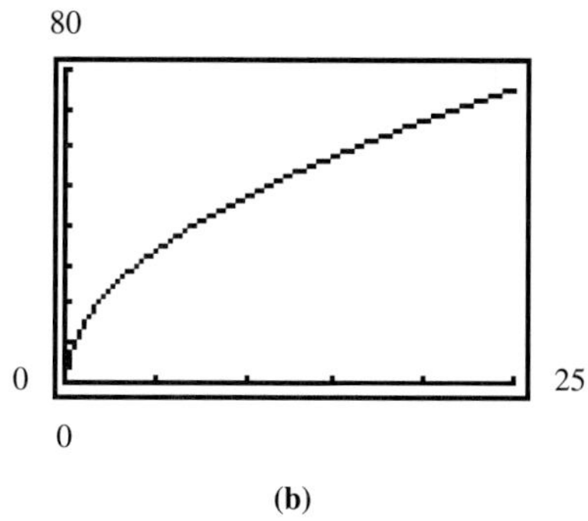

(b)

FIGURE 12.21

Confirming your calculations numerically or graphically, as in part (e) of Example 3, is a good way to detect algebraic errors. If you compute the rule of the derivative $f'(x)$, but its graph differs from the graph of the numerical derivative of $f(x)$, then you've made a mistake. If the two graphs appear to be identical, then you are *probably* correct. (The fact that two graphs appear identical on a calculator screen does not *prove* that they really are identical.)

The final rule in this section is for the derivative of a function that is a sum or difference of functions.

SUM OR DIFFERENCE RULE

If $f(x) = u(x) + v(x)$, and if $u'(x)$ and $v'(x)$ exist, then

$$f'(x) = u'(x) + v'(x).$$

If $f(x) = u(x) - v(x)$, then

$$f'(x) = u'(x) - v'(x).$$

(The derivative of a sum or difference of two functions is the sum or difference of the derivatives of the functions.)

For a proof of this rule, see Exercise 68 at the end of this section. This rule can be generalized to sums and differences with more than two terms.

EXAMPLE 4 Find the derivatives of the following functions.

(a) $y = 6x^3 + 15x^2$

Let $u(x) = 6x^3$ and $v(x) = 15x^2$; then $y = u(x) + v(x)$. Since $u'(x) = 18x^2$ and $v'(x) = 30x$,

$$\frac{dy}{dx} = 18x^2 + 30x.$$

(b) $p(t) = 8t^4 - 6\sqrt{t} + \dfrac{5}{t}$

Rewrite $p(t)$ as $p(t) = 8t^4 - 6t^{1/2} + 5t^{-1}$; then $p'(t) = 32t^3 - 3t^{-1/2} - 5t^{-2}$, which also may be written as $p'(t) = 32t^3 - \dfrac{3}{\sqrt{t}} - \dfrac{5}{t^2}$. 5

5 Find the derivatives of the following.

(a) $y = -4x^5 - 8x + 6$

(b) $y = 8t^{3/2} + 2t^{1/2}$

(c) $f(t) = -\sqrt{t} + 6/t$

Answers:

(a) $y' = -20x^4 - 8$

(b) $y' = 12t^{1/2} + t^{-1/2}$ or $12t^{1/2} + 1/t^{1/2}$

(c) $f'(t) = -1/(2\sqrt{t}) - 6/t^2$

6 Confirm your answer to part (c) graphically by graphing $D_x(f(x))$ and the numerical derivative of $f(x)$ on the same screen.

Answer:
Both graphs look like this.

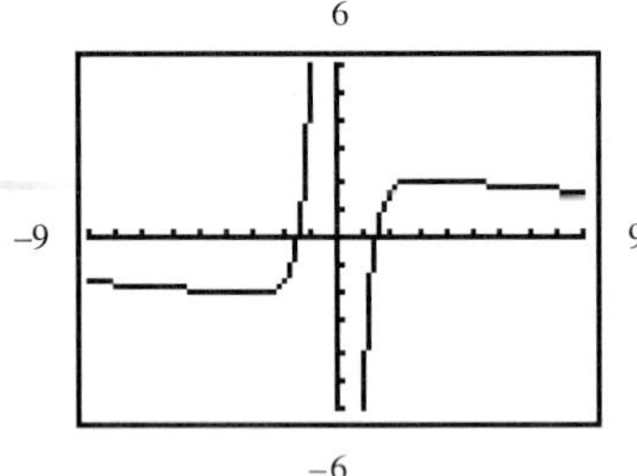

(c) $f(x) = 5\sqrt[3]{x^2} + 4x^{-2} + 7$
Rewrite $f(x)$ as $f(x) = 5x^{2/3} + 4x^{-2} + 7$. Then

$$D_x[f(x)] = \frac{10}{3}(x^{-1/3}) - 8x^{-3},$$

or

$$D_x[f(x)] = \frac{10}{3\sqrt[3]{x}} - \frac{8}{x^3}.$$ ■ 6

The rules developed in this section make it possible to find the derivative of a function more directly, so that applications of the derivative can be dealt with more effectively. The following examples illustrate some business applications.

MARGINAL ANALYSIS In business and economics the rates of change of such variables as cost, revenues, and profit are important considerations. Economists use the word marginal to refer to rates of change: for example, *marginal cost* refers to the rate of change of cost. Since the derivative of a function gives the rate of change of the function, a marginal cost (or revenue, or profit) function is found by taking the derivative of the cost (or revenue, or profit) function. Roughly speaking, the marginal cost at some level of production x is the cost to produce the $(x + 1)$st item, as we now show. (Similar statements could be made for revenue or profit.)

Look at Figure 12.22, where $C(x)$ represents the cost of producing x units of some item. Then the cost of producing $x + 1$ units is $C(x + 1)$. The cost of the $(x + 1)$st unit is, therefore, $C(x + 1) - C(x)$. This quantity is shown on the graph in Figure 12.22.

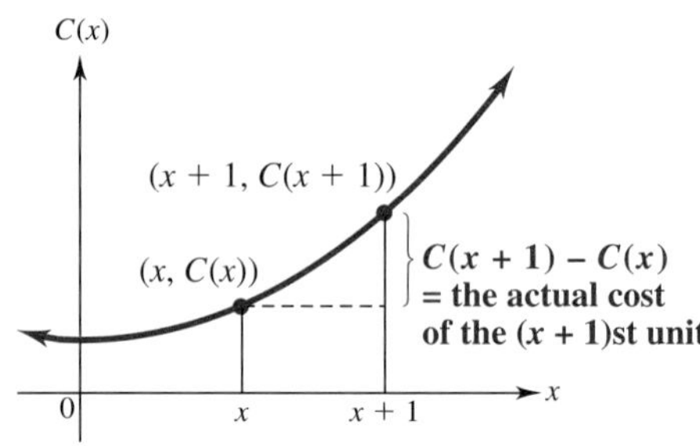

FIGURE 12.22

Now if $C(x)$ is the cost function, then the marginal cost $C'(x)$ represents the slope of the tangent line at any point $(x, C(x))$. The graph in Figure 12.23 shows the cost function $C(x)$ and the tangent line at point $P = (x, C(x))$. We know that the slope of the tangent line is $C'(x)$ and that the slope can be computed using the triangle PQR in Figure 12.23.

$$C'(x) = \text{slope} = \frac{QR}{PR} = \frac{QR}{1} = QR$$

So the length of the line segment QR is the number $C'(x)$.

Superimposing the graphs from Figures 12.22 and 12.23 as in Figure 12.24 shows that $C'(x)$ is indeed very close to $C(x + 1) - C(x)$. The two values are closest when $C'(x)$ is very large, so that 1 unit is relatively small.

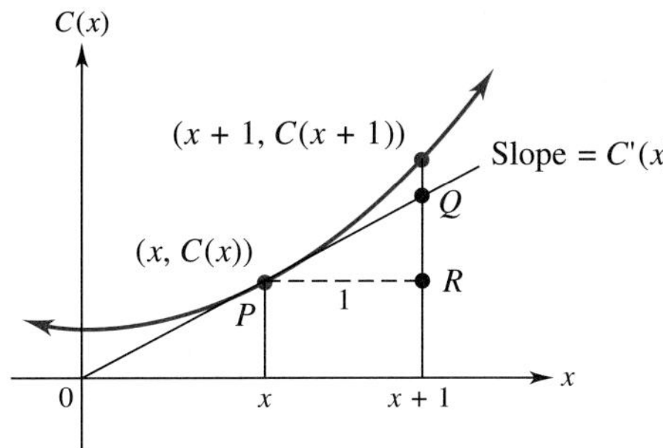

FIGURE 12.23

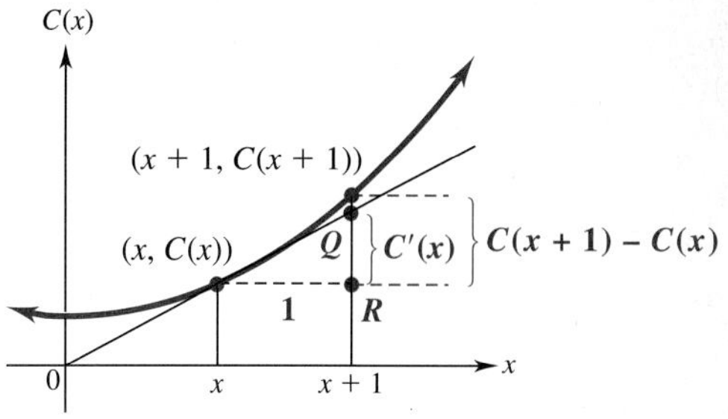

FIGURE 12.24

Therefore, we have the following conclusion.

MARGINAL COST

If $C(x)$ is the cost function, then the marginal cost (rate of change of cost) is given by the derivative $C'(x)$.

$$C'(x) \approx \text{cost of making one more item after } x \text{ have been made.}$$

The marginal revenue $R'(x)$ and marginal profit $P'(x)$ are interpreted similarly.

EXAMPLE 5 Suppose that the total cost in hundreds of dollars to produce x thousand barrels of a beverage is given by

$$C(x) = 4x^2 + 100x + 500 \quad (0 \le x \le 50).$$

Find the marginal cost for the following values of x.

(a) $x = 5$

To find the marginal cost, first find $C'(x)$, the derivative of the total cost function.

$$C'(x) = 8x + 100$$

When $x = 5$,

$$C'(5) = 8(5) + 100 = 140.$$

After 5 thousand barrels of the beverage have been produced, the cost to produce 1 thousand more barrels will be *approximately* 140 hundred dollars, or \$14,000.

The *actual* cost to produce 1 thousand more barrels is $C(6) - C(5)$.

$$\begin{aligned} C(6) - C(5) &= (4 \cdot 6^2 + 100 \cdot 6 + 500) - (4 \cdot 5^2 + 100 \cdot 5 + 500) \\ &= 1244 - 1100 \\ &= 144 \end{aligned}$$

The actual cost is 144 hundred dollars, or \$14,400.

(b) $x = 30$

After 30 thousand barrels have been produced, the cost to produce 1 thousand more barrels will be approximately

$$C'(30) = 8(30) + 100 = 340,$$

or \$34,000. Notice that the cost to produce an additional thousand barrels of beverage has increased by approximately \$20,000 at a production level of 30 thousand barrels, compared with a production level of 5 thousand barrels. Management must be careful to keep track of marginal costs. If the marginal cost of producing an extra unit exceeds the revenue received from selling it, then the company will lose money on that unit. ■ 7

7 The cost in dollars to produce x units of wheat is given by

$$C(x) = 5000 + 20x + 10\sqrt{x}.$$

Find the marginal cost when

(a) $x = 9$;

(b) $x = 16$;

(c) $x = 25$.

(d) As more wheat is produced, what happens to the marginal cost?

Answers:

(a) $65/3 \approx$ \$21.67

(b) $85/4 =$ \$21.25

(c) \$21

(d) It decreases and approaches \$20.

DEMAND FUNCTIONS The **demand function,** defined by $p = f(x)$, relates the number of units x of an item that consumers are willing to purchase at the price p. (Demand functions were also discussed in Chapter 1.) The total revenue $R(x)$ is related to price per unit and the amount demanded (or sold) by the equation

$$R(x) = xp = x \cdot f(x).$$

EXAMPLE 6 The demand function for a certain product is given by

$$p = \frac{50{,}000 - x}{25{,}000}.$$

Find the marginal revenue when $x = 10{,}000$ units and p is in dollars.

From the given function for p, the revenue function is given by

$$\begin{aligned} R(x) &= xp \\ &= x\left(\frac{50{,}000 - x}{25{,}000}\right) \\ &= \frac{50{,}000x - x^2}{25{,}000} = 2x - \frac{1}{25{,}000}x^2. \end{aligned}$$

The marginal revenue is

$$R'(x) = 2 - \frac{2}{25{,}000}x.$$

When $x = 10{,}000$, the marginal revenue is

$$R'(10{,}000) = 2 - \frac{2}{25{,}000}(10{,}000) = 1.2,$$

or \$1.20 per unit. Thus, the next unit sold (at sales of 10,000) will produce additional revenue of about \$1.20 per unit. ■ 8

8 Suppose the demand function for x units of an item is

$$p = 5 - \frac{x}{1000},$$

where x is the price in dollars. Find

(a) the marginal revenue;

(b) marginal revenue at $x = 500$;

(c) marginal revenue at $x = 1000$.

Answers:

(a) $R'(x) = 5 - \frac{x}{500}$

(b) \$4

(c) \$3

In economics, the demand function is written in the form $p = f(x)$, as shown above. From the perspective of a consumer, it is probably more reasonable to think of the quantity demanded as a function of price. Mathematically, these two viewpoints are equivalent. In Example 6, the demand function could have been written from the consumer's viewpoint as

$$x = 50{,}000 - 25{,}000p.$$

EXAMPLE 7 Suppose that the cost function for the product in Example 6 is given by

$$C(x) = 2100 + .25x, \quad \text{where } 0 \le x \le 30{,}000.$$

Find the marginal profit from the production of the following numbers of units.

(a) 15,000
From Example 6, the revenue from the sale of x units is

$$R(x) = 2x - \frac{1}{25{,}000}x^2.$$

Since profit, P, is given by $P = R - C$,

$$\begin{aligned} P(x) &= R(x) - C(x) \\ &= \left(2x - \frac{1}{25{,}000}x^2\right) - (2100 + .25x) \\ &= 2x - \frac{1}{25{,}000}x^2 - 2100 - .25x \\ &= 1.75x - \frac{1}{25{,}000}x^2 - 2100. \end{aligned}$$

The marginal profit from the sale of x units is

$$P'(x) = 1.75 - \frac{2}{25{,}000}x = 1.75 - \frac{1}{12{,}500}x.$$

At $x = 15{,}000$, the marginal profit is

$$P'(15{,}000) = 1.75 - \frac{1}{12{,}500}(15{,}000) = .55,$$

or \$.55 per unit.

(b) 21,875
When $x = 21{,}875$, the marginal profit is

$$P'(21{,}875) = 1.75 - \frac{1}{12{,}500}(21{,}875) = 0.$$

(c) 25,000
When $x = 25{,}000$, the marginal profit is

$$P'(25{,}000) = 1.75 - \frac{1}{12{,}500}(25{,}000) = -.25,$$

or $-$\$.25 per unit.

As shown by parts (b) and (c), if more than 21,875 units are sold, the marginal profit is negative. This indicates that increasing production beyond that level will *reduce* profit. ■ 9

9 For a certain product, the cost is $C(x) = 1250 + .75x$, and the revenue is

$$R(x) = 5x - \frac{x^2}{10{,}000}$$

for x units.

(a) Find the profit $P(x)$.

(b) Find $P'(20{,}000)$.

(c) Find $P'(30{,}000)$.

(d) Interpret the results of (b) and (c).

Answers:

(a) $P(x) = 4.25x - x^2/10{,}000 - 1250$

(b) .25

(c) -1.75

(d) Profit is increasing by \$.25 per unit at 20,000 units in (b) and decreasing by \$1.75 per unit at 30,000 units in (c).

The final example shows a medical application of the derivative as the rate of change of a function.

EXAMPLE 8 A tumor has the approximate shape of a cone. See Figure 12.25 on the next page. The radius of the tumor is fixed by the bone structure at 2 centimeters, but the tumor is growing along the height of the cone. The formula for the volume of a cone is $V = \frac{1}{3}\pi r^2 h$, where r is the radius of the base and h is the height of the cone. Find the rate of change in the volume of the tumor with respect to the height.

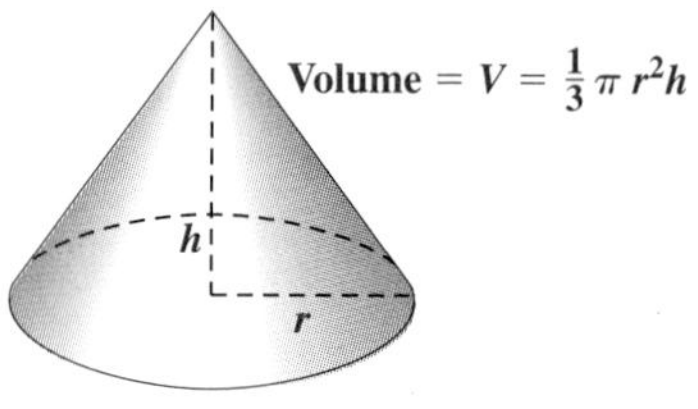

FIGURE 12.25

To emphasize that the rate of change of the volume is found with respect to the height, we use the symbol dV/dh for the derivative. For this tumor, r is fixed at 2 cm. By substituting 2 for r,

$$V = \frac{1}{3}\pi r^2 h \quad \text{becomes} \quad V = \frac{1}{3}\pi \cdot 2^2 \cdot h \quad \text{or} \quad V = \frac{4}{3}\pi h.$$

Since $4\pi/3$ is constant,

$$\frac{dV}{dh} = \frac{4\pi}{3} \approx 4.2 \text{ cu cm per cm.}$$

For each additional centimeter that the tumor grows in height, its volume will increase approximately 4.2 cubic centimeters. ■ 10

10 A balloon is spherical. The formula for the volume of a sphere is $V = (4/3)\pi r^3$, where r is the radius of the sphere. Find the following.

(a) dV/dr

(b) The rate of change of the volume when $r = 3$ inches

Answers:

(a) $4\pi r^2$

(b) 36π cubic inches per inch

12.4 EXERCISES

Find the derivatives of these functions. (See Examples 1–4.)

1. $f(x) = 4x^2 - 6x + 5$

2. $g(x) = 8x^2 + x - 12$

3. $y = 2x^3 + 3x^2 - 5x + 2$

4. $y = 4x^3 + 4x + 4$

5. $g(x) = x^4 + 3x^3 - 6x - 7$

6. $f(x) = 5x^6 - 3x^4 + x^3 - 3x + 9$

7. $f(x) = 6x^{1.5} - 4x^{.5}$

8. $f(x) = -2x^{2.5} + 8x^{.5}$

9. $y = -15x^{3.2} + 2x^{1.9}$

10. $y = 18x^{1.6} - 4x^{3.1}$

11. $y = 24t^{3/2} + 4t^{1/2}$

12. $y = -24t^{5/2} - 6t^{1/2}$

13. $y = 8\sqrt{x} + 6x^{3/4}$

14. $y = -100\sqrt{x} - 11x^{2/3}$

15. $g(x) = 6x^{-5} - x^{-1}$

16. $y = 4x^{-3} + x^{-1} + 5$

17. $y = 10x^{-2} + 3x^{-4} - 6x$

18. $y = x^{-5} - x^{-2} + 5x^{-1}$

19. $f(t) = \frac{6}{t} - \frac{8}{t^2}$

20. $f(t) = \frac{4}{t} + \frac{2}{t^3}$

21. $y = \frac{9 - 8x + 2x^3}{x^4}$

Find the derivatives of these functions. Confirm your answer graphically by graphing the derivative you find and the numerical derivative of the original function on the same screen. (See Example 3(e).)

22. $y = \frac{3 + x - 7x^4}{x^6}$

23. $g(x) = 8x^{-1/2} - 5x^{1/2} + x$

24. $f(x) = -12x^{-1/2} + 12x^{1/2} - 12x$

25. $y = 4x^{-3/2} + 8x^{-1/2} + x^2$

26. $y = 2x^{1/2} + 5 + 2x^{-1/2} + x^{-3/2}$

27. $y = \frac{6}{\sqrt[4]{x}}$

28. $y = \frac{-2}{\sqrt[3]{x}}$

29. $y = \frac{-5t}{\sqrt[3]{t^2}}$

30. $g(t) = \frac{9t}{\sqrt{t^3}}$

Find each of the following. (See Examples 1–4.)

31. $\frac{dy}{dx}$ if $y = 8x^{-5} - 9x^{-4}$

32. $\frac{dy}{dx}$ if $y = -3x^{-2} - 4x^{-5}$

33. $D_x\left(9x^{-1/2} + \frac{2}{x^{3/2}}\right)$

34. $D_x\left(\frac{8}{\sqrt[4]{x}} - \frac{3}{\sqrt{x^3}}\right)$

35. $f'(-2)$ if $f(x) = 6x^2 - 4x$

36. $f'(3)$ if $f(x) = 9x^3 - 8x^2$

37. $f'(4)$ if $f(t) = 2\sqrt{t} - \frac{3}{\sqrt{t}}$

38. $f'(8)$ if $f(t) = -5\sqrt[3]{t} + \frac{6}{\sqrt[3]{t}}$

39. If $f(x) = -\frac{(3x^2 + x)^2}{7}$, which of the following is *closest* to $f'(1)$?
(a) -12 **(b)** -9 **(c)** -6
(d) -3 **(e)** 0 **(f)** 3

40. If $g(x) = -3x^{3/2} + 4x^2 - 9x$, which of the following is *closest* to $g'(4)$?
(a) 3 **(b)** 6 **(c)** 9
(d) 12 **(e)** 15 **(f)** 18

Find the slope and the equation of the tangent line to the graph of each function at the given value of x.

41. $f(x) = x^4 - 2x^2 + 1; x = 1$

42. $g(x) = -x^5 + 4x^2 - 2x + 2; x = 2$

43. $y = 4x^{1/2} + 2x^{3/2} + 1; x = 4$

44. $y = -x^{-3} + 5x^{-1} + x; x = 2$

45. What is the y-intercept of the tangent line to the graph of $y = x^3 - 2x^2 - 3$ at the point where $x = 1$?
(a) -12 **(b)** -9 **(c)** -6
(d) -3 **(e)** 0 **(f)** 3

Work the following exercises. (See Examples 5–8.)

46. Management The profit in dollars from the sale of x expensive cassette recorders is

$$P(x) = x^3 - 5x^2 + 7x + 10.$$

Find the marginal profit for the following values of x.
(a) $x = 4$ **(b)** $x = 8$ **(c)** $x = 10$
(d) $x = 12$

47. Natural Science Insulation workers who were exposed to asbestos and employed before 1960 experienced an increased likelihood of lung cancer. If a group of insulation workers have a cumulative total of 100,000 years of work experience with their first date of employment t years ago, then the number of lung cancer cases occurring within the group can be modeled using the function

$$N(t) = .00437t^{3.2}*.$$

Find the rate of growth of the number of workers with lung cancer in the group when the first date of employment is:
(a) 5 years ago; **(b)** 10 years ago.

48. Management The total cost to produce x handcrafted weathervanes is

$$C(x) = 100 + 8x - x^2 + 4x^3.$$

Find the marginal cost for the following values of x.
(a) $x = 0$ **(b)** $x = 4$ **(c)** $x = 6$ **(d)** $x = 8$

49. Management The cost (in thousands of dollars) of manufacturing x sailboats is given by

$$C(x) = 600 + x + 42x^{2/3} \quad (0 \le x \le 100).$$

(a) Find the marginal cost function.
(b) What is the marginal cost at $x = 40$?
(c) What is the actual cost of manufacturing the 41st sailboat?
(d) Is the marginal cost at $x = 40$ a reasonable approximation of the actual cost of making the 41st sailboat?

50. Management Often sales of a new product grow rapidly at first and then level off with time. This is the case with the sales represented by the function

$$S(t) = 100 - 100t^{-1},$$

where t represents time in years. Find the rate of change of sales for the following values of t.
(a) $t = 1$ **(b)** $t = 10$

51. Management The revenue from selling x wallets is given by

$$R(x) = 201\sqrt[3]{x} + 2x \quad (4 \le x \le 80).$$

The cost of manufacturing x wallets is given by

$$C(x) = .1x^2 + 5x + 40.$$

(a) Find the profit function.
(b) What is the profit from selling 10 wallets? 20 wallets? 30 wallets? 50 wallets?
(c) Find the marginal profit function.
(d) What is the marginal profit at $x = 10$? at $x = 20$? at $x = 30$? at $x = 50$?
(e) What is the relationship between your answers in parts (b) and (d)?

52. Management An analyst has found that a company's costs and revenues for one product are given by

$$C(x) = 2x \quad \text{and} \quad R(x) = 6x - \frac{x^2}{1000},$$

respectively, where x is the number of items produced.

(exercise continues)

*Walker, A., *Observation and Inference: An Introduction to the Methods of Epidemiology,* Epidemiology Resources Inc., 1991.

(a) Find the marginal cost function.
(b) Find the marginal revenue function.
(c) Using the fact that profit is the difference between revenue and costs, find the marginal profit function.
(d) What value of x makes marginal profit equal 0?
(e) Find the profit when the marginal profit is 0.
(As we shall see in the next chapter, this process is used to find *maximum* profit.)

53. Natural Science Suppose $P(t) = 100/t$ represents the percent of acid in a chemical solution after t days of exposure to an ultraviolet light source. Find the percent of acid in the solution after the following number of days.
(a) 1 day **(b)** 100 days
(c) Find and interpret $P'(100)$.

54. Social Science Based on population trends from 1990 to 1995, it is predicted that the population of a certain city in year t will be given by

$$P(t) = 4t^2 + 2000\sqrt{t} + 50{,}000 \quad (0 \le t \le 30),$$

where $t = 0$ corresponds to 1990.
(a) At what rate (in people per year) is the population changing in year t?
(b) Use part (a) to explain why the population is growing during this 30-year period.
(c) What is the population growth rate in the years 1996, 2000, and 2010?
(d) Does the population of the city in 1990 affect the growth rate in subsequent years? Why?

55. Social Science According to the U.S. Census Bureau, the number of Americans (in thousands) who are expected to be over 100 years old in year x is approximated by the function

$$f(x) = .4018x^2 + 2.039x + 50.071,$$

where $x = 0$ corresponds to 1994 and the formula is valid through 2004.
(a) Find a formula giving the rate of change in the number of Americans over 100 years old.
(b) What is the rate of change in the number of Americans expected to be over 100 years old in the year 2000?
(c) In 2000 is the number of Americans expected to be over 100 years old increasing or decreasing?

56. Natural Science A short length of blood vessel has a cylindrical shape. The volume of a cylinder is given by $V = \pi r^2 h$. Suppose an experimental device is set up to measure the volume of blood in a blood vessel of fixed length 80 mm as the radius changes.
(a) Find dV/dr.
Suppose a drug is administered which causes the blood vessel to expand. Evaluate dV/dr for the following values of r and interpret your answers.
(b) 4 mm **(c)** 6 mm **(d)** 8 mm

57. Management Assume that a demand equation is given by $x = 5000 - 100p$. Find the marginal revenue for the following production levels (values of x). (*Hint:* Solve the demand equation for p and use $R(x) = xp$.)
(a) 1000 units **(b)** 2500 units **(c)** 3000 units

58. Management Suppose that for the situation in Exercise 57, the cost of producing x units is given by $C(x) = 3000 - 20x + .03x^2$. Find the marginal profit for each of the following production levels.
(a) 500 units **(b)** 815 units **(c)** 1000 units

59. Natural Science In an experiment testing methods of sexually attracting male insects to sterile females, equal numbers of males and females of a certain species are permitted to intermingle. Assume that

$$M(t) = 4t^{3/2} + 2t^{1/2}$$

approximates the number of matings observed among the insects in an hour, where t is the temperature in degrees Celsius. (This formula is only valid for certain temperature ranges.) Find each of the following.
(a) $M(16)$ **(b)** $M(25)$
(c) The rate of change of M when $t = 16$
(d) Interpret your answer for part (c).

60. Social Science Living standards are defined by the total output of goods and services divided by the total population. In the United States during the 1980s, living standards were closely approximated by

$$f(x) = -.023x^3 + .3x^2 - .4x + 11.6,$$

where $x = 0$ corresponds to 1981. Find the derivative of f. Use the derivative to find the rate of change in living standards in the following years.
(a) 1981 **(b)** 1983 **(c)** 1988
(d) 1989 **(e)** 1990
(f) What do your answers to parts (a)–(e) tell you about living standards in those years?

Physical Science *We saw earlier that the velocity of a particle moving in a straight line is given by*

$$\lim_{h \to 0} \frac{s(t+h) - s(t)}{h},$$

where $s(t)$ gives the position of the particle at time t. This limit is the derivative of $s(t)$, so the velocity of a particle is given by $s'(t)$. If $v(t)$ represents velocity at time t, then $v(t) = s'(t)$. For each of the following position functions, find **(a)** *$v(t)$;* **(b)** *the velocity when $t = 0$, $t = 5$, and $t = 10$.*

61. $s(t) = 8t^2 + 3t + 1$
62. $s(t) = 10t^2 - 5t + 6$
63. $s(t) = 2t^3 + 6t^2$
64. $s(t) = -t^3 + 3t^2 + t - 1$

65. Physical Science If a rock is dropped from a 144-ft-high building, its position (in feet above the ground) is given by $s(t) = -16t^2 + 144$, where t is the time in seconds since it was dropped.
(a) What is its velocity 1 second after being dropped? 2 seconds after being dropped?
(b) When will it hit the ground?
(c) What is its velocity upon impact?

66. Physical Science A ball is thrown vertically upward from the ground at a velocity of 64 feet per second. Its distance from the ground at t seconds is given by $s(t) = -16t^2 + 64t$.
(a) How fast is the ball moving 2 seconds after being thrown? 3 seconds after being thrown?
(b) How long after the ball is thrown does it reach its maximum height?
(c) How high will it go?

67. Perform each step and give reasons for your results in the following proof that the derivative of $y = x^n$ is $y' = n \cdot x^{n-1}$. (We prove this result only for positive integer values of n, but it is valid for all values of n.)
(a) Recall the binomial theorem from algebra:
$$(p + q)^n = p^n + n \cdot p^{n-1}q + \frac{n(n-1)}{2}p^{n-2}q^2 + \cdots + q^n.$$
Evaluate $(x + h)^n$.
(b) Find the quotient $\dfrac{(x+h)^n - x^n}{h}$.
(c) Use the definition of derivative to find y'.

68. Perform each step and give reasons for your result in the proof that the derivative of $y = f(x) + g(x)$ is
$$y' = f'(x) + g'(x).$$
(a) Let $s(x) = f(x) + g(x)$. Show that
$$s'(x) = \lim_{h\to 0} \frac{[f(x+h) + g(x+h)] - [f(x) + g(x)]}{h}.$$
(b) Show that
$$s'(x) = \lim_{h\to 0}\left[\frac{f(x+h) - f(x)}{h} + \frac{g(x+h) - g(x)}{h}\right].$$
(c) Finally, show that $s'(x) = f'(x) + g'(x)$.

Graph each function and its derivative on the same screen. Determine the values of x where the derivative is (a) *positive,* (b) *zero, and* (c) *negative.* (d) *What is true of the graph of the function in each case?*

69. $g(x) = 6 - 4x + 3x^2 - x^3$

70. $k(x) = 2x^4 - 3x^3 + x$

12.5 DERIVATIVES OF PRODUCTS AND QUOTIENTS

In the last section we saw that the derivative of the sum of two functions can be obtained by taking the sum of the derivatives. What about products? Is the derivative of a product of two functions equal to the product of their derivatives? For example, if
$$u(x) = 2x + 4 \quad \text{and} \quad v(x) = 3x^2,$$
then the product of u and v is
$$f(x) = (2x + 4)(3x^2) = 6x^3 + 12x^2.$$
Using the rules of the last section, we have
$$u'(x) = 2, \quad v'(x) = 6x, \quad \text{and} \quad f'(x) = 18x^2 + 24x,$$
so that
$$u'(x) \cdot v'(x) = 12x \qquad \text{and} \quad f'(x) = 18x^2 + 24x.$$
Obviously, these two functions are *not* the same, which shows that the derivative of the product is *not* equal to the product of the derivatives. For graphical confirmation of this fact, work the problem in the margin. 1

1 Let $u(x) = \ln x$ and $v(x) = \sqrt{x^2 + x}$. Using the viewing window with $0 \le x \le 5$ and $-2 \le y \le 4$, graph these two functions on the same screen:

NDeriv($u(x) \cdot v(x)$)

NDeriv($u(x)$) · NDeriv($v(x)$),

where NDeriv denotes the numerical derivative. What can you conclude from the graphs?

Answer:

Since the two graphs are not the same, the derivative y' of the product function $y = (\ln x)\sqrt{x^2 + x}$ is not equal to the product of the derivatives $u'(x) \cdot v'(x)$.

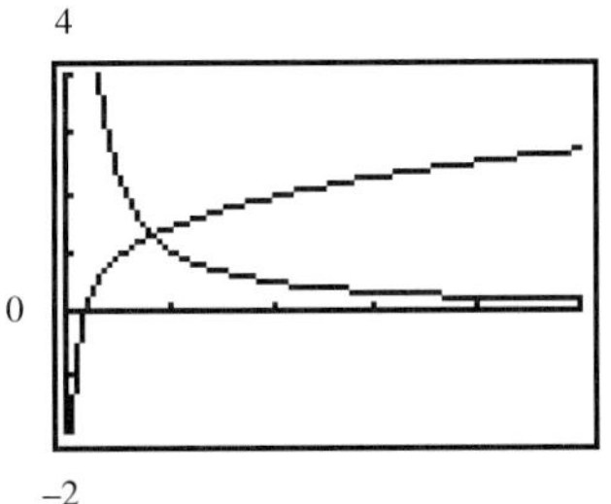

The correct rule for finding the derivative of a product is as follows.

PRODUCT RULE

If $f(x) = u(x) \cdot v(x)$, and if both $u'(x)$ and $v'(x)$ exist, then
$$f'(x) = u(x) \cdot v'(x) + v(x) \cdot u'(x).$$
(The derivative of a product of two functions is the first function times the derivative of the second, plus the second function times the derivative of the first.)

To sketch the method used to prove the product rule, let

$$f(x) = u(x) \cdot v(x).$$

Then $f(x+h) = u(x+h) \cdot v(x+h)$, and, by definition, $f'(x)$ is given by

$$\begin{aligned} f'(x) &= \lim_{h\to 0} \frac{f(x+h) - f(x)}{h} \\ &= \lim_{h\to 0} \frac{u(x+h)\cdot v(x+h) - u(x)\cdot v(x)}{h}. \end{aligned}$$

Now subtract and add $u(x+h) \cdot v(x)$ in the numerator, giving

$$\begin{aligned} f'(x) &= \lim_{h\to 0} \frac{u(x+h)\cdot v(x+h) - \boldsymbol{u(x+h)\cdot v(x)} + \boldsymbol{u(x+h)\cdot v(x)} - u(x)\cdot v(x)}{h} \\ &= \lim_{h\to 0} \frac{u(x+h)[v(x+h) - v(x)] + v(x)[u(x+h) - u(x)]}{h} \\ &= \lim_{h\to 0} u(x+h)\left[\frac{v(x+h) - v(x)}{h}\right] + \lim_{h\to 0} v(x)\left[\frac{u(x+h) - u(x)}{h}\right] \\ &= \lim_{h\to 0} u(x+h) \cdot \lim_{h\to 0} \frac{v(x+h) - v(x)}{h} + \lim_{h\to 0} v(x) \cdot \lim_{h\to 0} \frac{u(x+h) - u(x)}{h} \qquad (*) \end{aligned}$$

If u' and v' both exist, then

$$\lim_{h\to 0} \frac{u(x+h) - u(x)}{h} = u'(x) \quad \text{and} \quad \lim_{h\to 0} \frac{v(x+h) - v(x)}{h} = v'(x).$$

The fact that u' exists can be used to prove

$$\lim_{h\to 0} u(x+h) = u(x),$$

and since no h is involved in $v(x)$,

$$\lim_{h\to 0} v(x) = v(x).$$

Substituting these results into equation (*) gives

$$f'(x) = u(x) \cdot v'(x) + v(x) \cdot u'(x),$$

the desired result.

EXAMPLE 1 Let $f(x) = (2x+4)(3x^2)$. Use the product rule to find $f'(x)$.

Here f is given as the product of $u(x) = 2x + 4$ and $v(x) = 3x^2$. By the product rule and the fact that $u'(x) = 2$ and $v'(x) = 6x$,

$$\begin{aligned} f'(x) &= u(x) \cdot v'(x) + v(x) \cdot u'(x) \\ &= (2x+4)(6x) + (3x^2)(2) \\ &= 12x^2 + 24x + 6x^2 = 18x^2 + 24x. \end{aligned}$$

This result is the same as that found at the beginning of the section. ■ 2

2 Use the product rule to find the derivatives of the following.

(a) $f(x) = (5x^2 + 6)(3x)$

(b) $g(x) = (8x)(4x^2 + 5x)$

Answers:

(a) $45x^2 + 18$

(b) $96x^2 + 80x$

3 Find the derivatives of the following.

(a) $f(x) = (x^2 - 3)(\sqrt{x} + 5)$

(b) $g(x) = (\sqrt{x} + 4)(5x^2 + x)$

Answers:

(a) $\frac{5}{2}x^{3/2} + 10x - \frac{3}{2}x^{-1/2}$

(b) $\frac{25}{2}x^{3/2} + 40x + \frac{3}{2}x^{1/2} + 4$

EXAMPLE 2 Find the derivative of $y = (\sqrt{x} + 3)(x^2 - 5x)$.

Let $u(x) = \sqrt{x} + 3 = x^{1/2} + 3$, and $v(x) = x^2 - 5x$. Then

$$\begin{aligned} y' &= u(x) \cdot \mathbf{v'(x)} + v(x) \cdot \mathbf{u'(x)} \\ &= (x^{1/2} + 3)(\mathbf{2x - 5}) + (x^2 - 5x)\left(\frac{\mathbf{1}}{\mathbf{2}}\mathbf{x^{-1/2}}\right) \\ &= 2x^{3/2} + 6x - 5x^{1/2} - 15 + \frac{1}{2}x^{3/2} - \frac{5}{2}x^{1/2} \\ &= \frac{5}{2}x^{3/2} + 6x - \frac{15}{2}x^{1/2} - 15. \end{aligned}$$

■ 3

We could have found the derivatives above by multiplying out the original functions. The product rule then would not have been needed. In the next section, however, we shall see products of functions where the product rule is essential.

What about *quotients* of functions? To find the derivative of the quotient of two functions, use the next rule.

QUOTIENT RULE

If $f(x) = \frac{u(x)}{v(x)}$, if all indicated derivatives exist, and if $v(x) \neq 0$, then

$$f'(x) = \frac{v(x) \cdot u'(x) - u(x) \cdot v'(x)}{[v(x)]^2}.$$

(The derivative of a quotient is the denominator times the derivative of the numerator, minus the numerator times the derivative of the denominator, all divided by the square of the denominator.)

The proof of the quotient rule is similar to that of the product rule and is omitted here.

4 Confirm that the derivative found in Example 3 is correct by graphing $f'(x) = 10/(4x + 3)^2$ and the numerical derivative of $f(x)$ on the same screen.

Answer:

The two graphs appear to be identical, as they should if the computation of the derivative is correct.

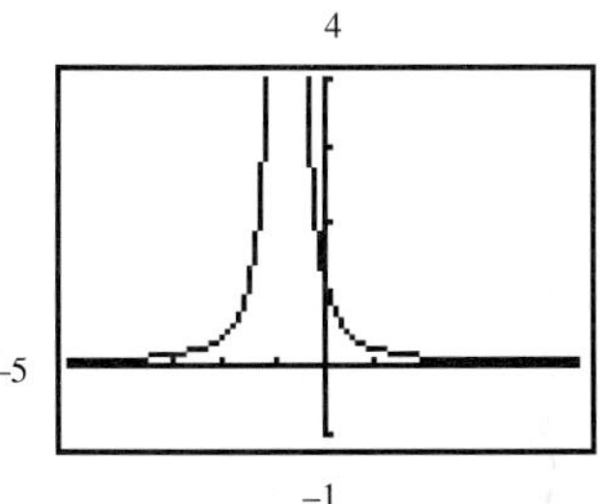

EXAMPLE 3 Find $f'(x)$ if $f(x) = \frac{2x - 1}{4x + 3}$.

Let $u(x) = 2x - 1$, with $u'(x) = 2$. Also, let $v(x) = 4x + 3$, with $v'(x) = 4$. Then, by the quotient rule,

$$\begin{aligned} f'(x) &= \frac{v(x) \cdot \mathbf{u'(x)} - u(x) \cdot \mathbf{v'(x)}}{[v(x)]^2} \\ &= \frac{(4x + 3)(\mathbf{2}) - (2x - 1)(\mathbf{4})}{(4x + 3)^2} \\ &= \frac{8x + 6 - 8x + 4}{(4x + 3)^2} \\ f'(x) &= \frac{10}{(4x + 3)^2}. \end{aligned}$$

You can confirm this result graphically by working Side Problem 4. ■ 4

EXAMPLE 4 Find $D_x\left(\frac{x^{-1} - 2}{x^{-2} + 4}\right)$.

Use the quotient rule.

$$D_x\left(\frac{x^{-1} - 2}{x^{-2} + 4}\right) = \frac{(x^{-2} + 4) \cdot D_x(x^{-1} - 2) - (x^{-1} - 2) \cdot D_x(x^{-2} + 4)}{(x^{-2} + 4)^2}$$

$$= \frac{(x^{-2} + 4)(-x^{-2}) - (x^{-1} - 2)(-2x^{-3})}{(x^{-2} + 4)^2}$$

$$= \frac{-x^{-4} - 4x^{-2} + 2x^{-4} - 4x^{-3}}{(x^{-2} + 4)^2} = \frac{x^{-4} - 4x^{-3} - 4x^{-2}}{(x^{-2} + 4)^2}$$

When derivatives are used to solve practical problems, the work is easier if the derivatives are first simplified. This derivative, for example, can be simplified if the negative exponents are removed by multiplying numerator and denominator by x^4, and using $(x^{-2} + 4)^2 = x^{-4} + 8x^{-2} + 16$.

$$\frac{x^4(x^{-4} - 4x^{-3} - 4x^{-2})}{x^4(x^{-2} + 4)^2} = \frac{1 - 4x - 4x^2}{x^4(x^{-4} + 8x^{-2} + 16)} = \frac{1 - 4x - 4x^2}{1 + 8x^2 + 16x^4}$$ ■ 5

5 Find each derivative. Write answers with positive exponents.

(a) $D_x\left(\frac{x^{-2} - 1}{x^{-1} + 2}\right)$

(b) $g(x) = \frac{2x + 11}{5x - 1}$

Answers:

(a) $\frac{-1 - 4x - x^2}{x^2 + 4x^3 + 4x^4}$

(b) $\frac{-57}{(5x - 1)^2}$

EXAMPLE 5 Find $D_x\left(\frac{(3 - 4x)(5x + 1)}{7x - 9}\right)$.

This function has a product within a quotient. Instead of multiplying the factors in the numerator first (which is an option), we can use the quotient rule together with the product rule, as follows. Use the quotient rule first to get

$$D_x\left(\frac{(3 - 4x)(5x + 1)}{7x - 9}\right)$$

$$= \frac{(7x - 9)[\mathbf{D_x(3 - 4x)(5x + 1)}] - [(3 - 4x)(5x + 1)D_x(7x - 9)]}{(7x - 9)^2}$$

Now use the product rule to find $D_x(3 - 4x)(5x + 1)$ in the numerator.

$$= \frac{(7x - 9)[\mathbf{(3 - 4x)5 + (5x + 1)(-4)}] - (3 + 11x - 20x^2)(7)}{(7x - 9)^2}$$

$$= \frac{(7x - 9)(15 - 20x - 20x - 4) - (21 + 77x - 140x^2)}{(7x - 9)^2}$$

$$= \frac{(7x - 9)(11 - 40x) - 21 - 77x + 140x^2}{(7x - 9)^2}$$

$$= \frac{-280x^2 + 437x - 99 - 21 - 77x + 140x^2}{(7x - 9)^2}$$

$$= \frac{-140x^2 + 360x - 120}{(7x - 9)^2}$$ ■ 6

6 Find each derivative.

(a) $D_x\left(\frac{(3x - 1)(4x + 2)}{2x}\right)$

(b) $D_x\left(\frac{5x^2}{(2x + 1)(x - 1)}\right)$

Answers:

(a) $\frac{6x^2 + 1}{x^2}$

(b) $\frac{-5x^2 - 10x}{(2x + 1)^2(x - 1)^2}$

AVERAGE COST Suppose $y = C(x)$ gives the total cost to manufacture x items. As mentioned earlier, the average cost per item is found by dividing the total cost by the number of items. The rate of change of average cost, called the *marginal average cost,* is the derivative of the average cost.

AVERAGE COST

If the total cost to manufacture x items is given by $C(x)$, then the **average cost per item** is

$$\overline{C}(x) = \frac{C(x)}{x}.$$

The **marginal average cost** is the derivative of the average cost function, $\overline{C}'(x)$.

A company naturally would be interested in making the average cost as small as possible. We will see in the next chapter that this can be done by using the derivative of $C(x)/x$. The derivative often can be found with the quotient rule, as in the next example.

EXAMPLE 6 The total cost in thousands of dollars to manufacture x electrical generators is given by $C(x)$, where

$$C(x) = -x^3 + 15x^2 + 1000.$$

(a) Find the average cost per generator.

The average cost is given by the total cost divided by the number of items, or

$$\frac{C(x)}{x} = \frac{-x^3 + 15x^2 + 1000}{x}.$$

(b) Find the marginal average cost.

The marginal average cost is the derivative of the average cost function. Using the quotient rule,

$$\frac{d}{dx}\left(\frac{C(x)}{x}\right) = \frac{x(-3x^2 + 30x) - (-x^3 + 15x^2 + 1000)(1)}{x^2}$$

$$= \frac{-3x^3 + 30x^2 + x^3 - 15x^2 - 1000}{x^2}$$

$$= \frac{-2x^3 + 15x^2 - 1000}{x^2}. \quad ■ \quad \boxed{7}$$

$\boxed{7}$ The total revenue in thousands of dollars from the sale of x dozen CB radios is given by

$$R(x) = 32x^2 + 7x + 80.$$

(a) Find the average revenue.

(b) Find the marginal average revenue.

Answers:

(a) $\dfrac{32x^2 + 7x + 80}{x}$

(b) $\dfrac{32x^2 - 80}{x^2}$

EXAMPLE 7 Suppose the cost in dollars of manufacturing x hundred items is given by

$$C(x) = 3x^2 + 7x + 12.$$

(a) Find the average cost.

The average cost is

$$\overline{C}(x) = \frac{C(x)}{x} = \frac{3x^2 + 7x + 12}{x} = 3x + 7 + \frac{12}{x}.$$

(b) Find the marginal average cost.

The marginal average cost is

$$\frac{d}{dx}(\overline{C}(x)) = \frac{d}{dx}\left(3x + 7 + \frac{12}{x}\right) = 3 - \frac{12}{x^2}.$$

(c) Find the marginal cost.
The marginal cost is

$$\frac{d}{dx}(C(x)) = \frac{d}{dx}(3x^2 + 7x + 12) = 6x + 7.$$

(d) Find the level of production at which the marginal average cost is zero.
Set the derivative $\overline{C}'(x) = 0$ and solve for x.

$$3 - \frac{12}{x^2} = 0$$

$$\frac{3x^2 - 12}{x^2} = 0$$

$$3x^2 - 12 = 0$$

$$x^2 = 4$$

$$x = \pm 2$$

You can't make a negative number of items, so the answer is $x = 2$. Since x is in hundreds, production of 200 items will produce a marginal average cost of zero dollars. ■ 8

8 If the cost in Example 7 is given by

$$C(x) = x^2 + 10x + 16,$$

find the production level at which the marginal average cost is zero.

Answer:
400 items

12.5 EXERCISES

Use the product rule to find the derivatives of the following functions. (See Examples 1 and 2.) (Hint for Exercises 6–9: Write the quantity as a product.)

1. $y = (x^2 - 2)(3x + 1)$

2. $y = (2x^2 + 3)(4x + 5)$

3. $y = (6x^3 + 2)(5x - 3)$

4. $y = (2x^2 + 4x - 3)(5x^3 + x + 2)$

5. $y = (x^4 - 2x^3 + 2x)(4x^2 + x - 3)$

6. $y = (3x - 2)^2$

7. $y = (6x^2 + 4x)^2$

8. $y = (x^2 - 1)^2$

9. $y = (3x^3 + x^2)^2$

Use the quotient rule to find the derivatives of the following functions. (See Examples 3 and 4.)

10. $y = \frac{x + 1}{2x - 1}$

11. $y = \frac{3x - 5}{x - 4}$

12. $f(x) = \frac{7x + 1}{3x + 8}$

13. $f(t) = \frac{t^2 - 4t}{t + 3}$

14. $y = \frac{4x + 11}{x^2 - 3}$

15. $g(x) = \frac{3x^2 + x}{2x^3 - 1}$

16. $k(x) = \frac{-x^2 + 6x}{4x^3 + 1}$

17. $y = \frac{x^2 - 4x + 2}{x + 3}$

18. $y = \frac{x^2 + 7x - 2}{x - 2}$

19. $r(t) = \frac{\sqrt{t}}{2t + 3}$

20. $y = \frac{5x + 6}{\sqrt{x}}$

21. $y = \frac{9x - 8}{\sqrt{x}}$

Find the derivative of the function and confirm your answer graphically by graphing the derivative you found and the numerical derivative of the original function on the same screen. (See Example 3.)

22. $y = (x^2 + 3x)(x^2 + 2)$

23. $y = (7x^4 + 2x)(x^2 - 4)$

24. $y = (x^3 + 4x^2 + 2x)(x^2 - 1)$

25. $y = (2x - 3)(\sqrt{x} - 1)$

26. $y = (5\sqrt{x} - 1)(2\sqrt{x} + 1)$

27. $y = (-3\sqrt{x} + 6)(4\sqrt{x} - 2)$

28. $y = \frac{2}{3x - 5}$

29. $y = \frac{9 - 7x}{1 - x}$

30. $f(t) = \frac{t^2 + t}{t - 1}$

Find the derivative of each of the following. (See Example 5.)

31. $f(p) = \frac{(2p + 3)(4p - 1)}{3p + 2}$

32. $g(t) = \frac{(5t - 2)(2t + 3)}{t - 4}$

33. $g(x) = \dfrac{x^3 + 1}{(2x + 1)(5x + 2)}$

34. $f(x) = \dfrac{x^3 - 4}{(2x + 1)(3x - 2)}$

35. Find the error in the following work.

$$D_x\left(\frac{2x + 5}{x^2 - 1}\right) = \frac{(2x + 5)(2x) - (x^2 - 1)2}{(x^2 - 1)^2} = \frac{4x^2 + 10x - 2x^2 + 2}{(x^2 - 1)^2} = \frac{2x^2 + 10x + 2}{(x^2 - 1)^2}$$

36. Find the error in the following work.

$$D_x\left(\frac{x^2 - 4}{x^3}\right) = x^3(2x) - (x^2 - 4)(3x^2) = 2x^4 - 3x^4 + 12x^2 = -x^4 + 12x^2$$

37. Find an equation of the line tangent to the graph of $f(x) = \dfrac{x}{x - 2}$ at (3, 3).

38. If $f(x) = 6 - 7x$ and $g(x) = 4x^3 - 9$, then which of the following is closest to $(fg)'(1)$?

(a) 0 **(b)** 6 **(c)** 12 **(d)** 18
(e) 24 **(f)** 30

Work the following exercises. (See Examples 6 and 7.)

39. Management The total cost (in hundreds of dollars) to produce x units of perfume is

$$C(x) = \frac{3x + 2}{x + 4}.$$

Find the average cost for each of the following production levels.

(a) 10 units **(b)** 20 units **(c)** x units
(d) Find the marginal average cost function.

40. Management The total profit (in tens of dollars) from selling x self-help books is

$$P(x) = \frac{5x - 6}{2x + 3}.$$

Find the average profit from each of the following sales levels.

(a) 8 books **(b)** 15 books **(c)** x books
(d) Find the marginal average profit function.
(e) Is this a reasonable function for profit? Why?

41. Social Science After t hours of instruction, a typical typing student can type

$$N(t) = \frac{70t^2}{30 + t^2}$$

words per minute.

(a) Find $N'(t)$, the rate at which the student is improving after t hours.
(b) At what rate is the student improving after 3 hours? 5 hours? 7 hours? 10 hours? 15 hours?
(c) Describe the student's progress during the first 15 hours of instruction.

42. Management Suppose you are the manager of a trucking firm, and one of your drivers reports that, according to her calculations, her truck burns fuel at the rate of

$$G(x) = \frac{1}{200}\left(\frac{800}{x} + x\right)$$

gallons per mile when traveling at x miles per hour on a smooth, dry road.

(a) If the driver tells you that she wants to travel 20 miles per hour, what should you tell her? (*Hint:* Take the derivative of G and evaluate it for $x = 20$. Then interpret your results.)
(b) If the driver wants to go 40 miles per hour, what should you say? (*Hint:* Find $G'(40)$.)

43. Physical Science The distance (in feet) from a cat to a string he is stalking is given by

$$f(t) = \frac{8}{t + 1} + \frac{20}{t^2 + 1},$$

where t is the time in seconds since he began.

(a) What is the cat's average velocity between 1 sec and 3 sec?
(b) What is the cat's instantaneous velocity at 3 sec?

44. Natural Science When a certain drug is introduced into a muscle, the muscle responds by contracting. The amount of contraction, s, in millimeters, is related to the concentration of the drug, x, in milliliters, by

$$s(x) = \frac{x}{m + nx},$$

where m and n are constants.

(a) Find $s'(x)$.
(b) Evaluate $s'(x)$ when $x = 50$, $m = 10$, and $n = 3$.
(c) Interpret your results in part (b).

45. Management The average number of vehicles waiting in line to enter a parking lot can be modeled by the function

$$f(x) = \frac{x^2}{2(1 - x)},$$

where x is a quantity between 0 and 1 known as the traffic intensity.* Find the rate of change of the waiting time with respect to the traffic intensity for the following values of the intensity.

(a) $x = .1$ **(b)** $x = .6$

*Mannering, F., and W. Kilareski, *Principles of Highway Engineering and Traffic Control,* John Wiley and Sons, 1990.

46. Natural Science Assume that the total number (in millions) of bacteria present in a culture at a certain time t (in hours) is given by

$$N(t) = (t - 10)^2(2t) + 50.$$

(a) Find $N'(t)$.

Find the rate at which the population of bacteria is changing at each of the following times.

(b) 8 hr **(c)** 11 hr

(d) The answer in part (b) is negative, and the answer in part (c) is positive. What does this mean in terms of the population of bacteria?

12.6 THE CHAIN RULE

Many of the most useful functions for applications are created by combining simpler functions. Viewing complex functions as combinations of simpler functions often makes them easier to understand and use.

COMPOSITION OF FUNCTIONS Consider the function h whose rule is $h(x) = \sqrt{x^3}$. To compute $h(4)$, for example, you first find $4^3 = 64$ and then take the square root: $\sqrt{64} = 8$. So the rule of h may be rephrased as:

First apply the function $f(x) = x^3$,
then apply the function $g(x) = \sqrt{x}$ to the result.

The same idea can be expressed in functional notation like this:

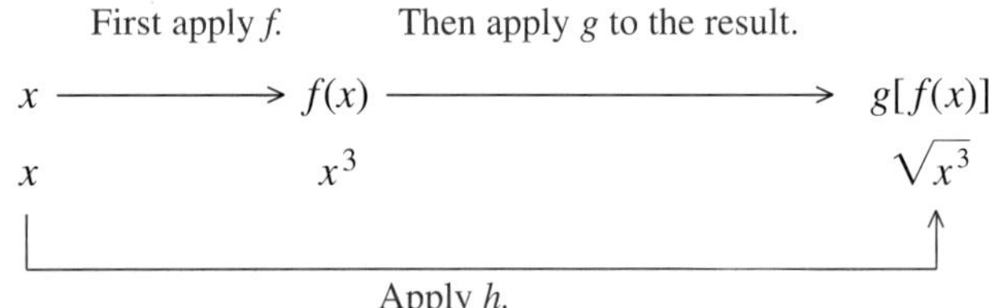

So the rule of h may be written as $h(x) = g[f(x)]$, where $f(x) = x^3$ and $g(x) = \sqrt{x}$. We can think of the functions g and f as being "composed" to create the function h. Here is a formal definition of this idea.

> **COMPOSITE FUNCTION**
>
> Let f and g be functions. The **composite function,** or **composition,** of g and f is the function whose values are given by $g[f(x)]$ for all x in the domain of f such that $f(x)$ is in the domain of g.

EXAMPLE 1 Let $f(x) = 2x - 1$ and $g(x) = \sqrt{3x + 5}$. Find each of the following.

(a) $g[f(4)]$
Find $f(4)$ first.

$$f(4) = 2 \cdot 4 - 1 = 8 - 1 = 7$$

Then

$$g[f(4)] = g[7] = \sqrt{3 \cdot 7 + 5} = \sqrt{26}.$$

(b) $f[g(4)]$
Since $g(4) = \sqrt{3 \cdot 4 + 5} = \sqrt{17}$,

$$f[g(4)] = 2 \cdot \sqrt{17} - 1 = 2\sqrt{17} - 1.$$

(c) $f[g(-2)]$ does not exist since -2 is not in the domain of g. ■ 1

1 Let $f(x) = 3x - 2$ and $g(x) = (x - 1)^5$. Find the following.

(a) $g[f(2)]$

(b) $f[g(2)]$

Answers:

(a) 243

(b) 1

EXAMPLE 2 Let $f(x) = 4x + 1$ and $g(x) = 2x^2 + 5x$. Find each of the following.

(a) $g[f(x)]$

Using the given functions,

$$\begin{aligned} g[f(\mathbf{x})] &= g[\mathbf{4x + 1}] \\ &= 2(\mathbf{4x + 1})^2 + 5(\mathbf{4x + 1}) \\ &= 2(16x^2 + 8x + 1) + 20x + 5 \\ &= 32x^2 + 16x + 2 + 20x + 5 \\ &= 32x^2 + 36x + 7. \end{aligned}$$

(b) $f[g(x)]$

By the definition above, with f and g interchanged,

$$\begin{aligned} f[g(\mathbf{x})] &= f[\mathbf{2x^2 + 5x}] \\ &= 4(\mathbf{2x^2 + 5x}) + 1 \\ &= 8x^2 + 20x + 1. \end{aligned}$$ ■ 2

2 Let $f(x) = \sqrt{x + 4}$ and $g(x) = x^2 + 5x + 1$. Find $f[g(x)]$ and $g[f(x)]$.

Answers:

$f[g(x)] = \sqrt{x^2 + 5x + 5}$,

$g[f(x)] = (\sqrt{x + 4})^2 + 5\sqrt{x + 4} + 1$
$= x + 5 + 5\sqrt{x + 4}$

As Example 2 shows, $f[g(x)]$ usually is *not* equal to $g[f(x)]$. In fact, it is rare to find two functions f and g for which $f[g(x)] = g[f(x)]$.

It is often necessary to write a given function as the composite of two other functions, as illustrated in the next example.

EXAMPLE 3 **(a)** Express the function $h(x) = (x^3 + x^2 - 5)^4$ as the composite of two functions.

One way to do this is to let $f(x) = x^3 + x^2 - 5$ and $g(x) = x^4$; then

$$g[f(x)] = g[x^3 + x^2 - 5] = (x^3 + x^2 - 5)^4 = h(x).$$

(b) Express the function $h(x) = \sqrt{4x^2 + 5}$ as the composite of two functions in two different ways.

One way is to let $f(x) = 4x^2 + 5$ and $g(x) = \sqrt{x}$, so that

$$g[f(x)] = g[4x^2 + 5] = \sqrt{4x^2 + 5} = h(x).$$

Another way is to let $k(x) = 4x^2$ and $t(x) = \sqrt{x + 5}$; then

$$t[k(x)] = t[4x^2] = \sqrt{4x^2 + 5} = h(x).$$ ■ 3

3 Express the given function as a composition of two other functions.

(a) $h(x) = (7x^2 + 5)^4$

(b) $h(x) = \sqrt{15x^2 + 1}$

Answers:

There are several correct answers, including:

(a) $h(x) = f[g(x)]$, where $f(x) = x^4$ and $g(x) = 7x^2 + 5$.

(b) $h(x) = f[g(x)]$, where $f(x) = \sqrt{x}$ and $g(x) = 15x^2 + 1$.

THE CHAIN RULE The product and quotient rules tell how to find the derivative of fg and f/g from the derivatives of f and g. Similarly, the **chain rule,** which is given below, tells how to find the derivative of the composite function $f[g(x)]$ from the derivatives of f and g. The proof of the chain rule is beyond the scope of this book, but we can illustrate the idea with some examples.

Metal expands or contracts as the temperature changes and the temperature changes over a period of time. Suppose the length of a metal bar is increasing at the rate of 2 mm for every degree increase in temperature and that temperature is increasing at the rate of 4° per hour. Then during the course of an hour, the length of the bar will increase by $2 \cdot 4 = 8$ mm. In other words, the rate of change of length with respect to time is the following product.

$$\begin{pmatrix} \text{rate of change} \\ \text{of length with} \\ \text{respect to time} \end{pmatrix} = \begin{pmatrix} \text{rate of change} \\ \text{of length with} \\ \text{respect to temperature} \end{pmatrix} \cdot \begin{pmatrix} \text{rate of change} \\ \text{of temperature with} \\ \text{respect to time} \end{pmatrix} \quad (*)$$

If we think of length as a function of temperature, say $L = f(d)$, and temperature as a function of time, say $d = g(t)$, then the composite function $L = f(d) = f[g(t)]$ gives length as a function of time. Since the derivative of a function is its rate of change, statement (*) says

$$L'(t) = f'(d) \cdot g'(t) = f'[g(t)] \cdot g'(t).$$

We shall see that a similar result holds for any composite function. For instance, if $f(x) = x^2$ and $g(x) = x^3 + x$, then the composite function is

$$f[g(x)] = f[x^3 + x] = [x^3 + x]^2 = (x^3)^2 + 2(x^3)x + x^2 = x^6 + 2x^4 + x^2.$$

The derivative of the composite function $y = x^6 + 2x^4 + x^2$ is

$$y' = 6x^5 + 8x^3 + 2x$$

and the derivatives of $f(x) = x^2$ and $g(x) = x^3 + x$ are

$$f'(x) = 2x \quad \text{and} \quad g'(x) = 3x^2 + 1.$$

The relationship of these three derivatives can be seen when we factor.

$$\begin{aligned} y' &= 6x^5 + 8x^3 + 2x \\ &= 2(3x^5 + 4x^3 + x) \\ &= 2(x^3 + x)(3x^2 + 1) \\ &= [2 \cdot g(x)] \cdot g'(x) \end{aligned}$$

Since $f'(x) = 2x$, then $f'[g(x)] = 2g(x)$, so that the last line can be written as

$$y' = [2 \cdot g(x)] \cdot g'(x) = f'[g(x)] \cdot g'(x).$$

Although there are different letters for the variables, this is the same result as in the case of the expanding metal bar: the derivative of the composite function $y = f[g(x)]$ is the product of the derivative of f, evaluated at $g(x)$, and the derivative of g. This same relationship holds in all cases.

CHAIN RULE

If f and g are functions and $y = f[g(x)]$, then

$$\mathbf{y' = f'[g(x)] \cdot g'(x),}$$

provided $f'[g(x)]$ and $g'(x)$ exist.

(To find the derivative of $f[g(x)]$, find the derivative of $f(x)$, replace each x with $g(x)$, and multiply the result by the derivative of $g(x)$.)

4 Let $y = \sqrt{2x^4 + 3}$.

(a) Find dy/dx.

(b) Confirm your answer graphically by graphing dy/dx and the numerical derivative of y on the same screen.

Answers:

(a) $\dfrac{dy}{dx} = \dfrac{4x^3}{\sqrt{2x^4 + 3}}$

(b) The two graphs appear to be identical.

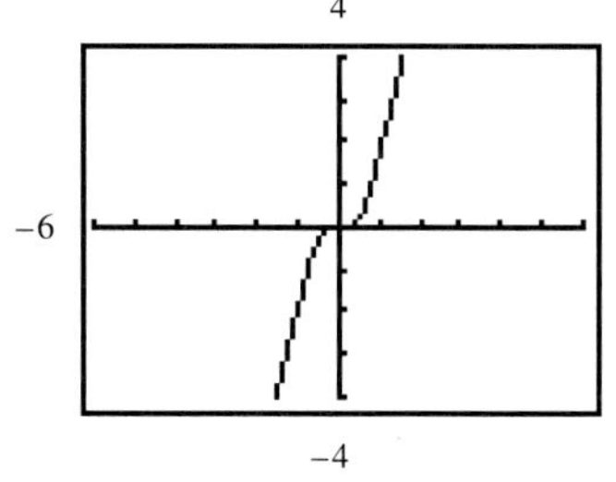

EXAMPLE 4 Use the chain rule to find $D_x\sqrt{15x^2 + 1}$.

Write $\sqrt{15x^2 + 1}$ as $(15x^2 + 1)^{1/2}$. Let $f(x) = x^{1/2}$ and $g(x) = 15x^2 + 1$. Then $\sqrt{15x^2 - 1} = f[g(x)]$ and

$$D_x(15x^2 + 1)^{1/2} = f'[g(x)] \cdot g'(x).$$

Here $f'(x) = \frac{1}{2}x^{-1/2}$, with $f'[g(x)] = \frac{1}{2}[g(x)]^{-1/2} = \frac{1}{2}(15x^2 + 1)^{-1/2}$, and

$$\begin{aligned} D_x\sqrt{\mathbf{15x^2 + 1}} &= \frac{1}{2}[\mathbf{g(x)}]^{-1/2} \cdot g'(x) \\ &= \frac{1}{2}(\mathbf{15x^2 + 1})^{-1/2} \cdot (30x) \\ &= \frac{15x}{(15x^2 + 1)^{1/2}}. \end{aligned}$$

You can confirm this result graphically by graphing $y = 15x/(15x^2 + 1)^{1/2}$ and the numerical derivative of $\sqrt{15x^2 + 1}$ on the same screen; the graphs will appear identical. ■ 4

The chain rule can also be stated using the Leibnitz notation for derivatives. If y is a function of u, say $y = f(u)$, and u is a function of x, say $u = g(x)$, then

$$f'(u) = \frac{dy}{du} \quad \text{and} \quad g'(x) = \frac{du}{dx}.$$

Now y can be considered as a function of x, namely, $y = f(u) = f(g(x))$. According to the chain rule, the derivative of y is

$$\frac{dy}{dx} = f'(g(x)) \cdot g'(x) = f'(u) \cdot g'(x) = \frac{dy}{du} \cdot \frac{du}{dx}.$$

Thus we have this alternative version of the chain rule.

THE CHAIN RULE (ALTERNATIVE FORM)

If y is a function of u, say $y = f(u)$, and if u is a function of x, say $u = g(x)$, then $y = f(u) = f[g(x)]$, and

$$\frac{dy}{dx} = \frac{dy}{du} \cdot \frac{du}{dx}$$

provided dy/du and du/dx exist.

One way to remember the chain rule is to *pretend* that dy/du and du/dx are fractions, with du "canceling out."

EXAMPLE 5 Find dy/dx if $y = (3x^2 - 5x)^{1/2}$.

Let $y = u^{1/2}$, and $u = 3x^2 - 5x$. Then

$$\begin{aligned} \frac{dy}{dx} &= \frac{dy}{du} \cdot \frac{du}{dx} \\ &= \frac{1}{2}u^{-1/2} \cdot (6x - 5). \end{aligned}$$

5 Use the chain rule to find dy/dx if $y = 10(2x^2 + 1)^4$.

Answer:
$160x(2x^2 + 1)^3$

Replacing u with $3x^2 - 5x$ gives

$$\frac{dy}{dx} = \frac{1}{2}(3x^2 - 5x)^{-1/2}(6x - 5) = \frac{6x - 5}{2(3x^2 - 5x)^{1/2}}$$ ■ 5

While the chain rule is essential for finding the derivatives of some of the functions discussed later, the derivatives of the algebraic functions discussed so far can be found by the following *generalized power rule,* a special case of the chain rule.

GENERALIZED POWER RULE

Let u be a function of x, and let $y = u^n$, for any real number n. Then

$$y' = n \cdot u^{n-1} \cdot u',$$

provided that u' exists.

(The derivative of $y = u^n$ is found by decreasing the exponent on u by 1 and multiplying the result by the exponent n and by the derivative of u with respect to x.)

EXAMPLE 6 **(a)** Use the generalized power rule to find the derivative of $y = (3 + 5x)^2$.

Let $u = 3 + 5x$, and $n = 2$. Then $u' = 5$. By the generalized power rule,

$$y' = \frac{dy}{dx} = n \cdot u^{n-1} \cdot u'$$

$$\begin{aligned} &= \underset{\downarrow}{\overset{n}{2}} \cdot (\underset{\downarrow}{\overset{u}{3 + 5x}})^{\overset{n-1}{2-1}} \cdot \overbrace{\frac{d}{dx}(3 + 5x)}^{u'} \\ &= 2(3 + 5x)^{2-1} \cdot 5 \\ &= 10(3 + 5x) \\ &= 30 + 50x. \end{aligned}$$

6 Find dy/dx for the following.

(a) $y = (2x + 5)^6$

(b) $y = (4x^2 - 7)^3$

(c) $f(x) = \sqrt{3x^2 - x}$

(d) $g(x) = (2 - x^4)^{-3}$

Answers:

(a) $12(2x + 5)^5$

(b) $24x(4x^2 - 7)^2$

(c) $\dfrac{6x - 1}{2\sqrt{3x^2 - x}}$

(d) $\dfrac{12x^3}{(2 - x^4)^4}$

(b) Find y' if $y = (3 + 5x)^{-3/4}$.

Use the generalized power rule with $n = -\frac{3}{4}$, $u = 3 + 5x$, and $u' = 5$.

$$\begin{aligned} y' &= -\frac{3}{4}(3 + 5x)^{(-3/4)-1}(5) \\ &= -\frac{15}{4}(3 + 5x)^{-7/4} \end{aligned}$$

This result could not have been found by any of the rules given earlier. ■ 6

EXAMPLE 7 Find the derivative of the following.

(a) $y = 2(7x^2 + 5)^4$

Let $u = 7x^2 + 5$. Then $u' = 14x$, and

$$y' = \overset{n}{\downarrow}2 \cdot 4(\overset{u}{\downarrow}7x^2 + 5)^{\overset{n-1}{\downarrow}4-1} \cdot \overbrace{\frac{d}{dx}(7x^2 + 5)}^{u'}$$

$$= 2 \cdot 4(7x^2 + 5)^3(14x)$$

$$= 112x(7x^2 + 5)^3.$$

(b) $y = \sqrt{9x + 2}$

Write $y = \sqrt{9x + 2}$ as $y = (9x + 2)^{1/2}$. Then

$$y' = \frac{1}{2}(9x + 2)^{-1/2}(9) = \frac{9}{2}(9x + 2)^{-1/2}.$$

The derivative also can be written as

$$y' = \frac{9}{2(9x + 2)^{1/2}} \quad \text{or} \quad y' = \frac{9}{2\sqrt{9x + 2}}. \blacksquare \quad \boxed{7}$$

$\boxed{7}$ Find dy/dx for the following.

(a) $y = 12(x^2 + 6)^5$

(b) $y = 8(4x^2 + 2)^{3/2}$

Answers:

(a) $120x(x^2 + 6)^4$

(b) $96x(4x^2 + 2)^{1/2}$

Sometimes both the generalized power rule and either the product or quotient rule are needed to find a derivative, as the next examples show.

EXAMPLE 8 Find the derivative of $y = 4x(3x + 5)^5$.

Write $4x(3x + 5)^5$ as the product

$$4x \cdot (3x + 5)^5.$$

To find the derivative of $(3x + 5)^5$, let $u = 3x + 5$ with $u' = 3$. Now use the product rule and the generalized power rule.

$$y' = 4x\overbrace{[5(3x + 5)^4 \cdot 3]}^{\text{Derivative of }(3x+5)^5} + (3x + 5)^5\overbrace{(4)}^{\text{Derivative of }4x}$$

$$= 60x(3x + 5)^4 + 4(3x + 5)^5$$

$$= 4(3x + 5)^4[15x + (3x + 5)^1] \quad \text{Factor out the greatest common factor, } 4(3x + 5)^4.$$

$$= 4(3x + 5)^4(18x + 5). \blacksquare \quad \boxed{8}$$

$\boxed{8}$ Find the derivatives of the following.

(a) $y = 6x(x + 2)^2$

(b) $y = -9x(2x^2 + 1)^3$

Answers:

(a) $6(x + 2)(3x + 2)$

(b) $-9(2x^2 + 1)^2(14x^2 + 1)$

EXAMPLE 9 Find the derivative of $y = \dfrac{(3x + 2)^7}{x - 1}$.

Use the quotient rule and the generalized power rule.

$$\frac{dy}{dx} = \frac{(x - 1)[7(3x + 2)^6 \cdot 3] - (3x + 2)^7(1)}{(x - 1)^2}$$

$$= \frac{21(x - 1)(3x + 2)^6 - (3x + 2)^7}{(x - 1)^2}$$

$$= \frac{(3x + 2)^6[21(x - 1) - (3x + 2)]}{(x - 1)^2} \quad \text{Factor out the greatest common factor, } (3x + 2)^6.$$

$$= \frac{(3x + 2)^6[21x - 21 - 3x - 2]}{(x - 1)^2} \quad \text{Simplify inside brackets.}$$

$$\frac{dy}{dx} = \frac{(3x + 2)^6(18x - 23)}{(x - 1)^2} \blacksquare \quad \boxed{9}$$

$\boxed{9}$ Find the derivatives of the following.

(a) $y = \dfrac{(2x + 1)^3}{3x}$

(b) $y = \dfrac{(x - 6)^5}{3x - 5}$

Answers:

(a) $\dfrac{(2x + 1)^2(4x - 1)}{3x^2}$

(b) $\dfrac{(x - 6)^4(12x - 7)}{(3x - 5)^2}$

Some applications requiring the use of the chain rule or the generalized power rule are illustrated in the next examples.

EXAMPLE 10 The revenue realized by a small city from the collection of fines from parking tickets is given by

$$R(n) = \frac{8000n}{n + 2},$$

where n is the number of work hours each day that can be devoted to parking patrol. At the outbreak of a flu epidemic, 30 work hours are used daily in parking patrol, but during the epidemic that number is decreasing at the rate of 6 work hours per day. Thus, $dn/dt = -6$. How fast is revenue from parking fines decreasing during the epidemic?

We want to find dR/dt, the change in revenue with respect to time. By the chain rule,

$$\frac{dR}{dt} = \frac{dR}{dn} \cdot \frac{dn}{dt}.$$

First find dR/dn, as follows.

$$\frac{dR}{dn} = \frac{(n + 2)(8000) - 8000n(1)}{(n + 2)^2} = \frac{16{,}000}{(n + 2)^2}$$

Since $n = 30$, $dR/dn = 15.625$. Also, $dn/dt = -6$. Thus,

$$\frac{dR}{dt} = (15.625)(-6) = -93.75.$$

Revenue is being lost at the rate of \$93.75 per day. ■ 10

10 Suppose the revenue in Example 10 is given by

$$R(n) = \frac{4500n}{n + 5}$$

and the work hours are decreasing at the rate of 4 per day. How fast is the revenue decreasing?

Answer:
About \$73.47 per day

EXAMPLE 11 Suppose a sum of \$500 is deposited in an account with an interest rate of r percent per year compounded monthly. At the end of 10 years, the balance in the account is given by

$$A = 500\left(1 + \frac{r}{1200}\right)^{120}.$$

Find the rate of change of A with respect to r if $r = 5$, 4.2, or 3.

First find dA/dr using the generalized power rule.

$$\frac{dA}{dr} = (120)(500)\left(1 + \frac{r}{1200}\right)^{119}\left(\frac{1}{1200}\right) = 50\left(1 + \frac{r}{1200}\right)^{119}$$

If $r = 5$,

$$\frac{dA}{dr} = 50\left(1 + \frac{5}{1200}\right)^{119} \approx 82.01,$$

or \$82.01 per percentage point. If $r = 4.2$

$$\frac{dA}{dr} = 50\left(1 + \frac{4.2}{1200}\right)^{119} \approx 75.78,$$

or \$75.78 per percentage point. If $r = 3$,

$$\frac{dA}{dr} = 50\left(1 + \frac{3}{1200}\right)^{119} \approx 67.30,$$

or \$67.30 per percentage point. ■

The chain rule can be used to develop the formula for **marginal revenue product,** an economic concept that approximates the change in revenue when a manufacturer hires an additional employee. Start with $R = px$, where R is total revenue from the daily production of x units and p is the price per unit. The demand function is $p = f(x)$, as before. Also, x can be considered a function of the number of employees, n. Since $R = px$, and x and therefore p depend on n, R can also be considered a function of n. To find an expression for dR/dn, use the product rule for derivatives on the function $R = px$ to get

$$\frac{dR}{dn} = p \cdot \frac{dx}{dn} + x \cdot \frac{dp}{dn}. \tag{1}$$

By the chain rule,

$$\frac{dp}{dn} = \frac{dp}{dx} \cdot \frac{dx}{dn}.$$

Substituting for dp/dn in equation (1) gives

$$\frac{dR}{dn} = p \cdot \frac{dx}{dn} + x\left(\frac{dp}{dx} \cdot \frac{dx}{dn}\right)$$

$$= \left(p + x \cdot \frac{dp}{dx}\right)\frac{dx}{dn}. \qquad \text{Factor out } \frac{dx}{dn}.$$

The expression for dR/dn gives the marginal revenue product.

EXAMPLE 12 Find the marginal revenue product dR/dn (in dollars) when $n = 20$ if the demand function is $p = 600/\sqrt{x}$ and $x = 5n$.

As shown above,

$$\frac{dR}{dn} = \left(p + x \cdot \frac{dp}{dx}\right)\frac{dx}{dn}.$$

Find dp/dx and dx/dn. From

$$p = \frac{600}{\sqrt{x}} = 600x^{-1/2},$$

we have the derivative

$$\frac{dp}{dx} = -300x^{-3/2}.$$

Also, from $x = 5n$,

$$\frac{dx}{dn} = 5.$$

Then, by substitution,

$$\frac{dR}{dn} = \left[\frac{600}{\sqrt{x}} + x(-300x^{-3/2})\right]5 = \frac{1500}{\sqrt{x}}.$$

If $n = 20$, then $x = 100$ and

$$\frac{dR}{dn} = \frac{1500}{\sqrt{100}} = 150.$$

This means that hiring an additional employee when production is at a level of 20 items will produce an increase in revenue of \$150. ■ 11

11 Find marginal revenue product at $n = 10$ if the demand function is $p = 1000/x^2$ and $x = 8n$. Interpret your answer.

Answer:
$-\$1.25$; hiring an additional employee will produce a decrease in revenue of \$1.25

12.6 EXERCISES

Let $f(x) = 2x^2 + 3x$ and $g(x) = 4x - 1$. Find each of the following. (See Example 1.)

1. $f[g(3)]$ **2.** $f[g(-4)]$

3. $g[f(3)]$ **4.** $g[f(-4)]$

Find $f[g(x)]$ and $g[f(x)]$ in each of the following. (See Example 2.)

5. $f(x) = 8x + 12$; $g(x) = 3x - 1$

6. $f(x) = -6x + 9$; $g(x) = 5x + 7$

7. $f(x) = -x^3 + 2$; $g(x) = 4x$

8. $f(x) = 2x$; $g(x) = 6x^2 - x^3$

9. $f(x) = \frac{1}{x}$; $g(x) = x^2$

10. $f(x) = \frac{2}{x^4}$; $g(x) = 2 - x$

11. $f(x) = \sqrt{x + 2}$; $g(x) = 8x^2 - 6$

12. $f(x) = 9x^2 - 11x$; $g(x) = 2\sqrt{x + 2}$

Write each function as a composition of two functions. (There may be more than one way to do this.) (See Example 3.)

13. $y = (4x + 3)^5$

14. $y = (x^2 + 2)^{1/3}$

15. $y = \sqrt{6 + 3x}$

16. $y = \sqrt{x + 3} - \sqrt[3]{x + 3}$

17. $y = \frac{\sqrt{x} + 3}{\sqrt{x} - 3}$

18. $y = \frac{2}{\sqrt{x} + 5}$

19. $y = (x^{1/2} - 3)^2 + (x^{1/2} - 3) + 5$

20. $y = (x^2 + 5x)^{1/3} - 2(x^2 + 5x)^{2/3} + 7$

Find the derivative of each of the following functions. (See Examples 4–7.)

21. $y = (3x + 4)^3$ **22.** $y = (6x - 1)^3$

23. $y = 6(3x + 2)^4$ **24.** $y = -5(2x - 1)^4$

25. $y = -2(8x^2 + 6)^4$ **26.** $y = -4(x^3 + 5x^2)^4$

27. $y = 12(2x + 5)^{3/2}$ **28.** $y = 45(3x - 8)^{3/2}$

Find the derivative of the function and confirm your answer graphically. (See Example 4.)

29. $y = -7(4x^2 + 9x)^{3/2}$ **30.** $y = 11(5x^2 + 6x)^{3/2}$

31. $y = 8\sqrt{4x + 7}$ **32.** $y = -3\sqrt{7x - 1}$

33. $y = -2\sqrt{x^2 + 4x}$ **34.** $y = 4\sqrt{2x^2 + 3}$

Use the product or quotient rule or the generalized power rule to find the derivative of each of the following functions. (See Examples 8–9.)

35. $y = (x + 1)(x - 3)^2$ **36.** $y = (2x + 1)^2(x - 5)$

37. $y = 5(x + 3)^2(2x - 1)^5$ **38.** $y = -9(x + 4)^2(2x - 3)^2$

39. $y = (3x + 1)^3\sqrt{x}$ **40.** $y = (3x + 5)^2\sqrt{x}$

41. $y = \frac{1}{(x - 4)^2}$ **42.** $y = \frac{-5}{(2x + 1)^2}$

43. $y = \frac{(4x + 3)^2}{2x - 1}$ **44.** $y = \frac{(x - 6)^2}{3x + 4}$

45. $y = \frac{x^2 + 4x}{(5x + 2)^3}$ **46.** $y = \frac{3x^2 - x}{(x - 1)^2}$

47. $y = (x^{1/2} + 1)(x^{1/2} - 1)^{1/2}$ **48.** $y = (3 - x^{2/3})(x^{2/3} + 2)^{1/2}$

Consider the following table of values of the functions f and g and their derivatives at various points:

x	1	2	3	4
$f(x)$	2	4	1	3
$f'(x)$	−6	−7	−8	−9
$g(x)$	2	3	4	1
$g'(x)$	2/7	3/7	4/7	5/7

Find each of the following.

49. **(a)** $D_x(f[g(x)])$ at $x = 1$ **(b)** $D_x(f[g(x)])$ at $x = 2$

50. **(a)** $D_x(g[f(x)])$ at $x = 1$ **(b)** $D_x(g[f(x)])$ at $x = 2$

51. If $f(x) = (2x^2 + 3x + 1)^{50}$, then which of the following is closest to $f'(0)$?
(a) 1 **(b)** 50 **(c)** 100 **(d)** 150
(e) 200 **(f)** 250

52. The graphs of $f(x) = 3x + 5$ and $g(x) = 4x - 1$ are straight lines.
(a) Show that the graph of $f[g(x)]$ is also a straight line.
(b) How are the slopes of the graphs of $f(x)$ and $g(x)$ related to the slope of the graph of $f[g(x)]$?

Work the following exercises. (See Examples 10–12.)

53. Management Suppose the demand for a certain brand of vacuum cleaner is given by

$$D(p) = \frac{-p^2}{100} + 500,$$

where p is the price in dollars. If the price, in terms of the cost c, is expressed as

$$p(c) = 2c - 10,$$

find the demand in terms of the cost.

54. Natural Science Suppose the population P of a certain species of fish depends on the number x (in hundreds) of a smaller fish that serves as its food supply, so that

$$P(x) = 2x^2 + 1.$$

Suppose, also, that the number x (in hundreds) of the smaller species of fish depends upon the amount a (in appropriate units) of its food supply, a kind of plankton. Suppose

$$x = f(a) = 3a + 2.$$

Find $P[f(a)]$, the relationship between the population P of the large fish and the amount a of plankton available.

55. Natural Science An oil well off the Gulf Coast is leaking, with the leak spreading oil over the surface as a circle. At any time t, in minutes, after the beginning of the leak, the radius of the circular oil slick on the surface is $r(t) = t^2$ feet. Let $A(r) = \pi r^2$ represent the area of a circle of radius r. Find and interpret $A[r(t)]$.

56. Natural Science When there is a thermal inversion layer over a city (as happens often in Los Angeles), pollutants cannot rise vertically but are trapped below the layer and must disperse horizontally. Assume that a factory smokestack begins emitting a pollutant at 8 A.M. Assume that the pollutant disperses horizontally, forming a circle. If t represents the time, in hours, since the factory began emitting pollutants ($t = 0$ represents 8 A.M.), assume that the radius of the circle of pollution is $r(t) = 2t$ miles. Let $A(r) = \pi r^2$ represent the area of a circle of radius r. Find and interpret $A[r(t)]$.

57. Management The Acme Company's total cost for producing x widgets is given by

$$C(x) = 600 + \sqrt{50 + 15x^2} \quad (0 \le x \le 200).$$

Find the marginal cost function.

58. Management Find the marginal revenue product for a manufacturer with 8 workers if the demand function is $p = 300/x^{1/3}$ and if $x = 8n$.

59. Management Suppose the demand function for a product is $p = 200/x^{1/2}$. Find the marginal revenue product if there are 25 employees and if $x = 15n$.

60. Management A manufacturer's weekly profit from the sales of x souvenir cups is given by

$$P(x) = (x^3 + 12x + 120)^{1/3} - 200,$$

where $(0 \le x \le 2000)$.
(a) Use a calculator to find $P(50)$, $P(100)$, $P(200)$, and $P(1000)$.
(b) Explain why it is reasonable that some of the numbers found in part (a) are negative.
(c) Find the marginal profit function.

61. Management The revenue from the sale of x items is given by $R(x) = 10\sqrt{300x - 2x^2}$ $(0 \le x \le 150)$.
(a) Find the marginal revenue function.
(b) Evaluate the marginal revenue function at $x = 30$, 60, 90, and 120.
(c) Explain the significance of the answers found in part (b).

62. Management Suppose a demand function is given by

$$x = 30\left(5 - \frac{p}{\sqrt{p^2 + 1}}\right),$$

where x is the demand for a product and p is the price per item in dollars. Find the rate of change in the demand for the product (i.e., find dx/dp).

63. Social Science Studies show that after t hours on the job, the number of items a supermarket cashier can ring up per minute is given by

$$F(t) = 60 - \frac{150}{\sqrt{8 + t^2}}.$$

(a) Find $F'(t)$, the rate at which the cashier's speed is increasing.
(b) At what rate is the cashier's speed increasing after 5 hours? 10 hours? 20 hours? 40 hours?
(c) Are your answers in part (b) increasing or decreasing with time? Is this reasonable? Explain.

64. Natural Science The total number of bacteria (in millions) present in a culture is given by

$$N(t) = 2t(5t + 9)^{1/2} + 12,$$

where t represents time in hours after the beginning of an experiment. Find the rate of change of the population of bacteria with respect to time for each of the following.
(a) $t = 0$ **(b)** $t = 7/5$
(c) $t = 8$ **(d)** $t = 11$

65. **Natural Science** To test an individual's use of calcium, a researcher injects a small amount of radioactive calcium into the person's bloodstream. The calcium remaining in the bloodstream is measured each day for several days. Suppose the amount of the calcium remaining in the bloodstream in milligrams per cubic centimeter t days after the initial injection is approximated by

$$C(t) = \frac{1}{2}(2t + 1)^{-1/2}.$$

Find the rate of change of C with respect to time for each of the following.

(a) $t = 0$ **(b)** $t = 4$
(c) $t = 6$ **(d)** $t = 7.5$

66. **Natural Science** The strength of a person's reaction to a certain drug is given by

$$R(Q) = Q\left(C - \frac{Q}{3}\right)^{1/2},$$

where Q represents the quantity of the drug given to the patient and C is a constant.

(a) The derivative $R'(Q)$ is called the *sensitivity* to the drug. Find $R'(Q)$.

(b) Find $R'(Q)$ if $Q = 87$ and $C = 59$.

Graph each function and its derivative on the same axes. Determine the values of x where the derivative is (a) *positive,* (b) *zero, and* (c) *negative.* (d) *What is true of the graph of the function in each case?*

67. $G(x) = \dfrac{2x}{(x - 1)^2}$

68. $K(x) = \sqrt[3]{(2x - 1)^2}$

12.7 DERIVATIVES OF EXPONENTIAL AND LOGARITHMIC FUNCTIONS

The exponential function $f(x) = e^x$ and the logarithmic function to the base e, $g(x) = \ln x$, were studied in Chapter 5. (Recall that $e \approx 2.71828$.) In this section we shall find the derivatives of these functions. In order to do this, we must first find a limit that will be needed in our calculations.

We claim that

$$\lim_{h \to 0} \frac{e^h - 1}{h} = 1.$$

Although a rigorous proof of this fact is beyond the scope of this book, a calculator provides both graphical and numerical support, as shown in Figure 12.26.*

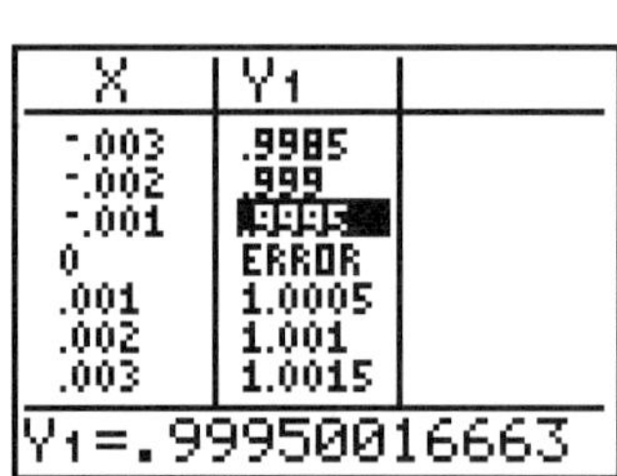

X	Y1
-.003	.9985
-.002	.999
-.001	.9995
0	ERROR
.001	1.0005
.002	1.001
.003	1.0015

Y1=.99950016663

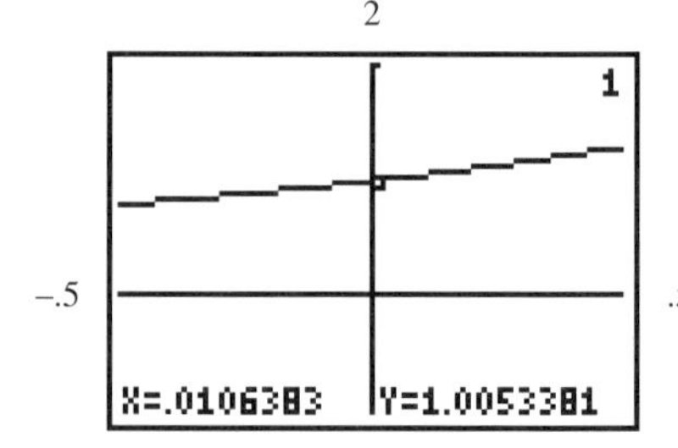

$y_1 = \dfrac{e^h - 1}{h}$

FIGURE 12.26

To find the derivative of $f(x) = e^x$, we use the definition of the derivative function:

$$f'(x) = \lim_{h \to 0} \frac{f(x + h) - f(x)}{h},$$

*As usual, the variable X is used in place of h on a calculator.

provided this limit exists. (Remember that h is the variable here and x is treated as a constant.)

For $f(x) = e^x$, we see that

$$f'(x) = \lim_{h\to 0} \frac{e^{x+h} - e^x}{h}$$

$$= \lim_{h\to 0} \frac{e^x e^h - e^x}{h} \qquad \text{Product property of exponents}$$

$$= \lim_{h\to 0} \frac{e^x(e^h - 1)}{h}$$

$$= \lim_{h\to 0} e^x \cdot \lim_{h\to 0} \frac{e^h - 1}{h}, \qquad \text{Product property of limits}$$

provided that both of these last limits exist. But h is the variable here and x is constant and therefore,

$$\lim_{h\to 0} e^x = e^x.$$

Combining this fact with our previous work, we see that

$$f'(x) = \lim_{h\to 0} e^x \cdot \lim_{h\to 0} \frac{e^h - 1}{h} = e^x \cdot 1 = e^x.$$

In other words, *the exponential function* $f(x) = e^x$ *is its own derivative.*

EXAMPLE 1 Find each derivative.

(a) $y = x^3 e^x$

The product rule and the fact that $f(x) = e^x$ is its own derivative show that

$$y' = x^3 \cdot D_x(e^x) + D_x(x^3) \cdot e^x$$
$$= x^3 \cdot e^x + 3x^2 \cdot e^x = e^x(x^3 + 3x^2).$$

(b) $y = (2e^x + x)^5$

By the generalized power, sum, and constant rules,

$$y' = 5(2e^x + x)^4 \cdot D_x(2e^x + x)$$
$$= 5(2e^x + x)^4 \cdot [D_x(2e^x) + D_x(x)]$$
$$= 5(2e^x + x)^4 \cdot [2D_x(e^x) + 1]$$
$$= 5(2e^x + x)^4(2e^x + 1).$$ ■ 1

1 Differentiate the following.

(a) $(2x^2 - 1)e^x$

(b) $(1 - e^x)^{1/2}$

Answers:

(a) $(2x^2 - 1)e^x + 4xe^x$

(b) $\dfrac{-e^x}{2(1 - e^x)^{1/2}}$

EXAMPLE 2 Find the derivative of $y = e^{x^2-3x}$.

Let $f(x) = e^x$ and $g(x) = x^2 - 3x$. Then

$$y = e^{x^2-3x} = e^{g(x)} = f[g(x)]$$

and $f'(x) = e^x$ and $g'(x) = 2x - 3$. By the chain rule,

$$y' = f'[g(x)] \cdot g'(x)$$
$$= e^{g(x)} \cdot (2x - 3)$$
$$= e^{x^2-3x} \cdot (2x - 3) = (2x - 3)e^{x^2-3x}.$$ ■

The argument used in Example 2 can be used to find the derivative of $y = e^{g(x)}$ for any differentiable function g. Let $f(x) = e^x$; then $y = e^{g(x)} = f[g(x)]$. By the chain rule,

$$y' = f'[g(x)] \cdot g'(x) = e^{g(x)} \cdot g'(x) = g'(x)e^{g(x)}.$$

We can summarize these results as follows.

DERIVATIVE OF e^x AND $e^{g(x)}$

If $y = e^x$, then $y' = e^x$.

If $y = e^{g(x)}$, then $y' = g'(x) \cdot e^{g(x)}$.

EXAMPLE 3 Find derivatives of the following functions.

(a) $y = 4e^{5x}$

Let $g(x) = 5x$, with $g'(x) = 5$. Then

$$y' = 4 \cdot 5e^{5x} = 20e^{5x}.$$

(b) $y = 3e^{-4x}$

$$y' = 3(-4e^{-4x}) = -12e^{-4x}$$

(c) $y = 10e^{3x^2}$

$$y' = 6x(10e^{3x^2}) = 60xe^{3x^2}$$ ■ 2

2 Find each derivative.

(a) $y = 3e^{12x}$

(b) $y = -6e^{(-10x+1)}$

(c) $y = e^{-x^2}$

Answers:

(a) $y' = 36e^{12x}$

(b) $y' = 60e^{(-10x+1)}$

(c) $y' = -2xe^{-x^2}$

EXAMPLE 4 Let $y = \dfrac{100{,}000}{1 + 100e^{-.3x}}$. Find y'.

Use the quotient rule.

$$y' = \frac{(1 + 100e^{-.3x})(0) - 100{,}000(-30e^{-.3x})}{(1 + 100e^{-.3x})^2}$$

$$= \frac{3{,}000{,}000e^{-.3x}}{(1 + 100e^{-.3x})^2}$$ ■ 3

3 Find the derivative of

$$y = \frac{e^x}{1 + x}.$$

Confirm your answer by graphing the derivative you find and the numerical derivative of y on the same screen.

Answer:

$$y' = \frac{xe^x}{(1 + x)^2}$$

The two graphs appear to be identical.

DERIVATIVES OF LOGARITHMIC FUNCTIONS To find the derivative of $g(x) = \ln x$, we use the definitions and properties of natural logarithms that were developed in Section 5.4:

$$g(x) = \ln x \text{ means } e^{g(x)} = x$$

and for all $x > 0$, $y > 0$ and every real number r,

$$\ln xy = \ln x + \ln y, \quad \ln \frac{x}{y} = \ln x - \ln y, \quad \ln x^r = r \ln x.$$

Note that $x > 0$, $y > 0$ because logarithms of negative numbers are not defined. Differentiating with respect to x on each side of $e^{g(x)} = x$ shows that

$$D_x(e^{g(x)}) = D_x(x)$$
$$e^{g(x)} \cdot g'(x) = 1.$$

Because $e^{g(x)} = x$, this last equation becomes

$$x \cdot g'(x) = 1$$
$$g'(x) = \frac{1}{x}$$
$$\frac{d}{dx}(\ln x) = \frac{1}{x} \quad \text{for all } x > 0.$$

EXAMPLE 5 **(a)** Assume $x > 0$ and use properties of logarithms to find the derivative of $y = \ln 6x$.

$$y' = \frac{d}{dx}(\ln 6x)$$

$$= \frac{d}{dx}(\ln 6 + \ln x) \qquad \text{Product rule for logarithms}$$

$$= \frac{d}{dx}(\ln 6) + \frac{d}{dx}(\ln x) \qquad \text{Sum rule for derivatives}$$

Be careful here: ln 6 is a *constant* ($\ln 6 \approx 1.79$), so its derivative is 0 (*not* 1/6). Hence

$$y' = \frac{d}{dx}(\ln 6) + \frac{d}{dx}(\ln x) = 0 + \frac{1}{x} = \frac{1}{x}.$$

(b) Assume $x > 0$ and use the chain rule to find the derivative of $y = \ln 6x$.

Let $f(x) = \ln x$ and $g(x) = 6x$, so that $y = \ln 6x = \ln g(x) = f(g(x))$. Then by the chain rule,

$$y' = f'[g(x)] \cdot g'(x) = \frac{1}{g(x)} \cdot \frac{d}{dx}(6x) = \frac{1}{6x} \cdot 6 = \frac{1}{x}. \quad \blacksquare$$

The argument used in Example 5(b), applies equally well in the general case. The derivative of $y = \ln g(x)$, where $g(x)$ is a function and $g(x) > 0$, can be found by letting $f(x) = \ln x$, so that $y = f[g(x)]$, and applying the chain rule:

$$y' = f'[g(x)] \cdot g'(x) = \frac{1}{g(x)} \cdot g'(x) = \frac{g'(x)}{g(x)}.$$

We can summarize these results as follows.

DERIVATIVE OF ln x AND ln $g(x)$

If $y = \ln x$, then $y' = \dfrac{1}{x}$ $\quad (x > 0)$.

If $y = \ln g(x)$, then $y' = \dfrac{g'(x)}{g(x)}$ $\quad (g(x) > 0)$.

EXAMPLE 6 Find the derivatives of the following functions.

(a) $y = \ln 5x$

Let $g(x) = 5x$, so that $g'(x) = 5$. From the formula above,

$$y' = \frac{g'(x)}{g(x)} = \frac{5}{5x} = \frac{1}{x}.$$

(b) $y = \ln(3x^2 - 4x)$

$$y' = \frac{6x - 4}{3x^2 - 4x}$$

4 Find y' for the following.

(a) $y = \ln(7 + x)$

(b) $y = \ln(4x^2)$

(c) $y = \ln(8x^3 - 3x)$

(d) $y = x^2 \ln x$

Answers:

(a) $y' = \frac{1}{7 + x}$

(b) $y' = \frac{2}{x}$

(c) $y' = \frac{24x^2 - 3}{8x^3 - 3x}$

(d) $y' = x(1 + 2 \ln x)$

(c) $y = 3x \ln x^2$

Since $3x \ln x^2$ is the product of $3x$ and $\ln x^2$, use the product rule.

$$y' = (3x)\left(\frac{d}{dx} \ln x^2\right) + (\ln x^2)\left(\frac{d}{dx} 3x\right)$$

$$= 3x\left(\frac{2x}{x^2}\right) + (\ln x^2)(3) \quad \text{Take derivatives.}$$

$$= 6 + 3 \ln x^2$$

$$= 6 + \ln(x^2)^3 \quad \text{Property of logarithms}$$

$$y' = 6 + \ln x^6 \quad \text{Property of exponents}$$ ■ 4

The function $y = \ln(-x)$ is defined for all $x < 0$ (since $-x > 0$ when $x < 0$). Its derivative can be found by applying the derivative rule for $\ln g(x)$ with $g(x) = -x$.

$$y' = \frac{g'(x)}{g(x)} = \frac{-1}{-x} = \frac{1}{x}$$

This is the same as the derivative of $y = \ln x$, with $x > 0$. Since

$$|x| = \begin{cases} x & \text{if } x > 0 \\ -x & \text{if } x < 0, \end{cases}$$

we can combine two results into one, as follows.

> If $y = \ln|x|$, then $y' = \frac{1}{x}$ $(x \neq 0)$.

5 Find each derivative.

(a) $y = e^{x^2} \ln|x|$

(b) $y = x^2/\ln|x|$

Answers:

(a) $e^{x^2}\left(\frac{1}{x} + 2x \ln|x|\right)$

(b) $\frac{2x \ln|x| - x}{(\ln|x|)^2}$

EXAMPLE 7 Let $y = e^x \cdot \ln|x|$. Find y'.

Use the product rule.

$$y' = e^x \cdot \frac{1}{x} + \ln|x| \cdot e^x$$

$$= e^x\left(\frac{1}{x} + \ln|x|\right)$$ ■ 5

Often a population, or the sales of a certain product, will start growing slowly, then grow more rapidly, and then gradually level off. Such growth can often be approximated by a mathematical model of the form

$$f(x) = \frac{b}{1 + ae^{kx}}$$

for appropriate constants a, b, and k.

6 Suppose a deer population is given by

$$f(x) = \frac{10{,}000}{1 + 2e^x},$$

where x is time in years. Find the rate of change of the population when

(a) $x = 0$;

(b) $x = 5$.

(c) Is the population increasing or decreasing?

Answers:

(a) About -2200

(b) About -33

(c) Decreasing

EXAMPLE 8 Suppose that the sales of a new product can be approximated for its first few years on the market by

$$S(x) = \frac{100{,}000}{1 + 100e^{-.3x}},$$

where x is time in years since the introduction of the product. Find the rate of change of the sales when $x = 4$.

The derivative was given in Example 4. Using this derivative and a calculator,

$$S'(4) = \frac{3{,}000{,}000e^{-.3(4)}}{(1 + 100e^{-.3(4)})^2} = \frac{3{,}000{,}000e^{-1.2}}{(1 + 100e^{-1.2})^2} \approx 933.$$

The rate of change of sales at time $x = 4$ is an increase of about 933 units per year. ■ 6

12.7 EXERCISES

Find the derivatives of the following functions. (See Examples 1–7.)

1. $y = e^{3x}$

2. $y = e^{-4x}$

3. $f(x) = 5e^{2x}$

4. $f(x) = 4e^{-3x}$

5. $g(x) = -4e^{-5x}$

6. $g(x) = 6e^{x/2}$

7. $y = e^{x^2}$

8. $y = e^{-x^2}$

9. $f(x) = e^{x^2/2}$

10. $y = 4e^{2x^2-4}$

11. $y = -3e^{3x^2+5}$

12. $y = xe^x$

13. $y = \ln(-8x^2 + 6x)$

14. $y = \ln\sqrt{x + 5}$

15. $y = \ln\sqrt{2x + 1}$

16. $y = \ln[(3x - 1)(5x + 2)]$

17. $f(x) = \ln[(2x - 3)(x^2 + 4)]$

18. $f(x) = \ln\left(\frac{4x + 3}{5x - 2}\right)$

Find the derivatives of each of these functions. Confirm your answer by graphing the derivative you find and the numerical derivative of the function on the same screen.

19. $y = x^2e^{-2x}$

20. $y = (x - 3)^2e^{2x}$

21. $y = (3x^2 - 4x)e^{-3x}$

22. $y = \ln(3 - x)$

23. $y = \ln(1 + x^2)$

24. $y = \ln(2x^2 - 7x)$

Find the derivative of each of these functions. (See Examples 1–7.)

25. $y = \ln\left(\frac{6 - x}{3x + 5}\right)$

26. $y = \ln(x^4 + 5x^2)^{3/2}$

27. $y = \ln(5x^3 - 2x)^{3/2}$

28. $y = -3x\ln(x + 2)$

29. $y = x\ln(2 - x^2)$

30. $y = \frac{x^2}{e^x}$

31. $y = \frac{e^x}{2x + 1}$

32. $y = (2x^3 - 1)\ln|x|$

33. $y = \frac{\ln|x|}{x^3}$

34. $y = \frac{3\ln|x|}{3x + 4}$

35. $y = \frac{-4\ln|x|}{5 - 2x}$

36. $y = \frac{3x^2}{\ln|x|}$

37. $y = \frac{x^3 - 1}{2\ln|x|}$

38. $y = [\ln(x + 1)]^4$

39. $y = \sqrt{\ln(x-3)}$

40. $y = \dfrac{e^x}{\ln|x|}$

41. $y = \dfrac{e^x - 1}{\ln|x|}$

42. $y = \dfrac{e^x + e^{-x}}{x}$

43. $y = \dfrac{e^x - e^{-x}}{x}$

44. $y = e^{x^3}\ln|x|$

45. $f(x) = e^{3x+2}\ln(4x-5)$

46. $f(x) = \dfrac{2400}{3 + 8e^{.2x}}$

47. $y = \dfrac{500}{7 - 10e^{.4x}}$

48. $y = \dfrac{10{,}000}{9 + 4e^{-.2x}}$

49. $y = \dfrac{500}{12 + 5e^{-.5x}}$

50. $y = \ln(\ln|x|)$

51. If $f(x) = x^2e^{-2x}$, which of the following is closest to $f'(-1)$?
(a) 0 **(b)** −10
(c) −20 **(d)** −30
(e) −40 **(f)** −50

52. If $g(x) = 10e^x + 3\ln(x+1)$, which of the following is closest to $g'(0)$?
(a) 6 **(b)** 9
(c) 12 **(d)** 15
(e) 18 **(f)** 21

53. If $f(x) = e^{2x}$, find $f'[\ln(1/4)]$.

54. If $g(x) = 3e\ln[\ln x]$, find $g'(e)$.

Work the following exercises.

55. Management Suppose the demand function for x thousand of a certain item is

$$p = 100 + \frac{50}{\ln x}, \quad x > 1,$$

where p is in dollars.
(a) Find the marginal revenue.
(b) Find the revenue from the next thousand items at a demand of 8000 ($x = 8$).

56. Management Assume that the total revenue received from the sale of x items is given by

$$R(x) = 30\ln(2x+1),$$

while the total cost to produce x items is $C(x) = x/2$. Find the number of items that should be manufactured so that marginal profit is 0.

57. Management If the cost function in dollars for x thousand of the item in Exercise 55 is $C(x) = 100x + 100$, find the following.
(a) The marginal cost
(b) The profit function $P(x)$
(c) The profit from the next thousand items at a demand of 8000 ($x = 8$)

58. Management The demand function for x units of a product is

$$p = 100 - 10\ln x, \quad 1 < x < 20{,}000,$$

where $x = 6n$ and n is the number of employees producing the product.
(a) Find the revenue function $R(x)$.
(b) Find the marginal revenue product function. (See Example 12 in Section 12.6.)
(c) Evaluate and interpret the marginal revenue product when $x = 20$.

59. Social Science Based on data from 1980 to the present, the population of a certain city in year t is expected to be

$$P(t) = 50{,}000(1 + .2t)e^{-.04t} \quad (0 \le t \le 40),$$

where $t = 0$ corresponds to 1980.
(a) At what rate is the population changing in year t?
(b) Is the city gaining or losing population in the years 1985, 1995, 2005, and 2015?

60. Management Suppose $P(x) = e^{-.02x}$ represents the proportion of cars manufactured by a given company that are still free of defects after x months of use. Find the proportion of cars free of defects after
(a) 1 month; **(b)** 10 months; **(c)** 100 months.
(d) Calculate and interpret $P'(100)$.

61. Management A child is waiting at a street corner for a gap in traffic so that she can safely cross the street. A mathematical model for traffic shows that if the child's expected waiting time is to be at most one minute, then the maximum traffic flow (in cars per hour) is given by

$$f(x) = \frac{67{,}338 - 12{,}595\ln x}{x},$$

where x is the width of the street in feet.* Find the maximum traffic flow and the rate of change of the maximum traffic flow with respect to street width when $x =$
(a) 30 ft
(b) 40 ft.

*Bender, Edward A., *An Introduction to Mathematical Modeling,* John Wiley and Sons, 1978, p. 213.

62. **Natural Science** Suppose that the population of a certain collection of rare Brazilian ants is given by

$$P(t) = 1000e^{.2t},$$

where t represents the time in days. Find the rate of change of the population when $t = 2$; when $t = 8$. Does the ant population ever decrease?

63. **Management** A timber company plans to sell a certain stand of timber and invest the proceeds. The timber is increasing in value, but waiting to sell may result in lost interest. Taking interest rates and inflation into account, the company projects that its revenue (in dollars) from selling in year t will be

$$R(t) = 600{,}000e^{-.07t+\sqrt{t}/2}.$$

At what rate will this revenue increase or decrease in
(a) year 5
(b) year 10
(c) year 15
(d) year 20
(e) Based on your answers to parts (a)–(d), approximately when should the company sell?

64. **Natural Science** Assume that the amount of a radioactive substance present at time t is given by

$$A(t) = 500e^{-.25t}$$

grams. Find the rate of change of the quantity present when
(a) $t = 0$;
(b) $t = 4$;
(c) $t = 6$;
(d) $t = 10$.
(e) Does the substance decay more slowly or more quickly as time goes on?

65. **Natural Science** Certain types of food are placed in a controlled environment in which the temperature is just above freezing. As the temperature increases, some of the food begins to spoil. Assume that for $1 \le t \le 30$,

$$M(t) = (e^{.1t} + 1)\ln \sqrt{t}$$

represents the percent of the food that has spoiled when the temperature reaches t degrees Celsius. Find
(a) $M(15)$; **(b)** $M(25)$.
(c) Find the rate of change of $M(t)$ when $t = 15$.

66. **Natural Science** Suppose that the population of a certain colony of honey bees is given by

$$P(t) = (t + 100)\ln(t + 2),$$

where t represents the time in days. Find the rates of change of the population when $t = 2$, $t = 8$, and $t = 20$. Is the population increasing or decreasing?

67. **Natural Science** The concentration of pollutants, in grams per liter, in the east fork of the Big Weasel River is approximated by

$$P(x) = .04e^{-4x},$$

where x is the number of miles downstream from a paper mill where the measurement is taken. Find
(a) $P(.5)$; **(b)** $P(1)$; **(c)** $P(2)$.
Find the rate of change of the concentration with respect to distance at
(d) $x = .5$; **(e)** $x = 1$; **(f)** $x = 2$.

68. **Social Science** According to work by the psychologist C. L. Hull, the strength of a habit is a function of the number of times the habit is repeated. If N is the number of repetitions and $H(N)$ is the strength of the habit, then

$$H(N) = 1000(1 - e^{-kN}),$$

where k is a constant. Find $H'(N)$ if $k = .1$ and
(a) $N = 10$; **(b)** $N = 100$; **(c)** $N = 1000$.
(d) Show that $H'(N)$ is always positive. What does this mean?

12.8 CONTINUITY AND DIFFERENTIABILITY

Intuitively speaking, a function is **continuous** at a point if you can draw the graph of the function near that point without lifting your pencil from the paper. Conversely, a function is **discontinuous** at a point if the pencil *must* be lifted from the paper in order to draw the graph on both sides of the point.

Looking first at graphs having points of discontinuity will clarify the idea of continuity at a point. For example, the graph of the function in Figure 12.27(a) on the next page has an open circle at (2, 3), which indicates that there is a "hole" in the graph at that point. Therefore the function is discontinuous at $x = 2$ because to draw the graph from $x = 1$ to $x = 3$, you must lift the pencil for an instant as you pass through (2, 3).

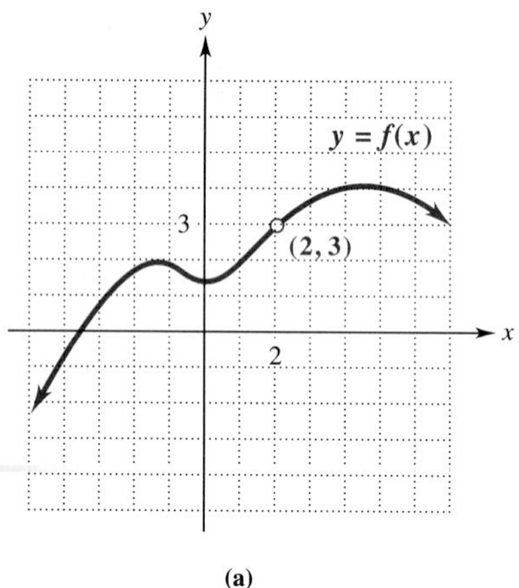

(a)

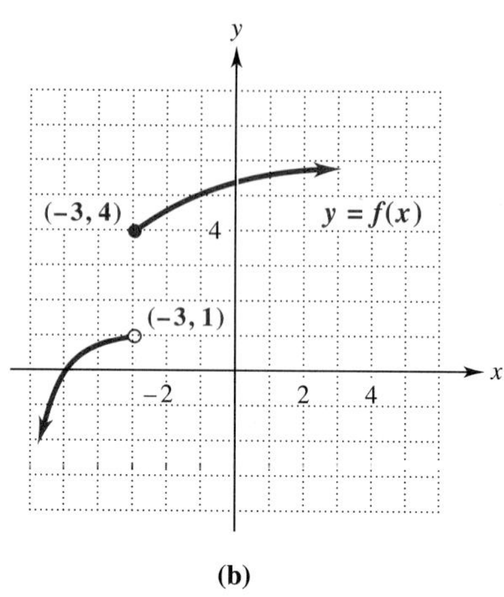

(b)

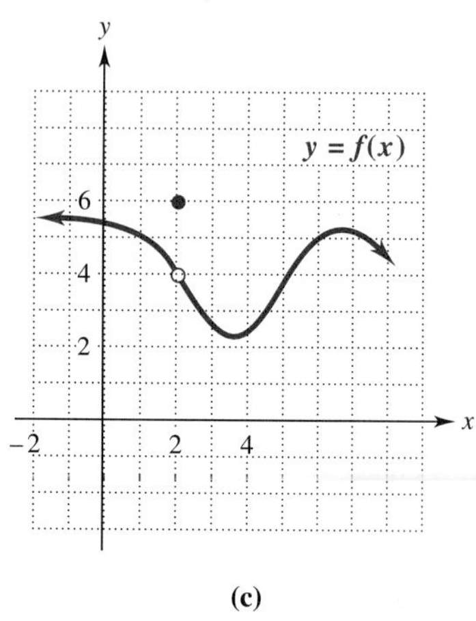

(c)

FIGURE 12.27

1 Find any points of discontinuity for the following functions.

(a)

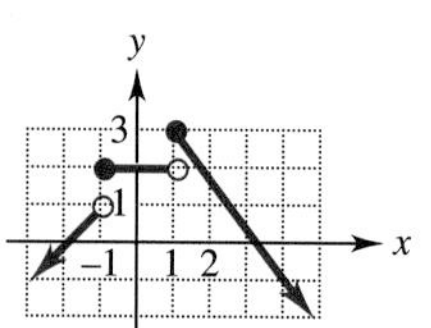

(b)

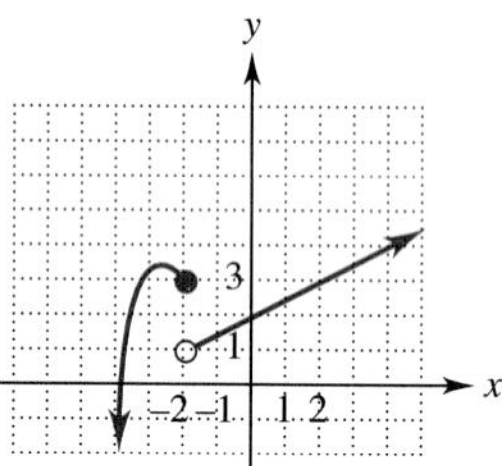

(c)

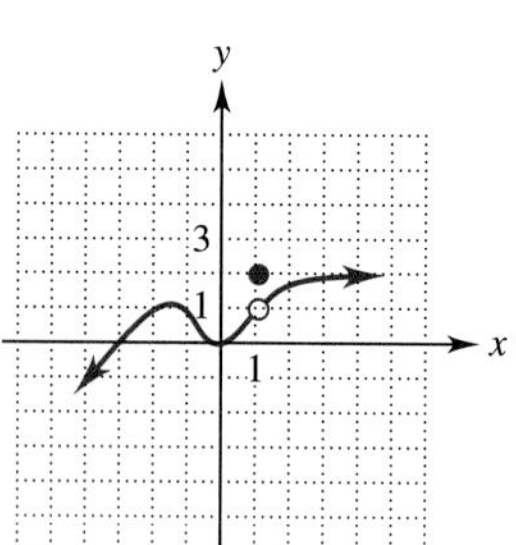

Answers:

(a) $-1, 1$

(b) -2

(c) 1

The function in Figure 12.27(b) is discontinuous at $x = -3$ because of the "jump" in the graph there (which necessitates lifting the pencil to draw the graph on both sides of $x = -3$). Although the function is not continuous at $x = -3$, it *is* continuous at $x = -1$ because you can draw the graph from $x = -2$ to $x = 0$, say, without lifting pencil from paper.

Finally, the function in Figure 12.27(c) is discontinuous at $x = 2$. When x is near (but not equal to) 2, all of the corresponding values of $f(x)$ are very near 4, so that on either side of $x = 2$, the graph is very near the point (2, 4) and can be drawn without lifting pencil from paper. But the instant $x = 2$, you must lift the pencil to the point $(2, f(2)) = (2, 6)$. Looked at from another point of view, as x gets closer and closer to 2, $f(x)$ gets closer and closer to 4, that is, $\lim_{x\to 2} f(x) = 4$. But $f(2) = 6$ and, hence,

$$\lim_{x\to 2} f(x) \neq f(2).$$ 1

Now let's consider what it means for a function f to be continuous at $x = c$. If you *can* draw the graph of f around $x = c$ without lifting pencil from paper, then at the very least, $f(c)$ must be defined (otherwise there would be a hole in the graph). But the last example shows that this is not enough to guarantee continuity: as x gets very close to c, $f(x)$ must get very close to $f(c)$ (otherwise you have to lift the pencil at $x = c$). These considerations lead to this definition.

DEFINITION OF CONTINUITY AT A POINT

A function f is **continuous** at $x = c$ if

(a) $f(c)$ is defined;

(b) $\lim_{x\to c} f(x)$ exists;

(c) $\lim_{x\to c} f(x) = f(c)$.

If f is not continuous at $x = c$, it is **discontinuous** there.

EXAMPLE 1 Tell why the following functions are discontinuous at the indicated points.

(a) $f(x)$ in Figure 12.28 at $x = 3$

The open circle on the graph of Figure 12.28 at the point where $x = 3$ means that $f(3)$ does not exist. Because of this, part (a) of the definition fails.

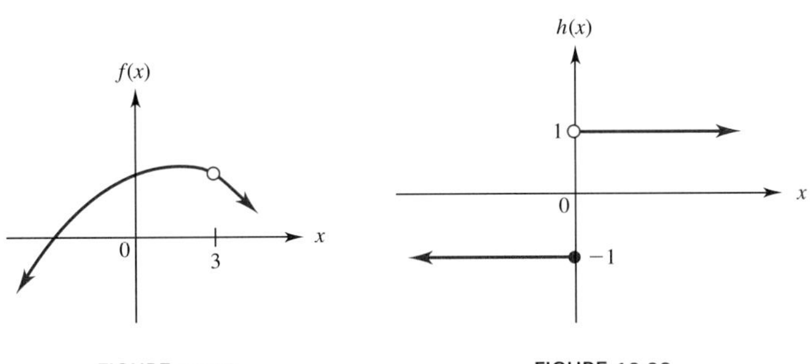

FIGURE 12.28

FIGURE 12.29

(b) $h(x)$ in Figure 12.29 at $x = 0$

The graph of Figure 12.29 shows that $h(0) = -1$. Also, as x approaches 0 from the left, $h(x)$ is -1. However, as x approaches 0 from the right, $h(x)$ is 1. As mentioned in Section 12.1, for a limit to exist at a particular value of x, the values of $h(x)$ must approach a single number. Since no single number is approached by the values of $h(x)$ as x approaches 0, $\lim_{x \to 0} h(x)$ does not exist, and part (b) of the definition fails.

(c) $g(x)$ at $x = 4$ in Figure 12.30

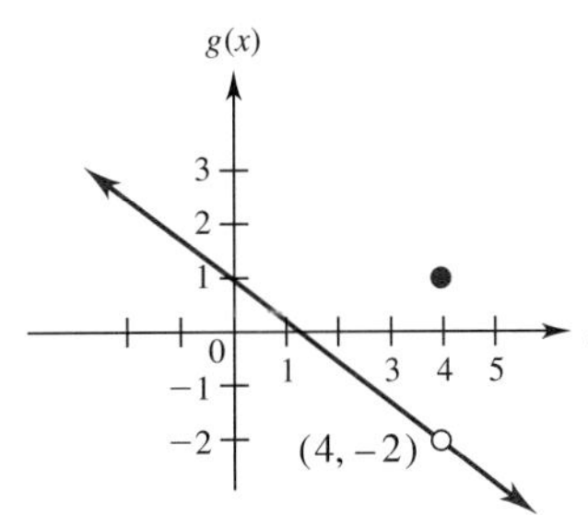

FIGURE 12.30

In Figure 12.30, the heavy dot above 4 shows that $g(4)$ is defined. In fact, $g(4) = 1$. However, the graph also shows that

$$\lim_{x \to 4} g(x) = -2,$$

so $\lim_{x \to 4} g(x) \neq g(4)$, and part (c) of the definition fails.

2 Tell why the following functions are discontinuous at the indicated points.

(a)

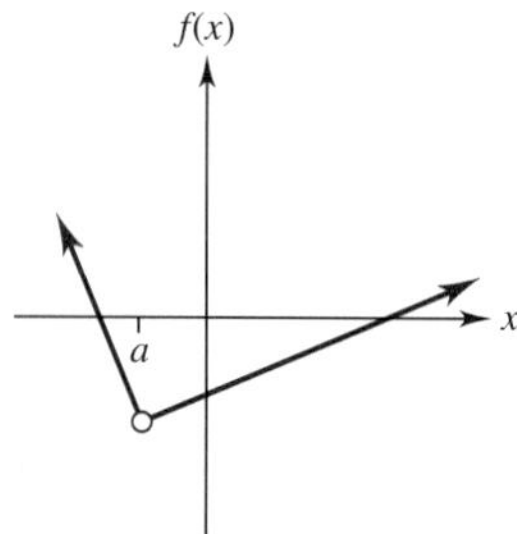

(b)

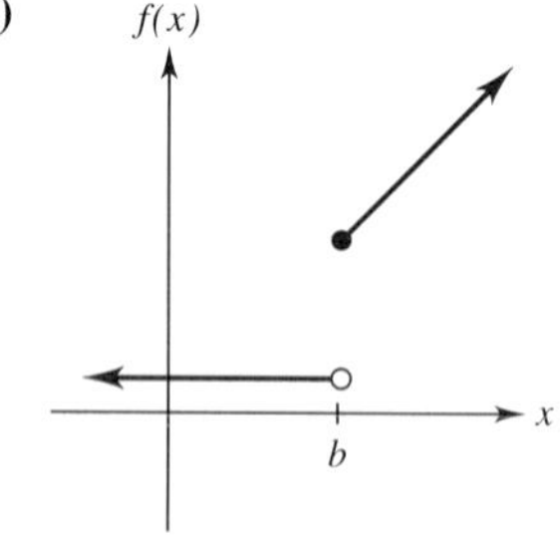

Answers:

(a) $f(a)$ does not exist.

(b) $\lim_{x \to b} f(x)$ does not exist.

3 Write each of the following using interval notation.

(a) open interval from −5 to 3 (number line)

(b) closed interval from 4 to 7 (number line)

(c) 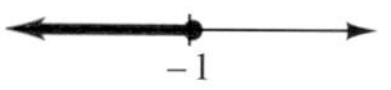 ray extending left to −1, closed at −1 (number line)

Answers:

(a) $(-5, 3)$

(b) $[4, 7]$

(c) $(-\infty, -1]$

(d) $f(x)$ in Figure 12.31 at $x = -2$

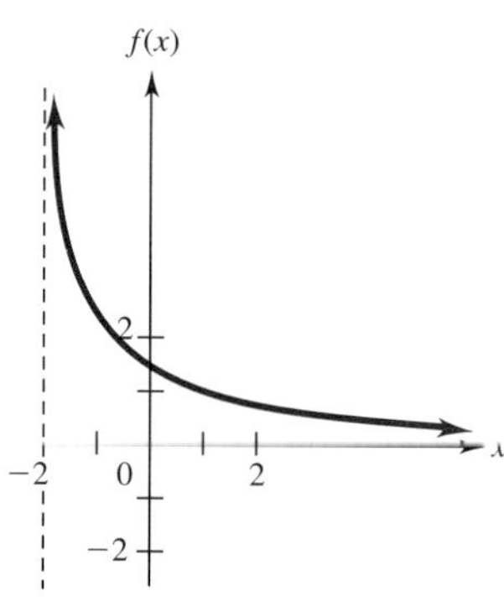

FIGURE 12.31

The function f graphed in Figure 12.31 is not defined at -2, and $\lim_{x \to -2} f(x)$ does not exist. Either of these reasons is sufficient to show that f is not continuous at -2. (Function f *is* continuous at any value of x greater than -2, however.) ■ 2

When discussing the continuity of a function, it is often helpful to use interval notation, which was introduced in Chapter 1. The following chart should help you recall how it is used.

Interval	*Name*	*Description*	*Interval Notation*
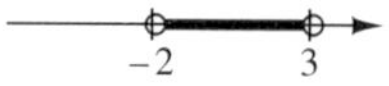 open circles at −2 and 3	Open interval	$-2 < x < 3$	$(-2, 3)$
 solid dots at −2 and 3	Closed interval	$-2 \le x \le 3$	$[-2, 3]$
 arrow left to open circle at 3	Open interval	$x < 3$	$(-\infty, 3)$
open circle at −5, arrow right	Open interval	$x > -5$	$(-5, \infty)$

Remember, the symbol ∞ does not represent a number; ∞ is used for convenience in interval notation to indicate that the interval extends without bound in the positive direction. Also, $-\infty$ indicates no bound in the negative direction. 3

Continuity at a point was defined above; *continuity on an open interval* is defined as follows.

> If a function is continuous at each point of an open interval, it is said to be **continuous on the open interval.**

Intuitively, the function f is continuous on the interval (a, b) if you can draw the graph between $x = a$ and $x = b$ without lifting your pencil from the paper.

4 Are the functions with graphs as shown continuous on the indicated intervals?

(a) $(-4, -2)$; $(-3, 0)$

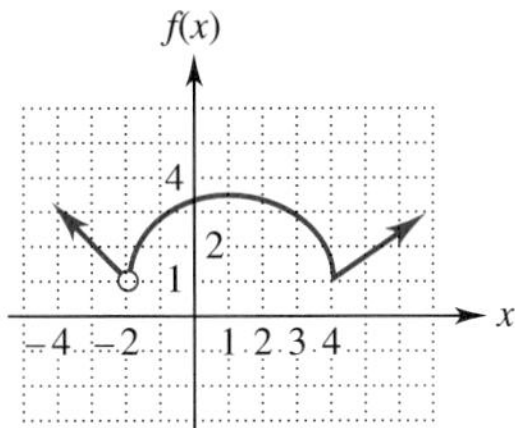

(b) $(-1, 1)$; $(0, 2)$

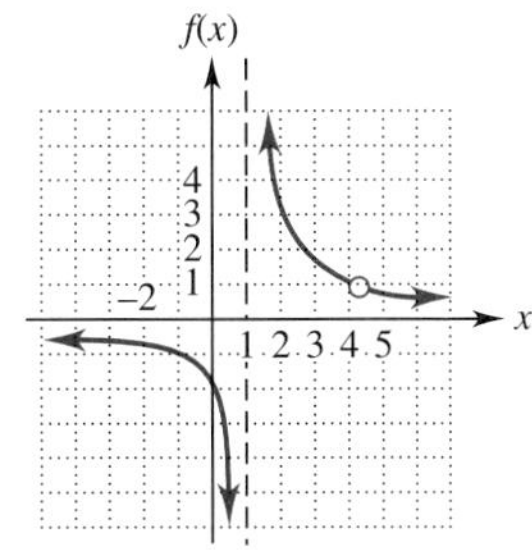

Answers:

(a) Yes; no

(b) Yes; no

EXAMPLE 2 Is the function of Figure 12.32 continuous on the x-intervals listed below?

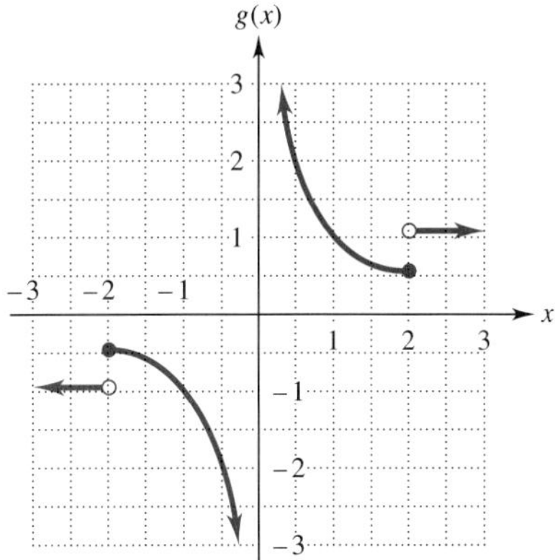

FIGURE 12.32

(a) $(-2, -1)$

The function is discontinuous only at $x = -2$, 0, and 2. Thus, it is continuous at every point of the open interval $(-2, -1)$, and, therefore, is continuous on the open interval.

(b) $(1, 3)$

Since this interval includes the point of discontinuity at $x = 2$, the function is not continuous on the open interval $(1, 3)$. ■ 4

EXAMPLE 3 A trailer rental firm charges a flat $4 to rent a hitch. The trailer itself is rented for $11 per day or fraction of a day. Let $C(x)$ represent the cost of renting a hitch and trailer for x days.

(a) Graph C.

The charge for 1 day is $4 for the hitch and $11 for the trailer, or $15. In fact, in the interval $(0, 1]$, $C(x) = 15$. To rent the trailer for more than 1 day, but not more than 2 days, the charge is $4 + 2 \cdot 11 = 26$ dollars. For any value of x in the interval $(1, 2]$, $C(x) = 26$. Also, in $(2, 3]$ $C(x) = 37$. These results lead to the graph of Figure 12.33.

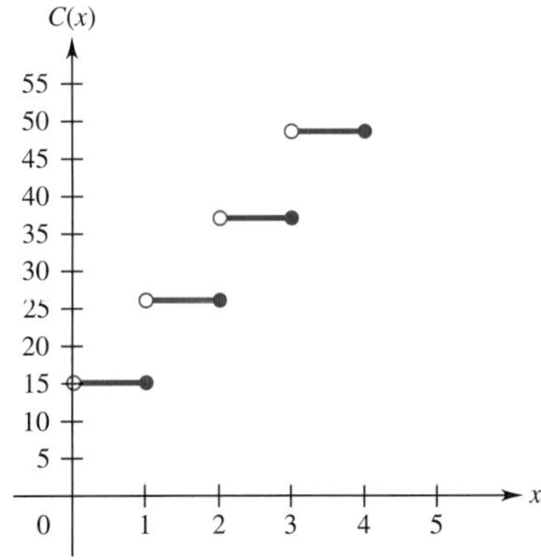

FIGURE 12.33

5 Suppose the cost is \$2.25 to mail a package weighing up to 1 pound plus \$.50 for each additional pound or fraction of a pound. Let $P(x)$ represent the cost of mailing a package weighing x pounds. Find any points of discontinuity for P.

Answers:

$x = 1, 2, 3, \ldots$

(b) Find any points of discontinuity for C.

As the graph suggests, C is discontinuous at 1, 2, 3, 4, and all other positive integers. ■ 5

CONTINUITY AND CALCULATORS Because of the way a calculator or computer graphs functions, the graph of a continuous function may look like disconnected, closely spaced line segments (Figure 12.34). Furthermore, calculators often have trouble accurately portraying graphs at points of discontinuity. For instance, "jump discontinuities" (such as those at $x = 1, 2, 3$ in Figure 12.33), may appear as "stair steps" with vertical line segments connecting separate pieces of the graph (Figure 12.35). Similarly, a hole in the graph (such as the one at $x = 4$ in Figure 12.30) may not be visible on a calculator screen, depending on what viewing window is used. Nor can a calculator indicate whether or not an "endpoint" is included in the graph.

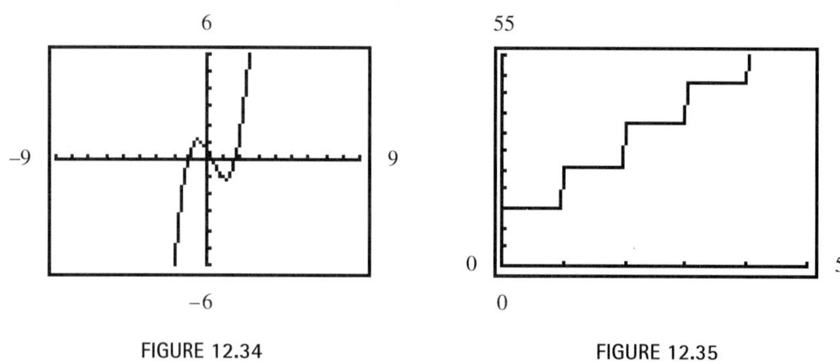

FIGURE 12.34

FIGURE 12.35

One reason these inaccuracies appear is due to the manner in which a calculator graphs: it plots points and connects them with line segments. In effect, the calculator assumes the function is continuous unless it actually computes a function value and determines it is undefined. In that case, it will skip a pixel and not connect points on either side of it.

The moral of this story is that a calculator or computer is only a tool. In order to use it correctly and effectively, you must understand the mathematics involved. When you do, it's usually easy to interpret screen images correctly.

CONTINUITY AND DIFFERENTIABILITY As shown earlier in this chapter, a function fails to have a derivative at a point where the function is not defined, where the graph of the function has a "sharp point," or where the graph has a vertical tangent line. (See Figure 12.36.)

The function graphed in Figure 12.36 is continuous on the interval (x_1, x_2) and has a derivative at each point on this interval. On the other hand, the function is also continuous on the interval $(0, x_2)$ but does *not* have a derivative at each point on the interval (see x_1 on the graph).

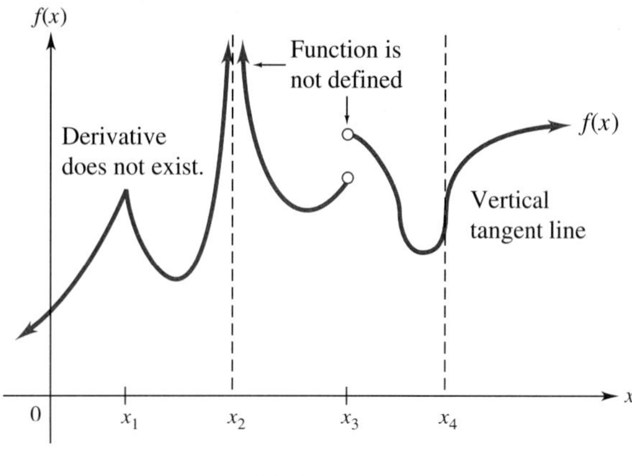

FIGURE 12.36

A similar situation holds in the general case.

> If the derivative of a function exists at a point, then the function is continuous at that point. However, a function may be continuous at a point and not have a derivative there.

EXAMPLE 4 A nova is a star whose brightness suddenly increases and then gradually fades. The cause of the sudden increase in brightness is thought to be an explosion of some kind. The intensity of light emitted by a nova as a function of time is shown in Figure 12.37.* Notice that although the graph is a continuous curve, it is not differentiable at the point of the explosion. ■

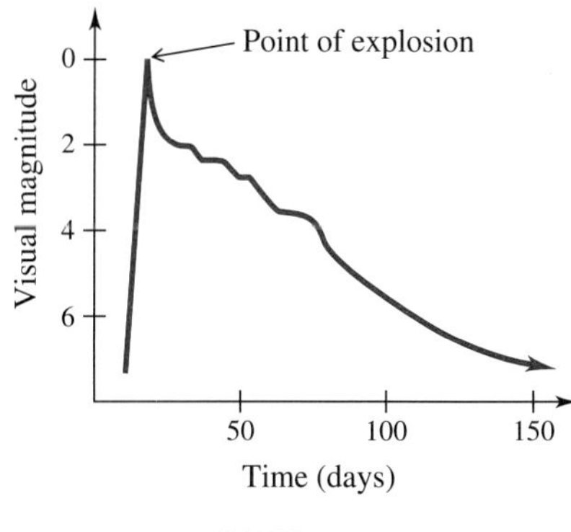

FIGURE 12.37

CAUTION In some viewing windows a calculator graph may appear to have a sharp corner, when in fact the graph is differentiable at that point. When in doubt try a different window to see if the corner disappears. ◆

---

*Reprinted with permission of Macmillan Publishing Company from *Astronomy: The Structure of the Universe* by William J. Kaufmann, III. Copyright © 1977 by William J. Kaufmann, III.

12.8 EXERCISES

Find all points of discontinuity for the functions whose graphs are shown below. (See Example 1.)

1.

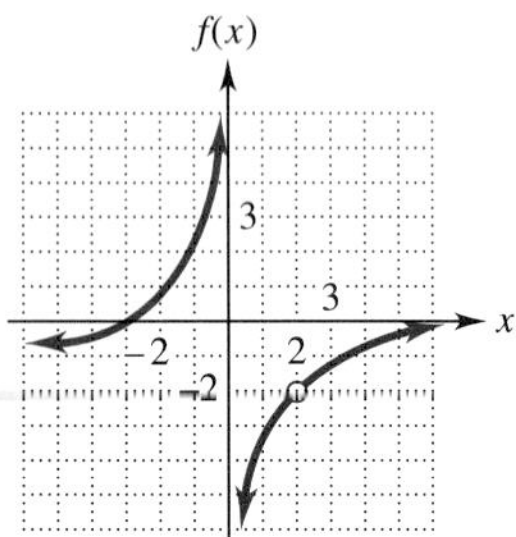

2.

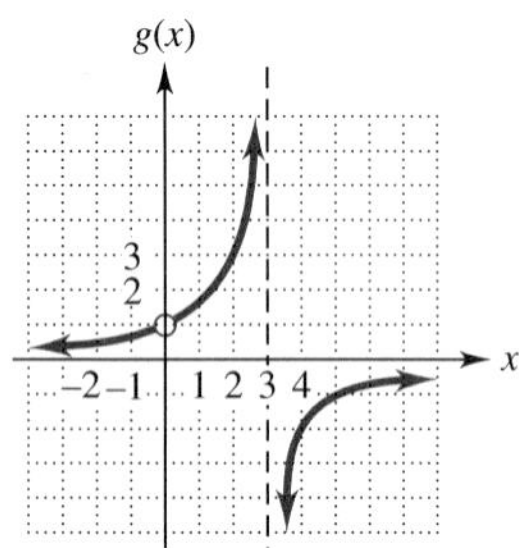

3.

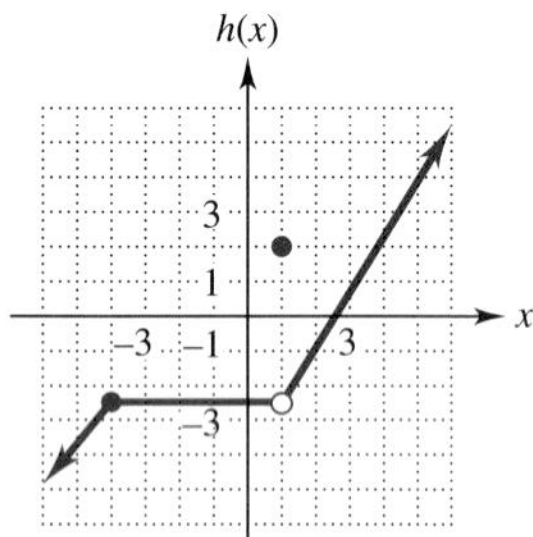

4.

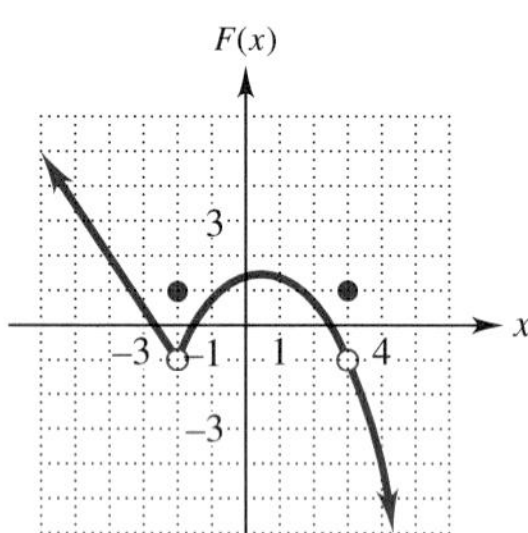

5.

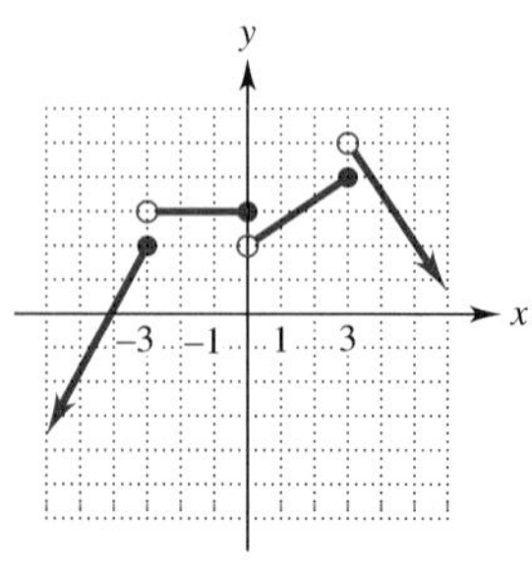

6.

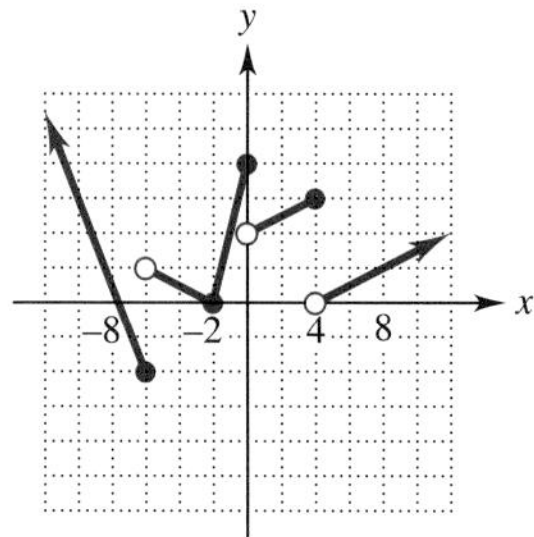

7.

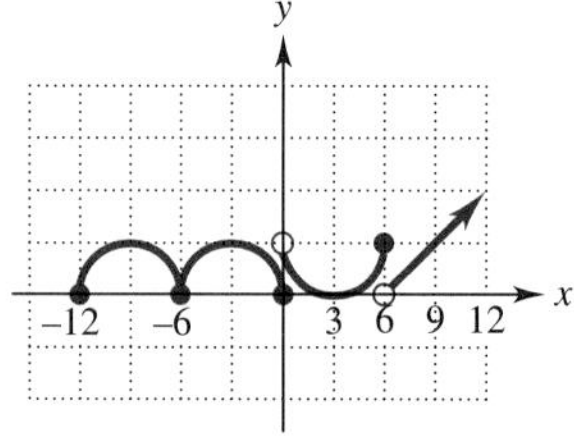

8.

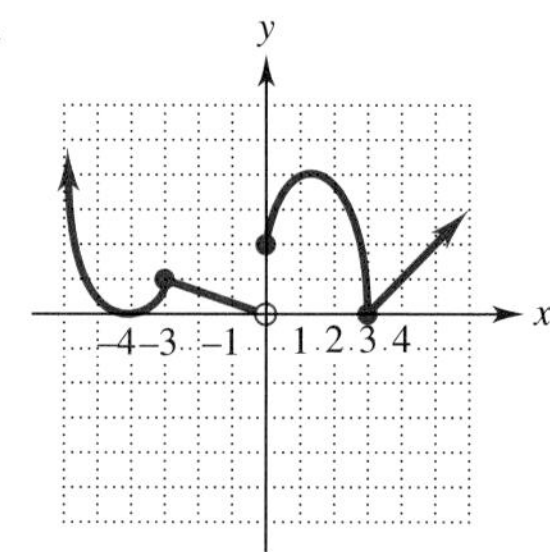

Are the following functions continuous at the given values of x?

9. $f(x) = \dfrac{4}{x-2}$; $x = 0, x = 2$

10. $g(x) = \dfrac{5}{x+5}$; $x = -5, x = 5$

11. $h(x) = \dfrac{1}{x(x-3)}$; $x = 0, x = 3, x = 5$

12. $h(x) = \dfrac{-1}{(x-2)(x+3)}$; $x = 0, x = 2, x = 3$

13. $g(x) = \dfrac{x+2}{x^2-x-2}$; $x = 1, x = 2, x = -2$

14. $h(x) = \dfrac{3x}{6x^2+15x+6}$; $x = 0, x = -1/2, x = 3$

15. $g(x) = \dfrac{x^2-4}{x-2}$; $x = 0, x = 2, x = -2$

16. $h(x) = \dfrac{x^2-25}{x+5}$; $x = 0, x = 5, x = -5$

17. $p(x) = \dfrac{|x+2|}{x+2}$; $x = -2, x = 0, x = 2$

18. $r(x) = \dfrac{|5 - x|}{x - 5}$; $x = -5, x = 0, x = 5$

19. $f(x) = \begin{cases} x - 2 & \text{if } x \le 3 \\ 2 - x & \text{if } x > 3 \end{cases}$; $x = 2, x = 3$

20. $g(x) = \begin{cases} e^x & \text{if } x < 0 \\ x + 1 & \text{if } 0 \le x \le 3; \\ 2x - 3 & \text{if } x > 3 \end{cases}$ $x = 0, x = 3$

In Exercises 21–22, find the constant k that makes the given function continuous at x = 2.

21. $f(x) = \begin{cases} x + k & \text{if } x \le 2 \\ 5 - x & \text{if } x > 2 \end{cases}$

22. $g(x) = \begin{cases} x^k & \text{if } x \le 2 \\ 2x + 4 & \text{if } x > 2 \end{cases}$

Work the following problems. (See Example 4.)

23. **Social Science** With certain skills (such as music) learning is rapid at first and then levels off. Sudden insights may cause learning to speed up sharply. A typical graph of such learning is shown in the figure. Where is the function discontinuous? Where is it differentiable?

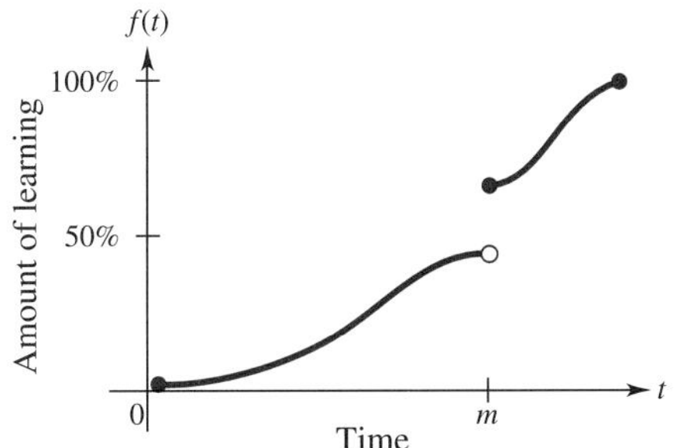

24. **Natural Science** Suppose a gram of ice is at a temperature of −100°C. The graph below shows the temperature of the ice as an increasing number of calories of heat are applied. It takes 80 calories to melt 1 gram of ice at 0°C into water, and 539 calories to boil 1 gram of water at 100°C into steam. Where is this graph discontinuous? Where is it differentiable?

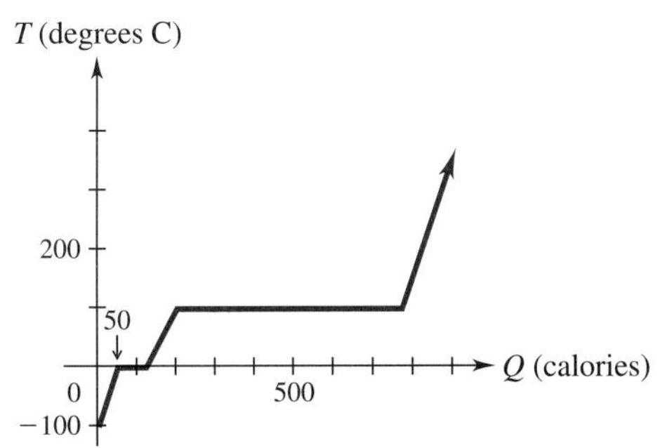

25. **Management** Like many states, California suffered a large budget deficit in 1991. As part of the solution, officials raised the sales tax by \$.0125. The graph shows the California state sales tax since it was first established in 1933. Let $T(x)$ represent the sales tax in year x. Find the following.

(a) $\lim_{x\to 80} T(x)$

(b) $\lim_{x\to 73} T(x)$

(c) List three years for which the graph indicates a discontinuity.

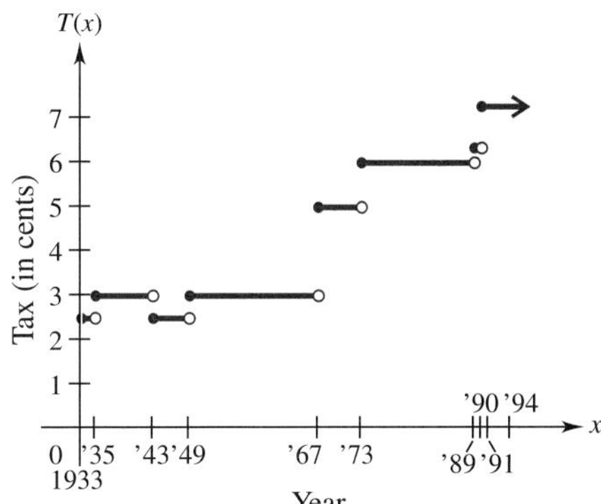

Work the following problems. (See Example 3.)

26. **Management** The cost to transport a mobile home depends on the distance, x, in miles that the home is moved. Let $C(x)$ represent the cost to move a mobile home x miles. One firm charges as follows.

Cost per Mile	*Distance in Miles*
\$2	if $0 < x \le 150$
1.50	if $150 < x \le 400$
1.25	if $x > 400$

(a) Find $C(130)$. (b) Find $C(210)$.
(c) Find $C(350)$. (d) Find $C(500)$.
(e) Graph $y = C(x)$.
(f) For what positive values of x is C discontinuous?

27. **Management** A company charges \$1.50 per pound for fertilizer on orders of less than 20 pounds. For orders of 20 pounds or more, the company charges \$25 plus \$1.25 for each pound over 20. On orders of more than 50 pounds, the company rebates .25 for each pound over 50. Let $F(x)$ represent the net cost (after any rebates) of buying x pounds of fertilizer. What is the net cost of buying

(a) 10 lb (b) 20 lb (c) 40 lb (d) 80 lb?

(e) Where is the function F discontinuous?

28. **Management** Recently, a car rental firm charged \$30 per day or portion of a day to rent a car for a period of 1 to 5 days. Days 6 and 7 were then "free," while the charge for days 8 through 12 was again \$30 per day. Let $C(t)$ represent the total cost to rent the car for t days, where $0 < t \le 12$. Find the total cost of a rental for the following number of days:
(a) 4 **(b)** 5 **(c)** 6 **(d)** 7 **(e)** 8.
(f) Find $\lim_{t \to 5} C(t)$. **(g)** Find $\lim_{t \to 6} C(t)$.

Write each of the following in interval notation.

29. 

30. −9 15

31. −2

32. 10

33. $\{x \mid -25 \le x \le 0\}$

34. $\{x \mid -5 \le x \le 14\}$

35. $\{x \mid \pi < x < 10\}$

36. $\{x \mid -7 \le x \le -3\}$

37. $\{x \mid x > -4\}$

38. $\{x \mid x < 3\}$

39. $\{x \mid x < 0\}$

40. $\{x \mid x > -10\}$

41. On which of the following intervals is the function in Exercise 5 continuous: $(-3, 0)$, $(0, 3)$, $(0, 4)$?

42. On which of the following intervals is the function in Exercise 6 continuous: $(-6, 0)$, $(0, 3)$, $(4, 8)$?

CHAPTER 12 SUMMARY

Key Terms and Symbols

12.1 $\lim_{x \to a} f(x)$ limit of a function as x approaches a

12.2 average rate of change
velocity
instantaneous rate of change
marginal cost, revenue, profit

12.3 y' derivative of y
$f'(x)$ derivative of $f(x)$
secant line
tangent line
derivative
differentiable
numerical derivative

12.4 $\frac{dy}{dx}$ derivative of $y = f(x)$
$D_x[f(x)]$ derivative of $f(x)$
$\frac{d}{dx}[f(x)]$ derivative of $f(x)$
demand function

12.5 $\overline{C}(x)$ average cost per item
marginal average cost

12.6 $g[f(x)]$ composite function
chain rule
marginal revenue product

12.8 continuous at a point
discontinuous
interval notation
continuous on an open interval

Key Concepts

Limit of a Function

Let f be a function and let a and L be real numbers. Suppose that as x takes values very close (but not equal) to a (on both sides of a), the corresponding values of $f(x)$ are very close (and possibly equal) to L; and that the values of $f(x)$ can be made arbitrarily close to L for all values of x that are close enough to a. Then L is the **limit** of f as x approaches a, written $\lim_{x \to a} f(x) = L$.

Properties of Limits

Let a, k, A, and B be real numbers, and let f and g be functions such that

$$\lim_{x \to a} f(x) = A \quad \text{and} \quad \lim_{x \to a} g(x) = B.$$

1. $\lim_{x \to a} k = k$ (for any constant k)
2. $\lim_{x \to a} x = a$ (for any real number a)

3. $\lim_{x\to a} [f(x) \pm g(x)] = A \pm B = \lim_{x\to a} f(x) \pm \lim_{x\to a} g(x)$

4. $\lim_{x\to a} [f(x) \cdot g(x)] = A \cdot B = \lim_{x\to a} f(x) \cdot \lim_{x\to a} g(x)$

5. $\lim_{x\to a} \frac{f(x)}{g(x)} = \frac{A}{B} = \frac{\lim_{x\to a} f(x)}{\lim_{x\to a} g(x)} \quad (B \neq 0)$

6. For any real number r for which A^r exists,

$$\lim_{x\to a} [f(x)]^r = A^r = [\lim_{x\to a} f(x)]^r.$$

Polynomial Limits If $f(x)$ is a polynomial function, then $\lim_{x\to a} f(x) = f(a)$.

Limit Theorem If f and g are functions that have limits as x approaches a, and $f(x) = g(x)$ for all $x \neq a$, then $\lim_{x\to a} f(x) = \lim_{x\to a} g(x)$.

The **instantaneous rate of change** of a function f when $x = x_0$ is

$$\lim_{h\to 0} \frac{f(x_0 + h) - f(x_0)}{h},$$

provided this limit exists.

The **tangent line** to the graph of $y = f(x)$ at the point $(x_0, f(x_0))$ is the line through this point having slope $\lim_{h\to 0} \frac{f(x_0 + h) - f(x_0)}{h}$, provided this limit exists.

The **derivative** of the function f is the function denoted f' whose value at the number x is $f'(x) = \lim_{h\to 0} \frac{f(x + h) - f(x)}{h}$, provided this limit exists.

Rules for Derivatives (Assume all indicated derivatives exist.)

Constant Function If $f(x) = k$, where k is any real number, then $\mathbf{f'(x) = 0}$.

Power Rule If $f(x) = x^n$, for any real number n, then $\mathbf{f'(x) = n \cdot x^{n-1}}$.

Constant Times a Function Let k be a real number. Then the derivative of $y = k \cdot f(x)$ is $\mathbf{y' = k \cdot f'(x)}$.

Sum or Difference Rule If $y = f(x) \pm g(x)$, then $\mathbf{y' = f'(x) \pm g'(x)}$.

Product Rule If $f(x) = g(x) \cdot k(x)$, then $\mathbf{f'(x) = g(x) \cdot k'(x) + k(x) \cdot g'(x)}$.

Quotient Rule If $f(x) = \frac{g(x)}{k(x)}$, and $k(x) \neq 0$, then $\mathbf{f'(x) = \frac{k(x) \cdot g'(x) - g(x) \cdot k'(x)}{[k(x)]^2}}$.

Chain Rule Let $y = f[g(x)]$. Then $\mathbf{y' = f'[g(x)] \cdot g'(x)}$.

Chain Rule (alternative form) If y is a function of u, say $y = f(u)$, and if u is a function of x, say $u = g(x)$, then $y = f(u) = f[g(x)]$, and

$$\mathbf{\frac{dy}{dx} = \frac{dy}{du} \cdot \frac{du}{dx}}.$$

Generalized Power Rule	Let u be a function of x, and let $y = u^n$ for any real number n. Then $$\boldsymbol{y' = n \cdot u^{n-1} \cdot u'}.$$
Exponential Function	If $y = e^{g(x)}$, then $\boldsymbol{y' = g'(x) \cdot e^{g(x)}}$.
Natural Logarithmic Function	If $y = \ln[g(x)]$, then $\boldsymbol{y' = \dfrac{g'(x)}{g(x)}}$.
	If $y = \ln\lvert x \rvert$, then $\boldsymbol{y' = \dfrac{1}{x}}$.

A function f is **continuous** at $x = c$ if $f(c)$ is defined, $\lim_{x\to c} f(x)$ exists, and $\lim_{x\to c} f(x) = f(c)$.

Chapter 12 Review Exercises

In Exercises 1–6, determine graphically or numerically if the limit exists. If a limit exists, find its (approximate) value.

1. $\lim_{x\to -3} f(x)$

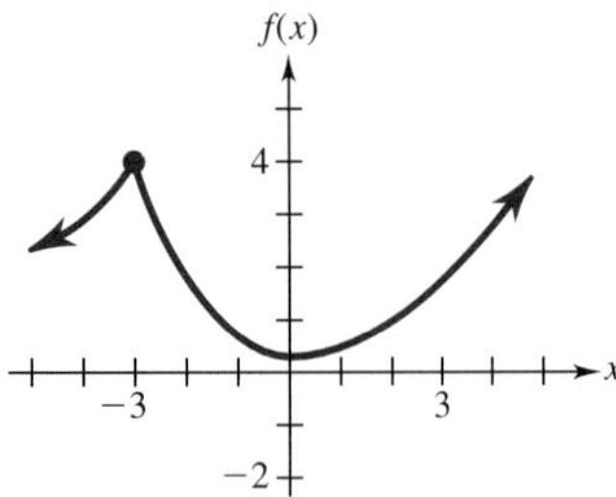

2. $\lim_{x\to -1} g(x)$

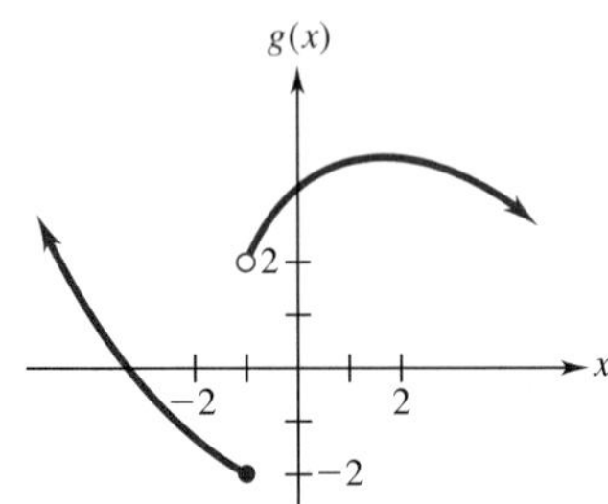

3. $\lim_{x\to 1} \dfrac{x^3 - 1.1x^2 - 2x + 2.1}{x - 1}$

4. $\lim_{x\to 2} \dfrac{x^4 + .5x^3 - 4.5x^2 - 2.5x + 3}{x - 2}$

5. $\lim_{x\to 0} \dfrac{\sqrt{2 - x} - \sqrt{2}}{x}$

6. $\lim_{x\to -1} \dfrac{10^x - .1}{x + 1}$

In Exercises 7–16, find the limit if it exists.

7. $\lim_{x\to 2} (x^2 \quad 3x + 1)$

8. $\lim_{x\to -1} (\quad 2x^2 + x \quad 5)$

9. $\lim_{x\to 4} \dfrac{3x + 1}{x - 2}$

10. $\lim_{x\to 3} \dfrac{4x + 7}{x - 3}$

11. $\lim_{x\to 2} \dfrac{x^2 - 4}{x - 2}$

12. $\lim_{x\to -3} \dfrac{x^2 + 2x - 3}{x + 3}$

13. $\lim_{x\to -4} \dfrac{2x^2 + 3x - 20}{x + 4}$

14. $\lim_{x\to 3} \dfrac{3x^2 - 2x - 21}{x - 3}$

15. $\lim_{x\to 9} \dfrac{\sqrt{x} - 3}{x - 9}$

16. $\lim_{x\to 16} \dfrac{\sqrt{x} - 4}{x - 16}$

Use the graph to find the average rate of change of f on the following intervals.

17. $x = 0$ to $x = 4$

18. $x = 2$ to $x = 8$

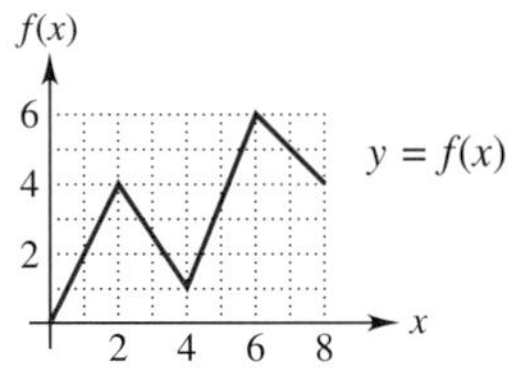

Find the average rate of change for each of the following functions.

19. $f(x) = 3x^2 - 5$, from $x = 1$ to $x = 6$

20. $g(x) = -x^3 + 2x^2 + 1$, from $x = -3$ to $x = 3$

21. $h(x) = \dfrac{6 - x}{2x + 3}$, from $x = 0$ to $x = 5$

22. $f(x) = e^{2x} + 5 \ln x$, from $x = 1$ to $x = 4$

Use the definition of the derivative to find the derivative of each of the following functions.

23. $y = 2x + 3$

24. $y = x^2 + 2x$

25. $y = 2x^2 - x + 1$

26. $y = x^3 + 5$

Find the slope of the tangent line to the given curve at the given value of x. Find the equation of each tangent line.

27. $y = x^2 - 6x$; at $x = 2$

28. $y = 8 - x^2$; at $x = 1$

29. $y = \frac{-2}{x + 5}$; at $x = -2$

30. $y = \sqrt{6x - 2}$; at $x = 3$

31. Management A company charges \$1.50 per pound when a certain chemical is bought in lots of 125 pounds or less, with a price per pound of \$1.35 if more than 125 pounds are purchased. Let $C(x)$ represent the cost of x pounds. Find each of the following.
(a) $C(100)$ **(b)** $C(125)$ **(c)** $C(140)$
(d) Graph $y = C(x)$.
(e) Where is C discontinuous?

32. Management Use the information in Exercise 31 to find the average cost per pound if the following number of pounds are bought.
(a) 100 **(b)** 125 **(c)** 140 **(d)** 200

33. Management Suppose hardware store customers are willing to buy $T(p)$ boxes of nails at p dollars per box, where

$$T(p) = .06p^4 - 1.25p^3 + 6.5p^2 - 18p + 200 \quad (0 < p \leq 11).$$

(a) Find the average rate of change in demand for a change in price from \$5 to \$8.
(b) Find the instantaneous rate of change in demand when the price is \$5.
(c) Find the instantaneous rate of change in demand when the price is \$8.

34. Suppose the average rate of change of a function $f(x)$ from $x = 0$ to $x = 4$ is 0. Does this mean that f is constant between $x = 0$ and $x = 4$? Explain.

Find the derivative of each of the following.

35. $y = 5x^2 - 7x - 9$

36. $y = x^3 - 4x^2$

37. $y = 6x^{7/3}$

38. $y = -3x^{-2}$

39. $f(x) = x^{-3} + \sqrt{x}$

40. $f(x) = 6x^{-1} - 2\sqrt{x}$

41. $y = (3t^2 + 7)(t^3 - t)$

42. $y = (-5t + 4)(t^3 - 2t^2)$

43. $y = 8x^{3/4}(2x + 3)$

44. $y = 25x^{-3/5}(x^2 + 5)$

45. $f(x) = \frac{2x}{x^2 + 2}$

46. $g(x) = \frac{-4x^2}{3x + 4}$

47. $y = \frac{\sqrt{x} - 1}{x + 2}$

48. $y = \frac{\sqrt{x} + 6}{x - 3}$

49. $y = \frac{x^2 - x + 1}{x - 1}$

50. $y = \frac{2x^3 - 5x^2}{x + 2}$

51. $f(x) = (3x - 2)^4$

52. $k(x) = (5x - 1)^6$

53. $y = \sqrt{2t - 5}$

54. $y = -3\sqrt{8t - 1}$

55. $y = 2x(3x - 4)^3$

56. $y = 5x^2(2x + 3)^5$

57. $f(u) = \frac{3u^2 - 4u}{(2u + 3)^3}$

58. $g(t) = \frac{t^3 + t - 2}{(2t - 1)^5}$

59. $y = e^{-2x^3}$

60. $y = -4e^{x^2}$

61. $y = 5x \cdot e^{2x}$

62. $y = -7x^2 \cdot e^{-3x}$

63. $y = \ln(x^2 + 4x + 1)$

64. $y = \ln(4x^3 + 2x)$

65. $y = \frac{\ln 4x}{x^2 - 1}$

66. $y = \frac{\ln(3x + 5)}{x^2 + 5x}$

Find the derivatives of each of these functions. Confirm your answer by graphing the derivative you find and the numerical derivative of the function on the same screen.

67. $y = \frac{x^2 + 3x - 10}{x - 3}$

68. $y = \frac{x^2 - x - 6}{x - 2}$

69. $y = -6e^{2x}$

70. $y = 8e^{.5x}$

Find each of the following.

71. $D_x\left(\frac{\sqrt{x} + 1}{\sqrt{x} - 1}\right)$

72. $D_x\left(\frac{2x + \sqrt{x}}{1 - x}\right)$

73. $\frac{dy}{dt}$ if $y = \sqrt{t^{1/2} + t}$

74. $\frac{dy}{dx}$ if $y = \frac{\sqrt{x - 1}}{x}$

75. $f'(1)$ if $f(x) = \frac{\sqrt{8 + x}}{x + 1}$

76. $f'(-2)$ if $f(t) = \frac{2 - 3t}{\sqrt{2 + t}}$

Find all points of discontinuity for the following.

77.

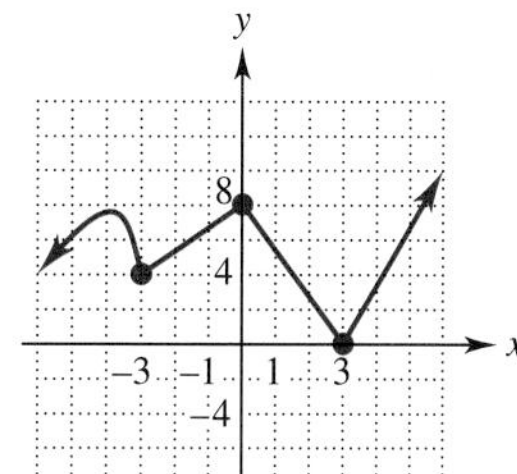

78.

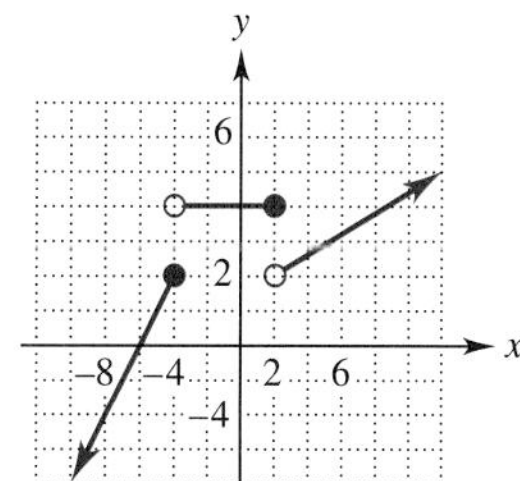

Are the following functions continuous at the given points?

79. $f(x) = \frac{2x - 3}{2x + 3}$; $x = -3/2, x = 0, x = 3/2$

80. $g(x) = \frac{2x - 1}{x^3 + x^2}$; $x = -1, x = 0, x = 1/2$

81. $h(x) = \frac{2 - 3x}{2 - x - x^2}$; $x = -2, x = 2/3, x = 1$

82. $f(x) = \dfrac{x^2 - 4}{x^2 - x - 6}$; $x = 2, x = 3, x = 4$

83. $f(x) = \dfrac{x - 6}{x + 5}$; $x = 6, x = -5, x = 0$

84. $f(x) = \dfrac{x^2 - 9}{x + 3}$; $x = 3, x = -3, x = 0$

Management *Work the following exercises.*

85. The owner of a new pizza shop projects that her profit (in dollars) from selling x hundred pizzas will be given by

$$P(x) = -.0009x^4 + .11x^3 - 2.2x^2 + 212x - 5000.$$

Find the marginal profit from selling
(a) 5000 pizzas;
(b) 7500 pizzas;
(c) 10,000 pizzas.

86. In Exercise 85, find the average profit function and the marginal average profit function.

87. The sales of a company are related to its expenditures on research by

$$S(x) = 1000 + 50\sqrt{x} + 10x,$$

where $S(x)$ gives sales in millions when x thousand dollars is spent on research. Find and interpret dS/dx if the following amounts are spent on research.
(a) \$9000 **(b)** \$16,000 **(c)** \$25,000
(d) As the amount spent on research increases, what happens to sales?

88. Suppose that the profit (in hundreds of dollars) from selling x units of a product is given by

$$P(x) = \frac{x^2}{x - 1}, \quad \text{where } x > 1.$$

Find and interpret the marginal profit when the following numbers of units are sold.
(a) 4 **(b)** 12 **(c)** 20
(d) What is happening to the marginal profit as the number sold increases?

89. A company finds that its costs are related to the amount spent on training programs by

$$T(x) = \frac{1000 + 50x}{x + 1},$$

where $T(x)$ is costs in thousands of dollars when x hundred dollars are spent on training. Find and interpret $T'(x)$ if the following amounts are spent on training.
(a) \$900 **(b)** \$1900
(c) Are costs per dollar spent on training always increasing or decreasing?

90. O'Brien Incorporated has found that its revenue is related to advertising expenditures by the function

$$R(x) = \frac{20{,}000}{1 + 24e^{-5x/9}} - 800,$$

where $R(x)$ is the revenue (in dollars) when x hundred dollars is spent on advertising. Use numerical methods to find the marginal revenue when the amount spent on advertising is:
(a) \$500; **(b)** \$900; **(c)** \$1300; **(d)** \$1500.
(e) Graph the revenue function.
(f) Explain why it is not worthwhile to spend more than \$1500 on advertising.

91. Physical Science The graph shows how the velocity of the hands and baseball bat vary with the time of the swing.* Estimate and interpret the value of the derivative functions for the hands and for the bat at the time when the velocity of the two are equal. (*Note:* The rate of change of velocity is called *acceleration.*)

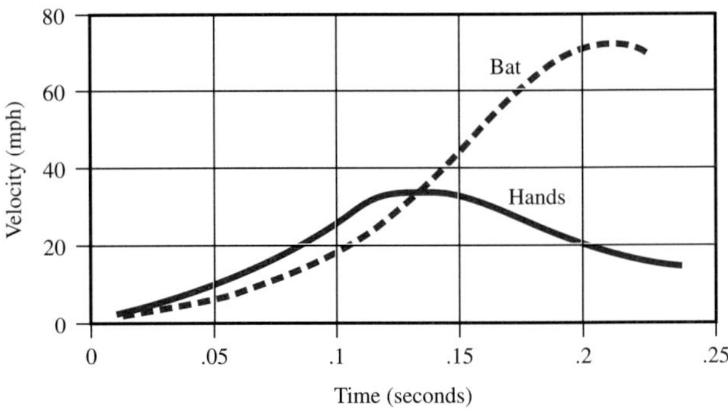

92. Natural Science Under certain conditions, the length of the monkeyface prickleback, a west coast game fish, can be approximated by

$$L = 71.5(1 - e^{-.1t})$$

and its weight by

$$W = .01289 \cdot L^{2.9},$$

where L is the length in cm, t is the age in years, and W is the weight in grams.†
(a) Find the approximate length of a 5-year-old monkeyface.
(b) Find how fast the length of a 5-year-old monkeyface is growing.
(c) Find the approximate weight of a 5-year-old monkeyface. (*Hint:* Use your answer from part (a).)
(d) Find the rate of change of the weight with respect to length for a 5-year-old monkeyface.
(e) Using the chain rule and your answers to parts (b) and (d), find how fast the weight of a 5-year-old monkeyface is growing.

*Adair, Robert K., *The Physics of Baseball,* copyright © 1990 by HarperCollins, p. 82.

†Marshall, William H., and Tina Wyllie Echeverria, "Characteristics of the Monkeyface Prickleback," *California Fish & Game,* Vol. 78, No. 2, Spring 1992. For more details, see Case 5 on page 223.

CASE 12

Price Elasticity of Demand

Anyone who sells a product or service is concerned with how a change in price affects demand. The sensitivity of demand to price changes varies with different items. For items such as soft drinks, pepper, and light bulbs, relatively small percentage changes in price will not change the demand for the item much. For cars, home loans, furniture, and computer equipment, however, small percentage changes in price have significant effects on demand.

One way to measure the sensitivity of demand to changes in price is by the ratio of percent change in demand to percent change in price. If q represents the quantity demanded and p the price, this ratio can be written as

$$\frac{\Delta q/q}{\Delta p/p},$$

where Δq represents the change in q and Δp represents the change in p. This ratio is always negative, because q and p are positive, while Δq and Δp have opposite signs. (An *increase* in price causes a *decrease* in demand.) If the absolute value of this ratio is large, it suggests that a relatively small increase in price causes a relatively large drop (decrease) in demand.

This ratio can be rewritten as

$$\frac{\Delta q/q}{\Delta p/p} = \frac{\Delta q}{q} \cdot \frac{p}{\Delta p} = \frac{p}{q} \cdot \frac{\Delta q}{\Delta p}.$$

Suppose $q = f(p)$. (Note that this is the inverse of the way our demand functions have been expressed so far; previously we had $p = D(q)$.) Then $\Delta q = f(p + \Delta p) - f(p)$, and

$$\frac{\Delta q}{\Delta p} = \frac{f(p + \Delta p) - f(p)}{\Delta p}.$$

As $\Delta p \to 0$, this quotient becomes

$$\lim_{\Delta p \to 0} \frac{\Delta q}{\Delta p} = \lim_{\Delta p \to 0} \frac{f(p + \Delta p) - f(p)}{\Delta p} = \frac{dq}{dp},$$

and

$$\lim_{\Delta p \to 0} \frac{p}{q} \cdot \frac{\Delta q}{\Delta p} = \frac{p}{q} \cdot \frac{dq}{dp}.$$

The quantity

$$E = -\frac{p}{q} \cdot \frac{dq}{dp}$$

is positive because dq/dp is negative. E is called the **elasticity of demand** and measures the instantaneous responsiveness of demand to price. For example, E may be .2 for medical services, but may be 1.2 for stereo equipment. The demand for essential medical services is much less responsive to price changes than is the demand for nonessential commodities, such as stereo equipment.

If $E < 1$, the relative change in demand is less than the relative change in price, and the demand is called **inelastic.** If $E > 1$, the relative change in demand is greater than the relative change in price, and the demand is called **elastic.** When $E = 1$, the percentage changes in price and demand are relatively equal and the demand is said to have **unit elasticity.**

Addiction to an illicit drug such as crack is an example of almost perfect inelastic demand. The quantity of the drug demanded by addicts does not change much no matter what the price. This fact is often used to support those who believe that increased law enforcement and longer prison terms will have little effect on the use of illicit drugs.

EXAMPLE 1 The demand for distilled spirits is given by $q = -.00375p + 7.87$, where p is the retail price (in dollars) of a case of liquor and q is the average number of cases purchased per year by a consumer.*

(a) Calculate and interpret the elasticity of demand when $p = \$118$ per case and when $p = \$1200$ per case.

Since $q = -.00375p + 7.87$, we have $dq/dp = -.00375$, so that

$$\begin{aligned} E &= -\frac{p}{q} \cdot \frac{dq}{dp} \\ &= -\frac{p}{-.00375p + 7.87} \cdot (-.00375) \\ &= \frac{.00375p}{-.00375p + 7.87}. \end{aligned}$$

Let $p = 118$ to get

$$E = \frac{.00375(118)}{-.00375(118) + 7.87} \approx .06.$$

Since $.06 < 1$, the demand is inelastic, and a percentage change in price will result in a smaller percentage change in demand. For example, a 10% increase in price will cause a small .6% decrease in demand.

*Wales, Terrance J., "Distilled Spirits and Interstate Consumption Efforts," *The American Economic Review,* 57(4): 853–863, 1968.

If $p = 1200$, then

$$E = \frac{.00375(1200)}{-.00375(1200) + 7.87} \approx 1.34.$$

Since $1.34 > 1$, demand is elastic. At this point a percentage increase in price will result in a *greater* percentage decrease in demand. Here a 10% price increase will cause a 13.4% decrease in demand.

(b) Determine the price per case at which demand would have unit elasticity (that is, $E = 1$). What is the significance of this price?

Demand will have unit elasticity at the price p that makes $E = 1$, so we must solve this equation:

$$E = \frac{.00375p}{-.00375p + 7.87} = 1$$

$$.00375p = -.00375p + 7.87$$

$$.0075p = 7.87$$

$$p = 1049.33.$$

Demand would have unit elasticity at a price of $1049.33 per case. At this price the percentage changes in price and demand are about the same. ■

The definitions from this discussion can be summarized as follows.

ELASTICITY OF DEMAND

Let $q = f(p)$, where q is demand at a price p. The **elasticity of demand** is

$$E = -\frac{p}{q} \cdot \frac{dq}{dp}.$$

Demand is **inelastic** if $E < 1$.

Demand is **elastic** if $E > 1$.

Demand has **unit elasticity** if $E = 1$.

EXERCISES

1. Some years ago research indicated that the demand for heroin was given by $q = 100p^{-.17}$.*
   (a) Find the elasticity of demand E.
   (b) Is the demand for heroin elastic or inelastic?
2. The demand for marijuana among UCLA students was found to be given by $q = -.225p + 3.74$, where p is the price per ounce (in dollars) and q is the average number of ounces purchased monthly per customer.†
   (a) Find the elasticity of demand E.
   (b) Compute the elasticity at a price of $10 (the prevailing price at the time of the research).
   (c) Determine the price at which the demand for marijuana is unit elastic.
3. For some products, the demand function is actually increasing. For example, the most expensive colleges in the United States also tend to have the greatest number of applicants for each student accepted. What is true about the elasticity in this case?
4. What must be true about the demand function if $E = 0$?

*Brown, George F., Jr. and Lester R. Silverman, *The Retail Price of Heroin: Estimation and Applications.* Washington DC: The Drug Abuse Council, Inc., 1973.

†Nievergelt, Yves, UMAP Module 674, *Price Elasticity of Demand: Gambling, Heroin, Marijuana, Whiskey, Prostitution, and Fish,* COMAP, Inc., 1987.

CHAPTER 13

Applications of the Derivative

In the last chapter, the derivative was defined and interpreted, and formulas were developed for the derivatives of many functions. In this chapter, we investigate the connection between the derivative of a function and the graph of the function. In particular, we shall see how to use the derivative to determine algebraically the maximum and minimum values of a function, as well as the intervals where the function is increasing or decreasing.

13.1 DERIVATIVES AND GRAPHS

Informally, we say that a function is **increasing** on an interval if its graph is *rising* from left to right over the interval and that a function is **decreasing** on an interval if its graph is *falling* from left to right over the interval.

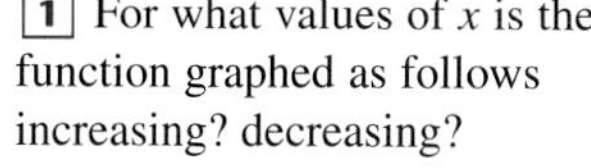

1 For what values of x is the function graphed as follows increasing? decreasing?

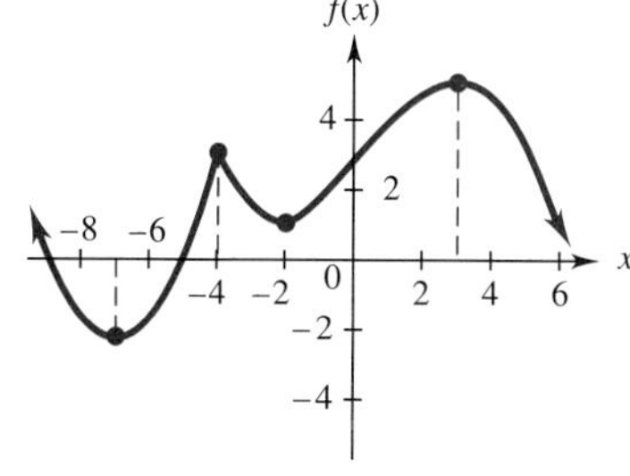

Answer:
Increasing on $(-7, -4)$ and $(-2, 3)$; decreasing on $(-\infty, -7)$, $(-4, -2)$, and $(3, \infty)$

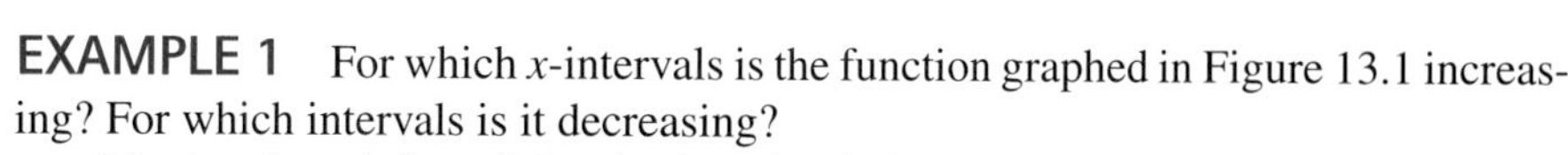

EXAMPLE 1 For which x-intervals is the function graphed in Figure 13.1 increasing? For which intervals is it decreasing?

Moving from left to right, the function is increasing up to -4, then decreasing from -4 to 0, constant (neither increasing nor decreasing) from 0 to 4, increasing from 4 to 6, and finally, decreasing from 6 on. In interval notation, the function is increasing on $(-\infty, -4)$ and $(4, 6)$, decreasing on $(-4, 0)$ and $(6, \infty)$, and constant on $(0, 4)$. ■ 1

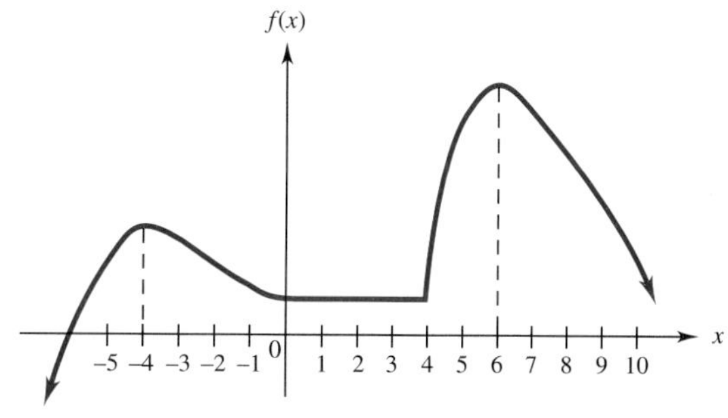

FIGURE 13.1

In order to examine the connection between the graph of a function f and the derivative of f, it is sometimes helpful to think of the graph of f as a roller coaster track, with a roller coaster car moving from left to right along the graph, as shown in Figure 13.2. At any point along the graph, the floor of the car (a straight line segment) represents the tangent line to the graph at that point.

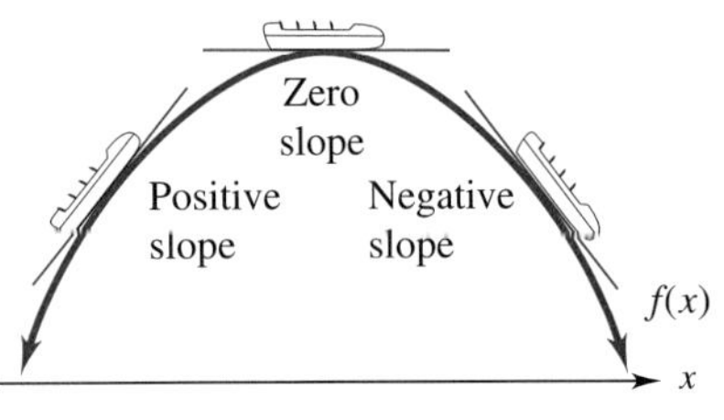

FIGURE 13.2

The slope of the tangent line is positive when the car travels uphill (the function is *increasing*) and the slope of the tangent line is negative when the car travels downhill (the function is *decreasing*). Since the slope of the tangent line at the point $(x, f(x))$ is given by the derivative $f'(x)$, we have these useful facts.

Suppose a function f has a derivative at each point in an open interval:

1. If $f'(x) > 0$ for each x in the interval, f is *increasing* on the interval.
2. If $f'(x) < 0$ for each x in the interval, f is *decreasing* on the interval.
3. If $f'(x) = 0$ for each x in the interval, f is *constant* on the interval.

EXAMPLE 2 Find the intervals on which the function

$$f(x) = x^3 + 3x^2 - 9x + 4,$$

whose graph is shown in Figure 13.3, is increasing or decreasing.

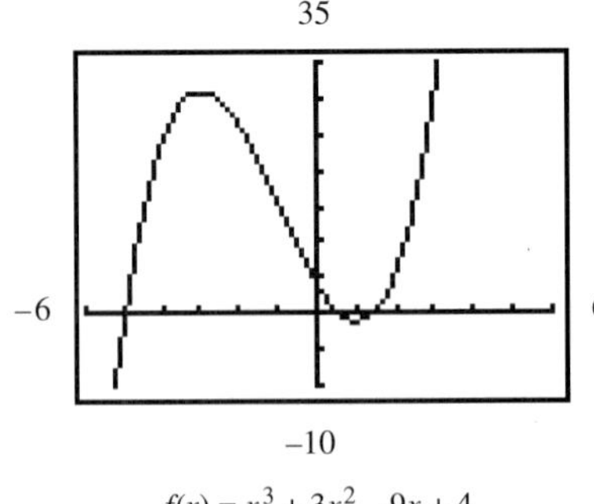

$f(x) = x^3 + 3x^2 - 9x + 4$

FIGURE 13.3

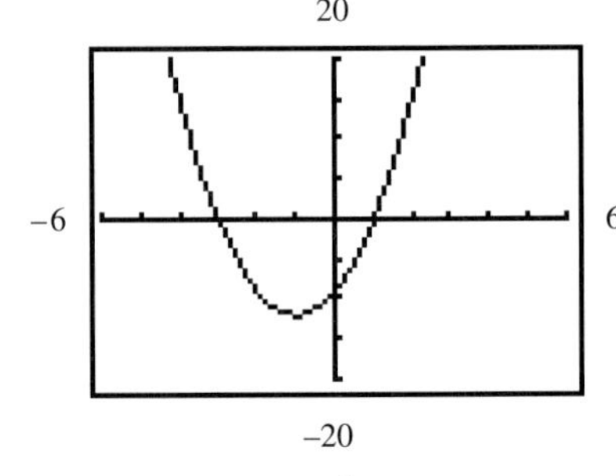

$f'(x) = 3x^2 + 6x - 9$

FIGURE 13.4

The graph of f in Figure 13.3 does not clearly show the intervals on which f is increasing or decreasing and suggests that f is constant near $x = -3$. We can use the derivative $f'(x) = 3x^2 + 6x - 9$ to get more precise information. According to the facts in the box above, the solutions of the inequalities $f'(x) > 0$ and $f'(x) < 0$, that is,

$$3x^2 + 6x - 9 > 0 \quad \text{and} \quad 3x^2 + 6x - 9 < 0,$$

are the intervals on which f is increasing or decreasing. As we saw in Section 2.4, the solutions of these inequalities are the intervals where the graph of $f'(x) = 3x^2 + 6x - 9$ lies above the x-axis and the intervals where the graph of $f'(x)$ lies below the x-axis. So we graph $f'(x)$ (Figure 13.4) and algebraically determine the x-intercepts by solving the equation

$$\begin{aligned} 3x^2 + 6x - 9 &= 0 \\ 3(x^2 + 2x - 3) &= 0 \\ 3(x + 3)(x - 1) &= 0 \\ x = -3 \quad \text{or} \quad x &= 1. \end{aligned}$$

2 Find all intervals on which $f(x) = 4x^3 + 3x^2 - 18x + 1$ is increasing or decreasing.

Answer:
Increasing on $(-\infty, -3/2)$ and $(1, \infty)$; decreasing on $(-3/2, 1)$

Hence, the x-intercepts of the graph of $f'(x)$ are $x = -3$ and $x = 1$. This fact and Figure 13.4 show that the graph lies above the x-axis on the intervals $(-\infty, -3)$ and $(1, \infty)$ and below the x-axis on $(-3, 1)$. Therefore, the original function $f(x) = x^3 + 3x^2 - 9x + 4$ is increasing on $(-\infty, -3)$ and $(1, \infty)$, and decreasing on $(-3, 1)$. In particular, f is *not* constant near $x = -3$; the "flat" portion of the graph in Figure 13.3 is not actually horizontal (as you can confirm by using the trace feature). ■ 2

In Example 2, the numbers for which $f'(x) = 0$ were essential for determining exactly where the function was increasing and decreasing. The situation is a bit different with the absolute value function $f(x) = |x|$, whose graph is shown in Figure 13.5. Clearly, f is decreasing on the left of $x = 0$ and increasing on the right of $x = 0$. But as we saw on page 579, the derivative of $f(x) = |x|$ does not exist at $x = 0$. These examples suggest that the points where the derivative is 0 or undefined play an important role.

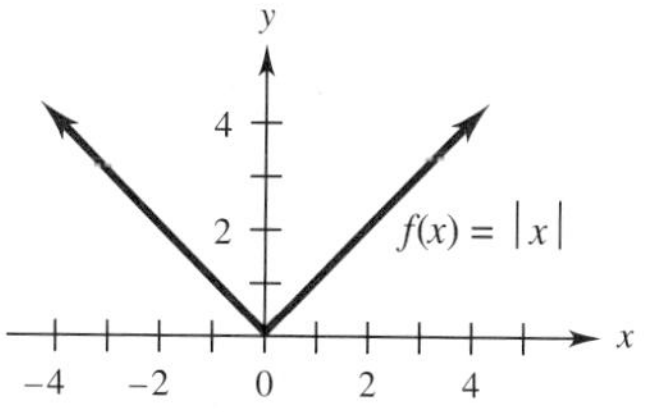

FIGURE 13.5

In view of the preceding discussion, we have this definition.

> If f is a function, then a number c for which $f(c)$ is defined and
>
> $$\text{either } f'(c) = 0 \quad \text{or} \quad f'(c) \text{ does not exist}$$
>
> is called a **critical number** of f. The corresponding point $(c, f(c))$ on the graph of f is called a **critical point.**

The procedure used in Example 2, which applies to all functions treated in this book, can now be summarized as follows.

> *Step 1* Compute the derivative f'.
>
> *Step 2* Find the critical numbers of f.
>
> *Step 3* Solve the inequalities $f'(x) > 0$ and $f'(x) < 0$ either algebraically or graphically (by finding the intervals where the graph of f' is above or below the x-axis).
>
> The solutions of $f'(x) > 0$ are intervals on which f is increasing and the solutions of $f'(x) < 0$ are intervals on which f is decreasing.

MAXIMA AND MINIMA We have seen that the graph of a typical function may have "peaks" or "valleys," as illustrated in Figure 13.6.

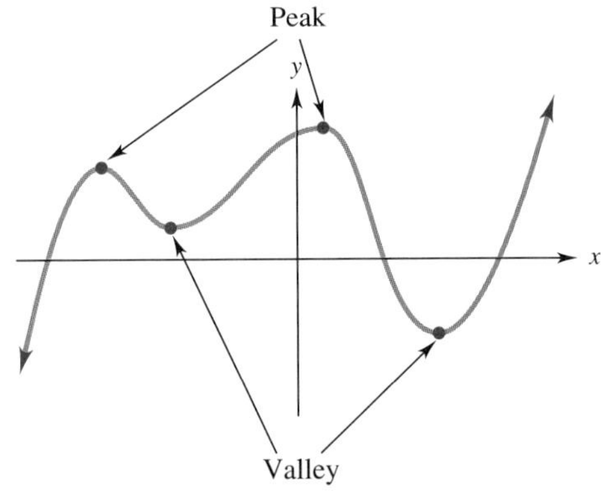

FIGURE 13.6

A peak is the highest point in its neighborhood, but not necessarily the highest point on the graph. Similarly, a valley is the lowest point in its neighborhood, but not necessarily the lowest point on the graph. Consequently, a peak is called a *local maximum* and a valley a *local minimum.* More precisely,

> Let c be a number in the domain of a function f.
>
> 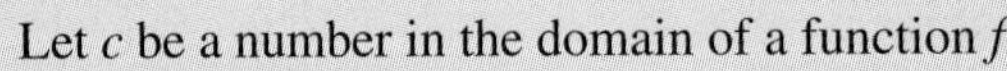
>
> **1.** f has a **local maximum** at c if $f(x) \leq f(c)$ for all x near c.
>
> **2.** f has a **local minimum** at c if $f(x) \geq f(c)$ for all x near c.
>
> The function f is said to have a **local extremum** at c if it has a local maximum or minimum there.

NOTE The plurals of maximum, minimum, and extremum, respectively, are maxima, minima, and extrema. ◆

EXAMPLE 3 Identify the local extrema of the function whose graph is shown in Figure 13.7.

The function has local maxima at x_1 and x_3 and local minima at x_2 and x_4. ■ 3

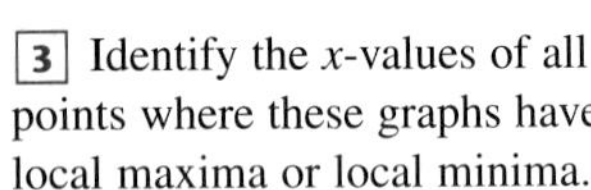

3 Identify the x-values of all points where these graphs have local maxima or local minima.

(a)

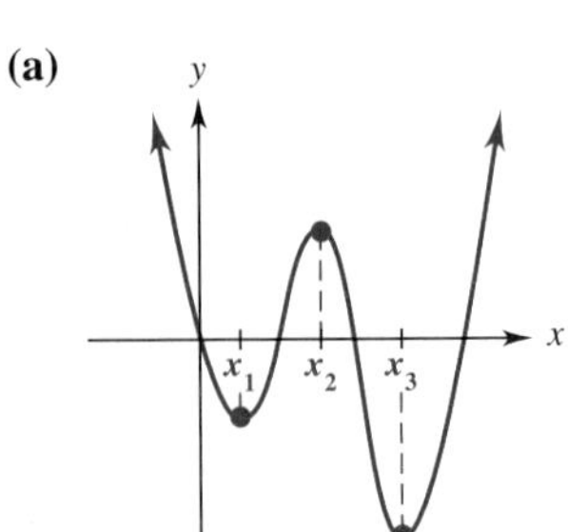

(b)

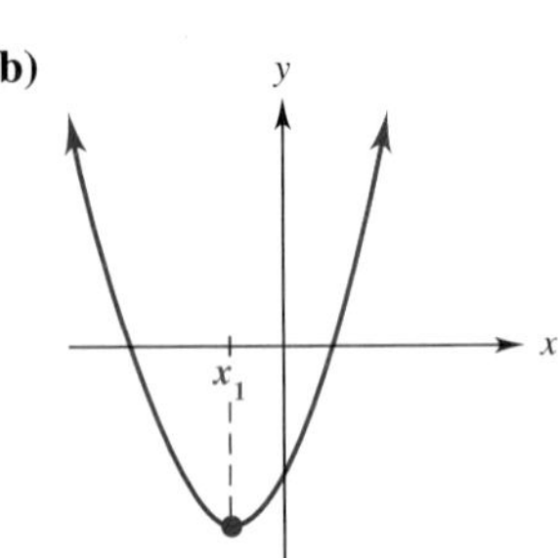

(c)

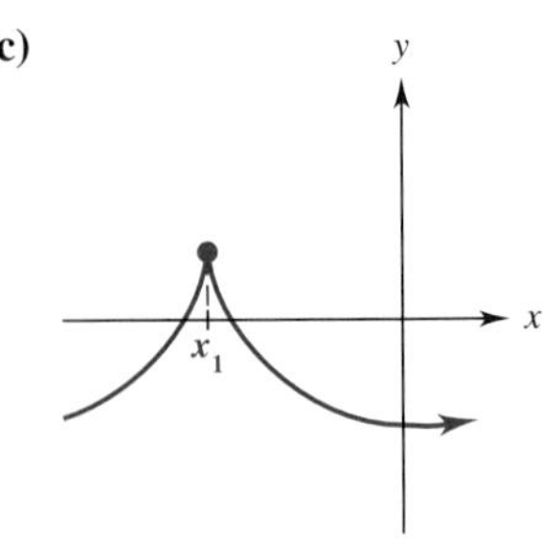

Answers:

(a) Local maximum at x_2; local minima at x_1 and x_3

(b) No local maximum; local minimum at x_1

(c) Local maximum at x_1; no local minimum

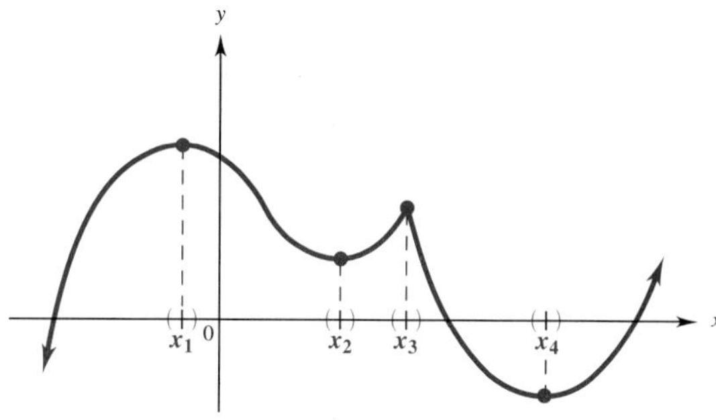

FIGURE 13.7

The maximum/minimum finder on a calculator can readily *approximate* the location of local extrema. To see how derivatives can be used to determine their *exact* location, consider the roller coaster analogy again, as shown in Figure 13.8.

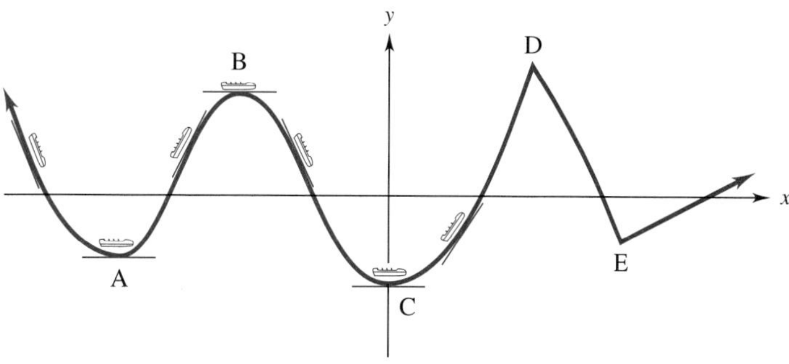

FIGURE 13.8

As the car passes through the local extrema at A, B, and C, the tangent line is horizontal and has slope 0. At D and E, however, a real roller coaster car would have trouble. It would fly off the track at D and be unable to make the 90° change of direction at E. Notice that the graph does not have tangent lines at points D and E (see the discussion of the existence of derivatives in Section 12.3). Thus, the points where local extrema occur have this property: the tangent line is horizontal and has slope 0 *or* there is no tangent line, that is, $f'(c) = 0$ or $f'(c)$ is not defined. In other words,

> If f has a local extremum at $x = c$, then c is a critical number of f.

CAUTION This result says that every local extremum occurs at a critical number, but *not* that every critical number produces a local extremum. Thus, the critical numbers provide a list of *possibilities*: if there is a local extremum, it must occur at a number on the list, but the list may include numbers at which there is no local extremum. ◆

EXAMPLE 4 Find the critical numbers of the following functions.

(a) $f(x) = 2x^3 - 3x^2 - 72x + 15$

We have $f'(x) = 6x^2 - 6x - 72$, so $f'(x)$ exists for every x. Setting $f'(x) = 0$ shows that

$$6x^2 - 6x - 72 = 0$$
$$6(x^2 - x - 12) = 0$$
$$x^2 - x - 12 = 0$$
$$(x + 3)(x - 4) = 0$$
$$x + 3 = 0 \quad \text{or} \quad x - 4 = 0$$
$$x = -3 \quad \text{or} \quad x = 4.$$

Therefore, -3 and 4 are the critical numbers of f; these are the only places where local extrema could possibly occur. The graph of f in Figure 13.9 shows that there is a local maximum at $x = -3$ and a local minimum at $x = 4$.

(b) $f(x) = 3x^{4/3} - 12x^{1/3}$.

We first compute the derivative.

$$f'(x) = 3 \cdot \frac{4}{3}x^{1/3} - 12 \cdot \frac{1}{3}x^{-2/3} = 4x^{1/3} - \frac{4}{x^{2/3}}$$
$$= \frac{4x^{1/3}x^{2/3}}{x^{2/3}} - \frac{4}{x^{2/3}} = \frac{4x - 4}{x^{2/3}}$$

The derivative fails to exist when $x = 0$. Since the original function f is defined when $x = 0$, 0 is a critical number of f. If $x \neq 0$, then $f'(x)$ is 0 only when the numerator $4x - 4 = 0$; that is, when $x = 1$. So the critical numbers of f are 0 and 1. These numbers are the *possible* locations for local extrema. However, the graph of f in Figure 13.10 suggests that while there is a local minimum at $x = 1$, there is no local extremum at $x = 0$. ■ 4

4 Find the critical numbers for each of these functions.

(a) $\frac{1}{3}x^3 - x^2 - 15x + 6$

(b) $6x^{2/3} - 4x$

Answers:

(a) $-3, 5$

(b) 0, 1

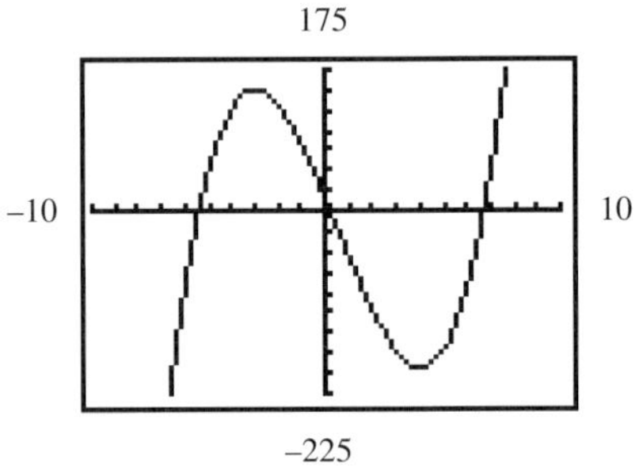

175

−10 10

−225

$f(x) = 2x^3 - 3x^2 - 72x + 15$

FIGURE 13.9

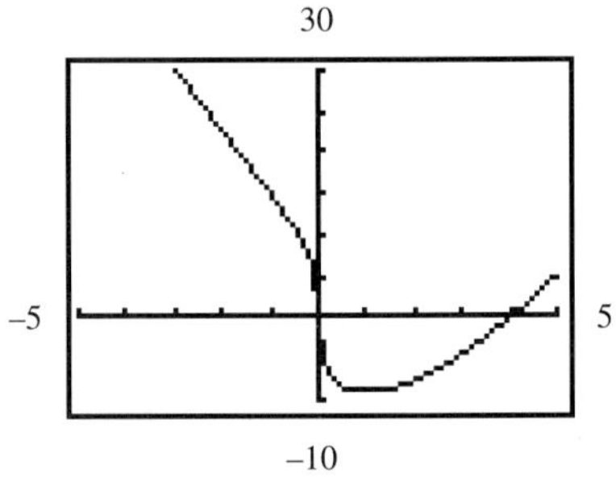

30

−5 5

−10

$f(x) = 3x^{4/3} - 12x^{1/3}$

FIGURE 13.10

When all the critical numbers of a function have been found, you must then determine which ones lead to local extrema. Sometimes this can be done graphically, as in Example 4. It can also be done algebraically by using the following observation: At a local maximum f changes from increasing to decreasing and at a local minimum f changes from decreasing to increasing, as illustrated in Figure 13.11.

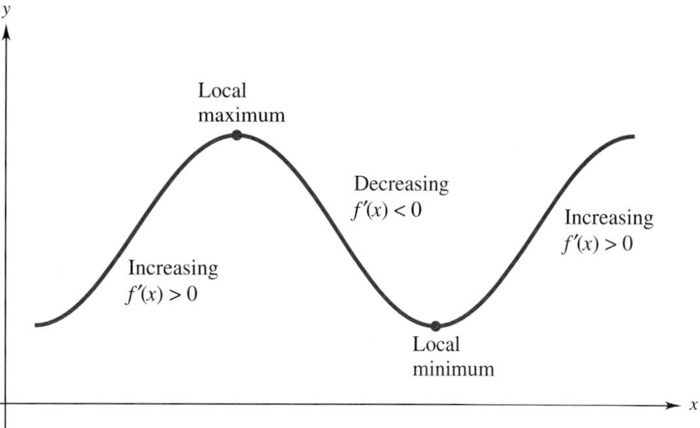

FIGURE 13.11

As we have seen, when f changes from increasing to decreasing, its derivative f' changes from positive to negative. Similarly, when f changes from decreasing to increasing, f' changes from negative to positive. These facts lead to the following test for local extrema, whose formal proof will be omitted.

FIRST DERIVATIVE TEST

Assume that $a < c < b$ and that c is the only critical number for a function f in the interval $[a, b]$. Assume that f is differentiable for all x in $[a, b]$, except possibly at $x = c$.

1. If $f'(a) > 0$ and $f'(b) < 0$, then there is a local maximum at c.
2. If $f'(a) < 0$ and $f'(b) > 0$, then there is a local minimum at c.
3. If $f'(a)$ and $f'(b)$ are both positive, or both negative, then there is no local extremum at c.

The sketches in the following table (which continues on the next page) show how the first derivative test works. Assume the same conditions on a, b, c as those stated in the box.

$f(x)$ has:	*Sign of $f'(a)$*	*Sign of $f'(b)$*	*Sketches*
Local maximum	+	−	+ − $(c, f(c))$ a c b $(c, f(c))$ + − a c b
Local minimum	−	+	$(c, f(c))$ − + a c b − + $(c, f(c))$ a c b

(Continued)

$f(x)$ *has:*	*Sign of* $f'(a)$	*Sign of* $f'(b)$	*Sketches*
No local extrema	+	+	
No local extrema	−	−	

EXAMPLE 5 Find all local extrema of $f(x) = 10x^3 + 15x^2 - 900x + 325$ without graphing the function.

First find the critical numbers. We have $f'(x) = 30x^2 + 30x - 900$, which is defined for every x. Setting $f'(x) = 0$, we see that

$$30x^2 + 30x - 900 = 0$$
$$x^2 + x - 30 = 0 \qquad \text{Divide both sides by 30.}$$
$$(x + 6)(x - 5) = 0$$
$$x = -6 \quad \text{or} \quad x = 5.$$

In order to test the critical number -6, choose any interval that contains -6, but not 5, say $[-10, 0]$.* Now apply the first derivative test with $a = -10$ and $b = 0$.

$$f'(-10) = 30(-10)^2 + 30(-10) - 900 = 1800$$
$$f'(0) = 30(0^2) + 30(0) - 900 = -900$$

Since $f'(-10)$ is positive and $f'(0)$ is negative (as shown schematically in Figure 13.12), there is a local maximum at -6 by part 1 of the first derivative test.

To test the critical number 5, we use the interval $[0, 10]$. We have just seen that $f'(0) = -900$ and we compute: $f'(10) = 30(10^2) + 30(10) - 900 = 2400$. Since $f'(0)$ is negative and $f'(10)$ is positive (see Figure 13.12), there is a local minimum at 5 by part 2 of the first derivative test. ■ 5

5 Find all local extrema of these functions.

(a) $f(x) = 2x^2 - 8x + 1$

(b) $g(x) = x^3 - 9x^2 - 48x + 195$

Answers:

(a) Local minimum at 2

(b) Local maximum at -2; local minimum at 8

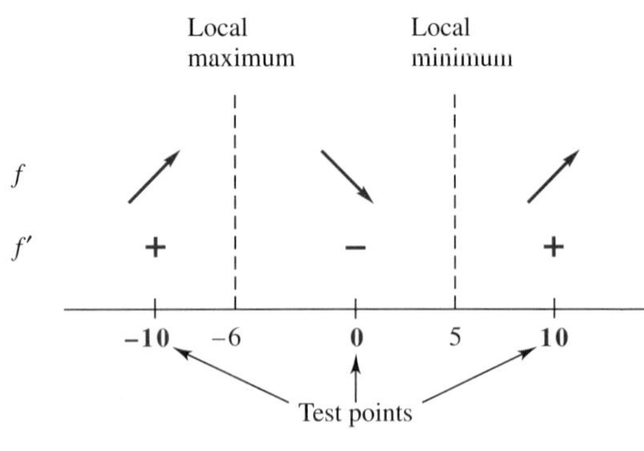

FIGURE 13.12

*When working by hand, it's best to choose endpoints that make the computations easy. When using a calculator, that isn't necessary.

EXAMPLE 6 Find all local extrema of $g(x) = x^3 - 1.8x^2 + x + 2$.

Although the graph of $g(x)$ in Figure 13.13 suggests that there are no local extrema, algebraic analysis shows otherwise. We have

$$g'(x) = 3x^2 - 3.6x + 1,$$

so the critical numbers are the solutions of

$$3x^2 - 3.6x + 1 = 0.$$

The quadratic formula shows that the critical numbers are

$$x = \frac{3.6 \pm \sqrt{(-3.6)^2 - 4 \cdot 3 \cdot 1}}{2 \cdot 3} = \frac{3.6 \pm \sqrt{.96}}{6} \approx \begin{cases} .4367 \\ .7633 \end{cases}.$$

We choose the interval [0, .5] to test .4367 and the interval [.5, 1] to test .7633. Using the table feature to compute the values of $y_1 = g'(x)$, we obtain Figure 13.14.

[6] Find a viewing window that clearly shows the local maximum and minimum of the function g in Example 6.

Answer:
Many possibilities, including $0 \le x \le 1$ and $2.1 \le y \le 2.2$

[7] Find the location of all local extrema of these functions.

(a) $f(x) = x^3 - 2.5x^2 + 2x - 1$

(b) $g(x) = x^3 + 2.5x^2 + 2.2x - 2$

Answers:
(a) Local maximum at 2/3; local minimum at 1

(b) No local extrema

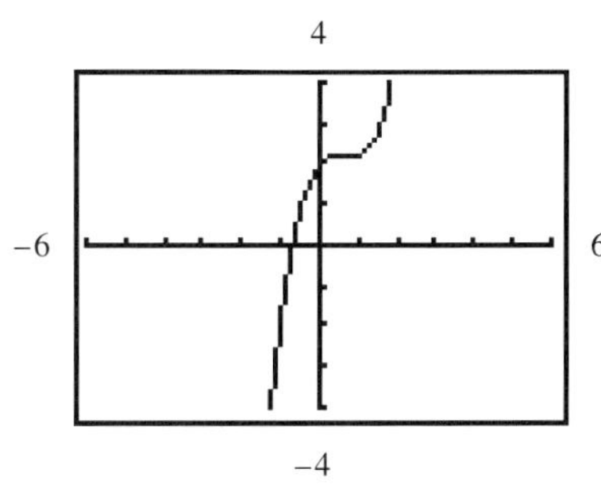

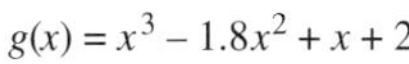
$g(x) = x^3 - 1.8x^2 + x + 2$

FIGURE 13.13

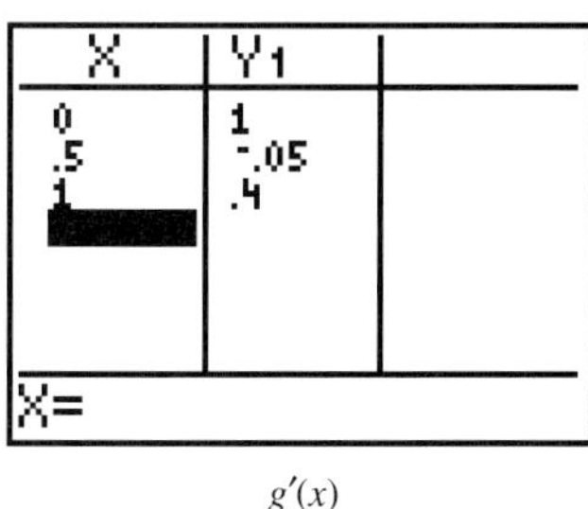

X	Y1
0	1
.5	-.05
1	.4

X=

$g'(x)$

FIGURE 13.14

The results are shown schematically in Figure 13.15. According to the first derivative test, there is a local maximum at $x \approx .4367$ and a local minimum at $x \approx .7633$. ■ [6] [7]

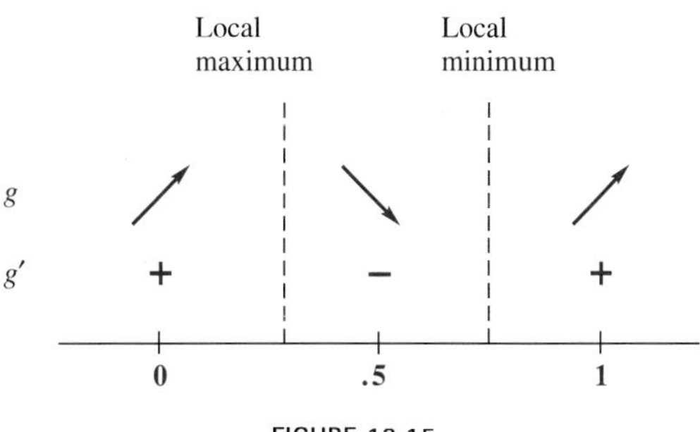

FIGURE 13.15

EXAMPLE 7 Find all local extrema of $f(x) = 3x^{5/3} - 9x^{2/3}$.

Note that $f(0) = 0$, so that (0, 0) is on the graph. However, this isn't at all clear in many viewing windows (Figure 13.16 on the next page). We can find out what's going on by determining the critical numbers. We have

$$f'(x) = 3 \cdot \frac{5}{3}x^{2/3} - 9 \cdot \frac{2}{3}x^{-1/3} = 5x^{2/3} - \frac{6}{x^{1/3}} = \frac{5x - 6}{x^{1/3}}.$$

8 Find all local extrema of $f(x) = x^2e^x$.

Answer:
Local minimum at 0; local maximum at -2

Therefore, the critical numbers are 0 (where f' is not defined, but f is) and 6/5 (where the numerator, and hence the derivative, is 0). Using the intervals $[-1, 1]$ and $[1, 2]$ to test the critical numbers, we obtain Figure 13.17, which shows that

$$f'(-1) > 0, \quad f'(1) < 0, \quad f'(2) > 0.$$

Hence, there is a local maximum at $x = 0$ and a local minimum at $x = 6/5$. 

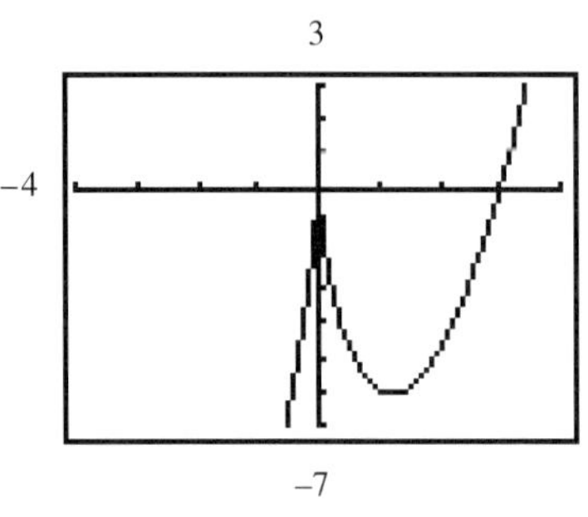

$f(x) = 3x^{5/3} - 9x^{2/3}$

FIGURE 13.16

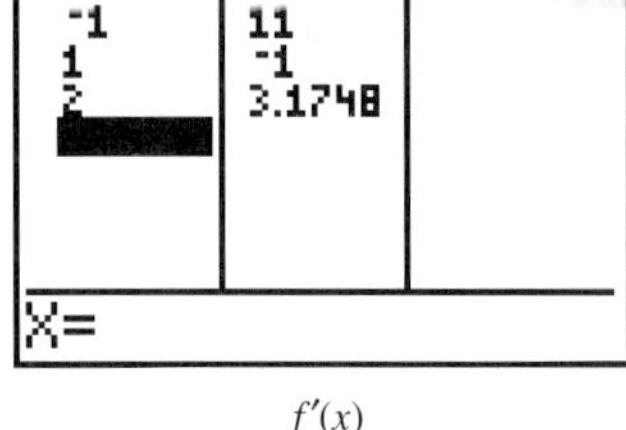

$f'(x)$

FIGURE 13.17

EXAMPLE 8 A company that makes digital alarm clocks has the following cost and revenue functions.

$$R(x) = 36x - .0015x^2 \qquad 0 \le x \le 12{,}000$$
$$C(x) = .00000034x^3 - .005x^2 + 27x + 25{,}000 \qquad 0 \le x \le 12{,}000$$

Determine when the profit function is increasing and find the maximum possible profit.

The profit function is $P(x) = R(x) - C(x)$, so

$$\begin{aligned} P(x) &= (36x - .0015x^2) - (.00000034x^3 - .005x^2 + 27x + 25{,}000) \\ &= -.00000034x^3 + .0035x^2 + 9x - 25{,}000. \end{aligned}$$

To determine the critical numbers we find $P'(x)$ and use the quadratic formula to solve $P'(x) = 0$.

$$P'(x) = -.00000102x^2 + .007x + 9 = 0$$
$$x = \frac{-.007 \pm \sqrt{(.007)^2 - 4(-.00000102)(9)}}{2(-.00000102)} \approx \begin{cases} 7969.86 \\ -1107.11 \end{cases}$$

Since $x \ge 0$ here, the only relevant critical number is 7969.86. Applying the first derivative test with $a = 0$ and $b = 10{,}000$ shows that

$$P'(0) = 9 > 0 \quad \text{and} \quad P'(10{,}000) \approx -23 < 0.$$

Therefore, $P(x)$ is increasing on the (approximate) interval (0, 7969.86), decreasing on (7969.86, 12000), and has a local maximum at approximately 7969.86. Hence maximum profit occurs when about 7970 clocks are manufactured and sold. As the graphs in Figure 13.18 show, profit increases as long as the revenue function increases faster than the cost function. ■ 9

9 Find the intervals where profit is increasing and $P(x) > 0$ if the profit function is defined as $P(x) = 1000 + 90x - x^2$.

Answer:
(0, 45)

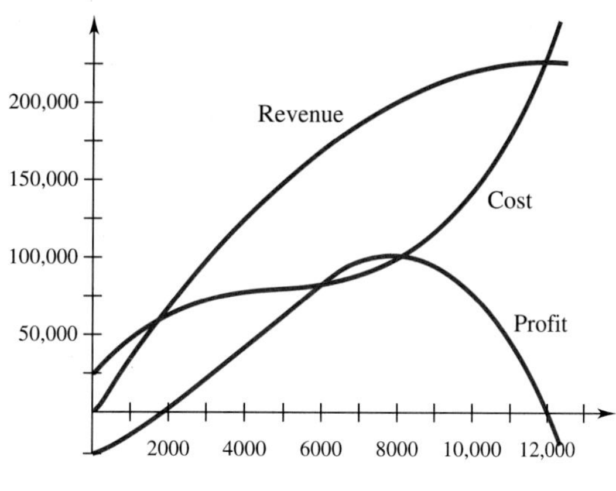

FIGURE 13.18

13.1 EXERCISES

For each function, list the intervals on which the function is increasing, the intervals on which it is decreasing, and the location of all local extrema. (See Examples 1 and 3.)

1.

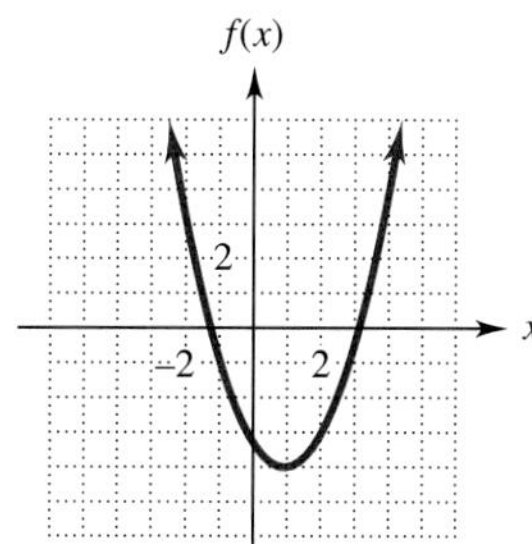

2.

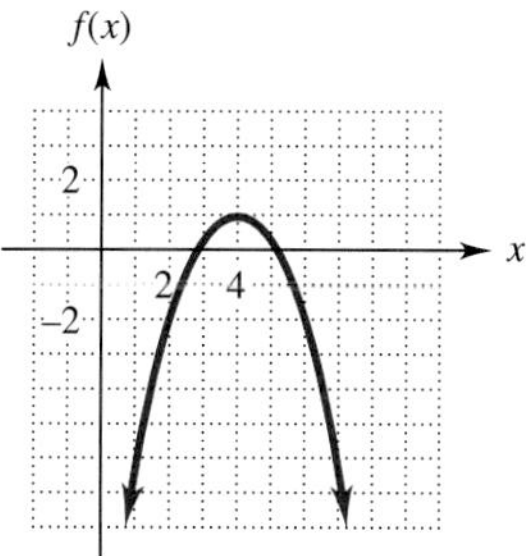

3.

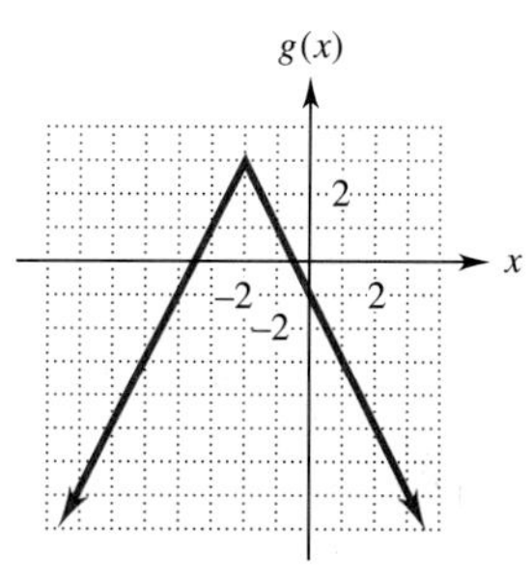

4.

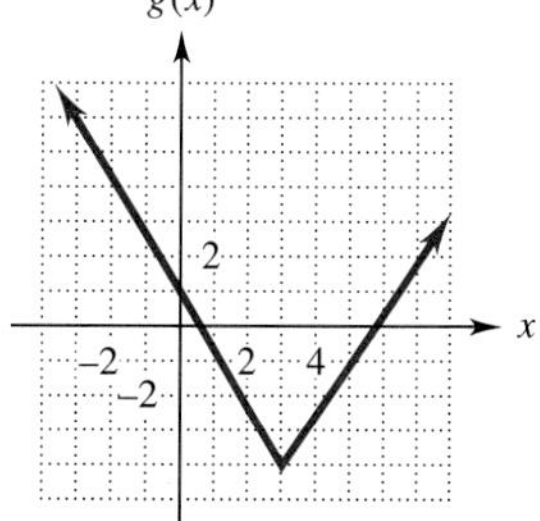

5.

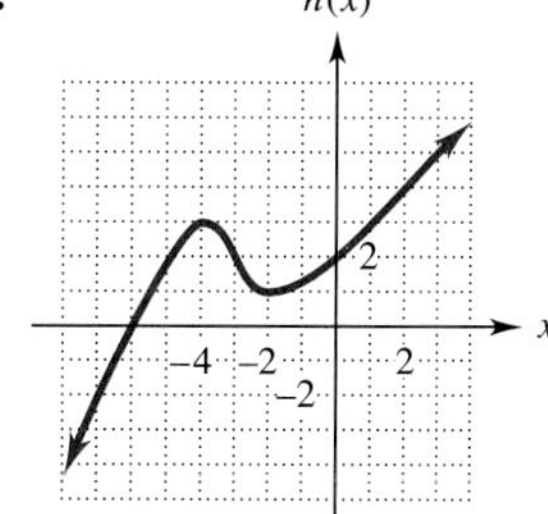

6.

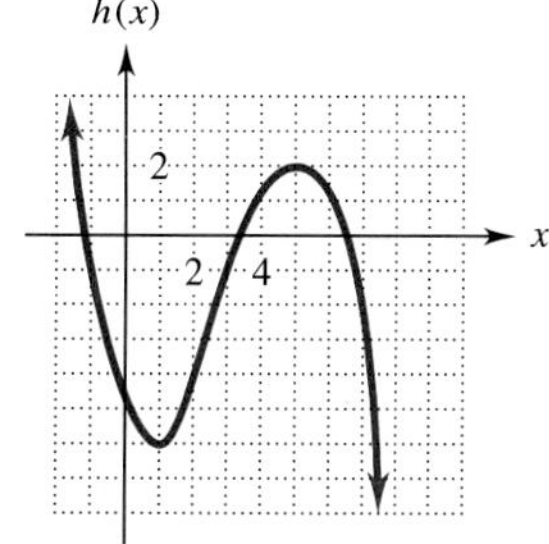

7.

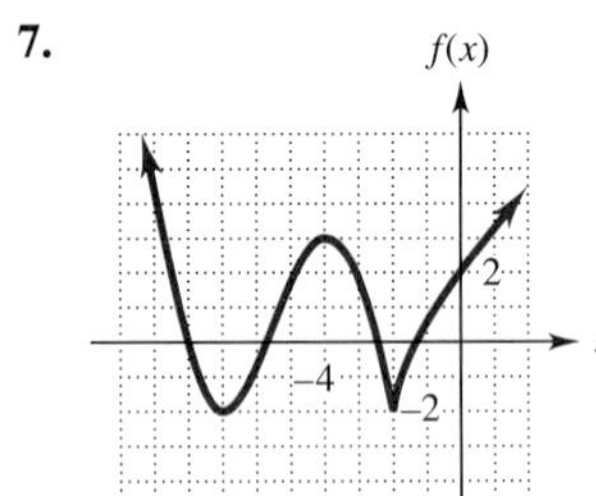

8.

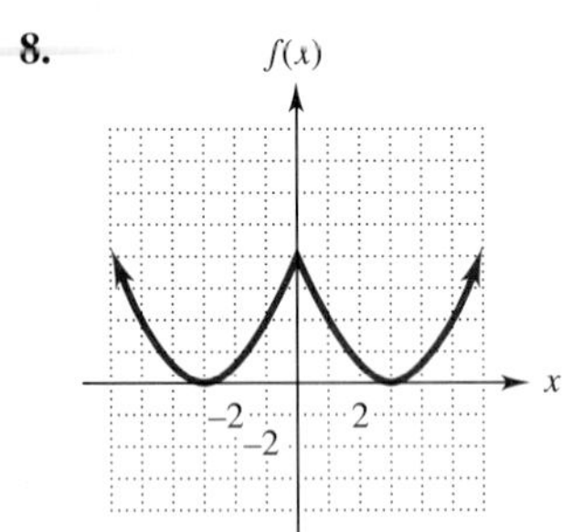

Find the intervals on which each function is increasing or decreasing. (See Example 2.)

9. $f(x) = 2x^3 - 5x^2 - 4x + 2$

10. $f(x) = 4x^3 - 9x^2 - 12x + 7$

11. $f(x) = \dfrac{x + 1}{x + 4}$

12. $f(x) = \dfrac{x^2 + 1}{x}$

13. $f(x) = \sqrt{5 - x}$

14. $f(x) = \sqrt{x^2 + 1}$

15. $f(x) = 2x^3 - 3x^2 - 12x + 2$

16. $f(x) = 4x^3 - 15x^2 - 72x + 5$

The graph of the derivative function f' is given; list the critical numbers of the function f.

17.

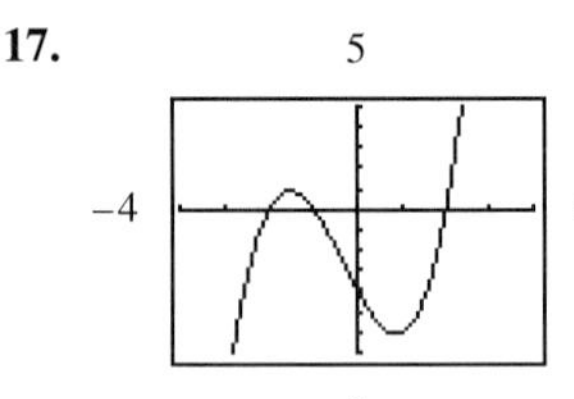

18.

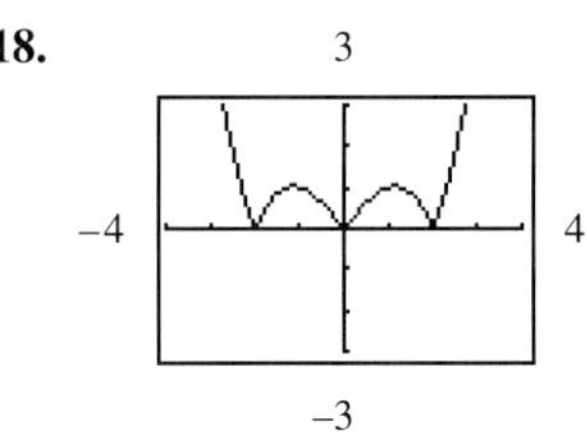

Find each critical number of the function and determine graphically whether there is a local extremum there. (See Example 4.)

19. $f(x) = x^3 - 3x^2 + 1$

20. $f(x) = x^3 - x^2 - 5x + 1$

21. $f(x) = x^3 + 6x^2 + 9x + 2$

22. $f(x) = x^3 + 3x^2 - 24x + 2$

23. $f(x) = -\dfrac{4}{3}x^3 - \dfrac{21}{2}x^2 - 5x + 8$

24. $f(x) = -\dfrac{2}{3}x^3 - \dfrac{1}{2}x^2 + 3x - 4$

25. $f(x) = \dfrac{2}{3}x^3 - x^2 - 12x + 2$

26. $f(x) = \dfrac{4}{3}x^3 - 10x^2 + 24x - 1$

27. $f(x) = x^5 - 20x^2 + 3$

28. $f(x) = 3x^3 - 18.5x^2 - 4.5x - 45$

Use the first derivative test to determine the location of each local extremum and the value of the function at this extremum. Be alert for hidden behavior that may not be visible in some viewing windows. (See Examples 5–7.)

29. $f(x) = x^{11/5} - x^{6/5} + 1$

30. $f(x) = (7 - 2x)^{2/3} - 2$

31. $f(x) = -(3 - 4x)^{2/5} + 4$

32. $f(x) = .1x^3 - .1x^2 - .005x + 1$

33. $f(x) = 2x^3 - .33x^2 - .006x + 5$

34. $f(x) = x^2 + \dfrac{1}{x}$

35. $f(x) = \dfrac{x^2}{x^2 + 1}$

36. $f(x) = \dfrac{x^2 - 2x + 1}{x - 3}$

37. $f(x) = -xe^x$

38. $f(x) = xe^{-x}$

39. $f(x) = x \cdot \ln|x|$

40. $f(x) = x - \ln|x|$

41. $f(x) = xe^{3x} - 2$

42. $f(x) = x^3e^{4x} + 1$

Use the maximum/minimum finder on a calculator to determine the approximate location of all local extrema of these functions.

43. $f(x) = .1x^4 - x^3 - 12x^2 + 99x - 10$

44. $f(x) = x^5 - 12x^4 - x^3 + 232x^2 + 260x - 600$

45. $f(x) = .01x^5 + x^4 - x^3 - 6x^2 + 5x + 4$

46. $f(x) = .1x^5 + 3x^4 - 4x^3 - 11x^2 + 3x + 2$

47. Let f be a continuous function whose graph has no horizontal segments. If c and d are the only critical numbers of f, explain why the graph of f must always rise or always fall between $x = c$ and $x = d$.

48. Let f be a continuous function that has only one critical number c. If f has a local minimum at $x = c$, explain why $f(c) \leq f(x)$ for all x in the domain of f.

Work the following exercises. (See Example 8.)

49. **Management** The total profit $P(x)$ (in thousands of dollars) from the sale of x thousand units of a new prescription drug is given by

$$P(x) = -x^3 + 3x^2 + 72x \quad (0 \leq x \leq 10).$$

(a) Find the number of units that should be sold in order to maximize the total profit.
(b) What is the maximum profit?

50. **Social Science** The standard normal probability function is used to describe many different populations. Its graph is the well-known normal curve. This function is defined by

$$f(x) = \frac{1}{\sqrt{2\pi}}e^{-x^2/2}.$$

Give the intervals where the function is increasing and decreasing.

51. **Natural Science** The graph shows the amount of air pollution removed by trees in the Chicago urban region for each month of the year.* From the graph we see that the ozone level increases up to June, and then abruptly decreases.

(a) At what points are the derivatives of the functions whose graphs are shown undefined?
(b) Look at the graph for particulates. Where is the function increasing? decreasing? constant?
(c) On what intervals do all four lower graphs indicate the corresponding functions are constant? Why do you think the functions are constant on those intervals?

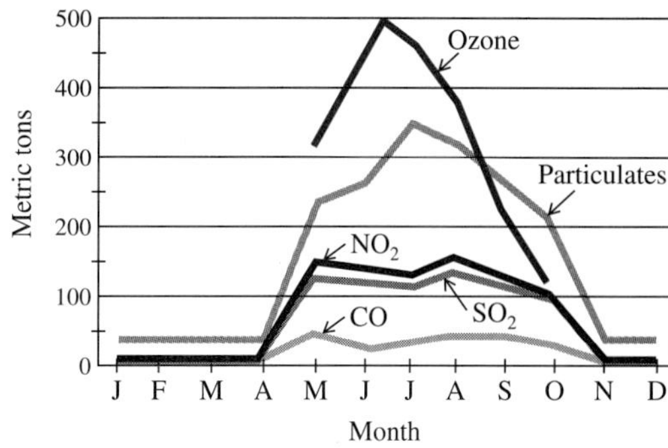

52. **Management** A county realty group estimates that the number of housing starts per year over the next 3 years will be

$$H(r) = \frac{300}{1 + .03r^2},$$

where r is the mortgage rate (in percent).
(a) Where is $H(r)$ increasing?
(b) Where is $H(r)$ decreasing?

53. **Management** A manufacturer sells cutlery with the following cost and revenue functions, where x is the number of sets sold.

$$C(x) = 4000 + 4x, \qquad 0 \leq x \leq 17{,}000$$
$$R(x) = 20x - x^2/1000, \quad 0 \leq x \leq 17{,}000$$

Determine the intervals on which the profit function is increasing.

54. **Management** A manufacturer of compact disc players has determined that the profit $P(x)$ (in thousands of dollars) is related to the quantity x of players produced (in hundreds) per month by

$$P(x) = \frac{1}{3}x^3 - \frac{7}{2}x^2 + 10x - 2,$$

as long as the number of units produced is fewer than 800 per month.
(a) At what production levels is the profit increasing?
(b) At what levels is it decreasing?

55. **Natural Science** During a four-week long flu epidemic, the number of people $P(t)$ infected t days after the epidemic begins is approximated by

$$P(t) = t^3 - 60t^2 + 900t + 20 \quad (0 \leq t \leq 28).$$

When will the number of people infected start to decline?

56. **Natural Science** The function

$$A(x) = -.15x^3 + 1.058x$$

approximates the alcohol concentration (in tenths of a percent) in an average person's bloodstream x hours after

(exercise continues)

*National Arbor Day Foundation, 100 Arbor Ave., Nebraska City, NE 68410 ad in *Chicago Tribune*, Sun. 2/4/96. Sect. 2, p. 11.

drinking 8 ounces of 100-proof whiskey. The function applies only for the interval [0, 8].

(a) On what time intervals is the alcohol concentration increasing?

(b) On what intervals is it decreasing?

57. Natural Science The percent of concentration of a drug in the bloodstream x hours after the drug is administered is given by

$$K(x) = \frac{4x}{3x^2 + 27}.$$

(a) On what time intervals is the concentration of the drug increasing?

(b) On what intervals is it decreasing?

58. Natural Science Suppose a certain drug is administered to a patient, with the percent of concentration of the drug in the bloodstream t hours later given by

$$k(t) = \frac{5t}{t^2 + 1}.$$

(a) On what time intervals is the concentration of the drug increasing?

(b) On what intervals is it decreasing?

59. Management The figure shows the average monthly transactions (in thousands) per ATM in the U.S. for the years 1985 through 1995.* Consider the closed interval [1985, 1995]. Give all approximate local maxima and minima of this function and when they occur on the interval.

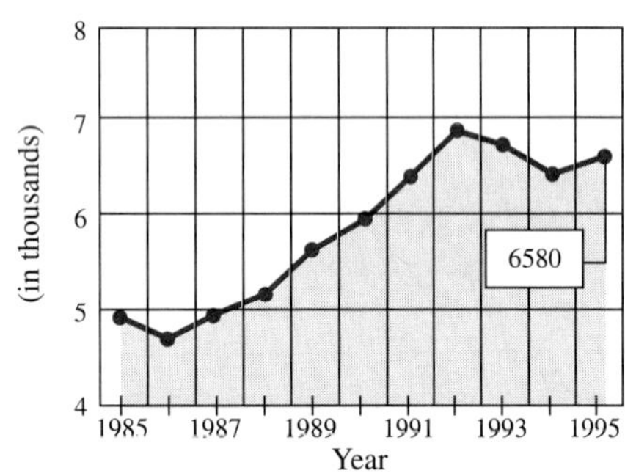

Sources: Bank Network News, Synergistics Research Corp., Electronic Data Systems Corp., Cash Station Inc.

60. Management The figure in the next column shows the losses due to fraud for each $100 charged on Mastercard International cards for the years 1982 through 1995.† Consider the closed interval [1982, 1995]. Give all local maxima and minima on the interval and the year when they occur.

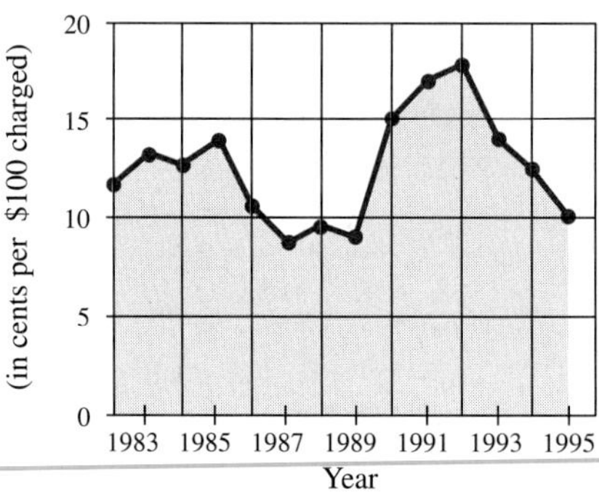

Source: Mastercard International.

61. Social Science The graph shows the stockpile of nuclear weapons held by the United States and by the Soviet Union and its successor states from 1945 to 1993.*

(a) On what intervals was the stockpile of United States weapons increasing?

(b) On what intervals was the stockpile of Soviet weapons increasing?

(c) In what years was the United States stockpile of weapons at a local maximum?

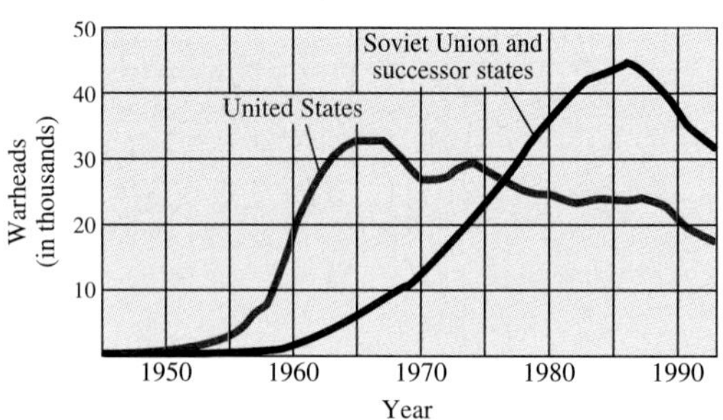

62. Social Science The number of murders in Chicago (in hundreds) from 1986 through 1995 is approximated by $f(x) = -.028x^3 + .413x^2 - 1.39x + 8.26$, where x corresponds to the number of years after 1985—that is, 1986 corresponds to $x = 1$, 1987 corresponds to $x = 2$, and so on.†

(a) In what year did a local maximum or a local minimum number of murders occur? How many murders occurred in those years?

(b) In what year did the rate of increase in murders start to slow down?

*From "Telling Future of ATMs," *Chicago Tribune,* December 18, 1995, A1, Sec. 4.

†From "Stop, Thief! Return My Name." *The New York Times,* Sunday, January 28, 1996, Section 3.

**The New York Times,* Sept. 26, 1993.

†*Chicago Tribune,* Sunday, Dec. 31, 1995, Section 4, page 3.

63. **Management** Suppose that the cost function for a product is given by $C(x) = .002x^3 - 9x + 4000$. Find the production level (i.e., value of x) that will produce the minimum average cost per unit $\overline{C}(x)$.

64. **Management** A company has found through experience that increasing its advertising also increases its sales, up to a point. The company believes that the mathematical model connecting profit in hundreds of dollars, $P(x)$, and expenditures on advertising in thousands of dollars, x, is

$$P(x) = 80 + 108x - x^3, \quad 0 \le x \le 10.$$

(a) Find the expenditure on advertising that leads to maximum profit.
(b) Find the maximum profit.

65. **Management** The total profit $P(x)$ (in thousands of dollars) from the sale of x hundred thousands of automobile tires is approximated by

$$P(x) = -x^3 + 9x^2 + 120x - 400, \quad 3 \le x \le 15.$$

Find the number of hundred thousands of tires that must be sold to maximize profit. Find the maximum profit.

66. **Natural Science** A marshy region used for agricultural drainage has become contaminated with selenium. It has been determined that flushing the area with clean water will reduce the selenium for a while, but it will then begin to build up again. A biologist has found that the percent of selenium in the soil x months after the flushing begins is given by

$$f(x) = \frac{x^2 + 36}{2x}, \quad 1 \le x \le 12.$$

When will the selenium be reduced to a minimum? What is the minimum percent?

67. **Natural Science** The number of salmon swimming upstream to spawn is approximated by

$$S(x) = -x^3 + 3x^2 + 400x + 5000, \quad 6 \le x \le 20,$$

where x represents the temperature of the water in degrees Celsius. Find the water temperature that produces the maximum number of salmon swimming upstream.

68. **Natural Science** In the summer the activity level of a certain type of lizard varies according to the time of day. A biologist has determined that the activity level is given by the function

$$a(t) = .008t^3 - .27t^2 + 2.02t + 7,$$

where t is the number of hours after 12 noon and $0 \le t \le 24$. When is the activity level highest? When is it lowest?

69. **Social Science** Social psychologists have found that as the discrepancy between the views of a speaker and those of an audience increases, the attitude change in the audience also increases to a point, but decreases when the discrepancy becomes too large, particularly if the communicator is viewed by the audience as having low credibility.* Suppose that the degree of change can be approximated by the function

$$D(x) = -x^4 + 8x^3 + 80x^2, \quad 0 \le x \le 13,$$

where x is the discrepancy between the views of the speaker and those of the audience, as measured by scores on a questionnaire. Find the amount of discrepancy the speaker should aim for to maximize the attitude change in the audience.

70. **Natural Science** The microbe concentration, $B(x)$, in appropriate units, of Lake Tom depends approximately on the oxygen concentration, x, again in appropriate units, according to the function

$$B(x) = x^3 - 7x^2 - 160x + 1800, \quad 0 \le x \le 20.$$

(a) Find the oxygen concentration that will lead to the minimum microbe concentration.
(b) What is the minimum concentration?

*See Eagly, A. H., and K. Telaak, "Width of the Latitude of Acceptance as a Determinant of Attitude Change" in *Journal of Personality and Social Psychology*, vol. 23, 1972, pp. 388–97.

13.2 THE SECOND DERIVATIVE

A salesman says he invested \$1200 in a certain mutual fund when it began two years ago and his investment is now worth \$1690, a two-year increase of 41%. Over the past two years he says the price of a share of this fund (in dollars) has been given by the function

$$P(t) = 12 + t^{1/2},$$

where t is the number of months since the fund began. Since you know some calculus, he points out that the derivative of this function,

$$P'(t) = \frac{1}{2}t^{-1/2} = \frac{1}{2\sqrt{t}},$$

is always positive (because $\sqrt{t}$ is positive for $t > 0$), so the price of a share is always increasing. If you take his advice and invest, will you, too, make a huge profit?

Although the past performance of a mutual fund is not necessarily a good guide to its future price, let us assume that the salesman is right and the price function remains valid for the next two years. Now it is true that the positive derivative means the function is increasing. The catch is in *how fast* it is increasing. For example, when $t = 1$, $P'(1) = 1/2$, meaning that the price per share is increasing at a rate of 1/2 dollar (50¢) per month. At 9 months, $P'(9) = 1/6$, or about 17¢ per month. When you buy at $t = 24$ months, the price is increasing at $P'(24) \approx 10$¢ per month and the *rate* of increase appears to be steadily decreasing.

The rate of increase of the derivative function $P'(t)$ is given by *its* derivative, which is denoted $P''(t)$. Since $P'(t) = (1/2)t^{-1/2}$,

$$P''(t) = -\frac{1}{4}t^{-3/2} = \frac{-1}{4\sqrt{t^3}}.$$

$P''(t)$ is negative whenever t is positive; therefore, the *rate* at which the price increases is always decreasing for $t > 0$. So the price of a share will continue to grow, but at a smaller and smaller rate. For instance, at $t = 24$, when you would buy, the price would be \$16.90 per share. Two years later ($t = 48$), the price would be \$18.93, a two-year increase of only 12%—hardly the "huge profit" the salesman predicts. The only investors to make huge profits on this fund would be those who got in early, when the rate of increase was much greater.

This example shows that it is important to know not only whether a function is increasing or decreasing, but also the rate at which this is occurring. As we have seen this rate is given by the derivative of the derivative of the original function. In order to deal with such situations we need some additional terminology and notation.

HIGHER DERIVATIVES If a function f has a derivative f', then the derivative of f', if it exists, is the **second derivative** of f, written $f''(x)$. The derivative of $f''(x)$, if it exists, is called the **third derivative** of f, and so on. By continuing this process, we can find **fourth derivatives** and other higher derivatives. For example, if $f(x) = x^4 + 2x^3 + 3x^2 - 5x + 7$, then

$$f'(x) = 4x^3 + 6x^2 + 6x - 5, \qquad \text{First derivative of } f$$

$$f''(x) = 12x^2 + 12x + 6, \qquad \text{Second derivative of } f$$

$$f'''(x) = 24x + 12, \qquad \text{Third derivative of } f$$

and

$$f^{(4)}(x) = 24. \qquad \text{Fourth derivative of } f$$

> The second derivative of $y = f(x)$ can be written with any of the following notations:
>
> $$f''(x),\quad y'',\quad \frac{d^2y}{dx^2},\quad \text{or}\quad D_x^2[f(x)].$$
>
> The third derivative can be written in a similar way. For $n \geq 4$, the nth derivative is written $f^{(n)}(x)$.

1 Let $f(x) = 4x^3 - 12x^2 + x - 1$. Find

(a) $f''(0)$;

(b) $f''(4)$;

(c) $f''(-2)$.

Answers:

(a) -24

(b) 72

(c) -72

EXAMPLE 1 Let $f(x) = x^3 + 6x^2 - 9x + 8$. Find the following.

(a) $f''(0)$

Here $f'(x) = 3x^2 + 12x - 9$, so that $f''(x) = 6x + 12$. Then

$$f''(0) = 6(0) + 12 = 12.$$

(b) $f''(-3) = 6(-3) + 12 = -6$ ■ 1

2 Find the second derivatives of the following.

(a) $y = -9x^3 + 8x^2 + 11x - 6$

(b) $y = -2x^4 + 6x^2$

(c) $y = \dfrac{x + 2}{5x - 1}$

(d) $y = e^x + \ln x$

Answers:

(a) $y'' = -54x + 16$

(b) $y'' = -24x^2 + 12$

(c) $y'' = \dfrac{110}{(5x - 1)^3}$

(d) $y'' = e^x - \dfrac{1}{x^2}$

EXAMPLE 2 Find the second derivative of the following functions.

(a) $y = 8x^3 - 9x^2 + 6x + 4$

Here $y' = 24x^2 - 18x + 6$. The second derivative is the derivative of y', or

$$y'' = 48x - 18.$$

(b) $y = \dfrac{4x + 2}{3x - 1}$

Use the quotient rule to find y'.

$$y' = \frac{(3x - 1)(4) - (4x + 2)(3)}{(3x - 1)^2} = \frac{12x - 4 - 12x - 6}{(3x - 1)^2} = \frac{-10}{(3x - 1)^2}$$

Use the quotient rule again to find y''.

$$y'' = \frac{(3x - 1)^2(0) - (-10)(2)(3x - 1)(3)}{[(3x - 1)^2]^2}$$

$$= \frac{60(3x - 1)}{(3x - 1)^4} = \frac{60}{(3x - 1)^3}$$

(c) $y = xe^x$

Using the product rule gives

$$y' = x \cdot e^x + e^x \cdot 1 = xe^x + e^x.$$

Differentiate this result to get y''.

$$y'' = (xe^x + e^x) + e^x = xe^x + 2e^x = (x + 2)e^x$$ ■ 2

In the previous chapter we saw that the first derivative of a function represents the rate of change of the function. The second derivative, then, represents the rate of change of the first derivative. This fact has a variety of applications. For instance, in the introduction to this section we saw that a negative second derivative showed that the value of a mutual fund was increasing at a slower and slower rate.

The second derivative also plays a role in the physics of a moving particle. If a function describes the position of a moving object (along a straight line) at time t, then the first derivative gives the velocity of the object. That is, if $y = s(t)$ describes the position (along a straight line) of the object at time t, then $v(t) = s'(t)$ gives the velocity at time t.

The rate of change of velocity is called **acceleration.** Since the second derivative gives the rate of change of the first derivative, the acceleration is the derivative of the velocity. Thus, if $a(t)$ represents the acceleration at time t, then

$$\boldsymbol{a(t) = \frac{d}{dt}v(t) = s''(t).}$$

EXAMPLE 3 Suppose that an object is moving along a straight line, with its position in feet at time t in seconds given by

$$s(t) = t^3 - 2t^2 - 7t + 9.$$

Find the following.

(a) The velocity at any time t
The velocity is given by

$$v(t) = s'(t) = 3t^2 - 4t - 7.$$

(b) The acceleration at any time t
Acceleration is given by

$$a(t) = v'(t) = s''(t) = 6t - 4.$$

(c) The object stops when velocity is zero. For $t \geq 0$, when does that occur?
Set $v(t) = 0$.

$$3t^2 - 4t - 7 = 0$$
$$(3t - 7)(t + 1) = 0$$
$$3t - 7 = 0 \quad \text{or} \quad t + 1 = 0$$
$$t = \frac{7}{3} \qquad\qquad t = -1$$

Since we want $t \geq 0$, only $t = 7/3$ is acceptable here. The object will stop at 7/3 seconds. ■ 3

3 Rework Example 3 if $s(t) = t^4 - t^3 + 10$.

Answers:
(a) $v(t) = 4t^3 - 3t^2$
(b) $a(t) = 12t^2 - 6t$
(c) At 0 and 3/4 second

CONCAVITY We shall now see how the second derivative provides information about how the graph of the function "bends," which is often hard to see on a calculator or computer screen. A graph is **concave upward** on an interval if it bends upward over the interval and **concave downward** if it bends downward, as shown in Figure 13.19. The graph is concave downward on the interval (a, b) and concave upward on the interval (b, c).* A point on the graph where the concavity changes (such as the point where $x = b$ in Figure 13.19) is called a **point of inflection.**

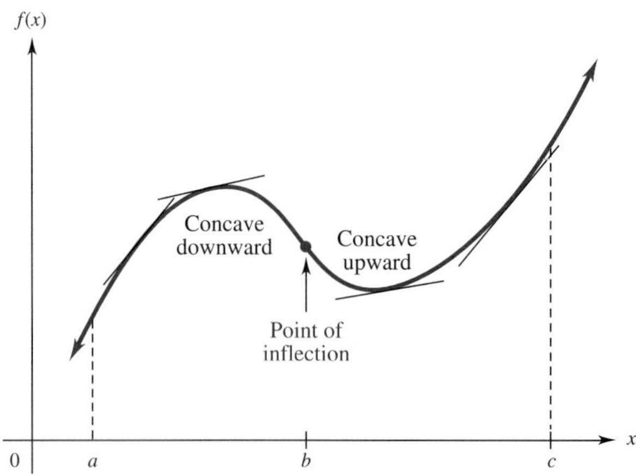

FIGURE 13.19

*Figure 13.19 also illustrates the formal definition of concavity: a function is *concave downward* on an interval if its graph lies below the tangent line at each point in the interval and *concave upward* if its graph is above the tangent line at each point in the interval.

A function that is increasing on an interval may have either kind of concavity; the same is true for a decreasing function. Some of the possibilities are illustrated in Figure 13.20.

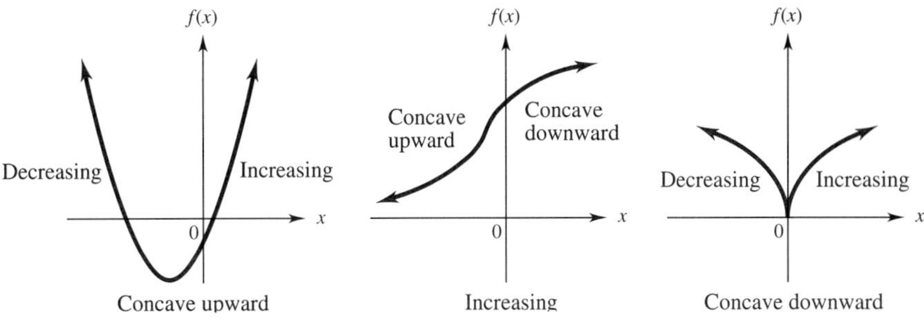

FIGURE 13.20

Next we examine the relationship between the second derivative of a function f and the concavity of the graph of f. We have seen that when the derivative of any function is positive, then that function is increasing. Consequently, if the *second* derivative of f (the derivative of the first derivative) is positive, then the *first* derivative of f is increasing. Since the first derivative gives the slope of the tangent line to the graph of f at each point, the fact that the first derivative is increasing means that the tangent line slopes are increasing as you move from left to right along the graph of f, as illustrated in Figure 13.21.

In Figure 13.21(a), the slopes of the tangent lines increase from negative at the left, to 0 in the center, to positive at the right. In Figure 13.21(b), the slopes are all positive, but increasing as the tangent lines get steeper. Note that both graphs in Figure 13.21 are *concave upward.*

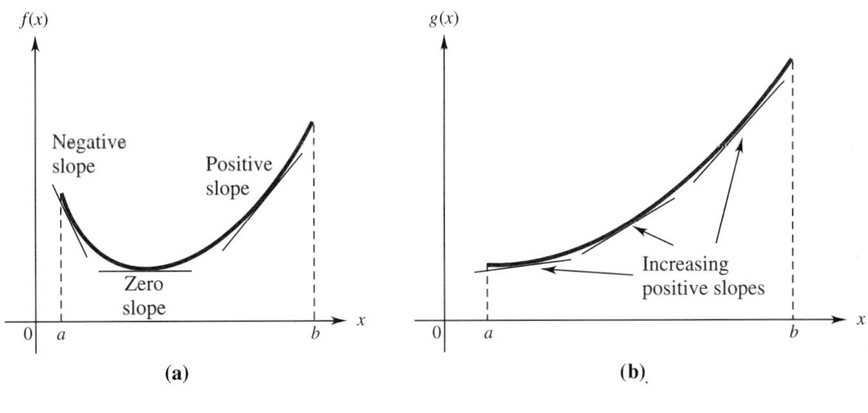

FIGURE 13.21

Similarly, when the second derivative is negative, then the first derivative (slope of the tangent line) is decreasing, as illustrated in Figure 13.22 on the next page. In Figure 13.22(a), the tangent line slopes decrease from positive, to 0, to negative.

In Figure 13.22(b), the slopes get more and more negative as the tangent lines drop downward more steeply. Note that both graphs are *concave downward.*

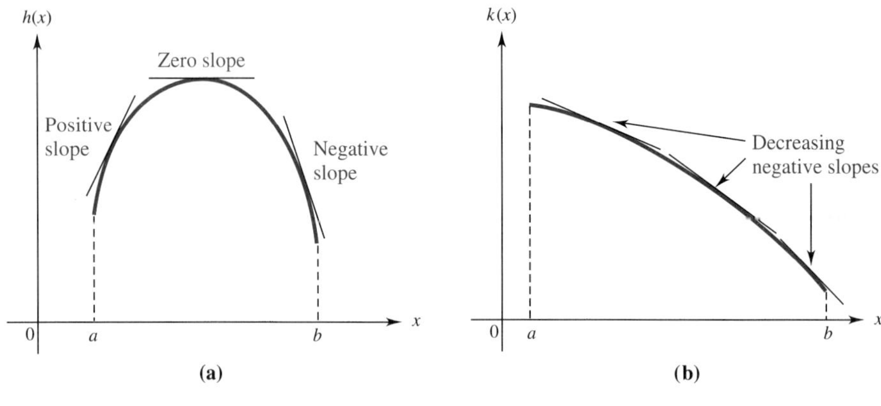

FIGURE 13.22

The preceding discussion suggests the following result.

CONCAVITY TEST

Let f be a function whose first and second derivatives exist at all points in the interval (a, b).

1. If $f''(x) > 0$ for all x in (a, b), then f is concave upward on (a, b).
2. If $f''(x) < 0$ for all x in (a, b), then f is concave downward on (a, b).

EXAMPLE 4 Find the intervals over which the function is concave upward or downward, and find any points of inflection.

(a) $f(x) = .5x^3 - 2x^2 + 5x + 1$

The graph of f in the standard window (Figure 13.23) suggests that f is concave upward to the right of the y-axis, but the concavity to the left of the y-axis isn't clear. Even in a window where the concavity is visible, the location of the point of inflection is not clear (try it!). So we use the test in the box above. The first derivative is $f'(x) = 1.5x^2 - 4x + 5$ and the second derivative is $f''(x) = 3x - 4$. The function is concave upward when $f''(x) > 0$, that is, when

$$3x - 4 > 0$$
$$3x > 4$$
$$x > 4/3.$$

Similarly, f is concave downward when $3x - 4 < 0$, that is, when $x < 4/3$. Therefore, f is concave downward on $(-\infty, 4/3)$ and concave upward on $(4/3, \infty)$, with a point of inflection when $x = 4/3$.

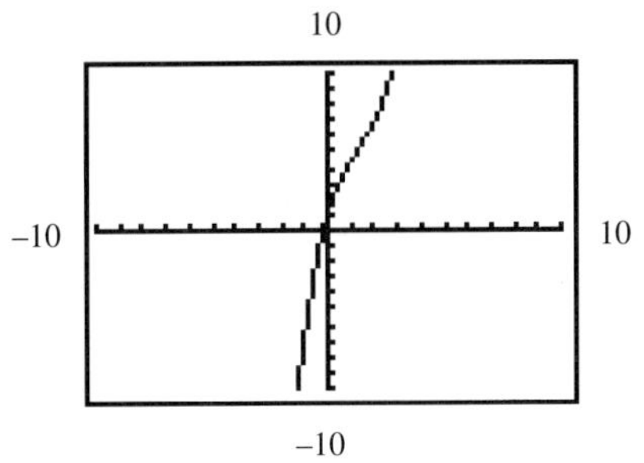

10

−10 10

−10

FIGURE 13.23

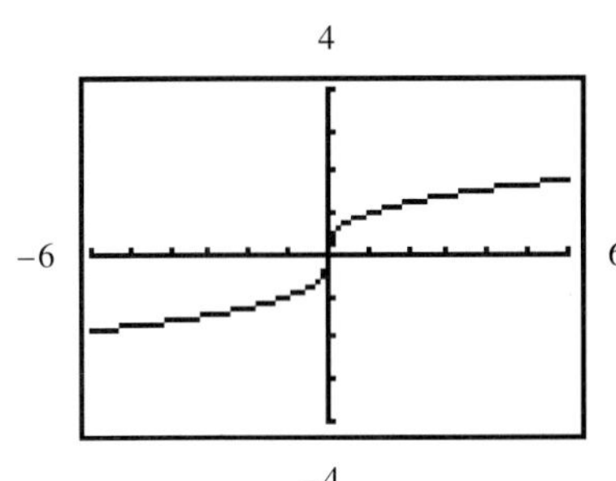

FIGURE 13.24

(b) $g(x) = x^{1/3}$

The graph of g in Figure 13.24 suggests that g is concave upward when $x < 0$ and concave downward when $x > 0$. We can confirm this conclusion algebraically by noting that $g'(x) = \frac{1}{3}x^{-2/3}$ and

$$g''(x) = -\frac{2}{9}x^{-5/3} = \frac{-2}{9\sqrt[3]{x^5}}.$$

When $x < 0$, then the denominator of $g''(x)$ is negative (why?), so $g''(x)$ is positive and g is concave upward on $(-\infty, 0)$. When $x > 0$, then the denominator of $g''(x)$ is positive, so $g''(x)$ is negative and g is concave downward on $(0, \infty)$. The graph changes concavity at $(0, 0)$, which is a point of inflection. ■

In Example 4(a) the point of inflection on the graph of f occurs at $x = 4/3$, the number at which the second derivative $f''(x) = 3x - 4$ is 0. In Example 4(b), the point of inflection occurs when $x = 0$, the number at which the second derivative $g''(x) = \frac{-2}{9\sqrt[3]{x^5}}$ is not defined. These facts suggest the following result.

4 Find the intervals where the following are concave upward. Identify any inflection points.

(a) $f(x) = 6x^3 - 24x^2 + 9x - 3$

(b) $f(x) = 2x^2 - 4x + 8$

Answers:

(a) Concave upward on $(4/3, \infty)$; point of inflection is $(4/3, -175/9)$.

(b) $f''(x) = 4$, which is always positive; function is always concave upward, no inflection point.

> If a function f has a point of inflection at $x = c$, then $f''(c) = 0$ or $f''(c)$ does not exist.

CAUTION The reverse of this fact is not always true. The second derivative may be 0 at a point that is not a point of inflection. For an example, if $f(x) = x^4$, then $f'(x) = 4x^3$ and $f''(x) = 12x^2$. Hence $f''(x) = 0$ when $x = 0$. However, the graph of $f(x)$ in Figure 13.25 on the next page is always concave upward, so it has no point of inflection at $x = 0$ (or anywhere else). ◆ 4

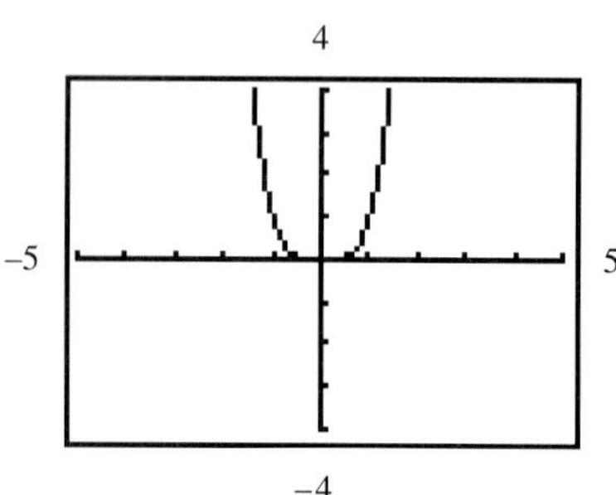

FIGURE 13.25

The **law of diminishing returns** in economics is related to the idea of concavity. The graph of the function f in Figure 13.26 shows the output y from a given input x. For instance, the input might be advertising costs and the output the corresponding revenue from sales.

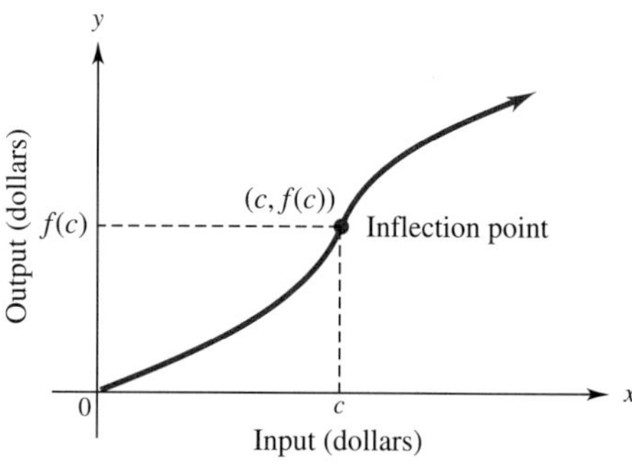

FIGURE 13.26

The graph in Figure 13.26 shows an inflection point at $(c, f(c))$. For $x < c$, the graph is concave upward, so the rate of change of the slope is increasing. This indicates that the output y is increasing at a faster rate with each additional dollar spent. When $x > c$, however, the graph is concave downward, the rate of change of the slope is decreasing, and the increase in y is smaller with each additional dollar spent. Thus, further input beyond c dollars produces diminishing returns. Thc point of inflection at $(c, f(c))$ is called the **point of diminishing returns.** Any investment beyond the value c is not considered a good use of capital.

EXAMPLE 5 The revenue $R(x)$ generated from sales of a certain product is related to the amount x spent on advertising by the function

$$R(x) = \frac{2x^2}{375} - \frac{x^3}{150{,}000} \qquad 0 \leq x \leq 500,$$

where x and $R(x)$ are in thousands of dollars. Is there a point of diminishing returns for this function? If so, what is it?

The graph of R in Figure 13.27 appears to change from concave upward to concave downward somewhere between $x = 200$ and $x = 400$. So there is a point of inflection (that is, a point of diminishing returns). We can locate it exactly as follows. Find $R'(x)$ and $R''(x)$.

$$R'(x) = \frac{4x}{375} - \frac{3x^2}{150{,}000} = \frac{4x}{375} - \frac{x^2}{50{,}000}$$

$$R''(x) = \frac{4}{375} - \frac{x}{25{,}000}$$

Set $R''(x) = 0$ and solve for x.

$$\frac{4}{375} - \frac{x}{25{,}000} = 0$$

$$\frac{4}{375} = \frac{x}{25{,}000}$$

$$375x = 4 \cdot 25{,}000$$

$$x = \frac{100{,}000}{375}$$

$$= \frac{800}{3}$$

$$\approx 266.667$$

5 In Example 5,

$$R(x) = \frac{x^4}{20{,}000} - \frac{x^5}{5{,}000{,}000}$$

$$(0 \le x \le 200)$$

for another product. What is the point of diminishing returns?

Answer:
(150, 10125)

The graph of R'' in Figure 13.28 is above the x-axis to the left of $x = 800/3$ and below it to the right, which means that $R''(x)$ changes from positive to negative there. So there is a point of inflection at $x = 800/3 \approx 266.667$, where the graph changes from concave upward to concave downward. This is the point of diminishing returns. Any investment beyond \$266,667 will not pay off. ■ 5

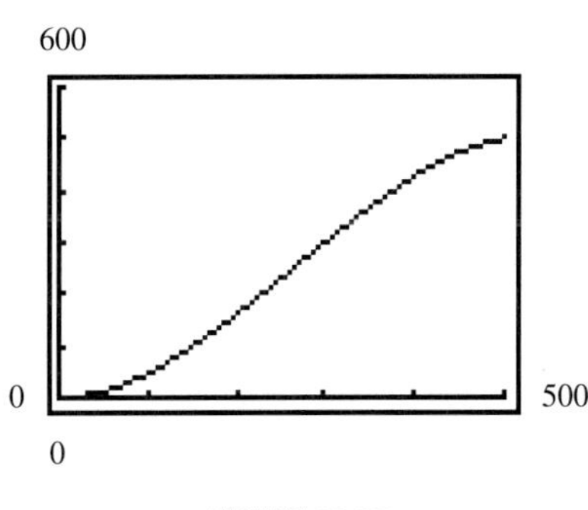

FIGURE 13.27

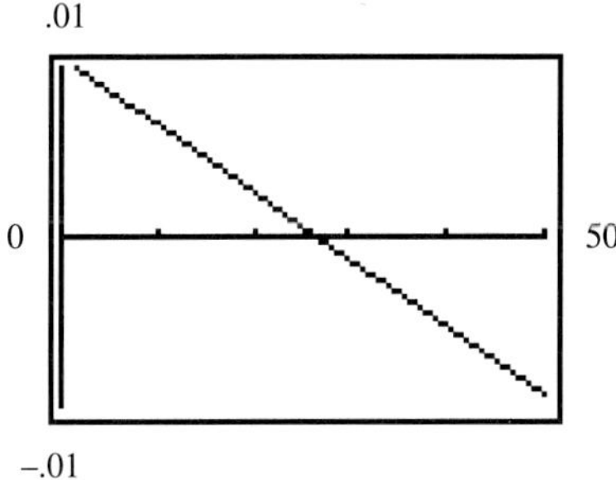

FIGURE 13.28

MAXIMA AND MINIMA If a function f has a local maximum at c and $f'(c)$ is defined, then the graph of f is necessarily concave downward near $x = c$. Similarly, if f has a local minimum at d and $f'(d)$ exists, then the graph is concave upward near $x = d$, as shown in Figure 13.29 on the next page.

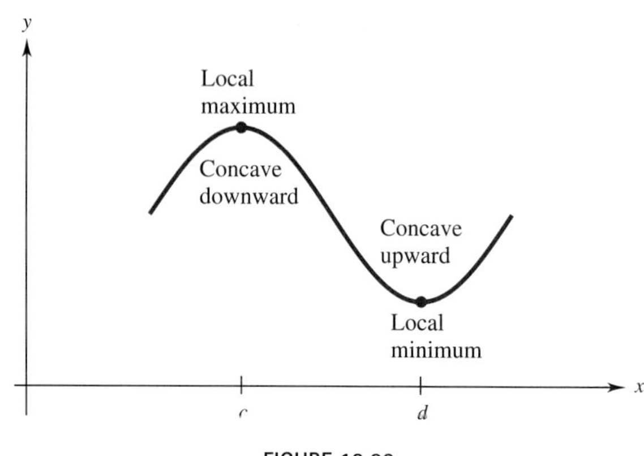

FIGURE 13.29

These facts should make the following result plausible.

THE SECOND DERIVATIVE TEST

Let c be a critical number of the function f such that $f'(c) = 0$ and $f''(x)$ exists for all x in some open interval containing c.

1. If $f''(c) > 0$, then f has a local minimum at c.
2. If $f''(c) < 0$, then f has a local maximum at c.
3. If $f''(c) = 0$, then this test gives no information; use the first derivative test.

EXAMPLE 6 Find all local extrema for

$$f(x) = 4x^3 + 7x^2 - 10x + 8.$$

First, find the critical points. Here $f'(x) = 12x^2 + 14x - 10$. Solve the equation $f'(x) = 0$.

$$12x^2 + 14x - 10 = 0$$
$$2(6x^2 + 7x - 5) = 0$$
$$2(3x + 5)(2x - 1) = 0$$
$$3x + 5 = 0 \quad \text{or} \quad 2x - 1 = 0$$
$$3x = -5 \qquad 2x = 1$$
$$x = -\frac{5}{3} \qquad x = \frac{1}{2}$$

Now use the second derivative test. The second derivative is $f''(x) = 24x + 14$. The critical points are $-5/3$ and $1/2$. Since

$$f''\left(-\frac{5}{3}\right) = 24\left(-\frac{5}{3}\right) + 14 = -40 + 14 = -26 < 0,$$

$-5/3$ leads to a local maximum of $f(-5/3) = 691/27 \approx 25.593$. Also,

$$f''\left(\frac{1}{2}\right) = 24\left(\frac{1}{2}\right) + 14 = 12 + 14 = 26 > 0,$$

so $1/2$ gives a local minimum of $f(1/2) = 21/4 = 5.25$. ■ 6

6 Find all local maxima and local minima for the following functions. Use the second derivative test.

(a) $f(x) = 6x^2 + 12x + 1$

(b) $f(x) = x^3 - 3x^2 - 9x + 8$

Answers:

(a) Local minimum of -5 at $x = -1$

(b) Local maximum of 13 at $x = -1$; local minimum of -19 at $x = 3$

The second derivative test works only for those critical points c that make $f'(c) = 0$. This test does not work for those critical points c for which $f'(c)$ does not exist (since $f''(c)$ would not exist either). Also, the second derivative test does not work for critical points c that make $f''(c) = 0$. In both of these cases, use the first derivative test.

13.2 EXERCISES

For each of these functions, find $f''(x)$, $f''(0)$, $f''(2)$, and $f''(-3)$. (See Examples 1 and 2.)

1. $f(x) = x^3 - 5x^2 + 1$

2. $f(x) = 2x^4 + x^3 - 3x^2 + 2$

3. $f(x) = (x + 2)^4$

4. $f(x) = \dfrac{2x + 5}{x - 3}$

5. $f(x) = \dfrac{x^2}{1 + x}$

6. $f(x) = \dfrac{-x}{1 - x^2}$

7. $f(x) = \sqrt{x + 4}$

8. $f(x) = \sqrt{2x + 9}$

9. $f(x) = 5x^{3/5}$

10. $f(x) = -2x^{2/3}$

11. $f(x) = 2e^x$

12. $f(x) = \ln(2x - 3)$

13. $f(x) = 5e^{2x}$

14. $f(x) = 2 + e^{-x}$

15. $f(x) = \ln|x|$

16. $f(x) = \dfrac{1}{x}$

17. $f(x) = x \ln|x|$

18. $f(x) = \dfrac{\ln|x|}{x}$

For each of the following, find $f'''(x)$, the third derivative, and $f^{(4)}(x)$, the fourth derivative.

19. $f(x) = 3x^4 + 2x^3 - x^2 + 5$

20. $f(x) = -2x^5 + 3x^3 - 4x + 7$

21. $f(x) = \dfrac{x - 1}{x}$

22. $f(x) = \dfrac{x + 2}{x - 2}$

Physical Science *Each of the functions in Exercises 23–26 gives the distance from a starting point at time t of a particle moving along a line. Find the velocity and acceleration functions. Then find the velocity and acceleration at $t = 0$ and $t = 4$. Assume that time is measured in seconds and distance is measured in centimeters. Velocity will be in centimeters per second (cm/sec) and acceleration in centimeters per second per second (cm/sec^2). (See Example 3.)*

23. $s(t) = 6t^2 + 2t$

24. $s(t) = 4t^3 - 6t^2 + 3t - 4$

25. $s(t) = 3t^3 - 4t^2 + 8t - 9$

26. $s(t) = \dfrac{-2}{3t + 4}$

In Exercises 27–28, $P(t)$ is the price of a certain stock at time t during a particular day.

27. If the price of the stock is falling faster and faster, are $P'(t)$ and $P''(t)$ positive or negative? Explain your answer.

28. When the stock reaches its highest price of the day, are $P'(t)$ and $P''(t)$ positive or negative? Explain your answer.

Find the largest open intervals on which each function is concave upward or concave downward and find the location of any points of inflection. (See Example 4.)

29. $f(x) = x^2 + 3x - 5$

30. $f(x) = -x^2 + 8x - 7$

31. $f(x) = x^3 + 4x^2 - 6x + 3$

32. $f(x) = 5x^3 + 12x^2 - 32x + 14$

33. $f(x) = \dfrac{2}{x - 3}$

34. $f(x) = \dfrac{-2}{x + 1}$

35. $f(x) = x^4 + 8x^3 - 30x^2 + 24x - 3$

36. $f(x) = x^4 + 8x^3 + 18x^2 + 12x - 84$

Management *In Exercises 37 and 38, find the point of diminishing returns for the given functions, where $R(x)$ represents revenue in thousands of dollars and x represents the amount spent on advertising in thousands of dollars. (See Example 5.)*

37. $R(x) = 10{,}000 - x^3 + 42x^2 + 800x$; $0 \le x \le 20$

38. $R(x) = \dfrac{4}{27}(-x^3 + 66x^2 + 1050x - 400)$; $0 \le x \le 25$

Find all critical numbers of the following functions. Then use the second derivative test on each critical number to determine whether it leads to a local maximum or minimum. (See Example 6.)

39. $f(x) = -2x^3 - 3x^2 - 72x + 1$

40. $f(x) = \frac{2}{3}x^3 + \frac{1}{2}x^2 - x - \frac{1}{4}$

41. $f(x) = x^3 + \frac{3}{2}x^2 - 60x + 100$

42. $f(x) = (x - 2)^5$

43. $f(x) = x^4 - 8x^2$

44. $f(x) = x^4 - 32x^2 + 7$

45. $f(x) = x + \frac{3}{x}$

46. $f(x) = x - \frac{1}{x}$

47. $f(x) = \frac{x^2 + 9}{2x}$

48. $f(x) = \frac{x^2 + 16}{2x}$

49. $f(x) = \frac{2 - x}{2 + x}$

50. $f(x) = \frac{x + 2}{x - 1}$

In Exercises 51–54, the rule of the derivative of a function f is given (but not the rule of f itself). Find the location of all local extrema and points of inflection of the function f.

51. $f'(x) = (x - 1)(x - 2)(x - 4)$

52. $f'(x) = (x^2 - 1)(x - 2)$

53. $f'(x) = (x - 2)^2(x - 1)$

54. $f'(x) = (x - 1)^2(x - 3)$

In Exercises 55–60, sketch the graph of a single function f that has all the properties listed. There are many correct answers and your graph need not be given by an algebraic formula.

55. **(a)** The domain of f is $[0, 10]$.
(b) $f'(x) > 0$ and $f''(x) > 0$ for all x in the domain of f.

56. **(a)** The domain of f is $[0, 10]$.
(b) $f'(x) > 0$ and $f''(x) < 0$ for all x in the domain of f.

57. **(a)** Continuous and differentiable for all real numbers
(b) Increasing on $(-\infty, -3)$ and $(1, 4)$
(c) Decreasing on $(-3, 1)$ and $(4, \infty)$
(d) Concave downward on $(-\infty, -1)$ and $(2, \infty)$
(e) Concave upward on $(-1, 2)$
(f) $f'(-3) = f'(4) = 0$
(g) Inflection points at $(-1, 3)$ and $(2, 4)$

58. **(a)** Continuous for all real numbers
(b) Increasing on $(-\infty, -2)$ and $(0, 3)$
(c) Decreasing on $(-2, 0)$ and $(3, \infty)$
(d) Concave downward on $(-\infty, 0)$ and $(0, 5)$
(e) Concave upward on $(5, \infty)$
(f) $f'(-2) = f'(3) = 0$

59. **(a)** Continuous for all real numbers
(b) Decreasing on $(-\infty, -6)$ and $(1, 3)$
(c) Increasing on $(-6, 1)$ and $(3, \infty)$
(d) Concave upward on $(-\infty, -6)$ and $(3, \infty)$
(e) Concave downward on $(-6, 3)$
(f) A y-intercept at $(0, 2)$

60. **(a)** Continuous and differentiable everywhere except at $x = 1$, where it has a vertical asymptote
(b) Decreasing everywhere it is defined
(c) Concave downward on $(-\infty, 1)$ and $(2, 4)$
(d) Concave upward on $(1, 2)$ and $(4, \infty)$

Work these problems. (See Example 3.)

61. Physical Science When an object is dropped straight down, the distance in feet that it falls in t seconds is given by

$$s(t) = -16t^2,$$

where negative distance (or velocity) indicates downward motion. Find the velocity at each of the following times.
(a) After 3 seconds
(b) After 5 seconds
(c) After 8 seconds
(d) Find the acceleration. (The answer here is a constant, the acceleration due to the influence of gravity alone.)

62. Physical Science If an object is thrown directly upward with a velocity of 256 ft/sec, its height above the ground after t seconds is given by $s(t) = 256t - 16t^2$. Find the velocity and the acceleration after t seconds. What is the maximum height the object reaches? When does it hit the ground?

Work these problems. (See Example 5.)

63. Management A national chain has found that advertising produces sales, but that too much advertising for a product tends to make consumers "turn off" so that sales are reduced. Based on past experience the chain expects that the number $N(x)$ of cameras sold during a week is related to the amount spent on advertising by the function

$$N(x) = -3x^3 + 135x^2 + 3600x + 12{,}000,$$

where x (with $0 \le x \le 40$) is the amount spent on advertising in thousands of dollars. What is the point of diminishing returns?

64. Management Because of raw material shortages, it is increasingly expensive to produce fine cigars. In fact, the profit in thousands of dollars from producing x hundred thousand cigars is approximated by

$$P(x) = -x^3 + 28x^2 + 20x - 60,$$

where $0 \le x \le 20$. Find the point of diminishing returns.

Work these problems. (See Example 6.)

65. Management A small company must hire expensive temporary help to supplement its full-time staff. It estimates that the weekly costs $C(x)$ of salaries and benefits are related to the number x of full-time employees by the function

$$C(x) = 250x + \frac{16{,}000}{x} + 1000 \quad (1 \le x \le 30).$$

How many full-time employees should the company have on its staff to minimize these costs?

66. Natural Science The percent of concentration of a certain drug in the bloodstream x hours after the drug is administered is given by

$$K(x) = \frac{3x}{x^2 + 4}.$$

For example, after 1 hour the concentration is given by $K(1) = 3(1)/(1^2 + 4) = (3/5)\% = .6\% = .006$.

(a) Find the time at which concentration is a maximum.
(b) Find the maximum concentration.

67. Management When a company has to pay large amounts of overtime, or build a larger factory, its profits may go down even though sales are going up. The Wizard Widget Company expects that its profit (in hundreds of dollars) during the next six months will be given by

$$P(x) = -x + 200\sqrt{x} - 2000 \quad (0 \le x \le 35{,}000),$$

where x is the number of units sold. Find the number of units that produce maximum profit.

68. Natural Science The percent of concentration of another drug in the bloodstream x hours after the drug is administered is given by

$$K(x) = \frac{4x}{3x^2 + 27}.$$

(a) Find the time at which the concentration is a maximum.
(b) Find the maximum concentration.

13.3 OPTIMIZATION APPLICATIONS

In most applications, the domains of the functions involved are restricted to numbers in a particular interval. For example, a factory that can produce a maximum of 40 units (because of market conditions, availability of labor, etc.) might have this cost function

$$C(x) = -3x^3 + 135x^2 + 3600x + 12{,}000 \quad (0 \le x \le 40).$$

Even though the rule of C is defined for all numbers x, only the numbers in the interval $[0, 40]$ are relevant because the factory can't produce a negative number of units or more than 40 units. In such applications, we often want to find a smallest or largest quantity—for instance, the minimum cost or the maximum profit—when x is restricted to the relevant interval. So we begin with the mathematical description of such a situation.

Let f be a function that is defined for all x in the closed interval $[a, b]$. Let c be a number in the interval. We say that f has an **absolute maximum on the interval** at c if

$$f(x) \le f(c) \quad \text{for all } x \text{ with } a \le x \le b,$$

that is, if $(c, f(c))$ is the highest point on the graph of f over the interval $[a, b]$. Similarly, f has an **absolute minimum on the interval** at c if

$$f(x) \ge f(c) \quad \text{for all } x \text{ with } a \le x \le b,$$

that is, if $(c, f(c))$ is the lowest point on the graph of f over the interval $[a, b]$.

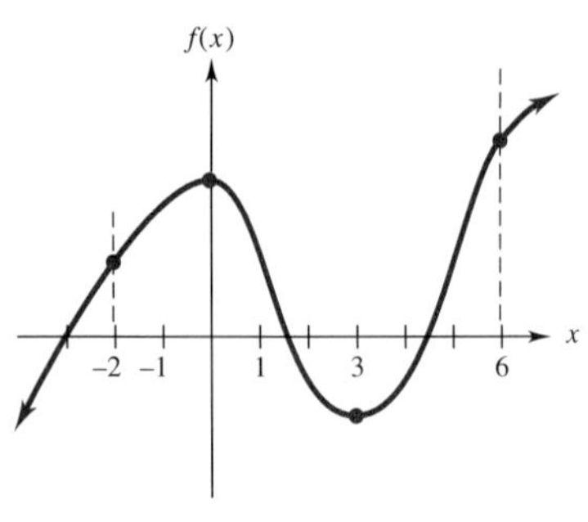

FIGURE 13.30

EXAMPLE 1 Figure 13.30 shows the graph of a function *f*. Consider the function *f* on the interval $[-2, 6]$. Since we are interested only in the interval $[-2, 6]$, the values of the function outside this interval are irrelevant. On the interval $[-2, 6]$, *f* has an absolute minimum at 3 (which is also a local minimum) and an absolute maximum at 6 (which is not a local maximum of the entire function). ■ 1

1 Find the location of the absolute maximum and absolute minimum of the function *f* in Figure 13.30 on the interval $[-2, 1]$.

Answer:

Absolute maximum at 0; absolute minimum at -2

The absolute maximum in Example 1 occurred at $x = 6$, which is an endpoint of the interval and the absolute minimum occurred at $x = 3$, which is a critical number of *f* (because *f* has a local minimum there). Similarly, in Problem 1 in the margin, the absolute maximum occurred at a critical number and the absolute minimum at an endpoint. These examples illustrate the following result, whose proof is omitted.

EXTREME VALUE THEOREM

If a function *f* is continuous on a closed interval $[a, b]$, then *f* has both an absolute maximum and an absolute minimum on the interval. Each of these occurs either at an endpoint of the interval or at a critical number of *f*.

CAUTION The Extreme Value Theorem may not hold on intervals that are not closed (that is, intervals that do not include one or both endpoints). For example, $f(x) = 1/x$ does not have an absolute maximum on the interval $(0, 1)$; the values of $f(x)$ get larger and larger as x approaches 0, as you can easily verify with a calculator. ◆

EXAMPLE 2 Find the absolute extrema of the function on the given interval.

(a) $f(x) = 4x + \frac{36}{x}$ on $[1, 6]$

According to the Extreme Value Theorem we need only consider the critical numbers of *f* and the endpoints, 1 and 6, of the interval. Begin by finding the derivative and determining the critical numbers.

$$f'(x) = 4 - \frac{36}{x^2} = 0$$

$$\frac{4x^2 - 36}{x^2} = 0$$

Since we are looking for critical numbers in $(1, 6)$, $x \neq 0$. When $f'(x) = 0$ and $x \neq 0$, then

$$4x^2 - 36 = 0$$
$$4x^2 = 36$$
$$x^2 = 9$$
$$x = -3 \quad \text{or} \quad x = 3.$$

Since -3 is not in the interval $[1, 6]$, disregard it; 3 is the only critical number of interest. By the Extreme Value Theorem, the absolute maximum and minimum must occur at critical numbers or endpoints, that is, at 1, 3, or 6. The graph of f in Figure 13.31 suggests that the absolute maximum occurs at $x = 1$ and the absolute minimum at $x = 3$. We can confirm this algebraically by evaluating f at these three numbers to see which ones give the largest and smallest values.

x-value	*Value of Function*	
1	40	← Absolute maximum
3	24	← Absolute minimum
6	30	

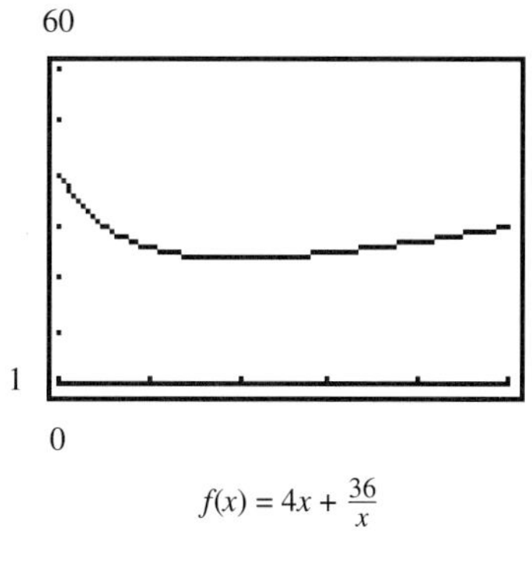

$f(x) = 4x + \frac{36}{x}$

FIGURE 13.31

25,000

60

135

0

$g(x) = -.02x^3 + 600x - 20{,}000$

FIGURE 13.32

(b) $g(x) = -.02x^3 + 600x - 20{,}000 \quad (60 \leq x \leq 135)$
Here $g'(x) = -.06x^2 + 600$ and the critical numbers are the solutions of

$$-.06x^2 + 600 = 0$$
$$-.06x^2 = -600$$
$$x^2 = 10{,}000$$
$$x = 100 \quad \text{or} \quad x = -100.$$

Disregard $x = -100$ since it is not in the interval $[60, 135]$. The absolute extrema occur at 60 or 100 or 135 (why?). The graph of g in Figure 13.32 shows that the absolute maximum occurs at 100 and the absolute minimum at one of the endpoints. Determine which one, by evaluating g at each.

x-value	*Value of Function*	
60	11,680	← Absolute minimum
100	20,000	← Absolute maximum
135	11,793	

■ 2

2 Find the absolute maximum and absolute minimum values.

(a) $f(x) = -x^2 + 4x - 8$ on $[-4, 4]$

(b) $g(x) = x^3 - 15x^2 + 48x + 50$ on $[1, 6]$

Answers:

(a) Absolute maximum of -4 at $x = 2$; absolute minimum of -40 at $x = -4$

(b) Absolute maximum of 94 at $x = 2$; absolute minimum of 14 at $x = 6$

APPLICATIONS When solving applied problems that involve maximum and minimum values, follow these guidelines:

SOLVING APPLIED PROBLEMS

Step 1 Read the problem carefully. Make sure you understand what is given and what is asked for.

Step 2 If possible, sketch a diagram and label the various parts.

Step 3 Decide which variable is to be maximized or minimized. Express that variable as a function of *one* other variable. Be sure to determine the domain of this function.

Step 4 Find the critical numbers for the function in Step 3.

Step 5 If the domain is a closed interval, evaluate the function at the endpoints and at each critical number to see which yields the maximum or minimum. If the domain is an open interval, test each critical number either graphically or by using the first or second derivative test to see which yields a maximum or a minimum.

CAUTION Do not skip Step 5 in the box above. If you are looking for a maximum and you find a critical number in Step 4, do not automatically assume that the maximum occurs there. It may occur at an endpoint or may not exist at all. ◆

EXAMPLE 3 When Power & Money, Inc. charges \$600 for a seminar on management techniques, it attracts 1000 people. For each \$20 decrease in the charge, an additional 100 people will attend the seminar. However, due to limited facilities, no more than 2500 people can be accommodated.

(a) Find an expression for the total revenue, if there are x \$20 decreases in the price.
The price charged will be

$$\text{Price per person} = 600 - 20x,$$

and the number of people at the seminar will be

$$\text{Number of people} = 1000 + 100x.$$

The maximum possible number of people, 2500, occurs when $1000 + 100x = 2500$. Verify that the solution of this equation is $x = 15$. So we must have $0 \le x \le 15$. The total revenue $R(x)$ is given by the product of the price per person and the number of people attending, that is,

$$\begin{aligned} R(x) &= (600 - 20x)(1000 + 100x) \\ &= 600{,}000 + 40{,}000x - 2000x^2 \quad (0 \le x \le 15). \end{aligned}$$

(b) Find the value of x that leads to maximum revenue, the amount of maximum revenue, and the number of people attending in this case.
Set the derivative, $R'(x) = 40{,}000 - 4000x$, equal to 0.

$$\begin{aligned} 40{,}000 - 4000x &= 0 \\ -4000x &= -40{,}000 \\ x &= 10 \end{aligned}$$

3 An investor has built a series of self-storage units near a group of apartment houses. She must now decide on the monthly rental. From past experience, she feels that 200 units will be rented for \$15 per month, with 5 additional rentals for each \$.25 reduction in the rental price. Let x be the number of \$.25 reductions in the price and find

(a) an expression for the number of units rented;

(b) an expression for the price per unit;

(c) an expression for the total revenue;

(d) the value of x leading to maximum revenue;

(e) the maximum revenue.

Answers:

(a) $200 + 5x$

(b) $15 - .25x$

(c) $(200 + 5x)(15 - .25x)$
$= 3000 + 25x - 1.25x^2$

(d) $x = 10$

(e) \$3125

Therefore, the maximum revenue occurs either at the critical number 10 or at one of the endpoints, 0 or 15. Look at the graph of R or note that

$$R(0) = 600{,}000, \quad R(10) = 800{,}000, \quad R(15) = 750{,}000.$$

Hence, the maximum revenue of \$800,000 occurs when $x = 10$, that is, when $1000 + 100(10) = 2000$ people attend. In this case the price per person is $600 - 20(10) =$ \$400. ■ 3

EXAMPLE 4 An open box is to be made by cutting a square from each corner of a 12-inch by 12-inch piece of metal and then folding up the sides. The finished box must be at least 1.5 inches deep, but not deeper than 3 inches. What size square should be cut from each corner in order to produce a box of maximum volume?

Let x represent the length of a side of the square that is cut from each corner, as shown in Figure 13.33(a). The width of the box is $12 - 2x$, while the length is also $12 - 2x$. As shown in Figure 13.33(b), the depth of the box will be x inches.

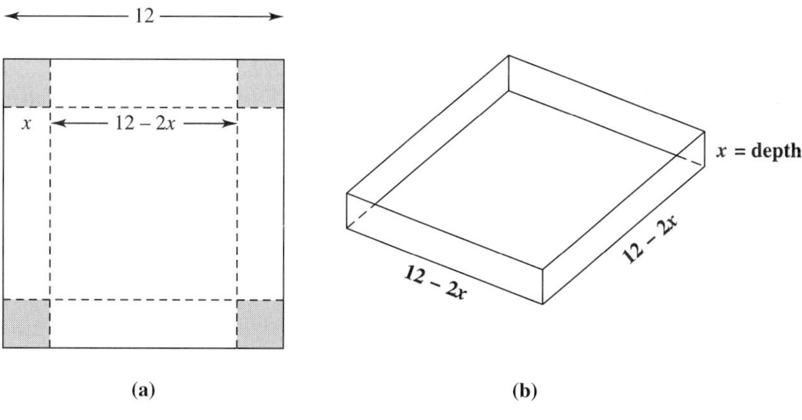

FIGURE 13.33

We must maximize the volume $V(x)$ of the box, which is given by

$$\text{Volume} = \text{length} \cdot \text{width} \cdot \text{height}$$
$$V(x) = (12 - 2x) \cdot (12 - 2x) \cdot x = 144x - 48x^2 + 4x^3.$$

Since the height x must be between 1.5 and 3 inches, the domain of this volume function is the closed interval [1.5, 3]. First find the critical numbers by setting the derivative equal to 0:

$$V'(x) = 12x^2 - 96x + 144 = 0$$
$$12(x^2 - 8x + 12) = 0$$
$$12(x - 2)(x - 6) = 0$$
$$x - 2 = 0 \quad \text{or} \quad x - 6 = 0$$
$$x = 2 \quad \text{or} \quad x = 6.$$

Since 6 is not in the domain, the only critical number of interest here is $x = 2$. The maximum volume must occur at $x = 2$ or at the endpoints $x = 1.5$ or $x = 3$. So we

4 An open box is to be made by cutting squares from each corner of a 20 cm by 32 cm piece of metal and folding up the sides. Let x represent the length of the side of the square to be cut out. Find

(a) an expression for the volume of the box, $V(x)$;

(b) $V'(x)$;

(c) the value of x that leads to maximum volume; (*Hint:* The solutions of the equation $V'(x) = 0$ are 4 and 40/3.)

(d) the maximum volume.

Answers:

(a) $V(x) = 640x - 104x^2 + 4x^3$

(b) $V'(x) = 640 - 208x + 12x^2$

(c) $x = 4$

(d) $V(4) = 1152$ cubic centimeters

use the following table and graph.

x	$V(x)$
1.5	121.5
2	128 ← Maximum
3	108

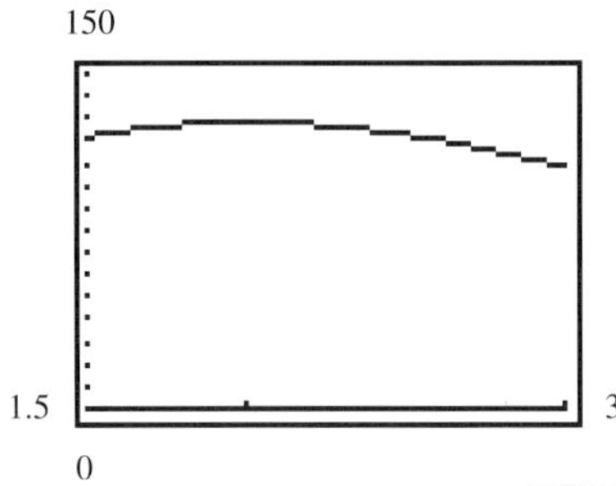

FIGURE 13.34

Both the table and the graph in Figure 13.34 show that the box has maximum volume when $x = 2$. The table shows that this maximum volume is 128 cubic inches. ■ 4

EXAMPLE 5 A truck burns fuel at the rate of

$$G(x) = \frac{1}{200}\left(\frac{800 + x^2}{x}\right) \quad (x > 0)$$

gallons per mile when traveling x miles per hour on a straight, level road. If fuel costs \$2 per gallon, find the speed that will produce the minimum total cost for a 1000-mile trip. Find the minimum total cost.

The total cost of the trip, in dollars, is the product of the number of gallons per mile, the number of miles, and the cost per gallon. If $C(x)$ represents this cost, then

$$C(x) = \left[\frac{1}{200}\left(\frac{800 + x^2}{x}\right)\right](1000)(2)$$

$$C(x) = \frac{2000}{200}\left(\frac{800 + x^2}{x}\right) = \frac{8000 + 10x^2}{x}.$$

Since x represents speed, only positive values of x make sense here. Thus, the domain of $C(x)$ is the open interval $(0, \infty)$ and there are no endpoints to check. To find the critical numbers, first find the derivative.

$$C'(x) = \frac{10x^2 - 8000}{x^2}$$

Set this derivative equal to 0 (and remember $x > 0$).

$$\frac{10x^2 - 8000}{x^2} = 0$$

$$10x^2 - 8000 = 0$$

$$10x^2 = 8000$$

$$x^2 = 800$$

Take the square root on both sides to get

$$x = \pm\sqrt{800} \approx \pm 28.3 \text{ mph.}$$

5 A diesel generator burns fuel at the rate of

$$G(x) = \frac{1}{48}\left(\frac{300}{x} + 2x\right)$$

gallons per hour when producing x thousand kilowatt hours of electricity. Suppose that fuel costs \$2.25 a gallon. Find the value of x that leads to minimum total cost if the generator is operated for 32 hours. Find the minimum cost.

Answer:
$x = \sqrt{150} \approx 12.2$; minimum cost is \$73.50

The only critical number in the domain is $x \approx 28.3$. Confirm that it leads to a minimum value of C either graphically or by using the second derivative test. The second derivative is

$$C''(x) = \frac{16{,}000}{x^3}.$$

Since $C''(28.3) > 0$, the second derivative test shows that 28.3 leads to a minimum. (It is not necessary to calculate $C''(28.3)$; just check that it is positive.) The minimum total cost is found by using the original function $C(x)$ at $x = 28.3$:

$$C(28.3) = \frac{8000 + 10(28.3)^2}{28.3} \approx 565.69 \text{ dollars.}$$ ■ 5

EXAMPLE 6 The U.S. Postal Service requires that boxes to be mailed have a length plus girth of no more than 108 inches, as shown in Figure 13.35. Find the dimensions of the box with largest volume that can be mailed, assuming its width and height are equal.

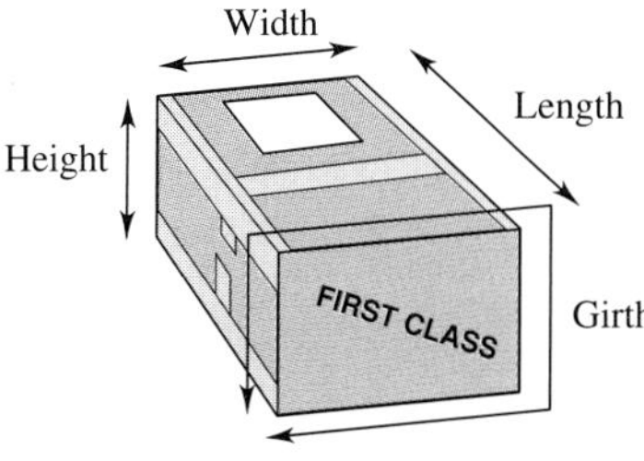

FIGURE 13.35

Let x be the width and y the length of the box. Since width and height are the same, the volume of the box is

$$V = y \cdot x \cdot x = yx^2.$$

Now express V in terms of just *one* variable. Use the facts that the girth is $x + x + x + x = 4x$ and that the length plus girth is 108, so that

$$y + 4x = 108, \quad \text{or equivalently,} \quad y = 108 - 4x.$$

Substitute for y in the expression for V to get

$$V = (108 - 4x)x^2 = 108x^2 - 4x^3.$$

Since x and y are dimensions, we must have $x > 0$ and $y > 0$. Now $y = 108 - 4x > 0$ implies that

$$4x < 108, \quad \text{or equivalently,} \quad x < 27.$$

Therefore, the domain of the volume function V (the values of x that make sense in the situation) is the open interval (0, 27). Since the domain is an open interval, we need not test the endpoints. Find the critical numbers for V by setting its derivative equal to 0 and solving the equation.

$$V' = 216x - 12x^2 = 0$$
$$x(216 - 12x) = 0$$
$$x = 0 \quad \text{or} \quad 12x = 216$$
$$x = 18$$

Use the graph of V or the second derivative test to check $x = 18$, the only critical number in the domain of V. Since $V'(x) = 216x - 12x^2$,

$$V''(x) = 216 - 24x.$$

Hence, $V''(18) = 216 - 24 \cdot 18 = -216$ and V is maximized when $x = 18$. In this case, $y = 108 - 4 \cdot 18 = 36$. Therefore, a box with dimensions 18 by 18 by 36 inches satisfies postal regulations and yields the maximum volume of $18^2 \cdot 36 = 11{,}664$ cubic inches. ■

The preceding examples illustrate some of the factors that may affect applications in the real world. First, you must be able to find a function that models the situation. The rule of this function may be defined for values of x that do not make sense in the context of the application, so the domain must be restricted to the relevant values of x. For instance, if x represents speeds or distances, x must be nonnegative. If x represents the number of employees on a production line, x must be restricted to the positive integers, or possibly to a few fractional values (we can conceive of a half-time employee, but probably not a 7/43-time employee).

The techniques of calculus apply to functions that are defined and continuous at every real number in some interval, so the maximum or minimum for the mathematical model (function) may not be feasible in the setting of the problem. For instance, if $C(x)$ has a minimum at $x = 80\sqrt{3}$ ($\approx$138.564), where $C(x)$ is the cost of hiring x employees, then the real-life minimum occurs at either 138 or 139, whichever one leads to lower cost. Similarly, if $V(x)$ has a maximum at $x = \sqrt{5}$, where $V(x)$ is the volume of a cylindrical can of radius x, then some decimal approximation for $\sqrt{5}$ (= 2.236067977 . . .) must be used. Depending on the manufacturing machinery, there may be several possibilities between 2.2 and 2.3.

ECONOMIC LOT SIZE Suppose that a company manufactures a constant number of units of a product per year and that the product can be manufactured in several batches of equal size during the year. If the company were to manufacture the item only once per year, it would minimize setup costs but incur high warehouse costs. On the other hand, if it were to make many small batches, this would increase setup costs. Calculus can be used to find the number of batches per year that should be manufactured in order to minimize total cost. This number is called the **economic lot size.**

Figure 13.36 shows several of the possibilities for a product having an annual demand of 12,000 units. The top graph shows the results if only one batch of the product is made annually; in this case, an average of 6000 items will be held in a warehouse. If four batches (of 3000 each) are made at equal time intervals during a year, the average number of units in the warehouse falls to only 1500. If twelve batches are made, an average of 500 items will be in the warehouse.

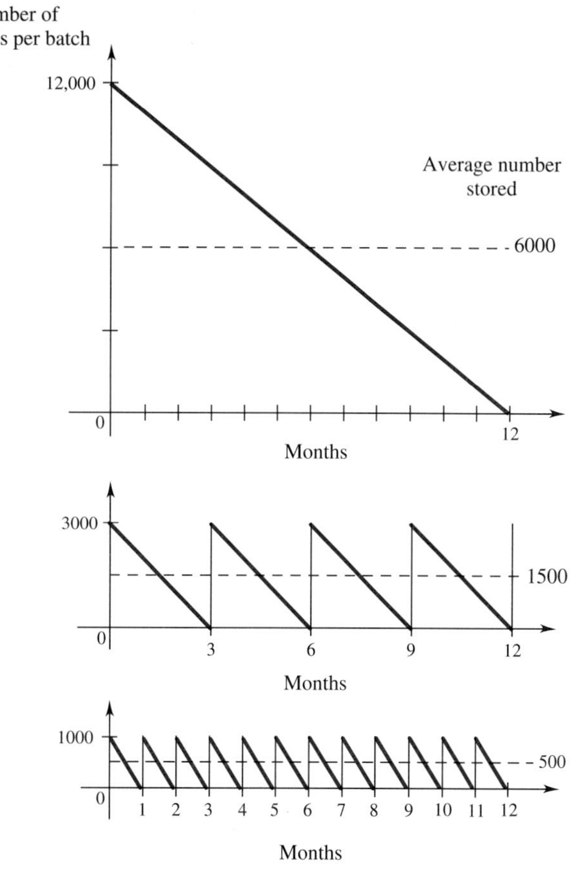

FIGURE 13.36

The following variables will be used in our discussion of economic lot size.

x = number of batches to be manufactured annually

k = cost of storing 1 unit of the product for 1 year

a = fixed setup cost to manufacture the product

b = variable cost of manufacturing a single unit of the product

M = total number of units produced annually

The company has two types of costs associated with the production of its product: a cost associated with manufacturing the item, and a cost associated with storing the finished product.

During a year the company will produce x batches of the product, with M/x units of the product produced per batch. Each batch has a fixed cost a and a variable cost b per unit, so that the manufacturing cost per batch is

$$a + b\left(\frac{M}{x}\right).$$

There are x batches per year, so the total annual manufacturing cost is

$$\left[a + b\left(\frac{M}{x}\right)\right]x. \tag{1}$$

Each batch consists of M/x units and demand is constant; therefore, it is common to assume an average inventory of

$$\frac{1}{2}\left(\frac{M}{x}\right) = \frac{M}{2x}$$

units per year. The cost to store 1 unit of the product for a year is k, so the total storage cost is

$$k\left(\frac{M}{2x}\right) = \frac{kM}{2x}. \qquad (2)$$

The total production cost is the sum of the manufacturing and storage costs, or the sum of expressions (1) and (2). If $T(x)$ is the total cost of producing x batches,

$$T(x) = \left[a + b\left(\frac{M}{x}\right)\right]x + \frac{kM}{2x} = ax + bM + \left(\frac{kM}{2}\right)x^{-1}.$$

Now find the value of x that will minimize $T(x)$. (Remember that a, b, k, and M are constants.) Find $T'(x)$.

$$T'(x) = a - \frac{kM}{2}x^{-2}$$

Set this derivative equal to 0 and solve for x (remember that $x > 0$).

$$a - \frac{kM}{2}x^{-2} = 0$$

$$a = \frac{kM}{2x^2}$$

$$2ax^2 = kM$$

$$x^2 = \frac{kM}{2a}$$

$$x = \sqrt{\frac{kM}{2a}} \qquad (3)$$

The second derivative test can be used to show that $\sqrt{kM/(2a)}$ is the annual number of batches that gives minimum total production cost.

6 A manufacturer of business forms has an annual demand for 30,720 units of form letters to people delinquent in their payments of installment debt. It costs \$5 per year to store 1 unit of the letters and \$1200 to set up the machines to produce them. Find the number of batches that should be made annually to minimize total cost.

Answer:
8 batches

EXAMPLE 7 A paint company has a steady annual demand for 24,500 cans of automobile primer. The cost accountant for the company says that it costs \$2 to store 1 can of paint for 1 year and \$500 to set up the plant for the production of the primer. Find the number of batches of primer that should be produced for the minimum total production cost.

Use equation (3) above.

$$x = \sqrt{\frac{kM}{2a}}$$

$$x = \sqrt{\frac{2(24{,}500)}{2(500)}} \qquad \text{Let } k = 2,\ M = 24{,}500,\ a = 500.$$

$$x = \sqrt{49} = 7$$

Seven batches of primer per year will lead to minimum production costs. ■ 6 7

7 An office uses 576 cases of copy-machine paper during the year. It costs \$3 per year to store 1 case. Each reorder costs \$24. Find the number of orders that should be placed annually. (*Hint:* Use the formula for economic lot size with reordering cost in place of setup cost.)

Answer:
6

13.3 EXERCISES

Find the location of the absolute maximum and absolute minimum of the function on the given interval. (See Example 1.)

1. $[0, 4]$

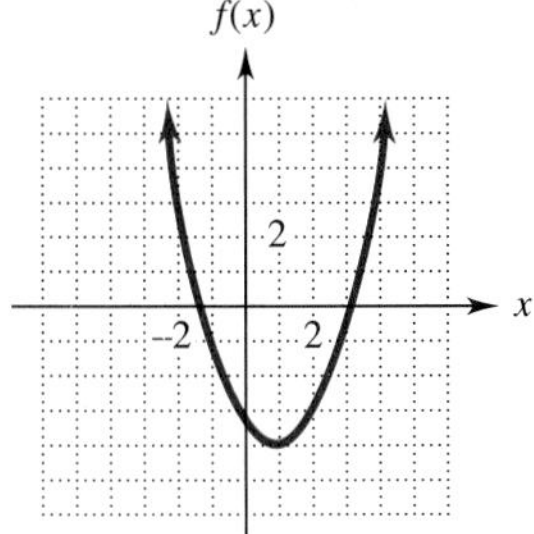

2. $[2, 5]$

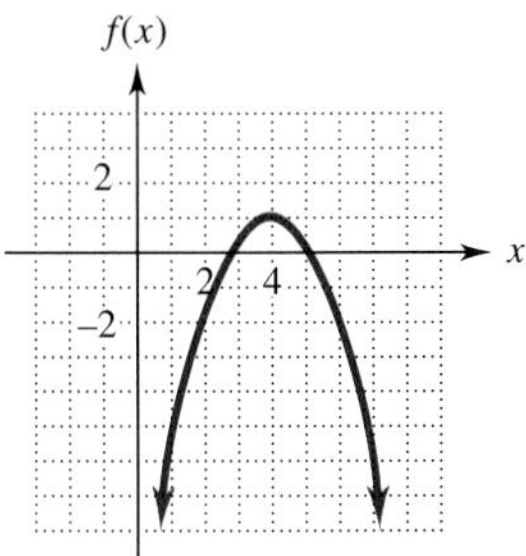

3. $[-4, 2]$

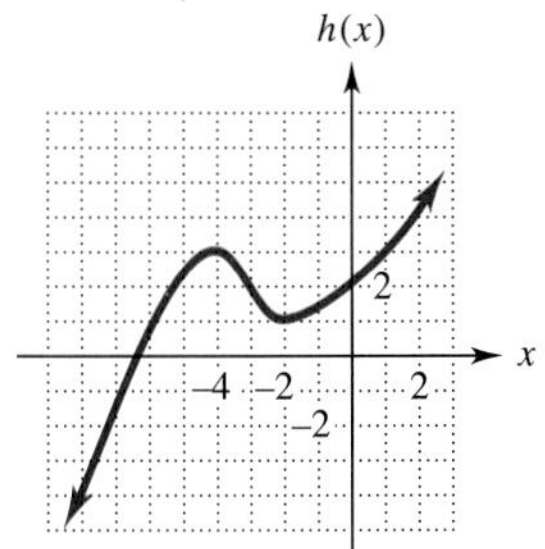

4. $[-1, 2]$

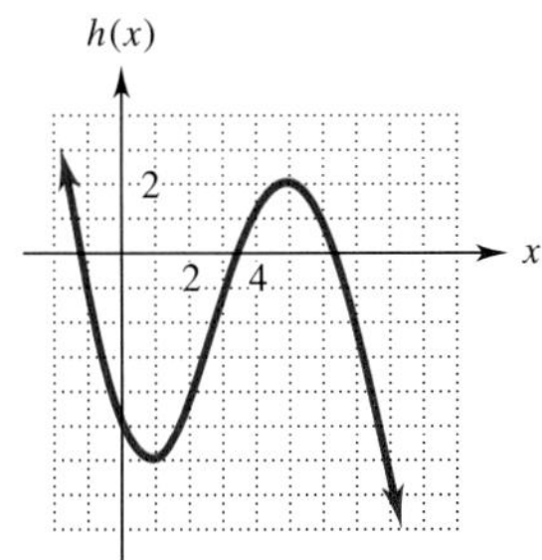

5. $[-8, 0]$

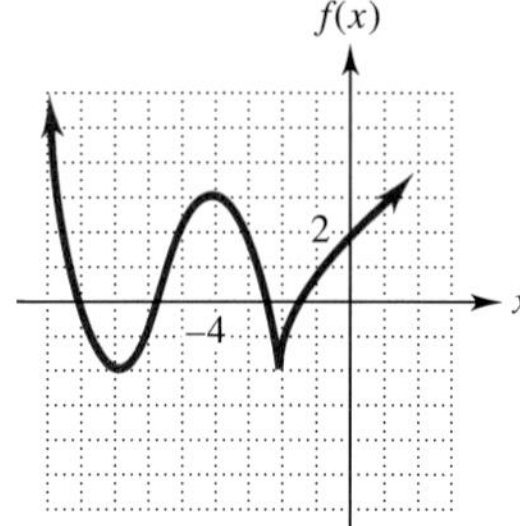

6. $[-4, 4]$

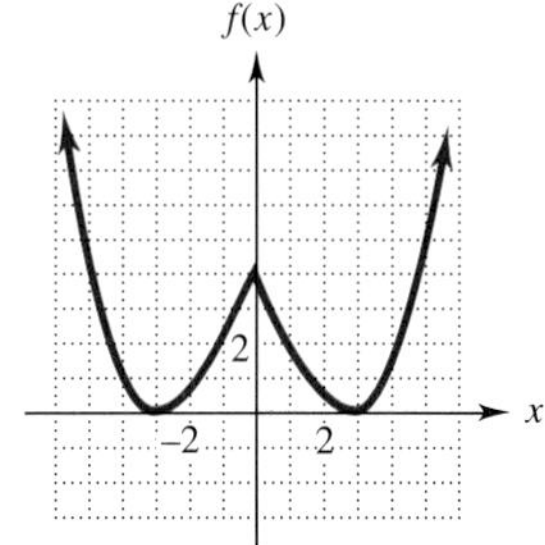

Find the absolute extrema of each function on the given interval. (See Example 2.)

7. $f(x) = x^4 - 32x^2 - 7; [-5, 6]$

8. $f(x) = x^4 - 18x^2 + 1; [-4, 4]$

9. $f(x) = \dfrac{8 + x}{8 - x}; [4, 6]$

10. $f(x) = \dfrac{1 - x}{3 + x}; [0, 3]$

11. $f(x) = \dfrac{x}{x^2 + 2}; [0, 4]$

12. $f(x) = \dfrac{x - 1}{x^2 + 1}; [1, 5]$

13. $f(x) = (x^2 + 18)^{2/3}; [-3, 3]$

14. $f(x) = (x^2 + 4)^{1/3}; [-2, 2]$

15. $f(x) = \dfrac{1}{\sqrt{x^2 + 1}}; [-1, 1]$

16. $f(x) = \dfrac{3}{\sqrt{x^2 + 4}}; [-2, 2]$

Work these problems. (See Example 3.)

17. Management The manager of an 80-unit apartment complex is trying to decide on the rent to charge. It is known from experience that at a rent of \$200, all the units will be full. However, on the average, 1 additional unit will remain vacant for each \$20 increase in rent.

(exercise continues)

(a) Let x represent the number of \$20 increases. Find an expression for the rent for each apartment.
(b) Find an expression for the number of apartments rented.
(c) Find an expression for the total revenue from all rented apartments.
(d) What value of x leads to maximum revenue?
(e) What is the maximum revenue?

18. **Management** The manager of a peach orchard is trying to decide when to have the peaches picked. If they are picked now, the average yield per tree will be 100 pounds, which can be sold for 40¢ per pound. Past experience shows that the yield per tree will increase about 5 pounds per week, while the price will decrease about 2¢ per pound per week.
(a) Let x represent the number of weeks that the manager should wait. Find the revenue per pound.
(b) Find the number of pounds per tree.
(c) Find the total revenue from a tree.
(d) When should the peaches be picked in order to produce maximum revenue?
(e) What is the maximum revenue?

19. **Management** In planning a small restaurant, it is estimated that a profit of \$5 per seat will be made if the number of seats is between 60 and 80, inclusive. On the other hand, the profit on each seat will decrease by 5¢ for each seat above 80.
(a) Find the number of seats that will produce the maximum profit.
(b) What is the maximum profit?

20. **Management** A local club is arranging a charter flight to Hawaii. The cost of the trip is \$425 each for 75 passengers, with a refund of \$5 per passenger for each passenger in excess of 75.
(a) Find the number of passengers that will maximize the revenue received from the flight.
(b) Find the maximum revenue.

Work these problems. (See Examples 4–6.)

21. An open box is to be made by cutting a square from each corner of a 3 ft by 8 ft piece of cardboard and then folding up the sides. What size square should be cut from each corner in order to produce a box of maximum volume?

22. **Management** A truck burns fuel at the rate of $G(x)$ gallons per mile, where

$$G(x) = \frac{1}{32}\left(\frac{64}{x} + \frac{x}{50}\right),$$

while traveling x miles per hour.
(a) If fuel costs \$1.60 per gallon, find the speed that will produce minimum total cost for a 400-mile trip.
(b) Find the minimum total cost.

23. **Management** A rock-and-roll band travels from engagement to engagement in a large bus. This bus burns fuel at the rate of $G(x)$ gallons per mile, where

$$G(x) = \frac{1}{50}\left(\frac{200}{x} + \frac{x}{15}\right),$$

while traveling x miles per hour.
(a) If fuel costs \$2 per gallon, find the speed that will produce minimum total cost for a 250-mile trip.
(b) Find the minimum total cost.

24. **Management** In Example 5 we found the speed in miles per hour that minimized cost when we considered only the cost of the fuel. Rework the problem taking into account the driver's salary of \$8 per hour. (*Hint:* If the trip is 1000 miles at x miles per hour, the driver will be paid for $1000/x$ hours.)

Management *Work these problems.*

25. A farmer has 1200 m of fencing. He wants to enclose a rectangular field bordering a river, with no fencing needed along the river. (See the sketch.) Let x represent the width of the field.

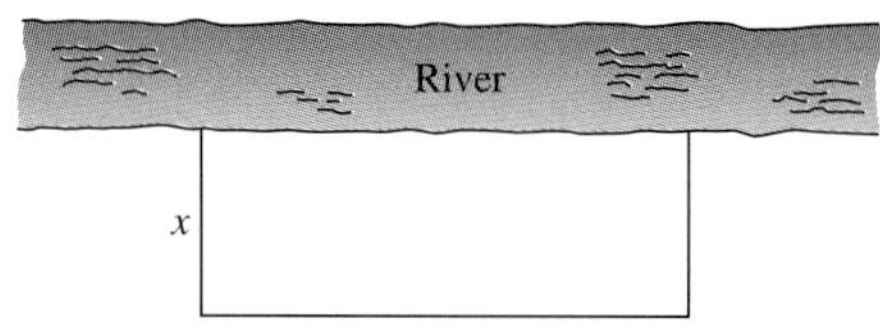

(a) Write an expression for the length of the field.
(b) Find the area of the field.
(c) Find the value of x leading to the maximum area.
(d) Find the maximum area.

26. A rectangular field is to be enclosed with a fence. One side of the field is against an existing fence, so that no fence is needed on that side. If material for the fence costs \$2 per foot for the two ends and \$4 per foot for the side parallel to the existing fence, find the dimensions of the field of largest area that can be enclosed for \$1000.

27. A rectangular field is to be enclosed on all four sides with a fence. Fencing material costs \$3 per foot for two opposite sides, and \$6 per foot for the other two sides. Find the maximum area that can be enclosed for \$2400.

28. A fence must be built to enclose a rectangular area of 20,000 ft^2. Fencing material costs \$3 per foot for the two sides facing north and south, and \$6 per foot for the other two sides. Find the cost of the least expensive fence.

29. A fence must be built in a large field to enclose a rectangular area of 15,625 m^2. One side of the area is bounded by an existing fence; no fence is needed there. Material for the fence costs \$2 per meter for the two ends, and \$4 per meter for the side opposite the existing fence. Find the cost of the least expensive fence.

30. Management If the price charged for a candy bar is $p(x)$ cents, then x thousand candy bars will be sold in a certain city, where

$$p(x) = 100 - \frac{x}{10}.$$

(a) Find an expression for the total revenue from the sale of x thousand candy bars. (*Hint:* Find the product of $p(x)$, x, and 1000.)
(b) Find the value of x that leads to maximum revenue.
(c) Find the maximum revenue.

31. Natural Science A lake polluted by bacteria is treated with an antibacterial chemical. After t days, the number N of bacteria per ml of water is approximated by

$$N(t) = 20\left(\frac{t}{12} - \ln\left(\frac{t}{12}\right)\right) + 30 \quad (1 \le t \le 15).$$

(a) When during this period will the number of bacteria be a minimum?
(b) What is this minimum number of bacteria?
(c) When during this period will the number of bacteria be a maximum?
(d) What is this maximum number of bacteria?

32. Management The sale of cassette tapes of "lesser" performers is very sensitive to price. If a tape manufacturer charges $p(x)$ dollars per tape, where

$$p(x) = 6 - \frac{x}{8},$$

then x thousand tapes will be sold.
(a) Find an expression for the total revenue from the sale of x thousand tapes. (*Hint:* Find the product of $p(x)$, x, and 1000.)
(b) Find the value of x that leads to maximum revenue.
(c) Find the maximum revenue.

33. Management A television manufacturing firm needs to design an open-topped box with a square base. The box must hold 32 cubic inches. Find the dimensions of the box that can be built with the minimum amount of materials.

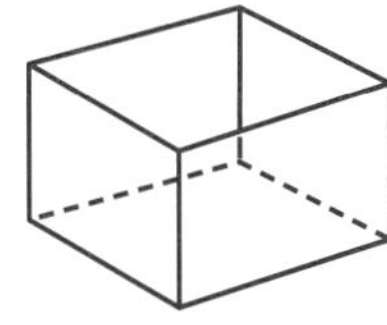

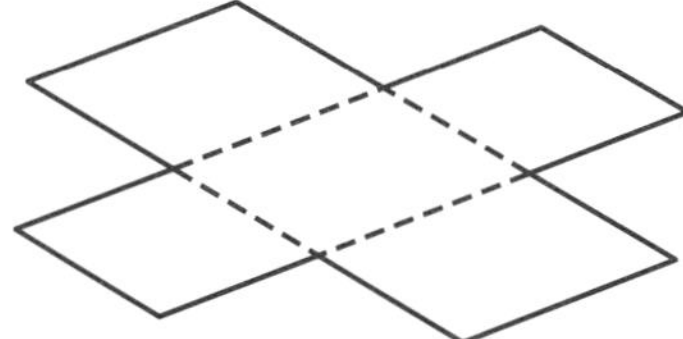

34. Management An artist makes a closed box with a square base which is to have a volume of 16,000 cubic centimeters. The material for the top and bottom of the box costs 3 cents per square centimeter, while the material for the sides costs 1.5 cents per square centimeter. Find the dimensions of the box that will lead to minimum total cost. What is the minimum total cost?

35. Management A cylindrical box will be tied up with ribbon as shown in the figure. The longest piece of ribbon available is 130 cm long, and 10 cm of that are required for the bow. Find the radius and height of the box with the largest possible volume.

36. Management A company wishes to manufacture a box with a volume of 36 cubic feet that is open on top and that is twice as long as it is wide. Find the dimensions of the box produced from the minimum amount of material.

37. Management A mathematics book is to contain 36 square inches of printed matter per page, with margins of 1 inch along the sides, and $1\frac{1}{2}$ inches along the top and bottom. Find the dimensions of the page that will lead to the minimum amount of paper being used for a page.

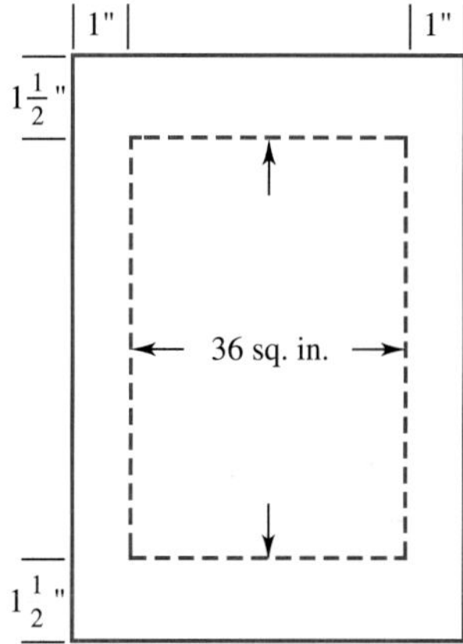

38. Management Decide what you would do if your assistant brought you the following contract to sign:

> Your firm offers to deliver 300 tables to a dealer, at \$90 per table, and to reduce the price per table on the entire order by 25¢ for each additional table over 300.

Find the dollar total involved in the largest possible transaction between you and the dealer; find the smallest possible dollar amount.

39. Management A company wishes to run a utility cable from point A on the shore to an installation at point B on the island (see figure on next page). The island is 6 miles from the shore (at point C) and point A is 9 miles from point C.

(exercise continues)

It costs $400 per mile to run the cable on land and $500 per mile underwater. Assume that the cable starts at A and runs along the shoreline, then angles and runs underwater to the island. Find the point at which the line should begin to angle in order to yield the minimum total cost. (*Hint:* The length of the line underwater is $\sqrt{x^2 + 36}$.)

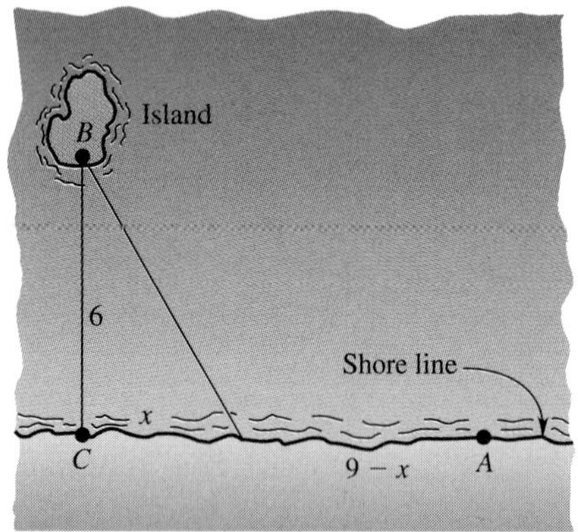

40. Natural Science Homing pigeons avoid flying over large bodies of water, preferring to fly around them instead. (One possible explanation is the fact that extra energy is required to fly over water because air pressure drops over water in the daytime.) Assume that a pigeon released from a boat 1 mi from the shore of a lake (point B in the figure) flies first to point P on the shore and then along the straight edge of the lake to reach its home at L. Assume that L is 2 mi from point A, the point on the shore closest to the boat, and that a pigeon needs 4/3 as much energy to fly over water as over land. Find the location of point P if the pigeon uses the least possible amount of energy.

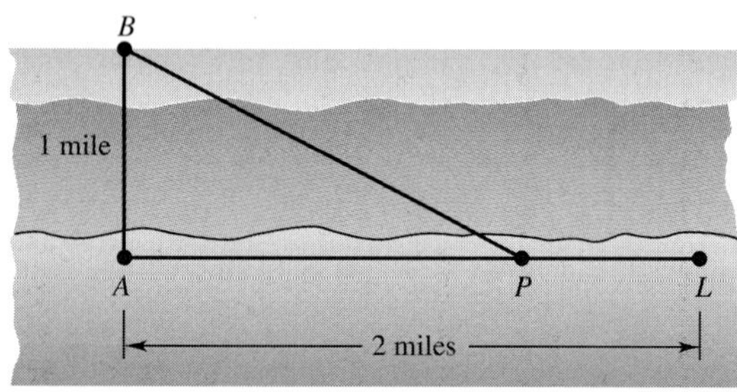

41. Management Suppose a manufacturer's cost to produce x units is given by $c(x) = .13x^3 - 70x^2 + 10{,}000x$ and that no more than 300 units can be produced each week. What production level should be used in order to minimize the average cost per unit, and what is that minimum average cost? (Average cost was defined on page 601.)

42. Management A company uses widgets throughout the year. It costs $20 every time an order for widgets is placed and $10 to store a widget until it is used. When widgets are ordered x times per year, then an average of $300/x$ widgets are in storage at any given time. How often should the company order widgets each year in order to minimize its total ordering and storage costs? (Be careful: the answer must be an integer.)

43. Management A company makes novelty bookmarks that sell for $142 per hundred. The cost (in dollars) of making x hundred bookmarks is $x^3 - 8x^2 + 20x + 40$. Assume that the company can sell all the bookmarks it makes.

(a) Because of other projects a maximum of 600 bookmarks per day can be manufactured. How many should the company make per day to maximize its profits?

(b) As a result of change in other orders, as many as 1600 bookmarks can now be made each day. How many should be made in order to maximize profits?

44. Management A cylindrical can of volume 58 cubic inches (approximately one quart) is to be designed. For convenient handling, it must be at least one inch high and two inches in diameter. What dimensions (radius of top, height of can) will use the least amount of material?

Management *The following exercises refer to economic lot size. (See Example 7.)*

45. Find the approximate number of batches that should be produced annually if 100,000 units are to be manufactured. It costs $1 to store a unit for 1 year and it costs $500 to set up the factory to produce each batch.

46. How many units per batch will be manufactured in Exercise 45?

47. A market has a steady annual demand for 16,800 cases of sugar. It costs $3 to store 1 case for 1 year. The market pays $7 for each order that is placed. Find the number of orders for sugar that should be placed each year.

48. Find the number of cases per order in Exercise 47.

49. A bookstore has an annual demand for 100,000 copies of a best-selling book. It costs $.50 to store one copy for one year, and it costs $60 to place an order. Find the optimum number of copies per order.

50. A restaurant has an annual demand for 900 bottles of a California wine. It costs $1 to store 1 bottle for 1 year, and it costs $5 to place a reorder. Find the number of orders that should be placed annually.

51. Choose the correct answer:* The economic order quantity formula assumes that

(a) Purchase costs per unit differ due to quantity discounts.
(b) Costs of placing an order vary with quantity ordered.
(c) Periodic demand for the goods is known.
(d) Erratic usage rates are cushioned by safety stocks.

*Question from the Uniform CPA Examination of the American Institute of Certified Public Accountants, May, 1991. Reprinted by permission of the Institute of Certified Public Accountants.

CHAPTER 13 SUMMARY

Key Terms and Symbols

13.1 increasing function on an interval
decreasing function on an interval
critical number
critical point
local maximum (maxima)
local minimum (minima)
local extremum (extrema)

13.2 $f''(x)$ or y'' or $\frac{d^2y}{dx^2}$ or $D_x^2[f(x)]$ second derivative of f
$f'''(x)$ third derivative of f
$f^{(n)}(x)$ nth derivative of f
acceleration
concave upward
concave downward
point of inflection
point of diminishing returns

13.3 absolute maximum on an interval
absolute minimum on an interval
Extreme Value Theorem
economic lot size

Key Concepts

If $f'(x) > 0$ for each x in an interval, then f is **increasing** on the interval; if $f'(x) < 0$ for each x in the interval, then f is **decreasing** on the interval; if $f'(x) = 0$ for each x in the interval, then f is **constant** on the interval.

Local Extrema Let c be a number in the domain of a function f. Then f has a **local maximum** at c if $f(x) \le f(c)$ for all x near c, and f has a **local minimum** at c if $f(x) \ge f(c)$ for all x near c. If f has a local extremum at c, then $f'(c) = 0$ or $f'(c)$ does not exist.

First Derivative Test Let f be a differentiable function for all x in $[a, b]$, except possibly at $x = c$. Assume $a < c < b$ and that c is the only critical number for f in $[a, b]$. If $f'(a) > 0$ and $f'(b) < 0$ then there is a local maximum at c. If $f'(a) < 0$ and $f'(b) > 0$, then there is a local minimum at c.

Concavity Let f have derivatives f' and f'' for all x in (a, b). f is **concave upward** on (a, b) if $f''(x) > 0$ for all x in (a, b). f is **concave downward** on (a, b) if $f''(x) < 0$ for all x in (a, b). f has a **point of inflection** at $x = c$ if $f''(x)$ changes sign at $x = c$.

Second Derivative Test Let c be a critical number of f such that $f'(c) = 0$ and $f''(x)$ exists for all x in some open interval containing c. If $f''(c) > 0$, then there is a local minimum at c. If $f''(c) < 0$, then there is a local maximum at c. If $f''(c) = 0$, then the test gives no information.

Absolute Extrema Let c be in an interval $[a, b]$ where f is defined. Then f has an **absolute maximum** on the interval at c if $f(x) \le f(c)$ for all x in $[a, b]$ and f has an **absolute minimum** on the interval at c if $f(x) \ge f(c)$ for all x in $[a, b]$.

Chapter 13 Review Exercises

1. When the rule of a function is given, how can you determine where it is increasing and where it is decreasing?
2. When the rule of a function is given, how can you determine where the local extrema are located? State two algebraic ways to test whether a local extremum is a maximum or a minimum.
3. What is the difference between a local extremum and an absolute extremum? Can a local extremum be an absolute extremum? Is a local extremum necessarily an absolute extremum?
4. What information about a graph can be found from the first derivative? From the second derivative?

Find the largest open intervals on which the following functions are increasing or decreasing.

5. $f(x) = x^2 + 7x - 9$
6. $f(x) = -3x^2 + 2x + 11$
7. $g(x) = 2x^3 - x^2 - 4x + 7$
8. $g(x) = -4x^3 + 5x^2 + 8x + 1$
9. $f(x) = \dfrac{4}{x - 3}$
10. $f(x) = \dfrac{6}{3x + 2}$

Find the locations and the values of all local maxima and minima for the following functions.

11. $f(x) = 2x^3 + 3x^2 - 36x + 20$
12. $f(x) = 2x^3 + 3x^2 - 12x + 5$
13. $f(x) = x^4 + \dfrac{8}{3}x^3 - 6x^2 + 1$
14. $f(x) = x \cdot e^x$
15. $f(x) = 3x \cdot e^{-x}$
16. $f(x) = \dfrac{e^x}{x - 1}$

Find the second derivatives of the following functions; then find $f''(1)$ and $f''(-2)$.

17. $f(x) = 2x^5 - 4x^3 + 2x - 1$
18. $f(x) = \dfrac{3 - 2x}{x + 2}$
19. $f(x) = -5e^{4x}$
20. $f(x) = \ln|5x + 2|$

For each of these functions, find a viewing window (or windows) that shows a complete graph. Then list the location of each local extremum and point of inflection. List the intervals on which the function is increasing and decreasing and the intervals on which it is concave upward and concave downward.

21. $f(x) = -2x^3 - \dfrac{1}{2}x^2 + x - 3$
22. $f(x) = -\dfrac{4}{3}x^3 + x^2 + 30x - 7$
23. $f(x) = x^4 - \dfrac{4}{3}x^3 - 4x^2 + 1$
24. $f(x) = -\dfrac{2}{3}x^3 + \dfrac{9}{2}x^2 + 5x + 1$
25. $f(x) = \dfrac{x - 1}{2x + 1}$
26. $f(x) = \dfrac{2x - 5}{x + 3}$
27. $f(x) = -4x^3 - x^2 + 4x + 5$
28. $f(x) = x^3 + \dfrac{5}{2}x^2 - 2x - 3$
29. $f(x) = x^4 + 2x^2$
30. $f(x) = 6x^3 - x^4$
31. $f(x) = \dfrac{x^2 + 4}{x}$
32. $f(x) = x + \dfrac{8}{x}$

Find the locations and values of all absolute maxima and absolute minima for the following functions on the given intervals.

33. $f(x) = -x^2 + 5x + 1$; $[1, 4]$
34. $f(x) = 4x^2 - 8x - 3$; $[-1, 2]$
35. $f(x) = x^3 + 2x^2 - 15x + 3$; $[-4, 2]$
36. $f(x) = -2x^3 - x^2 + 4x - 1$; $[-3, 1]$

Work the following exercises.

37. **Management** Suppose the profit from a product is $P(x) = 40x - x^2$, where x is the price in hundreds of dollars.
    (a) At what price will the maximum profit occur?
    (b) What is the maximum profit?

38. **Management** The total profit in hundreds of dollars from the sale of x hundred cartons of candy is given by

    $$P(x) = -x^3 + 10x^2 - 12x - 4.$$

    (a) Find the number of cartons of candy that should be sold in order to produce maximum profit.
    (b) Find the maximum profit.

39. **Management** The packaging department of a corporation is designing a box with a square base and top. The volume is to be 27 cubic meters. To reduce cost, the box is to have minimum surface area. What dimensions (height, length, and width) should the box have?

40. **Management** Another product (see Exercise 39) will be packaged in a closed cylindrical tin can with a volume of 54π cubic inches. Find the radius and height of the can if it is to have minimum surface area.

41. **Social Science** The city park department is planning an enclosed play area in a new park. One side of the area will be against an existing building, with no fence needed there. Find the dimensions of the rectangular space of maximum area that can be enclosed with 900 meters of fence.

42. **Management** A company plans to package its product in a cylinder which is open at one end. The cylinder is to have a volume of 27π cubic inches. What radius should the circular bottom of the cylinder have to minimize the cost of the material? (*Hint:* The volume of a circular cylinder is $\pi r^2 h$, where r is the radius of the circular base and h is the height; the surface area of an open circular cylinder is $2\pi rh + \pi r^2$.)

43. Management In 1 year, a health food manufacturer produces and sells 240,000 cases of vitamins. It costs \$2 to store a case for 1 year and \$15 to produce each batch. Find the number of batches that should be produced annually.

44. Management A company produces 128,000 cases of a soft drink annually. It costs \$1 to store a case for 1 year and \$10 to produce one lot. Find the number of lots that should be produced annually.

45. Social Science If the play area referred to in Exercise 41 needs fencing on all four sides, find the dimensions of the maximum rectangular area that can be made with 900 meters of fence.

CASE 13

A Total Cost Model for a Training Program*

In this application, we set up a mathematical model for determining the total costs in setting up a training program. Then we use calculus to find the time between training programs that produces the minimum total cost. The model assumes that the demand for trainees is constant and that the fixed cost of training a batch of trainees is known. Also, it is assumed that people who are trained, but for whom no job is readily available, will be paid a fixed amount per month while waiting for a job to open up.

The model uses the following variables.

D = demand for trainees per month
N = number of trainees per batch
C_1 = fixed cost of training a batch of trainees
C_2 = variable cost of training per trainee per month
C_3 = salary paid monthly to a trainee who has not yet been given a job after training
m = time interval in months between successive batches of trainees
t = length of training program in months
$Z(m)$ = total monthly cost of program

The total cost of training a batch of trainees is given by $C_1 + NtC_2$. However, $N = mD$, so that the total cost per batch is $C_1 + mDtC_2$.

After training, personnel are given jobs at the rate of D per month. Thus, $N - D$ of the trainees will not get a job the first month, $N - 2D$ will not get a job the second month, and so on. The $N - D$ trainees who do not get a job the first month produce total costs of $(N - D)C_3$, those not getting jobs during the second month produce costs of $(N - 2D)C_3$, and so on. Since $N = mD$, the costs during the first month can be written as

$$(N - D)C_3 = (mD - D)C_3 = (m - 1)DC_3,$$

while the costs during the second month are $(m - 2)DC_3$, and so on. The total cost for keeping the trainees without a job is thus

$$(m - 1)DC_3 + (m - 2)DC_3 + (m - 3)DC_3 + \cdots + 2DC_3 + DC_3,$$

which can be factored to give

$$DC_3[(m - 1) + (m - 2) + (m - 3) + \cdots + 2 + 1].$$

The expression in brackets is the sum of the terms of an arithmetic sequence. Using formulas for arithmetic sequences, the expression in brackets can be shown to equal $m(m - 1)/2$, so that we have

$$DC_3\left[\frac{m(m - 1)}{2}\right] \qquad (1)$$

as the total cost for keeping jobless trainees.

The total cost per batch is the sum of the training cost per batch, $C_1 + mDtC_2$, and the cost of keeping trainees without a proper job, given by (1). Because we assume that a batch of trainees is trained every m months, the total cost per month, $Z(m)$, is given by

$$Z(m) = \frac{C_1 + mDtC_2}{m} + \frac{DC_3\left[\frac{m(m - 1)}{2}\right]}{m}$$

$$= \frac{C_1}{m} + DtC_2 + DC_3\left(\frac{m - 1}{2}\right).$$

*Based on "A Total Cost Model for a Training Program" by P. L. Goyal and S. K. Goyal, Department of Mathematics and Computer Science, The Polytechnic of Wales, Treforest, Pontypridd. Used with permission.

EXERCISES

1. Find $Z'(m)$.
2. Solve the equation $Z'(m) = 0$.

Note: As a practical matter, it is usually required that m be a whole number. If m does not come out to be a whole number, then m^+ and m^-, the two whole numbers closest to m, must be chosen. Calculate both $Z(m^+)$ and $Z(m^-)$; the smaller of the two provides the optimum value of Z.

3. Suppose a company finds that its demand for trainees is 3 per month, that a training program requires 12 months, that the fixed cost of training a batch of trainees is \$15,000, that the variable cost per trainee per month is \$100, and that trainees are paid \$900 per month after training but before going to work. Use your result from Exercise 2 and find m.
4. Since m is not a whole number, find m^+ and m^-.
5. Calculate $Z(m^+)$ and $Z(m^-)$.
6. What is the optimum time interval between successive batches of trainees? How many trainees should be in a batch?
7. Write a brief essay describing other considerations, perhaps not quantifiable, that a manager might want to consider in this situation.

CHAPTER 14

Integral Calculus

In the previous two chapters, we studied the derivative of a function and various applications of derivatives. That material belongs to the branch of calculus called *differential calculus.* In this chapter we will study another branch of calculus, called *integral calculus.* Like the derivative of a function, the definite integral of a function is a special limit with many diverse applications. Geometrically, the derivative is related to the slope of the tangent line to a curve, while the definite integral is related to the area under a curve.

14.1 ANTIDERIVATIVES

Functions used in applications in previous chapters have provided information about a *total amount* of a quantity, such as cost, revenue, profit, temperature, gallons of oil, or distance. Derivatives of these functions provided information about the rate of change of these quantities and allowed us to answer important questions about the extrema of the functions. It is not always possible to find ready-made functions that provide information about the total amount of a quantity, but it is often possible to collect enough data to come up with a function that gives the *rate* of *change* of a quantity. We know that derivatives give the rate of change when the total amount is known. Is it possible to reverse the process and use a known rate of change to get a function that gives the total amount of a quantity? The answer is yes; this reverse process, called *antidifferentiation,* is the topic of this section. The *antiderivative* of a function is defined as follows.

If $F'(x) = f(x)$, then $F(x)$ is an **antiderivative** of $f(x)$.

EXAMPLE 1 **(a)** If $F(x) = 10x$, then $F'(x) = 10$, so $F(x) = 10x$ is an antiderivative of $f(x) = 10$.

(b) For $F(x) = x^5$, $F'(x) = 5x^4$, which means that $F(x) = x^5$ is an antiderivative of $f(x) = 5x^4$. ■

1 Find an antiderivative for each of the following.

(a) $3x^2$

(b) $5x$

(c) $8x^7$

Answers:

Only one possible antiderivative is given for each.

(a) x^3

(b) $\frac{5}{2}x^2$

(c) x^8

EXAMPLE 2 Find an antiderivative of $f(x) = 2x$.

By remembering formulas for derivatives, it's easy to see that $F(x) = x^2$ is an antiderivative of $f(x)$ because $F'(x) = 2x = f(x)$. Note that $G(x) = x^2 + 2$ and $H(x) = x^2 - 4$ are also antiderivatives of $f(x)$ because

$$G'(x) = 2x + 0 = f(x) \quad \text{and} \quad H'(x) = 2x - 0 = f(x). \quad \blacksquare \quad \boxed{1}$$

Any two of the antiderivatives of $f(x) = 2x$ that were found in Example 2 differ by a constant. For instance, $G(x) - F(x) = 2$ and $H(x) - G(x) = -6$. The same thing is true in the general case.

> If $F(x)$ and $G(x)$ are both antiderivatives of $f(x)$, then there is a constant C such that
>
> $$\mathbf{F(x) - G(x) = C.}$$
>
> (Two antiderivatives of a function can differ only by a constant.)

The statement in the box reflects a geometric fact about derivatives, namely, that the derivative of a function gives the slope of the tangent line at any number x. For example, if you graph the three antiderivatives of $f(x) = 2x$ found in Example 2, you will see that the graphs all have the same shape because at any x-value, their tangent lines all have the same slope, as shown in Figure 14.1.

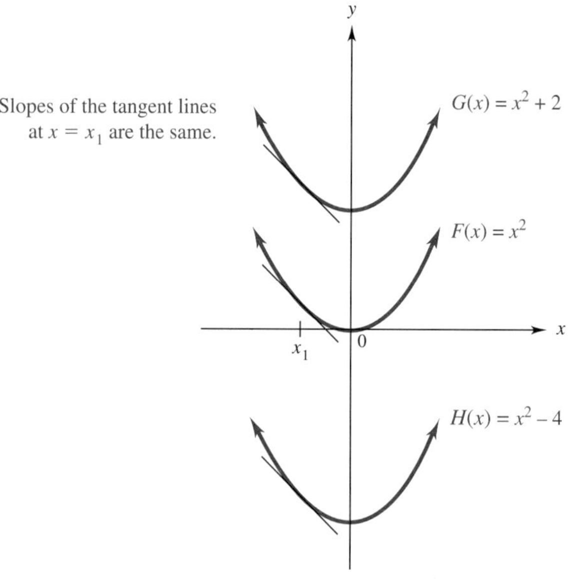

FIGURE 14.1

The family of all antiderivatives of the function f is indicated by

$$\int f(x)\, dx.$$

The symbol $\int$ is the **integral sign,** $f(x)$ is the **integrand,** and $\int f(x)\,dx$ is called an **indefinite integral.** Since any two antiderivatives of $f(x)$ differ by a constant (which means that one is a constant plus the other), we can describe the indefinite integral as follows.

INDEFINITE INTEGRAL

If $F'(x) = f(x)$, then

$$\int f(x)\,dx = F(x) + C,$$

for any real number C.

For example, using this notation,

$$\int 2x\,dx = x^2 + C.$$

NOTE The dx in the indefinite integral $\int f(x)\,dx$ indicates that x is the variable of the function whose antiderivative is to be found, in the same way that dy/dx denotes the derivative when y is a function of the variable x. For example, in the indefinite integral $\int 2ax\,dx$, the variable of the function is x, whereas in the indefinite integral $\int 2ax\,da$, the variable is a. ◆

The symbol $\int f(x)\,dx$ was created by G. W. Leibniz (1646–1716) in the latter part of the seventeenth century. The $\int$ is an elongated S from *summa,* the Latin word for *sum.* The word *integral* as a term in the calculus was coined by Jakob Bernoulli (1654–1705), a Swiss mathematician who corresponded frequently with Leibniz. The relationship between sums and integrals will be clarified in Section 14.3.

Because finding an antiderivative is the inverse of finding a derivative, each formula for derivatives leads to a rule for antiderivatives. For instance, the power rule for derivatives tells us that

$$\text{if } F(x) = x^4, \text{ then } F'(x) = 4x^3.$$

Consequently,

$$\text{if } F(x) = \frac{1}{4}x^4, \text{ then } F'(x) = \frac{1}{4}(4x^3) = x^3.$$

In other words, an antiderivative of $f(x) = x^3$ is $F(x) = \frac{1}{4}x^4$. Similarly, an antiderivative of $g(x) = x^7$ is $G(x) = \frac{1}{8}x^8$ because $G'(x) = \frac{1}{8}(8x^7) = x^7$. The same pattern holds in the general case: to find the antiderivative of x^n, increase the exponent by 1 and divide by that same number.

POWER RULE FOR ANTIDERIVATIVES

For any real number $n \neq -1$,

$$\int x^n\,dx = \frac{1}{n+1}x^{n+1} + C.$$

This result can be verified by differentiating the expression on the right above.

$$\frac{d}{dx}\left(\frac{1}{n+1}x^{n+1} + C\right) = \frac{n+1}{n+1}x^{(n+1)-1} + 0 = x^n$$

(If $n = -1$, the expression in the denominator is 0, and the above rule cannot be used. We will see later how to find an antiderivative in this case.)

EXAMPLE 3 Find each antiderivative.

(a) $\int x^3\, dx$

Use the power rule with $n = 3$.

$$\int x^3\, dx = \frac{1}{\mathbf{3+1}}x^{\mathbf{3+1}} + C = \frac{1}{4}x^4 + C$$

(b) $\int \frac{1}{t^2}\, dt$

First, write $1/t^2$ as t^{-2}. Then

$$\int \frac{1}{t^2}\, dt = \int t^{-2}\, dt = \frac{1}{-2+1}t^{-2+1} = \frac{t^{-1}}{-1} + C = \frac{-1}{t} + C.$$

(c) $\int \sqrt{u}\, du$

Since $\sqrt{u} = u^{1/2}$,

$$\int \sqrt{u}\, du = \int u^{1/2}\, du = \frac{1}{1/2+1}u^{1/2+1} + C = \frac{1}{3/2}u^{3/2} = \frac{2}{3}u^{3/2} + C.$$

To check this, differentiate $(2/3)u^{3/2} + C$; the derivative is $u^{1/2}$, the original function.

(d) $\int dx$

Writing dx as $1 \cdot dx$, and using the fact that $x^0 = 1$ for any nonzero number x,

$$\int dx = \int \mathbf{1}\, dx = \int \mathbf{x^0}\, dx = \frac{1}{1}x^1 + C = x + C. \quad \blacksquare \quad \boxed{2}$$

$\boxed{2}$ Find each of the following.

(a) $\int x^5\, dx$

(b) $\int \sqrt[3]{x}\, dx$

(c) $\int 5\, dx$

Answers:

(a) $\frac{1}{6}x^6 + C$

(b) $\frac{3}{4}x^{4/3} + C$

(c) $5x + C$

As shown in Chapter 12, the derivative of the product of a constant and a function is the product of the constant and the derivative of the function. A similar rule applies to antiderivatives. Also, since derivatives of sums or differences are found term by term, antiderivatives can also be found term by term.

PROPERTIES OF ANTIDERIVATIVES: CONSTANT MULTIPLE RULE; SUM OR DIFFERENCE RULE

If all indicated antiderivatives exist,

$$\int k \cdot f(x)\, dx = k\int f(x)\, dx, \quad \text{for any real number } k;$$

$$\int [f(x) \pm g(x)]\, dx = \int f(x)\, dx \pm \int g(x)\, dx.$$

CAUTION The constant multiple rule requires that k be a *number.* The rule does not apply to a *variable.* For example,

$$\int x\sqrt{x-1}\,dx \neq x\int \sqrt{x-1}\,dx. \blacklozenge$$

EXAMPLE 4 Find each of the following.

(a) $\int 2x^3\,dx$

By the constant multiple rule and the power rule,

$$\int 2x^3\,dx = 2\int x^3\,dx = 2\left(\frac{1}{4}x^4\right) + C = \frac{1}{2}x^4 + C.$$

Since C represents any real number, it is not necessary to multiply it by 2 in the next-to-last step.

(b) $\int \frac{12}{z^5}\,dz$

Use negative exponents.

$$\begin{aligned}\int \frac{12}{z^5}\,dz &= \int 12z^{-5}\,dz \\ &= 12\int z^{-5}\,dz && \text{Constant multiple rule} \\ &= 12\left(\frac{z^{-4}}{-4}\right) + C && \text{Power rule} \\ &= -3z^{-4} + C \\ &= \frac{-3}{z^4} + C\end{aligned}$$

(c) $\int (3z^2 - 4z + 5)\,dz$

By extending the sum or difference property given above to more than two terms,

$$\begin{aligned}\int (3z^2 - 4z + 5)\,dz &= 3\int z^2\,dz - 4\int z\,dz + 5\int dz \\ &= 3\left(\frac{1}{3}z^3\right) - 4\left(\frac{1}{2}z^2\right) + 5z + C \\ &= z^3 - 2z^2 + 5z + C.\end{aligned}$$

Only one constant C is needed in the answer: the three constants from the term by term antiderivatives are combined. ■ 3

3 Find each of the following.

(a) $\int (-6x^4)\,dx$

(b) $\int 9x^{2/3}\,dx$

(c) $\int \frac{8}{x^3}\,dx$

(d) $\int (5x^4 - 3x^2 + 6)\,dx$

(e) $\int \left(3\sqrt{x} + \frac{2}{x^2}\right)dx$

Answers:

(a) $-\frac{6}{5}x^5 + C$

(b) $\frac{27}{5}x^{5/3} + C$

(c) $-4x^{-2} + C$ or $-\frac{4}{x^2} + C$

(d) $x^5 - x^3 + 6x + C$

(e) $2x^{3/2} - \frac{2}{x} + C$

The nice thing about working with antiderivatives is that you can always check your work by taking the derivative of the result. For instance, in Example 4(c) check that $z^3 - 2z^2 + 5z + C$ is the required antiderivative by taking the derivative:

$$\frac{d}{dz}(z^3 - 2z^2 + 5z + C) = 3z^2 - 4z + 5.$$

The result is the original function to be integrated, so the work checks.

EXAMPLE 5 Find each of the following.

(a) $\int \frac{x^2 + 1}{\sqrt{x}}\, dx$

First rewrite the integrand as follows.

$$\int \frac{x^2 + 1}{\sqrt{x}}\, dx = \int \left(\frac{x^2}{\sqrt{x}} + \frac{1}{\sqrt{x}}\right) dx$$

$$= \int \left(\frac{x^2}{x^{1/2}} + \frac{1}{x^{1/2}}\right) dx$$

$$= \int (x^{3/2} + x^{-1/2})\, dx \quad \text{Quotient rule for exponents}$$

Now find the antiderivative.

$$\int (x^{3/2} + x^{-1/2})\, dx = \frac{x^{5/2}}{5/2} + \frac{x^{1/2}}{1/2} + C$$

$$= \frac{2}{5}x^{5/2} + 2x^{1/2} + C$$

(b) $\int (x^2 - 1)^2\, dx$

Square the binomial first, and then find the antiderivative.

$$\int (x^2 - 1)^2\, dx = \int (x^4 - 2x^2 + 1)\, dx$$

$$= \frac{x^5}{5} - \frac{2x^3}{3} + x + C \quad ■ \quad \boxed{4}$$

$\boxed{4}$ Find each of the following.

(a) $\int \frac{\sqrt{x} + 1}{x^2}\, dx$

(b) $\int (\sqrt{x} + 2)^2\, dx$

Answers:

(a) $-\frac{2}{\sqrt{x}} - \frac{1}{x} + C$

(b) $\frac{x^2}{2} + \frac{8}{3}x^{3/2} + 4x + C$

As shown in Chapter 12, the derivative of $f(x) = e^x$ is $f'(x) = e^x$. Also, the derivative of $f(x) = e^{kx}$ is $f'(x) = k \cdot e^{kx}$. These results lead to the following formulas for antiderivatives of exponential functions.

ANTIDERIVATIVES OF EXPONENTIAL FUNCTIONS

If k is a real number, $k \neq 0$, then

$$\int e^x\, dx = e^x + C;$$

$$\int e^{kx}\, dx = \frac{1}{k} \cdot e^{kx} + C.$$

EXAMPLE 6 Here are some antiderivatives of exponential functions.

(a) $\int 9e^x\, dx = 9\int e^x\, dx = 9e^x + C$

(b) $\int e^{9t}\, dt = \frac{1}{9}e^{9t} + C$

5 Find each of the following.

(a) $\int (-4e^x)\,dx$

(b) $\int e^{3x}\,dx$

(c) $\int (e^{2x} - 2e^x)\,dx$

(d) $\int (-11e^{-x})\,dx$

Answers:

(a) $-4e^x + C$

(b) $\frac{1}{3}e^{3x} + C$

(c) $\frac{1}{2}e^{2x} - 2e^x + C$

(d) $11e^{-x} + C$

6 Find each of the following.

(a) $\int (-9/x)\,dx$

(b) $\int (8e^{4x} - 3x^{-1})\,dx$

Answers:

(a) $-9 \cdot \ln|x| + C$

(b) $2e^{4x} - 3 \cdot \ln|x| + C$

(c) $$\int 3e^{(5/4)u}\,du = 3\left(\frac{1}{5/4}e^{(5/4)u}\right) + C = 3\left(\frac{4}{5}\right)e^{(5/4)u} + C$$

$$= \frac{12}{5}e^{(5/4)u} + C$$ ■ 5

The restriction $n \neq -1$ was necessary in the formula for $\int x^n\,dx$ because $n = -1$ made the denominator of $1/(n + 1)$ equal to 0. To find $\int x^n\,dx$ when $n = -1$, that is, to find $\int x^{-1}\,dx$, recall the differentiation formula for the logarithmic function: the derivative of $f(x) = \ln|x|$, where $x \neq 0$, is $f'(x) = 1/x = x^{-1}$. This formula for the derivative of $f(x) = \ln|x|$ gives a formula for $\int x^{-1}\,dx$.

ANTIDERIVATIVE OF x^{-1}

$$\int x^{-1}\,dx = \int \frac{1}{x}\,dx = \ln|x| + C, \quad \text{where } x \neq 0.$$

CAUTION The domain of the logarithmic function is the set of positive real numbers. However, $y = x^{-1} = 1/x$ has as domain the set of all nonzero real numbers, so the absolute value of x *must* be used in the antiderivative. ◆

EXAMPLE 7 Here are some antiderivatives of logarithmic functions.

(a) $$\int \frac{4}{x}\,dx = 4\int \frac{1}{x}\,dx = 4 \cdot \ln|x| + C$$

(b) $$\int \left(-\frac{5}{x} + e^{-2x}\right)dx = -5 \cdot \ln|x| - \frac{1}{2}e^{-2x} + C$$ ■ 6

In all the examples above, the family of antiderivative functions was found. In many applications, however, the given information allows us to determine the value of the integration constant C. The next examples illustrate this idea.

EXAMPLE 8 According to the Cellular Telecommunications Industry Association, the rate of increase of the number of cellular phone subscribers (in millions) since service began is given by

$$S'(x) = .38x + .04,$$

where x is the number of years since 1985, when the service started. There were .25 million subscribers in 1985, year 0. Find a function that gives the number of subscribers in year x.

Since $S'(x)$ gives the rate of change in the number of subscribers,

$$S(x) = \int (.38x + .04)\,dx$$

$$= .38\frac{x^2}{2} + .04x + C$$

$$= .19x^2 + .04x + C.$$

To find the value of C, use the fact that the number of subscribers (in millions) $S(0) = .25$.

$$S(x) = .19x^2 + .04x + C$$
$$.25 = .19(0)^2 + .04(0) + C$$
$$C = .25$$

Thus, the number of subscribers (in millions) in year x is

$$S(x) = .19x^2 + .04x + .25. \quad \blacksquare$$

EXAMPLE 9 Suppose the marginal revenue from a product is given by $40/e^{.05x} + 10$. Find the demand function for the product.

The marginal revenue is the derivative of the revenue function.

$$\frac{dR}{dx} = \frac{40}{e^{.05x}} + 10$$

$$R = \int\left(\frac{40}{e^{.05x}} + 10\right)dx = \int(40e^{-.05x} + 10)\,dx$$

$$= 40\left(\frac{-1}{.05}\right)e^{-.05x} + 10x + k = -800e^{-.05x} + 10x + k$$

If $x = 0$, then $R = 0$ (no items sold means no revenue), and

$$0 = -800e^0 + 10 \cdot 0 + k$$
$$800 = k.$$

Thus,

$$R = -800e^{-.05x} + 10x + 800$$

gives the revenue function. Now, recall that $R = xp$, where p is the demand function.

$$-800e^{-.05x} + 10x + 800 = xp$$
$$\frac{-800e^{-.05x} + 10x + 800}{x} = p$$

The demand function is $p = \dfrac{-800e^{-.05x} + 10x + 800}{x}$. ■ 7

7 The marginal cost at a level of production of x items is

$$C'(x) = 2x^3 + 6x - 5.$$

The fixed cost is \$800. Find the cost function $C(x)$.

Answer:

$$C(x) = \frac{1}{2}x^4 + 3x^2 - 5x + 800$$

EXAMPLE 10 The rate at which the population of Mexico has been growing in recent years is given by $f(t) = 1.7e^{.025t}$, where $t = 0$ corresponds to 1980 and $f(t)$ is in millions per year. Assume the population was 68 million in 1980 and that the growth rate remains the same.

(a) Find the rule of the population function $F(t)$ that gives the population (in millions) in year t.

The derivative of the population function $F(t)$ is the rate at which the population is growing, that is, $F'(t) = 1.7e^{.025t}$. Therefore,

$$F(t) = \int 1.7e^{.025t}\,dt = 1.7 \cdot \frac{1}{.025}e^{.025t} + C = 68e^{.025t} + C.$$

Since the population is 68 million in 1980 (that is, when $t = 0$), we have

$$68 = 68e^{.025(0)} + C = 68e^0 + C = 68 + C,$$

so that $C = 0$. Therefore, the population function is $F(t) = 68e^{.025t}$.

(b) What is the population in the year 2000?
Since 2000 corresponds to $t = 20$, the population is

$$F(20) = 68e^{.025(20)} = 68e^{.5} \approx 112.1 \text{ million.} \quad \blacksquare$$

14.1 EXERCISES

1. What must be true of $F(x)$ and $G(x)$ if both are antiderivatives of $f(x)$?

2. How is the antiderivative of a function related to the function?

3. In your own words, describe what is meant by an integrand.

4. Explain why the restriction $n \neq -1$ is necessary in the rule $\int x^n\,dx = \frac{1}{n+1}x^{n+1} + C$.

Find each of the following. (See Examples 3–7.)

5. $\int 10x\,dx$

6. $\int 25r\,dr$

7. $\int 8p^2\,dp$

8. $\int 5t^3\,dt$

9. $\int 100\,dx$

10. $\int 35\,dt$

11. $\int (5z - 1)\,dz$

12. $\int (2m + 3)\,dm$

13. $\int (z^2 - 4z + 2)\,dz$

14. $\int (2y^2 + 4y + 7)\,dy$

15. $\int (x^3 - 14x^2 + 20x + 3)\,dx$

16. $\int (x^3 + 5x^2 - 10x - 4)\,dx$

17. $\int 6\sqrt{y}\,dy$

18. $\int 8z^{1/2}\,dz$

19. $\int (6t\sqrt{t} + 3\sqrt{t})\,dt$

20. $\int (12\sqrt{x} - x\sqrt{x})\,dx$

21. $\int (56t^{1/2} + 18t^{7/2})\,dt$

22. $\int (10u^{3/2} - 14u^{5/2})\,du$

23. $\int \frac{24}{x^3}\,dx$

24. $\int \frac{-20}{x^2}\,dx$

25. $\int \left(\frac{1}{y^2} - \frac{2}{\sqrt{y}}\right)dy$

26. $\int \left(\frac{3}{\sqrt{u}} + \frac{2u}{\sqrt{u}}\right)du$

27. $\int (6x^{-3} + 4x^{-1})\,dx$

28. $\int (3x^{-1} - 10x^{-2})\,dx$

29. $\int 4e^{3u}\,du$

30. $\int -e^{-4x}\,dx$

31. $\int 3e^{-.2x}\,dx$

32. $\int -4e^{.2v}\,dv$

33. $\int \left(\frac{3}{x} + 4e^{-.5x}\right)dx$

34. $\int \left(\frac{9}{x} - 3e^{-.4x}\right)dx$

35. $\int \frac{1 + 2t^3}{t}\,dt$

36. $\int \frac{2y^{1/2} - 3y^2}{y}\,dy$

37. $\int \left(e^{2u} + \frac{u}{4}\right)du$

38. $\int \left(\frac{2}{v} - e^{3v}\right)dv$

39. $\int (x + 1)^2\,dx$

40. $\int (2y - 1)^2\,dy$

41. $\int \frac{\sqrt{x} + 1}{\sqrt[3]{x}}\,dx$

42. $\int \frac{1 - 2\sqrt[3]{z}}{\sqrt[3]{z}}\,dz$

43. The slope of the tangent line to a curve is given by

$$f'(x) = 6x^2 - 4x + 3.$$

If the point $(0, 1)$ is on the curve, find the equation of the curve.

44. Find the equation of the curve whose tangent line has a slope of

$$f'(x) = x^{2/3},$$

if the point (1, 3/5) is on the curve.

Management *Find the cost function for each of the following marginal cost functions. (See Example 8.)*

45. $C'(x) = .2x^2 + 5x$; fixed cost is \$10.

46. $C'(x) = .8x^2 - x$; fixed cost is \$5.

47. $C'(x) = x^{1/2}$; 16 units cost \$40.

48. $C'(x) = x^{2/3} + 2$; 8 units cost \$58.

49. $C'(x) = x^2 - 2x + 3$; 3 units cost \$15.

50. $C'(x) = .2x^2 + .4x + .2$; 6 units cost \$29.60.

51. $C'(x) = .0015x^3 + .033x^2 + .044x + .25$; 10 units cost \$25.

52. $C'(x) = -\dfrac{40}{e^{.05x}} + 100$; 5 units cost \$1200.

53. $C'(x) = .03e^{.01x}$; no units cost \$8.

54. $C'(x) = 1.2e^{.02x}$; 2 units cost \$95.

Work the following problems. (See Examples 8–10.)

55. Management The marginal revenue from a product is given by

$$50 - 3x - x^2.$$

Find the demand function for the product. (*Hint:* Recall $R = xp$. Also, if $x = 0$, $R = 0$.)

56. Management The marginal profit from the sale of x hundred items of a product is $P'(x) = 4 - 6x + 3x^2$, and the "profit" when no items are sold is −\$40. Find the profit function.

57. Natural Science If the rate of excretion of a biochemical compound is given by

$$f'(t) = .01e^{-.01t},$$

the total amount excreted by time t (in minutes) is $f(t)$.

(a) Find an expression for $f(t)$.

(b) If 0 units are excreted at time $t = 0$, how many units are excreted in 10 minutes?

58. Social Science Imports (in billions of dollars) to the United States from Canada since 1988 have changed at a rate given by $f(x) = 1.26x^2 - 5.5x + 8.33$, where x is the number of years since 1988. The United States imported \$82 billion in 1988.

(a) Find a function giving the imports in year x.

(b) What was the value of imports from Canada in 1993?

14.2 INTEGRATION BY SUBSTITUTION

In Section 14.1 we saw how to integrate a few simple functions. More complicated functions can sometimes be integrated by *substitution.* The technique depends on the idea of a differential. If $u = f(x)$, the **differential** of u, written du, is defined as

$$du = f'(x)\,dx.$$

For example, if $u = 6x^4$, then $du = 24x^3\,dx$. 1

> 1 Find du for the following.
>
> **(a)** $u = 9x$
>
> **(b)** $u = 5x^3 + 2x^2$
>
> **(c)** $u = e^{-2x}$
>
> Answers:
>
> **(a)** $du = 9\,dx$
>
> **(b)** $du = (15x^2 + 4x)\,dx$
>
> **(c)** $du = -2e^{-2x}\,dx$

Differentials have many useful interpretations which are studied in more advanced courses. We shall only use them as a convenient notational device when finding an antiderivative such as

$$\int (3x^2 + 4)^4\, 6x\, dx.$$

The function $(3x^2 + 4)^4 6x$ is reminiscent of the chain rule and so we shall try to use differentials and the chain rule in *reverse* to find the antiderivative. Let $u = 3x^2 + 4$; then $du = 6x\,dx$. Now substitute u for $3x^2 + 4$ and du for $6x\,dx$ in the indefinite integral above.

$$\int (3x^2 + 4)^4\, 6x\, dx = \int \overbrace{(3x^2 + 4)}^{u}{}^4 \overbrace{(6x\, dx)}^{du}$$

$$= \int u^4\, du$$

This last integral can now be found by the power rule.

$$\int u^4\, du = \frac{u^5}{5} + C$$

Finally, substitute $3x^2 + 4$ for u.

$$\int (3x^2 + 4)^4\, 6x\, dx = \frac{u^5}{5} + C = \frac{(3x^2 + 4)^5}{5} + C$$

We can check the accuracy of this result by using the chain rule to take the derivative.

$$\frac{d}{dx}\left[\frac{(3x^2 + 4)^5}{5} + C\right] = \frac{1}{5} \cdot 5(3x^2 + 4)^4(6x) + 0$$
$$= (3x^2 + 4)^4\, 6x,$$

which is the original function.

This method of integration is called **integration by substitution.** As shown above, it is simply the chain rule for derivatives in reverse. The results can always be verified by differentiation.

2 Find the following.

(a) $\int 8x(4x^2 - 1)^5\, dx$

(b) $\int (3x - 8)^5\, dx$

(c) $\int 18x^2(x^3 - 5)^{3/2}\, dx$

Answers:

(a) $\frac{(4x^2 - 1)^6}{6} + C$

(b) $\frac{(3x - 8)^6}{18} + C$

(c) $\frac{12(x^3 - 5)^{5/2}}{5} + C$

EXAMPLE 1 Find $\int (4x + 5)^9\, dx$.

We choose $4x + 5$ as u. Then $du = 4\, dx$. We are missing the constant 4. We can rewrite the integral by using the fact that $4(1/4) = 1$, as follows.

$$\int (4x + 5)^9\, dx = \frac{1}{4} \cdot 4 \int (4x + 5)^9\, dx$$

$$= \frac{1}{4}\int (4x + 5)^9(4\, dx) \qquad k\int f(x)\, dx = \int kf(x)\, dx$$

$$= \frac{1}{4}\int u^9\, du \qquad \text{Substitute.}$$

$$= \frac{1}{4} \cdot \frac{u^{10}}{10} + C = \frac{u^{10}}{40} + C$$

$$= \frac{(4x + 5)^{10}}{40} + C \qquad \text{Substitute.}$$

■ 2

CAUTION When changing the x-problem to the u-problem, make sure that the change is complete; that is, that no x's are left in the u-problem. ◆

EXAMPLE 2 Find $\int x^2\sqrt{x^3 + 1}\, dx$.

An expression raised to a power is usually a good choice for u, so because of the square root or 1/2 power, let $u = x^3 + 1$; then $du = 3x^2\, dx$. The integrand does not contain the constant 3, which is needed for du. To take care of this, solve the differential $du = 3x^2\, dx$ for $x^2\, dx$.

$$du = 3x^2\, dx$$

$$\frac{1}{3}\, du = x^2\, dx$$

Substitute $(1/3)\,du$ for $x^2\,dx$.

$$\int x^2\sqrt{x^3+1}\,dx = \int \sqrt{x^3+1}(x^2\,dx) = \int \sqrt{u}\cdot\frac{1}{3}\,du$$

Now use the constant multiple rule to bring the 1/3 outside the integral sign.

$$\int x^2\sqrt{x^3+1}\,dx = \int \sqrt{u}\cdot\frac{1}{3}\,du = \frac{1}{3}\int u^{1/2}\,du$$

$$= \frac{1}{3}\cdot\frac{u^{3/2}}{3/2} + C = \frac{2}{9}u^{3/2} + C$$

Since $u = x^3 + 1$,

$$\int x^2\sqrt{x^3+1}\,dx = \frac{2}{9}(x^3+1)^{3/2} + C. \quad \blacksquare \quad \boxed{3}$$

3 Find the following.

(a) $\int x(5x^2+6)^4\,dx$

(b) $\int x\sqrt{x^2+16}\,dx$

Answers:

(a) $\frac{1}{50}(5x^2+6)^5 + C$

(b) $\frac{1}{3}(x^2+16)^{3/2} + C$

CAUTION The substitution method given in the examples above *will not always work.* For example, we might try to find

$$\int x^3\sqrt{x^3+1}\,dx$$

by substituting $u = x^3 + 1$, so that $du = 3x^2\,dx$. However, there is no *constant* that can be inserted inside the integral sign to give $3x^2$. This integral, and a great many others, cannot be evaluated by substitution. ◆

With practice, choosing u will become easy if you keep two principles in mind. First, u should equal some expression in the integral that, when replaced with u, tends to make the integral simpler. Second and most important, u must be an expression whose derivative is also present in the integral. The substitution should include as much of the integral as possible, so long as its derivative is still present. In Example 2, we could have chosen $u = x^3$, but $u = x^3 + 1$ is better, because it has the same derivative as x^3 and captures more of the original integral. If we carry this reasoning further, we might try $u = \sqrt{x^3+1} = (x^3+1)^{1/2}$, but this is a poor choice because $du = (1/2)(x^3+1)^{-1/2}(3x^2)\,dx$, an expression not present in the original integral.

EXAMPLE 3 Find $\int \frac{x+3}{(x^2+6x)^2}\,dx$.

Let $u = x^2 + 6x$, so that $du = (2x+6)\,dx = 2(x+3)\,dx$. The integral is missing the 2, so multiply by 2/2, putting 2 inside the integral sign and 1/2 outside.

$$\int \frac{x+3}{(x^2+6x)^2}\,dx = \frac{1}{2}\int \frac{2(x+3)}{(x^2+6x)^2}\,dx$$

$$= \frac{1}{2}\int \frac{du}{u^2} = \frac{1}{2}\int u^{-2}\,du$$

$$= \frac{1}{2}\cdot\frac{u^{-1}}{-1} + C = \frac{-1}{2u} + C$$

Substituting $x^2 + 6x$ for u gives

$$\int \frac{x+3}{(x^2+6x)^2}\,dx = \frac{-1}{2(x^2+6x)} + C. \quad \blacksquare \quad \boxed{4}$$

4 Find the following.

(a) $\int z(z^2+1)^2\,dz$

(b) $\int \frac{x^2+3}{\sqrt{x^3+9x}}\,dx$

Answers:

(a) $\frac{(z^2+1)^3}{6} + C$

(b) $\frac{2}{3}\sqrt{x^3+9x} + C$

Recall the formula for $\frac{d}{dx}(e^u)$, where $u = f(x)$.

$$\frac{d}{dx}(e^u) = e^u \frac{d}{dx}(u)$$

For example, if $u = x^2$ then $\frac{d}{dx}(u) = \frac{d}{dx}(x^2) = 2x$, and

$$\frac{d}{dx}(e^{x^2}) = e^{x^2} \cdot 2x.$$

Working backwards, if $u = x^2$, then $du = 2x\,dx$, so

$$\int e^{x^2} \cdot 2x\,dx = \int e^u\,du = e^u + C$$
$$= e^{x^2} + C.$$

EXAMPLE 4 Find the following.

(a) $\int e^{-11x}\,dx$

Choose $u = -11x$, so $du = -11\,dx$. Multiply the integral by $(-1/11)(-11)$, and use the rule for $\int e^u\,du$.

$$\int e^{-11x}\,dx = -\frac{1}{11} \cdot -11 \int e^{-11x}\,dx$$
$$= -\frac{1}{11}\int e^{-11x}(-11\,dx)$$
$$= -\frac{1}{11}\int e^u\,du$$
$$= -\frac{1}{11}e^u + C$$
$$= -\frac{1}{11}e^{-11x} + C$$

(b) $\int x^2 \cdot e^{x^3}\,dx$

Let $u = x^3$, the exponent on e. Then $du = 3x^2\,dx$, and $(1/3)\,du = x^2\,dx$,

$$\int x^2 \cdot e^{x^3}\,dx = \int e^{x^3}(x^2\,dx)$$
$$= \int e^u\left(\frac{1}{3}\,du\right) \quad \text{Substitute.}$$
$$= \frac{1}{3}\int e^u\,du \quad \text{Constant multiple rule}$$
$$= \frac{1}{3}e^u + C \quad \text{Integrate.}$$
$$= \frac{1}{3}e^{x^3} + C. \quad \text{Substitute.}$$ ■ 5

5 Find the following.

(a) $\int e^{5x}\,dx$

(b) $\int 8xe^{3x^2}\,dx$

(c) $\int 2x^3e^{x^4-1}\,dx$

Answers:

(a) $\frac{1}{5}e^{5x} + C$

(b) $\frac{4}{3}e^{3x^2} + C$

(c) $\frac{1}{2}e^{x^4-1} + C$

Recall that the antiderivative of $f(x) = 1/x$ is $\ln|x|$. The next example uses $\int x^{-1}\,dx = \ln|x| + C$, and the method of substitution.

EXAMPLE 5 Find the following.

(a) $\int \frac{dx}{9x+6}$

Choose $u = 9x + 6$, so $du = 9\,dx$. Multiply by (1/9)(9).

$$\int \frac{dx}{9x+6} = \frac{1}{9}\cdot 9\int \frac{dx}{9x+6} = \frac{1}{9}\int \frac{1}{9x+6}(9\,dx)$$

$$= \frac{1}{9}\int \frac{1}{u}\,du = \frac{1}{9}\ln|u| + C = \frac{1}{9}\ln|9x+6| + C$$

(b) $\int \frac{(2x-3)\,dx}{x^2-3x}$

Let $u = x^2 - 3x$, so that $du = (2x-3)\,dx$. Then

$$\int \frac{(2x-3)\,dx}{x^2-3x} = \int \frac{du}{u} = \ln|u| + C = \ln|x^2-3x| + C.$$ ■ 6

6 Find the following.

(a) $\int \frac{4\,dx}{x-3}$

(b) $\int \frac{(3x^2+8)\,dx}{x^3+8x+5}$

Answers:

(a) $4\ln|x-3| + C$

(b) $\ln|x^3+8x+5| + C$

EXAMPLE 6 Find $\int x\sqrt{1-x}\,dx$.

Let $u = 1 - x$. Then $x = 1 - u$ and $dx = -du$. Now substitute:

$$\int x\sqrt{1-x}\,dx = \int (1-u)\sqrt{u}(-du) = \int (u-1)u^{1/2}\,du$$

$$= \int (u^{3/2} - u^{1/2})\,du = \frac{2}{5}u^{5/2} - \frac{2}{3}u^{3/2} + C$$

$$= \frac{2}{5}(1-x)^{5/2} - \frac{2}{3}(1-x)^{3/2} + C.$$ ■ 7

7 Find

$$\int x(x+1)^{2/3}\,dx.$$

Answer:

$\frac{3}{8}(x+1)^{8/3} - \frac{3}{5}(x+1)^{5/3} + C$

The substitution method is useful if the integral can be written in one of the following forms, where $u(x)$ is some function of x.

SUBSTITUTION METHOD

Let $u(x)$ be some function of x.

Form of the Integral	*Form of the Antiderivative*
1. $\int [u(x)]^n \cdot u'(x)\,dx,\ n \neq -1$	$\frac{[u(x)]^{n+1}}{n+1} + C$
2. $\int e^{u(x)} \cdot u'(x)\,dx$	$e^{u(x)} + C$
3. $\int \frac{u'(x)\,dx}{u(x)}$	$\ln|u(x)| + C$

EXAMPLE 7 The research department for a hardware chain has determined that at one store the marginal price of x boxes per week of a particular type of nails is

$$p'(x) = \frac{-4000}{(2x + 15)^3}.$$

Find the demand function if the weekly demand for this type of nails is 10 boxes when the price of a box of nails is \$4.

To find the demand function $p(x)$, first integrate $p'(x)$ as follows.

$$p(x) = \int p'(x)\,dx$$
$$= \int \frac{-4000}{(2x + 15)^3}\,dx$$

Let $u = 2x + 15$. Then $du = 2\,dx$, and

$$p(x) = -2000 \int (2x + 15)^{-3}\, 2\,dx$$

$$= -2000 \int u^{-3}\,du \qquad \text{Substitute.}$$

$$= (-2000)\frac{u^{-2}}{-2} + C \qquad \text{Integrate.}$$

$$= \frac{1000}{u^2} + C \qquad \text{Simplify.}$$

$$p(x) = \frac{1000}{(2x + 15)^2} + C. \qquad \text{Substitute.} \qquad (1)$$

Find the value of C by using the given information that $p = 4$ when $x = 10$.

$$4 = \frac{1000}{(2 \cdot 10 + 15)^2} + C$$
$$4 = \frac{1000}{35^2} + C$$
$$4 = .82 + C$$
$$3.18 = C$$

Replacing C with 3.18 in equation (1) gives the demand function,

$$p(x) = \frac{1000}{(2x + 15)^2} + 3.18. \quad ■ \quad \boxed{8}$$

$\boxed{8}$ Sales of a new company, in thousands, are changing at a rate of

$$S'(t) = 27e^{-3t},$$

where t is time in months. Ten units were sold when $t = 0$. Find the sales function.

Answer:
$S(x) = 19 - 9e^{-3t}$

EXAMPLE 8 To determine the top 100 popular songs of each year since 1956, Jim Quirin and Barry Cohen developed a function that represents the rate of change on the charts of *Billboard* magazine required for a song to earn a "star" on the *Billboard* "Hot 100" survey.* They developed the function

$$f(x) = \frac{A}{B + x},$$

*Formula for the "Popularity Index" from *Chartmasters' Rock 100,* Fourth Edition, by Jim Quirin and Barry Cohen.

where $f(x)$ represents the rate of change in position on the charts, x is the position on the "Hot 100" survey, and A and B are appropriate constants. The function

$$F(x) = \int f(x)\,dx$$

is defined as the "Popularity Index." Find $F(x)$.

Integrating $f(x)$ gives

$$\begin{aligned} F(x) &= \int f(x)\,dx \\ &= \int \frac{A}{B + x}\,dx \\ &= A\int \frac{1}{B + x}\,dx. \qquad \text{Constant multiple rule} \end{aligned}$$

Let $u = B + x$, so that $du = dx$. Then

$$\begin{aligned} F(x) &= A\int \frac{1}{u}\,du = A\ln u + C \\ &= A\ln(B + x) + C. \end{aligned}$$

(Absolute value is not necessary, since $B + x$ is always positive here.) ■

14.2 EXERCISES

1. Integration by substitution is related to what differentiation method? What type of integrand suggests using integration by substitution?

2. For each of the following integrals, decide what factor should be u. Then find du.

   (a) $\int (3x^2 - 5)^4\, 2x\,dx$ (b) $\int \sqrt{1 - x}\,dx$

   (c) $\int \frac{x^2}{2x^3 + 1}\,dx$ (d) $\int (8x - 8)(4x^2 - 8x)\,dx$

Use substitution to find the following indefinite integrals. (See Examples 1–6.)

3. $\int 3(12x - 1)^2\,dx$

4. $\int 5(4 - 2t)^3\,dt$

5. $\int \frac{2}{(3t + 1)^2}\,dt$

6. $\int \frac{4}{\sqrt{5u - 1}}\,du$

7. $\int \frac{x + 1}{(x^2 + 2x - 4)^{3/2}}\,dx$

8. $\int \frac{3x^2 - 2}{(2x^3 - 4x)^{5/2}}\,dx$

9. $\int r^2\sqrt{r^3 + 3}\,dr$

10. $\int y^3\sqrt{y^4 - 6}\,dy$

11. $\int (-3e^{5k})\,dk$

12. $\int (-2e^{-3z})\,dz$

13. $\int 4w^2e^{2w^3}\,dw$

14. $\int 5ze^{-z^2}\,dz$

15. $\int (2 - t)e^{4t - t^2}\,dt$

16. $\int (3 - x^2)e^{9x - x^3}\,dx$

17. $\int \frac{e^{\sqrt{y}}}{\sqrt{y}}\,dy$

18. $\int \frac{e^{1/z^2}}{z^3}\,dz$

19. $\int \frac{-4}{2 + 5x}\,dx$

20. $\int \frac{7}{3 - 4x}\,dx$

21. $\int \frac{e^{2t}}{e^{2t} + 1}\,dt$

22. $\int \frac{e^{w+1}}{2 - e^{w+1}}\,dw$

23. $\int \frac{x + 2}{(2x^2 + 8x)^3}\,dx$

24. $\int \frac{4y - 2}{(y^2 - y)^4}\,dy$

25. $\int \left(\frac{1}{r} + r\right)\left(1 - \frac{1}{r^2}\right)dr$

26. $\int \left(\frac{2}{a} - a\right)\left(\frac{-2}{a^2} - 1\right)da$

27. $\int \frac{x^2 + 1}{(x^3 + 3x)^{2/3}}\,dx$

28. $\int \frac{B^3 - 1}{(2B^4 - 8B)^{3/2}}\,dB$

29. $\int \frac{x + 2}{3x^2 + 12x + 8}\,dx$

30. $\int \frac{x^2}{x^3 + 3}\,dx$

31. $\int 2x(x^2 + 1)^3\,dx$

32. $\int y^2(y^3 - 4)^3\,dy$

33. $\int (\sqrt{x^2 + 12x})(x + 6)\,dx$

34. $\int (\sqrt{x^2 - 6x})(x - 3)\,dx$

35. $\int \frac{(1 + \ln x)^2}{x}\,dx$

36. $\int \frac{1}{x(\ln x)}\,dx$

37. $\int \frac{u}{\sqrt{u-1}}\,du$

38. $\int \frac{2x}{(x+5)^6}\,dx$

39. $\int t\sqrt{5t-1}\,dt$

40. $\int 4r\sqrt{8-r}\,dr$

Work these exercises. (See Examples 7 and 8.)

41. **Social Science** In Sacramento County, California, the use of seat belts has risen steadily since the enactment of a seat belt law in 1986. The rate of change (in %) of drivers using seat belts in year x, where 1985 corresponds to $x = 0$, is modeled by $f'(x) = .116x^3 - 1.803x^2 + 6.86x + 3.24$.* In 1985 (year 0), 26% of drivers used seat belts.
    (a) Find the function that gives the percent of drivers using seat belts in year x.
    (b) According to this function, what percent of drivers used seat belts in 1993?

42. **Social Science** Vehicle-related deaths in Sacramento County have declined since 1986 when the California seat belt law was enacted. The rate of change in deaths per 100 million miles of vehicle travel is modeled by $g'(x) = -.00156x^3 + .0312x^2 - .264x + .137$, where $x = 0$ corresponds to 1985 and so on. There were 2.4 deaths per 100 million miles driven in 1985.*
    (a) Find the function giving the number of deaths per 100 million miles in year x.
    (b) How many deaths were there in 1986? in 1990?

*California Highway Patrol and National Highway Traffic Safety Administration.

43. **Social Science** The approximate rate of change in the number of new telephones per 1000 U.S. population is given by

$$f'(x) = \frac{1110}{x},$$

where x represents the number of years since 1900.* In 1990 ($x = 90$) there were 1000 phones per 1000 population.
    (a) Find the function that gives the total number of phones per 1000 people in year x.
    (b) According to this function, how many phones per 1000 people were there in 1995?

44. **Management** The rate of change of U.S. investment in Mexico (in billions of dollars) since 1987 is given by $f(x) = 1.52e^{.11x}$, where x is the number of years since 1987. In 1987, U.S. companies invested \$13.8 billion in Mexico.
    (a) Find a function that gives the amount invested in year x.
    (b) At this rate, when would the amount invested in Mexico be double the 1987 investment?

*Bellcore.

14.3 AREA AND THE DEFINITE INTEGRAL

Suppose a car travels along a straight road at a constant speed of 50 mph. Then the speed of the car at time t is given by the constant function $v(t) = 50$, whose graph is a horizontal straight line, as shown in Figure 14.2(a).

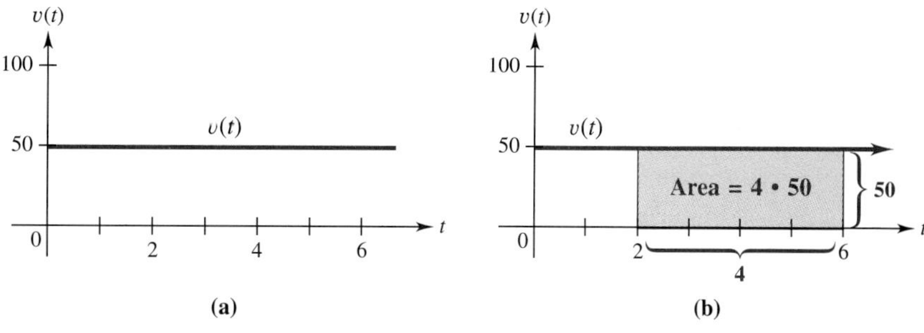

FIGURE 14.2

How far does the car travel from time $t = 2$ to $t = 6$? Since this is a 4-hour period, the answer, of course, is $4 \cdot 50 = 200$ miles. Note that 200 is precisely the *area* under the graph of the speed function $v(t)$ from $t = 2$ to $t = 6$, as shown in Figure 14.2(b) above.

As we saw in Chapter 13, the speed (or velocity) function $v(t)$ is just the rate of change of distance with respect to time, that is, the rate of change of the distance function $s(t)$ (which gives the distance traveled by the car at time t). Now the distance traveled from time $t = 2$ to $t = 6$ is just the amount that the distance has changed from $t = 2$ to $t = 6$. In other words, the *total change* in distance from $t = 2$ to $t = 6$ is the area under the graph of the speed (rate of change) function from $t = 2$ to $t = 6$.

A more complicated argument (that is omitted here) shows that a similar situation holds in the general case.

TOTAL CHANGE IN $F(x)$

Let f be a function such that f is continuous on the interval $[a, b]$ and $f(x) \geq 0$ for all x in $[a, b]$. If $f(x)$ is the rate of change of a function $F(x)$, then the **total change in $F(x)$** as x goes from a to b is the area between the graph of $f(x)$ and the x-axis from $x = a$ to $x = b$.

EXAMPLE 1 Figure 14.3 shows the graph of the function that gives the rate of change of the annual maintenance charges for a certain machine. The rate function is increasing because maintenance tends to cost more as the machine gets older. Estimate the total maintenance charges over the 10-year life of the machine.

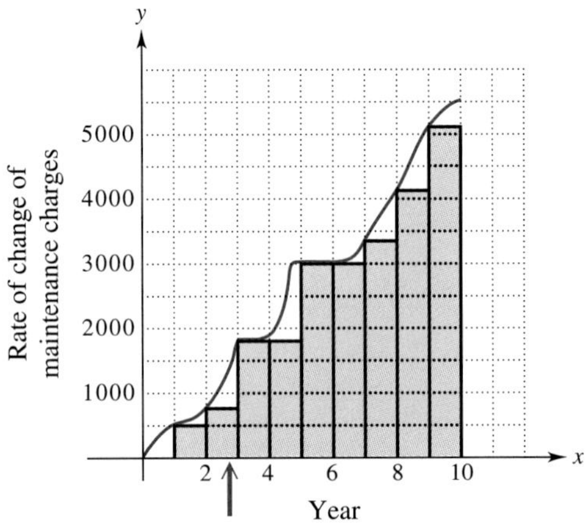

FIGURE 14.3

This is the situation described in the preceding box, with $F(x)$ being the maintenance cost function and $f(x)$, whose graph is given, the rate of change function. The total maintenance charges are the total change in $F(x)$ from $x = 0$ to $x = 10$, that is, the area between the graph of the rate function and the x-axis from $x = 0$ to $x = 10$. We can approximate this area by using the shaded rectangles in Figure 14.3. For instance, the rectangle marked with an arrow, has base 1 (from year 2 to year 3) and height 750 (the rate of change at $x = 2$), so its area is $1 \times 750 = 750$. Similarly, each of the other rectangles has base 1 and height determined by the rate of change at the beginning of the year. Consequently, we estimate the area to be the sum

$$1 \cdot 0 + 1 \cdot 500 + 1 \cdot 750 + 1 \cdot 1800 + 1 \cdot 1800 + 1 \cdot 3000 + 1 \cdot 3000 + 1 \cdot 3400 + 1 \cdot 4200 + 1 \cdot 5200 = 23{,}650.$$

1 Use Figure 14.3 to estimate the maintenance charge during

(a) the first 6 years of the machine's life;

(b) the first 8 years.

Answers:

(a) \$7850

(b) \$14,250

Hence, the total maintenance charges over the 10 years are at least \$23,650 (the unshaded areas under the rate graph have not been accounted for in this estimate). ■ 1

AREA The preceding examples show that the area between a graph and the x-axis has useful interpretations. In this section and the next, we develop a means of measuring such areas precisely when the function is given by an algebraic formula. The underlying idea is the same as in Example 1: Use rectangles to approximate the area under the graph.

EXAMPLE 2 Find the area under the graph of $f(x) = \sqrt{4 - x^2}$ from $x = 0$ to $x = 2$ (see Figure 14.4).

A very rough approximation of the area of this region can be found by using two rectangles, as in Figure 14.5. The height of the rectangle on the left is $f(0) = 2$ and the height of the rectangle on the right is $f(1) = \sqrt{3}$. The width of each rectangle is 1, making the total area of the two rectangles

$$1 \cdot f(0) + 1 \cdot f(1) = 2 + \sqrt{3} \approx 3.7321 \text{ square units.}$$

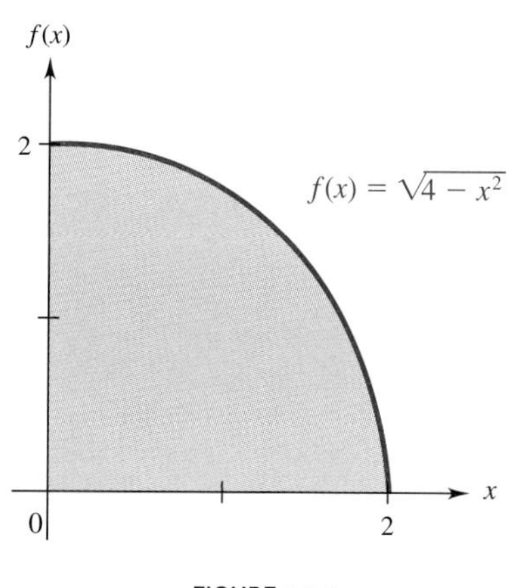

FIGURE 14.4

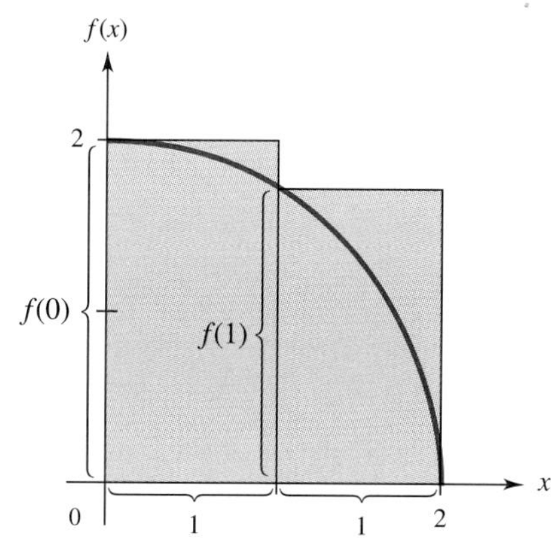

FIGURE 14.5

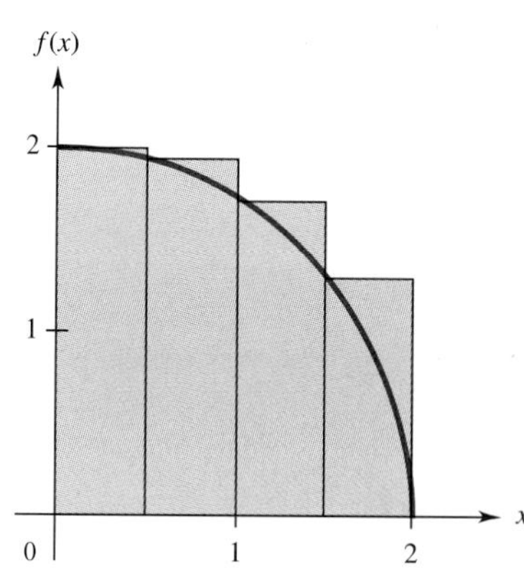

FIGURE 14.6

As Figure 14.5 suggests, this approximation is greater than the actual area. To improve the accuracy of the approximation, we could divide the interval from $x = 0$ to $x = 2$ into four equal parts, each of width 1/2, as shown in Figure 14.6. As before, the height of each rectangle is given by the value of f at the left-hand side of the rectangle, and its area is the width, 1/2, multiplied by the height. The total area of the four rectangles is

$$\begin{aligned}
&\frac{1}{2} \cdot f(0) + \frac{1}{2} \cdot f\left(\frac{1}{2}\right) + \frac{1}{2} \cdot f(1) + \frac{1}{2} \cdot f\left(\frac{3}{2}\right) \\
&\quad = \frac{1}{2}(2) + \frac{1}{2}\left(\frac{\sqrt{15}}{2}\right) + \frac{1}{2}(\sqrt{3}) + \frac{1}{2}\left(\frac{\sqrt{7}}{2}\right) \\
&\quad = 1 + \frac{\sqrt{15}}{4} + \frac{\sqrt{3}}{2} + \frac{\sqrt{7}}{4} \approx 3.4957 \text{ square units.}
\end{aligned}$$

2 Calculate the sum $\frac{1}{4} \cdot f(0) + \frac{1}{4} \cdot f\left(\frac{1}{4}\right) + \cdots + \frac{1}{4} \cdot f\left(\frac{7}{4}\right)$, using this information.

x	$f(x)$
0	2
1/4	1.98431
1/2	1.93649
3/4	1.85405
1	1.73205
5/4	1.56125
3/2	1.32288
7/4	.96825

Answer:
3.33982 square units

This approximation looks better, but it is still greater than the actual area desired. To improve the approximation, divide the interval from $x = 0$ to $x = 2$ into eight parts with equal widths of 1/4. (See Figure 14.7.) The total area of all these rectangles is

$$\frac{1}{4} \cdot f(0) + \frac{1}{4} \cdot f\left(\frac{1}{4}\right) + \frac{1}{4} \cdot f\left(\frac{1}{2}\right) + \frac{1}{4} \cdot f\left(\frac{3}{4}\right) + \frac{1}{4} \cdot f(1) + \frac{1}{4} \cdot f\left(\frac{5}{4}\right) + \frac{1}{4} \cdot f\left(\frac{3}{2}\right) + \frac{1}{4} \cdot f\left(\frac{7}{4}\right). \quad \boxed{2}$$

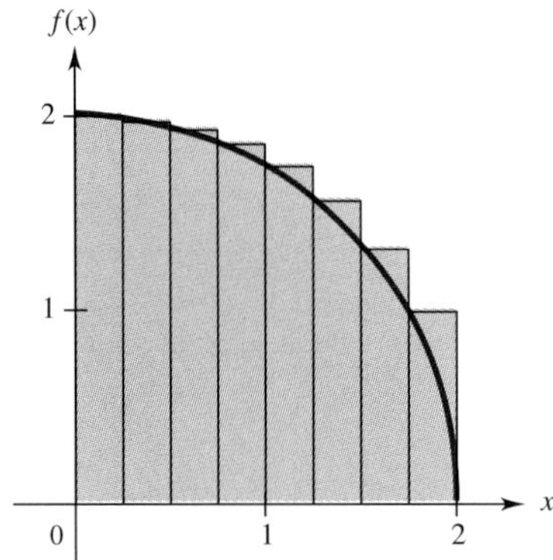

FIGURE 14.7

This process of approximating the area under a curve by using more and more rectangles to get a better and better approximation can be generalized. To do this, divide the interval from $x = 0$ to $x = 2$ into n equal parts. Each of these n intervals has width

$$\frac{2 - 0}{n} = \frac{2}{n},$$

so each rectangle has width $2/n$ and height determined by the function-value at the left side of the rectangle. A computer was used to find approximations of the area for several values of n given in the table at the side.

n	*Area*
125	3.15675
2000	3.14257
8000	3.14184
32,000	3.14165
128,000	3.14160
512,000	3.14159

As the number n of rectangles gets larger and larger, the sum of their areas gets closer and closer to the actual area of the region. In other words, the actual area is the *limit* of these sums as n gets larger and larger without bound, which can be written

$$\text{area} = \lim_{n \to \infty} (\text{sum of areas of } n \text{ rectangles}).$$

The table suggests that this limit is a number whose decimal expansion begins 3.14159 . . . , which is the same as the beginning of the decimal approximation of π. Therefore, it seems plausible that

$$\text{area} = \lim_{n \to \infty} (\text{sum of areas of } n \text{ rectangles}) = \pi. \quad \blacksquare$$

It can be shown that the region whose area was found in Example 2 is one-fourth of the interior of a circle of radius 2 with center at the origin (see Figure 14.4). Hence, its area is

$$\frac{1}{4}(\pi r^2) = \frac{1}{4}(\pi \cdot 2^2) = \pi,$$

which agrees with our answer in Example 2.

The method used in Example 2 can be generalized to find the area bounded by the curve $y = f(x)$, the x-axis, and the vertical lines $x = a$ and $x = b$, as shown in Figure 14.8. To approximate this area, we could divide the region under the curve first into ten rectangles (Figure 14.8(a)) and then into twenty rectangles (Figure 14.8(b)). In each case, the sum of the areas of the rectangles gives an approximation of the area under the curve.

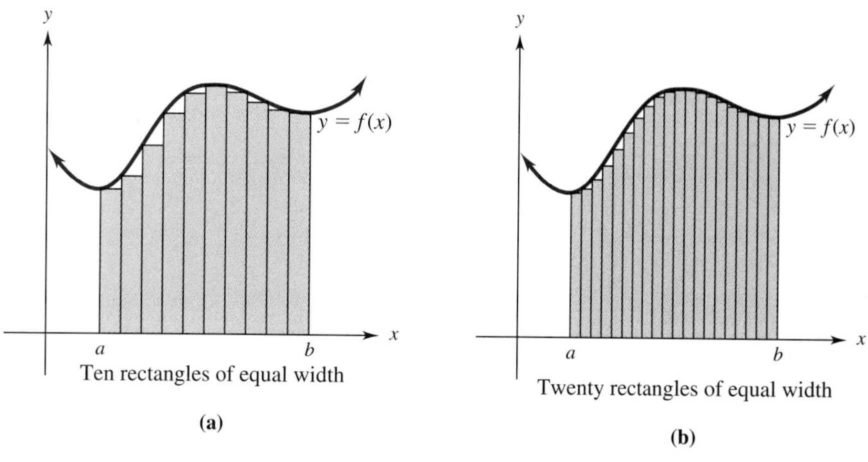

FIGURE 14.8

We can get better and better approximations by increasing the number n of rectangles. Here is a description of the general procedure. Let n be a positive integer. Divide the interval from a to b into n pieces of equal length. The symbol Δx is traditionally used to denote the length of each piece. Since the length of the entire interval is $b - a$, each of the n pieces has length

$$\Delta x = \frac{b - a}{n}.$$

Use each of these pieces as the base of a rectangle, as shown in Figure 14.9 on the next page, where the endpoints of the n intervals are labeled $x_1, x_2, x_3, \ldots, x_{n+1}$. A typical rectangle, the one whose lower left corner is at x_i, has darker shading. The base of this rectangle is Δx and its height is the height of the graph over x_i, namely $f(x_i)$, so

$$\text{Area of } i\text{th rectangle} = f(x_i) \cdot \Delta x.$$

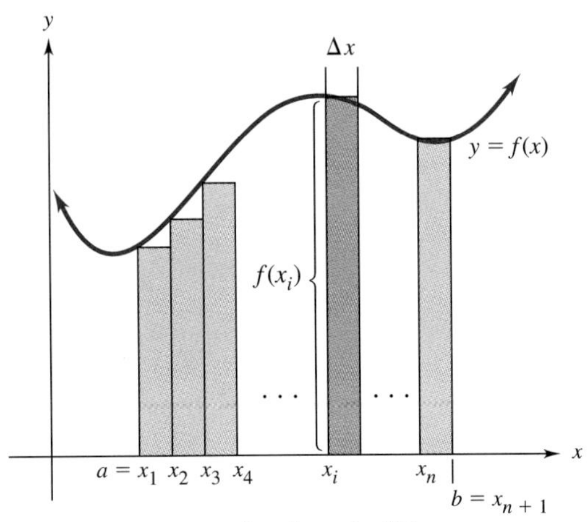

FIGURE 14.9

The total area under the curve is approximated by the sum of the areas of all n of the rectangles, namely,

$$f(x_1) \cdot \Delta x + f(x_2) \cdot \Delta x + f(x_3) \cdot \Delta x + \cdots + f(x_n) \cdot \Delta x.$$

The exact area is defined to be the limit of this sum (if it exists) as the number of rectangles gets larger and larger, without bound. Hence,

$$\begin{aligned}\text{Exact area} &= \lim_{n\to\infty} (f(x_1) \cdot \Delta x + f(x_2) \cdot \Delta x + f(x_3) \cdot \Delta x + \cdots + f(x_n) \cdot \Delta x) \\ &= \lim_{n\to\infty} ([f(x_1) + f(x_2) + f(x_3) + \cdots + f(x_n)] \cdot \Delta x).\end{aligned}$$

This limit is called the *definite integral* of $f(x)$ from a to b and is denoted by the symbol

$$\int_a^b f(x)\, dx.$$

The preceding discussion can be summarized as follows.

THE DEFINITE INTEGRAL

If f is a continuous function on the interval $[a, b]$, then the **definite integral** of f from a to b is the number

$$\int_a^b f(x)\, dx = \lim_{n\to\infty} [(f(x_1) + f(x_2) + f(x_3) + \cdots + f(x_n)) \cdot \Delta x],$$

where $\Delta x = (b - a)/n$ and x_i is the left-hand endpoint of the ith interval.

For instance, the area of the region in Example 2 could be written as the definite integral

$$\int_0^2 \sqrt{4 - x^2}\, dx = \pi.$$

Although the definition in the box is obviously motivated by the problem of finding areas, it is applicable to many other situations, as we shall see in later sections. In particular, *the definition of the definite integral is valid even when $f(x)$ takes negative values* (that is, when the graph goes below the x-axis). In that case, however, the resulting number is not the area between the graph and the x-axis. In this section we shall only deal with the area interpretation of the definite integral.

The elongated "S" in the notation for the definite integral stands for the word "Sum," which plays a crucial role in the definition. This notation looks very similar to that used for antiderivatives (also called *indefinite* integrals) in earlier sections. The connection between the definite integral and antiderivatives, which is the reason for the similar terminology and notation, will be explained in the next section.

CAUTION Children learning to read sometimes confuse b and d. Both consist of a half-circle and a vertical line segment, but the location of the line segment makes all the difference. Similarly, the symbols $\int f(x)\,dx$ and $\int_a^b f(x)\,dx$ have totally different meanings—the a and b make all the difference. The indefinite integral $\int f(x)\,dx$ denotes a set of *functions* (the antiderivatives of $f(x)$), whereas the definite integral $\int_a^b f(x)\,dx$ represents a *number* (that can be interpreted as the area under the graph when $f(x) \geq 0$). ◆

TECHNOLOGY TIP There are two ways to approximate a definite integral with a calculator, each of which is illustrated here for $\int_{-2}^{1} (x^3 - 5x + 6)\,dx$.

1. Approximate the limit in the definition by computing the sum for a large value of n, say $n = 100$. Then $\Delta x = (b - a)/n = (1 - (-2))/100 = 3/100 = .03$ and the sum is

$$[f(x_1) + f(x_2) + f(x_3) + \cdots + f(x_n)] \cdot \Delta x$$
$$= [f(x_1) + f(x_2) + f(x_3) + \cdots + f(x_{100})](.03).$$

To compute this sum automatically on TI-83/85/86/92, look in the submenus of the LIST menu and enter

sum(seq(x^3 − 5x + 6, x, −2, 1 − .03, .03)) × (.03).*

(−2: Left endpoint; 1 − .03: Right endpoint − Δx; .03: Δx)

On HP-38, look in the LIST submenu of the MATH menu and enter

ΣLIST(MAKELIST(x^3 − 5x + 6, x, −2, 1 − .03, .03)) × (.03).

On other calculators, use the RECTANGLE program in the Program Appendix. In each case, the calculator produces the approximation 21.8393.

2. Use **numerical integration.** This feature is available on most calculators; typically, it approximates the definite integral by using sums of areas of

*The same syntax works on TI-82 when $n \leq 99$, but not for larger values of n.

trapezoids rather than rectangles, as shown in Figure 14.10. On TI-82/83/85/86, look in the MATH or CALC menu and enter

$$\text{fnInt}(x^3 - 5x + 6, x, -2, 1).$$

On Casio, use the $\int dx$ key on the keyboard and enter

$$\int (x^3 - 5x + 6, x, -2, 1).$$

On HP-38, look for $\int$ in the CALCULUS submenu of the MATH menu and enter

$$\int (-2, 1, x^3 - 5x + 6, x).$$

On TI-81, use the NUMERICAL INTEGRATION program in the Program Appendix. In each case, the calculator approximates the integral as 21.75, which actually is its exact value, as we shall see in the next section. ✔

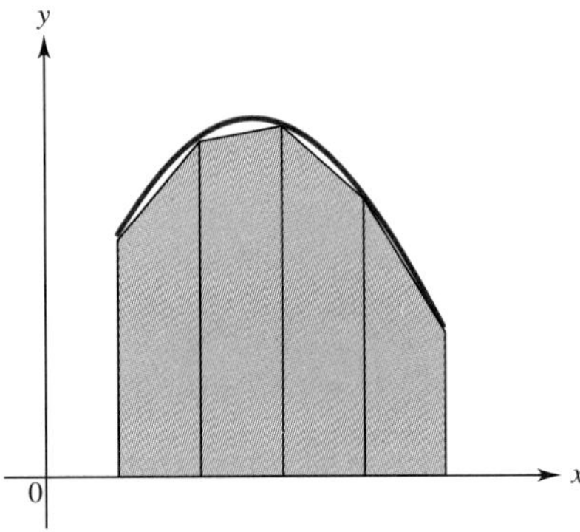

FIGURE 14.10

EXAMPLE 3 Figure 14.11(a) shows the graph of $f(x) = x^3 - 8x^2 + 18x + 5$. Approximate

$$\int_1^{4.5} (x^3 - 8x^2 + 18x + 5)\, dx,$$

which is the area under the graph of $f(x)$ from $x = 1$ to $x = 4.5$ (Figure 14.11(b)), in two ways.

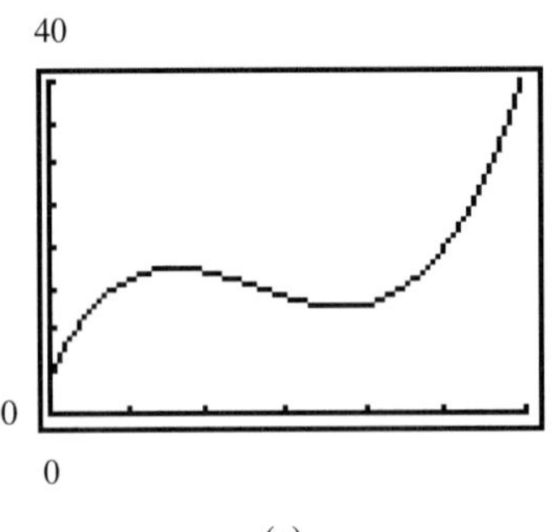

(a)

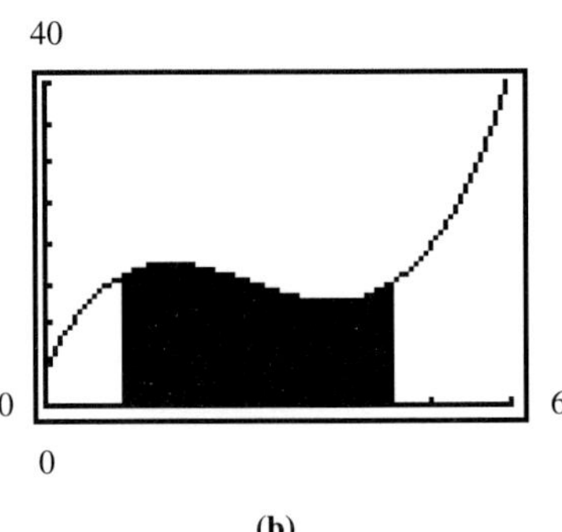

(b)

FIGURE 14.11

3 If $f(x) = x^3 - 8x^2 + 18x + 5$, use the first part of the Technology Tip to compute the sum

$$[f(1) + f(1.035) + f(1.07) + \cdots + f(4.465)](.035).$$

Answer:
52.6977

(a) Use the definition, with 100 rectangles.

For $n = 100$ rectangles, $\Delta x = (b - a)/n = (4.5 - 1)/100 = .035$. The left-hand endpoints of the bases of the rectangles are 1, 1.035, 1.07, 1.105, 1.14, . . . , 4.43, and 4.465 (the right-hand endpoint of the base of the last rectangle is 4.5). We must compute this sum:

$$[f(1) + f(1.035) + f(1.07) + \cdots + f(4.43) + f(4.465)](.035).$$

Compute this sum by doing Problem 3 in the margin. 3

(b) Use numerical integration.

The numerical integration program on a typical calculator (see part 2 of the Technology Tip above) produces 52.6823. ■

At the beginning of this section we saw that if $f(x)$ (with $f(x) \geq 0$) is the rate of change of a function $F(x)$, then the total change in $F(x)$ as x goes from a to b is the area between the graph of $f(x)$ and the x-axis from $x = a$ to $x = b$. In other words,

$$\text{Total Change in } F(x) = \int_a^b f(x)\,dx.$$

4 If the marginal revenue (in hundreds of dollars per year) is given by

$$MR(x) = .3x^3 - .5x^2 + x,$$

find the total revenue for the first six years (that is, from $x = 0$ to $x = 6$).

Answer:
Approximately $7920

EXAMPLE 4 The marginal revenue (in thousands of dollars per year) for sales of a certain product over a 12-year period is given by

$$MR(x) = .12x^3 - 2.5x^2 + 15x \quad (0 \leq x \leq 12).$$

Find the total sales revenue for the 12-year period.

Total revenue is the change in revenue from $x = 0$ to $x = 12$. Since the marginal revenue is the derivative of the revenue function,

$$\text{Total Revenue} = \int_0^{12} (.12x^3 - 2.5x^2 + 15x)\,dx.$$

Using numerical integration we find that revenue is approximately 262.08 thousands of dollars, that is, $262,080. ■ 4

14.3 EXERCISES

1. Explain the difference between an indefinite integral and a definite integral.
2. Complete the following statement.

$$\int_0^3 (x^2 + 2)\,dx = \lim_{n\to\infty} \_\_\_\_\_, \text{ where } \Delta x = \_\_\_\_\_.$$

For each function, (a) approximate the area between the graph and the x-axis over the given interval by using 4 rectangles, with the height of each rectangle given by the value of the function at the left side of the rectangle; (b) repeat the process, using 40 rectangles; (c) repeat the process, using 100 rectangles. (See Examples 1–3.)

3. $f(x) = 4 - x^2$; $[-2, 2]$
4. $f(x) = x^2 + 1$; $[-2, 2]$

5. $f(x) = e^x - 1$; $[0, 4]$

6. $f(x) = e^x + 1$; $[-2, 2]$

7. $f(x) = \frac{1}{x}$; $[1, 5]$

8. $f(x) = \frac{2}{x}$; $[1, 9]$

Use numerical integration to approximate the value of the definite integral. (See Example 3.)

9. $\int_5^0 (x^3 + 2x^2 - 15x + 2)\, dx$

10. $\int_{-1}^3 (-x^4 + 3x^3 - x^2 + 9)\, dx$

11. $\int_2^7 5 \ln(x^2 + 1)\, dx$

12. $\int_1^5 x \ln x\, dx$

13. $\int_{-1}^3 x^2 e^{-x}\, dx$

14. $\int_1^5 \frac{\ln x}{x}\, dx$

In Exercises 15–18, **(a)** *Graph the function in a square viewing window that includes the region between the graph of the function and the x-axis over the given interval.* **(b)** *Approximate the area of the region by using 100 rectangles.* **(c)** *Approximate the area using numerical integration.* **(d)** *Find the exact area by using either the formula for the area of a triangle or the formula for the area of a circle. (See Examples 2 and 3.)*

15. $f(x) = x/2$ from $x = 0$ to $x = 4$

16. $f(x) = 5 - x$ from $x = 0$ to $x = 5$

17. $f(x) = \sqrt{6x - x^2 - 5}$ from $x = 1$ to $x = 5$

18. $f(x) = \sqrt{-x^2 - 6x}$ from $x = -6$ to $x = 0$

In these exercises, estimate the required areas by using rectangles. Let the function value at the left side of each rectangle give the height. (See Example 1.)

19. **Management** The graph shows the average manufacturing hourly wage in the United States and Canada for 1987–1991.* All figures are in U.S. dollars. Assume that the average employee works 2000 hours per year. Estimate the total amount earned by an average U.S. worker during the four-year period from the beginning of 1987 to the beginning of 1991. Use rectangles with widths of 1 yr.

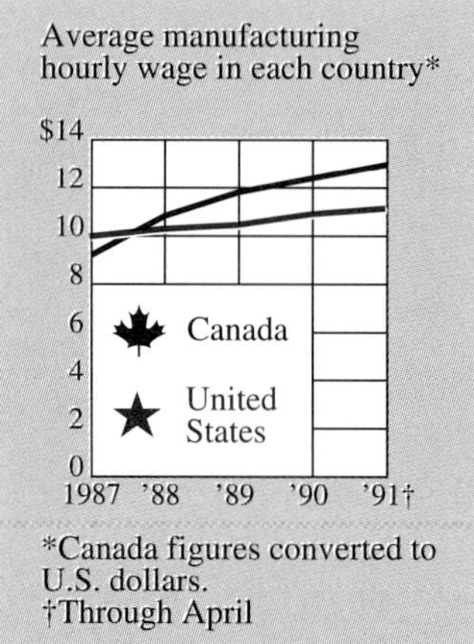

20. **Management** Estimate the total amount earned (in U.S. dollars) by an average Canadian worker during the four-year period from the beginning of 1987 to the beginning of 1991. Use rectangles with widths of 1 yr. (See Exercise 19.)

21. **Natural Science** The graph below shows the rate of inhalation of oxygen by a person riding a bicycle very rapidly for 10 minutes. Estimate the total volume of oxygen inhaled in the first 20 minutes after the beginning of the ride. Use rectangles of width 1 minute.

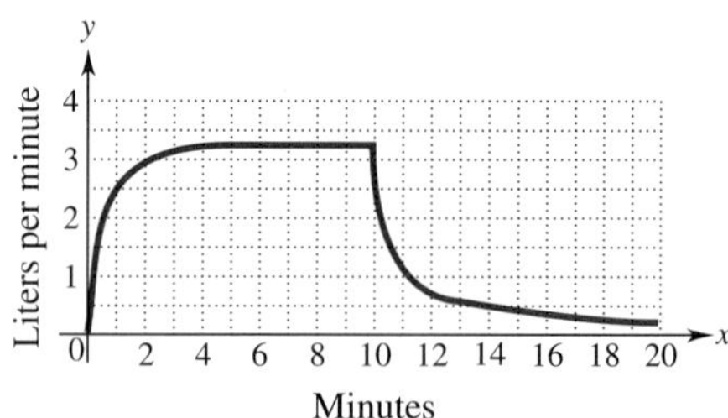

Physical Science *The next two graphs are from* Road and Track *magazine.* *The curve shows the velocity at time t, in seconds, when the car accelerates from a dead stop. To find the total distance traveled by the car in reaching 100 miles per hour, we must estimate the definite integral*

$$\int_0^T v(t)\, dt,$$

where T represents the number of seconds it takes for the car to reach 100 mph.

Use the graphs to estimate this distance by adding the areas of rectangles with widths of 5 seconds. The last rectangle has a width of 3. To adjust your answer to miles per hour, divide by 3600 (the number of seconds in an hour). You then have the number of miles that the car traveled in reaching 100 mph. Finally, multiply by 5280 feet per mile to convert the answers to feet.

*"Comparing Wages" from *The New York Times*. 1991. Copyright © 1991 by The New York Times Company. Reprinted by permission.

*From *Road & Track*, April and May, 1978. Reprinted with permission of *Road & Track*.

22. Estimate the distance traveled by the Porsche 928, using the graph below.

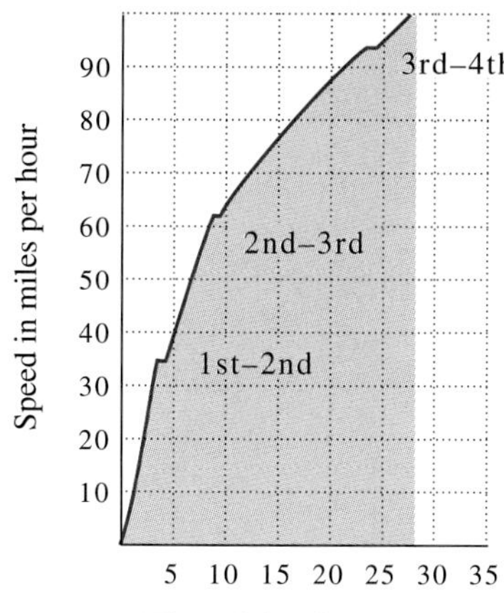

23. Estimate the distance traveled by the BMW 733i, using the graph below.

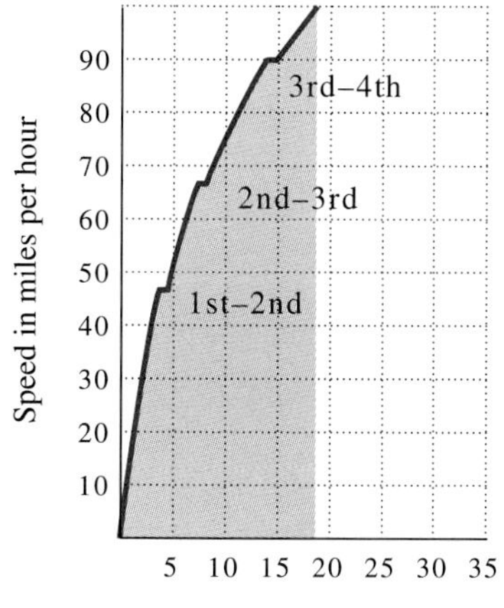

Physical Science *The graphs* in the right column show the typical heat gain, in BTUs per hour per square foot, for a window facing east and one facing south, with plain glass and with a black ShadeScreen. Estimate the total heat gain per square foot by summing the areas of the rectangles. Use rectangles with widths of 2 hr, and let the function value at the midpoint of the rectangle give the height of the rectangle.*

24. **(a)** Estimate the total heat gain per square foot for a plain glass window facing east.
    (b) Estimate the total heat gain per square foot for a window facing east with a ShadeScreen.

25. **(a)** Estimate the total heat gain per square foot for a plain glass window facing south.
    (b) Estimate the total heat gain per square foot for a window facing south with a ShadeScreen.

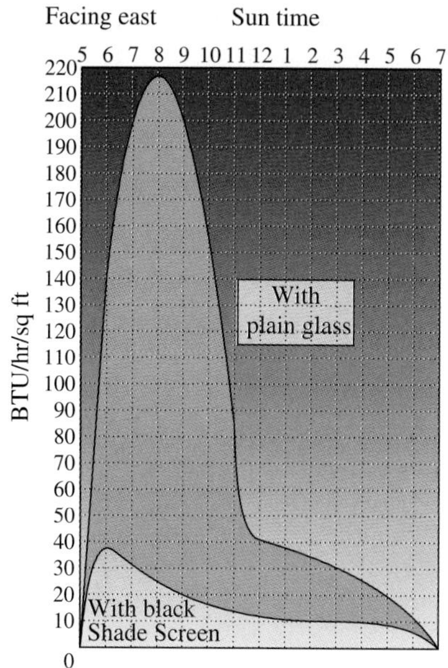

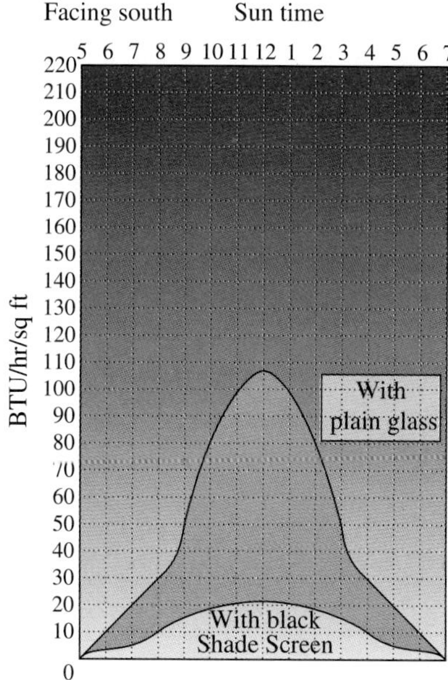

Each marginal revenue function below has x measured in years and MR(x) in hundreds of dollars per year. Find the total revenue over the given period. (See Example 4.)

26. $MR(x) = .04x^3 - .6x^2 + 3x \quad (0 \le x \le 12)$

27. $MR(x) = .04x^4 - .5x^3 + 2x^2 - x \quad (0 \le x \le 6)$

28. $MR(x) = .26x^4 - 6.25x^3 + 30.2x^2 + 87.5x \quad (0 \le x \le 5)$

---

*Two graphs, "Facing east, Sun time" and "Facing south, Sun time" from Phifer Wire Products. Reprinted by permission.

14.4 THE FUNDAMENTAL THEOREM OF CALCULUS

We now develop the connection between definite integrals and antiderivatives, which will explain the similar notation for these two concepts. More importantly, it provides a way to calculate definite integrals exactly.

In the last section we saw that when $f(x)$ is the rate of change of the function $F(x)$ and $f(x) \geq 0$ on $[a, b]$, then the definite integral has this interpretation:

$$\int_a^b f(x)\,dx = \text{Total Change in } F(x) \text{ as } x \text{ changes from } a \text{ to } b. \qquad (*)$$

Now to say that $f(x)$ is the rate of change of $F(x)$ means that $f(x)$ is the derivative of $F(x)$, or equivalently, that $F(x)$ is an antiderivative of $f(x)$. The total change in $F(x)$ as x changes from a to b is the difference between the value of F at the end and the value of F at the beginning, that is, $F(b) - F(a)$. So we can restate (*) by saying that

$$\int_a^b f(x)\,dx = F(b) - F(a).$$

This relationship is an example of the following result (in which $f(x)$ may not always be ≥ 0).

> **FUNDAMENTAL THEOREM OF CALCULUS**
>
> Suppose f is continuous on the interval $[a, b]$ and F is *any* antiderivative of f. Then
>
> $$\int_a^b f(x)\,dx = F(b) - F(a).$$

1 Let $C(x) = x^3 + 4x^2 - x + 3$. Find the following.

(a) $C(x)\Big|_1^5$

(b) $C(x)\Big|_3^4$

Answers:

(a) 216

(b) 64

CAUTION It is important to note that the Fundamental Theorem does not require $f(x) > 0$. The condition $f(x) > 0$ is necessary only when using the Fundamental Theorem to find area. Also, note that the Fundamental Theorem does not *define* the definite integral; it just provides a method for evaluating it. ◆

When evaluating definite integrals, the symbol $F(x)\big|_a^b$ is used to denote the number $F(b) - F(a)$. For example, if $F(x) = x^4$, then $x^4\big|_1^2$ means $F(2) - F(1) = 2^4 - 1^4$. 1

NOTE Because the definite integral is a number, there is no constant C added, as there is for the indefinite integral. Even if C were added to the antiderivative F, it would be eliminated in the final answer:

$$\begin{aligned}\int_a^b f(x)\,dx &= (F(x) + C)\Big|_a^b \\ &= (F(b) + C) - (F(a) + C) \\ &= F(b) - F(a). \ ◆\end{aligned}$$

EXAMPLE 1 Find $\int_1^2 4t^3\,dt.$

By the rules given earlier,

$$\int 4t^3\,dt = t^4 + C.$$

2 Find each of the following.

(a) $\int_4^6 5z\,dz$

(b) $\int_2^5 8t^3\,dt$

(c) $\int_1^9 \sqrt{z}\,dz$

Answers:

(a) 50

(b) 1218

(c) 52/3

By the Fundamental Theorem of Calculus, the value of $\int_1^2 4t^3\,dt$ is found by evaluating $t^4\Big|_1^2$.

$$\int_1^2 4t^3\,dt = t^4\Big|_1^2 = 2^4 - 1^4 = 15 \quad \blacksquare \quad \boxed{2}$$

Example 1 illustrates the difference between the definite integral and the indefinite integral. A definite integral is a real number; an indefinite integral is a family of functions in which all the functions are antiderivatives of a function f.

Although we cannot give a rigorous proof of the Fundamental Theorem of Calculus here, we can indicate why it is true when $f(x) \geq 0$ and the definite integral represents area. Given the function $f(x)$, define a new function $A(x)$ by the rule,

$$A(x) = \text{area between the graph of } f(x) \text{ and the } x\text{-axis from } a \text{ to } x,$$

as shown in Figure 14.12. For instance, if the area under the graph from a to 4 is 35, then $A(4) = 35$. We first show that A is an antiderivative of f.

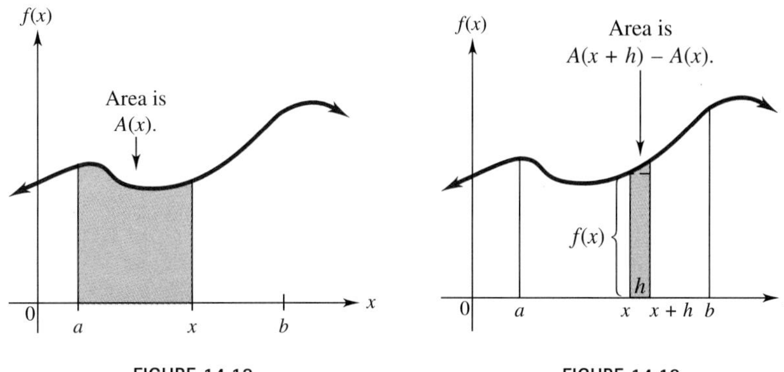

FIGURE 14.12

FIGURE 14.13

To compute $A'(x)$, let h be a small positive number. Then $A(x + h)$ is the area under the graph of f from a to $x + h$ and $A(x)$ is the area from a to x. Consequently, $A(x + h) - A(x)$ is the area of the shaded strip in Figure 14.13. This area can be approximated with a rectangle having base h and height $f(x)$. The area of the rectangle is $h \cdot f(x)$ and

$$A(x + h) - A(x) \approx h \cdot f(x).$$

Dividing both sides by h gives

$$\frac{A(x + h) - A(x)}{h} \approx f(x).$$

This approximation improves as h gets smaller and smaller. Take the limit on the left as h approaches 0.

$$\lim_{h \to 0} \frac{A(x + h) - A(x)}{h} = f(x)$$

This limit is simply $A'(x)$, so

$$A'(x) = f(x).$$

This result means that A is an antiderivative of f, as we set out to show.

Since $A(x)$ is the area under the graph of f from a to x, we see that $A(a) = 0$ and $A(b)$ is the area under the graph from a to b. But this last area is the definite integral $\int_a^b f(x)\,dx$. Putting these facts together we have

$$\int_a^b f(x)\,dx = A(b) = A(b) - 0 = A(b) - A(a).$$

This argument suggests that the Fundamental Theorem is true when $f(x) > 0$ and the area function $A(x)$ is used as the antiderivative. Other arguments, which are omitted here, handle the case when $f(x)$ may not be positive and any antiderivative $F(x)$ is used.

The Fundamental Theorem of Calculus certainly deserves its name, which sets it apart as the most important theorem of calculus. It is the key connection between differential calculus and integral calculus, which originally were developed separately without knowledge of this connection between them.

The variable used in the integrand does not matter; each of the following definite integrals represents the number $F(b) - F(a)$.

$$\int_a^b f(x)\,dx = \int_a^b f(t)\,dt = \int_a^b f(u)\,du$$

The definition of $\int_a^b f(x)\,dx$ assumed that $a < b$, that is, that the lower limit of integration is the smaller number. We now define $\int_a^b f(x)\,dx$ when $b < a$ to be $-\int_b^a f(x)\,dx$. For example, $\int_3^1 x^2\,dx = -\int_1^3 x^2\,dx$. The Fundamental Theorem remains valid for such integrals.

Key properties of definite integrals are listed below. Some of them are just restatements of properties from Section 14.1.

PROPERTIES OF DEFINITE INTEGRALS

For any real numbers a and b for which the definite integrals exist,

1. $\int_a^a f(x)\,dx = 0$;
2. $\int_a^b k \cdot f(x)\,dx = k \cdot \int_a^b f(x)\,dx$, for any real constant k (constant multiple of a function);
3. $\int_a^b [f(x) \pm g(x)]\,dx = \int_a^b f(x)\,dx \pm \int_a^b g(x)\,dx$ (sum or difference of functions);
4. $\int_a^b f(x)\,dx = \int_a^c f(x)\,dx + \int_c^b f(x)\,dx$, for any real number c.

For $f(x) \geq 0$, because the distance from a to a is 0, the first property says that the "area" under the graph of f bounded by $x = a$ and $x = a$ is 0. Also, since $\int_a^c f(x)\,dx$ represents the darker region in Figure 14.14 and $\int_c^b f(x)\,dx$ represents the lighter region,

$$\int_a^b f(x)\,dx = \int_a^c f(x)\,dx + \int_c^b f(x)\,dx,$$

as stated in the fourth property. While the figure shows $a < c < b$, the property is true for any value of c where both $f(x)$ and $F(x)$ are defined. Of course, the properties apply even if $f(x) < 0$.

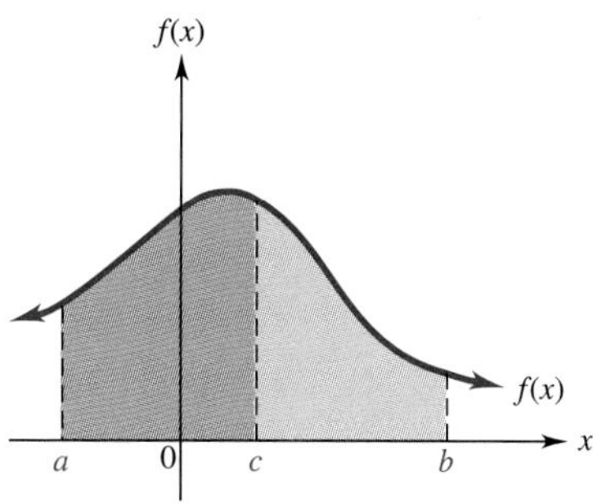

FIGURE 14.14

An algebraic proof is given here for the third property; proofs of the other properties are omitted. If $F(x)$ and $G(x)$ are antiderivatives of $f(x)$ and $g(x)$, respectively,

$$\begin{aligned}\int_a^b [f(x) + g(x)]\,dx &= [F(x) + G(x)]\Big|_a^b \\ &= [F(b) + G(b)] - [F(a) + G(a)] \\ &= [F(b) - F(a)] + [G(b) - G(a)] \\ &= \int_a^b f(x)\,dx + \int_a^b g(x)\,dx.\end{aligned}$$

3 Evaluate each definite integral.

(a) $\int_1^3 (x + 3x^2)\,dx$

(b) $\int_2^4 (6k^2 - 2k + 1)\,dk$

Answers:
(a) 30
(b) 102

EXAMPLE 2 Evaluate $\int_2^5 (6x^2 - 3x + 5)\,dx$.

Use the properties above, and the Fundamental Theorem, along with the power rule from Section 14.1.

$$\begin{aligned}\int_2^5 (6x^2 - 3x + 5)\,dx &= 6\int_2^5 x^2\,dx - 3\int_2^5 x\,dx + 5\int_2^5 dx && \text{Constant multiple; sum or difference} \\ &= 2x^3\Big|_2^5 - \frac{3}{2}x^2\Big|_2^5 + 5x\Big|_2^5 && \text{Integrate.} \\ &= 2(5^3 - 2^3) - \frac{3}{2}(5^2 - 2^2) + 5(5 - 2) && \text{Evaluate the limits.} \\ &= 2(125 - 8) - \frac{3}{2}(25 - 4) + 5(3) \\ &= 234 - \frac{63}{2} + 15 = \frac{435}{2}\end{aligned}$$ ■ 3

4 Evaluate the following.

(a) $\int_0^4 e^x\,dx$

(b) $\int_3^5 \frac{dx}{x}$

(c) $\int_2^8 \frac{4}{x}\,dx$

Answers:
(a) 53.59815
(b) .51083
(c) 5.54518

EXAMPLE 3 Find $\int_1^2 \frac{dy}{y}$.

Using a result from Section 14.1,

$$\int_1^2 \frac{dy}{y} = \ln|y|\Big|_1^2 = \ln|2| - \ln|1| \approx .6931 - 0 = .6931.$$ ■ 4

EXAMPLE 4 Evaluate $\int_0^5 x\sqrt{25 - x^2}\, dx$.

Use substitution. Let $u = 25 - x^2$, so that $du = -2x\, dx$. With a definite integral, the limits should be changed, too. The new limits on u are found as follows.

If $x = 5$, then $u = 25 - 5^2 = 0$; if $x = 0$, then $u = 25 - 0^2 = 25$.

$$\int_0^5 x\sqrt{25 - x^2}\, dx = -\frac{1}{2}\int_0^5 \sqrt{25 - x^2}\,(-2x\, dx)$$

$$= -\frac{1}{2}\int_{25}^{0} \sqrt{u}\, du \qquad \text{Substitute.}$$

$$= -\frac{1}{2}\int_{25}^{0} u^{1/2}\, du \qquad \text{Fractional exponent}$$

$$= -\frac{1}{2}\cdot\frac{u^{3/2}}{3/2}\bigg|_{25}^{0} \qquad \text{Integrate.}$$

$$= -\frac{1}{2}\cdot\frac{2}{3}[0^{3/2} - 25^{3/2}] \qquad \text{Evaluate limits.}$$

$$= -\frac{1}{3}(-125) = \frac{125}{3} \quad \blacksquare$$

5 Find $\int_0^2 \frac{x}{x^2 + 1}\, dx$.

Answer:

$\frac{1}{2}\ln 5$

CAUTION Whenever you use the substitution method, be sure to replace x by its equivalent in terms of u *everywhere.* In particular, remember that the limits of integration refer to x and must be changed, too. ◆ 5

AREA In the previous section we saw that when the graph of $f(x)$ lies above the x-axis between a and b, then the definite integral $\int_a^b f(x)\, dx$ gives the area between the graph of $f(x)$ and the x-axis from a to b. Now consider a function f whose graph lies below the x-axis from a to b. The shaded area in Figure 14.15 can be approximated by sums of areas of rectangles, that is, by sums of the form

$$f(x_1)\cdot\Delta x + f(x_2)\cdot\Delta x + f(x_3)\cdot\Delta x + \cdots + f(x_n)\cdot\Delta x,$$

with one difference: since $f(x)$ is negative, the sum represents the *negative* of the sum of the areas of the rectangles. Consequently, the definite integral $\int_a^b f(x)\, dx$, which is the limit of such sums as n gets larger and larger, is the *negative* of the shaded area in Figure 14.15.

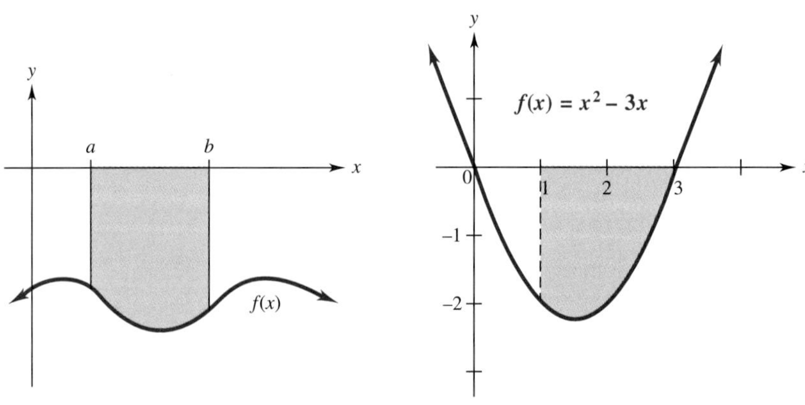

FIGURE 14.15

FIGURE 14.16

6 Find each area.

(a)

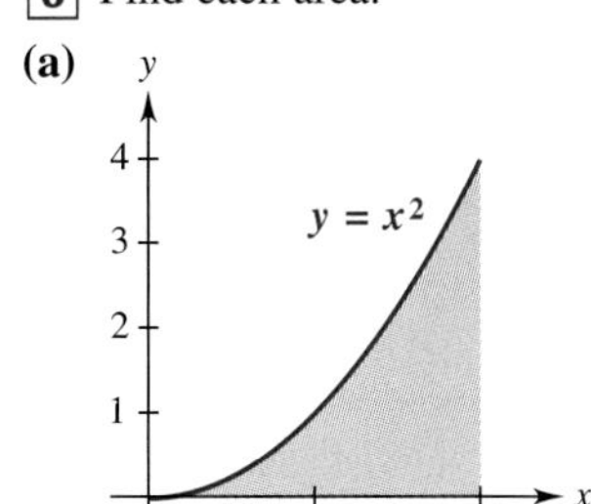

(b)

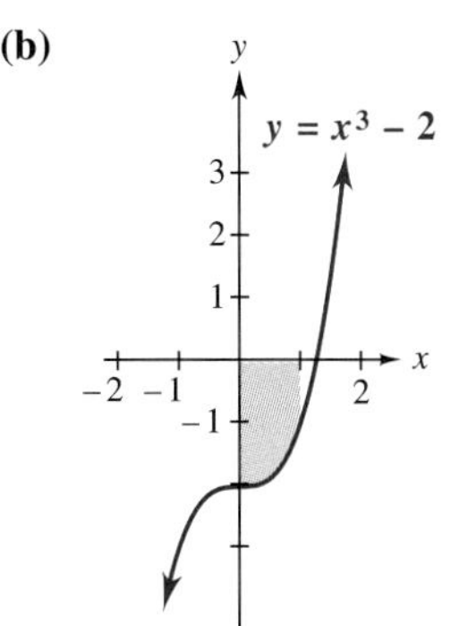

Answers:

(a) 8/3

(b) 7/4

EXAMPLE 5 Find the area between the x-axis and the graph of $f(x) = x^2 - 3x$ from $x = 1$ to $x = 3$.

The region, which is shaded in Figure 14.16, lies below the x-axis and the definite integral gives the negative of its area:

$$\int_1^3 (x^2 - 3x)\,dx = \left(\frac{x^3}{3} - \frac{3x^2}{2}\right)\Big|_1^3 = \left(\frac{27}{3} - \frac{27}{2}\right) - \left(\frac{1}{3} - \frac{3}{2}\right) = -\frac{10}{3}.$$

Therefore, the area of the region is 10/3. ■ 6

EXAMPLE 6 Find the area between the graph of $f(x) = 6x^2 - 7x - 3$ and the x-axis from $x = 0$ to $x = 2$, which is the shaded region in Figure 14.17.

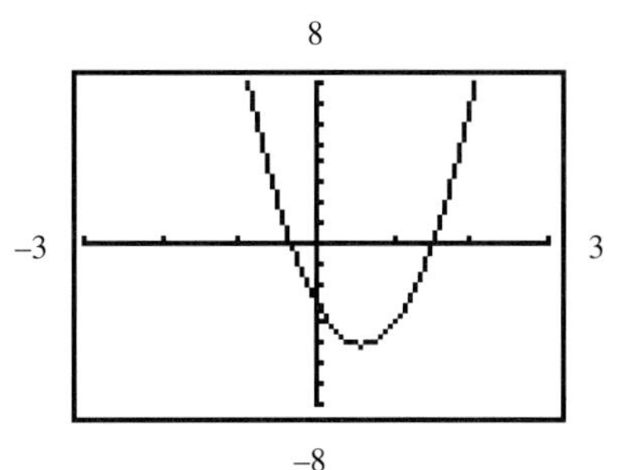

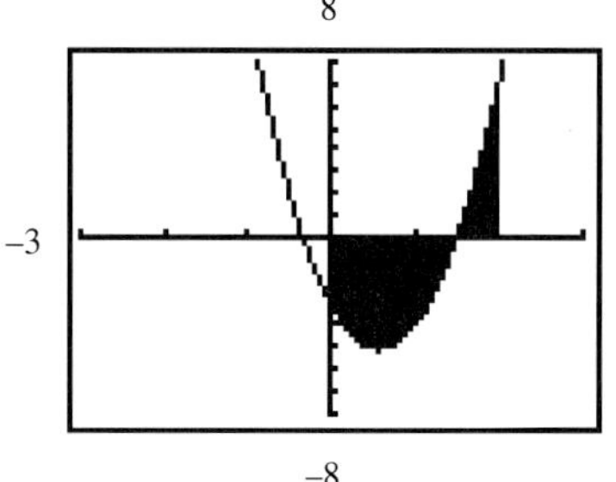

$f(x) = 6x^2 - 7x - 3$

FIGURE 14.17

To find the total area, compute the area under the x-axis and the area over the x-axis separately. Start by finding the x-intercepts of the graph by solving

$$6x^2 - 7x - 3 = 0$$
$$(2x - 3)(3x + 1) = 0$$
$$x = 3/2 \quad \text{or} \quad x = -1/3.$$

Since we are only concerned with the graph between 0 and 2, the only relevant x-intercept is 3/2. The area below the x-axis is the negative of

$$\int_0^{3/2} (6x^2 - 7x - 3)\,dx = \left(2x^3 - \frac{7}{2}x^2 - 3x\right)\Big|_0^{3/2}$$
$$= \left(2\left(\frac{3}{2}\right)^3 - \frac{7}{2}\left(\frac{3}{2}\right)^2 - 3\left(\frac{3}{2}\right)\right) - (0 - 0 - 0) = -\frac{45}{8}.$$

So the area of the lower region is 45/8. The area above the x-axis is

$$\int_{3/2}^2 (6x^2 - 7x - 3)\,dx = \left(2x^3 - \frac{7}{2}x^2 - 3x\right)\Big|_{3/2}^2$$
$$= \left(2(2^3) - \frac{7}{2}(2^2) - 3(2)\right) - \left(2\left(\frac{3}{2}\right)^3 - \frac{7}{2}\left(\frac{3}{2}\right)^2 - 3\left(\frac{3}{2}\right)\right) = \frac{13}{8}.$$

The area of the upper region is 13/8 and the total area between the graph and the x-axis is

$$\frac{45}{8} + \frac{13}{8} = \frac{58}{8} = 7.25 \text{ square units.} \quad ■$$

The procedure used in Example 6 may be summarized as follows.

FINDING AREA

To find the area bounded by $y = f(x)$, the vertical lines $x = a$ and $x = b$, and the x-axis, use the following steps.

Step 1 Sketch a graph.

Step 2 Find any x-intercepts in $[a, b]$. These divide the total region into subregions.

Step 3 The definite integral will be *positive* for subregions above the x-axis and *negative* for subregions below the x-axis. Use separate integrals to find the areas of the subregions.

Step 4 The total area is the sum of the areas of all of the subregions.

It is essential in Example 6 to compute the upper and lower areas separately. If you use a single integral over the entire interval, you obtain

$$\int_0^2 (6x^2 - 7x - 3)\,dx = \left(2x^3 - \frac{7}{2}x^2 - 3x\right)\Big|_0^2$$
$$= \left(2(2^3) - \frac{7}{2}(2^2) - 3(2)\right) - 0 = -4,$$

which is not the correct area. To see why, use property 4 of definite integrals.

$$\int_0^2 (6x^2 - 7x - 3)\,dx$$
$$= \int_0^{3/2} (6x^2 - 7x - 3)\,dx + \int_{3/2}^2 (6x^2 - 7x - 3)\,dx$$
$$= -\frac{45}{8} + \frac{13}{8} = \frac{13}{8} - \frac{45}{8}$$

But Example 6 shows that $\frac{13}{8} - \frac{45}{8}$ is

(area above the x-axis) $-$ (area below the x-axis),

which is not the same as the area between the graph and the axis. The same result holds in the general case.

If f is a continuous function on $[a, b]$, then

$$\int_a^b f(x)\,dx = \begin{pmatrix}\text{area between the}\\ \text{graph and the } x\text{-axis}\\ \textit{above}\text{ the axis}\end{pmatrix} - \begin{pmatrix}\text{area between the}\\ \text{graph and the } x\text{-axis}\\ \textit{below}\text{ the } x\text{-axis}\end{pmatrix}.$$

In the last section we saw that the area under the graph of a rate of change function $f'(x)$ from $x = a$ to $x = b$ gives the total change in $f(x)$ from a to b. We can now use the Fundamental Theorem to compute this change.

EXAMPLE 7 The yearly rate of consumption of natural gas in trillions of cubic feet for a certain city is

$$C'(t) = t + e^{.01t},$$

where t is time in years, and $t = 0$ corresponds to 1990. At this consumption rate, what is the total amount the city will use in the 10-year period of the nineties?

The amount used over the 10 years is the total change in consumption from year 0 to year 10, so it is given by the definite integral

$$\int_0^{10} (t + e^{.01t})\,dt = \left(\frac{t^2}{2} + \frac{e^{.01t}}{.01}\right)\Bigg|_0^{10}$$

$$= (50 + 100e^{.1}) - (0 + 100)$$

$$\approx -50 + 100(1.10517) \approx 60.5.$$

Therefore, a total of about 60.5 trillion cubic feet of natural gas will be used during the nineties if the consumption rate remains the same. ■ 7

7 In Example 7, suppose a conservation campaign and higher prices cause the rate of consumption to be given by $c'(t) = \frac{1}{2}t + e^{.005t}$. Find the total amount of gas used in the nineties.

Answer:
About 35.25 trillion cubic feet

14.4 EXERCISES

Evaluate each of the following definite integrals. (See Examples 1–4.)

1. $\int_{-1}^{3} (6x^2 - 4x + 3)\,dx$
2. $\int_{0}^{2} (-3x^2 + 2x + 5)\,dx$
3. $\int_{0}^{2} 3\sqrt{4u + 1}\,du$
4. $\int_{3}^{9} \sqrt{2r - 2}\,dr$
5. $\int_{0}^{1} 2(t^{1/2} - t)\,dt$
6. $\int_{0}^{4} -(3x^{3/2} + x^{1/2})\,dx$
7. $\int_{1}^{4} (5y\sqrt{y} + 3\sqrt{y})\,dy$
8. $\int_{4}^{9} (4\sqrt{r} - 3r\sqrt{r})\,dr$
9. $\int_{4}^{6} \frac{2}{(x - 3)^2}\,dx$
10. $\int_{1}^{4} \frac{-3}{(2p + 1)^2}\,dp$
11. $\int_{1}^{5} (5n^{-1} + n^{-3})\,dn$
12. $\int_{2}^{3} (3x^{-1} - x^{-4})\,dx$
13. $\int_{2}^{3} \left(2e^{-.1A} + \frac{3}{A}\right) dA$
14. $\int_{1}^{2} \left(\frac{-1}{B} + 3e^{.2B}\right) dB$
15. $\int_{1}^{2} \left(e^{5u} - \frac{1}{u^2}\right) du$
16. $\int_{.5}^{1} (p^3 - e^{4p})\,dp$
17. $\int_{-1}^{0} y(2y^2 - 3)^5\,dy$
18. $\int_{0}^{3} m^2(4m^3 + 2)^3\,dm$
19. $\int_{1}^{64} \frac{\sqrt{z} - 2}{\sqrt[3]{z}}\,dz$
20. $\int_{1}^{8} \frac{3 - y^{1/3}}{y^{2/3}}\,dy$
21. $\int_{1}^{2} \frac{\ln x}{x}\,dx$
22. $\int_{1}^{3} \frac{\sqrt{\ln x}}{x}\,dx$
23. $\int_{0}^{8} x^{1/3}\sqrt{x^{4/3} + 9}\,dx$
24. $\int_{1}^{2} \frac{3}{x(1 + \ln x)}\,dx$
25. $\int_{0}^{1} \frac{e^t}{(3 + e^t)^2}\,dt$
26. $\int_{0}^{1} \frac{e^{2z}}{\sqrt{1 + e^{2z}}}\,dz$
27. $\int_{1}^{49} \frac{(1 + \sqrt{x})^{4/3}}{\sqrt{x}}\,dx$
28. $\int_{1}^{8} \frac{(1 + x^{1/3})^6}{x^{2/3}}\,dx$
29. Suppose the function in Example 6, $f(x) = 6x^2 - 7x - 3$ from $x = 0$ to $x = 2$, represented the annual rate of profit of a company over a two-year period. What might the negative integral for the first year and a half indicate? What integral would represent the overall profit for the two-year period?
30. In your own words describe how the Fundamental Theorem relates definite and indefinite integrals.

Use the definite integral to find the area between the x-axis and f(x) over the indicated interval. Check first to see if the graph crosses the x-axis in the given interval. (See Examples 5 and 6.)

31. $f(x) = 4 - x^2$; [0, 3]
32. $f(x) = x^2 - 2x - 3$; [0, 4]
33. $f(x) = x^3 - 1$; [−2, 2]
34. $f(x) = x^3 - 2x$; [−2, 4]

35. $f(x) = e^x - 1$; $[-1, 2]$

36. $f(x) = 1 - e^{-x}$; $[-1, 2]$

37. $f(x) = \frac{1}{x}$; $[1, e]$

38. $f(x) = \frac{1}{x}$; $[e, e^2]$

Find the area of each shaded region.

39.

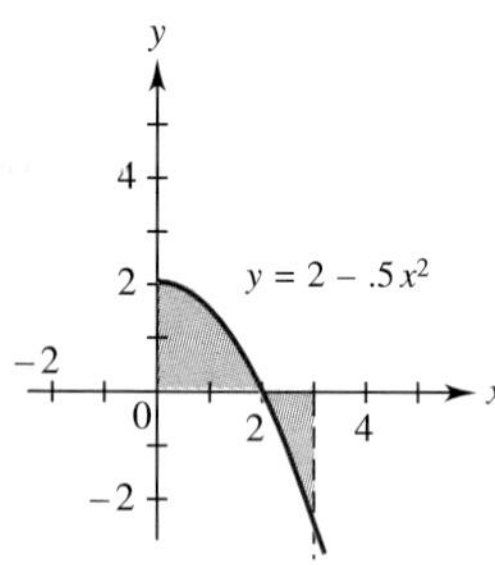

40.

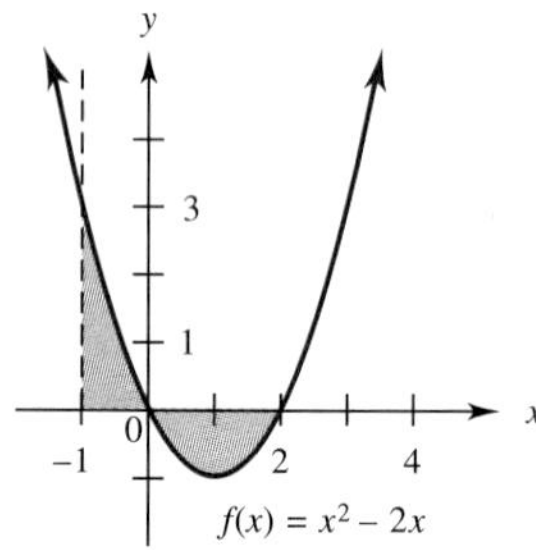

41.

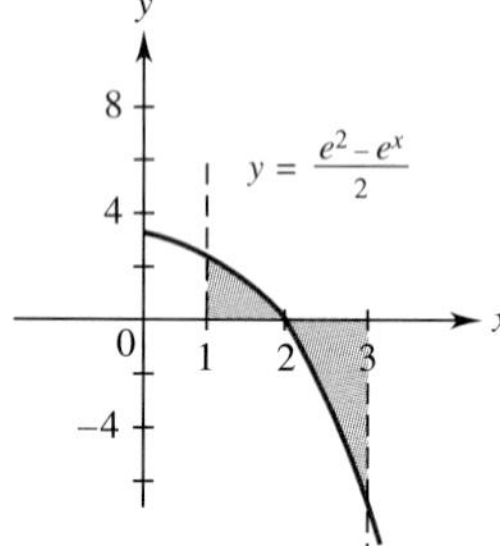

42.

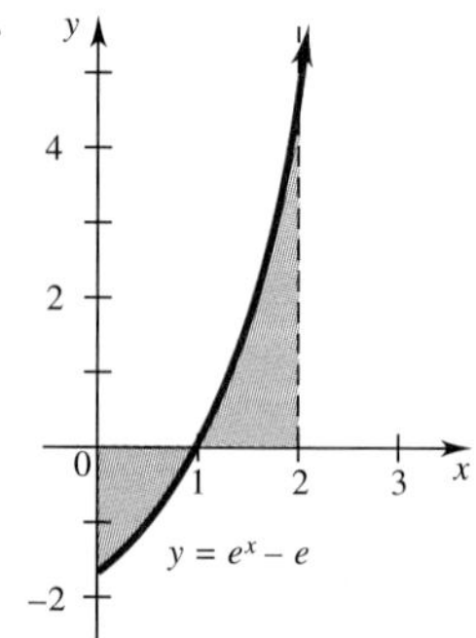

Use Property 4 of definite integrals to find $\int_1^4 f(x)\,dx$ for the following functions.

43. $f(x) = \begin{cases} 2x + 3 & \text{if } x \le 2 \\ -.5x + 8 & \text{if } x > 2 \end{cases}$

44. $f(x) = \begin{cases} x^2 - 2 & \text{if } x \le 3 \\ -x^2 + 16 & \text{if } x > 3 \end{cases}$

45. **(a)** Use the Fundamental Theorem to compute the definite integral in Exercise 22.
(b) Use numerical integration on your calculator to compute this integral.
(c) How do your answers in parts (a) and (b) compare? It may be possible to change the settings for your numerical integration program to make it more accurate (but slower); check your instruction manual.

46. **Management** De Win Enterprises has found that its expenditure rate per day (in hundreds of dollars) on a certain type of job is given by

$$E(x) = 4x + 2,$$

where x is the number of days since the start of the job.
(a) Find the total expenditure if the job takes 10 days.
(b) How much will be spent on the job from the 10th to the 20th day?
(c) If the company wants to spend no more than \$50,000 on the job, in how many days must they complete it?

47. **Management** Karla Harby Communications, a small company of science writers, found that its rate of profits (in thousands of dollars) after t years of operation is given by

$$P'(t) = (3t + 3)(t^2 + 2t + 2)^{1/3}.$$

(a) Find the total profits in the first three years.
(b) Find the profit in the fourth year of operation.
(c) What is happening to the annual profits over the long run?

48. **Management** A worker new to a job will improve his efficiency with time so that it takes him fewer hours to produce an item with each day on the job, up to a certain point. Suppose the rate of change of the number of hours it takes a worker in a certain factory to produce the xth item is given by

$$H'(x) = 20 - 2x.$$

(a) What is the total number of hours required to produce the first 5 items?
(b) What is the total number of hours required to produce the first 10 items?

49. **Management** The rate of depreciation for a certain truck is

$$f(t) = \frac{6000(.3 + .2t)}{(1 + .3t + .1t^2)^2},$$

where t is in years and $t = 0$ is the year of purchase.
(a) Find the total depreciation at the end of 3 years.
(b) In what year will the total depreciation be at least 3000?

50. Natural Science Pollution from a factory is entering a lake. The rate of concentration of the pollutant at time t is given by

$$P'(t) = 140t^{5/2},$$

where t is the number of years since the factory started introducing pollutants into the lake. Ecologists estimate that the lake can accept a total level of pollution of 4850 units before all the fish life in the lake ends. Can the factory operate for 4 yr without killing all the fish in the lake?

51. Natural Science An oil tanker is leaking oil at a rate given in barrels per hour by

$$L'(t) = \frac{80 \ln(t + 1)}{t + 1},$$

where t is the time in hours after the tanker hits a hidden rock (when $t = 0$).

(a) Find the total number of barrels that the ship will leak on the first day.

(b) Find the total number of barrels that the ship will leak on the second day.

(c) What is happening over the long run to the amount of oil leaked per day?

52. Natural Science After long study, tree scientists conclude that a eucalyptus tree will grow at the rate of $.2 + 4t^{-4}$ feet per year, where t is time in years.

(a) Find the number of feet that the tree will grow in the second year.

(b) Find the number of feet the tree will grow in the third year.

53. Management Suppose that the rate of consumption of a natural resource is $c'(t)$, where

$$c'(t) = ke^{rt}.$$

Here t is time in years, r is a constant, and k is the consumption in the year when $t = 0$. In 1990, an oil company sold 1.2 billion barrels of oil. Assume that $r = .04$.

(a) Set up a definite integral for the amount of oil that the company will sell in the next 10 years.

(b) Evaluate the definite integral of part (a).

(c) The company has about 20 billion barrels of oil in reserve. To find the number of years that this amount will last, solve this equation for T:

$$\int_0^T 1.2e^{.04t}\, dt = 20.$$

(d) Rework part (c), assuming that $r = .02$.

54. Management In Exercise 53 the rate of consumption of oil (in billions of barrels) was given as

$$1.2e^{.04t},$$

where $t = 0$ corresponds to 1990. Find the total amount of oil used from 1990 to year T. At this rate, how much will be used in 5 years?

14.5 APPLICATIONS OF INTEGRALS

Given a function that represents the total maintenance charge for a machine from the time it is installed, the rate of maintenance at any time t is given by the derivative of the total maintenance charge. Now, the total maintenance function can be found by finding the antiderivative of the rate of maintenance function. As we have seen in this chapter, if we graph the function giving the rate of maintenance, then the total maintenance is given by the area under the curve. Example 1 shows how this works.

EXAMPLE 1 Suppose a leasing company wants to decide on the yearly lease fee for a certain new printer. The company expects to lease the printer for 5 years, and it expects the *rate* of maintenance, $M(t)$ (in dollars), which it must supply, to be approximated by

$$M(t) = 10 + 2t + t^2,$$

where t is the number of years the printer has been used. How much should the company charge for maintenance on the printer for the 5-year period?

The definite integral can be used to find the total maintenance charge the company can expect over the life of the printer. Figure 14.18 shows the graph of $M(t)$. The total maintenance charge for the 5-year period will be given by the shaded area of the figure, which can be found as follows.

$$\int_0^5 (10 + 2t + t^2)\,dt = \left(10t + t^2 + \frac{t^3}{3}\right)\Bigg|_0^5$$
$$= 50 + 25 + \frac{125}{3} - 0$$
$$\approx 116.67$$

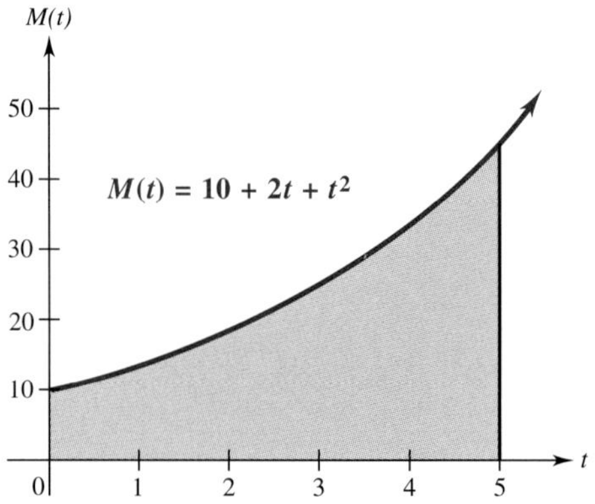

FIGURE 14.18

The company can expect the total maintenance charge for 5 years to be about \$117. Hence, the company should add about

$$\frac{\$117}{5} = \$23.40$$

to its annual lease price. ■ 1 2

1 Find the total maintenance charge for a lease of

(a) 1 year;

(b) 2 years.

Answers:

(a) \$11.33

(b) \$26.67

2 Suppose the rate of change of cost in dollars to produce x items is given by

$$C(x) = x^2 - 8x + 15.$$

Find the total cost to produce the first 10 items.

Answer:
\$83.33

EXAMPLE 2 Vonalaine Crowe, who runs a factory that makes signs, has been shown a new machine that staples the signs to the handles. She estimates that the rate of savings, $S(x)$, from the machine will be approximated by

$$S(x) = 3 + 2x,$$

where x represents the number of years the stapler has been in use. If the machine costs \$70, would it pay for itself in 5 years?

We need to find the area under the rate of savings curve shown in Figure 14.19 between the lines $x = 0$, $x = 5$, and the x-axis. Using a definite integral gives

$$\int_0^5 (3 + 2x)\,dx = 3x + x^2\Big|_0^5 = 40.$$

The total savings in 5 years is \$40, so the machine will not pay for itself in this time period. ■ 3

3 Find the amount of savings over the first 6 years for the machine in Example 2.

Answer:
\$54

FIGURE 14.19

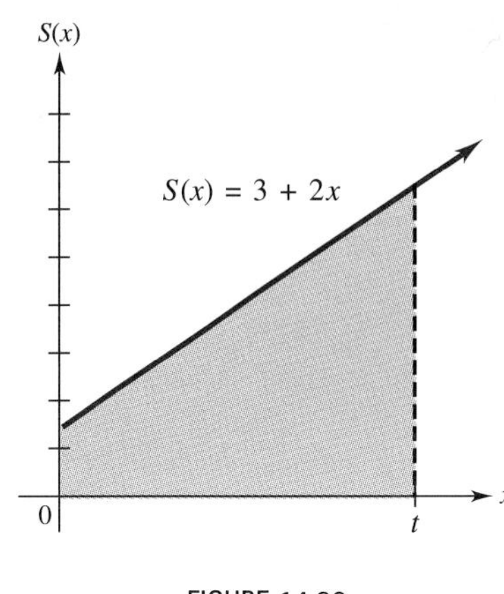

FIGURE 14.20

EXAMPLE 3 When will the machine in Example 2 pay for itself?

Because the machine in Example 2 costs a total of \$70, it will pay for itself when the area under the savings curve of Figure 14.20 equals 70, or at a time t such that

$$\int_0^t (3 + 2x)\,dx = 70.$$

Evaluating the definite integral gives

$$3x + x^2 \Big|_0^t = (3t + t^2) - (3 \cdot 0 + 0^2) = 3t + t^2.$$

Since the total savings must equal 70,

$$3t + t^2 = 70.$$

Solve this quadratic equation to verify that the solutions are 7 and -10. Since -10 cannot be used here, the machine will pay for itself in 7 years. ■ 4

4 Find the number of years in which the machine in Example 2 will pay for itself if the rate of savings is $S(x) = 5 + 4x$.

Answer:
4.8 years

In Section 14.3 we saw that a definite integral can be used to find the area *under* a curve. This idea can be extended to find the area *between* two curves, as shown in the next example.

EXAMPLE 4 A company is considering a new manufacturing process in one of its plants. The new process provides substantial initial savings, with the savings declining with time x according to the rate-of-savings function

$$S(x) = 100 - x^2,$$

where $S(x)$ is in thousands of dollars. At the same time, the cost of operating the new process increases with time x, according to the rate-of-cost function (in thousands of dollars)

$$C(x) = x^2 + \frac{14}{3}x.$$

(a) For how many years will the company realize savings?

Figure 14.21 shows the graphs of the rate-of-savings and the rate-of-cost functions. The rate-of-cost (marginal cost) is increasing, while the rate-of-savings (marginal savings) is decreasing. The company should use this new process until the difference between these quantities is zero—that is, until the time at which these graphs intersect. The intersection point can be found graphically or algebraically as follows. The graphs intersect when

$$S(x) = C(x),$$

or

$$100 - x^2 = x^2 + \frac{14}{3}x.$$

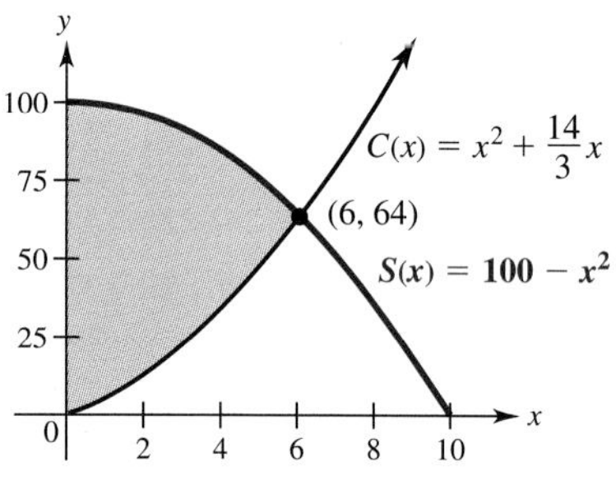

FIGURE 14.21

Solve this equation as follows.

$$0 = 2x^2 + \frac{14}{3}x - 100$$

$$0 = 3x^2 + 7x - 150 \qquad \text{Multiply by 3/2.}$$

$$0 = (x - 6)(3x + 25) \qquad \text{Factor.}$$

Set each factor equal to 0 and solve both equations to get

$$x = 6 \quad \text{or} \quad x = -\frac{25}{3}.$$

Only 6 is a meaningful solution here. The company should use the new process for 6 years.

(b) What will be the net total savings during this period?

Since the total savings over the 6-year period is given by the area under the rate-of-savings curve and the total additional cost by the area under the rate-of-cost curve, the net total savings over the 6-year period is given by the difference between these areas. This difference is the shaded region between the rate-of-cost and the rate-of-savings curves and the lines $x = 0$ and $x = 6$ shown in Figure 14.21. This area can be evaluated with a definite integral as follows.

$$\begin{aligned}
\text{Total savings} &= \int_0^6 [S(x) - C(x)]\, dx \\
&= \int_0^6 \left[(100 - x^2) - \left(x^2 + \frac{14}{3}x\right)\right] dx \\
&= \int_0^6 \left(100 - \frac{14}{3}x - 2x^2\right) dx \qquad \text{Combine terms.}
\end{aligned}$$

5 In Example 4, find the total savings if pollution control regulations permit the new process for only 4 years.

Answer:
\$320,000

6 If a company's marginal savings and marginal cost functions are

$$S(x) = 150 - 2x^2$$

and

$$C(x) = x^2 + 15x,$$

where $S(x)$ and $C(x)$ give amounts in thousands of dollars, find the following.

(a) Number of years until savings equal costs

(b) Total savings

Answers:

(a) 5

(b) \$437,500

$$= 100x - \frac{7}{3}x^2 - \frac{2}{3}x^3 \Big|_0^6 \qquad \text{Integrate.}$$

$$= 100(6) - \frac{7}{3}(36) - \frac{2}{3}(216) = 372.$$

The company will save a total of \$372,000 over the 6-year period. ■ 5 6

EXAMPLE 5 A farmer has been using a new fertilizer that gives him a better yield, but because it exhausts the soil of other nutrients he must use other fertilizers in greater and greater amounts, so that his costs increase each year. The new fertilizer produces a rate of increase in revenue (in hundreds of dollars) given by

$$R(t) = -.4t^2 + 8t + 10,$$

where t is measured in years. The rate of increase in yearly costs (also in hundreds of dollars) due to use of the fertilizer is given by

$$C(t) = 2t + 5.$$

How long can the farmer profitably use the fertilizer? What will be his net increase in revenue over this period?

The farmer should use the new fertilizer until the marginal costs equal the marginal revenue. Find this point by solving the equation $R(t) = C(t)$ as follows.

$$-.4t^2 + 8t + 10 = 2t + 5$$

$$-4t^2 + 80t + 100 = 20t + 50 \qquad \text{Multiply by 10.}$$

$$-4t^2 + 60t + 50 = 0$$

By the quadratic formula the only positive solution is

$$t = \frac{-60 - \sqrt{(-60)^2 - 4(-4)(50)}}{2(-4)} \approx 15.8.$$

The new fertilizer will be profitable for about 15.8 years.

To find the total amount of additional revenue over the 15.8-year period, find the area between the graphs of the rate of revenue and the rate of cost functions, as shown in Figure 14.22.

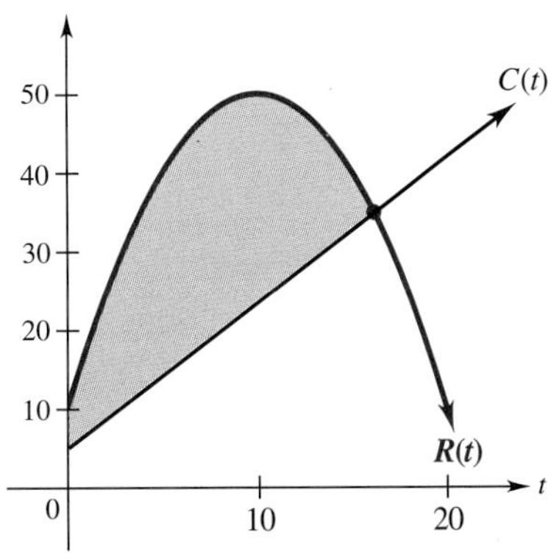

FIGURE 14.22

$$\begin{aligned}
\text{Total savings} &= \int_0^{15.8} [R(t) - C(t)]\, dt \\
&= \int_0^{15.8} [(-.4t^2 + 8t + 10) - (2t + 5)]\, dt \\
&= \int_0^{15.8} (-.4t^2 + 6t + 5)\, dt && \text{Combine terms.} \\
&= \left(\frac{-.4t^3}{3} + \frac{6t^2}{2} + 5t \right) \Bigg|_0^{15.8} && \text{Integrate.} \\
&\approx 302.01
\end{aligned}$$

The total savings will amount to about $30,000 over the 15.8-year period.

It is not realistic to say that the farmer will need to use the new process for 15.8 years—he will probably have to use it for 15 years or for 16 years. In this case, when the mathematical result is not in the domain of the function, it will be necessary to find the total savings after 15 years and after 16 years and then select the best result. ■

CONSUMERS' AND PRODUCERS' SURPLUS The market determines the price at which a product is sold. As indicated earlier, the point of intersection of the demand curve and the supply curve for a product gives the equilibrium price. At the equilibrium price, consumers will purchase the same amount of the product that the manufacturers want to sell. Some consumers, however, would be willing to spend more for an item than the equilibrium price. The total of the differences between the equilibrium price of the item and the higher prices all those individuals would be willing to pay is thought of as savings realized by those individuals and is called the **consumers' surplus.**

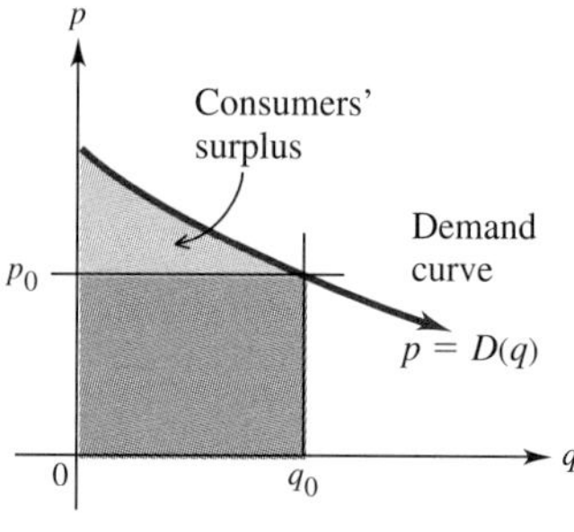

FIGURE 14.23

In Figure 14.23, the area under the demand curve is the total amount consumers are willing to spend for q_0 items. The heavily shaded area under the line $y = p_0$ shows the total amount consumers actually will spend at the equilibrium price of p_0. The lightly shaded area represents the consumers' surplus. As the figure suggests, the consumers' surplus is given by an area between the two curves $p = D(q)$ and $p = p_0$, so its value can be found with a definite integral as follows.

CONSUMERS' SURPLUS

If $D(q)$ is a demand function with equilibrium price p_0 and equilibrium demand q_0, then

$$\textbf{Consumers' surplus} = \int_0^{q_0} [D(q) - p_0]\, dq.$$

Similarly, if some manufacturers would be willing to supply a product at a price *lower* than the equilibrium price p_0, the total of the differences between the equilibrium price and the lower prices at which the manufacturers would sell the product is considered added income for the manufacturers and is called the **producers' surplus.** Figure 14.24 shows the (heavily shaded) total area under the supply curve from $q = 0$ to $q = q_0$, which is the minimum total amount the manufacturers are willing to realize from the sale of q_0 items. The total area under the line $p = p_0$ is the amount actually realized. The difference between these two areas, the producers' surplus, is also given by a definite integral.

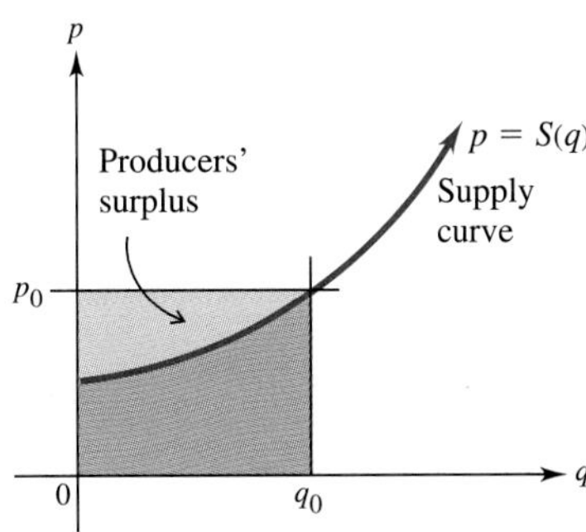

FIGURE 14.24

PRODUCERS' SURPLUS

If $S(q)$ is a supply function with equilibrium price p_0 and equilibrium supply q_0, then

$$\textbf{Producers' surplus} = \int_0^{q_0} [p_0 - S(q)]\, dq.$$

EXAMPLE 6 Suppose the price (in dollars per ton) for oat bran is

$$D(q) = 900 - 20q - q^2,$$

when the demand for the product is q tons. Also, suppose the function

$$S(q) = q^2 + 10q$$

gives the price (in dollars per ton) when the supply is q tons. Find the consumers' surplus and the producers' surplus.

We begin by finding the equilibrium quantity by setting the two equations equal.

$$\begin{aligned} 900 - 20q - q^2 &= q^2 + 10q \\ 0 &= 2q^2 + 30q - 900 \\ 0 &= q^2 + 15q - 450 \end{aligned}$$

Use the quadratic formula or factor to see that the only positive solution of this equation is $q = 15$. We could also find $q = 15$ by graphing $D(q)$ and $S(q)$ and finding the intersection point. At the equilibrium point where the supply and demand are both 15 tons, the price is

$$S(15) = 15^2 + 10(15) = 375,$$

or \$375. Verify that the same answer is found by computing $D(15)$. The consumers' surplus, represented by the area shown in Figure 14.25, is

$$\int_0^{15} [(900 - 20q - q^2) - 375]\, dq = \int_0^{15} (525 - 20q - q^2)\, dq.$$

Evaluating this definite integral gives

$$\left(525q - 10q^2 - \frac{1}{3}q^3\right)\Bigg|_0^{15} = \left[525(15) - 10(15)^2 - \frac{1}{3}(15)^3\right] - 0$$
$$= 4500.$$

7 Given the demand function $D(q) = 12 - .07q$ and the supply function $S(q) = .05q$, where $D(q)$ and $S(q)$ are in dollars, find

(a) the equilibrium point;

(b) the consumers' surplus;

(c) the producers' surplus.

Answers:

(a) $x = 100$

(b) \$350

(c) \$250

Here, the consumers' surplus is \$4500. The producers' surplus, also shown in Figure 14.25, is given by

$$\int_0^{15} [375 - (q^2 + 10q)]\, dq = \int_0^{15} (375 - q^2 - 10q)\, dq$$
$$= 325q - \frac{1}{3}q^3 - 5q^2 \Bigg|_0^{15}$$
$$= \left[375(15) - \frac{1}{3}(15)^3 - 5(15)^2\right] - 0$$
$$= 3375.$$

The producers' surplus is \$3375. ■ 7

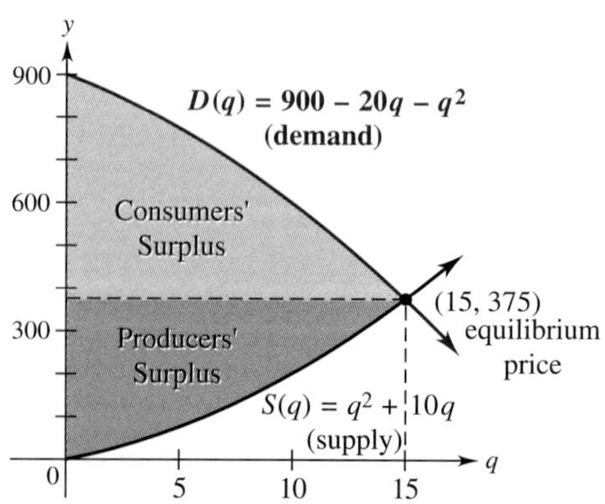

FIGURE 14.25

14.5 EXERCISES

Management *Work the following exercises. (See Examples 1–5.)*

1. A car-leasing firm must decide how much to charge for maintenance on the cars it leases. After careful study, the firm decides that the rate of maintenance, $M(x)$, on a new car will approximate $M(x) = 60(1 + x^2)$, where x is the number of years the car has been in use. What total maintenance charge can the company expect for a 2-year lease? What amount should be added to the monthly lease payments to pay for maintenance?

2. Using the function of Exercise 1, find the maintenance charge the company can expect during the third year. Find the total charge during the first 3 years. What monthly charge should be added to cover a 3-year lease?

3. A company is considering a new manufacturing process. It knows that the rate of savings from the process, $S(t)$, will be about $S(t) = 1000(t + 2)$, where t is the number of years the process has been in use. Find the total savings during the first year. Find the total savings during the first 6 years.

4. Assume that the new process in Exercise 3 costs \$16,000. About when will it pay for itself?

5. A company is introducing a new product. Production is expected to grow slowly because of difficulties in the start-up process. It is expected that the rate of production, $P(x)$, will be approximated by $P(x) = 1000e^{.2x}$, where x is the number of years since the introduction of the product. Will the company be able to supply 20,000 units during the first 4 years?

6. About when will the company of Exercise 5 be able to supply its 15,000th unit?

7. Suppose a company wants to introduce a new machine that will produce a rate of annual savings in dollars given by

$$S(x) = 150 - x^2,$$

where x is the number of years of operation of the machine, while producing a rate of annual costs in dollars of

$$C(x) = x^2 + \frac{11}{4}x.$$

(a) For how many years will it be profitable to use this new machine?
(b) What are the net total savings during the first year of use of the machine?
(c) What are the net total savings over the entire period of use of the machine?

8. **Natural Science** A new smog-control device will reduce the output of sulfur oxides from automobile exhausts. It is estimated that the rate of savings to the community from the use of this device will be approximated by

$$S(x) = -x^2 + 4x + 8,$$

where $S(x)$ is the rate of savings (in millions of dollars) after x years of use of the device. The new device cuts down on the production of sulfur oxides, but it causes an increase in the production of nitrous oxides. The rate of additional costs (in millions) to the community after x years is approximated by

$$C(x) = \frac{3}{25}x^2.$$

(a) For how many years will it pay to use the new device?
(b) What will be the net savings over this period of time?

9. **Management** De Win Enterprises had an expenditure rate of $E(x) = e^{.1x}$ dollars per day and an income rate of $I(x) = 98.8 - e^{.1x}$ dollars per day on a particular job, where x was the number of days from the start of the job. The company's profit on that job will equal total income less total expenditures. Profit will be maximized if the job ends at the optimum time, which is the point where the two curves meet. Find the following.
(a) The optimum number of days for the job to last
(b) The total income for the optimum number of days
(c) The total expenditures for the optimum number of days
(d) The maximum profit for the job

10. **Management** A factory at Harold Levinson Industries has installed a new process that will produce an increased rate of revenue (in thousands of dollars) of

$$R(t) = 104 - .4e^{t/2},$$

where t is time measured in years. The new process produces additional costs (in thousands of dollars) at the rate of

$$C(t) = .3e^{t/2}.$$

(a) When will it no longer be profitable to use this new process?
(b) Find the total net savings.

11. **Management** After t years, a mine is producing at the rate of

$$P(t) = \frac{15}{t + 1}$$

tons per year. At the same time, the ore produced is consumed at a rate of $C(t) = .1t + 2$ tons per year.
(a) In how many years will the rate of consumption equal the rate of production?
(b) What is the total excess production before consumption and production are equal?
(c) Consumption equals production when $t = 0$. Why is 0 not the correct answer in part (a)?

12. **Management** The rate of expenditure (in dollars) for maintenance of a certain machine is given by

$$M(x) = x^2 + 6x,$$

(exercise continues)

where x is time measured in years. The machine produces a rate of savings (in dollars) given by

$$S(x) = 360 - 2x^2.$$

(a) In how many years will the maintenance rate equal the savings rate?
(b) What will be the total net savings?

13. Natural Science Pollution from a factory is entering a lake. The rate of concentration of the pollutant at time t (in years) is $P'(t) = 140t^{.4}$. A cleaning substance is introduced into the lake that cleans it at a rate given by $C'(t) = 1.6t^{2.5}$. How long will it be before the total net effect is 0?

Management *Work the following supply and demand exercises, where the price is given in dollars. (See Example 6.)*

14. Find the producers' surplus if the supply function for pork bellies is given by

$$S(q) = q^{5/2} + 2q^{3/2} + 50.$$

Assume supply and demand are in equilibrium at $q = 16$.

15. Suppose the supply function for concrete is given by

$$S(q) = 100 + 3q^{3/2} + q^{5/2},$$

and that supply and demand are in equilibrium at $q = 9$. Find the producers' surplus.

16. Find the consumers' surplus if the demand function for grass seed is given by

$$D(q) = \frac{100}{(3q + 1)^2},$$

assuming supply and demand are in equilibrium at $q = 3$.

17. Find the consumers' surplus if the demand function for extra virgin olive oil is given by

$$D(q) = \frac{16{,}000}{(2q + 8)^3},$$

and if supply and demand are in equilibrium at $q = 6$.

18. Suppose the supply function of a certain item is given by

$$S(q) = e^{q/2} - 1,$$

and the demand function is given by

$$D(q) = 400 - e^{q/2}.$$

(a) Graph the supply and demand curves.
(b) Find the point at which supply and demand are in equilibrium.
(c) Find the consumers' surplus.
(d) Find the producers' surplus.

19. Repeat the four steps in Exercise 18 for the supply function

$$S(q) = q^2 + \frac{11}{4}q$$

and the demand function

$$D(q) = 150 - q^2.$$

20. Find the consumers' surplus and the producers' surplus for an item having supply function

$$S(q) = 3q^2$$

and demand function

$$D(q) = 144 - \frac{q^3}{6}.$$

21. Suppose the supply function of a certain item is given by

$$S(q) = \frac{7}{5}q$$

and the demand function is given by

$$D(q) = -\frac{3}{5}q + 10.$$

(a) Graph the supply and demand curves.
(b) Find the point at which supply and demand are in equilibrium.
(c) Find the consumers' surplus.
(d) Find the producers' surplus.

Work the following exercises.

22. Management If a large truck has been driven x thousand miles, the rate of repair costs in dollars per mile is given by $R(x)$, where

$$R(x) = .05x^{3/2}.$$

Find the total repair costs if the truck is driven
(a) 100,000 miles; **(b)** 400,000 miles.

23. Management In a recent inflationary period, costs of a certain industrial process, in millions of dollars, were increasing according to the function

$$i(t) = .45t^{3/2},$$

where $i(t)$ is the rate of increase in costs at time t measured in years. Find the total increase in costs during the first 4 years.

24. Natural Science From 1905 to 1920, most of the predators of the Kaibab Plateau of Arizona were killed by hunters. This allowed the deer population there to grow rapidly until they had depleted their food sources, which caused a rapid decline in population. The rate of change of this deer population during that time span is approximated by the function

$$D(t) = \frac{25}{2}t^3 - \frac{5}{8}t^4,$$

where t is the time in years ($0 \le t \le 25$).

(a) Find the function for the deer population if there were 4000 deer in 1905 ($t = 0$).
(b) What was the population in 1920?
(c) When was the population at a maximum?
(d) What was the maximum population?

25. **Social Science** Suppose that all the people in a country are ranked according to their incomes, starting at the bottom. Let x represent the fraction of the community making the lowest income ($0 \le x \le 1$); $x = .4$, therefore, represents the lower 40% of all income producers. Let $I(x)$ represent the proportion of the total income earned by the lowest x of all the people. Thus, $I(.4)$ represents the fraction of total income earned by the lowest 40% of the population. Suppose

$$I(x) = .9x^2 + .1x.$$

Find and interpret the following.
(a) $I(.1)$ **(b)** $I(.5)$ **(c)** $I(.9)$

If income were distributed uniformly, we would have $I(x) = x$. The area under this line of complete equality is 1/2. As $I(x)$ dips farther below $y = x$, there is less equality of income distribution. This inequality can be quantified by the ratio of the area between $I(x)$ and $y = x$ to 1/2. This ratio is called the *coefficient of inequality* and equals $2\int_0^1 (x - I(x))\,dx$.
(d) Graph $I(x) = x$ and $I(x) = .9x^2 + .1x$ for $0 \le x \le 1$ on the same axes.
(e) Find the area between the curves. What does this area represent?

26. **Social Science** Repeat Exercise 25 with $I(x) = .5x^2 + .5x$.

27. **Management** A worker new to a job will improve his efficiency with time so that it takes him fewer hours to produce an item with each day on the job up to a certain point. Suppose the rate of change of the number of hours it takes a worker in a certain factory to produce the xth item is given by

$$H(x) = 20 - 2x.$$

The production rate per item is a maximum when $\int_0^T H(x)\,dx$ is a maximum.
(a) How many items must be made to achieve the maximum production rate? Assume 0 items are made in 0 hours.
(b) What is the maximum production rate per item?

28. **Natural Science** After long study, tree scientists conclude that a poplar tree will grow at the rate of $4 + 4t^{-4}$ feet per year, where t is time in years. Find the number of feet that the tree will grow from the second to the tenth year.

29. **Natural Science** The function $\int_0^T (4 + 4t^{-4})\,dt$ from Exercise 28 is not realistic. Explain why.

30. **Natural Science** For a certain drug, the rate of reaction in appropriate units is given by

$$R(t) = \frac{5}{t} + \frac{2}{t^2},$$

where t is measured in hours after the drug is administered. Find the total reaction to the drug
(a) from $t = 1$ to $t = 12$;
(b) from $t = 12$ to $t = 24$.

Approximate the area between the graphs of each pair of functions on the given interval.

31. $y = \ln x$ and $y = xe^x$; $[1, 4]$
32. $y = \ln x$ and $y = 4 - x^2$; $[2, 4]$
33. $y = \sqrt{9 - x^2}$ and $y = \sqrt{x + 1}$; $[-1, 3]$
34. $y = \sqrt{4 - 4x^2}$ and $y = \sqrt{\dfrac{9 - x^2}{3}}$; $[-1, 1]$

14.6 DIFFERENTIAL EQUATIONS

Suppose that an economist wants to develop an equation that will forecast interest rates. By studying data on previous changes in interest rates, she hopes to find a relationship between the level of interest rates and their rate of change. A function giving the rate of change of interest rates would be the derivative of the function describing the level of interest rates. A **differential equation** is an equation that involves an unknown function, $y = f(x)$, and a finite number of its derivatives. Solving the differential equation for y would give the unknown function to be used for forecasting interest rates.

Usually a solution of an equation is a *number.* A solution of a differential equation, however, is a *function.* For example, the solutions of a differential equation such as

$$\frac{dy}{dx} = 3x^2 - 2x \tag{1}$$

consist of all functions y that satisfy the equation. Since the left side of the equation is the derivative of y with respect to x, we can solve the equation for y by finding an antiderivative on each side. On the left, the antiderivative is $y + C_1$. On the right side,

$$\int (3x^2 - 2x)\, dx = x^3 - x^2 + C_2.$$

The solutions of equation (1) are given by

$$y + C_1 = x^3 - x^2 + C_2$$

or

$$y = x^3 - x^2 + C_2 - C_1.$$

Replacing the constant $C_2 - C_1$ with the single constant C gives

$$y = x^3 - x^2 + C. \qquad (2)$$

(From now on we will add just one constant, with the understanding that it represents the difference between the two constants obtained in the two integrations.)

Each different value of C in equation (2) leads to a different solution of equation (1), showing that a differential equation can have an infinite number of solutions. Equation (2) is the **general solution** of the differential equation (1). Some of the solutions of equation (1) are graphed in Figure 14.26. 1

1 Find the general solution of

(a) $dy/dx = 4x$;

(b) $dy/dx = -x^3$;

(c) $dy/dx = 2x^2 - 5x$.

Answers:

(a) $y = 2x^2 + C$

(b) $y = -\frac{1}{4}x^4 + C$

(c) $y = \frac{2}{3}x^3 - \frac{5}{2}x^2 + C$

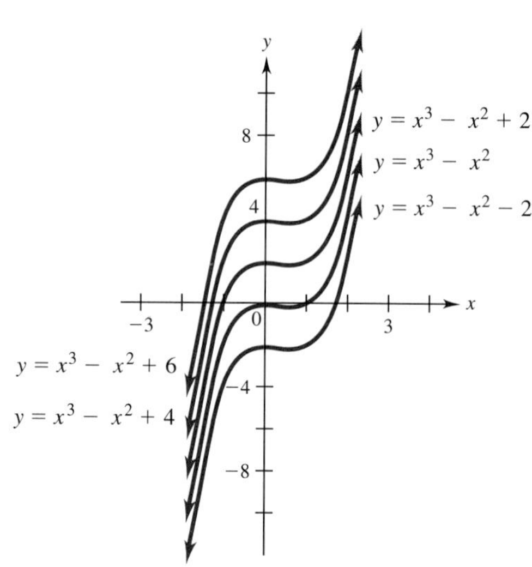

FIGURE 14.26

The simplest kind of differential equation has the form

$$\frac{dy}{dx} = f(x).$$

Equation (1) has this form, so the solution of equation (1) suggests the following generalization.

GENERAL SOLUTION OF $dy/dx = f(x)$

The general solution of the differential equation $dy/dx = f(x)$ is

$$y = \int f(x)\,dx.$$

EXAMPLE 1 The population P of a flock of birds is growing exponentially so that

$$\frac{dP}{dx} = 20e^{.05x},$$

where x is time in years. Find P in terms of x if there were 20 birds in the flock initially.

Solve the differential equation.

$$P = \int 20e^{.05x}\,dx = \frac{20}{.05}e^{.05x} + C = 400e^{.05x} + C$$

Since P is 20 when x is 0,

$$20 = 400e^{0} + C$$
$$-380 = C,$$

and

$$P = 400e^{.05x} - 380. \blacksquare$$

2 Find the particular solution in Example 1 if there were 100 birds in the flock after 2 years.

Answer:
$P = 400e^{.05x} - 342$

In Example 1, the given information was used to produce a solution with a specific value of C. Such a solution is called a **particular solution** of the given differential equation. The given information, $P = 20$ when $t = 0$, is called an **initial condition.** 2

Sometimes a differential equation must be rewritten in the form

$$\frac{dy}{dx} = f(x)$$

before it can be solved.

EXAMPLE 2 Find the particular solution of

$$\frac{dy}{dx} - 2x = 5,$$

given that $y = 2$ when $x = -1$.

Add $2x$ to both sides of the equation to get

$$\frac{dy}{dx} = 2x + 5.$$

The general solution is

$$y = \frac{2x^2}{2} + 5x + C = x^2 + 5x + C.$$

3 Find the particular solution of

$$2\frac{dy}{dx} - 4 = 6x^2,$$

given $y = 4$ when $x = 1$.

Answer:
$y = x^3 + 2x + 1$

Substituting 2 for y and -1 for x gives

$$2 = (-1)^2 + 5(-1) + C$$
$$C = 6.$$

The particular solution is $y = x^2 + 5x + 6$. ■ 3

Now let us consider solving the more general type of differential equation with the form

$$\frac{dy}{dx} = \frac{f(x)}{g(y)}.$$

Up to this point we have used the symbol dy/dx to denote the derivative function of the function y. In advanced courses it is shown that dy/dx can also be interpreted as a quotient of two differentials, dy divided by dx. (You may recall that differentials were used in integration by substitution.) Then we can multiply both sides of the equation above by $g(y)\,dx$ to obtain

$$g(y)\,dy = f(x)\,dx.$$

In this form all terms involving y (including dy) are on one side of the equation, and all terms involving x (and dx) are on the other side. A differential equation in this form is said to be **separable,** since the variables x and y can be separated. A separable differential equation may be solved by integrating each side.

EXAMPLE 3 Find the general solution of $\dfrac{dy}{dx} = -\dfrac{6x}{y}$.

Separate the variables by multiplying both sides by $y\,dx$:

$$y\,dy = -6x\,dx.$$

To solve this equation take antiderivatives on each side.

$$\int y\,dy = \int -6x\,dx$$
$$\frac{y^2}{2} = -3x^2 + C$$
$$3x^2 + \frac{y^2}{2} = C$$

Since powers of y are involved, it is better to leave the solution in this form rather than trying to solve for y. For each positive constant C, the graph of the solution is an ellipse, as shown in Figure 14.27. ■

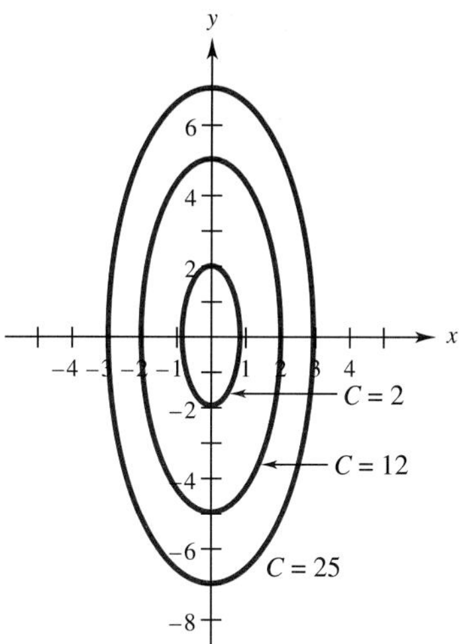

FIGURE 14.27

EXAMPLE 4 Find the general solution of $\frac{dy}{dx} = 5y$.

Separating variables leads to

$$\frac{1}{y}dy = 5\,dx.$$

To solve this equation, take antiderivatives on each side.

$$\int \frac{1}{y}\,dy = \int 5\,dx$$

$$\ln|y| = 5x + C$$

$$|y| = e^{5x+C} \qquad \text{Definition of logarithm}$$

$$|y| = e^{5x}e^{C} \qquad \text{Property of exponents}$$

$$y = e^{5x}e^{C} \quad \text{or} \quad y = -e^{5x}e^{C} \qquad \text{Definition of absolute value}$$

Since e^C and $-e^C$ are constants, replace them with the constant M, which may have any nonzero real-number value, to get the single equation

$$y = Me^{5x}.$$

The equation $y = Me^{5x}$ defines an exponential growth function, such as those considered in Section 5.3. ■

We can now explain how the exponential growth and decay functions presented in Section 5.3 were obtained. In the absence of inhibiting conditions, a population y (which might be human, animal, bacterial, etc.) grows in such a way that the rate of change of population is proportional to the population at time x, that is, there is a constant k such that

$$\frac{dy}{dx} = ky.$$

4 Find the particular solution of $\frac{dy}{dx} = .05y$ if y is 2000 when x is 0.

Answer:
$y = 2000e^{.05x}$

The constant k is called the **growth rate constant.** Example 4 is the case when $k = 5$. The same argument used there (with k in place of 5) shows that the population y at time x is given by

$$y = Me^{kx},$$

where M is the population at time $x = 0$. A positive value of k indicates growth, while a negative value of k indicates decay. 4

As a model of population growth, the equation $y = Me^{kx}$ is not realistic over the long run for most populations. As shown by graphs of functions of the form $y = Me^{kx}$, with both M and k positive, growth would be unbounded. Additional factors, such as space restrictions or a limited amount of food, tend to inhibit growth of populations as time goes on. In an alternative model that assumes a maximum population of size N, the rate of growth of a population is proportional to how close the population is to that maximum. These assumptions lead to the differential equation

$$\frac{dy}{dx} = k(N - y),$$

the limited growth function mentioned in Chapter 5. Graphs of limited growth functions look like the graph in Figure 14.28, where y_0 is the initial population.

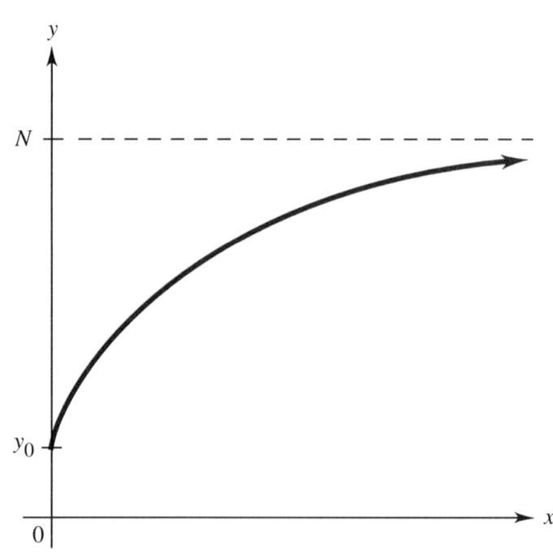

FIGURE 14.28

EXAMPLE 5 A certain area can support no more than 4000 mountain goats. There are 1000 goats in the area at present, with a growth constant of .20.

(a) Write a differential equation for the rate of growth of this population.
Let $N = 4000$ and $k = .20$. The rate of growth of the population is given by

$$\frac{dy}{dx} = .20(4000 - y).$$

To solve for y, first separate the variables.

$$\frac{dy}{4000 - y} = .2\,dx$$

$$\int \frac{dy}{4000 - y} = \int .2\,dx$$

$$-\ln(4000 - y) = .2x + C$$

$$\ln(4000 - y) = -.2x - C$$

$$4000 - y = e^{-.2x-C} = (e^{-.2x})(e^{-C})$$

The absolute value bars are not needed for $\ln(4000 - y)$ because y must be less than 4000 for this population so that $4000 - y$ is always nonnegative. Let $e^{-C} = B$. Then

$$4000 - y = Be^{-.2x}$$

$$y = 4000 - Be^{-.2x}.$$

Find B by using the fact that $y = 1000$ when $x = 0$.

$$1000 = 4000 - B$$

$$B = 3000$$

Notice that the value of B is the difference between the maximum population and the initial population. Substituting 3000 for B in the equation for y gives

$$y = 4000 - 3000e^{-.2x}.$$

5 An animal population is growing at a constant rate of 4%. The habitat will support no more than 10,000 animals. There are 3000 animals present now. Write an equation giving the population y in x years.

Answer:
$y = 10{,}000 - 7000e^{-.04x}$

(b) What will the goat population be in 5 years?
In 5 years, the population will be

$$y = 4000 - 3000e^{(-.2)(5)} = 4000 - 3000e^{-1}$$

$$= 4000 - 1103.6 = 2896.4,$$

or about 2900 goats. ■ 5

Marginal productivity is the rate at which production changes (increases or decreases) for a unit change in investment. Thus, marginal productivity can be expressed as the first derivative of the function which gives production in terms of investment.

EXAMPLE 6 Suppose the marginal productivity of a manufacturing process is given by

$$P'(x) = 3x^2 - 10, \qquad (3)$$

where x is the amount of the investment in hundreds of thousands of dollars. If the process produces 100 units per month with the present investment of \$300,000 (that is, $x = 3$), by how much would production increase if the investment is increased to \$500,000?

6 In Example 6, if marginal productivity is changed to

$$P'(x) = 3x^2 + 2x,$$

with the same initial conditions,

(a) find an equation for production;

(b) find the increase in production if investment increases to \$500,000.

Answers:

(a) $P(x) = x^3 + x^2 + 64$

(b) Production goes from 100 units to 214 units, an increase of 114 units.

To obtain an equation for production, we can take antiderivatives on both sides of equation (3) to get

$$P(x) = x^3 - 10x + C.$$

To find C, use the given initial values: $P(x) = 100$ when $x = 3$.

$$100 = 3^3 - 10(3) + C$$
$$C = 103$$

Production is thus given by

$$P(x) = x^3 - 10x + 103,$$

and if investment is increased to \$500,000, production becomes

$$P(5) = 5^3 - 10(5) + 103 = 178.$$

An increase to \$500,000 in investment will increase production from 100 units to 178 units. ■ 6

14.6 EXERCISES

Find general solutions for the following differential equations. (See Examples 1–4.)

1. $\dfrac{dy}{dx} = -2x + 3x^2$
2. $\dfrac{dy}{dx} = 3e^{-2x}$
3. $3x^3 - 2\dfrac{dy}{dx} = 0$
4. $3x^2 - 3\dfrac{dy}{dx} = 2$
5. $y\dfrac{dy}{dx} = x$
6. $y\dfrac{dy}{dx} = x^2 - 1$
7. $\dfrac{dy}{dx} = 2xy$
8. $\dfrac{dy}{dx} = x^2y$
9. $\dfrac{dy}{dx} = 3x^2y - 2xy$
10. $(y^2 - y)\dfrac{dy}{dx} = x$
11. $\dfrac{dy}{dx} = \dfrac{y}{x}, x > 0$
12. $\dfrac{dy}{dx} = \dfrac{y}{x^2}$
13. $\dfrac{dy}{dx} = y - 5$
14. $\dfrac{dy}{dx} = 3 - y$
15. $\dfrac{dy}{dx} = y^2e^x$
16. $\dfrac{dy}{dx} = \dfrac{e^x}{e^y}$

Find particular solutions for the following equations. (See Examples 1–4.)

17. $\dfrac{dy}{dx} + 2x = 3x^2$; $y = 2$ when $x = 0$
18. $\dfrac{dy}{dx} = 4x^3 - 3x^2 + x$; $y = 0$ when $x = 1$
19. $\dfrac{dy}{dx}(x^3 + 28) = \dfrac{x^2}{y}$; $y^2 = 6$ when $x = -3$
20. $\dfrac{y}{x-3}\dfrac{dy}{dx} = \sqrt{x^2 - 6x}$; $y^2 = 44$ when $x = 8$
21. $\dfrac{dy}{dx} = \dfrac{x^2}{y}$; $y = 3$ when $x = 0$
22. $x^2\dfrac{dy}{dx} = y$; $y = -1$ when $x = 1$
23. $(2x + 3)y = \dfrac{dy}{dx}$; $y = 1$ when $x = 0$
24. $x\dfrac{dy}{dx} - y\sqrt{x} = 0$; $y = 1$ when $x = 0$
25. $\dfrac{dy}{dx} = \dfrac{2x+1}{y-3}$; $y = 4$ when $x = 0$
26. $\dfrac{dy}{dx} = \dfrac{x^2+5}{2y-1}$; $y = 11$ when $x = 0$
27. What is the difference between a general solution and a particular solution of a differential equation?
28. What is meant by a separable differential equation?

Work the following problems. (See Examples 5 and 6.)

29. **Management** The marginal productivity of a process is given by
$$\frac{dy}{dx} = \frac{100}{32 - 4x},$$
where x represents the investment (in thousands of dollars). Find the productivity for each of the following investments if productivity is 100 units when the investment is \$1000.
(a) \$3000 **(b)** \$5000
(c) Can investments ever reach \$8000 according to this model? Why?
30. **Natural Science** The time dating of dairy products depends on the solution of a differential equation. The rate of growth of bacteria in such products increases with time.

If y is the number of bacteria (in thousands) present at a time t (in days), then the rate of growth of bacteria can be expressed as dy/dt and we have

$$\frac{dy}{dt} = kt,$$

where k is an appropriate constant. For a certain product, $k = 10$ and $y = 50$ (in thousands) when $t = 0$.

(a) Solve the differential equation for y.

(b) Suppose the maximum allowable value for y is 550 (thousand). How should the product be dated?

31. Management Sales (in thousands) of a certain product are declining at a rate proportional to the amount of sales, with a decay constant of 25% per year.

(a) Write a differential equation to express the rate of sales decline.

(b) Find a general solution to the equation in part (a).

(c) How much time will pass before sales become 30% of their original amount?

32. Management The rate of growth of an investment A is proportional to A, if money is compounded continuously; that is

$$\frac{dA}{dt} = kA,$$

where k is the interest rate.

(a) Solve the differential equation for A.

(b) Suppose inflation grows continuously at a rate of 4% per year. How long will it take for \$1 to lose half its value?

(c) How long would it take for \$1 to lose half its value at an inflation rate of 6% per year?

33. Management Suppose that the gross national product (GNP) of a particular country increases exponentially, with a growth constant of 2% per year. Ten years ago, the GNP was 10^5 dollars. What will the GNP be in 5 years?

34. Management In a certain area, 1500 small business firms are threatened by bankruptcy. Assume the rate of change in the number of bankruptcies is proportional to the number of small firms that are not yet bankrupt. If the growth constant is 6% and if 100 firms are bankrupt initially, how many will be bankrupt in 2 years?

35. Natural Science The rate at which the number of bacteria in a culture is changing after the introduction of a bactericide is given by

$$\frac{dy}{dx} = 50 - y,$$

where y is the number of bacteria (in thousands) present at time x. Find the number of bacteria present at each of the following times if there were 1000 thousand bacteria present at time $x = 0$.

(a) $x = 2$ **(b)** $x = 5$ **(c)** $x = 10$

36. Natural Science The amount of a tracer dye injected into the bloodstream decreases exponentially, with a decay constant of 3% per minute. If 6 cc are present initially, how many cc are present after 10 minutes? (Here k will be negative.)

37. Physical Science The amount of a radioactive substance decreases exponentially, with a decay constant of 5% a month. There are 90 grams at the start of an experiment. Find the amount left 10 months later.

38. Social Science Suppose the rate at which a rumor spreads—that is, the number of people who have heard the rumor over a period of time—increases with the number of people who have heard it. If y is the number of people who have heard the rumor, then

$$\frac{dy}{dt} = ky,$$

where t is the time in days and k is a constant.

(a) If y is 1 when $t = 0$, and y is 5 when $t = 2$, find k.

Using the value of k from part (a), find y for each of the following times.

(b) $t = 3$ **(c)** $t = 5$ **(d)** $t = 10$

39. Social Science A company has found that the rate at which a person new to the assembly line produces items is

$$\frac{dy}{dx} = 7.5e^{-.3y},$$

where x is the number of days the person has worked on the line. How many items can a new worker be expected to produce on the eighth day if he produces none when $x = 0$?

Physical Science *Newton's law of cooling states that the rate of change of temperature of an object is proportional to the difference in temperature between the object and the surrounding medium. Thus, if T is the temperature of the object after t hours and C is the (constant) temperature of the surrounding medium, then*

$$\frac{dT}{dt} = -k(T - C),$$

where k is a constant. When a dead body is discovered within 48 hours of the death and the temperature of the medium (air or water, for example) has been fairly constant, Newton's law of cooling can be used to determine the time of death. (The medical examiner does not actually solve the equation for each case, but uses a table which is based on the formula.) Use Newton's law of cooling to work the following problems.*

40. Assume the temperature of a body at death is 98.6°F, the temperature of the surrounding air is 68°F, and at the end of one hour the body temperature is 90°F.

(exercise continues)

*Callas, Dennis and Hildreth, David J., "Snapshots of Applications in Mathematics," *College Mathematics Journal,* Vol. 26, No. 2, March 1995.

(a) Find an equation that gives the body temperature T after t hours.
(b) What was the temperature of the body after two hours?
(c) When will the temperature of the body be 75°F?
(d) Approximately when will the temperature of the body be within .01° of the surrounding air?

41. Do Exercise 40 under these conditions: The temperature of the surrounding air is 38°F and after one hour the body temperature is 81°.

42. Under different conditions from those in Exercises 40 and 41, the equation that gives the body temperature T after t hours is $T = 10 + 88.6e^{-.24t}$.
(a) Graph the temperature equation for $0 \leq t \leq 30$.
(b) When does the temperature of the body decrease more rapidly: just after death or much later? How do you know?
(c) What will the temperature of the body be after 4 hours?
(d) How long will it take for the body to reach a temperature of 40°?

43. Management Rapid technological advancements make many products obsolete almost overnight. The phenomenon of a technically superior new product's replacing another product can be described by the equation

$$y = \frac{N}{1 + \frac{N - y_0}{y_0} e^{-kx}},$$

where y is the fraction of the total market share held by the new product, N is total market share, y_0 is the initial market share, and k is the growth or decay constant. Suppose $y_0 = .1$, $N = 1$, and $k = .2$.
(a) Graph the function for $0 \leq x \leq 25$, $0 < y < 1$.
(b) At what point does the market share of the new product appear to be growing most rapidly? (*Hint:* The most rapid growth occurs when $y = .5$.)

CHAPTER 14 SUMMARY

Key Terms and Symbols

14.1 $\int f(x)\,dx$ indefinite integral of f
antiderivative
integral sign
integrand
integration
power rule
constant multiple rule
sum or difference rule

14.2 differential
integration by substitution

14.3 $\int_a^b f(x)\,dx$ definite integral of f
total change in $F(x)$

14.4 $F(x)\Big|_a^b = F(b) - F(a)$

14.5 consumers' surplus
producers' surplus

14.6 differential equation
general solution
particular solution
initial condition
separable differential equation
growth rate constant
marginal productivity

Key Concepts

$F(x)$ is an antiderivative of $f(x)$ if $F'(x) = f(x)$.

Indefinite Integral If $F'(x) = f(x)$, then $\int f(x)\,dx = F(x) + C$, for any real number C.

Properties of Integrals $\int k \cdot f(x)\,dx = k \cdot \int f(x)\,dx$, for any real number k.

$$\int [f(x) \pm g(x)]\,dx = \int f(x)\,dx \pm \int g(x)\,dx.$$

Rules for Integrals For $u = f(x)$ and $du = f'(x)\,dx$,

$$\int u^n\,du = \frac{u^{n+1}}{n+1} + C; \qquad \int e^u\,du = e^u + C; \qquad \int u^{-1}\,du = \int \frac{du}{u} = \ln|u| + C$$

The Definite Integral

If f is continuous on $[a, b]$, the definite integral of f from a to b is

$$\int_a^b f(x)\,dx = \lim_{n\to\infty} ([f(x_1) + f(x_2) + f(x_3) + \cdots + f(x_n)] \cdot \Delta x),$$

provided the limit exists, where $\Delta x = \dfrac{b-a}{n}$ and x_i is the left endpoint of the ith interval.

Total Change in $F(x)$

Let f be continuous on $[a, b]$ and $f(x) \geq 0$ for all x in $[a, b]$. If $f(x)$ is the rate of change of $F(x)$, then the **total change** in $F(x)$ as x goes from a to b is given by

$$\int_a^b f(x)\,dx.$$

Fundamental Theorem of Calculus

Let f be continuous on $[a, b]$, and let F be any antiderivative of f. Then

$$\int_a^b f(x)\,dx = F(b) - F(a).$$

General Solution of $\dfrac{dy}{dx} = f(x)$

The general solution of the differential equation $dy/dx = f(x)$ is

$$y = \int f(x)\,dx.$$

General Solution of $\dfrac{dy}{dx} = ky$

The general solution of the differential equation $dy/dx = ky$ is

$$y = Me^{kx}.$$

Chapter 14 Review Exercises

Find each indefinite integral.

1. $\int (x^2 - 3x + 2)\,dx$
2. $\int (6 - x^2)\,dx$
3. $\int 3\sqrt{x}\,dx$
4. $\int \frac{\sqrt{x}}{2}\,dx$
5. $\int (x^{1/2} + 3x^{-2/3})\,dx$
6. $\int (2x^{4/3} + x^{-1/2})\,dx$
7. $\int \frac{-4}{x^3}\,dx$
8. $\int \frac{5}{x^4}\,dx$
9. $\int -3e^{2x}\,dx$
10. $\int 5e^{-x}\,dx$
11. $\int \frac{2}{x-1}\,dx$
12. $\int \frac{-4}{x+2}\,dx$
13. $\int xe^{3x^2}\,dx$
14. $\int 2xe^{x^2}\,dx$
15. $\int \frac{3x}{x^2-1}\,dx$
16. $\int \frac{-x}{2-x^2}\,dx$
17. $\int \frac{x^2\,dx}{(x^3+5)^4}$
18. $\int (x^2 - 5x)^4(2x - 5)\,dx$
19. $\int \frac{4x-5}{2x^2-5x}\,dx$
20. $\int \frac{12(2x+9)}{x^2+9x+1}\,dx$
21. $\int \frac{x^3}{e^{3x^4}}\,dx$
22. $\int e^{3x^2+4}\,x\,dx$
23. $\int -2e^{-5x}\,dx$
24. $\int e^{-4x}\,dx$
25. Explain how rectangles are used to approximate the area under a curve.
26. (a) Use 5 rectangles to approximate the area between the graph of $f(x) = 16x^2 - x^4 + 2$ and the x-axis from $x = -2$ to $x = 3$.
    (b) Use 50 rectangles to approximate this area.
    (c) Use numerical integration to approximate this area.
27. Do Exercise 26 for the function $g(x) = -x^4 + 12x^2 + x + 5$ from $x = -3$ to $x = 3$.
28. Approximate the area under the graph of $f(x) = 2x + 3$ and above the x-axis from $x = 0$ to $x = 4$ using four rectangles. Let the height of each rectangle be the function value on the left side.

29. Find $\int_0^4 (2x + 3)\,dx$ by using the formula for the area of a trapezoid: $A = \frac{1}{2}(B + b)h$, where B and b are the lengths of the parallel sides and h is the distance between them. Compare with Exercise 28. If the answers are different, explain why.

30. Explain under what circumstances substitution is useful in integration.

31. What does the Fundamental Theorem of Calculus state?

32. Explain why the limits of integration are changed when u is substituted for an expression in x in a definite integral.

Find each definite integral.

33. $\int_1^5 (3x^{-2} + x^{-3})\,dx$

34. $\int_2^3 (5x^{-2} + x^{-4})\,dx$

35. $\int_1^3 2x^{-1}\,dx$

36. $\int_1^6 8x^{-1}\,dx$

37. $\int_0^4 2e^x\,dx$

38. $\int_1^6 \frac{5}{2}e^{4x}\,dx$

39. $\int_{\sqrt{5}}^5 2x\sqrt{x^2 - 3}\,dx$

40. $\int_0^1 x\sqrt{5x^2 + 4}\,dx$

Find the area between the x-axis and f(x) over each of the given intervals.

41. $f(x) = e^x$; $[0, 2]$

42. $f(x) = 1 + e^{-x}$; $[0, 4]$

Management *Find the cost function for each of the marginal cost functions in Exercises 43–46.*

43. $C'(x) = 10 - 2x$; fixed cost is \$4.

44. $C'(x) = 2x + 3x^2$; 2 units cost \$12.

45. $C'(x) = 3\sqrt{2x - 1}$; 13 units cost \$270.

46. $C'(x) = \frac{1}{x + 1}$; fixed cost is \$18.

Work the following exercises.

47. **Management** The rate of change of sales of a new brand of tomato soup, in thousands, is given by
$$S(x) = \sqrt{x} + 2,$$
where x is the time in months that the new product has been on the market. Find the total sales after 9 months.

48. **Management** The curve shown at the top of the next column gives the rate that an investment accumulates income (in dollars per year). Use rectangles of width 2 units and height determined by the function value at the midpoint to find the total income accumulated over 10 yr.

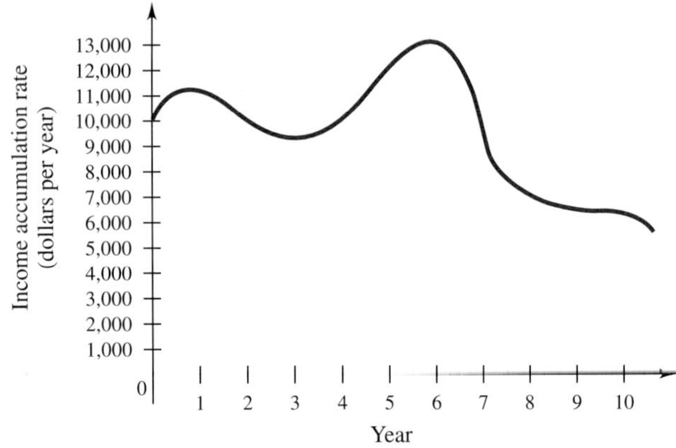

49. **Management** A manufacturer of electronic equipment requires a certain rare metal. He has a reserve supply of 4,000,000 units that he will not be able to replace. If the rate at which the metal is used is given by
$$f(t) = 100{,}000e^{.03t},$$
where t is the time in years, how long will it be before he uses up the supply? (*Hint:* Find an expression for the total amount used in t years and set it equal to the known reserve supply.)

50. **Management** A company has installed new machinery that will produce a savings rate (in thousands of dollars) of
$$S'(x) = 225 - x^2,$$
where x is the number of years the machinery is to be used. The rate of additional costs (in thousands of dollars) to the company due to the new machinery is expected to be
$$C'(x) = x^2 + 25x + 150.$$
For how many years should the company use the new machinery? Find the net savings (in thousands of dollars) over this period.

51. Explain what consumers' surplus and producers' surplus are.

52. **Management** Suppose that the supply function of some commodity is
$$S(q) = q^2 + 5q + 100$$
and the demand function for the commodity is
$$D(q) = 350 - q^2.$$
(a) Find the producers' surplus.
(b) Find the consumers' surplus.

53. **Natural Science** The rate of infection of a disease (in people per month) is given by the function
$$I'(t) = \frac{100t}{t^2 + 1},$$
where t is the time in months since the disease broke out. Find the total number of infected people over the first four months of the disease.

Use numerical integration to approximate the following.

54. $\int_8^{11} \frac{1}{\sqrt{x^2 - 64}}\,dx$ **55.** $\int_1^4 \frac{5}{x\sqrt{25 + x^2}}\,dx$

56. $\int_{-2}^{2} \frac{12}{x^2 - 9}\,dx$ **57.** $\int_{-4}^{0} \frac{15x}{2x - 5}\,dx$

58. What is a differential equation? What is it used for?

Find general solutions for the following differential equations.

59. $\frac{dy}{dx} = 2x^3 + 6x$ **60.** $\frac{dy}{dx} = x^2 + 5x^4$

61. $\frac{dy}{dx} = \frac{3x + 1}{y}$ **62.** $\frac{dy}{dx} = \frac{e^x + x}{y - 1}$

Find particular solutions for the following differential equations.

63. $\frac{dy}{dx} = 5(e^{-x} - 1)$; $y = 17$ when $x = 0$

64. $\frac{dy}{dx} = \frac{x}{x^2 - 3}$; $y = 52$ when $x = 2$

65. $(5 - 2x)y = \frac{dy}{dx}$; $y = 2$ when $x = 0$

66. $\sqrt{x}\frac{dy}{dx} = xy$; $y = 4$ when $x = 1$

67. Management A deposit of \$10,000 is made to a savings account at 5% interest compounded continuously. Assume that continuous *withdrawals* of \$1000 per year are made.
(a) Write a differential equation to describe the situation.
(b) How much will be left in the account after 1 year?

68. Management The marginal sales (in hundreds of dollars) of a computer software company are given by

$$\frac{dy}{dx} = 5e^{.2x},$$

where x is the number of months the company has been in business. Assume that sales were 0 initially.
(a) Find the sales after 6 months.
(b) Find the sales after 12 months.

69. Management The rate at which a new worker in a certain factory produces items is given by

$$\frac{dy}{dx} = .2(125 - y),$$

where y is the number of items produced by the worker per day, x is the number of days worked, and the maximum production per day is 125 items. Assume the worker produced 20 items the first day on the job ($x = 0$).
(a) Find the number of items the new worker will produce in 10 days.
(b) According to the function that is the solution of the differential equation, can the worker ever produce 125 items in a day?

70. Physical Science A roast at a temperature of 40° is put in a 300° oven. After 1 hr the roast has reached a temperature of 150°. Newton's law of cooling states that

$$\frac{dT}{dt} = k(T - T_F),$$

where T is the temperature of an object, the surrounding medium has temperature T_F at time t, and k is a constant.
(a) Use Newton's law to find the temperature of the roast after 2 hr.
(b) How long does it take for the roast to reach a temperature of 250°?

71. Natural Science Find an equation relating x to y given the following equations, which describe the interaction of two competing species and their growth rates.

$$\frac{dx}{dt} = .2x - .5xy$$

$$\frac{dy}{dt} = -.3y + .4xy$$

Find the values of x and y for which both growth rates are 0. (*Hint:* Solve the system of equations found by setting each growth rate equal to 0.)

72. Management The function defined by $f'(x) = 2.158e^{.0198x}$ approximates marginal U.S. nonfarm productivity from 1991 through 1995.* Productivity is measured as total output per hour compared to a measure of 100 for 1982, and x represents the end of the year with 1991 corresponding to $x = 1$, 1992 corresponding to $x = 2$, and so on.
(a) Give the function that describes total productivity in year x, if productivity was 115 in 1992.
(b) Use your function from part (a) to find productivity at the end of 1994. In 1994, productivity actually measured 118.6. How does your value using the function compare with this?

*Bureau of Labor Statistics.

CASE 14

Estimating Depletion Dates for Minerals

It is becoming more and more obvious that the earth contains only a finite quantity of minerals. The "easy and cheap" sources of minerals are being used up, forcing an ever more expensive search for new sources. For example, oil from the North Slope of Alaska would never have been used in the United States during the 1930s since there was so much Texas and California oil readily available.

Mineral usage tends to follow an exponential growth curve. Thus, if q represents the rate of consumption of a certain mineral at time t, while q_0 represents consumption when $t = 0$, then

$$q = q_0 e^{kt},$$

where k is the growth constant. For example, the world consumption of petroleum in a recent year was about 19,600 million barrels, with the value of k about 6%. Letting $t = 0$ correspond to this base year, then $q_0 = 19{,}600$, $k = .06$, and

$$q = 19{,}600e^{.06t}$$

is the rate of consumption at time t, assuming that all present trends continue.

Based on estimates of the National Academy of Science, 2,000,000 million barrels of oil are now in provable reserves or are likely to be discovered in the future. At the present rate of consumption, how many years would be necessary to deplete these estimated reserves? Use the integral calculus of this chapter to find out.

To begin, find the total quantity of petroleum that would be used between time $t = 0$ and some future time $t = t_1$. Figure 1 shows a typical graph of the function $q = q_0 e^{kt}$.

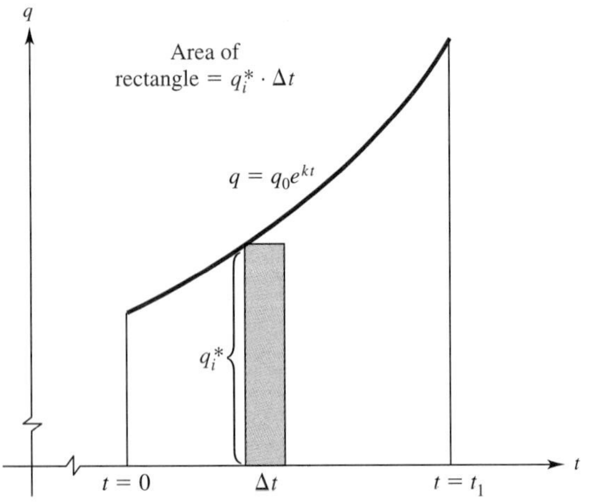

FIGURE 1

Following the work in Section 14.3, divide the time interval from $t = 0$ to $t = t_1$ into n equal subintervals. Let the ith subinterval have width Δt. Let the rate of consumption for the ith subinterval be approximated by q_i^*. Thus, the approximate total consumption for the subinterval is given by

$$q_i^* \cdot \Delta t,$$

and the total consumption over the interval from time $t = 0$ to $t = t_1$ is approximated by

$$q_i^* \Delta t_1 + \cdots + q_n^* \Delta t.$$

The limit of this sum as n approaches ∞ gives the total consumption from time $t = 0$ to $t = t_1$. That is,

$$\text{Total consumption} = \lim_{n\to\infty} (q_1^* + q_2^* + \cdots + q_n^*) \Delta t.$$

This limit is the definite integral of the function $q = q_0 e^{kt}$ from $t = 0$ to $t = t_1$, or

$$\text{Total consumption} = \int_0^{t_1} q_0 e^{kt}\, dt.$$

Evaluating this definite integral gives

$$\int_0^{t_1} q_0 e^{kt}\, dt = q_0 \int_0^{t_1} e^{kt}\, dt = q_0\left(\frac{1}{k}e^{kt}\right)\Bigg|_0^{t_1}$$

$$= \frac{q_0}{k}e^{kt}\Bigg|_0^{t_1} = \frac{q_0}{k}e^{kt_1} - \frac{q_0}{k}e^0$$

$$= \frac{q_0}{k}e^{kt_1} - \frac{q_0}{k}(1)$$

$$= \frac{q_0}{k}(e^{kt_1} - 1). \quad (1)$$

Now return to the numbers given for petroleum: $q_0 = 19{,}600$ million barrels, where q_0 represents consumption in the base year; $k = .06$; and total petroleum reserves are estimated as 2,000,000 million barrels. Thus, using equation (1),

$$2{,}000{,}000 = \frac{19{,}600}{.06}(e^{.06t_1} - 1).$$

Multiply both sides of the equation by .06.

$$120{,}000 = 19{,}600(e^{.06t_1} - 1)$$

Divide both sides of the equation by 19,600.

$$6.1 = e^{.06t_1} - 1$$

Add 1 to both sides.

$$7.1 = e^{.06t_1}$$

Take natural logarithms of both sides.

$$\ln 7.1 = \ln e^{.06t_1} = .06t_1 \ln e$$
$$= .06t_1 \quad (\text{since } \ln e = 1)$$

Finally,

$$t_1 = \frac{\ln 7.1}{.06}.$$

A calculator gives

$$t_1 \approx 33.$$

By this result, petroleum reserves will last the world for 33 years.

The results of mathematical analyses such as this must be used with great caution. By the analysis above, the world would use all the petroleum that it wants in the thirty-second year after the base year, but there would be none at all in 34 years. This is not at all realistic. As petroleum reserves decline, the price will increase, causing demand to decline and supplies to increase.

EXERCISES

1. Find the number of years that the estimated petroleum reserves would last if used at the same rate as in the base year.
2. How long would the estimated petroleum reserves last if the growth constant was only 2% instead of 6%?

Estimate the length of time until depletion for each of the following minerals.

3. Bauxite (the ore from which aluminum is obtained), estimated reserves in base year 15,000,000 thousand tons, rate of consumption 63,000 thousand tons, growth constant 6%.
4. Bituminous coal, estimated world reserves 2,000,000 million tons, rate of consumption 2200 million tons, growth constant 4%.

CHAPTER 15 Multivariate Calculus

Many of the ideas developed for functions of one variable also apply to functions of more than one variable. In particular, the fundamental idea of derivative generalizes in a very natural way to functions of more than one variable.

15.1 FUNCTIONS OF SEVERAL VARIABLES

If a company produces x items at a cost of \$10 per item, then the total cost $C(x)$ of producing the items is given by

$$C(x) = 10x.$$

The cost is a function of one independent variable, the number of items produced. If the company produces two products, with x of one product at a cost of \$10 each, and y of another product at a cost of \$15 each, then the total cost to the firm is a function of *two* independent variables, x and y. By generalizing $f(x)$ notation, the total cost can be written as $C(x, y)$, where

$$C(x, y) = 10x + 15y.$$

When $x = 5$ and $y = 12$, the total cost is written $C(5, 12)$, with

$$C(5, 12) = 10 \cdot 5 + 15 \cdot 12 = 230.$$

Here is a general definition.

> $z = f(x, y)$ is a **function of two independent variables** if a unique value of z is obtained from each ordered pair of real numbers (x, y). The variables x and y are **independent variables;** z is the **dependent variable.** The set of all ordered pairs of real numbers (x, y) such that $f(x, y)$ is a real number is the **domain** of f; the set of all values of $f(x, y)$ is the **range.**

EXAMPLE 1 Let $f(x, y) = 4x^2 + 2xy + 3/y$ and find each of the following.

(a) $f(-1, 3)$.

Replace x with -1 and y with 3.

$$f(-1, 3) = 4(-1)^2 + 2(-1)(3) + \frac{3}{3} = 4 - 6 + 1 = -1$$

1 Let $f(x, y) = x^3 - 4x^2 + xy$. Find

(a) $f(2, 4)$;

(b) $f(-2, 3)$.

Answers:

(a) 0

(b) -30

(b) $f(2, 0)$

Because of the quotient $3/y$, it is not possible to replace y with 0, so $f(2, 0)$ is undefined. By inspection we see that the domain of the function f consists of all ordered pairs (x, y) such that $y \neq 0$. ■ 1

EXAMPLE 2 Let x represent the number of milliliters (ml) of carbon dioxide released by the lungs in 1 minute. Let y be the change in the carbon dioxide content of the blood as it leaves the lungs (y is measured in ml of carbon dioxide per 100 ml of blood). The total output of blood from the heart in one minute (measured in ml) is given by C, where C is a function of x and y such that

$$C(x, y) = \frac{100x}{y}.$$

Find $C(320, 6)$.

Replace x with 320 and y with 6 to get

$$C(320, 6) = \frac{100(320)}{6}$$

$$\approx 5333 \text{ ml of blood per minute.}$$ ■

The definition given before Example 1 was for a function of two independent variables, but similar definitions could be given for functions of three, four, or more independent variables. Functions of more than one independent variable are called **multivariate functions.**

GRAPHING FUNCTIONS OF TWO INDEPENDENT VARIABLES Functions of one independent variable are graphed by using an x-axis and a y-axis to locate points in a plane. The plane determined by the x- and y-axes is called the ***xy*-plane.** A third axis is needed to graph functions of two independent variables—the z-axis, which goes through the origin in the xy-plane and is perpendicular to both the x-axis and the y-axis.

Figure 15.1 shows one possible way to draw the three axes. In Figure 15.1, the yz-plane is in the plane of the page, with the x-axis perpendicular to the plane of the page.

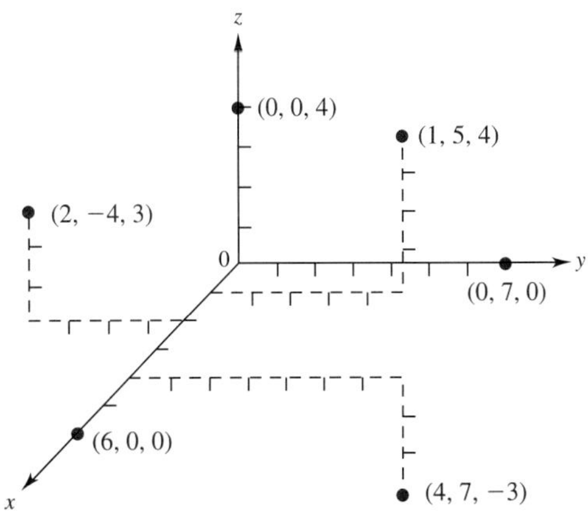

FIGURE 15.1

2 Locate $P(3, 2, 4)$ on the coordinate system below.

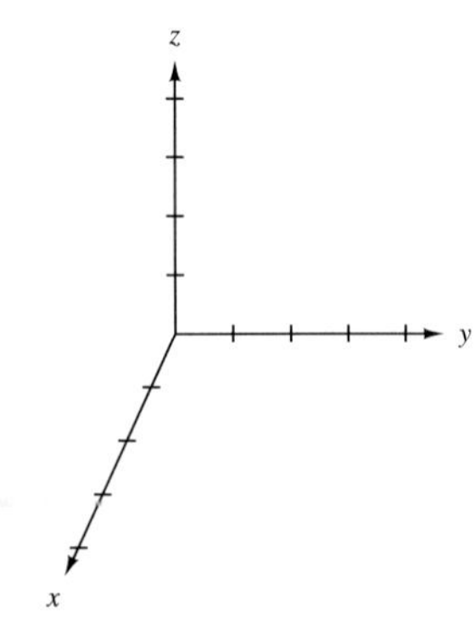

Answer:

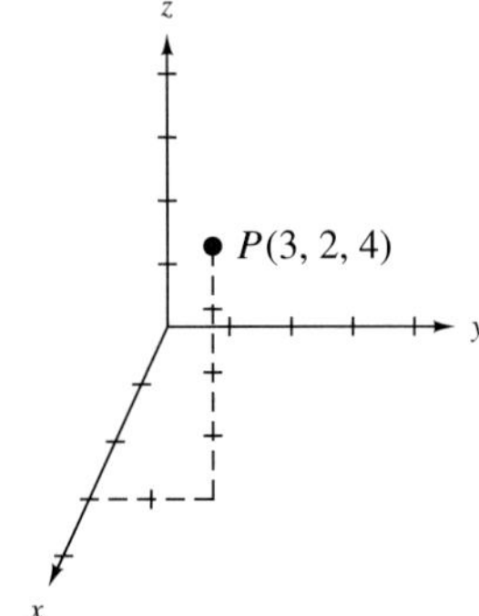

Just as we graphed ordered pairs earlier, we can now graph **ordered triples** of the form (x, y, z). For example, to locate the point corresponding to the ordered triple $(2, -4, 3)$, start at the origin and go 2 units along the positive x-axis. Then go 4 units in a negative direction (to the left), parallel to the y-axis. Finally, go up 3 units, parallel to the z-axis. The point representing $(2, -4, 3)$ is shown in Figure 15.1, along with several other points. The region of three-dimensional space where all coordinates are positive is called the **first octant.** 2

Some simple equations in three variables can be graphed by hand. In Chapter 1 we saw that the graph of $ax + by = c$ (where a, b, c are constants and not both of a and b are zero) is a straight line. This result generalizes to three dimensions.

PLANES

If a, b, c, and d are real numbers, with a, b, and c not all zero, then the graph of

$$ax + by + cz = d$$

is a plane.

EXAMPLE 3 Graph $2x + y + z = 6$.

By the result above, the graph of this equation is a plane. Earlier, we graphed straight lines by finding x- and y-intercepts. A similar idea helps graph a plane. To find the x-intercept, the point where the graph crosses the x-axis, let $y = 0$ and $z = 0$.

$$2x + 0 + 0 = 6$$
$$x = 3$$

The point $(3, 0, 0)$ is on the graph. Letting $x = 0$ and $z = 0$ gives the point $(0, 6, 0)$, while $x = 0$ and $y = 0$ lead to $(0, 0, 6)$. The plane through these three points includes the triangular surface shown in Figure 15.2. This region is the first-octant part of the plane that is the graph of $2x + y + z = 6$. ■

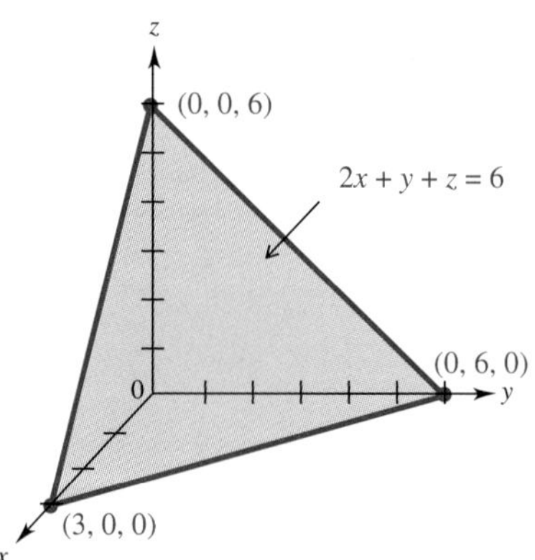

FIGURE 15.2

Throughout this discussion we assume that all equations involve three variables. Consequently, an equation such as $x + z = 6$ is understood to have a y-term with zero coefficient: $x + 0y + z = 6$.

EXAMPLE 4 Graph $x + z = 6$.

To find the x-intercept, let $z = 0$, giving (6, 0, 0). If $x = 0$, we get the point (0, 0, 6). Because there is no y in the equation $x + z = 6$, there can be no y-intercept. A plane that has no y-intercept is parallel to the y-axis. The first-octant portion of the graph of $x + z = 6$ is shown in Figure 15.3. ■

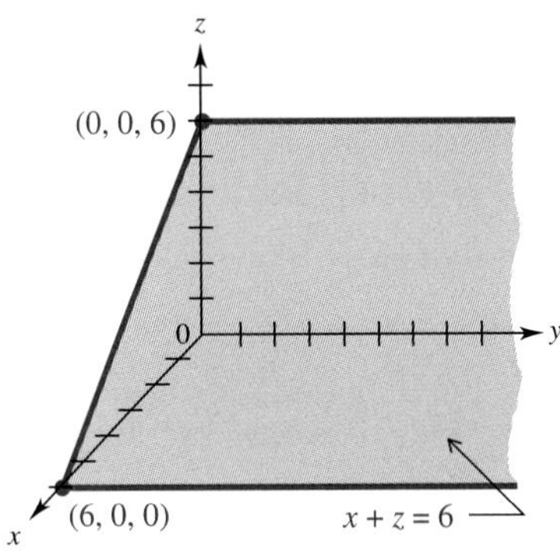

FIGURE 15.3

EXAMPLE 5 Graph each of the following functions in two independent variables.

(a) $x = 3$

This graph, which goes through (3, 0, 0), can have no y-intercept and no z-intercept. It is, therefore, a plane parallel to the y-axis and the z-axis and, therefore, to the yz-plane. The first-octant portion of the graph is shown in Figure 15.4.

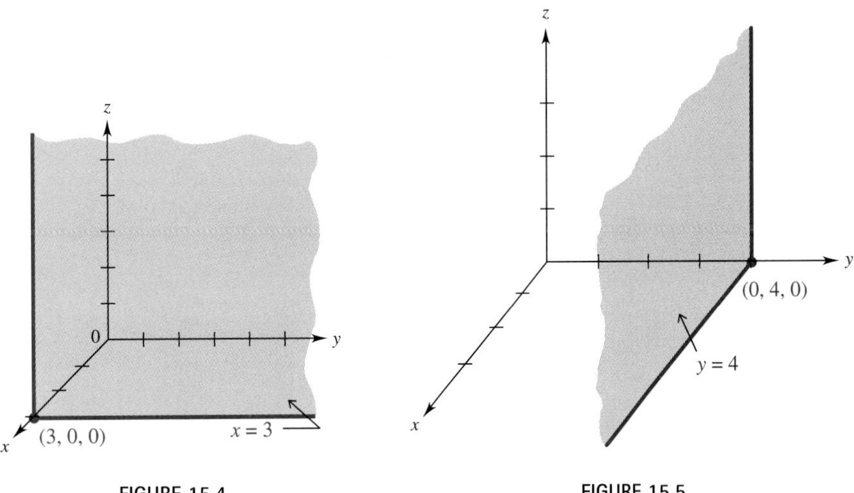

FIGURE 15.4

FIGURE 15.5

(b) $y = 4$

This graph goes through (0, 4, 0) and is parallel to the xz-plane. The first-octant portion of the graph is shown in Figure 15.5.

3 Describe each graph and give any intercepts.

(a) $2x + 3y - z = 4$

(b) $x + y = 3$

(c) $z = 2$

Answers:

(a) A plane; (2, 0, 0), (0, 4/3, 0), (0, 0, −4)

(b) A plane parallel to the z-axis; (3, 0, 0), (0, 3, 0)

(c) A plane parallel to the x-axis and the y-axis; (0, 0, 2)

(c) Graph $z = 1$.

The graph is a plane parallel to the xy-plane, passing through (0, 0, 1). Its first-octant portion is shown in Figure 15.6. ■ 3

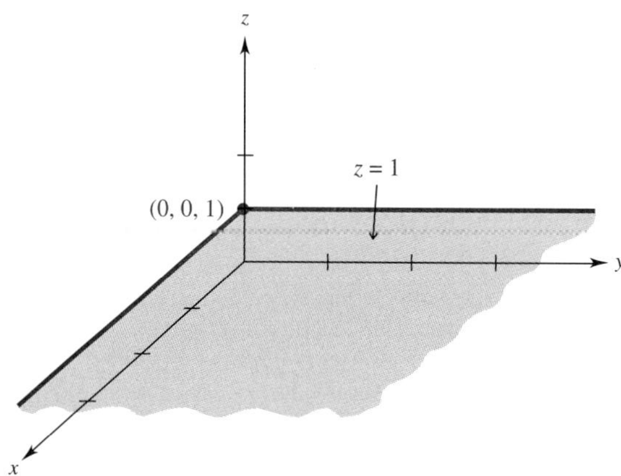

FIGURE 15.6

The graph of a function of one variable, $y = f(x)$, is a curve in the plane. If x_0 is in the domain of f, the point $(x_0, f(x_0))$ on the graph lies directly above, on, or below the number x_0 on the x-axis, as shown in Figure 15.7.

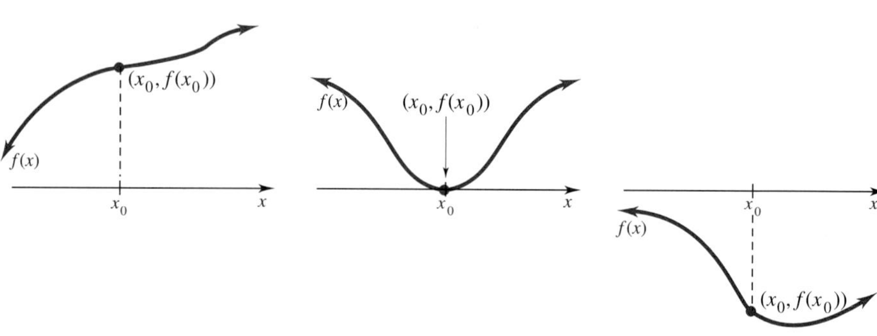

FIGURE 15.7

The graph of a function of two variables, $z = f(x, y)$, is a **surface** in three-dimensional space. If (x_0, y_0) is in the domain of f, the point $(x_0, y_0, f(x_0, y_0))$ lies directly above, on, or below the point (x_0, y_0) in the xy-plane, as shown in Figure 15.8.

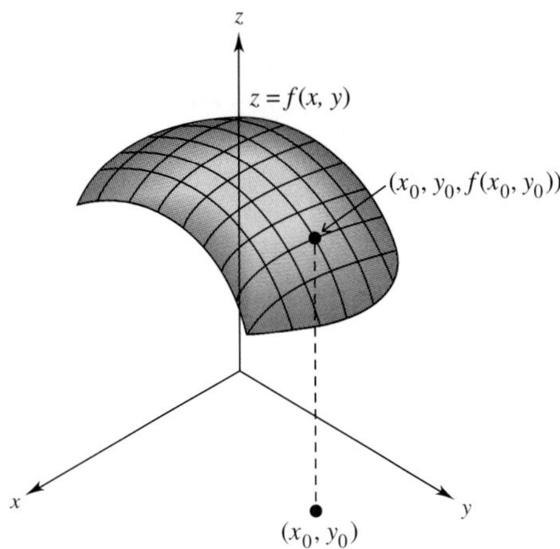

FIGURE 15.8

Most graphing calculators cannot be used for three-dimensional graphs, so more complicated graphs are usually done with appropriate graphing software on a computer. Figure 15.9 shows several computer generated graphs of functions of two variables.

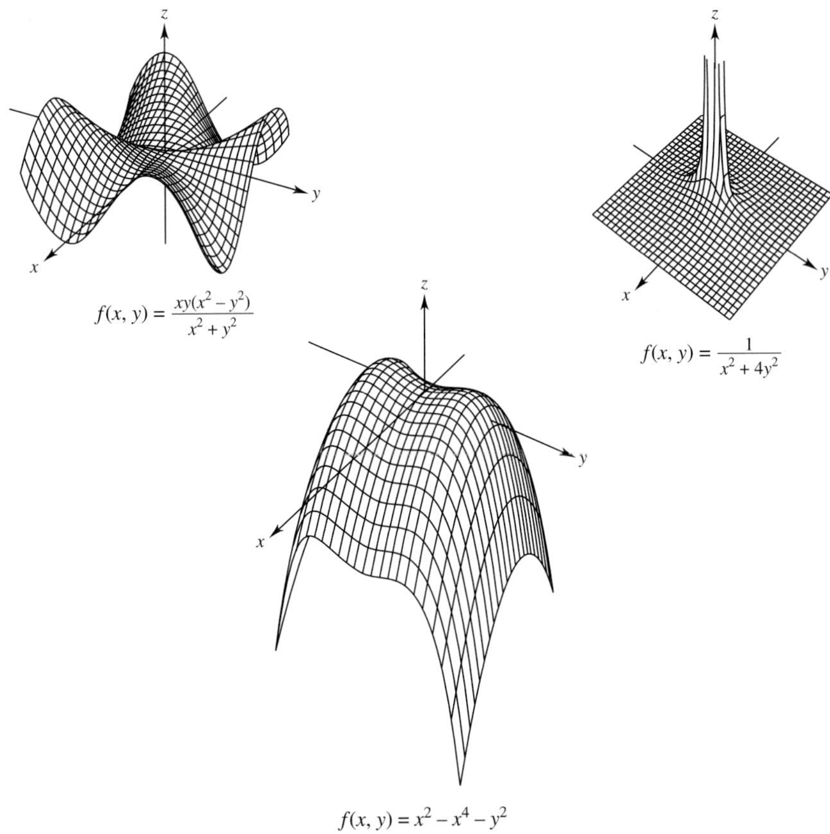

FIGURE 15.9

When computer graphing software is not available, you can sometimes get a good picture of a graph by finding various **traces**—the curves that result when a surface is cut by a plane. The ***xy*-trace** is the intersection of the surface with the xy-plane. The ***yz*-trace** and ***xz*-trace** are defined similarly. You can also determine the intersection of the surface with planes parallel to the xy-plane. Such planes are of the form $z = k$, where k is a constant and the curves that result when they cut the surface are called **level curves.**

EXAMPLE 6 Graph $z = x^2 + y^2$.

The yz-plane is the plane in which every point has first coordinate 0, so its equation is $x = 0$. When $x = 0$, the equation becomes $z = y^2$, which is the equation of a parabola in the yz-plane, as shown in Figure 15.10(a). Similarly, to find the intersection of the surface with the xz-plane (whose equation is $y = 0$), let $y = 0$ in the equation. It then becomes $z = x^2$, which is the equation of a parabola in the xz-plane (shown in Figure 15.10(a)). The xy-trace (the intersection of the surface with the plane $z = 0$) is the single point $(0, 0, 0)$ because $x^2 + y^2$ is never negative, and equal to 0 only when $x = 0$ and $y = 0$.

Next, we find the level curves by intersecting the surface with the planes $z = 1, z = 2$, $z = 3$, etc. (all of which are parallel to the xy-plane). In each case, the result is a circle

$$x^2 + y^2 = 1, \quad x^2 + y^2 = 2, \quad x^2 + y^2 = 3,$$

and so on, as shown in Figure 15.10(b). Drawing the traces and level curves on the same set of axes suggests that the graph of $z = x^2 + y^2$ is the bowl-shaped figure, called a **paraboloid,** that is shown in Figure 15.10(c). ■

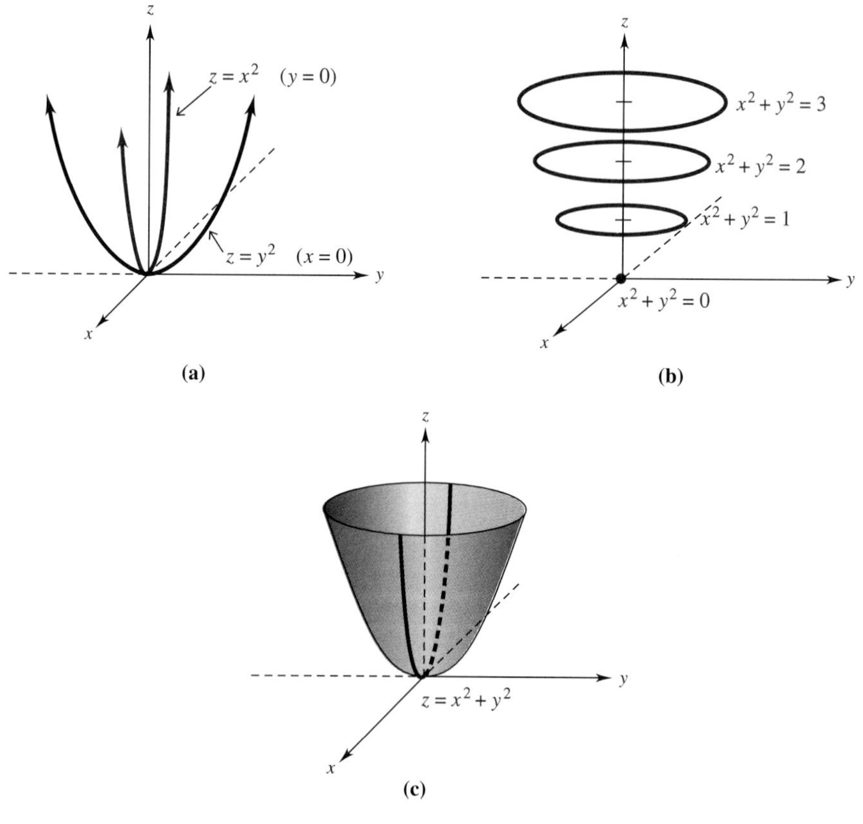

FIGURE 15.10

One application of level curves in economics occurs with production functions. A **production function** $z = f(x, y)$ is a function that gives the quantity z of an item produced as a function of x and y, where x is the amount of labor and y is the amount of capital (in appropriate units) needed to produce z units. If the production function has the special form $z = P(x, y) = Ax^a y^{1-a}$, where A is a constant and $0 < a < 1$, the function is called a **Cobb-Douglas production function.**

EXAMPLE 7 Find the level curve at a production of 100 items for the Cobb-Douglas production function $z = x^{2/3}y^{1/3}$.

Let $z = 100$ and solve for y to get

$$100 = x^{2/3}y^{1/3}$$

$$\frac{100}{x^{2/3}} = y^{1/3}.$$

Now cube both sides to express y as a function of x.

$$y = \frac{100^3}{x^2}$$

$$y = \frac{1{,}000{,}000}{x^2}$$

The level curve of height 100 is shown graphed in three dimensions in Figure 15.11(a) and on the familiar xy-plane in Figure 15.11(b). The points of the graph correspond to those values of x and y that lead to production of 100 items. ■ 4

4 Find the equation of the level curve for production of 100 items if the production function is $z = 5x^{1/4}y^{3/4}$.

Answer:

$$y = \frac{20^{4/3}}{x^{1/3}}$$

The curve in Figure 15.11 is called an *isoquant,* for *iso* (equal) and *quant* (amount). In Example 7, the "amounts" all "equal" 100.

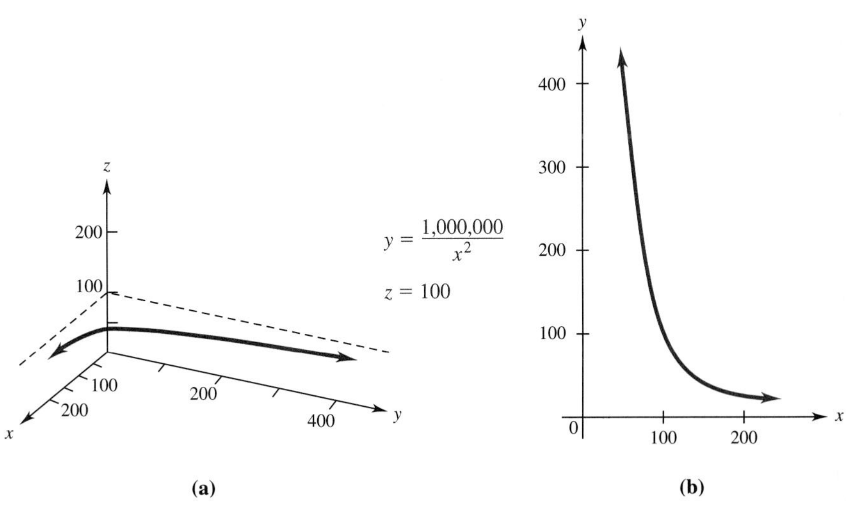

FIGURE 15.11

15.1 EXERCISES

1. What is meant by a multivariate function?

2. Describe how you would graph the function $x + y + z = 4$ and describe what the graph should look like.

For each of the following functions, find $f(2, -1)$, $f(-4, 1)$, $f(-2, -3)$, and $f(0, 8)$. (See Example 1.)

3. $f(x, y) = 5x + 2y - 4$

4. $f(x, y) = 2x^2 - xy + y^2$

5. $f(x, y) = \sqrt{y^2 + 2x^2}$

6. $f(x, y) = \dfrac{3x + 4y}{\ln |x|}$

7. What are *xy*-, *xz*-, and *yz*-traces of a graph?

8. What is a level curve?

Graph the first octant portion of each of the following planes. (See Examples 3–5.)

9. $3x + 2y + z = 12$

10. $2x + 3y + 3z = 18$

11. $x + y = 5$

12. $y + z = 3$

13. $z = 4$

14. $y = 3$

Graph the level curves in the first octant at heights of $z = 0$, $z = 2$, and $z = 4$ for the following equations. (See Example 6.)

15. $3x + 2y + z = 18$

16. $x + 3y + 2z = 8$

17. $y^2 - x = -z$

18. $2y - \dfrac{x^2}{3} = z$

Management *Find the level curve at a production of 500 for each of the production functions in Exercises 19–20. Graph each function on the xy-plane. (See Example 7.)*

19. The production function z for the United States was once estimated as $z = x^{.7}y^{.3}$, where x stands for the amount of labor and y stands for the amount of capital.

20. If x represents the amount of labor and y the amount of capital, a production function for Canada is approximately $z = x^{.4}y^{.6}$.

Management *The multiplier function*

$$M = \frac{(1 + i)^n(1 - t) + t}{[1 + (1 - t)i]^n}$$

compares the growth of an Individual Retirement Account (IRA) with the growth of the same deposit in a regular savings account. The function M depends on the three variables n, i, and t, where n represents the number of years an amount is left at interest, i represents the interest rate in both types of accounts, and t represents the income tax rate. Values of $M > 1$ indicate that the IRA grows faster than the savings account. Let $M = f(n, i, t)$ and find the following.

21. Find the multiplier when funds are left for 25 years at 5% interest and the income tax rate is 28%. Which account grows faster?

22. What is the multiplier when money is invested for 25 years at 6% interest and the income tax rate is 33%? Which account grows faster?

23. Extra postage is charged for parcels sent by U.S. mail that are more than 108 inches in length and girth combined. (Girth is the distance around the parcel perpendicular to its length. See the figure.) Express the combined length and girth as a function of L, W, and H.

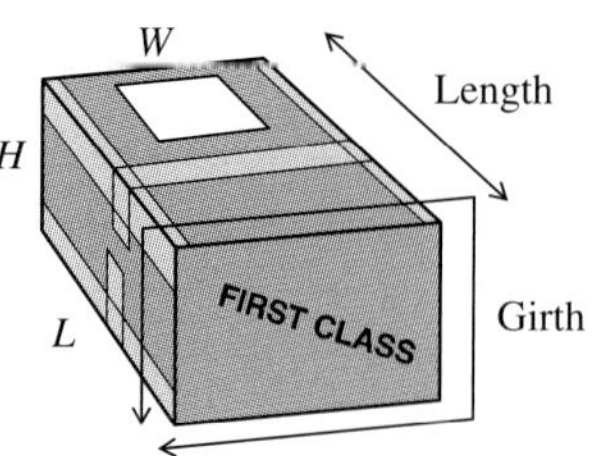

24. The holes cut in a roof for vent pipes require elliptical templates. A formula for determining the length of the major axis of the ellipse is $L = f(H, D) = \sqrt{H^2 + D^2}$, where D is the (outside) diameter of the pipe and H is the "rise" of the roof per D units of "run"; that is, the slope of the roof is H/D. (See the figure.) The width of the ellipse (minor axis) equals D. Find the length and width of the ellipse required to produce a hole for a vent pipe with a diameter of 3.75 inches in roofs with the following slopes.
(a) 3/4 **(b)** 2/5

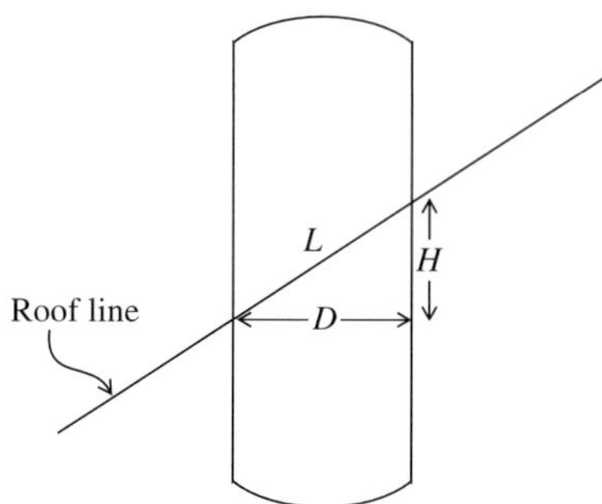

25. Let $f(x, y) = 9x^2 - 3y^2$, and find each of the following.
(a) $\dfrac{f(x + h, y) - f(x, y)}{h}$
(b) $\dfrac{f(x, y + h) - f(x, y)}{h}$

26. Let $f(x, y) = 7x^3 + 8y^2$, and find each of the following.
(a) $\dfrac{f(x + h, y) - f(x, y)}{h}$
(b) $\dfrac{f(x, y + h) - f(x, y)}{h}$

By considering traces, match each equation in Exercises 27–32 with its graph in (a)–(f).

27. $z = x^2 + y^2$

28. $z^2 - y^2 - x^2 = 1$

29. $x^2 - y^2 = z$

30. $z = y^2 - x^2$

31. $\dfrac{x^2}{16} + \dfrac{y^2}{25} + \dfrac{z^2}{4} = 1$

32. $z = 5(x^2 + y^2)^{-1/2}$

(a)

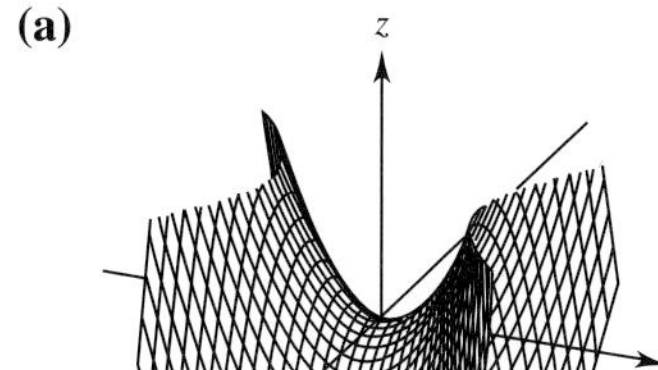

(b)

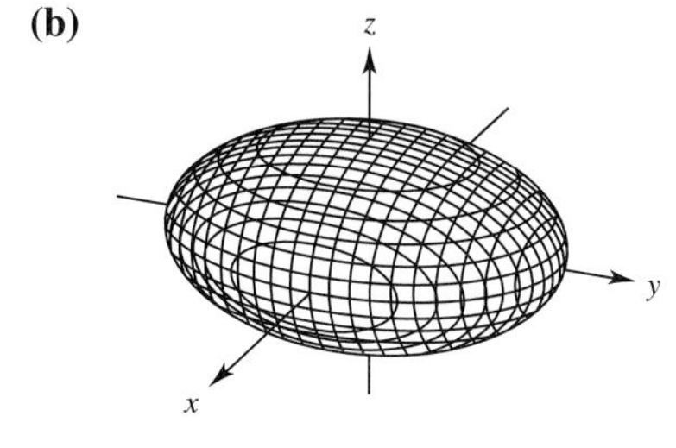

(c)

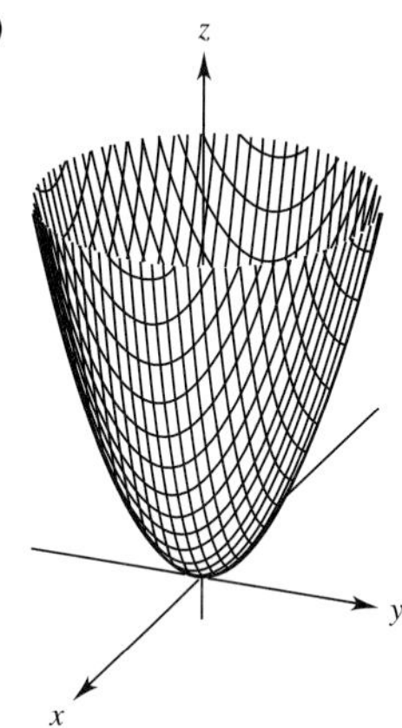

(d)

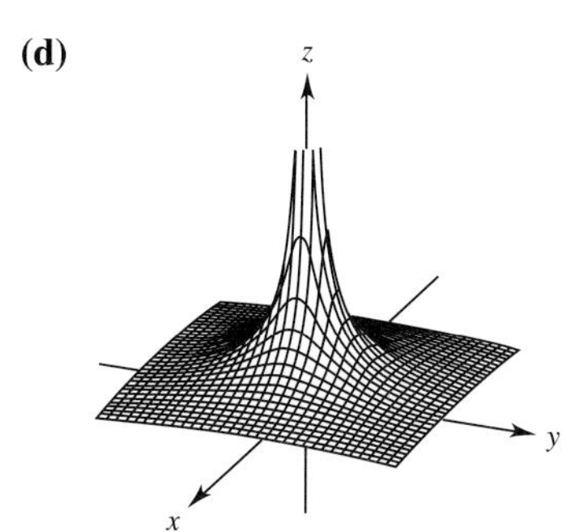

(e)

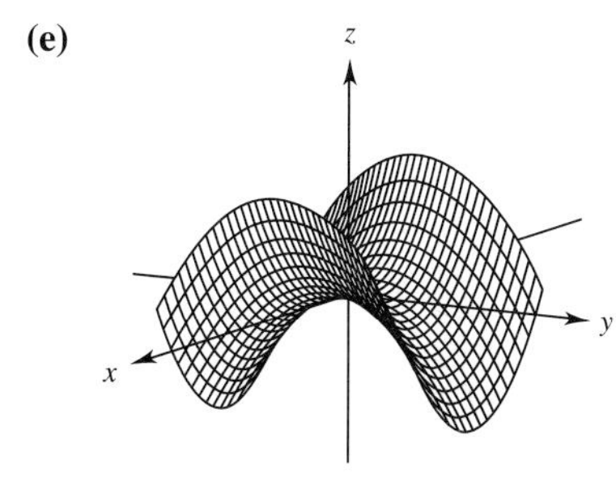

(f)

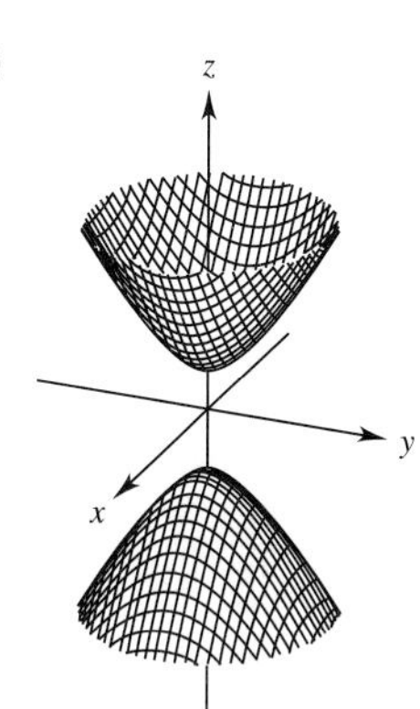

15.2 PARTIAL DERIVATIVES

A small firm makes only two products, radios and audiocassette recorders. The profits of the firm are given by

$$P(x, y) = 40x^2 - 10xy + 5y^2 - 80,$$

where x is the number of units of radios sold and y is the number of units of recorders sold. How will a change in x or y affect P?

Suppose that sales of radios have been steady at 10 units; only the sales of recorders vary. The management would like to find the marginal profit with respect to y, the number of recorders sold. Recall that marginal profit is given by the derivative of the profit function. Here, x is fixed at 10. Using this information, we begin by finding a new function, $f(y) = P(10, y)$. Let $x = 10$ to get

$$\begin{aligned} f(y) = P(\mathbf{10}, y) &= 40(\mathbf{10})^2 - 10(\mathbf{10})y + 5y^2 - 80 \\ &= 3920 - 100y + 5y^2. \end{aligned}$$

The function $f(y)$ shows the profit from the sale of y recorders, assuming that x is fixed at 10 units. Find the derivative df/dy to get the marginal profit with respect to y.

$$\frac{df}{dy} = -100 + 10y$$

In this example, the derivative of the function $f(y)$ was taken with respect to y only; we assumed that x was fixed. To generalize, let $z = f(x, y)$. An intuitive definition of the *partial derivatives* of f with respect to x and y follows.

PARTIAL DERIVATIVES (INFORMAL DEFINITION)

The **partial derivative of f with respect to x** is the derivative of f obtained by treating x as a variable and y as a constant.

The **partial derivative of f with respect to y** is the derivative of f obtained by treating y as a variable and x as a constant.

The symbols $f_x(x, y)$ (no prime used), $\partial z/\partial x$, and $\partial f/\partial x$ are used to represent the partial derivative of $z = f(x, y)$ with respect to x, with similar symbols used for the partial derivative with respect to y. The symbol $f_x(x, y)$ is often abbreviated as just f_x, with $f_y(x, y)$ abbreviated f_y.

Generalizing from the definition of derivative given earlier, partial derivatives of a function $z = f(x, y)$ are formally defined as follows.

PARTIAL DERIVATIVES (FORMAL DEFINITION)

Let $z = f(x, y)$ be a function of two variables. Then the **partial derivative of f with respect to x** is

$$f_x(x, y) = \lim_{h \to 0} \frac{f(x + h, y) - f(x, y)}{h};$$

the **partial derivative of f with respect to y** is

$$f_y(x, y) = \lim_{h \to 0} \frac{f(x, y + h) - f(x, y)}{h};$$

provided these limits exist.

Similar definitions could be given for functions of more than two independent variables.

EXAMPLE 1 Let $f(x, y) = 4x^2 - 9xy + 6y^3$. Find f_x and f_y.

To find f_x, treat y as a constant and x as a variable. The derivative of the first term, $4x^2$, is $8x$. In the second term, $-9xy$, the constant coefficient of x is $-9y$, so the derivative with x as the variable is $-9y$. The derivative of $6y^3$ is zero, since we are treating y as a constant. Thus,

$$f_x = 8x - 9y.$$

1 Find f_x and f_y.

(a) $f(x, y) = -x^2y + 3xy + 2xy^2$

(b) $f(x, y) = x^3 + 2x^2y + xy$

Answers:

(a) $f_x = -2xy + 3y + 2y^2$; $f_y = -x^2 + 3x + 4xy$

(b) $f_x = 3x^2 + 4xy + y$; $f_y = 2x^2 + x$

2 Find f_x and f_y.

(a) $f(x, y) = \ln(2x + 3y)$

(b) $f(x, y) = e^{xy}$

Answers:

(a) $f_x = \frac{2}{2x + 3y}$; $f_y = \frac{3}{2x + 3y}$

(b) $f_x = ye^{xy}$; $f_y = xe^{xy}$

3 Let $f(x, y) = x^2 + xy^2 + 5y - 10$. Find the following.

(a) $f_x(2, 1)$

(b) $\frac{\partial f}{\partial y}(-1, 0)$

Answers:

(a) 5

(b) 5

Now, to find f_y, treat y as a variable and x as a constant. Since x is a constant, the derivative of $4x^2$ is zero. In the second term, the coefficient of y is $-9x$ and the derivative of $-9xy$ is $-9x$. The derivative of the third term is $18y^2$. Thus,

$$f_y = -9x + 18y^2. \quad \blacksquare \quad \boxed{1}$$

EXAMPLE 2 Let $f(x, y) = \ln(x^2 + y)$. Find f_x and f_y.

Recall the formula for the derivative of a natural logarithmic function. If $y = \ln(g(x))$, then $y' = g'(x)/g(x)$. Using this formula,

$$f_x = \frac{D_x(x^2 + y)}{x^2 + y} = \frac{2x}{x^2 + y},$$

and

$$f_y = \frac{D_y(x^2 + y)}{x^2 + y} = \frac{1}{x^2 + y}. \quad \blacksquare \quad \boxed{2}$$

The notation

$$f_x(a, b) \quad \text{or} \quad \frac{\partial f}{\partial x}(a, b)$$

represents the value of a partial derivative when $x = a$ and $y = b$, as shown in the next example.

EXAMPLE 3 Let $f(x, y) = 2x^2 + 3xy^3 + 2y + 5$. Find the following.

(a) $f_x(-1, 2)$

First, find f_x by holding y constant.

$$f_x = 4x + 3y^3$$

Now let $x = -1$ and $y = 2$.

$$f_x(-1, 2) = 4(-1) + 3(2)^3 = -4 + 24 = 20$$

(b) $\frac{\partial f}{\partial y}(-4, -3)$

Since $\partial f/\partial y = 9xy^2 + 2$,

$$\frac{\partial f}{\partial y}(-4, -3) = 9(-4)(-3)^2 + 2 = 9(-36) + 2 = -322. \quad \blacksquare \quad \boxed{3}$$

The derivative of a function of one variable can be interpreted as the slope of the tangent line to the graph at that point. With some modification, the same is true of partial derivatives of functions of two variables. At a point on the graph of a function of two variables, $z = f(x, y)$, there may be many tangent lines, all of which lie in the same tangent plane, as shown in Figure 15.12.

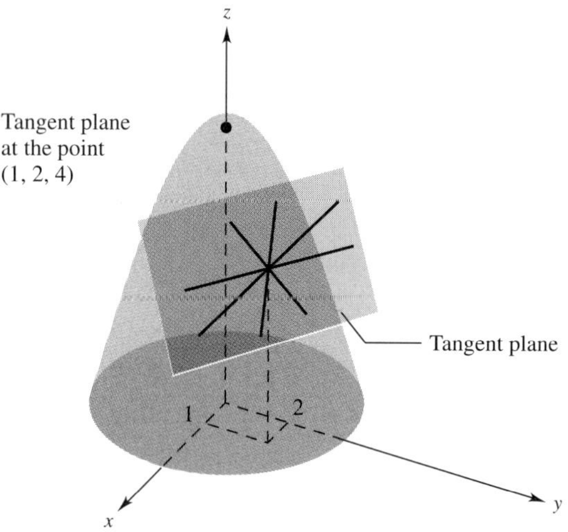

FIGURE 15.12

In any particular direction, however, there will be only one tangent line. We use partial derivatives to find the slope of the tangent lines in the x- and y-directions as follows.

Figure 15.13 shows a surface $z = f(x, y)$ and a plane that is parallel to the xz-plane. The equation of the plane is $y = a$. (This corresponds to holding y fixed.)

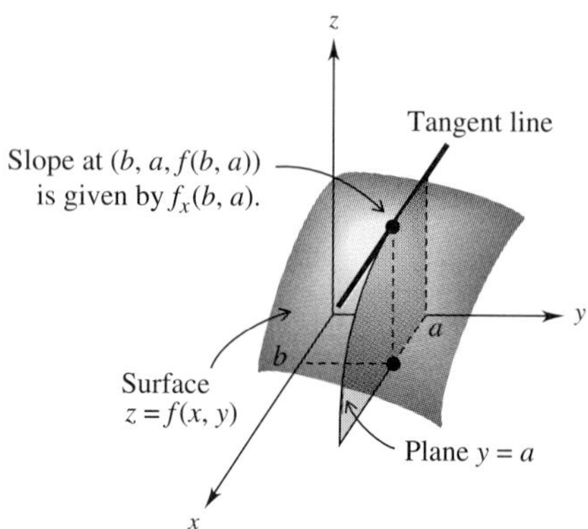

FIGURE 15.13

Because $y = a$ for points on the plane, any point on the curve that represents the intersection of the plane and the surface must have the form $(x, a, f(x, a))$. Thus, this curve can be described as $z = f(x, a)$. Since a is constant, $z = f(x, a)$ is a function of one variable. When the derivative of $z = f(x, a)$ is evaluated at $x = b$, it gives the slope of the line tangent to this curve at the point $(b, a, f(b, a))$, as shown in Figure 15.13. Thus, the partial derivative of f with respect to x, $f_x(b, a)$, gives the rate of change of the surface $z = f(x, y)$ in the x-direction at the point $(b, a, f(b, a))$. In the same way, the partial derivative with respect to y will give the slope of the line tangent to the surface in the y-direction at the point $(b, a, f(b, a))$.

RATE OF CHANGE The derivative of $y = f(x)$ gives the rate of change of y with respect to x. In the same way, if $z = f(x, y)$, then f_x gives the rate of change of z with respect to x, if y is held constant.

EXAMPLE 4 Suppose that the temperature of the water at the point on a river where a nuclear power plant discharges its hot waste water is approximated by

$$T(x, y) = 2x + 5y + xy - 40.$$

Here, x represents the temperature of the river water in degrees Celsius before it reaches the power plant and y is the number of megawatts (in hundreds) of electricity being produced by the plant.

(a) Find and interpret $T_x(9, 5)$.
First, find the partial derivative T_x.

$$T_x = 2 + y$$

This partial derivative gives the rate of change of T with respect to x. Replacing x with 9 and y with 5 gives

$$T_x(9, 5) = 2 + 5 = 7.$$

Just as marginal cost is the approximate cost of one more item, this result, 7, is the approximate change in temperature of the output water if input water temperature changes by 1 degree, from $x = 9$ to $x = 9 + 1 = 10$, while y remains constant at 5 (500 megawatts of electricity produced).

(b) Find and interpret $T_y(9, 5)$.
The partial derivative T_y is

$$T_y = 5 + x.$$

This partial derivative gives the rate of change of T with respect to y, with

$$T_y(9, 5) = 5 + 9 = 14.$$

This result, 14, is the approximate change in temperature resulting from a 1-unit increase in production of electricity from $y = 5$ to $y = 5 + 1 = 6$ (from 500 to 600 megawatts), while the input water temperature x remains constant at 9°C. ■ 4

4 Use the function of Example 4 to find and interpret the following.

(a) $T_x(5, 4)$

(b) $T_y(8, 3)$

Answers:

(a) $T_x(5, 4) = 6$; the approximate increase in temperature if the input temperature increases from 5 to 6 degrees

(b) $T_y(8, 3) = 13$; the approximate increase in temperature if the production of electricity increases from 300 to 400 megawatts

As mentioned in the previous section, if $P(x, y)$ gives the output P produced by x units of labor and y units of capital, $P(x, y)$ is a production function. The partial derivatives of this production function have practical implications. For example, $\partial P/\partial x$ gives the marginal productivity of labor. This represents the rate at which the output is changing with respect to changes in labor for a fixed capital investment. That is, if the capital investment is held constant and labor is increased by 1 work hour, $\partial P/\partial x$ will yield the approximate change in the production level. Likewise, $\partial P/\partial y$ gives the marginal productivity of capital, which represents the rate at which the output is changing with respect to changes in capital for a fixed labor value. So if the labor force is held constant and the capital investment is increased by 1 unit, $\partial P/\partial y$ will approximate the corresponding change in the production level.

EXAMPLE 5 A company that manufactures computers has determined that its production function is given by

$$P(x, y) = 500x + 800y + 3x^2y - x^3 - \frac{y^4}{4},$$

where x is the size of the labor force (in work hours per week) and y is the amount of capital (in units of \$1000) invested. Find the marginal productivity of labor and the marginal productivity of capital when $x = 50$ and $y = 20$, and interpret the results.

The marginal productivity of labor is found by taking the derivative of P with respect to x.

$$\frac{\partial P}{\partial x} = 500 + 6xy - 3x^2$$

$$\frac{\partial P}{\partial x}(50, 20) = 500 + 6(50)(20) - 3(50)^2$$

$$= -1000$$

Thus, if the capital investment is held constant at \$20,000 and labor is increased from 50 to 51 work hours per week, production will decrease by about 1000 units. In the same way, the marginal productivity of capital is $\partial P/\partial y$.

$$\frac{\partial P}{\partial y} = 800 + 3x^2 - y^3$$

$$\frac{\partial P}{\partial y}(50, 20) = 800 + 3(50)^2 - 20^3$$

$$= 300$$

If work hours are held constant at 50 hours per week and the capital investment is increased from \$20,000 to \$21,000, production will increase by about 300 units. ■ 5

5 Suppose a production function is given by $P(x, y) = 10x^2y + 100x + 400y - 5xy^2$, where x and y are defined as in Example 5. Find the marginal productivity of labor and capital when $x = 30$ and $y = 50$.

Answer:
Marginal productivity of labor is 17,600. Marginal productivity of capital is -5600.

SECOND-ORDER PARTIAL DERIVATIVES The second derivative of a function of one variable is very useful in determining relative maxima and minima. **Second-order partial derivatives** (partial derivatives of a partial derivative) are used in a similar way for functions of two or more variables. The situation is somewhat more complicated, however, with more independent variables. For example, $f(x, y) = 4x + x^2y + 2y$ has two first-order partial derivatives,

$$f_x = 4 + 2xy \quad \text{and} \quad f_y = x^2 + 2.$$

Because each of these has two partial derivatives, one with respect to y and one with respect to x, there are *four* second-order partial derivatives of function f. The notations for these four second-order partial derivatives are given below.

SECOND-ORDER PARTIAL DERIVATIVES

For a function $z = f(x, y)$, if all indicated partial derivatives exist, then

$$\frac{\partial}{\partial x}\left(\frac{\partial z}{\partial x}\right) = \frac{\partial^2 z}{\partial x^2} = f_{xx} \qquad \frac{\partial}{\partial y}\left(\frac{\partial z}{\partial y}\right) = \frac{\partial^2 z}{\partial y^2} = f_{yy}$$

$$\frac{\partial}{\partial y}\left(\frac{\partial z}{\partial x}\right) = \frac{\partial^2 z}{\partial y\,\partial x} = f_{xy} \qquad \frac{\partial}{\partial x}\left(\frac{\partial z}{\partial y}\right) = \frac{\partial^2 z}{\partial x\,\partial y} = f_{yx}.$$

As seen above, f_{xx} is used as an abbreviation for $f_{xx}(x, y)$, with f_{yy}, f_{xy}, and f_{yx} used in a similar way. The symbol f_{xx} is read "the partial derivative of f_x with respect to x," and f_{xy} is read "the partial derivative of f_x with respect to y." Also, the symbol $\partial^2 z/\partial y^2$ is read "the partial derivative of $\partial z/\partial y$ with respect to y."

NOTE For most functions found in applications and all the functions in this book, the second-order partial derivatives f_{xy} and f_{yx} are equal. Therefore, it is not necessary for us to be particular about the order in which these derivatives are found. ◆

EXAMPLE 6 Find all second-order partial derivatives for

$$f(x, y) = -4x^3 - 3x^2y^3 + 2y^2.$$

First find f_x and f_y.

$$f_x = -12x^2 - 6xy^3 \quad \text{and} \quad f_y = -9x^2y^2 + 4y$$

To find f_{xx}, take the partial derivative of f_x with respect to x.

$$f_{xx} = -24x - 6y^3$$

Take the partial derivative of f_y with respect to y; this gives f_{yy}.

$$f_{yy} = -18x^2y + 4$$

Find f_{xy} by starting with f_x, then taking the partial derivative of f_x with respect to y.

$$f_{xy} = -18xy^2$$

Finally, find f_{yx} by starting with f_y; take its partial derivative with respect to x.

$$f_{yx} = -18xy^2 \quad ■ \quad \boxed{6}$$

6 Let $f(x, y) = 4x^2y^2 - 9xy + 8x^2 - 3y^4$. Find all second-order partial derivatives.

Answer:
$f_{xx} = 8y^2 + 16$
$f_{yy} = 8x^2 - 36y^2$
$f_{xy} = 16xy - 9$
$f_{yx} = 16xy - 9$

EXAMPLE 7 Let $f(x, y) = 2e^x - 8x^3y^2$. Find all second-order partial derivatives.

Here $f_x = 2e^x - 24x^2y^2$ and $f_y = -16x^3y$. (Recall: if $g(x) = e^x$, then $g'(x) = e^x$.) Now find the second-order partial derivatives.

$$f_{xx} = 2e^x - 48xy^2 \qquad f_{xy} = -48x^2y$$
$$f_{yy} = -16x^3 \qquad f_{yx} = -48x^2y \quad ■ \quad \boxed{7}$$

7 Let $f(x, y) = 4e^{x+y} + 2x^3y$. Find all second-order partial derivatives.

Answer:
$f_{xx} = 4e^{x+y} + 12xy$
$f_{yy} = 4e^{x+y}$
$f_{xy} = 4e^{x+y} + 6x^2$
$f_{yx} = 4e^{x+y} + 6x^2$

Partial derivatives of multivariate functions with more than two independent variables are found in a way similar to that for functions with two independent variables. For example, to find f_x for $w = f(x, y, z)$ treat y and z as constants and differentiate with respect to x.

EXAMPLE 8 Let $f(x, y, z) = xy^2z + 2x^2y - 4xz^2$. Find f_x, f_y, f_z, f_{xy}, and f_{yz}.

$$f_x = y^2z + 4xy - 4z^2$$
$$f_y = 2xyz + 2x^2$$
$$f_z = xy^2 - 8xz$$

To find f_{xy}, differentiate f_x with respect to y.

$$f_{xy} = 2yz + 4x$$

In the same way, differentiate f_y with respect to z to get

$$f_{yz} = 2xy. \quad ■ \quad \boxed{8}$$

8 Let $f(x, y, z) = xyz + x^2yz + xy^2z^3$. Find f_x, f_y, f_z, and f_{xz}.

Answer:
$f_x = yz + 2xyz + y^2z^3$
$f_y = xz + x^2z + 2xyz^3$
$f_z = xy + x^2y + 3xy^2z^2$
$f_{xz} = y + 2xy + 3y^2z^2$

15.2 EXERCISES

For each of these functions, find

(a) $\frac{\partial z}{\partial x}$ (b) $\frac{\partial z}{\partial y}$ (c) $f_x(2, 3)$ (d) $f_y(1, -2)$.

1. $z = f(x, y) = 8x^3 - 4x^2y + 9y^2$

2. $z = f(x, y) = -3x^2 - 2xy^2 + 5y^3$

In Exercises 3–14, find f_x and f_y. Then find $f_x(2, -1)$ and $f_y(-4, 3)$. Leave the answers in terms of e in Exercises 5–8 and 13–14. (See Examples 1–3.)

3. $f(x, y) = -x^2y + 3x^4 + 8$

4. $f(x, y) = 5y^2 - 6xy^2 + 7$

5. $f(x, y) = e^{2x+y}$

6. $f(x, y) = -4e^{x-y}$

7. $f(x, y) = \frac{-2}{e^{x+2y}}$

8. $f(x, y) = \frac{6}{e^{4x-y}}$

9. $f(x, y) = \frac{x + 3y^2}{x^2 + y^3}$

10. $f(x, y) = \frac{8x^2y}{x^3 - y}$

11. $f(x, y) = \ln|2x - x^2y|$

12. $f(x, y) = \ln|4xy^2 + 3y|$

13. $f(x, y) = x^2e^{2xy}$

14. $f(x, y) = ye^{5x+2y}$

Find all second-order partial derivatives. (See Examples 6 and 7.)

15. $f(x, y) = 10x^2y^3 - 5x^3 + 3y$

16. $g(x, y) = 8x^3y + 2x^4 + 6y^3$

17. $h(x, y) = -3y^2 - 4x^2y^2 + 7xy^2$

18. $P(x, y) = -16x^3 + 3xy^2 - 12x^4y^2$

19. $R(x, y) = \frac{3y}{2x + y}$

20. $C(x, y) = \frac{8x}{x - 4y}$

21. $z = 4xe^y$

22. $z = -3ye^x$

23. $r = \ln(x + y)$

24. $k = \ln(5x - 7y)$

25. $z = x\ln(xy)$

26. $z = (y + 1)\ln(x^3y)$

In Exercises 27 and 28, evaluate $f_{xy}(2, 1)$ and $f_{yy}(1, 2)$.

27. $f(x, y) = x\ln(xy)$

28. $f(x, y) = (y + 1)\ln(x^3y)$

Find values of x and y such that both $f_x(x, y) = 0$ and $f_y(x, y) = 0$.

29. $f(x, y) = 6x^2 + 6y^2 + 6xy + 36x - 5$

30. $f(x, y) = 50 + 4x - 5y + x^2 + y^2 + xy$

31. $f(x, y) = 9xy - x^3 - y^3 - 6$

32. $f(x, y) = 2200 + 27x^3 + 72xy + 8y^2$

Find f_x, f_y, f_z, and f_{yz} for these functions. In Exercises 33 and 34, also find $f_y(2, -1, 3)$ and $f_{yz}(-1, 1, 0)$. (See Example 8.)

33. $f(x, y, z) = x^2 + yz + z^4$

34. $f(x, y, z) = 3x^5 - x^2 + y^5$

35. $f(x, y, z) = \frac{6x - 5y}{4z + 5}$

36. $f(x, y, z) = \frac{2x^2 + xy}{yz - 2}$

37. $f(x, y, z) = \ln(x^2 - 5xz^2 + y^4)$

38. $f(x, y, z) = \ln(8xy + 5yz - x^3)$

39. How many partial derivatives does a function with three independent variables have? How many second-order partial derivatives? Explain why.

40. Suppose $z = f(x, y)$ describes the cost to build a certain structure, where x represents the labor costs and y represents the cost of materials. Describe what f_x and f_y represent.

41. Social Science A developmental mathematics instructor at a large university has determined that a student's probability of success in the university's pass/fail remedial algebra course is a function of s, n, and a, where s is the student's score on the departmental placement exam, n is the number of semesters of mathematics passed in high school, and a is the student's mathematics SAT score. She estimates that p, the probability of passing the course (in percent), will be

$$p = f(s, n, a) = .003a + .1(sn)^{1/2}$$

for $200 \le a \le 800$, $0 \le s \le 10$, and $0 \le n \le 8$. Assuming that the above model has some merit, find the following.

(a) If a student scores 8 on the placement exam, has taken 6 semesters of high-school math, and has an SAT score of 450, what is the probability of passing the course?

(b) Find p for a student with 3 semesters of high school mathematics, a placement score of 3, and an SAT score of 320.

(c) Find and interpret $f_n(3, 3, 320)$ and $f_a(3, 3, 320)$. (See Example 4.)

42. A weight-loss counselor has prepared a program of diet and exercise for a client. If the client sticks to the program, the weight loss that can be expected (in pounds per week) is given by

$$\text{Weight loss} = f(n, c) = \frac{1}{8}n^2 - \frac{1}{5}c + \frac{1937}{8},$$

where c is the average daily calorie intake for the week and n is the number of 40-min aerobic workouts per week.

(a) How many pounds can the client expect to lose by eating an average of 1200 cal per day and participating in four 40-min workouts in a week?

(b) Find and interpret $\partial f/\partial n$.

(c) The client currently averages 1100 cal per day and does three 40-minute workouts each week. What would be the approximate impact on weekly weight loss of adding a fourth workout per week?

43. Management A car dealership estimates that the total weekly sales of its most popular model is a function of the car's list price, p, and the interest rate in percent, i, offered by the manufacturer. The approximate weekly sales are given by

$$f(p, i) = 132p - 2pi - .01p^2.$$

(a) Find the weekly sales if the average list price is \$9400 and the manufacturer is offering an 8% interest rate.

(b) Find and interpret f_p and f_i.

(c) What would be the effect on weekly sales if the price is \$9400 and interest rates rise from 8% to 9%?

44. Management Suppose the production function of a company is given by

$$P(x, y) = 100\sqrt{x^2 + y^2},$$

where x represents units of labor and y represents units of capital. (See Example 5.) Find the following when $x = 4$ and $y = 3$.

(a) The marginal productivity of labor

(b) The marginal productivity of capital

45. Management A manufacturer estimates that production (in hundreds of units) is a function of the amounts x and y of labor and capital used, as follows.

$$f(x, y) = \left[\frac{1}{3}x^{-1/3} + \frac{2}{3}y^{-1/3}\right]^{-3}$$

(a) Find the number of units produced when 27 units of labor and 64 units of capital are utilized.

(b) Find and interpret $f_x(27, 64)$ and $f_y(27, 64)$.

(c) What would be the approximate effect on production of increasing labor by 1 unit?

46. Management A manufacturer of automobile batteries estimates that his total production in thousands of units is given by

$$f(x, y) = 3x^{1/3}y^{2/3},$$

where x is the number of units of labor and y is the number of units of capital utilized.

(a) Find and interpret $f_x(64, 125)$ and $f_y(64, 125)$ if the current level of production uses 64 units of labor and 125 units of capital.

(b) What would be the approximate effect on production of increasing labor to 65 units while holding capital at the current level?

(c) Suppose that sales have been good and management wants to increase either capital or labor by 1 unit. Which option would result in a larger increase in production?

47. Management The production function z for the United States was once estimated as

$$z = x^{.7}y^{.3},$$

where x stands for the amount of labor and y stands for the amount of capital. Find the marginal productivity of labor (find $\partial z/\partial x$) and of capital.

48. Management A similar production function for Canada is

$$z = x^{.4}y^{.6},$$

with x, y, and z as in Exercise 47. Find the marginal productivity of labor and of capital.

49. Natural Science In one method of computing the quantity of blood pumped through the lungs in 1 minute, a researcher first finds each of the following (in milliliters).

b = quantity of oxygen used by body in 1 minute

a = quantity of oxygen per liter of blood that has just gone through the lungs

v = quantity of oxygen per liter of blood that is about to enter the lungs

In 1 minute,

Amount of oxygen used
= amount of oxygen per liter
× number of liters of blood pumped.

If C is the number of liters pumped through the blood in 1 minute, then

$$b = (a - v) \cdot C \quad \text{or} \quad C = \frac{b}{a - v}.$$

(a) Find C if $a = 160$, $b = 200$, and $v = 125$.

(b) Find C if $a = 180$, $b = 260$, and $v = 142$.

Find the following partial derivatives.

(c) $\partial C/\partial b$ **(d)** $\partial C/\partial v$

50. Natural Science The reaction to x units of a drug t hr after it was administered is given by

$$R(x, t) = x^2(a - x)t^2e^{-t},$$

for $0 \le x \le a$ (where a is a constant). Find the following.

(a) $\dfrac{\partial R}{\partial x}$ **(b)** $\dfrac{\partial R}{\partial t}$ **(c)** $\dfrac{\partial^2 R}{\partial x^2}$ **(d)** $\dfrac{\partial^2 R}{\partial x \partial t}$

(e) Interpret your answers to parts (a) and (b).

51. Physical Science The gravitational attraction F on a body a distance r from the center of the earth, where r is greater

(exercise continues)

than the radius of the earth, is a function of its mass m and the distance r as follows:

$$F = \frac{mgR^2}{r^2},$$

where R is the radius of the earth and g is the force of gravity—about 32 feet per second per second (ft/sec^2).

(a) Find and interpret F_m and F_r.

(b) Show that $F_m > 0$ and $F_r < 0$. Why is this reasonable?

15.3 EXTREMA OF FUNCTIONS OF SEVERAL VARIABLES

One of the most important applications of calculus is in finding maxima and minima for functions. Earlier, we studied this idea extensively for functions of a single independent variable; now we shall see that extrema can be found for functions of two variables. In particular, an extension of the second derivative test can be derived and used to identify maxima or minima. We begin with the definitions of local maxima and minima.

LOCAL MAXIMA AND MINIMA

Let (a, b) be in the domain of a function f.

1. f has a **local maximum** at (a, b) if there is a circular region in the xy-plane with (a, b) in its interior such that
$$f(a, b) \geq f(x, y)$$
for all points (x, y) in the circular region.
2. f has a **local minimum** at (a, b) if there is a circular region in the xy-plane with (a, b) in its interior such that
$$f(a, b) \leq f(x, y)$$
for all points (x, y) in the circular region.

As before, the word *extremum* is used for either a local maximum or a local minimum. Examples of a local maximum and a local minimum are given in Figures 15.14 and 15.15.

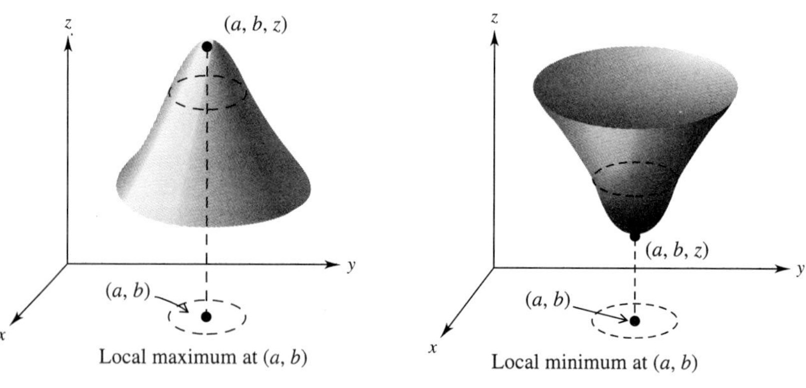

FIGURE 15.14

FIGURE 15.15

NOTE With functions of a single variable, we made a distinction between local extrema and absolute extrema. The methods for finding absolute extrema are quite involved for functions of two independent variables, so we will discuss only local extrema. ◆

As suggested by Figure 15.16, at a local maximum, the tangent line parallel to the x-axis has a slope of 0, as does the tangent line parallel to the y-axis. (Notice the similarity to functions of one variable.) That is, if the function $z = f(x, y)$ has a local extremum at (a, b), then $f_x(a, b) = 0$ and $f_y(a, b) = 0$, as stated in the theorem below.

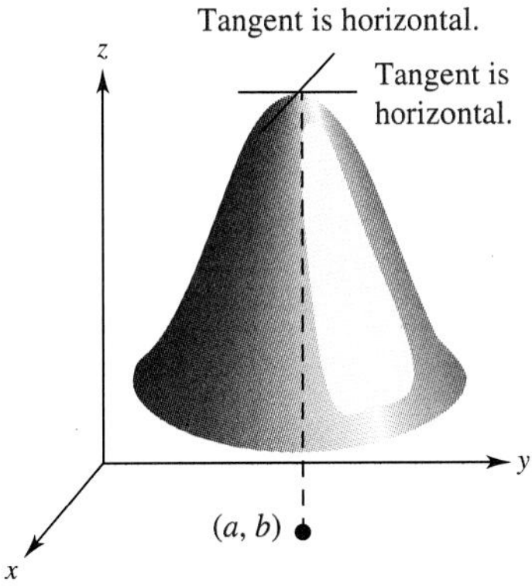

FIGURE 15.16

LOCATION OF EXTREMA

If a function $z = f(x, y)$ has a local maximum or local minimum at the point (a, b), and $f_x(a, b)$ and $f_y(a, b)$ both exist, then

$$\boldsymbol{f_x(a, b) = 0 \quad \text{and} \quad f_y(a, b) = 0.}$$

Just as with functions of one variable, the fact that the slopes of the tangent lines are 0 is no guarantee that a local extremum has been located. For example, Figure 15.17 shows the graph of $z = f(x, y) = x^2 - y^2$. Both $f_x(0, 0) = 0$ and $f_y(0, 0) = 0$, and yet $(0, 0)$ leads to neither a local maximum nor a local minimum for the function. The point $(0, 0, 0)$ on the graph of this function is called a **saddle point;** it is a minimum when approached from one direction but a maximum when approached from another direction. A saddle point is neither a maximum nor a minimum.

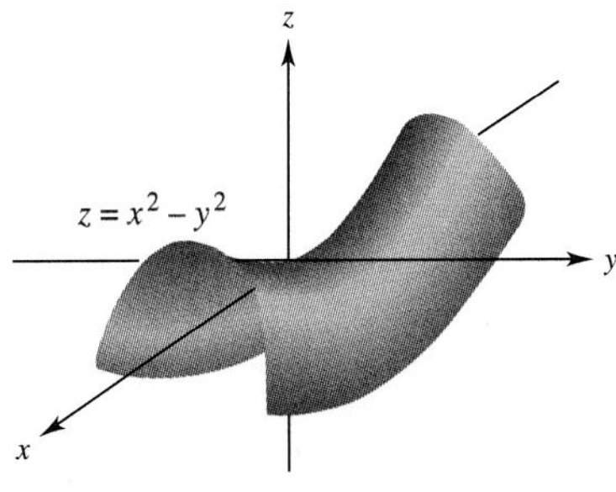

FIGURE 15.17

The theorem on location of extrema suggests a useful strategy for finding extrema. First, locate all points (a, b) where $f_x(a, b) = 0$ and $f_y(a, b) = 0$. Then test each of these points separately, using the test given after the next example. For a function $f(x, y)$, the points (a, b) such that $f_x(a, b) = 0$ and $f_y(a, b) = 0$ (or such that $f_x(a, b)$ or $f_y(a, b)$ does not exist) are called **critical points.**

EXAMPLE 1 Find all critical points for

$$f(x, y) = 6x^2 + 6y^2 + 6xy + 36x - 54y - 5.$$

We must find all points (a, b) such that $f_x(a, b) = 0$ and $f_y(a, b) = 0$. Here

$$f_x = 12x + 6y + 36 \quad \text{and} \quad f_y = 12y + 6x - 54.$$

Set each of these two partial derivatives equal to 0.

$$12x + 6y + 36 = 0 \quad \text{and} \quad 12y + 6x - 54 = 0$$

These two equations form a system of linear equations that we can rewrite as

$$\begin{aligned} 12x + 6y &= -36 \\ 6x + 12y &= 54. \end{aligned}$$

To solve this system by elimination, multiply the first equation by -2 and add.

$$\begin{array}{rcr} -24x - 12y &=& 72 \\ 6x + 12y &=& 54 \\ \hline -18x &=& 126 \\ x &=& -7 \end{array}$$

Substituting $x = -7$ in the first equation of the system, we have

$$\begin{aligned} 12(-7) + 6y &= -36 \\ 6y &= 48 \\ y &= 8. \end{aligned}$$

Therefore, $(-7, 8)$ is the solution of the system. Since this is the only solution, $(-7, 8)$ is the only critical point for the given function. By the theorem above, if the function has a local extremum, it must occur at $(-7, 8)$. ■ 1

1 Find all critical points for the following.

(a) $f(x, y) = 4x^2 + 3xy + 2y^2 + 7x - 6y - 6$

(b) $f(x, y) = e^{-2x} + xy$

Answers:

(a) $(-2, 3)$

(b) $(0, 2)$

The results of the next theorem can be used to decide whether $(-4, 2)$ in Example 1 leads to a local maximum, a local minimum, or neither. The proof of this theorem is beyond the scope of this course.

TEST FOR LOCAL EXTREMA

Suppose $f(x, y)$ is a function such that f_{xx}, f_{yy}, f_{xy} all exist. Let (a, b) be a critical point for which

$$f_x(a, b) = 0 \quad \text{and} \quad f_y(a, b) = 0.$$

Let M be the number defined by

$$M = f_{xx}(a, b) \cdot f_{yy}(a, b) - [f_{xy}(a, b)]^2.$$

1. If $M > 0$ and $f_{xx}(a, b) < 0$, then f has a **local maximum** at (a, b).
2. If $M > 0$ and $f_{xx}(a, b) > 0$, then f has a **local minimum** at (a, b).
3. If $M < 0$, then f has a **saddle point** at (a, b).
4. If $M = 0$, the test gives **no information.**

The chart below summarizes the conclusions of the theorem.

	$f_{xx}(a, b) < 0$	$f_{xx}(a, b) > 0$
$M > 0$	Local maximum	Local minimum
$M = 0$	No information	
$M < 0$	Saddle point	

EXAMPLE 2 Example 1 showed that the only critical point for the function

$$f(x, y) = 6x^2 + 6y^2 + 6xy + 36x - 54y - 5$$

is $(-7, 8)$. Does $(-7, 8)$ lead to a local maximum, a local minimum, or neither?

We can find out by using the test above. From Example 1,

$$f_x(-7, 8) = 0 \quad \text{and} \quad f_y(-7, 8) = 0.$$

Now find the various second-order partial derivatives used in finding M. From $f_x = 12x + 6y + 36$ and $f_y = 12y + 6x - 54$,

$$f_{xx} = 12, \quad f_{yy} = 12, \quad \text{and} \quad f_{xy} = 6.$$

(If these second-order partial derivatives had not all been constants, we would have had to evaluate them at the point $(-7, 8)$.) Now

$$M = f_{xx}(-7, 8) \cdot f_{yy}(-7, 8) - [f_{xy}(-7, 8)]^2 = 12 \cdot 12 - 6^2 = 108.$$

Since $M > 0$ and $f_{xx}(-7, 8) = 12 > 0$, Part 2 of the theorem applies, showing that $f(x, y) = 6x^2 + 6y^2 + 6xy + 36x - 54y - 5$ has a local minimum at $(-7, 8)$. This local minimum value is $f(-7, 8) = -347$. ■ 2

2 Find any local maxima or minima for the functions defined in Problem 1 at the side.

Answers:

(a) Local minimum at $(-2, 3)$

(b) Neither a local minimum nor a local maximum at $(0, 2)$

EXAMPLE 3 Find all points where the function

$$f(x, y) = 9xy - x^3 - y^3 - 6$$

has any local maxima or local minima.

First find any critical points. Here

$$f_x = 9y - 3x^2 \quad \text{and} \quad f_y = 9x - 3y^2.$$

Set each of these partial derivatives equal to 0.

$$\begin{aligned} f_x &= 0 & \qquad f_y &= 0 \\ 9y - 3x^2 &= 0 & 9x - 3y^2 &= 0 \\ 9y &= 3x^2 & 9x &= 3y^2 \\ 3y &= x^2 & 3x &= y^2 \end{aligned}$$

In the first equation ($3y = x^2$), notice that since $x^2 \geq 0$, $y \geq 0$. Also, in the second equation ($3x = y^2$), $y^2 \geq 0$, so $x \geq 0$.

The substitution method can be used to solve the system of equations

$$\begin{aligned} 3y &= x^2 \\ 3x &= y^2. \end{aligned}$$

The first equation, $3y = x^2$, can be rewritten as $y = x^2/3$. Substitute this into the second equation to get

$$3x = y^2 = \left(\frac{x^2}{3}\right)^2$$
$$3x = \frac{x^4}{9}.$$

Solve this equation as follows.

$$27x = x^4 \quad \text{Multiply both sides by 9.}$$
$$x^4 - 27x = 0$$
$$x(x^3 - 27) = 0 \quad \text{Factor.}$$
$$x = 0 \quad \text{or} \quad x^3 - 27 = 0 \quad \text{Set each factor equal to 0.}$$
$$x^3 = 27$$
$$x = 3 \quad \text{Take the cube root on each side.}$$

Use these values of x, along with the equation $3x = y^2$, to find y.

If $x = 0$,	If $x = 3$,
$3x = y^2$	$3x = y^2$
$3(0) = y^2$	$3(3) = y^2$
$0 = y^2$	$9 = y^2$
$0 = y.$	$3 = y$ or $-3 = y.$

The points (0, 0), (3, 3), and (3, −3) appear to be critical points; however, (3, −3) does not have $y \geq 0$. The only possible local extrema for $f(x, y) = 9xy - x^3 - y^3 - 6$ occur at the critical points (0, 0) or (3, 3). To identify any extrema, use the test. Here

$$f_{xx} = -6x, \quad f_{yy} = -6y, \quad \text{and} \quad f_{xy} = 9.$$

Test each of the critical points.

For (0, 0):

$$f_{xx}(0, 0) = -6(0) = 0, \quad f_{yy}(0, 0) = -6(0) = 0, \quad f_{xy}(0, 0) = 9,$$

so that $M = 0 \cdot 0 - 9^2 = -81$. Since $M < 0$, there is a saddle point at (0, 0).

For (3, 3):

$$f_{xx}(3, 3) = -6(3) = -18, \quad f_{yy}(3, 3) = -6(3) = -18, \quad f_{xy}(3, 3) = 9,$$

so that $M = (-18)(-18) - 9^2 = 243$. Since $M > 0$, and $f_{xx}(3, 3) = -18 < 0$, there is a local maximum at (3, 3). ■ 3

3 Find any local extrema for

$$f(x, y) = \frac{2\sqrt{2}}{3}x^3 - xy + \frac{1}{3}y^3 - 10.$$

Answer:

Local minimum at $\left(\frac{1}{2}, \frac{\sqrt{2}}{2}\right)$

EXAMPLE 4 A company is developing a new soft drink. The cost in dollars to produce a batch of the drink is approximated by

$$C(x, y) = 2200 + 27x^3 - 72xy + 8y^2,$$

where x is the number of kilograms of sugar per batch and y is the number of grams of flavoring per batch.

(a) Find the amounts of sugar and flavoring that result in minimum cost for a batch. Start with the following partial derivatives.

$$C_x = 81x^2 - 72y \quad \text{and} \quad C_y = -72x + 16y$$

Set each of these equal to 0 and solve for y.

$$\begin{aligned} 81x^2 - 72y &= 0 \\ -72y &= -81x^2 \\ y &= \frac{9}{8}x^2 \end{aligned} \qquad\qquad \begin{aligned} -72x + 16y &= 0 \\ 16y &= 72x \\ y &= \frac{9}{2}x \end{aligned}$$

From the equation on the left, $y \geq 0$. Since $(9/8)x^2$ and $(9/2)x$ both are equal to y, they are equal to each other. Set $(9/8)x^2$ and $(9/2)x$ equal and solve the resulting equation for x.

$$\begin{aligned} \frac{9}{8}x^2 &= \frac{9}{2}x \\ 9x^2 &= 36x \\ 9x^2 - 36x &= 0 \\ 9x(x - 4) &= 0 \\ 9x = 0 \quad &\text{or} \quad x - 4 = 0 \end{aligned}$$

The equation $9x = 0$ leads to $x = 0$, which is not a useful answer for our problem. Substitute $x = 4$ from $x - 4 = 0$ into $y = (9/2)x$ to find y.

$$y = \frac{9}{2}x = \frac{9}{2}(4) = 18$$

Now check to see if the critical point (4, 18) leads to a local minimum. For (4, 18),

$$C_{xx} = 162x = 162(4) = 648, \quad C_{yy} = 16, \quad \text{and} \quad C_{xy} = -72.$$

Also,

$$M = (648)(16) - (-72)^2 = 5184.$$

Since $M > 0$ and $C_{xx}(4, 18) > 0$, the cost at (4, 18) is a minimum.

(b) What is the minimum cost?

To find the minimum cost, go back to the cost function and evaluate $C(4, 18)$.

$$\begin{aligned} C(x, y) &= 2200 + 27x^3 - 72xy + 8y^2 \\ C(4, 18) &= 2200 + 27(4)^3 - 72(4)(18) + 8(18)^2 = 1336 \end{aligned}$$

The minimum cost for a batch is \$1336. ■

15.3 EXERCISES

1. Compare and contrast the way critical points are found for functions with one independent variable and functions with more than one independent variable.

2. Compare and contrast the second derivative test for $y = f(x)$ and the test for local extrema for $z = f(x, y)$.

Find all points where these functions have any local extrema. Give the values of any local extrema. Identify any saddle points. (See Examples 1–3.)

3. $f(x, y) = 2x^2 + 4xy + 6y^2 - 8x - 10$

4. $f(x, y) = x^2 + xy + y^2 - 6x - 3$

5. $f(x, y) = x^2 - xy + 2y^2 + 2x + 6y + 8$
6. $f(x, y) = 3x^2 + 6xy + y^2 - 6x - 3y$
7. $f(x, y) = 2x^2 + 4xy + y^2 - 4x + 4y$
8. $f(x, y) = 4xy - 4x^2 - 2y^2 + 4x - 8y - 7$
9. $f(x, y) = 4xy - 10x^2 - 4y^2 + 8x + 8y + 9$
10. $f(x, y) = x^2 + xy + 3x + 2y - 6$
11. $f(x, y) = x^2 + xy - 2x - 2y + 2$
12. $f(x, y) = x^2 + xy + y^2 - 3x - 5$
13. $f(x, y) = x^2 - y^2 - 2x + 4y - 7$
14. $f(x, y) = 4x + 2y - x^2 + xy - y^2 + 3$
15. $f(x, y) = 2x^3 + 2y^2 - 12xy + 15$
16. $f(x, y) = 2x^2 + 4y^3 - 24xy + 18$
17. $f(x, y) = 3x^2 + 6y^3 - 36xy + 27$
18. $f(x, y) = 2y^3 + 5x^2 + 60xy + 25$
19. $f(x, y) = e^{xy}$
20. $f(x, y) = x^2 + e^y$

Figures (a)–(f) show the graphs of the functions defined in Exercises 21–26. Find all local extrema for each function, and then match the equation to its graph.

21. $z = -3xy + x^3 - y^3 + \frac{1}{8}$
22. $z = \frac{3}{2}y - \frac{1}{2}y^3 - x^2y + \frac{1}{16}$
23. $z = y^4 - 2y^2 + x^2 - \frac{17}{16}$
24. $z = -2x^3 - 3y^4 + 6xy^2 + \frac{1}{16}$
25. $z = -x^4 + y^4 + 2x^2 - 2y^2 + \frac{1}{16}$
26. $z = -y^4 + 4xy - 2x^2 + \frac{1}{16}$

(a)
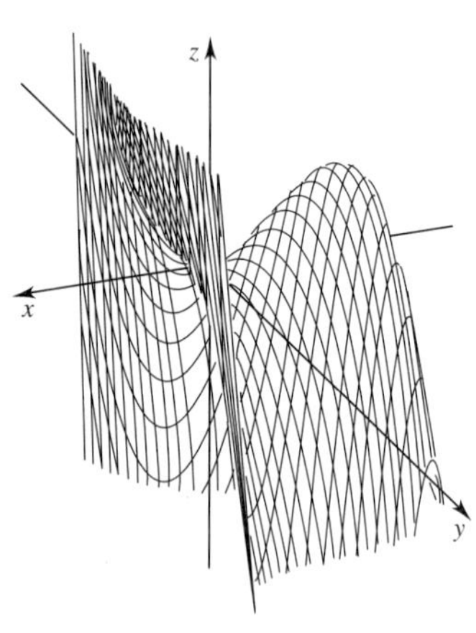

(b)
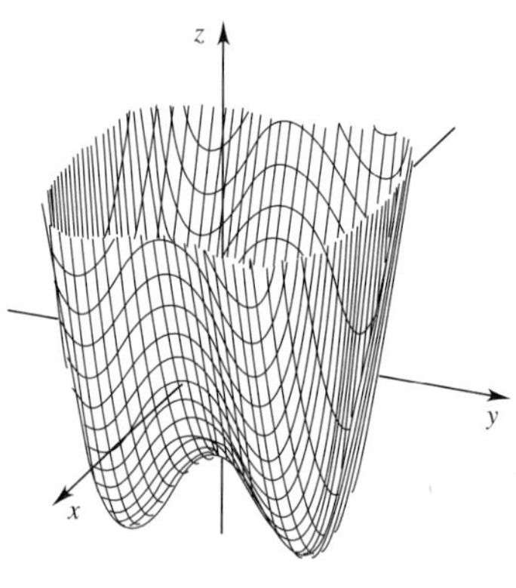

(c)
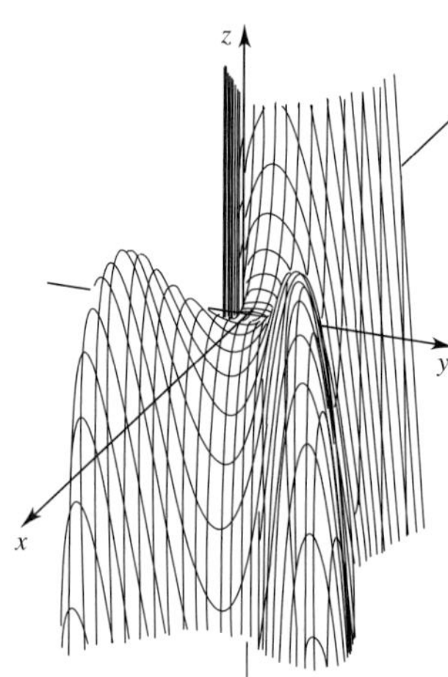

(d)
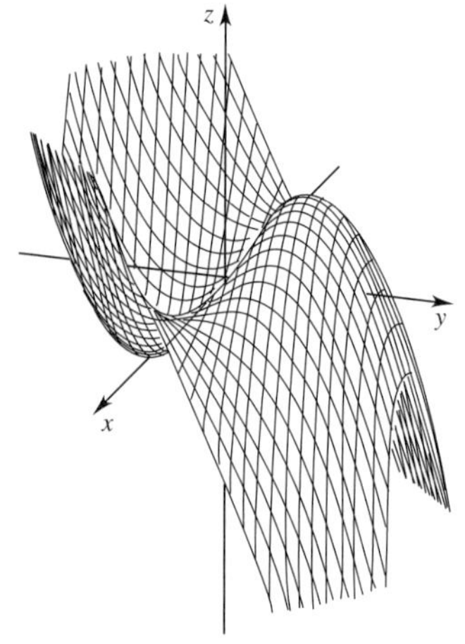

(e)
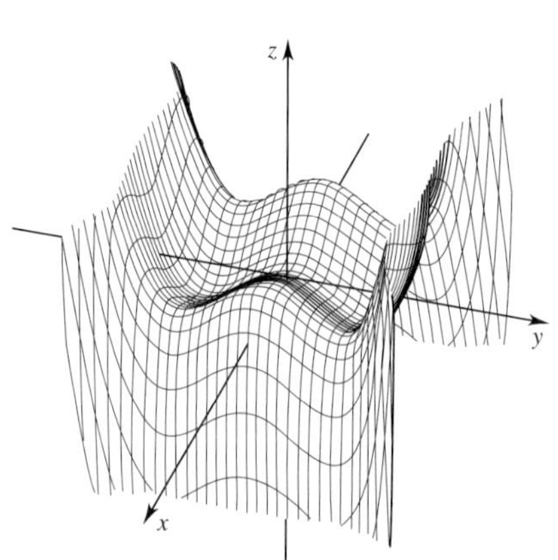

(f)
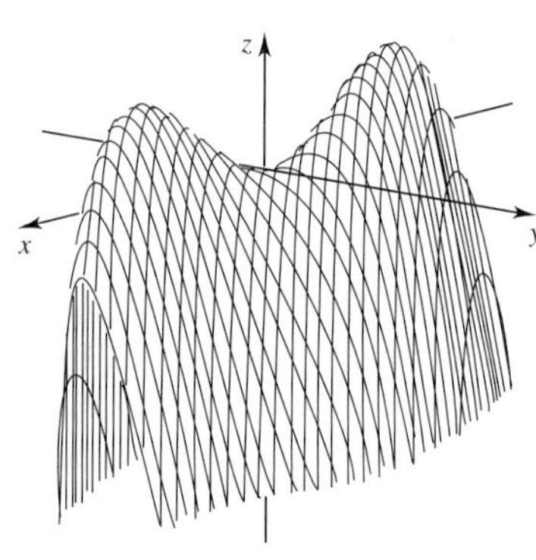

Management *Work the following exercises. (See Example 4.)*

27. Suppose that the profit of a certain firm is approximated by

$$P(x, y) = 1000 + 24x - x^2 + 80y - y^2,$$

where x is the cost of a unit of labor and y is the cost of a unit of goods. Find values of x and y that maximize profit. Find the maximum profit.

28. The labor cost in dollars for manufacturing a precision camera can be approximated by

$$L(x, y) = \frac{3}{2}x^2 + y^2 - 2x - 2y - 2xy + 68,$$

where x is the number of hours required by a skilled craftsperson and y is the number of hours required by a semi-skilled person. Find values of x and y that minimize the labor charge. Find the minimum labor charge.

29. The profit (in thousands of dollars) from the sales of graphing calculators is approximated by $P(x, y) = 800 - 2x^3 + 12xy - y^2$, where x is the cost of a unit of chips and y is the cost of a unit of labor. Find the maximum profit and the cost of chips and labor that produce the maximum profit.

30. The total profit from one acre of a certain crop depends on the amount spent on fertilizer, x, and hybrid seed, y, according to the model.

$$P(x, y) = -x^2 + 3xy + 160x - 5y^2 + 200y + 2{,}600{,}000.$$

Find values of x and y that lead to maximum profit. Find the maximum profit.

31. The total cost to produce x units of electrical tape and y units of packing tape is given by

$$C(x, y) = 2x^2 + 3y^2 - 2xy + 2x - 126y + 3800.$$

Find the number of units of each kind of tape that should be produced so that the total cost is a minimum. Find the minimum total cost.

32. The total revenue in thousands of dollars from the sale of x spas and y solar heaters is approximated by

$$R(x, y) = 12 + 74x + 85y - 3x^2 - 5y^2 - 5xy.$$

Find the number of each that should be sold to produce maximum revenue. Find the maximum revenue.

33. A rectangular closed box is to be built at minimum cost to hold 27 cubic meters. Since the cost will depend on the surface area, find the dimensions that will minimize the surface area of the box.

34. Find the dimensions that will minimize the surface area (and, hence, the cost) of a rectangular fish aquarium, open on top, with a volume of 32 cubic feet.

35. The U.S. Postal Service requires that any box sent through the mail must have a length plus girth (distance around) totaling no more than 108 inches. (See Example 6 on page 669 for a special case.) Find the dimensions of the box with maximum volume that can be sent.

36. Find the dimensions of the circular tube with maximum volume that can be sent through the U.S. mail. See Exercise 35.

37. The monthly revenue in hundreds of dollars from production of x thousand tons of grade A iron ore and y thousand tons of grade B iron ore is given by

$$R(x, y) = 2xy + 2y + 12,$$

and the corresponding cost in hundreds of dollars is given by

$$C(x, y) = 2x^2 + y^2.$$

Find the amount of each grade of ore that will produce maximum profit.

38. Suppose the revenue and cost in thousands of dollars from the manufacture of x units of one product and y units of another is

$$R(x, y) = 6xy + 3 - x^2 \quad \text{and} \quad C(x, y) = x^2 + 3y^3.$$

How many units of each product will produce maximum profit? What is the maximum profit?

CHAPTER 15 SUMMARY

Key Terms and Symbols

15.1 $z = f(x, y)$ function of two independent variables
multivariate function
xy-plane
ordered triple
first octant
surface
trace
level curves
paraboloid
production function
Cobb-Douglas production function

15.2 f_x or $\frac{\partial f}{\partial x}$ partial derivative of f with respect to x

$\frac{\partial}{\partial x}\left(\frac{\partial z}{\partial x}\right)$ or $\frac{\partial^2 z}{\partial x^2}$ or f_{xx} second-order partial derivative of $\partial z/\partial x$ (or f_x) with respect to x

$\frac{\partial}{\partial y}\left(\frac{\partial z}{\partial x}\right)$ or $\frac{\partial^2 z}{\partial y \partial x}$ or f_{xy} second-order partial derivative of $\partial z/\partial x$ (or f_x) with respect to y

15.3 local maximum
local minimum
saddle point
critical point

Key Concepts

The graph of $ax + by + cz = d$ is a **plane.**

The graph of $z = f(x, y)$ is a **surface** in three-dimensional space.

The graph of $z = ax^2 + by^2$ is a **paraboloid.**

Partial Derivatives

The **partial derivative of f with respect to x** is the derivative of f found by treating x as a variable and y as a constant.

The **partial derivative of f with respect to y** is the derivative of f found by treating y as a variable and x as a constant.

Second-Order Partial Derivatives

For a function $z = f(x, y)$, if all indicated partial derivatives exist, then

$$\frac{\partial}{\partial x}\left(\frac{\partial z}{\partial x}\right) = \frac{\partial^2 z}{\partial x^2} = f_{xx} \qquad \frac{\partial}{\partial y}\left(\frac{\partial z}{\partial y}\right) = \frac{\partial^2 z}{\partial y^2} = f_{yy}$$

$$\frac{\partial}{\partial y}\left(\frac{\partial z}{\partial x}\right) = \frac{\partial^2 z}{\partial y \partial x} = f_{xy} \qquad \frac{\partial}{\partial x}\left(\frac{\partial z}{\partial y}\right) = \frac{\partial^2 z}{\partial x \partial y} = f_{yx}.$$

Local Extrema

Let (a, b) be in the domain of a function f.

1. f has a **local maximum** at (a, b) if there is a circular region in the xy-plane with (a, b) in its interior such that
$$f(a, b) \geq f(x, y)$$
for all points (x, y) in the circular region.
2. f has a **local minimum** at (a, b) if there is a circular region in the xy-plane with (a, b) in its interior such that
$$f(a, b) \leq f(x, y)$$
for all points (x, y) in the circular region.

If $f(a, b)$ is a local extremum, then $f_x(a, b) = 0$ and $f_y(a, b) = 0$.

Test for Local Extrema

Suppose $f(x, y)$ is a function such that f_{xx}, f_{yy}, and f_{xy} all exist. Let (a, b) be a critical point for which $f_x(a, b) = 0$ and $f_y(a, b) = 0$. Let $M = f_{xx}(a, b) \cdot f_{yy}(a, b) - [f_{xy}(a, b)]^2$.

If $M > 0$ and $f_{xx}(a, b) < 0$, then f has a **local maximum** at (a, b).

If $M > 0$ and $f_{xx}(a, b) > 0$, then f has a **local minimum** at (a, b).

If $M < 0$, the graph of f has a **saddle point** at (a, b). ($f(a, b)$ is neither a maximum nor a minimum.)

If $M = 0$, the test gives **no information.**

Chapter 15 Review Exercises

Find $f(-1, 2)$ and $f(6, -3)$ for each of the following.

1. $f(x, y) = 6y^2 - 5xy + 2x$
2. $f(x, y) = -3x + 2x^2y^2 + 5y$
3. $f(x, y) = \dfrac{2x - 4}{x + 3y}$
4. $f(x, y) = x\sqrt{x^2 + y^2}$
5. Describe the graph of $2x + y + 4z = 12$.
6. Describe the graph of $y = 2$ on a three-dimensional grid.

Graph the first-octant portion of each plane.

7. $x + 2y + 4z = 4$
8. $3x + 2y = 6$
9. $4x + 5y = 20$
10. $x = 6$
11. Let $z = f(x, y) = -2x^2 + 5xy + y^2$. Find the following.
    (a) $\dfrac{\partial z}{\partial x}$ (b) $\dfrac{\partial z}{\partial y}(-1, 4)$ (c) $f_{xy}(2, -1)$
12. Let $z = f(x, y) = \dfrac{2y + x^2}{3y - x}$. Find the following.
    (a) $\dfrac{\partial z}{\partial y}$ (b) $\dfrac{\partial z}{\partial x}(0, 2)$ (c) $f_{yy}(-1, 0)$
13. Explain the difference between $\dfrac{\partial z}{\partial x}$ and $\dfrac{\partial z}{\partial y}$.

Find f_x and f_y.

14. $f(x, y) = 3y - 7x^2y^3$
15. $f(x, y) = 4x^3y + 10xy^4$
16. $f(x, y) = \sqrt{3x^2 + 2y^2}$
17. $f(x, y) = \dfrac{3x - 2y^2}{x^2 + 4y}$
18. $f(x, y) = x^3e^{3y}$
19. $f(x, y) = (y + 1)^2e^{2x+y}$
20. $f(x, y) = \ln|x^2 - 4y^3|$
21. $f(x, y) = \ln|1 + x^3y^2|$
22. Explain the difference between f_{xx} and f_{xy}.

Find f_{xx} and f_{xy}.

23. $f(x, y) = 4x^3y^2 - 8xy$
24. $f(x, y) = -6xy^4 + x^2y$
25. $f(x, y) = \dfrac{2x}{x - 2y}$
26. $f(x, y) = \dfrac{3x + y}{x - 1}$
27. $f(x, y) = x^2e^y$
28. $f(x, y) = ye^{x^2}$
29. $f(x, y) = \ln(2 - x^2y)$
30. $f(x, y) = \ln(1 + 3xy^2)$

Find all points where these functions have any local extrema. Find any saddle points.

31. $z = x^2 + 2y^2 - 4y$
32. $z = x^2 + y^2 + 9x - 8y + 1$
33. $f(x, y) = x^2 + 5xy - 10x + 3y^2 - 12y$
34. $z = x^3 - 8y^2 + 6xy + 4$
35. $z = x^3 + y^2 + 2xy - 4x - 3y - 2$
36. $f(x, y) = 7x^2 + y^2 - 3x + 6y - 5xy$
37. Write a function in terms of L, W, and H that gives the total material required to build the closed box shown in the figure.

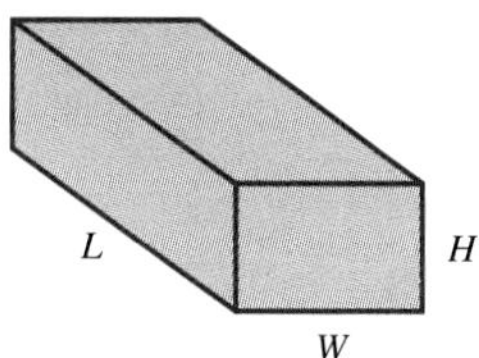

38. **Management** The manufacturing cost in dollars for a medium-sized business computer is given by
$$c(x, y) = 2x + y^2 + 4xy + 25,$$
where x is the memory capacity (RAM) of the computer in megabytes and y is the number of hours of labor required. Find each of the following.
    (a) $\dfrac{\partial c}{\partial x}(64, 6)$ (b) $\dfrac{\partial c}{\partial y}(128, 12)$
39. **Management** The total cost in dollars to manufacture x solar cells and y solar collectors is
$$c(x, y) = x^2 + 5y^2 + 4xy - 70x - 164y + 1800.$$
    (a) Find values of x and y that produce minimum total cost.
    (b) Find the minimum total cost.
40. **Management** The total profit from 1 acre of a certain crop depends on the amount spent on fertilizer, x, and on hybrid seed, y, according to the model
$$P(x, y) = .01(-x^2 + 3xy + 160x - 5y^2 + 200y + 2600).$$
The budget for fertilizer and seed is limited to \$280.
    (a) Use the budget constraint to express one variable in terms of the other. Then substitute into the profit function to get a function with one independent variable. Use the method shown in Chapter 13 to find the amounts spent on fertilizer and seed that will maximize profit. What is the maximum profit per acre? (*Hint:* Throughout this problem you may ignore the coefficient of .01 until you need to find the maximum profit.)
    (b) Find the amounts spent on fertilizer and seed that will maximize profit using the method shown in this chapter. (*Hint:* You will not need to use the budget constraint.)
    (c) Discuss any relationships between these methods.

APPENDIX A

Program Appendix

CONTENTS

The programs listed here are of two types: programs to give older calculators some of the features that are built-in on newer ones (such as a root finder) and programs to do specific tasks discussed in this book (such as linear programming). Each program is preceded by a *Description,* which describes, in general terms, how the program operates and what it does. Some programs require that certain things be done before the program is run (such as entering a function in the function memory); these requirements are listed as *Preliminaries.* Occasionally, italic remarks appear in brackets after a program step; they are *not* part of the program, but are intended to provide assistance when you are entering the program into your calculator. A remark such as "[*MATH NUM menu*]" means that the symbols or commands needed for that step of the program are in the NUM submenu of the MATH menu.

FRACTION CONVERSION FOR TI-81, CASIO, AND SHARP

Description: Enter a repeating decimal; the program converts it into a fraction. The denominator is displayed on the last line and the numerator on the line above.

TI-81

```
:ClrHome
:Lbl 2
:Input N
:0 → D
:Lbl 1
:D + 1 → D
:If fPart round (ND, 7) ≠ 0    [MATH NUM menu]
:Goto 1
```

```
:Int (ND + .5) → N
:Disp N
:Disp D
```

CASIO

```
Fix 7
Lbl 2
"N =" ? → N
0 → D
Lbl 1
D + 1 → D
N × D
Rnd   [MATH NUM menu]
(Frc Ans) ≠ 0 ⇒ Goto 1   [MATH NUM menu]
(Ans + .5) → N
Norm   [DISP menu]
(Int N)◢
D
```

SHARP

```
Input n
d = 0
Label 1
d = d + 1
If fpart (10^7 · n · d) ≥ .5 Goto 3   [MATH menu]
t = ipart (10^7 · n · d)/10^7   [MATH menu]
Goto 4
Label 3
t = (ipart (10^7 · n · d) + 1)/10^7
Label 4
If fpart t ≠ 0 Goto 1
n = ipart (n · d + .5)
Print n
Print d
```

GRAPHICAL ROOT FINDER, MAX/MIN FINDER, AND INTERSECTION FINDER FOR TI-81

Preliminaries: Enter the function whose roots or extrema are to be found in the function memory as Y_1. If an intersection point is to be found, enter the other function as Y_2. Set the RANGE so that the desired portions of the graph(s) will be displayed.
Description: Select root, intersection, or min/max. The appropriate function(s) are graphed. Use the arrow keys to move the cursor close to the desired root (x-intercept), intersection point, or extremum. Press ENTER, and its approximate coordinates are displayed. (If the calculator continues working for a long time without displaying an answer, press ON to quit the program. Then run it again, but pick a different point than before near the point you want to find.)

```
:ClrHome
:Disp "SELECT NUMBER, PRESS ENTER"
```

```
:Disp "1 = ROOT"
:Disp "2 = INTERSECTION"
:Disp "3 = MIN/MAX"
:Input C
:If C = 1
:Goto 1
:If C = 2
:Goto 2
:Goto 3
:Lbl 2
:"Y1 − Y2" → Y4   [Y-VARS menu]
:Y1 − On   [Y-VARS ON menu]
:Y2 − On
:Y3 − Off   [Y-VARS OFF menu]
:Y4 − Off
:Input
:Goto 4
:Lbl 3
:"NDeriv(Y1, .000001)" → Y4   [MATH menu]
:Y1 − On
:Y2 − Off
:Y3 − Off
:Y4 − Off
:Input
:Goto 4
:Lbl 1
:Y2 − Off
:Y3 − Off
:"Y1" → Y4
:Input
:Lbl 4
:X − Y4/NDeriv(Y4, .000001) → G   [Use the X|T key for X.]
:If abs (X − G) < .0000000001
:Goto 5
:G → X
:Goto 4
:Lbl 5
:ClrHome   [Optional]
:G → X
:Disp "X = "
:Disp X
:Disp "Y = "
:Disp Y1
```

ROOT FINDER FOR CASIO 7700/8700

Preliminaries: Enter the function whose roots are to be found in the equation memory as f_1.

Description: Enter two numbers; the program uses the bisection method to find a root (x-intercept) of the function that lies between the two numbers (if there is one).

```
"LOWER BOUND"? → A
"UPPER BOUND"? → B
0 → K
Lbl 1
B → X   [Use the variable key for X.]
f1 → C   [7700/8700 FMEM menu]
C = 0 ⇒ Goto 5
((A + B) ÷ 2) → M
M → X
f1 → D
CD < 0 ⇒ Goto 2
M → A
Goto 3
Lbl 2
1 → K
M → B
Lbl 3
abs(B − A) < .000000001 ⇒ Goto 4
Goto 1
Lbl 4
(B + A) ÷ 2 → M
K = 0 ⇒ Goto 7
Lbl 8
"ROOT = "
M
Goto 6
Lbl 7
"NO SIGN CHANGE"
Goto 6
Lbl 5
A → M
Goto 8
Lbl 9
B → M
Goto 8
Lbl 6
```

QUADRATIC FORMULA

Description: Enter the coefficients of the quadratic equation $ax^2 + bx + c = 0$; the program finds all real solutions.

TI-81/82/83

```
:ClrHome
:Disp "AX² + BX + C = 0"   [Optional]
```

```
:Prompt A†
:Prompt B†
:Prompt C†
:(B² − 4AC) → S
:If S < 0
:Goto 1
:Disp (−B + √S)/2A
:Disp (−B − √S)/2A
:Stop
:Lbl 1
:Disp "NO REAL ROOTS"
```

SHARP 9300

[*Gives both real and complex solutions when complex mode is selected.*]

```
Print "ax² + bx + c = 0"
x1 = (1/(2a))(−b + √(b² − 4ac) )
Print x1
x2 = (1/(2a))(−b − √(b² − 4ac) )
Print x2
```

CASIO 7700/8700

```
"AX² + BX + C = 0"   [Optional]
"A =" ? → A
"B =" ? → B
"C =" ? → C
B² − 4AC → D
D < 0 ⇒ Goto 1
(−B + √D) ÷ (2A)
(−B − √D) ÷ (2A)
Goto 2
Lbl 1
"NO REAL ROOTS"
Lbl 2
```

†*On TI-81, replace* Prompt A *by two lines:* :Disp "A = " *and* :Input A.

TABLE MAKER FOR TI-81 AND 85

Preliminaries: Enter the function to be evaluated in the function memory as Y_1. *Description:* Select a starting point and an increment (the amount by which adjacent *x* entries differ); the program displays a table of function values. To scroll through the table a page at a time, press "down" or "up" on TI-85, and "0 ENTER" or "1 ENTER" on TI-81. To end the program, press "quit" on TI-85 or "2 ENTER" on TI-81. (*Note:* An error message will occur if the calculator attempts to evaluate the function at a number for which it is not defined. In this case, change the starting point or increment to avoid the undefined point.)

TI-81

```
:ClrHome
:Disp "START AT"
:Input A
:Disp "INCREMENT"
:Input D
:6 → Arow   [VARS DIM menu]
:2 → Acol   [VARS DIM menu]
:A → X   [Use the variable key for X.]
:1 → J
:Lbl 1
:X → [A](J,1)   [Second function of 1]
:Y1 → [A](J,2)   [Y-VARS menu]
:J + 1 → J
:If J > 6
:Goto 2
:X + D → X
:Goto 1
:Lbl 2
:Disp [A]
:Disp "0 = DN 1 = UP 2 = QT"
:Input K
:If K = 2
:Stop
:If K = 1
:Goto 4
:1 → J
:X + D → X
:Goto 1
:Lbl 4
:1 → J
:X − 11D → X
:Goto 1
```

TI-85

```
:Lbl SETUP
:ClLCD
:Disp "TABLE SETUP"
:Input "TblMin = ", tblmin
:Input "ΔTbl = ", dtbl   [CHAR GREEK menu]
:tblmin → x   [Use the x-var key for x.]
:Lbl CONTD
:ClLCD
:Outpt(1,1,"x")   [I/O menu]
:Outpt(1,10,"y1")
:For (cnt,2,7.1)
:Outpt(cnt,1,x)
:Outpt(cnt,8," ")
:Outpt(cnt,9,y1)
:x + dtbl → x
```

```
:End
:Menu(1,"Down", CONTD, 2, "UP", CONTU, 4, "SETUP", SETUP, 5, "quit",
  TQUIT)
:Lbl CONTU
:x − 12*dtbl → x
:Goto CONTD
:Lbl TQUIT
:ClLCD
:Stop
```

PRESENT AND FUTURE VALUE OF AN ANNUITY

Description: Enter the requested information about the ordinary annuity: the periodic payment, the interest rate per period, and the number of payments. The program displays the present value and future value of this annuity.

TI

```
ClrHome   [labeled ClLCD on TI-85/86]
Disp "PAYMENT"
Input R
Disp "RATE"
Input I
Disp "NUMBER OF PYMTS"
Input N
Disp "PRESENT VALUE"
Disp round (R(1 − (1 + I)^−N)/I,2)†   [MATH NUM menu]
Disp "FUTURE VALUE"
Disp round(R((1 + I)^N − 1)/I,2)
```

CASIO

```
Fix 2   [DISP or SETUP DISPLAY menu]
"PAYMENT"? → R
"RATE"? → I
"NUMBER OF PYMTS"? → N
"PRESENT VALUE"
R(1 − (1 + I)^−N)/I
"FUTURE VALUE"
R((1 + I)^N − 1)/I
```

SHARP

```
Print "p = payment"
Print "i = interest"
Print "n = number of pymts"
presentvalue = p(1 − (1 + i)^−n)/i
Print presentvalue
futurevalue = p((1 + i)^n − 1)/i
```

†On TI-81, replace this line (and ones like it) by two lines: round(R(1 − (1 + I)$^{-N}$)/I,2) → F *and* Disp F.

LOAN PAYMENT

Description: Enter the amount of the loan, the interest rate per payment period, and the number of payments; the program displays the periodic payment.

TI

```
ClrHome   [labeled ClLCD on TI-85/86]
Disp "AMOUNT"
Input P
Disp "RATE PER PERIOD"
Input I
Disp "NUMBER OF PYMTS"
Input N
Disp "PAYMENT"
Disp round (P((1 − (1 + I)^−N)/I)^−1, 2)†   [MATH NUM menu]
```

CASIO

```
Fix 2   [DISP or SETUP DISPLAY menu]
"AMOUNT"? → P
"RATE"? → I
"NUMBER OF PYMTS"? → N
P((1 − (1 + I)^−N)/I)^−1
```

SHARP

```
Print "p = amount"
Print "i = rate per period"
Print "n = number of pymts"
payment = p((1 − (1 + i)^−n)/i)^−1
```

†On TI-81, replace this line by two lines: round (P((1 − (1 + I)$^{-N}$)/I)$^{-1}$, 2) → F *and* Disp F.

LOAN BALANCE AFTER *n* PAYMENTS

Description: Enter the amount of the loan (starting balance), the interest rate per payment period, and the number of payments; the program displays the remaining balance. This is useful for calculating the payoff amount when a loan is repaid early.

TI

```
ClrHome   [labeled ClLCD on TI-85/86]
Disp "STARTING BALANCE"
Input b
Disp "RATE PER PERIOD"
Input I
Disp "PAYMENT"
Input P
Disp "NUMBER OF PYMTS"
Input N
1 → K
Lbl 1
(B − P + round(B · I,2)) → B   [MATH NUM menu]
K + 1 → K
```

```
If K ≤ N
Goto 1
Disp "ENDING BALANCE"
Disp B
```

CASIO

```
Fix 2   [DISP or SETUP DISPLAY menu]
"STARTING BALANCE"? → B
"RATE PER PERIOD"? → I
"PAYMENT"? → P
"NUMBER OF PYMTS"? → N
1 → K
Lbl 1
B · I
Rnd   [MATH NUM or OPTN NUM menu]
Ans → S
B − P + S → B
K + 1 → K
K ≤ N ⇒ Goto 1
"ENDING BALANCE"
B
```

SHARP

```
Print "starting balance"
Input b
Print "rate per period"
Input i
Print "payment"
Input p
Print "number of payments"
Input n
k = 1
Label 1
If fpart(100 · b · i) ≥ .5 Goto 2   [MATH menu]
t = ipart(100 · b · i)/100   [MATH menu]
Goto 3
Label 2
t = (ipart(100 · b · i) + 1)/100
Label 3
b = b − p + t
k = k + 1
If k ≤ n Goto 1
Print "ending balance"
Print b
```

AMORTIZATION TABLE (IN MATRIX FORM) FOR TI (EXCEPT TI-81) AND CASIO 9850

Preliminaries: No preliminaries are needed for TI calculators. Before running the program on Casio 9850, open the matrix editor and change the dimensions of Mat A to $N \times 5$, where N is the number of payments.

Description: Enter the appropriate information about the loan; the program displays an amortization table for the loan in the form of a matrix, which you can scroll through by using the arrow keys. In this table, the five vertical columns are as follows.

payment number	amount of payment	interest for period	portion to principal	new balance

To complete the program, press ENTER, and the total payments made and the total interest paid will be displayed. When the program is finished, the table will be stored as matrix A, so that you can call it up and examine it further (until the program is run again and a new table takes its place).

When the regular payment is too small, the final payment may be quite large. When the regular payment is too large, the final payment may occur before N is reached, where N is the number of payments entered at the beginning of the program. In this case the matrix will either have fewer than N rows (TI) or will have all zero entries in the rows below row N (Casio).

TI

```
ClrHome   [labeled ClLCD on TI-85/86]
Disp "STARTING BALANCE"
Input B
Disp "RATE PER PERIOD"
Input I
Disp "PAYMENT"
Input P
Disp "NUMBER OF PYMTS"
Input N
{N, 5} → dim [A]
1 → K
0 → W
Lbl 1
If K = N + 1
Then
Pause [A]
ClrHome
Disp "TOTAL PAYMENTS"
Disp (J – 1) · P + [A](J, 2)
Disp "TOTAL INTEREST"
Disp W + [A] (J, 3)
Stop
End
K → [A](K, 1)
P → [A](K, 2)
round (I · B, 2) → [A](K, 3)
[A](K, 3) + W → W
P – [A](K, 3) → [A](K, 4)
B – [A](K, 4) → [A](K, 5)
[A](K, 5) → B
K + 1 → K
If K = N
Goto 2
```

```
If B ≤ P
Goto 2
Goto 1
Lbl 2
K → [A](K, 1)
B + round(B · I, 2) → [A](K, 2)
round (B · I, 2) → [A](K, 3)
[A](K, 2) − [A](K, 3) → [A](K, 4)
B − [A](K, 4) → [A](K, 5)
{K, 5} → dim [A]
K → J
N + 1 → K
Goto 1
```

CASIO 9850

```
Fill (0, Mat A)
Fix 2
"STARTING BALANCE"? → B
"RATE PER PERIOD"? → I
"PAYMENT"? → P
"NUMBER OF PYMTS"? → N
1 → K
0 → W
Lbl 1
If K = N + 1
Then Mat A◢
Clr Text
"TOTAL PAYMENTS"
(J − 1) · P + Mat A[J, 2]◢
"TOTAL INTEREST"
W + Mat A[J, 3]
Norm
Stop
IfEnd
K → Mat A[K, 1]
P → Mat A[K, 2]
I · B
rnd
Ans → Mat A[K, 3]
Mat A[K, 3] + W → W
P − Mat A[K, 3] → Mat A[K, 4]
B − Mat A[K, 4] → Mat A[K, 5]
Mat A[K, 5] → B
K + 1 → K
K = N ⇒ Goto 2
B ≤ P ⇒ Goto 2
Goto 1
Lbl 2
K → Mat A[K, 1]
B · I
```

```
rnd
Ans → S
B + S → Mat A[K, 2]
S → Mat A[K, 3]
Mat A[K, 2] − Mat A[K, 3] → Mat A[K, 4]
B − Mat A[K, 4] → Mat A[K, 5]
K → J
N + 1 → K
Goto 1
```

AMORTIZATION TABLE (ONE LINE AT A TIME) FOR TI-81, CASIO, AND SHARP

Description: Enter the appropriate information about the loan; the program displays the following entries from the first line of the amortization table.

payment number   interest for period   portion to principal   new balance

On Casio and Sharp, only one or two pieces of information will appear at a time (press ENTER to see the remaining ones). Press ENTER and the same information is displayed for the second line of the amortization table. Continue in this fashion through the remaining lines of the table. Then press ENTER again to see the total payments made and the total interest paid.

TI-81

```
ClrHome
Disp "STARTING BALANCE"
Input B
Disp "RATE PER PERIOD"
Input I
Disp "PAYMENT"
Input P
Disp "NUMBER OF PYMTS"
Input N
1 → K
0 → W
Lbl 1
ClrHome
Disp K
round (I · B, 2) → R
Disp "INTEREST"
Disp R
B + W → W
P − R → S
Disp "PRINCIPAL"
Disp S
B − S → T
Disp "NEW BALANCE"
Disp T
Pause
T → B
```

```
K + 1 → K
If K = N
Goto 2
If B ≤ P
Goto 2
Goto 1
Lbl 2
ClrHome
B + round (B · I, 2) → Q
Disp "LAST PAYMENT"
Disp Q
Disp "INTEREST"
round (I · B, 2) → S
Disp S
Q − S → T
Disp "PRINCIPAL"
Disp T
Pause
ClrHome
Disp "TOTAL PAYMENTS"
Disp (K − 1) · P + Q
Disp "TOTAL INTEREST"
Disp W + S
```

CASIO

```
Fix 2
"STARTING BALANCE"? → B
"RATE PER PERIOD"? → I
"PAYMENT"? → P
"NUMBER OF PYMTS"? → N
1 → K
0 → W
Lbl 1
"PAYMENT NUMBER"
K◢
"INTEREST"
I · B → R◢
R + W → W
P − R → S
"PRINCIPAL"
S◢
B − S → T
"NEW BALANCE"
T◢
T → B
K + 1 → K
K = N ⇒ Goto 2
B ≤ P ⇒ Goto 2
Goto 1
Lbl 2
```

```
"LAST PAYMENT"
B
rnd
Ans → B
B × I
rnd
Ans → S
B + S → Q◢
"INTEREST"
S◢
"PRINCIPAL"
Q − S → T◢
"TOTAL PAYMENTS"
(K − 1) · P + Q◢
"TOTAL INTEREST"
W + S
```

SHARP

```
Print "starting balance"
Input b
Print "rate per period"
Input i
Print "payment"
Input p
Print "number of pymts"
Input n
k = 1
w = 0
j = 0
Label 1
ClrT
Print "payment number"
Print K
Label 6
If fpart(100 · b · i) < .5 goto 3    [MATH menu]
r = (ipart(100 · b · i) + 1)/100    [MATH menu]
If j = 0 goto 4
If j = 1 goto 7
Label 3
r = ipart(100 · b · i)/100
If j = 0 goto 4
If j = 1 goto 7
Label 4
Print "interest"
Print r
Wait
w = r + w
s = p − r
Print "principal"
Print s
```

```
t = b − s
Print "new balance"
Print t
Wait
b = t
k = k + 1
If k = n goto 5
If b ≤ p goto 5
Goto 1
Label 5
j = 1
Goto 6
Label 7
ClrT
Print "last payment"
f = b + r
Print f
Print "interest"
Print r
Wait
Print "principal"
Print b
Wait
ClrT
Print "total payments"
t = (k − 1) · p + b + r
Print t
Print "total interest"
m = w + r
Print m
```

SIMPLEX METHOD FOR TI (EXCEPT TI-81) AND CASIO 9850

Preliminaries: Before running the program, enter the initial simplex matrix in the matrix memory as matrix A. It remains there, unchanged, when the program is run.
Description: When the initial simplex matrix is entered, the program does the first round of pivoting, and displays the resulting simplex matrix, which can be examined by using the arrow keys to scroll through it. When you press ENTER, the next round of pivoting is performed, and so on, until the final simplex matrix is reached. The final simplex matrix is stored in the matrix memory as matrix B.

TI

NOTE The program is written for TI-82/83, in which the matrix memories are denoted [A], [B], etc. For TI-85/86/92, use A, B in place of [A], [B]. Similarly, on TI-82/83, the list memories are labeled L_1, L_2, etc. and are on the keyboard. For TI-85/86/92, simply type in L1, L2, etc. ◆

ClrHome [*labeled ClLCD on TI-85/86*]
[A] → [B]
dim [B] → L_1 [*MATRIX MATH or MATRIX OPS menu*]
L_1(1) → R

$L_1(2) \rightarrow S$
seq([B](R,I,1,S − 1)) → L_2 [*LIST OPS menu*]
min(L_2) → T [*LIST MATH or LIST OPS menu*]
If T ≥ 0 [*TEST menu*]
Goto 1 [*Here and below on TI-85/86, use P1, P2, etc. in place of 1, 2 for label numbers.*]
Lbl 13 [*P13 in place of 13 on TI-85/86*]
1 → J
Lbl 2
If [B](R,J) = T [*TEST menu; here and below, use = = in place of = on TI-85/86.*]
Goto 3
J + 1 → J
Goto 2
Lbl 3
1 → K
Lbl 6
If [B](K,J) ≤ 0
Goto 4
[[[B](K,S)/[B](K,J)]] → [E]
K + 1 → K
Lbl 7
If [B](K,J) ≤ 0
Goto 5
augment ([E], [[[B](K, S)/[B](K, J)]]) → [E] [*"aug" on TI-85/86; in MATRIX MATH or OPS menu*]
K + 1 → K
Goto 7
Lbl 8
dim ([E]) → L_3
seq([E] (1, I), I, 1, L_3 (2)) → L_4
min (L_4) → M
1 → I
Lbl 10
If [B](I, J) = 0
Goto 14
If [B](I, S)/[B](I, J) = M
Goto 11
I + 1 → I
Goto 10
Lbl 11
If I = 1
Goto 12
∗row ([B](I, J)$^{-1}$, [B],I) → [B] [*MATRIX MATH or MATRIX OPS menu; on TI-85/86 ∗row is labeled MultR.*]
For (K, 1, I − 1, 1)
∗row+ (−[B](K, J), [B], I, K) → [B] [*MATRIX MATH or MATRIX OPS menu; on TI-85/86 ∗row+ is labeled mRAdd.*]
End
For (K, I + 1, R, 1)
∗row+ (−[B](K, J), [B], I, K) → [B]

```
End
round ([B], 9) → [B]   [MATH NUM menu; use 11 in place of 9 on TI-85/86.]
seq ([B] (R, I), I, 1, S – 1) → L2
min (L2) → T
If T ≥ 0
Goto 1
ClrHome
Pause [B]▶FRAC   [MATH or MATH MISC menu]
Goto 13
Lbl 12
*row ([B](I, J)^-1, [B], 1) → [B]
For (K, 2, R, 1)
*row + (−[B](K, J), [B], 1, K) → [B]
End
round ([B], 9) → [B]
seq ([B] (R, I), I, 1, S − 1) → L2
min (L2) → T
If T ≥ 0
Goto 1
ClrHome
Pause [B]▶FRAC
Goto 13
Lbl 4
K + 1 → K
If K > (R − 1)
Goto 9
Goto 6
Lbl 5
K + 1 → K
If K > (R − 1)
Goto 8
Goto 7
Lbl 1
ClrHome
Disp "FINAL SIMPLEX"
Disp "MATRIX"
Disp "      "
Pause [B]▶FRAC
Stop
Lbl 9
Disp "NO MAXIMUM SOLUTION"
Stop
Lbl 14
I + 1 → I
Goto 10
```

CASIO 9850

```
Mat A → Mat B
"INITIAL SIMPLEX"
"MATRIX"
"NUMBER OF ROWS"? → R
```

```
"NUMBER OF COLS"? → S
1 → J
1 → I
Lbl 2
Mat B[R, I] → T
Lbl 1
I + 1 → I
I > (S − 1) ⇒ Goto 3
Mat B[R,I] ≥ T ⇒ Goto 1
I → J
Goto 2
Lbl 3
T ≥ 0 ⇒ Goto 4
10^10 → u
0 → K
Lbl 5
K + 1 → K
K > (R − 1) ⇒ Goto 6
Mat B[K, J] ≤ 0 ⇒ Goto 5
Mat B[K, S]/Mat B[K, J] < u ⇒ K → I
Mat B[K, S]/Mat B[K, J] < u ⇒ Mat B[K, S]/Mat B[K, J] → u
Goto 5
Lbl 6
u ≤ 10^10 ⇒ Goto 8
I = 1 ⇒ Goto 7
*Row Mat B[I, J]^-1, B, I
For 1 → K to I − 1
*Row+ −Mat B[K, J], B, I, K
Next
For I + 1 → K to R
*Row+ −Mat B[K, J], B, I, K
Next
1 → J
1 → I
Mat B[R, I] → T
Lbl 9
I + 1 → I
I > (S − 1) ⇒ Goto 0
Mat B[R, I] ≥ T ⇒ Goto 9
I → J
Mat B[R, I] → T
Goto 9
Lbl 0
T ≥ 0 ⇒ Goto 4
Mat B◢
Goto 3
Lbl 7
*Row Mat B[1, J]^-1, B, 1
For 2 → K to R
*Row+ −Mat B[K, J], B, 1, K
Next
1 → I
```

```
Mat B[R, I] → T
Goto 9
Lbl 4
"FINAL SIMPLEX MATRIX"
Mat B◢
STOP
Lbl 8
"NO MAXIMUM SOLUTION"
```

NUMERICAL DERIVATIVE FOR CASIO 7700/8700

Preliminaries: Before running the program, enter the function in the function memory as f_1.
Description: The program approximates the value of the derivative of a function at a specified value of x.

```
"X"? → A   [Use the x, θ, τ key for X.]
A + .0001 → X
f1 → B
A − .0001 → X
f1 → C
(B − C)/.0002
```

RECTANGLE APPROXIMATION OF $\int_a^b f(x)\,dx$ (USING LEFT ENDPOINTS)

Preliminaries: Enter the function $f(x)$ in the function memory as Y_1 or f_1.
Description: Enter the endpoints a and b and the number of rectangles to be used. The program approximates the value of the integral by using left endpoints.

TI

```
ClrHome   [labeled ClLCD on TI-85/86]
Disp "A = "
Input A
Disp "B = "
Input B
Disp "N = "
Input N
(B − A)/N → 0
0 → S
For (K, 0, N − 1, 1)  ┐
(A + K · D) → X       │
Y1 + S → S            ├  [On TI-81, replace these five lines by:
End                   │      K → 0
Disp D · S            ┘      Lbl 1
                             A + K · D → X
                             Y1 + S → S
                             K + 1 → K
                             If K < N
                             Goto 1
                             Disp D · S]
```

CASIO

```
"A = "? → A
"B = "? → B
"N = "? → N
(B − A)/N → D
0 → S
0 → K
Lbl 1
A + K · D → X
f1 + S → S
K + 1 → K
K < N ⇒ Goto 1
D · S
```

NUMERICAL INTEGRATION (SIMPSON'S RULE) FOR TI-81

Preliminaries: Enter the function to be integrated in the function memory as Y_1.

Description: Enter a, b, and n (the number of subdivisions to be used); the program calculates the approximate value of $\int_a^b f(x)\,dx$.

```
ClrHome
Disp "A = "
Input A
Disp "B = "
Input B
Disp "N = "
Input N
(B − A)/N → D
0 → S
A → X
Y1 → S
B → X
(Y1 + S) → S
For (K, 1, N/2, 1)
(A + (2K − 1) · D) → X
(4Y1 + S) → S
End
For (K, 1, N/2 − 1, 1)
(A + 2K · D) → X
(2Y1 + S) → S
End
Disp S · D/3
```

APPENDIX B Tables

TABLE 1 Combinations $_nC_r = \binom{n}{r} = \frac{n!}{(n-r)!\,r!}$

n	$\binom{n}{0}$	$\binom{n}{1}$	$\binom{n}{2}$	$\binom{n}{3}$	$\binom{n}{4}$	$\binom{n}{5}$	$\binom{n}{6}$	$\binom{n}{7}$	$\binom{n}{8}$	$\binom{n}{9}$	$\binom{n}{10}$
0	1										
1	1	1									
2	1	2	1								
3	1	3	3	1							
4	1	4	6	4	1						
5	1	5	10	10	5	1					
6	1	6	15	20	15	6	1				
7	1	7	21	35	35	21	7	1			
8	1	8	28	56	70	56	28	8	1		
9	1	9	36	84	126	126	84	36	9	1	
10	1	10	45	120	210	252	210	120	45	10	1
11	1	11	55	165	330	462	462	330	165	55	11
12	1	12	66	220	495	792	924	792	495	220	66
13	1	13	78	286	715	1287	1716	1716	1287	715	286
14	1	14	91	364	1001	2002	3003	3432	3003	2002	1001
15	1	15	105	455	1365	3003	5005	6435	6435	5005	3003
16	1	16	120	560	1820	4368	8008	11440	12870	11440	8008
17	1	17	136	680	2380	6188	12376	19448	24310	24310	19448
18	1	18	153	816	3060	8568	18564	31824	43758	48620	43758
19	1	19	171	969	3876	11628	27132	50388	75582	92378	92378
20	1	20	190	1140	4845	15504	38760	77520	125970	167960	184756

For $r > 10$, it may be necessary to use the identity

$$\binom{n}{r} = \binom{n}{n-r}.$$

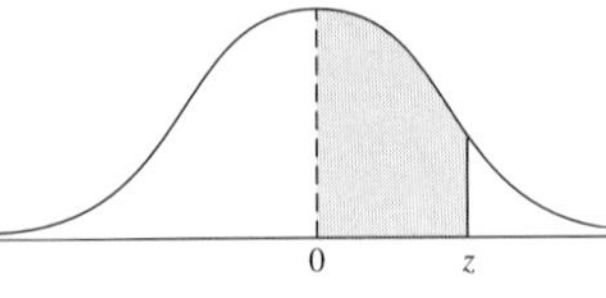

TABLE 2 Areas under the Normal Curve

The column under A gives the proportion of the area under the entire curve that is between $z = 0$ and a positive value of z.

z	A	z	A	z	A	z	A
.00	.0000	.49	.1879	.98	.3365	1.47	.4292
.01	.0040	.50	.1915	.99	.3389	1.48	.4306
.02	.0080	.51	.1950	1.00	.3413	1.49	.4319
.03	.0120	.52	.1985	1.01	.3438	1.50	.4332
.04	.0160	.53	.2019	1.02	.3461	1.51	.4345
.05	.0199	.54	.2054	1.03	.3485	1.52	.4357
.06	.0239	.55	.2088	1.04	.3508	1.53	.4370
.07	.0279	.56	.2123	1.05	.3531	1.54	.4382
.08	.0319	.57	.2157	1.06	.3554	1.55	.4394
.09	.0359	.58	.2190	1.07	.3577	1.56	.4406
.10	.0398	.59	.2224	1.08	.3599	1.57	.4418
.11	.0438	.60	.2258	1.09	.3621	1.58	.4430
.12	.0478	.61	.2291	1.10	.3643	1.59	.4441
.13	.0517	.62	.2324	1.11	.3665	1.60	.4452
.14	.0557	.63	.2357	1.12	.3686	1.61	.4463
.15	.0596	.64	.2389	1.13	.3708	1.62	.4474
.16	.0636	.65	.2422	1.14	.3729	1.63	.4485
.17	.0675	.66	.2454	1.15	.3749	1.64	.4495
.18	.0714	.67	.2486	1.16	.3770	1.65	.4505
.19	.0754	.68	.2518	1.17	.3790	1.66	.4515
.20	.0793	.69	.2549	1.18	.3810	1.67	.4525
.21	.0832	.70	.2580	1.19	.3830	1.68	.4535
.22	.0871	.71	.2612	1.20	.3849	1.69	.4545
.23	.0910	.72	.2642	1.21	.3869	1.70	.4554
.24	.0948	.73	.2673	1.22	.3888	1.71	.4564
.25	.0987	.74	.2704	1.23	.3907	1.72	.4573
.26	.1026	.75	.2734	1.24	.3925	1.73	.4582
.27	.1064	.76	.2764	1.25	.3944	1.74	.4591
.28	.1103	.77	.2794	1.26	.3962	1.75	.4599
.29	.1141	.78	.2823	1.27	.3980	1.76	.4608
.30	.1179	.79	.2852	1.28	.3997	1.77	.4616
.31	.1217	.80	.2881	1.29	.4015	1.78	.4625
.32	.1255	.81	.2910	1.30	.4032	1.79	.4633
.33	.1293	.82	.2939	1.31	.4049	1.80	.4641
.34	.1331	.83	.2967	1.32	.4066	1.81	.4649
.35	.1368	.84	.2996	1.33	.4082	1.82	.4656
.36	.1406	.85	.3023	1.34	.4099	1.83	.4664
.37	.1443	.86	.3051	1.35	.4115	1.84	.4671
.38	.1480	.87	.3079	1.36	.4131	1.85	.4678
.39	.1517	.88	.3106	1.37	.4147	1.86	.4686
.40	.1554	.89	.3133	1.38	.4162	1.87	.4693
.41	.1591	.90	.3159	1.39	.4177	1.88	.4700
.42	.1628	.91	.3186	1.40	.4192	1.89	.4706
.43	.1664	.92	.3212	1.41	.4207	1.90	.4713
.44	.1700	.93	.3238	1.42	.4222	1.91	.4719
.45	.1736	.94	.3264	1.43	.4236	1.92	.4726
.46	.1772	.95	.3289	1.44	.4251	1.93	.4732
.47	.1808	.96	.3315	1.45	.4265	1.94	.4738
.48	.1844	.97	.3340	1.46	.4279	1.95	.4744

TABLE 2 *(continued)*

z	A	z	A	z	A	z	A
1.96	.4750	2.45	.4929	2.94	.4984	3.43	.4997
1.97	.4756	2.46	.4931	2.95	.4984	3.44	.4997
1.98	.4762	2.47	.4932	2.96	.4985	3.45	.4997
1.99	.4767	2.48	.4934	2.97	.4985	3.46	.4997
2.00	.4773	2.49	.4936	2.98	.4986	3.47	.4997
2.01	.4778	2.50	.4938	2.99	.4986	3.48	.4998
2.02	.4783	2.51	.4940	3.00	.4987	3.49	.4998
2.03	.4788	2.52	.4941	3.01	.4987	3.50	.4998
2.04	.4793	2.53	.4943	3.02	.4987	3.51	.4998
2.05	.4798	2.54	.4945	3.03	.4988	3.52	.4998
2.06	.4803	2.55	.4946	3.04	.4988	3.53	.4998
2.07	.4808	2.56	.4948	3.05	.4989	3.54	.4998
2.08	.4812	2.57	.4949	3.06	.4989	3.55	.4998
2.09	.4817	2.58	.4951	3.07	.4989	3.56	.4998
2.10	.4821	2.59	.4952	3.08	.4990	3.57	.4998
2.11	.4826	2.60	.4953	3.09	.4990	3.58	.4998
2.12	.4830	2.61	.4955	3.10	.4990	3.59	.4998
2.13	.4834	2.62	.4956	3.11	.4991	3.60	.4998
2.14	.4838	2.63	.4957	3.12	.4991	3.61	.4999
2.15	.4842	2.64	.4959	3.13	.4991	3.62	.4999
2.16	.4846	2.65	.4960	3.14	.4992	3.63	.4999
2.17	.4850	2.66	.4961	3.15	.4992	3.64	.4999
2.18	.4854	2.67	.4962	3.16	.4992	3.65	.4999
2.19	.4857	2.68	.4963	3.17	.4992	3.66	.4999
2.20	.4861	2.69	.4964	3.18	.4993	3.67	.4999
2.21	.4865	2.70	.4965	3.19	.4993	3.68	.4999
2.22	.4868	2.71	.4966	3.20	.4993	3.69	.4999
2.23	.4871	2.72	.4967	3.21	.4993	3.70	.4999
2.24	.4875	2.73	.4968	3.22	.4994	3.71	.4999
2.25	.4878	2.74	.4969	3.23	.4994	3.72	.4999
2.26	.4881	2.75	.4970	3.24	.4994	3.73	.4999
2.27	.4884	2.76	.4971	3.25	.4994	3.74	.4999
2.28	.4887	2.77	.4972	3.26	.4994	3.75	.4999
2.29	.4890	2.78	.4973	3.27	.4995	3.76	.4999
2.30	.4893	2.79	.4974	3.28	.4995	3.77	.4999
2.31	.4896	2.80	.4974	3.29	.4995	3.78	.4999
2.32	.4898	2.81	.4975	3.30	.4995	3.79	.4999
2.33	.4901	2.82	.4976	3.31	.4995	3.80	.4999
2.34	.4904	2.83	.4977	3.32	.4996	3.81	.4999
2.35	.4906	2.84	.4977	3.33	.4996	3.82	.4999
2.36	.4909	2.85	.4978	3.34	.4996	3.83	.4999
2.37	.4911	2.86	.4979	3.35	.4996	3.84	.4999
2.38	.4913	2.87	.4980	3.36	.4996	3.85	.4999
2.39	.4916	2.88	.4980	3.37	.4996	3.86	.4999
2.40	.4918	2.89	.4981	3.38	.4996	3.87	.5000
2.41	.4920	2.90	.4981	3.39	.4997	3.88	.5000
2.42	.4922	2.91	.4982	3.40	.4997	3.89	.5000
2.43	.4925	2.92	.4983	3.41	.4997		
2.44	.4927	2.93	.4983	3.42	.4997		

Answers to Selected Exercises

CHAPTER 1

Section 1.1 (page 9)

1. True **3.** True **5.** Identity property (addition) **7.** Commutative property (addition) **9.** Associative property (multiplication) **11.** Distributive property and commutative property (multiplication) **15.** -54 **17.** $-\frac{1}{2}$ **19.** 2 **21.** 4 **23.** -4 **25.** -1 **27.** Irrational; 9.4248 **29.** Irrational; 1.7321 **31.** Rational **33.** $5 < 7$ **35.** $y \le 8.3$ **37.** $t > 0$

39. −4 −2 0 2 4

41. −2 0 2 4 6

43. −4 −2 0 2 4

45. 3

47. −2

49. −8 −1

51. −2 2

53. 42° **55.** 36° **57.** 4 **59.** -19 **61.** = **63.** = **65.** = **67.** = **69.** = **71.** $-(a - 7) = -a + 7$ **77.** Let x represent the number of dollars contributed annually by foreign students to the California economy. Then $x > 1{,}000{,}000{,}000$. **79.** Let x represent the percent of foreign students now in the U.S. from Middle Eastern countries. Then $0 \le x < 7.5$. **81.** Let x represent the percent of foreign students in the U.S. that are in California. Then $x > 13$. **83.** 100; 0 **85.** 67; 11

Section 1.2 (page 19)

1. 5 **3.** 7 **5.** $-19/52$ **7.** $-9/8$ **9.** 2 **11.** $40/7$ **13.** $26/3$ **15.** $-12/5$ **17.** $-59/6$ **19.** $-9/4$ **21.** $x = .72$ **23.** $r \approx -13.26$ **25.** $x = (5a - b)/6$ **27.** $x = 3b/(5 + a)$ **29.** $x = (-3a + 3)/(1 - a^2 - a)$ or $x = (3a - 3)/(a^2 + a - 1)$ **31.** $V = k/P$ **33.** $g = (V - V_0)/t$ **35.** $B = (2A/h) - b$ or $B = (2A - bh)/h$ **37.** $R = (r_1 r_2)/(r_1 + r_2)$ **39.** $2, -3$ **41.** $-2, 8$ **43.** 5/2, 7/2 **45.** $-4/3$, 2/9 **47.** $-7, -3/7$ **49.** **(a)** .0352 **(b)** Approximately .015 or 1.5% **(c)** Approximately one case **51.** 13% **53.** \$4000 **55.** \$205.41 **57.** **(a)** Let x represent the height. **(b)** $16x + 288 + 36x = 496$ **(c)** 4 ft **59.** 6 cm **61.** About 6.42 hr. **63.** 20 min **65.** \$21,000 **67.** \$70,000 for land that made a profit, \$50,000 for land that produced a loss **69.** \$800 **71.** 400/3 liters

Section 1.3 (page 25)

1. 118,587,876,497 **3.** 289.099133864 **7.** 2^7 **9.** $(-5)^7 = -5^7$ **11.** -3^9 **13.** $(2z)^{11}$ **15.** $-x^3 + x^2 + 3x$ **17.** $-6y^2 + 3y + 10$ **19.** $-10x^2 + 4x - 2$ **21.** $-18m^3 - 27m^2 + 9m$ **23.** $12z^3 + 14z^2 - 7z + 5$ **25.** $12k^2 - 20k + 3$ **27.** $6y^2 + 7y - 5$ **29.** $18k^2 - 7kq - q^2$ **31.** $4.34m^2 + 5.68m - 4.42$ **33.** $-k + 3$ **35.** $7x^2 - 4x - 12$ **37.** **(a)** 4.2 million **(b)** 4.269 million **39.** **(a)** 19.5 million **(b)** 19.281 million **41.** **(a)** $\frac{1}{3}hb^2$ (This is the correct formula.) **(b)** Approximately 91.6 million cubic feet; slightly smaller **(c)** Approximately 13.1 acres **43.** **(a)** 4 **(b)** 4 **(c)** 7 **47.** $5x^3 - 4x^2 + 2x + 1$ **49.** $x^2 - x + 40$

Section 1.4 (page 30)

1. $12x(x - 2)$ **3.** $r(r^2 - 5r + 1)$ **5.** Cannot be factored **7.** $6z(z^2 - 2z + 3)$ **9.** $5p^2(5p^2 - 4pq + 20q^2)$ **11.** $2(2y - 1)^2(5y - 1)$ **13.** $(x + 5)^4(x^2 + 10x + 28)$ **15.** $(2a + 5)(a - 1)$ **17.** $(x + 8)(x - 8)$ **19.** $(3p - 4)^2$ **21.** $(r + 2t)(r - 5t)$ **23.** $(m - 3n)^2$ **25.** $(2p + 3)(2p - 3)$ **27.** $3(x - 4z)^2$ **29.** Cannot be factored **31.** $(-x + 4)(x - 3)$ or $(x - 4)(-x + 3)$ **33.** $(3a + 5)(a - 6)$ **35.** $(7m + 2n)(3m + n)$ **37.** $(4y - x)(5y + 11x)$ **39.** Cannot be factored **41.** $(y - 7z)(y + 3z)$ **43.** $(n + 2)(n - 2)(m^2 + 3)$ **45.** $(11x + 8)(11x - 8)$ **47.** $2a^2(4a - b)(3a + 2b)$ **49.** $3x^3(3x - 5z)(2x + 5z)$ **51.** $m^3(m - 1)^2(m^2 + m + 1)^2(5 + 3m^2 - 3m^5)$ **55.** $(a - 6)(a^2 + 6a + 36)$ **57.** $(2r - 3s)(4r^2 + 6rs + 9s^2)$ **59.** $(4m + 5)(16m^2 - 20m + 25)$ **61.** $(10y - z)(100y^2 + 10yz + z^2)$

Section 1.5 (page 40)

1. **(a)** No **(b)** Answers vary depending on the calculator, but 20–30 is typical. **(c)** No; the y-axis is shorter than the x-axis on a calculator screen. **3.** **(a)** The one that appears first in the equation memory **(b)** The cursor moves to the other graph. **5.** Xscl = 1, Yscl = 1; $P = (3, 5)$; $Q = (-6, 2)$ **7.** Xscl = 2, Yscl = 2; $P = (-12, 8)$; $Q = (-3, -8.5)$ **9.** Yes **11.** No **13.** $0x + y = 0$, or equivalently, $y = 0$

15.

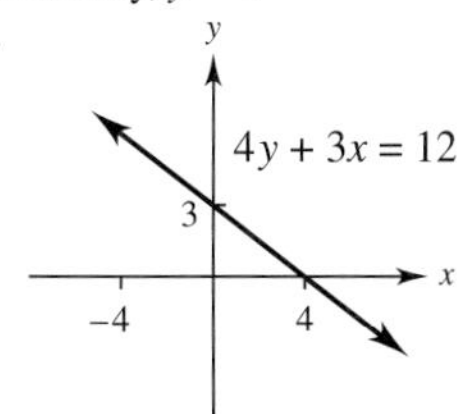

17.
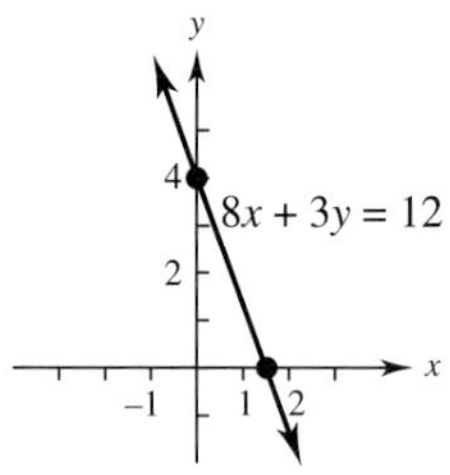

19.
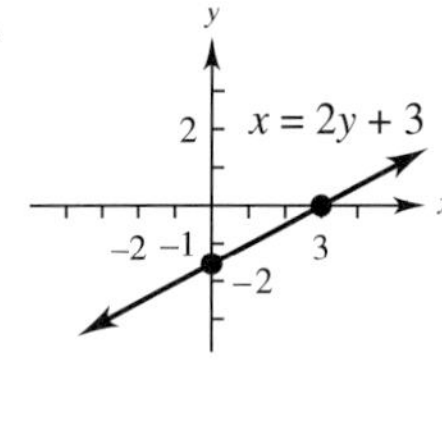

21. x-intercepts $-1, 3.5$; y-intercept 1 **23.** x-intercepts $-2, 0, 2$; y-intercept 0

25.
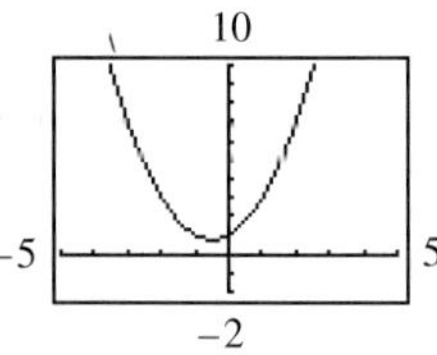

27.
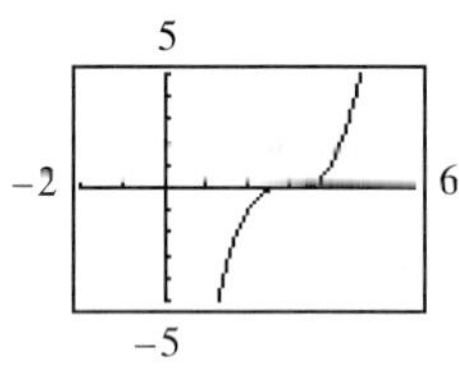

29.
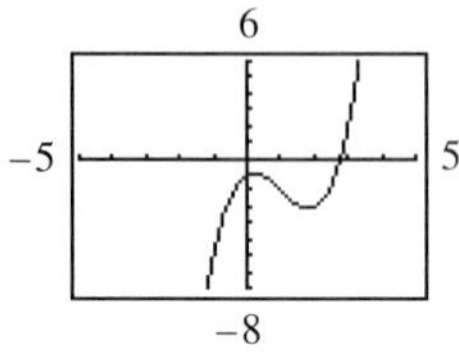

31.
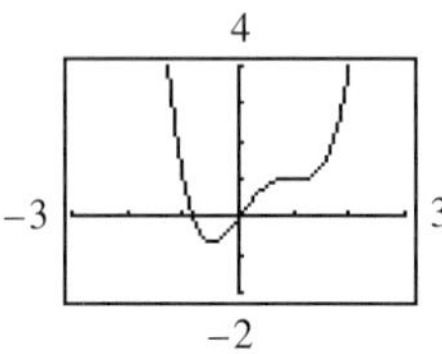

No

33. $0 \le x \le 42$ and $0 \le y \le 4500$, with Xscl = 5, Yscl = 500. Both x (time) and y (concentration) must be nonnegative and this window shows the part of the graph where they are. **35.** $0 \le x \le 4000$ and $0 \le y \le 100$, with Xscl = 500, Yscl = 10. Both x and y (numbers of barrels) must be nonnegative and this window shows the part of the graph where they are. **37.** Correct **39.** Incorrect **41.** Correct **43.** False **45.** False **47.** (c) **49.** (d) **51.** (e) **53.** $-4 \le x \le 4$; $-50 \le y \le 50$ **55.** $-6 \le x \le 12$; $-100 \le y \le 250$ **57.** Approximately 12 seconds **59.** **(a)** \$84.499 million; \$144.475 million **(b)** 1993 **61.** About 269; about \$576.92 **63.** 12

Section 1.6 (page 51)

1. **(a)** 188 **(b)** $-47 \le x \le 47$ **(c)** $-4.7 \le x \le 4.7$ **(d)** 260; $-65 \le x \le 65$; $-6.5 \le x \le 6.5$ **(e)** 252; $-63 \le x \le 63$; $-6.3 \le x \le 6.3$ **3.** -1 **5.** $-3/2$ **7.** Undefined **9.** $y = 3x + 5$ **11.** $y = -2.3x + 1.5$ **13.** $y = -3x/4 + 4$ **15.** $m = 2$; $b = -7$ **17.** $m = 3$; $b = -2$ **19.** $m = 2/3$; $b = -14/9$ **21.** $m = 2/3$; $b = 0$

23. Many correct answers, including:

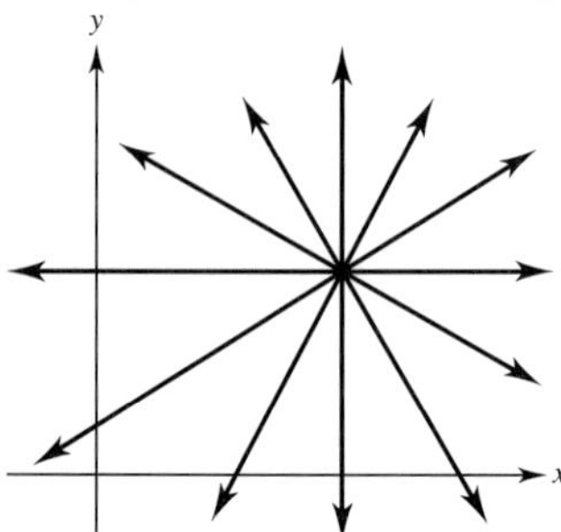

25. **(a)**
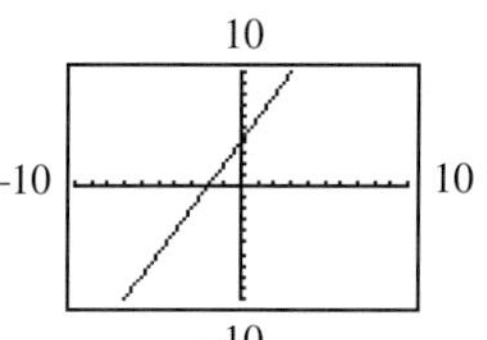

(b)
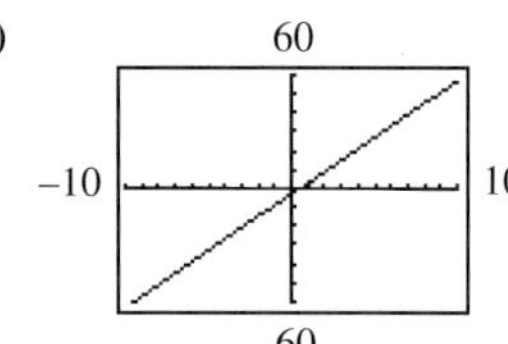

(c) The line in part (a); the line in part (b)

27.
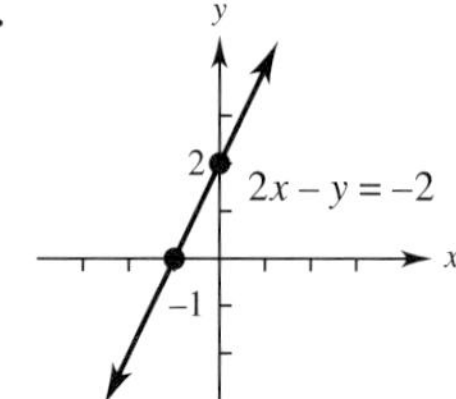

29.
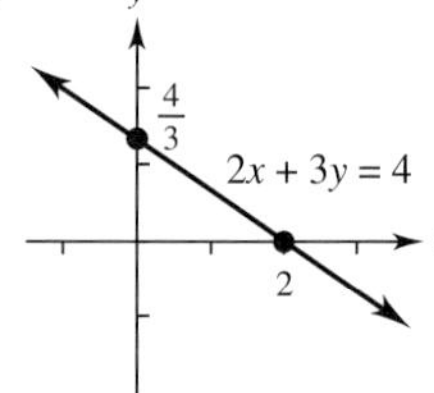

31.
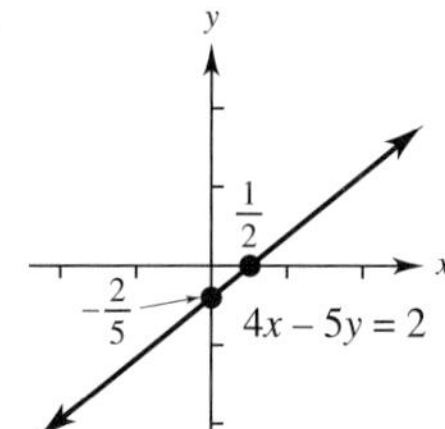

33. Perpendicular **35.** Parallel **37.** Neither **39.** **(a)** 2/5, 9/8, $-5/2$ **(b)** Yes **41.** **(a)** The slope of $-.0221$ indicates that on the average from 1912 to 1992 the 5000-meter run is being run .0221 second faster every Olympic Game. It is negative because the times are generally decreasing as time progresses. **(b)** World War II occurred during the years 1940 and 1944, and no Olympic Games were held. **43.** $3y = -2x + 4$ **45.** $y = 2x + 2$ **47.** $y = 2$ **49.** $x = 6$ **51.** $3y = 4x + 7$ **53.** $2y = 5x - 1$ **55.** $y = 7x$ **57.** $x = 5$ **59.** $y = 2x - 2$ **61.** $y = x - 5$ **63.** $y = -x + 2$ **65.** (b) **67.** \$3308.33 **69.** **(a)** \$135 **(b)** \$205 **(c)** \$275 **(d)** \$345 **(e)**

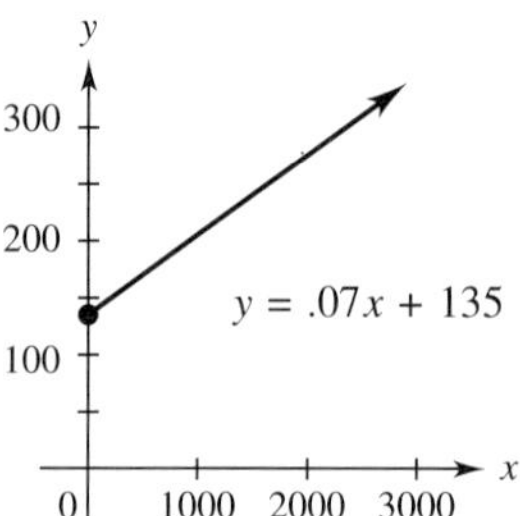

71. 48 liters per second **73.** 1989

Section 1.7 (page 62)

1. **(a)** 14.4° **(b)** 122° **(c)** 14° **(d)** $-28.9°$ **3.** $-40°$ **5.** **(a)** $y = 82{,}500x + 850{,}000$ **(b)** \$1,840,000 **(c)** 2003 **7.** $y = (-65/7)x + 504$; \$439 **9.** $y = 4x + 120$; 4 ft

11. $y = 806{,}400x$; 24,192,000 gallons **13.** $y = .0985x$; time would be 1 hour, 9 minutes, 16.2 seconds, which is faster than the marathon record. **15.** $y = 900x$; 27,000 cu ft
17. Approximately $y = 4.43x - 381.7$ **19.** $(3, -1)$
21. $(-11/4, -61/4)$ **23.** Approximately $(-1.3593, -2.5116)$
25. $(0, -3)$ and $(20, 87)$ **27.** **(a)** 200,000 policies ($x = 200$)
(b)

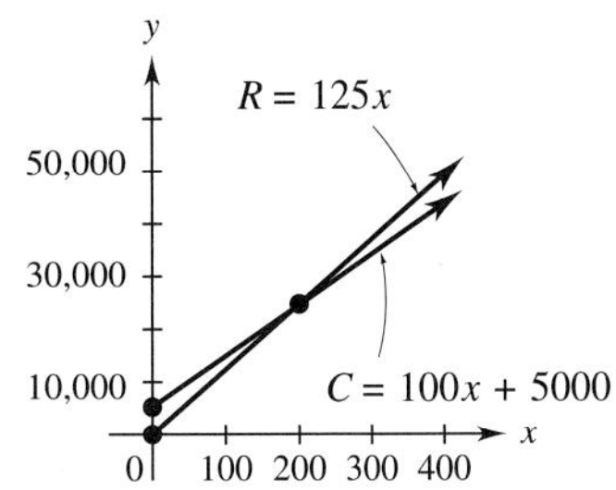

(c) Revenue: \$12,500; Cost: \$15,000
29. **(a)** $c = .126x + 1.5$ **(b)** 2.382 million **(c)** About 17.857 units
31. Break-even point is about 467; do not produce the item.
33. Break-even point is about 1037; produce the item. **35.** About 95 units in 1976 **37.** **(a)** Canada: $y = 1.56x + 12.1$; Japan: $y = 10.34x + 4.7$
(b)

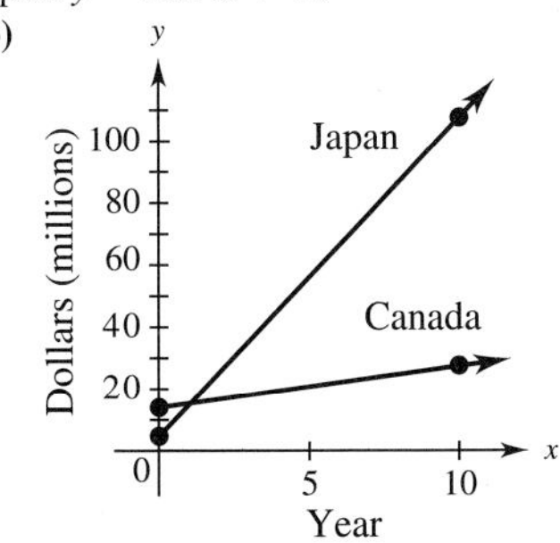

(c) (.84, 13.4); The investments of the Canadians and Japanese were both about \$13.4 million near the end of 1980. **39.** \$140
41. 10 items, 10 items **43.** **(a)** \$16 **(b)** \$11 **(c)** \$6 **(d)** 8 **(e)** 4 **(f)** 0
(g)

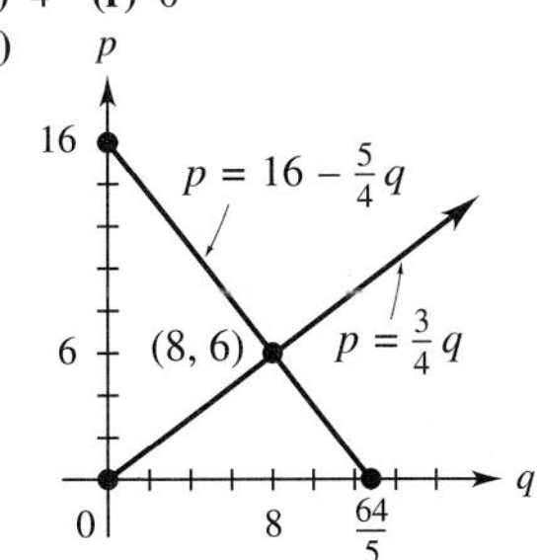

(h) 0 **(i)** 40/3 **(j)** 80/3 **(k)** See part (g). **(l)** 8 **(m)** \$6
45. **(a)**

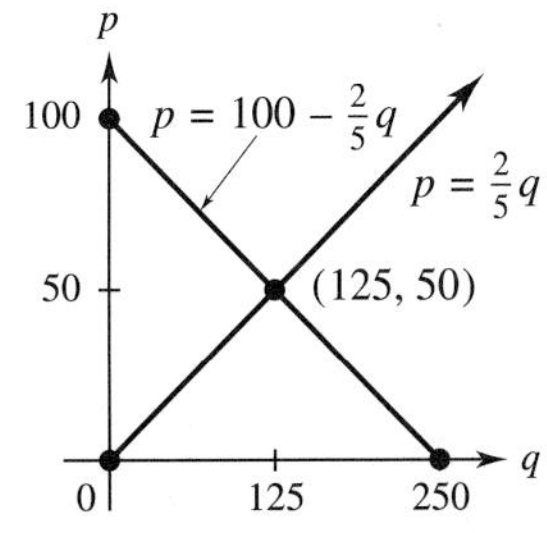

(b) 125 **(c)** 50¢ **(d)** [0, 125)
47. **(a)–(b)**

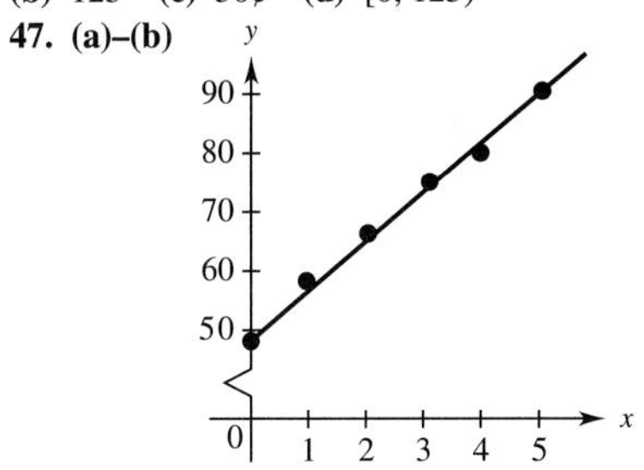

(c) $y = 8x + 50$
(d)

Year	*Sales (actual)*	*Sales (predicted from equation of (c))*	*Difference, Actual Minus Predicted*
0	48	50	−2
1	59	58	1
2	66	66	0
3	75	74	1
4	80	82	−2
5	90	90	0

(e) 106 **(f)** 122

Chapter 1 Review Exercises (page 67)

1. 0, 6 **3.** $-12, -6, -9/10, -\sqrt{4}, 0, 1/8, 6$
5. Commutative multiplication **7.** Distributive **9.** $x \geq 6$
11. $-7, -3, -2, 0, \pi, 8$ **13.** $-|3 - (-2)|, -|-2|, |6 - 4|, |8 + 1|$ **15.** -3 **17.** -1
19.
−3
21.
−2

23. -8 **25.** $-3/4$ **27.** 3 **29.** -2 **31.** No solution
33. $x = 1/(5a - 1)$ **35.** $x = (c - 3)/(3a - ac - 2)$
37. 12, -6 **39.** $-38, 42$ **41.** 2, 1/5 **43.** 20 lb of hearts, 10 lb of kisses **45.** $4x^4 - 4x^2 + 13x$ **47.** $2q^4 + 14q^3 - 4q^2$
49. $15z^2 - 4z - 4$ **51.** $16k^2 - 9h^2$ **53.** $36x^2 + 36xy + 9y^2$
55. $(-2, 3), (0, -5), (3, -2), (4, 3)$ **57.** $0 \leq x \leq 5.5$; $179 \leq y \leq 181$ **59.** 265 **61.** $-80 \leq x \leq 40$; $-20 \leq y \leq 30$
63. $k(2h^2 - 4h + 5)$ **65.** $a^2(3a + 1)(a + 4)$
67. $(2y - 1)(5y - 3)$ **69.** $(12p + 13q)(12p - 13q)$
71. $(2y - 1)(4y^2 + 2y + 1)$ **73.** Possibly true
75.

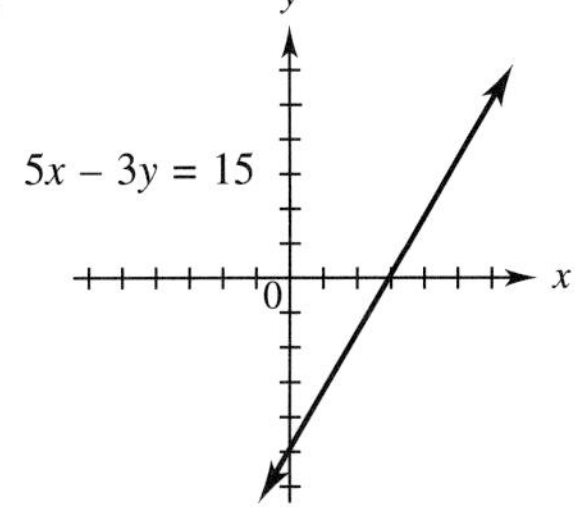

77.

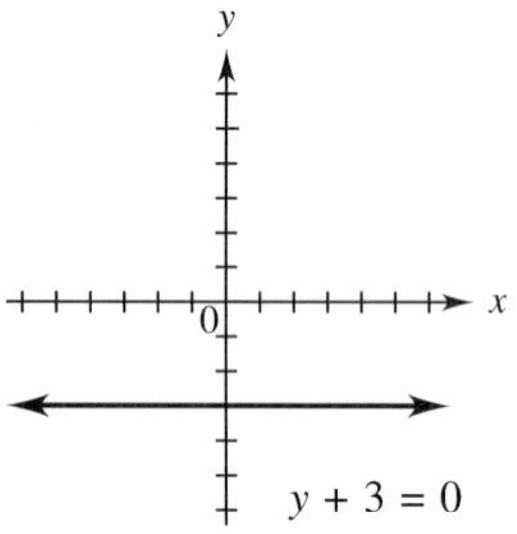

81. $-5/6$ **83.** 1/4 **85.** 4 **87.** 0 **89.** -3

91.

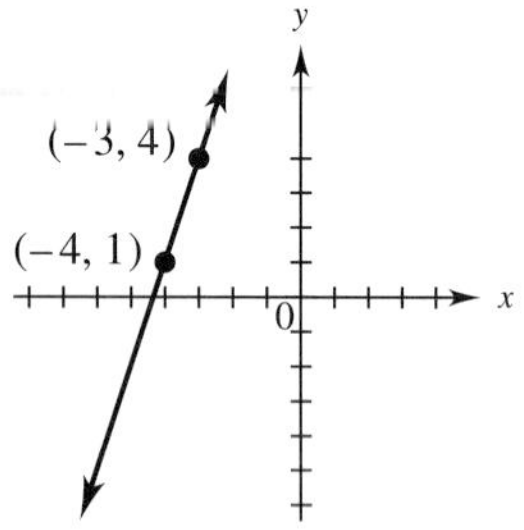

93. $3y = 2x - 13$ **95.** $4y = -5x + 17$ **97.** $x = -1$
99. $3y = 5x + 15$ **101.** **(a)** $y = .88x + 4.2$
(b)

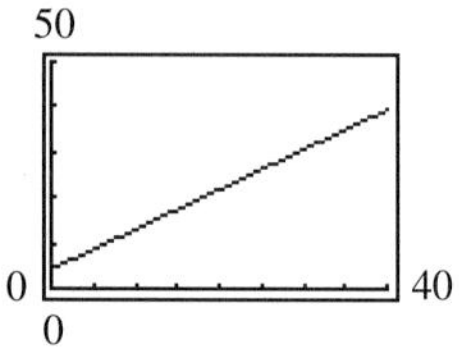

(c) Positive; percent is increasing, so line moves upward from left to right. **103.** **(a)** $r = 40x$
(b)

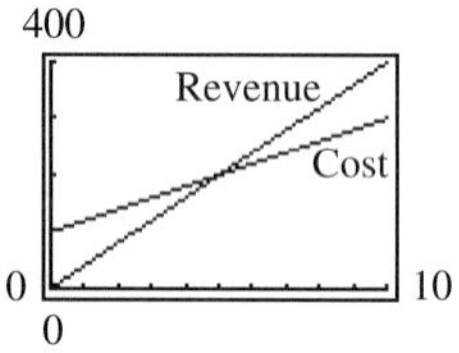

(c) 5 units **(d)** \$200 **(e)** $p = 20x - 100$ **105.** About 4.2
107. **(a)** $y = .57x$ **(b)** No, because there is 79.8 ppb remaining.
(c) About 87.7 ppb **109.** **(a)** $p = .5q - 2$ **(b)** \$5 for 14 units

Case 1 (page 71)

1. $c = 700 + 85x$ **3.** The \$700 refrigerator costs \$300 more over 10 years.

CHAPTER 2

Section 2.1 (page 77)

1. **(a)** The graph of $y = x^5 - 2x^4 - x^3 + 3x + 1$ has an intercept between -1 and 0, so the equation has a solution there.
(b) $x \approx -.3360527$ **(c)** Answers vary depending on the calculator, but the solutions usually agree to at least six decimal places.
3. $x \approx 1.3843$ **5.** $x \approx 1.1113$ **7.** $x = -5$ or -3 or -1 or 1
9. $x = 1$ or 4 or $x \approx -.3723$ or 5.3723 **11.** $x \approx 1.1640$
13. $x \approx -1.1043$ **15.** 3 **17.** 3 **19.** 2
21. $x \approx -1.1038$ **23.** $x \approx 2.1017$ **25.** $x \approx -1.7521$
27. $x \approx .9505$ **29.** $x \approx 0$ or 2.2074 **31.** $x \approx -.4125$ or 1.1211 **33.** $x = 2/3$ **35.** $x = \sqrt{3}$ **37.** $r \approx 4.6580$
39. **(a)** $p = -.0002x^2 + 1.4x - 300$ **(b)** About 1209
41. **(a)** $y = 30$
(b)

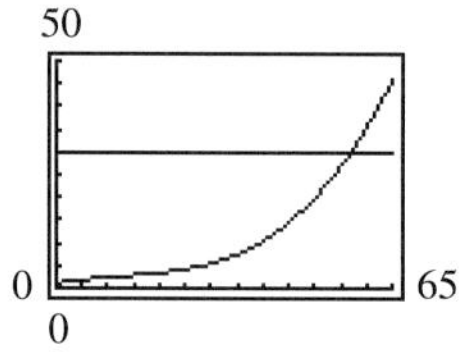

(c) Near the end of 1986 ($x = 56.9$)
43. **(a)** About 19.2 hr **(b)** About 84.3 ppm
45. 21.7 cm by 21.7 cm by 63.7 cm **47.** 25 inches by 26 inches by 27 inches

Section 2.2 (page 86)

1. 2 **3.** 0 **5.** 2 (Try a viewing window with $-.1 \le y \le .1$ to see what's going on.) **7.** $-7, -8$ **9.** 3/2, 1 **11.** $-1/2$, 1/3
13. 5/2, 4 **15.** 5, 2 **17.** 4/3, $-4/3$ **19.** 0, 1
21. $2 \pm \sqrt{7}$ **23.** $(1 \pm 2\sqrt{5})/4$ **25.** $(-5 \pm \sqrt{17})/4$; $-.219$, -2.281 **27.** $(-1 \pm \sqrt{5})/4$; .309, $-.809$ **29.** $(-3 \pm \sqrt{19})/5$; .272, -1.472 **31.** No real number solutions **33.** 5/2, 1
35. 4/3, 1/2 **37.** No real number solutions **39.** 1 **41.** 2
43. $x \approx .4701$ or 1.8240 **45.** $x \approx -1.0376$ or .67196
47. $\pm\sqrt{5}$ **49.** $\pm\sqrt{6}/2$ **51.** 11/3, 3/2 **53.** -5, 3/2
55. $-4 \pm 3\sqrt{2}$ **57.** **(a)** $(-r^2 + 3r - 12)/[r(r - 2)]$ **(b)** 4, -3
59. **(a)** $150 - x$ or $5000/x$ **(b)** $x(150 - x) = 5000$ or $2(5000/x) + 2x = 300$ **(c)** Length: 100 m; width: 50 m **61.** 1 ft
63. 176 mph **65.** 30 bicycles **67.** **(a)** 2 sec **(b)** 1/2 sec or 7/2 sec **(c)** It reaches the given height twice—once on the way up and once on the way down. **69.** $t = \pm\sqrt{2Sg}/g$
71. $h = (\pm d^2\sqrt{kL})/L$
73. $R = (-2Pr + E^2 \pm E\sqrt{E^2 - 4Pr})/(2P)$

Section 2.3 (page 93)

3. $[-4, \infty)$

5. $(-\infty, 0)$

7. $(-\infty, 8/3]$

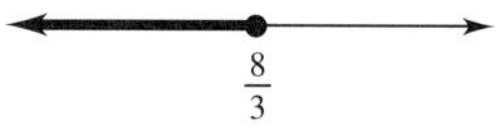

9. $(-\infty, -7]$

11. $(-\infty, 3)$

13. $(-1, \infty)$

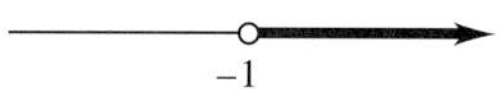

15. $(-\infty, 1]$

17. $(1/5, \infty)$

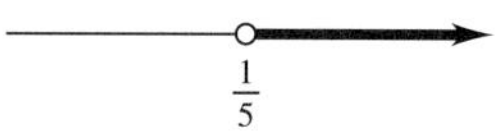

19. $(-5, 6)$

21. $[7/3, 4]$

23. $[-11/2, 7/2]$

25. $[-17/7, \infty)$ (tick label: $-\frac{17}{7}$)

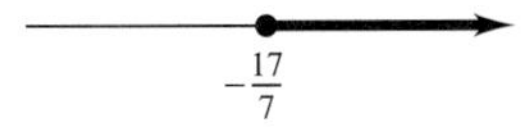

27. $(.1745, \infty)$ (tick label: .1745)

29. $(-\infty, 1.50)$ (tick label: 1.50)

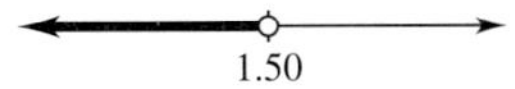

31. $(-\infty, .50]$ (tick label: .50)

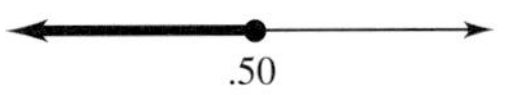

33. (a) Let x represent the number of mg per liter of lead in the water. (b) $.038 \le x \le .042$ (c) Yes 35. (a) $.0015 \le R \le .006$ (b) $.00002 \le R/75 \le .00008$

37. $(-1, 1)$ (tick labels: -1, 1)

39. No solution

41. $(-4, -1)$ (tick labels: -4, -1)

43. $(-\infty, -8/3]$ or $[2, \infty)$ (tick labels: $-\frac{8}{3}$, 2)

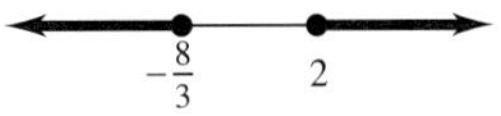

45. $(-3/2, 13/10)$ (tick labels: $-\frac{3}{2}$, $\frac{13}{10}$)

47. $-140 \le C \le -28$ 49. $|F - 730| \le 50$ 51. (a) $25.33 \le R_L \le 28.17$; $36.58 \le R_E \le 40.92$ (b) $5699.25 \le T_L \le 6338.25$; $8230.5 \le T_E \le 9207$ 53. At most 14 min 55. At least 629 mi 57. $[500, \infty)$ 59. $[45, \infty)$ 61. Impossible to break even 63. $|x - 2| \le 4$ 65. $|z - 12| \ge 2$ 67. If $|x - 2| \le .0004$, then $|y - 7| \le .00001$.

Section 2.4 (page 102)

1. $(-\infty, -1/2)$ or $(1/3, \infty)$ 3. $[-3, 1/2]$ 5. $[-5, 5]$ 7. $(-\infty, -2.1196)$ or $(.7863, \infty)$ 9. $(-.0806, 2.4806)$ 11. $[-3, 0]$ or $[3, \infty)$ 13. $(-\infty, -1/2)$ or $(0, 4/3)$ 15. $[-2.2635, .7556]$ or $[3.5079, \infty)$ 17. $(.5, .8393)$ 19. $(2.1931, \infty)$ 21. $[-2, 1/4]$ 23. $(-\infty, -1)$ or $(1/4, \infty)$ 25. $[-6, -1]$ or $[4, \infty)$ 29. Both excluded 31. $(7/2, 5)$ 33. $(-\infty, 2)$ or $(5, \infty)$ 35. $(-\infty, -3/2)$ or $[-13/9, \infty)$ 37. $(-\infty, .5)$ or $(5, 6)$ 39. $(-2, 0)$ or $(2, \infty)$ 41. $(-2, -1)$ or $(1, 3)$ 43. $(0, 5/3)$ or $(10, \infty)$ 45. $(100, 150)$ 47. More than \$4.77 per hour 49. Any width greater than 23 inches

Chapter 2 Review Exercises (page 104)

1. $x = -1$ or 5 3. $x \approx -2.3553$ 5. $x \approx 2.7644$ 7. $x \approx 2.8284$ 9. $x \approx -3.2843$ 11. $x \approx 1.6511$ 13. About 25 15. 2 17. 1 19. $-7 \pm \sqrt{5}$ 21. $1/2, -2$ 23. $1 \pm \sqrt{3}$ 25. $(6 \pm \sqrt{58})/2$ 27. $5/2, -3$ 29. $7, -3/2$ 31. $\pm\sqrt{3}/3$ 33. $\pm\sqrt{5}$ 35. $5, -2/3$ 37. $-5, -1/2$ 39. $r = (-Rp \pm E\sqrt{Rp})/p$ 41. $s = (a \pm \sqrt{a^2 + 4k})/2$ 43. 4.5 ft 45. 50 m by 225 m or 112.5 m by 100 m 47. $(3/8, \infty)$ 49. $(-\infty, 1/4]$ 51. $[-1/2, 2]$ 53. $[-8, 8]$ 55. $(-\infty, 2]$ or $[5, \infty)$ 57. $[-9/5, 1]$ 59. $5.5 \le y \le 9.5$ 61. $0 \le m < 500$, where m is the number of miles driven. 63. $(-3, 2)$ 65. $(-\infty, -5]$ or $[3/2, \infty)$ 67. $(-\infty, -5]$ or $[-2, 3]$ 69. $(-5.1623, 0)$ or $(1.1623, \infty)$ 71. $(-1.1903, 1.8850)$ 73. $[-2, 0)$ 75. $(-1, 3/2)$ 77. $[-19, -5)$ or $(2, \infty)$

Case 2 (page 106)

1.

Year	Straight-Line	Sum-of-the-Years'-Digits	Double Declining Balance
1	\$11,000	\$18,333.33	\$22,000
2	11,000	14,666.67	13,200
3	11,000	11,000.00	7920
4	11,000	7333.33	5940
5	11,000	3666.67	5940

3. Either the sum-of-the-years'-digits method or the double declining balance method gives the largest early years' deductions.

CHAPTER 3

Section 3.1 (page 114)

1. Function 3. Function 5. Not a function 7. Function 9. $(-\infty, \infty)$ 11. $(-\infty, \infty)$ 13. $(-\infty, 0]$ 15. All real numbers except 1 17. $(-\infty, \infty)$ 19. (a) 6 (b) 6 (c) 6 (d) 6 21. (a) 48 (b) 6 (c) 25.38 (d) 28.42 23. (a) $\sqrt{7}$ (b) 0 (c) $\sqrt{5.7} \approx 2.3875$ (d) Not defined 25. (a) -18.2 (b) -97.3 (c) -14.365 (d) -289.561 27. (a) 12 (b) 23 (c) 12.91 (d) 49.41 29. (a) $\sqrt{3}/15 \approx .1155$ (b) Not defined (c) $\sqrt{1.7}/6.29 \approx .2073$ (d) Not defined

31.

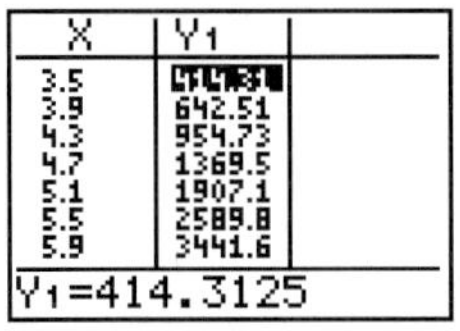

X	Y1
3.5	[illegible]
3.9	642.51
4.3	954.73
4.7	1369.5
5.1	1907.1
5.5	2589.8
5.9	3441.6

Y1=414.3125

33. (a) $5 - p$ (b) $5 + r$ (c) $2 - m$ 35. (a) $\sqrt{4 - p}$ $(p \le 4)$ (b) $\sqrt{4 + r}$ $(r \ge -4)$ (c) $\sqrt{1 - m}$ $(m \le 1)$ 37. (a) $p^3 + 1$ (b) $-r^3 + 1$ (c) $m^3 + 9m^2 + 27m + 28$ 39. Assume all denominators are nonzero. (a) $3/(p - 1)$ (b) $3/(-r - 1)$ (c) $3/(m + 2)$ 41. 2 43. $2x + h$ 45. (a) About 89% (b) About 47% 47. (a) Function h approximates the data best. (b) Approximately 157,000 49. $f(t) = 2000 - 475t$

Section 3.2 (page 123)

In Exercises 1–6, consider your answer correct if it shows the shape and graph features that appear in the window listed here.

1. $-16 \le x \le 0$ and $0 \le y \le 4$ 3. $-4 \le x \le 10$ and $-20 \le y \le 22$ 5. $-5 \le x \le 5$ and $-80 \le y \le 0$

7.

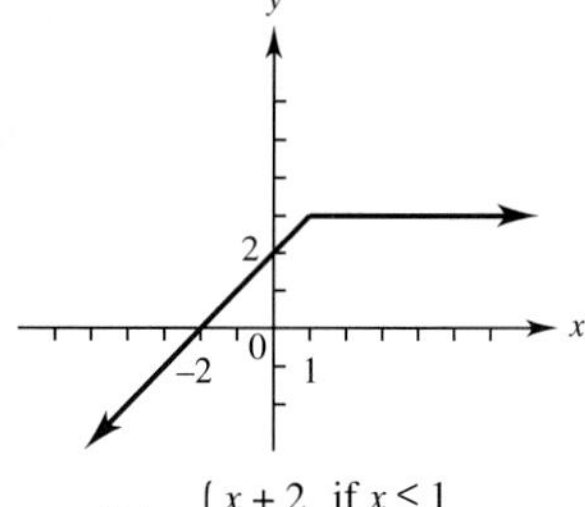

9.

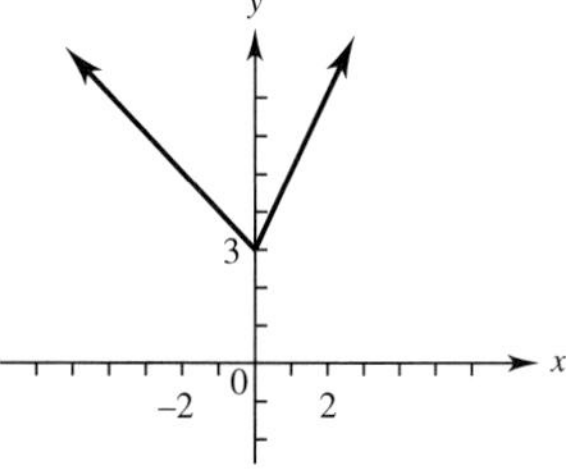

11.

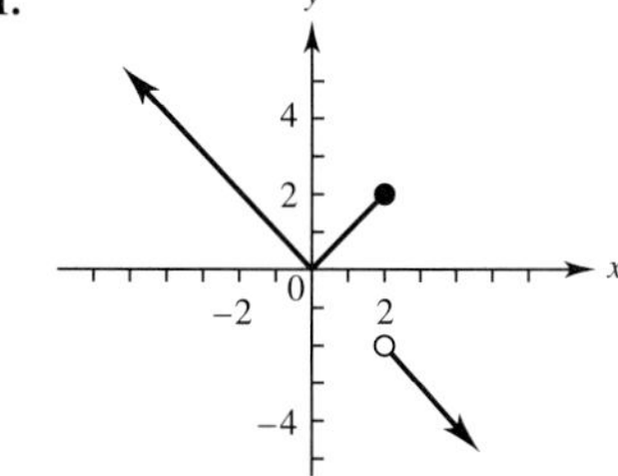

13.

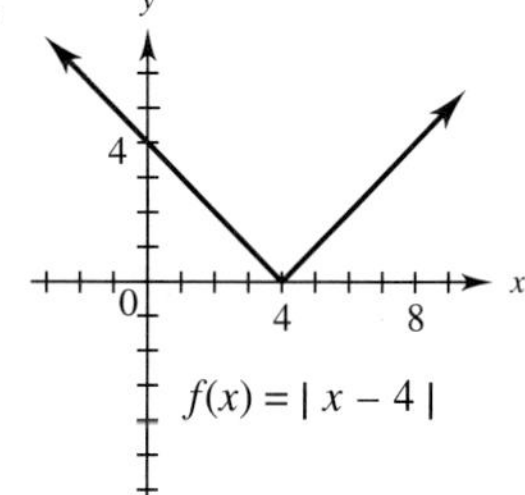

15.

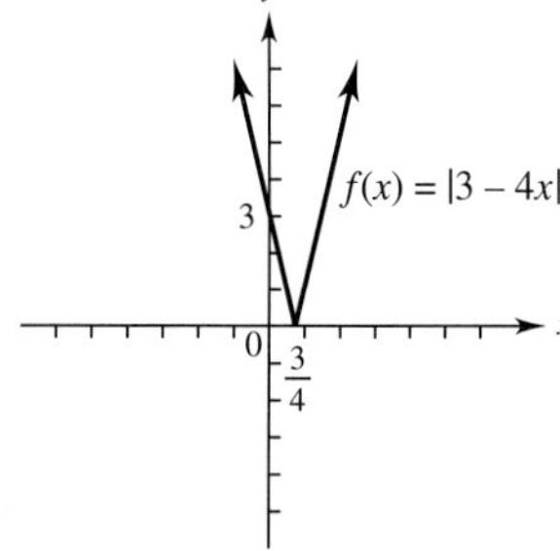

17.

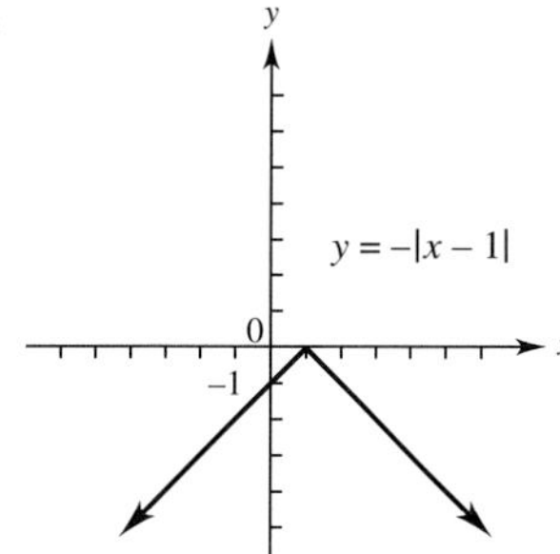

19.

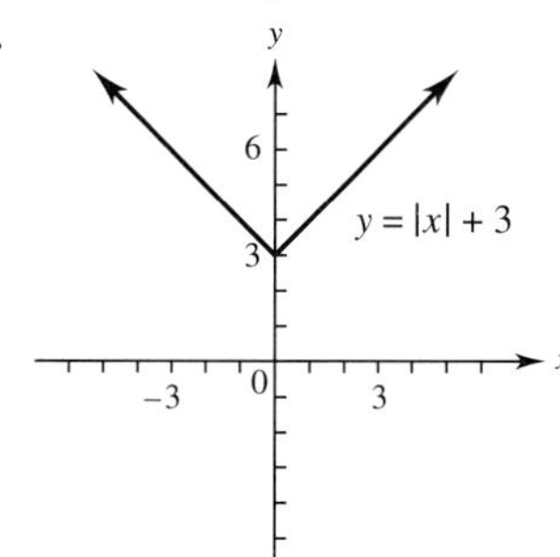

21.

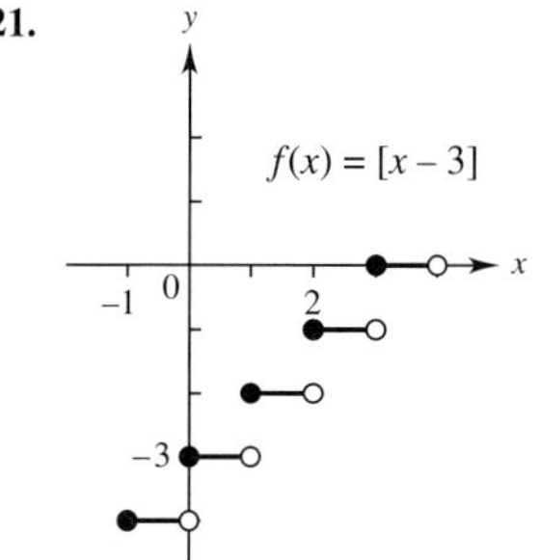

23.

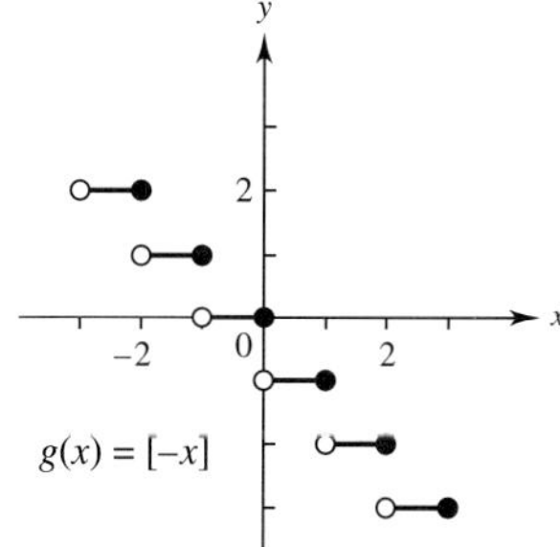

25.

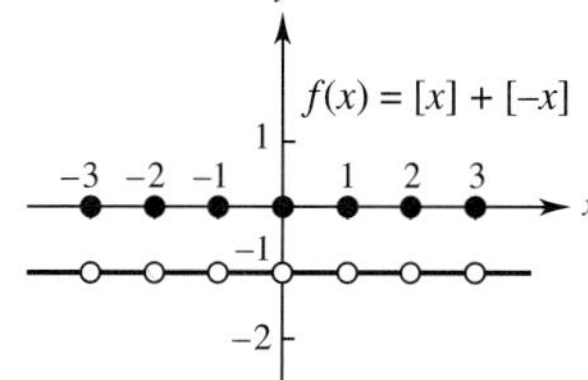

27. Function **29.** Not a function **31.** Function **33.** Not horizontal; there is a tiny peak and valley; window: $-2 \le x \le 2$ and $-.6 \le y \le -.4$. **35.** Not horizontal; the graph slowly falls when $-.5 \le x \le 0$ to a low point at $(0, -1)$, then slowly rises when $0 \le x \le .5$. However, every viewing window displays a horizontal

segment across the y-axis and in very small windows (such as $-.05 \le x \le .05$ and $-1.05 \le y \le -.95$), round-off may cause the trace feature to indicate that all the y-coordinates are -1, which is not the case.

37. 

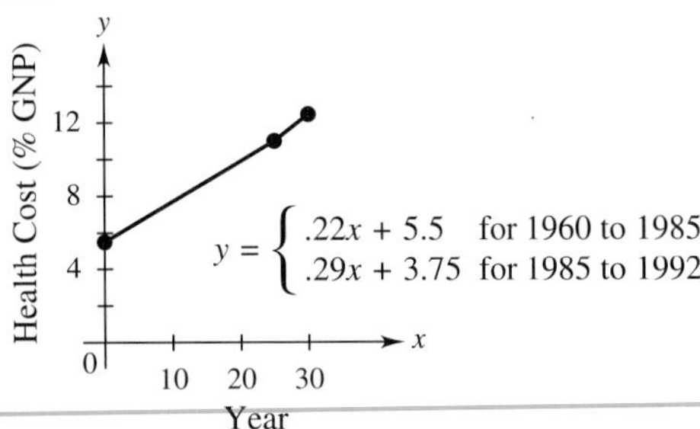

They rose faster from 1985 to 1992 than from 1960 to 1985.

39. **(a)**

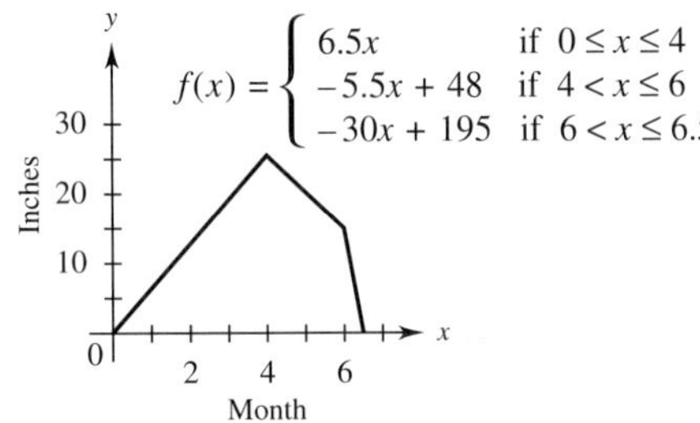

(b) At the beginning of February; 26 in. **(c)** Begins in early October; ends in mid-April

41. **(a)** $f(x) = \begin{cases} .012x + .05 & \text{if } 0 \le x \le 10 \\ .006x + .11 & \text{if } 10 < x \le 20 \end{cases}$

(b)

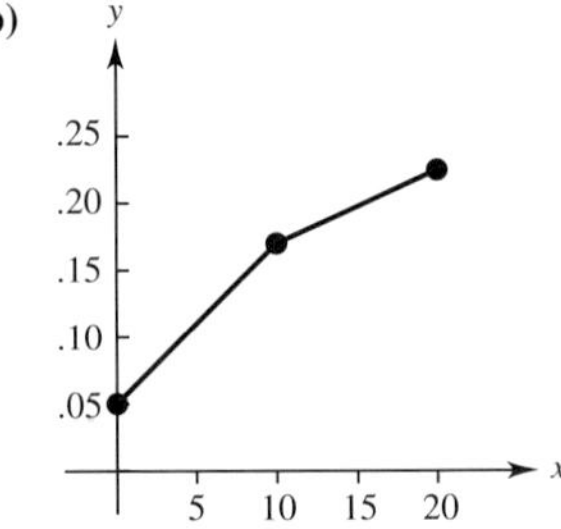

(c) 11% in 1975; 18.2% in 1982 **43.** **(a)** 26,300 BTU per dollar **(b)** $120 billion **(c)** 23,500 BTU per dollar, $85 billion; 1981 **(d)** None

45. **(a)**

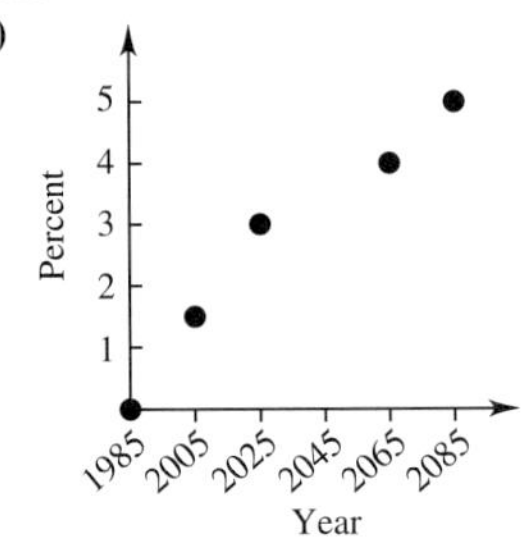

(b) $y = .04375x - 86.21875$ **(c)** $f(x) = .04375x - 86.21875$ **(d)** 4.125; yes; yes

47. Many correct answers, including:

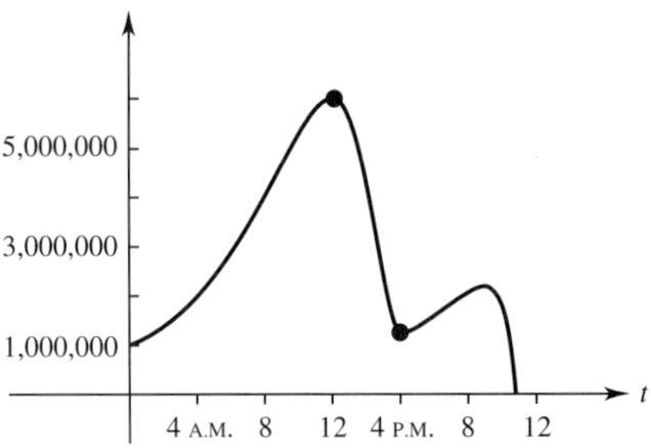

49. **(a)** $29 **(b)** $29 **(c)** $33 **(d)** $33

(e)

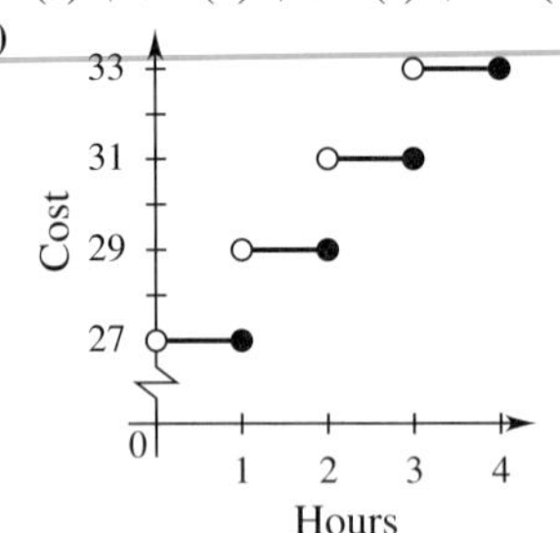

51.

53. **(a)** 1993 **(b)** $195 million

(c)

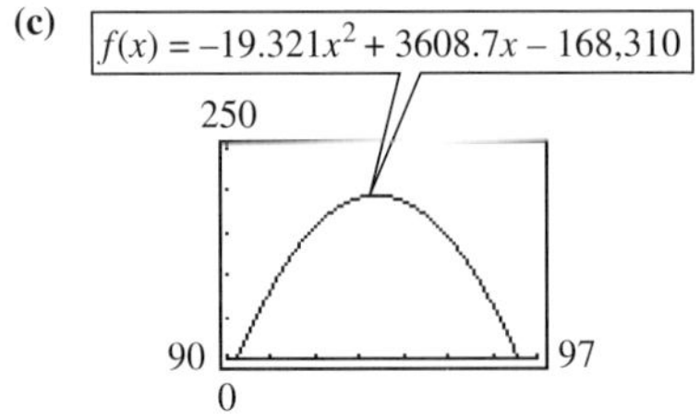

55. 49 yr

Section 3.3 (page 132)

1. **(a)** $f(x) = -.15x + 31.2 \quad (0 \le x \le 6)$ **(b)** $-.15$ million

3. **(a)** The data appear linear.

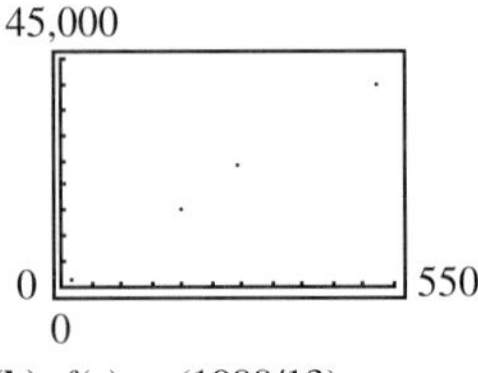

(b) $f(x) = (1000/13)x$

(c) 45,000

0 550

0

(d) About 780 megaparsecs (approximately 1.5×10^{22} miles) **(e)** About 12.4 billion years **5. (a)** $f(x) = (4/75)x - (13/300)$ **(b)** Approximately 10.2 years **7. (a)** $u(x) = 187 - .85x$; $l(x) = 154 - .7x$ **(b)** 140 to 170 beats per minute **(c)** 126 to 153 beats per minute **(d)** 16 and 52; 143 beats per minute **9. (a)** 2000 **(b)** 2900 **(c)** 3200 **(d)** Yes **(e)** 300 **11. (a)** The number of new car dealers selling used cars was decreasing at the rate of 2720 per year. **(b)** The slope of .3 indicates that the sales at superstores are increasing at the rate of 300,000 per year. **(c)** As the number of new car dealers selling used cars decreased, the number sold in superstores increased, suggesting that used car buyers are changing to this new way of buying used cars. **13. (a)** 3 **(b)** 3.5 **(c)** 1 **(d)** 0 **(e)** -2 **(f)** -2 **(g)** -3 **(h)** -1 **15.** Let $C(x)$ be the cost of renting a saw for x hours; $C(x) = 12 + x$. **17.** Let $P(x)$ be the cost (in cents) of parking for x half-hours; $P(x) = 30x + 35$. **19.** $C(x) = 30x + 100$ **21.** $C(x) = 120x + 3800$ **23. (a)** \$5.25 **(b)** \$66,250 **25. (a)** $C(x) = 10x + 500$ **(b)** $R(x) = 35x$ **27. (a)** $C(x) = 18x + 250$ **(b)** $R(x) = 28x$ **29.** (c)

Section 3.4 (page 141)

1. (5, 2); upward **3.** (1, 2); downward **5.** $(-6, -35)$; upward **7.** $(-1, -1)$; upward **9.** x-intercepts 1, 3; y-intercept 9 **11.** x-intercepts $-1, -3$; y-intercept 6 **13.** $f(x) = -(x - 3)^2 - 5$ **15.** $f(x) = (1/4)(x - 1)^2 + 2$ **17.** $f(x) = (x + 1)^2 - 2$ **19.** $(-2, 0)$, $x = -2$

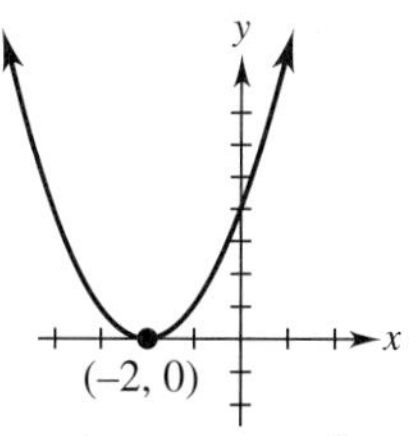

$f(x) = (x + 2)^2$

21. $(1, -3)$, $x = 1$

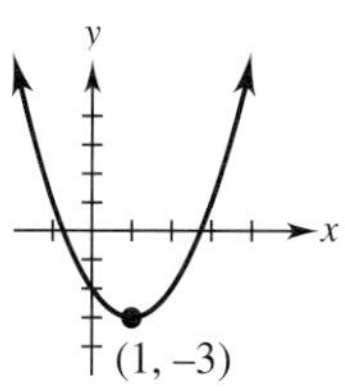

$f(x) = (x - 1)^2 - 3$

23. (2, 2), $x = 2$

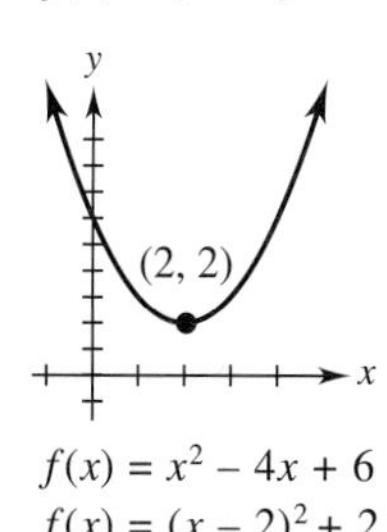

$f(x) = x^2 - 4x + 6$
$f(x) = (x - 2)^2 + 2$

25. (1, 3), $x = 1$

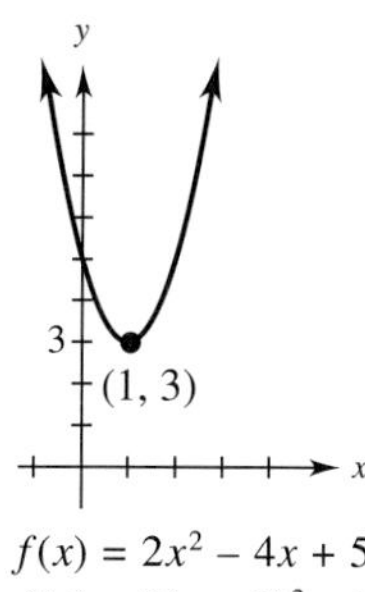

$f(x) = 2x^2 - 4x + 5$
$f(x) = 2(x - 1)^2 + 3$

27. (3, 3), $x = 3$

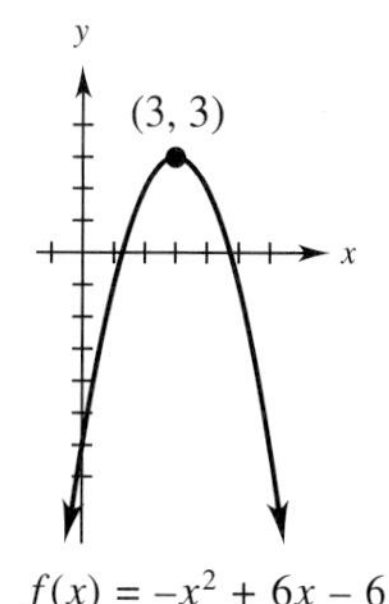

$f(x) = -x^2 + 6x - 6$
$f(x) = -(x - 3)^2 + 3$

In Exercises 29 and 31, one possible window is given.

29. Vertex (7.2, 12); window: $-2 \le x \le 10$; $-5 \le y \le 30$ **31.** Vertex $(95, -2695.5)$; window: $-30 \le x \le 220$; $-3000 \le y \le 3000$ **33. (a)–(d)**

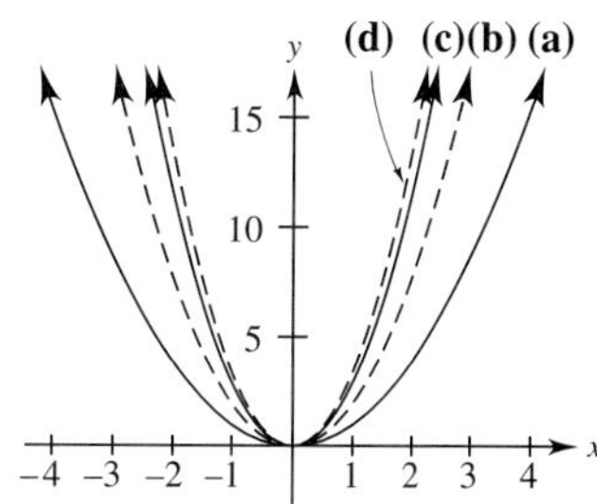

(e) The graph of $f(x) = ax^2$ is the graph of $k(x) = x^2$ stretched away from the x-axis by a factor of a.

35. (a)–(d)

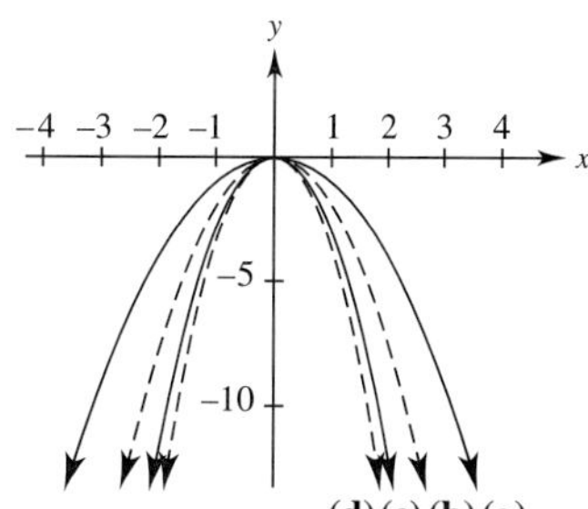

(e) Changing the sign of a reflects the graph in the x-axis.

37. (a)–(d)

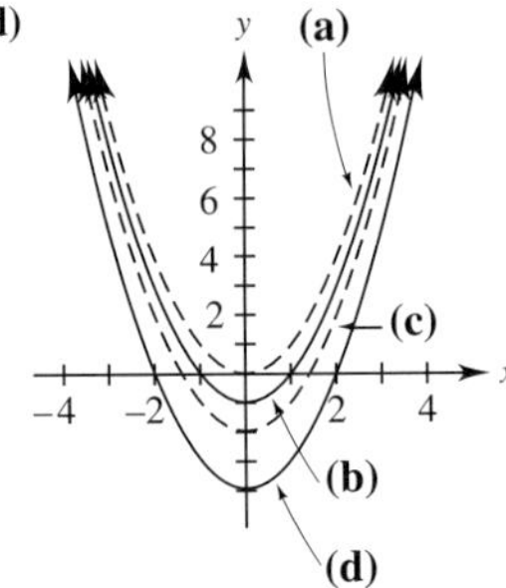

(e) The graph of $f(x) = x^2 - c$ is the graph of $k(x) = x^2$ shifted c units downward. **39.** $f(x) = 3x^2$

Section 3.5 (page 146)

1. (a) \$16; \$8; \$32 **(b)**

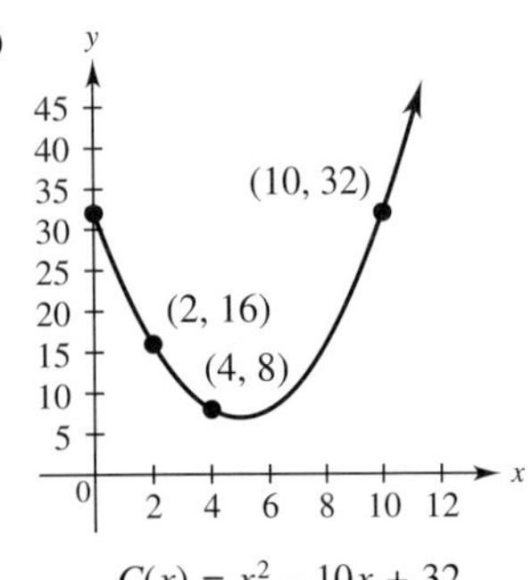

(c) (5, 7) **(d)** 5; \$7 per box **3. (a)** \$.60 **(b)** \$800 **5.** 16 ft; 2 sec **7. (a)** $R(x) = 150x - x^2/4$ **(b)** 300 **(c)** \$22,500 **9. (a)** $R(x) = x(500 - x)$
(b)

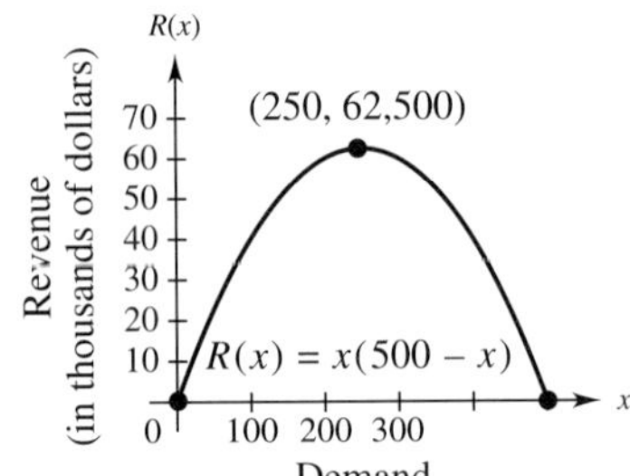

(c) \$250 **(d)** \$62,500 **11. (a)** About 12 **(b)** 10 **(c)** About 7 **(d)** 0 **(e)** 5 **(f)** About 7 **(g)** 10 **(h)** About 12
(i)

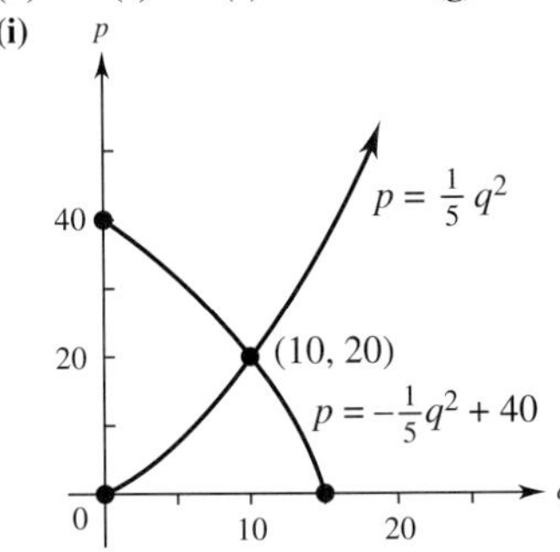

13. (a) $R(x) = (100 - x)(200 + 4x) = 20{,}000 + 200x - 4x^2$
(b) **(c)** 25 **(d)** \$22,500

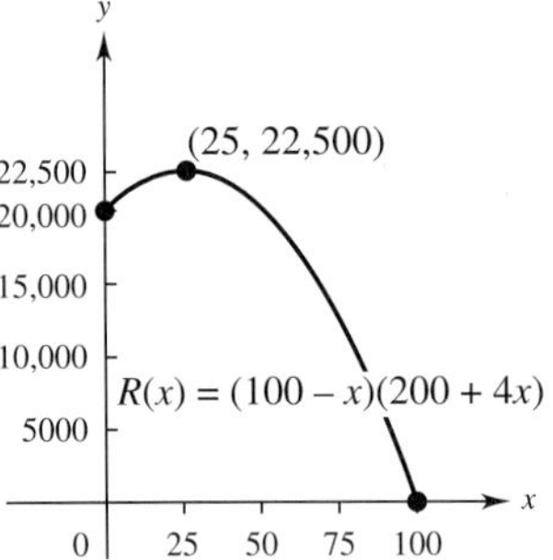

15. 13 weeks; \$96.10
17. (a) 250,000

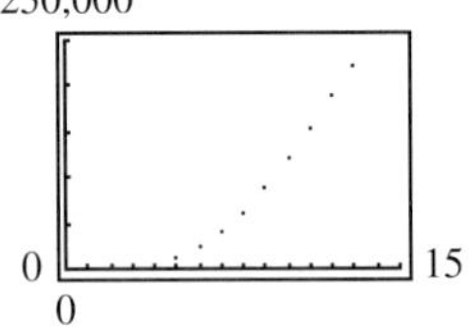

(b) $g(x) = 1817.95(x - 2)^2 + 620$ **(c)** There is a relatively good fit.

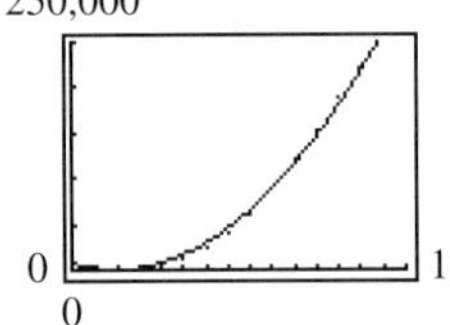

(d) Approximately 589,636 **19.** 80 ft by 160 ft **21.** 2.5 in. **23. (a)** 2.3 or 17.7 **(b)** 15 **(c)** 10 **(d)** \$120 **(e)** $0 < x < 2.3$ or $x > 17.7$ **(f)** $2.3 < x < 17.7$

Chapter 3 Review Exercises (page 149)

1. Not a function **3.** Function **5.** Not a function **7. (a)** 23 **(b)** -9 **(c)** $4p - 1$ **(d)** $4r + 3$ **9. (a)** -28 **(b)** -12 **(c)** $-p^2 + 2p - 4$ **(d)** $-r^2 - 3$ **11. (a)** -13 **(b)** 3 **(c)** $-k^2 - 4k$ **(d)** $-9m^2 + 12m$ **(e)** $-k^2 + 14k - 45$ **(f)** $12 - 5p$
13.

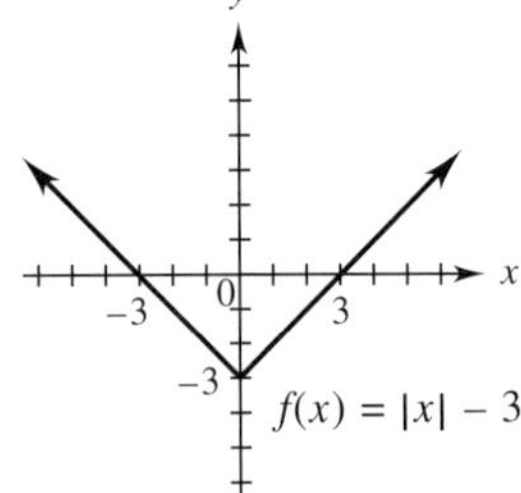

15.

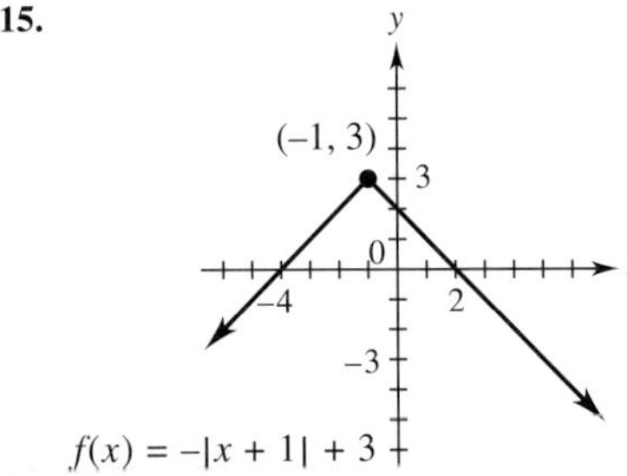

17.

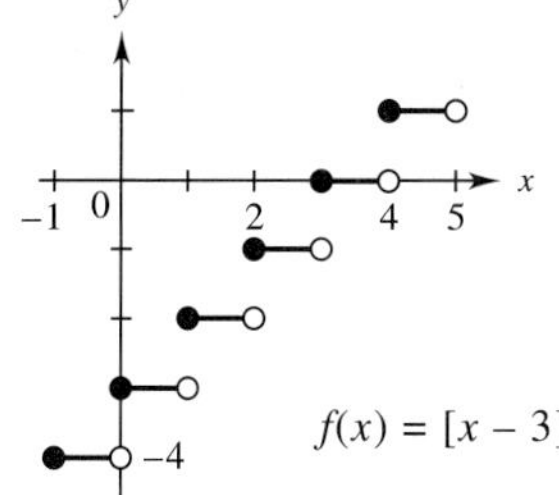

19.

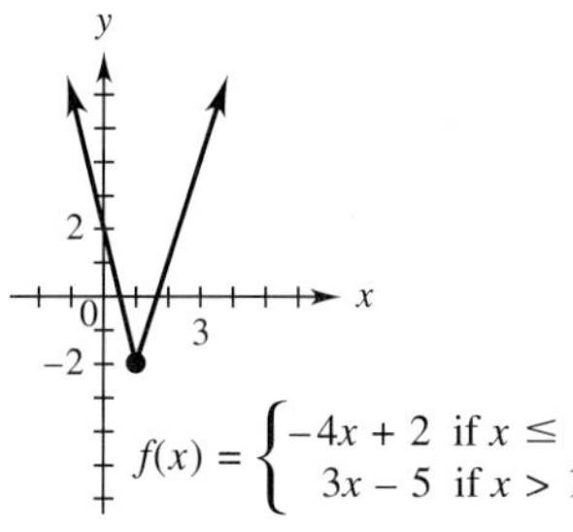

21.

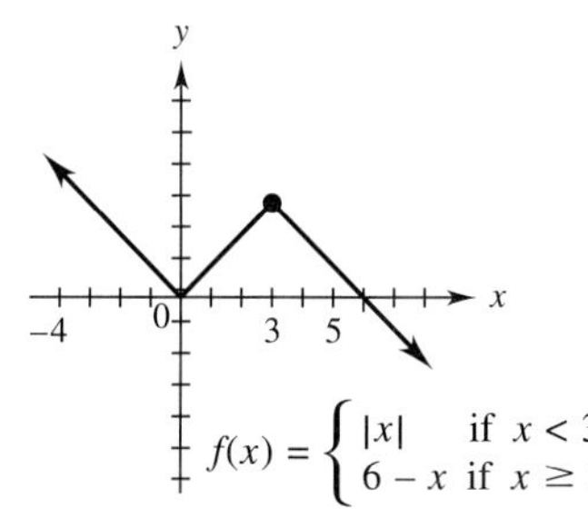

23. There is a tiny peak and valley to the right of the y-axis, which is visible in the window with $-.1 \le x \le .2$ and $.999 \le y \le 1.001$.
25. (a) $C(x) = 30x + 60$ **(b)** \$30 **(c)** \$30.60
27. (a) $C(x) = 30x + 85$ **(b)** \$30 **(c)** \$30.85
29. (a) 1.4 **(b)** $-.75$ **(c)** .8 **(d)** 1.25
31. (a) Yes **(b)**

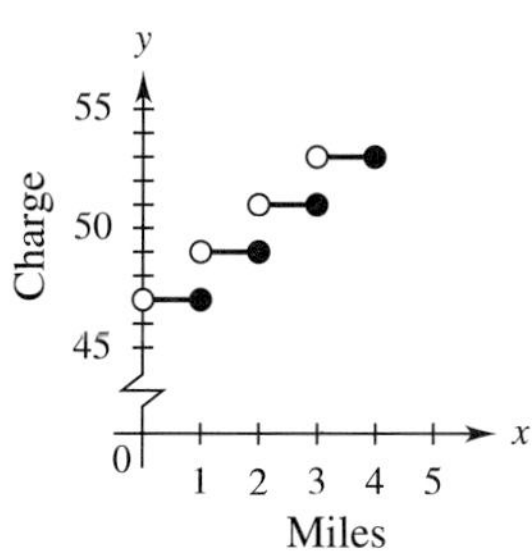

(c) Domain: $(0, \infty)$; range: $\{47, 49, 51, 53, \dots\}$
33. Upward; (2, 6) **35.** Downward; $(-1, 8)$

37.

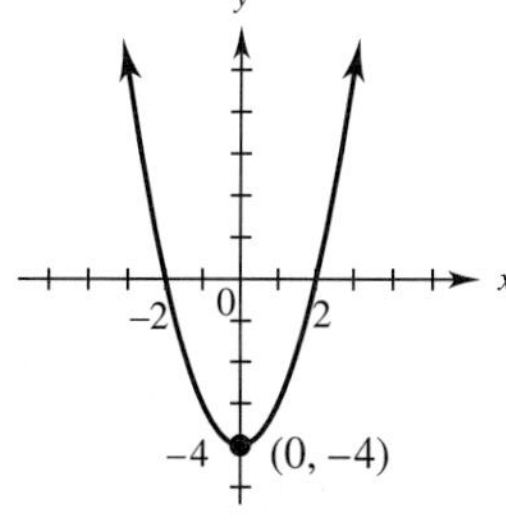

$f(x) = x^2 - 4$

39.

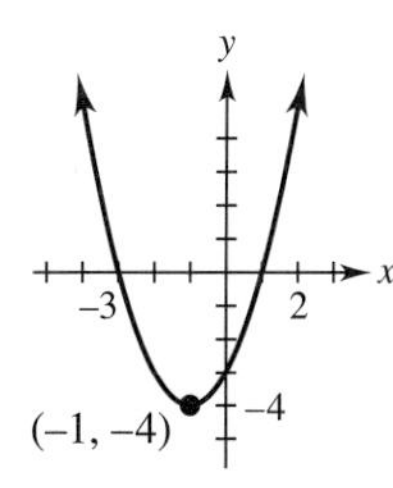

$f(x) = x^2 + 2x - 3$
$f(x) = (x + 1)^2 - 4$

41.

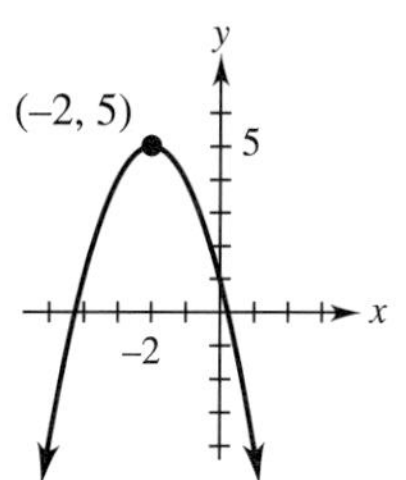

$f(x) = -x^2 - 4x + 1$
$f(x) = -(x + 2)^2 + 5$

43.

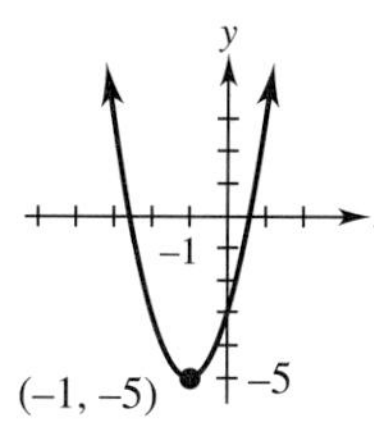

$f(x) = 2x^2 + 4x - 3$
$f(x) = 2(x + 1)^2 - 5$

45. Minimum value, -11 **47.** Maximum value, 7
49. Four months after she began **51.** Between 350 and 1850
53. 50 m $\times$ 50 m

Case 3 (page 151)

1. 4.8 million units **3.** In the interval under discussion (3.1 to 5.7 million units), the marginal cost always exceeds the selling price.

CHAPTER 4

Section 4.1 (page 157)

1. Many correct answers including $-12 \le x \le 12$ and $-3500 \le y \le 3500$ **3. (a)** Yes **(b)** No **(c)** No **(d)** Yes
5. (a) Yes **(b)** Yes **(c)** No **(d)** Yes **7. (a)** Yes **(b)** No **(c)** No **(d)** No **9. (a)** Yes **(b)** No **(c)** Yes **(d)** No
11. $-3 \le x \le 5$ and $-20 \le y \le 5$ **13.** $-3 \le x \le 4$ and $-35 \le y \le 20$

15.

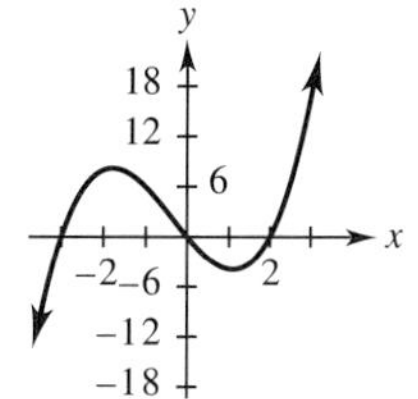

$f(x) = x^3 + x^2 - 6x$

17.

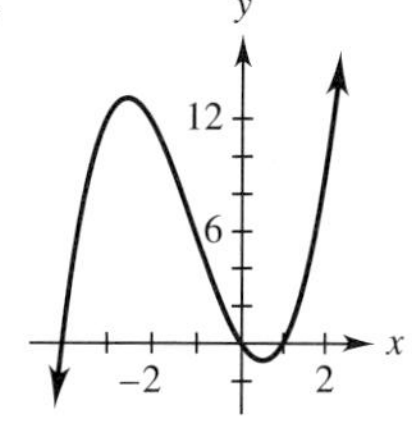

$f(x) = x^3 + 3x^2 - 4x$

19.

$f(x) = x^4 - 2x^2$

21.

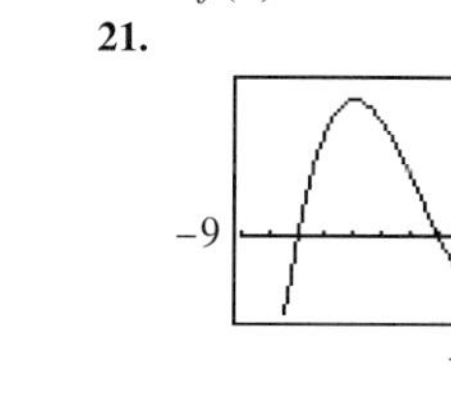

23.

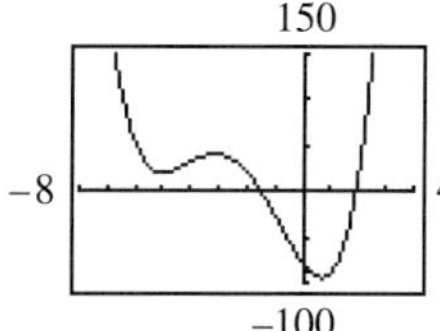

25.

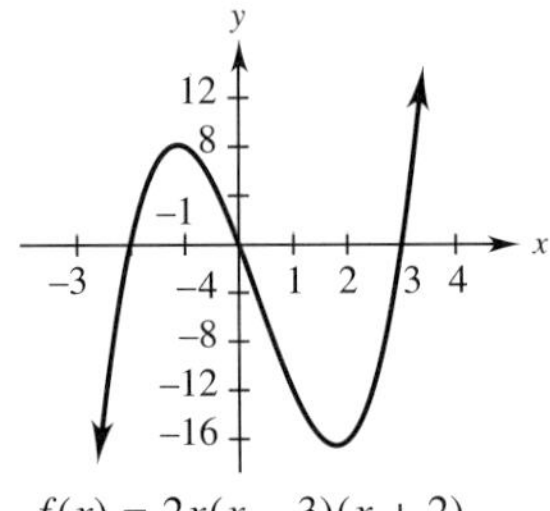

$f(x) = 2x(x - 3)(x + 2)$

27.

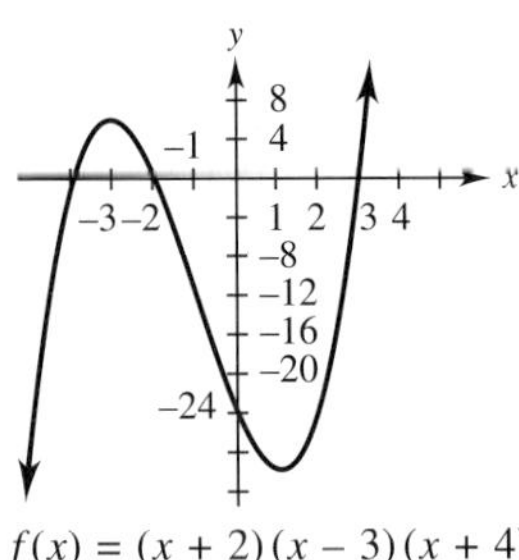

$f(x) = (x + 2)(x - 3)(x + 4)$

29.

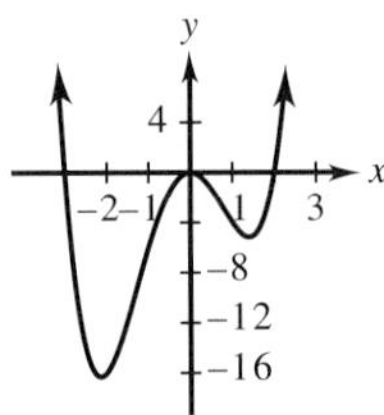

$f(x) = x^2(x - 2)(x + 3)$

31.

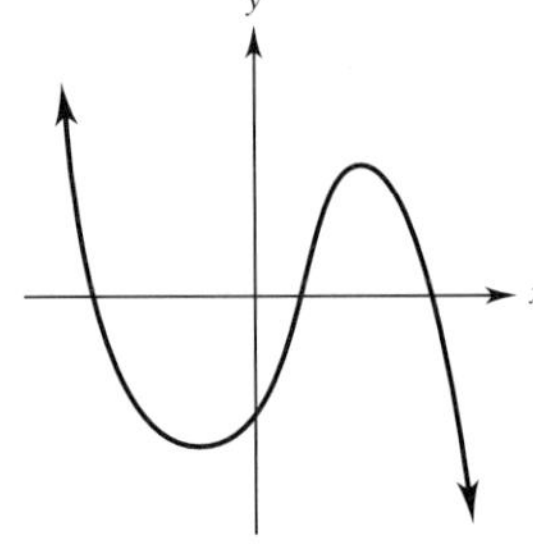

33. **(a)** 0; 1.871; 4.392; 8.187
(b)

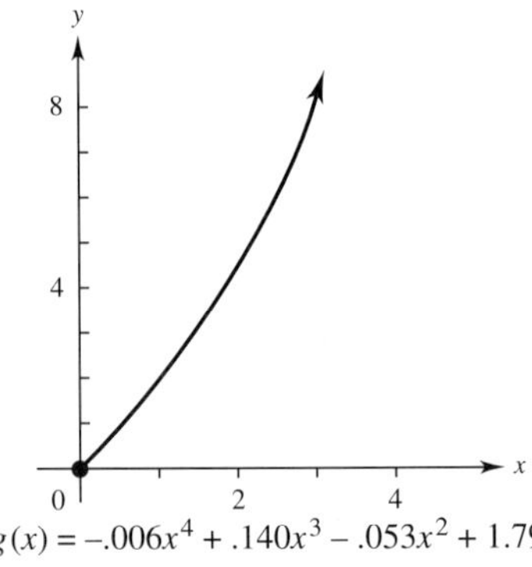

$g(x) = -.006x^4 + .140x^3 - .053x^2 + 1.79x$

35. **(a)** 4000; 5562.5; 22,750; 67,281.25; 104,000; 4000
(b)

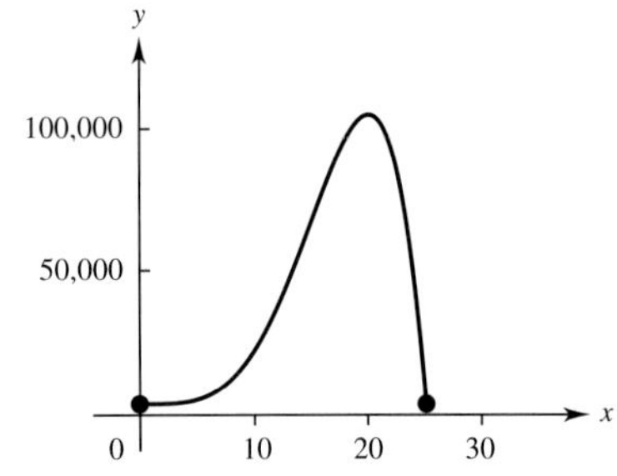

$D(x) = -.125x^5 + 3.125x^4 + 4000$

(c) The population was increasing from 1905 to 1925 and was decreasing from 1925 to 1930. It was relatively stable from 1905 to 1910. **37.** **(a)** $g(t) = 30$
(b)

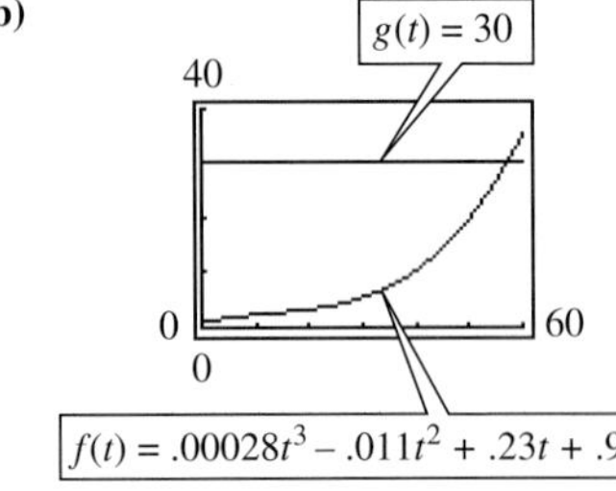

(c) 1986

Section 4.2 (page 162)

1. Equilibrium demand 123.122; equilibrium price \$40.03
3. Equilibrium demand 441.100; equilibrium price \$84.67
5. About 6671; about \$29.75
7. **(a)**

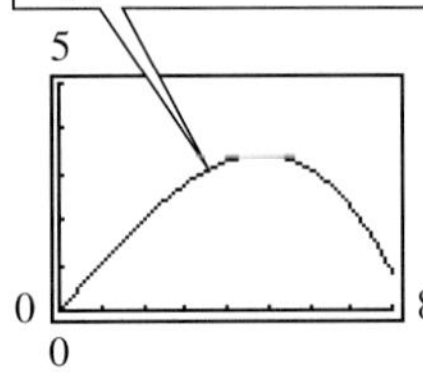

(b)

X	Y1
1	1.043
3	2.769
5	3.415
7	2.261

X=

(c) After about 4.85 hours **(d)** From about 1.46 hours to 7.57 hours
9. **(a)** $R(x) = 350x$; $P(x) = -.01x^2 + 375x - 600{,}000$ **(b)** 1675
(c) 35,825 **(d)** 18,750
11. **(a)** $C(x) = .000025x^3 - .008x^2 + x + 30$

160
0
250
0

(b) \$63,125; \$84,375; \$110,000 **(c)** \$18,875; \$44,625; loss of \$22,000 **(d)** About 119,320 **13.** **(a)** About 3.79 by 3.79 by 6.98 cm **(b)** About 6.32 by 6.32 by 3.16 cm **15.** About 9.66 by 9.66 by 24.15 cm; about 2254.21 sq cm **17.** **(a)** About 52.4%; about 78.8%; about 81.2% **(b)** Age 67; 81.5% **19.** 6

Section 4.3 (page 168)

1. $x/5$ **3.** $4/(7p)$ **5.** $5/4$ **7.** $4/(w + 3)$
9. $(y - 4)/(3y^2)$ **11.** $2(x + 2)/x$ **13.** $(m - 2)/(m + 3)$
15. $(x + 4)/(x + 1)$ **17.** $2p/7$ **19.** $9a^3/4$ **21.** $15/(8c)$
23. $3/4$ **25.** $2/9$ **27.** $3/10$ **29.** $2(a + 4)/(a - 3)$
31. $(k + 2)/(k + 3)$ **35.** $-1/(15z)$ **37.** $4/3$
39. $(12 + x)/(3x)$ **41.** $(8 - y)/(4y)$ **43.** $137/(30m)$
45. $(3m - 2)/[m(m - 1)]$ **47.** $14/[3(a - 1)]$
49. $23/[20(k - 2)]$ **51.** $(7x + 9)/[(x - 3)(x + 1)(x + 2)]$
53. $y^2/[(y + 4)(y + 3)(y + 2)]$
55. $(k^2 - 13k)/[(2k - 1)(k + 2)(k - 3)]$ **57.** $(x + 1)/(x - 1)$
59. $-1/[x(x + h)]$ **61.** $(2 + b - b^2)/(b - b^2)$

Section 4.4 (page 176)

1. $x = -5, y = 0$

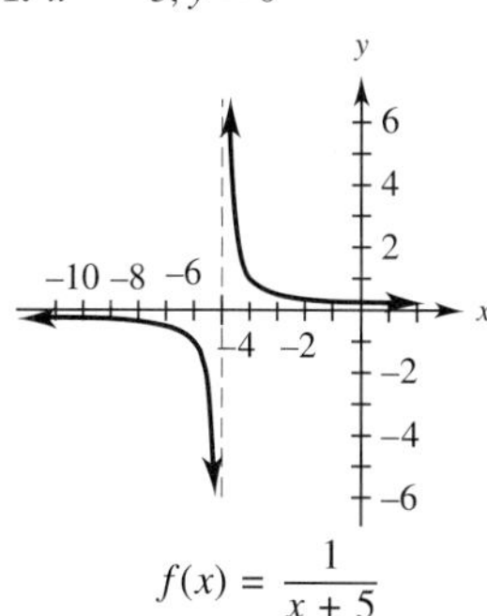

$f(x) = \dfrac{1}{x + 5}$

3. $x = -5/2, y = 0$

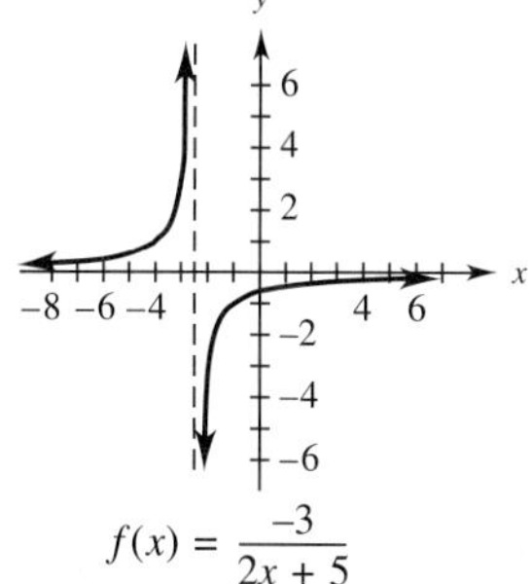

$f(x) = \dfrac{-3}{2x + 5}$

5. $x = 3, y = -1$

$f(x) = \dfrac{2 - x}{x - 3}$

7. $x = -1/2, y = 1/2$

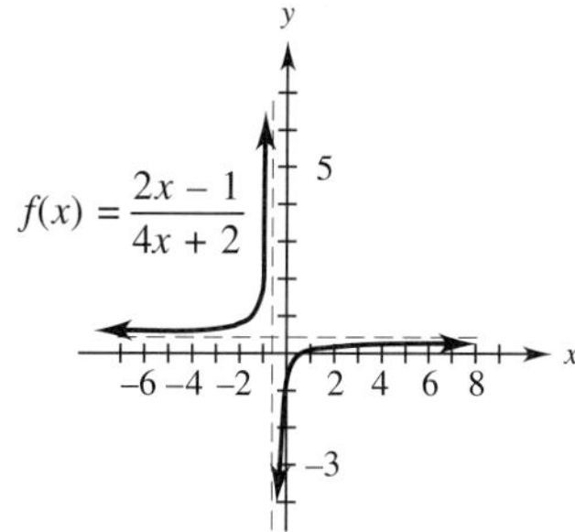

$f(x) = \dfrac{2x - 1}{4x + 2}$

9. $x = -4, x = 1, y = 0$

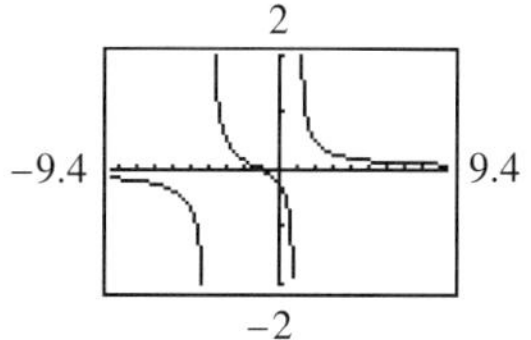

11. $x = -1, x = 1, y = 1$

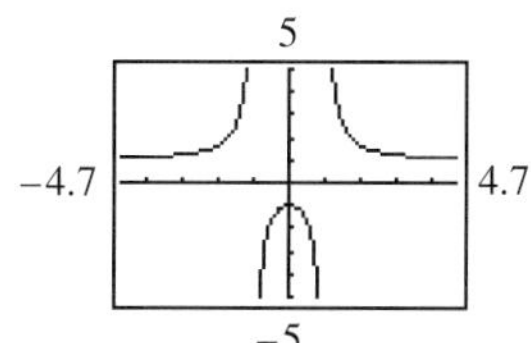

13. $y = 1$ (no vertical asymptote)

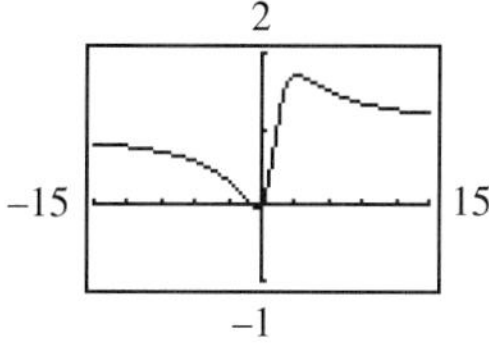

15. $-9.4 \le x \le 9.4$ and $-4 \le y \le 4$ (On wide screens, such as TI-85/92 or HP-38, this window may show erroneous vertical lines; try the decimal window to eliminate them.) **17.** A decimal window with longer y-axis (such as $-4.7 \le x \le 4.7$ and $-4 \le y \le 4$ on standard screens) shows the general shape of the graph. For the hidden behavior near $x = 3$, use $2 \le x \le 30$ and $-.2 \le y \le .2$.
19. A decimal window (such as $-4.7 \le x \le 4.7$ and $-4 \le y \le 4$ on standard screens) shows the general shape of the graph. For the hidden behavior near $x = 4$, use $3 \le x \le 15$ and $-.02 \le y \le .01$.
21. **(a)** \$4300 **(b)** \$10,033.33 **(c)** \$17,200 **(d)** \$38,700 **(e)** \$81,700 **(f)** \$210,700 **(g)** \$425,700 **(h)** No
(i)

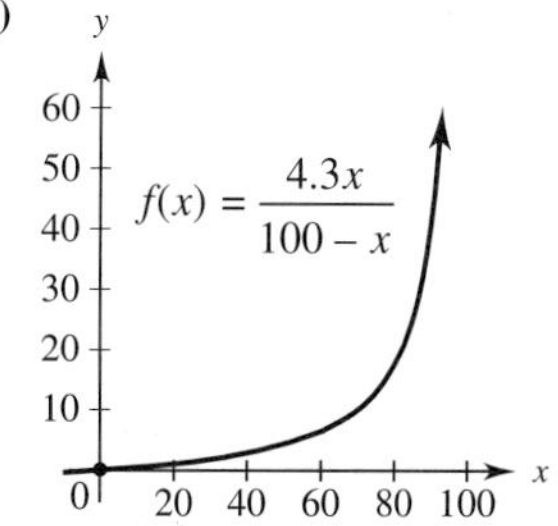

$f(x) = \dfrac{4.3x}{100 - x}$

23. **(a)** 125,000 **(b)** 187,500 **(c)** 200,000
(d)

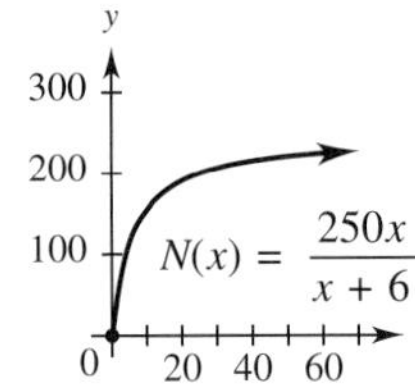

(e) The part in the first quadrant, because x and $N(x)$ are both positive
(f) $y = 250$; 250,000
25. **(a)**

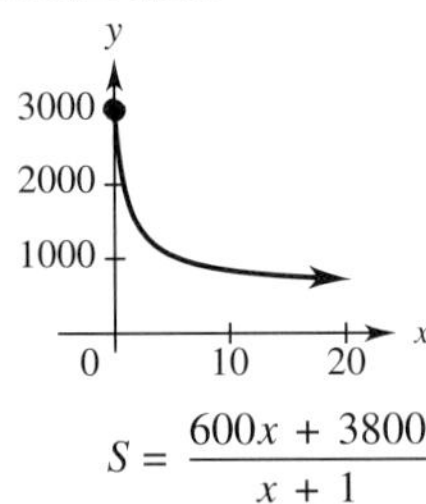

(b) Yes; \$600; the horizontal asymptote **(c)** After 7 days; the cost of ads will be more than the sales they generate.
27. 30,000 reds; 10,000 blues

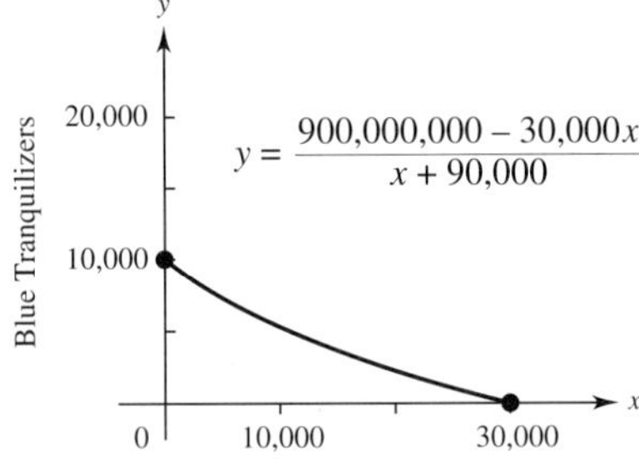

29. About 73.9 **31.** About 12.6 by 12.6 by 6.3 inches
33. **(a)**

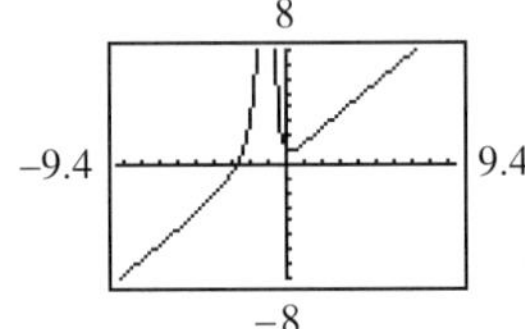

(b) No; yes
(c) Yes

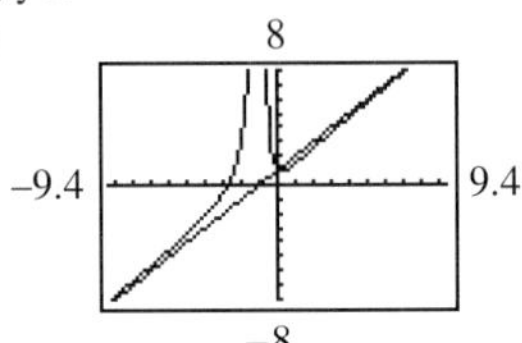

Chapter 4 Review Exercises (page 178)

1.

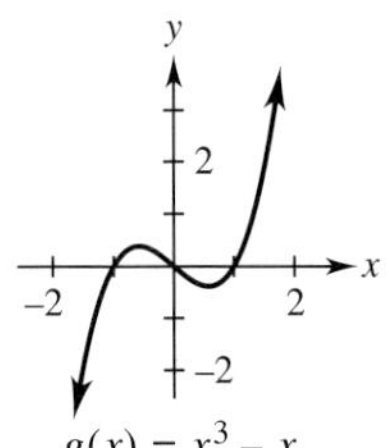

3.

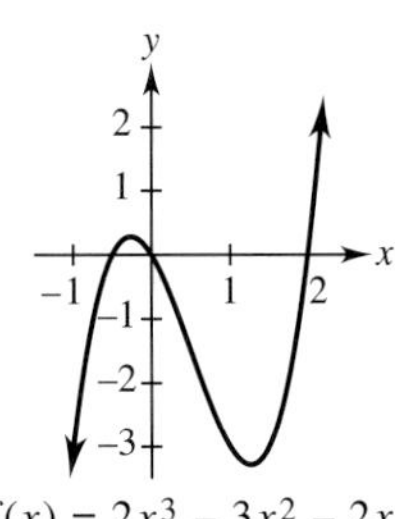

5.

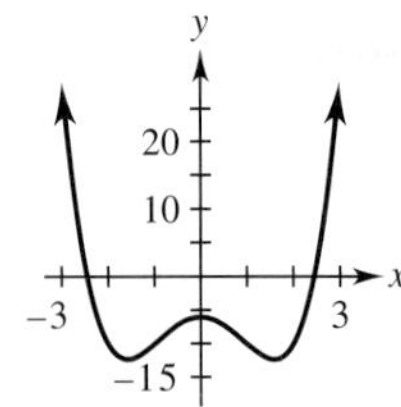

7. $-3 \leq x \leq 9$ and $-35 \leq y \leq 15$ **9.** Overall: $-10 \leq x \leq 15$ and $-1500 \leq y \leq 1000$; hidden behavior near $x = 7$: $6 \leq x \leq 8$ and $404 \leq y \leq 408$ **11.** About 313,152; about \$690.72 per thousand **13.** **(a)** $R(x) = 23x$; $P(x) = .000006x^3 - .07x^2 + 21x - 1200$ **(b)** About 76.54, which means that 77 must be made to earn a profit (you can't make .54 of a rack). **(c)** 230 **(d)** 153; about \$395.86 **15.** $(7x^2)/3$ **17.** 4 **19.** $[(y - 5)(4y - 5)]/(6y)$ **21.** $(m - 1)^2/[3(m + 1)]$ **23.** $1/(6z)$ **25.** $64/(35q)$
27. $x = 3, y = 0$

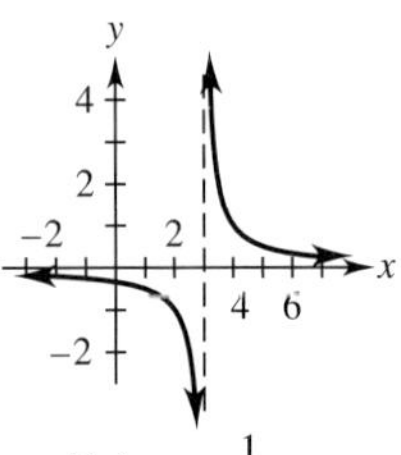

29. $x = 2, y = 0$

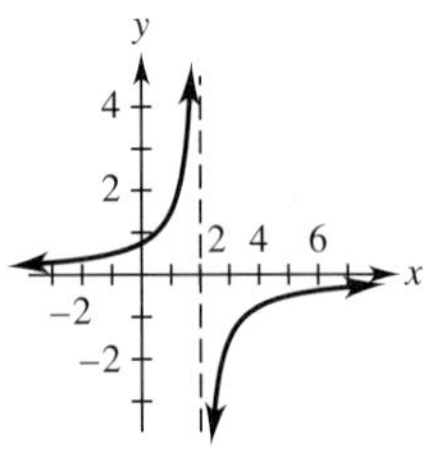

31. $x = -1/2, x = 3/2, y = 0$

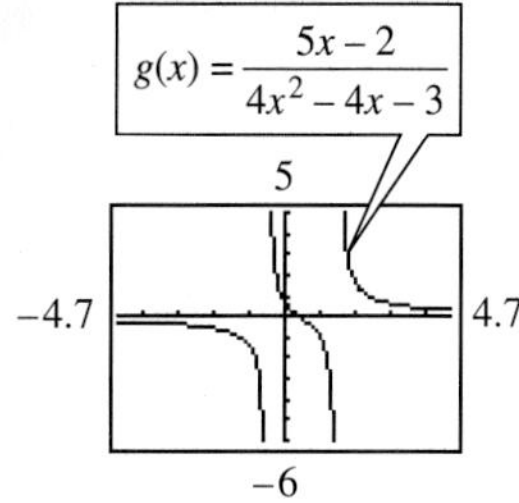

33. $x = -1/2, x = 1, y = 3/2$

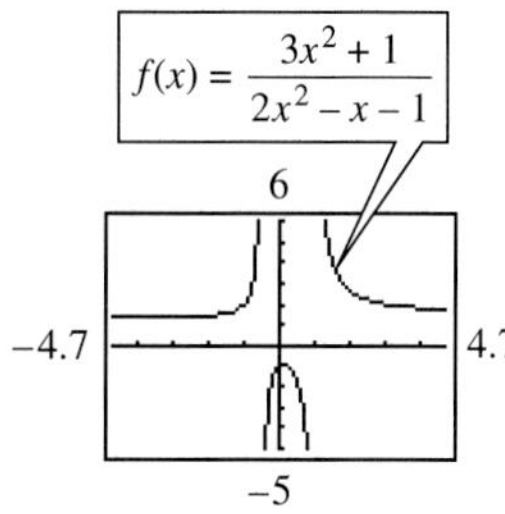

35. Overall: $-18.8 \le x \le 18.8$ and $-10 \le y \le 10$; near the origin: $-6 \le x \le 6$ and $-.5 \le y \le .5$ **37. (a)** About \$10.83 **(b)** About \$4.64 **(c)** About \$3.61 **(d)** About \$2.71
(e)

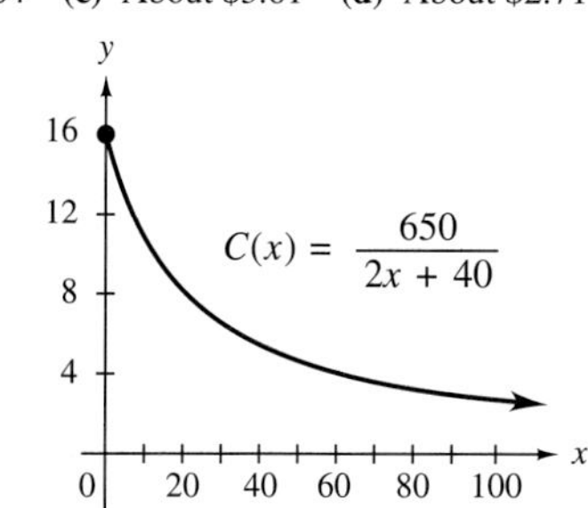

39. (a) (10, 50)

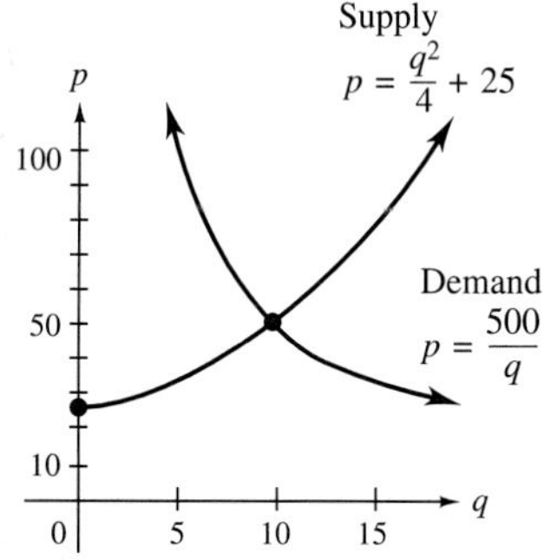

(b) $(10, \infty)$ **(c)** (0, 10)

Case 4 (page 180)

1. (2.9, 5.7, 8.5, 11.3, 14.1, 16.9)
3. (2.3, 1.1, 1.7, 2.4, 1.5, −2.7, −11.9, −27.8)

CHAPTER 5

Section 5.1 (page 188)

1. 1 **3.** 1/6 **5.** 1/32 **7.** −1/64 **9.** .001998 **11.** 9 **13.** 625/16 **17.** 7 **19.** 1.7 **21.** 9 **23.** 15.5 **25.** −16 **27.** 3/5 **29.** 27/64 **33.** 1/9 **35.** 5 **37.** $1/12^{1/2}$ **39.** 5^3 **41.** $3^{7/6}$ **43.** k^3 **45.** $1/(5^2x^{10})$ **47.** $z^6/(2^3y^6)$ **49.** $5^3 \cdot 3^4/m^{14}$ **51.** $5^{9/4}k^{13/4}$ **53.** $6 + 2z$ **55.** (b) **57.** (d) **59.** (a) **61.** (e) **65.** 5 **67.** −2 **69.** 9 **71.** $\sqrt{77}$ **73.** 7 **79. (a)** 2.130668582 **(b)** 2.130668582 **81.** 73.8 inches **83. (a)** −60.9° **(b)** −64.4° **85.** −63°; −47°; The expression in Exercise 84 provides a better model.

Section 5.2 (page 195)

1. Quadratic **3.** Exponential **5. (a)** The graph lies entirely above the x-axis and falls from left to right. It falls relatively steeply until it reaches the y-intercept 1 and then falls slowly, with the positive x-axis as a horizontal asymptote. **(b)** (0, 1), (1, .8) **7. (a)** The graph lies entirely above the x-axis and rises from left to right. The negative x-axis is a horizontal asymptote. The graph rises slowly until it reaches the y-intercept 1 and then rises quite steeply.
(b) (0, 1), $(1, 5^{.4})$

9.

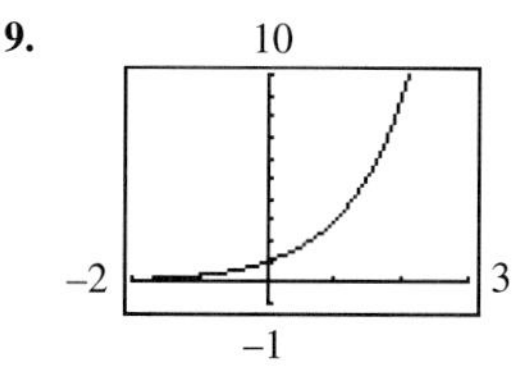

11.

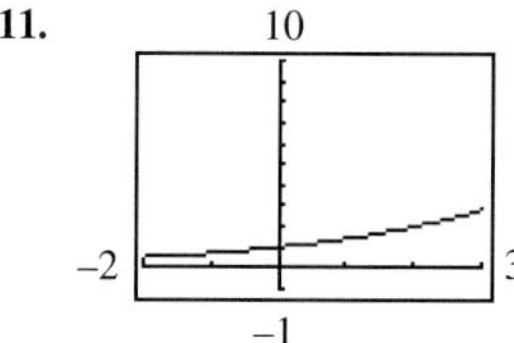

13.

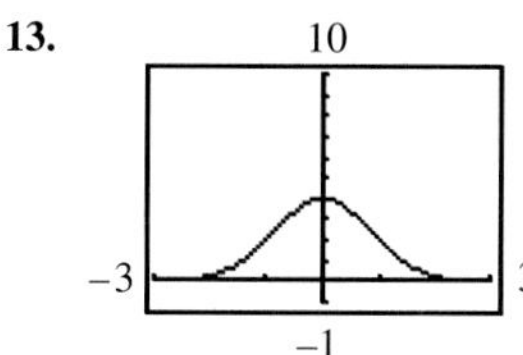

15.

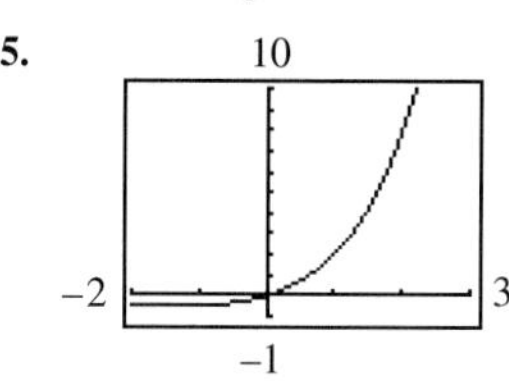

17. 2.3 **19.** .75 **21.** .31 **23. (a)** $a > 1$ **(b)** Domain: $(-\infty, \infty)$; range: $(0, \infty)$
(c)

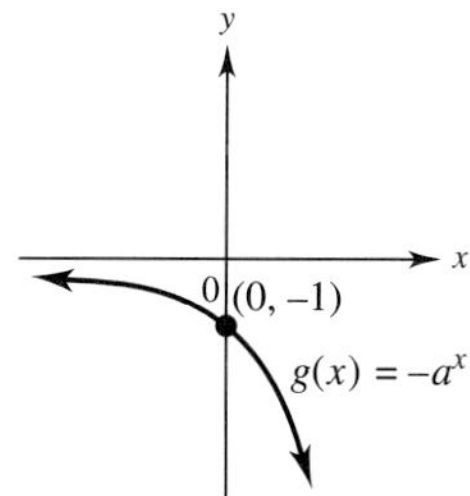

(d) Domain: $(-\infty, \infty)$; range: $(-\infty, 0)$
(e)

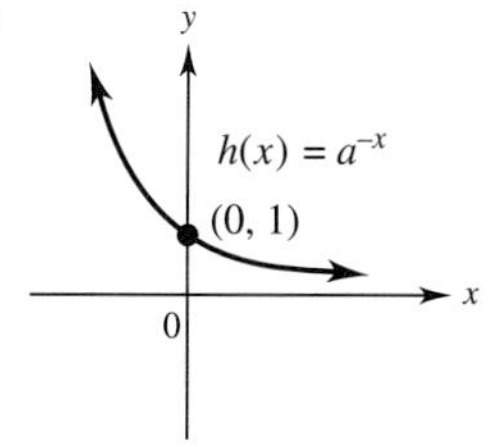

(f) Domain: $(-\infty, \infty)$; range: $(0, \infty)$

25. **(a)–(c)**

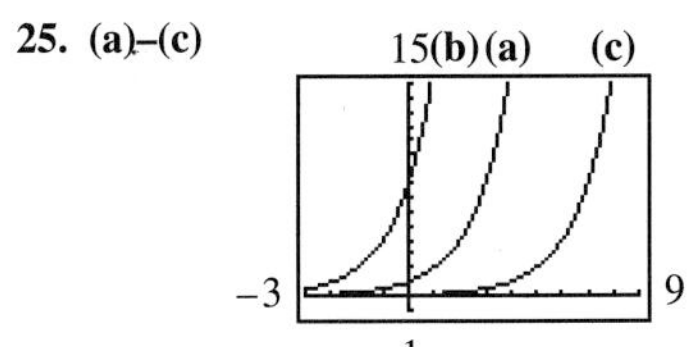

29. $f(x) = 2^x$ **31.** 2 **33.** 3 **35.** 1.5 **37.** 1 **39.** 1/4 **41.** 1/9 **43.** 4, −4 **45.** 2 **47.** 1.28 **49.** 4.17 **55.** **(a)** 4.2 billion **(b)** About 6.24 billion; about 13.74 billion **(c)** In 2056 **57.** $19,420.26
59. **(a)**

(b) 100 **(c)** About $1,400,000 **(d)** Total sales approach $2,500,000. **61.** **(a)** About 520 **(b)** About 1559 **(c)** About 32.4 days **63.** $y = 78.51(1.115)^x$

Section 5.3 (page 201)

1. **(a)** 14,700 **(b)** About 22,400 **(c)** About 34,100 **3.** **(a)** 10 g **(b)** About 12.2 g **(c)** About 18.2 g **(d)** About 73.9 g **5.** **(a)** 100,000 units **(b)** About 83,527 units and 58,275 units **(c)** No. The graph lies entirely above the x-axis and falls from left to right. It falls very rapidly until it reaches the y-intercept at 100,000. Then it falls more slowly until the positive x-axis is an asymptote. **7.** A new dose should be given at 8 hr. **9.** About 375 billion dollars **11.** 11.6 lb per square inch **13.** 1999 **15.** **(a)** 12 **(b)** About 20 **(c)** About 27 **(d)** 27 **17.** **(a)** About 6 **(b)** About 23 **(c)** 25 **(d)** On the 5th day **19.** **(a)** 1000 **(b)** About 1882 **21.** **(a)** 11% **(b)** 45.2% **(c)** 61.0% **(d)** 74.8% **(e)** 77.8% **(f)** 79.5% **(g)** No; $y = 80$ is a horizontal asymptote. **23.** **(a)** 446 (actual 383) billion **(b)** 1227 (actual 1000) billion **(c)** 4075 (actual 4077) billion **25.** **(a)** 77 **(b)** 72; 62 **(c)** Not much; the average score is about 4.

Section 5.4 (page 212)

1. a^y **3.** It is missing the value that equals b^y. If that value is x, then it should read $y = \log_b x$. **5.** $10^5 = 100,000$ **7.** $3^4 = 81$ **9.** $\log 75 = 1.8751$ **11.** $\log_3(1/9) = -2$ **13.** 2 **15.** 2 **17.** 3 **19.** −2 **21.** 1/2 **23.** 3.78 **25.** 1.672 **27.** −1.047 **31.** log 16 **33.** ln 5 **35.** $\log\left(\frac{u^2w^3}{v^6}\right)$ **37.** $\ln\left(\frac{(x+1)^2}{x+2}\right)$ **39.** $\log 5 + 2\log x + 3\log y$ **41.** $\ln 3 + \ln x - \ln 5 - \ln y$ **43.** $2u + 5v$ **45.** $3u - 2v$ **47.** 3.5145 **49.** 2.4851 **51.** There are many correct answers, including $b = 1$, $c = 2$. **53.** 1/5 **55.** 3/2 **57.** 16 **59.** 8/5 **61.** 1/3 **63.** 10 **65.** 5.2378 **67.** 5
71.

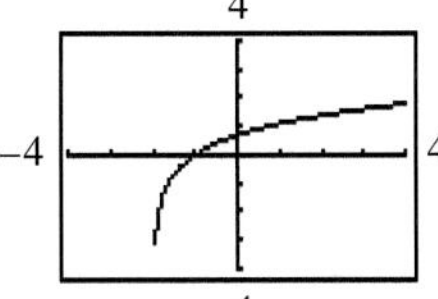

73.

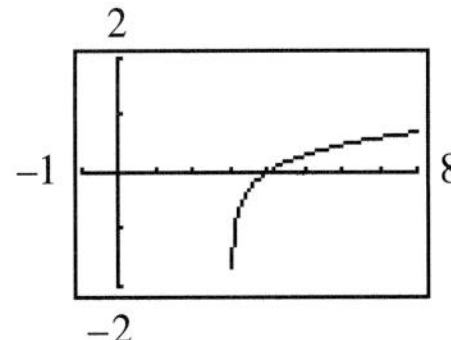

75. About 4.316 **77.** $\ln 2.75 = 1.0116009$ and $e^{1.0116009} = 2.75$

81. **(a)** About 8 **(b)** About 12 **83.** **(a)** The percent of change in rents increased rapidly from 1992 to 1993, leveled off to a slow increase from 1993 to 1994, and then increased rapidly again from 1994 to 1996. From 1996 to 1999 (estimated) the percent of increase slowed and became constant at about 7%. **(b)** $f(92) = -3.4$; $f(99) = 7.1$; $f(92) = -3.4$ agrees closely with the y-value on the graph of about −3; $f(99) = 7.1$ is also reasonably close to the y-value on the graph of about 7.5.

Section 5.5 (page 218)

1. 1.465 **3.** 2.710 **5.** −1.825 **7.** .805 **9.** −.123 **11.** ± 2.141 **13.** 1.386 **15.** $\frac{\log d + 3}{4}$ **17.** $\frac{\ln b + 1}{2}$ **19.** 5 **21.** No solution **23.** 11 **25.** 3 **27.** No solution **29.** −2, 2 **31.** 1, 10 **33.** $\frac{4+b}{4}$ **35.** $\frac{10^{2-b} - 5}{6}$ **39.** **(a)** 25 g **(b)** About 4.95 yr **41.** About 3606 years old **43.** **(a)** 3 **(b)** 5 **(c)** 7 **(d)** k **45.** **(a)** 21 **(b)** 70 **(c)** 120 **(d)** 140 **47.** **(a)** 27.5% **(b)** $130.14 **49.** **(a)** About 527 **(b)** About 3466 **(c)** About 6020 **(d)** About 1783 **(e)** $r \approx .8187$ **51.** **(a)** 77% **(b)** In 1989 **53.** **(a)** The exponential curve

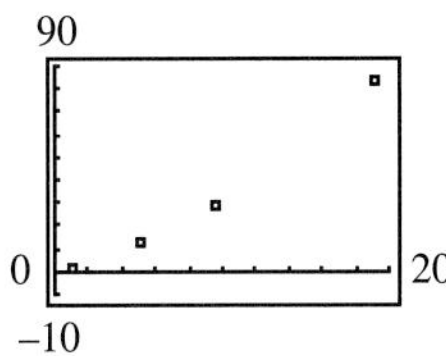

(b) The data appear to be linear.

PLANET	ln D	ln P
Earth	0	0
Jupiter	1.65	2.48
Saturn	2.26	3.38
Uranus	2.95	4.43

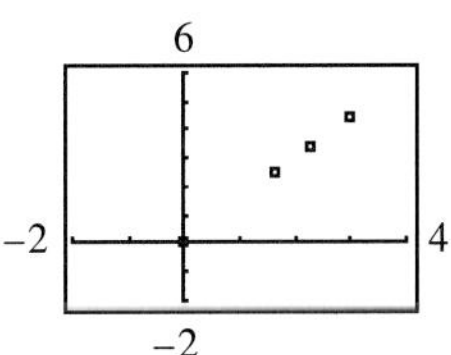

(c) $y = 1.5x$ or $\ln P = 1.5 \ln D$ **(d)** 248.2 years, which is close to the true value **55.** 590; 589

Chapter 5 Review Exercises (page 221)

1. $5^{7/3}$ **3.** $2^{19/6} \cdot p^{31/6}$ **5.** $\frac{n\sqrt{30m}}{6m}$ **7.** (c) **9.** (d) **11.** −1
13.

15.

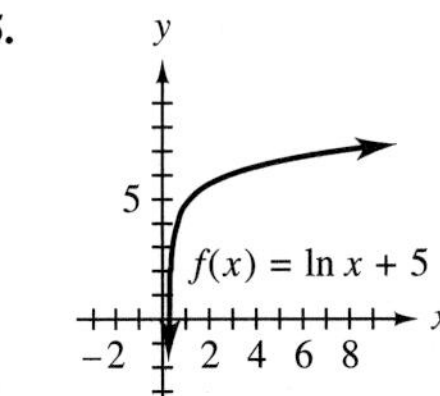

17. **(a)** 207 **(b)** 235 **(c)** 249
(d)

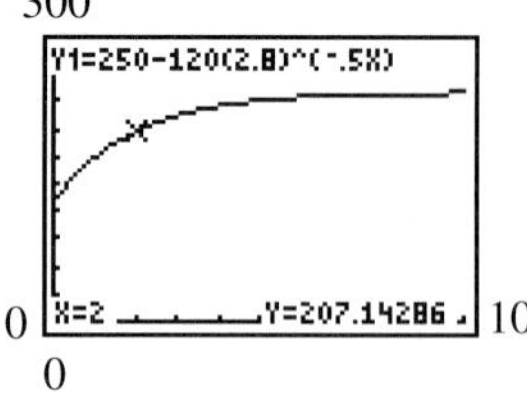

When $t = x = 2$, $y = p(t) \approx 207$.

19. log 47 = 1.6721 **21.** ln 39 = 3.6636 **23.** $10^3 = 1000$ **25.** $e^{4.5581} = 95.4$ **27.** 3 **29.** 7.4 **31.** 4/3 **33.** $\log 20k^4$ **35.** $\log\left(\frac{b^2}{c^3}\right)$ **37.** 1.416 **39.** −2.807 **41.** −3.305 **43.** .747 **45.** 28.463 **47.** 8 **49.** 6 **51.** 2 **53.** 3 **55.** **(a)** $15 million **(b)** $15.6 million **(c)** $16.4 million **57.** **(a)** 10 g **(b)** About 140 days **(c)** About 243 days **59.** 81.25°C **61.** About 20 min

Case 5 (page 224)

1. 23.6; 47.7; 58.4; the estimates are a bit low.

CHAPTER 6

Section 6.1 (page 230)

1. Time and interest rate **3.** $231.00 **5.** $286.75 **7.** $119.15 **9.** $241.56 **11.** $304.38 **13.** $3654.10 **17.** $46,265.06 **19.** $28,026.37 **21.** $8898.75 **23.** $48,140.65 **25.** 10.7% **27.** 11.8% **29.** $27,894.30 **31.** 6.8% **33.** $34,438.29 **35.** $6550.92 **37.** 11.4% **39.** $13,683.48; yes **41.** (c)

Section 6.2 (page 238)

3. $1593.85 **5.** $1515.80 **7.** $13,213.16 **9.** $10,466.35 **11.** $2307.95 **13.** $1968.48 **15.** $26,545.91 **17.** $45,552.97 **21.** 4.04% **23.** 8.16% **25.** 12.36% **27.** $8954.58 **29.** $3255.55 **31.** $11,572.58 **33.** $1000 now **35.** $13,693.34 **37.** $7743.93 **39.** $142,886.40 **41.** $123,506.50 **43.** 4.91, 5.20, 5.34, 5.56, 5.63 **45.** $8763.47 **47.** $30,611.30 **49.** About $1.946 million **51.** $11,940.52 **53.** About 12 yr **55.** About 18 yr **57.** 10.00% **59.** (a)

Section 6.3 (page 248)

1. 135 **3.** 6 **5.** 2315.25 **7.** 15 **9.** 6.24 **11.** 594.048 **13.** 15.91713 **15.** 21.82453 **17.** 22.01900 **21.** $4625.30 **23.** $327,711.81 **25.** $112,887.43 **27.** $1,391,304.39 **29.** $7118.38 **31.** $447,053.44 **33.** $36,752.01 **35.** $137,579.79 **37.** $3750.91 **39.** $236.61 **41.** $775.08 **43.** $4462.94 **45.** $148.02 **47.** $79,679.68 **49.** $66,988.91 **51.** $130,159.72 **53.** $284,527.35 **55.** $1349.48 **57.** 6.5% **59.** **(a)** 7 yr **(b)** 5 yr **61.** **(a)** $120 **(b)** $681.83 except the last payment of $681.80

(c)

Payment Number	*Amount of Deposit*	*Interest Earned*	*Total*
1	$681.83	$ 0.00	$ 681.83
2	681.83	54.55	1418.21
3	681.83	113.46	2213.50
4	681.83	177.08	3072.41
5	681.80	245.79	4000.00

Section 6.4 (page 254)

1. (c) **3.** 9.71225 **5.** 12.65930 **7.** 14.71787 **11.** $8415.93 **13.** $9420.83 **15.** $210,236.40 **17.** $103,796.58 **21.** $1603.01 **23.** $3109.71 **25.** $12.43 **27.** $681.02 **29.** $916.07 **31.** $86.24 **33.** $13.02 **35.** $48,677.34 **37.** **(a)** $158 **(b)** $1584 **39.** $573,496.06 **41.** About $77,790

The computer program, "Explorations in Finite Mathematics," was used for the following amortization schedules. Answers found using other computer programs or calculators may differ slightly.

43.

Payment Number	*Amount of Payment*	*Interest for Period*	*Portion to Principal*	*Principal at End of Period*
0	—	—	—	$72,000.00
1	$9247.24	$2160.00	$7087.24	64,912.76
2	9247.24	1947.38	7299.85	57,612.91
3	9247.24	1728.39	7518.85	50,094.06
4	9247.24	1502.82	7744.42	42,349.64

45.

Payment Number	*Amount of Payment*	*Interest for Period*	*Portion to Principal*	*Principal at End of Period*
0	—	—	—	$20,000.00
1	$2404.83	$700.00	$1704.83	18,295.17
2	2404.83	640.33	1764.50	16,530.68
3	2404.83	578.57	1826.25	14,704.42
4	2404.83	514.65	1890.17	12,814.25

47. $280.46; $32,310.40 **49.** **(a)** $2349.51; $197,911.80 **(b)** $2097.30; $278,352 **(c)** $1965.82; $364,746 **(d)** After 170 payments **51.** **(a)** $1352.45 **(b)** $156,428.83 **(c)** $14,216.35 **(d)** 20.5 years (246 payments) **53.** $432.53

Section 6.5 (page 257)

1. $45,401.41 **3.** $350.26 **5.** $5958.68 **7.** $2036.46 **9.** $8258.80 **11.** $47,650.97; $14,900.97 **13.** $16,876.98 **15.** $23,243.61 **17.** $32,854.98 **19.** $8362.60 **21.** $1228.20 **23.** $9843.39 **25.** $6943.65 **27.** $26,850.21

29.

Payment Number	Amount of Payment	Interest for Period	Portion to Principal	Principal at End of Period
0	—	—	—	$8500.00
1	$1416.18	$340.00	$1076.18	7423.82
2	1416.18	296.95	1119.23	6304.59
3	1416.18	252.18	1164.00	5140.59
4	1416.18	205.62	1210.56	3930.03
5	1416.18	157.20	1258.98	2671.05
6	1416.18	106.84	1309.34	1361.71
7	1416.18	54.47	1361.71	0

31. 5.1% **33.** $8017.02 **35.** $2572.38 **37.** $89,659.63; $14,659.63 **39.** $6659.79 **41.** $4587.64 **43.** $212,026

Chapter 6 Review Exercises (page 260)

1. $426.88 **3.** $62.91 **7.** $78,717.19 **9.** $739.09 **13.** $70,538.38; $12,729.04 **15.** $5282.19; $604.96 **17.** $12,857.07 **19.** $1923.09 **21.** 4, 2, 1, 1/2 **23.** −32 **25.** 5500 **29.** $137,925.91 **31.** $25,396.38 **35.** $2619.29 **37.** $916.12 **39.** $31,921.91 **41.** $14,222.42 **43.** $3628.00 **45.** $546.93 **47.** $896.06 **49.** $2696.12 **51.** $10,550.54 **53.** 8.21% **55.** $5596.62 **57.** $24,818.76; $2418.76 **59.** $3560.61 **61.** **(a)** $571.28 **(b)** $532.50 **(c)** Method 1: $56,324.44; method 2: $56,325.43 **(d)** $7100 **(e)** Method 1: $72,575.56; method 2: $72,574.57 **63.** $64,826.57

Case 6 (page 264)

1.

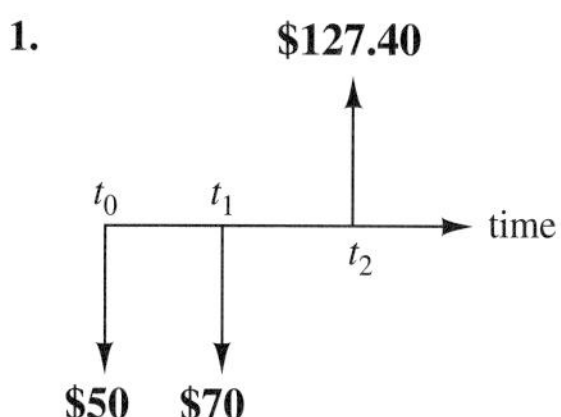

$50(1 + i)^2 + 70(1 + i) - 127.40 = 0$; 4.3%

3. **(a)**

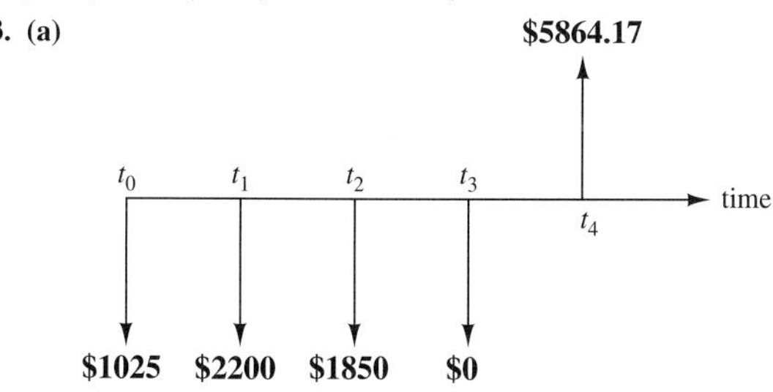

(b) 5.2%

5. **(a)**

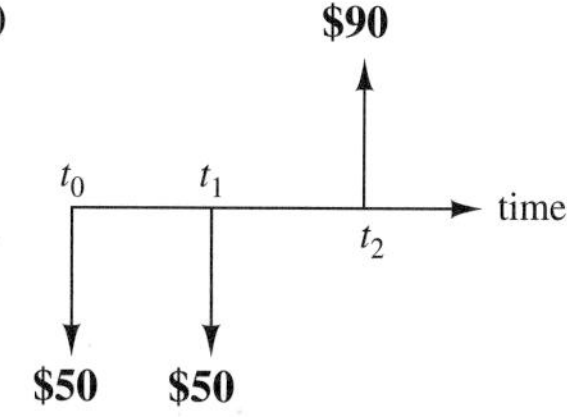

$50(1 + i)^2 + 50(1 + i) - 90 = 0$; −.068, −2.932 **(b)** −.068 is reasonable, −2.932 is not.

CHAPTER 7

Section 7.1 (page 276)

1. Yes **3.** (11/5, −7/5) **5.** (28, 22) **7.** (2, −1) **9.** No solution **11.** $(4y + 1, y)$ for any real number y **13.** No solution **15.** (a) **17.** (5, 10) **19.** (−5, −3) **21.** Dependent **23.** Inconsistent **25.** Independent **27.** (2, 1, 4) **29.** (−1, 4, 2) **31.** No solution **33.** (2, 0, 1) **35.** $((-7 - 2z)/5, (11z + 21)/5, z)$ for any real number z **37.** (1, 2) **39.** **(a)** $y = x + 1$ **(b)** $y = 3x + 4$ **(c)** (−3/2, −1/2) **43.** $W_1 = \dfrac{300}{1 + \sqrt{3}} = 110$ pounds; $W_2 = \dfrac{300 - W_1}{\sqrt{2}} = 134$ pounds **45.** Eastward: 7 hours; difference in time zones: 6 hours **47.** $27 **49.** 5 model 201, 8 model 301 **51.** $3000 at 8%, $6000 at 9%, $1000 at 5% **53.** 5 bags of brand A, 2 bags of brand B, 3 bags of brand C **55.** **(a)** 12; 5, 6, 7, . . . , 46 **(b)** The solution with 1 knife, 34 forks, and 5 spoons

Section 7.2 (page 284)

1. $\left[\begin{array}{ccc|c} 2 & 1 & 1 & 3 \\ 3 & -4 & 2 & -5 \\ 1 & 1 & 1 & 2 \end{array}\right]$ **3.** $\begin{aligned} 2x + 3y + 8z &= 20 \\ x + 4y + 6z &= 12 \\ 3y + 5z &= 10 \end{aligned}$

5. $\left[\begin{array}{ccc|c} 1 & 2 & 3 & -1 \\ 2 & 0 & 7 & -4 \\ 6 & 5 & 4 & 6 \end{array}\right]$ **7.** $\left[\begin{array}{cccc|c} -4 & -3 & 1 & -1 & 2 \\ 0 & -4 & 7 & -2 & 10 \\ 0 & -2 & 9 & 4 & 5 \end{array}\right]$

9. (−3, 4, 0) **11.** (1, 0, −1) **13.** $((-9z + 5)/23, (10z - 3)/23, z)$ for any real number z **15.** (−1, 23, 16) **17.** No solution **19.** (−7, 5) **21.** $(-3, z - 17, z)$ for any real number z **23.** (−1, 1, −3, −2) **25.** No solution **27.** Garcia 20 hr, Wong 15 hr **29.** 5 trucks, 2 vans, 3 station wagons **31.** **(a)** Let x_1 be the units purchased from the first supplier for Canoga Park, x_2 be the units from the first supplier for Wooster, x_3 be the units from the second supplier for Canoga Park, and x_4 be the units from the second supplier for Wooster. **(b)** $x_1 + x_2 = 75$; $x_3 + x_4 = 40$; $x_1 + x_3 = 40$; $x_2 + x_4 = 75$; $70x_1 + 90x_2 + 80x_3 + 120x_4 = 10{,}750$ **(c)** (40, 35, 0, 40) **33.** Three possibilities: 7 trucks, no vans, 2 station wagons; or 7 trucks, 1 van, 1 station wagon; or 7 trucks, 2 vans, no station wagons **35.** **(a)** $12,000 at 6%, $7000 at 7%, and $6000 at 10% **(b)** $10,000 at 6%, $15,000 at 7%, and $5000 at 10% **(c)** $20,000 at 6%, $10,000 at 7%, and $10,000 at 10% **37.** **(a)** $y = .01x^2 - .3x + 4.24$ **(b)** 15 platters; $1.99 **39.** **(a)** No **(b)** Yes; 150 acres for honeydews, 50 acres for onions, and 20 acres for lettuce **41.** **(a)** $C = .0378t^2 + .1t + 315$ **(b)** 2048

Section 7.3 (page 293)

1. 2×3; $\begin{bmatrix} -7 & 8 & -4 \\ 0 & -13 & -9 \end{bmatrix}$ **3.** 3×3; square matrix; $\begin{bmatrix} 3 & 0 & -11 \\ -1 & -\frac{1}{4} & 7 \\ -5 & 3 & -9 \end{bmatrix}$ **5.** 2×1; column matrix; $\begin{bmatrix} -7 \\ -11 \end{bmatrix}$

7. B is a 5×3 zero matrix. **9.** $\begin{bmatrix} 9 & 12 & 0 & 2 \\ 1 & -1 & 2 & -4 \end{bmatrix}$

11. $\begin{bmatrix} 5 & 13 & 0 \\ 3 & 1 & 8 \end{bmatrix}$ **13.** $\begin{bmatrix} 3 & -7 & 7 \\ 4 & 4 & -8 \end{bmatrix}$ **15.** $\begin{bmatrix} -4 & 8 \\ 0 & 6 \end{bmatrix}$

17. $\begin{bmatrix} 24 & -8 \\ -16 & 0 \end{bmatrix}$ **19.** $\begin{bmatrix} -22 & -6 \\ 20 & -12 \end{bmatrix}$ **21.** $\begin{bmatrix} 4 & -\frac{7}{2} \\ 4 & \frac{21}{2} \end{bmatrix}$

23. $X + T = \begin{bmatrix} x & y \\ z & w \end{bmatrix} + \begin{bmatrix} r & s \\ t & u \end{bmatrix} = \begin{bmatrix} x+r & y+s \\ z+t & w+u \end{bmatrix}$ (a 2×2 matrix)

25. $X + (T + P) = \begin{bmatrix} x + (r+m) & y + (s+n) \\ z + (t+p) & w + (u+q) \end{bmatrix} =$

$\begin{bmatrix} (x+r)+m & (y+s)+n \\ (z+t)+p & (w+u)+q \end{bmatrix} = (X+T)+P$

27. $P + 0 = \begin{bmatrix} m+0 & n+0 \\ p+0 & q+0 \end{bmatrix} = \begin{bmatrix} m & n \\ p & q \end{bmatrix} = P$

29. $\begin{bmatrix} 18 & 2.7 \\ 10 & 1.5 \\ 8 & 1.0 \\ 10 & 2.0 \\ 10 & 1.7 \end{bmatrix}$; $\begin{bmatrix} 18 & 10 & 8 & 10 & 10 \\ 2.7 & 1.5 & 1.0 & 2.0 & 1.7 \end{bmatrix}$

31. **(a)** $\begin{bmatrix} 5.6 & 6.4 & 6.9 & 7.6 & 6.1 \\ 144 & 138 & 149 & 152 & 146 \end{bmatrix}$

(b) $\begin{bmatrix} 10.2 & 11.4 & 11.4 & 12.7 & 10.8 \\ 196 & 196 & 225 & 250 & 230 \end{bmatrix}$

(c) $\begin{bmatrix} 4.6 & 5.0 & 4.5 & 5.1 & 4.7 \\ 52 & 58 & 76 & 98 & 84 \end{bmatrix}$

(d) $\begin{bmatrix} 12.0 & 12.9 & 13.7 & 14.5 & 12.8 \\ 221 & 218 & 254 & 283 & 250 \end{bmatrix}$

33. **(a)** Chicago: $\begin{bmatrix} 4.05 & 7.01 \\ 3.27 & 3.51 \end{bmatrix}$; Seattle: $\begin{bmatrix} 4.40 & 6.90 \\ 3.54 & 3.76 \end{bmatrix}$

(b) $\begin{bmatrix} 4.24 & 6.95 \\ 3.42 & 3.64 \end{bmatrix}$ **(c)** $\begin{bmatrix} 4.42 & 7.43 \\ 3.38 & 3.62 \end{bmatrix}$ **(d)** $\begin{bmatrix} 4.41 & 7.17 \\ 3.46 & 3.69 \end{bmatrix}$

Section 7.4 (page 304)

1. 2×2; 2×2 **3.** 3×2; BA does not exist. **5.** AB does not exist; 3×2 **7.** Columns; rows **9.** $\begin{bmatrix} 13 \\ 25 \end{bmatrix}$ **11.** $\begin{bmatrix} -2 & 10 \\ 0 & 8 \end{bmatrix}$

13. $\begin{bmatrix} -4 & 1 \\ 2 & -3 \end{bmatrix}$ **15.** $\begin{bmatrix} 3 & -5 & 7 \\ -2 & 1 & 6 \\ 0 & -3 & 4 \end{bmatrix}$ **17.** $\begin{bmatrix} 16 & 11 \\ 37 & 32 \\ 58 & 53 \end{bmatrix}$

19. $AB = \begin{bmatrix} -30 & -45 \\ 20 & 30 \end{bmatrix}$, but $BA = \begin{bmatrix} 0 & 0 \\ 0 & 0 \end{bmatrix}$

21. $(A+B)(A-B) = \begin{bmatrix} -7 & -24 \\ -28 & -33 \end{bmatrix}$, but $A^2 - B^2 = \begin{bmatrix} -37 & -69 \\ -8 & -3 \end{bmatrix}$

23. $(PX)T =$

$\begin{bmatrix} (mx+nz)r + (my+nw)t & (mx+nz)s + (my+nw)u \\ (px+qz)r + (py+qw)t & (px+qz)s + (py+qw)u \end{bmatrix}$

$P(XT)$ is the same so $(PX)T = P(XT)$.

25. $k(X+T) = k\begin{bmatrix} x+r & y+s \\ z+t & w+u \end{bmatrix} = \begin{bmatrix} k(x+r) & k(y+s) \\ k(z+t) & k(w+u) \end{bmatrix}$

$= \begin{bmatrix} kx+kr & ky+ks \\ kz+kt & kw+ku \end{bmatrix} = \begin{bmatrix} kx & ky \\ kz & kw \end{bmatrix} + \begin{bmatrix} kr & ks \\ kt & ku \end{bmatrix} = kX + kT$

27. No **29.** Yes **31.** No **33.** $\begin{bmatrix} 2 & -3 \\ -1 & 2 \end{bmatrix}$

35. No inverse **37.** $\begin{bmatrix} 2 & -3 \\ -\frac{1}{2} & 1 \end{bmatrix}$ **39.** $\begin{bmatrix} 3 & 3 & -1 \\ -2 & -2 & 1 \\ -4 & -5 & 2 \end{bmatrix}$

41. $\begin{bmatrix} 2 & 1 & -1 \\ 8 & 2 & -5 \\ -11 & -3 & 7 \end{bmatrix}$ **43.** No inverse

45. $\begin{bmatrix} \frac{7}{4} & \frac{5}{2} & 3 \\ -\frac{1}{4} & -\frac{1}{2} & 0 \\ -\frac{1}{4} & -\frac{1}{2} & -1 \end{bmatrix}$ **47.** $\begin{bmatrix} \frac{1}{2} & \frac{1}{2} & -\frac{1}{4} & \frac{1}{2} \\ -1 & 4 & -\frac{1}{2} & -2 \\ -\frac{1}{2} & \frac{5}{2} & -\frac{1}{4} & -\frac{3}{2} \\ \frac{1}{2} & -\frac{1}{2} & \frac{1}{4} & \frac{1}{2} \end{bmatrix}$

49. **(a)** $\begin{bmatrix} 900 & 1500 & 1150 \\ 600 & 950 & 800 \\ 750 & 900 & 825 \end{bmatrix}$ **(b)** $[1.50 \quad .90 \quad .60]$

(c) $[1.50 \quad .90 \quad .60]\begin{bmatrix} 900 & 1500 & 1150 \\ 600 & 950 & 800 \\ 750 & 900 & 825 \end{bmatrix} = [2340 \quad 3645 \quad 2940]$

(d) \$8925 **51.** **(a)**

	CC	MM	AD
S	.5	.4	.3
C	.2	.3	.3

(b)

	S	C
SD	3	3
MC	2	3
M	1	4

(c)

	CC	MM	AD
SD	2.1	2.1	1.8
MC	1.6	1.7	1.5
M	1.3	1.6	1.5

(d) \$1.60 **(e)** \$1200 in Managua

53. **(a)** $\begin{bmatrix} .027 & .009 \\ .030 & .007 \\ .015 & .009 \\ .013 & .011 \\ .019 & .011 \end{bmatrix}$; $\begin{bmatrix} 1596 & 218 & 199 & 425 & 214 \\ 1996 & 286 & 226 & 460 & 243 \\ 2440 & 365 & 252 & 484 & 266 \\ 2906 & 455 & 277 & 499 & 291 \end{bmatrix}$

(b)

	Births	Deaths
1960	62.208	24.710
1970	76.459	29.733
1980	91.956	35.033
1990	108.283	40.522

55. $X = \begin{bmatrix} 0 \\ \frac{3}{2} \end{bmatrix}$

Section 7.5 (page 314)

1. $\begin{bmatrix} 8 \\ 6 \end{bmatrix}$ **3.** $\begin{bmatrix} \frac{1}{2} & 1 \\ \frac{3}{2} & 1 \end{bmatrix}$ **5.** $\begin{bmatrix} 11 \\ -3 \\ 5 \end{bmatrix}$ **7.** $(-31, 24, -4)$

9. $(-31, -131, 181)$ **11.** $(15, 5, -1)$ **13.** $(-7, -34, -19, 7)$

15. $\begin{bmatrix} -6 \\ -14 \end{bmatrix}$ **17.** $\begin{bmatrix} \frac{32}{3} \\ \frac{25}{3} \end{bmatrix}$ **19.** $\begin{bmatrix} 6.43 \\ 26.12 \end{bmatrix}$ **21.** $\begin{bmatrix} 6.67 \\ 20 \\ 10 \end{bmatrix}$

23. Either 10 buffets, 5 chairs, no tables, or 11 buffets, 1 chair, 1 table

25. 2340 of the first species, 10,128 of the second species, 224 of the third species (rounded) **27.** About 1073 metric tons of wheat, about 1431 metric tons of oil **29.** Gas \$98 million, electric \$123 million **31. (a)** 7/4 bushels of yams, 15/8 pigs **(b)** 167.5 bushels of yams, 153.75 pigs **33.** Agriculture 4100/23, manufacturing 4080/23, transportation 3790/23

35. $\begin{bmatrix} 23 \\ 51 \end{bmatrix}, \begin{bmatrix} 13 \\ 30 \end{bmatrix}, \begin{bmatrix} 45 \\ 96 \end{bmatrix}, \begin{bmatrix} 69 \\ 156 \end{bmatrix}, \begin{bmatrix} 87 \\ 194 \end{bmatrix}, \begin{bmatrix} 23 \\ 51 \end{bmatrix}, \begin{bmatrix} 51 \\ 110 \end{bmatrix}, \begin{bmatrix} 45 \\ 102 \end{bmatrix}, \begin{bmatrix} 69 \\ 157 \end{bmatrix}$

37. (a) 3 **(b)** 3 **(c)** 5 **(d)** 3 **39. (a)** $B = \begin{bmatrix} 0 & 2 & 3 \\ 2 & 0 & 4 \\ 3 & 4 & 0 \end{bmatrix}$

(b) $B^2 = \begin{bmatrix} 13 & 12 & 8 \\ 12 & 20 & 6 \\ 8 & 6 & 25 \end{bmatrix}$ **(c)** 12 **(d)** 14

41. (a)

	Dogs	Rats	Cats	Mice
Dogs	0	1	1	1
Rats	0	0	0	1
Cats	0	1	0	1
Mice	0	0	0	0

$= C$

(b) $C^2 = \begin{bmatrix} 0 & 1 & 0 & 2 \\ 0 & 0 & 0 & 0 \\ 0 & 0 & 0 & 1 \\ 0 & 0 & 0 & 0 \end{bmatrix}$;

C^2 gives the number of food sources once removed from the feeder. Thus, since dogs eat rats and rats eat mice, mice are an indirect as well as a direct food source for dogs.

Chapter 7 Review Exercises (page 318)

1. $(-5, 7)$ **3.** $(0, -2)$ **5.** No solution; inconsistent system **7.** $(-35, 140, 22)$ **9.** 8000 standard, 6000 extra large **11.** \$7000 in the first; \$11,000 in the second **13.** 50 from source I, 150 from source II, 100 from source III **15.** $(0, 3, 3)$ **17.** No solution **19.** $(-79, 99, -8)$ **21.** 2×2; square **23.** 1×4; row **25.** 2×3 **27.** $\begin{bmatrix} 8 & 8 & 8 \\ 10 & 5 & 9 \\ 7 & 10 & 7 \\ 8 & 9 & 7 \end{bmatrix}$ **29.** $\begin{bmatrix} -2 & -3 & 2 \\ -2 & -4 & 0 \\ 0 & -1 & -2 \end{bmatrix}$

31. $\begin{bmatrix} 2 & 30 \\ -4 & -15 \\ 10 & 13 \end{bmatrix}$ **33.** Not possible

35. Next day $\begin{bmatrix} 2310 & -\frac{1}{4} \\ 1258 & -\frac{1}{4} \\ 5061 & \frac{1}{2} \\ 1812 & \frac{1}{2} \end{bmatrix}$; two-day total $\begin{bmatrix} 4842 & -\frac{1}{2} \\ 2722 & -\frac{1}{8} \\ 10{,}035 & -1 \\ 3566 & 1 \end{bmatrix}$

37. $\begin{bmatrix} 18 & 80 \\ -7 & -28 \\ 21 & 84 \end{bmatrix}$ **39.** $\begin{bmatrix} 13 & 43 \\ 17 & 46 \end{bmatrix}$ **41.** $\begin{bmatrix} 222 & 632 \\ -77 & -224 \\ 231 & 672 \end{bmatrix}$

43. (a) $\begin{bmatrix} \frac{1}{4} & \frac{1}{2} \\ \frac{1}{3} & \frac{1}{3} \end{bmatrix}$ **(b)** Cutting 34 hr; shaping 46 hr **45.** There are many correct answers, including $\begin{bmatrix} 1 & 2 \\ 3 & 4 \end{bmatrix}$.

47. $\begin{bmatrix} -\frac{1}{4} & \frac{1}{6} \\ 0 & \frac{1}{3} \end{bmatrix}$ **49.** No inverse **51.** $\begin{bmatrix} \frac{1}{4} & \frac{1}{2} & \frac{1}{2} \\ \frac{1}{4} & -\frac{1}{2} & \frac{1}{2} \\ \frac{1}{8} & -\frac{1}{4} & -\frac{1}{4} \end{bmatrix}$

53. No inverse **55.** $\begin{bmatrix} -\frac{2}{3} & -\frac{17}{3} & -\frac{14}{3} & -3 \\ \frac{1}{3} & \frac{1}{3} & \frac{1}{3} & 0 \\ -\frac{1}{3} & -\frac{10}{3} & -\frac{7}{3} & -2 \\ 0 & 2 & 1 & 1 \end{bmatrix}$

57. $\begin{bmatrix} -\frac{7}{19} & \frac{4}{19} \\ \frac{3}{19} & \frac{1}{19} \end{bmatrix}$ **59.** $\begin{bmatrix} 1 & 1 \\ -2 & -3 \end{bmatrix}$ **61.** No inverse **63.** $\begin{bmatrix} 18 \\ -7 \end{bmatrix}$

65. $\begin{bmatrix} -22 \\ -18 \\ 15 \end{bmatrix}$ **67.** $(2, 2)$ **69.** $(2, 1)$ **71.** $(-1, 0, 2)$

73. No inverse; no solution for the system **75.** 18 liters of the 8%; 12 liters of the 18% **77.** 30 liters of 40% solution, 10 liters of 60% solution **79.** 80 bowls, 120 plates **81.** \$12,750 at 8%, \$27,250 at 8 1/2%, \$10,000 at 11% **83.** $\begin{bmatrix} 218.09 \\ 318.27 \end{bmatrix}$ **85. (a)** $\begin{bmatrix} 1 & -\frac{1}{4} \\ -\frac{1}{2} & 1 \end{bmatrix}$

(b) $\begin{bmatrix} \frac{8}{7} & \frac{2}{7} \\ \frac{4}{7} & \frac{8}{7} \end{bmatrix}$ **(c)** $\begin{bmatrix} 2800 \\ 2800 \end{bmatrix}$ **87.** Agriculture \$140,909, manufacturing \$95,455 **89. (a)** $\begin{bmatrix} 54 \\ 32 \end{bmatrix}, \begin{bmatrix} 134 \\ 89 \end{bmatrix}, \begin{bmatrix} 172 \\ 113 \end{bmatrix}, \begin{bmatrix} 118 \\ 74 \end{bmatrix}, \begin{bmatrix} 208 \\ 131 \end{bmatrix}$

(b) $\begin{bmatrix} 2 & -3 \\ -\frac{1}{2} & 1 \end{bmatrix}$

Case 7 (page 323)

1. (a) $A = \begin{bmatrix} .245 & .102 & .051 \\ .099 & .291 & .279 \\ .433 & .372 & .011 \end{bmatrix}$; $D = \begin{bmatrix} 2.88 \\ 31.45 \\ 30.91 \end{bmatrix}$; $X = \begin{bmatrix} x_1 \\ x_2 \\ x_3 \end{bmatrix}$

(b) $I - A = \begin{bmatrix} .755 & -.102 & -.051 \\ -.099 & .709 & -.279 \\ -.433 & -.372 & .989 \end{bmatrix}$ **(d)** $\begin{bmatrix} 18.2 \\ 73.2 \\ 66.8 \end{bmatrix}$

\$18.2 billion of agriculture, \$73.2 billion of manufacturing, and \$66.8 billion of household would be required (rounded to three significant digits).

CHAPTER 8

Section 8.1 (page 331)

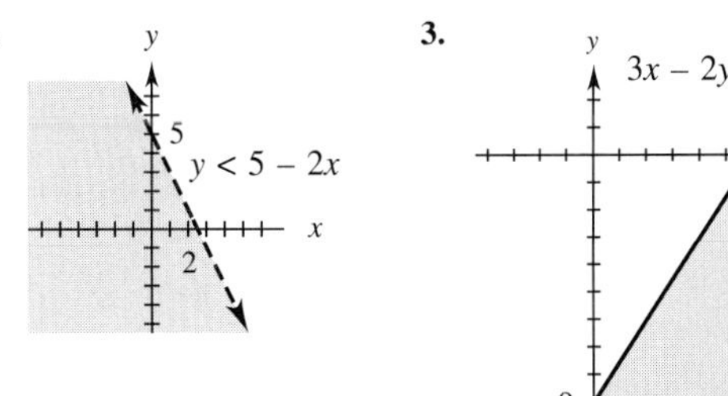

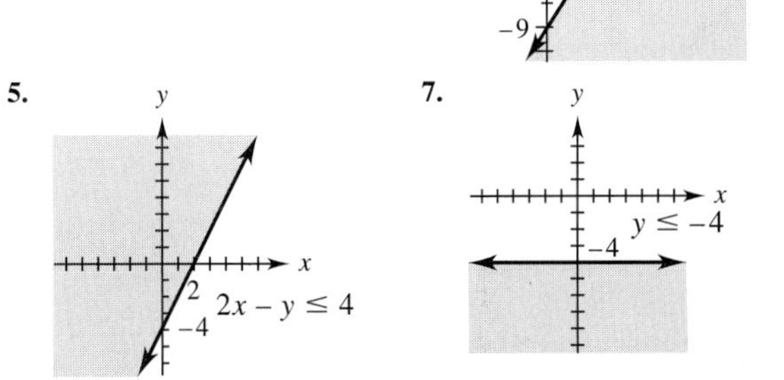

9.

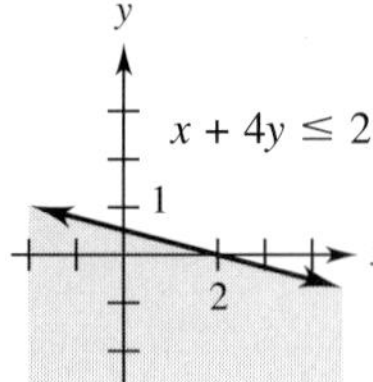

11.

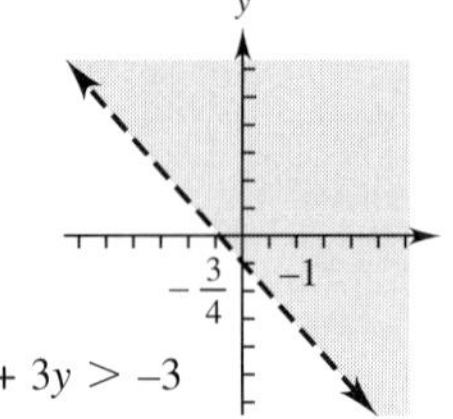

13.

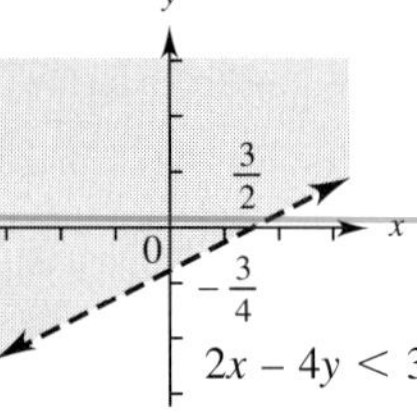

15.

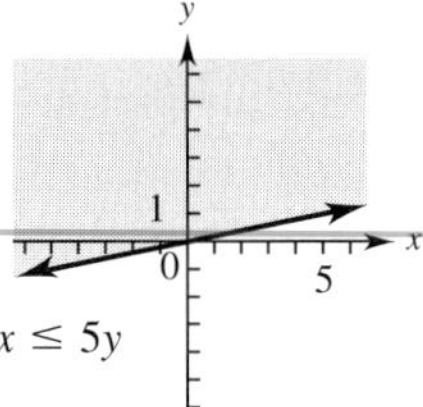

17.

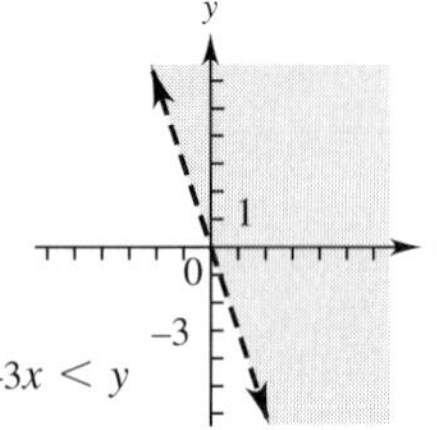

19.

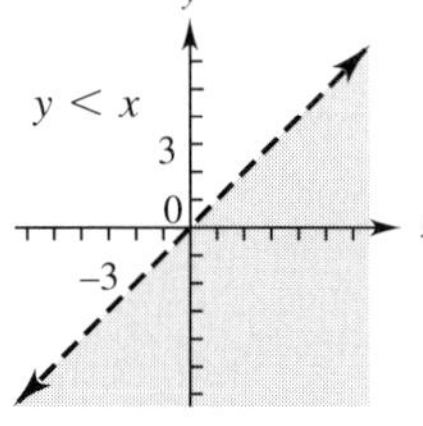

23.

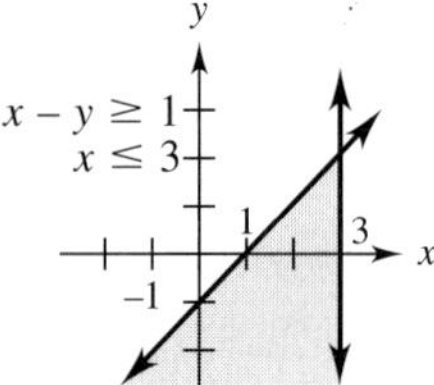

25.

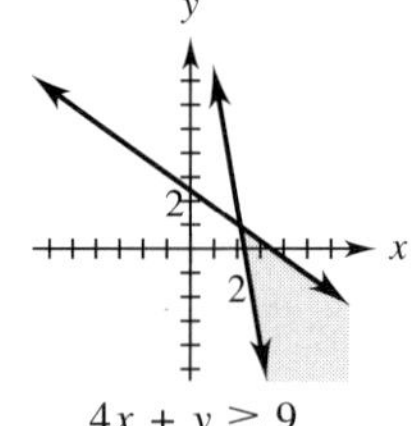

27.

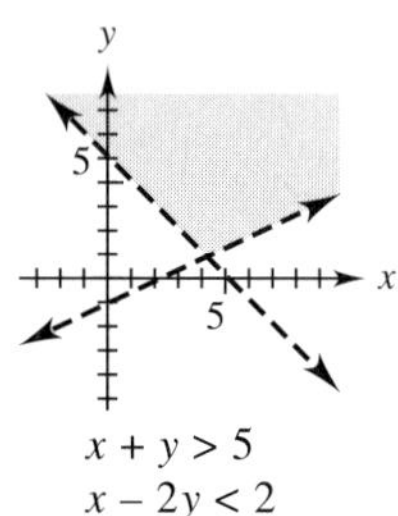

29.

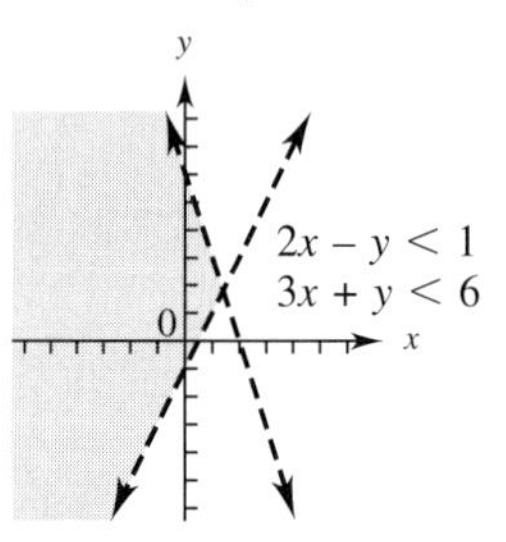

31.

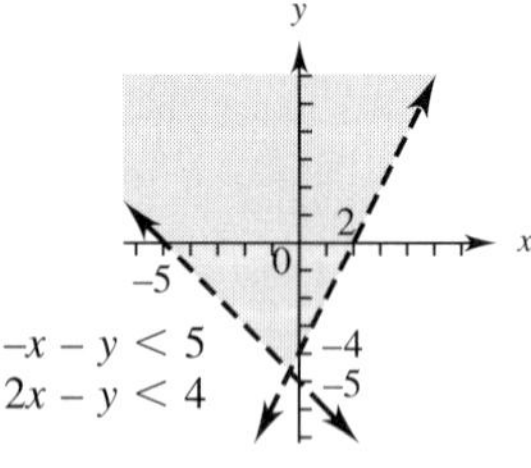

33.

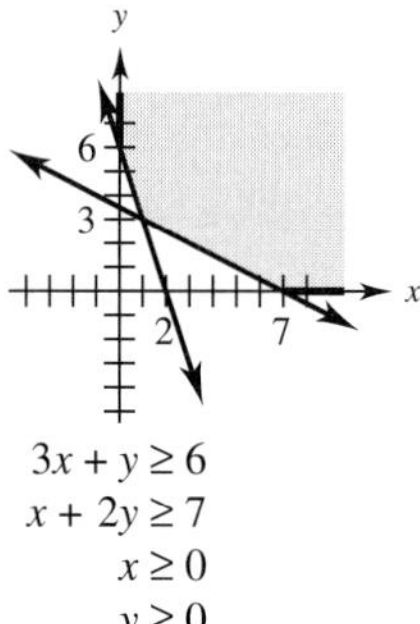

35.

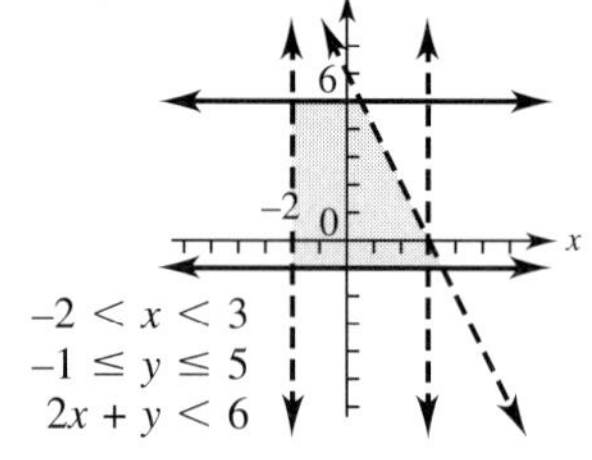

37. $2y - x \ge -5$
$y \le 3 + x$
$x \ge 0$
$y \ge 0$

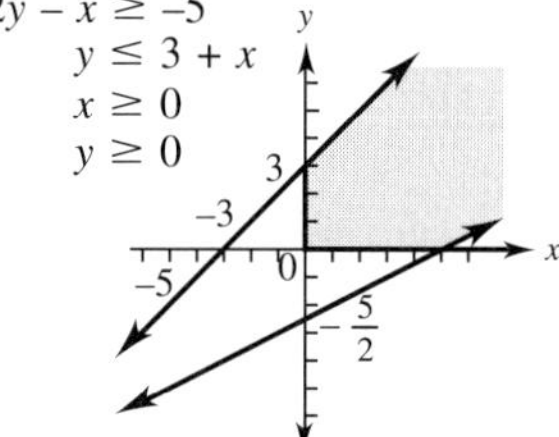

39. $3x + 4y > 12$
$2x - 3y < 6$
$0 \le y \le 2$
$x \ge 0$

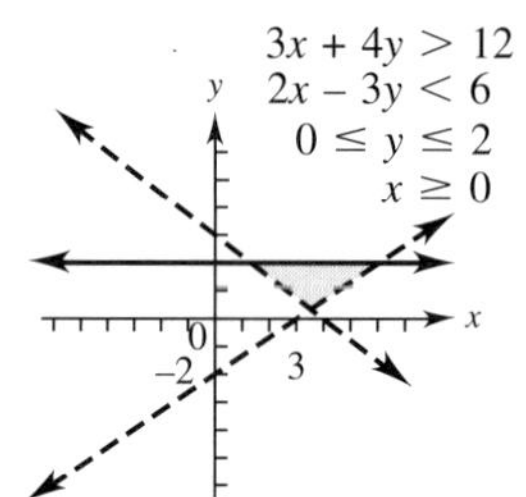

41. $2 < x < 7$
$-1 < y < 3$

43. (a)

	Number	*Hours Spinning*	*Hours Dyeing*	*Hours Weaving*
Shawls	x	1	1	1
Afghans	y	2	1	4
Maximum number of hours available		8	6	14

(b) $x + 2y \le 8$; $x + y \le 6$; $x + 4y \le 14$; $x \ge 0$; $y \ge 0$

(c)

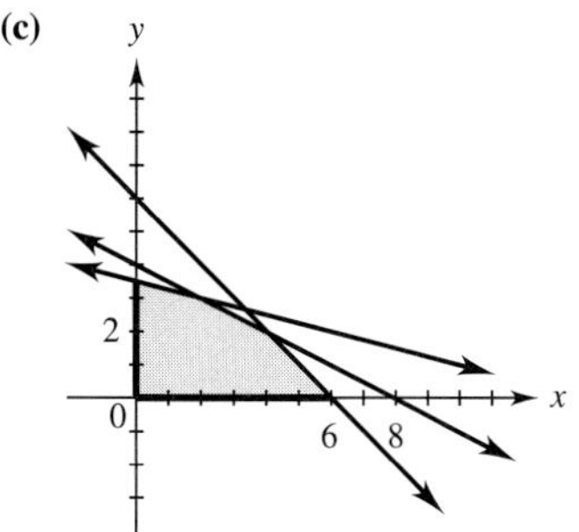

45. $x \geq 3000$; $y \geq 5000$; $x + y \leq 10{,}000$

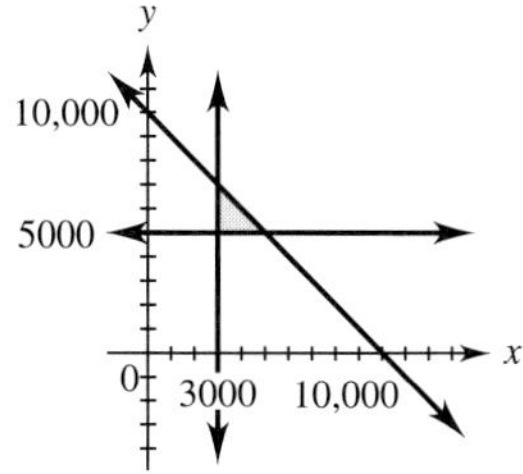

47. $x + y \geq 3.2$; $.5x + .3y \leq 1.8$; $.16x + .20y \leq .8$; $x \geq 0$; $y \geq 0$

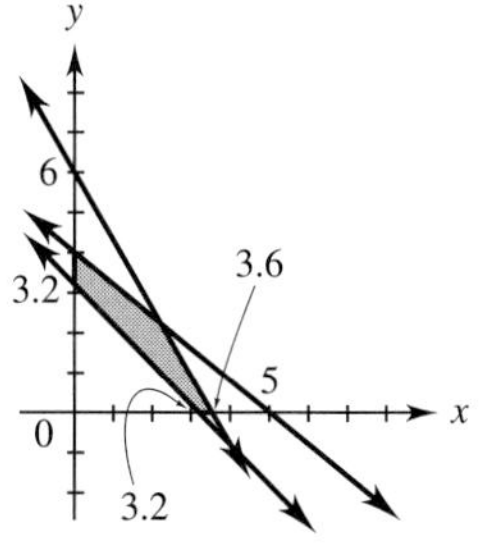

Section 8.2 (page 338)

1. Maximum of 65 at (5, 10); minimum of 8 at (1, 1) **3.** Maximum of 9 at (0, 12); minimum of 0 at (0, 0) **5. (a)** No maximum; minimum of 16 at (0, 8) **(b)** No maximum; minimum of 18 at (3, 4) **(c)** No maximum; minimum of 21 at (13/2, 2) **(d)** No maximum; minimum of 12 at (12, 0) **7.** Maximum of 42/5 at $x = 6/5$, $y = 6/5$ or (6/5, 6/5) **9.** Minimum of 13 at $x = 5$, $y = 3$ or (5, 3) **11.** Maximum of 235/4 at $x = 105/8$, $y = 25/8$ or (105/8, 25/8) **13.** No maximum; minimum of 9 at (1, 3/2) **15.** Maximum 22; no minimum **17. (a)** (18, 2) **(b)** (12/5, 39/5) **(c)** No maximum

Section 8.3 (page 344)

1. $6x + 4y \leq 90$, where x = number of canoes, y = number of rowboats. **3.** $150x + 750y \leq 8500$, where x = number of radio spots, y = number of TV ads. **5.** $x + y \geq 30$, where x = number of pounds of cashews, y = number of pounds of peanuts. **7.** Send 35 systems from Meadville to Superstore, 45 from Meadville to ValueHouse, 15 from Cambridge to ValueHouse, and none from Cambridge to Superstore for a minimum cost of $1015. **9. (a)** 6 units of policy A and 16 units of policy B for a minimum cost of $940 **(b)** 30 units of policy A and no units of policy B for a minimum cost of $750 **11.** 6.4 million gal of gasoline and 3.05 million gal of fuel oil for maximum revenue of $11,050,000 **13.** 800 Type 1 and 1600 Type 2 for maximum revenue of $272 **15.** 250,000 hectares to each crop for a maximum profit of $132,500,000 **17.** From warehouse I ship 60 boxes to San Jose and 300 boxes to Memphis. From warehouse II ship 290 boxes to San Jose and none to Memphis, for a minimum cost of $147.70. **19.** 8/7 units of Species I and 10/7 units of Species II will meet the requirements with a minimum expenditure of 6.57 units of energy; however, a predator probably can catch and digest only whole numbers of prey. **21.** 5 humanities, 12 science **23.** (b) **25.** (c)

Section 8.4 (page 357)

1. (a) 3 **(b)** x_3, x_4, x_5 **(c)**
$$\begin{aligned} 4x_1 + 2x_2 + x_3 &= 20 \\ 5x_1 + x_2 + x_4 &= 50 \\ 2x_1 + 3x_2 + x_5 &= 25 \end{aligned}$$

3. (a) 3 **(b)** x_4, x_5, x_6 **(c)**
$$\begin{aligned} 3x_1 - x_2 + 4x_3 + x_4 &= 95 \\ 7x_1 + 6x_2 + 8x_3 + x_5 &= 118 \\ 4x_1 + 5x_2 + 10x_3 + x_6 &= 220 \end{aligned}$$

5.
$$\begin{array}{cccccc|c} x_1 & x_2 & x_3 & x_4 & x_5 & z & \\ \hline 2 & 3 & 1 & 0 & 0 & 0 & 6 \\ 4 & 1 & 0 & 1 & 0 & 0 & 6 \\ 5 & 2 & 0 & 0 & 1 & 0 & 15 \\ \hline -5 & -1 & 0 & 0 & 0 & 1 & 0 \end{array}$$

7.
$$\begin{array}{ccccccc|c} x_1 & x_2 & x_3 & x_4 & x_5 & x_6 & z & \\ \hline 1 & 2 & 3 & 1 & 0 & 0 & 0 & 10 \\ 2 & 1 & 1 & 0 & 1 & 0 & 0 & 8 \\ 3 & 0 & 2 & 0 & 0 & 1 & 0 & 6 \\ \hline -1 & -5 & -10 & 0 & 0 & 0 & 1 & 0 \end{array}$$

9. 3 in row 2, column 1 **11.** 6 in row 1, column 1

13.
$$\begin{array}{cccccc|c} x_1 & x_2 & x_3 & x_4 & x_5 & z & \\ \hline -1 & 0 & 3 & 1 & -1 & 0 & 16 \\ 1 & 1 & \frac{1}{2} & 0 & \frac{1}{2} & 0 & 20 \\ \hline 2 & 0 & -\frac{1}{2} & 0 & \frac{3}{2} & 1 & 60 \end{array}$$

15.
$$\begin{array}{ccccccc|c} x_1 & x_2 & x_3 & x_4 & x_5 & x_6 & z & \\ \hline -\frac{1}{2} & \frac{1}{2} & 0 & 1 & -\frac{1}{2} & 0 & 0 & 10 \\ \frac{3}{2} & \frac{1}{2} & 1 & 0 & \frac{1}{2} & 0 & 0 & 50 \\ -\frac{7}{2} & \frac{1}{2} & 0 & 0 & -\frac{3}{2} & 1 & 0 & 50 \\ \hline 2 & 0 & 0 & 0 & 1 & 0 & 1 & 100 \end{array}$$

17. (a) Basic: x_3, x_5; nonbasic: x_1, x_2, x_4 **(b)** $x_1 = 0, x_2 = 0, x_3 = 16, x_4 = 0, x_5 = 29, z = 11$ **(c)** Not maximum
19. (a) Basic: x_1, x_2, x_5; nonbasic: x_3, x_4, x_6 **(b)** $x_1 = 6, x_2 = 13, x_3 = 0, x_4 = 0, x_5 = 21, x_6 = 0, z = 18$ **(c)** Maximum
21. Maximum is 30 when $x_1 = 0, x_2 = 10, x_3 = 0, x_4 = 0, x_5 = 16$
23. Maximum is 8 when $x_1 = 4, x_2 = 0, x_3 = 8, x_4 = 2, x_5 = 0$
25. No maximum **27.** No maximum **29.** Maximum is 34 when $x_1 = 17, x_2 = 0, x_3 = 0, x_4 = 0, x_5 = 14$ or when $x_1 = 0, x_2 = 17, x_3 = 0, x_4 = 0, x_5 = 14$. **31.** Maximum is 26,000 when $x_1 = 60, x_2 = 40, x_3 = 0, x_4 = 0, x_5 = 80, x_6 = 0$. **33.** Maximum is 64 when $x_1 = 28, x_2 = 16, x_3 = 0, x_4 = 0, x_5 = 28, x_6 = 0$.
35. Maximum is 250 when $x_1 = 0, x_2 = 0, x_3 = 0, x_4 = 50, x_5 = 0, x_6 = 50$. **37. (a)** Maximum is 24 when $x_1 = 12, x_2 = 0, x_3 = 0, x_4 = 0, x_5 = 6$. **(b)** Maximum is 24 when $x_1 = 0, x_2 = 12, x_3 = 0, x_4 = 0, x_5 = 18$. **(c)** The unique maximum value of z is 24, but this occurs at two different basic feasible solutions.

Section 8.5 (page 363)

1.
$$\begin{array}{c} \begin{matrix} x_1 & x_2 & x_3 & x_4 & x_5 & \end{matrix} \\ \left[\begin{array}{ccccc|c} 2 & 1 & 1 & 0 & 0 & 90 \\ 1 & 2 & 0 & 1 & 0 & 80 \\ 1 & 1 & 0 & 0 & 1 & 50 \\ \hline -12 & -10 & 0 & 0 & 0 & 0 \end{array}\right] \end{array}$$
where x_1 is the number of Siamese cats and x_2 is the number of Persian cats.

3.
$$\begin{array}{c} \begin{matrix} x_1 & x_2 & x_3 & x_4 & x_5 & x_6 & \end{matrix} \\ \left[\begin{array}{cccccc|c} -2 & 3 & 1 & 0 & 0 & 0 & 0 \\ 1 & 0 & 0 & 1 & 0 & 0 & 6700 \\ 0 & 1 & 0 & 0 & 1 & 0 & 5500 \\ 1 & 1 & 0 & 0 & 0 & 1 & 12{,}000 \\ \hline -8.5 & -12.10 & 0 & 0 & 0 & 0 & 0 \end{array}\right] \end{array}$$
where x_1 is the number of trucks and x_2 the number of fire engines.
5. Make no 1-speed or 3-speed bicycles; make 2295 10-speed bicycles; maximum profit is \$55,080. **7.** 48 loaves of bread and 6 cakes for a maximum gross income of \$168 **9.** 100 Basic Sets, no Regular Sets, and 200 Deluxe Sets for a maximum profit of \$15,000 **11.** 4 radio ads, 6 TV ads, and no newspaper ads for a maximum exposure of 64,800 **13. (a)** (3) **(b)** (4) **(c)** (3) **15.** 40 Siamese and 10 Persian for a maximum gross income of \$580 **17.** 6700 trucks, 4466 fire engines for a maximum profit of \$110,989

Section 8.6 (page 372)

1. $\begin{bmatrix} 3 & 1 & 0 \\ -4 & 10 & 3 \\ 5 & 7 & 6 \end{bmatrix}$ **3.** $\begin{bmatrix} 3 & 4 \\ 0 & 17 \\ 14 & 8 \\ -5 & -6 \\ 3 & 1 \end{bmatrix}$

5. Maximize $z = 4x_1 + 6x_2$
subject to: $3x_1 - x_2 \le 3$
$x_1 + 2x_2 \le 5$
$x_1 \ge 0, x_2 \ge 0.$

7. Maximize $z = 18x_1 + 15x_2 + 20x_3$
subject to: $x_1 + 4x_2 + 5x_3 \le 2$
$7x_1 + x_2 + 3x_3 \le 8$
$x_1 \ge 0, x_2 \ge 0, x_3 \ge 0.$

9. Maximize $z = -8x_1 + 12x_2$
subject to: $3x_1 + x_2 \le 1$
$4x_1 + 5x_2 \le 2$
$6x_1 + 2x_2 \le 6$
$x_1 \ge 0, x_2 \ge 0.$

11. Maximize $z = 5x_1 + 4x_2 + 15x_3$
subject to: $x_1 + x_2 + 2x_3 \le 8$
$x_1 + x_2 + x_3 \le 9$
$x_1 + 3x_3 \le 3$
$x_1 \ge 0, x_2 \ge 0, x_3 \ge 0.$

13. $y_1 = 0, y_2 = 100, y_3 = 0$; minimum is 100. **15.** $y_1 = 0, y_2 = 12, y_3 = 0$; minimum is 12. **17.** $y_1 = 0, y_2 = 0, y_3 = 2$; minimum is 4. **19.** $y_1 = 10, y_2 = 10, y_3 = 0$; minimum is 320. **21.** $y_1 = 0, y_2 = 0, y_3 = 4$; minimum is 4. **23.** 4 servings of A, 2 servings of B for a minimum cost of \$1.76 **25.** Make 15 tables and 45 chairs for a minimum cost of \$4080. **27. (a)** 1 bag of Feed 1, 2 bags of Feed 2 **(b)** \$6.60 per day for 1.4 bags of Feed 1 and 1.2 bags of Feed 2

29. (a) Minimize $w = 100y_1 + 20{,}000y_2$
subject to: $y_1 + 400y_2 \ge 120$
$y_1 + 160y_2 \ge 40$
$y_1 + 280y_2 \ge 60$
$y_1 \ge 0, y_2 \ge 0.$

(b) \$6300 **(c)** \$5700

Section 8.7 (page 383)

1. (a) Maximize $z = 5x_1 + 2x_2 - x_3$
subject to: $2x_1 + 3x_2 + 5x_3 - x_4 = 8$
$4x_1 - x_2 + 3x_3 + x_5 = 7$
$x_1 \ge 0, x_2 \ge 0, x_3 \ge 0, x_4 \ge 0, x_5 \ge 0.$

(b)
$$\begin{array}{c} \begin{matrix} x_1 & x_2 & x_3 & x_4 & x_5 & \end{matrix} \\ \left[\begin{array}{ccccc|c} 2 & 3 & 5 & -1 & 0 & 8 \\ 4 & -1 & 3 & 0 & 1 & 7 \\ \hline -5 & -2 & 1 & 0 & 0 & 0 \end{array}\right] \end{array}$$

3. (a) Maximize $z = 2x_1 - 3x_2 + 4x_3$
subject to: $x_1 + x_2 + x_3 + x_4 = 100$
$x_1 + x_2 + x_3 - x_5 = 75$
$x_1 + x_2 - x_6 = 27$
$x_1 \ge 0, x_2 \ge 0, x_3 \ge 0, x_4 \ge 0, x_5 \ge 0, x_6 \ge 0.$

(b)
$$\begin{array}{c} \begin{matrix} x_1 & x_2 & x_3 & x_4 & x_5 & x_6 & \end{matrix} \\ \left[\begin{array}{cccccc|c} 1 & 1 & 1 & 1 & 0 & 0 & 100 \\ 1 & 1 & 1 & 0 & -1 & 0 & 75 \\ 1 & 1 & 0 & 0 & 0 & -1 & 27 \\ \hline -2 & 3 & -4 & 0 & 0 & 0 & 0 \end{array}\right] \end{array}$$

5. Maximize $z = -2y_1 - 5y_2 + 3y_3$
subject to: $y_1 + 2y_2 + 3y_3 \ge 115$
$2y_1 + y_2 + y_3 \le 200$
$y_1 + y_3 \ge 50$
$y_1 \ge 0, y_2 \ge 0, y_3 \ge 0.$

$$\begin{array}{c} \begin{matrix} y_1 & y_2 & y_3 & y_4 & y_5 & y_6 & \end{matrix} \\ \left[\begin{array}{cccccc|c} 1 & 2 & 3 & -1 & 0 & 0 & 115 \\ 2 & 1 & 1 & 0 & 1 & 0 & 200 \\ 1 & 0 & 1 & 0 & 0 & -1 & 50 \\ \hline 2 & 5 & -3 & 0 & 0 & 0 & 0 \end{array}\right] \end{array}$$

7. Maximize $z = -y_1 + 4y_2 - 2y_3$
subject to: $7y_1 - 6y_2 + 8y_3 \ge 18$
$4y_1 + 5y_2 + 10y_3 \ge 20$
$y_1 \ge 0, y_2 \ge 0, y_3 \ge 0.$

$$\begin{array}{c} \begin{matrix} y_1 & y_2 & y_3 & y_4 & y_5 & \end{matrix} \\ \left[\begin{array}{ccccc|c} 7 & -6 & 8 & -1 & 0 & 18 \\ 4 & 5 & 10 & 0 & -1 & 20 \\ \hline 1 & -4 & 2 & 0 & 0 & 0 \end{array}\right] \end{array}$$

9. Maximum is 480 when $x_1 = 40, x_2 = 0$. **11.** Maximum is 114 when $x_1 = 38, x_2 = 0, x_3 = 0$. **13.** Maximum is 90 when $x_1 = 12, x_2 = 3$ or when $x_1 = 0, x_2 = 9$. **15.** Minimum is 40 when $y_1 = 10, y_2 = 0$. **17.** Minimum is 26 when $y_1 = 6, y_2 = 2$.

19.

y_1	y_2	y_3	y_4	y_5	y_6	y_7	y_8	
1	0	1	0	−1	0	0	0	32
0	1	0	1	0	−1	0	0	20
1	1	0	0	0	0	1	0	25
0	0	1	1	0	0	0	1	30
14	22	12	10	0	0	0	0	0

21.

y_1	y_2	y_3	y_4	y_5	y_6	y_7	
1	1	1	−1	0	0	0	10
1	1	1	0	1	0	0	15
1	$-\frac{1}{4}$	0	0	0	−1	0	0
−1	0	1	0	0	0	−1	0
.30	.09	.27	0	0	0	0	0

23. Ship 5000 barrels of oil from supplier 1 to distributor 2; ship 3000 barrels of oil from supplier 2 to distributor 1. Minimum cost is \$175,000. **25.** Make \$3,000,000 in commercial loans and \$22,000,000 in home loans for a maximum return of \$2,940,000. **27.** Use 1,060,000 kg for whole tomatoes and 80,000 kg for sauce for a minimum cost of \$4,500,000. **29.** Order 1000 small test tubes and 500 large ones for a minimum cost of \$210.

Chapter 8 Review Exercises (page 386)

1.

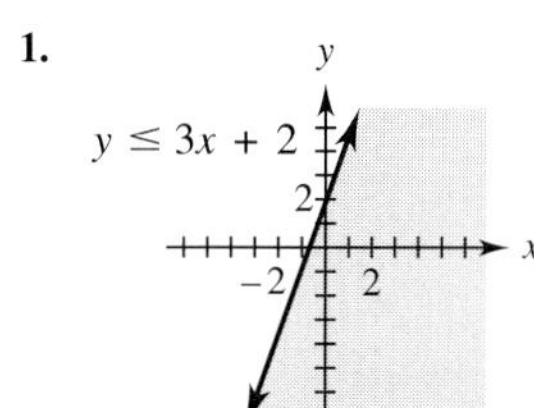

3.

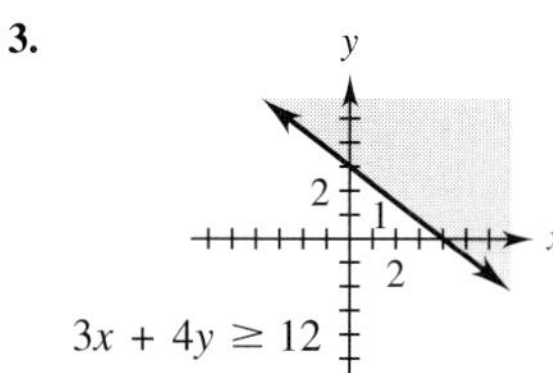

5.

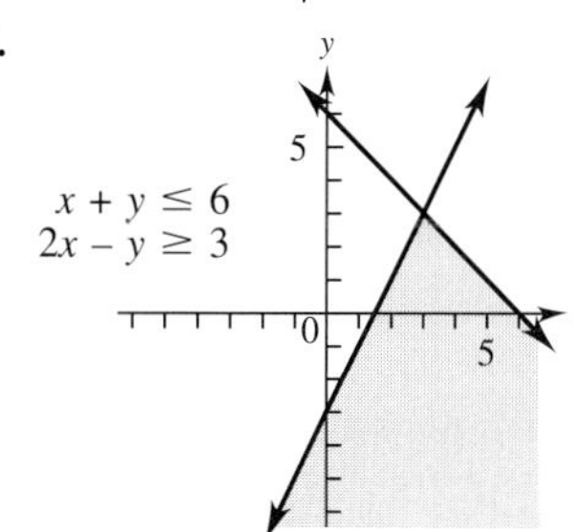

7.

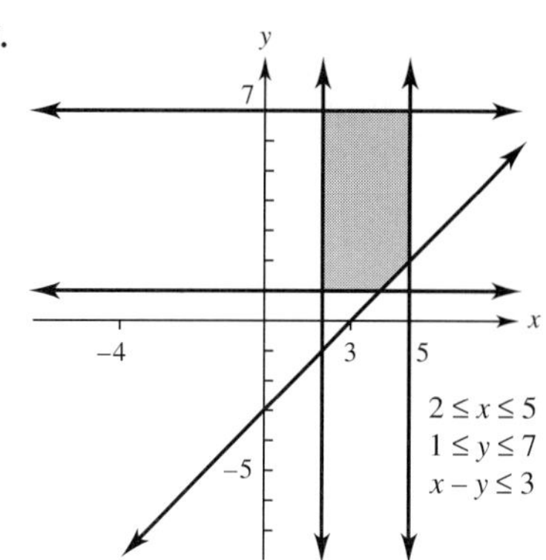

9. Let x represent the number of batches of cakes, and let y represent the number of batches of cookies. Then

$$2x + (3/2)y \le 15$$
$$3x + (2/3)y \le 13$$
$$x \ge 0$$
$$y \ge 0.$$

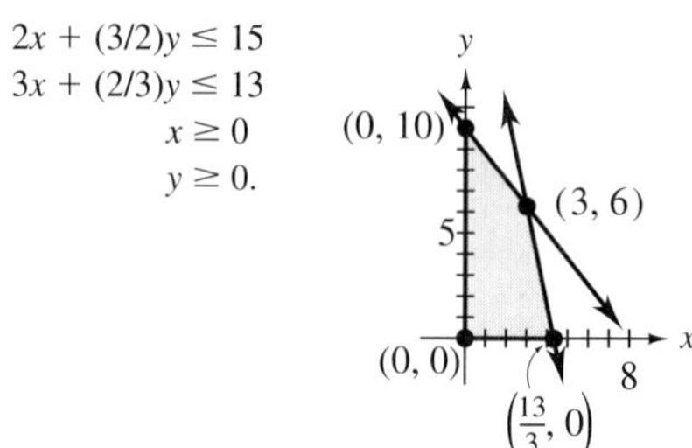

11. Minimum of 8 at (2, 1); maximum of 40 at (6, 7) **13.** Maximum is 15 when $x = 5$, $y = 0$. **15.** Minimum is 60 when $x = 0$, $y = 20$. **17.** Make 3 batches of cakes and 6 of cookies for a maximum profit of \$210. **19. (a)** Let x_1 = number of item A, x_2 = number of item B, x_3 = number of item C. **(b)** $z = 4x_1 + 3x_2 + 3x_3$ **(c)**

$$\begin{aligned} 2x_1 + 3x_2 + 6x_3 &\le 1200 \\ x_1 + 2x_2 + 2x_3 &\le 800 \\ 2x_1 + 2x_2 + 4x_3 &\le 500 \\ x_1 \ge 0, x_2 \ge 0, x_3 &\ge 0 \end{aligned}$$

21. (a) Let x_1 = number of gallons of Fruity and x_2 = number of gallons of Crystal. **(b)** $z = 12x_1 + 15x_2$ **(c)**

$$\begin{aligned} 2x_1 + x_2 &\le 110 \\ 2x_1 + 3x_2 &\le 125 \\ 2x_1 + x_2 &\le 90 \\ x_1 \ge 0, x_2 &\ge 0 \end{aligned}$$

23. When there are more than two variables
25. Any standard minimization problem
27. (a)

$$\begin{aligned} 3x_1 + 5x_2 + x_3 \qquad\qquad\qquad &= 47 \\ x_1 + x_2 \qquad + x_4 \qquad\qquad &= 25 \\ 5x_1 + 2x_2 \qquad\qquad + x_5 \qquad &= 35 \\ 2x_1 + x_2 \qquad\qquad\qquad + x_6 &= 30 \end{aligned}$$

(b)

x_1	x_2	x_3	x_4	x_5	x_6	
3	5	1	0	0	0	47
1	1	0	1	0	0	25
5	2	0	0	1	0	35
2	1	0	0	0	1	30
−2	−7	0	0	0	0	0

29. (a)

$$\begin{aligned} x_1 + x_2 + x_3 + x_4 \qquad\qquad &= 100 \\ 2x_1 + 3x_2 \qquad\qquad + x_5 \qquad &= 500 \\ x_1 \qquad + 2x_3 \qquad\qquad + x_6 &= 350 \end{aligned}$$

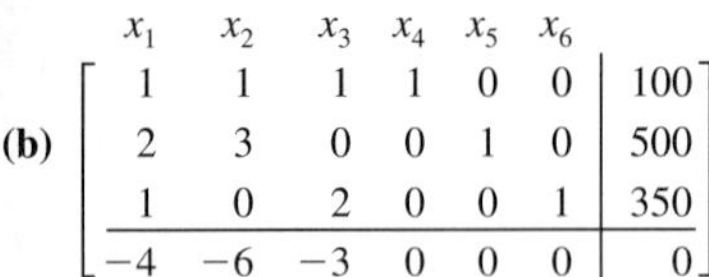

$$\text{(b)}\quad \begin{array}{cccccc|c} x_1 & x_2 & x_3 & x_4 & x_5 & x_6 & \\ 1 & 1 & 1 & 1 & 0 & 0 & 100 \\ 2 & 3 & 0 & 0 & 1 & 0 & 500 \\ 1 & 0 & 2 & 0 & 0 & 1 & 350 \\ \hline -4 & -6 & -3 & 0 & 0 & 0 & 0 \end{array}$$

31. Maximum is 80 when $x_1 = 16, x_2 = 0, x_3 = 0, x_4 = 12, x_5 = 0$. **33.** Maximum is 35 when $x_1 = 5, x_2 = 0, x_3 = 5, x_4 = 35, x_5 = 0, x_6 = 0$. **35.** Maximize $z = -18y_1 - 10y_2$ with the same constraints. **37.** Maximize $z = -6y_1 + 3y_2 - 4y_3$ with the same constraints. **39.** The simplex method gives a minimum of 40 at (10, 0). (The graphical method gives (34, 12) as another solution.) **41.** Minimum of 1957 at (47, 68, 0, 92, 35, 0, 0) **43.** (9, 5, 8, 0, 0, 0); minimum is 62. **45.** Get 250 of A, none of B, none of C for a maximum profit of $1000. **47.** Make 36.25 gal of Fruity and 17.5 gal of Crystal for a maximum profit of $697.50. **49.** Build 3 atlantic and 3 pacific models for a minimum cost of $21,000.

CHAPTER 9

Section 9.1 (page 398)

1. False **3.** True **5.** True **7.** True **9.** False **13.** $\subseteq$ **15.** $\not\subseteq$ **17.** $\subseteq$ **19.** $\subseteq$ **21.** 8 **23.** 64 **27.** $\cap$ **29.** $\cap$ **31.** $\cup$ **33.** $\cup$ **35.** {3, 5} **37.** {7, 9} **39.** $\emptyset$ **41.** U or {2, 3, 4, 5, 7, 9} **43.** All students in this school not taking this course **45.** All students in this school taking accounting and zoology **47.** C and D, A and E, C and E, D and E **49.** B' is the set of all stocks in the list with a last price less than $75 or greater than $100; B' = {ATT, GnMill, PepsiCo}. **51.** $(A \cup B)'$ is the set of all stocks with a high price less than $100 and a last price less than $75 or more than $100; $(A \cup B)'$ = {ATT, GnMill, PepsiCo}. **53.** $M \cap E$ is the set of all male, employed applicants. **55.** $M' \cup S'$ is the set of all female or married applicants. **57.** {1989, 1993, 1995} **59.** {HBO, The Disney Channel} **61.** {Spice} **63.** {The Disney Channel, Spice} **65.** {s, d, c} **67.** {g} **69.** {s, d, c}

Section 9.2 (page 406)

1.

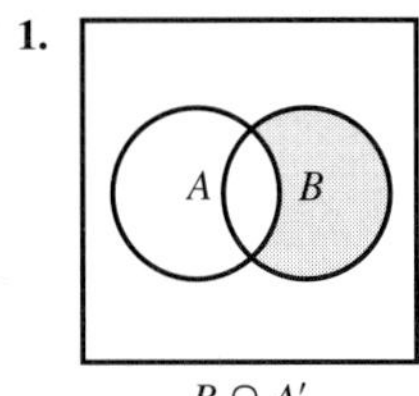

$B \cap A'$

3.

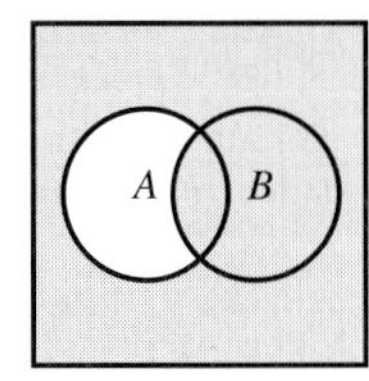

$A' \cup B$

5.

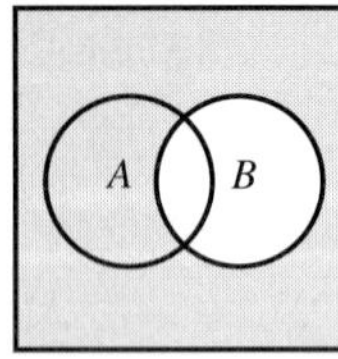

$B' \cup (A' \cap B')$

7. $\emptyset$

9.

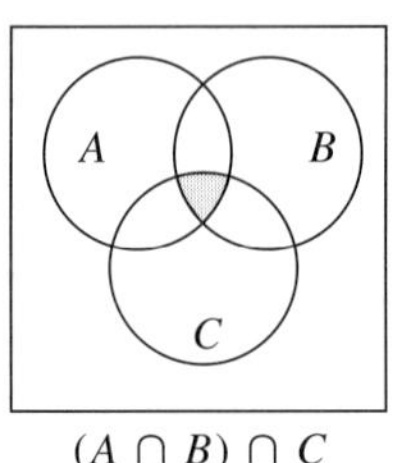

$(A \cap B) \cap C$

11.

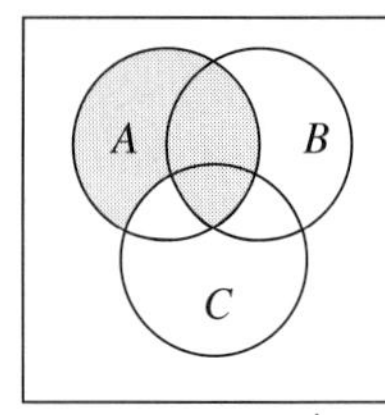

$A \cap (B \cup C')$

13.

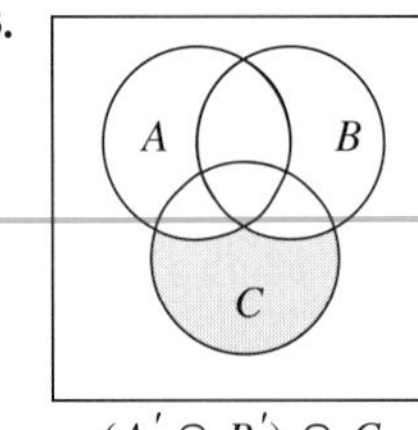

$(A' \cap B') \cap C$

15.

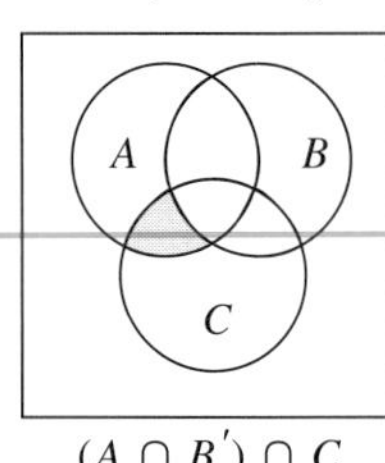

$(A \cap B') \cap C$

17. (a) 342 **(b)** 192 **(c)** 72 **(d)** 86 **19. (a)** 89% **(b)** 66% **(c)** 4% **(d)** 1% **(e)** 4% **21. (a)** 50 **(b)** 2 **(c)** 14 **23. (a)** 54 **(b)** 17 **(c)** 10 **(d)** 7 **(e)** 15 **(f)** 3 **(g)** 12 **(h)** 1 **25. (a)** 124.5 million **(b)** 74.2 million **(c)** 53.8 million **(d)** 37.1 million **(e)** 228.6 million **(f)** 30.7 million **29.** 9 **31.** 27

33.

A 20, 6, B 4, 13

35.

A 17, 12, B 13, 15

37.

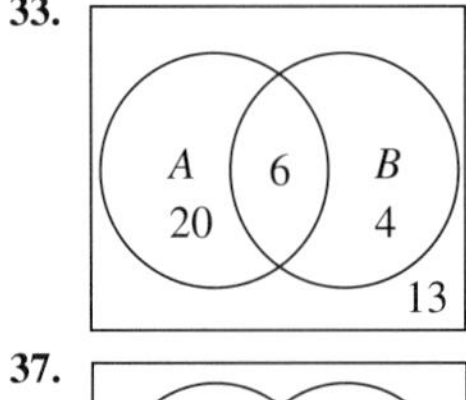

39.

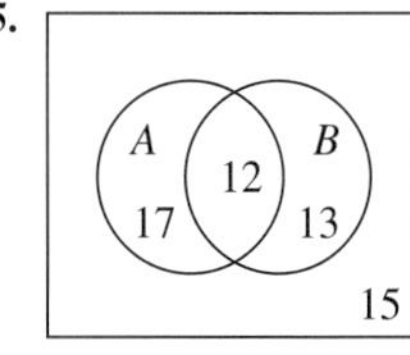

Section 9.3 (page 414)

3. {1, 2, 3, 4, . . . , 30} **5.** {buy, lease} **7.** {January, February, March, . . . , December} **11.** $\{y_1, y_2, y_3, w_1, w_2, w_3, w_4, b_1, b_2, b_3, b_4, b_5, b_6, b_7, b_8\}$ **(a)** $\{y_1, y_2, y_3\}$ **(b)** $\{b_1, b_2, b_3, b_4, b_5, b_6, b_7, b_8\}$ **(c)** $\{w_1, w_2, w_3, w_4\}$ **(d)** $\emptyset$ **13.** {ccc, ccw, cwc, cww, wcc, wcw, wwc, www} **(a)** {www} **(b)** {ccw, cwc, wcc} **(c)** {cww} **15.** {(1, 1), (1, 2), (1, 3), (1, 4), (1, 5), (2, 1), (2, 2), (2, 3), (2, 4), (2, 5), (3, 1), (3, 2), (3, 3), (3, 4), (3, 5), (4, 1), (4, 2), (4, 3), (4, 4), (4, 5)} **(a)** {(2, 1), (2, 2), (2, 3), (2, 4), (2, 5), (4, 1), (4, 2), (4, 3), (4, 4), (4, 5)} **(b)** {(1, 2), (1, 4), (2, 2), (2, 4), (3, 2), (3, 4), (4, 2), (4, 4)} **(c)** {(1, 4), (2, 3), (3, 2), (4, 1)} **(d)** $\emptyset$ **17.** 1/6 **19.** 1/3 **21.** 1/13 **23.** 1/26 **25.** 1/52 **27.** 1/13 **29.** 1/5 **31.** 9/25 **33.** 21/25 **35.** 9/25 **37. (a)** .197 **(b)** .228 **(c)** .229

Section 9.4 (page 423)

1. No **3.** No **5.** Yes **7.** .143 **9.** **(a)** 1/2 **(b)** 1/2 **(c)** 7/10 **(d)** 0 **11.** **(a)** 3/5 **(b)** 7/10 **(c)** 3/10 **13.** **(a)** 3/13 **(b)** 7/13 **(c)** 3/13 **15.** **(a)** .72 **(b)** .70 **(c)** .79 **17.** 0 **19.** .90 **21.** .84 **23.** **(a)** 1 to 5 **(b)** 1 to 2 **(c)** 1 to 1 **(d)** 1 to 5 **25.** 13 to 37 **27.** 8/25 **31.** Possible **33.** Not possible because the sum of the probabilities is less than 1 **35.** Not possible because one probability is negative **37.** **(a)** .187 **(b)** .540 **(c)** .769 **39.** **(a)** .45 **(b)** .75 **(c)** .35 **(d)** .46 **41.** .527 **43.** .466 **45.** .515 **47.** 1/4 **49.** 1/2 **51.** .90

In Exercises 53–57, answers will vary. Theoretical probabilities are given.

53. The theoretical probability is 5/32 = .15625. **55.** The theoretical probability is 1/221 = .004525. **57.** The theoretical probability is 7/8.

Section 9.5 (page 437)

1. 1/3 **3.** 1 **5.** 1/6 **7.** 4/17 **9.** 11/51 **11.** .012 **13.** .245 **19.** .815 **21.** .875 **23.** **(a)** .94 **(b)** .1282 **25.** .7456 **27.** .154 **29.** .43 **31.** The probability that a person in that group is white, given that the person is male is .956. **33.** The probability that a person in that group is black, given that the person is a woman is .083. **35.** .527 **37.** .042 **39.** 6/7 or .857 **41.** Yes **43.** .05 **45.** .25 **47.** .287 **49.** .248 **51.** .084 **53.** .4955 **55.** .0361 **57.** **(a)** $(.98)^3 \approx .94$ **(b)** Not very realistic **59.** **(a)** 3 backups **(b)** Yes **61.** No

Section 9.6 (page 444)

1. 1/3 **3.** 2/41 ≈ .0488 **5.** 21/41 ≈ .5122 **7.** 8/17 ≈ .4706 **9.** .0135 **11.** .342 **13.** .006 **15.** .091 **17.** .556 **19.** .706 **21.** 82.4% **23.** (c) **25.** .481 **27.** **(a)** .161 **29.** .030 **31.** **(a)** .53 **(b)** .1623

Chapter 9 Review Exercises (page 447)

1. False **3.** False **5.** True **7.** True **9.** {New Year's Day, Martin Luther King's Birthday, Washington's Birthday (President's Day), Memorial Day, Independence Day, Labor Day, Columbus Day, Veteran's Day, Thanksgiving, Christmas} **11.** {1, 2, 3, 4} **13.** $\{B_1, B_2, B_3, B_6, B_{12}\}$ **15.** {A, C, E} **17.** $\{A, B_3, B_6, B_{12}, C, D, E\}$ **19.** The set of all students in the class who are redheaded males **21.** The set of all students in the class who are male or younger than 21 **23.** The set of all students in the class who are not A students and do not have red hair

25.

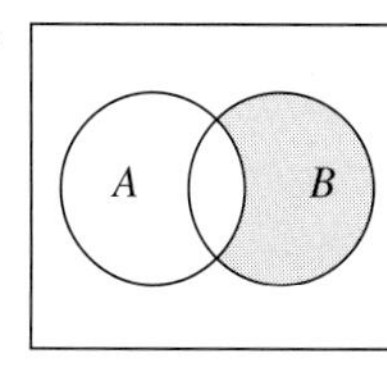

27.

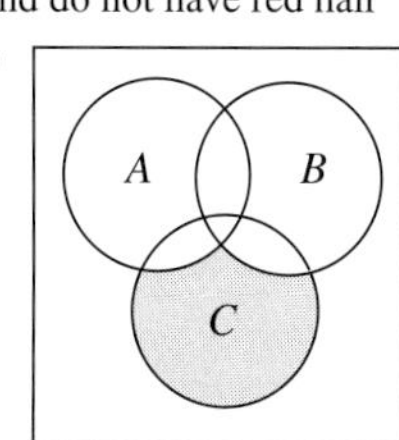

29. 5 **31.** {1, 2, 3, 4, 5, 6} **33.** {(red, 10), (red, 20), (red, 30), (blue, 10), (blue, 20), (blue, 30), (green, 10), (green, 20), (green, 30)} **35.** {(2, blue), (4, blue), (6, blue), (8, blue), (10, blue)} **37.** No **39.** $E \cup F$ **45.** 3/13 **47.** 1/2 **49.** 1 **51.** 1 to 25 **53.** .86

55.

	N_2	T_2
N_1	N_1N_2	N_1T_2
T_1	T_1N_2	T_1T_2

57. 1/2 **59.** 5/36 ≈ .139 **61.** 5/18 ≈ .278 **63.** 1/3 **65.** .66 **67.** .71 **69.** **(a)** 3/11 **(b)** 7/39 **73.** 3/22 **75.** 2/3 **77.** 5/11 **79.** **(a)** Row 1: 400; row 2: 150; row 3: 750, 1000 **(b)** 1000 **(c)** 300 **(d)** 250 **(e)** 600 **(f)** 150 **(g)** Those who purchased a used car, given that the buyer was not satisfied **(h)** 3/5 **(i)** 1/4

Case 9 (page 450)

1. .076 **3.** .051

CHAPTER 10

Section 10.1 (page 460)

1. 12 **3.** 56 **5.** 8 **7.** 24 **9.** 792 **11.** 156 **13.** 6,375,600 **15.** 240,240 **17.** 352,716 **19.** 2,042,975 **21.** 10^9 = 1,000,000,000; yes **23.** 10^9 = 1,000,000,000 **25.** 840 **27.** **(a)** 17,576,000 **(b)** 17,576,000 **(c)** 456,976,000 **29.** 800 **31.** 72,000,000 **33.** 60,949,324,800 **35.** 132 **37.** 210 **39.** 6840 **41.** 2,118,760 **43.** 1,621,233,900 **45.** **(a)** 9 **(b)** 6 **(c)** 3; yes, from both **49.** **(a)** 84 **(b)** 10 **(c)** 40 **(d)** 74 **51.** **(a)** 961 **(b)** 29,791 **53.** 5040 **55.** 81 **57.** 1 **59.** 55,440 **61.** **(a)** 7,059,052 **(b)** $3,529,526 **(c)** No **63.** 5.524×10^{26} **65.** **(a)** 840 **(b)** 180 **(c)** 420 **67.** **(a)** 362,880 **(b)** 6 **(c)** 1260

Section 10.2 (page 468)

1. .424 **3.** 7/9 **5.** 5/12 **7.** .147 **9.** .020 **11.** .314 **13.** 1326 **15.** .851 **17.** .765 **19.** .941

23. $\dfrac{\binom{4}{2}\binom{4}{3}\binom{44}{8}}{\binom{52}{13}}$ **25.** **(a)** 8.9×10^{-10} **(b)** 1.2×10^{-12}

27. 3.3×10^{-16} **29.** **(a)** .218 **(b)** .272 **(c)** .728 **31.** **(a)** .003 **(b)** .005 **(c)** .057 **(d)** .252 **33.** $(1 - {}_{365}P_{100})/(365)^{100}$ **35.** .350 **37.** There were 10 balls with 9 of them blue. **39.** Answers will vary. The theoretical answers are: **(a)** .0399 **(b)** .5191 **(c)** .0226.

Section 10.3 (page 473)

1. .067 **3.** .066 **5.** .934 **7.** .0000000005 **9.** .269 **11.** .875 **13.** 1/32 **15.** 13/16 **19.** .129 **21.** .549 **23.** .337 **25.** .349 **27.** .736 **29.** .218 **31.** .000729 **33.** .118 **35.** .121 **37.** **(a)** .001 **(b)** .088 **39.** .6930 **41.** **(a)** .199 **(b)** .568 **(c)** .133 **(d)** .794 **43.** **(a)** .047822 **(b)** .976710 **(c)** .897110 **45.** **(a)** 0 **(b)** .002438

Section 10.4 (page 480)

1. No **3.** Yes **5.** No **7.** No

9. Yes

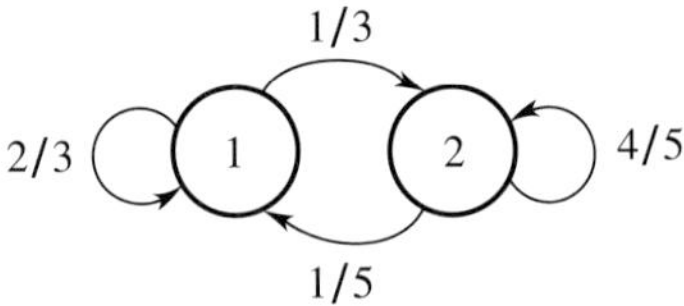

11. No **13.** Not a transition diagram

15. $\begin{array}{c} \\ A \\ B \\ C \end{array}\begin{array}{c} \begin{array}{ccc} A & B & C \end{array} \\ \begin{bmatrix} .6 & .2 & .2 \\ .9 & .02 & .08 \\ .4 & 0 & .6 \end{bmatrix} \end{array}$

17. No **19.** Yes **21.** No **23.** $\begin{bmatrix} \frac{1}{3} & \frac{2}{3} \end{bmatrix}$ **25.** $\begin{bmatrix} \frac{3}{11} & \frac{8}{11} \end{bmatrix}$

27. [.4633 .1683 .3684] **29.** $\begin{bmatrix} \frac{1}{4} & \frac{1}{4} & \frac{1}{2} \end{bmatrix}$

31. The first power is the given transition matrix;

$$\begin{bmatrix} .23 & .21 & .24 & .17 & .15 \\ .26 & .18 & .26 & .16 & .14 \\ .23 & .18 & .24 & .19 & .16 \\ .19 & .19 & .27 & .18 & .17 \\ .17 & .20 & .26 & .19 & .18 \end{bmatrix};$$

$$\begin{bmatrix} .226 & .192 & .249 & .177 & .156 \\ .222 & .196 & .252 & .174 & .156 \\ .219 & .189 & .256 & .177 & .159 \\ .213 & .192 & .252 & .181 & .162 \\ .213 & .189 & .252 & .183 & .163 \end{bmatrix};$$

$$\begin{bmatrix} .2205 & .1916 & .2523 & .1774 & .1582 \\ .2206 & .1922 & .2512 & .1778 & .1582 \\ .2182 & .1920 & .2525 & .1781 & .1592 \\ .2183 & .1909 & .2526 & .1787 & .1595 \\ .2176 & .1906 & .2533 & .1787 & .1598 \end{bmatrix};$$

$$\begin{bmatrix} .21932 & .19167 & .25227 & .17795 & .15879 \\ .21956 & .19152 & .25226 & .17794 & .15872 \\ .21905 & .19152 & .25227 & .17818 & .15898 \\ .21880 & .19144 & .25251 & .17817 & .15908 \\ .21857 & .19148 & .25253 & .17824 & .15918 \end{bmatrix}; .17794$$

33. 24.0% 30-year fixed rates, 69.7% 15-year fixed rates, 6.3% adjustable **35.** 17/18

37. $\begin{array}{c} \\ R \\ P \\ W \end{array}\begin{array}{c} \begin{array}{ccc} R & P & W \end{array} \\ \begin{bmatrix} \frac{1}{2} & \frac{1}{2} & 0 \\ \frac{1}{4} & \frac{1}{2} & \frac{1}{4} \\ 0 & \frac{1}{2} & \frac{1}{2} \end{bmatrix} \end{array}; \begin{bmatrix} \frac{1}{4} & \frac{1}{2} & \frac{1}{4} \end{bmatrix}$

39. Homeowners: .769; renters: .231; homeless: 0 **41. (a)** 42,500 in G_0; 5000 in G_1; 2500 in G_2 **(b)** 37,125 in G_0; 8750 in G_1; 4125 in G_2 **(c)** 33,281 in G_0; 11,513 in G_1; 5206 in G_2 **(d)** $\begin{bmatrix} \frac{28}{59} & \frac{22}{59} & \frac{9}{59} \end{bmatrix}$ or [.475 .373 .152]; in the long run, the probabilities of no accidents, one accident, and more than one accident are .475, .373, and .152, respectively. **43. (a)** $\begin{bmatrix} .348 & .379 & .273 \\ .320 & .378 & .302 \\ .316 & .360 & .323 \end{bmatrix}$ **(b)** .348 **(c)** .320

45. (b) $\begin{bmatrix} \frac{5}{12} & \frac{13}{36} & \frac{2}{9} \\ \frac{5}{12} & \frac{13}{36} & \frac{2}{9} \\ \frac{1}{4} & \frac{5}{12} & \frac{1}{3} \end{bmatrix}$ **(c)** 2/9 **47.** [0 0 .102273 .897727]

Section 10.5 (page 492)

1. (a)

Number of accidents	0	1	2	3	4
Probability	$\frac{2}{7}$	$\frac{3}{7}$	$\frac{1}{7}$	0	$\frac{1}{7}$

(b)

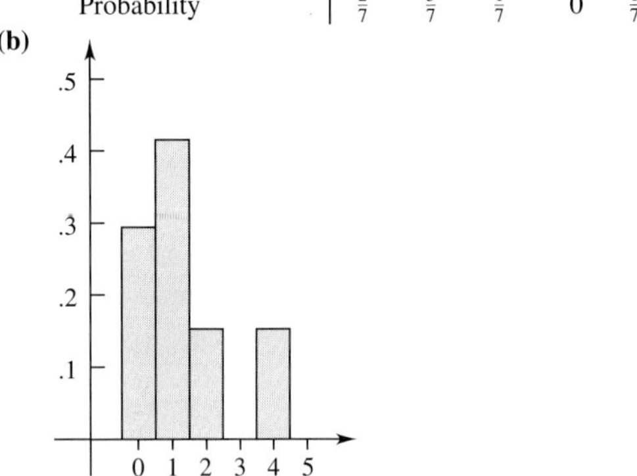

3. (a)

Number	0	1	2	3	4	5	6
Probability	0	.04	0	.16	.40	.32	.08

(b)

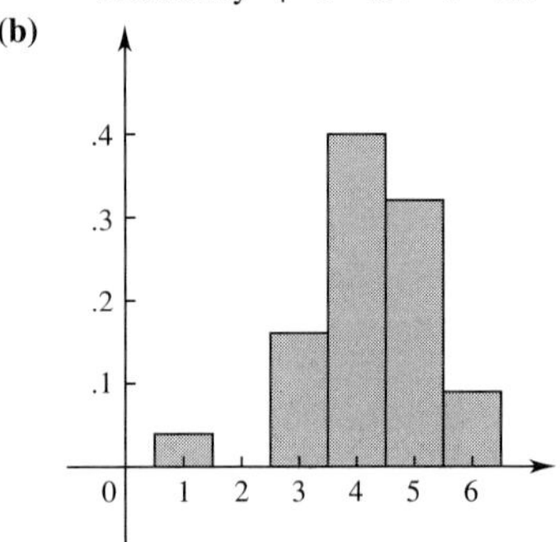

5.

Number of even numbers	0	1	2
Probability	$\frac{3}{10}$	$\frac{3}{5}$	$\frac{1}{10}$

7.

Number of points	2	3	4	5	6	7	8	9	10	11	12
Probability	$\frac{1}{36}$	$\frac{1}{18}$	$\frac{1}{12}$	$\frac{1}{9}$	$\frac{5}{36}$	$\frac{1}{6}$	$\frac{5}{36}$	$\frac{1}{9}$	$\frac{1}{12}$	$\frac{1}{18}$	$\frac{1}{36}$

9.

Number of black balls	0	1	2
Probability	$\frac{2}{5}$	$\frac{8}{15}$	$\frac{1}{15}$

11.

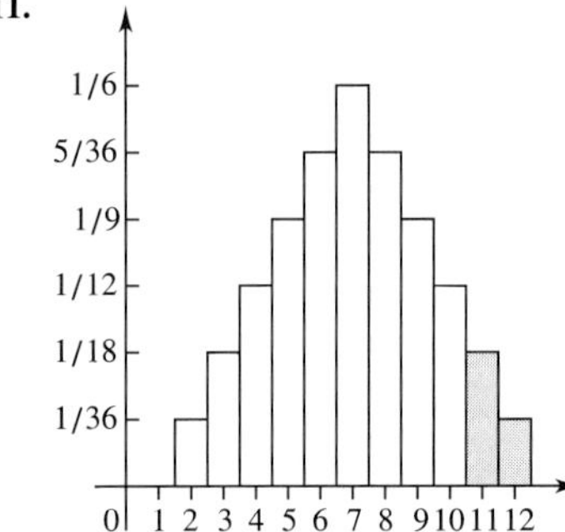

13.

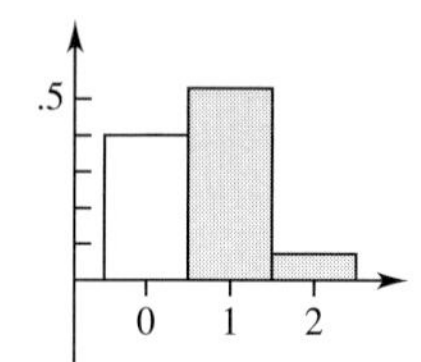

15.

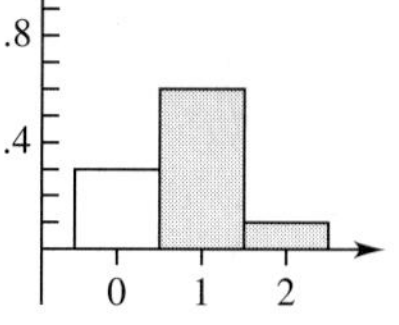

17. 6.5 **19.** 23.83

21. (a)

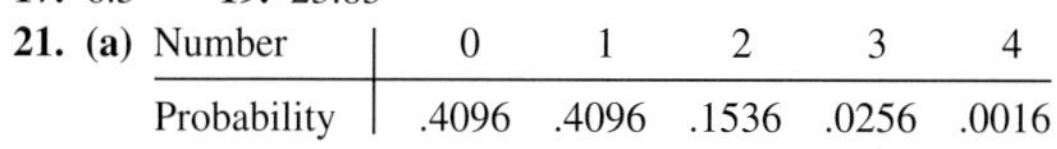

Number	0	1	2	3	4
Probability	.4096	.4096	.1536	.0256	.0016

(b)

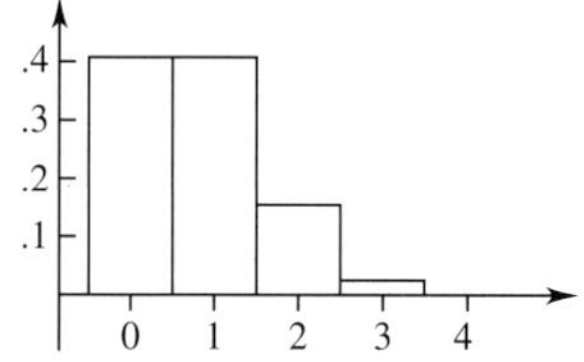

(c) .8

23. (a) Yes; the probability of a match is still 1/2. **(b)** 60¢ **(c)** −60¢ **25.** 5.6 **27.** 30 **29.** −32¢ **31.** 1 **33.** 1/2 **35.** 4.4435 **37.** −82¢ **39.** −5¢ **41.** −50¢ **45.** (c) **47.** $30,000 at age 55

49.

Account Number	*Expected Value*	*Total*	*Class*
3	2,000	22,000	*C*
4	1,000	51,000	*B*
5	25,000	30,000	*C*
6	60,000	60,000	*A*
7	16,000	46,000	*B*

51. (a)

Number	0	1	2	3	4	5
Probability	.0000	.0000	.0000	.0003	.0024	.0141

Number	6	7	8	9	10
Probability	.0573	.1600	.2929	.3178	.1552

(b) .0027 **(d)** 8, 3

Section 10.6 (page 498)

1. (a) Choose the coast. **(b)** Choose the highway. **(c)** Choose the highway; $38,000. **(d)** Choose the coast. **3. (a)** Make no repairs. **(b)** Make repairs. **(c)** Make no repairs; $10,750.

5. (a)

$$\begin{array}{r} \\ \text{Overhaul} \\ \text{Don't} \end{array} \begin{array}{c} \begin{array}{cc} \text{Fails} & \text{Doesn't} \end{array} \\ \begin{bmatrix} -8600 & -2600 \\ -6000 & 0 \end{bmatrix} \end{array}$$

(b) Do not overhaul before shipping.
7. (a) No campaign **(b)** Campaign for all **(c)** Campaign for all
9. Emphasize the environment; 14.25.

Chapter 10 Review Exercises (page 501)

1. 120 **3.** 220 **5.** 120 **7. (a)** 72 **(b)** 72 **11.** 3/8 **13.** 11/16 **15.** .245 **17.** .362 **19.** .091 **21.** .455 **23.** Yes **25.** No **27.** .000041 **29.** .182 **31. (a)** [.54 .46] **(b)** [.6464 .3536] **(c)** 2/3

33. (a)

x	1	2	3	4	5	6
$P(x)$	.05	0	.1	.25	.4	.2

(b)

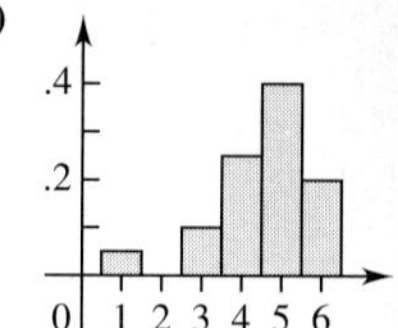

35. (a)

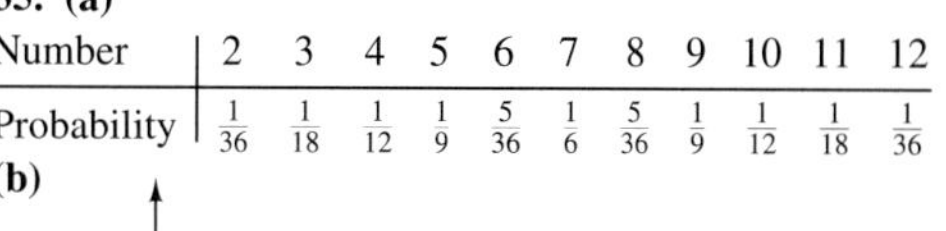

Number	2	3	4	5	6	7	8	9	10	11	12
Probability	$\frac{1}{36}$	$\frac{1}{18}$	$\frac{1}{12}$	$\frac{1}{9}$	$\frac{5}{36}$	$\frac{1}{6}$	$\frac{5}{36}$	$\frac{1}{9}$	$\frac{1}{12}$	$\frac{1}{18}$	$\frac{1}{36}$

(b)

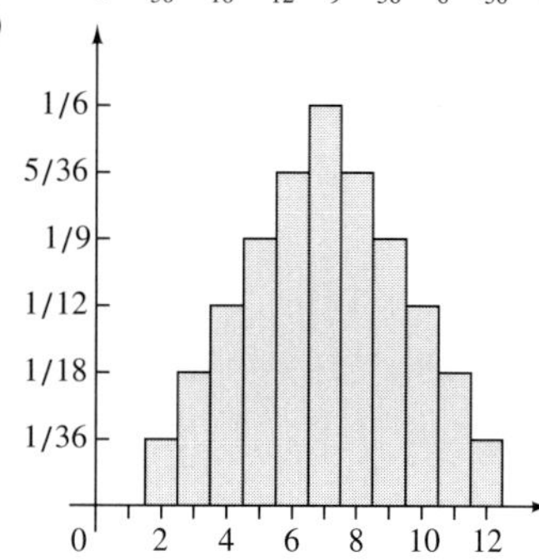

37. .6 **39.** $1.29 **41.** −28¢ **43. (a)** 3/13 or .23 **(b)** 3/4 or .75 **45. (a)** Oppose **(b)** Oppose **(c)** Oppose; 2700 **(d)** Oppose; 1400 **47.** (c)

Case 10 (page 505)

1. (a) $69.01 **(b)** $79.64 **(c)** $58.96 **(d)** $82.54 **(e)** $62.88 **(f)** $64.00 **3.** The events of needing parts 1, 2, and 3 are not the only events in the sample space.

CHAPTER 11

Section 11.1 (page 514)

1. (a)–(b)

Interval	*Frequency*
0–24	4
25–49	3
50–74	6
75–99	3
100–124	5
125–149	9

(c)–(d)

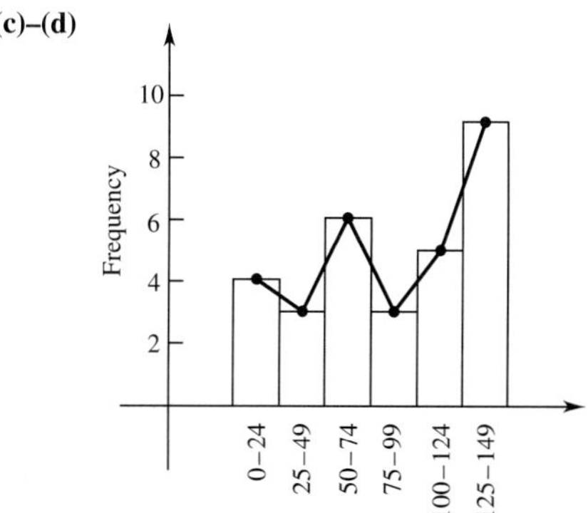

3. (a)–(b)

Interval	*Frequency*
70–74	2
75–79	1
80–84	3
85–89	2
90–94	6
95–99	5
100–104	6
105–109	4
110–114	2

(c)–(d)

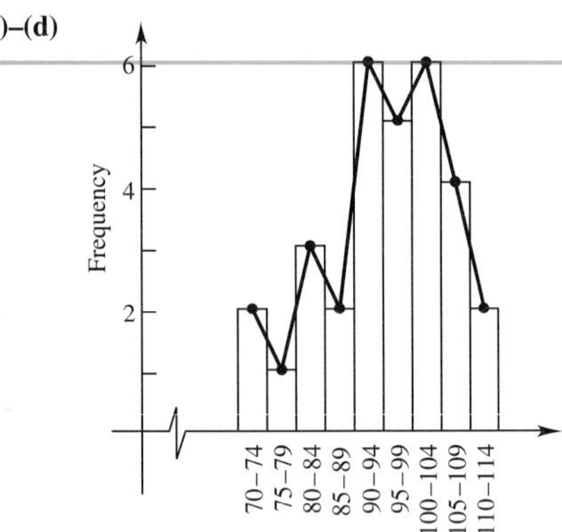

7. 16 **9.** 27,955 **11.** 7.7 **13.** 6.7 **15.** 17.2 **17.** 51 **19.** 130 **21.** 29.1 **23.** 9 **25.** 68 and 74 **27.** 6.3 **31.** 94.9; 90–94 and 100–104 **33. (a)** Mean = 1.9; median = 1; mode = 1 **35. (a)** Mean = 17.2; median = 17.5; no mode

37.

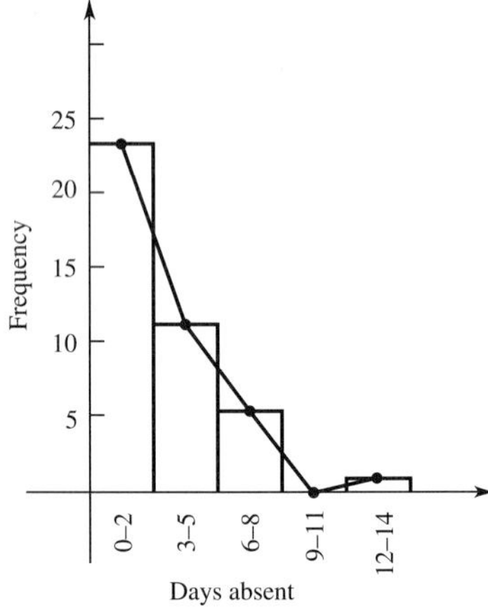

39. (a) About 17.5% **(b)** About 8% **(c)** 20–29 **41.** $3.29 **43. (a)** 23.98 **(b)** 21.47 **45. (a)** The mean wealth is $999,900.01 or roughly $1 million. **(b)** $0 **(c)** $0 **(d)** Median or mode

Section 11.2 (page 522)

3. 6; 2.2 **5.** 12; 4.7 **7.** 53; 21.8 **9.** 46; 16.1 **11.** 45.2 **13.** Mean: 5.0876; standard deviation: .1087 **15.** At least 3/4 **17.** At least 24/25 **19.** At least 93.8% **21.** No more than 11.1% **23.** Britelite: $\bar{x} = 26.2$, $s = 4.4$; Brand X: $\bar{x} = 25.5$, $s = 7.2$ **(a)** Britelite **(b)** Britelite **25. (a)** 7.77; 1991 **(b)** 1.22 **(c)** 4 **27. (a)** 1.83; .76 **(b)** 1.09 **(c)** .88 **29. (a)** 188.3; Mexico **(b)** 123.9; No; Yes, Canada and Asia **31. (a)** 1/3; 2; −1/3; 0; 5/3; 7/3; 1; 4/3; 7/3; 2/3 **(b)** 2.1; 2.6; 1.5; 2.6; 2.5; .6; 1.0; 2.1; .6; 1.2 **(c)** 1.13 **(d)** 1.68 **(e)** 4.41; −2.15; the process is out of control. **33.** Mean = 80.17; standard deviation = 12.2

Section 11.3 (page 533)

5. 9.10% **7.** 48.21% **9.** 7.7% **11.** 47.35% **13.** 92.42% **15.** 1.64 or 1.65 **17.** −1.04 **19.** .0796 **21.** .9933 **23.** .1527 **25.** .0051 **27.** .4052 **29.** .8186 **31.** .0475 **33.** .0021 **35.** 60.4 mph **37.** 6.68% **39.** 38.3% **41.** 625 **43.** 189 **45.** 15.87% **47.** 82 **49.** 70 **51.** .5000 **53.** .9050 **55.** .8106 **57.** .6736 **59.** .1820 **61.** .5398

Section 11.4 (page 540)

3. (a)

x	0	1	2	3	4	5	6
$P(x)$	.016	.094	.234	.313	.234	.094	.016

(b) 3 **(c)** 1.2

5. (a)

x	0	1	2	3	4	5
$P(x)$	.470	.383	.125	.020	.002	5×10^{-5}

(b) .7 **(c)** .78 **7.** 12.5; 3.49 **9.** 24.5; 3.53 **11. (a)** 3.95 **(b)** .409 **(c)** .9919 **13.** .1747 **15.** .0240 **17.** .9032 **19.** .8665 **21.** .0956 **23.** .0760 **25.** .6443 **27.** .0146 **29.** .0222 **31.** .3798 **33. (a)** .0001 **(b)** .0002 **(c)** .0000 **35. (a)** .1686 **(b)** .0304 **(c)** .9575

Chapter 11 Review Exercises (page 543)

3. (a)

Interval	*Frequency*
450–474	5
475–499	6
500–524	5
525–549	2
550–574	2

(b)–(c)

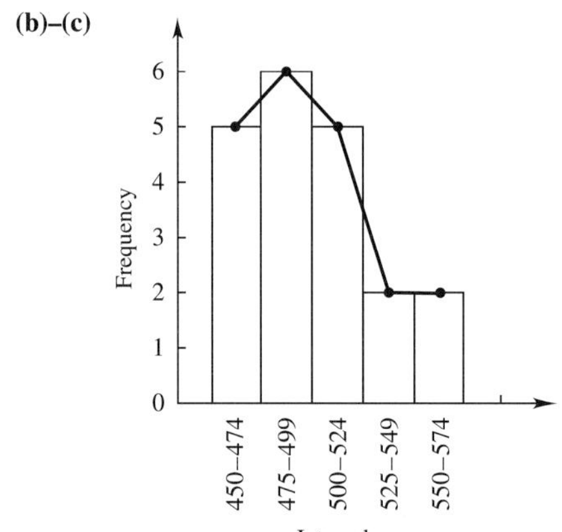

5. 73 **7.** 34.9 **11.** 38; 36 and 38 **13.** 55–59 **17.** 67; 23.9 **19.** 6.2 **23.** .3980 **25.** .9521 **29. (a)** .008 **(b)** $\mu = 1.014$; $\sigma = .9180$ **31. (a)** Diet A (mean = 2.7) **(b)** Diet B ($s = .95$) **33.** 2.27% **35.** 68.26% **37.** .8315 **39.** .0305 **41.** 1.000 **43.** .1428 **45.** .0806 **47.** .7357

Case 11 (page 546)

1. (a) 1/3; 2; −1/3; 0; 5/3; 7/3; 1; 4/3; 7/3; 2/3 **(b)** 2.1; 2.6; 1.5; 2.6; 2.5; .6; 1.0; 2.1; .6; 1.2 **(c)** 1.13 **(d)** 1.68 **(e)** 4.41; −2.15 **(f)** 4.31; 0

CHAPTER 12

Section 12.1 (page 555)

1. (a) 3 **(b)** 0 **3. (a)** Does not exist **(b)** −1/2 **5. (a)** 2 **(b)** Does not exist **7. (a)** 1 **(b)** −1 **11.** 1 **13.** 2 **15.** 0 **17.** 8 **19.** Does not exist **21.** 8 **23.** 2 **25.** 4 **27.** 3/2 **29. (a)**

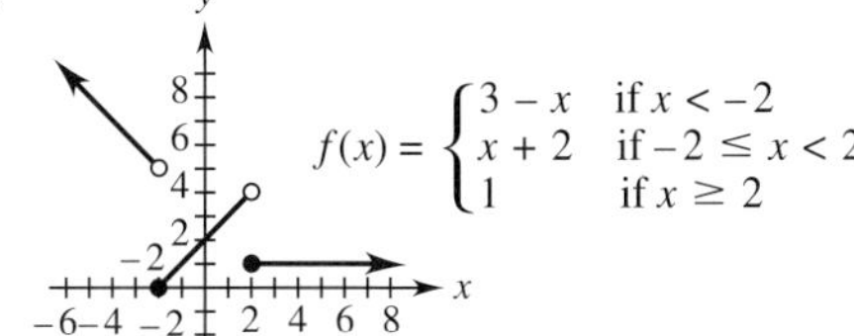

(b) Does not exist **(c)** 3 **(d)** Does not exist **31.** 41 **33.** 9/7 **35.** 6 **37.** −5 **39.** 1/2 **41.** Does not exist **43.** $\sqrt{5}$ **45.** Does not exist **47.** −1/9 **49.** 1/10 **51.** $1/(2\sqrt{5})$ **53. (a)** 25 **(b)** 5.2 **(c)** 7 **55. (a)** 3 **(b)** Does not exist **(c)** 2 **(d)** 16 months **57. (a)** Approx. .0444 **(b)** Approx. .0667 **(c)** Approx. .0667

Section 12.2 (page 565)

1. 7 **3.** 8 **5.** 1/3 **7.** −1/3 **9. (a)** 2 **(b)** 3 **(c)** 2 **(d)** 1/2 **(e)** 1/2 **11. (a)** 3 **(b)** 0 **(c)** −9/5 **(d)** Sales increase in years 0–4, stay constant until year 7, and then decrease. **13. (a)** 73.7/yr **(b)** 261.4/yr **(c)** 362/yr **(d)** 398.1/yr **(e)** 273.8/yr **(f)** It is increasing. **(g)** Average the answers to parts (a)–(d). **15. (a)** \$11 million, −\$1 million **(b)** −\$1 million, \$9 million **(c)** Civil penalties were increasing from 1987 to 1988 and decreasing from 1988 to 1989. Criminal penalties decreased slightly from 1987 to 1988, then increased from 1988 to 1989. This indicates that criminal penalties began to replace civil penalties in 1988. **(d)** About a \$3.5 million increase; the general trend was upward. More is being done to impose penalties for polluting. **19.** 20 ft per sec **21.** 60 ft per sec **23.** 7 ft per sec **25. (a)** $x_0^2 + 2x_0h + h^2 + 1$ **(b)** $2x_0 + h$ **(c)** 10 **27. (a)** $x_0^2 + 2x_0h + h^2 - x_0 - h - 1$ **(b)** $2x_0 + h - 1$ **(c)** 9 **29. (a)** $x_0^3 + 3x_0^2h + 3x_0h^2 + h^3$ **(b)** $3x_0^2 + 3x_0h + h^2$ **(c)** 75 **31. (a)** \$5998 **(b)** \$6000 **(c)** \$5998 **(d)** They are the same. **33. (a)** 12.4 ft/sec **(b)** 12.1 ft/sec **(c)** 12.025 ft/sec **(d)** 12.001 ft/sec **(e)** 12 ft/sec **35. (a)** \$555 per year **(b)** About \$119 per year **(c)** About \$1247 per year

Section 12.3 (page 581)

1. 35 **3.** 1/8 **5.** 1/8 **7.** $y = 6x - 4$

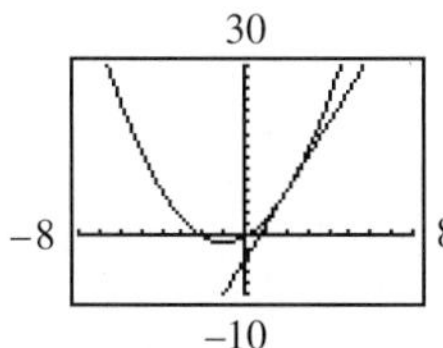

9. $y = 5 - 1.25x$

8
−9 9
−4

11. $y = (2/3)x + 6$

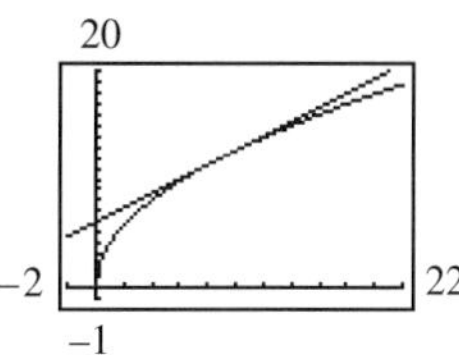

13. −6; 6 **15.** −5; −3; 0; 2; 4 **17. (a)** x_5 **(b)** x_4 **(c)** x_3 **(d)** x_2 **19.**

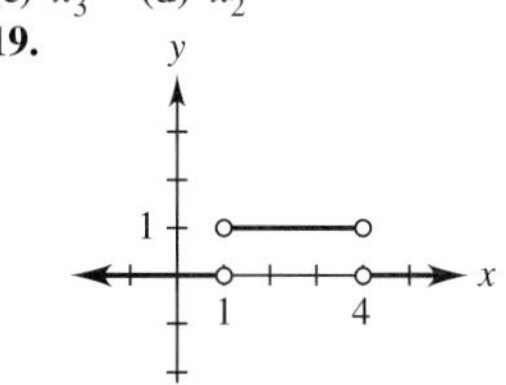

21. (a) Distance **(b)** Velocity **23.** $f'(x) = -8x + 11$; −5; 11; 35 **25.** $f'(x) = 8$; 8; 8; 8 **27.** $f'(x) = 2/x^2$; 1/2; does not exist; 2/9 **29.** $f'(x) = -4/(x-1)^2$; −4; −4; −1/4

31.

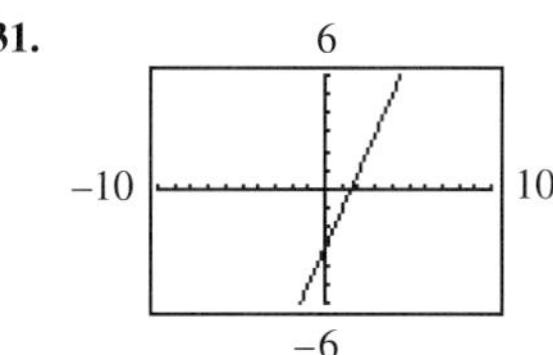

33. 6
0 9
−1

35. (a)

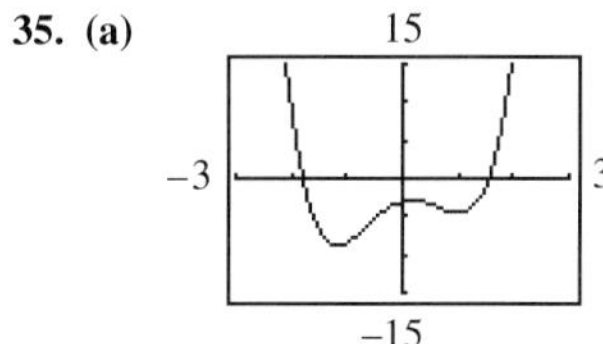

(b) 15
−3 3
−15

(c) The graphs appear identical, which suggests that $f'(x) = g(x)$. **37.** (d) **39. (a)** \$16 per table **(b)** \$15.998 or \$16 **(c)** The marginal revenue found in part (a) approximates the actual revenue from the sale of the 1001st item found in part (b). **41. (a)** $-4p + 4$ **(b)** −36; demand is decreasing at the rate of about 36 items for each increase in price of \$1. **43. (a)** 20 **(b)** 0 **(c)** −10 **(d)** At 5 hr **45.** $T'(1) \approx -3.764$; $T'(4) \approx 3.184$; $T'(8) \approx -2.448$. At an altitude of 1000 ft the temperature is decreasing at a rate of 3.764° per thousand ft. At 4000 ft it is increasing at a rate of 3.184° per thousand ft and at 8000 ft it is decreasing at 2.448° per thousand ft. **47.** About \$5000 per month; about \$453.59 per month; about \$41.15 per month; about \$3.73 per month; costs are decreasing at a slower and slower rate and are almost constant at the end of three years.

49. (a) Just past 3/4 of an hour (at $x = .775$) and just before 3 hours (at $x = 2.975$) **(b)** 1000; the oven temperature is increasing at 1000° per hour. **(c)** 0; the oven temperature is not changing. **(d)** -1000; the oven temperature is decreasing at 1000° per hour.

Section 12.4 (page 594)

1. $f'(x) = 8x - 6$ **3.** $y' = 6x^2 + 6x - 5$ **5.** $g'(x) = 4x^3 + 9x^2 - 6$ **7.** $f'(x) = 9x^{.5} - 2x^{-.5}$ or $9x^{.5} - 2/x^{.5}$ **9.** $y' = -48x^{2.2} + 3.8x^{.9}$ **11.** $y' = 36t^{1/2} + 2t^{-1/2}$ or $36t^{1/2} + 2/t^{1/2}$ **13.** $y' = 4x^{-1/2} + (9/2)x^{-1/4}$ or $4/x^{1/2} + 9/(2x^{1/4})$ **15.** $g'(x) = -30x^{-6} + x^{-2}$ or $-30/x^6 + 1/x^2$ **17.** $y' = -20x^{-3} - 12x^{-5} - 6$ or $-20/x^3 - 12/x^5 - 6$ **19.** $f'(t) = -6t^{-2} + 16t^{-3}$ or $-6/t^2 + 16/t^3$ **21.** $y' = -36x^{-5} + 24x^{-4} - 2x^{-2}$ or $-36/x^5 + 24/x^4 - 2/x^2$ **23.** $g'(x) = -4/x^{3/2} - 5/(2x^{1/2}) + 1$

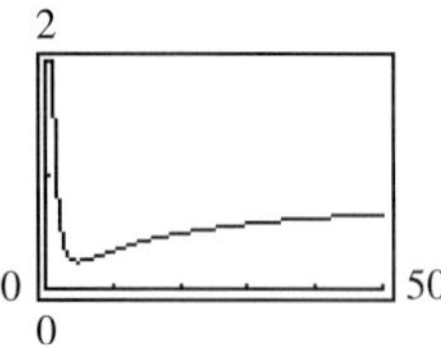

25. $y' = -6/x^{5/2} - 4/x^{3/2} + 2x$

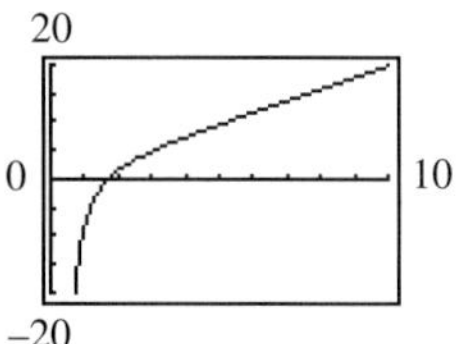

27. $y' = -3/(2x^{5/4})$

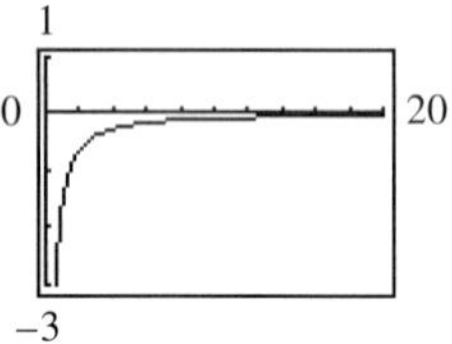

29. $y' = -5/(3t^{2/3})$

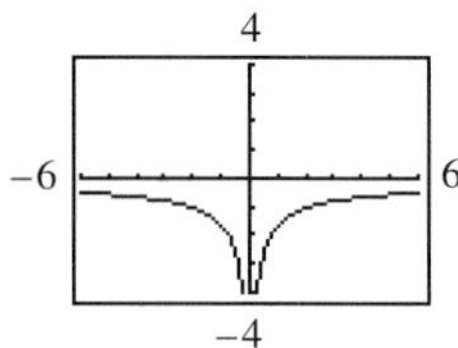

31. $dy/dx = -40x^{-6} + 36x^{-5}$ or $-40/x^6 + 36/x^5$ **33.** $(-9/2)x^{-3/2} - 3x^{-5/2}$ or $-9/(2x^{3/2}) - 3/x^{5/2}$ **35.** -28 **37.** 11/16 **39.** (b) **41.** 0; $y = 0$ **43.** 7; $y = 7x - 3$ **45.** (d) **47. (a)** .4824 **(b)** 2.216 **49. (a)** $C'(x) = 1 + 28x^{-1/3}$ **(b)** About \$9190 **(c)** About \$9150 **(d)** Yes

51. (a) $P(x) = 201\sqrt[3]{x} - .1x^2 - 3x - 40$ **(b)** About \$353; about \$406; about \$405; about \$300 **(c)** $P'(x) = 67x^{-2/3} - .2x - 3$ **(d)** About \$9.43; about \$2.09; about $-\$2.06$; about $-\$8.06$

53. (a) 100 **(b)** 1 **(c)** $-.01$; the percent of acid is decreasing at the rate of .01 per day after 100 days.

55. (a) $f'(x) = .8036x + 2.039$ **(b)** 6.8606 **(c)** Increasing because $f'(6)$ is positive. **57. (a)** 30 **(b)** 0 **(c)** -10

59. (a) 264 **(b)** 510 **(c)** 97/4 or 24.25 **(d)** The number of matings per hour is increasing by about 24.25 matings at a temperature of 16°C. **61. (a)** $v(t) = 16t + 3$ **(b)** 3; 83; 163

63. (a) $v(t) = 6t^2 + 12t$ **(b)** 0; 210; 720 **65. (a)** -32 ft per sec; -64 ft per sec **(b)** In 3 sec **(c)** -96 ft per sec **69. (a)** None **(b)** None **(c)** $(-\infty, \infty)$ **(d)** The derivative is always negative, so the graph of $g(x)$ is always decreasing.

Section 12.5 (page 602)

1. $y' = 9x^2 + 2x - 6$ **3.** $y' = 120x^3 - 54x^2 + 10$ **5.** $y' = 24x^5 - 35x^4 - 20x^3 + 42x^2 + 4x - 6$ **7.** $y' = 144x^3 + 144x^2 + 32x$ **9.** $y' = 54x^5 + 30x^4 + 4x^3$ **11.** $y' = -7/(x - 4)^2$ **13.** $f'(t) = (t^2 + 6t - 12)/(t + 3)^2$ **15.** $g'(x) = (-6x^4 - 4x^3 - 6x - 1)/(2x^3 - 1)^2$ **17.** $y' = (x^2 + 6x - 14)/(x + 3)^2$ **19.** $r'(t) = [-\sqrt{t} + 3/(2\sqrt{t})]/(2t + 3)^2$ or $(3 - 2t)/[2\sqrt{t}(2t + 3)^2]$ **21.** $y' = (9\sqrt{x}/2 + 4/\sqrt{x})/x$ or $(9x + 8)/(2x\sqrt{x})$ **23.** $y' = 42x^5 - 112x^3 + 6x^2 - 8$

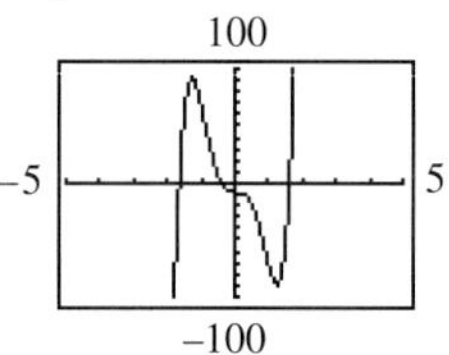

25. $y' = 3\sqrt{x} - 3/(2\sqrt{x}) - 2$

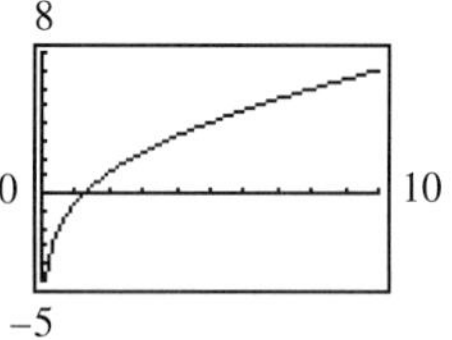

27. $y' = -12 + 15/\sqrt{x}$

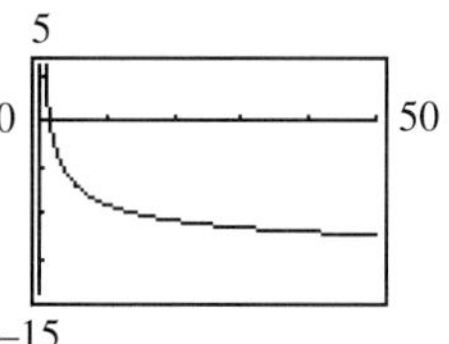

29. $y' = \dfrac{2}{(1 - x)^2}$

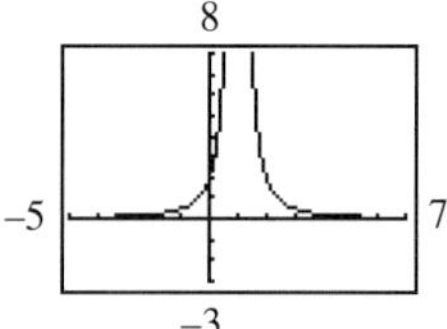

31. $f'(p) = (24p^2 + 32p + 29)/(3p + 2)^2$ **33.** $g'(x) = (10x^4 + 18x^3 + 6x^2 - 20x - 9)/[(2x + 1)^2(5x + 2)^2]$ **35.** In the first step, the numerator should be $(x^2 - 1)2 - (2x + 5)(2x)$. **37.** $y = -2x + 9$

39. **(a)** \$22.86 per unit **(b)** \$12.92 per unit **(c)** $(3x + 2)/(x^2 + 4x)$ hundred dollars per unit **(d)** $\overline{C}'(x) = (-3x^2 - 4x - 8)/(x^2 + 4x)^2$ **41.** **(a)** $N'(t) = \dfrac{4200t}{(30 + t^2)^2}$ **(b)** 8.28 words per min; 6.94 wpm; 4.71 wpm; 2.49 wpm; .97 wpm **43.** **(a)** −5 ft/sec **(b)** −1.7 ft/sec **45.** **(a)** .1173 **(b)** 2.625

Section 12.6 (page 612)

1. 275 **3.** 107 **5.** $24x + 4$; $24x + 35$ **7.** $-64x^3 + 2$; $-4x^3 + 8$ **9.** $1/x^2$; $1/x^2$ **11.** $\sqrt{8x^2 - 4}$; $8x + 10$

In Exercises 13–19 other answers are possible.

13. If $f(x) = x^5$ and $g(x) = 4x + 3$, then $y = f[g(x)]$.
15. If $f(x) = \sqrt{x}$ and $g(x) = 6 + 3x$, then $y = f[g(x)]$.
17. If $f(x) = (x + 3)/(x - 3)$ and $g(x) = \sqrt{x}$, then $y = f[g(x)]$.
19. If $f(x) = x^2 + x + 5$ and $g(x) = x^{1/2} - 3$, then $y = f[g(x)]$.
21. $y' = 9(3x + 4)^2$ **23.** $y' = 72(3x + 2)^3$
25. $y' = -128x(8x^2 + 6)^3$ **27.** $y' = 36(2x + 5)^{1/2}$
29. $y' = (-21/2)(8x + 9)(4x^2 + 9x)^{1/2}$

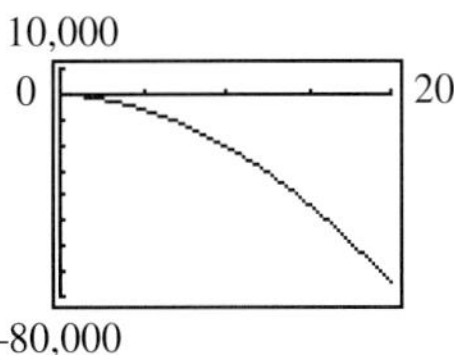

31. $y' = 16/\sqrt{4x + 7}$

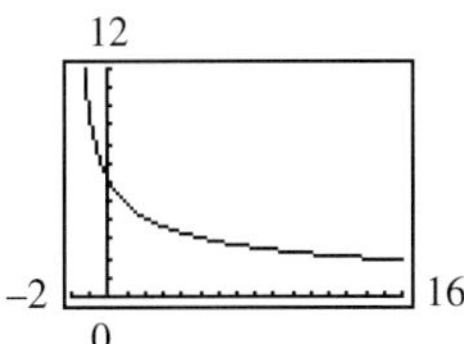

33. $y' = -\dfrac{2x + 4}{\sqrt{x^2 + 4x}}$

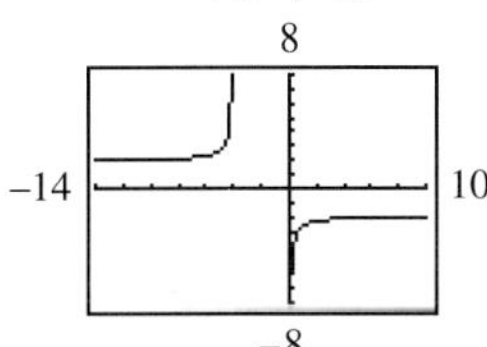

35. $y' = 2(x + 1)(x - 3) + (x - 3)^2$
37. $y' = 70(x + 3)(2x - 1)^4(x + 2)$
39. $y' = [(3x + 1)^2(21x + 1)]/(2\sqrt{x})$
41. $y' = -2(x - 4)^{-3}$ or $-2/(x - 4)^3$
43. $y' = [2(4x + 3)(4x - 7)]/(2x - 1)^2$
45. $y' = (-5x^2 - 36x + 8)/(5x + 2)^4$
47. $y' = (3x^{1/2} - 1)/[4x^{1/2}(x^{1/2} - 1)^{1/2}]$
49. **(a)** −2 **(b)** −24/7 **51.** (d)
53. $D(c) = (-c^2 + 10c - 25)/25 + 500$
55. $A[r(t)] = A(t^2) = \pi t^4$; this function represents the area of the oil slick as a function of time t after the beginning of the leak.
57. $C'(x) = \dfrac{15x}{\sqrt{50 + 15x^2}}$ **59.** \$77.46 per additional employee
61. **(a)** $R'(x) = \dfrac{5(300 - 4x)}{\sqrt{300x - 2x^2}}$ **(b)** \$10.61; \$2.89; −\$2.89; −\$10.61 **63.** **(a)** $F'(t) = \dfrac{150t}{(8 + t^2)^{3/2}}$ **(b)** About 3.96; 1.34; .36; .09 **65.** **(a)** −.5 **(b)** $-1/54 \approx -.02$ **(c)** −.011 **(d)** $-1/128 \approx -.008$ **67.** **(a)** $(-1, 1)$ **(b)** $x = -1$ **(c)** $(-\infty, -1)$, $(1, \infty)$ **(d)** The derivative is 0 when the graph of $G(x)$ is at a low point. It is positive where $G(x)$ is increasing and negative where $G(x)$ is decreasing.

Section 12.7 (page 619)

1. $y' = 3e^{3x}$ **3.** $f'(x) = 10e^{2x}$ **5.** $g'(x) = 20e^{-5x}$
7. $y' = 2xe^{x^2}$ **9.** $f'(x) = xe^{x^2/2}$ **11.** $y' = -18xe^{3x^2+5}$
13. $y' = (-8x + 3)/(-4x^2 + 3x)$ **15.** $y' = 1/(2x + 1)$
17. $f'(x) = \dfrac{6x^2 - 6x + 8}{(2x - 3)(x^2 + 4)}$
19. $y' = 2x(1 - x)e^{-2x}$

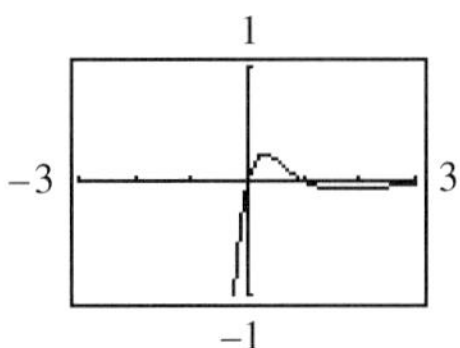

21. $y' = (-9x^2 + 18x - 4)e^{-3x}$

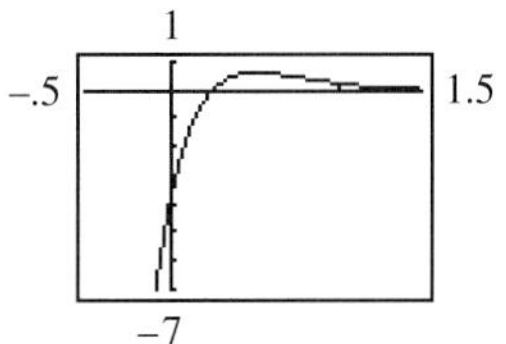

23. $y' = \dfrac{2x}{1 + x^2}$

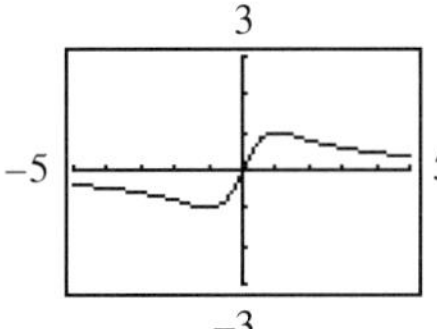

25. $y' = -23/[(6 - x)(3x + 5)]$
27. $y' = 3(15x^2 - 2)/[2(5x^3 - 2x)]$
29. $y' = -2x^2/(2 - x^2) + \ln(2 - x^2)$
31. $y' - (2x - 1)e^x/(2x + 1)^2$ **33.** $y' = (1 - 3\ln|x|)/x^4$
35. $y' = \dfrac{-20/x + 8 - 8\ln|x|}{(5 - 2x)^2}$
37. $y' = [3x^3\ln|x| - (x^3 - 1)]/[2x(\ln|x|)^2]$
39. $y' = 1/[2(x - 3)\sqrt{\ln(x - 3)}]$
41. $y' = (xe^x\ln|x| - e^x + 1)/[x(\ln|x|)^2]$
43. $y' = (xe^x + xe^{-x} - e^x + e^{-x})/x^2$ or $[e^x(x - 1) + e^{-x}(x + 1)]/x^2$
45. $f'(x) = \dfrac{4e^{3x+2}}{4x - 5} + 3e^{3x+2}\ln(4x - 5)$ **47.** $y' = \dfrac{2000e^{.4x}}{(7 - 10e^{.4x})^2}$
49. $y' = 1250e^{-.5x}/(12 + 5e^{-.5x})^2$ **51.** (d) **53.** 1/8
55. **(a)** $dR/dx = 100 + 50(\ln x - 1)/(\ln x)^2$ **(b)** \$112.48
57. **(a)** $C'(x) = 100$ **(b)** $P(x) = (50x/\ln x) - 100$ **(c)** \$12.48
59. **(a)** $P'(t) = 50{,}000[(1 + .2t)(-.04)e^{-.04t} + .2e^{-.04t}]$ **(b)** Gaining in 1985 and 1995; losing in 2005 and 2015
61. **(a)** About 817 vehicles/hr; −41.2 vehicles/hr per ft **(b)** About 522 vehicles/hr; −20.9 vehicles/hr per ft **63.** **(a)** Increase at \$54,065 per year **(b)** Increase at \$13,116 per year

(c) Decrease at \$7935 per year **(d)** Decrease at \$19,517 per year **(e)** Between years 10 and 15 **65. (a)** 7.42 **(b)** 21.22 **(c)** .79 **67. (a)** .005 **(b)** .0007 **(c)** .000013 **(d)** −.022 **(e)** −.0029 **(f)** −.000054

Section 12.8 (page 628)

1. $x = 0, 2$ **3.** $x = 1$ **5.** $x = -3, 0, 3$ **7.** $x = 0, 6$ **9.** Yes, no **11.** No, no, yes **13.** Yes, no, yes **15.** Yes, no, yes **17.** No, yes, yes **19.** Yes, no **21.** 1 **23.** Discontinuous at $t = m$; differentiable everywhere except $t = m$ and the endpoints **25. (a)** 6 cents **(b)** Does not exist **(c)** Any three of the years 1935, 1943, 1949, 1967, 1973, 1989, or 1991 **27. (a)** \$15 **(b)** \$25 **(c)** \$50 **(d)** \$92.50 **(e)** At $t = 20$ **29.** $(-4, 6)$ **31.** $(-\infty, -2]$ **33.** $[-25, 0]$ **35.** $(\pi, 10)$ **37.** $(-4, \infty)$ **39.** $(-\infty, 0)$ **41.** $(-3, 0), (0, 3)$

Chapter 12 Review Exercises (page 632)

1. 4 **3.** −1.2 **5.** .3536 **7.** −1 **9.** 13/2 **11.** 4 **13.** −13 **15.** 1/6 **17.** 1/4 **19.** 21 **21.** About −.3846 **23.** $y' = 2$ **25.** $y' = 4x - 1$ **27.** -2; $y + 2x = -4$ **29.** 2/9; $2x - 9y = 2$ **31. (a)** \$150 **(b)** \$187.50 **(c)** \$189

(d)

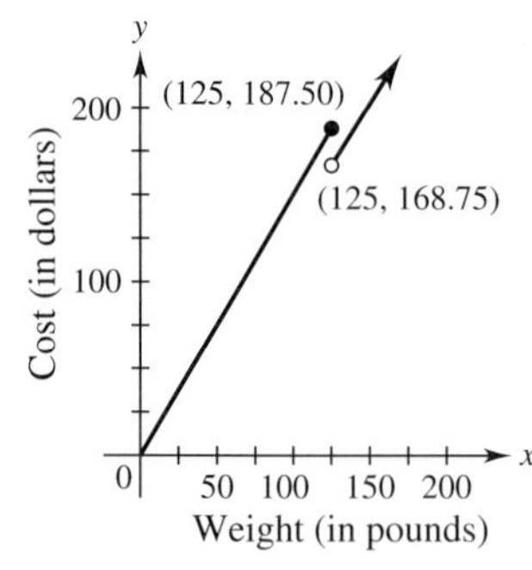

(e) At $x = \$125$ **33. (a)** −25.33 per dollar **(b)** −16.75 per dollar **(c)** −31.12 per dollar **35.** $y' = 10x - 7$ **37.** $y' = 14x^{4/3}$ **39.** $f'(x) = -3x^{-4} + (1/2)x^{-1/2}$ or $-3/x^4 + 1/(2x^{1/2})$ **41.** $y' = 15t^4 + 12t^2 - 7$

43. $y' = 16x^{3/4} + 6x^{-1/4}(2x + 3)$ **45.** $f'(x) = \dfrac{-2x^2 + 4}{(x^2 + 2)^2}$

47. $y' = (2 - x + 2\sqrt{x})/[2\sqrt{x}(x + 2)^2]$

49. $y' = (x^2 - 2x)/(x - 1)^2$ **51.** $f'(x) = 12(3x - 2)^3$

53. $y' = 1/\sqrt{2t - 5}$ **55.** $y' = 18x(3x - 4)^2 + 2(3x - 4)^3$

57. $f'(u) = \dfrac{(2u + 3)(6u - 4) - 6(3u^2 - 4u)}{(2u + 3)^4}$

59. $y' = -6x^2e^{-2x^3}$ **61.** $y' = 10xe^{2x} + 5e^{2x}$ or $5e^{2x}(2x + 1)$

63. $y' = \dfrac{2x + 4}{x^2 + 4x + 1}$ **65.** $y' = \dfrac{x - 1/x - 2x \ln 4x}{(x^2 - 1)^2}$

67. $y' = \dfrac{x^2 - 6x + 1}{(x - 3)^2}$

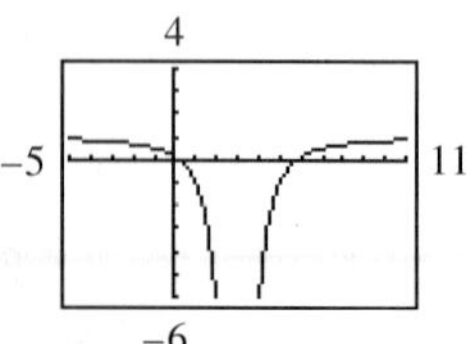

69. $y' = -12e^{2x}$

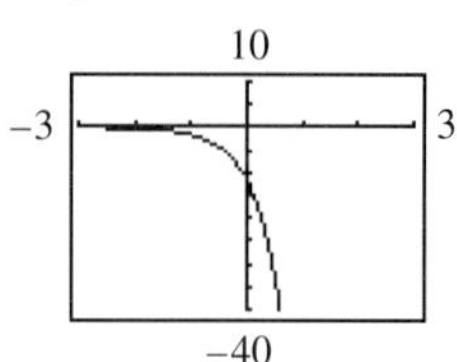

71. $-1/[x^{1/2}(x^{1/2} - 1)^2]$ **73.** $dy/dt = (1 + 2t^{1/2})/[4t^{1/2}(t^{1/2} + t)^{1/2}]$ **75.** −2/3 **77.** None **79.** No, yes, yes **81.** No, yes, no **83.** Yes, no, yes **85. (a)** \$367 per hundred **(b)** \$219.50 per hundred **(c)** −\$528 per hundred **87. (a)** 55/3; sales will increase by 55 million dollars when 3 thousand more dollars are spent on research. **(b)** 65/4; sales will increase by 65 million dollars when 4 thousand more dollars are spent on research. **(c)** 15; sales will increase by 15 million dollars when 1 thousand more dollars are spent on research. **(d)** As more is spent on research, the increase in sales is decreasing. **89. (a)** −9.5; costs will decrease by \$9500 for the next \$100 spent on training. **(b)** −2.375; costs will decrease by \$2375 for the next \$100 spent on training. **(c)** Decreasing **91.** 0 mph per sec for the hands and approximately 640 mph per sec for the bat. This represents the acceleration of the hands and the bat at the moment when their velocities are equal.

Case 12 (page 636)

1. (a) .17 **(b)** Inelastic **3.** The elasticity is negative.

CHAPTER 13

Section 13.1 (page 647)

1. Increasing on $(1, \infty)$; decreasing on $(-\infty, 1)$; local minimum at 1 **3.** Increasing on $(-\infty, -2)$; decreasing on $(-2, \infty)$; local maximum at −2 **5.** Increasing on $(-\infty, -4)$ and $(-2, \infty)$; decreasing on $(-4, -2)$; local maximum at −4; local minimum at −2 **7.** Increasing on $(-7, -4)$ and $(-2, \infty)$; decreasing on $(-\infty, -7)$ and $(-4, -2)$; local maximum at −4; local minima at −7 and −2 **9.** Increasing on $(-\infty, -1/3)$ and $(2, \infty)$; decreasing on $(-1/3, 2)$ **11.** Increasing on $(-\infty, -4)$ and $(-4, \infty)$ **13.** Decreasing on $(-\infty, 5)$ **15.** Increasing on $(-\infty, -1)$ and $(2, \infty)$; decreasing on $(-1, 2)$ **17.** −2, −1, 2 **19.** Local maximum at 0; local minimum at 2 **21.** Local maximum at −3; local minimum at −1 **23.** Local maximum at −1/4; local minimum at −5 **25.** Local maximum at −2; local minimum at 3 **27.** Local maximum at 0; local minimum at 2 **29.** Local maximum at 0; $f(0) = 1$; local minimum at 6/11; $f(6/11) \approx .7804$ **31.** Local maximum at 3/4; $f(3/4) = 4$ **33.** Local maximum at $\dfrac{.66 - \sqrt{.5796}}{12} \approx -.0084$; $f(-.0084) \approx 5$; local minimum at $\dfrac{.66 + \sqrt{.5796}}{12} \approx .1184$; $f(.1184) \approx 4.9980$ **35.** Local minimum at 0; $f(0) = 0$ **37.** Local maximum at −1; $f(-1) = 1/e$ **39.** Local maximum at $-1/e$; $f(-1/e) = 1/e$; local minimum at $1/e$; $f(1/e) = -1/e$ **41.** Local minimum at −1/3; $f(-1/3) \approx -2.1226$ **43.** Approximate local maximum: (3.35, 161.98); approximate local minima: (−6.77, −709.87) and (10.92, −240.08) **45.** Approximate local maxima: (−80.7064, 8671701.6) and (.3982, 5.0017); approximate local minima: (−1.6166, −8.8191) and (1.9249, −1.7461)

49. **(a)** 6000 **(b)** \$324,000
51. **(a)** The derivative is undefined at any point where the graph shows a "peak"—that is, a sharp change from increasing to decreasing. **(b)** From April to July; from July to November; from January to April and from November to December **(c)** From January to April and for November and December; air pollution is greatly reduced when the temperature is low, as is the case during these months.
53. (0, 8000) **55.** After 10 days **57.** **(a)** (0, 3) **(b)** $(3, \infty)$ (*Note: x* must be at least 0.) **59.** Local maxima of 4900 in 1985, 6900 in 1992, 6580 in 1995; local minima of 4700 in 1986 and 6500 in 1994 **61.** **(a)** [1945, 1965], [1970, 1974] **(b)** [1945, 1986] **(c)** 1965–1967, 1974; 1987 **63.** 100 units
65. 1,000,000 tires; \$700,000 **67.** About 12.6°C **69.** 10

Section 13.2 (page 661)

1. $f''(x) = 6x - 10$; -10; 2; -28 **3.** $f''(x) = 12(x + 2)^2$; 48; 192; 12 **5.** $f''(x) = 2/(1 + x)^3$; 2; 2/27; $-1/4$ **7.** $f''(x) = -(x + 4)^{-3/2}/4$ or $-1/[4(x + 4)^{3/2}]$; $-1/32$; $-1/(4 \cdot 6^{3/2})$; $-1/4$
9. $f''(x) = (-6/5)x^{-7/5}$ or $-6/(5x^{7/5})$; $f''(0)$ does not exist; $-6/(5 \cdot 2^{7/5})$; $-6/[5(-3)^{7/5}]$ **11.** $f''(x) = 2e^x$; 2; $2e^2$; $2e^{-3}$ or $2/e^3$
13. $f''(x) = 20e^{2x}$; 20; $20e^4$; $20e^{-6}$ **15.** $f''(x) = -1/x^2$; not defined; $-1/4$; $-1/9$ **17.** $f''(x) = 1/x$; not defined; 1/2; $-1/3$
19. $f'''(x) = 72x + 12$; $f^{(4)}(x) = 72$ **21.** $f'''(x) = 6/x^4$; $f^{(4)}(x) = -24/x^5$ **23.** $v(t) = 12t + 2$; $a(t) = 12$; $v(0) = 2$ cm/sec; $v(4) = 50$ cm/sec; $a(0) = a(4) = 12$ cm/sec^2
25. $v(t) = 9t^2 - 8t + 8$; $a(t) = 18t - 8$; $v(0) = 8$ cm/sec; $v(4) = 120$ cm/sec; $a(0) = -8$ cm/sec^2; $a(4) = 64$ cm/sec^2 **29.** Concave upward on $(-\infty, \infty)$; no points of inflection **31.** Concave upward on $(-4/3, \infty)$; concave downward on $(-\infty, -4/3)$; point of inflection at $(-4/3, 425/27)$ **33.** Concave upward on $(3, \infty)$; concave downward on $(-\infty, 3)$; no points of inflection **35.** Concave upward on $(-\infty, -5)$ and $(1, \infty)$; concave downward on $(-5, 1)$; points of inflection at $(-5, -1248)$ and $(1, 0)$ **37.** (14, 26688)
39. No critical numbers; no local extrema **41.** Local maximum at $x = -5$; local minimum at $x = 4$ **43.** Local maximum at $x = 0$; local minima at $x = 2$ and $x = -2$ **45.** Local maximum at $x = -\sqrt{3}$; local minimum at $x = \sqrt{3}$ **47.** Local maximum at $x = -3$; local minimum at $x = 3$ **49.** No critical numbers; no local extrema **51.** Local maximum at 2; local minima at 1 and 4; points of inflection at $x = (7 + \sqrt{7})/3$ and $x = (7 - \sqrt{7})/3$
53. Local minimum at 1; points of inflection at 4/3 and 2
55–59: Many correct answers, including the following.

55.

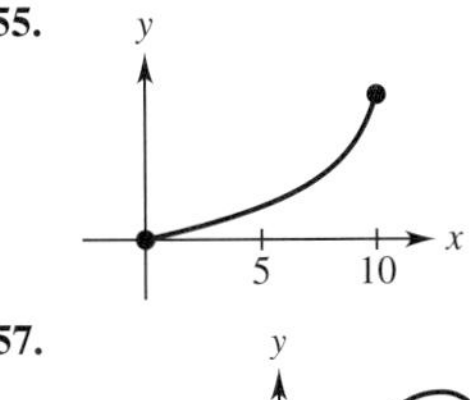

57.

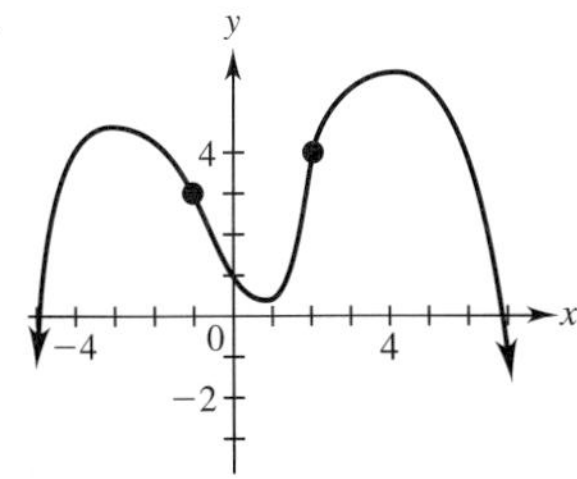

59.

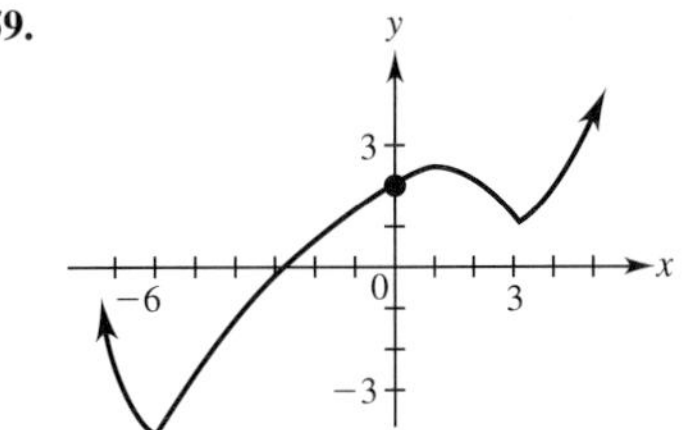

61. **(a)** -96 ft/sec **(b)** -160 ft/sec **(c)** -256 ft/sec **(d)** -32 ft/sec^2 **63.** (15, 86250) **65.** 8 **67.** 10,000

Section 13.3 (page 673)

1. Absolute maximum at 4; absolute minimum at 1 **3.** Absolute maximum at 2; absolute minimum at -2 **5.** Absolute maximum at -4; absolute minima at -7 and -2 **7.** Absolute maximum at $x = 6$; absolute minima at $x = -4$ and $x = 4$ **9.** Absolute maximum at $x = 6$; absolute minimum at $x = 4$ **11.** Absolute maximum at $x = \sqrt{2}$; absolute minimum at $x = 0$ **13.** Absolute maxima at $x = -3$ and $x = 3$; absolute minimum at $x = 0$
15. Absolute maximum at $x = 0$; absolute minima at $x = -1$ and $x = 1$ **17.** **(a)** $200 + 20x$ **(b)** $80 - x$ **(c)** $R(x) = 16{,}000 + 1400x - 20x^2$ **(d)** 35 **(e)** \$40,500 **19.** **(a)** 90 **(b)** \$405 **21.** 8 in. by 8 in. **23.** **(a)** 54.8 mph **(b)** \$73.03
25. **(a)** $1200 - 2x$ **(b)** $A(x) = 1200x - 2x^2$ **(c)** 300 m **(d)** 180,000 m^2 **27.** 20,000 ft^2 **29.** \$1000
31. **(a)** 12 days **(b)** 50 per ml **(c)** Day 1 **(d)** 81.365
33. 4 in. by 4 in. by 2 in. **35.** 10 cm; 10 cm **37.** Width $= 2\sqrt{6} + 2$ in. ≈ 6.90 in.; length $= 3\sqrt{6} + 3$ in. ≈ 10.35 in. **39.** 1 mile from *A* **41.** About 269; about \$577 **43.** **(a)** 600 **(b)** 958
45. 10 **47.** 60 **49.** 5000 **51.** (c)

Chapter 13 Review Exercises (page 677)

5. Increasing on $(-7/2, \infty)$; decreasing on $(-\infty, -7/2)$
7. Increasing on $(-\infty, -2/3)$ and $(1, \infty)$; decreasing on $(-2/3, 1)$
9. Decreasing on $(-\infty, 3)$ and $(3, \infty)$ **11.** Local maximum of 101 at $x = -3$; local minimum of -24 at $x = 2$ **13.** Local maximum of 1 at $x = 0$; local minima of -44 at $x = -3$ and $-4/3$ at $x = 1$
15. Local maximum of $3/e$ at $x = 1$ **17.** $f''(x) = 40x^3 - 24x$; 16; -272 **19.** $f''(x) = -80e^{4x}$; $-80e^4$; $-80e^{-8}$ **21.** Window: $-6 \le x \le 6$ and $-5 \le y \le 3$; local maximum at $x = 1/3$; local minimum at $x = -1/2$; point of inflection at $x = -1/12$; increasing on $(-1/2, 1/3)$; decreasing on $(-\infty, -1/2)$ and $(1/3, \infty)$; concave upward on $(-\infty, -1/12)$; concave downward on $(-1/12, \infty)$ **23.** Window: $-4 \le x \le 4$ and $-10 \le y \le 10$; local maximum at $x = 0$; local minima at $x = -1$ and $x = 2$; points of inflection at $x = (1 - \sqrt{7})/3$ and $x = (1 + \sqrt{7})/3$; increasing on $(-1, 0)$ and $(2, \infty)$; decreasing on $(-\infty, -1)$ and $(0, 2)$; concave upward on $(-\infty, (1 - \sqrt{7})/3)$ and $((1 + \sqrt{7})/3, \infty)$; concave downward on $((1 - \sqrt{7})/3, (1 + \sqrt{7})/3)$
25. Window: $-6 \le x \le 5$ and $-4 \le y \le 4$; no local extrema or points of inflection; increasing on $(-\infty, -1/2)$ and $(-1/2, \infty)$; concave upward on $(-\infty, -1/2)$; concave downward on $(-1/2, \infty)$
27. Window: $-6 \le x \le 6$ and $-1 \le y \le 7$; local maximum at $x = 1/2$; local minimum at $x = -2/3$; point of inflection at $x = -1/12$; increasing on $(-2/3, 1/2)$; decreasing on $(-\infty, -2/3)$ and $(1/2, \infty)$; concave upward on $(-\infty, -1/12)$; concave downward on $(-1/12, \infty)$
29. Window: $-6 \le x \le 6$ and $-1 \le y \le 7$; local minimum at $x = 0$; concave upward on $(-\infty, \infty)$

31. Window: $-6 \le x \le 6$ and $-10 \le y \le 10$; local maximum at $x = -2$; local minimum at $x = 2$; no point of inflection; increasing on $(-\infty, -2)$ and $(2, \infty)$; decreasing on $(-2, 0)$ and $(0, 2)$; concave upward on $(0, \infty)$; concave downward on $(-\infty, 0)$ **33.** Absolute maximum of 29/4 at $x = 5/2$; absolute minima of 5 at $x = 1$ and $x = 4$ **35.** Absolute maximum of 39 at $x = -3$; absolute minimum of $-319/27$ at $x = 5/3$ **37. (a)** \$2000 **(b)** \$400 **39.** 3 m by 3 m by 3 m **41.** 225 m by 450 m **43.** 126 **45.** 225 m by 225 m

Case 13 (page 680)

1. $Z'(m) = -C_1/m^2 + DC_3/2$ **3.** About 3.33 **5.** $Z(m^+) = Z(4) = \$11{,}400$; $Z(m^-) = Z(3) = \$11{,}300$

CHAPTER 14

Section 14.1 (page 689)

1. They differ only by a constant. **5.** $5x^2 + C$ **7.** $8p^3/3 + C$ **9.** $100x + C$ **11.** $5z^2/2 - z + C$ **13.** $z^3/3 - 2z^2 + 2z + C$ **15.** $x^4/4 - 14x^3/3 + 10x^2 + 3x + C$ **17.** $4y^{3/2} + C$ **19.** $12t^{5/2}/5 + 2t^{3/2} + C$ **21.** $112t^{3/2}/3 + 4t^{9/2} + C$ **23.** $-12/x^2 + C$ **25.** $-1/y - 4\sqrt{y} + C$ **27.** $-3x^{-2} + 4\ln|x| + C$ **29.** $4e^{3u}/3 + C$ **31.** $-15e^{-.2x} + C$ **33.** $3\ln|x| - 8e^{-.5x} + C$ **35.** $\ln|t| + 2t^3/3 + C$ **37.** $e^{2u}/2 + u^2/8 + C$ **39.** $x^3/3 + x^2 + x + C$ **41.** $6x^{7/6}/7 + 3x^{2/3}/2 + C$ **43.** $f(x) = 2x^3 - 2x^2 + 3x + 1$ **45.** $C(x) = .2x^3/3 + 5x^2/2 + 10$ **47.** $C(x) = 2x^{3/2}/3 - 52/3$ **49.** $C(x) = x^3/3 - x^2 + 3x + 6$ **51.** $C(x) = .000375x^4 + .011x^3 + .022x^2 + .25x + 5.55$ **53.** $C(x) = 3e^{.01x} + 5$ **55.** $p = 50 - 3x/2 - x^2/3$ **57. (a)** $f(t) = -e^{-.01t} + k$ **(b)** .095 unit

Section 14.2 (page 696)

3. $(12x - 1)^3/12 + C$ **5.** $-2/[3(3t + 1)] + C$ **7.** $-1/\sqrt{x^2 + 2x - 4} + C$ **9.** $2(r^3 + 3)^{3/2}/9 + C$ **11.** $-3e^{5k}/5 + C$ **13.** $2e^{2w^3}/3 + C$ **15.** $e^{4t - t^2}/2 + C$ **17.** $2e^{\sqrt{y}} + C$ **19.** $-4\ln|2 + 5x|/5 + C$ **21.** $(1/2)\ln|e^{2t} + 1| + C$ **23.** $-1/[8(2x^2 + 8x)^2] + C$ **25.** $\left(\frac{1}{r} + r\right)^2/2 + C$ **27.** $(x^3 + 3x)^{1/3} + C$ **29.** $(1/6)\ln|3x^2 + 12x + 8| + C$ **31.** $(x^2 + 1)^4/4 + C$ **33.** $(x^2 + 12x)^{3/2}/3 + C$ **35.** $(1 + \ln x)^3/3 + C$ **37.** $2(u - 1)^{3/2}/3 + 2(u - 1)^{1/2} + C$ **39.** $2(5t - 1)^{5/2}/125 + 2(5t - 1)^{3/2}/75 + C$ **41. (a)** $f(x) = .029x^4 - .601x^3 + 3.43x^2 + 3.24x + 26$ **(b)** 82.5% **43. (a)** $f(x) = 1110\ln|x| - 3994.8$ **(b)** 1060 per 1000 people

Section 14.3 (page 705)

3. 10; 10.66; 10.6656 **5.** 27.1929; 46.9629; 48.5333 **7.** 2.0833, 1.6502, 1.6256 **9.** 124.5833 **11.** 74.0439 **13.** 1.8719 **15. (a)**

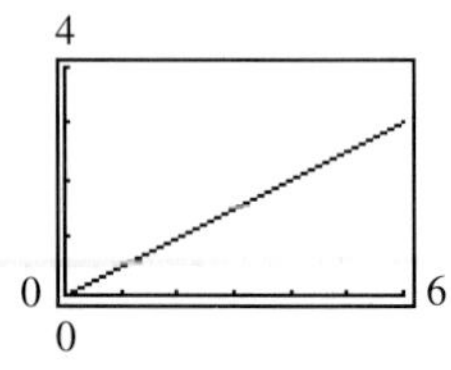

(b) 3.96 **(c)** 4 **(d)** 4

17. (a)

4
0
6
0

(b) 6.2765 **(c)** 6.2832 **(d)** 2π **19.** About \$83,000 **21.** About 35 liters **23.** About 1300 ft **25. (a)** About 690 BTUs **(b)** About 180 BTUs **27.** About \$2621

Section 14.4 (page 715)

1. 52 **3.** 13 **5.** 1/3 **7.** 76 **9.** 4/3 **11.** $5\ln 5 + (12/25) \approx 8.527$ **13.** $20e^{-.2} - 20e^{-.3} + 3\ln 3 - 3\ln 2 \approx 2.775$ **15.** $e^{10}/5 - e^5/5 - 1/2 \approx 4375.1$ **17.** 91/3 **19.** $447/7 \approx 63.857$ **21.** $(\ln 2)^2/2 \approx .24023$ **23.** 49 **25.** $1/4 - 1/(3 + e) \approx .075122$ **27.** $(6/7)(128 - 2^{7/3}) \approx 105.39$ **29.** A loss for the first year and a half; $\int_0^2 (6x^2 - 7x - 3)\,dx$ **31.** 23/3 **33.** 9.5 **35.** $e^2 + e^{-1} - 3 \approx 4.757$ **37.** 1 **39.** 23/6 **41.** $(e + e^3 - 2e^2)/2 \approx 4.01$ **43.** 19 **45. (a)** $(2/3)(\ln 3)^{3/2} \approx .767671503862$ **47. (a)** $(9000/8)(17^{4/3} - 2^{4/3}) \approx \$46{,}341$ **(b)** $(9000/8)(26^{4/3} - 17^{4/3}) \approx \$37{,}477$ **(c)** It is slowly increasing without bound. **49. (a)** \$3857 **(b)** When $t = 2$ (year 2) **51. (a)** About 414 barrels **(b)** About 191 barrels **(c)** Decreasing to 0 **53. (a)** $\int_0^{10} 1.2e^{.04t}\,dt$ **(b)** $30e^{.4} - 30 \approx 14.75$ billion **(c)** About 12.8 years **(d)** About 14.4 years

Section 14.5 (page 725)

1. \$280; \$11.67 **3.** \$2500; \$30,000 **5.** No **7. (a)** 8 yr **(b)** About \$148 **(c)** About \$771 **9. (a)** 39 days **(b)** \$3369.18 **(c)** \$484.02 **(d)** \$2885.16 **11. (a)** 5 **(b)** About 15.6 tons **13.** 13 yr **15.** \$1999.54 **17.** \$40.50

19. (a)

p
$S(q) = q^2 + \left(\frac{11}{4}\right)q$
150
120
90
60
30
$D(q) = 150 - q^2$
2 4 6 8 10 12
q

(b) (8, 86) **(c)** \$341.33 **(d)** \$429.33

21. (a)

p
$S(q) = \frac{7}{5}q$
10
5
(5, 7)
$D(q) = -\frac{3}{5}q + 10$
5 10
q

(b) (5, 7) **(c)** \$7.50 **(d)** \$17.50 **23.** \$5.76 million **25. (a)** .019; the lower 10% of the income producers earn 1.9% of the total income of the population. **(b)** .275; the lower 50% of the income producers earn 27.5% of the total income of the population.

(c) .819; the lower 90% of the income producers earn 81.9% of the total income of the population.

(d)

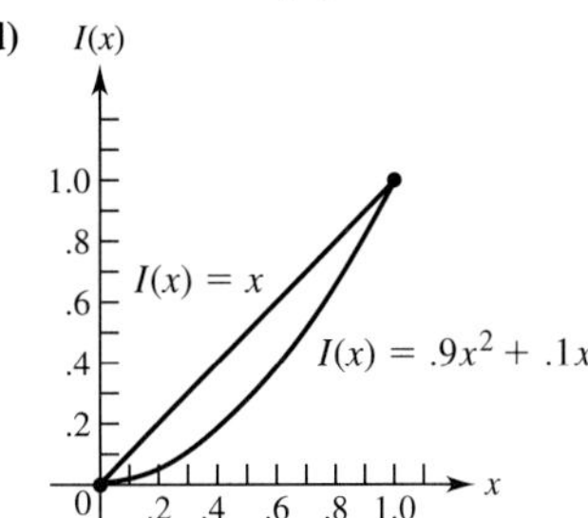

(e) .15; the amount of inequality of income distribution

27. (a) 10 items **(b)** 10 hr

The answers in Exercises 31 and 33 may vary slightly.

31. 161.2 **33.** 5.516

Section 14.6 (page 734)

1. $y = -x^2 + x^3 + C$ **3.** $y = 3x^4/8 + C$ **5.** $y^2 = x^2 + C$ **7.** $y = Me^{x^2}$ **9.** $y = Me^{x^3-x^2}$ **11.** $y = Mx$ **13.** $y = Me^x + 5$ **15.** $-1/(e^x + C)$ **17.** $y = x^3 - x^2 + 2$ **19.** $y^2 = \dfrac{2 \ln |x^3 + 28|}{3} + 6$ **21.** $y^2 = 2x^3/3 + 9$ **23.** $y = e^{x^2+3x}$ **25.** $y^2/2 - 3y = x^2 + x - 4$ **29. (a)** 108.4 **(b)** 121.2 **(c)** No; if $x = 8$, the denominator becomes 0. **31. (a)** $dy/dt = -.25y$ **(b)** $y = Me^{-.25t}$ **(c)** 4.8 yr **33.** About $\$1.35 \times 10^5$ **35. (a)** About 178.6 thousand **(b)** About 56.4 thousand **(c)** About 50.0 thousand **37.** 54.6 g **39.** About 10 **41. (a)** $T = 38 + 60.6e^{-.343t}$ **(b)** About 68.5° **(c)** About 1.44 hours **(d)** About 25.4 hours **43. (a)** $0 \le x \le 25, 0 \le y \le 1$

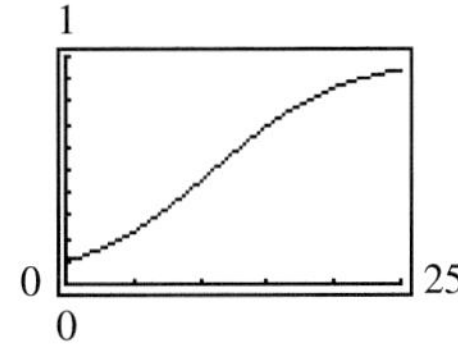

(b) At (11.0, .5)

Chapter 14 Review Exercises (page 737)

1. $x^3/3 - 3x^2/2 + 2x + C$ **3.** $2x^{3/2} + C$ **5.** $2x^{3/2}/3 + 9x^{1/3} + C$ **7.** $2x^{-2} + C$ **9.** $-3e^{2x}/2 + C$ **11.** $2 \ln |x - 1| + C$ **13.** $e^{3x^2}/6 + C$ **15.** $(3 \ln |x^2 - 1|)/2 + C$ **17.** $-(x^3 + 5)^{-3}/9 + C$ **19.** $\ln |2x^2 - 5x| + C$ **21.** $-e^{-3x^4}/12 + C$ **23.** $2e^{-5x}/5 + C$ **27. (a)** About 136.97 **(b)** About 148.35 **(c)** 148.8 **29.** 28 **33.** $72/25 \approx 2.88$ **35.** $2 \ln 3$ or $\ln 9 \approx 2.1972$ **37.** $2e^4 - 2 \approx 107.1963$ **39.** $(2/3)(22^{3/2} - 2^{3/2}) \approx 66.907$ **41.** $e^2 - 1 \approx 6.3891$ **43.** $C(x) = 10x - x^2 + 4$ **45.** $C(x) = (2x - 1)^{3/2} + 145$ **47.** 36,000 **49.** About 26.3 yr **53.** About 142 **55.** 1.2648 **57.** 12.0842 **59.** $y = x^4/2 + 3x^2 + C$ **61.** $y^2 = 3x^2 + 2x + C$ **63.** $y = -5e^{-x} - 5x + 22$ **65.** $y = 2e^{5x - x^2}$ **67. (a)** $dA/dt = .05A - 1000$ **(b)** \$9487.29 **69. (a)** About 111 items **(b)** Not exactly, but for practical purposes, yes **71.** $.2 \ln y - .5y = -.3 \ln x + .4x + C$; $x = 3/4$ unit, $y = 2/5$ unit

Case 14 (page 741)

1. About 102 years **3.** About 45.4 years

CHAPTER 15

Section 15.1 (page 750)

3. 4; −22; −20; 12 **5.** 3; $\sqrt{33}$; $\sqrt{17}$; 8

9.

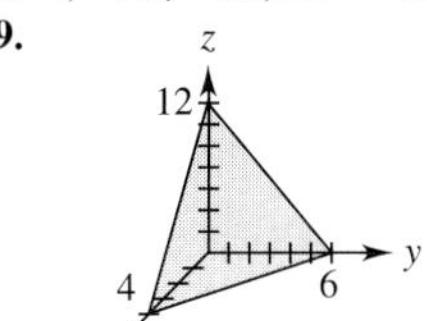

11.

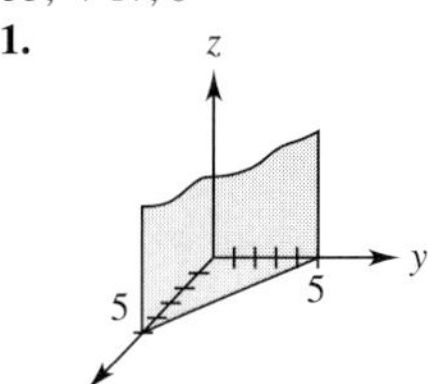

13.

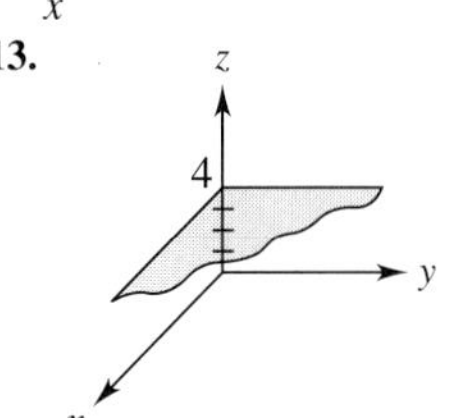

15.

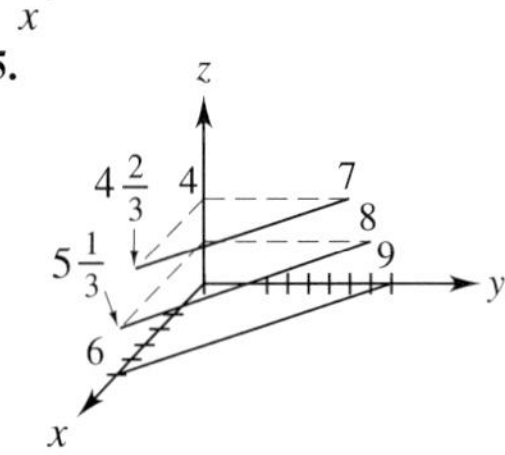

17.

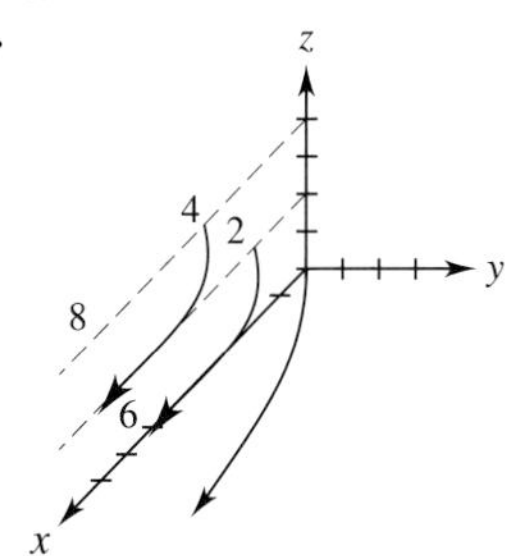

19. $y = 500^{10/3}x^{-7/3} \approx 10^9/x^{7/3}$

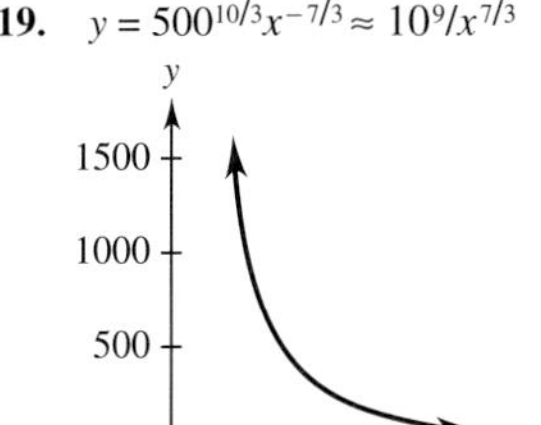
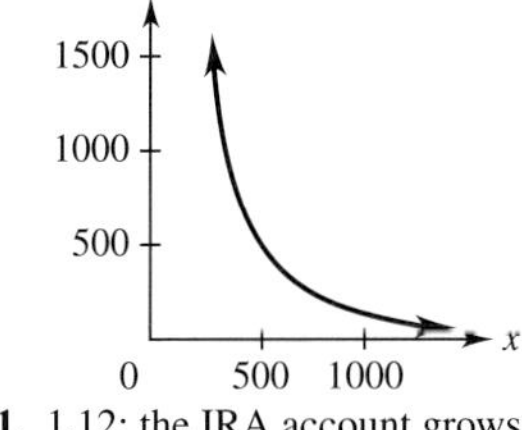

21. 1.12; the IRA account grows faster. **23.** $f(L, W, H) = L + 2H + 2W$ **25. (a)** $18x + 9h$ **(b)** $-6y - 3h$ **27.** (c) **29.** (e) **31.** (b)

Section 15.2 (page 758)

1. (a) $24x^2 - 8xy$ **(b)** $-4x^2 + 18y$ **(c)** 48 **(d)** −40 **3.** $f_x = -2xy + 12x^3$; $f_y = -x^2$; 100; −16 **5.** $f_x = 2e^{2x+y}$; $f_y = e^{2x+y}$; $2e^3$; e^{-5} **7.** $f_x = 2/(e^{x+2y})$; $f_y = 4/(e^{x+2y})$; 2; $4/e^2$ **9.** $f_x = (y^3 - x^2 - 6xy^2)/(x^2 + y^3)^2$; $f_y = (6x^2y - 3xy^2 - 3y^4)/(x^2 + y^3)^2$; −17/9; about .083 **11.** $f_x = \dfrac{2 - 2xy}{2x - x^2y}$; $f_y = \dfrac{-x}{2 - xy}$; 3/4; 2/7 **13.** $f_x = 2x^2ye^{2xy} + 2xe^{2xy}$; $f_y = 2x^3e^{2xy}$; $-4e^{-4}$; $-128e^{-24}$ **15.** $f_{xx} = 20y^3 - 30x$; $f_{xy} = f_{yx} = 60xy^2$; $f_{yy} = 60x^2y$

17. $h_{xx} = -8y^2$; $h_{xy} = h_{yx} = -16xy + 14y$; $h_{yy} = -6 - 8x^2 + 14x$
19. $R_{xx} = \dfrac{24y}{(2x + y)^3}$; $R_{xy} = R_{yx} = \dfrac{-12x + 6y}{(2x + y)^3}$; $R_{yy} = \dfrac{-12x}{(2x + y)^3}$
21. $z_{xx} = 0$; $z_{yy} = 4xe^y$; $z_{xy} = z_{yx} = 4e^y$ **23.** $r_{xx} = -1/(x + y)^2$; $r_{yy} = -1/(x + y)^2$; $r_{xy} = r_{yx} = -1/(x + y)^2$ **25.** $z_{xx} = 1/x$; $z_{yy} = -x/y^2$; $z_{xy} = z_{yx} = 1/y$ **27.** 1; $-1/4$ **29.** $x = -4$, $y = 2$
31. $x = 0, y = 0$ or $x = 3, y = 3$ **33.** $f_x = 2x$; $f_y = z$; $f_z = y + 4z^3$; $f_{yz} = 1$; 3; 1 **35.** $f_x = 6/(4z + 5)$; $f_y = -5/(4z + 5)$; $f_z = -4(6x - 5y)/(4z + 5)^2$; $f_{yz} = 20/(4z + 5)^2$
37. $f_x = (2x - 5z^2)/(x^2 - 5xz^2 + y^4)$; $f_y = 4y^3/(x^2 - 5xz^2 + y^4)$; $f_z = -10xz/(x^2 - 5xz^2 + y^4)$; $f_{yz} = 40xy^3z/(x^2 - 5xz^2 + y^4)^2$
41. **(a)** 2.04% **(b)** 1.26% **(c)** .05%: the rate of change of the probability for an additional semester of high school math; .003%: the rate of change of the probability per unit of change in the SAT score
43. **(a)** \$206,800 **(b)** $f_p = 132 - 2i - .02p$; $f_i = -2p$; the rate at which sales revenue is changing per unit of change in price (f_p) or interest rate (f_i) **(c)** A sales revenue drop of \$18,800
45. **(a)** 46.656 **(b)** $f_x(27, 64) = .6912$ and is the rate at which production is changing when labor changes by 1 unit from 27 to 28 and capital remains constant; $f_y(27, 64) = .4374$ and is the rate at which production is changing when capital changes by 1 unit from 64 to 65 and labor remains constant. **(c)** Production would be increased by about 69 units when labor is increased by 1 unit.
47. $.7x^{-.3}y^{.3}$ or $.7y^{.3}/x^{.3}$; $.3x^{.7}y^{-.7}$ or $.3x^{.7}/y^{.7}$ **49.** **(a)** About 5.71 **(b)** About 6.84 **(c)** $1/(a - v)$ **(d)** $b/(a - v)^2$
51. **(a)** $F_m = (gR^2)/r^2$; the rate of change in force per unit change in mass; $F_r = (-2mgR^2)/r^3$; the rate of change in force per unit change in distance

Section 15.3 (page 765)

3. Local minimum of -22 at $(3, -1)$ **5.** Local minimum of 0 at $(-2, -2)$ **7.** Saddle point at $(-3, 4)$ **9.** Local maximum of 17 at (2/3, 4/3) **11.** Saddle point at $(2, -2)$ **13.** Saddle point at (1, 2) **15.** Saddle point at (0, 0); local minimum of -201 at (6, 18) **17.** Saddle point at (0, 0); local minimum of -5157 at (72, 12) **19.** Saddle point at (0, 0) **21.** Local maximum of 9/8 at $(-1, 1)$; saddle point at (0, 0); (a) **23.** Local minima of $-33/16$ at (0, 1) and $(0, -1)$; saddle point at (0, 0); (b) **25.** Local maxima of 17/16 at (1, 0) and $(-1, 0)$; local minima of $-15/16$ at (0, 1) and $(0, -1)$; saddle points at (0, 0), $(-1, 1)$, $(1, -1)$, (1, 1), and $(-1, -1)$; (e) **27.** $P(12, 40) = 2744$ **29.** $P(12, 72) = \$2,528,000$
31. $C(12, 25) = 2237$ **33.** 3 m by 3 m by 3 m **35.** 18 inches by 18 inches by 36 inches **37.** 1000 tons of grade A ore and 2000 tons of grade B ore for maximum profit of \$1400

Chapter 15 Review Exercises (page 769)

1. 32; 156 **3.** $-6/5$; $-8/3$
7. **9.**

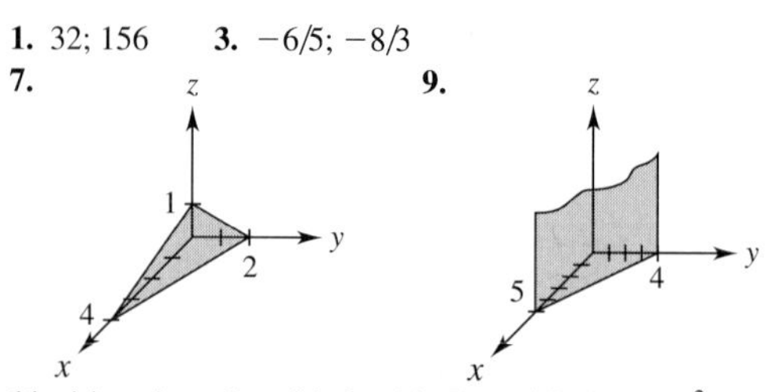

11. **(a)** $-4x + 5y$ **(b)** 3 **(c)** 5 **15.** $f_x = 12x^2y + 10y^4$; $f_y = 4x^3 + 40xy^3$ **17.** $f_x = (12y - 3x^2 + 4xy^2)/(x^2 + 4y)^2$; $f_y = (-4x^2y - 8y^2 - 12x)/(x^2 + 4y)^2$ **19.** $f_x = 2(y + 1)^2e^{2x+y}$; $f_y = (y + 1)(y + 3)e^{2x+y}$ **21.** $f_x = 3x^2y^2/(1 + x^3y^2)$; $f_y = 2x^3y/(1 + x^3y^2)$ **23.** $f_{xx} = 24xy^2$; $f_{xy} = 24x^2y - 8$
25. $f_{xx} = 8y/(x - 2y)^3$; $f_{xy} = (-4x - 8y)/(x - 2y)^3$ **27.** $f_{xx} = 2e^y$; $f_{xy} = 2xe^y$ **29.** $f_{xx} = (-2x^2y^2 - 4y)/(2 - x^2y)^2$; $f_{xy} = -4x/(2 - x^2y)^2$ **31.** Local minimum at (0, 1)
33. Saddle point at (0, 2) **35.** Local minimum at (1, 1/2); saddle point at $(-1/3, 11/6)$ **37.** $F(L, W, H) = 2LW + 2WH + 2LH$
39. **(a)** Local minimum at (11, 12) **(b)** \$431

Index of Applications

Natural Science

Physical Science

Social Science

Index

T

The **derivative** of the function f is the function denoted f' whose value at the number x is defined to be the number

$$f'(x) = \lim_{h \to 0} \frac{f(x+h) - f(x)}{h},$$

provided this limit exists.

RULES FOR DERIVATIVES

Assume all indicated derivatives exist.

Constant Function If $f(x) = k$, where k is any real number, then

$$f'(x) = 0.$$

Power Rule If $f(x) = x^n$, for any real number n, then

$$f'(x) = n \cdot x^{n-1}.$$

Constant Times a Function Let k be a real number. Then the derivative of $y = k \cdot f(x)$ is

$$y' = k \cdot f'(x).$$

Sum or Difference Rule If $y = f(x) \pm g(x)$, then

$$y' = f'(x) \pm g'(x).$$

Product Rule If $f(x) = g(x) \cdot k(x)$, then

$$f'(x) = g(x) \cdot k'(x) + k(x) \cdot g'(x).$$

Quotient Rule If $f(x) = \frac{g(x)}{k(x)}$, and $k(x) \neq 0$, then

$$f'(x) = \frac{k(x) \cdot g'(x) - g(x) \cdot k'(x)}{[k(x)]^2}.$$

Chain Rule Let $y = f[g(x)]$. Then

$$y' = f'[g(x)] \cdot g'(x).$$

Chain Rule (Alternative Form) If y is a function of u, say $y = f(u)$, and if u is a function of x, say $u = g(x)$, then $y = f[g(x)]$, and

$$\frac{dy}{dx} = \frac{dy}{du} \cdot \frac{du}{dx}.$$

Generalized Power Rule Let u be a function of x, and let $y = u^n$ for any real number n. Then

$$y' = n \cdot u^{n-1} \cdot u'.$$

Exponential Function If $y = e^{g(x)}$, then

$$y' = g'(x) \cdot e^{g(x)}.$$

Natural Logarithmic Function If $y = \ln|g(x)|$, then

$$y' = \frac{g'(x)}{g(x)}.$$